ROTHMANS
FOOTBALL
YEARBOOK
2001-2002

ROTHMANS

EDITORS: GLENDA ROLLIN AND **JACK ROLLIN**

In association with

HEADLINE

First published in 2001
by HEADLINE BOOK PUBLISHING

10 9 8 7 6 5 4 3 2 1

Front cover photographs: (left) Jimmy Floyd Hasselbaink (Chelsea); (centre) Emile Heskey (Liverpool) and Alain Goma (Newcastle United, now Fulham); (right) Thierry Henry (Arsenal); (spine and background) Mark Viduka (Leeds United) and Wes Brown (Manchester United) – all *Colorsport*.

Back cover photographs: (top and background) Barry Ferguson (Rangers) and Henrik Larsson (Celtic); (bottom) Joe Cole (West Ham United) – both *Actionimages*.

British Library Cataloguing in Publication Data
Rothmans Football Yearbook.—2001–2002
1. Association Football—Serials
796.334'05

ISBN 0 7472 7256 5   (hardback)
ISBN 0 7472 7260 3   (trade paperback)

All calls to Club Call
cost 60p per minute

Typeset by Wearset, Boldon, Tyne and Wear

Printed and bound in Great Britain by
Mackays of Chatham PLC,
Chatham, Kent

HEADLINE BOOK PUBLISHING
A division of Hodder Headline
338 Euston Road
London NW1 3BH

www.headline.co.uk
www.hodderheadline.com

CONTENTS

INTERNATIONAL FOOTBALL

NON-LEAGUE FOOTBALL

INFORMATION AND RECORDS

INTRODUCTION

In this 32nd edition of Rothmans Football Yearbook, we are delighted to announce a new association with both the FA Premier League and the Football League, which will certainly help sustain and indeed improve the excellent relationship which we have enjoyed with these two bodies over a number of years. Once again, our new edition features historical and record information for the 92 clubs. An important innovation sees a new who's who style players directory which incorporates the total of appearances and goals for each player as in earlier editions, but additionally, features more personal information and a season-by-season account of the individual player's record. There is also each club's full record in the previous ten seasons and the latest sequences recorded for wins, draws and defeats, etc.

Detailed and varied coverage involves the FA Premier League, Football League, Scottish, Welsh and Irish football, amateur, schools, university, reserve team, extensive non-league information, awards, records and an international directory, the Football Foundation, Football and the Law, coaching, women's football, referees and the work of chaplains.

Transfer fees are given where known. When two clubs have differed as to the amount of a record move, the lower figure has been quoted in both instances. For certain entries, the figure quoted in the list of transfers may be the original one without extra finance built in for appearances and other reasons, which would appear subsequently as a record fee on the relevant club page. Also the date when a player is signed often varies from the one given as his registration and the diary occasionally refers to the transfer fee originally discussed.

A frequent question asked is why Football League records have not been changed since the advent of the Premier League. The answer is simple: the Football League still considers its First Division to be a championship which has existed for over 100 years.

The Editors would like to thank Alan Elliott for the Scottish Section, Bob Hennessy for the Milestones Diary, Tony Brown for instances of match results in the Records Section and Tony Lynch for the Obituaries. Thanks are also due to John English, who provided invaluable and conscientious reading of the proofs. The Editors would like to pay tribute to the various organisations who have helped to make this edition complete, especially Mike Foster, Adrian Cook and Zoe Ward of the FA Premier League, Debbie Birch, Louise Standing and Andrea Stock of the Football League and David C. Thomson of the Scottish League.

ACKNOWLEDGEMENTS

The Editors would like to express appreciation of the following individuals and organisations for their cooperation: Heather Elliott, Malcolm Brodie, Wally Goss (AFA), Paul Reaney for Nationwide Conference information, Rev. Nigel Sands, Edward Grayson, Ken Goldman, Grahame Lloyd, Marshall Gillespie, Ben Jerram, Valery Karpoushkin, Steven Meeson and Wendy McCance (Headline Book Publishing).

Special thanks are due to Lorraine Jerram, Headline's Senior Editor for her generosity, expertise, constant support, unflagging patience, sincerity, understanding, perspicacity and appreciation, not to mention her unfailing humour, stoicism, quick-wittedness and understated authority.

Finally, sincere thanks to John Anderson, Simon Dunnington, Geoff Turner, Brian Tait and the staff at Wearset for their efforts in the production of this book, which was much appreciated throughout the year.

EDITORIAL

Football has never been more popular than it is today. Premier League attendances reached a new high in 2000–01, top foreign players are attracted to the clubs, sponsors queue to inject finance and television continues to offer the armchair fan more and more coverage.

In the Premier League which is to have a new sponsor in Barclaycard, the final crowd figures for the season showed an increase of 6.89 percent on 1999–2000. The aggregate attendances were 12,472,094 compared with 11,668,497. The weekend of 5 May 2001 produced 362,784, a record for the competition. It beat the previous one of 359,168 established over the weekend of 20 January.

The French squad which won the Confederations Cup in June had eight players with English clubs, another two current caps were not called up! Reported salaries of leading players now compare with the best paid in the world and if figures quoted are to be believed, Sol Campbell's situation after moving from Tottenham Hotspur the short distance to Arsenal, puts a whole new meaning into a 'Bosman free' . . .

As far as the ever wider choice of viewing is concerned it will be possible for football to appear every night of the week.

Naturally with a note of caution: where there is boom, comes the risk of bust. Doubtless market forces will determine the eventual outcome.

But on a matter crucial to actual play, most people would agree timing is as essential in football as in everything, except it seems when any form of accuracy is required over the exact moment a goal is scored. While armies of anoraks can provide all manner of statistics involving every conceivable facet of play, they have to be content with the erroneous fact that there are more goals scored in the last minute of the game, than at any other time. All this when the these 60 seconds can last up to seven or eight minutes.

The answer is simple enough: use the fourth official to take the responsibility of keeping watch on legitimate interruptions and time-wasting. Perhaps we are frightened that being deprived of the injury-time will lessen the excitement.

Surely we are in danger of ignoring the most essential aspect of the game, obtaining more justifiable playing time. We do not want to trail the same path as the Americans, where it seems they produce a set of figures and then change a game to fit them. But they do manage to keep time correctly!

Holding up a board with the number of minutes to be added on is really not something which should be concerning football in the 21st century. Injury time has to be spread throughout the 90 minutes and this can only be handled by an official whose chief *raison d'etre* would be clocking on and off.

There really is a mental block in this area because we also find it difficult to accept that while a player who scores in the last minute of the first half does so in the 45th minute, a substitute coming on at the beginning of the second half should do so in the 46th not 45th minute.

The Football Association can be congratulated over the timely appointment of Sven-Goran Eriksson as England manager judging by his first five matches in charge, which produced a nap hand of wins. There was criticism when it was announced that a Swede was to take charge of the national team. Much of this drifted away during the second half of the international season when the chances of qualifying for the World Cup 2002 improved. There is nothing like a win, except when they come in bunches of five.

However, he will have to go some to emulate the achievements of George Raynor the Englishman in charge of Sweden in the post-war period. He lost only one of his first 11 matches and then ironically 4-2 to England. Raynor, the former Aldershot right-winger who took over Sweden after being assistant trainer with the Hampshire club, his only other experience as a coach was in the Army in Iraq at the end of the war. He went on to win the Gold Medal at the 1948 Olympics, finish third in the 1950 World Cup, third in the 1952 Olympics and then runners-up to Brazil in the 1958 World Cup. He also had a spell in charge of Lazio, Eriksson's former club.

Not such praise for our FA over the decision to abandon artificial pitches in 1994. Much of the pioneering work on improving 'plastic' was shelved as a result, but with Mother Nature apparently undergoing a mid-life crisis, fixtures are at risk with the vageries of the elements as witnessed last season. While there is nothing like the real thing to play on, there is room certainly at grass roots level for such artificial use. This elemental PMT (pitch maintenance tweaking) is crucial to the situation which has been developing in non-league football since the FA virtually scrubbed amateur football in 1974. This created the potential for a vast swathe of semi-professional football which continues to grow and with it a clamour for more recognition by its elders.

While it was a positive move by the Football League to co-opt Nationwide Conference clubs into its LDV Vans Trophy, (unfairly called the Dads Army Cup) the competition for associate members, turning down two up from the Conference on financial grounds was a knock-back to the aspirations of many progressive clubs. Hopefully a way can be found to cushion these concerns of Third Division clubs at risk.

A more imaginative use of fixtures outside the television-controlled professional game with an increased programme early in the campaign would be ideal. If the rains come later, there will be fewer games to fit in. There is the machinery available to sweep water off artificial surfaces and it even helped on grass last season. More money needs to be spent on pitches.

It's not a miscalculated risk. Gambling is invariably getting nothing for something; surface improvements would reap obvious awards.

ROTHMANS FOOTBALL YEARBOOK HONOURS

For the sixth consecutive year, members of the Football Writers' Association selected their team of the season for Rothmans Football Yearbook. As in previous years, players eligible had to have appeared in FA Carling Premiership matches during the season.

For the 2000–01 Premiership, the majority of members again preferred selecting players in a 4-4-2 formation. Despite achieving their seventh such title in nine years and a record hat-trick for the competition, Manchester United's representation on the final selection was matched by Liverpool whose triple cup triumph in taking the Worthington, UEFA and FA trophies clearly impressed those voting.

Runners-up Arsenal were able to have two representatives and the remaining place was taken by a Leeds United representative.

In terms of the personalities involved, the Manchester United quartet consisted of French international goalkeeper Fabien Barthez, midfield players David Beckham and Ryan Giggs plus striker Teddy Sheringham. The Liverpool foursome was made up by full-back Markus Babbel, central defender Sami Hyypia, midfield player Steve Gerrard and striker Michael Owen. Arsenal's French international midfield player Patrick Vieira and the club's promising full-back Ashley Cole were the Highbury representatives and Rio Ferdinand, the Leeds central defender, completed the team.

The three substitutes all pressed for full recognition by themselves and here United had two further players chosen in Roy Keane and Paul Scholes, while Ipswich Town's striker Marcus Stewart reflected the fine season enjoyed by the East Anglian club.

It is interesting to note that there were 52 different players concerned in the voting and of those who finally made the team, Giggs was in the first selection six years ago, as was Keane, who had been selected in every previous line-up, apart from three years ago. Beckham has appeared in four of the last five.

Ipswich Manager George Burley was just edged out of the voting for Manager of the Season by Gerard Houllier of Liverpool while other votes were cast for Sir Alex Ferguson at Manchester United and Terry Venables, who made a significant contribution to Middlesbrough escaping relegation.

Rothmans Football Yearbook Team of the Season

Fabien Barthez
(*Manchester U*)

Markus Babbel	Rio Ferdinand	Sami Hyypia	Ashley Cole
(*Liverpool*)	(*Leeds U*)	(*Liverpool*)	(*Arsenal*)
David Beckham	Patrick Vieira	Steve Gerrard	Ryan Giggs
(*Manchester U*)	(*Arsenal*)	(*Liverpool*)	(*Manchester U*)

Teddy Sheringham   Michael Owen
(*Manchester U*)   (*Liverpool*)

Manager:
Gerard Houllier (*Liverpool*)

Substitutes:
Roy Keane (*Manchester U*)
Paul Scholes (*Manchester U*)
Marcus Stewart (*Ipswich T*)

ROTHMANS FOOTBALL RECORDS

● **TOP TEN**

ALL-TIME PREMIER LEAGUE GOALSCORERS

Alan Shearer	Newcastle U	181
Andy Cole	Manchester U	132
Les Ferdinand	Tottenham H	123
Robbie Fowler	Liverpool	117
Ian Wright	Arsenal	113
Teddy Sheringham	Manchester U	107
Dwight Yorke	Manchester U	107
Matthew Le Tissier	Southampton	101
Dion Dublin	Aston Villa	94
Chris Sutton	Chelsea	81

ALL-TIME PREMIER LEAGUE APPEARANCES

Gary Speed	Newcastle U	323
Peter Atherton	Bradford C	318
Tim Sherwood	Tottenham H	309
Nigel Winterburn	West Ham U	303
Gary McAllister	Liverpool	300
Kevin Dixon	Arsenal	292
Denis Irwin	Manchester U	284
Tim Flowers	Leicester C	282
David James	Aston Villa	281
Ryan Giggs	Manchester U	281

PREMIER LEAGUE AVERAGE ATTENDANCES 2000–01

Manchester U	67,544
Newcastle U	51,290
Sunderland	45,069
Liverpool	43,699
Leeds U	39,016
Arsenal	37,975
Tottenham H	35,216
Chelsea	34,698
Everton	34,130
Manchester C	34,058

PREMIER LEAGUE TURNOVER 1999–2000
Figures in £000's

Manchester U	116,005
Arsenal	61,260
Chelsea	59,246
Leeds U	57,064
Liverpool	46,609
Newcastle U	45,090
Tottenham H	42,442
Sunderland	37,309
Aston Villa	35,773
West Ham U	31,102

Source: The Times.

PREMIER LEAGUE WAGES 1999-2000
Figures in £000's

Manchester U	39,977
Chelsea	36,932
Liverpool	35,813
Arsenal	29,692
Leeds U	24,265
Tottenham H	22,645
Aston Villa	21,551
Newcastle U	21,389
West Ham U	21,287
Everton	19,780

Source: The Times

PREMIER LEAGUE ANNUAL AVERAGE SEASON TICKET SALES
Figures in £'s

Chelsea	1746
Arsenal	1505
Manchester U	1454
Tottenham H	1246
West Ham U	1065
Leeds U	1041
Newcastle U	1022
Liverpool	1002
Sunderland	957
Aston Villa	944

Source: Sir Norman Chester Centre for Football Research at Leicester University 1999-2000.

AVERAGE ATTENDANCES

Manchester U	2000–2001	67,544
Manchester U	1999–2000	58,017
Manchester U	1967–68	57,552
NewcastleU	1947–48	56,283
Tottenham H	1950–51	55,509
Manchester U	1998–99	55,188
Manchester U	1997–98	55,168
Manchester U	1996–97	55,081
Arsenal	1947–48	54,982
Manchester U	1947–48	54,890

PREMIER LEAGUE SEASON TICKET HOLDERS EARNING MORE THAN £50,000

Chelsea	33
Wimbledon	23
Arsenal	20
Watford	20
Tottenham H	18
Southampton	14
West Ham U	14
Manchester U	13
Leeds U	10
Aston Villa	9

Source: Sir Norman Chester Centre for Football Research at Leicester University 1999-2000.

FOOTBALL MILLIONAIRES
(Personal fortunes or family wealth)
Figures in £m's

Joseph Lewis	Tottenham H/Rangers	2,200
The Moores Family	Liverpool	800
Mohamed al-Fayed	Fulham	750
Trevor Hemmings	Rangers	600
Sir Alan Sugar	Tottenham H	544
David Sullivan	Birmingham C	500
David & Ralph Gold	Birmingham C	370
Steve Morgan	Liverpool	355
Dave Whelan	Wigan Ath	325
David Murray	Rangers	300

Source: Sunday Times

PREMIER LEAGUE WEEKLY WAGES
Figures in £'s

Juan Sebastian Veron	Manchester U	80,000
Sol Campbell	Arsenal	80,000
Alen Boksic	Middlesbrough	62,000
Jimmy Floyd Hasselbaink	Chelsea	60,000
Andy Cole	Manchester U	60,000
Ryan Giggs	Manchester U	60,000
Roy Keane	Manchester U	52,000
Alan Shearer	Newcastle U	40,000
David Ginola	Aston Villa	40,000
Marcel Desailly	Chelsea	40,000
Thierry Henry	Arsenal	35,000
Dennis Bergkamp	Arsenal	35,000
Jaap Stam	Manchester U	35,000
Robbie Fowler	Liverpool	35,000

Source: national press

WORLD STARS WEEKLY WAGES
Figures in £'s

Francesco Totti	Roma	107,000
Juan Sebastian Veron	Manchester U	80,000
Sol Campbell	Arsenal	80,000
Luis Figo	Real Madrid	80,000
Rivaldo	Barcelona	75,000
Alessandro Del Piero	Juventus	75,000
Gabriel Batistuta	Roma	71,000
Steve McManaman	Real Madrid	70,000
Alen Boksic	Middlesbrough	62,000
Jimmy Floyd Hasselbaink	Chelsea	60,000
Andy Cole	Manchester U	60,000
Ryan Giggs	Manchester U	60,000

Source: national press.

WORLD TRANSFERS

		£	Year
Zinedine Zidane	Juventus to Real Madrid	47.7m	2001
Luis Figo	Barcelona to Real Madrid	37.4m	2000
Hernan Crespo	Parma to Lazio	35.7m	2000
Gianluigi Buffon	Parma to Juventus	34m	2001
Christian Vieri	Lazio to Internationale	31m	1999
Juan Sebastian Veron	Lazio to Manchester United	28.1m	2001
Rui Costa	Fiorentina to AC Milan	25.9m	2001
Lilian Thuram	Parma to Juventus	25.9m	2001
Filippo Inzaghi	Juventus to AC Milan	25.9m	2001
Pavel Nedved	Lazio to Juventus	25.9m	2001

Source: Daily Telegraph July 2001

● HIGHEST WINS

First-Class Match		Arbroath (*Scottish Cup 1st Round*)	36	Bon Accord	0	12 Sept 1885
International Match		England	13	Ireland	0	18 Feb 1882
FA Cup		Preston NE (*1st Round*)	26	Hyde U	0	15 Oct 1887
League Cup		West Ham U (*2nd Round, 2nd Leg*)	10	Bury	0	25 Oct 1983
		Liverpool (*2nd Round, 1st Leg*)	10	Fulham	0	23 Sept 1986
FA PREMIER LEAGUE	(*Home*)	Manchester U	9	Ipswich T	0	4 March 1995
	(*Away*)	Nottingham F	1	Manchester U	8	6 Feb 1999
FOOTBALL LEAGUE						
Division 1	(*Home*)	WBA	12	Darwen	0	4 April 1892
		Nottingham F	12	Leicester Fosse	0	21 April 1909
	(*Away*)	Newcastle U	1	Sunderland	9	5 Dec 1908
		Cardiff C	1	Wolverhampton W	9	3 Sept 1955
Division 2	(*Home*)	Newcastle U	13	Newport Co	0	5 Oct 1946
	(*Away*)	Burslem PV	0	Sheffield U	10	10 Dec 1892
Division 3	(*Home*)	Gillingham	10	Chesterfield	0	5 Sept 1987
	(*Away*)	Halifax T	0	Fulham	8	16 Sept 1969
Division 3(S)	(*Home*)	Luton T	12	Bristol R	0	13 April 1936
	(*Away*)	Northampton T	0	Walsall	8	2 Feb 1947
Division 3(N)	(*Home*)	Stockport Co	13	Halifax T	0	6 Jan 1934
	(*Away*)	Accrington S	0	Barnsley	9	3 Feb 1934
Division 4	(*Home*)	Oldham Ath	11	Southport	0	26 Dec 1962
	(*Away*)	Crewe Alex	1	Rotherham U	8	8 Sept 1973
Aggregate Division 3(N)		Tranmere R	13	Oldham Ath	4	26 Dec 1935
SCOTTISH LEAGUE						
Premier Division	(*Home*)	Aberdeen	8	Motherwell	0	26 March 1979
	(*Away*)	Hamilton A	0	Celtic	8	5 Nov 1988
Division 1	(*Home*)	Celtic	11	Dundee	0	26 Oct 1895
	(*Away*)	Airdrieonians	1	Hibernian	11	24 Oct 1950
Division 2	(*Home*)	Airdrieonians	15	Dundee Wanderers	1	1 Dec 1894
	(*Away*)	Alloa Ath	0	Dundee	10	8 March 1947
Aggregate Division 2		Airdrieonians	15	Dundee Wanderers	1	1 Dec 1894

● MOST GOALS FOR IN A SEASON

	Season	Team	Goals	Games
FA PREMIER LEAGUE	1999–2000	Manchester U	97	38
FOOTBALL LEAGUE				
Division 1	1930–31	Aston V	128	42
Division 2	1926–27	Middlesbrough	122	42
Division 3(S)	1927–28	Millwall	127	42
Division 3(N)	1928–29	Bradford C	128	42
Division 3	1961–62	QPR	111	46
Division 4	1960–61	Peterborough U	134	46
SCOTTISH PREMIER LEAGUE	2000–01	Celtic	90	38
SCOTTISH LEAGUE				
Premier Division	1991–92	Rangers	101	44
	1982–83	Dundee U	90	36
	1982–83	Celtic	90	36
	1986–87	Celtic	90	44
Division 1	1957–58	Hearts	132	34
Division 2	1937–38	Raith R	142	34
New Division 1	1993–94	Dunfermline Ath	93	44
	1981–82	Motherwell	92	39
New Division 2	1987–88	Ayr U	95	39
New Division 3	1997–98	Alloa	78	36

● FEWEST GOALS FOR IN A SEASON

	Season	Team	Goals	Games
FA PREMIER LEAGUE	1996–97	Leeds U	28	38
FOOTBALL LEAGUE (minimum 42 games)				
Division 1	1984–85	Stoke C	24	42
Division 2	1971–72	Watford	24	42
	1994–95	Leyton Orient	30	46
Division 3(S)	1950–51	Crystal Palace	33	46
Division 3(N)	1923–24	Crewe Alex	32	42
Division 3	1969–70	Stockport Co	27	46
Division 4	1981–82	Crewe Alex	29	46
SCOTTISH PREMIER LEAGUE	1998–99	Dunfermline Ath	28	36
SCOTTISH LEAGUE (minimum 30 games)				
Premier Division	1988–89	Hamilton A	19	36
	1991–92	Dunfermline Ath	22	44
Division 1	1993–94	Brechin C	30	44
	1966–67	Ayr U	20	34
Division 2	1923–24	Lochgelly U	20	38
New Division 1	1980–81	Stirling Alb	18	39
	1995–96	Dumbarton	23	36
New Division 2	1994–95	Brechin C	22	36
New Division 3	1995–96	Alloa	26	36

● MOST GOALS AGAINST IN A SEASON

	Season	Team	Goals	Games
FA PREMIER LEAGUE	1993–94	Swindon T	100	42
FOOTBALL LEAGUE				
Division 1	1930–31	Blackpool	125	42
Division 2	1898–99	Darwen	141	34
Division 3(S)	1929–30	Merthyr T	135	42
Division 3(N)	1927–28	Nelson	136	42
Division 3	1959–60	Accrington S	123	46
Division 4	1959–60	Hartlepools U	109	46
SCOTTISH PREMIER LEAGUE	1999–2000	Aberdeen	83	36
SCOTTISH LEAGUE				
Premier Division	1984–85	Morton	100	36
	1987–88	Morton	100	44
Division 1	1931–32	Leith Ath	137	38
Division 2	1931–32	Edinburgh C	146	38
New Division 1	1988–89	Queen of the S	99	39
	1992–93	Cowdenbeath	109	44
New Division 2	1977–78	Meadowbank T	89	39
New Division 3	1994–95	Albion R	82	36

● FEWEST GOALS AGAINST IN A SEASON

	Season	Team	Goals	Games
FA PREMIER LEAGUE	1998–99	Arsenal	17	38
FOOTBALL LEAGUE (minimum 42 games)				
Division 1	1978–79	Liverpool	16	42
Division 2	1924–25	Manchester U	23	42
	1990–91	West Ham U	34	46
Division 3(S)	1921–22	Southampton	21	42
Division 3(N)	1953–54	Port Vale	21	46
Division 3	1995–96	Gillingham	20	46
Division 4	1980–81	Lincoln C	25	46
SCOTTISH PREMIER LEAGUE	1999–2000	Rangers	26	36
SCOTTISH LEAGUE (minimum 30 games)				
Premier Division	1989–90	Rangers	19	36
	1986–87	Rangers	23	44
	1987–88	Celtic	23	44
Division 1	1913–14	Celtic	14	38
Division 3	1966–67	Morton	20	38
New Division 1	1996–97	St Johnstone	23	36
	1980–81	Hibernian	24	39
	1993–94	Falkirk	32	44
New Division 2	1987–88	St Johnstone	24	39
	1990–91	Stirling Alb	24	39
New Division 3	1995–96	Brechin C	21	36

● **MOST POINTS IN A SEASON** *(under old system of two points for a win)*

	Season	Team	Points	Games
FOOTBALL LEAGUE				
Division 1	1978–79	Liverpool	68	42
Division 2	1919–20	Tottenham H	70	42
Division 3	1971–72	Aston V	70	46
Division 3(S)	1950–51	Nottingham F	70	46
	1954–55	Bristol C	70	46
Division 3(N)	1946–47	Doncaster R	72	42
Division 4	1975–76	Lincoln C	74	46
SCOTTISH LEAGUE				
Premier Division	1984–85	Aberdeen	59	36
	1992–93	Rangers	73	44
Division 1	1920–21	Rangers	76	42
Division 2	1966–67	Morton	69	38
New Division 1	1976–77	St Mirren	62	39
	1993–94	Falkirk	66	44
New Division 2	1983–84	Forfar Ath	63	39

(three points for a win)

	Season	Team	Points	Games
FA PREMIER LEAGUE	1993–94	Manchester U	92	42
FOOTBALL LEAGUE				
Division 1	1998–99	Sunderland	105	46
	1984–85	Everton	90	42
	1987–88	Liverpool	90	40
Division 2	1998–99	Fulham	101	46
Division 3	1997–98	Notts Co	99	46
Division 4	1985–86	Swindon T	102	46
SCOTTISH PREMIER LEAGUE	2000–01	Celtic	97	38
SCOTTISH LEAGUE				
Premier League	1995–96	Rangers	87	36
New Division 1	1998–99	Hibernian	89	36
New Division 2	1995–96	Stirling Alb	81	36
New Division 3	1994–95	Forfar Ath	80	36

● **FEWEST POINTS IN A SEASON**

	Season	Team	Points	Games
FA PREMIER LEAGUE	1999–2000	Watford	24	38
FOOTBALL LEAGUE (minimum 34 games)				
Division 1	1984–85	Stoke C	17	42
Division 2	1904–05	Doncaster R	8	34
	1899–1900	Loughborough T	8	34
Division 3	1997–98	Doncaster R	20	46
Division 3(S)	1924–25 & 1929–30	Merthyr T	21	42
	1925–26	QPR	21	42
Division 3(N)	1931–32	Rochdale	11	40
Division 4	1976–77	Workington	19	46
SCOTTISH PREMIER LEAGUE	1998–99	Dunfermline Ath	28	36
SCOTTISH LEAGUE (minimum 30 games)				
Premier Division	1975–76	St Johnstone	11	36
	1987–88	Morton	16	44
Division 1	1954–55	Stirling Alb	6	30
Division 2	1936–37	Edinburgh C	7	34
New Division 1	1988–89	Queen of the S	10	39
	1992–93	Cowdenbeath	13	44
New Division 2	1987–88	Berwick R	16	39
	1987–88	Stranraer	16	39
New Division 3	1994–95	Albion R	18	36

● **LEAGUE CHAMPIONSHIP HAT-TRICKS**

Huddersfield T	1923–24 to 1925–26
Arsenal	1932–33 to 1934–35
Liverpool	1981–82 to 1983–84
Manchester U	1998–99 to 2000–01

● MOST WINS IN A SEASON

	Season	Team	Wins	Games
FA PREMIER LEAGUE	1999–2000	Manchester U	28	38
FOOTBALL LEAGUE				
Division 1	1960–61	Tottenham H	31	42
Division 2	1919–20	Tottenham H	32	42
Division 3(S)	1927–28	Millwall	30	42
	1929–30	Plymouth Arg	30	42
	1946–47	Cardiff C	30	42
	1950–51	Nottingham F	30	46
	1954–55	Bristol C	30	46
Division 3(N)	1946–47	Doncaster R	33	42
Division 3	1971–72	Aston V	32	46
Division 4	1975–76	Lincoln C	32	46
	1985–86	Swindon T	32	46
SCOTTISH PREMIER LEAGUE	2000–01	Celtic	31	38
SCOTTISH LEAGUE				
Premier Division	1995–96	Rangers	27	36
	1984–85	Aberdeen	27	36
	1991–92	Rangers	33	44
	1992–93	Rangers	33	44
Division 1	1920–21	Rangers	35	42
Division 2	1966–67	Morton	33	38
New Division 1	1998–99	Hibernian	28	36
New Division 2	1983–84	Forfar Ath	27	39
	1987–88	Ayr U	27	39
New Division 3	1994–95	Forfar Ath	25	36

● RECORD HOME WINS IN A SEASON

Brentford won all 21 games in Division 3(S), 1929–30

● UNDEFEATED AT HOME

Liverpool 85 games (63 League, 9 League Cup, 7 European, 6 FA Cup), Jan 1978–Jan 1981

● RECORD AWAY WINS IN A SEASON

Doncaster R won 18 of 21 games in Division 3(N), 1946–47

● FEWEST WINS IN A SEASON

	Season	Team	Wins	Games
FA PREMIER LEAGUE	1993–94	Swindon T	5	42
FOOTBALL LEAGUE				
Division 1	1889–90	Stoke C	3	22
	1912–13	Woolwich Arsenal	3	38
	1984–85	Stoke C	3	42
Division 2	1899–1900	Loughborough T	1	34
	1983–84	Cambridge U	4	42
Division 3(S)	1929–30	Merthyr T	6	42
	1925–26	QPR	6	42
Division 3(N)	1931–32	Rochdale	4	40
Division 3	1973–74	Rochdale	2	46
Division 4	1976–77	Southport	3	46
SCOTTISH PREMIER LEAGUE	1998–99	Dunfermline Ath	4	36
SCOTTISH LEAGUE				
Premier Division	1975–76	St Johnstone	3	36
	1982–83	Kilmarnock	3	36
	1987–88	Morton	3	44
Division 1	1891–92	Vale of Leven	0	22
Division 2	1905–06	East Stirlingshire	1	22
	1974–75	Forfar Ath	1	38
New Division 1	1988–89	Queen of the S	2	39
	1992–93	Cowdenbeath	3	44
New Division 2	1975–76	Forfar Ath	4	26
	1987–88	Stranraer	4	39
New Division 3	1994–95	Albion R	5	36
	2000–01	Elgin C	5	36

● MOST DEFEATS IN A SEASON

	Season	Team	Defeats	Games
FA PREMIER LEAGUE	1994–95	Ipswich T	29	42
FOOTBALL LEAGUE				
Division 1	1984–85	Stoke C	31	42
Division 2	1938–39	Tranmere R	31	42
	1992–93	Chester C	33	46
	2000–01	Oxford U	33	46
Division 3	1997–98	Doncaster R	34	46
Division 3(S)	1924–25	Merthyr T	29	42
	1952–53	Walsall	29	46
	1953–54	Walsall	29	46
Division 3(N)	1931–32	Rochdale	33	40
Division 4	1987–88	Newport Co	33	46
SCOTTISH PREMIER LEAGUE	2000–01	St Mirren	24	38
SCOTTISH LEAGUE				
Premier Division	1984–85	Morton	29	36
Division 1	1920–21	St Mirren	31	42
Division 2	1962–63	Brechin C	30	36
	1923–24	Lochgelly	30	38
New Division 1	1988–89	Queen of the S	29	39
	1995–96	Dumbarton	31	36
	1992–93	Cowdenbeath	34	44
New Division 2	1987–88	Berwick R	29	39
New Division 3	1994–95	Albion R	28	36

● FEWEST DEFEATS IN A SEASON *(Minimum 20 games)*

	Season	Team	Defeats	Games
FA PREMIER LEAGUE	1999–2000	Manchester U	3	38
	1998–99	Manchester U	3	38
	1998–99	Chelsea	3	38
FOOTBALL LEAGUE				
Division 1	1888–89	Preston NE	0	22
	1990–91	Arsenal	1	38
	1987–88	Liverpool	2	40
	1968–69	Leeds U	2	42
Division 2	1893–94	Liverpool	0	28
	1897–98	Burnley	2	30
	1905–06	Bristol C	2	38
	1963–64	Leeds U	3	42
	1988–89	Chelsea	5	46
Division 3	1966–67	QPR	5	46
	1989–90	Bristol R	5	46
	1997–98	Notts Co	5	46
Division 3(S)	1921–22	Southampton	4	42
	1929–30	Plymouth Arg	4	42
Division 3(N)	1953–54	Port Vale	3	46
	1946–47	Doncaster R	3	42
	1923–24	Wolverhampton W	3	42
Division 4	1975–76	Lincoln C	4	46
	1981–82	Sheffield U	4	46
	1981–82	Bournemouth	4	46
SCOTTISH PREMIER LEAGUE	2000–01	Celtic	3	38
SCOTTISH LEAGUE				
Premier Division	1995–96	Rangers	3	36
	1987–88	Celtic	3	44
Division 1	1898–99	Rangers	0	18
	1920–21	Rangers	1	42
Division 2	1956–57	Clyde	1	36
	1962–63	Morton	1	36
	1967–68	St Mirren	1	36
New Division 1	1975–76	Partick T	2	26
	1976–77	St Mirren	2	39
	1992–93	Raith R	4	44
	1993–94	Falkirk	4	44
New Division 2	1975–76	Raith R	1	26
	1975–76	Clydebank	3	26
	1983–84	Forfar Ath	3	39
	1986–87	Raith R	3	39
	1998–99	Livingston	3	36
New Division 3	2000–01	Hamilton A	4	36

● HAT-TRICKS

Career   34 Dixie Dean (Tranmere R, Everton, Notts Co, England)
Division 1 (one season post-war)   6 Jimmy Greaves (Chelsea), 1960–61
Three for one team one match
West, Spouncer, Hooper, Nottingham F v Leicester Fosse, Division 1, 21 April 1909
Barnes, Ambler, Davies, Wrexham v Hartlepools U, Division 4, 3 March 1962
Adcock, Stewart, White, Manchester C v Huddersfield T, Division 2, 7 Nov 1987
Loasby, Smith, Wells, Northampton T v Walsall, Division 3S, 5 Nov 1927
Bowater, Hoyland, Readman, Mansfield T v Rotherham U, Division 3N, 27 Dec 1932

● MOST DRAWN GAMES IN A SEASON

	Season	Team	Draws	Games
FA PREMIER LEAGUE	1993–94	Manchester C	18	42
	1993–94	Sheffield U	18	42
	1994–95	Southampton	18	42
FOOTBALL LEAGUE Division 1	1978–79	Norwich C	23	42
Division 3	1997–98	Cardiff C	23	46
	1997–98	Hartlepool U	23	46
Division 4	1986–87	Exeter C	23	46
SCOTTISH LEAGUE Premier Division	1993–94	Aberdeen	21	44
New Division 1	1986–87	East Fife	21	44

● MOST GOALS IN A GAME

FA PREMIER LEAGUE	19 Sept 1999	Alan Shearer (Newcastle U) 5 goals v Sheffield W
	4 Mar 1995	Andy Cole (Manchester U) 5 goals v Ipswich T
FOOTBALL LEAGUE Division 1	14 Dec 1935	Ted Drake (Arsenal) 7 goals v Aston V
	6 Oct 1888	James Ross (Preston NE) 7 goals v Stoke
Division 2	5 Feb 1955	Tommy Briggs (Blackburn R) 7 goals v Bristol R
	23 Feb 1957	Neville Coleman (Stoke C) 7 goals v Lincoln C
Division 3(S)	13 April 1936	Joe Payne (Luton T) 10 goals v Bristol R
Division 3(N)	26 Dec 1935	Bunny Bell (Tranmere R) 9 goals v Oldham Ath
Division 3	16 Sept 1969	Steve Earle (Fulham) 5 goals v Halifax T
	24 April 1965	Barrie Thomas (Scunthorpe U) 5 goals v Luton T
	20 Nov 1965	Keith East (Swindon T) 5 goals v Mansfield T
	2 Oct 1971	Alf Wood (Shrewsbury T) 5 goals v Blackburn R
	10 Sept 1983	Tony Caldwell (Bolton W) 5 goals v Walsall
	4 May 1987	Andy Jones (Port Vale) 5 goals v Newport Co
	3 April 1990	Steve Wilkinson (Mansfield T) 5 goals v Birmingham C
Division 4	26 Dec 1962	Bert Lister (Oldham Ath) 6 goals v Southport
FA CUP	20 Nov 1971	Ted MacDougall (Bournemouth) 9 goals v Margate (*1st Round*)
LEAGUE CUP	25 Oct 1989	Frankie Bunn (Oldham Ath) 6 goals v Scarborough
SCOTTISH LEAGUE Premier Division	17 Nov 1984	Paul Sturrock (Dundee U) 5 goals v Morton
Division 1	14 Sept 1928	Jimmy McGrory (Celtic) 8 goals v Dunfermline Ath
Division 2	1 Oct 1927	Owen McNally (Arthurlie) 8 goals v Armadale
	2 Jan 1930	Jim Dyet (King's Park) 8 goals v Forfar Ath
	18 April 1936	John Calder (Morton) 8 goals v Raith R
	20 Aug 1937	Norman Hayward (Raith R) 8 goals v Brechin C
SCOTTISH CUP	12 Sept 1885	John Petrie (Arbroath) 13 goals v Bon Accord (*1st Round*)

● MOST LEAGUE GOALS IN A SEASON

	Season	Player	Goals	Games
FA PREMIER LEAGUE	1993–94	Andy Cole (Newcastle U)	34	40
	1994–95	Alan Shearer (Blackburn R)	34	42
Division 1	1927–28	Dixie Dean (Everton)	60	39
Division 2	1926–27	George Camsell (Middlesbrough)	59	37
Division 3(S)	1936–37	Joe Payne (Luton T)	55	39
Division 3(N)	1936–37	Ted Harston (Mansfield T)	55	41
Division 3	1959–60	Derek Reeves (Southampton)	39	46
Division 4	1960–61	Terry Bly (Peterborough U)	52	46
FA CUP	1887–88	Jimmy Ross (Preston NE)	20	8
LEAGUE CUP	1986–87	Clive Allen (Tottenham H)	12	9
SCOTTISH PREMIER LEAGUE	2000–01	Henrik Larsson Celtic	35	37
SCOTTISH LEAGUE Division 1	1931–32	William McFadyen (Motherwell)	52	34
Division 2	1927–28	Jim Smith (Ayr U)	66	38

● MOST LEAGUE GOALS IN A CAREER

Player	Team	Goals	Games	Season
FOOTBALL LEAGUE				
Arthur Rowley	WBA	4	24	1946–48
	Fulham	27	56	1948–50
	Leicester C	251	303	1950–58
	Shrewsbury T	152	236	1958–65
		434	619	
SCOTTISH LEAGUE				
Jimmy McGrory	Celtic	1	3	1922–23
	Clydebank	13	30	1923–24
	Celtic	396	375	1924–38
		410	408	

● MOST CUP GOALS IN A CAREER

FA CUP (post-war)
Ian Rush   43   (Chester, Liverpool)
Pre-Second World war: Henry Cursham   48   (Notts Co)

LEAGUE CUP
Geoff Hurst   49   (West Ham U, Stoke C)
Ian Rush   49   (Chester, Liverpool, Newcastle U)

● A CENTURY OF LEAGUE AND CUP GOALS IN CONSECUTIVE SEASONS

George Camsell	Middlesbrough	59 Lge	5 Cup	1926–27
(101 goals)		33	4	1927–28
Steve Bull	Wolverhampton W	34 Lge	18 Cup	1987–88
(102 goals)		37	13	1988–89

(Camsell's cup goals were all scored in the FA Cup; Bull had 12 in the Sherpa Van Trophy, 3 Littlewoods Cup, 3 FA Cup in 1987–88; 11 Sherpa Van Trophy, 2 Littlewoods Cup in 1988–89.)

● LONGEST SEQUENCE OF CONSECUTIVE SCORING (Individual)

FA PREMIER LEAGUE
Mark Stein (Chelsea)	9 in 7 games	1993–94
Alan Shearer (Newcastle U)	7 in 7 games	1996–97
Thierry Henry (Arsenal)	9 in 7 games	1999–2000

FOOTBALL LEAGUE RECORD
Tom Phillipson (Wolverhampton W)	23 in 13 games	1926–27

● LONGEST WINNING SEQUENCE

FOOTBALL LEAGUE	Season	Team	Games
Division 1	1959–60 (2) and 1960–61 (11)	Tottenham H	13
	1891–92	Preston NE	13
	1891–92	Sunderland	13
Division 2	1904–05	Manchester U	14
	1905–06	Bristol C	14
	1950–51	Preston NE	14
Division 3	1985–86	Reading	13
FROM SEASON'S START			
Division 1	1960–61	Tottenham H	11
	1992–93	Newcastle U	11
	2000–01	Fulham	11
Division 3	1985–86	Reading	13

● LONGEST UNBEATEN SEQUENCE

FOOTBALL LEAGUE	Season	Team	Games
Division 1	Nov 1977–Dec 1978	Nottingham F	42

● LONGEST UNBEATEN CUP SEQUENCE

Liverpool   25 rounds   League/Milk Cup   1980–84

● LONGEST UNBEATEN SEQUENCE IN A SEASON

FOOTBALL LEAGUE	Season	Team	Games
Division 1	1920–21	Burnley	30

● LONGEST UNBEATEN START TO A SEASON

FOOTBALL LEAGUE Division 1	*Season* 1973–74 1987–88	*Team* Leeds U Liverpool	*Games* 29 29

● LONGEST SEQUENCE WITHOUT A WIN IN A SEASON

FOOTBALL LEAGUE Division 2	*Season* 1983–84	*Team* Cambridge U	*Games* 31

● LONGEST SEQUENCE WITHOUT A WIN FROM SEASON'S START

FOOTBALL LEAGUE Division 1	*Season* 1990–91	*Team* Sheffield U	*Games* 16

● LONGEST SEQUENCE OF CONSECUTIVE DEFEATS

FOOTBALL LEAGUE Division 2	*Season* 1898–99	*Team* Darwen	*Games* 18

● GOALKEEPING RECORDS (without conceding a goal)

BRITISH RECORD (all competitive games)
Chris Woods, Rangers, in 1196 minutes from 26 November 1986 to 31 January 1987.

FOOTBALL LEAGUE
Steve Death, Reading, 1103 minutes from 24 March to 18 August 1979.

● PENALTIES

Most in a Season (individual) *Goals*		*Season*	
Division 1	Francis Lee (Manchester C)	13	1971–72
Most awarded in one game			
Five	Crystal Palace (4 – 1 scored, 3 missed) v Brighton & HA (1 scored), Div 2		1988–89
Most saved in a Season			
Division 1	Paul Cooper (Ipswich T)	8 (of 10)	1979–80

● MOST LEAGUE APPEARANCES (750+ matches)

1005 Peter Shilton (286 Leicester City, 110 Stoke City, 202 Nottingham Forest, 188 Southampton, 175 Derby County, 34 Plymouth Argyle, 1 Bolton Wanderers, 9 Leyton Orient) 1966–97

914 Tony Ford (355 Grimsby T, 9 Sunderland (loan), 112 Stoke C, 114 WBA, 68 Grimsby T, 5 Bradford C (loan), 76 Scunthorpe U, 103 Mansfield T, 72 Rochdale) 1975–2001

879 Graeme Armstrong (204 Stirling A, 83 Berwick R, 353 Meadowbank T, 239 Stenhousemuir) 1975–99

863 Tommy Hutchison (165 Blackpool, 314 Coventry City, 46 Manchester City, 92 Burnley, 178 Swansea City, 68 Alloa) 1965–91

824 Terry Paine (713 Southampton, 111 Hereford United) 1957–77

782 Robbie James (484 Swansea C, 48 Stoke C, 87 QPR, 23 Leicester C, 89 Bradford C, 51 Cardiff C) 1973–94

777 Alan Oakes (565 Manchester C, 211 Chester C, 1 Port Vale) 1959–84

771 John Burridge (27 Workington, 134 Blackpool, 65 Aston Villa, 6 Southend U (loan), 88 Crystal Palace, 39 QPR, 74 Wolverhampton W, 6 Derby Co (loan), 109 Sheffield U, 62 Southampton, 67 Newcastle U, 65 Hibernian, 3 Scarborough, 4 Lincoln C, 3 Aberdeen, 3 Dumbarton, 3 Falkirk, 4 Manchester C, 3 Darlington, 6 Queen of the South) 1968–96

770 John Trollope (all for Swindon Town) 1960–80†

764 Jimmy Dickinson (all for Portsmouth) 1946–65

761 Roy Sproson (all for Port Vale) 1950–72

760 Mick Tait (64 Oxford U, 106 Carlisle U, 33 Hull C, 240 Portsmouth, 99 Reading, 79 Darlington, 139 Hartlepool U)

758 Ray Clemence (48 Scunthorpe United, 470 Liverpool, 240 Tottenham Hotspur) 1966–87

758 Billy Bonds (95 Charlton Ath, 663 West Ham U) 1964–88

757 Pat Jennings (48 Watford, 472 Tottenham Hotspur, 237 Arsenal) 1963–86

757 Frank Worthington (171 Huddersfield T, 210 Leicester C, 84 Bolton W, 75 Birmingham C, 32 Leeds U, 19 Sunderland, 34 Southampton, 31 Brighton & HA, 59 Tranmere R, 23 Preston NE, 19 Stockport Co) 1966–88

† record for one club

CONSECUTIVE
401 Harold Bell (401 Tranmere R; 459 in all games) 1946–55

FA CUP
88 Ian Callaghan (79 Liverpool, 7 Swansea C, 2 Crewe Alex)

MOST SENIOR MATCHES
1390 Peter Shilton (1005 League, 86 FA Cup, 102 League Cup, 125 Internationals, 13 Under-23, 4 Football League XI, 20 European Cup, 7 Texaco Cup, 5 Simod Cup, 4 European Super Cup, 4 UEFA Cup, 3 Screen Sport Super Cup, 3 Zenith Data Systems Cup, 2 Autoglass Trophy, 2 Charity Shield, 2 Full Members Cup, 1 Anglo-Italian Cup, 1 Football League play-offs, 1 World Club Championship)

● MOST FA CUP FINAL GOALS

Ian Rush (Liverpool) 5: 1986(2), 1989(2), 1992(1)

● MOST LEAGUE MEDALS

Phil Neal (Liverpool) 8: 1976, 1977, 1979, 1980, 1982, 1983, 1984, 1986
Alan Hansen (Liverpool) 8: 1979, 1980, 1982, 1983, 1984, 1986, 1988, 1990

● OTHER RECORDS

YOUNGEST PLAYERS
FA Premier League   Andy Campbell, 16 years, 352 days, Middlesbrough v Sheffield W, 5.4.96.
FA Premier League scorer   Michael Owen, 17 years 144 days, Liverpool v Wimbledon, 6.5.97.
Football League   Albert Geldard, 15 years 158 days, Bradford Park Avenue v Millwall, Division 2, 16.9.29; and
Ken Roberts, 15 years 158 days, Wrexham v Bradford Park Avenue, Division 3N, 1.9.51
Football League scorer   Ronnie Dix, 15 years 180 days, Bristol Rovers v Norwich City, Division 3S, 3.3.28.
Division 1   Derek Forster, 15 years 185 days, Sunderland v Leicester City, 22.8.64.
Division 1 scorer   Jason Dozzell, 16 years 57 days as substitute Ipswich Town v Coventry City, 4.2.84
Division 1 hat-tricks   Alan Shearer, 17 years 240 days, Southampton v Arsenal, 9.4.88
   Jimmy Greaves, 17 years 10 months, Chelsea v Portsmouth, 25.12.57
FA Cup (any round)   Andy Awford, 15 years 88 days as substitute Worcester City v Boreham Wood, 3rd Qual. rd,
10.10.87
FA Cup proper   Scott Endersby, 15 years 288 days, Kettering v Tilbury, 1st rd, 26.11.77
FA Cup Final   James Prinsep, 17 years 245 days, Clapham Rovers v Old Etonians, 1879
FA Cup Final scorer   Norman Whiteside, 18 years 18 days, Manchester United v Brighton & Hove Albion, 1983
FA Cup Final captain   David Nish, 21 years 212 days, Leicester City v Manchester City, 1969
League Cup Final scorer   Norman Whiteside, 17 years 324 days, Manchester United v Liverpool, 1983
League Cup Final captain   Barry Venison, 20 years 7 months 8 days, Sunderland v Norwich City, 1985

OLDEST PLAYERS
Football League   Neil McBain, 52 years 4 months, New Brighton v Hartlepools United, Div 3N, 15.3.47 (McBain was
New Brighton's manager and had to play in an emergency)
Division 1   Stanley Matthews, 50 years 5 days, Stoke City v Fulham, 6.2.65

● SENDINGS-OFF

Season	371 (League alone)	1998–99
Day	15 (all League)	31 Oct 1998
	15 (3 League, 12 FA Cup*)	20 Nov 1982
	worst overall FA Cup total	
	26 (14 English, 12 Scottish)	16 Oct 1999
	(On 17 Oct 1999 a further 1 English made it 27 for the weekend)	
Weekend	15 (League alone)	22/23 Dec 1990
FA Cup Final	Kevin Moran, Manchester U v Everton	1985
Quickest	Walter Boyd, Swansea C v Darlington Div 3 as substitute in zero seconds	23 Nov 1999
Most in one game	Five: Chesterfield (2) v Plymouth Arg (3)	22 Feb 1997
	Five: Wigan Ath (1) v Bristol R (4)	2 Dec 1997
Most in one team	Wigan Ath (1) v Bristol R (4)	2 Dec 1997
	Hereford U (4) v Northampton T (0)	11 Nov 1992

● RECORD ATTENDANCES

FA Premier League	67,637	Manchester U v Coventry C, Old Trafford	14.4.2001
Football League	83,260	Manchester U v Arsenal, Maine Road	17.1.1948
Scottish League	118,567	Rangers v Celtic, Ibrox Stadium	2.1.1939
FA Cup Final	126,047*	Bolton W v West Ham U, Wembley	28.4.1923
European Cup	135,826	Celtic v Leeds U, semi-final at Hampden Park	15.4.1970
Scottish Cup	146,433	Celtic v Aberdeen, Hampden Park	24.4.37
World Cup	199,854†	Brazil v Uruguay, Maracana, Rio	16.7.50

* It has been estimated that as many as 70,000 more broke in without paying.
† 173,830 paid.

● MANAGERS

Most successful	Sir Alex Ferguson CBE	(Manchester U)	14 major trophies in 12 seasons: 7 Premier League, 4 FA Cup, 1 European Cup, 1 Cup-Winners' Cup, 1 League Cup.
		(Aberdeen)	1976–86 – 9 trophies: 3 League, 4 Scottish League, 1 League Cup, 1 Cup-Winners' Cup.
	Bob Paisley	(Liverpool)	1974–83 – 13 trophies: 6 League, 3 European Cup, 3 League Cup, 1 UEFA Cup,

● OCCURRENCES OF EACH SCORE

	From 1992/93:				Football League to 1991/92:						
Score	Premier	Div 1	Div 2	Div 3	Div 1	Div 2	Div 3	Div 4	Div 3(S)	Div 3(N)	Totals
0-0	332	431	420	389	2465	2665	1446	1438	997	803	11386
1-0	409	554	550	527	3469	3670	1991	1928	1343	1203	15644
0-1	275	369	389	383	2137	2166	1234	1178	730	711	9572
2-0	289	412	400	372	2912	3196	1638	1556	1267	1143	13184
1-1	468	636	648	626	4165	4206	2337	2253	1613	1384	18336
0-2	148	214	235	205	1198	1208	594	632	434	412	5280
3-0	144	209	210	191	1846	2008	833	964	827	795	8027
2-1	325	480	490	431	3275	3319	1701	1785	1241	1249	14297
1-2	212	270	323	320	2046	2028	1011	1041	762	699	8712
0-3	62	67	66	71	564	486	239	251	166	179	2151
4-0	58	65	73	62	945	1019	397	434	423	455	3931
3-1	151	236	225	201	2192	2062	981	948	855	844	8695
2-2	170	259	240	228	2024	1881	1008	946	768	718	8242
1-3	96	124	99	102	898	802	386	384	336	336	3563
0-4	26	20	20	17	171	133	65	72	63	57	644
5-0	35	28	28	20	403	484	139	162	235	237	1771
4-1	64	87	65	85	1108	1011	435	433	505	523	4316
3-2	74	122	114	116	1149	1073	571	484	455	451	4609
2-3	60	102	94	73	747	711	287	302	237	255	2868
1-4	22	32	36	20	288	303	120	111	104	106	1142
0-5	4	2	7	6	56	52	14	14	18	27	200
6-0	5	12	6	9	144	190	47	49	81	91	634
5-1	22	30	29	26	473	493	154	168	218	247	1860
4-2	49	44	32	38	622	555	248	250	256	255	2349
3-3	53	52	46	46	487	443	196	195	187	190	1895
2-4	17	24	16	27	285	225	85	86	83	104	952
1-5	6	5	6	7	113	87	33	33	40	38	368
0-6	2	1	2	0	13	14	6	5	5	5	53
7-0	2	2	3	2	57	76	17	12	42	38	251
6-1	7	7	4	4	210	220	55	47	117	115	786
5-2	7	15	14	16	300	294	93	112	123	144	1118
4-3	20	15	20	23	251	193	95	91	83	101	892
3-4	12	11	22	15	137	122	64	49	33	37	502
2-5	6	6	6	7	103	66	26	19	38	20	297
1-6	3	2	0	0	31	22	7	5	14	5	89
0-7	0	1	0	0	3	8	0	1	1	1	15
8-0	1	0	0	1	27	21	4	6	12	19	91
7-1	7	3	2	6	75	71	15	21	40	41	281
6-2	6	2	4	4	133	87	35	35	51	58	415
5-3	3	3	6	3	127	93	27	37	51	40	390
4-4	3	8	7	5	82	47	30	27	34	28	271
3-5	1	0	1	1	50	35	14	12	14	27	155
2-6	2	0	1	1	31	16	5	3	3	6	68
1-7	1	1	0	2	16	5	4	2	3	2	36
0-8	0	0	0	0	1	1	1	0	1	0	4
9-0	1	0	0	0	8	13	3	1	5	2	33
8-1	0	0	0	0	25	19	7	5	12	16	84

● **OCCURRENCES OF EACH SCORE –** *continued*

	From 1992/93:				Football League to 1991/92:						
Score	Premier	Div 1	Div 2	Div 3	Div 1	Div 2	Div 3	Div 4	Div 3(S)	Div 3(N)	Totals
7-2	2	0	1	1	37	44	10	4	18	24	141
6-3	1	1	1	2	45	32	18	10	20	25	155
5-4	1	1	1	3	37	29	12	7	8	17	116
4-5	1	0	2	0	21	15	7	4	4	11	65
3-6	0	1	0	0	17	8	5	2	5	5	43
2-7	0	0	1	0	6	4	2	1	3	0	17
1-8	1	0	1	1	1	0	0	1	1	1	7
0-9	0	0	0	0	0	0	0	0	0	1	1
10-0	0	0	0	0	5	5	1	1	2	1	15
9-1	0	0	0	0	8	10	1	1	4	6	30
8-2	0	0	0	0	14	9	1	2	5	7	38
7-3	0	0	0	1	17	14	3	1	5	14	55
6-4	0	0	1	0	10	14	2	2	8	7	44
5-5	0	1	0	0	15	7	0	0	4	4	31
4-6	0	1	1	0	5	5	3	1	1	1	18
3-7	0	0	0	0	6	2	1	0	2	3	14
2-8	0	0	0	0	1	1	1	0	2	2	7
1-9	0	0	0	1	2	0	0	0	0	0	3
0-10	0	0	0	0	0	1	0	0	0	0	1
11-0	0	0	0	0	0	0	0	1	0	0	1
10-1	0	0	0	0	4	3	0	2	0	2	11
9-2	0	0	0	0	7	5	1	1	5	5	24
8-3	0	0	0	0	5	5	1	1	3	3	18
7-4	0	0	0	1	9	3	0	1	3	2	19
6-5	0	0	0	0	7	0	0	0	1	0	8
5-6	0	0	0	0	2	1	0	0	2	2	7
4-7	0	0	0	0	2	2	0	1	1	1	7
3-8	0	0	0	0	1	0	0	0	0	0	1
12-0	0	0	0	0	2	4	0	0	1	1	8
11-1	0	0	0	0	0	2	0	0	1	4	7
10-2	0	0	0	0	0	2	0	0	4	0	6
9-3	0	0	0	0	3	4	0	0	1	1	9
8-4	0	0	0	0	2	2	0	0	0	1	5
7-5	0	0	0	0	3	0	1	0	0	1	5
6-6	0	0	0	0	1	1	0	0	0	0	2
5-7	0	0	0	0	1	1	0	0	0	0	2
3-9	0	0	0	0	0	1	0	0	0	0	1
13-0	0	0	0	0	0	1	0	0	0	1	2
12-1	0	0	0	0	0	0	0	0	0	1	1
11-2	0	0	0	0	1	0	0	0	0	1	2
10-3	0	0	0	0	2	1	0	0	0	0	3
9-4	0	0	0	0	0	0	0	0	2	0	2
8-5	0	0	0	0	1	1	0	0	0	1	3
7-6	0	0	0	0	0	1	0	0	0	0	1
12-2	0	0	0	0	1	0	0	0	0	0	1
11-3	0	0	0	0	0	1	0	0	0	0	1
10-4	0	0	0	0	1	0	0	0	0	0	1
13-4	0	0	0	0	0	0	0	0	0	1	1
	3666	**4968**	**4968**	**4698**	**38164**	**38140**	**18768**	**18631**	**15042**	**14374**	**161419**

● **COMMON RESULTS** – the season given is the final year of the season.

Season	Games	Score 0-0		Score 1-0		Score 0-1		Score 2-0		Score 1-1		Score 2-1		Other	
		No.	%	No.	%	No.	%	No.	%	No.	%	No.	%	No.	%
1889	132	2	1.52	5	3.79	1	0.76	6	4.55	6	4.55	16	12.12	96	72.73
1890	132	1	0.76	1	0.76	4	3.03	5	3.79	11	8.33	9	6.82	101	76.52
1891	132	4	3.03	9	6.82	5	3.79	7	5.30	7	5.30	8	6.06	92	69.70
1892	182	1	0.55	11	6.04	7	3.85	10	5.49	12	6.59	11	6.04	130	71.43
1893	372	6	1.61	22	5.91	15	4.03	25	6.72	23	6.18	26	6.99	255	68.55
1894	450	10	2.22	21	4.67	18	4.00	24	5.33	31	6.89	37	8.22	309	68.67
1895	480	9	1.88	25	5.21	11	2.29	25	5.21	25	5.21	44	9.17	341	71.04
1896	480	12	2.50	41	8.54	14	2.92	32	6.67	37	7.71	49	10.21	295	61.46
1897	480	22	4.58	30	6.25	22	4.58	36	7.50	39	8.13	31	6.46	300	62.50
1898	480	21	4.38	31	6.46	21	4.38	34	7.08	53	11.04	47	9.79	273	56.88
1899	612	32	5.23	53	8.66	29	4.74	57	9.31	64	10.46	48	7.84	329	53.76
1900	612	44	7.19	63	10.29	27	4.41	63	10.29	48	7.84	44	7.19	323	52.78
1901	612	51	8.33	78	12.75	44	7.19	59	9.64	60	9.80	58	9.48	262	42.81
1902	612	44	7.19	71	11.60	29	4.74	65	10.62	61	9.97	43	7.03	299	48.86
1903	612	32	5.23	58	9.48	43	7.03	57	9.31	48	7.84	57	9.31	317	51.80
1904	612	46	7.52	53	8.66	32	5.23	46	7.52	53	8.66	55	8.99	327	53.43
1905	612	44	7.19	54	8.82	37	6.05	62	10.13	45	7.35	57	9.31	313	51.14
1906	760	41	5.39	69	9.08	46	6.05	68	8.95	63	8.29	58	7.63	415	54.61
1907	760	42	5.53	74	9.74	40	5.26	74	9.74	67	8.82	70	9.21	393	51.71
1908	760	49	6.45	66	8.68	42	5.53	69	9.08	71	9.34	70	9.21	393	51.71
1909	760	44	5.79	76	10.00	44	5.79	73	9.61	85	11.18	62	8.16	376	49.47
1910	760	53	6.97	62	8.16	44	5.79	63	8.29	61	8.03	69	9.08	408	53.68
1911	760	49	6.45	90	11.84	47	6.18	77	10.13	87	11.45	64	8.42	346	45.53
1912	760	59	7.76	93	12.24	45	5.92	65	8.55	71	9.34	63	8.29	364	47.89
1913	760	57	7.50	62	8.16	41	5.39	71	9.34	83	10.92	58	7.63	388	51.05
1914	760	58	7.63	81	10.66	53	6.97	70	9.21	73	9.61	78	10.26	347	45.66
1915	760	52	6.84	81	10.66	37	4.87	57	7.50	73	9.61	64	8.42	396	52.11
1920	924	73	7.90	97	10.50	63	6.82	85	9.20	76	8.23	79	8.55	451	48.81
1921	1386	147	10.61	169	12.19	102	7.36	133	9.60	180	12.99	94	6.78	561	40.48
1922	1766	159	9.00	214	12.12	144	8.15	188	10.65	187	10.59	135	7.64	739	41.85
1923	1766	183	10.36	225	12.74	126	7.13	186	10.53	182	10.31	154	8.72	710	40.20
1924	1848	225	12.18	241	13.04	117	6.33	176	9.52	220	11.90	140	7.58	729	39.45
1925	1848	171	9.25	238	12.88	140	7.58	184	9.96	232	12.55	136	7.36	747	40.42
1926	1848	86	4.65	117	6.33	96	5.19	153	8.28	153	8.28	137	7.41	1106	59.85
1927	1848	77	4.17	137	7.41	77	4.17	127	6.87	158	8.55	144	7.79	1128	61.04
1928	1848	100	5.41	104	5.63	73	3.95	109	5.90	166	8.98	143	7.74	1153	62.39
1929	1848	73	3.95	137	7.41	66	3.57	109	5.90	174	9.42	153	8.28	1136	61.47
1930	1848	71	3.84	126	6.82	63	3.41	127	6.87	181	9.79	146	7.90	1134	61.36
1931	1848	84	4.55	123	6.66	57	3.08	131	7.09	165	8.93	137	7.41	1151	62.28
1932	1806	59	3.27	115	6.37	74	4.10	126	6.98	166	9.19	152	8.42	1114	61.68
1933	1848	80	4.33	131	7.09	69	3.73	141	7.63	188	10.17	155	8.39	1084	58.66
1934	1848	100	5.41	134	7.25	82	4.44	136	7.36	188	10.17	142	7.68	1066	57.68
1935	1848	91	4.92	123	6.66	74	4.00	142	7.68	181	9.79	159	8.60	1078	58.33
1936	1848	120	6.49	142	7.68	79	4.27	141	7.63	183	9.90	154	8.33	1029	55.68
1937	1848	90	4.87	145	7.85	65	3.52	146	7.90	202	10.93	159	8.60	1041	56.33
1938	1848	130	7.03	177	9.58	97	5.25	162	8.77	211	11.42	173	9.36	898	48.59
1939	1848	128	6.93	150	8.12	84	4.55	164	8.87	192	10.39	149	8.06	981	53.08
1947	1848	88	4.76	146	7.90	92	4.98	133	7.20	172	9.31	152	8.23	1065	57.63
1948	1848	136	7.36	176	9.52	116	6.28	132	7.14	222	12.01	155	8.39	911	49.30
1949	1848	155	8.39	179	9.69	106	5.74	157	8.50	222	12.01	174	9.42	855	46.27
1950	1848	143	7.74	201	10.88	113	6.11	159	8.60	227	12.28	162	8.77	843	45.62
1951	2028	114	5.62	203	10.01	103	5.08	158	7.79	227	11.19	187	9.22	1036	51.08

● COMMON RESULTS – *continued*

Season	Games	Score 0-0 No.	%	Score 1-0 No.	%	Score 0-1 No.	%	Score 2-0 No.	%	Score 1-1 No.	%	Score 2-1 No.	%	Other No.	%
1952	2028	99	4.88	186	9.17	96	4.73	159	7.84	221	10.90	181	8.93	1086	53.55
1953	2028	119	5.87	160	7.89	85	4.19	163	8.04	245	12.08	161	7.94	1095	53.99
1954	2028	106	5.23	155	7.64	111	5.47	151	7.45	222	10.95	193	9.52	1090	53.75
1955	2028	100	4.93	178	8.78	110	5.42	147	7.25	210	10.36	173	8.53	1110	54.73
1956	2028	100	4.93	136	6.71	104	5.13	153	7.54	190	9.37	185	9.12	1160	57.20
1957	2028	112	5.52	152	7.50	70	3.45	127	6.26	203	10.01	166	8.19	1198	59.07
1958	2028	102	5.03	143	7.05	73	3.60	125	6.16	208	10.26	181	8.93	1196	58.97
1959	2028	99	4.88	142	7.00	89	4.39	124	6.11	201	9.91	173	8.53	1200	59.17
1960	2028	84	4.14	152	7.50	114	5.62	149	7.35	214	10.55	175	8.63	1140	56.21
1961	2028	84	4.14	140	6.90	96	4.73	145	7.15	190	9.37	178	8.78	1195	58.93
1962	1982	100	5.05	134	6.76	86	4.34	153	7.72	193	9.74	181	9.13	1135	57.27
1963	2028	119	5.87	156	7.69	70	3.45	145	7.15	209	10.31	189	9.32	1140	56.21
1964	2028	113	5.57	173	8.53	97	4.78	155	7.64	221	10.90	150	7.40	1119	55.18
1965	2028	114	5.62	147	7.25	105	5.18	158	7.79	208	10.26	177	8.73	1119	55.18
1966	2028	107	5.28	198	9.76	128	6.31	168	8.28	222	10.95	179	8.83	1026	50.59
1967	2028	137	6.76	202	9.96	116	5.72	144	7.10	241	11.88	204	10.06	984	48.52
1968	2028	139	6.85	186	9.17	127	6.26	181	8.93	272	13.41	179	8.83	944	46.55
1969	2028	202	9.96	239	11.79	143	7.05	178	8.78	275	13.56	180	8.88	811	39.99
1970	2028	174	8.58	214	10.55	140	6.90	178	8.78	287	14.15	179	8.83	856	42.21
1971	2028	173	8.53	252	12.43	148	7.30	182	8.97	283	13.95	181	8.93	809	39.89
1972	2028	206	10.16	220	10.85	138	6.80	194	9.57	232	11.44	201	9.91	837	41.27
1973	2028	181	8.93	247	12.18	140	6.90	208	10.26	281	13.86	201	9.91	770	37.97
1974	2027	205	10.11	256	12.63	146	7.20	164	8.09	290	14.31	190	9.37	776	38.28
1975	2028	184	9.07	254	12.52	129	6.36	207	10.21	267	13.17	194	9.57	793	39.10
1976	2028	179	8.83	251	12.38	144	7.10	171	8.43	265	13.07	177	8.73	841	41.47
1977	2028	169	8.33	248	12.23	133	6.56	179	8.83	255	12.57	192	9.47	852	42.01
1978	2028	207	10.21	221	10.90	104	5.13	188	9.27	272	13.41	202	9.96	834	41.12
1979	2028	185	9.12	243	11.98	144	7.10	185	9.12	288	14.20	179	8.83	804	39.64
1980	2028	187	9.22	227	11.19	125	6.16	190	9.37	261	12.87	189	9.32	849	41.86
1981	2028	207	10.21	246	12.13	153	7.54	199	9.81	225	11.09	189	9.32	809	39.89
1982	2028	183	9.02	222	10.95	147	7.25	162	7.99	253	12.48	196	9.66	865	42.65
1983	2028	159	7.84	206	10.16	118	5.82	177	8.73	246	12.13	196	9.66	926	45.66
1984	2028	153	7.54	214	10.55	149	7.35	160	7.89	244	12.03	203	10.01	905	44.63
1985	2028	161	7.94	221	10.90	141	6.95	169	8.33	223	11.00	196	9.66	917	45.22
1986	2028	123	6.07	209	10.31	137	6.76	167	8.23	259	12.77	177	8.73	956	47.14
1987	2028	158	7.79	246	12.13	140	6.90	184	9.07	274	13.51	178	8.78	848	41.81
1988	2030	178	8.77	188	9.26	163	8.03	150	7.39	251	12.36	202	9.95	898	44.24
1989	2036	153	7.51	221	10.85	153	7.51	159	7.81	263	12.92	194	9.53	893	43.86
1990	2036	160	7.86	218	10.71	173	8.50	167	8.20	263	12.92	191	9.38	864	42.44
1991	2036	168	8.25	222	10.90	143	7.02	171	8.40	254	12.48	207	10.17	871	42.78
1992	2028	157	7.74	249	12.28	152	7.50	170	8.38	265	13.07	185	9.12	1017	50.15
1993	2028	158	7.79	195	9.62	152	7.50	175	8.63	252	12.43	178	8.78	1072	52.86
1994	2028	157	7.74	213	10.50	148	7.30	153	7.54	276	13.61	205	10.11	1054	51.97
1995	2028	189	9.32	215	10.60	157	7.74	173	8.53	246	12.13	180	8.88	1016	50.10
1996	2036	182	8.94	244	11.98	146	7.17	141	6.93	294	14.44	185	9.09	1040	51.08
1997	2036	191	9.38	234	11.49	147	7.22	189	9.28	267	13.11	190	9.33	987	48.48
1998	2036	192	9.43	246	12.08	152	7.47	146	7.17	257	12.62	215	10.56	987	48.48
1999	2036	178	8.74	230	11.30	173	8.50	168	8.25	253	12.43	179	8.79	855	41.99
2000	2036	164	8.06	236	11.59	178	8.74	153	7.51	260	12.77	211	10.36	834	40.96
2001	2036	161	7.91	227	11.15	163	8.01	175	8.60	273	13.41	183	8.99	854	41.94
	161419	11386	7.05	15644	9.69	9572	5.93	13184	8.17	18336	11.36	14297	8.86	80171	49.67

The season is the final year of the season.

● GOALS PER GAME

(from 1992–93)

Goals per game	Premier Games	Goals	Division 1 Games	Goals	Division 2 Games	Goals	Division 3 Games	Goals
0	332	0	431	0	420	0	389	0
1	684	684	923	923	939	939	910	910
2	905	1810	1262	2524	1283	2566	1203	2406
3	743	2229	1026	3078	1089	3267	1013	3039
4	501	2004	704	2816	657	2628	610	2440
5	259	1295	373	1865	344	1720	320	1600
6	154	924	168	1008	137	822	153	918
7	57	399	59	413	69	483	67	469
8	24	192	17	136	21	168	23	184
9	7	63	3	27	7	63	7	63
10	0	0	2	20	2	20	2	20
11	0	0	0	0	0	0	1	11
12	0	0	0	0	0	0	0	0
13	0	0	0	0	0	0	0	0
14	0	0	0	0	0	0	0	0
17	0	0	0	0	0	0	0	0
	3666	**9600**	**4968**	**12810**	**4968**	**12676**	**4698**	**12060**

(Football League to 1991–92)

Goals per game	Division 1 Games	Goals	Division 2 Games	Goals	Division 3 Games	Goals	Division 4 Games	Goals	Division 3(S) Games	Goals	Division 3(N) Games	Goals
0	2465	0	2665	0	1446	0	1438	0	997	0	803	0
1	5606	5606	5836	5836	3225	3225	3106	3106	2073	2073	1914	1914
2	8275	16550	8609	17218	4569	9138	4441	8882	3314	6628	2939	5878
3	7731	23193	7842	23526	3784	11352	4041	12123	2996	8988	2922	8766
4	6230	24920	5897	23588	2837	11348	2784	11136	2445	9780	2410	9640
5	3751	18755	3634	18170	1566	7830	1506	7530	1554	7770	1599	7995
6	2137	12822	2007	12042	769	4614	786	4716	870	5220	930	5580
7	1092	7644	1001	7007	357	2499	336	2352	451	3157	461	3227
8	542	4336	376	3008	135	1080	143	1144	209	1672	221	1768
9	197	1773	164	1476	64	576	35	315	76	684	102	918
10	83	830	68	680	13	130	8	80	33	330	45	450
11	37	407	19	209	2	22	7	77	15	165	15	165
12	12	144	17	204	1	12	0	0	7	84	8	96
13	4	52	4	52	0	0	0	0	2	26	4	52
14	2	28	1	14	0	0	0	0	0	0	0	0
17	0	0	0	0	0	0	0	0	0	0	1	17
	38164	**117060**	**38140**	**113030**	**18768**	**51826**	**18631**	**51461**	**15042**	**46577**	**14374**	**46466**

New Overall Totals (since 1992)

Games	18300
Goals	47146

Complete Overall Totals (since 1888–89)

Games	161419
Goals	473566

INTERNATIONAL RECORDS

● MOST GOALS IN AN INTERNATIONAL

Record/World Cup	Archie Thompson (Australia) 13 goals v American Samoa		11.4.2001
England	Malcolm Macdonald (Newcastle U) 5 goals v Cyprus, at Wembley		16.4.1975
	Willie Hall (Tottenham H) 5 goals v Ireland, at Old Trafford		16.11.1938
	Steve Bloomer (Derby Co) 5 goals v Wales, at Cardiff		16.3.1896
	Howard Vaughton (Aston Villa) 5 goals v Ireland, at Belfast		18.2.1882
Northern Ireland	Joe Bambrick (Linfield) 6 goals v Wales, at Belfast		1.2.1930
Wales	John Price (Wrexham) 4 goals v Ireland, at Wrexham		25.2.1882
	Mel Charles (Cardiff C) 4 goals v Ireland, at Cardiff		11.4.1962
	Ian Edwards (Chester) 4 goals v Malta, at Wrexham		25.10.1978

● MOST GOALS IN AN INTERNATIONAL CAREER

		Goals	Games
England	Bobby Charlton (Manchester U)	49	106
Scotland	Denis Law (Huddersfield T, Manchester C, Torino, Manchester U)	30	55
	Kenny Dalglish (Celtic, Liverpool)	30	102
Northern Ireland	Colin Clarke (Bournemouth, Southampton, QPR, Portsmouth)	13	38
Wales	Ian Rush (Liverpool, Juventus)	28	73
Republic of Ireland	Frank Stapleton (Arsenal, Manchester U, Ajax, Derby Co, Le Havre, Blackburn R)	20	70
	Niall Quinn (Arsenal, Manchester C, Sunderland)	20	79

● HIGHEST SCORES

Record/World Cup Match	Australia	31	American Samoa	0	2001
European Championship	Spain	12	Malta	1	1983
Olympic Games	Denmark	17	France	1	1908
	Germany	16	USSR	0	1912
Other International Match	Libya	21	Oman	0	1966
European Cup	Feyenoord	12	K R Reykjavik	2	1969
European Cup-Winners' Cup	Sporting Lisbon	16	Apoel Nicosia	1	1963
Fairs & UEFA Cups	Ajax	14	Red Boys	0	1984

● GOALSCORING RECORDS

World Cup Final	Geoff Hurst (England) 3 goals v West Germany	1966
World Cup Final tournament	Just Fontaine (France) 13 goals	1958
Career	Artur Friedenreich (Brazil) 1329 goals	1910–30
	Pele (Brazil) 1281 goals	*1956–78
	Franz 'Bimbo' Binder (Austria, Germany) 1006 goals	1930–50

Pele subsequently scored two goals in Testimonial matches making his total 1283.

● MOST CAPPED INTERNATIONALS IN BRITISH ISLES

England	Peter Shilton	125 appearances	1970–90
Northern Ireland	Pat Jennings	119 appearances	1964–86
Scotland	Kenny Dalglish	102 appearances	1971–86
Wales	Neville Southall	92 appearances	1982–97
Republic of Ireland	Steve Staunton	89 appearances	1998–01

FOOTBALL AWARDS 2001

FOOTBALLER OF THE YEAR

The Football Writers' Association Sir Stanley Matthews Trophy for the Footballer of the Year went to Teddy Sheringham of Manchester United and England.

THE PFA AWARDS 2001

Player of the Year: Teddy Sheringham, Manchester United.
Young Player of the Year: Steve Gerrard, Liverpool.
Merit Award: Jimmy Hill.

THE SCOTTISH FOOTBALL WRITERS' ASSOCIATION

Player of the Year: Henrik Larsson, Celtic.
Young Player of the Year: Stilian Petrov, Celtic.
Division One: David Bingham, Livingston.
Division Two: Scott McLean, Partick Thistle.
Division Three: Steve Hislop, East Stirling.

EUROPEAN FOOTBALLER OF THE YEAR 2000

Luis Figo, Real Madrid and Portugal.

WORLD PLAYER OF THE YEAR 2000

Zinedine Zidane, Juventus and France.

PLAYER OF THE CENTURY

Pele (Brazil)/Diego Maradona (Argentina).

CARLING PLAYER OF THE YEAR

Patrick Vieira, Arsenal and France.

CARLING MANAGER OF THE YEAR

George Burley, Ipswich Town.

Teddy Sheringham with his two awards: Football Writers' and PFA. (Colorsport)

MILESTONES DIARY 2000–2001

June 2000
BBC lose MOTD to ITV ... Houllier's 5-year deal ... Shearer shoots down Germans ... Bristol City appoint Wilson ... Turkey end England hopes ... Jewell lands Owls post ... Winterburn's Gunners goodbye ... Suker is a Hammer ... Holland pay the penalty

14 BBC suffer devastating blow being outbid for Premier League football highlights by ITV and bringing an end to *Match of the Day* as a regular Saturday night fixture. The corporation's offer of £41m a year is £20m less than independent television which wins the 3-season deal with £183m for 2 'showcase programmes' on Saturday and Sunday evenings. BskyB keeps the right to show 66 live matches on Sunday and Monday. Italy beat Belgium virtually ensuring their Euro 2000 quarter-final place.

15 Sweden and Turkey provide dreary scoreless draw in Eindhoven. Spurs give Villa permission to talk to David Ginola after agreeing £3m fee. Fulham coach Jean Tigana makes his first signing paying £2.1m for Metz striker Louis Saha.

16 Czech Republic bow out, in style, losing 2-1 to France, while Holland's assault breaks down Denmark's wall 3-0 in Rotterdam. Football League agree a new television deal worth more than £315m in 3-year link with Ondigital and ITV. Liverpool's Gerard Houllier signs new 5-year contract.

17 Shearer's stunning header in Charleroi ends 34 years of hurt as England beat Germany in a competitive fixture for the first time since 1966 World Cup. Portugal clinch added-time winner against Romania.

18 FA is stunned by UEFA's statement threatening to expel England if fans continue leaving a trail of destruction. Over 800 hooligans were arrested in Brussels and Charleroi, leaving Lennart Johansson to say: 'This cannot go on.' Spain beat Slovenia 2-1 and Norway lose 1-0 to Yugoslavia.

19 Italy, already qualified, field numerous reserves and beat Sweden 2-1. Nightmare display from Belgium's goalie gifts Turkey 2-1 win. Chelsea splash £4m for Bolton's Icelandic forward Eidur Gudjohnsen. Bradford order Paul Jewell to stay away on 'gardening leave' after the manager hands in a letter of resignation.

20 England's Euro 2000 hopes end when an 89th min pen, rashly conceded by Phil Neville, gives Romania a 3-2 win when Keegan's team only needed a draw to advance into the quarter-final against Italy. Defeat means skipper Shearer, cautioned and also a scorer, has played his last international after netting 30 times in 63 appearances. Germany head home whipped 3-0 by a Portuguese 'B' side.

21 In the wake of England's exit Keegan sums up: 'We had the spirit, endeavour and honesty but didn't quite pass the ball well enough.' Erick Ribbeck, 63, stands down as German coach. Holland beat World Champions France 3-2 in entertaining clash. Two stoppage-time goals snatch Spain a 4-3 win over Yugoslavia. Sheff Wed appoint former Bradford boss Paul Jewell as Owls manager on a 3-year contract. Sam Hammam makes verbal offer to buy 80 per cent of Cardiff City. Booked Shearer owns up to diving in the box 'for the sake of my country'.

22 Geoff Thompson, FA chairman, admits Kevin Keegan could benefit from some coaching help. Bradford fill their managerial vacancy by promoting Chris Hutchings. Nigel Winterburn ends his 13-year link with Arsenal by moving to W Ham. Man U will begin the defence of the title at home to Newcastle U. Fans at Chelsea are being charged £24.99 for a photo with the FA Cup.

23 England suffer final humiliation being demoted from UEFA's Euro 2000 Fair Play League along with Turkey, because of fans' poor behaviour. Man City's Shaun Goater is awarded the Freedom of his home town, Hamilton in Bermuda.

24 Irresistible Luis Figo leads Portugal into the semi-final after a 2-0 success over Turkey. Italy see off Romania 2-0. Beckham is the only English player picked in UEFA's top 50 at Euro 2000. Keegan's honesty to the end of England's spluttering campaign is reflected in his summing up: 'I've not set the world on fire with my management skills so far.'

25 Kluivert scores 4 as the Dutch dream team tear Yugoslavia to shreds in sensational fashion wining 6-1. Striker Raul misses a last min pen as Spain crash 2-1 to France.

26 Ex-Norwich boss Bruce Rioch replaces John Benson as Wigan manager. UEFA rule Kluivert's 3rd score for Holland against Yugoslavia was an own goal.

27 Bristol City confirm the appointment of manager Danny Wilson. Nigel Worthington is the assistant to Bryan Hamilton at Norwich. Mal Shotton gets a similar role at Bradford replacing Terry Yorath who heads to Sheff Wed.

28 France reach the final of Euro 2000 with an extra-time 2-1 match-settling pen from Zidane. The golden goal triggers disgraceful scenes from Portuguese players after match officials spot a handball against Xavier, resulting in the dismissal of Nuno Gomes and shortly afterwards the resignation of coach Coelho. Arsenal's Davor Suker joins W Ham on a free with his Croatian international colleague Mario Stanic completing a £5.6m move from Parma to Chelsea. Gillingham confirm popular Andy Hessenthaler as player/manager to succeed Peter Taylor. Former Dundee boss Jocky Scott takes charge at Notts Co.

29 Holland's dream of capturing the European Championship on home soil is shattered in Amsterdam, losing to 10-man Italy, after missing 2 pens in normal time and another 3 in the shoot-out following extra-time. It proves far too much for coach Frank Rijkaard who promptly resigns. The Italians will now meet France in Sunday's final. Celtic terminate the contract of Kenny Dalglish, their former director of football operations. Brighton are to remain at their Withdean Stadium for another 2 years.

30 A huge 11.8 million audience watches ITV's coverage of France's semi-final win over Portugal. Newcastle's Alessandro Pistone completes a £3m move to Everton.

July 2000
World Champs take Euro crown ... Lawrence leaves Luton ... Germany win WC 2006 vote ... Millennium Stadium is FA choice ... Lazio splash £35.7m ... Delaney's 3 reds ... Gazza joins Everton ... Barmby's Mersey switch ... Charlton's £4m buy ... Viduka gets clearance ... Anelka moves again ... Figo's World record move ... Akinbiyi joins Leicester ... Keane costs Inter £13m ... Au revoir to Deschamps ... Ginola joins Villa

1 Premiership refs are to arrange their own boot deals following sponsors Umbro withdrawing their support.

2 In Rotterdam's De Kuip Stadium, France, led by Chelsea's Deschamps, add the continental crown to their world title standing. In thrilling style their late recovery shocks Italy with Trezeguet's dramatic 2-1 (103 min golden goal) sealing the triumph. The Italians, leading through Delvecchio's 56th min effort, were on the brink of claiming the prize until Wiltord's 90th min equaliser set up a pulsating finale. Portugal's Xavier is banned from all European competitions for 9 months, colleagues Gomes (8 months) and Bento (6 months) while their association is fined £70,300.

3 Liverpool's Phil Babb and Tranmere's Alan Mahon join Sporting Lisbon. French super sub Robert Pires declines Real Madrid and joins Arsenal in a £6m transfer from Marseille.

4 Disappointed Italian coach Dino Zoff quits his post, the 6th Euro 2000 boss so to do. Lennie Lawrence leaves Luton after 5 years fighting to keep them in Div 2. Ex-Man City striker Uwe Rosler links with Southampton. Everton pay £2.5m to take Villa's Steve Watson. George Weah leaves Chelsea.

5 Newcastle pay £7m for the Dons' U-21 striker Carl Cort. Palace's future is assured following £10m take-over by Simon Jordan, 32, a mobile phone industry businessman. Joe Royle signs 4-year extension to his Man City contract.

6 Despite interventions by Nelson Mandela, the King of Belgium and amidst talk of death threats to one member of the FIFA committee, S Africa fail, by one vote, to take the 2006 World Cup to Africa. An extraordinary day in Zurich sees Germany get the 12-11 vote, with New Zealand's Charles Dempsey abstaining. After a campaign costing £10m England is eliminated after securing just two votes in the 2nd ballot. Derby pay £2m for Man U reserve defender Danny Higginbotham.

7 Louis Van Gaal takes the Dutch national post. Former Republic of Ireland skipper Andy Townsend, 37 this month, announces his retirement. Wembley is making 30,000 pieces of turf available free to clubs and charities. Bradford smash their club record signing David Hopkin from Leeds for £2.5m. Tottenham complete £5m signing of Ben Thatcher from the Dons. Misfit goalie Massimo Taibi ends his traumatic 10-month spell at Man U by joining Reggina for £2.5m.

8 Tony Banks, a key member of the failed England bid for 2006 World Cup, reveals that a trembling Charles Dempsey, who abstained from voting, was effectively handing the World Cup bid to Germany but had been put under intense pressure. S Africa plan to mount a legal challenge to FIFA's decision to award 2006 World Cup to the Germans. FA announce the Millennium Stadium in Cardiff is their preferred option for next season's FA Cup final.

9 Twelve people in a new capacity 60,000 stadium are crushed to death during a stampede 7 min from the end of S Africa's World Cup qualifier with Zimbabwe in Harare. In his first game in charge Martin O'Neill's Celtic win at Bray Wanderers.

10 Craig Hignett joins Blackburn from Barnsley for £2.25m. Brum splash a club record £2.25m on Fulham striker Geoff Horsfield. Luton appoint former crowd favourite Ricky Hill as boss.

11 Ex-Welsh skipper Barry Horne links with newcomers Kidderminster Harriers. Lazio pay a world record £35.7m fee to land Parma's Argentine striker Hernan Crespo. Chris Sutton completes his Scottish transfer record £6m switch from Chelsea to Celtic. Arsenal's new £6m signing Edu flies into Heathrow but is deported to Brazil having been found with a counterfeit passport.

12 Paul Rideout joins Tranmere after 3 years in China and the US. Stoke snap up experienced former England defender Tony Dorigo. Spurs lose appeal against a record £150,000 fine imposed after brawl at Leeds. A Labour MP's report brands Leeds U as having the worst trouble-makers in English football, three-times worse than the next offenders, Chelsea. League of Wales side Total Network Solutions, representing a village population of just 954, bring dash of romance to the 1st qualifying rd of Champions League, at Wrexham, twice pegging back Levadia of Estonia for 2-2 draw.

13 Everton accept around £2m for John Collins who moves on to Fulham as player/coach.

14 Don Hutchison leaves Everton for Sunderland in £2.5m deal.

15 Villa's England midfielder Lee Hendrie is lucky to be alive according to his father Paul, after the 23 year old wrote off his Porsche in an M6 crash.

16 Villa's Mark Delaney is sent-off for the 3rd time in 10 games in the 0-0 Inter-Toto tie at Czech Republic side Marila Pribram.

17 Boro's Gascoigne completes a surprise move to Everton getting a 2-year contract and vowing to repay Walter Smith, his former boss at Rangers. Injury-plagued Liverpool skipper Jamie Redknapp is out until Christmas requiring more knee surgery.

18 Villa's Mark Draper heads to Southampton for £1.25 fee. Nick Barmby makes a Merseyside switch after Everton finalise a £6m move to Liverpool, with both clubs quick to announce an amicable transaction. It is the first Goodison Park club sale to their near rivals in 40 years. Chelsea's Jody Morris is sentenced to 150 hours community service for attacking a stranger in a street brawl. Crocked Chelsea striker Pierluigi Casiraghi has his 10th knee operation, the last shot to try and salvage his career.

19 Everton complete £2.2m signing of Swede Niclas Alexandersson from Sheff Wed. Charlton snap up Bolton's Danish international, Claus Jensen, 23, for £4m club record fee. Newcastle off-load Silvio Maric to FC Porto for £2m.

20 Everton obtain work permit for Ghana midfielder Alex Nyarko who completes his £4.5m switch from Lens. Villa sign Fehmi Alpay Ozalan (known as Alfie Alpay) for £5.6m from Fenerbahce.

21 Leeds draw TSV 1860 Munich in Champions League qualifier. Gills chairman Paul Scally gets FA fine of £10,000 for breaching betting rules. Arsene Wenger says Arsenal will not be releasing Nigerian striker Kanu for the Olympics. Leeds new boy Mark Viduka gets his work permit following his £6m move from Celtic. Former Arsenal striker Anelka leaves Real Madrid to join Paris St Germain for £21.7m.

22 Merson is sent-off during Villa's win against Czech side Pribram, Sergei Rebrov, Spurs' £11m recruit gets off the mark in Finland.

23 W Ham's Joe Cole plays his first game since breaking his leg in April, on tour in Dublin. Fulham skipper Chris Coleman says new boss Tigana's team talks last 60 sec – at half time and at the end.

24 Luis Figo becomes the world's most expensive player completing his £37.4m move to Real Madrid, a decision greeted with dismay and anger in Barcelona. Millionaire printer Terry Brady, father of Brum's managing director Karren, takes control of Swindon in £2m take-over.

25 Tony Blair and Kevin Keegan unveil a new body, the Football Foundation, which aims to put £60m a year into football facilities in parks and schools. Liverpool and Granada Media announce £20m deal for delayed coverage

of Premiership matches, on the internet, on WAP-emblem mobile phones and through digital television. Christian Ziege has a secret get-out clause in his Boro contract which could enable the German to move to Liverpool in a £5.5m deal. Sunderland wrap up the £3.5m signing of Argentine defender Julio Arca. FA ask Brighton to explain their poor discipline record of last season, collecting 76 yellow cards and 9 reds.

26 Under tough new punishment guidelines FA threaten lengthy bans, with at least a 12-match ban, if players jostle or hold refs. WBA break club record paying £2m for Bristol City striker Jason Roberts. Rangers take a 4-1 lead into the away leg after beating Zalgiris Kaunas. A report by UK Sport shows 7 English footballers tested positive for using recreational drugs last season. Football League appoint David Burns as its new chief executive.

27 Ade Akinbiyi is unveiled as Leicester's new £5m striker from Wolves. Palace take experienced Neil Ruddock on a free from W Ham.

28 Inter swoop and pay £13m to Coventry for lively Irish striker Robbie Keane less than a year after Alex Ferguson said he was worth £500,000 and would play him only in the reserves. The Sky Blues double their money in less than 12 months with Inter shelling out £1m for each of Keane's 12 goals. Three weeks before the Premiership start Arsenal pair Overmars and Petit, as expected, join Barcelona for a £30m joint fee. Didier Deschamps who failed to settle at Chelsea moves to Valencia in £2.3m deal. Belgian Joos Val Gaeres moves to Celtic from Roda JC for £3.8m.

29 India end their 3-game English tour beating Bangladesh 1-0 at Filbert St, a match beamed to a 20 million audience across India. Ivano Bonetti, Dundee's new player/manager, is sent off 50 min into his debut at Motherwell.

30 Spurs' crowd favourite David Ginola joins Villa in a £3m move, adamant he was forced out from the London club. Chelsea's Dan Petrescu joins Bradford for £1m. Coventry's weekend takings top £15m selling Noel Whelan to Boro for £2.2m. Sutton scores for Celtic on his debut at Dundee U.

31 Cameroon's Joseph-Desire Job links with Boro in £3m move from Lens. Spurs off-load Allan Neilsen and Espen Baardsen to Watford for a combined £3m fee. Charlton strengthen their Premiership return paying £3.75 for Rangers striker Jonatan Johansson. Trafford council step up campaign to force supporters to sit down during Man U games or see the new 67,000 capacity reduced by up to 6,000.

August 2000

City get Weah ... Coppell quits the Palace ... Boksic heads to Boro ... Rotation for WC ... Sutton's red debut ... Sturrock out at Dundee U ... Bluebirds for Gould ... Bradford entice Carbone ... Wembley costs rise ... Sir Stanley Matthews award ... Chelsea lift Charity Shield ... £100,000 wage looms ... Refs go ex-directory ... Ferguson's Goodison return ... Blackburn's sad loss ... Vieira's red-opener ... Buckley out at Grimsby ... Ref alters view ... Gunners grab Wiltord ... McCarthy sends two home ... Boro's Maddren dies

1 Man City turn to George Weah, 33, giving the former AC Milan forward a 2-year deal and a reported £30,000 weekly wage. For the 4th time Steve Coppell relinquishes the manager's seat at Crystal Palace with Alan Smith replacing him.

2 Using the Hawthorns ground Villa exit the Inter-Toto Cup losing to Celta Vigo. Bradford's first European adventure ends, losing to Zenit St Petersburg. Darlington's David Hodgson quits after row with his chairman. Coventry splash £3m on Liverpool's David Thompson.

3 Alen Boksic completes £2.5m Lazio to Boro switch with chairman Steve Gibson ridiculing speculation the Croatian striker will pick up £63,000 a week in wages. In Amsterdam friendly Barcelona field new recruits, Overmars and Petit, in the 2-1 win over Arsenal. FIFA announce the World Cup will be rotated between 6 continents from 2010.

4 Solskjaer's goal clinches Man U win over Real Madrid in Munich's Opel Masters 2000. Sunderland's Quinn signs 3-year contract. S Africa drop legal fight against FIFA over failed World Cup 2006 bid.

5 Ajax end Arsenal's participation in Amsterdam tournament. New Man City signing Weah nets on debut at Stockport. Fabien Barthez makes Man U debut in defeat by Bayern Munich in Opel Masters clash. Celtic's Sutton red-carded against Motherwell.

6 Paul Sturrock quits after Dundee U's bad start. Robbie Mustoe's testimonial attracts 15,500 with 3 sent-off in the Boro defeat to Borussia Dortmund.

7 Keegan attacks the decision which means England's vital World Cup clash against Finland is being beamed from Helsinki to the UK on an obscure pay-per-view TV station, U>Direct, which is charging £10 to watch.

8 Former Wales boss Bobby Gould makes a surprise return to management by linking with Sam Hammam, Cardiff's new owner.

9 Man City finally agree £3.65m signing of Paulo Wanchope from W Ham. In Champions League, at home, Leeds beat 1860 Munich but have Olivier Dacourt, their record £7.2m summer signing, and Eirik Bakke red-carded. Rangers see-off robust Danes, Herfolge BK. Benito Carbone, a free agent, signs a 4-year contract at Bradford reportedly giving him £30,000 a week salary.

10 Indications show the cost of rebuilding Wembley has jumped to £600m, a staggering £125m increase in just 6 months, a rise which represents the entire cost of the less elaborate Cardiff Millennium Stadium. Former Real Madrid defender Christian Panucci leaves Inter and becomes Chelsea's 6th summer signing, in a £5m package deal with built-in conditions. Sir Bobby Charlton is first recipient of the Sir Stanley Matthews award for services to football, selected by a panel of judges from the FA, Premier League, Football League, PFA and Football Writers' Association.

11 Newcastle off-load Steve Howey to Man City for £2m.

12 As new season opens, League newcomers Kidderminster clinch an historic 2-0 home win over Torquay before a 5,122 gate. Fulham's new coach Tigana supervises a winning start over Crewe.

13 Wolves manager Colin Lee agrees a 1-year roll-on contract. Chelsea lift the Charity Shield beating Man U, who have Keane dismissed, for the 7th time. Sheff Wed goalie Kevin Pressman makes history being sent-off just 13 sec into the new season at Wolves.

14 Charlton's Alan Curbishley takes his summer spending past the £10m mark recruiting Iranian 68-times capped midfielder Karim Bagheri, 26, from Piroozi for £1m.

15 A Deloitte & Touche report says the average Premiership player now receives £350,000 per year compared to £37,000 each season in Div 3, and predicts the £100,000 per week barrier will be reached next season. Man City's Robert Taylor, 29, joins Wolves for £1.55m.

16   Heavily depleted N Ireland lose 2-1 to Yugoslavia in Belfast. Many lose their cool in the Mancheser derby testi-
      monial clash for Denis Irwin which attracts 45,000. Unsung Irwin, a £625,000 purchase in 1990, lasts just 36 min
      having been tackled hard by Weah. England will play their World Cup qualifier with Finland at Anfield. FA
      instruct all refs on the national list to ensure their home telephone number is ex-directory, while their home towns
      will not appear in Premiership or Football League programmes.

17   Newcastle's injury-prone striker Duncan Ferguson finally completes his £3.75m return to Everton, the club he left
      2 years ago. Harry Kewell puts pen to paper on a new 4-year Leeds contract worth £6m. Sheff Wed are one of the
      first clubs to suffer from a new FA discipline ruling, with a £5,000 fine for picking up 6 cards, 1 red and 5 yellow,
      against Wolves. Coventry pay £6.5m for Norwich's Wales striker Craig Bellamy.

18   On eve of Premiership start Glenn Hoddle warns Southampton players mere survival no longer takes priority.
      Gerard Houllier calls upon his players to finally end Liverpool's trophy failure. George Graham admits he could
      be forced out at Tottenham if he fails to meet supporters' expectations. Blackburn fans gather outside Ewood
      Park mourning the loss of Jersey-based generous benefactor and local man Jack Walker, 71, who dies of cancer.
      Bournemouth move Mel Machin upstairs putting long-serving ex-player Sean O'Driscoll in charge of team affairs.
      The new Premier League season kicking off tomorrow sees the start of an experiment designed to stop players
      mobbing refs; the so-called 10-yard rule comes into play.

19   Arsenal's Vieira is sent off, his 5th club dismissal, in the last min at Sunderland. Everton, who have not won a
      League match at Elland Road for 49 years, fail to break the trend, going under 2-0. Boro's Boksic nets twice and
      makes the third in win over Coventry. Mario Stanic grabs 2 on his Chelsea debut win over W Ham. Jorg Albertz,
      in his 200th competitive match for Rangers, strokes home a pen in win over Dunfermline watched by 47,452. The
      lowest crowd, 304, witnesses East Stirling and East Fife.

20   Champions Man U resume normal service with a comfy home win over Newcastle. Palace and QPR ends 1-1
      before 19,020 at Selhurst Park.

21   In bad-tempered affair Vieira is dismissed again, 3 days after his red card at Sunderland, as Arsenal chalk up
      win over a Liverpool side which has McAllister and Dietmar Hamann also sent off. Injuries force former
      England B defender John Beresford, currently with Southampton, to retire. Peter Kenyon, Man U's chief exec-
      utive, denies interest in proposals for a Euro Super League, pledging support for UEFA and the Champions
      League concept.

22   Grimsby sack Alan Buckley after 2 games, the first managerial casualty of the season. Newcomers Ipswich hold
      Man U 1-1 with the Old Trafford bosses claiming refs are 'prima donnas'. Inspirational Carbone spearheads
      Bradford's 2-0 success over Chelsea. In Worthington Cup Sheff Utd trounce Lincoln 6-1.

23   After re-viewing the video ref Graham Poll feels he was 'too severe' and rescinds the 2nd yellow card to
      Liverpool's Hamann meaning the German will not have to serve a ban. Coventry clinch their 1st away win in 22
      matches winning at Southampton. Ferguson's Everton homecoming is crowned by coming off the subs bench to
      score 2 late goals and help defeat Charlton. Barton sees red on his 350th League appearance but Newcastle clinch
      win over Derby before 51,000, their biggest gate for 24 years. Leeds advance to group stages of the Champions
      League beating 1860 Munich (agg 3-1). Rangers see off Herfolge (agg 6-0).

24   In UEFA Cup Dublin side Bohemians, down to 10 men before half-time, knock out Aberdeen (2-2) on away
      goals. Adams is new skipper and Campbell his deputy, but no surprises in Keegan's 24-man squad for Sept 2
      friendly with France in Paris. Celtic bring in John Robertson to link with close pal Martin O'Neill. Gunners agree
      'provisional terms' to land Bordeaux striker Sylvain Wiltord in £13m transfer. Despite failure at Euro 2000
      Keegan insists he will not walk out on the England job and warns that the FA will have to sack him if they want
      him out at Lancaster Gate.

25   Leeds draw Besiktas meaning a return to Turkey where 2 fans were murdered by Galatasaray supporters. Arsenal
      are grouped with Lazio, Sparta Prague and Shakhtar Donetsk. Man U must meet Anderlecht, PSV Eindhoven
      and Dynamo Kiev. In UEFA Cup Liverpool clash with Rapid Bucharest; Leicester against Red Star; Celtic tackle
      HJK Helsinki; Chelsea meet Swiss club St Gallen and Hearts travel to Stuttgart. A High Court decision means
      Boro reluctantly agree to let German defender Christian Ziege link with Liverpool for a £5.5m fee.

26   Arsenal bad boy Vieira bounces back after the worst week in his football life with 2 goals in the 5-3 win over
      Charlton. Southampton, 3 goals down to Liverpool and 18 min remaining, stage remarkable comeback to share
      the points. Sir Alex Ferguson informs BBC Radio 5 Live it is no longer welcome to interview him. Millwall finish
      with 9 men in the draw with Wycombe. Two red cards and 11 bookings mar Cheltenham's win over Torquay.
      Alloa concede 6 goals to Livingston.

27   Celtic, with 3 goals in the opening 11 min, celebrate a 6-2 rout of rivals Rangers.

28   Palace and Forest face £50,000 fines after mass brawl breaks out following the dismissal of goalie Beasant. When
      leading 2-1 at Torquay an excited Blackpool fan bares all and runs on the pitch, but in the 4 min 'streaking time'
      added the home side rally to snatch two scores and grab all 3 points. Icy relations between Tranmere and Bolton
      reaches a low point when Sam Allardyce refuses to use Prenton Park dressing-rooms, ordering his players,
      instead, to turn up in their kit 35 min before kick-off. His players were whisked away afterwards, still in dirty kit,
      without showering!

29   Republic boss Mick McCarthy sends home Mark Kennedy and Phil Babb after they appear in court following an
      incident in Dublin in the early hours. Former Boro defender Willie Maddren, 49, dies after a long battle against
      Motor Neurone disease. Birmingham's Trevor Francis believes there is a witch hunt to get him the sack, saying he
      knows who is behind it.

30   Rangers clinch the signing of Barcelona's Dutch international Ronald de Boer for £4.7m in time to meet tomor-
      row's Champions League deadline. W Ham receive notification of an FA charge to 4 players for harassing a ref –
      on Ceefax.

31   Sunderland pay a record £4.5m to snap up Chelsea's Emerson Thome, 8 months after the Brazilian defender had
      left Sheff Wed for £2.7m. England U-21's beat Germany 6-1 on Teesside. In Zurich FIFA and UEFA agree to
      scrap fees for players over 24 in the light of the European Commission declaring clubs could no longer demand a
      fee. Rangers pull out of £7m deal for John Hartson after the Dons target man fails a medical.

September 2000
England draw in France ... ROI shock Holland ... Blair backs transfer debate ... Geordies sit top ... Gunners' Granada link ... Horror break for Nilis ... Vialli out at Chelsea ... Ranieri in at the Bridge ... Lions sack management duo ... Leeds stun AC Milan ... Kelly is a Hatter ... Bould bows out ... McGhee's New Den return ... Collymore on list ... Di Matteo leg break

1   Celtic complete £2.7m signing of Villa's Alan Thompson. FA call in government help to eradicate unscrupulous business practices that tarnish the game's image, with prospective club owners or major shareholders needing approval.

2   Sub Owen rescues dispirited England with equaliser 4 min from time for a creditable 1-1 friendly draw in France. In World Cup action, attack-minded Irish shock the Dutch in Amsterdam taking a 2-goal lead through Robbie Keane and McAteer but wobble late on allowing Holland to snatch a draw. McCann's 81st min winner in Latvia saves blushes and nets Scotland full points. Sub Gray's strike gives N Ireland victory in Malta. Wales' qualifying hopes start badly suffering a one-sided 2-1 defeat in Belarus and having Craig Bellamy sent off.

3   WBA celebrate 100 years at the Hawthorns with a second successive victory beating Palace. Hammers boss Redknapp says his club has turned down another offer, of £15m, from Leeds for Rio Ferdinand.

4   Villa receive £5,200 fine for improper conduct during two legs of their Inter-Toto matches with Celta Vigo. Real Madrid president reports the club in grave financial crisis saying the European Champions are over £165m in debt. Leicester believe their UEFA tie with Red Star Belgrade could be switched to a neutral venue.

5   Man U, skippered by Sheringham and in front of 66,447, dish out a 6-0 hiding to Bradford. Man City surprise Leeds winning 2-1 at Elland Road. Everton's Gascoigne is upstaged at White Hart Lane as Rebrov, Spurs' £11m signing, nets twice. Sir Alex Ferguson reveals that he has received a lucrative job offer involving travel when he steps down in 2002.

6   Trailing to Chelsea's 2 goals Arsenal fight back for a point. Tony Blair launches attempt to enlist fellow European premiers behind a campaign to save the football transfer system. Shearer's 200th League goal in 375 games in service for Southampton, Blackburn and Newcastle ensures a Geordie win at Coventry putting Bobby Robson's revitalised team top of the Premiership, a spot last enjoyed under Keegan in Nov 1996. Owen hits a hat-trick for Liverpool. A Worthington Cup hat-trick of pens from David Dunn helps Blackburn to 6-1 drubbing of Rochdale. Chairman Derek Pavis sells his interest in Notts Co for £3.5m.

7   Chelsea's Vialli admits his side cannot handle pressure. Martin O'Neill wins the first Scottish Manager of the Month award. Leeds will be without Kewell for 3 months as he undergoes achilles tendon surgery. A £47m Granada deal taking a stake in Arsenal boosts plans for the proposed move to a nearby 60,000 all-seater stadium.

8   FA launch investigation into players' agent Dennis Roach. Henning Berg returns on loan to Blackburn after 3 years with Man U. UEFA bring forward Leicester's tie with Red Star Belgrade to 3 days before elections in Serbia. Newcastle's Robson is Carling Manager of the Month.

9   Wasteful Gunners, with £13m Wiltord making his debut, drop 2 points at Bradford. Leicester jump into 2nd spot. After 5-0 home thrashing embarassed boss Paul Jewell says Sheff Wed players are ashamed of themselves. Cambridge hit 6 past Rotherham. Villa's Luc Nilis suffers a shocking compound fracture of his left leg in a sickening 5th min collision with Ipswich goalie Richard Wright.

10   Leicester's Tony Cottee links with Norwich. Real Madrid tell out of favour Steve McManaman he can remain, if he wishes. Table-topping Fulham net 5 against Barnsley.

11   Sol Campbell's 1st goal in 18 months for Spurs sinks W Ham. Dublin side Bohemians lose at home to Kaiserslautern.

12   Chelsea sack manager Gianluca Vialli amid rumours of a dressing-room revolt. The popular Italian has spent £57m during his two and a half years in charge, winning Coca-Cola Cup, European Cup Winners Cup and the FA Cup. An outstanding individual Silvinho goal earns Arsenal a win at Sparta Prague. Rangers sweep away Sturm Graz 5-0. Manager Mark Lillis is relieved of duties at Halifax. Bury is put up for sale.

13   In a boys against men experience Leeds take a battering in Barcelona losing 4-0 before 85,000. Overcoming the fuel crisis 65,500 witness Man U run riot beating Anderlecht 5-1 with Cole's hat-trick, and 17th European score, smashing the goalscoring club record of Denis Law.

14   Vialli's name is shouted aloud as shaky Chelsea beat St Gallen in UEFA tie. Barmby nets Liverpool's winner at Rapid Bucharest.

15   Chelsea quickly install a replacement for Vialli giving the managerial hot seat at Stamford Bridge to relatively unknown Claudio Ranieri who has coached at Napoli, Fiorentina, Valencia and Atletico Madrid.

16   Sacked Vialli is greeted warmly whilst watching Harlequins at the Stoop. Man U stay top after totally controlling a 3-1 easy win at Everton. Ipswich chalk up a first away win at Leeds. Hibs go back top after beating Motherwell.

17   Ken Bates reveals in his national newspaper column that Vialli had to go because as chairman he could not allow the Chelsea club to decay and disintegrate. Millwall's joint-managers Stevens and McLeary are dismissed with coach Ray Harford taking temporary charge. The Potteries derby ends 1-1.

18   Stamford Bridge personnel changes as Ranieri brings in an assistant coach, fitness instructor and goalkeeping coach.

19   Resilient Leeds overcome AC Milan after Brazilian goalie Dida makes a hash of collecting Bowyer's 89th min shot. Man U get a valuable point in Ukraine against Dynamo Kiev. In Worthington Cup Boro are jeered off by their lowest gate, 5,244 after 2 late scores secure a 2-1 win over Maccesfield. Just 1,941, the lowest since leaving Plough Lane 9 years ago, witness the Dons end scoreless against Wigan.

20   Two goals in the last 5 min from Keown rescue Arsenal with win at Shakhtar Donetsk. Graham Kelly, ex-FA chief executive, joins the Luton board. Jaap Stam's achilles tendon injury may put him out for 3 months. Brighton's Alan Cork is to link with Cardiff as Bobby Gould's assistant.

21   England will wear red shirts against Germany in Wembley's final match, a World Cup qualifier, next month. Bohemians pull off a shock 1-0 UEFA Cup 2nd leg win in Kaiserslautern but go out on aggregate 3-2.

22   Colchester's Lomano Lua Lua, 19, completes his £2.25m move to Newcastle. Dennis Bergkamp claims he is ready to quit Highbury if he continues to remain on the subs bench.

23   Derby's 10 men hold Leeds 1-1. W Ham finally break their Premiership duck winning 3-0 at Coventry. Yorke, not selected, storms out of Old Trafford, as Man U conjure a draw after being 3-1 down to Chelsea. James Thomas takes just 53 sec to put Blackburn in front against Bolton.

24   Wolves beat Norwich 4-0. Prospective coaches will soon have to obtain a coaching licence before being allowed to manage top clubs in England. Sunderland's ex-Arsenal stalwart, Steve Bould, 37, is to retire on medical advice.

25   Mark McGhee, former boss at Leicester and Wolves, gets the Millwall job with a 2-year contract claiming he was frozen out of the game for 2 years.

26   Leeds run inept Besiktas ragged at home winning 6-0. Man U gamble on resting 6 players but the team selection backfires losing 3-1 at PSV Eindhoven. Leicester boss Peter Taylor puts Collymore on the list after the striker reportedly was asking for £40,000 weekly wages. Stoke claim the 1st Premiership scalp, on away goals, in the Worthington Cup defeat of Charlton. Ref Andy Hill orders Millwall to send an injured player back on as they were reduced to 7 men in a bizarre finish at Ipswich. With 2 players already red-carded and having used their subs, Christopher Kinet and Tim Cahill limped off 2 min from the end of extra-time.

27   Arsenal embarrass Champions League favourites Lazio thanks to a Ljungberg double. But Rangers go under 3-2 at Galatasaray. Man U agree a staggering £300m sponsorship deal with sportswear giant Nike. Preston field Andy Lonergan, 16, in goal for the cup tie at Coventry.

28   In UEFA Cup action Chelsea's Di Matteo breaks his left leg as their adventure embarassingly ends with 2-0 defeat to minnows St Gallen. Leicester go out to Red Star. Liverpool advance against Rapid Bucharest, and Celtic scramble through against HJK Helsinki. Southend sack boss Alan Little.

29   Ahead of Sunday's Arsenal v Man U clash, Sir Alex Ferguson warns ref Graham Barber not to be intimidated by the pressure-cooker Highbury atmosphere. Reading boss Alan Pardew gets new 3-year deal.

30   Patched-up Leeds put down Spurs 4-3. Pre-match announcement that Saints' boss Glenn Hoddle has a contract extension until July 2002 is followed by a defeat to Boro. A 'bride and groom' take part in a stunt at the interval in the Charlton v Coventry game promoting the Valley's new licence to conduct marriages. Charlton's Jonatan Johansson nets his 7th goal in 8 games since joining from the reserves at Rangers.

October 2000

Shrimpers catch Webb again ... Bluebirds exit for Ayres ... Halifax appoint Bracewell ... Hodges out at Pilgrims ... Keegan's shock resignation ... Wilko's England draw in Finland ... Pompey push out Pulis ... McLean punches reporter ... Bruce leaves Huddersfield ... Cork in charge at Cardiff ... City and Weah part ... Vieira's racial abuse ... Venables is non-runner ... Kinnear links with Oxford ... Taylor is temporary boss ... Blackburn land Hughes ... Todd quits Robins ... Bantams take Collymore ... FA name Eriksson as boss ... Sturrock in at Argyle

1   Man U slump to their 1st League defeat since February losing 1-0 at Arsenal. Chelsea beat Liverpool 3-0 with Ranieri claiming his side 'electric' in the opening half.

2   David Webb who left Yeovil over the weekend returns to manage Southend for the 3rd time. Oxford U boss Denis Smith resigns. Cardiff sack head coach Billy Ayres after twice demoting him under the club's new ownership.

3   Sacked Fulham boss Paul Bracewell is back in management with bottom club Halifax. The threat of a complete restructuring of the system has a calming influence in transfers with just £8.5m spent in September compared to £21m a year earlier and £27m in 1998. Mike Ford gets the caretaker role at Oxford.

4   At Derby's AGM Jim Smith says he pulled out of signing Jonatan Johansson, now with Charlton, because he would not pay an extra £250,000 to agent Dennis Roach who denies the claim. Plymouth sack manager Kevin Hodges. Former Argentine striker Claudio Caniggia, 33, joins Dundee.

5   Glentoran suspend N Ireland striker Rory Hamill until further notice after a positive drug test following a UEFA tie against Lillestrom.

6   Rochdale's Tony Ford plays at Kidderminster, the 100th League ground of his 25-year career. John Toshack takes the post at struggling St Etienne. Ahead of tomorrow's World Cup clash England and Germany U-21's finish 1-1 at Pride Park. Upbeat Keegan pleads for fans to cheer on England to victory for the final match in Wembley's 77-year history.

7   Kevin Keegan stuns England by quitting his 19-month reign as coach minutes after his side loses depressingly 1-0 to Germany in World Cup qualifier. Leaving the pitch to a chorus of boos he is immediately locked in discussion with FA officials then, close to tears, Keegan, 49, admits: 'I have no complaints. I have not been quite good enough. I blame no one but myself.' Howard Wilkinson is put in charge for Wednesday's tie in Finland. Scotland win in San Marino. Wales are held 1-1 at home by Norway. N Ireland hold Denmark 1-1 at Windsor Park. Ireland snatch a vital 1-1 away point in Portugal.

8   England's squad, still reeling following Keegan's resignation, arrive at their Bucks HQ with stand-in boss Wilkinson appealing to everyone to rally round him in preparing for Finland. Brian Kidd is brought into the England coaching set-up. Bobby Robson admits that, if asked, he could not refuse an offer to assist England. According to FA's Adam Crozier, an overseas coach to manage England is not to be ruled out. Terry Venables, Arsene Wenger, Roy Hodgson, Gerard Houllier, Bobby Robson and Peter Taylor are mooted as likely contenders.

9   Martin Keown is England's new captain taking the armband from absent Arsenal colleague Adams. Defender Gareth Southgate says he was as surprised as anyone at being pushed into midfield, by Keegan, against Germany.

10   FA form a 6-man think-tank to help select a new national coach who also must groom a successor. Leeds striker Alan Smith sees red as England and Finland U-21's draw. Gunners' boss Wenger is hit with 12-match touchline ban.

11   With Wilkinson playing striker Emile Heskey on the left wing England's 0-0 World Cup qualifier in Finland is anything but the start of a bright new age. Goalie Niemi should have gone in 6 min for cynically upending Sheringham, while Parlour's 87th min shot which struck the cross-bar crossed the line, but was disallowed. Wales draw in Poland, Scotland do well to get a point in Croatia. N Ireland lose out in the last min in Iceland. The Republic's good start continues beating Estonia. Portsmouth sack Tony Pulis 24 hours after receiving the 'full support' of the chairman, with Steve Claridge getting the player/manager role.

12   UEFA fine Beckham £4,000 for spitting at ref Markus Merk, and Chelsea's Hasselbaink and Leboeuf each pick up 2-match bans. Coach Wilkinson calls for long-term policy suggesting it would be best to forget 2002 World Cup and instead target 2006.

13   FA take steps to prevent any more England games being shown on obscure pay TV channels. Wenger admits interest in the England job but only when his Arsenal contract expires in June 2002.

14   Kilbane and Le Saux sent-off in Sunderland's win over Chelsea. Tottenham fans call for Graham's head following 2-1 defeat at Coventry. Man U reclaim top spot from Leicester winning comfortably at Filbert Street. The Dons and Gills share 8 goals. Dundee U chairman Jim McLean resigns after allegedly punching a BBC reporter in the face during an after-match interview.

15   Liverpool run riot at Derby with a Heskey hat-trick in 4-0 win. Unbeaten Fulham go top beating Blackburn and requiring 4 more victories for a record 14 successive League wins at the start to a season.

16   Neil Lennon receives £4,000 fine after 4 of his 75 tickets for Leicester's Worthington Cup Final fell into the hands of Tottenham supporters. Huddersfield boss Steve Bruce is sacked with caretaker Lou Macari stepping in. Alan Cork is the new boss at Cardiff replacing Bobby Gould whilst Newcastle win the Tees-Tyne derby. George Weah tells Man City he is off after lasting just 11 weeks on a £23,000 weekly wage.

17   An equaliser 2 min from time by Pires, at Lazio, ensures Arsenal's Champions League qualification. Gunners goalie John Lukic, 40 in December, becomes the oldest to play in the Champions League. Collymore is under investigation by Leicester following an alleged dressing-room fracas with colleague Trevor Benjamin.

18   Befitting their 100th Champions League Cup appearance, Man U's late goal seals 3-1 triumph over PSV Eindhoven. Leeds hold on for a precious point in scoreless tie at Besiktas. Cable company NTL withdraw from a proposed £328m 3-year deal to televise live Premiership matches. Arsenal's Vieira accuses Lazio's Mihajlovic of calling him 'a black monkey' during their clash in Rome. Man City pay £3m for Everton defender Richard Dunne.

19   After 4-hour FA discussion on likely contenders the hint emerges that neither Venables or Wilkinson will figure for the England post. Former Dons boss Joe Kinnear joins struggling Oxford U as a consultant.

20   UEFA give 3-game ban to Arsenal's Grimandi.

21   Newcastle block any prospect of Bobby Robson returning to England management in a part-time capacity. Jimmy Floyd Hasselbaink scores 4 in Chelsea's 6-1 thrashing of Coventry. Man U and Arsenal are level on 21 Premiership points. Fulham, Walsall and Chesterfield top their divisions. Ugo Ehiogu, Boro's £8m recent buy from Villa, limps off 5 min into his debut at Charlton.

22   Peter Taylor is England's new caretaker coach replacing Howard Wilkinson who ironically forced Taylor's departure from the U-21 set-up last year. Assisted by Man U's Steve McClaren, Taylor will be in charge for the Nov 15 friendly with Italy. But Arsene Wenger, Sven Goran Eriksson and Roy Hodgson make up the FA's shortlist to eventually replace Kevin Keegan. Hibs beat Edinburgh rivals Hearts 6-2 to stay second.

23   Bradford's chairman warns manager Chris Hutchings results must improve immediately. New England caretaker boss Taylor says he will include some youngsters in his first line-up.

24   Wenger states that he will honour his Highbury contract expiring in 2002 ruling him out of England consideration. Man U's immediate future in Europe is in jeopardy after 2-1 defeat at Anderlecht. Rivaldo's stoppage-time strike for Barcelona cruelly denies Leeds a sensational victory in a rip-roaring tie. Fulham suffer their 1st defeat, at home to Preston. Wales national boss Mark Hughes links with Blackburn who take over his Everton 18-month contract on a reported £20,000 a week wage.

25   Colin Todd suddenly quits Swindon to become assistant to Derby's Jim Smith. Arsenal win comfortably 4-2 against Sparta Prague securing top spot in their group, and ensuring the benefit of being seeded. Rangers' task looks difficult after losing at Sturm Graz.

26   At Anfield Liverpool make heavy weather of beating Slovan Liberec playing only their 3rd European tie. Larsson's pen gives Celtic a draw in Bordeaux.

27   Gunners' boss Wenger appeals against his FA 12-match touchline ban. PFA chief Gordon Taylor has a bust-up with FIFA's Sepp Blatter over the transfer system.

28   Before the biggest crowd in Premiership history, 67,581, Man U hit 5 past Southampton. Closest rivals Arsenal repeat the same score over Man City. Rangers lose 3-0 at home to Kilmarnock. In FA Cup 4th qualifying rd Barrow put 6 past Whitley Bay and Rushden & Diamonds knock out Grantham 5-4.

29   Liverpool overcome their Merseyside rivals Everton 3-1. New signing Collymore hits a spectacular Bradford goal in the drawn Yorkshire clash with Leeds. Motherwell hold Celtic 3-3. The FAI is to investigate claims by 88-times capped Tony Cascarino, in his book, that he may not have been qualified to play for the Republic after discovering recently his mother was adopted.

30   Highly regarded Sven Goran Eriksson agrees to become England's new national coach, from July 1, intending first of all to see out his Lazio contract. The Swedish-born boss, 52, the FA's first foreign manager, has lifted championships in Sweden, Portugal and Italy, and is to be engaged on a 5-year deal worth a reported £15m salary.

31   In front of 3,666, the poorly supported Dons knock-out Premiership strugglers Boro from the Worthington Cup. Man U goalie Raimond van der Gouw is sent-off at Watford. Spurs go out at home to Birmingham. Tranmere put out Leeds. Paul Sturrock gets the Plymouth post. Howard Kendall accepts, then rejects, the coaching post at Omonia Nicosia.

November 2000

Cottee's Barnet post ... Huddersfield name Macari ... Oxford opt for Kemp ... Armstrong's sudden death ... Bradford axe Hutchings ... Swindon appoint King ... Earle bows out ... Keane slams quiet OT ... Kinsella tops poll ... Hatters part with Hill ... Jefferies is Bantams boss ... Canvey cup heroics ... Noades sacks himself ... Ferdinand's £18m fee agreed ... Flo's Ibrox move ... Iran's scoring record ... Souness has US operation ... Chelsea dismiss coaches ... Shack dies ... Stoke's embarassing defeat ... FL internet link

1   Tony Cottee takes charge at Barnet. Lou Macari is new boss at Huddersfield. David Kemp takes over at struggling Oxford U. Watford's Graham Taylor, Ronnie Moore (Rotherham) and Steve McMahon of Blackpool are Managers of the Month. Arsenal mourn the sudden loss of popular ex-winger George Armstrong, 56, who made 621 appearances. Palace win League Cup tie at Leicester. Liverpool book 4th rd spot beating Chelsea. Owls overcome Blades in 110th Sheffield derby.

2   Graham says he intends staying at Spurs despite growing protests from some supporters. Leicester unveil plans for £35m 32,000 all-seater stadium close to Filbert Street.

3   Boro chairman Steve Gibson promises his full backing to beleaguered boss Robson who is considering bringing in Terry Venables to help stop the slump.

4   Viduka hits 4 in 4-3 Leeds win over Liverpool. Kenny Miller nets 5 as Rangers put 7 past S Mirren. Preston finish with 9 men at Forest.

5   Merson's 90th min long-range winner gives Villa success at Everton. Celtic maintain their dominance and unbeaten record, winning at Kilmarnock. Wolves owner Sir Jack Hayward sparks a row by telling the club to get rid of a Mercedes because it was built by 'evil' Germans.

6   Heading to Donetsk Arsenal stock up on bed linen, towels, food and water. They also take a chef plus 2 people to clean the hotel kitchen reported 'thick with grease' by an advance party rep who looked over the base which is in the heart of a Ukraine mining area. Bradford axe Chris Hutchings after 12 League games in charge, handing the temporary role to midfielder Stuart McCall. Andy King takes the manager's job at Swindon.

7   Arsenal crash to an embarassing 3-0 defeat to Donetsk, a tie which means nothing in terms of qualification. Rangers once again fail to realise their dream of reaching the 2nd stage drawing 2-2 with Monaco at Ibrox. Gunners unveil a computer-generated image of their proposed new 60,000 all-seater stadium at nearby Ashburton Grove. Long-serving Dons midfielder Robbie Earle, 35, is forced to call it a day.

8   Leeds progress to Champions League 2nd stage after surviving a 1st half onslaught by AC Milan. They pinch a lead through Matteo but concede a 67th min equaliser. At home to Dynamo Kiev Man U succumb to nerves but advance thanks to Sheringham's 18th min score. However, they might have gone out when Old Trafford held its breath seeing sub Demetradze miss the simplest of tap-ins close to the finish. Hearts confirm manager Jim Jefferies' departure by mutual consent. Danish striker Mikkel Beck, now with Lille, claims gay slurs forced him out of Boro.

9   Liverpool go behind at Slovan Liberec but recover to win 3-2 and advance on aggregate. Peter Taylor's first England squad to face Italy includes a quartet yet to be blooded, Michael Ball, Seth Johnson, Paul Robinson and Alan Smith. Bordeaux win 2-1 at Parkhead and eliminate Celtic from UEFA Cup. Wolves report a £77,000 loss on each Molineux game, with attendances falling from the break-even of 25,000 to nearly 18,000. Roy Keane blames Old Trafford's poor vocal support on corporate-type visitors more concerned with entertaining, labelling them the 'drinks and prawn sandwich' brigade.

10 In UEFA Cup draw, Liverpool get Greek champions Olympiakos. Rangers entertain Kaiserslautern. In Champions League group stage, Man U must meet Sturm Graz, Valencia and Panathinaikos. Leeds are grouped with Real Madrid, Anderlecht and Lazio. Arsenal will tackle Bayern Munich, Olympique Lyon and Spartak Moscow.

11 PFA open the door to admit women for the 1st time in their 93-year history by accepting 14 full-time professionals of Fulham Ladies. Lowly Derby reveal battling qualities by grabbing a point at Highbury. Leicester remain 3rd after 1-1 with Newcastle. In-form Sheringham nets his 13th in Man U win over Boro. Barnet put 7 past Blackpool. FA offer to pay Keegan's costs in legal proceedings with a national newspaper alleging the England boss acted as 'bookmaker' in heavy-duty gambling during Euro 2000.

12 Chelsea's late equaliser denies a win to a Leeds team missing 9 regulars. Liverpool beat Coventry 4-1. Celtic extend their unbeaten run to 15 matches against St Johnstone. Chairman Alan Sugar tells David Sullivan that he will have to come up with £70m to take control at Spurs.

13 Charlton's Mark Kinsella celebrates his selection as Ireland Player of the Year by being named captain for tomorrow's friendly against Finland. Four pull out of Taylor's 1st England panel to face Italy in Turin where Beckham will lead the side.

14 England's U-21 game with Italy in Monza is abandoned after 10 min because of fog – but the 11 who started will all receive caps. Long-serving Colin Hendry, 2 short of his 50th appearance, is dropped for the 1st time by Scotland. Man U have 6 nominated for European Footballer of the Year award: Barthez, Keane, Giggs, Stam, Scholes and Beckham, runner-up last year.

15 Before sparsely populated stands at the Stadio Delle Alpi, England give an overall encouraging performance despite losing 1-0 to Italy. Scotland are humiliated 2-0 at Hampden Park by a lively Australian side. Republic of Ireland defeat Finland 3-0 in low-key friendly. Ricky Hill's short term as Luton boss ends having won just 2 of their 17 League matches.

16 Luton quickly announce a new boss, former player Lil Fuccillo. Premiership bookings go down 25 per cent on this stage last season, totalling 397 with 20 dismissals. England demand UEFA launch an investigation into racism in Italian football after Emile Heskey's abusive treatment from the Turin crowd. Notts County must dig up their pitch because it has been contaminated by recent flash flooding leaving bacteria on the surface.

17 Former Hearts boss Jim Jefferies agrees in principle to take over as manager at Bradford. Hoddle admits he attempted to lure sacked Chelsea coach Gianluca Vialli to Southampton, as a Premiership player.

18 With Sir Alex Ferguson in S Africa attending his son's wedding, Beckham's 2nd min free kick goal at Maine Road seals the win in the lively, long-awaited Manchester clash. Robson calls a crisis meeting after Boro lose 3-0 at home to Leicester, their 7th consecutive defeat. Shearer's late pen is saved as Newcastle lose 2-1 to Sunderland at St James' Park. In FA Cup Yeovil take top honours thrashing Colchester 5-1, the club's 17th League scalp. Kingstonian dump out near neighbours Brentford.

19 Fowler ends his 11-month goal drought but Liverpool lose 2-1 at Spurs. Trailing 4-2 with 1 min remaining Canvey Island snatch stoppage-time draw to earn a replay at Port Vale.

20 Surprise team Ipswich climb to 5th winning at Coventry. Brentford's chairman Ron Noades dismisses himself from the role of manager following the FA Cup exit to non-League Kingstonian.

21 Scholes nets twice to give Man U 3-1 win over Panathinaikos providing the perfect start to the 2nd phase of the Champions League. Sheff Utd manager Neil Warnock receives 3-match touchline ban and £2,000 fine. Marc McGregor's late FA Cup strike, in dreadful conditions at Nuneaton, puts out Stoke. Leeds and W Ham agree an £18m fee for defender Rio Ferdinand. Tore Andre Flo officially requests a transfer from Chelsea clearing the way for an expected £12m move to Rangers. Jack Dyson, a member of Man City's 1956 FA Cup-winning team, dies aged 66.

22 Leeds survive for an hour at Elland Road but Real Madrid's classy skills eventually tell, winning 2-0. On the coldest day in Moscow, minus 15, Arsenal suffer their heaviest away defeat in Europe losing 4-0 to Spartak. In a local newspaper poll 89 per cent of Boro fans say Robson should quit. W Ham reject £8m Chelsea offer for Frederic Kanoute.

23 A 2-2 draw against Olympiakos in Athens with priceless goals from Barmby and Gerrard sets Liverpool up nicely for the UEFA return leg. Chelsea's Flo completes his record-breaking £12m switch to Rangers signing a 4 and a half year contract, and insisting he was given no choice following Ranieri's arrival. Maradona accuses FIFA of excluding him from the Player of the Century award. Leicester reject £4m Celtic bid for Neil Lennon. Blackburn snap up Sheffield U's Marcus Bent for £2.1m. Alick Jeffrey, Doncaster's youngest ever player at 15, dies aged 61.

24   In an Asian Zone World Cup qualifier Iran set a scoring record with a 19-0 victory over a Guam side making their debut in the competition. Arsenal's Wenger sparks a row accusing clubs of lying down when playing Man U.

25   Eight years after a triple by-pass, Graeme Souness reveals he flew to the US 5 weeks ago for a 3-hour operation at a clinic in Ohio after specialists discovered one of his arteries leading to his heart was still blocked. A Marcus Stewart double helps put Ipswich into the top 3 for the 1st time since the days under Bobby Robson.

26   In compelling scrap, Leeds beat an Arsenal side collecting 7 bookings. Newcastle's industry secures 2-1 win over Liverpool. New signing Flo scores as Rangers get revenge on Celtic with 5-1 Ibrox win. Guam take another trouncing, this time 16-0 by Tajikistan.

27   The poor state of the pitch at Cardiff's Millennium Stadium could jeopardise plans to hold the FA Cup Final, Worthington Cup Final and the Charity Shield at the arena. Everton supporters give the green light to pursue plans to move to Merseyside's Kings Dock, a decision which could end the club's 108-year association with Goodison Park. Sven Goran Eriksson and Peter Taylor meet up in Rome for the 1st time. Celtic's Alan Stubbs is back in hospital after suffering a relapse in his bid to beat cancer.

28   Chelsea's Ranieri axes the coaching staff linked to former boss Vialli by releasing Graham Rix, Ray Wilkins, Eddie Niedzwiecki and fitness trainer Antonio Pintus. W Ham spend £2.5m on Liverpool defender Rigobert Song. Football mourns the loss of Len Shackleton, 78, a legendary figure in the NE having played with Sunderland and Newcastle. BBC Radio 5 Live secure rights to continue broadcasting Premiership matches until the end of 2003-2004 season. Yorke is dismissed as Sunderland knock out a Man U 'reserve' side from the Worthington Cup in extra time. In FA Cup replay Canvey Island journey to the Potteries and knock out Vale. Northwich eliminate Bury.

29   In League Cup before 27,000, Stoke suffer their heaviest home defeat in 97 years being thrashed by Liverpool 8-0. Birmingham knock out Newcastle. Wasteful W Ham lose at home to Sheff Wed. Man City get deserved win over the Dons. Dundee U doctor, Derek McCormack, claims that on-the-pitch treatment to Jamie Fullarton prevented his foot being amputated as the blood supply to the midfielder's foot had been cut when he broke his ankle during the match with Kilmarnock.

30   Jorge Albertz's low drive 2 min from time gives Rangers a 1-0 lead for the testing UEFA 3rd rd return in Kaiserslautern. Football League sign a £105m, 20-year Internet deal with NTL.

December 2000

Venables teams with Boro … Hamilton leaves Canaries … Leeds lord it over Lazio … Man U is richest club … Celtic get Lennon … Law is Scotland's greatest … Player of Century awards … Zidane is FIFA's man … Cormack hired and fired … Sugar selling up … Lee leaves Wolves … Bassett goodbye at Barnsley … Figo rules Europe … Leeds entice back Keane … ENIC own Spurs … Gregory jibe hurts Ellis … Villa get prestige fixtures … Schmeichel's New Year recognition

1   Steve Gibson reluctantly pulls the plug on his plans to have Venables take over as manager, and allows Robson to stay at the helm, at least in the short term. At their shareholders AGM, managing director Colin Hutchinson says Chelsea would be in deeper trouble had they not sacked Vialli.

2   Resilient Derby notch their 200th Premiership goal to pull off a shock win at third-placed Ipswich. Bradford win the basement battle over Coventry. Leicester stun Leeds to go 3rd making it a miserable day for £18m Ferdinand on his debut. Deepdale's biggest gate of the season, 16,047, witness Preston and Fulham share the points.

3   Zola-inspired Chelsea defeat Man City turning out in silver shirts, black shorts and fluorescent yellow socks. Two defensive mistakes hand Bolton an early Christmas present of full points over Watford. Rangers have Reyna and Numan ordered off in win at Hearts.

4   After much speculation former England boss Venables, 57, finally agrees a position as head coach to work alongside Robson for 6 months at struggling Boro, with the main stumbling block to joining permanently being his television commitments. The immediate task, says chairman Gibson is '40-odd points to secure this club for next season'. Bryan Hamilton resigns after 9 months as Norwich manager and the side dropping to 20th spot.

5   Smith's coolly-taken goal against Lazio gives Leeds their greatest European win since the glory days of Don Revie. The win in Rome turns up the heat on new English coach Sven Goran Eriksson's club position. In bad-tempered clash wasteful Arsenal surrender a 2-nil advantage as Bayern Munich stage a comeback to draw.

6   Man U is confirmed as the world's richest club for the 3rd year running with an annual (1998-99) turnover at £110.9m putting them ahead of nearest rivals, Bayern Munich, on £83.5m. Showing their old hunger for battle on foreign fields, and Scholes taking his Champions League tally to 14, Man U win comfortably at Sturm Graz. Liverpool's Staunton re-joins Villa. Sacked Chelsea coach Eddie Niedzwiecki is engaged as Arsenal's reserve manager replacing the late George Armstrong.

7   In UEFA Cup action Liverpool see off Olympiakos 2-0. Rangers crash out losing 3-0 (agg 3-1) at Kaiserslautern. Neil Lennon finally leaves Leicester to link with his former boss Martin O'Neill at Celtic in £5.75m transfer. At stormy AGM Spurs chairman Alan Sugar hits out at Chelsea's big-spending foreign policy claiming their team sheet is more like a wine list! Huddersfield spent nearly £6.7m on wages last season with ex-boss Steve Bruce picking up £196,818 as a director.

8   Palace pick up £100 fine after Neil Ruddock wears his nickname Razor on his shirt. Sir Alex Ferguson confirms he will remain at Old Trafford beyond his tenure as manager. A Scottish national newspaper poll on the nation's greatest footballer votes Denis Law into top spot, narrowly ahead of Jim Baxter and Kenny Dalglish.

9   Venables see Boro hit rock-bottom of the Premiership following defeat at Sunderland. Parlour's hat-trick in 5-0 win floors Newcastle. Man City follow their 6 straight defeats by walloping Everton 5-0. Trailing to Man U by 2 goals and with just 11 min remaining Charlton stage a late comeback to snatch a draw. Southampton bring Leeds back down to earth with a win. In FA Cup Northwich draw with Leyton Orient. Morecambe shock Cambridge U with 2-1 win.

10   Renowned giant-killers and current Conference leaders Yeovil travel to Bloomfield Road and knock out Blackpool. Canvey Island's dream ends in the 'jellied-eel' clash at Southend. Houllier blames his strikers as Ipswich seal a memorable 1-0 win at Anfield. Beckham is in the top 6 but Olympic champion rower Steve Redgrave is the BBC Sports Personality of the Year.

11   Red-faced FIFA get themselves off the hook in the Player of the Century row by giving awards to both Pele and Maradona. Cash-strapped Lincoln is under a transfer embargo after borrowing from the PFA to pay the wage bill. Leeds U's S African defender Lucas Radebe collects FIFA's Fair Play prize. Walter Smith cancels Everton's Christmas party and sits the squad through a video re-run of their 5-0 hammering by Man City.

12 Rangers will seek compensation, a reported £500,000, from the Dutch FA for injury to Giovanni Bronckhorst, which puts the midfielder out of action for the season. Man City's Worthington Cup quarter-final clash with Ipswich (1-1) is abandoned after 23 min because of a saturated pitch. Sunderland will give around 2,000 fans who travelled to their postponed tie at Crystal Palace a free ticket for their FA Cup tie against the same opposition on Jan 6.

13 Liverpool defeat Fulham in extra-time of their Worthington Cup tie. First season Premiership ref Paul Taylor is charged with misconduct for allegedly using 'insulting language' towards a Notts Co player. Welsh international Matthew Jones completes £3m Leeds to Leicester move. UEFA Cup draw pairs Liverpool and Roma, a repeat of their 1984 European Cup Final which the Merseysiders won. Zinedine Zidane wins FIFA's World Player of the Year award, polled by each national coach from the 150 registered countries selecting 3 players.

14 Inter reject W Ham's £10m offer for Robbie Keane. Cowdenbeath sack Peter Cormack just 10 days after giving him the managerial job, and without him seeing the team perform.

15 Villa's England goalie David James drops a bombshell by requesting a transfer. Spurs' Ramon Vega joins Celtic until the end of the season. FA are considering options other than the Millennium Stadium in Cardiff for the FA Cup Final on May 12.

16 Everton, and football in particular, applaud sporting Paolo Di Canio for catching a goal-mouth cross and stopping play after seeing goalie Paul Gerrard prostrate and lying injured on the edge of the box. Boro, under the influence of Venables, beat Chelsea, their 1st victory in 10 matches and the 1st home success. Stoke's Peter Thorne grabs a hat-trick at Bristol Rovers, his 4th this year. Sheffield steel city clash before 25,156, at Bramall Lane ends 1-1. Celtic put 6 past Aberdeen.

17 Liverpool throw open the title chase in Houllier's 100th match by inflicting on Man U a first home League defeat for a year and 363 days, thanks to Murphy's spectacular free kick. The 1st League meeting in 17 years between two famous northern clubs, Burnley and Blackburn, attracts 21,369 to Turf Moor with Rovers winning 2-1.

18 Arsenal snatch a valuable point with late equaliser at Tottenham. Spurs chairman Sir Alan Sugar, preparing for his farewell, confirms his intention to sell, after 10 years, his 40 per cent stake in the club. Villa's James has a re-think and withdraws his transfer request. Colin Lee parts company with Wolves.

19 Ken Bates is replaced as chairman of Wembley National Stadium Ltd. Dave Bassett, who took Barnsley to last season's Wembley play-off final, leaves the club after 18 months in charge. Luis Figo is crowned European Footballer of the Year. FA confirm the departure of coach Derek Fazackerley who worked alongside Keegan. Exclusive *Daily Telegraph* survey shows that 5 years of frantic activity in the Premiership leaves just W Ham in profit – thanks to Rio Ferdinand.

20 Significant coup for Leeds as they win the 7-club battle to snap up Inter's Robbie Keane for the rest of the season with 1st option to buy the Irish striker for £12m in the summer. Northwich Victoria look all set for a shock win leading 2-nil at Leyton Orient but squander the advantage, then lose 3-2 in extra time. Tottenham's new owners will be ENIC, an investment company led by sports executive Daniel Levy, which has interests in several European clubs including Rangers, Slavia Prague, AEK Athens, Vicenza and FC Basle. FA set a January deadline for Sven Goran Eriksson to commit himself to England's World Cup campaign for the rest of the season.

21 W Ham sign Liverpool's Titi Camara for £1.5m. Houllier says Liverpool have rejected a Chelsea £12m bid for Fowler. Bradford goalie Matt Clarke requests a transfer. A competition in Thailand run by Pepsi for 20 people to spend a weekend at Old Trafford attracts an entry of 10 million. With their popularity so high Man U intend returning next summer with games planned for Bangkok, Singapore and Kuala Lumpur.

22 City win a lively Bristol derby against Rovers at Ashton Gate before a 17,000 attendance.

23 Liverpool stir up the title pot with a fine 4-0 victory over Arsenal. Man U open up an 8-point lead after beating Ipswich. Robbie Keane appears as sub as Leeds slip up to visitors Villa. The League Managers' Association is refusing to defend members if the outbreak of dugout dismissals continues. Sunderland chalk up 50th League win at the Stadium of Light. Sir Alex Ferguson claims Old Trafford's present team is the best Man U has ever had. Motherwell's Steven Hammell becomes the 1st player in Scottish football to be charged with racially abusing a fellow pro, St Johnstone's Momo Sylla.

24 No Christmas truce in Spain between rivals Barcelona and Real Madrid after the Catalan club president, Joan Gaspart, claims: 'We are the best club in the universe.' Tranmere's John Aldridge says he remains committed to the club although hounded by some fans after the 4-0 home defeat to the Dons. Real Sociedad want former coach John Toshack, currently at St Etienne, to return after the club slips to the bottom of the Spanish League.

25 Going into the Boxing Day programme, Man U, Fulham, Millwall, Chesterfield and Conference side Yeovil head their respective divisions. Celtic sit top of the SPL with Livingston, Partick Thistle and Cowdenbeath all in pole position. Christmas Day arrest for Rangers' Fernando Ricksen on a drink-drive offence.

26 After losing to Man U, Villa's John Gregory concedes that the Premiership title is as good as over. Everton face relegation fears as Coventry fight to grab the points at Goodison. With the result now all-important defensive Boro dent Liverpool ambitions with 1-0 win. Bradford's 20,370 gate for the visit of Sunderland is their highest in 30 years with Phillips firing a hat-trick for the Wearsiders. Henry notches a hat-trick in Arsenal's 6-1 beating of Leicester. W Ham put 5 past Charlton.

27 The arrival of Villa's £9.5m record signing Colombian Juan Pablo Angel is held up by work-permit processing and the Christmas shutdown of government departments. A detailed *Daily Telegraph* survey shows no fewer than 48 managerial changes took place in 2000. Most startling is the statistic that of the 92 employed 10 years ago, only 20 are still in the Premiership and Football League, but the bulk of the other 72 are out of work. Southampton beat Spurs still without an away win since April. Angry Villa chairman Doug Ellis is hurt by jibe that he is 'in a time-warp' and demands an immediate meeting with his team boss Gregory.

28 Big spending Chelsea splash out again completing the £8m transfer of Ajax's Jesper Gronkjaer. Coventry pay £350,000 to IFK Hasselholm for Sweden's U-16 captain, midfielder Andreas Dahl. Villa Park will host the FA Trophy on May 13, a week after the FA Vase takes place at the same venue, and England will also be using the Villa ground for the Feb 28 friendly with Spain.

29 Darren Huckerby leaves Leeds for Man City for a provisional £2.5m fee rising to £3m on appearances. After a 2-hour meeting Villa boss Gregory issues an apology to his chairman, through his solicitor, for some remarks he had made. The winter's first cold snap brings over 30 casualties to the fixture list. Former Man U goalie Peter Schmeichel who spent 8 years at Old Trafford is made an honorary MBE.

30 Arsenal fail to close the gap surrendering a 2-goal lead, allowing Sunderland back into the game and a share of the points. Boss Graham says sorry to supporters for a woeful Spurs display losing 3-0 at Ipswich. No change at

the top but battling Newcastle take a point off Man U. Peter Davenport is sacked at Macclesfield after refusing to work alongside the club's director of football, in a new managerial set-up.

31 Sol Campbell, sought after Spurs and England defender, clears up doubts about his future by pledging his loyalty to the club.

January 2001

Red again for Hughes ... Worthington lands Canaries job ... Ibrox remembers ... Jones in at Molineux ... Millennium Stadium will host finals ... Spending through the roof ... Daggers shock Charlton ... No future at Bradford for Collymore ... England finally entice Eriksson ... Liverpool snub Fowler enquiry ... Taylor is Eriksson's No 2 ... Villa's Angel appears ... Sir Alex to step down ... Mancini for Filbert Street ... Bosnich out at OT ... Grobbelaar Court shock ... Carling end link ... Adams ends England duty ... Taylor honoured ... Keegan wins damages ... Ferguson excuses as Reds lose ... Pirates dismiss Holloway ... Kinnear quits Manor

1 Arsenal lose at Charlton while Man U open up an 11-point gap beating W Ham with Alex Ferguson admitting it would be embarrassing to let slip such a Premiership lead. Robbie Keane marks his full debut for Leeds with a penalty score against Boro. Blackburn's Mark Hughes is red-carded for the ninth time at Norwich. Bristol City and Cardiff both hit 6 against Cambridge U and Exeter.

2 In stormy Tottenham affair goalie Sullivan and Newcastle pair Solano and Dyer are dismissed. St Etienne confirm John Toshack is quitting after 10 weeks to commence a third spell at Real Sociedad. Norwich appoint Nigel Worthington as manager. Celtic trounce Kilmarnock 6-0 to go into the winter break 9 points clear of Hibs. An emotional tribute service is held outside Ibrox, and relayed to 5,000 inside, to commemorate 66 fans who died on a stairway terracing exit 30 years ago.

3 Former Southampton boss David Jones is installed as Wolves' fifth manager in 6 years. Pompey axe Tony Pulis for alleged misconduct. Carlisle's controversial chairman Michael Knighton sells his 93 per cent shareholding to a consortium. Robbie Fowler is beaten up outside a Liverpool bar in the early hours. Huddersfield's Lou Macari is the December Nationwide Manager of the Month with Jocky Scott (Notts Co) and Nicky Law (Chesterfield) taking Divs 2 and 3 awards. FIFA will retain the Golden Goal ruling for the 2002 World Cup.

4 Cardiff's 72,000 capacity Millennium Stadium is the venue for the FA Cup final and Worthington Cup final for the next 3 years. A Daily Telegraph survey details transfer spending in 2000 reached a new record with English clubs involved in deals worth £423m (£100m in 1991), a figure inflated by the £30m sale of Arsenal's Petit and Overmars to Barcelona and Leeds paying £18m for Ferdinand. Current Premiership clubs have spent £1.8 billion over the last 5 years. Liverpool capture one of Europe's finest footballers, Finland international Jari Litmanen, 29, on a free from Barcelona.

5 St Johnstone sack George O'Boyle and Kevin Thomas for gross misconduct after they were reported for allegedly using cocaine in a Perth bar.

6 Dagenham & Redbridge are cruelly denied a history-making FA Cup win at Charlton through Salako's face-saving equaliser. The Conference side was just 4 min from becoming the first non-Leaguers to dump a Premiership team from the competition. Tottenham leave it late at Leyton Orient before snatching an injury-time winner and Arsenal hang on for victory in a bruising clash at Carlisle. But Geoff Chapple's Kingstonian keep the romance of the Cup alive by winning at Southend. Highland minnows Buckie Thistle claim their first League club scalp in 21 years, bouncing Hamilton Academicals out of the Scottish Cup.

7 Sheringham's late strike seals FA Cup 2-1 win at Fulham. Newcastle and Villa must meet again but Wolves advance winning at Forest. In the 4th rd draw Leeds will host Liverpool while holders Chelsea face a tricky tie at the Gills. Collymore is told he can leave Bradford. Brechin, watched by 395 while crushing Coldstream 6-2, draw a cash-spinning trip to Rangers in the Scottish Cup.

8 Nigel Spackman is the new Barnsley boss after being out of club management since quitting Sheffield U in March 1998. Benito Carbone is top of the Bradford clear-out as manager Jefferies, desperate to reduce an annual £11m wage bill, wields the axe on 10 under-achievers. Newcastle's goalie Shay Given requests a transfer. Egyptian striker Hossam Hassan becomes the world's most capped player making his 151st appearance against Zambia in Cairo. He equalled German Lothar Matthaus' 150th cap record last Saturday.

9 England's new coach-elect Sven-Goran Eriksson, 52, resigns from Lazio after three and a half years and will start his new job tomorrow, becoming the nation's first foreign national coach, succeeding Kevin Keegan. Swedish-born Eriksson, who has captured 16 trophies in Sweden, Portugal and Italy, has an FA contract to run five and a half years, reportedly worth £12.5m His first match in charge is a friendly against Spain at Villa Park. "The first job is to qualify for World Cup 2002 and Sven believes he can do that", says FA chief executive Adam Crozier.

10 Palace take 2-1 lead over Liverpool in League Cup semi-final. In eagerly awaited 1st League derby for 20 years Blackburn beat Lancashire rivals Preston 3-2. Italian press lay the blame for Sven-Goran Eriksson's abrupt departure from Lazio on FA's Adam Crozier.

11 Liverpool knock back Villa's enquiry for £12m rated Fowler. Stephen Brown, paraded as Carlisle's new owner, escapes to Spain after his credibility is queried.

12 Sven-Goran Eriksson is introduced to the media at FA headquarter in Soho and recalls that starting out he watched training sessions under Bob Paisley at Liverpool and Bobby Robson at Ipswich. "I also went to Germany and Italy to learn."

13 England coach Eriksson chooses the W Ham–Sunderland clash for his opening scouting match as Hutchison seals victory to take the Black Cats into second spot. Peter Taylor's appointment as assistant to Eriksson is confirmed in an Ipswich hotel room during the evening.

14 In front of Eriksson 13 eligible Englishmen start the Ipswich–Leicester fixture, and one candidate, Marcus Stewart, hits his 14th League goal to top the Premiership charts.

15 At last, Villa parade new £9.5m record signing, Colombian striker Juan Pablo Angel, 25, from Argentina's River Plate club. Brentford announce ground-sharing possibilities with Woking or Kingstonian for next season. FIFA back down from their controversial proposal that players could walk out in the middle of their contracts.

16 Sir Alex Ferguson intends retiring next summer, after 16 years, and reveals his continued involvement with Man U taking in the monitoring of the club's football academies in S Africa, China and the Far East. A win at Grimsby secures Wycombe an FA Cup 4th rd place for the first time. Brazilian midfielder Edu finally slips on an Arsenal shirt, in sub-zero conditions, for the reserves at Forest, ending one of football's most drawn-out transfer sagas following his £6m deal.

17   Villa see off Newcastle's FA Cup challenge. Extra-time goals take Sunderland through at Palace. Encouraged by his friend Vialli, Roberto Mancini, capped 36 times and who quit Lazio when coach Eriksson left, is taking up a short term offer with Leicester.

18   Frozen out at Man U, Mark Bosnich agrees to join Chelsea after a "mutual agreement" terminates his £35,000 weekly contract. Bruce Grobbelaar is facing a lifetime ban after 3 Appeal Court judges strip him of £85,000 libel damages, taking the unprecedented step of overturning a jury's unanimous verdict that he had libelled the *Sun* newspaper which had accused him of match-fixing. The former Liverpool goalie, 43, now a coach in S Africa, faces financial ruin with a legal bill of up to £1.2m.

19   Skipper Sammy Hyypia commits himself to Liverpool for the next 4 years. Newcastle's Didier Domi rejoins Paris St Germain for £3m. After 8 years Carling decide to end their association with the Premier League at the end of this season.

20   Zola chalks up his 200th appearance for Chelsea in the win over Ipswich. Tony Adams, 34, decides to end his England career after 66 appearances. Mancini makes his Leicester debut against Arsenal. Chairman Bryan Richardson says hounded boss Gordon Strachan will remain in charge even if Coventry go down.

21   An attendance of 50,002 turn up at Ibrox for a special charity clash between Rangers and Celtic "oldies" with plans to make it an annual affair.

22   Di Canio hits a stunning goal to rescue W Ham in draw at Charlton. Gascoigne, who has missed Everton's last 12 matches, will need another operation on a torn thigh muscle.

23   Collymore heads to Real Oviedo for talks. Coach Eriksson spends his first day at the FA's London HQ. Celtic legend Kenny Dalglish blames John Barnes for their disastrous season last year at Parkhead stating there were more bad signings than good ones.

24   Liverpool reach the Worthington Cup final inflicting a 5-0 (agg 6-2) hammering on Palace. Barnsley's Spackman appoints former England coach Derek Fazackerley as his No 2 replacing Peter Shirtliff. Joe Royle, who bought and sold Andrei Kanchelskis while at Everton, signs the Ukraine winger on loan for Man City from Rangers. Villa's Luc Nilis announces his retirement after failing to recover fully from a right leg double fracture.

25   Graham Taylor is recognised with a Carling No 1 award, and presented with a silver chalice by the League Managers' Association, to mark 1,000 matches as a manager. FA launch an investigation into the financial dealings of Div 3 leaders Chesterfield. Steve Burtenshaw, the QPR scout, suffers a stroke. Chelsea announce a £24m sponsorship over 4 years with Emirates, a Dubai-based airline. Blackburn's push for promotion is boosted by news they will receive £80m from their late benefactor, Jack Walker. More than 70 per cent of seats at Cardiff's Millennium Stadium will go to the FA Cup finalists, an increase of 10 per cent on recent years at Wembley.

26   WBA boss Gary Megson signs a new 5-year deal. At the High Court Kevin Keegan accepts £150,000 damages from the *News of the World* over a betting slur whilst he was England boss.

27   Kingstonian's dream of a last 16 place in the FA Cup is wrenched from their grasp in the dying seconds at Ashton Gate as Tony Thorpe's injury-time goal earns Bristol City a 1-1 draw. Wycombe march into the 5th rd for the first time beating Wolves. Dagenham & Redbridge, 4 min from winning at Charlton, lose the replay 1-0 after extra time. Tranmere take the scalp of Everton at Goodison Park. QPR concede 6 to Arsenal. Lowest Ibrox crowd for 10 years, 22,309, see Rangers shake off Brechin.

28   Boss Ferguson blames the pitch, his defenders, strikers, the ref's watch and rugby use of Old Trafford, after W Ham breach the offside trap to send Man U crashing out of the FA Cup. Arsenal v Chelsea is the pick of the FA Cup 5th rd draw.

29   Ian Holloway is sacked at Bristol Rovers after serving as a player, coach and manager for nearly 20 years. Man City slap £3.6m record signing Paulo Wanchope on the transfer list. Former Millwall boss Keith Stevens takes charge of Dr Martens League club Fisher Ath.

30   Premier League's dubious-goal panel deny Paolo di Canio a back-heel effort deflected in against Charlton on Boxing Day giving the final touch to Richard Rufus, so ruling it an o.g. Celtic's Alan Stubbs is given the all-clear after twice battling back from cancer. Arsenal's David Dein, dismayed by agents' lack of discretion, is commanding they sign a "good behaviour" agreement on the Holy Bible.

31   Ipswich's 26 year old captain Matt Holland makes his 200th consecutive appearance at St Andrews but Brum go through to their first League Cup final for 38 years to meet Liverpool. Thirteen of the leading clubs from Holland, Scotland, Denmark, Sweden, Portugal and Belgium sign a declaration agreeing to break away from their domestic Leagues to form an Atlantic League to start in July 2002. Joe Kinnear shocks struggling Oxford U by quitting his role as Director of Football, after just 4 months. Man U's Cole, and Sunderland pair Rae and Gray are red-carded at the Stadium of Light. Ian Rush is Barnsley's new part-time striker coach.

February 2001

Hatters appoint Kinnear ... Booze ban for Eriksson's men ... Collymore's La Liga debut ... Unique deal for Allardyce ... Hull lock-out ... Man U–Yankees tie-up ... Sky Blues get Hartson ... Owls sack Jewell ... Owen rocks Roma ... Francis bows out at QPR ... Cantona is tops of Man U poll ... Tranmere's amazing comeback ... Schmeichel calls it a day ... Roma rumpus at Anfield ... Rix is Pompey boss ... Liverpool win League cup ... Rioch quits ... McFarland is sacked ... Lincoln name Buckley ... Bees to ground-share

1   Bolton's Sam Allardyce is Nationwide Manager of the Month. The new Wembley will not now be ready until December 2004 meaning a further 6-month delay.

2   QPR chairman Chris Wright resigns after fans give continued abuse. FA drop 12-match touchline ban on Arsene Wenger, imposing instead a reprimand, a £10,000 fine and appeal costs.

3   Man U maintain a 15-point lead at the top with 1-0 win against Everton. Joe Kinnear is the new boss at struggling Luton. The first pay-per-view match in the SPL see Rangers beat Dunfermline. Sven-Goran Eriksson says he will not tolerate alcohol during international preparations.

4   Four Magpie fans travel 3,800 miles from New York to see their heroes but Newcastle's match with Southampton is cancelled 2 hours before start after snow falls on Tyneside. In blizzard-conditions Larsson fires a Celtic hat-trick against Hearts. Collymore makes a 67th min appearance for Real Oviedo at Las Palmas.

5   Swansea City is put up for sale by owners First Floor PLC who value the club at £3m. Ref Jeff Winter reports Brum after a number of crowd invasions against Ipswich. Sam Allardyce signs a 10-year Bolton contract, the longest management deal in British football.

6   Ref Paul Taylor, in trouble for alleged insulting comments to a Notts Co player, has his charge dismissed by the FA. Staff and officials of hard-up Hull find themselves locked out at Boothferry Park after bailiffs, under orders from landlord David Lloyd, change the locks.

7   Man U clinch a unique multi-million pound tie-up with American baseball giants, New York Yankees. In a stormy clash, 3 off and 8 cautioned, Celtic sweep past Rangers for the second time this season. Bristol City end the Kingstonian FA Cup dream. Coventry finally hammer out a £15,000-a-game deal with The Dons for striker John Hartson.

8   Controversial Chelsea chairman Ken Bates quits the new Wembley Stadium project with a bitter blast at leading FA figures.

9   Wimbledon's Norwegian chairman Bjorn Gjelsten steps down. Rochdale's chief executive Francis Collins camps overnight at Spotland to attend hired hot-air blowers brought in to beat the freeze. Boro's coach Venables becomes the first non-manager to win the Carling Manager of the Month award. PFA chief Gordon Taylor calls for points deduction if clubs found guilty. Hartlepool's Chris Turner, the Div 3 Manager of the Month, is presented with the award by local MP and former cabinet minister Peter Mandelson.

10   Cole's equaliser rescues Man U at Chelsea. Rebrov's winner at Man City ends Tottenham's 10-month away travel jinx, and is the club's first League goal in 7 hours and 42 min, home or away. Boro's unbeaten run under Venables extends to 12 League and cup matches, at Villa. Hull's financial problems spark a public response with 8,782, up 3,000 on the average, turning out to witness a 1-0 win over Leyton Orient.

11   Swansea goalie Roger Freestone chalks up his 500th appearance in draw with Millwall. Martin O'Neill refutes talk that the League is won despite beating closest rivals Rangers and setting up a 12-point Celtic lead.

12   Sheff Wed sack Paul Jewell after 8 months and hand the caretaker-reins to No 2 Peter Shreeves. Leicester sign a £2.5m shirt deal with LC Electronics, backers of the French international team. Arsenal's Wenger will quit club management if UEFA, FIFA and the EU decide to scrap the transfer system.

13   Bowyer's late strike gives Leeds a 2-1 win over Anderlecht. Henry's header in Lyon breathes life into Arsenal's Champions League campaign. Just 5,991 witness the Dons knock out Boro in FA Cup replay. England's new training home is to be a 360-acre site at Rangemoor, near Burton-upon-Trent, Staffs, with the £30m project opening in 2003.

14   Cole is targeted for racial abuse in Valencia as Man U come away with scoreless draw. Replays for 4 of this weekend's FA Cup ties are scheduled for next week after police drop their regular demands for a 10-day break. Pepsi pull out of the running to sponsor the Premier League next season.

15   Owen's double sinks Italian giants Roma in Liverpool's win at the Olympic Stadium. Roberto Mancini ends his short stay at Leicester to pursue a coaching post in Italy. With Airdrie facing a winding-up order and team manager Steve Archibald sacked by the liquidators, the players train in a public park because Broomfield is padlocked.

16   Gerry Francis steps down from the managerial seat at troubled QPR, anchored at the bottom of Division 1, and up for sale. Jaap Stam signs a new contract reportedly in the £50,000 a week bracket which keeps the Dutchman at Man U until 2006.

17   Spurs cruise into the FA Cup quarter-finals crushing Stockport 4-0. Wycombe come from 2-down to force a replay at Wimbledon. In Red Rose clash Burnley fail to make it count (1-1) against Blackburn's 10 men. Following their eclipse of Man U, W Ham see off Sunderland. Cup specialists Leicester put 3 past Bristol City. Spirited Tranmere get a draw at Southampton. Larsson hits goal No 40 for Celtic. Dario Gradi marks his 800th League game in charge of Crewe with a win over Watford. The 40th Potteries derby at the Britannia Stadium attracts 22,133, the highest in Division 2 this season.

18   Sub Wiltord backs his claim for an Arsenal starting place with 2 goals in FA Cup defeat of Chelsea. Liverpool brush aside Man City's challenge. Barry Ferguson spares the blushes for Rangers grabbing the 3-2 winner at Ross County.

19   Eric Cantona wins the vote as Man U's greatest player of all time in club's official magazine survey. Best is second with Giggs at three and Charlton fourth. Sacked Chelsea boss Vialli, taking his UEFA B coaching badge, is being taught by FA's Les Reed, whilst studying the practical side at Forest where the manager David Platt is a close friend.

20   Man U's dream is put on hold when Wes Brown's 88th min o.g. gives Valencia a last gasp 1-1 draw at Old Trafford. Tranmere stage one of the FA Cup's classic comebacks overturning a 3-goal deficit and securing a dramatic 4-3 replay win over Saints to advance to a quarter-final clash with neighbours Liverpool. Wycombe, down to 10 men from the 69th min, finish 2-2 (after extra time) and then in pulsating drama dump the Dons from the FA Cup 8-7 on penalty decider. Peter Schmeichel, 37, announces his retirement from international action with Denmark, after playing a record 128 times, and scoring, a penalty, in a friendly against Belgium.

21   Leeds book a Champions League quarter-final spot with a magnificent 4-1 home win over Anderlecht. Arsenal concede 90th min equaliser (1-1) at home to Lyon.

22   Nerve-wracking night at Anfield as Liverpool lose 1-0 to Roma but advance 2-1 on aggregate. The Italians go beserk when the ref clearly points, twice, for a 76th min pen after Babbel handles, then alters the direction of his finger and points for a corner to cause uproar. Premier League chairmen agree to put back the deadline for negotiation on a new sponsor. Carling, the current sponsors, withdraw while Coca-Cola, Pepsi and Budweiser decide against proceeding, but £178m will be netted from overseas broadcasting rights for Premiership games over the next 3 years. Twenty players and officials at Chesterfield are charged over financial irregularities.

23   Graham Rix signs a three and a half-year contract as new Portsmouth boss replacing Steve Claridge. After spending the last 41 days home and abroad watching 25 matches, Sven-Goran Eriksson names a 31-man squad, including some surprises, to face Spain at Villa Park. Roma lodge protest with UEFA demanding a replay, citing ref Jose Maria Garcia-Aranda's handling of their tie at Liverpool.

24   Venables-led Boro suffer first Premiership defeat in 11 games, at home to Southampton. Coventry's Hartson marks his home debut with a priceless equaliser against Charlton. The Dons put 5 past QPR while Hearts hit Dunfermline for 7.

25   Deadlocked at 1-1 after extra time, Liverpool capture their first trophy in 6 years winning the Worthington Cup at Cardiff's Millennium Stadium. Westerveld's (5-4) penalty shoot-out save from Brum's Andrew Johnson clinches it. Before 67,603, lethal Man U, assisted by Yorke's hat-trick, humiliate Arsenal 6-1, and storm 16 pts clear.

26   South Wales police will meet football authorities to try to prevent the centre of Cardiff becoming gridlocked on FA Cup final day as thousands of supporters, mainly from Birmingham, miss the League Cup start – which was delayed 10 min. Former Bristol Rovers boss Ian Holloway is appointed manager at struggling QPR.

Sven-Goran Eriksson started his England managerial career with a 3-0 win over Spain. Here Emile Heskey scores the second goal. (ASP)

27   Bruce Rioch resigns after 8 months at Wigan. Lincoln, on the verge of dropping into the Conference for the second time, sack manager Phil Stant. Roy McFarland is dismissed at Cambridge U. UEFA rule out a replay between Roma and Liverpool following the Italian club's appeal. Spain's U-21 side hand out a 4-0 lesson to England at St Andrews.
28   England make a bright start under new coach Eriksson, netting 3 times without reply against Spain at Villa Park. In Belfast, NI lose 4-0 to Norway in match marred by sectarian abuse at Neil Lennon. The ROI's Dublin friendly with Denmark is snowed off. In Scotland's WC group Belgium swamp San Marino 10-1. Former Grimsby boss Alan Buckley is Lincoln's 11th manager in 11 years. Luton purchase 5 acres of land near junction 10 of the M1 to build a new stadium. Fulham get permission for a 30,000 capacity all-seat stadium on their Craven Cottage site, a project costing £70m, and ready for the 2003–04 season. While they seek a new home Brentford are planning to groundshare with Woking during 2002–03.

March 2001
Cambridge recall Beck ... Promotion for Kidd ... Transfer system retained ... Wycombe's Cup glory ... Spurs axe boss Graham ... Aldridge parts with Tranmere ... Goram answers OT call ... Keane lashes FAI ... Saints' Hoddle leaves ... Saunders out and Lee in at Torquay ... Hornets' Taylor says he'll retire ... Spurs name Hoddle ... Rocastle sadness

1   John Beck returns to take charge at Cambridge U. Bristol Rovers appoint Garry Thompson as manager. League Managers' Association invite Sven-Goran Eriksson to become their new president succeeding Kevin Keegan. Former Man U and Wales winger Colin Webster, 65, dies in Swansea after a long illness.
2   Wigan break their club record paying £700,000 for Motherwell's Lee McCulloch. Leeds announce Brian Kidd is being promoted to head coach just 24 hours before entertaining Man U.
3   Wiltord's hat-trick in 39 min gives the Gunners victory over W Ham. In 100th competitive match at Pride Park, Derby's win over Spurs lifts them 8 pts clear of the drop-zone. Eight bookings as Barthez saves penalty to earn Man U a point at Leeds.
4   Dutchman Reuser nets twice and lays on a third for an Ipswich win over Bradford. Fulham's Luis Boa Morte is dismissed for spitting in the top of the table clash with Bolton.
5   Peter Reid's 250th game in charge of Sunderland ends in draw with Villa. Port Vale pip Stoke in the LDV Vans Trophy Northern section semi-final with 105th min golden goal. FIFA and UEFA reach agreement with EU commissioners in Brussels to save the transfer system, but Arsenal's David Dein says it will encourage players to change clubs "at the drop of a wallet".
6   Henry's late header against dogged opponents Spartak Moscow keeps Arsenal's Champions League destiny still in their own hands. Depleted Leeds lose 3-2 in the Bernabeu stadium, but Raul's blatant Maradona-like "Hand of God" 7th min goal should not have stood as the unsighted Polish ref indicated – afterwards!
7   Scholes' 90th min 1-1 equaliser at Panathinaikos disguises yet another inept Man U performance on the continent. Blackburn crush Lancashire rivals Bolton to secure an FA Cup quarter-final at Highbury. Collymore decides to retire from football at the age of 30. Coventry give former defender Roland Nilsson a coaching post.
8   Liverpool remain determined and disciplined to see out a scoreless clash at Porto. Former Sports minister Tony Banks admits the fiasco of the new Wembley has damaged the country and the government.
9   England will play their final World Cup qualifier in October at Old Trafford, with the clash against Albania in September expected to be staged at St James' Park.
10   Much-travelled striker Roy Essandoh, who answered a request on teletext, sweeps Wycombe into the FA Cup semi-final with a stoppage-time headed winner at Leicester. Arsenal end Blackburn's Cup hopes winning in a canter 3-0. FIFA give go-ahead for all England matches at next year's finals to be shown live on terrestrial television.

11 Goalie Sullivan is the Spurs hero as they knock out W Ham to set up an FA Cup semi-final clash with Arsenal. Anfield's Houllier admits relief after his superstars survive an FA Cup scare, to go through against giant-killers Tranmere.

12 Leeds commercial director Adam Pearson heads the consortium to purchase Hull City and leaves Elland Road to become chairman and chief executive at Boothferry Park. FA announce Old Trafford will host the FA Cup semi-final meeting of Arsenal and Tottenham, with a 1.30 pm start. Liverpool and Wycombe play at Villa Park, 4 pm.

13 A shaken-up Man U reach the quarter-final of the Champions League for a fifth successive season, defeating Sturm Graz 3-0. Fulham complete a club record £4m transfer for Newcastle's French international Alain Goma. England's friendly against Italy next year will be at Elland Road on March 27.

14 Thanks to their superior head-to-head record against Lyon, Arsenal have an agonising wait with news from Moscow before squeezing into the Champions League quarter-finals despite losing 1-0 to Bayern in Munich. Lazio's 90th min equaliser (3-3) spoils what would have been a momentous Elland Road occasion, but the Italian club was already out. Real Madrid striker Raul's 1-match ban and £8,000 fine for his handball goal against Leeds is strangely overturned by UEFA's appeal body.

15 Thanks to Murphy and Owen Liverpool progress into UEFA Cup semi-final beating Porto. George Graham is told by Tottenham's owners ENIC to direct budget-talk comments to the club and not the media. David Hopkin becomes the seventh player to leave Bradford recently making a shock £1.5m return to Palace. FIFA hand Africa the right to stage 2010 World Cup.

16 Graham is hastily dismissed at Tottenham following a stormy 15-minute meeting with the new executive vice-chairman, David Buchler. Graham's attitude, say Spurs, was called to account. Appointed in October 1998 the club won the Worthington Cup 4 months later, and most believe Graham was nurturing young players into his workmanlike side. Tony Cottee leaves his player/manager post at Barnet after 4 months. Bristol City's 2-1 win over Millwall ends as a ludicrous 9-a-side encounter.

17 Chelsea lose to Sunderland who had not won at Stamford Bridge since 1957. With David Pleat as caretaker boss Spurs beat Coventry 3-0. Preston captain Sean Gregan scores a long-range effort at Norwich reminiscent of the famous Beckham and Nayim goals. John Aldridge quits at rock-bottom Tranmere shortly after the shattering home defeat to Barnsley.

18 Larsson nets a hat-trick as Celtic win the CIS Cup final beating Kilmarnock despite losing sent-off Sutton after an hour. In front of 25,069 Wolves win the Black Country derby.

19 Newcastle pay £1.5m for Bradford centre back Andy O'Brien. Palace promote Ray Houghton to assistant manager. Neil Redfearn is Halifax's new player/coach. UEFA allow Man U sign a replacement loan to cover a goalkeeping crisis. Sacked Tottenham boss Graham asks the League Managers' Association to take up his case.

20 Brian Kidd resigns from his post as a coach with the England U-21 set-up. After clinching a place in the LDV Vans Trophy final Brentford's caretaker boss Ray Lewington gets the job full-time. Chelsea, Leeds, Villa, Newcastle, Coventry, W Ham, Everton and Leicester apply to enter next season's Inter-Toto Cup.

21 With UEFA's approval Andy Goram answers Man U's distress call joining on a 3-month loan with Motherwell receiving a £100,000 rental fee. Pakistan lose 3-0 to a reserve-strength Bury featuring the Nationwide's only Indian player Bhaichung Bhutia. Former Pompey boss Steve Claridge links with Millwall as a player.

22 The agreed £500,000 fee by WBA for Leicester's Phil Gilchrist tops a quiet transfer deadline day with loans the most popular transaction. In-demand Tony Cottee receives no less than 22 enquiries before opting for Millwall. Beckham pleads with Liverpool fans not to abuse his wife and son in Saturday's World Cup qualifier with Finland. Former Arsenal and Everton winger Anders Limpar retires.

23 Darren Brown, chairman of Chesterfield who face a Football League tribunal investigation, steps down. England U-21's have a comfortable 4-0 win over Finland at Oakwell. FA ban radio station Century FM from tomorrow's World Cup tie following an early morning hoax call to England coach Eriksson.

24 An England side at Anfield sporting Liverpool red come from behind to get a vital World Cup 2-1 win over awkward Finnish opposition who are denied a late equaliser by Seaman's agility. England's day was almost made even better in Germany when Albania were level at 1-1 until the 88th min before the Germans scrambled the winner. Scotland's hopes suffer a blow when 10-man Belgium peg back a 2-goal deficit to level in injury-time. Hartson's double is not enough as Wales draw in Armenia. N Ireland's faint hopes evaporate losing 1-0 at home to Czech Republic. The Republic notch up 4-0 win in Cyprus.

25 FA are to ask Man U if they will continue releasing coach Steve McClaren for future England duty. Roy Keane slams the state of the FAI's training facilities in Dublin. Fulham, Chesterfield and Rotherham top their respective divisions.

26 Liverpool's Litmanen will be out for 6 weeks after breaking his wrist. An UEFA official declares as dangerous the deeply rutted pitch at the Selman Stermasi stadium, Tirana, so England's U-21 switch to the Quemal Stafa ground where the seniors will also play. Derby's Jim Smith says he will continue next season, his 33rd in management. Wales send home 4 U-21 players for a breach of discipline in Armenia.

27 W Ham's Suker appears in a Croatian court to answer charges of avoiding mandatory military service. Sir Norman Wisdom, the 86 year old comedian who shot to fame in Albania when the government banned all films containing violence and sex, is mobbed at England's training session in Tirana. Southampton agree permission for managerless Spurs to speak with Glenn Hoddle who, later that evening, informs chairman Rupert Lowe he will be leaving the Dell. Angry FA officials lodge protest to UEFA over racist abuse directed at some England U-21 players in Tirana.

28 Andy Cole gets a late goal, his first, as England survive a disappointing start to overcome Albanian resistance 3-1. Hendry nets twice in Scotland win over San Marino. The Republic top their group after finally overcoming a stubborn Andorra rearguard 3-0. Wales get an early lead from Hartson but draw with Ukraine. N Ireland crash out of contention for a possible place in the finals losing in Bulgaria. Fulham get go-ahead to redevelop Craven Cottage. Lowly Torquay sack manager Wes Saunders with Colin Lee taking temporary charge.

29 Despite second-rate coverage Channel 5 claim 11.4 million switched on with a peak audience of 7.9m during England's WC win in Albania. Watford boss Graham Taylor, 56, announces he will bow out at the end of the season after 29 years in management.

30 Hoddle is confirmed the boss at Tottenham agreeing a 5-year contract and takes with him his Saints assistant John Gorman. Stuart Gray is put in temporary charge at the Dell. Man U block coach McClaren continuing with the England set-up. Oldham, losing £30,000 a month, is up for sale.

31 In Wenger's 250th game at the helm – a dress rehearsal for their FA Cup semi-final clash – Arsenal win at Spurs with new boss Hoddle an observer. Helped by Gerrard's thunderbolt Liverpool complete a League double over Man U for the first time in 22 years. Former Arsenal favourite David Rocastle who won 2 championship medals at Highbury loses his battle against cancer.

April 2001

QPR cash crisis ... Bayern's valuable lead ... Bruce's Wigan post ... Liverpool draw at Barca ... London fans kept apart ... Celtic glory ... North-South Cup final ... Fans acclaim Cantona ... Aussies hit cricket score! ... Premiership clubs' cash loss ... Chesterfield lose points ... Man U claim prize again ... Fulham in big time ... "Slim" Jim loses battle ... Southend ref sadness ... Bayern's red revenge ... Anfield ends Euro wait ... Sheringham wins the vote ... Horror tackle by Keane ... Van Nistelrooy is £19m man ... New pitch needed at Cardiff ... Bradford drop ... Palace relieve Smith of duties

1   Gascoigne's agent denies his Everton career is in the balance. Blackburn trounce East Lancashire rivals Burnley. The Nationwide's biggest attendance, 38,433, watch the 100th League clash between the Sheffield clubs which ends in an away win for United. The score now stands 38-31 in favour of the red half of the city.

2   Administrators are called in as debt crisis engulfs relegation-threatened QPR. Ipswich's Marcus Stewart nets a hat-trick at Southampton.

3   Before 66,584, sub Sergio's late score stuns lacklustre Man U giving Bayern sweet revenge and a precious lead for the return in Munich. Wycombe's Lawrie Sanchez gets a 3-match touchline ban and £2,000 fine. Peter Shreeves, caretaker boss at Sheff Wed, wins the Nationwide League Div 1 Manager of the Month award, with Brian Horton (Vale) and Scunthorpe's Brian Laws also named.

4   Arsenal take a slender 2-1 lead for their away leg at Valencia who are unbeaten at home in 16 Champions League ties. Leeds stand within touching distance of a semi-final with a 3-0 home win over Deportivo La Coruna. Steve Bruce is the new manager at Wigan. The first 2 rds of next season's Worthington Cup will be contested over 1 leg.

5   Ultra-cautious Liverpool are slammed for their negative approach but come away from Barcelona with a scoreless draw. Ronnie Whelan takes modest Olympiakos Nicosia into third spot and is then dismissed.

6   Villa's John Gregory, himself on the end of hurtful comments from Sir Alan Sugar, comes to George Graham's defence lashing the Tottenham chairman for "blaming all his managers for his lack of success". With concerns about clashes at motorway service stations police issue separate routes for fans of Arsenal and Spurs travelling to Old Trafford for Sunday's FA Cup semi-final.

7   Oxford U who lose 29 of their 39 League matches become the first in England to be relegated, going under at home to Oldham. Coventry's £15,000-a-game John Hartson nets his fifth goal in 4 matches at Leicester. Celtic wrest the League Championship from arch rivals Rangers before a record 60,440 home crowd, beating St Mirren. It is Celtic's 37th title but only their second in the last 13 seasons, and with 88 pts from 33 games, is the quickest for 26 years. Arsenal miss a hatful yet outclass Spurs to reach the FA Cup final where they meet Liverpool who secure their place by ending, not without a fight, the dream of shock side Wycombe.

8   Ruud van Nistelrooy plays down talk of a move to Man U, despite the presence of manger Ferguson at the Amsterdam Arena where PSV defeat Ajax 1-0.

9   The Tees-Wearside clash ends scoreless. Davor Suker says he will quit W Ham in the summer. Bristol ref Steve Dunn is given the FA Cup final task. Coventry's John Aloisi bags 6 and Australia go into the record books with a massive 22-0 World Cup win over Tonga.

10 Liverpool's third match in 6 days gets them a point at Ipswich. In a £12m deal the Football League sign a 3-year extension to their sponsorship agreement with Nationwide Building Society. Hoddle celebrates his return to the Spurs club he left 14 years ago with a win over Bradford. Eric Cantona receives the fans' award on the pitch after being voted the greatest player in Man U's history.

11 At Ellis Park, Johannesburgh. 43 people attending the Kaiser Chiefs–Orlando Pirates clash are crushed to death in a stampede. International football is reduced to a farce when Australia set a world record beating American Samoa (effectively a youth team) 31-0 in New South Wales, with the confused scoreboard operator flashing up an extra goal in error; Archie Thompson from the Marconi Stallions club nets a record 13! A review of clubs' accounts by Deloitte & Touche paints a bleak picture as wages turn profit into loss. Last season the 20 clubs in the Premiership – average salary £400,000 a year – made a collective loss of £34.5m with Chelsea topping the table as highest payers. FIFA ranking lists show England rising 2 places to 14th. Scotland (23), Republic of Ireland (30), Northern Ireland (98) and Wales (109).

12 Football League disciplinary panel dock Div 3 leaders Chesterfield 9 points for financial irregularities after facing 90 allegations of breaches of regulations, most of which were found not proven, but 8 charges upheld. In addition, a £20,000 fine is imposed.

13 Gerrard gets red-carded in Liverpool's eve of Grand National defeat by Leeds completing the first double for 30 years over the Anfield club. Man U's Ferguson says supporters have only themselves to blame if areas of tier two in the West Stand section at Old Trafford is closed by Trafford Council following a refusal by the fans to remain seated during the Euro tie with Bayern Munich.

14 A postwar record for Old Trafford of 67,637 witness Man U wrap up their third successive Premiership crown, equalling Liverpool's record of 7 titles in 9 seasons achieved between 1976 and 1984. Fulham win promotion – and a £5,000 Harrods hamper apiece for the players – with 2-1 win at Huddersfield, returning to the top flight for the first time in over 30 years. Troubled Chesterfield gain promotion. Brighton secure their place in Div 2. Rangers and Scotland legend Jim Baxter, 61, loses his fight against cancer.

15 Celtic hit-man Larsson's 48th and 49th strikes against Dundee U in Tennents Cup passes Charlie Nicholas' post-war Scottish scoring record of 48 in season 1982–83.

16 Five goals and 12 cautions including a dismissal in contentious stoppage-time Liverpool win at Everton with disrespect in a minute silence for the Hillsborough dead and the Ellis Park tragedy last week, leaves a sour taste in the 164th Merseyside clash. Southend's game with Mansfield is abandoned in tragic circumstances when Dorset ref Mike North, 42, collapses in the centre circle and later dies from a suspected heart attack. Paul Alcock dismisses 3 Carlisle players for professional fouls in the 3-0 defeat at Scunthorpe. Alex Stock, the former boss of Leyton Orient, QPR, Luton and Fulham dies, aged 84, at a Dorset nursing home.

17 Carew's header 15 min from time evicts Arsenal from a Champions League semi-final place. Nervous Leeds ride their luck and survive an onslaught to reach the semi-final (agg 3-2) despite losing at Deportivo La Coruna. Former Leicester midfielder Theo Zagorakis is dropped by Greece after testing positive for drug abuse.

18 In quarter-final 2nd leg Man U crash from the Champions League losing 2-1 (agg 3-1) at Bayern Munich who take revenge for their final defeat in 1999. A bare-faced trickster kitted out in the United strip and working for a men's magazine, cheekily cons his way into the official team photo before kick-off standing alongside Andy Cole completely oblivious to the stunt. Arsenal's Vieira breaks rank to publicly criticise the £30m sale last summer of Petit and Overmars.

19 McAllister's spot-kick winner over Barcelona gives Liverpool a famous UEFA victory and their first European final for 16 years. Houllier's team, already Worthington Cup winners, have an FA Cup final date against Arsenal,

and will now meet Spanish surprise side Alaves in Dortmund. Brighton's Bobby Zamora wins the Nationwide Player of the Month award for March. FA fine Forest and Preston for a mass confrontation on Nov 4.

20 Teddy Sheringham pips Beckham to win the Footballer of the Year award voted for by the Football Writers' Association. Sheringham, 35, is the first English player since Alan Shearer (1994) to collect the prize.

21 Roy Keane picks up his eighth red card as a Man U player shaming football with a savage over-the-top challenge which poleaxes Alfie Haaland, and with the Man City player writhing in agony the fiery Keane is seen spitting abuse at his opponent, believed to be "that's for 3 years ago". Grim-faced boss Ferguson comments, "I've not seen it but our secretary says it was a sending-off." Everton's Alex Nyarko requests to be withdrawn and says he is leaving football, after a fan runs on at Arsenal taunting the £4.5m signing to swap shirts. Fans of Tranmere and QPR are put out of their misery with both clubs being relegated. Cardiff gain promotion but Swansea drop into Div 3. The largest Conference crowd for 13 years – 8868 – see Yeovil and Rushden in scoreless all-action affair.

22 An exciting LDV Vans Trophy final sees Vale beat Brentford 2-1 before 25,654. Sub Moravcik's goal against Hearts uncorks the Championship celebrations at Celtic.

23 Man U finally seal a record £19m deal for PSV Eindhoven striker Ruud Van Nistelrooy, 24, on a 5-year contract. Van Nistelrooy, who failed a medical a year ago when all set to sign, will now be unveiled at an Old Trafford press conference later in the week, but not until July 1 will the Dutch ace actually become a United player. Juventus confirm Holland midfielder Edgar Davids has failed a drugs test after a fixture against Udinese.

24 The majority of Div 3 chairmen who believe Chesterfield should have been expelled, and not given a 9-point deduction and £20,000 fine, for financial irregularities, force the League to review the situation. Luton's defeat to Rotherham means Joe Kinnear's new club drops into Div 3 for the first time in 33 years. FA order Millennium Stadium pitch to be relaid in time for the Cup final on May 12. Ryan, the 9 year old son of the late Arsenal favourite David Rocastle, will lead out the Gunners in the Cup final.

25 Leeds wrap up the £12m signing of Robbie Keane ahead of schedule by agreeing with Inter to stagger payments over 3 years. Andorra take a shock World Cup lead in Dublin but eventually their 10-man defensive approach wilts to allow the Republic to score 3. Peter Schmeichel bows out of international action following his 129th Danish appearance.

26 FIFA impose 6-match ban and £4,500 fine on Scotland's Colin Hendry for elbowing a San Marino player in the throat. Peter Taylor is to continue his part-time coaching duties with England after FA receive permission from Leicester. FA Cup shock side Kingstonian are relegated from the Nationwide Conference. Wycombe ease relegation fears at Notts Co, their 60th game so far. Bryon Butler, 66, the respected BBC radio football correspondent from 1968–1991, loses his battle with cancer.

27 Lazio's Fernando Couto is suspended by the Italian League after testing positive for the banned steroid Nandrolone. Chelsea apply to join the increasingly powerful G 14 group of European clubs with a view to ensuring that players who break contracts do not prosper. Man U unveil new £19m recruit Ruud Van Nistelrooy at Old Trafford.

28 Bradford's 2-season fling with Premiership's elite ends after defeat at Everton. Leicester's defeat at Newcastle is their ninth straight loss – the worst sequence in City's 107-year history. At Wrexham, Millwall earn the point needed to secure promotion despite a pitch invasion from their supporters holding up play for 20 min. Rotherham will join the Londoners in Div 1. Watford's retiring boss Graham Taylor says farewell at his final home game against Tranmere. Petrol bombs are thrown at police during the Oldham–Stoke match. Livingston celebrate promotion into the SPL.

29 Teddy Sheringham, 35, completes an awards double adding the PFA Player of the Year trophy to the Football Writers' prize. Liverpool's Steven Gerrard takes the Young Player award. Premiership footballers did not vote for a single representative from Leeds U to make it into their all-star line-up. Champions Celtic humiliate sad Rangers on home soil with 3-0 win. Palace relieve manager Alan Smith and assistant Ray Houghton of duties and appoint Steve Kember for the remaining 2 matches.

30 Troubled Chesterfield get their 2nd owners in months when a supporters' society buy the club for £6,240. Barclaycard, replacing Carling, are named new sponsors of the Premier League, paying £48m over 3 years. Northampton reject a take-over bid from a consortium led by an Italian businessman.

May 2001
Wembley worries ... Watford welcome Vialli ... Zola stays ... Gloomy Sky Blues ... Man City drop down ... Euro end for Leeds ... Coppell is Bees boss ... Harry and Hammers in shock parting ... African fans perish ... Liverpool lift FA Cup ... Scribes acknowledge Larsson ... TV coverage increases ... 3 cups for Anfield cabinet ... Ferguson's OT bombshell ... MOTD farewell ... Goodbye to the Dell ... Surprise Royle parting ... Tractor team boss is tops ... Keegan returns at Maine Road ... Teddy is a Spur again ... McCoist links with TV ... Campbell's demands shock Spurs ... Premiership beckons Bolton ... Villa appoint board man Taylor ... Bruce reports for Palace duties

1 Plans to rebuild Wembley collapses after the government refuse to rescue the project with taxpayers' money. The FA, which recently requested £150m, says it is unable to raise the £660m, more than 3 times the original estimate in 1996. Brighton are crowned Div 3 champions. Graeme Souness is Nationwide Div 1 Manager of the Month with Millwall's Mark McGhee and Steve Parkin (Rochdale) also recognised. Relegated Oxford U dismiss David Kemp. Everton's Richard Gough, 39, announces his retirement after a 20-year career taking in Dundee U, Tottenham, Rangers and Kansas City Chiefs.

2 Leeds fail to get the home win badly needed over Valencia in scoreless Champions League tie. Watford introduce former Chelsea boss Gianluca Vialli, 36, as successor to Graham Taylor, on a 3-year deal. Blackburn clinch promotion to the Premiership winning at neighbours Preston. Defeat at home to Wycombe drops Bristol Rovers into the basement for the first time in their 118-year history.

3 QPR owner Chris Wright admits a proposed merger with Wimbledon is doomed because supporters would be against the move. Zola is to see out his career at Chelsea with the promise of a coaching post later.

4 Dave Watson, the former Everton stalwart, is the new boss at Tranmere. Ray Wilkins is to join the coaching staff at Watford. Liverpool's McAllister wins the Carling Player of the Month award. For the second successive month David O'Leary takes the Manager of the Month prize. Everton unveil a statue at Goodison's Park end in tribute to their greatest player, Dixie Dean, who scored a record 349 times in 399 games, during the 1920s and 30s.

5 Rochdale's Tony Ford who will be 42 later this month chalks up his 1064th senior outing at Plymouth. He is the only outfield player whose appearances run into four figures commencing from his days as a £10-a-week apprentice in 1975 and a Grimsby debut aged 16. Derby spoil the title script with an improbable win at Man U, a victory which secures their own top flight safety. Villa come from 2 goals down to beat Coventry ending the 34-year Sky Blues affair in the top flight. In bottom of the table clash Barnet lose at home to Torquay and drop into the Conference. Rushden & Diamonds clinch the Conference title moving into the League 9 years after forming.

Tony Adams is to retire after 1 more season. Before an acrimonious Arsenal–Leeds encounter – 7 bookings – David O'Leary, who made 722 appearances for the Highbury club, is roundly booed.

6   Hibs lose to Celtic in dress rehearsal for the Scottish Cup final with Larsson equalling Brian McClair's 35 goal post-war scoring record in a season for the club. Alan Stubbs marks his return since being diagnosed with cancer for a second time with a goal and a Celtic title medal. Huddersfield drop into Div 2 but Palace's last-gasp winner at Stockport keeps them up. Pompey, favoured by other results, wait anxiously to learn their 3-0 win over Barnsley safeguards their status.

7   On the eve of their Champions League semi-final clash in Valencia, Leeds receive an unexpected blow when UEFA dish out a 3-match suspension to Lee Bowyer for a stamping offence on Juan Sanchez in the first leg. Brentford boss Ray Lewington is taking up a coaching post at Vialli's Watford. A year to the day after beating Blackburn to gain promotion to the Premiership, Man City are relegated after losing at Ipswich. Arsenal Ladies beat Fulham, the only fully professional womens' outfit, to lift the FA Cup before 13,824 at Selhurst Park. Adam Crozier apologises to Gerard Houllier for ill-chosen remarks in a recent after dinner speech.

8   Leeds U's superb European adventure ends at the Mestalla stadium as Valencia, always a threat on the counter-attack, reach a second successive Champions League final. Shaven-headed to display a note of solidarity, Leeds finish with 10 men after Smith's instant dismissal for scything down Vicente. Brentford's chairman Ron Noades appoints the former Palace boss Steve Coppell as manager. Malcolm Allison, 73, is in hospital suffering from alcoholism.

9   Amidst shock and whispers of disagreements over monies available to improve the side, Harry Redknapp abruptly departs W Ham with 2 years remaining on his contract; his coach Frank Lampard also quits. Geoff Chapple, one of the most successful non-League bosses, quits Kingstonian a week after relegation. Mark Wright takes his first Football League post returning to manage Oxford U, his former club. In the fourth sporting tragedy in which African fans perish, up to 135 fans die in a stampede at the Accra stadium, Ghana, after police fire tear-gas to break up fighting between rivals fans of Heart of Oak and Ashanti Kotoko.

10   Alan Curbishley is a strong candidate for the W Ham post but Charlton state their intention to keep him. Arsenal's Patrick Vieira admits he was on the verge of leaving after early season dismissals. Promoted Chesterfield's winding-up order is deferred to allow the club's new owners to bring in administrators.

11   FA play down suggestions the FA Cup final could be moved to Twickenham after the contract to play in Cardiff's Millennium Stadium is fulfilled. UEFA's Lennart Johansson says he would like to see entry to the Champions League restricted to clubs who have won their Leagues.

12   Stunning late strikes from in-form Owen give Liverpool an AXA-sponsored FA Cup final 2-1 win over an Arsenal side which takes a stranglehold of the game, enjoys a lead from Ljungberg, but misses a hatful of opportunities to wrap it all up.

13   Frustrated Bradford team-mates McCall and Myers exchange blows during 6-1 hammering at Leeds. Southampton, their safety assured, surprise weakened Man U with 2-1 win. Celtic lose their first game at home to 10-man Dundee. Henrik Larsson is the Scottish Writers' Association Player of the Year.

14   The FA Cup final was watched by the smallest television audience since the present method of calculation began, in 1982, with only 6.8 million viewers tuning to ITV's coverage. Sky Sports 2 had 840,000 with 318,000 on Sky Sports Extra. BBC's 1997 broadcast attracted 11.1 million terrestrial viewers. Domestic football will become a 7-day event next season when ITV join Sky Sports to broadcast Premiership and Nationwide League fixtures. Sundays will see a live Nationwide fixture with further live matches on a Thursday and Friday.

15   Bobby Murdock, 56, one of Celtic's Lisbon Lions side, dies after suffering a stroke. Charlton's former Newcastle and WBA striker Andy Hunt is forced to retire. A crowd of 57,268 gives Celtic captain Tom Boyd a massive testimonial pay-day against Man U. In scoreless draw at Newcastle, Arsenal secure an automatic Champions League place as Premiership runners-up for the third year in succession. Mick Harford returns to Luton as first team coach.

16   Liverpool, triumphant in Worthington and FA Cups, seal an historic treble snatching a golden goal (5-4) winner against Alaves to take the UEFA Cup, the club's first European trophy victory for 17 years, in a thrilling clash in Dortmund. After semi-final play-off ties Walsall meet Reading for a Div 1 spot, while Blackpool and Leyton Orient contest a place in Div 2. Edgar Davids fails a second drugs test.

17   Preston advance to the Div 1 play-off final after defeating Birmingham in a penalty shoot-out at Deepdale. The match ends 2-1 in Preston's favour making the aggregate 2-2. But Trevor Francis disputes the choice of shoot-out ends, and twice leads his team from the pitch in an angry protest. Bolton cruise through, seeing off WBA 3-0 (agg 5-2) to thwart their Lancs rivals for a Premiership place.

18   Sir Alex Ferguson stuns football by revealing he will now sever all links with Man U at the end of his contract next summer following a bust-up with the board over his future role, while intimating Steve McClaren will also quit Old Trafford. FIFA postpone this summer's Club World Championship until 2003 in the wake of financial problems incurred by its marketing company ISL. Sunderland pay £3.5m for Argentine Nicolas Medina. Spurs complete £5m capture of Red Star Belgrade defender Goran Bunjevcevic.

19   *Match of the Day*, one of sport's great institutions and the nation's favourite soccer show, finally bows out after 37 years on the BBC. Liverpool's Sammy Lee replaces Steve McClaren on England's coaching staff. Liverpool ensure Champions League action sweeping aside Charlton 4-0 at the Valley. Chelsea clinch a UEFA spot. Leeds' win over Leicester will bring UEFA Cup action to Elland Road. Saints say a nostalgic farewell to the Dell, their traditional home for 103 years, with Matt Le Tissier appropriately notching the last goal in 3-2 victory over Arsenal.

20   Chelsea pay £6.2m for Marseille defender William Gallas, and agree to Gustavo Poyet's transfer request. The 55-year stranglehold by Benfica, Sporting Lisbon and FC Porto ends with Boavista taking the Portuguese title. Bayern Munich lift their 17th club championship. Over 500,000 line a 17-mile route through Merseyside streets to welcome Liverpool's treble-winning team. Boro make Terry Venables an offer which would allow him keep his job as an ITV soccer pundit. Kilmarnock clinch a UEFA Cup place by beating Celtic.

21   Joe Royle's 3-year reign as Man City boss ends with his surprise sacking amidst allegations of a drinking culture among some of his players. Ipswich's George Burley is presented with the Carling Manager of the Year award at the League Managers' Association dinner.

22   Arsenal's youngsters, 5-0 up from the first leg, lose at Blackburn but lift the FA Youth Cup (agg 6-3). David Seaman's testimonial, his 497th appearance, attracts 33,297 and a £600,000 tax-free reward, as Arsenal lose to Barcelona. Patrick Vieira is Carling's Player of the Year. Multi-millionaire businessman Chris Moore completes take-over of Oldham.

23   Bayern Munich lift the Champions League trophy against Valencia at the San Siro, holding their nerve in a nail-biting 5-4 penalty shoot-out after the sides finish 1-1.

24   Seven months after quitting England Kevin Keegan returns as Man City's new boss, signing a £6m deal over 5 years. England U-21's have 3-0 win over Mexico at Filbert Street.

25   Adventurous England sweep aside a modest Mexican side 4-0, giving Sven-Goran Eriksson his fourth win on the bounce, watched by 33,597 at Pride Park. Sacked Joe Royle considers legal action against Man City over claims he ran the side like a pub team.

26   Teddy Sheringham rejoins Tottenham on a free after 4 years at Man U. Eric Cantona is to make a sensational part-time return role as a coach to the Man U youngsters. Celtic complete a trophy hat-trick seeing off Hibs in a one-sided Scottish Cup final, the club's first treble since 1969. Former Scottish striker Ally McCoist retires and signs £1m deal to star in ITV's takeover of Premiership football coverage next season. Blackpool win the play-off final with Leyton Orient and will play in Div 2.

27   Tottenham, confronted by figures of £130,000 a week wages over 3 years – and a get-out clause – brand Sol Campbell's demands "ridiculous and unacceptable". Walsall snatch play-off final extra time goals to deflate Reading 3-2 and will now join Millwall and Rotherham in Div 1.

28   Bolton return to the big time brushing aside Lancashire rivals Preston 3-0 in one-sided Div 1 play-off final.

29   Steve Bruce informs Wigan he has had an offer to manage elsewhere, believed to be at Palace. Hibs boss Alex McLeish says linking him with the vacant W Ham job is just speculation. WBA knock back a £3.5m Birmingham bid for striker Lee Hughes.

30   Phil Neville signs a £35,000-a-week contract with Man U which keeps him at the club for another 6 years. Banned midfielder Lee Bowyer will miss Leeds' opening 2 UEFA games of next season. Scotland unveil plans to make a bid for the 2008 European Championships. After viewing a clutch of match videos new boss Vialli releases 7 Watford players. Graham Taylor joins the board at Villa.

31   Steve Bruce is confirmed boss at Palace, their 10th manager in 8 years. Next season's FA Cup final is pencilled in for May 4 – a week before the last Premiership games. Under a new agreement Premiership refs will earn £50,000 next season, a significant step towards full-time officials.

June

Ossie loses job ... Man U entice Fergie ... Robbo rolls out at Riverside ... England see off Albania ... McCarthy's men stay top ... Jail for N Irish players ... Charlton sign up Curbishley ... Chairmen snub Conference ... Poyet heads to Spurs ... Jewell's job ... McClaren is Boro boss ... Refs go full-time

1   Gretna, who currently play in the Unibond League, want to join the Scottish Football League if troubled Morton's demise is confirmed. York's chairman urges the FA and FL to allow Div 3 teams to become feeder clubs to the Premiership. Leicester's Filbert Street, their home ground for 110 years, is put up for sale.

2   Republic of Ireland survive early home mauling by Portugal in 1-1 draw. Wales who have not won a World Cup game for 5 years lose to Poland in Cardiff. N Ireland slump to their fifth successive defeat at home to Bulgaria. Ossie Ardiles is fired by Japanese side, Yokohama.

3   Neil Harris whose 28 goals helped Millwall win the Div 2 title is diagnosed with testicular cancer. At a beach tournament in Dublin Eric Cantona says he is not certain to accept a coaching job at Man U.

4   A Man U board peace initiative, and a pay-rise, looks set to heal the rift and help reverse manager Ferguson's decision to quit the club completely after his last season. Villa recruit Peter Bonetti to coach their goalies. Everton state that Paul Gascoigne is preparing himself "mentally and physically" at the Meadows Alcohol rehabilitation clinic in Arizona.

5   Bryan Robson steps down from his 7-year reign at Boro admitting the booing he received on the final day of the season had signalled his time was up at the Riverside. England U21's lose their heads, and have 2 dismissed, in defeat in Athens.

6   On the eve of the Election a fifth successive England World Cup win in Greece spreads the "feel-good" factor across the country although, after their victory in Albania, Germany maintain a 6-point advantage. Wales get a well-deserved draw against Ukraine in Kiev. N Ireland come within 3 min of holding the Czech Republic to a 1-1 draw before conceding 2 late goals. On a rutted surface well below international standard the Republic overcome Estonia to remain undefeated top of their group. Colin Lee is to take over on a permanent basis at Torquay. Coca-Cola are to sponsor for £50m the ITV Premiership highlights package for 3 years.

7   Five red-faced N Ireland players are released without charge after being detained in police cells following an incident in a Prague nightclub. Ray Graydon rules himself out of the race to succeed Glenn Hoddle at Southampton by agreeing a new contract with Div 1 newcomers Walsall.

8   Steve Bould is returning to Arsenal next season to coach the youths. Charlton's sought-after boss Alan Curbishley signs a new 4-year deal.

9   League chairmen vote almost unanimously (71-1) to reject proposals for two-up, two-down, promotion and relegation with the Conference, although with FA backing the Conference offers both relegated clubs a parachute fee of £260,000 a year for 2 seasons. Terry Venables says he has been sounded out about taking charge of the Greek national team.

10   Tottenham complete the £1.5m signing of Gustavo Poyet, surplus to requirements at Chelsea. The Uruguayan midfielder, 33, agrees a 3-year deal leaving Stamford Bridge after a 4-season spell. Vieira's header gives France a 1-0 win over Japan in Confederation Cup final in Yokohama. In front of a sell-out 42,000 home crowd, former Blackburn boss Roy Hodgson guides FC Copenhagen to the Danish title, the third country in which he has experienced a championship success.

11   Paul Jewell, former boss at Bradford and Sheff Wed, is named Wigan's eighth manager in 6 years. Former England and W Brom striker Ronnie Allen, 72, loses his long battle with Alzheimer's Disease. Ipswich are seeded for the 2001–02 UEFA Cup despite being absent from all European competition for 19 years. Sports Minister, Kate Hoey, an Arsenal fan and an enthusiast, loses her post in a government reshuffle to Richard Caborn, a keen supporter of Sheff U.

12   Highly rated Steve McClaren, 40, leaves Man U to take up a 5-year £8m post as the new manager of Boro, replacing Bryan Robson and short-term coach Venables. Luiz Felipe Scolari becomes Brazil's third national team coach in 9 months.

13   In a fundamental reorganisation the top 24 refs will become full-time earning up to £70,000 a year. The elite officials are to receive £33,000 plus a Premiership fee of £900 and bonuses based on good performances. A "National Group" with 50 refs and 188 assistants will officiate in the FL, and the venture, announced by the FA, will be governed by the Professional Game Match Official Board.

ENGLISH LEAGUE TABLES 2000–2001

FA CARLING PREMIERSHIP

			Home			Goals		Away			Goals			
		P	W	D	L	F	A	W	D	L	F	A	GD	Pts
1	Manchester U	38	15	2	2	49	12	9	6	4	30	19	48	80
2	Arsenal	38	15	3	1	45	13	5	7	7	18	25	25	70
3	Liverpool	38	13	4	2	40	14	7	5	7	31	25	32	69
4	Leeds U	38	11	3	5	36	21	9	5	5	28	22	21	68
5	Ipswich T	38	11	5	3	31	15	9	1	9	26	27	15	66
6	Chelsea	38	13	3	3	44	20	4	7	8	24	25	23	61
7	Sunderland	38	9	7	3	24	16	6	5	8	22	25	5	57
8	Aston Villa	38	8	8	3	27	20	5	7	7	19	23	3	54
9	Charlton Ath	38	11	5	3	31	19	3	5	11	19	38	−7	52
10	Southampton	38	11	2	6	27	22	3	8	8	13	26	−8	52
11	Newcastle U	38	10	4	5	26	17	4	5	10	18	33	−6	51
12	Tottenham H	38	11	6	2	31	16	2	4	13	16	38	−7	49
13	Leicester C	38	10	4	5	28	23	4	2	13	11	28	−12	48
14	Middlesbrough	38	4	7	8	18	23	5	8	6	26	21	0	42
15	West Ham U	38	6	6	7	24	20	4	6	9	21	30	−5	42
16	Everton	38	6	8	5	29	27	5	1	13	16	32	−14	42
17	Derby Co	38	8	7	4	23	24	2	5	12	14	35	−22	42
18	Manchester C	38	4	3	12	20	31	4	7	8	21	34	−24	34
19	Coventry C	38	4	7	8	14	23	4	3	12	22	40	−27	34
20	Bradford C	38	4	7	8	20	29	1	4	14	10	41	−40	26

NATIONWIDE FOOTBALL LEAGUE DIVISION 1

			Home			Goals		Away			Goals			
		P	W	D	L	F	A	W	D	L	F	A	GD	Pts
1	Fulham	46	16	5	2	49	14	14	6	3	41	18	58	101
2	Blackburn R	46	15	5	3	43	20	11	8	4	33	19	37	91
3	Bolton W	46	10	10	3	40	28	14	5	4	36	17	31	87
4	Preston NE	46	12	6	5	32	18	11	3	9	32	34	12	78
5	Birmingham C	46	14	3	6	34	22	9	6	8	25	26	11	78
6	WBA	46	13	5	5	37	23	8	6	9	23	29	8	74
7	Burnley	46	14	5	4	30	17	7	4	12	20	37	−4	72
8	Wimbledon	46	7	11	5	33	26	10	7	6	38	24	21	69
9	Watford	46	11	6	6	46	29	9	3	11	30	38	9	69
10	Sheffield U	46	14	4	5	34	18	5	7	11	18	31	3	68
11	Nottingham F	46	11	3	9	28	24	9	5	9	27	29	2	68
12	Wolverhampton W	46	7	9	7	25	20	7	4	12	20	28	−3	55
13	Gillingham	46	9	6	8	32	28	4	10	9	29	38	−5	55
14	Crewe Alex	46	12	5	6	30	24	3	5	15	17	38	−15	55
15	Norwich C	46	10	7	6	25	18	4	5	14	21	40	−12	54
16	Barnsley	46	11	3	9	32	26	4	6	13	17	36	−13	54
17	Sheffield W	46	9	4	10	34	38	6	4	13	18	33	−19	53
18	Grimsby T	46	10	4	9	26	27	4	6	13	17	35	−19	52
19	Stockport Co	46	6	11	6	29	26	5	7	11	29	39	−7	51
20	Portsmouth	46	9	8	6	31	25	1	11	11	16	34	−12	49
21	Crystal Palace	46	6	6	11	28	34	6	7	10	29	36	−13	49
22	Huddersfield T	46	7	6	10	29	26	4	9	10	19	31	−9	48
23	QPR	46	6	9	8	24	28	1	10	12	21	47	−30	40
24	Tranmere R	46	8	7	8	30	33	1	4	18	16	44	−31	38

NATIONWIDE FOOTBALL LEAGUE DIVISION 2

		P	W	D	L	F	A	W	D	L	F	A	GD	Pts
			Home			**Goals**		**Away**			**Goals**			
1	Millwall	46	17	2	4	49	11	11	7	5	40	27	51	93
2	Rotherham U	46	16	4	3	50	26	11	6	6	29	29	24	91
3	Reading	46	15	5	3	58	26	10	6	7	28	26	34	86
4	Walsall	46	15	5	3	51	23	8	7	8	28	27	29	81
5	Stoke C	46	12	6	5	39	21	9	8	6	35	28	25	77
6	Wigan Ath	46	12	9	2	29	18	7	9	7	24	24	11	75
7	AFC Bournemouth	46	11	6	6	37	23	9	7	7	42	32	24	73
8	Notts Co	46	10	6	7	37	33	9	6	8	25	33	−4	69
9	Bristol C	46	11	6	6	47	29	7	8	8	23	27	14	68
10	Wrexham	46	10	6	7	33	28	7	6	10	32	43	−6	63
11	Port Vale	46	9	8	6	35	22	7	6	10	20	27	6	62
12	Peterborough U	46	12	6	5	38	27	3	8	12	23	39	−5	59
13	Wycombe W	46	8	7	8	24	23	7	7	9	22	30	−7	59
14	Brentford	46	9	10	4	34	30	5	7	11	22	40	−14	59
15	Oldham Ath	46	11	5	7	35	26	4	8	11	18	39	−12	58
16	Bury	46	10	6	7	25	22	6	4	13	20	37	−14	58
17	Colchester U	46	10	5	8	32	23	5	7	11	23	36	−4	57
18	Northampton T	46	9	6	8	26	28	6	6	11	20	31	−13	57
19	Cambridge U	46	8	6	9	32	31	6	5	12	29	46	−16	53
20	Swindon T	46	6	8	9	30	35	7	5	11	17	30	−18	52
21	Bristol R	46	6	10	7	28	26	6	5	12	25	31	−4	51
22	Luton T	46	5	6	12	24	35	4	7	12	28	45	−28	40
23	Swansea C	46	5	9	9	26	24	3	4	16	21	49	−26	37
24	Oxford U	46	5	4	14	23	34	2	2	19	30	66	−47	27

NATIONWIDE FOOTBALL LEAGUE DIVISION 3

		P	W	D	L	F	A	W	D	L	F	A	GD	Pts
			Home			**Goals**		**Away**			**Goals**			
1	Brighton & HA	46	19	2	2	52	14	9	6	8	21	21	38	92
2	Cardiff C	46	16	7	0	56	20	7	6	10	39	38	37	82
3	Chesterfield	46	16	5	2	46	14	9	9	5	33	28	37	80*
4	Hartlepool U	46	12	8	3	40	23	9	6	8	31	31	17	77
5	Leyton Orient	46	13	7	3	31	18	7	8	8	28	33	8	75
6	Hull C	46	12	7	4	27	18	7	10	6	20	21	8	74
7	Blackpool	46	14	4	5	50	26	8	2	13	24	32	16	72
8	Rochdale	46	11	8	4	36	25	7	9	7	23	23	11	71
9	Cheltenham T	46	12	5	6	37	27	6	9	8	22	25	7	68
10	Scunthorpe U	46	13	7	3	42	16	5	4	14	20	36	10	65
11	Southend U	46	10	8	5	29	23	5	10	8	26	30	2	63
12	Plymouth Arg	46	13	5	5	33	17	2	8	13	21	44	−7	58
13	Mansfield T	46	12	7	4	40	26	3	6	14	24	46	−8	58
14	Macclesfield T	46	10	5	8	23	21	4	9	10	28	41	−11	56
15	Shrewsbury T	46	12	5	6	30	26	3	5	15	19	39	−16	55
16	Kidderminster H	46	10	6	7	29	27	3	8	12	18	34	−14	53
17	York C	46	9	6	8	23	26	4	7	12	19	37	−21	52
18	Lincoln C	46	9	9	5	36	28	3	6	14	22	38	−8	51
19	Exeter C	46	8	9	6	22	20	4	5	14	18	38	−18	50
20	Darlington	46	10	6	7	28	23	2	7	14	16	33	−12	49
21	Torquay U	46	8	9	6	30	29	4	4	15	22	48	−25	49
22	Carlisle U	46	8	8	7	26	26	3	7	13	16	39	−23	48
23	Halifax T	46	7	6	10	33	32	5	5	13	21	36	−14	47
24	Barnet	46	9	8	6	44	29	3	1	19	23	52	−14	45

* 9pts deducted for breach of rules.

FOOTBALL LEAGUE PLAY-OFFS 2000–2001

DIV 1 SEMI-FINALS FIRST LEG

13 MAY

Birmingham C (0) 1 *(Eaden 55)*
Preston NE (0) 0   29,072
Birmingham C: Bennett; Atherton, Woodhouse
(Hughes), Sonner, Purse, Johnson M, Eaden (McCarthy),
O'Connor (Holdsworth), Horsfield, Marcelo, Lazaridis.
Preston NE: Lucas; Alexander, Edwards, Murdock,
Gregan, Kidd, McKenna, Cresswell, Macken
(Anderson), Healy, Cartwright.

WBA (1) 2 *(Roberts 44, Hughes 55 (pen))*
Bolton W (0) 2 *(Bergsson 81, Frandsen 88 (pen))*   18.167
WBA: Hoult; Lyttle, Clement, Gilchrist, Butler,
Appleton, Fox (Jordao), Sneekes, Roberts (Taylor),
Hughes, Van Blerk (Chambers A).
Bolton W: Clarke; Barness, Charlton, Hendry (Whitlow),
Bergsson, Elliott, Farrelly, Ricketts (Marshall), Hansen,
Holdsworth (Frandsen), Gardner.

DIV 2 SEMI-FINALS FIRST LEG

13 MAY

Stoke C (0) 0
Walsall (0) 0   23,689
Stoke C: Ward; Hansson (Petty), Clarke, Thomas
(Dadason), Kippe, Gunnarsson, Gudjonsson, Kavanagh,
Cooke, Thorne, O'Connor.
Walsall: Walker; Brightwell, Aranalde, Tillson, Barras,
Bennett, Hall (Gadsby), Simpson (Keates), Leitao,
Goodman, Matias.

Wigan Ath (0) 0
Reading (0) 0   12,638
Wigan Ath: Carroll; Bradshaw, Sharp, Green, McGibbon,
De Zeeuw, Martinez, Nicholls, McCulloch (Haworth),
Liddell (Ashcroft), Beagrie (Roberts).
Reading: Whitehead; Gurney, Robinson, Viveash,
Hunter, Parkinson, McIntyre, Jones (Caskey), Cureton
(Forster), Butler, Igoe.

DIV 3 SEMI-FINALS FIRST LEG

13 MAY

Blackpool (0) 2 *(Ormerod 61, 78)*
Hartlepool U (0) 0   5720
Blackpool: Barnes; Parkinson, Jaszczun, Wellens
(Bushell), Shittu, Reid, Coid, Clarkson, Ormerod,
Murphy J, Simpson (Milligan J).
Hartlepool U: Williams; Knowles, Clark (Sharp), Barron,
Westwood, Lee, Tinkler, Miller, Lormor (Easter),
Midgley (Henderson), Stephenson.

Hull C (0) 1 *(Eyre 69)*
Leyton Orient (0) 0   13,310
Hull C: Musselwhite; Edwards, Whitney, Goodison
(Atkins), Whittle, Greaves, Holt, Brabin, Rowe, Francis
(Eyre), Matthews (Philpott).
Leyton Orient: Bayes; Joseph, Lockwood, McGhee,
Smith, Downer, Walschaerts, Castle, Watts (Tate),
Houghton (Martin), Ibehre.

DIV 1 SEMI-FINALS SECOND LEG

17 MAY

Bolton W (1) 3 *(Bergsson 10, Gardner 63, Ricketts 90)*
WBA (0) 0   23,515
Bolton W: Clarke; Barness, Charlton, Hendry (Whitlow),
Bergsson, Nolan (Ricketts), Farrelly, Frandsen, Hansen,
Holdsworth (Marshall), Gardner.
WBA: Hoult; Lyttle, Clement, Gilchrist (Sigurdsson),
Butler, Appleton, Fox, Sneekes (Jordao), Roberts,
Hughes, Van Blerk (Taylor).

Preston NE (1) 2 *(Healy 24, Rankine 90)*
Birmingham C (0) 1 *(Horsfield 58)*   16,928
Preston NE: Lucas; Alexander, Edwards, Murdock,
Gregan, Kidd, Cartwright, Rankine, Macken (Cresswell),
Healy, Anderson (McKenna).
Birmingham C: Bennett; Atherton (Lazaridis), Grainger,
Sonner, Purse, Johnson M, McCarthy (Eaden),
O'Connor (Hughes), Horsfield, Marcelo, Woodhouse.
aet; Preston NE won 4-2 on penalties.

An own goal by Reading's Tony Rougier makes it all square against Walsall, but not for long. (Colorsport)

Blackpool's four goalscorers celebrate victory over Leyton Orient: Ian Hughes, Brian Reid, Paul Simpson and Brett Ormerod. (Actionimages/Tony O'Brien)

DIV 2 SEMI-FINALS SECOND LEG

16 MAY

Reading (0) 2 *(Butler 86, Forster 90)*
Wigan Ath (1) 1 *(Nicholls 26)*   22,034
Reading: Whitehead; Gurney, Robinson, Viveash, Williams, Parkinson, McIntyre (Rougier), Caskey (Harper), Cureton, Butler, Igoe (Forster).
Wigan Ath: Carroll; Bradshaw, Sharp, Green, McGibbon, De Zeeuw, Martinez, Nicholls, Haworth, Liddell (Ashcroft), Beagrie.

Walsall (1) 4 *(Ward 42 (og), Matias 47, 61, Keates 50)*
Stoke C (1) 2 *(Kavanagh 31, Thorne 85)*   8993
Walsall: Walker; Brightwell, Aranalde, Tillson, Barras, Keates, Hall (Gadsby), Bennett, Leitao (Angell), Goodman (Byfield), Matias.
Stoke C: Ward; Thomas (Thorne), Dorigo (Thordarson), Mohan (Cooke), Kippe, Gunnarsson, Gudjonsson, Kavanagh, Dadason, Clarke, O'Connor.

DIV 3 SEMI-FINALS SECOND LEG

16 MAY

Hartlepool U (0) 1 *(Henderson 48)*
Blackpool (1) 3 *(Ormerod 21, 68, Hills 50)*   5836
Hartlepool U: Williams; Knowles (Easter), Clark, Barron, Westwood, Sharp, Tinkler, Miller, Lormor (Lee), Henderson, Stephenson.
Blackpool: Barnes; Parkinson, Jaszczun, Wellens, Shittu, Reid (Hughes), Coid, Clarkson, Ormerod, Murphy J, Hills (Milligan J).

Leyton Orient (1) 2 *(Watts 44, Lockwood 70)*
Hull C (0) 0   9419
Leyton Orient: Bayes; Joseph, Lockwood, McGhee, Smith, Downer, Walschaerts, Castle (Harris), Watts, Houghton (Brkovic), Ibehre (Tate).
Hull C: Musselwhite; Edwards, Whitney, Greaves, Whittle, Atkins, Holt (Philpott), Brabin, Eyre, Francis (Rowe), Matthews (Brown).

DIV 3 FINAL (at Millennium Stadium)

26 MAY

Blackpool (2) 4 *(Hughes 35, Reid 45, Simpson 77, Ormerod 88)*
Leyton Orient (2) 2 *(Tate 1, Houghton 37)*   23,600
Blackpool: Barnes; Parkinson, Hills, Wellens (Milligan M), Hughes, Reid, Clarkson, Simpson (Milligan J), Ormerod (Thompson), Murphy J, Coid.
Leyton Orient: Bayes; Joseph, Lockwood, McGhee, Smith, Downer, Walschaerts (Castle), Harris, Tate (Brkovic), Houghton (Martin), Ibehre.

DIV 2 FINAL (at Millennium Stadium)

27 MAY

Reading (1) 2 *(Cureton 31, Butler 91)*
Walsall (0) 3 *(Goodman 48, Rougier 108 (og), Byfield 109)*   50,496
Reading: Whitehead; Murty, Robinson, Viveash, Williams (Hunter), Parkinson, McIntyre (Rougier), Harper, Cureton, Butler, Igoe (Forster).
Walsall: Walker; Brightwell, Aranalde, Tillson, Barras, Bennett (Bukran), Hall (Gadsby), Keates, Leitao (Byfield), Goodman, Matias.
aet.

DIV 1 FINAL (at Millennium Stadium)

28 MAY

Bolton W (1) 3 *(Farrelly 17, Ricketts 89, Gardner 90)*
Preston NE (0) 0   54,328
Bolton W: Clarke; Barness, Charlton, Hendry, Nolan, Farrelly, Frandsen (Elliott), Hansen (Ricketts), Holdsworth (Whitlow), Gardner.
Preston NE: Lucas; Alexander, Edwards, Murdock, Gregan, Kidd, McKenna (Cresswell), Rankine, Macken, Healy, Cartwright (Anderson).

LEADING GOALSCORERS 2000–2001

FA CARLING PREMIERSHIP	League	FA Cup	Worthington Cup	Other	Total
Jimmy Floyd Hasselbaink *(Chelsea)*	23	2	0	0	25
Marcus Stewart *(Ipswich T)*	19	1	1	0	21
Thierry Henry *(Arsenal)*	17	1	0	4	22
Mark Viduka *(Leeds U)*	17	1	0	4	22
Michael Owen *(Liverpool)*	16	3	1	4	24
Teddy Sheringham *(Manchester U)*	15	1	0	5	21
Emile Heskey *(Liverpool)*	14	5	0	3	22
Kevin Phillips *(Sunderland)*	14	2	2	0	18
Alen Boksic *(Middlesbrough)*	12	0	0	0	12
Alan Smith *(Leeds U)*	11	0	0	7	18
Jonatan Johansson *(Charlton Ath)*	11	0	3	0	14
Frederic Kanoute *(West Ham U)*	11	3	0	0	14
James Beattie *(Southampton)*	11	1	0	0	12
Gustavo Poyet *(Chelsea)*	11	1	0	0	12
Ole Gunnar Solskjaer *(Manchester U)*	10	1	2	0	13
Eidur Gudjohnsen *(Chelsea)*	10	3	0	0	13
Les Ferdinand *(Tottenham H)*	10	0	0	0	10

NATIONWIDE DIVISION 1

	League	FA Cup	Worthington Cup	Other	Total
Louis Saha *(Fulham)*	27	0	5	0	32
Matt Jansen *(Blackburn R)*	23	1	0	0	24
Lee Hughes *(WBA)*	21	1	0	1	23
Michael Ricketts *(Bolton W)*	19	2	1	2	24
Tommy Mooney *(Watford)*	19	1	2	0	22
Jon Macken *(Preston NE)*	19	0	3	0	22
Jason Euell *(Wimbledon)*	19	1	0	0	20
Luis Boa Morte *(Fulham)*	18	0	3	0	21
Barry Hayles *(Fulham)*	18	0	1	0	19
Iwan Roberts *(Norwich C)*	15	1	3	0	19
Bruce Dyer *(Barnsley)*	15	0	1	0	16
Marlon King *(Gillingham)*	15	0	0	0	15
Clint Morrison *(Crystal Palace)*	14	1	4	0	19
Jason Roberts *(WBA)*	14	0	2	1	17
Chris Bart-Williams *(Nottingham F)*	14	0	1	0	15
Neil Shipperley *(Barnsley)*	14	0	0	0	14
Gerald Sibon *(Sheffield W)*	13	1	1	0	15
Mikael Forssell *(Crystal Palace)*	13	0	2	0	15

NATIONWIDE DIVISION 2

	League	FA Cup	Worthington Cup	Other	Total
Jamie Cureton *(Reading)*	27	1	1	2	31
(Including 1 League goal for Bristol R)					
Neil Harris *(Millwall)*	27	1	0	0	28
Martin Butler *(Reading)*	24	2	0	2	28
Mark Robins *(Rotherham U)*	24	0	1	1	26
Tony Thorpe *(Bristol C)*	19	3	1	0	23
Jorge Leitao *(Walsall)*	18	1	2	0	21
Andy Scott *(Oxford U)*	18	0	2	0	20
(Including 13 League goals for Brentford)					
Jemaine Defoe *(Bournemouth)*	18	1	0	0	19
Mark Stallard *(Notts Co)*	17	3	3	0	23
Jamie Forrester *(Northampton T)*	17	2	0	0	19
Peter Thorne *(Stoke C)*	16	0	0	0	16
Nathan Ellington *(Bristol R)*	15	0	2	1	18
Tony Naylor *(Port Vale)*	14	1	0	5	20
Tom Youngs *(Cambridge U)*	14	1	0	0	15
Lee Peacock *(Bristol C)*	13	1	1	0	15
Alan Lee *(Rotherham U)*	13	1	0	1	15
Brett Angell *(Notts Co)*	13	1	0	0	14
Paul Moody *(Millwall)*	13	1	0	0	14
Danny Allsopp *(Notts Co)*	13	0	0	0	13
Leon McKenzie *(Peterborough U)*	13	0	0	0	13

NATIONWIDE DIVISION 3

	League	FA Cup	Worthington Cup	Other	Total
Bobby Zamora *(Brighton & HA)*	28	2	0	1	31
Robert Earnshaw *(Cardiff C)*	19	6	0	0	25
Chris Greenacre *(Mansfield T)*	19	1	1	0	21
Steve Kerrigan *(Halifax T)*	19	0	0	1	20
John Murphy *(Blackpool)*	18	1	5	0	24
Brett Ormerod *(Blackpool)*	17	2	1	6	26
Kevin Henderson *(Hartlepool U)*	17	0	0	2	19
Tommy Miller *(Hartlepool U)*	16	0	2	2	20
Luke Beckett *(Chesterfield)*	16	0	2	0	18
Paul Brayson *(Cardiff C)*	15	0	0	0	15
Nigel Jemson *(Shrewsbury T)*	15	0	0	0	15
Carl Griffiths *(Leyton Orient)*	14	4	0	0	18
Guy Ipoua *(Scunthorpe U)*	14	4	0	0	18
David Reeves *(Chesterfield)*	13	0	1	2	16
Neil Grayson *(Cheltenham T)*	13	2	0	0	15
Steve Flack *(Exeter C)*	13	0	0	0	13

Other matches consist of European games, LDV Vans Trophy, Charity Shield and Football League play-offs. Only goals scored in the respective divisions count in the table. Players listed in order of League goals total.

REVIEW OF THE SEASON

Manchester United will be poorly served by the record books in years to come when the margin of their seventh FA Premier League title in nine years fails to tell the full story of the 2000–01 season. By 14 April with five matchees still to be played, the trophy was on its way back to Old Trafford for the third time in a row, a record hat-trick since the Premiership began in 1992.

With the title wrapped up, United then lost three of their remaining fixtures to give entirely the wrong picture of the campaign as a whole. Such a shame because Sir Alex Ferguson had manipulated the squad system to perfection.

This can best be illustrated by the fact that not one player was ever present and Gary Neville with 32 full appearances was the highest in terms of selection. Top scorer Teddy Sheringham with 15 League goals made only 29 appearances and six of these were as substitute. Next highest marksman Ole Gunnar Solskjaer scored 10 goals from 31 outings, 12 of which were after coming off the bench.

With only one major signing for the entire season in France's international goalkeeper Fabien Barthez, the tried and tested formula which has served the club so well in nearly a decade of Premiership play, again proved a winner. Not that it was free from hiccups. There was a slow start with just one win in the first three matches and Liverpool completed the double over their great rivals. But Arsenal the runners-up were comprehensively beaten 6-1 on 25 February, a telling result in many ways as United were then 16 points ahead.

For Arsenal in second place they topped the table just in that brief opening spell when United were still sorting themselves out. In a bizarre event Arsenal handed the title to United by losing their first home game of the season to Middlesbrough, courtesy of two own goals. And in many respects Arsenal, with a hard core of the successful French national team in tow, were overshadowed by third placed Liverpool, who as mentioned above had twice beaten the champions elect and achieved a trio of cup successes with the League Cup, UEFA Cup and FA Cup finding their way to the Anfield trophy room. Arsenal disappointed in Europe, but Leeds United did well to reach the semi-finals of the European Cup before losing to Valencia who had put out the Gunners in the previous round.

Fourth place for Leeds was further indication of the progress they have been making in recent years, but had it not been for Ipswich Town dropping points in their last three matches, an even better season that fifth could

Liverpool completed a rare win at Manchester United's Old Trafford ground in December. Sami Hyypia and Ole Gunnar Solskjaer challenge for the ball. (Colorsport)

have come the way of the team which most had predicted would go straight back to the First Division after one season. Manager George Burley was Manager of the Season, a deserved if narrow verdict in view of Gerard Houllier's performance at the head of Liverpool.

Chelsea by tradition had their good moments and some bad ones, under new manager Claudio Ranieri. Four straight wins from late March was the highlight but to find an English manager you had to look at Sunderland in seventh place and Peter Reid. Five games without a win late on cost them a better finishing position.

Aston Villa were never higher than fifth throughout and Charlton Athletic proved they had learned a lesson from their previous sojurn among the elite. Southampton, awaiting a move to a new ground, were tenth the best position since 1994–95 and though the first two places in the table were secured already, the Saints did beat both United and Arsenal to pull down the curtain at The Dell.

Newcastle United fitfully flitted around but tailed off in the second half of the season and Tottenham Hotspur who welcomed back Glenn Hoddle, this time as manager, were unconvincing on travel and did not record their first away win until February.

Yet for Leicester a pre-Christmas third placing was eroded by a club record eight consecutive defeats from March. In contrast a late surge by Middlesbrough including that outstanding win at Highbury pulled them clear of the relegation zone.

West Ham United managed only three wins from the turn of the year and Everton's chopping and changing around kept them with the real threat of relegation hovering over Goodison Park. Derby County, who did not win a game until 18 November, squeezed out enough points to stay clear, but the trio who finally dropped out of the Premier League were the three City teams of Manchester, Coventry and Bradford.

For Manchester City it was a short-lived return to the top, but for once Coventry's successful struggle against relegation was to no avail after appearing in the top flight continuously since 1967. Bradford, who had just escaped the previous season, ended eight points adrift of Coventry.

Fulham were the only team in the four divisions to top a century of points in winning the championship of the Football League, First Division. They benefited from a flyer of a start with 11 consecutive wins, with one from the end of the 1999–2000 term tacked on, it was a club record run.

Match No.13 was their downfall at Preston North End, but this was their only reverse until the New Year. Again sealing promotion at Easter saw them ease off and their record would have been all the more impressive without it.

Blackburn Rovers ten points behind, lost only one of their last 16, to Fulham of course and stayed the course well to achieve automatic promotion. From the play-offs came Bolton Wanderers who had finished one place above the persistent Preston North End in the League and beat them in the final play-off. Quite a good season for Lancashire overall.

Birmingham City missed out in the play-offs, but showed in the Worthington Cup final against Liverpool they were capable of better things. Further disappointment for neighbours West Bromwich Albion, and though one win in the last six matches was unhelpful, Bolton were probably out of reach.

Burnley were unable to make the cut though they were fourth in November and Wimbledon's finishing position of eighth was their best of the season and four consective draws at the death were crucial.

Watford leaders in early November then took just one point from a possible 24 and just one win in nine ending late into April robbed Sheffield United of a possible play-off berth.

James Scowcroft (hidden right), scores for Ipswich against Chelsea. Ace marksman Marcus Stewart (11) is also on hand. (Actionimages/John Sibley)

Leeds United's Alan Smith tries to find a way through Patrick Vieira of Arsenal. (Actionimages/Darren Walsh)

Nottingham Forest also slipped out of contention the same month, but Wolverhampton Wanderers's mid-table look was confirmed by a solitary win from the last nine games. On the other hand, Gillingham could be congratulated for consolidating after promotion.

Crewe Alexandra, bottom in January, pulled away impressively but Norwich City's five consecutive defeats to December, knocked them back at the wrong time. For Barnsley, they lost the art of scoring goals at one stage. In a spell of 12 games they managed to find the net just four times.

In mid-October and again in mid-February, Sheffield Wednesday found themselves propping up the table, but fought clear of trouble and three straight wins in April put the smiles back on Grimsby Town faces.

Stockport County with spells of 12 and ten games without victory were always likely to be concerned and Portsmouth needed to beat Barnsley in the last game for insurance against the drop. Crystal Palace having appeared to put the skids under Pompey with a 4-2 win escaped themselves by winning 1-0 at Stockport.

Not so fortunate were Huddersfield Town, Queens Park Rangers and Tranmere Rovers, the relegated trio. Huddersfield had made it difficult for themselves with an early run of 17 games without a win and a mere seven wins in the season was obviously insufficient for Rangers survival. Tranmere, too, with a sole win in the last 15, were rooted to the foot.

Millwall won the Second Division title heading the division for much of the second half of the season. Six wins in the last seven outings clinched it for them. Rotherham United joined them thanks largely to nine wins from a sequence of ten games. Reading, Walsall, Stoke City and Wigan Athletic reached the play-offs. Reading's best was an unbeaten run of 11 games, but they were beaten at the Millennium Stadium by Walsall who had never been out of the top four all season.

Stoke were handicapped by being unable to sustain a series of victories, three in a row being their best, but of not strategic value at the end of the season. However, it was galling for Wigan riding high top on 11 November having lost just once to Walsall.

Bournemouth made a valiant effort with five wins out of the last six, but seven games without a win bonus from early March cost Notts County dearly. Two wins from the last nine did nothing for Bristol City after they put a bad start behind them.

Five wins out of six matches was Wrexham's best all through, but steady improvement by Port Vale from the turn of the year saw them out of danger. Runs of six and five games without a win kept Peterborough United in check and Wycombe Wanderers had to be content with their exemplary FA Cup semi-final place while they scrambled for points.

Eight games early in the New Year with just one win and three goals put Brentford's situation in perspective and a single win on the opening day for Oldham Athletic followed by 11 without success posed problems. Two points from a possible 27 for Bury ended their serious aspirations into December after being in third place.

A sequence of eight matches minus a win after a useful start put Colchester United out of their stride and just one success in the last ten made the play-offs out of reach for Northampton Town. For Cambridge United twelve games without a win from mid-October reduced their immediate options and left them battling against relegation.

Swindon Town, too, had similar problems and 18th was their highest all term. But it was worse for Bristol Rovers, Luton Town, Swansea City and Oxford United, the quartet headed for Division Three.

Rovers mid-season goalscoring famine when only six goals came from 14 matches underlined their problems while Luton were never out of the bottom three from the end of September. Swansea went from 17 October until early March with just one win and Oxford produced a single victory in their first 17 attempts.

The situation with Division Three was clouded by the Chesterfield story. In the end the points deducted from their total may have robbed them of the title, not promotion. The honour of taking the prize went to Brighton & Hove Albion.

Brighton were never out of the top three from mid-October, while runners-up Cardiff City were in a similar position from January. Undoubtedly off-field problems contributed to Chesterfield losing touch as a mere two matches were won from the last ten.

Hartlepool United, Leyton Orient, Hull City and Blackpool fought out the play-offs, with Blackpool emerging having finished in the lowest position of the foursome. Hartlepool enjoyed a club record unbeaten run of 21 matches, but had too many of them drawn.

Leyton Orient were only briefly out of the top six, but suffered one win in a period of nine games. For Hull, they shrugged off financial worries and climbed into respectability, but it was Blackpool who came through in the final play-off with Orient. They had even survived a 7-0 hammering at Barnet!

Rochdale, too, had a couple of odd results: winning 4-0 at Shrewsbury and losing 7-1 at home in the return! This in a period of scoring only two goals in eight games.

Cheltenham Town for the second season came close to the play-offs, but the last half of the term was worse than the opening. One victory in 13 was untimely for Scunthorpe United and Southend United drifted away steadily from mid-November.

The first table of the season had Mansfield Town in 12th spot; so did the last, while Plymouth Argyle were never alble to soar above 11th place and those other mid-table huggers Macclesfield Town, just one notch higher than that.

For Shrewsbury Town some inconsistency (see earlier) and just two spells of three wins in a row, while after a promising start to their Football League career, the second half of the season was less rewarding for new-comers Kidderminster Harriers.

Five wins in the last 13 hauled York City to safety and despite one run of seven and two of six without wins, Lincoln City were out of trouble. Bottom on 10 February, Exeter City looked doomed, but revived and Darlington in semi-freefall, just avoided a similar fate after showing up well initially.

While Carlisle United and Halifax Town had vied for the role subsequently handed them by Exeter, it was left to the last fixture to decide who went out of the League. Barnet at home to Torquay had to win. Torquay could escape with a draw. Three down at half-time, Barnet clawed back two goals, but it was not enough. Their replacements for 2001–02 are Rushden & Diamonds.

Bolton super-sub Michael Ricketts wraps it up for the Wanderers with the third goal in the play-off victory over Preston North End. (Colorsport)

INTRODUCTION TO THE CLUB SECTION

For this year's Rothmans Football Yearbook, an important innovation sees a new who's who style players directory which incorporates the total of appearances and goals for each player as in earlier editions but, additionally, features more personal information and a season-by-season account of the individual player's record. It is again featured in A to Z form for easy reference (see pages 424 to 556). There is also each club's full record in the previous ten seasons and the latest sequences recorded for wins, draws and defeats, etc.

The club section again comprises four pages as last year, the first two feature new entries in the 'It's a fact!' and 'Did you know?' series. Record transfer fees are usually left to the discretion of the club concerned.

The third and fourth pages of this section present a complete record of the League season, including date, venue, opponents, results, half-time score, League position, goalscorers, attendances and complete line-ups including substitutes where used, for every League game in the 2000–2001 season. Again goal times have been added, though not official they give an indication of when goals were scored. These appear as superior figures [10, 20, 30].

Squad numbers have not been included; those used are the familiar ones, 1–11 while the introduction of a third outfield substitute has been recognised as follows:- the first substitute No. 12, the second No. 13 and the third No. 14. However, if there is a substitute goalkeeper he is represented by No. 15 but *only* if he replaces the first choice goalkeeper. Otherwise he adopts one of the other three substitute numbers, as there have been several instances where a goalkeeper has been used as an outfield player because of injuries during the game. Players replaced are respectively noted with superior figures [1], [2], [3] and [g] for goalkeeper. These third and fourth pages also include consolidated lists of goalscorers for the club in League, Worthington Cup and FA Cup matches plus a summary of results in these two main domestic competitions.

The continued increase in the number of matches played on Sundays has resulted in the League positions shown after every League result being taken on that day. Full holiday programmes are also recorded, but the position after mid-week fixtures will not normally have been updated. Attendance figures quoted for the Nationwide Football League are those which appeared in the Press at the time. But those in the FA Carling Premiership are official. The attendance statistics published on pages 582–583 are those officially issued by the FA Premier League but not the Football League at the end of the season.

In the totals at the top of each column on page 4, substitute appearances are listed separately by the '+', but have been amalgamated in the totals which feature in the players historical section in the directory mentioned above. Thus these appearances include those as substitute. In fact the directory again features those names appearing on the FA Premier League and Football League's Retained list, which is published at the end of May. Each player's height and weight where known, plus birth place, birth date and source together with total League goals and appearances for each club he has represented, can be found as in previous editions. The player's details remain under the club which retained him at the end of the season. An asterisk '*' by a player's name indicates that he was given a free transfer at the end of the 2000–2001 season, a dagger '†' against a name means that he is a non-contract player, a double dagger '‡' indicates that the player's registration was cancelled during the season and a section mark '§' shows the player to be a trainee or associated schoolboy who has made League appearances. The symbol # indicates players aged 24 and over who are out of contract but who were offered re-engagement by their clubs. Appearances by players in the play-offs are not included in their career totals.

ARSENAL   FA Premiership

FOUNDATION

Formed by workers at the Royal Arsenal, Woolwich in 1886, they began as Dial Square (name of one of the workshops), and included two former Nottingham Forest players, Fred Beardsley and Morris Bates. Beardsley wrote to his old club seeking help and they provided the new club with a full set of red jerseys and a ball. The club became known as the 'Woolwich Reds' although their official title soon after formation was Woolwich Arsenal.

Arsenal Stadium, Highbury, London N5 1BU.

Telephone: (020) 7704 4000. *Fax:* (020) 7704 4001.
Box Office: (020) 7704 4040. *Commercial & Marketing:* (020) 7704 4100. *Recorded Information:* (020) 7704 4242.
Clubline: 09068 202 021.

Ground Capacity: 38,500 all seated.

Record Attendance: 73,295 v Sunderland, Div 1, 9 March 1935.

At Wembley: 73,455 v Panathinaikos, European Cup Group E, 30 September 1998.

Record Receipts: £392,726.50 v Sampdoria, European Cup-Winners' Cup, semi-final first leg, 6 April 1995.

Pitch Measurements: 110yd x 73yd.

Life President: Sir Robert Bellinger GBE, D.SC.
Chairman: P. D. Hill-Wood. *Vice-Chairman:* D. Dein.
Directors: R. G. Gibbs, C. E. B. L. Carr, R. C. L. Carr, D. D. Fiszman, K. J. Friar.

Managing Director: K. Edelman.

Manager: Arsène Wenger.

Assistant Manager: Pat Rice.

First Team Coach: Boro Primorac.

Head Youth Coach: Don Howe.

Head of Youth Development: Liam Brady.

Physio: Gary Lewin.

Reserve Coach: Eddie Niedzwiecki.

Company Secretary: David Miles.

Commercial Manager: John Hazell.

Stadium Manager: John Beattie.

Colours: Red shirts with white sleeves, white shorts, red and white hooped stockings.

Change Colours: Gold shirts, blue shorts and stockings.

Year Formed: 1886.

Turned Professional: 1891.

Ltd Co: 1893.

HONOURS

FA Premier League: Champions 1997–98. Runners-up 1998–99, 1999–2000, 2000–01.

Football League: Division 1 – Champions 1930–31, 1932–33, 1933–34, 1934–35, 1937–38, 1947–48, 1952–53, 1970–71, 1988–89, 1990–91; Runners-up 1925–26, 1931–32, 1972–73; Division 2 – Runners-up 1903–04.

FA Cup: Winners 1930, 1936, 1950, 1971, 1979, 1993, 1998; Runners-up 1927, 1932, 1952, 1972, 1978, 1980, 2001.

Double performed: 1970–71, 1997–98.

Football League Cup: Winners 1987, 1993; Runners-up 1968, 1969, 1988.

European Competitions: Fairs Cup: 1963–64, 1969–70 (winners), 1970–71. *European Cup:* 1971–72, 1991–92, 1998–99, 1999–2000, 2000–01. *UEFA Cup:* 1978–79, 1981–82, 1982–83, 1996–97, 1997–98, 1999–2000 (runners-up). *European Cup-Winners' Cup:* 1979–80 (runners-up), 1993–94 (winners), 1994–95 (runners-up).

IT'S A FACT !

Arsenal established a Premier League record by completing eight League games without conceding a goal during the 1997–98 season. The total number of minutes involved was 833.

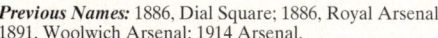

Previous Names: 1886, Dial Square; 1886, Royal Arsenal; 1891, Woolwich Arsenal; 1914 Arsenal.

Club Nickname: 'Gunners'.

Previous Grounds: 1886, Plumstead Common; 1887, Sportsman Ground; 1888, Manor Ground; 1890, Invicta Ground; 1893, Manor Ground; 1913, Highbury.

First Football League Game: 2 September 1893, Division 2, v Newcastle U (h) D 2–2 – Williams; Powell, Jeffrey; Devine, Buist, Howat; Gemmell, Henderson, Shaw (1), Elliott (1), Booth.

Record League Victory: 12–0 v Loughborough T, Division 2, 12 March 1900 – Orr; McNichol, Jackson; Moir, Dick (2), Anderson (1); Hunt, Cottrell (2), Main (2), Gaudie (3), Tennant (2).

Record Cup Victory: 11–1 v Darwen, FA Cup 3rd rd, 9 January 1932 – Moss; Parker, Hapgood; Jones, Roberts, John; Hulme (2), Jack (3), Lambert (2), James, Bastin (4).

Record Defeat: 0–8 v Loughborough T, Division 2, 12 December 1896.

Most League Points (2 for a win): 66, Division 1, 1930–31.

Most League Points (3 for a win): 83, Division 1, 1990–91.

Most League Goals: 127, Division 1, 1930–31.

Highest League Scorer in Season: Ted Drake, 42, 1934–35.

Most League Goals in Total Aggregate: Cliff Bastin, 150, 1930–47.

Most League Goals in One Match: 7, Ted Drake v Aston Villa, Division 1, 14 December 1935.

Most Capped Player: Kenny Sansom, 77 (86), England, 1981–1988.

Most League Appearances: David O'Leary, 558, 1975–93.

Youngest League Player: Gerry Ward, 16 years 321 days v Huddersfield T, 22 August 1953 (Jermaine Pennant, 16 years 319 days v Middlesbrough, League Cup, 30 November 1999).

Record Transfer Fee Received: A reported £22,900,000 from Real Madrid for Nicolas Anelka, August 1999.

Record Transfer Fee Paid: A reported £11,000,000 to Bordeaux for Sylvain Wiltord, August 2000.

Football League Record: 1893 Elected to Division 2; 1904–13 Division 1; 1913–19 Division 2; 1919–92 Division 1; 1992– FA Premier League.

MANAGERS
Sam Hollis 1894–97
Tom Mitchell 1897–98
George Elcoat 1898–99
Harry Bradshaw 1899–1904
Phil Kelso 1904–08
George Morrell 1908–15
Leslie Knighton 1919–25
Herbert Chapman 1925–34
George Allison 1934–47
Tom Whittaker 1947–56
Jack Crayston 1956–58
George Swindin 1958–62
Billy Wright 1962–66
Bertie Mee 1966–76
Terry Neill 1976–83
Don Howe 1984–86
George Graham 1986–95
Bruce Rioch 1995–96
Arsène Wenger September 1996–

LATEST SEQUENCES

Longest Sequence of League Wins: 10, 11.3.98 – 3.5.98.

Longest Sequence of League Defeats: 7, 12.2.77 – 12.3.77.

Longest Sequence of League Draws: 6, 4.3.61 – 1.4.61.

Longest Sequence of Unbeaten League Matches: 26, 28.4.90 – 19.1.91.

Longest Sequence Without a League Win: 23, 28.9.12 – 1.3.13.

TEN YEAR LEAGUE RECORD

		P	W	D	L	F	A	Pts	Pos
1990-91	Div 1	38	24	13	1	74	18	83	1
1991-92	Div 1	42	19	15	8	81	46	72	4
1992-93	PR Lge	42	15	11	16	40	38	56	10
1993-94	PR Lge	42	18	17	7	53	28	71	4
1994-95	PR Lge	42	13	12	17	52	49	51	12
1995-96	PR Lge	38	17	12	9	49	32	63	5
1996-97	PR Lge	38	19	11	8	62	32	68	3
1997-98	PR Lge	38	23	9	6	68	33	78	1
1998-99	PR Lge	38	22	12	4	59	17	78	2
1999-2000	PR Lge	38	22	7	9	73	43	73	2

DID YOU KNOW ?

Arsenal won the FA Cup in 1950 playing seven matches in London. They defeated Sheffield Wednesday, Swansea Town, Burnley and Leeds United at Highbury; Chelsea after a replay – both matches at White Hart Lane – and Liverpool 2–0 in the Final at Wembley.

ARSENAL 2000–01 LEAGUE RECORD

Match No.	Date	Venue	Opponents	Result	H/T Score	Lg. Pos.	Goalscorers	Attendance
1	Aug 19	A	Sunderland	L	0-1	0-0	—	45,820
2	21	H	Liverpool	W	2-0	1-0	—	Lauren [8], Henry [90]	38,014
3	26	H	Charlton Ath	W	5-3	1-2	1	Vieira 2 [19, 61], Henry 2 [46, 67], Silvinho [89]	38,025
4	Sept 6	A	Chelsea	D	2-2	0-1	—	Henry [76], Silvinho [86]	34,923
5	9	A	Bradford C	D	1-1	0-1	5	Cole [66]	17,160
6	16	H	Coventry C	W	2-1	1-0	3	Wiltord [24], Vernazza [72]	37,794
7	23	A	Ipswich T	D	1-1	0-0	3	Bergkamp [84]	22,028
8	Oct 1	H	Manchester U	W	1-0	1-0	3	Henry [30]	38,146
9	14	A	Aston Villa	W	1-0	0-0	2	Henry [61]	38,042
10	21	A	West Ham U	W	2-1	2-0	2	Pires [12], Ferdinand (og) [21]	26,034
11	28	H	Manchester C	W	5-0	1-0	2	Cole [44], Bergkamp [52], Wiltord [75], Henry 2 [82, 88]	38,049
12	Nov 4	A	Middlesbrough	W	1-0	1-0	2	Henry (pen) [25]	29,541
13	11	H	Derby Co	D	0-0	0-0	2		37,679
14	18	A	Everton	L	0-2	0-0	2		33,106
15	26	A	Leeds U	L	0-1	0-0	2		38,084
16	Dec 2	H	Southampton	W	1-0	0-0	2	Kachloul (og) [85]	38,036
17	9	H	Newcastle U	W	5-0	2-0	2	Henry [13], Parlour 3 [16, 86, 90], Kanu [52]	38,052
18	18	A	Tottenham H	D	1-1	0-1	—	Vieira [89]	36,062
19	23	A	Liverpool	L	0-4	0-1	2		44,144
20	26	H	Leicester C	W	6-1	1-0	2	Henry 3 [35, 66, 82], Vieira [50], Ljungberg [75], Adams [90]	38,007
21	30	H	Sunderland	D	2-2	2-0	2	Vieira [5], Dixon [40]	38,026
22	Jan 1	A	Charlton Ath	L	0-1	0-1	2		20,043
23	13	H	Chelsea	D	1-1	1-0	3	Pires [3]	38,071
24	20	A	Leicester C	D	0-0	0-0	3		21,872
25	30	H	Bradford C	W	2-0	2-0	—	Parlour [17], Lauren [26]	37,318
26	Feb 3	A	Coventry C	W	1-0	0-0	2	Bergkamp [78]	22,034
27	10	H	Ipswich T	W	1-0	0-0	2	Henry [67]	38,011
28	25	A	Manchester U	L	1-6	1-5	2	Henry [16]	67,535
29	Mar 3	H	West Ham U	W	3-0	3-0	2	Wiltord 3 [6, 13, 39]	38,076
30	18	A	Aston Villa	D	0-0	0-0	2		36,111
31	31	H	Tottenham H	W	2-0	0-0	2	Pires [70], Henry [87]	38,121
32	Apr 11	A	Manchester C	W	4-0	4-0	—	Ljungberg 2 [8, 16], Wiltord [9], Kanu [36]	33,444
33	14	H	Middlesbrough	L	0-3	0-2	2		37,879
34	21	H	Everton	W	4-1	1-1	2	Ljungberg [21], Grimandi [55], Wiltord [67], Henry [87]	38,029
35	28	A	Derby Co	W	2-1	1-1	2	Kanu [21], Pires [80]	29,567
36	May 5	H	Leeds U	W	2-1	1-0	2	Ljungberg [17], Wiltord [56]	38,142
37	15	A	Newcastle U	D	0-0	0-0	—		50,729
38	19	A	Southampton	L	2-3	1-0	2	Cole [26], Ljungberg [54]	15,252

Final League Position: 2

GOALSCORERS

League (63): **Henry 17 (1 pen), Wiltord 8, Ljungberg 6, Vieira 5, Parlour 4, Pires 4, Bergkamp 3, Cole 3, Kanu 3, Lauren 2, Silvinho 2, Adams 1, Dixon 1, Grimandi 1, Vernazza 1, own goals 2.**
Worthington Cup (1): Stepanovs 1.
FA Cup (16): Wiltord 6, Pires 3, Adams 1, Bergkamp 1, Henry 1 (pen), Ljungberg 1, Vieira 1, own goals 2.

Seaman D 24	Dixon L 26 + 3	Silvinho 23 + 1	Vieira P 28 + 2	Keown M 28	Adams T 26	Parlour R 28 + 5	Grimandi G 28 + 2	Kanu N 13 + 14	Henry T 27 + 8	Ljungberg F 25 + 5	Lauren E 15 + 3	Bergkamp D 19 + 6	Pires R 29 + 4	Luzhny O 16 + 3	Wiltord S 20 + 7	Cole A 15 + 2	Vernazza P — + 2	Vivas N 3 + 9	Lukic J 3	Manninger A 11	Upson M — + 2	Stepanovs I 9	Danilevicius T — + 2	Malz S — + 1	Edu 2 + 3	Match No.
1	2^1	3	4	5	6	7	8^2	9	10	11^3	12	13	14													1
1		3	4	5	6		8	12	9		7	10^1	11	2												2
1	2	3	4	5	6		8	9	10		7^1	12	11													3
1	2^1	3		5		7^3	4	9	10	13	8	12	11^2	6	14											4
1	2			5		7	4	12	9	8		11		6	10^1	3										5
1		3		5	6	7^2	4	12	13	8		10^1	11	2	9^2		14									6
1		3		5		7	4^2	12	9	11		10		6	8^1		13	2								7
1		3		5	6	7	4	8^2	9	11		10^1		2	12		13									8
1	2	3	4		6	7	5	12	9^3		8	10^2	11^1	13	14											9
1		3	4	5		12	6	13	14	8^1	7	10^2	11	2	9^3											10
	12		4	5	6	7^2	8		9	13		10	11^2	2^1	14	3				1						11
	2	3	4	5	6	7	8		9	11	12	10^1								1						12
	12	3	4	5		7	6^1	13	9	11^2		10		2	8					1						13
	2^1			5		7		9		4			10	11	6	8	3			1	12					14
	3	4	5	6	7			12	10		8^1		11	2	9					1						15
	12	3^1	4	5	6		8	13	14	7		10	11^2	2	9^3					1						16
	2		5	6	7	4^1	8^2	9	10^3	12	13	11	14				3			1						17
	2	3	12	5	6	7	4^1	9^3	10	8		13	11^2		14					1						18
	2	3	4	5		7	8	12	9	11^3		10^1	13	6^2	14					1						19
	2	3	4		6	7	8^2	9^1	10	12		11^2			13		14		1	5						20
	2	3	4		6	12	8	9^1	10^2	7		11							1	5	13					21
	2	3^1	4			7	6^3	9		10			11^2		12	8			1	5	13	14				22
1	2	3	4	6		7			10	8^1		11	9		12					5						23
1	2	3	4	5	6	7			10	8^1	13	11	9							5			12^2			24
1	2		4		6	7	12	13	9	8^1	10^2	11			3					5						25
1	2		4		6	7	12		8^1	10	11^2		9	3	13					5						26
1	2			6	7	4		12	13	8^1	10	11		9^2	3					5						27
1	11	4		7^2	6		10	12		8	2	9	3^1	13						5						28
1	2	4		6		5	12	11	8	10	7^1		9^1	3^2	13										14	29
	2	3	4		7^1	6		12	11^1	8	10	13	5	9^1			14	1								30
1	2^2		4	5	6	7		12	10		8^1		11	13	9	3				5						31
1		12	5		7^3		9	13	11	8		2	10^2	3	14					6		4^1				32
1	2	3	4	5	6	12		9	10	11^1		7	13										8^2			33
1	2	12	4	5	6		8^2		10	11		7^1		9	3	13										34
1	2		4	5	6	12	8		9^1	13	11^3	7^2		14	10	3										35
1	2		4	5	6	12	8		10	11		7			9^1	3										36
1	2		4	5	6	7		12	9		8	10^1	11			3										37
	4	5	6	7	2	12	9	8^2		10^1	11^3		3							1	14			13		38

Worthington Cup

Third Round	Ipswich T	(h)	1-2

FA Cup

Third Round	Carlisle U	(a)	1-0
Fourth Round	QPR	(a)	6-0
Fifth Round	Chelsea	(h)	3-1
Sixth Round	Blackburn R	(h)	3-0
Semi-Final (at Old Trafford)	Tottenham H		2-1
Final (at Millennium Stadium)	Liverpool		1-2

ASTON VILLA

FA Premiership

FOUNDATION

Cricketing enthusiasts of Villa Cross Wesleyan Chapel, Aston, Birmingham decided to form a football club during the winter of 1874–75. Football clubs were few and far between in the Birmingham area and in their first game against Aston Brook St Mary's Rugby team they played one half rugby and the other soccer. In 1876 they were joined by a Scottish soccer enthusiast George Ramsay who was immediately appointed captain and went on to lead Aston Villa from obscurity to one of the country's top clubs in a period of less than 10 years.

Villa Park, Trinity Rd, Birmingham B6 6HE.
Telephone: (0121) 327 2299. **Fax:** (0121) 322 2107.
Commercial Dept: (0121) 327 5399.
ClubCall: 09068 121 148. **Commercial Fax:** (0121) 328 2099. **Ticket Information:** (0121) 327 5353.
Ticketline: 09068 121 848. **Club Shop:** (0121) 327 2800.

Ground Capacity: 42,584.

Record Attendance: 76,588 v Derby Co, FA Cup 6th rd, 2 March 1946.

Record Receipts: £1,196,712 Portugal v Czech Republic, Euro '96, 23 June 1996.

Pitch Measurements: 115yd × 72yd.

President: J. A. Alderson. **Chairman:** H. D. Ellis.
Deputy Chief Executive and Finance Director: M. J. Ansell. **Operations Director and Secretary:** S. M. Stride.

Non Executive Directors: D. M. Owen, A. J. Hales, G. Taylor, P. D. Ellis.

Manager: John Gregory. **First Team Coach:** Steve Harrison. **Coaches:** Kevin MacDonald, Gordon Cowans.

Physio: Jim Walker. **Reserve Team Manager:** Kevin MacDonald. **Chief Scout:** Ross MacLaren. **Fitness Consultant:** Paul Barron. **Youth Team Manager:** Tony McAndrew. **Youth Team Coach:** Gordon Cowans.
Youth Development Officer: Alan Miller.

Commercial Manager: Abdul Rashid.

Stadium Manager: Tony Diffley.

Football Academy Director: Bryan Jones.

Assistant Academy Director: Steve Burns.

Colours: Claret shirts with blue and yellow trim, white shorts with claret and blue side trim, sky blue and claret stockings with white turnover.

Change Colours: Silver shirts with navy and lime green trim, navy and grey shorts with lime green side trim, navy and lime green stockings with grey turnover.

Year Formed: 1874. **Turned Professional:** 1885. **Ltd Co.:** 1896.

Club Nickname: 'The Villans'.

HONOURS

FA Premier League: Runners-up 1992–93.

Football League: Division 1 – Champions 1893–94, 1895–96, 1896–97, 1898–99, 1899–1900, 1909–10, 1980–81; Runners-up 1888–89, 1902–03, 1907–08, 1910–11, 1912–13, 1913–14, 1930–31, 1932–33, 1989–90; Division 2 – Champions 1937–38, 1959–60; Runners-up 1974–75, 1987–88; Division 3 – Champions 1971–72.

FA Cup: Winners 1887, 1895, 1897, 1905, 1913, 1920, 1957; Runners-up 1892, 1924, 2000.

Double Performed: 1896–97.

Football League Cup: Winners 1961, 1975, 1977, 1994, 1996; Runners-up 1963, 1971.

European Competitions: *European Cup:* 1981–82 (winners), 1982–83. *UEFA Cup:* 1975–76, 1977–78, 1983–84, 1990–91, 1993–94, 1994–95, 1996–97, 1997–98, 1998–99. *World Club Championship:* 1982. *European Super Cup:* 1982–83 (winners).

IT'S A FACT !

One of the first players to move clubs in exchange for a fee was Jimmy Crabtree a wing-half transferred from Burnley to Aston Villa for £250 in August 1895. He won 14 England caps as a wing-half and was an all-round sportsman.

Previous Grounds: 1874 Wilson Road and Aston Park (also used Aston Lower Grounds for some matches); 1876 Wellington Road, Perry Barr; 1897 Villa Park.

First Football League Game: 8 September 1888, Football League, v Wolverhampton W (a) D 1–1 – Warner; Cox, Coulton; Yates, H. Devey, Dawson; A. Brown, Green (1), Allen, Garvey, Hodgetts.

Record League Victory: 12–2 v Accrington S, Division 1, 12 March 1892 – Warner; Evans, Cox; Harry Devey, Jimmy Cowan, Baird; Athersmith (1), Dickson (2), John Devey (4), L. Campbell (4), Hodgetts (1).

Record Cup Victory: 13–0 v Wednesbury Old Ath, FA Cup 1st rd, 30 October 1886 – Warner; Coulton, Simmonds; Yates, Robertson, Burton (2); R. Davis (1), A. Brown (3), Hunter (3), Loach (2), Hodgetts (2).

Record Defeat: 1–8 v Blackburn R, FA Cup 3rd rd, 16 February 1889.

Most League Points (2 for a win): 70, Division 3, 1971–72.

Most League Points (3 for a win): 78, Division 2, 1987–88.

Most League Goals: 128, Division 1, 1930–31.

Highest League Scorer in Season: 'Pongo' Waring, 49, Division 1, 1930–31.

Most League Goals in Total Aggregate: Harry Hampton, 215, 1904–15.

Most League Goals in One Match: 5, Harry Hampton v Sheffield W, Division 1, 5 October 1912; 5, Harold Halse v Derby Co, Division 1, 19 October 1912; 5, Len Capewell v Burnley, Division 1, 29 August 1925; 5, George Brown v Leicester C, Division 1, 2 January 1932; 5, Gerry Hitchens v Charlton Ath, Division 2, 18 November 1959.

Most Capped Player: Paul McGrath, 51 (83), Republic of Ireland.

Most League Appearances: Charlie Aitken, 561, 1961–76.

Youngest League Player: Jimmy Brown, 15 years 349 days v Bolton W, 17 September 1969.

Record Transfer Fee Received: £12,600,000 from Manchester U for Dwight Yorke, August 1998.

Record Transfer Fee Paid: A reported figure of £9,500,000 to River Plate for Juan Pablo Angel, January 2001.

Football League Record: 1888 Founder Member of the League; 1936–38 Division 2; 1938–59 Division 1; 1959–60 Division 2; 1960–67 Division 1; 1967–70 Division 2; 1970–72 Division 3; 1972–75 Division 2; 1975–87 Division 1; 1987–88 Division 2; 1988–92 Division 1; 1992– FA Premier League.

MANAGERS

George Ramsay 1884–1926
(Secretary-Manager)
W. J. Smith 1926–34
(Secretary-Manager)
Jimmy McMullan 1934–35
Jimmy Hogan 1936–44
Alex Massie 1945–50
George Martin 1950–53
Eric Houghton 1953–58
Joe Mercer 1958–64
Dick Taylor 1964–67
Tommy Cummings 1967–68
Tommy Docherty 1968–70
Vic Crowe 1970–74
Ron Saunders 1974–82
Tony Barton 1982–84
Graham Turner 1984–86
Billy McNeill 1986–87
Graham Taylor 1987–90
Dr Jozef Venglos 1990–91
Ron Atkinson 1991–94
Brian Little 1994–1998
John Gregory February 1998–

LATEST SEQUENCES

Longest Sequence of League Wins: 9, 15.10.10 – 10.12.10.

Longest Sequence of League Defeats: 11, 23.3.63 – 4.5.63.

Longest Sequence of League Draws: 6, 12.9.81 – 10.10.81.

Longest Sequence of Unbeaten League Matches: 15, 12.3.49 – 27.8.49.

Longest Sequence Without a League Win: 12, 27.12.86 – 25.3.87.

TEN YEAR LEAGUE RECORD

		P	W	D	L	F	A	Pts	Pos
1990-91	Div 1	38	9	14	15	46	58	41	17
1991-92	Div 1	42	17	9	16	48	44	60	7
1992-93	PR Lge	42	21	11	10	57	40	74	2
1993-94	PR Lge	42	15	12	15	46	50	57	10
1994-95	PR Lge	42	11	15	16	51	56	48	18
1995-96	PR Lge	38	18	9	11	52	35	63	4
1996-97	PR Lge	38	17	10	11	47	34	61	5
1997-98	PR Lge	38	17	6	15	49	48	57	7
1998-99	PR Lge	38	15	10	13	51	46	55	6
1999-2000	PR Lge	38	15	13	10	46	35	58	6

DID YOU KNOW ?

Up to the start of the Second World War in 1939, Aston Villa had had more players capped at international level than any other League club. Their 58 with such honours were 41 for England; nine for Wales; seven Scots and one from Northern Ireland.

ASTON VILLA 2000–01 LEAGUE RECORD

Match No.	Date	Venue	Opponents	Result		H/T Score	Lg. Pos.	Goalscorers	Atten- dance
1	Aug 19	A	Leicester C	D	0-0	0-0	—		21,455
2	27	H	Chelsea	D	1-1	1-1	17	Nilis [10]	27,056
3	Sept 6	A	Liverpool	L	1-3	0-3	—	Stone [83]	43,360
4	9	A	Ipswich T	W	2-1	1-0	14	Hendrie [28], Dublin [54]	22,064
5	16	H	Bradford C	W	2-0	1-0	7	Southgate [5], Dublin (pen) [75]	27,849
6	23	A	Middlesbrough	D	1-1	0-0	9	Joachim [74]	27,556
7	30	H	Derby Co	W	4-1	2-0	5	Joachim 2 [28, 87], Merson [37], Wright [54]	27,941
8	Oct 14	A	Arsenal	L	0-1	0-0	7		38,042
9	22	H	Sunderland	D	0-0	0-0	11		27,215
10	28	H	Charlton Ath	W	2-1	2-0	7	Taylor [33], Merson [41]	27,461
11	Nov 5	A	Everton	W	1-0	0-0	5	Merson [90]	27,670
12	11	H	Tottenham H	W	2-0	1-0	5	Taylor 2 [22, 57]	33,608
13	18	A	Southampton	L	0-2	0-2	5		14,979
14	25	A	Coventry C	D	1-1	1-0	6	Dublin [8]	21,455
15	Dec 2	H	Newcastle U	D	1-1	1-0	7	Dublin [4]	34,255
16	9	A	West Ham U	D	1-1	1-1	8	Hendrie [37]	25,888
17	16	H	Manchester C	D	2-2	0-0	9	Dublin [71], Ginola [86]	29,281
18	23	A	Leeds U	W	2-1	1-0	7	Southgate [43], Boateng [88]	39,714
19	26	H	Manchester U	L	0-1	0-0	9		40,889
20	Jan 1	A	Chelsea	L	0-1	0-1	11		33,159
21	13	H	Liverpool	L	0-3	0-2	13		41,366
22	20	A	Manchester U	L	0-2	0-0	13		67,533
23	24	H	Leeds U	L	1-2	1-1	—	Merson [24]	29,335
24	Feb 3	A	Bradford C	W	3-0	0-0	12	Vassell 2 [50, 56], Joachim [87]	19,591
25	10	H	Middlesbrough	D	1-1	0-0	13	Stone [38]	28,912
26	24	A	Derby Co	L	0-1	0-1	14		27,289
27	Mar 5	A	Sunderland	D	1-1	0-0	—	Joachim [52]	44,114
28	10	H	Ipswich T	W	2-1	0-1	12	Joachim 2 [53, 71]	28,216
29	18	H	Arsenal	D	0-0	0-0	12		36,111
30	31	A	Manchester C	W	3-1	2-1	11	Merson [14], Dublin [45], Hendrie [65]	34,243
31	Apr 4	A	Leicester C	W	2-1	1-1	—	Dublin [30], Hendrie [72]	29,043
32	7	H	West Ham U	D	2-2	0-0	8	Ginola [71], Hendrie [78]	31,432
33	14	H	Everton	W	2-1	1-1	8	Dublin [2], Taylor [81]	31,272
34	17	A	Charlton Ath	D	3-3	0-2	—	Ginola [59], Vassell [75], Hendrie [90]	20,043
35	21	A	Southampton	D	0-0	0-0	7		29,336
36	28	A	Tottenham H	D	0-0	0-0	8		36,096
37	May 5	H	Coventry C	W	3-2	0-2	8	Vassell [61], Angel [81], Merson [86]	39,761
38	19	A	Newcastle U	L	0-3	0-2	8		51,306

Final League Position: 8

GOALSCORERS

League (46): Dublin 8 (1 pen), Joachim 7, Hendrie 6, Merson 6, Taylor 4, Vassell 4, Ginola 3, Southgate 2, Stone 2, Angel 1, Boateng 1, Nilis 1, Wright 1.
Worthington Cup (0).
FA Cup (3): Joachim 1, Stone 1, Vassell 1.

James D 38	Stone S 33+1	Wright A 35+1	Southgate G 31	Alpay O 33	Barry G 29+1	Merson P 38	Boateng G 29+4	Dublin D 29+4	Hendrie L 27+5	Ginola D 14+13	Vassell D 5+18	Nilis L 3	Joachim J 11+9	Taylor I 25+4	Ehiogu U 1+1	Delaney M 12+7	De Bilde G 4	Samuel J 1+2	Staunton S 13+1	McGrath J —+3	Hitzsperger T —+1	Angel J 7+2	Match No
1	2	3	4	5	6	7	8	9	10	11¹	12												1
1	2	3	4	5	6	11	8	9	7¹				10²	13	12								2
1	2		4	6¹	3	11	8²	9	13	12			10	7	5								3
1	2	3	4¹	5	6	11	8	9	7	14	13³	10²			12								4
1	2	3	4	5	6	7	8	9	10¹	11²			13	12									5
1	2	3	4	5	6	10	8¹	9	12	11²			13	7									6
1	2	3	4	5	6	10	12	9	8¹	11²	14		13³	7									7
1	2	3⁴	4	5	6	11	12	9¹	8		13		10	7									8
1	2	3	4	5	6	11	12	9²	8¹		13		10	7									9
1	2	3	4	5	6	11	8	9			12		10¹	7									10
1	2²	3	4	5	6	11	8				12		10	7		13	9¹						11
1	2	3	4²	5	6	11	8	9			12		10¹	7		13							12
1	2²	3	4	5	6¹	11²	8	9	13	12			10	7		14							13
1	2	3	4	5	6	11	8	9	10					7¹		12							14
1	2	3	4	5	6	7	8	9	10	11¹								12					15
1	2	3	4	5	6	7	8	9	10	11													16
1	2	3	4	5	6¹	7	8	9	10	11						12							17
1	2	3	4	5	6	7	8		10	11²	12						9¹		13				18
1	2	3	4	5¹	6²	7	8	12	10	11	13					14	9¹						19
1	2	3	4			11	8	9¹		12				7		5	10		6²	13			20
1	2	3	4	5¹	10	7		9		11²	12						8¹		6	13	14		21
1	2	3		5	6¹	11	8	9	7	12	13								4			10²	22
1	2³	3¹		5	6	11	8		10	12	13			7²	14				4			9	23
1		3		5	6¹	7³	8		10		11	13	12			2			4	14		9²	24
1	2	3		5		7	8	12	10²	11	13					6			4			9¹	25
1	2	3¹		5	6	11	8²	9		12	13		14	7					4			10³	26
1	2	3		5	6	11		9	8				10	7					4				27
1	2		4	5	12	7		9	6	11¹			10	8		3							28
1	2	3	4	5		7		12	8	11	13		10¹						6			9²	29
1	2	3	4	5		11²	8	9¹	10		12		13	7³					6	14			30
1	7¹	3	4	5		11	8²	9	10		12		13			2			6				31
1	7²	12	4		5	8		10	11		13		9			2	3¹		6				32
1	7²	3	4	5		11	8	9³	10¹	12	13					2			6	14			33
1	7²	3		5		11	8¹	9	10	12	13				6	2			4				34
1		3	4		5	11	8	9	10	12				7		2			6¹				35
1		3	4		5	11	8	9		12	10²		13	7		2			6¹				36
1		3	4		5	11	8¹	9	12	13	10³			7		2			6²	14			37
1	12	3	4	5		7	13	14	10	11²	8³					2			6			9¹	38

Worthington Cup
Third Round   Manchester C   (h)   0-1

FA Cup
Third Round   Newcastle U   (a) 1-1   (h) 1-0
Fourth Round   Leicester C   (h) 1-2

BARNET

Conference

FOUNDATION

Barnet Football Club was formed in 1888 as an amateur organisation and they played at a ground in Queen's Road until they disbanded in 1901. A club known as Alston Works FC was then formed and they played at Totteridge Lane until changing to Barnet Alston FC in 1906. They moved to their present ground a year later, combining with The Avenue to form Barnet and Alston in 1912. The club progressed to senior amateur football by way of the Athenian and Isthmian Leagues, turning professional in 1965. It was as a Southern League and Conference club that they made their name.

Underhill Stadium, Barnet Lane, Barnet, Herts EN5 2BE.

Telephone: (020) 8441 6932.

Fax: (020) 8447 0655.

Ticket Office: (020) 8449 6325.

ClubCall: 09068 121 544.

Ground Capacity: 5560.

Record Attendance: 11,026 v Wycombe Wanderers, FA Amateur Cup 4th Round 1951–52.

Record Receipts: £31,202 v Portsmouth, FA Cup 3rd Round, 5 January 1991.

Pitch Measurements: 113yd × 72yd.

Chairman: A. Kleanthous.

Director/Chief Executive: Andrew Adie.

Manager: John Still.

Physio: John Stannard.

Colours: Amber shirts with black trim, amber shorts, amber stockings.

Change Colours: Yellow and blue.

Year Formed: 1888.

Turned Professional: 1965.

Previous Names: 1906, Barnet Alston FC; 1919 Barnet.

Club Nickname: The Bees.

Previous Grounds: 1888, Queens Road; 1901, Totteridge Lane, 1907 Barnet Lane.

HONOURS

Football League: Division 2 best season: 24th, 1993–94.
FA Amateur Cup: Winners 1946.
FA Trophy: Finalists 1972.
GM Vauxhall Conference: Winners 1990–91.
FA Cup: never past 3rd rd.
League Cup: never past 2nd rd.

IT'S A FACT !

Despite the disappointment at losing their League status at the end of the season, Barnet could claim a club record, having beaten Blackpool 7-0 on 11 November 2000.

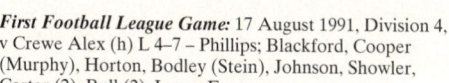
First Football League Game: 17 August 1991, Division 4, v Crewe Alex (h) L 4–7 – Phillips; Blackford, Cooper (Murphy), Horton, Bodley (Stein), Johnson, Showler, Carter (2), Bull (2), Lowe, Evans.

Record League Victory: 7–0 v Blackpool, Division 3, 11 November 2000 – Naisbitt; Stockley, Sawyers, Niven (Brown), Heald, Arber (1), Currie (3), Doolan, Richards (2) (McGleish), Cottee (1) (Riza), Toms.

Record Cup Victory: 6–1 v Newport Co, FA Cup 1st rd, 21 November 1970 – McClelland; Lye, Jenkins, Ward, Embery, King, Powell (1), Ferry, Adams (1), Gray, George (3), (1 og).

Record Defeat: 1–9 v Peterborough U, Division 3, 5 September 1998.

Most League Points (3 for a win): 79, Division 3, 1992–93.

Most League Goals: 81, Division 4, 1991–92.

Highest League Scorer in Season: Dougie Freedman, 24, Division 3, 1994–95.

Most League Goals in Total Aggregate: Sean Devine, 47, 1995–99.

Most League Goals in One Match: 4, Dougie Freedman v Rochdale, Division 3, 13 September 1994; 4, Lee Hodges v Rochdale, Division 3, 8 April 1996.

Most Capped Player: Ken Charlery, 4, St. Lucia.

Most League Appearances: Paul Wilson, 263, 1991–2000.

Youngest League Player: Kieran Adams, 17 years 71 days v Mansfield T, 31 December 1994.

Record Transfer Fee Received: £800,000 from Crystal Palace for Dougie Freedman, September 1995.

Record Transfer Fee Paid: £130,000 to Peterborough U for Greg Heald, August 1997.

Football League Record: Promoted to Division 4 from GMVC 1991; 1991–92 Division 4; 1992–93 Division 3; 1993–94 Division 2; 1994–2001 Division 3; 2001– Conference.

MANAGERS

Lester Finch
George Wheeler
Dexter Adams
Tommy Coleman
Gerry Ward
Gordon Ferry
Brian Kelly
Bill Meadows
Barry Fry
Roger Thompson
Don McAllister
Barry Fry
Edwin Stein
Gary Phillips *(Player-Manager)* 1993–94
Ray Clemence 1994–96
Alan Mullery *(Director of Football)* 1996–97
Terry Bullivant 1997
John Still 1997–2000
Tony Cottee 2000–01
John Still March 2001–

LATEST SEQUENCES

Longest Sequence of League Wins: 6, 28.8.93 – 25.9.99.

Longest Sequence of League Defeats: 11, 8.5.93 – 2.10.93.

Longest Sequence of League Draws: 4, 22.1.94 – 12.2.94.

Longest Sequence of Unbeaten League Matches: 12, 8.5.99 – 9.10.99.

Longest Sequence Without a League Win: 14, 11.12.93 – 8.3.94.

TEN YEAR LEAGUE RECORD

		P	W	D	L	F	A	Pts	Pos
1990-91	Conf	42	26	9	7	103	52	87	1
1991-92	Div 4	42	21	6	15	81	61	69	7
1992-93	Div 3	42	23	10	9	66	48	79	3
1993-94	Div 2	46	5	13	28	41	86	28	24
1994-95	Div 3	42	15	11	16	56	63	56	11
1995-96	Div 3	46	18	16	12	65	45	70	9
1996-97	Div 3	46	14	16	16	46	51	58	15
1997-98	Div 3	46	19	13	14	61	51	70	7
1998-99	Div 3	46	14	13	19	54	71	55	16
1999-2000	Div 3	46	21	12	13	59	53	75	6

DID YOU KNOW ?

In the 1930's, Tottenham Hotspur arranged for four of their junior players to be loaned to Barnet. They were Taffy O'Callaghan, Willie Evans, Alf Day and Bill Whatley, all of whom subsequently won caps for Wales.

BARNET 2000–01 LEAGUE RECORD

Match No.	Date	Venue	Opponents	Result	H/T Score	Lg. Pos.	Goalscorers	Attendance
1	Aug 12	H	Shrewsbury T	W 3-0	2-0	—	McGleish [21], Currie [42], Purser [89]	2090
2	19	H	Mansfield T	D 3-3	3-1	4	Arber [23], Stockley [28], McGleish [33]	1732
3	26	H	Cardiff C	D 2-2	1-0	6	McGleish [28], Charlery [81]	2264
4	28	A	York C	L 0-1	0-0	8		1981
5	Sept 2	A	Chesterfield	W 2-1	1-0	7	Sawyers [44], Charlery [51]	4340
6	9	H	Kidderminster H	D 0-0	0-0	7		2103
7	12	H	Exeter C	D 1-1	1-0	—	Charlery [41]	1322
8	16	A	Darlington	L 0-1	0-1	10		3929
9	23	H	Hull C	D 1-1	0-1	11	Strevens [75]	2109
10	30	A	Plymouth Arg	W 3-2	0-1	10	Richards 2 [49, 59], Arber [71]	3423
11	Oct 8	H	Macclesfield T	L 0-2	0-1	12		1841
12	14	A	Carlisle U	W 2-0	1-0	9	Niven [1], McGleish [54]	2487
13	17	A	Southend U	L 0-2	0-1	—		4124
14	21	H	Halifax T	W 1-0	1-0	9	Doolan (pen) [32]	1580
15	24	A	Leyton Orient	L 1-3	0-1	—	Riza [49]	4707
16	28	H	Lincoln C	W 4-3	1-3	9	Niven [28], Goodhind [53], Riza [77], Richards [80]	1642
17	Nov 4	A	Rochdale	D 0-0	0-0	10		3657
18	11	H	Blackpool	W 7-0	4-0	8	Cottee [18], Richards 2 [25, 42], Currie 3 [45, 80, 83], Arber [76]	2520
19	25	A	Torquay U	L 1-2	1-2	9	Richards [41]	1735
20	Dec 2	A	Cheltenham T	L 3-4	2-2	11	Currie [25], Cottee [27], Riza [60]	3599
21	16	H	Scunthorpe U	W 4-2	0-1	9	Cottee 3 [47, 67, 90], Riza [80]	2086
22	23	H	Hartlepool U	L 1-6	0-3	12	Richards [86]	3133
23	26	H	Brighton & HA	L 0-1	0-1	13		3908
24	Jan 1	A	Shrewsbury T	L 2-3	0-2	13	Arber [71], McGleish [78]	2991
25	13	H	York C	W 2-0	1-0	11	Richards [5], Cottee [63]	2731
26	27	H	Hartlepool U	L 1-3	0-1	12	Cottee [62]	2565
27	Feb 3	H	Chesterfield	D 1-1	0-1	13	Arber [65]	2372
28	10	A	Kidderminster H	L 1-2	1-0	16	Cottee [14]	2585
29	17	H	Darlington	W 3-0	1-0	15	Cottee [13], Currie [68], Arber [86]	1818
30	20	A	Exeter C	L 0-1	0-0	—		3572
31	24	A	Hull C	L 1-2	1-0	16	Gower [23]	7268
32	27	A	Mansfield T	L 1-4	0-2	—	Strevens [61]	1623
33	Mar 3	H	Plymouth Arg	D 1-1	0-1	16	Currie [61]	2879
34	6	H	Carlisle U	L 0-1	0-1	—		1480
35	11	A	Macclesfield T	L 0-3	0-2	17		2060
36	14	A	Brighton & HA	L 1-4	0-2	—	Doolan (pen) [82]	6587
37	17	H	Southend U	W 2-1	1-0	16	Strevens [25], Currie [64]	2654
38	24	A	Halifax T	L 0-3	0-1	18		1639
39	31	A	Scunthorpe U	L 1-2	1-2	20	Heald [2]	2963
40	Apr 4	A	Cardiff C	L 0-1	0-0	—		6209
41	7	H	Cheltenham T	D 2-2	1-1	20	Currie (pen) [29], Strevens [89]	1977
42	14	H	Leyton Orient	L 1-2	0-0	21	Currie (pen) [65]	3759
43	16	A	Lincoln C	L 1-2	0-2	22	Doolan [57]	3391
44	21	H	Rochdale	W 3-0	2-0	21	Heald 2 [16, 57], Arber [32]	2381
45	28	A	Blackpool	L 2-3	1-0	24	Purser [36], Parkinson (og) [64]	5289
46	May 5	H	Torquay U	L 2-3	0-3	24	Green (og) [60], Purser [76]	5523

Final League Position: 24

GOALSCORERS

League (67): Currie 10 (2 pens), Cottee 9, Richards 8, Arber 7, McGleish 5, Riza 4, Strevens 4, Charlery 3, Doolan 3 (2 pens), Heald 3, Purser 3, Niven 2, Goodhind 1, Gower 1, Sawyers 1, Stockley 1, own goals 2.
Worthington Cup (3): Doolan 1, McGleish 1, Richards 1.
FA Cup (3): Cottee 1, Currie 1, Richards 1.

Harrison L 30	Stockley S 45	Sawyers R 25 + 4	Basham M 8	Heald G 39	Arber M 45	Currie D 43 + 2	Doolan J 31	McGleish S 14 + 5	Richards T 27 + 6	Brown D 22 + 7	Darcy R — + 3	Purser W 4 + 14	Toms F 19 + 7	Charlery K 6 + 1	Strevens B 13 + 15	Newton E 2 + 2	Bell L 7 + 4	Naisbitt D 16 + 3	Goodhind W 30 + 1	Niven S 20 + 4	Riza O 7 + 3	Cottee T 16	Gledhill L 1 + 4	Flynn L 17	Gower M 10 + 4	Pluck L — + 1	Dawson K 5	Collis D 1 + 1	Midgley N 3 + 1	Match No.
1	2	3^1	4	5	6	7	8	9	10^2	11^3	12	13	14																	1
1	2		4	5	6	7	8	10^1		3			12	11	9^2	13														2
1	2	3		5	6	7	8		10	11^2	13		12		9^1	4														3
1	2	3		5	6	7	8	10^2			12	14		11^1	9	13	4^3													4
1	2	3	4	5	6	7	8	10		11				9																5
1	2	3	4^3	5	6	7	8	10^2	12			11		9^1	13	14														6
1	2	3	4	5	6	7	8	10	12			11^2	9^1		13															7
1	2	3	4^1	5	6	7	8	10		12			11^3	9^2	13	14														8
1^6	2			5	6	7		9^1	10		8			11		12	4	15	3											9
1	2			5	6	7	8	9^1	10					11^2		12	4	1	3	13										10
1	2			5	6	7	8	12	9			13	11		10^2		4^1	1	3											11
	2	3		5	6	7		8	9	10	11^1					12	1		4											12
	2	3		5	6	7		9	10^1		8			11		12	1		4											13
	2	3		5	6	7	8	12	9^1					11		13	1		4	10^2										14
	2	3		5	6	7		9			8	12		11^1			1		4	10										15
	2	3			6	7	8		9					11			1	5	4	10										16
	2			5	6	7	8	12	9^1					11			1	3	4	10										17
	2	3		5	6	7	8	12	9^1	13				11			1		4^2	14	10^3									18
	2	3^2		5	6	7	8		9	13				11			1		4	10^1										19
	2	3			6	7	8					12	11				1	5	4	10^2	9^1	13								20
	2	3		5		7	8^1			12			11				1	6	4	10	9									21
	2	3^1		5	6	7		9	11^3			12	13				1	8	4	10^2		14								22
1	2	3^1		5	6	7		9^2	12			11^3					8	4	13	10	14									23
1	2	3		5	6	7		12				11		9		8	4^1	13	10^2											24
1^9	2	12	4	5	6	7		9	13						3^1		8	15		10^2	11									25
1	2		4	5	6	7		9				12		8^2	3			10		11^1	13									26
1	2			5	6	12		9^2	11						4	8		10	3	7^1										27
1	2			5	6	12		9^2	11			13	8		4			10	3	7^1										28
1	2				6	7		9	11			12		5^3	4^2		10^1	13	3	8	14									29
1	2				6	7		9	11			12		5	4		10^1	3	8											30
1	2				6	7		9	11			12		5	4^1		10	3	8											31
1	2	12		5	6	7		9^2	11^1		13		10	14	4		3	8^3												32
1				5	6	7		12	11		9			3	4	10^1	2	8												33
1	2			5	6	7		11^1	13	12	9	14		3	4^3	10	8^2													34
1	2	12		5	6		8			9	13		10		3	7^2		4	11^1											35
1	2	3		5	6	7	8	9^1		12		10		4^2							11	13								36
1	2	3^2			6	7	8	9^1		12		10		5							11	13	4							37
1	2	3			6	7	8	9^1		10		5								11		4	12							38
1	2	3		5	6	7	8	12		13		9		4^3	14					11^{12}	10^1									39
1	2	3		5	6	7	8	12		10		9		4						11^1										40
1	2	3^2		5	6	7	8	11		12		9		4	13								10^1							41
1	2			5	6	7	8	12	11^1	13		10		4					3				9^2							42
	2			5	6	7	8	9	11^2	12		13		1	4^5					3	14		10^1							43
	2			5	6	7	8	9	11^1	10^2	12	13		1	4^5	14				3										44
	2	12		5	6	7	8	9	11^1	10	13			1	4^2					3										45
1^9	2			5	6	7	8	9	11^2	10	12			15	4					3^1	13									46

Worthington Cup
First Round   Wycombe W   (h)   2-1
                                      (a)   1-3

FA Cup
First Round   Hampton & Richmond B (h)   2-1
Second Round   Walsall   (a)   1-2

BARNSLEY

Division 1

FOUNDATION

Many clubs owe their inception to the church and Barnsley are among them, for they were formed in 1887 by the Rev. T. T. Preedy, curate of Barnsley St Peter's and went under that name until it was dropped in 1897 a year before being admitted to the Second Division of the Football League.

Oakwell Stadium, Barnsley, South Yorkshire S71 1ET

Telephone: (01226) 211 211. *Fax:* (01226) 211 444.
Website: barnsleyfc.co.uk
Email: thereds@barnsleyfc.co.uk
ClubCall: 09068 121 152.

Ground Capacity: 23,186.

Record Attendance: 40,255 v Stoke C, FA Cup 5th rd, 15 February 1936.

Record Receipts: undisclosed.

Pitch Measurements: 110yd × 75yd.

Chairman: J. A. Dennis. *Directors:* C. B. Taylor (Vice-Chairman), M. Hanson, C. H. Harrison, M. R. Hayselden, J. N. Kelly, I. D. Potter.

Manager: Nigel Spackman. *First Team Coach:* Derek Fazackerley.
Physio: Jim Webb.

General Manager/Secretary: Michael Spinks. *Lotteries Manager:* Gerry Whewall.
Sales and Marketing Manager: Graham Barlow.

Colours: Red shirts, white shorts, red stockings.

Change Colours: Royal blue and black striped shirts, black shorts, black stockings.

Year Formed: 1887. *Turned Professional:* 1888. *Ltd Co.:* 1899.

Previous Name: 1887, Barnsley St Peter's; 1897, Barnsley.

Club Nickname: 'The Tykes', 'Reds' or 'Colliers'.

First Football League Game: 1 September 1898, Division 2, v Lincoln C (a) L 0–1 – Fawcett; McArtney, Nixon; King, Burleigh, Porteous; Davis, Lees, Murray, McCullough, McGee.

Record League Victory: 9–0 v Loughborough T, Division 2, 28 January 1899 – Greaves; McArtney, Nixon; Porteous, Burleigh, Howard; Davis (4), Hepworth (1), Lees (1), McCullough (1), Jones (2). 9–0 v Accrington S, Division 3 (N), 3 February 1934 – Ellis; Cookson, Shotton; Harper, Henderson, Whitworth; Spence (2), Smith (1), Blight (4), Andrews (1), Ashton (1).

Record Cup Victory: 6–0 v Blackpool, FA Cup 1st rd replay, 20 January 1910 – Mearns; Downs, Ness; Glendinning, Boyle (1), Utley; Bartrop, Gadsby (1), Lillycrop (2), Tufnell (2), Forman. 6–0 v Peterborough U, League Cup 1st rd 2nd leg, 15 September 1981 – Horn; Joyce, Chambers, Glavin (2), Banks, McCarthy, Evans, Parker (2), Aylott (1), McHale, Barrowclough (1).

HONOURS

Football League: Division 1 – Runners-up 1996–97; Division 3 (N) – Champions 1933–34, 1938–39, 1954–55; Runners-up 1953–54; Division 3 – Runners-up 1980–81; Division 4 – Runners-up 1967–68; Promoted 1978–79.

FA Cup: Winners 1912; Runners-up 1910.

Football League Cup: best season: 5th rd, 1982.

IT'S A FACT !

George Donkin, a diminutive winger who joined Barnsley in 1913 and stayed 11 years, was one of the club's most popular players. Though a non-swimmer, he was awarded the Humane Society Certificate for Bravery after saving the life of a small girl in a nearby canal.

Record Defeat: 0–9 v Notts Co, Division 2, 19 November 1927.

Most League Points (2 for a win): 67, Division 3 (N), 1938–39.

Most League Points (3 for a win): 82, Division 1, 1999–2000.

Most League Goals: 118, Division 3 (N), 1933–34.

Highest League Scorer in Season: Cecil McCormack, 33, Division 2, 1950–51.

Most League Goals in Total Aggregate: Ernest Hine, 123, 1921–26 and 1934–38.

Most League Goals in One Match: 5, Frank Eaton v South Shields, Division 3N, 9 April 1927; 5, Peter Cunningham v Darlington, Division 3N, 4 February 1933; 5, Beau Asquith v Darlington, Division 3N, 12 November 1938; 5, Cecil McCormack v Luton T, Division 2, 9 September 1950.

Most Capped Player: Gerry Taggart, 35 (50), Northern Ireland.

Most League Appearances: Barry Murphy, 514, 1962–78.

Youngest League Player: Alan Ogley, 16 years 226 days v Bristol R, 18 September 1962.

Record Transfer Fee Received: £4,250,000 from Blackburn R for Ashley Ward, December 1998.

Record Transfer Fee Paid: £1,500,000 to Partizan Belgrade for Georgi Hristov, June 1997.

Football League Record: 1898 Elected to Division 2; 1932–34 Division 3 (N); 1934–38 Division 2; 1938–39 Division 3 (N); 1946–53 Division 2; 1953–55 Division 3 (N); 1955–59 Division 2; 1959–65 Division 3; 1965–68 Division 4; 1968–72 Division 3; 1972–79 Division 4; 1979–81 Division 3; 1981–92 Division 2; 1992–97 Division 1; 1997–98 FA Premier League; 1998– Division 1.

MANAGERS

Arthur Fairclough 1898–1901
(Secretary-Manager)
John McCartney 1901–04
(Secretary-Manager)
Arthur Fairclough 1904–12
John Hastie 1912–14
Percy Lewis 1914–19
Peter Sant 1919–26
John Commins 1926–29
Arthur Fairclough 1929–30
Brough Fletcher 1930–37
Angus Seed 1937–53
Tim Ward 1953–60
Johnny Steele 1960–71
(continued as General Manager)
John McSeveney 1971–72
Johnny Steele *(General Manager)* 1972–73
Jim Iley 1973–78
Allan Clarke 1978–80
Norman Hunter 1980–84
Bobby Collins 1984–85
Allan Clarke 1985–89
Mel Machin 1989–93
Viv Anderson 1993–94
Danny Wilson 1994–98
John Hendrie 1998–99
Dave Bassett 1999–2000
Nigel Spackman January 2001–

LATEST SEQUENCES

Longest Sequence of League Wins: 10, 5.3.55 – 23.4.55.

Longest Sequence of League Defeats: 9, 14.3.53 – 25.4.53.

Longest Sequence of League Draws: 7, 28.3.11 – 22.4.11.

Longest Sequence of Unbeaten League Matches: 21, 1.1.34 – 5.5.34.

Longest Sequence Without a League Win: 26, 13.12.52 – 26.8.53.

TEN YEAR LEAGUE RECORD

		P	W	D	L	F	A	Pts	Pos
1990-91	Div 2	46	19	12	15	63	48	69	8
1991-92	Div 2	46	16	11	19	46	57	59	16
1992-93	Div 1	46	17	9	20	56	60	60	13
1993-94	Div 1	46	16	7	23	55	67	55	18
1994-95	Div 1	46	20	12	14	63	52	72	6
1995-96	Div 1	46	14	18	14	60	66	60	10
1996-97	Div 1	46	22	14	10	76	55	80	2
1997-98	PR Lge	38	10	5	23	37	82	35	19
1998-99	Div 1	46	14	17	15	59	56	59	13
1999-2000	Div 1	46	24	10	12	88	67	82	4

DID YOU KNOW ?

On 11 January 1947, Barnsley won a see-saw third round FA Cup tie at Huddersfield Town, after taking a seventh minute lead through Gavin Smith and scoring the winner with a 25 yard lob from Jimmy Baxter.

BARNSLEY 2000–01 LEAGUE RECORD

Match No.	Date	Venue	Opponents	Result		H/T Score	Lg. Pos.	Goalscorers	Attendance
1	Aug 12	H	Norwich C	W	1-0	0-0	—	Jones [64]	15,640
2	19	A	Watford	L	0-1	0-0	11		13,186
3	26	H	WBA	W	4-1	0-1	5	Jones 2 [53, 60], Shipperley 2 [75, 90]	14,321
4	28	A	Birmingham C	L	1-4	0-2	8	Appleby [71]	17,160
5	Sept 10	A	Fulham	L	1-5	0-3	15	Appleby [73]	10,437
6	12	A	Crystal Palace	L	0-1	0-1	—		16,297
7	16	H	QPR	W	4-2	3-0	14	Darlington (og) [23], Shipperley [34], Van der Laan [45], Dyer [88]	12,763
8	23	A	Crewe Alex	D	2-2	0-1	15	Barnard (pen) [80], Dyer [89]	5738
9	30	H	Grimsby T	W	2-0	1-0	11	Dyer [32], Shipperley [50]	13,096
10	Oct 6	A	Huddersfield T	D	1-1	0-0	—	Kozluk (og) [67]	13,556
11	14	H	Nottingham F	L	3-4	0-2	11	Shipperley 2 [67, 68], Dyer [80]	14,831
12	17	H	Tranmere R	D	1-1	0-1	—	Barnard (pen) [83]	12,412
13	21	A	Gillingham	D	0-0	0-0	13		9030
14	24	H	Wolverhampton W	L	1-2	1-2	—	McClare [8]	13,393
15	27	A	Preston NE	W	2-1	1-0	—	Dyer [33], Sheron [53]	13,566
16	Nov 5	H	Wimbledon	L	0-1	0-0	13		13,641
17	8	H	Blackburn R	L	1-2	1-0	—	Ripley [19]	13,622
18	11	A	Bolton W	L	0-2	0-2	14		13,406
19	18	H	Sheffield W	W	1-0	1-0	13	Dyer [24]	19,989
20	25	H	Portsmouth	W	1-0	0-0	12	Dyer [58]	12,853
21	Dec 2	A	Wolverhampton W	L	0-2	0-1	13		17,340
22	9	H	Sheffield U	D	0-0	0-0	14		16,780
23	16	A	Stockport Co	L	0-2	0-0	14		5383
24	23	A	Norwich C	D	0-0	0-0	14		16,581
25	26	H	Burnley	W	1-0	0-0	12	Morgan [90]	18,725
26	29	H	Watford	L	0-1	0-0	—		13,820
27	Jan 1	A	WBA	L	0-1	0-0	15		19,423
28	13	H	Birmingham C	L	2-3	0-2	16	Dyer [75], Jones [86]	13,631
29	20	A	Burnley	L	1-2	0-1	17	Hayward [77]	15,380
30	Feb 3	A	Blackburn R	D	0-0	0-0	17		18,573
31	10	H	Fulham	D	0-0	0-0	17		14,654
32	17	A	QPR	L	0-2	0-1	19		9388
33	20	H	Crystal Palace	W	1-0	1-0	—	Shipperley [36]	12,909
34	24	H	Crewe Alex	W	3-0	1-0	14	Jones [34], Wright (og) [66], Shipperley [86]	13,175
35	Mar 3	A	Grimsby T	W	2-0	1-0	13	Dyer 2 [27, 56]	5996
36	7	A	Nottingham F	L	0-1	0-1	—		18,788
37	10	H	Huddersfield T	W	3-1	1-1	—	Dyer 2 [27, 55], Shipperley [78]	15,290
38	17	A	Tranmere R	W	3-2	0-2	12	Dyer [65], Shipperley [82], Rankin [90]	8484
39	25	H	Gillingham	W	3-1	1-1	12	Dyer 2 [9, 83], Shipperley (pen) [73]	13,609
40	31	H	Stockport Co	L	0-2	0-1	12		13,203
41	Apr 7	A	Sheffield U	W	2-1	1-1	12	Bullock [32], Shipperley [63]	22,811
42	14	A	Wimbledon	D	1-1	0-1	12	Shipperley [68]	7609
43	16	H	Preston NE	L	0-4	0-2	12		16,361
44	21	A	Sheffield W	L	1-2	1-0	12	Shipperley [19]	23,498
45	28	H	Bolton W	L	0-1	0-0	14		13,979
46	May 6	A	Portsmouth	L	0-3	0-1	16		13,064

Final League Position: 16

GOALSCORERS

League (49): Dyer 15, Shipperley 14 (1 pen), Jones 5, Appleby 2, Barnard 2 (2 pens), Bullock 1, Hayward 1, McClare 1, Morgan 1, Rankin 1, Ripley 1, Sheron 1, Van der Laan 1, own goals 3.
Worthington Cup (13): Sheron 5, Barnard 2, Shipperley 2, Corbo 1, Dyer 1, Jones 1, Van der Laan 1.
FA Cup (0).

Miller K 46	Moses A 11 + 3	Regan C 25 + 2	Morgan C 40	Chettle S 35	Kay A 3 + 4	Appleby M 17 + 2	Jones L 15 + 12	Shipperley N 38 + 1	Sheron M 21 + 13	Barnard D 26 + 4	O'Callaghan B 20 + 6	Dyer B 27 + 11	McClare S 5 + 5	Ward M 34 + 2	Thomas G 1 + 10	Barker C 39 + 1	Van der Laan R 16 + 2	Neil A 19 + 13	Brown K 1	Corbo M 10 + 7	Woan I 2 + 1	Maddison N 3	Ripley S 8 + 2	Satli J 6 + 1	Bullock M 15 + 3	Hayward S 10	Rankin I 6 + 3	Barrowclough C 2 + 5	Parkin J 4	Fallon R 1	Bertos L — + 2	Match No.
1	2	3	4	5	6^1	7	8^2	9	10^3	11	12	13	14																			1
1	2	3	4	5		7^2	8^1	9	10	11			12		6	13																2
1	2		4	5			8^1	9	10^1	11			12		6	13	3	7^2	14													3
1			4	5		12	8	9		11		2	10		6^3	7^1	14	13	3^2													4
1	12	2	4^1			7	13	9^2	10	11	5				6		8	14		3^3												5
1	4	2			10^2	7^1	8	9	12	11^3	5				6		3	13		14												6
1	4	2				7^3		9	10^1	11	5	12	14		6		13	8		3^2												7
1	2^1		4	5^2		7	13	12	9^2	11		14	10		6		8			3												8
1	12		4	5^1				9	13	11^3		2	10	7	6^2		3	8		14												9
1	5		4			12		9	13			2	10^1	8^1	6		3	7				11										10
1		2	4	5		7		9	12	13		14	10		6^1			8^3				3	11^2									11
1	2		4	5		7^1	12	9	10^2	11	6	8			13		3^3			14												12
1	2		4			12	7	9		11	5		10		6^1		3	8														13
1	2	12	4			7^3		9		11	5		10		6^2	13	3	8^1	14													14
1		2	4	5		7		9^1	12	11^3		13	10^2		6		3	8		14												15
1	12	2^1	4	5			8	9							6	13	3	7	14				11^3	10^2								16
1			4	5			8^1	9				2	12		6		3	10^3	14				13	11	7^2							17
1			4	5		12		9				2	10^1		6^3	13	3			8				14	11^2	7						18
1			4	5				9				2	10	12	6	13	3			8^1			11^2		7							19
1			4	5				9		12		2	10		6	13	3			8^2			11^1		7							20
1			4	5^2		12		9		11		2	10		6^2	13	3			8					7^1	14						21
1	2		4			12		9		11^3		13			6		3	8^1		10^2			14		7	5						22
1	2		4			8	12	9	10^1			13			6		3	14					11^3		7^2	5						23
1			4	5		7		9		10		11^2			6^1		3	8					12	2	13							24
1			4	5		7	12	9	10^1			13			6^2		3	8					14		11^3	2						25
1			4	5		7	12	9	10					8^3		13	3	6^2		14					11^1	2						26
1			4	5		7	8^1	9	10				6	12			3			11					2^2	13						27
1			4	5			12	9	10^3			2		8	6^2	13	3			7					11^1		14					28
1	12		4	5			8	9^2				2		13			3			6					7^1	11	10					29
1	2			5			8	9^1		4	12			13	14		3			6^3					7	11	10^2					30
1	2			5			8	9		4					6		3			10					7	11						31
1	2			5			8	9		4	12				6		3								7	11	10^1					32
1	2		4	5			8^3	9^1	12	13					6		3	14							7^2	11	10					33
1	2		4	5^1			8^2	9		13	14	12			6		3								7	11	10^1					34
1	2		4	5				9	12	11		10^1			6		3	13							8^2	7						35
1	2		4	5			8^2	9		11		10^1			6^3		3	14							13	7	12					36
1	2		4	5			12	9		11^1		10^3			6		3	13							8^2	7	14					37
1	2		4	5			8^2	9		11^1		10			6		3	12								7	13					38
1	2		4	5			12	9^2		13			10		6		3	7							11^3	8^1	14					39
1	2		4	5	12			9		13		11^3	10^2		6		3	7^1							8		14					40
1	2			5				9		11			10		6		3	7							8				4			41
1	2		4	5				9	12	11			10^1		6		3	7							8^2		13					42
1	2		4	5	12			9^2		13		11^3			6^1		3	7							8				10	14		43
1	2		4					9		11			10		6		3	7							8^1		12	5				44
1	2		4		6			9	12	11			10^1				3	7							8^2		13	5				45
1			4	12	2			9		13		11^3	10^2				3	7							8		6^1	5			14	46

Worthington Cup

First Round	Rotherham U	(a)	1-0
		(h)	3-2
Second Round	Crewe Alex	(h)	4-0
		(a)	3-0
Third Round	Stoke C	(a)	2-3

FA Cup

Third Round	Leeds U	(a)	0-1

BIRMINGHAM CITY   Division 1

FOUNDATION

In 1875 cricketing enthusiasts who were largely members of
Trinity Church, Bordesley, determined to continue their sporting
relationships throughout the year by forming a football club which
they called Small Heath Alliance. For their earliest games played
on waste land in Arthur Street, the team included three Edden
brothers and two James brothers.

St Andrews, Birmingham B9 4NH.

Telephone: 0709 111 25837. *Fax:* (0121) 766 7866.
Website: www.bcfc.com *ClubCall:* 09068 121 188.
Club Soccer Shop: 0709 111 25837 (ext. 8).

Ground Capacity: 30,009.

Record Attendance: 66,844 v Everton, FA Cup 5th rd,
11 February 1939.

Record Receipts: £396,113 v Preston NE, (play off
semi-final 1st leg), 13 May 2001.

Pitch Measurements: 110yd × 74yd.

Chairman: D. Gold. *Vice-Chairman:* J. F. Wiseman.
Directors: D. Sullivan, R. Gold, B. Gold, H. Brandman,
A. G. Jones, M. Wiseman.
Managing Director: K. R. Brady.

Manager: Trevor Francis. *Coach:* Mick Mills.
Physio: John Pryce.

Commercial Manager: Simon Bradley. *Stadium
Manager:* Brian Tew. *Secretary:* A. G. Jones BA, MBA.

Colours: Blue shirts, white shorts, blue and white
stockings.

Change Colours: Yellow and navy shirts, yellow shorts and stockings.

Year Formed: 1875.

Turned Professional: 1885.

Ltd Co.: 1888.

Previous Names: 1875, Small Heath Alliance; 1888, dropped 'Alliance'; 1905, Birmingham;
1945, Birmingham City.

Club Nickname: 'Blues'.

Previous Grounds: 1875, waste ground near Arthur St; 1877, Muntz St, Small Heath; 1906, St
Andrews.

First Football League game: 3 September 1892, Division 2, v Burslem Port Vale (h) W 5–1 – Charsley;
Bayley, Speller; Ollis, Jenkyns, Devey; Hallam (1), Edwards (1), Short (1), Wheldon (2), Hands.

Record League Victory: 12–0 v Walsall T Swifts, Division 2, 17 December 1892 – Charsley; Bayley,
Jones; Ollis, Jenkyns, Devey; Hallam (2), Walton (3), Mobley (3), Wheldon (2), Hands (2). 12–0 v
Doncaster R, Division 2, 11 April 1903 – Dorrington; Goldie, Wassell; Beer, Dougherty (1), Howard;
Athersmith (1), Leonard (3), McRoberts (1), Wilcox (4), Field (1). Aston, (1 og).

HONOURS

Football League: Division 1 best
season: 4th, 1998–99; Division 2 –
Champions 1892–93, 1920–21,
1947–48, 1954–55, 1994–95; Runners-
up 1893–94, 1900–01, 1902–03,
1971–72, 1984–85; Division 3
Runners-up 1991–92.

FA Cup: Runners-up 1931, 1956.

Football League Cup: Winners 1963;
Runners-up 2001.

Leyland Daf Cup: Winners 1991.

Auto Windscreens Shield: Winners
1995.

European Competitions: European
Fairs Cup: 1955–58, 1958–60
(runners-up), 1960–61 (runners-up),
1961–62.

IT'S A FACT !

Joe Bradford of the then Birmingham FC, scored three
hat-tricks in eight days during September 1929. Three
goals against Newcastle United, five for the Football
League and three against Blackburn Rovers.

Record Cup Victory: 9–2 v Burton W, FA Cup 1st rd, 31 October 1885 – Hedges; Jones, Evetts (1); F. James, Felton, A. James (1); Davenport (2), Stanley (4), Simms, Figures, Morris (1).

Record Defeat: 1–9 v Sheffield W, Division 1, 13 December 1930. 1–9 v Blackburn R, Division 1, 5 January 1895.

Most League Points (2 for a win): 59, Division 2, 1947–48.

Most League Points (3 for a win): 89, Division 2, 1994–95.

Most League Goals: 103, Division 2, 1893–94 (only 28 games).

Highest League Scorer in Season: Joe Bradford, 29, Division 1, 1927–28.

Most League Goals in Total Aggregate: Joe Bradford, 249, 1920–35.

Most League Goals in One Match: 5, Walter Abbott v Darwen, Division 2, 26 November, 1898; 5, John McMillan v Blackpool, Division 2, 2 March 1901; 5, James Windridge v Glossop, Division 2, 23 January 1915.

Most Capped Player: Malcolm Page, 28, Wales.

Most League Appearances: Frank Womack, 491, 1908–28.

Youngest League Player: Trevor Francis, 16 years 7 months v Cardiff C, 5 September 1970.

Record Transfer Fee Received: £2,500,000 from Coventry C for Gary Breen, January 1997.

Record Transfer Fee Paid: £2,250,000 to Fulham for Geoff Horsfield, July 2000.

MANAGERS

Alfred Jones 1892–1908
  (Secretary-Manager)
Alec Watson 1908–10
Bob McRoberts 1910–15
Frank Richards 1915–23
Billy Beer 1923–27
Leslie Knighton 1928–33
George Liddell 1933–39
Harry Storer 1945–48
Bob Brocklebank 1949–54
Arthur Turner 1954–58
Pat Beasley 1959–60
Gil Merrick 1960–64
Joe Mallett 1965
Stan Cullis 1965–70
Fred Goodwin 1970–75
Willie Bell 1975–77
Jim Smith 1978–82
Ron Saunders 1982–86
John Bond 1986–87
Garry Pendrey 1987–89
Dave Mackay 1989–1991
Lou Macari 1991
Terry Cooper 1991–93
Barry Fry 1993–96
Trevor Francis May 1996–

Football League Record: 1892 elected to Division 2; 1894–96 Division 1; 1896–1901 Division 2; 1901–02 Division 1; 1902–03 Division 2; 1903–08 Division 1; 1908–21 Division 2; 1921–39 Division 1; 1946–48 Division 2; 1948–50 Division 1; 1950–1955 Division 2; 1955–65 Division 1; 1965–72 Division 2; 1972–79 Division 1; 1979–80 Division 2; 1980–84 Division 1; 1984–85 Division 2; 1985–86 Division 1; 1986–89 Division 2; 1989–92 Division 3; 1992–94 Division 1; 1994–95 Division 2; 1995– Division 1.

LATEST SEQUENCES

Longest Sequence of League Wins: 13, 17.12.1892 – 16.9.1893.

Longest Sequence of League Defeats: 8, 28.9.85 – 23.11.85.

Longest Sequence of League Draws: 8, 18.9.90 – 23.10.90.

Longest Sequence of Unbeaten League Matches: 20, 3.9.94 – 2.1.95.

Longest Sequence Without a League Win: 17, 28.9.85 – 18.1.86.

TEN YEAR LEAGUE RECORD

		P	W	D	L	F	A	Pts	Pos
1990-91	Div 3	46	16	17	13	45	49	65	12
1991-92	Div 3	46	23	12	11	69	52	81	2
1992-93	Div 1	46	13	12	21	50	72	51	19
1993-94	Div 1	46	13	12	21	52	69	51	22
1994-95	Div 2	46	25	14	7	84	37	89	1
1995-96	Div 1	46	15	13	18	61	64	58	15
1996-97	Div 1	46	17	15	14	52	48	66	10
1997-98	Div 1	46	19	17	10	60	35	74	7
1998-99	Div 1	46	23	12	11	66	37	81	4
1999-2000	Div 1	46	22	11	13	65	44	77	5

DID YOU KNOW ?

On 13 May 2001, Nicky Eaden scored the play-off goal by which Birmingham City beat Preston North End 1-0. On 13 May 2000 he had been in the Barnsley team which beat Birmingham City 4-0 in the corresponding fixture.

BIRMINGHAM CITY 2000–01 LEAGUE RECORD

Match No.	Date	Venue	Opponents	Result	H/T Score	Lg. Pos.	Goalscorers	Attendance
1	Aug 12	A	QPR	D 0-0	0-0	—		13,926
2	18	H	Fulham	L 1-3	1-3	—	Sonner [38]	21,659
3	26	A	Nottingham F	W 2-1	2-0	14	Marcelo [16], Eaden [45]	18,820
4	28	H	Barnsley	W 4-1	2-0	5	Ndlovu [9], Grainger (pen) [35], Holdsworth [51], Hughes [90]	17,160
5	Sept 9	H	Sheffield U	W 1-0	1-0	6	O'Connor (pen) [9]	21,493
6	12	H	Preston NE	W 3-1	0-1	—	Ndlovu [58], Johnson A [65], O'Connor (pen) [78]	16,464
7	17	A	WBA	D 1-1	0-1	4	Horsfield [61]	19,858
8	23	H	Tranmere R	W 2-0	0-0	4	Grainger [73], Horsfield [90]	17,640
9	Oct 1	A	Watford	L 0-2	0-0	5		12,355
10	8	A	Crewe Alex	W 2-0	0-0	4	Hughes [54], Marcelo [81]	6829
11	14	H	Crystal Palace	W 2-1	0-0	4	Burchill [72], Adebola [85]	17,191
12	17	H	Stockport Co	W 4-0	1-0	—	Horsfield [13], Grainger (pen) [70], Burchill 2 [80, 87]	15,579
13	22	A	Sheffield W	L 0-1	0-0	3		14,695
14	25	H	Gillingham	W 1-0	0-0	—	Marcelo [90]	26,044
15	28	A	Portsmouth	D 1-1	0-1	3	Adebola [48]	15,218
16	Nov 4	H	Bolton W	D 1-1	0-0	3	Grainger (pen) [50]	20,043
17	7	A	Norwich C	L 0-1	0-1	—		13,900
18	18	H	Burnley	W 3-2	0-0	4	Adebola [48], O'Connor [50], Burchill [86]	19,641
19	25	H	Huddersfield T	W 2-1	2-0	3	Lazaridis [26], Horsfield [45]	22,120
20	Dec 2	A	Gillingham	W 2-1	0-1	2	Johnson M [78], Horsfield [90]	9247
21	9	H	Wimbledon	L 0-3	0-2	3		16,778
22	17	A	Wolverhampton W	W 1-0	1-0	3	Adebola [32]	19,938
23	23	H	QPR	D 0-0	0-0	3		24,311
24	26	A	Blackburn R	L 1-2	0-0	4	Purse [88]	24,899
25	Jan 1	H	Nottingham F	L 0-2	0-0	6		20,034
26	13	A	Barnsley	W 3-2	2-0	6	Marcelo [16], Johnson M [40], Lazaridis [46]	13,631
27	27	A	Fulham	W 1-0	0-0	5	Grainger [49]	17,077
28	Feb 3	H	Norwich C	W 2-1	1-0	5	Hughes [9], Purse (pen) [62]	18,551
29	10	A	Sheffield U	L 1-3	0-2	6	Horsfield [89]	19,313
30	17	H	WBA	W 2-1	1-1	4	Adebola [36], O'Connor [57]	25,025
31	20	A	Preston NE	W 2-0	1-0	—	Grainger [11], Johnson A [71]	14,864
32	Mar 2	H	Watford	W 2-0	1-0	—	Eaden [45], Hughes [79]	20,724
33	6	A	Crystal Palace	W 2-1	0-0	—	Upson (og) [48], Adebola [58]	13,987
34	10	H	Crewe Alex	W 2-0	0-0	3	Purse (pen) [61], Johnson A [77]	28,042
35	14	H	Blackburn R	L 0-2	0-1	—		29,150
36	17	A	Stockport Co	L 0-2	0-1	4		7176
37	20	A	Grimsby T	D 1-1	1-1	—	Johnson A [16]	4843
38	24	H	Sheffield W	L 1-2	0-1	—	Horsfield [60]	19,733
39	Apr 1	H	Wolverhampton W	L 0-1	0-1	4		24,003
40	7	A	Wimbledon	L 1-3	0-1	4	Marcelo [86]	6619
41	10	A	Tranmere R	L 0-1	0-0	—		8004
42	13	A	Bolton W	D 2-2	1-0	—	O'Connor [14], Marcelo [57]	15,025
43	16	H	Portsmouth	D 0-0	0-0	4		23,304
44	21	A	Burnley	D 0-0	0-0	6		17,057
45	28	H	Grimsby T	W 1-0	0-0	5	Marcelo [84]	24,822
46	May 6	A	Huddersfield T	W 2-1	2-1	5	Woodhouse 2 [21, 45]	19,290

Final League Position: 5

GOALSCORERS

League (59): Horsfield 7, Marcelo 7, Adebola 6, Grainger 6 (3 pens), O'Connor 5 (2 pens), Burchill 4, Hughes 4, Johnson A 4, Purse 3 (2 pens), Eaden 2, Johnson M 2, Lazaridis 2, Ndlovu 2, Woodhouse 2, Holdsworth 1, Sonner 1, own goal 1.
Worthington Cup (22): Adebola 5, Horsfield 3, Johnson A 3, Johnson M 2, Burchill 1, Eaden 1, Grainger 1, Hughes 1, Marcelo 1, Ndlovu 1, Purse 1 (pen), Sonner 1, 1 own goal.
FA Cup (2): Adebola 1, Grainger 1.

Bennett I 45	Eaden N 44 + 1	Johnson M 39	Hughes B 38 + 7	Purse D 34 + 3	Holdsworth D 24 + 5	Grainger M 35	Sonner D 22 + 4	Horsfield G 25 + 9	Ndlovu P 10 + 2	Lazaridis S 26 + 5	Marcelo 16 + 15	Williams J 1 + 2	Johnson A 20 + 14	Gill J 21 + 8	O'Connor M 28 + 2	Adebola D 16 + 15	Burrows D 8 + 5	Robinson S — + 4	Charles G 3	Hyde G 1 + 2	Burchill M 4 + 9	Edghill R 3	Jenkins S 3	Poole K 1	McCarthy J 7 + 8	Woodhouse C 17	Tiler C 1	Atherton P 10	Furlong P — + 4	Pollock J 4 + 1	Bass J — + 1	Match No.
1	2	3	4	5	6	7	8	9	10	11[1]	12																					1
1	2	3	4[2]	5	6	7	8	9[1]	10	11[3]	12	13	14																			2
1	7	6	4		5	3	11		10		9[1]				13	2	8	12														3
1	7	6	4		5	3	11		10[1]		9[2]			13	2	8	12															4
1	2	6	4	12	5	7	11[1]	13	10		9[2]	14			8		3[3]															5
1	2	6[1]	4	12	5	3		9	11		10[2]	7[3]	13		8			14														6
1	7		4	5	6	3	11	9[2]	10[3]				13		8	12		14	2[1]													7
1	7		4	5	6	3	11	9	12				10[1]	13					2[2]	8[3]	14											8
1	7[3]	6	4		5	3	8	9	12	11[1]	14		13	2							10[2]											9
1	2	3	4	5	6		8	9[2]	10[1]	11[3]	13		14		7	12																10
1	7	6	4		5	3	11[1]	9[3]	12				10[2]		8	13		2			14											11
1	7	6	4[1]		5	3	11	9[2]	12	13				2	8	12					14											12
1	7	6	4	12	5	3		9[2]		11[1]	13		14	2[3]	8	10																13
1	7		4	5	6	3		10[2]	11	12			13	2[1]	8	9[1]					14											14
1	7	6	12	5	4	3	11			9[3]			10[1]	2[2]	8	13					14											15
1	7	6	4	5	12	3		13		11	14			2	8[1]	9[3]					10[2]											16
1	7	6	8	5	4	3		12		11[2]			13	2[3]		9		14	10[1]													17
1	7	6	4	5		11		9[3]		12			10[2]		8	13	3[1]				14	2										18
1	7	6	4	5		3	12	9		11[2]					8	10[3]	13				14	2[1]										19
1	7[3]	6	12	5		3	4[2]	9		11[1]					2	8	10	13			14											20
1	7	6[1]	4	5		3		9[3]		11			12		8	10	13				14	2[2]										21
1	7	6	4	5		8		11	12		13	14		9[1]	3						10[2]	2[3]										22
1	7[2]	6	4	5		8	12	11		10[3]	2	13	9	3[1]	14																	23
1	7[2]	6	4[1]	5		10	9[3]	11	13		2	8	12	3	14																	24
1	7[1]	6	4	5		3	11[3]	9[2]		12	13			8	10	14						2										25
	7	6	12	5		3	4	13	10[3]	11[1]	9[2]		14	8								2	1									26
1	7	6	12	5		3	4[1]	9		11			13	2	8	10[2]																27
1	7[3]	6	4	5		3		9		11[2]			10[1]	2	13	12									14	8						28
1	7	6	12			3	4	9		11[1]			13	2[3]	10[2]										14	8	5					29
1	7[2]	6	4	5					9[1]		12		8	10	3										13	11		2				30
1		6	4[2]	5		3	13			9[1]			10		8	12									7	11		2				31
1	7[3]	6	4	5		3	12	9					10[2]		8[1]	13									14	11		2				32
1	7	6	4	5		3[2]		9[1]					10[3]	13	12										8	11		2				33
1	7[1]	6	4	5		3		9[3]		10	12	8[2]													13	11		2	14			34
1	7	6[1]	4	5	12	3		9[3]		13	10														8[2]	11		2	14			35
1	7[2]		4	5	6	3		9		10[3]	12														13	11		2	14	8[1]		36
1	7[3]		12	5	6	3		13		11[1]			10		9[2]										14	4		2		8		37
1	7[3]		4	5	6	3		9		11	12		2		10[1]		13												8[2]	14		38
1	12	6	4		5			9[2]		11	13		10	3		14									7[3]			2[1]	8			39
1	7	6	4		5	3[3]		13		11[1]	9		10	2		12[2]	14									8						40
1	7[1]	6	4		5			12		11	9		10	2		3										8						41
1	2	6	12	5	13					11	9		10[2]	14	8[1]		3[3]								7	4						42
1	2	6		5	12	13				11	9		10[1]	3	8										7[2]	4						43
1	2	3	4[1]	5	6	10[2]				12	9			8											7	11				13		44
1	2[1]	6	4	5	12	3	7			9			10	14	8[2]	13[3]										11						45
1	7		4	5	6			12		11[2]	9[1]		10[3]	3											13	8		2	14			46

Worthington Cup

First Round	Southend U	(a)	5-0
		(h)	0-0
Second Round	Wycombe W	(a)	4-3
		(h)	1-0
Third Round	Tottenham H	(a)	3-1
Fourth Round	Newcastle U	(h)	2-1
Fifth Round	Sheffield W	(h)	2-0
Semi-Final	Ipswich T	(a)	0-1
		(h)	4-1
Final	Liverpool		1-1
(at Millennium Stadium)			

FA Cup

Third Round	Manchester C	(a)	2-3

BLACKBURN ROVERS FA Premiership

FOUNDATION

It was in 1875 that some Public School old boys called a meeting at which the Blackburn Rovers club was formed and the colours blue and white adopted. The leading light was John Lewis, later to become a founder of the Lancashire FA, a famous referee who was in charge of two FA Cup Finals, and a vice-president of both the FA and the Football League.

Ewood Park, Blackburn BB2 4JF.

Telephone: (01254) 698 888. *Fax:* (01254) 671 042.
Website: www.rovers.co.uk *Email:* enquiries@rovers.co.uk
Ticket Hotline: (01254) 671 666. *ClubCall:* 09068 121 179.
Mail Order: 08080 20 20 20. *Club Shop:* (01254) 665 606.

Ground Capacity: 31,367.

Record Attendance: 62,522 v Bolton W, FA Cup 6th rd, 2 March 1929.

Record Receipts: £438,868 (gross) v Newcastle U, FA Cup 5th rd, 31 January 2000.

Pitch Measurements: 115yd × 72yd.

Chairman: R. D. Coar BSc.
Vice-Chairman: R. L. Matthewman.
Directors: R. D. Coar BSc, R. L. Matthewman, J. O. Williams BSc (Chief Executive), Tom Finn, K. C. Lee, G. R. Root, I. R. Stanners.

Manager: Graeme Souness. *Physio:* Dave Fevre.
Assistant Manager: Tony Parkes. *Coach:* Phil Boersma.

Commercial Manager: Ken Beamish.

Secretary: Tom Finn.

Stadium Manager: M. Highmore.

Colours: Blue and white halved shirts, white shorts with navy blue strip, white stockings with navy blue trim.

Change Colours: Red and black striped shirts, red shorts with black panel, red and black stockings.

Year Formed: 1875.

Turned Professional: 1880.

Ltd Co.: 1897.

Club Nickname: Rovers.

Previous Grounds: 1875, all matches played away; 1876, Oozehead Ground; 1877, Pleasington Cricket Ground; 1878, Alexandra Meadows; 1881, Leamington Road; 1890, Ewood Park.

First Football League Game: 15 September 1888, Football League, v Accrington (h) D 5–5 – Arthur; Beverley, James Southworth; Douglas, Almond, Forrest; Beresford (1), Walton, John Southworth (1), Fecitt (1), Townley (2).

HONOURS

FA Premier League: Champions 1994–95; Runners-up 1993–94.

Football League: Division 1 – Champions 1911–12, 1913–14; Runners-up 2000–01; Division 2 – Champions 1938–39; Runners-up 1957–58; Division 3 – Champions 1974–75; Runners-up 1979–80.

FA Cup: Winners 1884, 1885, 1886, 1890, 1891, 1928; Runners-up 1882, 1960.

Football League Cup: Semi-final 1962, 1993.

Full Members' Cup: Winners 1987.

European Competitions: *European Cup:* 1995–96. *UEFA Cup:* 1994–95, 1998–99.

IT'S A FACT !

David Dunn's hat-trick of penalties for Blackburn Rovers v Rochdale on 6 September 2000 was a record for the League Cup competition. His first shot was to the goalkeeper's right, the next two to his left.

Record League Victory: 9–0 v Middlesbrough, Division 2, 6 November 1954 – Elvy; Suart, Eckersley; Clayton, Kelly, Bell; Mooney (3), Crossan (2), Briggs, Quigley (3), Langton (1).

Record Cup Victory: 11–0 v Rossendale, FA Cup 1st rd, 13 October 1884 – Arthur; Hopwood, McIntyre; Forrest, Blenkhorn, Lofthouse; Sowerbutts (2), J. Brown (1), Fecitt (4), Barton (3), Birtwistle (1).

Record Defeat: 0–8 v Arsenal, Division 1, 25 February 1933.

Most League Points (2 for a win): 60, Division 3, 1974–75.

Most League Points (3 for a win): 91, Division 1, 2000–01.

Most League Goals: 114, Division 2, 1954–55.

Highest League Scorer in Season: Ted Harper, 43, Division 1, 1925–26.

Most League Goals in Total Aggregate: Simon Garner, 168, 1978–92.

Most League Goals in One Match: 7, Tommy Briggs v Bristol R, Division 2, 5 February 1953.

Most Capped Player: Bob Crompton, 41, England.

Most League Appearances: Derek Fazackerley, 596, 1970–86.

Youngest League Player: Harry Dennison, 16 years 155 days v Bristol C, 8 April 1911.

Record Transfer Fee Received: £15,000,000 from Newcastle U for Alan Shearer, July 1996.

Record Transfer Fee Paid: £7,250,000 to Southampton for Kevin Davies, June 1998.

Football League Record: 1888 Founder Member of the League; 1936–39 Division 2; 1946–48 Division 1; 1948–58 Division 2; 1958–66 Division 1; 1966–71 Division 2; 1971–75 Division 3; 1975–79 Division 2; 1979–80 Division 3; 1980–92 Division 2; 1992–99 FA Premier League; 1999– Division 1.

LATEST SEQUENCES

Longest Sequence of League Wins: 8, 1.3.80 – 7.4.80.

Longest Sequence of League Defeats: 7, 12.3.66 – 16.4.66.

Longest Sequence of League Draws: 5, 11.10.75 – 1.11.75.

Longest Sequence of Unbeaten League Matches: 23, 30.9.87 – 27.3.88.

Longest Sequence Without a League Win: 16, 11.11.78 – 24.3.79.

MANAGERS

Thomas Mitchell 1884–96
(Secretary-Manager)
J. Walmsley 1896–1903
(Secretary-Manager)
R. B. Middleton 1903–25
Jack Carr 1922–26
(Team Manager under Middleton to 1925)
Bob Crompton 1926–30
(Hon. Team Manager)
Arthur Barritt 1931–36
(had been Secretary from 1927)
Reg Taylor 1936–38
Bob Crompton 1938–41
Eddie Hapgood 1944–47
Will Scott 1947
Jack Bruton 1947–49
Jackie Bestall 1949–53
Johnny Carey 1953–58
Dally Duncan 1958–60
Jack Marshall 1960–67
Eddie Quigley 1967–70
Johnny Carey 1970–71
Ken Furphy 1971–73
Gordon Lee 1974–75
Jim Smith 1975–78
Jim Iley 1978
John Pickering 1978–79
Howard Kendall 1979–81
Bobby Saxton 1981–86
Don Mackay 1987–91
Kenny Dalglish 1991–95
Ray Harford 1995–97
Roy Hodgson 1997–98
Brian Kidd 1998–99
Tony Parkes 1999–2000
Graeme Souness March 2000–

TEN YEAR LEAGUE RECORD

		P	W	D	L	F	A	Pts	Pos
1990-91	Div 2	46	14	10	22	51	66	52	19
1991-92	Div 2	46	21	11	14	70	53	74	6
1992-93	PR Lge	42	20	11	11	68	46	71	4
1993-94	PR Lge	42	25	9	8	63	36	84	2
1994-95	PR Lge	42	27	8	7	80	39	89	1
1995-96	PR Lge	38	18	7	13	61	47	61	7
1996-97	PR Lge	38	9	15	14	42	43	42	13
1997-98	PR Lge	38	16	10	12	57	52	58	6
1998-99	PR Lge	38	7	14	17	38	52	35	19
1999-2000	Div 1	46	15	17	14	55	51	62	11

DID YOU KNOW ?

On 18 November 2000, Blackburn Rovers celebrated their 125th anniversary with an important 1-0 victory over visiting Wolverhampton Wanderers at Ewood Park.

BLACKBURN ROVERS 2000–01 LEAGUE RECORD

Match No.	Date	Venue	Opponents	Result	H/T Score	Lg. Pos.	Goalscorers	Attendance
1	Aug 12	H	Crystal Palace	W 2-0	2-0	—	Blake [41], Jansen [44]	18,733
2	19	A	Crewe Alex	D 0-0	0-0	6		7500
3	26	H	Norwich C	W 3-2	1-0	3	Dunn (pen) [25], Blake [52], Jansen [82]	19,542
4	28	A	Sheffield W	D 1-1	1-1	4	Taylor [44]	15,646
5	Sept 9	A	Nottingham F	W 3-0	2-0	4	Jansen [17], Dunn (pen) [20], Blake [66]	18,471
6	12	H	Watford	L 3-4	2-3	—	Dunn [6], Blake 2 [16, 87]	17,258
7	15	A	Sheffield U	L 0-2	0-2	—		10,816
8	23	H	Bolton W	D 1-1	1-0	10	Thomas [1]	23,660
9	30	A	WBA	L 0-1	0-0	13		16,794
10	Oct 15	A	Fulham	L 1-2	1-1	15	Jansen [4]	15,247
11	18	A	Wimbledon	W 2-0	2-0	—	Ostenstad [22], Flitcroft [45]	6019
12	21	H	Grimsby T	W 2-0	0-0	10	Flitcroft [56], Jansen [90]	16,397
13	25	H	Tranmere R	W 3-2	3-1	—	Hughes 2 [26, 31], Ostenstad [36]	17,010
14	28	A	Huddersfield T	W 1-0	0-0	8	Ostenstad [73]	12,287
15	Nov 4	H	Stockport Co	W 2-1	0-1	8	Hughes [52], Hignett [90]	17,404
16	8	A	Barnsley	W 2-1	0-1	—	Jansen [73], Dunn [82]	13,622
17	11	A	Portsmouth	D 2-2	1-1	6	Bjornebye [45], Jansen [82]	14,141
18	18	H	Wolverhampton W	W 1-0	0-0	5	Dunn (pen) [64]	20,380
19	25	H	Gillingham	L 1-2	1-2	7	Hughes [12]	18,061
20	Dec 2	A	Tranmere R	D 1-1	0-0	8	Dunn [47]	10,063
21	9	H	QPR	D 0-0	0-0	9		16,886
22	17	A	Burnley	W 2-0	1-0	6	McAteer [45], Bent [90]	21,369
23	22	A	Crystal Palace	W 3-2	3-0	—	Dunn 2 (1 pen) [12 (p), 16], Taylor [44]	15,010
24	26	H	Birmingham C	W 2-1	0-0	3	Jansen 2 [65, 90]	24,899
25	30	A	Crewe Alex	W 1-0	0-0	3	Jansen [67]	18,554
26	Jan 1	A	Norwich C	D 1-1	0-1	4	Bent [64]	16,695
27	10	H	Preston NE	W 3-2	3-0	—	Jansen 2 [6, 19], Hughes [9]	23,983
28	13	H	Sheffield W	W 2-0	2-0	3	Bent [30], Taylor [40]	19,308
29	Feb 3	H	Barnsley	D 0-0	0-0	3		18,573
30	10	A	Nottingham F	L 1-2	0-0	3	Jansen [89]	22,455
31	20	A	Watford	W 1-0	0-0	—	Bent [72]	15,970
32	23	A	Bolton W	W 4-1	1-0	—	Bent [45], Dunn [74], Jansen [81], Hignett [89]	20,017
33	Mar 3	H	WBA	W 1-0	0-0	3	Bent [47]	23,926
34	14	A	Birmingham C	W 2-0	1-0	—	Bent [41], Duff [53]	29,150
35	17	H	Wimbledon	D 1-1	0-0	3	Jansen [73]	19,000
36	Apr 1	H	Burnley	W 5-0	2-0	2	Short [15], Davis (og) [29], Jansen 2 [55, 70], Hignett [82]	23,442
37	4	H	Sheffield U	D 1-1	1-0	—	Berg [4]	26,276
38	7	A	QPR	W 3-1	2-1	2	Dunn [25], Jansen [45], Berkovic [86]	12,449
39	11	H	Fulham	L 1-2	1-1	—	Jansen [6]	21,578
40	14	A	Stockport Co	D 0-0	0-0	2		9705
41	16	H	Huddersfield T	W 2-0	1-0	2	Flitcroft [30], Jansen [90]	29,426
42	21	A	Wolverhampton W	D 0-0	0-0	2		20,018
43	24	A	Grimsby T	W 4-1	2-0	—	Dunn [35], Berkovic [39], Jansen 2 [58, 87]	6507
44	29	H	Portsmouth	W 3-1	0-1	2	Hiley (og) [61], Dunn [79], Bent [86]	24,257
45	May 2	A	Preston NE	W 1-0	0-0	—	Jansen [72]	16,975
46	6	A	Gillingham	D 1-1	1-0	2	Blake [5]	10,319

Final League Position: 2

GOALSCORERS

League (76): Jansen 23, Dunn 12 (4 pens), Bent 8, Blake 6, Hughes 5, Flitcroft 3, Hignett 3, Ostenstad 3, Taylor 3, Berkovic 2, Berg 1, Bjornebye 1, Duff 1, McAteer 1, Short 1, Thomas 1, own goals 2.
Worthington Cup (12): Dunn 4 (3 pens), Duff 2, Thomas 2, Blake 1, Carsley 1, Diawara 1, Ostenstad 1.
FA Cup (11): Bent 3, Dunn 2 (1 pen), Flitcroft 2, Hignett 2 (1 pen), Jansen 1, Taylor 1.

Kelly J 7	Curtis J 46	Bjornebye S 30 + 3	Short C 35	Dailly C 3 + 7	Dunn D 41 + 1	McAteer J 20 + 7	Flitcroft G 41	Blake N 11 + 1	Jansen M 31 + 9	Duff D 31 + 1	Johnson D 12 + 4	Gillespie K 12 + 6	Carsley L 3 + 5	Diawara K 1 + 4	Taylor M 12 + 4	Broomes M 1	Berg H 41	Ostenstad E 7 + 6	Thomas J 1 + 3	Filan J 12 + 1	Kenna J 5 + 1	Hignett C 15 + 15	Hughes M 21 + 8	Friedel B 27	Bent M 21 + 7	Mahon A 14 + 4	Keller M — + 2	Berkovic E 4 + 7	Dunning D 1	Match No.
1	2	3	4	5	6^1	7	8	9	10	11	12																			1
1	2	3	4	5	6	7^1	8	9	10	11		12																		2
1	2	3	4	5	6	7	8	9	10	11^2			12	13																3
1	2	3	4^3		6	7^1	8	9	10	11^2	12				13	14	5													4
1	2	3	4		6	7	8^2	9^1	10^3	11	13	12					5	14												5
1	2	3	4		6	7^1	8	9	10^2	11	12	13^3					5	14												6
1	2	3	12		6	7	8	9		11	10^2	4^1					5		13											7
	2	3	4		12	7^2	8^1	9		11	13		6				5	14	10^3	1										8
		4	3		10	7^1		9	8	11^2		12			6		5		13	1	2									9
	7	3	4^2		11		8	9	10^1	12		6^3		13	5				1	2	14									10
	2	3	4		6	12	8			11^1	10		13				5	9^2		1		7								11
	2	3	4		6	7^1	8		12	11		13					5	9		1		10^2								12
	2	3	4		6	12	7			11^1		13					5	9^2		1		8	10							13
3			4		6	12	7			11							5	9		1	2	8^1	10							14
	2	3	4	12	6	13	7			11^2							5	9^1		1		8	10							15
	2	3	4	12	6		7		13	11^1							5	9^2		1		8	10							16
	2	3	4	12	6		7		13	11^1							5	9^2		1		8	10							17
	2	3^3	4	12	11	13			9		7^1	6					5		14			8^2	10	1						18
	2	3^2	4	14	6		7		9^1	11							5			13^3	8^1	10	1	12						19
	2		4		6	12	7	13	11								5			3	8^1	10^2	1	9						20
	2		4			7^1	6		8	11							5	12		3^2	13	10	1	9						21
	2	3			6	7	8		12	11^2			4				5					10^1	1	9	13					22
	2	3			6	7	8		12	11^2			4				5					10^1	1	9	13					23
	2	3			6	7	8		12	11			4	5	13			15				10^2	1^8	9^1						24
	2	3			6	7			8	11			4	5					1			12	10	9^1						25
	2	3^2		12	6	7^1			8^2	11			4	5	13				1			14	10	9						26
	2	3			6		8		9	11^2			4	5								7	10^1	1	12	13				27
	2	3				8		10	11				4	5								7^1		1	9	6	12			28
4			11	2^3	7	12	9	3					6	5								10^2	1	13	8^1	14			29
4			11	2^2	8		12	3		13			6	5								10^1	1	9	7^3		14		30
4	6		11		7^3		8^1	3		2^2				5							13	12	1	9	10		14		31
4	6		11		7	10^1	3		2^2					5							13	12	1	9	8				32
4	6		11			8^1	3		2^2					5							13	12	1	9	7		10		33
2	3	4		6		8		10	11	7				5									1	9^1	12				34
2	3^3	4			8		10	11	7				5							12	13	1	9^2	6^1		14			35
4	12	6		11	2^3	7		8	3^1					5^2							14	13	1	9	10				36
4	12	6		11		7		8		13^3	2^2			5							14		1	9	3	10¹			37
4		6		11		7		8^2	3		2^1			5							12	13	1	9	10^3		14		38
4	12	6^3		11		7		8	3^1		2^1			5							13		1	9	10		14		39
4	3	6		11		8		9			2			5								10^1	1	12	7				40
4	3^1	6		11		7		8			2^1			5							13	12	1	9^1	10		14		41
2	3^3	4		6		7		8			12			5							11	13	1	9^2	10^1		14		42
4	6^2		11		7		9		2	12		13		5							3^1	10^3	1	14			8		43
4	6		3	12	8		9		7	14				5							2^2	10^3	1	13			11^1		44
4	6		11		8		9	3	2^1	7				5							12	10^2	1	13					45
4	6			7	8	10^1	12		3^1	2			5								13		1	9				11	46

Worthington Cup

First Round	Rochdale	(a)	1-1
		(h)	6-1
Second Round	Portsmouth	(h)	4-0
		(a)	1-1
Third Round	West Ham U	(a)	0-2

FA Cup

Third Round	Chester C	(h)	2-0
Fourth Round	Derby Co	(h)	0-0
		(a)	5-2
Fifth Round	Bolton W	(a)	1-1
		(h)	3-0
Sixth Round	Arsenal	(a)	0-3

BLACKPOOL

Division 2

FOUNDATION

Old boys of St John's School who had formed themselves into a football club decided to establish a club bearing the name of their town and Blackpool FC came into being at a meeting at the Stanley Arms Hotel in the summer of 1887. In their first season playing at Raikes Hall Gardens, the club won both the Lancashire Junior Cup and the Fylde Cup.

Bloomfield Rd Ground, Blackpool FY1 6JJ.

Telephone: (01253) 404 331 (Ticket/Credit Bookings), (01253) 405 331 (Shop/General Enquiries). *Fax:* (01253) 405 011. *Website:* www.blackpoolfc.co.uk *Email:* info@blackpoolfc.co.uk *ClubCall:* 09068 121 648

Ground Capacity: 6100.

Record Attendance: 38,098 v Wolverhampton W, Division 1, 17 September 1955.

Record Receipts: £79,420 v Preston NE, Division 2, 21 November 1998.

Pitch Measurements: 112yd × 74yd.

Chairman: Mr K. Oyston.

Directors: C. Muir OBE, O. J. Oyston, G. Warburton, P. Smith, P. Whitehead.

Manager: Steve McMahon.

Secretary: Carol Banks.

Commercial Director: Geoff Warburton.

Physio: Phil Horner.

Stadium Manager: John Turner.

Colours: Tangerine shirts, white shorts, tangerine stockings.

Change Colours: White shirts, tangerine shorts, white stockings.

Year Formed: 1887.

Turned Professional: 1887.

Ltd Co.: 1896.

Previous Name: 'South Shore' combined with Blackpool in 1899, twelve years after the latter had been formed on the breaking up of the old 'Blackpool St John's' club.

Club Nickname: 'The Seasiders'.

Previous Grounds: 1887, Raikes Hall Gardens; 1897, Athletic Grounds; 1899, Raikes Hall Gardens; 1899, Bloomfield Road.

First Football League game: 5 September 1896, Division 2, v Lincoln C (a) L 1–3 – Douglas; Parr, Bowman; Stuart, Stirzaker, Norris; Clarkin, Donnelly, R. Parkinson, Mount (1), J. Parkinson.

HONOURS

Football League: Division 1 – Runners-up 1955–56; Division 2 – Champions 1929–30; Runners-up 1936–37, 1969–70; Promoted from Division 3 – 2000–01 (play-offs); Division 4 – Runners-up 1984–85.

FA Cup: Winners 1953; Runners-up 1948, 1951.

Football League Cup: Semi-final 1962.

Anglo-Italian Cup: Winners 1971; Runners-up 1972.

IT'S A FACT !

Jimmy Hampson was the only Blackpool player chosen for the Football League XI in a match to celebrate His Majesty's Silver Jubilee on 11 May 1935 against a combined Welsh-Irish XI. The game was controlled by two referees, the League side winning 10-2.

Record League Victory: 7–0 v Reading, Division 2, 10 November 1928 – Mercer; Gibson, Hamilton, Watson, Wilson, Grant, Ritchie, Oxberry (2), Hampson (5), Tufnell, Neal. 7–0 v Preston NE (away), Division 1, 1 May 1948 – Robinson; Shimwell, Crosland; Buchan, Hayward, Kelly; Hobson, Munro (1), McIntosh (5), McCall, Rickett (1). 7–0 v Sunderland, Division 1, 5 October 1957 – Farm; Armfield, Garrett, Kelly (J), Gratrix, Kelly (H), Matthews, Taylor (2), Charnley (2), Durie (2), Perry (1).

Record Cup Victory: 7–1 v Charlton Ath, League Cup 2nd rd, 25 September 1963 – Harvey; Armfield, Martin; Crawford, Gratrix, Cranston; Lea, Ball (1), Charnley (4), Durie (1), Oates (1).

Record Defeat: 1–10 v Small Heath, Division 2, 2 March 1901 and v Huddersfield T, Division 1, 13 December 1930.

Most League Points (2 for a win): 58, Division 2, 1929–30 and Division 2, 1967–68.

Most League Points (3 for a win): 86, Division 4, 1984–85.

Most League Goals: 98, Division 2, 1929–30.

Highest League Scorer in Season: Jimmy Hampson, 45, Division 2, 1929–30.

Most League Goals in Total Aggregate: Jimmy Hampson, 246, 1927–38.

Most League Goals in One Match: 5, Jimmy Hampson v Reading, Division 2, 10 November 1928; 5, Jimmy McIntosh v Preston NE, Division 1, 1 May 1948.

Most Capped Player: Jimmy Armfield, 43, England.

Most League Appearances: Jimmy Armfield, 568, 1952–71.

Youngest League Player: Trevor Sinclair, 16 years 170 days v Wigan Ath, 19 August 1989.

Record Transfer Fee Received: £750,000 from QPR for Trevor Sinclair, August 1993.

Record Transfer Fee Paid: £275,000 to Millwall for Chris Malkin, October 1996.

Football League Record: 1896 Elected to Division 2; 1899 Failed re-election; 1900 Re-elected; 1900–30 Division 2; 1930–33 Division 1; 1933–37 Division 2; 1937–67 Division 1; 1967–70 Division 2; 1970–71 Division 1; 1971–78 Division 2; 1978–81 Division 3; 1981–85 Division 4; 1985–90 Division 3; 1990–92 Division 4; 1992–2000 Division 2; 2000–01 Division 3; 2001– Division 2.

MANAGERS

Tom Barcroft 1903–33
(Secretary-Manager)
John Cox 1909–11
Bill Norman 1919–23
Maj. Frank Buckley 1923–27
Sid Beaumont 1927–28
Harry Evans 1928–33
(Hon. Team Manager)
Alex 'Sandy' Macfarlane 1933–35
Joe Smith 1935–58
Ronnie Suart 1958–67
Stan Mortensen 1967–69
Les Shannon 1969–70
Bob Stokoe 1970–72
Harry Potts 1972–76
Allan Brown 1976–78
Bob Stokoe 1978–79
Stan Ternent 1979–80
Alan Ball 1980–81
Allan Brown 1981–82
Sam Ellis 1982–89
Jimmy Mullen 1989–90
Graham Carr 1990
Bill Ayre 1990–94
Sam Allardyce 1994–96
Gary Megson 1996–97
Nigel Worthington 1997–99
Steve McMahon January 2000–

LATEST SEQUENCES

Longest Sequence of League Wins: 9, 21.11.36 – 1.1.37.

Longest Sequence of League Defeats: 8, 26.11.1898 – 7.1.1899.

Longest Sequence of League Draws: 5, 4.12.76 – 1.1.77.

Longest Sequence of Unbeaten League Matches: 17, 6.4.68 – 21.9.68.

Longest Sequence Without a League Win: 19, 19.12.70 – 24.4.71.

TEN YEAR LEAGUE RECORD

		P	W	D	L	F	A	Pts	Pos
1990-91	Div 4	46	23	10	13	78	47	79	5
1991-92	Div 4	42	22	10	10	71	45	76	4
1992-93	Div 2	46	12	15	19	63	75	51	18
1993-94	Div 2	46	16	5	25	63	75	53	20
1994-95	Div 2	46	18	10	18	64	70	64	12
1995-96	Div 2	46	23	13	10	67	40	82	3
1996-97	Div 2	46	18	15	13	60	47	69	7
1997-98	Div 2	46	17	11	18	59	67	62	12
1998-99	Div 2	46	14	14	18	44	54	56	14
1999-2000	Div 2	46	8	17	21	49	77	41	22

DID YOU KNOW ?

John Murphy, 24 hours after a family bereavement, scored a hat-trick v Stockport County in a first round, second leg League Cup tie in a 4-2 aggregate victory. The third goal came from a five-man beating run by Richard Wellens.

BLACKPOOL 2000–01 LEAGUE RECORD

Match No.	Date	Venue	Opponents	Result		H/T Score	Lg. Pos.	Goalscorers	Attendance
1	Aug 12	H	Hull C	W	3-1	1-1	—	Ormerod [33], Murphy J [85], Simpson [86]	5862
2	19	A	Cardiff C	D	1-1	0-1	5	Murphy J [90]	11,019
3	26	H	Leyton Orient	D	2-2	1-2	7	Simpson [18], Clarkson [83]	4816
4	28	A	Torquay U	L	2-3	1-0	10	Ormerod [17], Wellens [59]	2384
5	Sept 2	A	Scunthorpe U	L	0-1	0-1	14		3822
6	9	H	Hartlepool U	L	1-2	0-1	20	Morrison [73]	4562
7	12	H	Brighton & HA	L	0-2	0-2	—		3406
8	16	A	Lincoln C	D	1-1	0-1	23	Murphy J [52]	2753
9	23	H	Chesterfield	L	1-3	0-2	23	Bushell [75]	3970
10	29	A	Kidderminster H	W	4-1	2-0	—	Simpson 2 [20, 47], Ormerod 2 [27, 60]	3891
11	Oct 8	H	Southend U	D	2-2	2-0	19	Murphy J [17], Ormerod [45]	3915
12	14	A	Plymouth Arg	L	0-2	0-0	21		3651
13	17	H	Mansfield T	W	1-0	0-0	—	Wellens [77]	2328
14	21	H	Macclesfield T	W	2-1	0-0	16	Hills [54], Coid [62]	3700
15	24	H	Carlisle U	W	3-2	2-0	—	Hills [6], Murphy J [44], Clarkson [71]	4744
16	28	A	Cheltenham T	W	1-0	1-0	10	Murphy J [7]	3798
17	Nov 4	H	Shrewsbury T	L	0-1	0-0	11		4850
18	11	A	Barnet	L	0-7	0-4	15		2520
19	25	H	Darlington	W	2-1	1-0	12	Ormerod [37], Simpson [50]	3683
20	Dec 2	A	Rochdale	L	0-1	0-0	13		4186
21	16	H	Exeter C	W	3-0	2-0	13	Murphy J 2 [5, 27], Ormerod [51]	2907
22	22	A	York C	W	2-0	1-0	—	Ormerod [27], Hughes [83]	2705
23	26	H	Halifax T	L	0-1	0-1	12		5044
24	Jan 13	H	Torquay U	W	5-0	2-0	10	Ormerod [14], Simpson 2 (1 pen) [37 (p), 82], Reid [50], Clarkson [81]	3549
25	16	A	Hull C	W	1-0	0-0	—	Murphy J [72]	4450
26	27	H	York C	W	1-0	0-0	8	Wellens [73]	3938
27	Feb 3	H	Scunthorpe U	W	6-0	3-0	8	Simpson (pen) [11], Murphy J 2 [13, 66], Wellens [14], Reid [59], Milligan M [62]	4161
28	10	A	Hartlepool U	L	1-3	0-1	8	Ormerod [82]	3973
29	13	H	Cardiff C	W	1-0	0-0	—	Ormerod [50]	4417
30	17	H	Lincoln C	W	2-0	1-0	7	Shittu [40], Murphy J [90]	4596
31	20	A	Brighton & HA	L	0-1	0-0	—		6756
32	24	A	Chesterfield	L	1-2	0-1	6	Wellens [56]	4812
33	Mar 3	H	Kidderminster H	W	5-1	2-1	6	Murphy J 3 (1 pen) [7, 26, 66 (p)], Wellens [61], Ormerod [85]	4624
34	6	H	Plymouth Arg	W	1-0	0-0	—	Walker [90]	4570
35	10	A	Southend U	W	3-0	1-0	5	Wellens [11], Simpson [59], Walker [63]	4810
36	17	H	Mansfield T	D	2-2	1-1	5	Murphy J [35], Ormerod [68]	5241
37	20	A	Leyton Orient	L	0-1	0-0	—		4086
38	24	A	Macclesfield T	L	1-2	0-2	6	Walker [86]	3045
39	31	A	Exeter C	L	0-2	0-0	6		3836
40	Apr 10	H	Halifax T	W	2-1	1-0	—	Simpson [4], Clarkson [84]	3311
41	14	A	Carlisle U	L	0-1	0-0	8		6096
42	16	H	Cheltenham T	D	2-2	1-1	9	Murphy J [45], Ormerod [62]	5192
43	21	A	Shrewsbury T	L	0-1	0-1	9		3129
44	26	H	Rochdale	W	3-1	1-0	—	Clarkson [43], Ormerod [64], Murphy J [85]	5470
45	28	H	Barnet	W	3-2	0-1	7	Ormerod [46], Simpson 2 [53, 61]	5289
46	May 5	A	Darlington	W	3-1	1-0	7	Ormerod [8], Shittu [56], Wellens [60]	5428

Final League Position: 7

GOALSCORERS

League (74): Murphy J 18 (1 pen), Ormerod 17, Simpson 12 (2 pens), Wellens 8, Clarkson 5, Walker 3, Hills 2, Reid 2, Shittu 2, Bushell 1, Coid 1, Hughes 1, Milligan M 1, Morrison 1.
Worthington Cup (7): Murphy J 5, Nowland 1, Ormerod 1.
FA Cup (3): Ormerod 2, Murphy J 1.

Caig T 6	Murphy N 3+3	Collins L 23+5	Bushell S 16+8	Hughes I 31+3	Hawe S 2	Milligan M 24+2	Simpson P 44	Ormerod B 36+5	Newell M 4+1	Coid D 45+1	Clarkson P 16+12	Murphy J 44+2	Jaszczun T 32+3	Jones E 4+3	Nowland A —+10	Wellens R 34+2	Morrison A 6	Barnes P 34	Reid B 29	Maley M 2	Hills J 18	O'Connor J 10+1	Thompson P 6+2	Kennedy J 6	Walker R 6+12	Shittu D 15+2	Parkinson G 9	Milligan J 1+5	Match No.
1	2	3	4	5	6	7¹	8	9	10²	11	12	13																	1
1	2		4	5	6³	7¹	8	9	10²	11	12	13	3	14															2
1	2		4	5		12	8¹	9		11	7	10	3		6²	13													3
1	12		4	5		7²	8¹	9¹		11	13	10	3	6	14	2													4
1			4	5		7¹	8		10	11		9	3		12	2	6												5
12			4	5		7¹		9	10²	11	13	8	3		2	6	1												6
			4	5			8	9		2	7	10	3		12	11¹	6	1											7
	2		4	5			8	9		11		10	3			7	6	1											8
	2¹		4	5²			8	9		11		10	3	13	12	7	6	1											9
	2		4	5			8	9¹		11		10	3	7	12		6	1											10
	7		4	5¹			8	9		2		10	3	12				1	6	11									11
	7		4				8	9¹		2	13	10	3	5	12²	14		1	6	11³									12
1				7	8			2	10	9					11		6		3	4	5								13
	2	12			8			11	10	9					7		6		3	4¹	5	1							14
	2	12			8			11	10	9	13				7		6		3²	4	5¹	1							15
	2		5		8¹	12		11	10	9	13				7		6		3²	4		1							16
	2		5		8	12		11	10	9	3				7		6			4¹		1							17
	2		5		8	9		11		10					7		6		3	4		1							18
	2	5¹			8	9		11	12	10					7		6		3	4		1							19
	7	5			8	9		2	11	10							1	6	3	4									20
	4		5¹		8	9		7	10	11	3						1	6	2		12								21
	4		5		8	9		11	7	10	3						1	6	2										22
	4¹	13²	5		8	9		7	11	10	3		14	12			1	6	2²										23
			5		7	8	9		4	12	10²	3	13	11			1	6	2¹										24
			5		7	8¹	9		2	11	10	3		4			1	6			12								25
	13		5		7¹		9		11	12	10	3		8²			1	6	2		4								26
	12		5		7¹	8²	9		11	13	10	3	14	4			1	6	2³										27
			5		7	8	9		2		10	3¹		11			1	6			12	4²		13					28
	12		5		7¹	8²	9		3	13	10		2				1				4	6		11					29
	14	12	5¹		7³	8	9		3	13	10		2				1					4		11²	6				30
	6	12			7	8	9		11		10	3	4²				1		2¹					13	5				31
	2	12	5		7²	8		13	11		9	3¹	4				1							10	6				32
	12		4		7	8	9²		11	13	10³	3¹	2				1	6						14	5				33
	2		4		7¹	8	9		11		10	3					1	6						12	5				34
	2	12			7	8	9²		11		10	3	4¹				1	6						13	5				35
	4	12			7²	8	9		2		10	3	11¹				1	6						13	5				36
	2	4¹			7	8	9		11		10	3					1	6						12	5				37
			12		4	8²	9		11		10	3²	7				1	6						13	5¹	2	14		38
			5		4	8¹	12		11³		9	3	7				1	6²						10	13	2	14		39
			5			8²	12		11	7	9	13	4				1			3				10¹	6	2			40
			5			8²	9¹		11	7	10		4				1			3				12	6	2	13		41
	13		5			8²	9		12	7	10	11	4¹				1			3				14	6	2⁸			42
	4³		5			8	12		11		9		7				1	6		3²				10¹	14	2	13		43
			12		8³	9²		11	7¹	10	3		4				1	6						13	5	2	14		44
		12			7	8	9		11		10	3¹		4				1	6						5	2			45
		12			7	8	9		3		10²			4				1	6						13	5	2	11¹	46

Worthington Cup

First Round	Stockport Co	(a)	1-0
		(h)	3-2
Second Round	Norwich C	(a)	3-3
		(h)	0-5

FA Cup

First Round	Telford U	(h)	3-1
Second Round	Yeovil T	(h)	0-1

BOLTON WANDERERS FA Premiership

FOUNDATION

In 1874 boys of Christ Church Sunday School, Blackburn Street, led by their master Thomas Ogden, established a football club which went under the name of the school and whose president was Vicar of Christ Church. Membership was 6d (two and a half pence). When their president began to lay down too many rules about the use of church premises, the club broke away and formed Bolton Wanderers in 1877, holding their earliest meetings at the Gladstone Hotel.

Reebok Stadium, Burnden Way, Lostock, Bolton BL6 6JW.

Telephone: (01204) 673 673. *Fax:* (01204) 673 773.
Ticket Office: (01204) 673 601. *ClubCall:* 09068 121 164.

Ground Capacity: 27,879.

Record Attendance: 69,912 v Manchester C, FA Cup 5th rd, 18 February 1933.

Record Receipts: £335,468 v WBA, Division 1, play-off semi-final, 17 May 2001.

Pitch Measurements: 114yd × 74yd.

President: Nat Lofthouse OBE. *Chairman:* P. A. Gartside.
Directors: G. Seymour, G. Warburton, W. B. Warburton, I. Currie, E. Davies OBE, D. Speakman, D. McBain.

Team Manager: Sam Allardyce.

Physio: Mark Taylor.

Chief Executive & Secretary: Simon Marland.

Commercial Director: G. Moores.

Colours: White shirts, navy blue shorts, blue stockings.

Change Colours: Blue shirts with white sash, white shorts, blue stockings.

Year Formed: 1874.

Turned Professional: 1880.

Ltd Co.: 1895.

Previous Name: 1874, Christ Church FC; 1877, Bolton Wanderers.

Club Nickname: 'The Trotters'.

Previous Grounds: Park Recreation Ground and Cockle's Field before moving to Pike's Lane ground 1881; 1895, Burnden Park; 1997, Reebok Stadium.

First Football League Game: 8 September 1888, Football League, v Derby Co (h) L 3–6 – Harrison; Robinson, Mitchell; Roberts, Weir, Bullough, Davenport (2), Milne, Coupar, Barbour, Brogan (1).

Record League Victory: 8–0 v Barnsley, Division 2, 6 October 1934 – Jones; Smith, Finney; Goslin, Atkinson, George Taylor; George T. Taylor (2), Eastham, Milsom (1), Westwood (4), Cook, (1 og).

HONOURS

Football League: Division 1 – Champions 1996–97; Promoted from Division 1 (play-offs) 2000–01.
Division 2 – Champions 1908–09, 1977–78; Runners-up 1899–1900, 1904–05, 1910–11, 1934–35, 1992–93; Division 3 – Champions 1972–73.
FA Cup: Winners 1923, 1926, 1929, 1958; Runners-up 1894, 1904, 1953.
Football League Cup: Runners-up 1995.
Freight Rover Trophy: Runners-up 1986.
Sherpa Van Trophy: Winners 1989.

IT'S A FACT !

Three years after scoring the goal for Everton which effectively relegated Bolton Wanderers, Gareth Farrelly opened the scoring for Bolton in their 3-0 play-off win against Preston North End on 28 May 2001, which put them back in the Premier League.

Record Cup Victory: 13–0 v Sheffield U, FA Cup 2nd rd, 1 February 1890 – Parkinson; Robinson (1), Jones; Bullough, Davenport, Roberts; Rushton, Brogan (3), Cassidy (5), McNee, Weir (4).

Record Defeat: 1–9 v Preston NE, FA Cup 2nd rd, 10 December 1887.

Most League Points (2 for a win): 61, Division 3, 1972–73.

Most League Points (3 for a win): 98, Division 1, 1996–97.

Most League Goals: 100, Division 1, 1996–97.

Highest League Scorer in Season: Joe Smith, 38, Division 1, 1920–21.

Most League Goals in Total Aggregate: Nat Lofthouse, 255, 1946–61.

Most League Goals in One Match: 5, Tony Caldwell v Walsall, Division 3, 10 September 1983.

Most Capped Player: Mark Fish, 34, South Africa.

Most League Appearances: Eddie Hopkinson, 519, 1956–70.

Youngest League Player: Ray Parry, 15 years 267 days v Wolverhampton W, 13 October 1951.

Record Transfer Fee Received: £4,500,000 from Liverpool for Jason McAteer, September 1995.

Record Transfer Fee Paid: £3,500,000 for Dean Holdsworth from Wimbledon, October 1997.

Football League Record: 1888 Founder Member of the League; 1899–1900 Division 2; 1900–03 Division 1; 1903–05 Division 2; 1905–08 Division 1; 1908–09 Division 2; 1909–10 Division 1; 1910–11 Division 2; 1911–33 Division 1; 1933–35 Division 2; 1935–64 Division 1; 1964–71 Division 2; 1971–73 Division 3; 1973–78 Division 2; 1978–80 Division 1; 1980–83 Division 2; 1983–87 Division 3; 1987–88 Division 4; 1988–92 Division 3; 1992–93 Division 2; 1993–95 Division 1; 1995–96 FA Premier League; 1996–97 Division 1; 1997–98 FA Premier League; 1998–2001 Division 1; 2001– FA Premier League.

LATEST SEQUENCES

Longest Sequence of League Wins: 11, 5.11.04 – 2.1.05.

Longest Sequence of League Defeats: 11, 7.4.02 – 18.10.02.

Longest Sequence of League Draws: 6, 25.1.13 – 8.3.13.

Longest Sequence of Unbeaten League Matches: 23, 13.10.90 – 9.3.91.

Longest Sequence Without a League Win: 26, 7.4.02 – 10.1.03.

MANAGERS

Tom Rawthorne 1874–85
(Secretary)
J. J. Bentley 1885–86
(Secretary)
W. G. Struthers 1886–87
(Secretary)
Fitzroy Norris 1887
(Secretary)
J. J. Bentley 1887–95
(Secretary)
Harry Downs 1895–96
(Secretary)
Frank Brettell 1896–98
(Secretary)
John Somerville 1898–1910
Will Settle 1910–15
Tom Mather 1915–19
Charles Foweraker 1919–44
Walter Rowley 1944–50
Bill Ridding 1951–68
Nat Lofthouse 1968–70
Jimmy McIlroy 1970
Jimmy Meadows 1971
Nat Lofthouse 1971
    (then Admin. Manager to 1972)
Jimmy Armfield 1971–74
Ian Greaves 1974–80
Stan Anderson 1980–81
George Mulhall 1981–82
John McGovern 1982–85
Charlie Wright 1985
Phil Neal 1985–92
Bruce Rioch 1992–95
Roy McFarland 1995–96
Colin Todd 1996–99
Sam Allardyce October 1999–

TEN YEAR LEAGUE RECORD

		P	W	D	L	F	A	Pts	Pos
1990-91	Div 3	46	24	11	11	64	50	83	4
1991-92	Div 3	46	14	17	15	57	56	59	13
1992-93	Div 2	46	27	9	10	80	41	90	2
1993-94	Div 1	46	15	14	17	63	64	59	14
1994-95	Div 1	46	21	14	11	67	45	77	3
1995-96	PR Lge	38	8	5	25	39	71	29	20
1996-97	Div 1	46	28	14	4	100	53	98	1
1997-98	PR Lge	38	9	13	16	41	61	40	18
1998-99	Div 1	46	20	16	10	78	59	76	6
1999-2000	Div 1	46	21	13	12	69	50	76	6

DID YOU KNOW ?

Bolton Wanderers scored in every one of their 22 League games in 1888-89. Yet their highest of the season came from their reserves in a 9-0 FA Cup win over West Manchester, on the same day as a League fixture.

BOLTON WANDERERS 2000–01 LEAGUE RECORD

Match No.	Date	Venue	Opponents	Result		H/T Score	Lg. Pos.	Goalscorers	Attendance
1	Aug 12	H	Burnley	D	1-1	1-0	—	Frandsen (pen) [28]	20,662
2	19	A	WBA	W	2-0	1-0	5	Rankin [23], Farrelly [75]	17,316
3	26	H	Preston NE	W	2-0	1-0	2	Rankin [42], Ricketts [82]	19,954
4	28	A	Tranmere R	W	1-0	0-0	3	Whitlow [53]	9350
5	Sept 9	A	Huddersfield T	W	3-2	0-0	2	Holdsworth [51], Ricketts 2 [70, 76]	12,248
6	12	A	Grimsby T	W	1-0	0-0	—	Ricketts [71]	3732
7	16	H	Portsmouth	W	2-0	1-0	3	Holdsworth [42], Ricketts [85]	14,113
8	23	A	Blackburn R	D	1-1	0-1	3	Hansen [88]	23,660
9	30	H	Fulham	L	0-2	0-1	3		19,924
10	Oct 6	A	Gillingham	D	2-2	2-0	—	Hansen [8], O'Kane [32]	9311
11	14	H	Wolverhampton W	W	2-1	1-0	3	Holdsworth [28], Bergsson [68]	15,585
12	17	H	Nottingham F	D	0-0	0-0	—		13,017
13	21	A	Stockport Co	L	3-4	0-3	4	Marshall 2 [59, 84], Ricketts [69]	8266
14	24	A	Watford	L	0-1	0-0	—		11,799
15	28	H	Crystal Palace	D	3-3	1-1	6	Bergsson [20], Ricketts [75], Frandsen [77]	12,879
16	31	H	QPR	W	3-1	1-1	—	Bergsson [45], Elliott [62], Ricketts [65]	10,180
17	Nov 4	A	Birmingham C	D	1-1	0-0	4	Ricketts [66]	20,043
18	11	H	Barnsley	W	2-0	2-0	3	Ricketts [14], Gardner [28]	13,406
19	18	A	Norwich C	W	2-0	0-0	3	Ricketts [58], Bergsson [74]	15,224
20	25	A	Sheffield U	L	0-1	0-0	5		14,962
21	Dec 3	H	Watford	W	2-1	0-1	5	Gardner [71], Marshall [79]	13,904
22	9	H	Crewe Alex	W	4-1	3-1	2	Frandsen [20], Marshall [22], Bergsson [44], Nolan [89]	12,836
23	16	A	Wimbledon	W	1-0	0-0	2	Holdsworth [78]	6076
24	23	A	Burnley	W	2-0	0-0	2	Ricketts 2 [53, 72]	19,552
25	26	H	Sheffield W	W	2-0	1-0	2	Holdsworth [15], Hendry [51]	21,316
26	30	H	WBA	L	0-1	0-1	2		18,985
27	Jan 1	A	Preston NE	W	2-0	1-0	2	Farrelly [8], Ricketts [84]	15,863
28	13	H	Tranmere R	W	2-0	2-0	2	Hansen [16], Hill (og) [20]	15,493
29	20	A	Sheffield W	W	3-0	2-0	2	Gardner [19], Ricketts [40], Marshall [88]	17,638
30	Feb 3	A	QPR	D	1-1	0-0	2	Frandsen [87]	10,293
31	10	H	Huddersfield T	D	2-2	0-2	2	Bergsson [60], Frandsen [90]	14,866
32	13	A	Portsmouth	W	2-1	0-0	—	Ricketts [48], Hansen [71]	11,377
33	20	H	Grimsby T	D	2-2	0-1	—	Bergsson [61], Hansen [74]	24,249
34	23	H	Blackburn R	L	1-4	0-1	—	Ricketts [84]	20,017
35	Mar 4	A	Fulham	D	1-1	0-1	2	Frandsen [51]	16,468
36	10	H	Gillingham	D	3-3	2-1	2	Frandsen [30], Patterson (og) [45], Holdsworth [51]	13,161
37	17	A	Nottingham F	W	2-0	0-0	2	Holdsworth [61], Farrelly [90]	22,162
38	31	H	Wimbledon	D	2-2	1-1	3	Elliott [28], Hendry [66]	14,562
39	Apr 3	A	Stockport Co	D	1-1	1-0	—	Hendry [11]	12,492
40	13	H	Birmingham C	D	2-2	0-1	—	Bergsson [53], Holdsworth [55]	15,025
41	16	A	Crystal Palace	W	2-0	1-0	3	Marshall [12], Summerbee [68]	16,268
42	18	A	Crewe Alex	L	1-2	0-0	—	Holdsworth [62]	8054
43	21	A	Norwich C	W	1-0	0-0	3	Holdsworth [66]	17,967
44	28	A	Barnsley	W	1-0	0-0	3	Ricketts [56]	13,979
45	May 1	A	Wolverhampton W	W	2-0	1-0	—	Holdsworth [20], Ricketts [70]	16,242
46	6	H	Sheffield U	D	1-1	0-0	3	Holden [90]	14,836

Final League Position: 3

GOALSCORERS

League (76): Ricketts 19, Holdsworth 11, Bergsson 8, Frandsen 7 (1 pen), Marshall 6, Hansen 5, Farrelly 3, Gardner 3, Hendry 3, Elliott 2, Rankin 2, Holden 1, Nolan 1, O'Kane 1, Summerbee 1, Whitlow 1, own goals 2.
Worthington Cup (2): Holdsworth 1, Ricketts 1.
FA Cup (8): Holdsworth 3, Nolan 2, Ricketts 2, O'Kane 1.

Jaaskelainen J 27	O'Kane J 25 + 2	Charlton S 18 + 4	Bergsson G 44	Barness A 17 + 3	Fish M 13 + 1	Passi F 14 + 9	Frandsen P 35 + 4	Hansen B 38 + 3	Rankin J 9 + 7	Farrelly G 36 + 5	Richardson L 5 + 7	Marshall I 13 + 23	Holdsworth D 22 + 9	Whitlow M 7 + 1	Ricketts M 24 + 15	Nolan K 25 + 6	Banks S 8 + 1	Elliott R 31 + 2	Gardner R 27 + 5	Warhurst P 19 + 1	Morini E 1 + 1	Fredgaard C 1 + 4	Gope-Fenepej J — + 2	Hendry C 22	Summerbee N 9 + 3	Wright T 3 + 1	Campbell A 3 + 3	Clarke M 8	Holden D 1	Hunt N — + 1	Downey C — + 1	Smith J 1	Match No.
1	2[1]	3	4	5	6	7	8	9[2]	10	11	12	13																					1
1	2[2]	3[1]	4	5	6	7	8	9	10[1]	11	13	12	14																				2
1			5	2	6	7	4	9[2]	8[3]	11	13	12	10[1]	3	14																		3
1			5	2	6	7	4	9[1]	12	11	14	10[2]	13	3	8[1]																		4
1	2		5	6		7	4	9[1]	8[3]	11	12	13	10[2]	3	14																		5
1	2		4	5		7	6	9[3]	8		12	11	10[2]	3[1]	13	14																	6
1	2		5	3	6[1]	7	4	9	8[2]	11		12	10[3]		13	14																	7
1	2		5	3	6	7[3]	4	9	12	11		13	10[2]		8[1]	14																	8
1	2	12	5	3[1]	6	7	4	9[2]	13	11		14	10[3]		8																		9
	2	3	5				12	4	9	8[2]	7[1]		11	10	13	6[3]	1	14															10
1	2	3	5[2]		12		4	9	8[3]	7		11	10[1]		14	6		13															11
1	2	3			6		4	9	10[2]	7		5			8	12		11[1]	13														12
1	2[1]	3	5	12	6		4	9[3]		7[2]		11			8	13		10	14														13
1		3	5	2	6	12	4	9[2]	13	14		10[3]	7		8[1]	11																	14
1		3[2]	5	2[1]	6		4	9	12	13		10	7[3]		8	11																	15
1	2		5		6		4	9	12	7					8[1]	10		3	11														16
1	2		5		6[2]		4	9	12	7					8	10		3	11	13													17
1	2		5				4	9[2]		7			12		8	10		3	11	6	13												18
1	2		5	7			12	4	9[1]						8	10[2]		3	11[3]	6		13	14										19
1	2		5				7[2]	4	9[1]				12		8	10		3	11	6		13											20
1	2		5				7		9[2]	10		12			8[1]	6		3	11	4			13										21
1	2		5				4	9[2]	11[1]			10[2]	12		13	8		3	7	6	14												22
1	2		5						8			9[1]	12		13	10		3	11	6		7[2]	4										23
1	2		5			7		9[2]		8			10[1]		12	6		3	11			13	4										24
1	2	12	5			13		9[2]	7			14	10[3]		8[1]	6		3	11				4										25
1	2[1]	12	5			13		9[2]	7			14	10		8[2]	6		3	11				4										26
1		2				12	8	9[2]	7			14	10[1]		13	6[1]		3	11	5			4										27
1[d]		2				10	9[2]	7		12			13	8[1]	6	15	3	11	5			4											28
		2	12				10	9[3]				13		3[1]	8[2]	7	1	6	11	5			4	14									29
		2					8	9		11[2]		12	10			1	3	13	5[1]			4	7[6]	15									30
12		2					8	9[1]		11		13			10	6[2]	1	3	14	5[1]			4	7									31
2[1]		5	12			14	8	9		7		13[3]			10[2]	6	1	3	14	5[4]			4										32
2		5					6	9		10			12		8[2]	13	1	3	11				4	7[1]									33
2[1]	12	5				13	8	9[2]		7			10		14	6[3]	1	3	11				4										34
	3	2				7	8	9[3]		11[1]		13	10[2]			6			5				4	14	1								35
	3	2				12	7[1]	9		11		13	10[2]		8[3]			6		5			4		1	14							36
	3	5					12	2		9[1]		13	7[3]			6	11	8					4	14	1	10[2]							37
	3	5					12			13	2	14	9[3]			8	11	6					4	7[2]		10[1]	1						38
	3	5					12			13	2	14	9			8	11	6[2]					4	7[3]		10[1]	1						39
	3	5				8		9[1]		7	2	13	12		10[1]	6[2]		11					4				14	1					40
	3	5	2			12				8		10[1]	9[2]		13			11	6				4	7			1						41
	3	5	2			13				8		10[1]	12		9			11[3]	6[2]				4	7		14	1						42
	5	2	12		6	13		8		10[2]	9				3	11							4	7[1]			1						43
	3	5	2			8[2]	9[3]	11	14			12			10			6	13	4				7[1]			1						44
	3	4	2			12	9	7		13	10[1]	5	8[2]			6	11										1						45
12						7	8					3[1]	10	5	8[2]	6	1		9[3]		4[2]				2	13	14	11					46

Worthington Cup

First Round	Macclesfield T	(h)	1-0
		(a)	1-3

FA Cup

Third Round	Yeovil T	(h)	2-1
Fourth Round	Scunthorpe U	(h)	5-1
Fifth Round	Blackburn R	(h)	1-1
		(a)	0-3

AFC BOURNEMOUTH

Division 2

FOUNDATION

There was a Bournemouth FC as early as 1875, but the present club arose out of the remnants of the Boscombe St John's club (formed 1890). The meeting at which Boscombe FC came into being was held at a house in Gladstone Road in 1899. They began by playing in the Boscombe and District Junior League.

Dean Court Ground, Bournemouth, Dorset BH7 7AF.

Telephone: (01202) 395 381. *Fax:* (01202) 309 797.
Website: http://www.afcb.co.uk *Fansline:* tba.
Ticket Office: (01202) 397 939.

Ground Capacity: 9,600 seats, rising to 12,000 all-seater.

Record Attendance: 28,799 v Manchester U, FA Cup 6th rd, 2 March 1957.

Record Receipts: £80,267 v Walsall, Auto Windscreens Shield Southern Area Final, 17 March 1998.

Pitch Measurements: 105m × 78m.

Chairman: A. Swaisland. *Directors:* A. H. Kaye (Vice-Chairman), A. Dawson (Managing Director), Mel Machin (Director of Football).

Secretary: K. R. J. MacAlister.

Manager: Sean O'Driscoll. *Assistant Manager:* John Williams. *Head Coach:* Peter Grant.
Physio: John Cooper.

Corporate Manager: Mrs D. Rackley. *Groundsman:* D. Edwards.

Colours: Red and black striped shirts, black shorts, black stockings.

Change Colours: White shirts with red and black trim, black or white shorts, black or white stockings.

Year Formed: 1899.

Turned Professional: 1912.

Ltd Co.: 1914.

Previous Names: 1890, Boscombe St Johns; 1899, Boscombe FC; 1923, Bournemouth & Boscombe Ath FC; 1971, AFC Bournemouth.

Club Nickname: 'Cherries'.

Previous Grounds: 1899, Castlemain Road, Pokesdown; 1910, Dean Court.

First Football League Game: 25 August 1923, Division 3 (S), v Swindon T (a), L 1–3 – Heron; Wingham, Lamb, Butt, C. Smith, Voisey; Miller, Lister (1), Davey, Simpson, Robinson.

Record League Victory: 7–0 v Swindon T, Division 3 (S), 22 September 1956 – Godwin; Cunningham, Keetley; Clayton, Crosland, Rushworth; Siddall (1), Norris (2), Arnott (1), Newsham (2), Cutler (1). 10–0 win v Northampton T at start of 1939–40 expunged from the records on outbreak of war.

HONOURS

Football League: Division 3 – Champions 1986–87; Division 3 (S) – Runners-up 1947–48; Division 4 – Runners-up 1970–71; Promotion from Division 4 1981–82 (4th).

FA Cup: best season: 6th rd, 1957.

Football League Cup: best season: 4th rd, 1962, 1964.

Associate Members' Cup: Winners 1984.

Auto Windscreens Shield: Runners-up 1998.

IT'S A FACT !

On 1 January 2001, Jermaine Defoe broke a 74 year old Bournemouth club record by scoring in his eighth consecutive game. He went on to register in ten successive matches.

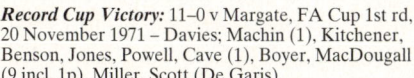

Record Cup Victory: 11–0 v Margate, FA Cup 1st rd, 20 November 1971 – Davies; Machin (1), Kitchener, Benson, Jones, Powell, Cave (1), Boyer, MacDougall (9 incl. 1p), Miller, Scott (De Garis).

Record Defeat: 0–9 v Lincoln C, Division 3, 18 December 1982.

Most League Points (2 for a win): 62, Division 3, 1971–72.

Most League Points (3 for a win): 97, Division 3, 1986–87.

Most League Goals: 88, Division 3 (S), 1956–57.

Highest League Scorer in Season: Ted MacDougall, 42, 1970–71.

Most League Goals in Total Aggregate: Ron Eyre, 202, 1924–33.

Most League Goals in One Match: 4, Jack Russell v Clapton Orient, Division 3S, 7 January 1933; 4, Jack Russell v Bristol C, Division 3S, 28 January 1933; 4, Harry Mardon v Southend U, Division 3S, 1 January 1938; 4, Jack McDonald v Torquay U, Division 3S, 8 November 1947; 4 James Hayter v Bury, Division 2, 21 October 2000.

Most Capped Player: Gerry Peyton, 7 (33), Republic of Ireland.

Most League Appearances: Sean O'Driscoll, 423, 1984–95.

Youngest League Player: Jimmy White, 15 years 321 days v Brentford, 30 April 1958.

Record Transfer Fee Received: £800,000 from Everton for Joe Parkinson, March 1994.

Record Transfer Fee Paid: £210,000 to Gillingham for Gavin Peacock, August 1989.

Football League Record: 1923 Elected to Division 3 (S) and remained a Third Division club for record number of years until 1970; 1970–71 Division 4; 1971–75 Division 3; 1975–82 Division 4; 1982–87 Division 3; 1987–90 Division 2; 1990–92 Division 3; 1992– Division 2.

MANAGERS

Vincent Kitcher 1914–23
(Secretary-Manager)
Harry Kinghorn 1923–25
Leslie Knighton 1925–28
Frank Richards 1928–30
Billy Birrell 1930–35
Bob Crompton 1935–36
Charlie Bell 1936–39
Harry Kinghorn 1939–47
Harry Lowe 1947–50
Jack Bruton 1950–56
Fred Cox 1956–58
Don Welsh 1958–61
Bill McGarry 1961–63
Reg Flewin 1963–65
Fred Cox 1965–70
John Bond 1970–73
Trevor Hartley 1974–75
John Benson 1975–78
Alec Stock 1979–80
David Webb 1980–82
Don Megson 1983
Harry Redknapp 1983–92
Tony Pulis 1992–94
Mel Machin 1994–2000
Sean O'Driscoll August 2000–

LATEST SEQUENCES

Longest Sequence of League Wins: 7, 22.8.70 – 23.9.70.

Longest Sequence of League Defeats: 7, 13.8.94 – 13.9.94.

Longest Sequence of League Draws: 5, 25.4.00 – 12.8.00.

Longest Sequence of Unbeaten League Matches: 18, 6.3.82 – 28.8.82.

Longest Sequence Without a League Win: 14, 6.3.74 – 27.4.74.

TEN YEAR LEAGUE RECORD

		P	W	D	L	F	A	Pts	Pos
1990-91	Div 3	46	19	13	14	58	58	70	9
1991-92	Div 3	46	20	11	15	52	48	71	8
1992-93	Div 2	46	12	17	17	45	52	53	17
1993-94	Div 2	46	14	15	17	51	59	57	17
1994-95	Div 2	46	13	11	22	49	69	50	19
1995-96	Div 2	46	16	10	20	51	70	58	14
1996-97	Div 2	46	15	15	16	43	45	60	16
1997-98	Div 2	46	18	12	16	57	52	66	9
1998-99	Div 2	46	21	13	12	63	41	76	7
1999-2000	Div 2	46	16	9	21	59	62	57	16

DID YOU KNOW ?

Alf White, who had been spasmodically used in four different positions, was restored to lead the Bournemouth attack in the last eight games of the 1934-35 season and scored eight of the club's nine goals.

AFC BOURNEMOUTH 2000–01 LEAGUE RECORD

Match No.	Date	Venue	Opponents	Result	H/T Score	Lg. Pos.	Goalscorers	Attendance
1	Aug 12	A	Bristol R	D	1-1	1-1	—	Eribenne [27]	8046
2	19	H	Cambridge U	D	1-1	0-1	16	Fletcher S [88]	4869
3	26	A	Luton T	L	0-1	0-0	21		5221
4	Sept 2	A	Colchester U	L	1-3	1-2	22	Jorgensen [44]	3459
5	9	H	Port Vale	D	1-1	0-1	23	Fletcher C [86]	3859
6	12	H	Swindon T	W	3-0	2-0	—	Fletcher S 2 [17, 25], Hayter [51]	3673
7	16	A	Walsall	D	1-1	0-1	17	Elliott [90]	5054
8	23	H	Oldham Ath	D	1-1	0-1	16	Fletcher S [62]	3976
9	26	H	Wrexham	L	1-2	1-0	—	Jorgensen [5]	3004
10	30	A	Brentford	L	2-3	1-2	19	Jorgensen [10], Hughes (pen) [90]	4210
11	Oct 6	A	Bristol C	D	3-3	2-3	—	Fletcher C [31], Jorgensen [45], O'Connor [89]	8936
12	14	H	Rotherham U	L	0-1	0-1	21		3878
13	17	H	Wigan Ath	D	0-0	0-0	—		3035
14	21	A	Bury	W	5-2	2-0	19	Jorgensen [6], Hayter 4 [14, 55, 60, 61]	2892
15	24	H	Notts Co	L	0-1	0-0	—		3556
16	28	A	Stoke C	L	1-2	1-2	21	Defoe [45]	11,572
17	Nov 4	H	Peterborough U	W	2-1	1-0	20	Defoe [20], Cummings [84]	3936
18	11	A	Northampton T	W	3-0	1-0	18	Fletcher S [36], Defoe 2 [60, 78]	5692
19	Dec 2	A	Wycombe W	W	3-0	1-0	18	Fletcher C 2 [23, 90], Defoe [61]	5185
20	16	H	Swansea C	W	2-0	1-0	15	Hughes (pen) [31], Defoe [49]	3738
21	23	H	Millwall	L	1-2	0-1	16	Defoe [54]	6843
22	26	A	Oxford U	W	2-1	1-0	14	Defoe 2 [7, 64]	6200
23	Jan 1	A	Luton T	W	3-2	1-2	13	Fletcher S [39], Hughes (pen) [83], Defoe [86]	5411
24	13	A	Wrexham	D	2-2	1-0	13	Defoe [6], Hayter [62]	2852
25	23	A	Cambridge U	W	2-0	0-0	—	Defoe [64], Hayter [84]	3027
26	27	A	Millwall	W	1-0	1-0	10	Jorgensen [6]	12,713
27	Feb 3	H	Colchester U	D	2-2	0-2	10	Hughes (pen) [63], Fletcher C [86]	4407
28	10	A	Port Vale	L	1-2	0-1	12	Tindall [68]	3956
29	17	H	Walsall	D	2-2	2-0	11	Howe [6], Defoe [33]	4564
30	20	A	Swindon T	D	1-1	0-0	—	Hughes [83]	5948
31	24	A	Oldham Ath	L	1-2	0-0	12	Hayter [53]	4845
32	27	H	Bristol R	L	1-2	1-2	—	Jorgensen [35]	3466
33	Mar 3	A	Brentford	W	2-0	2-0	11	Fletcher S [7], Elliott [36]	4438
34	6	A	Rotherham U	L	1-3	0-1	—	Hayter [89]	6488
35	10	A	Bristol C	W	4-0	3-0	11	Elliott 2 [12, 55], Hughes [17], Fletcher C [39]	4028
36	17	A	Wigan Ath	D	1-1	0-0	11	Howe [68]	5878
37	24	H	Bury	W	1-0	1-0	10	Defoe [22]	3325
38	31	A	Swansea C	W	3-0	1-0	9	Hayter [33], Elliott [49], Feeney [87]	4013
39	Apr 3	H	Oxford U	W	4-3	1-1	—	Hayter [3], Hughes 2 (1 pen) [56, 62 (p)], Feeney [83]	3747
40	10	H	Reading	L	1-2	1-2	—	Defoe [3]	6603
41	14	A	Notts Co	W	2-0	2-0	8	Fletcher S 2 [14, 21]	5186
42	17	H	Stoke C	W	1-0	1-0	—	Defoe [38]	5373
43	21	A	Peterborough U	W	2-1	0-1	7	Feeney [79], Defoe [82]	6318
44	23	H	Wycombe W	W	2-0	0-0	—	Feeney [64], Elliott [70]	5026
45	28	H	Northampton T	W	2-0	1-0	7	Elliott [35], Jorgensen [52]	6511
46	May 5	A	Reading	D	3-3	3-1	7	Elliott 2 [4, 33], Defoe [24]	20,589

Final League Position: 7

GOALSCORERS

League (79): Defoe 18, Hayter 11, Elliott 9, Fletcher S 9, Hughes 8 (5 pens), Jorgensen 8, Fletcher C 6, Feeney 4, Howe 2, Cummings 1, Eribenne 1, O'Connor 1, Tindall 1.
Worthington Cup (1): Jorgensen 1.
FA Cup (7): Elliott 2, Defoe 1, Fletcher C 1, Hayter 1, Hughes 1, O'Connor 1.

Menetrier M 11 + 1	Young N 7	Purches S 25 + 9	Fenton N 4 + 1	Angus S 7 + 2	Day J 6 + 1	Jorgensen C 43	Fletcher C 43	Eribenne C 6 + 11	Fletcher S 45	Hughes R 44	Elliott W 27 + 9	Hayter J 29 + 11	Tindall J 44 + 1	Huck W 1 + 7	Grant P 14 + 1	O'Connor G 1 + 21	Smith D 7 + 7	Stewart G 35	Woozley D 6	Ford J — + 3	Broadhurst K 25 + 5	O'Neill J — + 3	Cummings W 10	Howe E 30 + 1	Defoe J 27 + 2	Stock B — + 1	Bernard N 6 + 8	Keeler J — + 1	Feeney W 3 + 7	Match No.
1	2	3	4	5	6	7[1]	8	9	10	11	12																			1
1	2	3[1]	4	5[2]	6[3]	7	8	9	10	11	12	13	14																	2
1	2	3	4	12		7	8[1]	9[2]	10	11			14	5	13	6[2]														3
1		3	4	2	12	7	8	9[2]	10				5	11[2]	6[1]	14	13													4
1	2	3	12			7[2]	8	9[1]	10	11			14	5	6	13	4[1]													5
	2[1]	3		12		7[1]	8	9	10	11		13	5		6	4	14	1												6
	2	3		5		8[3]	12	9	10	11	13			6[2]	4[1]	14		1	7											7
	2	3		5		8[1]	12	9[3]	10	11	13			6[2]	7	14		1	4											8
		3		2		7	8	9[2]	10	11[1]	13			5	6[2]	14		1	4											9
1		3		2[4]		7	8[3]	9	10	11			5		6[1]	13	4	14												10
		3		2[3]		7	8	9	10		5[2]	6	12	11[1]		1	4	13	14											11
						7	8	9	10	11	12		5		6[1]	2[2]	1	4		3	13									12
		3				7[2]	8	9[1]	10	11	4		5		6	2	1				12	13								13
		3				7[1]	8	9[3]	10	11	13	12	5		6	2	1				14	4[2]								14
		3				7	8	9	10	11		5	13		6[1]	2[3]	1				12[2]	4	14							15
		3				7	6	12[2]	10	11	13	8[3]	5	14		1					2[1]		4	9						16
		3				7[1]	6		10	11	8	12	5	13		1					2		4	9[2]						17
		3				7[3]	6		10	11	8[1]	5[2]	12			1		13			2		4	9	14					18
		3				7[3]	6	8[1]		11[2]	10	12	5			13		1		14	2		4	9						19
		3		5		7			10	11	8[2]	12	6			13		1		14	2[3]		4	9[1]						20
		3[1]				7	6[2]	12	10	11	8		5			13		1			2		4	9						21
		3		6		7			10	11	8	12	5			13		1			2[4]		4	9[1]						22
		3[2]				7			10	11	8	12	5		6[1]	13		1			2		4	9						23
						7	6		10	11	8		5					1		3	2		4	9						24
						7	8		10	11	6	12	5			13		1			2[2]		4	9[1]	3					25
						7	6		10	11	8	13	5			12[2]		1			2		4	9[1]	3					26
						7	6		10	11	8[3]	12	5	13		14		1			2[2]		4	9	3[1]					27
	4[3]					7[1]	6		10	11		8	5			12	13	1			2			9	3[2]			14		28
	3					7	6		10	11		8	5			13		1			2		4	9						29
	3[2]					7[3]	6	12	10	11		8	5[1]	13		14		1			2		4	9						30
15						7	6	12	10	11	13	8[2]	5					1[1]			2		4	9[1]	3					31
1						7	6	12	10	11	8	9	5[1]			13					2		4		3[2]					32
1		3[1]				7	6		10	11	8	9[2]	5								2		4	9	12	13				33
1						7	6		10	11	3	8	5[1]								2		4	9	12					34
1	12					7[3]	6		10	11	3[1]	8[3]	5			13					2		4	9	14					35
1						7	6		10[2]	11	3	8	5			12					2		4	9[1]	13					36
						7	6		10	11	3	8[2]	5					1			2		4	9[2]	12	13				37
	12					7	6		10	11	3	8[2]	5					1			2[1]		4	9[3]	13	14				38
	12					7[4]	6		10	11	3	8[2]	5					1			2[1]		4	9	13	14				39
						7[2]	6	12	10	11	3	8	5[1]					1			2		4	9	13					40
	12						6	13	10	11	3	8	5					1			2		4	9[2]	7[1]					41
	12					7	6		10	11	3	8[1]	5					1			2		4	9	13					42
	12					7[1]	6		10	11	3	8	5[2]	13				1			2		4	9	14					43
	12					7[3]	6	13	10	11	3	9[1]	5	14				1			2		4		8[2]					44
	12					7	6		10	11	3	9[1]	5					1			2		4	13	14		8[2]			45
	12					7[3]	6		10	11	3	8[1]	5[2]			13		1			2		4	9	14					46

Worthington Cup
First Round   Norwich C   (a) 0-0
                               (h) 1-2

FA Cup
First Round   Swansea C   (h) 2-0
Second Round   Nuneaton B   (h) 3-0
Third Round   Gillingham   (h) 2-3

BRADFORD CITY   Division 1

FOUNDATION

Bradford was a rugby stronghold around the turn of the century but after Manningham RFC held an archery contest to help them out of financial difficulties in 1903, they were persuaded to give up the handling code and turn to soccer. So they formed Bradford City and continued at Valley Parade. Recognising this as an opportunity of spreading the dribbling code in this part of Yorkshire, the Football League immediately accepted the new club's first application for membership of the Second Division.

Bradford & Bingley Stadium, Valley Parade, Bradford BD8 7DY.

Telephone: (01274) 773 355 (Office). *Fax:* (01274) 773 356.
Ticket Office: (01274) 770 022.
Website: www.bradfordcity.co.uk
Email: bradfordcityfc@compuserve.com
ClubCall: 09068 888 640.

Ground Capacity: 25,000.

Record Attendance: 39,146 v Burnley, FA Cup 4th rd, 11 March 1911.

Record Receipts: £164,567 v Sheffield Wednesday, FA Cup 5th rd, 16 February 1997.

Pitch Measurements: 110yd × 73yd.

HONOURS

Football League: Division 1 – Runners-up 1998–99; Division 2 – Champions 1907–08; Promoted from Division 2 1995–96 (play-offs); Division 3 – Champions 1984–85; Division 3 (N) – Champions 1928–29; Division 4 – Runners-up 1981–82.
FA Cup: Winners 1911.
Football League Cup: best season: 5th rd, 1965, 1989.

Chairman: Geoffrey Richmond. *Vice-Chairman:* David Thompson FCA. *Directors:* David Richmond, Elizabeth Richmond, Terry Goddard, Michael Richmond, Julian Rhodes, Prof. David Rhodes.

Managing Director: Shaun Harvey.

Manager: Jim Jefferies. *Assistant Manager:* Billy Brown. *Reserve/Youth Coach:* Walter Kidd.
Physio: Steve Redmond.

Secretary: Jon Pollard.

Stadium Manager: Allan Gilliver.

Colours: Claret and amber shirts, black shorts, amber stockings.

Change Colours: Burgundy and navy shirts, navy shorts and stockings with burgundy trim.

Year Formed: 1903.

Turned Professional: 1903.

Ltd Co.: 1908.

Club Nickname: 'The Bantams'.

First Football League Game: 1 September 1903, Division 2, v Grimsby T (a) L 0–2 – Seymour; Wilson, Halliday; Robinson, Millar, Farnall; Guy, Beckram, Forrest, McMillan, Graham.

Record League Victory: 11–1 v Rotherham U, Division 3 (N), 25 August 1928 – Sherlaw; Russell, Watson; Burkinshaw (1), Summers, Bauld; Harvey (2), Edmunds (3), White (3), Cairns, Scriven (2).

IT'S A FACT !

Left-back George Mulholland made a club record 231 consecutive League appearances for Bradford City between August 1953 and September 1958. With FA Cup games it was a total of 246 from an overall tally of 304.

Record Cup Victory: 11–3 v Walker Celtic, FA Cup 1st rd (replay), 1 December 1937 – Parker; Rookes, McDermott; Murphy, Mackie, Moore; Bagley (1), Whittingham (1), Deakin (4 incl. 1p), Cooke (1), Bartholomew (4).

Record Defeat: 1–9 v Colchester U, Division 4, 30 December 1961.

Most League Points (2 for a win): 63, Division 3 (N), 1928–29.

Most League Points (3 for a win): 94, Division 3, 1984–85.

Most League Goals: 128, Division 3 (N), 1928–29.

Highest League Scorer in Season: David Layne, 34, Division 4, 1961–62.

Most League Goals in Total Aggregate: Bobby Campbell, 121, 1981–84, 1984–86.

Most League Goals in One Match: 7, Albert Whitehurst v Tranmere R, Division 3N, 6 March 1929.

Most Capped Player: Harry Hampton, 9, Northern Ireland.

Most League Appearances: Cec Podd, 502, 1970–84.

Youngest League Player: Robert Cullingford, 16 years 141 days v Mansfield T, 22 April 1970.

Record Transfer Fee Received: £2,000,000 from Newcastle U for Des Hamilton, March 1997 and £2,000,000 from Newcastle U for Andrew O'Brien, March 2001.

Record Transfer Fee Paid: £2,500,000 to Leeds U for David Hopkin, July 2000.

Football League Record: 1903 Elected to Division 2; 1908–22 Division 1; 1922–27 Division 2; 1927–29 Division 3 (N); 1929–37 Division 2; 1937–61 Division 3; 1961–69 Division 4; 1969–72 Division 3; 1972–77 Division 4; 1977–78 Division 3; 1978–82 Division 4; 1982–85 Division 3; 1985–90 Division 2; 1990–92 Division 3; 1992–96 Division 2; 1996–99 Division 1; 1999–2001 FA Premier League; 2001– Division 1.

MANAGERS

Robert Campbell 1903–05
Peter O'Rourke 1905–21
David Menzies 1921–26
Colin Veitch 1926–28
Peter O'Rourke 1928–30
Jack Peart 1930–35
Dick Ray 1935–37
Fred Westgarth 1938–43
Bob Sharp 1943–46
Jack Barker 1946–47
John Milburn 1947–48
David Steele 1948–52
Albert Harris 1952
Ivor Powell 1952–55
Peter Jackson 1955–61
Bob Brocklebank 1961–64
Bill Harris 1965–66
Willie Watson 1966–69
Grenville Hair 1967–68
Jimmy Wheeler 1968–71
Bryan Edwards 1971–75
Bobby Kennedy 1975–78
John Napier 1978
George Mulhall 1978–81
Roy McFarland 1981–82
Trevor Cherry 1982–87
Terry Dolan 1987–89
Terry Yorath 1989–90
John Docherty 1990–91
Frank Stapleton 1991–94
Lennie Lawrence 1994–95
Chris Kamara 1995–98
Paul Jewell 1998–2000
Chris Hutchings 2000
Jim Jefferies November 2000–

LATEST SEQUENCES

Longest Sequence of League Wins: 10, 26.11.83 – 3.2.84.

Longest Sequence of League Defeats: 8, 21.1.33 – 11.3.33.

Longest Sequence of League Draws: 6, 30.1.76 – 13.3.76.

Longest Sequence of Unbeaten League Matches: 21, 11.1.69 – 2.5.69.

Longest Sequence Without a League Win: 16, 28.8.48 – 20.11.48.

TEN YEAR LEAGUE RECORD

		P	W	D	L	F	A	Pts	Pos
1990-91	Div 3	46	20	10	16	62	54	70	8
1991-92	Div 3	46	13	19	14	62	61	58	16
1992-93	Div 2	46	18	14	14	69	67	68	10
1993-94	Div 2	46	19	13	14	61	53	70	7
1994-95	Div 2	46	16	12	18	57	64	60	14
1995-96	Div 2	46	22	7	17	71	69	73	6
1996-97	Div 1	46	12	12	22	47	72	48	21
1997-98	Div 1	46	14	15	17	46	59	57	13
1998-99	Div 1	46	26	9	11	82	47	87	2
1999-2000	PR Lge	38	9	9	20	38	68	36	17

DID YOU KNOW ?

Bradford City's FA Cup winning. team of 1911 included eight Scots. The side conceded just one goal in six rounds, Norwich City 2–1 in the second round. In all they played seven games including the 1–0 replay final win over Newcastle United.

BRADFORD CITY 2000–01 LEAGUE RECORD

Match No.	Date	Venue	Opponents	Result	H/T Score	Lg. Pos.	Goalscorers	Attendance
1	Aug 19	A	Liverpool	L	0-1	0-0	—		44,183
2	22	H	Chelsea	W	2-0	1-0	—	Windass [24], Carbone [74]	17,872
3	26	H	Leicester C	D	0-0	0-0	9		16,766
4	Sept 5	A	Manchester U	L	0-6	0-2	—		67,447
5	9	H	Arsenal	D	1-1	1-0	15	McCall [10]	17,160
6	16	A	Aston Villa	L	0-2	0-1	18		27,849
7	23	H	Southampton	L	0-1	0-1	20		16,163
8	30	A	West Ham U	D	1-1	0-1	19	Petrescu [90]	25,407
9	Oct 14	A	Manchester C	L	0-2	0-2	19		34,229
10	21	A	Ipswich T	L	0-2	0-1	19		17,045
11	29	H	Leeds U	D	1-1	1-0	19	Collymore [21]	17,364
12	Nov 4	A	Charlton Ath	L	0-2	0-2	19		19,633
13	11	H	Everton	L	0-1	0-0	20		17,276
14	18	A	Derby Co	L	0-2	0-0	20		31,614
15	25	A	Middlesbrough	D	2-2	2-0	20	Windass [3], Carbone [10]	28,525
16	Dec 2	H	Coventry C	W	2-1	0-0	20	Collymore [80], Beagrie [83]	15,523
17	9	H	Tottenham H	D	3-3	1-2	19	Lawrence [9], Windass [69], Carbone [89]	17,225
18	16	A	Newcastle U	L	1-2	0-1	20	Molenaar [83]	50,470
19	23	A	Chelsea	L	0-3	0-1	20		33,377
20	26	H	Sunderland	L	1-4	0-1	20	Blake [75]	20,370
21	Jan 1	A	Leicester C	W	2-1	2-1	20	Jess [25], Jacobs [30]	19,278
22	13	H	Manchester U	L	0-3	0-0	20		20,551
23	21	A	Sunderland	D	0-0	0-0	20		45,288
24	30	A	Arsenal	L	0-2	0-2	—		37,318
25	Feb 3	H	Aston Villa	L	0-3	0-0	20		19,591
26	10	A	Southampton	L	0-2	0-0	20		14,651
27	24	H	West Ham U	L	1-2	0-1	20	Jess [62]	20,469
28	Mar 4	A	Ipswich T	L	1-3	1-0	20	Carbone [27]	21,816
29	17	H	Manchester C	D	2-2	0-1	20	Blake [52], Ward [57]	19,117
30	31	H	Newcastle U	D	2-2	2-1	20	Wetherall [6], Blake (pen) [10]	20,160
31	Apr 10	A	Tottenham H	L	1-2	1-1	—	Jess [44]	28,300
32	13	H	Charlton Ath	W	2-0	0-0	—	Blake (pen) [74], Carbone [80]	17,511
33	21	H	Derby Co	W	2-0	1-0	20	Ward 2 [16, 87]	18,564
34	28	A	Everton	L	1-2	1-0	20	Myers [3]	34,256
35	May 1	H	Liverpool	L	0-2	0-0	—		22,057
36	5	H	Middlesbrough	D	1-1	1-0	20	Jacobs [38]	20,921
37	13	A	Leeds U	L	1-6	1-5	—	Ward [22]	38,300
38	19	A	Coventry C	D	0-0	0-0	20		20,299

Final League Position: 20

GOALSCORERS

League (30): Carbone 5, Blake 4 (2 pens), Ward 4, Jess 3, Windass 3, Collymore 2, Jacobs 2, Beagrie 1, Lawrence 1, McCall 1, Molenaar 1, Myers 1, Petrescu 1, Wetherall 1.
Worthington Cup (11): Carbone 2, Ward 2, Whalley 2, Windass 2, Grant 1, Halle 1, Nolan 1.
FA Cup (0).

Clarke M 17	Atherton P 25	Nolan I 17 + 4	McCall S 36 + 1	Wetherall D 18	O'Brien A 17 + 1	Petrescu D 16 + 1	Hopkin D 8 + 3	Windass D 22 + 2	Whalley G 17 + 2	Sharpe L 6 + 5	Carbone B 29 + 2	Ward A 24 + 9	Beagrie P 9 + 10	Myers A 15 + 5	Halle G 10 + 3	Jacobs W 19 + 2	Lawrence J 15 + 2	Grant G — + 5	Saunders D 4 + 6	Collymore S 5 + 2	McKinlay B 10 + 1	Molenaar R 21	Blake R 14 + 7	Walsh G 19	Jess E 17	Rankin I — + 1	Locke G 6 + 1	Davison A 2	Kerr S — + 1	Match No.
1	2	3	4	5	6	7^1	8^2	9	10	11^3	12	13	14																	1
1	2	3	4	5	6	7^2	8	9	12	11^1	10^3	13				14														2
1	2	3	4	5	6^3	7	8	9^2	12	11^1	10	13				14														3
1	6	3	4	5		7		9	8	11^1	10	12				2														4
1	6	2	4	5		7	8				12	10	9	11^1		3^2	13													5
1	5	3^2	4	6		2	7	8	11^1			10	9	12			13													6
1	6		4	5		7^1		8		11^2		10	9			2	3	12	13											7
1	6		4	5		7		8	11^2	14		10	9	12		13^3	3^1	2												8
1	5	3	4	6		7		8				10	9	11				2												9
1	6		4	5		2^1						10	9	11		7		12											10
1	6	3	4	5		2			8	12	10^2	13	11^1			7		14	9^3										11
1	6	3	4	5		2^1		12	8		13	9	11^3			7	14	10^2												12
1	6	3	4	5		2^1		12	11		10^2	9^3	13			7		14	8											13
1	6	3	5^1	12		2		8^2	4	13		9	11^2			7		14	10											14
1	5	3	4		6	2^2		8			10^1	9^3	12	13		7				14	11									15
1	2	3	7	6				8			10			12	4^1					9	11	5								16
1	2		4		6	12		8			13	10		11^3	3^2		7^1			9		5	14							17
		4	3	7	6	2^2		8			10^5		12	14			13		11	5	9^1	1								18
		4	12	8	6	2^1		9			3^1	10^5	13			7			11	5	14	1								19
	2^1	12	4	6				9			10^2	13	11			3	7^3			8	5	14	1							20
	2^1		4	6			8						12		3			9^3	13	11	5	10^2	1	7	14					21
	2		4	6			8				9				3			12		7	5	10^1	1	11						22
	2		4	6			8				12	13			3		7	9^1			5	10^2	1	11						23
	2		8	6	12	7					9^2		4		3			11			5	13	1	10^1						24
	2		4	6		7^2	8				13	12			3^1					11	5	9	1	10						25
		7^2		6	12	8					13	3^3	4				9^1			11	5	14	1	10	2					26
		12	6	8	13						10	9	4		3^3	2				5^1	14	1	11	10	7^1					27
		8	6	4	7						10	9	3	12^2						5	13	1	11	2^1						28
		4	6			7					10	9	3							5	8	1	11	2						29
		4	6			7					10	9	12	3	13					5	8^2	1	11	2^1						30
		4				7					10	9	6	2	3					5	8	1	11							31
	12	4				7^1					10	9	6	2	3		13		5	8^2	1	11							32
		4				7					10	9	6	2	3	12				5	8^1	1	11							33
		4									10	9	6	2	3	7				5	8	1	11							34
		4				7					10	9	6	2	3					5	8	1	11							35
	12	4				7^2					10	9	6	2	3	13				5^1	8	1	11							36
	2^1	4						8			10	9	6	5	3	7						11				12	1		37
	2^4	4						7			10	9	6	5	3	12					8^1				11	1	13		38

Worthington Cup

Second Round	Darlington	(a)	1-0
		(h)	7-2
Third Round	Newcastle U	(a)	3-4

FA Cup

Third Round	Middlesbrough	(h)	0-1

BRENTFORD

Division 2

FOUNDATION

Formed as a small amateur concern in 1889 they were very successful in local circles. They won the championship of the West London Alliance in 1893 and a year later the West Middlesex Junior Cup before carrying off the Senior Cup in 1895. After winning both the London Senior Amateur Cup and the Middlesex Senior Cup in 1898 they were admitted to the Second Division of the Southern League.

Griffin Park, Braemar Rd, Brentford, Middlesex TW8 0NT.

Telephone: (020) 8847 2511. *Fax:* (020) 8568 9940.
Commercial Dept: (020) 8847 2511
Press Office: (020) 8847 2511. *ClubCall:* 09068 121 108.

Ground Capacity: 12,763.

Record Attendance: 38,678 v Leicester C, FA Cup 6th rd, 26 February 1949.

Record Receipts: £162,314 v Tottenham H, Worthington Cup 2nd rd, 15 September 1998.

Pitch Measurements: 111yd × 74yd.

Chairman: Ron Noades. *President:* E. J. Radley-Smith.
Managing Director: G. Hargraves.
Directors: S. R. Ebbs MS FRCS, J. Herting, D. Miller, E. Rogers, D. Tana.

Manager: Steve Coppell.
Coaches: Terry Bullivant, Wally Downes.
Director of Youth Football: Geoff Taylor.
Youth Coach: Bob Booker. *Physio:* Phil McLoughlin.

Community Officer: Lee Doyle. *Secretary:* Polly Kates.

Safety Officer: Jill Dawson.

Communications Manager: Peter Gilham.

Corporate Sales Manager: Samantha Marmara.

Colours: Red and white vertical striped shirts, black shorts, black stockings.

Change Colours: Blue and yellow shirts, blue shorts, yellow stockings.

Year Formed: 1889.

Turned Professional: 1899.

Ltd Co.: 1901.

Club Nickname: 'The Bees'.

Previous Grounds: 1889, Clifden Road; 1891, Benns Fields, Little Ealing; 1895, Shotters Field; 1898, Cross Road, S. Ealing; 1900, Boston Park; 1904, Griffin Park.

First Football League Game: 28 August 1920, Division 3, v Exeter C (a) L 0–3 – Young; Hodson, Rosier, Elliott J, Levitt, Amos, Smith, Thompson, Spreadbury, Morley, Henery.

HONOURS

Football League: Division 1 best season: 5th, 1935–36; Division 2 – Champions 1934–35; Division 3 – Champions 1991–92, 1998–99; Division 3 (S) – Champions 1932–33, Runners-up 1929–30, 1957–58; Division 4 – Champions 1962–63.

FA Cup: best season: 6th rd, 1938, 1946, 1949, 1989.

Football League Cup: best season: 4th rd, 1983.

Freight Rover Trophy: Runners-up 1985.

LDV Vans Trophy: Runners-up 2001.

IT'S A FACT !

After promotion to the First Division in the 1930's, Brentford achieved the feat of remaining unbeaten against Arsenal in their first two such seasons and then in 1937-38 won 2-0 at Highbury and 3-0 at Griffin Park.

Record League Victory: 9–0 v Wrexham, Division 3,
15 October 1963 – Cakebread; Coote, Jones; Slater, Scott,
Higginson; Summers (1), Brooks (2), McAdams (2),
Ward (2), Hales (1), (1 og).

Record Cup Victory: 7–0 v Windsor & Eton (away), FA
Cup 1st rd, 20 November 1982 – Roche; Rowe, Harris
(Booker), McNichol (1), Whitehead, Hurlock (2), Kamara,
Joseph (1), Mahoney (3), Bowles, Roberts.

Record Defeat: 0–7 v Swansea T, Division 3 (S),
8 November 1924 and v Walsall, Division 3 (S), 19 January
1957.

Most League Points (2 for a win): 62, Division 3 (S),
1932–33 and Division 4, 1962–63.

Most League Points (3 for a win): 85, Division 2, 1994–95
and Division 3, 1998–99.

Most League Goals: 98, Division 4, 1962–63.

Highest League Scorer in Season: Jack Holliday, 38,
Division 3 (S), 1932–33.

Most League Goals in Total Aggregate: Jim Towers, 153,
1954–61.

Most League Goals in One Match: 5, Jack Holliday v
Luton T, Division 3S, 28 January 1933; Billy Scott v
Barnsley, Division 2, 15 December 1934; Peter McKennan v
Bury, Division 2, 18 February 1949.

Most Capped Player: John Buttigieg, 22 (85), Malta.

Most League Appearances: Ken Coote, 514, 1949–64.

Youngest League Player: Danis Salman, 15 years 243 days v
Watford, 15 November 1975.

Record Transfer Fee Received: £720,000 from Wimbledon
for Dean Holdsworth, August 1992.

Record Transfer Fee Paid: £850,000 to Crystal Palace for
Hermann Hreidarsson, September 1998.

Football League Record: 1920 Original Member of Division 3; 1921–33 Division 3 (S); 1933–35
Division 2; 1935–47 Division 1; 1947–54 Division 2; 1954–62 Division 3 (S); 1962–63 Division 4;
1963–66 Division 3; 1966–72 Division 4; 1972–73 Division 3; 1973–78 Division 4; 1978–92 Division 3;
1992–93 Division 1; 1993–98 Division 2; 1998 –99 Division 3; 1999– Division 2.

MANAGERS

Will Lewis 1900–03
(Secretary-Manager)
Dick Molyneux 1903–06
W. G. Brown 1906–08
Fred Halliday 1908–26
(only Secretary to 1922)
Ephraim Rhodes 1912–15
Archie Mitchell 1921–22
Harry Curtis 1926–49
Jackie Gibbons 1949–52
Jimmy Blain 1952–53
Tommy Lawton 1953
Bill Dodgin Snr 1953–57
Malcolm Macdonald 1957–65
Tommy Cavanagh 1965–66
Billy Gray 1966–67
Jimmy Sirrel 1967–69
Frank Blunstone 1969–73
Mike Everitt 1973–75
John Docherty 1975–76
Bill Dodgin Jnr 1976–80
Fred Callaghan 1980–84
Frank McLintock 1984–87
Steve Perryman 1987–90
Phil Holder 1990–93
David Webb 1993–97
Micky Adams 1997–98
Ron Noades 1998–2000
Steve Coppell May 2001–

LATEST SEQUENCES

Longest Sequence of League Wins: 9, 30.4.32 – 24.9.32.

Longest Sequence of League Defeats: 9, 20.10.28 – 25.12.28.

Longest Sequence of League Draws: 5, 16.3.57 – 6.4.57.

Longest Sequence of Unbeaten League Matches: 26, 20.2.99 – 16.10.99.

Longest Sequence Without a League Win: 16, 19.2.94 – 7.5.94.

TEN YEAR LEAGUE RECORD

		P	W	D	L	F	A	Pts	Pos
1990-91	Div 3	46	21	13	12	59	47	76	6
1991-92	Div 3	46	25	7	14	81	55	82	1
1992-93	Div 1	46	13	10	23	52	71	49	22
1993-94	Div 2	46	13	19	14	57	55	58	16
1994-95	Div 2	46	25	10	11	81	39	85	2
1995-96	Div 2	46	15	13	18	43	49	58	15
1996-97	Div 2	46	20	14	12	56	43	74	4
1997-98	Div 2	46	11	17	18	50	71	50	21
1998-99	Div 3	46	26	7	13	79	56	85	1
1999-2000	Div 2	46	13	13	20	47	61	52	17

DID YOU KNOW ?

On 1 February 1933,
Brentford were 4-1 down at
Luton Town in a Division
Three (South) fixture but
fought back to draw 5-5 with
Jack Holliday, scoring all five
for them.

BRENTFORD 2000–01 LEAGUE RECORD

Match No.	Date	Venue	Opponents	Result	H/T Score	Lg. Pos.	Goalscorers	Attendance
1	Aug 12	A	Northampton T	D	1-1	0-0	—	Ingimarsson [82]	6379
2	19	H	Swansea C	D	0-0	0-0	17		5036
3	26	A	Oxford U	W	1-0	1-0	8	Folan [20]	4756
4	28	H	Bristol R	L	2-6	0-3	13	Evans (pen) [68], Scott [88]	5434
5	Sept 2	H	Wycombe W	D	0-0	0-0	13		4699
6	9	A	Reading	L	0-4	0-3	17		10,222
7	16	H	Millwall	D	1-1	0-0	19	Scott [51]	5495
8	23	A	Notts Co	D	2-2	0-1	18	McCammon [46], Partridge [90]	4164
9	30	H	Bournemouth	W	3-2	2-1	16	Scott 2 [13, 28], Pinamonte [55]	4210
10	Oct 14	H	Peterborough U	W	1-0	0-0	15	Scott [80]	4479
11	17	H	Colchester U	W	1-0	0-0	—	Scott [89]	3595
12	21	A	Luton T	L	1-3	0-3	14	Scott [73]	5382
13	24	A	Port Vale	D	1-1	0-0	—	Owusu [89]	3338
14	28	H	Walsall	W	2-1	2-1	14	Scott [2], Evans [19]	4007
15	Nov 4	A	Cambridge U	D	1-1	0-1	12	Scott [90]	4083
16	11	H	Rotherham U	L	0-3	0-3	15		4544
17	Dec 2	H	Wigan Ath	D	2-2	0-1	17	Evans (pen) [69], Scott [87]	4144
18	12	A	Bristol C	W	2-1	1-1	—	Mahon [41], Partridge [86]	8096
19	16	A	Wrexham	L	1-2	1-1	14	Rowlands [13]	2228
20	23	H	Oldham Ath	D	1-1	0-0	15	Rowlands [90]	5317
21	26	A	Swindon T	W	3-2	0-1	13	Owusu [46], Scott [66], Evans (pen) [73]	6649
22	Jan 1	H	Oxford U	W	3-0	2-0	12	Scott 2 [22, 45], Partridge [88]	5020
23	6	H	Northampton T	D	1-1	0-1	11	Owusu [90]	5361
24	13	A	Bristol R	D	0-0	0-0	11		6933
25	17	A	Stoke C	L	0-1	0-1	—		9350
26	23	A	Bury	W	1-0	0-0	—	Owusu [56]	2274
27	27	A	Oldham Ath	L	0-3	0-0	11		4964
28	Feb 3	A	Wycombe W	D	0-0	0-0	11		6604
29	10	H	Reading	L	1-2	0-1	13	McCammon [85]	7550
30	16	A	Millwall	L	0-1	0-1	—		10,233
31	20	H	Bristol C	W	2-1	1-1	—	O'Connor [3], Partridge [68]	4823
32	24	H	Notts Co	W	3-1	1-0	10	Evans [27], Owusu [59], Partridge [66]	4366
33	Mar 3	A	Bournemouth	L	0-2	0-2	10		4438
34	6	A	Peterborough U	D	1-1	0-1	—	Ingimarsson [65]	4479
35	10	A	Stoke C	D	2-2	0-1	12	Williams [72], Owusu [79]	5518
36	16	A	Colchester U	L	1-3	1-1	—	Owusu [9]	3420
37	31	H	Wrexham	W	1-0	1-0	13	Powell [28]	4449
38	Apr 7	A	Wigan Ath	W	3-1	0-0	13	Gibbs [50], Owusu [53], Partridge [61]	6502
39	10	H	Swindon T	L	0-1	0-0	—		4180
40	14	H	Port Vale	D	1-1	1-0	13	Evans [2]	3671
41	17	A	Walsall	L	2-3	1-2	—	McCammon [37], Roper (og) [53]	4540
42	25	H	Cambridge U	D	2-2	1-0	—	Owusu [22], Evans [80]	3062
43	28	A	Rotherham U	L	1-2	1-1	18	Owusu [6]	9760
44	May 1	A	Swansea C	L	0-6	0-2	—		2002
45	3	H	Luton T	D	2-2	0-1	—	Partridge [55], Williams [66]	3287
46	5	H	Bury	W	3-1	0-0	14	Partridge [51], Folan [62], Ingimarsson [81]	4596

Final League Position: 14

GOALSCORERS

League (56): Scott 13, Owusu 10, Partridge 8, Evans 7 (3 pens), Ingimarsson 3, McCammon 3, Folan 2, Rowlands 2, Williams 2, Gibbs 1, Mahon 1, O'Connor 1, Pinamonte 1, Powell 1, own goal 1.
Worthington Cup (4): Scott 2, McCammon 1, Rowlands 1.
FA Cup (1): Pinamonte 1.

Gottskalksson O 45	Gibbs P 26 + 1	Anderson I 1	Mahon G 40	Quinn R 22	Marshall S 29	Ingimarsson I 42	Evans P 43	Owusu L 24 + 9	McCammon M 14 + 10	Scott A 22	Folan T 11 + 10	Pinamonte L 3 + 5	Rowlands M 32	Javary J 4 + 2	Dobson M 23 + 3	Partridge S 29 + 7	Marsh S 3 + 1	Crowe J 9	Williams M 6 + 24	Kennedy R 1	Theobald D 15	Lovett J 2 + 4	Austin K 3	O'Connor K 5 + 6	Powell D 18	Smith P 1 + 1	Charles J 4 + 6	Hutchinson E 5 + 2	Smith J 2 + 1	Somner M 2 + 1	Tabb J 1 + 1	Graham G —— + 1	Match No.
1	2	3	4[1]	5	6	7	8	9[2]	10	11	12	13																					1
1	2		4	5[1]	6	7	8	9	10[2]	11[3]		14	3	12	13																		2
1			4	5	6	7	8		10	3	11[1]		2	9		12																	3
1			4	5	6	7	8		10	3	11[2]	13	2	9[1]	12																		4
1			4	5	6	7	8		10	3	12	11[1]		9	13	2[2]																	5
1			4[3]	5	6	7	8		10	3	12	13	2[1]	9	11[2]	14																	6
1			4	5	6	7	8		10	9		11[1]			3	2			12														7
1			4	5	6	7	8		10[3]	9[2]	12	11			13	2			14		3[1]												8
1			4	5	6	7	8	9		13	11		10[2]		12	3	2																9
1	2		4[2]	5	6	7	8		9		11[1]	10			12	3			13														10
1			4[2]	5	6	7	8		9		12	10[1]			11	2			13				3										11
1	2		4	5	6	7	8[3]		9		12	13			10	11[2]			3[1]		14												12
1	2		4	5	6[3]	7	8[2]	12	9[1]	13					3	14					10												13
1	2		4	5		7	8	12	9						10						11[1]			6									14
1	2[2]		4	5		7	8[1]	12	9	13					10	14			3		11[3]			6									15
1	2		4	5[2]		7	8[1]	9	12		11				10	3					13			6									16
1	2[3]		4	5	6[1]	7	8	12	9						14	10			13		3			11[2]									17
1			4	5	6	7	8	12	9						10	2[1]			11		3												18
1	2		4	5	6[2]	7[1]	8	12	9						10				11		14			3[3]			13						19
1	2		4	5	6	7[1]	8	9[2]							10				3		11			12			13						20
1	2		4	5	6	7[1]	8	12	9						3				11					13			10[2]						21
1	2		4	5	6	7	8		9						10[1]				3		11						12						22
1	2[2]		4	5[1]	6	7	8[1]	12	9						3				11		14			13									23
1	2[2]		4		6	7	8	9[1]	12						10				3		11			13	5								24
1			4[3]		6	7	8	9[1]	12						10				3		13			2[2]	5		14						25
1	12		4		6	7	8		9	13					10				3		11[2]			2	5[1]		15						26
1	2[1]		4		6	7	8		9	12					10				3		11			13	5[2]								27
1			4		6	7	8	9[1]	12						10				3		11[2]			13	5		2						28
1	2				6	7		9		12					10				3		11	13	8[1]	4[2]	5								29
1	2[1]		4		6	7	8		9						10				3		11			12	5								30
1	2		4		6	7	8	9[1]	12										3		11			13	10[2]		5						31
1	2		4			7	8[2]		9	12									3		11		6	13	10[1]		5						32
1	2		4			7	8[2]		9	12					10				3		11	13	6[1]		5								33
1	2		4			7	8		9						10		6		3		11[1]				5		12						34
1	2		4			7	8	12	9[1]						10				13		6		3[3]		5		11						35
1			4			7	8		9	12					3				11[1]		13		6	2[2]	10		5						36
1			4			7	8		9						10[1]		6		3		11[2]		2	12	5		13						37
1	2		4				8		9						10		6		11[1]		7		5	3			12						38
1	2		4				8		9			7[1]					6		11		10[2]		5	3			12	13					39
1	2[2]		4				8		9[1]			10					6		12		7		3		5		11	13					40
1			4				8		10			9[1]			3		12		6		2		5		7		11[2]	13					41
1						7	8		9						10				3		11[1]		4		6	2	5	12					42
1						7	8		9						10[1]				3		11			12	6	2	5				4		43
1						7	8		9						10[1]				3[3]		12	13			6	2	5[2]	1	11	4	14		44
1						7			9						10				11		12				6	2	4	8	3[1]	5[2]	13		45
1						7		9[2]	10										3		11[1]			12	6	2[3]	13	4	8	5	14		46

Worthington Cup

First Round	Bristol C	(a)	2-2
		(h)	2-1
Second Round	Tottenham H	(h)	0-0
		(a)	0-2

FA Cup

First Round	Kingstonian	(h)	1-3

BRIGHTON & HOVE ALBION — Division 2

FOUNDATION

A professional club Brighton United was formed in November 1897 at the Imperial Hotel, Queen's Road, but folded in March 1900 after less than two seasons in the Southern League at the County Ground. An amateur team, Brighton & Hove Rangers was then formed by some prominent United supporters and after one season at Withdean, decided to turn semi-professional and play at the County Ground. Rangers were accepted into the Southern League but then also folded June 1901. John Jackson the former United manager organised a meeting at the Seven Stars public house, Ship Street on 24 June 1901 at which a new third club Brighton & Hove United was formed. They took over Rangers' place in the Southern League and pitch at County Ground. The name was changed to Brighton & Hove Albion before a match was played because of objections by Hove FC.

Offices: Fifth floor, Hanover House, 118 Queens Road, Brighton BN1 3XG.

Ground Address: Withdean Stadium, Tongdean Lane, Brighton BN1 5JD.

Telephone: (01273) 778 855. *Fax:* (01273) 321 095.
ClubCall: 09068 800 609.

Ground Capacity: 6960.

Record Attendance: 36,747 v Fulham, Division 2, 27 December 1958.

Record Receipts: £109,615.65 v Crawley T, FA Cup 3rd rd, 4 January 1992.

Pitch Measurements: 110yd × 70yd.

Directors: Dick Knight (Chairman), Ray Bloom, Derek Chapman, Martin Perry, Bob Pinnock FCA, Kevin Griffiths
Non-Executive Director: Lord Faulkner of Worcester.

HONOURS

Football League: Division 1 best season: 13th, 1981–82; Division 2 – Runners-up 1978–79; Division 3 (S) – Champions 1957–58; Runners-up 1953–54, 1955–56; Division 3 – Champions 2000–01; Runners-up 1971–72, 1976–77, 1987–88; Division 4 – Champions 1964–65.

FA Cup: Runners-up 1983.

Football League Cup: best season: 5th rd, 1979.

Manager: Micky Adams. *Assistant Manager:* Bob Booker. *Physio:* Malcolm Stuart.
Youth Team Coach: Dean Wilkins.

Chief Executive: Martin Perry. *Secretary:* Derek Allan. *Director of Youth:* Martin Hinshelwood.

Colours: Blue and white striped shirts, white shorts, blue stockings.

Change Colours: Red and black striped shirts, black shorts, black stockings.

Year Formed: 1901.

Turned Professional: 1901.

Ltd Co.: 1904.

Previous Grounds: 1901, County Ground; 1902, Goldstone Ground.

Club Nickname: 'The Seagulls'.

First Football League Game: 28 August 1920, Division 3, v Southend U (a) L 0–2 – Hayes; Woodhouse, Little; Hall, Comber, Bentley; Longstaff, Ritchie, Doran, Rodgerson, March.

IT'S A FACT !

During excavation work carried out for the building of the North stand at Brighton & Hove Albion's Goldstone ground in 1930, an 18th century cannonball was unearthed.

Record League Victory: 9–1 v Newport Co, Division 3 (S), 18 April 1951 – Ball; Tennant (1p), Mansell (1p); Willard, McCoy, Wilson; Reed, McNichol (4), Garbutt, Bennett (2), Keene (1). 9–1 v Southend U, Division 3, 27 November 1965 – Powney; Magill, Baxter; Leck, Gall, Turner; Gould (1), Collins (1), Livesey (2), Smith (3), Goodchild (2).

Record Cup Victory: 10–1 v Wisbech, FA Cup 1st rd, 13 November 1965 – Powney; Magill, Baxter; Collins (1), Gall, Turner; Gould, Smith (2), Livesey (3), Cassidy (2), Goodchild (1), (1 og).

Record Defeat: 0–9 v Middlesbrough, Division 2, 23 August 1958.

Most League Points (2 for a win): 65, Division 3 (S), 1955–56 and Division 3, 1971–72.

Most League Points (3 for a win): 92, Division 3, 2000–01.

Most League Goals: 112, Division 3 (S), 1955–56.

Highest League Scorer in Season: Peter Ward, 32, Division 3, 1976–77.

Most League Goals in Total Aggregate: Tommy Cook, 114, 1922–29.

Most League Goals in One Match: 5, Jack Doran v Northampton T, Division 3S, 5 November 1921; 5, Adrian Thorne v Watford, Division 3S, 30 April 1958.

Most Capped Player: Steve Penney, 17, Northern Ireland.

Most League Appearances: 'Tug' Wilson, 509, 1922–36.

Youngest League Player: Ian Chapman, 16 years 259 days v Birmingham C, 14 February 1987.

Record Transfer Fee Received: £900,000 from Liverpool for Mark Lawrenson, August 1981.

Record Transfer Fee Paid: £500,000 to Manchester U for Andy Ritchie, October 1980.

Football League Record: 1920 Original Member of Division 3; 1921–58 Division 3 (S); 1958–62 Division 2; 1962–63 Division 3; 1963–65 Division 4; 1965–72 Division 3; 1972–73 Division 2; 1973–77 Division 3; 1977–79 Division 2; 1979–83 Division 1; 1983–87 Division 2; 1987–88 Division 3; 1988–96 Division 2; 1996–2001 Division 3; 2001– Division 2.

MANAGERS

John Jackson 1901–05
Frank Scott-Walford 1905–08
John Robson 1908–14
Charles Webb 1919–47
Tommy Cook 1947
Don Welsh 1947–51
Billy Lane 1951–61
George Curtis 1961–63
Archie Macaulay 1963–68
Fred Goodwin 1968–70
Pat Saward 1970–73
Brian Clough 1973–74
Peter Taylor 1974–76
Alan Mullery 1976–81
Mike Bailey 1981–82
Jimmy Melia 1982–83
Chris Cattlin 1983–86
Alan Mullery 1986–87
Barry Lloyd 1987–93
Liam Brady 1993–95
Jimmy Case 1995–96
Steve Gritt 1996–98
Brian Horton 1998–99
Jeff Wood 1999
Micky Adams February 1999–

LATEST SEQUENCES

Longest Sequence of League Wins: 9, 2.10.26 – 20.11.26.

Longest Sequence of League Defeats: 12, 11.11.72 – 27.1.73.

Longest Sequence of League Draws: 6, 16.2.80 – 15.3.80.

Longest Sequence of Unbeaten League Matches: 16, 8.10.30 – 28.1.31.

Longest Sequence Without a League Win: 15, 21.10.72 – 27.1.73

TEN YEAR LEAGUE RECORD

		P	W	D	L	F	A	Pts	Pos
1990-91	Div 2	46	21	7	18	63	69	70	6
1991-92	Div 2	46	12	11	23	56	77	47	23
1992-93	Div 2	46	20	9	17	63	59	69	9
1993-94	Div 2	46	15	14	17	60	67	59	14
1994-95	Div 2	46	14	17	15	54	53	59	16
1995-96	Div 2	46	10	10	26	46	69	40	23
1996-97	Div 3	46	13	10	23	53	70	47	23
1997-98	Div 3	46	6	17	23	38	66	35	23
1998-99	Div 3	46	16	7	23	49	66	55	17
1999-2000	Div 3	46	17	16	13	64	46	67	11

DID YOU KNOW ?

On 3 May 1970, Brighton & Hove Albion on tour in Spain, defeated Paiporta a third division club from Valencia 2-0. The pitch was in the middle of a dried-up riverbed.

BRIGHTON & HOVE ALBION 2000–01 LEAGUE RECORD

Match No.	Date	Venue	Opponents	Result	H/T Score	Lg. Pos.	Goalscorers	Attendance
1	Aug 12	A	Southend U	L	0-2	0-1	—	7492
2	19	H	Rochdale	W	2-1	2-1	11	Zamora 2 [18, 45]	6076
3	26	A	Lincoln C	L	0-2	0-2	15		3024
4	28	H	Kidderminster H	L	0-2	0-0	20		6274
5	Sept 2	H	Torquay U	W	6-2	4-2	13	Zamora 3 [10, 64, 85], Hart [20], Jones 2 [30, 45]	5804
6	9	A	Cardiff C	D	1-1	0-0	15	Wicks [59]	6741
7	12	A	Blackpool	W	2-0	2-0	—	Rogers [33], Hart [45]	3406
8	16	H	Cheltenham T	W	3-0	0-0	6	Wicks [58], Watson (pen) [74], Zamora [88]	6325
9	23	A	York C	W	1-0	1-0	4	Jones [35]	3178
10	30	H	Leyton Orient	W	2-0	1-0	4	Rogers [42], Mayo [65]	6731
11	Oct 6	A	Hull C	W	2-0	0-0	—	Wicks [65], Rogers [74]	6225
12	14	H	Scunthorpe U	D	0-0	0-0	3		6567
13	18	H	Hartlepool U	W	4-2	3-1	—	Hart [7], Zamora 2 [22, 68], Carpenter [30]	6528
14	21	A	Chesterfield	L	0-1	0-0	3		7014
15	24	H	Plymouth Arg	W	2-0	1-0	—	Carpenter [37], Zamora [85]	6724
16	28	A	Darlington	W	2-1	1-1	2	Jones [4], Steele [63]	3637
17	Nov 4	A	Carlisle U	W	4-1	1-1	2	Watson 2 (1 pen) [21, 62 (p)], Zamora [49], Steele [65]	6746
18	11	A	Macclesfield T	D	0-0	0-0	2		2654
19	25	A	Shrewsbury T	W	4-0	2-0	2	Hart [7], Zamora 2 [36, 82], Carpenter [55]	6556
20	Dec 2	H	Halifax T	W	2-1	1-0	2	Zamora 2 [35, 52]	6995
21	16	A	Mansfield T	L	0-2	0-0	2		2668
22	22	H	Exeter C	W	2-0	1-0	—	Rogers [17], Campbell (og) [61]	6758
23	26	A	Barnet	W	1-0	1-0	2	Hart [31]	3908
24	Jan 1	H	Southend U	L	0-2	0-0	2		6503
25	13	A	Kidderminster H	W	2-0	1-0	2	Smith (og) [37], Zamora (pen) [78]	4056
26	27	A	Exeter C	L	0-1	0-1	3		4490
27	Feb 3	A	Torquay U	W	1-0	0-0	2	Zamora [75]	2909
28	10	H	Cardiff C	W	1-0	1-0	2	Zamora [15]	6922
29	17	A	Cheltenham T	L	1-3	1-2	2	Cullip [14]	4533
30	20	H	Blackpool	W	1-0	0-0	2	Crosby [57]	6756
31	24	A	York C	D	1-1	0-0	3	Hart [55]	6555
32	Mar 3	A	Leyton Orient	W	2-0	1-0	3	Brooker [29], Zamora [46]	7958
33	6	A	Scunthorpe U	L	1-2	1-2	—	Brooker [4]	2581
34	10	H	Hull C	W	3-0	1-0	2	Watson [42], Melton [69], Stant [88]	6823
35	14	H	Barnet	W	4-1	2-0	—	Crosby [36], Zamora 2 [37, 62], Rogers [54]	6587
36	17	A	Hartlepool U	D	2-2	1-0	3	Carpenter [37], Zamora (pen) [56]	4410
37	31	H	Mansfield T	W	2-0	1-0	2	Zamora [18], Hart [90]	6703
38	Apr 3	A	Rochdale	D	1-1	0-0	—	Carpenter [87]	2444
39	10	A	Lincoln C	W	2-0	1-0	—	Rogers [34], Zamora [67]	6716
40	14	A	Plymouth Arg	W	2-0	2-0	2	Brooker [3], Zamora [16]	7490
41	16	H	Darlington	W	2-0	2-0	2	Carpenter [28], Zamora [29]	6639
42	21	A	Carlisle U	D	0-0	0-0	2		4727
43	28	H	Macclesfield T	W	4-1	2-1	1	Zamora 3 (1 pen) [20, 34 (p), 80], Watson [87]	6731
44	May 1	H	Chesterfield	W	1-0	0-0	—	Cullip [78]	6847
45	3	A	Halifax T	D	0-0	0-0	—		3979
46	5	A	Shrewsbury T	L	0-3	0-2	1		5360

Final League Position: 1

GOALSCORERS

League (73): Zamora 28 (3 pens), Hart 7, Carpenter 6, Rogers 6, Watson 5 (2 pens), Jones 4, Brooker 3, Wicks 3, Crosby 2, Cullip 2, Steele 2, Mayo 1, Melton 1, Stant 1, own goals 2.
Worthington Cup (2): Jones 1, Watson 1.
FA Cup (7): Watson 2 (2 pens), Zamora 2, Carpenter 1, Oatway 1, Wicks 1.

Kuipers M 34	Watson P 46	Mayo K 43 + 2	Carr D 2	Crosby A 28 + 6	Carpenter R 42	Zamora B 42 + 1	Rogers P 41 + 4	Hart G 43 + 2	Oatway C 36 + 2	Brooker P 25 + 16	Freeman D 5 + 11	Steele L 4 + 19	Cartwright M 12 + 1	Aspinall W — + 1	Ramsay S 2 + 9	Cullip D 38	Jones N 27 + 13	Thomas R — + 2	Melton S 10 + 18	Wicks M 23 + 1	Virgo M 2 + 4	Stant P — 7	Wilkinson S — + 1	Thomas M 1 + 7	Packham W — + 1	Match No.
1^8	2	3	4	5	6	7	8^1	9^2	10	11	12	13	15													1
	2	3	4	5	6	9^1	12	8^2	10	11		7^1		1	13	14										2
	2	3		5		7	8	9	10	6			1		11^1	4	12									3
	2	12		5		11	8^3	9	10	6^1	7^2		1			4	3	13	14							4
	2	3		6	7	12	9^3	10	8^2				1		14	4	11	13		5^1						5
	2	3		6	7^2	8^1	9^3	10	12				1		13	4	11		14	5						6
	2	3		6	7	8	9	10	12				1			4	11^1			5						7
	2	3		6^1	7	8	9	10	13		12	1				4	11^2			5						8
	2	3	12	6	7^1	8	9^2	10	14		13	1				4	11^3			5						9
	2	3		6	7	8^2	9^1	10	12			1				4	11		13	5						10
1	2	3	12	6	7^3	8	9	10	13		14					4	11^2			5^1						11
1	2	3		6	7	8	9^2	10^1	12		13					4	11^1		14	5						12
1	2	3		6	7	8^2	9^1	10	12		13					4	11^1		14	5						13
1	2	3	12	6	7^2	8	9	10			13					4	11^3			5						14
1	2	3		6^1	7	8^3	9^1	10	13		12					4	11		14	5						15
1	2	3		6	7^2	8	9	10^1	13		12					4	11^3		14	5						16
1	2	3	12	6	7	8^9	9		13		10					4	11^2		14	5^1						17
1	2	3		6	7	8	9^1	12	13		10					4	11^2			5						18
1	2	3		6	7^3	8^1	9^2	10	12		13		14			4	11			5						19
1	2	3	12	6	7	8	9^1	10^1			13					4	11^2		14	5						20
1	2	3		6	7	8^2	9^2	10	12	13			14			4	11^1			5						21
1	2	3	12	6	7	8	9^2	10	11^3	13						4	14			5^1						22
1	2	3		5	6	8	9^2	10	7^3	12			13			4	11^1		14							23
1	2	3		5	6	12	8^3	9	10	7^1	13					4	11^2		14							24
1	2	3		5	6	7^3	8	9^2	10	11^1	12		14			4	13									25
1	2	3	4	6	7	8^1	9^2	10	11^3	12			14			13				5						26
	2	3	4		9^2	8		10		7	12	1				11^1		6	5	13						27
	2	3	4	6	9^2	8	12	10	11^2	7^1	13	1						14	5							28
	2	3^3		5	11	9	8^1	12	10	14	7			1		4	13			6^2						29
1	2	3		5	6	7^2	8	9^1	10		12				13	4	11^3		14							30
1	2	3^1		5	6	7	8^2	9	10	12						4	11		13							31
1	2			5	6	7^3	8	9	10^1	11^4		12				4	13		3			14				32
1	2	12		5^1	6	7	8^1	9		10		11^1				4			3	13	14					33
1	2	3		5	6	7^3	8	9^1		10^2	12					4	13		11				14			34
1	2	3		5	6	7^2	8^3	9		10	12					4	11^1						13	14		35
1	2	3		5	6	7	8	9		10^1	12					4^3	11^2		13	14						36
1	2	3		5	6	7^2	8^3	9		10^1	12					13	4		11					14		37
1	2	3		5	6			8	9^2	10^1						11	4		7	13				12		38
1	2	3		5	6^1	7	8	9	12	10^2						4	13		11^3					14		39
1	2	3		5	6^1	7^3	12	9^2	10	8						4	13		11				14			40
1	2	3		5	6^2	7	8	9^3	10	11^1						4	12						14			41
1	2	3		5	6	7	12	9^3	10	11^2	13					4			8^1				14			42
1	2	3		5	6	7^3	8	9^2	10^1	11	12					4	13						14			43
1	2	3		5	6	7	8	9^1	10^2	11^3	12					4			13				14			44
1^8	2^1	3	5			9^2			8			7			11		6	4	12	13				10	15	45
1	2^3	3	5	6	7	8^1	9^2	10	11			12				4	13		14							46

Worthington Cup
First Round   Millwall   (h)   1-2
                                        (a)   1-1

FA Cup
First Round   Aldershot T   (a)   6-2
Second Round   Scunthorpe U   (a)   1-2

BRISTOL CITY

Division 2

FOUNDATION

The name Bristol City came into being in 1897 when the Bristol South End club, formed three years earlier, decided to adopt professionalism and apply for admission to the Southern League after competing in the Western League. The historic meeting was held at The Albert Hall, Bedminster. Bristol City employed Sam Hollis from Woolwich Arsenal as manager and gave him £40 to buy players. In 1901 they merged with Bedminster, another leading Bristol club.

Ashton Gate, Bristol BS3 2EJ.

Telephone: (0117) 963 0630 (5 lines).
Fax: (0117) 963 0700. *Website:* www.bcfc.co.uk
Commercial: (0117) 963 0600. *Shop:* (0117) 963 0637.
ClubCall: 09068 121 176. *Supporters Club:* (0117) 966 5554. *Community Dept:* (0117) 963 0636.

Ground Capacity: 21,479.

Record Attendance: 43,335 v Preston NE, FA Cup 5th rd, 16 February 1935.

Record Receipts: £251,612 v Everton, FA Cup 4th rd, 23 January 1999.

Pitch Measurements: 115yd × 75yd.

Chairman: J. Laycock.

Directors: S. Lansdown, K. Dawe, A. Gooch.

Chief Executive: Colin Sexstone.

Football Secretary: Michelle McDonald.

Manager: Danny Wilson. *Physio:* Gill O'Shea.

Stadium Manager: Dave Lewis.

Sales Manager: Elaine White.

Safety Officer: Keith Draisey.

Colours: Red shirts, red shorts, white stockings.

Change Colours: White shirts, white shorts, white stockings.

Year Formed: 1894.

Turned Professional: 1897.

Ltd Co.: 1897. Bristol City Football Club Ltd.

Previous Name: 1894, Bristol South End; 1897, Bristol City.

Club Nickname: 'Robins'.

Previous Grounds: 1894, St John's Lane; 1904, Ashton Gate.

First Football League Game: 7 September 1901, Division 2, v Blackpool (a) W 2–0 – Moles; Tuft, Davies; Jones, McLean, Chambers; Bradbury, Connor, Boucher, O'Brien (2), Flynn.

HONOURS

Football League: Division 1 – Runners-up 1906–07; Division 2 – Champions 1905–06; Runners-up 1975–76, 1997–98; Division 3 (S) – Champions 1922–23, 1926–27, 1954–55; Runners-up 1937–38; Division 3 – Runners-up 1964–65, 1989–90.
FA Cup: Runners-up 1909.
Football League Cup: Semi-final 1971, 1989.
Welsh Cup: Winners 1934.
Anglo-Scottish Cup: Winners 1978.
Freight Rover Trophy: Winners 1986; Runners-up 1987.
Auto Windscreens Shield: Runners-up 2000.

IT'S A FACT !

Tony Thorpe scored the 100th goal of his career during Bristol City's 4-0 win over Notts County on 4 November 2000.

Record League Victory: 9–0 v Aldershot, Division 3 (S), 28 December 1946 – Eddols; Morgan, Fox; Peacock, Roberts, Jones (1); Chilcott, Thomas, Clark (4 incl. 1p), Cyril Williams (1), Hargreaves (3).

Record Cup Victory: 11–0 v Chichester C, FA Cup 1st rd, 5 November 1960 – Cook; Collinson, Thresher; Connor, Alan Williams, Etheridge; Tait (1), Bobby Williams (1), Atyeo (5), Adrian Williams (3), Derrick, (1 og).

Record Defeat: 0–9 v Coventry C, Division 3 (S), 28 April 1934.

Most League Points (2 for a win): 70, Division 3 (S), 1954–55.

Most League Points (3 for a win): 91, Division 3, 1989–90.

Most League Goals: 104, Division 3 (S), 1926–27.

Highest League Scorer in Season: Don Clark, 36, Division 3 (S), 1946–47.

Most League Goals in Total Aggregate: John Atyeo, 314, 1951–66.

Most League Goals in One Match: 6, Tommy 'Tot' Walsh v Gillingham, Division 3S, 15 January 1927.

Most Capped Player: Billy Wedlock, 26, England.

Most League Appearances: John Atyeo, 597, 1951–66.

Youngest League Player: Nyrere Kelly, 16 years 213 days v Hartlepool U, 16 October 1982.

Record Transfer Fee Received: £3,000,000 from Wolverhampton W for Ade Akinbiyi, September 1999.

Record Transfer Fee Paid: £1,200,000 to Gillingham for Ade Akinbiyi, May 1998.

MANAGERS
Sam Hollis 1897–99
Bob Campbell 1899–1901
Sam Hollis 1901–05
Harry Thickett 1905–10
Sam Hollis 1911–13
George Hedley 1913–15
Jack Hamilton 1915–19
Joe Palmer 1919–21
Alex Raisbeck 1921–29
Joe Bradshaw 1929–32
Bob Hewison 1932–49
(under suspension 1938–39)
Bob Wright 1949–50
Pat Beasley 1950–58
Peter Doherty 1958–60
Fred Ford 1960–67
Alan Dicks 1967–80
Bobby Houghton 1980–82
Roy Hodgson 1982
Terry Cooper 1982–88
(Director from 1983)
Joe Jordan 1988–90
Jimmy Lumsden 1990–92
Denis Smith 1992–93
Russell Osman 1993–94
Joe Jordan 1994–97
John Ward 1997–98
Benny Lennartsson 1998–99
Tony Pulis 1999
Tony Fawthrop 2000
Danny Wilson June 2000–

Football League Record: 1901 Elected to Division 2; 1906–11 Division 1; 1911–22 Division 2; 1922–23 Division 3 (S); 1923–24 Division 2; 1924–27 Division 3 (S); 1927–32 Division 2; 1932–55 Division 3 (S); 1955–60 Division 2; 1960–65 Division 3; 1965–76 Division 2; 1976–80 Division 1; 1980–81 Division 2; 1981–82 Division 3; 1982–84 Division 4; 1984–90 Division 3; 1990–92 Division 2; 1992–95 Division 1; 1995–98 Division 2; 1998–99 Division 1; 1999– Division 2.

LATEST SEQUENCES

Longest Sequence of League Wins: 14, 9.9.05 – 2.12.05.

Longest Sequence of League Defeats: 7, 3.10.70 – 7.11.70.

Longest Sequence of League Draws: 4, 6.11.99 – 27.11.99.

Longest Sequence of Unbeaten League Matches: 24, 9.9.05 – 10.2.06.

Longest Sequence Without a League Win: 15, 29.4.33 – 4.11.33.

TEN YEAR LEAGUE RECORD

		P	W	D	L	F	A	Pts	Pos
1990-91	Div 2	46	20	7	19	68	71	67	9
1991-92	Div 2	46	13	15	18	55	71	54	17
1992-93	Div 1	46	14	14	18	49	67	56	15
1993-94	Div 1	46	16	16	14	47	50	64	13
1994-95	Div 1	46	11	12	23	42	63	45	23
1995-96	Div 2	46	15	15	16	55	60	60	13
1996-97	Div 2	46	21	10	15	69	51	73	5
1997-98	Div 2	46	25	10	11	69	39	85	2
1998-99	Div 1	46	9	15	22	57	80	42	24
1999-2000	Div 2	46	15	19	12	59	57	64	9

DID YOU KNOW ?

On 18 September 1973, Bristol City beat Hull City 3-1 at Ashton Gate. They went ahead 2-1 in a wet and windswept second half when City goalkeeper Ray Cashley, from fully 98 yards, scored with a freak clearance.

BRISTOL CITY 2000–01 LEAGUE RECORD

Match No.	Date	Venue	Opponents	Result		H/T Score	Lg. Pos.	Goalscorers	Attendance
1	Aug 12	A	Wrexham	W	2-0	1-0	—	Thorpe [6], Holland [62]	5852
2	19	H	Stoke C	L	1-2	0-0	9	Thomas (og) [65]	12,590
3	26	A	Cambridge U	L	0-1	0-0	14		3716
4	28	H	Rotherham U	L	0-1	0-0	20		8280
5	Sept 9	A	Swindon T	L	0-1	0-0	22		10,110
6	16	A	Oldham Ath	D	0-0	0-0	22		4095
7	23	H	Colchester U	D	1-1	1-1	23	Thorpe [20]	7411
8	30	A	Oxford U	W	1-0	1-0	18	Murray [10]	5308
9	Oct 6	H	Bournemouth	D	3-3	3-2	—	Thorpe 3 [24, 30, 38]	8936
10	14	A	Walsall	D	0-0	0-0	20		6576
11	17	A	Millwall	D	1-1	0-1	—	Murray [90]	9694
12	21	H	Reading	W	4-0	3-0	17	Peacock 2 [9, 60], Murray [18], Bell [30]	11,134
13	24	A	Peterborough U	W	2-1	0-1	—	Peacock [63], Thorpe [89]	9219
14	28	A	Wycombe W	W	2-1	1-1	15	Thorpe 2 (1 pen) [2 (p), 70]	6051
15	31	A	Swansea C	D	2-2	1-1	—	Carey [35], Smith S (og) [74]	5286
16	Nov 4	H	Notts Co	W	4-0	2-0	9	Clist [33], Murray [37], Thorpe [61], Peacock [88]	10,250
17	11	A	Luton T	W	3-0	0-0	8	Murray [56], Peacock [64], Bell [67]	6595
18	25	H	Wigan Ath	D	1-1	1-1	8	Peacock [7]	12,708
19	Dec 2	H	Bury	W	4-1	1-0	6	Carey [45], Thorpe [52], Clist [73], Murray [90]	9416
20	12	H	Brentford	L	1-2	1-1	—	Peacock [32]	8096
21	16	H	Port Vale	W	2-1	1-0	6	Peacock 2 (1 pen) [19, 88 (p)]	4113
22	22	H	Bristol R	W	3-2	0-1	—	Millen [49], Beadle [55], Thorpe [74]	16,696
23	26	A	Northampton T	L	0-2	0-2	6		6064
24	30	A	Stoke C	L	0-1	0-0	7		14,629
25	Jan 1	H	Cambridge U	W	6-2	1-1	7	Murray 2 [31, 48], Thorpe 3 (1 pen) [61 (p), 79, 82], Tinnion [86]	10,637
26	13	A	Rotherham U	D	1-1	0-1	7	Beadle [89]	5654
27	20	H	Northampton T	W	2-0	0-0	7	Clist [54], Bell [73]	11,630
28	Feb 3	H	Swansea C	W	3-1	1-1	7	Bell [20], Beadle [89], Thorpe [90]	10,379
29	10	A	Swindon T	D	1-1	1-1	7	Beadle [45]	10,031
30	13	H	Wrexham	W	2-1	0-0	—	Peacock [57], Millen [66]	9500
31	20	A	Brentford	L	1-2	1-1	—	Thorpe [36]	4823
32	24	A	Colchester U	L	0-4	0-2	7		3430
33	Mar 3	H	Oxford U	D	0-0	0-0	7		9681
34	6	H	Walsall	L	1-3	1-2	—	Thorpe [32]	9263
35	10	A	Bournemouth	L	0-4	0-3	9		4028
36	16	H	Millwall	W	2-1	1-0	—	Carey [4], Matthews (pen) [90]	10,395
37	23	A	Reading	W	3-1	1-1	—	Thorpe [45], Peacock [54], Matthews [71]	15,716
38	27	H	Oldham Ath	D	2-2	1-1	—	Maddison [2], Peacock [89]	9568
39	31	H	Port Vale	D	1-1	0-1	7	Murray [80]	11,782
40	Apr 3	A	Bristol R	D	1-1	0-0	—	Peacock (pen) [79]	9361
41	7	A	Bury	W	1-0	0-0	7	Lourenco [53]	3729
42	14	A	Peterborough U	L	1-2	1-1	7	Matthews [23]	6560
43	16	H	Wycombe W	L	1-2	0-0	7	Murray [49]	11,643
44	21	A	Notts Co	L	1-2	1-0	8	Clist [33]	5369
45	28	H	Luton T	W	3-1	1-0	8	Brown A 2 [34, 65], Thorpe [78]	9161
46	May 5	A	Wigan Ath	D	0-0	0-0	9		10,048

Final League Position: 9

GOALSCORERS

League (70): Thorpe 19 (2 pens), Peacock 13 (2 pens), Murray 10, Beadle 4, Bell 4, Clist 4, Carey 3, Matthews 3 (1 pen), Brown A 2, Millen 2, Lourenco 1, Holland 1, Maddison 1, Tinnion 1, own goals 2.
Worthington Cup (3): Holland 1, Peacock 1 (pen), Thorpe 1 (pen).
FA Cup (8): Thorpe 3, Clist 2, Beadle 1, Murray 1, Peacock 1.

Miller A 4	Testimitanui 14 + 7	Bell M 41	Holland P 5	Lever M 2	Carey L 46	Murray S 46	Dunning D 9	Peacock L 31 + 4	Thorpe T 33 + 6	Tinnion B 40 + 2	Spencer D 2 + 2	Goodridge G 1 + 6	Lavin G 3	Hulbert R 14 + 5	Jordan A 1 + 1	Brown A 27 + 8	Millen K 28 + 1	Odejav K + 3	Phillips S 42	Matessa A — + 1	Beadle P 18 + 15	Amankwaah R 8 + 6	Brown M — + 5	Clist S 36 + 2	Hill M 32 + 2	Rodrigues D 3 + 1	Burnell J 19 + 4	Woodman C 1 + 1	Coles D 1 + 1	Matthews L 4 + 2	Maddison N 4 + 3	Laurenco 1 + 2	Match No.
1	2	3	4	5	6	7[1]	8	9	10[2]	11	12	13																					1
1	2	3	4[1]	5	6	7	8	9	10	11	12																						2
1	12	3			6	7	8		10	11		9[2]	2	4[1]	5	13																	3
1		3	4		6	7[1]	8	9	10[2]	11	12		2				5	13															4
	12	3	4		6	7	8		10	11				2[1]	5	13	1[6]	15			9[2]												5
	2	3	4[2]		6	7	8		10	11	12	13			5				1		9[1]												6
	12	3			6	7	8		10	11				4[1]	5				1		9[2]	2	13										7
	12	3			6	7	8	13	10[2]	11					5				1		9[2]	2		4[1]	14								8
		3			6	7	8	12	10[2]	11					5				1		9[1]	2		4	13								9
		3			6	7	8[1]	9		11	12				5				1			2		4	10								10
		3			6	7	8[1]	9[2]		11	12				5				1		13	2[3]		4	10	14							11
		3			6	7	8[2]	9[1]	12	11					5				1		14			4	10[1]	2							12
		3			6	7	8[4]	9[1]	10	11					5				1		13			4	2								13
		3			6	7	8	9[2]	10	11	12								1		13			4[1]	5	2							14
		3			6	2	8[1]	9	10	11	12					13			1			7		4	5[2]								15
		3			6	7[1]		9	10[2]	11	12					8	5		1		13			4	2								16
	12	3			6	7		9	10[2]	11[1]						8[3]	5		1		13			4	2	14							17
		3			6	7		9	10[1]	11						8	5		1		12			4	2								18
		3			6	7		9	10	11[1]	12					8	5		1					4	2								19
		3			6	7		9	10	11						8	5		1		12			4	2								20
		3			6	7[4]		9	10[1]	11	13					8	5		1		12			4[3]	2	14							21
		3			6	7		9[1]	10	11						8	5		1		12			4	2								22
4[1]		3			6	7			10							8	5		1		9	2		12	11								23
	12	3			6	7			10	11		9[2]				8	5	13	1					4[1]	2								24
	12	3[1]			6	7			10	11						8	5		1		9			4	2								25
		3			6	7			10	11						8	5		1		9	12		4[1]	2								26
		3			6	7		9	12	11						8	5		1		10[1]			4	2								27
		3			6	7		9[2]	10	11						8	5		1		13	14	12	4[1]	2[3]								28
	3[2]				6	7		12	10	11						8	5		1		9[1]			4	2	13							29
					6	7		12	10	11						8	5		1		9[1]	13		4	3	2[2]							30
	3				6	2		9	10[1]	11						8	5		1		12			7	4								31
					6	7		9	12	11						8	5		1		10	2[8]		4[1]	13		3						32
					6	2		9	10	11[1]				7		8			1		12	3[1]		4			5[2]	13	14				33
					6	7			10	11[1]					8		5		1		9	12		4	3		2						34
					6	7			10						11	8			1		9	12		4	3		2		5[1]				35
		3[2]			6	2		9[1]	10					13		8			1		12			7[3]	4		5			14	11		36
		3			6	2		9	10[2]		12			13		8[1]			1					7[4]	4		5			14	11		37
		3			6	2		9	10	11				12					1		13			7[4]	4		5				8[1]		38
		3			6	2		9		12				14		8[1]			1		13			7	4		5			10[2]	11[3]		39
		3			6	2		9		11						8			1					7	4		5			10			40
		3			6	2		9[1]		11						8			1					7	4		5			10	12		41
		3			6	2			12	11				8[2]		13			1		9	14		7[3]	4		5			10[1]			42
		3			6	2			10	11[3]				12		8[2]			1		9	13		7[1]	4		5			14			43
		3			6	2		9		12	11					8			1		10[2]			7[1]	4		5			13			44
		3			6	2		9		12	11					8			1		13			7[3]	4		5[2]			14	10[1]		45
		3			6	2		9		11[13]				7[1]		8			1		10	12			4		5			13			46

Worthington Cup
First Round   Brentford   (h)   2-2   (a)   1-2

FA Cup
First Round   Chesterfield   (a)   1-0
Second Round   Kettering T   (h)   3-1
Third Round   Huddersfield T   (a)   2-0
Fourth Round   Kingstonian   (h)   1-1   (a)   1-0
Fifth Round   Leicester C   (a)   0-3

BRISTOL ROVERS

Division 3

FOUNDATION

Bristol Rovers were formed at a meeting in Stapleton Road, Eastville, in 1883. However, they first went under the name of the Black Arabs (wearing black shirts). Changing their name to Eastville Rovers in their second season, they won the Gloucestershire Senior Cup in 1888–89. Original members of the Bristol & District League in 1892, this eventually became the Western League and Eastville Rovers adopted professionalism in 1897.

Registered Offices: The Memorial Stadium, Filton Avenue, Horfield, Bristol BS7 0BF. (0117) 909 6648.

Ground: The Memorial Stadium.

Training Ground: (0117) 977 2000.

Matchday Ticket Office: (0117) 909 8848.
ClubCall: 09068 121 131. *Fax:* (0117) 908 5530.
Community Office: (0117) 907 6555.
Ticket Office: (0117) 924 7474.

Ground Capacity: 11,976.

Record Attendance: 11,433 v Sunderland, Worthington Cup 3rd rd, 31 October 2000 (Memorial Stadium). 9464 v Liverpool, FA Cup 4th rd, 8 February 1992 (Twerton Park). 38,472 v Preston NE, FA Cup 4th rd, 30 January 1960 (Eastville).

Record Receipts: £115,000 v Sunderland, Worthington Cup 3rd rd, 31 October 2000.

Pitch Measurements: 101m × 68m.

HONOURS

Football League: Division 2 best season: 4th, 1994–95; Division 3 (S) – Champions 1952–53; Division 3 – Champions 1989–90; Runners-up 1973–74.

FA Cup: best season: 6th rd, 1951, 1958.

Football League Cup: best season: 5th rd, 1971, 1972.

Vice-Presidents: Dr W. T. Cussen, A. I. Seager, R. Redmond. *Chairman:* D. H. A. Dunford.
Vice-Chairman: G. M. H. Dunford. *Directors:* R. Craig, B. Andrews, V. Stokes, B. Bradshaw.

Director of Football and Team Manager: Gerry Francis. *Assistant Manager:* Gary Thompson.

First Team Coach: Gary Penrice. *Physio:* Phil Kite. *Director of Youth:* Phil Bater.

Community Scheme Organiser: Peter Aitken.

Club Secretary: Roger Brinsford. *Office Manager:* Mrs Angela Mann.

Commercial Manager: Ralph Ellis.

Colours: Blue and white quartered shirts, blue shorts, blue stockings.

Change Colours: Black and stone quartered shirts, black shorts and stockings.

Year Formed: 1883. *Turned Professional:* 1897. *Ltd Co.:* 1896.

Previous Names: 1883, Black Arabs; 1884, Eastville Rovers; 1897, Bristol Eastville Rovers; 1898, Bristol Rovers. *Club Nickname:* 'Pirates'.

Previous Grounds: 1883, Purdown; Three Acres, Ashley Hill; Rudgeway, Fishponds; 1897, Eastville; 1986, Twerton Park; 1996, The Memorial Stadium.

First Football League Game: 28 August 1920, Division 3, v Millwall (a) L 0–2 – Stansfield; Bethune, Panes; Boxley, Kenny, Steele; Chance, Bird, Sims, Bell, Palmer.

IT'S A FACT !

Wally McArthur, a wing-half, was a Bristol Rovers' ever-present in 1938-39 and again in 1948-49, his best years lost in the Second World War. Signed in 1932, he spent 18 years at Eastville and still made 261 peacetime League appearances.

Record League Victory: 7–0 v Brighton & HA, Division 3 (S), 29 November 1952 – Hoyle; Bamford, Fox; Pitt, Warren, Sampson; McIlvenny, Roost (2), Lambden (1), Bradford (1), Petherbridge (2), (1 og). 7–0 v Swansea T, Division 2, 2 October 1954 – Radford; Bamford, Watkins; Pitt, Muir, Anderson; Petherbridge, Bradford (2), Meyer, Roost (1), Hooper (2), (2 og). 7–0 v Shrewsbury T, Division 3, 21 March 1964 – Hall; Hillard, Gwyn Jones; Oldfield, Stone (1), Mabbutt; Jarman (2), Brown (1), Biggs (1p), Hamilton, Bobby Jones (2).

Record Cup Victory: 6–0 v Merthyr Tydfil, FA Cup 1st rd, 14 November 1987 – Martyn; Alexander (Dryden), Tanner, Hibbitt, Twentyman, Jones, Holloway, Meacham (1), White (2), Penrice (3) (Reece), Purnell.

Record Defeat: 0–12 v Luton T, Division 3 (S), 13 April 1936.

Most League Points (2 for a win): 64, Division 3 (S), 1952–53.

Most League Points (3 for a win): 93, Division 3, 1989–90.

Most League Goals: 92, Division 3 (S), 1952–53.

Highest League Scorer in Season: Geoff Bradford, 33, Division 3 (S), 1952–53.

Most League Goals in Total Aggregate: Geoff Bradford, 242, 1949–64.

Most League Goals in One Match: 4, Sidney Leigh v Exeter C, Division 3S, 2 May 1921; 4, Jonah Wilcox v Bournemouth, Division 3S, 12 December 1925; 4, Bill Culley v QPR, Division 3S, 5 March 1927; Frank Curran v Swindon T, Division 3S, 25 March 1939; Vic Lambden v Aldershot, Division 3S, 29 March 1947; George Petherbridge v Torquay U, Division 3S, 1 December 1951; Vic Lambden v Colchester U, Division 3S, 14 May 1952; Geoff Bradford v Rotherham U, Division 2, 14 March 1959; Robin Stubbs v Gillingham, Division 2, 10 October 1970; Alan Warboys v Brighton & HA, Division 3, 1 December 1973; Jamie Cureton v Reading, Division 2, 16 January 1999.

Most Capped Player: Neil Slatter, 10 (22), Wales.

Most League Appearances: Stuart Taylor, 546, 1966–80.

Youngest League Player: Ronnie Dix, 15 years 180 days v Norwich C, 3 March 1928.

Record Transfer Fee Received: £2,000,000 from Fulham for Barry Hayles, November 1998 and £2,000,000 from WBA for Jason Roberts, July 2000.

Record Transfer Fee Paid: £370,000 to QPR for Andy Tillson, November 1992.

Football League Record: 1920 Original Member of Division 3; 1921–53 Division 3 (S); 1953–62 Division 2; 1962–74 Division 3; 1974–81 Division 2; 1981–90 Division 3; 1990–92 Division 2. 1992–93 Division 1; 1993–2001 Division 2; 2001– Division 3.

MANAGERS

Alfred Homer 1899–1920
  (continued as Secretary to 1928)
Ben Hall 1920–21
Andy Wilson 1921–26
Joe Palmer 1926–29
Dave McLean 1929–30
Albert Prince-Cox 1930–36
Percy Smith 1936–37
Brough Fletcher 1938–49
Bert Tann 1950–68
  (continued as General Manager to 1972)
Fred Ford 1968–69
Bill Dodgin Snr 1969–72
Don Megson 1972–77
Bobby Campbell 1978–79
Harold Jarman 1979–80
Terry Cooper 1980–81
Bobby Gould 1981–83
David Williams 1983–85
Bobby Gould 1985–87
Gerry Francis 1987–91
Martin Dobson 1991
Dennis Rofe 1992
Malcolm Allison 1992–93
John Ward 1993–96
Ian Holloway 1996–2001
Gary Thompson 2001
Gerry Francis July 2001–

LATEST SEQUENCES

Longest Sequence of League Wins: 12, 18.10.52 – 17.1.53.

Longest Sequence of League Defeats: 8, 29.4.61 – 9.9.61.

Longest Sequence of League Draws: 5, 1.11.75 – 22.11.75.

Longest Sequence of Unbeaten League Matches: 32, 7.4.73 – 27.1.74.

Longest Sequence Without a League Win: 20, 5.4.80 – 1.11.80.

TEN YEAR LEAGUE RECORD

		P	W	D	L	F	A	Pts	Pos
1990-91	Div 2	46	15	13	18	56	59	58	13
1991-92	Div 2	46	16	14	16	60	63	62	13
1992-93	Div 1	46	10	11	25	55	87	41	24
1993-94	Div 2	46	20	10	16	60	59	70	8
1994-95	Div 2	46	22	16	8	70	40	82	4
1995-96	Div 2	46	20	10	16	57	60	70	10
1996-97	Div 2	46	15	11	20	47	50	56	17
1997-98	Div 2	46	20	10	16	70	64	70	5
1998-99	Div 2	46	13	17	16	65	56	56	13
1999-2000	Div 2	46	23	11	12	69	45	80	7

DID YOU KNOW ❓

Bristol Rovers' Eastville ground attendance record was broken in the space of three weeks in January 1955 in successive Cup ties: 35,921 v Portsmouth and 35,972 v Chelsea.

BRISTOL ROVERS 2000–01 LEAGUE RECORD

Match No.	Date	Venue	Opponents	Result	H/T Score	Lg. Pos.	Goalscorers	Attendance
1	Aug 12	H	Bournemouth	D	1-1	1-1	—	Cureton (pen) [9]	8046
2	20	A	Peterborough U	D	2-2	1-1	15	Evans [28], Ellington [59]	6997
3	28	A	Brentford	W	6-2	3-0	11	Astafjevs 2 [5, 84], Ellington [33], Hogg 2 [39, 70], Jones [86]	5434
4	Sept 9	A	Notts Co	D	1-1	0-0	15	Ellington [59]	5511
5	12	A	Wycombe W	W	1-0	1-0	—	Foster [34]	4718
6	16	H	Wigan Ath	D	0-0	0-0	12		8109
7	23	A	Cambridge U	W	3-0	2-0	8	Bryant [20], Evans [42], Jones [53]	4624
8	30	H	Luton T	D	3-3	2-1	9	Foster [14], Ellington 2 [31, 61]	7901
9	Oct 6	A	Bury	L	0-1	0-0	—		3279
10	14	H	Northampton T	L	0-1	0-0	11		7704
11	17	H	Rotherham U	D	1-1	0-1	—	Evans [66]	6910
12	21	A	Swindon T	W	3-1	3-0	11	Andreasson [14], Williams M (og) [31], Evans (pen) [37]	8097
13	24	A	Colchester U	L	1-2	0-1	—	Ellis [87]	2951
14	28	H	Oldham Ath	L	0-2	0-1	16		6110
15	Nov 4	A	Oxford U	W	1-0	1-0	13	Foster [17]	5407
16	11	H	Walsall	D	0-0	0-0	12		7540
17	22	A	Millwall	L	1-2	0-1	—	Cameron [50]	5502
18	25	A	Wrexham	L	0-1	0-0	15		2575
19	Dec 2	A	Swansea C	D	0-0	0-0	16		5563
20	16	H	Stoke C	L	0-3	0-3	18		6838
21	22	H	Bristol C	L	2-3	1-0	—	Bignot [1], Cameron [78]	16,696
22	26	H	Reading	D	2-2	1-2	19	Ellington [30], Thomson [81]	8029
23	Jan 13	H	Brentford	D	0-0	0-0	19		6933
24	20	A	Reading	L	0-1	0-1	19		11,767
25	Feb 3	A	Millwall	L	0-3	0-1	20		10,828
26	10	H	Notts Co	D	0-0	0-0	21		6914
27	17	A	Wigan Ath	D	0-0	0-0	21		7271
28	24	H	Cambridge U	W	2-1	1-1	21	Astafjevs [33], Ellington [47]	7079
29	27	A	Bournemouth	W	2-1	2-1	—	Ellington 2 [14, 16]	3466
30	Mar 3	A	Luton T	D	0-0	0-0	20		7405
31	6	A	Northampton T	L	1-2	0-1	—	Ellington [80]	4552
32	10	H	Bury	W	2-0	1-0	21	Foster [32], Plummer [81]	7065
33	17	A	Rotherham U	L	0-3	0-1	21		7098
34	24	H	Swindon T	D	0-0	0-0	21		8114
35	31	A	Stoke C	L	1-4	0-2	21	Gall [88]	12,274
36	Apr 3	H	Bristol C	D	1-1	0-0	—	Lee [53]	9361
37	7	H	Swansea C	W	1-0	1-0	21	Hogg [8]	6505
38	9	A	Port Vale	L	0-1	0-0	—		3962
39	11	H	Peterborough U	L	1-2	0-2	—	Jones [48]	6540
40	14	H	Colchester U	W	2-0	0-0	21	Astafjevs [85], Ellington [90]	6551
41	16	A	Oldham Ath	L	0-1	0-0	21		6883
42	21	A	Oxford U	W	6-2	1-1	20	Lee [28], Ellington 2 [50, 80], Astafjevs [67], Walters 2 (1 pen) [86, 90 (p)]	7554
43	28	A	Walsall	L	1-2	0-2	21	Ellington [90]	7130
44	30	H	Port Vale	L	0-3	0-0	—		7340
45	May 2	H	Wycombe W	L	1-2	0-0	—	Gall [80]	8264
46	5	H	Wrexham	W	4-0	2-0	21	Walters 2 (1 pen) [29 (p), 44], Partridge [51], Ellington [66]	6418

Final League Position: 21

GOALSCORERS

League (53): Ellington 15, Astafjevs 5, Evans 4 (1 pen), Foster 4, Walters 4 (2 pens), Hogg 3, Jones 3, Cameron 2, Gall 2, Lee 2, Andreasson 1, Bignot 1, Bryant 1, Cureton 1 (pen), Ellis 1, Partridge 1, Plummer 1, Thomson 1, own goal 1.
Worthington Cup (6): Bignot 2, Ellington 2, Cameron 1, Hogg 1.
FA Cup (1): own goal 1.

Culkin N 45	Pethick R 11+2	Wilson C 36+1	Foster S 44	Foran M 9+3	Jones S 37+2	Bignot M 26	Thomson A 31+1	Ellington N 36+6	Cureton J 1	Astafjevs V 34+7	Cameron M 6+8	Bryant S 27+3	Hogg L 31+3	Evans M 19+2	Ellis C 2+13	Walters M 11+15	Parkin B —+2	Glennon M 1	Andreasson M 4	Dagnogo M —+2	Plummer D 17+3	Challis T 19+3	Meaker M 2+3	Allsopp D 4+2	Hillier D 3+1	Johansen R —+2	Barrett G —+1	Mauge R 14+2	Richards J 3+4	McKeever M 7+5	Owusu A 11+6	Partridge R 4+2	Lee C 8+1	Gall K 3+7	Match No.
1	2¹	3²	4	5	6	7	8	9¹	10	11	12	13	14																						1
1	12	3	4		6	2	5	9³		7	13	11	10¹	8³	14																				2
1		3	4		6	2	5	9¹		7	12²	11	10	8³	14	13																			3
1		3¹	4		6	2	5	9		7		11	10	8	12	13																			4
1⁸		3	4		6	2	5	9¹		7		11	10	8	12	15																			5
	5¹	3³	4	12	6	2		9²		7		11	10	8	13	14		1																	6
1		3	4		6	2		9¹		7		11	10	8	12				5																7
1		3	4		6	2		9²		7		11		8	10¹	5¹				14	13	12													8
1⁸		3	4	12	6	2		9						8	10¹		15		5²		11	7	13												9
1		3¹	4	5	6	2				7			10²	8	12	11					13	9													10
1		3¹	4	5		2		9		7		11		8	12						10²	6	13												11
1			5	6		2				7				8²	12	10¹		1	4	13		3		9³	14										12
1	12		4		6					7		11	10²	8		13					2¹	5		3	9³										13
1		3	4	5	6	2	12			7	13	11	10²	8¹	14							9³													14
1		3	4	5	6	2		9		7¹		11	10	8²	12							13													15
1	2	12	4		6		5	9		7		11¹	10²	8								3					13								16
1			4	5		2¹	6³	9²			12	10	11	8	13	14						3					7								17
1	2		4		6		5	12		13		9³	11	8	10¹							3					7²	14							18
1			4		6	2	5	9		7		11	10¹	8	12							3													19
1			4	5²	6	2	11	9		7			10		12							3¹		8		13									20
1	3¹		5		6	2	4	9¹		12		7	11	10	8²							13						14							21
1			4	12		2	5	9		7³	8²		10	13		11¹						3	14					6							22
1	2	3	4				5	9¹		7		11²		8	12	13						10						6							23
1		3	4			2	5	9		7	12	11²		8³								13		10¹				6	14						24
1		3	4			2¹	5			7	12			8		13						10						6	9						25
1		3	4				5	9¹			12		7	2														6		10	11				26
1		3	4	12			5¹	13		7²		14	8	2								4						6	11¹²	10	9				27
1		3	5		6	2¹		12		7		11	14	13								4							10³	8²	9				28
1		3	5		6	2	12	9²		7			8									4¹							13	10	11				29
1		3	5		6			9		12		7¹				13						11	4						6	10²					30
1	3¹		5		6	2		9		7												11	4					13	12	8²	10				31
1	3³	4			6	2	5	9		12		8¹	13									11						7		14	10²				32
1		3	4		2²		5	9		7			8			12						11	13					6¹		14	10³				33
1		3	4		6		5	9				10										2	13						8¹	12²	11	7			34
1		3	4		6		5	9		12		7										11							13	8¹	2²	10³	14		35
1	11	3	4		6		5	9⁴		7			8¹									7	2					11		12		10	12		36
1	11¹	3	4		6		5	9⁴		7		12	8²									2							13			10	14		37
1		3	4		6		5	9¹		7			8									2						11²		12		10	13		38
1	3¹	4			6		5	12		2	9¹	11²	8		14							7							13			10			40
1		4			6		5	12		2	9¹	7¹	8		14						11								13			10⁸			41
1	3³	4			6		5	9¹		2	12		8		14						11							7		13		10²			42
1	2	3	4		6²		5	9		7			8¹			12						11									13	10³	14		43
1			4		6¹		5	9		2²						8						11						7		13	10	3	12		44
1	2	3	4¹	12			5	9		13						8						11						7²		10³	6		14		45
1	2¹	3		5	6²			9		7		8³	12			4						11								13		14	10		46

Worthington Cup

First Round	Plymouth Arg	(a)	2-1	
		(h)	1-1	
Second Round	Everton	(a)	1-1	
		(h)	1-1	
Third Round	Sunderland	(h)	1-2	

FA Cup

First Round	Cardiff C	(a)	1-5

BURNLEY

Division 1

FOUNDATION

The majority of those responsible for the formation of the Burnley club in 1881 were from the defunct rugby club Burnley Rovers. Indeed, they continued to play rugby for a year before changing to soccer and dropping 'Rovers' from their name. The changes were decided at a meeting held in May 1882 at the Bull Hotel.

Turf Moor, Burnley BB10 4BX.

Telephone: (01282) 700 000. *Fax:* (01282) 700 014.
ClubCall: 09068 121 153. *Ticket Office:* (01282) 700 010.
Community Programme: (01282) 700 081.
Commercial Department: (01282) 700 007.

Ground Capacity: 22,546.

Record Attendance: 54,775 v Huddersfield T, FA Cup 3rd rd, 23 February 1924.

Record Receipts: £183,000 v Preston NE, Division 2, 4 March 2000.

Pitch Measurements: 114yd × 72yd.

Chairman: B. Kilby. *Vice-Chairman:* R. Ingleby.
President: Dr R. D. Iven MRCS (Eng), LRCP (Lond), MRCGP.
Directors: C. Holt, R. Blakeborough, J. Turkington, M. Hobbs, C. Duckworth.

Manager: Stan Ternent. *Chief Executive:* A. Watson.

Company Secretary: Cathy Pickup.

Coaches: Ronnie Jepson, Michael Docherty, James Robson.

Sales Manager: Anthony Fairclough.

Colours: Claret body with blue sleeves, white shorts, white stockings.

Change Colours: White shirts, blue shorts, blue stockings.

Year Formed: 1882.

Turned Professional: 1883.

Ltd Co.: 1897.

Previous Name: 1881, Burnley Rovers; 1882, Burnley.

Club Nickname: 'The Clarets'.

Previous Grounds: 1881, Calder Vale; 1882, Turf Moor.

First Football League Game: 8 September 1888, Football League, v Preston NE (a) L 2–5 – Smith; Lang, Bury, Abrams, Friel, Keenan, Brady, Tait, Poland (1), Gallocher (1), Yates.

Record League Victory: 9–0 v Darwen, Division 1, 9 January 1892 – Hillman; Walker, McFettridge, Lang, Matthews, Keenan, Nicol (3), Bowes, Espie (1), McLardie (3), Hill (2).

HONOURS

Football League: Division 1 –
Champions 1920–21, 1959–60;
Runners-up 1919–20, 1961–62;
Division 2 – Champions 1897–98,
1972–73; Runners-up 1912–13,
1946–47, 1999–2000; Promoted from
Division 2, 1993–94 (play-offs);
Division 3 – Champions 1981–82;
Division 4 – Champions 1991–92.
Record 30 consecutive Division 1
games without defeat 1920–21.
FA Cup: Winners 1914; Runners-up
1947, 1962.
Football League Cup: Semi-final 1961,
1969, 1983.
Anglo–Scottish Cup: Winners 1979.
Sherpa Van Trophy: Runners-up
1988.
European Competitions: European
Cup: 1960–61. European Fairs Cup:
1966–67.

IT'S A FACT !

On 11 March 1961, Burnley fielded a virtual reserve team against Chelsea, but still managed to draw 4-4. It was four days before their European Cup third round tie in Hamburg.

Record Cup Victory: 9–0 v Crystal Palace, FA Cup 2nd rd (replay), 10 February 1909 – Dawson; Barron, McLean; Cretney (2), Leake, Moffat; Morley, Ogden, Smith (3), Abbott (2), Smethams (1). 9–0 v New Brighton, FA Cup 4th rd, 26 January 1957 – Blacklaw; Angus, Winton; Seith, Adamson, Miller; Newlands (1), McIlroy (3), Lawson (3), Cheesebrough (1), Pilkington (1). 9–0 v Penrith, FA Cup 1st rd, 17 November 1984 – Hansbury; Miller, Hampton, Phelan, Overson (Kennedy), Hird (3 incl. 1p), Grewcock (1), Powell (2), Taylor (3), Biggins, Hutchison.

Record Defeat: 0–10 v Aston Villa, Division 1, 29 August 1925 and v Sheffield U, Division 1, 19 January 1929.

Most League Points (2 for a win): 62, Division 2, 1972–73.

Most League Points (3 for a win): 88, Division 2, 1999–2000.

Most League Goals: 102, Division 1, 1960–61.

Highest League Scorer in Season: George Beel, 35, Division 1, 1927–28.

Most League Goals in Total Aggregate: George Beel, 178, 1923–32.

Most League Goals in One Match: 6, Louis Page v Birmingham C, Division 1, 10 April 1926.

Most Capped Player: Jimmy McIlroy, 51 (55), Northern Ireland.

Most League Appearances: Jerry Dawson, 522, 1907–28.

Youngest League Player: Tommy Lawton, 16 years 174 days v Doncaster R, 28 March 1936.

Record Transfer Fee Received: £750,000 from Luton T for Steve Davis, August 1995.

Record Transfer Fee Paid: £1,000,000 to Stockport C for Ian Moore, October 2000.

Football League Record: 1888 Original Member of the Football League; 1897–98 Division 2; 1898–1900 Division 1; 1900–13 Division 2; 1913–30 Division 1; 1930–47 Division 2; 1947–71 Division 1; 1971–73 Division 2; 1973–76 Division 1; 1976–80 Division 2; 1980–82 Division 3; 1982–83 Division 2; 1983–85 Division 3; 1985–92 Division 4; 1992–94 Division 2; 1994–95 Division 1; 1995–2000 Division 2; 2000– Division 1.

MANAGERS

Arthur F. Sutcliffe 1893–96
(Secretary-Manager)
Harry Bradshaw 1896–99
(Secretary-Manager)
Ernest Magnall 1899–1903
(Secretary-Manager)
Spen Whittaker 1903–10
R. H. Wadge 1910–11
(Secretary-Manager)
John Haworth 1911–25
Albert Pickles 1925–32
Tom Bromilow 1932–35
Alf Boland 1935–39
(Secretary-Manager)
Cliff Britton 1945–48
Frank Hill 1948–54
Alan Brown 1954–57
Billy Dougall 1957–58
Harry Potts 1958–70
(General Manager to 1972)
Jimmy Adamson 1970–76
Joe Brown 1976–77
Harry Potts 1977–79
Brian Miller 1979–83
John Bond 1983–84
John Benson 1984–85
Martin Buchan 1985
Tommy Cavanagh 1985–86
Brian Miller 1986–89
Frank Casper 1989–91
Jimmy Mullen 1991–96
Adrian Heath 1996–97
Chris Waddle 1997–98
Stan Ternent June 1998–

LATEST SEQUENCES

Longest Sequence of League Wins: 10, 16.11.12 – 18.1.13.
Longest Sequence of League Defeats: 8, 2.1.95 – 25.2.95.
Longest Sequence of League Draws: 6, 21.2.31 – 28.3.31.
Longest Sequence of Unbeaten League Matches: 30, 6.9.20 – 25.3.21.
Longest Sequence Without a League Win: 24, 16.4.79 – 17.11.79.

TEN YEAR LEAGUE RECORD

		P	W	D	L	F	A	Pts	Pos
1990-91	Div 4	46	23	10	13	70	51	79	6
1991-92	Div 4	42	25	8	9	79	43	83	1
1992-93	Div 2	46	15	16	15	57	59	61	13
1993-94	Div 2	46	21	10	15	79	58	73	6
1994-95	Div 1	46	11	13	22	49	74	46	22
1995-96	Div 2	46	14	13	19	56	68	55	17
1996-97	Div 2	46	19	11	16	71	55	68	9
1997-98	Div 2	46	13	13	20	55	65	52	20
1998-99	Div 2	46	13	16	17	54	73	55	15
1999-2000	Div 2	46	25	13	8	69	47	88	2

DID YOU KNOW ?

On 8 February 1967, Burnley drew their Fairs Cup tie 0-0 in Italy. The bruising match known as the Battle of Naples produced a hero in goalkeeper Harry Thomson, who made 13 outstanding saves including one from the penalty spot.

BURNLEY 2000–01 LEAGUE RECORD

Match No.	Date	Venue	Opponents	Result	H/T Score	Lg. Pos.	Goalscorers	Attendance
1	Aug 12	A	Bolton W	D	1-1	0-1	—	Gray [56]	20,662
2	19	H	Wimbledon	W	1-0	1-0	8	Weller [27]	15,124
3	26	A	Wolverhampton W	L	0-1	0-0	11		20,156
4	28	H	Gillingham	D	1-1	0-0	12	Ashby (og) [70]	15,611
5	Sept 9	A	Crystal Palace	W	1-0	0-0	8	Branch [77]	18,531
6	12	A	Fulham	L	1-3	1-0	—	Cook [10]	11,863
7	16	H	Grimsby T	D	1-1	1-1	12	Cooke [18]	15,413
8	23	A	Huddersfield T	W	1-0	1-0	11	Payton [17]	14,016
9	30	H	Portsmouth	D	1-1	0-0	10	Weller [88]	15,494
10	Oct 6	A	Tranmere R	W	3-2	1-0	—	Davis 2 [45, 55], Payton [90]	10,153
11	14	H	Stockport Co	W	2-1	2-0	7	Payton [20], Branch [25]	16,107
12	17	H	Sheffield W	W	1-0	0-0	—	Davis [74]	16,372
13	21	A	QPR	W	1-0	0-0	6	Mullin [70]	11,427
14	25	A	Nottingham F	L	0-5	0-2	—		17,195
15	31	H	Crewe Alex	W	1-0	1-0	—	Cooke [39]	13,189
16	Nov 4	A	WBA	D	1-1	1-0	5	Branch [23]	17,828
17	11	H	Sheffield U	W	2-0	0-0	4	Payton 2 (1 pen) [55 (p), 67]	16,635
18	18	A	Birmingham C	L	2-3	0-0	8	Cox [61], Weller [90]	19,641
19	21	H	Norwich C	W	2-0	0-0	—	Payton [56], Davis [66]	15,017
20	Dec 2	H	Nottingham F	W	1-0	0-0	6	Payton (pen) [79]	17,876
21	9	A	Preston NE	L	1-2	0-0	8	Moore [26]	17,355
22	17	H	Blackburn R	L	0-2	0-1	9		21,369
23	23	H	Bolton W	L	0-2	0-0	9		19,552
24	26	A	Barnsley	L	0-1	0-0	10		18,725
25	Jan 1	H	Wolverhampton W	L	1-2	1-1	10	Branch [9]	15,483
26	13	A	Gillingham	D	0-0	0-0	10		9331
27	20	H	Barnsley	W	2-1	1-0	9	Johnrose [23], Payton [61]	15,380
28	Feb 3	A	Crewe Alex	L	2-4	1-3	10	Branch [12], Cook (pen) [60]	6994
29	10	H	Crystal Palace	L	1-2	1-0	10	Cook [13]	14,973
30	17	A	Grimsby T	L	0-1	0-0	10		6044
31	20	H	Fulham	W	2-1	0-0	—	Moore [73], Little [88]	15,737
32	24	A	Huddersfield T	W	1-0	0-0	10	Davis [48]	16,191
33	Mar 3	A	Portsmouth	L	0-2	0-0	10		12,941
34	6	A	Stockport Co	D	0-0	0-0	—		7087
35	13	A	Watford	W	1-0	0-0	—	Taylor [73]	13,653
36	17	A	Sheffield W	L	0-2	0-1	10		20,184
37	24	H	QPR	W	2-1	2-0	10	Smith [13], Taylor [42]	14,018
38	Apr 1	A	Blackburn R	L	0-5	0-2	10		23,442
39	6	H	Preston NE	W	3-0	2-0	—	Moore [3], Ball [45], Little [73]	16,591
40	10	A	Wimbledon	W	2-0	2-0	—	Taylor [1], Moore [45]	6132
41	14	H	WBA	D	1-1	0-0	9	Little [46]	18,199
42	16	A	Norwich C	W	3-2	1-2	8	Ball [24], Taylor [48], Moore [62]	17,507
43	21	H	Birmingham C	D	0-0	0-0	8		17,057
44	24	H	Tranmere R	W	2-1	1-1	—	Roberts (og) [23], Mullin [59]	13,717
45	28	A	Sheffield U	L	0-2	0-1	7		20,013
46	May 6	H	Watford	W	2-0	0-0	7	Payton [74], Mullin [90]	18,283

Final League Position: 7

GOALSCORERS

League (50): Payton 9 (2 pens), Branch 5, Davis 5, Moore 5, Taylor 4, Cook 3 (1 pen), Little 3, Mullin 3, Weller 3, Ball 2, Cooke 2, Cox 1, Gray 1, Johnrose 1, Smith 1, own goals 2.
Worthington Cup (9): Payton 5 (2 pens), Cooke 3, Davis 1.
FA Cup (3): Johnrose 1, Moore 1, Payton 1.

Crichton P 7 + 1	Weller P 39 + 5	Briscoe L 25 + 4	Cox I 35 + 3	Davis S 44	Thomas M 41 + 2	Ball K 40	Cook P 38 + 2	Cooke A 10 + 1	Gray P 5	Mullin J 11 + 25	Branch G 26 + 9	Little G 27 + 7	Payton A 18 + 22	Armstrong G 14 + 5	Mellon M 19 + 3	Jepson R — + 13	Michopoulos N 39	Robinson P — + 4	Johnrose L 9 + 10	Moore I 26 + 1	Maylett B 2 + 10	Smith C 10 + 4	Shandran A — + 1	Taylor G 15	West D 6 + 1	Match No.
1	2	3	4	5	6	7	8	9^1	10	11^2	12	13														1
1	2	3	4	5	6	11	8	9^3	10^2	12	13		7^1	14												2
1	2^3	3	4	5	6	7	8	9^1	10^2	12	13	11	14													3
1	2^1	3	4	5	6	7	8	9^2	10^2	12	13	11	14													4
1	2	3	4	5^1	6	7	8	9^2	10^2	12	13	11	14													5
1	2	3	4		6	7	8^1	9		11^3	12	10	13	5^2	14											6
1	2^1	3	4	5	6	7	8^2	9^3		12	13	11	10			14										7
		3	4	5	6	7	8	9^2		12	13	2^1	10^3	11		14	1									8
	12	3	4	5	6^3	11	8^1	9^2			13	2	10	7	14		1									9
	12	3	4	5	6	7	8^3	9^2		11^1	13	2	10	14			1									10
	12	3	4	5	2	7	8^2	9		11^1	13		10^3	6	14		1									11
	7	3	4	5	2	11	8^1	12		9^2	13		10^3	6	14		1									12
	2	3	4	5	6	7	8^3	9^1		12	13		10^2	11	14		1									13
	2	3	4	5^4	6	7	8^1	9^2		12	13		10	11	14		1									14
15	2		4	5	6	7	8^2	9^4		12	13	3	10^1	11	14		1									15
	2	3	4	5	6	7	8^2	9		12	13		10^1	11	13		1^6									16
	7^1	3	4	5	2	11				12	9^2	13	10^1		6	14	1		8							17
	12	3	4	5	6	7				13	9	2	10^3	11^2			1	14	8							18
	12	3^1	4	5	6	7	8^2			13	9	2	10	11			1		14							19
	2		4	5	6	7	8^3			12	3		10^1	11	13		1		14	9^2						20
	2		4	5	6			12		10	13	11	14				1		7^2	9	3^1					21
	2		4	5	6	7	3^2			12	9^3	10	11^1				1		13	8	14					22
	2^1		4	5	6	7	3^2			11	9	12	8^3	14			1		13	10						23
	2		4	5	6	7				9^1	12^2	14		8^3	14		1		8	10^3		3				24
	2		4		6					12	9		10^3	5	7	13	1		11^2	8^1	14	3				25
	2		4	5	6		8			11^1	9	12					1		7	10	3					26
	2		4	5	6	7	8^3			12	3^2	13	10^1	14			1		11	9						27
	2			5	6	7	8			11^1	3	10	12				1		9^2	13	4^2	14				28
	2		4	5		8^2				12	3	7	10^1	11			1		6	9	14	13^3				29
	2		4^2	5	6		12			11^3	3	8	13	10			1		7^1	9	14					30
	2			5	6		8			3		7^2	11	12			1		13	9^1				10		31
	2			5	6^2	7^1	8^3			3	11	13	4	12			1		14	9				10		32
	2	12	13	5	6	7^2	8^3			14	3^1	11	4				1		9					10		33
	2	3	4	5	6	7	8			12	11	13					1		9^2					10^1		34
	2	3	4	5	6	7	8^2			11^3	12	13					1		9^1	14				10		35
	2	3^1	4	5	6	7^3	8			11^1	12	13					1		9	14				10		36
	2			5	6	7	8^1			3	11	13	12				1		9^2	14	4^2			10		37
	2		4	5	6	7^2	8			3^3	11	13	12				1		9^1	14				10		38
	6		4	5		7	8			12	11	13					1		9^1	14	3			10^2	2^3	39
	4	12		5		7	8			13	11^3	14	6^1				1		9^2		3			10	2	40
	4	12		5	13	7	8^1			14	11^3		6^2				1		9		3		3^1	10	2	41
	4	12		5	13	7	8^2			11	14		6				1		9^2		3^1			10	2	42
	8	3^2	12	5	6	7				11	13	4^2					1		9	14				10	2^1	43
	8^3	3		5	6	7	12			11^2	10	13	4				1		9	14					2^1	44
		3^3		5	6	7	8^2			11	12	4					1		9	2^1	13		10	14		45
	2	3	12	5	6	7	8^1			13	11^3	14	4				1		9^2					10		46

Worthington Cup
First Round — Hartlepool U — (h) 4-1 / (a) 2-3
Second Round — Crystal Palace — (h) 2-2 / (a) 1-1

FA Cup
Third Round — Scunthorpe U — (h) 2-2 / (a) 1-1

BURY

Division 2

FOUNDATION

A meeting at the Waggon & Horses Hotel, attended largely by members of Bury Wesleyans and Bury Unitarians football clubs, decided to form a new Bury club. This was officially formed at a subsequent gathering at the Old White Horse Hotel, Fleet Street, Bury on 24 April 1885.

Gigg Lane, Bury BL9 9HR.

Telephone: (0161) 764 4881. *Fax:* (0161) 764 5521.
Commercial Dept: (0161) 705 2144. *Fax:* (0161) 762 9620.
Community Programme: (0161) 797 5423.
ClubCall: 09068 121 197.

Social Club: (0161) 764 6771.

Ground Capacity: 11,669.

Record Attendance: 35,000 v Bolton W, FA Cup 3rd rd, 9 January 1960.

Record Receipts: £86,000 v Manchester C, Division 1, 12 September 1997.

Pitch Measurements: 112yd × 72yd.

HONOURS

Football League: Division 1 best season: 4th, 1925–26; Division 2 – Champions 1894–95, 1996–97; Runners-up 1923–24; Division 3 – Champions 1960–61; Runners-up 1967–68; Promoted from Division 3 (3rd) 1995–96.

FA Cup: Winners 1900, 1903.

Football League Cup: Semi-final 1963.

Chairman: T. Robinson. *Directors:* J. Smith, F. Mason, N. Neville.

Manager: Andy Preece. *Assistant Manager:* Kevin Blackwell. *Coach:* Billy Ayre.
Physios: Alan Raw, Lee Nobes. *Youth Development:* Wayne Joyce.

Safety Officer: Wilf Linton.

Secretary: Jill Neville.

Commercial Manager: Peter Young.

Colours: White shirts, royal blue shorts, royal blue stockings.

Change Colours: Gold and blue.

Year Formed: 1885.

Turned professional: 1885.

Ltd Co.: 1897.

Club Nickname: 'Shakers'.

Club Sponsors: Birthdays.

First Football League Game: 1 September 1894, Division 2, v Manchester C (h) W 4–2 – Lowe; Gillespie, Davies; White, Clegg, Ross; Wylie, Barbour (2), Millar (1), Ostler (1), Plant.

Record League Victory: 8–0 v Tranmere R, Division 3, 10 January 1970 – Forrest; Tinney, Saile; Anderson, Turner, McDermott; Hince (1), Arrowsmith (1), Jones (4), Kerr (1), Grundy, (1 og).

Record Cup Victory: 12–1 v Stockton, FA Cup 1st rd (replay), 2 February 1897 – Montgomery; Darroch, Barbour; Hendry (1), Clegg, Ross (1); Wylie (3), Pangbourn, Millar (4), Henderson (2), Plant, (1 og).

IT'S A FACT !

Jack Acquroff, a centre or inside-forward signed by Bury from Hull City in October 1936 for a club record £2,250 was born in Chelsea of Scottish parentage and Russian ancestry. Later with Norwich City he eventually emigrated to Tasmania ...

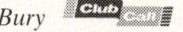
Record Defeat: 0–10 v West Ham U, Milk Cup 2nd rd 2nd leg, 25 October 1983.

Most League Points (2 for a win): 68, Division 3, 1960–61.

Most League Points (3 for a win): 84, Division 4, 1984–85 and Division 2, 1996–97.

Most League Goals: 108, Division 3, 1960–61.

Highest League Scorer in Season: Craig Madden, 35, Division 4, 1981–82.

Most League Goals in Total Aggregate: Craig Madden, 129, 1978–86.

Most League Goals in One Match: 5, Eddie Quigley v Millwall, Division 2, 15 February 1947; 5, Ray Pointer v Rotherham U, Division 2, 2 October 1965.

Most Capped Player: Bill Gorman, 11 (13), Republic of Ireland and (4), Northern Ireland.

Most League Appearances: Norman Bullock, 506, 1920–35.

Youngest League Player: Brian Williams, 16 years 133 days v Stockport Co, 18 March 1972.

Record Transfer Fee Received: £1,100,000 from Ipswich T for David Johnson, November 1997.

Record Transfer Fee Paid: £200,000 to Ipswich T for Chris Swailes, November 1997 and to Swindon T for Darren Bullock, February 1999.

Football League Record: 1894 Elected to Division 2; 1895–1912 Division 1; 1912–24 Division 2; 1924–29 Division 1; 1929–57 Division 2; 1957–61 Division 3; 1961–67 Division 2; 1967–68 Division 3; 1968–69 Division 2; 1969–71 Division 3; 1971–74 Division 4; 1974–80 Division 3; 1980–85 Division 4; 1985–96 Division 3; 1996–97 Division 2; 1997–99 Division 1; 1999– Division 2.

MANAGERS

T. Hargreaves 1887
   (Secretary-Manager)
H. S. Hamer 1887–1907
   (Secretary-Manager)
Archie Montgomery 1907–15
William Cameron 1919–23
James Hunter Thompson 1923–27
Percy Smith 1927–30
Arthur Paine 1930–34
Norman Bullock 1934–38
Jim Porter 1944–45
Norman Bullock 1945–49
John McNeil 1950–53
Dave Russell 1953–61
Bob Stokoe 1961–65
Bert Head 1965–66
Les Shannon 1966–69
Jack Marshall 1969
Les Hart 1970
Tommy McAnearney 1970–72
Alan Brown 1972–73
Bobby Smith 1973–77
Bob Stokoe 1977–78
David Hatton 1978–79
Dave Connor 1979–80
Jim Iley 1980–84
Martin Dobson 1984–89
Sam Ellis 1989–90
Mike Walsh 1990–95
Stan Ternent 1995–98
Neil Warnock 1998–99
Andy Preece May 2000–

LATEST SEQUENCES

Longest Sequence of League Wins: 9, 26.9.60 – 19.11.60.

Longest Sequence of League Defeats: 6, 14.1.67 – 4.3.67.

Longest Sequence of League Draws: 6, 6.3.99 – 3.4.99.

Longest Sequence of Unbeaten League Matches: 18, 4.2.61 – 29.4.61.

Longest Sequence Without a League Win: 19, 1.4.11 – 2.12.11.

TEN YEAR LEAGUE RECORD

		P	W	D	L	F	A	Pts	Pos
1990-91	Div 3	46	20	13	13	67	56	73	7
1991-92	Div 3	46	13	12	21	55	74	51	21
1992-93	Div 3	42	18	9	15	63	55	63	7
1993-94	Div 3	42	14	11	17	55	56	53	13
1994-95	Div 3	42	23	11	8	73	36	80	4
1995-96	Div 3	46	22	13	11	66	48	79	3
1996-97	Div 2	46	24	12	10	62	38	84	1
1997-98	Div 1	46	11	19	16	42	58	52	17
1998-99	Div 1	46	10	17	19	35	60	47	22
1999-2000	Div 2	46	13	18	15	61	64	57	15

DID YOU KNOW ?

The Griffiths brothers Bill and George both defenders, each served Bury for 13 years, Bill from 1939-40, George the younger the following season when he made his debut at 16 years 296 days.

BURY 2000–01 LEAGUE RECORD

Match No.	Date		Venue	Opponents	Result		H/T Score	Lg. Pos.	Goalscorers	Attendance
1	Aug	12	A	Cambridge U	W	1-0	1-0	—	Barnes [44]	3654
2		19	H	Wrexham	L	1-4	0-2	14	Crowe [59]	3613
3		26	A	Rotherham U	W	2-1	1-1	7	Bhutia [43], Littlejohn [65]	3739
4		28	H	Northampton T	W	1-0	0-0	2	Bullock [72]	3182
5	Sept	2	A	Peterborough U	D	1-1	0-1	2	Bullock [78]	5286
6		9	H	Walsall	W	2-0	0-0	2	Swailes C [56], Collins [76]	4755
7		12	H	Colchester U	D	0-0	0-0	—		2577
8		16	A	Oxford U	L	0-1	0-0	4		3676
9		23	H	Port Vale	W	2-0	1-0	3	Carragher (og) [33], Daws [71]	3176
10		30	A	Swansea C	W	2-0	1-0	2	Littlejohn [5], Jarrett [83]	5362
11	Oct	6	H	Bristol R	W	1-0	0-0	—	Daws [81]	3279
12		14	A	Millwall	L	0-4	0-2	3		10,203
13		17	A	Notts Co	L	0-1	0-0	—		3461
14		21	H	Bournemouth	L	2-5	0-2	7	Redmond [49], Preece (pen) [80]	2892
15		24	H	Reading	L	0-2	0-0	—		2808
16		28	A	Wigan Ath	L	0-1	0-0	9		6622
17	Nov	4	H	Luton T	D	1-1	0-0	10	Littlejohn [47]	2861
18		11	A	Wycombe W	L	1-2	0-0	11	Reid (pen) [81]	4488
19	Dec	2	A	Bristol C	L	1-4	0-1	14	Reid [50]	9416
20		16	H	Oldham Ath	D	1-1	0-1	17	Barnes [56]	4976
21		23	H	Swindon T	W	1-0	1-0	14	Barnes [30]	2921
22		26	A	Stoke C	L	1-2	1-1	17	Barnes [19]	16,499
23	Jan	1	H	Rotherham U	D	0-0	0-0	17		3743
24		6	H	Cambridge U	L	0-1	0-1	18		2629
25		13	A	Northampton T	L	1-2	1-1	18	Swailes C [36]	5127
26		23	H	Brentford	L	0-1	0-0	—		2274
27		27	A	Swindon T	L	0-3	0-2	18		4960
28	Feb	3	H	Peterborough U	W	2-1	0-0	18	Newby [56], Collins [69]	2725
29		10	A	Walsall	W	2-1	1-1	17	Daws [4], Redmond [69]	4839
30		17	A	Oxford U	W	3-1	1-0	15	Newby 2 [18, 70], Armstrong [76]	3320
31		20	A	Colchester U	D	1-1	0-0	—	Preece [82]	2755
32		24	A	Port Vale	D	1-1	0-1	16	Cramb [57]	4331
33	Mar	3	H	Swansea C	W	3-0	1-0	14	Reid 2 (2 pens) [9, 65], Connell [88]	3443
34		6	H	Millwall	W	2-1	1-1	—	Cramb [35], Newby [90]	3587
35		10	A	Bristol R	L	0-2	0-1	13		7065
36		17	H	Notts Co	D	1-1	0-0	12	Littlejohn [87]	3487
37		20	A	Wrexham	W	1-0	0-0	—	Newby [90]	3388
38		24	A	Bournemouth	L	0-1	0-1	12		3325
39		27	H	Stoke C	W	1-0	0-0	—	Swailes C [62]	4224
40		31	A	Oldham Ath	D	1-1	0-0	10	Cramb [46]	5787
41	Apr	7	H	Bristol C	L	0-1	0-0	12		3729
42		14	A	Reading	L	1-4	1-2	14	Cramb [8]	16,829
43		16	H	Wigan Ath	L	0-1	0-0	16		4915
44		21	A	Luton T	W	2-1	1-1	13	Swailes C [9], Cramb [90]	4902
45		28	H	Wycombe W	D	1-1	0-0	13	Nelson [52]	4096
46	May	5	A	Brentford	L	1-3	0-0	16	Jarrett [53]	4596

Final League Position: 16

GOALSCORERS

League (45): Cramb 5, Newby 5, Barnes 4, Littlejohn 4, Reid 4 (3 pens), Swailes C 4, Daws 3, Bullock 2, Collins 2, Jarrett 2, Preece 2 (1 pen), Redmond 2, Armstrong 1, Bhutia 1, Connell 1, Crowe 1, Nelson 1, own goal 1.
Worthington Cup (3): Bullock 2 (1 pen), Littlejohn 1.
FA Cup (1): Daws 1.

Kenny P 46	Unsworth L 12 + 3	Barrick D 9 + 1	Daws N 44	Collins S 33 + 1	Swailes C 43	Billy C 46	Reid P 42 + 1	Barnes P 12 + 4	Preece A 13 + 17	Littlejohn A 24 + 13	Bullock D 9 + 1	Swailes D 10 + 1	Bhutia B 11 + 9	Crowe D 1 + 6	Redmond S 39	James L 7 + 21	Forrest M 20 + 7	Barrass M 4 + 1	Jarrett J 13 + 12	Halford S 2 + 1	Smith A 2	Armstrong C 22	Newby J 17	Hill N 8 + 2	Cramb C 15	Connell L — + 1	Peyton W — + 1	Nelson M 2	Match No.
1	2	3	4	5	6	7	8	9	10	11[1]	12																		1
1	2	3[2]	4	5	6	7	8	9[3]	10	11[1]			13	14	12														2
1	2		4	3	5	7	8		11[1]	10	12		9[2]		6	13													3
1	2[3]		4	3	5	7	8		11[2]	10	12		9[1]	14	6	13													4
1			4	3	5	7	8		10	11[1]	12		9[2]		6	13					2								5
1			4	3	5	7	8	9[1]	10[3]	11[2]	12			14	6	13					2								6
1			4	3	5	7	8	9[2]	10[3]	11	12			14	6	13					2[1]								7
1			4	3	5	7	8[1]		10[3]	11	12		9[2]	14	6	13					2								8
1	12		4	3	5	7[3]	8		10[1]	11			9[2]	14	6	13	2												9
1		3	4	2	5[3]	7	8[2]		10	11			9[1]	14	6	13	12												10
1		3	4	2	5	7	8[1]		10	11[2]	12		9[3]	14	6	13													11
1		3[1]	4	2	5	7	8		10	11	12		9		6[2]	13													12
1	2		4	3	5	7	8		10	11	12		9[1]		6[2]	13													13
1	2	3	4	5		7	8	9[1]	10	11[3]	12			14	6[2]	13													14
1	2	3[1]	4	5		7	8	9		11[2]	12				6	13	10												15
1	2	3	4	5		7	8[2]	9		11	12				6[1]	13	10												16
1	2[2]	3	4	5		7	8	9		11	12				6	13	10												17
1	2		4	3	5	7	8	9[1]		11	12				6	13	10[2]												18
1	2	3	4	5		7	8	9[1]	10[2]	11[3]	12			14	6	13													19
1	2		4	5		7	8	9[1]		11[2]	12			14	6	13	3	10[3]											20
1	2		4	5		7	8	9[1]		11	12				6		3	10											21
1	12		4	2	5	7	8	9[1]		11[3]				14	6[3]	13	3	10											22
1	12		4	2	5	7	8	9[1]		11[2]				14	6	13	3[1]	10											23
1	12		4	2	5	7	8	9		11				14	6[1]	13	3[3]	10[2]											24
1	2[3]		4	5		7	8	9	10[1]	11	12				6	13	3												25
1	2			5		7[3]	8	9[1]		11	12			14	6[2]	13						3		4	10				26
1	2[2]			5		7	8	9	10	11[1]	12			14	6	13						3		4[3]					27
1	2			5[1]		7	8	9[2]		11[3]	12			14	6	13						3		4	10				28
1	2			5		7	8	9[2]		11[1]	12			14	6	13						3		4[3]	10				29
1	2		4	5			8				12				6		7			11		3	9		10[1]				30
1	2		4	5		7	8				12			14	6[1]	13				11[3]		3	9		10[2]				31
1	2		4	5		7	8								6					11		3	9		10				32
1	2[3]		4	5		7	8				12			14	6	13				11		3	9[1]		10[2]				33
1	2		4	5		7	8								6					11		3	9		10				34
1	2[3]		4	5		7	8				12				6	13				11[1]		3	9		10				35
1	2		4[3]	5		7	8				12				6[1]	13				11[2]		3	9	14	10				36
1	2[1]			5		7	8				12				6	13				11[1]		3	9	4[3]	10				37
1	2[1]		4	5		7	8				12				6[2]	13				11[3]		3	9	14	10				38
1	2		4	5		7	8								6					11		3	9	4	10				39
1	2		4	5		7	8				12				6	13				11[3]		3	9[1]	14	10[2]				40
1	2			5		7	8				12				6[2]	13				11[1]		3	9	4	10				41
1	2[1]		4	5		7	8				12				6					11		3	9		10				42
1	2		4	5[1]		7	8				12				6[2]	13				11[3]		3	9	14	10				43
1	2		4	5		7	8				12				6					11		3	9		10[1]				44
1			4	5		7	8								6					11		3	9		10			2	45
1			4	5		7[1]	8				12				6[2]	13				11		3	9		10			2	46

Worthington Cup
First Round   Crewe Alex   (a)   2-2
                                 (h)   1-2

FA Cup
First Round   Northwich Vic   (h)   1-1
                                 (a)   0-1

CAMBRIDGE UNITED   Division 2

FOUNDATION

The football revival in Cambridge began soon after World War II when the Abbey United club (formed 1912) decided to turn professional in 1949. In 1951 they changed their name to Cambridge United. They were competing in the United Counties League before graduating to the Eastern Counties League in 1951 and the Southern League in 1958.

Abbey Stadium, Newmarket Rd, Cambridge, CB5 8LN.

Telephone: (01223) 566 500. *Fax:* (01223) 566 502.
ClubCall: 09068 555 885.
Website: cambridge-united.co.uk

Ground Capacity: 9247.

Record Attendance: 14,000 v Chelsea, Friendly,
1 May 1970.

Record Receipts: £86,308 v Manchester U,
Rumbelows Cup 2nd rd 2nd leg, 9 October 1991.

Pitch Measurements: 110yd × 74yd.

Chairman: R. H. Smart. *Vice-Chairman:* R. F. Hunt.

Directors: G. Harwood, J. Howard, R. Hunt, G. Lowe,
R. Summerfield, P. S. Barry, R. L. Sargent.

Manager: John Beck. *Assistant Manager:* Shane Westley.

Youth Manager: Dale Brooks. *Physio:* Stuart Ayres.

Secretary: Andrew Pincher.

Stadium Manager: Ian Darler.

Colours: Amber shirts with black trim, black shorts, amber stockings.

Change Colours: All navy with sky blue trim.

Year Formed: 1912.

Turned Professional: 1949.

Ltd Co.: 1948.

Previous Name: 1919, Abbey United; 1951, Cambridge United.

Club Nickname: The 'U's'.

First Football League Game: 15 August 1970, Division 4, v Lincoln C (h) D 1–1 – Roberts;
Thompson, Meldrum (1), Slack, Eades, Hardy, Leggett, Cassidy, Lindsey, McKinven, Harris.

HONOURS

Football League: Division 2 best season: 5th, 1991–92; Division 3 – Champions 1990–91; Runners-up 1977–78, 1998–99; Division 4 – Champions 1976–77; Promoted from Division 4 1989–90 (play-offs).

FA Cup: best season: 6th rd, 1990 (shared record for Fourth Division club), 1991.

Football League Cup: best season: 5th rd, 1993.

IT'S A FACT !

On 21 October 1957, Cambridge United staged their first match under floodlights. It was an East Anglian Cup first round replay against Great Yarmouth Town. United won 3-0. The lights were attached to telegraph poles and had a combined power of 32,000 watts.

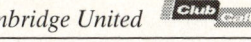

Record League Victory: 6–0 v Darlington, Division 4, 18 September 1971 – Roberts; Thompson, Akers, Guild, Eades, Foote, Collins (1p), Horrey, Hollett, Greenhalgh (4), Phillips, (1 og). 6–0 v Hartlepool U, Division 4, 11 February 1989 – Vaughan; Beck, Kimble, Turner, Chapple (1), Daish, Clayton, Holmes, Taylor (3 incl. 1p), Bull (1), Leadbitter (1).

Record Cup Victory: 5–1 v Bristol C, FA Cup 5th rd second replay, 27 February 1990 – Vaughan; Fensome, Kimble, Bailie (O'Shea), Chapple, Daish, Cheetham (Robinson), Leadbitter (1), Dublin (2), Taylor (1), Philpott (1).

Record Defeat: 0–6 v Aldershot, Division 3, 13 April 1974; v Darlington, Division 4, 28 September 1974. 0–6 v Chelsea, Division 2, 15 January 1983 and v Brentford, Division 2, 28 January 1995.

Most League Points (2 for a win): 65, Division 4, 1976–77.

Most League Points (3 for a win): 86, Division 3, 1990–91.

Most League Goals: 87, Division 4, 1976–77.

Highest League Scorer in Season: David Crown, 24, Division 4, 1985–86.

MANAGERS
Bill Whittaker 1949–55
Gerald Williams 1955
Bert Johnson 1955–59
Bill Craig 1959–60
Alan Moore 1960–63
Roy Kirk 1964–66
Bill Leivers 1967–74
Ron Atkinson 1974–78
John Docherty 1978–83
John Ryan 1984–85
Ken Shellito 1985
Chris Turner 1985–90
John Beck 1990–1992
Ian Atkins 1992–93
Gary Johnson 1993–95
Tommy Taylor 1995–96
Roy McFarland 1996–2001
John Beck February 2001–

Most League Goals in Total Aggregate: John Taylor, 86, 1988–92; 1996–2001.

Most League Goals in One Match: 5, Steve Butler v Exeter C, Division 2, 4 April 1994.

Most Capped Player: Tom Finney, 7 (15), Northern Ireland.

Most League Appearances: Steve Spriggs, 416, 1975–87.

Youngest League Player: Andy Sinton, 16 years 228 days v Wolverhampton W, 2 November 1982.

Record Transfer Fee Received: £1,000,000 from Manchester U for Dion Dublin, August 1992.

Record Transfer Fee Paid: £190,000 to Luton T for Steve Claridge, November 1992.

Football League Record: 1970 Elected to Division 4; 1973–74 Division 3; 1974–77 Division 4; 1977–78 Division 3; 1978–84 Division 2; 1984–85 Division 3; 1985–90 Division 4; 1990–91 Division 3; 1991–92 Division 2; 1992–93 Division 1; 1993–95 Division 2; 1995–99 Division 3; 1999– Division 2.

LATEST SEQUENCES

Longest Sequence of League Wins: 7, 19.2.77 – 1.4.77.

Longest Sequence of League Defeats: 7, 8.4.85 – 30.4.85.

Longest Sequence of League Draws: 6, 6.9.86 – 30.9.86.

Longest Sequence of Unbeaten League Matches: 14, 9.9.72 – 10.11.72.

Longest Sequence Without a League Win: 31, 8.10.83 – 23.4.84.

TEN YEAR LEAGUE RECORD

		P	W	D	L	F	A	Pts	Pos
1990-91	Div 3	46	25	11	10	75	45	86	1
1991-92	Div 2	46	19	17	10	65	47	74	5
1992-93	Div 1	46	11	16	19	48	69	49	23
1993-94	Div 2	46	19	9	18	79	73	66	10
1994-95	Div 2	46	11	15	20	52	69	48	20
1995-96	Div 3	46	14	12	20	61	71	54	16
1996-97	Div 3	46	18	11	17	53	59	65	10
1997-98	Div 3	46	14	18	14	63	57	60	16
1998-99	Div 3	46	23	12	11	78	48	81	2
1999-2000	Div 2	46	12	12	22	64	65	48	19

DID YOU KNOW ?

On 3 October 1986, Cambridge United ended a club record of seven consecutive draws, with a 5-0 home win against Stockport County, their biggest victory for nine years.

CAMBRIDGE UNITED 2000–01 LEAGUE RECORD

Match No.	Date	Venue	Opponents	Result		H/T Score	Lg. Pos.	Goalscorers	Attendance
1	Aug 12	H	Bury	L	0-1	0-1	—		3654
2	19	A	Bournemouth	D	1-1	1-0	19	Abbey [8]	4869
3	26	H	Bristol C	W	1-0	0-0	11	Wanless (pen) [57]	3716
4	28	A	Notts Co	W	1-0	1-0	6	Abbey [42]	5020
5	Sept 2	A	Oxford U	D	1-1	1-1	7	Youngs [25]	4479
6	9	H	Rotherham U	W	6-1	3-1	4	Ashbee 2 [16, 25], Youngs 2 [38, 76], Abbey [52], Axeldal [70]	3925
7	12	H	Port Vale	W	4-0	1-0	—	Wanless (pen) [20], Russell [64], Youngs [71], Slade [87]	3660
8	23	H	Bristol R	L	0-3	0-2	6		4624
9	30	A	Oldham Ath	W	3-1	1-0	6	Youngs 2 [45, 62], Russell [82]	3888
10	Oct 13	H	Luton T	W	2-1	0-1	—	Youngs [54], Abbey [79]	6191
11	17	H	Stoke C	D	1-1	0-1	—	Taylor (pen) [90]	4433
12	21	A	Colchester U	L	0-2	0-1	8		3761
13	24	H	Northampton T	L	1-2	0-2	—	Youngs [58]	5394
14	28	A	Millwall	L	1-3	1-3	10	Axeldal [45]	10,104
15	31	A	Swindon T	L	1-3	1-2	—	Abbey [29]	3452
16	Nov 4	H	Brentford	D	1-1	1-0	11	Taylor [33]	4083
17	11	A	Wigan Ath	L	1-2	1-0	13	Mustoe (pen) [40]	6537
18	21	A	Wrexham	D	2-2	1-0	—	Connor 2 [31, 90]	1584
19	25	H	Swansea C	D	3-3	3-0	11	Wanless [10], Youngs [29], Connor [36]	3269
20	Dec 2	A	Reading	L	0-3	0-2	12		9601
21	15	A	Peterborough U	D	0-0	0-0	—		7505
22	23	A	Walsall	L	1-3	0-2	17	Connor [72]	5277
23	26	H	Wycombe W	W	1-0	0-0	15	Youngs [65]	4758
24	Jan 1	A	Bristol C	L	2-6	1-1	18	Wanless [32], Connor [59]	10,637
25	6	A	Bury	W	1-0	1-0	14	Cowan [20]	2629
26	13	H	Notts Co	D	2-2	1-0	14	Wanless (pen) [58], Taylor [90]	4029
27	23	H	Bournemouth	L	0-2	0-0	—		3027
28	27	H	Walsall	L	0-1	0-1	16		3888
29	Feb 6	A	Wycombe W	W	2-0	1-0	—	Logan [19], Youngs [69]	4524
30	10	A	Rotherham U	L	0-3	0-2	16		4497
31	17	H	Swindon T	L	0-1	0-0	18		4046
32	20	A	Port Vale	L	2-4	1-3	—	Humphreys 2 [7, 51]	3558
33	24	A	Bristol R	L	1-2	1-1	18	Humphreys [39]	7079
34	Mar 3	H	Oldham Ath	W	2-0	2-0	18	Guttridge [2], Riza [32]	3762
35	6	A	Luton T	L	0-1	0-0	—		6370
36	10	H	Wrexham	L	2-3	1-0	20	Wanless [45], Fleming [65]	3737
37	17	A	Stoke C	W	3-2	2-0	19	Riza [10], Wanless [33], Richardson [90]	11,939
38	27	H	Oxford U	W	1-0	0-0	—	Wanless [90]	3502
39	31	A	Peterborough U	L	1-4	1-1	19	Youngs [26]	10,086
40	Apr 7	H	Reading	D	1-1	0-1	13	Wanless [83]	4745
41	13	A	Northampton T	W	2-0	1-0	—	Ashbee [24], Riza [84]	6063
42	17	H	Millwall	L	1-5	0-1	—	Youngs [65]	5223
43	25	A	Brentford	D	2-2	0-1	—	Youngs [84], Duncan [90]	3062
44	28	H	Wigan Ath	L	1-2	1-1	20	Wanless [25]	4776
45	May 1	H	Colchester U	W	2-1	0-0	—	Richardson [48], Cowan [56]	5317
46	5	A	Swansea C	D	1-1	1-1	19	Kitson [4]	3383

Final League Position: 19

GOALSCORERS

League (61): Youngs 14, Wanless 10 (3 pens), Abbey 5, Connor 5, Ashbee 3, Humphreys 3, Riza 3, Taylor 3 (1 pen), Axeldal 2, Cowan 2, Richardson 2, Russell 2, Duncan 1, Fleming 1, Guttridge 1, Kitson 1, Logan 1, Mustoe 1 (pen), Slade 1.
Worthington Cup (0).
FA Cup (3): Axeldal 1, Hansen 1, Youngs 1.

Perez L 36+1	Ashbee I 43+1	Cowan T 41	Duncan A 39	McAnespie S 20+3	Dreyer J 40	Wanless P 42+1	Taylor J 12+18	Abbey Z 14	Russell A 22+7	Youngs T 32+6	Mustoe N 15+12	Hansen J 7+5	Revell A 2+2	Lamey N —+3	Tann A 1	Slade S 4+5	Axeldal J 12+6	MacKenzie N 1+5	Joseph M 29+1	Connor P 12+1	Gudmundsson J 3	Oakes S 7+11	Preece D —+2	Wilson S 3+3	Marshall S 10+1	Traore D —+1	McNeil M 5+1	Butterworth A —+1	Logan R 5	Humphreys R 7	Guttridge L 1	Riza O 10+2	Chillingworth D —+1	Fleming T 9+1	Richardson M 3+7	Kitson D 6+2	Prokas R 1+2	Greene D 1	Pilvi T 3+2	Hanson C 8	Match No.
1	2	3	4	5	6	7^1	8	9^3	10	11^2	12	13	14																												1
1	2	3	4	5	6	7	12	9^1	10^2	11^3	13	14				8																									2
1	2		4	5	6	7		9	10	11	3					8^1	12																								3
1	2	3^1	4	5	6	7		9	12	13	10					14	8^3	11^2																							4
1	2	3	4	5	6	7		9	10^2	11	8						12	13																							5
1	2	3	4	5	6	7	12	9^1	10^2	11	14						8^3	13																							6
1	2	3^1	4	5	6	7		9	10^3	11	12					13	8	14																							7
1	2	3	4	5^1	6	7		9	10	11^2	13					12	8^1	14																							8
1	2	3	4	5	6	7	12	9^1	10	11^3						13	8^3	14																							9
1	2	3	4	5	6	7	12	9^1	10	11	13						8^2																								10
1	2	3	4	5	6^3	7	12	9	10^1	11						13	8^1	14																							11
1	2	3	4^2	5	6	7	12	9^3	10^1	11	14						8	13																							12
1	2	3	4	5^2	6	7	8		10	9	12			13		11^1																									13
1	2	3	4	5	6	7	12		11^3	9^2	13					14	10^1	8																							14
1	4	3^2		2	6	7^1	12		9	13	11^3	10				8			5			14																			15
1	2		4	5	6		8	9	10	11^1	7	12							3																						16
1	2		4	5	6	12	13		10	11^2	7							14	3	8^1	9^3																				17
1	2	3	4	5^1	6	7			12	11	13								10^1		9	8^2	14																		18
1	2	3^1	4	5	6	7	12		10^2	11	8	13									9																				19
1	2	3	4		6				10	11^1	7								5	9		8^2	12	13																	20
1	2	3	4		6	7		8	11	12	10^1							13	5	9^2																					21
1		3	4		6	7			11	2^1	10^3						8^2		5	9					13	12	14														22
1	2	3	4		6	7		8											5	9		9			10																23
1	2	3	4		6	7		8											5	9		10^2			11^1	15	13														24
1	2^1	3	4		6^2	7	8	12											5	9		10			11	13															25
1	2	3	4		6	7	8	12											5	9		10^1			11																26
	2	3^1	4		6	7	8^1	13	11		12								5	9		10^2			14		1														27
1	2	3	4	12	6	7	13												5^1	9^2		11			8^3				10												28
1	2			12	6	7			10^3	11	8								5^1	13					14					3	4	9^2									29
1	2			12	6	7	13		10^3	11^2	4^1								5						14				8	3		9									30
1	12	3			6	7	13		8^3	11	4								5^2						14				2	9^1		10									31
1	2	3			6	7	8												5						12				4			10									32
1	2	3		5^2	6	7	12												8^1			13			14				4	9^1		10									33
1	2	3	4		6	7	12												5						11^1							9	8	10^2	13						34
1	2	3	4		6	7	12	13		8									5						11^2							9^1		10							35
	2	3	4		6	7	12	9^3		14									5						11^1		1							10^2	11	13					36
	2	3	4		6	7	8^2	9^3											5						12		1							10^1	11	13	14				37
	2	3^1	4		6	7	8^2	9											5						12		1							10^3	11	13	14				38
	2	11	4			7	8^2	9											5								1					10^3		12	13	6	14		3		39
	6^1	11^2	4			7	8^3	9											5								1					10		2	14	13	12		3		40
	6	11	4			7			12	13									5								1					10		9^1	2	8^2			3		41
	4	11^1	6			7			12	13									5								1					10		9	2	8^2			3		42
1	6	11	4			7			12										5								1					10^2		9	2	8^1	13		3		43
	6	11^1	4			7			9^2										5								1					12		10	2	13	8		3		44
	6	11^1	4			7						10^2							5								1					12		9	2	13	8^1		3		45
15		11	4		6^2						10^3		2						5								1^0		13			12		7	2	9			3		46

Worthington Cup

First Round   Portsmouth   (h) 0–0
(a) 0–1

FA Cup

First Round   Rochdale   (h) 2–1
Second Round   Morecambe   (a) 1–2

CARDIFF CITY

Division 2

FOUNDATION

Credit for the establishment of a first class professional football club in such a rugby stronghold as Cardiff, is due to members of the Riverside club formed in 1899 out of a cricket club of that name. Cardiff became a city in 1905 and in 1908 the South Wales and Monmouthshire FA granted Riverside permission to call themselves Cardiff City.

Ninian Park, Cardiff CF1 8SX.

Telephone: (029) 2022 1001. *Fax:* (029) 2034 1148.
Ticket Office: (029) 2022 2857/2022 2858.
ClubCall: 09068 121 171. *Website:* www.cardiffcityfc.co.uk
Email: ccafc@baynet.co.uk

Ground Capacity: 15,585.

Record Attendance: 62,634, Wales v England, 17 October 1959.

Club Record Attendance: 57,893 v Arsenal, Division 1, 22 April 1953.

Record Receipts: £141,756 v Manchester C, FA Cup 4th rd, 29 January 1994.

Pitch Measurements: 120yd × 72yd.

Owner: Sam Hammam. *Vice-Chairman:* Steve Borley.
Chief Executive: David Temme.

Directors: Sam Hammam, Steve Borley, Paul Guy, Kim Walker, Samesh Kumar, Michael Isaac, Jonathan Crystal QC. *Advisor:* Tony Clemo.

Manager: Alan Cork.
Assistant Head Coaches: Ian Atkins, Ian Butterworth.
Physios: Clive Goodyear, Jimmy Goodfellow.

Club Secretary: Jason Turner.
Commercial Manager: Neil Hughes.

Colours: Blue shirts, white shorts, blue stockings.

Change Colours: Yellow shirts, blue shorts, yellow stockings.

Year Formed: 1899. *Turned Professional:* 1910. *Ltd Co.:* 1910.

Previous Names: 1899, Riverside; 1902, Riverside Albion; 1908, Cardiff City.

Club Nickname: 'Bluebirds'.

Previous Grounds: Riverside, Sophia Gardens, Old Park and Fir Gardens. Moved to Ninian Park, 1910.

First Football League Game: 28 August 1920, Division 2, v Stockport Co (a) W 5–2 – Kneeshaw; Brittan, Leyton; Keenor (1), Smith, Hardy; Grimshaw (1), Gill (2), Cashmore, West, Evans (1).

Record League Victory: 9–2 v Thames, Division 3 (S), 6 February 1932 – Farquharson; E. L. Morris, Roberts; Galbraith, Harris, Ronan; Emmerson (1), Keating (1), Jones (1), McCambridge (1), Robbins (5).

HONOURS

Football League: Division 1 – Runners-up 1923–24; Division 2 – Runners-up 1920–21, 1951–52, 1959–60; Division 3 (S) – Champions 1946–47; Division 3 – Champions 1992–93. Runners-up 1975–76, 1982–83, 2000–01; Division 4 – Runners-up 1987–88.

FA Cup: Winners 1927 (only occasion the Cup has been won by a club outside England); Runners-up 1925.

Football League Cup: Semi-final 1966.

Welsh Cup: Winners 21 times.

Charity Shield: Winners 1927.

European Competitions: *European Cup-Winners' Cup:* 1964–65, 1965–66, 1967–68 (semi-finalists), 1968–69, 1969–70, 1970–71, 1971–72, 1973–74, 1974–75, 1976–77, 1977–78, 1988–89, 1991–92, 1992–93, 1993–94.

IT'S A FACT !

Tom Farquharson, Cardiff City's goalkeeper in their 1927 FA Cup triumph, played 519 matches for the club including 445 in the League before retiring in May 1935. Capped by both Northern and the Republic of Ireland he always carried a hand gun with him!

Record Cup Victory: 8–0 v Enfield, FA Cup 1st rd, 28 November 1931 – Farquharson; Smith, Roberts; Harris (1), Galbraith, Ronan; Emmerson (2), Keating (3); O'Neill (2), Robbins, McCambridge.

Record Defeat: 2–11 v Sheffield U, Division 1, 1 January 1926.

Most League Points (2 for a win): 66, Division 3 (S), 1946–47.

Most League Points (3 for a win): 86, Division 3, 1982–83.

Most League Goals: 95, Division 3, 2000–01.

Highest League Scorer in Season: Stan Richards, 30, Division 3 (S), 1946–47.

Most League Goals in Total Aggregate: Len Davies, 128, 1920–31.

Most League Goals in One Match: 5, Hugh Ferguson v Burnley, Division 1, 1 September 1928; 5, Walter Robbins v Thames, Division 3S, 6 February 1932; 5, William Henderson v Northampton T, Division 3S, 22 April 1933.

Most Capped Player: Alf Sherwood, 39 (41), Wales.

Most League Appearances: Phil Dwyer, 471, 1972–85.

Youngest League Player: John Toshack, 16 years 236 days v Leyton Orient, 13 November 1965.

Record Transfer Fee Received: £500,000 from Coventry C for Simon Haworth, June 1997.

Record Transfer Fee Paid: £180,000 to San Jose Earthquakes for Godfrey Ingram, September 1982.

Football League Record: 1920 Elected to Division 2; 1921–29 Division 1; 1929–31 Division 2; 1931–47 Division 3 (S); 1947–52 Division 2; 1952–57 Division 1; 1957–60 Division 2; 1960–62 Division 1; 1962–75 Division 2; 1975–76 Division 3; 1976–82 Division 2; 1982–83 Division 3; 1983–85 Division 2; 1985–86 Division 3; 1986–88 Division 4; 1988–90 Division 3; 1990–92 Division 4; 1992–93 Division 3; 1993–95 Division 2; 1995–99 Division 3; 1999–2000 Division 2; 2000–01 Division 3; 2001– Division 2.

MANAGERS

Davy McDougall 1910–11
Fred Stewart 1911–33
Bartley Wilson 1933–34
B. Watts-Jones 1934–37
Bill Jennings 1937–39
Cyril Spiers 1939–46
Billy McCandless 1946–48
Cyril Spiers 1948–54
Trevor Morris 1954–58
Bill Jones 1958–62
George Swindin 1962–64
Jimmy Scoular 1964–73
Frank O'Farrell 1973–74
Jimmy Andrews 1974–78
Richie Morgan 1978–82
Len Ashurst 1982–84
Jimmy Goodfellow 1984
Alan Durban 1984–86
Frank Burrows 1986–89
Len Ashurst 1989–91
Eddie May 1991–94
Terry Yorath 1994–95
Eddie May 1995
Kenny Hibbitt *(Chief Coach)* 1995
Phil Neal 1996
Russell Osman 1996–97
Kenny Hibbitt 1996–98
Frank Burrows 1998–99
Billy Ayre 1999–2000
Bobby Gould 2000
Alan Cork October 2000–

LATEST SEQUENCES

Longest Sequence of League Wins: 9, 26.10.46 – 28.12.46.

Longest Sequence of League Defeats: 7, 4.11.33 – 25.12.33.

Longest Sequence of League Draws: 6, 29.11.80 – 17.1.81.

Longest Sequence of Unbeaten League Matches: 21, 21.9.46 – 1.3.47.

Longest Sequence Without a League Win: 15, 21.11.36 – 6.3.37.

TEN YEAR LEAGUE RECORD

		P	W	D	L	F	A	Pts	Pos
1990-91	Div 4	46	15	15	16	43	54	60	13
1991-92	Div 4	42	17	15	10	66	53	66	9
1992-93	Div 3	42	25	8	9	77	47	83	1
1993-94	Div 2	46	13	15	18	66	79	54	19
1994-95	Div 2	46	9	11	26	46	74	38	22
1995-96	Div 3	46	11	12	23	41	64	45	22
1996-97	Div 3	46	20	9	17	56	54	69	7
1997-98	Div 3	46	9	23	14	48	52	50	21
1998-99	Div 3	46	22	14	10	60	39	80	3
1999-2000	Div 2	46	9	17	20	45	67	44	21

DID YOU KNOW

In 1946-47, Cardiff City's Division Three (South) championship winning season was given considerable impetus by a remarkable run of 21 games without defeat in which they scored 63 times and conceded only 12 goals.

CARDIFF CITY 2000–01 LEAGUE RECORD

Match No.	Date	Venue	Opponents	Result	H/T Score	Lg. Pos.	Goalscorers	Attendance
1	Aug 12	A	Exeter C	W 2-1	1-0	—	Brayson [34], Low [62]	3929
2	19	H	Blackpool	D 1-1	1-0	8	Nugent [36]	11,019
3	26	A	Barnet	D 2-2	0-1	9	Low [84], Earnshaw [90]	2264
4	28	H	Southend U	D 2-2	2-0	7	Nugent [4], Brayson [42]	7628
5	Sept 2	A	Rochdale	D 1-1	1-0	11	Brayson [10]	2824
6	9	H	Brighton & HA	D 1-1	0-0	10	Hill [74]	6741
7	12	H	Halifax T	W 4-2	3-0	—	Young [5], Bowen [26], Earnshaw [32], Fortune-West [81]	5087
8	16	A	Scunthorpe U	W 2-0	0-0	3	Nugent [70], Earnshaw [72]	3263
9	23	A	Kidderminster H	D 0-0	0-0	6		8003
10	30	H	Hull C	L 0-2	0-1	8		5503
11	Oct 14	A	Leyton Orient	L 1-2	0-2	13	Fortune-West [55]	4649
12	17	A	Carlisle U	D 2-2	1-2	—	Legg [39], Nugent [50]	1309
13	21	H	Mansfield T	W 2-0	0-0	11	Earnshaw [52], Brayson [85]	4625
14	24	H	Darlington	W 2-0	1-0	—	Earnshaw [5], Evans [90]	5440
15	28	A	Chesterfield	D 2-2	1-0	8	Evans [24], Bowen [49]	5378
16	Nov 4	H	York C	W 4-0	3-0	8	Bowen 2 [2, 7], Young [41], Earnshaw [90]	6101
17	22	H	Lincoln C	W 3-2	1-2	—	Earnshaw [5], Brayson [88], Barnett (og) [90]	4786
18	25	H	Hartlepool U	W 3-2	1-1	5	Fortune-West [20], Bonner [89], Nogan [90]	6251
19	Dec 2	A	Torquay U	W 4-1	0-1	5	Earnshaw 3 [46, 60, 71], Brayson [79]	2427
20	16	H	Cheltenham T	W 3-1	1-0	4	Fortune-West [31], Earnshaw [52], Brayson [80]	6764
21	23	H	Macclesfield T	W 2-0	1-0	3	Young [6], Bowen [49]	8088
22	26	A	Plymouth Arg	L 1-2	1-0	4	Fortune-West [15]	8543
23	Jan 1	H	Exeter C	W 6-1	1-0	3	Young [21], Gordon [48], Legg [60], Bowen [63], Brazier [66], Brayson [87]	9038
24	13	A	Southend U	D 1-1	1-0	4	Fortune-West [45]	4601
25	20	H	Plymouth Arg	W 4-1	1-0	3	Earnshaw 2 [38, 88], Fortune-West [69], McCulloch [90]	9157
26	27	A	Macclesfield T	W 5-2	2-1	2	Bowen [4], Young 2 [43, 46], Earnshaw 2 [49, 83]	2376
27	Feb 2	H	Rochdale	D 0-0	0-0	—		11,912
28	10	A	Brighton & HA	L 0-1	0-1	3		6922
29	13	A	Blackpool	L 0-1	0-0	—		4417
30	17	H	Scunthorpe U	W 3-0	2-0	3	Gabbidon 2 [35, 42], Brazier [61]	6057
31	20	H	Halifax T	W 2-1	1-0	—	Brayson 2 [21, 52]	1991
32	25	A	Kidderminster H	W 4-2	2-1	2	Young [41], Bowen [45], Gabbidon [86], Earnshaw [90]	4317
33	Mar 2	H	Hull C	W 2-0	0-0	—	Legg [60], Edwards (og) [75]	10,074
34	6	A	Leyton Orient	D 1-1	0-0	—	Earnshaw [89]	9022
35	10	A	Lincoln C	L 0-2	0-0	3		4451
36	13	A	Shrewsbury T	W 4-0	0-0	—	Low [56], Fortune-West [64], Boland (pen) [79], Bowen [82]	3847
37	17	H	Carlisle U	W 4-1	3-0	2	Brayson 2 [2, 14], Bowen 2 [44, 57]	7130
38	Apr 1	A	Cheltenham T	L 1-3	1-2	3	Young [6]	5139
39	4	H	Barnet	W 1-0	0-0	—	Low [69]	6209
40	7	H	Torquay U	W 2-1	0-1	2	Brayson [60], Fortune-West [76]	8210
41	14	A	Darlington	L 0-2	0-2	3		3683
42	16	H	Chesterfield	D 3-3	1-2	3	Brayson 2 (1 pen) [27, 49 (p)], Evans [90]	13,602
43	21	A	York C	D 3-3	2-1	3	Fortune-West 3 [37, 45, 71]	3881
44	24	A	Mansfield T	L 1-2	0-1	—	Bowen [86]	2204
45	28	H	Shrewsbury T	W 3-1	1-1	3	Young 2 [11, 72], Earnshaw [72]	12,188
46	May 5	A	Hartlepool U	L 1-3	1-1	2	Earnshaw [10]	5324

Final League Position: 2

GOALSCORERS

League (95): Earnshaw 19, Brayson 15 (1 pen), Bowen 12, Fortune-West 12, Young 10, Low 4, Nugent 4, Evans 3, Gabbidon 3, Legg 3, Brazier 2, Boland 1 (pen), Bonner 1, Gordon 1, Hill 1, McCulloch 1, Nogan 1, own goals 2.
Worthington Cup (1): Young 1.
FA Cup (10): Earnshaw 6 (1 pen), Evans 2, Fortune-West 1, Young 1.

Walton M 40	Thompson A 5 + 2	Brazier M 23 + 3	Fowler J 3 + 2	Greene D 10	Young S 45	Bowen J 35 + 5	Boland W 25	Brayson P 25 + 15	Nugent K 14	Low J 31 + 5	Bonner M 17 + 7	Legg A 39	Gabbidon D 42 + 1	Hill D 7 + 2	Earnshaw R 21 + 15	Eckhardt J 6 + 2	McCulloch S 9 + 12	Evans K 24 + 6	Nogan K — + 12	Jones G — + 2	Fortune-West L 28 + 9	Jordan A 3 + 2	Weston R 25 + 3	Collins J — + 3	Gordon G 4 + 6	Harper J 3	Hughes D 11 + 1	Lightbourne K 2 + 1	Giles M 1 + 4	Muggleton C 6	Perrett R 2	Match No.
1	2	3	4^1	5	6	7	8	9	10	11	12																					1
1	2^1	3		5	6		8	9	10	7	4	11	12																			2
1		3	12	5	6		8^1	9	10	7	4^2	11^3	2	13	14																	3
1		3	4^1	5	6		9^2	10	7	8	11	2^3	12	13	14																	4
1		3^2	4	5	6		9^1	10	8	11	2	7^3					13	14	12													5
1				5	6		9	10	7^2	4^1	11	2	8^2	12			3	13	14													6
1			5^2	6	9^3		10		12	11	2	7	8		3^1	4		13	14													7
1	3		5	6	9^3		12	10		11^1	2	4	7^2		13	8		14														8
1	3		5	6	9^3		12	10^1		13	11	2	4^2	7		8		14														9
1	3		5	6	12		13			7^1	8	11	2	4	10^2			9														10
1	3		6	7^1			13		12	8	11	2	10^3	14	5	4^2		9														11
1	3		6	12			13	10^2	7	4	11^1	2		8		5^3	14	9														12
1			6	9^1			12	10^2	7	4	3	2	8	5		11		13														13
1			6	9^1			12	10^2	7	4	3	2	8	5		11		13														14
1			6	9^1				10^2	7	4	3	2	8	5	12	11		13														15
1	12		6	9				10^2	7^1	4	3	2	8	5		11^3		13	14													16
1			5	9^1			12		2	8		3^2	7			11	13	10	4	6												17
1			5	9^1			12		2	8		3	7^2		14	11	13	10	4	6^3												18
1			5	9^1			12		2	8		3	7^2		4	11	13	10^3		6	14											19
1	12		5	9^2			13		2	8	11	3^1		7	14	4^3		10		6												20
1			5	9^1			12		2	8^2	11	3	7^3		4	13		10		6	14											21
1			6			8^1	9^2		2		11	3	7^3	5	12	4		10		13	14											22
1	3		5^3	9			12		13		11	2	7		4^2				14	6	10^1	8										23
1	3		5	7^2				12		11	2^1		13		14	8^3		10		6		9	4									24
1	3		5^1	9	8^3	12		7		11	2^2		13	14				10		6			4									25
1	3		5^1	9	8			12		11	2	7		13	4^2			10	6^3	14												26
1	3	12	5	8^1	6	9		7		11	2				4^2			10^3		13	14											27
1	3		5	7^2	8	9		2		6	4				12	13		10^3		11^1	14											28
1	3		5	12	7	9^2		2		11	4				8^1	13		14				10^3	6									29
1	12		5	7	8	9		2^1		6	3^2				13		14	10^3		11				4								30
1			5	7	8	9		2		11	3						12	10^1		4		6										31
1			5	7^1	8	9		2		11	3	12				13		4				6	10^2	14								32
1	3^3		5	7	8	9				11	2	12^2				13		4				6	10^1	14								33
1	3^3		5^2	7^1	8	9				2	12				11	13		10		4			6		14							34
1	3^3		5	12	8	9				2		7^1				11		10		4			6	13								35
1	12		5	7	8	9		2^1		3					13	11^2	14	10^3		4			6^1									36
1			5	7	8	9		2		11	3						12	10^1		4			6									37
1			5	9^1	8	12		2		11	3	7						10^3		4	14		6^2		13							38
			5^2	9	8			2		11	3^3	7		6				10^1		4		12	13		14	1						39
			5	7	8	9		2^1	12	11	3	13						14		4	10^3		6^2			1						40
			5	7^3	8	9		2^2		11	3	12		13				10		4	14				6^1	1						41
	2	11		7	8	9^1			5	3	12			6				10		4						1						42
	2	3	5	7^1	8	9			11				12	13	6^2			10		4						1						43
	2	3^3	5	7^2	8	9		12	11				13	14	6^1			10								1		4				44
1			5	7	8	9^1	12	13	11	2	14							10^2		4									3^2			45
1	12		5	13		9		2^1	14	11	3	7		8	6^2			10		4^2												46

Worthington Cup

First Round	Crystal Palace	(a)	1-2
		(h)	0-0

FA Cup

First Round	Bristol R	(h)	5-1
Second Round	Cheltenham T	(h)	3-1
Third Round	Crewe Alex	(h)	1-1
		(a)	1-2

CARLISLE UNITED

Division 3

FOUNDATION

Carlisle United came into being in 1903 through the amalgamation of Shaddongate United and Carlisle Red Rose. The new club was admitted to the Second Division of the Lancashire Combination in 1905–06, winning promotion the following season. Devonshire Park was officially opened on 2 September 1905, when St Helens Town were the visitors. Despite defeat in a disappointing 3-2 start, a respectable mid-table position was achieved.

Brunton Park, Carlisle CA1 1LL.

Telephone: (01228) 526 237. *Fax:* (01228) 530 138.
Commercial Dept: (01228) 524 014.
Information Line: 09068 230 011.

Ground Capacity: 16,651.

Record Attendance: 27,500 v Birmingham C, FA Cup 3rd rd, 5 January 1957 and v Middlesbrough, FA Cup 5th rd, 7 February 1970.

Record Receipts: £146,000 v Tottenham H, Coca-Cola Cup 2nd rd, 30 September 1997.

Pitch Measurements: 117yd × 72yd.

Directors: A. Doweck (Chairman), R. McKnight, H. A. Jenkins, P. Fletcher, S. Pattison, G. Crooks.

Physio: Neil Dalton.

Secretary: Sarah McKnight.

Colours: Blue shirts, blue shorts, blue stockings.

Change Colours: All white with green and red trim.

Year Formed: 1903.

Ltd Co.: 1921.

Previous Name: 1903, Shaddongate United; 1904, Carlisle United.

Club Nickname: 'Cumbrians' or 'The Blues'.

Previous Grounds: 1903, Milholme Bank; 1905, Devonshire Park; 1909, Brunton Park.

First Football League Game: 25 August 1928, Division 3 (N), v Accrington S (a) W 3–2 – Prout; Coulthard, Cook; Harrison, Ross, Pigg; Agar (1), Hutchison, McConnell (1), Ward (1), Watson.

Record League Victory: 8–0 v Hartlepool U, Division 3 (N), 1 September 1928 – Prout; Smiles, Cook; Robinson (1) Ross, Pigg; Agar (1), Hutchison (1), McConnell (4), Ward (1), Watson. 8–0 v Scunthorpe U, Division 3 (N), 25 December 1952 – MacLaren; Hill, Scott; Stokoe, Twentyman, Waters; Harrison (1), Whitehouse (5), Ashman (2), Duffett, Bond.

HONOURS

Football League: Division 1 best season: 22nd, 1974–75; Promoted from Division 2 (3rd) 1973–74; Division 3 – Champions 1964–65, 1994–95; Runners-up 1981–82; Promoted from Division 3 1996–97; Division 4 – Runners-up 1963–64.

FA Cup: best season: 6th rd 1975.

Football League Cup: Semi-final 1970.

Auto Windscreens Shield: Winners 1997; Runners-up 1995.

IT'S A FACT !

Despite an erratic season of scoring in 1937-38, twelfth placed Carlisle United were encouraged when Hugh Mills scored all five goals for them in a 5-2 win over Halifax Town on 11 September.

Record Cup Victory: 6–0 v Shepshed Dynamo, FA Cup
1st rd, 16 November 1996 – Caig; Hopper, Archdeacon
(pen), Walling, Robinson, Pounewatchy, Peacock (1),
Conway (1) (Jansen), Smart (McAlindon (1)), Hayward,
Aspinall (Thorpe), (2 og).

Record Defeat: 1–11 v Hull C, Division 3 (N), 14 January 1939.

Most League Points (2 for a win): 62, Division 3 (N), 1950–51.

Most League Points (3 for a win): 91, Division 3, 1994–95.

Most League Goals: 113, Division 4, 1963–64.

Highest League Scorer in Season: Jimmy McConnell, 42,
Division 3 (N), 1928–29.

Most League Goals in Total Aggregate: Jimmy McConnell,
126, 1928–32.

Most League Goals in One Match: 5, Hugh Mills v Halifax T,
Division 3N, 11 September 1937; 5, Jim Whitehouse v
Scunthorpe U, Division 3N, 25 December 1952.

Most Capped Player: Eric Welsh, 4, Northern Ireland.

Most League Appearances: Allan Ross, 466, 1963–79.

Youngest League Player: Rory Delap, 16 years 306 days v
Scarborough, 8 May 1993.

Record Transfer Fee Received: £1,500,000 from Crystal
Palace for Matt Jansen, February 1998.

Record Transfer Fee Paid: £121,000 to Notts Co for David
Reeves, December 1993.

Football League Record: 1928 Elected to Division 3 (N);
1958–62 Division 4; 1962–63 Division 3; 1963–64 Division 4;
1964–65 Division 3; 1965–74 Division 2; 1974–75 Division 1;
1975–77 Division 2; 1977–82 Division 3; 1982–86 Division 2;
1986–87 Division 3; 1987–92 Division 4; 1992–95 Division 3;
1995–96 Division 2; 1996–97 Division 3; 1997–98 Division 2;
1998– Division 3.

LATEST SEQUENCES

Longest Sequence of League Wins: 6, 27.8.94 – 17.9.94.

Longest Sequence of League Defeats: 8, 8.11.86 – 3.1.87.

Longest Sequence of League Draws: 6, 11.2.78 – 11.3.78.

Longest Sequence of Unbeaten League Matches: 19, 1.10.94
– 11.2.95.

Longest Sequence Without a League Win: 14, 19.1.35 –
19.4.35.

MANAGERS

Harry Kirkbride 1904–05
(Secretary-Manager)
McCumiskey 1905–06
(Secretary-Manager)
Jack Houston 1906–08
(Secretary-Manager)
Bert Stansfield 1908–10
Jack Houston 1910–12
Davie Graham 1912–13
George Bristow 1913–30
Billy Hampson 1930–33
Bill Clarke 1933–35
Robert Kelly 1935–36
Fred Westgarth 1936–38
David Taylor 1938–40
Howard Harkness 1940–45
Bill Clark 1945–46 *(Secretary-Manager)*
Ivor Broadis 1946–49
Bill Shankly 1949–51
Fred Emery 1951–58
Andy Beattie 1958–60
Ivor Powell 1960–63
Alan Ashman 1963–67
Tim Ward 1967–68
Bob Stokoe 1968–70
Ian MacFarlane 1970–72
Alan Ashman 1972–75
Dick Young 1975–76
Bobby Moncur 1976–80
Martin Harvey 1980
Bob Stokoe 1980–85
Bryan 'Pop' Robson 1985
Bob Stokoe 1985–86
Harry Gregg 1986–87
Cliff Middlemass 1987–91
Aidan McCaffery 1991–92
David McCreery 1992–93
Mick Wadsworth *(Director of Coaching)* 1993–96
Mervyn Day 1996–97
David Wilkes and John Halpin *(Directors of Coaching)*
Michael Knighton 1997–99
Martin Wilkinson 1999–2000
Ian Atkins 2000–01

TEN YEAR LEAGUE RECORD

		P	W	D	L	F	A	Pts	Pos
1990-91	Div 4	46	13	9	24	47	89	48	20
1991-92	Div 4	42	7	13	22	41	67	34	22
1992-93	Div 3	42	11	11	20	51	65	44	18
1993-94	Div 3	42	18	10	14	57	42	64	7
1994-95	Div 3	42	27	10	5	67	31	91	1
1995-96	Div 2	46	12	13	21	57	72	49	21
1996-97	Div 3	46	24	12	10	67	44	84	3
1997-98	Div 2	46	12	8	26	57	73	44	23
1998-99	Div 3	46	11	16	19	43	53	49	23
1999-2000	Div 3	46	9	12	25	42	75	39	23

DID YOU KNOW ?

Centre-forward Alf
Ackerman scored 12 goals in
seven FA Cup matches for
Carlisle United between
1956-57 and 1958-59.

CARLISLE UNITED 2000–01 LEAGUE RECORD

Match No.	Date	Venue	Opponents	Result	H/T Score	Lg. Pos.	Goalscorers	Attendance
1	Aug 12	H	Halifax T	D	2-2	0-2	—	Soley 2 (1 pen) [80 (p), 90]	4491
2	19	A	Leyton Orient	L	0-1	0-1	15		4320
3	25	H	York C	D	1-1	0-0	—	Soley [90]	4087
4	29	A	Shrewsbury T	W	1-0	0-0	—	Stevens [82]	2912
5	Sept 2	A	Kidderminster H	W	1-0	0-0	10	Stevens [63]	4052
6	9	H	Rochdale	L	1-2	1-1	12	Stevens [37]	3906
7	12	H	Chesterfield	L	2-4	1-3	—	Stevens [45], Heggs [84]	2929
8	16	A	Plymouth Arg	L	0-2	0-2	20		3378
9	23	H	Exeter C	L	0-1	0-1	20		2856
10	30	A	Darlington	L	0-1	0-0	21		4316
11	Oct 6	A	Cheltenham T	L	0-1	0-0	—		4264
12	14	H	Barnet	L	0-2	0-1	22		2487
13	17	H	Cardiff C	D	2-2	2-1	—	Lemarchand [7], Dobie [35]	1309
14	21	A	Torquay U	L	2-4	1-2	23	Heggs (pen) [14], Tracey [49]	1778
15	24	A	Blackpool	L	2-3	0-2	—	Dobie [72], Keen [78]	4744
16	28	H	Scunthorpe U	L	1-2	0-2	23	Darby [88]	2381
17	Nov 4	A	Brighton & HA	L	1-4	1-1	24	Mayo (og) [41]	6746
18	11	H	Southend U	W	3-1	2-0	24	Stevens [13], Dobie 2 [27, 88]	2201
19	25	A	Hull C	L	1-2	0-2	24	Connelly [71]	4677
20	Dec 2	H	Lincoln C	D	1-1	1-0	24	Dobie [21]	2539
21	16	A	Macclesfield T	L	0-1	0-0	24		1860
22	22	A	Mansfield T	D	1-1	1-1	—	Dobie [35]	2247
23	Jan 13	H	Shrewsbury T	W	1-0	1-0	24	Soley [10]	3328
24	20	A	Hartlepool U	D	2-2	1-0	24	Heggs [17], Dobie [90]	4473
25	27	H	Mansfield T	W	2-1	2-1	24	Morley [18], Whitehead [45]	3375
26	30	A	York C	D	0-0	0-0	—		2750
27	Feb 3	H	Kidderminster H	W	2-0	2-0	23	Stevens [9], Dobie [15]	3429
28	13	H	Hartlepool U	L	2-3	2-0	—	Galloway [19], Stevens [30]	4159
29	17	H	Plymouth Arg	D	1-1	0-0	23	Stevens [84]	3592
30	20	A	Chesterfield	D	1-1	1-0	—	Stevens [16]	3796
31	24	A	Exeter C	L	0-1	0-1	24		5150
32	Mar 3	H	Darlington	L	0-2	0-1	24		3726
33	6	A	Barnet	W	1-0	1-0	—	Stevens [38]	1480
34	10	A	Cheltenham T	D	1-1	1-0	24	McCann (og) [32]	3280
35	13	H	Leyton Orient	W	1-0	0-0	—	Dobie [52]	2610
36	17	A	Cardiff C	L	1-4	0-3	23	Halliday [90]	7130
37	23	H	Torquay U	W	1-0	0-0	—	Stevens [60]	4828
38	27	A	Halifax T	D	0-0	0-0	—		3723
39	31	H	Macclesfield T	W	1-0	0-0	21	Dobie [47]	3885
40	Apr 10	A	Rochdale	L	0-6	0-4	—		2892
41	14	H	Blackpool	W	1-0	0-0	20	Heggs [84]	6096
42	16	A	Scunthorpe U	L	0-3	0-1	20		4068
43	21	H	Brighton & HA	D	0-0	0-0	22		4727
44	28	A	Southend U	D	1-1	1-0	21	Stevens [6]	4175
45	May 2	A	Lincoln C	D	1-1	0-1	—	Heggs [66]	4245
46	5	H	Hull C	D	0-0	0-0	22		8194

Final League Position: 22

GOALSCORERS

League (42): Stevens 12, Dobie 10, Heggs 5 (1 pen), Soley 4 (1 pen), Connelly 1, Darby 1, Galloway 1, Halliday 1, Keen 1, Lemarchand 1, Morley 1, Tracey 1, Whitehead 1, own goals 2.
Worthington Cup (1): Stevens 1.
FA Cup (7): Stevens 4, Dobie 2, Connelly 1.

Weaver L 14	Birch M 44	Squires J 2+3	Whitehead S 45	Winstanley M 34+2	Darby J 15+3	Soley S 21+4	Stevens I 41	Heggs C 16+14	Hemmings T 16+6	Cars T 6+1	Dobie S 41+12	Lee D 1+12	Pitts M 1+4	Prokas R 26+3	Tracey R 4+2	McAughtrie C —+5	Inglis J 8	Lemarchand S 4+1	Maddison L 34	Halliday S 3+21	Thurston M 3+2	Keen P 3	Connelly G 21+7	Galloway M 26	Glennon M 29	Hore J 1	Morley D 23	Carr D 10	Hopper T 4+5	Cullen J 10+1	Match No.
1	2	3	4	5[1]	6	7	8	9	10	11[3]	12	13																			1
1	2	3[3]	4	5	6[1]	7	8	9	10	11	14	12	13[3]																		2
1	2		4	5	6[2]	7	8	9	10		12	11	3[1]	13																	3
1	2		4	5	6	7	8[1]	9	3[2]		10	12	13	11																	4
1	2		4	5	6	7	8[1]	9	3		10			11	12																5
1	2	12	4	5	6[1]	7	8	9	3		10			11																	6
1	2	12[2]	4	5	6[1]	7	8	9	3[2]	13	10	14		11[2]																	7
1	2	12[2]	4	5	6[1]	7	8	9	3[3]	11	10	14	13																		8
1	2[3]		4	5	6	7[2]	8	9[1]	3	11	10	12		13		14															9
1	2		4	5	6		8[3]	12	3[2]	11	10	13					9[1]		7	14											10
1	2		4	5	6[1]		8	12	3[2]	11	10		13				9		7												11
1	2		4	5	6[2]	7[2]	8	9[1]			10	12		13	14				11	3											12
1	2		4	5			8[1]	12			10			6			9		7	11	3										13
1	2		4	5				9[1]			10	12		6			8	11[2]	7[2]	3	14	13									14
	2[2]		4	5				9			10	12		6	13			11	7	3	8[1]	1									15
	2		4	5[1]			12	9[2]			10	13		6				11[3]	7	3	8	14	1								16
	2		4				8				10	12		6				5	3		12	7	1	9[1]	11						17
	2		4				8[2]		10[1]		9[3]	12		6			13		3	14			5	7	11	1					18
	2		4	5			8	12	10[1]		9			6					3				13	7	11	1					19
	2		4	5			8[2]	12	10[1]		9			6					3				13	7	11	1					20
	2		4	5	6		8[1]	12	13[3]		9							14	3					7	11	1	10[2]				21
	2		4	5	6			12			10			9[1]			8		3					7	11	1					22
	2		4	5		7	8[1]	12	13		9			6					3				10		11[2]	1					23
	2[3]		4	5	13	7		9	3		10			6								12[2]	14		11[1]	1	8				24
	2		4	5		7	8[1]	12			9			10					3				13		11[2]	1	6				25
	2		4	5		7	8[1]				9			10					3				12	13	11[2]	1	6				26
	2		4	5		7	8[1]	12			9			10					3						11	1	6				27
	2[3]		4			7	8[1]	12			9			10					3				13	14	11[2]	1	6	5			28
	2[2]		4			7	8	12			9			10[3]					3				13	14	11[1]	1	6	5[1]			29
	2		4	12			8[2]				9[1]			10					3				13	7	11	1	6	5			30
	2[2]		4	12	13		8[3]				9			10					3				14	7	11	1	6	5[1]			31
	2			5		7	8	4[1]			9			10					3				12		11[1]	1	6				32
	2		4	5		7	8				9			10					3				12		11[1]	1	6				33
	2[2]		4	5		7[4]	8[1]	12			9			10					3				13		11	1	6				34
	2		4	5			8[1]				9			10					3				12	7	11[2]	1	6	13			35
	2		4	5			8[1]				9			10[3]					3				12	7	11[2]	1	6	13		14	36
	2		4				8[1]				9								3				12	7	11	1	6	5		10	37
	2		4				8[1]				9								3				12	7	11	1	6	5		10	38
	2		4				8[1]				9								3				12	7	11	1	6	5	13	10[2]	39
	2		4				8[1]	12			9								3				13	7	11[2]	1	6	5	14	10	40
	2		4				8[1]	12			9								3				13	7	11[2]	1	6	5	14	10[3]	41
	2		4	14			8[2]	12			9								3				13[3]	7		1	6	5	11	10[1]	42
	2		4	5			8	12			9[1]								3				13		11[2]	1	6		7	10	43
			4	5	12		8[2]					13						14	3				9[3]	7		1	6		11	10[1]	44
			4	5	2	7	8	12			9[1]								3				11			1	6			10	45
			4	5	12		8				9								3				11			1	6		2	10[1]	46

Worthington Cup

First Round	Grimsby T	(a)	0-2
		(h)	1-1

FA Cup

First Round	Woking	(h)	5-1
Second Round	Kidderminster H	(a)	2-0
Third Round	Arsenal	(h)	0-1

CHARLTON ATHLETIC   FA Premiership

FOUNDATION

The club was formed on 9 June 1905, by a group of 14 and 15-year-old youths living in streets by the Thames in the area which now borders the Thames Barrier. The club's progress through local leagues was so rapid that after the First World War they joined the Kent League where they spent a season before turning professional and joining the Southern League in 1920. A year later they were elected to the Football League's Division 3 (South).

The Valley, Floyd Road, Charlton, London SE7 8BL.

Telephone: (020) 8333 4000. *Fax:* (020) 8333 4001.
Website: www.cafc.co.uk *Email:* info@cafc.co.uk
Box Office: (020) 8333 4010. *ClubCall:* 09068 121 146.

Ground Capacity: 20,043, rising to 26,500 December 2001.

Record Attendance: 75,031 v Aston Villa, FA Cup 5th rd, 12 February 1938 (at The Valley).

Record Receipts: £201,711 v QPR, FA Cup 5th rd, 8 January 2000.

Pitch Measurements: 111yd × 73yd.

Chairman: M. A. Simons.
Deputy Chairman: R. A. Murray.
Chief Executive: P. D. Varney.
Directors: R. N. Alwen, G. P. Bone, N. E. Capelin, R. D. Collins, D. J. Hughes, M. C. Stevens, D. C. Sumners, D. G. Ufton, R. C. Whitehand, G. B. C. Franklin, D. White.

HONOURS

Football League: Division 1 – Champions 1999–2000; Runners-up 1936–37; Promoted from Division 1, 1997–98 (play-offs); Division 2 – Runners-up 1935–36, 1985–86; Division 3 (S) – Champions 1928–29, 1934–35; Promoted from Division 3 (3rd) 1974–75, 1980–81.

FA Cup: Winners 1947; Runners-up 1946.

Football League Cup: best season: 4th rd, 1963, 1966, 1979.

Full Members' Cup: Runners-up 1987.

Manager: Alan Curbishley. *Assistant Manager:* Keith Peacock. *First Team Coach:* Mervyn Day.
Academy Director: Mick Browne. *Physio:* Andy Jones.

Football Secretary: Chris Parkes.

Safety Officer: John Little.

Media and PR: Rick Everitt.

Colours: Red shirts, white shorts, red stockings.

Change Colours: White shirts, red shorts, white stockings.

Year Formed: 1905.

Turned Professional: 1920. *Ltd Co.:* 1919.

Club Nickname: 'Addicks'.

Previous Grounds: 1906, Siemen's Meadow; 1907, Woolwich Common; 1909, Pound Park; 1913, Horn Lane; 1920, The Valley; 1923, Catford (The Mount); 1924, The Valley; 1985, Selhurst Park; 1991, Upton Park; 1992, The Valley.

First Football League Game: 27 August 1921, Division 3 (S), v Exeter C (h) W 1–0 – Hughes; Mitchell, Goodman; Dowling (1), Hampson, Dunn; Castle, Bailey, Halse, Green, Wilson.

IT'S A FACT !

On 1 October 1938 in the wake of the Munich Agreement, Charlton Athletic's guests in the 4–4 draw with Bolton Wanderers included Prime Minister Neville Chamberlain and the Rector of Charlton.

Record League Victory: 8–1 v Middlesbrough, Division 1, 12 September 1953 – Bartram; Campbell, Ellis; Fenton, Ufton, Hammond; Hurst (2), O'Linn (2), Leary (1), Firmani (3), Kiernan.

Record Cup Victory: 7–0 v Burton A, FA Cup 3rd rd, 7 January 1956 – Bartram; Campbell, Townsend; Hewie, Ufton, Hammond; Hurst (1), Gauld (1), Leary (3), White, Kiernan (2).

Record Defeat: 1–11 v Aston Villa, Division 2, 14 November 1959.

Most League Points (2 for a win): 61, Division 3 (S), 1934–35.

Most League Points (3 for a win): 91, Division 1, 1999–2000.

Most League Goals: 107, Division 2, 1957–58.

Highest League Scorer in Season: Ralph Allen, 32, Division 3 (S), 1934–35.

Most League Goals in Total Aggregate: Stuart Leary, 153, 1953–62.

Most League Goals in One Match: 5, Wilson Lennox v Exeter C, Division 3S, 2 February 1929; 5, Eddie Firmani v Aston Villa, Division 1, 5 February 1955; 5, John Summers v Huddersfield T, Division 2, 21 December 1957; 5, John Summers v Portsmouth, Division 2, 1 October 1960.

Most Capped Player: John Robinson, 26, Wales.

Most League Appearances: Sam Bartram, 583, 1934–56.

Youngest League Player: Paul Konchesky, 16 years 93 days v Oxford U, 16 August 1997.

Record Transfer Fee Received: £4,370,000 from Leeds U for Danny Mills, June 1999.

Record Transfer Fee Paid: £4,750,000 to Wimbledon for Jason Euell, July 2001.

Football League Record: 1921 Elected to Division 3 (S); 1929–33 Division 2; 1933–35 Division 3 (S); 1935–36 Division 2; 1936–57 Division 1; 1957–72 Division 2; 1972–75 Division 3; 1975–80 Division 2; 1980–81 Division 3; 1981–86 Division 2; 1986–90 Division 1; 1990–92 Division 2; 1992–98 Division 1; 1998–99 FA Premier League; 1999–2000 Division 1; 2000– FA Premier League.

MANAGERS

Bill Rayner 1920–25
Alex McFarlane 1925–27
Albert Lindon 1928
Alex McFarlane 1928–32
Jimmy Seed 1933–56
Jimmy Trotter 1956–61
Frank Hill 1961–65
Bob Stokoe 1965–67
Eddie Firmani 1967–70
Theo Foley 1970–74
Andy Nelson 1974–79
Mike Bailey 1979–81
Alan Mullery 1981–82
Ken Craggs 1982
Lennie Lawrence 1982–91
Steve Gritt/Alan Curbishley 1991–95
Alan Curbishley June 1995–

LATEST SEQUENCES

Longest Sequence of League Wins: 12, 26.12.99 – 7.3.00.

Longest Sequence of League Defeats: 10, 11.4.90 – 15.9.90.

Longest Sequence of League Draws: 6, 13.12.92 – 16.1.93.

Longest Sequence of Unbeaten League Matches: 15, 4.10.80 – 20.12.80.

Longest Sequence Without a League Win: 16, 26.2.55 – 22.8.55.

TEN YEAR LEAGUE RECORD

		P	W	D	L	F	A	Pts	Pos
1990-91	Div 2	46	13	17	16	57	61	56	16
1991-92	Div 2	46	20	11	15	54	48	71	7
1992-93	Div 1	46	16	13	17	49	46	61	12
1993-94	Div 1	46	19	8	19	61	58	65	11
1994-95	Div 1	46	16	11	19	58	66	59	15
1995-96	Div 1	46	17	20	9	57	45	71	6
1996-97	Div 1	46	16	11	19	52	66	59	15
1997-98	Div 1	46	26	10	10	80	49	88	4
1998-99	PR Lge	38	8	12	18	41	56	36	18
1999-2000	Div 1	46	27	10	9	79	45	91	1

DID YOU KNOW ?

When Charlton Athletic beat Cardiff City 5–2 on 26 October 1963, respective scorers on each side were Eddie Firmani and John Charles, whose last direct opposition had been in Italy with Genoa and Roma.

CHARLTON ATHLETIC 2000–01 LEAGUE RECORD

Match No.	Date	Venue	Opponents	Result		H/T Score	Lg. Pos.	Goalscorers	Attendance
1	Aug 19	H	Manchester C	W	4-0	2-0	—	Hunt [10], Robinson [42], Kinsella [72], Stuart (pen) [80]	20,039
2	23	A	Everton	L	0-3	0-0	—		36,300
3	26	A	Arsenal	L	3-5	2-1	14	Hunt 2 [24, 31], Stuart [58]	38,025
4	Sept 6	H	Southampton	D	1-1	0-0	—	Johansson [82]	20,021
5	10	A	Derby Co	D	2-2	0-2	13	Jensen [59], Johansson [62]	22,310
6	16	H	Tottenham H	W	1-0	1-0	8	Johansson [39]	20,043
7	23	A	Newcastle U	W	1-0	1-0	5	Stuart [8]	50,768
8	30	H	Coventry C	D	2-2	0-1	6	Hunt [60], Johansson [88]	20,043
9	Oct 14	A	Leeds U	L	1-3	0-1	9	Jensen [84]	38,837
10	21	H	Middlesbrough	W	1-0	0-0	7	Svensson [68]	20,043
11	28	A	Aston Villa	L	1-2	0-2	11	Dublin (og) [82]	27,461
12	Nov 4	H	Bradford C	W	2-0	2-0	9	Johansson [4], Stuart [16]	19,633
13	11	A	Ipswich T	L	0-2	0-0	9		22,287
14	18	H	Chelsea	W	2-0	1-0	7	Johansson [35], Pringle [90]	20,043
15	25	H	Sunderland	L	0-1	0-0	12		20,043
16	Dec 2	A	Liverpool	L	0-3	0-1	13		43,515
17	9	H	Manchester U	D	3-3	1-2	13	Bartlett 2 [10, 79], Robinson [85]	20,043
18	16	A	Leicester C	L	1-3	1-1	13	Johansson [6]	19,371
19	23	H	Everton	W	1-0	1-0	13	Svensson [9]	20,043
20	26	A	West Ham U	L	0-5	0-3	13		26,046
21	30	A	Manchester C	W	4-1	2-0	10	Johansson 2 [26, 37], Stuart (pen) [79], Jensen [89]	33,280
22	Jan 1	A	Arsenal	W	1-0	1-0	8	Johansson [39]	20,043
23	13	A	Southampton	D	0-0	0-0	8		15,220
24	22	H	West Ham U	D	1-1	1-0	—	Bartlett [7]	20,043
25	30	H	Derby Co	W	2-1	1-1	—	Mawene (og) [8], Parker [61]	20,043
26	Feb 3	A	Tottenham H	D	0-0	0-0	10		35,368
27	11	H	Newcastle U	W	2-0	2-0	7	Svensson [37], Bartlett [43]	20,043
28	24	A	Coventry C	D	2-2	1-1	8	Rufus [22], Johansson [46]	19,478
29	Mar 3	A	Middlesbrough	D	0-0	0-0	8		28,177
30	17	H	Leeds U	L	1-2	1-1	10	Bartlett [18]	20,043
31	Apr 1	H	Leicester C	W	2-0	1-0	8	Todd [33], Bartlett [82]	20,043
32	10	A	Manchester U	L	1-2	0-1	—	Fish [63]	67,505
33	13	A	Bradford C	L	0-2	0-0	—		17,511
34	17	H	Aston Villa	D	3-3	2-0	—	Boateng (og) [16], Jensen (pen) [45], Kinsella [89]	20,043
35	21	A	Chelsea	W	1-0	1-0	9	Bartlett [35]	34,976
36	30	H	Ipswich T	W	2-1	1-1	—	Svensson [12], Rufus [57]	20,043
37	May 5	A	Sunderland	L	2-3	1-2	9	Svensson [18], Jensen [60]	44,890
38	19	H	Liverpool	L	0-4	0-0	9		20,043

Final League Position: 9

GOALSCORERS

League (50): Johansson 11, Bartlett 7, Jensen 5 (1 pen), Stuart 5 (2 pens), Svensson 5, Hunt 4, Kinsella 2, Robinson 2, Rufus 2, Fish 1, Parker 1, Pringle 1, Todd 1, own goals 3.
Worthington Cup (5): Johansson 3, Lisbie 2.
FA Cup (4): Newton 1, Powell 1, Salako 1, Svensson 1.

Kiely D 25	Kishishev R 25 + 2	Powell C 31 + 2	Stuart G 33 + 2	Rufus R 32	Tiler C 7	Kinsella M 27 + 5	Jensen C 37 + 1	Hunt A 8	Lisbie K 5 + 13	Robinson J 21 + 8	Brown S 15 + 10	Newton S 1 + 9	Konchesky P 11 + 12	Parker S 15 + 5	Johansson J 27 + 4	Todd A 19 + 4	MacDonald C 1 + 2	Shields G 2 + 2	Salako J 4 + 13	Svensson M 18 + 4	Fish M 24	Bagheri K — + 1	Pringle M 1 + 7	Bartlett S 16 + 2	Caig T — + 1	Ilic S 13	Match No.
1	2	3	4	5	6	7	8^1	9	10^2	11^3	12	13	14														1
1	2	3	4	5	6	7	8^1	9	10^2	11^3	13	12			14												2
1	2	3	4	5	6	7^2	8^3	9	10^1	11			14		13	12											3
1	2	3	4	5		7	8^2	9	10^1	11^3	6	12			13	14											4
1	2^3	3	4	5	6	7	8	9^2	12	11^1	13		14		10												5
1		3	4	5		7	8^2	9^1	12	11		6	13	2	10												6
1		3	4^1	5		7	8	9^3		11		6	13	2	10^2	12	14										7
1		3	4	5		7	8	9^1	12	11^3	6			2^2	10			13	14								8
1		3	4	5		7	8	9^2		11^3	6			2^1	10		14	12	13								9
1		3	4		6	7	8				11	2			10^1	5		9^2	12	13							10
1		3^2	4		6	7	8		12	11^1		2		13	10	5		14	9^3								11
1		3	4	5		7	8^2		12	11		6			10^3	13		2	14	9^1							12
1		3	4			7	8		11^1			5			10			2	12	9^2	6	13					13
1	2	3	4	5		7	8^1					12			10	13			14	11^2	6			9^3			14
1	2	3^3	4	5		7	8		12				13		10				14	11^1	6			9^3			15
1	2^1	3	4	5		7	8		12				13		10				14	11^2	6			9^3			16
1	2^2	3	4	5		7	8		12				13		10				14	11^1	6			9^3			17
1	2	3	11^1	4^3		7	8		12			5			10	13			14	9^2	6						18
1	2^2	3	4	5		7	8		11			12			10^3	13			14	9	6^1						19
1	2^2	3	4	5		7	8		11		6	12			10	13			14	9^3							20
1	2		7	5		8			12	13		3	11		10^2	4					6		14	9^3			21
1	2	12	7^1	5		8				13		3	11^3		10	4					6		14	9^3			22
1	2		7	5			8^3		12	13		3	11^2		10	4			14		6			9^1			23
1	2	12	7	5			8^3			13		3^1	11		10^2	4			14		6			9			24
1	2	3	7	5			8		12	13			11^2		10^3	4					6		15	9			25
	2	3	7	5		8^1							11		10	4			12					9		1	26
	2^2	3	7	5	12	8			13				11^1	14	10	4					6			9^3		1	27
	2	3	7	5	11^2	8^2			12			14		13	10^1	4			9		6					1	28
	2^1	3	7	5	13	8^2			12			14	11		10	4					6			9^3		1	29
	2^3	3		5		8			12				11		7^3	4	13		14		6			9		1	30
	2^1	3	7	5	13	8			12				11^2		10^3	4			14		6			9		1	31
	2^3	3	7^2	5	12	8^1			13			14	11		10	4					6			9		1	32
	2^1			5		7	12		11			3		8^2	10	4	13		9^3		6		14			1	33
				5		7	8		12	13		3^3	11^2	2	10^1	4			14		6			9		1	34
	12	13	7	5		8						14	11^2	2^1	10	4			3		6			9		1	35
	12	3	7	5		8^3			13			14	11^1	2	10^2	4					6			9		1	36
	12	3	7	11		8			13			5		2^3	10^2	4^1			14		6			9		1	37
		3	4			7	8			11^3		13	14	2	5^2	10			12		6			9		1	38

Worthington Cup

Second Round	Stoke C	(a)	1-2
		(h)	4-3

FA Cup

Third Round	Dagenham & R	(h)	1-1
		(a)	1-0
Fourth Round	Tottenham H	(h)	2-4

CHELSEA   FA Premiership

FOUNDATION

Chelsea may never have existed but for the fact that Fulham rejected an offer to rent the Stamford Bridge ground from Mr H. A. Mears who had owned it since 1904. Fortunately he was determined to develop it as a football stadium rather than sell it to the Great Western Railway and got together with Frederick Parker, who persuaded Mears of the financial advantages of developing a major sporting venue. Chelsea FC was formed in 1905, and when admission to the Southern League was denied, they immediately gained admission to the Second Division of the Football League.

Stamford Bridge, London SW6 1HS.

Telephone: (020) 7385 5545. *Fax:* (020) 7381 4831. *ClubCall:* 09068 121 159. *Ticket News and Promotions:* 09068 121 011. *Ticket Credit Card Service:* (020) 7386 7799.

Ground Capacity: 42,420.

Record Attendance: 82,905 v Arsenal, Division 1, 12 October 1935.

Record Receipts: £488,960 v Liverpool, FA Premier League, 30 December 1995.

Pitch Measurements: 113yd × 74yd.

Chairman: K. W. Bates.
Directors: C. Hutchinson (Managing), Ms Y. S. Todd. *Financial Director:* M. Russell ACMA.

Head Coach: Claudio Ranieri. *Assistant Manager:* Gwyn Williams. *First Team Coach:* Angelo Antenucci. *Physio:* Michael Banks. *Reserve Team Manager:* Mick McGiven.

Company Secretary: Alan Shaw.

Assistant Secretary: Claire Lait.

Corporate Sales Manager: Carole Phair.

Safety Officer: Jill Dawson.

HONOURS

Football League: Division 1 – Champions 1954–55; Division 2 – Champions 1983–84, 1988–89; Runners-up 1906–07, 1911–12, 1929–30, 1962–63, 1976–77.

FA Cup: Winners 1970, 1997, 2000; Runners-up 1915, 1967, 1994.

Football League Cup: Winners 1965, 1998; Runners-up 1972.

Full Members' Cup: Winners 1986.

Zenith Data Systems Cup: Winners 1990.

European Competitions: *European Cup:* 1999–2000. *European Fairs Cup:* 1958–60, 1965–66, 1968–69. *European Cup-Winners' Cup:* 1970–71 (winners), 1971–72, 1994–95, 1997–98 (winners), 1998–99 (semi-finals). *Super Cup:* 1998–99 (winners).

Colours: Royal blue shirts and shorts with white trim, white stockings with royal blue trim.

Change Colours: White shirts and shorts with royal blue trim, royal blue stockings with white trim.

Year Formed: 1905. *Turned Professional:* 1905. *Ltd Co.:* 1905. *Club Nickname:* 'The Blues'.

First Football League Game: 2 September 1905, Division 2, v Stockport Co (a) L 0–1 – Foulke; Mackie, McEwan; Key, Harris, Miller; Moran, J. T. Robertson, Copeland, Windridge, Kirwan.

IT'S A FACT !

On 17 April 2001, Chelsea won 3–0 at Tottenham Hotspur to extend their unbeaten League record against Spurs to 11 years, since losing 2–0 at home on 10 February 1990.

Record League Victory: 9–2 v Glossop N E, Division 2, 1 September 1906 – Byrne; Walton, Miller; Key (1), McRoberts, Henderson; Moran, McDermott (1), Hilsdon (5), Copeland (1), Kirwan (1).

Record Cup Victory: 13–0 v Jeunesse Hautcharage, ECWC, 1st rd 2nd leg, 29 September 1971 – Bonetti; Boyle, Harris (1), Hollins (1p), Webb (1), Hinton, Cooke, Baldwin (3), Osgood (5), Hudson (1), Houseman (1).

Record Defeat: 1–8 v Wolverhampton W, Division 1, 26 September 1953.

Most League Points (2 for a win): 57, Division 2, 1906–07.

Most League Points (3 for a win): 99, Division 2, 1988–89.

Most League Goals: 98, Division 1, 1960–61.

Highest League Scorer in Season: Jimmy Greaves, 41, 1960–61.

Most League Goals in Total Aggregate: Bobby Tambling, 164, 1958–70.

Most League Goals in One Match: 5, George Hilsdon v Glossop, Division 2, 1 September 1906; 5, Jimmy Greaves v Wolverhampton W, Division 1, 30 August 1958; 5, Jimmy Greaves v Preston NE, Division 1, 19 December 1959; 5, Jimmy Greaves v WBA, Division 1, 3 December 1960; 5, Bobby Tambling v Aston Villa, Division 1, 17 September 1966; 5, Gordon Durie v Walsall, Division 2, 4 February 1989.

Most Capped Player: Dan Petrescu, 43 (95), Romania.

Most League Appearances: Ron Harris, 655, 1962–80.

Youngest League Player: Ian Hamilton, 16 years 138 days v Tottenham H, 18 March 1967.

Record Transfer Fee Received: £4,500,000 from Leeds U for Michael Duberry, July 1999 and a reported figure of £4,500,000 from Sunderland for Emerson, August 2000.

Record Transfer Fee Paid: £15,000,000 to Atletico Madrid for Jimmy Floyd Hasselbaink, June 2000.

Football League Record: 1905 Elected to Division 2; 1907–10 Division 1; 1910–12 Division 2; 1912–24 Division 1; 1924–30 Division 2; 1930–62 Division 1; 1962–63 Division 2; 1963–75 Division 1; 1975–77 Division 2; 1977–79 Division 1; 1979–84 Division 2; 1984–88 Division 1; 1988–89 Division 2; 1989–92 Division 1; 1992– FA Premier League.

MANAGERS

John Tait Robertson 1905–07
David Calderhead 1907–33
Leslie Knighton 1933–39
Billy Birrell 1939–52
Ted Drake 1952–61
Tommy Docherty 1962–67
Dave Sexton 1967–74
Ron Suart 1974–75
Eddie McCreadie 1975–77
Ken Shellito 1977–78
Danny Blanchflower 1978–79
Geoff Hurst 1979–81
John Neal 1981–85 *(Director to 1986)*
John Hollins 1985–88
Bobby Campbell 1988–91
Ian Porterfield 1991–93
David Webb 1993
Glenn Hoddle 1993–96
Ruud Gullit 1996–98
Gianluca Vialli 1998–2000
Claudio Ranieri September 2000–

LATEST SEQUENCES

Longest Sequence of League Wins: 8, 15.3.89 – 8.4.89.

Longest Sequence of League Defeats: 7, 1.11.52 – 20.12.52.

Longest Sequence of League Draws: 6, 20.8.69 – 13.9.69.

Longest Sequence of Unbeaten League Matches: 27, 29.10.88 – 8.4.89.

Longest Sequence Without a League Win: 21, 3.11.87 – 2.4.88.

TEN YEAR LEAGUE RECORD

		P	W	D	L	F	A	Pts	Pos
1990-91	Div 1	38	13	10	15	58	69	49	11
1991-92	Div 1	42	13	14	15	50	60	53	14
1992-93	PR Lge	42	14	14	14	51	54	56	11
1993-94	PR Lge	42	13	12	17	49	53	51	14
1994-95	PR Lge	42	13	15	14	50	55	54	11
1995-96	PR Lge	38	12	14	12	46	44	50	11
1996-97	PR Lge	38	16	11	11	58	55	59	6
1997-98	PR Lge	38	20	3	15	71	43	63	4
1998-99	PR Lge	38	20	15	3	57	30	75	3
1999-2000	PR Lge	38	18	11	9	53	34	65	5

DID YOU KNOW ?

Chelsea began the post-war transfer rush in 1945 by signing Len Goulden (West Ham U), Johnny Harris (Wolverhampton W) and Tommy Lawton (Everton) the latter for a then record fee of £11,500.

CHELSEA 2000–01 LEAGUE RECORD

Match No.	Date	Venue	Opponents	Result	H/T Score	Lg. Pos.	Goalscorers	Atten- dance
1	Aug 19	H	West Ham U	W 4-2	1-0	—	Hasselbaink (pen) [31], Zola [59], Stanic 2 [78, 90]	34,914
2	22	A	Bradford C	L 0-2	0-1	—		17,872
3	27	A	Aston Villa	D 1-1	1-1	10	Desailly [30]	27,056
4	Sept 6	H	Arsenal	D 2-2	1-0	—	Hasselbaink [31], Zola [58]	34,923
5	9	A	Newcastle U	D 0-0	0-0	10		51,687
6	17	H	Leicester C	L 0-2	0-1	17		33,697
7	23	A	Manchester U	D 3-3	2-3	16	Hasselbaink [8], Flo 2 [45, 70]	67,568
8	Oct 1	H	Liverpool	W 3-0	2-0	12	Westerveld (og) [10], Hasselbaink [11], Gudjohnsen [71]	34,966
9	14	A	Sunderland	L 0-1	0-0	15		43,185
10	21	H	Coventry C	W 6-1	2-0	10	Hasselbaink 4 (1 pen) [25 (p), 42, 52, 58], Zola [48], Flo [68]	34,646
11	28	H	Tottenham H	W 3-0	2-0	6	Hasselbaink 2 (1 pen) [13 (p), 87], Zola [39]	34,934
12	Nov 4	A	Southampton	L 2-3	0-2	11	Wise [69], Poyet [78]	15,236
13	12	H	Leeds U	D 1-1	0-0	10	Poyet [79]	35,121
14	18	A	Charlton Ath	L 0-2	0-1	14		20,043
15	25	A	Everton	L 1-2	1-0	14	Dalla Bona [45]	33,515
16	Dec 3	H	Manchester C	W 2-1	2-0	14	Zola [28], Hasselbaink [45]	34,971
17	9	H	Derby Co	W 4-1	3-0	11	Gudjohnsen 2 [10, 16], Poyet [37], Zola [54]	34,315
18	16	A	Middlesbrough	L 0-1	0-0	12		29,420
19	23	H	Bradford C	W 3-0	1-0	9	Poyet [22], Dalla Bona [68], Gudjohnsen [90]	33,377
20	26	A	Ipswich T	D 2-2	2-1	10	Gudjohnsen 2 [8, 17]	22,240
21	Jan 1	H	Aston Villa	W 1-0	1-0	9	Hasselbaink [45]	33,159
22	13	A	Arsenal	D 1-1	0-1	9	Terry [62]	38,071
23	20	A	Ipswich T	W 4-1	1-1	8	Poyet 2 [45, 65], Wise [58], Hasselbaink (pen) [73]	34,948
24	31	H	Newcastle U	W 3-1	1-1	—	Zola [37], Poyet [62], Gronkjaer [79]	35,108
25	Feb 3	A	Leicester C	L 1-2	0-1	8	Hasselbaink [75]	21,502
26	10	H	Manchester U	D 1-1	1-0	9	Hasselbaink [24]	34,960
27	Mar 3	A	Coventry C	D 0-0	0-0	10		21,708
28	7	A	West Ham U	W 2-0	2-0	—	Gudjohnsen [32], Hasselbaink [38]	26,016
29	17	H	Sunderland	L 2-4	2-1	9	Desailly [15], Gudjohnsen [38]	34,981
30	31	H	Middlesbrough	W 2-1	1-0	7	Zola [35], Gudjohnsen [63]	34,933
31	Apr 7	A	Derby Co	W 4-0	0-0	6	Zola [64], Hasselbaink [85], Poyet 2 [89, 90]	29,320
32	14	H	Southampton	W 1-0	1-0	5	Poyet [43]	35,136
33	17	A	Tottenham H	W 3-0	1-0	—	Hasselbaink [29], Poyet [60], Gudjohnsen [90]	36,079
34	21	H	Charlton Ath	L 0-1	0-0	6		34,976
35	28	A	Leeds U	L 0-2	0-0	6		39,253
36	May 5	H	Everton	W 2-1	2-1	6	Hasselbaink 2 [32, 35]	35,196
37	8	A	Liverpool	D 2-2	1-1	—	Hasselbaink 2 [13, 67]	43,588
38	19	A	Manchester C	W 2-1	1-1	6	Wise [19], Hasselbaink [62]	34,479

Final League Position: 6

GOALSCORERS

League (68): Hasselbaink 23 (4 pens), Poyet 11, Gudjohnsen 10, Zola 9, Flo 3, Wise 3, Dalla Bona 2, Desailly 2, Stanic 2, Gronkjaer 1, Terry 1, own goal 1.
Worthington Cup (1): Zola 1.
FA Cup (10): Gudjohnsen 3, Gronkjaer 2, Hasselbaink 2, Zola 2, Poyet 1.

De Goey E 15	Melchiot M 27 + 4	Babayaro C 19 + 5	Stanic M 8 + 4	Panucci C 7 + 1	Desailly M 34	Poyet G 22 + 8	Di Matteo R 7	Hasselbaink J 35	Zola G 31 + 5	Wise D 35 + 1	Le Saux G 18 + 2	Morris J 13 + 8	Flo T 5 + 9	Harley J 6 + 4	Emerson1	Cudicini C 23 + 1	Leboeuf F 23 + 2	Gudjohnsen E 17 + 13	Dalla Bona S 26 + 3	Bogarde W 2 + 7	Ferrer A 12 + 2	Jokanovic S 7 + 12	Terry J 19 + 3	Aleksidze R — + 2	Gronkjaer J 6 + 8	Lambourde B — + 1	Match No.
1	2	3^1	4	5	6	7^2	8	9	10^3	11	12	13	14														1
1	2^2	3^3	13		6	7	8	9^1	10	11			4	12	14	5											2
		3	4^1	2	6	7	8	9^2		11		12	10			1	5	13									3
12	3		2		6	7^1	4	9	10^2	8	11^3	14	13			1	5										4
7^2			2	6		4	9	12	8	3	13	10^1	11^1			1	5	14									5
12			2^1	6		8	9^2	7	11	3	4	10				1	13	5									6
12			2	6		8	9^3	7^2	3	4	10	11^1				1	5	13	14								7
1	4	12			6		9^2	10	11	3	14	13					5	7	8^3		2^1						8
1	4	12			6		9^3	10	11	3		13					5^3	7^1	8	14	2						9
1	4	3^2			6	7		9	10	11		12					5		8^3	13	2^1	14					10
1	4	3			6	7^1		9	10^2	11		12					5		8		2	13					11
1		3	2			7		9	10^2	11			8^1				5	12	6				13	4			12
1	4	3			6	7		9	10^1	11		13	12				5	14	8^2		2^3						13
1	2	3			6	7^2		9^3	10	11		4	12				5	13	8^1			14					14
1	2				6	12		9	10^3	11		13			14		5	7	8	3^1		4^2					15
1	2	3^2			6	12		9	10			11	13				5	7^1	8	14		4^3					16
1^6	4	3			6^1	7		10	2			11			15		9^2	8	12				5	13			17
1	4				6	7		10^2	2			11	3^1				12	9	8				5	13			18
1	2^2				6	7^3			10	11		12	3				5^1	9	8	13			14	4			19
1	2^2				6			9^3	10^1	3		11	12				5	7	8	13			14	4			20
2						7		9^1	12	13		11			3^2	1	5	10^3	8	14	6	4					21
					6	7		9	12	2			3			1	5^2	10^1	8	13	11^3	4			14		22
12	3				6	4		9	11	7						1		10^1	8^2		2^3	13	5		14		23
	4	6	12					7^1	9	10^2	7	3^3				1	5	13	8		2				14		24
	4	3	12					6^2	9	10^2	7					1	5	13	8		2	14			11^1		25
	3				6			9	10^1	7						1	5	12	8		2^3	13	4		11^{2}	14	26
	12				6	6^3	7^1	9	13	8	3					1	5	10^2			2	4	14		11		27
	4	4^1			6	12		9		7	3^3					1	5	10	13		2	8^1	14		11		28
	4	4^1			6	12		9	13	7	3					1	5	10			2^3	8	14		11^{2}		29
	2^1	4			6			9	10	7	12					1		13	8				5		11^{2}		30
	2^{12}	4			6	13		9	10^1	11	3^3					1		7^2	8				5		14		31
	2	4^1			6	7		9	10	11	3					1			8			12	5				32
	2	3^{12}	4		6	4^1		9	10^2	7	11^3					1		13	8				5		14		33
	2	4			6	7		9	10^1	11	3					1		13	8				5		13		34
	2	3			6	12		9	10^3	7	11^2	4^1				1		13	8				5		14		35
	2^{12}				6	7^1		9	10^2	11	3	4				1		8^3				13	5		14		36
	2^{12}				6	13		9	10^2	11	3	4^3				1		7^1	8			14	5				37
	2^2	3^1			6	12		9	10	7	11	8^9				1	13	14				4	5				38

Worthington Cup
Third Round   Liverpool   (a)   1-2

FA Cup
Third Round   Peterborough U   (h)   5-0
Fourth Round   Gillingham   (a)   4-2
Fifth Round   Arsenal   (a)   1-3

CHELTENHAM TOWN   Division 3

FOUNDATION

Although a scratch team representing Cheltenham played a match against Gloucester in 1884, the earliest recorded match for Cheltenham Town FC was a friendly against Dean Close School on 12 March 1892. The School won 4–3 and the match was played at Prestbury (half a mile from Whaddon Road). Cheltenham Town played Wednesday afternoon friendlies at a local cricket ground until entering the Mid Gloucester League. In those days the club played in deep red coloured shirts and were nicknamed 'the Rubies'. The club moved to Whaddon Lane for season 1901–02 and changed to red and white colours two years later.

Whaddon Road, Cheltenham, Gloucester GL52 5NA.

Telephone: (01242) 573 558.

Fax: (01242) 224 675.

ClubCall: 09066 555 833.

Website: www.cheltenham-town.co.uk

Ground Capacity: 6114.

Record Attendance: at Whaddon Road: 8326 v Reading, FA Cup 1st rd, 17 November 1956; at Cheltenham Athletic Ground: 10,389 v Blackpool, FA Cup 3rd rd, 13 January 1934.

Record Receipts: £40,000 v Yeovil T, Nationwide Conference, 22 April 1999.

Pitch Measurements: 111yd × 72yd.

Chairman: Paul Baker.

Directors: Rod Burge, Colin Farmer, Arthur Hayward, Brian Sandland, John Wood, Barrie Wood.

Manager: Steve Cotterill.

Assistant Manager: Mike Davis.

First Team Coach: Graham Allner.

Youth Team Manager: Bob Bloomer.

Secretary: Bob Hands.

Physio: Andy Mitchell. *Head of Youth:* Brian Forsbrook.

Colours: Red and white striped shirts, white shorts, red stockings.

Change Colours: All orange.

HONOURS

Football Conference: Champions 1998–99, runners-up 1997–98.

FA Trophy: Winners 1997–98.

Southern League: Champions 1984–85; *Southern League Cup:* Winners 1957–58, runners-up 1968–69, 1984–85; *Southern League Merit Cup:* Winners 1984–85; *Southern League Championship Shield:* Winners 1985.

Gloucestershire Senior Cup: Winners 1998–99; *Gloucestershire Northern Senior Professional Cup:* Winners 30 times; *Midland Floodlit Cup:* Winners 1985–86, 1986–87, 1987–88; *Mid Gloucester League:* Champions 1896–97; *Gloucester and District League:* Champions 1902–03, 1905–06; *Cheltenham League:* Champions 1910–11, 1913–14; *North Gloucestershire League:* Champions 1913–14; *Gloucestershire Northern Senior League:* Champions 1928–29, 1932–33; *Gloucestershire Northern Senior Amateur Cup:* Winners 1929–30, 1930–31, 1932–33, 1933–34, 1934–35; *Leamington Hospital Cup:* Winners 1934–35.

IT'S A FACT !

On 18 November 2000, Cheltenham Town's 4-1 win over Shrewsbury Town in the FA Cup first round was their first such success in the competition against League opposition since beating Carlisle United 2-1 in December 1933.

Year Formed: 1892.

Turned Professional: 1932.

Ltd Co.: 1937.

Club Nickname: 'The Robins'.

Previous Grounds: Grafton Cricket Ground, Whaddon Lane, Carter's Field (pre 1932).

Record League Victory: 11–0 v Bourneville Ath, Birmingham Combination, 29 April 1933 – Davis; Jones, Williams; Lang (1), Blackburn, Draper; Evans, Hazard (4), Haycox (4), Goodger (1), Hill (1).

Record Cup Victory: 12–0 v Chippenham R, FA Cup 3rd qual. rd, 2 November 1935 – Bowles; Whitehouse, Williams; Lang, Devonport (1), Partridge (2); Perkins, Hackett, Jones (4), Black (4), Griffiths (1).

Record Defeat: 1–10 v Merthyr T, Southern League, 8 March 1952.

Most League Points (2 for a win): 60, Southern League Division 1, 1963–64.

Most League Points (3 for a win): 86, Southern League Premier Division, 1994–95.

Most League Goals: 115, Southern League, 1957–58.

Highest League Scorer in Season: Dave Lewis, 33 (53 in all competitions), Southern League Division 1, 1974–75.

Most League Goals in Total Aggregate: Dave Lewis, 205 (290 in all competitions), 1970–83.

Most League Appearances: Roger Thorndale, 523 (702 in all competitions), 1958–76.

Record Transfer Fee Received: £60,000 from Southampton for Christer Warren, 1995.

Record Transfer Fee Paid: £25,000 to Kidderminster H for Kim Casey, 1991.

MANAGERS

George Blackburn 1932–34
George Carr 1934–37
Jimmy Brain 1937–48
Cyril Dean 1948–50
George Summerbee 1950–52
William Raeside 1952–53
Arch Anderson 1953–58
Ron Lewin 1958–60
Peter Donnelly 1960–61
Tommy Cavanagh 1961
Arch Anderson 1961–65
Harold Fletcher 1965–66
Bob Etheridge 1966–73
Willie Penman 1973–74
Dennis Allen 1974–79
Terry Paine 1979
Alan Grundy 1979–82
Alan Wood 1982–83
John Murphy 1983–88
Jim Barron 1988–90
John Murphy 1990
Dave Lewis 1990–91
Ally Robertson 1991–92
Lindsay Parsons 1992–95
Chris Robinson 1995–97
Steve Cotterill 1997–

LATEST SEQUENCES

Longest Sequence of League Wins: not more than 3.

Longest Sequence of League Defeats: 5, 13.1.01 – 13.2.01.

Longest Sequence of League Draws: not more than 2.

Longest Sequence of Unbeaten League Matches: 12, 24.2.01 – 16.4.01.

Longest Sequence Without a League Win: 5, 13.1.01 – 13.2.01.

TEN YEAR LEAGUE RECORD

		P	W	D	L	F	A	Pts	Pos
1990–91	Conf	42	12	12	18	54	72	48	16
1991–92	Conf	42	10	13	19	56	82	43	21
1992–93	Sth L	40	21	10	9	76	40	73	2
1993–94	Sth L	42	21	12	9	67	38	75	2
1994–95	Sth L	42	25	11	6	87	39	86	2
1995–96	Sth L	42	21	11	10	76	57	74	3
1996–97	Sth L	42	21	11	10	76	44	74	2
1997–98	Conf	42	23	9	10	63	43	78	2
1998-99	Conf	42	22	14	6	71	36	80	1
1999-2000	Div 3	46	20	10	16	50	42	70	8

DID YOU KNOW ?

On 13 January 1934, though a fine crowd of 10,389 watched Cheltenham Town play Blackpool in the third round of the FA Cup, it was the lowest attendance of the round.

CHELTENHAM TOWN 2000–01 LEAGUE RECORD

Match No.	Date	Venue	Opponents	Result		H/T Score	Lg. Pos.	Goalscorers	Attendance
1	Aug 12	H	Mansfield T	D	2-2	1-1	—	Blake (og) [16], Howarth [87]	4051
2	19	A	York C	W	2-0	1-0	6	Grayson 2 [19, 86]	2793
3	26	H	Torquay U	W	2-0	1-0	2	Victory [45], Howarth [68]	3568
4	28	A	Hartlepool U	D	0-0	0-0	4		2870
5	Sept 2	A	Hull C	W	2-0	0-0	1	Alsop [50], Devaney [66]	4750
6	9	H	Chesterfield	L	0-1	0-0	3		3870
7	12	H	Darlington	W	1-0	0-0	—	Duff [76]	2368
8	16	A	Brighton & HA	L	0-3	0-0	4		6325
9	23	H	Plymouth Arg	W	5-2	4-0	3	Griffin [8], Devaney 3 (1 pen) [24, 41, 79 (p)], Howells [36]	3665
10	30	A	Exeter C	W	2-0	0-0	3	Devaney 2 [62, 73]	3978
11	Oct 6	H	Carlisle U	W	1-0	0-0	—	Duff [53]	4264
12	14	A	Macclesfield T	L	1-2	0-0	4	Alsop [50]	2035
13	17	A	Halifax T	W	2-1	2-0	—	Yates [9], McAuley [33]	1382
14	21	H	Rochdale	L	0-2	0-1	4		4033
15	24	A	Lincoln C	L	0-1	0-0	—		2194
16	28	H	Blackpool	L	0-1	0-1	5		3798
17	Nov 4	A	Kidderminster H	D	1-1	0-1	7	Banks [68]	4162
18	11	H	Leyton Orient	D	1-1	0-0	7	Grayson [56]	3375
19	25	A	Southend U	W	1-0	1-0	7	Grayson [42]	4199
20	Dec 2	H	Barnet	W	4-3	2-2	6	McAuley 2 [9, 36], Alsop 2 [62, 89]	3599
21	16	A	Cardiff C	L	1-3	0-1	6	Devaney [80]	6764
22	23	A	Scunthorpe U	D	1-1	1-1	6	Grayson [37]	3275
23	26	H	Shrewsbury T	D	1-1	0-0	6	Devaney [84]	4439
24	Jan 6	A	Torquay U	W	2-1	0-1	6	Devaney 2 [53, 81]	2383
25	13	H	Hartlepool U	L	1-2	1-0	7	Yates [44]	3574
26	20	A	Shrewsbury T	L	0-1	0-1	8		2844
27	Feb 3	H	Hull C	L	0-1	0-1	9		3360
28	9	A	Chesterfield	L	0-2	0-2	—		4186
29	13	A	Mansfield T	L	1-2	0-2	—	Iwelumo [68]	1940
30	17	H	Brighton & HA	W	3-1	2-1	9	McCann [9], Alsop [10], Bloomer [70]	4533
31	20	A	Darlington	L	0-1	0-1	—		2689
32	24	A	Plymouth Arg	D	0-0	0-0	10		5209
33	27	H	Scunthorpe U	W	1-0	0-0	—	Howarth [70]	2481
34	Mar 3	H	Exeter C	W	1-0	1-0	9	Yates [6]	3913
35	6	H	Macclesfield T	D	1-1	0-0	—	Yates [57]	3091
36	10	A	Carlisle U	D	1-1	0-1	8	Grayson [65]	3280
37	17	H	Halifax T	W	4-2	3-1	8	Goodridge [10], Grayson [13], Yates [43], Milton [48]	3134
38	20	A	York C	D	1-1	1-0	—	Yates [90]	2669
39	23	A	Rochdale	D	1-1	1-0	—	Grayson [12]	2713
40	Apr 1	H	Cardiff C	W	3-1	2-1	7	Grayson 3 [37, 41, 49]	5139
41	7	A	Barnet	D	2-2	1-1	7	Duff [14], McCann [90]	1977
42	14	A	Lincoln C	W	2-1	2-1	—	Duff 2 [6, 17]	4012
43	16	A	Blackpool	D	2-2	1-1	8	MacDonald 2 [35, 76]	5192
44	21	H	Kidderminster H	L	1-3	0-2	8	Grayson [54]	4415
45	28	A	Leyton Orient	D	0-0	0-0	10		5640
46	May 5	H	Southend U	W	2-1	0-0	9	Grayson [48], McCann [86]	3637

Final League Position: 9

GOALSCORERS

League (59): Grayson 13, Devaney 10 (1 pen), Yates 6, Alsop 5, Duff 5, Howarth 3, McAuley 3, McCann 3, MacDonald 2, Banks 1, Bloomer 1, Goodridge 1, Griffin 1, Howells 1, Iwelumo 1, Milton 1, Victory 1, own goal 1.
Worthington Cup (0).
FA Cup (5): Grayson 2, Alsop 1, Howells 1, Milton 1.

Book S 46	Duff M 39	Victory J 3	Banks C 40	Brough J 4+6	Howarth N 19+4	Howells L 36	Walker R 35+1	Grayson N 23+8	McAuley H 30+5	Yates M 45	White J 8+19	Alsop J 29+10	Griffin A 14+8	Freeman M 25+2	Devaney M 23+11	Bloomer B 5+7	Jackson M 2+4	Hopkins G 1+3	McCann G 27+3	Milton R 18+1	Jones M 1+1	Clare D 4	Iwelumo C 2+2	Goodridge G 10+1	Sertori M 10	MacDonald C 7+1	Higgs S —+1	Match No.
1	2	3	4	5	6	7	8¹	9²	10	11	12	13																1
1	2	3	4	5	6		8	9¹	10	11	12	7																2
1	2	3¹	4	5¹	6		8		10	11		9	7	12	13													3
1	2		4		6		8				11	9²	7	12	5	3¹	10	13										4
1	2		4		6		8				11	9	7		5	3	10											5
1	2		4	12	6		8		10	11		9		13	5¹	3			7²									6
1	2		4	12	6		3		10¹	11		9	7		5	8												7
1	2		4	12	6		3		10	11		9²	7		5	8	13											8
1	2²		4	12	6	7²	3		10	11	13	9			5	8	14											9
1	2		4	12	6	7	3		10¹	11	13	9¹	14		5	8²												10
1	2³		4	12	6	7	3		10	11	13	9¹	14		5	8²												11
1	2		4	12	6	7	3³		10	11²	13	9	14		5¹	8												12
1	2		4	12	6	7	3		10¹	11	13	9²	14		5	8³												13
1	2		4	12	6	7	3³		10	11	13	9²			5¹	8	14											14
1	2		4		6²	7	3¹	9	10³	11	13			12	5	8	14											15
1	2		4		6²	7	3	12	10²	11		9			5	8¹			14	13								16
1	2		4			7³	3	12	10	11	13	9¹			5	8²			14	6								17
1	2		4	12		7	3	9	10	11	13				5	8²				6¹								18
1	2		4			7	3	9¹	10²	11	13			12	5	8				6								19
1	2		4			7	3	9¹	10	11	12				5	8				6								20
1	2		4			7	3	9¹	10²	11	12	13			5	8				6								21
1	2		4			7	3¹	9	10	11	12				5	8				6								22
1	2		4			7	3	9¹	10	11	12				5	8				6								23
1			4		10	7	3	9		11	12			5¹		8			2	6								24
1	2²		4	5	6	7	3	9	10¹	11	12	13				8												25
1	2¹		4	5	6	7	3	9	10	11	12					8												26
1	2		4		6	7	3	9	10¹	11		13		12²	5¹	8			14									27
1	2		4²	5		7	3	9	10	11	12	13				8				6¹								28
1	2¹		4		6	7	3	9	10²	11		13		12	5¹	8							14					29
1			4		6	7	3	9	10	11		13		12	5	8²			2									30
1			4		6	7	3	9	10	11¹		13		12	5¹	8			2									31
1	2¹		4		6	7	3	9	10³	11		13		12		8²				5			14					32
1	2³		4		6	7	3	9¹	10	11		13		12		8²				5			14					33
1	2		4			7¹	3	9¹	10	11		13		12		8²			6	5			14					34
1	2		4			7	3	9¹	10	11				12		8			6	5								35
1	2		4			7	3	9	10	11	12					8¹			6	5								36
1	2					7	3	9		11		13		12		8²			6	5			14	4¹		10²		37
1	2					7	3¹	9		11		13		12		8			6	5				4		10²		38
1	2					7	3	9		11		13		12		8			6	5²				4		10¹		39
1	2					7	3	9²		11		13		12		8			6	5				4		10¹		40
1³	2					7	3	9		11				12		8			6	5				4		10¹	15	41
1	2					7	3	9²		11		13		12		8			6	5				4		10¹		42
1	2					7	3	9		11²		13		12		8			6	5				4		10		43
1	2					7	3²	9		11		13		12		8			6	5¹			14	4³		10		44
1	2					7	3	9²	10	11		13		12		8			6	5				4¹				45
1	2					7³	3	9	10¹	11		13		12		8²			6	5			14	4				46

Worthington Cup

First Round	Watford		(a)	0-0
			(h)	0-3

FA Cup

First Round	Shrewsbury T		(h)	4-1
Second Round	Cardiff C		(a)	1-3

CHESTERFIELD

Division 2

FOUNDATION

Chesterfield are fourth only to Stoke, Notts County and Nottingham Forest in age for they can trace their existence as far back as 1866, although it is fair to say that they were somewhat casual in the first few years of their history playing only a few friendlies a year. However, their rules of 1871 are still in existence showing an annual membership of 2s (10p), but it was not until 1891 that they won a trophy (the Barnes Cup) and followed this a year later by winning the Sheffield Cup, Barnes Cup and the Derbyshire Junior Cup.

Recreation Ground, Chesterfield S40 4SX.

Telephone: (01246) 209 765. *Fax:* (01246) 550 930.
Commercial Dept: (01246) 231 535.
ClubCall: 09068 555 818.

Ground Capacity: 8960.

Record Attendance: 30,968 v Newcastle U, Division 2, 7 April 1939.

Record Receipts: £45,000 v Mansfield T, Division 3 play-off semi-final, 17 May 1995.

Pitch Measurements: 113yd × 71yd.

President: His Grace the Duke of Devonshire MC, DL, JP.

Chief Executive: John Green.

Manager: Nicky Law. *Assistant Manager:* Kevin Randall. *Physio:* Dave Rushbury.

Secretary: Stephanie Otter. *Commercial Manager:* Jim Brown. *Stadium Manager:* W. W. Kenworthy.

Colours: All blue.

Change Colours: White shirts, blue shorts, white stockings.

Year Formed: 1866.

Turned Professional: 1891.

Ltd Co: 1871.

Previous Name: Chesterfield Town.

Club Nickname: 'Blues' or 'Spireites'.

First Football League Game: 2 September 1899, Division 2, v Sheffield W (a) L 1–5 – Hancock; Pilgrim, Fletcher; Ballantyne, Bell, Downie; Morley, Thacker, Gooing, Munday (1), Geary.

Record League Victory: 10–0 v Glossop NE, Division 2, 17 January 1903 – Clutterbuck; Thorpe, Lerper; Haig, Banner, Thacker; Tomlinson (2), Newton (1), Milward (3), Munday (2), Steel (2).

Record Cup Victory: 5–0 v Wath Ath (a), FA Cup 1st rd, 28 November 1925 – Birch; Saxby, Dennis; Wass, Abbott, Thompson; Fisher (1), Roseboom (1), Cookson (2), Whitfield (1), Hopkinson.

HONOURS

Football League: Division 2 best season: 4th, 1946–47; Division 3 (N) – Champions 1930–31, 1935–36; Runners-up 1933–34; Promoted to Division 2 (3rd) – 2000–01; Division 4 – Champions 1969–70, 1984–85.
FA Cup: Semi-final 1997.
Football League Cup: best season: 4th rd, 1965.
Anglo-Scottish Cup: Winners 1981.

IT'S A FACT !

On 4 November 2000, Chesterfield drew 1-1 at Lincoln City to establish a club record of 13 games unbeaten away.

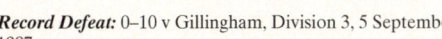
Record Defeat: 0–10 v Gillingham, Division 3, 5 September 1987.

Most League Points (2 for a win): 64, Division 4, 1969–70.

Most League Points (3 for a win): 91, Division 4, 1984–85.

Most League Goals: 102, Division 3 (N), 1930–31.

Highest League Scorer in Season: Jimmy Cookson, 44, Division 3 (N), 1925–26.

Most League Goals in Total Aggregate: Ernie Moss, 161, 1969–76, 1979–81 and 1984–86.

Most League Goals in One Match: 4, Jimmy Cookson v Accrington S, Division 3N, 16 January 1926; 4, Jimmy Cookson v Ashington, Division 3N, 1 May 1926; 4, Jimmy Cookson v Wigan Borough, Division 3N, 4 September 1926; 4, Tommy Lyon v Southampton, Division 2, 3 December 1938.

Most Capped Player: Walter McMillen, 4 (7), Northern Ireland; Mark Williams, 4 (11), Northern Ireland.

Most League Appearances: Dave Blakey, 613, 1948–67.

Youngest League Player: Dennis Thompson, 16 years 160 days v Notts Co, 26 December 1950.

Record Transfer Fee Received: £750,000 from Southampton for Kevin Davies, May 1997.

Record Transfer Fee Paid: £250,000 to Watford for Jason Lee, August 1998.

Football League Record: 1899 Elected to Division 2; 1909 failed re-election; 1921–31 Division 3 (N); 1931–33 Division 2; 1933–36 Division 3 (N); 1936–51 Division 2; 1951–58 Division 3 (N); 1958–61 Division 3; 1961–70 Division 4; 1970–83 Division 3; 1983–85 Division 4; 1985–89 Division 3; 1989–92 Division 4; 1992–95 Division 3; 1995–2000 Division 2; 2000–01 Division 3; 2001– Division 2.

MANAGERS

E. Russell Timmeus 1891–95
(Secretary-Manager)
Gilbert Gillies 1895–1901
E. F. Hind 1901–02
Jack Hoskin 1902–06
W. Furness 1906–07
George Swift 1907–10
G. H. Jones 1911–13
R. L. Weston 1913–17
T. Callaghan 1919
J. J. Caffrey 1920–22
Harry Hadley 1922
Harry Parkes 1922–27
Alec Campbell 1927
Ted Davison 1927–32
Bill Harvey 1932–38
Norman Bullock 1938–45
Bob Brocklebank 1945–48
Bobby Marshall 1948–52
Ted Davison 1952–58
Duggie Livingstone 1958–62
Tony McShane 1962–67
Jimmy McGuigan 1967–73
Joe Shaw 1973–76
Arthur Cox 1976–80
Frank Barlow 1980–83
John Duncan 1983–87
Kevin Randall 1987–88
Paul Hart 1988–91
Chris McMenemy 1991–93
John Duncan 1993– 2000
Nicky Law May 2000–

LATEST SEQUENCES

Longest Sequence of League Wins: 10, 6.9.33 – 4.11.33.

Longest Sequence of League Defeats: 9, 22.10.60 – 27.12.60.

Longest Sequence of League Draws: 5, 19.9.90 – 6.10.90.

Longest Sequence of Unbeaten League Matches: 21, 26.12.94 – 29.4.95.

Longest Sequence Without a League Win: 18, 11.9.99 – 3.1.00.

TEN YEAR LEAGUE RECORD

		P	W	D	L	F	A	Pts	Pos
1990-91	Div 4	46	13	14	19	47	62	53	18
1991-92	Div 4	42	14	11	17	49	61	53	13
1992-93	Div 3	42	15	11	16	59	63	56	12
1993-94	Div 3	42	16	14	12	55	48	62	8
1994-95	Div 3	42	23	12	7	62	37	81	3
1995-96	Div 2	46	20	12	14	56	51	72	7
1996-97	Div 2	46	18	14	14	42	39	68	10
1997-98	Div 2	46	16	17	13	46	44	65	10
1998-99	Div 2	46	17	13	16	46	44	64	9
1999-2000	Div 2	46	7	15	24	34	63	36	24

DID YOU KNOW ?

In 1891 Chesterfield won its first trophy, the Barnes Cup, put up by Alfred Barnes, the local Member of Parliament and local colliery owner. The club then recorded a hat-trick of these trophies.

CHESTERFIELD 2000–01 LEAGUE RECORD

Match No.	Date	Venue	Opponents	Result	H/T Score	Lg. Pos.	Goalscorers	Attendance
1	Aug 12	H	York C	W	4-1	0-1	—	Reeves [57], Parrish [66], Breckin [74], Williams R [80]	4745
2	19	A	Hartlepool U	W	2-1	1-1	1	Tutill [6], Willis [78]	3583
3	26	H	Shrewsbury T	W	3-0	2-0	1	Reeves 2 [13, 77], Parrish [31]	4338
4	28	A	Scunthorpe U	D	1-1	0-0	1	Willis [75]	5154
5	Sept 2	A	Barnet	L	1-2	0-1	3	Reeves [46]	4340
6	9	A	Cheltenham T	W	1-0	0-0	1	Beckett [66]	3870
7	12	A	Carlisle U	W	4-2	3-1	—	Ebdon [7], Willis 2 [30, 82], Williams R [38]	2929
8	16	H	Mansfield T	W	4-0	2-0	1	Edwards [4], Williams R 2 [39, 58], Beckett [52]	6793
9	23	H	Blackpool	W	3-1	2-0	1	Beckett [11], Williams R (pen) [12], Ebdon [73]	3970
10	30	H	Macclesfield T	W	4-1	3-1	1	Tinson (og) [27], Parrish 3 (1 pen) [30, 45, 62 (p)]	4904
11	Oct 7	H	Plymouth Arg	W	2-1	1-0	1	Parrish [38], Reeves (pen) [61]	4285
12	14	A	Exeter C	D	1-1	1-0	1	Payne [25]	2986
13	17	A	Rochdale	D	2-2	2-1	—	Monington (og) [36], Reeves [40]	5008
14	21	A	Brighton & HA	W	1-0	0-0	1	Ingledow [90]	7014
15	24	A	Kidderminster H	W	2-0	1-0	—	Breckin [38], Howard [67]	3844
16	28	H	Cardiff C	D	2-2	0-1	1	Williams R [54], Beckett [86]	5378
17	Nov 4	A	Lincoln C	D	1-1	0-0	1	Beckett [77]	4805
18	11	H	Hull C	W	1-0	0-0	1	Beckett [67]	5659
19	25	A	Halifax T	D	2-2	0-0	1	Willis [81], Edwards [85]	2769
20	Dec 2	H	Leyton Orient	W	4-1	4-1	1	Howard 2 [19, 34], Beckett [35], Parrish [39]	4985
21	9	H	Exeter C	W	2-0	1-0	1	Ebdon [4], Beckett [69]	4289
22	16	A	Southend U	L	2-3	1-2	1	Beckett 2 [2, 90]	3889
23	23	A	Torquay U	D	0-0	0-0	1		2248
24	26	H	Darlington	W	2-0	2-0	1	Parrish [26], Beckett [39]	5128
25	Jan 6	A	Shrewsbury T	D	0-0	0-0	1		3792
26	13	H	Scunthorpe U	W	1-0	0-0	1	Thom (og) [86]	4803
27	16	H	Hartlepool U	D	0-0	0-0	—		4240
28	20	A	Darlington	W	3-0	2-0	1	Reeves [34], Parrish [45], Dudfield [87]	3802
29	23	A	York C	W	1-0	0-0	—	Edwards [51]	2570
30	27	A	Torquay U	W	3-0	0-0	1	Ingledow [63], Reeves [74], Beckett [87]	4364
31	Feb 3	A	Barnet	D	1-1	1-0	1	Reeves (pen) [4]	2372
32	9	H	Cheltenham T	W	2-0	2-0	—	Reeves [10], Edwards [15]	4186
33	17	A	Mansfield T	W	1-0	1-0	1	Dudfield [6]	7899
34	20	H	Carlisle U	D	1-1	0-1	—	Beckett [90]	3796
35	24	H	Blackpool	W	2-1	1-0	1	Williams R [9], Dudfield [82]	4812
36	Mar 3	A	Macclesfield T	W	2-1	1-1	1	Beckett [41], Parrish [59]	2740
37	10	A	Plymouth Arg	L	0-3	0-1	1		5399
38	17	H	Rochdale	D	1-1	0-1	1	Howard [89]	4338
39	31	H	Southend U	D	1-1	0-1	1	Reeves [62]	4018
40	Apr 7	A	Leyton Orient	L	0-2	0-0	1		4793
41	14	H	Kidderminster H	W	1-0	1-0	1	Beckett [45]	4495
42	16	A	Cardiff C	D	3-3	2-1	1	Blatherwick [11], Reeves [42], Beckett [85]	13,602
43	21	H	Lincoln C	L	1-2	1-1	1	Williams R [26]	4856
44	28	A	Hull C	L	1-3	1-2	2	Breckin [16]	11,337
45	May 1	A	Brighton & HA	L	0-1	0-0	—		6847
46	5	H	Halifax T	W	3-0	0-0	3	Howard [52], Reeves [65], Ingledow [84]	5700

Final League Position: 3

GOALSCORERS

League (79): Beckett 16, Reeves 13 (2 pens), Parrish 10 (1 pen), Williams R 8 (1 pen), Howard 5, Willis 5, Edwards 4, Breckin 3, Dudfield 3, Ebdon 3, Ingledow 3, Blatherwick 1, Payne 1, Tutill 1, own goals 3.
Worthington Cup (5): Beckett 2, Breckin 1, Parrish 1, Reeves 1.
FA Cup (0).

Pollitt M 46	Breckin I 45	Parrish S 33+2	Tutill S 17+2	Blatherwick S 38	Simpkins J 14+2	Ebdon M 41	Williams R 39+6	Reeves D 34+3	Beckett L 38+3	Richardson L 30	Willis R 11+21	Ingledow J 14+10	Howard J 13+18	Perkins C 8	Galloway M 4+1	Payne S 33+2	Edwards R 34	Beaumont C 4+10	D'Auria D 4+2	Jones M —+3	Dudfield L 4+10	Williams D 1+1	Rushbury A —+2	Barrett D —+1	Pearce G 1	Armstrong J —+1	Match No.
1	2	3	4	5	6	7	8	9	10^1	11^1	12	13															1
1	2	3	4	5	6	7	8	9^1	10	11^1	12		13														2
1	6	8	4	5		7^1	2	9	10^2	11^1	12	13			14		3										3
1	6	8	4	5		7	2^2	9	10^1	11	12	13					3										4
1	6	8	4	5		7	2	9	10^2	11^1	12	13					3										5
1	6	8		5		7	2^1	9	10		12				11	4	3										6
1	6	8		5		7	2		10^1		9		12		11	4	3										7
1	6^1	8	12	5		7	2^3		10		9^2		13		11	4	3	14									8
1	6	8	12	5		7	2^3	13	10^2		9		14		11^1	4	3										9
1	6	8	4^3	5		7	2	9^1	10^2		12		13		11		3	14									10
1	6	8	4	5		7	2^1	9		11^2	12	13				10^1	3										11
1	6	8	4	5		7	2^1	9		11			12			10	3										12
1	2	6	4	5		7	12	9	10^1			8^2		3		11	13										13
1	2	6^1	4	5	3	7	8	9		11	12	13	10^2														14
1	2	6	4	5^2	3	7	8^1	9		11	12		10		13												15
1	2	6^1	4^3	5	3	7	8		12	11^2	9		10			14		13									16
1	2	6	4		3^1		8	9^2	10	11	13	7^3	12			5		14									17
1	2	7	4			5	8		10	11	9^1					6	3	12									18
1	6	11		4	5^2	2^1	7	8^3	10		9		12			3	13	14									19
1	5	6		4		7^2	12	10		9^3		8	2			3	13	11^1	14								20
1	6	4	5^1		12	7	13	14	10^3			8^2	2			3		11	9								21
1		6		5		7	12	13	10			8^2	2^3		4	3	14	11	9^2								22
1	2	3		5	12	7	8^3	10			14	13			4		6^2	11^1	9								23
1	2	6		5		7	8	10	11				9^1		4	3		12									24
1	2	6		5			8	10	11	9^1	12	7^2			4	3		13									25
1	2	6		5		7	8^3	9	10	11^1	12				4	3		13									26
1	2	6		5		7	8^3	9	10	11^2	12	13			4	3		14									27
1	2	6^1		5		7	8	9	10^2	11	12				4	3		13									28
1	6			5		7	2^2	9^1	10	11	12	8			4	3	13										29
1	2			5		7	8	9	10	11	6				4	3											30
1	4	12		5	6	7	2^3	9	10^2	11^3	13	8			3		14										31
1	6	12		5		7	2^1	9	10	11		8^2			4	3		13									32
1	2	6		5				9	10	11	7				4	3	12	8^1									33
1	2			5	6^2		8^3	9^1	10	11	12	7			4	3	14	13									34
1	2	6		5		7	8^1	9	10	11					4	3		12									35
1	2	6		5		7	8^2	9	10	11	12				4	3		13									36
1	2	6		5		7	8	9	10	11^1		12			4	3											37
1	2	6^1		5		7	8^2	9^3	12		13	14	10			4	3				11						38
1	2			5	7	12	9	10	11	13	6	8^1			3	4^2											39
1	2		5	6	7	12	9	10^2	11	13	14	8^1			4^3	3											40
1	6			5		7	2	9^1	10	11	12	8			4	3											41
1	6			5^1		7	2^2	9	10	11^1	12	8	13			4	3	14									42
1	6			5		7	2	9	10	11^1	12^2	8	14			4	3	5^3			13						43
1	6			5	2^1	7	8	9	10				11	12		4	3										44
1	6			5		7	8^3	9	12			11	10^1			4	3	5^2					14	13	2		45
1	6			5		7	2	9	10^2	11			8	12		4	3^1							13		15	46

Worthington Cup

First Round	Port Vale	(a)	2-1
		(h)	2-2
Second Round	Fulham	(h)	1-0
		(a)	0-4

FA Cup

First Round	Bristol C	(h)	0-1

COLCHESTER UNITED

Division 2

FOUNDATION

Colchester United was formed in 1937 when a number of enthusiasts of the much older Colchester Town club decided to establish a professional concern as a limited liability company. The new club continued at Layer Road which had been the amateur club's home since 1909.

Layer Rd Ground, Colchester, Essex CO2 7JJ.

Telephone: (01206) 508 800. *Fax:* (01206) 508 803.
Club Shop: (01206) 508 809.
Soccer Centre: (01206) 572 378. *Lottery:* (01206) 508 820.

Ground Capacity: 7556.

Record Attendance: 19,072 v Reading, FA Cup 1st rd, 27 November 1948.

Record Receipts: £26,330 v Barrow, GM Vauxhall Conference, 2 May 1992.

Pitch Measurements: 110yd × 71yd.

Patron: The Mayor of Colchester.

Chairman: Peter Heard.

Directors: John Worsp, Peter Powell.

Manager: Steve Whitton.

Assistant Manager/Coach: Geraint Williams.

Director of Youth: Micky Cook.

Physios: Brian Owen, Andy Hunt.

Consultant Physio: Ray Cole.

Secretary: Miss Sonia Constantine.

Corporate and Promotions Consultant: John Schultz.

Commercial and Marketing Manager: Jerry Carter.

Lottery Manager: John Cross.

Stadium Manager: David Blacknall.

Colours: Blue and white striped shirts, navy shorts, white stockings.

Change Colours: Red shirts with black side panels, black shorts with red side stripes, black stockings with red turnover.

Year Formed: 1937.

Turned Professional: 1937.

Ltd Co.: 1937.

Club Nickname: 'The U's'.

First Football League Game: 19 August 1950, Division 3 (S), v Gillingham (a) D 0–0 – Wright; Kettle; Allen; Bearryman, Stewart, Elder; Jones, Curry, Turner, McKim, Church.

HONOURS

Football League: Promoted from Division 3 – 1997–98 (play-offs); Division 4 – Runners-up 1961–62.

FA Cup: best season: 6th rd, 1971.

Football League Cup: best season: 5th rd, 1975.

Auto Windscreens Shield: Runners-up 1997.

GM Vauxhall Conference: Winners 1991–92.

FA Trophy: Winners 1992.

IT'S A FACT !

On 30 April 1962, Colchester United ensured promotion with a 5-3 win over Doncaster Rovers in front of a crowd of 6108. Leading scorer Bobby Hunt scored four times.

Record League Victory: 9–1 v Bradford C, Division 4, 30 December 1961 – Ames; Millar, Fowler; Harris, Abrey, Ron Hunt; Foster, Bobby Hunt (4), King (4), Hill (1), Wright.

Record Cup Victory: 7–1 v Yeovil T (away), FA Cup 2nd rd (replay), 11 December 1958 – Ames; Fisher, Fowler; Parker, Milligan, Hammond; Williams (1), McLeod (2), Langman (4), Evans, Wright. 7–1 v Yeading, FA Cup 1st rd (replay), 22 November 1994 – Cheesewright; Betts, English, Cawley, Caesar, Locke (Dennis), Fry, Brown (2), Whitton (2) (Thompson), Kinsella (1), Abrahams (2).

Record Defeat: 0–8 v Leyton Orient, Division 4, 15 October 1989.

Most League Points (2 for a win): 60, Division 4, 1973–74.

Most League Points (3 for a win): 81, Division 4, 1982–83.

Most League Goals: 104, Division 4, 1961–62.

Highest League Scorer in Season: Bobby Hunt, 38, Division 4, 1961–62.

Most League Goals in Total Aggregate: Martyn King, 130, 1956–64.

Most League Goals in One Match: 4, Bobby Hunt v Bradford C, Division 4, 30 December 1961; 4, Martyn King v Bradford C, Division 4, 30 December 1961; 4, Bobby Hunt v Doncaster R, Division 4, 30 April 1962.

Most Capped Player: None.

Most League Appearances: Micky Cook, 613, 1969–84.

Youngest League Player: Lindsay Smith, 16 years 218 days v Grimsby T, 24 April 1971.

Record Transfer Fee Received: £2,250,000 from Newcastle U for Lomano Lua-Lua, September 2000.

Record Transfer Fee Paid: £50,000 to Ipswich T for Neil Gregory, March 1998.

Football League Record: 1950 Elected to Division 3 (S); 1958–61 Division 3; 1961–62 Division 4; 1962–65 Division 3; 1965–66 Division 4; 1966–68 Division 3; 1968–74 Division 4; 1974–76 Division 3; 1976–77 Division 4; 1977–81 Division 3; 1981–90 Division 4; 1990–92 GM Vauxhall Conference; 1992–98 Division 3; 1998– Division 2.

MANAGERS

Ted Fenton 1946–48
Jimmy Allen 1948–53
Jack Butler 1953–55
Benny Fenton 1955–63
Neil Franklin 1963–68
Dick Graham 1968–72
Jim Smith 1972–75
Bobby Roberts 1975–82
Allan Hunter 1982–83
Cyril Lea 1983–86
Mike Walker 1986–87
Roger Brown 1987–88
Jock Wallace 1989
Mick Mills 1990.
Ian Atkins 1990–91
Roy McDonough 1991–94
George Burley 1994
Steve Wignall 1995–99
Mick Wadsworth 1999
Steve Whitton August 1999–

LATEST SEQUENCES

Longest Sequence of League Wins: 7, 29.11.68 – 1.2.69.

Longest Sequence of League Defeats: 8, 9.10.54 – 4.12.54.

Longest Sequence of League Draws: 6, 21.3.77 – 11.4.77.

Longest Sequence of Unbeaten League Matches: 20, 22.12.56 – 19.4.57.

Longest Sequence Without a League Win: 20, 2.3.68 – 31.8.68.

TEN YEAR LEAGUE RECORD

		P	W	D	L	F	A	Pts	Pos
1990-91	Conf	42	25	10	7	68	35	85	2
1991-92	Conf	42	28	10	4	98	40	94	1
1992-93	Div 3	42	18	5	19	67	76	59	10
1993-94	Div 3	42	13	10	19	56	71	49	17
1994-95	Div 3	42	16	10	16	56	64	58	10
1995-96	Div 3	46	18	18	10	61	51	72	7
1996-97	Div 3	46	17	17	12	62	51	68	8
1997-98	Div 3	46	21	11	14	72	60	74	4
1998-99	Div 2	46	12	16	18	52	70	52	18
1999-2000	Div 2	46	14	10	22	59	82	52	18

DID YOU KNOW ?

In the season before election to the Football League, Colchester United attracted a Southern League crowd of 14,718 for the visit of neighbours Chelmsford City. United won 4-1.

COLCHESTER UNITED 2000–01 LEAGUE RECORD

Match No.	Date	Venue	Opponents	Result	H/T Score	Lg. Pos.	Goalscorers	Attendance
1	Aug 12	A	Swindon T	D 0-0	0-0	—		7296
2	18	H	Rotherham U	L 0-1	0-1	—		3807
3	26	A	Swansea C	W 2-0	1-0	10	Lua-Lua 2 [15, 83]	6247
4	29	H	Oldham Ath	D 1-1	1-0	—	Duguid [37]	3675
5	Sept 2	H	Bournemouth	W 3-1	2-1	5	Skelton 2 [4, 40], Stockwell [62]	3459
6	9	A	Wigan Ath	L 1-3	1-2	10	Duguid [30]	5782
7	12	A	Bury	D 0-0	0-0	—		2577
8	16	H	Wrexham	D 1-1	0-1	14	Lock [63]	3724
9	23	ˋA	Bristol C	D 1-1	1-1	12	Lock [2]	7411
10	30	H	Stoke C	L 0-1	0-1	12		3758
11	Oct 6	H	Walsall	L 0-2	0-2	—		3428
12	14	A	Port Vale	L 1-3	0-1	17	Scott [63]	3192
13	17	A	Brentford	L 0-1	0-0	—		3595
14	21	H	Cambridge U	W 2-0	1-0	18	McGavin 2 (1 pen) [39, 63 (p)]	3761
15	24	H	Bristol R	W 2-1	1-0	—	Gregory [36], Duguid [62]	2951
16	28	A	Peterborough U	L 1-3	0-0	17	Duguid [48]	5469
17	Nov 4	H	Northampton T	L 0-2	0-1	19		3352
18	11	A	Reading	W 1-0	1-0	17	Johnson G [38]	11,549
19	25	H	Wycombe W	D 0-0	0-0	17		3646
20	Dec 2	H	Notts Co	W 2-0	1-0	13	Keeble [43], Conlon [78]	3280
21	16	A	Luton T	W 3-0	1-0	12	Conlon [28], Gregory [48], Pinault [76]	4791
22	22	H	Oxford U	W 3-2	2-0	—	Conlon [27], Stockwell 2 [35, 69]	3695
23	26	A	Millwall	L 1-6	0-2	12	Ryan (og) [87]	11,156
24	Jan 13	A	Oldham Ath	D 1-1	0-0	15	Stockwell [59]	4076
25	27	A	Oxford U	W 1-0	1-0	15	Dunne [45]	5064
26	Feb 3	A	Bournemouth	D 2-2	2-0	15	McGleish [22], Stockwell [28]	4407
27	6	H	Millwall	L 0-1	0-1	—		4523
28	10	A	Wigan Ath	L 0-2	0-1	15		3275
29	17	A	Wrexham	L 0-1	0-1	17		2492
30	20	H	Bury	D 1-1	0-0	—	Skelton (pen) [59]	2755
31	24	H	Bristol C	W 4-0	2-0	17	Gregory [7], Keith [42], Stockwell [57], Conlon [69]	3430
32	27	A	Rotherham U	L 2-3	1-0	—	Johnson G [35], Keith [74]	5864
33	Mar 3	A	Stoke C	L 1-3	1-2	17	Skelton (pen) [4]	11,714
34	7	H	Port Vale	L 0-1	0-0	—		2579
35	10	H	Walsall	W 1-0	0-0	17	Conlon [56]	4553
36	16	H	Brentford	W 3-1	1-1	—	Keith [41], Stockwell [51], Duguid [74]	3420
37	20	H	Swindon T	L 0-1	0-1	—		2736
38	31	H	Luton T	W 3-1	3-0	14	Stockwell 2 [17, 37], Skelton (pen) [43]	4271
39	Apr 3	A	Swansea C	W 3-0	1-0	—	Conlon 2 [20, 86], McGleish [64]	2886
40	14	A	Bristol R	L 0-2	0-0	17		6551
41	17	H	Peterborough U	D 2-2	1-1	—	Stockwell [18], Izzet [77]	4336
42	21	A	Northampton T	L 0-2	0-1	17		5012
43	28	H	Reading	W 2-1	2-1	16	Conlon [34], Skelton (pen) [43]	5010
44	May 1	A	Cambridge U	L 1-2	0-0	—	McGleish [81]	5317
45	3	A	Notts Co	D 2-2	1-1	—	Stockwell [9], McGleish [89]	2860
46	5	A	Wycombe W	D 1-1	0-0	17	McGleish [51]	7516

Final League Position: 17

GOALSCORERS

League (55): Stockwell 11, Conlon 8, Skelton 6 (4 pens), Duguid 5, McGleish 5, Gregory 3, Keith 3, Johnson G 2, Lock 2, Lua-Lua 2, McGavin 2 (1 pen), Dunne 1, Izzet 1, Keeble 1, Pinault 1, Scott 1, own goal 1.
Worthington Cup (4): Lua-Lua 3, McGavin 1.
FA Cup (1): Duguid 1.

Brown S 18	Dunne J 31+3	Keith J 21+6	Skelton A 43+1	White A 29+3	Clark S 33+1	Duguid K 34+7	Gregory D 27+1	Lua-Lua L 7	Stockwell M 46	Dozzell J 22	Lock T 3+11	Pinault T 3+2	McGavin G 19+22	Johnson G 33+4	Keeble C 10+6	Tanner A 1+3	Opara C —+2	Arnott A 1+2	Nicholls M 3+1	Scott K 8+1	Fitzgerald S 30	Morgan D —+4	Woodman A 28	Conlon B 23+3	Johnson R 17+1	McGleish S 11+10	Izzet K 5+1	Match No.
1	2	3	4	5	6	7[1]	8	9	10[2]	11[3]	12	13	14															1
1	2	3	4	5[1]	6	7	8[2]	9	10	11			12	13														2
1	2	3	4	5	6	7[2]	12	9	10[1]	11	13		8															3
1	2	3[2]	4	5	6	7[1]		9	10	11	12		8	13														4
1	12		4	5	6	7	2	9[2]	10	11	13		8	3[1]														5
1			4	5	6	7	2	9	10[2]	11	12		8[1]	3	13													6
1		4[2]		5	6	7	2	9[1]	10	11	12		8	3	13													7
1	12			5	6	7	2[2]		10	11	8		9	3	13	4[1]												8
1	2	12	4	5[1]	6	7[2]			10	11	8		9[3]	3	13	14												9
1	2	3	4	5					10[3]	11	8[2]		9[1]	6	7	12	13	14										10
1	2	3	4	5[1]		7[2]			10	11	12		6	8	13					9								11
1	2	12	4[2]	5		7			10[1]	11		13	14	3	6					8[3]	9							12
1		3	4	5		12	2		10	11			7	6						8[1]	9							13
1	12			5[1]	6	7	2		10	11			8	3							9	4						14
1			4		6	7	2		10	11			8	3							9	5						15
1			4		6	7	2		10	11			8	3						12	9[1]	5						16
1		4[2]			6	7[1]	8		10	11	12		9	3					2		5	13						17
	12		4	5		7	2[1]		10	11	13		8[2]	3							6		1	9				18
	2		4	5		7	8	3	10[1]	11	12										6		1	9				19
	2		4	5		7	8		10[1]	11			12	6			13				3		1	9[2]				20
	2[1]		4		12	7	8		10[3]	11[2]			14	13	3						6	5	1	9				21
			4	5	6	7	2		10[1]	11[2]			12	8							3		1	9	13			22
			4	5	6	7	2		10[2]	11			12	13	8[1]						3		1	9				23
	2				6	7	8		10[1]				11[2]	3	12						4		1	9	5	13		24
	2		4		6	12	8		10[1]				13	7							5		1	9	3	11[2]		25
	2		4		6	12	8		10[1]				13	3							5		1	9[2]	7	11		26
	2		7		6	12	8		10[2]				13	3							5		1	9	4	11[1]		27
	2[1]		7[3]		6	12	8		10				13	3	14						5		1	9	4	11		28
	2[2]	3	7	12	6	13	8		10[3]				9	14							5		1		4[1]	11		29
	2	3	7		6		8		10												5		1	9	4	11		30
	2	3	7		6	11[1]	8[2]		10				12	13							5		1	9	4	14		31
	2	3	7	12	6	11			10				8								5		1	9	4			32
	2	3	7	5		11			10				12	8							6		1	9[1]	4[2]	13		33
	2	3	7[1]			11[2]	8		10				12	6							5		1	9	4	13		34
	2	3	7	5		11			10				12	8							6		1	9[2]	4	13		35
	2	3	7	5		11[1]			10				12	8							6		1	9	4	13		36
	2	3	7[1]	5		11[2]			10				12	8						14	6		1	9[2]	4	13		37
		3[1]	7	5	6		2		10[1]				12	8						9[2]	4		1	13		11	14	38
	12	4[1]	5	3	2				10				13	8							6	14	1	9[1]		11[2]	7	39
	12	3[1]	7	5	6	2			10				13							9[3]	4		1	14		11[2]	8	40
	2		7	5	6	3			10[1]				12	8						9[2]	4		1	13			11	41
	2	12	7		6	3			10					11[1]							5		1	9	4[2]	13	8	42
	2	3	4[1]	12	6	11[2]			10					7							5		1	9	13	8		43
	2	3	4[1]	5	6	11			10			7	12	8									1	9[2]		13		44
1	2	3	4		6				10[1]				7	9	8							12			5	11		45
	2	12		5	6	13			10[3]				7	9[2]	8	3[1]						14	1		4	11		46

Worthington Cup

First Round	QPR		(h)	0-1
			(a)	4-1
Second Round	Sheffield U		(a)	0-3
			(h)	0-1

FA Cup

First Round	Yeovil T		(a)	1-5

COVENTRY CITY

Division 1

FOUNDATION

Workers at Singers' cycle factory formed a club in 1883. The first success of Singers' FC was to win the Birmingham Junior Cup in 1891 and this led in 1894 to their election to the Birmingham and District League. Four years later they changed their name to Coventry City and joined the Southern League in 1908 at which time they were playing in blue and white quarters.

Highfield Road Stadium, King Richard Street, Coventry CV2 4FW.

Telephone: (024) 7623 4000. *Fax:* (024) 7623 4099. *Ticket Office:* (024) 7623 4020. *Ticket Office Fax:* (024) 7623 4023. *Sales & Marketing:* (024) 7623 4010. *ClubCall:* 09068 121 166. *Website:* http://www.ccfc.co.uk *Email:* info@ccfc.co.uk

Ground Capacity: 23,633.

Record Attendance: 51,455 v Wolverhampton W, Division 2, 29 April 1967.

Record Receipts: £405,369 v Charlton Ath, FA Cup 5th rd, 29 January 2000.

Pitch Measurements: 110yd × 75yd.

President: G. Robinson MP.

Chairman: B. A. Richardson.
Deputy Chairman: M. C. McGinnity.
Directors: A. M. Jepson, J. F. W Reason, D. A. Higgs, Miss B. Price, G. P. Hover. *Company Secretary:* Graham Hover.

Manager: Gordon Strachan. *Coaches:* Garry Pendrey, Trevor Peake and Roland Nilsson. *Physio:* Stuart Collie.

Commercial: Ric Allison.

Stadium Manager: Don Blair.

Club Statistician: Jim Brown.

Colours: Sky blue shirts and shorts with black piping, sky blue stockings with black side tabs.

Change Colours: Navy blue shirts with sky blue chest panel and white piping, navy shorts with white piping, navy stockings with sky blue panel.

Year Formed: 1883.

Turned Professional: 1893.

Ltd Co.: 1907.

Previous Names: 1883, Singers FC; 1898, Coventry City FC.

Club Nickname: 'Sky Blues'.

Previous Grounds: 1883, Binley Road; 1887, Stoke Road; 1899, Highfield Road.

First Football League Game: 30 August 1919, Division 2, v Tottenham H (h) L 0–5 – Lindon; Roberts, Chaplin, Allan, Hawley, Clarke, Sheldon, Mercer, Sambrooke, Lowes, Gibson.

HONOURS

Football League: Division 1 best season: 6th, 1969–70; Division 2 – Champions 1966–67; Division 3 – Champions 1963–64; Division 3 (S) – Champions 1935–36; Runners-up 1933–34; Division 4 – Runners-up 1958–59.

FA Cup: Winners 1987.

Football League Cup: Semi-final 1981, 1990.

European Competitions: European Fairs Cup: 1970–71.

IT'S A FACT !

In 2000–01, Paul Telfer equalled the Coventry City club record of 191 Premier League appearances achieved by Steve Ogrizovic, but injury prevented him overhauling the target.

Record League Victory: 9–0 v Bristol C, Division 3 (S), 28 April 1934 – Pearson; Brown, Bisby; Perry, Davidson, Frith; White (2), Lauderdale, Bourton (5), Jones (2), Lake.

Record Cup Victory: 7–0 v Scunthorpe U, FA Cup 1st rd, 24 November 1934 – Pearson; Brown, Bisby; Mason, Davidson, Boileau; Birtley (2), Lauderdale (2), Bourton (1), Jones (1), Liddle (1).

Record Defeat: 2–10 v Norwich C, Division 3 (S), 15 March 1930.

Most League Points (2 for a win): 60, Division 4, 1958–59 and Division 3, 1963–64.

Most League Points (3 for a win): 63, Division 1, 1986–87.

Most League Goals: 108, Division 3 (S), 1931–32.

Highest League Scorer in Season: Clarrie Bourton, 49, Division 3 (S), 1931–32.

Most League Goals in Total Aggregate: Clarrie Bourton, 171, 1931–37.

Most League Goals in One Match: 5, Clarrie Bourton v Bournemouth, Division 3S, 17 October 1931; 5, Arthur Bacon v Gillingham, Division 3S, 30 December 1933.

Most Capped Player: Magnus Hedman 31 (36), Sweden.

Most League Appearances: Steve Ogrizovic, 507, 1984–2000.

Youngest League Player: Gary McSheffrey, 16 years 198 days v Aston Villa, 27 February 1999.

Record Transfer Fee Received: £12,500,000 from Internazionale for Robbie Keane, July 2000.

Record Transfer Fee Paid: £6,000,000 to Wolverhampton W for Robbie Keane, August 1999.

Football League Record: 1919 Elected to Division 2; 1925–26 Division 3 (N); 1926–36 Division 3 (S); 1936–52 Division 2; 1952–58 Division 3 (S); 1958–59 Division 4; 1959–64 Division 3; 1964–67 Division 2; 1967–92 Division 1; 1992–2001 FA Premier League; 2001– Division 1.

LATEST SEQUENCES

Longest Sequence of League Wins: 6, 25.4.64 – 5.9.64.

Longest Sequence of League Defeats: 9, 30.8.19 – 11.10.19.

Longest Sequence of League Draws: 6, 28.9.96 – 16.11.96.

Longest Sequence of Unbeaten League Matches: 25, 26.11.66 – 13.5.67.

Longest Sequence Without a League Win: 19, 30.8.19 – 20.12.19.

MANAGERS

H. R. Buckle 1909–10
Robert Wallace 1910–13
　(Secretary-Manager)
Frank Scott-Walford 1913–15
William Clayton 1917–19
H. Pollitt 1919–20
Albert Evans 1920–24
Jimmy Kerr 1924–28
James McIntyre 1928–31
Harry Storer 1931–45
Dick Bayliss 1945–47
Billy Frith 1947–48
Harry Storer 1948–53
Jack Fairbrother 1953–54
Charlie Elliott 1954–55
Jesse Carver 1955–56
Harry Warren 1956–57
Billy Frith 1957–61
Jimmy Hill 1961–67
Noel Cantwell 1967–72
Bob Dennison 1972
Joe Mercer 1972–75
Gordon Milne 1972–81
Dave Sexton 1981–83
Bobby Gould 1983–84
Don Mackay 1985–86
George Curtis 1986–87
　(became Managing Director)
John Sillett 1987–90
Terry Butcher 1990–92
Don Howe 1992
Bobby Gould 1992–93
Phil Neal 1993–95
Ron Atkinson 1995–96
　(became Director of Football)
Gordon Strachan November 1996–

TEN YEAR LEAGUE RECORD

		P	W	D	L	F	A	Pts	Pos
1990-91	Div 1	38	11	11	16	42	49	44	16
1991-92	Div 1	42	11	11	20	35	44	44	19
1992-93	PR Lge	42	13	13	16	52	57	52	15
1993-94	PR Lge	42	14	14	14	43	45	56	11
1994-95	PR Lge	42	12	14	16	44	62	50	16
1995-96	PR Lge	38	8	14	16	42	60	38	16
1996-97	PR Lge	38	9	14	15	38	54	41	17
1997-98	PR Lge	38	12	16	10	46	44	52	11
1998-99	PR Lge	38	11	9	18	39	51	42	15
1999-2000	PR Lge	38	12	8	18	47	54	44	14

DID YOU KNOW

Although John Aloisi's double hat-trick for Australia against Tonga on 9 April 2001 was an individual record for his country, it lasted only two days, but it remained the best international performance by a Coventry City player.

COVENTRY CITY 2000–01 LEAGUE RECORD

Match No.	Date	Venue	Opponents	Result	H/T Score	Lg. Pos.	Goalscorers	Attendance
1	Aug 19	H	Middlesbrough	L	1-3	1-1	—	Eustace [41]	20,623
2	23	A	Southampton	W	2-1	1-0	—	Bellamy (pen) [20], Roussel [62]	14,801
3	26	A	Manchester C	W	2-1	2-0	4	Edghill (og) [23], Bellamy [45]	34,140
4	Sept 6	H	Newcastle U	L	0-2	0-1	—		22,102
5	9	H	Leeds U	D	0-0	0-0	9		20,363
6	16	A	Arsenal	L	1-2	0-1	13	Hadji [80]	37,794
7	23	H	West Ham U	L	0-3	0-2	17		20,132
8	30	A	Charlton Ath	D	2-2	1-0	17	Aloisi [41], Bellamy (pen) [71]	20,043
9	Oct 14	H	Tottenham H	W	2-1	1-0	13	Aloisi [12], Eustace [26]	21,430
10	21	A	Chelsea	L	1-6	0-2	15	Roussel [89]	34,646
11	28	A	Sunderland	L	0-1	0-0	16		43,249
12	Nov 4	H	Manchester U	L	1-2	0-2	17	Zuniga [64]	21,077
13	12	A	Liverpool	L	1-4	0-1	17	Thompson [56]	43,701
14	20	H	Ipswich T	L	0-1	0-0	—		19,327
15	25	H	Aston Villa	D	1-1	0-1	17	Hadji [83]	21,455
16	Dec 2	A	Bradford C	L	1-2	0-0	18	Aloisi [64]	15,523
17	10	H	Leicester C	W	1-0	1-0	17	Bellamy [40]	17,275
18	16	A	Derby Co	L	0-1	0-1	18		27,869
19	22	H	Southampton	D	1-1	1-0	—	Thompson [33]	18,082
20	26	A	Everton	W	2-1	0-0	18	Hadji [69], Breen [87]	35,704
21	30	A	Middlesbrough	D	1-1	1-0	17	Whelan (og) [41]	30,499
22	Jan 1	H	Manchester C	D	1-1	0-0	17	Edworthy [72]	21,991
23	13	A	Newcastle U	L	1-3	0-1	18	Thompson [78]	50,159
24	20	H	Everton	L	1-3	0-3	19	Carsley (pen) [86]	19,172
25	31	A	Leeds U	L	0-1	0-0	—		36,555
26	Feb 3	H	Arsenal	L	0-1	0-0	19		22,034
27	12	A	West Ham U	D	1-1	0-0	—	Dailly (og) [90]	22,586
28	24	H	Charlton Ath	D	2-2	1-1	19	Bellamy [10], Hartson [67]	19,478
29	Mar 3	H	Chelsea	D	0-0	0-0	19		21,708
30	17	A	Tottenham H	L	0-3	0-2	19		35,606
31	31	H	Derby Co	W	2-0	1-0	19	Hadji [44], Hartson [49]	19,622
32	Apr 7	A	Leicester C	W	3-1	2-1	18	Bellamy [2], Carsley [19], Hartson [51]	19,545
33	14	A	Manchester U	L	2-4	2-2	19	Hartson 2 [10, 33]	67,637
34	16	H	Sunderland	W	1-0	1-0	18	Hartson [21]	20,934
35	21	A	Ipswich T	L	0-2	0-1	18		24,576
36	28	H	Liverpool	L	0-2	0-0	19		23,063
37	May 5	A	Aston Villa	L	2-3	2-0	19	Hadji 2 [18, 26]	39,761
38	19	H	Bradford C	D	0-0	0-0	19		20,299

Final League Position: 19

GOALSCORERS

League (36): Bellamy 6 (2 pens), Hadji 6, Hartson 6, Aloisi 3, Thompson 3, Carsley 2 (1 pen), Eustace 2, Roussel 2, Breen 1, Edworthy 1, Zuniga 1, own goals 3.
Worthington Cup (9): Aloisi 3 (1 pen), Eustace 2, Bellamy 1 (pen), Hall 1, Strachan 1 (pen), Zuniga 1.
FA Cup (2): Bellamy 1, Hadji 1.

Hedman M 15	Breen G 29+2	Hall M 21	Williams P 27+3	Hendry C 1+1	Chippo Y 18+14	Thompson D 22+3	Palmer C 12+3	Bellamy C 33+1	Eustace J 22+10	Roussel C 10+7	Aloisi J 8+11	Telfer P 27+4	Edworthy M 18+6	Shaw R 23+1	Zuniga Y 7+8	Hadji M 28+1	Kirkland C 23	Miller A —+1	Guerrero I 3	Quinn B 25	Bothroyd J 3+5	Strachan G 2	Konjic M 8	Carsley L 21	Hartson J 12	Davenport C —+1	Betts R —+1	Match No.
1	2^1	3	4	5	6	7	8	9	10^2	11	12	13																1
1		3	4		6		8	9^1	10	11			7	2		5	12											2
1		3	4		6^1	12	8	9	10	11			7	2		5												3
1		3	4		6		8	9	10^2	11	12	7		2		5	13											4
1		3	4		6		8	9^2	12	11		7		2		5	13	10										5
1	12	3	4		6		8	9^3	13	11		7^2		2^1		5	14	10										6
1	12	3^1	4		6	7^2	8	9	13		14			2		5	11^3	10										7
1		3	4		6		8	9	11		12	10^1	7	2		5												8
			4		12		6	8	9^1		11	13	10^2	2	3	5	1			7								9
	5		4				6	8	9		11^2	12	10^3	2	3	13	1		15	7								10
	6		4							11	12		9	14	13	10^2	1		5	8		7	2^1	3^3				11
	6		4					9^1		10	11^1		13	12	8	5	1		7	14			2	3^2				12
	3		4		6^1	7	8	9	13		12		14	5		11	1		2^3				10^2					13
	2		4		6		8	9	11^1		12	7	3			10	1							5				14
	2		4		6^2		8	12	14		11^3	13	7	3		10^1	9							1	5			15
	6		4		12	7^3	8	13	11			10	2			9	1			3				5^1	6			16
1	2		4			11	13	9		12	10^1	7^2				8				3				5	6			17
1	2	4^1			12			9	14	13	10^2	7				8				3				5	6			18
	2		4		12	8^3		9^3	13	11^1		7				14	10	1		3				5	6			19
	2		4		12	8		9^1			13	7	14			11^2	10	1		3				5^6	6			20
	5		4		12	8		9^1			13	7	2			11^2	10	1		3					6			21
	5		4		12	8		9^1	13		14	7	2			11^3	10	1		3^2					6			22
1	5		4			8		9	11			10^1	7	2						3	12				6			23
	4				12	8	13		10			14	7^2	2		11^3	9	1		3				5^2	6			24
1	6	3	4		12	2^2		9	8			13				5	10			11^2	14				7^1			25
1		4	2		7^1			9	8	11						5	10			3	12				6			26
1	4	3			12	7		9^2	11			13		5		10				2^3	14				6^1	8		27
1	4	3			6^1	8		9			12			2		5	11								7	10		28
	4	3			12	7		9	8		13			5		11^2	1			2					6^1	10		29
	4	3			12^2	7^3		9	8^1				14	13	5	11	1			2					6	10		30
	4	3			12			9	8			7		5		11	1			2					6	10		31
	4	3	12		13			9	8^2			7		5		11^1	1			2					6	10		32
	4	3	12		13	11		9	8^1			7^2		5			1			2					6	10		33
	4	3			12			9	8^1			7		5			1			2	11				6	10		34
	4	3	12					9	8			7	13	5	14		1			2^1	11^2				6^2	10		35
	5	3	4		6			9^1	8			7				12	11	1		2						10		36
	5	3^2	4					9	8			7^1	12			13	11	1		2					6	10		37
		4^3	7^1									2	5	11	9	1				3	12	8^2		6	10	14	13	38

Worthington Cup
Second Round   Preston NE   (a)   3-1
                (h)   4-1
Third Round   Southampton   (a)   1-0
Fourth Round   Ipswich T   (a)   1-2

FA Cup
Third Round   Swindon T   (a)   2-0
Fourth Round   Manchester C (a)   0-1

CREWE ALEXANDRA — Division 1

FOUNDATION

The first match played at Crewe was on 1 December 1877 against Basford, the leading North Staffordshire team of that time. During the club's history they have also played in a number of other leagues including the Football Alliance, Football Combination, Lancashire League, Manchester League, Central League and Lancashire Combination. Two former players, Aaron Scragg in 1899 and Jackie Pearson in 1911, had the distinction of refereeing FA Cup finals. Pearson was also capped for England against Ireland in 1892.

Football Ground, Gresty Road, Crewe CW2 6EB.

Telephone: (01270) 213 014. *ClubCall:* 09068 121 647.

Ground Capacity: 10,046.

Record Attendance: 20,000 v Tottenham H, FA Cup 4th rd, 30 January 1960.

Record Receipts: £41,093 v Liverpool, FA Cup 3rd rd, 6 January 1992.

Pitch Measurements: 112yd × 74yd.

President: N. Rowlinson.

Chairman: J. Bowler.

Vice-Chairman: N. Hassall.

Directors: D. Rowlinson, R. Clayton, J. McMillan, D. Gradi.

Manager: Dario Gradi MBE.

Secretary: Mrs Gill Palin.

Marketing Manager: Alison Bowler.

Colours: Red shirts, white shorts, red stockings.

Change Colours: Blue shirts, white shorts, blue stockings.

Year Formed: 1877.

Turned Professional: 1893.

Ltd Co.: 1892.

Club Nickname: 'Railwaymen'.

First Football League Game: 3 September 1892, Division 2, v Burton Swifts (a) L 1–7 – Hickton; Moore, Cope; Linnell, Johnson, Osborne; Bennett, Pearson (1), Bailey, Barnett, Roberts.

Record League Victory: 8–0 v Rotherham U, Division 3 (N), 1 October 1932 – Foster; Pringle, Dawson; Ward, Keenor (1), Turner (1); Gillespie, Swindells (1), McConnell (2), Deacon (2), Weale (1).

HONOURS

Football League: Promoted from Division 2 1996–97 (play-offs).
FA Cup: Semi-final 1888.
Football League Cup: best season: 3rd rd, 1975, 1976, 1979, 1993, 1999, 2000.
Welsh Cup: Winners 1936, 1937.

IT'S A FACT !

On 14 February 1997, Crewe Alexandra announced an alliance with Liverpool FC, thought to be the first of such co-operation between clubs to be put on an official basis.

Record Cup Victory: 8–0 v Hartlepool U, Auto Windscreens Shield 1st rd, 17 October 1995 – Gayle; Collins (1), Booty, Westwood (Unsworth), Macauley (1), Whalley (1), Garvey (1), Murphy (1), Savage (1) (Rivers (1p)), Lennon, Edwards, (1 og).

Record Defeat: 2–13 v Tottenham H, FA Cup 4th rd replay, 3 February 1960.

Most League Points (2 for a win): 59, Division 4, 1962–63.

Most League Points (3 for a win): 83, Division 2, 1994–95.

Most League Goals: 95, Division 3 (N), 1931–32.

Highest League Scorer in Season: Terry Harkin, 35, Division 4, 1964–65.

Most League Goals in Total Aggregate: Bert Swindells, 126, 1928–37.

Most League Goals in One Match: 5, Tony Naylor v Colchester U, Division 3, 24 April 1993.

Most Capped Player: Bill Lewis, 9 (27), Wales.

Most League Appearances: Tommy Lowry, 436, 1966–78.

Youngest League Player: Steve Walters, 16 years 119 days v Peterborough U, 6 May 1988.

Record Transfer Fee Received: £3,000,000 Derby Co for Seth Johnson, May 1999.

Record Transfer Fee Paid: £650,000 to Torquay U for Rodney Jack, June 1998.

Football League Record: 1892 Original Member of Division 2; 1896 Failed re-election; 1921 Re-entered Division 3 (N); 1958–63 Division 4; 1963–64 Division 3; 1964–68 Division 4; 1968–69 Division 3; 1969–89 Division 4; 1989–91 Division 3; 1991–92 Division 4; 1992–94 Division 3; 1994–97 Division 2; 1997– Division 1.

MANAGERS

W. C. McNeill 1892–94 *(Secretary-Manager)*
J. G. Hall 1895–96 *(Secretary-Manager)*
R. Roberts *(1st team Secretary-Manager)* 1897
J. B. Blomerley 1898–1911 *(Secretary-Manager, continued as Hon. Secretary to 1925)*
Tom Bailey *(Secretary only)* 1925–38
George Lillycrop *(Trainer)* 1938–44
Frank Hill 1944–48
Arthur Turner 1948–51
Harry Catterick 1951–53
Ralph Ward 1953–55
Maurice Lindley 1956–57
Willie Cook 1957–58
Harry Ware 1958–60
Jimmy McGuigan 1960–64
Ernie Tagg 1964–71 *(continued as Secretary to 1972)*
Dennis Viollet 1971
Jimmy Melia 1972–74
Ernie Tagg 1974
Harry Gregg 1975–78
Warwick Rimmer 1978–79
Tony Waddington 1979–81
Arfon Griffiths 1981–82
Peter Morris 1982–83
Dario Gradi June 1983–

LATEST SEQUENCES

Longest Sequence of League Wins: 7, 30.4.94 – 3.9.94.

Longest Sequence of League Defeats: 10, 16.4.79 – 22.8.79.

Longest Sequence of League Draws: 5, 31.8.87 – 18.9.87.

Longest Sequence of Unbeaten League Matches: 17, 25.3.95 – 16.9.95.

Longest Sequence Without a League Win: 30, 22.9.56 – 6.4.57.

TEN YEAR LEAGUE RECORD

		P	W	D	L	F	A	Pts	Pos
1990-91	Div 3	46	11	11	24	62	80	44	22
1991-92	Div 4	42	20	10	12	66	51	70	6
1992-93	Div 3	42	21	7	14	75	56	70	6
1993-94	Div 3	42	21	10	11	80	61	73	3
1994-95	Div 2	46	25	8	13	80	68	83	3
1995-96	Div 2	46	22	7	17	77	60	73	5
1996-97	Div 2	46	22	7	17	56	47	73	6
1997-98	Div 1	46	18	5	23	58	65	59	11
1998-99	Div 1	46	12	12	22	54	78	48	18
1999-2000	Div 1	46	14	9	23	46	67	51	19

DID YOU KNOW ?

Jimmy Scullion, in two seasons with Crewe Alexandra 1928-30, scored 41 goals in only 73 matches including four hat-tricks, before signing for Wigan Borough.

CREWE ALEXANDRA 2000–01 LEAGUE RECORD

Match No.	Date	Venue	Opponents	Result	Score	H/T Score	Lg. Pos.	Goalscorers	Attendance
1	Aug 12	A	Fulham	L	0-2	0-0	—		11,157
2	19	H	Blackburn R	D	0-0	0-0	22		7500
3	26	A	QPR	L	0-1	0-1	23		9415
4	29	H	Grimsby T	W	2-0	1-0	—	Rivers [13], Jack [75]	5305
5	Sept 9	H	Norwich C	D	0-0	0-0	16		5955
6	12	H	WBA	L	0-1	0-1	—		6222
7	16	A	Watford	L	0-3	0-1	22		13,784
8	23	H	Barnsley	D	2-2	1-0	21	Hulse [36], Jack [71]	5738
9	30	A	Tranmere R	W	3-1	2-0	17	Hulse 2 [28, 46], Little [40]	8162
10	Oct 8	A	Birmingham C	L	0-2	0-0	18		6829
11	14	A	Sheffield U	L	0-1	0-0	19		12,921
12	17	A	Portsmouth	L	1-2	0-0	—	Smith S (pen) [60]	14,621
13	21	A	Wimbledon	L	0-4	0-2	21		5469
14	24	H	Huddersfield T	W	1-0	0-0	—	Cramb [73]	5215
15	28	A	Gillingham	W	1-0	0-0	18	Little [52]	8347
16	31	A	Burnley	L	0-1	0-1	—		13,189
17	Nov 4	H	Wolverhampton W	W	2-0	2-0	15	Cramb 2 [27, 45]	7147
18	10	A	Preston NE	L	1-2	1-1	—	Rivers [36]	12,632
19	18	H	Stockport Co	L	1-2	0-1	18	Hulse [78]	6099
20	25	H	Sheffield W	W	1-0	0-0	15	Rivers [81]	7103
21	Dec 2	A	Huddersfield T	L	1-3	1-0	16	Cramb [43]	10,603
22	9	A	Bolton W	L	1-3	1-3	20	Sorvel [31]	12,836
23	16	H	Crystal Palace	D	1-1	1-0	22	Little [41]	5752
24	23	H	Fulham	L	1-2	1-0	22	Rivers [19]	6935
25	26	A	Nottingham F	L	0-1	0-1	22		20,903
26	30	A	Blackburn R	L	0-1	0-0	24		18,554
27	Jan 13	A	Grimsby T	W	3-1	2-0	24	Hulse 2 [29, 34], Rivers [62]	4495
28	Feb 3	H	Burnley	W	4-2	3-1	20	Street [5], Smith S 2 (2 pens) [40, 44], Ashton [85]	6994
29	10	A	Norwich C	D	1-1	0-0	20	Jack [52]	15,164
30	17	H	Watford	W	2-0	2-0	18	Jack [15], Ashton [24]	6757
31	20	A	WBA	D	2-2	1-1	—	Ashton [30], Hulse [76]	15,476
32	24	A	Barnsley	L	0-3	0-1	19		13,175
33	Mar 3	H	Tranmere R	W	3-1	0-1	18	Macauley [61], Hulse [63], Little [81]	7157
34	6	H	Sheffield U	W	1-0	0-0	—	Lunt [51]	6909
35	10	A	Birmingham C	L	0-2	0-0	17		28,042
36	13	H	Nottingham F	W	1-0	0-0	—	Rivers [76]	7916
37	17	H	Portsmouth	W	1-0	1-0	14	Ashton [11]	6182
38	31	H	Crystal Palace	L	0-1	0-0	16		20,872
39	Apr 10	A	QPR	D	2-2	0-2	—	Ashton [86], Smith S [90]	6354
40	14	A	Wolverhampton W	D	0-0	0-0	17		20,364
41	16	H	Gillingham	W	2-1	1-1	15	Navarro [9], Ashton [59]	7051
42	18	H	Bolton W	W	2-1	0-0	—	Hulse [67], Ashton [89]	8054
43	21	A	Stockport Co	L	0-3	0-0	13		7163
44	24	A	Wimbledon	D	3-3	1-2	—	Rivers [34], Hulse [57], Ashton [69]	5468
45	28	H	Preston NE	L	1-3	1-3	15	Hulse [19]	9415
46	May 6	A	Sheffield W	D	0-0	0-0	14		28,007

Final League Position: 14

GOALSCORERS

League (47): Hulse 11, Ashton 8, Rivers 7, Cramb 4, Jack 4, Little 4, Smith S 4 (3 pens), Lunt 1, Macauley 1, Navarro 1, Sorvel 1, Street 1.
Worthington Cup (4): Rivers 2, Foster 1, Little 1.
FA Cup (3): Rivers 1, Smith S 1 (pen), own goal 1.

Kearton J 25 + 1	Wright D 42	Smith S 44 + 1	Sodje E 29 + 3	Macauley S 30	Street K 16 + 7	Little C 24 + 3	Lunt K 46	Jack R 23 + 7	Rivers M 32 + 1	Sorvel N 42 + 4	Hulse R 22 + 11	Tait P 9 + 9	Collins J 2 + 2	Vaughan D 1	Foster S 21 + 9	Grant J — + 2	Walton D 17 + 3	Lumsdon C 14 + 2	Howell D — + 1	Smith P 2 + 3	Maybury A 6	Cramb C 10 + 3	Ashton D 12 + 9	Walker R 2 + 1	Bankole A 21	Gannon J 5 + 2	Charnock P 4 + 5	Ince C — + 1	Navarro A 5 + 3	Match No.
1	2	3	4	5	6^1	7^2	8	9	10^3	11	12	13	14																	1
1	2	3	4^3	5	12	7	8	13	10	11		9^1			6^2	14														2
1	2	3	4	5	6		8	9	10	11	7^1						12													3
1	2	3	4	5	6		8	9	10	11	7^1						12													4
1	2	3	4	5	6	9	8	12	10^1	11	7^2				13															5
1	2	3^1	4^2	5	6	10^1	8	9		11	7				12		13	14												6
1	2	3^2	4	5	6		8			11					9^1		12	7	13	10										7
1	2	3	4^1	5^1		10	6	9		8	7				12		13	11												8
1	2	3	4^1	5		9	8		10		7	13			12^2		6	11												9
1	4	3^1		5	12	9^2	8	13	10		7^3	14			6		11						2							10
1	5	3								4	9	10	11	12	8^1		6	7					2							11
1	5	3			12					4	9	10	11		8		6	7^1					2							12
1	2	3		5	12	9	4		10	11	8^2				6			7				13								13
1	2	3	12	5	13	9	4		10	11	8^1				6^1			7^2				14								14
1	4	3	6	5	7	9	8			11					10^1							12	2							15
1	2	3	4^1	5	6^2	9	8	12		11					13			7	10				2							16
1	5	3				9	8					10	12	14	13		4^1	7				2	11^3							17
1	5	3	6				2^2	8	12	10	11	13			14		7					9^1		4^3						18
1	2	3	6^1		13		4	9	10	11	12				5		7^2					8								19
1	2	3	6				4	9	10	11	12				5^2		7					8^1	13							20
1	2	3	6				12	4	9	10	11	13			5		7^2					8^1								21
1	3			6	5		4	9	10	11					2		7					8								22
1	3	12	6	5^1		11	4		10	8	7^2				2			13				9								23
1	2^1	3	6				9	4		10	11	7^1	12	13	5							8								24
	3	6	5			12	4			9	11				13				14			8^1			1	7^2				25
	3	6	5			9	4				11				8	7^1			10			12			1					26
		3	2	5					8	9	10	11	7^1		4							12			1	6			27
	2	3			5	6^1		8	9	10	11	7^2					4					13			1	12				28
	2	3			5	6^2		8	9	10	11	7^1					4					12			1	13				29
	2	3			5^1	6	12	8	9	10^1	11	13			14		4					7^2			1					30
	2	3				6^1		8	9		11	13	12		5		4					10^2			1	7^1				31
	2	3			5		9	8			11	7^1			6		4					10			1		12			32
	2	3			5	12	7	8		10^1	11	13			6		4					9^2			1					33
	2	3			5		9	8^2		10	11	7^2			14		4					13			1	6^1	12			34
	2	3			5		9^1	8^2		10	11	7			4		6					12	1^0				13	15		35
	2	3			5	12	9	8		10	11				13		4					7^2	1				6^1			36
	2	3			5	6^2		8	9	10	11				12		4					7^1	1				13			37
	2	3			5	6^2		8	9	10	11	12			4							7^1	1						13	38
	2	3	12		5^1	6	10	8	9	11^3	7				4							13	1					14		39
	2	3	5			6	10	8	9		11	7^1			4							12	1							40
	2	3	5				7	8	9^1	11		12			4							10	1				13	6^2		41
	2	3	5				8	9		11	7				4							10	1				6^1	12		42
	2	3	5				8^1	9^1	10	12	7^3	11			4			13				14	1				6			43
		3	5				8	12	10^1	11	7							9^4					1				6	2		44
15	2	3	5				8	12	10	13	7				4							9	1^0				6^1	11^2		45
1	2	3	5				8	12	10	13	7				4							9					6^1	11^2		46

Worthington Cup
First Round — Bury — (h) 2-2
— (a) 2-1
Second Round — Barnsley — (a) 0-4
— (h) 0-3

FA Cup
Third Round — Cardiff C — (a) 1-1
— (h) 2-1
Fourth Round — Stockport Co — (h) 0-1

CRYSTAL PALACE   Division 1

FOUNDATION

There was a Crystal Palace club as early as 1861 but the present organisation was born in 1905 after the formation of a club by the company that controlled the Crystal Palace (building), had been rejected by the FA who did not like the idea of the Cup Final hosts running their own club. A separate company had to be formed and they had their home on the old Cup Final ground until 1915.

Selhurst Park, London SE25 6PU.

Telephone: (020) 8768 6000. *Fax:* (020) 8771 5311.
Lottery Office: (020) 8768 6094.
Club Shop: (020) 8768 6100.
Dial-A-Seat Ticketline: (020) 8771 8841.
PR and Communications: (020) 8768 6020.
Fax: (020) 8768 6114. *ClubCall:* 09068 400 333.

Ground Capacity: 26,400.

Record Attendance: 51,482 v Burnley, Division 2, 11 May 1979.

Record Receipts: £327,124 v Manchester U, FA Premier League, 21 April 1993 (League); £336,583 v Chelsea, Coca-Cola Cup 5th rd, 6 January 1993.

Pitch Measurements: 110yd × 74yd.

Chairman: Simon Jordan.

Vice Chairman: Kevin Brummitt.

Director: S. Coppell.

Manager: Steve Bruce.

Physio: Gary Sadler.

Stadium Manager: Vic Worrall.

Club Secretary: Mike Hurst.

PR and Communications Manager: Terry Byfield.

Colours: Red and blue vertical striped shirts, red shorts, red stockings with blue tops.

Change Colours: All white with red and blue sash on shirt.

Year Formed: 1905. *Turned Professional:* 1905. *Ltd Co.:* 1905.

Club Nickname: 'The Eagles'.

Previous Grounds: 1905, Crystal Palace; 1915, Herne Hill; 1918, The Nest; 1924, Selhurst Park.

First Football League Game: 28 August 1920, Division 3, v Merthyr T (a) L 1–2 – Alderson; Little, Rhodes; McCracken, Jones, Feebury; Bateman, Conner, Smith, Milligan (1), Whibley.

Record League Victory: 9–0 v Barrow, Division 4, 10 October 1959 – Rouse; Long, Noakes; Truett, Evans, McNichol; Gavin (1), Summersby (4 incl. 1p), Sexton, Byrne (2), Colfar (2).

HONOURS

Football League: Division 1 – Champions 1993–94; Promoted from Division 1, 1996–97 (play-offs); Division 2 – Champions 1978–79; Runners-up 1968–69; Division 3 – Runners-up 1963–64; Division 3 (S) – Champions 1920–21; Runners-up 1928–29, 1930–31, 1938–39; Division 4 – Runners-up 1960–61.
FA Cup: Runners-up 1990.
Football League Cup: Semi-final 1993, 1995, 2001.
Zenith Data Systems Cup: Winners 1991.

IT'S A FACT !

On 18 November 2000, Steve Staunton scored with a left-foot curling shot from 55 yards against Tranmere Rovers in the 15th minute. Palace went on to win 3-2.

Record Cup Victory: 8–0 v Southend U, Rumbelows League Cup 2nd rd (1st leg), 25 September 1989 – Martyn; Humphrey (Thompson (1)), Shaw, Pardew, Young, Thorn, McGoldrick, Thomas, Bright (3), Wright (3), Barber (Hodges (1)).

Record Defeat: 0–9 v Burnley, FA Cup 2nd rd replay, 10 February 1909. 0–9 v Liverpool, Division 1, 12 September 1990.

Most League Points (2 for a win): 64, Division 4, 1960–61.

Most League Points (3 for a win): 90, Division 1, 1993–94.

Most League Goals: 110, Division 4, 1960–61.

Highest League Scorer in Season: Peter Simpson, 46, Division 3 (S), 1930–31.

Most League Goals in Total Aggregate: Peter Simpson, 153, 1930–36.

Most League Goals in One Match: 6, Peter Simpson v Exeter C, Division 3S, 4 October 1930.

Most Capped Player: Eric Young, 19 (21), Wales.

Most League Appearances: Jim Cannon, 571, 1973–88.

Youngest League Player: Phil Hoadley, 16 years 112 days v Bolton W, 27 April 1968.

Record Transfer Fee Received: £4,500,000 from Tottenham H for Chris Armstrong, June 1995.

Record Transfer Fee Paid: £2,750,000 to RC Strasbourg for Valerien Ismael, January 1998.

Football League Record: 1920 Original Members of Division 3; 1921–25 Division 2; 1925–58 Division 3 (S); 1958–61 Division 4; 1961–64 Division 3; 1964–69 Division 2; 1969–73 Division 1; 1973–74 Division 2; 1974–77 Division 3; 1977–79 Division 2; 1979–81 Division 1; 1981–89 Division 2; 1989–92 Division 1; 1992–93 FA Premier League; 1993–94 Division 1; 1994–95 FA Premier League; 1995–97 Division 1; 1997–98 FA Premier League; 1998– Division 1.

LATEST SEQUENCES

Longest Sequence of League Wins: 8, 9.2.21 – 26.3.21.

Longest Sequence of League Defeats: 8, 10.1.98 – 14.3.98.

Longest Sequence of League Draws: 5, 30.12.78 – 24.2.79.

Longest Sequence of Unbeaten League Matches: 18, 22.2.69 – 13.8.69.

Longest Sequence Without a League Win: 20, 3.3.62 – 8.9.62.

MANAGERS

John T. Robson 1905–07
Edmund Goodman 1907–25
(had been Secretary since 1905 and afterwards continued in this position to 1933)
Alec Maley 1925–27
Fred Mavin 1927–30
Jack Tresadern 1930–35
Tom Bromilow 1935–36
R. S. Moyes 1936
Tom Bromilow 1936–39
George Irwin 1939–47
Jack Butler 1947–49
Ronnie Rooke 1949–50
Charlie Slade and Fred Dawes _(Joint Managers)_ 1950–51
Laurie Scott 1951–54
Cyril Spiers 1954–58
George Smith 1958–60
Arthur Rowe 1960–62
Dick Graham 1962–66
Bert Head 1966–72
(continued as General Manager to 1973)
Malcolm Allison 1973–76
Terry Venables 1976–80
Ernie Walley 1980
Malcolm Allison 1980–81
Dario Gradi 1981
Steve Kember 1981–82
Alan Mullery 1982–84
Steve Coppell 1984–93
Alan Smith 1993–95
Steve Coppell _(Technical Director)_ 1995–96
Dave Bassett 1996–97
Steve Coppell 1997–98
Attilio Lombardo 1998
Terry Venables _(Head Coach)_ 1998–99
Steve Coppell 1999–2000
Alan Smith 2000–01
Steve Bruce May 2001–

TEN YEAR LEAGUE RECORD

		P	W	D	L	F	A	Pts	Pos
1990-91	Div 1	38	20	9	9	50	41	69	3
1991-92	Div 1	42	14	15	13	53	61	57	10
1992-93	PR Lge	42	11	16	15	48	61	49	20
1993-94	Div 1	46	27	9	10	73	46	90	1
1994-95	PR Lge	42	11	12	19	34	49	45	19
1995-96	Div 1	46	20	15	11	67	48	75	3
1996-97	Div 1	46	19	14	13	78	48	71	6
1997-98	PR Lge	38	8	9	21	37	71	33	20
1998-99	Div 1	46	14	16	16	58	71	58	14
1999-2000	Div 1	46	13	15	18	57	67	54	15

DID YOU KNOW ?

On 28 November 2000, youth team player Steve Kabba, a 106th minute substitute, secured a place in the League Cup quarter-finals for Crystal Palace with a successful shoot-out penalty kick.

CRYSTAL PALACE 2000–01 LEAGUE RECORD

Match No.	Date	Venue	Opponents	Result	H/T Score	Lg. Pos.	Goalscorers	Attendance
1	Aug 12	A	Blackburn R	L	0-2	0-2	—		18,733
2	20	H	QPR	D	1-1	1-0	20	Forssell [45]	19,020
3	26	A	Huddersfield T	W	2-1	1-1	15	Gray [44], Ruddock [51]	10,670
4	28	H	Nottingham F	L	2-3	0-3	17	Black [52], Zhiyi [82]	18,865
5	Sept 3	A	WBA	L	0-1	0-1	21		13,980
6	9	H	Burnley	L	0-1	0-0	23		18,531
7	12	H	Barnsley	W	1-0	1-0	—	Morrison C [1]	16,297
8	16	A	Norwich C	D	0-0	0-0	16		16,828
9	23	H	Sheffield U	L	0-1	0-1	18		17,521
10	30	A	Preston NE	L	0-2	0-1	19		13,028
11	Oct 14	A	Birmingham C	L	1-2	0-0	20	Morrison C [66]	17,191
12	18	A	Fulham	L	1-3	1-2	—	Ruddock [17]	16,040
13	21	H	Portsmouth	L	2-3	2-1	22	Black 2 [36, 40]	15,693
14	24	H	Grimsby T	L	0-1	0-1	—		16,685
15	28	A	Bolton W	D	3-3	1-1	23	Freedman 2 [41, 87], Morrison C [90]	12,879
16	Nov 4	H	Sheffield W	W	4-1	3-0	21	Freedman [3], Morrison C [33], Pollock 2 [36, 47]	15,333
17	11	A	Wolverhampton W	W	3-1	2-0	21	Freedman [23], Morrison C 2 [45, 72]	17,658
18	18	H	Tranmere R	W	3-2	1-2	17	Staunton [15], Pollock [83], Morrison C [86]	14,221
19	25	H	Stockport Co	D	2-2	0-1	18	Forssell 2 [50, 78]	18,819
20	Dec 2	A	Grimsby T	D	2-2	1-0	18	Forssell [42], Morrison C [81]	5802
21	5	H	Wimbledon	W	3-1	0-1	—	Forssell [47], Morrison C 2 [56, 78]	16,699
22	9	H	Watford	W	1-0	0-0	12	Morrison C [61]	16,049
23	16	A	Crewe Alex	D	1-1	0-1	12	Freedman [80]	5752
24	22	H	Blackburn R	L	2-3	0-3	—	Forssell [49], Mullins [63]	15,010
25	26	A	Gillingham	L	1-4	0-1	15	Freedman (pen) [73]	10,518
26	30	A	QPR	D	1-1	0-1	16	Morrison C [59]	14,439
27	Jan 14	A	Nottingham F	W	3-0	2-0	14	Forssell 2 [19, 45], Freedman [68]	21,198
28	20	H	Gillingham	D	2-2	0-1	15	Freedman [82], Forssell [84]	18,823
29	Feb 3	H	WBA	D	2-2	2-1	16	Forssell [2], Pollock [6]	16,692
30	10	A	Burnley	W	2-1	0-1	14	Forssell [75], Morrison C [90]	14,973
31	17	H	Norwich C	D	1-1	1-0	14	Forssell [34]	16,417
32	20	A	Barnsley	L	0-1	0-1	—		12,909
33	24	A	Sheffield U	L	0-1	0-0	16		18,924
34	Mar 3	H	Preston NE	L	0-2	0-2	17		15,160
35	6	H	Birmingham C	L	1-2	0-0	—	Austin [61]	13,987
36	10	A	Wimbledon	L	0-1	0-1	19		13,167
37	17	H	Fulham	L	0-2	0-1	20		21,133
38	31	A	Crewe Alex	W	1-0	0-0	19	Austin [61]	20,872
39	Apr 3	H	Huddersfield T	D	0-0	0-0	—		15,324
40	7	A	Watford	D	2-2	1-0	22	Austin (pen) [15], Black [90]	15,598
41	14	A	Sheffield W	L	1-4	1-3	22	Morrison C [2]	19,877
42	16	H	Bolton W	L	0-2	0-1	22		16,268
43	21	A	Tranmere R	D	1-1	1-0	22	Hopkin [25]	8119
44	28	H	Wolverhampton W	L	0-2	0-1	22		18,993
45	May 2	A	Portsmouth	W	4-2	3-1	—	Forssell [18], Riihilahti [25], Freedman 2 [45, 51]	19,013
46	6	A	Stockport Co	W	1-0	0-0	21	Freedman [87]	9782

Final League Position: 21

GOALSCORERS

League (57): Morrison C 14, Forssell 13, Freedman 11 (1 pen), Black 4, Pollock 4, Austin 3 (1 pen), Ruddock 2, Gray 1, Hopkin 1, Mullins 1, Riihilahti 1, Staunton 1, Zhiyi 1.
Worthington Cup (12): Morrison C 4, Forssell 2, Rubins 2, Black 1, Linighan 1, Ruddock 1, Thomson 1.
FA Cup (2): Morrison C 1, Thompson 1.

Taylor S 10	Smith J 25 + 4	Harrison C 30 + 2	Austin D 38 + 1	Zhiyi F 28	Ruddock N 19 + 1	Mullins H 40 + 1	Pollock J 29 + 2	Morrison C 41 + 4	Forssell M 31 + 8	Fullarton J 1 + 1	Black T 30 + 10	Carlisle W 4 + 10	Gray J 12 + 1	Rodger S 28 + 5	McKenzie L 2 + 6	Harris R 1 + 1	Kitson P 4	Linighan A — + 1	Kolinko A 35	Morrison A 5	Thomson S 12 + 6	Rubins A 17 + 5	Staunton S 6	Freedman D 16 + 10	Frampton A 8 + 2	Gregg M 1	Kabba S — + 1	Berhalter G 4 + 1	Fuller R 2 + 6	Karic A 3	Upson M 7	Hopkin D 8 + 1	Verhoene K — + 1	Riihilahti A 9	Evans S — + 1	Match No.
1	2^1	3	4	5	6	7	8	9^2	10	11^3	12	13	14																							1
1		3		5	6	7	11^1	9^3	10^2	12	2	4	13	8	14																					2
1		3		5	6	7	11	9	10^1		2	13	4	8	14																					3
1		3	12	5	6^1	7	11	9	10^3		2	13	4	8	14																					4
1	12	3		5	6	7		10	9		2		4	8^1	11^2	13																				5
1		3	4^1	5	6	7		10	9	12	2			8	13	11^2																				6
1		3	4		6	7		10	9	12	2			8	11^1																					7
1		3	4	5	6	7	11	9			2			8^1	12		10																			8
1		3	4	5	6	7	11	9	12		2^2			8^1	13	14	10^3																			9
1		3	4	5^1	6	7	11	12	9^3		2^1	13	8				10	14																		10
	2	3	4				11^1	9	12					7	8		10		1	5	6															11
	2	3	6^3			7	11	9	10^1		4^2	12	13	8					1	5		14														12
	2	3^1				7	11	9	10^2		4	13	12						1	5	8	6														13
	2	3^2				7^1	11	12	10^1		4	13	14						1	5	8	6	9													14
		3				7	11	9	12		2	13	8						1	5^1	4^2	6	10													15
		3	5			7	11	9			2^1	12	8						1	13	4^2	6	10													16
		4	5			7	11	9			2		8						1	12	3^1	6	10													17
12		3	5			7	11	9			2	13	4^1	8					1				6	10^2												18
12	3^1	4	5			7	11	9	10		2	13	6^2	8^3					1		14															19
	2	3	4	5	6	7	11^1	9	10		8								1		12															20
	2^2	12	4	5	6	7	11	9	10		8								1		13		3^1													21
	2		4	5	6	7	11^1	9	10^2		8								1					13	3											22
	2	3^1	4	5	6	7	11	9	10^2		8								1					13												23
12	13	2	5	6	6^3	7	11	9			3			8^2					1		4^1			14												24
	2	4^1	5	12		7	11	9	10		3^2	13							1		6	8														25
	2	3		5		7		9	10^1		4			8					1		11	6	12													26
	2	3	4		6	7	12	9^2	10		8								1		5^1	11^3		13	14											27
	2		4		6^3		12	9	10		8			7	13				1		5^1	11^3	14	3												28
	2	3	5		6		11	9^2				10							1		4^1	7	13													29
	2	3	4			7	11^3	9	10		12	13		8							14	6^2		5^1	1											30
	2	3	5			7	11		10		4			8					1		6			9^1	12											31
	4	3	5				2	11	9		10^1	12		7^2	8				1		13							6^1	14							32
	4		5				2^2	9	10		7	13		8					1		11	14		12	3^1			6								33
		3	4	5^3			12	9	10		8^2			7	13				1		11^1	14								2	6					34
	2	3	5^2			7	12		10^1		8	13							1		11			9^2							4	14	6			35
	2^1	3				7		9^3	10		12								1		11	6	8	13							4	14	5^2			36
	4					2	12	10^1	7					8					1		6		9^1	3					13			5		11		37
		3	2	5^2				9	10		12								1		11^1										4	7	13	6		38
		3	2	5				9	10		11^1								1		12										4	7		6		39
		3	2	5		7		9^1	12		14			8^3					1		13			10^1							4	11		6		40
	2^1	3	4	5		7		9^3	13		12			8					1		14			10^3								11		6		41
	2^2	3	4	5		7		9	12		13								1		8^1			10								11		6		42
		3	4				2	9				12							1		11			10^2	5				13		7			6		43
		3	2			7		9				4	12						1		8^1			10	5^3				13	14		11^2		6		44
	2		4			7		9	10					5^1					1		11			8					3					6	12	45
	2		4			7		9	10		12			5^2					1		11^1			8					3			13		6		46

Worthington Cup

First Round	Cardiff C	(h)	2-1	
		(a)	0-0	
Second Round	Burnley	(a)	2-2	
		(h)	1-1	
Third Round	Leicester C	(a)	3-0	
Fourth Round	Tranmere R	(h)	0-0	
Fifth Round	Sunderland	(h)	2-1	
Semi-Final	Liverpool	(h)	2-1	
		(a)	0-5	

FA Cup

Third Round	Sunderland	(a)	0-0
		(h)	2-4

DARLINGTON   Division 3

Feethams Ground, Darlington DL1 5JB.

Telephone: (01325) 240 240.

Fax: (01325) 240 500.

Ground Capacity: 8500.

Record Attendance: 21,023 v Bolton W, League Cup
3rd rd, 14 November 1960.

Record Receipts: £32,300 v Rochdale, Division 4,
11 May 1991.

Pitch Measurements: 110yd × 74yd.

President: A. Noble.

Chairman: George Reynolds.

Vice-Chairman: G. Hodgson.

Manager: Gary Bennett.

Assistant Manager: Mick Tait.

Football Secretary: Lisa Charlton.

Colours: White and black with red piping.

Change Colours: Red, black and white.

Year Formed: 1883.

Turned Professional: 1908.

Ltd Co.: 1891.

Club Nickname: 'The Quakers'.

First Football League Game: 27 August 1921, Division 3 (N), v Halifax T (h) W 2–0 – Ward; Greaves,
Barbour; Dickson (1), Sutcliffe, Malcolm; Dolphin, Hooper (1), Edmunds, Wolstenholme, Winship.

Record League Victory: 9–2 v Lincoln C, Division 3 (N), 7 January 1928 – Archibald; Brooks, Mellen;
Kelly, Waugh, McKinnell; Cochrane (1), Gregg (1), Ruddy (3), Lees (3), McGiffen (1).

HONOURS

Football League: Division 2 best
season: 15th, 1925–26; Division 3 (N)
– Champions 1924–25; Runners-up
1921–22; Division 4 – Champions
1990–91; Runners-up 1965–66.

FA Cup: best season: 5th rd, 1958.

Football League Cup: best season:
5th rd, 1968.

GM Vauxhall Conference: Champions
1989–90.

IT'S A FACT !

Despite failing to score in any of their opening three
League matches in 1965-66, and winning just one of the
first half dozen, Darlington won promotion from
Division 4 as runners-up, level on points with the
champions Doncaster Rovers.

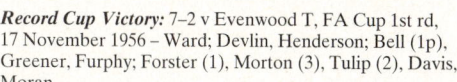
Record Cup Victory: 7–2 v Evenwood T, FA Cup 1st rd, 17 November 1956 – Ward; Devlin, Henderson; Bell (1p), Greener, Furphy; Forster (1), Morton (3), Tulip (2), Davis, Moran.

Record Defeat: 0–10 v Doncaster R, Division 4, 25 January 1964.

Most League Points (2 for a win): 59, Division 4, 1965–66.

Most League Points (3 for a win): 85, Division 4, 1984–85.

Most League Goals: 108, Division 3 (N), 1929–30.

Highest League Scorer in Season: David Brown, 39, Division 3 (N), 1924–25.

Most League Goals in Total Aggregate: Alan Walsh, 90, 1978–84.

Most League Goals in One Match: 5, Tom Ruddy v South Shields, Division 2, 23 April 1927; 5, Maurice Wellock v Rotherham U, Division 3N, 15 February 1930.

Most Capped Player: Jason Devos, 3, Canada.

Most League Appearances: Ron Greener, 442, 1955–68.

Youngest League Player: Dale Anderson, 16 years 254 days v Chesterfield, 4 May 1987.

Record Transfer Fee Received: £400,000 from Dundee U for Jason Devos, October 1998.

Record Transfer Fee Paid: £95,000 to Motherwell for Nick Cusack, January 1992.

Football League Record: 1921 Original Member Division 3 (N); 1925–27 Division 2; 1927–58 Division 3 (N); 1958–66 Division 4; 1966–67 Division 3; 1967–85 Division 4; 1985–87 Division 3; 1987–89 Division 4; 1989–90 GM Vauxhall Conference; 1990–91 Division 4; 1991– Division 3.

LATEST SEQUENCES

Longest Sequence of League Wins: 6, 6.2.00 – 7.3.00.

Longest Sequence of League Defeats: 8, 31.8.85 – 19.10.85.

Longest Sequence of League Draws: 5, 31.12.88 – 28.1.89.

Longest Sequence of Unbeaten League Matches: 17, 27.4.68 – 19.10.68.

Longest Sequence Without a League Win: 19, 27.4.88 – 8.11.88.

MANAGERS

Tom McIntosh 1902–11
W. L. Lane 1911–12
  (Secretary-Manager)
Dick Jackson 1912–19
Jack English 1919–28
Jack Fairless 1928–33
George Collins 1933–36
George Brown 1936–38
Jackie Carr 1938–42
Jack Surtees 1942
Jack English 1945–46
Bill Forrest 1946–50
George Irwin 1950–52
Bob Gurney 1952–57
Dick Duckworth 1957–60
Eddie Carr 1960–64
Lol Morgan 1964–66
Jimmy Greenhalgh 1966–68
Ray Yeoman 1968–70
Len Richley 1970–71
Frank Brennan 1971
Ken Hale 1971–72
Allan Jones 1972
Ralph Brand 1972–73
Dick Conner 1973–74
Billy Horner 1974–76
Peter Madden 1976–78
Len Walker 1978–79
Billy Elliott 1979–83
Cyril Knowles 1983–87
Dave Booth 1987–89
Brian Little 1989–91
Frank Gray 1991–92
Ray Hankin 1992
Billy McEwan 1992–93
Alan Murray 1993–95
Paul Futcher 1995
David Hodgson/Jim Platt
  (Director of Coaching) 1995
Jim Platt 1995–96
David Hodgson 1996–2000
Gary Bennett August 2000–

TEN YEAR LEAGUE RECORD

		P	W	D	L	F	A	Pts	Pos
1990-91	Div 4	46	22	17	7	68	38	83	1
1991-92	Div 3	46	10	7	29	56	90	37	24
1992-93	Div 3	42	12	14	16	48	53	50	15
1993-94	Div 3	42	10	11	21	42	64	41	21
1994-95	Div 3	42	11	8	23	43	57	41	20
1995-96	Div 3	46	20	18	8	60	42	78	5
1996-97	Div 3	46	14	10	22	64	78	52	18
1997-98	Div 3	46	14	12	20	56	72	54	19
1998-99	Div 3	46	18	11	17	69	58	65	11
1999-2000	Div 3	46	21	16	9	66	36	79	4

DID YOU KNOW ?

The intervention of the Second World War in September 1939 came after Darlington had had a three match unbeaten start and for eight of the 11 players involved, this was their only official games with the club.

DARLINGTON 2000–01 LEAGUE RECORD

Match No.	Date		Venue	Opponents	Result		H/T Score	Lg. Pos.	Goalscorers	Attendance
1	Aug	12	A	Rochdale	D	1-1	1-0	—	Nogan [10]	3255
2		19	H	Exeter C	D	1-1	1-0	14	Liddle [24]	4056
3		26	A	Southend U	W	2-0	0-0	8	Liddle [56], Nogan [67]	3444
4		29	H	Plymouth Arg	W	1-0	1-0	—	Kaak [4]	4415
5	Sept	2	H	York C	D	1-1	1-1	5	Kaak [8]	5170
6		9	A	Shrewsbury T	L	0-1	0-1	9		2597
7		12	A	Cheltenham T	L	0-1	0-0	—		2368
8		16	H	Barnet	W	1-0	1-0	8	Campbell [10]	3929
9		22	A	Macclesfield T	D	1-1	0-1	—	Nogan [71]	2389
10		30	H	Carlisle U	W	1-0	0-0	5	Beavers [88]	4316
11	Oct	7	A	Hartlepool U	L	1-2	0-1	8	Naylor [89]	3265
12		14	H	Torquay U	W	2-0	1-0	7	Naylor [5], Nogan [54]	3518
13		17	H	Kidderminster H	L	1-2	0-1	—	Naylor [66]	3713
14		21	A	Scunthorpe U	D	1-1	1-1	8	Naylor [41]	3298
15		24	A	Cardiff C	L	0-2	0-1	—		5440
16		28	H	Brighton & HA	L	1-2	1-1	14	Naylor [34]	3637
17	Nov	4	A	Hull C	L	0-2	0-1	15		5344
18		11	H	Halifax T	L	0-1	0-1	17		3288
19		25	A	Blackpool	L	1-2	0-1	18	Hjorth [80]	3683
20	Dec	2	H	Mansfield T	W	2-1	1-1	14	Kyle [21], Atkinson (pen) [62]	3087
21		16	H	Leyton Orient	L	0-0	0-0	17		4117
22		23	H	Lincoln C	W	3-0	2-0	14	McMahon [8], Heckingbottom [25], Atkinson (pen) [58]	3364
23		26	A	Chesterfield	L	0-2	0-2	14		5128
24	Jan	6	H	Rochdale	L	1-2	0-1	17	Hodgson [56]	3481
25		13	A	Plymouth Arg	D	1-1	0-1	18	Williams [68]	4278
26		20	H	Chesterfield	L	0-3	0-2	19		3802
27		27	A	Lincoln C	D	2-2	1-0	19	Atkinson (pen) [38], Schofield (og) [89]	2873
28	Feb	17	A	Barnet	L	0-3	0-1	21		1818
29		20	H	Cheltenham T	W	1-0	1-0	—	Freeman (og) [21]	2689
30		24	H	Macclesfield T	D	1-1	1-1	21	Ford (pen) [32]	3103
31	Mar	3	A	Carlisle U	W	2-0	1-0	18	Ford [14], Jackson [70]	3726
32		10	H	Hartlepool U	D	1-1	1-0	21	Naylor [37]	6717
33		13	A	York C	L	0-2	0-1	—		3244
34		17	A	Kidderminster H	D	0-0	0-0	20		2568
35		24	H	Scunthorpe U	W	2-1	1-0	19	Williams 2 [37, 74]	3125
36		27	A	Exeter C	D	1-1	0-0	—	Hodgson [64]	3530
37		31	H	Leyton Orient	D	1-1	1-1	19	Naylor (pen) [43]	3189
38	Apr	3	A	Southend U	D	1-1	0-0	—	Naylor [61]	2782
39		10	H	Shrewsbury T	W	3-0	3-0	—	Bernard [12], Kilty [25], Naylor [45]	2917
40		14	H	Cardiff C	W	2-0	2-0	14	Williams [12], Naylor [28]	3683
41		16	A	Brighton & HA	L	0-2	0-2	15		6639
42		21	H	Hull C	L	0-2	0-2	15		4998
43		24	A	Torquay U	L	1-2	0-0	—	Bernard [55]	2810
44		28	A	Halifax T	L	0-1	0-0	16		2287
45	May	1	A	Mansfield T	L	2-3	1-2	—	Atkinson (pen) [28], Naylor [69]	1878
46		5	H	Blackpool	L	1-3	0-1	20	Williams [51]	5428

Final League Position: 20

GOALSCORERS

League (44): Naylor 11 (1 pen), Williams 5, Atkinson 4 (4 pens), Nogan 4, Bernard 2, Ford 2 (1 pen), Hodgson 2, Kaak 2, Liddle 2, Beavers 1, Campbell 1, Heckingbottom 1, Hjorth 1, Jackson 1, Kilty 1, Kyle 1, McMahon 1, own goals 2.
Worthington Cup (6): Elliott 3 (1 pen), Angel 1, Campbell 1, Naylor 1.
FA Cup (6): Naylor 3, Hodgson 2, Kyle 1.

Collett A 37	Liddle C 45	Heckingbottom P 17 + 1	Reed A 28 + 6	Aspin N 21	Himsworth G 14 + 1	Gray M 25	Elliott S 20 + 4	Nogan L 18	Naylor G 42 + 2	Kaak T 7 + 1	Atkinson B 17 + 6	Hjorth J 8 + 15	Williamson G 1 + 5	Campbell P 11 + 5	Hodgson R 20 + 15	Angel M 1 + 4	Walklate S 2 + 4	Van der Geest F 2	Jeannin A 11	Zeghdane L 1 + 2	Beavers P 3 + 4	Butler T 8	Cau J — + 1	Tait J 2 + 1	Skelton C — + 1	Kyle K 5	Brunwell P 19 + 2	Marsh A 1 + 6	McMahon D 5 + 3	Kitty M 18	Williams J 23 + 1	Brightwell D 12 + 2	Harper S 17	Convery M 5 + 6	Ford M 11	Marcelle C 8 + 4	Jackson K 5 + 5	Keen P 7	Bernard O 9 + 1	Match No.
1	4	3	6	5	8¹	7	2	9²	10	11³	12	13	14																											1
1	4	3	6¹	5	8²	7	2	9	10	11³			14	12	13																									2
1	4	3	6	5	8	7	2	9¹	10	13				12	11²																									3
1	4	3	6	5¹	8	7	2	9	10	11³				12	14	13																								4
1	5	3	6		8	4	2³	9	10	11²				7¹	12	13		14																						5
1	4	3	6	5	8¹	7²	2	9	10	11³				12		13		14					1																	6
	2	3	4	5			6	9	10	11²				12		7	8¹		1	13																				7
1	4	3	6	5	12	8	2	9	10	11²				7¹				11²																						8
1	4		6	5	12	8	2	9	10	11²				7¹		13	12																							9
1	4		6	5	3²	7	2	9						12		10	8³	11³	13		14																			10
1	4	6²	5	3	8	2¹	9	10		13	12			7	14				11³																					11
1	4		5	3	8	2	9¹	10		13	12			7³	11				14	6²																				12
1	4		5	3²	8	2	9	10		12	7¹			11¹	13				14	6																				13
1	4	12	5	3¹		2	9	10		11	7			8					6																					14
1	4	3	5²		8	2	9	10		11³	12			7¹					6	13	14																			15
1	4	3	5		8	2	9¹	10			12			7	13				6	11²																				16
1	2	3	5		6		9	10		11¹	12				13				4	8²	7																			17
1	4	3	2	5			6	9¹	10		11	12			13	7²				8																				18
1	4	12	2¹	5	3³	6		9		11²	13				7	14			8		10																			19
1	4	3	2	5		7		9²		11				8¹					6			10	12	13																20
1	4	3	6	5	8¹	7	2	9		11												10		12																21
1	4	3		6²	12		10		11	9¹			14		13											2		7	5	8³										22
1	4			5		7¹	12	9	11						13	3										2		8	6	10²										23
1	4	3		6		2	9		11²			12			7											13		8¹	5	10										24
1	4	3	12	6		2	13		9³			7²			8											14		11¹	5	10										25
1	4	3		6		2¹	9		12			7			8											13		11²	5	10										26
1	2	3	14			12	9		11			8			7¹									4		6²	13		5³	10										27
1		3	4				9		11			8²			6	12				7										10¹	5	2	13							28
1	4	3¹	12						11²			8			13				9³							6	14		10	5	2		7							29
1	4						12		9²			7¹			13									11			14		10³	3	2		6	8						30
1	4			2			11¹					12												7					10²	5	3	13		6	8	9				31
1	2						7¹					13	12										4			5	10²	11	3			6	8	9					32
	5						7																3			6	12	4	2		8	10	9¹			1	11			33
	5	12															7²						3¹			6		4	2	13		8	10	9			1		34
	4						11											5								7	12	6	10	3	2		8	9¹			1		35
	4	12					11								13			5								7		6	10³	2¹	3		8	9²	14		1		36
	4	2					9²							12	11	5						14				7		6	10³		3	13	8¹				1		37
	4	2					9							11	8	5										7		6	10		3¹					1	12		38
	4	2					9¹							7		5										6		10³	3	13		8²	12	14	1	11			39
1	4	2					9							11									7			6		10¹		8				12	3		40
1	4	2					9¹				12			7		5²							6			10³	13	3	8		14	11						41
1	4	2					9		12					7		5										11	6¹	10³	3		14	13		14	3				42
1	4	2					8²	7						13		5							10			12		3	14	6³		9¹		11					43
1	4	2¹					9	7						8												6		10	5	3		12		11					44
1	4						12	11		13				7		5											10¹	6	2	8		9²		3					45
1	4						9³	11		7				5²		12	13									10	6	2	8¹		14		3					46

Worthington Cup

First Round	Nottingham F	(h)	2-2
		(a)	2-1
Second Round	Bradford C	(h)	0-1
		(a)	2-7

FA Cup

First Round	AFC Sudbury	(h)	6-1
		(h)	0-0
Second Round	Luton T	(a)	0-2

DERBY COUNTY   FA Premiership

FOUNDATION

Derby County was formed by members of the Derbyshire County Cricket Club in 1884, when football was booming in the area and the cricketers thought that a football club would help boost finances for the summer game. To begin with, they sported the cricket club's colours of amber, chocolate and pale blue, and went into the game at the top immediately entering the FA Cup.

Pride Park Stadium, Derby DE24 8XL.

Telephone: (01332) 202 202. *Fax:* (01332) 667 519.
ClubCall: 09068 121 187.

Ground Capacity: 33,597.

Record Attendance: 41,826 v Tottenham H, Division 1, 20 September 1969.

Record Receipts: £425,804 v Huddersfield T, FA Cup 5th rd replay, 24 February 1999.

Pitch Measurements: 110yd × 72yd.

Chairman: L. V. Pickering.

Vice-Chairman: P. J. Gadsby.

Directors: J. N. Kirkland OBE, R. Clarke.

Manager: Jim Smith. *Assistant Manager:* Colin Todd.

Chief Scout: Bobby Roberts.

First Team Coach: Steve Round.

Physio: Peter Melville.

Stadium Manager: David Goodwin.

Chief Executive: Keith Loring.

Secretary: Keith Pearson ACIS.

General Sales Manager: Gary Hodder.

Colours: White shirts with black piping, black shorts, white stockings.

Change Colours: Navy blue shirts, navy blue shorts with white trim, navy blue stockings.

Year Formed: 1884.

Turned Professional: 1884.

Ltd Co.: 1896.

Club Nickname: 'The Rams'.

Previous Grounds: 1884, Racecourse Ground; 1895, Baseball Ground; 1997, Pride Park.

First Football League Game: 8 September 1888, Football League, v Bolton W (a) W 6–3 – Marshall; Latham, Ferguson, Williamson; Monks, W. Roulstone; Bakewell (2), Cooper (2), Higgins, H. Plackett, L. Plackett (2).

HONOURS

Football League: Division 1 – Champions 1971–72, 1974–75; Runners-up 1895–96, 1929–30, 1935–36, 1995–96; Division 2 – Champions 1911–12, 1914–15, 1968–69, 1986–87; Runners-up 1925–26; Division 3 (N) Champions 1956–57; Runners-up 1955–56.

FA Cup: Winners 1946; Runners-up 1898, 1899, 1903.

Football League Cup: Semi-final 1968.

Texaco Cup: Winners 1972.

European Competitions: *European Cup:* 1972–73, 1975–76. *UEFA Cup:* 1974–75, 1976–77. *Anglo-Italian Cup:* Runners-up 1993.

IT'S A FACT !

Johnny Goodall became the first player to score hat-tricks in successive League games during the initial season of the competition in 1888–89. He achieved this feat against Wolverhampton Wanderers and Notts County.

Record League Victory: 9–0 v Wolverhampton W,
Division 1, 10 January 1891 – Bunyan; Archie Goodall,
Roberts; Walker, Chalmers, Roulston (1); Bakewell,
McLachlan, Johnny Goodall (1), Holmes (2), McMillan (5).
9–0 v Sheffield W, Division 1, 21 January 1899 – Fryer;
Methven, Staley; Cox, Archie Goodall, May; Oakden (1),
Bloomer (6), Boag, McDonald (1), Allen, (1 og).

Record Cup Victory: 12–0 v Finn Harps, UEFA Cup 1st rd
1st leg, 15 September 1976 – Moseley; Thomas, Nish,
Rioch (1), McFarland, Todd (King), Macken, Gemmill,
Hector (5), George (3), James (3).

Record Defeat: 2–11 v Everton, FA Cup 1st rd, 1889–90.

Most League Points (2 for a win): 63, Division 2, 1968–69
and Division 3 (N), 1955–56 and 1956–57.

Most League Points (3 for a win): 84, Division 3, 1985–86
and Division 3, 1986–87.

Most League Goals: 111, Division 3 (N), 1956–57.

Highest League Scorer in Season: Jack Bowers, 37,
Division 1, 1930–31; Ray Straw, 37 Division 3 (N), 1956–57.

Most League Goals in Total Aggregate: Steve Bloomer,
292, 1892–1906 and 1910–14.

MANAGERS
Harry Newbould 1896–1906
Jimmy Methven 1906–22
Cecil Potter 1922–25
George Jobey 1925–41
Ted Magner 1944–46
Stuart McMillan 1946–53
Jack Barker 1953–55
Harry Storer 1955–62
Tim Ward 1962–67
Brian Clough 1967–73
Dave Mackay 1973–76
Colin Murphy 1977
Tommy Docherty 1977–79
Colin Addison 1979–82
Johnny Newman 1982
Peter Taylor 1982–84
Roy McFarland 1984
Arthur Cox 1984–93
Roy McFarland 1993–95
Jim Smith June 1995–

Most League Goals in One Match: 6, Steve Bloomer v Sheffield W, Division 1, 2 January 1899.

Most Capped Player: Deon Burton, 35 (35), Jamaica.

Most League Appearances: Kevin Hector, 486, 1966–78 and 1980–82.

Youngest League Player: Steve Powell, 16 years 33 days v Arsenal, 23 October 1971.

Record Transfer Fee Received: £5,300,000 from Blackburn R for Christian Dailly, August 1998.

Record Transfer Fee Paid: £3,000,000 rising to £4,000,000 for Lee Morris from Sheffield U,
October 1999.

Football League Record: 1888 Founder Member of the Football League; 1907–12 Division 2;
1912–14 Division 1; 1914–15 Division 2; 1915–21 Division 1; 1921–26 Division 2; 1926–53 Division 1;
1953–55 Division 2; 1955–57 Division 3 (N); 1957–69 Division 2; 1969–80 Division 1; 1980–84
Division 2; 1984–86 Division 3; 1986–87 Division 2; 1987–91 Division 1; 1991–92 Division 2; 1992–96
Division 1; 1996– FA Premier League.

LATEST SEQUENCES

Longest Sequence of League Wins: 9, 15.3.69 – 19.4.69.

Longest Sequence of League Defeats: 8, 12.12.87 – 10.2.88.

Longest Sequence of League Draws: 6, 26.3.27 – 18.4.27.

Longest Sequence of Unbeaten League Matches: 22, 8.3.69 – 20.9.69.

Longest Sequence Without a League Win: 20, 15.12.90 – 23.4.91.

TEN YEAR LEAGUE RECORD

		P	W	D	L	F	A	Pts	Pos
1990-91	Div 1	38	5	9	24	37	75	24	20
1991-92	Div 2	46	23	9	14	69	51	78	3
1992-93	Div 1	46	19	9	18	68	57	66	8
1993-94	Div 1	46	20	11	15	73	68	71	6
1994-95	Div 1	46	18	12	16	66	51	66	9
1995-96	Div 1	46	21	16	9	71	51	79	2
1996-97	PR Lge	38	11	13	14	45	58	46	12
1997-98	PR Lge	38	16	7	15	52	49	55	9
1998-99	PR Lge	38	13	13	12	40	45	52	8
1999-2000	PR Lge	38	9	11	18	44	57	38	16

DID YOU KNOW ?

On 18 December 1950 Derby
County beat Sunderland 6–5
on a frozen Baseball Ground.
Jack Lee scored four goals
for the Rams who were
masterminded by Johnny
Morris signed for a then
record British fee of £24,500
from Manchester United.

DERBY COUNTY 2000–01 LEAGUE RECORD

Match No.	Date	Venue	Opponents	Result	H/T Score	Lg. Pos.	Goalscorers	Attendance
1	Aug 19	H	Southampton	D	2-2	1-2	—	Strupar [32], Burton [49]	27,223
2	23	A	Newcastle U	L	2-3	1-1	—	Strupar [45], Johnson [83]	51,327
3	26	A	Everton	D	2-2	0-2	18	Sturridge [52], Strupar [68]	34,840
4	Sept 6	H	Middlesbrough	D	3-3	0-1	—	Christie 2 [68, 88], Strupar [83]	24,290
5	10	H	Charlton Ath	D	2-2	2-0	16	Christie [7], Valakari [39]	22,310
6	16	A	Sunderland	L	1-2	0-1	19	Christie [83]	43,898
7	23	H	Leeds U	D	1-1	0-1	19	Kinkladze [75]	26,248
8	30	A	Aston Villa	L	1-4	0-2	20	Riggott [61]	27,941
9	Oct 15	H	Liverpool	L	0-4	0-1	20		30,532
10	21	A	Tottenham H	L	1-3	1-2	20	Riggott [39]	34,459
11	28	A	Leicester C	L	1-2	1-1	20	Delap [12]	20,525
12	Nov 6	H	West Ham U	D	0-0	0-0	—		24,621
13	11	A	Arsenal	D	0-0	0-0	19		37,679
14	18	H	Bradford C	W	2-0	0-0	19	Christie [55], Delap [68]	31,614
15	25	H	Manchester U	L	0-3	0-0	19		32,910
16	Dec 2	H	Ipswich T	W	1-0	1-0	17	Delap [28]	21,991
17	9	A	Chelsea	L	1-4	0-3	18	Riggott [56]	34,315
18	16	H	Coventry C	W	1-0	1-0	17	Christie [9]	27,869
19	23	H	Newcastle U	W	2-0	1-0	16	Carbonari [33], Burton [73]	29,978
20	26	A	Manchester C	D	0-0	0-0	16		34,321
21	30	A	Southampton	L	0-1	0-0	16		15,075
22	Jan 1	H	Everton	W	1-0	1-0	15	Burton [20]	27,358
23	13	A	Middlesbrough	L	0-4	0-1	17		29,041
24	20	H	Manchester C	D	1-1	0-0	17	Powell [49]	31,174
25	30	A	Charlton Ath	L	1-2	1-1	—	Burley [35]	20,043
26	Feb 3	H	Sunderland	W	1-0	1-0	16	Burley [42]	29,123
27	10	A	Leeds U	D	0-0	0-0	16		38,789
28	24	H	Aston Villa	W	1-0	1-0	16	Burton (pen) [42]	27,289
29	Mar 3	H	Tottenham H	W	2-1	2-0	14	Strupar 2 (1 pen) [12, 33 (p)]	29,410
30	18	A	Liverpool	D	1-1	1-0	15	Burton [9]	43,362
31	31	A	Coventry C	L	0-2	0-1	16		19,622
32	Apr 7	H	Chelsea	L	0-4	0-0	16		29,320
33	14	A	West Ham U	L	1-3	0-3	17	Gudjonsson [83]	25,319
34	16	H	Leicester C	W	2-0	1-0	16	Boertien [24], Eranio [90]	28,387
35	21	A	Bradford C	L	0-2	0-1	17		18,564
36	28	H	Arsenal	L	1-2	1-1	17	Eranio [45]	29,567
37	May 5	A	Manchester U	W	1-0	1-0	16	Christie [34]	67,526
38	19	H	Ipswich T	D	1-1	1-0	17	Christie [31]	33,239

Final League Position: 17

GOALSCORERS

League (37): Christie 8, Strupar 6 (1 pen), Burton 5 (1 pen), Delap 3, Riggott 3, Burley 2, Eranio 2, Boertien 1, Carbonari 1, Gudjonsson 1, Johnson 1, Kinkladze 1, Powell 1, Sturridge 1, Valakari 1.
Worthington Cup (10): Bragstad 2, Burley 2 (1 pen), Christie 2, Burton 1, Delap 1, Powell 1, Riggott 1.
FA Cup (5): Christie 2, Eranio 2, Riggott 1.

Poom M 32+1	Eranio S 25+3	Higginbotham D 23+3	Valakari S 9+2	Blatsis C 2	Bragstad B 10+2	Delap R 32+1	Morris L 4+16	Strupar B 7+2	Johnson S 30	Powell D 27	Elliott S 5+1	Burton D 25+7	Sturridge D 3+11	Riggott C 29+2	Schnoor S 6+2	Jackson R 1+1	Murray A 4+10	Kinkladze G 13+11	Christie M 29+5	Carbonari H 27	Burley C 24	Bohinen L 1+1	Martin L 7+2	West T 18	O'Neil B 3+1	Mawene Y 7+1	Oakes A 6	Boertien P 7+1	Gudjonsson T 2+8	Bolder A —+2	Evatt I —+1	Match No.
1	2	3	4	5	6	7^1	8^2	9^3	10	11	12	13	14																			1
1	7^1	3	4	2^8	5		13	9	10	11	6	8	12																			2
1	7^3	3^8	4		6			9	10		2	8	12	14	13	5^1	11															3
1	7^2	4^3		5	2			9^1	10		6	8	11			3	12	13	14													4
1	2^1	3	4		6	7			10		8	9^2				5	12	13	11													5
1	2^3	3	4		6		12		10		7^1	9	13	14			8^2	11	5													6
1	2^3	3	7		6^2				10		8	12	14	4			13	9^1	5	11												7
1	2^3	3			6		12		10	11	8^3	13	4	5^1				14	9^2	7												8
1	2^1	6		5		7				13	3	11	12	4^2					10	9	8											9
1	3^1			5	6		13		10^3	11	8	7	4	12					9^2	2	14											10
1	7^1	2			6				3	11	8	9	4	5^2					13	12	10											11
1	12						8	13		3	11^1	14	4	6				10	9^3	5	7		2^2									12
1	6	12					8	13		3	11	14	4					10^3	9^2	5	7		2^1									13
1	7^2						8	13		3	11	12	4					10	9^1	5			2	6								14
1	12						8	13		3	11	14	4					10	9	5^1			2^8	6	7^2							15
1	7^3	12							10	14	3	11	13	4					9^2	5	8		2^1	6								16
1	3						8	12			11	13	4	14				9	5^2	7	10^3		2^1	6								17
1	7^3						10	12		3	11	13	4	14				9^1	5	8			2^2	6								18
1	7^2						2	12		3	11	10^1	4					13	9	5	8			6								19
1	12						2			3	11^1	8	4					10^2	9	5	7	13	6									20
1	7^2	3					2				10	8	12	4				13	9^1	11			6		5							21
1	7^1	3					2				10	8	4	13	12			9	5	11^2			6									22
1	7^2	3^1					2	12	14		11	8	4	13				9^3	5	10			6									23
1	3^1						2	12			11	8					7^2	9	5	10	13	6	4									24
1	12	3^1	13				2				11	8	4					9	5	7			10	6^2								25
1	7						2^3	12			11^2	8	4	13				9^1	5	10		6	14				1	3				26
1	2^2	12					13	14	10		11	8	4					9^3	5	7		6	3^1		1							27
1	5						2	10^1	9^2		3	11	8	4				12		7		6		1	13							28
1	3						2		10	11	12	4						8^2	5	7		6		1				13				29
1	12	3^1					2		10	11	8	4						9^2	5	7		6		1				13				30
15	6						2				3	11	8	12	13		9	5	7^1			4	1^0		10^2							31
1							2		10	11	8	4		7^1	12	9	5^2				6			3	13							32
1	7^1	3^1					2	14	10	11	9	4		8^2	12	5					6				13							33
1	7						2		10	11^2	9	4		8^1	12	5					6	14		3	13^3							34
1	7^2						2	11^1	10		9	4		6	8	12	5							3	13							35
1	7	6					2		10	12	4	13		8^3	9^1	5	11^2							3	14							36
1	7	6					2	8					4		10^2	9^2	5					11		3	12	13						37
1	7	6					2					4^2	13	10	9	5					11		3	8^3	12	14					38

Worthington Cup

Second Round	WBA	(h)	1-2
		(a)	4-2
Third Round	Norwich C	(h)	3-0
Fourth Round	Fulham	(a)	2-3

FA Cup

Third Round	WBA	(h)	3-2
Fourth Round	Blackburn R	(a)	0-0
		(h)	2-5

EVERTON

FA Premiership

FOUNDATION

St Domingo Church Sunday School formed a football club in 1878 which played at Stanley Park. Enthusiasm was so great that in November 1879 they decided to expand membership and changed the name to Everton playing in black shirts with a scarlet sash and nicknamed the 'Black Watch'. After wearing several other colours, royal blue was adopted in 1901.

Goodison Park, Liverpool L4 4EL.

Telephone: (0151) 330 2200. **Fax:** (0151) 286 9112.
Ticket Infoline: 09068 121 599. **ClubCall:** 09068 121 199.

Ground Capacity: 40,170.

Record Attendance: 78,299 v Liverpool, Division 1, 18 September 1948.

Record Receipts: £730,000 v Manchester U, FA Premier League, 16 September 2000.

Pitch Measurements: 110yd × 70yd.

Chairman: Sir Philip Carter CBE.

Deputy-Chairman: Bill Kenwright CBE.

Directors: Keith Tamlin, Arthur Abercromby, Paul Gregg, Jon Woods.

Manager: Walter Smith OBE.

Assistant Manager: Archie Knox.

Physio: Steve Hardwick.

Chief Executive: Michael J. Dunford.

Stadium Manager: Alan Bowen.

Head of Marketing: Andy Oldknow.

Head of Media Publications: Alan Myers.

Colours: Royal blue shirts with white panels, white shorts with blue trim, blue stockings with white trim.

Change Colours: Silver shirts, black shorts, silver and black stockings.

Year Formed: 1878.

Turned Professional: 1885.

Ltd Co.: 1892.

Previous Name: 1878, St Domingo FC; 1879, Everton.

Club Nickname: 'The Toffees'.

Previous Grounds: 1878, Stanley Park; 1882, Priory Road; 1884, Anfield Road; 1892, Goodison Park.

HONOURS

Football League: Division 1 – Champions 1890–91, 1914–15, 1927–28, 1931–32, 1938–39, 1962–63, 1969–70, 1984–85, 1986–87; Runners-up 1889–90, 1894–95, 1901–02, 1904–05, 1908–09, 1911–12, 1985–86; Division 2 – Champions 1930–31; Runners-up 1953–54.

FA Cup: Winners 1906, 1933, 1966, 1984, 1995; Runners-up 1893, 1897, 1907, 1968, 1985, 1986, 1989.

Football League Cup: Runners-up 1977, 1984.

League Super Cup: Runners-up 1986.

Simod Cup: Runners-up 1989.

Zenith Data Systems Cup: Runners-up 1991.

European Competitions: *European Cup:* 1963–64, 1970–71. *European Cup-Winners' Cup:* 1966–67, 1984–85 (winners), 1995–96. *European Fairs Cup:* 1962–63, 1964–65, 1965–66. *UEFA Cup:* 1975–76, 1978–79, 1979–80.

IT'S A FACT !

Brazil were so impressed with Everton's training ground which they used during the 1966 World Cup, that they photographed the site and had a replica built after returning home.

First Football League Game: 8 September 1888, Football League, v Accrington (h) W 2–1 – Smalley; Dick, Ross; Holt, Jones, Dobson; Fleming (2), Waugh, Lewis, E. Chadwick, Farmer.

Record League Victory: 9–1 v Manchester C, Division 1, 3 September 1906 – Scott; Balmer, Crelley; Booth, Taylor (1), Abbott (1); Sharp, Bolton (1), Young (4), Settle (2), George Wilson. 9–1 v Plymouth Arg, Division 2, 27 December 1930 – Coggins; Williams, Cresswell; McPherson, Griffiths, Thomson; Critchley, Dunn, Dean (4), Johnson (1), Stein (4).

Record Cup Victory: 11–2 v Derby Co, FA Cup 1st rd, 18 January 1890 – Smalley; Hannah, Doyle (1); Kirkwood, Holt (1), Parry; Latta, Brady (3), Geary (3), Chadwick, Millward (3).

Record Defeat: 4–10 v Tottenham H, Division 1, 11 October 1958.

Most League Points (2 for a win): 66, Division 1, 1969–70.

Most League Points (3 for a win): 90, Division 1, 1984–85.

Most League Goals: 121, Division 2, 1930–31.

Highest League Scorer in Season: William Ralph 'Dixie' Dean, 60, Division 1, 1927–28 (All-time League record).

Most League Goals in Total Aggregate: William Ralph 'Dixie' Dean, 349, 1925–37.

MANAGERS
W. E. Barclay 1888–89 *(Secretary-Manager)*
Dick Molyneux 1889–1901 *(Secretary-Manager)*
William C. Cuff 1901–18 *(Secretary-Manager)*
W. J. Sawyer 1918–19 *(Secretary-Manager)*
Thomas H. McIntosh 1919–35 *(Secretary-Manager)*
Theo Kelly 1936–48
Cliff Britton 1948–56
Ian Buchan 1956–58
Johnny Carey 1958–61
Harry Catterick 1961–73
Billy Bingham 1973–77
Gordon Lee 1977–81
Howard Kendall 1981–87
Colin Harvey 1987–90
Howard Kendall 1990–93
Mike Walker 1994
Joe Royle 1994–97
Howard Kendall 1997–98
Walter Smith July 1998–

Most League Goals in One Match: 6, Jack Southworth v WBA, Division 1, 30 December 1893.

Most Capped Player: Neville Southall, 92, Wales.

Most League Appearances: Neville Southall, 578, 1981–98.

Youngest League Player: Joe Royle, 16 years 282 days v Blackpool, 15 January 1966.

Record Transfer Fee Received: £10,000,000 from Arsenal for Francis Jeffers, June 2001.

Record Transfer Fee Paid: £5,750,000 to Middlesbrough for Nick Barmby, October 1996.

Football League Record: 1888 Founder Member of the Football League; 1930–31 Division 2; 1931–51 Division 1; 1951–54 Division 2; 1954–92 Division 1; 1992– FA Premier League.

LATEST SEQUENCES

Longest Sequence of League Wins: 12, 24.3.1894 – 13.10.1894.

Longest Sequence of League Defeats: 6, 26.12.96 – 29.1.97.

Longest Sequence of League Draws: 5, 4.5.77 – 16.5.77.

Longest Sequence of Unbeaten League Matches: 20, 29.4.78 – 16.12.78.

Longest Sequence Without a League Win: 14, 6.3.37 – 4.9.37.

TEN YEAR LEAGUE RECORD

		P	W	D	L	F	A	Pts	Pos
1990-91	Div 1	38	13	12	13	50	46	51	9
1991-92	Div 1	42	13	14	15	52	51	53	12
1992-93	PR Lge	42	15	8	19	53	55	53	13
1993-94	PR Lge	42	12	8	22	42	63	44	17
1994-95	PR Lge	42	11	17	14	44	51	50	15
1995-96	PR Lge	38	17	10	11	64	44	61	6
1996-97	PR Lge	38	10	12	16	44	57	42	15
1997-98	PR Lge	38	9	13	16	41	56	40	17
1998-99	PR Lge	38	11	10	17	42	47	43	14
1999-2000	PR Lge	38	12	14	12	59	49	50	13

DID YOU KNOW ?

Centre-forward Dave Hickson signed by Everton from Ellesmere Port in 1948 at the age of 18 had received the best possible tuition for the position. At 15 he had been encouraged by Pongo Waring and was coached when an army cadet by Bill 'Dixie' Dean.

EVERTON 2000–01 LEAGUE RECORD

Match No.	Date	Venue	Opponents	Result	H/T Score	Lg. Pos.	Goalscorers	Attendance
1	Aug 19	A	Leeds U	L	0-2	0-2	—		40,010
2	23	H	Charlton Ath	W	3-0	0-0	—	Jeffers [54], Ferguson 2 [84, 90]	36,300
3	26	H	Derby Co	D	2-2	2-0	7	Jeffers [38], Gravesen [40]	34,840
4	Sept 5	A	Tottenham H	L	2-3	2-1	—	Jeffers [25], Nyarko [41]	35,923
5	9	A	Middlesbrough	W	2-1	0-1	7	Jeffers 2 [54, 87]	30,885
6	16	H	Manchester U	L	1-3	0-3	10	Gravesen [54]	38,541
7	24	A	Leicester C	D	1-1	0-1	11	Unsworth [52]	18,084
8	30	H	Ipswich T	L	0-3	0-1	15		32,597
9	Oct 14	H	Southampton	D	1-1	0-0	17	Ball (pen) [81]	29,491
10	21	A	Newcastle U	W	1-0	0-0	13	Campbell [80]	51,625
11	29	A	Liverpool	L	1-3	1-1	14	Campbell [17]	44,718
12	Nov 5	H	Aston Villa	L	0-1	0-0	15		27,670
13	11	A	Bradford C	W	1-0	0-0	14	Naysmith [87]	17,276
14	18	H	Arsenal	W	2-0	0-0	13	Cadamarteri [54], Campbell [73]	33,106
15	25	H	Chelsea	W	2-1	0-1	13	Cadamarteri [47], Campbell [74]	33,515
16	Dec 4	A	Sunderland	L	0-2	0-1	—		43,736
17	9	A	Manchester C	L	0-5	0-3	14		34,516
18	16	H	West Ham U	D	1-1	0-0	14	Cadamarteri [75]	31,246
19	23	A	Charlton Ath	L	0-1	0-1	14		20,043
20	26	H	Coventry C	L	1-2	0-0	14	Gemmill [85]	35,704
21	Jan 1	A	Derby Co	L	0-1	0-1	16		27,338
22	13	H	Tottenham H	D	0-0	0-0	16		32,290
23	20	A	Coventry C	W	3-1	3-0	15	Gemmill [8], Cadamarteri [15], Campbell [31]	19,172
24	31	H	Middlesbrough	D	2-2	0-1	—	Naysmith [49], Tal [79]	34,244
25	Feb 3	A	Manchester U	L	0-1	0-0	15		67,528
26	7	H	Leeds U	D	2-2	1-0	—	Ferguson [23], Campbell [73]	34,224
27	10	H	Leicester C	W	2-1	2-0	15	Jeffers [8], Campbell [43]	30,409
28	24	A	Ipswich T	L	0-2	0-0	15		22,211
29	Mar 3	A	Newcastle U	D	1-1	0-0	16	Unsworth (pen) [82]	35,779
30	17	A	Southampton	L	0-1	0-0	16		15,251
31	31	A	West Ham U	W	2-0	1-0	15	Unsworth (pen) [45], Alexandersson [71]	26,044
32	Apr 8	H	Manchester C	W	3-1	2-1	14	Ferguson [16], Ball [40], Weir [84]	36,561
33	14	A	Aston Villa	L	1-2	1-1	15	Unsworth [21]	31,272
34	16	H	Liverpool	L	2-3	1-1	15	Ferguson [42], Unsworth (pen) [84]	40,260
35	21	A	Arsenal	L	1-4	1-1	16	Campbell [24]	38,029
36	28	H	Bradford C	W	2-1	0-1	14	Ferguson [47], Alexandersson [64]	34,256
37	May 5	A	Chelsea	L	1-2	1-2	15	Campbell [3]	35,196
38	19	H	Sunderland	D	2-2	1-1	16	Tal [10], Ball (pen) [77]	37,444

Final League Position: 16

GOALSCORERS

League (45): Campbell 9, Ferguson 6, Jeffers 6, Unsworth 5 (3 pens), Cadamarteri 4, Ball 3 (2 pens), Alexandersson 2, Gemmill 2, Gravesen 2, Naysmith 2, Tal 2, Nyarko 1, Weir 1.
Worthington Cup (2): Campbell 1, Jeffers 1.
FA Cup (2): Hughes 1, Watson 1.

Gerrard P 32	Watson S 34	Pistone A 5 + 2	Unsworth D 17 + 12	Weir D 37	Ball M 29	Nyarko A 19 + 3	Gemmill S 25 + 3	Jeffers F 10 + 2	Hughes M 6 + 3	Hughes S 16 + 2	Gascoigne P 10 + 4	Moore J 8 + 13	Ferguson D 9 + 3	Gravesen T 30 + 2	Gough R 9	Alexandersson N 17 + 3	Cadamarteri D 7 + 9	Cleland A 2 + 3	Xavier A 10 + 1	Campbell K 27 + 2	Dunne R 3	McLeod K — + 5	Pembridge M 20 + 1	Tal I 12 + 10	Naysmith G 17 + 3	Simonsen S — + 1	Myhre T 6	Clarke P — + 1	Jevons P — + 4	Hibbert A 1 + 2	Match No.
1	2	3	4	5	6	7	8¹	9	10²	11³	12	13	14																		1
1	2	3¹	12	5		7	8²	9	10³	11		13	14	4	6																2
1	2	3		5		7	8	9¹	10³	11	12	13	14	4	6²																3
1	2	3		5		7	8	9	10¹	11³	12	13	14	4²	6																4
1	2	3		5		7¹	8	9	10²	11	12	13		4	6																5
1	2	3	12	5		7	8	9	10³	11¹		13	14	4²	6																6
1	2	3		5		7	8	9¹	10²	11	12	13		4	6																7
1	2	3²		5		7	8³	9	10	11¹	12	13	14	4	6																8
1	2	3		5		7	8	9	10²	11¹	12	13		4	6																9
1	2	3	12	5		7	8					13		4	6					9			4	10²	11¹						10
1	2	3²		5		7	8					13			6					9			4	10	11¹						11
1	2¹	6³		5						11	12	13				7				9			4	10	14					3	12
	6			5		7			12	11²		14		2			13			8			2	10¹	8²		1		3		13
				5	6	7				11				8	2			9		12			4	10²	3		1				14
1	2	12		5	6	7				11				8²						9			13	4	10¹	3					15
1	2			5	6	12	7¹			11		13					14			8²			9	4	10³	3					16
1	2	3¹		5	6	7	8							4						12			9	10	11						17
1⁸	2			5	6	7				11				4¹		12	8						9	10		3			15		18
	2	12		5	6	7					11¹		9³	13	4		8		10²						14	3		1			19
	2	12		5	6	13	7						14	10	4		9³							11²	8¹	3		1			20
	2	12		5	6	7¹	8					13	10	4²			9⁴							11	14	3		1			21
	2	3		5²	7				11			10¹		4		7³	12	13		9				8	14			1			22
	5	3			6		8							7²	10		2¹			9				4	11		1	12	13		23
	2			5	6	7				11¹	10		8²	4						12				9			1				24
1	2	12		5	6	7						10³		8		4	13			9				11³	3¹			14			25
1	2	12		5	6	7						11¹	10²	8	4					9				11	13	3					26
1	2	12		5	6	7	10³			11³		14		8	4¹		13			9						3					27
				5	6	7			10¹	11				4								2	9	12	8²	3	1		13		28
1	2	12		5	6	7¹	11	10				13		8						4²	9				14	3¹					29
1	2	12	13	5	6		10²					14		9	8	4	7³			3				11¹							30
1	4		3	5	6	7	11	12						9	8¹	10													2		31
1	4	2	3	5	6		11	12					10¹	8²		7³				9				13	14						32
1	4	2	3²	5	6	12	11					13		8¹		7³				9				10	14						33
1	2¹	12	3	5	6	7	8						10	4¹³			11			9											34
	3			5	6	7²	8					12		4		10¹				2	9			11³	13				14		35
1	2	3¹		5	6		8						10	12	4²	7				9				11					13		36
1	2	3		5	6		8					10²				7¹				9			14	11³	4	12			13		37
1	2	10		5	6		8							7¹		12	13			9				11	4²	3					38

Worthington Cup

Second Round	Bristol R	(h)	1-1	
		(a)	1-1	

FA Cup

Third Round	Watford	(a)	2-1	
Fourth Round	Tranmere R	(h)	0-3	

EXETER CITY

Division 3

FOUNDATION

Exeter City was formed in 1904 by the amalgamation of St. Sidwell's United and Exeter United. The club first played in the East Devon League and then the Plymouth & District League. After an exhibition match between West Bromwich Albion and Woolwich Arsenal was held to test interest as Exeter was then a rugby stronghold, Exeter City decided at a meeting at the Red Lion Hotel to turn professional in 1908.

St James Park, Exeter EX4 6PX.

Telephone: (01392) 254 073.

Fax: (01392) 425 885.

ClubCall: 09068 121 634.

Website: www.exetercityfc.co.uk

Training Ground: (01395) 232784.

Ground Capacity: 9036.

Record Attendance: 20,984 v Sunderland, FA Cup 6th rd (replay), 4 March 1931.

Record Receipts: £59,862.98 v Aston Villa, FA Cup 3rd rd, 8 January 1994.

Pitch Measurements: 114yd × 73yd.

Chairman: A. I. Doble.

Directors: P. Carter, I. M. Couch, S. W. Dawe, M. Vandale, J. Gadston.

Associate Directors: M. Shelbourne, P. Dobson, J. Tagg, S. Perryman, D. Newbery.

Manager: Noel Blake.

Physio: Damien Davey.

Chief Executive: Bernard Frowd OBE.

Secretary: Stuart Brailey.

Company Secretary: P. Carter.

Colours: Red and white striped shirts, black shorts and stockings.

Change Colours: Purple and white.

Year Formed: 1904.

Turned Professional: 1908.

Ltd Co.: 1908.

Club Nickname: 'The Grecians'.

First Football League Game: 28 August 1920, Division 3, v Brentford (h) W 3–0 – Pym; Coleburne, Feebury (1p); Crawshaw, Carrick, Mitton; Appleton, Makin, Wright (1), Vowles (1), Dockray.

HONOURS

Football League: Division 3 best season: 8th, 1979–80; Division 3 (S) – Runners-up 1932–33; Division 4 – Champions 1989–90; Runners-up 1976–77.

FA Cup: best season: 6th rd replay, 1931, 6th rd 1981.

Football League Cup: never beyond 4th rd.

Division 3 (S) Cup: Winners 1934.

IT'S A FACT !

In 1936-37, former Norwich City centre-forward Rod Williams, scored 29 of Exeter City's 59 League goals, plus seven more in the FA Cup but had to be transferred to Reading because of the club's financial situation.

Record League Victory: 8–1 v Coventry C, Division 3 (S), 4 December 1926 – Bailey; Pollard, Charlton; Pullen, Pool, Garrett; Purcell (2), McDevitt, Blackmore (2), Dent (2), Compton (2). 8–1 v Aldershot, Division 3 (S), 4 May 1935 – Chesters; Gray, Miller; Risdon, Webb, Angus; Jack Scott (1), Wrightson (1), Poulter (3), McArthur (1), Dryden (1), (1 og).

Record Cup Victory: 14–0 v Weymouth, FA Cup 1st qual rd, 3 October 1908 – Fletcher; Craig, Bulcock; Ambler, Chadwick, Wake; Parnell (1), Watson (1), McGuigan (4), Bell (6), Copestake (2).

Record Defeat: 0–9 v Notts Co, Division 3 (S), 16 October 1948. 0–9 v Northampton T, Division 3 (S), 12 April 1958.

Most League Points (2 for a win): 62, Division 4, 1976–77.

Most League Points (3 for a win): 89, Division 4, 1989–90.

Most League Goals: 88, Division 3 (S), 1932–33.

Highest League Scorer in Season: Fred Whitlow, 33, Division 3 (S), 1932–33.

Most League Goals in Total Aggregate: Tony Kellow, 129, 1976–78, 1980–83, 1985–88.

Most League Goals in One Match: 4, Harold 'Jazzo' Kirk v Portsmouth, Division 3S, 3 March 1923; 4, Fred Dent v Bristol R, Division 3S, 5 November 1927; 4, Fred Whitlow v Watford, Division 3S, 29 October 1932.

Most Capped Player: Dermot Curtis, 1 (17), Eire.

Most League Appearances: Arnold Mitchell, 495, 1952–66.

Youngest League Player: Cliff Bastin, 16 years 31 days v Coventry C, 14 April 1928.

Record Transfer Fee Received: £500,000 from Manchester C for Martin Phillips, November 1995.

Record Transfer Fee Paid: £65,000 to Blackpool for Tony Kellow, March 1980.

Football League Record: 1920 Elected Division 3; 1921–58 Division 3 (S); 1958–64 Division 4; 1964–66 Division 3; 1966–77 Division 4; 1977–84 Division 3; 1984–90 Division 4; 1990–92 Division 3; 1992–94 Division 2; 1994– Division 3.

MANAGERS
Arthur Chadwick 1910–22
Fred Mavin 1923–27
Dave Wilson 1928–29
Billy McDevitt 1929–35
Jack English 1935–39
George Roughton 1945–52
Norman Kirkman 1952–53
Norman Dodgin 1953–57
Bill Thompson 1957–58
Frank Broome 1958–60
Glen Wilson 1960–62
Cyril Spiers 1962–63
Jack Edwards 1963–65
Ellis Stuttard 1965–66
Jock Basford 1966–67
Frank Broome 1967–69
Johnny Newman 1969–76
Bobby Saxton 1977–79
Brian Godfrey 1979–83
Gerry Francis 1983–84
Jim Iley 1984–85
Colin Appleton 1985–87
Terry Cooper 1988–91
Alan Ball 1991–94
Terry Cooper 1994–95
Peter Fox 1995–2000
Noel Blake May 2000–

LATEST SEQUENCES

Longest Sequence of League Wins: 7, 23.4.77 – 20.8.77.

Longest Sequence of League Defeats: 7, 14.1.84 – 25.2.84.

Longest Sequence of League Draws: 6, 13.9.86 – 4.10.86.

Longest Sequence of Unbeaten League Matches: 13, 23.8.86 – 25.10.86.

Longest Sequence Without a League Win: 18, 21.2.95 – 19.8.95.

TEN YEAR LEAGUE RECORD

		P	W	D	L	F	A	Pts	Pos
1990-91	Div 3	46	16	9	21	58	52	57	16
1991-92	Div 3	46	14	11	21	57	80	53	20
1992-93	Div 2	46	11	17	18	54	69	50	19
1993-94	Div 2	46	11	12	23	52	83	45	22
1994-95	Div 3	42	8	10	24	36	70	34	22
1995-96	Div 3	46	13	18	15	46	53	57	14
1996-97	Div 3	46	12	12	22	48	73	48	22
1997-98	Div 3	46	15	15	16	68	63	60	15
1998-99	Div 3	46	17	12	17	47	50	63	12
1999-2000	Div 3	46	11	11	24	46	72	44	21

DID YOU KNOW ?

In successive weeks, Exeter City had home attendances of 20,000 against Chelsea in the first round of the FA Cup on 27 January 1951 (drawing 1-1) and in the League against Plymouth Argyle (won 3-2). They lost the Cup replay 2-0 at Chelsea before a crowd of 40,000.

EXETER CITY 2000–01 LEAGUE RECORD

Match No.	Date	Venue	Opponents	Result	H/T Score	Lg. Pos.	Goalscorers	Attendance
1	Aug 12	H	Cardiff C	L	1-2	0-1	—	Tomlinson [48]	3929
2	19	A	Darlington	D	1-1	0-1	16	Roscoe [53]	4056
3	26	H	Hartlepool U	D	1-1	0-1	18	Roberts C [79]	2967
4	28	A	Leyton Orient	L	1-2	1-0	23	Inglethorpe [2]	4098
5	Sept 2	H	Mansfield T	D	0-0	0-0	23		2737
6	9	A	Macclesfield T	W	2-0	1-0	17	Flack [45], Roberts C [81]	1793
7	12	A	Barnet	D	1-1	0-1	—	Roberts C [73]	1322
8	16	H	York C	W	3-1	3-1	11	Buckle [23], Roberts C 2 [28, 36]	2904
9	23	A	Carlisle U	W	1-0	1-0	8	Flack [37]	2856
10	30	H	Cheltenham T	L	0-2	0-0	13		3978
11	Oct 6	A	Shrewsbury T	L	0-2	0-1	—		2651
12	14	H	Chesterfield	D	1-1	0-1	16	Rawlinson (pen) [87]	2986
13	17	H	Hull C	L	0-1	0-0	—		2470
14	21	A	Kidderminster H	D	0-0	0-0	18		3269
15	24	A	Southend U	D	1-1	0-0	—	Flack [83]	4942
16	28	H	Rochdale	L	0-1	0-0	19		2606
17	Nov 4	A	Halifax T	L	1-3	0-0	19	Whitworth [66]	1836
18	11	H	Scunthorpe U	W	2-1	0-0	18	Tierney [70], Buckle [73]	2556
19	25	A	Lincoln C	L	1-3	0-0	19	Francis [76]	2304
20	Dec 2	H	Plymouth Arg	L	0-2	0-0	21		5145
21	9	A	Chesterfield	L	0-2	0-1	21		4289
22	16	A	Blackpool	L	0-3	0-2	22		2907
23	22	A	Brighton & HA	L	0-2	0-1	—		6758
24	26	H	Torquay U	D	1-1	1-0	23	Campbell [20]	4592
25	Jan 1	A	Cardiff C	L	1-6	0-1	23	Jordan (og) [79]	9038
26	6	A	Hartlepool U	L	0-2	0-0	23		3016
27	13	H	Leyton Orient	L	2-3	2-1	23	Read [3], Power [23]	3044
28	20	A	Torquay U	L	1-2	0-1	23	Rawlinson [69]	4053
29	27	H	Brighton & HA	W	1-0	1-0	23	Flack [34]	4490
30	Feb 2	A	Mansfield T	D	1-1	1-0	—	Flack [33]	3830
31	10	H	Macclesfield T	D	0-0	0-0	24		3458
32	17	A	York C	W	3-0	2-0	22	Roberts C [5], Flack 2 [39, 67]	3030
33	20	H	Barnet	W	1-0	0-0	—	Inglethorpe [90]	3572
34	24	H	Carlisle U	W	1-0	1-0	18	Roberts C [39]	5150
35	Mar 3	A	Cheltenham T	L	0-1	0-1	19		3913
36	10	H	Shrewsbury T	W	1-0	0-0	19	Flack [67]	3955
37	17	A	Hull C	L	1-2	0-1	21	Flack [47]	7536
38	24	H	Kidderminster H	W	2-1	2-0	20	Flack [9], Buckle [13]	3302
39	27	H	Darlington	D	1-1	0-0	—	Flack [60]	3530
40	31	H	Blackpool	W	2-0	0-0	17	Birch [71], Flack [74]	3836
41	Apr 7	A	Plymouth Arg	L	0-1	0-1	17		8671
42	14	A	Southend U	D	2-2	1-2	18	Flack [26], Campbell [82]	4535
43	16	A	Rochdale	L	0-3	0-2	19		2773
44	21	H	Halifax T	D	0-0	0-0	19		4235
45	28	A	Scunthorpe U	W	2-0	1-0	17	Roberts C [45], Birch [87]	3912
46	May 5	H	Lincoln C	D	0-0	0-0	19		4949

Final League Position: 19

GOALSCORERS

League (40): Flack 13, Roberts C 8, Buckle 3, Birch 2, Campbell 2, Inglethorpe 2, Rawlinson 2 (1 pen), Francis 1, Power 1, Read 1, Roscoe 1, Tierney 1, Tomlinson 1, Whitworth 1, own goal 1.
Worthington Cup (2): Ampadu 1, Rawlinson 1.
FA Cup (0).

Van Heusden A 41	Ashton J 7 + 6	Campbell J 42	Roscoe A 33 + 10	Curran C 26	Whitworth N 34	Cornforth J 11 + 1	Ampadu K 29 + 7	Roberts D 3 + 5	Tomlinson G 13 + 11	Inglethorpe A 11 + 7	Zabek L 26 + 5	Flack S 33 + 7	Roberts C 33 + 9	Burrows M 21 + 8	Fraser S 5 + 1	Rawlinson M 18 + 7	Power G 34 + 1	Buckle P 39 + 2	Breslan G — + 2	Holligan G 3	Rapley K 6 + 1	Francis K 3 + 4	Tierney F 4 + 3	Read P 10 + 1	Hutchings C 2	McConnell B 3 + 1	Holloway C — + 4	Blake N 3 + 2	Speakman R — + 1	Wilkinson J — + 1	Mudge J — + 3	Birch G 6 + 3	Epesse-Titi S 5 + 1	Spencer D 2 + 4	Match No.
1	2	3	4	5	6	7^1	8	9^2	10	11^3	12	13	14																						1
1		3	4	5	6	7^2	8	9	10^3	11	13	12	14		2																				2
1	12	3	4	5^1	6		8	13	10^2	11	7	9	14	2^3	1																				3
1	12	3	4	5	6		8	13	10^3	11^2	7	9	14	2																					4
	12	3		5	6		8^3	9	10^2	4	7	13	11	2^1	1	14																			5
1	2		7	5	6	12		13			10	9	11^2				8	3	4^1																6
1	2	3	7	5^3	6		12			10	9	11^2	13				8	14	4^1																7
1	2	3	7	5			12		13		10	9	11^2	14			8^3	6	4^1																8
1	12	3	7^2	5	6		13				10	9	11^1				8	2	4																9
1	12	3	7^1		6		8^3		14	13	10	9	11	5				2^2	4																10
1		3	7^2	5	6		8	12	13		10^2	9	11^1	14				2	4																11
1		3	7	5	6		13		10^3	8^2	9	11				7	2^1	4																	12
1		3	7^1	5	6		8^2	12	10^3	13	9		11				2		4	14															13
1		3	12	5	6		8		10^1	11^2		13	4^3			7	2	14		9															14
1		3	14	5	6		8^1		10^2	13		9	12			7	2	4		11^3															15
1		3	12	5	6		13		10^2	14	7	9	11				2	4^2		8^1															16
1		3	12	5	6				10	8^3	13	11	4^2			7	2^1	14			9														17
1			12	5	6						7	9^2	11^3	13			2	3^1	4		8	10	14												18
1	2^2	3	12	5	6^2							13	7				11^1	4			9	14	8	10											19
1^0		3	7	5				9^1		11		2	15				4				8	13	12	10^2	6										20
		3	4		5		8^3	13				12		1	2		7				9^2	10	11^1		6	14									21
1		3	7^2		6		8					12	5^1	11	2	4					14	10	13			9^8									22
1	2	4			6				10^3		11	12	5^1		8	3	7				9^2	13		14											23
1		2	7^2	5	6	8^1	12					9				3	4					13	11	10^1			14								24
1		2	7^3	5	6	8	12					9				3	4^2					11^1	10				13	14							25
1	2^3	3	7		6	11^2	8		9^1			12				13	4					10				14	5								26
1		3	12		6	8^2						9	11	2		13	4^1	7				10					5^3	14							27
1			4	6	8^1	12		13				9	11^2	14		2	3	7				10					5^3								28
1		2	12	5	6		8					9	11			7	3	4				10													29
1		2	12	5	4		8					9	11			6	3	7				10													30
1		5	3		6	7^2	8		12			9	11^1				4					10^3		2						13	14				31
1		5	7		6	10^3	8		12	13	14	9^2	11^1			2	3	4																	32
1		5	7		6	10^1	8			13	12	9	11			2^3	3	4																	33
1		2	7	5^1	6		8^2			10		9	11	12			3	4					13												34
1		5	7^1		6^3		8^2			12		10	9	11	2		3	4					13					14							35
1	13	5					8^1	10	7^2		9	11	2			3	4					6					12								36
1		5	4		8		12	10	7	9	11	2				3	6																		37
1		5	4		8			10^1	7	9^1	11	2	1			3	6	12													13				38
1		5	4		8			7	9	11	2	12				3	6														10^1				39
1		5	4		8			7	9	11	2	12				6															10	3			40
1		5	4^1		8^2			7	9	11	12					3	6														10	2	13		41
1		5	4		8			7	9	11						3	6														10^1	2	12		42
1		5	4		8^2			7^1	9	11	13			12		3	6														14	2	10		43
1		5	4		8			7^2	9	11	2			12		3	6														10^5		13		44
1		4	7	5	6		8			9^1	11^1	2^2				3	10														12	13	14		45
		5	7^3				8	12	13	14	11	6	1			3	4														10^2	2	9^1		46

Worthington Cup
First Round   Swindon T   (a)   1-1
                                         (h)   1-2

FA Cup
First Round   Walsall   (a)   0-4

FULHAM

FA Premiership

FOUNDATION

Churchgoers were responsible for the foundation of Fulham, which first saw the light of day as Fulham St Andrew's Church Sunday School FC in 1879. They won the West London Amateur Cup in 1887 and the championship of the West London League in its initial season of 1892–93. The name Fulham had been adopted in 1888.

Craven Cottage, Stevenage Rd, Fulham, London SW6 6HH.

Telephone: (020) 7893 8383. *Fax:* (020) 7384 4715.
Website: http://www.fulhamfc.co.uk
ClubCall: 09068 440 044.

Ground Capacity: 20,787.

Record Attendance: 49,335 v Millwall, Division 2, 8 October 1938.

Record Receipts: £139,235 v Watford, Division 2, 2 May 1998.

Pitch Measurements: 110yd × 75yd.

Chairman: M. Al Fayed.

HONOURS

Football League: Division 1 – Champions 2000–01; Division 2 – Champions 1948–49, 1998–99; Runners-up 1958–59; Division 3 (S) – Champions 1931–32; Division 3 – Runners-up 1970–71, 1996–97.

FA Cup: Runners-up 1975.

Football League Cup: best season: 5th rd, 1968, 1971, 2000.

Directors: W. F. Muddyman (Vice-Chairman), Stuart Benson, Mark Griffiths, Andy Muddyman, Tim Delaney, Lee Hoos, Andy Ambler, Juliet Slot, Jean Tigana.

Managing Director: Michael Fiddy. *Manager:* Jean Tigana. *Chief Scout:* John Marshall. *Director of Youth:* Steve Kean.

Community Officer: Gary Mulcahey (020) 7384 4759. *Stadium Manager:* Francis Broughton. *Club Secretary:* Lee Hoos. *Sales and Marketing Director:* Juliet Slot. *Communications Manager:* Sarah Brookes.

Colours: White shirts, black trim, black shorts, white stockings red and black trim.

Change Colours: Red and black striped shirts, red shorts and stockings.

Year Formed: 1879.

Turned Professional: 1898.

Ltd Co.: 1903.

Reformed: 1987.

Previous Name: 1879, Fulham St Andrew's; 1888, Fulham.

Club Nickname: 'Cottagers'.

Previous Grounds: 1879 Star Road, Fulham; c.1883 Eel Brook Common, 1884 Lillie Road; 1885 Putney Lower Common; 1886 Ranelagh House, Fulham; 1888 Barn Elms, Castelnau; 1889 Purser's Cross (Roskell's Field), Parsons Green Lane; 1891 Eel Brook Common; 1891 Half Moon, Putney; 1895 Captain James Field, West Brompton; 1896 Craven Cottage.

First Football League Game: 3 September 1907, Division 2, v Hull C (h) L 0–1 – Skene; Ross, Lindsay; Collins, Morrison, Goldie; Dalrymple, Freeman, Bevan, Hubbard, Threlfall.

Record League Victory: 10–1 v Ipswich T, Division 1, 26 December 1963 – Macedo; Cohen, Langley; Mullery (1), Keetch, Robson (1); Key, Cook (1), Leggat (4), Haynes, Howfield (3).

IT'S A FACT !

On Good Friday 1959, Fulham virtually clinched promotion to the First Division with a 6-2 win over Sheffield Wednesday. On Easter Monday 2001, the 1-1 draw with the same club came after they had already secured a place in the Premier League.

Record Cup Victory: 7–0 v Swansea C, FA Cup 1st rd, 11 November 1995 – Lange; Jupp (1), Herrera, Barkus (Brooker (1)), Moore, Angus, Thomas (1), Morgan, Brazil (Hamill), Conroy (3) (Bolt), Cusack (1).

Record Defeat: 0–10 v Liverpool, League Cup 2nd rd 1st leg, 23 September 1986.

Most League Points (2 for a win): 60, Division 2, 1958–59 and Division 3, 1970–71.

Most League Points (3 for a win): 101, Division 2, 1998–99.

Most League Goals: 111, Division 3 (S), 1931–32.

Highest League Scorer in Season: Frank Newton, 43, Division 3 (S), 1931–32.

Most League Goals in Total Aggregate: Gordon Davies, 159, 1978–84, 1986–91.

Most League Goals in One Match: 5, Fred Harrison v Stockport Co, Division 2, 5 September 1908; 5, Bedford Jezzard v Hull C, Division 2, 8 October 1955; 5, Jimmy Hill v Doncaster R, Division 2, 15 March 1958; 5, Steve Earle v Halifax T, Division 3, 16 September 1969.

Most Capped Player: Johnny Haynes, 56, England.

Most League Appearances: Johnny Haynes, 594, 1952–70.

Youngest League Player: Tony Mahoney, 17 years 38 days v Cardiff C, 6 November 1976.

Record Transfer Fee Received: £800,000 from Bristol C for Tony Thorpe, February 1998.

Record Transfer Fee Paid: £3,000,000 to Sunderland for Lee Clark, July 1999.

Football League Record: 1907 Elected to Division 2; 1928–32 Division 3 (S); 1932–49 Division 2; 1949–52 Division 1; 1952–59 Division 2; 1959–68 Division 1; 1968–69 Division 2; 1969–71 Division 1; 1971–80 Division 2; 1980–82 Division 3; 1982–86 Division 2; 1986–92 Division 3; 1992–94 Division 2; 1994–97 Division 3; 1997–99 Division 2; 1999–2001 Division 1; 2001– FA Premier League.

LATEST SEQUENCES

Longest Sequence of League Wins: 8, 6.3.99 – 13.4.99.

Longest Sequence of League Defeats: 11, 2.12.61 – 24.2.62.

Longest Sequence of League Draws: 6, 14.10.95 – 18.11.95.

Longest Sequence of Unbeaten League Matches: 15, 26.1.99 – 13.4.99.

Longest Sequence Without a League Win: 15, 25.2.50 – 23.8.50.

MANAGERS

Harry Bradshaw 1904–09
Phil Kelso 1909–24
Andy Ducat 1924–26
Joe Bradshaw 1926–29
Ned Liddell 1929–31
Jim MacIntyre 1931–34
Jimmy Hogan 1934–35
Jack Peart 1935–48
Frank Osborne 1948–64
 (was Secretary-Manager or
 General Manager for most of
 this period)
Bill Dodgin Snr 1949–53
Duggie Livingstone 1956–58
Bedford Jezzard 1958–64
 (General Manager for last two
 months)
Vic Buckingham 1965–68
Bobby Robson 1968
Bill Dodgin Jnr 1969–72
Alec Stock 1972–76
Bobby Campbell 1976–80
Malcolm Macdonald 1980–84
Ray Harford 1984–96
Ray Lewington 1986–90
Alan Dicks 1990–91
Don Mackay 1991–94
Ian Branfoot 1994–96
 (continued as General
 Manager)
Micky Adams 1996–97
Ray Wilkins 1997–98
Kevin Keegan 1998–99
 (Chief Operating Officer)
Paul Bracewell 1999–2000
Jean Tigana July 2000–

TEN YEAR LEAGUE RECORD

		P	W	D	L	F	A	Pts	Pos
1990-91	Div 3	46	10	16	20	41	56	46	21
1991-92	Div 3	46	19	13	14	57	53	70	9
1992-93	Div 2	46	16	17	13	57	55	65	12
1993-94	Div 2	46	14	10	22	50	63	52	21
1994-95	Div 3	42	16	14	12	60	54	62	8
1995-96	Div 3	46	12	17	17	57	63	53	17
1996-97	Div 3	46	25	12	9	72	38	87	2
1997-98	Div 2	46	20	10	16	60	43	70	6
1998-99	Div 2	46	31	8	7	79	32	101	1
1999-2000	Div 1	46	17	16	13	49	41	67	9

DID YOU KNOW ?

Fulham's first meeting with a French team came in August 1988 when Matra Racing Paris reserve team played at Craven Cottage and a Clive Walker goal beat them.

FULHAM 2000–01 LEAGUE RECORD

Match No.	Date	Venue	Opponents	Result	H/T Score	Lg. Pos.	Goalscorers	Attendance
1	Aug 12	H	Crewe Alex	W 2-0	0-0	—	Hayles [64], Saha [73]	11,157
2	18	A	Birmingham C	W 3-1	3-1	—	Collins J [1], Saha [31], Davis [45]	21,659
3	26	H	Stockport Co	W 4-1	1-1	1	Hayles 2 [3, 76], Collins J [59], Boa Morte [87]	11,009
4	28	A	Norwich C	W 1-0	0-0	1	Boa Morte [88]	16,678
5	Sept 10	A	Barnsley	W 5-1	3-0	1	Saha 3 (1 pen) [6, 31, 45 (p)], Hayles [60], Boa Morte [90]	10,437
6	12	H	Burnley	W 3-1	0-1	—	Goldbaek [53], Saha 2 [64, 81]	11,863
7	16	A	Nottingham F	W 3-0	0-0	1	Saha (pen) [58], Fernandes [82], Hayles [83]	18,737
8	23	H	Gillingham	W 3-0	1-0	1	Hayles 2 [45, 87], Clark [65]	13,032
9	30	A	Bolton W	W 2-0	1-0	1	Boa Morte 2 [1, 85]	19,924
10	Oct 15	H	Blackburn R	W 2-1	1-1	1	Fernandes [15], Saha (pen) [68]	15,247
11	18	H	Crystal Palace	W 3-1	2-1	—	Saha [10], Clark 2 [23, 59]	16,040
12	21	A	Wolverhampton W	D 0-0	0-0	1		21,080
13	24	A	Preston NE	L 0-1	0-0	1	—	14,354
14	28	A	Sheffield W	D 3-3	0-1	2	Saha [47], Hayles [55], Melville [82]	17,559
15	Nov 4	H	Huddersfield T	W 3-0	0-0	2	Saha [58], Goldbaek [89], Finnan [90]	13,108
16	11	A	Wimbledon	W 3-0	1-0	1	Saha 2 (1 pen) [32, 59 (p)], Hayles [86]	14,071
17	18	H	Portsmouth	W 3-1	1-1	1	Hayles 2 [11, 69], Clark [80]	19,005
18	21	A	Sheffield U	D 1-1	1-1	—	Finnan [4]	16,041
19	25	H	Grimsby T	W 2-1	0-0	1	Boa Morte [60], Saha [81]	12,107
20	Dec 2	A	Preston NE	D 1-1	0-1	1	Davis [60]	16,047
21	9	A	WBA	W 3-1	2-0	1	Davis 2 [4, 28], Stolcers [87]	22,301
22	16	H	Tranmere R	W 3-1	2-1	1	Clark [21], Boa Morte 2 [28, 50]	13,157
23	23	A	Crewe Alex	W 2-1	0-1	1	Boa Morte [46], Hayles [75]	6935
24	26	H	Watford	W 5-0	2-0	1	Saha (pen) [29], Hayles 3 [42, 56, 75], Stolcers [77]	19,373
25	Jan 1	H	Stockport Co	L 0-2	0-1	1		6100
26	13	A	Norwich C	W 2-0	1-0	1	Saha [39], Boa Morte [90]	16,052
27	20	A	Watford	W 3-1	0-0	1	Boa Morte 2 [60, 68], Saha [82]	18,333
28	27	H	Birmingham C	L 0-1	0-0	1		17,077
29	31	A	QPR	W 2-0	1-0	—	Moller [45], Riedle [77]	16,403
30	Feb 4	H	Sheffield U	D 1-1	1-1	1	Boa Morte [17]	12,480
31	10	A	Barnsley	D 0-0	0-0	1		14,654
32	17	H	Nottingham F	W 1-0	1-0	1	Saha [20]	17,425
33	20	A	Burnley	L 1-2	0-0	—	Hayles [49]	15,737
34	24	H	Gillingham	W 2-0	0-0	1	Collins J [74], Boa Morte [88]	9931
35	Mar 4	H	Bolton W	D 1-1	1-0	1	Hayles [42]	16,468
36	10	H	QPR	W 2-0	1-0	1	Saha (pen) [37], Clark [90]	16,021
37	17	A	Crystal Palace	W 2-0	1-0	1	Boa Morte 2 [15, 69]	21,133
38	30	A	Tranmere R	W 4-1	2-0	1	Saha 2 [3, 84], Hayles [28], Clark [65]	12,362
39	Apr 7	H	WBA	D 0-0	0-0	1		17,795
40	11	A	Blackburn R	W 2-1	1-1	—	Saha [45], Davis [90]	21,578
41	14	A	Huddersfield T	W 2-1	0-0	1	Saha (pen) [66], Boa Morte [85]	15,882
42	16	H	Sheffield W	D 1-1	0-1	1	Davis [90]	17,500
43	21	A	Portsmouth	D 1-1	0-1	1	Saha (pen) [79]	17,651
44	24	A	Wolverhampton W	W 2-0	1-0	—	Saha 2 (2 pens) [23, 70]	15,375
45	28	H	Wimbledon	D 1-1	0-0	1	Boa Morte (pen) [87]	18,576
46	May 6	A	Grimsby T	L 0-1	0-1	1		8706

Final League Position: 1

GOALSCORERS

League (90): Saha 27 (10 pens), Boa Morte 18 (1 pen), Hayles 18, Clark 7, Davis 6, Collins J 3, Fernandes 2, Finnan 2, Goldbaek 2, Stolcers 2, Melville 1, Moller 1, Riedle 1.
Worthington Cup (14): Saha 5, Boa Morte 3, Davis 1, Fernandes 1, Hayles 1, Hayward 1, Lewis 1.
FA Cup (1): Fernandes 1.

Taylor M 44	Finnan S 45	Brevett R 39	Melville A 42 + 1	Coleman C 25	Lewis E 1 + 6	Goldbaek B 41 + 3	Clark L 45	Saha L 39 + 4	Collins J 25 + 2	Boa Morte L 21 + 18	Fernandes F 23 + 6	Betsy K 2 + 3	Hayles B 28 + 7	Davis S 37 + 3	Hayward S — + 1	Collins W 3 + 2	Trollope P 5 + 5	Symons K 22 + 2	Willock C — + 1	Sahnoun N 2 + 5	Stolcers A 8 + 7	Phelan T 1 + 1	Moller P 2 + 3	Riedle K 1 + 13	Neilson A — + 3	Hahnemann M 2	Goma A 3	Morgan S — + 1	Match No.
1	2	3	4	5	6	7	8^1	9^2	10	11^3	12	13	14																1
1	2	3	4	5		7	8	9^1	10		12		11	6															2
1	2	3	4	5		7^1	8	9^2	10		12	13	11	6															3
1	2	3	4	5	12	7^1	8^2	9	10	13	14		11^2	6															4
1	2	3	4	5	12	7^2	8^1	9		13	10		11^2	6	14														5
1	2	3	4	5	12	7	8	9^1		13	10		11^2	6^3		14													6
1	2	3^2	4	5		7	8	9^1		12	10		11			6	13												7
1	2		4	5		7	8	9^1	10	12	6		11			3													8
1	2		4	5		7	8		10	11	6		9			3													9
1	2		4	5	12	7^1	8	13	10	11^2	6		9			3													10
1	2			5	12	7^2	8^1	9	10	11^2	6		13	14		3	4												11
1	2	3	4	5		7	8	9^1	10	12	6		11																12
1	2	3	4	5		7^1	8	9	12	13	6^2		10	11^3				14											13
1	2	3^3	4	5		12	8	9	10	13	6^1		11^2	7				14											14
1	2	3		5		7	8	9^2	10		12		11	6^1		4	13												15
1	2	3	4	5		7^1	8	9^2	10	11^2	12		13	6				14											16
1	2	3	4	5		7^1	8	9		12	6		10	11^2							13								17
1	2	3	4	5		7^3	8^2	9^1		12	6		10	11			13				14								18
1	2	3		5		7^1	8	12		9	6		10	11				4											19
1	2	3	4	5		7	8	9		10^1	6		12	11															20
1	2	3	4	5		7^1	8	9^2	12	13	6^3		10	11							14								21
1	2	3	4	5		12	8	9^2		11	6^1		13	14				10^3	7										22
1	2	3	4	5		7	8	12		11			9	10^2	13			6^1											23
1	2	3	4	5^1		7	8	9^1		12	6^3		10	11							13		14						24
1	2	3	4	5		7	8	9		12	6^2		10^1	11^3							13		14						25
1	2	3	4			7		9		11		8^1	10			5				12	6^2	13							26
1	2	3	4			7	8	9		10	6		11			5													27
1	2	3	4		12	7	8^1			6			11			5			10^2		9	13							28
1	2	3	4			7	8	9		6			11			5			10^1	12									29
1	2	3	4			7^1	8	9	10	6			11			5			12										30
1	2		4			7	8	9		10	6^1		11		3	5			12										31
1	2	3	4			7^1	8	9^2	10^1	11			6			5		12			13	14							32
1	2	3	4			7	8		10^1	11^2	12		9	6		5						13							33
1	2	3	4			7^1	8	9^2	10	12			11	6^3		5						13	14						34
1	2	3	4			7^1	8	9	10	12			11	6		5													35
1	2	3	4			7^2	8	9^2	10	12			11^1	6		5		14			13								36
1	2	3	4			7	8	12	10^2	11			9^1	6		5						13							37
1	2	3	4				8	9	10				11	6		5		7											38
1	2	3	4			12	8	9	10^2				11	6		5		7^1			13								39
1	2	3	4			7	8	9	10				11^1	6		5					12								40
1	2	3	4			7^2	8	9^3		11			12			5	10^1	6		14	13								41
	2	3	4			7^1	8^2	9	10^3	11			12	6		5				14	13			1				42
1	2	3	4			7^3	8	9	10	11^1	12		6			13				14			5^2						43
1		3	4				8	9	10^1		11		6	2^3	5	12		13	7^2						14				44
1	2		12			7^3	8	9^2	10	11			6		3	5		14			13		4^1						45
	2		4			7^2	8	9		11		13	12	6			10^1	3				1	5						46

Worthington Cup

First Round	Northampton T	(a)	0-1
		(h)	4-1
Second Round	Chesterfield	(a)	0-1
		(h)	4-0
Third Round	Wolverhampton W	(h)	3-2
Fourth Round	Derby Co	(h)	3-2
Fifth Round	Liverpool	(a)	0-3

FA Cup

Third Round	Manchester U	(h)	1-2

GILLINGHAM

Division 1

Priestfield Stadium, Gillingham, ME7 4DD.

Telephone: (01634) 851 854 or 300 000.
Fax: (01634) 850 986. *ClubCall:* 09068 332 211.

Ground Capacity: 10,600.

Record Attendance: 23,002 v QPR, FA Cup 3rd rd, 10 January 1948.

Record Receipts: £80,184 v Sheffield W, FA Cup 3rd rd, 7 January 1995.

Pitch Measurements: 114yd × 75yd.

Chairman/Chief Executive: P. D. P. Scally.

Director: P. A. Spokes.
Associate Director: Yvonne Paulley.

Player Manager: Andy Hessenthaler.

Assistant Manager: Richard Hill.

First Team Coach: Wayne Jones.

Physio: George Johnson.

Secretary: Mrs G. E. Poynter.

Sales and Marketing Manager: J. Swaby.

Colours: Blue and black.

Change Colours: Red and black.

Year Formed: 1893.

Turned Professional: 1894.

Ltd Co.: 1893.

Previous Name: 1893, New Brompton; 1913, Gillingham.

Club Nickname: 'The Gills'.

First Football League Game: 28 August 1920, Division 3, v Southampton (h) D 1–1 – Branfield; Robertson, Sissons; Battiste, Baxter, Wigmore; Holt, Hall, Gilbey (1), Roe, Gore.

Record League Victory: 10–0 v Chesterfield, Division 3, 5 September 1987 – Kite; Haylock, Pearce, Shipley (2) (Lillis), West, Greenall (1), Pritchard (2), Shearer (2), Lovell, Elsey (2), David Smith (1).

HONOURS

Football League: Promoted from Division 2 1999–2000 (play-offs); Division 3 – Runners-up 1995-96; Division 4 – Champions 1963–64; Runners-up 1973–74.

FA Cup: best season: 6th rd, 2000.

Football League Cup: best season: 4th rd, 1964, 1997.

IT'S A FACT

On Boxing Day 2000 in the first League meeting between Gillingham and Crystal Palace for 34 years, Gillingham won 4-1 with Carl Asaba scoring a hat-trick against the team he had supported as a youth.

Record Cup Victory: 10–1 v Gorleston, FA Cup 1st rd,
16 November 1957 – Brodie; Parry, Hannaway; Riggs,
Boswell, Laing; Payne, Fletcher (2), Saunders (5),
Morgan (1), Clark (2).

Record Defeat: 2–9 v Nottingham F, Division 3 (S),
18 November 1950.

Most League Points (2 for a win): 62, Division 4, 1973–74.

Most League Points (3 for a win): 85, Division 2,
1999–2000.

Most League Goals: 90, Division 4, 1973–74.

Highest League Scorer in Season: Ernie Morgan, 31,
Division 3 (S), 1954–55; Brian Yeo, 31, Division 4, 1973–74.

Most League Goals in Total Aggregate: Brian Yeo, 135,
1963–75.

Most League Goals in One Match: 6, Fred Cheesmur v
Merthyr T, Division 3S, 26 April 1930.

Most Capped Player: Tony Cascarino, 3 (88), Republic of
Ireland.

Most League Appearances: John Simpson, 571, 1957–72.

Youngest League Player: Billy Hughes, 15 years 275 days v
Southend U, 13 April 1976.

Record Transfer Fee Received: £1,500,000 from
Manchester C for Robert Taylor, November 1999.

Record Transfer Fee Paid: £600,000 to Reading for Carl
Asaba, August 1998.

Football League Record: 1920 Original Member of
Division 3; 1921 Division 3 (S); 1938 Failed re-election;
Southern League 1938–44; Kent League 1944–46; Southern
League 1946–50; 1950 Re-elected to Division 3 (S); 1958–64
Division 4; 1964–71 Division 3; 1971–74 Division 4;
1974–89 Division 3; 1989–92 Division 4; 1992–96; Division 3; 1996–2000 Division 2; 2000– Division 1.

MANAGERS

W. Ironside Groombridge
   1896–1906 *(Secretary-Manager)*
   (previously Financial Secretary)
Steve Smith 1906–08
W. I. Groombridge 1908–19
   (Secretary-Manager)
George Collins 1919–20
John McMillan 1920–23
Harry Curtis 1923–26
Albert Hoskins 1926–29
Dick Hendrie 1929–31
Fred Mavin 1932–37
Alan Ure 1937–38
Bill Harvey 1938–39
Archie Clark 1939–58
Harry Barratt 1958–62
Freddie Cox 1962–65
Basil Hayward 1966–71
Andy Nelson 1971–74
Len Ashurst 1974–75
Gerry Summers 1975–81
Keith Peacock 1981–87
Paul Taylor 1988
Keith Burkinshaw 1988–89
Damien Richardson 1989–93
Mike Flanagan 1993–95
Neil Smillie 1995
Tony Pulis 1995–99
Peter Taylor 1999–2000
Andy Hessenthaler June 2000–

LATEST SEQUENCES

Longest Sequence of League Wins: 7, 18.12.54 – 29.1.55.

Longest Sequence of League Defeats: 10, 20.9.88 – 5.11.88.

Longest Sequence of League Draws: 5, 28.8.93 – 18.9.93.

Longest Sequence of Unbeaten League Matches: 20, 13.10.73 – 10.2.74.

Longest Sequence Without a League Win: 15, 1.4.72 – 2.9.72.

TEN YEAR LEAGUE RECORD

		P	W	D	L	F	A	Pts	Pos
1990-91	Div 4	46	12	18	16	57	60	54	15
1991-92	Div 4	42	15	12	15	63	53	57	11
1992-93	Div 3	42	9	13	20	48	64	40	21
1993-94	Div 3	42	12	15	15	44	51	51	16
1994-95	Div 3	42	10	11	21	46	64	41	19
1995-96	Div 3	46	22	17	7	49	20	83	2
1996-97	Div 2	46	19	10	17	60	59	67	11
1997-98	Div 2	46	19	13	14	52	47	70	8
1998-99	Div 2	46	22	14	10	75	44	80	4
1999-2000	Div 2	46	25	10	11	79	48	85	3

DID YOU KNOW ?

On 25 August 1934,
Gillingham began the season
with a 3-0 win over Torquay
United with Simeon Raleigh
scoring a hat-trick. On 1
December he sustained an
accidental injury against
Brighton & Hove Albion and
died from concussion the
same evening.

GILLINGHAM 2000–01 LEAGUE RECORD

Match No.	Date	Venue	Opponents	Result		H/T Score	Lg. Pos.	Goalscorers	Attendance
1	Aug 12	H	Stockport Co	L	1-3	1-2	—	Butters [3]	9429
2	19	A	Tranmere R	L	2-3	1-3	23	Asaba [10], Southall (pen) [66]	8355
3	25	H	Portsmouth	D	1-1	1-0	—	Thomson [6]	8741
4	28	A	Burnley	D	1-1	0-0	21	Asaba [66]	15,611
5	Sept 2	H	Wolverhampton W	W	1-0	1-0	16	Lewis [4]	10,017
6	9	A	Grimsby T	L	0-1	0-1	17		4512
7	13	A	QPR	D	2-2	0-0	—	Asaba [46], Hessenthaler [74]	10,655
8	16	H	Huddersfield T	W	2-1	0-1	13	Butters [56], Smith [74]	8503
9	23	A	Fulham	L	0-3	0-1	16		13,032
10	30	H	Sheffield W	W	2-0	1-0	14	Butters [45], Thomson [83]	9099
11	Oct 6	H	Bolton W	D	2-2	0-2	—	Smith [75], Onuora [90]	9311
12	14	A	Wimbledon	D	4-4	3-2	12	Thomson 2 [19, 21], Saunders [25], Asaba [86]	9030
13	17	A	Watford	D	0-0	0-0	—		12,356
14	21	H	Barnsley	D	0-0	0-0	14		9030
15	25	A	Birmingham C	L	0-1	0-0	—		26,044
16	28	H	Crewe Alex	L	0-1	0-0	16		8347
17	Nov 4	A	Sheffield U	W	2-1	1-0	14	Smith [37], Thomson [62]	14,028
18	12	H	Nottingham F	L	1-3	1-2	15	Onuora [19]	9884
19	18	A	WBA	L	1-3	0-2	16	King [75]	16,410
20	25	A	Blackburn R	W	2-1	2-1	14	Hessenthaler [43], Curtis (og) [45]	18,061
21	Dec 2	H	Birmingham C	L	1-2	1-0	15	King [26]	9247
22	9	A	Norwich C	L	0-1	0-0	18		16,725
23	16	H	Preston NE	W	4-0	2-0	15	Asaba 2 [27, 34], Ashby [73], King [87]	8198
24	22	A	Stockport Co	D	2-2	1-1	—	Lewis [43], King [90]	6095
25	26	H	Crystal Palace	W	4-1	1-0	13	Asaba 3 [32, 62, 79], Onuora [90]	10,518
26	Jan 1	A	Portsmouth	D	0-0	0-0	13		14,526
27	13	H	Burnley	D	0-0	0-0	13		9331
28	20	A	Crystal Palace	D	2-2	1-0	14	Saunders 2 [43, 59]	18,823
29	Feb 3	A	Wolverhampton W	D	1-1	1-1	15	King [26]	26,627
30	10	H	Grimsby T	W	1-0	0-0	13	King [62]	8633
31	17	A	Huddersfield T	W	3-2	2-2	12	Saunders 2 [19, 25], King [64]	10,576
32	20	H	QPR	L	0-1	0-0	—		10,432
33	24	H	Fulham	L	0-2	0-0	13		9931
34	Mar 3	A	Sheffield W	L	1-2	0-1	15	Asaba [81]	18,702
35	6	H	Wimbledon	D	0-0	0-0	—		8841
36	10	A	Bolton W	D	3-3	1-2	16	King 2 [35, 85], Southall [68]	13,161
37	20	H	Tranmere R	W	2-1	1-1	—	King (pen) [42], Onuora [47]	7810
38	25	A	Barnsley	L	1-3	1-1	16	King [23]	13,609
39	31	A	Preston NE	D	0-0	0-0	15		13,550
40	Apr 7	H	Norwich C	W	4-3	2-0	14	Hope [32], Onuora 3 [38, 47, 52]	9608
41	14	H	Sheffield U	W	4-1	1-0	13	Onuora [32], King 2 [55, 58], Shaw [68]	9502
42	16	A	Crewe Alex	L	1-2	1-1	13	Hope [45]	7051
43	21	A	WBA	L	1-2	1-2	16	Onuora [35]	9920
44	28	A	Nottingham F	W	1-0	0-0	13	King [78]	20,670
45	May 1	H	Watford	L	0-3	0-0	—		9098
46	6	H	Blackburn R	D	1-1	0-1	13	King (pen) [90]	10,319

Final League Position: 13

GOALSCORERS

League (61): King 15 (2 pens), Asaba 10, Onuora 9, Saunders 5, Thomson 5, Butters 3, Smith 3, Hessenthaler 2, Hope 2, Lewis 2, Southall 2 (1 pen), Ashby 1, Shaw 1, own goal 1.
Worthington Cup (7): Thomson 3, Asaba 2, Smith 1, own goal 1.
FA Cup (5): Shaw 2, Hessenthaler 1, Hope 1, Onuora 1.

Bartram V 46	Southall N 40+4	Edge R 19+1	Hope C 46	Ashby B 38+2	Butters G 12	Smith P 42	Hessenthaler A 19+4	Asaba C 18+7	Shaw P 27+6	Gooden T 17+1	King M 26+12	Thomson A 12+12	Saunders M 24+11	Lewis J 10+7	Patterson M 26+2	Browning M 22+9	James K 1+6	Nosworthy N 8+2	McGlinchey B 1	Onuora I 17+14	Pennock A 34+1	Ipoua G —+9	Rose R 1+3	Lovell M —+1	Crofts A —+1	Phillips M —+1	Match No
1	2	3	4	5	6[1]	7	8	9	10[2]	11[3]	12	13	14														1
1	2	3	4	5	6		8	9		11	12	10[1]		7													2
1	12	3	4	5	6		8	9		11[2]		10[3]		13	2[1]	7	14										3
1	7	3[2]	4	5	6		8	9[1]		11	12	10			2			13									4
1	7	3	4		6		8[2]	9		11		10[1]		13	5	2	12										5
1	2	3	4	5	6		8	9			12	10			7[2]	13		11[1]									6
1	2	3	4	5	6	7	8[1]	9[2]			10	13			12	11											7
1	2	3	4	5	6	7	8	9[2]			10[3]	13	14		12	11[1]											8
1	2[3]	3	4	5	6	7	8[1]	9			10[2]	13			12	11	14										9
1	2		4	5	6	7	8[2]		9		12	10[1]	13	14	3	11[3]											10
1	2[2]		4	5	6	7	8	9			12	10[3]	13		11[1]	3				14							11
1	2[1]		4	5	6[3]	7	8	9			12	10	11[2]		13	3				14							12
1	2	12	4	5		7	8		10[2]		13	9[3]			11	3[1]				14	6						13
1	2[2]		4	5		7	8	9[3]	12	13		10[1]			11	3				14	6						14
1	12		4	5		7	13		2[3]	11		10[2]	8	14	3[1]					9	6						15
1	12		4	5		7	8		2	11	13		14	10	3[3]					9[4]	6[1]						16
1			4	5		7	8		2[2]	11	12	10[3]	13		3	14				9[1]	6						17
1	12		4	5		7	8		2[2]	11	13	10			3[1]					9	6						18
1			4	5		7	8[2]		2	11	12	10[1]	13		3	14				9[3]	6						19
1	2		4	5		7	8[2]		10		9[1]	11			3	13				12	6						20
1	2[3]		4	5		7			8[1]		9[2]	12	10		3	11	14			13	6						21
1	2		4	5		7	12	13			9[3]	10[2]	8		3	11[1]				14	6						22
1	2	3[1]	4	5		7			9[1]	10[2]		12	13	11	8			14			6						23
1	2	3	4	5		7			9[1]	10[2]		12			11	8				13	6						24
1	2	3	4	5		7[1]	12		9[3]	10[2]		13			11	8				14	6						25
1	2	3	4	5		7	12		9[3]	10[3]		13			11[1]	8				14	6						26
1	2	3	4	5		7			9	10[1]					11	8				12	6						27
1	2	3	4	5[1]		7			9	10					11	8		12			6						28
1	2	3	4	5		7		12	10[2]	11[3]	9[1]		8			14				13	6						29
1	2	3	4	5		7		12	10[3]	11[1]	9[2]	13	8			14					6						30
1	2	3	4	5		7		12	10[3]	11	9[1]		8[2]			13				14	6						31
1	2	3[1]	4	5		7		12	10[1]	11[2]	9		8		14	13					6						32
1	3		4	5		7		12	10[1]	11	9[2]				2	8				13	6						33
1	2		4	5		7		12	10	11	9[1]		3[2]		14	8				13	6						34
1	2		4	5		7			12	11	10[2]	13	3[3]		14	8				9[1]	6						35
1	11		4			7			10	12					2	5	8[1]	3		9	6						36
1	11		4	5		7		12		10[2]	13				2[1]	8		3		9	6						37
1	2		4	5		7	8[1]		10[2]		11		12			3				9	6	13					38
1	11		4			7	8		10[2]	12			2		5	3				9[1]	6	13					39
1	11			5		7	8[1]		10	12			2	4	14	3				9[2]	6	13[3]					40
1	11			5		7	8		10				2	4		3				9[1]	6	12					41
1	11	5	12			7	8[1]		10			3	2[3]	4						9[2]	6	13	14				42
1	11[2]	5	12			7	8[1]		10	13		2	4[3]		3					9	6	14					43
1	11	4	5			7			10	12		2[3]	8		3[1]					9[2]	6	13	14				44
1	11	4	5			7			10[3]	3[2]		8[1]								9	6	12	2	13	14		45
1	3	4	5			7			10	11[3]		2[2]	8[1]							9	6	12	13			14	46

Worthington Cup

First Round	Torquay U	(h)	2-0
		(a)	2-3
Second Round	Manchester C	(a)	1-1
		(h)	2-4

FA Cup

Third Round	Bournemouth	(a)	3-2
Fourth Round	Chelsea	(h)	2-4

GRIMSBY TOWN
Division 1

FOUNDATION

Grimsby Pelham FC as they were first known, came into being at a meeting held at the Wellington Arms in September 1878. Pelham is the family name of big landowners in the area, the Earls of Yarborough. The receipts for their first game amounted to 6s. 9d. (approx. 39p). After a year, the club name was changed to Grimsby Town.

Blundell Park, Cleethorpes, North East Lincolnshire DN35 7PY.

Telephone: (01472) 605 050. *Fax:* (01472) 693 665.
ClubCall: 09068 555 855.

Ground Capacity: 10,033.

Record Attendance: 31,657 v Wolverhampton W, FA Cup 5th rd, 20 February 1937.

Record Receipts: £119,799 v Aston Villa, FA Cup 4th rd, 29 January 1994.

Pitch Measurements: 111yd × 75yd.

Life President: T. J. Lindley.

Chairman: P. Furneaux.

Vice-Chairman: B. Huxford.

Directors: J. Arnell, C. Graves, R. Jackson, A. King, D. Ramsden.

Manager: Lennie Lawrence. *Assistant Manager:* John Cockerill. *Chief Executive/Company Secretary:* Ian Fleming. *Physio:* Paul Mitchell.

Commercial Manager: Tony Richardson.

Assistant Commercial Manager: Tim Harvey.

Colours: Black and white striped shirts, black shorts, black stockings with red turnover.

Change Colours: Red shirts with blue collar and arm stripe, red shorts with blue stripe, blue stockings with red band.

Year Formed. 1878.

Turned Professional: 1890.

Ltd Co.: 1890.

Previous Name: 1878, Grimsby Pelham; 1879, Grimsby Town.

Club Nickname: 'The Mariners'.

Previous Grounds: 1880, Clee Park; 1889, Abbey Park; 1899, Blundell Park.

First Football League Game: 3 September 1892, Division 2, v Northwich Victoria (h) W 2–1 – Whitehouse; Lundie, T. Frith; C. Frith, Walker, Murrell; Higgins, Henderson, Brayshaw, Riddoch (2), Ackroyd.

HONOURS

Football League: Division 1 best season: 5th, 1934–35; Division 2 – Champions 1900–01, 1933–34; Runners-up 1928–29; Promoted from Division 2 1997–98 (play-offs); Division 3 (N) – Champions 1925–26, 1955–56; Runners-up 1951–52; Division 3 – Champions 1979–80; Runners-up 1961–62; Division 4 – Champions 1971–72; Runners-up 1978–79; 1989–90.

FA Cup: Semi-finals, 1936, 1939.

Football League Cup: best season: 5th rd, 1980, 1985.

League Group Cup: Winners 1982.

Auto Windscreen Shield: Winners 1998.

IT'S A FACT !

Despite suffering relegation from Division One on 30 April 1932, Grimsby Town won 6-5 at West Bromwich Albion with hat-tricks from Max Holmes and Jimmy Dyson.

Record League Victory: 9–2 v Darwen, Division 2, 15 April 1899 – Bagshaw; Lockie, Nidd; Griffiths, Bell (1), Nelmes; Jenkinson (3), Richards (1), Cockshutt (3), Robinson, Chadburn (1).

Record Cup Victory: 8–0 v Darlington, FA Cup 2nd rd, 21 November 1885 – G. Atkinson; J. H. Taylor, H. Taylor; Hall, Kimpson, Hopewell; H. Atkinson (1), Garnham, Seal (3), Sharman, Monument (4).

Record Defeat: 1–9 v Arsenal, Division 1, 28 January 1931.

Most League Points (2 for a win): 68, Division 3 (N), 1955–56.

Most League Points (3 for a win): 83, Division 3, 1990–91.

Most League Goals: 103, Division 2, 1933–34.

Highest League Scorer in Season: Pat Glover, 42, Division 2, 1933–34.

Most League Goals in Total Aggregate: Pat Glover, 180, 1930–39.

Most League Goals in One Match: 6, Tommy McCairns v Leicester Fosse, Division 2, 11 April 1896.

Most Capped Player: Pat Glover, 7, Wales.

Most League Appearances: Keith Jobling, 448, 1953–69.

Youngest League Player: Tony Ford, 16 years 143 days v Walsall, 4 October 1975.

Record Transfer Fee Received: £1,500,000 from Everton for John Oster, July 1997.

Record Transfer Fee Paid: £400,000 to Preston NE for Lee Ashcroft, August 1998.

Football League Record: 1892 Original Member Division 2; 1901–03 Division 1; 1903 Division 2; 1910 Failed re-election; 1911 re-elected Division 2; 1920–21 Division 3; 1921–26 Division 3 (N); 1926–29 Division 2; 1929–32 Division 1; 1932–34 Division 2; 1934–48 Division 1; 1948–51 Division 2; 1951–56 Division 3 (N); 1956–59 Division 2; 1959–62 Division 3; 1962–64 Division 2; 1964–68 Division 3; 1968–72 Division 4; 1972–77 Division 3; 1977–79 Division 4; 1979–80 Division 3; 1980–87 Division 2; 1987–88 Division 3; 1988–90 Division 4; 1990–91 Division 3; 1991–92 Division 2; 1992–97 Division 1; 1997–98 Division 2; 1998– Division 1.

MANAGERS

H. N. Hickson 1902–20
(Secretary-Manager)
Haydn Price 1920
George Fraser 1921–24
Wilf Gillow 1924–32
Frank Womack 1932–36
Charles Spencer 1937–51
Bill Shankly 1951–53
Billy Walsh 1954–55
Allenby Chilton 1955–59
Tim Ward 1960–62
Tom Johnston 1962–64
Jimmy McGuigan 1964–67
Don McEvoy 1967–68
Bill Harvey 1968–69
Bobby Kennedy 1969–71
Lawrie McMenemy 1971–73
Ron Ashman 1973–75
Tom Casey 1975–76
Johnny Newman 1976–79
George Kerr 1979–82
David Booth 1982–85
Mike Lyons 1985–87
Bobby Roberts 1987–88
Alan Buckley 1988–94
Brian Laws 1994–96
Kenny Swain 1997
Alan Buckley 1997–2000
Lennie Lawrence August 2000–

LATEST SEQUENCES

Longest Sequence of League Wins: 11, 19.1.52 – 29.3.52.

Longest Sequence of League Defeats: 9, 30.11.07 – 18.1.08.

Longest Sequence of League Draws: 5, 6.2.65 – 6.3.65.

Longest Sequence of Unbeaten League Matches: 19, 16.2.80 – 30.8.80.

Longest Sequence Without a League Win: 18, 10.10.81 – 16.3.82.

TEN YEAR LEAGUE RECORD

		P	W	D	L	F	A	Pts	Pos
1990-91	Div 3	46	24	11	11	66	34	83	3
1991-92	Div 2	46	14	11	21	47	62	53	19
1992-93	Div 1	46	19	7	20	58	57	64	9
1993-94	Div 1	46	13	20	13	52	47	59	16
1994-95	Div 1	46	17	14	15	62	56	65	10
1995-96	Div 1	46	14	14	18	55	69	56	17
1996-97	Div 1	46	11	13	22	60	81	46	22
1997-98	Div 2	46	19	15	12	55	37	72	3
1998-99	Div 1	46	17	10	19	40	52	61	11
1999-2000	Div 1	46	13	12	21	41	67	51	20

DID YOU KNOW ?

William Andrews, a wing-half who joined Grimsby Town in the 1912-13 season, was probably the first native of North America to play in the Football League. Born in Kansas City, he was subsequently capped by Ireland.

GRIMSBY TOWN 2000–01 LEAGUE RECORD

Match No.	Date	Venue	Opponents	Result	H/T Score	Lg. Pos.	Goalscorers	Attendance
1	Aug 12	H	Preston NE	L 1-2	0-1	—	Livingstone [90]	5755
2	19	A	Portsmouth	D 1-1	0-0	16	Smith D [84]	12,511
3	26	H	Sheffield W	L 0-1	0-1	20		7755
4	29	A	Crewe Alex	L 0-2	0-1	—		5305
5	Sept 9	H	Gillingham	W 1-0	1-0	22	Livingstone [2]	4512
6	12	H	Bolton W	L 0-1	0-0	—		3732
7	16	A	Burnley	D 1-1	1-1	21	Butterfield [11]	15,413
8	23	H	Nottingham F	L 0-2	0-2	22		6467
9	30	A	Barnsley	L 0-2	0-1	23		13,096
10	Oct 14	H	Huddersfield T	W 1-0	1-0	21	Allen [27]	4911
11	17	H	QPR	W 3-1	0-1	—	Livingstone 2 [51, 73], Nielsen [54]	4428
12	21	A	Blackburn R	L 0-2	0-0	19		16,397
13	24	A	Crystal Palace	W 1-0	1-0	—	Allen [20]	16,685
14	29	A	WBA	W 2-0	0-0	14	Allen [59], Nielsen [84]	5429
15	Nov 4	A	Watford	L 0-4	0-2	17		11,600
16	18	A	Sheffield U	L 2-3	0-1	20	Livingstone [48], Nielsen [74]	12,861
17	21	A	Wolverhampton W	L 0-2	0-2	—		16,088
18	25	A	Fulham	L 1-2	0-0	21	Donovan [87]	12,107
19	Dec 2	H	Crystal Palace	D 2-2	0-1	21	Jeffrey [85], Donovan [88]	5802
20	9	A	Tranmere R	L 0-2	0-0	22		7119
21	13	A	Wimbledon	D 2-2	1-2	—	Smith R [20], Nielsen [58]	4489
22	16	H	Norwich C	W 2-0	1-0	20	Fleming (og) [23], Nielsen [90]	5618
23	23	H	Preston NE	W 2-1	1-1	17	Willems [31], Groves [81]	14,667
24	26	H	Stockport Co	D 1-1	0-1	18	Burnett [68]	6654
25	Jan 1	A	Sheffield W	L 0-1	0-0	19		17,004
26	13	H	Crewe Alex	L 1-3	0-2	20	Donovan [56]	4495
27	20	A	Stockport Co	D 1-1	0-1	19	Donovan [90]	6165
28	27	H	Portsmouth	W 2-1	2-0	18	Donovan [17], Livingstone [20]	4128
29	Feb 10	A	Gillingham	L 0-1	0-0	19		8633
30	17	H	Burnley	W 1-0	0-0	17	Enhua [55]	6044
31	20	A	Bolton W	D 2-2	1-0	—	Groves [35], Enhua [63]	24,249
32	24	A	Nottingham F	L 1-3	1-0	18	Campbell [16]	21,660
33	Mar 3	H	Barnsley	L 0-2	0-1	20		5996
34	6	A	Huddersfield T	D 0-0	0-0	—		9494
35	10	H	Wolverhampton W	L 0-2	0-0	20		4899
36	13	H	Wimbledon	D 1-1	0-1	—	Enhua [90]	4276
37	17	A	QPR	W 1-0	0-0	19	Groves [80]	17,608
38	20	H	Birmingham C	D 1-1	1-1	—	Pouton (pen) [45]	4843
39	31	A	Norwich C	L 1-2	1-1	21	Campbell [32]	17,461
40	Apr 7	H	Tranmere R	W 3-1	0-1	20	Cornwall 2 [65, 70], Livingstone [72]	5816
41	14	H	Watford	W 2-1	0-1	18	Handyside [58], Coldicott [72]	6110
42	16	A	WBA	W 1-0	1-0	17	Cornwall [22]	16,504
43	21	A	Sheffield U	L 0-1	0-1	18		6983
44	24	H	Blackburn R	L 1-4	0-2	—	Cornwall [60]	6507
45	28	A	Birmingham C	L 0-1	0-0	19		24,822
46	May 6	H	Fulham	W 1-0	1-0	18	Groves [27]	8706

Final League Position: 18

GOALSCORERS

League (43): Livingstone 7, Donovan 5, Nielsen 5, Cornwall 4, Groves 4, Allen 3, Enhua 3, Campbell 2, Burnett 1, Butterfield 1, Coldicott 1, Handyside 1, Jeffrey 1, Pouton 1 (pen), Smith D 1, Smith R 1, Willems 1, own goal 1.
Worthington Cup (6): Allen 3, Coldicott 1, Gallimore 1, Rowan 1.
FA Cup (2): Jeffrey 1, Nielsen 1.

Coyne D 46	McDermott J 36	Smith D 16 + 8	Livingstone S 27 + 5	Raven P 11 + 4	Pouton A 16 + 5	Donovan K 36 + 5	Black K 4 + 1	Clare D 6 + 11	Jeffrey M 15 + 14	Groves P 45	Allen B 15 + 6	Gallimore T 26 + 2	Coldicott S 34 + 3	Butterfield D 23 + 7	Chapman B — + 2	Campbell S 38	Bloomer M 3 + 3	Handyside P 17 + 2	Rowan J 2 + 3	Nielsen D 16 + 1	Burnett W 20 + 3	Murray N 1 + 1	Fostervold K 9 + 1	Willems M 17 + 7	Smith R 2 + 4	Enhua Z 16 + 1	Cornwall L 9 + 1	Match No.
1	2	3	4	5	6	7	8	9[1]	10	11	12																	1
1	2	11	10	5	8	7			12	9[2]	4	13	3[3]	6[1]	14													2
1	2	11	7	5	8		13	12	10	4	9[1]		6	3[2]														3
1	2	3	4	5	8	7[1]		12	10	11	9		6															4
1	2	3	4	5	8	7[3]		12	10[4]	11	9[1]		6	13	14													5
1	2	11	10	5	8	7[1]	13	12		4	9[2]		6	3														6
1	2	11	10[1]	5				12		4	9		6	3		7	8											7
1	11			5[1]	8[2]		13		10	14	4	9[3]	12	6	2	7	3											8
1	2								12	10[3]	13	4	9	3	6	8[3]		11	7[1]	5	14							9
1		12	10[3]		8[1]	7	13			4	9[2]	3	6			2		11		5	14							10
1		11	12				7		13	4	9	3	6	2		10[1]		5		8[3]								11
1	2[2]	11[5]	9	13		7[3]			10	12	3	6	4			5		8	14									12
1	2[2]		10	12		13			11	9[1]	3	6	4			7		5	8									13
1	2		10	12		13			11	9[1]	3	6	4[2]			7		5	8									14
1	2	12	10	4[3]		13			11	9[2]	3	6				7[1]		5	8	14								15
1	2		9			7		12		11		3[3]	6			10	13	5	8	4[1]								16
1	2	11[3]	9			7				4		12				10		5	8	13	6[1]	3						17
1	2	5[2]				7		12	4			6	10[1]			8	13		9	11[3]	3	14						18
1	2	13				7		12				9[1]	6			10		5	8[2]	11	3	4						19
1	2[1]		7		9	4		13				12	10	14		8	6		3[2]	11	5[3]							20
1			7					11			3[1]	6	2	12	10	8	4			9	5							21
1	12		7					4				6[1]	2	10		8	11		3	9	13	5[2]						22
1	12		7		13	4						6	2	10		8[2]	11[1]		3	9	14	5[3]						23
1	12							4				3[1]	6	2		8	11	10	9	13	5[2]							24
1	12							4				6[1]	2	8			10	11	3	9	13	5[2]						25
1	9		7		12	4						3[3]	6	2[1]		8		10	11[1]	14	13	5						26
1	12	9				7						6	2[1]	8[2]				4	3	10	11[1]		5					27
1	2	3	9		12	7				10[1]	4			8				6		11			5					28
1	2	3	12			7				10	4		6[1]	13		8		9[2]		11			5					29
1	2	3	9			7				10[3]	4		12	13		8[3]		14		6[1]	11		5					30
1	2	3	9			7				10	4		6			8		13			11		5					31
1	2	3[1]	9[2]			7				10	4		6	12		8		13			11		5					32
1	2					7			10[2]	4	13	3	12			8		14	9[3]	6[1]	11		5					33
1	2					7		9[1]		11	12	3		4		8		5		6	10							34
1	2	13	10					9[3]		4	12	3	7[2]			8		5		6	11[1]	14						35
1	2	12	7					13		4	9	3	6[3]			8				11[1]	14		5	10[2]				36
1	2	12	7					13		4	9[2]	3	6			8		14		11			5[3]	10[1]				37
1	2	12	7					13	10	4		3	6[3]			8		11[1]		14			5	9[2]				38
1	2	12	8[2]	7		14		10	4		3	6				11		13					5[1]	9[3]				39
1	2	12	8[2]	7		9[3]		10[1]	4	3		6				11		5		13						14		40
1	2	10	8	7		12		4		3	6					11		5								9[1]		41
1	2	10	8	7		12		4		3	6					11		5								9[1]		42
1	2	12	10	6[1]		7		13	4	3			14			11		5						8[3]		9[2]		43
1	2	10	8	7				4	3		6					11		5								9		44
1	2	10	5	8[1]		7		12	4	3		6				11								13		9[2]		45
1	2	12	10	5		8		7	4	3			6			11[1]					13			9[2]				46

Worthington Cup
First Round   Carlisle U   (h)   2-0
              (a)   1-1
Second Round   Wolverhampton W   (h)   3-2
              (a)   0-2

FA Cup
Third Round   Wycombe W   (a)   1-1
              (h)   1-3

HALIFAX TOWN Division 3

FOUNDATION

The real pioneer behind the setting up of the club was Mr A. E. Jones, who, using the *nom de plume* 'Old Sport', wrote to the *Halifax Evening Courier*. His letter suggesting a club be set up and inviting public opinion was published on 20 April 1911. A public meeting was held at the Saddle Hotel on 23 May 1911, whereafter Dr A. H. Muir became the club's first president and Joe McClelland its first secretary. Mr Jones proposed the following: "That this meeting of townsmen of Halifax heartily approves of the establishment of a town's Association football club on the basis of scheme 1 (the formation of a limited company) and pledges itself to adopt every legitimate means to that end". Mr Charles Deantry seconded the motion and the resolution was carried unanimously. The chairman asked for a show of hands of those willing to become guarantors of £1. There was an immediate response from 46 of the assembly.

The Shay Stadium, Shaw Hill, Halifax HX1 2YS.

Telephone: (01422) 345 543. **Fax:** (01422) 349 487. **Souvenir Shop:** (01422) 353 423. **ClubCall:** 09068 121 649.

Ground Capacity: 9900.

Record Attendance: 36,885 v Tottenham H, FA Cup 5th rd, 15 February 1953.

Record Receipts: £36,267 v Bradford C, Worthington Cup, 2nd rd, 1st leg, 15 September 1998.

Pitch Measurements: 110yd × 70yd.

President: Robert Holmes.

Vice-Presidents: Jack Haymer and Bill King.

Chairman: R. F. Walker. **Directors:** R. Crabtree, D. Tait. **General Manager:** Tony Kniveton.

Manager: Paul Bracewell. **Assistant Manager:** Richie Barker.

Youth Team Coach: Steve Thornber.

Secretary: Mike Riley.

Colours: Blue shirts, blue shorts, blue stockings with white band.

Change Colours: White shirts with blue trim, white shorts and stockings.

Year Formed: 1911.

Turned Professional: 1911. **Ltd Co.:** 1911.

Club Nickname: 'The Shaymen'.

Previous Grounds: 1911, Sandhall; 1919, Exley; 1921, The Shay.

Club Sponsors: Nationwide.

First Football League Game: 27 August 1921, Division 3 (N), v Darlington (a) L 0-2 – Haldane; Hawley, Mackrill; Hall, Wellock, Challinor; Pinkey, Hetherington, Woods, Dent, Phipps.

HONOURS

Football League: Division 3 best season: 3rd, 1970–71; Division 3 (N) – Runners-up 1934–35; Division 4: Runners-up 1968–69.

FA Cup: best season: 5th rd, 1933, 1953.

Football League Cup: best season: 4th rd, 1964.

Vauxhall Conference: Champions 1997–98.

IT'S A FACT !

Fred Tunstall, left-winger for Halifax Town against Stockport County on 2 September 1933, scored all his team's goals in a 27 minute spell in a 4-2 victory in Division Three (North).

Record League Victory: 6–0 v Bradford PA, Division 3 (N), 3 December 1955 – Johnson; Griffiths, Ferguson; Watson, Harris, Bell; Hampson (2), Baker (3), Watkinson (1), Capel, Lonsdale. 6–0 v Doncaster R, Division 4, 2 November 1976 – Gennoe; Trainer, Loska (Bradley), McGill, Dunleavy (1), Phelan, Hoy (2), Carroll (1), Bullock (1), Lawson (1), Johnston.

Record Cup Victory: 7–0 v Bishop Auckland, FA Cup 2nd rd (replay), 10 January 1967 – White; Russell, Bodell; Smith, Holt, Jeff Lee; Taylor (2), Hutchison (2), Parks (2), Atkins (1), McCarthy.

Record Defeat: 0–13 v Stockport Co, Division 3 (N), 6 January 1934.

Most League Points (2 for a win): 57, Division 4, 1968–69.

Most League Points (3 for a win): 66, Division 3, 1998–99.

Most League Goals: 83, Division 3 (N), 1957–58.

Highest League Scorer in Season: Albert Valentine, 34, Division 3 (N), 1934–35.

Most League Goals in Total Aggregate: Ernest Dixon, 129, 1922–30.

Most League Goals in One Match: 6, William Chambers v Hartlepools U, Division 3N, 7 April 1934.

Most Capped Player: None.

Most League Appearances: John Pickering, 367, 1965–74.

Youngest League Player: Robert Herbert, 16 years 13 days v Brighton & HA, 11 September 1999.

Record Transfer Fee Received: £350,000 from Fulham for Geoff Horsfield, October 1998.

Record Transfer Fee Paid: £150,000 to Scarborough for Chris Tate, July 1999.

Football League Record: 1921 Original Member of Division 3 (N); 1958–63 Division 3; 1963–69 Division 4; 1969–76 Division 3; 1976–92 Division 4; 1992–93 Division 3; 1993–98 Vauxhall Conference; 1998– Division 3.

MANAGERS

A. M. Ricketts 1911–12
(Secretary-Manager)
Joe McClelland 1912–30
Alec Raisbeck 1930–36
Jimmy Thomson 1936–47
Jack Breedon 1947–50
William Wootton 1951–52
Gerald Henry 1952–54
Willie Watson 1954–56
Billy Burnikell 1956
Harry Hooper 1957–62
Willie Watson 1964–66
Vic Metcalfe 1966–67
Alan Ball Snr 1967–70
George Kirby 1970–71
Ray Henderson 1971–72
George Mulhall 1972–74
Johnny Quinn 1974–76
Alan Ball Snr 1976–77
Jimmy Lawson 1977–78
George Kirby 1978–81
Mick Bullock 1981–84
Mick Jones 1984–86
Bill Ayre 1986–90
Jim McCalliog 1990–91
John McGrath 1991–92
Peter Wragg 1992–93
John Bird 1993–95
John Carroll 1996
George Mulhall 1996–98
Kieran O'Regan 1998–99
Mark Lillis 1999–2000
Paul Bracewell October 2000–

LATEST SEQUENCES

Longest Sequence of League Wins: 7, 22.2.64 – 21.3.64.

Longest Sequence of League Defeats: 8, 7.12.46 – 13.1.47.

Longest Sequence of League Draws: 7, 22.1.82 – 20.2.82.

Longest Sequence of Unbeaten League Matches: 17, 14.1.69 – 21.4.69.

Longest Sequence Without a League Win: 22, 26.8.78 – 10.2.79.

TEN YEAR LEAGUE RECORD

		P	W	D	L	F	A	Pts	Pos
1990-91	Div 4	46	12	10	24	59	79	46	22
1991-92	Div 4	42	10	8	24	34	75	38	20
1992-93	Div 3	42	9	9	24	45	68	36	22
1993-94	Conf	42	13	16	13	55	49	55	13
1994-95	Conf	42	17	12	13	68	54	63	8
1995-96	Conf	42	13	13	16	49	63	52	15
1996-97	Conf	42	12	12	18	55	74	48	19
1997-98	Conf	42	25	12	5	74	43	87	1
1998-99	Div 3	46	17	15	14	58	56	66	10
1999-2000	Div 3	46	15	9	22	44	58	54	18

DID YOU KNOW ?

Halifax Town's record cup win prior to the first round proper, occurred in 1913-14 when they defeated West Vale Ramblers 12-0, before reaching the fifth qualifying round and a tie against Norwich City.

HALIFAX TOWN 2000–01 LEAGUE RECORD

Match No.	Date	Venue	Opponents	Result	H/T Score	Lg. Pos.	Goalscorers	Attendance
1	Aug 12	A	Carlisle U	D	2-2	2-0	—	Bradshaw [28], Kerrigan [67]	4491
2	19	H	Lincoln C	D	1-1	0-0	13	Kerrigan [58]	2113
3	26	A	Kidderminster H	L	1-2	1-2	16	Gaughan [21]	2956
4	28	H	Rochdale	L	1-2	1-1	22	Bradshaw [18]	2783
5	Sept 2	H	Leyton Orient	D	2-2	0-2	22	Harrison [51], Kerrigan [69]	1592
6	9	A	Mansfield T	L	1-5	1-2	24	Fitzpatrick [33]	2397
7	12	A	Cardiff C	L	2-4	0-3	—	Middleton [47], Jones [77]	5087
8	16	H	Southend U	L	0-1	0-0	24		1447
9	23	A	Torquay U	W	2-1	2-1	24	Kerrigan [32], Fitzpatrick [45]	1921
10	30	H	Shrewsbury T	D	0-0	0-0	24		1606
11	Oct 7	A	Scunthorpe U	L	0-1	0-0	24		2640
12	14	H	Hull C	L	0-2	0-1	24		3003
13	17	H	Cheltenham T	L	1-2	0-2	—	Herbert [88]	1382
14	21	H	Barnet	L	0-1	0-1	24		1580
15	24	H	York C	L	1-3	0-2	—	Stoneman (pen) [80]	1984
16	28	A	Macclesfield T	D	0-0	0-0	24		1734
17	Nov 4	H	Exeter C	W	3-1	0-0	23	Kerrigan 2 [54, 55], Jones [84]	1836
18	11	A	Darlington	W	1-0	1-0	22	Jones [24]	3288
19	25	H	Chesterfield	D	2-2	0-0	23	Thompson [48], Kerrigan [74]	2769
20	Dec 2	A	Brighton & HA	L	1-2	0-1	23	Kerrigan [79]	6995
21	16	H	Hartlepool U	L	0-1	0-0	23		2042
22	23	H	Plymouth Arg	W	2-0	1-0	23	Stoneman [6], Kerrigan [85]	1670
23	26	A	Blackpool	W	1-0	1-0	22	Jones [26]	5044
24	Jan 6	H	Kidderminster H	W	3-2	2-0	21	Thompson [9], Murphy [36], Kerrigan [85]	1824
25	13	A	Rochdale	W	1-0	1-0	19	Kerrigan [31]	4123
26	27	A	Plymouth Arg	L	0-1	0-1	20		4176
27	Feb 3	A	Leyton Orient	L	0-3	0-1	20		3849
28	10	H	Mansfield T	L	3-4	3-2	21	Mitchell G [25], Asher (og) [36], Kerrigan [45]	1857
29	17	A	Southend U	W	3-0	2-0	19	Clarke M [5], Matthews [22], Kerrigan [70]	3746
30	20	H	Cardiff C	L	1-2	0-1	—	Middleton [64]	1991
31	24	H	Torquay U	W	2-1	2-0	19	Jones [37], Kerrigan [45]	1783
32	Mar 3	A	Shrewsbury T	L	1-2	0-2	20	Reilly [86]	2604
33	6	A	Hull C	L	0-1	0-1	—		6167
34	10	H	Scunthorpe U	L	3-4	1-3	23	Kerrigan 2 [40, 48], Reilly [89]	2352
35	17	A	Cheltenham T	L	2-4	1-3	24	Matthews [45], Proctor [60]	3134
36	24	H	Barnet	W	3-0	1-0	23	Clarke C [12], Kerrigan [70], Proctor [74]	1639
37	27	H	Carlisle U	D	0-0	0-0	—		3723
38	31	A	Hartlepool U	D	1-1	1-1	23	Proctor [40]	4198
39	Apr 10	H	Blackpool	L	1-2	0-1	—	Jules [50]	3311
40	14	A	York C	L	1-2	0-2	24	Proctor [57]	3465
41	16	H	Macclesfield T	W	3-0	2-0	24	Middleton [15], Kerrigan 2 [41, 54]	1945
42	21	A	Exeter C	D	0-0	0-0	23		4235
43	28	H	Darlington	W	1-0	0-0	23	Middleton [54]	2287
44	30	A	Lincoln C	D	1-1	0-1	—	Middleton [90]	3701
45	May 3	H	Brighton & HA	D	0-0	0-0	—		3979
46	5	A	Chesterfield	L	0-3	0-0	23		5700

Final League Position: 23

GOALSCORERS

League (54): Kerrigan 19, Jones 5, Middleton 5, Proctor 4, Bradshaw 2, Fitzpatrick 2, Matthews 2, Reilly 2, Stoneman 2 (1 pen), Thompson 2, Clarke C 1, Clarke M 1, Gaughan 1, Harrison 1, Herbert 1, Jules 1, Mitchell G 1, Murphy 1, own goal 1.
Worthington Cup (1): Holt 1.
FA Cup (0).

Butler L 33	Wilder C 20	Bradshaw M 15+2	Mitchell G 42	Stansfield J 2	Richards I 8+10	Jules M 16+4	Gaughan S 6+3	Jones G 30+3	Kerrigan S 40+1	Thompson S 35+1	Herbert R 3+6	Parks T 4+1	Stoneman P 29+1	Middleton C 35+2	Harrison G 7+2	Fitzpatrick J 9+3	Holt G —+2	Reilly A 15+8	Painter R 8+8	Clarke C 26	Morgan S 1	Brass C 6	Oleksewycz S —+3	Wainwright N 13	Rezai C 8+3	Potter L —+3	Parnaby S 6	Murphy P 18+3	Hawe S 6+2	Clarke M 12+7	Matthews R 8	Mika L 2+5	Mawson C 9	Myers P —+1	Redfearn N 12	Proctor M 11+1	Mitchell P 11	Match No.
1	2	3	4	5	6	7	8[1]	9	10	11	12	15																										1
	2[1]	3	4			8	12	9	10	11			1	5	7[2]	13																						2
	2	3	4		6	8[1]		9	10[2]	11[3]			1	5	7	12	13	14																				3
	2	3	4		12	6[4]	8[3]	9	10	11[1]			1	5	7	13		14																				4
		3	4		12	2[1]		9	10				1	5	7	6	11	8[2]	13																			5
1		3	4		6	12		9[2]	10	14				7	2[3]	8	13	11[1]		5																		6
1	2		4			3			12	10[1]	11			5	7	6		9																				7
1	2	3	4		12	13	14	10[3]	11[1]					5	7	6[2]	8		9																			8
1	2	3	4				12	10[1]					5	13	6	7		9				8[2]	11															9
1	2	3	4		13	12		10	8				5		6[2]	7		9[1]		11																		10
1	2	3	4					10	8		12		5	7		11		9[1]		6																		11
1	2	3	4					9[2]	10				5	7[1]	12	8					6	13	11															12
1	2[3]	3	4					9[1]	10	11	13		5		8[2]					6		7	14	12														13
1	2	3	4					10		11	8		5					9[2]			6[1]	13	7[1]	14	12													14
1	2	3	4[1]		12			10		11[2]	7		5					9[3]		14			6	13	8													15
1	2				6			9		11			5		8									7	3		4	10										16
1	2				6			9	8	11	12							5						7[1]	3		4	10										17
1	2				6			9	10	11			5											7	3		4	8[1]	12									18
1	2				6			9	10	11			5	8										7			4	3										19
1	2		4		6[1]			9	10	11			5	8				12						7[2]				3		13								20
1			4					9	10	11[1]			5	8										7	6			3	2	12								21
1	2		4					9	10	11			5	8				12						7[1]			6	3										22
1	2[1]		4					9	10	11			5	8							6			7				3	12									23
1			4					9[2]	10	11[1]			5	8				12		2				7				3	6	13								24
1			4		12			9[1]	10[2]	11				8				13		2				7				3	6	5								25
1			4					9		11	7			8	12			10[1]		2								3	6	5								26
1			4					9	10	11			5[1]	8				12	7	2								3	6[2]	13								27
1			4					12	9[2]	10	11[1]		5	8						2								3	6		7	13						28
1			4					6[2]	9	10[1]	11			8				12		2					13			3			5	7[1]	14					29
1	12		4						9[2]	10	11			8						2					6			3[1]			5	7	13					30
1	12		4						9[2]	10	11			8						2					6[1]			3			5	7	13					31
	3		4					12	9[2]	10	11[1]			8				2							6						5	7[3]	13	1	14			32
1			4		13			7[1]		10	11			8				3	12	6											5	2	9	1				33
1			4		13			7[2]		10	11[1]			8				3	12	6											5	2	9	1				34
			4							10	11			8				3		6											5	2		1		7	9	35
			4		12	3				10	11	13		7[2]				8		5													1		6	9[2]	2	36
			4		12	3				10	11[1]			7				8		5													1		6	9	2	37
			4		12	3				10	11[1]	13		7				8[1]		5[3]										14			1		6	9	2	38
			4			3				10	11			8						6										5			1		7	9	2	39
			4			3				10	11[1]		12	7[2]				14	13	5							9[1]						1		6	9	2	40
1			4		12	3				10			6[1]	7				8[2]	13	5							14						1		11	9[2]	2	41
1			4			3				10[1]			6	7				8[2]	12	5							13						1		11	9	2	42
1			4			3				10[1]			6	7				8[2]	12	5							13	14					1		11	9[1]	2	43
1			4			3				10	11			6	7			8		5								10					1		11	9	2	44
1			4			3				10[1]			6	7				8		5								12					1		11	9	2	45
1			4			3				9[3]	12	7[2]		6	13					5							8	10[1]					1		11	14	2	46

Worthington Cup
First Round   Tranmere R   (a)   0-3
                                                        (h)   1-2

FA Cup
First Round   Gateshead   (h)   0-2

HARTLEPOOL UNITED

Division 3

FOUNDATION

The inspiration for the launching of Hartlepool United was the West Hartlepool club which won the FA Amateur Cup in 1904–05. They had been in existence since 1881 and their Cup success led in 1908 to the formation of the new professional concern which first joined the North-Eastern League. In those days they were Hartlepools United and won the Durham Senior Cup in their first two seasons.

Victoria Park, Clarence Road, Hartlepool TS24 8BZ.

Telephone: (01429) 272 584. *Fax:* (01429) 863 007.
Commercial Dept: (01429) 272 584.
Website: www.hartlepoolunited.co.uk
Email: info@hartlepoolunited.co.uk
Football in the Community: (01429) 862 595.

Ground Capacity: 7229.

Record Attendance: 17,426 v Manchester U, FA Cup 3rd rd, 5 January 1957.

Record Receipts: £42,300 v Tottenham H, Rumbelows Cup 2nd rd, 2nd leg, 9 October 1990.

Pitch Measurements: 110yd × 75yd.

Chairman: K. Hodcroft.

Directors: H. Hornsey, I. Prescott.

Manager: Chris Turner.

Coach: Colin West.

Youth Coach: Martin Scott.

Physios: John Murray, Ian Gallagher.

Commercial Manager: John Breward.

Secretary: Maureen Smith.

Football in the Community Officers: Keith Nobbs, Peter Smith.

Safety Officer: Maurice Russell.

Colours: Royal blue and white striped shirts.

Change Colours: Yellow with blue trim.

Year Formed: 1908.

Turned Professional: 1908.

Ltd Co.: 1908.

Previous Names: 1908, Hartlepools United; 1968, Hartlepool; 1977, Hartlepool United.

Club Nickname: 'The Pool'.

First Football League Game: 27 August 1921, Division 3 (N), v Wrexham (a) W 2–0 – Gill; Thomas, Crilly; Dougherty, Hopkins, Short; Kessler, Mulholland (1), Lister (1), Robertson, Donald.

HONOURS

Football League: Division 3 (N) – Runners-up 1956–57.

FA Cup: best season: 4th rd, 1955, 1978, 1989, 1993.

Football League Cup, best season: 4th rd, 1975.

IT'S A FACT !

On 23 December 2000, Craig Midgley (5ft 7in) scored three headed goals for Hartlepool United in the 6-1 win over Barnet.

Record League Victory: 10–1 v Barrow, Division 4, 4 April 1959 – Oakley; Cameron, Waugh; Johnson, Moore, Anderson; Scott (1), Langland (1), Smith (3), Clark (2), Luke (2), (1 og).

Record Cup Victory: 6–0 v North Shields, FA Cup 1st rd, 30 November 1946 – Heywood; Brown, Gregory; Spelman, Lambert, Jones; Price, Scott (2), Sloan (4), Moses, McMahon.

Record Defeat: 1–10 v Wrexham, Division 4, 3 March 1962.

Most League Points (2 for a win): 60, Division 4, 1967–68.

Most League Points (3 for a win): 82, Division 4, 1990–91.

Most League Goals: 90, Division 3 (N), 1956–57.

Highest League Scorer in Season: William Robinson, 28, Division 3 (N), 1927–28; Joe Allon, 28, Division 4, 1990–91.

Most League Goals in Total Aggregate: Ken Johnson, 98, 1949–64.

Most League Goals in One Match: 5, Harry Simmons v Wigan Borough, Division 3N, 1 January 1931; 5, Bobby Folland v Oldham Ath, Division 3N, 15 April 1961.

Most Capped Player: Ambrose Fogarty, 1 (11), Republic of Ireland.

Most League Appearances: Wattie Moore, 447, 1948–64.

Youngest League Player: John McGovern, 16 years 205 days v Bradford C, 21 May 1966.

Record Transfer Fee Received: £800,000 from Ipswich T for Tommy Miller, July 2001.

Record Transfer Fee Paid: £60,000 to Barnsley for Andy Saville, March 1992.

Football League Record: 1921 Original Member of Division 3 (N); 1958–68 Division 4; 1968–69 Division 3; 1969–91 Division 4; 1991–92 Division 3; 1992–94 Division 2; 1994– Division 3.

LATEST SEQUENCES

Longest Sequence of League Wins: 7, 1.4.68 – 26.4.68.

Longest Sequence of League Defeats: 8, 27.1.93 – 27.2.93.

Longest Sequence of League Draws: 5, 24.2.01 – 17.3.01.

Longest Sequence of Unbeaten League Matches: 21, 2.12.00 – 31.3.01.

Longest Sequence Without a League Win: 18, 9.1.93 – 3.4.93.

MANAGERS

Alfred Priest 1908–12
Percy Humphreys 1912–13
Jack Manners 1913–20
Cecil Potter 1920–22
David Gordon 1922–24
Jack Manners 1924–27
Bill Norman 1927–31
Jack Carr 1932–35
(had been Player-Coach since 1931)
Jimmy Hamilton 1935–43
Fred Westgarth 1943–57
Ray Middleton 1957–59
Bill Robinson 1959–62
Allenby Chilton 1962–63
Bob Gurney 1963–64
Alvan Williams 1964–65
Geoff Twentyman 1965
Brian Clough 1965–67
Angus McLean 1967–70
John Simpson 1970–71
Len Ashurst 1971–74
Ken Hale 1974–76
Billy Horner 1976–83
Johnny Duncan 1983
Mike Docherty 1983
Billy Horner 1984–86
John Bird 1986–88
Bobby Moncur 1988–89
Cyril Knowles 1989–91
Alan Murray 1991–93
Viv Busby 1993
John MacPhail 1993–94
David McCreery 1994–95
Keith Houchen 1995–96
Mick Tait 1996–99
Chris Turner March 1999–

TEN YEAR LEAGUE RECORD

		P	W	D	L	F	A	Pts	Pos
1990-91	Div 4	46	24	10	12	67	48	82	3
1991-92	Div 3	46	18	11	17	57	57	65	11
1992-93	Div 2	46	14	12	20	42	60	54	16
1993-94	Div 2	46	9	9	28	41	87	36	23
1994-95	Div 3	42	11	10	21	43	69	43	18
1995-96	Div 3	46	12	13	21	47	67	49	20
1996-97	Div 3	46	14	9	23	53	66	51	20
1997-98	Div 3	46	12	23	11	61	53	59	17
1998-99	Div 3	46	13	12	21	52	65	51	22
1999-2000	Div 3	46	21	9	16	60	49	72	7

DID YOU KNOW ?

The first player to achieve individual honours while playing for Hartlepool United was George Luke who was selected to play for the Third Division (North) against the Third Division (South) at outside-left in 1957.

HARTLEPOOL UNITED 2000–01 LEAGUE RECORD

Match No.	Date	Venue	Opponents	Result	H/T Score	Lg. Pos.	Goalscorers	Attendance
1	Aug 12	A	Lincoln C	W 2-0	1-0	—	Fitzpatrick 2 [20, 90]	3588
2	19	H	Chesterfield	L 1-2	1-1	9	Henderson [2]	3583
3	26	A	Exeter C	D 1-1	1-0	10	Henderson [1]	2967
4	28	H	Cheltenham T	D 0-0	0-0	11		2870
5	Sept 2	H	Shrewsbury T	L 1-3	0-1	15	Lormor [75]	2710
6	9	A	Blackpool	W 2-1	1-0	11	Miller [26], Henderson [57]	4562
7	12	A	Torquay U	L 0-1	0-1	—		1538
8	16	H	Macclesfield T	D 2-2	0-0	16	Miller (pen) [48], Shilton [58]	2589
9	23	A	Mansfield T	L 3-4	1-1	17	Shilton [45], Lormor [74], Henderson [78]	2135
10	30	H	York C	W 1-0	1-0	14	Henderson [33]	2130
11	Oct 7	H	Darlington	W 2-1	1-0	11	Henderson [9], Miller [66]	3265
12	14	A	Rochdale	L 1-2	0-1	14	Lormor [59]	2813
13	18	A	Brighton & HA	L 2-4	1-3	—	Kuipers (og) [45], Sperrevik [48]	6528
14	21	H	Plymouth Arg	D 1-1	1-0	17	Henderson [22]	2581
15	24	A	Hull C	D 0-0	0-0	—		5294
16	28	H	Leyton Orient	W 2-1	0-0	15	Miller [64], Stephenson [78]	2133
17	Nov 4	A	Scunthorpe U	L 0-3	0-1	16		3241
18	11	H	Kidderminster H	W 3-1	0-1	12	Westwood [50], Midgley [56], Miller [64]	2726
19	25	A	Cardiff C	L 2-3	1-1	14	Henderson [17], Miller [89]	6251
20	Dec 2	H	Southend U	W 1-0	1-0	12	Miller (pen) [28]	2638
21	16	A	Halifax T	W 1-0	0-0	11	Midgley [71]	2042
22	23	H	Barnet	W 6-1	3-0	9	Stephenson [3], Midgley 3 [9, 38, 56], Henderson [71], Tinkler [77]	3133
23	Jan 6	H	Exeter C	W 2-0	0-0	8	Miller 2 (1 pen) [46, 67 (p)]	3016
24	13	A	Cheltenham T	W 2-1	0-1	8	Henderson [54], Sharp [66]	3574
25	16	A	Chesterfield	D 0-0	0-0	—		4240
26	20	H	Carlisle U	D 2-2	0-1	7	Midgley [46], Arnison [54]	4473
27	27	A	Barnet	W 3-1	1-0	7	Henderson 2 [17, 54], Shilton [65]	2565
28	Feb 3	A	Shrewsbury T	D 1-1	1-1	7	Seabury (og) [28]	2528
29	10	H	Blackpool	W 3-1	1-0	6	Henderson 2 [27, 60], Miller (pen) [70]	3973
30	13	A	Carlisle U	W 3-2	0-2	—	Miller (pen) [60], Shilton [74], Fitzpatrick [81]	4159
31	17	A	Macclesfield T	W 1-0	0-0	4	Tinkler [66]	2228
32	20	H	Torquay U	W 3-1	1-0	—	Henderson [25], Fitzpatrick [59], Midgley [69]	3932
33	24	H	Mansfield T	D 1-1	0-0	4	Lormor [87]	3699
34	Mar 3	A	York C	D 1-1	1-0	4	Henderson [9]	4553
35	6	H	Rochdale	D 1-1	0-1	—	Lormor [88]	3492
36	10	A	Darlington	D 1-1	0-1	4	Knowles [74]	6717
37	17	H	Brighton & HA	D 2-2	0-1	4	Lormor [46], Henderson [57]	4410
38	24	A	Plymouth Arg	W 2-0	2-0	4	Miller [28], Lormor [43]	4226
39	27	A	Lincoln C	W 1-0	0-0	4	Miller [49]	3584
40	31	H	Halifax T	D 1-1	1-1	4	Mawson (og) [43]	4198
41	Apr 7	A	Southend U	L 1-2	0-1	4	Tinkler [84]	3759
42	14	H	Hull C	L 0-1	0-0	4		4364
43	16	A	Leyton Orient	L 1-3	0-3	5	Miller [78]	5359
44	21	H	Scunthorpe U	W 1-0	1-0	4	Miller [8]	3897
45	28	A	Kidderminster H	W 1-0	0-0	4	Sharp [89]	3748
46	May 5	H	Cardiff C	W 3-1	1-1	4	Midgley [33], Lormor [62], Miller [83]	5324

Final League Position: 4

GOALSCORERS

League (71): Henderson 17, Miller 16 (5 pens), Lormor 8, Midgley 8, Fitzpatrick 4, Shilton 4, Tinkler 3, Sharp 2, Stephenson 2, Arnison 1, Knowles 1, Sperrevik 1, Westwood 1, own goals 3.
Worthington Cup (4): Miller 2 (1 pen), Fitzpatrick 1, Stephenson 1.
FA Cup (1): Midgley 1.

Holland M 5	Knowles D 22 + 3	Robinson M 5 + 1	Ferguson B 4	Westwood C 46	Sharp J 31 + 3	Fitzpatrick L 12 + 11	Miller T 46	Lormor T 22 + 9	Henderson K 40	Stephenson P 40	Shilton S 29 + 4	Midgley C 24 + 17	McAvoy A 2 + 3	Sperrevik T 4 + 11	Arnison P 26 + 1	Strodder G 17 + 2	Williams A 41	Tennebo T — + 2	Lee G 3 + 3	Baker S 9	Clark I 15 + 9	Tinkler M 28	Boyd A 3 + 2	Barron M 27 + 1	Aspin N 5 + 5	Easter J — + 4	Match No.
1	2	3¹	4	5	6	7	8	9	10	11	12																1
1	2	3	4	5	6¹	7²	8	9³	10	11	12	13	14														2
1	2	3¹	4	5	6	7²	8	9	10³	11	12	13			14												3
1	2³		4	5	6²	12	8	9	10	11	3	7¹			14	13											4
1	2			5		12	8	9	10¹	11	3	7¹			13	4	6										5
12				5	6	7¹	8	9¹	10²	11	3	13	14		2	4	1										6
				5	6	7³	8	9¹	10²	11	3	12	13		2	4	1	14									7
				5	6	7³	8	9¹	10²	11	3	12	13		2	4	1	14									8
	2¹			5	6²		8	9	10³	11	3	12		14	7	4	1		13								9
	2	13		5			8	9¹	10²	11	3	12		14	7¹	4	1			6							10
	2			5		12	8	9	10²	11	3	13			7¹	4	1			6							11
	2			5		12	8	9		11	3	13	10²		7¹	4	1			6							12
	2			5	10¹	7	8	9		11	3	12				4	1			6							13
	2			5		7	8		10	11	3	9				4	1			6							14
				5		7²	8		10¹	11	3	12	13	9	2	4	1			6							15
				5		7²	8			11	3	12	10	9¹	2	4	1			6	13						16
				5		12	8			11	3²	9	10³		2	4	1		14	6	13	7¹					17
				5			8			11	3¹	9			2	4	1		13	6	12	7²	10				18
				5			8		10	11		9			2	4	1				3	7		6			19
				5			8		10¹	11		9	12		2	4	1				3	7		6			20
				5	6		8		10	11		9			2		1				3	7		4			21
				5	6		8		10¹	11	12	9¹		13	2		1				3	7		4			22
				5	6		8		10	11	12	9			2		1				3¹	7		4			23
				5	6		8		10¹	11	12	9			2		1				3	7		4			24
				5	6		8		10	11	12	9			2		1				3	7¹		4			25
				5	6		8		10¹	11	12	9			2		1				3	7		4			26
				5	6		8		10	11	3	9			2		1					7		4			27
				5	6		8		10¹	11	12	9			2		1		13		3	7		4			28
12				5	6	13	8		10	11		9²			2¹		1		14		3²	7		4			29
				5	6		8		10	11²	12	9			2¹		1		13		3	7		4			30
				5	6		8		10	11	12	9			2¹		1				3	7		4			31
12				5	6	11³	8		10²			9		13	2		1		14		3¹	7		4			32
				5	6	11	8		10¹		12	9²			2		1		14		3²	7	13	4			33
				5	6	12	8		10²		13	9¹			2		1		14		3	7	11³	4			34
	2			5	6	12	8		10		13	9¹					1		14		3	7	11²	4³			35
	2			5	6		8	9¹	10	11		12					1				3	7		4			36
	2			5	6		8	9¹	10	11		12					1				3	7		4			37
	2²	3		5	6		8	9	10¹	11		12					1					7		4	13		38
		3¹		5	6		8	9	10²	11		12		13	2		1					7		4			39
	2			5	6		8	9¹	10²	11		12					1				3	7		4	13		40
	2³			5	6		8		10	11¹	12	9					1				3²	7		4	13	14	41
				5	6²		8	9¹	10	11	12				2		1				3	7¹		4	13	14	42
				5			8		10	11	12	9¹			2		1		14	6³	3	7		4²	13		43
	2			5			8	9¹	10¹	11	12			13			1		6		3	7		4			44
	2			5			8	9	10²	11	12			13			1		6¹		3	7		4			45
	2			5			8	9²	10	11	12						1		6¹		3	7		4	13		46

Worthington Cup
First Round   Burnley   (a) 1-4 (h) 3-2

FA Cup
First Round   Scunthorpe U   (a) 1-3

HUDDERSFIELD TOWN Division 2

The Alfred McAlpine Stadium, Leeds Rd, Huddersfield HD1 6PX.

Telephone: (01484) 484 100. *Fax:* (01484) 484 101.
ClubCall: 09068 121 635. *Ticket Office:* (01484) 484 123.
Club Shop: (01484) 484 144.

Ground Capacity: 24,500.

Record Attendance: 67,037 v Arsenal, FA Cup 6th rd, 27 February 1932 (at Leeds Road);
23,678 v Liverpool, FA Cup 3rd rd, 12 December 1999 (at Alfred McAlpine Stadium).

Record Receipts: £243,081 v Liverpool, FA Cup 3rd rd, 12 December 1999.

Pitch Measurements: 115yd × 76yd.

President: Lawrence Batley OBE.

Chairman: Barry Rubery.

Directors: B. Rubery, G. Rubery, T. Cherry, A. Tarrant.

Manager: Lou Macari. *Assistant Manager:* Joe Jordan.

First Team Coach: John Deehan

Secretary: Ann Hough.

Commercial Director: Wayne Elliott.

Physio: Alex Moreno.

Stadium Manager: Phil Armitage.

Colours: Blue and white striped shirts, white shorts, white stockings with blue trim.

Change Colours: Black shirts and shorts with royal blue trim, black stockings with royal blue turnover.

Year Formed: 1908.

Turned Professional: 1908.

Ltd Co.: 1908.

Club Nickname: 'The Terriers'.

Previous Ground: 1908, Leeds Road; 1994, The Alfred McAlpine Stadium.

First Football League Game: 3 September 1910, Division 2, v Bradford PA (a) W 1–0 – Mutch; Taylor, Morris; Beaton, Hall, Bartlett; Blackburn, Wood, Hamilton (1), McCubbin, Jee.

HONOURS

Football League: Division 1 – Champions 1923–24, 1924–25, 1925–26; Runners-up 1926–27, 1927–28, 1933–34; Division 2 – Champions 1969–70; Runners-up 1919–20, 1952–53; Promoted from Division 2 1994–95 (play-offs); Division 4 – Champions 1979–80.

FA Cup: Winners 1922; Runners-up 1920, 1928, 1930, 1938.

Football League Cup: Semi-final 1968.

Autoglass Trophy: Runners-up 1994.

IT'S A FACT !

W.H. Smith, known as Billy, was the first player to score direct from a corner kick playing for Huddersfield Town against Arsenal on 11 October 1924, the year this rule was introduced.

Record League Victory: 10–1 v Blackpool, Division 1, 13 December 1930 – Turner; Goodall, Spencer; Redfern, Wilson, Campbell; Bob Kelly (1), McLean (4), Robson (3), Davies (1), Smailes (1).

Record Cup Victory: 7–0 v Lincoln U, FA Cup 1st rd, 16 November 1991 – Clarke; Trevitt, Charlton, Donovan (2), Mitchell, Doherty, O'Regan (1), Stapleton (1) (Wright), Roberts (2), Onuora (1), Barnett (Ireland).

Record Defeat: 1–10 v Manchester C, Division 2, 7 November 1987.

Most League Points (2 for a win): 66, Division 4, 1979–80.

Most League Points (3 for a win): 82, Division 3, 1982–83.

Most League Goals: 101, Division 4, 1979–80.

Highest League Scorer in Season: Sam Taylor, 35, Division 2, 1919–20; George Brown, 35, Division 1, 1925–26.

Most League Goals in Total Aggregate: George Brown, 142, 1921–29; Jimmy Glazzard, 142, 1946–56.

Most League Goals in One Match: 5, Dave Mangnall v Derby Co, Division 1, 21 November 1931; 5, Alf Lythgoe v Blackburn R, Division 1, 13 April 1935.

Most Capped Player: Jimmy Nicholson, 31 (41), Northern Ireland.

Most League Appearances: Billy Smith, 520, 1914–34.

Youngest League Player: Denis Law, 16 years 303 days v Notts Co, 24 December 1956.

Record Transfer Fee Received: £2,700,000 from Sheffield W for Andy Booth, July 1996.

Record Transfer Fee Paid: £1,200,000 to Bristol R for Marcus Stewart, July 1996.

Football League Record: 1910 Elected to Division 2; 1920–52 Division 1; 1952–53 Division 2; 1953–56 Division 1; 1956–70 Division 2; 1970–72 Division 1; 1972–73 Division 2; 1973–75 Division 3; 1975–80 Division 4; 1980–83 Division 3; 1983–88 Division 2; 1988–92 Division 3; 1992–95 Division 2; 1995–2001 Division 1; 2001– Division 2.

MANAGERS

Fred Walker 1908–10
Richard Pudan 1910–12
Arthur Fairclough 1912–19
Ambrose Langley 1919–21
Herbert Chapman 1921–25
Cecil Potter 1925–26
Jack Chaplin 1926–29
Clem Stephenson 1929–42
David Steele 1943–47
George Stephenson 1947–52
Andy Beattie 1952–56
Bill Shankly 1956–59
Eddie Boot 1960–64
Tom Johnston 1964–68
Ian Greaves 1968–74
Bobby Collins 1974
Tom Johnston 1975–78
(had been General Manager since 1975)
Mike Buxton 1978–86
Steve Smith 1986–87
Malcolm Macdonald 1987–88
Eoin Hand 1988–92
Ian Ross 1992–93
Neil Warnock 1993–95
Brian Horton 1995–97
Peter Jackson 1997–99
Steve Bruce 1999–2000
Lou Macari October 2000–

LATEST SEQUENCES

Longest Sequence of League Wins: 11, 5.4.20 – 4.9.20.
Longest Sequence of League Defeats: 7, 8.10.55 – 19.11.55.
Longest Sequence of League Draws: 6, 3.3.87 – 3.4.87.
Longest Sequence of Unbeaten League Matches: 27, 24.1.25 – 17.10.25.
Longest Sequence Without a League Win: 22, 4.12.71 – 29.4.72.

TEN YEAR LEAGUE RECORD

		P	W	D	L	F	A	Pts	Pos
1990-91	Div 3	46	18	13	15	57	51	67	11
1991-92	Div 3	46	22	12	12	59	38	78	3
1992-93	Div 2	46	17	9	20	54	61	60	15
1993-94	Div 2	46	17	14	15	58	61	65	11
1994-95	Div 2	46	22	15	9	79	49	81	5
1995-96	Div 1	46	17	12	17	61	58	63	8
1996-97	Div 1	46	13	15	18	48	61	54	20
1997-98	Div 1	46	14	11	21	50	72	53	16
1998-99	Div 1	46	15	16	15	62	71	61	10
1999-2000	Div 1	46	21	11	14	62	49	74	8

DID YOU KNOW ?

In 1982-83, Huddersfield Town enjoyed their first Football League season without losing a home match, drawing only eight times. They obtained promotion to Division Two from finishing in third place.

HUDDERSFIELD TOWN 2000–01 LEAGUE RECORD

Match No.	Date	Venue	Opponents	Result	H/T Score	Lg. Pos.	Goalscorers	Attendance
1	Aug 12	H	Watford	L	1-2	1-1	—	Palmer (og) [16]	13,018
2	19	A	Sheffield W	W	3-2	3-1	10	Smith 2 [6, 39], Gallen [35]	22,704
3	26	H	Crystal Palace	L	1-2	1-1	17	Lucketti [25]	10,670
4	28	A	Stockport Co	D	0-0	0-0	16		6137
5	Sept 9	H	Bolton W	L	2-3	0-0	21	Smith [47], Dyson [76]	12,248
6	12	H	Wimbledon	L	0-2	0-1	—		7592
7	16	A	Gillingham	L	1-2	1-0	24	Gallen [26]	8503
8	23	H	Burnley	L	0-1	0-1	24		14,016
9	30	A	Norwich C	D	1-1	0-0	22	Gallen [58]	14,499
10	Oct 6	H	Barnsley	D	1-1	0-0	—	Smith [80]	13,556
11	14	A	Grimsby T	L	0-1	0-1	23		4911
12	17	A	Sheffield U	L	0-3	0-1	—		14,062
13	21	H	Preston NE	D	0-0	0-0	24		13,161
14	24	A	Crewe Alex	L	0-1	0-0	—		5215
15	28	H	Blackburn R	L	0-1	0-0	24		12,287
16	Nov 4	A	Fulham	L	0-3	0-0	24		13,108
17	11	H	WBA	L	0-2	0-2	24		11,801
18	18	A	QPR	D	1-1	1-1	24	Gallen [8]	11,543
19	25	A	Birmingham C	L	1-2	0-2	24	Armstrong [61]	22,120
20	Dec 2	H	Crewe Alex	W	3-1	0-1	24	Baldry [46], Smith [62], Gallen [68]	10,603
21	9	H	Wolverhampton W	W	3-0	0-0	24	Ndlovu 2 [49, 90], Facey [86]	11,506
22	13	A	Nottingham F	W	3-1	0-0	—	Ndlovu [57], Gallen 2 [61, 65]	28,372
23	16	A	Portsmouth	D	1-1	1-0	24	Dyson [40]	12,041
24	23	A	Watford	W	2-1	1-1	23	Ndlovu [29], Facey [60]	13,371
25	26	H	Tranmere R	W	3-0	1-0	19	Facey [44], Dyson [65], Gallen [71]	14,043
26	30	H	Sheffield W	D	0-0	0-0	19		18,931
27	Jan 13	H	Stockport Co	D	0-0	0-0	19		10,988
28	Feb 3	H	Nottingham F	D	1-1	1-1	21	Facey [45]	13,838
29	10	A	Bolton W	D	2-2	2-0	21	Smith [6], Gallen [23]	14,866
30	17	H	Gillingham	L	2-3	2-2	23	Armstrong [16], Smith (pen) [45]	10,576
31	24	A	Burnley	L	0-1	0-0	23		16,191
32	27	A	Tranmere R	L	0-2	0-2	—		10,621
33	Mar 3	H	Norwich C	W	2-0	1-0	23	Armstrong [8], Facey [71]	11,122
34	6	H	Grimsby T	D	0-0	0-0	—		9494
35	10	A	Barnsley	L	1-3	1-1	23	Morris [10]	15,290
36	17	H	Sheffield U	W	2-1	1-1	22	Smith [25], Facey [78]	13,918
37	31	H	Portsmouth	W	4-1	0-1	22	Booth [56], Facey [71], Gorre (pen) [89], Baldry [90]	13,199
38	Apr 3	A	Crystal Palace	D	0-0	0-0	—		15,324
39	7	A	Wolverhampton W	W	1-0	1-0	21	Facey [10]	19,423
40	10	A	Preston NE	D	0-0	0-0	—		15,185
41	14	H	Fulham	L	1-2	0-0	21	Facey [78]	15,882
42	16	A	Blackburn R	L	0-2	0-1	21		29,426
43	21	H	QPR	W	2-1	1-1	20	Gorre [33], Facey [90]	12,846
44	28	A	WBA	D	1-1	1-1	20	Booth [7]	17,542
45	May 1	A	Wimbledon	D	1-1	0-0	—	Gallen [74]	4956
46	6	H	Birmingham C	L	1-2	1-2	22	Booth [44]	19,290

Final League Position: 22

GOALSCORERS

League (48): Facey 10, Gallen 10, Smith 8 (1 pen), Ndlovu 4, Armstrong 3, Booth 3, Dyson 3, Baldry 2, Gorre 2 (1 pen), Lucketti 1, Morris 1, own goal 1.
Worthington Cup (0).
FA Cup (0).

Vaesen N 45	Jenkins S 30	Vincent J 14 + 2	Irons K 18 + 15	Lucketti C 40	Armstrong C 44	Holland C 29	Gallen K 30 + 8	Smith M 27 + 3	Gorre D 23 + 11	Winphard C 4	Baldry S 26 + 9	Thornley B 29 + 7	Hay C — + 4	Heary T 25 + 3	Sellars S 6 + 8	Facey D 22 + 12	Dyson J 25 + 5	Beresford D — + 2	Beech C 10	Koziuk R 14	Monkou K 2	Kyle K — + 4	Gray K 13 + 4	Senior M — + 4	Schofield D — + 1	Ndlovu P 6	Moses A 10 + 2	Morris L 5	Brennan J — + 2	Booth A 8	Margetson M 1 + 1	Match No.
1	2	3	4^1	5	6	7	8^2	9	10	11^3	12	13	14																			1
1		2	4	5		7	8^2	9^1	10^1	11					6	12	13	14														2
1		2^1	4^2	5	6		9			11	7		12		10^3	13	3	14														3
1		2	4	5		7^1	9		11^2	13	12			6		10	3		8													4
1		3^1		5	6	7	8	9^2	10						12		13		11		2	4^3	14									5
1		3^1		5	6	7	8	9	10						12				11		2	4^2	13									6
1		4^1	5	6		8	9^2	10			7				12		3		11		2	13										7
1		4^1	5	6		8	9	10			7				12		3		11^2		2	13										8
1		4	5	6		8	9^1	10^2		13	7^3				12		3		11		2		14									9
1		3	4	5	6		8	9	10						12		7^1		11		2											10
1		3^2	10^3	5	6		8	9							13		7^1		12	14	4	11	2									11
1	2^1	3	10	5	6	7^2	8	9							12				13		4^3	11					14					12
1	3	4	5	6		8^2				14	12				11	13^3			7	2												13
1	3^1	8^2	5	6			10				7		9	12	11			13		2		4^3	14								14
1	3	8	5	6			12	10^1			7		9	13	11^3				2		4^2	14										15
1	3^2		5	6			9	10^1			7		8	14	11				2		4^3	13	12									16
1	3^1	13	5	6			9^2	12	10		7		11^3	8					2		4	14										17
1	3		6	8	10	9					7		11^1		12	5			2		4											18
1	3	12	5	6		8^2	10	9	13		7		11^3		14	4			2^1													19
1	2	4^1		6	8	10	9^2	12			7		11^2		3	13	14			5												20
1	3^1	12	4		6	8	10^3	9^2			7		13		2	14				5					11							21
1	3	12			6	8	10^3		13		7		9^1		2	14				5					11^2							22
1		3			6	8	10^2		12		7		9		2	13	4			5					11^1							23
1		3			6	8	9				7				2	11	4			5					10							24
1		3	12	5	6	8	9^1				7^3				2	11	4^2			13					10	14						25
1		3		5		8	9^1				7		12		2	11	6								10	4						26
1		3		5	6	8	10^2	12	13		7		9^1		2	11	4^3								14							27
1		12	5	6		8	9^1	10	13		14		7^3		2	11	3^2								4							28
1	2		5	6	8	10^2	9	12			7			3	11	13									4							29
1	2	12	5	6	8	10^2	9	13			7			3^1	11	14									4							30
1	2	12	5	6	8	10	9				7^1			3	11										4							31
1	2	8	5	6		10	9	12			7			3	11										4^1							32
1	2	8	5	6		10^1	9	12	13		7^2			3	11	4																33
1	2	4	5	6		10^1	9	8			7	12		3	11	3																34
1	2	12	5	6		10^2	9	8			7^1			14	13	3^3									4	11						35
1	2	12	5	6		13	9^1	10			7			14	11	3									4^3	8^2						36
1	2		5	6			10				7^2	11^1		3	12	4											8	13	9		37
1	2	12	5	6		13		8			7^1			3	9^2	4										11^3	14	10			38
1	2	12	5	6	7		8^1					13		3	9	4										11^2		10			39
1	2		5	6	7	12		10				11		3	9	4												8^1			40
1	2		5	6	8	12		10			7			3	11^1	4												9			41
1	2	12	5	6	8	13		10^1			7			3	11^4								4^2							15	42
1	2^2	12	5	6	4			10			7			3	11^1								13					8			43
1	2	12	5	6	8	13					7^2			3	11^1								4					10			44
	3	12	5	4	8	13					7^1				11^2								6				2	10		1	45
1	2	12	5	6	8	13		14			7^2			3^1	11^3								4					10			46

Worthington Cup
First Round   Oldham Ath   (a) 0-1
    (h) 0-2

FA Cup
Third Round   Bristol C   (h) 0-2

HULL CITY

Division 3

FOUNDATION

The enthusiasts who formed Hull City in 1904 were brave men indeed. More than that they were audacious for they immediately put the club on the map in this Rugby League fortress by obtaining a three-year agreement with the Hull Rugby League club to rent their ground! They had obtained quite a number of conversions to the dribbling code, before the Rugby League forbade the use of any of their club grounds by Association Football clubs. By that time, Hull City were well away having entered the FA Cup in their initial season and the Football League, Second Division after only a year.

Boothferry Park, Hull HU4 6EU.

Telephone: (01482) 575 263. *Fax:* (01482) 565 752.
Club Shop: Ground: (01482) 575 263. Princes Quay: (01482) 227 654. *ClubCall:* 09068 888 688.

Ground Capacity: 8500.

Record Attendance: 55,019 v Manchester U, FA Cup 6th rd, 26 February 1949.

Record Receipts: £79,604 v Liverpool, FA Cup 5th rd, 18 February 1989.

Pitch Measurements: 115yd × 75yd.

Vice-President: S. Hinchliffe.

Chairman: Tom Belton.

Manager: Brian Little.

Physios: Keith Warner, Mick Mathews.

Director of Football Administration: David Capper. *Commercial Director:* Andy Daykin (01482) 575 263.

Football in the Community Office: John Davies (01482) 568 088. *Marketing Manager:* Rob Smith.
Ticket Office Manager: Carol Taylor. *Club Secretary:* Jackie Bell.

Hon. Medical Officers: Mr F. R. Howell MA, FRCS, Dr T. Jackson.

Colours: Black, amber and white shirts, black shorts, black stockings.

Change Colours: All white.

Year Formed: 1904.

Turned Professional: 1905.

Ltd Co.: 1905.

Club Nickname: 'The Tigers'.

Previous Grounds: 1904, Boulevard Ground (Hull RFC); 1905, Anlaby Road (Hull CC); 1944, Boulevard Ground; 1946, Boothferry Park.

First Football League Game: 2 September 1905, Division 2, v Barnsley (h) W 4–1 – Spendiff; Langley, Jones; Martin, Robinson, Gordon (2); Rushton, Spence (1), Wilson (1), Howe, Raisbeck.

HONOURS

Football League: Division 2 best season: 3rd, 1909–10; Division 3 (N) – Champions 1932–33, 1948–49; Division 3 – Champions 1965–66; Runners-up 1958–59; Division 4 – Runners-up 1982–83.

FA Cup: Semi-final 1930.

Football League Cup: best season: 4th, 1974, 1976, 1978.

Associate Members' Cup: Runners-up 1984.

IT'S A FACT !

Hull City bounced back in dramatic fashion on 14 January 1939 after losing two away games 6-1 at New Brighton and 6-2 at Bradford City. They trounced Carlisle United 11-1 in their record League win.

Record League Victory: 11–1 v Carlisle U, Division 3 (N), 14 January 1939 – Ellis; Woodhead, Dowen; Robinson (1), Blyth, Hardy; Hubbard (2), Richardson (2), Dickinson (2), Davies (2), Cunliffe (2).

Record Cup Victory: 8–2 v Stalybridge Celtic (a), FA Cup 1st rd, 26 November 1932 – Maddison; Goldsmith, Woodhead; Gardner, Hill (1), Denby; Forward (1), Duncan, McNaughton (1), Wainscoat (4), Sargeant (1).

Record Defeat: 0–8 v Wolverhampton W, Division 2, 4 November 1911.

Most League Points (2 for a win): 69, Division 3, 1965–66.

Most League Points (3 for a win): 90, Division 4, 1982–83.

Most League Goals: 109, Division 3, 1965–66.

Highest League Scorer in Season: Bill McNaughton, 39, Division 3 (N), 1932–33.

Most League Goals in Total Aggregate: Chris Chilton, 195, 1960–71.

Most League Goals in One Match: 5, Ken McDonald v Bristol C, Division 2, 17 November 1928; 5, Simon 'Slim' Raleigh v Halifax T, Division 3N, 26 December 1930.

Most Capped Player: Terry Neill, 15 (59), Northern Ireland.

Most League Appearances: Andy Davidson, 520, 1952–67.

Youngest League Player: Matthew Edeson, 16 years 63 days v Fulham, 10 October 1992.

Record Transfer Fee Received: £750,000 from Middlesbrough for Andy Payton, November 1991.

Record Transfer Fee Paid: £200,000 to Leeds U for Peter Swan, March 1989.

Football League Record: 1905 Elected to Division 2; 1930–33 Division 3 (N); 1933–36 Division 2; 1936–49 Division 3 (N); 1949–56 Division 2; 1956–58 Division 3 (N); 1958–59 Division 3; 1959–60 Division 2; 1960–66 Division 3; 1966–78 Division 2; 1978–81 Division 3; 1981–83 Division 4; 1983–85 Division 3; 1985–91 Division 2; 1991–92 Division 3; 1992–96 Division 2; 1996– Division 3.

MANAGERS

James Ramster 1904–05
   (Secretary-Manager)
Ambrose Langley 1905–13
Harry Chapman 1913–14
Fred Stringer 1914–16
David Menzies 1916–21
Percy Lewis 1921–23
Bill McCracken 1923–31
Haydn Green 1931–34
John Hill 1934–36
David Menzies 1936
Ernest Blackburn 1936–46
Major Frank Buckley 1946–48
Raich Carter 1948–51
Bob Jackson 1952–55
Bob Brocklebank 1955–61
Cliff Britton 1961–70
   (continued as General Manager to 1971)
Terry Neill 1970–74
John Kaye 1974–77
Bobby Collins 1977–78
Ken Houghton 1978–79
Mike Smith 1979–82
Bobby Brown 1982
Colin Appleton 1982–84
Brian Horton 1984–88
Eddie Gray 1988–89
Colin Appleton 1989
Stan Ternent 1989–91
Terry Dolan 1991–97
Mark Hateley 1997–98
Warren Joyce 1998–2000
Brian Little April 2000–

LATEST SEQUENCES

Longest Sequence of League Wins: 10, 23.2.66 – 20.4.66.

Longest Sequence of League Defeats: 8, 7.4.34 – 8.9.34.

Longest Sequence of League Draws: 5, 30.3.29 – 15.4.29.

Longest Sequence of Unbeaten League Matches: 15, 23.4.83 – 18.10.83.

Longest Sequence Without a League Win: 27, 27.3.89 – 4.11.89.

TEN YEAR LEAGUE RECORD

		P	W	D	L	F	A	Pts	Pos
1990-91	Div 2	46	10	15	21	57	85	45	24
1991-92	Div 3	46	16	11	19	54	54	59	14
1992-93	Div 2	46	13	11	22	46	69	50	20
1993-94	Div 2	46	18	14	14	62	54	68	9
1994-95	Div 2	46	21	11	14	70	57	74	8
1995-96	Div 2	46	5	16	25	36	78	31	24
1996-97	Div 3	46	13	18	15	44	50	57	17
1997-98	Div 3	46	11	8	27	56	83	41	22
1998-99	Div 3	46	14	11	21	44	62	53	21
1999-2000	Div 3	46	15	14	17	43	43	59	14

DID YOU KNOW ?

Goalkeeper Tony Norman made 226 consecutive League appearances for Hull City between 1983 and 1988 from a total of 372 before joining Sunderland.

HULL CITY 2000–01 LEAGUE RECORD

Match No.	Date		Venue	Opponents		Result	H/T Score	Lg. Pos.	Goalscorers	Attendance
1	Aug	12	A	Blackpool	L	1-3	1-1	—	Edwards [34]	5862
2		19	H	Plymouth Arg	D	1-1	1-0	20	Whitmore [16]	5431
3		26	A	Macclesfield T	D	0-0	0-0	21		1795
4		28	H	Lincoln C	D	1-1	1-1	19	Brown [39]	5780
5	Sept	2	A	Cheltenham T	L	0-2	0-0	24		4750
6		9	A	Leyton Orient	D	2-2	1-0	23	Whitmore 2 [14, 56]	5177
7		12	A	Mansfield T	D	1-1	0-0	—	Brightwell [64]	2629
8		16	H	Shrewsbury T	W	1-0	1-0	19	Brown [45]	4775
9		23	A	Barnet	D	1-1	1-0	18	Marcelle [18]	2109
10		30	H	Cardiff C	W	2-0	1-0	15	Gabbidon (og) [11], Greene (og) [69]	5503
11	Oct	6	H	Brighton & HA	L	0-2	0-0	—		6225
12		14	A	Halifax T	W	2-0	1-0	15	Whitmore [22], Marcelle [57]	3003
13		17	A	Exeter C	W	1-0	0-0	—	Greaves [85]	2470
14		21	A	Southend U	D	1-1	1-0	13	Eyre (pen) [11]	6701
15		24	H	Hartlepool U	D	0-0	0-0	—		5294
16		28	A	York C	D	0-0	0-0	12		5493
17	Nov	4	H	Darlington	W	2-0	1-0	9	Brabin [36], Whitmore [76]	5344
18		11	A	Chesterfield	L	0-1	0-0	10		5659
19		25	H	Carlisle U	W	2-1	2-0	10	Brown [7], Goodison [23]	4677
20	Dec	2	A	Scunthorpe U	W	1-0	0-0	8	Brightwell [80]	6101
21		16	H	Torquay U	L	1-2	0-0	10	Greaves [81]	4708
22		23	H	Kidderminster H	D	0-0	0-0	10		5470
23		26	A	Rochdale	L	0-1	0-1	11		4327
24	Jan	6	H	Macclesfield T	D	0-0	0-0	11		6217
25		13	A	Lincoln C	L	0-2	0-1	13		4600
26		16	H	Blackpool	L	0-1	0-0	—		4450
27		27	H	Kidderminster H	D	2-2	2-2	13	Brown [4], Francis [14]	3029
28	Feb	3	A	Cheltenham T	W	1-0	1-0	10	Francis [45]	3360
29		10	H	Leyton Orient	W	1-0	0-0	9	Rowe [69]	8782
30		17	A	Shrewsbury T	W	2-0	2-0	10	Rowe [8], Francis [37]	3004
31		20	H	Mansfield T	W	2-1	1-1	—	Francis [30], Rowe (pen) [68]	7248
32		24	H	Barnet	W	2-1	0-1	8	Eyre 2 [64, 86]	7268
33	Mar	2	A	Cardiff C	L	0-2	0-0	—		10,074
34		6	H	Halifax T	W	1-0	1-0	—	Philpott [4]	6167
35		10	A	Brighton & HA	L	0-3	0-1	10		6823
36		13	A	Plymouth Arg	D	1-1	0-1	—	Wotton (og) [84]	5482
37		17	H	Exeter C	W	2-1	1-0	7	Burrows (og) [35], Rowe (pen) [67]	7536
38		27	H	Rochdale	W	3-2	2-0	—	Brabin [26], Edwards [35], Rowe (pen) [69]	7365
39		31	H	Torquay U	D	1-1	0-0	8	Holt [79]	2779
40	Apr	7	H	Scunthorpe U	W	2-1	1-1	6	Whitney [28], Holt [64]	10,881
41		14	A	Hartlepool U	W	1-0	0-0	6	Eyre [68]	4364
42		16	H	York C	D	0-0	0-0	6		11,820
43		21	A	Darlington	W	2-0	2-0	6	Jeannin (og) [8], Eyre [45]	4998
44		28	H	Chesterfield	W	3-1	2-1	5	Edwards [5], Francis [22], Rowe (pen) [79]	11,337
45	May	1	A	Southend U	D	1-1	1-1	—	Edwards [4]	3573
46		5	A	Carlisle U	D	0-0	0-0	6		8194

Final League Position: 6

GOALSCORERS

League (47): Rowe 6 (4 pens), Eyre 5 (1 pen), Francis 5, Whitmore 5, Brown 4, Edwards 4, Brabin 2, Brightwell 2, Greaves 2, Holt 2, Marcelle 2, Goodison 1, Philpott 1, Whitney 1, own goals 5.
Worthington Cup (1): Eyre 1.
FA Cup (0).

Bracey L 9 + 1	Edwards M 40 + 2	Harper S 27	Goodison I 36	Whittle J 38	Greaves M 28 + 2	Swales S 20 + 6	Whitmore T 23 + 3	Wood J 2 + 13	Eyre J 19 + 9	Philpott L 36 + 6	Brumwell P 1 + 3	Brown D 24 + 13	Brightwell D 24 + 3	Harris J 1 + 8	Brabin G 31 + 6	Marcelle C 16 + 7	Musselwhite P 37	Perry J 6	Bradshaw G — + 2	Francis K 22	Rowe R 14 + 7	Whitney J 14 + 1	Mann N 11 + 2	Morley B — + 2	Holt A 10	Fletcher G 1 + 4	Matthews R 8	Atkins M 8	Match No
1	2	3	4	5	6	7[1]	8		9[2]	10	11	12	13																1
1	2	3[3]	4	5	6	7	8		9[2]	10[1]	11	12	14	13															2
1		3		5	6	2	8		11	12		9	4	10[1]	7														3
1		3	4	5	6		8		10[1]	11	13	9[2]	2	12	7														4
1	12		3		5	6	2		13	10[2]	11[1]	8[3]	9	4		7	14												5
1	2	3	4	5	6		8			11		9[1]	12		7	10													6
1	2	3	4	5			8			12	11	9[1]	6		7	10													7
1	2	3	4	5			8			12	11	9[2]	7		13	10[1]													8
	2	3	7	5	6		8[1]			12	11	9[1]	4		13	10	1												9
	4	3	7	5	6		8			12	10[1]	11	9		2		1												10
	2	3		5	6	7				12	10	11	9[1]		4	8	1												11
	2	3	7	5	6[3]	12	8[1]			9[2]	11	13	4	14		10	1												12
	2	3	7	5	6	12	8			11[1]		9[1]	4		13	10	1												13
	2	3	7			6	8	12	9	11[2]		4			13	10[1]	1	5											14
	2	3	7			6	8		9[1]	12		4			11	10	1	5											15
	2	3	7			6	11[1]	8		12		4			10	9	1	5											16
	2	3	7			6	12		13				4		10	9[1]	1	5											17
	2	3	7			6	12	8		11[2]		13	4		10	9	1	5[1]											18
	2	3	8			6	12		13	14	11[1]	9[2]	4		7	10[3]	1	5											19
	2	3	5		6	7	8	12	13	11[3]		9[1]	4		14	10[2]	1												20
	2[2]	3	4			6	7	8	12	10[1]	11	9	5				1		13										21
	3	4	5	6	7		12		11	9[2]	2	8		10[1]	1			13											22
	2	3	4	5	6	7	12				9	8	11	10[1]	1														23
		4	5	6	3	8			11		2		7	12	1					10	9[1]								24
	12	3	4	5	6	2	8			11[1]		13	7[3]	14	1					10[2]	9								25
	3		4	5	6	12	8			11[3]		13	2	7	14	1				10[1]	9[2]								26
	2	3		5	6				11		8[1]	7	12	13	1					10	9[2]	4							27
	2	3	4	5	6[1]	7			11		8				1				10[1]	12	9								28
	2	3	4	5	6	7[2]			11	12	13	8			1				10[1]	9[1]	14								29
	2		8	5	6[3]	3			11	12	13	14			1				10[2]	9[1]	4	7							30
	3		4	5	2				12	11[2]	13	7		14	1				10[3]	9[1]	6	8							31
	3		4	5	6[3]				12	14	11	13	7		1				10[2]	9[1]	2	8							32
	2		5						12	8	11	7		13	6	1			10[2]	9[3]	3	4[2]	14						33
	3		5						12	7[1]	11	8		13	4	1			10[2]	9	2	6							34
15	3		5				12		7	11	8[2]		13	4	1[6]				10[1]	9	2	6							35
1	2		5			4[1]	8[2]		12	11		9	6						10	13	3	7							36
	2		4	5						11	8		6	6	1				10[1]	9		7		3	12			37
	2		4	5						11[2]	12	8			1				10[1]	9[3]	13		3	14	7	6		38
	2		5				12			11	9	4			1				10[1]		8[2]		3	13	7	6		39
	2		4	5		12			9[1]		8				1				10[2]		3			7	13	11	6	40
	2		4	5					9[1]	13	12	8			1				10[3]	14	3			7		11	6[2]	41
	2		4	5		12			9		8				1				10[2]	13	3[1]			7		11	6	42
	2		4	5					9[2]	12	13	8[1]			1				10[3]	14	3			7		11	6	43
	2		4	5	12				9[3]	13		8			1				10[3]	14	3			7		11	6[1]	44
	2		4	5	12				9	13		8			1				10[3]	14	3			7		11[2]	6[1]	45
	2			5	6	8[1]	12		11			7			1				9	13	4[2]	14		3	10[1]			46

Worthington Cup
First Round   Notts Co   (h) 1-0
                           (a) 0-2

FA Cup
First Round   Kettering T   (a) 0-0
                              (h) 0-1

IPSWICH TOWN   FA Premiership

FOUNDATION

Considering that Ipswich Town only reached the Football League in 1938, many people outside of East Anglia may be surprised to learn that this club was formed at a meeting held in the Town Hall as far back as 1878 when Mr T. C. Cobbold, MP, was voted president. Originally it was the Ipswich Association FC to distinguish it from the older Ipswich Football Club which played rugby. These two amalgamated in 1888 and the handling game was dropped in 1893.

Portman Road, Ipswich, Suffolk IP1 2DA.

Telephone: (01473) 400 500 (4 lines).
Fax: (01473) 400 040. *Ticket Office:* (01473) 400 555.
Website: www.itfc.co.uk *Email:* enquiries@itfc.co.uk
Sales Dept: (01473) 400 523.
ClubCall: 09068 121 068.

Ground Capacity: 23,290 rising to 30,300 by April 2002.

Record Attendance: 38,010 v Leeds U, FA Cup 6th rd, 8 March 1975.

Record Receipts: £105,950 v AZ 67 Alkmaar, UEFA Cup Final 1st leg, 6 May 1981.

Pitch Measurements: 101m × 65m.

Chairman and Chief Executive: David Sheepshanks.

Vice-Presidents: Kenneth H. Brightwell, Harold R. Smith.

Directors: P. Hope-Cobbold, R. Moore, John Kerr MBE, R. J. Finbow, Lord Ryder OBE.

Manager: George Burley. *Assistant Manager:* Dale Roberts.
First Team Coach: Tony Mowbray.
Youth Team Coach: Paul Goddard.
Chief Scout: Colin Suggett. *Academy Director:* Bryan Klug. *Physio:* Dave Williams.

Secretary: David C. Rose.

Communications Director: Alesha Gooderham. *Publications Manager:* Mike Noye.

Commercial Director: Paul Clouting. *Finance Director:* Mike Cooper.

Colours: Blue shirts, white shorts, blue stockings.

Change Colours: White shirts, black shorts, white stockings.

Year Formed: 1878.

Turned Professional: 1936.

Ltd Co.: 1936.

Club Nickname: 'Blues' or 'Town'.

HONOURS

Football League: Division 1 – Champions 1961–62; Runners-up 1980–81, 1981–82; Promoted from Division 1 1999–2000 (play-offs); Division 2 – Champions 1960–61, 1967–68, 1991–92; Division 3 (S) – Champions 1953–54, 1956–57.

FA Cup: Winners 1978.

Football League Cup: Semi-final 1982, 1985.

Texaco Cup: Winners 1973.

European Competitions: *European Cup:* 1962–63. *European Cup-Winners' Cup:* 1978–79. *UEFA Cup:* 1973–74, 1974–75, 1975–76, 1977–78, 1979–80, 1980–81 (winners), 1981–82, 1982–83.

IT'S A FACT !

Ipswich Town players excelled themselves in goalscoring feats in Europe. Ray Crawford scored five in a European Cup tie, John Wark four in the UEFA Cup and Trevor Whymark four on two occasions in the same competition.

First Football League Game: 27 August 1938, Division 3 (S), v Southend U (h) W 4–2 – Burns; Dale, Parry; Perrett, Fillingham, McLuckie; Williams, Davies (1), Jones (2), Alsop (1), Little.

Record League Victory: 7–0 v Portsmouth, Division 2, 7 November 1964 – Thorburn; Smith, McNeil; Baxter, Bolton, Thompson; Broadfoot (1), Hegan (2), Baker (1), Leadbetter, Brogan (3). 7–0 v Southampton, Division 1, 2 February 1974 – Sivell; Burley, Mills (1), Morris, Hunter, Beattie (1), Hamilton (2), Viljoen, Johnson, Whymark (2), Lambert (1) (Woods). 7–0 v WBA, Division 1, 6 November 1976 – Sivell; Burley, Mills, Talbot, Hunter, Beattie (1), Osborne, Wark (1), Mariner (1) (Bertschin), Whymark (4), Woods.

MANAGERS
Mick O'Brien 1936–37
Scott Duncan 1937–55
(continued as Secretary)
Alf Ramsey 1955–63
Jackie Milburn 1963–64
Bill McGarry 1964–68
Bobby Robson 1969–82
Bobby Ferguson 1982–87
Johnny Duncan 1987–90
John Lyall 1990–94
George Burley December 1994–

Record Cup Victory: 10–0 v Floriana, European Cup prel. rd, 25 September 1962 – Bailey; Malcolm, Compton; Baxter, Laurel, Elsworthy (1); Stephenson, Moran (2), Crawford (5), Phillips (2), Blackwood.

Record Defeat: 1–10 v Fulham, Division 1, 26 December 1963.

Most League Points (2 for a win): 64, Division 3 (S), 1953–54 and 1955–56.

Most League Points (3 for a win): 87, Division 1, 1999–2000.

Most League Goals: 106, Division 3 (S), 1955–56.

Highest League Scorer in Season: Ted Phillips, 41, Division 3 (S), 1956–57.

Most League Goals in Total Aggregate: Ray Crawford, 203, 1958–63 and 1966–69.

Most League Goals in One Match: 5, Alan Brazil v Southampton, Division 1, 16 February 1981.

Most Capped Player: Allan Hunter, 47 (53), Northern Ireland.

Most League Appearances: Mick Mills, 591, 1966–82.

Youngest League Player: Jason Dozzell, 16 years 56 days v Coventry C, 4 February 1984.

Record Transfer Fee Received: £6,000,000 from Newcastle U for Kieron Dyer, July 1999.

Record Transfer Fee Paid: £4,500,000 to Wimbledon for Hermann Hreidarsson, August 2000.

Football League Record: 1938 Elected to Division 3 (S); 1954–55 Division 2; 1955–57 Division 3 (S); 1957–61 Division 2; 1961–64 Division 1; 1964–68 Division 2; 1968–86 Division 1; 1986–92 Division 2; 1992–95 FA Premier League; 1995–2000 Division 1; 2000– FA Premier League.

LATEST SEQUENCES

Longest Sequence of League Wins: 8, 23.9.53 – 31.10.53.

Longest Sequence of League Defeats: 10, 4.9.54 – 16.10.54.

Longest Sequence of League Draws: 7, 10.11.90 – 21.12.90.

Longest Sequence of Unbeaten League Matches: 23, 8.12.79 – 26.4.80.

Longest Sequence Without a League Win: 21, 28.8.63 – 14.12.63.

TEN YEAR LEAGUE RECORD

		P	W	D	L	F	A	Pts	Pos
1990-91	Div 2	46	13	18	15	60	68	57	14
1991-92	Div 2	46	24	12	10	70	50	84	1
1992-93	PR Lge	42	12	16	14	50	55	52	16
1993-94	PR Lge	42	9	16	17	35	58	43	19
1994-95	PR Lge	42	7	6	29	36	93	27	22
1995-96	Div 1	46	19	12	15	79	69	69	7
1996-97	Div 1	46	20	14	12	68	50	74	4
1997-98	Div 1	46	23	14	9	77	43	83	5
1998-99	Div 1	46	26	8	12	69	32	86	3
1999-2000	Div 1	46	25	12	9	71	42	87	3

DID YOU KNOW ?

Ray Crawford scored in seven consecutive League and League Cup games for Ipswich Town from 17 August to 7 September 1968. Marcus Stewart equalled the feat in 2000-01 from 26 December in all three major domestic competitions. Both players scored just once in each game.

IPSWICH TOWN 2000–01 LEAGUE RECORD

Match No.	Date		Venue	Opponents	Result		H/T Score	Lg. Pos.	Goalscorers	Atten- dance
1	Aug	19	A	Tottenham H	L	1-3	1-2	—	Venus [9]	36,044
2		22	H	Manchester U	D	1-1	1-1	—	Wilnis [6]	22,007
3		26	H	Sunderland	W	1-0	0-0	13	Bramble [52]	21,830
4	Sept	6	A	Leicester C	L	1-2	0-0	—	Magilton (pen) [89]	19,598
5		9	H	Aston Villa	L	1-2	0-1	17	Stewart [90]	22,064
6		16	A	Leeds U	W	2-1	1-1	11	Scowcroft [12], Wright J [47]	35,552
7		23	H	Arsenal	D	1-1	0-0	12	Stewart [49]	22,028
8		30	A	Everton	W	3-0	1-0	9	McGreal [19], Stewart 2 [49, 60]	32,597
9	Oct	14	H	West Ham U	D	1-1	1-0	8	Stewart [5]	22,246
10		21	A	Bradford C	W	2-0	1-0	6	Petrescu (og) [34], Clapham [89]	17,045
11		28	H	Middlesbrough	W	2-1	2-0	5	Naylor [25], Venus [28]	21,767
12	Nov	4	A	Newcastle U	L	1-2	1-1	7	Stewart [13]	50,922
13		11	H	Charlton Ath	W	2-0	0-0	6	Holland [80], Stewart [84]	22,287
14		20	A	Coventry C	W	1-0	0-0	—	Wilnis [90]	19,327
15		25	A	Manchester C	W	3-2	2-0	3	Stewart 2 [9, 53], Heidarsson [32]	33,741
16	Dec	2	H	Derby Co	L	0-1	0-1	5		21,991
17		10	H	Liverpool	W	1-0	1-0	3	Stewart [45]	43,509
18		16	H	Southampton	W	3-1	0-1	3	Scowcroft [48], Bridge (og) [51], Armstrong [90]	22,223
19		23	A	Manchester U	L	0-2	0-2	5		67,597
20		26	H	Chelsea	D	2-2	1-2	5	Scowcroft [43], Stewart [82]	22,240
21		30	H	Tottenham H	W	3-0	1-0	3	Stewart [9], Armstrong [62], Clapham [88]	22,234
22	Jan	1	A	Sunderland	L	1-4	1-1	4	Stewart [5]	43,314
23		14	H	Leicester C	W	2-0	0-0	4	Stewart [80], Scowcroft [90]	22,002
24		20	A	Chelsea	L	1-4	1-1	5	Stewart [23]	34,948
25	Feb	3	H	Leeds U	L	1-2	0-2	5	Venus [63]	22,016
26		10	A	Arsenal	L	0-1	0-0	6		38,011
27		24	H	Everton	W	2-0	0-0	5	Holland [82], Armstrong [84]	22,211
28	Mar	4	H	Bradford C	W	3-1	0-1	3	Reuser 2 [59, 72], Burchill [75]	21,816
29		10	A	Aston Villa	L	1-2	1-0	3	Armstrong [30]	28,216
30		17	A	West Ham U	W	1-0	0-0	3	Reuser [60]	26,046
31	Apr	2	A	Southampton	W	3-0	1-0	—	Stewart 3 (1 pen) [33, 68, 71 (p)]	15,244
32		10	H	Liverpool	D	1-1	0-0	—	Armstrong [77]	23,500
33		14	H	Newcastle U	W	1-0	0-0	3	Stewart (pen) [76]	24,026
34		16	A	Middlesbrough	W	2-1	0-1	3	Armstrong 2 [46, 50]	34,263
35		21	H	Coventry C	W	2-0	1-0	3	Reuser [20], Wright J [56]	24,576
36		30	A	Charlton Ath	L	1-2	1-1	—	Reuser [20]	20,043
37	May	7	H	Manchester C	W	2-1	0-0	—	Holland [78], Reuser [85]	24,888
38		19	A	Derby Co	D	1-1	0-1	5	Carbonari (og) [46]	33,239

Final League Position: 5

GOALSCORERS

League (57): Stewart 19 (2 pens), Armstrong 7, Reuser 6, Scowcroft 4, Holland 3, Venus 3, Clapham 2, Wilnis 2, Wright J 2, Bramble 1, Burchill 1, Hreidarsson 1, Magilton 1 (pen), McGreal 1, Naylor 1, own goals 3.
Worthington Cup (13): Johnson 3, Bramble 2, Holland 2, Scowcroft 2, Clapham 1, Magilton 1, Stewart 1, Venus 1.
FA Cup (3): Armstrong 1, Stewart 1, Wright J 1.

Wright R 36	Croft G 6+2	Clapham J 28+7	Bramble T 23+3	Hreidarsson H 35+1	Venus M 23+2	Holland M 38	Magilton J 32+1	Johnson D 6+8	Scowcroft J 22+12	Stewart M 33+1	Brown W —+4	Reuser M 13+13	Wilnis F 27+2	Wright J 35+2	Scales J 2	McGreal J 25+3	Naylor R 5+8	Branagan K 2	Armstrong A 15+6	Abidallah N —+2	Burchill M 2+5	Makin C 10	Match No
1	2	3	4	5	6¹	7	8	9	10²	11	12	13											1
1		3	4	5	6	7²	8		9	12	11¹		13	2		10							2
1		3	4	5	6	7	8		9	12	11¹			2		10							3
1		3	4	5		7	8		9	12	11			2		10¹	6						4
1		3	4	5	6³	7	8	9¹	10	12		13		2		11²			14				5
1		3	4	5		7	8		10	9				2		11	6						6
1		3	4	5	6	7	8		10¹	9				2		11	12						7
1		3	4	5		7	8	12	13	9¹				2		11	6		10²				8
1		3		5	4	7	8	12	13	9²				2		11	6		10¹				9
1		3		5	4	7	8²	12	13	9¹				2		11	6		10				10
1		3		5	4	7	8²	12	13	9¹				2		11	6		10				11
1		3		5³	4	7	8	12	13	9²		14		2		11	6		10¹				12
1		3	12	5	4	7	8	13	10³	9²				2¹		11	6		14				13
1		3	12	5	4	7	8		10	9		13		2		11¹	6³						14
1		3		5	6	7	8	12	10¹	9				2	11	4							15
1		3	12	5	4	7	8	9²	13	10		14		2¹	11³	6		1					16
1	12	3		5	4	7	8		10²	9¹				2		11	6		13				17
1	2	3		5	4	7	8		10¹	9	12			11²		6			13				18
1	3	5	12	4	8	7²		10	9			13	2¹	11¹		6			14				19
1	12	3⁴	4	5	6	7			10	9		13	2¹	8		11							20
1		12	4	5	6	7		13	10	9¹		3	2²	8		14			11²				21
1		3²	4	5	6	7			10	9		13	2¹	8		12			11				22
1		3²	4	5		7	8		10	9		13	2	12		6			11¹				23
1	3²	6		5		7	8		10	9	12		2	13					11¹				24
1	2²	3	4	5²	6	7			10	9	14	13	8			12			11¹				25
1	2¹	3	4		5	7	8		10	9	12	6²	11			13							26
1		3	4		5³	7	8²		10			14	2¹	11		6	12		13			9	27
1		12	5	3¹		7	8²		10			4	2	11³		6	13		14			9	28
1		11¹		5		7	12		10			4	2	8³		6			9		13	3	29
1		12		5		7	8			9²		4¹	2	11		6			10		13	3	30
1	6	4	3	12	7			10³	9²		8¹		11	5		14			13		2		31
1		4²	3		7	8		12	9		6	13	11¹	5		10					2		32
1	12		5	14	7	8²		13	9		6¹	2³	11	4		10					3		33
1	12	4	3	5	7	8			9³		6¹		11		13	10²		14	2				34
1		12	4	3		7	8			9²		6¹		11	5	13	1	10			2		35
1		4	3		7	8			9¹		6		11	5		10			12	2			36
1	12	4	3¹		7	8	10			6		11²	5	13	9				2				37
1		4	3		7	8		12	9²		6	13	11¹	5	14	10			2²				38

Worthington Cup

Second Round	Millwall	(a)	0-2
		(h)	5-0
Third Round	Arsenal	(a)	2-1
Fourth Round	Coventry C	(h)	2-1
Fifth Round	Manchester C	(a)	2-1
Semi-Final	Birmingham C	(h)	1-0
		(a)	1-4

FA Cup

Third Round	Morecambe	(a)	3-0
Fourth Round	Sunderland	(a)	0-1

KIDDERMINSTER HARRIERS Division 3

FOUNDATION

Kidderminster Harriers were originally formed as a rugby team and played their first game as a soccer club on 18 September 1886 away to Wilden. Harriers won 2-1 with goals from Arthur Millward and William Colsey. Millward was vice-captain and later Kidderminster's first representative on the executive of the Birmingham County FA in 1897. Colsey was to die in tragic circumstances following an accidental injury sustained in a match only two months later.

Aggborough Stadium, Hoo Road, Kidderminster DY10 1NB.

Telephone: (01562) 823 931.

Fax: (01562) 827 329.

Website: www.harriers.co.uk

E-mail: info@harriers.co.uk

Ground Capacity: 6,293 (1,100 seated).

Record Attendance: 9,155 v Hereford U, 27 November 1948.

Chairman: L. Newton.

Vice Chairman: C. C. Youngjohns.

Directors: P. Byrne, G. R. Lane, T. Murrant.

Chief Executive: N. Morris.

Manager: Jan Molby.

Assistant Manager: Gary Barnett.

Reserve and Youth Team Manager: Ian Britton.

Medical Officers: Dr. K. O'Connor, Dr. V. P. Schreiber.

Physio: Jim Conway.

Commercial Manager: Mark Searl.

Financial Controller: Alan Biggs.

IT'S A FACT !

Ted Croker, later to become secretary of the Football Association, made 27 League appearances for Kidderminster Harriers during the 1951-52 season when their attendances for 21 home games reached a total of 70,042.

Football and Community Development Officer:
Nick Griffiths.

Football Secretary: Roger Barlow.

Matchday Secretary: Dave Colwell.

Safety Officer: Peter Picken.

Stadium Manager: Roger Barlow.

Year Formed: 1886.

Club Nickname: 'Harriers'.

Record Transfer Fee Received: £380,000 from WBA for Lee Hughes, 1997.

Record Transfer Fee Paid: £100,000 to Nuneaton Borough for Andy Ducros, July 2000.

Colours: Red shirts with white flash, red shorts and stockings with white trim.

Change Colours: Blue shirts with yellow flash, blue shorts and stockings with yellow trim.

HONOURS
Conference: – Champions 1993–94, 1999–2000; Runners-up 1996–97.
FA Trophy: 1986–87 (winners); 1990–91, 1994–95 (runners-up).
League Cup: 1996–97 (winners).
Welsh FA Cup: 1985–86 (runners-up), 1988–89 (runners-up).
Southern League Cup: 1979–80 (winners).
Worcester Senior Cup: (21)
Birmingham Senior Cup: (7)
Staffordshire Senior Cup: (4)
West Midland League: Champions (6) Runners-up (3)
Southern Premier: Runners-up (1)
West Midland League Cup: Winners (7)
Keys Cup: Winners (7)
Border Counties Floodlit League: Champions: (3)
Camkin Floodlit Cup: Winners (3)
Bass County Vase: Winners (1)
Conference Fair Play Trophy: (5)

First Football League Game: 12 August 2000, Division 3, v Torquay U W 2–0 – Clarke; Clarkson, Stamps, Webb, Hinton, Smith, Bennett, Horne (1), Foster, Hadley (1), Ducros (Bird).

Record League Victory: 3–0 v Plymouth Arg, Division 3, 16 April 2001 – Clarke; Stamps, Medou-Otye, Skovbjerg (1) (Corbett), Hinton, Smith, Bennett, Doyle (Davies), Hadley (1), Ducros (Durnin), MacKenzie (1).

TEN YEAR LEAGUE RECORD

		P	W	D	L	F	A	Pts	Pos
1990-91	Conf.	42	14	10	18	56	67	52	13
1991-92	Conf.	42	12	9	21	56	77	45	19
1992-93	Conf.	42	14	16	12	60	60	58	9
1993-94	Conf.	42	22	9	11	63	35	75	1
1994-95	Conf.	42	16	9	17	63	61	57	11
1995-96	Conf.	42	18	10	14	78	66	64	7
1996-97	Conf.	42	26	7	9	84	42	85	2
1997-98	Conf.	42	11	14	17	56	63	47	17
1998-99	Conf.	42	14	9	19	56	52	51	15
1999-2000	Div 3	00	00	00	00	00	00	00	00

DID YOU KNOW

The highlight of Kidderminster Harriers first centenary season in 1985-86 was in reaching the final of the Welsh Cup. In total that season, the club played an incredible 76 games.

KIDDERMINSTER HARRIERS 2000–01 LEAGUE RECORD

Match No.	Date	Venue	Opponents	Result	H/T Score	Lg. Pos.	Goalscorers	Attendance
1	Aug 12	H	Torquay U	W 2-0	1-0	—	Hadley [16], Horne [62]	5122
2	19	A	Scunthorpe U	L 0-2	0-1	10		3761
3	26	H	Halifax T	W 2-1	2-1	5	Hadley 2 [38, 40]	2956
4	28	A	Brighton & HA	W 2-0	0-0	3	Foster [52], Bennett [67]	6274
5	Sept 2	H	Carlisle U	L 0-1	0-0	6		4052
6	9	A	Barnet	D 0-0	0-0	5		2103
7	12	A	Southend U	D 1-1	1-0	—	Shail [28]	2403
8	16	H	Leyton Orient	W 2-1	0-1	5	Hinton [77], Bennett [82]	3365
9	23	A	Cardiff C	D 0-0	0-0	7		8003
10	29	H	Blackpool	L 1-4	0-2	—	Ducros [77]	3891
11	Oct 6	H	Rochdale	D 0-0	0-0	—		3094
12	14	A	Lincoln C	D 3-3	0-1	12	Durnin [64], Ducros [67], Bennett [75]	2922
13	17	A	Darlington	W 2-1	1-0	—	Durnin 2 [34, 46]	3713
14	21	H	Exeter C	D 0-0	0-0	7		3269
15	24	H	Chesterfield	L 0-2	0-1	—		3844
16	Nov 4	H	Cheltenham T	D 1-1	1-0	12	Smith [14]	4162
17	11	A	Hartlepool U	L 1-3	1-0	14	Durnin [36]	2726
18	25	H	York C	W 3-1	3-1	11	Smith 2 [15, 30], Foster [18]	2602
19	Dec 2	H	Macclesfield T	W 2-1	2-1	10	Smith 2 [30, 44]	2638
20	23	A	Hull C	D 0-0	0-0	13		5470
21	26	H	Mansfield T	W 1-0	1-0	10	Durnin [9]	3842
22	Jan 1	A	Torquay U	D 1-1	0-0	9	Durnin [61]	2467
23	6	A	Halifax T	L 2-3	0-2	10	Durnin [53], MacKenzie [65]	1824
24	13	H	Brighton & HA	L 0-2	0-1	12		4056
25	23	A	Mansfield T	L 1-2	1-1	—	Broughton [17]	1712
26	27	H	Hull C	D 2-2	2-2	11	Durnin [34], Broughton [45]	3029
27	30	A	Plymouth Arg	L 0-4	0-1	—		5332
28	Feb 3	A	Carlisle U	L 0-2	0-2	16		3429
29	10	H	Barnet	W 2-1	0-1	13	MacKenzie [55], Broughton [74]	2585
30	17	A	Leyton Orient	D 0-0	0-0	14		4132
31	20	H	Southend U	W 2-1	0-1	—	Bogie [65], Hadley [89]	2781
32	25	H	Cardiff C	L 2-4	1-2	14	Broughton 2 [14, 90]	4317
33	Mar 3	A	Blackpool	L 1-5	1-2	15	Coid (og) [20]	4624
34	6	H	Lincoln C	L 1-3	0-2	—	Hadley [73]	2471
35	10	A	Rochdale	D 0-0	0-0	15		2552
36	13	H	Scunthorpe U	D 0-0	0-0	—		2438
37	17	H	Darlington	D 0-0	0-0	15		2568
38	20	A	Shrewsbury T	L 0-1	0-0	—		2761
39	24	A	Exeter C	L 1-2	0-2	16	Bennett [87]	3302
40	31	H	Shrewsbury T	W 3-1	1-0	14	Durnin [40], Hinton [53], Broughton [82]	4548
41	Apr 7	A	Macclesfield T	L 0-1	0-1	14		1585
42	14	A	Chesterfield	L 0-1	0-1	15		4495
43	16	H	Plymouth Arg	W 3-0	3-0	14	Hadley [5], MacKenzie [21], Skovbjerg [43]	3321
44	21	A	Cheltenham T	W 3-1	2-0	14	Webb [20], Bird [45], Broughton [65]	4415
45	28	H	Hartlepool U	L 0-1	0-0	14		3748
46	May 5	A	York C	L 0-1	0-0	16		3185

Final League Position: 16

GOALSCORERS

League (47): Durnin 9, Broughton 7, Hadley 6, Smith 5, Bennett 4, MacKenzie 3, Ducros 2, Foster 2, Hinton 2, Bird 1, Bogie 1, Horne 1, Shail 1, Skovbjerg 1, Webb 1, own goal 1.
Worthington Cup (1): Hadley 1.
FA Cup (4): Hadley 2, Bird 1, Bogie 1.

Clarke T 25	Clarkson I 37 + 1	Stamps S 34	Webb P 23 + 9	Hinton C 46	Smith A 32 + 2	Bennett D 35 + 7	Horne B 21 + 6	Hadley S 18 + 15	Foster I 9 + 1	Ducros A 29 + 5	Bird T 16 + 9	Bogie I 14 + 7	Brock S 21	Shail M 36	Barnett G 2	Corbett A 3 + 3	Kerr D — + 1	Durnin J 28 + 3	MacKenzie N 20 + 3	Medou-Otye P 16 + 1	Doyle D 13 + 2	Broughton D 19	Skovbjerg T 7 + 5	Davies B 2 + 1	Match No.
1	2	3	4	5	6	7	8	9	10	11[1]	12														1
1	2	3	4[2]	5	6	7	8	9	10[1]	11	12	13													2
1	2	3		5	6	7	8	9	12	11[1]	10	4													3
	2	3[2]	12	5	13	7	8	9	10[1]	11		4	1	6											4
	2		12	5	3	7	8	9		11	10[1]	4	1	6											5
	2		12	5	3	7	8	9		11[1]		4	1	6	10										6
	2	3	4	5		7	8	9		12	10[1]		1	6	11										7
	2	3	12	5	6	7	8[1]	9[2]	10	11[3]		4	1					13	14						8
	2	3	4	5		7	8	11	10		9		1	6											9
	2[1]	3	4[2]	5	12	13	8	9	10	11		7	1	6											10
		3	4	5	2	7	8	11	10		9		1	6											11
1	2	3	12	5		7	8	9[2]		11	13	4[1]		6				10							12
1	2	3	4	5	10	7[3]	12	13		11[1]	9[2]	14		6				8							13
1	2	3[1]	4	5	10	7	12	13		11	9[2]			6				8							14
1	2	3	4	5	10	12	8[1]	13		9[2]	11			6				7							15
	2	3	4	5	10	12		9		11		7[1]	1	6				8							16
	2[2]	3	4[3]	5	10	7	12	9[1]		11	13	14	1	6				8							17
	2[1]	3	12	5	4		8	13		9	11[2]	7[3]	1	6				10	14						18
	2	3		5	4		8	12		9[2]	11	7[1]	1	6				10	13						19
		3		5		7	8	12		9[1]	11		1	6				10	4	2					20
		3		5			12		4	9	11	10[1]	1	6				8	7	2					21
		3	12	5	4	7	8				11		1	6				9	10[1]	2					22
	12	3[1]		5	4		8				11		1	6	10			9	7	2					23
	2			5	4		12	8[1]		9[2]	11	13	1	6	10			7	3						24
	2			5	4		12			11			1	6	10			7	3[1]	8	9				25
	2	3[1]	12	5	6		8	13		11	14		1					10[3]	7[2]	4		9			26
	2	3[1]		5	4	7	12				11		1	6				8	11	10		9			27
	2		5	3		7				11			1	6				8	4	10		9			28
1		3		5	4	7				11[1]				6				8	10	2	12	9			29
1	2			5	4	7	12	13						6				8	11	3	10[1]	9[2]			30
1	2	12		5	6	7	4[1]	13				14						8[1]	11	3	10[2]	9			31
1	2	4[3]	5		8[1]	7	12	13						6				14	11	3	10[2]	9			32
1	2	4	5			7		11						6				10	8	3		9			33
1	2	3[2]	4	5		7	12			10[3]		8[1]		6				11	13			9	14		34
1	2	3	4	5		7	12			10				6							8[2]	9[1]	13	11	35
1	2	3	4	5		7	12			10[3]	8[2]			6				13			11[1]	9	14		36
1	2	3	4	5		7				10		8		6				11				9[1]	12		37
1	2	3	4	5		7				12				6				10[1]	11			9	8		38
1	2	3	4	5		7		13		12	11[2]			6				10				9[1]	8		39
1	2	3	4	5	11	7[2]		14		12		13		6				10				9[1]	8[3]		40
1	2		4	5	3	7				12				6				10	11			9[1]	8		41
1		3	4[2]	5	2			12		9	11			6				8[3]			10[1]	7	13	14	42
1		3		5	6	7				9	10[1]					13		12	11	2	4[3]		8[2]	14	43
1		3	4[1]	5	6	7	8				14	10				13		12	2	11[2]		9[3]			44
1		3		5	6	7	8			12								11	2	10	9		4[1]		45
1		3		5	6	12		13			14					9[3]		10	11	2	7		8[1]	4[2]	46

Worthington Cup
First Round   Walsall   (a)   1-1
                                           (h)   0-1

FA Cup
First Round   Burton Albion   (h)   0-0
                                           (a)   4-2
Second Round   Carlisle U   (h)   0-2

LEEDS UNITED   FA Premiership

FOUNDATION

Immediately the Leeds City club (founded in 1904) was wound up by the FA in October 1919, following allegations of illegal payments to players, a meeting was called by a Leeds solicitor, Mr Alf Masser, at which Leeds United was formed. They joined the Midland League playing their first game in that competition in November 1919. It was in this same month that the new club had discussions with the directors of a virtually bankrupt Huddersfield Town who wanted to move to Leeds in an amalgamation. But Huddersfield survived even that crisis.

Elland Road, Leeds LS11 0ES.

Telephone: (0113) 226 6000. *Fax:* (0113) 226 6050.

Website: www.lufc.co.uk

Ticket Information: 09068 121 680.

ClubCall: 09068 121 180.

Ground Capacity: 40,204.

Record Attendance: 57,892 v Sunderland, FA Cup 5th rd (replay), 15 March 1967.

Record Receipts: £781,445 v Liverpool, FA Cup 4th rd, 27 January 2001.

Pitch Measurements: 105m × 68m.

President: The Right Hon. The Earl of Harewood KBE, LLD.

Chairman: Peter Ridsdale.

Directors: A. Hudson, S. Harrison, D. Spencer, I. Silvester, D. Walker.

Manager: David O'Leary.

Assistant Manager: Eddie Gray MBE.

Club Secretary: Ian Silvester.

Physio: Dave Hancock.

Commercial Manager: Phil Brining.

Stadium Manager: Harry Stokey.

Colours: All white with yellow and royal blue trim.

Change Colours: All yellow with royal blue trim.

Year Formed: 1919, as Leeds United after disbandment (by FA order) of Leeds City (formed in 1904).

Turned Professional: 1920.

Ltd Co.: 1920.

Club Nickname: 'United'.

HONOURS

Football League: Division 1 – Champions 1968–69, 1973–74, 1991–92; Runners-up 1964–65, 1965–66, 1969–70, 1970–71, 1971–72; Division 2 – Champions 1923–24, 1963–64, 1989–90; Runners-up 1927–28, 1931–32, 1955–56.

FA Cup: Winners 1972; Runners-up 1965, 1970, 1973.

Football League Cup: Winners 1968; Runners-up 1996.

European Competitions: *European Cup:* 1969–70, 1974–75 (runners-up), 1992–93, 2000–01. *European Cup-Winners' Cup:* 1972–73 (runners-up). *European Fairs Cup:* 1965–66, 1966–67 (runners-up), 1967–68 (winners), 1968–69, 1970–71 (winners). *UEFA Cup:* 1971–72, 1973–74, 1979–80, 1995–96, 1998–99, 1999–2000 (semi-finalists).

IT'S A FACT !

Jack Charlton is not only the player with the most League appearances for Leeds United but with 96 goals in all senior games is also their ninth highest marksman.

First Football League Game: 28 August 1920, Division 2, v Port Vale (a) L 0–2 – Down; Duffield, Tillotson; Musgrove, Baker, Walton; Mason, Goldthorpe, Thompson, Lyon, Best.

Record League Victory: 8–0 v Leicester C, Division 1, 7 April 1934 – Moore; George Milburn, Jack Milburn; Edwards, Hart, Copping; Mahon (2), Firth (2), Duggan (2), Furness (2), Cochrane.

Record Cup Victory: 10–0 v Lyn (Oslo), European Cup 1st rd 1st leg, 17 September 1969 – Sprake; Reaney, Cooper, Bremner (2), Charlton, Hunter, Madeley, Clarke (2), Jones (3), Giles (2) (Bates), O'Grady (1).

Record Defeat: 1–8 v Stoke C, Division 1, 27 August 1934.

Most League Points (2 for a win): 67, Division 1, 1968–69.

Most League Points (3 for a win): 85, Division 2, 1989–90.

Most League Goals: 98, Division 2, 1927–28.

Highest League Scorer in Season: John Charles, 42, Division 2, 1953–54.

Most League Goals in Total Aggregate: Peter Lorimer, 168, 1965–79 and 1983–86.

Most League Goals in One Match: 5, Gordon Hodgson v Leicester C, Division 1, 1 October 1938.

Most Capped Player: Billy Bremner, 54, Scotland.

Most League Appearances: Jack Charlton, 629, 1953–73.

Youngest League Player: Peter Lorimer, 15 years 289 days v Southampton, 29 September 1962.

Record Transfer Fee Received: £12,000,000 from Atletico Madrid for Jimmy Floyd Hasselbaink, July 1999.

Record Transfer Fee Paid: £18,000,000 to West Ham United for Rio Ferdinand, November 2000.

Football League Record: 1920 Elected to Division 2; 1924–27 Division 1; 1927–28 Division 2; 1928–31 Division 1; 1931–32 Division 2; 1932–47 Division 1; 1947–56 Division 2; 1956–60 Division 1; 1960–64 Division 2; 1964–82 Division 1; 1982–90 Division 2; 1990–92 Division 1; 1992– FA Premier League.

MANAGERS

Dick Ray 1919–20
Arthur Fairclough 1920–27
Dick Ray 1927–35
Bill Hampson 1935–47
Willis Edwards 1947–48
Major Frank Buckley 1948–53
Raich Carter 1953–58
Bill Lambton 1958–59
Jack Taylor 1959–61
Don Revie OBE 1961–74
Brian Clough 1974
Jimmy Armfield 1974–78
Jock Stein CBE 1978
Jimmy Adamson 1978–80
Allan Clarke 1980–82
Eddie Gray MBE 1982–85
Billy Bremner 1985–88
Howard Wilkinson 1988–96
George Graham 1996–98
David O'Leary October 1998–

LATEST SEQUENCES

Longest Sequence of League Wins: 9, 26.9.31 – 21.11.31.

Longest Sequence of League Defeats: 6, 6.4.96 – 2.5.96.

Longest Sequence of League Draws: 5, 19.4.97 – 9.8.97.

Longest Sequence of Unbeaten League Matches: 34, 26.10.68 – 26.8.69.

Longest Sequence Without a League Win: 17, 1.2.47 – 26.5.47.

TEN YEAR LEAGUE RECORD

		P	W	D	L	F	A	Pts	Pos
1990-91	Div 1	38	19	7	12	65	47	64	4
1991-92	Div 1	42	22	16	4	74	37	82	1
1992-93	PR Lge	42	12	15	15	57	62	51	17
1993-94	PR Lge	42	18	16	8	65	39	70	5
1994-95	PR Lge	42	20	13	9	59	38	73	5
1995-96	PR Lge	38	12	7	19	40	57	43	13
1996-97	PR Lge	38	11	13	14	28	38	46	11
1997-98	PR Lge	38	17	8	13	57	46	59	5
1998-99	PR Lge	38	18	13	7	62	34	67	4
1999-2000	PR Lge	38	21	6	11	58	43	69	3

DID YOU KNOW ?

In 1929-30 fifth place in the First Division represented Leeds United's highest League position at the time and they also achieved a home and away double over champions Sheffield Wednesday respectively 3–0 and 2–1.

LEEDS UNITED 2000–01 LEAGUE RECORD

Match No.	Date	Venue	Opponents	Result	H/T Score	Lg. Pos.	Goalscorers	Attendance
1	Aug 19	H	Everton	W	2-0	2-0	—	Smith 2 [16,37]	40,010
2	26	A	Middlesbrough	W	2-1	2-0	2	Bowyer [6], Smith [12]	31,626
3	Sept 5	H	Manchester C	L	1-2	0-2	—	Bowyer [56]	40,055
4	9	A	Coventry C	D	0-0	0-0	6		20,363
5	16	H	Ipswich T	L	1-2	1-1	9	Bowyer [4]	35,552
6	23	A	Derby Co	D	1-1	1-0	10	Harte [34]	26,248
7	30	H	Tottenham H	W	4-3	0-1	8	Viduka 2 [52,55], Smith 2 [59,64]	37,562
8	Oct 14	H	Charlton Ath	W	3-1	1-0	5	Smith [38], Viduka 2 [73,90]	38,837
9	21	A	Manchester U	L	0-3	0-1	9		67,523
10	29	A	Bradford C	D	1-1	0-1	10	Viduka [80]	17,364
11	Nov 4	H	Liverpool	W	4-3	1-2	8	Viduka 4 [24,47,73,75]	40,055
12	12	A	Chelsea	D	1-1	0-0	8	Viduka [62]	35,121
13	18	H	West Ham U	L	0-1	0-1	11		40,005
14	26	H	Arsenal	W	1-0	0-0	13	Dacourt [56]	38,084
15	Dec 2	A	Leicester C	L	1-3	0-3	11	Viduka [75]	21,489
16	9	A	Southampton	L	0-1	0-1	12		15,225
17	16	H	Sunderland	W	2-0	1-0	10	Bowyer [23], Viduka [78]	40,053
18	23	H	Aston Villa	L	1-2	0-1	12	Woodgate [90]	39,714
19	26	A	Newcastle U	L	1-2	1-2	12	Dacourt [10]	52,118
20	Jan 1	H	Middlesbrough	D	1-1	0-1	13	Keane (pen) [55]	39,251
21	13	A	Manchester C	W	4-0	1-0	12	Bakke [31], Bowyer [80], Keane 2 [89,90]	34,288
22	20	H	Newcastle U	L	1-3	1-2	12	Keane [2]	40,005
23	24	A	Aston Villa	W	2-1	1-1	—	Bowyer [28], Harte (pen) [75]	29,335
24	31	A	Coventry C	W	1-0	0-0	—	Keane [69]	36,555
25	Feb 3	A	Ipswich T	W	2-1	2-0	7	Venus (og) [28], Keane [41]	22,016
26	7	A	Everton	D	2-2	0-1	—	Harte [66], Dacourt [76]	34,224
27	10	H	Derby Co	D	0-0	0-0	5		38,789
28	24	H	Tottenham H	W	2-1	1-1	6	Harte (pen) [45], Bowyer [57]	36,070
29	Mar 3	H	Manchester U	D	1-1	0-0	6	Viduka [84]	40,055
30	17	A	Charlton Ath	W	2-1	1-1	5	Viduka [1], Smith [46]	20,043
31	31	A	Sunderland	W	2-0	1-0	3	Smith [33], Viduka [90]	46,833
32	Apr 7	H	Southampton	W	2-0	1-0	3	Kewell [10], Keane [72]	39,267
33	13	A	Liverpool	W	2-1	2-0	—	Ferdinand [4], Bowyer [33]	44,116
34	21	A	West Ham U	W	2-0	1-0	4	Keane [8], Ferdinand [47]	26,041
35	28	H	Chelsea	W	2-0	0-0	3	Keane [86], Viduka [88]	39,253
36	May 5	A	Arsenal	L	1-2	0-1	4	Harte [58]	38,142
37	13	H	Bradford C	W	6-1	5-1	4	Viduka [14], Harte [19], Bakke [27], Smith [38], Kewell [43], Bowyer [84]	38,300
38	19	H	Leicester C	W	3-1	1-1	4	Smith 2 [27,90], Harte [77]	39,905

Final League Position: 4

GOALSCORERS

League (64): Viduka 17, Smith 11, Bowyer 9, Keane 9 (1 pen), Harte 7 (2 pens), Dacourt 3, Bakke 2, Ferdinand 2, Kewell 2, Woodgate 1, own goal 1.
Worthington Cup (2): Huckerby 2.
FA Cup (1): Viduka 1.

Martyn N 23	Kelly G 22 + 2	Harte I 29	Woodgate J 14	Radebe L 19 + 1	Bakke E 24 + 5	Dacourt O 33	Smith A 26 + 7	Bridges M 6 + 1	Viduka M 34	Bowyer L 38	Mills D 20 + 3	Huckerby D 2 + 5	Duberry M 5	Jones M 3 + 1	Evans G — + 1	McPhail S 3 + 4	Wilcox J 7 + 10	Matteo D 30	Hay D 2 + 2	Robinson P 15 + 1	Burns J 3 + 1	Ferdinand R 23	Kewell H 12 + 5	Batty D 13 + 3	Keane R 12 + 6	Match No
1	2	3	4	5	6[1]	7	8	9[2]	10	11	12	13														1
1	2	3	4[1]	12	6[2]	7	8	9	10	11	14			5	13[3]											2
1	2	3		5		7	8	9	10	11				6	4[1]	12										3
1	2	3		5		7	8	9		11	10[1]	6			4	12										4
1	2	3				7	8	9		11	5	10	6		4											5
1	2	3		5	6[2]	7	10	9		8	12		4[1]		13		11									6
1	2	3		5[1]	6	7[2]	9	12	10[1]	8	4			13		11	14									7
1[9]	2	3	4		6		9		10	8	5			11		15	7									8
	2		4			9[1]	10	11		12	8	7		3	5	1	6									9
	2	3	4		6	7	9	10	8[1]				11	5	1	12										10
	2	3	4[1]		6	7	9	10	11				5	12	1	8										11
	2	3		5	6	7	9	10[1]	8	4	12		11		1											12
	2	3		5	6[1]	7	9	10	8	4	12		11		1											13
	2	3	4	5	6	7	9	10	8				11		1											14
	2		4[1]	5		7	9	10	11			8[2]	12	3	1			6	13							15
	2		4		6	7	9	10	8				11[1]	3	1			5	12							16
	2		4		6	7[2]	9	10[1]	11	12			3		1			5	8	13						17
	2		4	5[1]	7		9	10	11				3		1			6	8		12					18
	2		4		6[1]	7	9	10	11				3		1			5	8[2]	12	13					19
	2			5		7	12	10	8				11	3	1			6		4	9[1]					20
		5	4	7	9[1]		10	8	2				11	3	1			6			12					21
		4	5	6	7	12	10	8	2				11[1]	3	1						9					22
	2	3	4		6	7[3]	12	10	8				13	11[2]	1			5		14	9[1]					23
1		3		5	6		10	8	2				11			4	7	9								24
1		3		5	12	7[3]	13	10	8	2			11			4	6	9[2]								25
1		3		5	12	7	13	10	8[1]	2			14	11[3]			6	4	9[2]							26
1	2		5	12	7	13	10[2]	8[1]					11[3]	3			6	14	4	9						27
1		3		8[1]	7		10	11	2				6			5	12	4	9							28
1		3		5		7	12	10	8	2			11[1]			6	13	4	9[2]							29
1		3			7	9	10	8	2			12	6			5	11[1]	4								30
1	12	3		5[1]	13	7[2]	9	10	8	2						6	11[3]	4	14							31
1		3		7			10	8	2			12	6			5	11[1]	4	9							32
1		3			7	9[2]	10	8	2			12	6			5	11[1]	4	13							33
1	12	3		11	7			8	2			13	6			5	10[2]	4	9[1]							34
1		3		12	7	9	10	8[1]	2				6			5	11[2]	4	13							35
1	2	3		4[1]	7		10	8			12	13	6			5	11		9[2]							36
1		3		4	7[1]	9	10	8	2			12				5	11									37
1		3		4	7[1]	9	10	8	2			12	6			5	11									38

Worthington Cup
Third Round   Tranmere R   (a)   2-3

FA Cup
Third Round   Barnsley   (h)   1-0
Fourth Round   Liverpool   (h)   0-2

LEICESTER CITY   FA Premiership

FOUNDATION

In 1884 a number of young footballers who were mostly old boys of Wyggeston School, held a meeting at a house on the Roman Fosse Way and formed Leicester Fosse FC. They collected 9d (less than 4p) towards the cost of a ball, plus the same amount for membership. Their first professional, Harry Webb from Stafford Rangers, was signed in 1888 for 2s 6d (12p) per week, plus travelling expenses.

City Stadium, Filbert St, Leicester LE2 7FL.

Telephone: (0116) 291 5000. *Fax:* (0116) 247 0585.
Ticket Office: (0116) 291 5232. *ClubCall:* 09068 121 185.
24hr Ticket Information: 09068 121 028.
Website: www.lcfc.co.uk

Ground Capacity: 22,868.

Record Attendance: 47,298 v Tottenham H, FA Cup 5th rd, 18 February 1928.

Record Receipts: £377,467 v Aston Villa, League Cup semi-final, 2nd leg, 2 February 2000.

Pitch Measurements: 110yd × 76yd.

President: T. W. Shipman. *Chairman:* J. M. Elsom FCA.
Finance Director and Chief Operating Officer: Steve Kind FCCA. *Directors:* J. M. Elsom FCA, S. A. Kind FCCA, M. F. George.

Manager: Peter Taylor. *First Team Coach:* Steve Butler.
Physios: David Rennie and Mick Yeoman.

HONOURS

Football League: Division 1 – Runners-up 1928–29; Promoted from Division 1 1993–94 (play-offs) and 1995–96 (play-offs); Division 2 – Champions 1924–25, 1936–37, 1953–54, 1956–57, 1970–71, 1979–80; Runners-up 1907–08.
FA Cup: Runners-up 1949, 1961, 1963, 1969.
Football League Cup: Winners 1964, 1997, 2000; Runners-up 1965, 1999.
European Competitions: European Cup-Winners' Cup: 1961–62. UEFA Cup: 1997–98, 2000–01.

Director of Media and Communications: Paul Mace. *Director of Football Administration and Club Secretary:* Andrew Neville. *Stadium Manager:* John Petherick.

Colours: Royal blue shirts, white shorts, blue stockings.

Change Colours: White shirts, royal blue shorts, white stockings.

Year Formed: 1884.

Turned Professional: 1888.

Ltd Co: 1897.

Previous Name: 1884, Leicester Fosse; 1919, Leicester City.

Club Nickname: 'Foxes'.

Previous Grounds: 1884, Victoria Park; 1887, Belgrave Road; 1888, Victoria Park; 1891, Filbert Street.

First Football League Game: 1 September 1894, Division 2, v Grimsby T (a) L 3–4 – Thraves; Smith, Bailey; Seymour, Brown, Henrys; Hill, Hughes, McArthur (1), Skea (2), Priestman.

Record League Victory: 10–0 v Portsmouth, Division 1, 20 October 1928 – McLaren; Black, Brown; Findlay, Carr, Watson; Adcock, Hine (3), Chandler (6), Lochhead, Barry (1).

IT'S A FACT !

Leicester City achieved a home and away double over Chelsea in 2000–01. It was their first such feat against these opponents since 1961–62 when it was respectively 2–0 and 3–1.

Record Cup Victory: 8–1 v Coventry C (a), League Cup 5th rd, 1 December 1964 – Banks; Sjoberg, Norman (2); Roberts, King, McDerment; Hodgson (2), Cross, Goodfellow, Gibson (1), Stringfellow (2), (1 og).

Record Defeat: 0–12 (as Leicester Fosse) v Nottingham F, Division 1, 21 April 1909.

Most League Points (2 for a win): 61, Division 2, 1956–57.

Most League Points (3 for a win): 77, Division 2, 1991–92.

Most League Goals: 109, Division 2, 1956–57.

Highest League Scorer in Season: Arthur Rowley, 44, Division 2, 1956–57.

Most League Goals in Total Aggregate: Arthur Chandler, 259, 1923–35.

Most League Goals in One Match: 6, John Duncan v Port Vale, Division 2, 25 December 1924; 6, Arthur Chandler v Portsmouth, Division 1, 20 October 1928.

Most Capped Player: John O'Neill, 39, Northern Ireland.

Most League Appearances: Adam Black, 528, 1920–35.

Youngest League Player: Dave Buchanan, 16 years 192 days v Oldham Ath, 1 January 1979.

Record Transfer Fee Received: £11,000,000 from Liverpool for Emile Heskey, March 2000.

Record Transfer Fee Paid: £5,000,000 to Wolverhampton W for Ade Akinbiyi, July 2000.

Football League Record: 1894 Elected to Division 2; 1908–09 Division 1; 1909–25 Division 2; 1925–35 Division 1; 1935–37 Division 2; 1937–39 Division 1; 1946–54 Division 2; 1954–55 Division 1; 1955–57 Division 2; 1957–69 Division 1; 1969–71 Division 2; 1971–78 Division 1; 1978–80 Division 2; 1980–81 Division 1; 1981–83 Division 2; 1983–87 Division 1; 1987–92 Division 2; 1992–94 Division 1; 1994–95 FA Premier League; 1995–96 Division 1; 1996– FA Premier League.

MANAGERS

Frank Gardner 1884–92
Ernest Marson 1892–94
J. Lee 1894–95
Henry Jackson 1895–97
William Clark 1897–98
George Johnson 1898–1912
Jack Bartlett 1912–14
Louis Ford 1914–15
Harry Linney 1915–19
Peter Hodge 1919–26
Willie Orr 1926–32
Peter Hodge 1932–34
Arthur Lochhead 1934–36
Frank Womack 1936–39
Tom Bromilow 1939–45
Tom Mather 1945–46
John Duncan 1946–49
Norman Bullock 1949–55
David Halliday 1955–58
Matt Gillies 1958–68
Frank O'Farrell 1968–71
Jimmy Bloomfield 1971–77
Frank McLintock 1977–78
Jock Wallace 1978–82
Gordon Milne 1982–86
Bryan Hamilton 1986–87
David Pleat 1987–91
Gordon Lee 1991
Brian Little 1991–94
Mark McGhee 1994–95
Martin O'Neill 1995–2000
Peter Taylor June 2000–

LATEST SEQUENCES

Longest Sequence of League Wins: 7, 28.2.93 – 27.3.93.

Longest Sequence of League Defeats: 8, 17.3.01 – 28.4.01.

Longest Sequence of League Draws: 6, 21.8.76 – 18.9.76.

Longest Sequence of Unbeaten League Matches: 19, 6.2.71 – 18.8.71.

Longest Sequence Without a League Win: 18, 12.4.75 – 1.11.75.

TEN YEAR LEAGUE RECORD

		P	W	D	L	F	A	Pts	Pos
1990-91	Div 2	46	14	8	24	60	83	50	22
1991-92	Div 2	46	23	8	15	62	55	77	4
1992-93	Div 1	46	22	10	14	71	64	76	6
1993-94	Div 1	46	19	16	11	72	59	73	4
1994-95	PR Lge	42	6	11	25	45	80	29	21
1995-96	Div 1	46	19	14	13	66	60	71	5
1996-97	PR Lge	38	12	11	15	46	54	47	9
1997-98	PR Lge	38	13	14	11	51	41	53	10
1998-99	PR Lge	38	12	13	13	40	46	49	10
1999-2000	PR Lge	38	16	7	15	55	55	55	8

DID YOU KNOW ?

Sep Smith of Leicester City was the first English player to appear as a substitute coming on in the second-half of the Jubilee Fund international against Scotland on 21 August 1935 at Hampden Park.

LEICESTER CITY 2000–01 LEAGUE RECORD

Match No.	Date		Venue	Opponents	Result	H/T Score	Lg. Pos.	Goalscorers	Attendance
1	Aug	19	H	Aston Villa	D 0-0	0-0	—		21,455
2		23	A	West Ham U	W 1-0	0-0	—	Eadie [54]	25,195
3		26	A	Bradford C	D 0-0	0-0	6		16,766
4	Sept	6	H	Ipswich T	W 2-1	0-0	—	Akinbiyi [57], Elliott [73]	19,598
5		9	H	Southampton	W 1-0	0-0	2	Taggart [66]	18,366
6		17	A	Chelsea	W 2-0	1-0	2	Izzet [6], Collymore [82]	33,697
7		24	H	Everton	D 1-1	1-0	2	Akinbiyi [23]	18,084
8	Oct	1	A	Sunderland	D 0-0	0-0	1		44,153
9		14	H	Manchester U	L 0-3	0-1	3		22,132
10		21	A	Liverpool	L 0-1	0-0	5		44,395
11		28	H	Derby Co	W 2-1	1-1	4	Izzet [31], Gunnlaugsson [76]	20,525
12	Nov	4	A	Manchester C	W 1-0	0-0	3	Savage [56]	34,279
13		11	H	Newcastle U	D 1-1	0-0	4	Gunnlaugsson [63]	21,406
14		18	A	Middlesbrough	W 3-0	2-0	3	Izzet (pen) [8], Benjamin [13], Eadie [57]	27,965
15		25	A	Tottenham H	L 0-3	0-2	4		35,638
16	Dec	2	H	Leeds U	W 3-1	3-0	3	Savage [8], Akinbiyi [17], Taggart [29]	21,489
17		10	A	Coventry C	L 0-1	0-1	4		17,275
18		16	H	Charlton Ath	W 3-1	1-1	4	Akinbiyi [35], Elliott [79], Gunnlaugsson [90]	19,371
19		23	H	West Ham U	W 2-1	1-1	3	Izzet [26], Savage [63]	21,524
20		26	A	Arsenal	L 1-6	0-1	4	Akinbiyi [54]	38,007
21	Jan	1	H	Bradford C	L 1-2	1-2	6	Izzet (pen) [38]	19,278
22		14	A	Ipswich T	L 0-2	0-0	6		22,002
23		20	H	Arsenal	D 0-0	0-0	7		21,872
24		31	A	Southampton	L 0-1	0-0	—		14,909
25	Feb	3	H	Chelsea	W 2-1	1-0	6	Izzet [24], Rowett [76]	21,502
26		10	A	Everton	L 1-2	0-2	8	Sturridge [79]	30,409
27		24	H	Sunderland	W 2-0	1-0	7	Sturridge [30], Akinbiyi [65]	21,086
28	Mar	3	H	Liverpool	W 2-0	0-0	5	Akinbiyi [51], Izzet [90]	21,924
29		17	A	Manchester U	L 0-2	0-0	7		67,539
30	Apr	1	A	Charlton Ath	L 0-2	0-1	9		20,043
31		4	A	Aston Villa	L 1-2	1-1	—	Davidson [27]	29,043
32		7	H	Coventry C	L 1-3	1-2	10	Akinbiyi [10]	19,545
33		14	H	Manchester C	L 1-2	1-1	11	Akinbiyi [41]	20,224
34		16	A	Derby Co	L 0-2	0-1	11		28,387
35		21	H	Middlesbrough	L 0-3	0-1	12		18,162
36		28	A	Newcastle U	L 0-1	0-0	13		50,501
37	May	5	H	Tottenham H	W 4-2	1-0	10	Rowett [42], Sturridge [56], Guppy [82], Savage (pen) [90]	21,056
38		19	A	Leeds U	L 1-3	1-1	13	Ferdinand (og) [32]	39,905

Final League Position: 13

GOALSCORERS

League (39): Akinbiyi 9, Izzet 7 (2 pens), Savage 4 (1 pen), Gunnlaugsson 3, Sturridge 3, Eadie 2, Elliott 2, Rowett 2, Taggart 2, Benjamin 1, Collymore 1, Davidson 1, Guppy 1, own goal 1.
Worthington Cup (0).
FA Cup (9): Izzet 3 (2 pens), Akinbiyi 1, Cresswell 1, Gunnlaugsson 1, Rowett 1, Sturridge 1, own goal 1.

Flowers T 22	Impey A 29 + 4	Davidson C 25 + 3	Elliott M 34	Rowett G 38	Taggart G 24	Lennon N 15	Izzet M 27	Akinbiyi A 33 + 4	Collymore S 1 + 4	Savage R 33	Eadie D 16 + 8	Walsh S — + 1	Guppy S 17 + 11	Cottee T — + 2	Gilchrist P 6 + 6	Oakes S 5 + 8	Cresswell R 3 + 5	Benjamin T 7 + 14	Sinclair F 14 + 3	Gunnlaugsson A 3 + 14	Royce S 16 + 3	Jones M 10 + 1	Sturridge D 12 + 1	Mancini R 3 + 1	Lewis J 15	Delaney D 3 + 2	Ellison K — + 1	Marshall L 7 + 2	Match No.
1	2	3^1	4	5^2	6	7	8	9	10	11	12	13																	1
1	2		4	5	6	7	8	9		11	10^1		3	12															2
1	2		4	5	6	7^1	8^1	9		11	10		3	12	13														3
1	2		4	5	6		8^1	9	12	11	10		3			7													4
1	2		4	5	6	7^1	8^2	9	12	11	10		3		13														5
1	2	12	4	5		7	8	9^2	13	11	10^2		3^1		6		14												6
1	2^1		4	5	6	7	8	9^2	12	11	10^3		3		13		14												7
1	2	3	4	5	6	7		9^2		8	11^1		12				13	10^2	14										8
1	2^1	3	4	5		7	8^3	9^1		11	10		12		6			13	14										9
1	2^1	3	4	5		7	8	13		11	10^3		12		6			9^2	14										10
1		2	4	5		7	8	9		11	12		3^2			10^1			6	13									11
1^8		3	4	5	6	7	8	9		11							10^2	2	12	15									12
1		3	4	5	6	7	8	9		11							10^1	2	12										13
1^8		3^1	4	5	6	7	8	9		11	12			13			10^2	2		15									14
	12	3	4	5	6	7	8	9^1		11^2	13						14	10^3	2		1								15
	12	3	4	5	6	7	8	9^2		11	10			13				2^1			1								16
	12	3	4	5			8^3	9		7	11^2	13		6	10		14	2^1			1								17
1	7	3^1	4	2	5			9^1		6	10	11^2			14		13		12		8								18
1	2		4^2	5	6		8^3	9^1		7	12	13			11		14	3		10									19
1	2		4	5	6^1		8	9		7		12			11^2	13	3		10										20
1^8	2		4	5			8	9		7	3^1	12		6			13		10	15	11^2								21
	2	6	4	5			8	9^2	11			3	12	13	7^1	14					1	10^2							22
	2	3	4	5	6		8^2	12		7			13			14					1	10	9^3	11^1					23
	2	6	4	5			8	9^1		7			3			12					1	13	10^2	11					24
	2	6	4	5			8	12		7	13		3								1	9^2	10^1	11					25
	2		4	5	6^2		8			11	12		3^1			13					1	10^3	9	14	7				26
		3^1	4	5	6		8	9^2		11^3			12			2	13		14	10	1				7				27
1^8	2		4	5	6		8	9^2		7						14	2^1	13		10^3	1	11							28
	2		4	5			9^2			11		12		6		13			2^3	1	10^1	8^3	7	3	14				29
	2	3^1	4	5	6		12			11^2			13	8	14						1	9^3	10					7	30
	2	3^1	4	5	6		9^2			12		11	13	14							1	8^3	10					7	31
	2	3^1	4^2	5	6		8^3	9		12		13	14	10							1	11						7	32
1	2	12	4	5	6		9^3		11	13	3	14	10^2	8														7^1	33
	2	3^1	4	5			9		6	10	11^3	12	8^2	13							1	7						14	34
	7	12		5	6^1		9	4		11			2^3	13							1	8^2	10	3	14				35
1	2	6		5			9^1			11	12	14	13	10^1	8^2	7	3	4											36
1	2	3		5^2			9^1	6		11	12	4	8	10^3	8^2	10	13	7											37
1	2^1	3		5			9	7		12	13	6	10^3	8^2	11	14	4												38

Worthington Cup

Third Round	Crystal Palace	(h)	0–3

FA Cup

Third Round	York C	(h)	3–0
Fourth Round	Aston Villa	(a)	2–1
Fifth Round	Bristol C	(h)	3–0
Sixth Round	Wycombe W	(h)	1–2

LEYTON ORIENT   Division 3

FOUNDATION

There is some doubt about the foundation of Leyton Orient, and, indeed, some confusion with clubs like Leyton and Clapton over their early history. As regards the foundation, the most favoured version is that Leyton Orient was formed originally by members of Homerton Theological College who established Glyn Cricket Club in 1881 and then carried on through the following winter playing football. Eventually many employees of the Orient Shipping Line became involved and so the name Orient was chosen in 1888.

Leyton Stadium, Brisbane Road, Leyton, London E10 5NE.

Telephone: (020) 8926 1111. *Fax:* (020) 8926 1110.
ClubCall: 09068 121 150.

Ground Capacity: 13,842.

Record Attendance: 34,345 v West Ham U, FA Cup 4th rd, 25 January 1964.

Record Receipts: £87,867.92 v West Ham U, FA Cup 3rd rd, 10 January 1987.

Pitch Measurements: 110yd × 80yd.

Chairman: Barry Hearn.

Chief Executive: Steve Dawson.

HONOURS

Football League: Division 1 best season: 22nd, 1962–63; Division 2 – Runners-up 1961–62; Division 3 – Champions 1969–70; Division 3 (S) – Champions 1955–56; Runners-up 1954–55; Promoted from Division 4 1988–89 (play-offs).

FA Cup: Semi-final 1978.

Football League Cup: best season: 5th rd, 1963.

Directors: Tony Wood OBE, John Goldsmith FRIBA, David Dodd, Steve Davis, Nick Levene.

Team Manager: Tommy Taylor. *First Team Coach:* Paul Clark. *Physio:* Tony Flynn.

Secretary: Kirstine Nicholson. *General Manager, Commercial and Stadium:* John Hines.

Colours: Red and white checked shirts, black shorts with red and white checked trim.

Change Colours: Blue and yellow.

Year Formed: 1881. *Turned Professional:* 1903. *Ltd Co.:* 1906.

Previous Names: 1881, Glyn Cricket and Football Club; 1886, Eagle Football Club; 1888, Orient Football Club; 1898, Clapton Orient; 1946, Leyton Orient; 1966, Orient; 1987, Leyton Orient.

Club Nickname: 'The O's'.

Previous Grounds: 1884, Glyn Road; 1896, Whittles Athletic Ground; 1900, Millfields Road; 1930, Lea Bridge Road; 1937, Brisbane Road.

First Football League Game: 2 September 1905, Division 2, v Leicester Fosse (a) L 1–2 – Butler; Holmes, Codling; Lamberton, Boden, Boyle; Kingaby (1), Wootten, Leigh, Evenson, Bourne.

Record League Victory: 8–0 v Crystal Palace, Division 3 (S), 12 November 1955 – Welton; Lee, Earl; Blizzard, Aldous, McKnight; White (1), Facey (3), Burgess (2), Heckman, Hartburn (2). 8–0 v Rochdale, Division 4, 20 October 1987 – Wells; Howard, Dickenson (1), Smalley (1), Day, Hull, Hales (2), Castle (Sussex), Shinners (2), Godfrey (Harvey), Comfort (2). 8–0 v Colchester U, Division 4, 15 October 1988 – Wells; Howard, Dickenson, Hales (1p), Day (1), Sitton (1), Baker (1), Ward, Hull (3), Juryeff, Comfort (1). 8–0 v Doncaster R, Division 3, 28 December 1997 – Hyde; Channing, Naylor, Smith (1p), Hicks, Clark, Ling, Joseph R, Griffiths (3) (Harris), Richards (2) (Baker (1)), Inglethorpe (1) (Simpson).

IT'S A FACT !

Frank Neary, a versatile forward who unusually played for five different London clubs: Fulham, Queens Park Rangers (two spells), West Ham United, Leyton Orient and Millwall, topped the Orient goalscorers for two seasons 1947-48 and 1948-49.

Record Cup Victory: 9–2 v Chester, League Cup 3rd rd, 15 October 1962 – Robertson; Charlton, Taylor; Gibbs, Bishop, Lea; Deeley (1), Waites (3), Dunmore (2), Graham (3), Wedge.

Record Defeat: 0–8 v Aston Villa, FA Cup 4th rd, 30 January 1929.

Most League Points (2 for a win): 66, Division 3 (S), 1955–56.

Most League Points (3 for a win): 75, Division 4, 1988–89.

Most League Goals: 106, Division 3 (S), 1955–56.

Highest League Scorer in Season: Tom Johnston, 35, Division 2, 1957–58.

Most League Goals in Total Aggregate: Tom Johnston, 121, 1956–58, 1959–61.

Most League Goals in One Match: 4, Wally Leigh v Bradford C, Division 2, 13 April 1906; 4, Albert Pape v Oldham Ath, Division 2, 1 September 1924; 4, Peter Kitchen v Millwall, Division 3, 21 April 1984.

Most Capped Players: Tunji Banjo, 7 (7), Nigeria; John Chiedozie, 7 (9), Nigeria; Tony Grealish, 7 (45), Eire.

Most League Appearances: Peter Allen, 432, 1965–78.

Youngest League Player: Paul Went, 15 years 327 days v Preston NE, 4 September 1965.

Record Transfer Fee Received: £600,000 from Notts Co, for John Chiedozie, August 1981.

Record Transfer Fee Paid: £175,000 to Wigan Ath for Paul Beesley, October 1989.

Football League Record: 1905 Elected to Division 2; 1929–56 Division 3 (S); 1956–62 Division 2; 1962–63 Division 1; 1963–66 Division 2; 1966–70 Division 3; 1970–82 Division 2; 1982–85 Division 3; 1985–89 Division 4; 1989–92 Division 3; 1992–95 Division 2; 1995– Division 3.

LATEST SEQUENCES

Longest Sequence of League Wins: 10, 21.1.56 – 30.3.56.

Longest Sequence of League Defeats: 9, 1.4.95 – 6.5.95.

Longest Sequence of League Draws: 6, 30.11.74 – 28.12.74.

Longest Sequence of Unbeaten League Matches: 13, 30.10.54 – 19.2.55.

Longest Sequence Without a League Win: 23, 6.10.62 – 13.4.63.

MANAGERS

Sam Omerod 1905–06
Ike Ivenson 1906
Billy Holmes 1907–22
Peter Proudfoot 1922–29
Arthur Grimsdell 1929–30
Peter Proudfoot 1930–31
Jimmy Seed 1931–33
David Pratt 1933–34
Peter Proudfoot 1935–39
Tom Halsey 1939
Bill Wright 1939–45
Willie Hall 1945
Bill Wright 1945–46
Charlie Hewitt 1946–48
Neil McBain 1948–49
Alec Stock 1949–59
Les Gore 1959–61
Johnny Carey 1961–63
Benny Fenton 1963–64
Dave Sexton 1965
Dick Graham 1966–68
Jimmy Bloomfield 1968–71
George Petchey 1971–77
Jimmy Bloomfield 1977–81
Paul Went 1981
Ken Knighton 1981
Frank Clark 1982–91
 (Managing Director)
Peter Eustace 1991–94
Chris Turner/John Sitton 1994–95
Pat Holland 1995–96
Tommy Taylor November 1996–

TEN YEAR LEAGUE RECORD

		P	W	D	L	F	A	Pts	Pos
1990-91	Div 3	46	18	10	18	55	58	64	13
1991-92	Div 3	46	18	11	17	62	52	65	10
1992-93	Div 2	46	21	9	16	69	53	72	7
1993-94	Div 2	46	14	14	18	57	71	56	18
1994-95	Div 2	46	6	8	32	30	75	26	24
1995-96	Div 3	46	12	11	23	44	63	47	21
1996-97	Div 3	46	15	12	19	50	58	57	16
1997-98	Div 3	46	19	12	15	62	47	66	11
1998-99	Div 3	46	19	15	12	68	59	72	6
1999-2000	Div 3	46	13	13	20	47	52	52	19

DID YOU KNOW ?

The majority of Leyton Orient players (then Clapton Orient), joined the Footballers Battalion in the First World War and Fred 'Spider' Parker, whose career spanned the war, was actually its first recruit.

LEYTON ORIENT 2000–01 LEAGUE RECORD

Match No.	Date	Venue	Opponents	Result		H/T Score	Lg. Pos.	Goalscorers	Attendance
1	Aug 12	A	Plymouth Arg	W	1-0	1-0	—	Griffiths [27]	5649
2	19	H	Carlisle U	W	1-0	1-0	3	Lockwood (pen) [33]	4320
3	26	A	Blackpool	D	2-2	2-1	3	Garcia 2 [11, 39]	4816
4	28	H	Exeter C	W	2-1	0-1	2	McGhee [59], Lockwood (pen) [66]	4098
5	Sept 2	A	Halifax T	D	2-2	2-0	2	Smith [11], Griffiths [23]	1592
6	9	H	Hull C	D	2-2	0-1	2	Griffiths [51], Christie [86]	5177
7	12	H	Scunthorpe U	D	1-1	1-1	—	Lockwood (pen) [13]	3581
8	16	A	Kidderminster H	L	1-2	1-0	7	Christie [9]	3365
9	23	H	Lincoln C	W	1-0	0-0	5	Griffiths [48]	3889
10	30	A	Brighton & HA	L	0-2	0-1	6		6731
11	Oct 8	A	Torquay U	W	2-1	1-0	5	Garcia [22], Griffiths [56]	1925
12	14	H	Cardiff C	W	2-1	2-0	5	Smith [9], Lockwood (pen) [38]	4649
13	17	H	Shrewsbury T	W	2-0	1-0	—	Walschaerts [9], Watts [90]	3554
14	21	A	York C	D	1-1	1-0	5	Garcia [37]	2744
15	24	H	Barnet	W	3-1	1-0	—	Griffiths [41], Lockwood (pen) [78], Walschaerts [90]	4707
16	28	A	Hartlepool U	L	1-2	0-0	4	Watts [90]	2133
17	Nov 4	H	Mansfield T	W	2-1	1-0	4	Lockwood (pen) [39], Griffiths [49]	4165
18	11	A	Cheltenham T	D	1-1	0-0	4	McGhee [82]	3375
19	25	H	Macclesfield T	W	2-1	1-1	3	Brkovic [8], Watts [81]	4013
20	Dec 2	A	Chesterfield	L	1-4	1-4	4	Watts [18]	4985
21	16	H	Darlington	W	1-0	0-0	3	Houghton [83]	4117
22	23	H	Rochdale	D	1-1	0-1	4	Walschaerts [76]	2200
23	26	A	Southend U	W	1-0	0-0	3	Griffiths [89]	9950
24	Jan 13	A	Exeter C	W	3-2	1-2	3	Tate [45], Griffiths 2 [48, 77]	3044
25	20	H	Southend U	L	0-2	0-0	4		6859
26	28	A	Rochdale	L	1-3	0-2	5	Smith [90]	3676
27	Feb 3	H	Halifax T	W	3-0	1-0	4	Pinamonte [19], Brkovic [68], Watts [86]	3849
28	10	A	Hull C	L	0-1	0-0	4		8782
29	17	H	Kidderminster H	D	0-0	0-0	5		4132
30	20	A	Scunthorpe U	D	1-1	0-1	—	Griffiths [77]	2523
31	24	A	Lincoln C	W	3-2	2-0	5	Watts [21], Brkovic [38], Pinamonte [56]	3027
32	Mar 3	H	Brighton & HA	L	0-2	0-1	5		7958
33	6	A	Cardiff C	D	1-1	0-0	—	Opinel [73]	9022
34	10	H	Torquay U	L	0-2	0-2	6		4390
35	13	A	Carlisle U	L	0-1	0-0	—		2610
36	17	A	Shrewsbury T	D	1-1	0-0	6	McLean [74]	2740
37	20	H	Blackpool	W	1-0	0-0	—	Lockwood [68]	4086
38	24	H	York C	D	1-1	1-1	5	Griffiths (pen) [30]	4085
39	31	A	Darlington	D	1-1	1-1	5	Smith [30]	3189
40	Apr 7	H	Chesterfield	W	2-0	0-0	5	McGhee [47], Griffiths (pen) [83]	4793
41	10	H	Plymouth Arg	D	1-1	0-1	—	Watts [51]	4520
42	14	A	Barnet	W	2-1	0-0	5	Tate 2 [73, 83]	3759
43	16	H	Hartlepool U	W	3-1	3-0	4	Smith [8], Watts [16], Griffiths [17]	5359
44	21	A	Mansfield T	L	0-2	0-0	5		3356
45	28	H	Cheltenham T	D	0-0	0-0	6		5640
46	May 5	A	Macclesfield T	W	2-0	1-0	5	Ibehre 2 [44, 79]	2527

Final League Position: 5

GOALSCORERS

League (59): Griffiths 14 (2 pens), Watts 8, Lockwood 7 (6 pens), Smith 5, Garcia 4, Brkovic 3, McGhee 3, Tate 3, Walschaerts 3, Christie 2, Ibehre 2, Pinamonte 2, Houghton 1, McLean 1, Opinel 1.
Worthington Cup (4): Brkovic 2, Christie 1, Watts 1.
FA Cup (8): Griffiths 4, Houghton 1, Tate 1, Watts 1, own goal 1.

Bayes A 39	Dorrian C 2	Lockwood M 31 + 1	McGhee D 39	Smith D 43	Harris A 44	Walschaerts W 44 + 1	Martin J 15 + 4	Griffiths C 35 + 2	Garcia R 18	Brkovic A 34 + 6	Downer S 20 + 11	Watts S 14 + 22	Brissett J 2 + 2	Joseph M 44	McElholm B 3 + 9	Christie I 1 + 6	Shorey N 8	Ibehre J 1 + 4	Houghton S 17 + 4	Cadou F — + 3	Beall B 12 + 5	Tate C 9 + 13	Opara C 3 + 3	Mansley C — + 1	Hatcher D — + 2	Pinamonte L 5 + 6	Vasseur E — + 2	Opinel S 9 + 2	Jones B 1	Castle S 2 + 7	McLean A 1 + 1	Forge N 1	Lee C 2 + 1	Barrett S 7	Match No.
1	2^1	3	4	5	6	7	8^2	9	10	11^3	12	13	14																						1
1		3	4	5	6	7	8^1	9	10^2	11^3	12	13		2	14																				2
1		3		5	6	7	8	9^3	10	11^1	4^2	12		2	13	14																			3
1		3	4	5	6	7	8^2	9	10	11^1	12			2		13																			4
1			4	5	6	7	8^2	9	10	11^1	12			2		13			3																5
1		3	4	5	6	7	12	9	10	11^2			14	2^1	8^3	13																			6
1		3	4	5	6	7	8^1	9	10	11				2		12																			7
1		3	4	5	6	7	12		10	11				2	9	13	8^2																		8
1		3	4	5	6	7	8^2	9^1	10	11^3	12			2	14	13																			9
1		3	4	5	6	12^2		9	10^3	11	13			2	14		8^1																		10
1	2	3	8	5^1	6	7	13	9	10	4	12								11^2																11
1		3	4	5	6	7		9^1	10^1	11^3	12	13		2				8	14																12
1		3	4	5	6	7		9^1	10^2	11	12			2				8^3			13	14													13
1		3	4	5	6	7^2		9	10	11^1	12	13		2				8																	14
1		3	4	5^2	6	7		9	10	11	12	13		2				8^1																	15
1		3	4	5	6	7		9	10	11^1	12			2							13	8^2													16
1		3	4	5	6	7^1		9	10	11	12			2				8^2				13													17
1		3	4	5	6	7		10^3	11^1	12				2				8^1	14		13	9													18
1		3	4	5		7	8	11^3	12	13				2		6			10^1		14	9^2													19
1		3	4	5	6	7	8	11^2	12	9^3				2					10^1		13	14													20
1		3	4	5	6	7	8	11	12					2					10			9^2	8^1	13											21
1		3	4	5	6	7	8	9^2						2					10		11^1	12	13												22
1		3	4		6	7	8^2	12	5	13				2					10		14	9^2	11^1												23
1		3^2		5	6	7	8^3	11	4	12				2					13			10	9^1		14										24
1			4	5	6	7	8	11^1	9					2			3		10^2			12				13									25
1		3	4	5	6	7	8	12	9^2	13				2					11^1			10^3	14												26
1			4	5	6	7	12	8	11^3	13				2			3		10^1									9^2	14						27
1			4	5	6	7	8	9	11^2	12				2			3^1					13								10					28
1			4	5	6	7	8^2	9	11	12				2^2								13								10^1	14	3			29
1			4	5	6	7	12	9	11	13				2			3^3					10^2						8^1	14						30
1			4	5	6	7	8	9^1	11	12				2^4					10									3		13					31
1	12		4	5	6	7	8^3	9^2	11					2					10			13						3^1	14						32
1	3^2			5	11	4		12	10	6				2					8^1							9^2				7				13	33
1	3			5	6^1	12	11	4	2										10^3							9^2				13	14		8	7	34
	3			5	6	7	8^1	9	11	4				2					12^2							14				13			10^3	1	35
	3			5	6	7	9		4	2									11^2		13	10^3				8^1					14			1	36
	3		4		6	7	9		5	2									11		10					8^1								1	37
	3^3		4		6	7	9	12	5	13				2		14			11		10^2					8^1								1	38
	4		6	3	7	8^1		5	12^2	2									11		9^1	14			13	10								1	39
	4		6	3	7	8	10		5	9^1	2								11		12													1	40
			5	3	7^1	8	10^3	12	4	9	2								11		14	6^1												1	41
1			4	5	3	7	8^1	11		6^2				2					12		10												13	14	42
1			4	5	3	7	8	12		6				2					10^1		11^3	13												14	43
1			4	5	3	7		9		11^2				2					10^1		8	12											6^3	14	44
1			4	5	3	7	8^3			11^1	6			2					12		13												10^2	14	45
1		3	4	5	6	7	12	8		9^2				2					11^1		10^3	13												14	46

Worthington Cup

First Round	Reading	(h)	1-1	
		(a)	2-0	
Second Round	Newcastle U	(a)	0-2	
		(h)	1-1	

FA Cup

First Round	Barrow	(a)	2-0	
Second Round	Northwich Vic	(a)	3-3	
		(h)	3-2	
Third Round	Tottenham H	(h)	0-1	

LINCOLN CITY

Division 3

FOUNDATION

Although there was a Lincoln club as far back as 1861, the present organisation was formed in 1884 winning the Lincolnshire Senior Cup in only their fourth season. They were founder members of the Midland League in 1889 and that competition's first champions.

Sincil Bank, Lincoln LN5 8LD.

Telephone: (01522) 880 011. *Fax:* (01522) 880 020.
Website: www.redimps.com *ClubCall:* 09066 555 900.

Ground Capacity: 10,147.

Record Attendance: 23,196 v Derby Co, League Cup 4th rd, 15 November 1967.

Record Receipts: £44,184.46 v Everton, Coca-Cola Cup 2nd rd 1st leg, 21 September 1993.

Pitch Measurements: 110yd × 71yd.

President: J. Jennison. *Chairman:* R. Bradley.
Vice-Chairman: J. Hicks. *Directors:* K. Roe, S. Wright, K. Cooke. *Chief Executive:* J. Lonsdale.
Hon. Consultant Surgeon: Mr Brian Smith.
Hon. Club Doctor: Chris Batty.
Company Secretary: J. Hicks.

Manager: Alan Buckley.

Physio: Keith Oakes.

Commercial Manager: K. France.

Secretary: F. J. Martin.

Stadium Manager: Nigel Dennis.

Colours: Red and white striped shirts, red shorts and stockings.

Change Colours: Gold and black.

Year Formed: 1884.

Turned Professional: 1892.

Ltd Co.: 1895.

Club Nickname: 'The Red Imps'.

Previous Grounds: 1883, John O'Gaunt's; 1894, Sincil Bank.

First Football League Game: 3 September 1892, Division 2, v Sheffield U (a) L 2–4 – W. Gresham; Coulton, Neill; Shaw, Mettam, Moore; Smallman, Irving (1), Cameron (1), Kelly, J. Gresham.

Record League Victory: 11–1 v Crewe Alex, Division 3 (N), 29 September 1951 – Jones; Green (1p); Varney; Wright, Emery, Grummett (1); Troops (1), Garvey, Graver (6), Whittle (1), Johnson (1).

HONOURS

Football League: Division 2 best season: 5th, 1901–02; Promotion from Division 3, 1997–98; Division 3 (N) – Champions 1931–32, 1947–48, 1951–52; Runners-up 1927–28, 1930–31, 1936–37; Division 4 – Champions 1975–76; Runners-up 1980–81.

FA Cup: best season: 1st rd of Second Series (5th rd equivalent), 1887, 2nd rd (5th rd equivalent), 1890, 1902.

Football League Cup: best season: 4th rd, 1968.

GM Vauxhall Conference: Champions 1987–88.

IT'S A FACT !

Andy Lincoln scored twice on his Football League debut for Lincoln City on 31 August 1931, one of only two first team games he played for the club that season. Yet he had turned out for the club in their Midland League days, ten years earlier.

Record Cup Victory: 8–1 v Bromley, FA Cup 2nd rd, 10 December 1938 – McPhail; Hartshorne, Corbett; Bean, Leach, Whyte (1); Hancock, Wilson (1), Ponting (3), Deacon (1), Clare (2).

Record Defeat: 3–11 v Manchester C, Division 2, 23 March 1895.

Most League Points (2 for a win): 74, Division 4, 1975–76.

Most League Points (3 for a win): 77, Division 3, 1981–82.

Most League Goals: 121, Division 3 (N), 1951–52.

Highest League Scorer in Season: Allan Hall, 42, Division 3 (N), 1931–32.

Most League Goals in Total Aggregate: Andy Graver, 144, 1950–55 and 1958–61.

Most League Goals in One Match: 6, Frank Keetley v Halifax T, Division 3N, 16 January 1932; 6, Andy Graver v Crewe Alex, Division 3N, 29 September 1951.

Most Capped Player: David Pugh, 3 (7), Wales; George Moulson, 3, Republic of Ireland.

Most League Appearances: Tony Emery, 402, 1946–59.

Youngest League Player: Shane Nicholson, 16 years 172 days v Burnley, 22 November 1986.

Record Transfer Fee Received: £500,000 from Port Vale for Gareth Ainsworth, September 1997.

Record Transfer Fee Paid: £75,000 to Carlisle U for Dean Walling, September 1997; £75,000 to Bury for Tony Battersby, August 1998.

Football League Record: 1892 Founder member of Division 2. Remained in Division 2 until 1920 when they failed re-election but also missed seasons 1908–09 and 1911–12 when not re-elected. 1921–32 Division 3 (N); 1932–34 Division 2; 1934–48 Division 3 (N); 1948–49 Division 2; 1949–52 Division 3 (N); 1952–61 Division 2; 1961–62 Division 3; 1962–76 Division 4; 1976–79 Division 3; 1979–81 Division 4; 1981–86 Division 3; 1986–87 Division 4; 1987–88 GM Vauxhall Conference; 1988–92 Division 4; 1992–98 Division 3; 1998–99 Division 2; 1999– Division 3.

MANAGERS

David Calderhead 1900–07
John Henry Strawson 1907–14
(had been Secretary)
George Fraser 1919–21
David Calderhead Jnr. 1921–24
Horace Henshall 1924–27
Harry Parkes 1927–36
Joe McClelland 1936–46
Bill Anderson 1946–65
(General Manager to 1966)
Roy Chapman 1965–66
Ron Gray 1966–70
Bert Loxley 1970–71
David Herd 1971–72
Graham Taylor 1972–77
George Kerr 1977–78
Willie Bell 1977–78
Colin Murphy 1978–85
John Pickering 1985
George Kerr 1985–87
Peter Daniel 1987
Colin Murphy 1987–90
Allan Clarke 1990
Steve Thompson 1990–93
Keith Alexander 1993–94
Sam Ellis 1994–95
Steve Wicks *(Head Coach)* 1995
John Beck 1995–98
Shane Westley 1998
John Reames 1998–99
Phil Stant 2000–2001
Alan Buckley February 2001–

LATEST SEQUENCES

Longest Sequence of League Wins: 10, 1.9.30 – 18.10.30.
Longest Sequence of League Defeats: 12, 21.9.1896 – 9.1.1897.
Longest Sequence of League Draws: 5, 21.2.81 – 7.3.81.
Longest Sequence of Unbeaten League Matches: 18, 11.3.80 – 13.9.80.
Longest Sequence Without a League Win: 19, 22.8.78 – 23.12.78.

TEN YEAR LEAGUE RECORD

		P	W	D	L	F	A	Pts	Pos
1990-91	Div 4	46	14	17	15	50	61	59	14
1991-92	Div 4	42	17	11	14	50	44	62	10
1992-93	Div 3	42	18	9	15	57	53	63	8
1993-94	Div 3	42	12	11	19	52	63	47	18
1994-95	Div 3	42	15	11	16	54	55	56	12
1995-96	Div 3	46	13	14	19	57	73	53	18
1996-97	Div 3	46	18	12	16	70	69	66	9
1997-98	Div 3	46	20	15	11	60	51	72	3
1998-99	Div 2	46	13	7	26	42	74	46	23
1999-2000	Div 3	46	15	14	17	67	69	59	15

DID YOU KNOW ?

In May 1960, Lincoln City undertook a five day tour of the Republic of Ireland, beating Limerick 4-1, Shelbourne 3-1 and Waterford 7-6. The latter game saw centre-forward Andy Graver taking over in goal from the injured Bill Heath.

LINCOLN CITY 2000–01 LEAGUE RECORD

Match No.	Date	Venue	Opponents	Result	H/T Score	Lg. Pos.	Goalscorers	Atten- dance
1	Aug 12	H	Hartlepool U	L	0-2	0-1	—	3588
2	19	A	Halifax T	D	1-1	0-0	21	Holmes [90]	2113
3	26	H	Brighton & HA	W	2-0	2-0	13	Holmes [34], Cameron [38]	3024
4	28	A	Hull C	D	1-1	1-1	13	Holmes [45]	5780
5	Sept 2	H	Southend U	W	3-0	0-0	8	Smith [64], Gordon [67], Holmes (pen) [90]	2691
6	9	A	Torquay U	D	1-1	1-0	8	Smith [35]	2131
7	12	A	Macclesfield T	L	0-2	0-1	—		1349
8	16	H	Blackpool	D	1-1	1-0	12	Gordon [32]	2753
9	23	A	Leyton Orient	L	0-1	0-0	15		3889
10	30	H	Mansfield T	L	0-2	0-0	18		3494
11	Oct 14	H	Kidderminster H	D	3-3	1-0	18	Gordon 2 [26, 65], Brown [70]	2922
12	17	H	York C	W	2-1	1-1	—	Brown [2], Gordon [87]	2051
13	21	A	Shrewsbury T	L	2-3	0-3	20	Thorpe [51], Holmes (pen) [79]	2476
14	24	H	Cheltenham T	W	1-0	0-0	—	Thorpe [66]	2194
15	28	A	Barnet	L	3-4	3-1	18	Peacock 2 [6, 24], Gordon [26]	1642
16	Nov 4	H	Chesterfield	D	1-1	0-0	18	Holmes (pen) [56]	4805
17	22	H	Cardiff C	L	2-3	2-1	—	Gordon 2 [10, 40]	4786
18	25	H	Exeter C	W	3-1	0-0	16	Smith [52], Gain 2 [61, 65]	2304
19	Dec 2	A	Carlisle U	D	1-1	0-1	16	Gordon [72]	2539
20	16	H	Rochdale	D	1-1	1-0	16	Dudgeon [17]	2320
21	23	A	Darlington	L	0-3	0-2	17		3364
22	26	H	Scunthorpe U	D	1-1	1-1	19	Smith [6]	5487
23	Jan 13	H	Hull C	W	2-0	1-0	16	Battersby [2], Barnett J [61]	4600
24	16	A	Plymouth Arg	L	0-1	0-0	—		4139
25	27	A	Darlington	D	2-2	0-1	18	Holmes (pen) [56], Battersby [58]	2873
26	Feb 3	A	Southend U	L	0-1	0-1	18		3889
27	10	H	Torquay U	L	1-2	1-1	19	Thorpe [35]	2392
28	17	A	Blackpool	L	0-2	0-1	20		4596
29	20	H	Macclesfield T	L	1-2	0-1	—	Thorpe [66]	1853
30	24	H	Leyton Orient	L	2-3	0-2	23	Holmes [63], Peacock [90]	3027
31	Mar 3	A	Mansfield T	W	3-2	1-0	22	Holmes [42], Smith [54], Thorpe [60]	3201
32	6	A	Kidderminster H	W	3-1	2-0	—	Smith [22], Gain [40], Dudgeon [77]	2471
33	10	H	Cardiff C	W	2-0	0-0	18	Smith [72], Battersby [79]	4451
34	17	A	York C	D	0-0	0-0	19		3506
35	23	H	Shrewsbury T	D	2-2	0-2	—	Battersby 2 [52, 57]	2828
36	27	A	Hartlepool U	L	0-1	0-0	—		3584
37	Apr 3	A	Scunthorpe U	L	1-2	1-0	—	Holmes (pen) [21]	4299
38	10	A	Brighton & HA	L	0-2	0-1	—		6716
39	14	A	Cheltenham T	L	1-2	1-2	23	Cameron [3]	4012
40	16	H	Barnet	W	2-1	2-0	21	Gain [28], Battersby [30]	3391
41	21	A	Chesterfield	W	2-1	1-1	20	Gain [45], Walker [71]	4856
42	23	A	Rochdale	L	1-3	0-1	—	Thorpe [55]	2592
43	28	H	Plymouth Arg	W	2-1	1-1	20	Thorpe [24], Dudgeon [84]	4277
44	30	H	Halifax T	D	1-1	1-0	—	Sedgemore [9]	3701
45	May 2	H	Carlisle U	D	1-1	1-0	—	Holmes [13]	4245
46	5	A	Exeter C	D	0-0	0-0	18		4949

Final League Position: 18

GOALSCORERS

League (58): Holmes 11 (5 pens), Gordon 9, Smith 7, Thorpe 7, Battersby 6, Gain 5, Dudgeon 3, Peacock 3, Brown 2, Cameron 2, Barnett J 1, Sedgemore 1, Walker 1.
Worthington Cup (2): Smith 1, Stergiopoulos 1.
FA Cup (4): Gain 1, Gordon 1, Peacock 1, own goal 1.

Marriott A 30	Smith P 35 + 5	Bimson S 17 + 3	Logan R 4 + 1	Holmes S 37 + 1	Brown G 20	Walker J 44 + 1	Miller P 10 + 9	Gordon G 18	Cameron D 10 + 6	Finnigan J 40	Gain P 19 + 5	Battersby T 24 + 11	Stergiopoulos M 2 + 5	Mayo P 26 + 1	Barnett J 27 + 6	Peacock R 22 + 12	Lewis G — + 2	Schofield J 13 + 6	Dudfield L 2 + 1	Eustace S — + 1	Black K 5	Thorpe L 29 + 2	Dudgeon J 20 + 2	Ghent M — + 1	Day C 14	Camm M 3	Carr D 3	Garratt M 2	Perkins C 11 + 1	Grant G 3	Welsh S 10 + 1	Sedgemore B 3 + 7	Henry A 1	Bullock T 2	Match No.
1	2	3	4	5	6	7[1]	8	9	10[2]	11	12	13																							1
1	2	3	4	5	6	7	8	9	10[1]	11				12																					2
1	2		4	5	6	7	8	9	10	11				3																					3
1	2		4[3]	5	6	7	8[1]	9	10[2]	11	12	13		3	14																				4
1	2			5	6	7[1]		9[3]	10[2]	11	12	13	8	3	14																				5
1	2[1]			5	6	7	8[2]		10[3]	11	9	13		3	4	12	14																		6
1	2			5	6	7		9	12	11	10	8[1]		3	4[2]	13																			7
1	2			5	6	7		9		11	10[1]			3	4						8	12													8
1	2	3		5	6[2]	7		9				13		4	10[2]	12					8	11[1]	14												9
1	2		12	5	6	7	8	9	13	11				3	4[1]						10[2]														10
1	2			5	6	7	8	9		4	12			3								10	11[1]												11
1	2			5	6	7[1]	8	9		4[2]			14	3	10	13						11[3]	12												12
1	2[3]			5	6	7	8[1]	9		4				3	14	10		13				11[2]	12												13
1				5	6	7		9		4	12			3	2	8		13				11[2]	10[1]												14
1				5	6	7		9		4	12			3	2	8		11[1]				10													15
1	2			5[2]	6	7		9		4	12			3	13	8		14				11[3]	10[1]												16
1	2				6	7		9	12	11	10[1]			3	4	13		8[3]			5														17
1	2	12			6	7[3]		9			4[2]	11		3	14	8		13				10[1]	5												18
1[6]	2			5[2]	6	7	12	9		11				3		13		8[1]				10	4	15											19
					6	7		9						3	4	8		11				10	5		1	2									20
	2					7			12	11	9[2]			3	4	13		8				10[1]	5		1	6									21
	2					7		9		11				3	4	8						10[1]	5		1	6									22
	2				6[2]	7		9[1]	12	11				3	4	13		8				10			1		5								23
	2			5	6	7		9						3	4	8						10			1			11[1]	12						24
	2			5		7		9		11[1]					4	8	12					10			1				6	3					25
	12			13		7	8	9	4			14		3	2[2]			10[2]				9	5		1				6	11[1]					26
					6	7	8	9	12	13					2	11[1]		4[2]				10	5		1				3						27
	2			5		7				11	12			3	4[2]	13		8[2]				10			1				3	9[1]	6	14			28
	2			4		7				11	12					8						10	5		1				3	9[1]	6				29
		3			6	7[3]		9[2]		11	12	13			14							10	5		1				2			8	4[1]		30
		3		4	6	7	8	9		11[1]												10	5		1				2		12				31
		3		4		7	8	9		11												10	5		1				2		6				32
		3		4		7	8	9		11												10	5		1				2		6				33
1		3		5		7[2]	8	9[1]		11	12				4	13						10							2		6				34
1		3		5		7	8	9		11					4							10							2		6				35
	2	3		5		7	8[2]	9[1]	10	11	12	13			4										1						6[3]	14			36
1	2[1]	3			6	7	8	9	10[2]	11[3]	12	13			4								5									14			37
1	2	3		5	6	7	8	9	10	11[1]					4	12															6				38
		3		5		7[2]	8		10[1]	11	12	13			4										1				2		6[3]	14			39
1	12	3		4	6	7[2]		9		11		13			2	8[1]						10	5												40
1	12			4	6	7		9	13	11[1]				3	2	8						10[2]	5												41
1	2[1]	12			6	7[3]		9	13	11				3[2]	4	8						10	5									14			42
1	12	3		4	6	7[1]		9	13	11	14				2	8[2]						10[3]	5												43
1	12	3		4	6	7[2]		9	13	11					2	8[1]						10	5												44
1		3		4	6	7		9	12	11[1]					2	8[2]						10	5[3]									14	13		45
1	12			5	6	7		9	13	11[2]	4			3[1]	14	8						10							2[3]		6				46

Worthington Cup
First Round   Sheffield U   (a)   1-6
                                    (h)   1-0

FA Cup
First Round   Bracknell T   (h)   4-0
Second Round   Dagenham & R   (h)   0-1

LIVERPOOL

FA Premiership

FOUNDATION

But for a dispute between Everton FC and their landlord at Anfield in 1892, there may never have been a Liverpool club. This dispute persuaded the majority of Evertonians to quit Anfield for Goodison Park, leaving the landlord, Mr. John Houlding, to form a new club. He originally tried to retain the name 'Everton' but when this failed, he founded Liverpool Association FC on 15 March 1892.

Anfield Road, Liverpool L4 0TH.
Telephone: (0151) 263 2361. *Fax:* (0151) 260 8813.
Website: www.liverpoolfc.tv *ClubCall:* 09068 121 184.
Ticket and Match Information: (0151) 260 9999
(24-hour service) or (0151) 260 8680 (office hours).
Credit Card Bookings: (0151) 263 5727.
International Supporters Club: (0151) 261 1444.
Museum and Stadium Tours: (0151) 260 6677.
LFC Direct Mail Order: (0990) 532 532.

Ground Capacity: 45,362.

Record Attendance: 61,905 v Wolverhampton W, FA Cup 4th rd, 2 February 1952.

Record Receipts: £604,048 v Celtic, UEFA Cup, 30 September 1997.

Pitch Measurements: 111yd × 74yd.

Chairman: D. R. Moores.

Chief Executive: Rick Parry BSC, FCA.

Director of Finance: Les Wheatley.

Directors: N. White FSCA, T. D. Smith, J. Burns, K. E. B. Clayton FCA.

Vice-Presidents: H. E. Roberts, J. T. Cross, T. W. Saunders, P. B. Robinson.

Manager: Gerard Houllier.

Assistant Manager: Phil Thompson.

Physio: Dave Galley.

Secretary: Bryce Morrison.

Press Officer: Ian Cotton.

Stadium Manager: Ged Poynton.

Academy Director: Steve Heighway.

Colours: All red.

Change Colours: White shirts with navy blue panels and gold tipping, navy blue woven shorts, white stockings.

Year Formed: 1892. *Turned Professional:* 1892.
Ltd Co.: 1892.

HONOURS

Football League: Division 1 – Champions 1900–01, 1905–06, 1921–22, 1922–23, 1946–47, 1963–64, 1965–66, 1972–73, 1975–76, 1976–77, 1978–79, 1979–80, 1981–82, 1982–83, 1983–84, 1985–86, 1987–88, 1989–90 (Liverpool have a record number of 18 League Championship wins); Runners-up 1898–99, 1909–10, 1968–69, 1973–74, 1974–75, 1977–78, 1984–85, 1986–87, 1988–89, 1990–91; Division 2 – Champions 1893–94, 1895–96, 1904–05, 1961–62.
FA Cup: Winners 1965, 1974, 1986, 1989, 1992, 2001; Runners-up 1914, 1950, 1971, 1977, 1988, 1996;
Football League Cup: Winners 1981, 1982, 1983, 1984, 1995, 2001; Runners-up 1978, 1987.
League Super Cup: Winners 1986.
European Competitions: *European Cup:* 1964–65, 1966–67, 1973–74, 1976–77 (winners), 1977–78 (winners), 1978–79, 1979–80, 1980–81 (winners), 1981–82, 1982–83, 1983–84 (winners), 1984–85 (runners-up). *European Cup-Winners' Cup:* 1965–66 (runners-up), 1971–72, 1974–75, 1992–93, 1996–97 (s-f.). *European Fairs Cup:* 1967–68, 1968–69, 1969–70, 1970–71. *UEFA Cup:* 1972–73 (winners), 1975–76 (winners), 1991–92, 1995–96, 1997–98, 1998–99, 2000–01 (winners). *Super Cup:* 1977 (winners), 1978, 1984.
World Club Championship: 1981 (runners-up), 1984 (runners-up).

IT'S A FACT !

In 2000–01 Liverpool achieved a unique Cup treble: UEFA Cup, FA Cup and League Cup. They played 63 first class matches scoring 127 goals. In 1983–84 they had won the European Cup, First Division and League Cup, scoring 118 goals in 67 games.

Club Nickname: 'Reds' or 'Pool'.

First Football League Game: 2 September 1893, Division 2, v Middlesbrough Ironopolis (a) W 2–0 – McOwen; Hannah, McLean; Henderson, McQue (1), McBride; Gordon, McVean (1), M. McQueen, Stott, H. McQueen.

Record League Victory: 10–1 v Rotherham T, Division 2, 18 February 1896 – Storer; Goldie, Wilkie; McCartney, McQue, Holmes; McVean (3), Ross (2), Allan (4), Becton (1), Bradshaw.

Record Cup Victory: 11–0 v Stromsgodset Drammen, ECWC 1st rd 1st leg, 17 September 1974 – Clemence; Smith (1), Lindsay (1p), Thompson (2), Cormack (1), Hughes (1), Boersma (2), Hall, Heighway (1), Kennedy (1), Callaghan (1).

Record Defeat: 1–9 v Birmingham C, Division 2, 11 December 1954.

Most League Points (2 for a win): 68, Division 1, 1978–79.

Most League Points (3 for a win): 90, Division 1, 1987–88.

Most League Goals: 106, Division 2, 1895–96.

MANAGERS
W. E. Barclay 1892–96
Tom Watson 1896–1915
David Ashworth 1920–23
Matt McQueen 1923–28
George Patterson 1928–36
(continued as Secretary)
George Kay 1936–51
Don Welsh 1951–56
Phil Taylor 1956–59
Bill Shankly 1959–74
Bob Paisley 1974–83
Joe Fagan 1983–85
Kenny Dalglish 1985–91
Graeme Souness 1991–94
Roy Evans January 1994–98
(then Joint Manager)
Gerard Houllier July 1998–

Highest League Scorer in Season: Roger Hunt, 41, Division 2, 1961–62.

Most League Goals in Total Aggregate: Roger Hunt, 245, 1959–69.

Most League Goals in One Match: 5, Andy McGuigan v Stoke C, Division 1, 4 January 1902; 5, John Evans v Bristol R, Division 2, 15 September 1954; 5, Ian Rush v Luton T, Division 1, 29 October 1983.

Most Capped Player: Ian Rush, 67 (73), Wales.

Most League Appearances: Ian Callaghan, 640, 1960–78.

Youngest League Player: Max Thompson, 17 years 128 days v Tottenham H, 8 May 1974.

Record Transfer Fee Received: £7,000,000 from Aston Villa for Stan Collymore, May 1997.

Record Transfer Fee Paid: £11,000,000 to Leicester C for Emile Heskey, March 2000.

Football League Record: 1893 Elected to Division 2; 1894–95 Division 1; 1895–96 Division 2; 1896–1904 Division 1; 1904–05 Division 2; 1905–54 Division 1; 1954–62 Division 2; 1962–92 Division 1; 1992– FA Premier League.

LATEST SEQUENCES

Longest Sequence of League Wins: 12, 21.4.90 – 6.10.90.

Longest Sequence of League Defeats: 9, 29.4.1899 – 14.10.1899.

Longest Sequence of League Draws: 6, 19.2.75 – 19.3.75.

Longest Sequence of Unbeaten League Matches: 31, 4.5.87 – 16.3.88.

Longest Sequence Without a League Win: 14, 12.12.53 – 20.3.54.

TEN YEAR LEAGUE RECORD

		P	W	D	L	F	A	Pts	Pos
1990-91	Div 1	38	23	7	8	77	40	76	2
1991-92	Div 1	42	16	16	10	47	40	64	6
1992-93	PR Lge	42	16	11	15	62	55	59	6
1993-94	PR Lge	42	17	9	16	59	55	60	8
1994-95	PR Lge	42	21	11	10	65	37	74	4
1995-96	PR Lge	38	20	11	7	70	34	71	3
1996-97	PR Lge	38	19	11	8	62	37	68	4
1997-98	PR Lge	38	18	11	9	68	42	65	3
1998-99	PR Lge	38	15	9	14	68	49	54	7
1999-2000	PR Lge	38	19	10	9	51	30	67	4

DID YOU KNOW ?

On 31 March 2001, Liverpool beat Manchester United 2–0 to complete their first home and away double against the Old Trafford club for 22 years. In 1978–79 Liverpool had won 2–0 at home and 3–0 away.

LIVERPOOL 2000–01 LEAGUE RECORD

Match No.	Date	Venue	Opponents	Result	H/T Score	Lg. Pos.	Goalscorers	Attendance
1	Aug 19	H	Bradford C	W 1-0	0-0	—	Heskey [67]	44,183
2	21	A	Arsenal	L 0-2	0-1	—		38,014
3	26	A	Southampton	D 3-3	1-0	12	Owen 2 [24, 64], Hyypia [55]	15,202
4	Sept 6	H	Aston Villa	W 3-1	3-0	—	Owen 3 [5, 14, 33]	43,360
5	9	H	Manchester C	W 3-2	1-0	4	Owen [11], Hamann 2 [56, 82]	44,692
6	17	A	West Ham U	D 1-1	1-0	4	Gerrard [12]	25,998
7	23	H	Sunderland	D 1-1	1-1	4	Owen [34]	44,713
8	Oct 1	A	Chelsea	L 0-3	0-2	7		34,966
9	15	A	Derby Co	W 4-0	1-0	4	Heskey 3 [17, 54, 67], Berger [80]	30,532
10	21	H	Leicester C	W 1-0	0-0	3	Heskey [69]	44,395
11	29	H	Everton	W 3-1	1-1	3	Barmby [12], Heskey [56], Berger (pen) [78]	44,718
12	Nov 4	A	Leeds U	L 3-4	2-1	4	Hyypia [2], Ziege [18], Smicer [61]	40,055
13	12	H	Coventry C	W 4-1	1-0	3	McAllister [13], Gerrard [51], Heskey 2 [82, 87]	43,701
14	19	A	Tottenham H	L 1-2	1-2	4	Fowler [18]	36,051
15	26	H	Newcastle U	L 1-2	0-1	5	Heskey [78]	51,949
16	Dec 2	H	Charlton Ath	W 3-0	1-0	4	Fish (og) [5], Heskey [78], Babbel [90]	43,515
17	10	H	Ipswich T	L 0-1	0-1	6		43,509
18	17	A	Manchester U	W 1-0	1-0	5	Murphy [43]	67,533
19	23	H	Arsenal	W 4-0	1-0	4	Gerrard [11], Owen [62], Barmby [71], Fowler [90]	44,144
20	26	A	Middlesbrough	L 0-1	0-1	6		34,696
21	Jan 1	H	Southampton	W 2-1	1-1	5	Gerrard [12], Babbel [86]	38,474
22	13	A	Aston Villa	W 3-0	2-0	5	Murphy 2 [24, 53], Gerrard [32]	41,366
23	20	A	Middlesbrough	D 0-0	0-0	4		43,042
24	31	A	Manchester C	D 1-1	1-0	—	Heskey [43]	34,629
25	Feb 3	H	West Ham U	W 3-0	2-0	3	Smicer [20], Fowler 2 [45, 57]	44,045
26	10	A	Sunderland	D 1-1	0-0	3	Litmanen (pen) [79]	46,231
27	Mar 3	A	Leicester C	L 0-2	0-0	4		21,924
28	18	H	Derby Co	D 1-1	0-1	6	Owen [52]	43,362
29	31	H	Manchester U	W 2-0	2-0	4	Gerrard [16], Fowler [41]	44,806
30	Apr 10	H	Ipswich T	D 1-1	0-0	—	Heskey [46]	23,500
31	13	A	Leeds U	L 1-2	0-2	4	Gerrard [55]	44,116
32	16	A	Everton	W 3-2	1-1	5	Heskey [5], Babbel [75], McAllister [90]	40,260
33	22	H	Tottenham H	W 3-1	1-1	5	Heskey [7], McAllister (pen) [73], Fowler [88]	43,547
34	28	A	Coventry C	W 2-0	0-0	5	Hyypia [83], McAllister [86]	23,063
35	May 1	A	Bradford C	W 2-0	0-0	—	Owen [47], McAllister [67]	22,057
36	5	H	Newcastle U	W 3-0	1-0	3	Owen 3 [25, 72, 81]	44,363
37	8	H	Chelsea	D 2-2	1-1	—	Owen 2 [8, 60]	43,588
38	19	A	Charlton Ath	W 4-0	0-0	3	Fowler 2 [55, 71], Murphy [61], Owen [80]	20,043

Final League Position: 3

GOALSCORERS

League (71): Owen 16, Heskey 14, Fowler 8, Gerrard 7, McAllister 5 (1 pen), Murphy 4, Babbel 3, Hyypia 3, Barmby 2, Berger 2 (1 pen), Hamann 2, Smicer 2, Litmanen 1 (pen), Ziege 1, own goal 1.
Worthington Cup (20): Fowler 6 (1 pen), Murphy 4, Smicer 4, Babbel 1, Barmby 1, Biscan 1, Hyypia 1, Owen 1, Ziege 1.
FA Cup (17): Heskey 5, Owen 3, Fowler 2 (1 pen), Babbel 1, Barmby 1, Gerrard 1, Hamann 1, Litmanen 1 (pen), Murphy 1, Smicer 1 (pen).

Westerveld S 38	Babbel M 38	Traore D 8	Hamann D 26 + 4	Henchoz S 32	Hyypia S 35	Gerrard S 29 + 4	Smicer V 16 + 11	Heskey E 33 + 3	Owen M 20 + 8	Barmby N 21 + 5	McAllister G 21 + 9	Berger P 11 + 3	Carragher J 30 + 4	Meijer E — + 3	Murphy D 13 + 14	Staunton S — + 1	Song R 3	Ziege C 11 + 5	Diomede B 1 + 1	Fowler R 15 + 12	Heggem V 1 + 2	Biscan I 8 + 5	Litmanen J 4 + 1	Wright S — + 2	Vignal G 4 + 2	Match No.
1	2	3	4	5	6	7¹	8	9²	10³	11	12	13	14													1
1	2	3	4	5	6		8¹	9³	12	7²	10		11	14	13											2
1	2	3	4	5	6	7	8¹		9	10²		11		12	13											3
1	2	3	4	5	6	7	8¹	9²	10	12		11	13													4
1	6	3	4	5			7²		9	10¹	8		11	12				2	13							5
1	6	3	4	5			7²		9		8		11		10¹		2	12			13					6
1	6		4¹	5			12		9²	10	8		11		13		2	3	7³	14						7
1	2		4	5	6	7			9	10	8¹		11²					3		12	13					8
1	4			6		12	9	10²	7¹	8	11	5		14				3		13	2³					9
1	5		4		6	2		9		7	10	11		12				3		8¹						10
1	5		4		6	2²	12	9		7	10	11	13					3		8¹						11
1	5		4		6	12	8	9		13	10¹	11²	2		7³			3		14						12
1	4	3		5	6	2¹	8³	9	10²	7	11		12	13				14								13
1	2	3¹	4	5	6	12	8²		10	13	11		14		7³					9						14
1	2		4	5	6	7²	12	11		10	13		3		8¹					9						15
1	4	12		5	6	7	13	11		8	10¹		2	14				3³		9²						16
1	2			5	6		12	13	10²	8¹	11		4	7				3³		9		14				17
1	4			5	6	7	12	9	10¹	8	13		2	11²							3					18
1	4			5	6	7²	12	9	10³	8	13		2	11¹						14	3					19
1	2³			5	6	7	8	9	10²	11	12		3	14						13	4¹					20
1	2			5	6	4	8¹	9³	12	7³	11		3	13						10	14					21
1	2		4	5	6	7¹	8	9³	13		12		3	11							14	10³				22
1	2		4	5	6	7	8	9³	12	11²			3	14						13		10³				23
1	2		4	5	6	3	8	9			10²							11³	14	12	13	7¹				24
1	2³		4	5	6	7	8	9	12²									13		10	11¹		14	3		25
1	2		4	5	6	7¹		9²	12		10									8	11³	13	14	3		26
1	2	12	5²	6	7			9	13	8⁴	4¹		3	14				11		10						27
1	2		4	5	6	12	13	9	10		7³		3							14	11¹	8²				28
1	2		4	5	6	7¹		9	12	14	13	11³	3		8					10²						29
1	5	12		6	7		9			13	10	2	8					11¹			4²			3		30
1	2		4²	5	6	7	12	13	10		14	11¹	3		8³					9						31
1	2		4	5	6		8	9			11		3							10¹	7			12		32
1	2	12	5	6	7	4¹	9²	10		8	11	3³								13				14		33
1	2		4	5	6		9³	12		8	11²	3		7				13		10¹	14					34
1	2		4	5	6	7	12	9	10		11²	13	3		8¹					14						35
1	2		4	5	6	7²	8¹	9³	10		11	12	3	13						14						36
1	2	4²	5	6	7	12	9³	10		8	11¹	3	13							14						37
1	5			6	7		12	10	4²	8	11¹	3	13							9				2		38

Worthington Cup

Third Round	Chelsea	(h)	2-1
Fourth Round	Stoke C	(a)	8-0
Fifth Round	Fulham	(h)	3-0
Semi-Final	Crystal Palace	(a)	1-2
		(h)	5-0
Final	Birmingham C		1-1
(at Millennium Stadium)			

FA Cup

Third Round	Rotherham U	(h)	3-0
Fourth Round	Leeds U	(a)	2-0
Fifth Round	Manchester C	(h)	4-2
Sixth Round	Tranmere R	(a)	4-2
Semi-Final	Wycombe W		2-1
(at Villa Park)			
Final	Arsenal		2-1
(at Millennium Stadium)			

LUTON TOWN

Division 3

FOUNDATION

Formed by an amalgamation of two leading local clubs, Wanderers and Excelsior a works team, at a meeting in Luton Town Hall in April 1885. The Wanderers had three months earlier changed their name to Luton Town Wanderers and did not take too kindly to the formation of another Town club but were talked around at this meeting. Wanderers had already appeared in the FA Cup and the new club entered in its inaugural season.

Kenilworth Road Stadium, 1 Maple Rd, Luton, Beds LU4 8AW.

Telephone: (01582) 411 622. *Ticket Office:* (01582) 416 976. *Credit Hotline:* (01582) 307 48 (24 hrs). *ClubCall:* 09068 121 123.

Ground Capacity: 9975.

Record Attendance: 30,069 v Blackpool, FA Cup 6th rd replay, 4 March 1959.

Record Receipts: £115,541.20 v West Ham U, FA Cup 6th rd, 23 March 1994.

Pitch Measurements: 110yd × 72yd.

Chairman: M. Watson-Challis.

Directors: E. Hood, J. Mitchell, C. Bassett, R. Stringer, Y. Fletcher, R. H. E. Kelly.

Manager: Joe Kinnear

Coach: Mick Harford. *Physio:* Bruce Sewell.

Secretary: Cherry Newbery.

Sales and Marketing Manager: John Bailey Jnr.

Safety Officer: Geoff Lovell.

Colours: White shirts with orange and black trim, black shorts with orange and white trim, black stockings with two white hoops.

Change Colours: Orange shirts with white and royal trim, royal shorts with orange and white trim, royal stockings with two white hoops.

Year Formed: 1885.

Turned Professional: 1890.

Ltd Co.: 1897.

Club Nickname: 'The Hatters'.

Previous Grounds: 1885, Excelsior, Dallow Lane; 1897, Dunstable Road; 1905, Kenilworth Road.

First Football League Game: 4 September 1897, Division 2, v Leicester Fosse (a) D 1–1 – Williams; McCartney, McEwen; Davies, Stewart, Docherty; Gallacher, Coupar, Birch, McInnes, Ekins (1).

HONOURS

Football League: Division 1 best season: 7th, 1986–87; Division 2 – Champions 1981–82; Runners-up 1954–55, 1973–74; Division 3 – Runners-up 1969–70; Division 4 – Champions 1967–68; Division 3 (S) – Champions 1936–37; Runners-up 1935–36.

FA Cup: Runners-up 1959.

Football League Cup: Winners 1988; Runners-up 1989.

Simod Cup: Runners-up 1988.

IT'S A FACT !

Luton Town of 12 goals fame against Bristol Rovers, had been involved with an earlier match of such a figure. On 2 September 1933 they had defeated Torquay United 10-2.

Record League Victory: 12–0 v Bristol R, Division 3 (S), 13 April 1936 – Dolman; Mackey, Smith; Finlayson, Nelson, Godfrey; Rich, Martin (1), Payne (10), Roberts (1), Stephenson.

Record Cup Victory: 9–0 v Clapton, FA Cup 1st rd (replay after abandoned game), 30 November 1927 – Abbott; Kingham, Graham; Black, Rennie, Fraser; Pointon, Yardley (4), Reid (2), Woods (1), Dennis (2).

Record Defeat: 0–9 v Small Heath, Division 2, 12 November 1898.

Most League Points (2 for a win): 66, Division 4, 1967–68.

Most League Points (3 for a win): 88, Division 2, 1981–82.

Most League Goals: 103, Division 3 (S), 1936–37.

Highest League Scorer in Season: Joe Payne, 55, Division 3 (S), 1936–37.

Most League Goals in Total Aggregate: Gordon Turner, 243, 1949–64.

Most League Goals in One Match: 10, Joe Payne v Bristol R, Division 3S, 13 April 1936.

Most Capped Player: Mal Donaghy, 58 (91), Northern Ireland.

Most League Appearances: Bob Morton, 494, 1948–64.

Youngest League Player: Mike O'Hara, 16 years 32 days v Stoke C, 1 October 1960.

Record Transfer Fee Received: £2,500,000 from Arsenal for John Hartson, January 1995.

Record Transfer Fee Paid: £850,000 to Odense for Lars Elstrup, August 1989.

MANAGERS

Charlie Green 1901–28
  (Secretary-Manager)
George Thomson 1925
John McCartney 1927–29
George Kay 1929–31
Harold Wightman 1931–35
Ted Liddell 1936–38
Neil McBain 1938–39
George Martin 1939–47
Dally Duncan 1947–58
Syd Owen 1959–60
Sam Bartram 1960–62
Bill Harvey 1962–64
George Martin 1965–66
Allan Brown 1966–68
Alec Stock 1968–72
Harry Haslam 1972–78
David Pleat 1978–86
John Moore 1986–87
Ray Harford 1987–89
Jim Ryan 1900–91
David Pleat 1991–95
Terry Westley 1995
Lennie Lawrence 1995–2000
Ricky Hill 2000
Lil Fuccillo 2000
Joe Kinnear January 2001–

Football League Record: 1897 Elected to Division 2; 1900 Failed re-election; 1920 Division 3; 1921–37 Division 3 (S); 1937–55 Division 2; 1955–60 Division 1; 1960–63 Division 2; 1963–65 Division 3; 1965–68 Division 4; 1968–70 Division 3; 1970–74 Division 2; 1974–75 Division 1; 1975–82 Division 2; 1982–96 Division 1; 1996–2001 Division 2; 2001– Division 3.

LATEST SEQUENCES

Longest Sequence of League Wins: 9, 22.1.77 – 8.3.77.

Longest Sequence of League Defeats: 8, 11.11.1899 – 6.1.1900.

Longest Sequence of League Draws: 5, 28.8.71 – 18.9.71.

Longest Sequence of Unbeaten League Matches: 19, 8.4.69 – 7.10.69.

Longest Sequence Without a League Win: 16, 9.9.64 – 6.11.64.

TEN YEAR LEAGUE RECORD

		P	W	D	L	F	A	Pts	Pos
1990-91	Div 1	38	10	7	21	42	61	37	18
1991-92	Div 1	42	10	12	20	38	71	42	20
1992-93	Div 1	46	10	21	15	48	62	51	20
1993-94	Div 1	46	14	11	21	56	60	53	20
1994-95	Div 1	46	15	13	18	61	64	58	16
1995-96	Div 1	46	11	12	23	40	64	45	24
1996-97	Div 2	46	21	15	10	71	45	78	3
1997-98	Div 2	46	14	15	17	60	64	57	17
1998-99	Div 2	46	16	10	20	51	60	58	12
1999-2000	Div 2	46	17	10	19	61	65	61	13

DID YOU KNOW ?

An unusual stastistic for Luton Town came in 1921-22 when they conceded only 35 goals in 42 Division Three (South) matches and drew only eight games in finishing fourth.

LUTON TOWN 2000–01 LEAGUE RECORD

Match No.	Date	Venue	Opponents	Result		H/T Score	Lg. Pos.	Goalscorers	Attendance
1	Aug 12	H	Notts Co	L	0-1	0-1	—		7059
2	19	A	Wigan Ath	L	1-2	0-1	23	Watts [53]	6518
3	26	H	Bournemouth	W	1-0	0-0	18	Spring (pen) [75]	5221
4	28	A	Wycombe W	D	1-1	0-1	17	Kandol [81]	6001
5	Sept 2	A	Rotherham U	D	1-1	1-0	17	Fotiadis [6]	4061
6	9	H	Northampton T	L	0-2	0-1	19		6712
7	12	H	Walsall	D	0-0	0-0	—		4362
8	16	A	Swansea C	L	0-4	0-2	20		6011
9	23	H	Swindon T	L	2-3	2-2	21	Stein [13], George [43]	4933
10	30	A	Bristol R	D	3-3	1-2	22	Kandol 2 [45, 72], George [84]	7901
11	Oct 8	H	Millwall	L	0-1	0-0	22		5345
12	13	A	Cambridge U	L	1-2	1-0	—	Stein [13]	6191
13	17	A	Oxford U	D	0-0	0-0	—		4537
14	21	H	Brentford	W	3-1	3-0	23	Douglas 2 [16, 30], Spring (pen) [36]	5382
15	28	H	Wrexham	L	3-4	2-0	23	Stein [39], Watts [44], George [55]	5341
16	Nov 4	A	Bury	D	1-1	0-0	23	Helin [56]	2861
17	11	H	Bristol C	L	0-3	0-0	23		6595
18	25	A	Port Vale	L	0-3	0-1	23		4194
19	Dec 2	A	Stoke C	W	3-1	1-1	23	McLaren [15], Thomson 2 [50, 61]	12,389
20	16	H	Colchester U	L	0-3	0-1	23		4791
21	23	A	Reading	L	1-4	0-2	23	Nogan [69]	10,771
22	26	H	Peterborough U	W	3-2	2-1	23	Spring [5], Holmes [14], Boyce [49]	7374
23	30	A	Wigan Ath	L	0-2	0-1	23		5322
24	Jan 1	A	Bournemouth	L	2-3	2-1	23	Fotiadis [44], Locke [45]	5411
25	12	H	Wycombe W	L	1-2	1-0	—	Locke [20]	4551
26	23	H	Oldham Ath	L	0-2	0-1	—		3011
27	Feb 10	A	Northampton T	W	1-0	1-0	23	Douglas [4]	6633
28	13	A	Notts Co	W	3-1	1-1	—	Boyce [23], George [55], Fotiadis [82]	4333
29	17	H	Swansea C	W	5-3	2-1	22	Mansell 2 [3, 51], Douglas [9], Rowland [70], George [82]	7085
30	20	A	Walsall	L	1-3	0-2	—	Spring [55]	4816
31	24	A	Swindon T	W	3-1	1-1	22	Rowland [42], Boyce [70], Mansell [90]	7160
32	Mar 3	H	Bristol R	D	0-0	0-0	22		7405
33	6	H	Cambridge U	W	1-0	0-0	—	Taylor [86]	6370
34	10	A	Millwall	L	0-1	0-1	22		11,691
35	27	A	Peterborough U	D	1-1	0-0	—	Mansell [79]	5425
36	31	A	Colchester U	L	1-3	0-3	22	Howard (pen) [84]	4271
37	Apr 3	H	Reading	D	1-1	1-1	—	Harper (og) [10]	6132
38	7	A	Stoke C	L	1-2	1-2	22	Mansell [4]	6456
39	10	H	Oxford U	D	1-1	1-0	—	Watts [18]	6010
40	14	H	Oldham Ath	D	0-0	0-0	22		4886
41	16	A	Wrexham	L	1-3	1-1	22	Watts [27]	3339
42	21	H	Bury	L	1-2	1-1	22	George [7]	4902
43	24	A	Rotherham U	L	0-1	0-0	—		4854
44	28	A	Bristol C	L	1-3	0-1	22	George [58]	9161
45	May 3	A	Brentford	D	2-2	1-0	—	Howard [26], McLaren [51]	3287
46	5	H	Port Vale	D	1-1	1-1	22	Howard [15]	5260

Final League Position: 22

GOALSCORERS

League (52): George 7, Mansell 5, Douglas 4, Spring 4 (2 pens), Watts 4, Boyce 3, Fotiadis 3, Howard 3 (1 pen), Kandol 3, Stein 3, Locke 2, McLaren 2, Rowland 2, Thomson 2, Helin 1, Holmes 1, Nogan 1, Taylor 1, own goal 1.
Worthington Cup (3): Kandol 1, Scarlett 1, Stein 1.
FA Cup (7): George 2, Douglas 1, Fotiadis 1, McLaren 1, Mansell 1, Nogan 1.

Ovendale M 26	Boyce E 42	Taylor M 45	Locke A 17 + 8	Watts J 26 + 2	Johnson M 9	George L 37 + 6	McLaren P 35	Stein M 19 + 11	Fotiadis A 12 + 10	Spring M 41	Holmes P 12 + 6	Fraser S 10 + 5	Brennan D 2 + 7	Scarlett A 5 + 4	Kandol T 6 + 7	Abbey N 20	Stirling J 5 + 4	Thomson P 4 + 7	McGowan G 5 + 1	Breitenfelder F 2 + 3	Douglas S 15 + 6	Helin P 23	Karlsen K 4 + 2	Baptiste R — + 3	Nogan L 7	Whitbread A 9	Mansell L 17 + 1	Dryden R 20	Rowland K 12	Howard K 12	Shepherd P 7	Ward S — + 1	Match No
1	2	3	4^1	5^5	6	7	8	9	10	11	12	13																					1
1	2	3	4^5	5	6^1	7	8	9	10		11^2	12	13	14																			2
1	2	3	12	5		7^2	8	9	10	11		4^1	6	13																			3
1	2	3		5		7^1	8	9	10^3	11				4	12	6	13																4
1	2	3	4	5		12	8	9^1	10^3	11	7^2		13	6	14																	5
	2	3		5		7	8	9		11^1	12	6	4^2	10	13	1																6
	2	3	4	5		12	8	9		11	13		6^1	10^2	14	1		7^1															7
1	2	3	4	5		12	8	9^1		11	7					10	6																8
1	2	3	12	5		7		9		11	4	6		10	8^2	13																	9
1	2	3	4	5		7	8	12		11^2	13	6^3		10					9^1	14													10
1	2	3	4	5		7	8	9		11						10			6														11
1	2	3	4	5		7	8	9		11	12		13			10^1			6^2														12
	2	3		5		7		9		11	8	4	12			10^1			6^2	13													13
	2	3	4^3	5		7^1	8	9		11	6		12			1		13		14	10^2												14
	2	3		5	6	7	8^1	9	10^2	11	12					1		13	4														15
	2	3		5		7^1	8	9		11	12					1					10^2	4	6	13									16
	2	3		5		7	8	9^2	12	11		13				1			6		10^1	5	4	13									17
	2	3		5		7	8			12	11		13			1					4^2	10		9^1	6								18
		3	4	5	6	7^2	8			12	11					1		9^1			2	13			10								19
		3	10^1	5	6	7	8			12	11					1					2			9	4								20
	5	3	12			6^2	7^3	8^1		10	11		13			1					2		14	9	4								21
	5	3	8							10	11	7^2	6	13	12	1					2			9^1	4								22
1		3	8	5						12	10	11	7^2	6					13		2			9^1	4								23
1		3	8	5^5						10^1	11	7	6^2		12			14			13	2		9	4								24
1	2^1	3	8			7					11		5	13	12		14	10^1		6^2	9		4										25
1	2						12			13	10^2	11	4^1					14	3		7		6	9^3	5	8							26
1		5	3			7					12	11				4					9^1	2						8	6	10			27
1		5	3			7					13	11			12^2	4					9^1	2						8	6	10			28
1		5	3	12		7					13	11				4					9^2	2						8^1	6	10			29
1		5	3	12		7^2					13	11				4	14				9^2	2						8^1	6	10			30
1		5	3	4^3		7	8	12^2	9^1		11					13					2							14	6	10			31
		5	3	11	4	7	8^2	9^1									1	13			12	2							6	10			32
		5	3		12	7	8	14	13^3	11							1				9^1	2						4	6	10^2			33
		5	3		12	7	8	13	14	11							1				9^3	2						4^2	6	10			34
		5	3			7^1	4	12		11							1				2							8	6	10	9		35
		5	3			7	4			11							1				12	2						8	6	10^1	9		36
		5	3			12	4	9^1		11							1				13	2						8	6	10^1	7		37
		5	3			12	4	9^1		11							1				13	2						8	6	10^2	7		38
		4	3		5	7	8	12		11^2							1	13				2^1						10	6		9		39
1		4	3		5	7	8														9							10	6	11	2		40
1		4	3	12	5	7	8^1														9							10	6	11	2		41
1		4	3		5	7	8			11											12							10^1	6	9	2		42
1		5	3		4	7^1	8	12		11											9								6	10	2		43
1		5	3	12	10	7^2	8	13		11										14	4^1								6	9^3	2		44
1		5	3	12	4	7	8			11																		10^1	6	9	2^9	15	45
1		5	3			7		4	12	11											9^1		13					8	6	10	2^2		46

Worthington Cup

First Round	Peterborough U	(h)	0-0
		(a)	2-2
Second Round	Sunderland	(a)	0-3
		(h)	1-2

FA Cup

First Round	Rushden & D	(h)	1-0
		(a)	0-0
Second Round	Darlington	(h)	2-0
Third Round	QPR	(h)	3-3
		(a)	1-2

MACCLESFIELD TOWN

Division 3

FOUNDATION

From the mid-19th Century until 1874, Macclesfield Town FC played under rugby rules. In 1891 they moved to the Moss Rose and finished champions of the Manchester & District League in 1906 and 1908. By 1911, they had carried off the Cheshire Senior Cup five times. Macclesfield were founder members of the Cheshire County League in 1919.

The Moss Rose Ground, London Road, Macclesfield, Cheshire SK11 7SP.

Telephone: (01625) 264 686. *Fax:* (01625) 264 692.

Website: www.mtfc.co.uk

Email: office@mtfc.co.uk

Commercial Office: (01625) 264 693.

Social Club: (01625) 424 324.

Press Box: (01625) 264 690/1.

ClubCall: 09066 555 835.

Ground Capacity: 6028 (seated 1053, standing 4975).

Record Attendance: 9008 v Winsford U, Cheshire Senior Cup 2nd rd, 4 February 1948.

Pitch Measurements: 100m × 66m.

Chief Executive: Colin Garlick.

Directors: E. Furlong, C. Garlick, M. Rance, J. Turner, A. Cash, M. Lenton, R. Bickerton, R. Higginbotham.

Director of Football: Gil Prescott.

Assistant Manager: Allan Preston.

Reserve Team Manager: John Askey.

Secretary: Colin Garlick.

Administration Manager: Dianne Hehir.

Commercial Manager: Jackie Birks.

Club Doctors: Dr Mike Whiteside, Mike Hughes.

Physio: Ewan Simpson.

Colours: Royal blue shirts, white shorts, blue stockings.

Change Colours: Old gold shirts, navy shorts, navy stockings.

HONOURS

Football League: Division 3 – Runners-up 1997–98.

FA Cup: best season: 3rd rd, 1968, 1988.

Vauxhall Conference: Champions 1994–95, 1996–97.

FA Trophy: Winners 1969–70, 1995–96; Runners-up 1988–89.

Bob Lord Trophy: Winners 1993–94; Runners-up 1995–96, 1996–97.

Vauxhall Conference Championship Shield: Winners 1996, 1997, 1998.

Northern Premier League: Winners 1968–69, 1969–70, 1986–87; Runners-up 1984–85.

Northern Premier League Challenge Cup: Winners 1986–87; Runners-up 1969–70, 1970–71, 1982–83.

Northern Premier League Presidents Cup: Winners 1986–87; Runners-up 1984–85.

Cheshire Senior Cup: Winners 19 times; Runners-up 11.

IT'S A FACT !

On 12 September 1950, Albert Mycock scored the only goal for Macclesfield Town in a 1-0 win over Mossley. Fifty years to the exact day, Macclesfield Town beat Lincoln City 2-0 with a Damian Whitehead brace of goals.

Year formed: 1874.

Club Nickname: 'The Silkmen'.

Previous Ground: 1874, Rostron Field; 1891, Moss Rose.

First Football League Game: 9 August 1997, Division 3, v Torquay U (h) W 2–1 – Price; Tinson, Rose, Payne (Edey), Howarth, Sodje (1), Askey, Wood, Landon (1) (Power), Mason, Sorvel.

Record League Victory: 5–2 v Mansfield T, Division 3, 2 November 1999 – Martin; Ingram, Rioch, Collins, Tinson, Sedgemore (1), Askey (1), Priest (1), Barker (2), Davies (Wood), Durkan.

Record Win: 15–0 v Chester St Marys, Cheshire Senior Cup, 2nd rd, 16 February 1886.

Record Defeat: 1–13 v Tranmere R reserves, 3 May 1929.

Most League Points (3 for a win): 82, Division 3, 1997–98.

Most League Goals: 66, Division 3, 1999–2000.

Highest League Scorer in Season: Richard Barker, 16, Division 3, 1999–2000.

Most League Goals in Total Aggregate: John Askey, 25, 1997–2000.

Most League Appearances: Darren Tinson, 127, 1997–2000.

Youngest League Player: Peter Griffiths, 18 years 44 days v Reading, 26 September 1998.

Record Transfer Fee Received: £40,000 from Sheffield U for Mike Lake, 1988.

Record Transfer Fee Paid: £30,000 to Stevenage Borough for Efetobore Sodje, August 1997.

Football League Record: Promoted to Division 3 1997; 1998–99 Division 2; 1999– Division 3.

MANAGERS

Since 1967
Keith Goalen 1967–68
Frank Beaumont 1968–72
Billy Haydock 1972–74
Eddie Brown 1974
John Collins 1974
Willie Stevenson 1974
John Collins 1975–76
Tony Coleman 1976
John Barnes 1976
Brian Taylor 1976
Dave Connor 1976–78
Derek Partridge 1978
Phil Staley 1978–80
Jimmy Williams 1980–81
Brian Booth 1981–85
Neil Griffiths 1985–86
Roy Campbell 1986
Peter Wragg 1986–93
Sammy McIlroy 1993–2000
Peter Davenport 2000
Gil Prescott January 2001–

LATEST SEQUENCES

Longest Sequence of League Wins: 5, 16.10.99 – 6.11.99.

Longest Sequence of League Defeats: 6, 26.12.98 –6.2.99.

Longest Sequence of League Draws: 3, 27.9.97 – 11.10.97.

Longest Sequence of Unbeaten League Matches: 8, 16.10.99 – 27.11.99.

Longest Sequence Without a League Win: 10, 21.11.98 – 6.2.99.

TEN YEAR LEAGUE RECORD

		P	W	D	L	F	A	Pts	Pos
1990-91	Conf	42	17	12	13	63	52	63	7
1991-92	Conf	42	13	13	16	50	50	52	13
1992-93	Conf	42	12	13	17	40	50	49	18
1993-94	Conf	42	16	11	15	48	49	59	7
1994-95	Conf	42	24	8	10	70	40	80	1
1995-96	Conf	42	22	9	11	66	49	75	4
1996-97	Conf	42	27	9	6	80	30	90	1
1997-98	Div 3	46	23	13	10	63	44	82	2
1998-99	Div 2	46	11	10	25	43	63	43	24
1999-2000	Div 3	46	18	11	17	66	61	65	13

DID YOU KNOW ?

Macclesfield Town were the first winners of the FA Challenge Trophy. They beat Telford United 2-0 at Wembley on 2 May 1970, after their semi-final victims had been Barnet, who preceded them into the League.

MACCLESFIELD TOWN 2000–01 LEAGUE RECORD

Match No.	Date		Venue	Opponents		Result	H/T Score	Lg. Pos.	Goalscorers	Atten- dance
1	Aug	12	H	Scunthorpe U	L	0-1	0-0	—		2561
2		19	A	Shrewsbury T	D	2-2	1-2	17	Sedgemore [40], Tinson [90]	2822
3		26	H	Hull C	D	0-0	0-0	19		1795
4		28	A	Mansfield T	D	4-4	2-2	17	Askey [9], Sedgemore [27], Barker [72], Whitehead [86]	3360
5	Sept	2	A	Plymouth Arg	W	1-0	0-0	12	Barker [84]	3888
6		9	H	Exeter C	L	0-2	0-1	18		1793
7		12	H	Lincoln C	W	2-0	1-0	—	Whitehead 2 [20, 57]	1349
8		16	A	Hartlepool U	D	2-2	0-0	13	Barker [76], Glover (pen) [90]	2589
9		22	H	Darlington	D	1-1	1-0	—	Sedgemore [16]	2389
10		30	A	Chesterfield	L	1-4	1-3	16	Barker [23]	4904
11	Oct	8	A	Barnet	W	2-0	1-0	14	Glover 2 [30, 70]	1841
12		14	H	Cheltenham T	W	2-1	0-0	11	Ingram [68], Wood [77]	2035
13		17	H	Torquay U	W	2-1	1-1	—	Tinson [15], Barker [56]	1681
14		21	A	Blackpool	L	1-2	0-0	10	Whitehead [70]	3700
15		24	A	Rochdale	D	2-2	2-0	—	Glover [6], Barker [33]	3608
16		28	H	Halifax T	D	0-0	0-0	11		1734
17	Nov	4	A	Southend U	L	1-3	0-0	13	Munroe [68]	4190
18		11	H	Brighton & HA	D	0-0	0-0	11		2654
19		25	A	Leyton Orient	L	1-2	1-1	13	Whitehead [45]	4013
20	Dec	2	A	Kidderminster H	L	1-2	1-2	15	Glover [15]	2638
21		16	H	Carlisle U	W	1-0	0-0	14	Barker [56]	1860
22		23	A	Cardiff C	L	0-2	0-1	15		8088
23		26	H	York C	L	0-1	0-0	15		2001
24	Jan	1	A	Scunthorpe U	D	2-2	1-1	14	Durkan [18], Keen [49]	3168
25		6	A	Hull C	D	0-0	0-0	14		6217
26		14	H	Mansfield T	L	0-1	0-1	15		1893
27		20	A	York C	W	3-1	1-1	14	Alcide (og) [15], Priest 2 [65, 84]	2287
28		27	H	Cardiff C	L	2-5	1-2	16	Keen [8], Tracey [55]	2376
29	Feb	3	H	Plymouth Arg	W	3-1	0-0	14	Priest 2 [70, 90], Whitehead [73]	1881
30		10	A	Exeter C	D	0-0	0-0	15		3458
31		13	H	Shrewsbury T	W	2-1	1-0	—	Whitehead 2 [3, 55]	1430
32		17	H	Hartlepool U	L	0-1	0-0	13		2228
33		20	A	Lincoln C	W	2-1	1-0	—	Tinson [3], Askey [89]	1853
34		24	A	Darlington	D	1-1	1-1	11	Durkan (pen) [3]	3103
35	Mar	3	H	Chesterfield	L	1-2	1-1	14	Glover [6]	2740
36		6	A	Cheltenham T	D	1-1	0-0	—	Rioch [67]	3091
37		11	H	Barnet	W	3-0	2-0	12	Durkan 2 [17, 56], Glover [30]	2060
38		24	H	Blackpool	W	2-1	2-0	12	Tracey [22], Askey [28]	3045
39		31	A	Carlisle U	L	0-1	0-0	12		3885
40	Apr	7	H	Kidderminster H	W	1-0	1-0	12	Shuker [42]	1585
41		10	A	Torquay U	L	0-2	0-1	—		2911
42		14	H	Rochdale	D	0-0	0-0	12		2255
43		16	A	Halifax T	L	0-3	0-2	12		1945
44		21	H	Southend U	W	1-0	1-0	13	Glover (pen) [29]	1594
45		28	A	Brighton & HA	L	1-4	1-2	13	Tracey [39]	6731
46	May	5	H	Leyton Orient	L	0-2	0-1	14		2527

Final League Position: 14

GOALSCORERS

League (51): Glover 8 (2 pens), Whitehead 8, Barker 7, Durkan 4 (1 pen), Priest 4, Askey 3, Sedgemore 3, Tinson 3, Tracey 3, Keen 2, Ingram 1, Munroe 1, Rioch 1, Shuker 1, Wood 1, own goal 1.
Worthington Cup (5): Barker 2, Sedgemore 2 (1 pen), Munroe 1.
FA Cup (0).

Bullock T 24	Hitchen S 37	Ingram R 32 + 1	Collins S 15 + 2	Tinson D 45	Wood S 27 + 3	Munroe K 19 + 4	Sedgemore B 23 + 4	Barker R 23	Glover L 29 + 8	Durkan K 26 + 5	Twynham G 5 + 4	Whitehead D 9 + 24	Bettney C — + 2	Priest C 14 + 1	Abbey G 13 + 5	Askey J 29 + 8	Adams D 36 + 1	O'Neill P 5 + 7	Keen K 30 + 2	Rioch G 16 + 1	Woolley M 1 + 1	Bamber M 2 + 3	Martin L 21	Came S 3 + 4	Tracey R 11 + 2	Tereskinas A — + 1	Connell D — + 1	Lambert R 4 + 5	Shuker C 6 + 3	Wilson S 1	Match No
1	2	3	4	5	6	7	8¹	9	10²	11³	12	13	14																		1
1	2	3	4	5	6		8²	9	10	11	7¹	12			13																2
1	2	3	4	5	6	7¹	12	9	10³	13	11				8²	14															3
1	2	3	4	5	6		8¹	9		11²	10	13	12			7															4
1	2	3¹	4	5	6	12	8	9²		11	10¹	13		14	7																5
1	2	12	4¹	5	6³	10	8	9		11		13			3	7²	14														6
1	2	4		5	6²	11	8	9	12		10¹				7	3	13														7
1	2	3		5	6	11¹	8	9	13	14	12³	10²			4	7															8
1	4			5	6³	10²	8	9	12	11¹	13				2	7	3		14												9
1	3			5		10	8	9	12		11³	13			4²	7¹	2		6	14											10
1	4			5	6	7²	8	9	10						12		2		3	13	11										11
1	4			5	6		8	9	10		12				13	7²	2		3			11¹									12
1	4			5	6	11	8	9	10²		12	13			7¹		2		3												13
1	4			5	6	11¹	8	9	10		12				13		2		7	3²											14
1	4			5	6		8	9	10¹						11	7	2		12	3											15
1	2²			5	6	12	8²	9	10¹		13				11	7	4	14		3											16
1	3		12	5	13	11	8	9	10²		14				4	7²	2	6¹													17
1	3	4²		5		11	8	9	10	12					6	7¹	2	13													18
	2		4	5		12	9	10³	13		11			8		14	3	6¹	7²				1								19
	2		4	5	13	7²	9	10¹			11			8		12	3	6					1								20
	3		4	5		7	9	10			11¹			8		12	2	6					1								21
	3		4	5		7	9	10²	13		11¹			8		12	2	6					1								22
	3		4¹	5		7²	9	12	11	10				8		13	2	6					1								23
1	3		4	5	6		10		11					8		9	2	7					1								24
1	3		4²	5	6	12	10¹							8		9	2	13	7				1								25
1	3¹			5	6²			10	11					8		9	2	4	7						13						26
1	4¹			5	6¹			12	11		14			8	3	9³	2	13	7	10											27
1	3	4¹		5				10²	11					8		9	2	12	7	6					13						28
1	3¹	4	12	5				13	11		14			8		9²	2		7	6					10²						29
	3	4		5	12					11		13		8		9²	2	7	6¹				1								30
	3	4		5	12					11		10¹		8		9²	2	7	6				1		13						31
	3	4		5	12					11		10		8²		9¹	2	7	6				1				13				32
	3	4		5	6	8				11		12				9²	2	7	10¹				1					13			33
	3	4		5	6	8				11		12		13	9¹		2	7	10²				1								34
	2	4		5		8			10			12				9	3	7	6¹			13	1					11²			35
	2	4		5		8				12	11				10¹	9	3	7	6				1								36
	2	4		5		8²			10	11		12			13	9¹	3		6				1		7³			14			37
	2	4		5		8			10	11						9²	3¹	12	6				1		7³			13	14		38
	2	4		5		8			10	11		12					3		6				1		9¹				7		39
	2			5³	6				10	11		12			13		3²	4	7				1		14	9¹			8		40
	2				6				10	11		12			3²			4	7				1	5	9¹			13	8		41
	2	3		5	6				10										7				1	4	9			11	8		42
	2	3		5	12				10			13							7	6²		14	1	4	9³			11¹	8		43
	2	4²		5	6				10								3		7				12	13	9			11¹	8	1	44
	2	4		5	6				10¹	11³		12				9	3		7				1		8²			13	14		45
	2	4¹		5	6²				10	11						9³	3		7				1		12	8		13	14		46

Worthington Cup
First Round   Bolton W   (a) 0-1
               (h) 3-1
Second Round   Middlesbrough   (a) 1-2
               (h) 1-3

FA Cup
First Round   Oxford U   (h) 0-1

MANCHESTER CITY

Division 1

FOUNDATION

Manchester City was formed as a Limited Company in 1894 after their predecessors Ardwick had been forced into bankruptcy. However, many historians like to trace the club's lineage as far back as 1880 when St Mark's Church, West Gorton added a football section to their cricket club. They amalgamated with Gorton Athletic in 1884 as Gorton FC. Because of a change of ground they became Ardwick in 1887.

Maine Road, Moss Side, Manchester M14 7WN.

Telephone: (0161) 232 3000. *Fax:* (0161) 232 8999.
Ticket Office: (0161) 226 2224. *ClubCall:* 09068 121 191.
Dial-A-Seat: (0161) 227 9229. *Development Office:*
(0161) 226 3143.

Ground Capacity: 34,026.

Record Attendance: 84,569 v Stoke C, FA Cup 6th rd,
3 March 1934 (British record for any game outside
London or Glasgow).

Record Receipts: £512,235 Manchester U v Oldham Ath,
FA Cup semi-final replay, 13 April 1994.

Pitch Measurements: 116.5yd × 75yd.

Chairman: D. A. Bernstein. *Directors:* J. Wardle,
D. Tueart, A. Lewis, A. Thomas, B. Bodek, C. Bird,
A. Mackintosh. *General Secretary:* J. B. Halford.

Manager: Kevin Keegan. *Head Coach:* Willie Donachie.
Reserve Team Coach: Asa Hartford. *Physio:* Rob Harris.
Youth Team Coach: Alex Gibson.
Youth Academy Director: Jim Cassell.

Colours: Lazer blue shirts, white shorts, lazer blue and
navy stockings.

HONOURS

Football League: Division 1 –
Champions 1936–37, 1967–68;
Runners-up 1903–04, 1920–21,
1976–77, 1999–2000; Division 2 –
Champions 1898–99, 1902–03,
1909–10, 1927–28, 1946–47, 1965–66;
Runners-up 1895–96, 1950–51,
1987–88; Promoted from Division 2
(play-offs) 1998–99.
FA Cup: Winners 1904, 1934, 1956,
1969; Runners-up 1926, 1933, 1955,
1981.
Football League Cup: Winners 1970,
1976; Runners-up 1974.
European Competitions: *European
Cup:* 1968–69. *European Cup-
Winners' Cup:* 1969–70 (winners),
1970–71. *UEFA Cup:* 1972–73,
1976–77, 1977–78, 1978–79.

Change Colours: Silver with yellow and navy striped shirts, navy shorts with yellow trim, yellow
stockings.

Year Formed: 1887 as Ardwick FC; 1894 as Manchester City.

Turned Professional: 1887 as Ardwick FC.

Ltd Co.: 1894.

Previous Names: 1887, Ardwick FC (formed through the amalgamation of West Gorton and Gorton
Athletic, the latter having been formed in 1880); 1894, Manchester City.

Club Nickname: 'Blues' or 'The Citizens'.

Previous Grounds: 1880, Clowes Street; 1881, Kirkmanshulme Cricket Ground; 1882, Queens Road;
1884, Pink Bank Lane; 1887, Hyde Road (1894–1923 as City); 1923, Maine Road.

First Football League Game: 3 September 1892, Division 2, v Bootle (h) W 7–0 – Douglas;
McVickers, Robson; Middleton, Russell, Hopkins; Davies (3), Morris (2), Angus (1), Weir (1),
Milarvie.

IT'S A FACT !

In the 1978–79 season, Manchester City installed a gas-
orientated Swedish system of undersoil heating and a
new public address system at Maine Road.

Record League Victory: 10–1 v Huddersfield T, Division 2, 7 November 1987 – Nixon; Gidman, Hinchcliffe, Clements, Lake, Redmond, White (3), Stewart (3), Adcock (3), McNab (1), Simpson.

Record Cup Victory: 10–1 v Swindon T, FA Cup 4th rd, 29 January 1930 – Barber; Felton, McCloy; Barrass, Cowan, Heinemann; Toseland, Marshall (5), Tait (3), Johnson (1), Brook (1).

Record Defeat: 1–9 v Everton, Division 1, 3 September 1906.

Most League Points (2 for a win): 62, Division 2, 1946–47.

Most League Points (3 for a win): 89, Division 1, 1999–2000.

Most League Goals: 108, Division 2, 1926–27.

Highest League Scorer in Season: Tommy Johnson, 38, Division 1, 1928–29.

Most League Goals in Total Aggregate: Tommy Johnson, 158, 1919–30.

Most League Goals in One Match: 5, Fred Williams v Darwen, Division 2, 18 February 1899; 5, Tom Browell v Burnley, Division 2, 24 October 1925; 5, Tom Johnson v Everton, Division 1, 15 September 1928; 5, George Smith v Newport Co, Division 2, 14 June 1947.

Most Capped Player: Colin Bell, 48, England.

Most League Appearances: Alan Oakes, 565, 1959–76.

Youngest League Player: Glyn Pardoe, 15 years 314 days v Birmingham C, 11 April 1961.

Record Transfer Fee Received: £4,925,000 from Ajax for Georgi Kinkladze, May 1998.

Record Transfer Fee Paid: £3,000,000 to Portsmouth for Lee Bradbury, July 1997.

Football League Record: 1892 Ardwick elected founder member of Division 2; 1894 Newly-formed Manchester C elected to Division 2; Division 1 1899–1902, 1903–09, 1910–26, 1928–38, 1947–50, 1951–63, 1966–83, 1985–87, 1989–92; Division 2 1902–03, 1909–10, 1926–28, 1938–47, 1950–51, 1963–66, 1983–85; 1987–89; 1992–96 FA Premier League; 1996–98 Division 1; 1998–99 Division 2; 1999–2000 Division 1; 2000–01 FA Premier League; 2001– Division 1.

MANAGERS

Joshua Parlby 1893–95
(Secretary-Manager)
Sam Omerod 1895–1902
Tom Maley 1902–06
Harry Newbould 1906–12
Ernest Magnall 1912–24
David Ashworth 1924–25
Peter Hodge 1926–32
Wilf Wild 1932–46
(continued as Secretary to 1950)
Sam Cowan 1946–47
John 'Jock' Thomson 1947–50
Leslie McDowall 1950–63
George Poyser 1963–65
Joe Mercer 1965–71
(continued as General Manager to 1972)
Malcolm Allison 1972–73
Johnny Hart 1973
Ron Saunders 1973–74
Tony Book 1974–79
Malcolm Allison 1979–80
John Bond 1980–83
John Benson 1983
Billy McNeill 1983–86
Jimmy Frizzell 1986–87
(continued as General Manager)
Mel Machin 1987–89
Howard Kendall 1990
Peter Reid 1990–93
Brian Horton 1993–95
Alan Ball 1995–96
Steve Coppell 1996
Frank Clark 1996–98
Joe Royle 1998–2001
Kevin Keegan May 2001–

LATEST SEQUENCES

Longest Sequence of League Wins: 9, 8.4.12 – 28.9.12.

Longest Sequence of League Defeats: 8, 23.8.95 – 14.10.95.

Longest Sequence of League Draws: 6, 5.4.13 – 6.9.13.

Longest Sequence of Unbeaten League Matches: 22, 16.11.46 – 19.4.47.

Longest Sequence Without a League Win: 17, 26.12.79 – 7.4.80.

TEN YEAR LEAGUE RECORD

		P	W	D	L	F	A	Pts	Pos
1990-91	Div 1	38	17	11	10	64	53	62	5
1991-92	Div 1	42	20	10	12	61	48	70	5
1992-93	PR Lge	42	15	12	15	56	51	57	9
1993-94	PR Lge	42	9	18	15	38	49	45	16
1994-95	PR Lge	42	12	13	17	53	64	49	17
1995-96	PR Lge	38	9	11	18	33	58	38	18
1996-97	Div 1	46	17	10	19	59	60	61	14
1997-98	Div 1	46	12	12	22	56	57	48	22
1998-99	Div 2	46	22	16	8	69	33	82	3
1999-2000	Div 1	46	26	11	9	78	40	89	2

DID YOU KNOW ?

Manchester City made a financial profit in each of their first nine post-war seasons culminating with a figure of £14,982 from the 1953–54 season.

MANCHESTER CITY 2000–01 LEAGUE RECORD

Match No.	Date	Venue	Opponents	Result	H/T Score	Lg. Pos.	Goalscorers	Attendance
1	Aug 19	A	Charlton Ath	L	0-4	0-2	—	20,039
2	23	H	Sunderland	W	4-2	2-0	—	Wanchope 3 [4, 78, 88], Haaland [23]	34,410
3	26	H	Coventry C	L	1-2	0-2	16	Horlock [78]	34,140
4	Sept 5	A	Leeds U	W	2-1	2-0	—	Howey [34], Wiekens [40]	40,055
5	9	A	Liverpool	L	2-3	0-1	11	Weah [67], Horlock (pen) [81]	44,692
6	17	H	Middlesbrough	D	1-1	0-0	12	Wanchope [67]	32,053
7	23	A	Tottenham H	D	0-0	0-0	13		36,065
8	30	H	Newcastle U	L	0-1	0-0	16		34,497
9	Oct 14	H	Bradford C	W	2-0	2-0	12	Dickov [30], Haaland [45]	34,229
10	23	A	Southampton	W	2-0	1-0	—	Dickov [38], Tiatto [90]	15,056
11	28	A	Arsenal	L	0-5	0-1	13		38,049
12	Nov 4	H	Leicester C	L	0-1	0-0	13		34,279
13	11	H	West Ham U	L	1-4	1-0	16	Prior [32]	26,022
14	18	H	Manchester U	L	0-1	0-1	16		34,429
15	25	H	Ipswich T	L	2-3	0-2	16	Wanchope [71], Howey [81]	33,741
16	Dec 3	A	Chelsea	L	1-2	0-2	16	Dickov [82]	34,971
17	9	H	Everton	W	5-0	3-0	16	Wanchope [14], Howey [23], Goater [42], Dickov [54], Naysmith (og) [67]	34,516
18	16	A	Aston Villa	D	2-2	0-0	16	Haaland [65], Wanchope [73]	29,281
19	23	A	Sunderland	L	0-1	0-1	17		45,686
20	26	H	Derby Co	D	0-0	0-0	17		34,321
21	30	H	Charlton Ath	L	1-4	0-2	19	Huckerby (pen) [90]	33,280
22	Jan 1	A	Coventry C	D	1-1	0-0	19	Wanchope [54]	21,991
23	13	A	Leeds U	L	0-4	0-1	19		34,288
24	20	A	Derby Co	D	1-1	0-0	18	Howey [51]	31,174
25	31	H	Liverpool	D	1-1	0-1	—	Tiatto [48]	34,629
26	Feb 3	A	Middlesbrough	D	1-1	1-0	18	Vickers (og) [28]	31,792
27	10	H	Tottenham H	L	0-1	0-0	18		34,399
28	24	A	Newcastle U	W	1-0	0-0	18	Goater [61]	51,981
29	Mar 3	H	Southampton	L	0-1	0-0	18		33,990
30	17	A	Bradford C	D	2-2	1-0	18	Wiekens [22], Goater [70]	19,117
31	31	H	Aston Villa	L	1-3	1-2	18	Goater [12]	34,243
32	Apr 8	A	Everton	L	1-3	1-2	19	Whitley [9]	36,561
33	11	H	Arsenal	L	0-4	0-4	—		33,444
34	14	A	Leicester C	W	2-1	1-1	18	Goater [17], Wanchope [67]	20,224
35	21	A	Manchester U	D	1-1	0-0	19	Howey [84]	67,535
36	28	H	West Ham U	W	1-0	1-0	18	Pearce I (og) [23]	33,737
37	May 7	A	Ipswich T	L	1-2	0-0	—	Goater [74]	24,888
38	19	H	Chelsea	L	1-2	1-1	18	Howey [39]	34,479

Final League Position: 18

GOALSCORERS

League (41): Wanchope 9, Goater 6, Howey 6, Dickov 4, Haaland 3, Horlock 2 (1 pen), Tiatto 2, Wiekens 2, Huckerby 1 (pen), Prior 1, Weah 1, Whitley 1, own goals 3.
Worthington Cup (9): Weah 3, Dickov 1, Goater 1, Horlock 1 (pen), Kennedy 1, Wanchope 1.
FA Cup (6): Goater 3 (1 pen), Huckerby 1, Kanchelskis 1, Morrison 1.

Weaver N 31	Edghill R 6	Tiatto D 31 + 2	Wiekens G 29 + 5	Howey S 36	Prior S 18 + 3	Kennedy M 15 + 10	Horlock K 14	Weah G 5 + 2	Wanchope P 25 + 2	Haaland A 35	Wright-Phillips S 9 + 6	Grant T 5 + 5	Dickov P 15 + 6	Ritchie P 11 + 1	Granville D 16 + 3	Whitley J 28 + 3	Crooks L — + 2	Bishop I 3 + 7	Wright T 1	Dunne R 24 + 1	Goater S 20 + 6	Charvat L 16 + 4	Allsopp D — + 1	Huckerby D 8 + 5	Morrison A 3	Kanchelskis A 7 + 3	Ostenstad E 1 + 3	Nash C 6	Dunfield T — + 1	Match No.
1	2	3	4	5	6	7	8¹	9	10	11	12																			1
1	2	3	4	5	6	7	8	9	10	11																				2
1	2¹	3	4	5	6	7¹	8	9	10	11			12	13																3
1		11	4¹	5	6	7²	8		9	2	13		3	12	10															4
1			4	5	6	7¹	8	12	9	2			11	3		10														5
1		12	4¹	5	6	7	8³		9²	10	2		13	3		11		14												6
1		11¹	4	5³	6	12	7	13	10	2			9²	3		8		14												7
		3	4		6	12	7¹		9²	10	2³		8	5		11	14	13	1											8
1		11	4	5¹	6	7			10	2			9	3		8		12												9
1		11	4	5	6				10¹	7			9	3		8				2	12									10
1		11	4	5	6	12			7				9	3		8					10¹	2								11
1		11	4²	5	6	12			10	7			9	3¹	13	8						2								12
1			4	5	6	7			9²	8	11		3¹			10					12	2	13							13
1		3	4¹	5	6	7²			8	11			9			10					12	13	2							14
1		12		5	6	3			13	7	11		9²		14	8				4¹	10²	2								15
1		3¹	12	5	6		8		9²	4	11		13			7					10	2								16
1		3	12	5			13	11	9	8¹	7²		14			6				4	10³	2								17
1		3	12	5			13	11¹	9	8	7					6				4	10²	2								18
1		3				7¹	6		8	11		12				10²		13		4	9	2								19
1		3	12	5		6¹			10	7	11					8				4	9	2								20
1		3	4	5		11¹			8	7		9²	13			12				6	10	2³		14						21
1	2	11		5			9	7	12		3					8¹				4	13			10²	6					22
1	2	11		5			9	7	12	13	14		3²	8						4	10³				6¹					23
1		11¹	4	5	6		10	7	12		3¹	13	8							2	14			9³						24
1		11	4	5			7			12	3	8								2	10			9¹	6²	13				25
1		11	6	5			2	12	13		3¹	8								4	10			9²		7				26
1		11	4¹	5			2		12		3	8				6				10				9		7²	13			27
1		11	8	5			2²		6		3	12				4				10	13			9¹		7				28
1		11	8	5			2		6		3¹					4				10	12			9²		7	13			29
1		11	8	5		12					6¹		3¹	13		4				10	2			9²		7	14			30
1		11	12				6	13		4			3²	8		5				10	2			14		7³	9¹			31
1		11	4	5		12			10	2		9				3¹	8			6				13		7²				32
		11	4	5		7			9²	2			3	8¹		6	10	12				13						1		33
			4²	5	12	7			9	11		13	3	8		6	10¹	2³					14					1		34
			4¹	5	12				10	7		8²	9	3	11	2	14	6					13³					1		35
		11	4	5		7			12	2³		9¹	3	8		6	10²	14				13						1		36
		11	4	5	13	14			10			7¹	9¹	3	8	6	12²	2										1		37
	2		4	5		7			8			9	3	11¹	6	10												1	12	38

Worthington Cup

Second Round	Gillingham	(h)	1-1	
		(a)	4-2	
Third Round	Aston Villa	(a)	1-0	
Fourth Round	Wimbledon	(h)	2-1	
Fifth Round	Ipswich T	(h)	1-2	

FA Cup

Third Round	Birmingham C	(h)	3-2
Fourth Round	Coventry C	(h)	1-0
Fifth Round	Liverpool	(a)	2-4

MANCHESTER UNITED FA Premiership

FOUNDATION

Manchester United was formed as comparatively recently as 1902 after their predecessors, Newton Heath, went bankrupt. However, it is usual to give the date of the club's foundation as 1878 when the dining room committee of the carriage and waggon works of the Lancashire and Yorkshire Railway Company formed Newton Heath L and YR Cricket and Football Club. They won the Manchester Cup in 1886 and as Newton Heath FC were admitted to the Second Division in 1892.

Sir Matt Busby Way, Old Trafford, Manchester M16 0RA.

Telephone: (0161) 868 8000. *Fax:* (0161) 868 8804.
Textphone for Deaf/Impaired Hearing: (0161) 868 8668.
Ticket and Match Information: (0161) 868 8020.
Membership and Supporters Club Enquiries:
(0161) 868 8450.

Ground Capacity: 68,174.

Record Attendance: 76,962 Wolverhampton W v Grimsby T, FA Cup semi-final, 25 March 1939.

Club record: 70,504 v Aston Villa, Division 1, 27 December 1920.

Record Receipts: £723,650.22 (net of VAT), £850,289 (including VAT) v Liverpool, FA Cup 4th rd, 24 January 1999.

Pitch Measurements: 116yd × 76yd.

Chairman/Chief Executive: C. M. Edwards.
Directors: J. M. Edelson, Sir Bobby Charlton CBE, E. M. Watkins LL.M., R. L. Olive, P. F. Kenyon, D. A. Gill.

Manager: Sir Alex Ferguson CBE. *Assistant Manager:* Jim Ryan. *First Team Coach:* Mike Phelan.
Reserve Team Coach: Brian McClair. *Secretary:* Kenneth Merrett. *Stadium Manager:* Alan Bird.

Colours: Red shirts, white shorts, black stockings.

Change Colours: All white.

Year Formed: 1878 as Newton Heath LYR; 1902, Manchester United.

Turned Professional: 1885. *Ltd Co.:* 1907.

Previous Name: 1880, Newton Heath; 1902, Manchester United. *Club Nickname:* 'Red Devils'.

Previous Grounds: 1880, North Road, Monsall Road; 1893, Bank Street; 1910, Old Trafford (played at Maine Road 1941–49).

HONOURS

FA Premier League – Champions 1992–93, 1993–94, 1995–96, 1996–97, 1998–99, 1999–2000, 2000–01; Runners-up 1994–95, 1997–98.

Football League: Division 1 – Champions 1907–08, 1910–11, 1951–52, 1955–56, 1956–57, 1964–65, 1966–67; Runners-up 1946–47, 1947–48, 1948–49, 1950–51, 1958–59, 1963–64, 1967–68, 1979–80, 1987–88, 1991–92. Division 2 – Champions 1935–36, 1974–75; Runners-up 1896–97, 1905–06, 1924–25, 1937–38.

FA Cup: Winners 1909, 1948, 1963, 1977, 1983, 1985, 1990, 1994, 1996, 1999; Runners-up 1957, 1958, 1976, 1979, 1995.

Football League Cup: Winners 1992; Runners-up 1983, 1991, 1994.

European Competitions: European Cup: 1956–57 (s-f), 1957–58 (s-f), 1965–66 (s-f), 1967–68 (winners), 1968–69 (s-f), 1993–94, 1994–95, 1996–97 (s-f), 1997–98, 1998–99 (winners), 1999–2000, 2000–01. *European Cup-Winners' Cup:* 1963–64, 1977–78, 1983–84, 1990–91 (winners). 1991–92. *European Fairs Cup:* 1964–65. *UEFA Cup:* 1976–77, 1980–81, 1982–83, 1984–85, 1992–93, 1995–96. *Super Cup:* 1991 (winners), 1999 (runners-up). *Inter-Continental Cup:* 1999 (winners), 1968 (runners-up).

IT'S A FACT !

Denis Irwin completed his 500th senior game for Manchester United against Liverpool on 17 March 2001 to become the sixth highest in the club's list of such appearances and top among their current players.

First Football League Game: 3 September 1892, Division 1,
v Blackburn R (a) L 3–4 – Warner; Clements, Brown;
Perrins, Stewart, Erentz; Farman (1), Coupar (1),
Donaldson (1), Carson, Mathieson.

Record League Victory (as Newton Heath): 10–1 v
Wolverhampton W, Division 1, 15 October 1892 – Warner;
Mitchell, Clements; Perrins, Stewart (3), Erentz; Farman (1),
Hood (1), Donaldson (3), Carson (1), Hendry (1).

Record League Victory (as Manchester U): 9–0 v Ipswich T,
FA Premier League, 4 March 1995 – Schmeichel; Keane (1)
(Sharpe), Irwin, Bruce (Butt), Kanchelskis, Pallister,
Cole (5), Ince (1), McClair, Hughes (2), Giggs.

Record Cup Victory: 10–0 v RSC Anderlecht, European
Cup prel. rd 2nd leg, 26 September 1956 – Wood; Foulkes,
Byrne; Colman, Jones, Edwards; Berry (1), Whelan (2),
Taylor (3), Viollet (4), Pegg.

Record Defeat: 0–7 v Blackburn R, Division 1, 10 April
1926. 0–7 v Aston Villa, Division 1, 27 December 1930. 0–7
v Wolverhampton W, Division 2, 26 December 1931.

Most League Points (2 for a win): 64, Division 1, 1956–57.

Most League Points (3 for a win): 92, FA Premier League,
1993–94.

Most League Goals: 103, Division 1, 1956–57 and 1958–59.

Highest League Scorer in Season: Dennis Viollet, 32, 1959–60.

Most League Goals in Total Aggregate: Bobby Charlton, 199, 1956–73.

Most Capped Player: Bobby Charlton, 106, England.

Most League Appearances: Bobby Charlton, 606, 1956–73.

Youngest League Player: Jeff Whitefoot, 16 years 105 days v Portsmouth, 15 April 1950.

Record Transfer Fee Received: £7,000,000 from Internazionale for Paul Ince, June 1995.

Record Transfer Fee Paid: £28,100,000 to Lazio for Juan Sebastian Veron, July 2001.

Football League Record: 1892 Newton Heath elected to Division 1; 1894–1906 Division 2;
1906–22 Division 1; 1922–25 Division 2; 1925–31 Division 1; 1931–36 Division 2; 1936–37 Division 1;
1937–38 Division 2; 1938–74 Division 1; 1974–75 Division 2; 1975–92 Division 1; 1992– FA Premier
League.

MANAGERS

J. Ernest Mangnall 1903–12
John Bentley 1912–14
John Robson 1914–21
    (Secretary-Manager from 1916)
John Chapman 1921–26
Clarence Hilditch 1926–27
Herbert Bamlett 1927–31
Walter Crickmer 1931–32
Scott Duncan 1932–37
Walter Crickmer 1937–45
    (Secretary-Manager)
Matt Busby 1945–69
    *(continued as General Manager
    then Director)*
Wilf McGuinness 1969–70
Sir Matt Busby 1970–71
Frank O'Farrell 1971–72
Tommy Docherty 1972–77
Dave Sexton 1977–81
Ron Atkinson 1981–86
Alex Ferguson November 1986–

LATEST SEQUENCES

Longest Sequence of League Wins: 14, 15.10.04 – 3.1.05.

Longest Sequence of League Defeats: 14, 26.4.30 – 25.10.30.

Longest Sequence of League Draws: 6, 30.10.88 – 27.11.88.

Longest Sequence of Unbeaten League Matches: 29, 26.12.98 – 25.9.99.

Longest Sequence Without a League Win: 16, 19.4.30 – 25.10.30.

TEN YEAR LEAGUE RECORD

		P	W	D	L	F	A	Pts	Pos
1990-91	Div 1	38	16	12	10	58	45	59	6
1991-92	Div 1	42	21	15	6	63	33	78	2
1992-93	PR Lge	42	24	12	6	67	31	84	1
1993-94	PR Lge	42	27	11	4	80	38	92	1
1994-95	PR Lge	42	26	10	6	77	28	88	2
1995-96	PR Lge	38	25	7	6	73	35	82	1
1996-97	PR Lge	38	21	12	5	76	44	75	1
1997-98	PR Lge	38	23	8	7	73	26	77	2
1998-99	PR Lge	38	22	13	3	80	37	79	1
1999-2000	PR Lge	38	28	7	3	97	45	91	1

DID YOU KNOW ?

On 26 April 1952,
Manchester United clinched
the League championship
with a 6–1 win over Arsenal.
Jack Rowley completed a
hat-trick, with two goals from
his less favoured right foot,
including a penalty. In 2000–01
United again beat Arsenal
6–1 on the way to the title.

MANCHESTER UNITED 2000–01 LEAGUE RECORD

Match No.	Date	Venue	Opponents	Result	H/T Score	Lg. Pos.	Goalscorers	Atten- dance
1	Aug 20	H	Newcastle U	W 2-0	1-0	—	Johnsen [21], Cole [70]	67,477
2	22	A	Ipswich T	D 1-1	1-1	—	Beckham [39]	22,007
3	26	A	West Ham U	D 2-2	1-0	5	Beckham [6], Cole [49]	25,998
4	Sept 5	H	Bradford C	W 6-0	2-0	—	Cole [11], Fortune 2 [23, 60], Sheringham 2 [71, 81], Beckham [85]	67,447
5	9	H	Sunderland	W 3-0	1-0	1	Scholes 2 [14, 82], Sheringham [76]	67,503
6	16	A	Everton	W 3-1	3-0	1	Butt [27], Giggs [29], Solskjaer [38]	38,541
7	23	H	Chelsea	D 3-3	3-2	1	Scholes [14], Sheringham [37], Beckham [39]	67,568
8	Oct 1	A	Arsenal	L 0-1	0-1	2		38,146
9	14	A	Leicester C	W 3-0	1-0	1	Sheringham 2 [37, 55], Solskjaer [90]	22,132
10	21	H	Leeds U	W 3-0	1-0	1	Yorke [41], Beckham [50], Jones (og) [83]	67,523
11	28	H	Southampton	W 5-0	2-0	1	Cole 2 [9, 73], Sheringham 3 [45, 51, 55]	67,581
12	Nov 4	A	Coventry C	W 2-1	2-0	1	Cole [27], Beckham [37]	21,077
13	11	H	Middlesbrough	W 2-1	0-1	1	Butt [62], Sheringham [65]	67,576
14	18	A	Manchester C	W 1-0	1-0	1	Beckham [2]	34,429
15	25	A	Derby Co	W 3-0	0-0	1	Sheringham [61], Butt [69], Yorke [76]	32,910
16	Dec 2	H	Tottenham H	W 2-0	1-0	1	Scholes [40], Solskjaer [84]	67,583
17	9	A	Charlton Ath	D 3-3	2-1	1	Giggs [42], Solskjaer [43], Keane [66]	20,043
18	17	A	Liverpool	L 0-1	0-1	1		67,533
19	23	H	Ipswich T	W 2-0	2-0	1	Solskjaer 2 [20, 32]	67,597
20	26	A	Aston Villa	W 1-0	0-0	1	Solskjaer [85]	40,889
21	30	A	Newcastle U	D 1-1	1-0	1	Beckham (pen) [25]	52,134
22	Jan 1	A	West Ham U	W 3-1	2-0	1	Solskjaer [3], Pearce S (og) [33], Yorke [58]	67,603
23	13	A	Bradford C	W 3-0	0-0	1	Sheringham [72], Giggs [75], Chadwick [87]	20,551
24	20	A	Aston Villa	W 2-0	0-0	1	Neville G [57], Sheringham [87]	67,533
25	31	A	Sunderland	W 1-0	0-0	—	Cole [46]	47,250
26	Feb 3	H	Everton	W 1-0	0-0	1	Watson (og) [52]	67,528
27	10	A	Chelsea	D 1-1	0-1	1	Cole [69]	34,960
28	25	H	Arsenal	W 6-1	5-1	1	Yorke 3 [3, 18, 22], Keane [26], Solskjaer [38], Sheringham [90]	67,535
29	Mar 3	A	Leeds U	D 1-1	0-0	1	Chadwick [64]	40,055
30	17	H	Leicester C	W 2-0	0-0	1	Yorke [88], Silvestre [90]	67,539
31	31	A	Liverpool	L 0-2	0-2	1		44,806
32	Apr 10	H	Charlton Ath	W 2-1	1-0	—	Cole [45], Solskjaer [82]	67,505
33	14	H	Coventry C	W 4-2	2-2	1	Yorke 2 [12, 27], Giggs [81], Scholes [87]	67,637
34	21	H	Manchester C	D 1-1	0-0	1	Sheringham (pen) [71]	67,535
35	28	A	Middlesbrough	W 2-0	1-0	1	Neville P [4], Beckham [84]	34,417
36	May 5	H	Derby Co	L 0-1	0-1	1		67,526
37	13	A	Southampton	L 1-2	0-2	—	Giggs [71]	15,246
38	19	A	Tottenham H	L 1-3	1-1	1	Scholes [22]	36,078

Final League Position: 1

GOALSCORERS

League (79): Sheringham 15 (1 pen), Solskjaer 10, Beckham 9 (1 pen), Cole 9, Yorke 9, Scholes 6, Giggs 5, Butt 3, Chadwick 2, Fortune 2, Keane 2, Johnsen 1, Neville G 1, Neville P 1, Silvestre 1, own goals 3.
Worthington Cup (4): Solskjaer 2, Yorke 2.
FA Cup (2): Sheringham 1, Solskjaer 1.

Barthez F 30	Neville G 32	Neville P 24 + 5	Johnsen R 11	Keane R 28	Stam J 15	Beckham D 29 + 2	Scholes P 28 + 4	Cole A 15 + 4	Sheringham T 23 + 6	Giggs R 24 + 7	Wallwork R 4 + 8	Solskjaer O 19 + 12	Yorke D 15 + 7	Silvestre M 25 + 5	Berg H — + 1	Butt N 24 + 4	Greening J 3 + 4	Fortune Q 6 + 1	Irwin D 20 + 1	Van der Gouw R 5 + 5	Brown W 25 + 3	Chadwick L 6 + 10	Healy D — + 1	Rachubka P 1	Goram A 2	Stewart M 3	May D 1 + 1	Djordjic B — + 1	Match No.
1	2	3	4^3	5	6	7	8	9^1	10^2	11	14	12	13																1
1	2	3^3		5	6	7	8	12	13	11	4	9^1	10^2	14															2
1	2	3		5	6^1	7	8	9	10	11					4	12													3
1	2	12	6^1		7	13	9	10			4	14			3			5^2	8	11									4
1	2	4		6^2	7	8	9^1	10	11		12	3		5						13									5
1^9	2	12			7	8^1		10	11^2		9	13	4		5			3	15	6									6
	2		6	5		7	8	9^1	10^2	11		12		4		13			3^3	1	14								7
1	2		6	5		7	8	9	10^2	11^1		12	13	4		3													8
1			6	5				10^1	12		11	9	4	8		7	3		2										9
1	2	3	6^2	5^1	12	10				11	9	4		8		7			13										10
1	6^3	2			7	8	9^1	10^2	11	14	12	13		5		3		4											11
1	6	2	5		7	8^1	9	10^2	11		12	13			3		4												12
1	6	2	5		7	11		12		13	9^1	10^3	3	8					4^2	14									13
1	6	2	5		7	11		10^1	12		9			8			3		4										14
1^8	6		5			11^1		10		12	9	3		8		13	2	15	4	7^2									15
1	2	3	5		7	11		10	12		13	9^2	6	8^1					4										16
	2	3	5^3		7^2	12		13	11		9		6	8	14			1	4	10^1									17
1	2		5		7	10		11		9			6	8^1	12		3^2		4	13									18
1	2	3	5^1		7^2	10		11^3	12	9		6		13	8				4	14									19
1	6	12	5		7	10		11	13	9		3^1	8				2^2		4										20
1	6	2	5		7	12		11	13	9^1	10	3^2		8^3					4	14									21
1	6	2	5^1		7	8^2		11^3	12	9^1	10	3		13	14				4										22
1	4	8^3	5	6^2	7		12	10	11	9^1		3						2		13	14								23
1	4	3	5	6			12	10	11	9^1				8	7^2			2		13									24
1	2	12	5	6	7	8^3		9	10^2	11		13		14															25
1		5		6	7^3	8^1	9	13	12	14		10	3					2		4	11^2								26
	2		5	6	7	8	9		11			10	3					1	4										27
1	2		5^2	6	7	11		12		9^1	10^1	3		8					4	13									28
1	2	5		6	7	11		10^1		9^1	12			8^2		3			4	13									29
	4	3^1	5	6		11		10		9^1	13	12	8^3	7^2			2			14		1							30
1	6	2	5		7	12		10^2	11			9^1	13	8^1			3^3		4	14									31
1	6	12	5		7	9	13	11		14	10^3	3		8^2			2^1		4										32
	2		5	6	12	7	9^2		11			13	10	3		8^1			15	4					1^9				33
1	2	3	5	6	7	8^3		10	12		9		13	14					4^2	11^1									34
	3	4		6	7		12	10	13	9^1			5	11^2			1	2	14			8^3							35
1^9	3^1	4		7		9	10	12	6			13	5			2	15		11			8^1							36
	3	6					11	5^1		9			10	2	15	4	7				1^9	8	12						37
	5	6			7	9	10	11			3		8			2^1	1						4	12					38

Worthington Cup

Third Round	Watford	(a)	3-0
Fourth Round	Sunderland	(a)	1-2

FA Cup

Third Round	Fulham	(a)	2-1
Fourth Round	West Ham U	(h)	0-1

MANSFIELD TOWN
Division 3

FOUNDATION

The club was formed as Mansfield Wesleyans in 1897, and changed their name to Mansfield Wesley in 1906 and Mansfield Town in 1910. This was after the Mansfield Wesleyan Chapel trustees had requested that the club change its name as 'it has no longer had any connection with either the chapel or school'. The new club participated in the Notts and Derby District League, but in the following season 1911–12 joined the Central Alliance.

Field Mill Ground, Quarry Lane, Mansfield NG18 5DA.

Telephone: (01623) 623 482 482. *Fax:* (01623) 482 495.
Marketing: (01623) 482 482. *ClubCall:* 09068 121 311.
Football in the Community: (07977) 428 147.

Ground Capacity: 9990.

Record Attendance: 24,467 v Nottingham F, FA Cup 3rd rd, 10 January 1953.

Record Receipts: £46,915 v Sheffield W, FA Cup 3rd rd, 5 January 1991.

Pitch Measurements: 115yd × 70yd.

Chairman/Chief Executive: Keith Haslam.

Associate Directors: K. Woodcock, S. Whetton, M. Murphy.

Manager: Bill Dearden.

Physio: Barry Statham.

Community Scheme Organiser: John Gannon.

Secretary: Christine Reynolds.

Marketing Manager: Alan Prince.

Colours: Amber shirts with royal blue trim, royal blue shorts with amber trim, amber stockings with blue trim.

Change Colours: All navy.

Year Formed: 1897.

Turned Professional: 1906.

Ltd Co.: 1922.

Previous Name: 1897, Mansfield Wesleyans; 1906, Mansfield Wesley; 1910, Mansfield Town.

Club Nickname: 'The Stags'.

First Football League Game: 29 August 1931, Division 3 (S), v Swindon T (h) W 3–2 – Wilson; Clifford, England; Wake, Davis, Blackburn; Gilhespy, Readman (1), Johnson, Broom (2), Baxter.

Record League Victory: 9–2 v Rotherham U, Division 3 (N), 27 December 1932 – Wilson; Anthony, England; Davies, S. Robinson, Slack; Prior, Broom, Readman (3), Hoyland (3), Bowater (3).

HONOURS

Football League: Division 2 best season: 21st, 1977–78; Division 3 – Champions 1976–77; Division 4 – Champions 1974–75; Division 3 (N) – Runners-up 1950–51.

FA Cup: best season: 6th rd, 1969.

Football League Cup: best season: 5th rd, 1976.

Freight Rover Trophy: Winners 1987.

IT'S A FACT !

Charlie 'Pop' Anthony, right-back and penalty taker for Mansfield Town in their 1928-29 FA Cup tie with Arsenal, refused to take the spot kick in this game.
A great admirer of Arsenal manager Herbert Chapman, he named a son after him.

Record Cup Victory: 8–0 v Scarborough (a), FA Cup 1st rd, 22 November 1952 – Bramley; Chessell, Bradley; Field, Plummer, Lewis; Scott, Fox (3), Marron (2), Sid Watson (1), Adam (2).

Record Defeat: 1–8 v Walsall, Division 3 (N), 19 January 1933.

Most League Points (2 for a win): 68, Division 4, 1974–75.

Most League Points (3 for a win): 81, Division 4, 1985–86.

Most League Goals: 108, Division 4, 1962–63.

Highest League Scorer in Season: Ted Harston, 55, Division 3 (N), 1936–37.

Most League Goals in Total Aggregate: Harry Johnson, 104, 1931–36.

Most League Goals in One Match: 7, Ted Harston v Hartlepools U, Division 3N, 23 January 1937.

Most Capped Player: John McClelland, 6 (53), Northern Ireland.

Most League Appearances: Rod Arnold, 440, 1970–83.

Youngest League Player: Cyril Poole, 15 years 351 days v New Brighton, 27 February 1937.

Record Transfer Fee Received: £655,000 from Tottenham H for Colin Calderwood, July 1993.

Record Transfer Fee Paid: £150,000 to Carlisle U for Lee Peacock, October 1997.

Football League Record: 1931 Elected to Division 3 (S); 1932–37 Division 3 (N); 1937–47 Division 3 (S); 1947–58 Division 3 (N); 1958–60 Division 3; 1960–63 Division 4; 1963–72 Division 3; 1972–75 Division 4; 1975–77 Division 3; 1977–78 Division 2; 1978–80 Division 3; 1980–86 Division 4; 1986–91 Division 3; 1991–92 Division 4; 1992–93 Division 2; 1993– Division 3.

MANAGERS

John Baynes 1922–25
Ted Davison 1926–28
Jack Hickling 1928–33
Henry Martin 1933–35
Charlie Bell 1935
Harold Wightman 1936
Harold Parkes 1936–38
Jack Poole 1938–44
Lloyd Barke 1944–45
Roy Goodall 1945–49
Freddie Steele 1949–51
George Jobey 1952–53
Stan Mercer 1953–55
Charlie Mitten 1956–58
Sam Weaver 1958–60
Raich Carter 1960–63
Tommy Cummings 1963–67
Tommy Eggleston 1967–70
Jock Basford 1970–71
Danny Williams 1971–74
Dave Smith 1974–76
Peter Morris 1976–78
Billy Bingham 1978–79
Mick Jones 1979–81
Stuart Boam 1981–83
Ian Greaves 1983–89
George Foster 1989–93
Andy King 1993–96
Steve Parkin 1996–99
Bill Dearden July 1999–

LATEST SEQUENCES

Longest Sequence of League Wins: 7, 13.9.91 – 26.10.91.

Longest Sequence of League Defeats: 7, 18.1.47 – 15.3.47.

Longest Sequence of League Draws: 5, 18.10.86 – 22.11.86.

Longest Sequence of Unbeaten League Matches: 20, 14.2.76 – 21.8.76.

Longest Sequence Without a League Win: 14, 25.3.00 – 2.9.00.

TEN YEAR LEAGUE RECORD

		P	W	D	L	F	A	Pts	Pos
1990-91	Div 3	46	8	14	24	42	63	38	24
1991-92	Div 4	42	23	8	11	75	53	77	3
1992-93	Div 2	46	11	11	24	52	80	44	22
1993-94	Div 3	42	15	10	17	53	62	55	12
1994-95	Div 3	42	18	11	13	84	59	65	6
1995-96	Div 3	46	11	20	15	54	64	53	19
1996-97	Div 3	46	16	16	14	47	45	64	11
1997-98	Div 3	46	16	17	13	64	55	65	12
1998-99	Div 3	46	19	10	17	60	58	67	8
1999-2000	Div 3	46	16	8	22	50	65	56	17

DID YOU KNOW ?

Joe Eaton, a promising inside-forward with Mansfield Town, had his career cut short with injury in 1954, but served the club until 1993 as secretary. He was born on the Duke of Portland's Welbeck Estate, where his father was employed.

MANSFIELD TOWN 2000–01 LEAGUE RECORD

Match No.	Date	Venue	Opponents	Result	H/T Score	Lg. Pos.	Goalscorers	Attendance
1	Aug 12	A	Cheltenham T	D	2-2	1-1	—	Greenacre [21], Blake [84]	4051
2	19	A	Barnet	D	3-3	1-3	12	Blake [5], Clarke [64], Greenacre [75]	1732
3	26	A	Plymouth Arg	L	0-2	0-0	20		4069
4	28	H	Macclesfield T	D	4-4	2-2	18	Blake [22], Clarke 2 [45, 64], Bradley [54]	3360
5	Sept 2	H	Exeter C	D	0-0	0-0	19		2737
6	9	H	Halifax T	W	5-1	2-1	14	Blake [5], Greenacre 3 [16, 72, 88], Williams [84]	2397
7	12	H	Hull C	D	1-1	0-0	—	Clarke [73]	2629
8	16	A	Chesterfield	L	0-4	0-2	17		6793
9	23	A	Hartlepool U	W	4-3	1-1	13	Greenacre 2 [21, 84], Boulding [82], Corden [86]	2135
10	30	A	Lincoln C	W	2-0	0-0	11	Boulding [64], Clarke [83]	3494
11	Oct 6	A	York C	L	1-2	1-1	—	Boulding [2]	2681
12	14	H	Shrewsbury T	W	1-0	1-0	10	Boulding [45]	2206
13	17	H	Blackpool	L	0-1	0-0	—		2328
14	21	A	Cardiff C	L	0-2	0-0	14		4625
15	24	A	Torquay U	D	2-2	1-0	—	Bacon [14], Greenacre [46]	1880
16	28	H	Southend U	D	1-1	1-1	16	Greenacre [7]	2200
17	Nov 4	A	Leyton Orient	L	1-2	0-1	17	Clarke [72]	4165
18	11	H	Rochdale	W	1-0	0-0	13	Greenacre [88]	2543
19	25	A	Scunthorpe U	L	0-6	0-3	15		3258
20	Dec 2	A	Darlington	L	1-2	1-1	17	Pemberton [6]	3087
21	16	H	Brighton & HA	W	2-0	0-0	15	Greenacre 2 [61, 89]	2668
22	22	A	Carlisle U	D	1-1	1-1	—	Barrett [16]	2247
23	26	A	Kidderminster H	L	0-1	0-1	16		3842
24	Jan 6	H	Plymouth Arg	D	0-0	0-0	15		2321
25	14	A	Macclesfield T	W	1-0	1-0	14	Blake [34]	1893
26	23	H	Kidderminster H	W	2-1	1-1	—	Greenacre [32], Boulding [69]	1712
27	27	A	Carlisle U	L	1-2	1-2	15	Bradley [26]	3375
28	Feb 2	H	Exeter C	D	1-1	0-1	—	Corden [50]	3830
29	10	A	Halifax T	W	4-3	2-3	12	Williams [17], Greenacre 2 [39, 75], Clarke C (og) [90]	1857
30	13	H	Cheltenham T	W	2-1	2-0	—	Blake [5], Book (og) [26]	1940
31	17	H	Chesterfield	L	0-1	0-1	11		7899
32	20	A	Hull C	L	1-2	1-1	—	Corden [34]	7248
33	24	A	Hartlepool U	D	1-1	0-0	13	Blake [54]	3699
34	27	A	Barnet	W	4-1	2-0	—	Bradley 2 [6, 37], Greenacre [88], Williams [90]	1623
35	Mar 3	H	Lincoln C	L	2-3	0-1	11	Bradley [75], Blake [77]	3201
36	6	A	Shrewsbury T	L	1-2	0-1	—	Williams [85]	2219
37	10	H	York C	L	1-3	1-0	14	Lawrence [25]	2405
38	17	A	Blackpool	D	2-2	1-1	14	Greenacre 2 (1 pen) [3 (p), 47]	5241
39	31	A	Brighton & HA	L	0-2	0-1	15		6703
40	Apr 14	H	Torquay U	D	0-0	0-0	16		2225
41	21	H	Leyton Orient	W	2-0	0-0	16	Lawrence [78], Bradley [90]	3356
42	24	H	Cardiff C	W	2-1	1-0	—	Bradley [6], Greenacre (pen) [82]	2204
43	28	A	Rochdale	L	0-1	0-1	15		3114
44	May 1	H	Darlington	W	3-2	2-1	—	Brightwell (og) [23], Hassell [35], Lawrence [46]	1878
45	5	H	Scunthorpe U	W	1-0	0-0	12	Boulding [87]	2938
46	8	A	Southend U	L	1-3	1-0	—	Lawrence [28]	3345

Final League Position: 13

GOALSCORERS

League (64): Greenacre 19 (2 pens), Blake 8, Bradley 7, Boulding 6, Clarke 6, Lawrence 4, Williams 4, Corden 3, Bacon 1, Barrett 1, Hassell 1, Pemberton 1, own goals 3.
Worthington Cup (4): Corden 2, Clarke 1, Greenacre 1.
FA Cup (1): Greenacre 1 (pen).

Bowling I 4	Asher A 23 + 5	Andrews J 5 + 3	Pemberton M 16 + 2	Hicks S 25	Robinson L 44	Corden W 31 + 3	Clarke D 30 + 2	Williams L 36 + 5	Blake M 38 + 3	Greenacre C 46	Lomas J 4 + 2	Boulding M 12 + 21	Bacon D 7 + 15	Sisson M 2 + 2	Bradley S 21 + 5	Mimms B 40	Fortune J 14	Hassell B 39 + 1	Williamson L 10 + 5	Jarvis D 17 + 5	Disley C 16 + 8	Barrett A 8	Lawrence L 7 + 11	Reddington S 9	White A — + 4	Pilkington K 2	Match No.
1	2	3	4	5	6	7	8^1	9	10	11^3	12	13															1
1	2^1	3	4	5	6	7	8	9	10^3	11		12^2	13	14													2
1	2	3		5	6	7^1	8	4^3	10	11			13	12	9												3
1	12	3		5	6	7	8^1	2	10	11^3	14		13	4	9^2												4
				5	6	7	8		10	11	3		12	4^2	9^1	1	2	13									5
				5^1	6	7		3^3	10	11	8	12	9^1		1	2	4	14	13								6
				5	6	7	12	8	10^1	11	3	13	9^2		1	2	4										7
				5	6	7	8	9	10	11	3^2		12	13	1	2	4										8
	3^3	12		5^1	6	7	8	9^2	10	11	13	4			1	2	14										9
	12			5	6	7^3	8	3	10	11	9^2	13		1	2	4	14										10
				5	6	7^2	8	3^1	10	11	9	12		1	2	4	13										11
				5	6	7	8	3	10	11	9			1	2	4											12
				5	6	7	8	3^1	10	11	9	12		1	2	4											13
				5	6	7^1	8	9	10	11	12			1	2^2	4	3	13									14
	12			5^1	6		8	9	10	11	7			1	2	4	3										15
					6	7	8	5	10	11	12	9^1		1	2	4	3										16
		12			6	7	8	5	10^2	11	13	9		1	2	4	3^1										17
	12			5^1	6	7	8		10^2	11	9	13		1	2	4	14	3^3									18
12	2^2	14		5	6	7		8	10	11^1		9^2			13	1		4	3								19
	2			5	6			12	10	11		9^2			13	1		4	8^1	3			7				20
	2	5			6		8^2		10	11		12				1		4		13			7				21
	2	5			6		8		10	11		12	9^1			1		4					7				22
	2^1	5		6	12		8		10^2	11		9^3	14			1		4		13			7				23
	2^2	5		6	7^1		3		10	11		9	12			1		4		13	8						24
	2	5		6	8		3		10	11^1		9	12			1		4					7				25
12				5	6	2	8	3^3	10	11		13	9^2			1		4	14				7^1				26
2	3			6	7^2	8	5		10	11		12				1		4		13							27
12	2	5^1		6	7	8^3	3		10	11		13	9^2			1		4	14								28
2				5	6	7^1		3	10	11		9				1		4	12	8^2			13				29
2	3				6	7^1	5^3		10^2	11	12	9				1		4		13	8		14				30
2^1	3				6	7	12	5^1	10	11		13	9^2			1		4			8		14				31
2	3				6	7	8^2	5^1	10	11		12	9^1			1		4		13			14				32
2	3				6	7		5	10	11		12	9^1			1		4			8						33
2	3				6	7		5^1	10	11		12	9^1			1		4			8		13				34
2^2					6	7^2		5	10	11		12	9			1		3	13		8^1	14					35
2				5^2	6	7^3		4	10	11		12	9^1			1		13	3		8	14					36
2					6	7^1		5^2	10	11		9	12			1		4	13	3	8						37
2					6		10			11						1		4	5	3	8		9	7			38
2					5	12	10	13		11					14			4^2	7	3^1	8		9^3	6			39
					6	12	10	5^1		11		9^2			13	1		4	7	3	8		2	3			40
	2^1				5		10			11		9				1		4	7	3	8		12	6			41
	2				5		10		12	11		9^3				1		4	7	3^2	8^1		13	6	14		42
	2				5		10		12	11		13	9			1		4	7^2	3^2	8		14	6			43
	2				5^1				12	13	11		9^3					4	10	3	8^2		7	6	14	1	44
	2^1								12	10	11^2	13	9^3					4	5	3	8		7	6	14	1	45
	2								12	10	11	13	9^2			1		4	5^1	3^2	8		7	6	14		46

Worthington Cup

First Round	Wrexham	(h)	0-1	
		(a)	3-0	
Second Round	Southampton	(a)	0-2	
		(h)	1-3	

FA Cup

First Round	Peterborough U	(h)	1-1
		(a)	0-4

MIDDLESBROUGH   FA Premiership

FOUNDATION

A previous belief that Middlesbrough Football Club was founded at a tripe supper at the Corporation Hotel has proved to be erroneous. In fact, members of Middlesbrough Cricket Club were responsible for forming it at a meeting in the gymnasium of the Albert Park Hotel in 1875.

BT Cellnet Riverside Stadium, Middlesbrough, TS3 6RS.

Telephone: (01642) 877 700. *Fax:* (01642) 877 840.
Website: www.mfc.co.uk *ClubCall:* 09068 121 181.
Ticket Office: (01642) 877 745.
Ticket Information Line: (01642) 877 809.
Club Tours: (01642) 877 730.
Stadium Store: (01642) 877 720.
Town Centre Store: (01642) 877 849.
Mail Order: (01642) 866 642.
Lottery Office: (01642) 877 790.

Ground Capacity: 35,049.

Record Attendance: Ayresome Park: 53,536 v Newcastle U, Division 1, 27 December 1949.
BT Cellnet Riverside Stadium: 34,800 v Leeds U, FA Premier League, 26 February 2000.

Record Receipts: £486,229 v Newcastle U, FA Premier League, 6 December 1998.

Pitch measurements: 105m × 68m.

Chairman: Steve Gibson. *Chief Executive:* Keith Lamb.
Secretary: Karen Nelson.

Manager: Steve McClaren. *First Team Coach:* Steve Harrison.
Reserve Team Coach: Steve Round. *Physio:* Bob Ward.
Youth Academy Director: David Parnaby *Chief Scout:* Ray Train.

Commercial Manager: Graham Fordy. *Communication Manager:* Dave Allan.
Stadium Manager: Terry Tasker. *Head of Finance & Administration:* Alan Barge.

Colours: Red and white.

Change Colours: Black and blue stripes.

Year Formed: 1876; re-formed 1986.

Turned Professional: 1889; became amateur 1892, and professional again, 1899.

Ltd Co: 1892. *Club Nickname:* 'Boro'.

Previous Grounds: 1877, Old Archery Ground, Albert Park; 1879, Breckon Hill; 1882, Linthorpe Road Ground; 1903, Ayresome Park; 1995, Cellnet Riverside Stadium.

First Football League Game: 2 September 1899, Division 2, v Lincoln C (a) L 0–3 – Smith; Shaw, Ramsey; Allport, McNally, McCracken; Wanless, Longstaffe, Gettins, Page, Pugh.

Record League Victory: 9–0 v Brighton & HA, Division 2, 23 August 1958 – Taylor; Bilcliff, Robinson; Harris (2p), Phillips, Walley; Day, McLean, Clough (5), Peacock (2), Holliday.

HONOURS

Football League: Division 1 – Champions 1994–95; Runners-up 1997–98; Division 2 – Champions 1926–27, 1928–29, 1973–74; Runners-up 1901–02, 1991–92; Division 3 – Runners-up 1966–67, 1986–87.

FA Cup: Runners-up 1997.

Football League Cup: Runners-up 1997, 1998.

Amateur Cup: Winners 1895, 1898.

Anglo-Scottish Cup: Winners 1976.

Zenith Data Systems Cup: Runners-up 1990.

IT'S A FACT !

On 14 April 2001, Middlesbrough won 3–0 at Arsenal. It was their first success on this ground since All-Fools Day 1939 when goals by Wilf Mannion and George Camsell gave them a 2–1 victory.

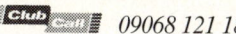
Record Cup Victory: 7–0 v Hereford U, Coca-Cola Cup
2nd rd, 1st leg, 18 September 1996 – Miller; Fleming (1),
Branco (1), Whyte, Vickers, Whelan, Emerson (1), Mustoe,
Stamp, Juninho, Ravanelli (4).

Record Defeat: 0–9 v Blackburn R, Division 2, 6 November
1954.

Most League Points (2 for a win): 65, Division 2, 1973–74.

Most League Points (3 for a win): 94, Division 3, 1986–87.

Most League Goals: 122, Division 2, 1926–27.

Highest League Scorer in Season: George Camsell, 59,
Division 2, 1926–27 (Second Division record).

Most League Goals in Total Aggregate: George Camsell,
325, 1925–39.

Most League Goals in One Match: 5, Andy Wilson v
Nottingham F, Division 1, 6 October 1923; 5, George
Camsell v Manchester C, Division 2, 25 December 1926;
5, George Camsell v Aston Villa, Division 1, 9 September
1935; 5, Brian Clough v Brighton & HA, Division 2, 22
August 1958.

Most Capped Player: Wilf Mannion, 26, England.

Most League Appearances: Tim Williamson, 563, 1902–23.

Youngest League Player: Stephen Bell, 16 years 323 days v
Southampton, 30 January 1982; Sam Lawrie, 16 years
323 days v Arsenal, 3 November 1951.

Record Transfer Fee Received: £12,000,000 from
Atletico Madrid for Juninho, July 1997.

Record Transfer Fee Paid: £8,000,000 to Aston Villa for Ugo Ehiogu, October 2000.

Football League Record: 1899 Elected to Division 2; 1902–24 Division 1; 1924–27 Division 2;
1927–28 Division 1; 1928–29 Division 2; 1929–54 Division 1; 1954–66 Division 2; 1966–67 Division 3;
1967–74 Division 2; 1974–82 Division 1; 1982–86 Division 2; 1986–87 Division 3; 1987–88 Division 2;
1988–89 Division 1; 1989–92 Division 2; 1992–93 FA Premier League; 1993–95 Division 1;
1995–97 FA Premier League; 1997–98 Division 1; 1998– FA Premier League.

MANAGERS

John Robson 1899–1905
Alex Mackie 1905–06
Andy Aitken 1906–09
J. Gunter 1908–10
  (Secretary-Manager)
Andy Walker 1910–11
Tom McIntosh 1911–19
Jimmy Howie 1920–23
Herbert Bamlett 1923–26
Peter McWilliam 1927–34
Wilf Gillow 1934–44
David Jack 1944–52
Walter Rowley 1952–54
Bob Dennison 1954–63
Raich Carter 1963–66
Stan Anderson 1966–73
Jack Charlton 1973–77
John Neal 1977–81
Bobby Murdoch 1981–82
Malcolm Allison 1982–84
Willie Maddren 1984–86
Bruce Rioch 1986–90
Colin Todd 1990–91
Lennie Lawrence 1991–94
Bryan Robson 1994–2001
Steve McClaren July 2001–

LATEST SEQUENCES

Longest Sequence of League Wins: 9, 16.2.74 – 6.4.74.
Longest Sequence of League Defeats: 8, 26.12.95 – 17.2.96.
Longest Sequence of League Draws: 8, 3.4.71 – 1.5.71.
Longest Sequence of Unbeaten League Matches: 24, 8.9.73 – 19.1.74.
Longest Sequence Without a League Win: 19, 3.10.81 – 6.3.82.

TEN YEAR LEAGUE RECORD

		P	W	D	L	F	A	Pts	Pos
1990-91	Div 2	46	20	9	17	66	47	69	7
1991-92	Div 2	46	23	11	12	58	41	80	2
1992-93	PR Lge	42	11	11	20	54	75	44	21
1993-94	Div 1	46	18	13	15	66	54	67	9
1994-95	Div 1	46	23	13	10	67	40	82	1
1995-96	PR Lge	38	11	10	17	35	50	43	12
1996-97	PR Lge	38	10	12	16	51	60	39	19
1997-98	Div 1	46	27	10	9	77	41	91	2
1998-99	PR Lge	38	12	15	11	48	54	51	9
1999-2000	PR Lge	38	14	10	14	46	52	52	12

DID YOU KNOW ?

On 18 November 1933
Middlesbrough beat Sheffield
United 10–3. It was the
highest score in a First
Division match since United
had beaten Cardiff City 11–2
seven years earlier.

MIDDLESBROUGH 2000–01 LEAGUE RECORD

Match No.	Date	Venue	Opponents	Result	H/T Score	Lg. Pos.	Goalscorers	Attendance
1	Aug 19	A	Coventry C	W 3-1	1-1	—	Job [20], Boksic 2 [59, 62]	20,623
2	22	H	Tottenham H	D 1-1	0-1	—	Summerbell [59]	31,254
3	26	H	Leeds U	L 1-2	0-2	8	Stamp [82]	31,626
4	Sept 6	A	Derby Co	D 3-3	1-0	—	Boksic (pen) [12], Job [51], Deane [59]	24,290
5	9	H	Everton	L 1-2	1-0	12	Watson (og) [7]	30,885
6	17	A	Manchester C	D 1-1	0-0	15	Festa [55]	32,053
7	23	H	Aston Villa	D 1-1	0-0	15	Alpay (og) [89]	27,556
8	30	A	Southampton	W 3-1	2-0	11	Boksic 2 [17, 82], Festa [32]	14,903
9	Oct 16	H	Newcastle U	L 1-3	0-1	—	Deane [90]	31,436
10	21	A	Charlton Ath	L 0-1	0-0	16		20,043
11	28	A	Ipswich T	L 1-2	0-2	17	Whelan [68]	21,767
12	Nov 4	H	Arsenal	L 0-1	0-1	18		29,541
13	11	H	Manchester U	L 1-2	1-0	18	Karembeu [32]	67,576
14	18	A	Leicester C	L 0-3	0-2	18		27,965
15	25	H	Bradford C	D 2-2	0-2	18	Ehiogu [48], Ince [89]	28,525
16	Dec 2	A	West Ham U	L 0-1	0-1	19		25,459
17	9	A	Sunderland	L 0-1	0-0	20		46,620
18	16	H	Chelsea	W 1-0	0-0	19	Gordon [71]	29,420
19	23	A	Tottenham H	D 0-0	0-0	19		35,638
20	26	H	Liverpool	W 1-0	1-0	19	Karembeu [41]	34,696
21	30	H	Coventry C	D 1-1	0-1	18	Boksic [86]	30,499
22	Jan 1	A	Leeds U	D 1-1	1-0	18	Boksic [27]	39,251
23	13	A	Derby Co	W 4-0	1-0	15	Boksic 2 (1 pen) [43 (p), 81], Ehiogu [60], Ricard (pen) [90]	29,041
24	20	A	Liverpool	D 0-0	0-0	16		43,042
25	31	A	Everton	D 2-2	1-0	—	Ricard [11], Cooper [63]	34,244
26	Feb 3	H	Manchester C	D 1-1	0-1	17	Cooper [62]	31,792
27	10	A	Aston Villa	D 1-1	0-1	17	Ehiogu [49]	28,912
28	24	H	Southampton	L 0-1	0-0	17		28,622
29	Mar 3	H	Charlton Ath	D 0-0	0-0	17		28,177
30	17	A	Newcastle U	W 2-1	2-0	17	Boksic 2 [28, 33]	51,751
31	31	H	Chelsea	L 1-2	0-1	17	Windass [54]	34,933
32	Apr 9	H	Sunderland	D 0-0	0-0	—		31,099
33	14	A	Arsenal	W 3-0	2-0	16	Edu (og) [34], Silvinho (og) [38], Ricard [58]	37,879
34	16	H	Ipswich T	L 1-2	1-0	17	Windass [39]	34,263
35	21	A	Leicester C	W 3-0	1-0	15	Ricard [12], Boksic [50], Ince [52]	18,162
36	28	H	Manchester U	L 0-2	0-1	16		34,417
37	May 5	A	Bradford C	D 1-1	0-1	17	Karembeu [81]	20,921
38	19	H	West Ham U	W 2-1	2-1	14	Job [21], Karembeu [45]	33,057

Final League Position: 14

GOALSCORERS

League (44): Boksic 12 (2 pens), Karembeu 4, Ricard 4 (1 pen), Ehiogu 3, Job 3, Cooper 2, Deane 2, Festa 2, Ince 2, Windass 2, Gordon 1, Stamp 1, Summerbell 1, Whelan 1, own goals 4.
Worthington Cup (5): Ricard 3, Summerbell 1, Whelan 1.
FA Cup (2): Ricard 2.

Schwarzer M 31	Fleming C 29 + 1	O'Neill K 14 + 1	Vickers S 29 + 1	Cooper C 26 + 1	Pallister G 8	Karembeu C 31 + 2	Job J 8 + 4	Boksic A 26 + 2	Deane B 13 + 12	Ince P 30	Gavin J 10 + 4	Okon P 23 + 1	Whelan N 13 + 14	Summerbell M 5 + 2	Ricard H 22 + 5	Campbell A 5 + 2	Stamp P 11 + 8	Festa G 21 + 4	Gordon D 12 + 8	Walsh G 3	Marinelli C 2 + 11	Mustoe R 13 + 12	Crossley M 4 + 1	Ehiogu U 21	Beresford M — + 1	Hudson M — + 3	Windass D 8	Match No.
1	2	3	4	5	6¹	7	8²	9¹	10	11	12	13	14															1
1	2	3	4		6	7	8¹		10			5	12	11	9²	13												2
1	2	3¹	4	5	6	7	12		10	11		8¹	13		9²	14												3
1		3		5	6³	7	8¹	9³	10	11	14				13	12		4	2									4
1	2		4³			7	8²	9	12	11¹	14		10		13		6	5	3									5
	2	3		6			8²		10	11	5		12		13	9¹		4		1		7						6
	2	3		6			8¹	9		11			12	7			4²	5		1	13	10						7
	2	3	4	6		7¹		9		11			13	12	8²			5	1⁰		10	15						8
	2¹			5	6	7		9	14	11		8			12²	4	3		13	10³	1							9
	2			5	6	7²			10	11			13		8³	9		12	3		14		1	4¹				10
	2		4	6		7	12		10³			13	11		9²	8¹		5	3		14		1					11
	2		4	3	6				10				8	11	9⁰	7¹	5	12			1		15					12
1	2		4	3²	6	7		12	10				11		8³	9¹	5		13		14							13
1	2		4			7	8³	9	10				11		6²	12	3		14	13		5						14
1	2			3			12	9²	13	11			10¹		6	4			7		8	5						15
1		3		4	6¹		12	13	10²	11			9		7	2			8			5						16
1	3	7	4	6		12			10	11			9		2¹				8			5						17
1		3	4	6		7			10	11		8¹	9				5	12			2							18
1	12	3²	4	2		7		9³	14	11		6	10¹				13		8			5						19
1	2	3		6		7²		9	12	11		8	10		4							5		13				20
1	2	3	12	6¹		7²			13	14	11	8	10³	9			4					5						21
1	2		4			7³		9	12			8	13		10²	14	6	3				11		5				22
1	2	3²	4			7		9	12	11		8²			10		6	14				13		5				23
1	2		4	12		7²		9		11		8³	10				13	6¹	3			14		5				24
1	2		4	6		7³		9		11		8	12		10¹			13	3²			14		5				25
1	2	3	4	6		7		9³		11		8³	12		10¹	13						14		5				26
1	2	3²		6		7³		9	12	11		8			10		14	4	13					5				27
1	3¹		4²			7		9		11	13	8			10³			2	12		14	6		5				28
1	2		4			7		9		11	6	8²			12			10¹				5	3²				14	29
1	2		4	3		7²		9¹		11		8	10		12		6	5				13						30
1	12		4	2¹		7²		9			3	8	10		13			5			14	6					11³	31
1	3²		4			7		9	13		2	8	10¹		12			5²	14			6					11	32
1			4			7		9¹	11	2		6	10²		13	3		3			12		5				8	33
1			4¹			7²		9	11	2		6	10		13		3	14	12		5						8³	34
1			6			7¹		9²	11	2		4	13		10³	14		3				12	5				8	35
1			4	3¹				9	11	2		8	10²		6³		12				14	13	5				7	36
1			4	3		7		9²	12	11		2³	6		10²			14	13				5				8	37
1			4	3		7³	10		12	11		2	6					9¹				5			13		8	38

Worthington Cup

Second Round	Macclesfield T	(h)	2-1
		(a)	3-1
Third Round	Wimbledon	(a)	0-1

FA Cup

Third Round	Bradford C	(a)	1-0
Fourth Round	Wimbledon	(h)	0-0
		(a)	1-3

MILLWALL

Division 1

FOUNDATION

Formed in 1885 as Millwall Rovers by employees of Morton & Co,
a jam and marmalade factory in West Ferry Road. The founders
were predominantly Scotsmen. Their first headquarters was The
Islanders pub in Tooke Street, Millwall. Their first trophy was the
East End Cup in 1887.

Millwall Football & Athletic Company (1985) plc,
The Den, Zampa Road, Bermondsey SE16 3LN.

Telephone: (020) 7232 1222. *Fax:* (020) 7231 3663.
Ticket Office: (020) 7231 9999. *ClubCall:* 09068 400 300.
Club Shop: (020) 7231 9845.

Ground Capacity: 20,146 (all-seater).

Record Attendance: 20,093 v Arsenal, FA Cup 3rd rd,
10 January 1994.

Record Receipts: undisclosed.

Pitch Measurements: 100m × 68m.

Life President: Reg Burr. *Chairman:* Theo Paphitis.
Directors: Reg Burr, Peter Mead, Doug Woodward,
David Sullivan. *Secretary:* Yvonne Haines.

Manager: Mark McGhee. *Assistant Manager:* Steve Gritt.
Physio: Gerry Docherty.

Youth Development Officer & Senior Scout: Bob Pearson.
Assistant Youth Development Officer: Dave Mehmet.
Hon. Medical Officer: Dr. Des Thompson.

Stadium Manager: Colin Sayer.
Sales and Promotions Manager: Mark Cole.

Colours: All blue.

Change Colours: All white.

Year Formed: 1885. *Turned Professional:* 1893. *Ltd Co.:* 1894.

Previous Names: 1885, Millwall Rovers; 1889, Millwall Athletic; 1985, Millwall Football & Athletic
Company.

Club Nickname: 'The Lions'.

Previous Grounds: 1885, Glengall Road, Millwall; 1886, Back of 'Lord Nelson'; 1890, East Ferry Road;
1901, North Greenwich; 1910, The Den, Cold Blow Lane; 1993, The Den, Bermondsey.

First Football League Game: 28 August 1920, Division 3, v Bristol R (h) W 2–0 – Lansdale; Fort,
Hodge; Voisey (1), Riddell, McAlpine; Waterall, Travers, Broad (1), Sutherland, Dempsey.

Record League Victory: 9–1 v Torquay U, Division 3 (S), 29 August 1927 – Lansdale; Tilling, Hill;
Amos, Bryant (3), Graham; Chance, Hawkins (3), Landells (1), Phillips (2), Black. 9–1 v Coventry C,
Division 3 (S), 19 November 1927 – Lansdale; Fort, Hill; Amos, Collins (1), Graham; Chance,
Landells (4), Cock (2), Phillips (2), Black.

HONOURS

Football League: Division 1 best
season: 3rd, 1993–94; Division 2 –
Champions 1987–88, 2000–01;
Division 3 (S) – Champions 1927–28,
1937–38; Runners-up 1952–53;
Division 3 – Runners–up 1965–66,
1984–85; Division 4 – Champions
1961–62; Runners-up 1964–65.

FA Cup: Semi-final 1900, 1903, 1937
(first Division 3 side to reach
semi-final).

Football League Cup: best season:
5th rd, 1974, 1977, 1995.

Football League Trophy: Winners
1983.

Auto Windscreens Shield: Runners-up
1999.

IT'S A FACT !

Despite winning the 1937-38 Division Three (South)
championship, Millwall's three leading scorers: Dave
Mangnall (16 goals), Syd Rawlings (14) and John Walsh
(11) missed a total of 57 matches between them!

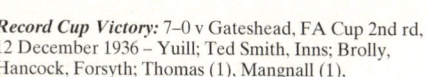
Record Cup Victory: 7–0 v Gateshead, FA Cup 2nd rd, 12 December 1936 – Yuill; Ted Smith, Inns; Brolly, Hancock, Forsyth; Thomas (1), Mangnall (1), Ken Burditt (2), McCartney (2), Thorogood (1).

Record Defeat: 1–9 v Aston Villa, FA Cup 4th rd, 28 January 1946.

Most League Points (2 for a win): 65, Division 3 (S), 1927–28 and Division 3, 1965–66.

Most League Points (3 for a win): 93, Division 2, 2000–01.

Most League Goals: 127, Division 3 (S), 1927–28.

Highest League Scorer in Season: Richard Parker, 37, Division 3 (S), 1926–27.

Most League Goals in Total Aggregate: Teddy Sheringham, 93, 1984–91.

Most League Goals in One Match: 5, Richard Parker v Norwich C, Division 3S, 28 August 1926.

Most Capped Player: Eamonn Dunphy, 22 (23), Republic of Ireland.

Most League Appearances: Barry Kitchener, 523, 1967–82.

Youngest League Player: David Mehmet, 16 years 163 days v Burnley, 14 May 1977.

Record Transfer Fee Received: £2,300,000 from Liverpool for Mark Kennedy, March 1995.

Record Transfer Fee Paid: £800,000 to Derby Co for Paul Goddard, December 1989.

Football League Record: 1920 Original Members of Division 3; 1921 Division 3 (S); 1928–34 Division 2; 1934–38 Division 3 (S); 1938–48 Division 2; 1948–58 Division 3 (S); 1958–62 Division 4; 1962–64 Division 3; 1964–65 Division 4; 1965–66 Division 3; 1966–75 Division 2; 1975–76 Division 3; 1976–79 Division 2; 1979–85 Division 3; 1985–88 Division 2; 1988–90 Division 1; 1990–92 Division 2; 1992–96 Division 1; 1996–2001 Division 2; 2001– Division 1.

MANAGERS

F. B. Kidd 1894–99
  (Hon. Treasurer/Manager)
E. R. Stopher 1899–1900
  (Hon. Treasurer/Manager)
George Saunders 1900–11
  (Hon. Treasurer/Manager)
Herbert Lipsham 1911–19
Robert Hunter 1919–33
Bill McCracken 1933–36
Charlie Hewitt 1936–40
Bill Voisey 1940–44
Jack Cock 1944–48
Charlie Hewitt 1948–56
Ron Gray 1956–57
Jimmy Seed 1958–59
Reg Smith 1959–61
Ron Gray 1961–63
Billy Gray 1963–66
Benny Fenton 1966–74
Gordon Jago 1974–77
George Petchey 1978–80
Peter Anderson 1980–82
George Graham 1982–86
John Docherty 1986–90
Bob Pearson 1990
Bruce Rioch 1990–92
Mick McCarthy 1992–96
Jimmy Nicholl 1996–97
John Docherty 1997
Billy Bonds 1997–98
Keith Stevens May 1998–2000
  (then Joint Manager)
(plus Alan McLeary 1999–2000)
Mark McGhee September 2000–

LATEST SEQUENCES

Longest Sequence of League Wins: 10, 10.3.28 – 25.4.28.

Longest Sequence of League Defeats: 11, 10.4.29 – 16.9.29.

Longest Sequence of League Draws: 5, 22.12.73 – 12.1.74.

Longest Sequence of Unbeaten League Matches: 19, 22.8.59 – 31.10.59.

Longest Sequence Without a League Win: 20, 26.12.89 – 5.5.90.

TEN YEAR LEAGUE RECORD

		P	W	D	L	F	A	Pts	Pos
1990-91	Div 2	46	20	13	13	70	51	73	5
1991-92	Div 2	46	17	10	19	64	71	61	15
1992-93	Div 1	46	18	16	12	65	53	70	7
1993-94	Div 1	46	19	17	10	58	49	74	3
1994-95	Div 1	46	16	14	16	60	60	62	12
1995-96	Div 1	46	13	13	20	43	63	52	22
1996-97	Div 2	46	16	13	17	50	55	61	14
1997-98	Div 2	46	14	13	19	43	54	55	18
1998-99	Div 2	46	17	11	18	52	59	62	10
1999-2000	Div 2	46	23	13	10	76	50	82	5

DID YOU KNOW ❓

On 28 April 1904, Millwall defeated the then Woolwich Arsenal 2-1 in the final of the Southern Professional Charity Cup, having beaten Tottenham Hotspur and Southampton on the way.

MILLWALL 2000–01 LEAGUE RECORD

Match No.	Date	Venue	Opponents	Result	H/T Score	Lg. Pos.	Goalscorers	Attendance
1	Aug 12	H	Reading	W 2-0	1-0	—	Cahill 2 [5, 50]	11,043
2	19	A	Notts Co	W 4-3	3-1	1	Moody [16], Reid [38], Harris [39], Bircham [90]	6046
3	26	H	Wycombe W	L 1-2	1-0	5	Harris [10]	10,139
4	Sept 9	H	Swansea C	W 1-0	0-0	8	Harris [89]	9550
5	12	H	Northampton T	L 0-1	0-0	—		7064
6	16	A	Brentford	D 1-1	0-0	13	Harris [80]	5495
7	23	H	Oxford U	W 5-0	3-0	9	Parkin 2 [2, 63], Harris 3 [36, 40, 66]	8565
8	30	A	Peterborough U	W 4-1	1-0	7	Dolan [23], Neill [64], Parkin [79], Cahill [89]	7126
9	Oct 8	A	Luton T	W 1-0	0-0	5	McGowan (og) [83]	5345
10	14	H	Bury	W 4-0	2-0	4	Harris 2 [28, 83], Neill [41], Livermore [77]	10,203
11	17	H	Bristol C	D 1-1	1-0	—	Parkin [3]	9694
12	21	A	Stoke C	L 2-3	2-2	6	Harris 2 [1, 44]	13,758
13	24	A	Swindon T	W 2-0	1-0	—	Sadlier 2 [43, 76]	5030
14	28	H	Cambridge U	W 3-1	3-1	5	Sadlier 2 [13, 21], Harris [33]	10,104
15	Nov 4	A	Port Vale	D 1-1	0-0	5	Livermore [66]	4559
16	7	A	Wigan Ath	L 0-1	0-0	—		5822
17	11	H	Wrexham	W 1-0	0-0	4	Moody [56]	9607
18	22	A	Bristol R	W 2-1	1-0	—	Harris [5], Reid [74]	5502
19	25	A	Oldham Ath	W 1-0	0-0	1	Cahill [79]	4779
20	Dec 2	A	Rotherham U	L 2-3	0-0	3	Reid 2 [55, 62]	7155
21	16	H	Walsall	W 2-0	1-0	1	Bircham [6], Reid [47]	11,737
22	23	A	Bournemouth	W 2-1	1-0	1	Kinet [41], Harris [70]	6843
23	26	H	Colchester U	W 6-1	2-0	1	Harris 3 (1 pen) [18, 76, 90 (p)], Moody 2 [26, 62], Ifill [88]	11,156
24	30	H	Notts Co	L 2-3	2-2	1	Ifill [17], Moody [38]	11,495
25	Jan 6	A	Reading	W 4-3	3-0	1	Harris 3 (1 pen) [17, 22, 50 (p)], Newman (og) [29]	14,743
26	13	H	Wigan Ath	W 3-1	2-0	1	Moody 3 [13, 26, 61]	15,317
27	27	H	Bournemouth	L 0-1	0-1	2		12,713
28	Feb 3	H	Bristol R	W 3-0	1-0	1	Cahill [31], Moody [60], Harris (pen) [89]	10,828
29	6	A	Colchester U	W 1-0	1-0	—	Ifill [21]	4523
30	11	A	Swansea C	D 0-0	0-0	1		6905
31	16	H	Brentford	W 1-0	1-0	—	Cahill [18]	10,233
32	20	A	Northampton T	D 3-3	1-0	—	Moody [13], Harris [54], Kinet [87]	5026
33	24	A	Oxford U	W 2-0	2-0	1	Moody [12], Livermore [45]	5795
34	Mar 3	H	Peterborough U	D 0-0	0-0	1		11,658
35	6	A	Bury	L 1-2	1-1	—	Harris [4]	3587
36	10	H	Luton T	W 1-0	1-0	1	Nethercott [41]	11,691
37	16	A	Bristol C	L 1-2	0-1	—	Harris (pen) [60]	10,395
38	27	A	Wycombe W	D 0-0	0-0	—		5094
39	31	A	Walsall	D 0-0	0-0	2		7073
40	Apr 3	H	Stoke C	W 2-0	1-0	—	Sadlier [6], Cahill [78]	11,639
41	7	H	Rotherham U	W 4-0	3-0	1	Cahill [13], Reid [31], Claridge 2 [42, 52]	16,015
42	11	H	Port Vale	W 1-0	1-0	—	Sadlier [17]	11,944
43	14	H	Swindon T	W 1-0	0-0	—	Harris [65]	12,266
44	17	A	Cambridge U	W 5-1	1-0	—	Nethercott [35], Ifill 3 [52, 79, 81], Claridge [74]	5223
45	28	A	Wrexham	D 1-1	0-1	1	Cahill [53]	5939
46	May 5	H	Oldham Ath	W 5-0	2-0	1	Moody 2 [21, 66], Harris 2 (1 pen) [30, 90 (p)], Reid [52]	18,510

Final League Position: 1

GOALSCORERS

League (89): Harris 27 (5 pens), Moody 13, Cahill 9, Reid 7, Ifill 6, Sadlier 6, Parkin 4, Claridge 3, Livermore 3, Bircham 2, Kinet 2, Neill 2, Nethercott 2, Dolan 1, own goals 2.
Worthington Cup (5): Braniff 1, Cahill 1, Ifill 1, Kinet 1, Livermore 1.
FA Cup (4): Bircham 1, Dolan 1, Harris 1 (pen), Moody 1.

Warner T 35	Lawrence M 45	Ryan R 42	Cahill T 40 + 1	Tuttle D 6 + 3	Dolan J 20	Livermore D 39	Moody P 21 + 6	Harris N 39 + 3	Reid S 27 + 10	Kinet C 18 + 9	Bircham M 13 + 7	Neill L 19 + 5	Gilkes M 2 + 1	Nethercott S 33 + 2	Braniff K 2 + 3	Tyne T — + 3	Bubb B 2 + 1	Odunsi L 2 + 6	Bowry B — + 1	Ifill P 28 + 7	Parkin S 5 + 2	Constantine L — + 1	Dyche S 33	Fitzgerald S — + + 1	Sadlier R 16 + 13	Bull R 2	Stuart J — + 1	Gueret W 11	Cottee T — + 2	Claridge S 6	Match No.
1	2	3	4¹	5	6	7	8	9	10	11²	12	13																			1
1	2	3	4	5	6	7	8	9	10		12				11¹																2
1	2	3	4	5³	6	7	8²	9¹	10	11				14	13	12															3
1	2	3	4	5	6			9		11		12			10²	13	7¹	8³	14												4
1	2	3	4	5	6	7		9	12	11							8²	13	10¹												5
1	2	3	4		6	7		9	10	11²				5	12	13				8¹											6
1	2	3	4		6	7		9¹	12	11³				5	13					14			10¹		8						7
1	2	3	4		6	7				11		9		5						10¹			8		12						8
1	2	3	4¹			7		9		11		10		5						12			8		6						9
1	2	3³	4			7		9		11¹		10		5						12	8²		6		14	13					10
1	2		4			7		9	10	11¹				5						12	8²		6		13	3²	14				11
1	2		4			7		9	10					5						11	12		6		8¹	3					12
1	2	3	4			7		9	10			11		5						12			6		8						13
1	2	3	4²					9	10			13		5	11¹			7		12			6		8						14
1	2	3	4			7		9	10			11		5						12			6		8¹						15
1	2	3	4			7		9	10¹			11²		5	13					12			6		8						16
1	2	3	4		6	7	12	9	10			11¹		5											8						17
1	2	3	4	12	6	7	8	9	10¹			13³		5	14					11²											18
1	2	3	4		6	7¹	8²	9	10	11				5						12					13						19
1	2	3	4		6	7	8¹	9	10					5						11					12						20
1	2	3	12		6	7	13	9²	10	4				5						11¹					8						21
1	2	3	4		6	7	12	9		11		10		5											8¹						22
1	2¹	3	4		6	7	8²	9	12	11		10		5											13						23
1	2	3	4		6	7	8²	9	12	11		10¹		5											13						24
1	2	3	4		6	7	8	9	12	11¹		10		5																	25
1		3	4		6	7	8¹	9	10		2			5						11					12						26
1	2	3³			6	7	8	9			4	10		5						11					12						27
	2	3	4		6²	7	8³	9	12					5						11	13		10¹		14			1			28
	2	3	4			7²	8	9	12			13		5						11¹			6		10			1			29
	2	3	4					9	11¹		12			5				7		10			6		8			1			30
	2	3	4		12			9	13	11²				5				7		10			6		8¹			1			31
	2	3¹				7	8³	9	10	12	4	13		5						11²			6		14			1			32
	2	3				7	8	9	10	12	4			5						11¹			6					1			33
	2	3²				7	8³	9	10	12	4	13		5						11¹			6		14			1			34
	2	3				7	8	9		11¹	4	10		5									6		12			1			35
	2	3	4²	5		7	8³	9	12			11			13					10¹			6		14			1			36
	2	3¹	4			7	8	9	13			11¹		5						10			6		12			1			37
	2	3	4			7		9²	10			11¹		5						12			6		8			1	13		38
1	2	3	4			7		9	10			11¹		5						12			6		8						39
1	2	3	4			7			10					5						11			6		8				12	9¹	40
1	2¹	3	4			7	12		10					5						11			6		8					9	41
1	2	3	4				12	13	10	14				5				7³		11			6		8					9²	42
1	2	3²	4				12	13	10	14				5				7		11¹			6		8					9³	43
1	2		4			7	12	13	10	14		3		5¹						11			6		8²					9³	44
1	2		4			7	12	9	10	14		13		5						11²			6				3³			9¹	45
1	2	3	4²			7	8	9	10¹	12		13		5						11			6								46

Worthington Cup

First Round	Brighton & HA	(a)	2-1
		(h)	1-1
Second Round	Ipswich T	(h)	2-0
		(a)	0-5

FA Cup

First Round (at Millwall)	Leigh RMI	(a)	3-0
Second Round	Wycombe W	(h)	0-0
		(a)	1-2

NEWCASTLE UNITED FA Premiership

FOUNDATION

It stemmed from a newly formed club called Stanley in 1881.
In October 1882 they changed their name to Newcastle East End to
avoid confusion with two other local clubs, Stanley Nops and
Stanley Albion. Shortly afterwards another club Rosewood merged
with them. Newcastle West End had been formed in August 1882
and they played on a pitch which was part of the Town Moor.
Moved to Brandling Park 1885 and St James' Park 1886 (home of
Newcastle Rangers). West End went out of existence after a bad
run and the remaining committee men invited East End to move to
St James' Park. They accepted and, at a meeting in Bath Lane Hall
in 1892, changed their name to Newcastle United.

St James' Park, Newcastle-upon-Tyne NE1 4ST.
Telephone: (0191) 201 8400. *Fax:* (0191) 201 8600.
ClubCall: 09068 121 190. *Box Office:* (0191) 261 1571.
Mail Order: 08705 501 892. *Club Shop:* (0191) 201 8426.
Football in the Community: (0191) 222 0134.
Travel Club: (0191) 201 8550.
Magpies Club: (0191) 201 8472.
Corporate Hospitality: (0191) 201 8421.
Conference and Banqueting: (0191) 201 8585.
Club United: (0191) 201 8581.
Press Office: (0191) 201 8544.
Commercial Department: (0191) 201 8715.
Lottery Office: (0191) 235 3901.
Junior Magpies: (0191) 201 8471.
Photographic Dept: (0191) 235 3906.

Ground Capacity: 52,218.

Record Attendance: 68,386 v Chelsea, Division 1,
3 September 1930.

Record Receipts: £830,271 v Everton, FA Cup 6th rd,
7 March 1999.

Pitch Measurements: 105m × 60m.

HONOURS

FA Premier League: Runners-up
1995–96, 1996–97; *Football League:*
Division 1 – Champions 1904–05,
1906–07, 1908–09, 1926–27, 1992–93;
Division 2 – Champions 1964–65;
Runners-up 1897–98, 1947–48.
FA Cup: Winners 1910, 1924, 1932,
1951, 1952, 1955; Runners-up 1905,
1906, 1908, 1911, 1974, 1998, 1999.
Football League Cup: Runners-up 1976.
Texaco Cup: Winners 1974, 1975.
European Competitions: European Cup:
1997–98. *European Fairs Cup:* 1968–69
(winners), 1969–70, 1970–71. *UEFA Cup:*
1977–78, 1994–95, 1996–97.
European Cup Winners' Cup: 1998–99.
Anglo-Italian Cup: Winners 1972–73.

President: Sir John Hall. *Patron:* T. Bennett. *Honorary President:* B. Young.

Chairman: W. F. Shepherd. *Deputy Chairman:* D. S. Hall.
Directors: W. F. Shepherd, D. S. Hall, R. Jones, R. Cushing, K. Slater (Finance Director).

Manager: Bobby Robson CBE. *Director of Football:* Gordon Milne. *Chief Scout:* Charlie Woods.
Coaches: John Carver, Tommy Craig, Simon Smith. *Academy Director:* Alan Irvine.
Senior Physio: Derek Wright. *Physio:* Paul Ferris. *Fitness Coach:* Paul Winsper.

Chief Operating Officer: Russell Cushing. *Director of Commercial Affairs:* Carole Beverley.
Safety Officer: Dave Pattison. *Team Administrator:* Tony Toward. *Assistant Secretary:* Lee Charnley.

Colours: Black and white striped shirts, black shorts and stockings.

Change Colours: Heron and raven shirts and shorts, heron stockings.

Year Formed: 1881. *Turned Professional:* 1889. *Ltd Co.:* 1890.

Previous Names: 1881, Stanley; 1882, Newcastle East End; 1892, Newcastle United.

IT'S A FACT !

When Gary Speed made his 318th Premier League
appearance for Newcastle United against Leicester City
on 28 April 2001, it was a record number in the history
of the competition.

Club Nickname: 'The Magpies'.

Previous Grounds: 1881, South Byker; 1886, Chillingham Road, Heaton, 1892, St James' Park.

First Football League Game: 2 September 1893, Division 2, v Royal Arsenal (a) D 2–2 – Ramsay; Jeffery, Miller; Crielly, Graham, McKane; Bowman, Crate (1), Thompson, Sorley (1), Wallace. Graham and not Crate scored according to some reports.

Record League Victory: 13–0 v Newport Co, Division 2, 5 October 1946 – Garbutt; Cowell, Graham; Harvey, Brennan, Wright; Milburn (2), Bentley (1), Wayman (4), Shackleton (6), Pearson.

Record Cup Victory: 9–0 v Southport (at Hillsborough), FA Cup 4th rd, 1 February 1932 – McInroy; Nelson, Fairhurst; McKenzie, Davidson, Weaver (1); Boyd (1), Jimmy Richardson (3), Cape (2), McMenemy (1), Lang (1).

Record Defeat: 0–9 v Burton Wanderers, Division 2, 15 April 1895.

Most League Points (2 for a win): 57, Division 2, 1964–65.

Most League Points (3 for a win): 96, Division 1, 1992–93.

Most League Goals: 98, Division 1, 1951–52.

Highest League Scorer in Season: Hughie Gallacher, 36, Division 1, 1926–27.

Most League Goals in Total Aggregate: Jackie Milburn, 177, 1946–57.

Most League Goals in One Match: 6, Len Shackleton v Newport Co, Division 2, 5 October 1946.

Most Capped Player: Alf McMichael, 40, Northern Ireland.

Most League Appearances: Jim Lawrence, 432, 1904–22.

Youngest League Player: Steve Watson, 16 years 223 days v Wolverhampton W, 10 November 1990.

MANAGERS

Frank Watt 1895–32
  (Secretary-Manager)
Andy Cunningham 1930–35
Tom Mather 1935–39
Stan Seymour 1939–47
  (Hon. Manager)
George Martin 1947–50
Stan Seymour 1950–54
  (Hon. Manager)
Duggie Livingstone 1954–56
Stan Seymour 1956–58
  (Hon. Manager)
Charlie Mitten 1958–61
Norman Smith 1961–62
Joe Harvey 1962–75
Gordon Lee 1975–77
Richard Dinnis 1977
Bill McGarry 1977–80
Arthur Cox 1980–84
Jack Charlton 1984
Willie McFaul 1985–88
Jim Smith 1988–91
Ossie Ardiles 1991–92
Kevin Keegan 1992–97
Kenny Dalglish 1997–98
Ruud Gullit 1998–1999
Bobby Robson September 1999–

Record Transfer Fee Received: £8,000,000 from Liverpool for Dieter Hamann, July 1999.

Record Transfer Fee Paid: £15,000,000 to Blackburn R for Alan Shearer, July 1996.

Football League Record: 1893 Elected to Division 2; 1898–1934 Division 1; 1934–48 Division 2; 1948–61 Division 1; 1961–65 Division 2; 1965–78 Division 1; 1978–84 Division 2; 1984–89 Division 1; 1989–92 Division 1; 1992–93 Division 1; 1993– FA Premier League.

LATEST SEQUENCES

Longest Sequence of League Wins: 13, 25.4.92 – 18.10.92.

Longest Sequence of League Defeats: 10, 23.8.77 – 15.10.77.

Longest Sequence of League Draws: 4, 20.1.90 – 24.2.90.

Longest Sequence of Unbeaten League Matches: 14, 22.4.50 – 30.9.50.

Longest Sequence Without a League Win: 21, 14.1.78 – 23.8.78.

TEN YEAR LEAGUE RECORD

		P	W	D	L	F	A	Pts	Pos
1990-91	Div 2	46	14	17	15	49	56	59	11
1991-92	Div 2	46	13	13	20	66	84	52	20
1992-93	Div 1	46	29	9	8	92	38	96	1
1993-94	PR Lge	42	23	8	11	82	41	77	3
1994-95	PR Lge	42	20	12	10	67	47	72	6
1995-96	PR Lge	38	24	6	8	66	37	78	2
1996-97	PR Lge	38	19	11	8	73	40	68	2
1997-98	PR Lge	38	11	11	16	35	44	44	13
1998-99	PR Lge	38	11	13	14	48	54	46	13
1999-2000	PR Lge	38	14	10	14	63	54	52	11

DID YOU KNOW ?

On 6th September 2000, Alan Shearer scored his 200th League goal in his 375th game with a penalty, as Newcastle United won 2–0 at Coventry City.

NEWCASTLE UNITED 2000–01 LEAGUE RECORD

Match No.	Date	Venue	Opponents	Result	H/T Score	Lg. Pos.	Goalscorers	Attendance
1	Aug 20	A	Manchester U	L	0-2	0-1	—		67,477
2	23	H	Derby Co	W	3-2	1-1	—	Cort [5], Cordone [46], Glass [55]	51,327
3	26	H	Tottenham H	W	2-0	1-0	3	Speed [9], Cordone [66]	51,503
4	Sept 6	A	Coventry C	W	2-0	1-0	—	Shearer (pen) [30], Gallacher [58]	22,102
5	9	H	Chelsea	D	0-0	0-0	3		51,687
6	16	A	Southampton	L	0-2	0-0	6		15,221
7	23	H	Charlton Ath	L	0-1	0-1	7		50,768
8	30	A	Manchester C	W	1-0	0-0	4	Shearer [74]	34,497
9	Oct 16	A	Middlesbrough	W	3-1	1-0	—	Shearer [38], Goma [55], Dyer [68]	31,436
10	21	H	Everton	L	0-1	0-0	4		51,625
11	28	A	West Ham U	L	0-1	0-0	8		26,044
12	Nov 4	H	Ipswich T	W	2-1	1-1	6	Shearer 2 (1 pen) [22, 67 (p)]	50,922
13	11	A	Leicester C	D	1-1	0-0	7	Speed [75]	21,406
14	18	H	Sunderland	L	1-2	1-0	8	Speed [4]	52,030
15	26	H	Liverpool	W	2-1	1-0	7	Solano [4], Dyer [70]	51,949
16	Dec 2	A	Aston Villa	D	1-1	0-1	8	Solano [82]	34,255
17	9	A	Arsenal	L	0-5	0-2	10		38,052
18	16	H	Bradford C	W	2-1	1-0	7	Speed [14], Dyer [70]	50,470
19	23	A	Derby Co	L	0-2	0-1	8		29,978
20	26	H	Leeds U	W	2-1	2-1	7	Solano [41], Acuna [44]	52,118
21	30	H	Manchester U	D	1-1	0-1	7	Glass [81]	52,134
22	Jan 2	A	Tottenham H	L	2-4	1-3	—	Solano [23], Dyer (pen) [49]	34,323
23	13	H	Coventry C	W	3-1	1-0	7	Speed [4], Ameobi [56], Dyer [66]	50,159
24	20	A	Leeds U	W	3-1	2-1	6	Solano (pen) [4], Acuna [44], Ameobi [86]	40,005
25	31	A	Chelsea	L	1-3	1-1	—	Bassedas [23]	35,108
26	Feb 11	A	Charlton Ath	L	0-2	0-2	10		20,043
27	24	H	Manchester C	L	0-1	0-0	11		51,981
28	Mar 3	A	Everton	D	1-1	0-0	11	Unsworth (og) [47]	35,779
29	17	H	Middlesbrough	L	1-2	0-2	13	Cort [60]	51,751
30	31	A	Bradford C	D	2-2	1-2	13	Cort [26], Acuna [77]	20,160
31	Apr 14	A	Ipswich T	L	0-1	0-0	14		24,026
32	16	H	West Ham U	W	2-1	1-0	13	Cort [32], Solano (pen) [56]	51,107
33	21	H	Sunderland	D	1-1	0-0	13	O'Brien [78]	47,213
34	28	H	Leicester C	W	1-0	0-0	10	Cort [90]	50,501
35	May 1	H	Southampton	D	1-1	1-0	—	Gallacher [26]	50,439
36	5	A	Liverpool	L	0-3	0-1	11		44,363
37	15	A	Arsenal	D	0-0	0-0	—		50,729
38	19	H	Aston Villa	W	3-0	2-0	11	Glass [9], Cort [13], Delaney (og) [74]	51,306

Final League Position: 11

GOALSCORERS

League (44): Cort 6, Solano 6 (2 pens), Dyer 5 (1 pen), Shearer 5 (2 pens), Speed 5, Acuna 3, Glass 3, Ameobi 2, Cordone 2, Gallacher 2, Bassedas 1, Goma 1, O'Brien 1, own goals 2.
Worthington Cup (8): Shearer 2, Caldwell 1, Cordone 1, Cort 1, Dyer 1, Gallacher 1, Speed 1.
FA Cup (1): Solano 1.

Given S 34	Barton W 27+2	Hughes A 34+1	Dabizas N 9	Marcelino E 5+1	Goma A 18+1	Lee R 21+1	Cort C 13	Shearer A 19	Cordone D 12+9	Speed G 35	Dyer K 25+1	Solano N 31+2	Domi D 11+3	Charvet L 6+1	Glass S 5+9	Griffin A 14+5	Coppinger J —+1	Gallacher K 12+7	Kerr B —+1	Ameobi F 12+8	Gavilan D —+1	Lua-Lua L 3+18	Caldwell S 5+4	Acuna C 23+3	Bassedas C 17+5	Harper S 4+1	Quinn W 14+1	O'Brien A 9	Match No.
1	2	3	4	5	6[1]	7[2]	8	9	10	11	12	13																	1
1	2	5	4[1]		12		8[3]	9	10	11	7	6[2]	3	13	14														2
1	2	5	4					9	10[2]	11	7	6	3		8[1]	12	13												3
1		5			6		8	9	10[3]	11	7		3[1]	2		4[2]		12		13	14								4
1	3	5			6			9	10	11	7		4[2]	2				8[1]		12	13								5
1		5	4					9	10	11	7	6		3[1]	2	12		8[2]		13									6
1		5	4			12	8	9	10[1]		7	6[2]	13		2[3]	3				14									7
1		5			6			9	10[2]	11	7[1]	12	3	4	2[3]			8		13	14								8
1		5	4				8	9	10[1]	11	7	6	3		2	12													9
1	2[1]	5	4				8	9	10[2]	11	7	6	3			13													10
1		5	4				6[2]	9	12	11	7		3	2				13		10[1]				8					11
1		5	4				6	9	10[1]	11	7	2[2]	3			12	13							8[1]	14				12
1		5	4				6[1]	9	12	11	7		3	2										8	10				13
1	12	5					6	9		11	7	2	3			13							4	8[1]	10[2]				14
1	2	5					8	9		11	7	6	3	4										12	10[1]				15
1	4	5[1]			6[1]		8[2]	9		11	7		3	2		12				10				13	14				16
1	2	5							9[3]	11	7[1]	6	13	3[2]				14		9				4	10				17
1	2	5	4				8	9		11	7	6	3			12									10[1]				18
1[1]	4	5	6				8[1]	9	12		7	13		3	2[2]					11				10	15				19
	3	5	4							11	7	6		2				9						8	10	1			20
	3	5	4						12	11	7	6		2				13		9[1]	14			8[2]	10[3]	1			21
	2	5	4							11	7	6		3[1]				12		9[2]	13			8	10	1			22
	2	5	4							11	7	6						12		9				8	10[1]	1		3	23
1	2	5				12				11	7[2]	6						10[3]		9[1]	14		4	8	13			3	24
1	2	5	4			12				11	7[2]	6								9[1]	13			8	10			3	25
1	2	5	4						10	11	7[2]	6[3]						12		9	14			8[1]	13			3	26
1	12	5	4						9		7	6		2				13		11[2]	10[3]			14	8[1]			3	27
1		5				7			9	12		6[1]		2				13		14	10[3]		4	8	11[2]			3	28
1	2[1]	5				7			10	11	12	6						13		9[3]	14		4	8[1]				3	29
1	2	5				7			10	11		6[1]						12		9				8[2]	13		3	4	30
1	2	5				7[2]			10	11		6						12		9[1]	13			8			3	4	31
1	2[1]	5				7[2]			10	11		6						9[3]			14		12	13	8		3	4	32
1	2	5				12			10	11		6[2]				14		9[1]					13	8[3]	7		3	4	33
1	2	5							10	11		6						9[1]		12			13	8	7		3	4	34
1	2				6[1]	12			10	11								9[2]					13	8	7		3	4	35
1	2		6		5	7			10[2]	11						14		9[1]		12			13	8[1]			3	4	36
1	2		5						10	11		6						9[1]					12	8	7		3	4	37
1	2		5						10	11		6[3]		7[2]				9[1]					12	8		14	3	4	38

Worthington Cup

Second Round	Leyton Orient	(h)	2-0
		(a)	1-1
Third Round	Bradford C	(h)	4-3
Fourth Round	Birmingham C	(a)	1-2

FA Cup

Third Round	Aston Villa	(h)	1-1
		(a)	0-1

NORTHAMPTON TOWN Division 2

FOUNDATION

Formed in 1897 by school teachers connected with the Northampton and District Elementary Schools' Association, they survived a financial crisis at the end of their first year when they were £675 in the red and became members of the Midland League – a fast move indeed for a new club. They achieved Southern League membership in 1901.

Sixfields Stadium, Upton Way, Northampton NN5 5QA.

Telephone: (01604) 757 773. *Fax:* (01604) 751 613.
TalkCobblers: 09066 130 906. *Website:* www.ntfc.co.uk
Email: secretary@ntfc.co.uk
Ticket Office: (01604) 588 338.

Ground Capacity: 7653 (all seated).

Record Attendance: (at County Ground): 24,523 v Fulham, Division 1, 23 April 1966. (at Sixfields Stadium): 7557 v Manchester C, Division 2, 26 September 1998.

Record Receipts (at Sixfields): £102,979 v Tottenham H, Worthington Cup 3rd rd, 27 October 1998.

Pitch Measurements: 116yd × 72yd.

Chairman: B. J. Stonhill. *Directors:* B. Hancock, D. Kerr, C. Smith, T. Clarke MP, P. Randall.

Secretary: Norman Howells. *Company Secretary:* B. J. Stonhill.

Manager: Kevin Wilson.

Coach: Russell Slade.

Physio: Denis Casey.

Commercial Manager: Eric Broad.

Stadium Manager: Tom Holland.

Colours: Claret shirts with thin white piping, white shorts, claret stockings.

Change Colours: Yellow shirts with claret, claret shorts with yellow, yellow stockings.

Year Formed: 1897.

Turned Professional: 1901.

Ltd Co.: 1901.

Previous Ground: 1897, County Ground; 1994, Sixfields Stadium.

Club Nickname: 'The Cobblers'.

First Football League Game: 28 August 1920, Division 3, v Grimsby T (a) L 0–2 – Thorpe; Sproston, Hewison; Jobey, Tomkins, Pease; Whitworth, Lockett, Thomas, Freeman, MacKechnie.

Record League Victory: 10–0 v Walsall, Division 3 (S), 5 November 1927 – Hammond; Watson, Jeffs; Allen, Brett, Odell; Daley, Smith (3), Loasby (3), Hoten (1), Wells (3).

HONOURS

Football League: Division 1 best season: 21st, 1965–66; Division 2 – Runners-up 1964–65; Division 3 – Champions 1962–63; Promoted from Division 3 1996–97 (play-offs); Division 3 (S) – Runners-up 1927–28, 1949–50; Division 4 – Champions 1986–87; Runners-up 1975–76.

FA Cup: best season: 5th rd, 1934, 1950, 1970.

Football League Cup: best season: 5th rd, 1965, 1967.

IT'S A FACT !

In 1920-21, Northampton Town's inaugural League season, George Whitworth scored 28 goals in his 40 Division Three matches. In one spell of six consecutive games, he scored 10 goals.

Record Cup Victory: 10–0 v Sutton T, FA Cup prel rd, 7 December 1907 – Cooch; Drennan, Lloyd Davies, Tirrell (1), McCartney, Hickleton, Badenock (3), Platt (3), Lowe (1), Chapman (2), McDiarmid.

Record Defeat: 0–11 v Southampton, Southern League, 28 December 1901.

Most League Points (2 for a win): 68, Division 4, 1975–76.

Most League Points (3 for a win): 99, Division 4, 1986–87.

Most League Goals: 109, Division 3, 1962–63 and Division 3 (S), 1952–53.

Highest League Scorer in Season: Cliff Holton, 36, Division 3, 1961–62.

Most League Goals in Total Aggregate: Jack English, 135, 1947–60.

Most League Goals in One Match: 5, Ralph Hoten v Crystal Palace, Division 3S, 27 October 1928.

Most Capped Player: E. Lloyd Davies, 12 (16), Wales.

Most League Appearances: Tommy Fowler, 521, 1946–61.

Youngest League Player: Adrian Mann, 16 years 297 days v Bury, 5 May 1984.

Record Transfer Fee Received: £265,000 from Watford for Richard Hill, July 1987.

Record Transfer Fee Paid: £150,000 to FC Utrecht for Jamie Forrester, July 2000.

Football League Record: 1920 Original Member of Division 3; 1921 Division 3 (S); 1958–61 Division 4; 1961–63 Division 3; 1963–65 Division 2; 1965–66 Division 1; 1966–67 Division 2; 1967–69 Division 3; 1969–76 Division 4; 1976–77 Division 3; 1977–87 Division 4; 1987–90 Division 3; 1990–92 Division 4; 1992–97 Division 3; 1997–99 Division 2; 1999–2000 Division 3; 2000– Division 2.

LATEST SEQUENCES

Longest Sequence of League Wins: 8, 27.8.60 – 19.9.60.

Longest Sequence of League Defeats: 8, 26.10.35 – 21.12.35.

Longest Sequence of League Draws: 6, 18.9.83 – 15.10.83.

Longest Sequence of Unbeaten League Matches: 21, 27.9.86 – 6.2.87.

Longest Sequence Without a League Win: 18, 26.3.69 – 20.9.69.

MANAGERS

Arthur Jones 1897–1907
(Secretary-Manager)
Herbert Chapman 1907–12
Walter Bull 1912–13
Fred Lessons 1913–19
Bob Hewison 1920–25
Jack Tresadern 1925–30
Jack English 1931–35
Syd Puddefoot 1935–37
Warney Cresswell 1937–39
Tom Smith 1939–49
Bob Dennison 1949–54
Dave Smith 1954–59
David Bowen 1959–67
Tony Marchi 1967–68
Ron Flowers 1968–69
Dave Bowen 1969–72
(continued as General Manager and Secretary to 1985 when joined the board)
Billy Baxter 1972–73
Bill Dodgin Jnr 1973–76
Pat Crerand 1976–77
Bill Dodgin Jnr 1977
John Petts 1977–78
Mike Keen 1978–79
Clive Walker 1979–80
Bill Dodgin Jnr 1980–82
Clive Walker 1982–84
Tony Barton 1984–85
Graham Carr 1985–90
Theo Foley 1990–92
Phil Chard 1992–93
John Barnwell 1993–95
Ian Atkins 1995–99
Kevin Wilson November 1999–

TEN YEAR LEAGUE RECORD

		P	W	D	L	F	A	Pts	Pos
1990-91	Div 4	46	18	13	15	57	58	67	10
1991-92	Div 4	42	11	13	18	46	57	46	16
1992-93	Div 3	42	11	8	23	48	74	41	20
1993-94	Div 3	42	9	11	22	44	66	38	22
1994-95	Div 3	42	10	14	18	45	67	44	17
1995-96	Div 3	46	18	13	15	51	44	67	11
1996-97	Div 3	46	20	12	14	67	44	72	4
1997-98	Div 2	46	18	17	11	52	37	71	4
1998-99	Div 2	46	10	18	18	43	57	48	22
1999-2000	Div 3	46	25	7	14	63	45	82	3

DID YOU KNOW ?

On 4 January 1958, Northampton Town beat Arsenal 3-1 in the third round of the FA Cup, watched by a crowd of 21,344. Their scorers were Barry Hawkings, Ken Leek and Robert Tebbutt.

NORTHAMPTON TOWN 2000–01 LEAGUE RECORD

Match No.	Date	Venue	Opponents	Result	H/T Score	Lg. Pos.	Goalscorers	Attendance
1	Aug 12	H	Brentford	D	1-1	0-0	—	Forrester [58]	6379
2	19	A	Wycombe W	L	0-1	0-0	20		4806
3	26	H	Reading	W	2-0	1-0	9	Forrester 2 [32, 76]	5728
4	28	A	Bury	L	0-1	0-0	15		3182
5	Sept 9	A	Luton T	W	2-0	1-0	13	Forrester [38], Howard [60]	6712
6	12	A	Millwall	W	1-0	0-0	—	Gabbiadini [60]	7064
7	16	H	Notts Co	W	1-0	0-0	6	Howard [69]	5703
8	23	A	Wigan Ath	L	1-2	1-2	11	Hendon (pen) [24]	6294
9	30	H	Wrexham	D	2-2	1-2	10	Howard [32], Forrester [87]	5595
10	Oct 14	A	Bristol R	W	1-0	0-0	9	Forrester [76]	7704
11	17	A	Port Vale	D	2-2	2-1	—	Forrester [5], Gabbiadini [32]	4215
12	21	H	Oldham Ath	W	2-1	1-0	9	Forrester [26], Hughes [81]	5677
13	24	A	Cambridge U	W	2-1	2-0	—	Forrester 2 [12, 20]	5394
14	28	H	Rotherham U	L	0-1	0-1	7		6478
15	Nov 4	A	Colchester U	W	2-0	1-0	6	Forrester [39], Howard [60]	3352
16	7	H	Stoke C	D	2-2	2-2	—	Forrester [13], Howard [45]	5475
17	11	H	Bournemouth	L	0-3	0-1	7		5692
18	25	A	Walsall	L	0-3	0-1	9		5894
19	Dec 2	H	Swindon T	L	0-1	0-1	9		5816
20	16	A	Oxford U	L	1-3	1-2	11	Savage (pen) [28]	4899
21	23	A	Peterborough U	W	2-1	0-1	9	Forrester [66], Sampson [83]	9868
22	26	H	Bristol C	W	2-0	2-0	8	Savage [29], Forrester [30]	6064
23	30	H	Wycombe W	D	2-2	1-1	8	Forrester [26], Howard [85]	5722
24	Jan 1	A	Reading	D	1-1	0-0	8	Gabbiadini [87]	10,599
25	6	A	Brentford	D	1-1	1-0	8	Savage (pen) [45]	5361
26	13	H	Bury	W	2-1	1-1	8	Hodge [2], Gabbiadini [79]	5127
27	20	A	Bristol C	L	0-2	0-0	8		11,630
28	27	H	Peterborough U	D	0-0	0-0	8		7079
29	Feb 3	A	Stoke C	D	1-1	0-0	8	Howard [74]	13,235
30	10	H	Luton T	L	0-1	0-1	9		6633
31	17	H	Notts Co	L	0-2	0-1	9		6320
32	20	H	Millwall	D	3-3	0-1	—	Gabbiadini [60], Savage 2 (2 pens) [67, 81]	5026
33	24	H	Wigan Ath	W	1-0	1-0	9	Forrester [45]	5571
34	27	H	Swansea C	W	2-1	0-1	—	Sampson [89], Gabbiadini [90]	4361
35	Mar 2	A	Wrexham	L	0-3	0-2	—		2940
36	6	H	Bristol R	W	2-1	1-0	—	Savage (pen) [13], Hunt [72]	4552
37	10	A	Swansea C	D	1-1	1-0	8	Howard [45]	4911
38	23	A	Oldham Ath	L	1-2	1-0	—	Frain [15]	4001
39	31	H	Oxford U	L	0-1	0-1	11		6115
40	Apr 7	A	Swindon T	D	1-1	1-1	11	Savage [39]	5932
41	13	H	Cambridge U	L	0-2	0-1	—		6063
42	16	A	Rotherham U	L	0-1	0-1	15		6714
43	21	H	Colchester U	W	2-0	1-0	12	Savage (pen) [35], Forrester [61]	5012
44	26	H	Port Vale	L	0-2	0-2	—		4775
45	28	A	Bournemouth	L	0-2	0-1	15		6511
46	May 5	H	Walsall	L	0-3	0-0	18		5389

Final League Position: 18

GOALSCORERS

League (46): Forrester 17, Howard 8, Savage 8 (6 pens), Gabbiadini 6, Sampson 2, Frain 1, Hendon 1 (pen), Hodge 1, Hughes 1, Hunt 1.
Worthington Cup (2): Gabbiadini 1, Sampson 1.
FA Cup (4): Forrester 2, Frain 1, Hunt 1.

Welch K 40	Hendon J 9	Frain J 27	Sampson I 41	Green R 34 + 4	Hope R 30 + 3	Savage D 37 + 6	Hunt J 41	Forrester J 42 + 1	Gabbiadini M 34 + 10	Hargreaves C 29 + 2	Howard S 23 + 10	Hodge J 24 + 9	Spedding D 17 + 4	Hughes G 12 + 4	Morrow A 2 + 2	Dryden R 9 + 1	Wilson K — + 6	Gould J — + 1	Maley M 2	Clare D 3 + 1	Sollitt A 6	Chivers L 7	Crooks L 3	Canoville L 2	Nicholson K 6 + 1	Thompson R — + 2	Whitley J 13	Ferguson B 1 + 2	Dempsey P 5 + 1	Lopes R 3 + 3	Hunter R 1 + 3	Lowe D — + 4	Howey L 2 + 1	Carruthers C 1 + 2	Match No.
1	2		4	5	6	7	8	9	10^1	11	12																								1
1	2^1	3	4	5	6	7^2	8	9^3	10	11	14	12	13																						2
1	2	3		5	6	12^2	8	9	10	11	7		13	4																					3
1	2^3	3		5	6	12	8^2	9^1	10		7		13	11	4	14																			4
1	2	3	4	5		12	8	9^2	10	11		7^1	13			6																			5
1	2	3^1	4	5		12	8	9^2	10	11		7	13			6																			6
1	2		4	5		3	8	9	10	11		7^2	13	12		6^1																			7
1	2		4	5		3	8	9	10	11		7^1	13	12		6^2																			8
1	2		4	5		3	8^2	9	10	11		7^1	13	12	14	6^1																			9
1			4	5		3	8	9	10	11	2^1	7		12		6																			10
1		3	4	5	12	2	8	9	10	11		7^1				6																			11
1		3	4	5	12	2	8	9	10^2	11	13	7				6^1																			12
1		3	4	5	12	2	8	9^2	10	11	13	7				6^1																			13
1		3	4	5		2	8	9	10^2	11	12	7	13			6^1																			14
1		3	4	5	6	2	8	9	10	11		7																							15
1		3	4	5^1	6	2	8	9	10	11		7		12																					16
1		3	4	5	6^3	2	8	9	10^2	11	2^1	7	13	12	14																				17
1		3	4	5	6	12	8^1	9	13	11^3		7^2		14					2	10															18
1		3^1	4	5	6	7	8	9	12	11		13	14						2^2	10^1															19
		3	4	5	6^1	12	8	9	10^2	11	2	7	13								1														20
1		3	4	5	6		8	9	10^1	11		7		12											2										21
1		3	4	5	6	7^1	8	9	10	11				12											2										22
1			4	5	6	7^1	8	9	10	11			13	12											2	3^2									23
1		3	4	5	6		8	9	10	11		7													2										24
1		3	4	5	6		8	9^1	10	11		7		12											2										25
1		3	4	5^1	6		8	9	10	11		7		12											2										26
1		3	4	5	6	7	8	9	10^1	11			13	12											2	3^2									27
1		3	4	5	6		8	9^1	10	11		7		12													2								28
1		2	4	5	6	7	8	9	10^1	11				12													3								29
1		3	4	5	6	12	8	9	10	11^3		7^2	13													2^1	14								30
1		3	4	5	6	2	8	9	10	11^1		7		12													3								31
1		2	4	5	6	7	8	9	10	11																	3								32
1		2	4	5	6		8	9	10			7		12													11^1		3						33
1		2	4	5^1	6		8	9	10			12															11^2		3	13	7				34
1		2	4	5^1	6^2	12	8	9	10^2				11	13														3		7	14				35
1		2	4		5	6	8	9^1	10	11		12															3		7						36
1		2	4^2	12	5	3	6	9	10	11	8	7^1	13																						37
1		2		12	4	7	8	9	10	13	6																11		5^1	3^2					38
1		2		5	6	4	8	9	10		7^2	3^1		12													11			13				39
		2	4	5	6	7	8	9	10			3									1						11								40
		2	4	5^1	6	7	8^2	9	10			12	3								1						11		13						41
		2	4	12	5	6	8^2	9	10^1			7	3^3								1						11		13	14					42
		2	4		5	8		9	10^3			7^1									1						11		3	6^2	12	13	14		43
		2	4		5	7		9	10^2												1						11^1		3	8	12	13	6^3	14	44
1		2	4		5	8^1		9	10			7^2									1						11		3	6^2	12	13	14		45
1		2	4		5			10	12			7^2															11		3	8	13	6	9^1		46

Worthington Cup
First Round   Fulham   (h) 1-0
                              (a) 1-4

FA Cup
First Round   Frickley Ath   (h) 4-0
Second Round   Rotherham U   (a) 0-1

NORWICH CITY   Division 1

FOUNDATION

Formed in 1902, largely through the initiative of two local
schoolmasters who called a meeting at the Criterion Cafe, they
were shocked by an FA Commission which in 1904 declared the
club professional and ejected them from the FA Amateur Cup.
However, this only served to strengthen their determination. New
officials were appointed and a professional club established at a
meeting in the Agricultural Hall in March 1905.

Carrow Road, Norwich NR1 1JE.

Telephone: (01603) 760 760. *Fax:* (01603) 613 886.
Box Office: (01603) 761 661. *ClubCall:* 09068 121 144.

Ground Capacity: 21,468.

Record Attendance: 43,984 v Leicester C, FA Cup 6th rd,
30 March 1963.

Record Receipts: £261,918 v Internazionale, UEFA Cup
3rd rd 1st leg, 24 November 1993.

Pitch Measurements: 114yd × 74yd.

President: G. C. Watling. *Chairman:* Bob Cooper.
Deputy Chairman: B. J. Skipper.
Company Secretary: N. A. Doncaster.
Directors: M. M. Foulger, M. Wynn Jones, D. Smith,
R. J. Munby, R. Stuart.

HONOURS

FA Premier League: best season: 3rd
1992–93.

Football League: Division 2 –
Champions 1971–72, 1985–86;
Division 3 (S) – Champions 1933–34;
Division 3 – Runners-up 1959–60.

FA Cup: Semi-finals 1959, 1989, 1992.

Football League Cup: Winners 1962,
1985; Runners-up 1973, 1975.

European Competitions: UEFA Cup:
1993–94.

First Team Manager: Nigel Worthington. *Assistant Manager:* Doug Livermore.

First Team Coach: Steve Foley. *Director of Academy:* Sammy Morgan.

Coach: Keith Webb.

Physio: Neil Reynolds, MCSP, SRP.

Club Secretary: Kevin Platt.

Colours: Yellow shirts, green shorts, yellow stockings.

Change Colours: All red.

Year Formed: 1902.

Turned Professional: 1905.

Ltd Co.: 1905.

Club Nickname: 'The Canaries'.

Previous Grounds: 1902, Newmarket Road; 1908, The Nest, Rosary Road; 1935, Carrow Road.

First Football League Game: 28 August 1920, Division 3, v Plymouth Arg (a) D 1–1 – Skermer; Gray,
Gadsden; Wilkinson, Addy, Martin; Laxton, Kidger, Parker, Whitham (1), Dobson.

Record League Victory: 10–2 v Coventry C, Division 3 (S), 15 March 1930 – Jarvie; Hannah, Graham;
Brown, O'Brien, Lochhead (1); Porter (1), Anderson, Hunt (5), Scott (2), Slicer (1).

IT'S A FACT !

Former England international Albert Sturgess became
Norwich City's oldest player in a competitve match on
14 February 1925 playing at left-half against Millwall at
the age of 42 years 249 days.

Record Cup Victory: 8–0 v Sutton U, FA Cup 4th rd, 28 January 1989 – Gunn; Culverhouse, Bowen, Butterworth, Linighan, Townsend (Crook), Gordon, Fleck (3), Allen (4), Phelan, Putney (1).

Record Defeat: 2–10 v Swindon T, Southern League, 5 September 1908.

Most League Points (2 for a win): 64, Division 3 (S), 1950–51.

Most League Points (3 for a win): 84, Division 2, 1985–86.

Most League Goals: 99, Division 3 (S), 1952–53.

Highest League Scorer in Season: Ralph Hunt, 31, Division 3 (S), 1955–56.

Most League Goals in Total Aggregate: Johnny Gavin, 122, 1945–54, 1955–58.

Most League Goals in One Match: 5, Tommy Hunt v Coventry C, Division 3S, 15 March 1930; 5, Roy Hollis v Walsall, Division 3S, 29 December 1951.

Most Capped Player: Mark Bowen, 35 (41), Wales.

Most League Appearances: Ron Ashman, 592, 1947–64.

Youngest League Player: Ian Davies, 17 years 29 days v Birmingham C, 27 April 1974.

Record Transfer Fee Received: £5,000,000 from Blackburn R for Chris Sutton, July 1994.

Record Transfer Fee Paid: £1,000,000 to Leeds U for Jon Newsome, June 1994.

Football League Record: 1920 Original Member of Division 3; 1921 Division 3 (S): 1934–39 Division 2; 1946–58 Division 3 (S); 1958–60 Division 3; 1960–72 Division 2; 1972–74 Division 1; 1974–75 Division 2; 1975–81 Division 1; 1981–82 Division 2; 1982–85 Division 1; 1985–86 Division 2; 1986–92 Division 1; 1992–95 FA Premier League; 1995– Division 1.

MANAGERS

John Bowman 1905–07
James McEwen 1907–08
Arthur Turner 1909–10
Bert Stansfield 1910–15
Major Frank Buckley 1919–20
Charles O'Hagan 1920–21
Albert Gosnell 1921–26
Bert Stansfield 1926
Cecil Potter 1926–29
James Kerr 1929–33
Tom Parker 1933–37
Bob Young 1937–39
Jimmy Jewell 1939
Bob Young 1939–45
Cyril Spiers 1946–47
Duggie Lochhead 1947–50
Norman Low 1950–55
Tom Parker 1955–57
Archie Macaulay 1957–61
Willie Reid 1961–62
George Swindin 1962
Ron Ashman 1962–66
Lol Morgan 1966–69
Ron Saunders 1969–73
John Bond 1973–80
Ken Brown 1980–87
Dave Stringer 1987–92
Mike Walker 1992–94
John Deehan 1994–95
Martin O'Neill 1995
Gary Megson 1995–96
Mike Walker 1996–98
Bruce Rioch 1998–2000
Bryan Hamilton 2000
Nigel Worthington January 2001–

LATEST SEQUENCES

Longest Sequence of League Wins: 10, 23.11.85 – 25.1.86.

Longest Sequence of League Defeats: 7, 1.4.95 – 6.5.95.

Longest Sequence of League Draws: 7, 15.1.94 – 26.2.94.

Longest Sequence of Unbeaten League Matches: 20, 31.8.50 – 30.12.50.

Longest Sequence Without a League Win: 25, 22.9.56 – 23.2.57.

TEN YEAR LEAGUE RECORD

		P	W	D	L	F	A	Pts	Pos
1990-91	Div 1	38	13	6	19	41	64	45	15
1991-92	Div 1	42	11	12	19	47	63	45	18
1992-93	PR Lge	42	21	9	12	61	65	72	3
1993-94	PR Lge	42	12	17	13	65	61	53	12
1994-95	PR Lge	42	10	13	19	37	54	43	20
1995-96	Div 1	46	14	15	17	59	55	57	16
1996-97	Div 1	46	17	12	17	63	68	63	13
1997-98	Div 1	46	14	13	19	52	69	55	15
1998-99	Div 1	46	15	17	14	62	61	62	9
1999-2000	Div 1	46	14	15	17	45	50	57	12

DID YOU KNOW ?

Norwich City reached the fifth round of the FA Cup in 1935 by beating Leeds United 2-1 at Elland Road on 30 January in a replay after being two goals down in the first game before drawing 3-3.

NORWICH CITY 2000–01 LEAGUE RECORD

Match No.	Date	Venue	Opponents	Result	H/T Score	Lg. Pos.	Goalscorers	Attendance
1	Aug 12	A	Barnsley	L	0-1	0-0	—	15,640
2	19	H	Nottingham F	D	0-0	0-0	17	18,059
3	26	A	Blackburn R	L	2-3	0-1	21	Roberts [55], Giallanza [90]	19,542
4	28	H	Fulham	L	0-1	0-0	23		16,678
5	Sept 9	A	Crewe Alex	D	0-0	0-0	24		5955
6	12	A	Stockport Co	W	3-1	2-0	—	Whitley [15], Roberts 2 (1 pen) [30 (p), 85]	5703
7	16	H	Crystal Palace	D	0-0	0-0	20		16,828
8	24	A	Wolverhampton W	L	0-4	0-3	20		15,105
9	30	H	Huddersfield T	D	1-1	0-0	20	Giallanza [80]	14,499
10	Oct 14	A	WBA	W	3-2	2-1	18	Derveld [10], Llewellyn [43], Kenton [86]	16,511
11	17	A	Preston NE	L	0-1	0-0	—		13,002
12	21	H	Sheffield U	W	4-2	2-2	16	Mulryne [28], Roberts [42], Cottee [62], Llewellyn [63]	15,504
13	24	H	Portsmouth	D	0-0	0-0	—		18,772
14	Nov 4	H	Tranmere R	W	1-0	0-0	16	Roberts [52]	13,688
15	7	H	Birmingham C	W	1-0	1-0	—	Forbes [45]	13,900
16	11	A	Sheffield W	L	2-3	1-1	13	Parker [42], Marshall L [90]	16,956
17	18	H	Bolton W	L	0-2	0-0	14		15,224
18	21	A	Burnley	L	0-2	0-0	—		15,017
19	25	H	Wimbledon	L	1-2	1-1	17	Roberts [39]	14,059
20	Dec 2	A	Portsmouth	L	0-2	0-1	20		13,409
21	9	H	Gillingham	W	1-0	0-0	17	Llewellyn [78]	16,725
22	16	A	Grimsby T	L	0-2	0-1	18		5618
23	23	H	Barnsley	D	0-0	0-0	18		16,581
24	26	A	QPR	W	3-2	1-2	16	Roberts 2 [41, 81], Marshall L [46]	12,338
25	30	A	Nottingham F	D	0-0	0-0	17		20,108
26	Jan 1	H	Blackburn R	D	1-1	1-0	16	Forbes [32]	16,695
27	13	A	Fulham	L	0-2	0-1	17		16,052
28	20	H	QPR	W	1-0	1-0	16	Abbey [33]	16,472
29	27	H	Watford	W	2-1	0-0	12	Nedergaard [81], Marshall L [88]	15,309
30	Feb 3	A	Birmingham C	L	1-2	0-1	12	Llewellyn [80]	18,551
31	10	H	Crewe Alex	D	1-1	0-0	15	Llewellyn [88]	15,164
32	17	A	Crystal Palace	D	1-1	0-1	15	Russell [55]	16,417
33	20	H	Stockport Co	W	4-0	3-0	—	Llewellyn [15], Roberts 3 [35, 38, 57]	19,768
34	24	H	Wolverhampton W	W	1-0	1-0	12	McVeigh [3]	17,288
35	Mar 3	A	Huddersfield T	L	0-2	0-1	12		11,122
36	6	H	WBA	L	0-1	0-1	—		16,372
37	10	A	Watford	L	1-4	1-1	14	Forbes [7]	15,123
38	17	H	Preston NE	L	1-2	1-1	14	Roberts [32]	16,282
39	31	H	Grimsby T	W	2-1	1-1	14	Roberts [3], Llewellyn [74]	17,461
40	Apr 7	A	Gillingham	L	3-4	0-2	15	Llewellyn [58], Russell [63], Roberts [81]	9608
41	10	A	Sheffield U	D	1-1	0-1	—	Kenton [86]	16,072
42	14	A	Tranmere R	W	1-0	0-0	15	McGovern [87]	9303
43	16	H	Burnley	L	2-3	2-1	16	Notman [13], Roberts (pen) [38]	17,507
44	21	A	Bolton W	L	0-1	0-0	17		17,967
45	28	H	Sheffield W	W	1-0	1-0	16	MacKay [18]	21,241
46	May 6	A	Wimbledon	D	0-0	0-0	15		7888

Final League Position: 15

GOALSCORERS

League (46): Roberts 15 (2 pens), Llewellyn 8, Forbes 3, Marshall L 3, Giallanza 2, Kenton 2, Russell 2, Abbey 1, Cottee 1, Derveld 1, MacKay 1, McGovern 1, McVeigh 1, Mulryne 1, Nedergaard 1, Notman 1, Parker 1, Whitley 1.
Worthington Cup (10): Giallanza 3, Roberts 3 (1 pen), Russell 2, Cottee 1, Marshall L 1.
FA Cup (1): Roberts 1.

Marshall A 41	Sutch D 39 + 1	Llewellyn C 41 + 1	Kenton D 24 + 5	Fleming C 39	Derveld F 15 + 3	Marshall L 34 + 2	Bellamy C 1	Roberts I 44	Mulryne P 27 + 1	Russell D 34 + 7	Forbes A 13 + 16	De Waard R — + 6	Giallanza G 5 + 6	Jackson M 26	McGovern B 3 + 9	Whitley J 7 + 1	McVeigh P 6 + 5	Brady G 2	Nedergaard S 10 + 5	Mackay M 34 + 4	Cottee T 5 + 2	Walsh S 1 + 3	Dalglish P — + 7	Granville D 6	Parker S 6	Coote A 3 + 11	Notman A 10 + 5	De Blasiis Y 2 + 5	Abbey Z 11 + 9	Drury A 6	Holt G 3 + 1	Peschisolido P 3 + 2	Green R 5	Match No.
1	2	3¹	4²	5	6	7	8	9	10	11³	12	13	14																					1
1	2	3	4	5	6¹	7		9	10	11		12		8																				2
1	7	11	2²	5	3	4		9	10¹	8	13		12	6²	14																			3
1	7	11¹	2	5	3	4		9		10	12²	13		8³																				4
1	2		5	3	4			9		7	12		8¹	6²	13	10			11³	14														5
1	2		5	3	4			9		8	12			6²	11				7¹	13	10													6
1	2		5	3	4			9		8	12	13	14	6	11²				7¹		10³													7
1	2		5	3	4			9		8	7	12	13	11²					14	10¹	6³													8
1	2	12	6	5	3	4¹		9		8				13		11		7³		10²	14													9
1	2	11	6	5	3	4		9	10¹	8³				13		14			7²	12														10
1	2	11²	6¹	5	3	4		9	10		13			8		7³				12	14													11
1	2	11	6	5	3	4		9	10					8¹						7	12													12
1	2	11	6²	5	3¹	4		9	10	12				13						7	8³	14												13
1	2	11		5		4		9	10	12	7²									6		13		3	8¹									14
1	2	11		5		4		9	10	12	8²									6			3	7¹	13									15
1	2	11¹		5	12	4		9	10	13	8³									6			3	7²	14									16
1	2	11¹		5	12	4³		9	10	13	8									6			3	7²	14									17
1	2	11²		5		4¹		9	10	12	8³	13								6			3	7	14									18
1	2	11²		5		4¹	12	9	10		8									6			3	7	13									19
1	2	11		5	3³	12		9	10²	4	7¹									6						14	8	13						20
1	2	11	12	5		7		9		8				6						4						10	3¹							21
1	2¹	11	12	5		4		9	10	7³	13			6						3						8²		14						22
1	2	11		5		4¹		9	10	7				6						3		12				8²		13						23
1	2	11	12	5		4		9	10	7¹				6						3						14	8²	13³						24
1	2	11	12	5		4		9¹	10¹	7				6						3		13				14		8²						25
1	2	11		5		4			12	7	8³			6						3		13				10²	14	9¹						26
1	2	11	3	5		4		9	10¹	7				6²	13					3						8³	12	14						27
1	2²	11	3		4			9		7				6						5	13					10¹	14	12	8³					28
1	2²	11	7		4			9						5		13	14	6		12			10¹	3¹	8									29
1	3	11	2²		4³			9		8				5		7¹		6		12			14	13	10									30
1	2	11	3		4				8	12				5	9²	7		6					13			10¹								31
1	2	11	3		4			9		8	12			5		7¹		6					13			10								32
1	2	11	3		4			9		7³	12			5		8²		14	6				13			10¹								33
1	2	11	3²	5				9		7	12			4	13	8¹		14	6							10³								34
1	2	3		5				9			11	12		4		8		7	6							10¹								35
1	3	2²	5		7			9			11	12		4³	13	8		6					14			10¹								36
1	2	3	5	8¹				9			11	10²		4		13	7³	6					12	14										37
1	2³	3	5	7				9			11	10²		4		8¹	14	6					12	13										38
1	2	11	12	5¹				9	8			7			4											13	3	6	10²					39
	2	11						9	8	12	7²			6					5						13		3	4	10¹	1				40
		11	2	5				9	8	7				6					4						10¹		3		12	1				41
		11	2	5				9¹	8	7	12			6	13				4						14		3⁴	10¹		1				42
		11	2¹	5				9	8	7	12			6²	13				4						10³		3	14		1				43
		11	2¹	5				9	8³	7				6	12				4						10²	13	3	14		1				44
1		3¹	2	5				9	8	11				6		12		7	4						10									45
1	12	11²	2¹	5				9³	8	10				3	13	7		4							14			6					46

Worthington Cup

First Round	Bournemouth	(h)	0-0	
		(a)	2-1	
Second Round	Blackpool	(h)	3-3	
		(a)	5-0	
Third Round	Derby Co	(a)	0-3	

FA Cup

Third Round	Sheffield W	(a)	1-2

NOTTINGHAM FOREST — Division 1

FOUNDATION

One of the oldest football clubs in the world, Nottingham Forest was formed at a meeting in the Clinton Arms in 1865. Known originally as the Forest Football Club, the game which first drew the founders together was 'shinney', a form of hockey. When they determined to change to football in 1865, one of their first moves was to buy a set of red caps to wear on the field.

City Ground, Nottingham NG2 5FJ.

Telephone: (0115) 982 4444. *Fax:* (0115) 982 4455.
Information Desk: (0115) 982 4449.
Commercial Office: (0115) 982 4450. *Fax:* (0115) 982 4410. *Ticket Office:* (0115) 982 4445. *Souvenir Shop:* (0115) 982 4447. *Junior Reds:* (0115) 982 4454.
ClubCall: 09068 121 174.

Ground Capacity: 30,602.

Record Attendance: 49,946 v Manchester U, Division 1, 28 October 1967.

Record Receipts: £499,099 v Bayern Munich, UEFA Cup quarter-final 2nd leg, 19 March 1996.

Pitch Measurements: 112yd × 74yd.

Chairman: E. M. Barnes. *Chief Executive:* M. A. Arthur.
Finance Director: J. D. Pelling.
Board of Directors: E. M. Barnes, M. A. Arthur, J. D. Pelling, N. G. Candeland, T. H. Farr, Sir David White.

Manager: Paul Hart. *First Team Coach:* Steve Wigley.
Reserve Team Coach: Jimmy Gilligan.
Physio: John Haselden.

Secretary: Paul White.

Public Relations Manager: Nick Lucy.

Football Press Officer: Fraser Nicholson.

Colours: Red shirts, white shorts, red stockings.

Change Colours: White shirts, red shorts, white stockings.

Year Formed: 1865. *Turned Professional:* 1889. *Ltd Co.:* 1982. *Club Nickname:* 'Reds'.

Previous Grounds: 1865, Forest Racecourse; 1879, The Meadows; 1880, Trent Bridge Cricket Ground; 1882, Parkside, Lenton; 1885, Gregory, Lenton; 1890, Town Ground; 1898, City Ground.

First Football League Game: 3 September 1892, Division 1, v Everton (a) D 2–2 – Brown; Earp, Scott; Hamilton, A. Smith, McCracken; McCallum, W. Smith, Higgins (2), Pike, McInnes.

Record League Victory: 12–0 v Leicester Fosse, Division 1, 12 April 1909 – Iremonger; Dudley, Maltby; Hughes (1), Needham, Armstrong; Hooper (3), Marrison, West (3), Morris (2), Spouncer (3 incl. 1p).

HONOURS

Football League: Division 1 – Champions 1977–78, 1997–98; Runners-up 1966–67, 1978–79; Division 2 – Champions 1906–07, 1921–22; Runners-up 1956–57; Division 3 (S) – Champions 1950–51.

FA Cup: Winners 1898, 1959; Runners-up 1991.

Football League Cup: Winners 1978, 1979, 1989, 1990; Runners-up 1980, 1992.

Anglo-Scottish Cup: Winners 1977;

Simod Cup: Winners 1989.

Zenith Data Systems Cup: Winners: 1992.

European Competitions: *European Fairs Cup:* 1961–62, 1967–68. *European Cup:* 1978–79 (winners), 1979–80 (winners), 1980–81. *Super Cup:* 1979–80 (winners), 1980–81 (runners-up). *World Club Championship:* 1980. *UEFA Cup:* 1983–84, 1984–85, 1995–96.

IT'S A FACT !

On 29 November 2000, injury-hit Nottingham Forest gave a debut to schoolboy Andrew Reid, who marked his appearance with an 83rd minute goal in the 2-0 win over Sheffield United.

Record Cup Victory: 14–0 v Clapton (away), FA Cup 1st rd, 17 January 1891 – Brown; Earp, Scott; A. Smith, Russell, Jeacock; McCallum (2), 'Tich' Smith (1), Higgins (5), Lindley (4), Shaw (2).

Record Defeat: 1–9 v Blackburn R, Division 2, 10 April 1937.

Most League Points (2 for a win): 70, Division 3 (S), 1950–51.

Most League Points (3 for a win): 94, Division 1, 1997–98.

Most League Goals: 110, Division 3 (S), 1950–51.

Highest League Scorer in Season: Wally Ardron, 36, Division 3 (S), 1950–51.

Most League Goals in Total Aggregate: Grenville Morris, 199, 1898–1913.

Most League Goals in One Match: 4, Enoch West v Sunderland, Division 1, 9 November 1907; 4, Tommy Gibson v Burnley, Division 2, 25 January 1913; 4, Tom Peacock v Port Vale, Division 2, 23 December 1933; 4, Tom Peacock v Barnsley, Division 2, 9 November 1935; 4, Tom Peacock v Port Vale, Division 2, 23 November 1935; 4, Tom Peacock v Doncaster R, Division 2, 26 December 1935; 4, Tommy Capel v Gillingham, Division 3S, 18 November 1950; 4, Wally Ardron v Hull C, Division 2, 26 December 1952; 4, Tommy Wilson v Barnsley, Division 2, 9 February 1957; 4, Peter Withe v Ipswich T, Division 1, 4 October 1977.

Most Capped Player: Stuart Pearce, 76 (78), England.

Most League Appearances: Bob McKinlay, 614, 1951–70.

Youngest League Player: Gary Mills, 16 years 302 days v Arsenal, 9 September 1978.

Record Transfer Fee Received: £8,500,000 from Liverpool for Stan Collymore, June 1995.

Record Transfer Fee Paid: £3,500,000 to Celtic for Pierre van Hooijdonk, March 1997.

Football League Record: 1892 Elected to Division 1; 1906–07 Division 2; 1907–11 Division 1; 1911–22 Division 2; 1922–25 Division 1; 1925–49 Division 2; 1949–51 Division 3 (S); 1951–57 Division 2; 1957–72 Division 1; 1972–77 Division 2; 1977–92 Division 1; 1992–93 FA Premier League; 1993–94 Division 1; 1994–97 FA Premier League; 1997–98 Division 1; 1998–99 FA Premier League; 1999– Division 1.

MANAGERS

Harry Radford 1889–97 *(Secretary-Manager)*
Harry Haslam 1897–1909 *(Secretary-Manager)*
Fred Earp 1909–12
Bob Masters 1912–25
John Baynes 1925–29
Stan Hardy 1930–31
Noel Watson 1931–36
Harold Wightman 1936–39
Billy Walker 1939–60
Andy Beattie 1960–63
Johnny Carey 1963–68
Matt Gillies 1969–72
Dave Mackay 1972
Allan Brown 1973–75
Brian Clough 1975–93
Frank Clark 1993–96
Stuart Pearce 1996–97
Dave Bassett 1997–98 *(previously General Manager from February)*
Ron Atkinson 1998–99
David Platt 1999–2001
Paul Hart July 2001–

LATEST SEQUENCES

Longest Sequence of League Wins: 7, 9.5.79 – 1.9.79.

Longest Sequence of League Defeats: 14, 21.3.13 – 27.9.13.

Longest Sequence of League Draws: 7, 29.4.78 – 2.9.78.

Longest Sequence of Unbeaten League Matches: 42, 26.11.77 – 25.11.78.

Longest Sequence Without a League Win: 19, 8.9.98 – 16.1.99.

TEN YEAR LEAGUE RECORD

		P	W	D	L	F	A	Pts	Pos
1990-91	Div 1	38	14	12	12	65	50	54	8
1991-92	Div 1	42	16	11	15	60	58	59	8
1992-93	PR Lge	42	10	10	22	41	62	40	22
1993-94	Div 1	46	23	14	9	74	49	83	2
1994-95	PR Lge	42	22	11	9	72	43	77	3
1995-96	PR Lge	38	15	13	10	50	54	58	9
1996-97	PR Lge	38	6	16	16	31	59	34	20
1997-98	Div 1	46	28	10	8	82	42	94	1
1998-99	PR Lge	38	7	9	22	35	69	30	20
1999-2000	Div 1	46	14	14	18	53	55	56	14

DID YOU KNOW ?

On 13 December 1987, Nigel Clough scored three goals in four minutes for Nottingham Forest against Queens Park Rangers, registering in the 81st, 82nd and 85th minutes, the last goal coming from the penalty spot.

NOTTINGHAM FOREST 2000–01 LEAGUE RECORD

Match No.	Date	Venue	Opponents	Result	H/T Score	Lg. Pos.	Goalscorers	Attendance
1	Aug 12	H	WBA	W 1-0	0-0	—	Hjelde [78]	21,209
2	19	A	Norwich C	D 0-0	0-0	9		18,059
3	26	H	Birmingham C	L 1-2	0-2	12	Bart-Williams [52]	18,820
4	28	A	Crystal Palace	W 3-2	3-0	7	Johnson A [12], Platt [31], Mullins (og) [40]	18,865
5	Sept 9	A	Blackburn R	L 0-3	0-2	9		18,471
6	13	A	Sheffield W	W 1-0	1-0	—	Lester [35]	15,700
7	16	H	Fulham	L 0-3	0-0	11		18,737
8	23	A	Grimsby T	W 2-0	2-0	9	Rogers [14], Lester [42]	6467
9	30	H	Wolverhampton W	D 0-0	0-0	8		19,110
10	Oct 14	A	Barnsley	W 4-3	2-0	9	Bart-Williams 2 (1 pen) [10 (p), 54], Rogers [24], Blake [69]	14,831
11	17	A	Bolton W	D 0-0	0-0	—		13,017
12	21	H	Watford	L 0-2	0-2	11		20,065
13	25	H	Burnley	W 5-0	2-0	—	Bart-Williams 2 (1 pen) [4, 54 (p)], Johnson A [45], Rogers [76], Scimeca [89]	17,195
14	28	A	Stockport Co	W 2-1	0-0	9	Lester 2 [75, 88]	6021
15	Nov 4	H	Preston NE	W 3-1	1-1	9	Bart-Williams 2 (2 pens) [23, 66], Olsen [58]	19,504
16	12	A	Gillingham	W 3-1	2-1	9	Lester 3 [9, 45, 77]	9884
17	18	H	Wimbledon	L 1-2	0-1	9	Vaughan [89]	18,159
18	25	H	Tranmere R	W 3-1	2-1	9	Bart-Williams (pen) [37], Foy [42], Scimeca [63]	19,678
19	29	H	Sheffield U	W 2-0	1-0	—	Olsen [10], Reid [64]	17,089
20	Dec 2	A	Burnley	L 0-1	0-0	7		17,876
21	9	H	Portsmouth	W 2-0	1-0	6	Scimeca [12], Bart-Williams [65]	19,284
22	13	H	Huddersfield T	L 1-3	0-0	—	Reid [69]	28,372
23	16	A	QPR	L 0-1	0-1	7		14,409
24	23	A	WBA	L 0-3	0-2	7		20,350
25	26	H	Crewe Alex	W 1-0	1-0	6	Jones [38]	20,903
26	30	H	Norwich C	D 0-0	0-0	7		20,108
27	Jan 1	A	Birmingham C	W 2-0	0-0	5	Bart-Williams (pen) [71], Prutton [86]	20,034
28	14	H	Crystal Palace	L 0-3	0-2	7		21,198
29	Feb 3	A	Huddersfield T	D 1-1	1-1	7	Scimeca [12]	13,838
30	10	H	Blackburn R	W 2-1	0-0	7	Bart-Williams [52], Edwards [66]	22,455
31	17	A	Fulham	L 0-1	0-1	7		17,425
32	21	H	Sheffield W	L 0-1	0-0	—		23,266
33	24	H	Grimsby T	W 3-1	0-1	7	Edds [55], Edwards [57], Johnson D [86]	21,660
34	Mar 3	A	Wolverhampton W	L 0-2	0-0	9		20,291
35	7	H	Barnsley	W 1-0	1-0	—	Bart-Williams [2]	18,788
36	10	A	Sheffield U	W 3-1	1-0	6	Edwards [3], Johnson A [65], Johnson D [87]	25,673
37	13	A	Crewe Alex	L 0-1	0-0	—		7916
38	17	H	Bolton W	L 0-2	0-0	7		22,162
39	31	H	QPR	D 1-1	1-0	7	Harewood [13]	22,208
40	Apr 3	A	Watford	L 0-3	0-1	—		13,651
41	7	A	Portsmouth	W 2-0	2-0	7	Bart-Williams 2 (1 pen) [11 (p), 38]	13,018
42	14	A	Preston NE	D 1-1	0-1	7	Hjelde [90]	16,842
43	16	H	Stockport Co	W 1-0	1-0	7	John [25]	23,500
44	21	A	Wimbledon	L 1-2	0-0	7	John [77]	10,027
45	28	H	Gillingham	L 0-1	0-0	10		20,670
46	May 6	A	Tranmere R	D 2-2	0-1	11	Harewood 2 [66, 78]	9891

Final League Position: 11

GOALSCORERS

League (55): Bart-Williams 14 (7 pens), Lester 7, Scimeca 4, Edwards 3, Harewood 3, Johnson A 3, Rogers 3, Hjelde 2, John 2, Johnson D 2, Olsen 2, Reid 2, Blake 1, Edds 1, Foy 1, Jones 1, Platt 1, Prutton 1, Vaughan 1, own goal 1.
Worthington Cup (3): Bart-Williams 1 (pen), John 1, Rogers 1.
FA Cup (0).

Beasant D 45	Scimeca R 34 + 2	Brennan J 9 + 3	Bart-Williams C 46	Hjelde J 10 + 1	Doig C 14 + 1	Prutton D 41 + 1	Johnson A 29 + 2	Jones G 22 + 9	Harewood M 13 + 20	Rogers A 16 + 1	Louis-Jean M 10 + 3	Lester J 18 + 1	Vaughan T 23 + 2	Gray A 11 + 7	John S 16 + 13	Blake R 9 + 2	Roche B 1 + 1	Platt D 2	Dawson K 1	Edwards C 35 + 1	Freedman D 2 + 3	Williams G 11 + 6	Foy K 17 + 3	Olsen B 14 + 4	Calderwood C 1 + 1	Reid A 9 + 5	Cooper R — + 2	Upson M 1	Edds G 9 + 4	Benali F 15	Jenas J 1	Freeman D 2 + 3	Johnson D 19	Match No.
1	2	3	4	5	6	7	8^1	9	10^2	11	12	13																						1
1	8^3	3	4	5^1	6	7		9		11	2	10^2	14	12	13																			2
1	8	3^1			6	7	13	9^3	12	11	2^2		14	5		10																		3
1			4		6	7	8	12			3	2	10^6	9^2	5					13	15	11^1												4
1			4		6	7	8	12			3	2	10	9^2				11^1	5^3	14	13													5
		11			6	7	8		9^1		3	2	10		5			1		4	12													6
1	3^3	4				7	8		9^1	11		2^2	10	12	5					6	13	14												7
1	12	4				7	8			13	11^1	2	10		5					6	9^2	3												8
1	12	4				7	8	13			11	2	10^2		5^1	14				6	9^3	3												9
1	7	4		6			8	12	13	11		2	10^1		9^2					5		3												10
1	2	4		6	7		8	12	13	11			10^2		9^1					5		3												11
1	7	4		6^2	12	8			14	11	13	10^2		9						5		3	2^1											12
1	2	4			7	8^1	9^2		3^3	12	10		5		11				6		13		14											13
1	2	4			7	8	9	12	3		10		5^2		11^1				6			13												14
1	2	4			7^1	8	9	12	3		10^6		5		11^1				6		13	14												15
1	2	4			7	8	9		3^2		10		5		11^1				6		12	13												16
1	2	4			7	8	9^2	12			10^1		5		11				6		13	14	3^3											17
1	2	4			7		9^1	12			10		5						6		8	3	11											18
1	2	4			7						10^1	12	5						6		8	3^3	11^2	14	9	13								19
1	8	13	4			7			10			2^3	12	5					6		11^1	3^2		9	14									20
1	8		4			7			10^1	13		5							6		3	2	9	11^2										21
1	2^2		4			7		8	12			9^1		13					6		3	11	5	10										22
1			4			7		9	10			12		2					6		3^1	11	8		5									23
1			4			7		9	10			12	5	13					6		11^2	3	2^1	14		8^1								24
1	3^1		4			7		8	10^3			9	5	12					6		11^2	13	2^1	14										25
1	3^1		4			7		8	10^2			9^3	5	13					6		11	12	2^1	14										26
1	12		4			7		8	10			5	2						6		11	3^2		9^1		13								27
1	7^1		4				8						12	5							11			10		2	3	6^2	13	9				28
1	5	12	4			7	13		8^3				14						6		11			10^1		2^2	3			9				29
1	11	3	4			7	8	10^1	12										6				2				5			9				30
1	11	3	4				8^2	7^1	10			12							6		13		2				5			9				31
1	7	3^1	4				8	11^2	10^1			12							6				2	14		13	5			9				32
1	2	11	4^2	7	8		12												6			3				13	5		10	9^1				33
1	11		4			7	8	13	12										5			3				2^2	6		10	9				34
1	11		4			7	8					10^2	12						6			3^1	2^3			14	5		13	9				35
1	2		4	14		7	8	11	12			10^2	5	13					6^3								3			9^1				36
1	2		4			7	8	11^2	12			10^1	5	13					6								3			9				37
1	2		4			7^1	13					10	5	11					6				8				3		12^2	9				38
1	2		4			7		8				12	11						6	10	3^2		13				5			9^1				39
1	2		4	5	12	7	10					8	11						6^1								3			9				40
1	2		4	5	6	7	8					10	11														3			9				41
1	2		4	5	6	7	8					10	11														3			9				42
1	2		4	5	6	7	8	12				10^1	11										3							9				43
1	2^2		4	5	6	7	8	13	12			10	11										3^1							9				44
1			4	5	6	7^1	8	12	13	14		10^2	2									11^3					3			9				45
1	2		4	5			7^1	8		12		10	11						6								3			9^1				46

Worthington Cup
First Round   Darlington   (a)   2-2
                              (h)   1-2

FA Cup
Third Round   Wolverhampton W   (h)   0-1

NOTTS COUNTY
Division 2

FOUNDATION

According to the official history of Notts County 'the true date of Notts' foundation has to be the meeting at the George Hotel on 7 December 1864'. However, in the same opening chapter is the following: The Nottingham Guardian on 28 November 1862 carried the following report: 'The opening of the Nottingham Football Club commenced on Tuesday last at Cremorne Gardens. A side was chosen by W. Arkwright and Chas Deakin. A very spirited game resulted in the latter scoring two goals and two rouges against one and one'.

County Ground, Meadow Lane, Nottingham NG2 3HJ.
Telephone: (0115) 952 9000. *Fax:* (0115) 955 3994.
Ticket Office: (0115) 955 7210. *ClubCall:* 09068 121 101.
Football in the Community: (0115) 955 7215.
Supporters Club: (0115) 955 7255.

Ground Capacity: 20,300.

Record Attendance: 47,310 v York C, FA Cup 6th rd, 12 March 1955.

Record Receipts: £124,539.10 v Manchester C, FA Cup 6th rd, 16 February 1991.

Pitch Measurements: 113yd × 72yd.

Chairman: D. C. Pavis. *Deputy Chairman:* P. Storrie.
Directors: W. Barrowcliffe, Mrs V. Pavis, G. Davey (Managing). D. Rhodes, A. Scardino
Executive Deputy Chairman: P. Storrie.

Manager: Jocky Scott. *Assistant Manager:* Gary Brazil.
Youth Coach: John Gaunt. *Secretary:* Tony Cuthbert.
Physio: Roger Cleary.

Commercial Manager: Clair Finnegan.
Conference & Banqueting Manager: Matthew Foote.
Stadium Manager: Bob Davy.

Colours: Black with white striped shirts, black shorts, black stockings.

Change Colours: All white.

Year Formed: 1862* (*see Foundation*).

Turned Professional: 1885. *Ltd Co.:* 1888. *Club Nickname:* 'Magpies'.

Previous Grounds: 1862, The Park; 1864, The Meadows; 1877, Beeston Cricket Ground; 1880, Castle Ground; 1883, Trent Bridge; 1910, Meadow Lane.

First Football League Game: 15 September 1888, Football League, v Everton (a) L 1–2 – Holland; Guttridge, McLean; Brown, Warburton, Shelton; Hodder, Harker, Jardine, Moore (1), Wardle.

Record League Victory: 11–1 v Newport Co, Division 3 (S), 15 January 1949 – Smith; Southwell, Purvis; Gannon, Baxter, Adamson; Houghton (1), Sewell (4), Lawton (4), Pimbley, Johnston (2).

Record Cup Victory: 15–0 v Rotherham T (at Trent Bridge), FA Cup 1st rd, 24 October 1885 – Sherwin; Snook, H. T. Moore; Dobson (1), Emmett (1), Chapman; Gunn (1), Albert Moore (2), Jackson (3), Daft (2), Cursham (4), (1 og).

HONOURS

Football League: Division 1 best season: 3rd, 1890–91, 1900–01; Division 2 – Champions 1896–97, 1913–14, 1922–23; Runners-up 1894–95, 1980–81; Promoted from Division 2 1990–91 (play-offs); Division 3 (S) – Champions 1930–31, 1949–50; Runners-up 1936–37; Division 3 – Champions 1997–98; Runners-up 1972–73; Promoted from Division 3 1989–90 (play-offs); Division 4 – Champions 1970–71; Runners-up 1959–60.

FA Cup: Winners 1894; Runners-up 1891.

Football League Cup: best season: 5th rd, 1964, 1973, 1976.

Anglo-Italian Cup: Winners 1995; Runners-up 1994.

IT'S A FACT !

By 1881 Notts County had had at least two members each from the following football families: Greenhalgh, Cursham, Ashwell, Morse, Dobson, Shelton, Jessop and Oswald.

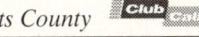
Record Defeat: 1–9 v Blackburn R, Division 1, 16 November 1889. 1–9 v Aston Villa, Division 1, 29 September 1888. 1–9 v Portsmouth, Division 2, 9 April 1927.

Most League Points (2 for a win): 69, Division 4, 1970–71.

Most League Points (3 for a win): 99, Division 3, 1997–98.

Most League Goals: 107, Division 4, 1959–60.

Highest League Scorer in Season: Tom Keetley, 39, Division 3 (S), 1930–31.

Most League Goals in Total Aggregate: Les Bradd, 124, 1967–78.

Most League Goals in One Match: 5, Robert Jardine v Burnley, Division 1, 27 October 1888; 5, Daniel Bruce v Port Vale, Division 2, 26 February 1895; 5, Bertie Mills v Barnsley, Division 2, 19 November 1927.

Most Capped Player: Kevin Wilson, 15 (42), Northern Ireland.

Most League Appearances: Albert Iremonger, 564, 1904–26.

Youngest League Player: Tony Bircumshaw, 16 years 54 days v Brentford, 3 April 1961.

Record Transfer Fee Received: £2,500,000 from Derby Co for Craig Short, September 1992.

Record Transfer Fee Paid: £685,000 to Sheffield U for Tony Agana, November 1991.

Football League Record: 1888 Founder Member of the Football League; 1893–97 Division 2; 1897–1913 Division 1; 1913–14 Division 2; 1914–20 Division 1; 1920–23 Division 2; 1923–26 Division 1; 1926–30 Division 2; 1930–31 Division 3 (S); 1931–35 Division 2; 1935–50 Division 3 (S); 1950–58 Division 2; 1958–59 Division 3; 1959–60 Division 4; 1960–64 Division 3; 1964–71 Division 4; 1971–73 Division 3; 1973–81 Division 2; 1981–84 Division 1; 1984–85 Division 2; 1985–90 Division 3; 1990–91 Division 2; 1991–95 Division 1; 1995–97 Division 2; 1997–98 Division 3; 1998– Division 2.

LATEST SEQUENCES

Longest Sequence of League Wins: 10, 3.12.97 – 31.1.98.

Longest Sequence of League Defeats: 7, 3.9.83 – 16.10.83.

Longest Sequence of League Draws: 5, 2.12.78 – 26.12.78.

Longest Sequence of Unbeaten League Matches: 19, 26.4.30 – 6.12.30.

Longest Sequence Without a League Win: 20, 3.12.96 – 31.3.97.

MANAGERS

Edwin Browne 1883–93 *(Secretary-Manager)*
Tom Featherstone 1893 *(Secretary-Manager)*
Tom Harris 1893–1913 *(Secretary-Manager)*
Albert Fisher 1913–27
Horace Henshall 1927–34
Charlie Jones 1934–35
David Pratt 1935
Percy Smith 1935–36
Jimmy McMullan 1936–37
Harry Parkes 1938–39
Tony Towers 1939–42
Frank Womack 1942–43
Major Frank Buckley 1944–46
Arthur Stollery 1946–49
Eric Houghton 1949–53
George Poyser 1953–57
Tommy Lawton 1957–58
Frank Hill 1958–61
Tim Coleman 1961–63
Eddie Lowe 1963–65
Tim Coleman 1965–66
Jack Burkitt 1966–67
Andy Beattie *(General Manager)* 1967
Billy Gray 1967–68
Jimmy Sirrel 1969–75
Ron Fenton 1975–77
Jimmy Sirrel 1978–82 *(continued as General Manager to 1984)*
Howard Wilkinson 1982–83
Larry Lloyd 1983–84
Richie Barker 1984–85
Jimmy Sirrel 1985–87
John Barnwell 1987–88
Neil Warnock 1989–93
Mick Walker 1993–94
Russell Slade 1994–95
Howard Kendall 1995
Colin Murphy June 1995 *(continued as General Manager to 1996)*
Steve Thompson 1996
Sam Allardyce 1997–1999
Gary Brazil 1999–2000
Jocky Scott June 2000–

TEN YEAR LEAGUE RECORD

		P	W	D	L	F	A	Pts	Pos
1990-91	Div 2	46	23	11	12	76	55	80	4
1991-92	Div 1	42	10	10	22	40	62	40	21
1992-93	Div 1	46	12	16	18	55	70	52	17
1993-94	Div 1	46	20	8	18	65	69	68	7
1994-95	Div 1	46	9	13	24	45	66	40	24
1995-96	Div 2	46	21	15	10	63	39	78	4
1996-97	Div 2	46	7	14	25	33	59	35	24
1997-98	Div 3	46	29	12	5	82	43	99	1
1998-99	Div 2	46	14	12	20	52	61	54	16
1999-2000	Div 2	46	18	11	17	61	55	65	8

DID YOU KNOW ?

In 1914, Notts County celebrated promotion with a trip to Spain for three matches against Barcelona. The non-stop journey by boat, train and coach took 39 hours! Notts won all three games, 3-1, 4-2 and 10-3 (after being 2-1 down at half-time).

NOTTS COUNTY 2000–01 LEAGUE RECORD

Match No.	Date	Venue	Opponents	Result		H/T Score	Lg. Pos.	Goalscorers	Attendance
1	Aug 12	A	Luton T	W	1-0	1-0	—	Stallard [24]	7059
2	19	H	Millwall	L	3-4	1-3	10	Ramage 2 [32, 58], Stallard [75]	6046
3	26	A	Stoke C	W	1-0	0-0	6	Stallard [86]	13,041
4	28	H	Cambridge U	L	0-1	0-1	9		5020
5	Sept 2	A	Oldham Ath	W	1-0	1-0	4	Owers [42]	4424
6	9	H	Bristol R	D	1-1	0-0	7	Stallard [89]	5511
7	12	H	Swansea C	L	0-1	0-1	—		3395
8	16	A	Northampton T	L	0-1	0-0	15		5703
9	23	H	Brentford	D	2-2	1-0	14	Joseph [12], Hughes [87]	4164
10	30	A	Walsall	L	1-5	0-2	15	Stallard [55]	5211
11	Oct 6	A	Wycombe W	L	1-3	1-2	—	Stallard [18]	5080
12	14	H	Wigan Ath	D	2-2	1-0	16	Farrell [45], Hughes [90]	4567
13	17	H	Bury	W	1-0	0-0	—	Stallard [60]	3461
14	21	A	Peterborough U	L	0-1	0-0	16		5889
15	24	A	Bournemouth	W	1-0	0-0	—	Stallard (pen) [85]	3556
16	28	H	Swindon T	W	3-2	2-1	13	Farrell [12], Ramage [42], Joseph (pen) [76]	4502
17	Nov 4	A	Bristol C	L	0-4	0-2	16		10,250
18	25	A	Oxford U	W	3-2	0-2	14	Allsopp 2 (1 pen) [49, 86 (p)], Newton [87]	4765
19	Dec 2	A	Colchester U	L	0-2	0-1	15		3280
20	16	H	Reading	W	3-2	2-1	13	Allsopp 2 [35, 89], Stallard (pen) [43]	5106
21	23	H	Wrexham	W	1-0	1-0	11	Liburd [2]	6206
22	26	A	Rotherham U	D	0-0	0-0	11		7673
23	30	A	Millwall	W	3-2	2-2	10	Hughes 2 [6, 36], Owers [90]	11,495
24	Jan 1	H	Stoke C	D	2-2	1-1	9	Liburd [17], Richardson [57]	9125
25	13	A	Cambridge U	D	2-2	1-0	10	Stallard [1], Allsopp (pen) [82]	4029
26	20	H	Rotherham U	W	4-1	0-1	9	Jacobsen [46], Liburd [60], Hughes [78], Stallard [82]	7010
27	Feb 3	H	Oldham Ath	W	1-0	1-0	9	Allsopp [44]	5212
28	10	A	Bristol R	D	0-0	0-0	8		6914
29	13	H	Luton T	L	1-3	1-1	—	Stallard [44]	4333
30	17	H	Northampton T	W	2-0	1-0	8	Stallard [13], Fenton [77]	6320
31	20	A	Swansea C	W	1-0	1-0	—	Brough [12]	4058
32	24	A	Brentford	L	1-3	0-1	8	Allsopp [82]	4366
33	Mar 3	H	Walsall	W	2-0	1-0	8	Farrell [38], Allsopp [90]	6077
34	6	A	Wigan Ath	D	1-1	0-0	—	Fenton [90]	5021
35	17	H	Bury	D	1-1	0-0	8	Allsopp [69]	3487
36	23	H	Peterborough U	D	3-3	2-1	—	Allsopp (pen) [11], Nicholson [40], Stallard [79]	6510
37	27	H	Port Vale	L	0-1	0-0	—		4603
38	31	A	Reading	L	1-2	0-0	8	Owers [81]	11,624
39	Apr 10	A	Wrexham	D	1-1	1-1	—	Thomas [26]	2741
40	14	H	Bournemouth	L	0-2	0-2	10		5186
41	16	A	Swindon T	W	2-1	0-1	10	Joseph [74], Stallard [80]	6207
42	21	H	Bristol C	W	2-1	0-1	9	Nicholson [69], Allsopp [78]	5369
43	26	A	Wycombe W	L	0-2	0-1	—		3522
44	28	A	Port Vale	W	3-2	2-1	9	Allsopp 2 (1 pen) [10, 83 (p)], Owers [45]	5236
45	May 3	H	Colchester U	D	2-2	1-1	—	Stallard [41], Jacobsen [60]	2860
46	5	H	Oxford U	W	2-1	1-1	8	Joseph [35], Stallard [82]	5513

Final League Position: 8

GOALSCORERS

League (62): Stallard 17 (2 pens), Allsopp 13 (4 pens), Hughes 5, Joseph 4 (1 pen), Owers 4, Farrell 3, Liburd 3, Ramage 3, Fenton 2, Jacobsen 2, Nicholson 2, Brough 1, Newton 1, Richardson 1, Thomas 1.
Worthington Cup (5): Stallard 3 (2 pens), Hughes 1, McDermott 1.
FA Cup (7): Stallard 3, Hughes 2, Liburd 2.

Ward D 35	McDermott A 20+5	Liburd R 28+3	Warren M 15+1	Redmile M 7+1	Dyer A 8+1	Owers G 40	Ramage C 14+1	Stallard M 42	Joseph D 13+14	Hughes A 20+10	Holmes R 3+2	McCann G 2	Hamilton I 23+2	Richardson I 24+1	Rapley K —+7	Farrell S 9+10	Gibson P 9	Cramb C 2+1	Bolland P 7	Lindley J 2	Fenton N 30	Jacobsen A 27+2	Pearce D 26+1	Heffernan P —+1	Murray S 7+4	Allsopp D 26+3	Newton A 13+7	Brough M 11+5	Ireland C 16	Jorgensen H 3+2	Thomas G 8	Calderwood C 5	Nicholson K 9+2	Moreau F 2+3	Match No.
1	2	3¹	4	5	6	7	8	9	10	11	12																								1
1	2	3	4	5	6	7	8	9	10				11¹	12																					2
1	2	3	4		6	7	8	9	10¹	13			11²	5	12																				3
1	2	3	4	5¹	12	7	8	9	10³	13			11²	6	14																				4
1	2	3	4		6	7	8¹	9	10²	12			11	5	13																				5
1		3	4	12	6³	7	8	9	10²	2			11¹	5	13	14																			6
1	12	3³	4	5		7	8	9		2¹			11	6	14	13			10¹																7
	12	3	4	5		7	8	9	13	2¹			11	6					1	10²															8
1	2	3	4	5³		7		9	10²	12			11	6	13			14	8¹																9
	2¹	3		5²	6	7		9	12	10			11				8		1		4	13													10
	5		2			7	12	9	10³	6¹			11		13			8²	1		4	14	3												11
	2		5		6²	7	8	9	12	13			11					10¹	1		4		3												12
	2		5			7	8	9		12			11					10¹	1		4	6	3												13
	12		5			7	8	9		3²			11	6				10	1		2¹	4			13										14
	2		5			7	8	9	12	10¹			11	6					1		4		3												15
	2		5²			7	8		10			14	11			12	9¹		1		4³	6	3		13										16
	2					7	8		10¹				11	5			9		1		4	6	3		12										17
	2					7			12				11	5			8¹		1	10²	4	6	3			9	13								18
	2					7	8		12				11²	5					1	10¹	4	6	3			9	13								19
1		3¹				7		9	8				11	5							4	6	2			10	12								20
1		3				7	8		12				11³	5							4	6	2		10²	9¹	13	14							21
1		3				7	8							5							4	6	2			9	10	11							22
1		3				7	8		12	11				5					2			6			13	9	10¹	4²							23
1		3²	12			7	8		13	10		2		5							4¹	6				9		11							24
1		3				7	8		12	10				5	13						4	6				9	2¹	11¹²							25
1		3				7	8		12	2¹				5							4	6			11	9	10								26
1		3				7³	8		10				11			12					2	6	13			9¹	4	14	5²						27
1	12	3					8		10				11								2	6¹	5			9	4	7							28
1	2	3					8		12				11		13						4	6	5¹		14	9²	10	7³							29
1	7					9	12			10²							8¹				2	6	3		11	13	4	5							30
1	7	12					8		10¹												2	6	3		11	9²	4	5	13						31
1	7	4					8						12								2²	6	3		10	9	13	11²	5						32
1	2		11				8		12								9¹					6²	3		4	7	13		5					10	33
1	2					7	8		12												4		3		11²	9	6¹	13	5					10	34
1	4					7	8						12								2		3			9			5		10	6	11¹		35
1	2					7	8		4				12										3			9			5		10²	6	11¹	13	36
1	4					7	8		11²				12								2³		3			9			5	14		6	13	10¹	37
1						7	8		10²	11³			12										3¹			9			5	2	4	6	13	14	38
1	12					7	8		13				4	8												9	11²	5	2	10		6		3¹	39
1	12					7	8		13	6			4								2					9²	14	5		3¹	10		11³		40
1	11¹	10				7	8	9²													2	6	4		12	13			5				3		41
1						7	8		12												2	6	4			9	11¹	13	5			10²	3		42
1						7	8	9							13						2	6	3²		12	4³	10¹		5				11	14	43
1	12					7	8							5		10					2	6	3			9	4¹						11		44
1	2					7	8							5		10						6	3			9	4						11		45
1	2						8		10				11	4								6				9	7		5				3		46

Worthington Cup

		(a)	0-1
First Round	Hull C		
		(h)	2-0
Second Round	Watford	(h)	1-3
		(a)	2-0

FA Cup

		(a)	2-1
First Round	Gravesend & N		
		(a)	1-1
Second Round	Wigan Ath	(h)	2-1
		(a)	2-2
Third Round	Wimbledon		
		(h)	0-1

OLDHAM ATHLETIC

Division 2

FOUNDATION

It was in 1895 that John Garland, the landlord of the Featherstall and Junction Hotel, decided to form a football club. As Pine Villa they played in the Oldham Junior League. In 1899 the local professional club Oldham County, went out of existence and one of the liquidators persuaded Pine Villa to take over their ground at Sheepfoot Lane and change their name to Oldham Athletic.

Boundary Park, Oldham OL1 2PA.

Telephone: (0161) 624 4972. **Fax:** (0161) 627 5915.
Website: www.oldhamathletic.co.uk
ClubCall: 09068 121 142. **Commercial Office:** (0161) 627 1802. **Fax:** (0161) 652 6501.

Ground Capacity: 13,559.

Record Attendance: 47,671 v Sheffield W, FA Cup 4th rd, 25 January 1930.

Record Receipts: £138,680 v Manchester U, FA Premier League, 29 December 1993.

Pitch Measurements: 110yd × 74yd.

Chairman: C. E. Moore. **Deputy-Chairman:** R. Telfer.
Directors: D. R. Taylor, P. Chadwick, N. Horn, M. Hogarty.

Manager: Andy Ritchie.

Chief Executive/Secretary: Alan Hardy. **Commercial Manager:** Bob Gorrill.

Marketing and Public Relations Manager: S. Jarvis.

Stadium Manager: Stuart Oddie.

Safety Officer: Frank Carlisle.

Senior Coach: Bill Urmson.

Physio: TBA.

Youth Coaches: David Cross, Tony Philliskirk.

Colours: White shirts with blue panel on front, blue shorts and stockings.

Change Colours: Burgundy shirts and shorts, navy stockings.

Year Formed: 1895.

Turned Professional: 1899.

Ltd Co.: 1906.

Previous Name: 1895, Pine Villa; 1899, Oldham Athletic.

Club Nickname: 'The Latics'.

Previous Grounds: 1895, Sheepfoot Lane; 1900, Hudson Field; 1906, Sheepfoot Lane; 1907, Boundary Park.

HONOURS

Football League: Division 1 – Runners-up 1914–15; Division 2 – Champions 1990–91; Runners-up 1909–10; Division 3 (N) – Champions 1952–53; Division 3 – Champions 1973–74; Division 4 – Runners-up 1962–63.
FA Cup: Semi-final 1913, 1990, 1994.
Football League Cup: Runners-up 1990.

IT'S A FACT !

In the three years leading up to the First World War, Oldham Athletic had six players capped at international level: Hugh Moffat and George Woodger (England); Joe Donnachie and Dave Wilson (Scotland) plus David Davies and Evan Jones (Wales).

First Football League Game: 9 September 1907, Division 2,
v Stoke (a) W 3–1 – Hewitson; Hodson, Hamilton; Fay,
Walders, Wilson; Ward, W. Dodds (1), Newton (1),
Hancock, Swarbrick (1).

Record League Victory: 11–0 v Southport, Division 4,
26 December 1962 – Hollands; Branagan, Marshall; McCall,
Williams, Scott; Ledger (1), Johnstone, Lister (6),
Colquhoun (1), Whitaker (3).

Record Cup Victory: 10–1 v Lytham, FA Cup 1st rd,
28 November 1925 – Gray; Wynne, Grundy; Adlam,
Heaton, Naylor (1), Douglas, Pynegar (2), Ormston (2),
Barnes (3), Watson (2).

Record Defeat: 4–13 v Tranmere R, Division 3 (N),
26 December 1935.

Most League Points (2 for a win): 62, Division 3, 1973–74.

Most League Points (3 for a win): 88, Division 2, 1990–91.

Most League Goals: 95, Division 4, 1962–63.

Highest League Scorer in Season: Tom Davis, 33,
Division 3 (N), 1936–37.

Most League Goals in Total Aggregate: Roger Palmer, 141,
1980–94.

Most League Goals in One Match: 7, Eric Gemmell v
Chester, Division 3N, 19 January 1952.

Most Capped Player: Gunnar Halle, 24 (63), Norway.

Most League Appearances: Ian Wood, 525, 1966–80.

MANAGERS

David Ashworth 1906–14
Herbert Bamlett 1914–21
Charlie Roberts 1921–22
David Ashworth 1923–24
Bob Mellor 1924–27
Andy Wilson 1927–32
Jimmy McMullan 1933–34
Bob Mellor 1934–45
    (continued as Secretary to 1953)
Frank Womack 1945–47
Billy Wootton 1947–50
George Hardwick 1950–56
Ted Goodier 1956–58
Norman Dodgin 1958–60
Jack Rowley 1960–63
Les McDowall 1963–65
Gordon Hurst 1965–66
Jimmy McIlroy 1966–68
Jack Rowley 1968–69
Jimmy Frizzell 1970–82
Joe Royle 1982–94
Graeme Sharp 1994–97
Neil Warnock 1997–98
Andy Ritchie May 1998–

Youngest League Player: Wayne Harrison, 15 years 11 months v Notts Co, 27 October 1984.

Record Transfer Fee Received: £1,700,000 from Aston Villa for Earl Barrett, February 1992.

Record Transfer Fee Paid: £750,000 to Aston Villa for Ian Olney, June 1992.

Football League Record: 1907 Elected to Division 2; 1910–23 Division 1; 1923–35 Division 2;
1935–53 Division 3 (N); 1953–54 Division 2; 1954–58 Division 3 (N); 1958–63 Division 4;
1963–69 Division 3; 1969–71 Division 4; 1971–74 Division 3; 1974–91 Division 2; 1991–92 Division 1;
1992–94 FA Premier League; 1994–97 Division 1; 1997– Division 2.

LATEST SEQUENCES

Longest Sequence of League Wins: 10, 12.1.74 – 12.3.74.

Longest Sequence of League Defeats: 8, 15.12.34 – 2.2.35.

Longest Sequence of League Draws: 5, 26.12.82 – 15.1.83.

Longest Sequence of Unbeaten League Matches: 20, 1.5.90 – 10.11.90.

Longest Sequence Without a League Win: 17, 4.9.20 – 18.12.20.

TEN YEAR LEAGUE RECORD

		P	W	D	L	F	A	Pts	Pos
1990-91	Div 2	46	25	13	8	83	53	88	1
1991-92	Div 1	42	14	9	19	63	67	51	17
1992-93	PR Lge	42	13	10	19	63	74	49	19
1993-94	PR Lge	42	9	13	20	42	68	40	21
1994-95	Div 1	46	16	13	17	60	60	61	14
1995-96	Div 1	46	14	14	18	54	50	56	18
1996-97	Div 1	46	10	13	23	51	66	43	23
1997-98	Div 2	46	15	16	15	62	54	61	13
1998-99	Div 2	46	14	9	23	48	66	51	20
1999-2000	Div 2	46	16	12	18	50	55	60	14

DID YOU KNOW ?

During his brief stay with
Oldham Athletic,
inside-forward Lawrie
Cumming, scored 11 goals in
25 appearances in 1929-30,
having cost £900 from
Huddersfield Town.

OLDHAM ATHLETIC 2000–01 LEAGUE RECORD

Match No.	Date		Venue	Opponents	Result		H/T Score	Lg. Pos.	Goalscorers	Atten- dance
1	Aug	12	H	Port Vale	W	4-1	2-0	—	Adams [29], Allott [36], Corazzin [69], Garnett [72]	5639
2		19	A	Walsall	L	2-3	2-1	7	Adams [40], Duxbury [44]	5952
3		26	H	Peterborough U	L	1-4	0-2	15	Tipton [81]	4967
4		29	A	Colchester U	D	1-1	0-1	—	Holt [52]	3675
5	Sept	2	H	Notts Co	L	0-1	0-1	19		4424
6		9	A	Wrexham	L	1-3	0-1	20	Corazzin [83]	3527
7		12	A	Reading	L	0-5	0-3	—		7768
8		16	H	Bristol C	D	0-0	0-0	21		4095
9		23	A	Bournemouth	D	1-1	1-0	22	Allott [11]	3976
10		30	H	Cambridge U	L	1-3	0-1	23	Dreyer (og) [87]	3888
11	Oct	8	A	Rotherham U	L	0-3	0-2	23		3774
12		14	H	Swindon T	W	1-0	0-0	22	Dudley [72]	4009
13		17	H	Wycombe W	W	2-0	1-0	—	Dudley 2 [12, 72]	3496
14		21	A	Northampton T	L	1-2	0-1	22	Dudley [65]	5677
15		28	A	Bristol R	W	2-0	1-0	20	Allott [5], Duxbury [76]	6110
16	Nov	4	H	Swansea C	D	1-1	0-0	21	Jones [77]	4282
17		11	A	Stoke C	W	1-0	0-0	19	Duxbury [15]	12,503
18		25	H	Millwall	L	0-1	0-0	20		4779
19	Dec	2	H	Oxford U	W	3-2	1-1	19	Corazzin [2], Eyres [52], Jones [69]	3986
20		16	A	Bury	D	1-1	1-0	19	Boshell [27]	4976
21		23	A	Brentford	D	1-1	0-0	18	Allott [54]	5317
22		26	H	Wigan Ath	W	2-1	1-0	18	Duxbury [41], Allott [73]	7750
23		30	H	Walsall	D	0-0	0-0	17		5267
24	Jan	1	A	Peterborough U	D	0-0	0-0	16		5039
25		6	A	Port Vale	D	0-0	0-0	16		4313
26		13	H	Colchester U	D	1-1	0-0	16	Tipton [90]	4076
27		20	A	Wigan Ath	L	1-3	1-1	16	Sheridan [22]	8274
28		23	H	Luton T	W	2-0	1-0	—	Rickers [30], Sheridan [67]	3011
29		27	H	Brentford	W	3-0	0-0	13	Eyres [80], Allott 2 [82, 90]	4964
30	Feb	3	A	Notts Co	L	0-1	0-1	13		5212
31		10	H	Wrexham	W	5-1	2-1	11	Corazzin 4 [10, 45, 48, 57], Rickers [56]	4703
32		20	H	Reading	L	0-2	0-2	—		4160
33		24	H	Bournemouth	W	2-1	0-0	11	Sheridan (pen) [61], Tipton [88]	4845
34	Mar	3	A	Cambridge U	L	0-2	0-2	13		3762
35		6	A	Swindon T	L	0-3	0-1	—		4168
36		10	H	Rotherham U	L	2-3	1-2	14	Duxbury 2 [9, 52]	5993
37		17	A	Wycombe W	L	1-2	1-1	17	Tipton [25]	5847
38		23	H	Northampton T	W	2-1	0-0	—	Duxbury 2 [48, 70]	4001
39		27	A	Bristol C	D	2-2	1-1	—	Carss [15], Sheridan (pen) [70]	9568
40		31	H	Bury	D	1-1	0-0	16	Tipton [90]	5787
41	Apr	7	A	Oxford U	W	1-0	0-0	15	Eyres [89]	4217
42		14	A	Luton T	D	0-0	0-0	15		4886
43		16	H	Bristol R	W	1-0	0-0	11	Carss [47]	6883
44		21	A	Swansea C	W	2-1	0-1	11	Parkin 2 [54, 63]	3261
45		28	H	Stoke C	L	1-2	1-0	12	Parkin [17]	9359
46	May	5	A	Millwall	L	0-5	0-2	15		18,510

Final League Position: 15

GOALSCORERS

League (53): Duxbury 8, Allott 7, Corazzin 7, Tipton 5, Dudley 4, Sheridan 4 (2 pens), Eyres 3, Parkin 3, Adams 2, Carss 2, Jones 2, Rickers 2, Boshell 1, Garnett 1, Holt 1, own goal 1.
Worthington Cup (5): Rickers 2, Boshell 1, Corazzin 1, Duxbury 1.
FA Cup (5): Dudley 2, Corazzin 1, Duxbury 1, Tipton 1.

Kelly G 45	Jones P 10+2	Holt A 12+8	Garnett S 39	Rickers P 38	Duxbury L 40	Adams N 18	Sheridan J 22+3	Allott M 26+13	Corazzin C 37+1	Hotte M 25+3	Innes M 27+3	Boshell D 11+7	McNiven S 43+2	Whitehall S —+2	Tipton M 15+15	Dudley C 10+16	Miskelly D 1+1	Prenderville B 6+3	Lightfoot C 3	Smith P 3+1	Watson M 1+1	Salt P 4+2	Carss T 35	Eyres D 30	Sugden R 1+1	Futcher B 1+4	Parkin S 3+4	Roach N —+1	Match No.
1	2	3	4	5	6	7^1	8^2	9	10	11	12	13																	1
1	2	3	4	5	6	7^1		9	10	8	11		12																2
1	2	3	4	5	6	7^3		9	10	11^1		8^2	12	14	13														3
1	2	3	4	5	6			9^1	10		12	8^1	7	14	13	11^2													4
1	2^1	3	4	5^1	6	7		9^2		12	11	13	8		10	14													5
1	2^2	3	4	5	6	7		9^1	10	11			8		12	13													6
1^8	2	3		5	6	7		9^1	10	11^2			4	8	12		15	13											7
1	2			5^3	6	7		9^2	10	12	11	8	3	13						14	4^1								8
1		3			6	7		9	10^1		11	4	2		12			13	5	8^2									9
1		3			6	7		12	10		11	4^3	2		13	8^1			5^2	9	14								10
1		3	4		6	7		12		11			2^2		9	8^3			13	5	10								11
1			4		6	7		11				3	12	2	9							10^1	8						12
1			4		6	7		12	10	5	3		2		9^1								8	11					13
1			4		6	7		12	10	5	3^1		2		9								8	11					14
1	12		4^1	5	6	7		9	10			3	2										8	11					15
1	2			5	6	7		9^1	10			3	4		12								8	11					16
1	12		4	5	6	7^2		13	10			3	2		9^1								8	11					17
1	12		4	5	6			9	10^2			3^1	2			13						7	8	11					18
1	2^1	12	4	5	6^3				10			3	14	7	13	9^2							8	11					19
1			4	5		7			10			3	6	2	9								8	11					20
1			4	5			8^2	9			12	3^1	6	2		10^3						13	7	11	14				21
1			4	5	6		8	9	10^1	11		3	2										7	11					22
1			4	5	6		8	9	10^1	11		3	2										7						23
1			4	5	6		8	9	10^1	11		3	2		12								7						24
1	12		4	5			8^3		10			6^2	2	9								13	7	11		3^1	14		25
1	12		4	5			8	13	10^2			6^1	3	2	9								7	11					26
1			4	5^1	6		8	12	10			3	2		9								7	11					27
1			4^1	5	6		8^3		10		3	12	14	2	9^4	13							7	11					28
1	12			5	6		8	13	10^2		4	3	2		9^1	14							7	11					29
1	12			5	6		8	9	4			3	2		10^2	13							7	11					30
1	12		4^1	5			8^3	9	10^2	6		3	14	2	13								7	11					31
1	12		4	5	6		8	9^2	10^3			3^1	2		13	14							7	11					32
1	3		4	5	6		8^2	9^3	10^1			13	2		12	14							7	11					33
1	3		4	5	6			9	10^1			8^2	2		12	13							7	11					34
1			4	5	6			9^2	10			3	8^1	2	12	13							7	11					35
1			4	5	6		8		10			3	2		9^1	12							7	11					36
1			4	5	6		8	12	10^1			3	2		9^2	13							7	11					37
1			4	5	6		8	9^1	10			3	2										7	11			12		38
1			4	5			8	9	10	6		3	2										7	11			12		39
1			4	5^1	6		12	9^2	10^3	8		3	2		13	14							7	11					40
1			4		6^3		8	12		10^2			3	2		9^1						5		7	11			13	14	41
1			4		6		12		10	5^2			2		9^3			3				8^1	7	11			13	14	42
1			4	5	6		8	9^1	10				2		12			3					7	11					43
			4	5	6	7	12	13					2		9^2		1	3				8^1		11			10		44
1			4	5	6	7		12	13				2		9^2			3				8		11^3			14	10^1	45
1			4^1	5	6		8	12	10^2				2					3				7					9	11 13	46

Worthington Cup

First Round	Huddersfield T	(h)	1-0
		(a)	2-0
Second Round	Sheffield W	(h)	1-3
		(a)	1-5

FA Cup

First Round	Hednesford T	(a)	4-2
Second Round	Peterborough U	(a)	1-1
		(h)	0-1

OXFORD UNITED

Division 3

FOUNDATION

There had been an Oxford United club around the time of World War I but only in the Oxfordshire Thursday League and there is no connection with the modern club which began as Headington in 1893, adding 'United' a year later. Playing first on Quarry Fields and subsequently Wootten's Fields, they owe much to a Dr. Hitchings for their early development.

The Kassam Stadium, Grenoble Road, Oxford OX4 4XP.

Telephone: (01865) 337500. *ClubCall:* 09068 440 055.
Website: www.oufc.co.uk
Email: oxford-united@community.co.uk
Supporters Club: (01865) 763 063.

Ground Capacity: 9650.

Record Attendance: 22,730 v Preston NE, FA Cup 6th rd, 29 February 1964.

Record Receipts: £136,423 v Chelsea, FA Cup 4th rd, 25 January 1999.

Pitch Measurements: 110yd × 75yd.

President: The Duke of Marlborough.
Chairman: Firoz Kassam. *Directors:* F. Higgins, A. Tawakley.

Manager: Mark Wright.

Assistant Manager: Ted McMinn.

Reserve Team Coach: Mike Ford.

Physio: Neal Reynolds.

Secretary: Mick Brown.

Stadium Manager: Mick Moore.

Colours: Yellow shirts with navy trim, navy shorts, navy stockings.

Change Colours: Navy shirts with white trim, white shorts, white stockings.

Year Formed: 1893.

Turned Professional: 1949.

Ltd Co.: 1949.

Club Nickname: 'The U's'.

Previous Names: 1893, Headington; 1894, Headington United; 1960, Oxford United.

Previous Grounds: 1893, Headington Quarry; 1894, Wootten's Field; 1898, Sandy Lane Ground; 1902, Britannia Field; 1909, Sandy Lane; 1910, Quarry Recreation Ground; 1914, Sandy Lane; 1922, The Paddock Manor Road; 1925, Manor Ground.

First Football League Game: 18 August 1962, Division 4, v Barrow (a) L 2–3 – Medlock; Beavon, Quartermain; R. Atkinson, Kyle, Jones; Knight, G. Atkinson (1), Houghton (1), Cornwell, Colfar.

HONOURS

Football League: Division 1 best season: 12th, 1997–98; Division 2 – Champions 1984–85; Runners-up 1995–96; Division 3 – Champions 1967–68, 1983–84; Division 4 – Promoted 1964–65 (4th).

FA Cup: best season: 6th rd, 1964 (shared record for 4th Division club).

Football League Cup: Winners 1986.

IT'S A FACT !

On 23 April 1996, Oxford United's successful scoring efforts in the 6-0 win over Shrewsbury Town were all achieved with headed goals.

Record League Victory: 7–0 v Barrow, Division 4,
19 December 1964 – Fearnley; Beavon, Quartermain;
R. Atkinson (1), Kyle, Jones; Morris, Booth (3), Willey (1),
G. Atkinson (1), Harrington (1).

Record Cup Victory: 9–1 v Dorchester T, FA Cup 1st rd,
11 November 1995 – Whitehead; Wood (2), Ford M (1),
Smith, Elliott, Gilchrist, Rush (1), Massey (Murphy),
Moody (3), Ford R (1), Angel (Beauchamp (1)).

Record Defeat: 0–7 v Sunderland, Division 1, 19 September
1998.

Most League Points (2 for a win): 61, Division 4, 1964–65.

Most League Points (3 for a win): 95, Division 3, 1983–84.

Most League Goals: 91, Division 3, 1983–84.

Highest League Scorer in Season: John Aldridge, 30,
Division 2, 1984–85.

Most League Goals in Total Aggregate: Graham Atkinson,
77, 1962–73.

Most League Goals in One Match: 4, Tony Jones v
Newport Co, Division 4, 22 September 1962; 4, Arthur
Longbottom v Darlington, Division 4, 26 October 1963; 4,
Richard Hill v Walsall, Division 2, 26 December 1988; 4,
John Durnin v Luton T, 14 November 1992.

MANAGERS
Harry Thompson 1949–58
(Player-Manager) 1949-51
Arthur Turner 1959–69
(continued as General Manager
to 1972)
Ron Saunders 1969
George Summers 1969–75
Mike Brown 1975–79
Bill Asprey 1979–80
Ian Greaves 1980–82
Jim Smith 1982–85
Maurice Evans 1985–88
Mark Lawrenson 1988
Brian Horton 1988–93
Denis Smith 1993–97
Malcolm Crosby 1997
Malcolm Shotton 1998–99
Denis Smith 2000
David Kemp 2000–01
Mark Wright May 2001–

Most Capped Player: Jim Magilton, 18 (47), Northern Ireland.

Most League Appearances: John Shuker, 478, 1962–77.

Youngest League Player: Jason Seacole, 16 years 149 days v Mansfield T, 7 September 1976.

Record Transfer Fee Received: £1,600,000 from Leicester C for Matt Elliott, January 1997.

Record Transfer Fee Paid: £475,000 to Aberdeen for Dean Windass, August 1998.

Football League Record: 1962 Elected to Division 4; 1965–68 Division 3; 1968–76 Division 2;
1976–84 Division 3; 1984–85 Division 2; 1985–88 Division 1; 1988–92 Division 2; 1992–94 Division 1;
1994–96 Division 2; 1996–99 Division 1; 1999–2001 Division 2; 2001– Division 3.

LATEST SEQUENCES

Longest Sequence of League Wins: 6, 6.4.85 – 24.4.85.

Longest Sequence of League Defeats: 7, 4.5.91 – 7.9.91.

Longest Sequence of League Draws: 5, 7.10.78 – 28.10.78.

Longest Sequence of Unbeaten League Matches: 20, 17.3.84 – 29.9.84.

Longest Sequence Without a League Win: 27, 14.11.87 – 27.8.88.

TEN YEAR LEAGUE RECORD

		P	W	D	L	F	A	Pts	Pos
1990-91	Div 2	46	14	19	13	69	66	61	10
1991-92	Div 2	46	13	11	22	66	73	50	21
1992-93	Div 1	46	14	14	18	53	56	56	14
1993-94	Div 1	46	13	10	23	54	75	49	23
1994-95	Div 2	46	21	12	13	66	52	75	7
1995-96	Div 2	46	24	11	11	76	39	83	2
1996-97	Div 1	46	16	9	21	64	68	57	17
1997-98	Div 1	46	16	10	20	60	64	58	12
1998-99	Div 1	46	10	14	22	48	71	44	23
1999-2000	Div 2	46	12	9	25	43	73	45	20

DID YOU KNOW ?

Of the first ten players who
won full international
honours for Oxford United,
four represented the
Republic of Ireland and three
each for Wales and Northern
Ireland.

OXFORD UNITED 2000–01 LEAGUE RECORD

Match No.	Date	Venue	Opponents	Result	H/T Score	Lg. Pos.	Goalscorers	Attendance
1	Aug 12	H	Peterborough U	L 0-1	0-1	—		5870
2	19	A	Port Vale	L 0-3	0-1	24		3814
3	26	H	Brentford	L 0-1	0-1	24		4756
4	29	A	Walsall	L 2-3	2-1	—	Beauchamp 2 [3, 33]	5678
5	Sept 2	H	Cambridge U	D 1-1	1-1	23	Jarman [15]	4479
6	8	A	Wycombe W	L 1-3	0-1	—	Tait [86]	5831
7	13	A	Stoke C	L 0-4	0-3	—		9600
8	16	H	Bury	W 1-0	0-0	24	Cook [81]	3676
9	23	A	Millwall	L 0-5	0-3	24		8565
10	30	A	Bristol C	L 0-1	0-1	24		5308
11	Oct 8	A	Swindon T	L 1-2	0-1	24	Whittingham [61]	7975
12	14	H	Wrexham	L 3-4	1-1	24	Tait [7], Beauchamp [86], McGregor (og) [90]	3884
13	17	H	Luton T	D 0-0	0-0	—		4537
14	21	A	Rotherham U	L 1-3	0-0	24	Lilley [84]	3983
15	24	H	Wigan Ath	L 0-2	0-1	—		4030
16	28	A	Reading	L 3-4	1-1	24	Lilley [40], Viveash (og) [69], Richardson [73]	16,022
17	Nov 4	H	Bristol R	L 0-1	0-1	24		5407
18	11	H	Swansea C	W 2-1	2-1	24	Beauchamp [17], Andrews [34]	4892
19	25	H	Notts Co	L 2-3	2-0	24	Murphy 2 [41, 45]	4765
20	Dec 2	A	Oldham Ath	L 2-3	1-1	24	Gray (pen) [16], Innes (og) [68]	3986
21	16	H	Northampton T	W 3-1	2-1	24	Anthrobus [6], Murphy [36], Hackett [59]	4899
22	22	A	Colchester U	L 2-3	0-2	—	Gray [56], Beauchamp [57]	3695
23	26	H	Bournemouth	L 1-2	1-1	24	Fear [12]	6200
24	Jan 1	A	Brentford	L 0-3	0-2	24		5020
25	13	H	Walsall	W 2-1	2-0	24	Gray 2 [26, 31]	5184
26	27	H	Colchester U	L 0-1	0-1	24		5064
27	30	A	Peterborough U	L 2-4	1-2	—	Murphy [19], Fear [88]	4004
28	Feb 10	H	Wycombe W	L 1-2	1-1	24	Hackett [13]	5384
29	17	A	Bury	L 1-3	0-1	24	Beauchamp [89]	3320
30	20	H	Stoke C	D 1-1	1-0	—	Patterson [7]	4856
31	24	A	Millwall	L 0-2	0-2	24		5795
32	Mar 3	A	Bristol C	D 0-0	0-0	24		9681
33	6	A	Wrexham	L 3-5	2-1	—	Gray (pen) [2], Powell [45], Murphy [77]	3009
34	10	H	Swindon T	L 0-2	0-1	24		7480
35	24	H	Rotherham U	W 4-3	2-1	24	Quinn [6], Omoyinmi 2 [27, 59], Scott [67]	4493
36	27	A	Cambridge U	L 0-1	0-0	—		3502
37	31	A	Northampton T	W 1-0	1-0	24	Tait [12]	6115
38	Apr 3	A	Bournemouth	L 3-4	1-1	—	Gray 2 (1 pen) [1, 60 (p)], Quinn [68]	3747
39	7	H	Oldham Ath	L 0-1	0-0	24		4217
40	10	A	Luton T	D 1-1	0-1	—	Scott [78]	6010
41	14	A	Wigan Ath	L 2-3	1-2	24	Beauchamp [40], Scott [90]	5322
42	17	H	Reading	L 0-2	0-1	—		6886
43	21	H	Bristol R	L 2-6	1-1	24	Richardson [21], Scott [73]	7554
44	28	H	Swansea C	W 3-1	1-1	24	Omoyinmi [10], Brooks [61], Murphy [63]	4148
45	May 1	H	Port Vale	D 1-1	0-0	—	Scott [82]	7080
46	5	A	Notts Co	L 1-2	1-1	24	Folland [18]	5513

Final League Position: 24

GOALSCORERS

League (53): Beauchamp 7, Gray 7 (3 pens), Murphy 6, Scott 5, Omoyinmi 3, Tait 3, Fear 2, Hackett 2, Lilley 2, Quinn 2, Richardson 2, Andrews 1, Anthrobus 1, Brooks 1, Cook 1, Folland 1, Jarman 1, Patterson 1, Powell 1, Whittingham 1, own goals 3.
Worthington Cup (2): Murphy 1, Shepheard 1.
FA Cup (3): Gray 2, Murphy 1.

Knight R 33	Robertson J 37 + 3	Powell P 15 + 5	Fear P 14 + 5	Richardson J 41	McGuckin I 6 + 1	Omoyinmi E 16 + 8	Tait P 22 + 4	Murphy M 37 + 3	Weatherstone S 6 + 1	Jarman L 15 + 6	Wilson P 1 + 1	Lilley D 15 + 4	Anthrobus S 13 + 7	Beauchamp J 32 + 11	McGowan N 11	Cook J 4 + 5	Whitehead D 16 + 4	Shepheard J 5	Hackett C 10 + 6	Folland R 1 + 4	Busby H — + 1	Glass J 1	King S 2	Mike L 1 + 2	Ford M 1	Ricketts S 13 + 1	Brooks J 3 + 1	Whittingham G 1	Linighan A 12 + 1	Holder J — + 2	Brown K 3	Andrews K 4	Gray P 21 + 2	Hatswell W 26 + 1	Cutler N 11	Weatherstone R 1	Monk G 5	Quinn R 12 + 1	Scott A 21	Patterson D 18	Match No.
1	2	3	4^1	5	6	7	8	9	10^2	11^3	12	13	14																												1
1	2	3	4^1	5	6^2	7	8	9				10^3	13	12	11	14																									2
1	2	3		5		7	8	9^2		10	12	11^1		4	6	13																									3
1	2	3^2		5		7	8	12	10	13		9	11^2	4^1	6	14																									4
1	2			5	6	7	8			10		9	11	3	4																										5
1^3	2					4	9	10	7	8^1	11	3	12		6		15																								6
	2			5	6	7	8	9^2		13	12	10^1	11	3^2		4		14	1																						7
1	2	12	5	6^2	8^3	4	9		13	7	10^1	11^1	3	14																											8
1	2			5	6^1	8^2	4	9		12	7	10^3	11	3	13									14																	9
1	2	12	5		8^2	4^1		10	7			11		13	6									9	3																10
1	12			5		6^3	9	10	7		11^2	3^1		4										13		2	14	8													11
1	12			5		13	8	9^3		10	7	14	11	3	6^3	4										2^1															12
1	12			5		13	8^1			9	7		11	3	10^2	4										2		6													13
1	2			5				9	10		7		12	3^2	8	11^1	4									13		6													14
1	2	4		5				9	10^2	12	7		13		8^3		11^1	14								3		6													15
1	2^1	4		5				9	10	8	7	11		3					12									6													16
1	2	3	4^1	5		13		9	10^2	12	7	8^3	11				14											6													17
1	2			5		4		9			7		11																6	3	8	10									18
1	2			5				9	10^1	12	7^2		11			13												6	3	4	8										19
1	2^3	12	4^1	5		13		9			7^2		11															6	3	8	10	14									20
			5					9		10		7	11			2												6		4	8	3	1							21
		12	4	5				9		3		7	11			10												6^1		8	2	1								22
		13	4	5	7			9	12				11			10												6		8^1	2	1					3^2			23
		3^1	4	5				9		10		7	11			12	8											6			2	1								24
	2			5				9					11			7														8	3	1				6	4	10		25
	2	12		5				9		4^1			11			7														8	3	1				6	5	10		26
	2		4	13	12			9		7^2			11^3			14														8	3	1				6	5^1	10		27
		2	12	5				9					11^1			4	7													8	3	1				6	5	10		28
		5		12				9^3				13	11			14	7											8			8^2	3	1				6	4^1	10	2	29
	2		6					12	9				11				7^1											10			8	3	1				5	10	4	30
	2		6					12	9				11^1			13	7											10			8	3	1				5^2	10	4	31
1	2	11^1	5					7	9				12			4												8			8	3						10	6	32
1	2	11	5					7	9				12			6												8			8	3						10^1	4	33
1	2	11^2	14	5				12	7^1	9			10^3	13		4												8			8	3						6	4	34
1	2	11^1		5				7	10				12											8							3					6	9	4	35
1	2	11^1		5				7	8				12											10							3					6	9	4	36
1	2	11^1		5				7^2	8				12											10			13	3								6	9	4	37
1	2	11^2		5					10	12			13											7^1				8	3						6	9	4	38
1	2			5					10	12			11			13								7^2				8	3						6^1	9	4	39
1	2	11^1	13	5				6^2	9				12											7				8	3							10	4	40
1	2		6	5					9				12	11										7^1				8	3							10	4	41
1	2	14	6	5		12			9				13	11										7^3				8^1	3^2							10	4	42
1	2		6^2	5^6	7			9	15				11	12										8^1				13	3							10	4	43
1	2	3^1		7				9					11	5												8	12	6									10	4	44
1	2			7^1	12	9				11			5			13				6^4					8^2		14	3									10	4	45
	2	12				9	1			11			5			8^3			6						7^1		14	3								13	10^2	4	46

Worthington Cup
First Round   Wolverhampton W   (a) 1-0
                                           (h) 1-3

FA Cup
First Round   Macclesfield T   (a) 1-0
Second Round   Chester C   (a) 2-3

PETERBOROUGH UNITED   Division 2

FOUNDATION

The old Peterborough & Fletton club, founded in 1923, was suspended by the FA during season 1932–33 and disbanded. Local enthusiasts determined to carry on and in 1934 a new professional club Peterborough United was formed and entered the Midland League the following year. Peterborough's first success came in 1939–40, but from 1955–56 to 1959–60 they won five successive titles. During the 1958–59 season they were undefeated in the Midland League. They reached the third round of the FA Cup, won the Northamptonshire Senior Cup, the Maunsell Cup and were runners-up in the East Anglian Cup.

London Road Ground, Peterborough PE2 8AL.

Telephone: (01733) 563 947. *Fax:* (01733) 344 140.
ClubCall: 09068 121 654. *Website:* www.theposh.com
Email: management@theposh.net

Ground Capacity: 15,314.

Record Attendance: 30,096 v Swansea T, FA Cup 5th rd, 20 February 1965.

Record Receipts: £51,315 v Brighton & HA, FA Cup 5th rd, 15 February 1986.

Pitch Measurements: 112yd × 71yd.

Chairman: Peter Boizot MBE, DL.
Vice-Chairman: Roger Terrell. *Directors:* A. Hand, P. Sagar.

Chief Executive: Nigel Hards.

Company Secretary: Timothy Warren.

Club Secretary: Julie Etherington.

First Team Manager: Barry Fry.

Assistant Manager: Wayne Turner.

Youth Academy Director: Dan Ashworth.

Physio: Paul Showler.

Colours: Royal blue shirts, white shorts, blue stockings with white tops.

Change Colours: Green shirts with navy trim, navy shorts, navy stockings.

Year Formed: 1934.

Turned Professional: 1934.

Ltd Co.: 1934.

Club Nickname: 'The Posh'.

First Football League Game: 20 August 1960, Division 4, v Wrexham (h) W 3–0 – Walls; Stafford, Walker; Rayner, Rigby, Norris; Hails, Emery (1), Bly (1), Smith, McNamee (1).

HONOURS

Football League: Division 1 best season: 10th, 1992–93. Promoted from Division 3 1999–2000 (play-offs); Division 4 – Champions 1960–61, 1973–74.

FA Cup: best season: 6th rd, 1965.

Football League Cup: Semi-final 1966.

IT'S A FACT !

When Peterborough United beat Derby County 1-0 on 15 August 1992 in a Division One match, it was the 10th consecutive season the club had remained unbeaten in the opening game.

Record League Victory: 9–1 v Barnet (a) Division 3, 5 September 1998 – Griemink; Hooper (1), Drury (Farell), Gill, Bodley, Edwards, Davies, Payne, Grazioli (5), Quinn (2) (Rowe), Houghton (Etherington) (1).

Record Cup Victory: 7–0 v Harlow T, FA Cup 1st rd, 16 November 1991 – Barber; Luke, Johnson, Halsall (1), Robinson D, Welsh, Sterling (1) (Butterworth), Cooper G (2 incl. 1p), Riley (1) (Culpin (1)), Charlery (1), Kimble.

Record Defeat: 1–8 v Northampton T, FA Cup 2nd rd (2nd replay), 18 December 1946.

Most League Points (2 for a win): 66, Division 4, 1960–61.

Most League Points (3 for a win): 82, Division 4, 1981–82.

Most League Goals: 134, Division 4, 1960–61.

Highest League Scorer in Season: Terry Bly, 52, Division 4, 1960–61.

Most League Goals in Total Aggregate: Jim Hall, 122, 1967–75.

Most League Goals in One Match: 5, Guiliano Grazioli v Barnet, Division 3, 5 September 1998.

Most Capped Player: Tony Millington, 8 (21), Wales.

Most League Appearances: Tommy Robson, 482, 1968–81.

Youngest League Player: Matthew Etherington, 15 years 262 days v Brentford, 3 May 1997.

Record Transfer Fee Received: £700,000 from Tottenham H for Simon Davies, December 1999.

Record Transfer Fee Paid: £350,000 to Walsall for Martin O'Connor, July 1996.

Football League Record: 1960 Elected to Division 4; 1961–68 Division 3, when they were demoted for financial irregularities; 1968–74 Division 4; 1974–79 Division 3; 1979–91 Division 4; 1991–92 Division 3; 1992–94 Division 1; 1994–97 Division 2; 1997–2000 Division 3; 2000– Division 2.

MANAGERS

Jock Porter 1934–36
Fred Taylor 1936–37
Vic Poulter 1937–38
Sam Madden 1938–48
Jack Blood 1948–50
Bob Gurney 1950–52
Jack Fairbrother 1952–54
George Swindin 1954–58
Jimmy Hagan 1958–62
Jack Fairbrother 1962–64
Gordon Clark 1964–67
Norman Rigby 1967–69
Jim Iley 1969–72
Noel Cantwell 1972–77
John Barnwell 1977–78
Billy Hails 1978–79
Peter Morris 1979–82
Martin Wilkinson 1982–83
John Wile 1983–86
Noel Cantwell 1986–88
(continued as General Manager)
Mick Jones 1988–89
Mark Lawrenson 1989–90
Chris Turner 1991–92
Lil Fuccillo 1992–93
John Still 1994–95
Mick Halsall 1995–96
Barry Fry May 1996–

LATEST SEQUENCES

Longest Sequence of League Wins: 9, 1.2.92 – 14.3.92.

Longest Sequence of League Defeats: 5, 8.10.96 – 26.10.96.

Longest Sequence of League Draws: 8, 18.12.71 – 12.2.72.

Longest Sequence of Unbeaten League Matches: 17, 17.12.60 – 8.4.61.

Longest Sequence Without a League Win: 17, 23.9.78 – 30.12.78.

TEN YEAR LEAGUE RECORD

		P	W	D	L	F	A	Pts	Pos
1990-91	Div 4	46	21	17	8	67	45	80	4
1991-92	Div 3	46	20	14	12	65	58	74	6
1992-93	Div 1	46	16	14	16	55	63	62	10
1993-94	Div 1	46	8	13	25	48	76	37	24
1994-95	Div 2	46	14	18	14	54	69	60	15
1995-96	Div 2	46	13	13	20	59	66	52	19
1996-97	Div 2	46	11	14	21	55	73	47	21
1997-98	Div 3	46	18	13	15	63	51	67	10
1998-99	Div 3	46	18	12	16	72	56	66	9
1999-2000	Div 3	46	22	12	12	63	54	78	5

DID YOU KNOW

Dennis Emery scored 22 FA Cup goals for Peterborough United over seven seasons from 1955-56 to 1961-62 including one spell of scoring in seven consecutive matches.

Tyler M 40
Scott R 18 + 2

1   2
1   2
1   2
1   2¹
1   2¹
1   3
1   2¹
1
1
1
1
1
1
1
1
1
1
1
1
1
1   2
1   2
1   2
1   4
1   2¹

12
4
1
1
1
1
1
1   4
1   4
1   2
1   12
1   4
1   2

Worthi
First R

PLYMOUTH ARGYLE

Division 3

FOUNDATION

The club was formed in September 1886 as the Argyle Football Club by former public and private school pupils who wanted to continue playing the game. The meeting was held in a room above the Borough Arms (a Coffee House), Bedford Street, Plymouth. It was common then to choose a local street/terrace as a club name and Argyle or Argyll was a fashionable name throughout the land due to Queen Victoria's great interest in Scotland.

Home Park, Plymouth, Devon PL2 3DQ.

Telephone: (01752) 562 561. *Fax:* (01752) 606 167.
Pilgrim Shop: (01752) 558 292.

Ground Capacity: 19,630.

Record Attendance: 43,596 v Aston Villa, Division 2, 10 October 1936.

Record Receipts: £128,000 v Burnley, Division 2 play-off, 18 May 1994.

Pitch Measurements: 110yd × 72yd.

President: S. J. Rendell.

Chairman: D. McCauley. *Vice-Chairman:* P. Bloom.

Directors: Paul Stapleton, John McNulty, Ken Jones, Roy Griggs.

Manager: Paul Sturrock.
Assistant Manager: Steve McCall.
Physio: Norman Medhurst.

Secretary/Chief Executive: Roger Matthews.

Colours: Green and white shirts, white shorts, green, black and white stockings.

Change Colours: All white.

Year Formed: 1886.

Turned Professional: 1903.

Ltd Co.: 1903.

Previous Name: 1886, Argyle Athletic Club; 1903, Plymouth Argyle.

Club Nickname: 'The Pilgrims'.

First Football League game: 28 August 1920, Division 3, v Norwich C (h) D 1–1 – Craig; Russell, Atterbury; Logan, Dickinson, Forbes; Kirkpatrick, Jack, Bowler, Heeps (1), Dixon.

Record League Victory: 8–1 v Millwall, Division 2, 16 January 1932 – Harper; Roberts, Titmuss; Mackay, Pullan, Reed; Grozier, Bowden (2), Vidler (3), Leslie (1), Black (1), (1 og). 8–1 v Hartlepool U (a), Division 2, 7 May 1994 – Nicholls; Patterson (Naylor), Hill, Burrows, Comyn, McCall (1), Barlow, Castle (1), Landon (3), Marshall (1), Dalton (2).

HONOURS

Football League: Division 2 best season: 4th, 1931–32, 1952–53; Division 3 (S) – Champions 1929–30, 1951–52; Runners-up 1921–22, 1922–23, 1923–24, 1924–25, 1925–26, 1926–27 (record of six consecutive years); Division 3 – Champions 1958–59; Runners-up 1974–75, 1985–86, Promoted 1995–96 (play-offs).

FA Cup: Semi-final 1984.

Football League Cup: Semi-final 1965, 1974.

IT'S A FACT ❗

In 1930-31 Plymouth Argyle completed a League double over West Bromwich Albion, FA Cup winners and Division Two promotion winners, 2-1 away and 5-1 at Home Park.

Record League Victory: 9–1 v Barnet (a) Division 3, 5 September 1998 – Griemink; Hooper (1), Drury (Farell), Gill, Bodley, Edwards, Davies, Payne, Grazioli (5), Quinn (2) (Rowe), Houghton (Etherington) (1).

Record Cup Victory: 7–0 v Harlow T, FA Cup 1st rd, 16 November 1991 – Barber; Luke, Johnson, Halsall (1), Robinson D, Welsh, Sterling (1) (Butterworth), Cooper G (2 incl. 1p), Riley (1) (Culpin (1)), Charlery (1), Kimble.

Record Defeat: 1–8 v Northampton T, FA Cup 2nd rd (2nd replay), 18 December 1946.

Most League Points (2 for a win): 66, Division 4, 1960–61.

Most League Points (3 for a win): 82, Division 4, 1981–82.

Most League Goals: 134, Division 4, 1960–61.

Highest League Scorer in Season: Terry Bly, 52, Division 4, 1960–61.

Most League Goals in Total Aggregate: Jim Hall, 122, 1967–75.

Most League Goals in One Match: 5, Guiliano Grazioli v Barnet, Division 3, 5 September 1998.

Most Capped Player: Tony Millington, 8 (21), Wales.

Most League Appearances: Tommy Robson, 482, 1968–81.

Youngest League Player: Matthew Etherington, 15 years 262 days v Brentford, 3 May 1997.

Record Transfer Fee Received: £700,000 from Tottenham H for Simon Davies, December 1999.

Record Transfer Fee Paid: £350,000 to Walsall for Martin O'Connor, July 1996.

MANAGERS

Jock Porter 1934–36
Fred Taylor 1936–37
Vic Poulter 1937–38
Sam Madden 1938–48
Jack Blood 1948–50
Bob Gurney 1950–52
Jack Fairbrother 1952–54
George Swindin 1954–58
Jimmy Hagan 1958–62
Jack Fairbrother 1962–64
Gordon Clark 1964–67
Norman Rigby 1967–69
Jim Iley 1969–72
Noel Cantwell 1972–77
John Barnwell 1977–78
Billy Hails 1978–79
Peter Morris 1979–82
Martin Wilkinson 1982–83
John Wile 1983–86
Noel Cantwell 1986–88
    (continued as
    General Manager)
Mick Jones 1988–89
Mark Lawrenson 1989–90
Chris Turner 1991–92
Lil Fuccillo 1992–93
John Still 1994–95
Mick Halsall 1995–96
Barry Fry May 1996–

Football League Record: 1960 Elected to Division 4; 1961–68 Division 3, when they were demoted for financial irregularities; 1968–74 Division 4; 1974–79 Division 3; 1979–91 Division 4; 1991–92 Division 3; 1992–94 Division 1; 1994–97 Division 2; 1997–2000 Division 3; 2000– Division 2.

LATEST SEQUENCES

Longest Sequence of League Wins: 9, 1.2.92 – 14.3.92.

Longest Sequence of League Defeats: 5, 8.10.96 – 26.10.96.

Longest Sequence of League Draws: 8, 18.12.71 – 12.2.72.

Longest Sequence of Unbeaten League Matches: 17, 17.12.60 – 8.4.61.

Longest Sequence Without a League Win: 17, 23.9.78 – 30.12.78.

TEN YEAR LEAGUE RECORD

		P	W	D	L	F	A	Pts	Pos
1990-91	Div 4	46	21	17	8	67	45	80	4
1991-92	Div 3	46	20	14	12	65	58	74	6
1992-93	Div 1	46	16	14	16	55	63	62	10
1993-94	Div 1	46	8	13	25	48	76	37	24
1994-95	Div 2	46	14	18	14	54	69	60	15
1995-96	Div 2	46	13	13	20	59	66	52	19
1996-97	Div 2	46	11	14	21	55	73	47	21
1997-98	Div 3	46	18	13	15	63	51	67	10
1998-99	Div 3	46	18	12	16	72	56	66	9
1999-2000	Div 3	46	22	12	12	63	54	78	5

DID YOU KNOW

Dennis Emery scored 22 FA Cup goals for Peterborough United over seven seasons from 1955-56 to 1961-62 including one spell of scoring in seven consecutive matches.

PETERBOROUGH UNITED 2000–01 LEAGUE RECORD

Match No.	Date	Venue	Opponents	Result	H/T Score	Lg. Pos.	Goalscorers	Atten- dance
1	Aug 12	A	Oxford U	W 1-0	1-0	—	Farrell [30]	5870
2	20	H	Bristol R	D 2-2	1-1	3	Green [20], Clarke [51]	6997
3	26	A	Oldham Ath	W 4-1	2-0	2	Clarke [28], Green [29], Jones (og) [84], Whittingham [90]	4967
4	28	H	Swansea C	L 0-2	0-1	5		6428
5	Sept 2	H	Bury	D 1-1	1-0	6	Green [30]	5286
6	9	A	Stoke C	L 0-3	0-0	11		13,011
7	12	A	Wigan Ath	L 0-1	0-0	—		4798
8	16	H	Reading	W 1-0	0-0	11	Cullen (pen) [89]	5767
9	23	A	Wycombe W	L 0-2	0-1	15		4980
10	30	A	Millwall	L 1-4	0-1	17	Shields [71]	7126
11	Oct 8	H	Port Vale	W 2-0	0-0	12	Lee [67], Clarke [87]	4752
12	14	A	Brentford	L 0-1	0-0	14		4479
13	17	A	Walsall	D 1-1	1-0	—	Oldfield [15]	4716
14	21	H	Notts Co	W 1-0	0-0	12	Clarke [69]	5889
15	24	A	Bristol C	L 1-2	1-0	—	Farrell [23]	9219
16	28	H	Colchester U	W 3-1	0-0	12	McKenzie [56], Lee [87], Clarke [89]	5469
17	Nov 4	A	Bournemouth	L 1-2	0-1	15	Farrell [74]	3936
18	11	H	Swindon T	W 4-0	2-0	10	Farrell [26], McKenzie 2 [38, 65], Forsyth [85]	5700
19	25	A	Rotherham U	L 0-3	0-1	12		5519
20	Dec 2	H	Wrexham	W 1-0	1-0	10	McKenzie [41]	5381
21	15	A	Cambridge U	D 0-0	0-0	—		7505
22	23	H	Northampton T	L 1-2	1-0	13	McKenzie [26]	9868
23	26	A	Luton T	L 2-3	1-2	16	Farrell [41], McKenzie (pen) [69]	7374
24	Jan 1	H	Oldham Ath	D 0-0	0-0	15		5039
25	13	A	Swansea C	D 2-2	2-0	17	McKenzie [34], Clarke [43]	5288
26	27	A	Northampton T	D 0-0	0-0	17		7079
27	30	H	Oxford U	W 4-2	2-1	—	Oldfield [27], Clarke [31], Gill [80], McKenzie [90]	4004
28	Feb 3	A	Bury	L 1-2	0-0	16	Forinton [76]	2725
29	10	H	Stoke C	L 0-4	0-2	18		7568
30	17	A	Reading	D 1-1	0-1	16	Lee [54]	10,342
31	20	H	Wigan Ath	W 2-0	0-0	—	Rea [51], Williams M [68]	4111
32	24	H	Wycombe W	W 3-2	3-2	14	McKenzie 2 [15, 21], Lee [34]	4731
33	Mar 3	A	Millwall	D 0-0	0-0	15		11,658
34	6	H	Brentford	D 1-1	1-0	—	Williams M [32]	4479
35	10	H	Port Vale	L 0-5	0-1	15		4787
36	23	A	Notts Co	D 3-3	1-2	—	Green [21], McKenzie [53], Farrell [69]	6510
37	27	H	Luton T	D 1-1	0-0	—	Clarke [75]	5425
38	31	H	Cambridge U	W 4-1	1-1	15	Forsyth (pen) [25], Green [79], Farrell [84], Lee [90]	10,086
39	Apr 7	A	Wrexham	L 1-2	0-1	16	Edwards [74]	2678
40	11	A	Bristol R	W 2-1	2-0	—	Hanlon [18], Lee [38]	6540
41	14	H	Bristol C	W 2-1	1-1	11	McKenzie (pen) [29], Green [64]	6560
42	17	A	Colchester U	D 2-2	1-1	—	Lee [11], Oldfield [53]	4336
43	21	H	Bournemouth	L 1-2	1-0	14	Clarke [19]	6318
44	24	H	Walsall	W 2-0	1-0	—	Lee [45], Rea [57]	5549
45	28	A	Swindon T	L 1-2	0-1	11	Reeves (og) [76]	8145
46	May 5	H	Rotherham U	D 1-1	1-1	12	McKenzie [11]	11,274

Final League Position: 12

GOALSCORERS

League (61): McKenzie 13 (2 pens), Clarke 9, Lee 8, Farrell 7, Green 6, Oldfield 3, Forsyth 2 (1 pen), Rea 2, Williams M 2, Cullen 1 (pen), Edwards 1, Forinton 1, Gill 1, Hanlon 1, Shields 1, Whittingham 1, own goals 2.
Worthington Cup (2): Clarke 1, Farrell 1.
FA Cup (7): Clarke 1, Edwards 1, Farrell 1, Forsyth 1, Lee 1, Oldfield 1, Shields 1.

Tyler M 40	Scott R 18 + 2	Drury A 29	Shields T 28 + 5	Rea S 35 + 1	Edwards A 43	Farrell D 39 + 5	Green F 18 + 14	Clarke A 36 + 6	Cullen J 12 + 6	Hanlon R 21 + 5	Forinton H 2 + 6	Forsyth R 25 + 5	Oldfield D 32 + 7	Whittingham G 1 + 4	Hooper D 28 + 5	Jelleyman G 6 + 2	Lee J 14 + 16	McKenzie L 30	Rogers D 1 + 2	Gill M 11 + 6	Danielsson H 3 + 3	Williams M 13 + 2	Murray D 1 + 2	Taylor S 6	Morrow S 11	French D 1 + 1	Williams T 1 + 1	MacDonald G 1	Match No.
1	2	3	4	5	6	7	8	9	10^2	11^3	12	13	14																1
1	2	3	4	5	6	7	8^2	9	10^1	11	13		12																2
1	2	3	4	5	6	7	8^3	9	10^1	11		12			14	13													3
1	2^2	3	4	5	6	7	8^3	9	10^1	11		12			14	13													4
1	2^2	3	4	5	6	7^1	8^3	9	10	11		12			14	13													5
1	3	2	4		5	7	6^3	9	10^2	8^1		12	13	14		11													6
1	2^2	3	6^1		5	7	8^2	9	10	12		4	13		14	11													7
1		3	6^2		5	7^1	12	8	9	13	10	4		8^1	2	11	14												8
1		3	12		5	7	8^3	9	6^1	10^3		4	13		2	11	14												9
1		3	10		5	6	7	8^2	9	12	13	4		11^3	2^1		14												10
1		3^3	8^1		5	6	7	10^2	9	12		4		11	2	14	13												11
1			5^3		6	7		9	10	12		4^1		8^2	2	3	13	11	14										12
1		3			5	6	7	9		10		4		8	2			11											13
1		3	12		5	6	7^1	13	9	10^2		4		8	2		14	11^3											14
1		3	10^3		5	6	7	8^2	9			4	11		2^1		13		12	14									15
1		3	12		5	6	7	13	9			4	8		2^2		10^1	11^2	14										16
1		3	12		5	6	7	13	9			4	8^1		2^2		10	11^2	14										17
1		3	12		5	6	7	13	9^2	14		4	8		2^2		10	11^1											18
1		3	8		5	6	7	12	9^1	13		4	10^2		2		14	11^3											19
1		8	5^3		6	7		10^2	12			4	11		2		9	3^1	14	13									20
1		3	8		5	6	7		9			4	10		12		11^1	2											21
1		3	8		6	12	13	9^1				4	7		2^2		10	11	5										22
1		3	8		5	7	12	9^2		13		4		2^1	14		11	10^3	6										23
1		3			5	7	6	9				4	8			11		10	2										24
1	2	3			5	7		9		10		4	8			11		6											25
1	2			5	6	7^1		9	4	12		8			11		3	10											26
1	2			5	6	7		9	4			8			11		3	10											27
1	4	12	3^3	5	7		9	11^2	6	13		8			2		10^1	14											28
1	2^1		4^2	5	6	7		9	11	14		8	13	12	3		10^3												29
		3		5	6		12		10^1	11^2	4	8	2	13	7		9		1										30
		3		5	6	12	13		11^1		4^3	8	2		9	7^2	14	10	1										31
		3	4	5	6	7^3	12	13				8	2		9^2	11^1	14	10	1										32
		3	4	5	6		9					8	2		7	11		10	1										33
	12	3	4	5	6^3	13		9^2				8	2		7	11	2^1	10	14	1									34
	4	3	6	5		7	12	9^2	13		11^1			2	14	10^2	8	1											35
1			7	5	6	12	9^2		10		4	8^1	2		11		13		3										36
1			8	5	6	7	9		4		2	12	11		10^1			3											37
1			8^1	5	6	7	10	9		4	12	2		13	11^2			3											38
1			5	6	7	10^3	9	12		4^1	8	2		13	11^2	14		3											39
1			4	5	6	7		10		8	2		9	11				3											40
1	4	6		5	7	12	13	10		8	2		9^2	11^1				3											41
1	4		5	7	12	13	6		8	2		9^2	11^1		14	10^3		3											42
1	2	6	12	4^1	9	10		8	2	13	11^2		7^3				3	14											43
1	12	4	5	6^1	7	13	9^2		8	2		10				3	11												44
1	4	5^2	7	8^1	10	12	2	13	11		6	9^2	3	14															45
1	2	4^2	7	12	13	8	9	11	6^1	3	5	10																	46

Worthington Cup
First Round   Luton T   (a) 0-0
                                     (h) 2-2

FA Cup
First Round   Mansfield T   (a) 1-1
                                       (h) 4-0
Second Round   Oldham Ath   (h) 1-1
                                       (a) 1-0
Third Round   Chelsea   (a) 0-5

PLYMOUTH ARGYLE

Division 3

FOUNDATION

The club was formed in September 1886 as the Argyle Football Club by former public and private school pupils who wanted to continue playing the game. The meeting was held in a room above the Borough Arms (a Coffee House), Bedford Street, Plymouth. It was common then to choose a local street/terrace as a club name and Argyle or Argyll was a fashionable name throughout the land due to Queen Victoria's great interest in Scotland.

Home Park, Plymouth, Devon PL2 3DQ.

Telephone: (01752) 562 561. *Fax:* (01752) 606 167.
Pilgrim Shop: (01752) 558 292.

Ground Capacity: 19,630.

Record Attendance: 43,596 v Aston Villa, Division 2, 10 October 1936.

Record Receipts: £128,000 v Burnley, Division 2 play-off, 18 May 1994.

Pitch Measurements: 110yd × 72yd.

President: S. J. Rendell.

Chairman: D. McCauley. *Vice-Chairman:* P. Bloom.

Directors: Paul Stapleton, John McNulty, Ken Jones, Roy Griggs.

Manager: Paul Sturrock.
Assistant Manager: Steve McCall.
Physio: Norman Medhurst.

Secretary/Chief Executive: Roger Matthews.

Colours: Green and white shirts, white shorts, green, black and white stockings.

Change Colours: All white.

Year Formed: 1886.

Turned Professional: 1903.

Ltd Co.: 1903.

Previous Name: 1886, Argyle Athletic Club; 1903, Plymouth Argyle.

Club Nickname: 'The Pilgrims'.

First Football League game: 28 August 1920, Division 3, v Norwich C (h) D 1–1 – Craig; Russell, Atterbury; Logan, Dickinson, Forbes; Kirkpatrick, Jack, Bowler, Heeps (1), Dixon.

Record League Victory: 8–1 v Millwall, Division 2, 16 January 1932 – Harper; Roberts, Titmuss; Mackay, Pullan, Reed; Grozier, Bowden (2), Vidler (3), Leslie (1), Black (1), (1 og). 8–1 v Hartlepool U (a), Division 2, 7 May 1994 – Nicholls; Patterson (Naylor), Hill, Burrows, Comyn, McCall (1), Barlow, Castle (1), Landon (3), Marshall (1), Dalton (2).

HONOURS

Football League: Division 2 best season: 4th, 1931–32, 1952–53; Division 3 (S) – Champions 1929–30, 1951–52; Runners-up 1921–22, 1922–23, 1923–24, 1924–25, 1925–26, 1926–27 (record of six consecutive years); Division 3 – Champions 1958–59; Runners-up 1974–75, 1985–86, Promoted 1995–96 (play-offs).
FA Cup: Semi-final 1984.
Football League Cup: Semi-final 1965, 1974.

IT'S A FACT !

In 1930-31 Plymouth Argyle completed a League double over West Bromwich Albion, FA Cup winners and Division Two promotion winners, 2-1 away and 5-1 at Home Park.

Record Cup Victory: 6–0 v Corby T, FA Cup 3rd rd, 22 January 1966 – Leiper; Book, Baird; Williams, Nelson, Newman; Jones (1), Jackson (1), Bickle (3), Piper (1), Jennings.

Record Defeat: 0–9 v Stoke C, Division 2, 17 December 1960.

Most League Points (2 for a win): 68, Division 3 (S), 1929–30.

Most League Points (3 for a win): 87, Division 3, 1985–86.

Most League Goals: 107, Division 3 (S), 1925–26 and 1951–52.

Highest League Scorer in Season: Jack Cock, 32, Division 3 (S), 1925–26.

Most League Goals in Total Aggregate: Sammy Black, 180, 1924–38.

Most League Goals in One Match: 5, Wilf Carter v Charlton Ath, Division 2, 27 December 1960.

Most Capped Player: Moses Russell, 20 (23), Wales.

Most League Appearances: Kevin Hodges, 530, 1978–92.

Youngest League Player: Lee Phillips, 16 years 43 days v Gillingham, 29 October 1996.

Record Transfer Fee Received: £750,000 from Southampton for Mickey Evans, March 1997.

Record Transfer Fee Paid: £250,000 to Hartlepool U for Paul Dalton, June 1992.

Football League Record: 1920 Original Member of Division 3; 1921–30 Division 3 (S); 1930–50 Division 2; 1950–52 Division 3 (S); 1952–56 Division 2; 1956–58 Division 3 (S); 1958–59 Division 3; 1959–68 Division 2; 1968–75 Division 3; 1975–77 Division 2; 1977–86 Division 3; 1986–95 Division 2; 1995–96 Division 3; 1996–98 Division 2; 1998– Division 3.

MANAGERS

Frank Brettell 1903–05
Bob Jack 1905–06
Bill Fullerton 1906–07
Bob Jack 1910–38
Jack Tresadern 1938–47
Jimmy Rae 1948–55
Jack Rowley 1955–60
Neil Dougall 1961
Ellis Stuttard 1961–63
Andy Beattie 1963–64
Malcolm Allison 1964–65
Derek Ufton 1965–68
Billy Bingham 1968–70
Ellis Stuttard 1970–72
Tony Waiters 1972–77
Mike Kelly 1977–78
Malcolm Allison 1978–79
Bobby Saxton 1979–81
Bobby Moncur 1981–83
Johnny Hore 1983–84
Dave Smith 1984–88
Ken Brown 1988–90
David Kemp 1990–92
Peter Shilton 1992–95
Steve McCall 1995
Neil Warnock 1995–97
Mick Jones 1997–98
Kevin Hodges 1998–2000
Paul Sturrock October 2000–

LATEST SEQUENCES

Longest Sequence of League Wins: 9, 8.3.86 – 12.4.86.

Longest Sequence of League Defeats: 9, 12.10.63 – 7.12.63.

Longest Sequence of League Draws: 5, 26.2.00 – 14.3.00.

Longest Sequence of Unbeaten League Matches: 22, 20.4.29 – 21.12.29.

Longest Sequence Without a League Win: 13, 27.4.63 – 2.10.63.

TEN YEAR LEAGUE RECORD

		P	W	D	L	F	A	Pts	Pos
1990-91	Div 2	46	12	17	17	54	68	53	18
1991-92	Div 2	46	13	9	24	42	64	48	22
1992-93	Div 2	46	16	12	18	59	64	60	14
1993-94	Div 2	46	25	10	11	88	56	85	3
1994-95	Div 2	46	12	10	24	45	83	46	21
1995-96	Div 3	46	22	12	12	68	49	79	4
1996-97	Div 2	46	12	18	16	47	58	54	19
1997-98	Div 2	46	12	13	21	55	70	49	22
1998-99	Div 3	46	17	10	19	58	54	61	13
1999-2000	Div 3	46	16	18	12	55	51	66	12

DID YOU KNOW ?

Harry Raymond an inside-forward was 16 years with Plymouth Argyle 1908-24. He achieved three England amateur caps in 1914, the first player to achieve such honours with the club.

PLYMOUTH ARGYLE 2000–01 LEAGUE RECORD

Match No.	Date	Venue	Opponents	Result	H/T Score	Lg. Pos.	Goalscorers	Attendance
1	Aug 12	H	Leyton Orient	L	0-1	0-1	—	5649
2	19	A	Hull C	D	1-1	0-1	19	Gritton [90]	5431
3	26	H	Mansfield T	W	2-0	0-0	11	Hicks (og) [52], McGregor [71]	4069
4	29	A	Darlington	L	0-1	0-1	—		4415
5	Sept 2	H	Macclesfield T	L	0-1	0-0	18		3888
6	9	A	Southend U	D	2-2	2-1	21	McCarthy [13], McGregor [38]	3417
7	12	A	Shrewsbury T	L	1-4	0-2	—	Peake [67]	2361
8	16	H	Carlisle U	W	2-0	2-0	18	McCarthy [9], Peake [17]	3378
9	23	A	Cheltenham T	L	2-5	0-4	19	McCarthy [45], Mardon [55]	3665
10	30	H	Barnet	L	2-3	1-0	20	McCarthy [45], Guinan [79]	3423
11	Oct 7	A	Chesterfield	L	1-2	0-1	21	McGregor [47]	4285
12	14	H	Blackpool	W	2-0	0-0	19	Wotton (pen) [58], McGregor [86]	3651
13	17	H	Scunthorpe U	L	0-1	0-0	—	McGregor [45]	3437
14	21	A	Hartlepool U	D	1-1	0-1	19	Nancekivell [69]	2581
15	24	A	Brighton & HA	L	0-2	0-1	—		6724
16	Nov 4	A	Torquay U	D	1-1	1-0	20	McCarthy [5]	3936
17	Dec 2	H	Exeter C	W	2-0	0-0	20	McCarthy 2 [47, 75]	5145
18	16	H	York C	W	1-0	1-0	18	Taylor [3]	3830
19	23	A	Halifax T	L	0-2	0-1	18		1670
20	26	H	Cardiff C	W	2-1	0-1	17	McCarthy 2 [74, 86]	8543
21	Jan 6	A	Mansfield T	D	0-0	0-0	16		2321
22	13	A	Darlington	D	1-1	1-0	17	Taylor [39]	4278
23	16	H	Lincoln C	W	1-0	0-0	—	Stonebridge [90]	4139
24	20	A	Cardiff C	L	1-4	0-1	15	Stonebridge [51]	9157
25	27	H	Halifax T	W	1-0	1-0	14	O'Sullivan [33]	4176
26	30	H	Kidderminster H	W	4-0	1-0	—	Taylor [38], Stonebridge 2 [62, 80], Wotton (pen) [90]	5332
27	Feb 3	A	Macclesfield T	L	1-3	0-0	11	Stonebridge [50]	1881
28	17	A	Carlisle U	D	1-1	0-0	16	Friio [53]	3592
29	20	H	Shrewsbury T	W	3-1	0-0	—	Friio [56], Stonebridge 2 [73, 78]	5007
30	24	A	Cheltenham T	D	0-0	0-0	12		5209
31	Mar 3	H	Barnet	D	1-1	1-0	13	Wotton [13]	2879
32	6	A	Blackpool	L	0-1	0-0	—		4570
33	10	H	Chesterfield	W	3-0	1-0	13	Friio [20], Phillips M [61], McCarthy [80]	5399
34	13	H	Hull C	D	1-1	1-0	—	McGregor [3]	5482
35	17	A	Scunthorpe U	L	1-4	0-2	12	Stonebridge [90]	3844
36	24	H	Hartlepool U	L	0-2	0-2	13		4226
37	31	A	York C	W	2-1	1-1	13	Evans 2 [45, 51]	3083
38	Apr 7	H	Exeter C	W	1-0	1-0	13	Friio [20]	8671
39	10	A	Leyton Orient	D	1-1	1-0	—	Meaker [27]	4520
40	14	H	Brighton & HA	L	0-2	0-2	13		7490
41	16	A	Kidderminster H	L	0-3	0-3	13		3321
42	21	H	Torquay U	W	3-1	0-1	12	Stonebridge 2 [52, 60], Wills [54]	5711
43	24	A	Southend U	D	3-3	2-1	—	Friio 2, Evans [23], Wotton (pen) [86]	3619
44	28	A	Lincoln C	L	1-2	1-1	12	Stonebridge [25]	4277
45	May 1	A	Rochdale	L	1-2	1-0	—	Evans [34]	4027
46	5	H	Rochdale	D	0-0	0-0	13		5125

Final League Position: 13

GOALSCORERS

League (54): Stonebridge 11, McCarthy 10, McGregor 6, Friio 5, Evans 4, Wotton 4 (3 pens), Taylor 3, Peake 2, Gritton 1, Guinan 1, Mardon 1, Meaker 1, Nancekivell 1, O'Sullivan 1, Phillips M 1, Wills 1, own goal 1.
Worthington Cup (2): McCarthy 1, McGregor 1.
FA Cup (2): McGregor 1, Peake 1.

Sheffield J 29	O'Sullivan W 38 + 2	Beswetherick J 44 + 1	Barrett A 9	Wotton P 38 + 4	McCarthy S 31 + 6	Fleming T 15 + 2	Barlow M 17 + 3	Stonebridge I 17 + 14	Gunan S 7 + 15	Peake J 7 + 3	Phillips L 4 + 2	Phillips M 36 + 6	Taylor C 38 + 1	Gritton M 1 + 9	Nancekivell K — + 6	McGregor P 31 + 2	Mardon P 3	Leadbitter C 9	Heathcote M 4 + 1	Wills K 4 + 6	Adams S 12 + 5	Hodges J 2	Worrell D 14	McGlinchey B 17 + 3	Friio D 26	Wilkie L 2	Meaker M 5 + 6	Betts R 3 + 1	Larrieu R 14 + 1	Javary J 4	Elliott S 11 + 1	Evers S 2 + 5	Evans M 10	Bance D 1	McCormick L 1	Connolly P — + 1	Trudgian R — + 1	Match No.
1	2	3	4	5	6	7	8	9	10	11²	12	13																										1
1	2	3	4	5	6³	7	8	12	9¹				10²	11	14	13																						2
1	2	3	4		9²	6	8			12			11¹	7	5	13		10																				3
1	2	3¹	4		6	8				10	12	11³	7	5	13	14	9³																					4
1	2	3	4		9	6	8			10¹	11²		7	5	12	13																						5
1	2	3	4	12	9³	6	8	13	14	11			7²	5		10¹																						6
1	2	3	4	12	9²	6	8			13	11		7	5¹		10																						7
1	2	3¹	4	12	9	6	8			11			7			10	5																					8
1	2²	3¹	4	13	9	7³	8			12	11		14			10	5	6																				9
1	4			9	2	8³	12	13	11¹				7	6		14	10²	5	3																			10
1	2¹	3		11	9	8⁹				13	12		7	6		10²		4	5	14																		11
1	2	3		11		7	9	8		12			6			10¹		4	5																			12
1	2	3		11	9	8				12			7	6		10¹		4	5²	13																		13
1	2	3		11	9	8							7	6	12	10		4¹		5																		14
	2²	3		11	9	8				12			7¹	6	13	10		4		5	1																	15
	3		2	9¹		8				12	13	11³	7	6		10²		4		14	5	1																16
1	8	3		4	9	11		12					7²	5		10¹							2	13	6													17
1	8	3		5	9¹			13					7³	6	12²	10					14		2	11	4													18
1	8²	3		5	9	12		14					7¹	6		10		2			13			11¹³	4													19
1	8	3		5	9	12							7	6		10				11¹			2	4														20
1		3		5	9	8							7¹	6		10	4			12			2	11														21
1		3		5	9¹	8		13					7²	6	12	10				14			2	11	4³													22
1	11²	3		5	9¹	8¹		12					7	6	13	10							2	14	4													23
1	7³	3		5	9			10²					12	6	13					14			2	11	4	8¹												24
1	8	3		5		12	9						7¹	6		10							2	11	4													25
1	8	3		5	12	13	9³	14					7	6		10¹							2	11²	4													26
1	8	3¹		5		13	9	12					7²	6		10							2		4	11												27
1	8	3		5		7	11	9³	12				6			10¹		13					2		4													28
1	8²	3		5		9¹	12						7³	6		10							2	11	4		14	13										29
1⁸	8	3		5	9								7	6		10							2	11	4	12		15										30
	3		5	12		9¹		13	6				10			14		2³	11	4	7²		1	8														31
	8	3		5	7		9									10		2		11	4		6	1														32
	8	3		5	9	12							7²	6		10¹				4		13	11³	1		2	14											33
	8	3		5	9	12							7¹	6		10²				4		13	11³	1		2	14											34
	8¹	3		5²	9	12							13	6		14				11³	4	10		1		2	7											35
	8	3		5	12	9¹							13	6		4³		7²				1	11	2	14	10												36
	12	3		5		9							7	6		13		4		11		1	8¹	2	10²													37
	8	3		5	12	13							7	6		10²		14		11	4³	1		2	9¹													38
	8	3		5	12		10						13	6		4		11²		7³		1		2	14	9¹												39
	8	3		5	9¹	12							7	6		4²		11³		13		1		2	14	10												40
1	13	12		5	9³								14			7	6	4							8²	2	11	10	3¹									41
	8	3		5		9¹							7	6	12			11	2		4				1		10											42
	8	3		5	12	9¹							7	6²				11	2		4			13	1		10											43
	8²	3		5	11	9¹	12						7			6					4		13	1		2	10											44
	3		5	9	12	8¹							7			14	6			13	4	11²	1		2³	10												45
	3		5	6	9								7	8²		10	2			11	4¹	1	12	13											1	12	13	46

Worthington Cup
First Round   Bristol R   (h)   1-2
                                (a)   1-1

FA Cup
First Round   Chester C   (a)   1-1
                                (h)   1-2

PORTSMOUTH

Division 1

Fratton Park, Frogmore Rd, Portsmouth PO4 8RA.

Telephone: (023) 9273 1204. *Fax:* (023) 9273 4129

Ticket Office: (023) 9261 8777.

ClubCall: 09068 121 182.

Ground Capacity: 19,179.

Record Attendance: 51,385 v Derby Co, FA Cup 6th rd, 26 February 1949.

Record Receipts: £233,000 v Chelsea, FA Cup 6th rd, 9 March 1997.

Pitch Measurements: 110yd × 72yd.

Chairman: Milan Mandaric. *Director:* F. Dinenage. *Managing Director:* David Deacon.

Manager: Graham Rix.

Director of Football: Harry Redknapp.

Coach: Alan Knight.

Secretary: Paul Weld.

Youth Team Manager: Neil McNab.

Physio: Jonathan Trigg.

Colours: Blue shirts, white shorts, red stockings.

Change Colours: Gold shirts, blue shorts, white stockings.

Year Formed: 1898.

Turned Professional: 1898.

Ltd Co.: 1898.

Club Nickname: 'Pompey'.

First Football League Game: 28 August 1920, Division 3, v Swansea T (h) W 3–0 – Robson; Probert, Potts; Abbott, Harwood, Turner; Thompson, Stringfellow (1), Reid (1), James (1), Beedie.

Record League Victory: 9–1 v Notts Co, Division 2, 9 April 1927 – McPhail; Clifford, Ted Smith; Reg Davies (1), Foxall, Moffat; Forward (1), Mackie (2), Haines (3), Watson, Cook (2).

HONOURS

Football League: Division 1 – Champions 1948–49, 1949–50; Division 2 – Runners-up 1926–27, 1986–87; Division 3 (S) – Champions 1923–24; Division 3 – Champions 1961–62, 1982–83.

FA Cup: Winners 1939; Runners-up 1929, 1934.

Football League Cup: best season: 5th rd, 1961, 1986.

IT'S A FACT !

Since the advent of the Premier League in 1992-93, the highest number of individual goals scored in Division One has been by Guy Whittingham for Portsmouth with 42 goals in the same season.

Record Cup Victory: 7–0 v Stockport Co, FA Cup 3rd rd, 8 January 1949 – Butler; Rookes, Ferrier; Scoular, Flewin, Dickinson; Harris (3), Barlow, Clarke (2), Phillips (2), Froggatt.

Record Defeat: 0–10 v Leicester C, Division 1, 20 October 1928.

Most League Points (2 for a win): 65, Division 3, 1961–62.

Most League Points (3 for a win): 91, Division 3, 1982–83.

Most League Goals: 91, Division 4, 1979–80.

Highest League Scorer in Season: Guy Whittingham, 42, Division 1, 1992–93.

Most League Goals in Total Aggregate: Peter Harris, 194, 1946–60.

Most League Goals in One Match: 5, Alf Strange v Gillingham, Division 3, 27 January 1923; 5, Peter Harris v Aston Villa, Division 1, 3 September 1958.

Most Capped Player: Jimmy Dickinson, 48, England.

Most League Appearances: Jimmy Dickinson, 764, 1946–65.

Youngest League Player: Clive Green, 16 years 259 days v Wrexham, 21 August 1976.

Record Transfer Fee Received: £3,500,000 from Manchester C for Lee Bradbury, August 1997.

Record Transfer Fee Paid: £1,000,000 to Tottenham H for Rory Allen, July 1999.

Football League Record: 1920 Original Member of Division 3; 1921 Division 3 (S); 1924–27 Division 2; 1927–59 Division 1; 1959–61 Division 2; 1961–62 Division 3; 1962–76 Division 2; 1976–78 Division 3; 1978–80 Division 4; 1980–83 Division 3; 1983–87 Division 2; 1987–88 Division 1; 1988–92 Division 2; 1992– Division 1.

MANAGERS

Frank Brettell 1898–1901
Bob Blyth 1901–04
Richard Bonney 1905–08
Bob Brown 1911–20
John McCartney 1920–27
Jack Tinn 1927–47
Bob Jackson 1947–52
Eddie Lever 1952–58
Freddie Cox 1958–61
George Smith 1961–70
Ron Tindall 1970–73
   (General Manager to 1974)
John Mortimore 1973–74
Ian St. John 1974–77
Jimmy Dickinson 1977–79
Frank Burrows 1979–82
Bobby Campbell 1982–84
Alan Ball 1984–89
John Gregory 1989–90
Frank Burrows 1990–1991
Jim Smith 1991–95
Terry Fenwick 1995–98
Alan Ball 1998–99
Tony Pulis 2000
Steve Claridge 2000–01
Graham Rix February 2001–

LATEST SEQUENCES

Longest Sequence of League Wins: 7, 22.1.83 – 26.2.83.

Longest Sequence of League Defeats: 9, 21.10.75 – 6.12.75.

Longest Sequence of League Draws: 5, 6.12.00 – 13.1.01.

Longest Sequence of Unbeaten League Matches: 15, 18.4.24 – 18.10.24.

Longest Sequence Without a League Win: 25, 29.11.58 – 22.8.59.

TEN YEAR LEAGUE RECORD

		P	W	D	L	F	A	Pts	Pos
1990-91	Div 2	46	14	11	21	58	70	53	17
1991-92	Div 2	46	19	12	15	65	51	69	9
1992-93	Div 1	46	26	10	10	80	46	88	3
1993-94	Div 1	46	15	13	18	52	58	58	17
1994-95	Div 1	46	15	13	18	53	63	58	18
1995-96	Div 1	46	13	13	20	61	69	52	21
1996-97	Div 1	46	20	8	18	59	53	68	7
1997-98	Div 1	46	13	10	23	51	63	49	20
1998-99	Div 1	46	11	14	21	57	73	47	19
1999-2000	Div 1	46	13	12	21	55	66	51	18

DID YOU KNOW ?

When Portsmouth won the Football League Championship in 1948-49, the team did not contain one full international player, however this omission was remedied in subsequent seasons.

PORTSMOUTH 2000–01 LEAGUE RECORD

Match No.	Date	Venue	Opponents	Result	H/T Score	Lg. Pos.	Goalscorers	Attendance
1	Aug 12	A	Sheffield U	L	0-2	0-1	—	15,816
2	19	H	Grimsby T	D	1-1	0-0	21	Bradbury [73]	12,511
3	25	A	Gillingham	D	1-1	0-1	—	Moore [68]	8741
4	28	H	Wolverhampton W	W	3-1	3-1	10	Claridge 3 (1 pen) [2, 30, 32 (p)]	14,124
5	Sept 2	A	Preston NE	L	0-1	0-0	15		13,343
6	9	H	Watford	L	1-3	0-2	18	Quashie [75]	14,012
7	12	H	Tranmere R	W	2-0	0-0	—	Mills [81], Bradbury [86]	9235
8	16	A	Bolton W	L	0-2	0-1	15		14,113
9	23	A	WBA	L	0-1	0-0	17		11,937
10	30	A	Burnley	D	1-1	0-0	18	Claridge [74]	15,494
11	Oct 8	A	Stockport Co	D	1-1	1-0	17	Mills [16]	6212
12	14	H	Sheffield W	W	2-1	1-0	13	Thogersen [24], Claridge [48]	13,376
13	17	H	Crewe Alex	W	2-1	0-0	13	Thogersen [67], Claridge (pen) [81]	14,621
14	21	A	Crystal Palace	W	3-2	1-2	10	Claridge [45], Thogersen [59], Panopoulos [80]	15,693
15	24	A	Norwich C	D	0-0	0-0	—		18,772
16	28	H	Birmingham C	D	1-1	1-0	11	Bradbury [41]	15,218
17	Nov 4	A	QPR	D	1-1	0-1	11	Bradbury [50]	12,036
18	11	H	Blackburn R	D	2-2	1-1	11	Quashie [44], Panopoulos [61]	14,141
19	18	A	Fulham	L	1-3	1-1	12	Claridge [44]	19,005
20	25	A	Barnsley	L	0-1	0-0	13		12,853
21	Dec 2	H	Norwich C	W	2-0	1-0	12	Panopoulos [13], Quashie [57]	13,409
22	9	A	Nottingham F	L	0-2	0-1	13		19,284
23	16	H	Huddersfield T	D	1-1	0-1	13	Claridge [77]	12,041
24	23	H	Sheffield U	D	0-0	0-0	12		13,606
25	26	A	Wimbledon	D	1-1	1-0	14	Claridge [45]	9245
26	Jan 1	H	Gillingham	D	0-0	0-0	14		14,526
27	13	A	Wolverhampton W	D	1-1	1-1	15	Lescott (og) [27]	20,869
28	20	H	Wimbledon	W	2-1	2-1	12	Bradbury (pen) [16], Quashie [28]	12,488
29	27	A	Grimsby T	L	1-2	0-2	13	Bradbury [72]	4128
30	Feb 3	H	Preston NE	L	0-1	0-1	14		13,331
31	10	A	Watford	D	2-2	2-2	16	Quashie [39], Claridge [45]	16,051
32	13	H	Bolton W	L	1-2	0-0	—	Panopoulos [89]	11,377
33	24	A	WBA	L	0-2	0-1	17		17,645
34	Mar 3	H	Burnley	W	2-0	0-0	16	Nightingale [56], Panopoulos (pen) [69]	12,941
35	7	A	Sheffield W	D	0-0	0-0	—		20,503
36	10	H	Stockport Co	W	2-1	0-0	15	Bradbury [76], Lovell [85]	12,202
37	14	A	Tranmere R	D	1-1	0-1	—	Harper [57]	9872
38	17	A	Crewe Alex	L	0-1	0-1	15		6182
39	31	A	Huddersfield T	L	1-4	1-0	18	Mills [33]	13,199
40	Apr 7	H	Nottingham F	L	0-2	0-2	19		13,018
41	14	H	QPR	D	1-1	1-0	20	Bradbury [2]	13,426
42	16	A	Birmingham C	D	0-0	0-0	19		23,304
43	21	H	Fulham	D	1-1	1-0	21	Bradbury [10]	17,651
44	29	A	Blackburn R	L	1-3	1-0	21	Panopoulos [11]	24,257
45	May 2	H	Crystal Palace	L	2-4	1-3	—	Mills [45], Tiler [87]	19,013
46	6	H	Barnsley	W	3-0	1-0	20	Bradbury [17], O'Neil [63], Harper [75]	13,064

Final League Position: 20

GOALSCORERS

League (47): Claridge 11 (2 pens), Bradbury 10 (1 pen), Panopoulos 6 (1 pen), Quashie 5, Mills 4, Thogersen 3, Harper 2, Lovell 1, Moore 1, Nightingale 1, O'Neil 1, Tiler 1, own goal 1.
Worthington Cup (2): Mills 1, Nightingale 1.
FA Cup (1): Bradbury 1.

Hoult R 22	Derry S 27 + 1	Edinburgh J 16 + 1	Curtis T 4	Primus L 23	Awford A 2	Harper K 15 + 9	Thogersen T 32 + 2	Bradbury L 35 + 4	Mills L 22 + 2	Hughes C 16 + 3	Rudonja M 2 + 9	Waterman D 12 + 10	Quashie N 29 + 2	Moore D 31 + 1	Claridge S 24 + 7	O'Neil G 7 + 3	Lambourde B 6	Keller M 3	Hiley S 34	Nightingale L 7 + 12	Panopoulos M 26 + 4	Miglioranzi S 8 + 4	Crowe J 21 + 2	Flahavan A 20	Vine R — + 2	Whittingham G — + 1	Sharpe L 17	Tardif C 2 + 2	Vincent J 14	Brady G 8	Lovell S 5 + 4	Wolleaston R 5 + 1	Tiler C 9	Pettefer C — + 1	Petterson A 2	Match No.
1	2	3	4¹	5	6²	7	8	9	10	11³	12	13	14																							1
1	2	3		5			8	9	10¹	11¹			4	7	6	12	13																			2
1	2	3	4	5			8	9¹	10		12			7	6	13	11¹																		3
1	2	3	4	5		11³	8	12	10¹				13	7²	6	9	14																		4
1	2	3	4	5			8²	12	10				13	7	6	9	11¹																		5
1	2	3		5²			8	12	10	13	11¹			7	6	9		4																	6
1	2	3		5			8¹	9	10		12			7	6	11		4																	7
1	2	3		5			8	9	10	11¹				7	6	12		4																	8
1			4	5			8	9	10	12				7	6	13	3	11¹																	9
1			4	5		12	8		10				2	7	6	9	3	11¹																	10
1		3¹	4	5		12	8	13	10²				14	7	6	9³	2	11¹																	11
1		3	4	5		11³	8	9						7	6	10¹			2	12	13														12
1		3	4	5			8	9²					12		6¹	10			2	13	11														13
1		3	4	5			8	9¹			12²			7	6¹	10			2	14	11	13													14
1		3	4	5			8	9¹				7²			6	10			2	12	11	13													15
1		3¹	4	5²			8	9					7	12	6	10			2	11	13														16
1				5			8	9					7	3	6	10			2	11	4														17
1			4	5			8	9					3		6	10			2	11															18
1			4¹	5			8	9	11				12	7	6	10			2		3														19
1			4	5¹		12	8	9²	11					7	6	10			2	13	3														20
1		3	4				8	9¹						7	6	10			5	12	11			2											21
1		3¹	4			12	8					7		10	13	9			5	6	11²			2											22
			4			12	8	9		11				7	6	10			5		3¹			2	1										23
							8	9		11				7	6	10			5¹		3	4	2	1	12										24
			4			12	8	9¹		11²				7	6	10			5		3	2		1		13									25
			4			12	8	9³				13		7	6	10			5	14	3¹	11²		2	1										26
						7	3	9				11¹	12	13	4	6			5	10		8	2²	1											27
						3	8	9				11¹	12	13	7	6	14		5	10³		4	2²	1											28
				12		3²	8¹	9				11¹			7	6	14		5	10	13	4	2	1											29
				4			12	9				13			7	6	10		5		3	8¹	2	1					11²						30
				4				8	9						6	7	10		5		3	2		1					11						31
								8¹	9	12					4	7	10		5		3	6	2						11	1					32
			4³			12		9					5¹	7	6	13				8²	11	14	2	1			10	3							33
						12		9				13			6				5	8¹	7		2	1			10	3	4	11²					34
						11¹	8³	9			12	13			6²				5		7	4	1				3	2	10	14					35
						12		9	4			10¹	2						5		7		1				11	3	8	13	6²				36
						7		9		6									5	11		4	1				3	2	8	12	10¹				37
						7		9											5	12	11	4	1				3	2¹	8²	10	13	6			38
						8		9											5	12	7		2	1⁸			11¹	15	3	6²	13	10	4		39
						7		9⁵											5	13	12		2				11	1	3	6¹	8	10²	4	14	40
			4					9	10								13		5	12	7¹		2	1			11	3		8²		6			41
						12		9	10				4				7		5	8¹			2	1⁶			11	15	3			6			42
				5				9	10²				4	12		7			2			13					11	3		8¹	6		1		43
				5		8		9	12				4			10³			2		7¹	13					11	3			6		1		44
				5		8		9	10²				4³			7			2	13	12		1				11	3		6¹					45
				5		8		9					7						2				12	1			11	3	4	10¹	6				46

Worthington Cup

First Round	Cambridge U	(a)	0-0
		(h)	1-0
Second Round	Blackburn R	(a)	0-4
		(h)	1-1

FA Cup

Third Round	Tranmere R	(h)	1-2

PORT VALE

Division 2

FOUNDATION

Formed in 1876 as Port Vale, adopting the prefix 'Burslem' in 1884 upon moving to that part of the city. It was dropped in 1909.

Vale Park, Hamil Road, Burslem, Stoke-on-Trent ST6 1AW.

Telephone: (01782) 814 134. *Fax:* (01782) 834 981.
ClubCall: 09068 121 636. *Club Shop:* (01782) 833 545.
Community: (01782) 575 594. *Marketing Dept:* (01782) 835 524. *Marketing Fax:* (01782) 836 875.

Ground Capacity: 22,356.

Record Attendance: 49,768 v Aston Villa, FA Cup 5th rd, 20 February 1960.

Record Receipts: £170,349 v Everton, FA Cup 4th rd, 14 February 1996.

Pitch Measurements: 114yd × 77yd.

President: J. Burgess.

Chairman: W. T. Bell LAE, TECH. ENG, MIMI.

Directors: A. Belfield, I. McPherson, P. Wright, N. Hughes (Marketing Director).

Manager: Brian Horton. *Physio:* Alan Rankin.

Medical Officer: Dr D. Phillips.

Secretary: F. W. Lodey.

Safety Officer: W. Stevenson.

Groundsman: S. Speed.

Community Scheme Officer: Jim Cooper (01782 575594).

Colours: White shirts, black shorts, black and white stockings.

Change Colours: All yellow.

Year Formed: 1876.

Turned Professional: 1885.

Ltd Co.: 1911.

Previous Name: 1876, Burslem Port Vale; 1909, Port Vale.

Club Nickname: 'Valiants'.

Previous Grounds: 1876, Limekin Lane, Longport; 1881, Westport; 1884, Moorland Road, Burslem; 1886, Athletic Ground, Cobridge; 1913, Recreation Ground, Hanley; 1950, Vale Park.

First Football League Game: 3 September 1892, Division 2, v Small Heath (a) L 1–5 – Frail; Clutton, Elson; Farrington, McCrindle, Delves; Walker, Scarratt, Bliss (1). Jones. (Only 10 men).

Record League Victory: 9–1 v Chesterfield, Division 2, 24 September 1932 – Leckie; Shenton, Poyser; Sherlock, Round, Jones; McGrath, Mills, Littlewood (6), Kirkham (2), Morton (1).

HONOURS

Football League: Division 2 – Runners-up 1993–94; Division 3 (N) – Champions 1929–30, 1953–54; Runners-up 1952–53; Division 4 – Champions 1958–59; Promoted 1969–70 (4th).

FA Cup: Semi-final 1954, when in Division 3.

Football League Cup: best season: 3rd rd 1992, 1997.

Autoglass Trophy: Winners 1993.

Anglo-Italian Cup: Runners-up 1996.

LDV Vans Trophy: Winners 2001.

IT'S A FACT !

Port Vale lost only five matches in their Third Division (North) championship winning season of 1929-30, drawing seven times and failing to score in only four.

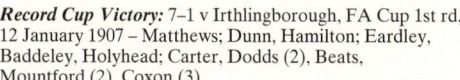

Record Cup Victory: 7–1 v Irthlingborough, FA Cup 1st rd, 12 January 1907 – Matthews; Dunn, Hamilton; Eardley, Baddeley, Holyhead; Carter, Dodds (2), Beats, Mountford (2), Coxon (3).

Record Defeat: 0–10 v Sheffield U, Division 2, 10 December 1892. 0–10 v Notts Co, Division 2, 26 February 1895.

Most League Points (2 for a win): 69, Division 3 (N), 1953–54.

Most League Points (3 for a win): 89, Division 2, 1992–93.

Most League Goals: 110, Division 4, 1958–59.

Highest League Scorer in Season: Wilf Kirkham 38, Division 2, 1926–27.

Most League Goals in Total Aggregate: Wilf Kirkham, 154, 1923–29, 1931–33.

Most League Goals in One Match: 6, Stewart Littlewood v Chesterfield, Division 2, 24 September 1922.

Most Capped Player: Tony Rougier, Trinidad & Tobago.

Most League Appearances: Roy Sproson, 761, 1950–72.

Youngest League Player: Malcolm McKenzie, 15 years 347 days v Newport Co, 12 April 1966.

Record Transfer Fee Received: £2,000,000 from Wimbledon for Gareth Ainsworth, October 1998.

Record Transfer Fee Paid: £500,000 to Lincoln C for Gareth Ainsworth, September 1997.

Football League Record: 1892 Original Member of Division 2. Failed re-election in 1896; Re-elected 1898; Resigned 1907; Returned in Oct, 1919, when they took over the fixtures of Leeds City; 1929–30 Division 3 (N); 1930–36 Division 2; 1936–38 Division 3 (N); 1938–52 Division 3 (S); 1952–54 Division 3 (N); 1954–57 Division 2; 1957–58 Division 3 (S); 1958–59 Division 4; 1959–65 Division 3; 1965–70 Division 4; 1970–78 Division 3; 1978–83 Division 4; 1983–84 Division 3; 1984–86 Division 4; 1986–89 Division 3; 1989–94 Division 2; 1994–2000 Division 1; 2000– Division 2.

MANAGERS

Sam Gleaves 1896–1905
(Secretary-Manager)
Tom Clare 1905–11
A. S. Walker 1911–12
H. Myatt 1912–14
Tom Holford 1919–24
(continued as Trainer)
Joe Schofield 1924–30
Tom Morgan 1930–32
Tom Holford 1932–35
Warney Cresswell 1936–37
Tom Morgan 1937–38
Billy Frith 1945–46
Gordon Hodgson 1946–51
Ivor Powell 1951
Freddie Steele 1951–57
Norman Low 1957–62
Freddie Steele 1962–65
Jackie Mudie 1965–67
Sir Stanley Matthews
(General Manager) 1965–68
Gordon Lee 1968–74
Roy Sproson 1974–77
Colin Harper 1977
Bobby Smith 1977–78
Dennis Butler 1978–79
Alan Bloor 1979
John McGrath 1980–83
John Rudge 1984–99
Brian Horton February 1999–

LATEST SEQUENCES

Longest Sequence of League Wins: 8, 8.4.1893 – 30.9.1893.

Longest Sequence of League Defeats: 9, 9.3.57 – 20.4.57.

Longest Sequence of League Draws: 6, 26.4.81 – 12.9.81.

Longest Sequence of Unbeaten League Matches: 19, 5.5.69 – 8.11.69.

Longest Sequence Without a League Win: 17, 7.12.91 – 21.3.92.

TEN YEAR LEAGUE RECORD

		P	W	D	L	F	A	Pts	Pos
1990-91	Div 2	46	15	12	19	56	64	57	15
1991-92	Div 2	46	10	15	21	42	59	45	24
1992-93	Div 2	46	26	11	9	79	44	89	3
1993-94	Div 2	46	26	10	9	79	46	88	2
1994-95	Div 1	46	15	13	18	58	64	58	17
1995-96	Div 1	46	15	15	16	59	66	60	12
1996-97	Div 1	46	17	16	13	58	55	67	8
1997-98	Div 1	46	13	10	23	56	66	49	19
1998-99	Div 1	46	13	8	25	45	75	47	21
1999-2000	Div 1	46	7	15	24	48	69	36	23

DID YOU KNOW ?

The first League game staged at Vale Park on 24 August 1950 produced a 1-0 win for Port Vale over Newport County and despite inadequate cover, and other parts of the ground incomplete, an encouraging crowd of 30,196 were present.

PORT VALE 2000–01 LEAGUE RECORD

Match No.	Date	Venue	Opponents	Result		H/T Score	Lg. Pos.	Goalscorers	Attendance
1	Aug 12	A	Oldham Ath	L	1-4	0-2	—	Twiss [67]	5639
2	19	H	Oxford U	W	3-0	1-0	11	Naylor [29], Bridge-Wilkinson 2 [65, 67]	3814
3	28	H	Swindon T	W	3-0	1-0	7	Naylor 2 [27, 90], Smith [55]	3926
4	Sept 2	H	Reading	L	0-1	0-1	12		4701
5	9	A	Bournemouth	D	1-1	1-0	12	Viljanen [34]	3859
6	12	A	Cambridge U	L	0-4	0-1	—		3660
7	17	H	Stoke C	D	1-1	1-1	16	Bridge-Wilkinson [11]	8948
8	23	A	Bury	L	0-2	0-1	17		3176
9	30	A	Wycombe W	L	0-1	0-1	20		3615
10	Oct 8	A	Peterborough U	L	0-2	0-0	21		4752
11	14	H	Colchester U	W	3-1	1-0	18	Tankard [4], Naylor 2 [68, 76]	3192
12	17	H	Northampton T	D	2-2	1-2	—	Tankard [11], Viljanen [61]	4215
13	21	A	Wigan Ath	L	0-1	0-0	20		6275
14	24	H	Brentford	D	1-1	0-0	—	Widdrington [65]	3338
15	28	A	Swansea C	W	1-0	1-0	18	Cummins [19]	3715
16	Nov 4	H	Millwall	D	1-1	0-0	17	Brammer [79]	4559
17	25	A	Luton T	W	3-0	1-0	18	Walsh [34], Naylor [64], Minton [70]	4194
18	Dec 2	A	Walsall	L	1-2	0-1	20	O'Callaghan [78]	5597
19	16	H	Bristol C	L	1-2	0-1	21	Bridge-Wilkinson [59]	4113
20	22	H	Rotherham U	L	0-2	0-1	—		4110
21	26	A	Wrexham	L	0-1	0-1	22		4941
22	Jan 6	H	Oldham Ath	D	0-0	0-0	22		4313
23	13	A	Swindon T	W	1-0	0-0	20	Widdrington [83]	5175
24	27	A	Rotherham U	L	2-3	0-1	21	Cummins [62], Brooker [85]	5044
25	Feb 3	A	Reading	L	0-1	0-0	21		9026
26	10	H	Bournemouth	W	2-1	1-0	20	Naylor [7], Brisco [90]	3956
27	17	A	Stoke C	D	1-1	0-0	20	Brammer [81]	22,133
28	20	H	Cambridge U	W	4-2	3-1	—	Bridge-Wilkinson (pen) [31], Lowe [33], Naylor [45], Brooker [90]	3558
29	24	H	Bury	D	1-1	1-0	19	Bridge-Wilkinson [41]	4331
30	Mar 3	A	Wycombe W	W	1-0	0-0	19	Brooker [57]	4828
31	7	A	Colchester U	W	1-0	0-0	—	Brammer [54]	2579
32	10	H	Peterborough U	W	5-0	1-0	18	Naylor [20], Tankard [57], Smith [59], Bridge-Wilkinson (pen) [82], Twiss [90]	4787
33	24	H	Wigan Ath	D	0-0	0-0	19		5017
34	27	A	Notts Co	W	1-0	0-0	—	Brooker [86]	4603
35	31	A	Bristol C	D	1-1	1-0	17	Brooker [29]	11,782
36	Apr 3	H	Wrexham	D	1-1	0-1	—	Naylor [67]	4234
37	9	H	Bristol R	W	1-0	0-0	—	Naylor [73]	3962
38	11	A	Millwall	L	0-1	0-1	—		11,944
39	14	A	Brentford	D	1-1	0-1	16	Bridge-Wilkinson (pen) [83]	3671
40	16	H	Swansea C	W	1-0	1-0	12	Brooker [10]	4396
41	26	A	Northampton T	W	2-0	2-0	—	Naylor [13], Brooker [15]	4775
42	28	H	Notts Co	L	2-3	1-2	14	Brooker [16], Twiss [75]	5236
43	30	A	Bristol R	W	3-0	0-0	—	Plummer (og) [72], Bridge-Wilkinson [79], Naylor [90]	7340
44	May 1	A	Oxford U	D	1-1	0-0	—	Naylor [89]	7080
45	3	H	Walsall	L	0-2	0-0	—		6027
46	5	A	Luton T	D	1-1	1-1	11	Tankard [16]	5260

Final League Position: 11

GOALSCORERS

League (55): Naylor 14, Bridge-Wilkinson 9 (3 pens), Brooker 8, Tankard 4, Brammer 3, Twiss 3, Cummins 2, Smith 2, Viljanen 2, Widdrington 2, Brisco 1, Lowe 1, Minton 1, O'Callaghan 1, Walsh 1, own goal 1.
Worthington Cup (3): Bridge-Wilkinson 1, Burton 1, Minton 1.
FA Cup (5): Minton 2, Brammer 1, Bridge-Wilkinson 1, Naylor 1.

Goodlad M 39 + 1	Tankard A 28 + 5	Carragher M 45	Brammer D 33 + 2	Burton S 24 + 5	Widdrington T 31 + 4	Twiss M 15 + 3	Cummins M 43 + 2	Viljanen V 15 + 4	Naylor T 41 + 1	Minton J 11 + 2	Bridge-Wilkinson M 40 + 2	Olaoye D — + 1	Eyre R 1 + 5	Burns L 5 + 8	Smith A 36 + 1	Walsh M 38 + 1	Freeman D 2 + 1	Beresford D 4	O'Callaghan G 2 + 6	Gray W 2 + 1	Delany D 7 + 1	Brooker S 20 + 3	Lowe O 4 + 1	Brisco N 16 + 1	Burgess R — + 1	Donnelly P — + 1	Dodd A 3	Byrne P 1	Paynter B — + 1	Match No.
1	2	3	4¹	5	6	7	8	9	10	11	12																			1
1	2	3		5	6	7	8	9	10¹	11	4²	12	13																	2
1	2	3		5¹	6	7	8	9	10	4					12	11														3
1	2	3			6	7	8¹	9	10	4		13			12	5	11²													4
1	2	3	12	5²	6	7	8	9		4	11					13	10¹													5
1		3	12	5	6	11¹	8	9		4	10					2	7													6
1	2¹	3	4	5³	11	12	13	9	10		8				14	6	7													7
1		3	4		6¹	7	12	9²	10	13	8				5	2	11													8
1		3		5¹	6²	7	8		9	10	4				12	2	13	11	14											9
1		3			6	7	8	12	10¹		4²				5	13	2		11	9										10
1	2	3	4		6		8	12	10		7				11	5			9¹											11
1	2	3	4		6		8	9	10		7				11	5														12
1	2	3	4		6		8	9	10¹		7²			12	11	5								13						13
1	2	3	4		6		8	9	10		7				11	5														14
1	2	3	4		6		8	9	10		7				11	5														15
1	2	3	4		6		8	9	10¹		7				11	5														16
1	2¹	3	4²	12	6		8	9³	10		7		14		11	5								13						17
1	2	3	4	12	6		8	9	10		7²				11	5¹								13						18
1	2	3	4	12	6		8	9¹	10		7				11	5														19
1		3	4	2	6		8	9	10¹		7				11	5								12						20
1	2	3	4	12	6		8¹		10²		7		13³		11	5			9					14						21
1	2	3	4		6		8	9¹	12		7				11	5						10								22
1	2¹	3	4		6	11	8	9			7				12	5						10								23
1	2	3	4		6		8	9			7				11	5						10								24
1	2	3	4		6¹		8	9	12		7				11	5						10²		13						25
1	2	3	4²		6		8	9¹			7				11	5					12	10		13						26
1	2	3	4				8	9			7				11	5					12	10¹	6							27
1	2	3	4	12			8	9			7²				11	5					13	10	6¹							28
1	2¹	3	4	5			8	9			7				12	11					13	10²	6							29
1	2	3	4		6		8	9			7				11	5						10								30
1	2	3	4		6		8	9			7				11	5						10								31
1	12	3²	4	2	13	14	8	9³			7				11	5¹						10	6							32
1⁸		3	4	2			8	9			7			15	11	5						10	6							33
		3	4	2			8	9			7				11	5					1	10	6							34
		3	4	2	12	7¹	8	9¹							11	5					1	10	6							35
	12	3	4	2		7¹	8	9							11	5					1	10	6							36
1		3	4	2			8	9			7				11	5						10	6							37
1		3	4	2			8	9¹			7				11	5						10	6			12				38
1		3		2	6	7	8	12	9	13					11	5					4²	10¹								39
1	12	3	4	2			8	9			7				11¹	5						10	6							40
1		3	4¹	2	12		8	9			7				11	5						10	6							41
	12	3	2	4	13		8	9			7				11	5¹					1	10	6²							42
	12	3	2		13		8	9			7				11	5					1	10	6²	4¹						43
	2	3			6	7	12	9	10		8				5²	11					1			13			4¹			44
	2	3			11	7	8	9		4				15		5					1⁸	10	6¹	12						45
1	2	3	5	4			8¹	9			7				12	11						10	6							46

Worthington Cup
First Round   Chesterfield   (h) 1-2
                                             (a) 2-2

FA Cup
First Round   Canvey Island   (a) 4-4
                                             (h) 1-2

PRESTON NORTH END Division 1

Deepdale, Preston PR1 6RU.
Telephone: (01772) 902 020. *Fax:* (01772) 653 266.
Website: www.pnefc.net
Email: enquiries@pnefc.net
Ticket Enquiries: (01772) 902 000.
Ticket Office Credit Card Bookings: (01772) 902 222.
Corporate Hospitality: (01772) 902 030.
Publishing: (01772) 902 002.
Community: (01772) 902 030.
Kit 1 Shop at Deepdale: (01772) 902 040.
Kit 2 Shop, Preston Town Centre: (01772) 887 088.
Kit 3 Shop, Leyland: (01772) 624 600.
ClubCall: 09068 121 173.

Ground Capacity: 21,412.

Record Attendance: 42,684 v Arsenal, Division 1, 23 April 1938.

Record Receipts: £108,920 v Stockport C, FA Cup 3rd rd, 11 January 2001.

Pitch Measurements: 110yd × 77yd.

President: Sir Tom Finney OBE, JP.

Chairman: Bryan M. Gray.

Directors: K. W. Leeming and M. J. Woodhouse (snr), D. Shaw (Deputy Chairman), T. Scholes (Chief Executive). *Non-Executive:* D. Taylor, H. Nash.

Manager: David Moyes. *Assistant Manager:* Kelham O'Hanlon.

Coach: Jimmy Lumsden. *Secretary:* G. E. Harrison.

Colours: White shirts, navy shorts, white stockings.

Change Colours: Navy shirts, white shorts, navy stockings.

Year Formed: 1881.

Turned Professional: 1885.

Ltd Co.: 1893.

Club Nicknames: 'The Lilywhites' or 'North End'.

First Football League Game: 8 September 1888, Football League, v Burnley (h) W 5–2 – Trainer; Howarth, Holmes; Robertson, W. Graham, J. Graham; Gordon (1), Ross (2), Goodall, Dewhurst (2), Drummond.

HONOURS

Football League: Division 1 – Champions 1888–89 (first champions) 1889–90; Runners-up 1890–91, 1891–92, 1892–93, 1905–06, 1952–53, 1957–58; Division 2 – Champions 1903–04, 1912–13, 1950–51, 1999–2000; Runners-up 1914–15, 1933–34; Division 3 – Champions 1970–71, 1995–96; Division 4 – Runners-up 1986–87.

FA Cup: Winners 1889, 1938; Runners-up 1888, 1922, 1937, 1954, 1964.

Double Performed: 1888–89.

Football League Cup: best season: 4th rd, 1963, 1966, 1972, 1981.

IT'S A FACT !

On Boxing Day 2000, Preston North End won 1-0 away to Wolverhampton Wanderers. It was their first win at Molineux since 22 November 1952 when they won 2-0, with goals from Jimmy Baxter and Angus Morrison.

Record League Victory: 10–0 v Stoke, Division 1,
14 September 1889 – Trainer; Howarth, Holmes; Kelso,
Russell (1), Graham; Gordon, Jimmy Ross (2),
Nick Ross (3), Thomson (2), Drummond (2).

Record Cup Victory: 26–0 v Hyde, FA Cup 1st rd,
15 October 1887 – Addison; Howarth, Nick Ross;
Russell (1), Thomson (5), Graham (1); Gordon (5), Jimmy
Ross (8), John Goodall (1), Dewhurst (3), Drummond (2).

Record Defeat: 0–7 v Blackpool, Division 1, 1 May 1948.

Most League Points (2 for a win): 61, Division 3, 1970–71.

Most League Points (3 for a win): 95, Division 2, 1999–2000.

Most League Goals: 100, Division 2, 1927–28 and
Division 1, 1957–58.

Highest League Scorer in Season: Ted Harper, 37,
Division 2, 1932–33.

Most League Goals in Total Aggregate: Tom Finney, 187,
1946–60.

Most League Goals in One Match: 7, Jimmy Ross v Stoke,
Division 1, 6 October 1888.

Most Capped Player: Tom Finney, 76, England.

Most League Appearances: Alan Kelly, 447, 1961–75.

Youngest League Player: Steve Doyle, 16 years 166 days v
Tranmere R, 15 November 1974.

Record Transfer Fee Received: £1,250,000 from WBA for
Kevin Kilbane, June 1997.

Record Transfer Fee Paid: £1,500,000 to Manchester U for
David Healy, December 2000.

MANAGERS

Charlie Parker 1906–15
Vincent Hayes 1919–23
Jim Lawrence 1923–25
Frank Richards 1925–27
Alex Gibson 1927–31
Lincoln Hayes 1931–1932
Run by committee 1932–36
Tommy Muirhead 1936–37
Run by committee 1937–49
Will Scott 1949–53
Scot Symon 1953–54
Frank Hill 1954–56
Cliff Britton 1956–61
Jimmy Milne 1961–68
Bobby Seith 1968–70
Alan Ball Sr 1970–73
Bobby Charlton 1973–75
Harry Catterick 1975–77
Nobby Stiles 1977–81
Tommy Docherty 1981
Gordon Lee 1981–83
Alan Kelly 1983–85
Tommy Booth 1985–86
Brian Kidd 1986
John McGrath 1986–90
Les Chapman 1990–92
John Beck 1992–94
Gary Peters 1994–98
David Moyes January 1998–

Football League Record: 1888 Founder Member of League;
1901–04 Division 2; 1904–12 Division 1; 1912–13 Division 2; 1913–14 Division 1; 1914–15 Division 2;
1919–25 Division 1; 1925–34 Division 2; 1934–49 Division 1; 1949–51 Division 2; 1951–61 Division 1;
1961–70 Division 2; 1970–71 Division 3; 1971–74 Division 2; 1974–78 Division 3; 1978–81 Division 2;
1981–85 Division 3; 1985–87 Division 4; 1987–92 Division 3; 1992–93 Division 2; 1993–96 Division 3;
1996–2000 Division 2; 2000– Division 1.

LATEST SEQUENCES

Longest Sequence of League Wins: 14, 25.12.50 – 27.3.51.

Longest Sequence of League Defeats: 8, 22.9.84 – 27.10.84.

Longest Sequence of League Draws: 6, 24.2.79 – 20.3.79.

Longest Sequence of Unbeaten League Matches: 23, 8.9.1888 – 14.9.1889.

Longest Sequence Without a League Win: 15, 14.4.23 – 20.10.23.

TEN YEAR LEAGUE RECORD

		P	W	D	L	F	A	Pts	Pos
1990-91	Div 3	46	15	11	20	54	67	56	17
1991-92	Div 3	46	15	12	19	61	72	57	17
1992-93	Div 2	46	13	8	25	65	94	47	21
1993-94	Div 3	42	18	13	11	79	60	67	5
1994-95	Div 3	42	19	10	13	58	41	67	5
1995-96	Div 3	46	23	17	6	78	38	86	1
1996-97	Div 2	46	18	7	21	49	55	61	15
1997-98	Div 2	46	15	14	17	56	56	59	15
1998-99	Div 2	46	22	13	11	78	50	79	5
1999-2000	Div 2	46	28	11	7	74	37	95	1

DID YOU KNOW ?

The 1969-70 season was the
first in which at least one goal
was scored by Preston North
End players wearing numbers
2 to 11 inclusive, though the
event was repeated several
times in later seasons.

PRESTON NORTH END 2000–01 LEAGUE RECORD

Match No.	Date	Venue	Opponents	Result	H/T Score	Lg. Pos.	Goalscorers	Attendance
1	Aug 12	A	Grimsby T	W 2-1	1-0	—	Appleton [35], Macken [87]	5755
2	19	H	Sheffield U	W 3-0	2-0	2	Appleton [2], Macken 2 [6, 71]	13,948
3	26	A	Bolton W	L 0-2	0-1	6		19,954
4	28	H	Wimbledon	D 1-1	0-1	6	Appleton [46]	13,519
5	Sept 2	H	Portsmouth	W 1-0	0-0	4	Basham [47]	13,343
6	9	A	QPR	D 0-0	0-0	5		11,092
7	12	A	Birmingham C	L 1-3	1-0	—	Rankine [34]	16,464
8	16	H	Stockport Co	D 1-1	1-1	6	McKenna [14]	12,735
9	23	A	Sheffield W	W 3-1	0-1	5	Alexander [57], Anderson [69], Walker (og) [76]	17,379
10	30	H	Crystal Palace	W 2-0	1-0	4	Macken [15], McKenna [61]	13,028
11	Oct 14	H	Tranmere R	W 1-0	0-0	5	Basham [57]	14,511
12	17	H	Norwich C	W 1-0	0-0	—	Gunnlaugsson [90]	13,002
13	21	A	Huddersfield T	D 0-0	0-0	5		13,161
14	24	A	Fulham	W 1-0	0-0	—	Appleton [68]	14,354
15	27	H	Barnsley	L 1-2	0-1	—	Macken [86]	13,566
16	Nov 4	A	Nottingham F	L 1-3	1-1	6	Macken [3]	19,504
17	10	H	Crewe Alex	W 2-1	1-1	—	Appleton [12], Rankine [73]	12,632
18	18	A	Watford	W 3-2	2-2	6	Macken [31], Rankine [41], Anderson [54]	13,066
19	25	A	WBA	L 1-3	0-1	8	Anderson [52]	20,043
20	Dec 2	H	Fulham	D 1-1	1-0	9	Jackson [4]	16,047
21	9	H	Burnley	W 2-1	0-1	7	Macken [51], Alexander [67]	17,355
22	16	A	Gillingham	L 0-2	0-2	8		8198
23	23	H	Grimsby T	L 1-2	1-1	8	Macken [1]	14,667
24	26	A	Wolverhampton W	W 1-0	1-0	7	Anderson [14]	24,306
25	30	A	Sheffield U	L 2-3	2-1	9	Healy [4], Rankine [20]	22,316
26	Jan 1	H	Bolton W	L 0-2	0-1	9		15,863
27	10	A	Blackburn R	L 2-3	0-3	—	Macken [54], Healy (pen) [73]	23,983
28	13	A	Wimbledon	L 1-3	0-1	9	Robinson [63]	7242
29	Feb 3	A	Portsmouth	W 1-0	1-0	9	Healy [26]	13,331
30	10	H	QPR	W 5-0	0-0	9	Macken 2 [51, 61], McBride [68], Healy [71], Anderson [87]	14,423
31	13	A	Stockport Co	W 1-0	0-0	—	Healy [74]	7590
32	20	H	Birmingham C	L 0-2	0-1	—		14,864
33	24	H	Sheffield W	W 2-0	0-0	9	McKenna [49], Macken [52]	14,379
34	Mar 3	A	Crystal Palace	W 2-0	2-0	7	Healy [8], Alexander (pen) [24]	15,160
35	6	A	Tranmere R	D 1-1	1-0	—	Macken [8]	10,335
36	14	H	Wolverhampton W	W 2-0	1-0	—	McKenna [43], Cresswell [78]	15,457
37	17	A	Norwich C	W 2-1	1-1	5	Healy [34], Gregan [48]	16,282
38	31	H	Gillingham	D 0-0	0-0	6		13,550
39	Apr 6	H	Burnley	L 0-3	0-2	—		16,591
40	10	H	Huddersfield T	D 0-0	0-0	—		15,185
41	14	H	Nottingham F	D 1-1	1-0	6	Healy [11]	16,842
42	16	A	Barnsley	W 4-0	2-0	6	Macken [14], Anderson [38], McKenna [57], Cresswell [70]	16,361
43	22	H	Watford	W 3-2	2-1	5	Alexander (pen) [25], Macken 2 [34, 61]	14,071
44	28	A	Crewe Alex	W 3-1	3-1	4	Healy [5], Macken 2 [13, 45]	9415
45	May 2	H	Blackburn R	L 0-1	0-0	—		16,975
46	6	H	WBA	W 2-1	1-1	4	Gregan [3], Alexander (pen) [53]	16,226

Final League Position: 4

GOALSCORERS

League (64): Macken 19, Healy 9 (1 pen), Anderson 6, Alexander 5 (3 pens), Appleton 5, McKenna 5, Rankine 4, Basham 2, Cresswell 2, Gregan 2, Gunnlaugsson 1, Jackson 1, McBride 1, Robinson 1, own goal 1.
Worthington Cup (6): Macken 3, Alexander 2 (1 pen), Rankine 1.
FA Cup (0).

Moilanen T 17	Alexander G 34	Edwards R 41 + 1	Murdock C 33 + 4	Gregan S 39 + 2	Appleton M 25 + 1	McKenna P 43 + 1	Rankine M 43 + 1	Macken J 37 + 1	Basham S 11	Anderson I 19 + 12	Eyres D — + 5	Robinson S 6 + 16	Cartwright L 29 + 9	Jackson M 27 + 3	Parkinson G 11	Lucas D 28 + 1	Gunnlaugsson B 5 + 14	O'Hanlon K — + 1	McBride B 8 + 1	Mayer E 9	Kidd R 13 + 2	Ludden D — + 2	Barry-Murphy B 2 + 12	Healy D 19 + 3	Cresswell R 5 + 6	Lonergan A 1	Keane M — + 2	Eaton A 1	Match No.
1	2	3	4	5	6	7	8	9	10[1]	11[2]	12	13																	1
1	2	3	4	5	6	7	8	9	10	11																			2
1	2[2]	3	4		6	7[1]	8	9	10	11			12	13	5														3
1		3	4	6	11	7	8	9	10		12			5[1]	2														4
1	2	3	6	4	7[1]	8	9	10[2]	11[3]	12	13	14	5																5
	2	3	4	5	6	7	8	9[1]	10	11[2]		13				1													6
	2	3	4	5	6[3]	7	8	9	10[2]			13	11[1]	12		1	14												7
	2	3	4	5	6	7[2]	8		10[1]		12	13	11			1[1]		15	9										8
	2	3	4	5	6	7[2]	8		10[3]	13	12	14	11			1			9[1]										9
	2	3		4	6	7[1]	8	9[2]	10		12		13	11	5	1													10
	2	3	4	5	6	7	8[1]	9[2]	12				10	11		1	13												11
	2	3	4	5	6	7		11[1]		10	8		12			1	9												12
	2	3	4	5	6	7[1]	8		12		10	11[2]		13		1	9												13
	2	3	4	5	6	7	8	10[1]		12	11			13		1	9												14
	2	3	4[1]	5	6	7	8	10		13[3]			11[2]	12		1	14				9								15
	2	3	4	5	6	7	8	10[1]		11[2]		14		13		1	12		9[3]										16
	2		4	5	6	7	8	10[1]		11		13				1	12		9[2]	3									17
	12			5	6	7	8	10[3]		11[2]		14	13	4	3	1		9	2[1]										18
	3			5	6	7	8[1]	10		11		13		4	2[2]	1	12		9										19
	3			5		7	8	10		11[1]			6[3]	12	4	2	1	13	9[2]	14									20
	2	3	4	5		7	8	10		12			11	6		1	9[1]												21
	2	3	4	5	12	7	8	10		13			11[2]	6[1]		1	9												22
1	2	3	12	5	6	7	8[3]	10		13			11[1]	4			9[2]					14							23
	2[1]	3	12	5	6	7	8	9		11[3]			10[2]	13	4		1						14						24
	3[2]			5	6	7	8		12				11[1]	4	2	1		9		13			14	10[3]					25
		4[1]	5	6	7	12	10[3]			11[2]		13		8	2	1		9	3					14					26
		12	5	6	7[3]	8	9			11			4	2[1]	1			13	3[2]				14	10					27
	3	4		6	12	8[2]	9			7	11[1]	5		1			2						13	10	11[2]				28
1	3	4			7	8	10[1]			6	5	2					12							13	11[2]				29
1	3	4			6[3]	8	9[2]	12		7	5	2	13		11[1]								14	10					30
1	3	4			6	8	9			7	5	2		11										10					31
1	3	4	12		6	8[1]		11[2]		7[3]	5	2	13		9								14	10					32
1	2	3	4	12		6	8	9		7	5		11[1]										13	10[2]					33
1	2	3	4	5		7	8	9		11	6												12	10[1]					34
1	2	3	4	5		7	8	9		11	6													10					35
1	2	3	4	5		7	8	9		11	6												10[1]	12					36
1	2	3	4[1]	5		7	8	9[2]		11	6						12						10	13					37
1	2	3		5		7	8	9	12	11[1]	6						4						13	10[2]					38
1[3]	2	3	4	5		7	11	9[1]	12	6				15									10	8					39
	2	3	4	5		7	8[1]	12	13	11[3]			1				6					14	10[4]	9					40
	2	3	4	5		7	8	9	11[1]	12			1				6						10[2]	13					41
	2	3	4	5		7	8[2]	9[1]	11				1	12			6					13	10[3]	14					42
	2	3	4	5		7	8	9	11[2]			12					6						10[1]	13	1				43
	2	3		5		7	8	9	11[1]			12	4[2]			1	6						13	10[3]	14				44
	2	3		5			8[1]	9	11[1]			7				1	12					4	6	13	10[2]		14		45
	2	12		5[3]					13			7	4			1	11[2]					6		8	10	9	14	3[1]	46

Worthington Cup
First Round   Shrewsbury T   (a)   0-1   (h)   4-1
Second Round   Coventry C   (h)   1-3   (a)   1-4

FA Cup
Third Round   Stockport Co   (h)   0-1

QUEENS PARK RANGERS Division 2

There is an element of doubt about the date of the foundation of this club, but it is believed that in either 1885 or 1886 it was formed through the amalgamation of Christchurch Rangers and St Jude's Institute FC. The leading light was George Wodehouse, whose family maintained a connection with the club until comparatively recent times. Most of the players came from the Queen's Park district so this name was adopted after a year as St Jude's Institute.

South Africa Road, London W12 7PA.

Telephone: (020) 8743 0262. *Fax:* (020) 8749 0994.
Club Shop: (020) 8749 2509. *Box Office:* (020) 8740 2575.
Supporters Club: (020) 8740 2534.
Commercial: (020) 8740 2588.
ClubCall: 09068 121 162.

Ground Capacity: 19,148.

Record Attendance: 35,353 v Leeds U, Division 1, 27 April 1974.

Record Receipts: £218,475 v Manchester U, FA Premier League, 5 February 1994.

Pitch Measurements: 111yd × 73yd.

Directors: Nick Blackburn, David Davies, Chris Wright, Ross Jones, Charles Levison.

Manager: Ian Holloway. *Secretary:* Sheila Marson.
Physio: Prav Mathema.

Commercial and Marketing Director: Mark Devlin.

Year Formed: 1885* (*see Foundation*). *Turned Professional:* 1898. *Ltd Co.:* 1899.

Previous Name: 1885, St Jude's; 1887, Queens Park Rangers. *Club Nicknames:* 'Rangers' or 'Rs'.

Colours: Blue and white hooped shirts, white shorts and stockings.

Change Colours: Black shirts and silver hoops, black shorts, black stockings.

Previous Grounds: 1885* (*see Foundation*), Welford's Fields; 1888–99; London Scottish Ground, Brondesbury, Home Farm, Kensal Rise Green, Gun Club Wormwood Scrubs, Kilburn Cricket Ground; 1899, Kensal Rise Athletic Ground; 1901, Latimer Road, Notting Hill; 1904, Agricultural Society, Park Royal; 1907, Park Royal Ground; 1917, Loftus Road; 1931, White City; 1933, Loftus Road; 1962, White City; 1963, Loftus Road.

First Football League Game: 28 August 1920, Division 3, v Watford (h) L 1–2 – Price; Blackman, Wingrove; McGovern, Grant, O'Brien; Faulkner, Birch (1), Smith, Gregory, Middlemiss.

Record League Victory: 9–2 v Tranmere R, Division 3, 3 December 1960 – Drinkwater; Woods, Ingham; Keen, Rutter, Angell; Lazarus (2), Bedford (2), Evans (2), Andrews (1), Clark (2).

Football League: Division 1 – Runners-up 1975–76; Division 2 – Champions 1982–83; Runners-up 1967–68, 1972–73; Division 3 (S) – Champions 1947–48; Runners-up 1946–47; Division 3 – Champions 1966–67.

FA Cup: Runners-up 1982.

Football League Cup: Winners 1967; Runners-up 1986. (In 1966–67 won Division 3 and Football League Cup.)

European Competitions: UEFA Cup: 1976–77, 1984–85.

IT'S A FACT !

On 9 December 2000, Ludek Miklosko celebrated his 39th birthday by keeping a clean sheet for Queens Park Rangers at Blackburn Rovers in a goalless draw, his feat including a penalty save.

Record Cup Victory: 8–1 v Bristol R (away), FA Cup 1st rd, 27 November 1937 – Gilfillan; Smith, Jefferson; Lowe, James, March; Cape, Mallett, Cheetham (3), Fitzgerald (3) Bott (2). 8–1 v Crewe Alex, Milk Cup 1st rd, 3 October 1983 – Hucker; Neill, Dawes, Waddock (1), McDonald (1), Fenwick, Micklewhite (1), Stewart (1), Allen (1), Stainrod (3), Gregory.

Record Defeat: 1–8 v Mansfield T, Division 3, 15 March 1965. 1–8 v Manchester U, Division 1, 19 March 1969.

Most League Points (2 for a win): 67, Division 3, 1966–67.

Most League Points (3 for a win): 85, Division 2, 1982–83.

Most League Goals: 111, Division 3, 1961–62.

Highest League Scorer in Season: George Goddard, 37, Division 3 (S), 1929–30.

Most League Goals in Total Aggregate: George Goddard, 172, 1926–34.

Most League Goals in One Match: 4, George Goddard v Merthyr T, Division 3S, 9 March 1929; 4, George Goddard v Swindon T, Division 3S, 12 April 1930; 4, George Goddard v Exeter C, Division 3S, 20 December 1930; 4, George Goddard v Watford, Division 3S, 19 September 1931; 4, Tom Cheetham v Aldershot, Division 3S, 14 September 1935; 4, Tom Cheetham v Aldershot, Division 3S, 12 November 1938.

Most Capped Player: Alan McDonald, 52, Northern Ireland.

Most League Appearances: Tony Ingham, 519, 1950–63.

Youngest League Player: Frank Sibley, 16 years 97 days v Bristol C, 10 March 1964.

Record Transfer Fee Received: £6,000,000 from Newcastle U for Les Ferdinand, June 1995.

Record Transfer Fee Paid: £2,750,000 to Stoke C for Mike Sheron, July 1997.

Football League Record: 1920 Original Members of Division 3; 1921–48 Division 3 (S); 1948–52 Division 2; 1952–58 Division 3 (S); 1958–67 Division 3; 1967–68 Division 2; 1968–69 Division 1; 1969–73 Division 2; 1973–79 Division 1; 1979–83 Division 2; 1983–92 Division 1; 1992–96 FA Premier League; 1996–2001 Division 1; 2001– Division 2.

LATEST SEQUENCES

Longest Sequence of League Wins: 8, 7.11.31 – 28.12.31.

Longest Sequence of League Defeats: 9, 25.2.69 – 5.4.69.

Longest Sequence of League Draws: 6, 29.1.00 – 5.3.00.

Longest Sequence of Unbeaten League Matches: 20, 11.3.72 – 23.9.72.

Longest Sequence Without a League Win: 20, 7.12.68 – 7.4.69.

MANAGERS

James Cowan 1906–13
Jimmy Howie 1913–20
Ted Liddell 1920–24
Will Wood 1924–25
    (had been Secretary since 1903)
Bob Hewison 1925–30
John Bowman 1930–31
Archie Mitchell 1931–33
Mick O'Brien 1933–35
Billy Birrell 1935–39
Ted Vizard 1939–44
Dave Mangnall 1944–52
Jack Taylor 1952–59
Alec Stock 1959–65
    (General Manager to 1968)
Bill Dodgin Jnr 1968
Tommy Docherty 1968
Les Allen 1968–71
Gordon Jago 1971–74
Dave Sexton 1974–77
Frank Sibley 1977–78
Steve Burtenshaw 1978–79
Tommy Docherty 1979–80
Terry Venables 1980–84
Gordon Jago 1984
Alan Mullery 1984
Frank Sibley 1984–85
Jim Smith 1985–88
Trevor Francis 1988–90
Don Howe 1990–91
Gerry Francis 1991–94
Ray Wilkins 1994–96
Stewart Houston 1996–97
Ray Harford 1997–98
Gerry Francis 1998–2001
Ian Holloway February 2001–

TEN YEAR LEAGUE RECORD

		P	W	D	L	F	A	Pts	Pos
1990-91	Div 1	38	12	10	16	44	53	46	12
1991-92	Div 1	42	12	18	12	48	47	54	11
1992-93	PR Lge	42	17	12	13	63	55	63	5
1993-94	PR Lge	42	16	12	14	62	61	60	9
1994-95	PR Lge	42	17	9	16	61	59	60	8
1995-96	PR Lge	38	9	6	23	38	57	33	19
1996-97	Div 1	46	18	12	16	64	60	66	9
1997-98	Div 1	46	10	19	17	51	63	49	21
1998-99	Div 1	46	12	11	23	52	61	47	20
1999-2000	Div 1	46	16	18	12	62	53	66	10

DID YOU KNOW ?

Queens Park Rangers FA Cup record in pre-Football League days included a fine 7-0 win over Fulham on 3 November 1900, in a third qualifying round tie when Rangers were in the Southern League.

QUEENS PARK RANGERS 2000–01 LEAGUE RECORD

Match No.	Date	Venue	Opponents	Result		H/T Score	Lg. Pos.	Goalscorers	Atten- dance
1	Aug 12	H	Birmingham C	D	0-0	0-0	—		13,926
2	20	A	Crystal Palace	D	1-1	0-1	14	Carlisle 67	19,020
3	26	H	Crewe Alex	W	1-0	1-0	9	Furlong 13	9415
4	28	A	WBA	L	1-2	1-0	13	Kiwomya 28	14,831
5	Sept 9	H	Preston NE	D	0-0	0-0	12		11,092
6	13	H	Gillingham	D	2-2	0-0	—	Crouch 79, Kiwomya 83	10,655
7	16	A	Barnsley	L	2-4	0-3	17	Kiwomya 2 60, 71	12,763
8	23	H	Wimbledon	W	2-1	0-0	14	Wardley 54, Crouch 65	11,720
9	30	A	Sheffield U	D	1-1	0-1	16	Koejoe 52	13,803
10	Oct 14	A	Watford	L	1-3	0-2	17	Connolly 56	17,488
11	17	A	Grimsby T	L	1-3	1-0	—	Connolly 18	4428
12	21	H	Burnley	L	0-1	0-0	18		11,427
13	25	H	Sheffield W	L	1-2	1-0	—	Peacock (pen) 38	10,353
14	28	A	Tranmere R	D	1-1	0-0	20	Connolly 83	7263
15	31	A	Bolton W	L	1-3	1-1	—	Crouch 42	10,180
16	Nov 4	H	Portsmouth	D	1-1	1-0	20	Peschisolido 10	12,036
17	11	A	Stockport Co	D	2-2	1-1	22	Carlisle 2, Langley 88	6356
18	18	H	Huddersfield T	D	1-1	1-1	22	Connolly 30	11,543
19	25	H	Wolverhampton W	D	2-2	1-2	22	Peacock 2 (1 pen) 36 ipl, 86	11,156
20	Dec 2	A	Sheffield W	L	2-5	1-3	22	Crouch 2 11, 71	21,782
21	9	A	Blackburn R	D	0-0	0-0	23		16,886
22	16	H	Nottingham F	W	1-0	1-0	23	Crouch 41	14,409
23	23	A	Birmingham C	D	0-0	0-0	24		24,311
24	26	H	Norwich C	L	2-3	2-1	24	Carlisle 11, Wardley 42	12,338
25	30	H	Crystal Palace	D	1-1	1-0	23	Crouch 14	14,439
26	Jan 13	H	WBA	W	2-0	1-0	23	Plummer 29, Koejoe 72	11,881
27	20	A	Norwich C	L	0-1	0-1	23		16,472
28	31	H	Fulham	L	0-2	0-1	—		16,403
29	Feb 3	H	Bolton W	D	1-1	0-0	23	Ngonge 53	10,293
30	10	A	Preston NE	L	0-5	0-0	23		14,423
31	17	H	Barnsley	W	2-0	1-0	21	Kiwomya 45, Crouch 62	9388
32	20	A	Gillingham	W	1-0	0-0	—	Kiwomya 83	10,432
33	24	A	Wimbledon	L	0-5	0-1	21		9446
34	Mar 3	H	Sheffield U	L	1-3	1-0	22	Ngonge 34	11,024
35	7	H	Watford	D	1-1	0-0	—	Ngonge (pen) 51	12,436
36	10	A	Fulham	L	0-2	0-1	22		16,021
37	17	H	Grimsby T	L	0-1	0-0	23		17,608
38	24	A	Burnley	L	1-2	0-2	23	Bignot 56	14,018
39	31	A	Nottingham F	D	1-1	0-1	23	Wardley 85	22,208
40	Apr 7	H	Blackburn R	L	1-3	1-2	23	Plummer 15	12,449
41	10	A	Crewe Alex	D	2-2	2-0	—	Crouch 15, Thomson 34	6354
42	14	A	Portsmouth	D	1-1	0-1	23	Thomson 56	13,426
43	16	H	Tranmere R	W	2-0	1-0	23	Thomson 14, Crouch 63	9696
44	21	A	Huddersfield T	L	1-2	1-1	23	Thomson 43	12,846
45	28	H	Stockport Co	L	0-3	0-0	23		10,608
46	May 6	A	Wolverhampton W	D	1-1	0-1	23	Bruce 62	17,447

Final League Position: 23

GOALSCORERS

League (45): Crouch 10, Kiwomya 6, Connolly 4, Thomson 4, Carlisle 3, Ngonge 3 (1 pen), Peacock 3 (2 pens), Wardley 3, Koejoe 2, Plummer 2, Bignot 1, Bruce 1, Furlong 1, Langley 1, Peschisolido 1.
Worthington Cup (2): Kiwomya 2.
FA Cup (5): Crouch 2, Kiwomya 2, Peacock 1 (pen).

Harper L 29	Darlington J 32 + 1	Baraclough I 26 + 3	Morrow S 18 + 6	Ready K 19 + 4	Carlisle C 27	Langley R 26	Peacock G 31 + 1	Crouch P 38 + 4	Wardley S 26 + 8	Kiwumya C 20 + 6	Perry M 23 + 6	Furlong P 3	Connolly K 17 + 6	Heinola A — + 1	Warren C 16 + 6	Breacker T 8 + 2	Plummer C 24 + 1	Rose M 27	Rowland K 4	McFlynn T 1 + 1	Koejoe S 8 + 13	Kulcsar G 9 + 5	Murray P 4 + 2	Walshe B — + 1	Broomes M 5	Peschisolido P 5	Cochrane J — + 1	Miklosko L 17	Lisbie K 1 + 1	Higgins A — + 1	Ngonge M 7 + 6	Bruce P 5 + 2	Dowie I — + 1	Scully T 1 + 1	Maddix D 1 + 1	Bubb A — + 1	Knight L 10 + 1	Bignot M 8 + 1	Brown W 2	Thomson A 7 + 1	Burgess O — + 1	Pacquette R 1 + 1	Match No
1	2	3¹	4	5	6	7	8	9	10	11	12																																1
1		3	4	5	6	7	8	12	10	11²	2	9¹	13																														2
1		3	4	5²	6	7	8		10	11	2	9	12	13																													3
1	2³		4		6	7	12		10	11	3²	9¹	13		8	14	5																										4
1	2	12			6	7	13		10	11	3				5¹		4	8	9²																								5
1	2		4¹		6	7	12		10	11	3				5			8	9																								6
1	2		4¹		6	7		9	10	11	3				12		5²	8	13																								7
1	2		4		6	7		9¹	10	11	3²		13		5			8¹	12	14																							8
1	2		4		6			9	10	11	12				3		5¹	8	7																								9
1	2		4		6	7	12	9	10		5¹	13	3		9		11²																										10
1	2		4		6	7	8	9	12		5¹	11	3		10																												11
1	2				6	7²	8	9	10		5¹	11	3		4		13	12																									12
1	2¹				6	7	8	9	11	12²	10		3		4		13	5																									13
1		12			6	7²	8	9	13	11	2³		10		3¹		4	14	5																								14
1		6²		5	7	8	9	12		11	3		2		10		13	4																									15
1					6	7	8	9	12		11¹	3	2		4		5	10																									16
1		12	13		6	7	8	9		11	3³		2		4		14	5²	10																								17
	3	4	5		7	8	9			11	12		2		6		10			1																							18
		5²	6	7	8	9	12			11	3		2		4		13	10¹		1																							19
	13	4	5	6³	8	9				11¹	3²		2		7		12	10		1	14																						20
	2	3			6	7	8		10				12		5		4	11¹		1	9																						21
	2	3	12		6	7		9	10	11¹					5		4	13		1	8²																						22
	2	3	4		6	7		9	10	12		13			5¹		14	11²		1	8³																						23
	2	3	4²		6	7		9	10	12		13			5		8			1	11¹																						24
	2	3			6	7		9	10¹	12		11			5		4	8		1																							25
	2	3	12		6	7	8	9		13		4			11¹		5	10²		1																							26
	3	5	8¹		6	7		9	10	11	2²		4		12					1	13																						27
		3			6³	7¹	8	9		11	2	10²			5		4	12		1	13	14																					28
	2	3	4				8	9¹	10	11					5		6			1	7	12																					29
	2	3	4¹	12			8		10	11			9²		5		6			1	7	13																					30
	2	12		5			8	9	10	11	3		7²				13	4¹		1	6																						31
	2	12	13	5			8	9	10	11²	3¹		6				4	7		1																							32
	2			5			8	9	10	11	3¹		6				4	7		1	12																						33
		12		5			8	9	10³	2	13	3			6²		4	7¹	14	1	11																						34
1	7²	3		5			8	9		12	2	13			6³						11								10¹					4	14								35
1	10	3		5			8	9	14		2		12		6		4²				13	11³														7¹							36
1	10	3		5			8	9		11	2		6								14	11²														7¹	4	12					37
1	10	3						9²	11³	6					12		8¹				13													5	7	2	4	14					38
1	10	3		12			8²	9	13	11					5³		6				14															7	2	4¹					39
1	3³	5					8	9²	10		6¹		4		12																	7				13	2	11	14				40
1	3	5					8	9	12		6		4		13							14							11²					7²	2	10¹							41
1	12	3¹		5			8	9	13		6		4²								11													7	2	10¹							42
1	4	3		5			8	9			6				12						11													7	2	10¹							43
1	11	3¹		5			8	9	12	13			4³		6																			7²	2	10						14	44
1	8	3						10³	4		5²		6		12		13				14										7	2¹					9	11					45
1	2	3²		5				9	10	12			6		11		13				4	14									7¹						8³						46

Worthington Cup
First Round — Colchester U — (a) 1-0 (h) 1-4

FA Cup
Third Round — Luton T — (a) 3-3 (h) 2-1
Fourth Round — Arsenal — (h) 0-6

READING

Division 2

FOUNDATION

Reading was formed as far back as 1871 at a public meeting held at the Bridge Street Rooms. They first entered the FA Cup as early as 1877 when they amalgamated with the Reading Hornets. The club was further strengthened in 1889 when Earley FC joined them. They were the first winners of the Berks and Bucks Cup in 1878–79.

Madejski Stadium, Junction 11, M4, Reading, Berks RG2 0FL.

Telephone: (0118) 968 1100. *Fax:* (0118) 968 1101.

ClubCall: 09068 121 000. *Website:* www.readingfc.co.uk
Email: comments@readingfc.co.uk
Ticket Office: (0118) 968 1000.
Ticket Office Fax: (0118) 968 1001.

Ground Capacity: 24,200.

Record Attendance: 33,042 v Brentford, FA Cup 5th rd, 19 February 1927.

Record Receipts: £171,203 v Manchester C, Division 2, 27 March 1999.

Pitch Measurements: 112yd × 77yd.

President: F. Orton.

Chairman: John Madejski OBE, DL.

Director: I. Wood-Smith.

Manager: Alan Pardew.

Chief Executive: Nigel Howe.

Physio: Jon Fearn.

Commercial Manager: Kevin Girdler.

Secretary: Ms Sue Hewett.

HONOURS

Football League: Division 1 – Runners-up 1994–95; Division 2 – Champions 1993–94; Division 3 – Champions 1985–86; Division 3 (S) – Champions 1925–26; Runners-up 1931–32, 1934–35, 1948–49, 1951–52; Division 4 – Champions 1978–79.

FA Cup: Semi-final 1927.

Football League Cup: best season: 5th rd, 1996.

Simod Cup: Winners 1988.

Colours: Blue and white hooped shirts, blue shorts, blue stockings with white bands.

Change Colours: Burgundy shirts with navy and gold trim, navy shorts with gold trim, navy stockings with gold bands.

Year Formed: 1871.

Turned Professional: 1895.

Ltd Co.: 1895.

Club Nickname: 'The Royals'.

Previous Grounds: 1871, Reading Recreation; Reading Cricket Ground; 1882, Coley Park; 1889, Caversham Cricket Ground; 1896, Elm Park; 1998, Madejski Stadium.

First Football League Game: 28 August 1920, Division 3, v Newport Co (a) W 1–0 – Crawford; Smith, Horler; Christie, Mavin, Getgood; Spence, Weston, Yarnell, Bailey (1), Andrews.

IT'S A FACT !

Reading's consistency in Division Three (South) during the 1930's was such that from 1931-32 to 1938-39 they were never out of the top six and their finishing positions were respectively 2 4 3 2 3 5 6 5.

Record League Victory: 10–2 v Crystal Palace, Division 3 (S), 4 September 1946 – Groves; Glidden, Gulliver; McKenna, Ratcliffe, Young; Chitty, Maurice Edelston (3), McPhee (4), Barney (1), Deverell (2).

Record Cup Victory: 6–0 v Leyton, FA Cup 2nd rd, 12 December 1925 – Duckworth; Eggo, McConnell; Wilson, Messer, Evans; Smith (2), Braithwaite (1), Davey (1), Tinsley, Robson (2).

Record Defeat: 0–18 v Preston NE, FA Cup 1st rd, 1893–94.

Most League Points (2 for a win): 65, Division 4, 1978–79.

Most League Points (3 for a win): 94, Division 3, 1985–86.

Most League Goals: 112, Division 3 (S), 1951–52.

Highest League Scorer in Season: Ronnie Blackman, 39, Division 3 (S), 1951–52.

Most League Goals in Total Aggregate: Ronnie Blackman, 158, 1947–54.

Most League Goals in One Match: 6, Arthur Bacon v Stoke C, Division 2, 3 April 1931.

Most Capped Player: Jimmy Quinn, 17 (46), Northern Ireland.

Most League Appearances: Martin Hicks, 500, 1978–91.

Youngest League Player: Steve Hetzke, 16 years 184 days v Darlington, 4 December 1971.

Record Transfer Fee Received: £1,575,000 from Newcastle U for Shaka Hislop, August 1995.

Record Transfer Fee Paid: £800,000 to Brentford for Carl Asaba, August 1997 and £800,000 to Cambridge U for Martin Butler, February 2000.

Football League Record: 1920 Original Member of Division 3; 1921–26 Division 3 (S); 1926–31 Division 2; 1931–58 Division 3 (S); 1958–71 Division 3; 1971–76 Division 4; 1976–77 Division 3; 1977–79 Division 4; 1979–83 Division 3; 1983–84 Division 4; 1984–86 Division 3; 1986–88 Division 2; 1988–92 Division 3; 1992–94 Division 2; 1994–98 Division 1; 1998– Division 2.

MANAGERS

Thomas Sefton 1897–1901
  (Secretary-Manager)
James Sharp 1901–02
Harry Matthews 1902–20
Harry Marshall 1920–22
Arthur Chadwick 1923–25
H. S. Bray 1925–26
  (Secretary only since 1922 and 1926–35)
Andrew Wylie 1926–31
Joe Smith 1931–35
Billy Butler 1935–39
John Cochrane 1939
Joe Edelston 1939–47
Ted Drake 1947–52
Jack Smith 1952–55
Harry Johnston 1955–63
Roy Bentley 1963–69
Jack Mansell 1969–71
Charlie Hurley 1972–77
Maurice Evans 1977–84
Ian Branfoot 1984–89
Ian Porterfield 1989–91
Mark McGhee 1991–94
Jimmy Quinn/Mick Gooding 1994–97
Terry Bullivant 1997–98
Tommy Burns 1998–99
Alan Pardew October 1999–

LATEST SEQUENCES

Longest Sequence of League Wins: 13, 17.8.85 – 19.10.85.

Longest Sequence of League Defeats: 7, 10.4.98 – 15.8.98.

Longest Sequence of League Draws: 5, 11.10.97 – 1.11.97.

Longest Sequence of Unbeaten League Matches: 19, 21.4.73 – 27.10.73.

Longest Sequence Without a League Win: 14, 30.4.27 – 29.10.27.

TEN YEAR LEAGUE RECORD

		P	W	D	L	F	A	Pts	Pos
1990-91	Div 3	46	17	8	21	53	66	59	15
1991-92	Div 3	46	16	13	17	59	62	61	12
1992-93	Div 2	46	18	15	13	66	51	69	8
1993-94	Div 2	46	26	11	9	81	44	89	1
1994-95	Div 1	46	23	10	13	58	44	79	2
1995-96	Div 1	46	13	17	16	54	63	56	19
1996-97	Div 1	46	15	12	19	58	67	57	18
1997-98	Div 1	46	11	9	26	39	78	42	24
1998-99	Div 2	46	16	13	17	54	63	61	11
1999-2000	Div 2	46	16	14	16	57	63	62	10

DID YOU KNOW ?

In achieving the Championship of Division Three (South) in 1925-26, Reading were unbeaten at home, failing to score in only four League games. Yet surprisingly, they had a sequence of nine matches overall in which only once did they score more than one goal.

READING 2000–01 LEAGUE RECORD

Match No.	Date	Venue	Opponents	Result	H/T Score	Lg. Pos.	Goalscorers	Attendance
1	Aug 12	A	Millwall	L	0-2	0-1	—	11,043
2	19	H	Swindon T	W	2-0	1-0	13	Butler [17], Caskey [47]	14,134
3	26	A	Northampton T	L	0-2	0-1	19		5728
4	29	H	Stoke C	D	3-3	1-2	—	Butler [45], Caskey (pen) [84], Cureton [90]	10,668
5	Sept 2	A	Port Vale	W	1-0	1-0	10	Cureton [5]	4701
6	9	H	Brentford	W	4-0	3-0	5	Cureton 3 [19, 38, 69], Caskey (pen) [45]	10,222
7	12	H	Oldham Ath	W	5-0	3-0	—	Butler [3], Igoe 2 [5, 43], Hodges [49], McIntyre [80]	7768
8	16	A	Peterborough U	L	0-1	0-0	5		5767
9	23	H	Swansea C	W	5-1	1-0	4	Cureton [29], Butler 3 [53, 57, 88], Hodges [70]	11,003
10	30	A	Rotherham U	W	3-1	1-1	3	Butler [6], Cureton [49], McIntyre [79]	4288
11	Oct 6	A	Wigan Ath	D	1-1	1-1	—	Butler [10]	7021
12	14	H	Wycombe W	W	2-0	0-0	2	Butler [59], Viveash [73]	15,443
13	17	H	Wrexham	W	4-1	4-0	—	Butler 2 [6, 43], Caskey 2 [21, 45]	10,350
14	21	A	Bristol C	L	0-4	0-3	2		11,134
15	24	A	Bury	W	2-0	0-0	—	Butler [54], Cureton [60]	2808
16	28	H	Oxford U	W	4-3	1-1	1	Caskey (pen) [28], Cureton [68], Rougier 2 [78, 87]	16,022
17	Nov 4	A	Walsall	L	1-2	0-0	2	McIntyre [90]	7772
18	11	H	Colchester U	L	0-1	0-1	5		11,549
19	Dec 2	H	Cambridge U	W	3-0	2-0	5	Viveash [1], Parkinson [35], Gurney [70]	9601
20	16	A	Notts Co	L	2-3	1-2	5	Richardson (og) [45], Parkinson [64]	5106
21	23	H	Luton T	W	4-1	2-0	5	Hunter [22], Cureton 3 [35, 80, 89]	10,771
22	26	A	Bristol R	D	2-2	2-1	5	Smith [38], Parkinson [44]	8029
23	Jan 1	H	Northampton T	D	1-1	0-0	6	Caskey [90]	10,599
24	6	H	Millwall	L	3-4	0-3	6	Igoe [65], Caskey (pen) [76], Cureton [90]	14,743
25	13	A	Stoke C	D	0-0	0-0	6		14,154
26	20	H	Bristol R	W	1-0	1-0	6	Cureton [42]	11,767
27	Feb 3	A	Port Vale	W	1-0	0-0	6	Butler [78]	9026
28	10	A	Brentford	W	2-1	1-0	6	Parkinson [30], Igoe [58]	7550
29	17	H	Peterborough U	D	1-1	1-0	6	Cureton [24]	10,342
30	20	A	Oldham Ath	W	2-0	2-0	—	Butler [3], Cureton [45]	4160
31	24	A	Swansea C	W	1-0	1-0	5	Cureton [42]	5073
32	Mar 3	H	Rotherham U	W	2-0	0-0	3	Harper [60], Butler [80]	13,103
33	6	A	Wycombe W	D	1-1	0-1	—	Igoe [87]	6788
34	9	A	Wigan Ath	W	1-0	0-0	—	McIntyre [69]	12,307
35	17	H	Wrexham	W	2-1	1-0	3	Butler 2 [12, 83]	5080
36	23	H	Bristol C	L	1-3	1-1	—	Murty [9]	15,716
37	27	A	Swindon T	W	1-0	0-0	—	Cureton [51]	9674
38	31	H	Notts Co	W	2-1	0-0	3	Butler [55], Cureton [74]	11,624
39	Apr 3	A	Luton T	D	1-1	1-1	—	Butler [4]	6132
40	7	A	Cambridge U	D	1-1	1-0	3	Cureton [33]	4745
41	10	A	Bournemouth	W	2-1	2-1	—	Cureton [4], Butler [9]	6603
42	14	A	Bury	W	4-1	2-1	2	Igoe [11], Cureton [23], Butler 2 [55, 62]	16,829
43	17	A	Oxford U	W	2-0	1-0	—	Cureton [20], Butler [71]	6886
44	21	H	Walsall	D	2-2	2-1	2	Cureton 2 [15, 27]	16,710
45	28	A	Colchester U	L	1-2	1-2	3	Cureton [24]	5010
46	May 5	H	Bournemouth	D	3-3	1-3	3	Butler [26], Caskey [72], Forster [88]	20,589

Final League Position: 3

GOALSCORERS

League (86): Cureton 26, Butler 24, Caskey 9 (4 pens), Igoe 6, McIntyre 4, Parkinson 4, Hodges 2, Rougier 2, Viveash 2, Forster 1, Gurney 1, Harper 1, Hunter 1, Murty 1, Smith 1, own goal 1.
Worthington Cup (1): Cureton 1.
FA Cup (7): Butler 2, Caskey 1, Cureton 1, Hodges 1, Jones 1, Newman 1.

Whitehead P 46	Newman R 37 + 2	Robinson M 29 + 3	Viveash A 40	Hunter B 21 + 2	Parkinson P 44	Hodges L 23 + 6	Caskey D 35 + 8	McIntyre J 25 + 8	Scott K 1	Rougier T 14 + 17	Igoe S 15 + 16	Henderson D —+ 4	Smith N 4 + 11	Gurney A 15 + 6	Butler M 42 + 3	Murty G 18 + 5	Mackie J 7 + 3	Cureton J 37 + 6	Gamble J —+ 1	Haddow A —+ 1	Ashdown J —+ 1	Williams A 5	Jones K 18 + 5	Gray S 2 + 1	Whitbread A 19	Harper J 9 + 3	Forster N —+ 9	Match No.
1	2	3	4	5	6	7¹	8	9²	10³	11	12	13	14															1
1	10	3	4	5	6	7	8¹			11	13	12			2	9²												2
1	10	3	4¹	5	6²	7	8			11					2³	9	14	12	13									3
1	10³	3	4	5	6	12	8	13		11²	14				2¹	7		9										4
1	2	3	4	5	6	7	8³	12		11²				13	10			9¹	14									5
1		3	4	5¹	6²	7	8			11			13		2³	10	12	9		14								6
1⁸		3	4	5	6²	7	8	12		11			13		2	10¹		9			15							7
1		3	4	5	6	7	8	12		11²			13		2	10¹		9										8
1		3	4	5	6	7	8³	11¹				12	13		2	10	14	9²										9
1		3	4		6	7	8	11				12			2	10²	13	9¹				5³	14					10
1		3	4		6	7	8³	9¹					13		2	10	14	12				5	11²					11
1		3	12	4	6	7²	8	11³			14		13		2¹			9				5	10					12
1	2²	3	4			7¹	8	11				12	14			10	13	9³				5	6					13
1	2	3	4			7	8	9²			12			14	10	11¹		13				5³	6					14
1	2	3⁸	4		6	7¹	8	12				13		14	10		5	9²					11					15
1		3	4		6	7	8	12				13	14		2²	10	5	9¹					11³					16
1		3	4		6	7²	8	12		11				14	2¹	9	5	13					10³					17
1		3	4		6	7	8³	12				13	14		2²	10¹	5	9					11					18
1		3	4		6	7²					12	13	11¹	14	2	10	5	9					8¹					19
1	2	3	4		6	7				11	12			13	10		5	9¹					8²					20
1	2	3	4	5	6	7²	8					12	13	11	10			9¹										21
1	2	3	4	5	6²	7	8					12	13	11	10¹			9										22
1	2	3	4	5	6	7	8					12	13	11²	10			9										23
1	2	3⁸		5	6	7¹	8					12	13	11²	10	14	4	9										24
1	2		4	5	6	12	8	10¹		11³			13				7	9²					14	3				25
1	2		4	5	6		8³	10		11¹		12	13				7	9²					14	3				26
1	2		4	5	6		8	10		11		12	7¹	3³				9²					13	14				27
1		3	4		6		8	7		11²		12			2	10		9¹					13		5			28
1		3	4		6		8²	7¹		11	12	13			2	10		9							5			29
1		3	5		6		8	7¹			12	13			2	10		9					11²		4			30
1		3	4		6	12	8	7							2	10		9¹					11		5			31
1		3	5		6	7¹	8	12							2	10		9					11		4			32
1	2³	3	4²	14	6	7	8	12		11		13				10		9¹							5			33
1		3	4		6	7	8	12							2	10		9¹					11		5			34
1	12	3	5		6		8²	9¹		11³		13			2	10							14		4	7		35
1	2	3	5²		6¹	12		9		11³		13				10	7						14		4	8		36
1	2	3	5		6		8					12				10	7	9¹							4	11		37
1		3	4¹	12	6	7²	8					13			2	10		9³							5	11	14	38
1	12	3	4		6	7²	8¹					13			2	10		9³							5	11	14	39
1	2	3	4	12	6	7¹				11		13³				10		9²					8		5		14	40
1	2	3	4		6	12		7²		11¹		13				10		9³					8		5		14	41
1	2	3	4		6¹	12				11						10	7	9²					8³		5	13	14	42
1	2	3	4		6	12				11²						10	7	9³					8¹		5	13	14	43
1	2¹		4		6					11³		12		3		10	7	9					8²		5	13	14	44
1		3³	4		6	12				11		13			2	10	7³	9					8¹		5		14	45
1		3	4		6²	12				11³		13			2	10		9					8¹		5	7	14	46

Worthington Cup
First Round   Leyton Orient   (a)   1-1
                                            (h)   0-2

FA Cup
First Round   Grays Ath   (h)   4-0
Second Round   York C   (a)   2-2
                                        (h)   1-3

ROCHDALE

Division 3

Spotland, Sandy Lane, Rochdale OL11 5DS.

Telephone: (01706) 644 648.

Fax: (01706) 648 466.

Commercial: (01706) 647 521.

Ground Capacity: 10,249 (from October 2000).

Record Attendance: 24,231 v Notts Co, FA Cup 2nd rd, 10 December 1949.

Record Receipts: £46,000 v Burnley, Division 4, 5 May 1992.

Pitch Measurements: 114yd × 76yd.

President: Mrs L. Stoney.

Chairman: D. F. Kilpatrick.

Chief Executive: Francis Collins.

Directors: G. R. Brierley, C. Dunphy, J. Marsh, G. Morris, R. Bott.

Manager: Steve Parkin.

Secretary: Hilary Molyneux Dearden.

Youth Development Manager: David Hamilton.

Lottery and Merchandising Manager: R. Wild.

Advertising & Sponsorship Manager: L. Duckworth.

Stadium Manager: Ronnie Cowgill.

Physio: Andy Thorpe.

Colours: Blue shirts with white trim, blue shorts, blue stockings with white hoop on turnover.

Change Colours: Jade green and black shirts, white shorts, black socks.

Year Formed: 1907.

Turned Professional: 1907.

Ltd Co.: 1910.

Club Nickname: 'The Dale'.

First Football League Game: 27 August 1921, Division 3 (N), v Accrington Stanley (h) W 6–3 – Crabtree; Nuttall, Sheehan; Hill, Farrer, Yarwood; Hoad, Sandiford, Dennison (2), Owens (3), Carney (1).

HONOURS

Football League: Division 3 best season: 9th, 1969–70; Division 3 (N) – Runners-up 1923–24, 1926–27.
FA Cup: best season: 5th rd, 1990.
Football League Cup: Runners-up 1962 (record for 4th Division club).

IT'S A FACT !

Rochdale's promotion season of 1968-69 was achieved even though they failed to score in 17 matches. Moreover, in the first 16 games, their goals total of 23 included two 6-0 wins.

Record League Victory: 8–1 v Chesterfield, Division 3 (N),
18 December 1926 – Hill; Brown, Ward; Hillhouse, Parkes,
Braidwood; Hughes, Bertram, Whitehurst (5), Schofield (2),
Martin (1).

Record Cup Victory: 8–2 v Crook T, FA Cup 1st rd,
26 November 1927 – Moody; Hopkins, Ward; Braidwood,
Parkes, Barker; Tompkinson, Clennell (3) Whitehurst (4),
Hall, Martin (1).

Record Defeat: 1–9 v Tranmere R, Division 3 (N),
25 December 1931.

Most League Points (2 for a win): 62, Division 3 (N),
1923–24.

Most League Points (3 for a win): 71, Division 3, 2000–01.

Most League Goals: 105, Division 3 (N), 1926–27.

Highest League Scorer in Season: Albert Whitehurst, 44,
Division 3 (N), 1926–27.

Most League Goals in Total Aggregate: Reg Jenkins, 119,
1964–73.

Most League Goals in One Match: 6, Tommy Tippett v
Hartlepools U, Division 3N, 21 April 1930.

Most Capped Player: None.

Most League Appearances: Graham Smith, 317, 1966–74.

Youngest League Player: Zac Hughes, 16 years 105 days v
Exeter C, 19 September 1987.

Record Transfer Fee Received: £400,000 from West Ham U
for Stephen Bywater, August 1998.

Record Transfer Fee Paid: £100,000 to Walsall for
Clive Platt, September 1999.

Football League Record: 1921 Elected to Division 3 (N);
1958–59 Division 3; 1959–69 Division 4; 1969–74 Division 3;
1974–92 Division 4; 1992– Division 3.

MANAGERS

Billy Bradshaw 1920
Run by committee 1920–22
Tom Wilson 1922–23
Jack Peart 1923–30
Will Cameron 1930–31
Herbert Hopkinson 1932–34
Billy Smith 1934–35
Ernest Nixon 1935–37
Sam Jennings 1937–38
Ted Goodier 1938–52
Jack Warner 1952–53
Harry Catterick 1953–58
Jack Marshall 1958–60
Tony Collins 1960–68
Bob Stokoe 1967–68
Len Richley 1968–70
Dick Conner 1970–73
Walter Joyce 1973–76
Brian Green 1976–77
Mike Ferguson 1977–78
Doug Collins 1979
Bob Stokoe 1979–80
Peter Madden 1980–83
Jimmy Greenhoff 1983–84
Vic Halom 1984–86
Eddie Gray 1986–88
Danny Bergara 1988–89
Terry Dolan 1989–91
Dave Sutton 1991–94
Mick Docherty 1995–96
Graham Barrow 1996–99
Steve Parkin June 1999–

LATEST SEQUENCES

Longest Sequence of League Wins: 8, 29.9.69 – 3.11.69.
Longest Sequence of League Defeats: 17, 14.11.31 – 12.3.32.
Longest Sequence of League Draws: 6, 17.8.68 – 14.9.68.
Longest Sequence of Unbeaten League Matches: 20, 15.9.23 – 19.1.24.
Longest Sequence Without a League Win: 28, 14.11.31 – 29.8.32.

TEN YEAR LEAGUE RECORD

		P	W	D	L	F	A	Pts	Pos
1990-91	Div 4	46	15	17	14	50	53	62	12
1991-92	Div 4	42	18	13	11	57	53	67	8
1992-93	Div 3	42	16	10	16	70	70	58	11
1993-94	Div 3	42	16	12	14	63	51	60	9
1994-95	Div 3	42	12	14	16	44	67	50	15
1995-96	Div 3	46	14	13	19	57	61	55	15
1996-97	Div 3	46	14	16	16	58	58	58	14
1997-98	Div 3	46	17	7	22	56	55	58	18
1998-99	Div 3	46	13	15	18	42	55	54	19
1999-2000	Div 3	46	18	14	14	57	54	68	10

DID YOU KNOW ?

Tony Ford, who holds the
record of Football League
appearances among current
players, reached another
milestone when Rochdale
played Kidderminster
Harriers. It was the 100th
League club he had played
against.

ROCHDALE 2000–01 LEAGUE RECORD

Match No.	Date	Venue	Opponents	Result		H/T Score	Lg. Pos.	Goalscorers	Attendance
1	Aug 12	H	Darlington	D	1-1	0-1	—	Davies (pen) [54]	3255
2	19	A	Brighton & HA	L	1-2	1-2	18	Ford [14]	6076
3	26	H	Scunthorpe U	W	3-2	1-1	12	Ellis [35], Platt [54], Ware [63]	2561
4	28	H	Halifax T	W	2-1	1-1	6	Platt [4], Jones [61]	2783
5	Sept 2	H	Cardiff C	D	1-1	0-1	9	Hadland [81]	2824
6	9	A	Carlisle U	W	2-1	1-1	4	Platt [16], Todd [90]	3906
7	12	A	York C	W	2-0	2-0	—	Platt [8], Monington [41]	2215
8	16	H	Torquay U	W	2-1	2-0	2	Monington [3], Ellis [24]	2871
9	23	A	Shrewsbury T	W	4-0	1-0	2	Ellis [18], Platt [55], Monington [63], Bayliss [69]	3427
10	30	H	Southend U	L	0-1	0-1	2		3264
11	Oct 6	A	Kidderminster H	D	0-0	0-0	—		3094
12	14	H	Hartlepool U	W	2-1	1-0	2	Ford [17], Jones (pen) [79]	2813
13	17	H	Chesterfield	D	2-2	1-2	—	Jones (pen) [20], Monington [70]	5008
14	21	A	Cheltenham T	W	2-0	1-0	2	Monington 2 [34, 63]	4033
15	24	H	Macclesfield T	D	2-2	0-2	—	Lee [76], Ware [83]	3608
16	28	A	Exeter C	W	1-0	0-0	3	Platt [89]	2606
17	Nov 4	H	Barnet	D	0-0	0-0	3		3657
18	11	A	Mansfield T	L	0-1	0-0	3		2543
19	Dec 2	H	Blackpool	W	1-0	0-0	3	Jones [79]	4186
20	16	H	Lincoln C	D	1-1	0-1	5	Ellis [56]	2320
21	23	A	Leyton Orient	D	1-1	1-0	5	Jones (pen) [21]	2200
22	26	H	Hull C	W	1-0	1-0	5	Jones [19]	4327
23	Jan 6	A	Darlington	W	2-1	1-0	4	Ellis [21], Evans [77]	3481
24	13	A	Halifax T	L	0-1	0-1	5		4123
25	28	H	Leyton Orient	W	3-1	2-0	4	Ellis [17], Jones [41], Hadland [48]	3676
26	Feb 2	A	Cardiff C	D	0-0	0-0	—		11,912
27	13	A	Scunthorpe U	D	0-0	0-0	—		2821
28	17	H	Torquay U	L	0-1	0-1	6		2195
29	20	H	York C	L	0-1	0-0	—		2807
30	24	H	Shrewsbury T	L	1-7	1-2	7	Lancashire [11]	2647
31	Mar 3	A	Southend U	L	0-3	0-2	8		3681
32	6	A	Hartlepool U	D	1-1	1-0	—	Lancashire [43]	3492
33	10	H	Kidderminster H	D	0-0	0-0	7		2552
34	17	A	Chesterfield	D	1-1	1-0	10	Connor [45]	4338
35	23	H	Cheltenham T	D	1-1	0-1	—	Connor [73]	2713
36	27	A	Hull C	L	2-3	0-2	—	Bayliss [74], Connor [77]	7365
37	Apr 3	H	Brighton & HA	D	1-1	0-0	—	Todd [90]	2444
38	10	H	Carlisle U	W	6-0	4-0	—	Jones [8], Todd [22], Connor 3 [30, 34, 64], Evans [61]	2892
39	14	A	Macclesfield T	D	0-0	0-0	10		2255
40	16	H	Exeter C	W	3-0	2-0	10	Connor 2 [6, 55], Bayliss [22]	2773
41	21	A	Barnet	L	0-3	0-2	10		2381
42	23	H	Lincoln C	W	3-1	1-0	—	Platt [9], Connor [60], Monington [71]	2592
43	26	A	Blackpool	L	1-3	0-1	—	Lancashire [80]	5470
44	28	H	Mansfield T	W	1-0	1-0	8	Platt [32]	3114
45	May 1	H	Plymouth Arg	W	2-1	0-1	—	Elliott (og) [54], Connor [58]	4027
46	5	A	Plymouth Arg	D	0-0	0-0	8		5125

Final League Position: 8

GOALSCORERS

League (59): Connor 10, Jones 8 (3 pens), Platt 8, Monington 7, Ellis 6, Bayliss 3, Lancashire 3, Todd 3, Evans 2, Ford 2, Hadland 2, Ware 2, Davies 1 (pen), Lee 1, own goal 1.
Worthington Cup (2): Ellis 1, Platt 1.
FA Cup (1): Platt 1.

Edwards N 44	Evans W 45	Todd L 40	Ware P 17+13	Bayliss D 41	Hill K 22+3	Ford T 36+2	Flitcroft D 40+1	Platt C 39+4	Ellis T 25+3	Davies S 7+5	Oliver M 25+13	Hadland P 12+20	Hamilton G —+3	Lancashire G 6+10	Jones G 44	Monington M 31+3	Coleman S 5	Bugpie L —+2	Lee C 2+3	Kyle K 3+3	McAuley S 1	Howell D 2+1	Townson K 1+2	Connor P 14	Gilks M 2+1	Turner A 2+2	Match No.
1	2	3	4^1	5	6	7^2	8	9	10^3	11	12	13	14														1
1	2	3	4	5^2	6	7	8^1	9	10	11^2	13	12			14												2
1	2	3	12	5	6	7	4^1	9	10	13	11^2				8												3
1	2	3	12	5	6	7	4	9	10^2	11^1		13			8												4
1	2	3	12	5	6	7^2	4^3	9		11	10^1	13	14		8												5
1	2	3	4	5	6^2		8	9	12	11^1	7	10	13														6
1	2	3	4	5			8	9	10		12	7^1			11	6											7
1	2	3	4	5			8	9	10		11	7				6											8
1	2	3	4^1	5	12		8	9^1	10	13	7^2				11	6			14								9
1	2	3	4^1	5	12		8	9^2	10	13	7^2				11	6			14								10
1	2	3	4	5		7^1	8	9	10		12				11	6											11
1	2	3	4^1	5		7	8	9	10		12				11	6											12
1	2	3		5		7	4	9	10	11^1	12				8	6											13
1	2	3	12	5		7^1	4	9	10^3	13	11^2				8	6			14								14
1	2	3	12	5		7	4^2	9^1	10	13	11^3				8	6			14								15
1	2	3	4	5		7^1		9		11	12				8	6			10								16
1	2	3	4		6	7		9		11	12				8	5			10^1								17
1	2	3	4	5		7^1		9	10^2	11	12				8	6			13								18
1	2	3	4	5		7		9	10^2	11^1	12	13			8	6											19
1	2	3	4	5		7	12	9	10	11^1					8	6											20
1	2	3	4	5		7^1		9	13	11^2	10	12			8	6											21
1	2	3	12	5		7^2	8	9	10	11^1		13			4	6											22
1	2	3		5		7	8	9	10	11^1	12				4	6											23
1	2	3		5		7^2	8	9	10	11^1	13	12			4	6											24
1	2	3		5	12	7	8	9	10	13	11^1				4	6^1				14							25
1	2	3		5	6	7^1	8	9	10		12				4					11							26
1	2	3		5	6	7	8	9^1		11^1	12	13			4	14				10^2							27
1	2	3		5	6	7^1	8	9	10	11^2	12				4					13							28
1	2	3		5	6^2	7^1	8	9^1	10	11	12				4	13				14							29
1	2^3	3	12	5	13		8		10			14			9	7	6^2	4	11^1								30
1	2		12	5	6		8		10						11	7^2	9^3	4				3^1	13	14			31
1	2	3		5	6		8								11	9		4					7	10			32
1	2	3			6		8	12		11		13			9^1		5	4				7^1	14	10^3			33
	2	3			6	7	8	12		11					9^1		5	4						10	1		34
1^6	2	3			6	7^2	8	12		11					9^1		5	4						10	15	13	35
	2	3	4^1	5			8	12	11	13		7			6	9								10^2	1		36
1	2	3		5		7^1	8	9^3	12	13		14			4	6								10		11^2	37
1	2	3	12	5		7^2	8^1	9		11	13	14			4	6								10^3			38
1	2	3		5		7	8	9		11					4	6								10			39
1	2	3	12	5		7	8^2	9		11	13	14			4	6								10^3			40
1	2		4^3	5	12	7^1	8	9		3		13		11	6									10		14	41
1	2			5	6	7	8	9		3	12			11	4									10^1			42
1	2		12	5	6	7^3	8^1	9		3		13	14	11	4									10^2			43
1	2			5	6	7	8	9		3	12			11	4									10^1			44
1	2		12	5	6	7	8	9			11^1	13		3	4									10^2			45
1	2		12	5	6	7^2	8^1	9		3		13^3	14	11	4									10			46

Worthington Cup
First Round Blackburn R (h) 1-1
  (a) 1-6

FA Cup
First Round Cambridge U (a) 1-2

ROTHERHAM UNITED

Division 1

Millmoor Ground, Rotherham S60 1HR.

Telephone: (01709) 512 434. *Fax:* (01709) 512 762.
Commercial Dept: (01709) 512 760.
Fax: (01709) 512 763. *ClubCall:* 09068 121 637.

Football in the Community: (01709) 512 761.

Ground Capacity: 11,514.

Record Attendance: 25,170 v Sheffield U, Division 2, 13 December 1952 and v Sheffield W, Division 2, 26 January 1952.

Record Receipts: £79,155 v Newcastle U, FA Cup 4th rd, 23 January 1993.

Pitch Measurements. 115yd × 75yd.

Chairman: K. F. Booth. *Directors:* R. Hull (Vice-Chairman), C. A. Luckock, J. A. Webb, N. Freeman.

Chief Executive: Phil Henson.

Manager: Ronnie Moore.

Assistant Manager: John Breckin.

Coach: Billy Russell.

Youth Development Officer: Fraser Foster. *Physios:* Paul Smith, Ian Bailey.

Stadium Manager/Safety Officer: David Sumner.

Commercial Manager: D. Nicholls.

Year Formed: 1870. *Turned Professional:* 1905. *Ltd Co.:* 1920. *Club Nickname:* 'The Merry Millers'.

Colours: Red and white.

Change Colours: White shirts, black shorts, black stockings.

Previous Names: 1877, Thornhill United; 1905, Rotherham County; 1925, amalgamated with Rotherham Town under Rotherham United.

Previous Ground: 1870, Red House Ground; 1907, Millmoor.

First Football League Game: 2 September 1893, Division 2, Rotherham T v Lincoln C (a) D 1–1 – McKay; Thickett, Watson; Barr, Brown, Broadhead; Longden, Cutts, Leatherbarrow, McCormick, Pickering, (1 og). 30 August 1919, Division 2, Rotherham Co v Nottingham F (h) W 2–0 – Branston; Alton, Baines; Bailey, Coe, Stanton; Lee (1), Cawley (1), Glennon, Lees, Lamb.

Record League Victory: 8–0 v Oldham Ath, Division 3 (N), 26 May 1947 – Warnes; Selkirk, Ibbotson; Edwards, Horace Williams, Danny Williams; Wilson (2), Shaw (1), Ardron (3), Guest (1), Hainsworth (1).

HONOURS

Football League: Division 2 – runners-up 2000–01; Division 3 – Champions 1980–81; Runners-up 1999–2000; Division 3 (N) – Champions 1950–51; Runners-up 1946–47, 1947–48, 1948–49; Division 4 – Champions 1988–89; Runners-up 1991–92.

FA Cup: best season: 5th rd, 1953, 1968.

Football League Cup: Runners-up 1961.

Auto Windscreens Shield: Winners 1996.

IT'S A FACT !

When Rotherham United defeated Darlington 7-2 in an FA Cup first round tie on 25 November 1950, Jack Shaw scored five goals.

Record Cup Victory: 6–0 v Spennymoor U, FA Cup 2nd rd,
17 December 1977 – McAlister; Forrest, Breckin, Womble,
Stancliffe, Green, Finney, Phillips (3), Gwyther (2) (Smith),
Goodfellow, Crawford (1). 6–0 v Wolverhampton W, FA Cup
1st rd, 16 November 1985 – O'Hanlon; Forrest, Dungworth,
Gooding (1), Smith (1), Pickering, Birch (2), Emerson,
Tynan (1), Simmons (1), Pugh. 6–0 v Kings Lynn, FA Cup
2nd rd, 6 December 1997 – Mimms; Clark, Hurst (Goodwin),
Garner (1) (Hudson) (1), Warner (Bass), Richardson (1),
Berry (1), Thompson, Druce (1), Glover (1), Roscoe.

Record Defeat: 1–11 v Bradford C, Division 3 (N),
25 August 1928.

Most League Points (2 for a win): 71, Division 3 (N), 1950–51.

Most League Points (3 for a win): 91, Division 2, 2000–01.

Most League Goals: 114, Division 3 (N), 1946–47.

Highest League Scorer in Season: Wally Ardron, 38,
Division 3 (N), 1946–47.

Most League Goals in Total Aggregate: Gladstone Guest,
130, 1946–56.

Most League Goals in One Match: 4, Roland Bastow v
York C, Division 3N, 9 November 1935; 4, Roland Bastow v
Rochdale, Division 3N, 7 March 1936; 4, Wally Ardron v
Crewe Alex, Division 3N, 5 October 1946; 4, Wally Ardron
v Carlisle U, Division 3N, 13 September 1947; 4, Wally
Ardron v Hartlepools U, Division 3N, 13 October 1948.

Most Capped Player: Shaun Goater, 19, Bermuda.

Most League Appearances: Danny Williams, 459, 1946–62.

Youngest League Player: Kevin Eley, 16 years 72 days v Scunthorpe U, 15 May 1984.

Record Transfer Fee Received: £325,000 from Sheffield W for Matt Clarke, July 1996.

Record Transfer Fee Paid: £150,000 to Millwall for Tony Towner, August 1980; £150,000 to Port Vale
for Lee Glover, August 1996.

Football League Record: 1893 Rotherham Town elected to Division 2; 1896 Failed re-election;
1919 Rotherham County elected to Division 2; 1923–51 Division 3 (N); 1951–68 Division 2;
1968–73 Division 3; 1973–75 Division 4; 1975–81 Division 3; 1981–83 Division 2; 1983–88 Division 3;
1988–89 Division 4; 1989–91 Division 3; 1991–92 Division 4; 1992–97 Division 2; 1997–2001 Division 3;
2001– Division 2.

MANAGERS

Billy Heald 1925–29 *(Secretary
   only for long spell)*
Stanley Davies 1929–30
Billy Heald 1930–33
Reg Freeman 1934–52
Andy Smailes 1952–58
Tom Johnston 1958–62
Danny Williams 1962–65
Jack Mansell 1965–67
Tommy Docherty 1967–68
Jimmy McAnearney 1968–73
Jimmy McGuigan 1973–79
Ian Porterfield 1979–81
Emlyn Hughes 1981–83
George Kerr 1983–85
Norman Hunter 1985–87
Dave Cusack 1987–88
Billy McEwan 1988–91
Phil Henson 1991–94
Archie Gemmill/John McGovern
   1994–96
Danny Bergara 1996–97
Ronnie Moore May 1997–

LATEST SEQUENCES

Longest Sequence of League Wins: 9, 2.2.82 – 6.3.82.

Longest Sequence of League Defeats: 8, 7.4.56 – 18.8.56.

Longest Sequence of League Draws: 6, 13.10.69 – 22.11.69.

Longest Sequence of Unbeaten League Matches: 18, 13.10.69 – 7.2.70.

Longest Sequence Without a League Win: 14, 8.10.77 – 2.1.78.

TEN YEAR LEAGUE RECORD

		P	W	D	L	F	A	Pts	Pos
1990-91	Div 3	46	10	12	24	50	87	42	23
1991-92	Div 4	42	22	11	9	70	37	77	2
1992-93	Div 2	46	17	14	15	60	60	65	11
1993-94	Div 2	46	15	13	18	63	60	58	15
1994-95	Div 2	46	14	14	18	57	61	56	17
1995-96	Div 2	46	14	14	18	54	62	56	16
1996-97	Div 2	46	7	14	25	39	70	35	23
1997-98	Div 3	46	16	19	11	67	61	67	9
1998-99	Div 3	46	20	13	13	79	61	73	5
1999-2000	Div 3	46	24	12	10	72	36	84	2

DID YOU KNOW ?

In front of a crowd of 33,481
at Villa Park on 17 February
1968, a headed goal by Jim
Storrie put Rotherham
United into the fifth round of
the FA Cup against Aston
Villa for only the second time
in their history.

ROTHERHAM UNITED 2000–01 LEAGUE RECORD

Match No.	Date	Venue	Opponents	Result	H/T Score	Lg. Pos.	Goalscorers	Attendance
1	Aug 12	H	Walsall	L	2-3	1-0	—	Robins 2 (1 pen) [43 (p), 53]	5200
2	18	A	Colchester U	W	1-0	1-0	—	Robins [34]	3807
3	26	H	Bury	L	1-2	1-1	17	Scott [45]	3739
4	28	A	Bristol C	W	1-0	0-0	10	Fortune-West [64]	8280
5	Sept 2	H	Luton T	D	1-1	0-1	9	Robins [65]	4061
6	9	A	Cambridge U	L	1-6	1-3	14	Robins [8]	3925
7	12	A	Wrexham	W	3-1	1-0	—	Warne 2 [2, 79], Scott [56]	2126
8	16	H	Wycombe W	W	1-0	0-0	7	Branston [48]	3545
9	23	A	Stoke C	D	1-1	1-0	7	Artell [26]	13,472
10	30	H	Reading	L	1-3	1-1	11	Robins (pen) [28]	4288
11	Oct 8	H	Oldham Ath	W	3-0	2-0	8	Warne [1], Artell [6], Talbot [79]	3774
12	14	A	Bournemouth	W	1-0	1-0	8	Watson [11]	3878
13	17	A	Bristol R	D	1-1	1-0	—	Watson [16]	6910
14	21	H	Oxford U	W	3-1	0-0	5	Warne 2 [76, 90], Watson [82]	3983
15	24	H	Swansea C	W	4-2	2-1	—	Robins [5], Garner [28], Watson [50], Lee [58]	3892
16	28	A	Northampton T	W	1-0	1-0	4	Talbot [30]	6478
17	Nov 4	H	Wigan Ath	D	1-1	0-0	4	Robins [80]	6192
18	11	A	Brentford	W	3-0	3-0	3	Talbot 2 [3, 43], Lee [33]	4544
19	25	H	Peterborough U	W	3-0	1-0	4	Branston [33], Hurst [46], Robins [87]	5519
20	Dec 2	H	Millwall	W	3-2	0-0	2	Artell [49], Lee 2 [70, 87]	7155
21	16	A	Swindon T	L	1-2	1-1	4	Branston [15]	4740
22	22	A	Port Vale	W	2-0	1-0	—	Robins [33], Hurst [77]	4110
23	26	H	Notts Co	D	0-0	0-0	3		7673
24	Jan 1	A	Bury	D	0-0	0-0	4		3743
25	13	H	Bristol C	D	1-1	1-0	4	Robins [34]	5654
26	20	A	Notts Co	L	1-4	1-0	4	Branston [35]	7010
27	23	A	Walsall	D	1-1	0-0	—	Sedgwick [81]	4437
28	27	H	Port Vale	W	3-2	1-0	4	Robins [24], Lee [74], Warne [90]	5044
29	Feb 10	H	Cambridge U	W	3-0	2-0	4	Lee 3 (1 pen) [2, 28, 89 (p)]	4497
30	20	H	Wrexham	W	2-0	1-0	—	Lee [45], Wilsterman [64]	4528
31	24	H	Stoke C	W	2-1	0-0	3	Robins 2 [54, 64]	8211
32	27	A	Colchester U	W	3-2	0-1	—	Robins [48], Artell [50], Hurst [84]	5864
33	Mar 3	A	Reading	L	0-2	0-0	2		13,103
34	6	H	Bournemouth	W	3-1	1-0	—	Lee [45], Robins 2 (1 pen) [51 (p), 79]	6488
35	10	A	Oldham Ath	W	3-2	2-1	2	Branston [23], Robins [33], Garnett (og) [89]	5993
36	17	H	Bristol R	W	3-0	1-0	2	Barker [44], Minton 2 [53, 88]	7098
37	20	A	Wycombe W	W	1-0	0-0	—	Lee [83]	5254
38	24	A	Oxford U	L	3-4	1-2	1	Robins [24], Branston [61], Lee [80]	4493
39	31	H	Swindon T	W	4-3	2-2	1	Reeves (og) [13], Robins 3 [25, 67, 84]	7106
40	Apr 7	A	Millwall	L	0-4	0-3	2		16,015
41	14	A	Swansea C	D	0-0	0-0	3		4327
42	16	H	Northampton T	W	1-0	1-0	3	Robins (pen) [45]	6714
43	21	A	Wigan Ath	W	2-0	1-0	3	Watson [16], Robins [77]	8836
44	24	A	Luton T	W	1-0	0-0	—	Sedgwick [76]	4854
45	28	H	Brentford	W	2-1	1-1	2	Talbot [34], Lee [90]	9760
46	May 5	A	Peterborough U	D	1-1	1-1	2	Warne [16]	11,274

Final League Position: 2

GOALSCORERS

League (79): Robins 24 (4 pens), Lee 13 (1 pen), Warne 7, Branston 6, Talbot 5, Watson 5, Artell 4, Hurst 3, Minton 2, Scott 2, Sedgwick 2, Barker 1, Fortune-West 1, Garner 1, Wilsterman 1, own goals 2.
Worthington Cup (2): Robins 1, Watson 1.
FA Cup (2): Lee 1, own goal 1.

Gray I 33	Bryan M 23 + 5	Beech C 8 + 7	Scott R 39	Varty W 5 + 1	Branston G 41	Watson K 46	Robins M 42	Fortune-West L 5	Warne P 44	Talbot S 37 + 1	Hurst P 42 + 2	Monkhouse A 1 + 11	Garner D 30 +	Berry T 5 + 6	Wilsterman B 9 + 1	Artell D 35 + 1	Turner A 3 + 1	Lee A 29 + 2	Hudson D 1 + 4	Bolima C — + 1	Pettinger P 13	Carr D 1	Sedgwick C 2 + 19	Barker R 7 + 12	Minton J 5 + 4	Match No
1	2^1	3	4	5	6	7	8	9	10	11^2	12	13														1
1	2	3	4		6	7	8	9	10^1	11				5	12											2
1	2	3	4^1	12	6	7^1	8	9^2	10	11			14	5	13											3
1	2	3			6	7	8	9	10	11^1	12			5		4										4
1	2				6	7	8	9	10^2	11	3	12		5^1	13	4										5
1		4	3		6	7	8^1		10	11	2	13	12	9		5^2										6
1	12		2		6	7	8		10	11^1	3		4	9^3		5^2	13	14								7
1	12		2		6	7	8	9^2	10	11^1	3		4		13	5										8
1	12		2		6	7	8^1		10	11^2	3	13	4			5		9								9
1	2				6	7	8^2		10	11^1	3	12	4			5		9	13							10
1		3	4		6	7	8^1		10	11	2	12				5		9								11
1	12		2		6	7	8^1		10	11	3		4			5		9^2	13							12
1	2^1	12	4		6	7	8		10	11	3					5		9								13
1	2				6	7	8^1		10	11	3	12	4			5		9								14
1	2				6	7	8		10	11^1	3		4			5		9	12							15
1	12		2		6	7	8^1		10	11	3		4			5		9								16
		2			6	7	8		10	11	3		4			5		9			1					17
1		3			6	7	8		10	11	2		4			5		9								18
1		2			6	7	8		10	11	3		4			5		9								19
1		2				7	8		10	11^1	3		4	12		5		9				6				20
1	12		2		6	7	8^1		10^2	11	3	13	4	14		5		9^3								21
1	2		4		6	7	8	9	11		3	10				5										22
1	12		2		6	7^1	8		10	11	3	9^2	4			5							13			23
1	2		4		6	7	8^1		10	11	3		9			5							12			24
1	2				6	7	8^2		10	11	3		4			5		9^1					12	13		25
1		2			6	7^1	8			11^2	3		4	9		5			13				12	10		26
1	2				6	7	8^1		10	11	3		4			5	9						12	13		27
1	2^1	11			6	7	8		10		3		4			5		9					12			28
1		3	4			7	8^1		10	11	2			6		5		9^2					12	13		29
		12	2			7	8^1		10	11	3		4			5		9^2			1			13		30
		12	2		6	7^1	8		10	11	3		4			5					1		13	9		31
			4		6	7	8^1		10	11	3		2			5		13			1		12	9^2		32
		12	4		6	7	8^2		10	11	3		2^1			5		9			1			13		33
			2		6	7	8		10^1		3					5	9^2	11			1		12	13		34
			2		6	7	8		10^1	11^2	3					5	9^1	13			1			12		35
1	2		4		6	7	8^1		10		3					5							12	9	11	36
1	2		4		6	7	8^2		10		3				12	5^1	14						13	9^2	11	37
1	2^2	12	4		6	7	8^3		10		3				5^1	9							13	14	11	38
1	2		4	5^1	6	7	8		10	12	3					9							13		11^2	39
1	2^1		4		6	7^1	8^2		10	11	3					5		9					12	13		40
1	2		4^1		6	7^1	8		10	11	3					5		9			1		12		13	41
1	2				6	7	8		10^1	11	3					5		9			1		4	12		42
	2		4		6	7	8		10^1	11^2	3					5					1		12	9	13	43
	2		4		6	7	8^2			11^1	3	13				5					1		10	9	12	44
	2^1		4		6	7	8^2		10	11^3	3					5		9			1		12	13	14	45
	2	4			6	7	8^1		10^2		3	13				5	9^2				1		12	14	11	46

Worthington Cup
First Round   Barnsley   (h) 0-1
               (a) 2-3

FA Cup
First Round   Wrexham   (a) 1-0
Second Round   Northampton T (h) 1-0
Third Round   Liverpool   (a) 0-3

RUSHDEN & DIAMONDS   Division 3

FOUNDATION

Rushden & Diamonds were formed in 1992 from an amalgamation of Rushden Town and Earthlingborough Diamonds. At the end of 1990-91, Rushden Town had been relegated to the Southern League Midland Division as their ground was unfit for Premier Division football. Earthlingborough Diamonds were competing in the United Counties League at the time. The idea for this merger came from Max Griggs (owner of Doc Martens) a local multi-millionaire businessman. He invested several million pounds and they have been able to achieve Football League status in nine years.

Nene Park, Diamond Way, Earthlingborough, Northants NN9 5QF.

Telephone: (01933) 652 000.

Fax: (01933) 650 418.

Website: www.thediamondsfc.com.

RDFC ClubCall: 09068 440033.

Radio Diamonds: (01933) 653 535.

Ground Capacity: 6,553

Record Attendance: 6,431 v Leeds U, F.A. Cup 3rd rd, 2 January 1999.

Record Receipts: £38,276 v Leeds U, F.A. Cup 3rd rd, 2 January 1999.

Pitch Measurements: 111yd x 75yd.

HONOURS

Conference – Champions 2000-01.
Southern League Midland Division – Champions 1993-94.
Premier Division – Champions 1995–96.
FA Trophy – Semi-finalists 1994.
Northants FA Hillier Senior Cup – Winners 1993–94, 1998–99.
Maunsell Premier Cup –Winners 1994–95, 1998–99

Directors: W.M. Griggs CBE, MA (Chairman), M.G. Darnell (Managing), S.W. Griggs, H.M. Johnstone, A.C. Jones, R.W. Langley, C.M. Smith.

President: D. Attley.

Manager: Brian Talbot. *First Team Coach:* Terry Westley.
Youth Team Coach: Steve Spooner. *Physio:* Simon Parsell.

Secretary: David Joyce.

Colours: White shirts with blue sleeves, blue shorts with white trim, white stockings.

Change Colours: Yellow shirts with black sleeves, black shorts, yellow stockings.

Year formed: 1992.

Turned Professional: 1992.

Ltd Co.: 1992.

Club Nickname: 'The Diamonds'.

Record League Victory: 7–0 v Redditch U, Southern League, Midland Division, 7 May 1994:– Fox; Wooding (1), Johnson, Flower (1), Beech, Page, Coe, Mann (2), Nuttell (1), Watkins (1), Keast (1).

Record Cup Victory: 8–0 v Desborough T, Northants F.A. Hillier Senior Cup, 1st rd, 27 September 1994:– Fox; Wooding, Johnson, Flower, Keast, Page, Collins, Butterworth, Nuttell (2), Watkins (2), Mann (2). Subs:– Capone (2), Mason.

Record Defeat: 0–5 v Slough Town, GM Vauxhall Conference, 20 August 1996.

Most League Points (3 for a win): 98, Southern League Midland Division, 1993–94.

Most League Goals: 109, Southern League Midland Division, 1993–94.

IT'S A FACT !

Manager Brian Talbot's 200th game in charge of Rushden & Diamonds was away at Doncaster Rovers on 11 November 2000. At the time, the club had won 104 matches, drawn 48 and lost 48.

Highest League Scorer in Season: Darren Collins, 30 (40 in all competitions), Southern League Premier Division, 1995–96.

Most League Goals in Total Aggregate: Darren Collins, 112 (153 in all competitions), 1994–2000.

Most League Appearances: Garry Butterworth, 254 (335 in all competitions), 1994–2001.

Record Transfer Fee Received: £25,000 from Kettering T for Darren Collins, November 2000.

Record Transfer Fee Paid: Undisclosed to Morecambe for Justin Jackson, July 2000.

MANAGERS
Roger Ashby 1992–1997
Brian Talbot 1997–

RUSHDEN & DIAMONDS ROLL CALL 2000–2001

Player	Date of Birth	Signed from	Debut
Jon Brady	14-01-75	Hayes	v Forest Green R (15-08-98)
Andy Burgess	10-08-81	Youth	v Farnborough T (22-12-98)
Richard Butcher	22-01-81	Northampton T	v Kettering T (25-01-00)
Garry Butterworth	08-06-69	Dagenham & R	v Peterborough U (03-08-94)
Shaun Carey	13-05-76	Norwich C	v Hednesford T (21-08-00)
Duane Darby	17-10-73	Notts Co	v Chester C (19-08-00)
Justin Jackson	10-12-74	Morecambe	v Chester C (19-08-00)
Michael McElhatton	16-04-75	Scarborough	v Kingstonian (25-08-98)
Gary Mills	20-05-81	Youth	v Farnborough T (22-12-98)
Tarkan Mustafa	28-08-73	Kingstonian	v Chester C (19-08-00)
Stuart Naylor	06-12-62	Exeter C	v Southport (22-04-00)
Mark Peters	06-07-72	Mansfield T	v Northampton T (31-07-99)
Jim Rodwell	20-11-70	Halesowen T	v Altrincham (17-08-96)
Mark Sale	27-02-72	Colchester U	v Northampton T (31-07-99)
Gary Setchell	08-05-75	Kettering T	v Hednesford T (21-08-00)
Jean-Michel Sigere	26-01-77	Bordeaux	v Kidderminster H (08-04-00)
Brett Solkhan			v Stevenage B (24-10-00)
Matt Stowell	01-03-77	Bristol C	v Havant & W (27-11-00)
Daniel Talbot		Youth	v Stevenage B (24-10-00)
Billy Turley	15-07-72	Northampton T	v Northampton T (31-07-99)
Paul Underwood	16-08-73	Enfield	v Northwich Vic (16-08-97)
Ray Warburton	07-10-67	Northampton T	v Leatherhead (09-11-98)
Simon Wormull	01-12-76	Dover Ath	v Sutton U (18-03-00)

Appearances: Bradshaw, 0+1; Brady, 39+2; Burgess, 37+3; Butterworth, 40+1; Carey, 32+1; Collins, 0+1; Darby, 38; Essandoh, 0+2; Gray, 4+2; Iga, 0+1; Jackson, 40; Mills, 12+9; Mustafa, 41; Naylor, 0+1; Peters, 20+2; Rogers, 1; Rodwell, 28+2; Sale, 0+2; Setchell, 19+10; Sigere, 5+15; Solkhon, 1; Town, 1+2; Turley, 41; Underwood, 23+2; Warburton, 37; Wormull, 3+5.

Goals (78): Darby 24 (3 pens), Jackson 18 (1 pen), Brady 11, Burgess 7, Sigere 6, Underwood 3 (2 pens), Peters 2, Butterworth 1, Carey 1, Setchell 1, Town 1, Warburton 1, Wormull 1, own goal 1.

TEN YEAR LEAGUE RECORD

		P	W	D	L	F	A	Pts	Pos
1990-91	Rushden T in Sl pr; Diamonds in UCL								
1991-92	Rushden T in Sl mid; Diamonds in UCL								
1992-93	SL mid	42	25	10	7	85	41	85	3
1993-94	SL mid	42	29	11	2	109	37	98	1
1994-95	SL pr	42	19	11	12	99	65	68	5
1995-96	SL pr	42	29	7	6	99	41	94	1
1996-97	Conf.	42	14	11	17	61	63	53	12
1997-98	Conf.	42	23	5	14	79	57	74	4
1998-99	Conf.	42	20	12	10	71	42	72	4
1999-2000	Conf.	42	21	13	8	71	42	76	2

DID YOU KNOW ?

Possibly the only thing Rushden & Diamonds lost out on from its merger was the fact that Rushden Town used to be known as the Russians and appropriately enough, their colours were all red.

SCUNTHORPE UNITED   Division 3

*Glanford Park, Scunthorpe, North Lincolnshire
DN15 8TD.*

Telephone: (01724) 848 077. *Fax:* (01724) 857 986.
ClubCall: 09068 121 652.

Ground Capacity: 9183.

Record Attendance: Old Showground: 23,935 v
Portsmouth, FA Cup 4th rd, 30 January 1954.
Glanford Park: 8775 v Rotherham U, Division 4,
1 May 1989.

Record Receipts: £47,252 v Burnley, Division 2,
6 May 2000.

Pitch Measurements: 110yd × 71yd.

HONOURS

Football League: Division 2 best
season: 4th, 1961–62; Division 3 (N) –
Champions 1957–58. Promoted from
Division 3 1998–99 (play-offs).

FA Cup: best season: 5th rd, 1958,
1970.

Football League Cup: never past
3rd rd.

Vice-Presidents: I. T. Botham, G. Johnson, A. Harvey, R. Ashman, K. Waters, J. Brownsword,
B. Heywood, Dr J. Zacarias. *Chairman:* K. Wagstaff. *Vice-Chairman:* R. Garton.

Directors: J. B. Borrill, B. Collen, J. A. C. Godfrey CBE, J. S. Wharton, C. Holland.

Team Manager: Brian Laws.

Chief Executive/Secretary: A. D. Rowing.

Commercial Manager: A. D. Rowing.

Colours: White shirt with claret and blue trim, white shorts with claret and blue trim, white stockings
with claret and blue top.

Change Colours: Lime green shirt with navy trim, navy shorts with lime trim, navy stockings with
lime top.

Year Formed: 1899. *Turned Professional:* 1912.

Ltd Co.: 1912.

Club Nickname: 'The Iron'.

Previous Names: Amalgamated first with Brumby Hall then North Lindsey United to become
Scunthorpe & Lindsey United, 1910; dropped '& Lindsey' in 1958.

Previous ground: 1899, Old Showground; 1988, Glanford Park.

First Football League Game: 19 August 1950, Division 3 (N), v Shrewsbury T (h) D 0–0 – Thompson;
Barker, Brownsword; Allen, Taylor, McCormick; Mosby, Payne, Gorin, Rees, Boyes.

IT'S A FACT !

Steve Cammack was top scorer for Scunthorpe United
in five out of six seasons in the 1980's and in 1984-85 was
the recipient of the club's Ernie Storey Player of the
Season award.

Record League Victory: 8–1 v Luton T, Division 3,
24 April 1965 – Sidebottom; Horstead, Hemstead; Smith,
Neale, Lindsey; Bramley (1), Scott, Thomas (5), Mahy (1),
Wilson (1). 8–1 v Torquay U (a), Division 3, 28 October
1995 – Samways; Housham, Wilson, Ford (1), Knill (1),
Hope (Nicholson), Thornber, Bullimore (Walsh),
McFarlane (4) (Young), Eyre (2), Paterson.

Record Cup Victory: 9–0 v Boston U, FA Cup 1st rd,
21 November 1953 – Malan; Hubbard, Brownsword;
Sharpe, White, Bushby; Mosby (1), Haigh (3), Whitfield (2),
Gregory (1), Mervyn Jones (2).

Record Defeat: 0–8 v Carlisle U, Division 3 (N),
25 December 1952.

Most League Points (2 for a win): 66, Division 3 (N),
1956–57, 1957–58.

Most League Points (3 for a win): 83, Division 4, 1982–83.

Most League Goals: 88, Division 3 (N), 1957–58.

Highest League Scorer in Season: Barrie Thomas, 31,
Division 2, 1961–62.

Most League Goals in Total Aggregate: Steve Cammack,
110, 1979–81, 1981–86.

Most League Goals in One Match: 5, Barrie Thomas v
Luton T, Division 3, 24 April 1965.

Most Capped Player: None.

Most League Appearances: Jack Brownsword, 595, 1950–65.

Youngest League Player: Mike Farrell, 16 years 240 days v
Workington, 8 November 1975.

Record Transfer Fee Received: £350,000 from Aston Villa for Neil Cox, February 1991.

Record Transfer Fee Paid: £200,000 to Bristol C for Steve Torpey, February 2000.

Football League Record: 1950 Elected to Division 3 (N); 1958–64 Division 2; 1964–68 Division 3;
1968–72 Division 4; 1972–73 Division 3; 1973–83 Division 4; 1983–84 Division 3; 1984–92 Division 4;
1992–99 Division 3; 1999–2000 Division 2; 2000– Division 3.

MANAGERS

Harry Allcock 1915–53
(Secretary-Manager)
Tom Crilly 1936–37
Bernard Harper 1946–48
Leslie Jones 1950–51
Bill Corkhill 1952–56
Ron Suart 1956–58
Tony McShane 1959
Bill Lambton 1959
Frank Soo 1959–60
Dick Duckworth 1960–64
Fred Goodwin 1964–66
Ron Ashman 1967–73
Ron Bradley 1973–74
Dick Rooks 1974–76
Ron Ashman 1976–81
John Duncan 1981–83
Allan Clarke 1983–84
Frank Barlow 1984–87
Mick Buxton 1987–91
Bill Green 1991–93
Richard Money 1993–94
David Moore 1994–96
Mick Buxton 1996–97
Brian Laws February 1997–

LATEST SEQUENCES

Longest Sequence of League Wins: 6, 18.10.69 – 25.11.69.

Longest Sequence of League Defeats: 8, 29.11.97 – 20.1.98.

Longest Sequence of League Draws: 6, 2.1.84 – 25.2.84.

Longest Sequence of Unbeaten League Matches: 15, 13.11.71 – 26.2.72.

Longest Sequence Without a League Win: 14, 22.3.75 – 6.9.75.

TEN YEAR LEAGUE RECORD

		P	W	D	L	F	A	Pts	Pos
1990-91	Div 4	46	20	11	15	71	62	71	8
1991-92	Div 4	42	21	9	12	64	59	72	5
1992-93	Div 3	42	14	12	16	57	54	54	14
1993-94	Div 3	42	15	14	13	64	56	59	11
1994-95	Div 3	42	18	8	16	68	63	62	7
1995-96	Div 3	46	15	15	16	67	61	60	12
1996-97	Div 3	46	18	9	19	59	62	63	13
1997-98	Div 3	46	19	12	15	56	52	69	8
1998-99	Div 3	46	22	8	16	69	58	74	4
1999-2000	Div 2	46	9	12	25	40	74	39	23

DID YOU KNOW ?

Scunthorpe & Lindsey
United reached the FA Cup
first round proper for the first
time in 1928 and a then
record crowd of 5305 saw
Rochdale beaten 1-0.

SCUNTHORPE UNITED 2000–01 LEAGUE RECORD

Match No.	Date	Venue	Opponents	Result	H/T Score	Lg. Pos.	Goalscorers	Attendance
1	Aug 12	A	Macclesfield T	W	1-0	0-0	—	Hodges [58]	2561
2	19	H	Kidderminster H	W	2-0	1-0	2	Torpey [17], Graves [76]	3761
3	26	A	Rochdale	L	2-3	1-1	4	Sheldon [43], Hodges (pen) [47]	2561
4	28	H	Chesterfield	D	1-1	0-0	5	Torpey [85]	5154
5	Sept 2	H	Blackpool	W	1-0	1-0	4	Torpey [40]	3822
6	9	A	York C	L	0-2	0-0	6		3370
7	12	A	Leyton Orient	D	1-1	1-1	—	Hodges [26]	3581
8	16	H	Cardiff C	L	0-2	0-0	9		3263
9	23	A	Southend U	L	0-1	0-1	14		3110
10	30	H	Torquay U	W	3-0	2-0	12	Ipoua 2 [22, 76], Dawson [31]	2922
11	Oct 7	H	Halifax T	W	1-0	0-0	6	Ipoua [82]	2640
12	14	A	Brighton & HA	D	0-0	0-0	8		6567
13	17	A	Plymouth Arg	L	0-1	0-1	—		3437
14	21	H	Darlington	D	1-1	1-1	12	Elliott (og) [9]	3298
15	24	H	Shrewsbury T	W	2-0	0-0	—	Ipoua [52], Dawson [56]	2552
16	28	A	Carlisle U	W	2-1	2-0	7	Larusson [11], Hodges (pen) [24]	2381
17	Nov 4	H	Hartlepool U	W	3-0	1-0	6	Hodges 2 [5, 49], Ipoua [55]	3241
18	11	A	Exeter C	L	1-2	0-0	6	Torpey [57]	2556
19	25	H	Mansfield T	W	6-0	3-0	6	Larusson [2], Torpey [6], Ipoua 4 (1 pen) [27, 56, 61 ip, 88]	3258
20	Dec 2	H	Hull C	L	0-1	0-0	7		6101
21	16	A	Barnet	L	2-4	1-0	8	Torpey [14], Ipoua [88]	2086
22	23	H	Cheltenham T	D	1-1	1-1	8	Torpey [12]	3275
23	26	A	Lincoln C	D	1-1	1-1	8	Ipoua [23]	5487
24	Jan 1	H	Macclesfield T	D	2-2	1-1	8	Ipoua [43], Stamp [88]	3168
25	13	A	Chesterfield	L	0-1	0-0	9		4803
26	Feb 3	A	Blackpool	L	0-6	0-3	12		4161
27	10	H	York C	W	4-0	1-0	11	Ipoua 2 [23, 77], Calvo-Garcia [61], Larusson [64]	3164
28	13	H	Rochdale	D	0-0	0-0	—		2821
29	17	A	Cardiff C	L	0-3	0-2	12		6057
30	20	H	Leyton Orient	D	1-1	1-0	—	Hodges [21]	2523
31	24	H	Southend U	D	1-1	0-1	15	Berry [80]	2631
32	27	A	Cheltenham T	L	0-1	0-0	—		2481
33	Mar 3	A	Torquay U	W	2-0	2-0	12	Sparrow 2 [12, 34]	1868
34	6	H	Brighton & HA	W	2-1	2-1	—	Cullip (og) [35], Sparrow [42]	2581
35	10	A	Halifax T	W	4-3	3-1	11	Jackson [11], Calvo-Garcia [20], Harsley [21], Quailey [58]	2352
36	13	A	Kidderminster H	D	0-0	0-0	—		2438
37	17	H	Plymouth Arg	W	4-1	2-0	9	Calvo-Garcia [7], Dawson [31], Quailey 2 [62, 90]	3844
38	24	A	Darlington	L	1-2	0-1	9	Calvo-Garcia [85]	3125
39	31	H	Barnet	W	2-1	2-1	9	Larusson [14], Torpey [26]	2963
40	Apr 3	A	Lincoln C	W	2-1	0-1	—	Graves [69], Hodges [90]	4299
41	7	A	Hull C	L	1-2	1-1	9	Dawson [41]	10,881
42	14	A	Shrewsbury T	W	2-0	2-0	9	Torpey [32], Wilcox [39]	2717
43	16	H	Carlisle U	W	3-0	1-0	7	Sparrow [28], Carruthers [50], Torpey [78]	4068
44	21	A	Hartlepool U	L	0-1	0-1	7		3897
45	28	H	Exeter C	L	0-2	0-1	9		3912
46	May 5	A	Mansfield T	L	0-1	0-0	10		2938

Final League Position: 10

GOALSCORERS

League (62): Ipoua 14 (1 pen), Torpey 10, Hodges 8 (2 pens), Calvo-Garcia 4, Dawson 4, Larusson 4, Sparrow 4, Quailey 3, Graves 2, Berry 1, Carruthers 1, Harsley 1, Jackson 1, Sheldon 1, Stamp 1, Wilcox 1, own goals 2.
Worthington Cup (1): Torpey 1.
FA Cup (9): Ipoua 4, Calvo-Garcia 1, Dawson 1, Hodges 1, Sheldon 1, Torpey 1.

Evans T 46	Stanton N 34 + 4	Dawson A 41	Pepper N 2	Jackson M 28 + 4	Thom S 17 + 4	Calvo-Garcia A 30 + 4	Hodges L 32 + 6	Sheldon G 33 + 6	Torpey S 40	Morrison P 8 + 10	Quailey B 11 + 16	Harsley P 22 + 11	Wilcox R 33 + 3	Sparrow M 9 + 2	Graves W 25 + 9	Mamoun B — + 1	Fickling A 3 + 6	Stamp D 4 + 8	Larusson B 33	Woodward A 12	Ipoua G 22 + 3	Shepherd P — + 1	Banger N — + 1	Brough S — + 4	Berry T 6	Rogers D 1	Cotterill J 4	Rapley K 1 + 4	Ridley L 1 + 1	Carruthers M 8	Match No
1	2	3	4	5	6	7^1	8	9	10	11^2	12	13																			1
1	5	3	4		6		8^1	9^2	10	11^3	13	7		2	12	14															2
1	5	3			6	7		9	10	11^2	12			2	4		8	13													3
1	5	3			6	11^1	7	9^2	10	12				2	4^2		8	13	14												4
1	5	3			6	7		9	10	12				2	4^2		8	13													5
1		3			11	7^1	9	10	12	13	5	2^2	8		4		6														6
1	5	3			6	7	9^3	10	12	13	2				8		4	11^2													7
1	5	3			6	7	9^1	10	11	12		2^2			8^3		13	14	4												8
1	5	3			6	8	9^2	10	11^1	12	7						4	2	13												9
1	5	3^2			6^3		7		11	10	12	13		8^1			4	2	9	14											10
1	5	3			12	8		11^1	10^3	7	6^2				13	14	4	2	9												11
1	4	3^3	14	11	7^2	12		13			5		8		10	6	2	9^1													12
1	4	3	12	13	11	7		14			5^2		8^3		10	6	2	9													13
1	4	3	12		11^1	7	8^2	10	13		5^1		14			6	2	9													14
1	4	3	12	5^1	11^2	7	8	10			13					6	2	9													15
1		3^2	4	11	7	8	10	14			5		13^3	12		6	2	9^1													16
1	4		2	11	7	8^1	10	12		14	5	6				3	9^2		13^3												17
1	4		2	11	7	8	10		12	5	6^1		3	13			9^2														18
1	4	3	2	11	7^3	8^1	10	12			5^2		13			6	9		14												19
1	4	3	2	11	7^1	8	10				5					6	9		12												20
1	4	3	2	12	7^2	8	10	13	11	5^1						6	9														21
1	4		3^1	11	7	8	10		6	5	12						6	9													22
1	4	3		11	7	8	10			5						6	2	9													23
1	4^2	3		11	7	8^1	10	12		13^3	5				14	6	2	9													24
1	4	3	2	5	11	7^1	8	10			12	6					9														25
1	4	3	2	12	11^2	8^1	10			13	5	14				6	9														26
1	4	3	2	5	11	7		10^3	12	13					14	6^2	9					8^1									27
1	4	3	2	5	11	7		10	12	6						13	9^2					8^1									28
1	4	3	2	5^2	11	7^1	8		12		13		14			10	6	9^3													29
1	4	3	2		11	7	12			13		5			14	10	6^1	9^2					8^3								30
1	4	3	2		11	7^1	12	10	13			5				6	9^2					8									31
1	4	3	2	11^3		9^2	10		7	12	5^1		14			6	13					8									32
1		3	4		14	10		11	2		7	9					6	12			13^3	8^2	5^1								33
1		3	5	12	13	8	10		11	2		7^2	9				6^1										4				34
1		3	5	11		8	10		7	2			9				6										4				35
1		3	5	11^1		8	10		7	2			9				6							12			4				36
1		3	5^2	11	12	8^3	10		7	2	13		9				6^1										4	14			37
1	12		5	11	13	14	10		7^3	2	4	8^1					6											3^2	9		38
1	4		3	11	12	8^1	10		2	5			7				6												9		39
1		3	4	11^1	12	8	10		13	2	5	14	7				6^3												9^2		40
1	4	3	6	12		7	13	10		14	2^2	5^3	11	8															9^1		41
1	4^2	3	2		12	7^3	6^1	10	11	13	5	8	9															14			42
1	12	3	4		13	7^3		10		2^1	5	11	8				6^2											14	9		43
1	12	3	4		13		10		14	2^3	5	11	8				6^2											7^1	9		44
1	12	3	4	6	11^2		10		13	2	5	7^1	8																9		45
1	4	3^2	6				10		11^1	2	5	7	8															12	13	9	46

Worthington Cup

First Round	Wigan Ath	(a)	0-1
		(h)	1-4

FA Cup

First Round	Hartlepool U	(h)	3-1
Second Round	Brighton & HA	(h)	2-1
Third Round	Burnley	(a)	2-2
		(h)	1-1
Fourth Round	Bolton W	(a)	1-5

SHEFFIELD UNITED   Division 1

FOUNDATION

In March 1889, Yorkshire County Cricket Club formed Sheffield United six days after an FA Cup semi-final between Preston North End and West Bromwich Albion had finally convinced Charles Stokes, a member of the cricket club, that the formation of a professional football club would prove successful at Bramall Lane. The United's first secretary, Mr J. B. Wostinholm was also secretary of the cricket club.

Bramall Lane Ground, Sheffield S2 4SU.

Telephone: (0114) 221 5757. **Fax:** (0114) 272 3030.
ISDN: (0114) 221 3148. **Website:** http://www.sufc.co.uk
Email: info@sufc.co.uk **Box Office:** (0114) 221 1889.
Box Office Promotions: (0114) 221 3131.
ClubCall: 09068 888 650. **Club Shop:** (0114) 221 3132.
Executive Suite: (0114) 221 3195.
Football in the Community: (0114) 276 9314.

Ground Capacity: 30,936.

Record Attendance: 68,287 v Leeds U, FA Cup 5th rd, 15 February 1936.

Record Receipts: £298,364 v Coventry C, FA Cup 6th rd replay, 17 March 1998.

Pitch Measurements: 112yd × 72yd.

Chairman: D. Dooley.

Directors: K. McCabe, B. Proctor, A. Laver, M. Dudley, A. Bamford.

Manager: Neil Warnock. **Assistant Manager:** Kevin Blackwell. **Player/Coach:** Keith Curle.

Physios: Dennis Pettitt, Nigel Cox.

Estates Manager: Rob McRobbie.

General Manager, Commercial: Andy Daykin.

Community Programme Organiser: Tony Currie, Tel: (0114) 2769314.

Colours: Red and white striped shirts with black trim, black shorts and stockings with red trim.

Change Colours: All gold with purple trim, or all white with black trim.

Year Formed: 1889.

Turned Professional: 1889.

Ltd Co.: 1899.

Club Nickname: 'The Blades'.

First Football League Game: 3 September 1892, Division 2, v Lincoln C (h) W 4–2 – Lilley; Witham, Cain; Howell, Hendry, Needham (1); Wallace, Dobson, Hammond (3), Davies, Drummond.

Record League Victory: 10–0 v Burslem Port Vale (a), Division 2, 10 December 1892 – Howlett; Witham, Lilley; Howell, Hendry, Needham; Drummond (1), Wallace (1), Hammond (4), Davies (2), Watson (2).

HONOURS

Football League: Division 1 – Champions 1897–98; Runners-up 1896–97, 1899–1900; Division 2 – Champions 1952–53; Runners-up 1892–93, 1938–39, 1960–61, 1970–71, 1989–90; Division 4 – Champions 1981–82.

FA Cup: Winners 1899, 1902, 1915, 1925; Runners-up 1901, 1936.

Football League Cup: best season: 5th rd, 1962, 1967, 1972.

IT'S A FACT !

On 6 May 1939, Harry Hampson scored after ten seconds for Sheffield United against Tottenham Hotspur in a Division Two match at Bramall Lane. At the time, it was the second fastest recorded from the kick-off.

Record Cup Victory: 5–0 v Newcastle U (a), FA Cup 1st rd, 10 January 1914 – Gough; Cook, English; Brelsford, Howley, Sturgess; Simmons (2), Gillespie (1), Kitchen (1), Fazackerley, Revill (1). 5–0 v Corinthians, FA Cup 1st rd, 10 January 1925 – Sutcliffe; Cook, Milton; Longworth, King, Green; Partridge, Boyle (1), Johnson (4), Gillespie, Tunstall. 5–0 v Barrow, FA Cup 3rd rd, 7 January 1956 – Burgin; Coldwell, Mason; Fountain, Johnson, Iley; Hawksworth (1), Hoyland (2), Howitt, Wragg (1), Grainger (1).

Record Defeat: 0–13 v Bolton W, FA Cup 2nd rd, 1 February 1890.

Most League Points (2 for a win): 60, Division 2, 1952–53.

Most League Points (3 for a win): 96, Division 4, 1981–82.

Most League Goals: 102, Division 1, 1925–26.

Highest League Scorer in Season: Jimmy Dunne, 41, Division 1, 1930–31.

Most League Goals in Total Aggregate: Harry Johnson, 205, 1919–30.

Most League Goals in One Match: 5, Harry Hammond v Bootle, Division 2, 26 November 1892; 5, Harry Johnson v West Ham U, Division 1, 26 December 1927.

Most Capped Player: Billy Gillespie, 25, Northern Ireland.

Most League Appearances: Joe Shaw, 629, 1948–66.

Youngest League Player: Julian Broddle, 17 years 62 days v Halifax T, 2 January 1982.

Record Transfer Fee Received: £2,700,000 from Leeds U for Brian Deane, July 1993.

Record Transfer Fee Paid: £1,200,000 to West Ham U for Don Hutchison, January 1996.

Football League Record: 1892 Elected to Division 2; 1893–1934 Division 1; 1934–39 Division 2; 1946–49 Division 1; 1949–53 Division 2; 1953–56 Division 1; 1956–61 Division 2; 1961–68 Division 1; 1968–71 Division 2; 1971–76 Division 1; 1976–79 Division 2; 1979–81 Division 3; 1981–82 Division 4; 1982–84 Division 3; 1984–88 Division 2; 1988–89 Division 3; 1989–90 Division 2; 1990–92 Division 1; 1992–94 FA Premier League; 1994– Division 1.

MANAGERS

J. B. Wostinholm 1889–1899
  (Secretary-Manager)
John Nicholson 1899–1932
Ted Davison 1932–52
Reg Freeman 1952–55
Joe Mercer 1955–58
Johnny Harris 1959–68
  (continued as General Manager to 1970)
Arthur Rowley 1968–69
Johnny Harris *(General Manager resumed Team Manager duties)* 1969–73
Ken Furphy 1973–75
Jimmy Sirrel 1975–77
Harry Haslam 1978–81
Martin Peters 1981
Ian Porterfield 1981–86
Billy McEwan 1986–88
Dave Bassett 1988–95
Howard Kendall 1995–97
Nigel Spackman 1997–98
Steve Bruce 1998–99
Adrian Heath 1999
Neil Warnock December 1999–

LATEST SEQUENCES

Longest Sequence of League Wins: 8, 14.9.60 – 22.10.60.

Longest Sequence of League Defeats: 7, 19.8.75 – 20.9.75.

Longest Sequence of League Draws: 5, 16.12.95 – 20.1.96.

Longest Sequence of Unbeaten League Matches: 22, 2.9.1899 – 13.1.1900.

Longest Sequence Without a League Win: 19, 27.9.75 – 7.2.76.

TEN YEAR LEAGUE RECORD

		P	W	D	L	F	A	Pts	Pos
1990-91	Div 1	38	13	7	18	36	55	46	13
1991-92	Div 1	42	16	9	17	65	63	57	9
1992-93	PR Lge	42	14	10	18	54	53	52	14
1993-94	PR Lge	42	8	18	16	42	60	42	20
1994-95	Div 1	46	17	17	12	74	55	68	8
1995-96	Div 1	46	16	14	16	57	54	62	9
1996-97	Div 1	46	20	13	13	75	52	73	5
1997-98	Div 1	46	19	17	10	69	54	74	6
1998-99	Div 1	46	18	13	15	71	66	67	8
1999-2000	Div 1	46	13	15	18	59	71	54	16

DID YOU KNOW ?

Herbert Chapman was the 100th player to appear in Sheffield United's League team when he made his debut on the opening day of the 1902-03 season.

SHEFFIELD UNITED 2000–01 LEAGUE RECORD

Match No.	Date		Venue	Opponents	Result		H/T Score	Lg. Pos.	Goalscorers	Atten-dance
1	Aug	12	H	Portsmouth	W	2-0	1-0	—	Devlin (pen) [13], Primus (og) [81]	15,816
2		19	A	Preston NE	L	0-3	0-2	12		13,948
3		26	H	Tranmere R	W	2-0	1-0	7	Bent 2 [19, 57]	12,074
4		28	A	Watford	L	1-4	1-2	9	Quinn [42]	12,675
5	Sept	9	A	Birmingham C	L	0-1	0-1	14		21,493
6		12	A	Wolverhampton W	D	0-0	0-0	—		14,853
7		15	H	Blackburn R	W	2-0	2-0	—	Kelly [5], Devlin [25]	10,816
8		23	A	Crystal Palace	W	1-0	1-0	7	Bent [45]	17,521
9		30	H	QPR	D	1-1	1-0	7	Murphy [36]	13,803
10	Oct	14	H	Crewe Alex	W	1-0	0-0	8	Santos [89]	12,921
11		17	H	Huddersfield T	W	3-0	1-0	—	Kelly 2 [45, 75], Devlin [64]	14,062
12		21	A	Norwich C	L	2-4	2-2	8	Kelly [7], Brown [24]	15,504
13		24	H	Stockport Co	W	1-0	0-0	—	Murphy [68]	13,542
14		28	A	Wimbledon	D	0-0	0-0	10		7327
15	Nov	4	H	Gillingham	L	1-2	0-1	10	D'Jaffo [78]	14,028
16		11	A	Burnley	L	0-2	0-0	10		16,635
17		18	H	Grimsby T	W	3-2	1-0	10	Santos [44], Bent 2 [50, 59]	12,861
18		21	H	Fulham	D	1-1	1-1	—	D'Jaffo [8]	16,041
19		25	H	Bolton W	W	1-0	0-0	10	Sandford [81]	14,962
20		29	A	Nottingham F	L	0-2	0-1	—		17,089
21	Dec	2	A	Stockport Co	W	2-0	1-0	10	Devlin [45], Quinn (pen) [88]	6460
22		9	A	Barnsley	D	0-0	0-0	10		16,780
23		16	H	Sheffield W	D	1-1	0-0	10	Ford (pen) [56]	25,156
24		23	A	Portsmouth	D	0-0	0-0	10		13,606
25		26	H	WBA	W	2-0	1-0	9	Ford (pen) [26], Kelly [53]	22,281
26		30	H	Preston NE	W	3-2	1-2	8	Ford (pen) [30], Kelly [70], Thomas [80]	22,316
27	Jan	1	A	Tranmere R	L	0-1	0-1	8		8474
28		13	H	Watford	L	0-1	0-0	8		17,551
29		20	A	WBA	L	1-2	0-0	8	Peschisolido [75]	16,778
30	Feb	4	A	Fulham	D	1-1	1-1	8	D'Jaffo [41]	12,480
31		10	H	Birmingham C	W	3-1	2-0	8	Murphy [31], Devlin (pen) [40], Peschisolido [64]	19,313
32		20	H	Wolverhampton W	W	1-0	1-0	—	D'Jaffo [21]	20,282
33		24	H	Crystal Palace	W	1-0	0-0	8	Suffo [51]	18,924
34	Mar	3	A	QPR	W	3-1	0-1	6	Murphy [48], Santos 2 [57, 76]	11,024
35		6	A	Crewe Alex	L	0-1	0-0	—		6909
36		10	H	Nottingham F	L	1-3	0-1	9	Murphy [73]	25,673
37		17	A	Huddersfield T	L	1-2	1-1	9	Asaba [35]	13,918
38	Apr	1	A	Sheffield W	W	2-1	0-0	8	D'Jaffo [51], Asaba [71]	38,433
39		4	A	Blackburn R	D	1-1	0-1	—	Ndlovu [74]	26,276
40		7	H	Barnsley	L	1-2	1-1	9	Asaba [45]	22,811
41		10	H	Norwich C	D	1-1	1-0	—	Roberts (og) [31]	16,072
42		14	A	Gillingham	L	1-4	0-1	10	Ndlovu [49]	9502
43		17	A	Wimbledon	L	0-1	0-0	—		14,527
44		21	A	Grimsby T	W	1-0	1-0	11	Ndlovu [42]	6983
45		28	H	Burnley	W	2-0	1-0	9	Ndlovu [21], Asaba [90]	20,013
46	May	6	A	Bolton W	D	1-1	0-0	10	Asaba [52]	14,836

Final League Position: 10

GOALSCORERS

League (52): Kelly 6, Asaba 5, Bent 5, D'Jaffo 5, Devlin 5 (2 pens), Murphy 5, Ndlovu 4, Santos 4, Ford 3 (3 pens), Peschisolido 2, Quinn 2 (1 pen), Brown 1, Sandford 1, Suffo 1, Thomas 1, own goals 2.
Worthington Cup (11): Bent 3, Devlin 3 (1 pen), Kelly 2, Brown 1, own goals 2.
FA Cup (0).

Tracey S 40	Uhlenbeek G 28 + 3	Weber N 3 + 1	Ford B 33 + 2	Murphy S 46	Santos G 23 + 8	Devlin P 41	Brown M 36	Bent M 16	Kelly D 21 + 14	Quinn W 21 + 3	Woodhouse C 23 + 2	Newby J 3 + 10	Sandford L 20 + 2	Kozluk R 23 + 4	Smith A — + 6	Burley A — + 1	Cryan C — + 1	Ribeiro B 3 + 2	Jagielka P 3 + 12	Curle K 23 + 2	Montgomery N 14 + 13	D'Jaffo L 16 + 6	Suffo P 6 + 10	Thomas J 3 + 7	Ullathorne R 13 + 1	Peschisolido P 4 + 1	Ndlovu P 15	Asaba C 10	Bullock D 6	Talia C 10	Thetis M — + 1	Morrison A 3 + 1	Doane B 3	Tonge M 1 + 1	Ward M — + 1	Match No.
1	2	3	4	5	6	7	8^1	9	10^2	11	12	13																								1
1	2	3	4^1	5	6	7	8	9	10^2	11	12	13																								2
1	2		11	5	12	7	8^1	9	10^2	3	4	13	6																							3
1	2^2	3	4	5		7	8^1	9	11	10	12		6	13																						4
1	2		4^2	5	6	7	8	9	10^1	3	11				12	13																				5
1	2	12	11	5	6^2	7^1	8	9	10^3	3	4				13	14																				6
1	2		11	5	6	7^1	8	9	10^1	3	4	12			13																					7
1	2		11	5	6	7^1		9	10^1	3	4				12			13		8^2	14															8
1	2		11	5	6	7	8	9	10^1	3	4^2	12			13																					9
1	2		11^1	5	6	7	8^3	9^1	10	3	4	13			14																					10
1	2		11^1	5	6	7	8^2	9	10	3	4				13																					11
1	2		4^3	5		7	8^1	9	10	3	11	12			6^2					13	14															12
1	2		4^1	5	12	7	8	9^2	10^1	3		13							11	6	14															13
1	2^3		4	5	14	7	8	9^1	10	3	12								11	6	13															14
1	2		4	5	12	7	8	9^2	10^1	3^2	11				13					6	14	4														15
1	2		4^3	5	12	7	8	9	10^2	3^1	11				14					6	13	4														16
1	2		4	5		7	8	9	10^1	3	12				11^2					6	13															17
1	2		4	5		7	8	9	10^1	3	11									6	12															18
1	2		4	5		7	8		10^1	3	12				13					6^2		9^3	14													19
1	2		4	5	12	7	8		10^3	3	11^1									6	9^2	14														20
1	10		4	5		7	8		3	2	12								13	6	11^1	9^2														21
1	10		4^1	5		7	8	9^1	3	2	11									6		12														22
1	11		4^1	5	12	7	8		3	2	13									6	10^2	9^3	14													23
1	11		4^2	5	12	7	8	9^1	3	2	13								14	6																24
1	11		4^1	5	12	7	8		3	2	10									6	9^2	13														25
1	2		4^1	5	6	7	8		10^2	3	4								13		9^1	12														26
1	11		4	5		7	8	9^3	3^2	2	12									13		14	10^1													27
1	11		5			7^2	8	9^1	4	2	12								13		10^1	3														28
1			4^1	5			8		11	2	14				12					13	7^3	9^2	3	10												29
1	2		11^2	5			8		3		12								13	6	4	7	9			10^1										30
1			4	5		7	8		3		12								13	6	9^1					10^1	11									31
1	12		4	5		7	8		6^3	2	13								3		9^2		14			10^3	11									32
1	11		4	5		7	8			2	14								6	12	9^2	13^3			3^1	10^2										33
1	11^3		4	5		7	8		13	2									6	14	9^2				3	10^1										34
1	11		5	4			8		12	2									6	7^2	9^1	13			3	10										35
1	3		4^1	5		7	8		10^3	2									12^2	14	13				6		9									36
1	11		5		7	8^2				2								13	6	4^3	12				3	14	10	9^1								37
1	12	4	5		7				13	2									6	14	9^2				3^1	10	8	11^3								38
1	3		11	5	7					2									6	4						10	9	8								39
1	3	4	5		7					2^1								12	6	13	9^3	14				10	8	11^2								40
1	3		11	5	7					2								12	6	4	13					10^2	9	8^1	1							41
	3^3		11	5	9					2								12	6^1	7	13					10	8^2		1		14	4				42
	3^2	4	5		7					2									6	9^1	12					10	8		1		13		14		43
			11	5	7				12									13	8	6	14				3^2	10^3	9^1		1		4	2			44
			11	5	7				12									12	8	6	14	13^3	3			10	9^1		1		4^2	2			45
			4	5	7^1				12									12	8	6	13		3			10^3	9		1		2		11^2	14	46

Worthington Cup

First Round	Lincoln C	(h)	6-1
		(a)	0-1
Second Round	Colchester U	(h)	3-0
		(a)	1-0
Third Round	Sheffield W	(a)	1-2

FA Cup

Third Round	Southampton	(a)	0-1

SHEFFIELD WEDNESDAY

Division 1

FOUNDATION

Sheffield, being one of the principal centres of early Association Football, this club was formed as long ago as 1867 by the Sheffield Wednesday Cricket Club (formed 1825) and their colours from the start were blue and white. The inaugural meeting was held at the Adelphi Hotel and the original committee included Charles Stokes who was subsequently a founder member of Sheffield United.

Hillsborough, Sheffield S6 1SW.

Telephone: (0114) 221 2121. *Fax:* (0114) 221 2122.
ClubCall: 09068 121 186. *Website:* www.swfc.co.uk
Email: enquiries@swfc.co.uk
Ticket Office: (0114) 221 2400.

Ground Capacity: 39,859.

Record Attendance: 72,841 v Manchester C, FA Cup 5th rd, 17 February 1934.

Record Receipts: £533,918 Sunderland v Norwich C, FA Cup semi-final, 5 April 1992.

Pitch Measurements: 115yd × 74yd.

President: K. T. Addy.

Chairman: G. K. Hulley. *Vice-Chairman:* K. T. Addy.

Directors: G. K. Hulley, R. M. Grierson FCA, K. T. Addy, G. A. Thorpe, H. E. Culley, D. E. D. Allen, M. G. Wright.

Manager: Peter Shreeves. *Physio:* John Dickens.

Secretary: Alan D. Sykes.

Commercial Manager: Kaven Walker.

Stadium Manager: Trevor Grayson.

Colours: Blue and white striped shirts, black shorts, blue stockings.

Change Colours: Yellow shirts, light blue shorts, white/light blue stockings.

Year Formed: 1867 (fifth oldest League club).

Turned Professional: 1887.

Ltd Co.: 1899.

Former Names: The Wednesday until 1929.

Club Nickname: 'The Owls'.

Previous Grounds: 1867, Highfield; 1869, Myrtle Road; 1877, Sheaf House; 1887, Olive Grove; 1899, Owlerton (since 1912 known as Hillsborough). Some games were played at Endcliffe in the 1880s. Until 1895 Bramall Lane was used for some games.

First Football League Game: 3 September 1892, Division 1, v Notts Co (a) W 1–0 – Allan; Tom Brandon (1), Mumford; Hall, Betts, Harry Brandon; Spiksley, Brady, Davis, R. N. Brown, Dunlop.

HONOURS

Football League: Division 1 – Champions 1902–03, 1903–04, 1928–29, 1929–30; Runners-up 1960–61; Division 2 – Champions 1899–1900, 1925–26, 1951–52, 1955–56, 1958–59; Runners-up 1949–50, 1983–84.

FA Cup: Winners 1896, 1907, 1935; Runners-up 1890, 1966, 1993.

Football League Cup: Winners 1991; Runners-up 1993.

European Competitions: *European Fairs Cup:* 1961–62, 1963–64. *UEFA Cup:* 1992–93.

IT'S A FACT !

In 1925-26, centre-half Frank Froggatt captained Sheffield Wednesday to the Division Two Championship. In 1958-59 his son, Redfearn, skippered the Owls to the same title from inside-forward.

Record League Victory: 9–1 v Birmingham, Division 1, 13 December 1930 – Brown; Walker, Blenkinsop; Strange, Leach, Wilson; Hooper (3), Seed (2), Ball (2), Burgess (1), Rimmer (1).

Record Cup Victory: 12–0 v Halliwell, FA Cup 1st rd, 17 January 1891 – Smith; Thompson, Brayshaw; Harry Brandon (1), Betts, Cawley (2); Winterbottom, Mumford (2), Bob Brandon (1), Woolhouse (5), Ingram (1).

Record Defeat: 0–10 v Aston Villa, Division 1, 5 October 1912.

Most League Points (2 for a win): 62, Division 2, 1958–59.

Most League Points (3 for a win): 88, Division 2, 1983–84.

Most League Goals: 106, Division 2, 1958–59.

Highest League Scorer in Season: Derek Dooley, 46, Division 2, 1951–52.

Most League Goals in Total Aggregate: Andy Wilson, 199, 1900–20.

Most League Goals in One Match: 6, Doug Hunt v Norwich C, Division 2, 19 November 1938.

Most Capped Player: Nigel Worthington, 50 (66), Northern Ireland.

Most League Appearances: Andy Wilson, 502, 1900–20.

Youngest League Player: Peter Fox, 15 years 269 days v Orient, 31 March 1973.

Record Transfer Fee Received: £2,650,000 from Blackburn R for Paul Warhurst, September 1993.

Record Transfer Fee Paid: £4,700,000 to Celtic for Paolo Di Canio, August 1997.

Football League Record: 1892 Elected to Division 1; 1899–1900 Division 2; 1900–20 Division 1; 1920–26 Division 2; 1926–37 Division 1; 1937–50 Division 2; 1950–51 Division 1; 1951–52 Division 2; 1952–55 Division 1; 1955–56 Division 2; 1956–58 Division 1; 1958–59 Division 2; 1959–70 Division 1; 1970–75 Division 2; 1975–80 Division 3; 1980–84 Division 2; 1984–90 Division 1; 1990–91 Division 2; 1991–92 Division 1; 1992–2000 FA Premier League; 2000– Division 1.

MANAGERS

Arthur Dickinson 1891–1920
(Secretary-Manager)
Robert Brown 1920–33
Billy Walker 1933–37
Jimmy McMullan 1937–42
Eric Taylor 1942–58
(continued as General Manager to 1974)
Harry Catterick 1958–61
Vic Buckingham 1961–64
Alan Brown 1964–68
Jack Marshall 1968–69
Danny Williams 1969–71
Derek Dooley 1971–73
Steve Burtenshaw 1974–75
Len Ashurst 1975–77
Jackie Charlton 1977–83
Howard Wilkinson 1983–88
Peter Eustace 1988–89
Ron Atkinson 1989–91
Trevor Francis 1991–95
David Pleat 1995–97
Ron Atkinson 1997–98
Danny Wilson 1998–2000
Peter Shreeves (Acting) 2000
Paul Jewell 2000–2001
Peter Shreeves February 2001–

LATEST SEQUENCES

Longest Sequence of League Wins: 9, 23.4.04 – 15.10.04.

Longest Sequence of League Defeats: 8, 9.9.2000 – 17.10.2000.

Longest Sequence of League Draws: 5, 24.10.92 – 28.11.92.

Longest Sequence of Unbeaten League Matches: 19, 10.12.60 – 8.4.61.

Longest Sequence Without a League Win: 20, 11.1.75 – 30.8.75.

TEN YEAR LEAGUE RECORD

		P	W	D	L	F	A	Pts	Pos
1990-91	Div 2	46	22	16	7	80	51	82	3
1991-92	Div 1	42	21	12	9	62	49	75	3
1992-93	PR Lge	42	15	14	13	55	51	59	7
1993-94	PR Lge	42	16	16	10	76	54	64	7
1994-95	PR Lge	42	13	12	17	49	57	51	13
1995-96	PR Lge	38	10	10	18	48	61	40	15
1996-97	PR Lge	38	14	15	9	50	51	57	7
1997-98	PR Lge	38	12	8	18	52	67	44	16
1998-99	PR Lge	38	13	7	18	41	42	46	12
1999-2000	PR Lge	38	8	7	23	38	70	31	19

DID YOU KNOW ?

The Jim Smith who played as goalkeeper in 22 consecutive FA Cup matches for Sheffield Wednesday from 1884 to 1891, was actually Clarke, preferring to use the anonymity for the purposes of playing football.

SHEFFIELD WEDNESDAY 2000–01 LEAGUE RECORD

Match No.	Date	Venue	Opponents	Result	H/T Score	Lg. Pos.	Goalscorers	Attendance
1	Aug 13	A	Wolverhampton W	D 1-1	0-1	—	Booth [79]	19,086
2	19	H	Huddersfield T	L 2-3	1-3	15	Booth [45], Hinchcliffe (pen) [64]	22,704
3	26	A	Grimsby T	W 1-0	1-0	10	Di Piedi [22]	7755
4	28	H	Blackburn R	D 1-1	1-1	11	Westwood [2]	15,646
5	Sept 9	H	Wimbledon	L 0-5	0-0	20		15,856
6	13	H	Nottingham F	L 0-1	0-1	—		15,700
7	16	A	Tranmere R	L 0-2	0-1	23		9352
8	23	H	Preston NE	L 1-3	1-0	23	Morrison [35]	17,379
9	30	A	Gillingham	L 0-2	0-1	24		9099
10	Oct 8	H	WBA	L 1-2	1-1	24	Morrison [21]	15,338
11	14	A	Portsmouth	L 1-2	0-1	24	Morrison [67]	13,376
12	17	A	Burnley	L 0-1	0-0	—		16,372
13	22	H	Birmingham C	W 1-0	0-0	23	Harkness [58]	14,695
14	25	A	QPR	W 2-1	0-1	—	Cooke [48], Quinn [77]	10,353
15	28	H	Fulham	D 3-3	1-0	21	Sibon [41], Morrison [72], Westwood [90]	17,559
16	Nov 4	A	Crystal Palace	L 1-4	0-3	22	Sibon (pen) [83]	15,333
17	7	A	Watford	W 3-1	1-0	—	Haslam [37], Crane [66], Quinn [83]	11,166
18	11	H	Norwich C	W 3-2	1-1	18	Hinchcliffe (pen) [32], Crane [56], Di Piedi [62]	16,956
19	18	A	Barnsley	L 0-1	0-1	19		19,989
20	25	A	Crewe Alex	L 0-1	0-0	20		7103
21	Dec 2	H	QPR	W 5-2	3-1	17	Sibon 3 [6, 39, 51], Morrison [45], Ekoku [61]	21,782
22	9	H	Stockport Co	L 2-4	2-2	19	Morrison [9], Ekoku [15]	16,337
23	16	A	Sheffield U	D 1-1	0-0	21	Hendon [64]	25,156
24	23	H	Wolverhampton W	L 0-1	0-1	21		17,787
25	26	A	Bolton W	L 0-2	0-1	23		21,316
26	30	A	Huddersfield T	D 0-0	0-0	22		18,931
27	Jan 1	H	Grimsby T	W 1-0	0-0	21	Sibon [67]	17,004
28	13	A	Blackburn R	L 0-2	0-2	22		19,308
29	20	H	Bolton W	L 0-3	0-2	22		17,638
30	Feb 3	H	Watford	L 2-3	2-2	24	Sibon [15], Ekoku [45]	16,134
31	10	A	Wimbledon	L 1-4	1-2	24	Ekoku [17]	6741
32	13	H	Tranmere R	W 1-0	0-0	—	Ekoku [78]	15,444
33	21	A	Nottingham F	W 1-0	0-0	—	Sibon [76]	23,266
34	24	A	Preston NE	L 0-2	0-0	22		14,379
35	Mar 3	H	Gillingham	W 2-1	1-0	19	Ekoku [38], Di Piedi [59]	18,702
36	7	H	Portsmouth	D 0-0	0-0	—		20,503
37	10	A	WBA	W 2-1	1-1	18	Soltvedt [45], Booth [63]	18,662
38	17	H	Burnley	W 2-0	1-0	17	Hendon [42], Sibon (pen) [70]	20,184
39	24	A	Birmingham C	W 2-1	1-0	15	De Bilde [24], Di Piedi [87]	19,733
40	Apr 1	H	Sheffield U	L 1-2	0-0	17	Sibon [76]	38,433
41	7	A	Stockport Co	L 1-2	0-1	17	De Bilde [52]	9666
42	14	H	Crystal Palace	W 4-1	3-1	16	Ekoku [26], De Bilde [32], Sibon [45], Ripley [64]	19,877
43	16	A	Fulham	D 1-1	1-0	18	Sibon [45]	17,500
44	21	H	Barnsley	W 2-1	0-1	14	Sibon [79], Donnelly [84]	23,498
45	28	A	Norwich C	L 0-1	0-1	17		21,241
46	May 6	H	Crewe Alex	D 0-0	0-0	17		28,007

Final League Position: 17

GOALSCORERS

League (52): Sibon 13 (2 pens), Ekoku 7, Morrison 6, Di Piedi 4, Booth 3, De Bilde 3, Crane 2, Hendon 2, Hinchcliffe 2 (2 pens), Quinn 2, Westwood 2, Cooke 1, Donnelly 1, Harkness 1, Haslam 1, Ripley 1, Soltvedt 1.
Worthington Cup (12): Ekoku 2, Morrison 2, Westwood 2, Crane 1, De Bilde 1, Di Piedi 1, Hamshaw 1, Quinn 1, Sibon 1.
FA Cup (3): Booth 1, Hamshaw 1, Sibon 1.

Pressman K 38+1	Grayson S 5	Hinchcliffe A 9	Jonk W 2	Westwood A 32+1	Walker D 43	Cresswell R 4	Booth A 17+1	De Bilde G 13+8	Haslam S 24+3	Quinn A 37	Sibon G 32+9	Di Piedi M 6+19	Stringer C 4+1	O'Donnell P 7+4	Rudi P —+1	Hamshaw M 9+9	Muller A 1+4	Nicholson K —+1	Crane A 7+8	Stockdale R 6	Humphreys R 7	Morrison O 20+10	Cooke T 16+1	Geary D 1+4	Harkness S 28+2	Lescott A 17+13	Hendon I 31	Ekoku E 31+1	Bromby L 17+1	Blatsis C 6	Beresford M 4	Palmer C 12	Soltvedt T 15	Ripley S 5+1	Donnelly S —+3	Match No.
1	2	3^1	4	5	6	7^9	8	9^2	10	11	12	13	15																							1
1	2	3	4^1	5	6	7^2	8	9^3		11	13	12		10		14																				2
1	2	3		5	6	11	4	8	9^1					10		7	12																			3
	2	3^1		5	6	11	9		4	8				1	10	7			12																	4
1	2	3		5	6		8	12		4	10	9		11^1		7																				5
1				5	6		10	12	2^3	4	13	9^1		11^2		7			14	3	8															6
1				5	6		8	9^1		4	12			7^2		13			10	3	2	11														7
1				5	6		10^1	9		4	8^3	12		13					14	3	2	11^2	7													8
1				5	6			4	8	9^1	1	11^1			13				2^3	10	12	7	14	3												9
1				5	6		9^1		10	8^2	12	1	13			14			2	11	7^3		3	4												10
15					6			4	10		12	1^6	11^1						2^3	9	8	13		3	7	5										11
1					6			2	4		12		7^1	8^2		13			9	10	11		3		5											12
1				5	6			2	11	12			13			9^1	10^2	7		3		4	8													13
1				5	6			4	11	9			12			10^1	7			3		2	8													14
1				5	6			4	11	9^2						12				10^1	7	3	13	2	8											15
1					6			2	11	9	12					13				10^2	7	3	4^1	5	8											16
1	11				6		8		2	4	9^1	12				10					7	3^2	13	5												17
1	3				6		9^1	2			12					10					7		4	5	8											18
1	3^1				6			2	11	12	9^2					10					13	7		4	5	8										19
1				5	6		9		2^2	11	13	12				10						7	3^3	14	4	8^1										20
1				5	6		9^1		4	10	7^2	12									11		3	13	2	8^1										21
1				5^2	6		9^1		2	11	7	12									10		3	13	4	8										22
1				5	6		9^2		4						13			11^1			10	7	3	12	2	8										23
1					6			4	11	9	12		13	14							10^2	7	3		2	8^1	5^2									24
1				5	6			4^2	11	12			13					14			10	7^1	3	8^3	2	9										25
1				5^2	6			8	11	12			14	7^1							10^3	3	13	2	9		4									26
1					6			4	11	8	9^1	14	13								10^2	7^3	3	12	2		5									27
				5^2	6		12	13	7^1	11			14								10	3	8	2	9^2		4	1								28
				5			10^5	9^1	7	11	8		12								13	3	6	2^2	14		4	1								29
					6			12	10^3	11	8			7^1					14			13	3	4		9	2	5^1	1							30
			12	6				13	7^2	11	8			14							3	10	2	9	5^3	4^1	1									31
1				5	6			9^2		11	8										3^1	13	2	10	12			4	7							32
1				5	6					11	8										4	2	9	3			10	7							33
1				5	6			12		11^2	8								4^1		13		2	9	3		10	7								34
1				5	6			14	11^2	8	12			7^1							13		4^3	2	9	3			10							35
1				5	6	10^1			11^2	8	12										13		2	9	3		4	7								36
1				5	6	10^1			11^2	8												12	13	2	9	3		4	7							37
1				5	6	10			11^1	8												12		2	9	3		4	7							38
1				5	6			9^1		8	12										11	13	2^2	10	3		4	7	14							39
1				5	6			9^2		11^3	8	12									13	3^1		10	2		4	7	14							40
1	3^3				6			12	13		8								14		11^1		5^1	4		9	2		10	7							41
1					6			9^1	4^3		8	13									12		3	14		10	2		5	11	7^1					42
1					6			9^1	13		8	12										3	4		10	2		5	11^2	7						43
1					6			9^1		8											12		13	3^1	4^2	2	10	5		11		7	14			44
1		5						9^1		8		12											13	3^2	4^3	2	10	6		11		7	14			45
1		5						12		8													10^2	6		2	9^1	3		4	11	7	13			46

Worthington Cup

Second Round	Oldham Ath	(a)	3-1
		(h)	5-1
Third Round	Sheffield U	(h)	2-1
Fourth Round	West Ham U	(a)	2-1
Fifth Round	Birmingham C	(a)	0-2

FA Cup

Third Round	Norwich C	(h)	2-1
Fourth Round	Southampton	(a)	1-3

SHREWSBURY TOWN   Division 3

FOUNDATION

Shrewsbury School having provided a number of the early
England and Wales international players it is not surprising that
there was a Town club as early as 1876 which won the Birmingham
Senior Cup in 1879. However, the present Shrewsbury Town club
was formed in 1886 and won the Welsh FA Cup as early as 1891.

Gay Meadow, Shrewsbury SY2 6AB.

Telephone: (01743) 360 111. *Fax:* (01743) 236 384.
Commercial Dept: (01743) 356 316.
ClubCall: 09068 121 194.
Community Officer: Brian Williams (01743) 356 623.

Ground Capacity: 8000.

Record Attendance: 18,917 v Walsall, Division 3,
26 April 1961.

Record Receipts: £80,610 v Arsenal, FA Cup 5th rd,
27 February 1991.

Pitch Measurements: 114yd × 74yd.

President:

Life Vice-Presidents: Dr J. Millard Bryson, G. W. Nelson,
W.H. Richards.

Chairman: R. Wycherley.

HONOURS

Football League: Division 2 best
season: 8th, 1983–84, 1984–85;
Division 3 – Champions 1978–79,
1993–94; Division 4 – Runners-up
1974–75.

FA Cup: best season: 6th rd, 1979,
1982.

Football League Cup: Semi-final 1961.

Welsh Cup: Winners 1891, 1938, 1977,
1979, 1984, 1985; Runners-up 1931,
1948, 1980.

Auto Windscreens Shield: Runners-up
1996

Directors: A. Hopkins, M. J. Starkey, K. R. Woodhouse, T. J. Allen, K. J. Sayfritz. *Associate
Directors:* M. R. Ashton, H. J. Wilson, A. T. Jones.

Manager: Kevin Ratcliffe. *Physio:* Simon Shakeshaft. *Coach:* Dave Fogg.

Commercial Manager: M. Thomas. *Secretary:* M. J. Starkey. *Operations Manager:* M. R. Ashton.

Chaplain: Rev. Tim Welch.

Colours: Amber and blue shirts, blue shorts, blue stockings with amber trim.

Change Colours: All white.

Year Formed: 1886.

Turned Professional: 1896.

Ltd Co.: 1936.

Club Nickname: 'Town', 'Blues' or 'Salop'. The name 'Salop' is a colloquialism for the county of
Shropshire. Since Shrewsbury is the only club in Shropshire, cries of 'Come on Salop' are frequently
used!

Previous Ground: Old Shrewsbury Racecourse.

First Football League Game: 19 August 1950, Division 3 (N), v Scunthorpe U (a) D 0–0 – Egglestone;
Fisher, Lewis; Wheatley, Depear, Robinson; Griffin, Hope, Jackson, Brown, Barker.

IT'S A FACT !

Gary Shaw scored three goals in a two minute
forty-seven second spell within five minutes of the
second half for Shrewsbury Town against Bradford City
on 22 December 1990. Shrewsbury won 4-2.

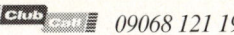

Record League Victory: 7–0 v Swindon T, Division 3 (S), 6 May 1955 – McBride; Bannister, Skeech; Wallace, Maloney, Candlin; Price, O'Donnell (1), Weigh (4), Russell, McCue (2).

Record Cup Victory: 11–2 v Marine, FA Cup 1st rd, 11 November 1995 – Edwards, Seabury (Dempsey (1)), Withe (1), Evans (1), Whiston (2), Scott (1), Woods, Stevens (1), Spink (3) (Anthrobus), Walton, Berkley, (1 og).

Record Defeat: 1–8 v Norwich C, Division 3 (S), 13 September 1952. 1–8 v Coventry C, Division 3, 22 October 1963.

Most League Points (2 for a win): 62, Division 4, 1974–75.

Most League Points (3 for a win): 79, Division 3, 1993–94.

Most League Goals: 101, Division 4, 1958–59.

Highest League Scorer in Season: Arthur Rowley, 38, Division 4, 1958–59.

Most League Goals in Total Aggregate: Arthur Rowley, 152, 1958–65 (thus completing his League record of 434 goals).

Most League Goals in One Match: 5, Alf Wood v Blackburn R, Division 3, 2 October 1971.

Most Capped Player: Jimmy McLaughlin, 5 (12), Northern Ireland; Bernard McNally, 5, Northern Ireland.

Most League Appearances: Colin Griffin, 406, 1975–89.

Youngest League Player: Jamie Tolley, 16 years 230 days v Rochdale, 28 December 1999.

Record Transfer Fee Received: £500,000 from Crewe Alex for Dave Walton, October 1997.

Record Transfer Fee Paid: £100,000 to Aldershot for John Dungworth, November 1979 and £100,000 to Southampton for Mark Blake, August 1990.

Football League Record: 1950 Elected to Division 3 (N); 1951–58 Division 3 (S); 1958–59 Division 4; 1959–74 Division 3; 1974–75 Division 4; 1975–79 Division 3; 1979–89 Division 2; 1989–94 Division 3; 1994– Division 2.

MANAGERS

W. Adams 1905–12
  (Secretary-Manager)
A. Weston 1912–34
  (Secretary-Manager)
Jack Roscamp 1934–35
Sam Ramsey 1935–36
Ted Bousted 1936–40
Leslie Knighton 1945–49
Harry Chapman 1949–50
Sammy Crooks 1950–54
Walter Rowley 1955–57
Harry Potts 1957–58
Johnny Spuhler 1958
Arthur Rowley 1958–68
Harry Gregg 1968–72
Maurice Evans 1972–73
Alan Durban 1974–78
Richie Barker 1978
Graham Turner 1978–84
Chic Bates 1984–87
Ian McNeill 1987–90
Asa Hartford 1990–91
John Bond 1991–93
Fred Davies 1994–97
  (previously Caretaker-Manager 1993–94)
Jake King 1997–99
Kevin Ratcliffe November 1999–

LATEST SEQUENCES

Longest Sequence of League Wins: 7, 28.10.95 – 16.12.95.

Longest Sequence of League Defeats: 7, 17.10.87 – 14.11.87.

Longest Sequence of League Draws: 6, 30.10.63 – 14.12.63.

Longest Sequence of Unbeaten League Matches: 16, 30.10.93 – 26.2.94.

Longest Sequence Without a League Win: 17, 25.1.92 – 11.4.92.

TEN YEAR LEAGUE RECORD

		P	W	D	L	F	A	Pts	Pos
1990-91	Div 3	46	14	10	22	61	68	52	18
1991-92	Div 3	46	12	11	23	53	68	47	22
1992-93	Div 3	42	17	11	14	57	52	62	9
1993-94	Div 3	42	22	13	7	63	39	79	1
1994-95	Div 2	46	13	14	19	54	62	53	18
1995-96	Div 2	46	13	14	19	58	70	53	18
1996-97	Div 2	46	11	13	22	49	74	46	22
1997-98	Div 3	46	16	13	17	61	62	61	13
1998-99	Div 3	46	14	14	18	52	63	56	15
1999-2000	Div 3	46	9	13	24	40	67	40	22

DID YOU KNOW ?

Seven survivors from the Shrewsbury Town team beaten 4-0 at home by Rochdale on 23 September 2000, were in the squad which won 7-0 in the return fixture on 24 February 2001!

SHREWSBURY TOWN 2000–01 LEAGUE RECORD

Match No.	Date	Venue	Opponents	Result		H/T Score	Lg. Pos.	Goalscorers	Attendance
1	Aug 12	A	Barnet	L	0-3	0-2	—		2090
2	19	H	Macclesfield T	D	2-2	2-1	23	Jemson 2 [7, 45]	2822
3	26	A	Chesterfield	L	0-3	0-2	24		4338
4	29	H	Carlisle U	L	0-1	0-0	—		2912
5	Sept 2	A	Hartlepool U	W	3-1	1-0	20	Jemson 2 (1 pen) [24, 60 (p)], Brown [90]	2710
6	9	H	Darlington	W	1-0	1-0	16	Jemson (pen) [20]	2597
7	12	H	Plymouth Arg	W	4-1	2-0	—	McCarthy (og) [9], Jemson 2 [44, 65], Brown [53]	2361
8	16	A	Hull C	L	0-1	0-1	14		4775
9	23	H	Rochdale	L	0-4	0-1	16		3427
10	30	H	Halifax T	D	0-0	0-0	17		1606
11	Oct 6	H	Exeter C	W	2-0	1-0	—	Jagielka [39], Wilding [87]	2651
12	14	A	Mansfield T	L	0-1	0-1	17		2206
13	17	A	Leyton Orient	L	0-2	0-1	—		3554
14	21	H	Lincoln C	W	3-2	3-0	15	Brown [19], Hughes [26], Tretton [35]	2476
15	24	A	Scunthorpe U	L	0-2	0-0	—		2552
16	28	H	Torquay U	D	1-1	0-0	17	Jemson (pen) [89]	2319
17	Nov 4	A	Blackpool	W	1-0	0-0	14	Jemson (pen) [78]	4850
18	25	A	Brighton & HA	L	0-4	0-2	17		6556
19	Dec 2	A	York C	L	1-2	1-1	19	Jemson [38]	2318
20	22	H	Southend U	L	0-1	0-0	—		2499
21	26	A	Cheltenham T	D	1-1	0-0	20	Tolley [88]	4439
22	Jan 1	H	Barnet	W	3-2	2-0	18	Brown [6], Hughes [34], Tolley [77]	2991
23	6	H	Chesterfield	D	0-0	0-0	18		3792
24	13	A	Carlisle U	L	0-1	0-1	20		3328
25	20	H	Cheltenham T	W	1-0	1-0	17	Redmile [36]	2844
26	27	A	Southend U	D	0-0	0-0	17		4289
27	Feb 3	H	Hartlepool U	D	1-1	1-1	17	Aiston [14]	2528
28	13	A	Macclesfield T	L	1-2	0-1	—	Jemson [79]	1430
29	17	H	Hull C	L	0-2	0-2	—		3004
30	20	A	Plymouth Arg	L	1-3	0-0	—	Rodgers [87]	5007
31	24	A	Rochdale	W	7-1	2-1	17	Rodgers 3 [2, 71, 77], Tretton [13], Redmile [46], Lowe [56], Jagielka (pen) [90]	2647
32	Mar 3	H	Halifax T	W	2-1	2-0	17	Jagielka [18], Jemson [39]	2604
33	6	H	Mansfield T	W	2-1	1-0	—	Jemson 2 [6, 82]	2219
34	10	A	Exeter C	L	0-1	0-0	16		3955
35	13	H	Cardiff C	L	0-4	0-0	—		3847
36	17	H	Leyton Orient	D	1-1	0-0	17	Jagielka [47]	2740
37	20	H	Kidderminster H	W	1-0	0-0	—	Redmile [90]	2761
38	23	A	Lincoln C	D	2-2	2-0	—	Aiston [22], Lowe [40]	2828
39	31	A	Kidderminster H	L	1-3	0-1	16	Rodgers (pen) [61]	4548
40	Apr 10	A	Darlington	L	0-3	0-3	—		2917
41	14	H	Scunthorpe U	L	0-2	0-2	19		2717
42	16	A	Torquay U	D	0-0	0-0	18		3482
43	21	H	Blackpool	W	1-0	1-0	17	Lowe [3]	3129
44	28	A	Cardiff C	L	1-3	1-1	19	Jemson [33]	12,188
45	May 1	A	York C	W	2-0	1-0	—	Lowe [20], Rodgers [90]	2058
46	5	H	Brighton & HA	W	3-0	2-0	15	Jemson 2 (1 pen) [23 (p), 72], Rodgers [45]	5360

Final League Position: 15

GOALSCORERS

League (49): Jemson 15 (5 pens), Rodgers 7 (1 pen), Jagielka 6 (1 pen), Brown 4, Lowe 4, Redmile 3, Aiston 2, Hughes 2, Tolley 2, Tretton 2, Wilding 1, own goal 1.
Worthington Cup (2): Davidson 1, Freestone 1.
FA Cup (1): Freestone 1.

Edwards P 26	Seabury K 9 + 2	Jenkins I 16	Tretton A 21 + 1	Wilding P 14 + 7	Hughes D 24	Thomas W 4	Jagielka S 21 + 10	Freestone C 16 + 4	Jemson N 41	Peer D 34 + 3	Tolley J 22 + 2	Davidson R 31 + 2	Brown M 20 + 14	Dunbavin J 20 + 2	Hanmer G 18 + 4	Alston S 40 + 2	Rodgers L 13 + 13	Lowe R 13 + 17	Murray K 29 + 6	Drysdale L 16 + 2	Jones M 5 + 1	Keister J 8	Gayle B — + 1	Redmile M 24	Collins S 12	Sertori M — + 1	Harris J 1 + 3	Rioch G 8	Murphy C — + 1	Match No.
1	2	3	4	5^1	6^2	7^1	8	9	10	11	12	13	14																	1
	2		4			7^1	8	9^3	10	6	12	5			1	3	11^2	13	14											2
	2		4			7	8	9	10	6^1		5			1	3	11^2		13	12										3
	2				6	7	8^1	9	10	4		5	12		1	3	11		7											4
	2		4		6		9	10^1	8			5	12		1	3	11		7											5
	2	13	6		12	9^3	10	4		5	7^1	1				11^2		14	8	3										6
	2	12	6		13	9	10^3	4		5	7^1	1				11^2		14	8	3										7
	2		4	6		9^2	10	7		5	12	1				11		13	8^1	3										8
	2	4		12	9^2	10	6		5	7	1		11^1	13		8	3													9
1	3^1	4		5	8	9^2	10		2		12	11		13	7	6														10
1	4	5	6	8^1	13	10		2	12	3	11	9^2	7																	11
1	4	6	8	10^2		2	7^1	11	13	9	3		5	12																12
1^6	4	5	8	9^1	10	2	7^2	15	13	12	11	3	6																	13
	4	12	6	8	9^1	10	2	7	1	3	11	5																		14
	4	6	8	9^1	10	2	7^2	1	3	13	12	11	5																	15
	3	4	6	8^1	9^2	10	2	12	1	11	13	7	5																	16
	3	4	6	8	9^1	7	2	12	1	11	13	10	5																	17
	3	4	6	8	12	10	7^2	2	13	1	11^1	14	9^1	5																18
1		6	9^1	10	4^2	2	7	3	11	12	13	8	5																	19
1	12	6	13	9	4	10^1	2	7	3	11^{13}	14	8^2	5																	20
1	6	8	10	4	11	7	3	12	9^1	2	5																			21
1	2	6	12	10	4	8	7	3	11^{11}	13	9^2	5																		22
1	3	6	10	4	8	7	11	9	2	5																				23
1	12	3^2	6	10	4	8	5	7	13	11	14	9^2	2^1																	24
1^8	2	6	10^1	9	8	4	7	15	3	11^2	13	12																		25
	2	4	6	10	8	9	5	7	1	3	11^1	12																		26
	2	5	6	12	9^2	8	4	7^1	1	3	11	13	10																	27
	2	4		12	9	10	8^3	3	7^1	1	11^2	6	13	14					5											28
	2^2			9	10	8	6	7^1	1	3	11	12	13						5	4										29
	12		6^1		9	7^2	8	2	1	3	11^{11}	10	14	13					5	4										30
1	4		7	9^1	8	13	3^3	12	10	11^2	2	14							5	6										31
1	4		7	12	9	13	8^2	11^1	10	3	6								5	2										32
1	4		6^2	12	9	13	8	11^1	10	7	2	5							3											33
1	4		6^3	9	10	13	8^2	12	11	7	2	5							3	14										34
1			10	9	4	8	2	12	11^1	7	13	3^2							5	6										35
1	12		10	4	8^2	2	11	9^3	13	7	3	5	6^1	14																36
1	12		10^1	4	2	11	9	13	7	3	5	6	8^2																	37
1	2		4	7	11	9	10	8	5	6	3																			38
1	2^1	12	4	7^2	11	9	10	8	5	6	13	3																		39
1	2^1	4^2	10	8	13	12	11	9^3	7	5	6	14	3																	40
1	4	10	6	8^1	2	12	11	9^2	13	7	5	3																		41
1	4	12	10	6^3	8	2^1	14	13	11	9	7	5	3^2																	42
1	4	2^1	14	10	6	8	13	3	11	9^2	7^3	12	5																	43
1	4	2	10	6	8	11	12	9^1	7	5	3																			44
1	4	12	10	6	8^2	1	11^1	9	7	13	2	5	3																	45
1	4	12	10	8	1	11^1	9^2	7	6	2	5	3	13																	46

Worthington Cup
First Round   Preston NE   (h) 1-0
                             (a) 1-4

FA Cup
First Round   Cheltenham T   (a) 1-4

SOUTHAMPTON — FA Premiership

The Friends Provident St Mary's Stadium, Britannia Road, Southampton SO14 5FP.

Telephone: (0870) 2200 000. *Fax:* (023) 8033 0360.
ClubCall: 09068 121 178. *Website:* www.soton.ac.uk/saints
Email: sfc@tcp.co.uk
Recorded Ticket Information: (023) 8022 8575.

Ground Capacity: 32,000.

Record Attendance: 31,044 v Manchester U, Division 1, 8 October 1969.

Record Receipts: £277,863 v Tranmere R, FA Cup 5th rd, 17 February 2001.

Pitch Measurements: 112yd × 74yd.

President: E. T. Bates. *Chairman:* R. J. G. Lowe.
Vice-Chairman: B. H. D. Hunt.
Directors: I. L. Gordon, K. St. J. Wiseman,
M. R. Richards FCA, A. Cowen, R. M. Withers.

Manager: Stuart Gray

Assistant Manager: John Mortimore.

First Team Coach: Mick Wadsworth.

Academy Director: Huw Jennings.

Physios: Don Taylor, Jim Joyce.

Secretary: Brian Truscott.

Colours: Red and white striped shirts, black shorts, white stockings with black and red trim.

Change Colours: All black.

Year Formed: 1885.

Turned Professional: 1894.

Ltd Co.: 1897.

Previous Name: 1885, Southampton St Mary's; 1897, Southampton.

Club Nickname: 'The Saints'.

Previous Grounds: 1885, Antelope Ground; 1897, County Cricket Ground; 1898, The Dell; 2001, St Mary's.

HONOURS

Football League: Division 1 – Runners-up 1983–84; Division 2 – Runners-up 1965–66, 1977–78; Division 3 (S) – Champions 1921–22; Runners-up 1920–21; Division 3 – Champions 1959–60.
FA Cup: Winners 1976; Runners-up 1900, 1902.
Football League Cup: Runners-up 1979.
Zenith Data Systems Cup: Runners-up 1992.
European Competitions: European Fairs Cup: 1969–70. UEFA Cup: 1971–72, 1981–82, 1982–83, 1984–85. European Cup-Winners' Cup: 1976–77.

IT'S A FACT !

Southampton completed eight matches without conceding a goal from 15 April until 28 August 1922. In 2000-01 they came close to equalling this sequence from 13 January to 17 March in seven matches.

First Football League Game: 28 August 1920, Division 3, v Gillingham (a) D 1–1 – Allen; Parker, Titmuss; Shelley, Campbell, Turner; Barratt, Dominy (1), Rawlings, Moore, Foxall.

Record League Victory: 9–3 v Wolverhampton W, Division 2, 18 September 1965 – Godfrey; Jones, Williams; Walker, Knapp, Huxford; Paine (2), O'Brien (1), Melia, Chivers (4), Sydenham (2).

Record Cup Victory: 7–1 v Ipswich T, FA Cup 3rd rd, 7 January 1961 – Reynolds; Davies, Traynor; Conner, Page, Huxford; Paine (1), O'Brien (3 incl. 1p), Reeves, Mulgrew (2), Penk (1).

Record Defeat: 0–8 v Tottenham H, Division 2, 28 March 1936. 0–8 v Everton, Division 1, 20 November 1971.

Most League Points (2 for a win): 61, Division 3 (S), 1921–22 and Division 3, 1959–60.

Most League Points (3 for a win): 77, Division 1, 1983–84.

Most League Goals: 112, Division 3 (S), 1957–58.

Highest League Scorer in Season: Derek Reeves, 39, Division 3, 1959–60.

Most League Goals in Total Aggregate: Mike Channon, 185, 1966–77, 1979–82.

Most League Goals in One Match: 5, Charlie Wayman v Leicester C, Division 2, 23 October 1948.

Most Capped Player: Peter Shilton, 49 (125), England.

Most League Appearances: Terry Paine, 713, 1956–74.

Youngest League Player: Danny Wallace, 16 years 313 days v Manchester U, 29 November 1980.

Record Transfer Fee Received: £7,250,000 from Blackburn R, for Kevin Davies, June 1998.

Record Transfer Fee Paid: £4,000,000 to Derby Co for Rory Delap, July 2001.

Football League Record: 1920 Original Member of Division 3; 1921–22 Division 3 (S); 1922–53 Division 2; 1953–58 Division 3 (S); 1958–60 Division 3; 1960–66 Division 2; 1966–74 Division 1; 1974–78 Division 2; 1978–92 Division 1; 1992– FA Premier League.

MANAGERS

Cecil Knight 1894–95
(Secretary-Manager)
Charles Robson 1895–97
E. Arnfield 1897–1911
(Secretary-Manager)
(continued as Secretary)
George Swift 1911–12
Ernest Arnfield 1912–19
Jimmy McIntyre 1919–24
Arthur Chadwick 1925–31
George Kay 1931–36
George Gross 1936–37
Tom Parker 1937–43
J. R. Sarjantson stepped down
from the board to act as
Secretary-Manager 1943–47
with the next two listed being
team Managers during this
period
Arthur Dominy 1943–46
Bill Dodgin Snr 1946–49
Sid Cann 1949–51
George Roughton 1952–55
Ted Bates 1955–73
Lawrie McMenemy 1973–85
Chris Nicholl 1985–91
Ian Branfoot 1991–94
Alan Ball 1994–95
Dave Merrington 1995–96
Graeme Souness 1996–97
Dave Jones 1997–2000
Glenn Hoddle 2000–01
Stuart Gray July 2001–

LATEST SEQUENCES

Longest Sequence of League Wins: 6, 3.3.92 – 4.4.92.

Longest Sequence of League Defeats: 5, 16.8.98 – 12.9.98.

Longest Sequence of League Draws: 7, 28.12.94 – 11.2.95.

Longest Sequence of Unbeaten League Matches: 19, 5.9.21 – 31.12.21.

Longest Sequence Without a League Win: 20, 30.8.69 – 27.12.69.

TEN YEAR LEAGUE RECORD

		P	W	D	L	F	A	Pts	Pos
1990-91	Div 1	38	12	9	17	58	69	45	14
1991-92	Div 1	42	14	10	18	39	55	52	16
1992-93	PR Lge	42	13	11	18	54	61	50	18
1993-94	PR Lge	42	12	7	23	49	66	43	18
1994-95	PR Lge	42	12	18	12	61	63	54	10
1995-96	PR Lge	38	9	11	18	34	52	38	17
1996-97	PR Lge	38	10	11	17	50	56	41	16
1997-98	PR Lge	38	14	6	18	50	55	48	12
1998-99	PR Lge	38	11	8	19	37	64	41	17
1999-2000	PR Lge	38	12	8	18	45	62	44	15

DID YOU KNOW ?

On 3 September 1898, Southampton beat the short-lived Brighton United 4–1 in the first game at The Dell. On 19 May 2001, Matt Le Tissier scored in the 89th minute. It was his 209th goal for the club in 534 appearances, in the last competitive match on the ground.

SOUTHAMPTON 2000–01 LEAGUE RECORD

Match No.	Date	Venue	Opponents	Result		H/T Score	Lg. Pos.	Goalscorers	Attendance
1	Aug 19	A	Derby Co	D	2-2	2-1	—	Kachloul 2 [15, 22]	27,223
2	23	H	Coventry C	L	1-2	0-1	—	Tessem [62]	14,801
3	26	H	Liverpool	D	3-3	0-1	19	Pakhar (Pahars) 2 [73, 90], El Khalej [85]	15,202
4	Sept 6	A	Charlton Ath	D	1-1	0-0	—	Pakhar (Pahars) [79]	20,021
5	9	A	Leicester C	L	0-1	0-0	18		18,366
6	16	H	Newcastle U	W	2-0	0-0	16	Pakhar (Pahars) 2 [47, 61]	15,221
7	23	A	Bradford C	W	1-0	1-0	8	Halle (og) [29]	16,163
8	30	H	Middlesbrough	L	1-3	0-2	13	Pakhar (Pahars) [81]	14,903
9	Oct 14	A	Everton	D	1-1	0-0	16	Dodd [76]	29,491
10	23	H	Manchester C	L	0-2	0-1	—		15,056
11	28	A	Manchester U	L	0-5	0-2	18		67,581
12	Nov 4	H	Chelsea	W	3-2	2-0	14	Beattie 2 [3, 90], Tessem [37]	15,236
13	11	A	Sunderland	D	2-2	1-1	15	Beattie [12], Richards [89]	43,711
14	18	H	Aston Villa	W	2-0	2-0	15	Beattie 2 [22, 24]	14,979
15	25	H	West Ham U	L	2-3	1-2	15	Oakley [20], Beattie [53]	15,232
16	Dec 2	A	Arsenal	L	0-1	0-0	15		38,036
17	9	H	Leeds U	W	1-0	0-0	15	Beattie [43]	15,225
18	16	H	Ipswich T	L	1-3	1-0	15	Beattie [3]	22,223
19	22	A	Coventry C	D	1-1	0-1	—	Tessem [51]	18,082
20	27	H	Tottenham H	W	2-0	2-0	—	Beattie [38], Davies [40]	15,237
21	30	H	Derby Co	W	1-0	0-0	12	Beattie [73]	15,075
22	Jan 1	A	Liverpool	L	1-2	1-1	12	Soltvedt [20]	38,474
23	13	H	Charlton Ath	D	0-0	0-0	14		15,220
24	20	A	Tottenham H	D	0-0	0-0	14		36,091
25	31	H	Leicester C	W	1-0	0-0	—	Petrescu [79]	14,909
26	Feb 10	A	Bradford C	W	2-0	0-0	12	Pakhar (Pahars) [60], Beattie [63]	14,651
27	24	A	Middlesbrough	W	1-0	0-0	10	Draper [49]	28,622
28	Mar 3	A	Manchester C	W	1-0	0-0	9	Petrescu [55]	33,990
29	17	H	Everton	W	1-0	0-0	8	Tessem [58]	15,251
30	Apr 2	H	Ipswich T	L	0-3	0-1	—		15,244
31	7	A	Leeds U	L	0-2	0-1	11		39,267
32	14	A	Chelsea	L	0-1	0-1	12		35,136
33	21	A	Aston Villa	D	0-0	0-0	10		29,336
34	28	H	Sunderland	L	0-1	0-0	12		15,249
35	May 1	H	Newcastle U	D	1-1	0-1	—	Pakhar (Pahars) [81]	50,439
36	5	A	West Ham U	L	0-3	0-0	13		26,041
37	13	H	Manchester U	W	2-1	2-0	—	Brown (og) [11], Pakhar (Pahars) [15]	15,246
38	19	H	Arsenal	W	3-2	0-1	10	Kachloul 2 [46, 61], Le Tissier [89]	15,252

Final League Position: 10

GOALSCORERS

League (40): Beattie 11, Pakhar (Pahars) 9, Kachloul 4, Tessem 4, Petrescu 2, Davies 1, Dodd 1, Draper 1, El Khalej 1,
Le Tissier 1, Oakley 1, Richards 1, Soltvedt 1, own goals 2.
Worthington Cup (5): Soltvedt 2, Le Tissier 1, Rosler 1, Tessem 1.
FA Cup (7): Dodd 2 (2 pens), Beattie 1, Davies 1, Kachloul 1, Richards 1, Tessem 1.

Jones P 35	Dodd J 29 + 2	Bridge W 38	Marsden C 19 + 4	Lundekvam C 38	El Khalej T 25 + 7	Davies K 21 + 6	Oakley M 35	Rosler U 6 + 14	Draper M 16 + 6	Kachloul H 26 + 6	Tessem J 27 + 6	Beattie J 29 + 8	Pakhar (Pahars) M 26 + 5	Moss N 3	Richards D 28	Le Tissier M 2 + 6	Ripley S 1 + 2	Soltvedt T 3 + 3	Benali F — + 4	Gibbens K 1 + 2	Petrescu D 8 + 1	Bleidelis I — + 1	Monk G 2	Match No.
1	2	3	4	5	6	7	8^1	9^2	10	11	12	13												1
1	2	3	4^5	5	6	7^3	8	9	10	11^1	13	12	14											2
	2^1	3		5	12		4	9^2	8	11^3	7	13	10	1	6	14								3
		3	4^1	5	2		8	9^2	11	12	7	13	10	1	6									4
		3	12	5	2		4	9^2	8^1	11	7	13	10	1	6									5
1	2	3		5	4		8	12		11^2	7	9	10^3		6	13	14							6
1	2	3	12	5	4		8	13		11^1	7^3	9^2	10		6		14							7
1	2	3		5	4		8	9^1		11^2	12	10			6^3	7	13	14						8
1	2	3	4	5	6	7	8			11		9				10								9
1	2	3	12	5	6	13	4^1			11		14	9		10^2	7^3	8							10
1	2	3	12	5	6^2	8	4^1		10	11	7^2	13	9				14							11
1	2	3	8	5	4	12	11^1			7		9	10		6									12
1	2	3	4	5	8^2		11	12		13	7	9	10^1		6									13
1	2	3		5		8^1	4			12	11	7	9	10^2		6						13			14
1	2	3	5^2	4			8	12	13	11	7^1	9	10		6									15
1	2	3		5	6	10	4	12		8^2	11	7	9^1								13			16
1	2	3		5	6	8	4			12	11	7	9		10^1									17
1	2^1	3		5	4	11^3	8	12	14	13	7	9	10		6									18
1		3	4	5	2	12				8	11	7	9		6						10^1			19
1	2	3	4^2	5	13	11		12	8^3		7	9^1	10		6		14							20
1	2	3		5	6	8	4			11	7	9	10											21
1	2	3		5	6	11	4	12		13	7^1	9	10^2						8					22
1	2	3	4^1	5	10^2	8		12	11	7	9				6						13			23
1	4	3		5	2	10	7		8	11^1		9	12		6									24
1	4	3	8	5^1	12	11^3	7		13	14		9	10		6						2^2			25
1	2^1	3	4^2	5	12		8	13		11		9	10		6						7^3	14		26
1		3	4	5		12	10		8	11^1	7	9			6						2			27
1		3	4	5	2	12	8	13	10	11^1	14	9^2			6						7^3			28
1	12	3		5	2^1	4		8		11		9	10		6						7			29
1	12	3	4^3	5	2		8	13		11		9	10^2		6	14					7			30
1	2	3	4	5		11	8		10^1			9	12		6						7			31
1	2	3		5	12	10^2	4^1	13	8^3	14	11	9			6						7			32
1	2	3		5	12	10^2	4^1		8	11	7	9	13		6									33
1	2^1	3		5	4	13	8	12		11	7	9^2	10^3		6	14								34
1	2	3	4	5	6^3	10	8	12		11	7^2	9^1	13				14							35
1	2	3	4	5	7	8	12^2			11^1	13	9	10^3		6	14								36
1		3	4	5		7	8			11^1	12	9	10		6					13		2^2		37
1		3	4	5	12	8^2				11^3	7	9	10		6	13				14		2^1		38

Worthington Cup

Second Round	Mansfield T	(h)	2-0
		(a)	3-1
Third Round	Coventry C	(h)	0-1

FA Cup

Third Round	Sheffield U	(h)	1-0
Fourth Round	Sheffield W	(h)	3-1
Fifth Round	Tranmere R	(h)	0-0
		(a)	3-4

SOUTHEND UNITED $\qquad$ Division 3

FOUNDATION

The leading club in Southend around the turn of the century was Southend Athletic, but they were an amateur concern. Southend United was a more ambitious professional club when they were founded in 1906, employing Bob Jack as secretary-manager and immediately joining the Second Division of the Southern League.

Roots Hall Football Ground, Victoria Avenue, Southend-on-Sea SS2 6NQ.

Telephone: (01702) 304 050. *Fax:* (01702) 304 124. *Commercial:* (01702) 304 147. *ClubCall:* 09068 121 105. *Ticket Office:* (01702) 304 090.

Ground Capacity: 12,392.

Record Attendance: 31,090 v Liverpool, FA Cup 3rd rd, 10 January 1979.

Record Receipts: £83,999 v West Ham U, Division 1, 7 April 1993.

Pitch Measurements: 110yd × 74yd.

HONOURS

Football League: Division 1 best season: 13th, 1994–95. Division 3 – Runners-up 1990–91; Division 4 – Champions 1980–81; Runners-up 1971–72, 1977–78.

FA Cup: best season: old 3rd rd, 1921; 5th rd, 1926, 1952, 1976, 1993.

Football League Cup: never past 3rd rd.

Deputy-Chairman: G. King.

Directors: D. M. Markscheffel, R. J. Osborne, P. Robinson, D. A. J. Wilshire, F. Van Wezel, R. Martin.

Secretary: Miss H. Giles.

Manager: David Webb.

Assistant Manager: Rob Newman.

Physio: John Gowens.

Commercial Manager: Brian Wheeler.

Safety Officer: David Jobson.

Club Nickname: 'The Blues' or 'The Shrimpers'.

Colours: Navy blue.

Change Colours: All white.

Year Formed: 1906.

Turned Professional: 1906.

Ltd Co.: 1919.

Previous Grounds: 1906, Roots Hall, Prittlewell; 1920, Kursaal; 1934, Southend Stadium; 1955, Roots Hall Football Ground.

First Football League Game: 28 August 1920, Division 3, v Brighton & HA (a) W 2–0 – Capper; Reid, Newton; Wileman, Henderson, Martin; Nicholls, Nuttall, Fairclough (2), Myers, Dorsett.

Record League Victory: 9–2 v Newport Co, Division 3 (S), 5 September 1936 – McKenzie; Nelson, Everest (1); Deacon, Turner, Carr; Bolan, Lane (1), Goddard (4), Dickinson (2), Oswald (1).

IT'S A FACT !

Full-back Arthur Williamson made a club record 219 consecutive League appearances for Southend United between 14 January 1956 and 14 September 1960 from a total of 287 League and Cup matches.

Record Cup Victory: 10–1 v Golders Green, FA Cup 1st rd, 24 November 1934 – Moore; Morfitt, Kelly; Mackay, Joe Wilson, Carr (1); Lane (1), Johnson (5), Cheesmuir (2), Deacon (1), Oswald. 10–1 v Brentwood, FA Cup 2nd rd, 7 December 1968 – Roberts; Bentley, Birks; McMillan (1) Beesley, Kurila; Clayton, Chisnall, Moore (4), Best (5), Hamilton. 10–1 v Aldershot, Leyland Daf Cup Prel rd, 6 November 1990 – Sansome; Austin, Powell, Cornwell, Prior (1), Tilson (3), Cawley, Butler, Ansah (1), Benjamin (1), Angell (4).

Record Defeat: 1–9 v Brighton & HA, Division 3, 27 November 1965.

Most League Points (2 for a win): 67, Division 4, 1980–81.

Most League Points (3 for a win): 85, Division 3, 1990–91.

Most League Goals: 92, Division 3 (S), 1950–51.

Highest League Scorer in Season: Jim Shankly, 31, 1928–29; Sammy McCrory, 1957–58, both in Division 3 (S).

Most League Goals in Total Aggregate: Roy Hollis, 122, 1953–60.

Most League Goals in One Match: 5, Jim Shankly v Merthyr T, Division 3S, 1 March 1930.

Most Capped Player: George Mackenzie, 9, Eire.

Most League Appearances: Sandy Anderson, 452, 1950–63.

Youngest League Player: Phil O'Connor, 16 years 76 days v Lincoln C, 26 December 1969.

Record Transfer Fee Received: £3,570,000 from Nottingham F, for Stan Collymore, June 1993.

Record Transfer Fee Paid: £750,000 to Crystal Palace for Stan Collymore, November 1992.

Football League Record: 1920 Original Member of Division 3; 1921–58 Division 3 (S); 1958–66 Division 3; 1966–72 Division 4; 1972–76 Division 3; 1976–78 Division 4; 1978–80 Division 3; 1980–81 Division 4; 1981–84 Division 3; 1984–87 Division 4; 1987–89 Division 3; 1989–90 Division 4; 1990–91 Division 3; 1991–92 Division 2; 1992–97 Division 1; 1997–98 Division 2; 1998– Division 3.

MANAGERS

Bob Jack 1906–10
George Molyneux 1910–11
O. M. Howard 1911–12
Joe Bradshaw 1912–19
Ned Liddell 1919–20
Tom Mather 1920–21
Ted Birnie 1921–34
David Jack 1934–40
Harry Warren 1946–56
Eddie Perry 1956–60
Frank Broome 1960
Ted Fenton 1961–65
Alvan Williams 1965–67
Ernie Shepherd 1967–69
Geoff Hudson 1969–70
Arthur Rowley 1970–76
Dave Smith 1976–83
Peter Morris 1983–84
Bobby Moore 1984–86
Dave Webb 1986–87
Dick Bate 1987
Paul Clark 1987–88
Dave Webb *(General Manager)* 1988–92
Colin Murphy 1992–93
Barry Fry 1993
Peter Taylor 1993–95
Steve Thompson 1995
Ronnie Whelan 1995–97
Alvin Martin 1997–99
Alan Little 1999–2000
David Webb October 2000–

LATEST SEQUENCES

Longest Sequence of League Wins: 7, 27.4.90 – 18.9.90.

Longest Sequence of League Defeats: 6, 29.8.87 – 19.9.87.

Longest Sequence of League Draws: 6, 30.1.82 – 19.2.82.

Longest Sequence of Unbeaten League Matches: 16, 20.2.32 – 29.8.32.

Longest Sequence Without a League Win: 17, 31.12.83 – 14.4.84.

TEN YEAR LEAGUE RECORD

		P	W	D	L	F	A	Pts	Pos
1990-91	Div 3	46	26	7	13	67	51	85	2
1991-92	Div 2	46	17	11	18	63	63	62	12
1992-93	Div 1	46	13	13	20	54	64	52	18
1993-94	Div 1	46	17	8	21	63	67	59	15
1994-95	Div 1	46	18	8	20	54	73	62	13
1995-96	Div 1	46	15	14	17	52	61	59	14
1996-97	Div 1	46	8	15	23	42	86	39	24
1997-98	Div 2	46	11	10	25	47	79	43	24
1998-99	Div 3	46	14	12	20	52	58	54	18
1999-2000	Div 3	46	15	11	20	53	61	56	16

DID YOU KNOW ?

Republic of Ireland international centre-half Charlie Turner had the honour of captaining his country on five occasions while with Southend United, before being transferred to West Ham United in June 1938.

SOUTHEND UNITED 2000–01 LEAGUE RECORD

Match No.	Date	Venue	Opponents	Result	H/T Score	Lg. Pos.	Goalscorers	Attendance
1	Aug 12	H	Brighton & HA	W 2-0	1-0	—	Carruthers [5], Lee [83]	7492
2	19	A	Torquay U	D 1-1	1-0	7	Houghton [7]	2528
3	26	H	Darlington	L 0-2	0-0	14		3444
4	28	A	Cardiff C	D 2-2	0-2	12	Maher [54], Tolson [74]	7628
5	Sept 2	A	Lincoln C	L 0-3	0-0	16		2691
6	9	H	Plymouth Arg	D 2-2	1-2	19	Fitzpatrick [9], Houghton [73]	3417
7	12	H	Kidderminster H	D 1-1	0-1	—	Roget [81]	2403
8	16	A	Halifax T	W 1-0	0-0	15	Roget [64]	1447
9	23	H	Scunthorpe U	W 1-0	1-0	10	Carruthers [14]	3110
10	30	A	Rochdale	W 1-0	1-0	7	Carruthers [31]	3264
11	Oct 8	A	Blackpool	D 2-2	0-2	7	Tinkler [71], Fitzpatrick [89]	3915
12	14	H	York C	W 1-0	1-0	6	Fitzpatrick [11]	4724
13	17	H	Barnet	W 2-0	1-0	—	Carruthers 2 [24, 90]	4124
14	21	A	Hull C	D 1-1	0-1	6	Roget [59]	6701
15	24	H	Exeter C	D 1-1	0-0	—	Lee [64]	4942
16	28	A	Mansfield T	D 1-1	1-1	6	Carruthers (pen) [16]	2200
17	Nov 4	H	Macclesfield T	W 3-1	0-0	5	Abbey 2 [67, 89], Forbes [90]	4190
18	11	A	Carlisle U	L 1-3	0-2	5	Lee [86]	2201
19	25	H	Cheltenham T	L 0-1	0-1	8		4199
20	Dec 2	A	Hartlepool U	L 0-1	0-1	9		2638
21	16	H	Chesterfield	W 3-2	2-1	7	Abbey 2 [4, 88], Forbes [36]	3889
22	22	A	Shrewsbury T	W 1-0	0-0	—	Abbey [76]	2499
23	26	H	Leyton Orient	L 0-1	0-0	7		9950
24	30	A	Torquay U	D 1-1	1-0	7	Roget [4]	3643
25	Jan 1	A	Brighton & HA	W 2-0	0-0	6	Carruthers [66], Lee [82]	6503
26	13	H	Cardiff C	D 1-1	0-1	6	Weston (og) [90]	4601
27	20	A	Leyton Orient	W 2-0	0-0	6	Abbey 2 [60, 64]	6859
28	27	H	Shrewsbury T	D 0-0	0-0	6		4289
29	Feb 3	H	Lincoln C	W 1-0	1-0	6	Abbey [38]	3889
30	17	H	Halifax T	L 0-3	0-2	8		3746
31	20	A	Kidderminster H	L 1-2	1-0	—	Black [31]	2781
32	24	A	Scunthorpe U	D 1-1	1-0	9	Lee [18]	2631
33	Mar 3	H	Rochdale	W 3-0	2-0	7	Whelan [30], Lee 2 (1 pen) [44 (pl), 57]	3681
34	6	A	York C	L 0-1	0-1	—		2144
35	10	H	Blackpool	L 0-3	0-1	9		4810
36	17	A	Barnet	L 1-2	0-1	11	Newman [62]	2654
37	31	A	Chesterfield	D 1-1	1-0	11	Johnson [39]	4018
38	Apr 3	A	Darlington	D 1-1	0-0	—	Bramble [85]	2782
39	7	H	Hartlepool U	W 2-1	1-0	10	Forbes [35], Bramble [51]	3759
40	14	A	Exeter C	D 2-2	2-1	11	Bramble 2 [5, 20]	4535
41	21	A	Macclesfield T	L 0-1	0-1	11		1594
42	24	H	Plymouth Arg	D 3-3	1-2	—	Webb [45], Maher (pen) [77], Newman [90]	3619
43	28	H	Carlisle U	D 1-1	0-1	11	Lee [86]	4175
44	May 1	H	Hull C	D 1-1	1-1	—	Bramble [45]	3573
45	5	A	Cheltenham T	L 1-2	0-0	11	Rawle [54]	3637
46	8	H	Mansfield T	W 3-1	0-1	—	Thurgood [62], Bramble [78], Searle [90]	3345

Final League Position: 11

GOALSCORERS

League (55): Abbey 8, Lee 8 (1 pen), Carruthers 7 (1 pen), Bramble 6, Roget 4, Fitzpatrick 3, Forbes 3, Houghton 2, Maher 2 (1 pen), Newman 2, Black 1, Johnson 1, Rawle 1, Searle 1, Thurgood 1, Tinkler 1, Tolson 1, Webb 1, Whelan 1, own goal 1.
Worthington Cup (0).
FA Cup (5): Williamson 2, Abbey 1, Forbes 1, Roget 1.

Woodman A 17	Booty M 32	Searle D 46	Tinkler M 14 + 1	Roget L 26	Morley D 8 + 9	Lee D 37 + 5	Maher K 40 + 1	Carruthers M 31 + 1	Tolson N 5	Houghton S 7 + 2	Connelly G 8 + 1	Whelan P 40 + 2	Forbes S 27 + 7	Cross G 4 + 4	Fitzpatrick T 8 + 3	Capleton M — + 1	McDonald T — + 1	Johnson L 19 + 1	McSweeney D 10 + 1	Newman R 3 + 3	Abbey B 15 + 9	Williamson R 9 + 3	Flahavan D 29	Webb D 6 + 9	Hutchings C 14	Black M 10 + 5	Bramble T 12 + 4	Rawle M 11 + 3	Thurgood S 8 + 5	Broad S 10	Wardley S — + 2	Edwards C — + 1	Match No.
1	2	3	4	5	6	7	8^1	9	10^2	11^3	12	13	14																				1
1	2	3	4	5	6	7	8	9	10^1	11^2		12	13																				2
1	2^3	3	4	5	12	7	8	9	10^2	11^1		6	13	14																			3
1	2	3	4	5	12	7^5	8	9	10			11	6																				4
1	2	3	4	5		7	8	9	10	12		11^1	6																				5
1	2^3	3	12	5	6^2	7^1	8	9		13		11		4	14	10																	6
1		3	4	5	12		8	9		11	10	6	13		2^1		7^1																7
1^8		3	4	5	7			8	9	11	10	6		2			15																8
1		3	4	5	7	12	8^3	9		11^1	10^2	6	13	2		14																	9
1	2	3	4	5	8	7		9		11^1	10	6		12																			10
1	2	3	4	5	8^2	7	12	9		11^1		6	10		13																		11
1	2	3		5		7	8	9			6	10	4^2	11^1				13	12														12
1	2	3	4^2	5	12	7	8	9			6	11	13	10^1																			13
1	2	3	4	5	12	7	8	9			6	11		10^1																			14
1	2	3	4	5	12	7	8	9			6	11		10^1																			15
1	2	3	4	5		7	8	9			6	11		10^1						12													16
1	2	3		5	12	7	8	9			6	11		10^2						13	4^1												17
	2	3				6	7	8	9			11		12			5			10	4^1	1											18
	2	3		5	12	7	8	9			6	11		13						10^2	4^1	1											19
		3		5	12	7		9^2			6	11	13				8	2		10	4^1	1											20
	2	3		5		7^1	8	9			6	11								10	4	1	12										21
	2	3		5		7	8	9			6	11								10	4	1											22
	2	3		5		7	8	9			6	11								10^1	4	1	12										23
	2	3		5		7^3	8	9			6	11								12		1	10^1	4	13								24
	2	3		5		12	8	9			6	11								10^1		1	7	4									25
	2	3		5		7	8	9			6	11								12	4^2	1	13	10^1									26
	2	3				7	8				6	11						5		10		1	12	4	9^1								27
	2	3				7^2	8				6	11						5		10		1	12	4	9^1	13							28
	2	3				7^1	8				6	11	9^2					5		10		1		4	12	13							29
	2	3		5		7	8	9			6							4		10^2		1	12	11		13							30
		3				7	8	9^3			6							5	2	12	13	1	14	4	10^1	11^2							31
		3				7	8				6							5	2	10^1		1		4	9	11	12						32
	2	3				7	8	9			6							5^1		13		1	4	10	11^1	12^2	14						33
	2	3				7		9^2			6							5		13	12	1	4	11^1	10	8							34
		3				7					6							5	2	12	10^3	1	13	4^1	14	11^2	9	8					35
	2	3				7	8	12			6	13						5		4	10^1	1				9^3			14				36
	2	3				7^2	8					11						5		4	10^1	1	12			9	13	6					37
	2	3				7^3	8					11^2						5		4	12	1	13	10	9^1			6	14				38
	2^3	3				12	8				6	11						5		13		1	7	10^1	9^2	14	4						39
		3				12	8				6	11						5	2			1	7^2	10	9^1	13	4						40
		3									6	11						5	2			1	7	9^2	10	12	8	4^1					41
		3					8				6							5	2	12		1	7	10	9	11	4						42
		3				12	8				6	13						5	2^2			1	7^1	10	9	11	4						43
		3				7	6				5	11						2				1	10	9	8	4							44
		3				7	6				11^2						2	12				1	13	5	10	9^1	8	4					45
		3				7^2	8				6	11^2						1	2^5	5			12	9	10	4	13	14					46

Worthington Cup
First Round — Birmingham C — (h) 0-5
— — (a) 0-0

FA Cup
First Round — Torquay U — (a) 1-1
— — (h) 2-1
Second Round (at Southend) — Canvey Island — (a) 2-1
Third Round — Kingstonian — (h) 0-1

STOCKPORT COUNTY

Division 1

Edgeley Park, Hardcastle Road, Stockport, Cheshire SK3 9DD.

Telephone: (0161) 286 8888. *Fax:* (0161) 286 8900.
Club Shop: (0161) 286 8899. *ClubCall:* 09068 121 638.
Website: www.stockportcounty.com

Ground Capacity: 11,541.

Record Attendance: 27,833 v Liverpool, FA Cup 5th rd, 11 February 1950.

Record Receipts: £181,449 v Middlesbrough, Coca-Cola Cup Semi-final 1st leg, 26 February 1997.

Pitch Measurements: 111yd × 72yd.

Hon. Vice-Presidents: Freddie Pye, Andrew Barlow.

Chairman: Brendan Elwood.

Vice-Chairman: Grahame White.

Directors: Mike Baker, Michael Rains, Brian Taylor, David Jolley.

Secretary: Gary Glendenning BA (HONS), FCCA.

Manager: Andy Kilner. *Assistant Manager:* David Moss. *Physio:* Rodger Wylde.

Assistant Secretary: Andrea Dawson. *Commercial Manager:* John Rutter.
Marketing Manager/Programme Editor: Steve Bellis.

Year Formed: 1883.

Turned Professional: 1891.

Ltd Co.: 1908.

Previous Names: 1883, Heaton Norris Rovers; 1888, Heaton Norris; 1890, Stockport County.

Club Nicknames: 'County' or 'Hatters'.

Colours: Blue shirts with vertical white chest band, blue shorts, white stockings.

Change Colours: Yellow shirts, yellow shorts, yellow stockings.

Previous Grounds: 1883 Heaton Norris Recreation Ground; 1884 Heaton Norris Wanderers Cricket Ground; 1885 Chorlton's Farm, Chorlton's Lane; 1886 Heaton Norris Cricket Ground; 1887 Wilkes' Field, Belmont Street; 1889 Nursery Inn, Green Lane; 1902 Edgeley Park.

First Football League Game: 1 September 1900, Division 2, v Leicester Fosse (a) D 2–2 – Moores; Earp, Wainwright; Pickford, Limond, Harvey; Stansfield, Smith (1), Patterson, Foster, Betteley (1).

Record League Victory: 13–0 v Halifax T, Division 3 (N), 6 January 1934 – McGann; Vincent (1p), Jenkinson; Robinson, Stevens, Len Jones; Foulkes (1), Hill (3), Lythgoe (2), Stevenson (2), Downes (4).

HONOURS

Football League: Division 1 best season: 8th, 1997–98; Division 2 – Runners-up 1996–97; Division 3 (N) – Champions 1921–22, 1936–37; Runners-up 1928–29, 1929–30; Division 4 – Champions 1966–67; Runners-up 1990–91.

FA Cup: best season: 5th rd, 1935, 1950.

Football League Cup: Semi-final 1997.

Autoglass Trophy: Runners-up 1992, 1993.

IT'S A FACT !

Alf Lythgoe, having scored five goals on the opening day of the 1934-35 season for Stockport County, was transferred to Huddersfield Town in October. Despite this, he remained County's joint leading scorer that season with 15 goals.

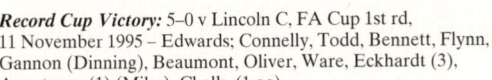

Record Cup Victory: 5–0 v Lincoln C, FA Cup 1st rd,
11 November 1995 – Edwards; Connelly, Todd, Bennett, Flynn,
Gannon (Dinning), Beaumont, Oliver, Ware, Eckhardt (3),
Armstrong (1) (Mike), Chalk, (1 og).

Record Defeat: 1–8 v Chesterfield, Division 2, 19 April 1902.

Most League Points (2 for a win): 64, Division 4, 1966–67.

Most League Points (3 for a win): 85, Division 2, 1993–94.

Most League Goals: 115, Division 3 (N), 1933–34.

Highest League Scorer in Season: Alf Lythgoe, 46, Division 3 (N),
1933–34.

Most League Goals in Total Aggregate: Jack Connor, 132,
1951–56.

Most League Goals in One Match: 5, Joe Smith v Southport,
Division 3N, 7 January 1928; 5, Joe Smith v Lincoln C,
Division 3N, 15 September 1928; 5, Frank Newton v
Nelson, Division 3N, 21 September 1929; 5, Alf Lythgoe v
Southport, Division 3N, 25 August 1934; 5, Billy McNaughton v
Mansfield T, Division 3N, 14 December 1935; 5, Jack Connor v
Workington, Division 3N, 8 November 1952; 5, Jack Connor v
Carlisle U, Division 3N, 7 April 1956.

Most Capped Player: Martin Nash, 8, Canada.

Most League Appearances: Andy Thorpe, 489, 1978–86, 1988–92.

Youngest League Player: Jimmy Collier, 16 years 227 days v
Bristol R, 8 April 1969.

Record Transfer Fee Received: £1,600,000 from Middlesbrough
for Alun Armstrong, February 1998.

Record Transfer Fee Paid: £800,000 to Nottingham F for
Ian Moore, July 1998.

Football League Record: 1900 Elected to Division 2; 1904 Failed
re-election; 1905–21 Division 2; 1921–22 Division 3 (N); 1922–26
Division 2; 1926–37 Division 3 (N); 1937–38 Division 2; 1938–58
Division 3 (N); 1958–59 Division 3; 1959–67 Division 4; 1967–70
Division 3; 1970–91 Division 4; 1991–92 Division 3; 1992–97
Division 2; 1997– Division 1.

LATEST SEQUENCES

Longest Sequence of League Wins: 8, 26.12.27 – 28.1.28.

Longest Sequence of League Defeats: 9, 19.12.08 – 13.2.09.

Longest Sequence of League Draws: 7, 17.3.89 – 14.4.89.

Longest Sequence of Unbeaten League Matches: 18, 28.1.33 – 28.8.33.

Longest Sequence Without a League Win: 19, 28.12.99 – 22.4.00.

MANAGERS

Fred Stewart 1894–1911
Harry Lewis 1911–14
David Ashworth 1914–19
Albert Williams 1919–24
Fred Scotchbrook 1924–26
Lincoln Hyde 1926–31
Andrew Wilson 1932–33
Fred Westgarth 1934–36
Bob Kelly 1936–38
George Hunt 1938–39
Bob Marshall 1939–49
Andy Beattie 1949–52
Dick Duckworth 1952–56
Billy Moir 1956–60
Reg Flewin 1960–63
Trevor Porteous 1963–65
Bert Trautmann
   (General Manager) 1965–66
Eddie Quigley *(Team
   Manager)* 1965–66
Jimmy Meadows 1966–69
Wally Galbraith 1969–70
Matt Woods 1970–71
Brian Doyle 1972–74
Jimmy Meadows 1974–75
Roy Chapman 1975–76
Eddie Quigley 1976–77
Alan Thompson 1977–78
Mike Summerbee 1978–79
Jimmy McGuigan 1979–82
Eric Webster 1982–85
Colin Murphy 1985
Les Chapman 1985–86
Jimmy Melia 1986
Colin Murphy 1986–87
Asa Hartford 1987–89
Danny Bergara 1989–95
Dave Jones 1995–97
Gary Megson 1997–99
Andy Kilner July 1999–

TEN YEAR LEAGUE RECORD

		P	W	D	L	F	A	Pts	Pos
1990-91	Div 4	46	23	13	10	84	47	82	2
1991-92	Div 3	46	22	10	14	75	51	76	5
1992-93	Div 2	46	19	15	12	81	57	72	6
1993-94	Div 2	46	24	13	9	74	44	85	4
1994-95	Div 2	46	19	8	19	63	60	65	11
1995-96	Div 2	46	19	13	14	61	47	70	9
1996-97	Div 2	46	23	13	10	59	41	82	2
1997-98	Div 1	46	19	8	19	71	69	65	8
1998-99	Div 1	46	12	17	17	49	60	53	16
1999-2000	Div 1	46	13	15	18	55	67	54	17

DID YOU KNOW ?

Harry Hardy, who for many
years was Stockport County's
only fully capped
international, had also been
honoured by selection for the
Football League in 1924.

STOCKPORT COUNTY 2000–01 LEAGUE RECORD

Match No.	Date	Venue	Opponents	Result		H/T Score	Lg. Pos.	Goalscorers	Atten- dance
1	Aug 12	A	Gillingham	W	3-1	2-1	—	Moore 2 [24, 84], Maxwell [39]	9429
2	19	H	Wolverhampton W	D	1-1	0-0	4	Moore [55]	7758
3	26	A	Fulham	L	1-4	1-1	13	Cooper [5]	11,009
4	28	H	Huddersfield T	D	0-0	0-0	14		6137
5	Sept 1	A	Tranmere R	L	1-2	1-2	—	Moore [12]	7229
6	9	H	WBA	D	0-0	0-0	13		6632
7	12	H	Norwich C	L	1-3	0-2	—	Smith [52]	5703
8	16	A	Preston NE	D	1-1	1-1	19	Moore [2]	12,735
9	23	H	Watford	L	2-3	0-1	19	Wilbraham [73], Moore [87]	6933
10	30	A	Wimbledon	L	0-2	0-1	21		6087
11	Oct 8	H	Portsmouth	D	1-1	0-1	20	Cooper [89]	6212
12	14	A	Burnley	L	1-2	0-2	22	Tod [56]	16,107
13	17	A	Birmingham C	L	0-4	0-1	—		15,579
14	21	H	Bolton W	W	4-3	3-0	20	Tod [22], Wiss [24], Moore [40], Wilbraham [90]	8266
15	24	A	Sheffield U	L	0-1	0-0	—		13,542
16	28	H	Nottingham F	L	1-2	0-0	22	Edwards (og) [48]	6021
17	Nov 4	A	Blackburn R	L	1-2	1-0	23	Wilbraham [8]	17,404
18	11	H	QPR	D	2-2	1-1	23	Bergersen [12], Wilbraham [52]	6356
19	18	A	Crewe Alex	W	2-1	1-0	23	Tod [24], Clark [70]	6099
20	25	A	Crystal Palace	D	2-2	1-0	23	Wilbraham [5], Fradin [67]	18,819
21	Dec 2	H	Sheffield U	L	0-2	0-1	23		6460
22	9	A	Sheffield W	W	4-2	2-2	21	Fradin 2 [14, 70], Cooper 2 [28, 56]	16,337
23	16	H	Barnsley	W	2-0	0-0	19	Wiss [49], Woodthorpe [60]	5383
24	22	H	Gillingham	D	2-2	1-1	—	Wiss [31], Maxwell [89]	6095
25	26	A	Grimsby T	D	1-1	1-0	20	Matthews [42]	6654
26	30	A	Wolverhampton W	L	2-3	1-3	20	Nicholson (pen) [45], Wiss [90]	16,667
27	Jan 1	H	Fulham	W	2-0	1-0	18	Wiss [40], Clark [47]	6100
28	13	A	Huddersfield T	D	0-0	0-0	18		10,988
29	20	H	Grimsby T	D	1-1	1-0	18	Wiss [9]	6165
30	Feb 3	H	Tranmere R	D	1-1	1-0	18	Wilbraham [39]	7804
31	10	A	WBA	D	1-1	0-1	18	Cooper [78]	16,385
32	13	H	Preston NE	L	0-1	0-0	—		7590
33	20	A	Norwich C	L	0-4	0-3	—		19,768
34	24	A	Watford	D	2-2	1-0	20	Wilbraham 2 [23, 90]	13,647
35	Mar 3	H	Wimbledon	D	2-2	1-1	21	Wilbraham [14], Fradin [59]	5519
36	6	H	Burnley	D	0-0	0-0	—		7087
37	10	A	Portsmouth	L	1-2	0-0	21	Kuqi [77]	12,202
38	17	H	Birmingham C	W	2-0	1-0	21	Kuqi 2 [41, 83]	7176
39	31	A	Barnsley	W	2-0	1-0	20	Kuqi [10], Wilbraham [62]	13,203
40	Apr 3	A	Bolton W	D	1-1	0-1	—	Kuqi [67]	12,492
41	7	H	Sheffield W	W	2-1	1-0	18	Harkness (og) [42], Carrigan [76]	9666
42	14	H	Blackburn R	D	0-0	0-0	18		9705
43	16	A	Nottingham F	L	0-1	0-1	20		23,500
44	21	H	Crewe Alex	W	3-0	0-0	19	Fradin [71], Nicholson (pen) [84], Wilbraham [90]	7163
45	28	A	QPR	W	3-0	0-0	18	Wilbraham [47], Fradin [55], Kuqi (pen) [83]	10,608
46	May 6	H	Crystal Palace	L	0-1	0-0	19		9782

Final League Position: 19

GOALSCORERS

League (58): Wilbraham 12, Moore 7, Fradin 6, Kuqi 6 (1 pen), Wiss 6, Cooper 5, Tod 3, Clark 2, Maxwell 2, Nicholson 2 (2 pens), Bergersen 1, Carrigan 1, Matthews 1, Smith 1, Woodthorpe 1, own goals 2.
Worthington Cup (2): Dinning 1, Moore 1.
FA Cup (2): Fradin 1, Wiss 1.

Jones L 27	Bryngelsson F 4+1	Clark P 33+4	Dinning T 6	Flynn M 44	Gray K 1	Cooper K 34	Moore I 17	Maxwell L 8+12	Fradin K 27+4	Gibb A 38+1	Wiss J 27+3	Woodthorpe C 14+10	Smith D 31+2	Connelly S 11+2	Bailey A 1+3	Clare R 19+3	Carrigan B 3+10	Hancock G 1+1	Matthews R 7+4	Lawson I 1+9	Nicholson S 31+4	Carratt P —+2	Wilbraham A 32+4	Nash C 8	Tod A 11	Brebner G 3+3	Bergersen K 8+1	Dibble A 9+1	Grayson S 13	Kuqi S 17	Hurst G 10+1	Flogel L 8+1	Kelly A 2	Byrne C —+1	Match No.
1	2¹	3²	4	5	6	7	8	9²	10	11	12	13	14																						1
1	2	3	4	5		7¹	8	9²	10	11	13	12		6																					2
1		3	4	5		7	8	9¹	10			2	11²		6	12	13																		3
1	2	3	4	5		7	8	12	10²	6		13				9¹	11³	14																4
1	2	3	4	5		7	8			6		11	10				9																	5
1		5				7	8	13	10	4¹		2	11		14	3	12²	6	9³															6
1		6	5			7	8	9¹	10	2²		4	11			3	12		13															7
1		6	4	5		7	8	9¹		10		2	11			3²	13	12																8
1		6		5		7	8	9¹		10²		4	11	2									3	12	13									9
		6	4			7		12		8¹	5		11	2			10³	13	3	14	9²		1											10
		6	4			7	8			10²			11	2			13	9¹	3		12	1	5											11
		3	4			7¹	8	9³			6		11	2				12	13		10²	1	5	14										12
		6	4				8			7¹			11	2³	12	14		13	3		9²	1	5	10										13
		5	4			7²	8						6	12	11		2		3		13	1	9	10¹										14
		5	4			7	8	12					6	13	11		2²		3		14	1	9³	10¹										15
			5			7	8						2	4	12	11			3		9	1	6		10¹									16
		3	5			7¹	8						2	4	12	11			13	14	9²		6		10³	1								17
		6	5			7	8		13	2			11						12	3	9¹		4		10²	1								18
		6	5			7²			12	2	8		11						13	3	9		4		10¹	1								19
		6	5			7		12	10	2	8²	13							3	3	9		4		11¹	1								20
		6	5			7		12	10	2	8²		13					14	3³	3	9		4		11¹	1								21
		6	5			7		12	10	2	4	13	11						3	3	9		8²	1										22
1		6	5			7¹		12		2	4	8	11					13	3	3	9		10²											23
1	12	5	4			7		13		2	6	10³	11					8²	3	9¹		14												24
1		5	4			7				2	6	10	11					8	3	9														25
1⁸		6	5			7				2	4	10¹	11					8	3	9		12	15											26
		6	5			7			12	2	4	10	11			3		8¹		9	1													27
1		6	5			7			10¹	8	4	12	11			3²		13		9					2									28
1		6	5			7			12	10²	2	4		11				8¹	13	9					3									29
1		3	5			7¹			10	2	4		12						11	9					6	8								30
1			5			7			12	13	8	4	11²			3			2	9¹					6	10								31
1			5						9¹	10		4	11	2		13	7²		12	3					6	8								32
1			5			7²			10	2	4		11	12			13		3¹						6	8	9							33
1	3		5						10	2¹			11	12		4	7²			9					6	8	13							34
1	6					7			10	4	11								3	9						8		5						35
			4			7			10		11			2					3	9					1	6	8	5						36
			4			7¹			10	12	11			2		13			3	9					1	6²	8	5						37
			4						10	2				6	12				3	9					1	7	8	11¹	5					38
1	12		4						10	2				6					3	9¹						7	8	11	5					39
			4						10	2				6	12				3	9						7	8	11¹	5	1				40
			4						10¹	2	12			6	13				3	9						7	8	11²	5	1				41
1	12		4						10	2	7			6	13				3¹	9							8	11²	5					42
1	5¹		4						10	2	7³			6	13				3	9						12	8	11²		14				43
1	12		4						10	2⁵		5	11	6					3	9							8	7						44
1	12		4					13	10	2²		5	11	6					3	9							8	7¹						45
1	5		4						10	2		3	11²	6					12	9							8	7¹	13					46

Worthington Cup
First Round Blackpool (h) 0-1
  (a) 2-3

FA Cup
Third Round Preston NE (a) 1-0
Fourth Round Crewe Alex (a) 1-0
Fifth Round Tottenham H (a) 0-4

STOKE CITY

Division 2

FOUNDATION

The date of the formation of this club has long been in doubt. The year 1863 was claimed, but more recent research by Wade Martin has uncovered nothing earlier than 1868, when a couple of Old Carthusians, who were apprentices at the local works of the old North Staffordshire Railway Company, met with some others from that works, to form Stoke Ramblers. It should also be noted that the old Stoke club went bankrupt in 1908 when a new club was formed.

Britannia Stadium, Stoke-on-Trent ST4 4EG.

Telephone: (01782) 592 222. *Fax:* (01782) 592 221.
Commercial Dept: (01782) 592 211.
Football in the Community: (01782) 592 255.
ClubCall: 09068 121 040.

Ground Capacity: 28,384.

Record Attendance: 51,380 v Arsenal, Division 1, 29 March 1937.

Record Receipts: £336,000 v Liverpool, Worthington Cup 4th rd, 29 November 2000.

Pitch Measurements: 116yd × 72yd.

Vice-President: Stefan Geir Thorisson.

Chairman: Gunnar Thor Gislason.

Directors: Asgeir Sigurvinsson, Peter Coates, Keith Humphreys.

Chief Executive: Jonathan Fuller.

Manager: Gudjon Thordarson *Physio:* Stefan Stefansson.

Stadium Manager/Safety Officer: J. Alcock.

Colours: Red and white striped shirts, white shorts, red and white hooped stockings.

Change Colours: Blue shirts and shorts with red and white stripe on left hand side, white stockings with blue turnover.

Year Formed: 1863 *(see Foundation).* *Turned Professional:* 1885. *Ltd Co.:* 1908.

Previous Names: 1868, Stoke Ramblers; 1870, Stoke; 1925, Stoke City.

Club Nickname: 'The Potters'.

Previous Grounds: 1875, Sweeting's Field; 1878, Victoria Ground (previously known as the Athletic Club Ground); 1997, Britannia Stadium.

First Football League Game: 8 September 1888, Football League, v WBA (h) L 0–2 – Rowley; Clare, Underwood; Ramsey, Shutt, Smith; Sayer, McSkimming, Staton, Edge, Tunnicliffe.

Record League Victory: 10–3 v WBA, Division 1, 4 February 1937 – Doug Westland; Brigham, Harbot; Tutin, Turner (1p), Kirton; Matthews, Antonio (2), Freddie Steele (5), Jimmy Westland, Johnson (2).

HONOURS

Football League: Division 1 best season: 4th, 1935–36, 1946–47; Division 2 – Champions 1932–33, 1962–63, 1992–93; Runners-up 1921–22; Promoted 1978–79 (3rd); Division 3 (N) – Champions 1926–27.

FA Cup: Semi-finals 1899, 1971, 1972.

Football League Cup: Winners 1972.

Autoglass Trophy: Winners: 1992.

Auto Windscreens Shield: Winners: 2000.

European Competitions: UEFA Cup: 1972–73, 1974–75.

IT'S A FACT !

The first player to score a hat-trick for Stoke was Alf Edge, who actually hit five in an FA Cup tie against Caernarvon Wanderers in a qualifying round match in October 1886. Stoke won 10-1.

Record Cup Victory: 7–1 v Burnley, FA Cup 2nd rd (replay), 20 February 1896 – Clawley; Clare, Eccles; Turner, Grewe, Robertson; Willie Maxwell, Dickson, A. Maxwell (3), Hyslop (4), Schofield.

Record Defeat: 0–10 v Preston NE, Division 1, 14 September 1889.

Most League Points (2 for a win): 63, Division 3 (N), 1926–27.

Most League Points (3 for a win): 93, Division 2, 1992–93.

Most League Goals: 92, Division 3 (N), 1926–27.

Highest League Scorer in Season: Freddie Steele, 33, Division 1, 1936–37.

Most League Goals in Total Aggregate: Freddie Steele, 142, 1934–49.

Most League Goals in One Match: 7, Neville Coleman v Lincoln C, Division 2, 23 February 1957.

Most Capped Player: Gordon Banks, 36 (73), England.

Most League Appearances: Eric Skeels, 506, 1958–76.

Youngest League Player: Peter Bullock, 16 years 163 days v Swansea C, 19 April 1958.

Record Transfer Fee Received: £2,750,000 from QPR for Mike Sheron, July 1997.

Record Transfer Fee Paid: £600,000 to Orgryte for Brnynjar Gunnarsson, December 1999.

Football League Record: 1888 Founder Member of Football League; 1890 Not re-elected; 1891 Re-elected; relegated in 1907, and after one year in Division 2, resigned for financial reasons; 1919 re-elected to Division 2; 1922–23 Division 1; 1923–26 Division 2; 1926–27 Division 3 (N); 1927–33 Division 2; 1933–53 Division 1; 1953–63 Division 2; 1963–77 Division 1; 1977–79 Division 2; 1979–85 Division 1; 1985–90 Division 2; 1990–92 Division 3; 1992–93 Division 2; 1993–98 Division 1; 1998– Division 2.

MANAGERS

Tom Slaney 1874–83
  (Secretary-Manager)
Walter Cox 1883–84
  (Secretary-Manager)
Harry Lockett 1884–90
Joseph Bradshaw 1890–92
Arthur Reeves 1892–95
William Rowley 1895–97
H. D. Austerberry 1897–1908
A. J. Barker 1908–14
Peter Hodge 1914–15
Joe Schofield 1915–19
Arthur Shallcross 1919–23
John 'Jock' Rutherford 1923
Tom Mather 1923–35
Bob McGrory 1935–52
Frank Taylor 1952–60
Tony Waddington 1960–77
George Eastham 1977–78
Alan A'Court 1978
Alan Durban 1978–81
Richie Barker 1981–83
Bill Asprey 1984–85
Mick Mills 1985–89
Alan Ball 1989–91
Lou Macari 1991–93
Joe Jordan 1993–94
Lou Macari 1994–97
Chic Bates 1997–98
Chris Kamara 1998
Brian Little 1998–99
Gary Megson 1999
Gudjon Thordarson
  November 1999–

LATEST SEQUENCES

Longest Sequence of League Wins: 8, 30.3.1895 – 21.9.1895.

Longest Sequence of League Defeats: 11, 6.4.85 – 17.8.85.

Longest Sequence of League Draws: 5, 21.3.87 – 11.4.87.

Longest Sequence of Unbeaten League Matches: 25, 5.9.92 – 20.2.93.

Longest Sequence Without a League Win: 17, 22.4.89 – 14.10.89.

TEN YEAR LEAGUE RECORD

		P	W	D	L	F	A	Pts	Pos
1990-91	Div 3	46	16	12	18	55	59	60	14
1991-92	Div 3	46	21	14	11	69	49	77	4
1992-93	Div 2	46	27	12	7	73	34	93	1
1993-94	Div 1	46	18	13	15	57	59	67	10
1994-95	Div 1	46	16	15	15	50	53	63	11
1995-96	Div 1	46	20	13	13	60	49	73	4
1996-97	Div 1	46	18	10	18	51	57	64	12
1997-98	Div 1	46	11	13	22	44	74	46	23
1998-99	Div 2	46	21	6	19	59	63	69	8
1999-2000	Div 2	46	23	13	10	68	42	82	6

DID YOU KNOW ❓

On 20 September 2000, Marc Goodfellow scored his first goal for Stoke City on his 19th birthday to establish a first leg lead in a second round League Cup tie.

STOKE CITY 2000–01 LEAGUE RECORD

Match No.	Date	Venue	Opponents	Result	H/T Score	Lg. Pos.	Goalscorers	Attendance
1	Aug 12	H	Wycombe W	D	0-0	0-0	—	14,532
2	19	A	Bristol C	W	2-1	0-0	4	Gudjonsson [76], O'Connor [87]	12,590
3	26	H	Notts Co	L	0-1	0-0	12		13,041
4	29	A	Reading	D	3-3	2-1	—	Hunter (og) [17], Thordarson [22], Fenton [75]	10,668
5	Sept 9	H	Peterborough U	W	3-0	0-0	9	Lightbourne [53], Thordarson [87], Kavanagh [90]	13,011
6	13	H	Oxford U	W	4-0	3-0	—	Thordarson [22], Gudjonsson [32], O'Connor [45], Robinson [71]	9600
7	17	A	Port Vale	D	1-1	1-1	8	Lightbourne [15]	8948
8	23	H	Rotherham U	D	1-1	0-1	10	Thorne [81]	13,472
9	30	A	Colchester U	W	1-0	1-0	8	Thorne [14]	3758
10	Oct 14	A	Swansea C	L	1-2	0-0	10	Lightbourne [88]	6498
11	17	A	Cambridge U	D	1-1	1-0	—	Thorne [41]	4433
12	21	H	Millwall	W	3-2	2-2	10	Thorne 2 [18, 13], Iwelumo [90]	13,758
13	24	A	Walsall	L	0-3	0-0	—		6996
14	28	H	Bournemouth	W	2-1	2-1	8	Gudjonsson [9], O'Connor [13]	11,572
15	Nov 4	A	Wrexham	W	2-1	2-0	7	Thorne [16], Thordarson (pen) [27]	6447
16	7	A	Northampton T	D	2-2	2-2	—	Kavanagh [10], O'Connor [24]	5475
17	11	H	Oldham Ath	L	0-1	0-1	9		12,503
18	25	A	Swindon T	W	3-0	2-0	6	Dryden (og) [8], Lightbourne 2 [11, 78]	4904
19	Dec 2	H	Luton T	L	1-3	1-1	7	Mohan [35]	12,389
20	16	A	Bristol R	W	3-0	3-0	7	Thorne 3 [3, 19, 40]	6838
21	23	A	Wigan Ath	D	1-1	0-0	7	O'Connor [65]	8957
22	26	H	Bury	W	2-1	1-1	7	Dadason [39], Gunnarsson [84]	16,499
23	30	H	Bristol C	W	1-0	0-0	5	Gudjonsson [82]	14,629
24	Jan 1	A	Notts Co	D	2-2	1-1	5	Gudjonsson [1], Cooke [60]	9125
25	13	H	Reading	D	0-0	0-0	5		14,154
26	17	H	Brentford	W	1-0	0-0	—	Dadason [22]	9350
27	27	H	Wigan Ath	W	2-0	1-0	5	Cooke [18], Thorne [60]	16,859
28	Feb 3	H	Northampton T	D	1-1	0-0	5	Cooke [59]	13,235
29	10	A	Peterborough U	W	4-0	2-0	5	Thorne [2], Gudjonsson [45], Dadason [72], O'Connor [89]	7568
30	17	H	Port Vale	D	1-1	0-1	4	O'Connor [55]	22,133
31	20	A	Oxford U	D	1-1	0-1	—	Cooke [69]	4856
32	24	A	Rotherham U	L	1-2	0-0	6	Thorne [53]	8211
33	Mar 3	H	Colchester U	W	3-1	2-1	6	Thorne 2 [9, 40], Kavanagh [88]	11,714
34	7	H	Swansea C	L	1-2	0-2	—	O'Connor [81]	10,091
35	10	A	Brentford	D	2-2	1-0	6	Cooke [17], Dadason [90]	5518
36	13	A	Wycombe W	W	1-0	1-0	—	Kavanagh (pen) [11]	5385
37	17	H	Cambridge U	L	2-3	0-2	5	Kavanagh (pen) [56], Dadason [57]	11,939
38	27	A	Bury	L	0-1	0-0	—		4224
39	31	H	Bristol R	W	4-1	2-0	6	Hansson 2 [4, 15], Thorne 2 [71, 86]	12,274
40	Apr 3	A	Millwall	L	0-2	0-1	—		11,639
41	7	A	Luton T	W	2-1	2-1	5	Kavanagh 2 [30, 40]	6456
42	14	H	Walsall	D	0-0	0-0	5		16,603
43	17	A	Bournemouth	L	0-1	0-1	—		5373
44	21	H	Wrexham	W	3-1	2-0	5	Hardy (og) [6], Gunnarsson 2 [44, 56]	12,687
45	28	A	Oldham Ath	W	2-1	0-1	5	Gunnarsson [73], Dadason [84]	9359
46	May 5	H	Swindon T	W	4-1	4-0	5	O'Halloran (og) [1], Gunnarsson [13], Cooke [23], Kavanagh (pen) [38]	20,591

Final League Position: 5

GOALSCORERS

League (74): Thorne 16, Kavanagh 8 (3 pens), O'Connor 6, Cooke 6, Dadason 6, Gudjonsson 6, Gunnarsson 5, Lightbourne 5, Thordarson 4 (1 pen), Hansson 2, Fenton 1, Iwelumo 1, Mohan 1, Robinson 1, own goals 4.
Worthington Cup (13): Connor 2, Gudjonsson 2, O'Connor 2, Thordarson 2 (1 pen), Dadason 1, Goodfellow 1, Gunnarsson 1, Heath 1, Iwelumo 1.
FA Cup (0).

Ward G 17	Hansson M 36+2	Petty B 10+12	Thomas W 33+1	Mohan N 37	Gunnarsson B 46	Risom H 9+16	Thordarson S 15+15	Lightbourne K 11+11	Gudjonsson B 41+1	O'Connor J 44	Fenton G 2+3	Connor P 1+6	Muggleton C 11+1	Dorigo T 34+2	Kavanagh G 42+1	Clarke C 12+9	Robinson N 3	Thorne P 35+3	Goodfellow M —+7	Kippe F 15+4	Iwelumo C —+2	Dadason R 13+15	Cooke A 21+1	Kristinsson B 18	Neal L —+1	Match No
1	2	3[1]	4	5	6	7	8	9[2]	10	11	12	13		15												1
1	2		4[2]	5	6	7	8	9[1]	10	11	13	12		3												2
1	2		4	5	6	7[2]		9[1]	10	11	12	13		3	8											3
1	2		4	5	6	7[2]		9	10[1]	11	12	13		3	8											4
1	2		4[2]	5	6	7		9[1]	10	11	12	13		3	8											5
1	2		4[2]	5	6	7		9	10[3]	11	12	13		3	8[1]	14										6
1	2		4[1]	5	6	7		9	10	11	12	13		3	8											7
1	2		4[3]	5	6	7		9[2]	10[1]	11	12	13		3	8	14										8
1	2	12	4	5	6	7		9[1]	10[2]	11		13		3	8											9
	2		4[1]	5	6	7		9	10	11	12	13	1	3[2]	8											10
	2			5	6	7[2]			10[1]	11	12	13	1	3	8	4		9								11
	2		4[2]	5	6	7		9[3]	10	11[1]	12	13	1	3	8	14										12
	2[1]		4[2]	5	6	7		9[3]	10	11	12	13	1	3	8	14										13
	2[3]	12	4	5	6	7			10[2]	11		13	1	3	8			9								14
	2	12	4[3]	5	6	7			10[1]	11		13	1	3	8	14		9[2]								15
	2	12	4	5	6	7			10[2]	11		13	1	3	8			9[1]								16
	2[1]	12	4	5	6	7			10[3]	11		13	1	3	8[2]	14		9								17
	2	12	4	5	6	7[3]			10[2]	11		13	1	3	8[1]	14		9								18
	2	12	4	5	6[1]	7			10	11		13	1	3[2]	8			9[3]								19
	2	12		5	6	7			10[2]	11[1]		13		3	8	4		9[3]				14		1		20
	2			5	6	7			10[1]	11				3	8	12		9						1		21
	2			5	6	7			10[3]	11		13		3[1]	8	4[2]		9				14		1		22
	2[1]	4	5	6	7			10[3]	11		13		3[2]	8	12		9				14		1			23
	2	4	5	6	7[1]				10	11		13		3[2]	8	12		9						1		24
	2	4	5[1]	6	7				10[2]	11		13		3	8	12		9						1		25
	2	4	5	6	7				10	11				3	8	12		9[1]						1		26
	2	12	4	5	6	7[2]			10	11		13		3[3]	8[1]			9				14		1		27
	2	4	5	6	7				10[1]	11		13		3[2]	8	12		9						1		28
	2	4	5	6	7				10[2]	11		13		3	8	12		9[1]						1		29
	2[1]	4	5	6	7				10	11		13		3	8	12		9[2]						1		30
	2[1]	12	4	5	6	7			10[3]	11		13		3	8			9						1		31
	2	4	5	6[1]	7				10	11		13		3[2]	8	12		9						1		32
	2	4	5	6	7[1]			11[2]	10			13		3	8	12		9[3]				14		1		33
	2[1]	4	5[2]	6	7				10	11		13		3	8	12		9						1		34
	2[1]	12	4	5	6	7			10[3]	11		13		3	8			9[2]				14		1		35
	2	4	5	6	7				10[3]	11		13		3[2]	8	12		9[1]				14		1		36
	2[1]	12	4	5	6	7			10	11		13		3[2]	8			9[3]				14		1		37
1	2	4	5[1]	6	7				10	11		13		3	8[2]	12		9[3]				14				38
1	2	4	5[2]	6	7[3]				10[1]	11		13		3	8	12		9				14				39
1	2	4	5	6	7[2]			11[1]	10[3]			13		3	8	12		9				14				40
1	2	4	5	6	7[2]			11	10			13		3	8	12		9[1]								41
1	2	4	5	6	7			11	10[1]			13		3	8	12		9[2]								42
1	2	4[1]	5	6	7[3]			11	10			13		3[2]	8	12		9				14				43
1	2[1]	4	5	6[2]	7			11	10			13		3[3]	8	12		9				14				44
1	2	4[2]	5	6	7			11	10[1]			13		3	8	12		9								45
1	2[1]	4	5	6	7			11	10			13		3	8[2]	12		9[3]				14				46

Worthington Cup

First Round	York C	(a)	5-1
		(h)	0-0
Second Round	Charlton Ath	(h)	2-1
		(a)	3-4
Third Round	Barnsley	(h)	3-2
Fourth Round	Liverpool	(h)	0-8

FA Cup

First Round	Nuneaton B	(h)	0-0
		(a)	0-1

SUNDERLAND   FA Premiership

FOUNDATION

A Scottish schoolmaster named James Allan, working at Hendon Board School, took the initiative in the foundation of Sunderland in 1879 when they were formed as The Sunderland and District Teachers' Association FC at a meeting in the Adults School, Norfolk Street. Due to financial difficulties, they quickly allowed members from outside the teaching profession and so became Sunderland AFC in October 1880.

Sunderland Stadium of Light, Sunderland, Tyne and Wear SR5 1SU.

Telephone: (0191) 551 5000. *Fax:* (0191) 551 5123.
Website: www.safc.com
ClubCall: 09068 121 140. *Ticket Office:* (0191) 551 5151.
Club Shop: (0191) 551 5050.
Tour Hotline: (0191) 551 5055.

Ground Capacity: 48,300.

Record Attendance: Stadium of Light: 48,285 v Leeds U, FA Premier League, 31 March 2001.
Roker Park: 75,118 v Derby Co, FA Cup 6th rd replay, 8 March 1933.

Record Receipts: £605,310 v Sheffield U, Division 1 play-off semi-final, 13 May 1998.

Pitch Measurements: 105m × 68m.

Chairman: R. S. Murray. *Vice Chairman:* John Fickling.
Directors: G. McDonnell. K. J. Slater.
Associate Directors: J. R. Featherstone, G. S. Wood, J. G. Wood. *Chief Executive:* Hugh Roberts.

Manager: Peter Reid. *Assistant Manager:* Bobby Saxton.
Reserve Team Manager: Ricky Sbragia. *Physio:* Mark Leather. *Academy Director:* Ian Branfoot.
Community Programme Officer: Bob Oates.

Secretary: Mark Blackbourne.

Marketing Director: Grahame McDonnell.

Safety Officer: John Davidson.

Colours: Red and white striped shirts, black shorts, black stockings.

Change Colours: Navy blue and royal blue vertical striped shirts with red piping, royal blue shorts and stockings.

Year Formed: 1879.

Turned Professional: 1886.

Ltd Co.: 1906.

Previous Name: 1879, Sunderland and District Teacher's AFC; 1880, Sunderland.

Previous Grounds: 1879, Blue House Field, Hendon; 1882, Groves Field, Ashbrooke; 1883, Horatio Street; 1884, Abbs Field, Fulwell; 1886, Newcastle Road; 1898, Roker Park; 1997, Stadium of Light.

HONOURS

Football League: Division 1 – Champions 1891–92, 1892–93, 1894–95, 1901–02, 1912–13, 1935–36, 1995–96, 1998–99; Runners-up 1893–94, 1897–98, 1900–01, 1922–23, 1934–35; Division 2 – Champions 1975–76; Runners-up 1963–64, 1979–80; Division 3 – Champions 1987–88.

FA Cup: Winners 1937, 1973; Runners-up 1913, 1992.

Football League Cup: Runners-up 1985.

European Competitions: European Cup-Winners' Cup: 1973–74.

IT'S A FACT !

When Sunderland won 4–2 at Chelsea on 17 March 2001, it was the first time they had scored as many goals there since a 4–1 win on 12 March 1910 when their scorers were Harry Low (2), Arthur Bridgett and George Holley.

First Football League Game: 13 September 1890, Football League, v Burnley (h) L 2–3 – Kirtley; Porteous, Oliver; Wilson, Auld, Gibson; Spence (1), Miller, Campbell (1), Scott, D. Hannah.

Record League Victory: 9–1 v Newcastle U (a), Division 1, 5 December 1908 – Roose; Forster, Melton; Daykin, Thomson, Low; Mordue (1), Hogg (3), Brown, Holley (3), Bridgett (2).

Record Cup Victory: 11–1 v Fairfield, FA Cup 1st rd, 2 February 1895 – Doig; McNeill, Johnston; Dunlop, McCreadie (1), Wilson; Gillespie (1), Millar (5), Campbell, Hannah (3), Scott (1).

Record Defeat: 0–8 v Sheff Wed, Division 1, 26 December 1911. 0–8 v West Ham U, Division 1, 19 October 1968. 0–8 v Watford, Division 1, 25 September 1982.

Most League Points (2 for a win): 61, Division 2, 1963–64.

Most League Points (3 for a win): 105, Division 1, 1998–99 (Football League Record).

Most League Goals: 109, Division 1, 1935–36.

Highest League Scorer in Season: Dave Halliday, 43, Division 1, 1928–29.

Most League Goals in Total Aggregate: Charlie Buchan, 209, 1911–25.

MANAGERS
Tom Watson 1888–96
Bob Campbell 1896–99
Alex Mackie 1899–1905
Bob Kyle 1905–28
Johnny Cochrane 1928–39
Bill Murray 1939–57
Alan Brown 1957–64
George Hardwick 1964–65
Ian McColl 1965–68
Alan Brown 1968–72
Bob Stokoe 1972–76
Jimmy Adamson 1976–78
Ken Knighton 1979–81
Alan Durban 1981–84
Len Ashurst 1984–85
Lawrie McMenemy 1985–87
Denis Smith 1987–91
Malcolm Crosby 1992–93
Terry Butcher 1993
Mick Buxton 1993–95
Peter Reid March 1995–

Most League Goals in One Match: 5, Charlie Buchan v Liverpool, Division 1, 7 December 1919; 5, Bobby Gurney v Bolton W, Division 1, 7 December 1935; 5, Dominic Sharkey v Norwich C, Division 2, 20 February 1962.

Most Capped Player: Charlie Hurley, 38 (40), Republic of Ireland.

Most League Appearances: Jim Montgomery, 537, 1962–77.

Youngest League Player: Derek Forster, 15 years 184 days v Leicester C, 22 August 1964.

Record Transfer Fee Received: £5,600,000 from Leeds U for Michael Bridges, July 1999.

Record Transfer Fee Paid: £4,500,000 to Chelsea for Emerson Thome, September 2000.

Football League Record: 1890 Elected to Division 1; 1958–64 Division 2; 1964–70 Division 1; 1970–76 Division 2; 1976–77 Division 1; 1977–80 Division 2; 1980–85 Division 1; 1985–87 Division 2; 1987–88 Division 3; 1988–90 Division 2; 1990–91 Division 1; 1991–92 Division 2; 1992–96 Division 1; 1996–97 FA Premier League; 1997– 99 Division 1; 1999– FA Premier League.

LATEST SEQUENCES

Longest Sequence of League Wins: 13, 14.11.1891 – 2.4.1892.

Longest Sequence of League Defeats: 9, 23.11.76 – 15.1.77.

Longest Sequence of League Draws: 6, 26.3.49 – 19.4.49.

Longest Sequence of Unbeaten League Matches: 19, 3.5.98 – 14.11.98.

Longest Sequence Without a League Win: 14, 16.4.85 – 14.9.85.

TEN YEAR LEAGUE RECORD

		P	W	D	L	F	A	Pts	Pos
1990-91	Div 1	38	8	10	20	38	60	34	19
1991-92	Div 2	46	14	11	21	61	65	53	18
1992-93	Div 1	46	13	11	22	50	64	50	21
1993-94	Div 1	46	19	8	19	54	57	65	12
1994-95	Div 1	46	12	18	16	41	45	54	20
1995-96	Div 1	46	22	17	7	59	33	83	1
1996-97	PR Lge	38	10	10	18	35	53	40	18
1997-98	Div 1	46	26	12	8	86	50	90	3
1998-99	Div 1	46	31	12	3	91	28	105	1
1999-2000	PR Lge	38	16	10	12	57	56	58	7

DID YOU KNOW ?

On 9 December 2000, Sunderland celebrated their 2000th home League game with a 1–0 win over north-east rivals Middlesbrough at the Stadium of Light.

SUNDERLAND 2000–01 LEAGUE RECORD

Match No.	Date	Venue	Opponents	Result	H/T Score	Lg. Pos.	Goalscorers	Attendance
1	Aug 19	H	Arsenal	W	1-0	0-0	—	Quinn [53]	45,820
2	23	A	Manchester C	L	2-4	0-2	—	Quinn [64], Phillips [67]	34,410
3	26	A	Ipswich T	L	0-1	0-0	15		21,830
4	Sept 5	A	West Ham U	D	1-1	1-1	—	Arca [25]	45,285
5	9	A	Manchester U	L	0-3	0-1	18		67,503
6	16	H	Derby Co	W	2-1	1-0	14	Kilbane [40], Phillips [74]	43,898
7	23	A	Liverpool	D	1-1	1-1	14	Phillips [14]	44,713
8	Oct 1	A	Leicester C	D	0-0	0-0	14		44,153
9	14	H	Chelsea	W	1-0	0-0	10	Phillips (pen) [63]	43,185
10	22	A	Aston Villa	D	0-0	0-0	12		27,215
11	28	H	Coventry C	W	1-0	0-0	9	Emerson [52]	43,249
12	Nov 4	H	Tottenham H	L	1-2	0-1	12	Hutchison [63]	36,079
13	11	H	Southampton	D	2-2	1-1	12	Quinn [23], Hutchison [80]	43,711
14	18	A	Newcastle U	W	2-1	0-1	10	Hutchison [68], Quinn [76]	52,030
15	25	A	Charlton Ath	W	1-0	0-0	9	Rae [58]	20,043
16	Dec 4	H	Everton	W	2-0	1-0	—	Rae [45], Phillips [65]	43,736
17	9	H	Middlesbrough	W	1-0	0-0	5	Gray [54]	46,620
18	16	A	Leeds U	L	0-2	0-1	6		40,053
19	23	H	Manchester C	W	1-0	1-0	6	Hutchison [19]	45,686
20	26	A	Bradford C	W	4-1	1-0	3	Quinn [45], Phillips 3 [48, 55, 85]	20,370
21	30	A	Arsenal	D	2-2	0-2	4	Phillips (pen) [53], McCann [83]	38,026
22	Jan 1	H	Ipswich T	W	4-1	1-1	3	Arca [25], Phillips [57], Dichio [63], Schwarz [88]	43,314
23	13	A	West Ham U	W	2-0	1-0	2	Varga [22], Hutchison [68]	26,014
24	21	H	Bradford C	D	0-0	0-0	2		45,288
25	31	H	Manchester U	L	0-1	0-0	—		47,250
26	Feb 3	A	Derby Co	L	0-1	0-1	4		29,123
27	10	H	Liverpool	D	1-1	0-0	4	Hutchison [51]	46,231
28	24	H	Leicester C	L	0-2	0-1	4		21,086
29	Mar 5	H	Aston Villa	D	1-1	0-0	—	McCann [84]	44,114
30	17	A	Chelsea	W	4-2	1-2	4	Hutchison 2 [28, 52], McCann [61], Phillips [79]	34,981
31	31	H	Leeds U	L	0-2	0-1	6		46,833
32	Apr 9	A	Middlesbrough	D	0-0	0-0	—		31,099
33	14	H	Tottenham H	L	2-3	2-0	7	Kilbane [3], Quinn [12]	45,826
34	16	A	Coventry C	L	0-1	0-1	7		20,934
35	21	H	Newcastle U	D	1-1	0-0	8	Carteron [67]	47,213
36	28	A	Southampton	W	1-0	0-0	7	Kilbane [54]	15,249
37	May 5	H	Charlton Ath	W	3-2	2-1	7	Kilbane [11], Quinn [20], Phillips [50]	44,890
38	19	A	Everton	D	2-2	1-1	7	Phillips 2 [21, 83]	37,444

Final League Position: 7

GOALSCORERS

League (46): Phillips 14 (2 pens), Hutchison 8, Quinn 7, Kilbane 4, McCann 3, Arca 2, Rae 2, Carteron 1, Dichio 1, Emerson 1, Gray 1, Schwarz 1, Varga 1.
Worthington Cup (10): Hutchison 2, Phillips 2 (1 pen), Arca 1, Butler 1, Oster 1, Rae 1, Reddy 1, Thirlwell 1.
FA Cup (5): Phillips 2, Dichio 1, Kilbane 1, Quinn 1.

Sorensen T 34	Makin C 21+2	Gray M 36	Holloway D 5	Varga S 9+3	Butler P 3	Roy E 1+2	Thirlwell P 3+2	Quinn N 32+2	Phillips K 34	Kilbane K 26+4	Williams D 21+7	Reddy M —+2	Macho J 4+1	Bould S —+1	Hutchison D 30+2	Oster J 2+6	Craddock J 33+1	Emerson 30+1	Arca J 26+1	Rae A 18	Dichio D 2+13	McCann G 22	Schwarz S 17+3	McCartney G 1+1	Butler T —+4	Carteron P 8	Kyle K —+3	Match No.
1	2	3	4	5	6	7¹	8	9²	10	11	12	13		15														1
	2	3	4²	5¹	6	12	8¹	9	10	11		13	1	14	7													2
	2	3	4		6		8¹	9	10	11			1		7	12	5											3
	2	3	4					9	10	11			1		7	13	5	6	8									4
	2	3	4¹				12	9	10	11			1		7	13	5	6	8²									5
1	2	3						9	10	11	4				7		5	6	8									6
1	2	3						9	10	11	4				7		5	6	8									7
1	2	3						9	10	11	4				7	12	5	6	8¹									8
1	2	3					12	9²	10	11	4						5	6	8	7¹	13							9
1	2	3						9	10¹	11	4				12		5	6	8	7								10
1	2	3						9¹	10		4				11		5	6	8	7	12							11
1	2	3	4					9	10	11	6				12		5		8¹	7								12
1	2	3						9	10	11	4				8		5	6	7									13
1	2²	3						9¹	10	11	4				8		5	6	13	7	12							14
1	2	3						9¹	10	11	4				8		5	6	7		12							15
1		3	12					9¹	10²	11		2			13		5	6	8	7³		4	14					16
1		3						9	10	11		2					5	6	8	7		4						17
1		3						9¹	10	11		2					5	6	8	7	12	4						18
1	12	3						9		11¹		2			10²		5	6	8	7	13	4						19
1	2	3						9¹	10	11							5	6	8	7	12	4	13					20
1	2	3	4					9¹	10	11							5	6	8	7	12							21
1	2	3	12						10	11		13					5¹	6	8³	7	9	4	14					22
1		3	4					9¹	10	11	12	2					5	6	8	7								23
1		3						9²	10	11	12	2					5	6		7	13	4	8¹					24
1	14	3	4					9¹	10	11	12	2					5	6	8²	7	13³							25
1		3	4						10	11	12	2					5	6	8¹	7	9							26
1	2	3	5					9	10	11	12				4			6	8¹	7								27
1		3						9		11¹		2			10		5	6	8²			4	7				13	28
1	2	3						9¹		11					10²		5	6	8			4	7				13	29
1		3						9²		11	12				10		5	6	8¹		13	4	7			2		30
1		3						9		11³	12				10²		5¹	6	8		13	4	7	14		2		31
1		3						9		11¹	12	13			10		5	6	8³			4²	7	14		2		32
1		3						9¹	10	11	12				7		5	6	8			4				2		33
1		5	12	13				9		11		2			10²			6	8³	7¹		4		14		3		34
1		3						9	10	11							5	6	8	7		4				2		35
1		3						9²		11					10		5	6	8¹	7		4			12	2	13	36
1		3						9¹	10	11	12				8		5	6		7¹		4				2	13	37
1		3²						9³	10	11	12	13					5	6	8¹	7		4				2	14	38

Worthington Cup

Second Round	Luton T	(h)	3-0	
		(a)	2-1	
Third Round	Bristol R	(a)	2-1	
Fourth Round	Manchester U	(h)	2-1	
Fifth Round	Crystal Palace	(a)	1-2	

FA Cup

Third Round	Crystal Palace	(h)	0-0
		(a)	4-2
Fourth Round	Ipswich T	(h)	1-0
Fifth Round	West Ham U	(h)	0-1

SWANSEA CITY

Division 3

Vetch Field, Swansea SA1 3SU.
Telephone: (01792) 633 400. *Fax:* (01792) 646 120.
ClubCall: 09068 121 639. *Website:* www.swansfc.co.uk
Email: swans.prom@btinternet.com
Club Shop: (01792) 633 425.
Commercial Department: (01792) 633 422.
Youth Development: (01792) 633 410.

Ground Capacity: 10,402.

Record Attendance: 32,796 v Arsenal, FA Cup 4th rd, 17 February 1968.

Record Receipts: £36,477.42 v Liverpool, Division 1, 18 September 1982.

Pitch Measurements: 112yd × 74yd.

Chairman: Mike Lewis. *Vice-Chairman:* Neil McClure.
Directors: M. Nurse, M. Burgess.

Manager: John Hollins MBE.

Assistant Manager: Alan Curtis.

Physio: Richard Evans.

Director of Youth Development: Malcolm Elias.

Centre of Excellence Director: Jeremy Charles.

Football Development Officer: Lyndon Jones.

Club Secretary: Jackie Rockey.

Commercial Manager: Dianne Griffiths. *Safety Officer:* Don Goss.

Programme Editor: Major Reg Pike (01792) 474114.

Colours: White shirts with maroon and black facing, white shorts with maroon and black trim, white stockings with maroon ring top.

Change Colours: Maroon shirts with black and white facings, maroon shorts with black and white trim, maroon stockings with white band.

Year Formed: 1912. *Turned Professional:* 1912. *Ltd Co.:* 1912.

Previous Name: Swansea Town until February 1970. *Club Nickname:* 'The Swans'.

First Football League Game: 28 August 1920, Division 3, v Portsmouth (a) L 0–3 – Crumley; Robson, Evans; Smith, Holdsworth, Williams; Hole, I. Jones, Edmundson, Rigsby, Spottiswood.

Record League Victory: 8–0 v Hartlepool U, Division 4, 1 April 1978 – Barber; Evans, Bartley, Lally (1) (Morris), May, Bruton, Kevin Moore, Robbie James (3 incl. 1p), Curtis (3), Toshack (1), Chappell.

HONOURS

Football League: Division 1 best season: 6th, 1981–82; Division 2 – Promoted 1980–81 (3rd); Division 3 (S) – Champions 1924–25, 1948–49; Division 3 – Champions 1999–2000; Promoted 1978–79 (3rd); Division 4 – Promoted 1969–70 (3rd), 1977–78 (3rd), 1987–88 (play-offs).

FA Cup: Semi-finals 1926, 1964.

Football League Cup: best season: 4th rd, 1965, 1977.

Welsh Cup: Winners 9 times; Runners-up 8 times.

Autoglass Trophy: Winners 1994.

European Competitions: European Cup-Winners' Cup: 1961–62, 1966–67, 1981–82, 1982–83, 1983–84, 1989–90, 1991–92.

IT'S A FACT !

On 15 April 1953, all five forwards in the Wales team against Northern Ireland in Belfast: Terry Medwin, John Charles, Trevor Ford, Ivor Allchurch and Harry Griffiths were Swansea born and had played for Swansea Town at one time or another.

Record Cup Victory: 12–0 v Sliema W (Malta), ECWC 1st rd 1st leg, 15 September 1982 – Davies; Marustik, Hadziabdic (1), Irwin (1), Kennedy, Rajkovic (1), Loveridge (2) (Leighton James), Robbie James, Charles (2), Stevenson (1), Latchford (1) (Walsh (3)).

Record Defeat: 0–8 v Liverpool, FA Cup 3rd rd, 9 January 1990. 0–8 v Monaco, ECWC, 1st rd 2nd leg, 1 October 1991.

Most League Points (2 for a win): 62, Division 3 (S), 1948–49.

Most League Points (3 for a win): 85, Division 3, 1999–2000.

Most League Goals: 90, Division 2, 1956–57.

Highest League Scorer in Season: Cyril Pearce, 35, Division 2, 1931–32.

Most League Goals in Total Aggregate: Ivor Allchurch, 166, 1949–58, 1965–68.

Most League Goals in One Match: 5, Jack Fowler v Charlton Ath, Division 3S, 27 December 1924.

Most Capped Player: Ivor Allchurch, 42 (68), Wales.

Most League Appearances: Wilfred Milne, 585, 1919–37.

Youngest League Player: Nigel Dalling, 15 years 289 days v Southport, 6 December 1974.

Record Transfer Fee Received: £400,000 from Bristol C for Steve Torpey, August 1997.

Record Transfer Fee Paid: £340,000 to Liverpool for Colin Irwin, August 1981.

Football League Record: 1920 Original Member of Division 3; 1921–25 Division 3 (S); 1925–47 Division 2; 1947–49 Division 3 (S); 1949–65 Division 2; 1965–67 Division 3; 1967–70 Division 4; 1970–73 Division 3; 1973–78 Division 4; 1978–79 Division 3; 1979–81 Division 2; 1981–83 Division 1; 1983–84 Division 2; 1984–86 Division 3; 1986–88 Division 4; 1988–92 Division 3; 1992–96 Division 2; 1996–2000 Division 3; 2000–01 Division 2; 2001– Division 3.

MANAGERS

Walter Whittaker 1912–14
William Bartlett 1914–15
Joe Bradshaw 1919–26
Jimmy Thomson 1927–31
Neil Harris 1934–39
Haydn Green 1939–47
Bill McCandless 1947–55
Ron Burgess 1955–58
Trevor Morris 1958–65
Glyn Davies 1965–66
Billy Lucas 1967–69
Roy Bentley 1969–72
Harry Gregg 1972–75
Harry Griffiths 1975–77
John Toshack 1978–83
    (resigned October re-appointed in December) 1983–84
Colin Appleton 1984
John Bond 1984–85
Tommy Hutchison 1985–86
Terry Yorath 1986–89
Ian Evans 1989–90
Terry Yorath 1990–91
Frank Burrows 1991–95
Kevin Cullis 1996
Jan Molby 1996–97
Micky Adams 1997
Alan Cork 1997–98
John Hollins July 1998–

LATEST SEQUENCES

Longest Sequence of League Wins: 9, 27.11.99 – 22.100.
Longest Sequence of League Defeats: 9, 26.1.91 – 19.3.91.
Longest Sequence of League Draws: 5, 5.1.93 – 5.2.93.
Longest Sequence of Unbeaten League Matches: 19, 19.10.70 – 9.3.71.
Longest Sequence Without a League Win: 15, 25.3.89 – 2.9.89.

TEN YEAR LEAGUE RECORD

		P	W	D	L	F	A	Pts	Pos
1990-91	Div 3	46	13	9	24	49	72	48	20
1991-92	Div 3	46	14	14	18	55	65	56	19
1992-93	Div 2	46	20	13	13	65	47	73	5
1993-94	Div 2	46	16	12	18	56	58	60	13
1994-95	Div 2	46	19	14	13	57	45	71	10
1995-96	Div 2	46	11	14	21	43	79	47	22
1996-97	Div 3	46	21	8	17	62	58	71	5
1997-98	Div 3	46	13	11	22	49	62	50	20
1998-99	Div 3	46	19	14	13	56	48	71	7
1999-2000	Div 3	46	24	13	9	51	30	85	1

DID YOU KNOW ?

Herbie Williams scored 102 league goals for Swansea City from 1958 to 1974, having starred for Swansea schoolboys when they won the Welsh Shield and English Schools Trophy in 1955.

SWANSEA CITY 2000–01 LEAGUE RECORD

Match No.	Date	Venue	Opponents	Result		H/T Score	Lg. Pos.	Goalscorers	Attendance
1	Aug 12	H	Wigan Ath	D	0-0	0-0	—		8391
2	19	A	Brentford	D	0-0	0-0	18		5036
3	26	H	Colchester U	L	0-2	0-1	22		6247
4	28	A	Peterborough U	W	2-0	1-0	12	Bound (pen) [39], Price [47]	6428
5	Sept 9	A	Millwall	L	0-1	0-0	18		9550
6	12	A	Notts Co	W	1-0	1-0	—	Thomas [28]	3395
7	16	H	Luton T	W	4-0	2-0	10	Bound (pen) [32], Boyd [45], Cusack [70], Roberts [89]	6011
8	23	A	Reading	L	1-5	0-1	13	Watkin [62]	11,003
9	30	H	Bury	L	0-2	0-1	14		5362
10	Oct 14	H	Stoke C	W	2-1	0-0	13	Savarese 2 [59, 75]	6498
11	17	H	Swindon T	D	0-0	0-0	—		6333
12	21	A	Wrexham	L	0-1	0-1	15		4008
13	24	A	Rotherham U	L	2-4	1-2	—	Watkin [18], Bound [81]	3892
14	28	H	Port Vale	L	0-1	0-1	19		3715
15	31	H	Bristol C	D	2-2	1-1	—	Savarese 2 [9, 65]	5286
16	Nov 4	A	Oldham Ath	D	1-1	0-0	18	Savarese [85]	4282
17	11	H	Oxford U	L	1-2	1-2	21	Watkin [12]	4892
18	25	A	Cambridge U	D	3-3	0-3	21	Savarese 2 [76, 89], Watkin [90]	3269
19	Dec 2	H	Bristol R	D	0-0	0-0	22		5563
20	16	A	Bournemouth	L	0-2	0-1	22		3738
21	23	A	Wycombe W	L	1-2	0-2	22	Roberts [68]	5001
22	26	H	Walsall	W	3-1	1-1	21	Savarese [20], Jones S [56], Watkin [76]	5795
23	Jan 6	A	Wigan Ath	L	0-2	0-1	21		5571
24	13	H	Peterborough U	D	2-2	0-2	21	Savarese [49], Casey [83]	5288
25	20	A	Walsall	L	1-5	0-1	21	Watkin (pen) [68]	5227
26	Feb 3	A	Bristol C	L	1-3	1-1	22	Roberts [11]	10,379
27	11	H	Millwall	D	0-0	0-0	22		6905
28	17	A	Luton T	L	3-5	1-2	23	Savarese 3 [18, 65, 80]	7085
29	20	H	Notts Co	L	0-1	0-1	—		4058
30	24	H	Reading	L	0-1	0-1	23		5073
31	27	A	Northampton T	L	1-2	1-0	—	Fabiano [39]	4361
32	Mar 3	A	Bury	L	0-3	0-1	23		3443
33	7	A	Stoke C	W	2-1	2-0	—	Price [18], O'Leary [31]	10,091
34	10	H	Northampton T	D	1-1	0-1	23	Watkin [53]	4911
35	17	A	Swindon T	D	1-1	0-0	23	Roberts [76]	6724
36	31	H	Bournemouth	L	0-3	0-1	23		4013
37	Apr 3	A	Colchester U	L	0-3	0-1	—		2886
38	7	A	Bristol R	L	0-1	0-1	23		6505
39	10	H	Wycombe W	W	3-1	0-1	—	Boyd 2 [75, 90], Price [87]	3010
40	14	H	Rotherham U	D	0-0	0-0	23		4327
41	16	A	Port Vale	L	0-1	0-1	23		4396
42	21	H	Oldham Ath	L	1-2	1-0	23	Roberts [22]	3261
43	24	H	Wrexham	L	0-1	0-1	—		2665
44	28	A	Oxford U	L	1-3	1-1	23	Price [25]	4148
45	May 1	H	Brentford	W	6-0	2-0	—	Verschave 2 [3, 66], O'Leary [11], Cusack [47], Coates [55], Todd [79]	2002
46	5	H	Cambridge U	D	1-1	1-1	23	Verschave [45]	3383

Final League Position: 23

GOALSCORERS

League (47): Savarese 12, Watkin 7 (1 pen), Roberts 5, Price 4, Bound 3 (2 pens), Boyd 3, Verschave 3, Cusack 2, O'Leary 2, Casey 1, Coates 1, Fabiano 1, Jones S 1, Thomas 1, Todd 1.
Worthington Cup (1): Bound 1 (pen).
FA Cup (0).

Freestone R 43	Jones S 13	Howard M 39 + 2	O'Leary K 22 + 2	Smith J 22	Bound M 39 + 1	Price J 41	Thomas M 12 + 9	Cusack N 30 + 10	Watkin S 27 + 8	Coates J 16 + 3	Jenkins L 29 + 10	Mutton T 3 + 2	Phillips G 9 + 6	Boyd W 14 + 3	Roberts S 21 + 15	Casey R 3 + 6	Morgan B — + 5	Keegan M 4	Romo D 28 + 5	Savarese G 28 + 3	De-Vulgt L 6 + 1	Appleby R — + 5	Lacey D 17 + 1	Fabiano N 12 + 4	Verschave M 12	Jones J 3	Davies A — + 1	Todd C 11	Mumford A 2 + 4	Match No.
1	2	3	4	5	6	7	8¹	9²	10	11³	12	13	14																	1
1	2	3		5	6	7	12	4	10	11¹	8		9																	2
1	2	3¹		5	6	7	12	4	10	11²	8		9³	14	13															3
1	2	3		5	6	7	8	4	10	11			9																	4
1	2	3	6		5		8¹	4		11	12	10		9²		13														5
1		3	6		5	2	8	4		11	12	10⁵		9²	13		14	7¹												6
1		3	6		5	2	8	4		11¹	7		10	9²	12		13													7
1		3	6		5	2	8	4	12	11	7²		10³	9¹	13		14													8
1	2¹	3	6		5	7⁴	8	4	10	12	13	14		9³	11															9
1		3		5	6	2			10	7	8				11				4	9										10
1		3		5	6	2	12	13	10	7	8				11¹				4	9²										11
1		3		5	6	2	12	13	10	7¹	8				11³	14			4	9²										12
1		3¹	12	5	6	2	8	4	10	13	7				11²					9¹	14									13
1		3	11²	5¹	6	2¹	8	4	9	7					10	12			13	14										14
1				5	6	2			4	10					8				7	9										15
1				5	6	2	12	4	10²		8¹			13	11³				7	9	3	14								16
1		3		5	6	2	12	4	10		8			13	11³				7¹	9²		14								17
1	2	3	6			7	8	4	12		11³			10²	13					9	5¹	14								18
1	2	3	6	5			8	4	10						11				12	9		7¹								19
1	2	3	6	5				12	4	10					9	11¹²	13		8			7¹								20
1	2	3		5	6	7	8¹	4	12					13	11				10²	9										21
1	2	3		5	6	7		4	10	12					11¹				8	9										22
1	2¹	3	12	5	6	7		4	10²	13				14	11				8¹	9										23
1		3	4	5		7		12	10¹	8				11	13				6	9			2²							24
1	2	3	4	5		7		12	10	8				13					11²	9¹		6								25
1		3	4	5		7		12	13	8				11					6¹	10	9²		2							26
1			4	5	12	2				8¹				11					6²	10	9		3	13	7					27
1			4		6	2¹	12	13		8³				11					10	9	5		3²	14	7					28
1			4		6	2	12	13					14		11		14		8¹	10	9	5	3²		7³					29
1		3	4¹		5	7		12	10³		8		13		11		14		6²	9			2							30
1		3		5	7	12	4	10		8									6				2	9	11¹					31
1		3		5	7		4	12		8⁶	13								6	9¹			2²	10	11	1	15			32
1		3	8	5¹	6	7	4	10¹		12									13				2	9	11					33
1		3²		6	7		4	10	13		12				8¹								2	9²		6				34
1		3		5	7		4	10	12						11				8¹	13			2	9²		6				35
1		3	6	5	7		4	12	13					14					8²	9			2¹	10	11³					36
1		3²	6²	5	7		4	10	13		14				12				8	9			2¹	11						37
1		3		5	2¹		4²	10		8		7	13	12						9				11				6		38
1		3		5	7			10²				6	9	11		14	13				12	2³	8¹					4		39
1		3		5	2		12					7²	6	10	13				8	9			11¹					4		40
1		3		5	2³						8		7	10	12				6	9²		13	11¹					4	14	41
1		3		5	2		12			7	8		6²	10	11							13		9¹	1			4¹	14	42
1		3		6					10²	8		7	9	11					12			5		13	1			4	2¹	43
1	12			6	2³		13		10¹	8²		7		11						9	5			14				4	3	44
1		2		5				4		3	8¹	12		13					11³	9			10²	7				6	14	45
1	12	2¹		5				4		3	8		13						11³	9			10²	7				6	14	46

Worthington Cup
First Round   WBA   (h) 0-0
                               (a) 1-2

FA Cup
First Round   Bournemouth   (a) 0-2

SWINDON TOWN

Division 2

FOUNDATION

It is generally accepted that Swindon Town came into being in 1881, although there is no firm evidence that the club's founder, Rev. William Pitt, captain of the Spartans (an offshoot of a cricket club) changed his club's name to Swindon Town before 1883, when the Spartans amalgamated with St Mark's Young Men's Friendly Society.

County Ground, Swindon, Wiltshire SN1 2ED.

Telephone: (01793) 333 700. *Fax:* (01793) 333 703.

Marketing: (01793) 333 718. *Fax:* (01793) 333 719.

Superstore: (01793) 333 778. *Fax:* (01793) 333 780.

Community Office: (01793) 421 303.

ClubCall: 09068 121 640.

Ground Capacity: 15,728.

Record Attendance: 32,000 v Arsenal, FA Cup 3rd rd, 15 January 1972.

Record Receipts: £149,371 v Bolton W, Coca-Cola Cup semi-final, 1st leg, 12 February 1995.

Pitch Measurements: 110yd × 70yd.

Chief Executive: Peter Rowe.

Chairman: Terry Brady.

Directors: C. Puffett, G. Lux.

Manager: Andy King.

Assistant Manager: Malcolm Crosby.

Physio: Dick Mackey.

Company Secretary: Mike Squires.

Colours: Red shirts, white shorts, red stockings.

Change Colours: Light blue/dark blue panelled shirts and shorts, light blue stockings.

Year Formed: 1881* (*see Foundation*).

Turned Professional: 1894.

Ltd Co.: 1894.

Club Nickname: 'Robins'.

Previous Ground: 1881, The Croft; 1896, County Ground.

First Football League Game: 28 August 1920, Division 3, v Luton T (h) W 9–1 – Nash; Kay, Macconachie; Langford, Hawley, Wareing; Jefferson (1), Fleming (4), Rogers, Batty (2), Davies (1), (1 og).

HONOURS

FA Premier League: best season: 22nd 1993–94.

Football League: Division 2 – Champions 1995–96; Division 3 – Runners-up 1962–63, 1968–69; Division 4 – Champions 1985–86 (with record 102 points).

FA Cup: Semi-finals 1910, 1912.

Football League Cup: Winners 1969.

Anglo-Italian Cup: Winners 1970.

IT'S A FACT !

Swindon Town were two goals down against Bournemouth on 2 January 1926, but recovered spectacularly to win 8-2, with Frank 'Swerver' Richardson scoring four times.

Record League Victory: 9–1 v Luton T, Division 3 (S),
28 August 1920 – Nash; Kay, Macconachie; Langford,
Hawley, Wareing; Jefferson (1), Fleming (4), Rogers,
Batty (2), Davies (1), (1 og).

Record Cup Victory: 10–1 v Farnham U Breweries (away),
FA Cup 1st rd (replay), 28 November 1925 – Nash;
Dickenson, Weston, Archer, Bew, Adey; Denyer (2),
Wall (1), Richardson (4), Johnson (3), Davies.

Record Defeat: 1–10 v Manchester C, FA Cup 4th rd
(replay), 25 January 1930.

Most League Points (2 for a win): 64, Division 3, 1968–69.

Most League Points (3 for a win): 102, Division 4, 1985–86.

Most League Goals: 100, Division 3 (S), 1926–27.

Highest League Scorer in Season: Harry Morris, 47,
Division 3 (S), 1926–27.

Most League Goals in Total Aggregate: Harry Morris, 216,
1926–33.

Most League Goals in One Match: 5, Harry Morris v QPR,
Division 3S, 18 December 1926; 5, Harry Morris v
Norwich C, Division 3S, 26 April 1930; 5, Keith East v
Mansfield T, Division 3, 20 November 1965.

Most Capped Player: Rod Thomas, 30 (50), Wales.

Most League Appearances: John Trollope, 770, 1960–80.

Youngest League Player: Paul Rideout, 16 years 107 days v Hull C, 29 November 1980.

Record Transfer Fee Received: £1,500,000 from Manchester C for Kevin Horlock, January 1997.

Record Transfer Fee Paid: £800,000 to West Ham U for Joey Beauchamp, August 1994.

Football League Record: 1920 Original Member of Division 3; 1921–58 Division 3 (S);
1958–63 Division 3; 1963–65 Division 2; 1965–69 Division 3; 1969–74 Division 2; 1974–82 Division 3;
1982–86 Division 4; 1986–87 Division 3; 1987–92 Division 2; 1992–93 Division 1; 1993–94 FA Premier
League; 1994–95 Division 1; 1995–96 Division 2; 1996–2000 Division 1; 2000– Division 2.

MANAGERS
Sam Allen 1902–33
Ted Vizard 1933–39
Neil Harris 1939–41
Louis Page 1945–53
Maurice Lindley 1953–55
Bert Head 1956–65
Danny Williams 1965–69
Fred Ford 1969–71
Dave Mackay 1971–72
Les Allen 1972–74
Danny Williams 1974–78
Bobby Smith 1978–80
John Trollope 1980–83
Ken Beamish 1983–84
Lou Macari 1984–89
Ossie Ardiles 1989–91
Glenn Hoddle 1991–93
John Gorman 1993–94
Steve McMahon 1994–99
Jimmy Quinn 1999–2000
Colin Todd 2000
Andy King October 2000–

LATEST SEQUENCES

Longest Sequence of League Wins: 8, 12.1.86 – 15.3.86.

Longest Sequence of League Defeats: 6, 2.5.93 – 25.8.93.

Longest Sequence of League Draws: 6, 22.11.91 – 28.12.91.

Longest Sequence of Unbeaten League Matches: 22, 12.1.86 – 23.8.86.

Longest Sequence Without a League Win: 19, 30.10.99 – 4.3.00.

TEN YEAR LEAGUE RECORD

		P	W	D	L	F	A	Pts	Pos
1990-91	Div 2	46	12	14	20	65	73	50	21
1991-92	Div 2	46	18	15	13	69	55	69	8
1992-93	Div 1	46	21	13	12	74	59	76	5
1993-94	PR Lge	42	5	15	22	47	100	30	22
1994-95	Div 1	46	12	12	22	54	73	48	21
1995-96	Div 2	46	25	17	4	71	34	92	1
1996-97	Div 1	46	15	9	22	52	71	54	19
1997-98	Div 1	46	14	10	22	42	73	52	18
1998-99	Div 1	46	13	11	22	59	81	50	17
1999-2000	Div 1	46	8	12	26	38	77	36	24

DID YOU KNOW ?

Ernie Hunt was leading
goalscorer for Swindon Town
for four consecutive seasons
from 1960-61 with 14, 18, 24
and 12 League goals
respectively.

SWINDON TOWN 2000–01 LEAGUE RECORD

Match No.	Date	Venue	Opponents	Result	H/T Score	Lg. Pos.	Goalscorers	Attendance
1	Aug 12	H	Colchester U	D	0-0	0-0	—		7296
2	19	A	Reading	L	0-2	0-1	22		14,134
3	26	H	Walsall	L	1-4	1-2	23	Invincible [17]	5492
4	28	A	Port Vale	L	0-3	0-1	23		3926
5	Sept 9	A	Bristol C	W	1-0	0-0	21	Reeves [81]	10,110
6	12	A	Bournemouth	L	0-3	0-2	—		3673
7	23	A	Luton T	W	3-2	2-2	20	Duke [29], Williams M 2 [41, 67]	4933
8	30	H	Wigan Ath	D	2-2	2-1	21	Alexander [21], Robinson M [22]	4895
9	Oct 8	H	Oxford U	W	2-1	1-0	18	Reeves [20], Grazioli [79]	7975
10	14	A	Oldham Ath	L	0-1	0-0	19		4009
11	17	A	Swansea C	D	0-0	0-0	—		6333
12	21	H	Bristol R	L	1-3	0-3	21	Robertson (pen) [90]	8097
13	24	H	Millwall	L	0-2	0-1	—		5030
14	28	A	Notts Co	L	2-3	1-2	22	Invincible 2 [35, 54]	4502
15	31	H	Cambridge U	W	3-1	2-1	—	Invincible 2 [11, 35], O'Halloran [56]	3452
16	Nov 4	A	Wycombe W	D	1-1	0-1	22	Reeves [90]	5226
17	7	H	Wrexham	D	2-2	1-1	—	Invincible [32], O'Halloran (pen) [75]	4423
18	11	A	Peterborough U	L	0-4	0-2	22		5700
19	25	H	Stoke C	L	0-3	0-2	22		4904
20	Dec 2	A	Northampton T	W	1-0	1-0	21	Alexander [24]	5816
21	16	H	Rotherham U	W	2-1	1-1	20	Woan [5], Invincible [53]	4740
22	23	A	Bury	L	0-1	0-1	20		2921
23	26	H	Brentford	L	2-3	1-0	20	Invincible [5], Howe [78]	6649
24	Jan 1	A	Walsall	L	0-1	0-0	20		5548
25	13	H	Port Vale	L	0-1	0-0	22		5175
26	27	H	Bury	W	3-0	2-0	19	Reddy [4], O'Halloran (pen) [13], Cowe [67]	4960
27	Feb 4	A	Wrexham	D	1-1	1-0	19	Van der Linden [26]	3004
28	10	H	Bristol C	D	1-1	1-1	19	Reddy [33]	10,031
29	17	A	Cambridge U	W	1-0	0-0	19	Reddy [73]	4046
30	20	A	Bournemouth	D	1-1	0-0	24	Alexander [67]	5948
31	24	H	Luton T	L	1-3	1-1	20	Alexander [39]	7160
32	Mar 3	A	Wigan Ath	D	0-0	0-0	21		6563
33	6	H	Oldham Ath	W	3-0	1-0	—	Kelly (og) [8], McAreavey [80], Grazioli [90]	4168
34	10	A	Oxford U	W	2-0	1-0	19	Robinson S 2 [29, 90]	7480
35	17	A	Swansea C	D	1-1	0-0	20	O'Halloran (pen) [81]	6724
36	20	A	Colchester U	W	1-0	1-0	—	Reddy [28]	2736
37	24	A	Bristol R	D	0-0	0-0	18		8114
38	27	H	Reading	L	0-1	0-0	—		9674
39	31	A	Rotherham U	L	3-4	2-2	20	Alexander 2 [6, 28], Woan [49]	7106
40	Apr 7	H	Northampton T	D	1-1	1-1	20	Woan [2]	5932
41	10	A	Brentford	W	1-0	0-0	—	Heywood [52]	4180
42	14	A	Millwall	L	0-1	0-0	19		12,266
43	16	A	Notts Co	L	1-2	1-0	20	Heywood [35]	6207
44	21	A	Wycombe W	D	0-0	0-0	19		6844
45	28	H	Peterborough U	W	2-1	1-0	19	Alexander [7], Invincible [90]	8145
46	May 5	A	Stoke C	L	1-4	0-4	20	O'Halloran (pen) [55]	20,591

Final League Position: 20

GOALSCORERS

League (47): Invincible 9, Alexander 7, O'Halloran 5 (4 pens), Reddy 4, Reeves 3, Woan 3, Grazioli 2, Heywood 2, Robinson S 2, Williams M 2, Cowe 1, Duke 1, Howe 1, McAreavey 1, Robertson 1 (pen), Robinson M 1, Van der Linden 1, own goal 1.
Worthington Cup (4): Howe 1, Invincible 1, Reeves 1, own goal 1.
FA Cup (9): Cowe 2, Howe 2, O'Halloran 2, Williams M 1, Willis 1, Young 1.

Gruenink B 24+1	Robinson M 29+5	Davis S 35+1	O'Halloran K 40	Reeves A 42+2	Willis A 21	Invincible D 32+10	Hewlett M 25+1	Alexander G 30+7	Grazioli G 10+18	Duke D 24+8	Cowe S 5+4	Howe B 17+2	Griffin C 1+1	Cobian J 3	Heiselberg K 1	Van der Linden A 17+16	Williams A 3+5	Williams M 17+2	Tuomela 1+1	Robertson M 4+6	Young A —+4	Woan A —+4	Mildenhall S 22+1	Drydan R 7	Whitley J 2	Hall G 3+4	Williams J 6+1	Lightbourne K 2	McHugh F 3+1	Heywood M 21	Reddy M 17+1	Robinson S 18	McAreavey P 2+1	Mills J —+2	Bakalli A 1	Match No.
1	2	3	4	5	6	7	8	9	10^1	11^2	12	13																								1
1	2	3	4	5	6	7	8	9	10^1	11^2				12	13																					2
1	12		4	5		7	8	9	10					11	2	3^1	6																			3
1	2	3	4^2	5	6		8		12	11		7		9	10^1			13																		4
1	2	3	4	5	6	7^1	8		12	11				9						10																5
1	2	3	4	5	6^3	7	8^2		12	11^1				9						10	14	13														6
1	12	3	4	5		13	8	9		11^2					2^1					10	6	7^3	14													7
1	2	3	4	5	6	7	8	9		11																										8
1	2	3	4	5	6	7^3	8	9^1	12	11^2						14	13	10																		9
1	2	3	4	5	6^3	7	8^2	9^1	12	11						14	13	10																		10
1	2	3	4	5	6	7		9^1	12	11^2				8				10^3		13	14															11
1	2	3	4	5^2	6	7			10	11^2				8		14	13	9^1	12																	12
1	2^3	3	4	12	6	7			13	14				8^2		5	11	9^1		10																13
1	2	3^1	4	5	6	7^2			12					8		10		9		13			11													14
1	2		4	5	3	7			12	11		13		6		9^1		8^2		10																15
1	2	3^2	4	5	6	7			12					8^1		10		9^1		13			11		15											16
1	2	3	4^3	5	6	7			12	13				8^2		10		9^1		14			11													17
1	2	3^2	4		6	7			12	13	14			8		10		9^1		5^3			11													18
1	2^3	3	4	5	6	7			12	13	14			8^2				9^1		11			10													19
1	2	3	4	5		7^1		9		11^2				8		13		12		10			6													20
1	2	3				7^2		9	12					8		13		10^1		11			6			4										21
1	2	3^1		5		7^2		9^1	12					8		14		13		11			6		10											22
1	2^3	3	4	5		7		9^2	12					8		13		10^1		11			6		14											23
1		3	4	5		7		9^2	11	12		8^1	2^3	13				10					6		14											24
	3	4	5		7			12	13	8^3				10^1					14	11		6	2		9^2											25
		8^2	5		2			12				3	7	6						14			1		13	10^1	11		4	9^3						26
13		8	5		12^2	9				3	2			6						11^1	1			7				4	10							27
	3	6		5	12				13	11	8^1			10						1				2^2	7			4	9						28
	6^1	7	5			8	12		3^2					11						1				2		13	4	9	10						29
15		3	6	5		12	8	9		11										1^6				7^1			4	10	2						30
		6	5		12	8^2	9	13	3					2						1				11^1			4	10^1	7						31
		5		7		9	12	3^2						6						1				13	11	8	4	10^1	2						32
12			5		7	11^3	9	10						2						1					3^1		6^2	4	8	13	14				33
	2	3		5		12	6	9	10^1											11	1						4	8	7						34
	2^1	3^2	6	5		12	8	9					13							11	1						4	10	7						35
	2	3	6	5			8	9	10^1				12							1							4	11	7						36
	2	3	6	5		12	8	9	10^2				13							11^1	1						4		7						37
	2^1	3	6	5		12	8	9^1	13				14							11	1						4	10^2	7						38
	2	3	6^2	5		12	8	9^1	13				14							11	1						4	10^3	7						39
	2	3	6	5		12	8	9^2					13							11	1						4	10^1	7						40
12		3	6^1	5			2	8	9											11^1	1						4	10	7						41
	2^1			5		8		9^1	10					3	12					11^1	1			14			4	13	7	6					42
12	3			5		7^1	8	9^1	13					14	2^1					1							4	10	11	6					43
		6	5	2		7	8	9	12	3										1							4	10^1	11						44
		6	5	2	11	8	9		3					12						13	1						4	10^1	7^2						45
		6	12	5	11		13	10	3					8^1	2^2					1							4		7		14	9^3			46

Worthington Cup

First Round	Exeter C	(h)	1-1	
		(a)	2-1	
Second Round	Tranmere R	(a)	1-1	
		(h)	0-1	

FA Cup

First Round	Ilkeston T	(h)	4-1
Second Round	Gateshead	(h)	5-0
Third Round	Coventry C	(h)	0-2

TORQUAY UNITED

Division 3

FOUNDATION

The idea of establishing a Torquay club was agreed by old boys of Torquay College and Torbay College, while sitting in Princess Gardens listening to the band. A proper meeting was subsequently held at Tor Abbey Hotel at which officers were elected. This was on 1 May 1899 and the club's first competition was the Eastern League (later known as the East Devon League). As an amateur club it played at Teignmouth Road, Torquay Recreation Ground and Cricket Field Road before settling down for four years at Torquay Cricket Ground where the rugby club now plays. They became Torquay United in 1921 after merging with Babbacombe FC.

Plainmoor Ground, Torquay, Devon TQ1 3PS.

Telephone: (01803) 328 666. *Fax:* (01803) 323 976.

Ground Capacity: 6283.

Record Attendance: 21,908 v Huddersfield T, FA Cup 4th rd, 29 January 1955.

Record Receipts: £30,824 v Plymouth Arg, Division 3, 25 March 2000.

Pitch Measurements: 112yd × 74yd.

Chairman/Managing Director: M. Bateson.

Financial Director: Mrs H. Kindeleit-Badcock.

Directors: Mrs S. Bateson, M. Benney, I. Hayman, B. Palk.

Manager:

Physio: Norman Medhurst.

Company Secretary: Mrs H. Kindeleit-Badcock.

Colours: Yellow shirts with navy and white inserts under arm and white V. neck, navy shorts with yellow stripe, yellow stockings.

Change Colours: Blue shirts with yellow sleeves, yellow shorts, yellow stockings with blue tops.

Year Formed: 1899.

Turned Professional: 1921.

Ltd Co.: 1921.

Previous Name: 1910, Torquay Town; 1921, Torquay United.

Club Nickname: 'The Gulls'.

Previous Grounds: 1899, Teignmouth Road; 1900, Torquay Recreation Ground; 1904, Cricket Field Road; 1906, Torquay Cricket Ground; 1910, Plainmoor Ground.

HONOURS

Football League: Division 3 best season: 4th, 1967–68; Division 3 (S) – Runners-up 1956–57; Division 4 – Promoted 1959–60 (3rd), 1965–66 (3rd), 1990–91 (play-offs).

FA Cup: best season: 4th rd, 1949, 1955, 1971, 1983, 1990.

Football League Cup: never past 3rd rd.

Sherpa Van Trophy: Runners-up 1989.

IT'S A FACT !

In 1989-90, Carl Airey equalled Sam Collins' record set during the 1954-55 season of scoring in seven successive League matches.

First Football League Game: 27 August 1927, Division 3 (S), v Exeter C (h) D 1–1 – Millsom; Cook, Smith; Wellock, Wragg, Connor, Mackey, Turner (1), Jones, McGovern, Thomson.

Record League Victory: 9–0 v Swindon T, Division 3 (S), 8 March 1952 – George Webber; Topping, Ralph Calland; Brown, Eric Webber, Towers; Shaw (1), Marchant (1), Northcott (2), Collins (3), Edds (2).

Record Cup Victory: 7–1 v Northampton T, FA Cup 1st rd, 14 November 1959 – Gill; Penford, Downs; Bettany, George Northcott, Rawson; Baxter, Cox, Tommy Northcott (1), Bond (3), Pym (3).

Record Defeat: 2–10 v Fulham, Division 3 (S), 7 September 1931. 2–10 v Luton T, Division 3 (S), 2 September 1933.

Most League Points (2 for a win): 60, Division 4, 1959–60.

Most League Points (3 for a win): 77, Division 4, 1987–88.

Most League Goals: 89, Division 3 (S), 1956–57.

Highest League Scorer in Season: Sammy Collins, 40, Division 3 (S), 1955–56.

Most League Goals in Total Aggregate: Sammy Collins, 204, 1948–58.

Most League Goals in One Match: 5, Robin Stubbs v Newport Co, Division 4, 19 October 1963.

Most Capped Player: Rodney Jack, St Vincent.

Most League Appearances: Dennis Lewis, 443, 1947–59.

Youngest League Player: David Byng, 16 years 36 days v Walsall, 14 August 1993.

Record Transfer Fee Received: £500,000 from Crewe Alex for Rodney Jack, July 1998.

Record Transfer Fee Paid: £70,000 to Barry T for Eifion Williams, March 1999.

Football League Record: 1927 Elected to Division 3 (S); 1958–60 Division 4; 1960–62 Division 3; 1962–66 Division 4; 1966–72 Division 3; 1972–91 Division 4; 1991– Division 3.

MANAGERS

Percy Mackrill 1927–29
A. H. Hoskins 1929
  (Secretary-Manager)
Frank Womack 1929–32
Frank Brown 1932–38
Alf Steward 1938–40
Billy Butler 1945–46
Jack Butler 1946–47
John McNeil 1947–50
Bob John 1950
Alex Massie 1950–51
Eric Webber 1951–65
Frank O'Farrell 1965–68
Alan Brown 1968–71
Jack Edwards 1971–73
Malcolm Musgrove 1973–76
Mike Green 1977–81
Frank O'Farrell 1981–82
  (continued as General Manager to 1983)
Bruce Rioch 1982–84
Dave Webb 1984–85
John Sims 1985
Stuart Morgan 1985–87
Cyril Knowles 1987–89
Dave Smith 1989–91
John Impey 1991–92
Ivan Golac 1992
Paul Compton 1992–93
Don O'Riordan 1993–95
Eddie May 1995–96
Kevin Hodges *(Head Coach)* 1996–98
Wes Saunders 1998–2001

LATEST SEQUENCES

Longest Sequence of League Wins: 8, 24.1.98 – 3.3.98.

Longest Sequence of League Defeats: 8, 30.9.95 – 18.11.95.

Longest Sequence of League Draws: 8, 25.10.69 – 13.12.69.

Longest Sequence of Unbeaten League Matches: 15, 5.5.90 – 3.11.90.

Longest Sequence Without a League Win: 17, 5.3.38 – 10.9.38.

TEN YEAR LEAGUE RECORD

		P	W	D	L	F	A	Pts	Pos
1990-91	Div 4	46	18	18	10	64	47	72	7
1991-92	Div 3	46	13	8	25	42	68	47	23
1992-93	Div 3	42	12	7	23	45	67	43	19
1993-94	Div 3	42	17	16	9	64	56	67	6
1994-95	Div 3	42	14	13	15	54	57	55	13
1995-96	Div 3	46	5	14	27	30	84	29	24
1996-97	Div 3	46	13	11	22	46	62	50	21
1997-98	Div 3	46	21	11	14	68	59	74	5
1998-99	Div 3	46	12	17	17	47	58	53	20
1999-2000	Div 3	46	19	12	15	62	52	69	9

DID YOU KNOW ?

Torquay United were deprived of a final place in the 1938-39 Third Division (South) Cup held over to the next season, but cancelled by the war. Their semi-final win had been an impressive 4-2 victory over Crystal Palace, who were runners-up in the division.

TORQUAY UNITED 2000–01 LEAGUE RECORD

Match No.	Date	Venue	Opponents	Result	H/T Score	Lg. Pos.	Goalscorers	Attendance
1	Aug 12	A	Kidderminster H	L	0-2	0-1	—	5122
2	19	H	Southend U	D	1-1	0-1	22	Hill [50]	2528
3	26	A	Cheltenham T	L	0-2	0-1	22		3568
4	28	H	Blackpool	W	3-2	0-1	15	Sissoko [51], Williams 2 [89, 90]	2384
5	Sept 2	A	Brighton & HA	L	2-6	2-4	21	Parker [33], Mendy [38]	5804
6	9	H	Lincoln C	D	1-1	0-1	22	Bedeau [71]	2131
7	12	H	Hartlepool U	W	1-0	1-0	—	Williams [29]	1538
8	16	A	Rochdale	L	1-2	0-2	22	Herrera [53]	2871
9	23	H	Halifax T	L	1-2	1-2	22	Hill [26]	1921
10	30	A	Scunthorpe U	L	0-3	0-2	23		2922
11	Oct 8	H	Leyton Orient	L	1-2	0-1	23	Hill [88]	1925
12	14	A	Darlington	L	0-2	0-1	23		3518
13	17	A	Macclesfield T	L	1-2	1-1	—	Williams [32]	1681
14	21	H	Carlisle U	W	4-2	2-1	22	Ford (pen) [6], Holmes [19], Tully [57], Hill [81]	1778
15	24	H	Mansfield T	D	2-2	0-1	—	Hill [49], Mendy [75]	1880
16	28	A	Shrewsbury T	D	1-1	0-0	22	O'Brien [84]	2319
17	Nov 4	H	Plymouth Arg	D	1-1	0-1	22	Williams [63]	3936
18	11	A	York C	L	2-3	2-2	23	Ford (pen) [31], Chalqi [45]	2415
19	25	H	Barnet	W	2-1	2-1	21	Bedeau [32], Sissoko [45]	1735
20	Dec 2	A	Cardiff C	L	1-4	1-0	22	Bedeau [43]	2427
21	16	A	Hull C	W	2-1	0-0	21	Bedeau [59], Williams [90]	4708
22	23	H	Chesterfield	D	0-0	0-0	21		2248
23	26	A	Exeter C	D	1-1	0-1	21	Williams [90]	4592
24	30	A	Southend U	D	1-1	0-1	20	Williams [60]	3643
25	Jan 1	H	Kidderminster H	D	1-1	0-0	21	Lyons [89]	2467
26	6	H	Cheltenham T	L	1-2	1-0	22	Hill [15]	2383
27	13	A	Blackpool	L	0-5	0-2	22		3549
28	20	H	Exeter C	W	2-1	1-0	21	Ford (pen) [45], Parker [90]	4053
29	27	A	Chesterfield	L	0-3	0-0	21		4364
30	Feb 3	H	Brighton & HA	L	0-1	0-0	21		2909
31	10	A	Lincoln C	W	2-1	1-1	18	Kell [12], Holmes [65]	2392
32	17	H	Rochdale	W	1-0	1-0	17	Hill [23]	2195
33	20	A	Hartlepool U	L	1-3	0-1	—	Hockley [87]	3932
34	24	A	Halifax T	L	1-2	0-0	20	Neil (pen) [81]	1783
35	Mar 3	H	Scunthorpe U	L	0-2	0-2	21		1868
36	10	A	Leyton Orient	W	2-0	2-0	22	Rees [24], Aggrey [30]	4390
37	23	A	Carlisle U	L	0-1	0-0	—		4828
38	31	H	Hull C	D	1-1	0-0	24	Kell (pen) [90]	2779
39	Apr 7	A	Cardiff C	L	1-2	1-0	24	Graham [31]	8210
40	10	H	Macclesfield T	W	2-0	1-0	—	Bedeau [18], Williams [79]	2911
41	14	A	Mansfield T	D	0-0	0-0	22		2225
42	16	H	Shrewsbury T	D	0-0	0-0	23		3482
43	21	A	Plymouth Arg	L	1-3	1-0	24	Kell (pen) [21]	5711
44	24	A	Darlington	W	2-1	0-0	—	Law [60], Gayle [88]	2810
45	28	H	York C	D	2-2	0-1	22	Hill [59], Aggrey [86]	4505
46	May 5	A	Barnet	W	3-2	3-0	21	Rees [10], Hill [25], Graham [66]	5523

Final League Position: 21

GOALSCORERS

League (52): Hill 9, Williams 9, Bedeau 5, Ford 3 (3 pens), Kell 3 (2 pens), Aggrey 2, Graham 2, Holmes 2, Mendy 2, Parker 2, Rees 2, Sissoko 2, Chalqi 1, Gayle 1, Herrera 1, Hockley 1, Law 1, Lyons 1, Neil 1 (pen), O'Brien 1, Tully 1.
Worthington Cup (3): Bedeau 2, Hill 1.
FA Cup (2): Chalqi 1, Ford 1 (pen).

Jones S 16	Holmes P 28 + 4	Platts M 2 + 2	Aggrey J 41	Tully S 28 + 1	Watson A 29 + 1	Brandon C 1 + 1	Ford M 28	Parker K 8 + 7	Sissoko H 7 + 7	Hill K 43 + 1	O'Brien M 7 + 14	Stocco T — + 2	Ashington R 9 + 5	Mendy J 7 + 14	Northmore R 24 + 1	Douglin T 3	Williams E 31 + 6	Herrera R 29	Benefield J — + 1	Neil G 9 + 4	Bedeau A 33 + 1	Russell L 27	Rowbotham J 4 + 1	Chalqk K 20 + 1	Hockley M 4 + 2	Rees J 25	Gayle J 5 + 8	Lyons S — + 9	Law G 2 + 8	Kell R 15	Green R 10	Petterson A 6	Graham D 5	Match No.
1	2[1]	3	4	5	6	7	8	9	10	11[2]	12	13																						1
1	2	3	4	5	6		8	9[2]	10[1]	11		12	7	13																				2
1[9]	2	12	4	5	6		8	9		11			7[1]	10	15	3[2]	13																	3
				5	6		4	9	10	11[2]	12		7	8[2]	1	2	13	3																4
1			4	5		2	8	9[2]		7[3]	11		13	12		6[1]	10	3	14															5
1			4[1]	5		6	8	9		11	7[2]			12			13	3		2	10													6
1	2		4			6	8	12		11	7[3]	13					10[1]	3[2]		14	9	5												7
1	2					6	8	12		11	7[2]		13				10[1]	3		4	9	5												8
1	2[1]	13	6	12		8	10[3]	11		7[2]			14				3			4	9	5												9
	2[2]	13	4	6		8	10[1]			11				12		1	14	3		7[3]	9	5												10
	2[1]		4	5		8[3]	12			11	7[2]		14	13	1		10	3			9	6												11
12		4[3]	2	5		8	13			11			7[1]	14			10[2]	3			9	6												12
12		4	2	6		8[1]	13			11[2]			7[3]	14			10	3			9	5												13
	2	4	5	6		8[1]				11	12		7[2]	13	1		10[2]	3		14	9													14
	2	4	5	6		8				11	12		7[1]	13	1		10	3		9[2]														15
	2	4	5	6						11	12		7	8	1		10	3[1]			9													16
	3	4	2	5		6				13	11	12	7[1]	8[1]	1		10				9													17
		4	2	6		8[1]				13	3[3]	12		9[2]	1		10			14		5	7	11										18
1		4	2	6		8				10[1]	11			12							9		7	3	5									19
1		4	2[1]	6		8				12	7[2]	13		14			10[3]	3			9			11	5									20
1		4	2	6		8				5							10	3			9						7	11[1]	12					21
1		4	2	5		8				6				11[1]			10	3			9						7	12						22
1		4	2	5		8				6[1]	12			11[3]			10	3			9						7[2]	13	14					23
1		4	2	5		8				12							10	3			9				6[8]		7	13	11[1]					24
1		4	2	5		8				6							10	3			9				11[1]		7	12						25
		4	2[1]	5		8				12	6	13					10	3[4]			9				11[3]		7	14						26
12		4	2[1]	5		8				9	11[2]						1	10		3	13	14	6	7[3]										27
12		4	2			8	13			11[2]							1	10		3[1]	7	9[3]	5	6	14									28
3		4	2[2]			8	12			11							1	9		10		5	6[1]	7	13									29
3		4	2							12				1			10			6	9	5	11[1]	7[2]	8	13								30
3		4	2	6						11							1	10			9	5		7					8					31
		4	2[1]	6						11							1	10		3	9[2]	5		12	7	13			8					32
		4	2[2]	6						11[1]							1	10		3	9	5		13	7	12			8					33
2			6							11				12			1	10		3	4[2]	5			7[1]	9[3]	13	14	8					34
2[2]		4								11							1	10		3	8[1]	9	5	13	7	12			6					35
		4								11							3	12		9	5	6		7	10[2]	13	8	2						36
		4								11							10	3			5	6[2]	2	7	9[1]	12	13	8	1					37
		4					9[1]			11							3			5	6	7	12	8	2	1	10							38
2		4						12	11				13				9	5		6	7		8[1]	3	1	10								39
2		4						11	13					12			9	5		6	7[2]		8	3	1	10[1]								40
2		4					12	11	13					10[1]			9[3]	5		6	7		14	8[2]	3	1								41
2		4					12	11						10[1]			9	5		6	7		8	3	1									42
2		4					10[2]	11	12								9	5		6	7[1]		13	8	3									43
3		4						11					1				9	5		6	2[1]	7	12	13	8				10[2]					44
3[1]		4						11					1				12	9	5	6	7		13	10[2]	8	2								45
1	3	4	12					6	13					10[3]			9	5		7[2]	14		8	2		11[1]								46

Worthington Cup
First Round   Gillingham   (a)   0-2
                                              (h)   3-2

FA Cup
First Round   Southend U   (h)   1-1
                                              (a)   1-2

TOTTENHAM HOTSPUR   FA Premiership

FOUNDATION

The Hotspur Football Club was formed from an older cricket club in 1882. Most of the founders were old boys of St John's Presbyterian School and Tottenham Grammar School. The Casey brothers were well to the fore as the family provided the club's first goalposts (painted blue and white) and their first ball. They soon adopted the local YMCA as their meeting place, but after a couple of moves settled at the Red House, which is still their headquarters, although now known simply as 748 High Road.

Bill Nicholson Way, 748 High Rd, Tottenham, London N17 0AP.

Telephone: (020) 8365 5000. *Fax:* (020) 8365 5005.
Spurs ticket line: 08700 112 222. *Ticket information line:* 09068 100 505. *Spurs Line:* 09068 100 500.
Members Office: (020) 8365 5150. *Commercial Dept:* (020) 8365 5010.

Ground Capacity: 36,236.

Record Attendance: 75,038 v Sunderland, FA Cup 6th rd, 5 March 1938.

Record Receipts: £336,702 v Manchester U, Division 1, 28 September 1991.

Pitch Measurements: 110yd × 73yd.

Executive Directors: D Buchler (Vice-Chairman), J. Sedgwick (Finance Director), David Pleat (Director of Football).

Non-Executive Directors: D. Levy (Chairman).
M. S. Peters MBE, I. Yawetz, C. T. Sandy.

President: W. E. Nicholson OBE.

Vice-Presidents: N. Solomon, D. A. Alexiou, A. G. Berry.

Manager: Glenn Hoddle. *Assistant Manager:* John Gorman.
First Team Coach: Chirs Hughton. *Reserve Team Manager:* Theo Foley. *Chief Physio:* Alasdair Beattie.

Club Secretary: John Alexander. *Sales Manager:* Scot Gardiner.

Public Relations Officer: John Fennelly.

Colours: White shirts, navy blue shorts, navy blue stockings.

Change Colours: Argentina blue shirts, white shorts and stockings.

Year Formed: 1882. *Turned Professional:* 1895. *Ltd Co.:* 1898.

Previous Name: 1882–84, Hotspur Football Club.

Club Nickname: 'Spurs'.

Previous Grounds: 1882, Tottenham Marshes; 1888, Northumberland Park; 1899, White Hart Lane.

HONOURS

Football League: Division 1 – Champions 1950–51, 1960–61; Runners-up 1921–22, 1951–52, 1956–57, 1962–63; Division 2 – Champions 1919–20, 1949–50; Runners-up 1908–09, 1932–33; Promoted 1977–78 (3rd).

FA Cup: Winners 1901 (as non-League club), 1921, 1961, 1962, 1967, 1981, 1982, 1991; Runners-up 1987.

Football League Cup: Winners 1971, 1973, 1999; Runners-up 1982.

European Competitions: *European Cup:* 1961–62. *European Cup-Winners' Cup:* 1962–63 (winners), 1963–64, 1967–68, 1981–82, 1982–83, 1991–92. *UEFA Cup:* 1971–72 (winners), 1972–73, 1973–74 (runners-up), 1983–84 (winners), 1984–85, 1999–2000.

IT'S A FACT !

In the last match of the 1909–10 season, Chelsea needed a win at Tottenham to avoid relegation. But Spurs won 2–1, the winning goal scored by Percy Humphreys who had been signed from Chelsea.

First Football League Game: 1 September 1908, Division 2, v Wolverhampton W (h) W 3–0 – Hewitson; Coquet, Burton; Morris (1), D. Steel, Darnell; Walton, Woodward (2), Macfarlane, R. Steel, Middlemiss.

Record League Victory: 9–0 v Bristol R, Division 2, 22 October 1977 – Daines; Naylor, Holmes, Hoddle (1), McAllister, Perryman, Pratt, McNab, Moores (3), Lee (4), Taylor (1).

Record Cup Victory: 13–2 v Crewe Alex, FA Cup 4th rd (replay), 3 February 1960 – Brown; Hills, Henry; Blanchflower, Norman, Mackay; White, Harmer (1), Smith (4), Allen (5), Jones (3 incl. 1p).

Record Defeat: 0–8 v Cologne, UEFA Inter Toto Cup, 22 July 1995.

Most League Points (2 for a win): 70, Division 2, 1919–20.

Most League Points (3 for a win): 77, Division 1, 1984–85.

Most League Goals: 115, Division 1, 1960–61.

Highest League Scorer in Season: Jimmy Greaves, 37, Division 1, 1962–63.

Most League Goals in Total Aggregate: Jimmy Greaves, 220, 1961–70.

Most League Goals in One Match: 5, Ted Harper v Reading, Division 2, 30 August 1930; 5, Alf Stokes v Birmingham C, Division 1, 18 September 1957; 5, Bobby Smith v Aston Villa, Division 1, 29 March 1958.

Most Capped Player: Pat Jennings, 74 (119), Northern Ireland.

Most League Appearances: Steve Perryman, 655, 1969–86.

Youngest League Player: Ally Dick, 16 years 301 days v Manchester C, 20 February 1982.

Record Transfer Fee Received: £5,500,000 from Lazio for Paul Gascoigne, May 1992.

Record Transfer Fee Paid: £11,000,000 to Dynamo Kiev for Sergei Rebrov, May 2000.

Football League Record: 1908 Elected to Division 2; 1909–15 Division 1; 1919–20 Division 2; 1920–28 Division 1; 1928–33 Division 2; 1933–35 Division 1; 1935–50 Division 2; 1950–77 Division 1; 1977–78 Division 2; 1978–92 Division 1; 1992– FA Premier League.

MANAGERS

Frank Brettell 1898–99
John Cameron 1899–1906
Fred Kirkham 1907–08
Peter McWilliam 1912–27
Billy Minter 1927–29
Percy Smith 1930–35
Jack Tresadern 1935–38
Peter McWilliam 1938–42
Arthur Turner 1942–46
Joe Hulme 1946–49
Arthur Rowe 1949–55
Jimmy Anderson 1955–58
Bill Nicholson 1958–74
Terry Neill 1974–76
Keith Burkinshaw 1976–84
Peter Shreeves 1984–86
David Pleat 1986–87
Terry Venables 1987–91
Peter Shreeves 1991–92
Ossie Ardiles 1993–94
Gerry Francis 1994–97
Christian Gross *(Head Coach)* 1997–98
George Graham 1998–2001
Glenn Hoddle April 2001–

LATEST SEQUENCES

Longest Sequence of League Wins: 13, 23.4.60 – 1.10.60.
Longest Sequence of League Defeats: 7, 1.1.94 – 27.2.94.
Longest Sequence of League Draws: 6, 9.1.99 – 27.2.99.
Longest Sequence of Unbeaten League Matches: 22, 31.8.49 – 31.12.49.
Longest Sequence Without a League Win: 16, 29.12.34 – 13.4.35.

TEN YEAR LEAGUE RECORD

		P	W	D	L	F	A	Pts	Pos
1990-91	Div 1	38	11	16	11	51	50	49	10
1991-92	Div 1	42	15	7	20	58	63	52	15
1992-93	PR Lge	42	16	11	15	60	66	59	8
1993-94	PR Lge	42	11	12	19	54	59	45	15
1994-95	PR Lge	42	16	14	12	66	58	62	7
1995-96	PR Lge	38	16	13	9	50	38	61	8
1996-97	PR Lge	38	13	7	18	44	51	46	10
1997-98	PR Lge	38	11	11	16	44	56	44	14
1998-99	PR Lge	38	11	14	13	47	50	47	11
1999-2000	PR Lge	38	15	8	15	57	49	53	10

DID YOU KNOW ?

During November–December 1995, Tottenham Hotspur completed 602 minutes without conceding a goal in the Premier League. The sequence began in a 2–1 win over Arsenal and ended in a 2–2 draw with Bolton Wanderers.

TOTTENHAM HOTSPUR 2000–01 LEAGUE RECORD

Match No.	Date	Venue	Opponents	Result		H/T Score	Lg. Pos.	Goalscorers	Attendance
1	Aug 19	H	Ipswich T	W	3-1	2-1	—	Anderton (pen) [30], Carr [31], Ferdinand [82]	36,044
2	22	A	Middlesbrough	D	1-1	1-0	—	Leonhardsen [41]	31,254
3	26	A	Newcastle U	L	0-2	0-1	11		51,503
4	Sept 5	H	Everton	W	3-2	1-2	—	Rebrov 2 (1 pen) [45, 61 (p)], Ferdinand [62]	35,923
5	11	H	West Ham U	W	1-0	0-0	—	Campbell [67]	33,133
6	16	A	Charlton Ath	L	0-1	0-1	5		20,043
7	23	H	Manchester C	D	0-0	0-0	6		36,065
8	30	A	Leeds U	L	3-4	1-0	10	Rebrov 2 [37, 74], Perry [60]	37,562
9	Oct 14	A	Coventry C	L	1-2	0-2	11	Rebrov [53]	21,430
10	21	H	Derby Co	W	3-1	2-1	8	Leonhardsen 2 [4, 48], Carr [45]	34,459
11	28	A	Chelsea	L	0-3	0-2	12		34,934
12	Nov 4	H	Sunderland	W	2-1	1-0	10	Sherwood [43], Armstrong [79]	36,079
13	11	A	Aston Villa	L	0-2	0-1	11		33,608
14	19	H	Liverpool	W	2-1	2-1	9	Ferdinand [32], Sherwood [41]	36,051
15	25	H	Leicester C	W	3-0	2-0	8	Ferdinand 3 [34, 39, 84]	35,638
16	Dec 2	A	Manchester U	L	0-2	0-1	9		67,583
17	9	A	Bradford C	D	3-3	2-1	9	King [1], Campbell [21], Armstrong [54]	17,225
18	18	H	Arsenal	D	1-1	1-0	—	Rebrov [31]	36,062
19	23	H	Middlesbrough	D	0-0	0-0	11		35,638
20	27	A	Southampton	L	0-2	0-2	—		15,237
21	30	A	Ipswich T	L	0-3	0-1	13		22,234
22	Jan 2	A	Newcastle U	W	4-2	3-1	-1	Doherty [27], Anderton (pen) [30], Rebrov [35], Ferdinand [77]	34,323
23	13	A	Everton	D	0-0	0-0	10		32,290
24	20	H	Southampton	D	0-0	0-0	10		36,091
25	31	A	West Ham U	D	0-0	0-0	—		26,048
26	Feb 3	A	Charlton Ath	D	0-0	0-0	11		35,368
27	10	A	Manchester C	W	1-0	0-0	11	Rebrov [89]	34,399
28	24	H	Leeds U	L	1-2	1-1	12	Ferdinand [33]	36,070
29	Mar 3	A	Derby Co	L	1-2	0-2	12	West (og) [70]	29,410
30	17	H	Coventry C	W	3-0	2-0	11	Iversen [29], Ferdinand [34], Rebrov [59]	35,606
31	31	A	Arsenal	L	0-2	0-0	12		38,121
32	Apr 10	H	Bradford C	W	2-1	1-1	—	Iversen [26], Davies [76]	28,300
33	14	A	Sunderland	W	3-2	0-2	9	Clemence [53], Doherty 2 [75, 88]	45,826
34	17	H	Chelsea	L	0-3	0-1	—		36,079
35	22	H	Liverpool	L	1-3	1-1	11	Korsten [24]	43,547
36	28	H	Aston Villa	D	0-0	0-0	11		36,096
37	May 5	A	Leicester C	L	2-4	0-1	12	Davies [54], Carr [61]	21,056
38	19	H	Manchester U	W	3-1	1-1	12	Korsten 2 [17, 67], Ferdinand [75]	36,078

Final League Position: 12

GOALSCORERS

League (47): Ferdinand 10, Rebrov 9 (1 pen), Carr 3, Doherty 3, Korsten 3, Leonhardsen 3, Anderton 2 (2 pens), Armstrong 2, Campbell 2, Davies 2, Iversen 2, Sherwood 2, Clemence 1, King 1, Perry 1, own goal 1.
Worthington Cup (3): Anderton 1 (pen), Iversen 1, Leonhardsen 1.
FA Cup (13): Doherty 3, Rebrov 3, Davies 2, Anderton 1, King 1, Leonhardsen 1, own goals 2.

Sullivan N 35	Carr S 27 + 1	Thatcher B 10 + 2	Freund S 19 + 2	Campbell S 21	Perry C 30 + 2	Anderton D 22 + 1	Sherwood T 31 + 2	Rebrov S 28 + 1	Iversen S 10 + 4	Leonhardsen O 23 + 2	Taricco M 2 + 3	Ferdinand L 25 + 3	Young L 19 + 4	Clemence S 27 + 2	Vega R 8 + 2	Doherty G 18 + 4	Walker 13 + 1	Dominguez J — + 2	Davies S 9 + 4	Korsten W 8 + 6	Armstrong C 3 + 6	Thelwell A 13 + 3	King L 18	McEwen D — + 3	Booth A 3 + 1	Etherington M 1 + 5	Gardner A 5 + 3	Piercy J — + 5	Match No
1	2	3^1	4	5	6	7	8	9	10^2	11	12	13																	1
1	2	3	4	5	6	7	8	9^1	10	11		12																	2
1	2	3^1	4	5	6	7	8	9	10^1	11^1	13	12	14																3
1	2	3^1	4	5	6	7^3	8	9	13	11	12	10^2		14															4
1	2	12	4	5		7	9	8	11	3^1	10	6^2		13															5
1	2		4	5	12	7^1	9	8	11^2	3	10			13	6														6
1	2	3^1	4		6	7	9	8	11			10^2	12	5	13														7
1	2	3	4		6	12	7	9	8	11		10^1		5															8
	2	3	4^1		6	7	8	9	12	11^3		10		5			1	13											9
1	2	3			6	7^3	8	9^2		11^1		10		4	5				12	14	13								10
1	2		4^1		6	7	8					9	3	11	5	13			12	10^2									11
1	2	3			6	7	8	9^1				10	4	11	5				12										12
1	2	3			6	7	8	9^1				10^2	4	11	5				12	13									13
1	2	12			6	7	8^1	9^2				10		5	11					13		3	4						14
1	2^2	12	13	5	6^1	7	8	9^1	10	3													14	4	11				15
1	2			5	6	7	8					10		11				12		9^1		3	4						16
1	2		7	5	6		8^1					10	3	12						9^2		4	11						17
1	2			5	6	7	8	9^1				10	3	12								4	11						18
1	2			5	6	7	8^1	9			12	10^2	3							13		4	11						19
1	2^1			5	6	7	12	9^3	8				3	14						13	10^2	4	11						20
1				5	6	7	8^1	12					4	3		9			13	10^1	2	11							21
1				5	6	7^1	8	9			2^9	10	12	3		4	15			11									22
1				6	2	8	9		11^1			4	3	5						12^2	10^2	7	13						23
		8^1	5	6	7		9		12			10^2	2	3		4	1				11	13							24
		8	5	6	2		9^2		7			12	3^1	4	1						11	13	10						25
1		8	5	6	2	12	9		7				3^1	4							11^1	10	13						26
1	12	7	5	6^2	2^1	8	9		11			3		10							4	13							27
1		7	5				8	9	12			10^1	2	3^1	4	11^2				13	6		14						28
1		7	5				8		12			10	2	3^1	4					6^2	11		9		13				29
1		7	5	6				9	8			10	2	3	4						11								30
1		7		5					2			9	3		4				11^1	10^2	8					12	6	13	31
1	2			6			8	9	10^2	7^1		4	3	5					11	12	13								32
1	2			6			8	9		7^1		5	3	10					11^3	12		4^2					13	14	33
1	2			6^2			4	9		3		7^1	10						11^3	8		5					12 13	14	34
1	2						8			4		3	7^1	9					11^1	10		5				6	12		35
1	2						8			4		9^1	3	7	5				11^{12}	10	13					12	6		36
1	2						8			4		10	3	7	9				11		5						6		37
1	2						12			4		9	3	7^1	5				11	8						10^2	6^1	13	38

Worthington Cup

Second Round	Brentford	(a)	0-0
		(h)	2-0
Third Round	Birmingham C	(h)	1-3

FA Cup

Third Round	Leyton Orient	(a)	1-0
Fourth Round	Charlton Ath	(a)	4-2
Fifth Round	Stockport Co	(h)	4-0
Sixth Round	West Ham U	(a)	3-2
Semi-Final	Arsenal		1-2
(at Old Trafford)			

TRANMERE ROVERS Division 2

FOUNDATION

Formed in 1884 as Belmont they adopted their present title the following year and eventually joined their first league, the West Lancashire League in 1889–90, the same year as their first success in the Wirral Challenge Cup. The club almost folded in 1899–1900 when all the players left en bloc to join a rival club, but they survived the crisis and went from strength to strength winning the 'Combination' title in 1907–08 and the Lancashire Combination in 1913–14. They joined the Football League in 1921 from the Central League.

Prenton Park, Prenton Road West, Prenton, Wirral CH42 9PY.

Telephone: (0151) 609 3333. *Fax:* (0151) 608 4385.
Shop: (0151) 609 3311. *Ticket Office:* (0151) 609 3322.
ClubCall: 09068 121 646

Ground Capacity: 16,587 (all seated).

Record Attendance: 24,424 v Stoke C, FA Cup 4th rd, 5 February 1972.

Record Receipts: £268,946 v Liverpool, FA Cup 6th rd, 11 March 2001.

Pitch Measurements: 110yd × 70yd.

Chairperson: Lorraine Rogers.

Directors: Lorraine Rogers, Mick Horton, Richard Hughes.

Secretary: Mick Horton.

Manager: Dave Watson

Assistant Manager: TBA.

Youth Development Officer: Warwick Rimmer.

Coach and Chief Scout: Dave Philpotts.

Reserve Team Coach: TBA.

Physio: Les Parry.

Colours: White shirts and shorts with blue trim.

Change Colours: Navy and royal blue shirt and shorts.

Year Formed: 1884.

Turned Professional: 1912.

Ltd Co.: 1920.

Previous Name: 1884, Belmont AFC; 1885, Tranmere Rovers.

Club Nickname: 'The Rovers'.

HONOURS

Football League Division 1 best season: 4th, 1992–93; Promoted from Division 3 1990–91 (play-offs); Division 3 (N) – Champions 1937–38; Promotion to 3rd Division: 1966–67, 1975–76; Division 4 – Runners-up 1988–89.

FA Cup: best season: 6th rd, 2000, 2001.

Football League Cup: Runners-up, 2000.

Welsh Cup: Winners 1935; Runners-up 1934.

Leyland Daf Cup: Winners 1990; Runners-up 1991.

IT'S A FACT !

On 20 February 2001, Tranmere Rovers were trailing 3-0 to Southampton in the first half of their FA Cup fifth round replay, when they staged a remarkable recovery to win 4-3.

Previous Grounds: 1884, Steeles Field; 1887, Ravenshaws Field/Old Prenton Park; 1912, Prenton Park.

First Football League Game: 27 August 1921, Division 3 (N), v Crewe Alex (h) W 4–1 – Bradshaw; Grainger, Stuart (1); Campbell, Milnes (1), Heslop; Moreton, Groves (1), Hyam, Ford (1), Hughes.

Record League Victory: 13–4 v Oldham Ath, Division 3 (N), 26 December 1935 – Gray; Platt, Fairhurst; McLaren, Newton, Spencer; Eden, MacDonald (1), Bell (9), Woodward (2), Urmson (1).

Record Cup Victory: 13–0 v Oswestry U, FA Cup 2nd prel rd, 10 October 1914 – Ashcroft; Stevenson, Bullough, Hancock, Taylor, Holden (1), Moreton (1), Cunningham (2), Smith (5), Leck (3), Gould (1).

Record Defeat: 1–9 v Tottenham H, FA Cup 3rd rd (replay), 14 January 1953.

Most League Points (2 for a win): 60, Division 4, 1964–65.

Most League Points (3 for a win): 80, Division 4, 1988–89 and Division 3, 1989–90.

Most League Goals: 111, Division 3 (N), 1930–31.

Highest League Scorer in Season: Bunny Bell, 35, Division 3 (N), 1933–34.

Most League Goals in Total Aggregate: Ian Muir, 142, 1985–95.

Most League Goals in One Match: 9, Bunny Bell v Oldham Ath, Division 3N, 26 December 1935.

Most Capped Player: John Aldridge, 30 (69), Republic of Ireland.

Most League Appearances: Harold Bell, 595, 1946–64 (incl. League record 401 consecutive appearances).

Youngest League Player: Iain Hume, 16 years 167 days v Swindon T, 15 April 2000.

Record Transfer Fee Received: £3,300,000 from Everton for Steve Simonsen, September 1998.

Record Transfer Fee Paid: £450,000 to Aston Villa for Shaun Teale, August 1995.

Football League Record: 1921 Original Member of Division 3 (N): 1938–39 Division 2; 1946–58 Division 3 (N); 1958–61 Division 3; 1961–67 Division 4; 1967–75 Division 3; 1975–76 Division 4; 1976–79 Division 3; 1979–89 Division 4; 1989–91 Division 3; 1991–92 Division 2; 1992–2001 Division 1; 2001– Division 2.

MANAGERS

Bert Cooke 1912–35
Jackie Carr 1935–36
Jim Knowles 1936–39
Bill Ridding 1939–45
Ernie Blackburn 1946–55
Noel Kelly 1955–57
Peter Farrell 1957–60
Walter Galbraith 1961
Dave Russell 1961–69
Jackie Wright 1969–72
Ron Yeats 1972–75
John King 1975–80
Bryan Hamilton 1980–85
Frank Worthington 1985–87
Ronnie Moore 1987
John King 1987–96
John Aldridge 1996–2001
Dave Watson April 2001–

LATEST SEQUENCES

Longest Sequence of League Wins: 9, 9.2.90 – 19.3.90.

Longest Sequence of League Defeats: 8, 29.10.38 – 17.12.38.

Longest Sequence of League Draws: 5, 26.12.97 – 31.1.98.

Longest Sequence of Unbeaten League Matches: 18, 16.3.70 – 4.9.70.

Longest Sequence Without a League Win: 16, 8.11.69 – 14.3.70.

TEN YEAR LEAGUE RECORD

		P	W	D	L	F	A	Pts	Pos
1990-91	Div 3	46	23	9	14	64	46	78	5
1991-92	Div 2	46	14	19	13	56	56	61	14
1992-93	Div 1	46	23	10	13	72	56	79	4
1993-94	Div 1	46	21	9	16	69	53	72	5
1994-95	Div 1	46	22	10	14	67	58	76	5
1995-96	Div 1	46	14	17	15	64	60	59	13
1996-97	Div 1	46	17	14	15	63	56	65	11
1997-98	Div 1	46	14	14	18	54	57	56	14
1998-99	Div 1	46	12	20	14	63	61	56	15
1999-2000	Div 1	46	15	12	19	57	68	57	13

DID YOU KNOW ?

Tranmere Rovers' successful action in winning the 1937-38 Third Division (North) championship was off the field directed by Jim Knowles in his role as the club's new secretary-manager. He was a former film extra.

TRANMERE ROVERS 2000–01 LEAGUE RECORD

Match No.	Date	Venue	Opponents	Result		H/T Score	Lg. Pos.	Goalscorers	Attendance
1	Aug 12	A	Wimbledon	D	0-0	0-0	—		8266
2	19	H	Gillingham	W	3-2	3-1	7	Gill [4], Flynn [9], Hill [45]	8355
3	26	A	Sheffield U	L	0-2	0-1	16		12,074
4	28	H	Bolton W	L	0-1	0-0	18		9350
5	Sept 1	H	Stockport Co	W	2-1	2-1	—	Allison [27], Gill (pen) [32]	7229
6	9	A	Wolverhampton W	W	2-1	1-1	7	Allison [43], Barlow (pen) [83]	17,252
7	12	A	Portsmouth	L	0-2	0-0	—		9235
8	16	H	Sheffield W	W	2-0	1-0	5	Taylor 2 [15, 90]	9352
9	23	A	Birmingham C	L	0-2	0-0	8		17,640
10	30	H	Crewe Alex	L	1-3	0-2	12	Parkinson [82]	8162
11	Oct 6	H	Burnley	L	2-3	0-1	—	Koumas [57], Hill [64]	10,153
12	14	A	Preston NE	L	0-1	0-0	14		14,511
13	17	A	Barnsley	D	1-1	1-0	—	Allison [42]	12,412
14	21	H	WBA	D	2-2	1-2	15	Butler (og) [28], Barlow [90]	8931
15	25	A	Blackburn R	L	2-3	1-3	—	Koumas [30], Taylor [90]	17,010
16	28	H	QPR	D	1-1	0-0	17	Koumas [58]	7263
17	Nov 4	A	Norwich C	L	0-1	0-0	19		13,688
18	11	H	Watford	W	2-0	1-0	16	Hill [19], Taylor [60]	8858
19	18	A	Crystal Palace	L	2-3	2-1	15	Koumas [12], Hill [26]	14,221
20	25	A	Nottingham F	L	1-3	1-2	19	Hill [3]	19,678
21	Dec 2	H	Blackburn R	D	1-1	0-0	19	Parkinson [59]	10,063
22	9	H	Grimsby T	W	2-0	0-0	16	Parkinson [52], Koumas [68]	7119
23	16	A	Fulham	L	1-3	1-2	17	Koumas [7]	13,157
24	23	H	Wimbledon	L	0-4	0-1	20		8058
25	26	A	Huddersfield T	L	0-3	0-1	21		14,043
26	Jan 1	H	Sheffield U	W	1-0	1-0	20	Parkinson [11]	8474
27	13	A	Bolton W	L	0-2	0-2	21		15,493
28	Feb 3	A	Stockport Co	D	1-1	0-1	22	Rideout [90]	7804
29	10	H	Wolverhampton W	L	0-2	0-1	22		9678
30	13	A	Sheffield W	L	0-1	0-0	—		15,444
31	27	H	Huddersfield T	W	2-0	2-0	—	Allison [1], Yates [38]	10,621
32	Mar 3	A	Crewe Alex	L	1-3	1-0	24	Parkinson [45]	7157
33	6	H	Preston NE	D	1-1	0-1	—	Allison [59]	10,335
34	14	H	Portsmouth	D	1-1	1-0	—	Allison [28]	9872
35	17	H	Barnsley	L	2-3	2-0	24	Taylor [1], Koumas [20]	8484
36	20	A	Gillingham	L	1-2	1-1	—	Koumas [10]	7810
37	25	A	WBA	L	1-2	0-1	24	Koumas [85]	17,151
38	30	H	Fulham	L	1-4	0-2	—	Osborn [90]	12,362
39	Apr 7	A	Grimsby T	L	1-3	1-0	24	Koumas [27]	5816
40	10	H	Birmingham C	W	1-0	0-0	—	N'Diaye [70]	8004
41	14	H	Norwich C	L	0-1	0-0	24		9303
42	16	A	QPR	L	0-2	0-1	24		9696
43	21	H	Crystal Palace	D	1-1	0-1	24	Parkinson [47]	8119
44	24	A	Burnley	L	1-2	1-1	—	Yates [20]	13,717
45	28	A	Watford	D	1-1	0-0	24	N'Diaye [61]	16,063
46	May 6	H	Nottingham F	D	2-2	1-0	24	Rideout [14], Mellon [90]	9891

Final League Position: 24

GOALSCORERS

League (46): Koumas 10, Allison 6, Parkinson 6, Hill 5, Taylor 5, Barlow 2 (1 pen), Gill 2 (1 pen), N'Diaye 2, Rideout 2, Yates 2, Flynn 1, Mellon 1, Osborn 1, own goal 1.
Worthington Cup (10): Parkinson 2, Rideout 2, Allison 1, Barlow 1, Gill 1, Hill 1, Taylor 1, Yates 1.
FA Cup (11): Yates 4, Rideout 3, Allison 1, Barlow 1, Koumas 1, Parkinson 1.

Achterberg J 24 + 1	Yates S 41 + 2	Roberts G 33 + 1	Flynn S 35	Challinor D 18 + 4	Hill C 34	Gill W 7 + 9	Henry N 17 + 3	Rideout P 28 + 3	Allison W 32 + 4	Taylor S 24 + 13	Hinds R 24 + 5	Aldridge P — + 2	Koumas J 34 + 5	Parkinson A 29 + 10	Barlow S 12 + 15	Hazell R 11 + 2	Morgan A 3 + 4	Murphy J 19 + 1	Allen G 21 + 1	Hamilton D 5 + 1	Hume I — + 10	Myhre T 3	Jobson R 16	Mellon M 11 + 2	Kenna J 11	N'Diaye S 5 + 3	Osborn S 9	Olsen J — + 1	Match No.
1	2	3	4	5	6	7	8^1	9	10	11^2	12	13																	1
1	2	3	4	5	6	7	8^1	9	10	11	12																		2
1	2	3		5	6	7^1	8^2	9	10	11^1	4		12	13	14														3
1	2	3		5	6	7^2	4	9	10	11^1	13		8^3	14	12														4
1		3	4	5	6	7^1	8	9^2	10	11	2		12	13															5
1	2	3	4	5	6		8	9	10	11^1	7		12																6
1		3	4^2	5	6		8^3	9	10	11^1	7		12	14		2	13												7
1		3	4	5	6	12	8^1	9	10	11	2^3		13	7^2	14														8
1	2	3	4^3	5	6		8^2	9	10	11^1	7		12	13		14													9
1	2	3	4	5	6	7^2	8^1	9	10	11		14	12	13															10
1		3		4	5	6		9^1	10	11	2		12	8		7													11
	2	3	4	12	6			13	14	7			11	10^3	9^2	8		1	5^1										12
	2	3	4		6			9	10	12	7		11	8^1		5		1											13
	2	3	4	5				9^1	10	11			7^2	8^3	14	6	13	1											14
	2^1	3	4	12	6			10^2	13	7			11	8		5		1	9										15
	2	3	4	5	6			9		7			11	12	8^1			1	10										16
		3	4	5	6	12		10	9^2	7			11	8	13	2^1		1											17
	2	3	4	5	6	12		13	10	9^2	7		11	8^1															18
	2	3	4	5	6	12		9	10	11^2			7	8^1	13			1											19
	2	3	4	5^2	6		12		10	9^3	7		11	8^1				1	13	14									20
12		3	4		6	13	9^2	10	11^3	2			7^1	8		5			14	1									21
	2	3	4			12		9	10^1	11^2			7	8		6			5	13		1							22
	2	3					4^2	9	12	11^1	7	13	10	8^3		6			5	14		1							23
12	3^1	4		6				9	10	11			7	8		2^2		1	5	13									24
	2^1	12	4		6	13	10^3	9		14	7^2		11	8		3		1	5										25
1	2	3	4		6	12		9		13	7^3		11^2	8	10^1	14			3				5						26
1	2	3	4		6	7^3		12	9	13			10^1	8		11^2	14						5						27
1		3	7		6			9			2		10	8		4^1	11		12				5						28
1		3	7^1	5	6			9^2	12		2		11	8		10	13			4									29
1	2		4^1		6			9	12	7			10	8^2		3	11		13				5						30
1	2	3			12	4			10	13	7		11^1	8	9^2			6						5					31
1	2	3			12	4			10	13	7^1		11^2	8	9			6						5					32
1	2	3				4			10				11	8	9			6						5	7				33
1	2	3	12						10	13	7		11	8	9^2			6						5^1	4				34
1	2	3				4			10		9		11	8^1	12			6						5	7				35
1		3				4	12	10^1	9^3				11	8^2	13			6						5	7	2	14		36
1		3	4					9^1	12				11	10^2				6						5	7	2	13	8	37
		3	4					9^2	10^1				11		12			1	6					5	7	2	13	8	38
1^6	5	3	4						12				11	8^1	13	15	6							7		2	9^1	10	39
	3	7		6				10^2					11	12	13			1	4					5		2	9^8	8	40
	3	7	12	6				10^2					11		13			1	4^1					5	14	2	9	8^3	41
	3	7		6				12	9^1				11	8^2	13			1	4^2	14				5	10	2			42
	5	3	4		6			9^1		12			11	13	10			1							7^2	2	8		43
15	5	3	4^2		6			9		12			11	8^1	10			1^8						13	2		7		44
	5	3			6			9^1		12				10	4	1								7	2	11	8		45
	5	3^3			6^1			9		12				10^2	4	1				13				7	2	11	8	14	46

Worthington Cup

First Round	Halifax T	(h)	3-0
		(a)	2-1
Second Round	Swindon T	(h)	1-1
		(a)	1-0
Third Round	Leeds U	(h)	3-2
Fourth Round	Crystal Palace	(a)	0-0

FA Cup

Third Round	Portsmouth	(a)	2-1
Fourth Round	Everton	(a)	3-0
Fifth Round	Southampton	(a)	0-0
		(h)	4-3
Sixth Round	Liverpool	(h)	2-4

WALSALL Division 1

FOUNDATION

Two of the leading clubs around Walsall in the 1880s were Walsall Swifts (formed 1877) and Walsall Town (formed 1879). The Swifts were winners of the Birmingham Senior Cup in 1881, while the Town reached the 4th round (5th round modern equivalent) of the FA Cup in 1883. These clubs amalgamated as Walsall Town Swifts in 1888, becoming simply Walsall in 1895.

Bescot Stadium, Bescot Crescent, Walsall WS1 4SA.

Telephone: (01922) 622 791. *Fax:* (01922) 613 202.
ClubCall: 09068 555 800. *Website:* www.saddlers.co.uk
Email: wfc@saddlers.co.uk
Commercial Dept: (01922) 651 412.

Ground Capacity: 9000.

Record Attendance: 10,628 B International, England v Switzerland, 20 May 1991.

Record Receipts: £98,828 v Leeds U, FA Cup 3rd rd, 7 January 1995.

Pitch Measurements: 110yd × 73yd.

HONOURS

Football League: Division 2: Runners-up, 1998–99, Promoted to Division 1 – 2000–01 (play-offs); Division 3 – Runners-up 1960–61, 1994–95; Division 4 – Champions 1959–60; Runners-up 1979–80.

FA Cup: best season: 5th rd, 1939, 1975, 1978, 1987 and last 16 1889.

Football League Cup: Semi-final 1984.

Chairman and Managing Director: M. N. Lloyd.
Directors: J. W. Bonser, R. E. Tisdale, C. Welch, K. R. Whalley. *Chief Executive:* K. R. Whalley.
Director of Finance: K. Avery. *Director of Football:* P. Taylor. *Director of Conference and Banqueting Services:* C. Deakin.

Manager: Ray Graydon. *General Manager:* Paul Taylor. *Physio:* Duncan Russell.

Secretary/Commercial Manager: Roy Whalley.

Year Formed: 1888. *Turned Professional:* 1888. *Ltd Co.:* 1921.

Previous Names: Walsall Swifts (founded 1877) and Walsall Town (founded 1879) amalgamated in 1888 and were known as Walsall Town Swifts until 1895.

Club Nickname: 'The Saddlers'.

Colours: Red shirts with black shoulder panel, black shorts with white trim, red stockings with white band.

Change Colours: Royal blue shirts with yellow side panel, royal blue shorts with yellow side panel, royal blue stockings with white band.

Previous Grounds: 1888, Fellows Park; 1990, Bescot Stadium.

First Football League Game: 3 September 1892, Division 2, v Darwen (h) L 12 – Hawkins; Withington, Pinches; Robinson, Whitrick, Forsyth; Marshall, Holmes, Turner, Gray (1), Pangbourn.

Record League Victory: 10–0 v Darwen, Division 2, 4 March 1899 – Tennent; E. Peers (1), Davies; Hickinbotham, Jenkyns, Taggart; Dean (3), Vail (2), Aston (4), Martin, Griffin.

Record Cup Victory: 7–0 v Macclesfield T (a), FA Cup 2nd rd, 6 December 1997 – Walker; Evans, Marsh, Viveash (1), Ryder, Peron, Boli (2 incl. 1p) (Ricketts), Porter (2), Keates, Watson (Platt), Hodge (2 incl. 1p).

IT'S A FACT !

Three Walsall players: Tom Johnson (4 goals), Alf Griffin and George Johnson all scored hat-tricks in Walsall's 11-0 FA Cup win against Dresden United in a third qualifying round FA Cup tie on 21 November 1896.

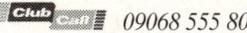

Record Defeat: 0–12 v Small Heath, 17 December 1892. 0–12 v Darwen, 26 December 1896, both Division 2.

Most League Points (2 for a win): 65, Division 4, 1959–60.

Most League Points (3 for a win): 87, Division 2, 1998–99.

Most League Goals: 102, Division 4, 1959–60.

Highest League Scorer in Season: Gilbert Alsop, 40, Division 3 (N), 1933–34 and 1934–35.

Most League Goals in Total Aggregate: Tony Richards, 184, 1954–63; Colin Taylor, 184, 1958–63, 1964–68, 1969–73.

Most League Goals in One Match: 5, Gilbert Alsop v Carlisle U, Division 3N, 2 February 1935; 5, Bill Evans v Mansfield T, Division 3N, 5 October 1935; 5, Johnny Devlin v Torquay U, Division 3S, 1 September 1949.

Most Capped Player: Mick Kearns, 15 (18), Republic of Ireland.

Most League Appearances: Colin Harrison, 467, 1964–82.

Youngest League Player: Geoff Morris, 16 years 218 days v Scunthorpe U, 14 September 1965.

Record Transfer Fee Received: £600,000 from West Ham U for David Kelly, July 1988.

Record Transfer Fee Paid: £175,000 to Birmingham C for Alan Buckley, June 1979.

Football League Record: 1892 Elected to Division 2; 1895 Failed re-election; 1896–1901 Division 2; 1901 Failed re-election; 1921 Original Member of Division 3 (N); 1927–31 Division 3 (S); 1931–36 Division 3 (N); 1936–58 Division 3 (S); 1958–60 Division 4; 1960–61 Division 3; 1961–63 Division 2; 1963–79 Division 3; 1979–80 Division 4; 1980–88 Division 3; 1988–89 Division 2; 1989–90 Division 3; 1990–92 Division 4; 1992–95 Division 3; 1995–99 Division 2; 1999–2000 Division 1; 2000–01 Division 2; 2001– Division 1.

LATEST SEQUENCES

Longest Sequence of League Wins: 7, 10.10.59 – 21.11.59.

Longest Sequence of League Defeats: 15, 29.10.88 – 4.2.89.

Longest Sequence of League Draws: 5, 7.5.88 – 17.9.88.

Longest Sequence of Unbeaten League Matches: 21, 6.11.79 – 22.3.80.

Longest Sequence Without a League Win: 18, 15.10.88 – 4.2.89.

MANAGERS

H. Smallwood 1888–91
(Secretary-Manager)
A. G. Burton 1891–93
J. H. Robinson 1893–95
C. H. Ailso 1895–96
(Secretary-Manager)
A. E. Parsloe 1896–97
(Secretary-Manager)
L. Ford 1897–98
(Secretary-Manager)
G. Hughes 1898–99
(Secretary-Manager)
L. Ford 1899–1901
(Secretary-Manager)
J. E. Shutt 1908–13
(Secretary-Manager)
Haydn Price 1914–20
Joe Burchell 1920–26
David Ashworth 1926–27
Jack Torrance 1927–28
James Kerr 1928–29
Sid Scholey 1929–30
Peter O'Rourke 1930–32
Bill Slade 1932–34
Andy Wilson 1934–37
Tommy Lowes 1937–44
Harry Hibbs 1944–51
Tony McPhee 1951
Brough Fletcher 1952–53
Major Frank Buckley 1953–55
John Love 1955–57
Billy Moore 1957–64
Alf Wood 1964
Reg Shaw 1964–68
Dick Graham 1968
Ron Lewin 1968–69
Billy Moore 1969–72
John Smith 1972–73
Doug Fraser 1973–77
Dave Mackay 1977–78
Alan Ashman 1978
Frank Sibley 1979
Alan Buckley 1979–86
Neil Martin *(Joint Manager with Buckley)* 1981–82
Tommy Coakley 1986–88
John Barnwell 1989–90
Kenny Hibbitt 1990–94
Chris Nicholl 1994–97
Jan Sorensen 1997–98
Ray Graydon May 1998–

TEN YEAR LEAGUE RECORD

		P	W	D	L	F	A	Pts	Pos
1990-91	Div 4	46	12	17	17	48	51	53	16
1991-92	Div 4	42	12	13	17	48	58	49	15
1992-93	Div 3	42	22	7	13	76	61	73	5
1993-94	Div 3	42	17	9	16	48	53	60	10
1994-95	Div 3	42	24	11	7	75	40	83	2
1995-96	Div 2	46	19	12	15	60	45	69	11
1996-97	Div 2	46	19	10	17	54	53	67	12
1997-98	Div 2	46	14	12	20	43	52	54	19
1998-99	Div 2	46	26	9	11	63	47	87	2
1999-2000	Div 1	46	11	13	22	52	77	46	22

DID YOU KNOW ?

Eddie Holding made his debut for Walsall in September 1950 at right-half, subsequently appeared at right-back and even scored a Christmas Day hat-trick from centre-forward against Brighton & Hove Albion in 1953.

WALSALL 2000–01 LEAGUE RECORD

Match No.	Date		Venue	Opponents	Result		H/T Score	Lg. Pos.	Goalscorers	Attendance
1	Aug	12	A	Rotherham U	W	3-2	0-1	—	Angell 2 [54, 78], Bryan (og) [71]	5200
2		19	H	Oldham Ath	W	3-2	1-2	2	Byfield 2 [11, 89], Wrack [75]	5952
3		26	A	Swindon T	W	4-1	2-1	1	Wrack [5], Keates [38], Byfield [62], Leitao [75]	5492
4		29	H	Oxford U	W	3-2	1-2	—	Hall [14], Leitao [65], Angell [82]	5678
5	Sept	2	A	Wigan Ath	W	2-0	2-0	1	Leitao [10], Keates [16]	7156
6		9	A	Bury	L	0-2	0-0	1		4755
7		12	A	Luton T	D	0-0	0-0	—		4362
8		16	H	Bournemouth	D	1-1	1-0	1	Angell [28]	5054
9		23	A	Wrexham	W	1-0	1-0	1	Leitao [29]	3766
10		30	H	Notts Co	W	5-1	2-0	1	Matias [4], Angell [38], Bennett [62], Leitao [67], Byfield [72]	5211
11	Oct	6	A	Colchester U	W	2-0	2-0	—	Angell [20], Leitao [43]	3428
12		14	H	Bristol C	D	0-0	0-0	1		6576
13		17	A	Peterborough U	D	1-1	0-1	—	Matias [81]	4716
14		21	A	Wycombe W	L	1-3	1-1	1	Wrack [32]	5564
15		24	H	Stoke C	W	3-0	0-0	—	Leitao [47], Gunnarsson (og) [61], Hall [66]	6996
16		28	A	Brentford	L	1-2	1-2	2	Byfield [12]	4007
17	Nov	4	H	Reading	W	2-1	0-0	1	Matias [58], Byfield [86]	7772
18		11	A	Bristol R	D	0-0	0-0	2		7540
19		25	H	Northampton T	W	3-0	1-0	2	Leitao [3], Hall [52], Angell [88]	5894
20	Dec	2	H	Port Vale	W	2-1	1-0	1	Matias [35], Keates (pen) [50]	5597
21		16	A	Millwall	L	0-2	0-1	3		11,737
22		23	H	Cambridge U	W	3-1	2-0	2	Bukran 2 [9, 42], Matias [90]	5277
23		26	A	Swansea C	L	1-3	1-1	2	Angell [3]	5795
24		30	A	Oldham Ath	D	0-0	0-0	3		5267
25	Jan	1	H	Swindon T	W	1-0	0-0	2	Leitao [89]	5548
26		13	H	Oxford U	L	1-2	0-2	3	Keates [85]	5184
27		20	H	Swansea C	W	5-1	1-0	3	Angell 2 [33, 51], Leitao [65], Hall 2 [74, 88]	5227
28		23	A	Rotherham U	D	1-1	0-0	—	Byfield [73]	4437
29		27	A	Cambridge U	W	1-0	1-0	1	Leitao [13]	3888
30	Feb	2	A	Wigan Ath	D	1-1	0-1	—	Leitao [90]	9586
31		10	A	Bury	L	1-2	1-1	3	Wrack [23]	4839
32		17	H	Bournemouth	D	2-2	0-2	3	Ekelund (pen) [59], Byfield [88]	4564
33		20	H	Luton T	W	3-1	2-0	—	Leitao [13], Bennett [36], Byfield [67]	4816
34		24	H	Wrexham	L	2-3	2-0	2	Bennett 2 [14, 36]	4958
35	Mar	3	A	Notts Co	L	0-2	0-1	4		6077
36		6	A	Bristol C	W	3-1	2-1	—	Leitao [15], Simpson [17], Carey (og) [73]	9263
37		10	H	Colchester U	L	0-1	0-0	4		4553
38		24	H	Wycombe W	W	5-1	1-0	4	Matias 3 [42, 61, 83], Hall [67], Leitao [70]	4530
39		31	H	Millwall	D	0-0	0-0	4		7073
40	Apr	14	A	Stoke C	D	0-0	0-0	4		16,603
41		17	H	Brentford	W	3-2	2-1	—	Leitao 2 [8, 61], Bennett [35]	4540
42		21	A	Reading	D	2-2	1-2	4	Leitao [28], Barras [53]	16,710
43		24	A	Peterborough U	L	0-2	0-1	—		5549
44		28	H	Bristol R	W	2-1	2-0	4	Matias [6], Goodman [10]	7130
45	May	3	A	Port Vale	W	2-0	0-0	—	Goodman [50], Tillson [67]	6027
46		5	A	Northampton T	W	3-0	0-0	4	Angell 3 [63, 80, 81]	5389

Final League Position: 4

GOALSCORERS

League (79): Leitao 18, Angell 13, Byfield 9, Matias 9, Hall 6, Bennett 5, Keates 4 (1 pen), Wrack 4, Bukran 2, Goodman 2, Barras 1, Ekelund 1 (pen), Simpson 1, Tillson 1, own goals 3.
Worthington Cup (3): Leitao 2, Byfield 1.
FA Cup (8): Tillson 2, Angell 1, Barras 1, Hall 1, Leitao 1, Matias 1, Wrack 1.

Walker J 43 + 1	Brightwell I 43 + 1	Aranalde Z 45	Tillson A 42	Roper I 20 + 5	Bukran G 30 + 6	Hall P 36 + 6	Bennett T 34 + 4	Angell B 23 + 18	Leitao J 40 + 4	Matias P 36 + 4	Wrack D 11 + 17	Byfield D 21 + 19	Keates D 21 + 12	Barras T 33 + 3	Gadsby M 2 + 3	Carter A — + 1	Wright M — + 4	Emberson C 3	Marsh C 4 + 3	Ekelund R 2 + 7	Simpson F 8 + 2	Horne B 1 + 2	Goodman D 8	Scott D — + 1	Match No.
1	2	3	4	5	6	7¹	8	9	10¹	11	12	13													1
1	2	3	4	5	6	7	8²	9¹	12	11³	13	10	14												2
1	2	3	4	5	6¹	7²	12	13	9³	14	11	10	8												3
1	2	3	4	5³	6	7		12	9	13	8²	10¹	11	14											4
1	2	3	4		6	7	12	9³	10¹	13	11²	14	8	5											5
1	2	3	4		6	7	12	9	13	11³	14	10²	8¹	5											6
1	2	3	4	12		13	8	14	9³	11	7²	10	6	5¹											7
1	2	3	4		12	7³	8	9¹	13	11		10⁴	6	5	14										8
1	2	3	4		6	7³	8	12	9²	11		10¹	13	5		14									9
1	2	3	4		6	7²	8	9	10¹	11		12		5			13								10
1	2	3	4	12	6³	7	8	9¹	10²	11		13	14	5											11
1	2	3	4		6	7²	8	9¹	10	11	13	12		5											12
1	2	3	4		6	7¹	8	9²	10	11	12	13		5											13
1	2	3	4	5	6	12	8	13	9	11	7¹	10²													14
	2	3	4		6²	7³	8	12	9¹	11		10	13	5		14	1								15
	2	3	4		6²	7³	8	12	9¹	11		10¹	13	5		14	1								16
15	2	3	4		6	7	8	12	9¹	11		10²		5				16	13						17
1	2	3	4		6	7²	8	12	9	11		10¹		5					13						18
1	2	3	4	12	6	7²		14	9	11	13	10¹	8	5¹											19
1	2	3	4		6³	7		12	9²	11	13	10¹	8	5							14				20
1		3	4		6³	7²	8	12	9	11	13	10¹		5						2	14				21
1	12	3	4		6	7	8	9³	10²	11		13	14	5						2¹					22
1	2	3	4	5	6		8	9	12	11²	7	10¹									13				23
1	2	3	4		6¹	7	12	9²	10		11	13	8	5											24
1	2	3	4		6	7²	8	9	10³	11	12	13	14	5											25
1	2		4¹	12	6²		8	9		11³	7	10	13	5					3	14					26
1	2	3	4	5	12	7	8¹	9³	10²	11	14	13	6												27
1	2	3	4	5	12	7	8¹	9²	10	11³	14	13	6												28
1	2	3	4	5		7		9³	10¹	11²	13	12	8	14				6							29
1	2	3	4		12	7	8¹	9	10	11²	13	14	6	5											30
1	2	3	4¹	5	6	7	8	9²	10		11			12					13						31
1	2	3	4	5		7	8	9	10	12	11²	13	14						6²						32
1	2	3		5		7¹	8²	9	10²	11	12	13		6	4				14						33
1	2	3		5		7	8³	9	10	11³	12	13		6	4				14						34
1	2	3	4			7²	8	12	9¹	11	13	10		6	5										35
1	2¹	3	4	5			8		9			10	7	6					12		11				36
1		3	4	5	12	13	7¹	14	9			10³	8	6²					2		11				37
1	2	3	4		6³	7		12	9	11¹			8	5								13	14	10²		38
1	2	3	4		6	7²		12	9¹	11			8	5								13		10		39
1	2	3	4	5	11	12	8²		9					6							7	13	10¹		40
1	2	3	4	5		7²	6		9¹	11		12			13						8		10		41
1	2	3	4¹	5		12	7³	13	9²	11		14	6								8		10		42
1	2	3		5		12	6³		9	11	7²	13	14	4							8		10¹		43
1	2	3	4		6	7³		12	9²	11			13	5	14						8		10¹		44
1	2	3	4¹	12	13		8		9³			14	6²	5	11						7		10		45
1	2	3		5³	6	7²		9		11	12	10¹		4			13					8		14	46

Worthington Cup

First Round	Kidderminster H	(h)	1-1
		(a)	1-0
Second Round	West Ham U	(h)	0-1
		(a)	1-1

FA Cup

First Round	Exeter C	(h)	4-0
Second Round	Barnet	(h)	2-1
Third Round	West Ham U	(h)	2-3

WATFORD

Division 1

Vicarage Road Stadium, Watford WD18 0ER.

Telephone: (01923) 496 000. **Fax:** (01923) 496 001. **Ticket and Prizeline:** 09068 400 401. **Ticket Office:** (01923) 496 010. **Ticket Office Fax:** (01923) 351 145. **ClubCall:** 09068 104 104. **Club Shop:** (01923) 229 859. **Club Shop Fax:** (01923) 496 238. **Catering:** (01923) 252 323. **Football in the Community:** (01923) 440 449. **Junior Hornets Club:** (01923) 496 256. **Marketing:** (01923) 496 006. **Press Office:** (01923) 496 234.

Ground Capacity: 20,800.

Record Attendance: 34,099 v Manchester U, FA Cup 4th rd (replay), 3 February 1969.

Record Receipts: £440,349 v Chelsea, FA Premier League, 18 September 1999.

Pitch Measurements: 113yd × 73yd.

Life Presidents: Sir Elton John CBE, Geoff Smith, Graham Taylor.

HONOURS

Football League: Division 1 – Runners-up 1982–83, promoted from Division 1 1998–99 (play-offs); Division 2 – Champions 1997–98; Runners-up 1981–82; Division 3 – Champions 1968–69; Runners-up 1978–79; Division 4 – Champions 1977–78; Promoted 1959–60 (4th).

FA Cup: Runners-up 1984.

Football League Cup: Semi- final 1979.

European Competitions: UEFA Cup: 1983–84.

Chairman: Sir Elton John CBE. **Vice Chairman:** Haig Oundjian. **Directors:** B. Anderson, D. Meller, D. Lester, C. Lissack, C. Norton, G. Simpson, M. Sherwood, N. Wray. **Chief Executive:** Tim Shaw. **Football Secretary:** Catherine Alexander.

Football Manager: Gianluca Vialli. **First Team Coach:** Ray Wilkins. **Assistant Manager:** Terry Byrne. **Reserve Team Manager:** Ray Lewington. **Academy Director:** John McDermott. **Academy Assistant Directors:** Chris Cummins, David Hockaday.

Press and Publications Officer: Andrew French. **Director of Marketing:** Ed Coan. **Safety Officer:** Paul Dumpleton. **Stadium Manager:** Paddy Flavin.

Colours: Yellow shirts, red shorts, red stockings with black and yellow turnover.

Change Colours: Black shirts with red and yellow trim around cuffs and collar, black shorts, black stockings with thick red and thin yellow bands on turnover.

Year Formed: 1881.

Turned Professional: 1897.

Ltd Co.: 1909.

Club Nickname: 'The Hornets'.

Previous Names: 1881, Watford Rovers; 1893, West Herts; 1898, Watford.

Previous Grounds: 1883, Vicarage Meadow, Rose and Crown Meadow; 1889, Colney Butts; 1890, Cassio Road; 1922, Vicarage Road.

First Football League Game: 28 August 1920, Division 3, v QPR (a) W 2–1 – Williams; Horseman, F. Gregory; Bacon, Toone, Wilkinson; Bassett, Ronald (1), Hoddinott, White (1), Waterall.

IT'S A FACT !

After a goalless first half on 20 December 1933, Watford scored four goals in the first five minutes of the restart in a 6-0 win over Clapton Orient.

Record League Victory: 8–0 v Sunderland, Division 1, 25 September 1982 – Sherwood; Rice, Rostron, Taylor, Terry, Bolton, Callaghan (2), Blissett (4), Jenkins (2), Jackett, Barnes.

Record Cup Victory: 10–1 v Lowestoft T, FA Cup 1st rd, 27 November 1926 – Yates; Prior, Fletcher (1); F. Smith, 'Bert' Smith, Strain; Stephenson, Warner (3), Edmonds (3), Swan (1), Daniels (1), (1 og).

Record Defeat: 0–10 v Wolverhampton W, FA Cup 1st rd (replay), 24 January 1912.

Most League Points (2 for a win): 71, Division 4, 1977–78.

Most League Points (3 for a win): 88, Division 2, 1997–98.

Most League Goals: 92, Division 4, 1959–60.

Highest League Scorer in Season: Cliff Holton, 42, Division 4, 1959–60.

Most League Goals in Total Aggregate: Luther Blissett, 148, 1976–83, 1984–88, 1991–92.

Most League Goals in One Match: 5, Eddie Mummery v Newport Co, Division 3S, 5 January 1924.

Most Capped Player: John Barnes, 31 (79), England and Kenny Jackett, 31, Wales.

Most League Appearances: Luther Blissett, 415, 1976–83, 1984–88, 1991–92.

Youngest League Player: Keith Mercer, 16 years 125 days v Tranmere R, 16 February 1973.

Record Transfer Fee Received: £2,300,000 from Chelsea for Paul Furlong, May 1994.

Record Transfer Fee Paid: £2,250,000 to Tottenham H for Allan Nielson, August 2000.

MANAGERS

John Goodall 1903–10
Harry Kent 1910–26
Fred Pagnam 1926–29
Neil McBain 1929–37
Bill Findlay 1938–47
Jack Bray 1947–48
Eddie Hapgood 1948–50
Ron Gray 1950–51
Haydn Green 1951–52
Len Goulden 1952–55
  (General Manager to 1956)
Johnny Paton 1955–56
Neil McBain 1956–59
Ron Burgess 1959–63
Bill McGarry 1963–64
Ken Furphy 1964–71
George Kirby 1971–73
Mike Keen 1973–77
Graham Taylor 1977–87
Dave Bassett 1987–88
Steve Harrison 1988–90
Colin Lee 1990
Steve Perryman 1990–93
Glenn Roeder 1993–96
Kenny Jackett 1996–97
Graham Taylor 1997–2001
Gianluca Vialli July 2001–

Football League Record: 1920 Original Member of Division 3; 1921–58 Division 3 (S); 1958–60 Division 4; 1960–69 Division 3; 1969–72 Division 2; 1972–75 Division 3; 1975–78 Division 4; 1978–79 Division 3; 1979–82 Division 2; 1982–88 Division 1; 1988–92 Division 2; 1992–96 Division 1; 1996–98 Division 2; 1998–99 Division 1; 1999–2000 FA Premier League; 2000– Division 1.

LATEST SEQUENCES

Longest Sequence of League Wins: 7, 28.8.00 – 14.10.00.

Longest Sequence of League Defeats: 9, 26.12.72 – 27.2.73.

Longest Sequence of League Draws: 7, 30.11.96 – 27.1.97.

Longest Sequence of Unbeaten League Matches: 22, 1.10.96 – 1.3.97.

Longest Sequence Without a League Win: 19, 27.11.71 – 8.4.72.

TEN YEAR LEAGUE RECORD

		P	W	D	L	F	A	Pts	Pos
1990-91	Div 2	46	12	15	19	45	59	51	20
1991-92	Div 2	46	18	11	17	51	48	65	10
1992-93	Div 1	46	14	13	19	57	71	55	16
1993-94	Div 1	46	15	9	22	66	80	54	19
1994-95	Div 1	46	19	13	14	52	46	70	7
1995-96	Div 1	46	10	18	18	62	70	48	23
1996-97	Div 2	46	16	19	11	45	38	67	13
1997-98	Div 2	46	24	16	6	67	41	88	1
1998-99	Div 1	46	21	14	11	65	56	77	5
1999-2000	PR Lge	38	6	6	26	35	77	24	20

DID YOU KNOW ?

In the 1997/98 Second Division Championship winning season, versatile defender Steve Palmer wore all 14 shirts during the campaign. In the penultimate game at home to Bournemouth he started in goal and switched with Alec Chamberlain after 5 seconds.

WATFORD 2000–01 LEAGUE RECORD

Match No.	Date	Venue	Opponents	Result	H/T Score	Lg. Pos.	Goalscorers	Attendance
1	Aug 12	A	Huddersfield T	W 2-1	1-1	—	Cox [45], Smith [47]	13,018
2	19	H	Barnsley	W 1-0	0-0	3	Foley [90]	13,186
3	26	A	Wimbledon	D 0-0	0-0	4		8447
4	28	A	Sheffield U	W 4-1	2-1	2	Helguson [8], Mooney [45], Noel-Williams [47], Hyde [69]	12,675
5	Sept 9	A	Portsmouth	W 3-1	2-0	2	Nielsen [27], Mooney [45], Helguson [59]	14,012
6	12	H	Blackburn R	W 4-3	3-2	—	Hyde 2 [18, 37], Helguson [35], Mooney [65]	17,258
7	16	H	Crewe Alex	W 3-0	1-0	2	Smith [22], Noel-Williams [57], Hyde [89]	13,784
8	23	A	Stockport Co	W 3-2	1-0	2	Smith [45], Noel-Williams [49], Nielsen [86]	6933
9	Oct 1	H	Birmingham C	W 2-0	0-0	2	Nielsen [58], Cox [76]	12,355
10	14	H	QPR	W 3-1	2-0	2	Cox 2 [2, 22], Noel-Williams [86]	17,488
11	17	H	Gillingham	D 0-0	0-0	—		12,356
12	21	A	Nottingham F	W 2-0	2-0	2	Hyde 2 [9, 28]	20,065
13	24	H	Bolton W	W 1-0	0-0	—	Mooney (pen) [88]	11,799
14	28	A	Wolverhampton W	D 2-2	2-0	1	Cox [33], Mooney [39]	20,296
15	Nov 4	H	Grimsby T	W 4-0	2-0	1	Nielsen [30], Mooney 2 [33, 90], Noel-Williams [75]	11,600
16	7	H	Sheffield W	L 1-3	0-1	—	Smith [48]	11,166
17	11	A	Tranmere R	L 0-2	0-1	2		8858
18	18	H	Preston NE	L 2-3	2-2	2	Mooney [38], Palmer S [45]	13,066
19	Dec 3	A	Bolton W	L 1-2	1-0	4	Smith [4]	13,904
20	9	A	Crystal Palace	L 0-1	0-0	5		16,049
21	16	H	WBA	D 3-3	2-0	5	Butler (og) [2], Mooney 2 [27, 82]	14,601
22	23	H	Huddersfield T	L 1-2	1-1	6	Heary (og) [34]	13,371
23	26	A	Fulham	L 0-5	0-2	8		19,373
24	29	A	Barnsley	W 1-0	0-0	—	Nielsen [56]	13,820
25	Jan 2	A	Wimbledon	W 3-1	3-1	—	Mooney 2 [12, 20], Noel-Williams [36]	11,336
26	13	A	Sheffield U	W 1-0	0-0	5	Mooney [75]	17,551
27	20	H	Fulham	L 1-3	0-0	5	Helguson [79]	18,333
28	27	A	Norwich C	L 1-2	0-0	6	Helguson [50]	15,309
29	Feb 3	H	Sheffield W	W 3-2	2-2	6	Vernazza [10], Ward [25], Smith [49]	16,134
30	10	H	Portsmouth	D 2-2	2-2	5	Smith 2 [13, 17]	16,051
31	17	A	Crewe Alex	L 0-2	0-2	6		6757
32	20	H	Blackburn R	L 0-1	0-0	—		15,970
33	24	H	Stockport Co	D 2-2	0-1	6	Mooney [78], Nielsen [80]	13,647
34	Mar 2	A	Birmingham C	L 0-2	0-1	—		20,724
35	7	A	QPR	D 1-1	0-0	—	Nielsen [66]	12,436
36	10	H	Norwich C	W 4-1	1-1	7	Wooter [9], Smith [61], Helguson [76], Nielsen [86]	15,123
37	13	H	Burnley	L 0-1	0-0	—		13,653
38	31	A	WBA	L 0-3	0-0	9		17,261
39	Apr 3	A	Nottingham F	W 3-0	1-0	—	Noel-Williams [21], Mooney 2 [47, 73]	13,651
40	7	H	Crystal Palace	D 2-2	0-1	8	Nielsen [77], Mooney [79]	15,598
41	14	A	Grimsby T	L 1-2	1-0	8	Mooney [45]	6110
42	17	H	Wolverhampton W	W 3-2	2-1	—	Mooney [8], Smith [14], Helguson [90]	13,765
43	22	H	Preston NE	L 2-3	1-2	10	Noel-Williams [36], Page [60]	14,071
44	28	H	Tranmere R	D 1-1	0-0	11	Nielsen [90]	16,063
45	May 1	A	Gillingham	W 3-0	0-0	—	Helguson [51], Smith [54], Vernazza [66]	9098
46	6	A	Burnley	L 0-2	0-0	9		18,283

Final League Position: 9

GOALSCORERS

League (76): Mooney 19 (1 pen), Smith 11, Nielsen 10, Helguson 8, Noel-Williams 8, Hyde 6, Cox 5, Vernazza 2, Foley 1, Page 1, Palmer S 1, Ward 1, Wooter 1, own goals 2.
Worthington Cup (6): Mooney 2, Helguson 1, Palmer 1, Smith 1, Ward 1.
FA Cup (1): Mooney 1.

Baardsen E 27	Cox N 43 + 1	Robinson P 39	Palmer S 37 + 2	Page R 36	Ward D 40	Perpetuini D 4 + 1	Nielsen A 45	Mooney T 38 + 1	Wooter N 14 + 12	Smith T 38 + 5	Ngonge M — + 2	Gibbs N 3 + 3	Easton C 5 + 6	Foley D — + 5	Helguson H 23 + 10	Noel-Williams G 28 + 4	Hyde M 17 + 9	Chamberlain A 19 + 2	Smart A 1 + 7	Jobson R 2	Armstrong S — + 3	Palmer C 5	Vernazza P 20 + 3	Kennedy P 11 + 6	Panayi J 8 + 1	Cook L 2 + 2	Johnson R 1 + 2	Forde F — + 1	Match No.
1	2	3	4	5	6	7*	8	9	10	11²	12	13																	1
1	2	3	4	5	6		8	9	10¹	11	12²				7	13													2
1	2	3	4	5	6		8¹	9	10³	11	12	13			7²	14													3
1	2	3	4	5	6			9		11					7	10	8												4
1	2		4	5	6		8	9		11			3	12	7¹	10													5
1	2	3	4		6		8	5	11	12	9¹				10	7													6
1⁹	2	3	4	5	6		8	9		11					10	7	15												7
	2	3	4	5	6		8	9		11					7	10		1											8
	2	3	4	5	6		8	9	10						7	11		1											9
	2	3	4	5	6		8	10		12			13		7¹	9	11²	1											10
	2	3	4	5	6		8		12	11			13		7²	9	10¹	1											11
	2	3	4	5	6		8		12	11¹			13		7²	9³	10	1	14										12
	2	3	4		6		8		12	11¹			13		7²	9³	10	1	14										13
	2	3¹	4	5	6		8	7	10¹	12	13		14		9	11³		1											14
1	2		4	5	6¹	7	8						3		10	12	11	9											15
1	2		4	5		7³	8						3		10¹	12	13	11²	9		14		6						16
1	2	3	4	5	6		8								7	12	11	10¹			6								17
1	2	3	4	5	6		8	10¹	12	11²			13		9¹	7	14												18
1	2	3		5	6		8	7	10¹	11			13		9¹	4	12												19
1	2	3	4	5	6		8	9		11¹					7	12	10²		13										20
1	2	3	4	5²			8								7	12	11	9¹	10³				6	13	14				21
1	2	3	4		6		8	9	12				13		7²		14	10¹				5	11³						22
1	2²	3	4		6		8	9	12						7	13	11¹	10				5							23
	2	3		5	6		8	9		11						10		1					4	7					24
	2	3		5	6		8	9		11						10		1					4	7					25
	2	3¹	12	5	6		8	9			13				11³	14	10	1					4	7²					26
	2³		4		6		8	9	12	11¹			13		10²	14		1				5	7	3					27
	2	3		5	6		8	9							7	10	11	1					4						28
	2	3	4	5	6		8	9		11					7			1					10						29
		3	4	5	6		8		11						9	12		1					10	7			2¹		30
1	2		4	5	6		8	9		11			3		10²	12			13					7¹					31
1	2	3	4	5	6		8²	9³	12	11¹					7	13							10	14					32
1	2	3	4³	5	6		8	9	12	11¹					7¹	13							10²	14					33
1	2		4	5	6	3	8	9²	12	11			13		7¹								10²	14					34
1	12	3		5			8	9	10	11			2¹		13								6	7³	4				35
1	2	3		5			8	9	10¹	11					7	12							6		4				36
1	2	3		5			8	9		11					7²	10¹	12						6	13	4				37
1	2	3	4	5			8	10²							9¹	7	12	11					14	6	13				38
1	2	3	4	5	6		8	9	10²	11³					12	7							13	14					39
1	2²	3	4	5	6		8	9	10¹	11					7	12							13						40
1⁹		3	4	5	6		8	9		11²					7¹		15	12					10			2	13		41
	2	3	4	5			8	9		11					12	10¹		1					6	7					42
	2	3	4	5			8	9							12	11	10	1					6	7¹					43
	2	3¹	4	5			8	9								11	10²	1					6	7³	12	13	14		44
	2	3			6	12	8³		11²		13				9	10		1				5	4	7¹	14				45
	2	3		12	6		8		11						9²	13		1				5	4	7³	10¹	14			46

Worthington Cup

First Round	Cheltenham T	(h)	0-0	
		(a)	3-0	
Second Round	Notts Co	(a)	3-1	
		(h)	0-2	
Third Round	Manchester U	(h)	0-3	

FA Cup

Third Round	Everton	(h)	1-2

WEST BROMWICH ALBION   Division 1

The Hawthorns, West Bromwich B71 4LF.

Telephone: (0121) 525 8888 (all Depts).
Fax: (0121) 553 6634.

Registered Office: 'The Tom Silk Building', Halfords Lane, West Bromwich, West Midlands B71 4BR.

Ground Capacity: 25,396 (all seated).

Record Attendance: 64,815 v Arsenal, FA Cup 6th rd, 6 March 1937.

Record Receipts: £270,000 v Nottingham F, Division 1, 3 May 1998.

Pitch Measurements: 115yd × 74yd.

President: Sir F. A. Millichip.
Vice-President: John G. Silk LL.B (Lond).
Chairman: P. Thompson.
Directors: J. W. Brandrick, B. Hurst, C. Stapleton, J. D. Wile (Chief Executive), J. Peace.

Manager: Gary Megson.
Assistant Manager: Frank Burrows.

Reserve Coach: Gary Shelton.
Youth Coach: Richard O'Kelly. *Physio:* Nick Worth.

Secretary: Dr John J. Evans BA, PHD. (Wales).

Club Statistician: Tony Matthews.

Colours: Navy blue and white striped shirts, white shorts, blue and white stockings.

Change Colours: Yellow shirts with navy blue band, blue shorts with yellow stripe, yellow stockings.

Year Formed: 1878. *Turned Professional:* 1885.

Ltd Co.: 1892. *Plc:* 1996.

Previous Name: 1878, West Bromwich Strollers; 1871, West Bromwich Albion.

Club Nicknames: 'Throstles', 'Baggies', 'Albion'.

Previous Grounds: 1878, Coopers Hill; 1879, Dartmouth Park; 1881, Bunns Field, Walsall Street; 1882, Four Acres (Dartmouth Cricket Club); 1885, Stoney Lane; 1900, The Hawthorns.

First Football League Game: 8 September 1888, Football League, v Stoke (a) W 2–0 – Roberts; J. Horton, Green; E. Horton, Perry, Bayliss; Bassett, Woodhall (1), Hendry, Pearson, Wilson (1).

HONOURS

Football League: Division 1 – Champions 1919–20; Runners-up 1924–25, 1953–54; Division 2 – Champions 1901–02, 1910–11; Runners-up 1930–31, 1948–49; Promoted to Division 1 1975–76 (3rd).

FA Cup: Winners 1888, 1892, 1931, 1954, 1968; Runners-up 1886, 1887, 1895, 1912, 1935.

Football League Cup: Winners 1966; Runners-up 1967, 1970.

European Competitions: European Cup-Winners' Cup: 1968–69. European Fairs Cup: 1966–67. UEFA Cup: 1978–79, 1979–80, 1981–82.

IT'S A FACT !

On 3 September 2000, West Bromwich Albion celebrated their 100th anniversary at The Hawthorns by beating Crystal Palace 1-0. The previous century they had played their inaugural match on the ground against Derby County in a 1-1 draw; Chippy Simmons equalising for Albion in the 78th minute. The team sheet cost 1d.

Record League Victory: 12–0 v Darwen, Division 1, 4 April 1892 – Reader; J. Horton, McCulloch; Reynolds (2), Perry, Groves; Bassett (3), McLeod, Nicholls (1), Pearson (4), Geddes (1), (1 og).

Record Cup Victory: 10–1 v Chatham (away), FA Cup 3rd rd, 2 March 1889 – Roberts; J. Horton, Green; Timmins (1), Charles Perry, E. Horton; Bassett (2), Perry (1), Bayliss (2), Pearson, Wilson (3), (1 og).

Record Defeat: 3–10 v Stoke C, Division 1, 4 February 1937.

Most League Points (2 for a win): 60, Division 1, 1919–20.

Most League Points (3 for a win): 85, Division 2, 1992–93.

Most League Goals: 105, Division 2, 1929–30.

Highest League Scorer in Season: William 'Ginger' Richardson, 39, Division 1, 1935–36.

Most League Goals in Total Aggregate: Tony Brown, 218, 1963–79.

Most League Goals in One Match: 6, Jimmy Cookson v Blackpool, Division 2, 17 September 1927.

Most Capped Player: Stuart Williams, 33 (43), Wales.

Most League Appearances: Tony Brown, 574, 1963–80.

Youngest League Player: Charlie Wilson, 16 years 73 days v Oldham Ath, 1 October 1921.

Record Transfer Fee Received: £4,300,000 from Juventus for Enzo Maresca, January 2000.

Record Transfer Fee Paid: £1,250,000 to Preston NE for Kevin Kilbane, June 1997.

Football League Record: 1888 Founder Member of Football League; 1901–02 Division 2; 1902–04 Division 1; 1904–11 Division 2; 1911–27 Division 1; 1927–31 Division 2; 1931–38 Division 1; 1938–49 Division 2; 1949–73 Division 1; 1973–76 Division 2; 1976–86 Division 1; 1986–91 Division 2; 1991–92 Division 3; 1992–93 Division 2; 1993– Division 1.

LATEST SEQUENCES

Longest Sequence of League Wins: 11, 5.4.30 – 8.9.30.

Longest Sequence of League Defeats: 11, 28.10.95 – 26.12.95.

Longest Sequence of League Draws: 5, 30.8.99 – 3.10.99.

Longest Sequence of Unbeaten League Matches: 17, 7.9.57 – 7.12.57.

Longest Sequence Without a League Win: 14, 28.10.95 – 3.2.96.

MANAGERS

Louis Ford 1890–92
(Secretary-Manager)
Henry Jackson 1892–94
(Secretary-Manager)
Edward Stephenson 1894–95
(Secretary-Manager)
Clement Keys 1895–96
(Secretary-Manager)
Frank Heaven 1896–1902
(Secretary-Manager)
Fred Everiss 1902–48
Jack Smith 1948–52
Jesse Carver 1952
Vic Buckingham 1953–59
Gordon Clark 1959–61
Archie Macaulay 1961–63
Jimmy Hagan 1963–67
Alan Ashman 1967–71
Don Howe 1971–75
Johnny Giles 1975–77
Ronnie Allen 1977
Ron Atkinson 1978–81
Ronnie Allen 1981–82
Ron Wylie 1982–84
Johnny Giles 1984–85
Ron Saunders 1986–87
Ron Atkinson 1987–88
Brian Talbot 1988–91
Bobby Gould 1991–92
Ossie Ardiles 1992–93
Keith Burkinshaw 1993–94
Alan Buckley 1994–97
Ray Harford 1997
Denis Smith 1997–2000
Brian Little 2000
Gary Megson March 2000–

TEN YEAR LEAGUE RECORD

		P	W	D	L	F	A	Pts	Pos
1990-91	Div 2	46	10	18	18	52	61	48	23
1991-92	Div 3	46	19	14	13	64	49	71	7
1992-93	Div 2	46	25	10	11	88	54	85	4
1993-94	Div 1	46	13	12	21	60	69	51	21
1994-95	Div 1	46	16	10	20	51	57	58	19
1995-96	Div 1	46	16	12	18	60	68	60	11
1996-97	Div 1	46	14	15	17	68	72	57	16
1997-98	Div 1	46	16	12	17	50	56	61	10
1998-99	Div 1	46	16	11	19	69	76	59	12
1999-2000	Div 1	46	10	19	17	43	60	49	21

DID YOU KNOW ?

Goalkeeper Joe Reader was the only West Bromwich Albion player to appear for the club at their three major grounds: The Four Acres, Stoney Lane and The Hawthorns. He made 370 League and Cup appearances for the club.

WEST BROMWICH ALBION 2000–01 LEAGUE RECORD

Match No.	Date	Venue	Opponents	Result	H/T Score	Lg. Pos.	Goalscorers	Attendance
1	Aug 12	A	Nottingham F	L 0-1	0-0	—		21,209
2	19	H	Bolton W	L 0-2	0-1	24		17,316
3	26	A	Barnsley	L 1-4	1-0	24	Hughes [13]	14,321
4	28	H	QPR	W 2-1	0-1	20	Van Blerk [46], Hughes [83]	14,831
5	Sept 3	H	Crystal Palace	W 1-0	1-0	11	McInnes [8]	13,980
6	9	A	Stockport Co	D 0-0	0-0	10		6632
7	12	A	Crewe Alex	W 1-0	1-0	—	Hughes [14]	6222
8	17	H	Birmingham C	D 1-1	1-0	8	Taylor [2]	19,858
9	23	A	Portsmouth	W 1-0	0-0	6	Roberts [55]	11,937
10	30	H	Blackburn R	W 1-0	0-0	6	Hughes [57]	16,794
11	Oct 8	A	Sheffield W	W 2-1	1-1	5	Roberts 2 [23, 76]	15,338
12	14	H	Norwich C	L 2-3	1-2	6	Clement [38], Hughes (pen) [65]	16,511
13	17	H	Wolverhampton W	W 1-0	1-0	—	Hughes (pen) [19]	21,492
14	21	A	Tranmere R	D 2-2	2-1	7	Hughes [30], Roberts [35]	8931
15	24	H	Wimbledon	W 3-1	2-1	—	Roberts [9], Van Blerk [21], Sneekes [85]	15,570
16	29	A	Grimsby T	L 0-2	0-0	5		5429
17	Nov 4	A	Burnley	D 1-1	0-1	7	Roberts [87]	17,828
18	11	A	Huddersfield T	W 2-0	2-0	8	Jordao [30], Hughes [40]	11,801
19	18	H	Gillingham	W 3-1	2-0	7	Hughes 3 [2, 38, 62]	16,410
20	25	H	Preston NE	W 3-1	1-0	4	Hughes 3 [40, 63, 89]	20,043
21	Dec 2	A	Wimbledon	W 1-0	0-0	3	Williams (og) [70]	8608
22	9	H	Fulham	L 1-3	0-2	4	Lyttle [71]	22,301
23	16	A	Watford	D 3-3	0-2	4	Hughes [48], Sneekes [58], Roberts [63]	14,601
24	23	H	Nottingham F	W 3-0	2-0	4	Roberts 2 [8, 56], Olsen (og) [35]	20,350
25	26	A	Sheffield U	L 0-2	0-1	5		22,281
26	30	H	Bolton W	W 1-0	1-0	4	Roberts [45]	18,985
27	Jan 1	H	Barnsley	W 1-0	0-0	3	Morgan (og) [85]	19,423
28	13	A	QPR	L 0-2	0-1	4		11,881
29	20	H	Sheffield U	W 2-1	0-0	4	Fox [62], Hughes [84]	16,778
30	Feb 3	A	Crystal Palace	D 2-2	1-2	4	Sneekes [42], Hughes [55]	16,692
31	10	A	Stockport Co	D 1-1	1-0	4	Roberts [44]	16,385
32	17	A	Birmingham C	L 1-2	1-1	5	Butler [38]	25,025
33	20	H	Crewe Alex	D 2-2	1-1	—	Taylor [24], Roberts [69]	15,476
34	24	H	Portsmouth	W 2-0	1-0	5	Roberts [10], Chambers A [69]	17,645
35	Mar 3	A	Blackburn R	L 0-1	0-0	5		23,926
36	6	A	Norwich C	W 1-0	1-0	—	Hughes (pen) [33]	16,372
37	10	H	Sheffield W	L 1-2	1-1	5	Hughes [5]	18,662
38	18	A	Wolverhampton W	L 1-3	0-2	6	Clement [82]	25,069
39	25	A	Tranmere R	W 2-1	1-0	5	Taylor 2 [40, 63]	17,151
40	31	H	Watford	W 3-0	0-0	5	Quinn [52], Hughes [59], Clement [90]	17,261
41	Apr 7	A	Fulham	D 0-0	0-0	5		17,795
42	14	A	Burnley	D 1-1	0-0	5	Taylor [84]	18,199
43	16	H	Grimsby T	L 0-1	0-1	5		16,504
44	21	A	Gillingham	W 2-1	2-1	4	Hughes [11], Clement [18]	9920
45	28	H	Huddersfield T	D 1-1	1-1	6	Roberts [17]	17,542
46	May 6	A	Preston NE	L 1-2	1-1	6	Clement [31]	16,226

Final League Position: 6

GOALSCORERS

League (60): Hughes 21 (3 pens), Roberts 14, Clement 5, Taylor 5, Sneekes 3, Van Blerk 2, Butler 1, Chambers A 1, Fox 1, Jordao 1, Lyttle 1, McInnes 1, Quinn 1, own goals 3.
Worthington Cup (6): Clement 2, Roberts 2, Jordao 1, Sneekes 1.
FA Cup (2): Hughes 1, Taylor 1.

Jensen B 33	Lyttle D 38+2	Clement N 45	McInnes D 14	Butler T 44	Carbon M 19+5	Quinn J 3+11	Sneekes R 39+6	Roberts J 32+11	Hughes L 41	Van Blerk J 35+1	Oliver A 1+6	Taylor B 17+23	Chambers J 27+4	Jordao 28+7	Fox R 36+2	Chambers A 4+7	Burgess D 1+2	Grant T 3+2	Balis I 1+6	Sigurdsson L 7+5	Appleton M 15	Derveld F 1+1	Hoult R 13	Gilchrist P 8	Cummings W 1+2	Match No.
1	2	3	4¹	5	6	7²	8	9	10	11³	12	13	14													1
1	2	3	4	5	6	7²	8	9	10	11¹	13	12														2
1	2²	3	4	5	6	12	8³		10		7¹	9	13	11	14											3
1	2	3	4	5		12		10	11	13		9	6	8²	7¹											4
1	2	3	4	5	12	13	14	10³	11¹			9	6	8	7²											5
1	2²	3		5	6¹		8²	13	10	11	12	9	4	7		14										6
1	2	3	4	5			8	12	10	11		9¹	6	7												7
1	2	3	4	5			8²	12	10	11		9¹	6	7	13											8
1	2	3	4	5			12	9²	10	11		13	6	8	7¹											9
1	2	3	4	5			12	9²	10	11		13	6	8¹	7³	14										10
1	2	3	4	5			8	9	10	11			6		7											11
1	2¹	3	4	5	12		8	9³	10	11²		13	6	14	7											12
1		3	4	5	6		12	9²	10	11		13	2	8	7¹											13
1		3	4	5	6			9	10¹	11		12	2	8	7											14
1		3	4¹	5	6		12	9	10	11			2	8	7											15
1	12	3¹		5	6²		4	9	10	11		13	2²	8	7	14										16
1	2²	3		5¹		12	4	9		11		10	6	8	7	13										17
1	2	3		5		12	4	9	10	11	13		6	8	7											18
1	2	3		5	6	9¹	8		10		12		4	11	7											19
1	2	3		5¹	12		4	9²	10	11		13	6	8	7											20
1	2	3		5			4	9	10¹	11		12	6	8	7											21
1	2	3		5¹		12	4	9²	10	11³		13	6	8	7		14									22
1	2	3		5	12		4	9²	10	11¹		13	6	8³	7		14									23
1	2²	3		5			8	9	10	11		6	12	7¹				4	13							24
1	2³	3		5	12		8	9	10	11¹		13	6	7²				4	14							25
1	2	3		5	6		8	9	10¹			12	4²	7					11	13						26
1	2	3		5	6		8	9¹	10			12	4	7²11						13						27
1	2²	3		5	6		8	9	10			12	4¹	7 11						13						28
1	2¹	3		5	6		8	9	10			12	4³	11²					14	13	7					29
1	2	3		5			8	9	10	11		12	4	13	7²		5			6						30
1	2	3		5	6		8	9	10¹	11²		12		7						4	13					31
1	2	4		5	6		8	9²	10	12		13		14	11					7³	3¹					32
1		3		5	6		4	9		11¹		10		8	7	2				12						33
		3		5	6	12	8	9¹				10			11	2				4	7		1			34
12			5	2²			8²13		11			9	14	7	10	3¹				4	6		1			35
	2	6	5				8	9²10¹	3			13			12	11				4	7		1			36
	2	6	5¹				8³9	10	3			12			13	11¹14				4	7		1			37
	2²	4	5	6			8	9	10	3¹				12	11					14 13	7¹		1			38
	2	6	5				8	12	10	3		9¹	7	11²									1	4	13	39
	2	6	5		12		8	13	10			9²	7							11			1	4	3¹	40
	2	6	5				8	12	10	3		9¹	7²	13						11			1	4		41
	2	6	5³		13		8	12	10	3¹		9		11²						14	7		1	4		42
	2	6	5		12		8²13	10	3³			9		11¹14							7		1	4		43
	2	3	5		14		8	12	10³			9¹		11² 13						6	7		1	4		44
	2²	3	5		12		8	9¹	10²			13		11 14						6	7		1	4		45
		3¹			13		8³9		11³			10	12	7		6			2	5			1	4	14	46

Worthington Cup					FA Cup			
First Round	Swansea C	(a)	0-0		Third Round	Derby Co	(a)	2-3
		(h)	2-1					
Second Round	Derby Co	(a)	2-1					
		(h)	2-4					

WEST HAM UNITED   FA Premiership

FOUNDATION

Thames Iron Works FC was formed by employees of this famous shipbuilding company in 1895 and entered the FA Cup in their initial season at Chatham and the London League in their second. The committee wanted to introduce professional players, so Thames Iron Works was wound up in June 1900 and relaunched a month later as West Ham United.

Boleyn Ground, Green Street, Upton Park, London E13 9AZ.

Telephone General Office: (020) 8548 2748.
Fax: (020) 8548 2758. *Ticket Office:* (020) 8548 2700.
Sportswear Shop: (020) 8548 2722.
Membership Office: (020) 8548 2727.
Commercial: (020) 8548 2777.
Dial-a-seat: (020) 8548 2700.

Football in the Community: (020) 8548 2707.

ClubCall: 09068 121 110.

Hammers Line: 09065 861 966.

Website: www.whufc.co.uk

Ground Capacity: 26,054 (35,000 after December 2001).

Record Attendance: 42,322 v Tottenham H, Division 1, 17 October 1970.

Record Receipts: £840,307 v Tottenham H, FA Cup 6th rd, 11 March 2001.

Pitch Measurements: 112yd × 72yd.

HONOURS

Football League: Division 1 best season: 3rd, 1985–86; Division 2 – Champions 1957–58, 1980–81; Runners-up 1922–23, 1990–91.

FA Cup: Winners 1964, 1975, 1980; Runners-up 1923.

Football League Cup: Runners-up 1966, 1981.

European Competitions: European Cup-Winners' Cup: 1964–65 (winners), 1965–66, 1975–76 (runners-up), 1980–81. *UEFA Cup:* 1999–2000. *Intertoto Cup* (winners) 1999.

Chairman: T. W. Brown FCIS, AII, FCCA. *Vice-Chairman:* M. W. Cearns ACIB. *Directors:* C. J. Warner, N. Igoe, C. Manhire, T. Brooking CBE (Non-executive), P. Aldridge (Managing).

Manager: Glenn Roeder. *Assistant Manager:* TBA. *Reserve Team Coach:* Roger Cross.

Physio: John Green BSC, MCSP, SRP.

Football Secretary: Peter Barnes.

Stadium Manager: John Ball.

Press Officer: Peter Stewart.

Colours: Claret shirts with sky blue sleeves, white shorts and stockings.

Change Colours: Sky blue shirts with two claret rings, sky blue shorts and stockings.

Year Formed: 1895.

Turned Professional: 1900.

Ltd Co.: 1900.

Previous Name: Thames Iron Works FC, 1895–1900.

Club Nicknames: 'The Hammers', 'The Irons'.

IT'S A FACT !

When West Ham United signed inside-forward Archie Macaulay from Glasgow Rangers in 1937, they were experiencing trouble with the centre-forward position. They experimented with him there in a reserve match against Queens Park Rangers and he scored six goals.

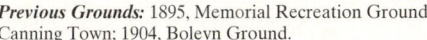
Previous Grounds: 1895, Memorial Recreation Ground, Canning Town; 1904, Boleyn Ground.

First Football League Game: 30 August 1919, Division 2, v Lincoln C (h) D 1–1 – Hufton; Cope, Lee; Lane, Fenwick, McCrae; D. Smith, Moyes (1), Puddefoot, Morris, Bradshaw.

Record League Victory: 8–0 v Rotherham U, Division 2, 8 March 1958 – Gregory; Bond, Wright; Malcolm, Brown, Lansdowne; Grice, Smith (2), Keeble (2), Dick (4), Musgrove. 8–0 v Sunderland, Division 1, 19 October 1968 – Ferguson; Bonds, Charles; Peters, Stephenson, Moore (1); Redknapp, Boyce, Brooking (1), Hurst (6), Sissons.

Record Cup Victory: 10–0 v Bury, League Cup 2nd rd (2nd leg), 25 October 1983 – Parkes; Stewart (1), Walford, Bonds (Orr), Martin (1), Devonshire (2), Allen, Cottee (4), Swindlehurst, Brooking (2), Pike.

Record Defeat: 2–8 v Blackburn R, Division 1, 26 December 1963.

Most League Points (2 for a win): 66, Division 2, 1980–81.

Most League Points (3 for a win): 88, Division 1, 1992–93.

Most League Goals: 101, Division 2, 1957–58.

Highest League Scorer in Season: Vic Watson, 42, Division 1, 1929–30.

Most League Goals in Total Aggregate: Vic Watson, 298, 1920–35.

Most League Goals in One Match: 6, Vic Watson v Leeds U, Division 1, 9 February 1929; 6, Geoff Hurst v Sunderland, Division 1, 19 October 1968.

Most Capped Player: Bobby Moore, 108, England.

Most League Appearances: Billy Bonds, 663, 1967–88.

Youngest League Player: Neil Finn, 17 years 3 days v Manchester C, 1 January 1996.

Record Transfer Fee Received: £18,000,000 from Leeds U for Rio Ferdinand, November 2000.

Record Transfer Fee Paid: £4,200,000 to Lens for Marc-Vivien Foe, January 1999.

Football League Record: 1919 Elected to Division 2; 1923–32 Division 1; 1932–58 Division 2; 1958–78 Division 1; 1978–81 Division 2; 1981–89 Division 1; 1989–91 Division 2; 1991–93 Division 1; 1993– FA Premier League.

MANAGERS
Syd King 1902–32
Charlie Paynter 1932–50
Ted Fenton 1950–61
Ron Greenwood 1961–74
(continued as General Manager to 1977)
John Lyall 1974–89
Lou Macari 1989–90
Billy Bonds 1990–94
Harry Redknapp 1994–2001
Glenn Roeder June 2001–

LATEST SEQUENCES

Longest Sequence of League Wins: 9, 19.10.85 – 14.12.85.

Longest Sequence of League Defeats: 9, 28.3.32 – 29.8.32.

Longest Sequence of League Draws: 5, 7.9.68 – 5.10.68.

Longest Sequence of Unbeaten League Matches: 27, 27.12.80 – 10.10.81.

Longest Sequence Without a League Win: 17, 31.1.76 – 21.8.76.

TEN YEAR LEAGUE RECORD

		P	W	D	L	F	A	Pts	Pos
1990-91	Div 2	46	24	15	7	60	34	87	2
1991-92	Div 1	42	9	11	22	37	59	38	22
1992-93	Div 1	46	26	10	10	81	41	88	2
1993-94	PR Lge	42	13	13	16	47	58	52	13
1994-95	PR Lge	42	13	11	18	44	48	50	14
1995-96	PR Lge	38	14	9	15	43	52	51	10
1996-97	PR Lge	38	10	12	16	39	48	42	14
1997-98	PR Lge	38	16	8	14	56	57	56	8
1998-99	PR Lge	38	16	9	13	46	53	57	5
1999-2000	PR Lge	38	15	10	13	52	53	55	9

DID YOU KNOW

West Ham United can claim two outstanding victories over London rivals Arsenal. On 7 March 1927 they beat the Gunners 7–0 in a First Division match and on 5 January 1946 took a 6–0 first leg lead over them in a third round FA Cup tie.

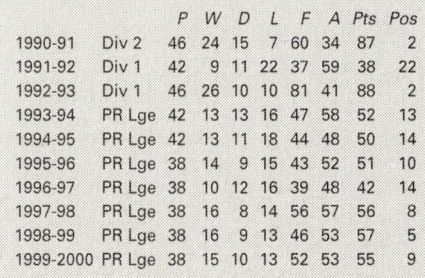

WEST HAM UNITED 2000–01 LEAGUE RECORD

Match No.	Date	Venue	Opponents	Result	H/T Score	Lg. Pos.	Goalscorers	Atten- dance
1	Aug 19	A	Chelsea	L	2-4	0-1	—	Di Canio [48], Kanoute [85]	34,914
2	23	H	Leicester C	L	0-1	0-0	—		25,195
3	26	H	Manchester U	D	2-2	0-1	20	Di Canio (pen) [86], Suker [89]	25,998
4	Sept 5	A	Sunderland	D	1-1	1-1	—	Suker [32]	45,285
5	11	A	Tottenham H	L	0-1	0-0	—		33,133
6	17	H	Liverpool	D	1-1	0-1	20	Di Canio (pen) [69]	25,998
7	23	A	Coventry C	W	3-0	2-0	18	Di Canio [38], Cole [40], Lampard [69]	20,132
8	30	H	Bradford C	D	1-1	1-0	18	Cole [26]	25,407
9	Oct 14	A	Ipswich T	D	1-1	0-1	18	Di Canio [72]	22,246
10	21	H	Arsenal	L	1-2	0-2	18	Pearce S [56]	26,034
11	28	H	Newcastle U	W	1-0	0-0	15	Kanoute [73]	26,044
12	Nov 6	A	Derby Co	D	0-0	0-0	—		24,621
13	11	H	Manchester C	W	4-1	0-1	13	Lomas [53], Sinclair [58], Pearce I [67], Di Canio (pen) [90]	26,022
14	18	A	Leeds U	W	1-0	1-0	12	Winterburn [45]	40,005
15	25	A	Southampton	W	3-2	2-1	11	Kanoute [41], Pearce S [43], Sinclair [69]	15,232
16	Dec 2	H	Middlesbrough	W	1-0	1-0	6	Di Canio [42]	25,459
17	9	H	Aston Villa	D	1-1	1-1	7	Carrick [15]	25,888
18	16	A	Everton	D	1-1	0-0	8	Kanoute [83]	31,246
19	23	A	Leicester C	L	1-2	1-1	10	Kanoute [8]	21,524
20	26	H	Charlton Ath	W	5-0	3-0	8	Rufus (og) [13], Kanoute 2 [18, 84], Lampard [45], Sinclair [71]	26,046
21	Jan 1	A	Manchester U	L	1-3	0-2	10	Kanoute [72]	67,603
22	13	H	Sunderland	L	0-2	0-1	11		26,014
23	22	A	Charlton Ath	D	1-1	0-1	—	Di Canio [74]	20,043
24	31	H	Tottenham H	D	0-0	0-0	—		26,048
25	Feb 3	A	Liverpool	L	0-3	0-2	14		44,045
26	12	H	Coventry C	D	1-1	0-0	—	Cole [83]	22,586
27	24	A	Bradford C	W	2-1	1-0	13	Lampard 2 [18, 75]	20,469
28	Mar 3	A	Arsenal	L	0-3	0-3	13		38,076
29	7	H	Chelsea	L	0-2	0-2	—		26,016
30	17	H	Ipswich T	L	0-1	0-0	14		26,046
31	31	H	Everton	L	0-2	0-1	14		26,044
32	Apr 7	A	Aston Villa	D	2-2	0-0	15	Kanoute [48], Lampard [87]	31,432
33	14	H	Derby Co	W	3-1	3-0	13	Kanoute [5], Lampard [7], Cole [45]	25,319
34	16	A	Newcastle U	L	1-2	0-0	14	Lampard (pen) [80]	51,107
35	21	H	Leeds U	L	0-2	0-1	14		26,041
36	28	A	Manchester C	L	0-1	0-1	15		33,737
37	May 5	H	Southampton	W	3-0	0-0	14	Cole [59], Di Canio [70], Kanoute [90]	26,041
38	19	A	Middlesbrough	L	1-2	1-2	15	Todorov [31]	33,057

Final League Position: 15

GOALSCORERS

League (45): Kanoute 11, Di Canio 9 (3 pens), Lampard 7 (1 pen), Cole 5, Sinclair 3, Pearce S 2, Suker 2, Carrick 1, Lomas 1, Pearce I 1, Todorov 1, Winterburn 1, own goal 1.
Worthington Cup (5): Defoe 1, Di Canio 1, Lampard 1, Lomas 1, Suker 1.
FA Cup (7): Kanoute 3, Di Canio 1, Lampard 1, Pearce S 1, Todorov 1.

Hislop S 34	Lomas S 20	Winterburn N 33	Margas J 3	Stimac I 19	Pearce S 34	Lampard F 30	Kanoute F 32	Suker D 7 + 4	Di Canio P 31	Carrick M 32 + 1	Cole J 24 + 6	Ferdinand R 12	Charles G — + 1	Kitson P — + 2	Bassila C — + 3	Moncur J 6 + 10	Sinclair T 19	Potts S 2 + 6	Diawara K 6 + 5	Pearce I 13 + 2	Song R 18 + 1	Camara T 5 + 1	Tihinen H 5 + 3	Forrest C 3 + 1	Schemmel 10 + 2	Dailly C 11 + 1	Soma R 2 + 2	Todorov S 2 + 6	Bywater S 1	Foxe H 3 + 2	McCann G — + 1	Defoe J — + 1	Minto S 1	Match No.
1	2	3	4	5	6	7	8	9	10	11[1]	12																							1
1	7	3	4[1]	5	6		8[2]	9[3]	10	11	12	2	14	13																				2
1	7	3	4[1]	5	6			9	10	11	8	2[2]	12	13																				3
1	4	3		5	6	7		9[1]	10	11	8					12	2																	4
1	4	3			6	7		9	10	11	8	5					2																	5
1	7	3	4		6			9	10	11	8	5					2																	6
1	11	3	4		6	7		9[3]	10	12	8	5[1]					2[2]	13	14															7
1	7	3	4		6			9	10	11	8	5					2																	8
1	11	3[1]	4[2]		6	7		9	10		8	5				12	2	13																9
1	4	3			6	7		9	12	10	8	5				11[1]	2																	10
1		3			6	7		9[1]	10	11	8[2]			5		12	2	13	14	4														11
1	2				6	7	8[1]	9[2]	10	11		5				12	3	13		4														12
1	8	3			6	7		9	10[1]	11		5					2		12	4														13
1	10	3			6	7	8			11		5					2	12	9	4[1]														14
1	2	3	4[1]	5	6		8		10	11	12						7	9																15
1		3		5[1]	6	7[2]	8		10	11		13					2	12	9		4													16
1	7				6		8		10	11						12	2	3	9[1]		4	5												17
1	8	3			6	7		9	10	11							2				4	5												18
1	10	3			6	7		9		11						12	2				4[1]	5	8											19
1	2	3			6	7		9	10[3]	11						12	13				4[2]	5	8[1]	14										20
1	2	3			6		8	9		11						12	10[1]			7	5	4[2]	13											21
1[6]	11	3			6	7	8	9	10							12	2				4[1]	5		15										22
		3				7	8[1]	9	10	11						12					4	5		1	2	6								23
1		3			6	7	8	9	10	11											4	2			5									24
		3			6	7	8[2]	9[3]	10	11						12			14		4	5	13	1	2[1]									25
		3			6	7	8	9	10	11											4	5		1	2									26
		3			6	7	8		10	11						12					4	5	13	1	2[2]			9[1]						27
1		3			6[2]	7	8	9	10[3]	11						12				5[1]	4		13		2			14						28
1		3			6[1]	7	8	9[3]	10	11			14			12					4	5	13		2			12[2]						29
1		3			6	7	8[2]	9	10	11						12					4	5	13		2[1]									30
1		3			6	7	8	9	10	11											4	5			2									31
1		3			6	7	8	9	10[2]	11						12					4	5	13		2[1]									32
1		3	4		6	7	8	9	10	11												5			2									33
1		3			6	7	8	9[3]		11						12					4[2]	5	13		2			10[1]						34
1		3			6	7	8	9[2]	10	11						12					4	5	13		2[1]			14						35
1		3[2]	4		6	7[3]	8	9[1]	10	11						12					4	5	13		2			14						36
1		3	4[2]		6	7[1]	8	9	10[2]	11						12					4	5	13		2									37
1					6	7	8	9	10[2]	11						12					4	5			2			7		10[2]	4	12	13	3[1]	38

Worthington Cup

Second Round	Walsall	(a)	1-0
		(h)	1-1
Third Round	Blackburn R	(h)	2-0
Fourth Round	Sheffield W	(h)	1-2

FA Cup

Third Round	Walsall	(a)	3-2
Fourth Round	Manchester U	(a)	1-0
Fifth Round	Sunderland	(a)	1-0
Sixth Round	Tottenham H	(h)	2-3

WIGAN ATHLETIC   Division 2

FOUNDATION

Following the demise of Wigan Borough and their resignation
from the Football League in 1931, a public meeting was called in
Wigan at the Queen's Hall in May 1932 at which a new club Wigan
Athletic, was founded in the hope of carrying on in the Football
League. With this in mind, they bought Springfield Park for
£2,250, but failed to gain admission to the Football League until 46
years later.

*JJB Stadium, Robin Park Complex, Newtown, Wigan
WN5 0UZ.*

Website: www.wiganlatics.co.uk

Ticket Office: (01942) 770 410.

Telephone: (01942) 774 000.

Fax: (01942) 770 477.

Commercial Dept: (01942) 774 000.

Latics ClubCall: 09068 121 655.

Football in the Community: (01942) 824 599.

Ground Capacity: 25,000.

Record Attendance: 27,526 v Hereford U, 12 December
1953.

Record Receipts: £140,000 v Preston NE, Division 2, 4 April 2000.

Pitch Measurements: 115yd × 75yd.

President: S. Jackson.

Chairman: David Whelan.

Directors: D. Whelan, J. Winstanley, D. Sharpe, P. Williams, B. Ashcroft, J. Benson, B. Spencer.

Chief Executive/Secretary: Mrs Brenda Spencer.

Assistant Secretary: Stuart Hayton.

Manager: Paul Jewell.

Physio: Alex Cribley.

Safety Officer: David Johnson.

Groundsman: David Pinch.

Colours: Blue shirts, blue shorts and stockings.

Change Colours: Gold shirts, black shorts and stockings.

Year Formed: 1932.

Club Nickname: 'The Latics'.

First Football League Game: 19 August 1978, Division 4, v Hereford U (a) D 0–0 – Brown; Hinnigan,
Gore, Gillibrand, Ward, Davids, Corrigan, Purdie, Houghton, Wilkie, Wright.

HONOURS

Football League: Division 3
Champions, 1996–97; Division 4 –
Promoted (3rd) 1981–82.

FA Cup: best season: 6th rd, 1987.

Football League Cup: best season:
4th rd, 1982.

Freight Rover Trophy: Winners 1985.

Auto Windscreens Shield: Winners
1999.

IT'S A FACT !

In 1932-33, Wigan Athletic's William Chambers scored
an incredible 60 goals in all matches, including 39 in the
Cheshire League alone.

Record League Victory: 7–1 v Scarborough, Division 3, 11 March 1997 – Butler L, Butler J, Sharp (Morgan), Greenall, McGibbon (Biggins (1)), Martinez (1), Diaz (2), Jones (Lancashire (1)), Lowe (2), Rogers, Kilford.

Record Cup Victory: 6–0 v Carlisle U (away), FA Cup 1st rd, 24 November 1934 – Caunce; Robinson, Talbot; Paterson, Watson, Tufnell; Armes (2), Robson (1), Roberts (2), Felton, Scott (1).

Record Defeat: 1–6 v Bristol R, Division 3, 3 March 1990.

Most League Points (2 for a win): 55, Division 4, 1978–79 and 1979–80.

Most League Points (3 for a win): 91, Division 4, 1981–82.

Most League Goals: 84, Division 3, 1996–97.

Highest League Scorer in Season: Graeme Jones, 31, Division 3, 1996–97.

Most League Goals in Total Aggregate: David Lowe, 66, 1982–87 and 1995–99.

Most League Goals in One Match: Not more than three goals by one player.

Most Capped Player: Roy Carroll, 9, Northern Ireland.

Most League Appearances: Kevin Langley, 317, 1981–86, 1990–94.

Youngest League Player: Steve Nugent, 16 years 132 days v Leyton Orient, 16 September 1989.

Record Transfer Fee Received: £329,000 from Coventry C for Peter Atherton, August 1991.

Record Transfer Fee Paid: £700,000 to Motherwell for Lee McCulloch, March 2001.

Football League Record: 1978 Elected to Division 4; 1982–92 Division 3; 1992–93 Division 2; 1993–97 Division 3; 1997– Division 2.

LATEST SEQUENCES

Longest Sequence of League Wins: 6, 26.12.87 – 23.1.88.

Longest Sequence of League Defeats: 7, 6.4.93 – 4.5.93.

Longest Sequence of League Draws: 4, 30.9.00 – 17.10.00.

Longest Sequence of Unbeaten League Matches: 25, 8.5.99 – 3.1.00.

Longest Sequence Without a League Win: 14, 9.5.89 – 17.10.89.

MANAGERS

Charlie Spencer 1932–37
Jimmy Milne 1946–47
Bob Pryde 1949–52
Ted Goodier 1952–54
Walter Crook 1954–55
Ron Suart 1955–56
Billy Cooke 1956
Sam Barkas 1957
Trevor Hitchen 1957–58
Malcolm Barrass 1958–59
Jimmy Shirley 1959
Pat Murphy 1959–60
Allenby Chilton 1960
Johnny Ball 1961–63
Allan Brown 1963–66
Alf Craig 1966–67
Harry Leyland 1967–68
Alan Saunders 1968
Ian McNeill 1968–70
Gordon Milne 1970–72
Les Rigby 1972–74
Brian Tiler 1974–76
Ian McNeill 1976–81
Larry Lloyd 1981–83
Harry McNally 1983–85
Bryan Hamilton 1985–86
Ray Mathias 1986–89
Bryan Hamilton 1989–93
Dave Philpotts 1993
Kenny Swain 1993–94
Graham Barrow 1994–95
John Deehan 1995–98
Ray Mathias 1998–99
John Benson 1999–2000
Bruce Rioch 2000–2001
Steve Bruce 2001
Paul Jewell June 2001–

TEN YEAR LEAGUE RECORD

		P	W	D	L	F	A	Pts	Pos
1990-91	Div 3	46	20	9	17	71	54	69	10
1991-92	Div 3	46	15	14	17	58	64	59	15
1992-93	Div 2	46	10	11	25	43	72	41	23
1993-94	Div 3	42	11	12	19	51	70	45	19
1994-95	Div 3	42	14	10	18	53	60	52	14
1995-96	Div 3	46	20	10	16	62	56	70	10
1996-97	Div 3	46	26	9	11	84	51	87	1
1997-98	Div 2	46	17	11	18	64	66	62	11
1998-99	Div 2	46	22	10	14	75	48	76	6
1999-2000	Div 2	46	22	17	7	72	38	83	4

DID YOU KNOW ❓

Full-back Harry Parkinson completed a club record 212 consecutive appearances in senior games for Wigan Athletic from 1946 from a total of 456 matches over 11 years.

WIGAN ATHLETIC 2000–01 LEAGUE RECORD

Match No.	Date		Venue	Opponents	Result		H/T Score	Lg. Pos.	Goalscorers	Attendance
1	Aug	12	A	Swansea C	D	0-0	0-0	—		8391
2		19	H	Luton T	W	2-1	1-0	5	McGibbon [10], Liddell [79]	6518
3		26	A	Wrexham	W	3-1	1-0	3	Liddell [34], Haworth [54], De Zeeuw [75]	5271
4	Sept	2	A	Walsall	L	0-2	0-2	8		7156
5		9	H	Colchester U	W	3-1	2-1	6	Haworth 3 [12, 42, 50]	5782
6		12	H	Peterborough U	W	1-0	0-0	—	Kilford [75]	4798
7		16	A	Bristol R	D	0-0	0-0	3		8109
8		23	H	Northampton T	W	2-1	2-1	2	Haworth [3], Liddell [45]	6294
9		30	A	Swindon T	D	2-2	1-2	4	Haworth [7], Green [86]	4895
10	Oct	6	H	Reading	D	1-1	1-1	—	Bradshaw [11]	7021
11		14	A	Notts Co	D	2-2	0-1	7	Roberts [75], Redfearn (pen) [88]	4567
12		17	A	Bournemouth	D	0-0	0-0	—		3035
13		21	H	Port Vale	W	1-0	0-0	3	Liddell [76]	6275
14		24	A	Oxford U	W	2-0	1-0	—	Green [11], Liddell [89]	4030
15		28	H	Bury	W	1-0	0-0	3	Kilford [61]	6622
16	Nov	4	A	Rotherham U	D	1-1	0-0	3	Griffiths [76]	6192
17		7	H	Millwall	W	1-0	0-0	—	Liddell [65]	5822
18		11	H	Cambridge U	W	2-1	0-1	1	Roberts [78], Wanless (og) [86]	6537
19		25	A	Bristol C	D	1-1	1-1	3	Carey (og) [3]	12,708
20	Dec	2	A	Brentford	D	2-2	1-0	4	Ashcroft 2 [29, 65]	4144
21		16	H	Wycombe W	W	2-1	1-0	2	Haworth [4], Roberts [86]	5779
22		23	H	Stoke C	D	1-1	0-0	4	Gunnarsson (og) [90]	8957
23		26	A	Oldham Ath	L	1-2	0-1	4	Haworth [62]	7750
24		30	A	Luton T	W	2-0	1-0	2	Haworth [11], Bidstrup [54]	5322
25	Jan	1	H	Wrexham	D	0-0	0-0	3		6515
26		6	H	Swansea C	W	2-0	1-0	2	Liddell 2 [28, 72]	5571
27		13	A	Millwall	L	1-3	0-2	2	Roberts [79]	15,317
28		20	H	Oldham Ath	W	3-1	1-1	2	Ashcroft [43], Roberts 2 [62, 79]	8274
29		27	A	Stoke C	L	0-2	0-1	3		16,859
30	Feb	2	H	Walsall	D	1-1	1-0	—	Ashcroft [35]	9586
31		10	A	Colchester U	W	2-0	1-0	2	Bidstrup [3], Liddell [77]	3275
32		17	H	Bristol R	D	0-0	0-0	2		7271
33		20	A	Peterborough U	L	0-2	0-0	—		4111
34		24	A	Northampton T	L	0-1	0-1	4		5571
35	Mar	3	H	Swindon T	D	0-0	0-0	5		6563
36		6	H	Notts Co	D	1-1	0-0	—	Bradshaw (pen) [69]	5021
37		9	A	Reading	L	0-1	0-0	—		12,307
38		17	A	Bournemouth	D	1-1	0-0	6	McGibbon [46]	5878
39		24	A	Port Vale	D	0-0	0-0	5		5017
40		31	A	Wycombe W	W	2-1	1-0	5	McCulloch [45], Beagrie [90]	4939
41	Apr	7	H	Brentford	L	1-3	0-0	6	Haworth [68]	6502
42		14	A	Oxford U	W	3-2	2-1	6	Haworth [6], Ashcroft (pen) [43], McCulloch [67]	5322
43		16	A	Bury	W	1-0	0-0	4	Balmer [48]	4915
44		21	H	Rotherham U	L	0-2	0-1	6		8836
45		28	A	Cambridge U	W	2-1	1-1	6	McCulloch [30], Bradshaw (pen) [59]	4776
46	May	5	H	Bristol C	D	0-0	0-0	6		10,048

Final League Position: 6

GOALSCORERS

League (53): Haworth 11, Liddell 9, Roberts 6, Ashcroft 5 (1 pen), Bradshaw 3 (2 pens), McCulloch 3, Bidstrup 2, Green 2, Kilford 2, McGibbon 2, Balmer 1, Beagrie 1, De Zeeuw 1, Griffiths 1, Redfearn 1 (pen), own goals 3.
Worthington Cup (6): Haworth 2, Kilford 1, Liddell 1, Roberts 1, Sharp 1.
FA Cup (5): Ashcroft 1, Bidstrup 1, Kilford 1, Roberts 1, own goal 1.

Carroll R 29	Green S 27 + 8	Bradshaw C 22 + 5	McGibbon P 38 + 2	Griffiths G 14 + 3	Redfearn N 6 + 4	Nicholls K 13 + 7	Sheridan D 25 + 2	Haworth S 25 + 5	Ashcroft L 23 + 7	Liddell A 37	Martinez R 25 + 9	De Zeeuw A 45	Mitchell P — + 1	McLaughlin B 13 + 5	Kilford I 23 + 1	Sharp K 29 + 2	McLoughlin A — + 4	Stillie D 17 + 1	Roberts N 17 + 17	Balmer S 22 + 2	Padula G 2 + 2	Bidstrup S 10 + 5	Gillespie K 4 + 1	Brannan G 12 + 1	Beagrie P 7 + 3	Dickson H — + 1	McCulloch L 10	McMillan S 6	Dalglish P 5 + 1	Match No
1	2	3	4	5	6	7	8	9	10[1]	11	12																			1
1	2[1]	3	4	5	11	7[1]	8	9	13	10	12	6																		2
1	2[1]	3	5	11[1]				9		10	8[2]	6	14	12	7	4	13													3
	2[2]		4	5	11[1]			9		10	8	6			7	3	12	1	13											4
1	2[1]		4		13			9		10	11[2]	6	8	7	3	12		5												5
1	2[1]		4		12			9		10	11	6	8[2]	7	3			5	13											6
1	2		4		8			9		10	11[1]	6		7	3	12		5												7
1	2[1]		4		8			9		10[2]	12	6	11	7	3			13	5											8
1	2	12	4		8[2]			9		11		6	10	7	3			13	5[1]											9
	2	3		5	8[1]			12		11		6	10	7	4		1	9												10
1	2[1]	3	4	5	12	13		10		11[2]	6		14	7	8[3]			9												11
1	12	2	4[1]	5	8			10		11	6		7	3				9												12
1	12	3	4	5[1]	8[2]			9[3]		10	11	6	13	7	2			14												13
1	2	3[1]	4	12		13				10	11	6	8[2]	7	5			9												14
1	2		4	5	12					10	11	6	8[1]	7	3			9												15
1		2	5	12	13			10[1]	11	8	6		4[1]	7	3	15		9[0]												16
1	2		4	5	12	7[1]	8		11		6	10[3]		7	3			9	13											17
1	2		4[3]	5			8[1]	13	11	12	6	10[2]	7	3		9		14												18
	2		4	5				10	11	6		7	3	1	9			8												19
1		2	5		12			9	10	11	6		7[1]	3	1			4	8											20
1	2	5	12			8	9[3]	10	11[2]	6		13	3	14			4	7[1]												21
	12	2	5			8	9[3]	13	10	6		7	3	1	14			4[2]	11[1]											22
	12	2[1]	5			8	9	10	11	4[3]	6		3	1	13			14	7[2]											23
	2		4			8	9	10[1]	11	6		3	1	12	5		7													24
	2[1]	12	4		13	8[3]	9	10	11[2]	6		3	1		5		7	14												25
	2	3				8	9[1]	10	11	4	6		7	1	12	5														26
	2[2]	3				8	9	10[1]	11	4	6		7	1	12	5	13													27
	12		2[1]			8[2]	4	9[3]	10	11	13	6		7	1	14	5	3												28
	12	13	2[1]			4[3]	8		10	11	6		14	7	1	9	5	3[2]												29
	2[1]	3	4			8		9	11	6	5		6	7	1	12														30
	2		5	12			9		11	7[2]	6		8[1]	3	1	10	13	4												31
	2		5				9[1]		8	12	6		13	3	1	10		4	7	11[2]										32
	2		5	12			9[3]		11	13	6		8	3	1	10[1]		4	7[2]	14										33
1		2		5			8	12	9[1]	10	11[2]	6		3		13	4			7										34
1	12	2					4		9[1]	8		6				13	5			7	10[2]			11	3					35
1		3					4	12	10	11		6				8	5			7				9[1]	2					36
1	12	3[1]	13					4[3]	10	8		6				9	5			14	7			11[1]	2					37
1	2	3	12					4[3]	10	8	13	6				9[1]	5			14	7	11[2]								38
	3[1]	2					8		12	10	13	6				1		5		4	7	11[3]		9[1]		14				39
1		2					3	12	10	11[3]	4	6						5		13	7	14		9[2]		8[1]				40
1		2					3	12	10		4[1]	6			13			5			7	11[2]		9		8				41
1	12	4					13	8	9[3]	10[2]		6				14	5			7				11[1]	3		2			42
1		4					7	8	9[3]	10[2]		6				12	5			13	14			11[1]	3		2			43
1	12	4					7	8	9	10[3]		6			13		11	5[1]			14				3[2]		2			44
1	5	2	4				8		9	12		6					3			13				7	11[1]		10[2]			45
1	5	2[1]	4				8		12	13	10[2]	7	6				3							11	9					46

Worthington Cup

First Round	Scunthorpe U	(h)	1-0
		(a)	4-1
Second Round	Wimbledon	(a)	0-0
		(h)	1-2

FA Cup

First Round	Dorchester T	(h)	3-1
Second Round	Notts Co	(h)	1-1
		(a)	1-2

WIMBLEDON

Division 1

Selhurst Park, South Norwood, London SE25 6PY.

Telephone: (020) 8771 2233.

Fax: (020) 8768 0641.

Website: www.wimbledon-fc.co.uk

Box Office: (020) 8771 8841.

ClubCall: 09068 121 175.

Ground Capacity: 26,297.

Record Attendance: 30,115 v Manchester U, FA Premier League, 9 May 1993.

Record Receipts: £531,976 v Tottenham H, Worthington Cup semi-final, 2nd leg, 16 February 1999.

Pitch Measurements: 110yd × 74yd.

Chairman: Charles Koppel.

Deputy Chairman: Peter Lloyd-Cooper.

Directors: K. I. Røkke, S. Reed, J. H. Lelliott, P. E. Cork, P. J. B. Miller, M. Hauger, C. Stromberg.

Manager: Terry Burton.

Head Coach: Stewart Robson.

Club Secretary: Steve Rooke.

Director of Media and Communications: Graham Thorley.

Marketing Manager: Sharon Sillitoe.

Press Manager: Reg Davis.

Chief Scout: Ron Suart.

Team Physio: Steve Allen. *Club Physio:* John Clinkard.

Stadium Manager: Vic Worrall.

Colours: All navy blue with yellow trim.

Change Colours: All yellow with navy blue trim.

Year Formed: 1889.

Turned Professional: 1964.

Ltd Co.: 1964.

Previous Name: Wimbledon Old Centrals, 1899–1905.

Previous Ground: 1899, Plough Lane; 1991, Selhurst Park.

HONOURS

FA Premier League: best season: 6th, 1993–94.

Football League: Division 3 – Runners-up 1983–84; Division 4 – Champions 1982–83.

FA Cup: Winners 1988.

Football League Cup: Semi-final 1996–97, 1998–99.

League Group Cup: Runners-up 1982.

Amateur Cup: Winners 1963; Runners-up 1935, 1947.

IT'S A FACT !

Despite suffering relegation from the Premier League in 1999-2000, Wimbledon achieved the feat of being the only team to stay unbeaten against the champions Manchester United, drawing 2-2 at home and 1-1 away.

Club Nickname: 'The Dons', 'The Crazy Gang'.

First Football League Game: 20 August 1977, Division 4, v Halifax T (h) D 3–3 – Guy; Bryant (1), Galvin, Donaldson, Aitken, Davies, Galliers, Smith, Connell (1), Holmes, Leslie (1).

Record League Victory: 6–0 v Newport Co, Division 3, 3 September 1983 – Beasant; Peters, Winterburn, Galliers, Morris, Hatter, Evans (2), Ketteridge (1), Cork (3 incl. 1p), Downes, Hodges (Driver).

Record Cup Victory: 7–2 v Windsor & Eton, FA Cup 1st rd, 22 November 1980 – Beasant; Jones, Armstrong, Galliers, Mick Smith (2), Cunningham (1), Ketteridge, Hodges, Leslie, Cork (1), Hubbick (3).

Record Defeat: 0–8 v Everton, League Cup 2nd rd, 29 August 1978.

Most League Points (2 for a win): 61, Division 4, 1978–79.

Most League Points (3 for a win): 98, Division 4, 1982–83.

Most League Goals: 97, Division 3, 1983–84.

Highest League Scorer in Season: Alan Cork, 29, 1983–84.

Most League Goals in Total Aggregate: Alan Cork, 145, 1977–92.

Most League Goals in One Match: 4, Alan Cork v Torquay U, Division 4, 28 February 1979.

Most Capped Player: Kenny Cunningham, 33, Republic of Ireland.

Most League Appearances: Alan Cork, 430, 1977–92.

Youngest League Player: Kevin Gage, 17 years 15 days v Bury, 2 May 1981.

Record Transfer Fee Received: £7,000,000 from Newcastle U for Carl Cort, July 2000.

Record Transfer Fee Paid: £7,500,000 to West Ham U for John Hartson, January 1999.

Football League Record: 1977 Elected to Division 4; 1979–80 Division 3; 1980–81 Division 4; 1981–82 Division 3; 1982–83 Division 4; 1983–84 Division 3; 1984–86 Division 2; 1986–92 Division 1; 1992–2000 FA Premier League; 2000– Division 1.

MANAGERS

Les Henley 1955–71
Mike Everitt 1971–73
Dick Graham 1973–74
Allen Batsford 1974–78
Dario Gradi 1978–81
Dave Bassett 1981–87
Bobby Gould 1987–90
Ray Harford 1990–91
Peter Withe 1991
Joe Kinnear 1992–99
Egil Olsen 1999–2000
Terry Burton May 2000–

LATEST SEQUENCES

Longest Sequence of League Wins: 7, 4.9.96 – 19.10.96.

Longest Sequence of League Defeats: 8, 19.3.00 – 30.4.00.

Longest Sequence of League Draws: 4, 26.10.96 – 23.11.96.

Longest Sequence of Unbeaten League Matches: 22, 15.1.83 – 14.5.83.

Longest Sequence Without a League Win: 14, 19.3.00 – 28.8.00.

TEN YEAR LEAGUE RECORD

		P	W	D	L	F	A	Pts	Pos
1990-91	Div 1	38	14	14	10	53	46	56	7
1991-92	Div 1	42	13	14	15	53	53	53	13
1992-93	PR Lge	42	14	12	16	56	55	54	12
1993-94	PR Lge	42	18	11	13	56	53	65	6
1994-95	PR Lge	42	15	11	16	48	65	56	9
1995-96	PR Lge	38	10	11	17	55	70	41	14
1996-97	PR Lge	38	15	11	12	49	46	56	8
1997-98	PR Lge	38	10	14	14	34	46	44	15
1998-99	PR Lge	38	10	12	16	40	63	42	16
1999-2000	PR Lge	38	7	12	19	46	74	33	18

DID YOU KNOW ?

In 1958-59, Wimbledon won the Isthmian League title for the first time in 23 years with a points record and unbeaten at home. Highest gate was 6946 v Tooting & Mitcham. Eddie Reynolds scored 41 goals that season.

WIMBLEDON 2000–01 LEAGUE RECORD

Match No.	Date	Venue	Opponents	Result		H/T Score	Lg. Pos.	Goalscorers	Attendance
1	Aug 12	H	Tranmere R	D	0-0	0-0	—		8266
2	19	A	Burnley	L	0-1	0-1	18		15,124
3	26	H	Watford	D	0-0	0-0	18		8447
4	28	A	Preston NE	D	1-1	1-0	19	Williams [45]	13,519
5	Sept 9	H	Sheffield W	W	5-0	0-0	11	Francis [50], Hartson 2 [64, 67], Euell 2 [76, 84]	15,856
6	12	A	Huddersfield T	W	2-0	1-0	—	Hartson 2 [21, 54]	7592
7	16	H	Wolverhampton W	D	1-1	0-0	9	Hartson [58]	8761
8	23	A	QPR	L	1-2	0-0	12	Euell [70]	11,720
9	30	H	Stockport Co	W	2-0	1-0	9	Ardley (pen) [40], Francis [88]	6087
10	Oct 14	H	Gillingham	D	4-4	2-3	10	Francis [5], Hartson 2 [23, 78], Euell [58]	9030
11	18	H	Blackburn R	L	0-2	0-2	—		6019
12	21	A	Crewe Alex	W	4-0	2-0	12	Harley 2 [12, 56], Gayle [26], Euell [80]	5469
13	24	A	WBA	L	1-3	1-2	—	Euell (pen) [45]	15,570
14	28	H	Sheffield U	D	0-0	0-0	13		7327
15	Nov 5	A	Barnsley	W	1-0	0-0	12	Francis [89]	13,641
16	11	H	Fulham	L	0-3	0-1	12		14,071
17	18	A	Nottingham F	W	2-1	1-0	11	Euell [13], Andersen [90]	18,159
18	25	A	Norwich C	W	2-1	1-1	11	Hartson [35], Francis [46]	14,059
19	Dec 2	H	WBA	L	0-1	0-0	11		8608
20	5	A	Crystal Palace	L	1-3	1-0	—	Roberts [27]	16,699
21	9	A	Birmingham C	W	3-0	2-0	11	Francis 2 [30, 78], Euell [42]	16,778
22	13	H	Grimsby T	D	2-2	2-1	—	Euell [40], Andersen [45]	4489
23	16	H	Bolton W	L	0-1	0-0	11		6076
24	23	A	Tranmere R	W	4-0	1-0	11	Andersen [40], Williams [54], Euell 2 [77, 85]	8058
25	26	H	Portsmouth	D	1-1	1-0	11	Francis [50]	9245
26	Jan 2	A	Watford	L	1-3	1-3	—	Gayle [11]	11,336
27	13	H	Preston NE	W	3-1	1-0	11	Euell 2 [15, 50], Williams [84]	7242
28	20	A	Portsmouth	L	1-2	1-2	11	Euell [20]	12,488
29	Feb 10	H	Sheffield W	W	4-1	2-1	11	Andersen 2 [5, 83], Euell [9], Beresford (og) [70]	6741
30	24	H	QPR	W	5-0	1-0	11	Williams 2 [42, 75], Gayle [52], Euell 2 [62, 80]	9446
31	Mar 3	A	Stockport Co	D	2-2	1-1	11	Agyemang [26], Wiss (og) [47]	5519
32	6	A	Gillingham	D	0-0	0-0	—		8841
33	10	H	Crystal Palace	W	1-0	1-0	10	Agyemang [22]	13,167
34	13	A	Grimsby T	D	1-1	1-0	—	Agyemang [6]	4276
35	17	A	Blackburn R	D	1-1	0-0	11	Euell [50]	19,000
36	31	A	Bolton W	D	2-2	1-1	11	Agyemang [31], Cooper [90]	14,562
37	Apr 4	A	Wolverhampton W	W	1-0	0-0	—	Ardley [53]	16,767
38	7	H	Birmingham C	W	3-1	1-0	10	Nielsen [15], Hughes [71], Williams [73]	6619
39	10	H	Burnley	L	0-2	0-2	—		6132
40	14	H	Barnsley	D	1-1	1-0	11	Ainsworth [19]	7609
41	17	A	Sheffield U	W	1-0	0-0	—	Roberts [46]	14,527
42	21	A	Nottingham F	W	2-1	0-0	9	Nielsen [48], Cooper [70]	10,027
43	24	H	Crewe Alex	D	3-3	2-1	—	Willmott [2], Cooper [4], Ardley [52]	5468
44	28	A	Fulham	D	1-1	0-0	8	Euell (pen) [74]	18,576
45	May 1	H	Huddersfield T	D	1-1	0-0	—	Ainsworth [51]	4956
46	6	H	Norwich C	D	0-0	0-0	8		7888

Final League Position: 8

GOALSCORERS

League (71): Euell 19 (2 pens), Francis 8, Hartson 8, Williams 6, Andersen 5, Agyemang 4, Ardley 3 (1 pen), Cooper 3, Gayle 3, Ainsworth 2, Harley 2, Nielsen 2, Roberts 2, Hughes 1, Willmott 1, own goals 2.
Worthington Cup (4): Hartson 2 (1 pen), Gayle 1, Roberts 1.
FA Cup (9): Ardley 2 (1 pen), Agyemang 1, Ainsworth 1, Andersen 1, Euell 1, Hunt 1, Karlsson 1, Williams 1.

Davis K 45	Jupp D 4	Kimble A 21 + 4	Andersen T 40 + 2	Williams M 42	Hreidarsson H 1	Ardley N 36 + 1	Francis D 29	Leaburn C 2 + 1	Agyemang P 16 + 13	Gayle M 24 + 8	Selley I 1 + 3	Robinson P —+ 3	Hawkins P 29 + 1	Thomas M 5 + 3	Willmott C 13 + 1	Morgan L 1 + 4	Euell J 33 + 3	Hartson J 19	Hunt J 8 + 4	Roberts A 25 + 2	Owusu A 1 + 3	Holloway D 30 + 1	Gier R 13 + 1	Harley J 6	Karlsson P 7 + 9	Blackwell D 5 + 1	Heald P 1 + 2	Ainsworth G 8 + 4	Gray W 1 + 10	Cunningham K 15	Hughes M 5 + 5	Cooper K 11	Nielsen D 9 + 2	Match No.
1	2	3	4	5	6	7	8^1	9	10^2	11	12	13																						1
1	2	3^2	4	5		7	8	9^1	10^2	11	6	13	12	14																				2
1		3^2	4	5		7	8			11	12		2	10^1	13	6^2	14	9																3
1			4	5		7	6			11	12	13	2^1	10	3		8	9^2																4
1	2		4	5		7	8			12	11		3			6	13	10^2	9^1															5
1			4	5		7	6			12	11		2				10	3	8	9^1														6
1			4	5		7	6^1			12	11^2		2				10	3	13	8	9													7
1	2		4	5		7	10			11			3				8	9				6												8
1			4	5		7	8			12	11		3				10^1	9^1	6^2	2		13	14											9
1			4				8			11			3	10	5	7	9	6		2														10
1		3	4^3	5			8^2			12	11^1		13	6		7	9	10	14	2														11
1		3^1	4^3	5			8	12		9			6		7		13		10^2	2	14	11												12
1		3^1	4	5			8			12	9		6		7^2		10			2		11	13											13
1		3	4	5			8			12	10						9^1	7^2		2	6	11	13											14
1		3	2	5			8			12	10						9^1	7^2	4	6^3	11	13	14											15
1		3^3	4^1	5			12	8^2		10			13	9		7				2		11	14	6										16
1		3	4	5		7	8			9			10^1							2		11	12	6										17
1		3^2	4	5		7	10			12	11		8	9^1						2		13	6											18
1			4^2	5		7	10			12	11^1		3^3				9	13	8	2		6	14											19
1			4^2	5		7	10			12	11^1		3				13	9^1	8	2		6	14											20
1		2		5		7	10			12			11^1	9			8			3		6	4											21
1		2		5		7	10			12		13					8	9	4^2	14		3^3	6		11^1									22
1		2		5		7	10			12							8	9	4			3	6		11^1									23
1			4	5		7	10^2			11^1	12		3				9			13	8	2	6											24
1			4	5		7	10			11^1	12		3				9			8		2	6											25
1			4	5		7	10			12	11		3				9			8^1		2	6											26
1^0		3	4	5		7	10			11^{12}	12		2				9			8^1	6				15	13								27
1		3	4	5			10			12			2				8	9							11^1	6		7						28
1		3^1	4	5			10			11^1	12		2				9^3					13	8					7	14	6				29
1		3	4	5			11			9^2	10^1		2				8					12						7	13	6				30
1		3	4				11			10	9		2	5			12								8^2			7^1	13	6				31
1			4			7				11	10		3	5	9		8			2		6												32
1	12	4	5			7				11^2			3				9			10^1	8	2						6	13					33
1	12		5			7				10^2			3				9			8^1	4	2						13	6	11				34
1			5			7				10^2			3				9			4		2						12	13	6	11	8^1		35
1	12	13	5			7				9^3			3				10			4		2^2							6	11^1	8	14		36
1	12		4	5		7				3							9^3			8		2						13	6	14	11^1	10^2		37
1			4	5		7				9^2			3				8			2								12	6	13	11	10^1		38
1^0			4^2	5		7				12			3				8			2^1						15	13	6	10	11	9		39
1			12	5		7				9			3				4			2							8	6	11^1	10			40
1		3	4	5		7				8			2															9^1	12	6	11	10		41
1		3	4	5		7				9			8							2									6	11	10			42
1		3		5		7				6	9		4				2^1											8^2	12	13	11	10		43
1		3	4			7				9			8				2	6										12	5	13	11^1	10^2		44
1				5			8^1			3			13	10			4			2	6							7	9^2	11	12			45
		3	4^2	5		7				2			12	9			8			6							1	13	14	11^1	10^3		46

Worthington Cup

Second Round	Wigan Ath	(h)	0-0	
		(a)	2-1	
Third Round	Middlesbrough	(h)	1-0	
Fourth Round	Manchester C	(a)	1-2	

FA Cup

Third Round	Notts Co	(h)	2-2	
		(a)	1-0	
Fourth Round	Middlesbrough	(a)	0-0	
		(h)	3-1	
Fifth Round	Wycombe W	(a)	2-2	
		(h)	1-1	

WOLVERHAMPTON WANDERERS Division 1

FOUNDATION

Enthusiasts of the game at St. Luke's School, Blakenhall formed a club in 1877. In the same neighbourhood a cricket club called Blakenhall Wanderers had a football section. Several St. Luke's footballers played cricket for them and shortly before the start of the 1879–80 season the two amalgamated and Wolverhampton Wanderers FC was brought into being.

Molineux Stadium, Wolverhampton WV1 4QR.

Telephone: (01902) 655 000. *Fax:* (01902) 687 006.
ClubCall: 09068 121 103.

Ground Capacity: 28,525.

Record Attendance: 61,315 v Liverpool, FA Cup 5th rd, 11 February 1939.

Record Receipts: £319,141 v Arsenal, FA Cup 4th rd, 24 January 1999.

Pitch Measurements: 110yd × 75yd.

President and Chairman: Sir Jack Hayward.

Deputy Chairman: Derek Harrington.

Chief Executive: Jez Moxey.

Directors: Jack Harris, John Harris, Rick Hayward, Rachael Heyhoe Flint, Michael Lister, Paul Manduca.

Manager: David Jones. *Assistant Manager:* John Ward.
Coach: Terry Connor. *Physio:* Barry Holmes.

Secretary: Richard Skirrow.

Stadium Manager: Steve Sutton.

Safety Officer: Bob Morrison.

Colours: Old gold shirts, black shorts, old gold stockings.

Change Colours: All silver.

Year Formed: 1877* (*see Foundation*).

Turned Professional: 1888. *Ltd Co.:* 1982.

Previous Names: 1879, St Luke's combined with Wanderers Cricket Club to become Wolverhampton Wanderers (1923) Ltd until 1982.

Club Nickname: 'Wolves'.

Previous Grounds: 1877, Goldthorn Hill; 1879, John Harper's Field; 1881, Dudley Road; 1889, Molineux.

First Football League Game: 8 September 1888, Football League, v Aston Villa (h) D 1–1 – Baynton; Baugh, Mason; Fletcher, Allen, Lowder; Hunter, Cooper, Anderson, White, Cannon, (1 og).

Record League Victory: 10–1 v Leicester C, Division 1, 15 April 1938 – Sidlow; Morris, Dowen; Galley, Cullis, Gardiner; Maguire (1), Horace Wright, Westcott (4), Jones (1), Dorsett (4).

HONOURS

Football League: Division 1 – Champions 1953–54, 1957–58, 1958–59; Runners-up 1937–38, 1938–39, 1949–50, 1954–55, 1959–60; Division 2 – Champions 1931–32, 1976–77; Runners-up 1966–67, 1982–83; Division 3 (N) – Champions 1923–24; Division 3 – Champions 1988–89; Division 4 – Champions 1987–88.

FA Cup: Winners 1893, 1908, 1949, 1960; Runners-up 1889, 1896, 1921, 1939.

Football League Cup: Winners 1974, 1980.

Texaco Cup: Winners 1971.

Sherpa Van Trophy: Winners 1988.

European Competitions: *European Cup:* 1958–59, 1959–60. *European Cup-Winners' Cup:* 1960–61. *UEFA Cup:* 1971–72 (runners-up), 1973–74, 1974–75, 1980–81.

IT'S A FACT !

Between May 1935 and May 1939, Wolverhampton Wanderers spent £110,658 on transfer fees and received £42,330 in similiar sales for a then profit record of £68,328.

Record Cup Victory: 14–0 v Cresswell's Brewery, FA Cup 2nd rd, 13 November 1886 – I. Griffiths; Baugh, Mason; Pearson, Allen (1), Lowder; Hunter (4), Knight (2), Brodie (4), B. Griffiths (2), Wood. Plus one goal 'scrambled through'.

Record Defeat: 1–10 v Newton Heath, Division 1, 15 October 1892.

Most League Points (2 for a win): 64, Division 1, 1957–58.

Most League Points (3 for a win): 92, Division 4, 1988–89.

Most League Goals: 115, Division 2, 1931–32.

Highest League Scorer in Season: Dennis Westcott, 38, Division 1, 1946–47.

Most League Goals in Total Aggregate: Steve Bull, 250, 1986–99.

Most League Goals in One Match: 5, Joe Butcher v Accrington, Division 1, 19 November 1892; 5, Tom Phillipson v Barnsley, Division 2, 26 April 1926; 5, Tom Phillipson v Bradford C, Division 2, 25 December 1926; 5, Billy Hartill v Notts Co, Division 2, 12 October 1929; 5, Billy Hartill v Aston Villa, Division 1, 3 September 1934.

Most Capped Player: Billy Wright, 105, England (70 consecutive).

Most League Appearances: Derek Parkin, 501, 1967–82.

Youngest League Player: Jimmy Mullen, 16 years 43 days v Leeds U, 18 February 1939.

Record Transfer Fee Received: £2,000,000 from Crystal Palace for Neil Emblen, August 1997.

MANAGERS

George Worrall 1877–85
  (Secretary-Manager)
John Addenbrooke 1885–1922
George Jobey 1922–24
Albert Hoskins 1924–26
  (had been Secretary since 1922)
Fred Scotchbrook 1926–27
Major Frank Buckley 1927–44
Ted Vizard 1944–48
Stan Cullis 1948–64
Andy Beattie 1964–65
Ronnie Allen 1966–68
Bill McGarry 1968–76
Sammy Chung 1976–78
John Barnwell 1978–81
Ian Greaves 1982
Graham Hawkins 1982–84
Tommy Docherty 1984–85
Bill McGarry 1985
Sammy Chapman 1985–86
Brian Little 1986
Graham Turner 1986–94
Graham Taylor 1994–95
Mark McGhee 1995–98
Colin Lee 1998–2000
David Jones January 2001–

Record Transfer Fee Paid: £3,000,000 to Bristol C for Ade Akinbiyi, September 1999.

Football League Record: 1888 Founder Member of Football League: 1906–23 Division 2; 1923–24 Division 3 (N); 1924–32 Division 2; 1932–65 Division 1; 1965–67 Division 2; 1967–76 Division 1; 1976–77 Division 2; 1977–82 Division 1; 1982–83 Division 2; 1983–84 Division 1; 1984–85 Division 2; 1985–86 Division 3; 1986–88 Division 4; 1988–89 Division 3; 1989–92 Division 2; 1992– Division 1.

LATEST SEQUENCES

Longest Sequence of League Wins: 8, 15.10.88 – 26.11.88.

Longest Sequence of League Defeats: 8, 5.12.81 – 13.2.82.

Longest Sequence of League Draws: 6, 22.4.95 – 20.8.95.

Longest Sequence of Unbeaten League Matches: 20, 24.11.23 – 5.4.24.

Longest Sequence Without a League Win: 19, 1.12.84 – 6.4.85.

TEN YEAR LEAGUE RECORD

		P	W	D	L	F	A	Pts	Pos
1990-91	Div 2	46	13	19	14	63	63	58	12
1991-92	Div 2	46	18	10	18	61	54	64	11
1992-93	Div 1	46	16	13	17	57	56	61	11
1993-94	Div 1	46	17	17	12	60	47	68	8
1994-95	Div 1	46	21	13	12	77	61	76	4
1995-96	Div 1	46	13	16	17	56	62	55	20
1996-97	Div 1	46	22	10	14	68	51	76	3
1997-98	Div 1	46	18	11	17	57	53	65	9
1998-99	Div 1	46	19	16	11	64	43	73	7
1999-2000	Div 1	46	21	11	14	64	48	74	7

DID YOU KNOW ?

Three days after selling Steve Daley to Manchester City for a record £1,437,500, Wolverhampton Wanderers shattered the record by paying Aston Villa £1,469,000 for Andy Gray in September 1979.

WOLVERHAMPTON WANDERERS 2000–01 LEAGUE RECORD

Match No.	Date		Venue	Opponents	Result	H/T Score	Lg. Pos.	Goalscorers	Attendance
1	Aug	13	H	Sheffield W	D 1-1	1-0	—	Ketsbaia [18]	19,086
2		19	A	Stockport Co	D 1-1	0-0	13	Bazeley [71]	7758
3		26	H	Burnley	W 1-0	0-0	8	Sedgley [74]	20,156
4		28	A	Portsmouth	L 1-3	1-3	15	Ketsbaia [45]	14,124
5	Sept	2	A	Gillingham	L 0-1	0-1	18		10,017
6		9	H	Tranmere R	L 1-2	1-1	19	Robinson [12]	17,252
7		12	H	Sheffield U	D 0-0	0-0	—		14,853
8		16	A	Wimbledon	D 1-1	0-0	18	Lescott [79]	8761
9		24	H	Norwich C	W 4-0	3-0	13	Proudlock [21], Dinning [26], Robinson [45], Branch [70]	15,105
10		30	A	Nottingham F	D 0-0	0-0	15		19,110
11	Oct	14	A	Bolton W	L 1-2	0-1	16	Dinning (pen) [53]	15,585
12		17	A	WBA	L 0-1	0-1	—		21,492
13		21	H	Fulham	D 0-0	0-0	17		21,080
14		24	A	Barnsley	W 2-1	2-1	—	Muscat [18], Ketsbaia [45]	13,393
15		28	H	Watford	D 2-2	0-2	15	Muscat (pen) [47], Dinning [75]	20,296
16	Nov	4	A	Crewe Alex	L 0-2	0-2	18		7147
17		11	H	Crystal Palace	L 1-3	0-2	20	Branch [60]	17,658
18		18	A	Blackburn R	L 0-1	0-0	21		20,380
19		21	H	Grimsby T	W 2-0	2-0	—	Dinning [6], Ndah [45]	16,088
20		25	A	QPR	D 2-2	2-1	16	Ndah [19], Pollet [43]	11,156
21	Dec	2	A	Barnsley	W 2-0	1-0	14	Robinson [28], Dinning [59]	17,340
22		9	A	Huddersfield T	L 0-3	0-0	15		11,506
23		17	H	Birmingham C	L 0-1	0-1	16		19,938
24		23	A	Sheffield W	W 1-0	1-0	15	Muscat [45]	17,787
25		26	H	Preston NE	L 0-1	0-1	17		24,306
26		30	H	Stockport Co	W 3-2	3-1	15	Proudlock [22], Wiss (og) [32], Branch [45]	16,667
27	Jan	1	A	Burnley	W 2-1	1-1	12	Proudlock [28], Naylor [85]	15,483
28		13	H	Portsmouth	D 1-1	1-1	12	Sinton [20]	20,869
29	Feb	3	H	Gillingham	D 1-1	1-1	13	Branch [45]	26,627
30		10	A	Tranmere R	W 2-0	1-0	12	Flynn (og) [21], Proudlock [47]	9678
31		20	A	Sheffield U	L 0-1	0-1	—		20,282
32		24	A	Norwich C	L 0-1	0-1	15		17,288
33	Mar	3	H	Nottingham F	W 2-0	0-0	14	Edds (og) [48], Proudlock [62]	20,291
34		10	H	Grimsby T	W 2-0	0-0	13	Dinning [66], Proudlock [83]	4899
35		14	A	Preston NE	L 0-2	0-1	—		15,457
36		18	H	WBA	W 3-1	2-0	13	Ndah 2 [23, 45], Pollet [66]	25,069
37	Apr	1	A	Birmingham C	W 1-0	1-0	13	Ndah [1]	24,003
38		4	H	Wimbledon	L 0-1	0-0	—		16,767
39		7	H	Huddersfield T	L 0-1	0-1	13		19,423
40		14	H	Crewe Alex	D 0-0	0-0	14		20,364
41		17	A	Watford	L 2-3	1-2	—	Ndah (pen) [44], Proudlock [80]	13,765
42		21	A	Blackburn R	D 0-0	0-0	15		20,018
43		24	A	Fulham	L 0-2	0-1	—		15,375
44		28	A	Crystal Palace	W 2-0	1-0	12	Sinton [16], Proudlock [49]	18,993
45	May	1	H	Bolton W	L 0-2	0-1	—		16,242
46		6	H	QPR	D 1-1	1-0	12	Lescott [36]	17,447

Final League Position: 12

GOALSCORERS

League (45): Proudlock 8, Dinning 6 (1 pen), Ndah 6 (1 pen), Branch 4, Ketsbaia 3, Muscat 3 (1 pen), Robinson 3, Lescott 2, Pollet 2, Sinton 2, Bazeley 1, Naylor 1, Sedgley 1, own goals 3.
Worthington Cup (9): Taylor 3, Proudlock 2, Ketsbaia 1, Muscat 1 (pen), Osborn 1, Robinson 1.
FA Cup (2): Proudlock 1, Robinson 1.

Oakes M 46	Muscat K 37	Naylor L 44+2	Lescott J 31+6	Pollet L 29	Emblen N 21+7	Bazeley D 23+1	Osborn S 16+4	Ketsbaia T 14+8	Branch M 31+7	Sinton A 28+2	Taylor S 3+1	Taylor R 5+4	Ndah G 23+6	Sedgley S 5	Thetis M 3	Camara M 4+14	Robinson C 36+4	Larkin C —+2	Green R 5+2	Proudlock A 28+7	Al-Jaber S —+4	Dinning T 31	Peacock D 2+2	Butler P 12	Tudor S —+1	Andrews K 20+2	Roussel C 3+6	Connelly S 6	Stowell M —+1	Match No
1	2	3	4	5	6	7	8	9	10	11																				1
1	2	3	4		5	7	8	9		11¹			6			10	12													2
1	2	3	4		8	7		9²		11¹			10			12	5		6	13										3
1	2	3	4			8	7³	12	9				13			10²	5¹		6	11		14								4
1	2	12	4			7²	13	8	9	11			10³			5	6	3¹		14										5
1	4	3	13		8	7	12		14				11¹			9	5			6		2³	10²							6
1	2	3	4		11	7	8¹	12					13			9²	5			6		10								7
1	5	3	4		8	7		9²	12				11¹				6			2		10	13							8
1		3			6	7		9	8³	11²			12			13	5		2	10¹		14	4							9
1	4	3	5			7		9¹		11			8				2		10	12		6								10
1		3	12	5¹	6²	2	8	13	9	11²			7				10		4	14										11
1		3	12	5¹	11³	7	8	9					13			14	2		10²	4		6								12
1	2	3	4	5	6²	7	8	9	11¹				12			13	10													13
1	2	3	4		7	8	9²	10¹	11				12			13	6		5											14
1	2	3	4	5²	7	8	9	10	11¹				12			6	13													15
1	2	3	4		11	7¹	8	9	10				13			5²	12		6											16
1	2	3	4	5¹	9	7⁴	8	10		12			11³			14	13		6											17
1	2	3		5	8¹	7		10²		9			12			11	13		4			6								18
1	2	3		5	10	7	8	12		9¹			11²			13	4		6											19
1	2	3		5	10	7	8			9¹			11			12	4		6											20
1	4	3²	5	11¹	2	8		12	9				13			7			10			6								21
1	2	3	12	5	7¹	8³		9²					13			10	4		14	11		6								22
1	2	3	4	5	6	7²	12	14	10³	9			13			11	8¹													23
1	2	3	4	5	7²		12	11		9¹			6			10	13									8				24
1	2	3	4	5	12		13	11³	9				14			7²	10		8							6¹				25
1	2	3	4	5	12		9	8²					13			7	10		11¹							6				26
1	2	3	4	5²	12		9	8²					13			7¹	14		10	11						6				27
1	2	3	4		12	8	13	9	11²				7			10	5									6¹				28
1	2	3		5	9	11¹	12	7	10				4													6	8			29
1	2	3	12	5¹	13	9²	11	7	10				8				6		4											30
1	2	3¹		5	9	11	12	13	7²	10			4				6		8											31
1	2	3		5	12	9	11²	10	7¹				4				6		8	13										32
1	2	3		5	9	11	8	7	10				4				6													33
1	2	3	12	5¹	9²	11	13	7	10				4				6		14	8³										34
1	2	3	4		9³	11¹	8	12	7	10			6²				5		13	14										35
1	2	3	4	5	9	11	8	7	10				6																	36
1		3	4	5	12	9	11¹	8	7	10			6															2		37
1		3	4	5		12	9¹	11	8	7			10²				6										13	2		38
1		3	4	5	12	13	9³	11²	8	7			10				6¹										14	2		39
1		3	4	5		12	11¹	8	7	10			6				9										2			40
1	12	4	5¹		11	9	8	3	7	13			6				10²		2											41
1	2	3	4		12	9¹	11²	8	13	7²			10				5		6											42
1	2	3	4	5	9	8	12	7	10²				6¹				11		13											43
1	2	3	4		12	8¹	9	11	7	10			5				6													44
1	2	3	4		12	8	9	11²	7¹	10			5				6		13											45
1⁸		3	4		7	8	9	11¹	12	10			5				6										2	15		46

Worthington Cup

First Round	Oxford U	(h)	0-1
		(a)	3-1
Second Round	Grimsby T	(a)	2-3
		(h)	2-0
Third Round	Fulham	(a)	2-3

FA Cup

Third Round	Nottingham F	(a)	1-0
Fourth Round	Wycombe W	(a)	1-2

WREXHAM

Division 2

FOUNDATION

The club was formed on 28 September 1872 by members of Wrexham Cricket Club, so they could continue playing a sport during the winter months. This meeting was held at the Turf Hotel, which although rebuilt since, still stands at one corner of the present ground. Their first game was a few weeks later and matches often included 17 players on either side! By 1875 team formations were reduced to 11 men and a year later the club was among the founder members of the Cambrian Football Association, which quickly changed its title to the Football Association of Wales.

Racecourse Ground, Mold Road, Wrexham LL11 2AH.

Telephone: (01978) 262 129. *Fax:* (01978) 357 821.
Commercial Dept: (01978) 352 536.
Community Office: (01978) 358 545.
ClubCall: 09068 121 642.

Ground Capacity: 15,500.

Record Attendance: 34,445 v Manchester U, FA Cup 4th rd, 26 January 1957.

Record Receipts: £126,012 v West Ham U, FA Cup 4th rd, 4 February 1992.

Pitch Measurements: 111yd × 71yd.

Chairman: W. P. Griffiths.

Managing Director: D. L. Rhodes.

Directors: C. Griffiths (Vice-Chairman), D. Griffiths, S. Mackarth, G. Farrell, G. Jones, B. DeRosa.

Manager: Brian Flynn.
Assistant Manager: Kevin Reeves.
Player-Coach: Joey Jones. *Physio:* Mel Pejic.

Secretary: D. L. Rhodes.

Commercial Manager: Christian Smith.

Colours: Red shirts, white shorts, red stockings.

Change Colours: Gold shirts, navy blue shorts, navy blue stockings.

Year Formed: 1872 (oldest club in Wales). *Turned Professional:* 1912. *Ltd Co.:* 1912.

Club Nickname: 'Robins'.

Previous Grounds: 1872, Racecourse Ground; 1883, Rhosddu Recreation Ground; 1887, Racecourse Ground.

First Football League Game: 27 August 1921, Division 3 (N), v Hartlepools U (h) L 0–2 – Godding; Ellis, Simpson; Matthias, Foster, Griffiths; Burton, Goode, Cotton, Edwards, Lloyd.

HONOURS

Football League: Division 2 best season: 7th, 1997–98; Division 3 – Champions 1977–78; Runners-up 1992–93; Division 3 (N) – Runners-up 1932–33; Division 4 – Runners-up 1969–70.

FA Cup: best season: 6th rd, 1974, 1978, 1997.

Football League Cup: best season: 5th rd, 1961, 1978.

Welsh Cup: Winners 23 times (record); Runners-up 22 times (record).

FAW Premier Cup: Winners 1998, 2000.

European Competition: European Cup-Winners' Cup: 1972–73, 1975–76, 1978–79, 1979–80, 1984–85, 1986–87, 1990–91, 1995–96.

IT'S A FACT !

On 28 October 2000, Wrexham scored five times in 28 second-half minutes to overhaul a 55th minute Luton Town lead of three goals.

Record League Victory: 10–1 v Hartlepool U, Division 4, 3 March 1962 – Keelan; Peter Jones, McGavan; Tecwyn Jones, Fox, Ken Barnes; Ron Barnes (3), Bennion (1), Davies (3), Ambler (3), Ron Roberts.

Record Cup Victory: 11–1 v New Brighton, Football League Northern Section Cup 1st rd, 3 January 1934 – Foster; Alfred Jones, Hamilton, Bulling, McMahon, Lawrence, Bryant (3), Findlay (1), Bamford (5), Snow, Waller (1), (o.g. 1).

Record Defeat: 0–9 v Brentford, Division 3, 15 October 1963.

Most League Points (2 for a win): 61, Division 4, 1969–70 and Division 3, 1977–78.

Most League Points (3 for a win): 80, Division 3, 1992–93.

Most League Goals: 106, Division 3 (N), 1932–33.

Highest League Scorer in Season: Tom Bamford, 44, Division 3 (N), 1933–34.

Most League Goals in Total Aggregate: Tom Bamford, 175, 1928–34.

Most League Goals in One Match: 5, Tom Bamford v Carlisle U, Division 3N, 17 March 1934.

Most Capped Player: Joey Jones, 29 (72), Wales.

Most League Appearances: Arfon Griffiths, 592, 1959–61, 1962–79.

Youngest League Player: Ken Roberts, 15 years 158 days v Bradford PA, 1 September 1951.

Record Transfer Fee Received: £800,000 from Birmingham C for Bryan Hughes, March 1997.

Record Transfer Fee Paid: £210,000 to Liverpool for Joey Jones, October 1978.

Football League Record: 1921 Original Member of Division 3 (N); 1958–60 Division 3; 1960–62 Division 4; 1962–64 Division 3; 1964–70 Division 4; 1970–78 Division 3; 1978–82 Division 2; 1982–83 Division 3; 1983–92 Division 4; 1992–93 Division 3; 1993– Division 2.

MANAGERS

Selection Committee 1872–1924
Charlie Hewitt 1924–25
Selection Committee 1925–1929
Jack Baynes 1929–31
Ernest Blackburn 1932–37
James Logan 1937–38
Arthur Cowell 1938
Tom Morgan 1938–42
Tom Williams 1942–49
Les McDowell 1949–50
Peter Jackson 1950–55
Cliff Lloyd 1955–57
John Love 1957–59
Cliff Lloyd 1959–60
Billy Morris 1960–61
Ken Barnes 1961–65
Billy Morris 1965
Jack Rowley 1966–67
Alvan Williams 1967–68
John Neal 1968–77
Arfon Griffiths 1977–81
Mel Sutton 1981–82
Bobby Roberts 1982–85
Dixie McNeil 1985–89
Brian Flynn November 1989–

LATEST SEQUENCES

Longest Sequence of League Wins: 7, 4.3.78 – 27.3.78.

Longest Sequence of League Defeats: 9, 2.10.63 – 30.10.63.

Longest Sequence of League Draws: 6, 12.11.99 – 26.12.99.

Longest Sequence of Unbeaten League Matches: 16, 3.9.66 – 19.11.66.

Longest Sequence Without a League Win: 16, 25.9.99 – 3.1.00.

TEN YEAR LEAGUE RECORD

		P	W	D	L	F	A	Pts	Pos
1990-91	Div 4	46	10	10	26	48	74	40	24
1991-92	Div 4	42	14	9	19	52	73	51	14
1992-93	Div 3	42	23	11	8	75	52	80	2
1993-94	Div 2	46	17	11	18	66	77	62	12
1994-95	Div 2	46	16	15	15	65	64	63	13
1995-96	Div 2	46	18	16	12	76	55	70	8
1996-97	Div 2	46	17	18	11	54	50	69	8
1997-98	Div 2	46	18	16	12	55	51	70	7
1998-99	Div 2	46	13	14	19	43	62	53	17
1999-2000	Div 2	46	17	11	18	52	61	62	11

DID YOU KNOW ?

On 3 January 1934 in the first round of the Third Division (North) Cup, Wrexham beat New Brighton 11-1 with Tommy Bamford scoring five goals and William Bryant a hat-trick. These two marksmen were transferred to Manchester United in October that same year.

WREXHAM 2000–01 LEAGUE RECORD

Match No.	Date	Venue	Opponents	Result	H/T Score	Lg. Pos.	Goalscorers	Attendance
1	Aug 12	H	Bristol C	L	0-2	0-1	—	5852
2	19	A	Bury	W	4-1	2-0	8	Faulconbridge 2 [5, 54], Sam [18], Williams [78]	3613
3	26	H	Wigan Ath	L	1-3	0-1	16	Sam [82]	5271
4	Sept 9	H	Oldham Ath	W	3-1	1-0	16	Sam 2 [9, 90], Killen [46]	3527
5	12	H	Rotherham U	L	1-3	0-1	—	Sam [89]	2126
6	16	A	Colchester U	D	1-1	1-0	18	Sam [12]	3724
7	23	H	Walsall	L	0-1	0-1	19		3766
8	26	A	Bournemouth	W	2-1	0-1	—	Morrell [87], Ferguson [88]	3004
9	30	A	Northampton T	D	2-2	2-1	13	Chalk [4], McGregor [18]	5595
10	Oct 14	A	Oxford U	W	4-3	1-1	12	Ferguson [26], McGregor [70], Chalk [81], Edwards [89]	3884
11	17	A	Reading	L	1-4	0-4	—	Faulconbridge [52]	10,350
12	21	H	Swansea C	W	1-0	1-0	13	Killen [27]	4008
13	24	H	Wycombe W	D	0-0	0-0	—		3014
14	28	A	Luton T	W	4-3	0-2	11	Faulconbridge [59], Killen [63], Chalk [83], Ferguson [87]	5341
15	Nov 4	H	Stoke C	L	1-2	0-2	14	Ferguson (pen) [66]	6447
16	7	A	Swindon T	D	2-2	1-1	—	Chalk [1], Edwards [68]	4423
17	11	A	Millwall	L	0-1	0-0	14		9607
18	21	H	Cambridge U	D	2-2	0-1	—	Owen 2 [53, 67]	1584
19	25	H	Bristol R	W	1-0	0-0	10	Faulconbridge [89]	2575
20	Dec 2	A	Peterborough U	L	0-1	0-1	11		5381
21	16	H	Brentford	W	2-1	1-1	9	Edwards [8], Russell [50]	2228
22	23	H	Notts Co	L	0-1	0-1	12		6206
23	26	H	Port Vale	W	1-0	1-0	10	Faulconbridge [9]	4941
24	Jan 1	A	Wigan Ath	D	0-0	0-0	11		6515
25	13	H	Bournemouth	D	2-2	0-1	—	Russell [64], McGregor [90]	2852
26	Feb 4	H	Swindon T	D	1-1	0-1	14	Phillips [72]	3004
27	10	A	Oldham Ath	L	1-5	1-2	14	Edwards [32]	4703
28	13	A	Bristol C	L	1-2	0-0	—	Russell [61]	9500
29	17	H	Colchester U	W	1-0	1-0	14	McGregor [36]	2492
30	20	A	Rotherham U	L	0-2	0-1	—		4528
31	24	A	Walsall	W	3-2	0-2	15	Trundle [60], Russell [69], Faulconbridge [90]	4958
32	Mar 2	H	Northampton T	W	3-0	2-0	—	Carey [14], Morrell [39], Trundle [90]	2940
33	6	H	Oxford U	W	5-3	1-2	—	Trundle 3 [13, 73, 79], Ferguson 2 (1 pen) [89 (p), 90]	3009
34	10	A	Cambridge U	W	3-2	0-1	10	Trundle [69], Ferguson (pen) [83], Morrell [90]	3737
35	17	H	Reading	L	1-2	0-1	10	Trundle [69]	5080
36	20	H	Bury	L	0-1	0-0	—		3388
37	31	A	Brentford	L	0-1	0-1	12		4449
38	Apr 3	A	Port Vale	D	1-1	1-0	—	Gibson [29]	4234
39	7	H	Peterborough U	W	2-1	1-0	10	Carey [9], Trundle [82]	2678
40	10	H	Notts Co	D	1-1	1-1	—	Williams [30]	2741
41	14	A	Wycombe W	D	1-1	0-0	9	Faulconbridge [52]	5482
42	16	H	Luton T	W	3-1	1-0	9	McGregor [18], Carey [83], Ferguson [85]	3339
43	21	A	Stoke C	L	1-3	0-2	10	Ferguson (pen) [86]	12,687
44	24	A	Swansea C	W	1-0	1-0	—	Faulconbridge [4]	2665
45	28	H	Millwall	D	1-1	1-0	10	Faulconbridge [9]	5939
46	May 5	A	Bristol R	L	0-4	0-2	10		6418

Final League Position: 10

GOALSCORERS

League (65): Faulconbridge 10, Ferguson 9 (4 pens), Trundle 8, Sam 6, McGregor 5, Chalk 4, Edwards 4, Russell 4, Carey 3, Killen 3, Morrell 3, Owen 2, Williams 2, Gibson 1, Phillips 1.
Worthington Cup (1): Ferguson 1.
FA Cup (0).

Rogers K 5	McGregor M 43	Roche L 41	Owen G 18+4	Carey B 33	Roberts S 6+1	Gibson R 17+11	Ferguson D 43	Sam H 11+9	Blackwood M 3+12	Faulconbridge C 33+6	Ridler D 22+2	Williams D 14+1	Edwards C 31+5	Morrell A 10+10	Barrett P 22+2	Killen C 11+1	Chalk M 22+2	Dearden K 36	Bouanane E 13+4	Mardon P 6+1	Moody A 2+1	Hardy P 13	Russell K 24+2	Phillips W 4+3	Trundle L 12+2	Lawrence D 1+2	Pejic S 1	Thomas S 4+2	Walsh D 5	Match No.
1	2	3	4	5	6	7	8	9	10	11																				1
1	2	3	4	5		12	8	9²		11	6	7	10¹	13																2
1	2²	3	4	5		12	8	9		11	6	7	10	13															3
1	2	3	4	5			8	9			6		10	12	7	11¹														4
1	2	3	4¹	5		12	8	9			6		10	13	7³	11²	14													5
	2	3		5	13	12	8	9²		11	6		10¹		7		4	1												6
	2	3	12	5			8	9	13	11	6²	7¹	10				4	1												7
	2	3		5			8	9¹	13	11	6²		10	12	7		4	1												8
	2	3			6		8	9		11			10		7		4	1	5											9
	2			5¹		12	8	9²		11	6		10¹	13	7		4	1	3											10
	2	3				12	8	9²		11	6		10¹	13	7	14	4	1	5³											11
	2	3		5	13	12	8	9¹		11	6²		10		7		4	1												12
	2	3		5			8	9		11	6		10		7		4	1												13
	2	3		5³		12	8	9	13	11	6¹		10		7	14	4²	1												14
	2	3		5		12	8	9¹		11	6		10		7		4	1												15
	2	3		5		12	8	9¹	13	11	6		10		7		4²	1												16
	2	3		5		12	8²	9¹	13	11	6		10		7		4	1												17
	2	3	4	5			8	9		11			10		7			1	6											18
		3	4	5		12	8²	9¹	13	11			10		7	14		1	6²		2									19
	2	3	4²	5¹	6	12	8	9¹	13	11			10		7	14		1												20
	2	3	4¹	5	6	12	8			11			10		7			1					9							21
	2	3	4²	5		12	8			11			10		7			1	6¹				9	13						22
	2	3	4	5		12	8¹		13	11²			10¹		7			1	6				9	14						23
	2	3	4	5			8			11			10		7			1	6				9							24
	2		4	5		12	8		13	11			10¹		7²			1	6			3	9							25
		3	4²	5		12	8		13	11			10¹		7			1	6		2		9							26
	2	3	4	5			8			11			10		7			1	6				9							27
	2	3	4¹	5		12	8		13	11²	6		10	14	7³			1					9							28
	2	3	4²	5		12	8		13	11³	6		10¹	14	7			1					9							29
	2	3	4¹	5		7	8		13	11³	6²		10	12	14			1					9							30
	2	3		5		7	8			11¹	6			12			4	1					9		10					31
	2	3		5		7	8			11	6						4	1					9		10					32
	2	3		5		7¹	8		13	11	6			12			4²	1					9		10					33
	2	3²		5		7	8		13	11	6			12	14		4¹	1					9³		10					34
	2	3		5		7	8		13	11²	6³			12			4¹	1					9		10			14		35
	2	3		5		7	8¹		13	11³	6			12²			4	1					9		10			14		36
	2	3		5		7	8²		13	11¹	6			12			4	1					9		10					37
	2	3				7	8			11¹				12			4	1					9	5	10		6			38
	2	3				7	8		13	11¹				12			4	1		6			9²	5	10					39
	2	3				7	8			11				12			4	1		6			9²	5	10¹	13				40
	2	3				7¹	8			11				12			4	1		6			9	5	10					41
	2	3				7²	8		13	11				12			4			6			9	5	10¹				1	42
	2	3				7¹	8			11			10	12			4²			6			9	5		13			1	43
	2	3					8		12	11			10				4			6			9¹	5				7	1	44
	2			5		12	8			11	6				7¹		4					3	9		10				1	45
		3		5		7³	8		13	11	6			12²			4				2		9¹		10	14		11	1	46

Worthington Cup
First Round Mansfield T (a) 1-0
  (h) 0-3

FA Cup
First Round Rotherham U (h) 0-1

WYCOMBE WANDERERS Division 2

FOUNDATION

In 1887 a group of young furniture trade workers called a meeting at the Steam Engine public house with the aim of forming a football club and entering junior football. It is thought that they were named after the famous FA Cup winners, The Wanderers who had visited the town in 1877 for a tie with the original High Wycombe club. It is also possible that they played informally before their formation, although there is no proof of this.

Adams Park, Hillbottom Road, Sands, High Wycombe HP12 4HJ.

Telephone: (01494) 472 100. *Fax:* (01494) 527 633.
Credit Card Hotline: (01494) 441 118.
Information Line: 0891 446 855.

Ground Capacity: 10,000; new stand now seats 7350.

Record Attendance: 9650 v Wimbledon, FA Cup 5th rd, 17 February 2001.

Pitch Measurements: 115yd × 77yd.

Patron: J. Adams. *President:* M. E. Seymour.

Chairman: I. L. Beeks JP.

Directors: G. Peart (Financial), M. Greatwood, R. Tomlin, A. Parry, A. Thibault, B. Kane, D. Vere.

Associate Directors: J. Goldsworthy, G. Cox, B. R. Lee, J. Goldsworthy. *Secretary:* Keith J. Allen.

Manager: Lawrie Sanchez. *Assistant Manager:* Terry Gibson.

Reserve Team Manager: Micky Forsyth. *Physio:* David Jones.

Youth Team Manager: Gary Goodchild.

Youth Development Officer: Adrian Cole.

Youth Physio: Terry Evans.

Marketing Manager: Mark Austin.

Promotions Manager: Mike Phillips.

Press Officer: Alan Hutchinson.

Colours: Light & dark blue quartered shirts, navy shorts, light blue stockings.

Change Colours: All orange.

Year Formed: 1887.

Turned Professional: 1974.

Club Nicknames: 'Chairboys' (after High Wycombe's tradition of furniture making), 'The Blues'.

Previous Grounds: 1887, The Rye; 1893, Spring Meadow; 1895, Loakes Park; 1899, Daws Hill Park; 1901, Loakes Park; 1990, Adams Park.

HONOURS

Football League: Division 2 best season: 6th, 1994–95.

FA Amateur Cup: Winners 1931.

FA Trophy: Winners 1991, 1993.

GM Vauxhall Conference: Winners 1992–93.

FA Cup: semi-final 2001.

Football League Cup: never beyond 2nd rd.

IT'S A FACT !

Wycombe Wanderers became the eighth club from the third ranked League competition to reach the Semi-Final of the FA Cup and the second from the Second Division since the start of the Premier League.

First Football League Game: 14 August 1993, Division 3 v Carlisle U (a) D 2–2: Hyde; Cousins, Horton (Langford), Kerr, Crossley, Ryan, Carroll, Stapleton, Thompson, Scott, Guppy (1) (Hutchinson), (1 og).

Record League Victory: 5–0 v Burnley, Division 2, 15 April 1997 – Parkin; Cousins, Bell, Kavanagh, McCarthy, Forsyth, Carroll (2p) (Simpson), Scott (Farrell), Stallard (1), McGavin (1) (Read (1)), Brown.

Record Cup Victory: 5–0 v Hitchin T (a), FA Cup 2nd rd, 3 December 1994 – Hyde; Cousins, Brown, Crossley, Evans, Ryan (1), Carroll, Bell (1), Thompson, Garner (3) (Hemmings), Stapleton (Langford).

Record Defeat: 0–5 v Walsall, Auto Windscreens Shield 1st rd, 7 November 1995.

Most League Points (3 for a win): 78, Division 2, 1994–95.

Most League Goals: 67, Division 3, 1993–94.

Highest League Goalscorer in Season: Sean Devine 23, 1999–2000.

Most League Goals in Total Aggregate: Dave Carroll, 40, 1993–2001.

Most League Goals in One Match: 3, Miguel Desouza v Bradford C, Division 2, 26 March 1996; 3, Mark Stallard v Walsall, Division 2, 21 October 1997; 3, Sean Devine v Reading, Division 2, 2 October 1999; 3, Sean Divine v Bury, Division 2, 26 February 2000.

Most Capped Player: None.

Most League Appearances: Dave Carroll, 290, 1993–2001.

Youngest League Player: Roger Johnson, 17 years 8 days v Cambridge U, 6 May 2000.

Record Transfer Fee Received: £375,000 from Swindon T for Keith Scott, November 1993.

Record Transfer Fee Paid: £220,000 to Barnet for Sean Devine, 15 April 1999.

Football League Record: Promoted to Division 3 from GMVC in 1993; 1993–94 Division 3; 1994– Division 2.

MANAGERS

First coach appointed 1951.
Prior to Brian Lee's appointment in 1969 the team was selected by a Match Committee which met every Monday evening.
James McCormack 1951–52
Sid Cann 1952–61
Graham Adams 1961–62
Don Welsh 1962–64
Barry Darvill 1964–68
Brian Lee 1969–76
Ted Powell 1976–77
John Reardon 1977–78
Andy Williams 1978–80
Mike Keen 1980–84
Paul Bence 1984–86
Alan Gane 1986–87
Peter Suddaby 1987–88
Jim Kelman 1988–90
Martin O'Neill 1990–95
Alan Smith 1995–96
John Gregory 1996–98
Neil Smillie 1998–99
Lawrie Sanchez February 1999–

LATEST SEQUENCES

Longest Sequence of League Wins: 4, 26.2.94 – 19.3.94.

Longest Sequence of League Defeats: 4, 2.1.99 – 30.1.99.

Longest Sequence of League Draws: 4, 16.9.95 – 7.10.95.

Longest Sequence of Unbeaten League Matches: 14, 29.8.95 – 18.11.95.

Longest Sequence Without a League Win: 12, 8.8.98 – 10.10.98.

TEN YEAR LEAGUE RECORD

		P	W	D	L	F	A	Pts	Pos
1990-91	Conf	42	21	11	10	75	46	74	5
1991-92	Conf	42	30	4	8	84	35	94	2
1992-93	Conf	42	24	11	7	84	37	83	1
1993-94	Div 3	42	19	13	10	67	53	70	4
1994-95	Div 2	46	21	15	10	60	46	78	6
1995-96	Div 2	46	15	15	16	63	59	60	12
1996-97	Div 2	46	15	10	21	51	56	55	18
1997-98	Div 2	46	14	18	14	51	53	60	14
1998-99	Div 2	46	13	12	21	52	58	51	19
1999-2000	Div 2	46	16	13	17	56	53	61	12

DID YOU KNOW ?

Roy Essandoh's historic FA Cup goal which took Wycombe Wanderers into the Semi-Final, was the only one he scored in any competition for any club during the 2000-01 season. Born in Belfast, raised in Ghana, his career had taken him to Austria, Finland and Scotland.

WYCOMBE WANDERERS 2000–01 LEAGUE RECORD

Match No.	Date	Venue	Opponents	Result	H/T Score	Lg. Pos.	Goalscorers	Atten-dance
1	Aug 12	A	Stoke C	D	0-0	0-0	—	14,532
2	19	H	Northampton T	W	1-0	0-0	6	Brown (pen) [51]	4806
3	26	A	Millwall	W	2-1	0-1	4	Baird [50], Bulman [70]	10,139
4	28	H	Luton T	D	1-1	1-0	3	Brown [17]	6001
5	Sept 2	A	Brentford	D	0-0	0-0	3		4699
6	8	H	Oxford U	W	3-1	1-0	—	Baird [4], McSporran [81], Brown (pen) [90]	5831
7	12	H	Bristol R	L	0-1	0-1	—		4718
8	16	A	Rotherham U	L	0-1	0-0	9		3545
9	23	H	Peterborough U	W	2-0	1-0	5	Bates [45], McSporran [46]	4980
10	30	A	Port Vale	W	1-0	1-0	5	Rammell [21]	3615
11	Oct 6	H	Notts Co	W	3-1	2-1	—	Baird [20], Rammell [26], McCarthy [78]	5080
12	14	A	Reading	L	0-2	0-0	5		15,443
13	17	A	Oldham Ath	L	0-2	0-1	—		3496
14	21	H	Walsall	W	3-1	1-1	4	Simpson [23], Rammell 2 [52, 56]	5564
15	24	A	Wrexham	D	0-0	0-0	—		3014
16	28	H	Bristol C	L	1-2	1-1	6	Rammell [45]	6051
17	Nov 4	A	Swindon T	D	1-1	1-0	8	Rammell [9]	5226
18	11	H	Bury	W	2-1	0-0	6	Bates 2 [63, 90]	4488
19	25	A	Colchester U	D	0-0	0-0	7		3646
20	Dec 2	H	Bournemouth	L	0-3	0-1	8		5185
21	16	A	Wigan Ath	L	1-2	0-1	8	Parkin [49]	5779
22	23	H	Swansea C	W	2-1	2-0	8	Rammell 2 [16, 22]	5001
23	26	A	Cambridge U	L	0-1	0-0	9		4758
24	30	A	Northampton T	D	2-2	1-1	9	Brown [7], Bulman [49]	5722
25	Jan 12	A	Luton T	W	2-1	0-1	—	Rammell 2 [50, 64]	4551
26	Feb 3	H	Brentford	D	0-0	0-0	12		6604
27	6	H	Cambridge U	L	0-2	0-1	—		4524
28	10	A	Oxford U	W	2-1	1-1	10	Rogers [41], Ryan [90]	5384
29	24	A	Peterborough U	L	2-3	2-3	13	Lee [13], Ryan [14]	4731
30	Mar 3	H	Port Vale	L	0-1	0-0	16		4828
31	6	H	Reading	D	1-1	1-0	—	Lee [39]	6788
32	13	H	Stoke C	L	0-1	0-1	—		5385
33	17	H	Oldham Ath	W	2-1	1-1	14	Simpson [37], Ryan [49]	5847
34	20	H	Rotherham U	L	0-1	0-0	—		5254
35	24	A	Walsall	L	1-5	0-1	16	Lee [81]	4530
36	27	H	Millwall	D	0-0	0-0	—		5094
37	31	H	Wigan Ath	L	1-2	0-1	18	McCarthy [72]	4939
38	Apr 10	A	Swansea C	L	1-3	1-0	—	Simpson [3]	3010
39	14	H	Wrexham	D	1-1	0-0	20	Vinnicombe [86]	5482
40	16	A	Bristol C	W	2-1	0-0	18	Senda [63], Whittingham [90]	11,643
41	21	H	Swindon T	D	0-0	0-0	18		6844
42	23	H	Bournemouth	L	0-2	0-0	—		5026
43	26	A	Notts Co	W	2-0	1-0	—	Carroll [22], Bulman [87]	3522
44	28	A	Bury	D	1-1	0-0	17	Carroll [72]	4096
45	May 2	A	Bristol R	W	2-1	0-0	—	Senda [73], Bulman [79]	8264
46	5	H	Colchester U	D	1-1	0-0	13	Ryan [70]	7516

Final League Position: 13

GOALSCORERS

League (46): Rammell 10, Brown 4 (2 pens), Bulman 4, Ryan 4, Baird 3, Bates 3, Lee 3, Simpson 3, Carroll 2, McCarthy 2, McSporran 2, Senda 2, Parkin 1, Rogers 1, Vinnicombe 1, Whittingham 1.
Worthington Cup (7): Baird 1, Bates 1, Castledine 1, McCarthy 1, McSporran 1, Rammell 1, Rogers 1.
FA Cup (17): McCarthy 4, Simpson 3 (1 pen), Bates 2, Rammell 2, Brown 1, Carroll 1, Essendoh 1, Parkin 1, Rogers 1, Ryan 1.

Taylor M 46	Rogers M 19 + 3	Vinnicombe C 42	Bulman D 36	McCarthy P 38	Bates J 37 + 2	Harkin M 10 + 5	Simpson M 45	McSporran J 20	Jones S 5	Brown S 30 + 2	Castledine S 6 + 11	Baird A 9 + 4	Senda D 12 + 19	Rammell A 25 + 1	Cousins J 26 + 6	Lee M 13 + 8	Townsend B 9 + 1	Ryan K 21 + 9	Brady M 2 + 3	Beeton A 3	Carroll D 8 + 4	Thompson N 6 + 2	Parkin S 5 + 3	Lavin G 2	Nutter J 1	Essandoh R 8 + 5	Clegg G 2 + 8	Johnson R — + 1	Phelan L — + 2	Whittingham G 9 + 3	Marsh C 11	Match No.
1	2	3	4	5	6	7[1]	8	9[2]	10	11	12	13																				1
1	2	3	4	5	6	7[1]	8	9	10	11			12																			2
1	2	3	4	5	6		8	9[2]	10	11[1]	12			7	13																	3
1	2	3	4[1]	5	6		8	9[2]	10	11	12			7	13																	4
1	2	3	4	5	6		8	9	10[1]	11					7	12																5
1	2	3	4	5	6	7[1]	8	9[2]		11				10[2]	12	13	14															6
1	2	3	4	5	6	7[1]	8	9		11[2]	13				12	10																7
1	2	3	4	5	6		8	9		11[2]	13		7[1]		12	10																8
1	2	3	4	5	6	7[2]	8	9[1]		11					12	10	13															9
1	2	3	4	5	6	7[1]	8	9[2]		11[3]		13			12	10	14															10
1		3	4[3]	5	6		8	9[2]		11	13		7[1]	12	10	14			2													11
1	2	3		5	6	7[1]	8	9		11		4[2]			12	10					13											12
1	2	3		5	6	7[3]	8	9		11[1]		4[2]			12	10	14				13											13
1	2[1]	3		5	6		8	9		11					7	10	12	4														14
1		3		5	6		8	9		11			12		7	10	2	4[1]														15
1		3		5	6		8	9			12				7	10	2	11	4[1]													16
1	2	3[2]		5[1]	6		8	9							7	10	12	11			4	13										17
1	2				6		8						7[1]			10	5	9			4	3	12	11								18
1	2		4		6		8	9								10	5	7			3	11[1]	12									19
1		4[1]		5	6	12	8	9		11						10	2				3	7										20
1	2	3		5	6[2]		8	9[1]		11			12			10	13				4	7										21
1		3	4[2]	5			8	9					12			10		6	2	13	7[3]	11[1]	14									22
1	12	3		5			8	9					13			10		6	2[1]	4[2]	7	14	11[3]									23
1	2	3	4	5		7[2]	8	9					12					6			13	11[1]	10									24
1	12	3	4	5			8	9[2]		11[3]							2	10			6	13				7[1]	14					25
1		3	4	6	12		8					13				10[3]	5	11			14					7[1]				9[2]	2	26
1	12	3	4		6[1]		13	8					14			7[3]	9	5			11[2]	10					2					27
1	2	3	4[1]	5			8			11				9[2]		6		7			10	12	13									28
1		5		12	7[2]		8				14					11		2	6[1]	13	4		10[3]	9	3							29
1		3[1]		6	12		8					9	13				5	11	2		10[3]					7[2]	14					30
1		3	4		6		8					11	7[2]			5	10	2[1]	8							12	9	13				31
1		3	7	4	6		8			11[1]						5	12	2[2]								10	9	13				32
1		3	7	4	6		8									5	11[1]	2	9[2]	12						10	13					33
1		3	7	4	6		8				2					5	11[2]		9[1]							10	12	13				34
1		3	2	4	6[1]		8							11[3]	5	13	12	9[2]			7					10			14			35
1		3	7	4	6		8									10[3]	5		9[1]		12					14	13		11[2]	2		36
1		3	7[3]	4	6		8			11				12	10[3]	5										14	13		9[1]	2		37
1		3	7	4	6		8					12		13	9[3]	5	11[1]	14											10[2]	2		38
1		3	4	6			8			11[2]				12	9	5		10[3]			7[1]						13		14	2		39
1		3	4	6			8			11[1]	13			10	9[3]	5	12				7[2]								14	2		40
1		3	4	6	12		8			11					10[2]	5		13			7[1]								9	2		41
1		3	7	4	6		8			11					12	5[2]		10[3]								14	13		9[1]	2		42
1		3	4	5	6		8			11							12				7					10[1]			9[1]	2		43
1		3	4	5	6		8			11				12	13		14				7[2]					10[3]			9[1]	2		44
1		3	4		6		8			11				5[1]	10	7[2]	12										13		9	2		45
1		3	4		6	13	8			11[1]				7			5									10	12[2]		9	2		46

Worthington Cup

First Round	Barnet	(a)	1-2
		(h)	3-1
Second Round	Birmingham C	(h)	3-4
		(a)	0-1

FA Cup

First Round	Harrow Borough	(h)	3-0
Second Round	Millwall	(a)	0-0
		(h)	2-1
Third Round	Grimsby T	(h)	1-1
		(a)	3-1
Fourth Round	Wolverhampton W	(h)	2-1
Fifth Round	Wimbledon	(h)	2-2
		(a)	1-1
Sixth Round	Leicester C	(a)	2-1
Semi-Final	Liverpool		1-2
(at Villa Park)			

YORK CITY

Division 3

FOUNDATION

Although there was a York City club formed in 1903 by a soccer enthusiast from Darlington, this has no connection with the modern club because it went out of existence during World War I. Unlike many others of that period who restarted in 1919, York City did not re-form until 1922 and the tendency now is to ignore the modern club's pre-1922 existence.

Bootham Crescent, York YO30 7AQ.

Telephone: (01904) 624 447.

Fax: (01904) 631 457.

ClubCall: 09068 121 643

Ground Capacity: 9534.

Record Attendance: 28,123 v Huddersfield T, FA Cup 6th rd, 5 March 1938.

Record Receipts: £63,680 v Manchester U, Coca-Cola Cup 2nd rd, 2nd leg, 3 October 1995.

Pitch Measurements: 115yd × 74yd.

Chairman: D. M. Craig OBE, JP, BSC, FICE, FI, MUN E, FCI ARB, M CONS E.

Directors: C. Webb, E. B. Swallow, J. E. H. Quickfall FCA.

Manager: Terry Dolan.

First Team Coach: Adie Shaw.

Secretary: Keith Usher.

Commercial Manager: James Richardson.

Physio: Jeff Miller.

Hon. Orthopaedic Surgeon: Mr Peter De Boer MA, FRCS.

Medical Officer: Dr R. Porter.

Colours: Red shirts, navy shorts, navy stockings.

Change Colours: All yellow.

Year Formed: 1922.

Turned Professional: 1922.

Ltd Co.: 1922.

Club Nickname: 'Minstermen'.

Previous Grounds: 1922, Fulfordgate; 1932, Bootham Crescent.

First Football League Game: 31 August 1929, Division 3 (N), v Wigan Borough (a) W 2–0 – Farmery; Archibald, Johnson; Beck, Davis, Thompson; Evans, Gardner, Cowie (1), Smailes, Stockhill (1).

HONOURS

Football League: Division 3 – Promoted 1973–74 (3rd); Division 4 – Champions 1983–84.

FA Cup: Semi-finals 1955, when in Division 3.

Football League Cup: best season: 5th rd, 1962.

IT'S A FACT !

On 18 January 1975, York City scored two goals within two minutes of the start of the Division Two match at Norwich City and went on to record a 3-2 win at Carrow Road.

Record League Victory: 9–1 v Southport, Division 3 (N), 2 February 1957 – Forgan; Phillips, Howe; Brown (1), Cairney, Mollatt; Hill, Bottom (4 incl. 1p), Wilkinson (2), Wragg (1), Fenton (1).

Record Cup Victory: 6–0 v South Shields (away), FA Cup 1st rd, 16 November 1968 – Widdowson; Baker (1p), Richardson; Carr, Jackson, Burrows; Taylor, Ross (3), MacDougall (2), Hodgson, Boyer.

Record Defeat: 0–12 v Chester, Division 3 (N), 1 February 1936.

Most League Points (2 for a win): 62, Division 4, 1964–65.

Most League Points (3 for a win): 101, Division 4, 1983–84.

Most League Goals: 96, Division 4, 1983–84.

Highest League Scorer in Season: Bill Fenton, 31, Division 3 (N), 1951–52; Arthur Bottom, 31, Division 3 (N), 1954–55 and 1955–56.

Most League Goals in Total Aggregate: Norman Wilkinson, 125, 1954–66.

Most League Goals in One Match: 5, Alf Patrick v Rotherham U, Division 3N, 20 November 1948.

Most Capped Player: Peter Scott, 7 (10), Northern Ireland.

Most League Appearances: Barry Jackson, 481, 1958–70.

Youngest League Player: Reg Stockill, 15 years 281 days v Wigan Borough, 31 August 1929.

Record Transfer Fee Received: £1,000,000 from Manchester U for Jonathan Greening, March 1998.

Record Transfer Fee Paid: £140,000 to Burnley for Adrian Randall, December 1995.

Football League Record: 1929 Elected to Division 3 (N); 1958–59 Division 4; 1959–60 Division 3; 1960–65 Division 4; 1965–66 Division 3; 1966–71 Division 4; 1971–74 Division 3; 1974–76 Division 2; 1976–77 Division 3; 1977–84 Division 4; 1984–88 Division 3; 1988–92 Division 4; 1992–93 Division 3; 1993–99 Division 2; 1999– Division 3.

MANAGERS

Bill Sherrington 1924–60
(was Secretary for most of this time but virtually Secretary-Manager for a long pre-war spell)
John Collier 1929–36
Tom Mitchell 1936–50
Dick Duckworth 1950–52
Charlie Spencer 1952–53
Jimmy McCormick 1953–54
Sam Bartram 1956–60
Tom Lockie 1960–67
Joe Shaw 1967–68
Tom Johnston 1968–75
Wilf McGuinness 1975–77
Charlie Wright 1977–80
Barry Lyons 1980–81
Denis Smith 1982–87
Bobby Saxton 1987–88
John Bird 1988–91
John Ward 1991–93
Alan Little 1993–99
Neil Thompson 1999–2000
Terry Dolan February 2000–

LATEST SEQUENCES

Longest Sequence of League Wins: 7, 31.10.64 – 26.12.64.

Longest Sequence of League Defeats: 8, 14.11.66 – 31.12.66.

Longest Sequence of League Draws: 6, 26.12.92 – 22.1.93.

Longest Sequence of Unbeaten League Matches: 21, 10.9.73 – 12.1.74.

Longest Sequence Without a League Win: 17, 4.5.87 – 24.10.87.

TEN YEAR LEAGUE RECORD

		P	W	D	L	F	A	Pts	Pos
1990-91	Div 4	46	11	13	22	45	57	46	21
1991-92	Div 4	42	8	16	18	42	58	40	19
1992-93	Div 3	42	21	12	9	72	45	75	4
1993-94	Div 2	46	21	12	13	64	40	75	5
1994-95	Div 2	46	21	9	16	67	51	72	9
1995-96	Div 2	46	13	13	20	58	73	52	20
1996-97	Div 2	46	13	13	20	47	68	52	20
1997-98	Div 2	46	14	17	15	52	58	59	16
1998-99	Div 2	46	13	11	22	56	80	50	21
1999-2000	Div 3	46	12	16	18	39	53	52	20

DID YOU KNOW ?

On 16 November 1935 just a week after losing 5-0 at Rotherham United, York City had a remarkable 7-5 victory over Mansfield Town. It was their highest score of the season.

YORK CITY 2000–01 LEAGUE RECORD

Match No.	Date	Venue	Opponents	Result	H/T Score	Lg. Pos.	Goalscorers	Atten- dance
1	Aug 12	A	Chesterfield	L 1-4	1-0	—	Duffield [1]	4745
2	19	H	Cheltenham T	L 0-2	0-1	24		2793
3	25	A	Carlisle U	D 1-1	0-0	—	Duffield (pen) [60]	4087
4	28	H	Barnet	W 1-0	0-0	16	Alcide [90]	1981
5	Sept 2	A	Darlington	D 1-1	1-1	17	Duffield (pen) [6]	5170
6	9	H	Scunthorpe U	W 2-0	0-0	13	McNiven [56], Agnew [83]	3370
7	12	H	Rochdale	L 0-2	0-2	—		2215
8	16	A	Exeter C	L 1-3	1-3	21	McNiven [45]	2904
9	23	H	Brighton & HA	L 0-1	0-1	21		3178
10	30	A	Hartlepool U	L 0-1	0-1	22		2130
11	Oct 6	H	Mansfield T	W 2-1	1-1	—	McNiven [18], Mathie [61]	2681
12	14	A	Southend U	L 0-1	0-1	20		4724
13	17	A	Lincoln C	L 1-2	1-1	—	McNiven [42]	2051
14	21	H	Leyton Orient	D 1-1	0-1	21	Tarrant [76]	2744
15	24	A	Halifax T	W 3-1	2-0	—	Sertori [20], Bullock [35], McNiven [90]	1984
16	28	H	Hull C	D 0-0	0-0	20		5493
17	Nov 4	A	Cardiff C	L 0-4	0-3	21		6101
18	11	H	Torquay U	W 3-2	2-2	19	Hulme 2 [33, 88], McNiven [39]	2415
19	25	A	Kidderminster H	L 1-3	1-3	20	Bullock [35]	2602
20	Dec 2	H	Shrewsbury T	W 2-1	1-1	18	McNiven [25], Hulme [78]	2318
21	16	A	Plymouth Arg	L 0-1	0-1	19		3830
22	22	H	Blackpool	L 0-2	0-1	—		2705
23	26	A	Macclesfield T	W 1-0	0-0	18	Iwelumo [75]	2001
24	Jan 13	A	Barnet	L 0-2	0-1	21		2731
25	20	H	Macclesfield T	L 1-3	1-1	22	Iwelumo [26]	2287
26	23	H	Chesterfield	L 0-1	0-0	—		2570
27	27	A	Blackpool	L 0-1	0-0	22		3938
28	30	H	Carlisle U	D 0-0	0-0	—		2750
29	Feb 10	A	Scunthorpe U	L 0-4	0-1	22		3164
30	17	H	Exeter C	L 0-3	0-2	24		3030
31	20	A	Rochdale	W 1-0	0-0	—	Emmerson [75]	2807
32	24	A	Brighton & HA	D 1-1	0-0	22	Agnew [68]	6555
33	Mar 3	H	Hartlepool U	D 1-1	0-1	23	McNiven [73]	4553
34	6	H	Southend U	W 1-0	1-0	—	Nogan [13]	2144
35	10	A	Mansfield T	W 3-1	0-1	20	Potter [56], Alcide [59], Nogan [69]	2405
36	13	H	Darlington	W 2-0	1-0	—	Richardson [41], Alcide [85]	3244
37	17	H	Lincoln C	D 0-0	0-0	18		3506
38	20	A	Cheltenham T	D 1-1	1-0	—	Nogan [18]	2669
39	24	A	Leyton Orient	D 1-1	1-1	17	Nogan [24]	4085
40	31	H	Plymouth Arg	L 1-2	1-1	18	Bower [34]	3083
41	Apr 14	H	Halifax T	W 2-1	2-0	17	Bullock [31], Nogan [45]	3465
42	16	A	Hull C	D 0-0	0-0	16		11,820
43	21	H	Cardiff C	D 3-3	1-2	18	Brass (pen) [41], Nogan [62], Alcide [67]	3881
44	28	A	Torquay U	D 2-2	1-0	18	Basham [11], Potter [90]	4505
45	May 1	A	Shrewsbury T	L 0-2	0-1	—		2058
46	5	H	Kidderminster H	W 1-0	0-0	17	Alcide [77]	3185

Final League Position: 17

GOALSCORERS
League (42): McNiven 8, Nogan 6, Alcide 5, Bullock 3, Duffield 3 (2 pens), Hulme 3, Agnew 2, Iwelumo 2, Potter 2, Basham 1, Bower 1, Brass 1 (pen), Emmerson 1, Mathie 1, Richardson 1, Sertori 1, Tarrant 1.
Worthington Cup (1): Jones 1.
FA Cup (9): McNiven 2, Agnew 1, Alcide 1, Bullock 1, Iwelumo 1, Jordan 1, Mathie 1, Potter 1.

Fettis A 46	Edmondson D 22 + 1	Porter G 34 + 4	Sertori M 26	Swan P 2	Hobson G 8 + 3	Fox C 3 + 5	Hulme K 11 + 4	Conlon B 2 + 6	Duffield P 6	Agnew S 37 + 2	Hall W 16 + 3	McNiven D 25 + 16	Alcide C 24 + 14	Thompson M 9 + 3	Jones B 28 + 1	Bullock L 29 + 4	Williams J 1 + 5	Hocking M 24 + 2	Turley J 5 + 5	Jordan S 6 + 6	Mathie A 13 + 6	Durkan K 7	Stamp N 12 + 1	Reed M 1 + 1	Tarrant N 6 + 1	Iwelumo C 11 + 1	Bower M 21	Patterson D 4 + 2	Emmerson S 3 + 5	Wood L 4 + 1	Darlow K — + 1	Richardson N 16 + 1	Nogan L 16	Cooper R 14	Brass C 8 + 2	Basham M 6 + 1	Match No.
1	2	3	4	5	6	7^1	8	9	10	11	12	13																									1
1	2	3	4	5	6	7^1	8	9^2	10	11		12	13																								2
1	2^3	3	4		6		8^1		9^2	7	11	10	13	14	5	12																					3
1	2	3^1	4		6		12	13	9	7	11	10^3	14		5^3	8																					4
1	2	3	4		6		8^1		9^2	7	11	10^3	13		5	12	14																			5
1	2	3	4		6		8	13	9^1	7	11	10	12^2		5																					6
1	2^3	3^1	4		6		8	12		7	11	10	9^2		5	13	14																			7
1	2	3^2	4		6^3		8	12		7	11	10	9^1		5	13	14																			8
1	2		4							7	11	10	13	12	5^3	8	9^2	3	14	6																9
1	2	12	4							7	11	10^2			5	8	13	3		6^1	9															10
1	2	3	4									8	11^1	10	12	6	13	5		9^2	7															11
1	2		12							7		10^1		9	5	6		3	13		8		11	4^2												12
1		3	12					13		7		10^2		9	5	6^1		2			8		11	4												13
1	2	3	12					13		7		10^1	14		5	6				9	8^2		11^3	4												14
1	2	3	4							7		10^2	12		5	6	13			9	8^1		11													15
1	2^3	3	4							7^1		10	14	12	5	6	13			9	8^2		11													16
1	3^2	2	4				12			7^1		10	14		5	6^3	13			9	8		11													17
1	12	3	4				8			7		10^3	14		5^2	6^1	13	2		9	8		11													18
1	2	3					12			7		10	14		5	6^2	13	4		9^3	8		11^1													19
1	2	3	4				12			7		10	14		5	6^1	13			9^2			11^3		6		5									20
1	2	3	4				12			7		10^2			5	6	13			9	8^1		11				5		13							21
1		3	4				12			7		10	14		5^1	6	13	2		9^1	8		11^2		14											22
1		3	4				12			7		10			5	6	13	2		9^2	8^1		11													23
1		3^3	4				12			7		10	14		5	6	13	2		9^2	8^1		11													24
1	3^2		4^1				12			7		10	13		5	6		2		9	8		11													25
1	3^2						12			7		10	13		5	6		2		9^1	8		11				4									26
1		3	4				12			7		10			5	6		2^1		9	8		11													27
1	12	3^1	4							7		10	13		5	6^2		2		9	8^1		11		14											28
1	3^2		4				12			7		10^3	13		5	6		2		9^1	8		11		14											29
1		3^2	4				12			7^1		10	13		5	6		2		9	8		11		14				6^3							30
1		3					12					10						2					11				5					6^1	9	7	4	31
1		3					12					10^2						2					11		14		5		13			6^1	9	7	8^3/4	32
1		3					12					10						2					11^1				5		13			6^2	9	7	8/4	33
1		3					12					10						2					11				5					6	9	7	8/4	34
1		3					12					10^3						2					11^2		14		5^1		13			6	9	7	8/4	35
1		3					12					10^1						2					11				5		13			6	9	7	8^2/4	36
1		3					12					10^2						2^3					11		14		5		13			6	9^1	7	8^1/4	37
1		3					12					10						2					11				5		13			6	9^1	7	8^2/4	38
1		3					12					10^2						2^1					11				5		13			6	9	7	8/4	39
1		3					12					10^1						2					11		14		5		13			6	9	7^2	8/4^3	40
1		3					12					10						2					11^1				5					6	9	7	8/4	41
1	2	3^1					12					10											11				5					6	9	7	8/4	42
1	2	3										10											11				5					6	9	7	8/4	43
1	2^3	3					12					10											11				5		13			6	9	7^1	8/4	44
1	2	3					12					10											11^2		14		5^3		13			6	9	7	8/4	45
1	2	3					12					10^1											11^2				5		13			6	9	7	8/4	46

Worthington Cup
First Round — Stoke C — (h) 1-5 / (a) 0-0

FA Cup
First Round — Radcliffe B — (a) 4-1
Second Round — Reading — (h) 2-2 / (a) 3-1
Third Round — Leicester C — (a) 0-3

ENGLISH LEAGUE PLAYERS DIRECTORY

*Free transfer, †Non-contract, ‡Registration cancelled, §Trainee/Scholar/Schoolboy
#Players over age 24, out of contract but who have been made an offer of re-engagement.
Players listed refer to the retain and transfer list May 2001.

ARSENAL

ADAMS, Tony (D) — 494 32
H: 6 3 W: 13 02 b.Romford 10-10-66
Source: Apprentice. *Honours:* England Youth, Under-21, B, 66 full caps, 5 goals.

Season	Club	Apps	Gls	Tot Apps	Tot Gls
1983–84	Arsenal	3	0		
1984–85	Arsenal	16	0		
1985–86	Arsenal	10	0		
1986–87	Arsenal	42	6		
1987–88	Arsenal	39	2		
1988–89	Arsenal	36	4		
1989–90	Arsenal	38	5		
1990–91	Arsenal	30	1		
1991–92	Arsenal	35	2		
1992–93	Arsenal	35	0		
1993–94	Arsenal	35	0		
1994–95	Arsenal	27	3		
1995–96	Arsenal	21	1		
1996–97	Arsenal	28	3		
1997–98	Arsenal	26	3		
1998–99	Arsenal	26	1		
1999–2000	Arsenal	21	0		
2000–01	Arsenal	26	1	494	32

ALIADIERE, Jeremie (F) — 0 0
H: 6 0 W: 11 00 b.Rambouillet 30-3-83
Source: Scholarship.

Season	Club	Apps	Gls
1999–2000	Arsenal	0	0
2000–01	Arsenal	0	0

BARRETT, Graham (F) — 3 0
H: 5 10 W: 11 07 b.Dublin 6-10-81
Source: Trainee. *Honours:* Eire Schools, Youth, Under-21.

Season	Club	Apps	Gls	Tot Apps	Tot Gls
1998–99	Arsenal	0	0		
1999–2000	Arsenal	2	0		
2000–01	Arsenal	0	0	2	0
2000–01	*Bristol R*	1	0	1	0

BERGKAMP, Dennis (F) — 409 174
H: 6 0 W: 12 05 b.Amsterdam 18-5-69
Honours: Holland 79 full caps, 36 goals.

Season	Club	Apps	Gls	Tot Apps	Tot Gls
1986–87	Ajax	14	2		
1987–88	Ajax	25	5		
1988–89	Ajax	30	13		
1989–90	Ajax	25	8		
1990–91	Ajax	33	25		
1991–92	Ajax	30	24		
1992–93	Ajax	28	26	185	103
1993–94	Internazionale	31	8		
1994–95	Internazionale	21	3	52	11
1995–96	Arsenal	33	11		
1996–97	Arsenal	29	12		
1997–98	Arsenal	28	16		
1998–99	Arsenal	29	12		
1999–2000	Arsenal	28	6		
2000–01	Arsenal	25	3	172	60

CANOVILLE, Lee* (D) — 2 0
H: 6 0 W: 11 04 b.Ealing 14-3-81
Source: Trainee. *Honours:* FA Schools, England Youth.

Season	Club	Apps	Gls	Tot Apps	Tot Gls
1998–99	Arsenal	0	0		
1999–2000	Arsenal	0	0		
2000–01	Arsenal	0	0		
2000–01	*Northampton T*	2	0	2	0

CHILVERS, Liam (D) — 7 0
H: 6 0 W: 12 04 b.Chelmsford 6-10-81
Source: Scholar.

Season	Club	Apps	Gls	Tot Apps	Tot Gls
2000–01	Arsenal	0	0		
2000–01	*Northampton T*	7	0	7	0

COLE, Ashley (D) — 32 4
H: 5 8 W: 10 10 b.Stepney 20-12-80
Source: Trainee. *Honours:* England Youth, Under-21, 3 full caps.

Season	Club	Apps	Gls	Tot Apps	Tot Gls
1998–99	Arsenal	0	0		
1999–2000	Arsenal	1	0		
1999–2000	*Crystal Palace*	14	1	14	1
2000–01	Arsenal	17	3	18	3

DANILEVICIUS, Tomas (F) — 20 0
H: 6 2 W: 12 06 b.Lithuania 18-7-78
Source: Baltai, Atlantas, Beveren, FC Brugge.
Honours: Lithuania 11 full caps, 1 goal.

Season	Club	Apps	Gls	Tot Apps	Tot Gls
1998	Dynamo Moscow	11	0	11	0

From Ingelmunster

Season	Club	Apps	Gls	Tot Apps	Tot Gls
1999–2000	Lausanne	7	0	7	0
2000–01	Arsenal	2	0	2	0

DEMEL, Guy (M) — 1 0
H: 6 1 W: 13 07 b.Orsay 13-6-81

Season	Club	Apps	Gls	Tot Apps	Tot Gls
1999–2000	Nimes	0	0		
2000–01	Nimes	0	0	1	0
2000–01	Arsenal	0	0		

DIXON, Lee (D) — 622 36
H: 5 9 W: 10 12 b.Manchester 17-3-64
Source: Local. *Honours:* England B, 22 full caps, 1 goal.

Season	Club	Apps	Gls	Tot Apps	Tot Gls
1982–83	Burnley	3	0		
1983–84	Burnley	1	0	4	0
1983–84	Chester C	16	1		
1984–85	Chester C	41	0	57	1
1985–86	Bury	45	5	45	5
1986–87	Stoke C	42	3		
1987–88	Stoke C	29	2	71	5
1987–88	Arsenal	6	0		
1988–89	Arsenal	33	1		
1989–90	Arsenal	38	5		
1990–91	Arsenal	38	5		
1991–92	Arsenal	38	4		
1992–93	Arsenal	29	0		
1993–94	Arsenal	33	0		
1994–95	Arsenal	39	1		
1995–96	Arsenal	38	2		
1996–97	Arsenal	32	2		
1997–98	Arsenal	28	0		
1998–99	Arsenal	36	0		
1999–2000	Arsenal	28	4		
2000–01	Arsenal	29	1	445	25

EDU (M) — 5 0
H: 6 1 W: 12 04 b.Sao Paulo 15-5-78
Source: Corinthians.

Season	Club	Apps	Gls	Tot Apps	Tot Gls
2000–01	Arsenal	5	0	5	0

GALLI, Niccolo‡ (M) — 0 0
b.Florence 22-5-83
Source: Scholar.

Season	Club	Apps	Gls
2000–01	Arsenal	0	0

GRIMANDI, Gilles (D) — 178 7
H: 5 11 W: 11 08 b.Gap 11-11-70
Source: FC Gap.

Season	Club	Apps	Gls	Tot Apps	Tot Gls
1991–92	Monaco	5	0		
1992–93	Monaco	8	0		
1993–94	Monaco	19	1		
1994–95	Monaco	9	0		
1995–96	Monaco	25	1		
1996–97	Monaco	24	1	90	3
1997–98	Arsenal	22	1		
1998–99	Arsenal	8	0		
1999–2000	Arsenal	28	2		
2000–01	Arsenal	30	1	88	4

GRONDIN, David (D) — 1 0
H: 5 9 W: 11 11 b.Paris 8-5-80
Source: St Etienne, France Youth.

Season	Club	Apps	Gls	Tot Apps	Tot Gls
1998–99	Arsenal	1	0		
1999–2000	Arsenal	0	0		
2000–01	Arsenal	0	0	1	0

HALLS, John (D) — 0 0
H: 6 0 W: 11 00 b.Islington 14-2-82
Source: Scholar. *Honours:* England Youth.

Season	Club	Apps	Gls
2000–01	Arsenal	0	0

HENRY, Thierry (F) — 187 57
H: 6 2 W: 13 01 b.Paris 17-8-77
Honours: France 29 full caps, 10 goals.

Season	Club	Apps	Gls	Tot Apps	Tot Gls
1994–95	Monaco	8	3		
1995–96	Monaco	18	3		
1996–97	Monaco	36	9		
1997–98	Monaco	30	4		
1998–99	Monaco	13	1	105	20
1998–99	Juventus	16	3	16	3
1999–2000	Arsenal	31	17		
2000–01	Arsenal	35	17	66	34

ISRAEL (D) — 0 0
H: 5 9 W: 10 03 b.Sao Paulo 9-7-83
Source: Scholar.

Season	Club	Apps	Gls
2000–01	Arsenal	0	0

KANU, Nwankwo (F) — 196 62
H: 6 5 W: 12 01 b.Owerri 1-8-76
Honours: Nigeria full caps.

Season	Club	Apps	Gls	Tot Apps	Tot Gls
1991–92	Federation Works	30	9	30	9
1992–93	Iwanyanwu	30	6	30	6
1993–94	Ajax	6	2		
1994–95	Ajax	18	10		
1995–96	Ajax	30	13	54	25
1996–97	Internazionale	11	0		
1997–98	Internazionale	11	1		
1998–99	Internazionale	1	0	12	1
1998–99	Arsenal	12	6		
1999–2000	Arsenal	31	12		
2000–01	Arsenal	27	3	70	21

KEOWN, Martin (D) — 507 8
H: 6 1 W: 12 04 b.Oxford 24-7-66
Source: Apprentice. *Honours:* England Youth, Under-21, B, 38 full caps, 2 goals.

Season	Club	Apps	Gls	Tot Apps	Tot Gls
1983–84	Arsenal	0	0		
1984–85	Arsenal	0	0		
1984–85	*Brighton & HA*	16	0		
1985–86	Arsenal	22	0		
1985–86	*Brighton & HA*	7	1	23	1
1986–87	Aston Villa	36	0		
1987–88	Aston Villa	42	3		
1988–89	Aston Villa	34	0	112	3
1989–90	Everton	20	0		
1990–91	Everton	24	0		
1991–92	Everton	39	0		
1992–93	Everton	13	0	96	0
1992–93	Arsenal	16	0		
1993–94	Arsenal	33	0		
1994–95	Arsenal	31	1		
1995–96	Arsenal	34	0		
1996–97	Arsenal	33	1		
1997–98	Arsenal	18	0		
1998–99	Arsenal	34	1		
1999–2000	Arsenal	27	1		
2000–01	Arsenal	28	0	276	4

LAUREN, Etame-Mayer (M) — 161 20
H: 5 11 W: 11 03 b.Londi Keisi 19-1-77
Honours: Cameroon full caps.

Season	Club	Apps	Gls	Tot Apps	Tot Gls
1995–96	Utrera	30	5	30	5
1996–97	Sevilla B	17	3	17	3
1997–98	Levante	34	6	34	6
1998–99	Mallorca	32	1		
1999–2000	Mallorca	30	3	62	4
2000–01	Arsenal	18	2	18	2

LINCOLN, Greg* (M) — 0 0
H: 5 9 W: 10 01 b.Cheshunt 23-3-80
Source: Trainee. *Honours:* England Youth.

Season	Club	Apps	Gls
1998–99	Arsenal	0	0
1999–2000	Arsenal	0	0
2000–01	Arsenal	0	0

LJUNGBERG, Frederik (M) — 151 23
H: 5 9 W: 10 13 b.Halmstad 16-4-77
Honours: Sweden 26 full caps, 2 goals.

Season	Club	Apps	Gls	Tot Apps	Tot Gls
1994	Halmstad	1	0		
1995	Halmstad	16	1		
1996	Halmstad	20	2		
1997	Halmstad	24	5		
1998	Halmstad	18	2	79	10
1998–99	Arsenal	16	1		
1999–2000	Arsenal	26	6		
2000–01	Arsenal	30	9	72	13

LUKIC, John* (G) — 596 0
H: 6 4 W: 13 07 b.Chesterfield 11-12-60
Source: Apprentice. *Honours:* England Youth, Under-21, B.

Season	Club	Apps	Gls	Tot Apps	Tot Gls
1978–79	Leeds U	0	0		
1979–80	Leeds U	33	0		
1980–81	Leeds U	42	0		
1981–82	Leeds U	42	0		
1982–83	Leeds U	29	0		
1983–84	Arsenal	4	0		
1984–85	Arsenal	27	0		
1985–86	Arsenal	40	0		
1986–87	Arsenal	36	0		
1987–88	Arsenal	40	0		
1988–89	Arsenal	38	0		
1989–90	Arsenal	38	0		
1990–91	Leeds U	38	0		
1991–92	Leeds U	42	0		
1992–93	Leeds U	39	0		
1993–94	Leeds U	20	0		
1994–95	Leeds U	42	0		
1995–96	Leeds U	28	0	355	0
1996–97	Arsenal	15	0		
1997–98	Arsenal	0	0		
1998–99	Arsenal	0	0		
1999–2000	Arsenal	0	0		
2000–01	Arsenal	3	0	241	0

LUZHNY, Oleg (D) — 280 11
H: 5 10 W: 12 01 b.Ukraine 5-8-68
Honours: Ukraine 41 full caps.

Season	Club	Apps	Gls
1989	Dynamo Kiev	27	0
1990	Dynamo Kiev	12	0
1991	Dynamo Kiev	28	0

1992–93	Dynamo Kiev	26	3		
1993–94	Dynamo Kiev	34	1		
1994–95	Dynamo Kiev	24	4		
1995–96	Dynamo Kiev	24	1		
1996–97	Dynamo Kiev	28	2		
1997–98	Dynamo Kiev	16	0		
1998–99	Dynamo Kiev	21	0	240	11
1999–2000	Arsenal	21	0		
2000–01	Arsenal	19	0	40	0

MALZ, Stefan (M)   42   3
H: 5 10 W: 12 01 b.Ludwigshafen 15-6-72
Source: Pfingstweide, Oppau, Ludwigshafen, Darmstadt, Mannheim.

1997–98	Munich 1860	14	1		
1998–99	Munich 1860	22	1	36	2
1999–2000	Arsenal	5	1		
2000–01	Arsenal	1	0	6	1

MANNINGER, Alex (G)   68   0
H: 6 2 W: 13 03 b.Salzburg 4-6-77
Honours: Austria Under-21, 7 full caps.

1995–96	Vorwaerts Steyr	5	0	5	0
1995–96	Salzburg	1	0	1	0
1996–97	Graz	23	0	23	0
1997–98	Arsenal	7	0		
1998–99	Arsenal	6	0		
1999–2000	Arsenal	15	0		
2000–01	Arsenal	11	0	39	0

MENDEZ, Alberto (M)   4   0
H: 5 11 W: 11 09 b.Nuremberg 24-10-74
Source: FC Feucht.

1997–98	Arsenal	3	0		
1998–99	Arsenal	1	0		
1999–2000	Arsenal	0	0		
2000–01	Arsenal	0	0	4	0

NOBLE, David (M)   0   0
H: 6 0 W: 12 04 b.Hitchin 2-2-82
Source: Scholar. *Honours:* England Youth.

2000–01	Arsenal	0	0

OATES, Greg (D)   0   0
H: 6 0 W: 12 04 b.Maldon 3-10-81
Source: Scholar.

2000–01	Arsenal	0	0

OSEI-KUFFOUR, Jo (F)   0   0
H: 5 7 W: 10 03 b.Edmonton 17-11-81
Source: Scholar.

2000–01	Arsenal	0	0

PARLOUR, Ray (M)   268   22
H: 5 10 W: 11 12 b.Romford 7-3-73
Source: Trainee. *Honours:* England Under-21, B, 10 full caps.

1990–91	Arsenal	0	0		
1991–92	Arsenal	6	1		
1992–93	Arsenal	21	1		
1993–94	Arsenal	27	2		
1994–95	Arsenal	30	0		
1995–96	Arsenal	22	0		
1996–97	Arsenal	30	2		
1997–98	Arsenal	34	5		
1998–99	Arsenal	35	6		
1999–2000	Arsenal	30	1		
2000–01	Arsenal	33	4	268	22

PENNANT, Jermaine (M)   0   0
H: 5 8 W: 10 01 b.Nottingham 15-1-83
Honours: England Schools, Youth, England Under-21.

1998–99	Notts Co	0	0
1998–99	Arsenal	0	0
1999–2000	Arsenal	0	0
2000–01	Arsenal	0	0

PIRES, Robert (M)   261   55
H: 6 1 W: 11 09 b.Reims 29-10-73
Honours: France 48 full caps, 7 goals.

1992–93	Metz	2	0		
1993–94	Metz	24	1		
1994–95	Metz	35	9		
1995–96	Metz	38	11		
1996–97	Metz	32	11		
1997–98	Metz	31	11	162	43
1998–99	Marseille	34	6		
1999–2000	Marseille	32	2	66	8
2000–01	Arsenal	33	4	33	4

SEAMAN, David (G)   667   0
H: 6 3 W: 13 00 b.Rotherham 19-9-63
Source: Apprentice. *Honours:* England Under-21, B, 65 full caps.

1981–82	Leeds U	0	0		
1982–83	Peterborough U	38	0		
1983–84	Peterborough U	45	0		
1984–85	Peterborough U	8	0	91	0
1984–85	Birmingham C	33	0		
1985–86	Birmingham C	42	0	75	0
1986–87	QPR	41	0		
1987–88	QPR	32	0		
1988–89	QPR	35	0		
1989–90	QPR	33	0	141	0

1990–91	Arsenal	38	0		
1991–92	Arsenal	42	0		
1992–93	Arsenal	39	0		
1993–94	Arsenal	39	0		
1994–95	Arsenal	31	0		
1995–96	Arsenal	38	0		
1996–97	Arsenal	22	0		
1997–98	Arsenal	31	0		
1998–99	Arsenal	32	0		
1999–2000	Arsenal	24	0		
2000–01	Arsenal	24	0	360	0

SILVINHO (D)   55   3
H: 5 7 W: 10 06 b.Sao Paulo 12-4-74
Source: Corinthians. *Honours:* Brazil 5 full caps.

1999–2000	Arsenal	31	1		
2000–01	Arsenal	24	2	55	3

STACK, Graham (G)   0   0
H: 6 2 W: 12 06 b.Hampstead 26-9-81

2000–01	Arsenal	0	0

STEPANOVS, Igor (D)   158   13
H: 6 4 W: 13 05 b.Ogre 21-1-76
Honours: Latvia 44 full caps, 2 goals.

1994	Interskonto	20	2	20	2
1995	Skonto Riga	23	1		
1996	Skonto Riga	22	2		
1997	Skonto Riga	22	2		
1998	Skonto Riga	24	0		
1999	Skonto Riga	20	4		
2000	Skonto Riga	18	2	129	11
2000–01	Arsenal	9	0	9	0

SVARD, Sebastian (D)   0   0
b.Hvidovre 15-1-82

2000–01	Arsenal	0	0

TAYLOR, Stuart (G)   20   0
H: 6 4 W: 13 06 b.Romford 28-11-80
Source: Trainee. *Honours:* FA Schools, England Youth.

1998–99	Arsenal	0	0		
1999–2000	*Bristol R*	4	0	4	0
2000–01	Arsenal	0	0		
2000–01	*Crystal Palace*	10	0	10	0
2000–01	*Peterborough U*	6	0	6	0

UPSON, Matthew (D)   29   0
H: 6 1 W: 11 04 b.Hartismere 18-4-79
Source: Trainee. *Honours:* England Youth, Under-21.

1995–96	Luton T	0	0		
1996–97	Luton T	1	0	1	0
1996–97	Arsenal	0	0		
1997–98	Arsenal	5	0		
1998–99	Arsenal	5	0		
1999–2000	Arsenal	8	0		
2000–01	Arsenal	2	0	20	0
2000–01	*Nottingham F*	1	0	1	0
2000–01	*Crystal Palace*	7	0	7	0

VIEIRA, Patrick (M)   209   16
H: 6 4 W: 13 00 b.Dakar 23-6-76
Honours: France Under-21, 43 full caps, 2 goals.

1993–94	Cannes	5	0		
1994–95	Cannes	31	2		
1995–96	Cannes	13	0	49	2
1995–96	AC Milan	2	0	2	0
1996–97	Arsenal	31	2		
1997–98	Arsenal	33	2		
1998–99	Arsenal	34	3		
1999–2000	Arsenal	30	2		
2000–01	Arsenal	30	5	158	14

VIVAS, Nelson* (D)   113   3
H: 5 5 W: 10 06 b.San Nicolas 18-10-69
Source: Quilmes, Boca Juniors, Lugano. *Honours:* Argentina 27 full caps, 1 goal.

1995–96	Boca Juniors	25	2		
1996–97	Boca Juniors	27	1		
1997–98	Boca Juniors	8	0	60	3
1998–99	Arsenal	23	0		
1999–2000	*Celta Vigo*	13	0	13	0
2000–01	Arsenal	12	0	40	0

VOLZ, Moritz (D)   0   0
H: 5 10 W: 12 06 b.Germany 21-1-83

1999–2000	Arsenal	0	0
2000–01	Arsenal	0	0

WILTORD, Sylvain (F)   251   66
H: 5 9 W: 12 04 b.Neuilly-sur-Marne 10-5-74
Honours: France 29 full caps, 12 goals.

1991–92	Rennes	0	0
1992–93	Rennes	2	0
1993–94	Rennes	26	8
1994–95	La Coruna	0	0
1994–95	Rennes	25	5
1995–96	Rennes	37	15

1996–97	Rennes	35	5	125	33
1997–98	Bordeaux	34	10		
1998–99	Bordeaux	33	2		
1999–2000	Bordeaux	32	13	99	25
2000–01	Arsenal	27	8	27	8

WREH, Christopher (F)   81   17
H: 5 9 W: 11 05 b.Monrovia 14-5-75
Honours: Liberia full caps.

1995–96	Monaco	13	3	13	3
1996–97	Guincamp	33	10	33	10
1997–98	Arsenal	16	3		
1998–99	Arsenal	12	0		
1999–2000	Arsenal	0	0		
1999–2000	*Birmingham*	7	1	7	1
2000–01	Arsenal	0	0	28	3

(Transferred to Al Hildal, December 2000).

Scholars
Bailey, Alex C; Bentley, David M; Brown, Jermaine A; Chorley, Benjamin F; Garry, Ryan FM; Hollington, Daniel H; Holloway, Craig D; Islam, Tafazzul; Itonga, Carlin D; Nicolau, Nicky G; Ricketts, Rohan A: Rouse, Matthew A; Santry, Stephen M; Sesto, Alexander C; Sidwell, Steven J; Smith, Michael K; Spicer, John W; Thomas, Jerome W

ASTON VILLA

ALPAY, Ozalan (D)   233   13
H: 6 2 W: 14 00 b.Izmir 29-5-73
Source: Soma Linyit. *Honours:* Turkey 56 full caps, 1 goal.

1992–93	Altay	23	1	23	1
1993–94	Besiktas	10	0		
1994–95	Besiktas	29	3		
1995–96	Besiktas	31	2		
1996–97	Besiktas	25	3		
1997–98	Besiktas	26	1		
1998–99	Besiktas	27	0	148	9
1999–2000	Fenerbahce	29	3	29	3
2000–01	Aston Villa	33	0	33	0

ANGEL, Juan Pablo (F)   100   46
H: 6 0 W: 12 10 b.Medellin 24-10-75
Source: Nacional. *Honours:* Colombia 21 caps, 5 goals.

1997–98	River Plate	12	2		
1998–99	River Plate	27	11		
1999–2000	River Plate	34	19		
2000–01	River Plate	18	13	91	45
2000–01	Aston Villa	9	1	9	1

BARRY, Gareth (D)   94   3
H: 5 11 W: 12 06 b.Hastings 23-2-81
Source: Trainee. *Honours:* England Youth, Under-21, 6 full caps.

1997–98	Aston Villa	2	0		
1998–99	Aston Villa	32	2		
1999–2000	Aston Villa	30	1		
2000–01	Aston Villa	30	0	94	3

BERKS, David (M)   0   0
H: 5 8 W: 10 07 b.Stoke 23-12-81
Source: Scholar.

2000–01	Aston Villa	0	0

BEWERS, Jonathan (D)   1   0
H: 5 8 W: 9 13 b.Kettering 10-9-82
Source: Trainee. *Honours:* England Youth.

1999–2000	Aston Villa	1	0		
2000–01	Aston Villa	0	0	1	0

BOATENG, George (M)   190   9
H: 5 9 W: 10 12 b.Nkawkaw 5-9-75

1994–95	Excelsior	9	0	9	0
1995–96	Feyenoord	24	1		
1996–97	Feyenoord	26	0		
1997–98	Feyenoord	18	0	68	1
1997–98	Coventry C	14	1		
1998–99	Coventry C	33	4	47	5
1999–2000	Aston Villa	33	2		
2000–01	Aston Villa	33	1	66	3

COOKE, Stephen (M)   0   0
H: 5 7 W: 9 00 b.Walsall 15-2-83

1999–2000	Aston Villa	0	0
2000–01	Aston Villa	0	0

CURTOLO, David‡ (M)   0   0
H: 5 9 W: 11 00 b.Stockholm 30-9-80

1997–98	Aston Villa	0	0
1998–99	Aston Villa	0	0
1999–2000	Aston Villa	0	0
2000–01	Aston Villa	0	0

CUTLER, Neil* (G)   41   0
H: 6 1 W: 12 00 b.Birmingham 3-9-76
Source: Trainee. *Honours:* England Schools, Youth.

1993–94	WBA	0	0
1994–95	WBA	0	0

1995–96	WBA	0	0		
1995–96	*Coventry C*	0	0		
1995–96	*Chester C*	1	0		
1996–97	Crewe Alex	0	0		
1996–97	*Chester C*	5	0		
1997–98	Crewe Alex	0	0		
1998–99	Chester C	23	0		
1999–2000	Chester C	0	0	**29**	**0**
1999–2000	Aston Villa	1	0		
2000–01	Aston Villa	0	0	**1**	**0**
2000–01	*Oxford U*	11	0	**11**	**0**

DELANEY, Mark (D) **77 1**
H: 6 1 W: 11 07 b.Haverfordwest 13-5-76
Source: Carmarthen T. *Honours:* Wales 9 full caps.

1998–99	Cardiff C	28	0	**28**	**0**
1998–99	Aston Villa	2	0		
1999–2000	Aston Villa	28	1		
2000–01	Aston Villa	19	0	**49**	**1**

DILLON, Sean (D) **0 0**
H: 6 0 W: 12 06 b.Dublin 30-7-83
Source: Scholar.

2000–01	Aston Villa	0	0

DUBLIN, Dion (F) **396 146**
H: 6 2 W: 12 04 b.Leicester 22-4-69
Source: Oakham U. *Honours:* England 4 full caps.

1987–88	Norwich C	0	0		
1988–89	Cambridge U	21	6		
1989–90	Cambridge U	46	15		
1990–91	Cambridge U	46	16		
1991–92	Cambridge U	43	15	**156**	**52**
1992–93	Manchester U	7	1		
1993–94	Manchester U	5	1	**12**	**2**
1994–95	Coventry C	31	13		
1995–96	Coventry C	34	14		
1996–97	Coventry C	34	13		
1997–98	Coventry C	36	18		
1998–99	Coventry C	10	3	**145**	**61**
1998–99	Aston Villa	24	11		
1999–2000	Aston Villa	26	12		
2000–01	Aston Villa	33	8	**83**	**31**

EDWARDS, Rob (D) **0 0**
H: 6 1 W: 11 10 b.Telford 25-12-82
Source: Trainee.

1999–2000	Aston Villa	0	0
2000–01	Aston Villa	0	0

ENCKELMAN, Peter (G) **89 0**
H: 6 2 W: 12 05 b.Turku 10-3-77
Source: TPS Turku. *Honours:* Finland 2 full caps.

1995	TPS Turku	6	0		
1996	TPS Turku	24	0		
1997	TPS Turku	25	0		
1998	TPS Turku	24	0	**79**	**0**
1998–99	Aston Villa	0	0		
1999–2000	Aston Villa	10	0		
2000–01	Aston Villa	0	0	**10**	**0**

ENNIS, Pierre (D) **0 0**
H: 5 10 W: 12 03 b.Dublin 25-2-84
Source: Scholar.

2000–01	Aston Villa	0	0

EVANS, Stephen* (F) **0 0**
H: 5 8 W: 10 08 b.Coventry 12-11-80
Source: Trainee.

1999–2000	Aston Villa	0	0
2000–01	Aston Villa	0	0

FAHEY, Keith (M) **0 0**
H: 5 10 W: 12 07 b.Dublin 15-1-83

1999–2000	Aston Villa	0	0
2000–01	Aston Villa	0	0

FOLDS, Liam (D) **0 0**
H: 5 11 W: 12 01 b.Bedford 21-1-82
Source: Scholar.

2000–01	Aston Villa	0	0

GHRAYIB, Najwan‡ (D) **132 27**
H: 5 8 W: 11 04 b.Nazareth 30-1-74
Honours: Israel 18 full caps, 4 goals.

1994–95	Maccabi Haifa	23	4	**23**	**4**
1995–96	Maccabi P-T	27	10		
1996–97	Maccabi P-T	22	4	**49**	**14**
1997–98	Hapoel Haifa	26	2		
1998–99	Hapoel Haifa	29	7	**55**	**9**
1999–2000	Aston Villa	5	0		
2000–01	Aston Villa	0	0	**5**	**0**

(Transferred to Hapoel Haifa, February 2001).

GINOLA, David (F) **492 75**
H: 5 10 W: 12 07 b.Gassin 25-1-67
Honours: France 17 full caps, 3 goals.

1985–86	Toulon	14	0		
1986–87	Toulon	34	0		
1987–88	Toulon	33	4	**81**	**4**
1988–89	Racing Paris	29	7		
1989–90	Racing Paris	32	1	**61**	**8**
1990–91	Brest	33	1		
1991–92	Brest	17	9	**50**	**10**
1991–92	Paris St Germain	15	2		
1992–93	Paris St Germain	34	6		
1993–94	Paris St Germain	38	13		
1994–95	Paris St Germain	28	11	**115**	**32**
1995–96	Newcastle U	34	5		
1996–97	Newcastle U	24	1	**58**	**6**
1997–98	Tottenham H	34	6		
1998–99	Tottenham H	30	3		
1999–2000	Tottenham H	36	3	**100**	**12**
2000–01	Aston Villa	27	3	**27**	**3**

HAYNES, Danny (D) **0 0**
H: 6 2 W: 12 02 b.Nuneaton 24-8-82
Source: Scholar.

2000–01	Aston Villa	0	0

HENDERSON, Wayne (G) **0 0**
H: 5 11 W: 12 02 b.Dublin 16-9-83
Source: Scholar.

2000–01	Aston Villa	0	0

HENDRIE, Lee (M) **117 13**
H: 5 10 W: 11 00 b.Birmingham 18-5-77
Source: Trainee. *Honours:* England Youth, Under-21, B, 1 full cap.

1993–94	Aston Villa	0	0		
1994–95	Aston Villa	0	0		
1995–96	Aston Villa	3	0		
1996–97	Aston Villa	4	0		
1997–98	Aston Villa	17	3		
1998–99	Aston Villa	32	3		
1999–2000	Aston Villa	29	1		
2000–01	Aston Villa	32	6	**117**	**13**

HITZISPERGER, Thomas (D) **1 0**
H: 6 0 W: 11 12 b.Germany 5-4-82
Source: Bayern Munich.

2000–01	Aston Villa	1	0	**1**	**0**

HYLTON, Leon (D) **0 0**
H: 5 9 W: 11 00 b.Birmingham 27-1-83

1999–2000	Aston Villa	0	0
2000–01	Aston Villa	0	0

HYNES, Peter (F) **0 0**
H: 5 9 W: 11 12 b.Dublin 28-11-83

2000–01	Aston Villa	0	0

JACKMAN, Daniel (D) **0 0**
H: 5 4 W: 9 08 b.Worcester 3-1-83
Source: Scholar.

2000–01	Aston Villa	0	0

JAMES, David (G) **370 0**
H: 6 5 W: 14 02 b.Welwyn 1-8-70
Source: Trainee. *Honours:* England Youth, Under-21, B, 4 full caps.

1988–89	Watford	0	0		
1989–90	Watford	0	0		
1990–91	Watford	46	0		
1991–92	Watford	43	0	**89**	**0**
1992–93	Liverpool	29	0		
1993–94	Liverpool	14	0		
1994–95	Liverpool	42	0		
1995–96	Liverpool	38	0		
1996–97	Liverpool	38	0		
1997–98	Liverpool	27	0		
1998–99	Liverpool	26	0	**214**	**0**
1999–2000	Aston Villa	29	0		
2000–01	Aston Villa	38	0	**67**	**0**

(Transferred to West Ham U, July 2001).

JOACHIM, Julian (F) **240 64**
H: 5 6 W: 12 00 b.Boston 20-9-74
Source: Trainee. *Honours:* England Youth, Under-21.

1992–93	Leicester C	26	10		
1993–94	Leicester C	36	11		
1994–95	Leicester C	15	3		
1995–96	Leicester C	22	1	**99**	**25**
1995–96	Aston Villa	11	1		
1996–97	Aston Villa	15	3		
1997–98	Aston Villa	26	8		
1998–99	Aston Villa	36	14		
1999–2000	Aston Villa	33	6		
2000–01	Aston Villa	20	7	**141**	**39**

(Transferred to Coventry C, July 2001).

MARFELL, Andrew (F) **0 0**
H: 6 1 W: 12 07 b.Gloucester 20-2-82
Source: Scholar.

2000–01	Aston Villa	0	0

McGRATH, John (F) **3 0**
H: 5 10 W: 10 04 b.Limerick 27-3-80
Source: Belvedere. *Honours:* Eire Under-21.

1999–2000	Aston Villa	0	0		
2000–01	Aston Villa	3	0	**3**	**0**

MELAUGH, Gavin (M) **0 0**
H: 5 7 W: 9 07 b.Derry 9-7-81
Source: Trainee.

1998–99	Aston Villa	0	0
1999–2000	Aston Villa	0	0
2000–01	Aston Villa	0	0

MERSON, Paul (F) **478 105**
H: 6 0 W: 13 02 b.Northolt 20-3-68
Source: Apprentice. *Honours:* England Youth, Under-21, B, 21 full caps, 3 goals.

1985–86	Arsenal	0	0		
1986–87	Arsenal	7	3		
1986–87	*Brentford*	7	0	**7**	**0**
1987–88	Arsenal	15	5		
1988–89	Arsenal	37	10		
1989–90	Arsenal	29	7		
1990–91	Arsenal	37	13		
1991–92	Arsenal	42	12		
1992–93	Arsenal	33	6		
1993–94	Arsenal	33	7		
1994–95	Arsenal	24	4		
1995–96	Arsenal	38	5		
1996–97	Arsenal	32	6	**327**	**78**
1997–98	Middlesbrough	45	11		
1998–99	Middlesbrough	3	0	**48**	**11**
1998–99	Aston Villa	26	5		
1999–2000	Aston Villa	32	5		
2000–01	Aston Villa	38	6	**96**	**16**

MOORE, Stefan (F) **0 0**
H: 5 10 W: 10 12 b.Birmingham 28-9-83
Source: Scholar.

2000–01	Aston Villa	0	0

MYHILL, Boaz (G) **0 0**
H: 6 3 W: 14 06 b.California 9-11-82
Source: Scholar. *Honours:* England Youth.

2000–01	Aston Villa	0	0

NICHOLAS, Alexis (M) **0 0**
b.London 13-2-83
Source: Scholar.

2000–01	Aston Villa	0	0

NILIS, Luc‡ (F) **391 238**
H: 6 0 W: 12 00 b.Hasselt 25-5-67
Honours: Belgium 56 full caps, 10 goals.

1986–87	Anderlecht	16	5		
1987–88	Anderlecht	32	14		
1988–89	Anderlecht	33	19		
1989–90	Anderlecht	27	10		
1990–91	Anderlecht	30	19		
1991–92	Anderlecht	27	16		
1992–93	Anderlecht	29	19		
1993–94	Anderlecht	30	25	**224**	**127**
1994–95	PSV Eindhoven	30	12		
1995–96	PSV Eindhoven	31	21		
1996–97	PSV Eindhoven	26	21		
1997–98	PSV Eindhoven	24	13		
1998–99	PSV Eindhoven	27	24		
1999–2000	PSV Eindhoven	26	19	**164**	**110**
2000–01	Aston Villa	3	1	**3**	**1**

NKUBI, Isaac* (F) **0 0**
b.Uganda 5-3-81
Source: Vasteras.

1998–99	Aston Villa	0	0
1999–2000	Aston Villa	0	0
2000–01	Aston Villa	0	0

SAMUEL, J Lloyd (D) **12 0**
H: 5 11 W: 11 04 b.Trinidad 29-3-81
Source: Charlton Ath Trainee. *Honours:* England Youth.

1998–99	Aston Villa	0	0		
1999–2000	Aston Villa	9	0		
2000–01	Aston Villa	3	0	**12**	**0**

SMITH, Jay (M) **0 0**
H: 5 7 W: 10 00 b.London 24-9-81
Source: Scholar.

2000–01	Aston Villa	0	0

SOUTHGATE, Gareth (D) **343 22**
H: 6 0 W: 12 06 b.Watford 3-9-70
Source: Trainee. *Honours:* England 42 full caps, 1 goal.

1988–89	Crystal Palace	0	0		
1989–90	Crystal Palace	0	0		
1990–91	Crystal Palace	1	0		
1991–92	Crystal Palace	30	0		
1992–93	Crystal Palace	33	3		
1993–94	Crystal Palace	46	9		
1994–95	Crystal Palace	42	3	**152**	**15**
1995–96	Aston Villa	31	1		
1996–97	Aston Villa	28	1		
1997–98	Aston Villa	32	0		
1998–99	Aston Villa	38	1		
1999–2000	Aston Villa	31	2		
2000–01	Aston Villa	31	2	**191**	**7**

(Transferred to Middlesbrough, July 2001).

STANDING, Michael (M) **0 0**
H: 5 10 W: 10 05 b.Shoreham 20-3-81
Source: Trainee. *Honours:* England Schools.

1997–98	Aston Villa	0	0
1998–99	Aston Villa	0	0
1999–2000	Aston Villa	0	0
2000–01	Aston Villa	0	0

STAUNTON, Steve (D)   345 17
H: 6 0   W: 12 12   b.Drogheda 19-1-69
Source: Dundalk. *Honours:* Eire Under-21, 89 full caps, 7 goals.

1986–87	Liverpool	0	0		
1987–88	Liverpool	0	0		
1987–88	*Bradford C*	8	0	8	0
1988–89	Liverpool	21	0		
1989–90	Liverpool	20	0		
1990–91	Liverpool	24	0		
1991–92	Aston Villa	37	4		
1992–93	Aston Villa	42	2		
1993–94	Aston Villa	24	2		
1994–95	Aston Villa	35	5		
1995–96	Aston Villa	13	0		
1996–97	Aston Villa	30	2		
1997–98	Aston Villa	27	1		
1998–99	Liverpool	31	0		
1999–2000	Liverpool	12	0		
2000–01	Liverpool	1	0	109	0
2000–01	*Crystal Palace*	6	0		
2000–01	Aston Villa	14	0	222	16

STONE, Steve (M)   261 26
H: 5 8   W: 12 07   b.Gateshead 20-8-71
Source: Trainee. *Honours:* England 9 full caps, 2 goals.

1989–90	Nottingham F	0	0		
1990–91	Nottingham F	0	0		
1991–92	Nottingham F	1	0		
1992–93	Nottingham F	12	1		
1993–94	Nottingham F	45	5		
1994–95	Nottingham F	41	5		
1995–96	Nottingham F	34	7		
1996–97	Nottingham F	5	0		
1997–98	Nottingham F	29	2		
1998–99	Nottingham F	26	3	193	23
1998–99	Aston Villa	10	0		
1999–2000	Aston Villa	24	1		
2000–01	Aston Villa	34	2	68	3

TARRANT, Neil (F)   53 21
H: 6 1   W: 11 05   b.Darlington 24-6-79
Honours: Scotland Under-21.

1997–98	Darlington	0	0		
1997–98	*Shamrock R*	2	0	2	0
1997–98	Ross Co	11	3		
1998–99	Ross Co	33	17	44	20
1998–99	Aston Villa	0	0		
1999–2000	Aston Villa	0	0		
2000–01	Aston Villa	0	0		
2000–01	*York C*	7	1	7	1

TAYLOR, Ian (M)   301 54
H: 6 1   W: 12 00   b.Birmingham 4-6-68
Source: Moor Green.

1992–93	Port Vale	41	15		
1993–94	Port Vale	42	13	83	28
1994–95	Sheffield W	14	1	14	1
1994–95	Aston Villa	22	1		
1995–96	Aston Villa	25	3		
1996–97	Aston Villa	34	2		
1997–98	Aston Villa	32	6		
1998–99	Aston Villa	33	4		
1999–2000	Aston Villa	29	5		
2000–01	Aston Villa	29	4	204	25

THOMPSON, Alan‡ (M)   219 37
H: 6 0   W: 12 08   b.Newcastle 22-12-73
Source: Trainee. *Honours:* England Youth, Under-21.

1990–91	Newcastle U	0	0		
1991–92	Newcastle U	14	0		
1992–93	Newcastle U	2	0	16	0
1993–94	Bolton W	27	6		
1994–95	Bolton W	37	7		
1995–96	Bolton W	26	1		
1996–97	Bolton W	34	10		
1997–98	Bolton W	33	9	157	33
1998–99	Aston Villa	25	2		
1999–2000	Aston Villa	21	2		
2000–01	Aston Villa	0	0	46	4

THORNLEY, Stuart‡ (D)   0 0
H: 5 8   W: 11 04   b.Wrexham 28-10-80
Source: Trainee.

| 1999–2000 | Aston Villa | 0 | 0 | | |
| 2000–01 | Aston Villa | 0 | 0 | | |

VASSELL, Darius (F)   40 4
H: 5 7   W: 12 00   b.Birmingham 13-6-80
Source: Trainee. *Honours:* England Youth, Under-21.

1998–99	Aston Villa	6	0		
1999–2000	Aston Villa	11	0		
2000–01	Aston Villa	23	4	40	4

WALKER, Richard (F)   45 8
H: 6 0   W: 12 04   b.Sutton Coldfield 8-11-77
Source: Trainee.

1995–96	Aston Villa	0	0		
1996–97	Aston Villa	0	0		
1997–98	Aston Villa	1	0		

1998–99	Aston Villa	0	0		
1998–99	*Cambridge U*	21	3	21	3
1999–2000	Aston Villa	5	2		
2000–01	Aston Villa	0	0	6	2
2000–01	*Blackpool*	18	3	18	3

WILLETTS, Ben (D)   0 0
H: 5 9   W: 11 05   b.West Bromwich 10-2-83
Source: Scholar.

| 1999–2000 | Aston Villa | 0 | 0 | | |
| 2000–01 | Aston Villa | 0 | 0 | | |

WRIGHT, Alan (D)   399 6
H: 5 4   W: 9 09   b.Ashton-under-Lyme 28-9-71
Source: Trainee. *Honours:* England Schools, Youth, Under-21.

1987–88	Blackpool	1	0		
1988–89	Blackpool	16	0		
1989–90	Blackpool	24	0		
1990–91	Blackpool	45	0		
1991–92	Blackpool	12	0	98	0
1991–92	Blackburn R	33	1		
1992–93	Blackburn R	24	0		
1993–94	Blackburn R	12	0		
1994–95	Blackburn R	5	0	74	1
1994–95	Aston Villa	8	0		
1995–96	Aston Villa	38	2		
1996–97	Aston Villa	38	1		
1997–98	Aston Villa	37	0		
1998–99	Aston Villa	38	0		
1999–2000	Aston Villa	32	1		
2000–01	Aston Villa	36	1	227	5

Scholars
Amoo, Ryan L; Andrewartha, David P; Cunnington, James J; Husbands, Michael P; McGuire, Lee A; Pawley, James D; Ridgewell, Liam M; Stuart, Cameron R; Wells, Andrew M

BARNET

ARBER, Mark (D)   125 15
H: 6 1   W: 12 11   b.Johannesburg 8-10-77
Source: Trainee.

1995–96	Tottenham H	0	0		
1996–97	Tottenham H	0	0		
1997–98	Tottenham H	0	0		
1998–99	Tottenham H	0	0		
1998–99	Barnet	35	2		
1999–2000	Barnet	45	6		
2000–01	Barnet	45	7	125	15

BELL, Leon (M)   12 0
H: 5 7   W: 9 07   b.Hitchin 19-12-80
Source: Trainee.

| 1999–2000 | Barnet | 1 | 0 | | |
| 2000–01 | Barnet | 11 | 0 | 12 | 0 |

BERKLEY, Austin (M)   176 12
H: 5 9   W: 10 10   b.Gravesend 24-1-73
Source: Trainee.

1990–91	Gillingham	0	0		
1991–92	Gillingham	3	0	3	0
1992–93	Swindon T	0	0		
1993–94	Swindon T	0	0		
1994–95	Swindon T	1	0	1	0
1995–96	Shrewsbury T	38	1		
1996–97	Shrewsbury T	24	0		
1997–98	Shrewsbury T	36	3		
1998–99	Shrewsbury T	41	8		
1999–2000	Shrewsbury T	33	0	172	12
2000–01	Barnet	0	0		

BOSSU, Bertrand (G)   0 0
H: 6 7   W: 14 00   b.Calais 14-10-80

| 1999–2000 | Barnet | 0 | 0 | | |
| 2000–01 | Barnet | 0 | 0 | | |

BROWN, Daniel (M)   53 3
H: 6 0   W: 12 06   b.Bethnal Green 12-9-80
Source: Trainee.

1997–98	Leyton Orient	0	0		
1998–99	Leyton Orient	0	0		
1999–2000	Barnet	24	3		
2000–01	Barnet	29	0	53	3

CHAPMAN, Danny‡ (D)   0 0
H: 6 2   W: 12 07   b.London 19-4-81
Source: Trainee.

| 1999–2000 Barnet | | 0 | 0 | | |
| 2000–01 Barnet | | 0 | 0 | | |

CHARLERY, Ken‡ (F)   438 120
H: 6 1   W: 13 12   b.Stepney 28-11-64
Source: Fisher Ath, Basildon U, Beckton U.
Honours: St Lucia full caps.

1989–90	Maidstone U	30	2		
1990–91	Maidstone U	29	9	59	11
1990–91	Peterborough U	8	0		
1991–92	Peterborough U	37	16		
1992–93	Peterborough U	10	3		

1992–93	Watford	32	11		
1993–94	Watford	16	2	48	13
1993–94	Peterborough U	26	8		
1994–95	Peterborough U	44	16		
1995–96	Birmingham C	17	4	17	4
1995–96	*Southend U*	3	0	3	0
1995–96	Peterborough U	19	7		
1996–97	Peterborough U	37	5	177	55
1996–97	Stockport Co	10	0	10	0
1997–98	Barnet	32	5		
1998–99	Barnet	42	16		
1999–2000	Barnet	43	13		
2000–01	Barnet	7	3	124	37

CURRIE, Darren (M)   227 29
H: 5 10   W: 12 07   b.Hampstead 29-11-74
Source: Trainee.

1993–94	West Ham U	0	0		
1994–95	West Ham U	0	0		
1994–95	*Shrewsbury T*	17	2		
1995–96	West Ham U	0	0		
1995–96	*Leyton Orient*	10	0	10	0
1995–96	Shrewsbury T	13	2		
1996–97	Shrewsbury T	37	2		
1997–98	Shrewsbury T	16	4	83	10
1997–98	Plymouth Arg	7	0	7	0
1998–99	Barnet	38	4		
1999–2000	Barnet	44	5		
2000–01	Barnet	45	10	127	19

DARCY, Ross (D)   6 0
H: 6 0   W: 12 02   b.Balbriggan 21-3-78
Source: Trainee. *Honours:* Eire Under-21.

1995–96	Tottenham H	0	0		
1996–97	Tottenham H	0	0		
1997–98	Tottenham H	0	0		
1998–99	Tottenham H	0	0		
1999–2000	Tottenham H	0	0		
1999–2000	Barnet	3	0		
2000–01	Barnet	3	0	6	0

DOOLAN, John (M)   265 17
H: 6 1   W: 13 00   b.Liverpool 7-5-74
Source: Trainee.

1992–93	Everton	0	0		
1993–94	Everton	0	0		
1994–95	Mansfield T	24	1		
1995–96	Mansfield T	42	2		
1996–97	Mansfield T	41	6		
1997–98	Mansfield T	24	1	131	10
1997–98	Barnet	17	0		
1998–99	Barnet	42	2		
1999–2000	Barnet	44	2		
2000–01	Barnet	31	3	134	7

FLYNN, Lee (D)   17 0
b.Hampstead 4-9-73
Source: Hayes.

| 2000–01 | Barnet | 17 | 0 | 17 | 0 |

GLEDHILL, Lee (D)   16 0
H: 5 10   W: 11 02   b.Bury 7-11-80
Source: Trainee.

1998–99	Barnet	1	0		
1999–2000	Barnet	10	0		
2000–01	Barnet	5	0	16	0

GOODHIND, Warren (D)   93 3
H: 5 11   W: 11 02   b.Johannesburg 16-8-77
Source: Trainee.

1996–97	Barnet	3	0		
1997–98	Barnet	35	1		
1998–99	Barnet	15	1		
1999–2000	Barnet	9	0		
2000–01	Barnet	31	1	93	3

GOWER, Mark (M)   23 2
H: 5 11   W: 11 12   b.Edmonton 5-10-78
Source: Trainee. *Honours:* England Schools, Youth.

1996–97	Tottenham H	0	0		
1997–98	Tottenham H	0	0		
1998–99	Tottenham H	0	0		
1998–99	*Motherwell*	9	1	9	1
1999–2000	Tottenham H	0	0		
2000–01	Tottenham H	0	0		
2000–01	Barnet	14	1	14	1

HACKETT, Warren* (D)   276 11
H: 6 0   W: 12 05   b.Plaistow 16-12-71
Source: Tottenham H Trainee. *Honours:* St Lucia full caps.

1990–91	Leyton Orient	0	0		
1991–92	Leyton Orient	22	0		
1992–93	Leyton Orient	17	0		
1993–94	Leyton Orient	33	3	72	3
1994–95	Doncaster R	39	2		
1995–96	Doncaster R	7	0	46	2
1995–96	Mansfield T	32	3		
1996–97	Mansfield T	36	1		
1997–98	Mansfield T	23	1		
1998–99	Mansfield T	26	0	117	5
1998–99	Barnet	7	0		
1999–2000	Barnet	34	1		
2000–01	Barnet	0	0	41	1

HARRISON, Lee (G) 197 0
H: 6 2 W: 12 07 b.Billericay 12-9-71
Source: Trainee.

1990–91	Charlton Ath	0	0		
1991–92	Charlton Ath	0	0		
1991–92	*Fulham*	0	0		
1991–92	*Gillingham*	2	0	**2**	**0**
1992–93	Charlton Ath	0	0		
1992–93	*Fulham*	0	0		
1993–94	Fulham	0	0		
1994–95	Fulham	7	0		
1995–96	Fulham	5	0	**12**	**0**
1996–97	Barnet	21	0		
1997–98	Barnet	46	0		
1998–99	Barnet	43	0		
1999–2000	Barnet	43	0		
2000–01	Barnet	30	0	**183**	**0**

HEALD, Greg (D) 246 19
H: 6 1 W: 13 01 b.Enfield 26-9-71
Source: Enfield. *Honours:* England Schools.

1994–95	Peterborough U	29	0		
1995–96	Peterborough U	40	4		
1996–97	Peterborough U	36	2	**105**	**6**
1997–98	Barnet	43	3		
1998–99	Barnet	19	2		
1999–2000	Barnet	40	5		
2000–01	Barnet	39	3	**141**	**13**

McCANN, Peter* (D) 0 0
H: 5 6 W: 10 09 b.Paisley 27-6-82
Source: Trainee.

1999–2000	Barnet	0	0		
2000–01	Barnet	0	0		

MIDGLEY, Neil (F) 18 4
H: 5 11 W: 11 02 b.Cambridge 21-10-78
Source: Trainee.

1997–98	Ipswich T	0	0		
1998–99	Ipswich T	0	0		
1999–2000	Ipswich T	4	1		
1999–2000	*Luton T*	10	3	**10**	**3**
2000–01	Ipswich T	0	0	**4**	**1**
2000–01	Barnet	4	0	**4**	**0**

NAISBITT, Danny (G) 23 0
H: 6 1 W: 11 12 b.Bishop Auckland 25-11-78
Source: Trainee.

1997–98	Walsall	0	0		
1998–99	Walsall	0	0		
1999–2000	Barnet	4	0		
2000–01	Barnet	19	0	**23**	**0**

NEWTON, Eddie‡ (M) 198 12
H: 5 11 W: 12 11 b.Hammersmith 13-12-71
Source: Trainee. *Honours:* England Under-21.

1990–91	Chelsea	0	0		
1991–92	Chelsea	1	1		
1991–92	*Cardiff C*	18	4	**18**	**4**
1992–93	Chelsea	34	5		
1993–94	Chelsea	36	0		
1994–95	Chelsea	30	1		
1995–96	Chelsea	24	1		
1996–97	Chelsea	15	0		
1997–98	Chelsea	18	0		
1998–99	Chelsea	7	0	**165**	**8**
1999–2000	Birmingham C	4	0	**4**	**0**
1999–2000	Oxford U	7	0	**7**	**0**
2000–01	Barnet	4	0	**4**	**0**

NIVEN, Stuart (M) 26 2
H: 5 11 W: 12 08 b.Glasgow 24-12-78
Source: Trainee.

1996–97	Ipswich T	2	0		
1997–98	Ipswich T	0	0		
1998–99	Ipswich T	0	0		
1999–2000	Ipswich T	0	0		
2000–01	Ipswich T	0	0	**2**	**0**
2000–01	Barnet	24	2	**24**	**2**

PLUCK, Lee (D) 1 0
b.Enfield 25-3-82
Source: Scholar.

2000–01	Barnet	1	0	**1**	**0**

PURSER, Wayne (F) 18 3
H: 5 9 W: 11 13 b.Basildon 13-4-80
Source: Trainee.

1996–97	QPR	0	0		
1997–98	QPR	0	0		
1998–99	QPR	0	0		
1999–2000	QPR	0	0		
2000–01	Barnet	18	3	**18**	**3**

RICHARDS, Tony (F) 138 24
H: 6 0 W: 13 06 b.Newham 17-9-73
Source: West Ham U Trainee, Sudbury T.

1995–96	Cambridge U	19	1		
1996–97	Cambridge U	23	4	**42**	**5**
1997–98	Leyton Orient	17	2		
1998–99	Leyton Orient	29	7		
1999–2000	Leyton Orient	17	2	**63**	**11**
2000–01	Barnet	33	8	**33**	**8**

SAWYERS, Robert (D) 84 3
H: 5 10 W: 11 03 b.Dudley 20-11-78
Source: Wolverhampton W Trainee.

1997–98	Barnet	1	0		
1998–99	Barnet	22	0		
1999–2000	Barnet	32	2		
2000–01	Barnet	29	1	**84**	**3**

SEARLE, Stevie (M) 84 5
H: 5 10 W: 11 08 b.Lambeth 7-3-77
Source: Sittingbourne.

1997–98	Barnet	30	2		
1998–99	Barnet	35	3		
1999–2000	Barnet	19	0		
2000–01	Barnet	0	0	**84**	**5**

STOCKLEY, Sam (D) 182 2
H: 6 0 W: 12 00 b.Tiverton 5-9-77
Source: Trainee.

1996–97	Southampton	0	0		
1996–97	Barnet	21	0		
1997–98	Barnet	41	0		
1998–99	Barnet	41	0		
1999–2000	Barnet	34	1		
2000–01	Barnet	45	1	**182**	**2**

STREVENS, Ben (F) 34 4
H: 6 1 W: 11 00 b.Islington 24-5-80
Source: Wingate & Finchley.

1998–99	Barnet	0	0		
1999–2000	Barnet	6	0		
2000–01	Barnet	28	4	**34**	**4**

TAYLOR, Mark (D) 0 0
H: 5 10 W: 12 00 b.Hertfordshire 14-7-82
Source: Trainee.

2000–01	Barnet	0	0		

TOMS, Frazer (M) 65 1
H: 6 1 W: 11 00 b.Ealing 13-9-79
Source: Trainee.

1998–99	Charlton Ath	0	0		
1999–2000	Barnet	39	1		
2000–01	Barnet	26	0	**65**	**1**

WILSON, Paul‡ (M) 263 24
H: 5 9 W: 12 00 b.Forest Gate 26-9-64
Source: West Ham U, Billericay, Barking.

1991–92	Barnet	25	1		
1992–93	Barnet	9	0		
1993–94	Barnet	34	3		
1994–95	Barnet	36	3		
1995–96	Barnet	33	4		
1996–97	Barnet	37	5		
1997–98	Barnet	39	5		
1998–99	Barnet	31	2		
1999–2000	Barnet	19	1		
2000–01	Barnet	0	0	**263**	**24**

Scholars
Cashman, Christopher S; Cattle, Lee CD; Langton, John J; Lee, Ryan RS; Lette Jellow, Bai M; Madden, Thomas D; Millard, Ricky A; Olayinka, Ade J; Oshitola, Oloruntobi O; Pope, Craig; Purches, John R; Still, Robert J; Williams, Gregg J; Wiper, Benjamin A
Non-Contract
May, Dean K; Simba, Amara S

BARNSLEY

APPLEBY, Matty (D) 248 15
H: 5 10 W: 11 08 b.Middlesbrough 16-4-72
Source: Trainee.

1989–90	Newcastle U	0	0		
1990–91	Newcastle U	1	0		
1991–92	Newcastle U	18	0		
1992–93	Newcastle U	0	0		
1993–94	Newcastle U	1	0	**20**	**0**
1993–94	*Darlington*	10	1		
1994–95	Darlington	36	1		
1995–96	Darlington	43	6	**89**	**8**
1996–97	Barnsley	35	0		
1997–98	Barnsley	15	0		
1998–99	Barnsley	34	0		
1999–2000	Barnsley	36	5		
2000–01	Barnsley	19	2	**139**	**7**

AUSTIN, Kevin (D) 244 5
H: 6 1 W: 15 00 b.Hackney 12-2-73
Source: Saffron Walden.

1993–94	Leyton Orient	30	0		
1994–95	Leyton Orient	39	2		
1995–96	Leyton Orient	40	1	**109**	**3**
1996–97	Lincoln C	44	1		
1997–98	Lincoln C	46	0		
1998–99	Lincoln C	39	1	**129**	**2**
1999–2000	Barnsley	3	0		
2000–01	Barnsley	0	0	**3**	**0**
2000–01	*Brentford*	3	0	**3**	**0**

AUSTIN, Neil (D) 0 0
H: 5 10 W: 11 00 b.Barnsley 26-4-83
Source: Trainee.

1999–2000	Barnsley	0	0		
2000–01	Barnsley	0	0		

BARKER, Christopher (D) 69 0
H: 6 0 W: 11 08 b.Sheffield 2-3-80
Source: Alfreton.

1998–99	Barnsley	0	0		
1999–2000	Barnsley	29	0		
2000–01	Barnsley	40	0	**69**	**0**

BARNARD, Darren (D) 243 38
H: 5 9 W: 12 03 b.Rinteln 30-11-71
Source: Wokingham T. *Honours:* England Schools, Wales 15 full caps.

1990–91	Chelsea	0	0		
1991–92	Chelsea	4	0		
1992–93	Chelsea	13	1		
1993–94	Chelsea	12	1		
1994–95	Chelsea	0	0		
1994–95	*Reading*	4	0	**4**	**0**
1995–96	Chelsea	0	0	**29**	**2**
1995–96	Bristol C	34	4		
1996–97	Bristol C	44	11	**78**	**15**
1997–98	Barnsley	35	2		
1998–99	Barnsley	26	4		
1999–2000	Barnsley	41	13		
2000–01	Barnsley	30	2	**132**	**21**

BARROWCLOUGH, Carl (M) 7 0
b.Doncaster 25-9-81
Source: Scholar.

2000–01	Barnsley	7	0	**7**	**0**

BERNARD, Curtis‡ (F) 0 0
H: 5 10 W: 12 05 b.Leeds 3-7-80
Source: Trainee.

1997–98	Barnsley	0	0		
1998–99	Barnsley	0	0		
1999–2000	Barnsley	0	0		
2000–01	Barnsley	0	0		

BERTOS, Leo (F) 2 0
H: 6 0 W: 12 00 b.Wellington 20-12-81

2000–01	Barnsley	2	0	**2**	**0**

BROWN, Keith (D) 14 0
H: 5 11 W: 11 02 b.Edinburgh 24-12-79
Source: trainee.

1996–97	Blackburn R	0	0		
1997–98	Blackburn R	0	0		
1998–99	Blackburn R	0	0		
1999–2000	Blackburn R	0	0		
1999–2000	Barnsley	10	0		
2000–01	Barnsley	1	0	**11**	**0**
2000–01	*Oxford U*	3	0	**3**	**0**

BULLOCK, Martin* (M) 191 5
H: 5 6 W: 9 04 b.Derby 5-3-75
Source: Eastwood T. *Honours:* England Under-21.

1993–94	Barnsley	0	0		
1994–95	Barnsley	29	0		
1995–96	Barnsley	41	1		
1996–97	Barnsley	28	0		
1997–98	Barnsley	33	0		
1998–99	Barnsley	32	2		
1999–2000	Barnsley	4	0		
1999–2000	*Port Vale*	6	1	**6**	**1**
2000–01	Barnsley	18	1	**185**	**4**

CHETTLE, Steve (D) 475 13
H: 6 1 W: 13 07 b.Nottingham 27-9-68
Source: Apprentice. *Honours:* England Under-21.

1986–87	Nottingham F	0	0		
1987–88	Nottingham F	30	0		
1988–89	Nottingham F	28	2		
1989–90	Nottingham F	22	1		
1990–91	Nottingham F	37	2		
1991–92	Nottingham F	22	1		
1992–93	Nottingham F	30	0		
1993–94	Nottingham F	46	1		
1994–95	Nottingham F	41	0		
1995–96	Nottingham F	37	0		
1996–97	Nottingham F	32	0		
1997–98	Nottingham F	45	1		
1998–99	Nottingham F	34	2		
1999–2000	Nottingham F	11	1	**415**	**11**
1999–2000	Barnsley	25	2		
2000–01	Barnsley	35	0	**60**	**2**

CORBO, Mateo (D) 91 2
H: 5 11 W: 12 08 b.Montevideo 21-4-76

1996	River Plate (Uru)	16	0		
1997	River Plate (Uru)	25	1		
1998	River Plate (Uru)	16	0		
1999	River Plate (Uru)	11	1	**68**	**2**
1999–2000	Oviedo	6	0	**6**	**0**
2000–01	Barnsley	17	0	**17**	**0**

CROOKS, Lee (D) — 79 2
H: 6 2 W: 13 13 b.Wakefield 14-1-78
Source: Trainee. *Honours:* England Youth.

Season	Club				
1994-95	Manchester C	0	0		
1995-96	Manchester C	0	0		
1996-97	Manchester C	15	0		
1997-98	Manchester C	5	0		
1998-99	Manchester C	34	1		
1999-2000	Manchester C	20	1		
2000-01	Manchester C	2	0	76	2
2000-01	*Northampton T*	3	0	3	0
2000-01	Barnsley	0	0		

DUDGEON, James (D) — 22 3
H: 6 2 W: 12 04 b.Newcastle 19-3-81
Source: Trainee.

Season	Club				
1999-2000	Barnsley	0	0		
2000-01	Barnsley	0	0		
2000-01	*Lincoln C*	22	3	22	3

DYER, Bruce (F) — 264 71
H: 5 11 W: 12 06 b.Ilford 13-4-75
Source: Trainee. *Honours:* England Under-21.

Season	Club				
1992-93	Watford	2	0		
1993-94	Watford	29	6	31	6
1993-94	Crystal Palace	11	0		
1994-95	Crystal Palace	16	1		
1995-96	Crystal Palace	35	13		
1996-97	Crystal Palace	43	17		
1997-98	Crystal Palace	24	4		
1998-99	Crystal Palace	6	2	135	37
1998-99	Barnsley	28	7		
1999-2000	Barnsley	32	6		
2000-01	Barnsley	38	15	98	28

EVANS, Andy (F) — 21 0
H: 6 2 W: 12 02 b.Aberystwyth 25-11-75
Source: Trainee.

Season	Club				
1993-94	Cardiff C	1	0		
1994-95	Cardiff C	12	0		
1995-96	Cardiff C	2	0	15	0
From Aberystwyth T.					
1999-2000	Barnsley	0	0		
1999-2000	*Mansfield T*	6	0	6	0
2000-01	Barnsley	0	0		

FALLON, Rory (F) — 1 0
H: 6 2 W: 12 06 b.Gisbourne 20-3-82
Source: North Shore U. *Honours:* England Youth.

Season	Club				
1998-99	Barnsley	0	0		
1999-2000	Barnsley	0	0		
2000-01	Barnsley	1	0	1	0

GARTLAND, Graham (M) — 0 0
b.Dublin 13-7-83

Season	Club		
2000-01	Barnsley	0	0

GOODYEAR, Craig‡ (M) — 0 0
H: 5 7 W: 10 07 b.Barnsley 7-11-80
Source: Trainee.

Season	Club		
1997-98	Barnsley	0	0
1998-99	Barnsley	0	0
1999-2000	Barnsley	0	0
2000-01	Barnsley	0	0

HAYWARD, Steve (M) — 241 22
H: 5 11 W: 13 00 b.Walsall 8-9-71
Source: Trainee. *Honours:* England Youth.

Season	Club				
1988-89	Derby Co	0	0		
1989-90	Derby Co	3	0		
1990-91	Derby Co	1	0		
1991-92	Derby Co	7	0		
1992-93	Derby Co	7	1		
1993-94	Derby Co	5	0		
1994-95	Derby Co	3	0	26	1
1994-95	Carlisle U	9	2		
1995-96	Carlisle U	38	4		
1996-97	Carlisle U	43	7	90	13
1997-98	Fulham	35	4		
1998-99	Fulham	42	3		
1999-2000	Fulham	37	0		
2000-01	Fulham	1	0	115	7
2000-01	Barnsley	10	1	10	1

HOOD, Nathan‡ (M) — 0 0
H: 5 5 W: 10 05 b.Rotherham 24-2-82

Season	Club		
1999-2000	Barnsley	0	0
2000-01	Barnsley	0	0

JACKSON, Paul (F) — 0 0
H: 5 8 W: 11 04 b.Rochdale 14-5-81
Source: Trainee.

Season	Club		
1999-2000	Barnsley	0	0
2000-01	Barnsley	0	0

JONES, Lee (F) — 189 41
H: 5 8 W: 10 06 b.Wrexham 29-5-73
Source: Trainee. *Honours:* Wales Under-21, 2 full caps.

Season	Club				
1990-91	Wrexham	18	5		
1991-92	Wrexham	21	5		
1991-92	Liverpool	0	0		
1992-93	Liverpool	0	0		
1993-94	Liverpool	0	0		
1993-94	Crewe Alex	8	1	8	1
1994-95	Liverpool	1	0		
1995-96	Liverpool	0	0		
1995-96	Wrexham	20	9		
1996-97	Liverpool	2	0	3	0
1996-97	Wrexham	6	0	65	19
1996-97	Tranmere R	8	5		
1997-98	Tranmere R	34	9		
1998-99	Tranmere R	30	2		
1999-2000	Tranmere R	14	0	86	16
2000-01	Barnsley	27	5	27	5

KAY, Antony (M) — 7 0
H: 5 11 W: 11 08 b.Barnsley 21-10-82
Source: Trainee.

Season	Club				
1999-2000	Barnsley	0	0		
2000-01	Barnsley	7	0	7	0

LAUCHLAN, James‡ (D) — 83 2
H: 6 1 W: 10 13 b.Glasgow 2-2-77
Source: Highbury BC. *Honours:* Scotland Under-21.

Season	Club				
1993-94	Kilmarnock	1	0		
1994-95	Kilmarnock	2	0		
1995-96	Kilmarnock	5	0		
1996-97	Kilmarnock	10	0		
1997-98	Kilmarnock	22	0		
1998-99	Kilmarnock	14	0		
1999-2000	Kilmarnock	29	2	83	2
2000-01	Barnsley	0	0		

MARRIOTT, Andy (G) — 256
H: 6 2 W: 13 04 b.Sutton-in-Ashfield 11-10-70
Source: Trainee. *Honours:* England Schools, FA Schools, Youth, Under-21, Wales 5 full caps.

Season	Club				
1988-89	Arsenal	0	0		
1989-90	Nottingham F	0	0		
1989-90	WBA	3	0	3	0
1989-90	Blackburn R	2	0	2	0
1989-90	Colchester U	10	0	10	0
1990-91	Nottingham F	0	0		
1991-92	Nottingham F	6	0		
1991-92	Burnley	15	0	15	0
1992-93	Nottingham F	5	0		
1993-94	Nottingham F	0	0	11	0
1993-94	Wrexham	36	0		
1994-95	Wrexham	46	0		
1995-96	Wrexham	46	0		
1996-97	Wrexham	43	0		
1997-98	Wrexham	42	0		
1998-99	Wrexham	0	0	213	0
1998-99	Sunderland	1	0		
1999-2000	Sunderland	1	0		
2000-01	Sunderland	0	0	2	0
2000-01	Wigan Ath	0	0		
2000-01	Barnsley	0	0		

McCLARE, Sean (M) — 59 6
H: 5 11 W: 11 08 b.Rotherham 12-1-78
Source: Trainee. *Honours:* Eire Under-21.

Season	Club				
1996-97	Barnsley	0	0		
1997-98	Barnsley	0	0		
1998-99	Barnsley	30	3		
1999-2000	Barnsley	10	2		
1999-2000	*Rochdale*	9	0	9	0
2000-01	Barnsley	10	1	50	6

MILLER, Christopher (M) — 0 0
b.Paisley 19-11-82
Source: Scholar.

Season	Club		
2000-01	Barnsley	0	0

MILLER, Kevin (G) — 468 0
H: 6 1 W: 16 00 b.Falmouth 15-3-69
Source: Newquay.

Season	Club				
1988-89	Exeter C	3	0		
1989-90	Exeter C	28	0		
1990-91	Exeter C	46	0		
1991-92	Exeter C	42	0		
1992-93	Exeter C	44	0	163	0
1993-94	Birmingham C	24	0	24	0
1994-95	Watford	44	0		
1995-96	Watford	42	0		
1996-97	Watford	42	0	128	0
1997-98	Crystal Palace	38	0		
1998-99	Crystal Palace	28	0		
1999-2000	Crystal Palace	0	0	66	0
1999-2000	Barnsley	41	0		
2000-01	Barnsley	46	0	87	0

MORGAN, Chris (D) — 107 1
H: 6 1 W: 12 09 b.Barnsley 9-11-77
Source: Trainee.

Season	Club				
1996-97	Barnsley	0	0		
1997-98	Barnsley	11	0		
1998-99	Barnsley	19	0		
1999-2000	Barnsley	37	0		
2000-01	Barnsley	40	1	107	1

MULLIGAN, David (M) — 0 0
b.Fazakerley 24-3-82
Source: Scholar.

Season	Club		
2000-01	Barnsley	0	0

NEIL, Alex (M) — 48 5
H: 5 9 W: 11 00 b.Coatbridge 9-6-81
Source: Dunfermline Ath.

Season	Club				
1999-2000	Airdrieonians	16	5	16	5
2000-01	Barnsley	32	0	32	0

O'CALLAGHAN, Brian (D) — 26 0
H: 6 1 W: 12 01 b.Limerick 24-2-81
Source: Pike Rovers.

Season	Club				
1998-99	Barnsley	0	0		
1999-2000	Barnsley	0	0		
2000-01	Barnsley	26	0	26	0

PARKIN, Jonathan (F) — 6 0
H: 6 4 W: 13 07 b.Barnsley 30-12-81
Source: Scholarship.

Season	Club				
1998-99	Barnsley	2	0		
1999-2000	Barnsley	0	0		
2000-01	Barnsley	4	0	6	0

PARRY, Craig (M) — 0 0
b.Barnsley 10-3-84
Source: Scholar.

Season	Club		
2000-01	Barnsley	0	0

RANKIN, Isiah (F) — 87 16
H: 5 10 W: 11 00 b.London 22-5-78
Source: Trainee.

Season	Club				
1995-96	Arsenal	0	0		
1996-97	Arsenal	0	0		
1997-98	Arsenal	1	0	1	0
1997-98	*Colchester U*	11	5	11	5
1998-99	Bradford C	27	4		
1999-2000	Bradford C	9	0		
1999-2000	*Birmingham C*	13	4	13	4
2000-01	Bradford C	1	0	37	4
2000-01	*Bolton W*	16	2	16	2
2000-01	Barnsley	9	1	9	1

RAVENHILL, Richard (M) — 0 0
H: 5 10 W: 11 01 b.Doncaster 16-1-81
Source: Trainee.

Season	Club		
1999-2000	Barnsley	0	0
2000-01	Barnsley	0	0

REGAN, Carl (D) — 27 0
H: 6 0 W: 11 05 b.Liverpool 9-9-80
Source: Trainee. *Honours:* England Youth.

Season	Club				
1997-98	Everton	0	0		
1998-99	Everton	0	0		
1999-2000	Everton	0	0		
2000-01	Barnsley	27	0	27	0

ROSE, Karl‡ (F) — 5 0
H: 5 10 W: 11 00 b.Barnsley 12-10-78

Season	Club				
1995-96	Barnsley	0	0		
1996-97	Barnsley	0	0		
1997-98	Barnsley	0	0		
1998-99	Barnsley	4	0		
1998-99	*Mansfield T*	1	0	1	0
1999-2000	Barnsley	0	0		
2000-01	Barnsley	0	0	4	0

SALLI, Janne (D) — 7 0
H: 6 2 W: 11 13 b.Finland 14-12-77
Honours: Finland 7 full caps, 1 goal.

Season	Club				
2000-01	Barnsley	7	0	7	0

SAVIC, Sinisa (M) — 0 0
b.Starnberg 8-11-80

Season	Club		
2000-01	Barnsley	0	0

SHERON, Mike (F) — 350 92
H: 5 10 W: 12 07 b.Liverpool 11-1-72
Source: Trainee. *Honours:* England Under-21.

Season	Club				
1990-91	Manchester C	0	0		
1990-91	Bury	5	1	5	1
1991-92	Manchester C	29	7		
1992-93	Manchester C	38	11		
1993-94	Manchester C	33	6	100	24
1994-95	Norwich C	21	1		
1995-96	Norwich C	7	1	28	2
1995-96	Stoke C	28	15		
1996-97	Stoke C	41	19	69	34
1997-98	QPR	40	11		
1998-99	QPR	23	8	63	19
1998-99	Barnsley	15	2		
1999-2000	Barnsley	36	9		
2000-01	Barnsley	34	1	85	12

SHIPPERLEY, Neil (F) — 268 68
H: 6 0 W: 14 01 b.Chatham 30-10-74
Source: Trainee. *Honours:* England Under-21.

Season	Club				
1992-93	Chelsea	3	1		
1993-94	Chelsea	24	4		
1994-95	Chelsea	10	2	37	7
1994-95	*Watford*	6	1	6	1
1994-95	Southampton	19	4		

Season	Club	Apps	Gls	Tot Apps	Tot Gls
1995–96	Southampton	37	7		
1996–97	Southampton	10	1	66	12
1996–97	Crystal Palace	32	12		
1997–98	Crystal Palace	26	7		
1998–99	Crystal Palace	3	1	61	20
1998–99	Nottingham F	20	1	20	1
1999–2000	Barnsley	39	13		
2000–01	Barnsley	39	14	78	27

SIDDALL, Richard‡ (G)   0 0
H: 6 1   W: 11 06   b.Sheffield 24-1-82
Source: Scholarship.

1998–99	Barnsley	0	0		
1999–2000	Barnsley	0	0		
2000–01	Barnsley	0	0		

TINKLER, Eric (M)   160 10
H: 6 2   W: 13 08   b.Roodepoort 30-7-70
Honours: South Africa full caps.

1993–94	Vitoria Setubal	21	0		
1994–95	Vitoria Setubal	17	1		
1995–96	Vitoria Setubal	19	0	57	1
1996–97	Cagliari	20	0	20	0
1997–98	Barnsley	25	2		
1998–99	Barnsley	25	3		
1999–2000	Barnsley	33	4		
2000–01	Barnsley	0	0	83	9

TURNER, Mike‡ (F)   13 1
H: 6 2   W: 13 03   b.Stoke 2-4-76
Source: Bilston T.

1998–99	Barnsley	13	1		
1999–2000	Barnsley	0	0		
1999–2000	*Lincoln C*	0	0		
2000–01	Barnsley	0	0	13	1

VAN DER LAAN, Robin‡ (M)   315 37
H: 5 11   W: 13 08   b.Schiedam 5-9-68
Source: Wageningen.

1990–91	Port Vale	18	4		
1991–92	Port Vale	43	5		
1992–93	Port Vale	38	6		
1993–94	Port Vale	33	4		
1994–95	Port Vale	44	5	176	24
1995–96	Derby Co	39	6		
1996–97	Derby Co	16	2		
1996–97	*Wolverhampton W*	7	0	7	0
1997–98	Derby Co	10	0	65	8
1998–99	Barnsley	17	1		
1999–2000	Barnsley	32	3		
2000–01	Barnsley	18	1	67	5

WALKER, Leigh‡ (G)   0 0
H: 5 10   W: 12 06   b.Sheffield 12-2-81
Source: Trainee.

1999–2000	Sheffield U	0	0		
1999–2000	Barnsley	0	0		
2000–01	Barnsley	0	0		

WARD, Mitch (D)   218 12
H: 5 8   W: 11 13   b.Sheffield 19-6-71
Source: Trainee.

1989–90	Sheffield U	0	0		
1990–91	Sheffield U	4	0		
1990–91	*Crewe Alex*	4	1	4	1
1991–92	Sheffield U	6	2		
1992–93	Sheffield U	26	0		
1993–94	Sheffield U	22	1		
1994–95	Sheffield U	14	2		
1995–96	Sheffield U	42	1		
1996–97	Sheffield U	34	4		
1997–98	Sheffield U	6	1	154	11
1997–98	Everton	8	0		
1998–99	Everton	6	0		
1999–2000	Everton	10	0	24	0
2000–01	Barnsley	36	0	36	0

WATSON, David‡ (G)   178 0
H: 6 0   W: 12 09   b.Barnsley 10-11-73
Source: Trainee. Honours: England Youth, Under-21.

1992–93	Barnsley	5	0		
1993–94	Barnsley	9	0		
1994–95	Barnsley	37	0		
1995–96	Barnsley	45	0		
1996–97	Barnsley	46	0		
1997–98	Barnsley	30	0		
1998–99	Barnsley	6	0		
1999–2000	Barnsley	0	0		
2000–01	Barnsley	0	0	178	0

YOUNG, Darren‡ (M)   0 0
H: 5 8   W: 10 07   b.Whitehaven 20-2-81

| 1999–2000 | Barnsley | 0 | 0 | | |
| 2000–01 | Barnsley | 0 | 0 | | |

Scholars
Black, Grant; Carrington, Richard J; Christie, Jeremy J; Cox, Christopher D; Jones, Griffith T; Pearce, Allan D; Reece, Gary L; Richards, Duncan; Sedgwick, Craig D; Selby, Callum S; Welch, Michael F
Non-Contract
Hendrie, John G; Rhodes, Andrew C

BIRMINGHAM C

ADEBOLA, Dele (F)   253 70
H: 6 3   W: 12 08   b.Lagos 23-6-75
Source: Trainee.

1992–93	Crewe Alex	6	0		
1993–94	Crewe Alex	0	0		
1994–95	Crewe Alex	30	8		
1995–96	Crewe Alex	29	8		
1996–97	Crewe Alex	32	16		
1997–98	Crewe Alex	27	7	124	39
1997–98	Birmingham C	17	7		
1998–99	Birmingham C	39	13		
1999–2000	Birmingham C	42	5		
2000–01	Birmingham C	31	6	129	31

BASS, Jonathan* (D)   78 0
H: 6 0   W: 12 02   b.Weston-Super-Mare 1-1-76
Source: Trainee. Honours: England Schools.

1994–95	Birmingham C	0	0		
1995–96	Birmingham C	5	0		
1996–97	Birmingham C	13	0		
1996–97	*Carlisle U*	3	0	3	0
1997–98	Birmingham C	30	0		
1998–99	Birmingham C	11	0		
1999–2000	Birmingham C	8	0		
1999–2000	*Gillingham*	7	0	7	0
2000–01	Birmingham C	1	0	68	0

BENNETT, Ian (G)   325 0
H: 6 0   W: 12 10   b.Worksop 10-10-71
Source: Newcastle U Trainee.

1991–92	Peterborough U	7	0		
1992–93	Peterborough U	46	0		
1993–94	Peterborough U	19	0	72	0
1993–94	Birmingham C	22	0		
1994–95	Birmingham C	46	0		
1995–96	Birmingham C	24	0		
1996–97	Birmingham C	40	0		
1997–98	Birmingham C	45	0		
1998–99	Birmingham C	10	0		
1999–2000	Birmingham C	21	0		
2000–01	Birmingham C	45	0	253	0

BURROWS, David (D)   364 5
H: 5 8   W: 11 08   b.Dudley 25-10-68
Source: Apprentice. Honours: England Under-21, B.

1985–86	WBA	1	0		
1986–87	WBA	15	1		
1987–88	WBA	21	0		
1988–89	WBA	9	0	46	1
1988–89	Liverpool	21	0		
1989–90	Liverpool	26	0		
1990–91	Liverpool	35	0		
1991–92	Liverpool	30	1		
1992–93	Liverpool	30	2		
1993–94	Liverpool	4	0	146	3
1993–94	West Ham U	25	1		
1994–95	West Ham U	4	0	29	1
1994–95	Everton	19	0	19	0
1994–95	Coventry C	11	0		
1995–96	Coventry C	11	0		
1996–97	Coventry C	18	0		
1997–98	Coventry C	33	0		
1998–99	Coventry C	23	0		
1999–2000	Coventry C	15	0	111	0
2000–01	Birmingham C	13	0	13	0

CAPALDI, Tony (D)   0 0
H: 6 0   W: 12 00   b.Porsgrunn 12-8-81
Source: Trainee.

| 1999–2000 | Birmingham C | 0 | 0 | | |
| 2000–01 | Birmingham C | 0 | 0 | | |

DYSON, James* (D)   2 0
H: 6 2   W: 12 00   b.Wordsley 20-4-79
Source: Trainee.

1997–98	Birmingham C	0	0		
1998–99	Birmingham C	0	0		
1999–2000	Birmingham C	2	0		
2000–01	Birmingham C	0	0	2	0

EADEN, Nicky (D)   338 12
H: 5 9   W: 12 02   b.Sheffield 12-12-72
Source: Trainee.

1991–92	Barnsley	0	0		
1992–93	Barnsley	2	0		
1993–94	Barnsley	37	2		
1994–95	Barnsley	45	1		
1995–96	Barnsley	46	2		
1996–97	Barnsley	46	3		
1997–98	Barnsley	35	0		
1998–99	Barnsley	40	1		
1999–2000	Barnsley	42	1	293	10
2000–01	Birmingham C	45	2	45	2

FURLONG, Paul (F)   303 104
H: 6 0   W: 11 00   b.London 1-10-68
Source: Enfield.

1991–92	Coventry C	37	4	37	4
1992–93	Watford	41	19		
1993–94	Watford	38	18	79	37
1994–95	Chelsea	36	10		
1995–96	Chelsea	28	3	64	13
1996–97	Birmingham C	43	10		
1997–98	Birmingham C	25	15		
1998–99	Birmingham C	29	13		
1999–2000	Birmingham C	19	11		
2000–01	Birmingham C	4	0	120	49
2000–01	*QPR*	3	1	3	1

GILL, Jeremy (D)   46 0
H: 5 11   W: 11 00   b.Clevedon 8-9-70
Source: Yeovil T.

1997–98	Birmingham C	3	0		
1998–99	Birmingham C	3	0		
1999–2000	Birmingham C	11	0		
2000–01	Birmingham C	29	0	46	0

GRAINGER, Martin (D)   320 39
H: 5 10   W: 11 07   b.Enfield 23-8-72
Source: Trainee.

1989–90	Colchester U	7	2		
1990–91	Colchester U	0	0		
1991–92	Colchester U	0	0		
1992–93	Colchester U	31	3		
1993–94	Colchester U	8	2	46	7
1993–94	Brentford	31	2		
1994–95	Brentford	37	7		
1995–96	Brentford	33	3	101	12
1995–96	Birmingham C	8	0		
1996–97	Birmingham C	23	3		
1997–98	Birmingham C	33	2		
1998–99	Birmingham C	40	4		
1999–2000	Birmingham C	34	5		
2000–01	Birmingham C	35	6	173	20

GRONDIN, Christophe (M)   0 0
b.Toulouse 2-9-83
Source: Toulouse.

| 2000–01 | Birmingham C | 0 | 0 | | |

HAARHOFF, Jimmy‡ (M)   1 0
H: 5 5   W: 10 02   b.Lusaka 25-7-81
Source: Trainee.

1998–99	Birmingham C	0	0		
1999–2000	Birmingham C	1	0		
2000–01	Birmingham C	0	0	1	0

HOLDSWORTH, David (D)   432 21
H: 6 1   W: 12 10   b.Walthamstow 8-11-68
Source: Trainee. Honours: England Youth, Under-21.

1986–87	Watford	0	0		
1987–88	Watford	0	0		
1988–89	Watford	33	1		
1989–90	Watford	44	3		
1990–91	Watford	15	2		
1991–92	Watford	33	2		
1992–93	Watford	39	0		
1993–94	Watford	28	0		
1994–95	Watford	39	1		
1995–96	Watford	27	1		
1996–97	Watford	40	0	258	10
1996–97	Sheffield U	37	1		
1997–98	Sheffield U	40	2		
1998–99	Sheffield U	16	1	93	4
1998–99	Birmingham C	8	1		
1999–2000	Birmingham C	44	5		
2000–01	Birmingham C	29	1	81	7

HORSFIELD, Geoff (F)   115 37
H: 6 1   W: 13 07   b.Barnsley 1-11-73

| 1992–93 | Scarborough | 6 | 1 | | |
| 1993–94 | Scarborough | 6 | 0 | 12 | 1 |

From Witton Alb

1998–99	Halifax T	7		10	7
1998–99	Fulham	28	15		
1999–2000	Fulham	31	7	59	22
2000–01	Birmingham C	34	7	34	7

HUGHES, Bryan (M)   263 34
H: 5 9   W: 10 00   b.Liverpool 19-6-76
Source: Trainee.

1993–94	Wrexham	11	0		
1994–95	Wrexham	38	9		
1995–96	Wrexham	22	0		
1996–97	Wrexham	23	3	94	12
1996–97	Birmingham C	11	0		
1997–98	Birmingham C	40	5		
1998–99	Birmingham C	28	3		
1999–2000	Birmingham C	45	10		
2000–01	Birmingham C	45	4	169	22

HUTCHINSON, Jonathan (M)   0 0
b.Middlesbrough 2-4-82
Source: Scholar.

| 2000–01 | Birmingham C | 0 | 0 | | |

HYDE, Graham (M)   219 12
H: 5 7   W: 12 04   b.Doncaster 10-11-70
Source: Trainee.

| 1988–89 | Sheffield W | 0 | 0 | | |
| 1989–90 | Sheffield W | 0 | 0 | | |

1990–91 Sheffield W 0 0
1991–92 Sheffield W 13 0
1992–93 Sheffield W 20 1
1993–94 Sheffield W 36 1
1994–95 Sheffield W 35 5
1995–96 Sheffield W 26 1
1996–97 Sheffield W 19 2
1997–98 Sheffield W 22 1
1998–99 Sheffield W 1 0 **172 11**
1998–99 Birmingham C 13 0
1999–2000 Birmingham C 31 1
2000–01 Birmingham C 3 0 **47 1**

JOHNSON, Andrew (F) 60 5
H: 5 7 W: 10 00 b.Bedford 10-2-81
Source: Trainee. *Honours:* England Youth.
1997–98 Birmingham C 0 0
1998–99 Birmingham C 4 0
1999–2000 Birmingham C 22 1
2000–01 Birmingham C 34 4 **60 5**

JOHNSON, Michael (D) 331 12
H: 5 11 W: 11 00 b.Nottingham 4-7-73
Source: Trainee.
1991–92 Notts Co 5 0
1992–93 Notts Co 37 0
1993–94 Notts Co 34 0
1994–95 Notts Co 31 0
1995–96 Notts Co 0 0 **107 0**
1995–96 Birmingham C 33 0
1996–97 Birmingham C 35 0
1997–98 Birmingham C 38 3
1998–99 Birmingham C 45 5
1999–2000 Birmingham C 34 2
2000–01 Birmingham C 39 2 **224 12**

LAZARIDIS, Stan (M) 131 7
H: 5 9 W: 12 00 b.Perth 16-8-72
Source: Adelaide Sharks 73 apps, 5 goals.
Honours: Australia 52 full caps.
1995–96 West Ham U 4 0
1996–97 West Ham U 22 1
1997–98 West Ham U 28 2
1998–99 West Ham U 15 0 **69 3**
1999–2000 Birmingham C 31 2
2000–01 Birmingham C 31 2 **62 4**

LUNTALA, Tresor (M) 0 0
H: 5 9 W: 11 00 b.Dreux 31-5-82
1999–2000 Birmingham C 0 0
2000–01 Birmingham C 0 0

MARCELO (F) 122 36
H: 6 0 W: 13 04 b.Niteroi 11-10-69
Source: Alaves.
1997–98 Sheffield U 21 6
1998–99 Sheffield U 35 16
1999–2000 Sheffield U 10 2 **66 24**
1999–2000 Birmingham C 25 5
2000–01 Birmingham C 31 7 **56 12**

MARSH, Simon‡ (D) 67 3
H: 5 11 W: 12 00 b.Ealing 29-1-77
Source: Trainee. *Honours:* England Under-21.
1994–95 Oxford U 8 0
1995–96 Oxford U 5 0
1996–97 Oxford U 8 1
1997–98 Oxford U 14 0
1998–99 Oxford U 21 2 **56 3**
1998–99 Birmingham C 7 0
1999–2000 Birmingham C 0 0
2000–01 Birmingham C 0 0 **7 0**
2000–01 *Brentford* 4 0 **4 0**

McCARTHY, Jon (M) 414 50
H: 5 9 W: 11 05 b.Middlesbrough 18-8-70
Honours: Northern Ireland 18 full caps.
1987–88 Hartlepool U 1 0 **1 0**
From Shepshed
1990–91 York C 27 2
1991–92 York C 42 6
1992–93 York C 42 7
1993–94 York C 44 7
1994–95 York C 44 9 **199 31**
1995–96 Port Vale 45 7
1996–97 Port Vale 45 4
1997–98 Port Vale 4 0 **94 11**
1997–98 Birmingham C 41 4
1998–99 Birmingham C 43 0
1999–2000 Birmingham C 21 4
2000–01 Birmingham C 15 0 **120 8**

O'CONNOR, Martin (M) 287 41
H: 5 8 W: 10 08 b.Walsall 10-12-67
Source: Bromsgrove R.
1992–93 Crystal Palace 0 0
1992–93 *Walsall* 10 1
1993–94 Crystal Palace 2 0 **2 0**
1993–94 Walsall 14 2
1994–95 Walsall 39 10
1995–96 Walsall 41 9 **104 22**
1996–97 Peterborough U 18 3 **18 3**
1996–97 Birmingham C 24 4
1997–98 Birmingham C 33 1
1998–99 Birmingham C 37 4
1999–2000 Birmingham C 39 2
2000–01 Birmingham C 30 5 **163 16**

PARKER, Sonny (M) 0 0
b.Middlesbrough 28-2-83
Source: Trainee.
1999–2000 Birmingham C 0 0
2000–01 Birmingham C 0 0

POOLE, Kevin* (G) 296 0
H: 5 10 W: 11 11 b.Bromsgrove 21-7-63
Source: Apprentice.
1981–82 Aston Villa 0 0
1982–83 Aston Villa 0 0
1983–84 Aston Villa 0 0
1984–85 Aston Villa 7 0
1984–85 *Northampton T* 3 0 **3 0**
1985–86 Aston Villa 11 0
1986–87 Aston Villa 10 0 **28 0**
1987–88 Middlesbrough 1 0
1988–89 Middlesbrough 12 0
1989–90 Middlesbrough 21 0
1990–91 Middlesbrough 0 0 **34 0**
1990–91 *Hartlepool U* 12 0 **12 0**
1991–92 Leicester C 42 0
1992–93 Leicester C 19 0
1993–94 Leicester C 14 0
1994–95 Leicester C 36 0
1995–96 Leicester C 45 0
1996–97 Leicester C 7 0 **163 0**
1997–98 Birmingham C 1 0
1998–99 Birmingham C 36 0
1999–2000 Birmingham C 18 0
2000–01 Birmingham C 1 0 **56 0**

PURSE, Darren (D) 217 13
H: 6 2 W: 13 08 b.Stepney 14-2-76
Source: Trainee. *Honours:* England Under-21.
1993–94 Leyton Orient 5 0
1994–95 Leyton Orient 38 3
1995–96 Leyton Orient 12 0 **55 3**
1996–97 Oxford U 31 1
1997–98 Oxford U 28 4 **59 5**
1997–98 Birmingham C 8 0
1998–99 Birmingham C 20 0
1999–2000 Birmingham C 38 2
2000–01 Birmingham C 37 3 **103 5**

RANDRIANANTOANINA, Marco (M) 0 0
b.Bourg La Reine 24-8-83
2000–01 Birmingham C 0 0

SABATHIER, Mickael (M) 0 0
b.Auch 14-4-82
Source: Toulouse.
2000–01 Birmingham C 0 0

SONNER, Danny (M) 146 10
H: 5 11 W: 12 08 b.Wigan 9-1-72
Source: Wigan Ath. *Honours:* Northern Ireland B, 7 full caps.
1990–91 Burnley 2 0
1991–92 Burnley 3 0
1992–93 Burnley 1 0 **6 0**
1992–93 *Bury* 5 3 **5 3**
From Erzgebirge Aue
1996–97 Ipswich T 29 2
1997–98 Ipswich T 23 1
1998–99 Ipswich T 4 0 **56 3**
1998–99 Sheffield W 26 3
1999–2000 Sheffield W 27 0 **53 3**
2000–01 Birmingham C 26 1 **26 1**

WARD, Christopher (M) 0 0
b.Preston 28-4-81
Source: Lancaster C.
2000–01 Birmingham C 0 0

WILLIAMS, Jacques (M) 3 0
H: 5 9 W: 11 00 b.Wallasey 25-4-81
1999–2000 Birmingham C 0 0
2000–01 Birmingham C 3 0 **3 0**

WOODHOUSE, Curtis (M) 121 8
H: 5 8 W: 11 06 b.Driffield 17-4-80
Source: Trainee. *Honours:* England Youth, Under-21.
1997–98 Sheffield U 9 0
1998–99 Sheffield U 33 3
1999–2000 Sheffield U 37 3
2000–01 Sheffield U 25 0 **104 6**
2000–01 Birmingham C 17 2 **17 2**

Scholars
Allen, Mark A; Barnes, Neil; Beauchamp, James FV; Carter, Darren A; Chisholm, Kelvin S; Davies, Clint; Diamond, Ross; Evans, Richard G; Fagan, Craig A; Gilbert, Peter; Hart, Steven; Hider, Allan J; Hipkiss, Robert J; Horrigan, Darren; Jameson, Michael; Robertson, Daniel; Tearney, Trevor L; Wood, Paul A

BLACKBURN R

BELL, Andrew (F) 0 0
b.Blackburn 12-2-84
Source: Scholar.
2000–01 Blackburn R 0 0

BENT, Marcus (F) 197 42
H: 6 2 W: 12 04 b.Hammersmith 19-5-78
Source: Trainee. *Honours:* England Under-21.
1995–96 Brentford 12 1
1996–97 Brentford 34 3
1997–98 Brentford 24 4 **70 8**
1997–98 Crystal Palace 16 5
1998–99 Crystal Palace 12 0 **28 5**
1998–99 Port Vale 15 0
1999–2000 Port Vale 8 1 **23 1**
1999–2000 Sheffield U 32 15
2000–01 Sheffield U 16 5 **48 20**
2000–01 Blackburn R 28 8 **28 8**

BERG, Henning (D) 266 7
H: 6 0 W: 12 04 b.Eidsvoll 1-9-69
Source: Lillestrom. *Honours:* Norway Under-21, 81 full caps, 8 goals.
1992–93 Blackburn R 4 0
1993–94 Blackburn R 41 1
1994–95 Blackburn R 40 1
1995–96 Blackburn R 38 0
1996–97 Blackburn R 36 2
1997–98 Manchester U 27 1
1998–99 Manchester U 16 0
1999–2000 Manchester U 22 1
2000–01 Manchester U 1 0 **66 2**
2000–01 Blackburn R 41 1 **200 5**

BERKOVIC, Eyal‡ (M) 264 51
H: 5 7 W: 10 02 b.Haifa 2-4-72
Honours: Israel 70 full caps, 9 goals.
1992–93 Maccabi Haifa 32 7
1993–94 Maccabi Haifa 38 10
1994–95 Maccabi Haifa 29 5
1995–96 Maccabi Haifa 29 3 **128 25**
1996–97 Southampton 28 4 **28 4**
1997–98 West Ham U 35 7
1998–99 West Ham U 30 3 **65 10**
1999–2000 Celtic 28 9
2000–01 Celtic 4 1 **32 10**
2000–01 Blackburn R 11 2 **11 2**

BINGHAM, Michael* (G) 0 0
H: 6 0 W: 12 05 b.Preston 21-5-81
Source: Trainee. *Honours:* England Schools.
1998–99 Blackburn R 0 0
1999–2000 Blackburn R 0 0
2000–01 Blackburn R 0 0

BJORNEBYE, Stig Inge (D) 287 11
H: 5 10 W: 11 09 b.Elverum 11-12-69
Honours: Norway 75 full caps, 1 goal.
1988 Strammen 19 0 **19 0**
1989 Kongsvinger 21 2
1990 Kongsvinger 20 0
1991 Kongsvinger 21 1 **62 3**
1992 Rosenborg 21 3 **21 3**
1992–93 Liverpool 11 0
1993–94 Liverpool 9 0
1994–95 Liverpool 31 0
1995–96 Liverpool 2 0
1996–97 Liverpool 38 2
1997–98 Liverpool 25 0
1998–99 Liverpool 23 0 **139 2**
1999–2000 Brondby 13 2 **13 2**
2000–01 Blackburn R 33 1 **33 1**

BLAKE, Nathan (F) 358 119
H: 5 11 W: 13 12 b.Cardiff 27-1-72
Source: Chelsea Trainee. *Honours:* Wales B, Under-21, 20 full caps, 4 goals.
1989–90 Cardiff C 6 0
1990–91 Cardiff C 40 4
1991–92 Cardiff C 31 6
1992–93 Cardiff C 34 11
1993–94 Cardiff C 20 14 **131 35**
1993–94 Sheffield U 12 5
1994–95 Sheffield U 35 17
1995–96 Sheffield U 22 12 **69 34**
1995–96 Bolton W 18 1
1996–97 Bolton W 42 19
1997–98 Bolton W 35 12
1998–99 Bolton W 12 6 **107 38**
1998–99 Blackburn R 11 3
1999–2000 Blackburn R 28 3
2000–01 Blackburn R 12 6 **51 12**

BLAKEMAN, Liam (M) 0 0
b.Southport 6-9-82
Source: Scholarship.
1999–2000 Blackburn R 0 0
2000–01 Blackburn R 0 0

BROOMES, Marlon (D)   48   2
H: 6 1   W: 13 00   b.Meriden 28-11-77
Source: Trainee. *Honours:* England Schools, Youth, Under-21.

1994-95	Blackburn R	0	0		
1995-96	Blackburn R	0	0		
1996-97	Blackburn R	0	0		
1996-97	Swindon T	12	1	12	1
1997-98	Blackburn R	4	0		
1998-99	Blackburn R	13	0		
1999-2000	Blackburn R	13	1		
2000-01	Blackburn R	1	0	31	1
2000-01	QPR	5	0	5	0

BURGESS, Ben (F)   2   0
H: 6 3   W: 14 04   b.Buxton 9-11-81
Source: Trainee.

1998-99	Blackburn R	0	0		
1999-2000	Blackburn R	2	0		
2000-01	Blackburn R	0	0	2	0

CHAMBERLAIN, Robert* (M)   0   0
b.Chester 5-6-82
Source: Trainee.

1999-2000	Blackburn R	0	0
2000-01	Blackburn R	0	0

CORBETT, Jimmy (F)   16   2
H: 5 10   W: 12 00   b.Hackney 6-7-80
Source: Trainee.

1997-98	Gillingham	16	2	16	2
1998-99	Blackburn R	0	0		
1999-2000	Blackburn R	0	0		
2000-01	Blackburn R	0	0		

CURTIS, John (D)   87   2
H: 5 10   W: 11 13   b.Nuneaton 3-9-78
Source: Trainee. *Honours:* England Schools, Youth, Under-21, B.

1995-96	Manchester U	0	0		
1996-97	Manchester U	0	0		
1997-98	Manchester U	8	0		
1998-99	Manchester U	4	0		
1999-2000	Manchester U	1	0	13	0
1999-2000	Barnsley	28	2	28	2
2000-01	Blackburn R	46	0	46	0

DANNS, Neil (F)   0   0
b.Liverpool 23-11-82
Source: Scholar.

2000-01	Blackburn R	0	0

DOUGLAS, Jonathan (M)   0   0
b.Monaghan 22-11-81
Source: Trainee.

1999-2000	Blackburn R	0	0
2000-01	Blackburn R	0	0

DOYLE, Robert (D)   0   0
b.Dublin 15-4-82
Source: Trainee.

1998-99	Blackburn R	0	0
1999-2000	Blackburn R	0	0
2000-01	Blackburn R	0	0

DUFF, Damien (F)   126   11
H: 5 9   W: 12 12   b.Ballyboden 2-3-79
Source: Lourdes Celtic. *Honours:* Eire Youth, 20 full caps.

1995-96	Blackburn R	0	0		
1996-97	Blackburn R	1	0		
1997-98	Blackburn R	26	4		
1998-99	Blackburn R	28	1		
1999-2000	Blackburn R	39	5		
2000-01	Blackburn R	32	1	126	11

DUNN, David (M)   79   15
H: 5 10   W: 12 06   b.Gt Harwood 27-12-79
Source: Trainee. *Honours:* England Youth, Under-21.

1997-98	Blackburn R	0	0		
1998-99	Blackburn R	15	1		
1999-2000	Blackburn R	22	2		
2000-01	Blackburn R	42	12	79	15

DUNNING, Darren (M)   10   0
H: 5 6   W: 11 12   b.Scarborough 8-1-81
Source: Trainee.

1998-99	Blackburn R	0	0		
1999-2000	Blackburn R	0	0		
2000-01	Blackburn R	1	0	1	0
2000-01	Bristol C	9	0	9	0

FILAN, John (G)   146   0
H: 6 2   W: 12 12   b.Sydney 8-2-70
Source: Budapest St George 52 apps, Wollongong Wolves 9 apps.Australia 3 full caps.

1992-93	Cambridge U	6	0		
1993-94	Cambridge U	46	0		
1994-95	Cambridge U	16	0	68	0
1994-95	Nottingham F	2	0		
1994-95	Coventry C	2	0		
1995-96	Coventry C	13	0		
1996-97	Coventry C	1	0	16	0

1997-98	Blackburn R	7	0		
1998-99	Blackburn R	26	0		
1999-2000	Blackburn R	16	0		
2000-01	Blackburn R	13	0	62	0

FITZGERALD, John (M)   0   0
b.Dublin 10-2-84
Source: Scholar.

2000-01	Blackburn R	0	0

FLITCROFT, Garry (M)   259   21
H: 6 0   W: 11 08   b.Bolton 6-11-72
Source: Trainee. *Honours:* England Schools, Under-21.

1991-92	Manchester C	0	0		
1991-92	Bury	12	0	12	0
1992-93	Manchester C	32	5		
1993-94	Manchester C	21	3		
1994-95	Manchester C	37	5		
1995-96	Manchester C	25	0	115	13
1995-96	Blackburn R	3	0		
1996-97	Blackburn R	28	3		
1997-98	Blackburn R	33	0		
1998-99	Blackburn R	8	2		
1999-2000	Blackburn R	19	0		
2000-01	Blackburn R	41	3	132	8

FORSYTH, Paul* (F)   0   0
H: 5 8   W: 10 05   b.Dublin 11-4-81
Source: Trainee.

1998-99	Blackburn R	0	0
1999-2000	Blackburn R	0	0
2000-01	Blackburn R	0	0

FOSTER, Steve* (F)   0   0
H: 5 9   W: 13 01   b.Manchester 30-12-81
Source: Trainee.

1998-99	Blackburn R	0	0
1999-2000	Blackburn R	0	0
2000-01	Blackburn R	0	0

FRIEDEL, Brad (G)   90   0
H: 6 3   W: 14 00   b.Lakewood 18-5-71
Honours: USA 68 full caps.

1996	Columbus Crew	9	0		
1997	Columbus Crew	29	0	38	0
1997-98	Liverpool	11	0		
1998-99	Liverpool	12	0		
1999-2000	Liverpool	2	0		
2000-01	Liverpool	0	0	25	0
2000-01	Blackburn R	27	0	27	0

GILLESPIE, Keith (F)   191   19
H: 5 10   W: 11 03   b.Bangor 18-2-75
Source: Trainee. *Honours:* Northern Ireland Youth, Under-21, 36 full caps, 1 goal.

1992-93	Manchester U	0	0		
1993-94	Manchester U	0	0		
1993-94	Wigan Ath	8	4		
1994-95	Manchester U	9	1	9	1
1994-95	Newcastle U	17	2		
1995-96	Newcastle U	28	4		
1996-97	Newcastle U	32	1		
1997-98	Newcastle U	29	4		
1998-99	Newcastle U	7	0	113	11
1998-99	Blackburn R	16	1		
1999-2000	Blackburn R	22	2		
2000-01	Blackburn R	18	0	56	3
2000-01	Wigan Ath	5	0	13	4

GRAYSON, Simon (D)   290   4
H: 6 0   W: 13 07   b.Ripon 16-12-69
Source: Trainee.

1987-88	Leeds U	2	0		
1988-89	Leeds U	0	0		
1989-90	Leeds U	0	0		
1990-91	Leeds U	0	0		
1991-92	Leeds U	0	0	2	0
1991-92	Leicester C	13	0		
1992-93	Leicester C	24	1		
1993-94	Leicester C	40	1		
1994-95	Leicester C	34	0		
1995-96	Leicester C	41	2		
1996-97	Leicester C	36	0	188	4
1997-98	Aston Villa	33	0		
1998-99	Aston Villa	15	0	48	0
1999-2000	Blackburn R	34	0		
2000-01	Blackburn R	0	0	34	0
2000-01	Sheffield W	5	0	5	0
2000-01	Stockport Co	13	0	13	0

HAMILTON, Gary‡ (F)   3   0
b.Bambridge 6-10-80
Source: Trainee. *Honours:* Northern Ireland Under-21.

1997-98	Blackburn R	0	0		
1998-99	Blackburn R	0	0		
1999-2000	Blackburn R	0	0		
2000-01	Blackburn R	0	0		
2000-01	Rochdale	3	0	3	0

HARDY, Lee* (M)   0   0
b.Blackpool 26-11-81
Source: Scholar.

2000-01	Blackburn R	0	0

HAWE, Steven* (F)   10   0
b.Machbrafelt 23-12-80
Source: Trainee. *Honours:* Northern Ireland Under-21.

1997-98	Blackburn R	0	0		
1998-99	Blackburn R	0	0		
1999-2000	Blackburn R	0	0		
2000-01	Blackburn R	0	0		
2000-01	Blackpool	2	0	2	0
2000-01	Halifax T	8	0	8	0

HIGNETT, Craig (M)   386   108
H: 5 9   W: 11 03   b.Whiston 12-1-70
Source: Liverpool Trainee.

1987-88	Crewe Alex	0	0		
1988-89	Crewe Alex	1	0		
1989-90	Crewe Alex	35	8		
1990-91	Crewe Alex	38	13		
1991-92	Crewe Alex	33	13		
1992-93	Crewe Alex	14	8	121	42
1992-93	Middlesbrough	21	4		
1993-94	Middlesbrough	29	5		
1994-95	Middlesbrough	26	8		
1995-96	Middlesbrough	22	5		
1996-97	Middlesbrough	22	4		
1997-98	Middlesbrough	36	7	156	33
1998-99	Aberdeen	13	2	13	2
1998-99	Barnsley	24	9		
1999-2000	Barnsley	42	19	66	28
2000-01	Blackburn R	30	3	30	3

HOWSON, Stuart (M)   0   0
b.Chorley 30-9-81
Source: Trainee.

1999-2000	Blackburn R	0	0
2000-01	Blackburn R	0	0

HUGHES, Mark (F)   585   162
H: 5 11   W: 13 00   b.Wrexham 1-11-63
Source: Apprentice. *Honours:* Wales Youth, Under-21, 72 full caps, 16 goals.

1980-81	Manchester U	0	0		
1981-82	Manchester U	0	0		
1982-83	Manchester U	0	0		
1983-84	Manchester U	11	4		
1984-85	Manchester U	38	16		
1985-86	Manchester U	40	17		
1986-87	Barcelona	28	4	28	4
1987-88	Bayern Munich	18	6	18	6
1988-89	Manchester U	38	14		
1989-90	Manchester U	37	13		
1990-91	Manchester U	31	10		
1991-92	Manchester U	39	11		
1992-93	Manchester U	41	15		
1993-94	Manchester U	36	11		
1994-95	Manchester U	34	8	345	119
1995-96	Chelsea	31	8		
1996-97	Chelsea	35	8		
1997-98	Chelsea	29	9	95	25
1998-99	Southampton	32	1		
1999-2000	Southampton	20	1	52	2
1999-2000	Everton	9	1		
2000-01	Everton	9	0	18	1
2000-01	Blackburn R	29	5	29	5

JANSEN, Matt (F)   149   49
H: 5 11   W: 12 06   b.Carlisle 20-10-77
Source: Trainee. *Honours:* England Under-21.

1995-96	Carlisle U	0	0		
1996-97	Carlisle U	19	1		
1997-98	Carlisle U	23	9	42	10
1997-98	Crystal Palace	8	3		
1998-99	Crystal Palace	18	7	26	10
1998-99	Blackburn R	11	2		
1999-2000	Blackburn R	30	4		
2000-01	Blackburn R	40	23	81	29

JOHNSON, Damien (M)   59   2
H: 5 9   W: 11 07   b.Lisburn 18-11-78
Source: Trainee. *Honours:* Northern Ireland Under-21, 12 full caps.

1995-96	Blackburn R	0	0		
1996-97	Blackburn R	0	0		
1997-98	Blackburn R	0	0		
1997-98	Nottingham F	6	0	6	0
1998-99	Blackburn R	21	1		
1999-2000	Blackburn R	16	1		
2000-01	Blackburn R	16	0	53	2

KELLER, Marc* (M)   377   68
H: 5 9   W: 12 03   b.Colmar 14-1-68
Honours: France 6 full caps, 1 goal.

1987-88	Mulhouse	27	1		
1988-89	Mulhouse	25	8		
1989-90	Mulhouse	36	2		
1990-91	Mulhouse	30	4	118	15
1991-92	Strasbourg	34	11		

1992–93	Strasbourg	34	8		
1993–94	Strasbourg	27	6		
1994–95	Strasbourg	21	2		
1995–96	Strasbourg	33	8	149	35
1996–97	Karlsruhe	33	9		
1997–98	Karlsruhe	28	4	61	13
1998–99	West Ham U	21	5		
1999–2000	West Ham U	23	0		
2000–01	West Ham U	0	0	44	5
2000–01	*Portsmouth*	3	0	3	0
2000–01	Blackburn R	2	0	2	0

KELLY, Alan (G) 397 0
H: 6 3 W: 14 02 b.Preston 11-8-68
Source: Trainee. *Honours:* Eire Youth,
Under-21, Under-23, 33 full caps.

1985–86	Preston NE	13	0		
1986–87	Preston NE	22	0		
1987–88	Preston NE	19	0		
1988–89	Preston NE	0	0		
1989–90	Preston NE	42	0		
1990–91	Preston NE	23	0		
1991–92	Preston NE	23	0	142	0
1992–93	Sheffield U	33	0		
1993–94	Sheffield U	30	0		
1994–95	Sheffield U	38	0		
1995–96	Sheffield U	35	0		
1996–97	Sheffield U	39	0		
1997–98	Sheffield U	19	0		
1998–99	Sheffield U	22	0	216	0
1999–2000	Blackburn R	30	0		
2000–01	Blackburn R	7	0	37	0
2000–01	*Stockport Co*	2	0	2	0

KENNA, Jeff (D) 280 5
H: 5 11 W: 12 03 b.Dublin 28-8-70
Source: Trainee. *Honours:* Eire Youth,
Under-21, B, 27 full caps.

1988–89	Southampton	0	0		
1989–90	Southampton	0	0		
1990–91	Southampton	2	0		
1991–92	Southampton	14	0		
1992–93	Southampton	29	2		
1993–94	Southampton	41	2		
1994–95	Southampton	28	0	114	4
1994–95	Blackburn R	9	1		
1995–96	Blackburn R	32	0		
1996–97	Blackburn R	37	0		
1997–98	Blackburn R	37	0		
1998–99	Blackburn R	23	0		
1999–2000	Blackburn R	11	0		
2000–01	Blackburn R	6	0	155	1
2000–01	*Tranmere R*	11	0	11	0

MAHON, Alan* (M) 138 13
H: 5 9 W: 11 05 b.Dublin 4-4-78
Source: Crumplin U. *Honours:* Eire
Under-21, 2 full caps.

1994–95	Tranmere R	0	0		
1995–96	Tranmere R	2	0		
1996–97	Tranmere R	25	2		
1997–98	Tranmere R	18	1		
1998–99	Tranmere R	39	6		
1999–2000	Tranmere R	36	4		
2000–01	Tranmere R	0	0	120	13

From Sporting Lisbon

2000–01	Blackburn R	18	0	18	0

MARTIN, Anthony (M) 0 0
b.Dublin 20-9-83
Source: Scholar.

2000–01	Blackburn R	0	0		

McATEER, Jason (M) 282 15
H: 5 11 W: 12 04 b.Birkenhead 18-6-71
Source: Marine. *Honours:* Eire B, 40 full caps,
2 goals.

1991–92	Bolton W	0	0		
1992–93	Bolton W	21	0		
1993–94	Bolton W	46	3		
1994–95	Bolton W	43	5		
1995–96	Bolton W	4	0	114	8
1995–96	Liverpool	29	0		
1996–97	Liverpool	37	1		
1997–98	Liverpool	21	2		
1998–99	Liverpool	13	0	100	3
1998–99	Blackburn R	13	1		
1999–2000	Blackburn R	28	2		
2000–01	Blackburn R	27	1	68	4

McCANN, Peter* (M) 0 0
H: 5 6 W: 10 13 b.Dublin 18-8-81
Source: Trainee.

1998–99	Blackburn R	0	0		
1999–2000	Blackburn R	0	0		
2000–01	Blackburn R	0	0		

McLEAN, Matthew (M) 0 0
b.Brighton 3-12-83
Source: School.

2000–01	Blackburn R	0	0		

McNAMEE, David (D) 31 0
H: 5 11 W: 11 02 b.Glasgow 10-10-80
Source: St Mirren BC.

1998–99	St Mirren	31	0	31	0
1998–99	Blackburn R	0	0		
1999–2000	Blackburn R	0	0		
2000–01	Blackburn R	0	0		

MILLER, Alan (G) 203 0
H: 6 3 W: 14 06 b.Epping 29-3-70
Source: Trainee. *Honours:* England Schools,
FA Schools, Under-21.

1987–88	Arsenal	0	0		
1988–89	Arsenal	0	0		
1988–89	*Plymouth Arg*	13	0	13	0
1989–90	Arsenal	0	0		
1990–91	Arsenal	0	0		
1991–92	Arsenal	3	0		
1991–92	*WBA*	0	0		
1991–92	*Birmingham C*	15	0	15	0
1992–93	Arsenal	4	0		
1993–94	Arsenal	4	0	8	0
1994–95	Middlesbrough	41	0		
1995–96	Middlesbrough	6	0		
1996–97	Middlesbrough	10	0	57	0
1996–97	*Huddersfield T*	0	0		
1996–97	*Grimsby T*	3	0	3	0
1996–97	WBA	12	0		
1997–98	WBA	41	0		
1998–99	WBA	20	0		
1999–2000	WBA	25	0	101	0
1999–2000	Blackburn R	1	0		
2000–01	*Blackburn R*	0	0	1	0
2000–01	*Bristol C*	4	0	4	0
2000–01	*Coventry C*	1	0	1	0

MORGAN, Alan (M) 0 0
b.Edinburgh 27-11-83
Source: Scholar.

2000–01	Blackburn R	0	0		

MURPHY, Peter* (D) 21 1
H: 5 11 W: 12 10 b.Dublin 27-10-80
Source: Trainee. *Honours:* Eire Under-21.

1998–99	Blackburn R	0	0		
1999–2000	Blackburn R	0	0		
2000–01	Blackburn R	0	0		
2000–01	*Halifax T*	21	1	21	1

MURRAY, Frederick (M) 0 0
b.Clonmel 22-5-82
Source: Trainee.

1998–99	Blackburn R	0	0		
1999–2000	Blackburn R	0	0		
2000–01	Blackburn R	0	0		

O'BRIEN, Burton (M) 22 1
H: 5 10 W: 10 12 b.South Africa 10-6-81
Source: S Form. *Honours:* Scotland Under-21.

1998–99	St Mirren	22	1	22	1
1998–99	Blackburn R	0	0		
1999–2000	Blackburn R	0	0		
2000–01	Blackburn R	0	0		

OSTENSTAD, Egil (F) 269 93
H: 5 11 W: 13 00 b.Haugesund 2-1-72
Honours: Norway 17 full caps, 6 goals.

1990	Viking	10	1		
1991	Viking	10	1		
1992	Viking	20	1		
1993	Viking	22	10		
1994	Viking	21	6		
1995	Viking	21	12		
1996	Viking	24	23	128	54
1996–97	Southampton	30	9		
1997–98	Southampton	29	11		
1998–99	Southampton	34	7		
1999–2000	Southampton	3	1	96	28
1999–2000	Blackburn R	28	8		
2000–01	Blackburn R	13	3	41	11
2000–01	*Manchester C*	4	0	4	0

PEACOCK, Darren‡ (D) 397 12
H: 6 2 W: 12 12 b.Bristol 3-2-68
Source: Apprentice.

1984–85	Newport Co	0	0		
1985–86	Newport Co	18	0		
1986–87	Newport Co	5	0		
1987–88	Newport Co	5	0	28	0
1988–89	Hereford U	8	0		
1989–90	Hereford U	36	3		
1990–91	Hereford U	15	1	59	4
1990–91	QPR	19	0		
1991–92	QPR	39	1		
1992–93	QPR	38	2		
1993–94	QPR	30	3	126	6
1993–94	Newcastle U	9	0		
1994–95	Newcastle U	35	1		
1995–96	Newcastle U	35	0		
1996–97	Newcastle U	35	1		
1997–98	Newcastle U	20	0	133	2

1998–99	Blackburn R	30	0		
1999–2000	Blackburn R	17	0		
2000–01	Blackburn R	0	0	47	0
2000–01	*West Ham U*	0	0		
2000–01	*Wolverhampton W*	4	0	4	0

RICHARDS, Marc (M) 0 0
b.Wolverhampton 8-7-82
Source: Trainee. *Honours:* England Youth.

1999–2000	Blackburn R	0	0		
2000–01	Blackburn R	0	0		

SHORT, Craig (D) 460 27
H: 6 1 W: 11 10 b.Bridlington 25-6-68
Source: Pickering T. *Honours:* England
Schools.

1987–88	Scarborough	21	2		
1988–89	Scarborough	42	5	63	7
1989–90	Notts Co	44	2		
1990–91	Notts Co	0	0		
1990–91	Notts Co	43	0		
1991–92	Notts Co	38	3		
1992–93	Notts Co	3	1	128	6
1992–93	Derby Co	38	3		
1993–94	Derby Co	43	3		
1994–95	Derby Co	37	3	118	9
1995–96	Everton	23	2		
1996–97	Everton	23	2		
1997–98	Everton	31	0		
1998–99	Everton	22	0	99	4
1999–2000	Blackburn R	17	0		
2000–01	Blackburn R	35	1	52	1

TAYLOR, Martin (D) 36 3
H: 6 4 W: 14 00 b.Ashington 9-11-79
Source: Trainee. *Honours:* England Youth,
Under-21.

1997–98	Blackburn R	0	0		
1998–99	Blackburn R	3	0		
1999–2000	Blackburn R	6	0		
1999–2000	*Darlington*	4	0	4	0
1999–2000	*Stockport Co*	7	0	7	0
2000–01	Blackburn R	16	3	25	3

TAYLOR, Michael (M) 0 0
b.Liverpool 21-11-82
Source: Scholarship.

1999–2000	Blackburn R	0	0		
2000–01	Blackburn R	0	0		

TAYLOR, Stuart* (M) 0 0
b.Rochdale 14-9-81
Source: Trainee.

1999–2000	Blackburn R	0	0		
2000–01	Blackburn R	0	0		

THOMAS, James (F) 26 4
H: 6 1 W: 13 04 b.Swansea 16-1-79
Source: Trainee. *Honours:* Wales Under-21.

1996–97	Blackburn R	0	0		
1997–98	Blackburn R	0	0		
1997–98	*WBA*	3	0	3	0
1998–99	Blackburn R	0	0		
1999–2000	Blackburn R	0	0		
1999–2000	*Blackpool*	9	2	9	2
2000–01	Blackburn R	4	1	4	1
2000–01	*Sheffield U*	10	1	10	1

Scholars
Byrne, Mark J; Cole, Michael J; Creasy, Neil;
Davey, Hugh CC; Derbyshire, Robert W;
Donnelly, Ciaran; Hevicon, Ryan; Hind,
Matthew; Hockenhull, Darren; Murray, Philip
D; Nelson, Adam E; Renton, Keiron;
Robinson, Ryan; Stone, Daniel JC; Walters,
Jonathan R; Willis, David J; Woodhead,
Robert A

BLACKPOOL

BARNES, Phil (G) 50 0
H: 6 1 W: 11 01 b.Rotherham 2-3-79
Source: Trainee.

1996–97	Rotherham U	2	0	2	0
1997–98	Blackpool	1	0		
1998–99	Blackpool	1	0		
1999–2000	Blackpool	12	0		
2000–01	Blackpool	34	0	48	0

BENT, Junior* (F) 338 34
H: 5 5 W: 10 06 b.Huddersfield 1-3-70
Source: Trainee.

1987–88	Huddersfield T	36	3		
1988–89	Huddersfield T	22	5		
1989–90	Huddersfield T	7	1	36	6
1989–90	Burnley	9	3	9	3
1989–90	Bristol C	1	0		
1990–91	Bristol C	20	2		
1991–92	Bristol C	17	2		
1991–92	Stoke C	1	0	1	0

Year	Club	App	Gls	Tot App	Tot Gls
1992–93	Bristol C	20	3		
1993–94	Bristol C	20	2		
1994–95	Bristol C	41	6		
1995–96	Bristol C	40	2		
1996–97	Bristol C	22	3		
1996–97	*Shrewsbury T*	6	0	6	0
1997–98	Bristol C	2	0	183	20
1997–98	Blackpool	36	3		
1998–99	Blackpool	39	1		
1999–2000	Blackpool	28	1		
2000–01	Blackpool	0	0	103	5

BUSHELL, Steve* (M)   253 16
H: 5 9 W: 11 06 b.Manchester 28-12-72
Source: Trainee.

1990–91	York C	15	0		
1991–92	York C	16	0		
1992–93	York C	8	0		
1993–94	York C	31	4		
1994–95	York C	10	1		
1995–96	York C	23	0		
1996–97	York C	31	3		
1997–98	York C	40	2	174	10
1998–99	Blackpool	31	3		
1999–2000	Blackpool	24	2		
2000–01	Blackpool	24	1	79	6

CLARKSON, Phil (M)   319 81
H: 5 10 W: 12 05 b.Garstang 13-11-68
Source: Fleetwood T.

1991–92	Crewe Alex	28	6		
1992–93	Crewe Alex	35	13		
1993–94	Crewe Alex	7	2		
1994–95	Crewe Alex	23	6		
1995–96	Crewe Alex	5	0	98	27
1995–96	Scunthorpe U	24	6		
1996–97	Scunthorpe U	28	13	52	19
1996–97	Blackpool	17	5		
1997–98	Blackpool	45	13		
1998–99	Blackpool	44	9		
1999–2000	Blackpool	35	3		
2000–01	Blackpool	28	5	169	35

COID, Danny (M)   68 2
H: 5 11 W: 11 07 b.Liverpool 3-10-81
Source: Trainee.

1998–99	Blackpool	1	0		
1999–2000	Blackpool	21	1		
2000–01	Blackpool	46	1	68	2

COLLINS, Lee (M)   136 3
H: 5 8 W: 10 08 b.Bellshill 3-2-74
Source: Possil U.

1993–94	Albion R	20	0		
1994–95	Albion R	17	0		
1995–96	Albion R	8	1	45	1
1995–96	Swindon T	5	0		
1996–97	Swindon T	4	0		
1997–98	Swindon T	26	1		
1998–99	Swindon T	4	0		
1999–2000	Swindon T	24	1	63	2
2000–01	Blackpool	28	0	28	0

GARVEY, Steve* (M)   128 7
H: 5 9 W: 11 01 b.Stalybridge 22-11-73
Source: Trainee.

1990–91	Crewe Alex	1	0		
1991–92	Crewe Alex	11	0		
1992–93	Crewe Alex	10	1		
1993–94	Crewe Alex	0	0		
1994–95	Crewe Alex	28	3		
1995–96	Crewe Alex	29	2		
1996–97	Crewe Alex	16	0		
1997–98	Crewe Alex	13	2	108	8
1997–98	*Chesterfield*	3	0	3	0
1998–99	Blackpool	15	1		
1999–2000	Blackpool	2	0		
2000–01	Blackpool	0	0	17	1

HILLS, Danny (D)   119 7
H: 5 8 W: 10 08 b.St Annes-on-Sea 21-4-78
Source: Trainee.

1995–96	Blackpool	0	0		
1995–96	Everton	0	0		
1996–97	Everton	3	0		
1996–97	*Swansea C*	11	0		
1997–98	Everton	0	0	3	0
1997–98	*Swansea C*	7	1	18	1
1997–98	Blackpool	19	1		
1998–99	Blackpool	28	1		
1999–2000	Blackpool	33	2		
2000–01	Blackpool	18	2	98	6

HUGHES, Ian (M)   297 3
H: 5 10 W: 12 08 b.Bangor 2-8-74
Source: Trainee. *Honours:* Wales Under-21.

1991–92	Bury	17	0		
1992–93	Bury	15	0		
1992–93	Bury	15	0		
1993–94	Bury	38	0		
1994–95	Bury	23	1		
1995–96	Bury	32	0		
1996–97	Bury	22	0		
1997–98	Bury	13	0	175	1
1997–98	Blackpool	21	0		
1998–99	Blackpool	33	1		
1999–2000	Blackpool	34	0		
2000–01	Blackpool	34	1	122	2

JASZCZUN, Tommy (D)   54 0
H: 5 11 W: 11 02 b.Kettering 16-9-77
Source: Trainee.

1996–97	Aston Villa	0	0		
1997–98	Aston Villa	0	0		
1998–99	Aston Villa	0	0		
1999–2000	Aston Villa	0	0		
1999–2000	Blackpool	19	0		
2000–01	Blackpool	35	0	54	0

JONES, Eifion (D)   8 0
H: 6 3 W: 13 00 b.Llanrug 28-9-80
Source: Trainee. *Honours:* Wales Under-21.

1997–98	Liverpool	0	0		
1998–99	Liverpool	0	0		
1999–2000	Liverpool	0	0		
1999–2000	Blackpool	1	0		
2000–01	Blackpool	7	0	8	0

MILLIGAN, Jamie (M)   10 0
H: 5 7 W: 9 12 b.Blackpool 3-1-80
Source: Trainee. *Honours:* England Youth.

1997–98	Everton	0	0		
1998–99	Everton	3	0		
1999–2000	Everton	1	0		
2000–01	Everton	0	0	4	0
2000–01	Blackpool	6	0	6	0

MILLIGAN, Mike (M)   446 30
H: 5 10 W: 11 06 b.Manchester 20-2-67
Source: Trainee. *Honours:* Eire Under-21, B, 1 full cap.

1984–85	Oldham Ath	0	0		
1985–86	Oldham Ath	5	1		
1986–87	Oldham Ath	38	2		
1987–88	Oldham Ath	39	1		
1988–89	Oldham Ath	39	6		
1989–90	Oldham Ath	41	7		
1990–91	Everton	17	1	17	1
1991–92	Oldham Ath	36	3		
1992–93	Oldham Ath	42	3		
1993–94	Oldham Ath	39	0	279	23
1994–95	Norwich C	26	2		
1995–96	Norwich C	28	2		
1996–97	Norwich C	37	1		
1997–98	Norwich C	20	0		
1998–99	Norwich C	2	0		
1999–2000	Norwich C	11	0	124	5
2000–01	Norwich C	26	1	26	1

MURPHY, John (F)   188 48
H: 6 2 W: 14 00 b.Whiston 18-10-76
Source: Trainee.

1994–95	Chester C	5	0		
1995–96	Chester C	18	3		
1996–97	Chester C	11	1		
1997–98	Chester C	27	4		
1998–99	Chester C	42	12	103	20
1999–2000	Blackpool	39	10		
2000–01	Blackpool	46	18	85	28

MURPHY, Neil (D)   6 0
H: 5 9 W: 11 00 b.Liverpool 19-5-80
Source: Trainee. *Honours:* England Youth.

1997–98	Liverpool	0	0		
1998–99	Liverpool	0	0		
1999–2000	Liverpool	0	0		
2000–01	Blackpool	6	0	6	0

NEWELL, Mike* (F)   512 116
H: 6 0 W: 13 00 b.Liverpool 27-1-65
Source: Liverpool Amateur. *Honours:* England Under-21, B.

1983–84	Crewe Alex	3	0		
1983–84	Wigan Ath	9	0		
1984–85	Wigan Ath	39	9		
1985–86	Wigan Ath	24	16	72	25
1985–86	Luton T	16	6		
1986–87	Luton T	42	12		
1987–88	Luton T	5	0	63	18
1987–88	Leicester C	36	8		
1988–89	Leicester C	45	13	81	21
1989–90	Everton	26	7		
1990–91	Everton	29	7		
1991–92	Everton	13	1	68	15
1991–92	Blackburn R	20	6		
1992–93	Blackburn R	40	13		
1993–94	Blackburn R	28	6		
1994–95	Blackburn R	12	0		
1995–96	Blackburn R	30	3	130	28
1996–97	Birmingham C	15	1	15	1
1996–97	*West Ham U*	7	0	7	0
1996–97	*Bradford C*	7	0	7	0
1997–98	Aberdeen	21	4		
1998–99	Aberdeen	23	2	44	6
1998–99	Crewe Alex	4	0		
1999–2000	Crewe Alex	0	0	7	0
1999–2000	Blackpool	13	2		
2000–01	Blackpool	5	0	18	2

NOWLAND, Adam (F)   69 5
H: 5 11 W: 11 06 b.Preston 6-7-81
Source: Trainee.

1997–98	Blackpool	1	0		
1998–99	Blackpool	37	2		
1999–2000	Blackpool	21	3		
2000–01	Blackpool	10	0	69	5

O'CONNOR, Jon (D)   20 0
H: 6 0 W: 12 03 b.Darlington 29-10-76
Source: Trainee. *Honours:* England Youth, Under-21.

1993–94	Everton	0	0		
1994–95	Everton	0	0		
1995–96	Everton	4	0		
1996–97	Everton	0	0		
1997–98	Everton	1	0	5	0
1997–98	Sheffield U	2	0		
1998–99	Sheffield U	2	0		
1999–2000	Sheffield U	0	0		
2000–01	Sheffield U	0	0	4	0
2000–01	Blackpool	11	0	11	0

ORMEROD, Brett (F)   107 32
H: 5 11 W: 11 04 b.Blackburn 18-10-76
Source: Blackburn R Trainee, Accrington S.

1996–97	Blackpool	4	0		
1997–98	Blackpool	9	2		
1998–99	Blackpool	40	8		
1999–2000	Blackpool	13	5		
2000–01	Blackpool	41	17	107	32

PARKINSON, Gary (D)   439 15
H: 5 10 W: 11 10 b.Middlesbrough 10-1-68
Source: Everton Amateur.

1985–86	Middlesbrough	0	0		
1986–87	Middlesbrough	46	0		
1987–88	Middlesbrough	38	0		
1988–89	Middlesbrough	36	2		
1989–90	Middlesbrough	41	2		
1990–91	Middlesbrough	10	1		
1991–92	Middlesbrough	27	0		
1992–93	Middlesbrough	4	0	202	5
1992–93	*Southend U*	6	0	6	0
1992–93	Bolton W	2	0		
1993–94	Bolton W	1	0	3	0
1993–94	Burnley	20	1		
1994–95	Burnley	43	2		
1995–96	Burnley	29	0		
1996–97	Burnley	43	1	135	4
1997–98	Preston NE	45	5		
1998–99	Preston NE	27	1		
1999–2000	Preston NE	0	0		
2000–01	Preston NE	11	0	84	6
2000–01	Blackpool	9	0	9	0

RACHEL, Adam* (G)   2 0
H: 5 11 W: 12 08 b.Birmingham 10-12-76
Source: Trainee.

1994–95	Aston Villa	0	0		
1995–96	Aston Villa	0	0		
1996–97	Aston Villa	0	0		
1997–98	Aston Villa	0	0		
1998–99	Aston Villa	1	0		
1999–2000	Aston Villa	0	0	1	0
1999–2000	Blackpool	1	0		
2000–01	Blackpool	0	0	1	0

REID, Brian (D)   85 8
H: 6 3 W: 13 08 b.Paisley 15-6-70

1998–99	Burnley	31	3	31	3
1999–2000	Dunfermline Ath	23	3		
2000–01	Dunfermline Ath	2	0	25	3
2000–01	Blackpool	29	2	29	2

SIMPSON, Paul (M)   563 128
H: 5 8 W: 11 11 b.Carlisle 26-7-66
Source: Apprentice. *Honours:* England Youth, Under-21.

1982–83	Manchester C	3	0		
1983–84	Manchester C	0	0		
1984–85	Manchester C	10	6		
1985–86	Manchester C	37	8		
1986–87	Manchester C	32	3		
1987–88	Manchester C	38	1		
1988–89	Manchester C	1	0	121	18
1988–89	Oxford U	25	8		
1989–90	Oxford U	42	9		
1990–91	Oxford U	46	17		
1991–92	Oxford U	31	9	144	43
1991–92	Derby Co	16	7		
1992–93	Derby Co	35	12		
1993–94	Derby Co	34	9		
1994–95	Derby Co	42	8		
1995–96	Derby Co	39	10		
1996–97	Derby Co	19	2		
1996–97	*Sheffield U*	6	0	6	0
1997–98	Derby Co	1	0	186	48
1997–98	Wolverhampton W	28	4		

1998–99 Wolverhampton W 11 2
1998–99 *Walsall* 10 1 **10 1**
1999–2000 Wolverhampton W 13 0
2000–01 Wolverhampton W 0 0 **52 6**
2000–01 Blackpool 44 12 **44 12**

THOMPSON, Phil (D) 34 2
H: 5 11 W: 12 00 b.Blackpool 1-4-81
Source: Trainee.
1997–98 Blackpool 1 0
1998–99 Blackpool 22 2
1999–2000 Blackpool 3 0
2000–01 Blackpool 8 0 **34 2**

WELLENS, Richard (M) 44 8
H: 5 9 W: 11 05 b.Manchester 26-3-80
Source: Trainee. *Honours:* England Youth.
1996–97 Manchester U 0 0
1997–98 Manchester U 0 0
1998–99 Manchester U 0 0
1999–2000 Manchester U 0 0
1999–2000 Blackpool 8 0
2000–01 Blackpool 36 8 **44 8**

Scholars
Burns, Jamie D; Carroll, John D; Connors, John J; Gordon, William D; Heffernan, Guy; Maden, Wayne T; McMahon, Stephen J; Robinson, Craig; Robinson, Daniel M; Watson, David L

Player who does not hold a current contract but his registration has been retained by the club
Baines, Christopher J

BOLTON W

BALDACCHINO, Ryan (F) 0 0
H: 5 9 W: 12 03 b.Leicester 13-1-81
Source: Trainee.
1998–99 Blackburn R 0 0
1999–2000 Blackburn R 0 0
2000–01 Blackburn R 0 0
2000–01 Bolton W 0 0

BANKS, Steve (G) 237 0
H: 6 0 W: 13 12 b.Hillingdon 9-2-72
Source: Trainee.
1991–92 West Ham U 0 0
1992–93 West Ham U 0 0
1993–94 Gillingham 29 0
1994–95 Gillingham 38 0 **67 0**
1995–96 Blackpool 24 0
1996–97 Blackpool 46 0
1997–98 Blackpool 45 0
1998–99 Blackpool 35 0 **150 0**
1998–99 Bolton W 9 0
1999–2000 Bolton W 2 0
2000–01 Bolton W 9 0 **20 0**

BARNESS, Anthony (D) 162 4
H: 5 11 W: 11 10 b.Lewisham 25-3-73
Source: Trainee.
1990–91 Charlton Ath 0 0
1991–92 Charlton Ath 22 1
1992–93 Charlton Ath 5 0
1992–93 Chelsea 2 0
1993–94 Chelsea 0 0
1993–94 *Middlesbrough* 0 0
1994–95 Chelsea 12 0
1995–96 Chelsea 0 0 **14 0**
1995–96 *Southend U* 5 0 **5 0**
1996–97 Charlton Ath 45 2
1997–98 Charlton Ath 29 1
1998–99 Charlton Ath 3 0
1999–2000 Charlton Ath 19 0 **123 4**
2000–01 Bolton W 20 0 **20 0**

BERGSSON, Gudni# (D) 280 23
H: 6 1 W: 12 11 b.Reykjavik 21-7-65
Source: Valur. *Honours:* Iceland Youth, Under-21, 77 full caps, 1 goal.
1988–89 Tottenham H 8 0
1989–90 Tottenham H 18 0
1990–91 Tottenham H 12 1
1991–92 Tottenham H 28 1
1992–93 Tottenham H 5 0
1993–94 Tottenham H 0 0 **71 2**
1994–95 Bolton W 8 0
1995–96 Bolton W 34 4
1996–97 Bolton W 33 3
1997–98 Bolton W 35 2
1998–99 Bolton W 17 0
1999–2000 Bolton W 38 4
2000–01 Bolton W 44 8 **209 21**

CHARLTON, Simon (D) 332 3
H: 5 8 W: 11 00 b.Huddersfield 25-10-71
Source: Trainee. *Honours:* FA Schools.
1989–90 Huddersfield T 3 0
1990–91 Huddersfield T 30 0
1991–92 Huddersfield T 45 0
1992–93 Huddersfield T 46 1 **124 1**
1993–94 Southampton 33 1
1994–95 Southampton 25 1
1995–96 Southampton 26 0
1996–97 Southampton 27 0
1997–98 Southampton 3 0 **114 2**
1998–99 Birmingham C 28 0
1997–98 Birmingham C 24 0
1999–2000 Birmingham C 20 0 **72 0**
2000–01 Bolton W 22 0 **22 0**

CRUMBLEHULME, Danny* (M) 0 0
H: 5 6 W: 10 07 b.Blackpool 7-2-82
Source: Trainee.
1999–2000 Bolton W 0 0
2000–01 Bolton W 0 0

DOWNEY, Chris§ (F) 1 0
b.Warrington 19-4-83
Source: Scholar.
2000–01 Bolton W 1 0 **1 0**

ELLIOTT, Robbie# (M) 165 14
H: 5 10 W: 12 03 b.Gosforth 25-12-73
Source: Trainee. *Honours:* England Under-21.
1990–91 Newcastle U 6 0
1991–92 Newcastle U 9 0
1992–93 Newcastle U 0 0
1993–94 Newcastle U 15 0
1994–95 Newcastle U 14 2
1995–96 Newcastle U 6 0
1996–97 Newcastle U 29 7 **79 9**
1997–98 Bolton W 4 0
1998–99 Bolton W 22 0
1999–2000 Bolton W 27 3
2000–01 Bolton W 33 2 **86 5**
(Transferred to Newcastle U, July 2001).

EVANS, James (G) 0 0
H: 6 0 W: 12 00 b.Glasgow 27-1-82
Source: Fortuna Dusseldorf.
1998–99 Bolton W 0 0
1999–2000 Bolton W 0 0
2000–01 Bolton W 0 0

FARRELLY, Gareth (M) 97 7
H: 6 1 W: 13 07 b.Dublin 28-8-75
Source: Home Farm. *Honours:* Eire Under-21, 6 full caps.
1992–93 Aston Villa 0 0
1993–94 Aston Villa 0 0
1994–95 Aston Villa 0 0
1994–95 *Rotherham U* 10 2 **10 2**
1995–96 Aston Villa 5 0
1996–97 Aston Villa 3 0 **8 0**
1997–98 Everton 26 1
1998–99 Everton 1 0
1999–2000 Everton 0 0 **27 1**
1999–2000 Bolton W 11 1
2000–01 Bolton W 41 3 **52 4**

FRANDSEN, Per (M) 389 82
H: 5 11 W: 12 10 b.Copenhagen 6-2-70
Honours: Denmark 20 full caps.
1990 B 1903 25 15 **25 15**
1990–91 Lille 19 4
1991–92 Lille 27 8
1992–93 Lille 32 3
1993–94 Lille 31 4 **109 19**
1994–95 FC Copenhagen 29 12
1995–96 FC Copenhagen 26 7 **55 19**
1996–97 Bolton W 41 5
1997–98 Bolton W 38 2
1998–99 Bolton W 44 8
1999–2000 Bolton W 7 2
1999–2000 Blackburn R 31 5 **31 5**
2000–01 Bolton W 39 7 **169 24**

GARDNER, Ricardo (M) 91 10
H: 5 9 W: 11 01 b.St Andrews 25-9-78
Source: Harbour View. *Honours:* Jamaica full caps.
1998–99 Bolton W 30 2
1999–2000 Bolton W 29 5
2000–01 Bolton W 32 3 **91 10**

GLENNON, Matthew (G) 30 0
H: 6 2 W: 14 09 b.Stockport 8-10-78
Source: Trainee.
1997–98 Bolton W 0 0
1998–99 Bolton W 0 0
1999–2000 Bolton W 0 0
1999–2000 *Port Vale* 0 0
1999–2000 *Stockport Co* 0 0
2000–01 Bolton W 0 0
2000–01 *Bristol R* 1 0 **1 0**
2000–01 *Carlisle U* 29 0 **29 0**

GOPE-FENEPEJ, John‡ (D) 2 0
H: 5 11 W: 12 08 b.Noumea 6-11-78
2000–01 Bolton W 2 0 **2 0**

HANSEN, Bo (F) 181 57
H: 6 1 W: 12 02 b.Jutland 16-6-72.
Honours: Denmark 1 full cap.
1994–95 Brondby 31 11
1995–96 Brondby 14 4
1996–97 Brondby 20 2
1997–98 Brondby 21 14
1998–99 Brondby 16 12 **102 43**
1998–99 Bolton W 8 0
1999–2000 Bolton W 30 9
2000–01 Bolton W 41 5 **79 14**

HAVERON, Gary* (D) 0 0
H: 6 1 W: 14 00 b.Belfast 6-3-81
Source: Wolverhampton W Trainee.
1999–2000 Bolton W 0 0
2000–01 Bolton W 0 0

HENDRY, Colin (D) 492 44
H: 6 1 W: 12 07 b.Keith 7-12-65
Source: Islavale. *Honours:* Scotland B, 51 full caps, 3 goals.
1983–84 Dundee 4 0
1984–85 Dundee 4 0
1985–86 Dundee 20 0
1986–87 Dundee 13 2 **41 2**
1986–87 Blackburn R 13 3
1987–88 Blackburn R 44 12
1988–89 Blackburn R 38 7
1989–90 Blackburn R 7 0
1989–90 Manchester C 25 3
1990–91 Manchester C 32 1
1991–92 Manchester C 6 1 **63 5**
1991–92 Blackburn R 30 4
1992–93 Blackburn R 41 1
1993–94 Blackburn R 23 0
1994–95 Blackburn R 38 4
1995–96 Blackburn R 33 1
1996–97 Blackburn R 35 1
1997–98 Blackburn R 34 1 **336 34**
1998–99 Rangers 19 0 **19 0**
1999–2000 Coventry C 9 0
2000–01 Coventry C 2 0 **11 0**
2000–01 Bolton W 22 3 **22 3**

HOLDEN, Dean (D) 13 1
H: 6 0 W: 12 03 b.Salford 15-9-79
Source: Trainee. *Honours:* England Youth.
1997–98 Bolton W 0 0
1998–99 Bolton W 0 0
1999–2000 Bolton W 12 0
2000–01 Bolton W 1 1 **13 1**

HOLDSWORTH, Dean# (F) 435 156
H: 5 11 W: 13 06 b.Walthamstow 8-11-68
Source: Trainee.
1986–87 Watford 2 0
1987–88 *Carlisle U* 4 1 **4 1**
1987–88 *Port Vale* 6 2 **6 2**
1988–89 Watford 10 2
1988–89 *Swansea C* 5 1 **5 1**
1988–89 *Brentford* 7 1
1989–90 Watford 4 1 **16 3**
1989–90 Brentford 39 24
1990–91 Brentford 30 5
1991–92 Brentford 41 24 **117 54**
1992–93 Wimbledon 36 19
1993–94 Wimbledon 42 17
1994–95 Wimbledon 28 7
1995–96 Wimbledon 33 10
1996–97 Wimbledon 25 5
1997–98 Wimbledon 5 0 **169 58**
1997–98 Bolton W 20 3
1998–99 Bolton W 32 12
1999–2000 Bolton W 35 11
2000–01 Bolton W 31 11 **118 37**

HUNT, Nicky§ (D) 1 0
b.Bolton 3-9-83
Source: Scholar.
2000–01 Bolton W 1 0 **1 0**

JAASKELAINEN, Jussi (G) 213 0
H: 6 3 W: 13 05 b.Mikkeli 19-4-75
Honours: Finland 7 full caps.
1992 MP 6 0
1993 MP 6 0
1994 MP 26 0
1995 MP 26 0 **64 0**
1996 VPS 27 0
1997 VPS 27 0 **54 0**
1997–98 Bolton W 0 0
1998–99 Bolton W 34 0
1999–2000 Bolton W 34 0
2000–01 Bolton W 27 0 **95 0**

KAPRIELIAN, Mickael* (F) 1 0
H: 5 10 W: 11 00 b.Marseille 6-10-80
1999–2000 Bolton W 1 0
2000–01 Bolton W 0 0 **1 0**

MARSHALL, Ian# (F) 388 93
H: 6 2 W: 14 09 b.Liverpool 20-3-66
Source: Apprentice.
1983–84 Everton 0 0
1984–85 Everton 0 0
1985–86 Everton 9 0
1986–87 Everton 2 1

1987–88	Everton	4	0	15 1
1987–88	Oldham Ath	10	0	
1988–89	Oldham Ath	41	4	
1989–90	Oldham Ath	25	3	
1990–91	Oldham Ath	26	17	
1991–92	Oldham Ath	41	10	
1992–93	Oldham Ath	27	2	170 36
1993–94	Ipswich T	29	10	
1994–95	Ipswich T	18	3	
1995–96	Ipswich T	35	19	
1996–97	Ipswich T	2	0	84 32
1996–97	Leicester C	28	8	
1997–98	Leicester C	24	7	
1998–99	Leicester C	10	3	
1999–2000	Leicester C	21	0	83 18
2000–01	Bolton W	36	6	36 6

MORINI, Emmanuelle (F) 2 0
b.Rome 31-1-82
Source: Roma.
| 2000–01 | Bolton W | 2 | 0 | 2 0 |

NOLAN, Kevin (D) 35 1
H: 6 0 W: 14 00 b.Liverpool 24-6-82
Source: Scholarship. Honours: England Youth.
| 1999–2000 | Bolton W | 4 | 0 | |
| 2000–01 | Bolton W | 31 | 1 | 35 1 |

NORRIS, David (M) 0 0
H: 5 7 W: 11 06 b.Peterborough 22-2-81
Source: Boston U.
| 1999–2000 | Bolton W | 0 | 0 | |
| 2000–01 | Bolton W | 0 | 0 | |

O'CONNOR, Kieran* (M) 0 0
b.Belfast 29-8-81
Source: Scholar. Honours: N.Ireland Youth.
| 2000–01 | Bolton W | 0 | 0 | |

O'KANE, John* (D) 82 5
H: 5 10 W: 12 06 b.Nottingham 15-11-74
Source: Trainee.
1992–93	Manchester U	0	0	
1993–94	Manchester U	0	0	
1994–95	Manchester U	0	0	
1994–95	Wimbledon	0	0	
1995–96	Manchester U	1	0	
1996–97	Manchester U	1	0	
1996–97	*Bury*	13	3	13 3
1997–98	Manchester U	0	0	2 0
1997–98	*Bradford C*	7	0	7 0
1997–98	Everton	12	0	
1998–99	Everton	2	0	
1998–99	*Burnley*	8	0	8 0
1999–2000	Everton	0	0	14 0
1999–2000	Bolton W	11	1	
2000–01	Bolton W	27	1	38 2

PASSI, Franck* (M) 272 6
H: 5 10 W: 12 08 b.Bergerac 28-3-66
1990–91	Toulon	36	0	
1991–92	Toulon	27	1	
1992–93	Toulon	14	1	77 2
1993–94	Monaco	15	0	15 0
1994–95	Compostela	34	2	
1995–96	Compostela	35	0	
1996–97	Compostela	38	1	
1997–98	Compostela	35	1	142 4
1999–2000	Bolton W	15	0	
From Compostela				
2000–01	Bolton W	23	0	38 0

PHILLIPS, Jimmy* (D) 572 19
H: 6 0 W: 13 06 b.Bolton 8-2-66
Source: Apprentice.
1983–84	Bolton W	1	0	
1984–85	Bolton W	40	1	
1985–86	Bolton W	33	1	
1986–87	Bolton W	34	0	
1986–87	Rangers	6	0	
1987–88	Rangers	19	0	25 0
1988–89	Oxford U	45	5	
1989–90	Oxford U	34	3	79 8
1989–90	Middlesbrough	12	0	
1990–91	Middlesbrough	44	2	
1991–92	Middlesbrough	43	2	
1992–93	Middlesbrough	40	2	139 6
1993–94	Bolton W	42	0	
1994–95	Bolton W	46	1	
1995–96	Bolton W	37	0	
1996–97	Bolton W	36	0	
1997–98	Bolton W	22	1	
1998–99	Bolton W	15	0	
1999–2000	Bolton W	23	1	
2000–01	Bolton W	0	0	329 5

RICHARDSON, Leam (D) 12 0
H: 5 8 W: 11 04 b.Leeds 19-11-79
Source: Trainee.
1997–98	Blackburn R	0	0	
1998–99	Blackburn R	0	0	
1999–2000	Blackburn R	0	0	
2000–01	Bolton W	12	0	12 0

RICKETTS, Michael (F) 115 33
H: 6 2 W: 11 12 b.Birmingham 4-12-78
Source: Trainee.
1995–96	Walsall	1	1	
1996–97	Walsall	11	1	
1997–98	Walsall	24	1	
1998–99	Walsall	8	0	
1999–2000	Walsall	32	11	76 14
2000–01	Bolton W	39	19	39 19

SMITH, Jeff (M) 4 0
H: 5 10 W: 11 01 b.Middlesbrough 28-6-80
Source: Trainee.
1998–99	Hartlepool U	3	0	
1999–2000	Hartlepool U	0	0	3 0
From Bishop Auckland				
2000–01	Bolton W	1	0	1 0

SNORRASON, Olaf (F) 0 0
H: 5 10 W: 11 00 b.Reykjavik 22-4-82
1998–99	Bolton W	0	0	
1999–2000	Bolton W	0	0	
2000–01	Bolton W	0	0	

STRONG, Greg (D) 73 6
H: 6 2 W: 14 04 b.Bolton 5-9-75
Source: Trainee. Honours: England Schools, Youth.
1992–93	Wigan Ath	0	0	
1993–94	Wigan Ath	18	1	
1994–95	Wigan Ath	17	2	35 3
1995–96	Bolton W	1	0	
1996–97	Bolton W	0	0	
1997–98	Bolton W	0	0	
1997–98	*Blackpool*	11	1	11 1
1998–99	Bolton W	5	1	
1998–99	*Stoke C*	5	1	5 1
1999–2000	Bolton W	6	0	
1999–2000	*Motherwell*	10	0	10 0
2000–01	Bolton W	0	0	12 1
(Transferred to Motherwell, July 2001)

SUMMERBEE, Nicky* (M) 348 20
H: 5 11 W: 12 03 b.Altrincham 26-8-71
Source: Trainee. Honours: England Under-21.
1989–90	Swindon T	1	0	
1990–91	Swindon T	7	0	
1991–92	Swindon T	27	0	
1992–93	Swindon T	39	3	
1993–94	Swindon T	38	3	112 6
1994–95	Manchester C	41	1	
1995–96	Manchester C	37	1	
1996–97	Manchester C	44	4	
1997–98	Manchester C	9	0	131 6
1997–98	Sunderland	25	3	
1998–99	Sunderland	36	3	
1999–2000	Sunderland	32	1	
2000–01	Sunderland	0	0	93 7
2000–01	Bolton W	12	1	12 1

WARHURST, Paul# (D) 276 16
H: 6 0 W: 13 07 b.Stockport 26-9-69
Source: Trainee. Honours: England Under-21.
1987–88	Manchester C	0	0	
1988–89	Oldham Ath	4	0	
1989–90	Oldham Ath	30	1	
1990–91	Oldham Ath	33	1	67 2
1991–92	Sheffield W	33	0	
1992–93	Sheffield W	29	6	
1993–94	Sheffield W	4	0	66 6
1993–94	Blackburn R	9	0	
1994–95	Blackburn R	27	2	
1995–96	Blackburn R	10	0	
1996–97	Blackburn R	11	2	57 4
1997–98	Crystal Palace	22	3	
1998–99	Crystal Palace	5	1	27 4
1998–99	Bolton W	20	0	
1999–2000	Bolton W	19	0	
2000–01	Bolton W	20	0	59 0

WHEATCROFT, Paul (F) 0 0
H: 5 9 W: 9 11 b.Manchester 22-11-80
Source: Trainee. Honours: England Schools, Youth.
1998–99	Manchester U	0	0	
1999–2000	Manchester U	0	0	
2000–01	Bolton W	0	0	

WHITLOW, Mike (D) 310 14
H: 6 1 W: 13 03 b.Northwich 13-1-68
Source: Witton Alb.
1988–89	Leeds U	20	1	
1989–90	Leeds U	29	1	
1990–91	Leeds U	18	1	
1991–92	Leeds U	10	1	77 4
1991–92	Leicester C	5	0	
1992–93	Leicester C	24	1	
1993–94	Leicester C	31	2	
1994–95	Leicester C	28	2	
1995–96	Leicester C	42	3	
1996–97	Leicester C	17	0	
1997–98	Leicester C	0	0	147 8
1997–98	Bolton W	13	0	
1998–99	Bolton W	28	0	
1999–2000	Bolton W	37	1	
2000–01	Bolton W	8	1	86 2

WRIGHT, Tommy* (G) 164 0
H: 6 2 W: 14 12 b.Belfast 29-8-63
Source: Linfield. Honours: Northern Ireland 31 full caps. Football League.
1987–88	Newcastle U	0	0	
1988–89	Newcastle U	9	0	
1989–90	Newcastle U	14	0	
1990–91	Newcastle U	0	0	
1990–91	*Hull C*	6	0	6 0
1991–92	Newcastle U	33	0	
1992–93	Newcastle U	14	0	
1993–94	Newcastle U	3	0	
1993–94	Nottingham F	10	0	
1994–95	Nottingham F	0	0	
1995–96	Nottingham F	0	0	
1996–97	Nottingham F	1	0	11 0
1996–97	*Reading*	17	0	17 0
1996–97	Manchester C	13	0	
1997–98	Manchester C	18	0	
1998–99	Manchester C	1	0	
1998–99	*Wrexham*	16	0	16 0
1999–2000	Manchester C	1	0	
1999–2000	*Newcastle U*	3	0	76 0
2000–01	Manchester C	1	0	34 0
2000–01	Bolton W	4	0	4 0

Scholars
Astle, Brook M; Bird, Michael E; Buchanan, Wayne B; Dootson, Shaun; Downey, Christopher A; Eckersley, Michael W; Flanagan, Daniel J; Hunt, Nicholas B; Laidlaw, Simon G; Letson, Craig W; Lyons, Bradley J; O'Hare, Alan PJ; Ross, Clive; Ryan, Ciaran P; Tagoe, Darrel J; Taylor, Cleveland KW; Tubbs, Mathew; Williams, Christopher

AFC BOURNEMOUTH

BAILEY, John‡ (M) 149 6
H: 5 8 W: 10 02 b.London 6-5-69
Source: Enfield.
1995–96	Bournemouth	44	4	
1996–97	Bournemouth	40	1	
1997–98	Bournemouth	32	1	
1998–99	Bournemouth	32	0	
1999–2000	Bournemouth	1	0	
2000–01	Bournemouth	0	0	149 6

BERNARD, Narada (M) 14 0
b.Bristol 30-1-81
Source: Trainee.
| 1999–2000 | Arsenal | 0 | 0 | |
| 2000–01 | Bournemouth | 14 | 0 | 14 0 |

BIRMINGHAM, David† (D) 2 0
H: 5 8 W: 11 01 b.Portsmouth 16-4-81
Source: Bournemouth Trainee.
1999–2000	Portsmouth	2	0	
2000–01	Portsmouth	0	0	2 0
2000–01	Bournemouth	0	0	

BROADHURST, Karl (D) 46 0
H: 6 1 W: 11 07 b.Portsmouth 18-3-80
Source: Trainee.
1998–99	Bournemouth	0	0	
1999–2000	Bournemouth	16	0	
2000–01	Bournemouth	30	0	46 0

DAY, Jamie* (M) 20 1
H: 5 10 W: 11 04 b.Sidcup 13-9-79
Source: Trainee. Honours: England Schools.
1997–98	Arsenal	0	0	
1998–99	Arsenal	0	0	
1998–99	Bournemouth	2	0	
1999–2000	Bournemouth	11	1	
2000–01	Bournemouth	7	0	20 1

ELLIOTT, Wade (M) 48 12
H: 5 9 W: 11 01 b.Southampton 14-12-78
| 1999–2000 | Bournemouth | 12 | 3 | |
| 2000–01 | Bournemouth | 36 | 9 | 48 12 |

ERIBENNE, Chukkie (F) 17 1
H: 5 10 W: 11 12 b.London 2-11-80
Source: Trainee.
1997–98	Coventry C	0	0	
1998–99	Coventry C	0	0	
1999–2000	Coventry C	0	0	
2000–01	Bournemouth	17	1	17 1

FLETCHER, Carl (M) 70 9
H: 5 10 W: 11 07 b.Camberley 7-4-80
Source: Trainee.

1997–98	Bournemouth	1	0		
1998–99	Bournemouth	1	0		
1999–2000	Bournemouth	25	3		
2000–01	Bournemouth	43	6	70	9

FLETCHER, Steve (F) 343 64
H: 6 2 W: 14 09 b.Hartlepool 26-6-72
Source: Trainee.

1990–91	Hartlepool U	14	2		
1991–92	Hartlepool U	18	2	32	4
1992–93	Bournemouth	31	4		
1993–94	Bournemouth	36	6		
1994–95	Bournemouth	40	6		
1995–96	Bournemouth	7	1		
1996–97	Bournemouth	35	7		
1997–98	Bournemouth	42	12		
1998–99	Bournemouth	39	8		
1999–2000	Bournemouth	36	7		
2000–01	Bournemouth	45	9	311	60

FORD, James (M) 5 0
H: 5 8 W: 11 00 b.Portsmouth 23-10-81
Source: Trainee.

1999–2000	Bournemouth	2	0		
2000–01	Bournemouth	3	0	5	0

GRANT, Peter (M) 475 19
H: 5 8 W: 11 07 b.Bellshill 30-8-65
Source: Celtic BC. *Honours:* Scotland Schools, Youth B, Under-21, 2 full caps.

1982–83	Celtic	0	0		
1983–84	Celtic	3	0		
1984–85	Celtic	20	4		
1985–86	Celtic	30	1		
1986–87	Celtic	37	1		
1987–88	Celtic	37	2		
1988–89	Celtic	21	0		
1989–90	Celtic	26	0		
1990–91	Celtic	27	0		
1991–92	Celtic	22	0		
1992–93	Celtic	31	2		
1993–94	Celtic	28	0		
1994–95	Celtic	28	2		
1995–96	Celtic	30	3		
1996–97	Celtic	23	0	363	15
1997–98	Norwich C	35	3		
1998–99	Norwich C	33	0		
1999–2000	Norwich C	0	0	68	3
1999–2000	Reading	29	1	29	1
2000–01	Bournemouth	15	0	15	0

HAYTER, James (F) 98 15
H: 5 9 W: 10 13 b.Newport (IW) 9-4-79
Source: Trainee.

1996–97	Bournemouth	2	0		
1997–98	Bournemouth	5	0		
1998–99	Bournemouth	20	2		
1999–2000	Bournemouth	31	2		
2000–01	Bournemouth	40	11	98	15

HOWE, Eddie (D) 162 6
H: 5 9 W: 11 02 b.Amersham 29-11-77
Source: Trainee.

1995–96	Bournemouth	5	0		
1996–97	Bournemouth	13	0		
1997–98	Bournemouth	40	1		
1998–99	Bournemouth	45	2		
1999–2000	Bournemouth	28	1		
2000–01	Bournemouth	31	2	162	6

HUCK, Willie (M) 33 0
H: 5 10 W: 11 09 b.Paris 17-3-79
Source: Monaco.

1998–99	Arsenal	0	0		
1998–99	Bournemouth	8	0		
1999–2000	Bournemouth	17	0		
2000–01	Bournemouth	8	0	33	0

HUGHES, Richard (M) 109 12
H: 6 2 W: 12 00 b.Glasgow 25-6-79
Source: Atalanta. *Honours:* Scotland Youth, Under-21.

1997–98	Arsenal	0	0		
1998–99	Bournemouth	44	2		
1999–2000	Bournemouth	21	2		
2000–01	Bournemouth	44	8	109	12

JORGENSEN, Claus# (M) 87 14
H: 5 10 W: 10 06 b.Holstebro 27-4-76
Source: Resen-Humlum, Struer BK, Holstebro, Aarhus, AC Horsens.

1999–2000	Bournemouth	44	6		
2000–01	Bournemouth	43	8	87	14

KEELER, Justin‡ (M) 4 0
H: 5 11 W: 11 06 b.Hillingdon 17-4-78
Source: Christchurch.

1999–2000	Bournemouth	3	0		
2000–01	Bournemouth	1	0	4	0

MENETRIER, Michael (G) 12 0
b.Reims 23-9-78
Source: Metz.

2000–01	Bournemouth	12	0	12	0

O'CONNOR, Gareth (F) 52 5
b.Dublin 10-11-78
Source: Bohemians.

1998–99	Shamrock R	8	0	8	0
1999–2000	Bohemians	22	4	22	4
2000–01	Bournemouth	22	1	22	1

O'NEILL, Jon‡ (F) 216 40
H: 5 11 W: 12 00 b.Glasgow 2-1-74
Source: Queen's Park BC.

1991–92	Queen's Park	25	6		
1992–93	Queen's Park	27	6		
1993–94	Queen's Park	39	18	91	30
1994–95	Celtic	1	0	1	0
1995–96	Bournemouth	6	0		
1996–97	Bournemouth	18	1		
1997–98	Bournemouth	43	3		
1998–99	Bournemouth	24	3		
1999–2000	Bournemouth	30	3		
2000–01	Bournemouth	3	0	124	10

PURCHES, Stephen (M) 34 0
b.Redbridge 14-1-80
Source: Trainee.

1998–99	West Ham U	0	0		
1999–2000	West Ham U	0	0		
2000–01	Bournemouth	34	0	34	0

SHEERIN, Joe‡ (F) 7 1
H: 6 1 W: 12 13 b.Hammersmith 1-2-79
Source: Trainee.

1996–97	Chelsea	1	0		
1997–98	Chelsea	0	0		
1998–99	Chelsea	0	0		
1999–2000	Chelsea	0	0	1	0
2000–01	Bournemouth	6	1	6	1

SMITH, Danny (D) 15 0
H: 5 11 W: 11 04 b.Southampton 17-8-82
Source: Trainee.

1999–2000	Bournemouth	1	0		
2000–01	Bournemouth	14	0	15	0

STEWART, Gareth (G) 38 0
H: 6 0 W: 12 08 b.Preston 3-2-80
Source: Trainee. *Honours:* England Schools, Youth.

1996–97	Blackburn R	0	0		
1997–98	Blackburn R	0	0		
1998–99	Blackburn R	0	0		
1999–2000	Bournemouth	3	0		
2000–01	Bournemouth	35	0	38	0

STOCK, Brian (M) 6 0
H: 5 11 W: 11 02 b.Winchester 24-12-81
Source: Trainee.

1999–2000	Bournemouth	5	0		
2000–01	Bournemouth	1	0	6	0

TINDALL, Jason (M) 70 2
H: 6 1 W: 12 01 b.Stepney 15-11-77
Source: Trainee.

1996–97	Charlton Ath	0	0		
1997–98	Charlton Ath	0	0		
1998–99	Bournemouth	17	1		
1999–2000	Bournemouth	8	0		
2000–01	Bournemouth	45	1	70	2

YOUNG, Neil (D) 249 3
H: 5 9 W: 12 00 b.Harlow 31-8-73
Source: Trainee.

1991–92	Tottenham H	0	0		
1992–93	Tottenham H	0	0		
1993–94	Tottenham H	0	0		
1994–95	Bournemouth	32	0		
1995–96	Bournemouth	41	0		
1996–97	Bournemouth	44	0		
1997–98	Bournemouth	44	2		
1998–99	Bournemouth	44	1		
1999–2000	Bournemouth	37	0		
2000–01	Bournemouth	7	0	249	3

Non-Contract
Birmingham, David P; Brinias, Dimitrios; Rayner, Simon C

BRADFORD C

ATHERTON, Peter (D) 512 10
H: 5 11 W: 13 12 b.Wigan 6-4-70
Source: Trainee. *Honours:* England Schools, Under-21.

1987–88	Wigan Ath	16	0		
1988–89	Wigan Ath	40	1		
1989–90	Wigan Ath	46	0		
1990–91	Wigan Ath	46	0		
1991–92	Wigan Ath	1	0	149	1
1991–92	Coventry C	35	0		
1992–93	Coventry C	39	0		
1993–94	Coventry C	40	0	114	0
1994–95	Sheffield W	41	1		
1995–96	Sheffield W	36	0		
1996–97	Sheffield W	37	2		
1997–98	Sheffield W	27	3		
1998–99	Sheffield W	38	2		
1999–2000	Sheffield W	35	1	214	9
2000–01	Bradford C	25	0	25	0
2000–01	Birmingham C	10	0	10	0

BLAKE, Robbie (F) 206 52
H: 5 8 W: 12 00 b.Middlesbrough 4-3-76
Source: Trainee.

1994–95	Darlington	9	0		
1995–96	Darlington	29	11		
1996–97	Darlington	30	10	68	21
1996–97	Bradford C	5	0		
1997–98	Bradford C	34	8		
1998–99	Bradford C	39	16		
1999–2000	Bradford C	28	2		
2000–01	Bradford C	21	4	127	30
2000–01	*Nottingham F*	11	1	11	1

BOWER, Mark (D) 39 2
H: 5 10 W: 11 00 b.Bradford 23-1-80
Source: Trainee.

1997–98	Bradford C	3	0		
1998–99	Bradford C	0	0		
1999–2000	Bradford C	0	0		
1999–2000	York C	15	1		
2000–01	Bradford C	0	0	3	0
2000–01	*York C*	21	1	36	2

CARBONE, Benito (F) 338 58
H: 5 6 W: 10 08 b.Begnara 14-8-71

1988–89	Torino	3	0		
1989–90	Torino	5	0		
1990–91	Reggina	31	5	31	5
1991–92	Casert	31	4	31	4
1992–93	Ascoli	28	6	28	6
1993–94	Torino	28	3	36	3
1994–95	Napoli	29	5	29	5
1995–96	Internazionale	31	2		
1996–97	Internazionale	1	0	32	2
1996–97	Sheffield W	25	6		
1997–98	Sheffield W	33	9		
1998–99	Sheffield W	31	8		
1999–2000	Sheffield W	7	2	96	25
1999–2000	Aston Villa	24	3	24	3
2000–01	Bradford C	31	5	31	5

CLARKE, Matthew (G) 174 0
H: 6 3 W: 11 07 b.Sheffield 3-11-73
Source: Trainee.

1992–93	Rotherham U	9	0		
1993–94	Rotherham U	30	0		
1994–95	Rotherham U	45	0		
1995–96	Rotherham U	40	0	124	0
1996–97	Sheffield W	1	0		
1997–98	Sheffield W	3	0		
1998–99	Sheffield W	0	0	4	0
1999–2000	Bradford C	21	0		
2000–01	Bradford C	17	0	38	0
2000–01	Bolton W	8	0	8	0

COLLYMORE, Stan‡ (F) 245 97
H: 6 3 W: 13 10 b.Cannock 22-1-71
Source: Stafford R. *Honours:* England 3 full caps.

1990–91	Crystal Palace	6	0		
1991–92	Crystal Palace	12	1		
1992–93	Crystal Palace	2	0	20	1
1992–93	Southend U	30	15	30	15
1993–94	Nottingham F	28	19		
1994–95	Nottingham F	37	22	65	41
1995–96	Liverpool	31	14		
1996–97	Liverpool	30	12	61	26
1996–97	Aston Villa	0	0		
1997–98	Aston Villa	25	6		
1998–99	Aston Villa	20	1		
1999–2000	Aston Villa	0	0	45	7
1999–2000	*Fulham*	6	0	6	0
1999–2000	Leicester C	6	4		
2000–01	Leicester C	5	1	11	5
2000–01	Bradford C	7	2	7	2

(Transferred to Oviedo, January 2001).

DAVISON, Aidan (G) 178 0
H: 6 1 W: 13 12 b.Sedgefield 11-5-68
Source: Billingham Synthonia. *Honours:* Northern Ireland 3 full caps.

1987–88	Notts Co	0	0		
1988–89	Notts Co	1	0		
1989–90	Notts Co	0	0	1	0
1989–90	*Leyton Orient*	0	0		
1989–90	Bury	0	0		
1989–90	*Chester C*	0	0		
1990–91	Bury	0	0		
1990–91	*Blackpool*	0	0		
1991–92	Millwall	33	0		
1992–93	Millwall	1	0	34	0
1993–94	Bolton W	31	0		

1994–95	Bolton W	4	0		
1995–96	Bolton W	2	0		
1996–97	Bolton W	0	0	**37**	**0**
1996–97	*Ipswich T*	0	0		
1996–97	*Hull C*	9	0	**9**	**0**
1996–97	Bradford C	10	0		
1997–98	Grimsby T	42	0		
1998–99	Grimsby T	35	0		
1999–2000	Grimsby T	0	0	**77**	**0**
1999–2000	Sheffield U	2	0	**2**	**0**
1999–2000	Bradford C	6	0		
2000–01	Bradford C	2	0	**18**	**0**

GRANT, Gareth (F) **20 0**
H: 6 1 W: 11 00 b.Leeds 6-9-80
Source: Trainee.

1997–98	Bradford C	3	0		
1998–99	Bradford C	5	0		
1998–99	*Halifax T*	3	0	**3**	**0**
1999–2000	Bradford C	1	0		
1999–2000	*Bolton W*	0	0		
2000–01	Bradford C	5	0	**14**	**0**
2000–01	*Lincoln C*	3	0	**3**	**0**

HALLE, Gunnar (D) **309 21**
H: 5 11 W: 11 00 b.Oslo 11-8-65
Source: Lillestrom. *Honours:* Norway 64 full caps, 5 goals.

1990–91	Oldham Ath	17	0		
1991–92	Oldham Ath	10	0		
1992–93	Oldham Ath	41	5		
1993–94	Oldham Ath	23	1		
1994–95	Oldham Ath	40	5		
1995–96	Oldham Ath	37	3		
1996–97	Oldham Ath	20	3	**188**	**17**
1996–97	Leeds U	20	0		
1997–98	Leeds U	33	2		
1998–99	Leeds U	17	2	**70**	**4**
1999–2000	Bradford C	38	0		
2000–01	Bradford C	13	0	**51**	**0**

JACOBS, Wayne (D) **407 17**
H: 5 9 W: 11 00 b.Sheffield 3-2-69
Source: Apprentice.

1986–87	Sheffield W	0	0		
1987–88	Sheffield W	6	0	**6**	**0**
1987–88	Hull C	6	0		
1988–89	Hull C	33	0		
1989–90	Hull C	46	3		
1990–91	Hull C	19	1		
1991–92	Hull C	25	0		
1992–93	Hull C	0	0	**129**	**4**
1993–94	Rotherham U	42	2	**42**	**2**
1994–95	Bradford C	38	1		
1995–96	Bradford C	28	0		
1996–97	Bradford C	39	3		
1997–98	Bradford C	36	2		
1998–99	Bradford C	44	3		
1999–2000	Bradford C	24	0		
2000–01	Bradford C	21	2	**230**	**11**

JESS, Eoin (F) **353 82**
H: 5 10 W: 11 06 b.Aberdeen 13-12-70
Source: Rangers 'S' Form. *Honours:* Scotland Under-21, 18 full caps, 2 goals.

1987–88	Aberdeen	0	0		
1988–89	Aberdeen	2	0		
1989–90	Aberdeen	11	3		
1990–91	Aberdeen	27	13		
1991–92	Aberdeen	39	12		
1992–93	Aberdeen	31	12		
1993–94	Aberdeen	41	6		
1994–95	Aberdeen	25	1		
1995–96	Aberdeen	25	3		
1995–96	Coventry C	12	1		
1996–97	Coventry C	27	0	**39**	**1**
1997–98	Aberdeen	34	9		
1998–99	Aberdeen	36	14		
1999–2000	Aberdeen	26	5		
2000–01	Aberdeen	0	0	**297**	**78**
2000–01	Bradford C	17	3	**17**	**3**

KERR, Scott (M) **1 0**
H: 5 9 W: 10 07 b.Leeds 11-12-81
Source: Scholar.

2000–01	Bradford C	1	0	**1**	**0**

LAWRENCE, Jamie (M) **194 13**
H: 6 0 W: 12 00 b.Balham 8-3-70
Source: Cowes.

1993–94	Sunderland	4	0	**4**	**0**
1993–94	Doncaster R	9	1		
1994–95	Doncaster R	16	2	**25**	**3**
1994–95	Leicester C	17	1		
1995–96	Leicester C	15	0		
1996–97	Leicester C	15	0	**47**	**1**
1997–98	Bradford C	43	3		
1998–99	Bradford C	35	2		
1999–2000	Bradford C	23	3		
2000–01	Bradford C	17	1	**118**	**9**

LOCKE, Gary (D) **148 5**
H: 6 1 W: 12 06 b.Edinburgh 16-6-75
Source: Whitehill Welfare. *Honours:* Scotland Under-21.

1992–93	Hearts	1	0		
1993–94	Hearts	33	0		
1994–95	Hearts	9	0		
1995–96	Hearts	29	4		
1996–97	Hearts	11	0		
1997–98	Hearts	21	0		
1998–99	Hearts	25	1		
1999–2000	Hearts	12	0		
2000–01	Hearts	0	0	**141**	**5**
2000–01	Bradford C	7	0	**7**	**0**

McCALL, Stuart (M) **649 62**
H: 5 8 W: 11 12 b.Leeds 10-6-64
Source: Apprentice. *Honours:* Scotland Under-21, 40 full caps, 1 goal.

1982–83	Bradford C	28	4		
1983–84	Bradford C	46	5		
1984–85	Bradford C	46	8		
1985–86	Bradford C	38	4		
1986–87	Bradford C	36	7		
1987–88	Bradford C	44	9		
1988–89	Everton	33	0		
1989–90	Everton	37	3		
1990–91	Everton	33	3	**103**	**6**
1991–92	Rangers	36	1		
1992–93	Rangers	36	5		
1993–94	Rangers	34	3		
1994–95	Rangers	30	2		
1995–96	Rangers	21	3		
1996–97	Rangers	7	0		
1997–98	Rangers	30	0	**194**	**14**
1998–99	Bradford C	43	3		
1999–2000	Bradford C	34	1		
2000–01	Bradford C	37	1	**352**	**42**

McKINLAY, Billy* (M) **323 26**
H: 5 8 W: 11 06 b.Glasgow 22-4-69
Source: Hamilton Th. *Honours:* Scotland Under-21, B, 29 full caps, 4 goals.

1986–87	Dundee U	3	0		
1987–88	Dundee U	12	1		
1988–89	Dundee U	30	1		
1989–90	Dundee U	13	0		
1990–91	Dundee U	34	2		
1991–92	Dundee U	22	1		
1992–93	Dundee U	37	1		
1993–94	Dundee U	39	9		
1994–95	Dundee U	27	4		
1995–96	Dundee U	5	4	**222**	**23**
1995–96	Blackburn R	19	2		
1996–97	Blackburn R	25	1		
1997–98	Blackburn R	30	0		
1998–99	Blackburn R	16	0		
1999–2000	Blackburn R	0	0		
2000–01	Blackburn R	0	0	**90**	**3**
2000–01	*Leicester C*	0	0		
2000–01	Bradford C	11	0	**11**	**0**

MOLENAAR, Robert (D) **196 9**
H: 6 2 W: 14 09 b.Zaandam 27-2-69

1992–93	Volendam	28	2		
1993–94	Volendam	27	1		
1994–95	Volendam	31	0		
1995–96	Volendam	21	0		
1996–97	Volendam	17	0	**124**	**3**
1996–97	Leeds U	12	1		
1997–98	Leeds U	22	2		
1998–99	Leeds U	17	2		
1999–2000	Leeds U	0	0		
2000–01	Leeds U	0	0	**51**	**5**
2000–01	Bradford C	21	1	**21**	**1**

MYERS, Andy (D) **125 3**
H: 5 10 W: 12 11 b.Isleworth 3-11-73
Source: Trainee. *Honours:* England Schools, Youth, Under-21.

1990–91	Chelsea	3	0		
1991–92	Chelsea	11	1		
1992–93	Chelsea	3	0		
1993–94	Chelsea	6	0		
1994–95	Chelsea	10	0		
1995–96	Chelsea	20	0		
1996–97	Chelsea	18	1		
1997–98	Chelsea	12	0		
1998–99	Chelsea	1	0	**84**	**2**
1999–2000	Bradford C	13	0		
1999–2000	*Portsmouth*	8	0	**8**	**0**
2000–01	Bradford C	20	1	**33**	**1**

NOLAN, Ian* (D) **274 5**
H: 6 0 W: 12 01 b.Liverpool 9-7-70
Source: Preston NE Trainee, Northwich Vic, Marine. *Honours:* Northern Ireland 17 full caps.

1991–92	Tranmere R	34	1		
1992–93	Tranmere R	14	0		
1993–94	Tranmere R	40	0	**88**	**1**
1994–95	Sheffield W	42	3		
1995–96	Sheffield W	29	0		
1996–97	Sheffield W	38	1		
1997–98	Sheffield W	27	0		
1998–99	Sheffield W	0	0		
1999–2000	Sheffield W	29	0	**165**	**4**
2000–01	Bradford C	21	0	**21**	**0**

SAUNDERS, Dean* (F) **618 190**
H: 5 8 W: 10 06 b.Swansea 21-6-64
Source: Apprentice. *Honours:* Wales 75 full caps, 22 goals.

1982–83	Swansea C	0	0		
1983–84	Swansea C	19	3		
1984–85	Swansea C	30	9	**49**	**12**
1984–85	*Cardiff C*	4	0	**4**	**0**
1985–86	Brighton & HA	42	15		
1986–87	Brighton & HA	30	6	**72**	**21**
1986–87	Oxford U	12	6		
1987–88	Oxford U	37	12		
1988–89	Oxford U	10	4	**59**	**22**
1988–89	Derby Co	30	14		
1989–90	Derby Co	38	11		
1990–91	Derby Co	38	17	**106**	**42**
1991–92	Liverpool	36	10		
1992–93	Liverpool	6	1	**42**	**11**
1992–93	Aston Villa	35	12		
1993–94	Aston Villa	38	10		
1994–95	Aston Villa	39	15	**112**	**37**
1995–96	Galatasaray	27	15	**27**	**15**
1996–97	Nottingham F	34	3		
1997–98	Nottingham F	9	2	**43**	**5**
1997–98	Sheffield U	24	10		
1998–99	Sheffield U	19	7	**43**	**17**
1998–99	Benfica	17	5	**17**	**5**
1999–2000	Bradford C	34	3		
2000–01	Bradford C	10	0	**44**	**3**

SHARPE, Lee (M) **295 31**
H: 6 0 W: 12 10 b.Halesowen 27-5-71
Source: Trainee. *Honours:* England Under-21, B, 8 full caps.

1987–88	Torquay U	14	3	**14**	**3**
1988–89	Manchester U	22	0		
1989–90	Manchester U	18	1		
1990–91	Manchester U	23	2		
1991–92	Manchester U	14	1		
1992–93	Manchester U	27	1		
1993–94	Manchester U	30	9		
1994–95	Manchester U	28	3		
1995–96	Manchester U	31	4	**193**	**21**
1996–97	Leeds U	26	5		
1997–98	Leeds U	0	0		
1998–99	Leeds U	4	0	**30**	**5**
1998–99	*Bradford C*	9	2		
1998–99	Sampdoria	3	0	**3**	**0**
1999–2000	Bradford C	18	0		
2000–01	Bradford C	11	0	**38**	**2**
2000–01	*Portsmouth*	17	0	**17**	**0**

WALSH, Gary (G) **217 0**
H: 6 3 W: 14 13 b.Wigan 21-3-68
Source: Apprentice. *Honours:* England Under-21.

1984–85	Manchester U	0	0		
1985–86	Manchester U	0	0		
1986–87	Manchester U	14	0		
1987–88	Manchester U	16	0		
1988–89	Manchester U	0	0		
1988–89	*Airdrieonians*	3	0	**3**	**0**
1989–90	Manchester U	0	0		
1990–91	Manchester U	5	0		
1991–92	Manchester U	2	0		
1992–93	Manchester U	0	0		
1993–94	Manchester U	3	0		
1993–94	*Oldham Ath*	6	0	**6**	**0**
1994–95	Manchester U	10	0	**50**	**0**
1995–96	Middlesbrough	32	0		
1996–97	Middlesbrough	12	0		
1997–98	Middlesbrough	0	0		
1997–98	Bradford C	35	0		
1998–99	Bradford C	46	0		
1999–2000	Bradford C	11	0		
2000–01	Bradford C	19	0	**111**	**0**
2000–01	*Middlesbrough*	3	0	**47**	**0**

WARD, Ashley (F) **304 92**
H: 6 1 W: 11 07 b.Manchester 24-11-70
Source: Trainee.

1989–90	Manchester C	1	0		
1990–91	Manchester C	0	0	**1**	**0**
1990–91	*Wrexham*	4	2	**4**	**2**
1991–92	Leicester C	10	0		
1992–93	Leicester C	0	0	**10**	**0**
1992–93	*Blackpool*	2	1	**2**	**1**
1992–93	Crewe Alex	20	4		
1993–94	Crewe Alex	25	13		
1994–95	Crewe Alex	16	8	**61**	**25**
1994–95	Norwich C	25	8		
1995–96	Norwich C	28	10	**53**	**18**
1995–96	Derby Co	7	1		
1996–97	Derby Co	30	8		
1997–98	Derby Co	3	0	**40**	**9**

1997–98	Barnsley	29	8		
1998–99	Barnsley	17	12	**46**	**20**
1998–99	Blackburn R	17	5		
1999–2000	Blackburn R	37	8	**54**	**13**
2000–01	Bradford C	33	4	**33**	**4**

WETHERALL, David (D)   **258**   **15**
H: 6 3   W: 13 02   b.Sheffield 14-3-71
Source: School. *Honours:* England Schools.

1989–90	Sheffield W	0	0		
1990–91	Sheffield W	0	0		
1991–92	Leeds U	1	0		
1992–93	Leeds U	13	1		
1993–94	Leeds U	32	1		
1994–95	Leeds U	38	3		
1995–96	Leeds U	34	4		
1996–97	Leeds U	29	0		
1997–98	Leeds U	34	3		
1998–99	Leeds U	21	0	**202**	**12**
1999–2000	Bradford C	38	2		
2000–01	Bradford C	18	1	**56**	**3**

WHALLEY, Gareth (M)   **260**   **12**
H: 5 10   W: 11 00   b.Manchester 19-12-73
Source: Trainee.

1992–93	Crewe Alex	25	1		
1993–94	Crewe Alex	15	1		
1994–95	Crewe Alex	40	1		
1995–96	Crewe Alex	44	2		
1996–97	Crewe Alex	38	3		
1997–98	Crewe Alex	18	1	**180**	**9**
1998–99	Bradford C	45	2		
1999–2000	Bradford C	16	1		
2000–01	Bradford C	19	0	**80**	**3**

Scholars
Brodie, Keith J; Emanuel, Lewis J; Fishlock, Craig C; Hardy, Adam N; Hatton, Philip D; Jones, Kingsley B; Lee, Andrew J; McGahey, Phillip M; Morgan, Robert D; Worsnop, Jon A

BRENTFORD

ANDERSON, Ijah (D)   **158**   **4**
H: 5 8   W: 10 06   b.Hackney 30-12-75
Source: Tottenham H Trainee.

1994–95	Southend U	0	0		
1995–96	Brentford	25	2		
1996–97	Brentford	46	1		
1997–98	Brentford	17	0		
1998–99	Brentford	38	1		
1999–2000	Brentford	31	0		
2000–01	Brentford	1	0	**158**	**4**

BOXALL, Danny (D)   **89**   **1**
H: 5 8   W: 11 06   b.Croydon 24-8-77
Source: Trainee. *Honours:* Eire Under-21.

1994–95	Crystal Palace	0	0		
1995–96	Crystal Palace	1	0		
1996–97	Crystal Palace	6	0		
1997–98	Crystal Palace	1	0	**8**	**0**
1997–98	*Oldham Ath*	18	0	**18**	**0**
1998–99	Brentford	38	1		
1999–2000	Brentford	25	0		
2000–01	Brentford	0	0	**63**	**1**

BRYAN, Derek (F)   **49**   **7**
H: 5 10   W: 11 05   b.London 11-11-74
Source: Hampton.

1997–98	Brentford	11	2		
1998–99	Brentford	20	4		
1999–2000	Brentford	18	1		
2000–01	Brentford	0	0	**49**	**7**

CHARLES, Julian (F)   **12**   **0**
H: 5 9   W: 11 00   b.Plaistow 5-2-77
Source: Hampton & Richmond B.

1999–2000	Brentford	2	0		
2000–01	Brentford	10	0	**12**	**0**

DOBSON, Michael (D)   **26**   **0**
H: 5 11   W: 12 04   b.Isleworth 9-4-81
Source: Trainee.

1999–2000	Brentford	0	0		
2000–01	Brentford	26	0	**26**	**0**

EVANS, Paul (M)   **288**   **43**
H: 5 8   W: 11 06   b.Oswestry 1-9-74
Source: Trainee. *Honours:* Wales Under-21.

1991–92	Shrewsbury T	2	0		
1992–93	Shrewsbury T	4	0		
1993–94	Shrewsbury T	13	0		
1994–95	Shrewsbury T	32	5		
1995–96	Shrewsbury T	34	3		
1996–97	Shrewsbury T	42	6		
1997–98	Shrewsbury T	39	6		
1998–99	Shrewsbury T	32	6	**198**	**26**
1998–99	Brentford	14	3		
1999–2000	Brentford	33	7		
2000–01	Brentford	43	7	**90**	**17**

FOLAN, Tony (F)   **60**   **7**
H: 5 11   W: 11 08   b.Lewisham 18-9-78
Source: Trainee. *Honours:* Eire Under-21.

1995–96	Crystal Palace	0	0		
1996–97	Crystal Palace	0	0		
1997–98	Crystal Palace	1	0		
1998–99	Crystal Palace	1	0	**1**	**0**
1998–99	Brentford	29	4		
1999–2000	Brentford	9	1		
2000–01	Brentford	21	2	**59**	**7**

GIBBS, Paul (D)   **155**   **14**
H: 5 10   W: 11 09   b.Gorleston 26-10-72
Source: Diss T.

1994–95	Colchester U	9	0		
1995–96	Colchester U	24	3		
1996–97	Colchester U	20	0	**53**	**3**
1997–98	Torquay U	41	7	**41**	**7**
1998–99	Plymouth Arg	27	3		
1999–2000	Plymouth Arg	7	0	**34**	**3**
2000–01	Brentford	27	1	**27**	**1**

GOTTSKALKSSON, Olafur (G)   **276**   **0**
H: 6 3   W: 13 12   b.Keflavik 12-3-68
Honours: Iceland 7 full caps.

1988	IA Akranes	18	0		
1989	IA Akranes	15	0	**33**	**0**
1990	KR	18	0		
1991	KR	18	0		
1992	KR	18	0		
1993	KR	17	0	**71**	**0**
1994	Keflavik	18	0		
1995	Keflavik	17	0		
1996	Keflavik	18	0		
1997	Keflavik	10	0	**63**	**0**
1997–98	Hibernian	16	0		
1998–99	Hibernian	36	0		
1999–2000	Hibernian	0	0		
2000–01	Hibernian	12	0	**64**	**0**
2000–01	Brentford	45	0	**45**	**0**

GRAHAM, Gareth* (M)   **15**   **0**
H: 5 7   W: 10 02   b.Belfast 6-12-78
Source: Trainee. *Honours:* Northern Ireland Under-21.

1996–97	Crystal Palace	0	0		
1997–98	Crystal Palace	0	0		
1998–99	Crystal Palace	1	0		
1999–2000	Crystal Palace	0	0	**1**	**0**
1999–2000	Brentford	13	0		
2000–01	Brentford	1	0	**14**	**0**

HUTCHINSON, Eddie (M)   **7**   **0**
H: 6 1   W: 13 00   b.Surrey 23-2-82
Source: Sutton U.

2000–01	Brentford	7	0	**7**	**0**

INGIMARSSON, Ivar (M)   **152**   **15**
H: 6 0   W: 12 07   b.Reykjavik 20-8-77
Honours: Iceland 1 full cap.

1995	Valur	12	0		
1996	Valur	17	2		
1997	Valur	16	3	**45**	**5**
1998	IBV	18	1		
1999	IBV	18	4	**36**	**5**
1999–2000	Torquay U	4	1	**4**	**1**
1999–2000	Brentford	25	1		
2000–01	Brentford	42	3	**67**	**4**

JOHNSON, Lee† (M)   **0**   **0**
H: 5 6   W: 10 07   b.Newmarket 7-6-81
Source: Trainee.

1998–99	Watford	0	0		
1999–2000	Watford	0	0		
2000–01	Brighton & HA	0	0		
2000–01	Brentford	0	0		

KENNEDY, Richard‡ (M)   **10**   **0**
H: 5 8   W: 10 05   b.Waterford 28-8-78
Source: Trainee.

1996–97	Crystal Palace	0	0		
1997–98	Crystal Palace	0	0		
1998–99	Wycombe W	0	0		
1999–2000	Brentford	9	0		
2000–01	Brentford	1	0	**10**	**0**

LOVETT, Jay (D)   **25**   **0**
H: 6 0   W: 12 00   b.Sussex 22-1-78
Source: Crawley T.

2000–01	Brentford	25	0	**25**	**0**

MAHON, Gavin (M)   **117**   **9**
H: 6 0   W: 13 02   b.Birmingham 2-1-77
Source: Trainee.

1995–96	Wolverhampton W	0	0		
1996–97	Hereford U	11	1		
1997–98	Hereford U	0	0		
1998–99	Hereford U	0	0	**11**	**1**
1998–99	Brentford	29	4		
1999–2000	Brentford	37	3		
2000–01	Brentford	40	1	**106**	**8**

MARSHALL, Scott (D)   **106**   **4**
H: 6 2   W: 12 12   b.Edinburgh 1-5-73
Source: Trainee. *Honours:* Scotland Under-21.

1992–93	Arsenal	2	0		
1993–94	Arsenal	0	0		
1993–94	Rotherham U	10	1	**10**	**1**
1993–94	Oxford U	0	0		
1994–95	Arsenal	0	0		
1994–95	Sheffield U	17	0	**17**	**0**
1995–96	Arsenal	11	1		
1996–97	Arsenal	8	0		
1997–98	Arsenal	3	0	**24**	**1**
1998–99	Southampton	2	0		
1998–99	Celtic	2	0	**2**	**0**
1999–2000	Southampton	0	0	**2**	**0**
1999–2000	Brentford	22	2		
2000–01	Brentford	29	0	**51**	**2**

McCAMMON, Mark (F)   **36**   **3**
H: 6 2   W: 14 06   b.Barnet 7-8-78
Source: Cambridge C.

1997–98	Cambridge U	2	0		
1998–99	Cambridge U	2	0	**4**	**0**
1998–99	Charlton Ath	0	0		
1999–2000	Charlton Ath	4	0	**4**	**0**
1999–2000	Swindon T	4	0	**4**	**0**
2000–01	Brentford	24	3	**24**	**3**

O'CONNOR, Kevin (F)   **17**   **1**
H: 5 11   W: 12 00   b.Blackburn 24-2-82
Source: Trainee.

1999–2000	Brentford	6	0		
2000–01	Brentford	11	1	**17**	**1**

OWUSU, Lloyd (F)   **120**   **44**
H: 6 0   W: 14 00   b.Slough 12-12-76
Source: Slough T.

1998–99	Brentford	46	22		
1999–2000	Brentford	41	12		
2000–01	Brentford	33	10	**120**	**44**

PARTRIDGE, Scott (F)   **243**   **46**
H: 5 9   W: 11 02   b.Leicester 13-10-74
Source: Trainee.

1992–93	Bradford C	4	0		
1993–94	Bradford C	1	0	**5**	**0**
1993–94	Bristol C	9	4		
1994–95	Bristol C	33	2		
1995–96	Bristol C	9	1		
1995–96	Torquay U	5	2		
1995–96	Plymouth Arg	7	2	**7**	**2**
1995–96	Scarborough	7	0	**7**	**0**
1996–97	Bristol C	6	0	**57**	**7**
1996–97	Cardiff C	15	0		
1997–98	Cardiff C	22	2	**37**	**2**
1997–98	Torquay U	5	0		
1998–99	Torquay U	29	12	**39**	**14**
1998–99	Brentford	14	7		
1999–2000	Brentford	41	6		
2000–01	Brentford	36	8	**91**	**21**

PEARCEY, Jason‡ (G)   **149**   **0**
H: 6 1   W: 13 12   b.Leamington Spa 23-7-71
Source: Trainee.

1988–89	Mansfield T	1	0		
1989–90	Mansfield T	5	0		
1990–91	Mansfield T	4	0		
1991–92	Mansfield T	22	0		
1992–93	Mansfield T	33	0		
1993–94	Mansfield T	9	0		
1994–95	Mansfield T	3	0	**77**	**0**
1994–95	Grimsby T	3	0		
1995–96	Grimsby T	2	0		
1996–97	Grimsby T	40	0		
1997–98	Grimsby T	4	0	**49**	**0**
1998–99	Brentford	17	0		
1999–2000	Brentford	6	0		
2000–01	Brentford	0	0	**23**	**0**

PINAMONTE, Lorenzo (F)   **50**   **7**
H: 6 3   W: 13 04   b.Foggia 9-5-78
Source: Foggia.

1998–99	Bristol C	1	1		
1999–2000	Bristol C	6	0	**7**	**1**
1999–2000	*Brighton & HA*	9	2	**9**	**2**
1999–2000	Brentford	15	1		
2000–01	Brentford	8	1	**23**	**2**
2000–01	*Leyton Orient*	11	2	**11**	**2**

POWELL, Darren (D)   **87**   **5**
H: 6 3   W: 13 02   b.Hammersmith 10-3-76
Source: Hampton.

1998–99	Brentford	33	2		
1999–2000	Brentford	36	2		
2000–01	Brentford	18	1	**87**	**5**

ROWLANDS, Martin (M)   **108**   **12**
H: 5 9   W: 10 10   b.Hammersmith 8-2-79
Source: Farnborough T. *Honours:* Eire Under-21.

1998–99	Brentford	36	4		
1999–2000	Brentford	40	6		
2000–01	Brentford	32	2	**108**	**12**

SAROYA, Nevin‡ (D) 1 0
H: 6 3 W: 14 00 b.Hillingdon 15-9-80
Source: Trainee.

1999–2000	Brentford	1	0	
2000–01	Brentford	0	0	1 0

SMITH, Jay (M) 3 0
H: 5 11 W: 12 00 b.London 29-12-81
Source: Trainee.

2000–01	Brentford	3	0	3 0

SMITH, Paul (G) 2 0
H: 6 3 W: 12 04 b.Epsom 17-12-79

1998–99	Charlton Ath	0	0	
1998–99	Brentford	0	0	
1999–2000	Charlton Ath	0	0	

From Carshalton Ath.

2000–01	Brentford	2	0	2 0

SOMNER, Matthew§ (M) 3 0
H: 5 11 W: 12 00 b.London 10-1-83
Source: Trainee.

2000–01	Brentford	3	0	3 0

TABB, Jay§ (M) 2 0
H: 5 7 W: 10 00 b.London 1-1-82
Source: Trainee.

2000–01	Brentford	2	0	2 0

THEOBALD, David (D) 25 0
H: 6 2 W: 11 00 b.Cambridge 15-12-78
Source: Trainee.

1997–98	Ipswich T	0	0	
1998–99	Ipswich T	0	0	
1999–2000	Brentford	10	0	
2000–01	Brentford	15	0	25 0

WILLIAMS, Mark (F) 30 2
H: 5 11 W: 12 00 b.London 9-4-82
Source: Scholar.

2000–01	Brentford	30	2	30 2

Trainees
Allen-Page, Danny L; Blackman, Lloyd J;
Fieldwick, Lee P; Hollands, Michael R;
Hughes, Stephen T; Johnson, Lee L; Johnson,
Paul; Julian, Alan J; Rehman, Rizwan;
Somner, Matthew J; Tabb, Jay A; Thomas,
Daniel K; Traynor, Robert T; Windell,
Gavin J

BRIGHTON & HA

ANDREWS, Ben‡ (D) 4 0
H: 6 1 W: 12 13 b.Burton-on-Trent
18-11-80
Source: Trainee.

1997–98	Brighton & HA	3	0	
1998–99	Brighton & HA	1	0	
1999–2000	Brighton & HA	0	0	
2000–01	Brighton & HA	0	0	4 0

ASPINALL, Warren‡ (M) 476 91
H: 5 9 W: 11 12 b.Wigan 13-9-67
Source: Apprentice. Honours: England
Youth.

1984–85	Wigan Ath	10	1	
1985–86	Wigan Ath	0	0	
1985–86	Everton	1	0	
1985–86	Wigan Ath	41	21	51 22
1986–87	Everton	6	0	7 0
1986–87	Aston Villa	12	3	
1987–88	Aston Villa	32	11	44 14
1988–89	Portsmouth	40	11	
1989–90	Portsmouth	3	0	
1990–91	Portsmouth	33	4	
1991–92	Portsmouth	24	4	
1992–93	Portsmouth	27	2	
1993–94	Portsmouth	5	0	132 21
1993–94	Swansea C	5	0	5 0
1993–94	Bournemouth	24	5	
1994–95	Bournemouth	9	4	33 9
1994–95	Carlisle U	7	1	
1995–96	Carlisle U	42	6	
1996–97	Carlisle U	40	5	
1997–98	Carlisle U	18	0	107 12
1997–98	Brentford	24	3	
1998–99	Brentford	19	2	43 5
1998–99	Colchester U	15	3	
1999–2000	Colchester U	7	2	22 5
1999–2000	Brighton & HA	31	3	
2000–01	Brighton & HA	1	0	32 3

BROOKER, Paul (F) 112 9
H: 5 8 W: 10 01 b.Hammersmith 25-11-76
Source: Trainee.

1995–96	Fulham	20	2	
1996–97	Fulham	26	2	
1997–98	Fulham	9	0	
1998–99	Fulham	1	0	
1999–2000	Fulham	0	0	56 4
1999–2000	Brighton & HA	15	2	
2000–01	Brighton & HA	41	3	56 5

CARPENTER, Richard (M) 297 19
H: 6 0 W: 13 01 b.Sheppey 30-9-72
Source: Trainee.

1990–91	Gillingham	9	1	
1991–92	Gillingham	3	0	
1992–93	Gillingham	28	0	
1993–94	Gillingham	40	3	
1994–95	Gillingham	29	0	
1995–96	Gillingham	12	0	
1996–97	Gillingham	1	0	122 4
1996–97	Fulham	34	5	
1997–98	Fulham	24	2	58 7
1998–99	Cardiff C	42	1	
1999–2000	Cardiff C	33	1	75 2
2000–01	Brighton & HA	42	6	42 6

CARR, Darren (D) 307 12
H: 6 2 W: 13 07 b.Bristol 4-9-68
Source: Trainee.

1985–86	Bristol R	1	0	
1986–87	Bristol R	20	0	
1987–88	Bristol R	9	0	30 0
1987–88	Newport Co	9	0	9 0
1987–88	Sheffield U	3	0	
1988–89	Sheffield U	10	1	
1989–90	Sheffield U	0	0	
1990–91	Sheffield U	0	0	13 1
1990–91	Crewe Alex	36	0	
1991–92	Crewe Alex	36	3	
1992–93	Crewe Alex	32	2	104 5
1993–94	Chesterfield	28	1	
1994–95	Chesterfield	35	2	
1995–96	Chesterfield	0	0	
1996–97	Chesterfield	12	0	
1997–98	Chesterfield	10	1	86 4
1998–99	Gillingham	30	2	30 2
1999–2000	Brighton & HA	19	0	
2000–01	Brighton & HA	2	0	21 0
2000–01	Rotherham U	1	0	1 0
2000–01	Lincoln C	3	0	3 0
2000–01	Carlisle U	10	0	10 0

CARTWRIGHT, Mark* (G) 50 0
H: 6 2 W: 13 06 b.Chester 13-1-73
Source: York C.

1994–95	Wrexham	0	0	
1995–96	Wrexham	0	0	
1996–97	Wrexham	3	0	
1997–98	Wrexham	4	0	
1998–99	Wrexham	30	0	
1999–2000	Wrexham	0	0	
2000–01	Wrexham	0	0	37 0
2000–01	Brighton & HA	13	0	13 0

CROSBY, Andy (D) 343 12
H: 6 2 W: 13 07 b.Rotherham 3-3-73
Source: Leeds U Trainee.

1991–92	Doncaster R	22	0	
1992–93	Doncaster R	29	0	
1993–94	Doncaster R	0	0	51 0
1993–94	Darlington	25	0	
1994–95	Darlington	35	0	
1995–96	Darlington	45	1	
1996–97	Darlington	42	1	
1997–98	Darlington	34	1	181 3
1998–99	Chester C	41	4	41 4
1999–2000	Brighton & HA	36	3	
2000–01	Brighton & HA	34	2	70 5

CULLIP, Danny (D) 136 6
H: 6 1 W: 12 07 b.Bracknell 17-9-76
Source: Trainee.

1995–96	Oxford U	0	0	
1996–97	Fulham	29	1	
1997–98	Fulham	21	1	50 2
1997–98	Brentford	13	0	
1998–99	Brentford	2	0	
1999–2000	Brentford	0	0	15 0
1999–2000	Brighton & HA	33	2	
2000–01	Brighton & HA	38	2	71 4

CULVERHOUSE, Ian‡ (D) 431 0
H: 5 10 W: 11 02 b.Bishop's Stortford
22-9-64
Source: Apprentice. Honours: England
Youth.

1982–83	Tottenham H	0	0	
1983–84	Tottenham H	2	0	
1984–85	Tottenham H	0	0	
1985–86	Tottenham H	0	0	2 0
1985–86	Norwich C	30	0	
1986–87	Norwich C	25	0	
1987–88	Norwich C	33	0	
1988–89	Norwich C	38	0	
1989–90	Norwich C	32	0	
1990–91	Norwich C	34	0	
1991–92	Norwich C	21	0	
1992–93	Norwich C	41	0	
1993–94	Norwich C	42	0	
1994–95	Norwich C	0	0	296 0
1994–95	Swindon T	9	0	
1995–96	Swindon T	46	0	

1996–97	Swindon T	31	0	
1997–98	Swindon T	11	0	97 0

From Kingstonian.

1998–99	Brighton & HA	35	0	
1999–2000	Brighton & HA	1	0	
2000–01	Brighton & HA	0	0	36 0

DAVIS, Danny‡ (M) 1 0
H: 5 10 W: 11 04 b.Brighton 3-10-80
Source: Trainee.

1998–99	Brighton & HA	1	0	
1999–2000	Brighton & HA	0	0	
2000–01	Brighton & HA	0	0	1 0

FREEMAN, Darren* (F) 134 27
H: 5 11 W: 13 00 b.Brighton 22-8-73
Source: Horsham T.

1994–95	Gillingham	2	0	
1995–96	Gillingham	10	0	12 0
1996–97	Fulham	39	9	
1997–98	Fulham	7	0	46 9
1998–99	Brentford	22	6	22 6
1999–2000	Brighton & HA	38	12	
2000–01	Brighton & HA	16	0	54 12

HART, Gary (F) 132 28
H: 5 9 W: 12 08 b.Harlow 6-11-75
Source: Stansted.

1998–99	Brighton & HA	44	12	
1999–2000	Brighton & HA	43	9	
2000–01	Brighton & HA	45	7	132 28

JONES, Nathan (D) 148 6
H: 5 7 W: 10 05 b.Rhondda 28-5-73
Source: Cardiff C Trainee, Maesteg Park, Ton
Pentre, Merthyr T.

1995–96	Luton T	0	0	

Badajoz, Numaicia

1997–98	Southend U	39	0	
1998–99	Southend U	17	0	
1998–99	Scarborough	9	0	9 0
1999–2000	Southend U	43	2	99 2
2000–01	Brighton & HA	40	4	40 4

KUIPERS, Michels (G) 35 0
H: 6 2 W: 14 03 b.Amsterdam 26-6-74

1998–99	Bristol R	1	0	
1999–2000	Bristol R	0	0	1 0
2000–01	Brighton & HA	34	0	34 0

MAYO, Kerry (D) 169 9
H: 5 8 W: 11 07 b.Cuckfield 21-9-77
Source: Trainee.

1996–97	Brighton & HA	24	0	
1997–98	Brighton & HA	44	6	
1998–99	Brighton & HA	25	1	
1999–2000	Brighton & HA	31	1	
2000–01	Brighton & HA	45	1	169 9

McARTHUR, Duncan (M) 3 0
H: 5 9 W: 12 06 b.Brighton 6-5-81
Source: Trainee.

1998–99	Brighton & HA	3	0	
1999–2000	Brighton & HA	0	0	
2000–01	Brighton & HA	0	0	3 0

McPHEE, Christopher§ (M) 4 0
b.Eastbourne 20-3-83
Source: Scholarship.

1999–2000	Brighton & HA	4	0	
2000–01	Brighton & HA	0	0	4 0

MELTON, Steve (M) 36 1
H: 5 10 W: 10 08 b.Lincoln 31-10-78
Source: Trainee.

1995–96	Nottingham F	0	0	
1996–97	Nottingham F	0	0	
1997–98	Nottingham F	0	0	
1998–99	Nottingham F	1	0	
1999–2000	Nottingham F	0	0	3 0
1999–2000	Stoke C	5	0	5 0
2000–01	Brighton & HA	28	1	28 1

OATWAY, Charlie (M) 239 5
H: 5 7 W: 10 10 b.Hammersmith 28-11-73
Source: Yeading.

1994–95	Cardiff C	30	0	
1995–96	Cardiff C	2	0	32 0
1995–96	Torquay U	24	0	
1996–97	Torquay U	41	1	
1997–98	Torquay U	2	0	67 1
1997–98	Brentford	33	0	
1998–99	Brentford	24	0	57 0
1998–99	Lincoln C	3	0	3 0
1999–2000	Brighton & HA	42	4	
2000–01	Brighton & HA	38	0	80 4

PACKHAM, Will (G) 1 0
H: 6 2 W: 13 00 b.Brighton 13-1-81
Source: Trainee.

1999–2000	Brighton & HA	0	0	
2000–01	Brighton & HA	1	0	1 0

RAMSAY, Scott (F) 35 2
H: 6 0 W: 13 00 b.Hastings 16-10-80
Source: Trainee.
1999–2000 Brighton & HA 24 2
2000–01 Brighton & HA 11 0 **35 2**

ROGERS, Paul# (M) 337 31
H: 6 0 W: 13 02 b.Portsmouth 21-3-65
Source: Sutton U.
1991–92 Sheffield U 13 0
1992–93 Sheffield U 27 3
1993–94 Sheffield U 25 3
1994–95 Sheffield U 44 4
1995–96 Sheffield U 16 0 **125 10**
1995–96 Notts Co 21 2
1996–97 Notts Co 1 0 **22 2**
1996–97 Wigan Ath 20 3
1997–98 Wigan Ath 38 0
1998–99 Wigan Ath 42 2 **100 5**
1999–2000 Brighton & HA 45 8
2000–01 Brighton & HA 45 6 **90 14**

STANT, Phil† (F) 433 170
H: 5 11 W: 12 07 b.Bolton 13-10-62
Source: Camberley.
1982–83 Reading 4 2 **4 2**
From Army
1986–87 Hereford U 9 1
1987–88 Hereford U 39 9
1988–89 Hereford U 41 28 **89 38**
1989–90 Notts Co 22 6
1990–91 Notts Co 0 0 **22 6**
1990–91 *Blackpool* 12 5 **12 5**
1990–91 *Lincoln C* 4 0
1990–91 *Huddersfield T* 5 1 **5 1**
1990–91 Fulham 19 5 **19 5**
1991–92 Mansfield T 40 26
1992–93 Mansfield T 17 6
1992–93 Cardiff C 24 11
1993–94 Cardiff C 36 10
1993–94 *Mansfield T* 4 1 **61 33**
1994–95 Cardiff C 19 13 **79 34**
1994–95 Bury 20 13
1995–96 Bury 34 9
1996–97 Bury 8 1 **62 23**
1996–97 *Northampton T* 5 2 **5 2**
1996–97 Lincoln C 22 15
1997–98 Lincoln C 21 2
1998–99 Lincoln C 3 0
1999–2000 Lincoln C 18 3
2000–01 Lincoln C 0 0 **68 20**
2000–01 Brighton & HA 7 1 **7 1**

STEELE, Lee (F) 136 39
H: 5 8 W: 12 05 b.Liverpool 2-12-73
Source: Bootle, Northwich V.
1997–98 Shrewsbury T 38 13
1998–99 Shrewsbury T 38 13
1999–2000 Shrewsbury T 37 11 **113 37**
2000–01 Brighton & HA 23 2 **23 2**

THOMAS, Martin* (M) 194 18
H: 5 8 W: 11 00 b.Lyndhurst 12-9-73
Source: Trainee.
1992–93 Southampton 0 0
1993–94 Southampton 0 0
1993–94 Leyton Orient 5 2 **5 2**
1994–95 Fulham 23 3
1995–96 Fulham 37 5
1996–97 Fulham 26 0
1997–98 Fulham 4 0 **90 8**
1998–99 Swansea C 30 3
1999–2000 Swansea C 40 4
2000–01 Swansea C 21 1 **91 8**
2000–01 Brighton & HA 8 0 **8 0**

THOMAS, Rod* (F) 330 37
H: 5 6 W: 11 11 b.London 10-10-70
Source: Trainee. *Honours:* England Schools, Youth, Under-21.
1987–88 Watford 4 0
1988–89 Watford 18 2
1989–90 Watford 32 6
1990–91 Watford 24 1
1991–92 Watford 5 0
1991–92 *Gillingham* 8 1 **8 1**
1992–93 Watford 1 0 **84 9**
1993–94 Carlisle U 38 9
1994–95 Carlisle U 36 6
1995–96 Carlisle U 36 1
1996–97 Carlisle U 36 0 **146 16**
1997–98 Chester C 38 4
1998–99 Chester C 6 3 **44 7**
1998–99 Brighton & HA 12 3
1999–2000 Brighton & HA 34 1
2000–01 Brighton & HA 2 0 **48 4**

VIRGO, Adam (D) 6 0
H: 6 1 W: 12 00 b.Brighton 25-1-83
2000–01 Brighton & HA 6 0 **6 0**

WATSON, Paul (D) 237 15
H: 5 8 W: 10 10 b.Hastings 4-1-75
Source: Trainee.
1992–93 Gillingham 1 0
1993–94 Gillingham 14 0
1994–95 Gillingham 39 2
1995–96 Gillingham 8 0 **62 2**
1996–97 Fulham 44 3
1997–98 Fulham 6 1 **50 4**
1997–98 Brentford 25 0
1998–99 Brentford 12 0 **37 0**
1999–2000 Brighton & HA 42 4
2000–01 Brighton & HA 46 5 **88 9**

WICKS, Matthew (D) 61 3
H: 6 2 W: 13 05 b.Reading 8-9-78
Source: Manchester U Trainee. *Honours:* England Youth.
1995–96 Arsenal 0 0
1996–97 Arsenal 0 0
1997–98 Arsenal 0 0
1998–99 Crewe Alex 6 0 **6 0**
1998–99 Peterborough U 11 0
1999–2000 Peterborough U 20 0
2000–01 Peterborough U 0 0 **31 0**
2000–01 Brighton & HA 24 3 **24 3**

WILKINSON, Shaun§ (M) 3 0
H: 5 7 W: 11 00 b.Portsmouth 12-9-81
Source: Scholarship.
1999–2000 Brighton & HA 2 0
2000–01 Brighton & HA 1 0 **3 0**

ZAMORA, Bobby (F) 53 34
H: 6 1 W: 11 08 b.Barking 16-1-81
Source: Trainee.
1999–2000 Bristol R 4 0 **4 0**
1999–2000 *Brighton & HA* 6 6
2000–01 Brighton & HA 43 28 **49 34**

Scholars
Bartholomew, Philip O; Beck, Daniel G; Beech, Andrew P; Bridle, Nicholas P; Davis, Adam R; Greatwich, Christopher R; Hammond, Dean J; Harding, Daniel A; Hemsley, Kevin C; Hinshelwood, Adam; Jackson, Mark A; Marney, Daniel G; McCurdy, Conor M; McPhee, Christopher SI; Sansom, Rupert; Wilkinson, Shaun F; Wojciechowski, Stefan
Non-Contract
Adams, Michael R; Wilkins, Dean M
Player who does not hold a current contract but his registration has been retained by the club
McArthur, Duncan E

BRISTOL C

AMANKWAAH, Kevin (D) 19 0
H: 6 1 W: 12 00 b.London 19-5-82
Source: Scholar. *Honours:* England Youth.
1999–2000 Bristol C 5 0
2000–01 Bristol C 14 0 **19 0**

ASHLEY, Neil* (M) 0 0
H: 5 9 W: 11 04 b.Chesterfield 16-9-80
Source: Nottingham F Trainee.
1997–98 Leicester C 0 0
1998–99 Leicester C 0 0
1999–2000 Bristol C 0 0
2000–01 Bristol C 0 0

BALL, Alex‡ (D) 0 0
H: 5 9 W: 10 06 b.Bristol 4-8-81
Source: Trainee.
1999–2000 Bristol C 0 0
2000–01 Bristol C 0 0

BEADLE, Peter (F) 319 76
H: 6 2 W: 14 07 b.Lambeth 13-5-72
Source: Trainee.
1988–89 Gillingham 2 0
1989–90 Gillingham 10 2
1990–91 Gillingham 22 7
1991–92 Gillingham 33 5 **67 14**
1992–93 Tottenham H 0 0
1992–93 *Bournemouth* 9 2 **9 2**
1993–94 Tottenham H 0 0
1993–94 *Southend U* 8 1 **8 1**
1994–95 Tottenham H 0 0
1994–95 Watford 20 1
1995–96 Watford 3 0 **23 1**
1995–96 Bristol R 27 12
1996–97 Bristol R 42 12
1997–98 Bristol R 40 15 **109 39**
1998–99 Port Vale 23 6 **23 6**
1998–99 Notts Co 14 3
1999–2000 Notts Co 8 0 **22 3**
1999–2000 Bristol C 25 6
2000–01 Bristol C 33 4 **58 10**

BELL, Mickey (D) 425 40
H: 5 8 W: 11 13 b.Newcastle 15-11-71
Source: Trainee.
1989–90 Northampton T 6 0
1990–91 Northampton T 28 0
1991–92 Northampton T 30 4
1992–93 Northampton T 39 5
1993–94 Northampton T 38 0
1994–95 Northampton T 12 1 **153 10**
1994–95 Wycombe W 31 3
1995–96 Wycombe W 41 1
1996–97 Wycombe W 46 2 **118 6**
1997–98 Bristol C 44 10
1998–99 Bristol C 33 5
1999–2000 Bristol C 36 5
2000–01 Bristol C 41 4 **154 24**

BROWN, Aaron (M) 67 5
H: 5 10 W: 11 12 b.Bristol 14-3-80
Source: Trainee. *Honours:* England Schools.
1997–98 Bristol C 0 0
1998–99 Bristol C 14 0
1999–2000 Bristol C 13 2
1999–2000 *Exeter C* 5 1 **5 1**
2000–01 Bristol C 35 2 **62 4**

BROWN, Marvin (F) 7 0
H: 5 9 W: 11 01 b.Bristol 6-7-83
1999–2000 Bristol C 2 0
2000–01 Bristol C 5 0 **7 0**

BURKE, Andrew (M) 0 0
b.Camden 9-1-83
2000–01 Bristol C 0 0

BURNELL, Joe (D) 40 0
H: 5 9 W: 11 11 b.Bristol 10-10-80
Source: Trainee.
1999–2000 Bristol C 17 0
2000–01 Bristol C 23 0 **40 0**

BURNS, John (M) 14 0
H: 5 8 W: 11 04 b.Dublin 4-12-77
Source: Belvedere, Trainee.
1994–95 Nottingham F 0 0
1995–96 Nottingham F 0 0
1996–97 Nottingham F 0 0
1997–98 Nottingham F 0 0
1998–99 Nottingham F 0 0
1999–2000 Nottingham F 3 0 **3 0**
1999–2000 Bristol C 11 0
2000–01 Bristol C 0 0 **11 0**

CAREY, Louis (D) 212 3
H: 5 10 W: 12 05 b.Bristol 22-1-77
Source: Trainee. *Honours:* Scotland Under-21.
1995–96 Bristol C 23 0
1996–97 Bristol C 42 0
1997–98 Bristol C 38 0
1998–99 Bristol C 41 0
1999–2000 Bristol C 22 0
2000–01 Bristol C 46 3 **212 3**

CLIST, Simon (M) 47 4
H: 5 9 W: 11 00 b.Bournemouth 13-6-81
Source: Tottenham H Trainee.
1999–2000 Bristol C 9 0
2000–01 Bristol C 38 4 **47 4**

COLES, Daniel (D) 3 0
H: 6 1 W: 11 05 b.Bristol 30-10-81
Source: Scholarship.
1999–2000 Bristol C 1 0
2000–01 Bristol C 2 0 **3 0**

CORREIA, Albano (M) 0 0
b.Guinea Bissau 18-10-81
2000–01 Bristol C 0 0

DEW, Simon (M) 0 0
b.Bristol 21-7-83
Source: Scholar.
2000–01 Bristol C 0 0

DOHERTY, Tom (M) 54 3
H: 5 8 W: 11 07 b.Bristol 17-3-79
Source: Trainee.
1997–98 Bristol C 30 2
1998–99 Bristol C 23 1
1999–2000 Bristol C 1 0
2000–01 Bristol C 0 0 **54 3**

EDWARDS, Jamie (M) 0 0
b.Hereford 18-2-83
Source: Scholarship.
1999–2000 Bristol C 0 0
2000–01 Bristol C 0 0

FORTUNE, Clayton (D) 0 0
b.Forest Gate 10-11-82
Source: Tottenham H Scholar.
2000–01 Bristol C 0 0

GOODRIDGE, Greg (M)   173 20
H: 5 6   W: 11 02   b.Barbados 10-7-71
Source: Lambada. *Honours:* Barbados full caps.

1993–94	Torquay U	8	1	
1994–95	Torquay U	30	3	38 4
1995–96	QPR	7	1	7 1
1996–97	Bristol C	28	6	
1997–98	Bristol C	31	6	
1998–99	Bristol C	30	2	
1999–2000	Bristol C	21	0	
2000–01	Bristol C	7	0	117 14
2000–01	*Cheltenham T*	11	1	11 1

HARRHY, Nicholas (M)   0 0
b.Abergavenny 14-9-82

2000–01	Bristol C	0	0

HILL, Matt (D)   51 0
H: 5 8   W: 11 09   b.Bristol 26-3-81
Source: Trainee.

1998–99	Bristol C	3	0	
1999–2000	Bristol C	14	0	
2000–01	Bristol C	34	0	51 0

HOLLAND, Paul (M)   313 38
H: 5 9   W: 13 05   b.Lincoln 8-7-73
Source: School. *Honours:* England Schools, Under-21.

1990–91	Mansfield T	1	0	
1991–92	Mansfield T	38	6	
1992–93	Mansfield T	39	3	
1993–94	Mansfield T	38	7	
1994–95	Mansfield T	33	9	149 25
1995–96	Sheffield U	1	1	18 1
1995–96	Chesterfield	17	2	
1996–97	Chesterfield	25	3	
1997–98	Chesterfield	35	3	
1998–99	Chesterfield	33	3	
1999–2000	Chesterfield	4	0	114 11
1999–2000	Bristol C	27	0	
2000–01	Bristol C	5	1	32 1

HULBERT, Robin (M)   50 0
H: 5 9   W: 10 05   b.Plymouth 14-3-80
Source: Trainee. *Honours:* England Youth.

1997–98	Swindon T	1	0	
1997–98	*Newcastle U*	0	0	
1998–99	Swindon T	16	0	
1999–2000	Swindon T	12	0	29 0
1999–2000	Bristol C	2	0	
2000–01	Bristol C	19	0	21 0

JONES, Darren (D)   0 0
b.Newport 26-8-83
Source: Scholar.

2000–01	Bristol C	0	0

JONES, Steve (F)   191 46
H: 6 1   W: 12 07   b.Cambridge 17-3-70
Source: Billericay T.

1992–93	West Ham U	6	2	
1993–94	West Ham U	8	2	
1994–95	West Ham U	2	0	
1994–95	Bournemouth	30	9	
1995–96	Bournemouth	44	17	
1995–96	West Ham U	8	0	
1996–97	West Ham U	8	0	24 4
1996–97	Charlton Ath	2	0	
1997–98	Charlton Ath	23	7	
1997–98	*Bournemouth*	5	4	79 30
1998–99	Charlton Ath	25	1	
1999–2000	Charlton Ath	0	0	52 8
1999–2000	Bristol C	14	2	
1999–2000	*Brentford*	8	0	8 0
1999–2000	*Southend U*	9	2	9 2
2000–01	Bristol C	0	0	14 2
2000–01	*Wycombe W*	5	0	5 0

JORDAN, Thomas (M)   0 0
b.Manchester 24-5-81
Source: School.

2000–01	Bristol C	0	0

LAVIN, Gerard (D)   224 3
H: 5 10   W: 11 10   b.Corby 5-2-74
Source: Trainee. *Honours:* Scotland Under-21.

1991–92	Watford	1	0	
1992–93	Watford	28	0	
1993–94	Watford	46	3	
1994–95	Watford	35	0	
1995–96	Watford	16	0	126 3
1995–96	Millwall	20	0	
1996–97	Millwall	9	0	
1997–98	Millwall	7	0	
1998–99	Millwall	38	0	74 0
1999–2000	Bristol C	19	0	
2000–01	Bristol C	3	0	22 0
2000–01	*Wycombe W*	2	0	2 0

LEVER, Mark (D)   363 8
H: 6 3   W: 14 03   b.Hull 29-3-70
Source: Trainee.

1987–88	Grimsby T	1	0	
1988–89	Grimsby T	37	2	
1989–90	Grimsby T	38	2	
1990–91	Grimsby T	40	2	
1991–92	Grimsby T	36	0	
1992–93	Grimsby T	14	1	
1993–94	Grimsby T	22	0	
1994–95	Grimsby T	31	0	
1995–96	Grimsby T	24	1	
1996–97	Grimsby T	21	0	
1997–98	Grimsby T	38	0	
1998–99	Grimsby T	24	0	
1999–2000	Grimsby T	35	0	361 8
2000–01	Bristol C	2	0	2 0

LOURENCO (F)   3 1
b.Luanda 5-6-83
Source: Sporting Lisbon.

2000–01	Bristol C	3	1	3 1

MALESSA, Antony* (G)   1 0
H: 5 11   W: 11 12   b.Ascot 13-11-80

1999–2000	Bristol C	0	0	
2000–01	Bristol C	1	0	1 0

MATTHEWS, Lee (F)   19 3
H: 6 2   W: 13 03   b.Middlesbrough 6-1-79
Source: Trainee. *Honours:* England Youth.

1995–96	Leeds U	0	0	
1996–97	Leeds U	0	0	
1997–98	Leeds U	3	0	
1998–99	Leeds U	0	0	
1998–99	*Notts Co*	5	0	5 0
1999–2000	Leeds U	0	0	
1999–2000	*Gillingham*	5	0	5 0
2000–01	Leeds U	0	0	3 0
2000–01	Bristol C	6	3	6 3

MEECHAN, Alex‡ (F)   14 4
H: 5 8   W: 10 06   b.Plymouth 29-1-80
Source: Trainee.

1997–98	Swindon T	1	0	1 0
1998–99	Bristol C	1	0	
1999–2000	Bristol C	12	4	
2000–01	Bristol C	0	0	13 4

MERCER, Billy (G)   282 0
H: 6 1   W: 11 00   b.Liverpool 22-5-69
Source: Trainee.

1987–88	Liverpool	0	0	
1988–89	Liverpool	0	0	
1988–89	Rotherham U	0	0	
1989–90	Rotherham U	2	0	
1990–91	Rotherham U	13	0	
1991–92	Rotherham U	35	0	
1992–93	Rotherham U	36	0	
1993–94	Rotherham U	17	0	
1994–95	Rotherham U	1	0	104 0
1994–95	Sheffield U	3	0	
1994–95	*Nottingham F*	0	0	
1995–96	Sheffield U	1	0	4 0
1995–96	Chesterfield	34	0	
1996–97	Chesterfield	35	0	
1997–98	Chesterfield	36	0	
1998–99	Chesterfield	44	0	
1999–2000	Chesterfield	0	0	149 0
1999–2000	Bristol C	25	0	
2000–01	Bristol C	0	0	25 0

MILLEN, Keith (D)   527 26
H: 6 1   W: 13 02   b.Croydon 26-9-66
Source: Juniors.

1984–85	Brentford	17	0	
1985–86	Brentford	32	2	
1986–87	Brentford	39	2	
1987–88	Brentford	40	3	
1988–89	Brentford	36	3	
1989–90	Brentford	32	0	
1990–91	Brentford	32	2	
1991–92	Brentford	34	1	
1992–93	Brentford	43	4	
1993–94	Brentford	0	0	305 17
1993–94	Watford	10	0	
1994–95	Watford	31	1	
1995–96	Watford	33	0	
1996–97	Watford	42	2	
1997–98	Watford	38	1	
1998–99	Watford	11	1	
1999–2000	Watford	0	0	165 0
1999–2000	Bristol C	28	2	
2000–01	Bristol C	29	2	57 4

MORTIMER, Paul* (M)   262 35
H: 5 9   W: 12 13   b.Kensington 8-5-68
Source: Fulham Apprentice. *Honours:* England Under-21.

1987–88	Charlton Ath	12	0	
1988–89	Charlton Ath	33	5	
1989–90	Charlton Ath	36	5	
1990–91	Charlton Ath	32	7	
1991–92	Aston Villa	12	1	12 1
1991–92	Crystal Palace	21	2	
1992–93	Crystal Palace	1	0	
1992–93	*Brentford*	6	0	6 0
1993–94	Crystal Palace	0	0	22 2
1994–95	Charlton Ath	26	4	
1995–96	Charlton Ath	19	5	
1996–97	Charlton Ath	11	1	
1997–98	Charlton Ath	13	4	
1998–99	Charlton Ath	17	1	199 32
1999–2000	Bristol C	23	0	
2000–01	Bristol C	0	0	23 0

MURRAY, Scott (M)   146 19
H: 5 8   W: 11 00   b.Aberdeen 26-5-74
Source: Fraserburgh.

1993–94	Aston Villa	0	0	
1994–95	Aston Villa	0	0	
1995–96	Aston Villa	3	0	
1996–97	Aston Villa	1	0	
1997–98	Aston Villa	0	0	4 0
1997–98	Bristol C	23	0	
1998–99	Bristol C	32	3	
1999–2000	Bristol C	41	6	
2000–01	Bristol C	46	10	142 19

ODEJAYI, Kayode (F)   6 0
H: 6 2   W: 12 02   b.Ibadon 21-2-82
Source: Scholarship.

1999–2000	Bristol C	3	0	
2000–01	Bristol C	3	0	6 0

PEACOCK, Lee (F)   208 53
H: 6 1   W: 13 12   b.Paisley 9-10-76
Source: Trainee.

1993–94	Carlisle U	1	0	
1994–95	Carlisle U	7	0	
1995–96	Carlisle U	22	2	
1996–97	Carlisle U	44	9	
1997–98	Carlisle U	2	0	76 11
1997–98	Mansfield T	32	5	
1998–99	Mansfield T	45	17	
1999–2000	Mansfield T	12	7	89 29
1999–2000	Manchester C	8	0	8 0
2000–01	Bristol C	35	13	35 13

PHILLIPS, Steve (G)   78 0
H: 6 1   W: 12 07   b.Bath 6-5-78
Source: Paulton R.

1996–97	Bristol C	0	0	
1997–98	Bristol C	0	0	
1998–99	Bristol C	15	0	
1999–2000	Bristol C	21	0	
2000–01	Bristol C	42	0	78 0

PIKE, James (F)   0 0
H: 5 9   W: 11 00   b.Bristol 15-11-82
Source: Scholarship.

1999–2000	Bristol C	0	0
2000–01	Bristol C	0	0

SCOPE, Tynan‡ (G)   0 0
H: 6 3   W: 13 08   b.Sydney 30-7-79

1997–98	Coventry C	0	0
1998–99	Coventry C	0	0
1999–2000	Bristol C	0	0
2000–01	Bristol C	0	0

SHANAHAN, Aaron (M)   0 0
b.Coventry 10-9-82
Source: Coventry C Scholar.

2000–01	Bristol C	0	0

SHEPPARD, Kyle (D)   0 0
b.Cardiff 4-12-82
Source: Chelsea Scholar.

2000–01	Bristol C	0	0

SPENCER, Damien (F)   19 1
H: 6 1   W: 14 05   b.Ascot 19-9-81
Source: Scholarship.

1999–2000	Bristol C	9	1	
2000–01	Bristol C	4	0	13 1
2000–01	*Exeter C*	6	0	6 0

TAYLOR, Shaun# (D)   517 53
H: 6 1   W: 12 10   b.Plymouth 26-2-63
Source: Bideford.

1986–87	Exeter C	23	0	
1987–88	Exeter C	41	1	
1988–89	Exeter C	46	6	
1989–90	Exeter C	45	5	
1990–91	Exeter C	45	4	200 16
1991–92	Swindon T	42	4	
1992–93	Swindon T	46	11	
1993–94	Swindon T	42	4	
1994–95	Swindon T	37	4	
1995–96	Swindon T	43	7	
1996–97	Swindon T	2	0	212 30
1996–97	Bristol C	29	1	
1997–98	Bristol C	43	2	
1998–99	Bristol C	8	0	
1999–2000	Bristol C	25	4	
2000–01	Bristol C	0	0	105 7

TESTIMITANU, Ivan (M) 114 26
H: 5 10 W: 11 02 b.Moldova 27-4-74
Honours: Moldova 35 full caps, 5 goals.

1995-96	Zimbru Chisinau	28	11		
1996-97	Zimbru Chisinau	25	4		
1997-98	Zimbru Chisinau	26	9	79	24
1998-99	Bristol C	8	0		
1999-2000	Bristol C	16	2		
2000-01	Bristol C	11	0	35	2

THORPE, Tony (F) 237 93
H: 5 8 W: 12 06 b.Leicester 10-4-74
Source: Leicester C.

1992-93	Luton T	0	0		
1993-94	Luton T	14	1		
1994-95	Luton T	4	0		
1995-96	Luton T	33	7		
1996-97	Luton T	41	28		
1997-98	Luton T	28	14		
1997-98	Fulham	13	3	13	3
1998-99	Bristol C	16	2		
1998-99	*Reading*	6	1	6	1
1998-99	*Luton T*	8	4		
1999-2000	Bristol C	31	13		
1999-2000	*Luton T*	14	9	132	55
2000-01	Bristol C	39	19	86	34

TINNION, Brian (M) 490 45
H: 5 11 W: 12 13 b.Stanley 23-2-68
Source: Apprentice.

1985-86	Newcastle U	0	0		
1986-87	Newcastle U	3	0		
1987-88	Newcastle U	16	1		
1988-89	Newcastle U	13	1	32	2
1988-89	Bradford C	14	1		
1989-90	Bradford C	37	5		
1990-91	Bradford C	41	5		
1991-92	Bradford C	26	8		
1992-93	Bradford C	37	3	145	22
1992-93	Bristol C	11	2		
1993-94	Bristol C	41	5		
1994-95	Bristol C	35	2		
1995-96	Bristol C	30	3		
1996-97	Bristol C	32	1		
1997-98	Bristol C	44	3		
1998-99	Bristol C	35	1		
1999-2000	Bristol C	43	3		
2000-01	Bristol C	42	1	313	21

TURNER, Danny‡ (M) 0 0
H: 6 3 W: 13 02 b.Maidstone 8-1-81

| 1999-2000 | Bristol C | 0 | 0 | | |
| 2000-01 | Bristol C | 0 | 0 | | |

WOODMAN, Craig (M) 2 0
b.Tiverton 22-12-82
Source: Trainee.

| 1999-2000 | Bristol C | 0 | 0 | | |
| 2000-01 | Bristol C | 2 | 0 | 2 | 0 |

WRIGHT, Ben‡ (F) 2 0
H: 6 1 W: 13 07 b.Munster 1-7-80

1998-99	Bristol C	0	0		
1999-2000	Bristol C	2	0		
2000-01	Bristol C	0	0	2	0

Scholars
Blake, David J; Burnett, Michael A; Claridge, Jamie L; Cleverley, Benjamin R; Gibbs, Stuart J; Hawkins, Darren; Horseman, David J; King, Rohan; Lindsay, Dean L; Palmer, Marc K; Platt, Daniel G; Reynolds, Nicholas; Rosenior, Liam J; Shorey, Adam C; Simpson, Sekani; Trace, Benjamin; Williams, Paul J; Wilson, Martin J

BRISTOL R

ANDREASSON, Marcus (D) 27 1
H: 6 4 W: 13 02 b.Liberia 13-7-78

1997	Osters	8	0		
1998	Osters	4	0	12	0
1998-99	Bristol R	5	0		
1999-2000	Bristol R	6	0		
2000-01	Bristol R	4	1	15	1

ASTAFJEVS, Vitalijs (M) 237 68
H: 5 11 W: 12 05 b.Riga 3-4-71
Honours: Latvia 75 full caps, 9 goals.

1992	Skonto Riga	21	0		
1993	Skonto Riga	11	5		
1994	Skonto Riga	21	7		
1995	Skonto Riga	28	19		
1996	Skonto Riga	18	12		
1996-97	*FK Austria*	26	1	26	1
1997	Skonto Riga	14	1		
1998	Skonto Riga	23	7		
1999	Skonto Riga	18	9	154	60
1999-2000	Bristol R	16	2		
2000-01	Bristol R	41	5	57	7

BRYANT, Simon (M) 45 1
H: 5 11 W: 12 11 b.Bristol 22-11-82
Source: Scholarship. *Honours:* England Youth.

| 1999-2000 | Bristol R | 15 | 0 | | |
| 2000-01 | Bristol R | 30 | 1 | 45 | 1 |

CAMERON, Martin (F) 14 2
H: 6 1 W: 12 12 b.Dunfermline 16-6-78

| 2000-01 | Bristol R | 14 | 2 | 14 | 2 |

CHALLIS, Trevor (D) 113 1
H: 5 8 W: 11 06 b.Paddington 23-10-75
Source: Trainee. *Honours:* England Youth, Under-21.

1994-95	QPR	0	0		
1995-96	QPR	11	0		
1996-97	QPR	2	0		
1997-98	QPR	0	0	13	0
1998-99	Bristol R	38	0		
1999-2000	Bristol R	40	1		
2000-01	Bristol R	22	0	100	1

DAGNOGO, Moussa‡ (F) 2 0
b.Paris 30-1-72

| 2000-01 | Bristol R | 2 | 0 | 2 | 0 |

ELLINGTON, Nathan (F) 89 20
H: 5 10 W: 12 10 b.Bradford 2-7-81
Source: Walton & Hersham.

1998-99	Bristol R	10	1		
1999-2000	Bristol R	37	4		
2000-01	Bristol R	42	15	89	20

ELLIS, Clinton (F) 15 1
H: 5 6 W: 12 06 b.Ealing 7-7-77

| 1999-2000 | Bristol R | 0 | 0 | | |
| 2000-01 | Bristol R | 15 | 1 | 15 | 1 |

FORAN, Mark (D) 90 3
H: 6 3 W: 13 04 b.Aldershot 30-10-73
Source: Trainee.

1991-92	Millwall	0	0		
1992-93	Millwall	0	0		
1993-94	Millwall	0	0		
1993-94	Sheffield U	0	0		
1994-95	Sheffield U	4	1		
1994-95	*Rotherham U*	3	0	3	0
1995-96	Sheffield U	7	0	11	1
1995-96	*Wycombe W*	5	0	5	0
1995-96	Peterborough U	17	1		
1996-97	Peterborough U	4	0		
1996-97	*Lincoln C*	2	0	2	0
1996-97	*Oldham Ath*	1	0	1	0
1997-98	Peterborough U	4	0	25	1
1997-98	Crewe Alex	12	1		
1998-99	Crewe Alex	6	0		
1999-2000	Crewe Alex	13	0	31	1
2000-01	Bristol R	12	0	12	0

FOSTER, Stephen (D) 169 6
H: 6 1 W: 13 00 b.Mansfield 3-12-74
Source: Trainee.

1993-94	Mansfield T	5	0	5	0
From Woking					
1997-98	Bristol R	34	0		
1998-99	Bristol R	43	1		
1999-2000	Bristol R	43	1		
2000-01	Bristol R	44	4	164	6

GALL, Kevin (F) 10 2
H: 5 9 W: 11 01 b.Merthyr 4-2-82
Source: Trainee.

1998-99	Newcastle U	0	0		
1999-2000	Newcastle U	0	0		
2000-01	Newcastle U	0	0		
2000-01	Bristol R	10	2	10	2

HARDCASTLE, Mark° (D) 0 0
b.Gloucester 21-4-83

| 2000-01 | Bristol R | 0 | 0 | | |

HILLIER, David (M) 227 6
H: 5 10 W: 12 07 b.Blackheath 19-12-69
Source: Trainee. *Honours:* England Under-21.

1987-88	Arsenal	0	0		
1988-89	Arsenal	0	0		
1989-90	Arsenal	0	0		
1990-91	Arsenal	16	0		
1991-92	Arsenal	27	1		
1992-93	Arsenal	30	1		
1993-94	Arsenal	15	0		
1994-95	Arsenal	9	0		
1995-96	Arsenal	5	0		
1996-97	Arsenal	2	0	104	2
1996-97	Portsmouth	21	2		
1997-98	Portsmouth	30	2		
1998-99	Portsmouth	16	0	67	4
1998-99	Bristol R	13	0		
1999-2000	Bristol R	39	0		
2000-01	Bristol R	4	0	56	0

HOGG, Lewis (M) 34 3
H: 5 8 W: 10 07 b.Bristol 13-9-82
Source: Trainee.

| 1999-2000 | Bristol R | 0 | 0 | | |
| 2000-01 | Bristol R | 34 | 3 | 34 | 3 |

JOHANSEN, Rune‡ (F) 22 8
H: 6 0 W: 12 02 b.Norway 1-4-78

1996	Tromso	3	0		
1997	Tromso	3	0		
1998	Tromso	0	0		
1999	Tromso	0	0		
2000	Tromso	14	8	20	8
2000-01	Bristol R	2	0	2	0

JONES, Scott (D) 128 7
H: 5 10 W: 12 01 b.Sheffield 1-5-75
Source: Trainee.

1993-94	Barnsley	0	0		
1994-95	Barnsley	0	0		
1995-96	Barnsley	4	0		
1996-97	Barnsley	18	0		
1997-98	Barnsley	12	1		
1997-98	*Mansfield T*	6	0	6	0
1997-98	*Notts Co*	0	0		
1998-99	Barnsley	29	3		
1999-2000	Barnsley	20	0		
2000-01	Barnsley	0	0	83	4
2000-01	Bristol R	39	3	39	3

LEE, Christian° (F) 79 11
H: 6 2 W: 11 07 b.Aylesbury 8-10-76
Source: Doncaster R.

1995-96	Northampton T	5	0		
1996-97	Northampton T	29	7		
1997-98	Northampton T	6	0		
1998-99	Northampton T	19	1	59	8
1999-2000	Gillingham	3	0		
2000-01	Gillingham	0	0	3	0
2000-01	*Rochdale*	5	1	5	1
2000-01	*Leyton Orient*	3	0	3	0
2000-01	Bristol R	9	2	9	2

MAUGE, Ronnie (M) 331 26
H: 5 10 W: 10 06 b.Islington 10-3-69
Source: Trainee. *Honours:* Trinidad & Tobago full caps.

1987-88	Charlton Ath	0	0		
1988-89	Fulham	13	0		
1989-90	Fulham	37	2	50	2
1990-91	Bury	29	6		
1991-92	Bury	22	0		
1991-92	*Manchester C*	0	0		
1992-93	Bury	13	1		
1993-94	Bury	26	3		
1994-95	Bury	18	0	108	10
1995-96	Plymouth Arg	37	7		
1996-97	Plymouth Arg	35	3		
1997-98	Plymouth Arg	31	1		
1998-99	Plymouth Arg	32	3	135	14
1999-2000	Bristol R	22	0		
2000-01	Bristol R	16	0	38	0

McKEEVER, Mark (M) 34 2
H: 5 9 W: 11 08 b.Derry 16-11-78
Source: Trainee. *Honours:* Eire Under-21.

1996-97	Peterborough U	3	0	3	0
1996-97	Sheffield W	0	0		
1997-98	Sheffield W	0	0		
1998-99	Sheffield W	3	0		
1998-99	*Bristol R*	7	0		
1998-99	*Reading*	7	2	7	2
1999-2000	Sheffield W	2	0		
2000-01	Sheffield W	0	0	5	0
2000-01	Bristol R	12	0	19	0

O'REILLY, Alex° (G) 7 0
b.Epping 15-9-79
Source: Trainee. *Honours:* Eire Youth, Under-21.

1998-99	West Ham U	0	0		
1999-2000	West Ham U	0	0		
1999-2000	*Northampton T*	7	0	7	0
2000-01	West Ham U	0	0		
2000-01	*Wigan Ath*	0	0		
2000-01	Bristol R	0	0		

PARKIN, Brian‡ (G) 396 0
H: 6 4 W: 14 05 b.Birkenhead 12-10-65
Source: Local.

1982-83	Oldham Ath	0	0		
1983-84	Oldham Ath	5	0		
1984-85	Oldham Ath	1	0	6	0
1984-85	Crewe Alex	12	0		
1985-86	Crewe Alex	39	0		
1986-87	Crewe Alex	44	0		
1987-88	Crewe Alex	3	0	98	0
1987-88	Crystal Palace	0	0		
1988-89	Crystal Palace	19	0		
1989-90	Crystal Palace	1	0	20	0
1989-90	Bristol R	30	0		
1990-91	Bristol R	39	0		
1991-92	Bristol R	43	0		

1992–93	Bristol R	26	0		
1993–94	Bristol R	43	0		
1994–95	Bristol R	40	0		
1995–96	Bristol R	20	0		
1996–97	Wycombe W	24	0		
1997–98	Wycombe W	1	0		
1998–99	Wycombe W	0	0	25	0
1998–99	Notts Co	1	0	1	0
1999–2000	Bristol R	3	0		
2000–01	Bristol R	2	0	246	0

PETHICK, Robbie* (D)   252   5
H: 5 10   W: 12 07   b.Tavistock 8-9-70
Source: Weymouth.

1993–94	Portsmouth	18	0		
1994–95	Portsmouth	44	1		
1995–96	Portsmouth	38	0		
1996–97	Portsmouth	35	0		
1997–98	Portsmouth	44	2		
1998–99	Portsmouth	10	0	189	3
1998–99	Bristol R	9	0		
1999–2000	Bristol R	41	2		
2000–01	Bristol R	13	0	63	2

PIERRE, Nigel (F)   3   0
H: 5 11   W: 11 11   b.Port of Spain 2-6-79
Source: Joe Public.

| 1999–2000 | Bristol R | 3 | 0 | | |
| 2000–01 | Bristol R | 0 | 0 | 3 | 0 |

PLUMMER, Dwayne (F)   34   1
H: 5 9   W: 10 12   b.Bristol 12-5-78
Source: Trainee.

1995–96	Bristol C	11	0		
1996–97	Bristol C	2	0		
1997–98	Bristol C	1	0		
1998–99	Bristol C	0	0		
1999–2000	Bristol C	0	0	14	0

From St'age, Cheshm

| 2000–01 | Bristol R | 20 | 1 | 20 | 1 |

PRITCHARD, David# (D)   163   1
H: 5 7   W: 12 00   b.Wolverhampton 27-5-72
Source: Telford U. Honours: Wales B.

1990–91	WBA	0	0		
1991–92	WBA	5	0	5	0
1993–94	Bristol R	11	0		
1994–95	Bristol R	43	0		
1995–96	Bristol R	12	0		
1996–97	Bristol R	26	0		
1997–98	Bristol R	33	0		
1998–99	Bristol R	12	0		
1999–2000	Bristol R	21	1		
2000–01	Bristol R	0	0	158	1

RICHARDS, Justin (F)   8   0
H: 6 0   W: 11 10   b.Sandwell 16-10-80
Source: Trainee.

1998–99	WBA	1	0		
1999–2000	WBA	0	0		
2000–01	WBA	0	0	1	0
2000–01	Bristol R	7	0	7	0

ROSE, Stephen* (D)   0   0
H: 6 00   W: 10 10   b.Salford 23-11-80
Source: Trainee.

| 1999–2000 | Manchester U | 0 | 0 | | |
| 2000–01 | Bristol R | 0 | 0 | | |

SHORE, Jamie (M)   24   2
H: 5 9   W: 12 05   b.Bristol 1-9-77
Source: Trainee. Honours: England Youth.

1994–95	Norwich C	0	0		
1995–96	Norwich C	0	0		
1996–97	Norwich C	0	0		
1997–98	Norwich C	0	0		
1998–99	Bristol R	24	2		
1999–2000	Bristol R	0	0		
2000–01	Bristol R	0	0	24	2

SMITH, Mark (D)   14   0
H: 6 0   W: 13 07   b.Bristol 13-9-79
Source: Trainee.

1998–99	Bristol R	14	0		
1999–2000	Bristol R	0	0		
2000–01	Bristol R	0	0	14	0

THOMSON, Andy (D)   211   8
H: 6 3   W: 14 03   b.Swindon 28-3-74
Source: Trainee.

1992–93	Swindon T	0	0		
1993–94	Swindon T	1	0		
1994–95	Swindon T	21	0		
1995–96	Swindon T	0	0	22	0
1995–96	Portsmouth	16	0		
1996–97	Portsmouth	28	1		
1997–98	Portsmouth	35	2		
1998–99	Portsmouth	14	0	93	3
1998–99	Bristol R	21	1		
1999–2000	Bristol R	43	3		
2000–01	Bristol R	32	1	96	5

TREES, Robert‡ (M)   46   1
H: 5 10   W: 12 07   b.Manchester 18-12-77
Source: Trainee.

| 1996–97 | Manchester U | 0 | 0 | | |

From Witton Alb.

1998–99	Bristol R	36	0		
1999–2000	Bristol R	10	1		
2000–01	Bristol R	0	0	46	1

TROUGHT, Michael (D)   13   0
H: 6 2   W: 14 03   b.Bristol 19-10-80
Source: Trainee.

1998–99	Bristol R	9	0		
1999–2000	Bristol R	4	0		
2000–01	Bristol R	0	0	13	0

VAALER, Roger‡ (G)   76   0
H: 6 3   W: 14 03   b.Lorenskog 23-1-71
Source: Lillestrom.

1996	Skeid	26	0		
1997	Skeid	23	0		
1998	Skeid	0	0		
1999	Skeid	26	0		
2000	Skeid	1	0	76	0
2000–01	Bristol R	0	0		

WALTERS, Mark (M)   574   128
H: 5 9   W: 11 05   b.Birmingham 2-6-64
Source: Apprentice. Honours: England Schools, Youth, Under-21, B. 1 full cap.

1981–82	Aston Villa	1	0		
1982–83	Aston Villa	22	1		
1983–84	Aston Villa	37	8		
1984–85	Aston Villa	36	10		
1985–86	Aston Villa	40	10		
1986–87	Aston Villa	21	3		
1987–88	Aston Villa	24	7	181	39
1987–88	Rangers	18	7		
1988–89	Rangers	31	8		
1989–90	Rangers	27	5		
1990–91	Rangers	30	12	106	32
1991–92	Liverpool	25	3		
1992–93	Liverpool	34	11		
1993–94	Liverpool	17	0		
1993–94	*Stoke C*	9	2	9	2
1994–95	Liverpool	18	0		
1994–95	*Wolverhampton W*	11	3	11	3
1995–96	Liverpool	0	0	94	14
1995–96	Southampton	5	0	5	0
1996–97	Swindon T	27	7		
1997–98	Swindon T	34	6		
1998–99	Swindon T	38	10		
1999–2000	Swindon T	13	2	112	25
1999–2000	Bristol R	30	9		
2000–01	Bristol R	26	4	56	13

WILSON, Che (D)   59   0
H: 5 11   W: 11 10   b.Ely 17-1-79
Source: Trainee.

1997–98	Norwich C	0	0		
1998–99	Norwich C	17	0		
1999–2000	Norwich C	5	0	22	0
2000–01	Bristol R	37	0	37	0

Scholars
Arndale, Neil D; Chambers, Andrew J; Clarke, Ryan J; Cordy, John D; Cozens, Leon; Crowley, Jonathan; Davis, Anthony S; Gilroy, David M; Greaves, Daniel G; Parker, Christian; Pope, Mark; Powell, Gary N; Scott, Robert T; Shore, Andrew J; Spencer, Lance JM; Zabek, James K

BURNLEY

ARMSTRONG, Gordon# (D)   511   58
H: 6 0   W: 13 04   b.Newcastle 15-7-67
Source: Apprentice.

1984–85	Sunderland	4	0		
1985–86	Sunderland	14	2		
1986–87	Sunderland	41	5		
1987–88	Sunderland	37	5		
1988–89	Sunderland	45	8		
1989–90	Sunderland	46	8		
1990–91	Sunderland	35	6		
1991–92	Sunderland	40	10		
1992–93	Sunderland	45	3		
1993–94	Sunderland	15	1		
1994–95	Sunderland	1	0	349	50
1995–96	*Bristol C*	6	0	6	0
1995–96	*Northampton T*	4	1	4	1
1996–97	Bury	32	2		
1997–98	Bury	37	2		
1998–99	Bury	2	0	71	4
1998–99	Burnley	40	2		
1999–2000	Burnley	22	1		
2000–01	Burnley	19	0	81	3

BALL, Kevin (M)   502   27
H: 5 10   W: 12 04   b.Hastings 12-11-64
Source: Apprentice.

1983–84	Portsmouth	1	0		
1984–85	Portsmouth	0	0		
1985–86	Portsmouth	9	0		
1986–87	Portsmouth	16	0		
1987–88	Portsmouth	29	1		
1988–89	Portsmouth	14	1		
1989–90	Sunderland	36	2	105	4
1990–91	Sunderland	33	3		
1991–92	Sunderland	33	1		
1992–93	Sunderland	43	3		
1993–94	Sunderland	36	0		
1994–95	Sunderland	42	2		
1995–96	Sunderland	36	4		
1996–97	Sunderland	32	3		
1997–98	Sunderland	31	3		
1998–99	Sunderland	42	2		
1999–2000	Sunderland	11	0	339	21
1999–2000	Fulham	18	0	18	0
2000–01	Burnley	40	2	40	2

BOARDMAN, John* (D)   0   0
b.Liverpool 6-9-80
Source: Trainee.

1998–99	Liverpool	0	0		
1999–2000	Liverpool	0	0		
2000–01	Burnley	0	0		

BRANCH, Graham (F)   222   23
H: 6 2   W: 12 02   b.Liverpool 12-2-72
Source: Heswall.

1991–92	Tranmere R	4	0		
1992–93	Tranmere R	3	0		
1992–93	Bury	4	1	4	1
1993–94	Tranmere R	13	0		
1994–95	Tranmere R	1	0		
1995–96	Tranmere R	21	2		
1996–97	Tranmere R	35	5		
1997–98	Tranmere R	25	3	102	10
1997–98	*Wigan Ath*	3	0	3	0
1998–99	Stockport Co	14	3	14	3
1998–99	Burnley	20	1		
1999–2000	Burnley	44	3		
2000–01	Burnley	35	5	99	9

BRISCOE, Lee (D)   112   2
H: 5 11   W: 11 12   b.Pontefract 30-9-75
Source: Trainee. Honours: England Under-21.

1993–94	Sheffield W	1	0		
1994–95	Sheffield W	6	0		
1995–96	Sheffield W	26	0		
1996–97	Sheffield W	6	0		
1997–98	Sheffield W	7	0		
1997–98	*Manchester C*	5	1	5	1
1998–99	Sheffield W	16	1		
1999–2000	Sheffield W	16	0	78	1
2000–01	Burnley	29	0	29	0

COOK, Paul (M)   524   50
H: 5 11   W: 11 00   b.Liverpool 22-6-67
Source: Marine.

1984–85	Wigan Ath	2	0		
1985–86	Wigan Ath	13	2		
1986–87	Wigan Ath	27	4		
1987–88	Wigan Ath	41	8	83	14
1988–89	Norwich C	4	0		
1989–90	Norwich C	2	0	6	0
1989–90	Wolverhampton W	28	2		
1990–91	Wolverhampton W	42	6		
1991–92	Wolverhampton W	43	8		
1992–93	Wolverhampton W	44	1		
1993–94	Wolverhampton W	36	2	193	19
1994–95	Coventry C	34	3		
1995–96	Coventry C	3	0	37	3
1995–96	Tranmere R	15	1		
1996–97	Tranmere R	36	3		
1997–98	Tranmere R	9	0	60	4
1997–98	Stockport Co	25	3		
1998–99	Stockport Co	24	0	49	3
1998–99	*Burnley*	12	1		
1999–2000	Burnley	44	3		
2000–01	Burnley	40	3	96	7

COX, Ian (D)   242   18
H: 6 0   W: 12 00   b.Croydon 25-3-71
Source: Carshalton Ath. Honours: Trinidad & Tobago full caps.

1993–94	Crystal Palace	0	0		
1994–95	Crystal Palace	11	0		
1995–96	Crystal Palace	4	0	15	0
1995–96	Bournemouth	8	0		
1996–97	Bournemouth	44	8		
1997–98	Bournemouth	46	3		
1998–99	Bournemouth	46	5		
1999–2000	Bournemouth	28	0	172	16
1999–2000	Burnley	17	1		
2000–01	Burnley	38	1	55	2

CRICHTON, Paul (G) 412 0
H: 6 1 W: 13 08 b.Pontefract 3-10-68
Source: Apprentice.

1986–87	Nottingham F	0	0		
1986–87	*Notts Co*	5	0	5	0
1986–87	*Darlington*	5	0		
1986–87	*Peterborough U*	4	0		
1987–88	Nottingham F	0	0		
1987–88	*Darlington*	3	0	8	0
1987–88	*Swindon T*	4	0	4	0
1987–88	*Rotherham U*	6	0	6	0
1988–89	Nottingham F	0	0		
1988–89	*Torquay U*	13	0	13	0
1988–89	Peterborough U	31	0		
1989–90	Peterborough U	16	0	51	0
1990–91	Doncaster R	20	0		
1991–92	Doncaster R	16	0		
1992–93	Doncaster R	41	0	77	0
1993–94	Grimsby T	46	0		
1994–95	Grimsby T	43	0		
1995–96	Grimsby T	44	0		
1996–97	Grimsby T	0	0	133	0
1996–97	WBA	30	0		
1997–98	WBA	2	0		
1997–98	*Aston Villa*	0	0		
1998–99	WBA	0	0	32	0
1998–99	Burnley	29	0		
1999–2000	Burnley	46	0		
2000–01	Burnley	8	0	83	0

DAVIS, Steve (D) 423 59
H: 6 2 W: 14 07 b.Hexham 30-10-68
Source: Trainee.

1987–88	Southampton	0	0		
1988–89	Southampton	0	0		
1989–90	Southampton	4	0		
1989–90	*Burnley*	0	0		
1990–91	Southampton	3	0	7	0
1990–91	*Notts Co*	2	0	2	0
1991–92	Burnley	40	6		
1992–93	Burnley	37	2		
1993–94	Burnley	42	7		
1994–95	Burnley	43	7		
1995–96	Luton T	36	2		
1996–97	Luton T	44	8		
1997–98	Luton T	38	5		
1998–99	Luton T	20	6	138	21
1998–99	Burnley	19	4		
1999–2000	Burnley	42	7		
2000–01	Burnley	44	5	276	38

DEVENNEY, Michael* (D) 0 0
H: 5 8 W: 10 05 b.Bolton 8-2-80
Source: Trainee.

1998–99	Burnley	0	0		
1999–2000	Burnley	0	0		
2000–01	Burnley	0	0		

JEPSON, Ronnie* (D) 354 86
H: 6 0 W: 14 00 b.Stoke 12-5-63
Source: Nantwich T.

1988–89	Port Vale	2	0		
1989–90	Port Vale	5	0		
1989–90	*Peterborough U*	18	5	18	5
1990–91	Port Vale	15	0	22	0
1990–91	Preston NE	14	3		
1991–92	Preston NE	24	5	38	8
1992–93	Exeter C	38	8		
1993–94	Exeter C	16	13	54	21
1993–94	Huddersfield T	23	5		
1994–95	Huddersfield T	41	19		
1995–96	Huddersfield T	31	9	107	36
1996–97	Bury	31	9		
1997–98	Bury	16	0	47	9
1997–98	*Oldham Ath*	9	4	9	4
1998–99	Burnley	15	1		
1999–2000	Burnley	31	2		
2000–01	Burnley	13	0	59	3

JOHNROSE, Lenny (M) 365 46
H: 5 11 W: 12 06 b.Preston 27-11-69
Source: Trainee.

1987–88	Blackburn R	1	0		
1988–89	Blackburn R	0	0		
1989–90	Blackburn R	8	3		
1990–91	Blackburn R	26	7		
1991–92	Blackburn R	7	1	42	11
1991–92	*Preston NE*	3	1	3	1
1991–92	Hartlepool U	15	2		
1992–93	Hartlepool U	38	6		
1993–94	Hartlepool U	13	3	66	11
1993–94	Bury	14	0		
1994–95	Bury	26	4		
1995–96	Bury	34	6		
1996–97	Bury	43	4		
1997–98	Bury	44	3		
1998–99	Bury	27	2	188	19
1998–99	Burnley	12	1		
1999–2000	Burnley	35	2		
2000–01	Burnley	19	1	66	4

KEVAN, Alex* (M) 0 0
H: 5 10 W: 11 00 b.Liverpool 23-2-81
Source: Trainee.

1999–2000	Burnley	0	0		
2000–01	Burnley	0	0		

LITTLE, Glen (M) 148 17
H: 6 3 W: 13 00 b.Wimbledon 15-10-75
Source: Trainee.

1994–95	Crystal Palace	0	0		
1995–96	Crystal Palace	0	0		
1996–97	*Glentoran*	6	2	6	2
1996–97	Burnley	9	0		
1997–98	Burnley	24	4		
1998–99	Burnley	34	5		
1999–2000	Burnley	41	3		
2000–01	Burnley	34	3	142	17

MAYLETT, Bradley (M) 29 0
H: 5 8 W: 10 07 b.Manchester 24-12-80
Source: Trainee.

1998–99	Burnley	17	0		
1999–2000	Burnley	0	0		
2000–01	Burnley	12	0	29	0

MICHOPOULOS, Nick (G) 141 0
H: 6 3 W: 14 00 b.Greece 20-2-70

1996–97	PAOK Salonika	34	0		
1997–98	PAOK Salonika	32	0		
1998–99	PAOK Salonika	19	0		
1999–2000	PAOK Salonika	17	0	102	0
2000–01	Burnley	39	0	39	0

MOORE, Ian (F) 200 38
H: 5 11 W: 12 02 b.Birkenhead 26-8-76
Source: Trainee. Honours: England Youth, Under-21.

1994–95	Tranmere R	1	0		
1995–96	Tranmere R	36	9		
1996–97	Tranmere R	21	3	58	12
1996–97	*Bradford C*	6	0	6	0
1996–97	Nottingham F	5	0		
1997–98	Nottingham F	10	1	15	1
1997–98	*West Ham U*	1	0	1	0
1998–99	Stockport Co	38	3		
1999–2000	Stockport Co	38	10		
2000–01	Stockport Co	17	7	93	20
2000–01	Burnley	27	5	27	5

MULLIN, John (F) 139 14
H: 6 0 W: 11 05 b.Bury 11-8-75
Source: School.

1992–93	Burnley	0	0		
1993–94	Burnley	6	1		
1994–95	Burnley	12	1		
1995–96	Sunderland	10	1		
1996–97	Sunderland	10	1		
1997–98	Sunderland	6	0		
1997–98	*Preston NE*	7	0	7	0
1997–98	*Burnley*	6	0		
1998–99	Sunderland	9	2	35	4
1999–2000	Burnley	37	5		
2000–01	Burnley	36	3	97	10

PAYTON, Andy (F) 489 195
H: 5 9 W: 11 13 b.Burnley 23-10-67
Source: Apprentice.

1985–86	Hull C	0	0		
1986–87	Hull C	2	0		
1987–88	Hull C	21	2		
1988–89	Hull C	28	4		
1989–90	Hull C	39	17		
1990–91	Hull C	43	25		
1991–92	Hull C	10	7	143	55
1991–92	Middlesbrough	19	12	19	3
1992–93	Celtic	29	13		
1993–94	Celtic	7	2	36	15
1993–94	Barnsley	25	12		
1994–95	Barnsley	43	12		
1995–96	Barnsley	40	17	108	41
1996–97	Huddersfield T	38	17		
1997–98	Huddersfield T	5	0	43	17
1997–98	Burnley	19	9		
1998–99	Burnley	40	19		
1999–2000	Burnley	41	27		
2000–01	Burnley	40	9	140	64

SCOTT, Christopher* (D) 14 0
H: 5 11 W: 12 05 b.Burnley 12-2-80
Source: Trainee.

1998–99	Burnley	14	0		
1999–2000	Burnley	0	0		
2000–01	Burnley	0	0	14	0

SHANDRAN, Anthony (F) 1 0
b.North Shields 17-9-81
Source: Scholar.

2000–01	Burnley	1	0	1	0

SMITH, Carl‡ (D) 11 0
H: 5 8 W: 11 00 b.Sheffield 15-1-79
Source: Trainee.

1997–98	Burnley	1	0		
1998–99	Burnley	10	0		
1999–2000	Burnley	0	0		
2000–01	Burnley	0	0	11	0

SMITH, Paul* (M) 116 5
H: 6 0 W: 13 03 b.Leeds 22-7-76
Source: Trainee.

1993–94	Burnley	1	0		
1994–95	Burnley	0	0		
1995–96	Burnley	10	0		
1996–97	Burnley	37	4		
1997–98	Burnley	14	0		
1998–99	Burnley	12	0		
1999–2000	Burnley	24	0		
2000–01	Burnley	14	1	112	5
2000–01	*Oldham Ath*	4	0	4	0

THOMAS, Mitchell (D) 574 15
H: 6 2 W: 14 00 b.Luton 2-10-64
Source: Apprentice. Honours: England Youth, Under-21, B.

1982–83	Luton T	4	0		
1983–84	Luton T	26	0		
1984–85	Luton T	36	0		
1985–86	Luton T	41	1		
1986–87	Tottenham H	39	4		
1987–88	Tottenham H	36	0		
1988–89	Tottenham H	25	1		
1989–90	Tottenham H	26	1		
1990–91	Tottenham H	31	0	157	6
1991–92	West Ham U	35	3		
1992–93	West Ham U	3	0		
1993–94	West Ham U	0	0	38	3
1993–94	Luton T	20	1		
1994–95	Luton T	36	0		
1995–96	Luton T	27	0		
1996–97	Luton T	42	3		
1997–98	Luton T	28	1		
1998–99	Luton T	32	0	292	6
1999–2000	Burnley	44	0		
2000–01	Burnley	43	0	87	0

WELLER, Paul (M) 147 9
H: 5 8 W: 11 02 b.Brighton 6-3-75
Source: Trainee.

1993–94	Burnley	0	0		
1994–95	Burnley	0	0		
1995–96	Burnley	25	1		
1996–97	Burnley	31	2		
1997–98	Burnley	39	2		
1998–99	Burnley	1	0		
1999–2000	Burnley	7	1		
2000–01	Burnley	44	3	147	9

WEST, Dean (D) 270 28
H: 5 10 W: 11 07 b.Leeds 5-12-72
Source: Leeds U Schoolboy.

1990–91	Lincoln C	1	1		
1991–92	Lincoln C	32	3		
1992–93	Lincoln C	19	3		
1993–94	Lincoln C	18	6		
1994–95	Lincoln C	41	6		
1995–96	Lincoln C	8	1	119	20
1995–96	Bury	37	1		
1996–97	Bury	46	4		
1997–98	Bury	4	0		
1998–99	Bury	23	3	110	8
1999–2000	Burnley	34	0		
2000–01	Burnley	7	0	41	0

WILLIAMSON, John (D) 1 0
H: 6 1 W: 11 06 b.Derby 3-3-81
Source: Trainee.

1998–99	Burnley	1	0		
1999–2000	Burnley	0	0		
2000–01	Burnley	0	0	1	0

Scholars
Barrett, Paul J; Bowden, Anthony; Clark, Christopher; Davis, Earl A; Eves, Liam J; Fogarty, Brian W; Hindle, Damien; Leary, Jonathan R; Leeson, Andrew; O'Neill, Matthew P; Paxton, Andrew J; Pilkington, Joel T; Robertshaw, Duncan; Salisbury; James A; Waine, Andrew P

BURY

ARMSTRONG, Christopher (D) 22 1
H: 5 9 W: 10 08 b.Newcastle 5-8-82
Source: Scholar.

2000–01	Bury	22	1	22	1

BARNES, Paul* (F) 390 140
H: 5 11 W: 13 00 b.Leeds 16-11-67
Source: Apprentice.

1985–86	Notts Co	14	4		
1986–87	Notts Co	0	0		
1987–88	Notts Co	11	2		
1988–89	Notts Co	15	7		
1989–90	Notts Co	13	0	53	14
1989–90	Stoke C	5	0		
1990–91	Stoke C	6	0		

1990–91	*Chesterfield*	1	0	1	0
1991–92	Stoke C	13	3	24	3
1992–93	York C	40	21		
1993–94	York C	42	24		
1994–95	York C	36	16		
1995–96	York C	30	15	148	76
1995–96	Birmingham C	15	7		
1996–97	Birmingham C	0	0	15	7
1996–97	Burnley	40	24		
1997–98	Burnley	25	6	65	30
1997–98	Huddersfield T	15	1		
1998–99	Huddersfield T	15	1	30	2
1998–99	Bury	8	0		
1999–2000	Bury	30	4		
2000–01	Bury	16	4	54	8

BARRASS, Matt (D) **30 1**
H: 5 11 W: 12 00 b.Bury 28-2-81
Source: Trainee.

1999–2000	Bury	25	1		
2000–01	Bury	5	0	30	1

BARRICK, Dean‡ (D) **368 14**
H: 5 8 W: 12 00 b.Hemsworth 30-9-69
Source: Trainee.

1987–88	Sheffield W	0	0		
1988–89	Sheffield W	8	2		
1989–90	Sheffield W	3	0		
1990–91	Sheffield W	0	0	11	2
1990–91	Rotherham U	19	2		
1991–92	Rotherham U	34	1		
1992–93	Rotherham U	46	4	99	7
1993–94	Cambridge U	44	1		
1994–95	Cambridge U	44	1		
1995–96	Cambridge U	3	1	91	3
1995–96	Preston NE	40	0		
1996–97	Preston NE	36	0		
1997–98	Preston NE	33	1	109	1
1998–99	Bury	20	1		
1998–99	*Ayr U*	11	0	11	0
1999–2000	Bury	17	0		
2000–01	Bury	10	0	47	1

BHUTIA, Baichung (F) **34 3**
H: 5 8 W: 10 02 b.Sikkim 15-6-76
Source: East Bengal. *Honours:* India full caps.

1999–2000	Bury	14	2		
2000–01	Bury	20	1	34	3

BILLY, Chris# (D) **337 17**
H: 5 11 W: 12 06 b.Huddersfield 2-1-71
Source: Trainee.

1991–92	Huddersfield T	10	2		
1992–93	Huddersfield T	13	0		
1993–94	Huddersfield T	34	0		
1994–95	Huddersfield T	37	2	94	4
1995–96	Plymouth Arg	32	4		
1996–97	Plymouth Arg	45	3		
1997–98	Plymouth Arg	41	2	118	9
1998–99	Notts Co	6	0	6	0
1998–99	Bury	37	0		
1999–2000	Bury	36	4		
2000–01	Bury	46	0	119	4

BUGGIE, Lee* (F) **3 0**
H: 5 9 W: 11 00 b.Bury 11-2-81
Source: Trainee.

1998–99	Bolton W	0	0		
1998–99	Bury	0	0		
1999–2000	Bury	1	0		
2000–01	Bury	0	0	1	0
2000–01	*Rochdale*	2	0	2	0

BULLOCK, Darren (M) **249 23**
H: 5 9 W: 12 10 b.Worcester 12-2-69
Source: Nuneaton Bor.

1993–94	Huddersfield T	20	3		
1994–95	Huddersfield T	39	6		
1995–96	Huddersfield T	42	6		
1996–97	Huddersfield T	27	1	128	16
1996–97	Swindon T	13	1		
1997–98	Swindon T	31	0		
1998–99	Swindon T	22	1	66	2
1998–99	Bury	12	1		
1999–2000	Bury	27	2		
2000–01	Bury	10	2	49	5
2000–01	*Sheffield U*	6	0	6	0

COLLINS, Sam (D) **90 2**
H: 6 2 W: 14 04 b.Pontefract 5-6-77
Source: Trainee.

1994–95	Huddersfield T	0	0		
1995–96	Huddersfield T	0	0		
1996–97	Huddersfield T	4	0		
1997–98	Huddersfield T	10	0		
1998–99	Huddersfield T	23	0	37	0
1999–2000	Bury	19	0		
2000–01	Bury	34	2	53	2

CONNELL, Lee (M) **3 1**
H: 6 0 W: 12 00 b.Bury 24-6-81
Source: Trainee.

1999–2000	Bury	2	0		
2000–01	Bury	1	1	3	1

CROSSLEY, Ryan‡ (D) **0 0**
H: 6 0 W: 11 00 b.Halifax 23-7-80
Source: Trainee.

1998–99	Huddersfield T	0	0		
1999–2000	Huddersfield T	0	0		
2000–01	Bury	0	0		

DAWS, Nick# (M) **369 16**
H: 5 11 W: 12 13 b.Salford 15-3-70
Source: Altrincham.

1992–93	Bury	36	1		
1993–94	Bury	37	1		
1994–95	Bury	34	2		
1995–96	Bury	37	1		
1996–97	Bury	46	2		
1997–98	Bury	46	2		
1998–99	Bury	46	2		
1999–2000	Bury	43	2		
2000–01	Bury	44	3	369	16

FORREST, Martyn (M) **43 0**
H: 5 10 W: 12 02 b.Bury 2-1-79

1997–98	Bury	0	0		
1998–99	Bury	1	0		
1999–2000	Bury	15	0		
2000–01	Bury	27	0	43	0

GARNER, Glyn (G) **0 0**
b.Pontypool 9-12-76
Source: Llanelli.

2000–01	Bury	0	0		

HALFORD, Stephen (D) **5 0**
H: 5 10 W: 12 10 b.Bury 21-9-80
Source: Trainee.

1999–2000	Bury	2	0		
2000–01	Bury	3	0	5	0

HILL, Nicky (D) **15 0**
H: 6 0 W: 12 03 b.Accrington 26-2-81
Source: Trainee.

1999–2000	Bury	5	0		
2000–01	Bury	10	0	15	0

JAMES, Lutel* (F) **74 4**
H: 5 8 W: 11 00 b.Manchester 2-6-72
Honours: St Kitts & Nevis full caps.

1992–93	Scarborough	6	0	6	0
From Hyde U.					
1998–99	Bury	17	2		
1999–2000	Bury	23	2		
2000–01	Bury	28	0	68	4

JARRETT, Jason (M) **28 2**
H: 6 0 W: 12 04 b.Bury 14-9-79
Source: Trainee.

1998–99	Blackpool	2	0		
1999–2000	Blackpool	0	0	2	0
1999–2000	Wrexham	1	0	1	0
2000–01	Bury	25	2	25	2

KENNY, Paddy (G) **92 0**
H: 6 1 W: 14 06 b.Halifax 17-5-78
Source: Bradford PA.

1998–99	Bury	0	0		
1999–2000	Bury	46	0		
2000–01	Bury	46	0	92	0

LITTLEJOHN, Adrian* (M) **343 61**
H: 5 10 W: 11 00 b.Wolverhampton 26-9-71
Source: WBA Trainee.

1989–90	Walsall	11	0		
1990–91	Walsall	33	1	44	1
1991–92	Sheffield U	7	0		
1992–93	Sheffield U	27	8		
1993–94	Sheffield U	19	3		
1994–95	Sheffield U	16	1	69	12
1995–96	Plymouth Arg	42	17		
1996–97	Plymouth Arg	37	6		
1997–98	Plymouth Arg	31	6	110	29
1997–98	Oldham Ath	5	3		
1998–99	Oldham Ath	16	2	21	5
1998–99	Bury	20	1		
1999–2000	Bury	42	9		
2000–01	Bury	37	4	99	14

NELSON, Michael† (D) **2 1**
b.Gateshead 28-3-80

2000–01	Bury	2	1	2	1

NEWBY, Jon (F) **37 5**
H: 6 0 W: 12 00 b.Warrington 28-11-78
Source: Trainee.

1998–99	Liverpool	0	0		
1999–2000	Liverpool	1	0		
1999–2000	*Crewe Alex*	6	0	6	0
2000–01	Liverpool	0	0	1	0
2000–01	*Sheffield U*	13	0	13	0
2000–01	Bury	17	5	17	5

PEYTON, Warren (M) **2 0**
H: 5 9 W: 11 03 b.Manchester 13-12-79

1999–2000	Rochdale	1	0	1	0
2000–01	Bury	1	0	1	0

PREECE, Andy# (F) **407 105**
H: 6 1 W: 12 00 b.Evesham 27-3-67
Source: Evesham U.

1988–89	Northampton T	1	0	1	0
From Worcester C					
1989–90	Wrexham	7	1		
1990–91	Wrexham	34	4		
1991–92	Wrexham	10	2	51	7
1991–92	Stockport Co	25	13		
1992–93	Stockport Co	29	8		
1993–94	Stockport Co	43	21	97	42
1994–95	Crystal Palace	20	4	20	4
1995–96	Blackpool	41	14		
1996–97	Blackpool	41	10		
1997–98	Blackpool	44	11	126	35
1998–99	Bury	39	3		
1999–2000	Bury	43	12		
2000–01	Bury	30	2	112	17

REDMOND, Steve# (D) **538 14**
H: 5 11 W: 13 00 b.Liverpool 2-11-67
Source: Apprentice. *Honours:* England Youth, Under-21.

1984–85	Manchester C	0	0		
1985–86	Manchester C	9	0		
1986–87	Manchester C	30	2		
1987–88	Manchester C	44	0		
1988–89	Manchester C	46	1		
1989–90	Manchester C	38	0		
1990–91	Manchester C	37	3		
1991–92	Manchester C	31	1	235	7
1992–93	Oldham Ath	31	0		
1993–94	Oldham Ath	33	1		
1994–95	Oldham Ath	43	0		
1995–96	Oldham Ath	40	1		
1996–97	Oldham Ath	24	2		
1997–98	Oldham Ath	34	0	205	4
1998–99	Bury	26	0		
1999–2000	Bury	33	1		
2000–01	Bury	39	2	98	3

REID, Paul# (M) **503 54**
H: 5 10 W: 10 12 b.Oldbury 19-1-68
Source: Apprentice.

1985–86	Leicester C	0	0		
1986–87	Leicester C	6	0		
1987–88	Leicester C	26	5		
1988–89	Leicester C	45	6		
1989–90	Leicester C	40	8		
1990–91	Leicester C	33	2		
1991–92	Leicester C	12	0	162	21
1991–92	*Bradford C*	7	0		
1992–93	Bradford C	44	6		
1993–94	Bradford C	38	9	89	15
1994–95	Huddersfield T	42	6		
1995–96	Huddersfield T	13	0		
1996–97	Huddersfield T	22	0	77	6
1996–97	Oldham Ath	9	1		
1997–98	Oldham Ath	44	4		
1998–99	Oldham Ath	40	1	93	6
1999–2000	Bury	39	2		
2000–01	Bury	43	4	82	6

SOUTER, Ryan* (M) **5 0**
H: 5 10 W: 12 00 b.Bedford 5-2-78
Source: Weston-Super-Mare.

1998–99	Bury	1	0		
1999–2000	Bury	4	0		
2000–01	Bury	0	0	5	0

SWAILES, Chris# (D) **208 11**
H: 6 2 W: 13 07 b.Gateshead 19-10-70
Source: Ipswich T Trainee, Peterborough U, Boston U, Birmingham C, Bridlington T.

1993–94	Doncaster R	17	0		
1994–95	Doncaster R	32	0	49	0
1995–96	Ipswich T	5	0		
1996–97	Ipswich T	23	1		
1997–98	Ipswich T	5	0	33	1
1997–98	Bury	13	1		
1998–99	Bury	43	3		
1999–2000	Bury	27	2		
2000–01	Bury	43	4	126	10

SWAILES, Danny (D) **35 3**
H: 6 3 W: 12 06 b.Bolton 1-4-79
Source: Trainee.

1997–98	Bury	0	0		
1998–99	Bury	0	0		
1999–2000	Bury	24	3		
2000–01	Bury	11	0	35	3

UNSWORTH, Lee# (D) **141 0**
H: 5 11 W: 11 02 b.Eccles 25-2-73
Source: Ashton U.

1994–95	Crewe Alex	0	0		
1995–96	Crewe Alex	29	0		
1996–97	Crewe Alex	29	0		
1997–98	Crewe Alex	36	0		
1998–99	Crewe Alex	24	0		

Season	Club	App	Gls	Tot	Tot
1999–2000	Crewe Alex	8	0	126	0
2000–01	Bury	15	0	15	0

Scholars
Abbiss, Graham P; Blackley, John A; Borley, David; Evans, Gary L; Gaynor, John; Gleaves, Carl M; Gunby, Stephen R; Joseph, Daniel; Lobban, Alexander; Martin, Adam T; Morris, James P; O'Shaughnessy, Paul J; Rowe, Sebastian; Thompson, David J; Thompson, James; Thompson, Nicholas A; Winstanley, Richard A
Non-Contract
Nelson, Michael J

CAMBRIDGE U

ASHBEE, Ian (M) 166 9
H: 6 1 W: 14 00 b.Birmingham 6-9-76
Source: Trainee. *Honours:* England Youth.

Season	Club	App	Gls	Tot	Tot
1994–95	Derby Co	1	0		
1995–96	Derby Co	0	0		
1996–97	Derby Co			1	0
1996–97	Cambridge U	18	0		
1997–98	Cambridge U	27	1		
1998–99	Cambridge U	31	4		
1999–2000	Cambridge U	45	1		
2000–01	Cambridge U	44	3	165	9

AXELDAL, Jonas* (F) 34 2
H: 5 11 W: 12 00 b.Holm 2-9-70

Season	Club	App	Gls	Tot	Tot
1999–2000	Ipswich T	16	0	16	0
2000–01	Cambridge U	18	2	18	2

BUTTERWORTH, Adam (D) 1 0
b.Paignton 9-8-82

Season	Club	App	Gls	Tot	Tot
2000–01	Cambridge U	1	0	1	0

CHILLINGWORTH, Daniel (F) 4 0
H: 6 0 W: 12 06 b.Cambridge 13-9-81
Source: Scholarship.

Season	Club	App	Gls	Tot	Tot
1999–2000	Cambridge U	3	0		
2000–01	Cambridge U	1	0	4	0

COCKRILL, Dale (D) 0 0
b.Great Yarmouth 23-11-81

Season	Club	App	Gls	Tot	Tot
2000–01	Cambridge U	0	0		

COWAN, Tom (D) 289 12
H: 5 8 W: 11 10 b.Bothwell 28-8-69
Source: Netherdale BC.

Season	Club	App	Gls	Tot	Tot
1988–89	Clyde	16	2	16	2
1988–89	Rangers	4	0		
1989–90	Rangers	3	0		
1990–91	Rangers	5	0	12	0
1991–92	Sheffield U	20	0		
1992–93	Sheffield U	21	0		
1993–94	Sheffield U	4	0	45	0
1993–94	Stoke C	14	0	14	0
1993–94	Huddersfield T	10	0		
1994–95	Huddersfield T	37	2		
1995–96	Huddersfield T	43	2		
1996–97	Huddersfield T	42	4		
1997–98	Huddersfield T	0	0		
1998–99	Huddersfield T	5	0	137	8
1998–99	Burnley	12	0		
1999–2000	Burnley	8	0	20	0
1999–2000	Cambridge U	4	0		
2000–01	Cambridge U	41	2	45	2

DREYER, John (D) 462 22
H: 6 1 W: 13 00 b.Alnwick 11-6-63
Source: Wallingford T.

Season	Club	App	Gls	Tot	Tot
1984–85	Oxford U	0	0		
1985–86	Oxford U	0	0		
1985–86	Torquay U	5	0	5	0
1985–86	Fulham	12	2	12	2
1986–87	Oxford U	25	2		
1987–88	Oxford U	35	0	60	2
1988–89	Luton T	18	1		
1989–90	Luton T	38	2		
1990–91	Luton T	38	3		
1991–92	Luton T	42	2		
1992–93	Luton T	38	2		
1993–94	Luton T	40	3	214	13
1994–95	Stoke C	18	2		
1994–95	Bolton W	2	0	2	0
1995–96	Stoke C	19	0		
1996–97	Stoke C	12	1	49	3
1996–97	Bradford C	28	1		
1997–98	Bradford C	17	0		
1998–99	Bradford C	21	0		
1999–2000	Bradford C	14	1	80	2
2000–01	Cambridge U	40	0	40	0

DUNCAN, Andy (D) 116 3
H: 5 11 W: 14 03 b.Hexham 20-10-77
Source: Trainee. *Honours:* England Schools.

Season	Club	App	Gls	Tot	Tot
1996–97	Manchester U	0	0		
1997–98	Manchester U	0	0		
1997–98	Cambridge U	19	0		
1998–99	Cambridge U	45	1		
1999–2000	Cambridge U	13	1		
2000–01	Cambridge U	39	1	116	3

FLEMING, Terry (M) 286 12
H: 5 8 W: 10 01 b.Marston Green 5-1-73
Source: Trainee.

Season	Club	App	Gls	Tot	Tot
1990–91	Coventry C	2	0		
1991–92	Coventry C	0	0		
1992–93	Coventry C	11	0	13	0
1993–94	Northampton T	31	1	31	1
1994–95	Preston NE	27	2		
1995–96	Preston NE	5	0	32	2
1995–96	Lincoln C	22	0		
1996–97	Lincoln C	37	0		
1997–98	Lincoln C	40	3		
1998–99	Lincoln C	43	0		
1999–2000	Lincoln C	41	5	183	8
2000–01	Plymouth Arg	17	0	17	0
2000–01	Cambridge U	10	1	10	1

GREENE, David (D) 208 16
H: 6 3 W: 14 03 b.Luton 26-10-73
Source: Trainee. *Honours:* Eire Under-21.

Season	Club	App	Gls	Tot	Tot
1991–92	Luton T	0	0		
1992–93	Luton T	1	0		
1993–94	Luton T	10	0		
1994–95	Luton T	8	0		
1995–96	Luton T	0	0	19	0
1995–96	Colchester U	14	1		
1995–96	Brentford	11	0	11	0
1996–97	Colchester U	44	2		
1997–98	Colchester U	38	4		
1998–99	Colchester U	42	8		
1999–2000	Colchester U	29	1	167	16
2000–01	Cardiff C	10	0	10	0
2000–01	Cambridge U	1	0	1	0

GUTTRIDGE, Luke (M) 2 1
H: 5 5 W: 8 06 b.Barnstaple 27-3-82

Season	Club	App	Gls	Tot	Tot
1999–2000	Torquay U	1	0		
2000–01	Torquay U	0	0	1	0
2000–01	Cambridge U	1	1	1	1

HANSEN, John (M) 34 3
H: 5 11 W: 13 01 b.Mannheim 17-9-73

Season	Club	App	Gls	Tot	Tot
1999–2000	Esbjerg	6	0	6	0
1999–2000	Cambridge U	16	3		
2000–01	Cambridge U	12	0	28	3

HUMPHREYS, Richie* (F) 89 11
H: 5 11 W: 14 07 b.Sheffield 30-11-77
Source: Trainee. *Honours:* England Youth, Under-21.

Season	Club	App	Gls	Tot	Tot
1995–96	Sheffield W	5	0		
1996–97	Sheffield W	29	3		
1997–98	Sheffield W	7	0		
1998–99	Sheffield W	19	1		
1999–2000	Sheffield W	0	0		
1999–2000	Scunthorpe U	6	2	6	2
1999–2000	Cardiff C	9	2	9	2
2000–01	Sheffield W	7	0	67	4
2000–01	Cambridge U	7	3	7	3

KITSON, Dave (F) 8 1
b.Hitchin 21-1-80
Source: Arlesey.

Season	Club	App	Gls	Tot	Tot
2000–01	Cambridge U	8	1	8	1

LAMEY, Nathan‡ (F) 6 0
H: 5 10 W: 13 04 b.Sandwell 14-10-80
Source: Trainee.

Season	Club	App	Gls	Tot	Tot
1997–98	Wolverhampton W	0	0		
1998–99	Wolverhampton W	0	0		
1999–2000	Cambridge U	3	0		
2000–01	Cambridge U	3	0	6	0

MARSHALL, Shaun (G) 57 0
H: 6 1 W: 13 03 b.Fakenham 3-10-78
Source: Trainee.

Season	Club	App	Gls	Tot	Tot
1996–97	Cambridge U	1	0		
1997–98	Cambridge U	2	0		
1998–99	Cambridge U	19	0		
1999–2000	Cambridge U	24	0		
2000–01	Cambridge U	11	0	57	0

McANESPIE, Steve (D) 101 0
H: 5 9 W: 10 09 b.Kilmarnock 1-2-72
Source: Aberdeen, Vasterhauringe.

Season	Club	App	Gls	Tot	Tot
1993–94	Raith R	3	0		
1994–95	Raith R	34	0		
1995–96	Raith R	3	0	40	0
1995–96	Bolton W	9	0		
1996–97	Bolton W	13	0		
1997–98	Bolton W	2	0	24	0
1997–98	Fulham	4	0		
1997–98	Bradford C	7	0	7	0
1998–99	Fulham	3	0		
1999–2000	Fulham	0	0	7	0
2000–01	Cambridge U	23	0	23	0

McCRACKEN, Gary* (D) 0 0
b.Belfast 22-7-81
Source: Fulham trainee.

Season	Club	App	Gls	Tot	Tot
2000–01	Cambridge U	0	0		

McNEIL, Martin (D) 41 0
H: 6 0 W: 13 02 b.Rutherglen 28-9-80
Source: Trainee.

Season	Club	App	Gls	Tot	Tot
1998–99	Cambridge U	6	0		
1999–2000	Cambridge U	29	0		
2000–01	Cambridge U	6	0	41	0

MUSTOE, Neil (M) 94 4
H: 5 9 W: 12 02 b.Gloucester 5-11-76
Source: Trainee.

Season	Club	App	Gls	Tot	Tot
1995–96	Manchester U	0	0		
1996–97	Manchester U	0	0		
1997–98	Manchester U	0	0		
1998–99	Cambridge U	34	3		
1999–2000	Cambridge U	33	0		
2000–01	Cambridge U	27	1	94	4

NACCA, Francesco (M) 0 0
b.Venezuela 9-11-81
Source: Scholar.

Season	Club	App	Gls	Tot	Tot
2000–01	Cambridge U	0	0		

OAKES, Scott† (M) 218 28
H: 6 2 W: 11 08 b.Leicester 5-8-72
Source: Trainee.

Season	Club	App	Gls	Tot	Tot
1989–90	Leicester C	2	0		
1990–91	Leicester C	0	0		
1991–92	Leicester C	1	0	3	0
1991–92	Luton T	21	2		
1992–93	Luton T	44	5		
1993–94	Luton T	36	8		
1994–95	Luton T	43	9		
1995–96	Luton T	29	3	173	27
1996–97	Sheffield W	19	1		
1997–98	Sheffield W	4	0		
1998–99	Sheffield W	1	0		
1999–2000	Sheffield W	0	0	24	1
2000–01	Cambridge U	18	0	18	0

PEREZ, Lionel (G) 303 0
H: 5 11 W: 13 04 b.Bagnols Coze 24-4-67

Season	Club	App	Gls	Tot	Tot
1989–90	Nimes	2	0		
1990–91	Nimes	34	0		
1991–92	Nimes	38	0		
1992–93	Nimes	36	0	111	0
1993–94	Bordeaux	9	0		
1994–95	Bordeaux	7	0	16	0
1995–96	Laval	42	0	42	0
1996–97	Sunderland	29	0		
1997–98	Sunderland	46	0	75	0
1998–99	Newcastle U	0	0		
1999–2000	Newcastle U	0	0		
1999–2000	Scunthorpe U	13	0	13	0
1999–2000	Cambridge U	9	0		
2000–01	Cambridge U	37	0	46	0

PILVI, Tero# (M) 14 2
b.Vihti 21-2-76

Season	Club	App	Gls	Tot	Tot
2000–01	Airdrieonians	9	2	9	2
2000–01	Cambridge U	5	0	5	0

PREECE, David (M) 548 30
H: 5 6 W: 11 05 b.Bridgnorth 28-5-63
Source: Apprentice. *Honours:* England B.

Season	Club	App	Gls	Tot	Tot
1980–81	Walsall	8	0		
1981–82	Walsall	8	0		
1982–83	Walsall	42	2		
1983–84	Walsall	41	3		
1984–85	Walsall	12	0	111	5
1984–85	Luton T	21	2		
1985–86	Luton T	41	2		
1986–87	Luton T	14	0		
1987–88	Luton T	13	0		
1988–89	Luton T	26	0		
1989–90	Luton T	32	1		
1990–91	Luton T	37	1		
1991–92	Luton T	38	3		
1992–93	Luton T	43	3		
1993–94	Luton T	29	5		
1994–95	Luton T	42	4	336	21
1995–96	Derby Co	13	1	13	1
1995–96	Birmingham C	6	0	6	0
1995–96	Swindon T	7	1	7	1
1996–97	Cambridge U	25	0		
1997–98	Cambridge U	22	0		
1998–99	Cambridge U	14	2		
1999–2000	Cambridge U	12	0		
2000–01	Cambridge U	2	0	75	2

PROKAS, Richard (M)   207   3
H: 5 9   W: 11 05   b.Penrith 22-1-76
Source: Trainee.

Season	Club	App	Gls	Tot	
1994-95	Carlisle U	39	1		
1995-96	Carlisle U	20	0		
1996-97	Carlisle U	13	1		
1997-98	Carlisle U	34	0		
1998-99	Carlisle U	34	0		
1999-2000	Carlisle U	35	1		
2000-01	Carlisle U	29	0	204	3
2000-01	Cambridge U	3	0	3	0

REVELL, Alexander (F)   4   0
b.Cambridge 7-7-83
Source: Scholar.

Season	Club	App	Gls	Tot	
2000-01	Cambridge U	4	0	4	0

RICHARDSON, Marcus (F)   10   2
b.Reading 31-8-77
Source: Harrow B.

Season	Club	App	Gls	Tot	
2000-01	Cambridge U	10	2	10	2

RUSSELL, Alex° (M)   183   22
H: 5 8   W: 11 12   b.Crosby 17-3-73
Source: Burscough.

Season	Club	App	Gls	Tot	
1994-95	Rochdale	7	1		
1995-96	Rochdale	25	0		
1996-97	Rochdale	39	9		
1997-98	Rochdale	31	4	102	14
1998-99	Cambridge U	37	6		
1999-2000	Cambridge U	15	0		
2000-01	Cambridge U	29	2	81	8

SLADE, Steve† (F)   86   7
H: 5 11   W: 11 00   b.Hackney 6-10-75
Source: Trainee. *Honours:* England Under-21.

Season	Club	App	Gls	Tot	
1994-95	Tottenham H	0	0		
1995-96	Tottenham H	5	0	5	0
1996-97	QPR	17	4		
1996-97	*Brentford*	4	0	4	0
1997-98	QPR	22	0		
1998-99	QPR	20	1		
1999-2000	QPR	9	1	68	6
2000-01	Cambridge U	9	1	9	1

TANN, Adam (D)   1   0
H: 6 0   W: 11 05   b.Fakenham 12-5-82
Source: Scholar. *Honours:* England Youth.

Season	Club	App	Gls	Tot	
1999-2000	Cambridge U	0	0		
2000-01	Cambridge U	1	0	1	0

TAYLOR, John (F)   506   151
H: 6 2   W: 15 00   b.Norwich 24-10-64
Source: Local.

Season	Club	App	Gls	Tot	
1982-83	Colchester U	0	0		
1983-84	Colchester U	0	0		
1984-85	Colchester U	0	0		
From Sudbury T					
1988-89	Cambridge U	40	12		
1989-90	Cambridge U	45	15		
1990-91	Cambridge U	40	14		
1991-92	Cambridge U	35	5		
1991-92	Bristol R	8	7		
1992-93	Bristol R	42	14		
1993-94	Bristol R	45	23	95	44
1994-95	Bradford C	36	11	36	11
1994-95	Luton T	9	3		
1995-96	Luton T	28	0		
1996-97	Luton T	0	0	37	3
1996-97	*Lincoln C*	5	2	5	2
1996-97	*Colchester U*	8	5	8	5
1996-97	Cambridge U	21	4		
1997-98	Cambridge U	34	10		
1998-99	Cambridge U	40	17		
1999-2000	Cambridge U	40	6		
2000-01	Cambridge U	30	3	325	86

TRAORE, Demba (F)   1   0
H: 6 0   W: 12 00   b.Sweden 24-4-82

Season	Club	App	Gls	Tot	
2000-01	Cambridge U	1	0	1	0

WANLESS, Paul (M)   256   33
H: 6 1   W: 14 08   b.Banbury 14-12-73
Source: Trainee.

Season	Club	App	Gls	Tot	
1991-92	Oxford U	6	0		
1992-93	Oxford U	7	0		
1993-94	Oxford U	9	0		
1994-95	Oxford U	10	0	32	0
1995-96	Lincoln C	8	0	8	0
1995-96	*Cambridge U*	14	1		
1996-97	Cambridge U	30	3		
1997-98	Cambridge U	42	8		
1998-99	Cambridge U	45	8		
1999-2000	Cambridge U	42	3		
2000-01	Cambridge U	43	10	216	33

WILSON, Stuart° (F)   34   3
H: 5 8   W: 10 03   b.Leicester 16-9-77
Source: Trainee.

Season	Club	App	Gls	Tot	
1996-97	Leicester C	2	1		
1997-98	Leicester C	11	2		
1998-99	Leicester C	9	0		
1999-2000	Leicester C	0	0		
1999-2000	*Sheffield U*	6	0	6	0
2000-01	Leicester C	0	0	22	3
2000-01	Cambridge U	6	0	6	0

YOUNGS, Tom (F)   73   22
H: 5 9   W: 11 01   b.Bury St Edmunds 31-8-79
Source: Trainee.

Season	Club	App	Gls	Tot	
1997-98	Cambridge U	4	0		
1998-99	Cambridge U	9	0		
1999-2000	Cambridge U	21	8		
2000-01	Cambridge U	38	14	73	22

Scholars
Bennett, Lee; Bridges, David S; George, Rikki; Haniver, Matthew G; Heathcote, Jonathan; Huggins, Daniel J; Kamara, Alim S; Mercer, James F; Paynter, Owen; Stephenson-Lowe, Jermaine J; Thornton, Robert I; Winkworth, Kevin P
Non-Contract
Rush, Graham P
Player who does not hold a current contract but his registration has been retained by the club
Millership, Jamie C

CARDIFF C

BOLAND, Willie (M)   116   2
H: 5 9   W: 11 02   b.Ennis 6-8-75
Source: Trainee. *Honours:* Eire Youth, Under-21s.

Season	Club	App	Gls	Tot	
1992-93	Coventry C	1	0		
1993-94	Coventry C	27	0		
1994-95	Coventry C	12	0		
1995-96	Coventry C	3	0		
1996-97	Coventry C	1	0		
1997-98	Coventry C	19	0		
1998-99	Coventry C	0	0	63	0
1999-2000	Cardiff C	28	1		
2000-01	Cardiff C	25	1	53	2

BONNER, Mark (M)   259   17
H: 5 8   W: 11 00   b.Ormskirk 7-6-74
Source: Trainee.

Season	Club	App	Gls	Tot	
1991-92	Blackpool	3	0		
1992-93	Blackpool	15	0		
1993-94	Blackpool	40	7		
1994-95	Blackpool	17	0		
1995-96	Blackpool	42	3		
1996-97	Blackpool	29	1		
1997-98	Blackpool	32	3	178	14
1998-99	Cardiff C	25	1		
1998-99	*Hull C*	1	1	1	1
1999-2000	Cardiff C	31	0		
2000-01	Cardiff C	24	1	80	2

BOWEN, Jason (F)   286   60
H: 5 8   W: 11 02   b.Merthyr 24-8-72
Source: Trainee. *Honours:* Wales Youth, Under-21, 2 full caps.

Season	Club	App	Gls	Tot	
1990-91	Swansea C	3	0		
1991-92	Swansea C	11	0		
1992-93	Swansea C	38	10		
1993-94	Swansea C	41	11		
1994-95	Swansea C	31	5	124	26
1995-96	Birmingham C	23	4		
1996-97	Birmingham C	25	3		
1997-98	Birmingham C	0	0	48	7
1997-98	*Southampton*	3	0	3	0
1997-98	Reading	14	1		
1998-99	Reading	1	0	15	1
1998-99	Cardiff C	17	2		
1999-2000	Cardiff C	39	12		
2000-01	Cardiff C	40	12	96	26

BRAYSON, Paul (F)   101   22
H: 5 4   W: 10 10   b.Newcastle 16-9-77
Source: Trainee. *Honours:* England Youth.

Season	Club	App	Gls	Tot	
1995-96	Newcastle U	0	0		
1996-97	Newcastle U	0	0		
1996-97	*Swansea C*	11	5	11	5
1997-98	Newcastle U	0	0		
1997-98	Reading	6	1		
1998-99	Reading	28	0		
1999-2000	Reading	7	0	41	1
1999-2000	*Cardiff C*	9	1		
2000-01	Cardiff C	40	15	49	16

BRAZIER, Matt (M)   125   8
H: 5 8   W: 11 08   b.Whipps Cross 2-7-76
Source: Trainee.

Season	Club	App	Gls	Tot	
1994-95	QPR	0	0		
1995-96	QPR	11	0		
1996-97	QPR	27	2		
1997-98	QPR	11	0	49	2
1997-98	Fulham	7	1		
1998-99	Fulham	2	0	9	1
1998-99	Cardiff C	11	2		
1999-2000	Cardiff C	30	1		
2000-01	Cardiff C	26	2	67	5

BUTTERY, Paul° (G)   0   0
H: 6 0   W: 12 00   b.Manchester 22-10-81
Source: Trainee.

Season	Club	App	Gls	Tot	
2000-01	Cardiff C	0	0		

COLLINS, James (F)   3   0
b.Newport 23-8-83
Source: Scholar.

Season	Club	App	Gls	Tot	
2000-01	Cardiff C	3	0	3	0

EARNSHAW, Robert (F)   55   23
H: 5 6   W: 9 09   b.Zambia 6-4-81
Source: Trainee. *Honours:* Wales Under-21.

Season	Club	App	Gls	Tot	
1997-98	Cardiff C	5	0		
1998-99	Cardiff C	5	1		
1998-99	*Middlesbrough*	0	0		
1999-2000	Cardiff C	6	1		
1999-2000	*Morton*	3	2	3	2
2000-01	Cardiff C	36	19	52	21

ECKHARDT, Jeff (D)   525   48
H: 6 0   W: 12 00   b.Sheffield 7-10-65

Season	Club	App	Gls	Tot	
1984-85	Sheffield U	7	0		
1985-86	Sheffield U	33	2		
1986-87	Sheffield U	22	0		
1987-88	Sheffield U	12	0	74	2
1987-88	Fulham	29	1		
1988-89	Fulham	43	2		
1989-90	Fulham	40	2		
1990-91	Fulham	29	2		
1991-92	Fulham	43	7		
1992-93	Fulham	30	6		
1993-94	Fulham	35	5	249	25
1994-95	Stockport Co	27	1		
1995-96	Stockport Co	35	6	62	7
1996-97	Cardiff C	35	5		
1997-98	Cardiff C	21	3		
1998-99	Cardiff C	35	5		
1999-2000	Cardiff C	41	1		
2000-01	Cardiff C	8	0	140	14

EVANS, Kevin (D)   32   3
H: 6 2   W: 12 10   b.Carmarthen 16-12-80
Source: Trainee. *Honours:* Wales Under-21.

Season	Club	App	Gls	Tot	
1997-98	Leeds U	0	0		
1998-99	Leeds U	0	0		
1999-2000	Leeds U	0	0		
1999-2000	*Swansea C*	2	0	2	0
2000-01	Cardiff C	30	3	30	3

FAERBER, Winston° (D)   61   1
H: 5 11   W: 12 06   b.Surinam 27-3-71

Season	Club	App	Gls	Tot	
1998-99	Den Haag	28	0	28	0
1999-2000	Cardiff C	33	1		
2000-01	Cardiff C	0	0	33	1

FORTUNE-WEST, Leo (F)   193   61
H: 6 4   W: 13 01   b.Stratford 9-4-71
Source: Tiptree, Dagenham, Dartford, Bishops Stortford, Stevenage Bor.

Season	Club	App	Gls	Tot	
1995-96	Gillingham	40	12		
1996-97	Gillingham	7	2		
1996-97	*Leyton Orient*	5	0	5	0
1997-98	Gillingham	20	4	67	18
1998-99	Lincoln C	9	1	9	1
1998-99	Brentford	11	0	11	0
1998-99	Rotherham U	20	12		
1999-2000	Rotherham U	39	17		
2000-01	Rotherham U	5	1	64	30
2000-01	Cardiff C	37	12	37	12

FOWLER, Jason (M)   170   14
H: 6 3   W: 12 04   b.Bristol 20-8-74
Source: Trainee.

Season	Club	App	Gls	Tot	
1992-93	Bristol C	1	0		
1993-94	Bristol C	1	0		
1994-95	Bristol C	13	0		
1995-96	Bristol C	10	0	25	0
1996-97	Cardiff C	37	5		
1997-98	Cardiff C	38	5		
1998-99	Cardiff C	37	3		
1999-2000	Cardiff C	28	1		
2000-01	Cardiff C	5	0	145	14

GABBIDON, Daniel (D)   63   3
H: 5 10   W: 11 02   b.Cwmbran 8-8-79
Source: Trainee. *Honours:* Wales Under-21.

Season	Club	App	Gls	Tot	
1998-99	WBA	2	0		
1999-2000	WBA	18	0		
2000-01	WBA	0	0	20	0
2000-01	Cardiff C	43	3	43	3

GILES, Martyn (D)   5   0
b.Cardiff 10-4-83
Source: Scholar.

Season	Club	App	Gls	Tot	
2000-01	Cardiff C	5	0	5	0

GORDON, Gavin (F) — 147 38
H: 6 2 W: 12 00 b.Manchester 24-6-79
Source: Trainee.

Season	Club				
1995–96	Hull C	13	3		
1996–97	Hull C	20	4		
1997–98	Hull C	5	2	38	9
1997–98	Lincoln C	13	3		
1998–99	Lincoln C	27	5		
1999–2000	Lincoln C	41	11		
2000–01	Lincoln C	18	9	99	28
2000–01	Cardiff C	10	1	10	1

GRAY, Matthew* (M) — 0 0
b.London 16-9-81

Season	Club		
2000–01	Cardiff C	0	0

HILL, Danny* (M) — 90 4
H: 5 8 W: 11 08 b.Edmonton 1-10-74
Source: Trainee. *Honours:* England Under-21.

Season	Club				
1992–93	Tottenham H	4	0		
1993–94	Tottenham H	3	0		
1994–95	Tottenham H	3	0		
1995–96	Tottenham H	0	0		
1995–96	*Birmingham C*	5	0	5	0
1995–96	*Watford*	1	0	1	0
1996–97	Tottenham H	0	0		
1997–98	Tottenham H	0	0	10	0
1997–98	*Cardiff C*	7	0		
1998–99	Oxford U	9	0	9	0
1998–99	Cardiff C	26	2		
1999–2000	Cardiff C	23	1		
2000–01	Cardiff C	9	1	65	4

HUGHES, David (D) — 66 3
H: 6 4 W: 13 06 b.Wrexham 1-2-78
Source: Trainee. *Honours:* Wales Under-21, B.

Season	Club				
1996–97	Aston Villa	7	0		
1997–98	Aston Villa	0	0		
1997–98	*Carlisle U*	1	0	1	0
1998–99	Aston Villa	0	0		
1999–2000	Aston Villa	0	0	7	0
1999–2000	Shrewsbury T	22	1		
2000–01	Shrewsbury T	24	2	46	3
2000–01	Cardiff C	12	0	12	0

JONES, Gethin (M) — 2 0
b.Carmarthen 8-8-81
Source: Carmarthen T.

Season	Club				
2000–01	Cardiff C	2	0	2	0

JORDAN, Andrew (D) — 16 0
H: 6 2 W: 13 04 b.Manchester 14-12-79
Source: Trainee. *Honours:* Scotland Under-21.

Season	Club				
1997–98	Bristol C	0	0		
1998–99	Bristol C	1	0		
1999–2000	Bristol C	8	0		
2000–01	Bristol C	2	0	11	0
2000–01	Cardiff C	5	0	5	0

KENDALL, Lee (G) — 0 0
H: 5 10 W: 10 05 b.Newport 8-1-81
Source: Trainee. *Honours:* Wales Under-21.

Season	Club		
1997–98	Crystal Palace	0	0
1998–99	Crystal Palace	0	0
1999–2000	Crystal Palace	0	0
2000–01	Crystal Palace	0	0
2000–01	Cardiff C	0	0

LEGG, Andy (D) — 425 51
H: 5 8 W: 11 01 b.Swansea 28-7-66
Source: Briton Ferry. *Honours:* Wales 6 full caps.

Season	Club				
1988–89	Swansea C	6	0		
1989–90	Swansea C	26	3		
1990–91	Swansea C	39	5		
1991–92	Swansea C	46	9		
1992–93	Swansea C	46	12	163	29
1993–94	Notts Co	30	2		
1994–95	Notts Co	34	3		
1995–96	Notts Co	25	4	89	9
1995–96	Birmingham C	12	1		
1996–97	Birmingham C	33	4		
1997–98	Birmingham C	0	0	45	5
1997–98	*Ipswich T*	6	1	6	1
1997–98	Reading	10	0		
1998–99	Reading	2	0	12	0
1998–99	*Peterborough U*	5	0	5	0
1998–99	Cardiff C	24	2		
1999–2000	Cardiff C	42	2		
2000–01	Cardiff C	39	3	105	7

LOW, Josh (F) — 80 7
H: 6 0 W: 14 00 b.Bristol 15-2-79
Source: Trainee. *Honours:* Wales Under-21.

Season	Club				
1995–96	Bristol R	1	0		
1996–97	Bristol R	3	0		
1997–98	Bristol R	10	0		
1998–99	Bristol R	8	0	22	0
1999–2000	Leyton Orient	5	1	5	1
1999–2000	Cardiff C	17	2		
2000–01	Cardiff C	36	4	53	6

McCULLOCH, Scott (D) — 130 6
H: 6 0 W: 13 04 b.Cumnock 29-11-75
Source: Rangers BC.

Season	Club				
1992–93	Rangers	0	0		
1993–94	Rangers	0	0		
1994–95	Hamilton A	8	1		
1995–96	Hamilton A	10	1		
1996–97	Hamilton A	24	1		
1997–98	Hamilton A	15	1	57	4
1997–98	Dunfermline Ath	18	0		
1998–99	Dunfermline Ath	19	1	37	1
1999–2000	Dundee U	15	0	15	0
2000–01	Cardiff C	21	1	21	1

NOGAN, Kurt (F) — 333 113
H: 5 10 W: 11 01 b.Cardiff 9-9-70
Source: Trainee. *Honours:* Wales Under-21.

Season	Club				
1989–90	Luton T	10	2		
1990–91	Luton T	9	0		
1991–92	Luton T	14	1	33	3
1992–93	Peterborough U	0	0		
1992–93	Brighton & HA	30	20		
1993–94	Brighton & HA	41	22		
1994–95	Brighton & HA	26	7	97	49
1994–95	Burnley	15	3		
1995–96	Burnley	46	20		
1996–97	Burnley	31	10	92	33
1996–97	Preston NE	7	0		
1997–98	Preston NE	22	5		
1997–98	Preston NE	42	18		
1999–2000	Preston NE	22	4	93	27
1999–2000	Cardiff C	6	0		
2000–01	Cardiff C	12	1	18	1

NUGENT, Kevin (F) — 393 95
H: 6 2 W: 13 00 b.Edmonton 10-4-69
Source: Trainee. *Honours:* Eire Youth.

Season	Club				
1987–88	Leyton Orient	11	3		
1988–89	Leyton Orient	3	0		
1989–90	Leyton Orient	11	0		
1990–91	Leyton Orient	33	5		
1991–92	Leyton Orient	36	12	94	20
1991–92	Plymouth Arg	4	0		
1992–93	Plymouth Arg	45	11		
1993–94	Plymouth Arg	39	14		
1994–95	Plymouth Arg	37	7		
1995–96	Plymouth Arg	6	0	131	32
1995–96	Bristol C	34	8		
1996–97	Bristol C	36	6	70	14
1997–98	Cardiff C	4	0		
1998–99	Cardiff C	41	15		
1999–2000	Cardiff C	39	10		
2000–01	Cardiff C	14	4	98	29

PERRETT, Russell (D) — 101 3
H: 6 2 W: 13 00 b.Barton-on-Sea 18-6-73
Source: AFC Lymington.

Season	Club				
1995–96	Portsmouth	9	0		
1996–97	Portsmouth	32	1		
1997–98	Portsmouth	16	1		
1998–99	Portsmouth	15	0	72	2
1999–2000	Portsmouth	27	1		
2000–01	Cardiff C	2	0	29	1

SHERIDAN, Tony‡ (F) — 161 25
H: 6 0 W: 11 08 b.Dublin 21-10-74
Honours: Eire Youth, Under-21.

Season	Club				
1991–92	Coventry C	0	0		
1992–93	Coventry C	1	0		
1993–94	Coventry C	8	0		
1994–95	Coventry C	0	0	9	0
1995–96	Shelbourne	29	5		
1996–97	Shelbourne	33	4		
1997–98	Shelbourne	27	2		
1998–99	Shelbourne	30	10	119	21
1999–2000	Portadown	33	4	33	4
2000–01	Cardiff C	0	0		

SKELLY, Lee‡ (D) — 0 0
H: 6 0 W: 12 00 b.Aberdare 10-12-81
Source: Trainee.

Season	Club		
2000–01	Cardiff C	0	0

THOMAS, Dai‡ (F) — 103 18
H: 5 11 W: 13 07 b.Caerphilly 26-9-75
Source: Trainee.

Season	Club				
1994–95	Swansea C	4	0		
1995–96	Swansea C	16	1		
1996–97	Swansea C	36	9	56	10
1997–98	Watford	16	3	16	3
1998–99	Cardiff C	24	4		
1999–2000	Cardiff C	7	1		
2000–01	Cardiff C	0	0	31	5

THOMPSON, Andy (D) — 503 48
H: 5 5 W: 10 06 b.Cannock 9-11-67
Source: Apprentice.

Season	Club				
1985–86	WBA	15	1		
1986–87	WBA	9	0	24	1
1986–87	Wolverhampton W	29	8		
1987–88	Wolverhampton W	42	2		
1988–89	Wolverhampton W	46	6		
1989–90	Wolverhampton W	33	4		
1990–91	Wolverhampton W	44	3		
1991–92	Wolverhampton W	17	0		
1992–93	Wolverhampton W	20	0		
1993–94	Wolverhampton W	37	3		
1994–95	Wolverhampton W	31	9		
1995–96	Wolverhampton W	45	6		
1996–97	Wolverhampton W	32	2	376	43
1997–98	Tranmere R	44	3		
1998–99	Tranmere R	37	1		
1999–2000	Tranmere R	15	0	96	4
2000–01	Cardiff C	7	0	7	0

WALTON, Mark (G) — 210 0
H: 6 4 W: 15 08 b.Merthyr 1-6-69
Source: Swansea C. *Honours:* Wales Under-21.

Season	Club				
1986–87	Luton T	0	0		
1987–88	Luton T	0	0		
1987–88	Colchester U	17	0		
1988–89	Colchester U	23	0	40	0
1989–90	Norwich C	1	0		
1990–91	Norwich C	4	0		
1991–92	Norwich C	17	0		
1992–93	Norwich C	0	0		
1993–94	Norwich C	0	0		
1993–94	*Wrexham*	6	0	6	0
1993–94	Dundee	0	0		
1993–94	*Bolton W*	3	0	3	0

From Fakenham T.

Season	Club				
1996–97	Fulham	28	0		
1997–98	Fulham	12	0	40	0
1997–98	*Gillingham*	1	0	1	0
1997–98	*Norwich C*	0	0	22	0
1998–99	Brighton & HA	19	0		
1999–2000	Brighton & HA	39	0	58	0
2000–01	Cardiff C	40	0	40	0

WESTON, Rhys (D) — 29 0
H: 6 0 W: 12 03 b.Kingston 27-10-80
Source: Trainee. *Honours:* Wales Under-21, 1 full cap.

Season	Club				
1999–2000	Arsenal	1	0		
2000–01	Arsenal	0	0	1	0
2000–01	Cardiff C	28	0	28	0

YOUNG, Scott (D) — 232 17
H: 6 2 W: 13 04 b.Llwynypia 14-1-76
Source: Trainee. *Honours:* Wales Under-21.

Season	Club				
1993–94	Cardiff C	6	0		
1994–95	Cardiff C	22	0		
1995–96	Cardiff C	41	0		
1996–97	Cardiff C	32	1		
1997–98	Cardiff C	31	3		
1998–99	Cardiff C	33	1		
1999–2000	Cardiff C	22	2		
2000–01	Cardiff C	45	10	232	17

Scholars
Anthony, Byron; Bailey, John; Brimble, Daniel; Busby, Dean C; Evans, Gari; Fish, Nicholas; Hajgato, Gezza; Hayward, Michael; Heal, Simon AF; Huggins, Kirk; Ingram, Richard G; Lewis, David MJ; Lippiett, Darren; Morley, Wayne; Parkins, Michael F; Porter, Marc A; Thomas, Daniel; Wallis, Tony

CARLISLE U

ALLAN, Jonathan (M) — 0 0
b.Carlisle 24-5-83
Source: Trainee.

Season	Club		
2000–01	Carlisle U	0	0

ANTONY, Paul (M) — 0 0
H: 5 10 W: 11 00 b.Barnet 4-3-82
Source: Trainee.

Season	Club		
2000–01	Carlisle U	0	0

BIRCH, Mark# (D) — 44 0
H: 5 11 W: 12 02 b.Stoke 5-1-77
Source: Trainee.

Season	Club				
1997–98	Stoke C	0	0		

From Northwich V.

Season	Club				
2000–01	Carlisle U	44	0	44	0

CONNELLY, Gordon# (F) — 131 8
H: 6 0 W: 12 04 b.Glasgow 1-11-76

Season	Club				
1995–96	Airdrieonians	8	0		
1996–97	Airdrieonians	4	0		
1997–98	Airdrieonians	21	1	33	1
1998–99	York C	28	4	28	4

1999–2000 Southend U 33 2
2000–01 Southend U 9 0 **42 2**
2000–01 Carlisle U 28 1 **28 1**

DARBY, Julian# (M) 420 44
H: 6 0 W: 11 04 b.Bolton 3-10-67
Source: Trainee. *Honours:* England Schools.
1984–85 Bolton W 0 0
1985–86 Bolton W 2 0
1986–87 Bolton W 28 0
1987–88 Bolton W 35 2
1988–89 Bolton W 44 5
1989–90 Bolton W 46 10
1990–91 Bolton W 45 9
1991–92 Bolton W 44 6
1992–93 Bolton W 21 4
1993–94 Bolton W 5 0 **270 36**
1993–94 Coventry C 26 5
1994–95 Coventry C 29 0
1995–96 Coventry C 0 0 **55 5**
1995–96 WBA 22 1
1996–97 WBA 17 0 **39 1**
1997–98 Preston NE 12 0
1997–98 *Rotherham U* 3 0 **3 0**
1998–99 Preston NE 20 1
1999–2000 Preston NE 3 0 **35 1**
2000–01 Carlisle U 18 1 **18 1**

DAWSON, Andrew† (D) 28 1
H: 6 0 W: 12 00 b.York 8-12-79
Source: Trainee.
1998–99 York C 11 1
1999–2000 York C 17 0
2000–01 York C 0 0 **28 1**
2000–01 Carlisle U 0 0

DOBIE, Scott (F) 142 24
H: 6 2 W: 12 09 b.Workington 10-10-78
Source: Trainee.
1996–97 Carlisle U 2 1
1997–98 Carlisle U 23 0
1998–99 Carlisle U 33 6
1998–99 *Clydebank* 6 0 **6 0**
1999–2000 Carlisle U 34 7
2000–01 Carlisle U 44 10 **136 24**

GALLOWAY, Mick (M) 147 7
H: 5 11 W: 11 05 b.Nottingham 13-10-74
Source: Trainee.
1993–94 Notts Co 0 0
1994–95 Notts Co 7 0
1995–96 Notts Co 9 0
1996–97 Notts Co 5 0 **21 0**
1996–97 *Gillingham* 9 1
1997–98 Gillingham 39 1
1998–99 Gillingham 25 3
1999–2000 Gillingham 2 0 **75 5**
1999–2000 *Lincoln C* 5 0 **5 0**
1999–2000 Chesterfield 15 1
2000–01 Chesterfield 5 0 **20 1**
2000–01 Carlisle U 26 1 **26 1**

HALLIDAY, Stephen (F) 184 33
H: 5 10 W: 12 07 b.Sunderland 3-5-76
Source: Charlton Ath.
1993–94 Hartlepool U 11 0
1994–95 Hartlepool U 28 5
1995–96 Hartlepool U 39 7
1996–97 Hartlepool U 31 8
1997–98 Hartlepool U 31 5 **140 25**
1998–99 *Motherwell* 4 0 **4 0**
1999–2000 Carlisle U 16 7
2000–01 Carlisle U 24 1 **40 8**

HARRIES, Paul‡ (F) 26 2
H: 6 1 W: 13 00 b.Sydney 19-11-77
Source: Wollongong Wolves 6 apps, 1 goal.
1997–98 Portsmouth 1 0 **1 0**
1998–99 Crystal Palace 0 0
1998–99 *Torquay U* 5 0 **5 0**
1999–2000 Carlisle U 20 2
2000–01 Carlisle U 0 0 **20 2**

HEGGS, Carl (F) 178 23
H: 6 1 W: 12 10 b.Leicester 11-10-70
Source: Doncaster R Trainee, Paget R.
1991–92 WBA 3 0
1992–93 WBA 17 2
1993–94 WBA 6 0
1994–95 WBA 14 1 **40 3**
1994–95 *Bristol R* 5 1 **5 1**
1995–96 Swansea C 32 5
1996–97 Swansea C 14 2 **46 7**
1997–98 Northampton T 33 4
1998–99 Northampton T 13 1 **46 5**
From Rushden & D.
1999–2000 Chester C 11 2 **11 2**
2000–01 Carlisle U 30 5 **30 5**

HEMMINGS, Tony# (M) 90 14
H: 5 10 W: 12 09 b.Burton 21-9-67
Source: Northwich Vic.
1993–94 Wycombe W 26 7

1994–95 Wycombe W 20 5
1995–96 Wycombe W 3 0 **49 12**
From Ilkeston T.
1999–2000 Chester C 19 2 **19 2**
2000–01 Carlisle U 22 0 **22 0**

HOPPER, Tony† (M) 109 1
H: 5 11 W: 12 08 b.Carlisle 31-5-76
Source: Trainee.
1992–93 Carlisle U 1 0
1993–94 Carlisle U 1 0
1994–95 Carlisle U 5 0
1995–96 Carlisle U 5 0
1996–97 Carlisle U 20 1
1997–98 Carlisle U 19 0
1998–99 Carlisle U 23 0
1999–2000 Carlisle U 27 0
2000–01 Carlisle U 9 0 **109 1**

HORE, John (F) 2 0
H: 5 11 W: 11 12 b.Liverpool 18-8-82
Source: Trainee.
1999–2000 Carlisle U 1 0
2000–01 Carlisle U 1 0 **2 0**

INGLIS, John‡ (D) 405 15
H: 6 0 W: 13 00 b.Edinburgh 16-10-66
Source: Hutchison Vale.
1983–84 East Fife 4 1
1984–85 East Fife 9 0
1985–86 East Fife 30 0
1986–87 East Fife 13 0 **56 1**
1986–87 Brechin C 15 0
1987–88 Brechin C 26 3
1988–89 Brechin C 12 1 **53 4**
1988–89 Meadowbank T 12 1
1989–90 Meadowbank T 38 3 **50 4**
1990–91 St Johnstone 31 1
1991–92 St Johnstone 40 0
1992–93 St Johnstone 39 0
1993–94 St Johnstone 25 1
1994–95 St Johnstone 5 0 **140 2**
1994–95 Aberdeen 17 1
1995–96 Aberdeen 24 1
1996–97 Aberdeen 15 0
1997–98 Aberdeen 25 1
1998–99 Aberdeen 17 1
1998–99 CSKA Sofia 0 0
1999–2000 Aberdeen 0 0
2000–01 Aberdeen 0 0 **98 4**
2000–01 Carlisle U 8 0 **8 0**

KEEN, Peter* (G) 16 1
H: 6 0 W: 11 10 b.Middlesbrough 16-11-76
Source: Trainee.
1995–96 Newcastle U 0 0
1996–97 Newcastle U 0 0
1997–98 Newcastle U 0 0
1998–99 Newcastle U 0 0
1999–2000 Carlisle U 6 0
2000–01 Carlisle U 3 1 **9 1**
2000–01 *Darlington* 7 0 **7 0**

LEE, David‡ (F) 488 64
H: 5 7 W: 11 00 b.Whitefield 5-11-67
Source: Blackburn Schools.
1984–85 Bury 0 0
1985–86 Bury 1 0
1986–87 Bury 30 4
1987–88 Bury 40 3
1988–89 Bury 45 4
1989–90 Bury 45 8
1990–91 Bury 45 15
1991–92 Bury 2 1 **208 35**
1991–92 Southampton 19 0
1992–93 Southampton 1 0 **20 0**
1992–93 Bolton W 32 5
1993–94 Bolton W 41 5
1994–95 Bolton W 39 4
1995–96 Bolton W 18 1
1996–97 Bolton W 25 2 **155 17**
1997–98 Wigan Ath 43 5
1998–99 Wigan Ath 36 6
1999–2000 Wigan Ath 4 0 **83 11**
1999–2000 *Blackpool* 9 1 **9 1**
2000–01 Carlisle U 13 0 **13 0**

MADDISON, Lee (D) 227 1
H: 6 0 W: 12 10 b.Bristol 5-10-72
Source: Trainee.
1991–92 Bristol R 10 0
1992–93 Bristol R 12 0
1993–94 Bristol R 37 0
1994–95 Bristol R 14 0
1995–96 Bristol R 0 0 **73 0**
1995–96 Northampton T 21 0
1996–97 Northampton T 34 0 **55 0**
1997–98 Dundee 24 1
1998–99 Dundee 21 0
1999–2000 Dundee 20 0
2000–01 Dundee 0 0 **65 1**

2000–01 Carlisle U 34 0 **34 0**

McAUGHTRIE, Craig (D) 5 0
H: 6 2 W: 14 07 b.Burton-on-Trent 3-3-81
Source: Trainee.
1999–2000 Sheffield U 0 0
2000–01 Carlisle U 5 0 **5 0**

MORLEY, David (D) 106 2
H: 6 2 W: 13 05 b.St Helens 25-9-77
Source: Trainee.
1995–96 Manchester C 0 0
1996–97 Manchester C 0 0
1997–98 Manchester C 3 1
1997–98 *Ayr U* 4 0 **4 0**
1998–99 Manchester C 0 0 **3 1**
1998–99 Southend U 27 0
1999–2000 Southend U 32 0
2000–01 Southend U 17 0 **76 0**
2000–01 Carlisle U 23 1 **23 1**

PITTS, Matthew‡ (D) 34 1
H: 5 11 W: 12 06 b.Middlesbrough 25-12-79
Source: Trainee.
1998–99 Sunderland 0 0
1999–2000 Carlisle U 29 1
2000–01 Carlisle U 5 0 **34 1**

PRUDHOE, Mark† (G) 350 0
H: 6 0 W: 14 00 b.Washington 8-11-63
Source: Apprentice.
1981–83 Sunderland 0 0
1982–83 Sunderland 7 0
1983–84 Sunderland 0 0
1983–84 *Hartlepool U* 3 0
1984–85 Sunderland 0 0 **7 0**
1984–85 *Birmingham C* 1 0 **1 0**
1985–86 Walsall 16 0
1986–87 Walsall 10 0
1986–87 *Doncaster R* 5 0 **5 0**
1986–87 *Sheffield W* 0 0
1986–87 *Grimsby T* 8 0 **8 0**
1987–88 Walsall 0 0 **26 0**
1987–88 *Hartlepool U* 13 0 **16 0**
1987–88 *Bristol C* 3 0 **3 0**
1987–88 Carlisle U 22 0
1988–89 Carlisle U 12 0
1988–89 Darlington 12 0
1989–90 Darlington 0 0
1990–91 Darlington 46 0
1991–92 Darlington 46 0
1992–93 Darlington 42 0
1993–94 Stoke C 30 0
1994–95 Stoke C 0 0
1994–95 *Peterborough U* 6 0 **6 0**
1994–95 *Liverpool* 0 0
1995–96 Stoke C 39 0
1996–97 Stoke C 13 0 **82 0**
1996–97 *York C* 2 0 **2 0**
1997–98 Bradford C 8 0
1998–99 Bradford C 0 0 **8 0**
1999–2000 *Darlington* 0 0 **146 0**
From Guiseley
1999–2000 Southend U 6 0
2000–01 Southend U 0 0 **6 0**
2000–01 Carlisle U 0 0 **34 0**

SKELTON, Gavin‡ (M) 7 0
H: 5 7 W: 10 00 b.Carlisle 27-3-81
Source: Trainee.
1999–2000 Carlisle U 7 0
2000–01 Carlisle U 0 0 **7 0**

SKINNER, Stephen‡ (F) 2 0
H: 6 0 W: 12 03 b.Whitehaven 25-11-81
Source: Trainee.
1999–2000 Carlisle U 2 0
2000–01 Carlisle U 0 0 **2 0**

SOLEY, Steve (M) 80 12
H: 5 11 W: 12 08 b.Widnes 22-4-71
Source: Warrington, Leek T.
1998–99 Portsmouth 8 0
1998–99 *Macclesfield T* 10 0 **10 0**
1999–2000 Portsmouth 0 0 **8 0**
1999–2000 Carlisle U 37 8
2000–01 Carlisle U 25 4 **62 12**

SQUIRES, Jamie* (D) 63 2
H: 6 2 W: 13 03 b.Preston 15-11-75
Source: Trainee.
1993–94 Preston NE 4 0
1994–95 Preston NE 11 0
1995–96 Preston NE 7 0
1996–97 Preston NE 9 0
1997–98 Preston NE 0 0 **31 0**
1997–98 *Mansfield T* 1 0 **1 0**
1997–98 Dunfermline Ath 0 0
1998–99 Dunfermline Ath 21 2
1999–2000 Dunfermline Ath 0 0 **26 2**
2000–01 Carlisle U 5 0 **5 0**

STEVENS, Ian# (F) 417 126
H: 5 10 W: 12 07 b.Malta 21-10-69
Source: Trainee.

Season	Club	A	G	A	G
1984–85	Preston NE	4	1		
1985–86	Preston NE	7	1	11	2
1986–87	Stockport Co	2	0	2	0
From Lancaster C					
1986–87	Bolton W	8	2		
1987–88	Bolton W	9	0		
1988–89	Bolton W	21	5		
1989–90	Bolton W	4	0		
1990–91	Bolton W	5	0	47	7
1991–92	Bury	45	17		
1992–93	Bury	32	14		
1993–94	Bury	33	7	110	38
1994–95	Shrewsbury T	38	8		
1995–96	Shrewsbury T	32	12		
1996–97	Shrewsbury T	41	17	111	37
1996–97	Carlisle U	0	0		
1997–98	Carlisle U	37	17		
1998–99	Carlisle U	41	9		
1999–2000	Wrexham	16	4	16	4
1999–2000	*Cheltenham T*	1	0	1	0
2000–01	Carlisle U	41	12	119	38

THURSTON, Mark (M) 5 0
H: 6 2 W: 11 08 b.Carlisle 10-2-80
Source: Trainee.

Season	Club	A	G	A	G
1998–99	Carlisle U	0	0		
1999–2000	Carlisle U	0	0		
2000–01	Carlisle U	5	0	5	0

THWAITES, Adam (M) 0 0
H: 5 10 W: 11 00 b.Kendal 0-0-0
Source: Trainee.

Season	Club	A	G
2000–01	Carlisle U	0	0

WEAVER, Luke (G) 58 0
H: 6 2 W: 13 02 b.Woolwich 26-6-79
Source: Trainee. *Honours:* England Schools, Youth.

Season	Club	A	G	A	G
1996–97	Leyton Orient	9	0		
1996–97	*West Ham U*	0	0		
1997–98	Leyton Orient	0	0	9	0
1997–98	Sunderland	0	0		
1998–99	*Scarborough*	6	0	6	0
1999–2000	Sunderland	0	0		
1999–2000	Carlisle U	29	0		
2000–01	Carlisle U	14	0	43	0

WHITEHEAD, Stuart (D) 111 1
H: 6 0 W: 12 02 b.Bromsgrove 17-7-76
Source: Bromsgrove R.

Season	Club	A	G	A	G
1995–96	Bolton W	0	0		
1996–97	Bolton W	0	0		
1997–98	Bolton W	0	0		
1998–99	Carlisle U	37	0		
1999–2000	Carlisle U	29	0		
2000–01	Carlisle U	45	1	111	1

WINSTANLEY, Mark# (D) 449 9
H: 6 1 W: 12 07 b.St Helens 22-1-68
Source: Trainee.

Season	Club	A	G	A	G
1984–85	Bolton W	0	0		
1985–86	Bolton W	3	0		
1986–87	Bolton W	13	0		
1987–88	Bolton W	8	1		
1988–89	Bolton W	44	0		
1989–90	Bolton W	43	1		
1990–91	Bolton W	32	0		
1991–92	Bolton W	27	0		
1992–93	Bolton W	29	1		
1993–94	Bolton W	21	0	220	3
1994–95	Burnley	44	2		
1995–96	Burnley	45	3		
1996–97	Burnley	35	0		
1997–98	Burnley	27	0		
1998–99	Burnley	1	0	152	5
1998–99	*Shrewsbury T*	0	0		
1998–99	*Scunthorpe U*	0	0		
1999–2000	Preston NE	0	0		
1999–2000	Shrewsbury T	33	1	41	1
2000–01	Carlisle U	36	0	36	0

Scholars
Andrews, Lee D; Bell, Stuart; Blades, Neil; Brown, Gary; Bruce, Paul R; Dickinson, Michael J; Hoolickin, Lee; Jack, Michael L; Johnston, Craig B; Lewis, Craig; May, Kyle; McKie, Michael J; Mitchell, Andrew R; Nicholson, Richard A; Nixon, Marc S; Robinson, Nicholas A; Rooke, Steven
Non-Contract
Dalton, Neil J

CHARLTON ATH

ALLMAN, Anthony* (D) 0 0
H: 5 9 W: 10 07 b.Sidcup 14-12-80
Source: Trainee. *Honours:* England Schools.

Season	Club	A	G
1997–98	Charlton Ath	0	0
1998–99	Charlton Ath	0	0
1999–2000	Charlton Ath	0	0
2000–01	Charlton Ath	0	0

BAGHERI, Karim (M) 52 6
H: 6 1 W: 12 04 b.Tabriz 20-2-74
Source: Teraktor Sazi, Keshavarz, Pirouzi. *Honours:* Iran 48 full caps.

Season	Club	A	G	A	G
1997–98	Arminia Bielefeld	18	3		
1998–99	Arminia Bielefeld	22	2		
1999–2000	Arminia Bielefeld	11	1	51	6
From Pirouzi					
2000–01	Charlton Ath	1	0	1	0

BARTLETT, Shaun (F) 152 49
H: 6 2 W: 12 04 b.Cape Town 31-10-72
Source: Cape Town Spurs. South Africa 46 full caps, 18 goals.

Season	Club	A	G	A	G
1996	Colorado Rapids	26	8		
1996–97	Amazulu	0	0		
1997	New York/New Jersey M	13	2	13	2
1997	Colorado Rapids	10	1	36	9
1998	Cape Town Spurs	18	8	18	8
1998–99	Zurich	27	13		
1999–2000	Zurich	20	2		
2000–01	Zurich	20	8	67	23
2000–01	Charlton Ath	18	7	18	7

BRENNAN, Martin (G) 0 0
b.0-0-0

Season	Club	A	G
2000–01	Charlton Ath	0	0

BROWN, Steve (M) 225 7
H: 6 1 W: 14 10 b.Brighton 13-5-72
Source: Trainee.

Season	Club	A	G	A	G
1990–91	Charlton Ath	0	0		
1991–92	Charlton Ath	1	0		
1992–93	Charlton Ath	0	0		
1993–94	Charlton Ath	19	0		
1994–95	Charlton Ath	42	3		
1995–96	Charlton Ath	19	0		
1996–97	Charlton Ath	27	0		
1997–98	Charlton Ath	34	2		
1998–99	Charlton Ath	18	0		
1999–2000	Charlton Ath	40	2		
2000–01	Charlton Ath	25	0	225	7

CAIG, Tony* (G) 273 0
H: 6 1 W: 12 00 b.Whitehaven 11-4-74
Source: Trainee.

Season	Club	A	G	A	G
1992–93	Carlisle U	1	0		
1993–94	Carlisle U	20	0		
1994–95	Carlisle U	40	0		
1995–96	Carlisle U	33	0		
1996–97	Carlisle U	46	0		
1997–98	Carlisle U	46	0		
1998–99	Carlisle U	37	0	223	0
1998–99	Blackpool	10	0		
1999–2000	Blackpool	33	0		
2000–01	Blackpool	6	0	49	0
2000–01	Charlton Ath	1	0	1	0

COLLIS, Dave (D) 2 0
H: 5 10 W: 10 12 b.London 8-11-81

Season	Club	A	G	A	G
2000–01	Charlton Ath	0	0		
2000–01	*Barnet*	2	0	2	0

DE BOLLA, Mark (F) 0 0
b.London 1-1-83
Source: Trainee.

Season	Club	A	G
1999–2000	Aston Villa	0	0
2000–01	Charlton Ath	0	0

DINCER, Fatih (M) 0 0
b.Stockholm 13-7-83

Season	Club	A	G
2000–01	Charlton Ath	0	0

FISH, Mark (D) 272 13
H: 6 4 W: 13 06 b.Cape Town 14-3-74
Source: Arcadia Shepherds. *Honours:* South Africa 59 full caps, 2 goals.

Season	Club	A	G	A	G
1992	Jomo Cosmos	14	1		
1993	Jomo Cosmos	41	1	55	2
1994	Orlando Pirates	37	5		
1995	Orlando Pirates	38	1	75	6
1996–97	Lazio	15	1	15	1
1997–98	Bolton W	22	2		
1998–99	Bolton W	36	1		
1999–2000	Bolton W	31	0		
2000–01	Bolton W	14	0	103	3
2000–01	Charlton Ath	24	1	24	1

FORTUNE, Jonathan (D) 18 0
H: 6 2 W: 12 12 b.Islington 23-8-80
Source: Trainee.

Season	Club	A	G
1998–99	Charlton Ath	0	0
1999–2000	Charlton Ath	0	0
1999–2000	Mansfield T	4	0
2000–01	Charlton Ath	0	0

Season	Club	A	G	A	G
2000–01	Mansfield T	14	0	18	0

GEORGE, Kevin (M) 0 0
H: 5 11 W: 12 04 b.London 21-11-82
Source: Scholar.

Season	Club	A	G
2000–01	Charlton Ath	0	0

GREENAWAY, James* (D) 0 0
H: 6 2 W: 12 08 b.Epsom 9-4-82

Season	Club	A	G
2000–01	Charlton Ath	0	0

HALES, Lee‡ (F) 0 0
H: 5 10 W: 11 00 b.Gillingham 1-5-81
Source: Trainee.

Season	Club	A	G
1998–99	Charlton Ath	0	0
1999–2000	Charlton Ath	0	0
2000–01	Charlton Ath	0	0

HOCKLEY, David‡ (M) 0 0
H: 5 11 W: 11 05 b.Gillingham 23-2-81
Source: Trainee.

Season	Club	A	G
1998–99	Charlton Ath	0	0
1999–2000	Charlton Ath	0	0
2000–01	Charlton Ath	0	0

HUNT, Andy (F) 341 122
H: 6 1 W: 12 08 b.Thurrock 9-6-70
Source: Kettering T.

Season	Club	A	G	A	G
1990–91	Newcastle U	16	2		
1991–92	Newcastle U	27	9		
1992–93	Newcastle U	0	0	43	11
1992–93	WBA	10	9		
1993–94	WBA	35	12		
1994–95	WBA	39	13		
1995–96	WBA	45	14		
1996–97	WBA	45	15		
1997–98	WBA	38	13	212	76
1998–99	Charlton Ath	34	7		
1999–2000	Charlton Ath	44	24		
2000–01	Charlton Ath	8	4	86	35

ILIC, Sasa (G) 52 0
H: 6 4 W: 14 12 b.Melbourne 18-7-72
Source: Partizan Belgrade, Radnicki, Ringwood, Daewoo Royals, St Leonards Stamcroft. *Honours:* Yugoslavia 1 full cap.

Season	Club	A	G	A	G
1997–98	Charlton Ath	14	0		
1998–99	Charlton Ath	23	0		
1999–2000	Charlton Ath	1	0		
1999–2000	*West Ham U*	1	0	1	0
2000–01	Charlton Ath	13	0	51	0

JENSEN, Claus (M) 190 27
H: 6 1 W: 13 04 b.Nykobing 29-4-77
Source: Stubbekobing, Nykobing. *Honours:* Denmark Under-21, 11 full caps, 1 goal.

Season	Club	A	G	A	G
1995–96	Naestved	4	0	4	0
1996–97	Lyngby	31	3		
1997–98	Lyngby	31	11	62	14
1998–99	Bolton W	44	2		
1999–2000	Bolton W	42	6	86	8
2000–01	Charlton Ath	38	5	38	5

JOHANSSON, Jonatan (F) 119 40
H: 6 2 W: 12 08 b.Stockholm 16-8-75
Source: Flora Tallinn. *Honours:* Finland 35 full caps, 9 goals.

Season	Club	A	G	A	G
1995	TPS Turku	9	0		
1996	TPS Turku	23	6	32	6
1996–97	Flora Tallinn	9	9	9	9
1997–98	Rangers	6	0		
1998–99	Rangers	25	8		
1999–2000	Rangers	16	6	47	14
2000–01	Charlton Ath	31	11	31	11

KIELY, Dean (G) 417 0
H: 6 0 W: 12 13 b.Salford 10-10-70
Source: WBA School. *Honours:* England Schools, FA Schools, Youth, Eire 4 full caps.

Season	Club	A	G	A	G
1987–88	Coventry C	0	0		
1988–89	Coventry C	0	0		
1989–90	Coventry C	0	0		
1989–90	*Ipswich T*	0	0		
1989–90	*York C*	0	0		
1990–91	York C	17	0		
1991–92	York C	21	0		
1992–93	York C	40	0		
1993–94	York C	46	0		
1994–95	York C	46	0		
1995–96	York C	40	0	210	0
1996–97	Bury	46	0		
1997–98	Bury	46	0		
1998–99	Bury	45	0	137	0
1999–2000	Charlton Ath	45	0		
2000–01	Charlton Ath	25	0	70	0

KINSELLA, Mark (M) 371 46
H: 5 8 W: 12 01 b.Dublin 12-8-72
Source: Home Farm. *Honours:* Eire 24 full caps, 2 goals.

Season	Club	A	G
1989–90	Colchester U	6	0
1990–91	Colchester U	0	0

1991–92	Colchester U	0	0		
1992–93	Colchester U	38	6		
1993–94	Colchester U	42	8		
1994–95	Colchester U	42	6		
1995–96	Colchester U	45	5		
1996–97	Colchester U	7	2	180	27
1996–97	Charlton Ath	37	6		
1997–98	Charlton Ath	38	4		
1998–99	Charlton Ath	38	2		
1999–2000	Charlton Ath	38	3		
2000–01	Charlton Ath	32	2	191	19

KISHISHEV, Radostin (D) 220 17
H: 5 10   W: 12 08   b.Bourgas 30-7-74
Honours: Bulgaria 41 full caps.

1991–92	Chernomorets	6	1		
1992–93	Chernomorets	23	2		
1993–94	Chernomorets	23	1	52	4
1994–95	Neftochimik	14	0		
1995–96	Neftochimik	30	6		
1996–97	Neftochimik	30	6		
1997–98	Neftochimik	1	0	75	6
1997–98	Bursaspor	20	3	20	3
1997–98	Litets Lovch	5	0	5	0
1998–99	Litets Lovch	26	2		
1999–2000	Litets Lovech	15	2	41	4
2000–01	Charlton Ath	27	0	27	0

KONCHESKY, Paul (D) 36 0
H: 5 10   W: 11 07   b.Barking 15-5-81
Source: Trainee. *Honours:* England Youth.

1997–98	Charlton Ath	3	0		
1998–99	Charlton Ath	2	0		
1999–2000	Charlton Ath	8	0		
2000–01	Charlton Ath	23	0	36	0

LISBIE, Kevin (F) 72 6
H: 5 10   W: 11 01   b.Hackney 17-10-78
Source: Trainee. *Honours:* England Youth.

1996–97	Charlton Ath	25	1		
1997–98	Charlton Ath	17	1		
1998–99	Charlton Ath	1	0		
1998–99	Gillingham	7	4	7	4
1999–2000	Charlton Ath	0	0		
1999–2000	Reading	2	0	2	0
2000–01	Charlton Ath	18	0	61	2
2000–01	QPR	2	0	2	0

MACDONALD, Charlie (F) 14 2
H: 5 8   W: 12 10   b.Southwark 13-2-81
Source: Trainee.

1998–99	Charlton Ath	0	0		
1999–2000	Charlton Ath	3	0		
2000–01	Charlton Ath	3	0	6	0
2000–01	Cheltenham T	8	2	8	2

MARTIN, Alex (M) 0 0
H: 5 8   W: 11 04   b.Harlow 2-5-83
Source: Scholar.

2000–01	Charlton Ath	0	0		

MENDONCA, Clive (F) 359 131
H: 5 10   W: 12 10   b.Islington 9-9-68
Source: Apprentice.

1986–87	Sheffield U	2	0		
1987–88	Sheffield U	11	4		
1987–88	Doncaster R	2	0	2	0
1987–88	Rotherham U	8	2		
1988–89	Rotherham U	10	1		
1989–90	Rotherham U	32	14		
1990–91	Rotherham U	34	10	84	27
1991–92	Sheffield U	10	1	23	5
1991–92	Grimsby T	10	3		
1992–93	Grimsby T	42	10		
1993–94	Grimsby T	39	14		
1994–95	Grimsby T	22	11		
1995–96	Grimsby T	8	4		
1996–97	Grimsby T	45	17	166	59
1997–98	Charlton Ath	40	23		
1998–99	Charlton Ath	25	8		
1999–2000	Charlton Ath	19	9		
2000–01	Charlton Ath	0	0	84	40

NEWTON, Shaun (F) 240 20
H: 5 8   W: 11 12   b.Camberwell 20-8-75
Source: Trainee. *Honours:* England Under-21.

1992–93	Charlton Ath	2	0		
1993–94	Charlton Ath	19	2		
1994–95	Charlton Ath	26	0		
1995–96	Charlton Ath	41	5		
1996–97	Charlton Ath	43	3		
1997–98	Charlton Ath	41	5		
1998–99	Charlton Ath	16	0		
1999–2000	Charlton Ath	42	5		
2000–01	Charlton Ath	10	0	240	20

PARKER, Scott (M) 48 3
H: 5 9   W: 10 12   b.Lambeth 13-10-80
Source: Trainee. *Honours:* England Schools, Youth, Under-21.

1997–98	Charlton Ath	3	0		
1998–99	Charlton Ath	4	0		
1999–2000	Charlton Ath	15	1		

2000–01	Charlton Ath	20	1	42	2
2000–01	Norwich C	6	1	6	1

POWELL, Chris (D) 464 4
H: 5 10   W: 11 13   b.Lambeth 8-9-69
Source: Trainee. *Honours:* England 3 full caps.

1987–88	Crystal Palace	0	0		
1988–89	Crystal Palace	3	0		
1989–90	Crystal Palace	0	0	3	0
1989–90	Aldershot	11	0	11	0
1990–91	Southend U	45	1		
1991–92	Southend U	44	0		
1992–93	Southend U	42	2		
1993–94	Southend U	46	0		
1994–95	Southend U	44	0		
1995–96	Southend U	27	0	248	3
1995–96	Derby Co	19	0		
1996–97	Derby Co	35	0		
1997–98	Derby Co	37	1	91	1
1998–99	Charlton Ath	38	0		
1999–2000	Charlton Ath	40	0		
2000–01	Charlton Ath	33	0	111	0

PRINGLE, Martin (F) 163 29
H: 6 2   W: 12 03   b.Gothenburg 18-11-70
Source: Stenungsund. *Honours:* Sweden 2 full caps, 1 goal.

1994	Helsingborg	21	3		
1995	Helsingborg	22	7		
1996	Helsingborg	21	5	64	15
1996–97	Benfica	15	3		
1997–98	Benfica	14	2		
1998–99	Benfica	12	1	41	6
1998–99	Charlton Ath	18	3		
1999–2000	Charlton Ath	32	4		
2000–01	Charlton Ath	8	1	58	8

ROBERTS, Ben (G) 62 0
H: 6 2   W: 13 00   b.Bishop Auckland 22-6-75
Source: Trainee. *Honours:* England Under-21.

1992–93	Middlesbrough	0	0		
1993–94	Middlesbrough	0	0		
1994–95	Middlesbrough	0	0		
1995–96	Middlesbrough	0	0		
1995–96	Hartlepool U	4	0	4	0
1995–96	Wycombe W	15	0	15	0
1996–97	Middlesbrough	10	0		
1996–97	Bradford C	2	0	2	0
1997–98	Middlesbrough	6	0		
1998–99	Middlesbrough	0	0		
1998–99	Millwall	11	0	11	0
1999–2000	Middlesbrough	0	0	16	0
1999–2000	Luton T	14	0	14	0
2000–01	Charlton Ath	0	0		

ROBINSON, John (F) 353 40
H: 5 10   W: 12 01   b.Bulawayo 29-8-71
Source: Apprentice. *Honours:* Wales Under-21, 26 full caps, 3 goals.

1989–90	Brighton & HA	5	0		
1990–91	Brighton & HA	15	0		
1991–92	Brighton & HA	36	6		
1992–93	Brighton & HA	6	0	62	6
1992–93	Charlton Ath	15	2		
1993–94	Charlton Ath	27	1		
1994–95	Charlton Ath	21	3		
1995–96	Charlton Ath	44	6		
1996–97	Charlton Ath	42	3		
1997–98	Charlton Ath	38	8		
1998–99	Charlton Ath	30	2		
1999–2000	Charlton Ath	45	7		
2000–01	Charlton Ath	29	2	291	34

ROYAL, Mark* (F) 0 0
H: 5 10   W: 12 03   b.Huddersfield 20-12-81

2000–01	Charlton Ath	0	0		

RUFUS, Richard (D) 248 9
H: 6 1   W: 12 12   b.Lewisham 12-1-75
Source: Trainee. *Honours:* England Under-21.

1993–94	Charlton Ath	0	0		
1994–95	Charlton Ath	28	0		
1995–96	Charlton Ath	41	0		
1996–97	Charlton Ath	34	0		
1997–98	Charlton Ath	40	0		
1998–99	Charlton Ath	27	1		
1999–2000	Charlton Ath	44	6		
2000–01	Charlton Ath	32	2	248	9

SALAKO, John (F) 361 32
H: 5 9   W: 11 12   b.Nigeria 11-2-69
Source: Trainee. *Honours:* England 5 full caps.

1986–87	Crystal Palace	4	0		
1987–88	Crystal Palace	31	0		
1988–89	Crystal Palace	28	0		
1989–90	Crystal Palace	17	2		
1989–90	Swansea C	13	3	13	3
1990–91	Crystal Palace	35	6		

1991–92	Crystal Palace	10	2		
1992–93	Crystal Palace	13	0		
1993–94	Crystal Palace	38	8		
1994–95	Crystal Palace	39	4	215	22
1995–96	Coventry C	37	3		
1996–97	Coventry C	24	1		
1997–98	Coventry C	11	0	72	4
1997–98	Bolton W	7	0	7	0
1998–99	Fulham	10	1		
1999–2000	Fulham	0	0	10	1
1999–2000	Charlton Ath	27	2		
2000–01	Charlton Ath	17	0	44	2

SHIELDS, Greg (D) 104 2
H: 5 10   W: 11 06   b.Falkirk 21-8-76
Source: Rangers BC. *Honours:* Scotland Under-21.

1994–95	Rangers	0	0		
1995–96	Rangers	1	0		
1996–97	Rangers	6	0	7	0
1997–98	Dunfermline Ath	36	4		
1998–99	Dunfermline Ath	36	0	72	0
1999–2000	Charlton Ath	21	2		
2000–01	Charlton Ath	4	0	25	2

SHITTU, Dan (D) 17 2
H: 6 2   W: 16 03   b.Lagos 2-9-80

1999–2000	Charlton Ath	0	0		
2000–01	Charlton Ath	0	0		
2000–01	Blackpool	17	2	17	2

STUART, Graham (M) 357 63
H: 5 8   W: 12 00   b.Tooting 24-10-70
Source: Trainee. *Honours:* FA Schools, England Under-21.

1989–90	Chelsea	2	1		
1990–91	Chelsea	19	4		
1991–92	Chelsea	27	0		
1992–93	Chelsea	39	9	87	14
1993–94	Everton	30	3		
1994–95	Everton	28	3		
1995–96	Everton	29	9		
1996–97	Everton	35	5		
1997–98	Everton	14	2	136	22
1997–98	Sheffield U	28	5		
1998–99	Sheffield U	25	6	53	11
1998–99	Charlton Ath	9	4		
1999–2000	Charlton Ath	37	7		
2000–01	Charlton Ath	35	5	81	16

SVENSSON, Mathias (F) 145 43
H: 6 1   W: 12 08   b.Boras 24-9-74
Honours: Sweden 3 full caps.

1996	Elfsborg	22	15	22	15
1996–97	Portsmouth	19	6		
1997–98	Portsmouth	26	4	45	10
1998–99	Innsbruck	6	1	6	1
1998–99	Crystal Palace	8	1		
1999–2000	Crystal Palace	24	9	32	10
1999–2000	Charlton Ath	18	2		
2000–01	Charlton Ath	22	5	40	7

TODD, Andy (D) 140 3
H: 5 11   W: 13 04   b.Derby 21-9-74
Source: Trainee.

1991–92	Middlesbrough	0	0		
1992–93	Middlesbrough	0	0		
1993–94	Middlesbrough	3	0		
1994–95	Middlesbrough	5	0	8	0
1994–95	Swindon T	13	0	13	0
1995–96	Bolton W	12	2		
1996–97	Bolton W	15	0		
1997–98	Bolton W	25	0		
1998–99	Bolton W	20	0		
1999–2000	Bolton W	12	0	84	2
1999–2000	Charlton Ath	12	0		
2000–01	Charlton Ath	23	1	35	1

YOUDS, Eddie (D) 217 13
H: 6 2   W: 14 10   b.Liverpool 3-5-70
Source: Trainee.

1988–89	Everton	0	0		
1989–90	Everton	0	0		
1989–90	Cardiff C	1	0	1	0
1989–90	Wrexham	20	2	20	2
1990–91	Everton	8	0		
1991–92	Everton	0	0	8	0
1991–92	Ipswich T	1	0		
1992–93	Ipswich T	16	0		
1993–94	Ipswich T	23	1		
1994–95	Ipswich T	10	0	50	1
1994–95	Bradford C	17	3		
1995–96	Bradford C	30	4		
1996–97	Bradford C	0	0		
1997–98	Bradford C	38	1	85	8
1997–98	Charlton Ath	8	0		
1998–99	Charlton Ath	22	2		
1999–2000	Charlton Ath	23	0		
2000–01	Charlton Ath	0	0	53	2

Scholars
Campbell-Ryce, Jamal; Cerroni, Christopher; Ford, Simon G; Lewis, Yohance; Martin,

Jamie N; McCafferty, Neil; McCarthy, Paul D; Tambue, Joe; Turner, Michael T

CHELSEA

ALEKSIDZE, Rati (F) 79 33
H: 6 0 W: 12 02 b.Georgia 3-8-78
Honours: Georgia 8 full caps.

Season	Club	Apps	Gls	Tot	Tot
1996-97	Dynamo Tbilisi	5	2		
1997-98	Dynamo Tbilisi	29	6		
1998-99	Dynamo Tbilisi	29	13		
1999-2000	Dynamo Tbilisi	14	12	77	33
2000-01	Chelsea	2	0	2	0

AMBROSETTI, Gabriele (M) 230 44
H: 5 11 W: 11 05 b.Varese 7-8-73

Season	Club	Apps	Gls	Tot	Tot
1990-91	Varese	8	0		
1991-92	Varese	16	2		
1992-93	Varese	26	9	50	11
1993-94	Brescia	25	8		
1994-95	Brescia	9	2		
1994-95	Venezia	18	3	18	3
1995-96	Brescia	9	2	43	12
1995-96	Vicenza	24	3		
1996-97	Vicenza	25	6		
1996-97	Vicenza	0	0		
1997-98	Vicenza	30	5		
1998-99	Vicenza	24	4	103	18
1999-2000	Chelsea	16	0		
2000-01	Chelsea	0	0	16	0

BABAYARO, Celestine (D) 160 11
H: 5 9 W: 11 09 b.Kaduna 29-8-78
Source: Plateau U. *Honours:* Nigeria full caps.

Season	Club	Apps	Gls	Tot	Tot
1994-95	Anderlecht	22	0		
1995-96	Anderlecht	28	5		
1996-97	Anderlecht	25	3	75	8
1997-98	Chelsea	8	0		
1998-99	Chelsea	28	3		
1999-2000	Chelsea	25	0		
2000-01	Chelsea	24	0	85	3

BOGARDE, Winston (D) 201 26
H: 6 3 W: 14 04 b.Rotterdam 22-10-70
Honours: Holland 20 full caps.

Season	Club	Apps	Gls	Tot	Tot
1988-89	SVV	9	1		
1989-90	SVV	2	0		
1989-90	Excelsior	10	1	10	1
1990-91	SVV	0	0	11	1
1991-92	Sparta	0	0		
1992-93	Sparta	32	3		
1993-94	Sparta	33	11	65	14
1994-95	Ajax	13	0		
1995-96	Ajax	33	2		
1996-97	Ajax	16	4	62	6
1997-98	AC Milan	3	0	3	0
1997-98	Barcelona	19	2		
1998-99	Barcelona	1	0		
1999-2000	Barcelona	21	2	41	4
2000-01	Chelsea	9	0	9	0

BOSNICH, Mark (G) 205 1
H: 6 2 W: 14 08 b.Fairfield 13-1-72
Source: Sydney United 5 apps.Australia 22 full caps, 1 goal.

Season	Club	Apps	Gls	Tot	Tot
1989-90	Manchester U	1	0		
1990-91	Manchester U	2	0		
1991-92	Aston Villa	1	0		
1992-93	Aston Villa	17	0		
1993-94	Aston Villa	28	0		
1994-95	Aston Villa	30	0		
1995-96	Aston Villa	38	1		
1996-97	Aston Villa	20	0		
1997-98	Aston Villa	30	0		
1998-99	Aston Villa	15	0	179	1
1999-2000	Manchester U	23	0		
2000-01	Manchester U	0	0	26	0
2000-01	Chelsea	0	0		

BROAD, Stephen* (D) 10 0
H: 6 0 W: 11 05 b.Epsom 10-6-80
Source: Trainee.

Season	Club	Apps	Gls	Tot	Tot
1997-98	Chelsea	0	0		
1998-99	Chelsea	0	0		
1999-2000	Chelsea	0	0		
2000-01	Chelsea	0	0		
2000-01	Southend U	10	0	10	0

COLE, Carlton (F) 0 0
H: 6 3 W: 12 13 b.Surrey 12-11-83
Source: Scholar.

Season	Club	Apps	Gls	Tot	Tot
2000-01	Chelsea	0	0		

CUDICINI, Carlo (G) 108 0
H: 6 1 W: 12 02 b.Milan 6-9-73

Season	Club	Apps	Gls	Tot	Tot
1991-92	AC Milan	0	0		
1992-93	AC Milan	0	0		
1993-94	Como	6	0	6	0
1994-95	AC Milan	0	0		
1995-96	AC Milan	0	0		
1995-96	Prato	30	0	30	0
1996-97	Lazio	1	0	1	0
1997-98	Castel di Sangro	14	0		
1998-99	Castel di Sangro	32	0	46	0
1999-2000	Chelsea	1	0		
2000-01	Chelsea	24	0	25	0

CUMMINGS, Warren (D) 13 1
H: 5 9 W: 11 05 b.Aberdeen 15-10-80
Source: Trainee. *Honours:* Scotland Under-21.

Season	Club	Apps	Gls	Tot	Tot
1999-2000	Chelsea	0	0		
2000-01	Chelsea	0	0		
2000-01	Bournemouth	10	1	10	1
2000-01	WBA	3	0	3	0

DALLA BONA, Samuele (M) 31 2
H: 6 0 W: 13 03 b.San Dona di Piave 6-2-81

Season	Club	Apps	Gls	Tot	Tot
1997-98	Atalanta	0	0		
1998-99	Chelsea	0	0		
1999-2000	Chelsea	2	0		
2000-01	Chelsea	29	2	31	2

DE GOEY, Ed (G) 461 0
H: 6 6 W: 14 05 b.Gouda 20-12-66
Honours: Holland 31 full caps.

Season	Club	Apps	Gls	Tot	Tot
1985-86	Sparta	12	0		
1986-87	Sparta	34	0		
1987-88	Sparta	34	0		
1988-89	Sparta	31	0		
1989-90	Sparta	34	0	145	0
1990-91	Feyenoord	34	0		
1991-92	Feyenoord	34	0		
1992-93	Feyenoord	33	0		
1993-94	Feyenoord	34	0		
1994-95	Feyenoord	32	0		
1995-96	Feyenoord	34	0	201	0
1997-98	Chelsea	28	0		
1998-99	Chelsea	35	0		
1999-2000	Chelsea	37	0		
2000-01	Chelsea	15	0	115	0

DEMETRIOUS, Shayne* (D) 0 0
H: 5 9 W: 10 01 b.Perivale 6-12-80
Source: Trainee.

Season	Club	Apps	Gls	Tot	Tot
1999-2000	Chelsea	0	0		
2000-01	Chelsea	0	0		

DESAILLY, Marcel (D) 435 14
H: 6 0 W: 13 05 b.Accra 7-9-68
Honours: France 84 full caps, 2 goals.

Season	Club	Apps	Gls	Tot	Tot
1986-87	Nantes	15	0		
1987-88	Nantes	11	0		
1988-89	Nantes	36	1		
1989-90	Nantes	36	1		
1990-91	Nantes	34	1		
1991-92	Nantes	32	2	164	5
1992-93	Marseille	31	1		
1993-94	Marseille	15	0	46	1
1993-94	AC Milan	21	1		
1994-95	AC Milan	22	1		
1995-96	AC Milan	32	2		
1996-97	AC Milan	29	1		
1997-98	AC Milan	33	0	137	5
1998-99	Chelsea	31	0		
1999-2000	Chelsea	23	1		
2000-01	Chelsea	34	2	88	3

DI CESARE, Valerio (M) 0 0
b.Rome 23-5-83

Season	Club	Apps	Gls	Tot	Tot
2000-01	Chelsea	0	0		

DI MATTEO, Roberto (M) 323 31
H: 5 10 W: 12 04 b.Schaffhausen 29-5-70
Honours: Italy 33 full caps, 1 goal.

Season	Club	Apps	Gls	Tot	Tot
1988-89	Schaffhausen	18	0		
1989-90	Schaffhausen	31	2		
1990-91	Schaffhausen	1	0	50	2
1991-92	Zurich	34	6	34	6
1992-93	Aarau	32	1	32	1
1993-94	Lazio	29	4		
1994-95	Lazio	28	1		
1995-96	Lazio	31	2	88	7
1996-97	Chelsea	34	7		
1997-98	Chelsea	30	4		
1998-99	Chelsea	30	2		
1999-2000	Chelsea	18	2		
2000-01	Chelsea	7	0	119	15

EVANS, Rhys (G) 4 0
H: 6 1 W: 11 12 b.Swindon 27-1-82
Source: Trainee. *Honours:* England Schools, Youth.

Season	Club	Apps	Gls	Tot	Tot
1998-99	Chelsea	0	0		
1999-2000	Chelsea	0	0		
1999-2000	Bristol R	4	0	4	0
2000-01	Chelsea	0	0		

FERRER, Albert (D) 291 1
H: 5 6 W: 12 02 b.Barcelona 6-6-70
Honours: Spain 36 full caps.

Season	Club	Apps	Gls	Tot	Tot
1989-90	Tenerife	17	0	17	0
1990-91	Barcelona	26	0		
1991-92	Barcelona	12	1		
1992-93	Barcelona	32	0		
1993-94	Barcelona	34	0		
1994-95	Barcelona	31	0		
1995-96	Barcelona	28	0		
1996-97	Barcelona	18	0		
1997-98	Barcelona	24	0	205	1
1998-99	Chelsea	30	0		
1999-2000	Chelsea	25	0		
2000-01	Chelsea	14	0	69	0

FLO, Tore Andre (F) 200 85
H: 6 4 W: 13 08 b.Strin 15-6-73
Honours: Norway 57 full caps, 21 goals.

Season	Club	Apps	Gls	Tot	Tot
1994	Sogndal	22	5	22	5
1995	Tromso	26	18	26	18
1996	Brann	24	19		
1997	Brann	16	9	40	28
1997-98	Chelsea	34	11		
1998-99	Chelsea	30	10		
1999-2000	Chelsea	34	10		
2000-01	Chelsea	14	3	112	34

(Transferred to Rangers, November 2000).

FORSSELL, Mikael (F) 79 18
H: 6 0 W: 12 08 b.Steinfurt 15-3-81
Honours: Finland 13 full caps, 3 goals.

Season	Club	Apps	Gls	Tot	Tot
1997	HJK Helsinki	1	0		
1998	HJK Helsinki	16	1	17	1
1998-99	Chelsea	10	1		
1999-2000	Chelsea	0	0		
1999-2000	Crystal Palace	13	3		
2000-01	Chelsea	0	0	10	1
2000-01	Crystal Palace	39	13	52	16

GRONKJAER, Jesper (M) 156 22
H: 6 2 W: 13 03 b.Nuuk 12-8-77
Honours: Denmark 19 full caps, 1 goal.

Season	Club	Apps	Gls	Tot	Tot
1995-96	Aalborg	29	3		
1996-97	Aalborg	28	1		
1997-98	Aalborg	29	6	86	10
1998-99	Ajax	25	8		
1999-2000	Ajax	25	3		
2000-01	Ajax	6	0	56	11
2000-01	Chelsea	14	1	14	1

GUDJOHNSEN, Eidur (F) 121 38
H: 6 1 W: 14 05 b.Reykjavik 15-9-78
Honours: Iceland Youth. Iceland 5 full caps, 3 goals.

Season	Club	Apps	Gls	Tot	Tot
1994-95	Valur	17	7	17	7
1995-96	PSV Eindhoven	13	3		
1996-97	PSV Eindhoven	0	0	13	3
1998	KR	6	0	6	0
1998-99	Bolton W	14	5		
1999-2000	Bolton W	41	13	55	18
2000-01	Chelsea	30	10	30	10

HARLEY, Jon (D) 36 4
H: 5 9 W: 11 05 b.Maidstone 26-9-79
Source: Trainee. *Honours:* England Under-21.

Season	Club	Apps	Gls	Tot	Tot
1996-97	Chelsea	0	0		
1997-98	Chelsea	3	0		
1998-99	Chelsea	0	0		
1999-2000	Chelsea	17	2		
2000-01	Chelsea	10	0	30	2
2000-01	Wimbledon	6	2	6	2

HASSELBAINK, Jimmy Floyd (F) 198 113
H: 5 11 W: 13 09 b.Paramaribo 27-3-72
Honours: Holland 13 full caps, 6 goals.

Season	Club	Apps	Gls	Tot	Tot
1995-96	Campomairorense	31	12	31	12
1996-97	Boavista	29	20	29	20
1997-98	Leeds U	33	16		
1998-99	Leeds U	36	18	69	34
1999-2000	Atletico Madrid	34	24	34	24
2000-01	Chelsea	35	23	35	23

HITCHCOCK, Kevin* (G) 295 0
H: 6 1 W: 12 13 b.Custom House 5-10-62
Source: Barking.

Season	Club	Apps	Gls	Tot	Tot
1983-84	Nottingham F	0	0		
1983-84	Mansfield T	14	0		
1984-85	Mansfield T	43	0		
1985-86	Mansfield T	46	0		
1986-87	Mansfield T	46	0		
1987-88	Mansfield T	33	0	182	0
1987-88	Chelsea	8	0		
1988-89	Chelsea	3	0		
1989-90	Chelsea	0	0		
1990-91	Chelsea	3	0		
1990-91	Northampton T	17	0	17	0
1991-92	Chelsea	21	0		
1992-93	Chelsea	20	0		
1992-93	West Ham U	0	0		
1993-94	Chelsea	2	0		
1994-95	Chelsea	12	0		
1995-96	Chelsea	12	0		
1996-97	Chelsea	12	0		
1997-98	Chelsea	0	0		
1998-99	Chelsea	3	0		
1999-2000	Chelsea	0	0		
2000-01	Chelsea	0	0	96	0

HOGH, Jes‡ (D) 312 29
H: 6 0 W: 11 11 b.Aalborg 7-5-66
Honours: Denmark 57 full caps, 1 goal.

1987	Aalborg	21	2		
1988	Aalborg	18	1		
1989	Aalborg	23	1		
1990	Aalborg	26	7		
1991	Aalborg	7	2		
1991–92	Aalborg	0	0		
1991–92	Brondby	7	1		
1992–93	Brondby	30	3		
1993–94	Brondby	29	2		
1994–95	Brondby	13	0	79	6
1994–95	Aalborg	14	4	109	17
1995–96	Fenerbahce	34	2		
1996–97	Fenerbahce	25	2		
1997–98	Fenerbahce	30	0		
1998–99	Fenerbahce	26	2	115	6
1999–2000	Chelsea	9	0		
2000–01	Chelsea	0	0	9	0

ISSA, Pierre (D) 46 0
H: 6 4 W: 13 07 b.Johannesburg 11-9-75
Source: Dunkerque. *Honours:* South Africa full caps.

1996–97	Marseille	9	0		
1997–98	Marseille	4	0		
1998–99	Marseille	16	0		
1999–2000	Marseille	8	0		
2000–01	Marseille	9	0	46	0
2000–01	Chelsea	0	0		

JOKANOVIC, Slavisa (M) 295 52
H: 6 3 W: 13 03 b.Novi Sad 16-8-68
Honours: Yugoslavia 58 full caps, 9 goals.

1990–91	Partizan Belgrade	20	4		
1991–92	Partizan Belgrade	16	4		
1992–93	Partizan Belgrade	32	13	68	21
1993–94	Oviedo	32	7		
1994–95	Oviedo	30	5	62	12
1995–96	Tenerife	34	2		
1996–97	Tenerife	30	10		
1997–98	Tenerife	30	3		
1998–99	Tenerife	29	2	123	17
1999–2000	La Coruna	23	2	23	2
2000–01	Chelsea	19	0	19	0

KEENAN, Joe (M) 0 0
H: 5 7 W: 10 00 b.Southampton 14-10-82
Source: Trainee. *Honours:* England Youth.

| 1999–2000 | Chelsea | 0 | 0 | | |
| 2000–01 | Chelsea | 0 | 0 | | |

KITAMIRIKE, Joel (D) 0 0
b.Uganda 5-4-84
Source: Scholar.

| 2000–01 | Chelsea | 0 | 0 | | |

KNEISSL, Sebastian (F) 0 0
H: 5 11 W: 11 05 b.Germany 13-1-83

| 2000–01 | Chelsea | 0 | 0 | | |

KNIGHT, Leon (F) 11 0
H: 5 4 W: 9 06 b.Hackney 16-9-82
Source: Trainee. *Honours:* England Youth.

1999–2000	Chelsea	0	0		
2000–01	Chelsea	0	0		
2000–01	QPR	11	0	11	0

LAMBOURDE, Bernard (D) 151 6
H: 6 0 W: 13 05 b.Pointe-A-Pitre 11-5-71

1991–92	Cannes	2	0		
1992–93	Cannes	5	0		
1993–94	Cannes	6	1		
1994–95	Angers	36	1	36	1
1995–96	Cannes	28	1	41	2
1996–97	Bordeaux	28	1	28	1
1997–98	Chelsea	7	0		
1998–99	Chelsea	17	0		
1999–2000	Chelsea	15	2		
2000–01	Chelsea	1	0	40	2
2000–01	*Portsmouth*	6	0	6	0

LE SAUX, Graeme (D) 304 16
H: 5 10 W: 11 09 b.Jersey 17-10-68
Source: St Pauls. *Honours:* England Under-21, B, 36 full caps, 1 goal.

1987–88	Chelsea	0	0		
1988–89	Chelsea	1	0		
1989–90	Chelsea	7	1		
1990–91	Chelsea	28	4		
1991–92	Chelsea	40	3		
1992–93	Chelsea	14	0		
1992–93	Blackburn	9	0		
1993–94	Blackburn	41	2		
1994–95	Blackburn	39	3		
1995–96	Blackburn	14	1		
1996–97	Blackburn	26	1	129	7
1997–98	Chelsea	26	1		
1998–99	Chelsea	31	0		
1999–2000	Chelsea	8	0		
2000–01	Chelsea	20	0	175	9

LEBOEUF, Franck (D) 455 80
H: 6 1 W: 11 11 b.Marseille 22-1-68
Honours: France 39 full caps, 3 goals.

1986–87	Hyeres	14	1	14	1
1986–87	Meaux	12	3		
1987–88	Meaux	27	0	39	3
1988–89	Laval	21	0		
1989–90	Laval	32	1		
1990–91	Laval	16	9	69	10
1990–91	Strasbourg	17	9		
1991–92	Strasbourg	31	11		
1992–93	Strasbourg	36	12		
1993–94	Strasbourg	36	6		
1994–95	Strasbourg	34	7		
1995–96	Strasbourg	35	4	189	49
1996–97	Chelsea	26	6		
1997–98	Chelsea	32	5		
1998–99	Chelsea	33	4		
1999–2000	Chelsea	28	2		
2000–01	Chelsea	25	0	144	17

MELCHIOT, Mario (D) 109 1
H: 6 2 W: 11 11 b.Amsterdam 4-11-76
Honours: Holland 4 full caps.

1996–97	Ajax	23	0		
1997–98	Ajax	26	0		
1998–99	Ajax	24	1	73	1
1999–2000	Chelsea	5	0		
2000–01	Chelsea	31	0	36	0

MORRIS, Jody (M) 94 5
H: 5 5 W: 10 03 b.Hammersmith 22-12-78
Source: Trainee. *Honours:* England Schools, Youth, Under-21.

1995–96	Chelsea	1	0		
1996–97	Chelsea	12	0		
1997–98	Chelsea	12	1		
1998–99	Chelsea	18	1		
1999–2000	Chelsea	30	3		
2000–01	Chelsea	21	0	94	5

NICHOLLS, Mark* (M) 51 4
H: 5 10 W: 10 12 b.Hillingdon 30-5-77
Source: Scholar.

1995–96	Chelsea	0	0		
1996–97	Chelsea	8	0		
1997–98	Chelsea	19	3		
1998–99	Chelsea	9	0		
1999–2000	Chelsea	0	0		
1999–2000	*Reading*	5	1	5	1
1999–2000	*Grimsby T*	6	0	6	0
2000–01	Chelsea	0	0	36	3
2000–01	*Colchester U*	4	0	4	0

PANUCCI, Christian‡ (D) 226 16
b.Savona 12-4-73
Honours: Italy 21 full caps, 1 goal.

1996–97	Real Madrid	19	2		
1997–98	Real Madrid	23	1		
1998–99	Real Madrid	31	0	73	3
1999–2000	Internazionale	26	1	26	1
1991–92	Genoa	1	0		
1992–93	Genoa	30	3	31	3
1993–94	AC Milan	19	2		
1994–95	AC Milan	28	2		
1995–96	AC Milan	29	5		
1996–97	AC Milan	12	0	88	9
1998–99	Chelsea	8	0	8	0

PARKIN, Sam (F) 22 8
H: 6 2 W: 13 03 b.Roehampton 14-3-81
Honours: England Schools.

1998–99	Chelsea	0	0		
1999–2000	Chelsea	0	0		
2000–01	Chelsea	0	0		
2000–01	*Millwall*	7	4	7	4
2000–01	*Wycombe W*	8	1	8	1
2000–01	*Oldham Ath*	7	3	7	3

PERCASSI, Luca‡ (M) 0 0
H: 5 9 W: 11 09 b.Milan 25-8-80

1997–98	Atalanta	0	0		
1998–99	Chelsea	0	0		
1999–2000	Chelsea	0	0		
2000–01	Chelsea	0	0		

PITT, Courtney (M) 0 0
H: 5 7 W: 10 08 b.London 17-12-81
Source: Scholar.

| 2000–01 | Chelsea | 0 | 0 | | |

POYET, Gustavo (M) 344 99
H: 6 1 W: 12 13 b.Montevideo 15-11-67
Source: River Plate, Grenoble, Bella Vista.
Honours: Uruguay 23 full caps, 3 goals.

1990–91	Zaragoza	31	7		
1991–92	Zaragoza	33	3		
1992–93	Zaragoza	33	6		
1993–94	Zaragoza	34	11		
1994–95	Zaragoza	34	11		
1995–96	Zaragoza	36	11		
1996–97	Zaragoza	38	14	239	63
1997–98	Chelsea				

1998–99 Chelsea 28 11
1999–2000 Chelsea 33 10
2000–01 Chelsea 30 11 **105 36**
(Transferred to Tottenham H, July 2001).

REDDINGTON, Stuart (D) 9 0
H: 6 3 W: 13 08 b.Lincoln 21-2-78
Source: Lincoln U.

1999–2000	Chelsea	0	0		
2000–01	Chelsea	0	0		
2000–01	*Mansfield T*	9	0	9	0

RICHARDSON, Jay* (D) 0 0
H: 5 9 W: 11 09 b.Keston 14-11-79
Source: Trainee.

1997–98	Chelsea	0	0		
1998–99	Chelsea	0	0		
1999–2000	Chelsea	0	0		
2000–01	Chelsea	0	0		

SLATTER, Danny (D) 0 0
H: 5 7 W: 10 01 b.Cardiff 15-11-80
Source: Trainee. *Honours:* Wales Under-21.

1998–99	Chelsea	0	0		
1999–2000	Chelsea	0	0		
2000–01	Chelsea	0	0		

STANIC, Mario (M) 277 83
H: 6 2 W: 13 00 b.Sarajevo 10-4-72
Honours: Croatia 38 full caps, 7 goals.

1988–89	Zeljeznicar	14	0		
1989–90	Zeljeznicar	14	0		
1990–91	Zeljeznicar	28	1		
1991–92	Zeljeznicar	21	11	77	12
1992–93	Croatia Zagreb	26	11	26	11
1993–94	Gijon	34	7	34	7
1994–95	Benfica	14	5	14	5
1995–96	FC Brugge	30	20		
1996–97	FC Brugge	7	7	37	27
1996–97	Parma	13	3		
1997–98	Parma	23	4		
1998–99	Parma	18	7		
1999–2000	Parma	23	5	77	19
2000–01	Chelsea	12	2	12	2

TERRY, John (D) 34 1
H: 6 1 W: 12 13 b.Barking 7-12-80
Source: Trainee. *Honours:* England Under-21.

1997–98	Chelsea	0	0		
1998–99	Chelsea	2	0		
1999–2000	Chelsea	4	0		
1999–2000	*Nottingham F*	6	0	6	0
2000–01	Chelsea	22	1	28	1

THORNTON, Paul (D) 0 0
H: 5 7 W: 11 00 b.Surrey 7-1-83
Source: Trainee.

| 1999–2000 | Chelsea | 0 | 0 | | |
| 2000–01 | Chelsea | 0 | 0 | | |

WISE, Dennis (M) 467 80
H: 5 6 W: 10 11 b.Kensington 16-12-66
Source: Southampton Apprentice. *Honours:* England Under-21, B, 21 full caps, 1 goal.

1984–85	Wimbledon	1	0		
1985–86	Wimbledon	4	0		
1986–87	Wimbledon	28	4		
1987–88	Wimbledon	30	10		
1988–89	Wimbledon	37	5		
1989–90	Wimbledon	35	8	135	27
1990–91	Chelsea	33	10		
1991–92	Chelsea	38	10		
1992–93	Chelsea	27	3		
1993–94	Chelsea	35	4		
1994–95	Chelsea	19	6		
1995–96	Chelsea	35	7		
1996–97	Chelsea	31	3		
1997–98	Chelsea	26	3		
1998–99	Chelsea	22	0		
1999–2000	Chelsea	30	4		
2000–01	Chelsea	36	3	332	53
(Transferred to Leicester C, June 2001).

WOLLEASTON, Robert (M) 11 0
H: 5 11 W: 11 07 b.Perivale 21-12-79
Source: Trainee.

1998–99	Chelsea	0	0		
1999–2000	Chelsea	1	0		
1999–2000	*Bristol R*	4	0	4	0
2000–01	Chelsea	0	0	1	0
2000–01	*Portsmouth*	6	0	6	0

ZOLA, Gianfranco (F) 482 154
H: 5 6 W: 10 08 b.Oliena 5-7-66
Honours: Italy 34 full caps, 9 goals.

1984–85	Nuorese	4	0		
1985–86	Nuorese	27	10	31	10
1986–87	Torres	30	8		
1987–88	Torres	24	2		
1988–89	Torres	34	11	88	21
1989–90	Napoli	18	2		
1990–91	Napoli	20	6		
1991–92	Napoli	34	12		
1992–93	Napoli	33	12	105	32
1993–94	Parma	33	18		

1994–95 Parma 32 19
1995–96 Parma 29 10
1996–97 Parma 8 2 **102 49**
1996–97 Chelsea 23 8
1997–98 Chelsea 27 8
1998–99 Chelsea 37 13
1999–2000 Chelsea 33 4
2000–01 Chelsea 36 9 **156 42**

Scholars
Baldwin, Patrick M; Cousins, Scott R; Huth, Robert; Ives, Nicholas L; Pidgeley, Leonard J; Ross, Andrew C; Stevenson, Ryan C; Woodards, Daniel M

CHELTENHAM T

ALSOP, Julian (F) **162 25**
H: 6 5 W: 14 08 b.Nuneaton 28-5-73
Source: Nuneaton, VS Rugby, RC Warwick, Tamworth, Halesowen T.
1996–97 Bristol R 16 3
1997–98 Bristol R 17 1 **33 4**
1997–98 Swansea C 12 3
1998–99 Swansea C 41 10
1999–2000 Swansea C 37 3 **90 16**
2000–01 Cheltenham T 39 5 **39 5**

BANKS, Chris (D) **192 3**
H: 5 11 W: 12 04 b.Stone 22-11-65
Source: local.
1982–83 Port Vale 0 0
1983–84 Port Vale 0 0
1984–85 Port Vale 7 0
1985–86 Port Vale 19 1
1986–87 Port Vale 25 0
1987–88 Port Vale 14 0 **65 1**
1988–89 Exeter C 45 1 **45 1**
From Bath C.
1999–2000 Cheltenham T 42 0
2000–01 Cheltenham T 40 1 **82 1**

BENBOW, Steve† (G) **0 0**
H: 5 10 W: 10 07 b.Cheltenham 5-4-82
1999–2000 Cheltenham T 0 0
2000–01 Cheltenham T 0 0

BLOOMER, Bob* (M) **186 16**
H: 5 10 W: 12 07 b.Sheffield 21-6-66
1985–86 Chesterfield 6 0
1986–87 Chesterfield 31 3
1987–88 Chesterfield 38 1
1988–89 Chesterfield 44 10
1989–90 Chesterfield 22 1 **141 15**
1989–90 Bristol R 0 0
1990–91 Bristol R 13 0
1991–92 Bristol R 9 0 **22 0**
1999–2000 Cheltenham T 11 0
2000–01 Cheltenham T 12 1 **23 1**

BOOK, Steve (G) **92 0**
H: 5 11 W: 11 02 b.Bournemouth 7-7-69
1997–98 Brighton & HA 0 0
1998–99 Lincoln C 0 0
From Forest Green R.
1999–2000 Cheltenham T 46 0
2000–01 Cheltenham T 46 0 **92 0**

BROUGH, John (D) **142 6**
H: 6 0 W: 12 11 b.Ilkeston 8-1-73
1991–92 Notts Co 0 0
1992–93 Shrewsbury T 14 1
1993–94 Shrewsbury T 2 0 **16 1**
From Telford U.
1994–95 Hereford U 18 1
1995–96 Hereford U 22 1
1996–97 Hereford U 39 1 **79 3**
1999–2000 Cheltenham T 37 2
2000–01 Cheltenham T 10 0 **47 2**

DEVANEY, Martin (F) **60 16**
H: 5 11 W: 12 06 b.Cheltenham 1-6-80
Source: Trainee.
1997–98 Coventry C 0 0
1998–99 Coventry C 0 0
1999–2000 Cheltenham T 26 6
2000–01 Cheltenham T 34 10 **60 16**

DUFF, Michael (D) **70 7**
H: 6 1 W: 11 08 b.Belfast 11-1-78
Source: Trainee.
1999–2000 Cheltenham T 31 2
2000–01 Cheltenham T 39 5 **70 7**

DUFF, Shane (D) **0 0**
b.Swindon 2-4-82
2000–01 Cheltenham T 0 0

FREEMAN, Mark (D) **65 2**
H: 6 2 W: 13 08 b.Walsall 27-1-70
Source: Bilston T.
1987–88 Wolverhampton W 0 0
From Bilston, Gloustr
1999–2000 Cheltenham T 38 2
2000–01 Cheltenham T 27 0 **65 2**

GRAYSON, Neil (F) **239 60**
H: 5 10 W: 12 09 b.York 1-11-64
Source: Rowntree Mackintosh.
1989–90 Doncaster R 6 1
1990–91 Doncaster R 23 5 **29 6**
1990–91 York C 1 0 **1 0**
1991–92 Chesterfield 15 0 **15 0**
From Gateshead, Boston U.
1994–95 Northampton
1995–96 Northampton T 42 11
1996–97 Northampton T 40 12 **120 31**
From Hereford U.
1999–2000 Cheltenham T 43 10
2000–01 Cheltenham T 31 13 **74 23**

GRIFFIN, Anthony (M) **52 1**
H: 5 11 W: 11 03 b.Bournemouth 22-3-79
Source: Trainee.
1997–98 Bournemouth 0 0
1998–99 Bournemouth 6 0 **6 0**
1999–2000 Cheltenham T 24 0
2000–01 Cheltenham T 22 1 **46 1**

HIGGS, Shane (G) **11 0**
H: 6 3 W: 14 02 b.Oxford 13-5-77
Source: Trainee.
1994–95 Bristol R 0 0
1995–96 Bristol R 0 0
1996–97 Bristol R 2 0
1997–98 Bristol R 8 0 **10 0**
From Worcester C.
1999–2000 Cheltenham T 0 0
2000–01 Cheltenham T 1 0 **1 0**

HOPKINS, Gareth (F) **5 0**
H: 6 2 W: 13 08 b.Cheltenham 14-6-80
Source: Trainee.
1999–2000 Cheltenham T 1 0
2000–01 Cheltenham T 4 0 **5 0**

HOWARTH, Neil (D) **128 8**
H: 6 2 W: 13 06 b.Bolton 15-11-71
Source: Trainee.
1989–90 Burnley 1 0 **1 0**
From Macclesfield T.
1997–98 Macclesfield T 41 3
1998–99 Macclesfield T 19 0 **60 3**
1999–2000 Cheltenham T 44 2
2000–01 Cheltenham T 23 3 **67 5**

HOWELLS, Lee (M) **81 4**
H: 5 11 W: 11 02 b.Fremantle 14-10-68
Source: Apprentice.
1986–87 Bristol R 0 0
From Brisbane Lions.
1999–2000 Cheltenham T 45 3
2000–01 Cheltenham T 36 1 **81 4**

JACKSON, Michael D (M) **8 0**
H: 5 7 W: 10 10 b.Cheltenham 26-6-80
Source: Trainee.
1999–2000 Cheltenham T 2 0
2000–01 Cheltenham T 6 0 **8 0**

JONES, Marcus‡ (M) **2 0**
H: 6 3 W: 13 00 b.Wolverhampton 24-6-74
Honours: From Stoke C, Chasetown, Bolehall Swifts, Willenhall T, Hinckley Ath, VS Rugby, Telford U, Scarborough.
2000–01 Cheltenham T 2 0 **2 0**

McAULEY, Hugh (F) **74 7**
H: 5 10 W: 11 06 b.Plymouth 13-5-77
Source: Leek T.
1999–2000 Cheltenham T 39 4
2000–01 Cheltenham T 35 3 **74 7**

MILTON, Russell (M) **57 10**
H: 5 8 W: 12 01 b.Folkestone 12-1-69
Source: Apprentice.
1986–87 Arsenal 0 0
1987–88 Arsenal 0 0
From Dover Ath.
1999–2000 Cheltenham T 38 9
2000–01 Cheltenham T 19 1 **57 10**

MITCHINSON, Stuart (F) **0 0**
H: 5 6 W: 10 08 b.Cheltenham 15-10-80
Source: Trainee.
1999–2000 Cheltenham T 0 0
2000–01 Cheltenham T 0 0

SERTORI, Mark‡ (D) **382 17**
H: 6 2 W: 14 02 b.Manchester 1-9-67
1986–87 Stockport Co 3 0
1987–88 Stockport Co 1 0 **4 0**
1987–88 Lincoln C 0 0
1988–89 Lincoln C 26 4
1989–90 Lincoln C 24 5 **50 9**
1989–90 Wrexham 18 2
1990–91 Wrexham 29 0
1991–92 Wrexham 36 0
1992–93 Wrexham 12 0
1993–94 Wrexham 15 1 **110 3**
1994–95 Bury 2 0
1995–96 Bury 11 1 **13 1**
1996–97 Scunthorpe U 42 1
1997–98 Scunthorpe U 41 1 **83 2**
1998–99 Halifax T 40 0
1999–2000 Halifax T 5 0 **45 0**
1999–2000 York C 40 1
2000–01 York C 26 1 **66 2**
2000–01 Shrewsbury T 1 0 **1 0**
2000–01 Cheltenham T 10 0 **10 0**

VICTORY, Jamie (D) **65 6**
H: 5 11 W: 12 02 b.London 14-11-75
Source: Trainee.
1994–95 West Ham U 0 0
1995–96 Bournemouth 16 1
1996–97 Bournemouth 0 0 **16 1**
1999–2000 Cheltenham T 46 4
2000–01 Cheltenham T 3 1 **49 5**

WALKER, Richard (D) **114 4**
H: 5 10 W: 11 09 b.Derby 9-11-71
Source: Trainee.
1991–92 Notts Co 0 0
1992–93 Notts Co 12 3
1993–94 Notts Co 21 1
1994–95 Notts Co 7 0
1994–95 *Mansfield T* 4 0 **4 0**
1995–96 Notts Co 11 0
1996–97 Notts Co 16 0 **67 4**
From Hereford U.
1999–2000 Cheltenham T 7 0
2000–01 Cheltenham T 36 0 **43 0**

WHITE, Jason (F) **312 77**
H: 6 1 W: 12 12 b.Meriden 19-10-71
Source: Derby Co Trainee.
1991–92 Scunthorpe U 22 11
1992–93 Scunthorpe U 37 5
1993–94 Scunthorpe U 9 0 **68 16**
1993–94 *Darlington* 4 1 **4 1**
1993–94 Scarborough 24 9
1994–95 Scarborough 39 11 **63 20**
1995–96 Northampton T 45 16
1996–97 Northampton T 32 2
1997–98 Northampton T 0 0 **77 18**
1997–98 Rotherham U 27 13
1998–99 Rotherham U 26 5
1999–2000 Rotherham U 20 4 **73 22**
2000–01 Cheltenham T 27 0 **27 0**

YATES, Mark (M) **211 19**
H: 5 11 W: 13 02 b.Birmingham 24-1-70
1987–88 Birmingham C 3 0
1988–89 Birmingham C 20 3
1989–90 Birmingham C 20 2
1990–91 Birmingham C 9 1
1991–92 Birmingham C 2 0 **54 6**
1991–92 Burnley 17 1
1992–93 Burnley 1 0 **18 1**
1992–93 *Lincoln C* 14 0 **14 0**
1993–94 Doncaster R 34 4 **34 4**
From Kidderminster H.
1999–2000 Cheltenham T 46 2
2000–01 Cheltenham T 45 6 **91 8**

Non-Contract
Benbow, Steven MJ; Williams, Alan R

CHESTERFIELD

ARMSTRONG, Joel§ (G) **4 0**
H: 5 11 W: 12 07 b.Chesterfield 25-9-81
Source: Scholarship.
1999–2000 Chesterfield 3 0
2000–01 Chesterfield 1 0 **4 0**

BARRETT, Danny (M) **3 0**
H: 6 0 W: 11 12 b.Bradford 25-9-80
Source: Trainee.
1999–2000 Chesterfield 2 0
2000–01 Chesterfield 1 0 **3 0**

BEAUMONT, Chris* (M) **450 52**
H: 5 11 W: 11 12 b.Sheffield 5-12-65
Source: Denaby U.
1988–89 Rochdale 34 7 **34 7**
1989–90 Stockport Co 22 5
1990–91 Stockport Co 45 15
1991–92 Stockport Co 34 2
1992–93 Stockport Co 44 14
1993–94 Stockport Co 32 1
1994–95 Stockport Co 38 2
1995–96 Stockport Co 43 0 **258 39**
1996–97 Chesterfield 33 1
1997–98 Chesterfield 39 1
1998–99 Chesterfield 39 2
1999–2000 Chesterfield 33 2
2000–01 Chesterfield 14 0 **158 6**

BECKETT, Luke (F)   115 41
H: 5 11   W: 11 06   b.Sheffield 25-11-76
Source: Trainee.

1995-96	Barnsley	0	0		
1996-97	Barnsley	0	0		
1997-98	Barnsley	0	0		
1998-99	Chester C	28	11		
1999-2000	Chester C	46	14	74	25
2000-01	Chesterfield	41	16	41	16

BLATHERWICK, Steve# (D)   141 3
H: 6 1   W: 15 00   b.Nottingham 20-9-73
Source: Notts Co.

1992-93	Nottingham F	0	0		
1993-94	Nottingham F	3	0		
1993-94	Wycombe W	2	0	2	0
1994-95	Nottingham F	0	0		
1995-96	Nottingham F	0	0		
1995-96	*Hereford U*	10	1	10	1
1996-97	Nottingham F	7	0	10	0
1996-97	*Reading*	7	0	7	0
1997-98	Burnley	21	0		
1998-99	Burnley	3	0	24	0
1998-99	Chesterfield	14	1		
1999-2000	Chesterfield	36	0		
2000-01	Chesterfield	38	1	88	2

BRECKIN, Ian (D)   302 13
H: 5 11   W: 11 07   b.Rotherham 24-2-75
Source: Trainee.

1993-94	Rotherham U	10	0		
1994-95	Rotherham U	41	2		
1995-96	Rotherham U	39	1		
1996-97	Rotherham U	42	3	132	6
1997-98	Chesterfield	43	1		
1998-99	Chesterfield	44	2		
1999-2000	Chesterfield	38	1		
2000-01	Chesterfield	45	3	170	7

D'AURIA, David (M)   269 36
H: 5 9   W: 11 11   b.Swansea 26-3-70
Source: Trainee.

1987-88	Swansea C	4	0		
1988-89	Swansea C	14	2		
1989-90	Swansea C	7	0		
1990-91	Swansea C	20	4	45	6
From Barry T.					
1994-95	Scarborough	34	7		
1995-96	Scarborough	18	1	52	8
1995-96	Scunthorpe U	27	5		
1996-97	Scunthorpe U	39	3		
1997-98	Scunthorpe U	41	10	107	18
1998-99	Hull C	42	4		
1999-2000	Hull C	12	0	54	4
1999-2000	Chesterfield	5	0		
2000-01	Chesterfield	6	0	11	0

EBDON, Marcus (M)   284 22
H: 5 10   W: 11 02   b.Pontypool 17-10-70
Source: Trainee. *Honours:* Wales Under-21.

1988-89	Everton	0	0		
1989-90	Everton	0	0		
1990-91	Everton	0	0		
1991-92	Peterborough U	15	2		
1992-93	Peterborough U	28	4		
1993-94	Peterborough U	10	0		
1994-95	Peterborough U	35	6		
1995-96	Peterborough U	39	2		
1996-97	Peterborough U	20	1	147	15
1996-97	Chesterfield	12	1		
1997-98	Chesterfield	33	2		
1998-99	Chesterfield	40	1		
1999-2000	Chesterfield	11	0		
2000-01	Chesterfield	41	3	137	7

EDWARDS, Rob (M)   327 62
H: 5 9   W: 12 04   b.Manchester 23-2-70
Source: Trainee.

1987-88	Crewe Alex	6	1		
1988-89	Crewe Alex	4	0		
1989-90	Crewe Alex	4	0		
1990-91	Crewe Alex	29	11		
1991-92	Crewe Alex	28	6		
1992-93	Crewe Alex	23	7		
1993-94	Crewe Alex	17	2		
1994-95	Crewe Alex	17	2		
1995-96	Crewe Alex	32	15	155	44
1995-96	Huddersfield T	13	7		
1996-97	Huddersfield T	33	3		
1997-98	Huddersfield T	38	1		
1998-99	Huddersfield T	45	2		
1999-2000	Huddersfield T	9	1		
2000-01	Huddersfield T	0	0	138	14
2000-01	Chesterfield	34	4	34	4

HEWITT, Jamie (M)   538 26
H: 5 10   W: 10 08   b.Chesterfield 17-5-68
Source: School.

1984-85	Chesterfield	0	0		
1985-86	Chesterfield	17	0		
1986-87	Chesterfield	42	2		
1987-88	Chesterfield	28	2		
1988-89	Chesterfield	40	1		
1989-90	Chesterfield	42	6		
1990-91	Chesterfield	43	0		
1991-92	Chesterfield	37	3		
1992-93	Chesterfield	27	0		
1993-94	Doncaster R	6	0	33	0
1993-94	Chesterfield	29	3		
1994-95	Chesterfield	38	3		
1995-96	Chesterfield	28	2		
1996-97	Chesterfield	37	1		
1997-98	Chesterfield	44	1		
1998-99	Chesterfield	40	2		
1999-2000	Chesterfield	40	0		
2000-01	Chesterfield	0	0	505	26

HOWARD, Jonathan# (F)   243 39
H: 5 11   W: 11 07   b.Sheffield 7-10-71
Source: Trainee.

1990-91	Rotherham U	1	0		
1991-92	Rotherham U	10	3		
1992-93	Rotherham U	17	2		
1993-94	Rotherham U	8	0		
1994-95	Rotherham U	0	0	36	5
1994-95	Chesterfield	12	1		
1995-96	Chesterfield	30	2		
1996-97	Chesterfield	35	9		
1997-98	Chesterfield	35	6		
1998-99	Chesterfield	37	9		
1999-2000	Chesterfield	27	2		
2000-01	Chesterfield	31	5	207	34

INGLEDOW, Jamie (M)   49 5
H: 5 7   W: 11 01   b.Barnsley 23-8-80
Source: Trainee.

1998-99	Rotherham U	21	2		
1999-2000	Rotherham U	4	0	25	2
2000-01	Chesterfield	24	3	24	3

JONES, Mark (F)   9 0
H: 5 10   W: 12 07   b.Walsall 7-9-79
Source: Trainee. *Honours:* England Schools.

1996-97	Wolverhampton W	0	0		
1997-98	Wolverhampton W	0	0		
1998-99	Wolverhampton W	2	0		
1999-2000	Wolverhampton W	1	0	3	0
1999-2000	*Cheltenham T*	3	0	3	0
2000-01	Chesterfield	3	0	3	0

PARRISH, Sean (M)   213 31
H: 5 10   W: 11 05   b.Wrexham 14-3-72
Source: Trainee.

1989-90	Shrewsbury T	2	0		
1990-91	Shrewsbury T	1	0	3	0
From Telford U.					
1994-95	Doncaster R	25	3		
1995-96	Doncaster R	41	5	66	8
1996-97	Northampton T	39	8		
1997-98	Northampton T	12	1		
1998-99	Northampton T	33	1		
1999-2000	Northampton T	25	3	109	13
2000-01	Chesterfield	35	10	35	10

PAYNE, Steve (D)   130 6
H: 5 11   W: 12 05   b.Castleford 1-8-75
Source: Trainee.

1993-94	Huddersfield T	0	0		
1994-95	Huddersfield T	0	0		
1995-96	Huddersfield T	0	0		
1996-97	Huddersfield T	0	0		
1997-98	Macclesfield T	39	0		
1998-99	Macclesfield T	38	2	77	2
1999-2000	Chesterfield	18	3		
2000-01	Chesterfield	35	1	53	4

PEARCE, Greg (M)   12 0
H: 6 0   W: 11 00   b.Bolton 26-5-80
Source: Trainee.

1997-98	Chesterfield	0	0		
1998-99	Chesterfield	1	0		
1999-2000	Chesterfield	10	0		
2000-01	Chesterfield	1	0	12	0

POLLITT, Mike (G)   287 0
H: 6 3   W: 14 12   b.Farnworth 29-2-72
Source: Trainee.

1990-91	Manchester U	0	0		
1990-91	*Oldham Ath*	0	0		
1991-92	*Bury*	0	0		
1992-93	Lincoln C	27	0		
1993-94	Lincoln C	30	0	57	0
1994-95	Darlington	40	0		
1995-96	Darlington	15	0	55	0
1995-96	Notts Co	0	0		
1996-97	Notts Co	8	0		
1997-98	Notts Co	2	0	10	0
1997-98	*Oldham Ath*	16	0	16	0
1997-98	*Gillingham*	6	0	6	0
1997-98	*Brentford*	5	0	5	0
1997-98	Sunderland	0	0		
1998-99	Rotherham U	46	0		
1999-2000	Rotherham U	46	0	92	0
2000-01	Chesterfield	46	0	46	0

REEVES, David (F)   510 149
H: 6 0   W: 12 06   b.Birkenhead 19-11-67
Source: Heswall.

1986-87	Sheffield W	0	0		
1986-87	Scunthorpe U	4	2		
1987-88	Sheffield W	0	0		
1987-88	Scunthorpe U	6	4	10	6
1987-88	*Burnley*	16	8	16	8
1988-89	Sheffield W	17	2	17	2
1989-90	Bolton W	41	10		
1990-91	Bolton W	44	10		
1991-92	Bolton W	35	8		
1992-93	Bolton W	14	1	134	29
1992-93	Notts Co	9	2		
1993-94	Notts Co	4	0	13	2
1993-94	Carlisle U	34	11		
1994-95	Carlisle U	42	21		
1995-96	Carlisle U	43	13		
1996-97	Carlisle U	8	3	127	48
1996-97	Preston NE	34	11		
1997-98	Preston NE	13	1	47	12
1997-98	Chesterfield	26	5		
1998-99	Chesterfield	40	10		
1999-2000	Chesterfield	43	14		
2000-01	Chesterfield	37	13	146	42

RICHARDSON, Lee J (M)   388 37
H: 5 11   W: 10 06   b.Halifax 12-3-69
Source: Trainee.

1986-87	Halifax T	1	0		
1987-88	Halifax T	30	1		
1988-89	Halifax T	25	1	56	2
1988-89	Watford	9	0		
1989-90	Watford	32	1	41	1
1990-91	Blackburn R	38	2		
1991-92	Blackburn R	24	1		
1992-93	Blackburn R	0	0	62	3
1992-93	Aberdeen	29	2		
1993-94	Aberdeen	35	4	64	6
1994-95	Oldham Ath	30	6		
1995-96	Oldham Ath	27	11		
1996-97	Oldham Ath	31	4		
1997-98	Oldham Ath	0	0	88	21
1997-98	*Stockport Co*	6	0	6	0
1997-98	Huddersfield T	21	3		
1998-99	Huddersfield T	15	0		
1999-2000	Huddersfield T	0	0	36	3
1999-2000	*Bury*	5	1	5	1
1999-2000	Livingston	0	0		
2000-01	Chesterfield	30	0	30	0

RUSHBURY, Andy§ (M)   2 0
b.Carlisle 7-3-83
Source: Scholar.

2000-01	Chesterfield	2	0	2	0

SIMPKINS, Mike (D)   26 0
H: 6 0   W: 11 11   b.Sheffield 28-11-78
Source: Trainee.

1997-98	Sheffield W	0	0		
1997-98	Chesterfield	0	0		
1998-99	Chesterfield	1	0		
1999-2000	Chesterfield	9	0		
2000-01	Chesterfield	16	0	26	0

TUTILL, Steve (D)   390 7
H: 5 10   W: 12 06   b.Derwent 1-10-69
Source: Trainee. *Honours:* England Schools.

1987-88	York C	21	0		
1988-89	York C	22	1		
1989-90	York C	42	0		
1990-91	York C	42	0		
1991-92	York C	39	1		
1992-93	York C	8	0		
1993-94	York C	46	4		
1994-95	York C	39	0		
1995-96	York C	25	0		
1996-97	York C	15	0		
1997-98	York C	2	0	301	6
1997-98	Darlington	7	0		
1998-99	Darlington	36	0		
1999-2000	Darlington	27	0	70	0
2000-01	Chesterfield	19	1	19	1

WILLIAMS, Danny (D)   7 0
H: 5 9   W: 9 13   b.Sheffield 2-3-81
Source: Trainee.

1999-2000	Chesterfield	5	0		
2000-01	Chesterfield	2	0	7	0

WILLIAMS, Ryan (F)   106 16
H: 5 4   W: 11 02   b.Chesterfield 31-8-78
Source: Trainee. *Honours:* England Youth.

1995-96	Mansfield T	10	3		
1996-97	Mansfield T	16	0	26	3
1997-98	Tranmere R	0	0		
1998-99	Tranmere R	5	0		
1999-2000	Tranmere R	0	0	5	0

| 1999–2000 | Chesterfield | 30 | 5 | | |
| 2000–01 | Chesterfield | 45 | 8 | 75 | 13 |

WILLIS, Roger# (M) 290 50
H: 6 0 W: 12 00 b.Islington 17-6-67
Source: Dunkirk.

1989–90	Grimsby T	9	0	9	0
From Barnet					
1991–92	Barnet	38	12		
1992–93	Barnet	6	1	44	13
1992–93	Watford	32	2		
1993–94	Watford	4	0	36	2
1993–94	Birmingham C	16	5		
1994–95	Birmingham C	3	0	19	5
1994–95	Southend U	21	4		
1995–96	Southend U	10	3	31	7
1996–97	Peterborough U	40	6	40	6
1997–98	Chesterfield	34	8		
1998–99	Chesterfield	17	0		
1999–2000	Chesterfield	28	4		
2000–01	Chesterfield	32	5	111	17

WOODS, Steve* (D) 64 0
H: 5 11 W: 11 13 b.Davenham 15-12-76
Source: Trainee.

1995–96	Stoke C	0	0		
1996–97	Stoke C	0	0		
1997–98	Stoke C	1	0		
1997–98	*Plymouth Arg*	5	0	5	0
1998–99	Stoke C	33	0	34	0
1999–2000	Chesterfield	25	0		
2000–01	Chesterfield	0	0	25	0

Scholars
Armstrong, Joel; Atkinson, Joe; Cooke, Nicholas J; Hall, Jordan; Hogg, Timothy G; James, Richard; Mitchell, Alistair; Renshaw, Lee; Richmond, Andrew J; Rushbury, Andrew J; Rushbury, Ian D; Shaw, Craig P; Smith, Mark; Stone, Joseph; Tuckwood, Stephen A; Wilding, Craig; Worthington, Matthew A; Young, Matthew P

COLCHESTER U

ARNOTT, Andy‡ (M) 167 20
H: 6 0 W: 13 07 b.Chatham 18-10-73
Source: Trainee.

1990–91	Gillingham	0	0		
1991–92	Gillingham	19	2		
1992–93	Gillingham	15	6		
1992–93	*Manchester U*	0	0		
1993–94	Gillingham	10	2		
1994–95	Gillingham	28	2		
1995–96	Gillingham	1	0	73	12
1995–96	Leyton Orient	19	3		
1996–97	Leyton Orient	31	3	50	6
1997–98	Fulham	1	0		
1998–99	Fulham	0	0	1	0
1998–99	Brighton & HA	27	2		
1999–2000	Brighton & HA	1	0	28	2
1999–2000	Colchester U	12	0		
2000–01	Colchester U	3	0	15	0

BROWN, Simon# (G) 57 0
H: 6 2 W: 15 01 b.Chelmsford 3-12-76
Source: Trainee.

1995–96	Tottenham H	0	0		
1996–97	Tottenham H	0	0		
1997–98	Tottenham H	0	0		
1997–98	*Lincoln C*	1	0	1	0
1998–99	Tottenham H	0	0		
1998–99	*Fulham*	0	0		
1999–2000	Colchester U	38	0		
2000–01	Colchester U	18	0	56	0

CLARK, Simon (D) 239 13
H: 6 0 W: 12 00 b.Boston 12-3-67
Source: Boston U, Holbeach, Kings Lynn, Hendon, Stevenage Borough.

1993–94	Peterborough U	1	0		
1994–95	Peterborough U	32	0		
1995–96	Peterborough U	40	1		
1996–97	Peterborough U	34	3	107	4
1997–98	Leyton Orient	39	4		
1998–99	Leyton Orient	40	4		
1999–2000	Leyton Orient	19	1	98	9
2000–01	Colchester U	34	0	34	0

DOZZELL, Jason# (M) 535 79
H: 6 2 W: 13 07 b.Ipswich 9-12-67
Source: School. *Honours:* England Youth, Under-21.

1983–84	Ipswich T	5	1		
1984–85	Ipswich T	14	2		
1985–86	Ipswich T	41	3		
1986–87	Ipswich T	42	2		
1987–88	Ipswich T	39	1		
1988–89	Ipswich T	29	11		
1989–90	Ipswich T	46	8		
1990–91	Ipswich T	30	6		
1991–92	Ipswich T	45	11		
1992–93	Ipswich T	41	7		
1993–94	Tottenham H	32	8		
1994–95	Tottenham H	7	0		
1995–96	Tottenham H	28	3		
1996–97	Tottenham H	17	2	84	13
1997–98	Ipswich T	8	1	340	53
1997–98	Northampton T	4	4	21	4
1998–99	Colchester U	29	4		
1999–2000	Colchester U	39	5		
2000–01	Colchester U	22	0	90	9

DUGUID, Karl (F) 172 28
H: 5 11 W: 11 00 b.Letchworth 21-3-78
Source: Trainee.

1995–96	Colchester U	16	1		
1996–97	Colchester U	20	3		
1997–98	Colchester U	21	3		
1998–99	Colchester U	33	4		
1999–2000	Colchester U	41	12		
2000–01	Colchester U	41	5	172	28

DUNNE, Joe# (D) 270 5
H: 5 9 W: 11 08 b.Dublin 25-5-73
Source: Trainee. *Honours:* Eire Youth, Under-21.

1990–91	Gillingham	26	0		
1991–92	Gillingham	11	0		
1992–93	Gillingham	4	0		
1993–94	Gillingham	37	0		
1994–95	Gillingham	35	1		
1995–96	Gillingham	2	0	115	1
1995–96	Colchester U	5	1		
1996–97	Colchester U	35	0		
1997–98	Colchester U	25	2		
1998–99	Colchester U	36	0		
From Dover Ath.					
1999–2000	Colchester U	20	0		
2000–01	Colchester U	34	1	155	4

FARLEY, Craig‡ (D) 14 0
H: 6 0 W: 11 00 b.Oxford 17-3-81

| 1999–2000 | Colchester U | 14 | 0 | | |
| 2000–01 | Colchester U | 0 | 0 | 14 | 0 |

FITZGERALD, Scott (D) 231 2
H: 5 11 W: 12 08 b.Westminster 13-8-69
Source: Trainee. *Honours:* Eire Under-21, B.

1988–89	Wimbledon	0	0		
1989–90	Wimbledon	1	0		
1990–91	Wimbledon	0	0		
1991–92	Wimbledon	36	1		
1992–93	Wimbledon	20	0		
1993–94	Wimbledon	28	0		
1994–95	Wimbledon	17	0		
1995–96	Wimbledon	4	0		
1995–96	*Sheffield U*	6	0	6	0
1996–97	Wimbledon	0	0	106	1
1996–97	*Millwall*	7	0		
1997–98	Millwall	18	0		
1998–99	Millwall	32	1		
1999–2000	Millwall	31	0		
2000–01	Millwall	1	0	89	1
2000–01	Colchester U	30	0	30	0

GREGORY, David# (M) 246 22
H: 5 10 W: 12 03 b.Polstead 23-1-70
Source: Trainee.

1987–88	Ipswich T	0	0		
1988–89	Ipswich T	2	0		
1989–90	Ipswich T	4	0		
1990–91	Ipswich T	21	1		
1991–92	Ipswich T	1	0		
1992–93	Ipswich T	3	1		
1993–94	Ipswich T	0	0		
1994–95	Ipswich T	1	0	32	2
1994–95	*Hereford U*	2	0	2	0
1995–96	*Peterborough U*	3	0	3	0
1995–96	Colchester U	10	0		
1996–97	Colchester U	38	1		
1997–98	Colchester U	44	5		
1998–99	Colchester U	44	11		
1999–2000	Colchester U	45	0		
2000–01	Colchester U	28	3	209	20

IZZET, Kemal (M) 6 1
H: 5 6 W: 10 03 b.Whitechapel 29-9-80
Source: Trainee.

1998–99	Charlton Ath	0	0		
1999–2000	Charlton Ath	0	0		
2000–01	Charlton Ath	0	0		
2000–01	Colchester U	6	1	6	1

JOHNSON, Gavin# (D) 303 21
H: 5 11 W: 11 07 b.Eye 10-10-70
Source: Trainee.

1988–89	Ipswich T	4	0		
1989–90	Ipswich T	6	0		
1990–91	Ipswich T	7	0		
1991–92	Ipswich T	42	5		
1992–93	Ipswich T	40	5		
1993–94	Ipswich T	16	1		
1994–95	Ipswich T	17	0	132	11
1995–96	Luton T	5	0	5	0
1995–96	Wigan Ath	27	3		
1996–97	Wigan Ath	37	3		
1997–98	Wigan Ath	20	2	84	8
1998–99	Dunfermline Ath	18	0	18	0
1999–2000	Colchester U	27	0		
2000–01	Colchester U	37	2	64	2

JOHNSON, Ross (D) 168 2
H: 6 0 W: 13 00 b.Brighton 2-1-76
Source: Trainee.

1993–94	Brighton & HA	2	0		
1994–95	Brighton & HA	0	0		
1995–96	Brighton & HA	20	0		
1996–97	Brighton & HA	29	0		
1997–98	Brighton & HA	38	0		
1998–99	Brighton & HA	34	2		
1999–2000	Brighton & HA	9	0	132	2
1999–2000	Colchester U	18	0		
2000–01	Colchester U	18	0	36	0

KEEBLE, Chris (M) 22 2
H: 5 9 W: 11 00 b.Colchester 17-9-78
Source: Trainee.

1997–98	Ipswich T	1	0		
1998–99	Ipswich T	0	0		
1999–2000	Ipswich T	0	0	1	0
1999–2000	Colchester U	5	1		
2000–01	Colchester U	16	1	21	2

KEITH, Joey (D) 72 4
H: 5 7 W: 10 06 b.London 1-10-78
Source: Trainee.

1997–98	West Ham U	0	0		
1998–99	West Ham U	0	0		
1999–2000	Colchester U	45	1		
2000–01	Colchester U	27	3	72	4

LOCK, Tony‡ (M) 102 13
H: 6 0 W: 12 04 b.Harlow 3-9-76
Source: Trainee.

1994–95	Colchester U	3	1		
1995–96	Colchester U	0	0		
1996–97	Colchester U	6	1		
1997–98	Colchester U	32	6		
1998–99	Colchester U	23	1		
From Kettering T.					
1999–2000	Colchester U	24	2		
2000–01	Colchester U	14	2	102	13

McGAVIN, Steve# (F) 287 52
H: 5 9 W: 12 08 b.North Walsham 24-1-69
Source: Sudbury T.

1990–91	Colchester U	0	0		
1991–92	Colchester U	0	0		
1992–93	Colchester U	37	9		
1993–94	Colchester U	21	8		
1993–94	Birmingham C	8	1		
1994–95	Birmingham C	15	1	23	2
1994–95	Wycombe W	12	1		
1995–96	Wycombe W	31	2		
1996–97	Wycombe W	35	9		
1997–98	Wycombe W	37	2		
1998–99	Wycombe W	5	0	120	15
1998–99	Southend U	11	0	11	0
1999–2000	Northampton T	0	0		
1999–2000	Colchester U	34	16		
2000–01	Colchester U	41	2	133	35

McGLEISH, Scott (F) 241 62
H: 5 10 W: 11 07 b.Camden Town 10-2-74
Source: Edgware T.

1994–95	Charlton Ath	6	0	6	0
1994–95	*Leyton Orient*	6	1		
1995–96	Peterborough U	12	0		
1995–96	*Colchester U*	15	6		
1996–97	Peterborough U	1	0	13	0
1996–97	*Cambridge U*	10	7	10	7
1996–97	Leyton Orient	28	7		
1997–98	Leyton Orient	8	0	42	8
1997–98	Barnet	37	13		
1998–99	Barnet	36	8		
1999–2000	Barnet	42	10		
2000–01	Barnet	19	5	134	36
2000–01	Colchester U	21	5	36	11

MORGAN, Dean§ (F) 4 0
b.Edmonton 3-10-83
Source: Scholar.

| 2000–01 | Colchester U | 4 | 0 | 4 | 0 |

OKAFOR, Samuel† (M) 1 0
H: 5 9 W: 12 00 b.Xtian 17-3-82

1998–99	Colchester U	1	0		
1999–2000	Colchester U	0	0		
2000–01	Colchester U	0	0	1	0

PINAULT, Thomas (M) 9 1
H: 5 10 W: 11 01 b.Grasse 4-12-81
Source: Cannes.

| 1999–2000 | Colchester U | 4 | 0 | | |
| 2000–01 | Colchester U | 5 | 1 | 9 | 1 |

SCOTT, Keith‡ (F) 253 61
H: 6 3 W: 14 03 b.Westminster 9-6-67
Source: Leicester U.

| 1989–90 | Lincoln C | 10 | 2 | | |
| 1990–91 | Lincoln C | 6 | 0 | 16 | 2 |

From Wycombe W.

1993–94	Wycombe W	15	10		
1993–94	Swindon T	27	4		
1994–95	Swindon T	24	8	51	12
1994–95	Stoke C	18	3		
1995–96	Stoke C	7	0	25	3
1995–96	Norwich C	12	2		
1995–96	Bournemouth	8	1	8	1
1996–97	Norwich C	13	3	25	5
1996–97	Watford	6	2	6	2
1996–97	Wycombe W	9	3		
1997–98	Wycombe W	29	11		
1998–99	Wycombe W	25	6	78	30
1998–99	Reading	9	2		
1999–2000	Reading	25	3		
2000–01	Reading	1	0	35	5
2000–01	Colchester U	9	1	9	1

SKELTON, Aaron# (M) 133 17
H: 6 0 W: 12 08 b.Welwyn 22-11-74
Source: Trainee.

1992–93	Luton T	0	0		
1993–94	Luton T	0	0		
1994–95	Luton T	5	0		
1995–96	Luton T	0	0		
1996–97	Luton T	3	0	8	0
1997–98	Colchester U	39	7		
1998–99	Colchester U	9	0		
1999–2000	Colchester U	33	4		
2000–01	Colchester U	44	6	125	17

STOCKWELL, Mick# (M) 552 46
H: 5 7 W: 11 07 b.Chelmsford 14-2-65
Source: Apprentice.

1982–83	Ipswich T	0	0		
1983–84	Ipswich T	0	0		
1984–85	Ipswich T	0	0		
1985–86	Ipswich T	8	0		
1986–87	Ipswich T	21	1		
1987–88	Ipswich T	43	1		
1988–89	Ipswich T	23	2		
1989–90	Ipswich T	34	3		
1990–91	Ipswich T	44	6		
1991–92	Ipswich T	46	2		
1992–93	Ipswich T	39	4		
1993–94	Ipswich T	42	1		
1994–95	Ipswich T	15	0		
1995–96	Ipswich T	37	1		
1996–97	Ipswich T	43	7		
1997–98	Ipswich T	46	3		
1998–99	Ipswich T	30	2		
1999–2000	Ipswich T	35	2	506	35
2000–01	Colchester U	46	11	46	11

TANNER, Adam‡ (M) 77 7
H: 6 0 W: 13 00 b.Maldon 25-10-73
Source: Trainee.

1992–93	Ipswich T	0	0		
1993–94	Ipswich T	0	0		
1994–95	Ipswich T	10	2		
1995–96	Ipswich T	16	4		
1996–97	Ipswich T	18	1		
1997–98	Ipswich T	19	0		
1998–99	Ipswich T	0	0		
1999–2000	Ipswich T	0	0	73	7
2000–01	Peterborough U	0	0		
2000–01	Colchester U	4	0	4	0

WALKER, Andy† (G) 3 0
b.Bexley 30-9-81

1998–99	Colchester U	1	0		
1999–2000	Colchester U	2	0		
2000–01	Colchester U	0	0	3	0

WHITE, Alan (D) 116 3
H: 6 1 W: 13 07 b.Darlington 22-3-76
Source: Derby Co Schoolboy.

1994–95	Middlesbrough	0	0		
1995–96	Middlesbrough	0	0		
1996–97	Middlesbrough	0	0		
1997–98	Middlesbrough	0	0		
1997–98	Luton T	28	1		
1998–99	Luton T	33	1		
1999–2000	Luton T	19	1	80	3
1999–2000	Colchester U	4	0		
2000–01	Colchester U	32	0	36	0

WIGNALL, Jack† (D) 1 0
H: 6 1 W: 11 00 b.Liverpool 26-9-81
Source: Trainee.

| 1999–2000 | Colchester U | 1 | 0 | | |
| 2000–01 | Colchester U | 0 | 0 | 1 | 0 |

WOODMAN, Andy (G) 275 0
H: 6 3 W: 13 07 b.Camberwell 11-8-71
Source: Apprentice.

1989–90	Crystal Palace	0	0		
1990–91	Crystal Palace	0	0		
1991–92	Crystal Palace	0	0		
1992–93	Crystal Palace	0	0		
1993–94	Crystal Palace	0	0		
1994–95	Exeter C	6	0	6	0
1994–95	Northampton T	10	0		
1995–96	Northampton T	44	0		
1996–97	Northampton T	45	0		
1997–98	Northampton T	46	0		
1998–99	Northampton T	18	0	163	0
1998–99	Brentford	22	0		
1999–2000	Brentford	39	0		
1999–2000	Peterborough U	0	0		
2000–01	Brentford	0	0	61	0
2000–01	Southend U	17	0	17	0
2000–01	Colchester U	28	0	28	0

Scholars
Canham, Marc D; Chambers, Tristan;
Cranfield, Ben MD; Gyoury, Nicky D;
Hadrava, David L; Hearn, Matthew J;
Heighway, George; Hillier, Sean E; Morgan,
Dean; Okafor, Samuel A; Opara, Lloyd;
Redmond, Gary SC; Snow, Alexander C;
Taylor, Andrew C; Walker, Andrew W;
Wignall, Jack D; Williamson, Glenn A

COVENTRY C

ALOISI, John (F) 128 37
H: 6 1 W: 12 06 b.Adelaide 5-2-76
Source: Adelaide City 1 app, Cremonese.
Honours: Australia 22 full caps, 15 goals.

1996–97	Cremonese	26	2	26	2
1997–98	Portsmouth	38	12		
1998–99	Portsmouth	22	13	60	25
1998–99	Coventry C	16	5		
1999–2000	Coventry C	7	2		
2000–01	Coventry C	19	3	42	10

BELLAMY, Craig (F) 118 38
H: 5 8 W: 11 00 b.Cardiff 13-7-79
Source: Trainee. *Honours:* Wales Under-21,
12 full caps, 2 goals.

1996–97	Norwich C	3	0		
1997–98	Norwich C	36	13		
1998–99	Norwich C	40	17		
1999–2000	Norwich C	4	2		
2000–01	Norwich C	1	0	84	32
2000–01	Coventry C	34	6	34	6

(Transferred to Newcastle U, July 2001.)

BETTS, Robert (D) 10 0
H: 5 10 W: 11 00 b.Doncaster 21-12-81
Source: School.

1997–98	Doncaster R	3	0	3	0
1998–99	Coventry C	0	0		
1999–2000	Coventry C	2	0		
2000–01	Coventry C	1	0	3	0
2000–01	Plymouth Arg	4	0	4	0

BOTHROYD, Jay (F) 8 0
H: 6 3 W: 13 00 b.Islington 7-5-82
Source: Trainee. *Honours:* England Youth,
Under-21.

| 1999–2000 | Arsenal | 0 | 0 | | |
| 2000–01 | Coventry C | 8 | 0 | 8 | 0 |

BRANCATI, Marco (M) 0 0
H: 5 10 W: 11 05 b.Rome 16-4-83

| 2000–01 | Coventry C | 0 | 0 | | |

BREEN, Gary (D) 295 5
H: 6 1 W: 11 12 b.London 12-12-73
Source: Charlton Ath. *Honours:* Eire
Under-21, 38 full caps, 5 goals.

1991–92	Maidstone U	19	0	19	0
1992–93	Gillingham	29	0		
1993–94	Gillingham	22	0	51	0
1994–95	Peterborough U	44	1		
1995–96	Peterborough U	25	0	69	1
1995–96	Birmingham C	18	1		
1996–97	Birmingham C	22	1	40	2
1996–97	Coventry C	9	0		
1997–98	Coventry C	30	1		
1998–99	Coventry C	25	0		
1999–2000	Coventry C	21	0		
2000–01	Coventry C	31	1	116	2

CARSLEY, Lee (M) 205 17
H: 5 10 W: 12 06 b.Birmingham 28-2-74
Source: Trainee. *Honours:* Eire 16 full caps.

1992–93	Derby Co	0	0		
1993–94	Derby Co	0	0		
1994–95	Derby Co	23	2		
1995–96	Derby Co	35	1		
1996–97	Derby Co	24	0		
1997–98	Derby Co	34	1		
1998–99	Derby Co	22	1	138	5
1998–99	Blackburn R	8	0		
1999–2000	Blackburn R	30	10		
2000–01	Blackburn R	8	0	46	10
2000–01	Coventry C	21	2	21	2

CHIPPO, Youssef (M) 95 4
H: 5 11 W: 12 00 b.Rabat 10-6-73
Source: Al Arabi. *Honours:* Morocco full
caps.

1997–98	Porto	18	2		
1998–99	Porto	12	0	30	2
1999–2000	Coventry C	33	2		
2000–01	Coventry C	32	0	65	2

CUDWORTH, Thomas (D) 1 0
H: 5 10 W: 11 00 b.Coventry 3-8-82
Source: Trainee.

| 1999–2000 | Coventry C | 0 | 0 | | |
| 2000–01 | Coventry C | 0 | 0 | | |

DAVENPORT, Calum (D) 1 0
H: 6 4 W: 14 00 b.Bedford 1-1-83
Source: Trainee.

| 1999–2000 | Coventry C | 0 | 0 | | |
| 2000–01 | Coventry C | 1 | 0 | 1 | 0 |

DELORGE, Laurent (M) 10 5
H: 5 10 W: 11 12 b.Leuven 21-7-79

1998–99	Gent	10	5	10	5
1998–99	Coventry C	0	0		
1999–2000	Coventry C	0	0		
2000–01	Coventry C	0	0		

EDWORTHY, Marc (D) 251 2
H: 5 11 W: 10 03 b.Barnstaple 24-12-72
Source: Trainee.

1990–91	Plymouth Arg	0	0		
1991–92	Plymouth Arg	15	0		
1992–93	Plymouth Arg	15	0		
1993–94	Plymouth Arg	12	0		
1994–95	Plymouth Arg	27	1	69	1
1995–96	Crystal Palace	44	0		
1996–97	Crystal Palace	45	0		
1997–98	Crystal Palace	34	0		
1998–99	Crystal Palace	3	0	126	0
1998–99	Coventry C	22	0		
1999–2000	Coventry C	10	0		
2000–01	Coventry C	24	1	56	1

EUSTACE, John (M) 59 4
H: 5 11 W: 11 12 b.Solihull 3-11-79
Source: Trainee.

1996–97	Coventry C	0	0		
1997–98	Coventry C	0	0		
1998–99	Coventry C	0	0		
1998–99	Dundee U	11	1	11	1
1999–2000	Coventry C	16	1		
2000–01	Coventry C	32	2	48	3

FAHLMAN, Per (G) 0 0
H: 6 0 W: 12 07 b.Sweden 26-4-84

| 2000–01 | Coventry C | 0 | 0 | | |

FERGUSON, Barry (D) 13 0
H: 6 3 W: 13 00 b.Dublin 7-9-79
Source: Home Farm. *Honours:* Eire
Under-21.

1998–99	Coventry C	0	0		
1999–2000	Coventry C	0	0		
1999–2000	Colchester U	6	0	6	0
2000–01	Coventry C	0	0		
2000–01	Hartlepool U	4	0	4	0
2000–01	Northampton T	3	0	3	0

FORD, Brian (D) 0 0
H: 5 11 W: 12 00 b.Edinburgh 23-9-82
Source: Trainee.

| 1999–2000 | Coventry C | 0 | 0 | | |
| 2000–01 | Coventry C | 0 | 0 | | |

FOWLER, Lee (M) 0 0
H: 5 7 W: 10 00 b.Cardiff 10-6-83
Source: Scholar.

| 2000–01 | Coventry C | 0 | 0 | | |

FROGGATT, Steve (F) 190 11
H: 5 11 W: 11 00 b.Lincoln 9-3-73
Source: Trainee. *Honours:* England
Under-21.

1990–91	Aston Villa	0	0		
1991–92	Aston Villa	9	0		
1992–93	Aston Villa	17	1		
1993–94	Aston Villa	9	1	35	2
1994–95	Wolverhampton W	20	2		
1995–96	Wolverhampton W	18	1		
1996–97	Wolverhampton W	27	2		
1997–98	Wolverhampton W	33	2		
1998–99	Wolverhampton W	8	0	106	7
1998–99	Coventry C	23	1		
1999–2000	Coventry C	26	1		
2000–01	Coventry C	0	0	49	2

GALLIERI, Antonio (F) 0 0
H: 5 8 W: 11 00 b.Rome 5-7-83

| 2000–01 | Coventry C | 0 | 0 | | |

GRANT, Martin* (F) 0 0
H: 5 7 W: 10 10 b.Kirkcaldy 16-1-82
Source: Trainee.

1998–99	Coventry C	0	0		
1999–2000	Coventry C	0	0		
2000–01	Coventry C	0	0		

GUERRERO, Ivan (D) 3 0
H: 5 7 W: 10 00 b.Comayagua 30-11-77
Source: Motagua. Honours: Honduras full caps.

| 2000–01 | Coventry C | 3 | 0 | 3 | 0 |

GUSTAFSSON, Tomas (D) 132 2
H: 5 10 W: 11 00 b.Stockholm 7-5-73
Honours: Sweden 5 full caps.

1995	Brommapojkarna	23	1		
1996	Brommapojkarna	24	0	47	0
1997	AIK Stockholm	26	1		
1998	AIK Stockholm	25	0		
1999	AIK Stockholm	24	1	75	2
1999–2000	Coventry C	10	0		
2000–01	Coventry C	0	0	10	0

HADJI, Mustapha (M) 268 48
H: 6 0 W: 12 00 b.Ifrane 16-11-71
Honours: Morocco full caps.

1992–93	Nancy	32	6		
1993–94	Nancy	37	11		
1994–95	Nancy	28	3		
1995–96	Nancy	42	11	139	31
1996–97	Sporting	27	3		
1997–98	Sporting	9	0	36	3
1997–98	La Coruna	10	0		
1998–99	La Coruna	21	2	31	2
1999–2000	Coventry C	33	6		
2000–01	Coventry C	29	6	62	12

(Transferred to Aston Villa, July 2001).

HALL, Daniel* (D) 0 0
H: 5 8 W: 10 06 b.Rugby 29-12-81
Source: Trainee. Honours: England Youth.

1998–99	Coventry C	0	0		
1999–2000	Coventry C	0	0		
2000–01	Coventry C	0	0		

HALL, Marcus (D) 103 1
H: 6 1 W: 12 02 b.Coventry 24-3-76
Source: Trainee. Honours: England Under-21, B.

1994–95	Coventry C	5	0		
1995–96	Coventry C	25	0		
1996–97	Coventry C	13	0		
1997–98	Coventry C	25	1		
1998–99	Coventry C	5	0		
1999–2000	Coventry C	9	0		
2000–01	Coventry C	21	0	103	1

HARTSON, John (F) 228 74
H: 6 0 W: 13 07 b.Swansea 5-4-75
Source: Trainee. Honours: Wales Under-21, 24 full caps, 5 goals.

1992–93	Luton T	0	0		
1993–94	Luton T	34	6		
1994–95	Luton T	20	5	54	11
1994–95	Arsenal	15	7		
1995–96	Arsenal	19	4		
1996–97	Arsenal	19	3	53	14
1996–97	West Ham U	11	5		
1997–98	West Ham U	32	15		
1998–99	West Ham U	17	4	60	24
1998–99	Wimbledon	14	2		
1999–2000	Wimbledon	16	9		
2000–01	Wimbledon	19	8	49	19
2000–01	Coventry C	12	6	12	6

HEDMAN, Magnus (G) 227 0
H: 6 3 W: 14 00 b.Stockholm 19-3-73
Honours: Sweden 36 full caps.

1990	AIK Stockholm	2	0		
1991	AIK Stockholm	2	0		
1992	AIK Stockholm	7	0		
1993	AIK Stockholm	26	0		
1994	AIK Stockholm	26	0		
1995	AIK Stockholm	25	0		
1996	AIK Stockholm	26	0		
1997	AIK Stockholm	13	0	127	0
1997–98	Coventry C	14	0		
1998–99	Coventry C	36	0		
1999–2000	Coventry C	35	0		
2000–01	Coventry C	15	0	100	0

HOPE, Shaun (D) 0 0
H: 5 11 W: 12 00 b.Hartlepool 15-12-82
Source: Scholar.

| 2000–01 | Coventry C | 0 | 0 | | |

HYLDGAARD, Morten (G) 5 0
H: 6 6 W: 14 00 b.Herning 26-1-78
Source: Ikast.

1999–2000	Coventry C	0	0		
1999–2000	Scunthorpe U	5	0	5	0
2000–01	Coventry C	0	0		
2000–01	Grimsby T	0	0		

KIRKLAND, Christopher (G) 23 0
H: 6 3 W: 11 07 b.Leicester 2-5-81
Source: Trainee. Honours: England Youth, Under-21.

1997–98	Coventry C	0	0		
1998–99	Coventry C	0	0		
1999–2000	Coventry C	0	0		
2000–01	Coventry C	23	0	23	0

KONJIC, Muhamed (D) 178 12
H: 6 3 W: 13 00 b.Bosnia 14-5-70
Honours: Bosnia 19 full caps, 2 goals.

1990–91	Tuzla	3	0		
1991–92	Tuzla	5	0	8	0
1992–93	Belisce	18	0	18	0
1993–94	Zagreb	29	3		
1994–95	Zagreb	19	1		
1995–96	Zagreb	15	1	63	5
1996–97	Zurich	29	2		
1997–98	Zurich	7	3	36	5
1997–98	Monaco	19	0		
1998–99	Monaco	18	2	37	2
1998–99	Coventry C	4	0		
1999–2000	Coventry C	4	0		
2000–01	Coventry C	8	0	16	0

MAGENNIS, Mark (M) 0 0
H: 5 7 W: 10 02 b.Newtonards 15-3-83
Source: Scholar.

| 2000–01 | Coventry C | 0 | 0 | | |

MARTINEZ, Jairo (F) 0 0
H: 5 9 W: 11 08 b.Honduras 14-5-78
Honours: Honduras full caps.

| 2000–01 | Coventry C | 0 | 0 | | |

MATHIE, Graeme‡ (D) 0 0
H: 6 1 W: 12 00 b.Lanark 17-10-82
Source: Trainee.

| 1999–2000 | Coventry C | 0 | 0 | | |
| 2000–01 | Coventry C | 0 | 0 | | |

McCONNELL, Peter‡ (M) 0 0
H: 5 10 W: 11 12 b.Rutherglen 16-9-82
Source: Trainee.

| 1999–2000 | Coventry C | 0 | 0 | | |
| 2000–01 | Coventry C | 0 | 0 | | |

McPHEE, Gary* (F) 0 0
H: 6 0 W: 12 00 b.Glasgow 18-4-80

1998–99	Coventry C	0	0		
1999–2000	Coventry C	0	0		
2000–01	Coventry C	0	0		

McPHEE, Stephen* (M) 0 0
H: 5 7 W: 10 08 b.Glasgow 5-6-81

1998–99	Coventry C	0	0		
1999–2000	Coventry C	0	0		
2000–01	Coventry C	0	0		

McSHEFFREY, Gary (F) 4 0
H: 5 8 W: 10 06 b.Coventry 13-8-82
Source: Trainee. Honours: England Youth.

1998–99	Coventry C	1	0		
1999–2000	Coventry C	3	0		
2000–01	Coventry C	0	0	4	0

MILLER, Kirk (D) 0 0
H: 5 10 W: 11 10 b.Coventry 15-9-83
Source: Scholar.

| 2000–01 | Coventry C | 0 | 0 | | |

MONTGOMERY, Gary (G) 0 0
H: 6 1 W: 13 07 b.Leamington Spa 8-10-82
Source: Scholar.

| 2000–01 | Coventry C | 0 | 0 | | |

NORMANN, Runar (M) 49 6
H: 5 11 W: 12 00 b.Harstad 1-3-78
Source: Harstad.

1997	Lillestrom	1	1		
1998	Lillestrom	23	2		
1999	Lillestrom	17	3	41	6
1999–2000	Lillestrom	8	0		
2000–01	Coventry C	0	0	8	0

PALMER, Carlton (M) 536 28
H: 6 3 W: 13 00 b.Oldbury 5-12-65
Source: Trainee. Honours: England Under-21, B, 18 full caps, 1 goal.

1984–85	WBA	0	0		
1985–86	WBA	20	0		
1986–87	WBA	37	1		
1987–88	WBA	38	3		
1988–89	WBA	26	0	121	4
1988–89	Sheffield W	13	1		
1989–90	Sheffield W	34	0		
1990–91	Sheffield W	45	2		
1991–92	Sheffield W	42	5		
1992–93	Sheffield W	34	1		
1993–94	Sheffield W	37	5		
1994–95	Leeds U	39	3		
1995–96	Leeds U	35	2		
1996–97	Leeds U	28	0		
1997–98	Leeds U	0	0	102	5
1997–98	Southampton	26	3		
1998–99	Southampton	19	0	45	3
1998–99	Nottingham F	13	0		
1999–2000	Nottingham F	3	1	16	1
1999–2000	Coventry C	15	1		
2000–01	Coventry C	15	0	30	1
2000–01	Watford	5	0	5	0
2000–01	Sheffield W	12	0	217	14

PEAD, Craig (M) 0 0
H: 5 9 W: 11 06 b.Bromsgrove 15-9-81
Source: Trainee. Honours: England Youth.

1998–99	Coventry C	0	0		
1999–2000	Coventry C	0	0		
2000–01	Coventry C	0	0		

PIPE, David (M) 0 0
H: 5 9 W: 12 01 b.Caerphilly 5-11-83
Source: Scholar.

| 2000–01 | Coventry C | 0 | 0 | | |

QUINN, Barry (M) 43 0
H: 6 0 W: 12 02 b.Dublin 9-5-79
Source: Trainee. Honours: Eire Under-21, 4 full caps.

1996–97	Coventry C	0	0		
1997–98	Coventry C	0	0		
1998–99	Coventry C	7	0		
1999–2000	Coventry C	11	0		
2000–01	Coventry C	25	0	43	0

SHAW, Richard (D) 390 3
H: 5 9 W: 12 08 b.Brentford 11-9-68
Source: Apprentice.

1986–87	Crystal Palace	0	0		
1987–88	Crystal Palace	3	0		
1988–89	Crystal Palace	14	0		
1989–90	Crystal Palace	21	0		
1989–90	Hull C	4	0	4	0
1990–91	Crystal Palace	36	1		
1991–92	Crystal Palace	10	0		
1992–93	Crystal Palace	33	0		
1993–94	Crystal Palace	34	2		
1994–95	Crystal Palace	41	0		
1995–96	Crystal Palace	15	0	207	3
1995–96	Coventry C	21	0		
1996–97	Coventry C	35	0		
1997–98	Coventry C	33	0		
1998–99	Coventry C	37	0		
1999–2000	Coventry C	29	0		
2000–01	Coventry C	24	0	179	0

SPONG, Richard (D) 0 0
H: 5 11 W: 11 09 b.Falun 23-9-83
Source: Scholar.

| 2000–01 | Coventry C | 0 | 0 | | |

STRACHAN, Craig (M) 0 0
H: 5 8 W: 10 06 b.Aberdeen 19-5-82
Source: Trainee.

| 1999–2000 | Coventry C | 0 | 0 | | |
| 2000–01 | Coventry C | 0 | 0 | | |

STRACHAN, Gavin (M) 20 0
H: 5 10 W: 11 07 b.Aberdeen 23-12-78
Source: Trainee. Honours: Scotland Under-21.

1996–97	Coventry C	0	0		
1997–98	Coventry C	9	0		
1998–99	Coventry C	0	0		
1998–99	Dundee	6	0	6	0
1999–2000	Coventry C	3	0		
2000–01	Coventry C	2	0	14	0

TELFER, Paul (M) 335 25
H: 5 9 W: 11 06 b.Edinburgh 21-10-71
Source: Trainee. Honours: Scotland Under-21, 1 full cap.

1988–89	Luton T	0	0		
1989–90	Luton T	0	0		
1990–91	Luton T	1	0		
1991–92	Luton T	20	1		
1992–93	Luton T	32	2		
1993–94	Luton T	45	7		
1994–95	Luton T	46	9	144	19
1995–96	Coventry C	31	1		
1996–97	Coventry C	34	0		
1997–98	Coventry C	33	3		
1998–99	Coventry C	32	2		
1999–2000	Coventry C	30	0		
2000–01	Coventry C	31	0	191	6

THOMPSON, David (M) 83 8
H: 5 7 W: 10 00 b.Birkenhead 12-9-77
Source: Trainee. Honours: England Youth, Under-21.

1994–95	Liverpool	0	0		
1995–96	Liverpool	2	0		
1996–97	Liverpool	2	0		
1997–98	Liverpool	5	1		
1997–98	Swindon T	10	0	10	0
1998–99	Liverpool	14	1		
1999–2000	Liverpool	27	3	48	5
2000–01	Coventry C	25	3	25	3

WILLIAMS, Paul (D)   327   31
H: 5 11   W: 12 10   b.Burton 26-3-71
Source: Trainee. *Honours:* England
Under-21.

1989–90	Derby Co	10	1		
1989–90	Lincoln C	3	0	3	0
1990–91	Derby Co	19	4		
1991–92	Derby Co	41	13		
1992–93	Derby Co	19	4		
1993–94	Derby Co	34	1		
1994–95	Derby Co	37	3	160	26
1995–96	Coventry C	32	2		
1996–97	Coventry C	32	2		
1997–98	Coventry C	20	0		
1998–99	Coventry C	22	0		
1999–2000	Coventry C	28	1		
2000–01	Coventry C	30	0	164	5

ZUNIGA, Ysrael (F)   46   22
H: 5 9   W: 11 00   b.Lima 27-8-76
Honours: Peru 18 full caps, 1 goal.

1999	Melgar	25	19	25	19
1999–2000	Coventry C	6	2		
2000–01	Coventry C	15	1	21	3

Scholars
Ashby, Jason C; Cook, Matthew; Cooney,
Sean P; Grant, Stephen; Jephcott, Avun C;
Nelson, Daniel M; Noon, Mark

CREWE ALEX

ASHTON, Dean (F)   21   8
b.Swindon 24-11-83
Source: Schoolboy.

| 2000–01 | Crewe Alex | 21 | 8 | 21 | 8 |

BANKOLE, Ademola (G)   28   0
H: 6 3   W: 14 11   b.Lagos 9-9-69
Source: Leyton Orient.

1996–97	Crewe Alex	3	0		
1997–98	Crewe Alex	3	0		
1998–99	QPR	0	0		
1998–99	Grimsby T	0	0		
1999–2000	QPR	1	0	1	0
1999–2000	Bradford C	0	0		
2000–01	Crewe Alex	21	0	27	0

BELL, Lee (M)   0   0
b.Crewe 26-1-83
Source: Scholar.

| 2000–01 | Crewe Alex | 0 | 0 | | |

BETTS, Thomas (M)   0   0
b.Stone 3-12-82
Source: Scholar.

| 2000–01 | Crewe Alex | 0 | 0 | | |

CHARLES, Anthony (D)   0   0
H: 6 0   W: 12 00   b.Isleworth 11-3-81
Source: Brook House.

| 1999–2000 | Crewe Alex | 0 | 0 | | |
| 2000–01 | Crewe Alex | 0 | 0 | | |

CHARNOCK, Phil (M)   138   7
H: 5 10   W: 11 03   b.Southport 14-2-75
Source: Trainee.

1992–93	Liverpool	0	0		
1993–94	Liverpool	0	0		
1994–95	Liverpool	0	0		
1995–96	Blackpool	4	0		
1996–97	Liverpool	0	0	4	0
1996–97	Crewe Alex	32	1		
1997–98	Crewe Alex	33	3		
1998–99	Crewe Alex	44	2		
1999–2000	Crewe Alex	16	1		
2000–01	Crewe Alex	9	0	134	7

COLLINS, James* (M)   24   1
H: 5 8   W: 10 00   b.Liverpool 28-5-78
Source: Trainee.

1996–97	Crewe Alex	0	0		
1997–98	Crewe Alex	1	0		
1998–99	Crewe Alex	6	1		
1999–2000	Crewe Alex	13	0		
2000–01	Crewe Alex	4	0	24	1

CRAMB, Colin (F)   250   65
H: 6 0   W: 12 09   b.Lanark 23-6-74
Source: Hamilton A BC.

1990–91	Hamilton A	3	2		
1991–92	Hamilton A	12	1		
1992–93	Hamilton A	33	7	48	10
1993–94	Southampton	1	0	1	0
1994–95	Falkirk	8	1	8	1
1994–95	Hearts	6	1	6	1
1995–96	Doncaster R	21	7		
1996–97	Doncaster R	41	18	62	25
1997–98	Bristol C	40	9		
1998–99	Bristol C	13	0		
1998–99	Walsall	4	4	4	4
1999–2000	Bristol C	0	0	53	9

1999–2000	Crewe Alex	37	6		
2000–01	Crewe Alex	13	4	50	10
2000–01	Notts Co	3	0	3	0
2000–01	Bury	15	5	15	5

EDWARDS, Paul (M)   0   0
b.Derby 10-11-82
Source: Scholar.

| 2000–01 | Crewe Alex | 0 | 0 | | |

FOSTER, Stephen (D)   31   0
H: 5 11   W: 11 00   b.Warrington 10-9-80
Source: Trainee. *Honours:* England Schools.

1998–99	Crewe Alex	1	0		
1999–2000	Crewe Alex	0	0		
2000–01	Crewe Alex	30	0	31	0

FROST, Carl (M)   0   0
b.Chester 19-7-83
Source: Scholar.

| 2000–01 | Crewe Alex | 0 | 0 | | |

GANNON, Jim# (D)   394   52
H: 6 2   W: 13 00   b.Southwark 7-9-68
Source: Dundalk.

1988–89	Sheffield U	0	0		
1989–90	Sheffield U	0	0		
1989–90	Halifax T	2	0	2	0
1989–90	Stockport Co	7	1		
1990–91	Stockport Co	41	6		
1991–92	Stockport Co	43	16		
1992–93	Stockport Co	46	12		
1993–94	Stockport Co	35	4		
1993–94	Notts Co	2	0	2	0
1994–95	Stockport Co	45	7		
1995–96	Stockport Co	23	1		
1996–97	Stockport Co	40	4		
1997–98	Stockport Co	36	1		
1998–99	Stockport Co	38	0		
1999–2000	Stockport Co	29	0		
2000–01	Stockport Co	0	0	383	52
2000–01	Crewe Alex	7	0	7	0

GRANT, John (F)   6   0
H: 5 11   W: 10 08   b.Manchester 9-8-81
Source: Trainee.

| 1999–2000 | Crewe Alex | 4 | 0 | | |
| 2000–01 | Crewe Alex | 2 | 0 | 6 | 0 |

HIGDON, Michael (M)   0   0
b.Liverpool 2-9-83
Source: School.

| 2000–01 | Crewe Alex | 0 | 0 | | |

HOWELL, Dean* (M)   5   0
H: 6 1   W: 12 05   b.Burton-on-Trent
29-11-80
Source: Trainee.

1999–2000	Notts Co	1	0	1	0
2000–01	Crewe Alex	1	0	1	0
2000–01	Rochdale	3	0	3	0

HULSE, Robert (F)   37   12
H: 6 1   W: 12 00   b.Crewe 25-10-79
Source: Trainee.

1998–99	Crewe Alex	0	0		
1999–2000	Crewe Alex	4	1		
2000–01	Crewe Alex	33	11	37	12

INCE, Clayton (G)   2   0
H: 6 3   W: 13 00   b.Trinidad 13-7-72
Source: Defence Force. *Honours:* Trinidad &
Tobago full caps.

| 1999–2000 | Crewe Alex | 1 | 0 | | |
| 2000–01 | Crewe Alex | 1 | 0 | 2 | 0 |

JACK, Rodney (F)   179   41
H: 5 7   W: 10 07   b.Kingston, Jamaica
28-9-72
Source: Lambada. *Honours:* St Vincent full
caps.

1995–96	Torquay U	14	2		
1996–97	Torquay U	33	10		
1997–98	Torquay U	40	12	87	24
1998–99	Crewe Alex	39	9		
1999–2000	Crewe Alex	23	4		
2000–01	Crewe Alex	30	4	92	17

JEFFS, Ian (M)   0   0
b.Chester 12-10-82
Source: Scholar.

| 2000–01 | Crewe Alex | 0 | 0 | | |

KEARTON, Jason (G)   237   0
H: 6 1   W: 12 03   b.Ipswich (Aus) 9-7-69
Source: Brisbane Lions 26 apps.Australia 1
full cap.

1988–89	Everton	0	0		
1989–90	Everton	0	0		
1990–91	Everton	0	0		
1991–92	Everton	0	0		
1991–92	Stoke C	16	0	16	0
1991–92	Blackpool	14	0	14	0
1992–93	Everton	5	0		
1993–94	Everton	0	0		
1994–95	Everton	1	0		

1994–95	Notts Co	10	0	10	0
1995–96	Everton	0	0		
1995–96	Preston NE	0	0		
1996–97	Everton	0	0	6	0
1996–97	Crewe Alex	30	0		
1997–98	Crewe Alex	43	0		
1998–99	Crewe Alex	46	0		
1999–2000	Crewe Alex	46	0		
2000–01	Crewe Alex	26	0	191	0

LIDDLE, Gareth (D)   0   0
H: 6 0   W: 12 00   b.Manchester 10-8-82
Source: Scholar.

| 2000–01 | Crewe Alex | 0 | 0 | | |

LIGHTFOOT, Chris* (D)   381   37
H: 6 1   W: 12 00   b.Penketh 1-4-70
Source: Trainee.

1987–88	Chester C	16	1		
1988–89	Chester C	36	7		
1989–90	Chester C	40	1		
1990–91	Chester C	37	2		
1991–92	Chester C	44	5		
1992–93	Chester C	39	2		
1993–94	Chester C	37	11		
1994–95	Chester C	28	3	277	32
1995–96	Wigan Ath	14	1	14	1
1995–96	Crewe Alex	6	0		
1996–97	Crewe Alex	25	0		
1997–98	Crewe Alex	13	1		
1998–99	Crewe Alex	22	2		
1999–2000	Crewe Alex	21	1		
2000–01	Crewe Alex	0	0	87	4
2000–01	Oldham Ath	3	0	3	0

LITTLE, Colin (F)   170   32
H: 5 10   W: 11 00   b.Wythenshaw 4-11-72
Source: Hyde U.

1995–96	Crewe Alex	12	1		
1996–97	Crewe Alex	17	0		
1997–98	Crewe Alex	40	13		
1998–99	Crewe Alex	37	10		
1999–2000	Crewe Alex	37	4		
2000–01	Crewe Alex	27	4	170	32

LUNT, Kenny (M)   148   7
H: 5 10   W: 10 00   b.Runcorn 20-11-79
Source: Trainee. *Honours:* England Schools,
Youth.

1997–98	Crewe Alex	41	2		
1998–99	Crewe Alex	18	1		
1999–2000	Crewe Alex	43	3		
2000–01	Crewe Alex	46	1	148	7

MACAULEY, Steve (D)   252   26
H: 6 1   W: 12 03   b.Lytham 4-3-69
Source: Fleetwood T.

1991–92	Crewe Alex	9	1		
1992–93	Crewe Alex	25	3		
1993–94	Crewe Alex	17	3		
1994–95	Crewe Alex	43	4		
1995–96	Crewe Alex	29	7		
1996–97	Crewe Alex	42	2		
1997–98	Crewe Alex	0	0		
1998–99	Crewe Alex	20	1		
1999–2000	Crewe Alex	37	4		
2000–01	Crewe Alex	30	1	252	26

McCREADY, Christopher (M)   0   0
b.Chester 5-9-81
Source: Scholar.

| 2000–01 | Crewe Alex | 0 | 0 | | |

MORRIS, Alexander (M)   0   0
b.Stoke 5-10-82
Source: Scholar.

| 2000–01 | Crewe Alex | 0 | 0 | | |

RIVERS, Mark (F)   203   43
H: 5 10   W: 11 00   b.Crewe 26-11-75
Source: Trainee.

1993–94	Crewe Alex	0	0		
1994–95	Crewe Alex	0	0		
1995–96	Crewe Alex	33	10		
1996–97	Crewe Alex	27	6		
1997–98	Crewe Alex	35	6		
1998–99	Crewe Alex	43	7		
1999–2000	Crewe Alex	32	7		
2000–01	Crewe Alex	33	7	203	43

RIX, Benjamin (M)   0   0
b.Wolverhampton 11-12-82
Source: Scholar.

| 2000–01 | Crewe Alex | 0 | 0 | | |

SMITH, Peter* (F)   34   3
H: 5 10   W: 10 00   b.Rhuddlan 15-9-78
Source: Trainee.

1996–97	Crewe Alex	1	0		
1997–98	Crewe Alex	6	0		
1998–99	Crewe Alex	4	0		
1998–99	Macclesfield T	12	3	12	3
1999–2000	Crewe Alex	6	0		
2000–01	Crewe Alex	5	0	22	0

SMITH, Shaun (D) — 367 40
H: 5 10 W: 11 00 b.Leeds 9-4-71
Source: Trainee.

Season	Club				
1988–89	Halifax T	1	0		
1989–90	Halifax T	6	0		
1990–91	Halifax T	0	0	7	0
1991–92	Crewe Alex	10	0		
1992–93	Crewe Alex	36	4		
1993–94	Crewe Alex	37	7		
1994–95	Crewe Alex	45	8		
1995–96	Crewe Alex	29	1		
1996–97	Crewe Alex	38	4		
1997–98	Crewe Alex	43	6		
1998–99	Crewe Alex	46	4		
1999–2000	Crewe Alex	31	2		
2000–01	Crewe Alex	45	4	360	40

SODJE, Efetobar# (D) — 127 6
H: 6 1 W: 12 00 b.Greenwich 5-10-72
Source: Delta Steel Pioneer, Stevenage Bor.
Honours: Nigeria full caps.

Season	Club				
1997–98	Macclesfield T	41	3		
1998–99	Macclesfield T	42	3	83	6
1999–2000	Luton T	9	0	9	0
1999–2000	Colchester U	3	0	3	0
2000–01	Crewe Alex	32	0	32	0

SORVEL, Neil (M) — 187 14
H: 6 0 W: 12 09 b.Widnes 2-3-73
Source: Trainee.

Season	Club				
1991–92	Crewe Alex	9	0		
1992–93	Crewe Alex	0	0		
1997–98	Macclesfield T	45	3		
1998–99	Macclesfield T	41	4	86	0
1999–2000	Crewe Alex	46	6		
2000–01	Crewe Alex	46	1	101	7

STREET, Kevin (M) — 106 8
H: 5 10 W: 11 00 b.Crewe 25-11-77
Source: Trainee.

Season	Club				
1996–97	Crewe Alex	0	0		
1997–98	Crewe Alex	32	4		
1998–99	Crewe Alex	23	2		
1999–2000	Crewe Alex	28	1		
2000–01	Crewe Alex	23	1	106	8

TAIT, Paul (F) — 56 6
H: 6 1 W: 11 00 b.Newcastle 24-10-74
Source: Trainee.

Season	Club				
1993–94	Everton	0	0		
1994–95	Wigan Ath	5	0		
1995–96	Wigan Ath	0	0	5	0

From Northwich Vic.

Season	Club				
1999–2000	Crewe Alex	33	6		
2000–01	Crewe Alex	18	0	51	6

TRAINER, Phil (M) — 0 0
H: 6 0 W: 12 00 b.Wolverhampton 3-7-81

Season	Club		
2000–01	Crewe Alex	0	0

VAUGHAN, David (M) — 1 0
b.St Asaph 18-2-83
Source: Scholar.

Season	Club				
2000–01	Crewe Alex	1	0	1	0

WALKER, Richard (D) — 3 0
H: 6 2 W: 13 00 b.Stafford 17-9-80
Source: Brook House.

Season	Club				
1999–2000	Crewe Alex	0	0		
2000–01	Crewe Alex	3	0	3	0

WALTON, David (D) — 224 11
H: 6 2 W: 14 07 b.Bellingham 10-4-73
Source: Trainee.

Season	Club				
1991–92	Sheffield U	0	0		
1992–93	Sheffield U	0	0		
1993–94	Sheffield U	0	0		
1993–94	Shrewsbury T	27	5		
1994–95	Shrewsbury T	36	3		
1995–96	Shrewsbury T	35	0		
1996–97	Shrewsbury T	24	1		
1997–98	Shrewsbury T	6	1	128	10
1997–98	Crewe Alex	27	0		
1998–99	Crewe Alex	38	1		
1999–2000	Crewe Alex	11	0		
2000–01	Crewe Alex	20	0	96	1

WELSBY, Kevin* (M) — 0 0
H: 6 0 W: 10 06 b.Crewe 27-8-80
Source: Trainee.

Season	Club		
1998–99	Crewe Alex	0	0
1999–2000	Crewe Alex	0	0
2000–01	Crewe Alex	0	0

WRIGHT, David (D) — 110 1
H: 5 11 W: 10 09 b.Warrington 1-5-80
Source: Trainee. *Honours:* England Youth.

Season	Club				
1997–98	Crewe Alex	3	0		
1998–99	Crewe Alex	20	1		
1999–2000	Crewe Alex	45	0		
2000–01	Crewe Alex	42	0	110	1

YATES, Adam (M) — 0 0
b.Stoke 28-5-83
Source: Scholar.

Season	Club		
2000–01	Crewe Alex	0	0

Scholars
Baylis, Philip; Blake, Mathew L; Booth, Martin T; Bostock, Andrew M; Clare, Craig G; Coverley, Neil; Harris, Paul J; Jenkins, Byron K; Lunt, Gary T; Malbon, Craig D; Marrow, James FJ; Marsh, Nicholas J; Platt, Matthew; Roberts, Mark A; Robinson, James G; Swiggs, Craig B; Westwood, Lee K; Whiting, Louie A; Wilcock, James W; Wilson, Nicholas D

CRYSTAL PALACE

AUSTIN, Dean (D) — 324 8
H: 5 11 W: 11 11 b.Hemel Hempstead 26-4-70
Source: St. *Honours:* Albans C.

Season	Club				
1989–90	Southend U	7	0		
1990–91	Southend U	44	0		
1991–92	Southend U	45	2	96	2
1992–93	Tottenham H	34	0		
1993–94	Tottenham H	23	0		
1994–95	Tottenham H	24	0		
1995–96	Tottenham H	28	0		
1996–97	Tottenham H	15	0		
1997–98	Tottenham H	0	0	124	0
1998–99	Crystal Palace	20	1		
1999–2000	Crystal Palace	45	2		
2000–01	Crystal Palace	39	3	104	6

BERHALTER, Gregg# (D) — 108 4
b.New Jersey 1-8-73
Honours: USA 20 full caps.

Season	Club				
1994–95	Zwolle	23	1		
1995–96	Zwolle	14	1	37	2
1996–97	Sparta	8	0		
1997–98	Sparta	2	0	10	0
1998–99	Cambuur	28	2		
1999–2000	Cambuur	28	0	56	2
2000–01	Crystal Palace	5	0	5	0

BLACK, Tommy (M) — 50 5
H: 5 7 W: 11 04 b.Chigwell 26-11-79
Source: Trainee.

Season	Club				
1998–99	Arsenal	0	0		
1999–2000	Arsenal	1	0	1	0
1999–2000	Carlisle U	5	1	5	1
1999–2000	Bristol C	4	0	4	0
2000–01	Crystal Palace	40	4	40	4

BOARDMAN, Jonathan (M) — 0 0
b.Reading 27-1-81
Source: Trainee.

Season	Club		
1999–2000	Crystal Palace	0	0
2000–01	Crystal Palace	0	0

BUSBY, Hubert‡ (G) — 1 0
b.Toronto 18-6-69
Source: Caldas.

Season	Club				
2000–01	Oxford U	1	0	1	0
2000–01	Crystal Palace	0	0		

CARLISLE, Wayne (M) — 46 3
H: 6 0 W: 11 06 b.Lisburn 9-9-79
Source: Trainee. *Honours:* Northern Ireland Under-21.

Season	Club				
1996–97	Crystal Palace	0	0		
1997–98	Crystal Palace	0	0		
1998–99	Crystal Palace	6	0		
1999–2000	Crystal Palace	26	3		
2000–01	Crystal Palace	14	0	46	3

DIGBY, Fraser‡ (G) — 473 0
H: 6 1 W: 12 12 b.Sheffield 23-4-67
Source: Apprentice. *Honours:* England Schools, Youth, Under-21.

Season	Club				
1984–85	Manchester U	0	0		
1985–86	Manchester U	0	0		
1985–86	Oldham Ath	0	0		
1985–86	Swindon T	0	0		
1986–87	Manchester U	0	0		
1986–87	Swindon T	39	0		
1987–88	Swindon T	31	0		
1988–89	Swindon T	46	0		
1989–90	Swindon T	45	0		
1990–91	Swindon T	41	0		
1991–92	Swindon T	21	0		
1992–93	Swindon T	33	0		
1992–93	Manchester U	0	0		
1993–94	Swindon T	28	0		
1994–95	Swindon T	39	0		
1995–96	Swindon T	25	0		
1996–97	Swindon T	31	0		
1997–98	Swindon T	38	0	417	0
1998–99	Crystal Palace	18	0		
1999–2000	Crystal Palace	38	0		
2000–01	Crystal Palace	0	0	56	0

DIMOND, Kristian (M) — 0 0
b.Cardiff 1-2-83
Source: Trainee.

Season	Club		
1999–2000	Crystal Palace	0	0
2000–01	Crystal Palace	0	0

DSANE, Roscoe* (M) — 0 0
b.Epsom 16-10-80
Source: Trainee.

Season	Club		
1999–2000	Crystal Palace	0	0
2000–01	Crystal Palace	0	0

EVANS, Stephen (M) — 6 0
H: 5 11 W: 11 02 b.Caerphilly 25-9-80
Source: Trainee. *Honours:* Wales Under-21.

Season	Club				
1998–99	Crystal Palace	4	0		
1999–2000	Crystal Palace	1	0		
2000–01	Crystal Palace	1	0	6	0

FOSTER, Craig‡ (M) — 68 5
H: 5 11 W: 12 00 b.Melbourne 15-4-69
Source: From Sydney United 41 apps, 2 goals, Sunshine George Cross, 33 apps, Adelaide City 50 apps, 15 goals, Marconi Stallions 26

Season	Club				
1997–98	Portsmouth	16	2		
1998–99	Portsmouth	0	0	16	2
1998–99	Crystal Palace	32	2		
1999–2000	Crystal Palace	20	1		
2000–01	Crystal Palace	0	0	52	3

FOWLER, Michael* (M) — 0 0
b.Cardiff 22-8-81
Source: Trainee.

Season	Club		
1999–2000	Crystal Palace	0	0
2000–01	Crystal Palace	0	0

FRAMPTON, Andrew (D) — 25 0
H: 5 11 W: 10 10 b.Wimbledon 3-9-79
Source: Trainee.

Season	Club				
1998–99	Crystal Palace	6	0		
1999–2000	Crystal Palace	9	0		
2000–01	Crystal Palace	10	0	25	0

FREEDMAN, Dougie (F) — 262 97
H: 5 9 W: 12 05 b.Glasgow 21-1-74
Source: Trainee. *Honours:* Scotland Under-21, B.

Season	Club				
1991–92	QPR	0	0		
1992–93	QPR	0	0		
1993–94	QPR	0	0		
1994–95	Barnet	42	24		
1995–96	Barnet	5	3	47	27
1995–96	Crystal Palace	39	20		
1996–97	Crystal Palace	44	11		
1997–98	Crystal Palace	7	0		
1997–98	Wolverhampton W	29	10	29	10
1998–99	Nottingham F	31	9		
1999–2000	Nottingham F	34	9		
2000–01	Nottingham F	5	0	70	18
2000–01	Crystal Palace	26	11	116	42

FULLARTON, Jamie (M) — 167 4
H: 5 9 W: 10 09 b.Bellshill 20-7-74

Season	Club				
1991–92	St Mirren	1	0		
1992–93	St Mirren	25	0		
1993–94	St Mirren	37	0		
1994–95	St Mirren	17	1		
1995–96	St Mirren	22	2	102	3
1996–97	Bastia	17	0	17	0
1997–98	Crystal Palace	25	1		
1998–99	Crystal Palace	7	0		
1998–99	Bolton W	1	0	1	0
1999–2000	Crystal Palace	13	0		
2000–01	Crystal Palace	2	0	47	1

(Transferred to Dundee, November 2000).

FULLER, Ricardo (F) — 8 0
b.Kingston, Jamaica 31-10-79
Source: Tivoli Gardens.

Season	Club				
2000–01	Crystal Palace	8	0	8	0

GRAY, Julian (M) — 24 1
H: 6 1 W: 11 00 b.Lewisham 21-9-79
Source: Trainee.

Season	Club				
1998–99	Arsenal	0	0		
1999–2000	Arsenal	1	0	1	0
2000–01	Crystal Palace	23	1	23	1

GREGG, Matt (G) — 44 0
H: 5 11 W: 12 00 b.Cheltenham 30-11-78
Source: Trainee.

Season	Club				
1995–96	Torquay U	1	0		
1996–97	Torquay U	1	0		
1997–98	Torquay U	19	0		
1998–99	Torquay U	11	0	32	0
1998–99	Crystal Palace	0	0		
1998–99	Swansea C	5	0	5	0
1999–2000	Crystal Palace	6	0		
2000–01	Crystal Palace	1	0	7	0

GWILLIM, Gareth (M) — 0 0
b.Farnborough 9-2-83

Season	Club		
2000–01	Crystal Palace	0	0

HANKIN, Sean (M) 1 0
H: 5 11 W: 12 04 b.Camberley 28-2-81
Source: Trainee.
1999–2000	Crystal Palace	1	0
2000–01	Crystal Palace	0	0	1	0

HARRIS, Richard (D) 9 0
H: 5 11 W: 10 09 b.Croydon 23-10-80
Source: Trainee.
1997–98	Crystal Palace	0	0
1998–99	Crystal Palace	1	0
1999–2000	Crystal Palace	6	0
2000–01	Crystal Palace	2	0	9	0

HARRISON, Craig (D) 62 0
H: 6 0 W: 11 08 b.Gateshead 10-11-77
Source: Trainee.
1996–97	Middlesbrough	0	0
1997–98	Middlesbrough	20	0
1998–99	Middlesbrough	4	0
1998–99	Preston NE	6	0	6	0
1999–2000	Middlesbrough	0	0
2000–01	Middlesbrough	0	0	24	0
2000–01	Crystal Palace	32	0	32	0

HIBBURT, James* (D) 6 0
H: 6 0 W: 12 08 b.Ashford 30-10-79
Source: Trainee. Honours: England Schools.
1996–97	Crystal Palace	0	0
1997–98	Crystal Palace	0	0
1998–99	Crystal Palace	2	0
1999–2000	Crystal Palace	4	0
2000–01	Crystal Palace	0	0	6	0

HOPKIN, David (M) 234 29
H: 6 1 W: 13 13 b.Greenock 21-8-70
Source: Pt Glasgow R BC. Honours: Scotland B, 7 full caps, 2 goals.
1989–90	Morton	8	0
1990–91	Morton	10	0
1991–92	Morton	0	0	18	0
1992–93	Chelsea	4	0
1993–94	Chelsea	21	0
1994–95	Chelsea	15	1	40	1
1995–96	Crystal Palace	42	8
1996–97	Crystal Palace	41	13
1997–98	Leeds U	25	1
1998–99	Leeds U	34	4
1999–2000	Leeds U	14	1	73	6
2000–01	Bradford C	11	0	11	0
2000–01	Crystal Palace	9	1	92	22

HOWELL, Richard (M) 0 0
b.Hitchin 29-8-82
1999–2000	Crystal Palace	0	0
2000–01	Crystal Palace	0	0

HUNT, Steve* (M) 3 0
H: 5 9 W: 12 06 b.Laois 1-8-81
Source: Trainee.
1999–2000	Crystal Palace	3	0
2000–01	Crystal Palace	0	0	3	0

KABBA, Steven (D) 2 0
H: 5 10 W: 11 12 b.Lambeth 7-3-81
Source: Trainee.
1999–2000	Crystal Palace	1	0
2000–01	Crystal Palace	1	0	2	0

KEMBER, Robert (M) 0 0
b.Wimbledon 21-8-81
2000–01	Crystal Palace	0	0

KOLINKO, Aleksandrs (G) 143 0
H: 6 3 W: 13 08 b.Latvia 18-6-75
Honours: Latvia 22 full caps.
1994	Interskonto	22	0	22	0
1995	Skonto Metals	25	0	25	0
1996	Skonto Riga	9	0
1997	Skonto Riga	12	0
1998	Skonto Riga	5	0
1999	Skonto Riga	18	0
2000	Skonto Riga	17	0	61	0
2000–01	Crystal Palace	35	0	35	0

MARTIN, Andrew (F) 22 2
H: 6 0 W: 10 12 b.Cardiff 28-2-80
Source: Trainee. Honours: Wales Under-21.
1996–97	Crystal Palace	0	0
1997–98	Crystal Palace	0	0
1998–99	Crystal Palace	3	0
1999–2000	Crystal Palace	19	2
2000–01	Crystal Palace	0	0	22	2

MORRISON, Clinton (F) 112 40
H: 6 1 W: 11 02 b.Tooting 14-5-79
Source: Trainee.
1996–97	Crystal Palace	0	0
1997–98	Crystal Palace	1	1
1998–99	Crystal Palace	37	12
1999–2000	Crystal Palace	29	13
2000–01	Crystal Palace	45	14	112	40

MULLINS, Hayden (M) 126 16
H: 6 0 W: 11 12 b.Reading 27-3-79
Source: Trainee. Honours: England Under-21.
1996–97	Crystal Palace	0	0
1997–98	Crystal Palace	0	0
1998–99	Crystal Palace	40	5
1999–2000	Crystal Palace	45	10
2000–01	Crystal Palace	41	1	126	16

POLLOCK, Jamie (M) 295 31
H: 6 0 W: 13 03 b.Stockton 16-2-74
Source: Trainee. Honours: England Youth, Under-21.
1990–91	Middlesbrough	1	0
1991–92	Middlesbrough	26	1
1992–93	Middlesbrough	22	1
1993–94	Middlesbrough	34	9
1994–95	Middlesbrough	41	5
1995–96	Middlesbrough	31	1	155	17
1996–97	Osasuna	1	0
1996–97	Bolton W	20	4
1997–98	Bolton W	26	1	46	5
1997–98	Manchester C	8	1
1998–99	Manchester C	26	1
1999–2000	Manchester C	24	3	58	5
2000–01	Crystal Palace	31	4	31	4
2000–01	Birmingham C	5	0	5	0

RHODES, Martin‡ (M) 0 0
b.Stoke Newington 17-2-82
Honours: England Schools.
2000–01	Crystal Palace	0	0

RIIHILAHTI, Aki (M) 9 1
H: 6 1 W: 12 06 b.Helsinki 9-6-76
Honours: Finland 30 full caps, 2 goals.
2000–01	Crystal Palace	9	1	9	1

RODGER, Simon# (M) 253 11
H: 5 9 W: 11 09 b.Shoreham 3-10-71
Source: Trainee.
1989–90	Crystal Palace	0	0
1990–91	Crystal Palace	0	0
1991–92	Crystal Palace	22	0
1992–93	Crystal Palace	23	2
1993–94	Crystal Palace	42	3
1994–95	Crystal Palace	4	0
1995–96	Crystal Palace	24	0
1996–97	Crystal Palace	0	0
1996–97	Manchester C	8	1	8	1
1996–97	Stoke C	5	0	5	0
1997–98	Crystal Palace	29	2
1998–99	Crystal Palace	18	1
1999–2000	Crystal Palace	34	2
2000–01	Crystal Palace	33	0	240	10

ROWLAND, Oliver‡ (M) 0 0
b.Brighton 6-8-82
Honours: England Schools.
2000–01	Crystal Palace	0	0

RUBINS, Andrejs (M) 89 14
H: 5 9 W: 10 03 b.Latvia 26-11-78
Honours: Latvia 23 full caps.
1998	Skonto Riga	19	1
1999	Skonto Riga	25	6
2000	Skonto Riga	23	7	67	14
2000–01	Crystal Palace	22	0	22	0

RUDDOCK, Neil (D) 340 28
H: 6 2 W: 12 12 b.Wandsworth 9-5-68
Source: Apprentice. Honours: England Youth, Under-21, B, 1 full cap.
1985–86	Millwall	0	0
1985–86	Tottenham H	0	0
1986–87	Tottenham H	4	0
1987–88	Tottenham H	5	0
1988–89	Millwall	2	1	2	1
1988–89	Southampton	13	3
1989–90	Southampton	29	3
1990–91	Southampton	35	3
1991–92	Southampton	30	0	107	9
1992–93	Tottenham H	38	3	47	3
1993–94	Liverpool	39	3
1994–95	Liverpool	37	2
1995–96	Liverpool	20	5
1996–97	Liverpool	17	1
1997–98	Liverpool	2	0	115	11
1997–98	QPR	7	0	7	0
1998–99	West Ham U	27	2
1999–2000	West Ham U	15	0	42	2
2000–01	Crystal Palace	20	2	20	2

SHARPLING, Christopher (F) 6 0
H: 5 11 W: 11 10 b.Bromley 21-4-81
Source: Trainee.
1998–99	Crystal Palace	0	0
1999–2000	Crystal Palace	6	0
2000–01	Crystal Palace	0	0	6	0

SMITH, Jamie# (D) 196 1
H: 5 8 W: 11 02 b.Birmingham 17-9-74
Source: Trainee.
1993–94	Wolverhampton W	0	0
1994–95	Wolverhampton W	25	0
1995–96	Wolverhampton W	13	0
1996–97	Wolverhampton W	38	0
1997–98	Wolverhampton W	11	0	87	0
1997–98	Crystal Palace	18	0
1998–99	Crystal Palace	26	0
1998–99	Fulham	9	1	9	1
1999–2000	Crystal Palace	27	0
2000–01	Crystal Palace	29	0	100	0

THOMSON, Steve (M) 55 0
H: 5 8 W: 10 04 b.Glasgow 23-1-78
Source: Trainee.
1995–96	Crystal Palace	0	0
1996–97	Crystal Palace	0	0
1997–98	Crystal Palace	0	0
1998–99	Crystal Palace	16	0
1999–2000	Crystal Palace	21	0
2000–01	Crystal Palace	18	0	55	0

VERHOENE, Kenny* (D) 135 13
H: 6 3 W: 14 07 b.Ghent 15-4-73
1994–95	Gent	20	0
1995–96	Gent	30	1
1996–97	Gent	17	1	67	2
1997–98	St Truiden	16	3	16	3
1998–99	Harelbeke	25	3
1999–2000	Harelbeke	26	5	51	8
2000–01	Crystal Palace	1	0	1	0

WALSH, Ronald* (M) 0 0
b.Glasnevin 15-9-82
Source: Scholarship.
1999–2000	Crystal Palace	0	0
2000–01	Crystal Palace	0	0

WARREN, Steven (M) 0 0
b.London 27-9-83
2000–01	Crystal Palace	0	0

WINDEGAARD, Stephen (M) 0 0
b.Chertsey 6-8-82
Honours: England Schools.
2000–01	Crystal Palace	0	0

WOOZLEY, David (D) 36 0
H: 6 0 W: 12 10 b.Berkshire 6-12-79
Source: Trainee.
1997–98	Crystal Palace	0	0
1998–99	Crystal Palace	7	0
1999–2000	Crystal Palace	23	0
2000–01	Crystal Palace	0	0	30	0
2000–01	Bournemouth	6	0	6	0

ZHIYI, Fan (M) 86 4
H: 6 0 W: 12 01 b.Shanghai 22-1-70
Source: Shanghai Shenhua. Honours: China full caps.
1998–99	Crystal Palace	29	2
1999–2000	Crystal Palace	29	1
2000–01	Crystal Palace	28	1	86	4

Scholars
Amoako, Adolf; Antwee, William; Dobson, Craig G; Elsegood, Christopher J; Gooding, Scott O; Hateley, Gary J; Hunt, David; Julius, Andrew; Leacock, Jamie H; Nicholas, Mark P; Smith, Robert; Surey, Ben D; Williams, Gareth A; Williams, Ryan

DARLINGTON

ANGEL, Mark‡ (M) 103 5
H: 5 8 W: 11 02 b.Newcastle 23-8-75
Source: Trainee.
1993–94	Sunderland	0	0
1994–95	Sunderland	0	0
1995–96	Oxford U	27	1
1996–97	Oxford U	24	2
1997–98	Oxford U	22	1	73	4
1998–99	WBA	22	1
1999–2000	WBA	3	0	25	1
2000–01	Darlington	5	0	5	0

ATKINSON, Brian (M) 301 14
H: 5 10 W: 12 10 b.Darlington 19-1-71
Source: Trainee. Honours: England Under-21.
1988–89	Sunderland	3	0
1989–90	Sunderland	13	0
1990–91	Sunderland	6	0
1991–92	Sunderland	30	2
1992–93	Sunderland	36	2
1993–94	Sunderland	29	0
1994–95	Sunderland	17	0
1995–96	Sunderland	7	0	141	4
1995–96	Carlisle U	2	0	2	0
1996–97	Darlington	30	3
1997–98	Darlington	32	1

1998–99 Darlington 43 2
1999–2000 Darlington 30 0
2000–01 Darlington 23 4 **158 10**

BEAVERS, Paul* (F) 27 3
H: 6 3 W: 14 07 b.Blackpool 2-10-78
Source: Trainee.
1996–97 Sunderland 0 0
1997–98 Sunderland 0 0
1998–99 Sunderland 0 0
1998–99 *Shrewsbury T* 2 0 2 0
1998–99 *Oldham Ath* 7 2
1999–2000 Oldham Ath 4 0
1999–2000 *Hartlepool U* 7 0 7 0
2000–01 Oldham Ath 0 0 11 2
2000–01 Darlington 7 1 7 1

BRIGHTWELL, David (D) 235 8
H: 6 2 W: 12 09 b.Lutterworth 7-1-71
Source: Trainee.
1987–88 Manchester C 0 0
1988–89 Manchester C 0 0
1989–90 Manchester C 0 0
1990–91 Manchester C 0 0
1990–91 *Chester C* 6 0 6 0
1991–92 Manchester C 4 0
1992–93 Manchester C 8 0
1993–94 Manchester C 22 1
1994–95 Manchester C 9 0
1995–96 Manchester C 0 0 43 1
1995–96 *Lincoln C* 5 0 5 0
1995–96 *Stoke C* 1 0 1 0
1995–96 Bradford C 22 0
1996–97 Bradford C 2 0 24 0
1996–97 *Blackpool* 2 0 2 0
1997–98 Northampton T 35 1 35 1
1998–99 Carlisle U 41 4
1999–2000 Carlisle U 37 0 78 4
2000–01 Hull C 27 2 27 2
2000–01 Darlington 14 0 14 0

BRUMWELL, Phil (M) 181 1
H: 5 8 W: 11 00 b.Darlington 8-8-75
Source: Trainee.
1994–95 Sunderland 0 0
1995–96 Darlington 28 0
1996–97 Darlington 38 1
1997–98 Darlington 35 0
1998–99 Darlington 37 0
1999–2000 Darlington 18 0
2000–01 Hull C 4 0 4 0
2000–01 Darlington 21 0 177 1

CAMPBELL, Paul (M) 40 5
H: 6 1 W: 11 00 b.Middlesbrough 29-1-80
Source: Trainee.
1997–98 Darlington 6 1
1998–99 Darlington 9 1
1999–2000 Darlington 9 2
2000–01 Darlington 16 1 40 5

CAU, Jean-Michel (F) 1 0
b.Corsica 27-10-80
Source: Gazelec.
2000–01 Darlington 1 0 1 0

COLLETT, Andy (G) 159 0
H: 6 0 W: 12 10 b.Stockton 28-10-73
Source: Trainee.
1991–92 Middlesbrough 0 0
1992–93 Middlesbrough 2 0
1993–94 Middlesbrough 0 0
1994–95 Middlesbrough 0 0 2 0
1994–95 Bristol R 4 0
1995–96 Bristol R 26 0
1996–97 Bristol R 44 0
1997–98 Bristol R 30 0
1998–99 Bristol R 3 0 107 0
1999–2000 Darlington 13 0
2000–01 Darlington 37 0 50 0

CONVERY, Mark (F) 11 0
H: 5 6 W: 10 05 b.Newcastle 29-5-81
Source: Trainee.
1998–99 Sunderland 0 0
1999–2000 Sunderland 0 0
2000–01 Sunderland 0 0
2000–01 Darlington 11 0 11 0

FORD, Mark (M) 131 7
H: 5 7 W: 10 08 b.Pontefract 10-10-75
Source: Trainee. *Honours:* England Youth, Under-21.
1992–93 Leeds U 0 0
1993–94 Leeds U 1 0
1994–95 Leeds U 0 0
1995–96 Leeds U 12 0
1996–97 Leeds U 16 1 29 1
1997–98 Burnley 36 1
1998–99 Burnley 12 0 48 1
1999–2000 Lommel 15 0 15 0
2000–01 Torquay U 28 3 28 3
2000–01 Darlington 11 2 11 2

GRAY, Martin (M) 262 5
H: 5 9 W: 11 05 b.Stockton 17-8-71
Source: Trainee.
1989–90 Sunderland 0 0
1990–91 Sunderland 0 0
1990–91 *Aldershot* 5 0 5 0
1991–92 Sunderland 1 0
1992–93 Sunderland 12 1
1993–94 Sunderland 22 0
1994–95 Sunderland 22 0
1995–96 Sunderland 7 0 64 1
1995–96 *Fulham* 6 0 6 0
1995–96 Oxford U 7 0
1996–97 Oxford U 43 2
1997–98 Oxford U 31 2
1998–99 Oxford U 40 0 121 4
1999–2000 Darlington 41 0
2000–01 Darlington 25 0 66 0

HARPER, Steve (M) 481 53
H: 5 10 W: 11 12 b.Newcastle-under-Lyme 3-2-69
Source: Trainee.
1987–88 Port Vale 21 2
1988–89 Port Vale 7 0 28 2
1988–89 Preston NE 5 0
1989–90 Preston NE 36 10
1990–91 Preston NE 36 0 77 10
1991–92 Burnley 35 3
1992–93 Burnley 34 5
1993–94 Burnley 0 0 69 8
1993–94 Doncaster R 31 2
1994–95 Doncaster R 33 9
1995–96 Doncaster R 1 0 65 11
1995–96 Mansfield T 29 5
1996–97 Mansfield T 40 2
1997–98 Mansfield T 46 5
1998–99 Mansfield T 45 6 160 18
1999–2000 Hull C 38 4
2000–01 Hull C 27 0 65 4
2000–01 Darlington 17 0 17 0

HECKINGBOTTOM, Paul (D) 107 3
H: 6 0 W: 12 03 b.Barnsley 17-7-77
Source: Manchester U Trainee.
1995–96 Sunderland 0 0
1996–97 Sunderland 0 0
1997–98 Sunderland 0 0
1997–98 *Scarborough* 29 0 29 0
1998–99 Sunderland 0 0
1998–99 *Hartlepool U* 5 1 5 1
1998–99 *Darlington* 10 0
1999–2000 Darlington 45 1
2000–01 Darlington 18 1 73 2

HIMSWORTH, Gary (M) 391 26
H: 5 8 W: 11 00 b.York 19-12-69
Source: Trainee.
1987–88 York C 31 2
1988–89 York C 32 2
1989–90 York C 23 4
1990–91 York C 2 0
1990–91 Scarborough 23 1
1991–92 Scarborough 36 4
1992–93 Scarborough 33 1 92 6
1993–94 Darlington 28 3
1994–95 Darlington 38 2
1995–96 Darlington 28 3
1995–96 York C 8 1
1996–97 York C 33 2
1997–98 York C 15 0
1998–99 York C 13 0 157 11
1998–99 Darlington 14 1
1999–2000 Darlington 19 0
2000–01 Darlington 15 0 142 9

HODGSON, Richard (M) 36 2
H: 5 10 W: 11 06 b.Sunderland 1-10-79
Source: Trainee.
1996–97 Nottingham F 0 0
1997–98 Nottingham F 0 0
1998–99 Nottingham F 0 0
1999–2000 Nottingham F 0 0
1999–2000 Scunthorpe U 1 0 1 0
2000–01 Darlington 35 2 35 2

JACKSON, Kirk (F) 10 1
H: 5 10 W: 11 07 b.Barnsley 16-10-76
Source: Trainee.
From Worksop T.
2000–01 Darlington 10 1 10 1

JEANNIN, Alex (D) 11 0
H: 6 0 W: 11 06 b.Troyes 30-12-77
Source: Troyes.
2000–01 Darlington 11 0 11 0

KAAK, Tom‡ (M) 23 3
H: 5 11 W: 12 04 b.Winterswijk 31-3-78
Source: Grol, De Graafschap.
1998–99 Heracles 15 1 15 1
2000–01 Darlington 8 2 8 2

KEITA, Abraham# (M) 0 0
b.Paris 10-2-75
Source: Choisy-le-Roi.
2000–01 Darlington 0 0

KILTY, Mark (D) 22 1
H: 6 0 W: 12 00 b.Sunderland 24-6-81
Source: Trainee.
1998–99 Darlington 2 0
1999–2000 Darlington 2 0
2000–01 Darlington 18 1 22 1

LIDDLE, Craig (D) 174 6
H: 5 11 W: 12 07 b.Chester-le-Street 21-10-71
Source: Blyth Spartans.
1994–95 Middlesbrough 1 0
1995–96 Middlesbrough 13 0
1996–97 Middlesbrough 5 0
1997–98 Middlesbrough 6 0 25 0
1997–98 *Darlington* 15 0
1998–99 Darlington 44 3
1999–2000 Darlington 45 1
2000–01 Darlington 45 2 149 6

MARCELLE, Clint (M) 165 13
H: 5 5 W: 10 00 b.Port of Spain 9-11-68
Source: Vitoria Setubal, Rio Ave. *Honours:* Trinidad & Tobago full caps.
1994–95 Falgueiras 30 3
1995–96 Falgueiras 21 0 51 3
1996–97 Barnsley 40 8
1997–98 Barnsley 20 0
1998–99 Barnsley 9 0
1999–2000 Barnsley 0 0
1999–2000 *Scunthorpe U* 10 0 10 0
2000–01 Barnsley 0 0 69 8
2000–01 *Hull C* 23 2 23 2
2000–01 Darlington 12 0 12 0

MARSH, Adam (F) 7 0
H: 5 11 W: 11 08 b.Derby 20-2-82
Source: Worksop T.
2000–01 Darlington 7 0 7 0

NAISBETT, Philip† (G) 2 0
b.Peterlee 12-1-79
Source: Trainee.
1996–97 Sunderland 0 0
1997–98 Sunderland 0 0
1998–99 Sunderland 0 0
1998–99 Scarborough 2 0 2 0
From Spennymoor T
1999–2000 Scunthorpe U 0 0
2000–01 Exeter C 0 0
2000–01 Darlington 0 0

NAYLOR, Glenn (F) 305 73
H: 5 10 W: 11 10 b.York 11-8-72
Source: Trainee.
1989–90 York C 1 0
1990–91 York C 20 5
1991–92 York C 21 8
1992–93 York C 4 0
1993–94 York C 10 1
1994–95 York C 29 9
1995–96 York C 25 7
1995–96 *Darlington* 4 1
1996–97 York C 1 0 111 30
1996–97 Darlington 37 11
1997–98 Darlington 42 8
1998–99 Darlington 42 9
1999–2000 Darlington 25 3
2000–01 Darlington 44 11 194 43

PEPPER, Carl‡ (D) 6 0
H: 5 11 W: 11 00 b.Darlington 26-7-80
Source: Trainee.
1998–99 Darlington 6 0
1999–2000 Darlington 0 0
2000–01 Darlington 0 0 6 0

RAYMOND, Christophe‡ (D) 0 0
b.Amiens 1-9-69
Source: Amiens F.C.
2000–01 Darlington 0 0

REED, Adam (D) 162 3
H: 6 1 W: 11 00 b.Bishop Auckland 18-2-77
Source: Trainee.
1991–92 Darlington 1 0
1992–93 Darlington 0 0
1993–94 Darlington 13 0

1994–95	Darlington	38	1		
1995–96	Blackburn R	0	0		
1996–97	Blackburn R	0	0		
1996–97	*Darlington*	14	0		
1997–98	Blackburn R	0	0		
1997–98	*Rochdale*	10	0	10	0
1998–99	Darlington	29	2		
1999–2000	Darlington	23	0		
2000–01	Darlington	34	0	152	3

SKELTON, Craig‡ (D)   1 0
H: 5 9 W: 11 11 b.Middlesbrough 14-9-80
Source: Trainee.

| 1999–2000 | Darlington | 0 | 0 | | |
| 2000–01 | Darlington | 1 | 0 | 1 | 0 |

TAIT, Jordan* (D)   4 0
H: 5 10 W: 11 05 b.Berwick 27-9-79
Source: Trainee.

1998–99	Newcastle U	0	0		
1999–2000	Oldham Ath	1	0		
2000–01	Oldham Ath	0	0	1	0
2000–01	Darlington	3	0	3	0

VAN DER GEEST, Frank (G)   61 0
H: 6 2 W: 11 06 b.Beverwijk 30-4-73

| 1993–94 | AZ | 1 | 0 | | |
| 1994–95 | AZ | 2 | 0 | 3 | 0 |

From ADO 20

1995–96	Sparta	0	0		
1996–97	Sparta	2	0	2	0
1997–98	Heracles	22	0		
1998–99	Heracles	32	0	54	0
2000–01	Darlington	2	0	2	0

WALKLATE, Steve‡ (M)   6 0
H: 5 11 W: 12 00 b.Durham 27-9-79
Source: Trainee.

1998–99	Middlesbrough	0	0		
1999–2000	Middlesbrough	0	0		
2000–01	Darlington	6	0	6	0

WELLS, David‡ (D)   0 0
H: 5 9 W: 12 00 b.Stockton 19-2-81
Source: Trainee.

| 1999–2000 | Darlington | 0 | 0 | | |
| 2000–01 | Darlington | 0 | 0 | | |

WILLIAMS, John# (F)   340 62
H: 6 2 W: 13 08 b.Birmingham 11-5-68
Source: Cradley T.

1991–92	Swansea C	39	11		
1992–93	Coventry C	41	8		
1993–94	Coventry C	32	3		
1994–95	Coventry C	7	0		
1994–95	*Notts Co*	5	2	5	2
1994–95	*Stoke C*	4	0	4	0
1994–95	*Swansea C*	7	2	46	13
1995–96	Coventry C	0	0	80	11
1995–96	Wycombe W	29	8		
1996–97	Wycombe W	19	1	48	9
1996–97	Hereford U	11	3	11	3
1997–98	Walsall	1	0	1	0
1997–98	Exeter C	36	4	36	4
1998–99	Cardiff C	43	12		
1999–2000	Cardiff C	0	0	43	12
1999–2000	York C	36	3		
2000–01	York C	6	0	42	3
2000–01	Darlington	24	5	24	5

WILLIAMSON, Garry§ (M)   6 0
b.Darlington 24-1-82
Source: Scholar.

| 2000–01 | Darlington | 6 | 0 | 6 | 0 |

ZEGHDANE, Lehit‡ (M)   3 0
b.Sedan 3-10-77

| 2000–01 | Darlington | 3 | 0 | 3 | 0 |

Scholars
Birrell, Adam P; Bromley, Kevin; Ellenden, John; Finch, Keith J; Hughes, Christopher; Jackson, Neil P; Jarvis, Mark; Liddle, Graham B; McGurk, David; Paxton, Richard J; Rundle, Adam; Scroggins, Lee P; Sheeran, Mark J; Trainer, Lee GE; Williamson, Garry

DERBY CO

BANNISTER, Patrick (M)   0 0
b.Walsall 3-12-83
Source: Scholar.

| 2000–01 | Derby Co | 0 | 0 | | |

BLATSIS, Con (D)   8 0
H: 6 3 W: 14 06 b.Australia 5-7-77
Source: South Melbourne 96 apps, 5 goals.
Honours: Australia 2 full caps.

| 2000–01 | Derby Co | 2 | 0 | 2 | 0 |
| 2000–01 | *Sheffield W* | 6 | 0 | 6 | 0 |

BOERTIEN, Paul (D)   30 2
H: 5 11 W: 11 11 b.Carlisle 21-1-79
Source: Trainee.

1996–97	Carlisle U	0	0		
1997–98	Carlisle U	9	0		
1998–99	Carlisle U	8	1	17	1
1998–99	Derby Co	1	0		
1999–2000	Derby Co	2	0		
1999–2000	*Crewe Alex*	2	0	2	0
2000–01	Derby Co	8	1	11	1

BOHINEN, Lars (M)   279 26
H: 6 1 W: 12 03 b.Vadso 8-9-69
Source: Young Boys. *Honours:* Norway 49 full caps, 10 goals.

1988	Valerengen	15	2		
1989	Valerengen	18	3	33	5
1990	Viking	10	0	10	0
1990–91	Young Boys	22	4		
1991–92	Young Boys	34	2		
1992–93	Young Boys	2	0	58	6
1993–94	Nottingham F	31	3		
1994–95	Nottingham F	34	6		
1995–96	Nottingham F	7	0	64	7
1995–96	Blackburn R	19	4		
1996–97	Blackburn R	23	2		
1997–98	Blackburn R	16	1	58	7
1997–98	Derby Co	9	1		
1998–99	Derby Co	32	0		
1999–2000	Derby Co	13	0		
2000–01	Derby Co	2	0	56	1

(Transferred to Lyngby, January 2001).

BOLDER, Adam (M)   22 0
H: 5 8 W: 11 13 b.Hull 25-10-80
Source: Trainee.

1998–99	Hull C	1	0		
1999–2000	Hull C	19	0	20	0
1999–2000	Derby Co	0	0		
2000–01	Derby Co	2	0	2	0

BRAGSTAD, Bjorn (D)   206 26
H: 6 3 W: 14 06 b.Trondheim 5-1-71
Honours: Norway 15 full caps.

1989	Rosenborg	1	0		
1990	Rosenborg	9	0		
1991	Rosenborg	6	1		
1992	Rosenborg	16	4		
1993	Rosenborg	20	4		
1994	Rosenborg	21	3		
1995	Rosenborg	25	6		
1996	Rosenborg	8	2		
1997	Rosenborg	22	0		
1998	Rosenborg	25	4		
1999	Rosenborg	25	1		
2000	Rosenborg	16	1	194	26
2000–01	Derby Co	12	0	12	0

BROWN, Karl* (M)   0 0
b.Liverpool 5-7-82
Source: Scholar.

| 2000–01 | Derby Co | 0 | 0 | | |

BURLEY, Craig (M)   211 33
H: 6 1 W: 13 03 b.Ayr 24-9-71
Source: Trainee. *Honours:* Scotland Schools, Youth, Under-21, 42 full caps, 3 goals.

1989–90	Chelsea	0	0		
1990–91	Chelsea	1	0		
1991–92	Chelsea	8	0		
1992–93	Chelsea	3	0		
1993–94	Chelsea	23	3		
1994–95	Chelsea	25	2		
1995–96	Chelsea	22	0		
1996–97	Chelsea	31	2	113	7
1997–98	Celtic	35	10		
1998–99	Celtic	21	9		
1999–2000	Celtic	0	0	56	19
1999–2000	Derby Co	18	5		
2000–01	Derby Co	24	2	42	7

BURTON, Deon (F)   171 33
H: 6 3 W: 12 08 b.Reading 25-10-77
Source: Trainee. *Honours:* Jamaica 35 full caps, 4 goals.

1993–94	Portsmouth	2	0		
1994–95	Portsmouth	7	2		
1995–96	Portsmouth	32	7		
1996–97	Portsmouth	21	1	62	10
1996–97	*Cardiff C*	5	2	5	2
1997–98	Derby Co	29	3		
1998–99	Derby Co	21	9		
1998–99	*Barnsley*	3	0	3	0
1999–2000	Derby Co	19	4		
2000–01	Derby Co	32	5	101	21

CARBONARI, Horace Angel (D)   85 8
H: 6 3 W: 14 08 b.Rosario 2-5-71
Source: Rosario Central.

1998–99	Derby Co	29	5		
1999–2000	Derby Co	29	2		
2000–01	Derby Co	27	1	85	8

CHRISTIE, Malcolm (F)   57 13
H: 6 0 W: 12 06 b.Peterborough 11-4-79
Source: Nuneaton B. *Honours:* England Under-21.

1998–99	Derby Co	2	0		
1999–2000	Derby Co	21	5		
2000–01	Derby Co	34	8	57	13

DELAP, Rory (D)   168 18
H: 6 1 W: 13 00 b.Sutton Coldfield 6-7-76
Source: Trainee. *Honours:* Eire 6 full caps.

1992–93	Carlisle U	1	0		
1993–94	Carlisle U	1	0		
1994–95	Carlisle U	3	0		
1995–96	Carlisle U	19	3		
1996–97	Carlisle U	32	4		
1997–98	Carlisle U	9	0	65	7
1997–98	Derby Co	13	0		
1998–99	Derby Co	23	0		
1999–2000	Derby Co	34	8		
2000–01	Derby Co	33	3	103	11

(Transferred to Southampton, July 2001).

DOHERTY, Gerard* (G)   0 0
H: 6 3 W: 12 06 b.Derry 24-8-81
Source: Derry C.

1998–99	Derby Co	0	0		
1999–2000	Derby Co	0	0		
2000–01	Derby Co	0	0		

ELLIOTT, Steve (D)   40 0
H: 6 2 W: 14 08 b.Derby 29-10-78
Source: Trainee.

1996–97	Derby Co	0	0		
1997–98	Derby Co	3	0		
1998–99	Derby Co	11	0		
1999–2000	Derby Co	20	0		
2000–01	Derby Co	6	0	40	0

ERANIO, Stefano* (M)   406 26
H: 5 11 W: 12 08 b.Genoa 29-12-66
Honours: Italy 20 full caps, 3 goals.

1984–85	Genoa	9	0		
1985–86	Genoa	13	0		
1986–87	Genoa	36	3		
1987–88	Genoa	34	0		
1988–89	Genoa	35	4		
1989–90	Genoa	25	0		
1990–91	Genoa	32	4		
1991–92	Genoa	29	2	213	13
1992–93	AC Milan	21	2		
1993–94	AC Milan	21	1		
1994–95	AC Milan	11	0		
1995–96	AC Milan	24	1		
1996–97	AC Milan	21	2	98	6
1997–98	Derby Co	23	5		
1998–99	Derby Co	25	0		
1999–2000	Derby Co	19	0		
2000–01	Derby Co	28	2	95	7

EVATT, Ian (D)   1 0
H: 6 3 W: 14 04 b.Coventry 23-11-81
Source: Trainee.

1998–99	Derby Co	0	0		
1999–2000	Derby Co	0	0		
2000–01	Derby Co	1	0	1	0

FLANAGAN, Martin (M)   0 0
b.Omagh 13-1-84
Source: Scholar.

| 2000–01 | Derby Co | 0 | 0 | | |

GRANT, Lee (G)   0 0
H: 6 2 W: 13 00 b.Watford 27-1-83
Source: Scholar.

| 2000–01 | Derby Co | 0 | 0 | | |

GUDJONSSON, Thordur (F)   192 60
H: 5 9 W: 12 04 b.Akranes 14-10-73
Honours: Iceland 41 full caps, 10 goals.

1990	KA	16	2	16	2
1991	IA Akranes	0	0		
1992	IA Akranes	18	6		
1993	IA Akranes	18	19	36	25
1994–95	Bochum	16	3		
1995–96	Bochum	0	0		
1996–97	Bochum	13	1	29	4
1997–98	Genk	33	9		
1998–99	Genk	28	9		
1999–2000	Genk	33	10	94	28
2000–01	Las Palmas	7	0	7	0
2000–01	Derby Co	10	1	10	1

HIGGINBOTHAM, Danny (D)   30 0
H: 6 1 W: 13 03 b.Manchester 29-12-78
Source: Trainee.

1997–98	Manchester U	1	0		
1998–99	Manchester U	0	0		
1999–2000	Manchester U	3	0	4	0
2000–01	Derby Co	26	0	26	0

HUNT, Lewis (D)   0 0
H: 5 11 W: 12 08 b.Birmingham 25-8-82
Source: Scholar.

| 2000–01 | Derby Co | 0 | 0 | | |

JACKSON, Richard (D) 26 0
H: 5 7 W: 11 02 b.Whitby 18-4-80
Source: Trainee.
1997–98	Scarborough	2	0	
1998–99	Scarborough	20	0	22 0
1998–99	Derby Co	0	0	
1999–2000	Derby Co	2	0	
2000–01	Derby Co	2	0	4 0

JOHNSON, Seth (M) 159 8
H: 5 11 W: 12 11 b.Birmingham 12-3-79
Source: Trainee. *Honours:* England Youth,
Under-21, 1 full cap.
1996–97	Crewe Alex	11	1	
1997–98	Crewe Alex	40	1	
1998–99	Crewe Alex	42	4	93 6
1999–2000	Derby Co	36	1	
2000–01	Derby Co	30	1	66 2

KINKLADZE, Georgiou (M) 315 81
H: 5 6 W: 11 05 b.Tbilisi 6-7-73
Source: Dynamo Tbilisi. *Honours:* Georgia 42
full caps, 8 goals.
1990	Mretebi	34	8	
1991	Mretebi	16	1	
1991–92	Mretebi	30	9	80 18
1992–93	Dynamo Tbilisi	30	14	
1993–94	Dynamo Tbilisi	14	13	
1993–94	Saarbrucken	11	0	11 0
1994–95	Dynamo Tbilisi	21	14	65 41
1995–96	Manchester C	37	4	
1996–97	Manchester C	39	12	
1997–98	Manchester C	30	4	106 20
1998–99	Ajax	12	0	12 0
1999–2000	Derby Co	17	1	
2000–01	Derby Co	24	1	41 2

MARTIN, Lilian‡ (D) 162 9
H: 5 11 W: 11 11 b.Marseille 28-5-71
1993–94	Dunkerque	37	3	
1994–95	Dunkerque	37	3	
1995–96	Dunkerque	34	3	108 9
1996–97	Monaco	26	0	
1997–98	Monaco	7	0	
1998–99	Monaco	10	0	43 0
1999–2000	Marseille	2	0	
2000–01	Marseille	0	0	2 0
2000–01	Derby Co	9	0	9 0

MAWENE, Youl (D) 14 0
H: 6 1 W: 13 05 b.Caen 16-7-79
1999–2000	Lens	6	0	6 0
2000–01	Derby Co	8	0	8 0

McARDLE, Fiachra (M) 0 0
b.Newry 18-8-83
Source: Scholar.
2000–01	Derby Co	0	0

MORRIS, Lee (F) 54 7
H: 5 9 W: 11 02 b.Driffield 30-4-80
Source: Trainee. *Honours:* England Youth.
1997–98	Sheffield U	5	0	
1998–99	Sheffield U	20	6	
1999–2000	Sheffield U	1	0	26 6
1999–2000	Derby Co	3	0	
2000–01	Derby Co	20	0	23 0
2000–01	*Huddersfield*	5	1	5 1

MOUKOKO, Tonton (M) 0 0
b.Congo 22-12-83
Source: Scholar.
2000–01	Derby Co	0	0

MURRAY, Adam (M) 26 0
H: 5 9 W: 11 11 b.Birmingham 30-9-81
Source: Trainee. *Honours:* England Youth.
1998–99	Derby Co	4	0	
1999–2000	Derby Co	8	0	
2000–01	Derby Co	14	0	26 0

O'NEIL, Brian (M) 208 12
H: 6 0 W: 13 10 b.Paisley 6-9-72
Source: X Form. *Honours:* Scotland
Under-21, 6 full caps.
1991–92	Celtic	28	1	
1992–93	Celtic	17	3	
1993–94	Celtic	28	2	
1994–95	Celtic	26	0	
1995–96	Celtic	5	0	
1996–97	Celtic	16	2	120 8
1996–97	*Nottingham F*	5	0	5 0
1997–98	Aberdeen	29	1	29 1
1998–99	Wolfsburg	26	2	
1999–2000	Wolfsburg	16	1	
2000–01	Wolfsburg	8	0	50 3
2000–01	Derby Co	4	0	4 0

OAKES, Andy (G) 25 0
H: 6 1 W: 12 04 b.Crewe 11-1-77
1995–96	Bury	0	0
1996–97	Bury	0	0
1997–98	Bury	0	0

From Winsford U.
1998–99	Hull C	19	0	19 0
1999–2000	Derby Co	0	0	
1999–2000	*Port Vale*	0	0	
2000–01	Derby Co	6	0	6 0

POOM, Mart (G) 163 0
H: 6 4 W: 14 03 b.Tallinn 3-2-72
Honours: Estonia 77 full caps.
1992–93	Flora Tallinn	11	0	
1993–94	Flora Tallinn	11	0	
1994–95	Portsmouth	0	0	
1995–96	Portsmouth	4	0	
1995–96	Flora Tallinn	7	0	
1996–97	Portsmouth	0	0	4 0
1996–97	Flora Tallinn	12	0	41 0
1996–97	Derby Co	4	0	
1997–98	Derby Co	36	0	
1998–99	Derby Co	17	0	
1999–2000	Derby Co	28	0	
2000–01	Derby Co	33	0	118 0

POWELL, Darryl (M) 316 25
H: 6 1 W: 13 03 b.Lambeth 15-11-71
Source: Trainee. *Honours:* Jamaica 5 full caps.
1988–89	Portsmouth	3	0	
1989–90	Portsmouth	0	0	
1990–91	Portsmouth	8	0	
1991–92	Portsmouth	36	6	
1992–93	Portsmouth	23	0	
1993–94	Portsmouth	28	5	
1994–95	Portsmouth	34	5	132 16
1995–96	Derby Co	37	5	
1996–97	Derby Co	33	1	
1997–98	Derby Co	23	0	
1998–99	Derby Co	33	0	
1999–2000	Derby Co	31	2	
2000–01	Derby Co	27	1	184 9

RIGGOTT, Chris (D) 32 3
H: 6 2 W: 13 09 b.Derby 1-9-80
Source: Trainee. *Honours:* England Youth,
Under-21.
1998–99	Derby Co	0	0	
1999–2000	Derby Co	1	0	
2000–01	Derby Co	31	3	32 3

ROBINSON, Marvin (F) 12 1
H: 6 0 W: 13 05 b.Crewe 11-4-80
Source: Trainee.
1998–99	Derby Co	1	0	
1999–2000	Derby Co	8	0	
2000–01	Derby Co	0	0	9 0
2000–01	*Stoke C*	3	1	3 1

SCHNOOR, Stefan (D) 191 10
H: 6 2 W: 12 11 b.Neumunster 24-4-71
1991–92	Hamburg	5	0	
1992–93	Hamburg	19	1	
1993–94	Hamburg	12	0	
1994–95	Hamburg	28	3	
1995–96	Hamburg	23	2	
1996–97	Hamburg	21	0	
1997–98	Hamburg	23	2	131 8
1998–99	Derby Co	23	2	
1999–2000	Derby Co	29	0	
2000–01	Derby Co	8	0	60 2
(Transferred to Wolfsburg, November 2000).

STRUPAR, Branko (F) 134 72
H: 6 3 W: 14 06 b.Zagreb 9-2-70
Source: Spansko. *Honours:* Belgium 12 full
caps, 5 goals.
1996–97	Genk	31	12	
1997–98	Genk	31	22	
1998–99	Genk	33	18	
1999–2000	Genk	15	9	110 61
1999–2000	Derby Co	15	5	
2000–01	Derby Co	9	6	24 11

TWIGG, Gary (M) 0 0
b.Glasgow 19-3-84
Source: Scholar.
2000–01	Derby Co	0	0

VALAKARI, Simo (M) 163 6
H: 5 11 W: 12 08 b.Helsinki 24-4-73
Honours: Finland 18 full caps.
1995	Finn PA	22	3	
1996	Finn PA	26	2	48 5
1996–97	Motherwell	28	0	
1997–98	Motherwell	28	0	
1998–99	Motherwell	35	0	
1999–2000	Motherwell	30	0	104 0
2000–01	Derby Co	11	1	11 1

WECKSTROM, Kristoffer (M) 0 0
b.Helsinki 26-5-83
Source: IFK Mariehamn.
2000–01	Derby Co	0	0

WEST, Taribo‡ (D) 139 5
H: 6 0 W: 12 08 b.Lagos 26-3-74
Source: Sharks, Julius Berger. *Honours:*
Nigeria 13 full caps.
1993–94	Auxerre	1	0

1994–95	Auxerre	23	0	
1995–96	Auxerre	22	0	
1996–97	Auxerre	27	1	73 1
1997–98	Internazionale	23	1	
1998–99	Internazionale	21	0	44 1
1999–2000	AC Milan	4	1	4 1
2000–01	Derby Co	18	0	18 0

Scholars
Camp, Lee MJ; Canning, Brendan; Cleary,
Sean J; Donnelly, Sean; Holmes, Gareth P;
Isik, Adam A; Lambert, Jordan K; McKeown,
Gareth D; Mills, Pablo; Molloy, Barry;
O'Halloran, Matthew V; Palmer, Christopher
L; Porter, Justin L; Tudgay, Marcus; Turner,
James J

EVERTON

ALEXANDERSSON, Niclas (M) 292 48
H: 5 9 W: 11 08 b.Halmstad 29-12-71
Honours: Sweden 51 full caps, 6 goals.
1989	Halmstad	4	0	
1990	Halmstad	22	2	
1991	Halmstad	16	3	
1992	Halmstad	27	7	
1993	Halmstad	25	4	
1994	Halmstad	25	4	
1995	Halmstad	26	5	145 25
1996	IFK Gothenburg	26	7	
1997	IFK Gothenburg	26	6	52 13
1997–98	Sheffield W	6	0	
1998–99	Sheffield W	32	3	
1999–2000	Sheffield W	37	5	75 8
2000–01	Everton	20	2	20 2

BALL, Michael (D) 121 8
H: 5 11 W: 11 12 b.Liverpool 2-10-79
Source: Trainee. *Honours:* England Schools,
Youth, Under-21, 1 full cap.
1996–97	Everton	5	0	
1997–98	Everton	25	1	
1998–99	Everton	37	3	
1999–2000	Everton	25	1	
2000–01	Everton	29	3	121 8

CADAMARTERI, Danny (F) 95 14
H: 5 10 W: 12 13 b.Bradford 12-10-79
Source: Trainee. *Honours:* England Youth,
Under-21.
1996–97	Everton	1	0	
1997–98	Everton	26	4	
1998–99	Everton	30	4	
1999–2000	Everton	17	1	
1999–2000	*Fulham*	5	1	5 1
2000–01	Everton	16	4	90 13

CAMPBELL, Kevin (F) 353 127
H: 6 0 W: 13 13 b.Lambeth 4-2-70
Source: Trainee. *Honours:* England
Under-21, B.
1987–88	Arsenal	1	0	
1988–89	Arsenal	0	0	
1988–89	*Leyton Orient*	16	9	16 9
1989–90	Arsenal	15	2	
1989–90	*Leicester C*	11	5	11 5
1990–91	Arsenal	22	9	
1991–92	Arsenal	31	13	
1992–93	Arsenal	37	4	
1993–94	Arsenal	37	14	
1994–95	Arsenal	4	4	166 46
1995–96	Nottingham F	21	3	
1996–97	Nottingham F	17	6	
1997–98	Nottingham F	42	23	80 32
1998–99	Trabzonspor	17	5	17 5
1998–99	Everton	8	9	
1999–2000	Everton	26	12	
2000–01	Everton	29	9	63 30

CARNEY, David (M) 0 0
b.Sydney 30-11-83
Source: Scholar.
2000–01	Everton	0	0

CHADWICK, Nick (F) 0 0
H: 6 0 W: 12 04 b.Stoke 26-10-82
1999–2000	Everton	0	0
2000–01	Everton	0	0

CLARKE, Peter (D) 1 0
H: 6 0 W: 12 00 b.Southport 3-1-82
Source: Trainee. *Honours:* England Youth.
1998–99	Everton	0	0	
1999–2000	Everton	0	0	
2000–01	Everton	1	0	1 0

CLELAND, Alec (D) 279 12
H: 5 10 W: 11 07 b.Glasgow 10-12-70
Source: 'S' Form. *Honours:* Scotland
Under-21, B.
1987–88	Dundee U	1	0
1988–89	Dundee U	9	0

1989–90	Dundee U	15	0		
1990–91	Dundee U	20	2		
1991–92	Dundee U	31	4		
1992–93	Dundee U	24	0		
1993–94	Dundee U	33	1		
1994–95	Dundee U	18	1	151	8
1994–95	Rangers	10	0		
1995–96	Rangers	25	1		
1996–97	Rangers	32	0		
1997–98	Rangers	29	3	96	4
1998–99	Everton	18	0		
1999–2000	Everton	9	0		
2000–01	Everton	5	0	32	0

CURRAN, Damien (M)   0 0
H: 5 9 W: 12 01 b.Antrim 17-10-81
Source: Trainee.

1999–2000	Everton	0	0
2000–01	Everton	0	0

DEGN, Peter (D)   80 5
H: 5 10 W: 12 06 b.Denmark 6-4-77

1995–96	Aarhus	9	0		
1996–97	Aarhus	31	2		
1997–98	Aarhus	23	0		
1998–99	Aarhus	13	3	76	5
1998–99	Everton	4	0		
1999–2000	Everton	0	0		
2000–01	Everton	0	0	4	0

FERGUSON, Duncan (F)   249 81
H: 6 4 W: 13 07 b.Stirling 27-12-71
Source: Carse T. *Honours:* Scotland Under-21, 7 full caps.

1990–91	Dundee U	9	1		
1991–92	Dundee U	38	15		
1992–93	Dundee U	30	12	77	28
1993–94	Rangers	10	1		
1994–95	Rangers	4	1	14	2
1994–95	Everton	23	7		
1995–96	Everton	18	5		
1996–97	Everton	33	10		
1997–98	Everton	29	11		
1998–99	Everton	13	4		
1998–99	Newcastle U	7	2		
1999–2000	Newcastle U	23	6	30	8
2000–01	Everton	12	6	128	43

GASCOIGNE, Paul (M)   354 80
H: 5 10 W: 11 12 b.Gateshead 27-5-67
Source: Apprentice. *Honours:* England, Under-21 B, 57 full caps, 10 goals.

1984–85	Newcastle U	2	0		
1985–86	Newcastle U	31	9		
1986–87	Newcastle U	24	5		
1987–88	Newcastle U	35	7	92	21
1988–89	Tottenham H	32	6		
1989–90	Tottenham H	34	6		
1990–91	Tottenham H	26	7		
1991–92	Tottenham H	0	0	92	19
1992–93	Lazio	22	4		
1993–94	Lazio	17	2		
1994–95	Lazio	2	0	41	6
1995–96	Rangers	28	14		
1996–97	Rangers	26	13		
1997–98	Rangers	20	3	74	30
1997–98	Middlesbrough	7	0		
1998–99	Middlesbrough	26	3		
1999–2000	Middlesbrough	8	1	41	4
2000–01	Everton	14	0	14	0

GEMMILL, Scotland (M)   294 25
H: 5 10 W: 11 08 b.Paisley 2-1-71
Source: School. *Honours:* Scotland Under-21, 17 full caps.

1989–90	Nottingham F	2	0		
1990–91	Nottingham F	4	0		
1991–92	Nottingham F	39	8		
1992–93	Nottingham F	33	1		
1993–94	Nottingham F	31	8		
1994–95	Nottingham F	19	1		
1995–96	Nottingham F	31	1		
1996–97	Nottingham F	24	0		
1997–98	Nottingham F	44	2		
1998–99	Nottingham F	20	0	245	21
1998–99	Everton	7	1		
1999–2000	Everton	14	1		
2000–01	Everton	28	2	49	4

GERRARD, Paul (G)   210 1
H: 6 2 W: 13 11 b.Heywood 22-1-73
Source: Trainee. *Honours:* England Under-21.

1991–92	Oldham Ath	0	0		
1992–93	Oldham Ath	25	0		
1993–94	Oldham Ath	16	0		
1994–95	Oldham Ath	42	0		
1995–96	Oldham Ath	36	1	119	1
1996–97	Everton	5	0		
1997–98	Everton	4	0		
1998–99	Everton	0	0		
1998–99	*Oxford U*	16	0	16	0
1999–2000	Everton	34	0		
2000–01	Everton	32	0	75	0

GOUGH, Richard* (D)   613 54
H: 6 1 W: 12 00 b.Stockholm 5-4-62
Source: Wits University. *Honours:* Scotland Under-21, 61 full caps, 6 goals.

1980–81	Dundee U	4	0		
1981–82	Dundee U	30	1		
1982–83	Dundee U	34	8		
1983–84	Dundee U	33	3		
1984–85	Dundee U	33	6		
1985–86	Dundee U	31	5	165	23
1986–87	Tottenham H	40	2		
1987–88	Tottenham H	9	0	49	2
1987–88	Rangers	31	5		
1988–89	Rangers	35	4		
1989–90	Rangers	26	0		
1990–91	Rangers	26	0		
1991–92	Rangers	33	2		
1992–93	Rangers	25	2		
1993–94	Rangers	37	3		
1994–95	Rangers	25	1		
1995–96	Rangers	29	3		
1996–97	Rangers	27	5		
1997	Kansas City W	17	0	17	0
1997–98	Rangers	24	1	318	26
1998	San Jose Clash	19	2	19	2
1998–99	Nottingham F	7	0	7	0
1999–2000	Everton	29	1		
2000–01	Everton	9	0	38	1

GRAVESEN, Thomas (M)   164 18
H: 5 11 W: 13 06 b.Vejle 11-3-76
Honours: Denmark 16 full caps.

1995–96	Vejle	28	2		
1996–97	Vejle	30	8	58	10
1997–98	Hamburg	26	2		
1998–99	Hamburg	22	3		
1999–2000	Hamburg	26	1	74	6
2000–01	Everton	32	2	32	2

HIBBERT, Tony (D)   3 0
H: 5 8 W: 11 01 b.Liverpool 20-2-81
Source: Trainee.

1998–99	Everton	0	0		
1999–2000	Everton	0	0		
2000–01	Everton	3	0	3	0

HOGG, Craig* (D)   0 0
H: 6 1 W: 11 12 b.Liverpool 8-10-81
Source: Trainee.

1999–2000	Everton	0	0
2000–01	Everton	0	0

HUGHES, Stephen* (M)   81 5
H: 6 0 W: 12 12 b.Wokingham 18-9-76
Source: Trainee. *Honours:* England Schools, Youth, Under-21.

1994–95	Arsenal	1	0		
1995–96	Arsenal	1	0		
1996–97	Arsenal	14	1		
1997–98	Arsenal	17	2		
1998–99	Arsenal	14	1		
1999–2000	Fulham	3	0	3	0
1999–2000	Arsenal	2	0	49	4
1999–2000	Everton	11	1		
2000–01	Everton	18	0	29	1

JEFFERS, Francis (F)   49 18
H: 5 10 W: 10 07 b.Liverpool 25-1-81
Source: Trainee. *Honours:* England Schools, Youth, Under-21.

1997–98	Everton	1	0		
1998–99	Everton	15	6		
1999–2000	Everton	21	6		
2000–01	Everton	12	6	49	18

(Transferred to Arsenal, June 2001.)

JEVONS, Phil (F)   8 0
H: 5 11 W: 12 00 b.Liverpool 1-8-79
Source: Trainee.

1996–97	Everton	0	0		
1997–98	Everton	0	0		
1998–99	Everton	1	0		
1999–2000	Everton	3	0		
2000–01	Everton	4	0	8	0

KEARNEY, Tom (M)   0 0
H: 5 9 W: 10 12 b.Liverpool 7-10-81
Source: Trainee.

1999–2000	Everton	0	0
2000–01	Everton	0	0

LESTER, John (M)   0 0
H: 5 11 W: 12 09 b.Dublin 5-8-82
Source: Trainee.

1999–2000	Everton	0	0
2000–01	Everton	0	0

McKAY, Matt (M)   5 0
H: 6 0 W: 11 05 b.Warrington 21-1-81
Source: Trainee.

1997–98	Chester C	5	0	5	0
1997–98	Everton	0	0		
1998–99	Everton	0	0		
1999–2000	Everton	0	0		
2000–01	Everton	0	0		

McLEOD, Kevin (M)   5 0
H: 5 11 W: 11 00 b.Liverpool 12-9-80
Source: Trainee.

1998–99	Everton	0	0		
1999–2000	Everton	0	0		
2000–01	Everton	5	0	5	0

MOOGAN, Alan (M)   0 0
b.Liverpool 22-2-84
Source: Scholar.

2000–01	Everton	0	0

MOORE, Joe-Max (F)   113 43
H: 5 8 W: 11 06 b.USA 23-2-71
Honours: USA 87 full caps, 22 goals.

1996	New England Rev	14	11		
1997	New England Rev	13	4		
1998	New England Rev	21	7		
1999	New England Rev	29	15	77	37
1999–2000	Everton	15	6		
2000–01	Everton	21	0	36	6

MYHRE, Thomas (G)   174 0
H: 6 3 W: 13 13 b.Sarpsborg 16-10-73
Honours: Norway 19 full caps.

1993	Viking	22	0		
1994	Viking	22	0		
1995	Viking	24	0		
1996	Viking	0	0		
1997	Viking	26	0	94	0
1997–98	Everton	22	0		
1998–99	Everton	38	0		
1999–2000	Everton	4	0		
1999–2000	*Birmingham C*	7	0	7	0
2000–01	Everton	6	0	70	0
2000–01	*Tranmere R*	3	0	3	0

NAYSMITH, Gary (D)   117 5
H: 5 7 W: 11 08 b.Edinburgh 16-11-78
Source: Whitehill Welfare Colts. *Honours:* Scotland Under-18, Under-21, 4 full caps.

1995–96	Hearts	1	0		
1996–97	Hearts	10	0		
1997–98	Hearts	16	2		
1998–99	Hearts	26	0		
1999–2000	Hearts	35	1		
2000–01	Hearts	9	0	97	3
2000–01	Everton	20	2	20	2

NYARKO, Alex (M)   144 14
H: 6 0 W: 13 00 b.Accra 15-10-73
Source: Asanti Kotoko, Deawe Youngsters. *Honours:* Ghana full caps.

1994–95	Sportul	1	0		
1995–96	Basle	26	3		
1996–97	Basle	29	5	55	8
1997–98	Karlsruhe	22	1	22	1
1998–99	Lens	24	3		
1999–2000	Lens	21	1	45	4
2000–01	Everton	22	1	22	1

O'HANLON, Sean (D)   0 0
H: 6 1 W: 12 02 b.Liverpool 2-1-83

1999–2000	Everton	0	0
2000–01	Everton	0	0

OSMAN, Leon (M)   0 0
H: 5 8 W: 9 11 b.Billinge 17-5-81
Source: Trainee. *Honours:* England Schools, Youth.

1998–99	Everton	0	0
1999–2000	Everton	0	0
2000–01	Everton	0	0

PEMBRIDGE, Mark (M)   334 48
H: 5 7 W: 11 09 b.Merthyr 29-11-70
Source: Trainee. *Honours:* Wales Under-21, B, 39 full caps, 6 goals.

1989–90	Luton T	0	0		
1990–91	Luton T	18	1		
1991–92	Luton T	42	5	60	6
1992–93	Derby Co	42	8		
1993–94	Derby Co	41	11		
1994–95	Derby Co	27	9	110	28
1995–96	Sheffield W	25	1		
1996–97	Sheffield W	34	6		
1997–98	Sheffield W	34	4	93	11
1998–99	Benfica	19	1	19	1
1999–2000	Everton	31	2		
2000–01	Everton	21	0	52	2

PENMAN, Craig (D)   0 0
H: 5 11 W: 11 06 b.Falkirk 9-9-82
Source: Trainee.

1999–2000	Everton	0	0
2000–01	Everton	0	0

PETTINGER, Andrew (G)   0 0
b.Scunthorpe 21-4-84
Source: Scunthorpe U.

2000–01	Everton	0	0

PILKINGTON, George (D) 0 0
H: 5 11 W: 11 00 b.Rugeley 7-11-81
Source: Trainee. Honours: England Youth.

Season	Club	Apps	Gls		
1998–99	Everton	0	0		
1999–2000	Everton	0	0		
2000–01	Everton	0	0		

PISTONE, Alessandro (D) 153 7
H: 5 11 W: 11 08 b.Milan 27-7-75

Season	Club	Apps	Gls		
1992–93	Vicenza	0	0		
1993–94	Solbiatese	20	1	20	1
1994–95	Crevalcore	29	4	29	4
1995–96	Vicenza	6	0	6	0
1995–96	Internazionale	19	1		
1996–97	Internazionale	26	0	45	1
1997–98	Newcastle U	28	0		
1998–99	Newcastle U	3	0		
1999–2000	Newcastle U	15	1	46	1
2000–01	Everton	7	0	7	0

PRICE, Michael* (D) 0 0
H: 5 8 W: 11 01 b.Wrexham 29-4-82
Source: Trainee. Honours: Wales Under-21.

Season	Club	Apps	Gls		
1999–2000	Everton	0	0		
2000–01	Everton	0	0		

SCHUMACHER, Steven (M) 0 0
b.Liverpool 30-4-84
Source: Scholar.

Season	Club	Apps	Gls		
2000–01	Everton	0	0		

SIMONSEN, Steve (G) 37 0
H: 6 2 W: 14 00 b.South Shields 3-4-79
Source: Trainee. Honours: England Youth, Under-21.

Season	Club	Apps	Gls		
1996–97	Tranmere R	0	0		
1997–98	Tranmere R	30	0		
1998–99	Tranmere R	5	0	35	0
1998–99	Everton	0	0		
1999–2000	Everton	1	0		
2000–01	Everton	1	0	2	0

SOUTHERN, Keith (M) 0 0
b.Gateshead 24-4-81
Source: Trainee.

Season	Club	Apps	Gls		
1998–99	Everton	0	0		
1999–2000	Everton	0	0		
2000–01	Everton	0	0		

SOUTHERN, Robert (M) 0 0
b.Gateshead 24-9-83
Source: Scholar.

Season	Club	Apps	Gls		
2000–01	Everton	0	0		

TAL, Idan (M) 143 19
H: 5 9 W: 11 07 b.Petah Tikva 13-9-75
Honours: Israel 22 full caps, 2 goals.

Season	Club	Apps	Gls		
1996–97	Maccabi Petah Tikva	27	1		
1997–98	Maccabi Petah Tikva	29	6		
1998–99	Maccabi Petah Tikva	15	3	71	10
1998–99	Hapoel Tel Aviv	14	2	14	2
1999–2000	Merida	36	5	36	5
2000–01	Everton	22	2	22	2

UNSWORTH, Dave (D) 244 25
H: 6 1 W: 15 02 b.Chorley 16-10-73
Source: Trainee. Honours: England Youth, Under-21, 1 full cap.

Season	Club	Apps	Gls		
1991–92	Everton	2	1		
1992–93	Everton	3	0		
1993–94	Everton	8	0		
1994–95	Everton	38	3		
1995–96	Everton	31	2		
1996–97	Everton	34	5		
1997–98	West Ham U	32	2	32	2
1998–99	Aston Villa	0	0		
1998–99	Everton	34	1		
1999–2000	Everton	33	6		
2000–01	Everton	29	5	212	23

VALENTINE, Ryan (D) 0 0
H: 5 10 W: 11 07 b.Wrexham 19-8-82
Source: Trainee. Honours: Wales Under-21.

Season	Club	Apps	Gls		
1999–2000	Everton	0	0		
2000–01	Everton	0	0		

WATSON, Dave* (D) 635 34
H: 6 0 W: 14 00 b.Liverpool 20-11-61
Source: Amateur. Honours: England Under-21, 12 full caps.

Season	Club	Apps	Gls		
1979–80	Liverpool	0	0		
1980–81	Liverpool	0	0		
1980–81	Norwich C	18	3		
1981–82	Norwich C	38	3		
1982–83	Norwich C	35	1		
1983–84	Norwich C	40	1		
1984–85	Norwich C	39	0		
1985–86	Norwich C	42	3	212	11
1986–87	Everton	35	4		
1987–88	Everton	37	4		
1988–89	Everton	32	3		
1989–90	Everton	29	1		
1990–91	Everton	32	2		
1991–92	Everton	35	3		
1992–93	Everton	40	1		
1993–94	Everton	28	1		
1994–95	Everton	38	2		
1995–96	Everton	34	1		
1996–97	Everton	29	1		
1997–98	Everton	26	0		
1998–99	Everton	22	0		
1999–2000	Everton	6	0		
2000–01	Everton	0	0	423	23

(Moved to Tranmere R as manager).

WATSON, Steve (D) 283 12
H: 6 0 W: 12 07 b.North Shields 1-4-74
Source: Trainee. Honours: England Youth, Under-21, B.

Season	Club	Apps	Gls		
1990–91	Newcastle U	24	0		
1991–92	Newcastle U	28	1		
1992–93	Newcastle U	2	0		
1993–94	Newcastle U	32	2		
1994–95	Newcastle U	27	4		
1995–96	Newcastle U	23	3		
1996–97	Newcastle U	36	1		
1997–98	Newcastle U	29	1		
1998–99	Newcastle U	7	0	208	12
1998–99	Aston Villa	27	0		
1999–2000	Aston Villa	14	0	41	0
2000–01	Everton	34	0	34	0

WEIR, David (D) 311 19
H: 6 5 W: 14 03 b.Falkirk 10-5-70
Source: Celtic BC. Honours: Scotland 27 full caps.

Season	Club	Apps	Gls		
1992–93	Falkirk	30	1		
1993–94	Falkirk	37	3		
1994–95	Falkirk	32	1		
1995–96	Falkirk	34	3	133	8
1996–97	Hearts	34	6		
1997–98	Hearts	35	1		
1998–99	Hearts	23	1	92	8
1998–99	Everton	14	0		
1999–2000	Everton	35	2		
2000–01	Everton	37	1	86	3

WILLIAMSON, Danny‡ (M) 79 6
H: 6 0 W: 13 13 b.West Ham 5-12-73
Source: Trainee.

Season	Club	Apps	Gls		
1992–93	West Ham U	0	0		
1993–94	West Ham U	3	1		
1993–94	Doncaster R	13	1	13	1
1994–95	West Ham U	4	0		
1995–96	West Ham U	29	4		
1996–97	West Ham U	15	0		
1997–98	West Ham U	0	0	51	5
1997–98	Everton	15	0		
1998–99	Everton	0	0		
1999–2000	Everton	0	0		
2000–01	Everton	0	0	15	0

XAVIER, Abel (D) 162 6
H: 6 2 W: 13 06 b.Mozambique 30-11-72
Honours: Portugal 18 full caps, 2 goals.

Season	Club	Apps	Gls		
1993–94	Benfica	24	1		
1994–95	Benfica	22	3	46	4
1995–96	Bari	8	0	8	0
1996–97	Oviedo	27	0		
1997–98	Oviedo	31	0	58	0
1998–99	PSV Eindhoven	19	2	19	2
1999–2000	Everton	20	0		
2000–01	Everton	11	0	31	0

Scholars
Beck, Steven R; Colbeck, Franklyn A; Crowder, Martin; Eaton, David F; Symes, Michael
Non-Contract
Woods, Christopher C

EXETER C

AMPADU, Kwame (M) 312 18
H: 5 10 W: 11 10 b.Bradford 20-12-70
Source: Belvedere, Trainee. Honours: Eire Youth, Under-21.

Season	Club	Apps	Gls		
1988–89	Arsenal	0	0		
1989–90	Arsenal	2	0		
1990–91	Arsenal	0	0	2	0
1990–91	Plymouth Arg	6	1	6	1
1990–91	WBA	7	1		
1991–92	WBA	21	3		
1992–93	WBA	10	0		
1993–94	WBA	11	0	49	4
1993–94	Swansea C	13	0		
1994–95	Swansea C	44	6		
1995–96	Swansea C	43	2		
1996–97	Swansea C	29	4		
1997–98	Swansea C	18	0	147	12
1998–99	Leyton Orient	29	1		
1999–2000	Leyton Orient	43	0	72	1
2000–01	Exeter C	36	0	36	0

ASHTON, Jon* (D) 47 0
H: 6 0 W: 13 00 b.Plymouth 4-8-79
Source: Trainee.

Season	Club	Apps	Gls		
1997–98	Plymouth Arg	0	0		
1998–99	Plymouth Arg	26	0		
1999–2000	Plymouth Arg	8	0	34	0
2000–01	Exeter C	13	0	13	0

BLAKE, Noel† (D) 602 37
H: 6 2 W: 14 05 b.Kingston, Jamaica 12-1-62
Source: Walsall Amateur, Sutton Coldfield T.

Season	Club	Apps	Gls		
1979–80	Aston Villa	3	0		
1980–81	Aston Villa	0	0		
1981–82	Aston Villa	1	0		
1981–82	Shrewsbury T	6	0	6	0
1982–83	Aston Villa	0	0	4	0
1982–83	Birmingham C	37	3		
1983–84	Birmingham C	39	2	76	5
1984–85	Portsmouth	42	3		
1985–86	Portsmouth	42	4		
1986–87	Portsmouth	41	3		
1987–88	Portsmouth	19	0	144	10
1988–89	Leeds U	44	4		
1989–90	Leeds U	7	0	51	4
1989–90	Stoke C	18	0		
1990–91	Stoke C	44	3		
1991–92	Stoke C	13	0	75	3
1991–92	Bradford C	6	0		
1992–93	Bradford C	32	3		
1993–94	Bradford C	7	0	45	3
1993–94	Dundee	23	2		
1994–95	Dundee	31	0	54	2
1995–96	Exeter C	44	2		
1996–97	Exeter C	46	6		
1997–98	Exeter C	38	1		
1998–99	Exeter C	7	0		
1999–2000	Exeter C	7	1		
2000–01	Exeter C	5	0	147	10

BRESLAN, Geoff (M) 66 4
H: 5 9 W: 10 05 b.Torbay 4-6-80
Source: Trainee.

Season	Club	Apps	Gls		
1997–98	Exeter C	1	0		
1998–99	Exeter C	34	4		
1999–2000	Exeter C	29	0		
2000–01	Exeter C	2	0	66	4

BUCKLE, Paul# (M) 311 23
H: 5 8 W: 11 08 b.Welwyn 16-12-70
Source: Trainee.

Season	Club	Apps	Gls		
1987–88	Brentford	1	0		
1988–89	Brentford	0	0		
1989–90	Brentford	10	0		
1990–91	Brentford	26	0		
1991–92	Brentford	15	1		
1992–93	Brentford	5	0		
1993–94	Brentford	0	0	57	1
1993–94	Torquay U	16	2		
1994–95	Torquay U	32	3		
1995–96	Torquay U	11	4	59	9
1995–96	Exeter C	22	2		
1996–97	Northampton T	0	0		
1996–97	Wycombe W	0	0		
1996–97	Colchester U	24	0		
1997–98	Colchester U	38	5		
1998–99	Colchester U	43	2	105	7
1999–2000	Exeter C	27	1		
2000–01	Exeter C	41	3	90	6

BURROWS, Mark (D) 29 0
H: 6 3 W: 12 08 b.Kettering 14-8-80
Source: Trainee.

Season	Club	Apps	Gls		
1997–98	Coventry C	0	0		
1998–99	Coventry C	0	0		
1999–2000	Coventry C	0	0		
2000–01	Exeter C	29	0	29	0

CAMPBELL, Jamie (D) 274 16
H: 6 1 W: 12 07 b.Birmingham 21-10-72
Source: Trainee.

Season	Club	Apps	Gls		
1991–92	Luton T	11	0		
1992–93	Luton T	9	1		
1993–94	Luton T	16	0		
1994–95	Luton T	0	0	36	1
1994–95	Mansfield T	3	1	3	1
1994–95	Cambridge U	12	0		
1995–96	Barnet	24	1		
1996–97	Barnet	43	4	67	5
1997–98	Cambridge U	46	2		
1998–99	Cambridge U	41	4	103	6
1999–2000	Brighton & HA	23	1	23	1
2000–01	Exeter C	42	2	42	2

COOPER, Michael* (D) 0 0
H: 5 11 W: 12 00 b.Yeovil 13-8-82
Source: Trainee.

Season	Club	Apps	Gls		
2000–01	Exeter C	0	0		

CORNFORTH, John* (M) 297 32
H: 5 11 W: 14 06 b.Whitley Bay 7-10-67
Source: Apprentice. *Honours:* Wales 2 full caps.

1984–85	Sunderland	1	0		
1985–86	Sunderland	0	0		
1986–87	Sunderland	0	0		
1986–87	Doncaster R	7	3	7	3
1987–88	Sunderland	12	2		
1988–89	Sunderland	15	0		
1989–90	Sunderland	2	0		
1989–90	Shrewsbury T	3	0	3	0
1989–90	Lincoln C	9	1	9	1
1990–91	Sunderland	2	0	32	2
1991–92	Swansea C	17	0		
1992–93	Swansea C	44	5		
1993–94	Swansea C	38	6		
1994–95	Swansea C	33	3		
1995–96	Swansea C	17	2	149	16
1995–96	Birmingham C	8	0		
1996–97	Birmingham C	0	0	8	0
1996–97	Wycombe W	10	0		
1997–98	Wycombe W	24	5		
1997–98	Peterborough U	4	0	4	0
1998–99	Wycombe W	13	1	47	6
1999–2000	Cardiff C	10	1	10	1
1999–2000	Scunthorpe U	4	1	4	1
1999–2000	Exeter C	12	2		
2000–01	Exeter C	12	0	24	2

CRONIN, Glenn (M) 0 0
H: 5 8 W: 10 11 b.Dublin 14-9-81
Source: Trainee.

2000–01	Exeter C	0	0		

CURRAN, Chris# (D) 289 9
H: 5 11 W: 12 12 b.Birmingham 17-9-71
Source: Trainee.

1989–90	Torquay U	1	0		
1990–91	Torquay U	13	0		
1991–92	Torquay U	17	0		
1992–93	Torquay U	34	0		
1993–94	Torquay U	41	1		
1994–95	Torquay U	27	2		
1995–96	Torquay U	19	1	152	6
1995–96	Plymouth Arg	8	0		
1996–97	Plymouth Arg	22	0	30	0
1997–98	Exeter C	9	0		
1998–99	Exeter C	34	4		
1999–2000	Exeter C	38	1		
2000–01	Exeter C	26	0	107	5

EPESSE-TITI, Steve* (M) 6 0
H: 6 1 W: 13 00 b.France 5-9-79

2000–01	Wolverhampton W	0	0		
2000–01	Exeter C	6	0	6	0

FLACK, Steve (F) 203 45
H: 6 1 W: 14 07 b.Cambridge 29-5-71
Source: Cambridge C.

1995–96	Cardiff C	10	1		
1996–97	Cardiff C	1	0	11	1
1996–97	Exeter C	27	4		
1997–98	Exeter C	41	14		
1998–99	Exeter C	44	11		
1999–2000	Exeter C	40	2		
2000–01	Exeter C	40	13	192	44

FRASER, Stuart (G) 7 0
H: 6 0 W: 12 00 b.Cheltenham 1-8-78
Source: Cheltenham T.

1996–97	Stoke C	0	0		
1997–98	Stoke C	0	0		
1998–99	Stoke C	1	0		
1999–2000	Stoke C	0	0	1	0
2000–01	Exeter C	6	0	6	0

HOLLOWAY, Chris* (M) 68 2
H: 5 10 W: 11 10 b.Swansea 5-2-80
Source: Trainee. *Honours:* Wales Under-21.

1997–98	Exeter C	6	0		
1998–99	Exeter C	34	1		
1999–2000	Exeter C	24	1		
2000–01	Exeter C	4	0	68	2

INGLETHORPE, Alex* (F) 160 39
H: 5 11 W: 11 04 b.Epsom 14-11-71
Source: School.

1990–91	Watford	1	0		
1991–92	Watford	2	0		
1992–93	Watford	0	0		
1993–94	Watford	9	2		
1994–95	Watford	0	0	12	2
1994–95	Barnet	6	3	6	3
1994–95	Leyton Orient	0	0		
1995–96	Leyton Orient	30	9		
1996–97	Leyton Orient	16	8		
1997–98	Leyton Orient	38	9		
1998–99	Leyton Orient	23	4		
1999–2000	Leyton Orient	16	2	123	32
1999–2000	Exeter C	1	0		
2000–01	Exeter C	18	2	19	2

McCONNELL, Barry (F) 109 12
H: 5 11 W: 10 10 b.Exeter 1-1-77
Source: Trainee.

1995–96	Exeter C	8	0		
1996–97	Exeter C	34	0		
1997–98	Exeter C	16	6		
1998–99	Exeter C	22	5		
1999–2000	Exeter C	25	1		
2000–01	Exeter C	4	0	109	12

MUDGE, James§ (F) 3 0
b.Exeter 25-3-83
Source: Scholar.

2000–01	Exeter C	3	0	3	0

POWER, Graeme# (D) 130 1
H: 5 11 W: 11 07 b.Northwick Park 7-3-77
Source: Trainee. *Honours:* England Schools, Youth.

1994–95	QPR	0	0		
1995–96	QPR	0	0		
1996–97	Bristol R	16	0		
1997–98	Bristol R	10	0	26	0
1998–99	Exeter C	40	0		
1999–2000	Exeter C	29	0		
2000–01	Exeter C	35	1	104	1

RAWLINSON, Mark* (M) 104 4
H: 5 10 W: 11 04 b.Bolton 9-6-75
Source: Trainee.

1993–94	Manchester U	0	0		
1994–95	Manchester U	0	0		
1995–96	Bournemouth	19	0		
1996–97	Bournemouth	25	2		
1997–98	Bournemouth	25	0		
1998–99	Bournemouth	7	0		
1999–2000	Bournemouth	3	0	79	2
2000–01	Exeter C	25	2	25	2

READ, Paul (F) 83 11
H: 5 8 W: 12 06 b.Harlow 25-9-73
Source: Trainee. *Honours:* England Schools.

1991–92	Arsenal	0	0		
1992–93	Arsenal	0	0		
1993–94	Arsenal	0	0		
1994–95	Arsenal	0	0		
1994–95	Leyton Orient	11	0	11	0
1995–96	Arsenal	0	0		
1995–96	Southend U	4	1	4	1
1996–97	Arsenal	0	0		
1996–97	Wycombe W	13	4		
1997–98	Wycombe W	28	4		
1998–99	Wycombe W	16	1		
1999–2000	Wycombe W	0	0	57	9
From OFK Östersund					
2000–01	Exeter C	11	1	11	1

ROBERTS, Chris (F) 65 11
H: 5 10 W: 12 03 b.Cardiff 22-10-79
Source: Trainee. *Honours:* Wales Under-21.

1997–98	Cardiff C	11	3		
1998–99	Cardiff C	4	0		
1999–2000	Cardiff C	8	0	23	3
2000–01	Exeter C	42	8	42	8

ROBERTS, Darren‡ (F) 177 47
H: 6 0 W: 12 04 b.Birmingham 12-10-69
Source: Burton Alb.

1991–92	Wolverhampton W	0	0		
1992–93	Wolverhampton W	21	5		
1993–94	Wolverhampton W	0	0	21	5
1993–94	Hereford U	6	5	6	5
1994–95	Doncaster R	0	0		
1994–95	Chesterfield	11	1		
1995–96	Chesterfield	14	0	25	1
1996–97	Darlington	44	16		
1997–98	Darlington	28	12		
1997–98	Peterborough U	3	0	3	0
1998–99	Darlington	44	5	96	33
1998–99	Scarborough	18	3		
1999–2000	Scarborough	0	0	18	3
2000–01	Exeter C	8	0	8	0

ROSCOE, Andy (M) 287 21
H: 5 9 W: 12 10 b.Liverpool 4-6-73
Source: Trainee.

1991–92	Liverpool	0	0		
1992–93	Bolton W	0	0		
1993–94	Bolton W	3	0		
1994–95	Bolton W	0	0	3	0
1994–95	Rotherham U	31	4		
1995–96	Rotherham U	45	2		
1996–97	Rotherham U	43	0		
1997–98	Rotherham U	45	7		
1998–99	Rotherham U	38	5	202	18
1999–2000	Mansfield T	39	2	39	2
2000–01	Exeter C	43	1	43	1

ROWBOTHAM, Darren‡ (F) 451 127
H: 5 10 W: 12 12 b.Cardiff 22-10-66
Source: Trainee.

1984–85	Plymouth Arg	7	0		
1985–86	Plymouth Arg	14	1		

1986–87	Plymouth Arg	16	1		
1987–88	Plymouth Arg	9	0	46	2
1987–88	Exeter C	23	2		
1988–89	Exeter C	45	20		
1989–90	Exeter C	32	21		
1990–91	Exeter C	13	3		
1991–92	Exeter C	5	1		
1991–92	Torquay U	14	3	14	3
1991–92	Birmingham C	22	4		
1992–93	Birmingham C	14	2	36	6
1992–93	Hereford U	8	2	8	2
1992–93	Mansfield T	4	0	4	0
1993–94	Crewe Alex	40	15		
1994–95	Crewe Alex	21	6	61	21
1995–96	Shrewsbury T	26	8		
1996–97	Shrewsbury T	14	1	40	9
1996–97	Exeter C	25	9		
1997–98	Exeter C	43	20		
1998–99	Exeter C	32	6		
1999–2000	Exeter C	18	2		
1999–2000	Leyton Orient	6	0	6	0
2000–01	Exeter C	0	0	236	84

SMITH, Peter‡ (M) 8 0
H: 5 10 W: 11 00 b.Skelmersdale 31-10-80
Source: Trainee.

1998–99	Exeter C	1	0		
1999–2000	Exeter C	7	0		
2000–01	Exeter C	0	0	8	0

SPEAKMAN, Robert* (M) 19 3
H: 5 10 W: 11 07 b.Swansea 5-12-80
Source: Trainee.

1998–99	Exeter C	1	0		
1999–2000	Exeter C	17	3		
2000–01	Exeter C	1	0	19	3

TIERNEY, Fran† (M) 127 15
H: 5 10 W: 12 07 b.Liverpool 10-9-75
Source: Trainee.

1992–93	Crewe Alex	1	0		
1993–94	Crewe Alex	8	1		
1994–95	Crewe Alex	20	4		
1995–96	Crewe Alex	22	2		
1996–97	Crewe Alex	32	3		
1997–98	Crewe Alex	4	0		
1998–99	Crewe Alex	0	0	87	10
1998–99	Notts Co	20	3		
1999–2000	Notts Co	13	1	33	4
2000–01	Exeter C	7	1	7	1

TOMLINSON, Graeme (F) 104 15
H: 5 10 W: 12 00 b.Watford 10-12-75
Source: Trainee.

1993–94	Bradford C	17	6	17	6
1994–95	Manchester U	0	0		
1995–96	Manchester U	0	0		
1995–96	Luton T	7	0	7	0
1996–97	Manchester U	0	0		
1997–98	Manchester U	0	0		
1997–98	Bournemouth	7	1	7	1
1997–98	Millwall	3	1	3	1
1998–99	Macclesfield T	28	4		
1999–2000	Macclesfield T	18	2	46	6
2000–01	Exeter C	24	1	24	1

VAN HEUSDEN, Arjan (G) 121 0
H: 6 4 W: 14 05 b.Alphen 11-12-72
Source: Noordwijk.

1994–95	Port Vale	2	0		
1995–96	Port Vale	7	0		
1996–97	Port Vale	13	0		
1997–98	Port Vale	5	0	27	0
1997–98	Oxford U	11	0	11	0
1998–99	Cambridge U	27	0		
1999–2000	Cambridge U	15	0	42	0
2000–01	Exeter C	41	0	41	0

VANNINEN, Jukka‡ (M) 5 0
H: 5 7 W: 12 01 b.Riihimaki 31-1-77
Source: Rops.

1999–2000	Exeter C	5	0		
2000–01	Exeter C	0	0	5	0

WHITWORTH, Neil (D) 164 7
H: 6 0 W: 12 13 b.Ince 12-4-72
Source: Trainee. *Honours:* England Youth.

1989–90	Wigan Ath	2	0		
1990–91	Manchester U	1	0		
1991–92	Manchester U	0	0		
1991–92	Preston NE	6	0	6	0
1991–92	Barnsley	11	0	11	0
1992–93	Manchester U	0	0		
1993–94	Manchester U	0	0	1	0
1993–94	Rotherham U	8	1	8	1
1993–94	Blackpool	3	0	3	0
1994–95	Kilmarnock	30	3		
1995–96	Kilmarnock	28	0		
1996–97	Kilmarnock	7	0		
1997–98	Kilmarnock	11	0	76	3
1997–98	Wigan Ath	4	0	6	0
1998–99	Hull C	18	2		
1999–2000	Hull C	1	0	19	2
2000–01	Exeter C	34	1	34	1

WILKINSON, John* (M) 20 2
H: 5 9 W: 10 06 b.Exeter 24-8-79
Source: Trainee.

1997–98	Exeter C	1	0	
1998–99	Exeter C	18	2	
1999–2000	Exeter C	0	0	
2000–01	Exeter C	1	0	20 2

ZABEK, Lee (M) 60 1
H: 6 0 W: 13 08 b.Bristol 13-10-78
Source: Trainee.

1996–97	Bristol R	1	0	
1997–98	Bristol R	13	1	
1998–99	Bristol R	11	0	
1999–2000	Bristol R	4	0	29 1
2000–01	Exeter C	31	0	31 0

Trainees
Afful, Leslie S; Arscott, Michael J; Bradford, Jamie; Bull, James J; Casey, Emmett R; Gillingham, Michael J; Goff, Shaun J; Gross, Marcus J; Hallam, Robin S; Johns, Steven S; Lock, Matthew J; Moor, Reinier S; Mudge, James RM; Price, Oliver
Associated Schoolboy
Hunt, Ben S

FULHAM

BETSY, Kevin (F) 21 1
H: 6 0 W: 12 03 b.Seychelles 20-3-78
Source: Woking.

1998–99	Fulham	7	1	
1999–2000	Fulham	2	0	
1999–2000	*Bournemouth*	5	0	5 0
1999–2000	*Hull C*	2	0	2 0
2000–01	Fulham	5	0	14 1

BREVETT, Rufus# (D) 379 5
H: 5 8 W: 11 11 b.Derby 24-9-69
Source: Trainee.

1987–88	Doncaster R	17	0	
1988–89	Doncaster R	23	0	
1989–90	Doncaster R	42	0	
1990–91	Doncaster R	27	3	109 3
1990–91	QPR	10	0	
1991–92	QPR	7	0	
1992–93	QPR	15	0	
1993–94	QPR	7	0	
1994–95	QPR	19	0	
1995–96	QPR	27	1	
1996–97	QPR	44	0	
1997–98	QPR	23	0	152 1
1997–98	Fulham	11	0	
1998–99	Fulham	45	1	
1999–2000	Fulham	23	0	
2000–01	Fulham	39	0	118 1

CLARK, Lee (M) 355 54
H: 5 8 W: 11 09 b.Wallsend 27-10-72
Source: Trainee. *Honours:* England Schools, Youth, Under-21.

1989–90	Newcastle U	0	0	
1990–91	Newcastle U	19	2	
1991–92	Newcastle U	29	5	
1992–93	Newcastle U	46	9	
1993–94	Newcastle U	29	2	
1994–95	Newcastle U	19	1	
1995–96	Newcastle U	28	2	
1996–97	Newcastle U	25	2	195 23
1997–98	Sunderland	46	13	
1998–99	Sunderland	27	3	73 16
1999–2000	Fulham	42	8	
2000–01	Fulham	45	7	87 15

COLEMAN, Chris (D) 478 23
H: 6 2 W: 14 04 b.Swansea 10-6-70
Source: Apprentice. *Honours:* Wales Under-21, 31 full caps, 4 goals.

1987–88	Swansea C	30	0	
1988–89	Swansea C	43	0	
1989–90	Swansea C	46	2	
1990–91	Swansea C	41	0	160 2
1991–92	Crystal Palace	18	4	
1992–93	Crystal Palace	38	5	
1993–94	Crystal Palace	46	3	
1994–95	Crystal Palace	35	1	
1995–96	Crystal Palace	17	0	154 13
1995–96	Blackburn R	20	0	
1996–97	Blackburn R	8	0	
1997–98	Blackburn R	0	0	28 0
1997–98	Fulham	26	1	
1998–99	Fulham	45	4	
1999–2000	Fulham	40	3	
2000–01	Fulham	25	0	136 8

COLLINS, John (M) 515 76
H: 5 7 W: 10 10 b.Galashiels 30-1-68
Source: Hutchison Vale BC. *Honours:* Scotland Youth, Under-21, 58 full caps, 12 goals.

1984–85	Hibernian	28	6	
1985–86	Hibernian	19	1	
1986–87	Hibernian	30	1	
1987–88	Hibernian	44	6	
1988–89	Hibernian	35	2	
1989–90	Hibernian	35	6	163 16
1990–91	Celtic	35	1	
1991–92	Celtic	38	11	
1992–93	Celtic	43	8	
1993–94	Celtic	38	8	
1994–95	Celtic	34	8	
1995–96	Celtic	29	11	217 47
1996–97	Monaco	28	6	
1997–98	Monaco	25	1	53 7
1998–99	Everton	20	1	
1999–2000	Everton	35	2	55 3
2000–01	Fulham	27	3	27 3

COLLINS, Wayne* (M) 206 24
H: 5 10 W: 12 01 b.Manchester 4-3-69
Source: Winsford U.

1993–94	Crewe Alex	35	2	
1994–95	Crewe Alex	40	11	
1995–96	Crewe Alex	42	1	117 14
1996–97	Sheffield W	12	1	
1997–98	Sheffield W	19	5	31 6
1997–98	Fulham	13	1	
1998–99	Fulham	21	2	
1999–2000	Fulham	19	1	
2000–01	Fulham	5	0	58 4

CORNWALL, Luke (F) 14 5
H: 5 9 W: 10 11 b.Lambeth 23-7-80
Source: Trainee.

1998–99	Fulham	4	1	
1999–2000	Fulham	0	0	
2000–01	Fulham	0	0	4 1
2000–01	*Grimsby T*	10	4	10 4

DAVIS, Sean (M) 73 6
H: 5 11 W: 12 10 b.Clapham 20-9-79
Source: Trainee. *Honours:* England Under-21.

1996–97	Fulham	1	0	
1997–98	Fulham	0	0	
1998–99	Fulham	6	0	
1999–2000	Fulham	26	0	
2000–01	Fulham	40	6	73 6

FERNANDES, Fabrice‡ (F) 61 5
H: 5 9 W: 11 00 b.Aubervilliers 10-10-79

1998–99	Rennes	15	2	
1999–2000	Rennes	17	1	32 3
2000–01	Fulham	29	2	29 2

FINNAN, Steve (D) 214 14
H: 6 0 W: 12 03 b.Limerick 20-4-76
Source: Welling U. *Honours:* Eire 7 full caps, 1 goal.

1995–96	Birmingham C	12	1	
1995–96	*Notts Co*	17	2	
1996–97	Birmingham C	3	0	15 1
1996–97	Notts Co	23	0	
1997–98	Notts Co	44	5	
1998–99	Notts Co	13	0	97 7
1998–99	Fulham	22	2	
1999–2000	Fulham	35	2	
2000–01	Fulham	45	2	102 6

GALBIATI, Jacopo* (M) 0 0
b.Fiorentina 10-8-82

2000–01	Fulham	0	0

GOLDBAEK, Bjarne (M) 274 40
H: 5 9 W: 12 08 b.Denmark 6-10-68
Honours: Denmark 28 full caps.

1991–92	Kaiserslautern	24	2	
1992–93	Kaiserslautern	28	5	
1993–94	Kaiserslautern	3	0	55 7
1993–94	Tennis Borussia	24	5	24 5
1994–95	Cologne	14	0	
1995–96	Cologne	16	2	30 2
1996–97	FC Copenhagen	32	7	
1997–98	FC Copenhagen	30	6	
1998–99	FC Copenhagen	12	3	74 16
1998–99	Chelsea	23	5	
1999–2000	Chelsea	6	0	29 5
1999–2000	Fulham	18	3	
2000–01	Fulham	44	2	62 5

GOMA, Alain (D) 232 5
H: 6 0 W: 12 08 b.Sault 5-10-72
Honours: France 2 full caps.

1990–91	Auxerre	1	0
1991–92	Auxerre	1	0
1992–93	Auxerre	15	1
1993–94	Auxerre	33	0
1994–95	Auxerre	28	0

1995–96	Auxerre	32	0	
1996–97	Auxerre	34	2	
1997–98	Auxerre	22	1	166 4
1998–99	Paris St Germain	30	0	30 0
1999–2000	Newcastle U	14	0	
2000–01	Newcastle U	19	1	33 1
2000–01	Fulham	3	0	3 0

HAHNEMANN, Marcus (G) 68 0
H: 6 3 W: 16 02 b.Seattle 15-6-72

1997	Colorado Rapids	25	0	
1998	Colorado Rapids	28	0	
1999	Colorado Rapids	13	0	66 0
1999–2000	Fulham	0	0	
2000–01	Fulham	2	0	2 0

HAMMOND, Elvis (F) 0 0
H: 5 11 W: 11 09 b.Accra 6-10-80
Source: Trainee.

1999–2000	Fulham	0	0
2000–01	Fulham	0	0

HAYLES, Barry (F) 162 63
H: 5 9 W: 13 00 b.London 17-5-72
Source: Stevenage Bor.

1997–98	Bristol R	45	23	
1998–99	Bristol R	17	9	62 32
1998–99	Fulham	30	8	
1999–2000	Fulham	35	5	
2000–01	Fulham	35	18	100 31

HUDSON, Mark (D) 0 0
H: 6 2 W: 12 08 b.Guildford 30-3-82
Source: Trainee.

1998–99	Fulham	0	0
1999–2000	Fulham	0	0
2000–01	Fulham	0	0

HUTCHINSON, Tom (D) 0 0
H: 6 0 W: 12 08 b.Kingston 23-2-82

1998–99	Fulham	0	0
1999–2000	Fulham	0	0
2000–01	Fulham	0	0

KEEVILL, Sam* (M) 0 0
H: 5 8 W: 10 01 b.Lewisham 8-5-81
Source: Trainee.

1999–2000	Fulham	0	0
2000–01	Fulham	0	0

KNIGHT, Zatyiah (D) 8 0
H: 6 6 W: 14 00 b.Solihull 2-5-80

1998–99	Fulham	0	0	
1999–2000	Fulham	0	0	
1999–2000	*Peterborough U*	8	0	8 0
2000–01	Fulham	0	0	

LEWIS, Eddie (M) 130 9
H: 5 9 W: 11 05 b.California 17-5-74
Honours: USA 24 full caps, 2 goals.

1996	San Jose Clash	25	0	
1997	San Jose Clash	29	2	
1998	San Jose Clash	32	3	
1999	San Jose Clash	29	4	115 9
1999–2000	Fulham	8	0	
2000–01	Fulham	7	0	15 0

McANESPIE, Kieran (D) 50 5
H: 5 8 W: 11 05 b.Gosport 11-9-79
Source: St Johnstone BC. *Honours:* Scotland Under-17, Under-21.

1995–96	St Johnstone	0	0	
1996–97	St Johnstone	9	2	
1997–98	St Johnstone	3	0	
1998–99	St Johnstone	18	2	
1999–2000	St Johnstone	20	1	50 5
2000–01	Fulham	0	0	

MELVILLE, Andy (D) 603 54
H: 6 1 W: 12 10 b.Swansea 29-11-68
Source: School. *Honours:* Wales Under-21, B, 46 full caps, 3 goals.

1985–86	Swansea C	5	0	
1986–87	Swansea C	42	3	
1987–88	Swansea C	37	4	
1988–89	Swansea C	45	10	
1989–90	Swansea C	46	5	175 22
1990–91	Oxford U	46	3	
1991–92	Oxford U	45	4	
1992–93	Oxford U	44	6	135 13
1993–94	Sunderland	44	2	
1994–95	Sunderland	36	3	
1995–96	Sunderland	40	4	
1996–97	Sunderland	30	2	
1997–98	Sunderland	10	1	
1997–98	*Bradford C*	6	1	6 1
1998–99	Sunderland	44	2	204 14
1999–2000	Fulham	40	3	
2000–01	Fulham	43	1	83 4

MOLLER, Peter* (F) 265 112
H: 6 3 W: 13 00 b.Gistrup 23-3-72
Honours: Denmark 17 full caps, 3 goals.

1990	Aalborg	19	9
1991–92	Aalborg	32	17

1992–93 Aalborg 30 20 81 46
1993–94 FC Copenhagen 29 7 29 7
1994–95 Zurich 14 4 14 4
1995–96 Brondby 33 15
1996–97 Brondby 33 22
1997–98 Brondby 3 5
1997–98 PSV Eindhoven 22 5 22 5
1998–99 Oviedo 26 2
1999–2000 Oviedo 1 0
1999–2000 *Brondby* 7 3 76 45
2000–01 Oviedo 11 2 38 4
2000–01 Fulham 5 1 5 1

MORGAN, Simon* (D) 513 51
H: 5 11 W: 12 05 b.Birmingham 5-9-66
Source: Trainee. *Honours:* England Under-21.
1984–85 Leicester C 0 0
1985–86 Leicester C 30 0
1986–87 Leicester C 41 1
1987–88 Leicester C 40 0
1988–89 Leicester C 32 0
1989–90 Leicester C 17 2
1990–91 Leicester C 0 0 160 3
1990–91 Fulham 32 0
1991–92 Fulham 36 3
1992–93 Fulham 39 8
1993–94 Fulham 37 6
1994–95 Fulham 42 11
1995–96 Fulham 41 6
1996–97 Fulham 44 6
1997–98 Fulham 19 1
1998–99 Fulham 34 5
1999–2000 Fulham 20 0
2000–01 Fulham 1 0 353 48

NEILSON, Alan* (D) 126 3
H: 5 11 W: 12 06 b.Wegburg 26-9-72
Source: Trainee. *Honours:* Wales Under-21, 5 full caps.
1990–91 Newcastle U 3 0
1991–92 Newcastle U 16 1
1992–93 Newcastle U 3 0
1993–94 Newcastle U 14 0
1994–95 Newcastle U 6 0 42 1
1995–96 Southampton 18 0
1996–97 Southampton 29 0
1997–98 Southampton 8 0 55 0
1997–98 Fulham 17 0
1998–99 Fulham 4 1
1999–2000 Fulham 5 1
2000–01 Fulham 3 0 29 2

PESCHISOLIDO, Paul (F) 273 81
H: 5 7 W: 11 03 b.Canada 25-5-71
Source: Toronto Blizzard. *Honours:* Canada 44 full caps, 9 goals.
1992–93 Birmingham C 19 7
1993–94 Birmingham C 24 9
1994–95 Stoke C 40 13
1995–96 Stoke C 26 6 66 19
1995–96 Birmingham C 9 1 52 17
1996–97 WBA 37 15
1997–98 WBA 8 3 45 18
1997–98 Fulham 32 13
1998–99 Fulham 33 7
1999–2000 Fulham 30 4
2000–01 Fulham 0 0 95 24
2000–01 *QPR* 5 1 5 1
2000–01 *Sheffield U* 5 2 5 2
2000–01 *Norwich C* 5 0 5 0

PHELAN, Terry* (D) 394 4
H: 5 6 W: 10 06 b.Manchester 16-3-67
Source: Trainee. *Honours:* Eire Youth, Under-21, Under-23, B, 42 full caps.
1984–85 Leeds U 0 0
1985–86 Leeds U 14 0 14 0
1986–87 Swansea U 45 0 45 0
1987–88 Wimbledon 30 0
1988–89 Wimbledon 29 0
1989–90 Wimbledon 34 0
1990–91 Wimbledon 29 0
1991–92 Wimbledon 37 1
1992–93 Wimbledon 0 0 159 1
1992–93 Manchester C 37 0
1993–94 Manchester C 30 1
1994–95 Manchester C 27 0
1995–96 Manchester C 9 0 103 1
1995–96 Chelsea 12 0
1996–97 Chelsea 3 0 15 0
1997–98 Everton 15 0
1997–98 Everton 9 0
1998–99 Everton 0 0
1999–2000 Everton 1 0 25 0
1999–2000 *Crystal Palace* 14 0 14 0
1999–2000 Fulham 17 2
2000–01 Fulham 2 0 19 2

RIEDLE, Karlheinz* (F) 386 119
H: 5 11 W: 11 07 b.Weiler 16-9-65
Source: Augsburg. *Honours:* Germany 42 full caps, 16 goals.
1986–87 Blau-Weiss 90 34 10 34 10
1987–88 Werder Bremen 33 17
1988–89 Werder Bremen 33 13
1989–90 Werder Bremen 20 8 86 38
1990–91 Lazio 33 9
1991–92 Lazio 29 13
1992–93 Lazio 22 8 84 30
1993–94 Borussia Dortmund 22 4
1994–95 Borussia Dortmund 29 6
1995–96 Borussia Dortmund 18 7
1996–97 Borussia Dortmund 18 7 87 24
1997–98 Liverpool 25 6
1998–99 Liverpool 34 5
1999–2000 Liverpool 1 0 60 11
1999–2000 Fulham 21 5
2000–01 Fulham 14 1 35 6

SAHA, Louis (F) 101 33
H: 6 0 W: 12 04 b.Paris 8-8-78
1997–98 Metz 21 1
1998–99 Metz 3 0
1998–99 Newcastle U 11 1 11 1
1999–2000 Metz 23 4 47 5
2000–01 Fulham 43 27 43 27

SAHNOUN, Nicolas* (M) 7 0
H: 6 2 W: 13 08 b.France 3-9-80
2000–01 Bordeaux 0 0
2000–01 Fulham 7 0 7 0

SHEVEL, David (M) 0 0
b.Croydon 14-9-83
Source: Scholar.
2000–01 Fulham 0 0

STOLCERS, Andrejs (M) 125 36
H: 5 8 W: 11 00 b.Latvia 8-7-74
Honours: Latvia 50 full caps, 6 goals.
1996 Skonto Riga 26 6
1997 Skonto Riga 23 9 49 15
1997–98 Shakhtar Donetsk 13 4
1998–99 Shakhtar Donetsk 21 6
1999–2000 Shakhtar Donetsk 15 4 49 14
2000 Spartak Moscow 12 5 12 5
2000–01 Fulham 15 2 15 2

SYMONS, Kit (D) 383 27
H: 6 3 W: 13 02 b.Basingstoke 8-3-71
Source: Trainee. *Honours:* Wales Under-21, 33 full caps, 2 goals.
1988–89 Portsmouth 2 0
1989–90 Portsmouth 1 0
1990–91 Portsmouth 1 0
1991–92 Portsmouth 46 1
1992–93 Portsmouth 41 2
1993–94 Portsmouth 29 3
1994–95 Portsmouth 40 4
1995–96 Portsmouth 1 0 161 10
1995–96 Manchester C 38 2
1996–97 Manchester C 44 0
1997–98 Manchester C 42 2 124 4
1998–99 Fulham 45 11
1999–2000 Fulham 29 2
2000–01 Fulham 24 0 98 13

TAYLOR, Maik (G) 252 0
H: 6 3 W: 14 02 b.Hildesheim 4-9-71
Source: Farnborough T. *Honours:* Northern Ireland Under-21, 15 full caps.
1995–96 Barnet 45 0
1996–97 Barnet 25 0 70 0
1996–97 Southampton 18 0
1997–98 Southampton 0 0 18 0
1997–98 Fulham 28 0
1998–99 Fulham 46 0
1999–2000 Fulham 46 0
2000–01 Fulham 44 0 164 0

THOMPSON, Glyn (G) 17 0
H: 6 3 W: 12 08 b.Shrewsbury 24-2-81
Source: Trainee.
1998–99 Shrewsbury T 1 0
1999–2000 Shrewsbury T 0 0
1999–2000 Fulham 0 0
1999–2000 *Mansfield T* 16 0 16 0
2000–01 Fulham 0 0
2000–01 *Shrewsbury T* 0 0 1 0

TROLLOPE, Paul (M) 263 27
H: 6 0 W: 11 05 b.Swindon 3-6-72
Source: Trainee. *Honours:* Wales 5 full caps.
1989–90 Swindon T 0 0
1990–91 Swindon T 0 0
1991–92 Swindon T 0 0
1991–92 *Torquay U* 10 0
1992–93 Torquay U 36 2
1993–94 Torquay U 42 10
1994–95 Torquay U 18 4 106 16
1994–95 Derby Co 24 4

1995–96 Derby Co 17 0
1996–97 Derby Co 14 1
1996–97 *Grimsby T* 7 1 7 1
1996–97 *Crystal Palace* 9 0 9 0
1997–98 Derby Co 10 0 65 5
1997–98 Fulham 24 3
1998–99 Fulham 20 2
1999–2000 Fulham 22 0
2000–01 Fulham 10 0 76 5

TUCKER, Anthony* (G) 0 0
H: 6 1 W: 11 13 b.Barking 12-10-81
Source: Trainee.
1999–2000 Fulham 0 0
2000–01 Fulham 0 0

WILLOCK, Calum (F) 1 0
H: 6 1 W: 12 08 b.London 29-10-81
Source: Scholar. *Honours:* England Schools.
2000–01 Fulham 1 0 1 0

Scholars
Browning, Robert; Buari, Malik; Clark, Darren; Davis, Thomas GR; Flitney, Ross D; Green, Adam; Howard, Antony D; Hunter, Jermaine A; Lampton, Neil J; Leacock, Dean; Lock, Christopher J; McClements, Edward J; Noble, Stuart W; Pomroy, John S; Read, Paul; Rehman, Zeshan; Upsher, Tom P; Wilson, Justin F; Yhdego, Esayes Y
Non-Contract
Kean, Steven; Nevin, Paul R

GILLINGHAM

ASHBY, Barry (D) 397 12
H: 6 2 W: 13 08 b.London 2-11-70
Source: Trainee.
1988–89 Watford 0 0
1989–90 Watford 18 1
1990–91 Watford 23 0
1991–92 Watford 21 0
1992–93 Watford 35 0
1993–94 Watford 17 2 114 3
1994–95 Brentford 8 1
1994–95 Brentford 40 1
1995–96 Brentford 33 1
1996–97 Brentford 40 1 121 4
1997–98 Gillingham 43 0
1998–99 Gillingham 38 1
1999–2000 Gillingham 41 3
2000–01 Gillingham 40 1 162 5

BARTRAM, Vince (G) 311 0
H: 6 2 W: 13 04 b.Birmingham 8-8-68
Source: Local.
1985–86 Wolverhampton W 0 0
1986–87 Wolverhampton W 1 0
1987–88 Wolverhampton W 0 0
1988–89 Wolverhampton W 0 0
1989–90 Wolverhampton W 0 0
1989–90 *Blackpool* 9 0 9 0
1990–91 Wolverhampton W 4 0
1990–91 *WBA* 0 0
1991–92 Bournemouth 46 0
1992–93 Bournemouth 45 0
1993–94 Bournemouth 41 0 132 0
1994–95 Arsenal 11 0
1995–96 Arsenal 0 0
1996–97 Arsenal 0 0
1996–97 *Wolverhampton W* 0 0 5 0
1997–98 Arsenal 0 0 11 0
1997–98 *Huddersfield T* 12 0 12 0
1997–98 Gillingham 9 0
1998–99 Gillingham 44 0
1999–2000 Gillingham 43 0
2000–01 Gillingham 46 0 142 0

BROWN, Jason (G) 0 0
b.Southwark 18-5-82
Source: Charlton Ath Scholar.
2000–01 Gillingham 0 0

BROWNING, Marcus (M) 250 18
H: 6 0 W: 12 10 b.Bristol 22-4-71
Source: Trainee. *Honours:* Wales 5 full caps.
1989–90 Bristol R 1 0
1990–91 Bristol R 0 0
1991–92 Bristol R 11 0
1992–93 Bristol R 19 1
1992–93 *Hereford U* 7 5 7 5
1993–94 Bristol R 31 4
1994–95 Bristol R 41 2
1995–96 Bristol R 45 4
1996–97 Bristol R 26 2 174 13
1996–97 Huddersfield T 13 0
1997–98 Huddersfield T 14 0
1998–99 Huddersfield T 6 0 33 0
1998–99 Gillingham 4 0
1999–2000 Gillingham 1 0
2000–01 Gillingham 31 0 36 0

BRYANT, Matthew* (D) 319 7
H: 6 1 W: 13 01 b.Bristol 21-9-70
Source: Trainee.

1989–90	Bristol C	0	0	
1990–91	Bristol C	22	1	
1990–91	*Walsall*	13	0	13 0
1991–92	Bristol C	43	2	
1992–93	Bristol C	41	1	
1993–94	Bristol C	28	0	
1994–95	Bristol C	37	3	
1995–96	Bristol C	32	0	203 7
1996–97	Gillingham	39	0	
1997–98	Gillingham	35	0	
1998–99	Gillingham	23	0	
1999–2000	Gillingham	6	0	
2000–01	Gillingham	0	0	103 0

BUTLER, Steve* (F) 401 128
H: 6 1 W: 12 02 b.Birmingham 21-1-62
Source: Windsor & Eton, Wokingham T.

1984–85	Brentford	3	1	
1985–86	Brentford	18	2	21 3
To Maidstone U (1986)				
1989–90	Maidstone U	44	21	
1990–91	Maidstone U	32	20	76 41
1990–91	Watford	10	1	
1991–92	Watford	43	8	
1992–93	Watford	9	0	62 9
1992–93	*Bournemouth*	1	0	1 0
1992–93	Cambridge U	23	6	
1993–94	Cambridge U	33	21	
1994–95	Cambridge U	37	14	
1995–96	Cambridge U	16	10	109 51
1995–96	Gillingham	20	5	
1996–97	Gillingham	38	9	
1997–98	Gillingham	43	6	
1998–99	Gillingham	7	0	
1998–99	Peterborough U	14	2	14 2
1999–2000	Gillingham	10	2	
2000–01	Gillingham	0	0	118 22

BUTTERS, Guy (D) 344 26
H: 6 3 W: 13 12 b.Hillingdon 30-10-69
Source: Trainee. *Honours:* England Under-21.

1988–89	Tottenham H	28	1	
1989–90	Tottenham H	7	0	35 1
1989–90	*Southend U*	16	3	16 3
1990–91	Portsmouth	23	0	
1991–92	Portsmouth	33	2	
1992–93	Portsmouth	15	1	
1993–94	Portsmouth	15	1	
1994–95	Portsmouth	24	0	
1994–95	*Oxford U*	3	1	3 1
1995–96	Portsmouth	37	2	
1996–97	Portsmouth	7	0	154 6
1996–97	Gillingham	30	0	
1997–98	Gillingham	31	7	
1998–99	Gillingham	23	3	
1999–2000	Gillingham	40	2	
2000–01	Gillingham	12	3	136 15

CROFTS, Andrew§ (D) 1 0
b.Chatham 29-5-84
Source: Trainee.

2000–01	Gillingham	1	0	1 0

EDGE, Roland (D) 54 1
H: 5 10 W: 11 10 b.Gillingham 25-11-78
Source: Trainee.

1997–98	Gillingham	0	0	
1998–99	Gillingham	8	0	
1999–2000	Gillingham	26	1	
2000–01	Gillingham	20	0	54 1

GOODEN, Ty (M) 180 13
H: 5 8 W: 12 06 b.Canvey Island 23-10-72
Source: Arsenal, Wycombe W.

1993–94	Swindon T	4	0	
1994–95	Swindon T	16	2	
1995–96	Swindon T	26	3	
1996–97	Swindon T	13	1	
1997–98	Swindon T	39	2	
1998–99	Swindon T	38	1	
1999–2000	Swindon T	10	0	146 9
1999–2000	Gillingham	16	4	
2000–01	Gillingham	10	0	34 4

HESSENTHALER, Andy# (M) 379 27
H: 5 7 W: 11 05 b.Gravesend 17-6-65
Source: Dartford, Redbridge Forest.

1991–92	Watford	35	1	
1992–93	Watford	45	3	
1993–94	Watford	42	5	
1994–95	Watford	43	2	
1995–96	Watford	30	0	195 11
1996–97	Gillingham	38	2	
1997–98	Gillingham	42	0	
1998–99	Gillingham	39	7	
1999–2000	Gillingham	42	5	
2000–01	Gillingham	23	2	184 16

HOPE, Chris (D) 333 21
H: 6 1 W: 12 08 b.Sheffield 14-11-73
Source: Darlington.

1991–92	Nottingham F	0	0	
1992–93	Nottingham F	0	0	
1993–94	Scunthorpe U	41	0	
1994–95	Scunthorpe U	24	0	
1995–96	Scunthorpe U	40	3	
1996–97	Scunthorpe U	46	3	
1997–98	Scunthorpe U	46	5	
1998–99	Scunthorpe U	46	5	
1999–2000	Scunthorpe U	44	3	287 19
2000–01	Gillingham	46	2	46 2

IPOUA, Guy (F) 98 26
H: 6 1 W: 13 02 b.Douala 14-1-76
Source: Atletico Madrid, Novelda.

1998–99	Bristol R	24	3	24 3
1999–2000	Scunthorpe U	40	9	
2000–01	Scunthorpe U	25	14	65 23
2000–01	Gillingham	9	0	9 0

JAMES, Kevin (F) 7 0
H: 5 9 W: 10 07 b.Southwark 3-1-80
Source: Trainee.

1998–99	Charlton Ath	0	0	
1999–2000	Charlton Ath	0	0	
2000–01	Gillingham	7	0	7 0

KING, Marlon (F) 91 29
H: 6 1 W: 12 03 b.Dulwich 26-4-80
Source: Trainee.

1998–99	Barnet	22	6	
1999–2000	Barnet	31	8	53 14
2000–01	Barnet	38	15	38 15

LOVELL, Mark§ (D) 1 0
b.Bromley 16-7-83
Source: Trainee.

2000–01	Gillingham	1	0	1 0

MILLER, Barry* (D) 4 0
H: 6 0 W: 11 07 b.Greenford Ealing 29-3-76

1999–2000	Gillingham	4	0	
2000–01	Gillingham	0	0	4 0

MITTEN, Charlie (G) 0 0
H: 6 2 W: 12 07 b.Woolwich 9-10-74
Source: Dover Ath.

1999–2000	Gillingham	0	0	
2000–01	Gillingham	0	0	

NOSWORTHY, Nayron (M) 42 1
H: 6 1 W: 12 07 b.London 11-10-80
Source: Trainee.

1998–99	Gillingham	3	0	
1999–2000	Gillingham	29	1	
2000–01	Gillingham	10	0	42 1

ONUORA, Iffy (F) 381 101
H: 6 1 W: 13 10 b.Glasgow 28-7-67
Source: British Univ.

1989–90	Huddersfield T	20	3	
1990–91	Huddersfield T	43	7	
1991–92	Huddersfield T	41	8	
1992–93	Huddersfield T	39	6	
1993–94	Huddersfield T	22	6	165 30
1994–95	Mansfield T	14	7	
1995–96	Mansfield T	14	1	28 8
1996–97	Gillingham	40	21	
1997–98	Gillingham	22	2	
1997–98	Swindon T	6	1	
1998–99	Swindon T	43	20	
1999–2000	Swindon T	24	4	73 25
1999–2000	Gillingham	22	6	
2000–01	Gillingham	31	9	115 38

PATTERSON, Mark (D) 309 8
H: 5 9 W: 12 04 b.Leeds 13-9-68
Source: Trainee.

1986–87	Carlisle U	6	0	
1987–88	Carlisle U	16	0	22 0
1987–88	Derby Co	0	0	
1988–89	Derby Co	1	0	
1989–90	Derby Co	9	0	
1990–91	Derby Co	11	1	
1991–92	Derby Co	12	2	
1992–93	Derby Co	18	0	51 3
1993–94	Plymouth Arg	41	0	
1994–95	Plymouth Arg	38	3	
1995–96	Plymouth Arg	43	0	
1996–97	Plymouth Arg	12	0	
1997–98	Plymouth Arg	0	0	134 3
1997–98	Gillingham	23	0	
1998–99	Gillingham	42	2	
1999–2000	Gillingham	9	0	
2000–01	Gillingham	28	0	102 2

PENNOCK, Adrian (M) 287 11
H: 6 1 W: 13 05 b.Ipswich 27-3-71
Source: Trainee.

1989–90	Norwich C	1	0	
1990–91	Norwich C	0	0	
1991–92	Norwich C	0	0	1 0
1992–93	Bournemouth	43	1	
1993–94	Bournemouth	40	3	
1994–95	Bournemouth	31	5	
1995–96	Bournemouth	17	0	
1996–97	Bournemouth	0	0	131 9
1996–97	Gillingham	26	2	
1997–98	Gillingham	20	0	
1998–99	Gillingham	40	0	
1999–2000	Gillingham	34	0	
2000–01	Gillingham	35	0	155 2

PHILLIPS, Michael§ (M) 1 0
b.Camberwell 22-1-83
Source: Trainee.

2000–01	Gillingham	1	0	1 0

PINNOCK, James* (F) 9 0
H: 5 9 W: 11 05 b.Dartford 1-8-78
Source: Trainee.

1996–97	Gillingham	2	0	
1997–98	Gillingham	1	0	
1998–99	Gillingham	4	0	
1999–2000	Gillingham	2	0	
2000–01	Gillingham	0	0	9 0

ROSE, Richard (D) 4 0
b.Tonbridge Wells 8-9-82
Source: Trainee.

2000–01	Gillingham	4	0	4 0

SAUNDERS, Mark (M) 167 21
H: 5 11 W: 11 12 b.Reading 23-7-71
Source: Tiverton.

1995–96	Plymouth Arg	10	1	
1996–97	Plymouth Arg	25	3	
1997–98	Plymouth Arg	37	7	72 11
1998–99	Gillingham	34	4	
1999–2000	Gillingham	26	1	
2000–01	Gillingham	35	5	95 10

SHAW, Paul (F) 181 38
H: 5 10 W: 12 10 b.Burnham 4-9-73
Source: Trainee.

1991–92	Arsenal	0	0	
1992–93	Arsenal	0	0	
1993–94	Arsenal	0	0	
1994–95	Arsenal	0	0	
1994–95	*Burnley*	9	4	9 4
1995–96	Arsenal	3	0	
1995–96	*Cardiff C*	6	0	6 0
1995–96	*Peterborough U*	12	5	12 5
1996–97	Arsenal	8	2	
1997–98	Arsenal	0	0	12 2
1997–98	Millwall	40	11	
1998–99	Millwall	34	10	
1999–2000	Millwall	35	5	109 26
2000–01	Gillingham	33	1	33 1

SMITH, Paul (M) 356 25
H: 5 11 W: 12 08 b.East Ham 18-9-71
Source: Trainee.

1989–90	Southend U	10	1	
1990–91	Southend U	2	0	
1991–92	Southend U	0	0	
1992–93	Southend U	8	0	20 1
1993–94	Brentford	32	3	
1994–95	Brentford	35	3	
1995–96	Brentford	46	4	
1996–97	Brentford	46	1	159 11
1997–98	Gillingham	46	3	
1998–99	Gillingham	45	6	
1999–2000	Gillingham	44	1	
2000–01	Gillingham	42	3	177 13

SOUTHALL, Nicky* (M) 364 46
H: 5 10 W: 12 12 b.Middlesbrough 28-1-72
Source: Trainee.

1990–91	Hartlepool U	0	0	
1991–92	Hartlepool U	22	3	
1992–93	Hartlepool U	39	6	
1993–94	Hartlepool U	40	9	
1994–95	Hartlepool U	37	6	138 24
1995–96	Grimsby T	33	2	
1996–97	Grimsby T	34	3	
1997–98	Grimsby T	5	0	72 5
1997–98	Gillingham	23	2	
1998–99	Gillingham	42	4	
1999–2000	Gillingham	45	9	
2000–01	Gillingham	44	2	154 17

SPILLER, Daniel (M) 0 0
b.Maidstone 10-10-81
Source: Trainee.

2000–01	Gillingham	0	0	

WHITE, Ben (D) 0 0
H: 6 1 W: 13 00 b.Hastings 2-6-82
Source: Trainee.

2000–01	Gillingham	0	0	

Trainees
Cornwall, Joseph M; Hafner, Stephen; Lovell, Mark; Phillips, Michael E; White, Liam JC

Scholars
Awuah, Jones; Beckwith, Dean S; Crofts, Andrew L; Flaherty, Darren S; Millar, James SBM; Peters, Ryan J

GRIMSBY T

ALLEN, Bradley (F)   177 48
H: 5 8 W: 11 00 b.Harold Wood 13-9-71
Source: School. *Honours:* England Youth, Under-21.

Season	Club				
1988–89	QPR	1	0		
1989–90	QPR	0	0		
1990–91	QPR	10	2		
1991–92	QPR	11	5		
1992–93	QPR	25	10		
1993–94	QPR	21	7		
1994–95	QPR	5	2		
1995–96	QPR	8	1	81	27
1995–96	Charlton Ath	10	3		
1996–97	Charlton Ath	18	4		
1997–98	Charlton Ath	12	2		
1998–99	Charlton Ath	0	0	40	9
1998–99	Colchester U	4	1	4	1
1999–2000	Grimsby T	31	8		
2000–01	Grimsby T	21	3	52	11

BLACK, Kingsley# (M)   385 51
H: 5 10 W: 12 00 b.Luton 22-6-68
Source: School. *Honours:* England Schools, Northern Ireland Under-21, 30 full caps, 1 goal.

Season	Club				
1986–87	Luton T	0	0		
1987–88	Luton T	13	0		
1988–89	Luton T	37	8		
1989–90	Luton T	36	11		
1990–91	Luton T	37	7		
1991–92	Luton T	4	0	127	26
1991–92	Nottingham F	25	4		
1992–93	Nottingham F	24	5		
1993–94	Nottingham F	37	3		
1994–95	Nottingham F	10	2		
1994–95	Sheffield U	11	2	11	2
1995–96	Nottingham F	2	0	98	14
1995–96	Millwall	3	1	3	1
1996–97	Grimsby T	24	0		
1997–98	Grimsby T	39	2		
1998–99	Grimsby T	42	4		
1999–2000	Grimsby T	31	2		
2000–01	Grimsby T	5	0	141	8
2000–01	Lincoln C	5	0	5	0

BLOOMER, Matthew* (D)   12 0
H: 6 0 W: 11 08 b.Cleethorpes 3-11-78
Source: Trainee.

Season	Club				
1997–98	Grimsby T	0	0		
1998–99	Grimsby T	4	0		
1999–2000	Grimsby T	2	0		
2000–01	Grimsby T	6	0	12	0

BUCKLEY, Adam (M)   15 0
H: 5 9 W: 11 07 b.Nottingham 2-8-79
Source: WBA schoolboy.

Season	Club				
1997–98	Grimsby T	0	0		
1998–99	Grimsby T	2	0		
1999–2000	Grimsby T	13	0		
2000–01	Grimsby T	0	0	15	0

BURNETT, Wayne# (M)   236 7
H: 5 11 W: 12 07 b.Lambeth 4-9-71
Source: Trainee.

Season	Club				
1989–90	Leyton Orient	3	0		
1990–91	Leyton Orient	1	0		
1991–92	Leyton Orient	36	0	40	0
1992–93	Blackburn R	0	0		
1993–94	Plymouth Arg	32	2		
1994–95	Plymouth Arg	32	1		
1995–96	Plymouth Arg	6	0	70	3
1995–96	Bolton W	1	0		
1996–97	Bolton W	1	0	2	0
1996–97	Huddersfield T	35	0		
1997–98	Huddersfield T	15	0	50	0
1997–98	Grimsby T	21	1		
1998–99	Grimsby T	20	2		
1999–2000	Grimsby T	10	0		
2000–01	Grimsby T	23	1	74	4

BUTTERFIELD, Danny (D)   78 1
H: 5 10 W: 11 06 b.Boston 21-11-79
Source: Trainee. *Honours:* England Youth.

Season	Club				
1997–98	Grimsby T	7	0		
1998–99	Grimsby T	12	0		
1999–2000	Grimsby T	29	0		
2000–01	Grimsby T	30	1	78	1

CHAPMAN, Ben (D)   4 0
H: 5 6 W: 11 05 b.Scunthorpe 2-3-79
Source: Trainee.

Season	Club				
1997–98	Grimsby T	0	0		
1998–99	Grimsby T	1	0		
1999–2000	Grimsby T	1	0		
2000–01	Grimsby T	2	0	4	0

CLARE, Daryl* (F)   97 12
H: 5 9 W: 12 05 b.Jersey 1-8-78
Source: Trainee. *Honours:* Eire Under-21.

Season	Club				
1995–96	Grimsby T	1	0		
1996–97	Grimsby T	0	0		
1997–98	Grimsby T	22	3		
1998–99	Grimsby T	22	3		
1999–2000	Grimsby T	17	3		
1999–2000	Northampton T	10	3		
2000–01	Grimsby T	17	0	79	9
2000–01	Northampton T	4	0	14	3
2000–01	Cheltenham T	4	0	4	0

COLDICOTT, Stacy# (M)   228 6
H: 5 8 W: 12 08 b.Worcester 29-4-74
Source: Trainee.

Season	Club				
1991–92	WBA	0	0		
1992–93	WBA	14	0		
1993–94	WBA	5	0		
1994–95	WBA	11	0		
1995–96	WBA	33	0		
1996–97	WBA	19	3		
1997–98	Cardiff C	6	0	6	0
1997–98	WBA	22	0	104	3
1998–99	Grimsby T	37	0		
1999–2000	Grimsby T	44	2		
2000–01	Grimsby T	37	1	118	3

COYNE, Danny (G)   201 0
H: 6 0 W: 13 04 b.Prestatyn 27-8-73
Source: Trainee. *Honours:* Wales Under-21, 1 full cap.

Season	Club				
1991–92	Tranmere R	0	0		
1992–93	Tranmere R	5	0		
1993–94	Tranmere R	5	0		
1994–95	Tranmere R	5	0		
1995–96	Tranmere R	46	0		
1996–97	Tranmere R	21	0		
1997–98	Tranmere R	16	0		
1998–99	Tranmere R	17	0	111	0
1999–2000	Grimsby T	44	0		
2000–01	Grimsby T	46	0	90	0

CRANLEY, Morgan (M)   0 0
b.Dublin 12-1-84

Season	Club			
2000–01	Grimsby T	0	0	

CROUDSON, Steve (G)   5 0
H: 6 0 W: 11 12 b.Grimsby 14-9-79
Source: Trainee.

Season	Club				
1998–99	Grimsby T	2	0		
1999–2000	Grimsby T	3	0		
2000–01	Grimsby T	0	0	5	0

DONOVAN, Kevin# (F)   350 44
H: 5 8 W: 11 13 b.Halifax 17-12-71
Source: Trainee.

Season	Club				
1989–90	Huddersfield T	1	0		
1990–91	Huddersfield T	6	1		
1991–92	Huddersfield T	10	0		
1991–92	Halifax T	6	0	6	0
1992–93	Huddersfield T	3	0	20	1
1992–93	WBA	32	6		
1993–94	WBA	37	8		
1994–95	WBA	33	5		
1995–96	WBA	34	0		
1996–97	WBA	32	0	168	19
1997–98	Grimsby T	46	16		
1998–99	Grimsby T	28	0		
1999–2000	Grimsby T	41	3		
2000–01	Grimsby T	41	5	156	24

ENHUA, Zhang‡ (D)   17 3
b.Dalian 28-4-73
Source: Dalian Shide. *Honours:* China full caps.

Season	Club				
2000–01	Grimsby T	17	3	17	3

FOSTERVOLD, Knut‡ (D)   150 10
H: 6 2 W: 13 10 b.Norway 4-10-71

Season	Club				
1995	Molde	22	0		
1996	Molde	24	0		
1997	Molde	23	6		
1998	Molde	23	1		
1999	Molde	24	2		
2000	Molde	24	1	140	10
2000–01	Grimsby T	10	0	10	0

GALLIMORE, Tony# (D)   348 13
H: 5 11 W: 13 04 b.Crewe 21-2-72
Source: Trainee.

Season	Club				
1989–90	Stoke C	1	0		
1990–91	Stoke C	7	0		
1991–92	Stoke C	3	0		
1991–92	Carlisle U	16	0		
1992–93	Stoke C	0	0	11	0
1992–93	Carlisle U	8	1		
1993–94	Carlisle U	40	1		
1994–95	Carlisle U	40	5		
1995–96	Carlisle U	36	2	140	9
1995–96	Grimsby T	10	1		
1996–97	Grimsby T	42	1		
1997–98	Grimsby T	35	2		
1998–99	Grimsby T	43	0		
1999–2000	Grimsby T	39	0		
2000–01	Grimsby T	28	0	197	4

GROVES, Paul# (M)   524 93
H: 5 11 W: 13 04 b.Derby 28-2-66
Source: Burton Alb.

Season	Club				
1987–88	Leicester C	1	1		
1988–89	Leicester C	15	0		
1989–90	Leicester C	0	0	16	1
1989–90	Lincoln C	8	1	8	1
1989–90	Blackpool	19	1		
1990–91	Blackpool	46	11		
1991–92	Blackpool	42	9	107	21
1992–93	Grimsby T	46	12		
1993–94	Grimsby T	46	11		
1994–95	Grimsby T	46	5		
1995–96	Grimsby T	46	10		
1996–97	WBA	29	4	29	4
1997–98	Grimsby T	46	7		
1998–99	Grimsby T	46	14		
1999–2000	Grimsby T	43	3		
2000–01	Grimsby T	45	4	364	66

HANDYSIDE, Peter# (D)   190 4
H: 6 1 W: 13 07 b.Dumfries 31-7-74
Source: Trainee. *Honours:* Scotland Under-21.

Season	Club				
1992–93	Grimsby T	11	0		
1993–94	Grimsby T	13	0		
1994–95	Grimsby T	35	0		
1995–96	Grimsby T	30	0		
1996–97	Grimsby T	9	1		
1997–98	Grimsby T	42	0		
1998–99	Grimsby T	31	2		
1999–2000	Grimsby T	0	0		
2000–01	Grimsby T	19	1	190	4

JEFFREY, Mike (F)   238 52
H: 6 1 W: 11 09 b.Liverpool 11-8-71
Source: Trainee.

Season	Club				
1988–89	Bolton W	9	0		
1989–90	Bolton W	4	0		
1990–91	Bolton W	0	0		
1991–92	Bolton W	2	0	15	0
1991–92	Doncaster R	11	6		
1992–93	Doncaster R	30	12		
1993–94	Doncaster R	8	1	49	19
1993–94	Newcastle U	2	0		
1994–95	Newcastle U	0	0	2	0
1994–95	Rotherham U	22	5	22	5
1995–96	Fortuna Sittard	19	4		
1996–97	Fortuna Sittard	28	5	103	25
1997–98	Fortuna Sittard	31	8		
1998–99	Fortuna Sittard	28	5		
1999–2000	Kilmarnock	18	2	18	2
2000–01	Grimsby T	29	1	29	1

LIVINGSTONE, Steve (F)   323 55
H: 6 1 W: 15 03 b.Middlesbrough 8-9-68
Source: Trainee.

Season	Club				
1986–87	Coventry C	3	0		
1987–88	Coventry C	4	0		
1988–89	Coventry C	1	0		
1989–90	Coventry C	13	3		
1990–91	Coventry C	10	2	31	5
1990–91	Blackburn R	18	9		
1991–92	Blackburn R	10	1		
1992–93	Blackburn R	2	0	30	10
1992–93	Chelsea	1	0		
1993–94	Chelsea	0	0	1	0
1993–94	Port Vale	5	0	5	0
1993–94	Grimsby T	27	3		
1994–95	Grimsby T	34	8		
1995–96	Grimsby T	38	11		
1996–97	Grimsby T	32	6		
1997–98	Grimsby T	41	5		
1998–99	Grimsby T	23	0		
1999–2000	Grimsby T	29	0		
2000–01	Grimsby T	32	7	256	40

McDERMOTT, John (D)   473 7
H: 5 7 W: 10 13 b.Middlesbrough 3-2-69
Source: Trainee.

Season	Club				
1986–87	Grimsby T	13	0		
1987–88	Grimsby T	28	0		
1988–89	Grimsby T	38	1		
1989–90	Grimsby T	39	0		
1990–91	Grimsby T	43	0		
1991–92	Grimsby T	39	1		
1992–93	Grimsby T	38	2		
1993–94	Grimsby T	26	0		
1994–95	Grimsby T	12	0		
1995–96	Grimsby T	28	1		
1996–97	Grimsby T	29	1		
1997–98	Grimsby T	41	1		
1998–99	Grimsby T	37	0		
1999–2000	Grimsby T	26	0		
2000–01	Grimsby T	36	0	473	7

MURRAY, Neil‡ (M) 68 1
H: 5 9 W: 10 10 b.Bellshill 21-2-73
Source: Rangers Amateur. *Honours:* Scotland Under-21.
1989-90	Rangers	0	0		
1990-91	Rangers	0	0		
1991-92	Rangers	0	0		
1992-93	Rangers	16	0		
1993-94	Rangers	22	0		
1994-95	Rangers	20	1		
1995-96	Rangers	5	0	63	1
From Lorient.					
1998-99	Dundee U	3	0		
1999-2000	Dundee U	0	0	3	0
2000-01	Grimsby T	2	0	2	0

POUTON, Alan (M) 146 9
H: 6 0 W: 12 10 b.Newcastle 1-2-77
Source: Newcastle U Trainee.
1995-96	Oxford U	0	0		
1995-96	York C	0	0		
1996-97	York C	22	1		
1997-98	York C	41	5		
1998-99	York C	27	1		
1999-2000	York C	0	0	90	7
1999-2000	Grimsby T	35	1		
2000-01	Grimsby T	21	1	56	2

RAVEN, Paul (D) 344 21
H: 6 1 W: 12 11 b.Salisbury 28-7-70
Source: School. *Honours:* England Schools, Youth.
1987-88	Doncaster R	17	3		
1988-89	Doncaster R	35	1		
1988-89	WBA	3	0		
1989-90	WBA	7	0		
1990-91	WBA	13	0		
1991-92	WBA	7	1		
1991-92	*Doncaster R*	7	0	59	4
1992-93	WBA	44	7		
1993-94	WBA	34	1		
1994-95	WBA	31	0		
1995-96	WBA	40	4		
1996-97	WBA	33	1		
1997-98	WBA	8	0		
1998-99	WBA	7	0		
1998-99	*Rotherham U*	11	2	11	2
1999-2000	Grimsby T	32	1	259	15
2000-01	Grimsby T	15	0	15	0

ROWAN, Jonathan (F) 5 0
H: 5 10 W: 11 00 b.Grimsby 29-11-81
| 2000-01 | Grimsby T | 5 | 0 | 5 | 0 |

SMITH, Andy* (M) 0 0
b.Blackpool 13-1-80
| 2000-01 | Grimsby T | 0 | 0 | | |

SMITH, David (M) 403 32
H: 5 7 W: 11 11 b.Gloucester 29-5-68
Source: Apprentice. *Honours:* England Under-21.
1986-87	Coventry C	0	0		
1987-88	Coventry C	16	4		
1988-89	Coventry C	35	3		
1989-90	Coventry C	37	6		
1990-91	Coventry C	36	1		
1991-92	Coventry C	24	4		
1992-93	Coventry C	6	1	154	19
1992-93	*Bournemouth*	1	0	1	0
1992-93	Birmingham C	13	1		
1993-94	Birmingham C	25	2	38	3
1993-94	WBA	18	0		
1994-95	WBA	22	0		
1995-96	WBA	16	0		
1996-97	WBA	24	2		
1997-98	WBA	22	0	102	2
1997-98	Grimsby T	17	1		
1998-99	Grimsby T	31	5		
1999-2000	Grimsby T	36	1		
2000-01	Grimsby T	24	1	108	8

SMITH, Richard# (D) 189 2
H: 6 0 W: 13 11 b.Leicester 3-10-70
Source: Trainee.
1988-89	Leicester C	0	0		
1989-90	Leicester C	4	0		
1989-90	*Cambridge U*	4	0	4	0
1990-91	Leicester C	4	0		
1991-92	Leicester C	25	1		
1992-93	Leicester C	44	1		
1993-94	Leicester C	8	0		
1994-95	Leicester C	12	0		
1995-96	Leicester C	1	0	98	1
1995-96	Grimsby T	18	0		
1996-97	Grimsby T	14	0		
1997-98	Grimsby T	0	0		
1998-99	Grimsby T	30	0		
1999-2000	Grimsby T	19	0		
2000-01	Grimsby T	6	1	87	1

WARD, Iain (M) 0 0
b.Cleethorpes 13-5-83
| 2000-01 | Grimsby T | 0 | 0 | | |

WILLEMS, Menno (M) 62 2
H: 6 0 W: 11 13 b.Amsterdam 10-3-77
1996-97	Ajax	2	0	2	0
1997-98	Vitesse	11	1		
1998-99	Vitesse	1	0		
1999-2000	Den Bosch	24	0	24	0
2000-01	Vitesse	0	0	12	1
2000-01	Grimsby T	24	1	24	1

Scholars
Beesley, Lee G; Butterwood, Michael S; Carchedi, Giovanni R; Gibson, Thomas W; Hildred, Ashley; Kirwin, Jonathan G; Moran, Gary; Soames, David M; Thorne, Sam; Wall, Christopher A; White, Russell

HALIFAX T

BRACEWELL, Paul† (M) 587 22
H: 5 9 W: 12 03 b.Heswall 19-7-62
Source: Apprentice. *Honours:* England Under-21, 3 full caps.
1979-80	Stoke C	6	0		
1980-81	Stoke C	40	2		
1981-82	Stoke C	42	1		
1982-83	Stoke C	41	2	129	5
1983-84	Sunderland	38	4		
1984-85	Everton	37	2		
1985-86	Everton	38	3		
1986-87	Everton	0	0		
1987-88	Everton	0	0		
1988-89	Everton	20	2		
1989-90	Everton	0	0	95	7
1989-90	Sunderland	37	2		
1990-91	Sunderland	37	0		
1991-92	Sunderland	39	0		
1992-93	Newcastle U	25	2		
1993-94	Newcastle U	32	1		
1994-95	Newcastle U	16	0	73	3
1995-96	Sunderland	38	0		
1996-97	Sunderland	38	0		
1997-98	Sunderland	1	0	228	6
1997-98	Fulham	36	0		
1998-99	Fulham	26	1		
1999-2000	Fulham	0	0	62	1
2000-01	Halifax T	0	0		

BRADSHAW, Mark* (D) 126 8
H: 5 10 W: 11 00 b.Ashton-under-Lyne 7-9-69
Source: Trainee.
1986-87	Blackpool	4	0		
1987-88	Blackpool	16	0		
1988-89	Blackpool	0	0		
1989-90	Blackpool	21	1		
1990-91	Blackpool	1	0	42	1
1990-91	York C	1	0	1	0
From Macclesfield T.					
1998-99	Halifax T	41	4		
1999-2000	Halifax T	25	1		
2000-01	Halifax T	17	2	83	7

BUTLER, Lee (G) 333 0
H: 6 1 W: 13 08 b.Sheffield 30-5-66
Source: Haworth Colliery.
1986-87	Lincoln C	30	0	30	0
1987-88	Aston Villa	4	0		
1988-89	Aston Villa	4	0		
1989-90	Aston Villa	4	0		
1990-91	Aston Villa	4	0	8	0
1990-91	Hull C	4	0	4	0
1991-92	Barnsley	43	0		
1992-93	Barnsley	28	0		
1993-94	Barnsley	37	0		
1994-95	Barnsley	9	0		
1995-96	Barnsley	3	0	120	0
1995-96	Scunthorpe U	2	0	2	0
1996-97	Wigan Ath	46	0		
1997-98	Wigan Ath	17	0	63	0
1998-99	Dunfermline Ath	35	0	35	0
1999-2000	Halifax T	38	0		
2000-01	Halifax T	33	0	71	0

BUTLER, Peter‡ (M) 450 23
H: 5 9 W: 11 01 b.Halifax 27-8-66
Source: Apprentice.
1984-85	Huddersfield T	4	0		
1985-86	Huddersfield T	1	0		
1985-86	*Cambridge U*	14	1		
1986-87	Bury	11	0	11	0
1986-87	Cambridge U	29	4		
1987-88	Cambridge U	26	5	69	10
1987-88	Southend U	15	3		
1988-89	Southend U	35	2		
1989-90	Southend U	41	2		
1990-91	Southend U	42	2		
1991-92	Southend U	9	0	142	9

1991-92	*Huddersfield T*	7	0	12	0
1992-93	West Ham U	39	2		
1993-94	West Ham U	26	1		
1994-95	West Ham U	5	0	70	3
1994-95	Notts Co	20	0		
1995-96	Notts Co	0	0	20	0
1995-96	*Grimsby T*	3	0	3	0
1995-96	WBA	9	0		
1996-97	WBA	17	0		
1997-98	WBA	34	0	60	0
1998-99	Halifax T	33	1		
1999-2000	Halifax T	30	0		
2000-01	Halifax T	0	0	63	1

CLARKE, Chris (D) 27 1
H: 6 3 W: 12 02 b.Leeds 18-12-80
Source: Wolverhampton W Trainee.
| 1999-2000 | Halifax T | 1 | 0 | | |
| 2000-01 | Halifax T | 26 | 1 | 27 | 1 |

CLARKE, Matthew (F) 38 1
H: 6 3 W: 13 00 b.Leeds 18-12-80
Source: Wolverhampton W Trainee.
| 1999-2000 | Halifax T | 19 | 0 | | |
| 2000-01 | Halifax T | 19 | 1 | 38 | 1 |

CROOKES, Peter* (G) 0 0
b.Liverpool 7-5-82
Source: Liverpool Scholar. *Honours:* England Schools.
| 2000-01 | Halifax T | 0 | 0 | | |

FITZPATRICK, Ian (F) 20 2
H: 5 9 W: 10 00 b.Manchester 22-9-80
Source: Trainee. *Honours:* England Schools.
1998-99	Manchester U	0	0		
1999-2000	Manchester U	0	0		
1999-2000	Halifax T	8	0		
2000-01	Halifax T	12	2	20	2

GAUGHAN, Steve* (M) 352 22
H: 5 11 W: 11 08 b.Doncaster 14-4-70
Source: Hatfield Main.
1987-88	Doncaster R	4	0		
1988-89	Doncaster R	34	2		
1989-90	Doncaster R	29	1	67	3
1990-91	Sunderland	0	0		
1991-92	Sunderland	0	0		
1991-92	Darlington	20	0		
1992-93	Darlington	37	1		
1993-94	Darlington	32	3		
1994-95	Darlington	41	8		
1995-96	Darlington	41	3		
1996-97	Chesterfield	18	0		
1997-98	Chesterfield	2	0	20	0
1997-98	Darlington	24	1		
1998-99	Darlington	23	2	218	18
1999-2000	Halifax T	38	0		
2000-01	Halifax T	9	1	47	1

HARRISON, Gerry‡ (M) 221 6
H: 5 10 W: 12 12 b.Lambeth 15-4-72
Source: Trainee. *Honours:* England Schools.
1989-90	Watford	3	0		
1990-91	Watford	6	0	9	0
1991-92	Bristol C	4	0		
1991-92	*Cardiff C*	10	1	10	1
1992-93	Bristol C	33	1		
1993-94	Bristol C	1	0	38	1
1993-94	*Hereford U*	6	0	6	0
1993-94	Huddersfield T	0	0		
1994-95	Burnley	19	2		
1995-96	Burnley	35	1		
1996-97	Burnley	35	0		
1997-98	Burnley	35	0		
1998-99	Sunderland	0	0		
1998-99	*Luton T*	14	0	14	0
1998-99	*Hull C*	8	0		
1999-2000	Sunderland	0	0		
1999-2000	*Hull C*	3	0	11	0
1999-2000	*Burnley*	0	0	124	3
2000-01	Halifax T	9	1	9	1

HERBERT, Robert (M) 13 1
H: 5 10 W: 11 00 b.Durham 29-8-83
Source: Scholarship.
| 1999-2000 | Halifax T | 4 | 0 | | |
| 2000-01 | Halifax T | 9 | 1 | 13 | 1 |

HOLT, Grant* (M) 6 0
H: 6 0 W: 12 06 b.Carlisle 12-4-81
Source: Workington.
| 1999-2000 | Halifax T | 4 | 0 | | |
| 2000-01 | Halifax T | 2 | 0 | 6 | 0 |

JONES, Gary (F) 308 76
H: 6 1 W: 12 08 b.Huddersfield 6-4-69
Source: Rossington Main.
1988-89	Doncaster R	17	2		
1989-90	Doncaster R	3	0	20	2
From Boston U.					
1993-94	Southend U	22	3		
1993-94	*Lincoln C*	4	2	4	2
1994-95	Southend U	25	11		

1995–96	Southend U	23	2	70	16
1995–96	Notts Co	18	5		
1996–97	Notts Co	27	3		
1996–97	*Scunthorpe U*	11	5	11	5
1997–98	Notts Co	44	28		
1998–99	Notts Co	28	2	117	38
1998–99	Hartlepool U	12	1		
1999–2000	Hartlepool U	33	6	45	7
1999–2000	*Halifax T*	8	1		
2000–01	Halifax T	33	5	41	6

JULES, Mark# (D)   325   21
H: 5 7   W: 10 09   b.Bradford 5-9-71
Source: Trainee.

1990–91	Bradford C	0	0		
1991–92	Scarborough	41	8		
1992–93	Scarborough	36	8	77	16
1993–94	Chesterfield	33	1		
1994–95	Chesterfield	23	0		
1995–96	Chesterfield	32	2		
1996–97	Chesterfield	42	0		
1997–98	Chesterfield	33	1		
1998–99	Chesterfield	23	0	186	4
1999–2000	Halifax T	42	0		
2000–01	Halifax T	20	1	62	1

KERRIGAN, Steve (F)   261   73
H: 6 1   W: 12 04   b.Bailleston 9-10-72
Source: Newmains J.

1992–93	Albion R	29	8		
1993–94	Albion R	24	6	53	14
1993–94	Clydebank	15	0		
1994–95	Clydebank	14	0		
1995–96	Clydebank	1	0	30	0
1995–96	Stranraer	21	5	21	5
1996–97	Ayr U	27	14		
1997–98	Ayr U	6	3	33	17
1997–98	Shrewsbury T	14	2		
1998–99	Shrewsbury T	37	10		
1999–2000	Shrewsbury T	25	3	76	15
1999–2000	Halifax T	7	3		
2000–01	Halifax T	41	19	48	22

MAWSON, Craig* (G)   9   0
H: 6 2   W: 13 04   b.Keighley 16-5-79
Source: Trainee.

1997–98	Burnley	0	0		
1998–99	Burnley	0	0		
1999–2000	Burnley	0	0		
2000–01	Burnley	0	0		
2000–01	*Lincoln C*	0	0		
2000–01	Halifax T	9	0	9	0

MIDDLETON, Craig (M)   234   26
H: 5 11   W: 12 00   b.Nuneaton 10-9-70
Source: Trainee.

1989–90	Coventry C	1	0		
1990–91	Coventry C	0	0		
1991–92	Coventry C	1	0		
1992–93	Coventry C	1	0	3	0
1993–94	Cambridge U	19	2		
1994–95	Cambridge U	0	0		
1995–96	Cambridge U	40	8	59	10
1996–97	Cardiff C	41	4		
1997–98	Cardiff C	33	0		
1998–99	Cardiff C	35	4		
1999–2000	Cardiff C	10	0	119	8
1999–2000	*Plymouth Arg*	6	2	6	2
1999–2000	Halifax T	10	1		
2000–01	Halifax T	37	5	47	6

MITCHELL, Graham (D)   469   6
H: 6 1   W: 13 01   b.Shipley 16-2-68
Source: Apprentice.

1986–87	Huddersfield T	17	0		
1987–88	Huddersfield T	29	1		
1988–89	Huddersfield T	34	0		
1989–90	Huddersfield T	37	1		
1990–91	Huddersfield T	46	0		
1991–92	Huddersfield T	43	0		
1992–93	Huddersfield T	4	0		
1993–94	Huddersfield T	22	0		
1993–94	*Bournemouth*	4	0	4	0
1994–95	Huddersfield T	12	0	244	2
1994–95	Bradford C	26	0		
1995–96	Bradford C	33	1		
1996–97	Bradford C	6	0	65	1
1996–97	Raith R	20	0		
1997–98	Raith R	3	0	23	0
1998–99	Cardiff C	46	0	46	0
1999–2000	Halifax T	45	2		
2000–01	Halifax T	42	1	87	3

MORGAN, Steve‡ (M)   416   21
H: 5 11   W: 12 00   b.Oldham 19-9-68
Source: Apprentice. *Honours:* England Youth.

1985–86	Blackpool	5	0		
1986–87	Blackpool	11	0		
1987–88	Blackpool	46	6		
1988–89	Blackpool	44	3		
1989–90	Blackpool	38	1	144	10
1990–91	Plymouth Arg	40	3		
1991–92	Plymouth Arg	45	2		
1992–93	Plymouth Arg	36	1	121	6
1993–94	Coventry C	40	2		
1994–95	Coventry C	28	0		
1995–96	Coventry C	0	0	68	2
1995–96	*Bristol R*	5	0	5	0
1996–97	Wigan Ath	23	1		
1997–98	Wigan Ath	13	1	36	2
1997–98	*Bury*	5	0	5	0
1998–99	Burnley	17	0	17	0
1999–2000	Hull C	19	1	19	1
2000–01	Halifax T	1	0	1	0

MYERS, Peter§ (M)   1   0
b.Dronfield 15-9-82
Source: Scholar.

2000–01	Halifax T	1	0	1	0

OLEKSEWYCZ, Stephen (F)   3   0
b.Halifax 24-2-83

2000–01	Halifax T	3	0	3	0

ORD, Michael‡ (M)   0   0
H: 6 1   W: 11 06   b.Huddersfield 22-5-81
Source: Ripon C.

1999–2000	Halifax T	0	0		
2000–01	Halifax T	0	0		

PAINTER, Robbie* (F)   425   81
H: 5 10   W: 12 02   b.Ince 26-1-71
Source: Trainee.

1987–88	Chester C	2	0		
1988–89	Chester C	8	1		
1989–90	Chester C	32	4		
1990–91	Chester C	42	3	84	8
1991–92	Maidstone U	30	5	30	5
1991–92	Burnley	9	2		
1992–93	Burnley	17	0		
1993–94	Burnley	0	0	26	2
1993–94	Darlington	36	11		
1994–95	Darlington	38	9		
1995–96	Darlington	35	8		
1996–97	Darlington	6	0	115	28
1996–97	Rochdale	27	7		
1997–98	Rochdale	45	17		
1998–99	Rochdale	40	6	112	30
1999–2000	Halifax T	42	8		
2000–01	Halifax T	16	0	58	8

PARKS, Tony (G)   264   0
H: 5 10   W: 11 05   b.Hackney 28-1-63
Source: Apprentice.

1980–81	Tottenham H	0	0		
1981–82	Tottenham H	2	0		
1982–83	Tottenham H	1	0		
1983–84	Tottenham H	16	0		
1984–85	Tottenham H	0	0		
1985–86	Tottenham H	0	0		
1986–87	Tottenham H	2	0		
1986–87	*Oxford U*	5	0	5	0
1987–88	Tottenham H	16	0	37	0
1987–88	*Gillingham*	2	0	2	0
1988–89	Brentford	33	0		
1989–90	Brentford	37	0		
1990–91	Brentford	1	0	71	0
1990–91	QPR	0	0		
1990–91	Fulham	2	0	2	0
1991–92	West Ham U	6	0	6	0
1992–93	Stoke C	2	0	2	0
1992–93	Falkirk	15	0		
1993–94	Falkirk	41	0		
1994–95	Falkirk	28	0		
1995–96	Falkirk	28	0	112	0
1996–97	Blackpool	0	0		
1997–98	Burnley	0	0		
1997–98	*Doncaster R*	6	0	6	0
1998–99	Burnley	0	0		
From Barrow					
1998–99	Scarborough	15	0	15	0
1999–2000	Halifax T	1	0		
2000–01	Halifax T	5	0	6	0

POTTER, Lee (F)   22   2
H: 5 11   W: 12 10   b.Salford 3-9-78
Source: Trainee.

1997–98	Bolton W	0	0		
1998–99	Bolton W	0	0		
1999–2000	Bolton W	0	0		
1999–2000	Halifax T	19	2		
2000–01	Halifax T	3	0	22	2

REDFEARN, Neil (M)   697   139
H: 5 8   W: 12 00   b.Dewsbury 20-6-65
Source: Nottingham F Apprentice.

1982–83	Bolton W	10	0		
1983–84	Bolton W	25	1	35	1
1983–84	Lincoln C	10	1		
1984–85	Lincoln C	45	4		
1985–86	Lincoln C	45	8	100	13
1986–87	Doncaster R	46	14	46	14
1987–88	Crystal Palace	42	0		
1988–89	Crystal Palace	15	2	57	10
1988–89	Watford	12	2		
1989–90	Watford	12	1	24	3
1989–90	Oldham Ath	17	2		
1990–91	Oldham Ath	45	14	62	16
1991–92	Barnsley	36	4		
1992–93	Barnsley	46	3		
1993–94	Barnsley	46	12		
1994–95	Barnsley	39	11		
1995–96	Barnsley	45	14		
1996–97	Barnsley	43	17		
1997–98	Barnsley	37	10	292	71
1998–99	Charlton Ath	30	3	30	3
1999–2000	Bradford C	17	1	17	1
1999–2000	Wigan Ath	12	6		
2000–01	Wigan Ath	10	1	22	7
2000–01	Halifax T	12	0	12	0

REILLY, Alan (M)   43   2
H: 5 11   W: 12 01   b.Dublin 22-8-80
Source: Trainee.

1998–99	Manchester C	0	0		
1999–2000	Manchester C	0	0		
1999–2000	Halifax T	20	0		
2000–01	Halifax T	23	2	43	2

REZAI, Carl (D)   11   0
H: 5 9   W: 11 00   b.Manchester 16-10-82

2000–01	Halifax T	11	0	11	0

RICHARDS, Ian* (M)   24   0
H: 5 8   W: 11 04   b.Barnsley 5-10-79
Source: Trainee.

1997–98	Blackburn R	0	0		
1998–99	Blackburn R	0	0		
1999–2000	Halifax T	6	0		
2000–01	Halifax T	18	0	24	0

SHANNON, Greg‡ (G)   0   0
H: 6 0   W: 11 00   b.Maghreafelt 15-2-81
Source: Trainee.

1997–98	Sunderland	0	0		
1998–99	Sunderland	0	0		
1999–2000	Sunderland	0	0		
2000–01	Halifax T	0	0		

STANSFIELD, James‡ (D)   26   1
H: 6 1   W: 13 04   b.Dewsbury 18-9-78
Source: Trainee.

1997–98	Huddersfield T	0	0		
1998–99	Halifax T	12	1		
1999–2000	Halifax T	12	0		
2000–01	Halifax T	2	0	26	1

STONEMAN, Paul (D)   153   12
H: 6 0   W: 13 06   b.Whitley Bay 26-2-73
Source: Trainee.

1991–92	Blackpool	19	0		
1992–93	Blackpool	10	0		
1993–94	Blackpool	10	0		
1994–95	Blackpool	4	0	43	0
1994–95	*Colchester U*	3	1	3	1
1998–99	Halifax T	40	5		
1999–2000	Halifax T	37	4		
2000–01	Halifax T	30	2	107	11

THOMPSON, Steve* (M)   655   84
H: 5 11   W: 13 00   b.Oldham 2-11-64
Source: Apprentice.

1982–83	Bolton W	3	0		
1983–84	Bolton W	40	3		
1984–85	Bolton W	34	4		
1985–86	Bolton W	35	8		
1986–87	Bolton W	44	7		
1987–88	Bolton W	44	7		
1988–89	Bolton W	43	9		
1989–90	Bolton W	45	6		
1990–91	Bolton W	45	5		
1991–92	Bolton W	2	0	335	49
1991–92	*Luton T*	5	0	5	0
1991–92	Leicester C	34	3		
1992–93	Leicester C	44	8		
1993–94	Leicester C	30	7		
1994–95	Leicester C	19	0	127	18
1994–95	Burnley	12	0		
1995–96	Burnley	18	0		
1996–97	Burnley	19	1	49	1
1997–98	Rotherham U	39	3		
1998–99	Rotherham U	33	5		
1999–2000	Rotherham U	31	6	103	14
2000–01	Halifax T	36	2	36	2

UNDERWOOD, Steven‡ (D)   0   0
H: 5 9   W: 11 00   b.Hull 16-3-82
Source: Scholar.

2000–01	Halifax T	0	0		

WILDER, Chris (D)   414   14
H: 5 11   W: 12 07   b.Stocksbridge 23-9-67
Source: Apprentice.

1985–86	Southampton	0	0		
1986–87	Sheffield U	11	0		
1987–88	Sheffield U	25	0		
1988–89	Sheffield U	29	1		
1989–90	Sheffield U	8	0		
1989–90	*Walsall*	4	0	4	0

1990–91	Sheffield U	16	0		
1990–91	*Charlton Ath*	1	0		
1991–92	Sheffield U	4	0		
1991–92	*Charlton Ath*	2	0	3	0
1991–92	*Leyton Orient*	16	1	16	1
1992–93	Rotherham U	32	8		
1993–94	Rotherham U	37	2		
1994–95	Rotherham U	45	1		
1995–96	Rotherham U	18	0	132	11
1995–96	Notts Co	9	0		
1996–97	Notts Co	37	0	46	0
1996–97	Bradford C	7	0		
1997–98	Bradford C	35	0	42	0
1997–98	Sheffield U	8	0		
1998–99	Sheffield U	4	0	105	1
1998–99	*Northampton T*	1	0	1	0
1998–99	*Lincoln C*	3	0	3	0
1999–2000	Brighton & HA	11	0	11	0
1999–2000	Halifax T	31	1		
2000–01	Halifax T	20	0	51	1

Scholars
Birchall, Gary N; Boulton, Matthew J; Dunnan, Ryan P; Farrell, Andrew; Harris, Chad; Lawler, Alex; Liversidge, Gareth J; Moores, Andrew M; Myers, Peter W; Smith, Craig M; Speight, Simon; Tyrell-Nestor, James A; Vincent, Alexander C; Winder, Nathan J; Woodcock, Gary R
Non-Contract
Bracewell, Paul W

HARTLEPOOL U

ARNISON, Paul (D) 35 2
H: 5 10 W: 11 08 b.Hartlepool 18-9-77
Source: Trainee.

1995–96	Newcastle U	0	0		
1996–97	Newcastle U	0	0		
1997–98	Newcastle U	0	0		
1998–99	Newcastle U	0	0		
1999–2000	Newcastle U	0	0		
1999–2000	Hartlepool U	8	1		
2000–01	Hartlepool U	27	1	35	2

ASPIN, Neil* (D) 615 8
H: 6 0 W: 13 00 b.Gateshead 12-4-65
Source: Apprentice.

1981–82	Leeds U	1	0		
1982–83	Leeds U	15	0		
1983–84	Leeds U	21	1		
1984–85	Leeds U	32	1		
1985–86	Leeds U	38	2		
1986–87	Leeds U	41	1		
1987–88	Leeds U	26	0		
1988–89	Leeds U	33	0	207	5
1989–90	Port Vale	42	0		
1990–91	Port Vale	41	1		
1991–92	Port Vale	42	0		
1992–93	Port Vale	35	0		
1993–94	Port Vale	40	1		
1994–95	Port Vale	37	0		
1995–96	Port Vale	22	1		
1996–97	Port Vale	33	0		
1997–98	Port Vale	26	0		
1998–99	Port Vale	30	0	348	3
1999–2000	Darlington	29	0		
2000–01	Darlington	21	0	50	0
2000–01	Hartlepool U	10	0	10	0

BARRON, Micky (D) 158 1
H: 5 11 W: 11 04 b.Lumley 22-12-74
Source: Trainee.

1992–93	Middlesbrough	0	0		
1993–94	Middlesbrough	2	0		
1994–95	Middlesbrough	0	0		
1995–96	Middlesbrough	1	0		
1996–97	Middlesbrough	0	0	3	0
1996–97	*Hartlepool U*	16	0		
1997–98	Hartlepool U	33	0		
1998–99	Hartlepool U	38	1		
1999–2000	Hartlepool U	40	0		
2000–01	Hartlepool U	28	0	155	1

BOYD, Adam (F) 9 1
H: 5 9 W: 10 12 b.Hartlepool 25-5-82
Source: Scholarship.

| 1999–2000 | Hartlepool U | 4 | 1 | | |
| 2000–01 | Hartlepool U | 5 | 0 | 9 | 1 |

BROWNRIGG, Andrew‡ (D) 8 0
H: 6 0 W: 11 11 b.Sheffield 2-8-76
Source: Trainee.

1994–95	Hereford U	8	0	8	0
1994–95	Norwich C	0	0		
1995–96	Norwich C	0	0		
1996–97	Norwich C	0	0		

From Kidderminster H.

| 2000–01 | Hartlepool U | 0 | 0 | | |

CLARK, Ian# (F) 176 18
H: 5 10 W: 11 04 b.Stockton 23-10-74
Source: Stockton.

1995–96	Doncaster R	23	1		
1996–97	Doncaster R	20	2		
1997–98	Doncaster R	2	0	45	3
1997–98	Hartlepool U	24	7		
1998–99	Hartlepool U	39	2		
1999–2000	Hartlepool U	44	6		
2000–01	Hartlepool U	24	0	131	15

EASTER, Jermaine (F) 4 0
H: 5 9 W: 11 04 b.Cardiff 15-1-82
Source: Trainee.

| 2000–01 | Wolverhampton W | 0 | 0 | | |
| 2000–01 | Hartlepool U | 4 | 0 | 4 | 0 |

FITZPATRICK, Lee* (M) 47 6
H: 5 10 W: 11 02 b.Manchester 31-10-78
Source: Trainee.

1996–97	Blackburn R	0	0		
1997–98	Blackburn R	0	0		
1998–99	Blackburn R	0	0		
1999–2000	Blackburn R	0	0		
1999–2000	Hartlepool U	24	2		
2000–01	Hartlepool U	23	4	47	6

HENDERSON, Kevin (F) 89 26
H: 5 11 W: 13 04 b.Ashington 8-6-74
Source: Morpeth Town.

1997–98	Burnley	7	0		
1998–99	Burnley	7	1	14	1
1999–2000	Hartlepool U	35	8		
2000–01	Hartlepool U	40	17	75	25

HOLLUND, Martin# (G) 138 0
H: 6 2 W: 12 09 b.Stord 11-8-74

1994	Brann	3	0		
1995	Brann	15	0		
1996	Brann	0	0		
1997	Brann	6	0	24	0
1997–98	Hartlepool U	28	0		
1998–99	Hartlepool U	41	0		
1999–2000	Hartlepool U	40	0		
2000–01	Hartlepool U	5	0	114	0

KNOWLES, Darren* (D) 375 4
H: 5 6 W: 11 02 b.Sheffield 8-10-70
Source: Trainee.

1989–90	Sheffield U	0	0		
1989–90	Stockport Co	9	0		
1990–91	Stockport Co	12	0		
1991–92	Stockport Co	31	0		
1992–93	Stockport Co	11	0	63	0
1993–94	Scarborough	42	1		
1994–95	Scarborough	39	0		
1995–96	Scarborough	46	1		
1996–97	Scarborough	17	0	144	2
1996–97	Hartlepool U	7	0		
1997–98	Hartlepool U	46	1		
1998–99	Hartlepool U	46	0		
1999–2000	Hartlepool U	44	0		
2000–01	Hartlepool U	25	1	168	2

LEE, Graeme (D) 135 13
H: 6 2 W: 13 07 b.Middlesbrough 31-5-78
Source: Trainee.

1995–96	Hartlepool U	6	0		
1996–97	Hartlepool U	24	0		
1997–98	Hartlepool U	37	3		
1998–99	Hartlepool U	24	3		
1999–2000	Hartlepool U	38	7		
2000–01	Hartlepool U	6	0	135	13

LORMOR, Tony (F) 350 99
H: 6 1 W: 14 02 b.Ashington 29-10-70
Source: Trainee.

1987–88	Newcastle U	5	2		
1988–89	Newcastle U	3	1		
1988–89	Norwich C	0	0		
1989–90	Newcastle U	0	0	8	3
1989–90	Lincoln C	21	8		
1990–91	Lincoln C	34	12		
1991–92	Lincoln C	35	9		
1992–93	Lincoln C	0	0		
1993–94	Lincoln C	10	1	100	30
1994–95	Peterborough U	5	0	5	0
1994–95	Chesterfield	23	10		
1995–96	Chesterfield	41	13		
1996–97	Chesterfield	36	8		
1997–98	Chesterfield	13	4	113	35
1997–98	Preston NE	12	3	12	3
1997–98	Notts Co	0	0	7	0
1998–99	Mansfield T	41	11		
1999–2000	Mansfield T	33	9	74	20
2000–01	Hartlepool U	31	8	31	8

McAVOY, Andy* (M) 21 0
H: 6 0 W: 13 06 b.Middlesbrough 28-8-79
Source: Trainee.

1997–98	Blackburn R	0	0		
1998–99	Blackburn R	0	0		
1999–2000	Blackburn R	0	0		
1999–2000	Hartlepool U	16	0		
2000–01	Hartlepool U	5	0	21	0

MIDGLEY, Craig* (F) 130 22
H: 5 7 W: 11 03 b.Bradford 24-5-76
Source: Trainee.

1994–95	Bradford C	3	0		
1995–96	Bradford C	5	1		
1995–96	Scarborough	16	1		
1996–97	Bradford C	1	0		
1996–97	Scarborough	6	2	22	3
1997–98	Bradford C	2	0	11	1
1997–98	Darlington	1	0	1	0
1997–98	Hartlepool U	9	3		
1998–99	Hartlepool U	29	7		
1999–2000	Hartlepool U	17	0		
2000–01	Hartlepool U	41	8	96	18

MILLER, Tommy (M) 137 35
H: 6 1 W: 12 01 b.Easington 8-1-79
Source: Trainee.

1997–98	Hartlepool U	13	1		
1998–99	Hartlepool U	34	4		
1999–2000	Hartlepool U	44	14		
2000–01	Hartlepool U	46	16	137	35

ROBINSON, Mark (D) 6 0
H: 5 9 W: 11 00 b.Guisborough 24-7-81
Source: Trainee.

| 1999–2000 | Hartlepool U | 0 | 0 | | |
| 2000–01 | Hartlepool U | 6 | 0 | 6 | 0 |

SHARP, James (D) 34 2
H: 6 2 W: 13 07 b.Reading 2-1-76
Source: Reading, Florida Tech, Aldershot T, Wokingham, Andover T.

| 2000–01 | Hartlepool U | 34 | 2 | 34 | 2 |

SHILTON, Sam* (M) 64 7
H: 5 11 W: 11 06 b.Nottingham 21-7-78
Source: School.

1994–95	Plymouth Arg	2	0		
1995–96	Plymouth Arg	1	0	3	0
1995–96	Coventry C	0	0		
1996–97	Coventry C	0	0		
1997–98	Coventry C	2	0		
1998–99	Coventry C	5	0		
1999–2000	Coventry C	0	0	7	0
1999–2000	Hartlepool U	21	3		
2000–01	Hartlepool U	33	4	54	7

SIMMS, Gordon (D) 0 0
H: 6 2 W: 12 06 b.Larne 23-3-81
Source: Trainee. *Honours:* Northern Ireland Under-21.

1997–98	Wolverhampton W	0	0		
1998–99	Wolverhampton W	0	0		
1999–2000	Wolverhampton W	0	0		
2000–01	Wolverhampton W	0	0		
2000–01	Hartlepool U	0	0		

SPERREVIK, Tim‡ (F) 15 1
b.Bergen 2-3-76
Source: Fana.

| 2000–01 | Hartlepool U | 15 | 1 | 15 | 1 |

STEPHENSON, Paul (M) 454 28
H: 5 10 W: 12 06 b.Wallsend 2-1-68
Source: Apprentice. *Honours:* England Youth.

1985–86	Newcastle U	22	1		
1986–87	Newcastle U	24	0		
1987–88	Newcastle U	7	0		
1988–89	Newcastle U	8	0	61	1
1989–90	Millwall	12	1		
1989–90	Millwall	23	2		
1990–91	Millwall	30	1		
1991–92	Millwall	28	2		
1992–93	Millwall	5	0	98	6
1992–93	*Gillingham*	12	2	12	2
1992–93	Brentford	11	0		
1993–94	Brentford	25	0		
1994–95	Brentford	34	2	70	2
1995–96	York C	27	2		
1996–97	York C	35	1		
1997–98	York C	35	5	97	8
1997–98	Hartlepool U	3	0		
1998–99	Hartlepool U	27	2		
1999–2000	Hartlepool U	46	5		
2000–01	Hartlepool U	40	2	116	9

STRODDER, Gary* (D) 522 26
H: 6 1 W: 13 07 b.Cleckheaton 1-4-65
Source: Apprentice.

1982–83	Lincoln C	8	0		
1983–84	Lincoln C	22	1		
1984–85	Lincoln C	26	2		
1985–86	Lincoln C	43	1		
1986–87	Lincoln C	33	2	132	6
1986–87	West Ham U	12	0		
1987–88	West Ham U	30	1		
1988–89	West Ham U	7	0		
1989–90	West Ham U	16	1	65	2
1990–91	WBA	34	1		

Season	Club				
1991–92	WBA	37	3		
1992–93	WBA	29	1		
1993–94	WBA	21	2		
1994–95	WBA	19	1	140	8
1995–96	Notts Co	43	3		
1996–97	Notts Co	28	2		
1997–98	Notts Co	39	4		
1998–99	Notts Co	11	1	121	10
1998–99	Rotherham U	3	0	3	0
1998–99	Hartlepool U	13	0		
1999–2000	Hartlepool U	29	0		
2000–01	Hartlepool U	19	0	61	0

TENNEBO, Thomas# (M) 13 0
H: 6 2 W: 12 00 b.Bergen 19-3-75
Source: Fana.

Season	Club				
1999–2000	Hartlepool U	11	0		
2000–01	Hartlepool U	2	0	13	0

TINKLER, Mark (M) 199 12
H: 6 2 W: 13 00 b.Bishop Auckland 24-10-74
Source: Trainee. *Honours:* England Schools, Youth.

Season	Club				
1991–92	Leeds U	0	0		
1992–93	Leeds U	7	0		
1993–94	Leeds U	3	0		
1994–95	Leeds U	3	0		
1995–96	Leeds U	9	0		
1996–97	Leeds U	3	0	25	0
1996–97	York C	9	1		
1997–98	York C	44	5		
1998–99	York C	37	2		
1999–2000	York C	0	0	90	8
1999–2000	Southend U	41	0		
2000–01	Southend U	15	1	56	1
2000–01	Hartlepool U	28	3	28	3

WEST, Colin* (F) 458 128
H: 6 1 W: 13 11 b.Wallsend 13-11-62
Source: Apprentice.

Season	Club				
1980–81	Sunderland	0	0		
1981–82	Sunderland	18	6		
1982–83	Sunderland	23	3		
1983–84	Sunderland	38	9		
1984–85	Sunderland	23	3	102	21
1984–85	Watford	12	7		
1985–86	Watford	33	13	45	20
1986–87	Rangers	9	2		
1987–88	Rangers	1	0	10	2
1987–88	Sheffield W	25	7		
1988–89	Sheffield W	20	1	45	8
1988–89	WBA	17	8		
1989–90	WBA	21	4		
1990–91	WBA	28	8		
1991–92	WBA	7	2	73	22
1991–92	Port Vale	5	1	5	1
1992–93	Swansea C	33	12	33	12
1993–94	Leyton Orient	43	14		
1994–95	Leyton Orient	30	9		
1995–96	Leyton Orient	39	16		
1996–97	Leyton Orient	23	3		
1997–98	Leyton Orient	7	0	142	42
1997–98	Northampton T	2	0	2	0

From Rushden, Northwich Vic.

Season	Club				
1999–2000	Hartlepool U	1	0		
2000–01	Hartlepool U	0	0	1	0

WESTWOOD, Chris (D) 91 2
H: 5 11 W: 12 03 b.Dudley 13-2-77
Source: Trainee.

Season	Club				
1995–96	Wolverhampton W	0	0		
1996–97	Wolverhampton W	0	0		
1997–98	Wolverhampton W	4	1		
1998–99	Wolverhampton W	0	0	4	1
1998–99	Hartlepool U	4	0		
1999–2000	Hartlepool U	37	0		
2000–01	Hartlepool U	46	1	87	1

WILLIAMS, Anthony (G) 67 0
H: 6 1 W: 12 13 b.Ogwr 20-9-77
Source: Trainee. *Honours:* Wales Under-21.

Season	Club				
1996–97	Blackburn R	0	0		
1997–98	Blackburn R	0	0		
1997–98	QPR	0	0		
1998–99	Blackburn R	0	0		
1998–99	Macclesfield T	4	0		
1998–99	Huddersfield T	0	0		
1998–99	Bristol R	9	0	9	0
1999–2000	Blackburn R	0	0		
1999–2000	Gillingham	2	0	2	0
1999–2000	Macclesfield T	11	0	15	0
2000–01	Hartlepool U	41	0	41	0

Scholars
Batey, Marc; Dunkerley, Mark G; Flett, Martyn J; Flockett, Stephen; Hill, Andrew S; Hill, Terence; Lawlor, Terence S; Manson, Stephen; McKenzie, Colin JF; McLean, Stephen; Nesbit, Mark A; Peachey, Lee G; Piggott, David J; Provett, Robert J; Ross, Brian S; Sweeney, Antony T; Wear, Jospeh M

HUDDERSFIELD T

ARMSTRONG, Craig (D) 179 4
H: 5 11 W: 12 10 b.South Shields 23-5-75
Source: Trainee.

Season	Club				
1992–93	Nottingham F	0	0		
1993–94	Nottingham F	0	0		
1994–95	Nottingham F	0	0		
1994–95	Burnley	4	0	4	0
1995–96	Nottingham F	0	0		
1995–96	Bristol R	14	0	14	0
1996–97	Nottingham F	0	0		
1996–97	Gillingham	10	0	10	0
1996–97	Watford	15	0	15	0
1997–98	Nottingham F	18	0		
1998–99	Nottingham F	22	0	40	0
1998–99	Huddersfield T	13	1		
1999–2000	Huddersfield T	39	0		
2000–01	Huddersfield T	44	3	96	4

BALDRY, Simon (M) 125 6
H: 5 10 W: 11 06 b.Huddersfield 12-2-76
Source: Trainee.

Season	Club				
1993–94	Huddersfield T	10	2		
1994–95	Huddersfield T	11	0		
1995–96	Huddersfield T	14	0		
1996–97	Huddersfield T	7	0		
1997–98	Huddersfield T	11	1		
1998–99	Huddersfield T	13	0		
1998–99	Bury	5	0	5	0
1999–2000	Huddersfield T	19	1		
2000–01	Huddersfield T	35	2	120	6

BEECH, Chris (M) 238 37
H: 5 10 W: 11 12 b.Blackpool 16-9-74
Source: Trainee.

Season	Club				
1992–93	Blackpool	1	0		
1993–94	Blackpool	35	2		
1994–95	Blackpool	28	2		
1995–96	Blackpool	18	0	82	4
1996–97	Hartlepool U	42	7		
1997–98	Hartlepool U	36	6		
1998–99	Hartlepool U	16	9	94	22
1998–99	Huddersfield T	17	2		
1999–2000	Huddersfield T	35	9		
2000–01	Huddersfield T	10	0	62	11

BERESFORD, David* (M) 113 5
H: 5 7 W: 10 06 b.Middleton 11-11-76
Source: Trainee. *Honours:* England Schools, Youth.

Season	Club				
1993–94	Oldham Ath	1	0		
1994–95	Oldham Ath	2	0		
1995–96	Oldham Ath	28	2		
1995–96	Swansea C	6	0	6	0
1996–97	Huddersfield T	6	1		
1997–98	Huddersfield T	8	0		
1998–99	Huddersfield T	19	2		
1999–2000	Huddersfield T	0	0		
1999–2000	Preston NE	4	0	4	0
2000–01	Huddersfield T	2	0	35	3
2000–01	Port Vale	4	0	4	0

BOOTH, Andy (F) 268 85
H: 6 0 W: 13 00 b.Huddersfield 6-12-73
Source: Trainee. *Honours:* England Under-21.

Season	Club				
1991–92	Huddersfield T	3	0		
1992–93	Huddersfield T	5	2		
1993–94	Huddersfield T	26	10		
1994–95	Huddersfield T	46	26		
1995–96	Huddersfield T	43	16		
1996–97	Sheffield W	35	10		
1997–98	Sheffield W	23	7		
1998–99	Sheffield W	34	6		
1999–2000	Sheffield W	23	2		
2000–01	Sheffield W	18	3	133	28
2000–01	Tottenham H	4	0	4	0
2000–01	Huddersfield T	8	3	131	57

BROWN, Nathaniel (F) 0 0
H: 6 2 W: 12 05 b.Sheffield 15-6-81
Source: Trainee.

Season	Club				
1999–2000	Huddersfield T	0	0		
2000–01	Huddersfield T	0	0		

DYSON, Jon# (D) 213 9
H: 6 1 W: 12 09 b.Mirfield 18-12-71
Source: School.

Season	Club				
1991–92	Huddersfield T	0	0		
1992–93	Huddersfield T	15	0		
1993–94	Huddersfield T	22	0		
1994–95	Huddersfield T	28	2		
1995–96	Huddersfield T	17	0		
1996–97	Huddersfield T	23	0		
1997–98	Huddersfield T	36	1		
1998–99	Huddersfield T	14	1		
1999–2000	Huddersfield T	28	2		
2000–01	Huddersfield T	30	3	213	9

FACEY, Delroy (F) 62 13
H: 6 0 W: 13 00 b.Huddersfield 22-4-80
Source: Trainee.

Season	Club				
1996–97	Huddersfield T	3	0		
1997–98	Huddersfield T	3	0		
1998–99	Huddersfield T	20	3		
1999–2000	Huddersfield T	2	0		
2000–01	Huddersfield T	34	10	62	13

GALLEN, Kevin* (F) 209 46
H: 5 11 W: 13 05 b.Hammersmith 21-9-75
Source: Trainee. *Honours:* England Schools, Youth, Under-21.

Season	Club				
1992–93	QPR	0	0		
1993–94	QPR	0	0		
1994–95	QPR	37	10		
1995–96	QPR	30	8		
1996–97	QPR	2	3		
1997–98	QPR	27	3		
1998–99	QPR	44	8		
1999–2000	QPR	31	4	171	36
2000–01	Huddersfield T	38	10	38	10

GORRE, Dean (M) 251 42
H: 5 8 W: 11 07 b.Surinam 10-9-70
Source: Trainee.

Season	Club				
1991–92	SVV/Dordrecht	32	8	32	8
1992–93	Feyenoord	25	2		
1993–94	Feyenoord	12	3		
1994–95	Feyenoord	5	1	42	6
1994–95	Groningen	12	3		
1995–96	Groningen	34	4		
1996–97	Groningen	34	11	80	18
1997–98	Ajax	21	3		
1998–99	Ajax	14	1	35	4
1999–2000	Huddersfield T	28	4		
2000–01	Huddersfield T	34	2	62	6

GRAY, Kevin (D) 328 8
H: 6 0 W: 14 00 b.Sheffield 7-1-72
Source: Trainee.

Season	Club				
1988–89	Mansfield T	1	0		
1989–90	Mansfield T	16	0		
1990–91	Mansfield T	31	1		
1991–92	Mansfield T	18	0		
1992–93	Mansfield T	33	0		
1993–94	Mansfield T	42	2	141	3
1994–95	Huddersfield T	5	0		
1995–96	Huddersfield T	38	0		
1996–97	Huddersfield T	39	1		
1997–98	Huddersfield T	35	1		
1998–99	Huddersfield T	34	1		
1999–2000	Huddersfield T	18	2		
2000–01	Stockport Co	1	0	1	0
2000–01	Huddersfield T	17	0	186	5

HAY, Chris (F) 130 34
H: 5 11 W: 11 07 b.Glasgow 28-8-74
Source: Giffnock N.

Season	Club				
1993–94	Celtic	2	0		
1994–95	Celtic	5	0		
1995–96	Celtic	4	0		
1996–97	Celtic	14	4	25	4
1997–98	Swindon T	36	14		
1998–99	Swindon T	27	6		
1999–2000	Swindon T	31	10	94	30
1999–2000	Huddersfield T	7	0		
2000–01	Huddersfield T	4	0	11	0

HEARY, Thomas (D) 40 0
H: 5 10 W: 11 03 b.Dublin 14-2-79
Source: Trainee. *Honours:* Eire Under-21.

Season	Club				
1995–96	Huddersfield T	0	0		
1996–97	Huddersfield T	5	0		
1997–98	Huddersfield T	3	0		
1998–99	Huddersfield T	3	0		
1999–2000	Huddersfield T	1	0		
2000–01	Huddersfield T	28	0	40	0

HOLLAND, Chris (M) 120 1
H: 5 9 W: 11 05 b.Whalley 11-9-75
Source: Trainee. *Honours:* England Youth, Under-21.

Season	Club				
1993–94	Preston NE	1	0	1	0
1993–94	Newcastle U	3	0		
1994–95	Newcastle U	0	0		
1995–96	Newcastle U	0	0		
1996–97	Newcastle U	0	0	3	0
1996–97	Birmingham C	32	0		
1997–98	Birmingham C	10	0		
1998–99	Birmingham C	14	0		
1999–2000	Birmingham C	14	0	70	0
1999–2000	Huddersfield T	17	1		
2000–01	Huddersfield T	29	0	46	1

IRONS, Kenny (M) 424 57
H: 5 10 W: 11 02 b.Liverpool 4-11-70
Source: Trainee.

Season	Club				
1989–90	Tranmere R	3	0		
1990–91	Tranmere R	32	6		
1991–92	Tranmere R	43	7		
1992–93	Tranmere R	42	7		
1993–94	Tranmere R	34	3		
1994–95	Tranmere R	38	4		

1995–96 Tranmere R 32 3
1996–97 Tranmere R 41 5
1997–98 Tranmere R 43 4
1998–99 Tranmere R 43 15 **351 54**
1999–2000 Huddersfield T 40 3
2000–01 Huddersfield T 33 0 **73 3**

JENKINS, Steve (D) 360 4
H: 5 11 W: 12 03 b.Merthyr 16-7-72
Source: Trainee. *Honours:* Wales Under-21, 14 full caps.
1990–91 Swansea C 1 0
1991–92 Swansea C 34 0
1992–93 Swansea C 33 0
1993–94 Swansea C 40 1
1994–95 Swansea C 42 0
1995–96 Swansea C 15 0 **165 1**
1995–96 Huddersfield T 31 1
1996–97 Huddersfield T 33 0
1997–98 Huddersfield T 29 1
1998–99 Huddersfield T 36 1
1999–2000 Huddersfield T 33 0
2000–01 Huddersfield T 30 0 **192 3**
2000–01 *Birmingham C* 3 0 **3 0**

LUCKETTI, Chris (D) 380 11
H: 6 1 W: 13 04 b.Littleborough 21-9-71
Source: Trainee.
1988–89 Rochdale 1 0
1989–90 Rochdale 0 0 **1 0**
1990–91 Stockport Co 0 0
1991–92 Halifax T 36 0
1992–93 Halifax T 42 2 **78 2**
1993–94 Bury 27 1
1994–95 Bury 39 3
1995–96 Bury 42 1
1996–97 Bury 38 0
1997–98 Bury 46 2
1998–99 Bury 43 1 **235 8**
1999–2000 Huddersfield T 26 0
2000–01 Huddersfield T 40 1 **66 1**

MACARI, Paul (F) 3 0
H: 5 8 W: 11 11 b.Manchester 23-8-76
Source: Trainee.
1993–94 Stoke C 0 0
1994–95 Stoke C 0 0
1995–96 Stoke C 0 0
1996–97 Stoke C 0 0
1997–98 Stoke C 3 0 **3 0**
1998–99 Sheffield U 0 0
1999–2000 Sheffield U 0 0
2000–01 Huddersfield T 0 0

MARGETSON, Martyn (G) 88 0
H: 6 0 W: 14 00 b.West Neath 8-9-71
Source: Trainee. *Honours:* Wales Under-21.
1990–91 Manchester C 2 0
1991–92 Manchester C 3 0
1992–93 Manchester C 1 0
1993–94 Manchester C 0 0
1993–94 *Bristol R* 3 0 **3 0**
1993–94 *Bolton W* 0 0
1994–95 Manchester C 0 0
1994–95 *Luton T* 0 0
1995–96 Manchester C 0 0
1996–97 Manchester C 17 0
1997–98 Manchester C 28 0 **51 0**
1998–99 Southend U 32 0 **32 0**
1999–2000 Huddersfield T 0 0
2000–01 Huddersfield T 2 0 **2 0**

MATTIS, Dwayne (M) 2 0
H: 5 10 W: 11 00 b.Huddersfield 31-7-81
Source: Trainee.
1998–99 Huddersfield T 2 0
1999–2000 Huddersfield T 0 0
2000–01 Huddersfield T 0 0 **2 0**

MONKOU, Ken‡ (D) 313 13
H: 6 3 W: 14 06 b.Surinam 29-11-64
Source: Feyenoord. *Honours:* Holland Under-21.
1988–89 Chelsea 2 0
1989–90 Chelsea 34 1
1990–91 Chelsea 27 1
1991–92 Chelsea 31 0
1992–93 Chelsea 0 0 **94 2**
1992–93 Southampton 33 1
1993–94 Southampton 35 4
1994–95 Southampton 31 1
1995–96 Southampton 32 2
1996–97 Southampton 13 0
1997–98 Southampton 32 1
1998–99 Southampton 22 1 **198 10**
1999–2000 Huddersfield T 19 1
2000–01 Huddersfield T 2 0 **21 1**

MOSES, Adi (D) 163 3
H: 6 0 W: 12 07 b.Doncaster 4-5-75
Source: School. *Honours:* England Under-21.
1993–94 Barnsley 0 0
1994–95 Barnsley 4 0
1995–96 Barnsley 24 1
1996–97 Barnsley 28 2
1997–98 Barnsley 35 0
1998–99 Barnsley 34 0
1999–2000 Barnsley 12 0
2000–01 Barnsley 14 0 **151 3**
2000–01 Huddersfield T 12 0 **12 0**

SCHOFIELD, Danny (F) 4 0
H: 5 10 W: 11 06 b.Doncaster 10-4-80
Source: Brodsworth.
1998–99 Huddersfield T 1 0
1999–2000 Huddersfield T 2 0
2000–01 Huddersfield T 1 0 **4 0**

SCOTT, Paul (M) 0 0
H: 5 11 W: 12 00 b.Wakefield 5-11-79
Source: Trainee.
1998–99 Huddersfield T 0 0
1999–2000 Huddersfield T 0 0
2000–01 Huddersfield T 0 0

SELLARS, Scott‡ (M) 505 68
H: 5 7 W: 9 10 b.Sheffield 27-11-65
Source: Apprentice. *Honours:* England Under-21.
1982–83 Leeds U 1 0
1983–84 Leeds U 19 3
1984–85 Leeds U 39 7
1985–86 Leeds U 17 2
1986–87 Blackburn R 32 4
1987–88 Blackburn R 42 7
1988–89 Blackburn R 46 2
1989–90 Blackburn R 43 14
1990–91 Blackburn R 9 1
1991–92 Blackburn R 30 7 **202 35**
1992–93 Leeds U 7 0 **83 12**
1992–93 Newcastle U 13 2
1993–94 Newcastle U 30 3
1994–95 Newcastle U 12 0
1995–96 Newcastle U 6 0 **61 5**
1995–96 Bolton W 22 3
1996–97 Bolton W 42 8
1997–98 Bolton W 22 2
1998–99 Bolton W 25 2 **111 15**
1999–2000 Huddersfield T 34 1
2000–01 Huddersfield T 14 0 **48 1**

SENIOR, Michael (M) 4 0
H: 5 9 W: 11 06 b.Huddersfield 3-3-81
Source: Trainee.
1999–2000 Huddersfield T 0 0
2000–01 Huddersfield T 4 0 **4 0**

SENIOR, Philip (M) 0 0
b.Huddersfield 30-10-82
Source: Trainee.
1999–2000 Huddersfield T 0 0
2000–01 Huddersfield T 0 0

SMITH, Martin (F) 187 47
H: 5 11 W: 12 00 b.Sunderland 13-11-74
Source: Trainee. *Honours:* England Schools, Under-21.
1992–93 Sunderland 0 0
1993–94 Sunderland 29 8
1994–95 Sunderland 35 10
1995–96 Sunderland 20 2
1996–97 Sunderland 11 0
1997–98 Sunderland 16 2
1998–99 Sunderland 8 3 **119 25**
1999–2000 Sheffield U 26 10 **26 10**
1999–2000 Huddersfield T 12 4
2000–01 Huddersfield T 30 8 **42 12**

THORNLEY, Ben* (F) 130 8
H: 5 9 W: 11 08 b.Bury 21-4-75
Source: Trainee. *Honours:* England Schools, Under-21.
1992–93 Manchester U 0 0
1993–94 Manchester U 1 0
1994–95 Manchester U 0 0
1995–96 Manchester U 1 0
1995–96 *Stockport Co* 10 1 **10 1**
1995–96 *Huddersfield T* 12 2
1996–97 Manchester U 2 0
1997–98 Manchester U 5 0 **9 0**
1998–99 Huddersfield T 35 4
1999–2000 Huddersfield T 28 1
2000–01 Huddersfield T 36 0 **111 7**

THORRINGTON, John (F) 0 0
H: 5 7 W: 10 05 b.Johannesburg 17-10-79
Source: US College.
1997–98 Manchester U 0 0
1998–99 Manchester U 0 0
1999–2000 Manchester U 0 0
2000–01 Huddersfield T 0 0

VAESEN, Nico (G) 184 0
H: 6 1 W: 13 08 b.Hasselt 28-9-69
Source: Tongeren.
1993–94 CS Brugge 13 0
1994–95 CS Brugge 3 0 **16 0**
1995–96 Aalst 20 0
1996–97 Aalst 0 0
1997–98 Aalst 14 0 **34 0**
1998–99 Huddersfield T 43 0
1999–2000 Huddersfield T 46 0
2000–01 Huddersfield T 45 0 **134 0**

WIJNHARD, Clyde (F) 173 55
H: 5 10 W: 13 04 b.Paramaribo 1-11-73
1992–93 Ajax 4 2
1993–94 Groningen 23 3 **23 3**
1994–95 Ajax 0 0 **4 2**
1995–96 RKC 33 8
1996–97 RKC 17 10 **50 18**
1997–98 Willem II 29 14 **29 14**
1998–99 Leeds U 18 3 **18 3**
1999–2000 Huddersfield T 45 15
2000–01 Huddersfield T 4 0 **49 15**

Scholars
Ahmed, Aadnan; Austin, Ben; Brown, Christopher T; Clapham, Daniel D; Clarke, Doni J; Clarke, Nathan; Fowler, Adam M; Greaves, Robert A; Hay, Nathan A; Holdsworth, Andrew; Kelly, Gregory; Kenworthy, Steven P; Lloyd, Anthony F; Padgett, Lee J; Senior, Christopher M; Simpson, Neil; Stead, Jonathan G; Trueman, Daniel P; Washington, Joe; Worthington, Jonathan A

HULL C

ATKINS, Mark* (M) 449 48
H: 6 1 W: 12 00 b.Doncaster 14-8-68
Honours: England Schools.
1986–87 Scunthorpe U 26 0
1987–88 Scunthorpe U 22 2 **48 2**
1988–89 Blackburn R 46 6
1989–90 Blackburn R 41 7
1990–91 Blackburn R 42 4
1991–92 Blackburn R 44 6
1992–93 Blackburn R 31 5
1993–94 Blackburn R 15 1
1994–95 Blackburn R 34 6
1995–96 Blackburn R 4 0 **257 35**
1995–96 Wolverhampton W 32 3
1996–97 Wolverhampton W 45 4
1997–98 Wolverhampton W 34 2
1998–99 Wolverhampton W 15 0 **126 9**
1999–2000 York C 10 2 **10 2**
2000–01 Doncaster R 0 0
2000–01 Hull C 8 0 **8 0**

BRABIN, Gary (M) 228 25
H: 5 11 W: 14 08 b.Liverpool 9-12-70
Source: Trainee.
1989–90 Stockport Co 1 0
1990–91 Stockport Co 1 0 **2 0**
From Runcorn
1994–95 Doncaster R 28 8
1995–96 Doncaster R 31 3 **59 11**
1995–96 Bury 5 0 **5 0**
1996–97 Blackpool 32 2
1997–98 Blackpool 24 3
1998–99 Blackpool 7 0 **63 5**
1998–99 *Lincoln C* 4 0 **4 0**
1998–99 Hull C 21 4
1999–2000 Hull C 37 3
2000–01 Hull C 37 2 **95 9**

BRACEY, Lee (G) 259 0
H: 6 2 W: 13 02 b.Barking 11-9-68
Source: Trainee.
1987–88 West Ham U 0 0
1988–89 Swansea C 30 0
1989–90 Swansea C 31 0
1990–91 Swansea C 35 0
1991–92 Swansea C 3 0 **99 0**
1991–92 Halifax T 32 0
1992–93 Halifax T 41 0 **73 0**
1993–94 Bury 40 0
1994–95 Bury 6 0
1995–96 Bury 21 0
1996–97 Bury 0 0 **67 0**
1996–97 *Ipswich T* 0 0
1997–98 Ipswich T 0 0
1998–99 Ipswich T 0 0
1999–2000 Hull C 10 0
2000–01 Hull C 10 0 **20 0**

BRADSHAW, Gary (F) 14 0
H: 5 6 W: 10 06 b.Beverley 30-12-82
Source: Scholarship.
1999–2000 Hull C 12 0
2000–01 Hull C 2 0 **14 0**

BROWN, David (F) — 131 23
H: 5 10 W: 12 07 b.Bolton 2-10-78
Source: Trainee.

Season	Club	App	Gls	Tot App	Tot Gls
1995–96	Manchester U	0	0		
1996–97	Manchester U	0	0		
1997–98	Manchester U	0	0		
1997–98	Hull C	7	2		
1998–99	Hull C	42	11		
1999–2000	Hull C	45	6		
2000–01	Hull C	37	4	131	23

EDWARDS, Mike (D) — 133 5
H: 6 1 W: 12 00 b.Hessle 25-4-80
Source: Trainee.

Season	Club	App	Gls	Tot App	Tot Gls
1997–98	Hull C	21	0		
1998–99	Hull C	30	0		
1999–2000	Hull C	40	1		
2000–01	Hull C	42	4	133	5

EYRE, John (F) — 235 65
H: 6 0 W: 12 00 b.Hull 9-10-74
Source: Trainee.

Season	Club	App	Gls	Tot App	Tot Gls
1993–94	Oldham Ath	2	0		
1994–95	Oldham Ath	8	1	10	1
1994–95	Scunthorpe U	9	8		
1995–96	Scunthorpe U	39	10		
1996–97	Scunthorpe U	42	8		
1997–98	Scunthorpe U	42	10		
1998–99	Scunthorpe U	41	15	173	51
1999–2000	Hull C	24	8		
2000–01	Hull C	28	5	52	13

FLETCHER, Gary‡ (F) — 5 0
b.Liverpool 4-6-81
Source: Northwich Vic. *Honours:* England Schools.

Season	Club	App	Gls	Tot App	Tot Gls
2000–01	Hull C	5	0	5	0

FRANCIS, Kevin* (F) — 304 115
H: 6 7 W: 16 12 b.Moseley 6-12-67
Source: Mile Oak R.

Season	Club	App	Gls	Tot App	Tot Gls
1988–89	Derby Co	0	0		
1989–90	Derby Co	8	0		
1990–91	Derby Co	2	0	10	0
1990–91	Stockport Co	13	5		
1991–92	Stockport Co	35	15		
1992–93	Stockport Co	42	28		
1993–94	Stockport Co	45	28		
1994–95	Stockport Co	17	12		
1994–95	Birmingham C	15	8		
1995–96	Birmingham C	19	3		
1996–97	Birmingham C	19	1		
1997–98	Birmingham C	20	1	73	13
1997–98	Oxford U	15	7		
1998–99	Oxford U	18	1		
1999–2000	Oxford U	3	0	36	8
1999–2000	Stockport Co	4	0		
2000–01	Stockport Co	0	0	156	88
2000–01	Exeter C	7	1	7	1
2000–01	Hull C	22	5	22	5

GOODISON, Ian (D) — 54 1
H: 6 1 W: 12 06 b.St James, Jamaica 5-8-72
Source: Olympic Gardens. *Honours:* Jamaica full caps.

Season	Club	App	Gls	Tot App	Tot Gls
1999–2000	Hull C	18	0		
2000–01	Hull C	36	1	54	1

GREAVES, Mark (D) — 148 9
H: 6 1 W: 13 00 b.Hull 22-1-75
Source: Brigg Town.

Season	Club	App	Gls	Tot App	Tot Gls
1996–97	Hull C	30	2		
1997–98	Hull C	25	2		
1998–99	Hull C	25	0		
1999–2000	Hull C	38	3		
2000–01	Hull C	30	2	148	9

HARRIS, Jason (F) — 122 19
H: 6 1 W: 11 07 b.Sutton 24-11-76
Source: Trainee.

Season	Club	App	Gls	Tot App	Tot Gls
1995–96	Crystal Palace	0	0		
1996–97	Crystal Palace	2	0		
1996–97	Bristol R	6	2	6	2
1997–98	Crystal Palace	0	0	2	0
1997–98	Lincoln C	1	0	1	0
1997–98	Leyton Orient	35	6		
1998–99	Leyton Orient	2	1	37	7
1998–99	Preston NE	34	6	34	6
1999–2000	Hull C	29	4		
2000–01	Hull C	9	0	38	4
2000–01	Shrewsbury T	4	0	4	0

JOYCE, Warren (M) — 608 78
H: 5 9 W: 12 00 b.Oldham 20-1-65
Source: School.

Season	Club	App	Gls	Tot App	Tot Gls
1982–83	Bolton W	8	0		
1983–84	Bolton W	45	3		
1984–85	Bolton W	45	5		
1985–86	Bolton W	31	4		
1986–87	Bolton W	44	5		
1987–88	Bolton W	11	0	184	17
1987–88	Preston NE	22	0		
1988–89	Preston NE	40	9		
1989–90	Preston NE	44	11		
1990–91	Preston NE	42	9		
1991–92	Preston NE	29	5	177	34
1992–93	Plymouth Arg	30	3	30	3
1993–94	Burnley	22	4		
1994–95	Burnley	5	0		
1994–95	Hull C	9	3		
1995–96	Burnley	43	5	70	9
1996–97	Hull C	45	5		
1997–98	Hull C	45	4		
1998–99	Hull C	29	2		
1999–2000	Hull C	19	1		
2000–01	Hull C	0	0	147	15

MANN, Neil (M) — 175 9
H: 5 10 W: 12 01 b.Nottingham 19-11-72
Source: Notts Co, Spalding U, Grantham T.

Season	Club	App	Gls	Tot App	Tot Gls
1993–94	Hull C	5	0		
1994–95	Hull C	31	2		
1995–96	Hull C	38	1		
1996–97	Hull C	32	2		
1997–98	Hull C	34	3		
1998–99	Hull C	20	1		
1999–2000	Hull C	2	0		
2000–01	Hull C	13	0	175	9

MATTHEWS, Rob (F) — 205 31
H: 6 0 W: 12 05 b.Slough 14-10-70
Source: Loughborough Univ. *Honours:* England Schools.

Season	Club	App	Gls	Tot App	Tot Gls
1991–92	Notts Co	5	3		
1992–93	Notts Co	8	2		
1993–94	Notts Co	12	3		
1994–95	Notts Co	18	3	43	11
1994–95	Luton T	11	0		
1995–96	Luton T	0	0	11	0
1995–96	York C	17	1	17	1
1995–96	Bury	16	4		
1996–97	Bury	27	5		
1997–98	Bury	15	0		
1998–99	Bury	16	2	74	11
1998–99	Stockport Co	23	2		
1999–2000	Stockport Co	4	1		
1999–2000	Blackpool	6	2	6	2
2000–01	Stockport Co	11	1	38	4
2000–01	Halifax T	8	2	8	2
2000–01	Hull C	8	0	8	0

MORLEY, Ben* (M) — 23 0
H: 5 9 W: 10 01 b.Hull 22-12-80
Source: Trainee.

Season	Club	App	Gls	Tot App	Tot Gls
1997–98	Hull C	8	0		
1998–99	Hull C	12	0		
1999–2000	Hull C	1	0		
2000–01	Hull C	2	0	23	0

MUSSELWHITE, Paul (G) — 481 0
H: 6 2 W: 14 04 b.Portsmouth 22-12-68
Source: Apprentice.

Season	Club	App	Gls	Tot App	Tot Gls
1987–88	Portsmouth	0	0		
1988–89	Scunthorpe U	41	0		
1989–90	Scunthorpe U	29	0		
1990–91	Scunthorpe U	38	0		
1991–92	Scunthorpe U	24	0	132	0
1992–93	Port Vale	41	0		
1993–94	Port Vale	46	0		
1994–95	Port Vale	44	0		
1995–96	Port Vale	39	0		
1996–97	Port Vale	33	0		
1997–98	Port Vale	41	0		
1998–99	Port Vale	38	0		
1999–2000	Port Vale	30	0	312	0
2000–01	Sheffield W	0	0		
2000–01	Hull C	37	0	37	0

PERRY, Jason* (D) — 333 5
H: 5 11 W: 11 12 b.Newport 2-4-70
Source: Trainee. *Honours:* Wales Under-21, B, 1 full cap.

Season	Club	App	Gls	Tot App	Tot Gls
1986–87	Cardiff C	1	0		
1987–88	Cardiff C	3	0		
1988–89	Cardiff C	0	0		
1989–90	Cardiff C	36	0		
1990–91	Cardiff C	43	0		
1991–92	Cardiff C	36	0		
1992–93	Cardiff C	39	3		
1993–94	Cardiff C	40	1		
1994–95	Cardiff C	34	1		
1995–96	Cardiff C	14	0		
1996–97	Cardiff C	35	0	281	5
1997–98	Bristol R	25	0	25	0
1998–99	Lincoln C	12	0	12	0
1998–99	Hull C	8	0		
1999–2000	Hull C	1	0		
2000–01	Hull C	6	0	15	0

PHILPOTT, Lee (M) — 373 29
H: 5 11 W: 11 08 b.Barnet 21-2-70
Source: Trainee.

Season	Club	App	Gls	Tot App	Tot Gls
1987–88	Peterborough U	1	0		
1988–89	Peterborough U	3	0	4	0
1989–90	Cambridge U	42	5		
1990–91	Cambridge U	45	5		
1991–92	Cambridge U	31	5		
1992–93	Cambridge U	16	2	134	17
1992–93	Leicester C	27	3		
1993–94	Leicester C	19	0		
1994–95	Leicester C	23	0		
1995–96	Leicester C	6	0	75	3
1995–96	Blackpool	10	0		
1996–97	Blackpool	26	3		
1997–98	Blackpool	35	2	71	5
1998–99	Lincoln C	24	0		
1999–2000	Lincoln C	23	3	47	3
2000–01	Hull C	42	1	42	1

ROWE, Rodney (F) — 200 35
H: 5 8 W: 12 08 b.Plymouth 30-7-75
Source: Trainee.

Season	Club	App	Gls	Tot App	Tot Gls
1993–94	Huddersfield T	13	1		
1994–95	Huddersfield T	0	0		
1994–95	Scarborough	14	1	14	1
1994–95	Bury	3	0	3	0
1995–96	Huddersfield T	14	1		
1996–97	Huddersfield T	7	0	34	2
1996–97	York C	10	3		
1997–98	York C	41	10		
1998–99	York C	39	7		
1999–2000	York C	7	0	97	20
1999–2000	Halifax T	9	2	9	2
1999–2000	Gillingham	22	4		
2000–01	Gillingham	0	0	22	4
2000–01	Hull C	21	6	21	6

SWALES, Steve* (D) — 165 2
H: 5 8 W: 10 06 b.Whitby 26-12-73
Source: Trainee.

Season	Club	App	Gls	Tot App	Tot Gls
1991–92	Scarborough	4	0		
1992–93	Scarborough	3	0		
1993–94	Scarborough	26	0		
1994–95	Scarborough	21	1	54	1
1995–96	Reading	9	0		
1996–97	Reading	3	0		
1997–98	Reading	31	1		
1998–99	Reading	0	0	43	1
1998–99	Hull C	22	0		
1999–2000	Hull C	20	0		
2000–01	Hull C	26	0	68	0

WHITMORE, Theodore (M) — 43 7
H: 6 2 W: 12 10 b.Jamaica 21-11-72
Source: Seba U. *Honours:* Jamaica full caps.

Season	Club	App	Gls	Tot App	Tot Gls
1999–2000	Hull C	17	2		
2000–01	Hull C	26	5	43	7

WHITNEY, Jon (D) — 188 11
H: 5 10 W: 13 08 b.Nantwich 23-12-70
Source: Winsford U.

Season	Club	App	Gls	Tot App	Tot Gls
1993–94	Huddersfield T	14	0		
1994–95	Huddersfield T	0	0		
1994–95	Wigan Ath	12	0	12	0
1995–96	Huddersfield T	4	0	18	0
1995–96	Lincoln C	26	2		
1996–97	Lincoln C	18	3		
1997–98	Lincoln C	44	1		
1998–99	Lincoln C	13	2	101	8
1998–99	Hull C	21	1		
1999–2000	Hull C	21	1		
2000–01	Hull C	15	1	57	3

WHITTLE, Justin (D) — 179 2
H: 6 1 W: 12 12 b.Derby 18-3-71
Source: Celtic.

Season	Club	App	Gls	Tot App	Tot Gls
1994–95	Stoke C	0	0		
1995–96	Stoke C	8	0		
1996–97	Stoke C	37	0		
1997–98	Stoke C	20	0		
1998–99	Stoke C	14	1	79	1
1998–99	Hull C	24	1		
1999–2000	Hull C	38	0		
2000–01	Hull C	38	0	100	1

WILSON, Steve* (G) — 182 0
H: 5 10 W: 10 12 b.Hull 24-4-74
Source: Trainee.

Season	Club	App	Gls	Tot App	Tot Gls
1990–91	Hull C	2	0		
1991–92	Hull C	3	0		
1992–93	Hull C	26	0		
1993–94	Hull C	9	0		
1994–95	Hull C	20	0		
1995–96	Hull C	19	0		
1996–97	Hull C	15	0		
1997–98	Hull C	37	0		
1998–99	Hull C	23	0		
1999–2000	Hull C	27	0		
2000–01	Hull C	0	0	181	0
2000–01	Macclesfield T	1	0	1	0

WOOD, Jamie* (F) 47 6
H: 5 10 W: 13 04 b.Salford 21-9-78
Source: Trainee.
1997–98	Manchester U	0	0	
1998–99	Manchester U	0	0	
1999–2000	Hull C	32	6	
2000–01	Hull C	15	0	47 6

Scholars
Bolder, Christopher J; Bowsley, Anthony J;
Burton, Steven PG; Chapman, Liam J;
Crutwell, Ian G; Dixon, Christopher;
Donaldson, Clayton A; Flower, Clayton J;
Kaveney, Glen; Lafferty, Mark A; McIntosh,
Neil G; Peat, Nathan NM; Poole, Philip J;
Van Der Ville, Lenuel N; Waslin, Daniel;
Woodward, Oliver

IPSWICH T

ABIDALLAH, Nabil (M) 2 0
H: 5 7 W: 9 00 b.Amsterdam 5-8-82
2000–01	Ipswich T	2	0	2 0

ARMSTRONG, Alun (F) 215 64
H: 6 0 W: 13 08 b.Gateshead 22-2-75
Source: School.
1993–94	Newcastle U	0	0	
1994–95	Stockport Co	45	14	
1995–96	Stockport Co	46	13	
1996–97	Stockport Co	39	9	
1997–98	Stockport Co	29	12	159 48
1997–98	Middlesbrough	11	7	
1998–99	Middlesbrough	6	1	
1999–2000	Middlesbrough	12	1	
1999–2000	*Huddersfield T*	6	0	6 0
2000–01	Middlesbrough	0	0	29 9
2000–01	Ipswich T	21	7	21 7

ARTUN, Erdem (D) 0 0
b.London 11-11-82
Source: Trainee.
1999–2000	Ipswich T	0	0
2000–01	Ipswich T	0	0

BEEVERS, Lee (D) 0 0
H: 6 2 W: 11 07 b.Doncaster 4-12-83
Source: Scholar.
2000–01	Ipswich T	0	0

BRAMBLE, Titus (D) 32 1
H: 6 2 W: 14 10 b.Ipswich 21-7-81
Source: Trainee. *Honours:* England
Under-21.
1998–99	Ipswich T	4	0	
1999–2000	Ipswich T	0	0	
1999–2000	*Colchester U*	2	0	2 0
2000–01	Ipswich T	26	1	30 1

BRANAGAN, Keith (G) 375 0
H: 6 0 W: 14 00 b.Fulham 10-7-66
Honours: Eire B. 1 full cap.
1983–84	Cambridge U	1	0	
1984–85	Cambridge U	19	0	
1985–86	Cambridge U	9	0	
1986–87	Cambridge U	46	0	
1987–88	Cambridge U	35	0	110 0
1987–88	Millwall	0	0	
1988–89	Millwall	0	0	
1989–90	Millwall	16	0	
1989–90	*Brentford*	2	0	2 0
1990–91	Millwall	18	0	
1991–92	Millwall	12	0	46 0
1991–92	*Gillingham*	1	0	1 0
1991–92	*Fulham*	0	0	
1992–93	Bolton W	46	0	
1993–94	Bolton W	10	0	
1994–95	Bolton W	43	0	
1995–96	Bolton W	31	0	
1996–97	Bolton W	36	0	
1997–98	Bolton W	34	0	
1998–99	Bolton W	3	0	
1999–2000	Bolton W	11	0	214 0
1999–2000	Ipswich T	0	0	
2000–01	Ipswich T	2	0	2 0

BROWN, Wayne (D) 35 0
H: 6 0 W: 12 06 b.Barking 20-8-77
Source: Trainee.
1995–96	Ipswich T	0	0	
1996–97	Ipswich T	0	0	
1997–98	Ipswich T	1	0	
1997–98	*Colchester U*	2	0	2 0
1998–99	Ipswich T	1	0	
1999–2000	Ipswich T	25	0	
2000–01	Ipswich T	4	0	31 0
2000–01	*QPR*	2	0	2 0

BURCHILL, Mark (F) 43 15
H: 5 8 W: 9 9 b.Broxburn 18-8-80
Source: Celtic BC. *Honours:* Scotland
Under-21, 6 full caps.
1997–98	Celtic	0	0	
1998–99	Celtic	21	9	
1999–2000	Celtic	0	0	
2000–01	Celtic	2	1	23 10
2000–01	*Birmingham C*	13	4	13 4
2000–01	*Ipswich T*	7	1	7 1

CLAPHAM, Jamie (M) 161 7
H: 5 9 W: 11 05 b.Lincoln 7-12-75
Source: Trainee.
1994–95	Tottenham H	0	0	
1995–96	Tottenham H	0	0	
1996–97	Tottenham H	1	0	
1996–97	*Leyton Orient*	6	0	6 0
1996–97	*Bristol R*	5	0	5 0
1997–98	Tottenham H	0	0	1 0
1997–98	Ipswich T	22	0	
1998–99	Ipswich T	46	3	
1999–2000	Ipswich T	46	2	
2000–01	Ipswich T	35	2	149 7

CROFT, Gary (D) 218 5
H: 5 8 W: 11 08 b.Stafford 17-2-74
Source: Trainee. *Honours:* England
Under-21.
1990–91	Grimsby T	1	0	
1991–92	Grimsby T	0	0	
1992–93	Grimsby T	32	0	
1993–94	Grimsby T	36	1	
1994–95	Grimsby T	44	1	
1995–96	Grimsby T	36	1	149 3
1995–96	Blackburn R	0	0	
1996–97	Blackburn R	5	0	
1997–98	Blackburn R	23	1	
1998–99	Blackburn R	12	0	
1999–2000	Blackburn R	0	0	40 1
1999–2000	Ipswich T	21	1	
2000–01	Ipswich T	8	0	29 1

DALY, Colm‡ (D) 0 0
H: 5 8 W: 10 07 b.Dublin 4-1-82
2000–01	Ipswich T	0	0

DICKINSON, Robert (M) 0 0
H: 5 9 W: 10 00 b.Leeds 27-11-83
Source: Scholar.
2000–01	Ipswich T	0	0

FRIARS, Sean* (F) 1 0
H: 5 8 W: 10 07 b.Derry 15-5-79
Source: Trainee. *Honours:* Northern Ireland
Under-21.
1995–96	Liverpool	0	0	
1996–97	Liverpool	0	0	
1997–98	Liverpool	0	0	
1998–99	Ipswich T	0	0	
1999–2000	Ipswich T	1	0	
2000–01	Ipswich T	0	0	1 0

GRAAVEN, Guillermo (M) 0 0
H: 6 0 W: 11 06 b.Amsterdam 17-1-82
2000–01	Ipswich T	0	0

HOLLAND, Matt (M) 280 45
H: 5 9 W: 12 07 b.Bury 11-4-74
Source: Trainee. *Honours:* Eire 11 full caps, 4
goals.
1992–93	West Ham U	0	0	
1993–94	West Ham U	0	0	
1994–95	West Ham U	0	0	
1994–95	Bournemouth	16	1	
1995–96	Bournemouth	43	10	
1996–97	Bournemouth	45	7	104 18
1997–98	Ipswich T	46	10	
1998–99	Ipswich T	46	5	
1999–2000	Ipswich T	46	10	
2000–01	Ipswich T	38	3	176 28

HREIDARSSON, Hermann (D) 204 15
H: 6 3 W: 13 01 b.Iceland 11-7-74
Honours: Iceland 37 full caps, 2 goals.
1993	IBV	2	0	
1994	IBV	18	2	
1995	IBV	18	1	
1996	IBV	17	2	
1997	IBV	11	0	66 5
1997–98	Crystal Palace	30	2	
1998–99	Crystal Palace	7	0	37 2
1998–99	Brentford	33	4	
1999–2000	Brentford	8	2	41 6
1999–2000	Wimbledon	24	1	24 1
2000–01	Ipswich T	36	1	36 1

KARIC, Amir (D) 3 0
H: 5 11 W: 12 07 b.Oramovica Ponja
31-12-73
Honours: Slovenia 33 full caps, 1 goal.
2000–01	Ipswich T	0	0	
2000–01	*Crystal Palace*	3	0	3 0

LOGAN, Richard (F) 8 1
H: 6 0 W: 12 05 b.Bury St Edmunds 4-1-82
Source: Trainee. *Honours:* England Youth.
1998–99	Ipswich T	2	0	
1999–2000	Ipswich T	1	0	
2000–01	Ipswich T	0	0	3 0
2000–01	*Cambridge U*	5	1	5 1

MAGILTON, Jim (M) 397 56
H: 6 0 W: 13 10 b.Belfast 6-5-69
Source: Apprentice. *Honours:* Northern
Ireland Under-21, 47 full caps, 5 goals.
Football League.
1986–87	Liverpool	0	0	
1987–88	Liverpool	0	0	
1988–89	Liverpool	0	0	
1989–90	Liverpool	0	0	
1990–91	Liverpool	0	0	
1990–91	Oxford U	37	6	
1991–92	Oxford U	44	12	
1992–93	Oxford U	40	11	
1993–94	Oxford U	29	5	150 34
1993–94	Southampton	15	0	
1994–95	Southampton	42	6	
1995–96	Southampton	31	3	
1996–97	Southampton	37	4	
1997–98	Southampton	5	0	130 13
1997–98	Sheffield W	21	1	
1998–99	Sheffield W	6	0	27 1
1998–99	Ipswich T	19	3	
1999–2000	Ipswich T	38	4	
2000–01	Ipswich T	33	1	90 8

MAKIN, Chris (D) 268 7
H: 5 11 W: 12 11 b.Manchester 8-5-73
Source: Trainee. *Honours:* England Schools.
Under-21.
1991–92	Oldham Ath	0	0	
1992–93	Oldham Ath	0	0	
1992–93	*Wigan Ath*	15	2	15 2
1993–94	Oldham Ath	27	1	
1994–95	Oldham Ath	28	1	
1995–96	Oldham Ath	39	2	94 4
1996–97	Marseille	29	0	29 0
1997–98	Sunderland	25	0	
1998–99	Sunderland	38	0	
1999–2000	Sunderland	34	1	
2000–01	Sunderland	23	0	120 1
2000–01	Ipswich T	10	0	10 0

McGREAL, John (D) 257 2
H: 5 11 W: 13 00 b.Birkenhead 2-6-72
Source: Trainee.
1990–91	Tranmere R	3	0	
1991–92	Tranmere R	0	0	
1992–93	Tranmere R	0	0	
1993–94	Tranmere R	15	1	
1994–95	Tranmere R	43	0	
1995–96	Tranmere R	32	0	
1996–97	Tranmere R	24	0	
1997–98	Tranmere R	42	0	
1998–99	Tranmere R	36	0	195 1
1999–2000	Ipswich T	34	0	
2000–01	Ipswich T	28	1	62 1

MILLER, Justin (D) 0 0
H: 6 0 W: 11 07 b.Johannesburg 16-12-80
Source: Academy.
1999–2000	Ipswich T	0	0
2000–01	Ipswich T	0	0

MOWBRAY, Tony* (D) 554 36
H: 6 1 W: 13 00 b.Saltburn 22-11-63
Source: Apprentice. *Honours:* England B.
1981–82	Middlesbrough	0	0	
1982–83	Middlesbrough	26	0	
1983–84	Middlesbrough	35	1	
1984–85	Middlesbrough	40	2	
1985–86	Middlesbrough	35	4	
1986–87	Middlesbrough	46	7	
1987–88	Middlesbrough	44	3	
1988–89	Middlesbrough	37	3	
1989–90	Middlesbrough	28	2	
1990–91	Middlesbrough	40	3	
1991–92	Middlesbrough	17	0	348 25
1991–92	Celtic	15	2	
1992–93	Celtic	26	2	
1993–94	Celtic	22	1	
1994–95	Celtic	15	1	78 6
1995–96	Ipswich T	19	2	
1996–97	Ipswich T	8	0	
1997–98	Ipswich T	25	0	
1998–99	Ipswich T	40	2	
1999–2000	Ipswich T	36	1	
2000–01	Ipswich T	0	0	128 5

NAYLOR, Richard (F) 111 20
H: 6 1 W: 13 07 b.Leeds 28-2-77
Source: Trainee.
1995–96	Ipswich T	0	0	
1996–97	Ipswich T	27	4	
1997–98	Ipswich T	5	2	

Season	Club				
1998–99	Ipswich T	30	5		
1999–2000	Ipswich T	36	8		
2000–01	Ipswich T	13	1	111	20

NICHOLLS, Ashley (M)   0 0
H: 5 11 W: 11 11 b.Suffolk 30-10-81
Source: Ipswich W. *Honours:* England Schools.

Season	Club				
2000–01	Ipswich T	0	0		

PULLEN, James (G)   0 0
H: 6 2 W: 14 00 b.Chelmsford 18-3-82
Source: Heybridge S.

Season	Club				
1999–2000	Ipswich T	0	0		
2000–01	Ipswich T	0	0		

REUSER, Martijn (M)   132 28
H: 5 7 W: 12 10 b.Amsterdam 1-2-75
Honours: Holland 1 full cap.

Season	Club				
1993–94	Ajax	2	0		
1994–95	Ajax	2	0		
1995–96	Ajax	18	3		
1996–97	Ajax	19	3		
1997–98	Ajax	1	0	42	6
1997–98	Vitesse	24	6		
1998–99	Vitesse	32	8	56	14
1999–2000	Ipswich T	8	2		
2000–01	Ipswich T	26	6	34	8

SALMON, Mike (G)   410 0
H: 6 2 W: 14 00 b.Leyland 14-7-64
Source: Local.

Season	Club				
1981–82	Blackburn R	0	0		
1982–83	Blackburn R	0	0	1	0
1982–83	*Chester C*	16	0	16	0
1983–84	Stockport Co	46	0		
1984–85	Stockport Co	46	0		
1985–86	Stockport Co	26	0	118	0
1986–87	Bolton W	26	0	26	0
1986–87	Wrexham	17	0		
1987–88	Wrexham	40	0		
1988–89	Wrexham	43	0	100	0
1989–90	Charlton Ath	0	0		
1990–91	Charlton Ath	7	0		
1991–92	Charlton Ath	0	0		
1992–93	Charlton Ath	19	0		
1993–94	Charlton Ath	41	0		
1994–95	Charlton Ath	20	0		
1995–96	Charlton Ath	27	0		
1996–97	Charlton Ath	25	0		
1997–98	Charlton Ath	9	0		
1998–99	Charlton Ath	0	0	148	0
1998–99	*Oxford U*	1	0	1	0
1999–2000	Ipswich T	0	0		
2000–01	Ipswich T	0	0		

SCALES, John‡ (D)   412 15
H: 6 2 W: 13 05 b.Harrogate 4-7-66
Honours: England B, 3 full caps.

Season	Club				
1984–85	Leeds U	1	0		
1985–86	Bristol R	29	1		
1986–87	Bristol R	43	1	72	2
1987–88	Wimbledon	25	1		
1988–89	Wimbledon	38	5		
1989–90	Wimbledon	28	2		
1990–91	Wimbledon	36	2		
1991–92	Wimbledon	41	0		
1992–93	Wimbledon	32	1		
1993–94	Wimbledon	37	0		
1994–95	Wimbledon	3	0	240	11
1994–95	Liverpool	35	2		
1995–96	Liverpool	27	0		
1996–97	Liverpool	3	0	65	2
1996–97	Tottenham H	12	0		
1997–98	Tottenham H	10	0		
1998–99	Tottenham H	7	0		
1999–2000	Tottenham H	4	0	33	0
2000–01	Ipswich T	2	0	2	0

SCOWCROFT, James (F)   202 47
H: 6 1 W: 14 02 b.Bury St Edmunds 15-11-75
Source: Trainee. *Honours:* England Under-21.

Season	Club				
1994–95	Ipswich T	0	0		
1995–96	Ipswich T	23	2		
1996–97	Ipswich T	41	9		
1997–98	Ipswich T	31	6		
1998–99	Ipswich T	32	13		
1999–2000	Ipswich T	41	13		
2000–01	Ipswich T	34	4	202	47

STEWART, Marcus (F)   348 136
H: 5 10 W: 11 08 b.Bristol 7-11-72
Source: Trainee. *Honours:* England Schools, Football League.

Season	Club				
1991–92	Bristol R	33	5		
1992–93	Bristol R	38	11		
1993–94	Bristol R	29	5		
1994–95	Bristol R	27	15		
1995–96	Bristol R	44	21	171	63
1996–97	Huddersfield T	20	7		
1997–98	Huddersfield T	41	15		
1998–99	Huddersfield T	43	22		
1999–2000	Huddersfield T	29	14	133	58
1999–2000	Ipswich T	10	2		
2000–01	Ipswich T	34	19	44	21

SUBRIN, Benoit* (D)   0 0
H: 5 8 W: 10 00 b.Lyon 29-3-83

Season	Club				
2000–01	Ipswich T	0	0		

VENUS, Mark (D)   463 23
H: 6 0 W: 13 02 b.Hartlepool 6-4-67

Season	Club				
1984–85	Hartlepool U	4	0	4	0
1985–86	Leicester C	1	0		
1986–87	Leicester C	39	0		
1987–88	Leicester C	21	1	61	1
1987–88	Wolverhampton W	4	0		
1988–89	Wolverhampton W	35	0		
1989–90	Wolverhampton W	44	2		
1990–91	Wolverhampton W	6	0		
1991–92	Wolverhampton W	46	1		
1992–93	Wolverhampton W	12	0		
1993–94	Wolverhampton W	39	1		
1994–95	Wolverhampton W	39	3		
1995–96	Wolverhampton W	22	0		
1996–97	Wolverhampton W	40	0	287	7
1997–98	Ipswich T	14	1		
1998–99	Ipswich T	44	9		
1999–2000	Ipswich T	28	2		
2000–01	Ipswich T	25	3	111	15

WILNIS, Fabian (D)   323 7
H: 5 8 W: 12 06 b.Paramaribo 23-8-70
Source: Het Noorden, NOC, De Zwervers, Sparta.

Season	Club				
1990–91	NAC	7	3		
1991–92	NAC	30	0		
1992–93	NAC	32	0		
1993–94	NAC	34	0		
1994–95	NAC	31	0	134	3
1995–96	De Graafschap	32	0		
1996–97	De Graafschap	23	0		
1997–98	De Graafschap	33	1		
1998–99	De Graafschap	19	0	107	1
1998–99	Ipswich T	18	1		
1999–2000	Ipswich T	35	0		
2000–01	Ipswich T	29	2	82	3

WRIGHT, Jermaine (M)   153 8
H: 5 10 W: 12 07 b.Greenwich 21-10-75
Source: Trainee. *Honours:* England Youth.

Season	Club				
1992–93	Millwall	0	0		
1993–94	Millwall	0	0		
1994–95	Millwall	0	0		
1994–95	Wolverhampton W	6	0		
1995–96	Wolverhampton W	7	0		
1995–96	*Doncaster R*	13	0	13	0
1996–97	Wolverhampton W	3	0		
1997–98	Wolverhampton W	4	0	20	0
1997–98	Crewe Alex	5	0		
1998–99	Crewe Alex	44	5	49	5
1999–2000	Ipswich T	34	1		
2000–01	Ipswich T	37	2	71	3

WRIGHT, Richard (G)   240 0
H: 6 2 W: 14 04 b.Ipswich 5-11-77
Source: Trainee. *Honours:* England Schools, Youth, Under-21, 1 full cap.

Season	Club				
1994–95	Ipswich T	3	0		
1995–96	Ipswich T	23	0		
1996–97	Ipswich T	40	0		
1997–98	Ipswich T	46	0		
1998–99	Ipswich T	46	0		
1999–2000	Ipswich T	46	0		
2000–01	Ipswich T	36	0	240	0

(Transferred to Arsenal, July 2001).

Scholars
Ambrose, Darren; Asiamah, Justin; Bent, Darren; Bloomfield, Matthew; Burton, Steven P; Chaffey, Lee; Chibogu, Edmund; Duncan, Fraser; Kelly, Darren; Mayes, Mark; Moffat, Stephen; Murkin, Carl T; O'Neill, Lee G; Riley, Dominic M; Robinson, Matthew A; Snowdon, William R; Wasylyczyn, Wayne; Westlake, Ian J

KIDDERMINSTER H

BARNETT, Gary (M)   397 59
H: 5 6 W: 9 13 b.Stratford upon Avon 11-3-63
Source: Apprentice.

Season	Club				
1980–81	Coventry C	0	0		
1981–82	Coventry C	0	0		
1982–83	Oxford U	22	2		
1982–83	*Wimbledon*	5	1	5	1
1983–84	Oxford U	19	7		
1984–85	Oxford U	2	0		
1984–85	*Fulham*	2	1		
1985–86	Oxford U	2	0	45	9
1985–86	Fulham	36	6		
1986–87	Fulham	42	9		
1987–88	Fulham	42	9		
1988–89	Fulham	28	5		
1989–90	Fulham	32	1	182	31
1990–91	Huddersfield T	22	1		
1991–92	Huddersfield T	31	3		
1992–93	Huddersfield T	46	7		
1993–94	Huddersfield T	1	0	100	11
1993–94	Leyton Orient	36	7		
1994–95	Leyton Orient	27	0	63	7
From Barry T.					
2000–01	Kidderminster H	2	0	2	0

BENNETT, Dean (F)   43 4
H: 5 10 W: 11 00 b.Wolverhampton 13-12-77

Season	Club				
1996–97	WBA	1	0		
1997–98	WBA	0	0	1	0
From Bromsgrove R.					
2000–01	Kidderminster H	42	4	42	4

BIRD, Tony (F)   186 32
H: 5 11 W: 12 10 b.Cardiff 1-9-74
Source: Trainee. *Honours:* Wales Youth, Under-21.

Season	Club				
1991–92	Cardiff C	0	0		
1992–93	Cardiff C	9	1		
1993–94	Cardiff C	35	5		
1994–95	Cardiff C	19	4		
1995–96	Cardiff C	12	3	75	13
From Barry T.					
1997–98	Swansea C	41	14		
1998–99	Swansea C	29	3		
1999–2000	Swansea C	16	1	86	18
2000–01	Kidderminster H	25	1	25	1

BOGIE, Ian‡ (M)   384 28
H: 5 7 W: 11 10 b.Newcastle 6-12-67
Source: Apprentice. *Honours:* England Schools.

Season	Club				
1985–86	Newcastle U	0	0		
1986–87	Newcastle U	1	0		
1987–88	Newcastle U	7	0		
1988–89	Newcastle U	6	0	14	0
1988–89	Preston NE	13	1		
1989–90	Preston NE	35	3		
1990–91	Preston NE	31	8	79	12
1991–92	Millwall	25	0		
1992–93	Millwall	22	0		
1993–94	Millwall	4	1	51	1
1993–94	Leyton Orient	34	3		
1994–95	Leyton Orient	31	2	65	5
1994–95	Port Vale	9	2		
1995–96	Port Vale	32	3		
1996–97	Port Vale	31	1		
1997–98	Port Vale	38	1		
1998–99	Port Vale	35	2		
1999–2000	Port Vale	9	0	154	9
2000–01	Kidderminster H	21	1	21	1

BROCK, Stuart (G)   21 0
H: 6 1 W: 13 03 b.Sandwell 26-9-76
Source: Trainee.

Season	Club				
1994–95	Aston Villa	0	0		
1995–96	Aston Villa	0	0		
1996–97	Aston Villa	0	0		
1996–97	Northampton T	0	0		
1997–98	Northampton T	0	0		
1998–99	Northampton T	0	0		
1999–2000	Northampton T	0	0		
2000–01	Kidderminster H	21	0	21	0

BROUGHTON, Drewe (F)   68 16
H: 6 3 W: 12 04 b.Hitchin 25-10-78
Source: Trainee.

Season	Club				
1996–97	Norwich C	8	1		
1997–98	Norwich C	1	0		
1997–98	*Wigan Ath*	4	0	4	0
1998–99	Norwich C	0	0	9	1
1998–99	Brentford	1	0	1	0
1998–99	Peterborough U	2	1		
1999–2000	Peterborough U	10	1		
2000–01	Peterborough U	0	0	35	8
2000–01	Kidderminster H	19	7	19	7

CLARKE, Tim* (G)   223 0
H: 6 3 W: 15 12 b.Stourbridge 19-9-68
Source: Halesowen T.

Season	Club				
1990–91	Coventry C	0	0		
1991–92	Huddersfield T	39	0		
1992–93	Huddersfield T	31	0	70	0
1992–93	*Rochdale*	2	0	2	0
1993–94	Shrewsbury T	0	0		
1994–95	Shrewsbury T	16	0		
1995–96	Shrewsbury T	15	0	31	0
From Witton Alb.					
1996–97	York C	17	0	17	0
1997–98	Scunthorpe U	15	0		
1997–98	Scunthorpe U	41	0		
1998–99	Scunthorpe U	22	0	78	0
2000–01	Kidderminster H	25	0	25	0

CLARKSON, Ian (D)   343   1
H: 5 10   W: 12 00   b.Solihull 4-12-70
Source: Trainee.

1988–89	Birmingham C	9	0	
1989–90	Birmingham C	20	0	
1990–91	Birmingham C	37	0	
1991–92	Birmingham C	42	0	
1992–93	Birmingham C	28	0	
1993–94	Birmingham C	0	0	136 0
1993–94	Stoke C	14	0	
1994–95	Stoke C	18	0	
1995–96	Stoke C	43	0	75 0
1996–97	Northampton T	45	0	
1997–98	Northampton T	42	1	
1998–99	Northampton T	5	0	
1999–2000	Northampton T	2	0	94 1
2000–01	Kidderminster H	38	0	38 0

CORBETT, Andy (F)   6   0
b.Worcester 20-2-82

2000–01	Kidderminster H	6	0	6 0

DAVIES, Ben (M)   3   0
b.Birmingham 27-5-81
Source: Walsall trainee.

2000–01	Kidderminster H	3	0	3 0

DOYLE, Daire (M)   15   0
H: 5 10   W: 11 06   b.Dublin 18-10-80
Source: Cherry Orchard.

1998–99	Coventry C	0	0	
1999–2000	Coventry C	0	0	
2000–01	Coventry C	0	0	
2000–01	Kidderminster H	15	0	15 0

DUCROS, Andy (F)   42   2
H: 5 6   W: 9 08   b.Evesham 16-9-77
Source: Trainee. *Honours:* England Schools, Youth.

1994–95	Coventry C	0	0	
1995–96	Coventry C	0	0	
1996–97	Coventry C	5	0	
1997–98	Coventry C	3	0	
1998–99	Coventry C	0	0	8 0
From Nuneaton B				
2000–01	Kidderminster H	34	2	34 2

DURNIN, John* (M)   405   89
H: 5 10   W: 12 08   b.Liverpool 18-8-65
Source: Waterloo Dock.

1985–86	Liverpool	0	0	
1986–87	Liverpool	0	0	
1987–88	Liverpool	0	0	
1988–89	Liverpool	0	0	
1988–89	*WBA*	5	2	5 2
1988–89	Oxford U	19	3	
1989–90	Oxford U	42	13	
1990–91	Oxford U	26	9	
1991–92	Oxford U	37	8	
1992–93	Oxford U	37	11	161 44
1993–94	Portsmouth	28	6	
1994–95	Portsmouth	16	2	
1995–96	Portsmouth	41	3	
1996–97	Portsmouth	34	3	
1997–98	Portsmouth	34	10	
1998–99	Portsmouth	26	7	
1999–2000	Portsmouth	2	0	181 31
1999–2000	*Blackpool*	5	1	5 1
1999–2000	Carlisle U	22	2	
2000–01	Carlisle U	0	0	22 2
2000–01	Kidderminster H	31	9	31 9

FOSTER, Ian (F)   29   2
H: 5 7   W: 10 07   b.Merseyside 11-11-76
Source: Liverpool Schoolboy. *Honours:* England Schools.

1996–97	Hereford U	19	0	19 0
From Barrow				
2000–01	Kidderminster H	10	2	10 2

HADLEY, Stewart (F)   157   37
H: 5 11   W: 13 05   b.Stourbridge 30-12-73
Source: Halesowen T.

1992–93	Derby Co	0	0	
1993–94	Derby Co	0	0	
1993–94	Mansfield T	14	5	
1994–95	Mansfield T	39	14	
1995–96	Mansfield T	33	8	
1996–97	Mansfield T	36	4	
1997–98	Mansfield T	2	0	124 31
2000–01	Kidderminster H	33	6	33 6

HINTON, Craig (D)   46   2
H: 5 11   W: 11 00   b.Wolverhampton 26-11-77
Source: Trainee.

1996–97	Birmingham C	0	0	
1997–98	Birmingham C	0	0	
2000–01	Kidderminster H	46	2	46 2

KERR, Dylan‡ (D)   197   10
H: 5 9   W: 11 04   b.Valletta 14-1-67
Source: Arcadia Shepherds.

1988–89	Leeds U	3	0	

1989–90	Leeds U	5	0	
1990–91	Leeds U	0	0	
1991–92	Leeds U	0	0	
1991–92	*Doncaster R*	7	1	7 1
1991–92	*Blackpool*	12	1	12 1
1992–93	Leeds U	5	0	13 0
1993–94	Reading	45	2	
1994–95	Reading	36	1	
1995–96	Reading	8	2	
1996–97	Reading	0	0	89 5
1996–97	Carlisle U	1	0	1 0
1996–97	Kilmarnock	27	0	
1997–98	Kilmarnock	14	0	
1998–99	Kilmarnock	16	0	
1999–2000	Kilmarnock	0	0	57 0
2000–01	Hamilton A	17	3	17 3
2000–01	Kidderminster H	1	0	1 0

MACKENZIE, Neil# (M)   97   5
H: 6 2   W: 13 06   b.Birmingham 15-4-76
Source: WBA schoolboy.

1996–97	Stoke C	22	1	
1997–98	Stoke C	12	0	
1998–99	Stoke C	6	0	
1998–99	*Cambridge U*	4	1	
1999–2000	Stoke C	2	0	42 1
1999–2000	Cambridge U	22	0	
2000–01	Cambridge U	6	0	32 1
2000–01	Kidderminster H	23	3	23 3

MEDOU-OTYE, Parfait (D)   27   0
H: 5 10   W: 12 00   b.Ekoundendi 29-11-76
Source: Trainee.

1998–99	Le Havre			
From Le Mans UC 72				
2000–01	Morton	10	0	10 0
2000–01	Kidderminster H	17	0	17 0

MURPHY, Brendan (G)   0   0
H: 5 11   W: 11 12   b.Wexford 19-8-75
Source: Bradford C Trainee. *Honours:* Eire Youth, Under-21, B.

1994–95	Wimbledon	0	0	
1995–96	Wimbledon	0	0	
1996–97	Wimbledon	0	0	
1997–98	Wimbledon	0	0	
1998–99	Wimbledon	0	0	
From Dundalk				
2000–01	Kidderminster H	0	0	

POPE, Steve* (D)   6   0
H: 5 11   W: 11 00   b.Stoke 8-9-76
Source: Trainee.

1995–96	Crewe Alex	0	0	
1996–97	Crewe Alex	0	0	
1997–98	Crewe Alex	6	0	6 0
2000–01	Kidderminster H	0	0	

SHAIL, Mark (D)   164   5
H: 6 1   W: 12 06   b.Sweden 15-10-66
Source: Yeovil T.

1992–93	Bristol C	4	0	
1993–94	Bristol C	36	2	
1994–95	Bristol C	38	2	
1995–96	Bristol C	12	0	
1996–97	Bristol C	11	0	
1997–98	Bristol C	2	0	
1998–99	Bristol C	24	0	
1999–2000	Bristol C	1	0	128 4
2000–01	Kidderminster H	36	1	36 1

SKOVBJERG, Thomas* (M)   12   1
b.Esbjerg 25-10-74
Source: Esbjerg.

2000–01	Kidderminster H	12	1	12 1

SMITH, Adie (D)   34   5
b.Birmingham 11-8-73
Source: Bromsgrove R.

2000–01	Kidderminster H	34	5	34 5

STAMPS, Scott (D)   176   6
H: 5 11   W: 11 09   b.Edgbaston 20-3-75
Source: Trainee.

1992–93	Torquay U	2	0	
1993–94	Torquay U	6	0	
1994–95	Torquay U	25	1	
1995–96	Torquay U	23	1	
1996–97	Torquay U	30	3	86 5
1996–97	Colchester U	8	0	
1997–98	Colchester U	27	1	
1998–99	Colchester U	21	0	56 1
2000–01	Kidderminster H	34	0	34 0

WEBB, Paul (D)   32   1
b.Wolverhampton 30-11-67
Source: Bromsgrove R.

2000–01	Kidderminster H	32	1	32 1

LEEDS U

ALLAWAY, Shaun (G)   0   0
H: 6 2   W: 11 06   b.Reading 16-2-83
Source: Trainee.

1999–2000	Reading	0	0	
1999–2000	Leeds U	0	0	
2000–01	Leeds U	0	0	

BAKKE, Eirik (M)   134   21
H: 6 1   W: 12 06   b.Sogndal 13-9-77
Honours: Norway 14 full caps.

1994	Sogndal	5	0	
1995	Sogndal	0	0	
1996	Sogndal	19	8	
1997	Sogndal	25	4	
1998	Sogndal	19	2	
1999	Sogndal	8	3	76 17
1999–2000	Leeds U	29	2	
2000–01	Leeds U	29	2	58 4

BATTY, David (M)   390   8
H: 5 8   W: 11 09   b.Leeds 2-12-68
Source: Trainee. *Honours:* England Under-21, B, 42 full caps.

1987–88	Leeds U	23	1	
1988–89	Leeds U	30	0	
1989–90	Leeds U	42	0	
1990–91	Leeds U	37	0	
1991–92	Leeds U	40	2	
1992–93	Leeds U	30	1	
1993–94	Leeds U	9	0	
1993–94	Blackburn R	26	0	
1994–95	Blackburn R	5	0	
1995–96	Blackburn R	23	1	54 1
1995–96	Newcastle U	11	1	
1996–97	Newcastle U	32	1	
1997–98	Newcastle U	32	1	
1998–99	Newcastle U	8	0	83 3
1998–99	Leeds U	10	0	
1999–2000	Leeds U	16	0	
2000–01	Leeds U	16	0	253 4

BOWYER, Lee (M)   209   38
H: 5 9   W: 10 07   b.London 3-1-77
Source: Trainee. *Honours:* England Youth, Under-21.

1993–94	Charlton Ath	0	0	
1994–95	Charlton Ath	5	0	
1995–96	Charlton Ath	41	8	46 8
1996–97	Leeds U	32	4	
1997–98	Leeds U	25	3	
1998–99	Leeds U	35	9	
1999–2000	Leeds U	33	5	
2000–01	Leeds U	38	9	163 30

BOYLE, Wes (F)   1   0
H: 5 10   W: 12 00   b.Portadown 30-3-79
Source: Trainee. *Honours:* Northern Ireland Under-21.

1995–96	Leeds U	0	0	
1996–97	Leeds U	1	0	
1997–98	Leeds U	0	0	
1998–99	Leeds U	0	0	
1999–2000	Leeds U	0	0	
2000–01	Leeds U	0	0	1 0

BREEN, Gerard (M)   0   0
H: 5 7   W: 11 08   b.County Louth 29-3-84
Source: Scholar.

2000–01	Leeds U	0	0	

BRIDGES, Michael (F)   120   35
H: 6 1   W: 12 04   b.North Shields 5-8-78
Source: Trainee. *Honours:* England Schools, Youth, Under-21.

1995–96	Sunderland	15	4	
1996–97	Sunderland	25	3	
1997–98	Sunderland	9	1	
1998–99	Sunderland	30	8	79 16
1999–2000	Leeds U	34	19	
2000–01	Leeds U	7	0	41 19

BURNS, Jacob (M)   4   0
H: 5 10   W: 11 06   b.Sydney 21-4-78
Honours: From Sydney United 57 apps, 5 goals, Paramatta Power 25 apps, 3 goals.Australia 4 full caps.

2000–01	Leeds U	4	0	4 0

CANDSELL-SHERIFF, Shane (M)   0   0
H: 6 0   W: 11 12   b.Sydney 10-11-82
Source: NSW Academy.

1999–2000	Leeds U	0	0	
2000–01	Leeds U	0	0	

CRAMER, Martin (M)   0   0
H: 5 4   W: 10 07   b.Dublin 15-11-82
Source: Maryland Boys.

1999–2000	Leeds U	0	0	
2000–01	Leeds U	0	0	

DACOURT, Olivier (M) 190 9
H: 5 10 W: 11 06 b.Montreuil 25-9-74
Honours: France 3 full caps.

1992–93	Strasbourg	6	0	
1993–94	Strasbourg	8	0	
1994–95	Strasbourg	18	0	
1995–96	Strasbourg	34	0	
1996–97	Strasbourg	31	1	
1997–98	Strasbourg	30	3	127 4
1998–99	Everton	30	2	30 2
1999–2000	Lens	0	0	
2000–01	Leeds U	33	3	33 3

DIXON, Kevin* (M) 3 0
H: 5 9 W: 12 03 b.Easington 27-6-80
Source: Trainee. *Honours:* England Youth.

1997–98	Leeds U	0	0	
1998–99	Leeds U	0	0	
1999–2000	Leeds U	0	0	
1999–2000	York C	3	0	3 0
2000–01	Leeds U	0	0	

DUBERRY, Michael (D) 111 2
H: 6 1 W: 14 00 b.Enfield 14-10-75
Source: Trainee. *Honours:* England Under-21.

1993–94	Chelsea	1	0	
1994–95	Chelsea	0	0	
1995–96	Chelsea	22	0	
1995–96	Bournemouth	7	0	7 0
1996–97	Chelsea	15	1	
1997–98	Chelsea	23	0	
1998–99	Chelsea	25	0	86 1
1999–2000	Leeds U	13	1	
2000–01	Leeds U	5	0	18 1

EVANS, Gareth (D) 1 0
H: 6 0 W: 12 00 b.Leeds 15-2-81
Source: Trainee. *Honours:* England Youth.

1997–98	Leeds U	0	0	
1998–99	Leeds U	0	0	
1999–2000	Leeds U	0	0	
2000–01	Leeds U	1	0	1 0

FARRELL, Craig (F) 0 0
H: 5 11 W: 12 13 b.Middlesbrough 5-12-82
Source: Trainee.

1999–2000	Leeds U	0	0	
2000–01	Leeds U	0	0	

FARREN, Larry (D) 0 0
H: 5 10 W: 11 09 b.Donegal 29-7-83
Source: Scholar.

2000–01	Leeds U	0	0	

FEENEY, Warren* (F) 10 4
H: 5 10 W: 11 05 b.Belfast 17-1-81
Source: Trainee.

1997–98	Leeds U	0	0	
1998–99	Leeds U	0	0	
1999–2000	Leeds U	0	0	
2000–01	Leeds U	0	0	
2000–01	Bournemouth	10	4	10 4

FERDINAND, Rio (D) 160 4
H: 6 3 W: 14 01 b.Peckham 7-11-78
Source: Trainee. *Honours:* England Youth, Under-21, 15 full caps.

1995–96	West Ham U	1	0	
1996–97	West Ham U	15	2	
1996–97	Bournemouth	10	0	10 0
1997–98	West Ham U	35	0	
1998–99	West Ham U	31	0	
1999–2000	West Ham U	33	0	
2000–01	West Ham U	12	0	127 2
2000–01	Leeds U	23	2	23 2

FERGUSON, Steven (M) 0 0
H: 5 6 W: 9 12 b.Newry 25-2-83
Source: St Andrew's.

1999–2000	Leeds U	0	0	
2000–01	Leeds U	0	0	

FOLAN, Caleb (F) 0 0
H: 6 1 W: 12 10 b.Leeds 26-10-82
Source: Trainee.

1999–2000	Leeds U	0	0	
2000–01	Leeds U	0	0	

HACKWORTH, Tony (F) 0 0
H: 6 1 W: 13 05 b.Durham 19-5-80
Source: Trainee. *Honours:* England Youth.

1997–98	Leeds U	0	0	
1998–99	Leeds U	0	0	
1999–2000	Leeds U	0	0	
2000–01	Leeds U	0	0	

HARPUR, Chad* (G) 0 0
H: 5 10 W: 12 11 b.Johannesburg 3-9-82

2000–01	Leeds U	0	0	

HARTE, Ian (D) 127 19
H: 6 0 W: 12 03 b.Drogheda 31-8-77
Source: Trainee. *Honours:* Eire 31 full caps, 5 goals.

1995–96	Leeds U	4	0	
1996–97	Leeds U	14	2	
1997–98	Leeds U	12	0	
1998–99	Leeds U	35	4	
1999–2000	Leeds U	33	6	
2000–01	Leeds U	29	7	127 19

HAY, Danny (D) 52 2
H: 6 4 W: 14 00 b.Auckland 15-5-75
Source: Waitakere, Central Utd.

1997–98	Perth Glory	24	1	
1998–99	Perth Glory	24	1	48 2
1999–2000	Leeds U	0	0	
2000–01	Leeds U	4	0	4 0

JOHNSON, Simon (F) 0 0
H: 5 9 W: 11 09 b.West Bromwich 9-3-83
Source: Scholar.

2000–01	Leeds U	0	0	

KAMARA, Christopher (D) 0 0
H: 5 6 W: 11 07 b.York 27-2-84
Source: Scholar.

2000–01	Leeds U	0	0	

KEANE, Robbie (F) 128 45
H: 5 9 W: 12 00 b.Dublin 8-7-80
Source: Trainee. *Honours:* Eire 25 full caps, 7 goals.

1997–98	Wolverhampton W	38	11	
1998–99	Wolverhampton W	33	11	
1999–2000	Wolverhampton W	2	2	73 24
1999–2000	Coventry C	31	12	31 12
2000–01	Internazionale	6	0	6 0
2000–01	Leeds U	18	9	18 9

KEEGAN, Paul (M) 0 0
H: 5 7 W: 11 04 b.Dublin 5-7-84
Source: Scholar.

2000–01	Leeds U	0	0	

KELLY, Gary (D) 245 2
H: 5 8 W: 11 00 b.Drogheda 9-7-74
Source: Home Farm. *Honours:* Eire Youth, 38 full caps, 2 goals.

1991–92	Leeds U	2	0	
1992–93	Leeds U	0	0	
1993–94	Leeds U	42	0	
1994–95	Leeds U	42	0	
1995–96	Leeds U	34	0	
1996–97	Leeds U	36	2	
1997–98	Leeds U	34	0	
1998–99	Leeds U	0	0	
1999–2000	Leeds U	31	0	
2000–01	Leeds U	24	0	245 2

KEWELL, Harry (F) 123 23
H: 6 0 W: 13 00 b.Sydney 22-9-78
Source: NSW Soccer Academy. *Honours:* Australia 10 full caps, 3 goals.

1995–96	Leeds U	2	0	
1996–97	Leeds U	1	0	
1997–98	Leeds U	29	5	
1998–99	Leeds U	38	6	
1999–2000	Leeds U	36	10	
2000–01	Leeds U	17	2	123 23

KILGALLON, Matthew (D) 0 0
H: 6 0 W: 12 00 b.York 8-1-84
Source: Scholar.

2000–01	Leeds U	0	0	

KINSELLA, Alan (F) 0 0
H: 5 6 W: 11 00 b.Dublin 2-2-84
Source: Scholar.

2000–01	Leeds U	0	0	

KRIEF, Dominique (M) 0 0
H: 5 7 W: 9 06 b.Leeds 15-9-83
Source: Scholar.

2000–01	Leeds U	0	0	

LAVERY, Sean (M) 0 0
H: 5 7 W: 10 08 b.Lurgan 16-11-83
Source: Scholar.

2000–01	Leeds U	0	0	

LENNON, Anthony (F) 0 0
H: 5 9 W: 10 08 b.Leeds 16-5-82
Source: Trainee.

1998–99	Leeds U	0	0	
1999–2000	Leeds U	0	0	
2000–01	Leeds U	0	0	
(Transferred to Celtic, December 2000).				

LYNCH, Damien* (D) 0 0
H: 5 10 W: 11 02 b.Dublin 31-7-79

1996–97	Leeds U	0	0	
1997–98	Leeds U	0	0	
1998–99	Leeds U	0	0	
1999–2000	Leeds U	0	0	

MARTIN, Alan‡ (D) 0 0
H: 5 10 W: 11 05 b.Dublin 21-11-81
Source: Trainee.

1998–99	Leeds U	0	0	
1999–2000	Leeds U	0	0	
2000–01	Leeds U	0	0	

MARTYN, Nigel (G) 542 0
H: 6 2 W: 14 08 b.St Austell 11-8-66
Source: St Blazey. *Honours:* England Under-21, B, 16 full caps.

1987–88	Bristol R	39	0	
1988–89	Bristol R	46	0	
1989–90	Bristol R	16	0	101 0
1989–90	Crystal Palace	25	0	
1990–91	Crystal Palace	38	0	
1991–92	Crystal Palace	38	0	
1992–93	Crystal Palace	42	0	
1993–94	Crystal Palace	46	0	
1994–95	Crystal Palace	37	0	
1995–96	Crystal Palace	46	0	272 0
1996–97	Leeds U	37	0	
1997–98	Leeds U	37	0	
1998–99	Leeds U	34	0	
1999–2000	Leeds U	38	0	
2000–01	Leeds U	23	0	169 0

MATTEO, Dominic (D) 158 1
H: 6 1 W: 12 07 b.Dumfries 28-4-74
Source: Trainee. *Honours:* England Youth, Under-21, B, Scotland 3 full caps.

1992–93	Liverpool	0	0	
1993–94	Liverpool	11	0	
1994–95	Liverpool	7	0	
1994–95	Sunderland	1	0	1 0
1995–96	Liverpool	5	0	
1996–97	Liverpool	26	0	
1997–98	Liverpool	26	0	
1998–99	Liverpool	20	1	
1999–2000	Liverpool	32	0	
2000–01	Liverpool	0	0	127 1
2000–01	Leeds U	30	0	30 0

MAYBURY, Alan (D) 27 0
H: 5 9 W: 11 05 b.Dublin 8-8-78
Source: Trainee. *Honours:* Eire Under-21, 2 full caps.

1995–96	Leeds U	1	0	
1996–97	Leeds U	0	0	
1997–98	Leeds U	12	0	
1998–99	Leeds U	0	0	
1998–99	Reading	8	0	8 0
1999–2000	Leeds U	0	0	
2000–01	Leeds U	0	0	13 0
2000–01	Crewe Alex	6	0	6 0

McCARGO, Gerard (F) 0 0
H: 5 4 W: 10 03 b.Belfast 3-11-82
Source: Celtic (Belfast) Boys.

1999–2000	Leeds U	0	0	
2000–01	Leeds U	0	0	

McMASTER, Jamie (M) 0 0
H: 5 10 W: 11 12 b.Sydney 29-11-82
Source: NSW Academy. *Honours:* England Youth.

1999–2000	Leeds U	0	0	
2000–01	Leeds U	0	0	

McPHAIL, Stephen (M) 52 2
H: 5 10 W: 12 00 b.London 9-12-79
Source: Trainee. *Honours:* Eire Under-21, 3 full caps, 1 goal.

1996–97	Leeds U	0	0	
1997–98	Leeds U	4	0	
1998–99	Leeds U	17	0	
1999–2000	Leeds U	24	2	
2000–01	Leeds U	7	0	52 2

MILLS, Danny (D) 151 4
H: 6 0 W: 12 05 b.Norwich 18-5-77
Source: Trainee. *Honours:* England Youth, Under-21, 1 full cap.

1994–95	Norwich C	0	0	
1995–96	Norwich C	14	0	
1996–97	Norwich C	32	0	
1997–98	Norwich C	20	0	66 0
1997–98	Charlton Ath	9	1	
1998–99	Charlton Ath	36	2	45 3
1999–2000	Leeds U	17	1	
2000–01	Leeds U	23	0	40 1

MILOSEVIC, Danny (G) 0 0
H: 6 3 W: 14 12 b.Carlton 26-6-78
Source: Canberra Cosmos 14 apps, Perth Glory 17 apps.

1999–2000	Leeds U	0	0	
2000–01	Leeds U	0	0	

MITCHELL, Peter (D) 0 0
H: 5 6 W: 10 03 b.Londonderry 10-4-84
Source: Scholar.

2000–01	Leeds U	0	0	

NEWEY, Tom (D) 0 0
H: 5 9 W: 10 07 b.Sheffield 31-10-82
Source: Scholar.

Season	Club	App	Gls	Tot	Gls
2000-01	Leeds U	0	0		

RADEBE, Lucas (D) 164 0
H: 6 1 W: 12 01 b.Johannesburg 12-4-69
Source: Kaiser Chiefs. *Honours:* South Africa full caps.

Season	Club	App	Gls	Tot	Gls
1994-95	Leeds U	12	0		
1995-96	Leeds U	13	0		
1996-97	Leeds U	32	0		
1997-98	Leeds U	27	0		
1998-99	Leeds U	29	0		
1999-2000	Leeds U	31	0		
2000-01	Leeds U	20	0	164	0

RICHARDSON, Frazer (D) 0 0
H: 5 11 W: 11 12 b.Rotherham 29-10-82
Source: Trainee. *Honours:* England Youth.

Season	Club	App	Gls	Tot	Gls
1999-2000	Leeds U	0	0		
2000-01	Leeds U	0	0		

ROBINSON, Paul (G) 21 0
H: 6 4 W: 14 04 b.Beverley 15-10-79
Source: Trainee. *Honours:* England Under-21.

Season	Club	App	Gls	Tot	Gls
1996-97	Leeds U	0	0		
1997-98	Leeds U	0	0		
1998-99	Leeds U	5	0		
1999-2000	Leeds U	0	0		
2000-01	Leeds U	16	0	21	0

SHIELDS, Robbie (M) 0 0
H: 5 5 W: 10 05 b.Dublin 1-5-84
Source: Scholar.

Season	Club	App	Gls	Tot	Gls
2000-01	Leeds U	0	0		

SINGH, Harpal (F) 0 0
H: 5 7 W: 10 09 b.Bradford 15-9-81
Source: Trainee.

Season	Club	App	Gls	Tot	Gls
1998-99	Leeds U	0	0		
1999-2000	Leeds U	0	0		
2000-01	Leeds U	0	0		

SMITH, Alan (F) 81 22
H: 5 9 W: 11 05 b.Leeds 28-10-80
Source: Trainee. *Honours:* England Youth, Under-21, 2 full caps.

Season	Club	App	Gls	Tot	Gls
1997-98	Leeds U	0	0		
1998-99	Leeds U	22	7		
1999-2000	Leeds U	26	4		
2000-01	Leeds U	33	11	81	22

STIENS, Craig (F) 0 0
H: 5 6 W: 11 07 b.Swansea 31-7-84
Source: Scholar.

VIDUKA, Marko (F) 177 105
H: 6 2 W: 14 08 b.Melbourne 9-10-75
Source: Melbourne Knights 48 apps, 40 goals, Croatia Zagreb. *Honours:* Australia 18 full caps, 2 goals.

Season	Club	App	Gls	Tot	Gls
1994-95	Melbourne Knights	22	18	22	18
1995-96	Croatia Zagreb	27	12		
1996-97	Croatia Zagreb	25	18		
1997-98	Croatia Zagreb	25	8		
1998-99	Croatia Zagreb	7	2	84	40
1998-99	Celtic	9	5		
1999-2000	Celtic	28	25	37	30
2000-01	Leeds U	34	17	34	17

WARD, Michael (F) 0 0
H: 5 6 W: 10 03 b.Omagh 17-4-84
Source: Scholar.

Season	Club	App	Gls	Tot	Gls
2000-01	Leeds U	0	0		

WATSON, Simon* (M) 0 0
H: 5 9 W: 10 02 b.Strabane 22-9-80
Source: Trainee.

Season	Club	App	Gls	Tot	Gls
1997-98	Leeds U	0	0		
1998-99	Leeds U	0	0		
1999-2000	Leeds U	0	0		
2000-01	Leeds U	0	0		

WILCOX, Jason (M) 306 34
H: 6 0 W: 12 00 b.Bolton 15-7-71
Source: Trainee. *Honours:* England B, 3 full caps.

Season	Club	App	Gls	Tot	Gls
1989-90	Blackburn R	1	0		
1990-91	Blackburn R	18	0		
1991-92	Blackburn R	38	4		
1992-93	Blackburn R	33	4		
1993-94	Blackburn R	33	6		
1994-95	Blackburn R	27	5		
1995-96	Blackburn R	10	3		
1996-97	Blackburn R	28	2		
1997-98	Blackburn R	31	4		
1998-99	Blackburn R	30	3		
1999-2000	Blackburn R	20	0	269	31
1999-2000	Leeds U	20	3		
2000-01	Leeds U	17	0	37	3

WOODGATE, Jonathan (D) 73 4
H: 6 2 W: 13 05 b.Middlesbrough 21-1-80
Source: Trainee. *Honours:* England Youth, Under-21, 1 full cap.

Season	Club	App	Gls	Tot	Gls
1996-97	Leeds U	0	0		
1997-98	Leeds U	0	0		
1998-99	Leeds U	25	2		
1999-2000	Leeds U	34	1		
2000-01	Leeds U	14	1	73	4

Scholars
Groves, Bradley M; Hitchcock, Thomas E; Keegan, Paul A; Krief, Dominique; Lavery, Sean P; Mitchell, Peter J; Stiens, Craig; Wray, Thomas

LEICESTER C

AKINBIYI, Ade (F) 244 83
H: 6 1 W: 13 09 b.Hackney 10-10-74
Source: Trainee. *Honours:* Nigeria full caps.

Season	Club	App	Gls	Tot	Gls
1992-93	Norwich C	0	0		
1993-94	Norwich C	2	0		
1993-94	Hereford U	4	2	4	2
1994-95	Norwich C	13	0		
1994-95	Brighton & HA	7	4	7	4
1995-96	Norwich C	22	3		
1996-97	Norwich C	12	0	49	3
1996-97	Gillingham	19	7		
1997-98	Gillingham	44	21	63	28
1998-99	Bristol C	44	19		
1999-2000	Bristol C	3	2	47	21
1999-2000	Wolverhampton W	37	16	37	16
2000-01	Leicester C	37	9	37	9

ASHTON, Jonathan (M) 0 0
b.Nuneaton 4-10-82
Source: Scholar.

Season	Club	App	Gls	Tot	Gls
2000-01	Leicester C	0	0		

BENJAMIN, Trevor (F) 144 36
H: 6 2 W: 14 02 b.Kettering 8-2-79
Source: Trainee. *Honours:* England Under-21.

Season	Club	App	Gls	Tot	Gls
1995-96	Cambridge U	5	0		
1996-97	Cambridge U	7	1		
1997-98	Cambridge U	2	0		
1998-99	Cambridge U	42	10		
1999-2000	Cambridge U	44	20	123	35
2000-01	Leicester C	21	1	21	1

BOATENG, Danny‡ (F) 0 0
H: 5 10 W: 12 07 b.London 14-11-80
Source: Arsenal Trainee.

Season	Club	App	Gls	Tot	Gls
1998-99	Leicester C	0	0		
1999-2000	Leicester C	0	0		
2000-01	Leicester C	0	0		

CAMPBELL, Stuart (M) 77 2
H: 5 10 W: 10 13 b.Corby 9-12-77
Source: Trainee. *Honours:* Scotland Under-21.

Season	Club	App	Gls	Tot	Gls
1996-97	Leicester C	10	0		
1997-98	Leicester C	11	0		
1998-99	Leicester C	12	0		
1999-2000	Leicester C	4	0		
1999-2000	Birmingham C	2	0	2	0
2000-01	Leicester C	0	0	37	0
2000-01	Grimsby T	38	2	38	2

CRESSWELL, Richard (F) 150 26
H: 6 0 W: 11 08 b.Bridlington 20-9-77
Source: Trainee. *Honours:* England Under-21.

Season	Club	App	Gls	Tot	Gls
1995-96	York C	16	1		
1996-97	York C	17	0		
1996-97	Mansfield T	5	1	5	1
1997-98	York C	26	4		
1998-99	York C	36	16	95	21
1998-99	Sheffield W	7	1		
1999-2000	Sheffield W	20	1		
2000-01	Sheffield W	4	0	31	2
2000-01	Leicester C	8	0	8	0
2000-01	Preston NE	11	2	11	2

DARBY, Brett (M) 0 0
b.Leicester 10-11-83
Source: Scholar.

Season	Club	App	Gls	Tot	Gls
2000-01	Leicester C	0	0		

DAVIDSON, Callum (D) 137 6
H: 5 10 W: 12 07 b.Stirling 25-6-76
Source: 'S' Form. *Honours:* Scotland Under-21, 14 full caps.

Season	Club	App	Gls	Tot	Gls
1994-95	St Johnstone	7	1		
1995-96	St Johnstone	2	0		
1996-97	St Johnstone	20	2		
1997-98	St Johnstone	15	1	44	4
1997-98	Blackburn R	1	0		
1998-99	Blackburn R	34	1		
1999-2000	Blackburn R	30	0	65	1
2000-01	Leicester C	28	1	28	1

DELANEY, Damien (D) 5 0
b.Cork 20-7-81
Source: Cork C.

Season	Club	App	Gls	Tot	Gls
2000-01	Leicester C	5	0	5	0

DUDFIELD, Lawrie (F) 19 3
H: 6 0 W: 12 04 b.London 7-5-80
Source: Kettering T.

Season	Club	App	Gls	Tot	Gls
1997-98	Leicester C	0	0		
1998-99	Leicester C	0	0		
1999-2000	Leicester C	2	0		
2000-01	Leicester C	0	0	2	0
2000-01	Lincoln C	3	0	3	0
2000-01	Chesterfield	14	3	14	3

EADIE, Darren (F) 208 37
H: 5 7 W: 10 09 b.Chippenham 10-6-75
Source: Trainee. *Honours:* England Youth, Under-21.

Season	Club	App	Gls	Tot	Gls
1992-93	Norwich C	0	0		
1993-94	Norwich C	15	3		
1994-95	Norwich C	26	2		
1995-96	Norwich C	31	6		
1996-97	Norwich C	42	17		
1997-98	Norwich C	19	3		
1998-99	Norwich C	22	3		
1999-2000	Norwich C	13	1	168	35
1999-2000	Leicester C	16	0		
2000-01	Leicester C	24	2	40	2

ELLIOTT, Matt (D) 494 65
H: 6 3 W: 15 00 b.Roehampton 1-11-68
Source: Epsom & Ewell. *Honours:* Scotland 15 full caps, 1 goal.

Season	Club	App	Gls	Tot	Gls
1988-89	Charlton Ath	0	0		
1988-89	Torquay U	13	2		
1989-90	Torquay U	33	2		
1990-91	Torquay U	45	6		
1991-92	Torquay U	33	5	124	15
1991-92	Scunthorpe U	8	1		
1992-93	Scunthorpe U	39	6		
1993-94	Scunthorpe U	14	1	61	8
1993-94	Oxford U	32	5		
1994-95	Oxford U	45	4		
1995-96	Oxford U	45	8		
1996-97	Oxford U	26	4	148	21
1996-97	Leicester C	16	4		
1997-98	Leicester C	37	7		
1998-99	Leicester C	37	2		
1999-2000	Leicester C	37	6		
2000-01	Leicester C	34	2	161	21

ELLISON, Kevin (F) 1 0
H: 6 3 W: 15 00 b.Liverpool 23-2-79
Source: Altrincham.

Season	Club	App	Gls	Tot	Gls
2000-01	Leicester C	1	0	1	0

FIELD, Declan* (M) 0 0
b.Dublin 26-7-82

Season	Club	App	Gls	Tot	Gls
2000-01	Leicester C	0	0		

FLOWERS, Tim (G) 490 0
H: 6 2 W: 14 00 b.Kenilworth 3-2-67
Source: Apprentice. *Honours:* England Youth, Under-21, 11 full caps.

Season	Club	App	Gls	Tot	Gls
1984-85	Wolverhampton W	38	0		
1985-86	Wolverhampton W	25	0	63	0
1985-86	Southampton	0	0		
1986-87	Southampton	9	0		
1986-87	Swindon T	2	0		
1987-88	Southampton	9	0		
1987-88	Swindon T	5	0	7	0
1988-89	Southampton	7	0		
1989-90	Southampton	35	0		
1990-91	Southampton	37	0		
1991-92	Southampton	41	0		
1992-93	Southampton	42	0		
1993-94	Southampton	12	0	192	0
1993-94	Blackburn R	29	0		
1994-95	Blackburn R	39	0		
1995-96	Blackburn R	37	0		
1996-97	Blackburn R	36	0		
1997-98	Blackburn R	25	0		
1998-99	Blackburn R	11	0	177	0
1999-2000	Leicester C	29	0		
2000-01	Leicester C	22	0	51	0

GOODWIN, Tommy* (D) 1 0
H: 6 0 W: 12 07 b.Leicester 8-11-79
Source: Trainee.

Season	Club	App	Gls	Tot	Gls
1998-99	Leicester C	0	0		
1999-2000	Leicester C	1	0		
2000-01	Leicester C	0	0	1	0

GUNNLAUGSSON, Arnar (F) 159 60
H: 5 10 W: 11 06 b.Akranes 6-3-73
Honours: Iceland 30 full caps, 3 goals.

Season	Club	App	Gls	Tot	Gls
1990	IA Akranes	12	3		
1991	IA Akranes	0	0		
1992	IA Akranes	18	15		
1992-93	Feyenoord	4	0		
1993-94	Feyenoord	5	0	9	0
1994-95	Nuremberg	28	8	28	8

1995   IA Akranes   7 15
From Sochaux.
1997   IA Akranes   2   1   **39 34**
1997–98 Bolton W   15   0
1998–99 Bolton W   27 13   **42 13**
1998–99 Leicester C 9   0
1999–2000 Leicester C 2   0
1999–2000 *Stoke C*   13   2   **13   2**
2000–01 Leicester C 17   3   **28   3**

GUPPY, Steve (M)   **292 29**
H:5 11 W:11 11 b.Winchester 29-3-69
Source: Southampton. Honours: England
Under-21, B, 1 full cap.
1993–94 Wycombe W   41   8   **41   8**
1994–95 Newcastle U 0   0
1994–95 Port Vale   27   2
1995–96 Port Vale   44   4
1996–97 Port Vale   34   6   **105 12**
1996–97 Leicester C 13   0
1997–98 Leicester C 37   2
1998–99 Leicester C 38   4
1999–2000 Leicester C 30   2
2000–01 Leicester C 28   1   **146   9**

HEATH, Matthew (M)   **0   0**
b.Leicester 1-11-81
Source: Scholar.
2000–01 Leicester C 0   0

IMPEY, Andrew (M)   **294 14**
H:5 8 W:11 06 b.Hammersmith 13-9-71
Source: Yeading. Honours: England
Under-21.
1990–91 QPR   0   0
1991–92 QPR   13   0
1992–93 QPR   40   2
1993–94 QPR   33   3
1994–95 QPR   40   3
1995–96 QPR   29   3
1996–97 QPR   32   2   **187 13**
1997–98 West Ham U 19   0
1998–99 West Ham U   8   0   **27   0**
1998–99 Leicester C 18   0
1999–2000 Leicester C 29   1
2000–01 Leicester C 33   0   **80   1**

IZZET, Muzzy (M)   **170 28**
H:5 10 W:11 02 b.Hackney 31-10-74
Source: Trainee. Honours: Turkey 4 full caps.
1993–94 Chelsea   0   0
1994–95 Chelsea   0   0
1995–96 Chelsea   0   0
1995–96 *Leicester C* 9   1
1996–97 Leicester C 35   3
1997–98 Leicester C 36   4
1998–99 Leicester C 31   5
1999–2000 Leicester C 32   8
2000–01 Leicester C 27   7   **170 28**

JONES, Matthew (M)   **34   0**
H:5 11 W:11 09 b.Llanelli 1-9-80
Source: Trainee. Honours: Wales Youth,
Under-21, B, 8 full caps.
1997–98 Leeds U   0   0
1998–99 Leeds U   8   0
1999–2000 Leeds U   11   0
2000–01 Leeds U   4   0   **23   0**
2000–01 Leicester C 11   0   **11   0**

LENNON, Neil (M)   **318 21**
H:5 9 W:13 02 b.Belfast 25-6-71
Source: Trainee. Honours: Northern Ireland
Under-21, 39 full caps, 2 goals.
1987–88 Manchester C 1   0
1988–89 Manchester C 0   0
1989–90 Manchester C 0   0   **1   0**
1990–91 Crewe Alex 34   3
1991–92 Crewe Alex   0   0
1992–93 Crewe Alex 24   0
1993–94 Crewe Alex 33   4
1994–95 Crewe Alex 31   6
1995–96 Crewe Alex 25   2   **147 15**
1995–96 Leicester C 15   1
1996–97 Leicester C 35   1
1997–98 Leicester C 37   2
1998–99 Leicester C 37   1
1999–2000 Leicester C 31   1
2000–01 Leicester C 15   0   **170   6**

LEWIS, Junior (F)   **80   8**
H:6 2 W:11 08 b.Wembley 9-10-73
Source: Trainee.
1992–93 Fulham   6   0   **6   0**
From Dover, Hendon
1999–2000 Gillingham 42   6
2000–01 Gillingham 17   2   **59   8**
2000–01 Leicester C 15   0   **15   0**

LYTH, Ashley (M)   **0   0**
b.Whitby 14-6-83
2000–01 Leicester C 0   0

MANCINI, Roberto‡ (M)   **545 156**
H:5 10 W:11 13 b.Jesi 27-11-64
Honours: Italy 36 full caps, 4 goals.
1981–82 Bologna   30   9   **30   9**
1982–83 Sampdoria   22   4
1983–84 Sampdoria   30   8
1984–85 Sampdoria   24   3
1985–86 Sampdoria   23   6
1986–87 Sampdoria   26   6
1987–88 Sampdoria   30   5
1988–89 Sampdoria   29   9
1989–90 Sampdoria   31 11
1990–91 Sampdoria   30 12
1991–92 Sampdoria   29   6
1992–93 Sampdoria   30 15
1993–94 Sampdoria   30 12
1994–95 Sampdoria   31   9
1995–96 Sampdoria   26 11
1996–97 Sampdoria   33 15   **424 132**
1997–98 Lazio   34   5
1998–99 Lazio   33 10
1999–2000 Lazio   20   0   **87 15**
2000–01 Leicester C 4   0   **4   0**

MARSHALL, Lee (M)   **126 11**
H:6 2 W:12 00 b.Islington 21-1-79
Source: Enfield. Honours: England Under-21.
1996–97 Norwich C   0   0
1997–98 Norwich C   4   0
1998–99 Norwich C   44   3
1999–2000 Norwich C   33   5
2000–01 Norwich C   36   3   **117 11**
2000–01 Leicester C 9   0   **9   0**

McCANN, Tim* (M)   **0   0**
H:5 9 W:12 00 b.Belfast 22-3-80
Source: Trainee.
1998–99 Leicester C 0   0
1999–2000 Leicester C 0   0
2000–01 Leicester C 0   0

MORTIMER, Alex (M)   **0   0**
H:5 10 W:10 06 b.Manchester 28-11-82
Source: Trainee.
1999–2000 Leicester C 0   0
2000–01 Leicester C 0   0

NURSE, Matt* (G)   **0   0**
H:6 1 W:13 02 b.Leicester 6-10-81
Source: Trainee.
2000–01 Leicester C 0   0

OAKES, Stefan (M)   **38   1**
H:5 11 W:12 08 b.Leicester 6-9-78
Source: Trainee.
1997–98 Leicester C 0   0
1998–99 Leicester C 3   0
1999–2000 Leicester C 22   1
2000–01 Leicester C 13   0   **38   1**

PIPER, Matt (M)   **0   0**
H:6 1 W:13 02 b.Leicester 29-9-81
Source: Trainee.
1999–2000 Leicester C 0   0
2000–01 Leicester C 0   0

PRICE, Michael (M)   **0   0**
b.Ashington 3-4-83
Source: Scholar.
2000–01 Leicester C 0   0

REEVES, Martin (M)   **0   0**
b.Birmingham 7-9-81
Source: Scholar.
2000–01 Leicester C 0   0

ROWETT, Gary (D)   **314 19**
H:6 0 W:12 10 b.Bromsgrove 6-3-74
Source: Trainee.
1991–92 Cambridge U 13   2
1992–93 Cambridge U 21   2
1993–94 Cambridge U 29   5   **63   9**
1993–94 Everton   2   0
1994–95 Everton   2   0   **4   0**
1994–95 *Blackpool* 17   0   **17   0**
1995–96 Derby Co   35   0
1996–97 Derby Co   35   1
1997–98 Derby Co   35   1
1998–99 Derby Co   0   0   **105   2**
1998–99 Birmingham C 42   5
1999–2000 Birmingham C 45   1   **87   6**
2000–01 Leicester C 38   2   **38   2**

ROYCE, Simon (G)   **176   0**
H:6 2 W:12 10 b.Newham 9-9-71
Source: Heybridge Swifts.
1991–92 Southend U   1   0
1992–93 Southend U   3   0
1993–94 Southend U   6   0
1994–95 Southend U 13   0
1995–96 Southend U 46   0
1996–97 Southend U 43   0
1997–98 Southend U 37   0   **149   0**
1998–99 Charlton Ath 8   0

1999–2000 Charlton Ath 0   0   **8   0**
2000–01 Leicester C 19   0   **19   0**

SAVAGE, Robbie (M)   **214 18**
H:5 11 W:11 02 b.Wrexham 18-10-74
Source: Trainee. Honours: Wales Under-21,
20 full caps, 1 goal.
1993–94 Manchester U 0   0
1994–95 Crewe Alex   6   2
1995–96 Crewe Alex 30   7
1996–97 Crewe Alex 41   1   **77 10**
1997–98 Leicester C 35   2
1998–99 Leicester C 34   1
1999–2000 Leicester C 35   1
2000–01 Leicester C 33   4   **137   8**

SHERMAN, David (D)   **0   0**
H:5 9 W:12 07 b.Wegberg 19-5-83
Source: Scholar.
2000–01 Leeds U   0   0
2000–01 Leicester C 0   0

SINCLAIR, Frank (D)   **257   9**
H:5 10 W:12 03 b.Lambeth 3-12-71
Source: Trainee. Honours: Jamaica full caps.
1989–90 Chelsea   0   0
1990–91 Chelsea   4   0
1991–92 Chelsea   8   1
1991–92 *WBA*   6   1   **6   1**
1992–93 Chelsea   32   0
1993–94 Chelsea   35   0
1994–95 Chelsea   35   3
1995–96 Chelsea   13   1
1996–97 Chelsea   20   1
1997–98 Chelsea   22   1   **169   7**
1998–99 Leicester C 31   1
1999–2000 Leicester C 34   0
2000–01 Leicester C 17   0   **82   1**

SMITH, Matthew (M)   **0   0**
b.Northampton 28-10-82
2000–01 Leicester C 0   0

STEVENSON, Jonathan (M)   **0   0**
b.Leicester 13-10-82
Source: Scholar.
2000–01 Leicester C 0   0

STEWART, Jordan (M)   **5   0**
H:6 0 W:12 04 b.Birmingham 3-3-82
Source: Trainee. Honours: England Youth.
1999–2000 Leicester C 1   0
1999–2000 *Bristol R* 4   0   **4   0**
2000–01 Leicester C 0   0   **1   0**

STURRIDGE, Dean (F)   **213 61**
H:5 8 W:12 02 b.Birmingham 27-7-73
Source: Trainee.
1991–92 Derby Co   1   0
1992–93 Derby Co   10   0
1993–94 Derby Co   0   0
1994–95 Derby Co   12   1
1994–95 *Torquay U* 10   5   **10   5**
1995–96 Derby Co   39 20
1996–97 Derby Co   30 11
1997–98 Derby Co   30   9
1998–99 Derby Co   29   5
1999–2000 Derby Co   25   6
2000–01 Derby Co   14   1   **190 53**
2000–01 Leicester C 13   3   **13   3**

TAGGART, Gerry (D)   **363 29**
H:6 2 W:14 01 b.Belfast 18-10-70
Source: Trainee. Honours: Northern Ireland
Under-23, 50 full caps, 7 goals.
1988–89 Manchester C 11   1
1989–90 Manchester C 1   0   **12   1**
1989–90 Barnsley   21   2
1990–91 Barnsley   30   2
1991–92 Barnsley   38   3
1992–93 Barnsley   44   4
1993–94 Barnsley   38   2
1994–95 Barnsley   41   3   **212 16**
1995–96 Bolton W   11   1
1996–97 Bolton W   43   3
1997–98 Bolton W   15   0   **69   4**
1998–99 Leicester C 15   0
1999–2000 Leicester C 31   6
2000–01 Leicester C 24   2   **70   8**

THOMAS, Danny (M)   **3   0**
H:5 7 W:10 10 b.Leamington Spa 1-5-81
Source: Trainee.
1997–98 Nottingham F 0   0
1998–99 Leicester C 0   0
1999–2000 Leicester C 3   0
2000–01 Leicester C 0   0   **3   0**

WEBB, Mark (M) 0 0
b.Wolverhampton 21-9-82
Source: Scholar.

2000-01	Leicester C	0	0	

Scholars
Frowen, Geraint; Hallows, Dominic K; Noble, Karl N; Purdie, Robert J; Savage, Michael J
Non-Contract
Andrews, Ian E

LEYTON ORIENT

AKONTOH, Ray‡ (F) 0 0
b.Clapham 23-11-81
Source: Trainee.

2000-01	Leyton Orient	0	0	

BARRETT, Scott# (G) 330 0
H: 5 11 W: 13 00 b.Ilkeston 2-4-63
Source: Ilkeston T.

1984-85	Wolverhampton W	4	0		
1985-86	Wolverhampton W	21	0		
1986-87	Wolverhampton W	5	0	30	0
1987-88	Stoke C	27	0		
1988-89	Stoke C	17	0		
1989-90	Stoke C	7	0	51	0
1989-90	*Colchester U*	13	0		
1989-90	*Stockport Co*	10	0	10	0
1990-91	Colchester U	0	0		
1991-92	Colchester U	0	0	13	0
1992-93	Gillingham	34	0		
1993-94	Gillingham	13	0		
1994-95	Gillingham	4	0	51	0
1995-96	Cambridge U	31	0		
1996-97	Cambridge U	45	0		
1997-98	Cambridge U	43	0		
1998-99	Cambridge U	0	0	119	0
1998-99	Leyton Orient	20	0		
1999-2000	Leyton Orient	29	0		
2000-01	Leyton Orient	7	0	56	0

BAYES, Ashley (G) 284 0
H: 6 1 W: 13 05 b.Lincoln 19-4-72
Source: Trainee.

1989-90	Brentford	1	0		
1990-91	Brentford	0	0		
1991-92	Brentford	1	0		
1992-93	Brentford	2	0	4	0
1993-94	Torquay U	32	0		
1994-95	Torquay U	37	0		
1995-96	Torquay U	28	0	97	0
1996-97	Exeter C	41	0		
1997-98	Exeter C	45	0		
1998-99	Exeter C	41	0	127	0
1999-2000	Leyton Orient	17	0		
2000-01	Leyton Orient	39	0	56	0

BEALL, Billy (M) 154 10
H: 5 6 W: 12 00 b.Enfield 4-12-77
Source: Trainee.

1995-96	Cambridge U	15	4		
1996-97	Cambridge U	36	2		
1997-98	Cambridge U	30	1		
1998-99	Cambridge U	0	0	81	7
1998-99	Leyton Orient	23	2		
1999-2000	Leyton Orient	33	1		
2000-01	Leyton Orient	17	0	73	3

BRISSETT, Jason‡ (F) 213 10
H: 5 10 W: 12 07 b.Redbridge 7-9-74
Source: Arsenal Trainee.

1993-94	Peterborough U	30	0		
1994-95	Peterborough U	5	0	35	0
1994-95	Bournemouth	25	0		
1995-96	Bournemouth	43	3		
1996-97	Bournemouth	25	4		
1997-98	Bournemouth	31	1	124	8
1998-99	Walsall	35	2		
1999-2000	Walsall	7	0	42	2
1999-2000	*Cheltenham T*	8	0	8	0
2000-01	Leyton Orient	4	0	4	0

BRKOVIC, Ahmet* (M) 69 8
H: 5 7 W: 10 02 b.Dubrovnik 23-9-74
Source: Dubrovnik.

1999-2000	Leyton Orient	29	5		
2000-01	Leyton Orient	40	3	69	8

CADIOU, Frederic‡ (F) 3 0
b.Paris 20-4-69
Source: Wasquehal.

2000-01	Leyton Orient	3	0	3	0

CARTER, Rob‡ (M) 2 0
H: 6 1 W: 12 01 b.Stepney 23-4-82
Source: Trainee.

1999-2000	Leyton Orient	2	0		
2000-01	Leyton Orient	0	0	2	0

CASTLE, Steve (M) 488 110
H: 5 11 W: 11 07 b.Ilford 17-5-66
Source: Apprentice.

1984-85	Orient	21	1		
1985-86	Orient	23	4		
1986-87	Orient	24	5		
1987-88	Orient	42	10		
1988-89	Orient	24	6		
1989-90	Orient	27	7		
1990-91	Orient	45	12		
1991-92	Orient	37	10	243	55
1992-93	Plymouth Arg	31	11		
1993-94	Plymouth Arg	44	21		
1994-95	Plymouth Arg	26	3	101	35
1995-96	Birmingham C	15	1		
1995-96	*Gillingham*	6	1	6	1
1996-97	Birmingham C	8	0	23	1
1996-97	*Leyton Orient*	4	1		
1996-97	Peterborough U	0	0		
1997-98	Peterborough U	37	3		
1998-99	Peterborough U	26	4		
1999-2000	Peterborough U	39	10	102	17
2000-01	Leyton Orient	9	0	13	1

CHRISTIE, Iyseden (F) 137 27
H: 5 10 W: 12 02 b.Coventry 14-11-76
Source: Trainee.

1994-95	Coventry C	0	0		
1995-96	Coventry C	1	0		
1996-97	Coventry C	0	0	1	0
1996-97	*Bournemouth*	4	0	4	0
1996-97	*Mansfield T*	8	0		
1997-98	Mansfield T	39	10		
1998-99	Mansfield T	36	8	89	18
1999-2000	Mansfield T	36	7		
2000-01	Leyton Orient	7	2	43	9

DORRIAN, Chris (D) 2 0
b.Harlow 3-4-82
Source: Trainee.

2000-01	Leyton Orient	2	0	2	0

DOWNER, Simon (D) 56 0
H: 5 11 W: 12 08 b.Romford 19-10-81
Source: Trainee.

1998-99	Leyton Orient	1	0		
1999-2000	Leyton Orient	24	0		
2000-01	Leyton Orient	31	0	56	0

FORGE, Nicolas† (D) 1 0
b.Roanne 13-5-77
Source: Trainee.

2000-01	Leyton Orient	1	0	1	0

GOUGH, Neil (F) 4 0
H: 5 11 W: 11 08 b.Harlow 1-9-81
Source: Trainee.

1999-2000	Leyton Orient	4	0		
2000-01	Leyton Orient	0	0	4	0

GOULD, Ronnie (M) 2 0
H: 5 11 W: 11 05 b.London 27-9-82
Source: Trainee.

1999-2000	Leyton Orient	2	0		
2000-01	Leyton Orient	0	0	2	0

GRIFFITHS, Carl (F) 321 116
H: 5 9 W: 11 04 b.Welshpool 15-7-71
Source: Trainee. *Honours:* Wales Youth, Under-21.

1988-89	Shrewsbury T	28	6		
1989-90	Shrewsbury T	18	4		
1990-91	Shrewsbury T	19	4		
1991-92	Shrewsbury T	27	8		
1992-93	Shrewsbury T	42	27		
1993-94	Shrewsbury T	9	5	143	54
1993-94	Manchester C	16	4		
1994-95	Manchester C	2	0		
1995-96	Manchester C	0	0	18	4
1995-96	*Portsmouth*	14	2	14	2
1995-96	Peterborough U	4	1		
1996-97	Peterborough U	12	1	16	2
1996-97	Leyton Orient	13	6		
1997-98	Leyton Orient	33	18		
1998-99	Leyton Orient	24	8		
1998-99	*Wrexham*	4	3	4	3
1998-99	Port Vale	3	1		
1999-2000	Port Vale	5	0	8	1
1999-2000	Leyton Orient	11	4		
2000-01	Leyton Orient	37	14	118	50

HARRIS, Andy# (D) 131 0
H: 5 10 W: 12 02 b.Springs 26-2-77
Source: Trainee.

1993-94	Liverpool	0	0		
1994-95	Liverpool	0	0		
1995-96	Liverpool	0	0		
1996-97	Southend U	44	0		
1997-98	Southend U	27	0		
1998-99	Southend U	44	0	72	0
1999-2000	Southend U	15	0		
2000-01	Leyton Orient	44	0	59	0

HATCHER, Daniel§ (F) 2 0
b.Newport 24-12-83
Source: Scholar.

2000-01	Leyton Orient	2	0	2	0

HOUGHTON, Scott (M) 291 41
H: 5 5 W: 12 02 b.Hitchin 22-10-71
Source: Trainee. *Honours:* England Schools, Youth.

1990-91	Tottenham H	0	0		
1990-91	*Ipswich T*	8	1	8	1
1991-92	Tottenham H	10	2		
1992-93	Tottenham H	0	0	10	2
1992-93	*Cambridge U*	0	0		
1992-93	*Gillingham*	3	0	3	0
1992-93	*Charlton Ath*	6	0	6	0
1993-94	Luton T	15	1		
1994-95	Luton T	1	0	16	1
1994-95	Walsall	38	8		
1995-96	Walsall	40	6	78	14
1996-97	Peterborough U	32	8		
1997-98	Peterborough U	30	4		
1998-99	Peterborough U	8	1	70	13
1998-99	Southend U	27	3		
1999-2000	Southend U	43	4		
2000-01	Southend U	9	2	79	9
2000-01	Leyton Orient	21	1	22	1

IBEHRE, Jabo§ (M) 8 2
H: 6 2 W: 12 10 b.London 28-1-83
Source: Trainee.

1999-2000	Leyton Orient	3	0		
2000-01	Leyton Orient	5	2	8	2

JONES, Billy§ (D) 1 0
b.Chatham 26-6-83
Source: Trainee.

1999-2000	Leyton Orient	1	0	1	0

JOSEPH, Matt (D) 292 7
H: 5 7 W: 10 02 b.Bethnal Green 30-9-72
Source: Trainee.

1991-92	Arsenal	0	0		
1992-93	Gillingham	0	0		
1993-94	Cambridge U	27	2		
1994-95	Cambridge U	39	2		
1995-96	Cambridge U	42	2		
1996-97	Cambridge U	44	0		
1997-98	Cambridge U	7	0	159	6
1997-98	Leyton Orient	14	1		
1998-99	Leyton Orient	34	0		
1999-2000	Leyton Orient	41	0		
2000-01	Leyton Orient	44	0	133	1

LING, Martin (M) 565 64
H: 5 7 W: 10 08 b.West Ham 15-7-66
Source: Apprentice.

1983-84	Exeter C	29	0		
1984-85	Exeter C	42	6		
1985-86	Exeter C	45	8	116	14
1986-87	Swindon T	2	0		
1986-87	Southend U	24	8		
1987-88	Southend U	42	7		
1988-89	Southend U	44	6		
1989-90	Southend U	25	10		
1990-91	Southend U	3	0	138	31
1990-91	*Mansfield T*	3	0	3	0
1990-91	Swindon T	1	0		
1991-92	Swindon T	21	3		
1992-93	Swindon T	43	3		
1993-94	Swindon T	33	1		
1994-95	Swindon T	36	3		
1995-96	Swindon T	16	0	152	10
1996-97	Leyton Orient	44	1		
1997-98	Leyton Orient	46	2		
1998-99	Leyton Orient	44	4		
1999-2000	Leyton Orient	14	1		
1999-2000	*Brighton & HA*	8	1	8	1
2000-01	Leyton Orient	0	0	148	8

LOCKWOOD, Matt (D) 173 17
H: 5 9 W: 10 12 b.Rochford 17-10-76
Source: Trainee.

1994-95	QPR	0	0		
1995-96	QPR	0	0		
1996-97	Bristol R	39	1		
1997-98	Bristol R	24	0	63	1
1998-99	Leyton Orient	37	3		
1999-2000	Leyton Orient	41	6		
2000-01	Leyton Orient	32	7	110	16

MANSLEY, Chad† (M) 1 0
b.Newcastle 13-11-80
Source: Watford.

2000-01	Leyton Orient	1	0	1	0

MARTIN, John (M) 29 0
H: 5 5 W: 10 00 b.Bethnal Green 15-7-81
Source: Trainee.

1997-98	Leyton Orient	1	0		
1998-99	Leyton Orient	1	0		
1999-2000	Leyton Orient	8	0		
2000-01	Leyton Orient	19	0	29	0

McELHOLM, Brendan (M) **15 0**
H: 5 11 W: 12 02 b.Omagh 7-7-82
Source: Trainee.
1999–2000 Leyton Orient 3 0
2000–01 Leyton Orient 12 0 **15 0**

McGHEE, Dave (D) **179 12**
H: 6 0 W: 12 01 b.Worthing 19-6-76
Source: Trainee.
1994–95 Brentford 7 1
1995–96 Brentford 36 5
1996–97 Brentford 45 1
1997–98 Brentford 29 1
1998–99 Brentford 0 0 **117 8**
From Stevenage Bor.
1999–2000 Leyton Orient 23 1
2000–01 Leyton Orient 39 3 **62 4**

McLEAN, Aaron§ (F) **5 1**
H: 5 6 W: 10 02 b.Hammersmith 25-5-83
Source: Trainee.
1999–2000 Leyton Orient 3 0
2000–01 Leyton Orient 2 1 **5 1**

MURRAY, Jade (F) **2 0**
H: 5 9 W: 11 05 b.Islington 23-9-81
Source: Trainee.
1999–2000 Leyton Orient 2 0
2000–01 Leyton Orient 0 0 **2 0**

OPARA, Chris-Santos§ (F) **25 0**
H: 6 0 W: 12 06 b.Oweri Imo State 21-12-81
Source: Trainee.
1998–99 Colchester U 1 0
1999–2000 Colchester U 16 0
2000–01 Colchester U 2 0 **19 0**
2000–01 Leyton Orient 6 0 **6 0**

OPINEL, Sasha# (D) **11 1**
H: 5 9 W: 12 00 b.Bourg 9-4-77
2000–01 Plymouth Arg 0 0
2000–01 Leyton Orient 11 1 **11 1**

PARSONS, David (M) **1 0**
H: 6 1 W: 12 07 b.Greenwich 25-2-82
Source: Trainee.
1999–2000 Leyton Orient 1 0
2000–01 Leyton Orient 0 0 **1 0**

SMITH, Dean (D) **426 48**
H: 6 0 W: 13 00 b.West Bromwich 19-3-71
Source: Trainee.
1988–89 Walsall 15 0
1989–90 Walsall 7 0
1990–91 Walsall 33 0
1991–92 Walsall 9 0
1992–93 Walsall 42 1
1993–94 Walsall 36 1 **142 2**
1994–95 Hereford U 35 3
1995–96 Hereford U 40 8
1996–97 Hereford U 42 8 **117 19**
1997–98 Leyton Orient 43 9
1998–99 Leyton Orient 37 9
1999–2000 Leyton Orient 44 4
2000–01 Leyton Orient 43 5 **167 27**

TATE, Chris (F) **89 20**
H: 6 0 W: 12 03 b.York 27-12-77
Source: York C Trainee.
1996–97 Sunderland 0 0
1997–98 Scarborough 24 1
1998–99 Scarborough 25 12 **49 13**
1999–2000 Halifax T 18 4 **18 4**
From Scarborough.
2000–01 Leyton Orient 22 3 **22 3**

UKA, Niam (M) **0 0**
H: 5 7 W: 10 01 b.Kosovo 26-10-81
Source: Partizani.
1999–2000 Leyton Orient 0 0
2000–01 Leyton Orient 0 0

VASSEUR, Emmanuel‡ (M) **2 0**
b.Calais 3-9-76
Source: Calais.
2000–01 Leyton Orient 2 0 **2 0**

WALSCHAERTS, Wim* (M) **125 9**
H: 5 11 W: 12 00 b.Antwerp 5-11-72
Source: FC Tielen.
1998–99 Leyton Orient 44 3
1999–2000 Leyton Orient 36 3
2000–01 Leyton Orient 45 3 **125 9**

WATTS, Steve (F) **96 20**
H: 6 1 W: 13 00 b.Peckham 11-7-76
Source: Fisher Ath.
1998–99 Leyton Orient 28 6
1999–2000 Leyton Orient 32 6
2000–01 Leyton Orient 36 8 **96 20**

Trainees
Goodfellow, Mark; Grimsdell, Daniel B; Ibehre, Jabo O; Jones, William K; McLean, Aaron; Morgan, Thomas

Scholars
Barnard, Donny G; Berry, Jimmie; Bray, Thomas J; Forbes, Boniek MG; Hatcher, Daniel I; Levy, Adam H; McGee, Paul; Morris, Glenn J; Opara, Kelechi C; Stephens, Kevin; Wild, Christopher

LINCOLN C

BARNETT, Dave‡ (D) **209 8**
H: 6 0 W: 12 08 b.Birmingham 16-4-67
Source: Windsor & Eton.
1988–89 Colchester U 20 0 **20 0**
1989–90 WBA 0 0
1990–91 Walsall 5 0 **5 0**
From Kidderminster H
1991–92 Barnet 4 0
1992–93 Barnet 36 2
1993–94 Barnet 19 1 **59 3**
1993–94 Birmingham C 9 0
1994–95 Birmingham C 31 0
1995–96 Birmingham C 0 0
1996–97 Birmingham C 6 0 **46 0**
1997–98 Dunfermline Ath 21 1 **21 1**
1997–98 Port Vale 9 1
1998–99 Port Vale 27 0 **36 1**
1999–2000 Lincoln C 22 3
2000–01 Lincoln C 0 0 **22 3**

BARNETT, Jason (D) **181 4**
H: 5 9 W: 10 10 b.Shrewsbury 21-4-76
Source: Trainee.
1994–95 Wolverhampton W 0 0
1995–96 Wolverhampton W 0 0
1995–96 Lincoln C 32 2
1996–97 Lincoln C 36 0
1997–98 Lincoln C 33 0
1998–99 Lincoln C 29 1
1999–2000 Lincoln C 18 0
2000–01 Lincoln C 33 1 **181 4**

BATTERSBY, Tony (F) **198 35**
H: 6 0 W: 12 09 b.Doncaster 30-8-75
Source: Trainee.
1993–94 Sheffield U 0 0
1994–95 Sheffield U 0 0
1994–95 *Southend U* 8 1 **8 1**
1995–96 Sheffield U 10 1 **10 1**
1995–96 Notts Co 21 7
1996–97 Notts Co 18 1 **39 8**
1996–97 *Bury* 11 2
1997–98 Bury 37 6
1998–99 Bury 0 0 **48 8**
1998–99 Lincoln C 39 7
1999–2000 Lincoln C 16 3
1999–2000 *Northampton T* 3 1 **3 1**
2000–01 Lincoln C 35 6 **90 16**

BIMSON, Stuart# (D) **134 3**
H: 5 11 W: 11 08 b.Liverpool 29-9-69
Source: Macclesfield T.
1994–95 Bury 19 0
1995–96 Bury 16 0
1996–97 Bury 1 0 **36 0**
1996–97 Lincoln C 15 1
1997–98 Lincoln C 12 0
1998–99 Lincoln C 31 2
1999–2000 Lincoln C 20 0
2000–01 Lincoln C 20 0 **98 3**

BROWN, Grant# (D) **385 15**
H: 6 0 W: 11 12 b.Sunderland 19-11-69
Source: Trainee.
1987–88 Leicester C 2 0
1988–89 Leicester C 12 0 **14 0**
1989–90 Lincoln C 34 2
1990–91 Lincoln C 32 1
1991–92 Lincoln C 37 1
1992–93 Lincoln C 40 1
1993–94 Lincoln C 38 3
1994–95 Lincoln C 39 3
1995–96 Lincoln C 34 0
1996–97 Lincoln C 34 1
1997–98 Lincoln C 15 0
1998–99 Lincoln C 22 1
1999–2000 Lincoln C 26 0
2000–01 Lincoln C 20 2 **371 15**

BULLOCK, Tony* (G) **64 0**
H: 6 1 W: 14 01 b.Warrington 18-2-72
Source: Northwich V, Leek T.
1996–97 Barnsley 0 0
1997–98 Barnsley 0 0
1998–99 Barnsley 32 0
1999–2000 Barnsley 6 0 **38 0**
2000–01 Macclesfield T 24 0 **24 0**
2000–01 Lincoln C 2 0 **2 0**

CAMERON, Dave (F) **44 4**
H: 6 1 W: 12 05 b.Bangor 24-8-75
1998–99 St Mirren 11 2 **11 2**
1999–2000 Brighton & HA 17 0 **17 0**
From Worthing.
2000–01 Lincoln C 16 2 **16 2**

CAMM, Mark (D) **3 0**
H: 5 8 W: 10 12 b.Mansfield 1-10-81
Source: Trainee.
1999–2000 Sheffield U 0 0
2000–01 Lincoln C 3 0 **3 0**

EUSTACE, Scott (D) **152 7**
H: 6 1 W: 15 03 b.Leicester 13-6-75
Source: Trainee.
1993–94 Leicester C 1 0
1994–95 Leicester C 0 0 **1 0**
1995–96 Mansfield T 27 1
1996–97 Mansfield T 42 4
1997–98 Mansfield T 29 1
1998–99 Mansfield T 0 0 **98 6**
1998–99 Cambridge U 16 0
1999–2000 Cambridge U 36 1 **52 1**
2000–01 Lincoln C 1 0 **1 0**

FINNIGAN, John (M) **120 3**
H: 5 8 W: 10 11 b.Wakefield 29-3-76
Source: Trainee.
1992–93 Nottingham F 0 0
1993–94 Nottingham F 0 0
1994–95 Nottingham F 0 0
1995–96 Nottingham F 0 0
1996–97 Nottingham F 0 0
1997–98 Nottingham F 0 0
1997–98 *Lincoln C* 6 0
1998–99 Lincoln C 37 1
1999–2000 Lincoln C 37 2
2000–01 Lincoln C 40 0 **120 3**

GAIN, Peter (M) **60 7**
H: 5 9 W: 11 00 b.Hammersmith 2-11-76
Source: Trainee.
1995–96 Tottenham H 0 0
1996–97 Tottenham H 0 0
1997–98 Tottenham H 0 0
1998–99 Tottenham H 0 0
1998–99 Lincoln C 4 0
1999–2000 Lincoln C 32 2
2000–01 Lincoln C 24 5 **60 7**

GARRATT, Martin‡ (M) **53 1**
H: 5 10 W: 11 00 b.York 22-2-80
1998–99 York C 38 1
1999–2000 York C 7 0 **45 1**
1999–2000 Mansfield T 6 0
2000–01 Mansfield T 0 0 **6 0**
2000–01 Lincoln C 2 0 **2 0**

GHENT, Matthew‡ (G) **1 0**
H: 6 3 W: 14 01 b.Burton 5-10-80
Source: Trainee. *Honours:* England Schools, Youth.
1997–98 Aston Villa 0 0
1998–99 Aston Villa 0 0
1999–2000 Aston Villa 0 0
2000–01 Aston Villa 0 0
2000–01 Lincoln C 1 0 **1 0**

HENRY, Anthony* (D) **18 1**
H: 6 0 W: 13 00 b.London 13-9-79
Source: Trainee.
1997–98 West Ham U 0 0
1998–99 West Ham U 0 0
1999–2000 Lincoln C 17 1
2000–01 Lincoln C 1 0 **18 1**

HOLMES, Steve (D) **199 32**
H: 6 2 W: 13 00 b.Middlesbrough 13-1-71
Source: Guisborough T.
1993–94 Preston NE 0 0
1994–95 Preston NE 5 1
1994–95 *Hartlepool U* 5 2 **5 2**
From Guisborough T.
1995–96 Preston NE 8 0 **13 1**
1995–96 Lincoln C 23 2
1996–97 Lincoln C 28 4
1997–98 Lincoln C 46 4
1998–99 Lincoln C 37 6
1999–2000 Lincoln C 9 2
2000–01 Lincoln C 38 11 **181 29**

LEWIS, Graham‡ (F) **7 0**
H: 5 10 W: 11 00 b.Reading 15-2-82
Source: Trainee.
1999–2000 Lincoln C 5 0
2000–01 Lincoln C 2 0 **7 0**

LOGAN, Richard (M) **216 20**
H: 6 0 W: 13 03 b.Barnsley 24-5-69
Source: Gainsborough T.
1993–94 Huddersfield T 16 0
1994–95 Huddersfield T 27 1
1995–96 Huddersfield T 2 0 **45 1**
1995–96 Plymouth Arg 31 4
1996–97 Plymouth Arg 28 4
1997–98 Plymouth Arg 27 4 **86 12**
1998–99 Scunthorpe U 41 6

MARRIOTT, Alan (G) — 48 0
H: 5 11 W: 12 05 b.Bedford 3-9-78
Source: Trainee.

1999-2000	Scunthorpe U	39	1	80	7
2000-01	Lincoln C	5	0	5	0
1997-98	Tottenham H	0	0		
1998-99	Tottenham H	0	0		
1999-2000	Lincoln C	18	0		
2000-01	Lincoln C	30	0	48	0

MAYO, Paul (D) — 46 0
H: 5 11 W: 11 09 b.Lincoln 13-10-81
Source: Scholarship.

1999-2000	Lincoln C	19	0		
2000-01	Lincoln C	27	0	46	0

MILLER, Paul* (M) — 309 45
H: 6 0 W: 11 07 b.Bisley 31-1-68
Source: Trainee.

1987-88	Wimbledon	5	0		
1987-88	Newport Co	6	2	6	2
1988-89	Wimbledon	18	5		
1989-90	Wimbledon	15	2		
1989-90	Bristol C	3	0	3	0
1990-91	Wimbledon	1	0		
1991-92	Wimbledon	22	2		
1992-93	Wimbledon	19	1		
1993-94	Wimbledon	0	0	80	10
1994-95	Bristol R	42	16		
1995-96	Bristol R	38	4		
1996-97	Bristol R	25	2	105	22
1997-98	Lincoln C	24	2		
1998-99	Lincoln C	32	2		
1999-2000	Lincoln C	40	7		
2000-01	Lincoln C	19	0	115	11

PEACOCK, Richard* (M) — 242 27
H: 6 1 W: 11 05 b.Sheffield 29-10-72
Source: Sheffield FC.

1993-94	Hull C	11	1		
1994-95	Hull C	37	5		
1995-96	Hull C	45	7		
1996-97	Hull C	40	4		
1997-98	Hull C	27	2		
1998-99	Hull C	14	2	174	21
1998-99	Lincoln C	10	0		
1999-2000	Lincoln C	24	3		
2000-01	Lincoln C	34	3	68	6

PERKINS, Chris* (D) — 214 3
H: 5 11 W: 10 09 b.Nottingham 9-1-74
Source: Trainee.

1992-93	Mansfield T	5	0		
1993-94	Mansfield T	3	0	8	0
1994-95	Chesterfield	18	0		
1995-96	Chesterfield	22	0		
1996-97	Chesterfield	30	0		
1997-98	Chesterfield	43	2		
1998-99	Chesterfield	34	1		
1999-2000	Hartlepool U	8	0	8	0
1999-2000	Chesterfield	31	0		
2000-01	Chesterfield	8	0	186	3
2000-01	Lincoln C	12	0	12	0

SCHOFIELD, Jon† (D) — 471 23
H: 5 10 W: 11 08 b.Barnsley 16-5-65
Source: Gainsborough T.

1988-89	Lincoln C	29	2		
1989-90	Lincoln C	29	2		
1990-91	Lincoln C	42	3		
1991-92	Lincoln C	39	1		
1992-93	Lincoln C	40	0		
1993-94	Lincoln C	40	2		
1994-95	Lincoln C	12	1		
1994-95	Doncaster R	27	1		
1995-96	Doncaster R	41	4		
1996-97	Doncaster R	42	7	110	12
1997-98	Mansfield T	44	0		
1998-99	Mansfield T	42	0	86	0
1999-2000	Hull C	25	0	25	0
2000-01	Lincoln C	19	0	250	11

SEDGEMORE, Ben (M) — 206 13
H: 6 0 W: 12 07 b.Wolverhampton 5-8-75
Source: Trainee. Honours: England Schools.

1993-94	Birmingham C	1	0		
1994-95	Birmingham C	0	0		
1994-95	*Northampton T*	1	0	1	0
1995-96	Birmingham C	0	0		
1995-96	*Mansfield T*	1	0		
1996-97	Peterborough U	17	0		
1996-97	Mansfield T	0	0	17	0
1996-97	Mansfield T	39	4		
1997-98	Mansfield T	28	2	76	6
1997-98	Macclesfield T	5	0		
1998-99	Macclesfield T	35	2		
1999-2000	Macclesfield T	35	1		
2000-01	Macclesfield T	27	3	102	6
2000-01	Lincoln C	10	1	10	1

SMITH, Paul (M) — 112 17
H: 5 11 W: 11 07 b.Hastings 25-1-76
Source: Hastings T.

1994-95	Nottingham F	0	0		
1995-96	Nottingham F	0	0		
1996-97	Nottingham F	0	0		
1997-98	Nottingham F	0	0		
1997-98	*Lincoln C*	17	3		
1998-99	Lincoln C	28	2		
1999-2000	Lincoln C	27	5		
2000-01	Lincoln C	40	7	112	17

STERGIOPOULOS, Marcus‡ (F) — 7 0
b.Melbourne 12-6-75
Honours: From Carlton 53 apps, 2 goals, Eastern Pride 89 apps, 2 goals, Football Kingz 28 apps, 1 goal.

2000-01	Lincoln C	7	0	7	0

THORPE, Lee (F) — 167 45
H: 6 0 W: 11 06 b.Wolverhampton 14-12-75
Source: Trainee.

1993-94	Blackpool	1	0		
1994-95	Blackpool	1	0		
1995-96	Blackpool	1	0		
1996-97	Blackpool	9	0	12	0
1997-98	Lincoln C	44	14		
1998-99	Lincoln C	38	8		
1999-2000	Lincoln C	42	16		
2000-01	Lincoln C	31	7	155	45

WALKER, Justin (M) — 177 3
H: 6 0 W: 13 03 b.Nottingham 6-9-75
Source: Trainee. Honours: England Schools, Youth.

1992-93	Nottingham F	0	0		
1993-94	Nottingham F	0	0		
1994-95	Nottingham F	0	0		
1995-96	Nottingham F	0	0		
1996-97	Nottingham F	0	0		
1996-97	Scunthorpe U	9	0		
1997-98	Scunthorpe U	40	1		
1998-99	Scunthorpe U	41	1		
1999-2000	Scunthorpe U	42	0	132	2
2000-01	Lincoln C	45	1	45	1

WELSH, Steve* (D) — 302 2
H: 6 0 W: 12 03 b.Glasgow 19-4-68
Source: Army.

1989-90	Cambridge U	1	0		
1990-91	Cambridge U	1	0	1	0
1991-92	Peterborough U	42	0		
1992-93	Peterborough U	45	1		
1993-94	Peterborough U	45	1		
1994-95	Peterborough U	14	0		
1994-95	*Preston NE*	0	0		
1994-95	Partick T	20	0		
1995-96	Partick T	35	0	55	0
1996-97	*Peterborough U*	6	0	152	2
1996-97	Dunfermline Ath	20	0		
1997-98	Dunfermline Ath	6	0	26	0
1998-99	Ayr U	25	0	25	0
1999-2000	Lincoln C	32	0		
2000-01	Lincoln C	11	0	43	0

Scholars
Bent, Daniel; Bone, Liam K; Byrne, Richard A; Cochrane, Gary J; Davies, Christopher M; Garfoot, Stephen R; Greenwood, David; Kinsella, Sean I; McConville, Christopher; Pinkney, Grant E
Non-Contract
Schofield, John D

LIVERPOOL

ARMSTRONG, Ian* (F) — 0 0
b.Fazackerley 16-11-81
Source: Trainee. Honours: England Schools, Youth.

1998-99	Liverpool	0	0		
1999-2000	Liverpool	0	0		
2000-01	Liverpool	0	0		

ARPHEXAD, Pegguy (G) — 24 0
H: 6 2 W: 13 07 b.Abymes 18-5-73
Source: Brest.

1994-95	Lens	0	0		
1995-96	Lens	3	0		
1996-97	Lens	0	0	3	0
1997-98	Leicester C	6	0		
1998-99	Leicester C	4	0		
1999-2000	Leicester C	11	0	21	0
2000-01	Liverpool	0	0		

BABBEL, Markus (D) — 280 13
H: 6 0 W: 13 03 b.Munich 8-9-72
Honours: Germany 51 full caps, 1 goal.

1991-92	Bayern Munich	0	0		
1992-93	Hamburg	27	1		
1993-94	Hamburg	33	0	60	1
1994-95	Bayern Munich	26	2		
1995-96	Bayern Munich	30	2		
1996-97	Bayern Munich	31	2		
1997-98	Bayern Munich	30	1		
1998-99	Bayern Munich	27	1		
1999-2000	Bayern Munich	26	1	182	9
2000-01	Liverpool	38	3	38	3

BARMBY, Nick (M) — 271 48
H: 5 6 W: 11 04 b.Hull 11-2-74
Source: Trainee. Honours: England Schools, Youth, Under-21, B, 19 full caps, 4 goals.

1991-92	Tottenham H	0	0		
1992-93	Tottenham H	22	6		
1993-94	Tottenham H	27	5		
1994-95	Tottenham H	39	9	87	20
1995-96	Middlesbrough	32	7		
1996-97	Middlesbrough	10	1	42	8
1996-97	Everton	25	4		
1997-98	Everton	30	2		
1998-99	Everton	24	3		
1999-2000	Everton	37	9	116	18
2000-01	Liverpool	26	2	26	2

BERGER, Patrik (M) — 239 55
H: 6 1 W: 13 00 b.Prague 10-11-73
Honours: Czech Republic 43 full caps, 18 goals.

1991-92	Slavia Prague	20	3		
1992-93	Slavia Prague	29	10		
1993-94	Slavia Prague	12	4		
1994-95	Slavia Prague	28	7	89	24
1995-96	Borussia Dortmund	25	4	25	4
1996-97	Liverpool	23	6		
1997-98	Liverpool	22	3		
1998-99	Liverpool	32	7		
1999-2000	Liverpool	34	9		
2000-01	Liverpool	14	2	125	27

BISCAN, Igor (M) — 78 9
H: 6 3 W: 12 08 b.Zagreb 4-5-78
Honours: Croatia 12 full caps, 1 goal.

1997-98	Samobor	12	1	12	1
1997-98	Dinamo Zagreb	5	0		
1998-99	Dinamo Zagreb	19	2		
1999-2000	Dinamo Zagreb	29	6	53	8
2000-01	Liverpool	13	0	13	0

CARRAGHER, Jamie (M) — 126 2
H: 6 1 W: 12 05 b.Liverpool 28-1-78
Source: Trainee. Honours: England Youth, Under-21, B, 3 full caps.

1995-96	Liverpool	0	0		
1996-97	Liverpool	2	1		
1997-98	Liverpool	20	0		
1998-99	Liverpool	34	1		
1999-2000	Liverpool	36	0		
2000-01	Liverpool	34	0	126	2

DIOMEDE, Bernard (M) — 178 30
H: 5 9 W: 12 04 b.Bourges 23-1-74
Honours: France 8 full caps.

1992-93	Auxerre	7	0		
1993-94	Auxerre	2	0		
1994-95	Auxerre	26	3		
1995-96	Auxerre	33	9		
1996-97	Auxerre	31	6		
1997-98	Auxerre	31	4		
1998-99	Auxerre	27	5		
1999-2000	Auxerre	19	3	176	30
2000-01	Liverpool	2	0	2	0

DOHERTY, Kevin* (M) — 0 0
b.Dublin 18-4-80

1998-99	Liverpool	0	0		
1999-2000	Liverpool	0	0		
2000-01	Liverpool	0	0		

FOLEY-SHERIDAN, Michael (M) — 0 0
b.Dublin 9-3-83

1999-2000	Liverpool	0	0		
2000-01	Liverpool	0	0		

FOWLER, Robbie (F) — 226 117
H: 5 11 W: 11 12 b.Liverpool 9-4-75
Source: Trainee. Honours: England Youth, B, Under-21, 18 full caps, 4 goals.

1991-92	Liverpool	0	0		
1992-93	Liverpool	0	0		
1993-94	Liverpool	28	12		
1994-95	Liverpool	42	25		
1995-96	Liverpool	38	28		
1996-97	Liverpool	32	18		
1997-98	Liverpool	20	9		
1998-99	Liverpool	25	14		
1999-2000	Liverpool	14	3		
2000-01	Liverpool	27	8	226	117

GERRARD, Steven (M) — 74 8
H: 6 1 W: 12 03 b.Whiston 30-5-80
Source: Trainee. Honours: England Youth, Under-21, 5 full caps.

1997-98	Liverpool	0	0		
1998-99	Liverpool	12	0		

1999–2000	Liverpool	29	1	
2000–01	Liverpool	33	7	74 8

HAMANN, Dietmar (M) 186 13
H: 6 2 W: 12 01 b.Waldasson 27-8-73
Source: Wacker Munich. *Honours:* Germany 32 full caps, 3 goals.

1993–94	Bayern Munich	5	1	
1994–95	Bayern Munich	30	0	
1995–96	Bayern Munich	20	2	
1996–97	Bayern Munich	22	1	
1997–98	Bayern Munich	28	2	105 6
1998–99	Newcastle U	23	4	23 4
1999–2000	Liverpool	28	1	
2000–01	Liverpool	30	2	58 3

HEGGEM, Vegard (D) 111 8
H: 5 11 W: 12 04 b.Trondheim 13-7-75
Honours: Norway 20 full caps, 1 goal.

1995	Rosenborg	15	1	
1996	Rosenborg	14	1	
1997	Rosenborg	23	3	
1998	Rosenborg	5	0	57 5
1998–99	Liverpool	29	2	
1999–2000	Liverpool	22	1	
2000–01	Liverpool	3	0	54 3

HENCHOZ, Stephane (D) 271 0
H: 6 1 W: 12 06 b.Billens 7-9-74
Source: Bulle. *Honours:* Switzerland 50 full caps.

1992–93	Neuchatel Xamax	35	0	
1993–94	Neuchatel Xamax	21	1	
1994–95	Neuchatel Xamax	35	0	91 1
1995–96	Hamburg	31	2	
1996–97	Hamburg	18	0	49 2
1997–98	Blackburn R	36	0	
1998–99	Blackburn R	34	0	70 0
1999–2000	Liverpool	29	0	
2000–01	Liverpool	32	0	61 0

HESKEY, Emile (F) 202 57
H: 6 1 W: 14 04 b.Leicester 11-1-78
Source: Trainee. *Honours:* England Youth, Under-21, B, 16 full caps, 2 goals.

1994–95	Leicester C	1	0	
1995–96	Leicester C	30	7	
1996–97	Leicester C	35	10	
1997–98	Leicester C	35	10	
1998–99	Leicester C	30	6	
1999–2000	Leicester C	23	7	154 40
1999–2000	Liverpool	12	3	
2000–01	Liverpool	36	14	48 17

HYYPIA, Sami (D) 236 11
H: 6 4 W: 13 11 b.Porvoo 7-10-73
Source: KuMu. *Honours:* Finland 39 full caps, 1 goal.

1993	MyPa 47	12	0	
1994	MyPa 47	25	0	
1995	MyPa 47	26	3	63 3
1995–96	Willem II	14	0	
1996–97	Willem II	30	1	
1997–98	Willem II	30	0	
1998–99	Willem II	26	2	100 3
1999–2000	Liverpool	38	2	
2000–01	Liverpool	35	3	73 5

KIPPE, Frode (D) 68 3
H: 6 4 W: 14 02 b.Oslo 17-1-78

1997	Lillestrom	9	0	
1998	Lillestrom	25	2	34 2
1998–99	Liverpool	0	0	
1999–2000	Liverpool	0	0	
1999–2000	Stoke C	15	1	
2000–01	Liverpool	0	0	
2000–01	Stoke C	19	0	34 1

LITMANEN, Jari (F) 316 145
H: 6 0 W: 12 10 b.Lahti 20-2-71
Honours: Finland 70 full caps, 18 goals.

1987	Reipas Lahti	9	0	
1988	Reipas Lahti	26	8	
1989	Reipas Lahti	25	6	
1990	Reipas Lahti	26	14	86 28
1991	HJK Helsinki	27	16	27 16
1992	MyPa	18	7	18 7
1992–93	Ajax	12	1	
1993–94	Ajax	30	26	
1994–95	Ajax	27	17	
1995–96	Ajax	26	13	
1996–97	Ajax	16	6	
1997–98	Ajax	25	16	
1998–99	Ajax	23	11	159 90
1999–2000	Barcelona	21	3	
2000–01	Barcelona	0	0	21 3
2000–01	Liverpool	5	1	5 1

MAXWELL, Leyton* (M) 20 2
H: 5 8 W: 11 00 b.St Asaph 3-10-79
Source: Trainee. *Honours:* Wales Under-21.

1997–98	Liverpool	0	0	
1998–99	Liverpool	0	0	
1999–2000	Liverpool	0	0	

2000–01	Liverpool	0	0	
2000–01	Stockport Co	20	2	20 2

McALLISTER, Gary (M) 640 109
H: 6 1 W: 11 11 b.Motherwell 25-12-64
Source: Fir Park BC. *Honours:* Scotland Under-21, B, 57 full caps, 5 goals.

1981–82	Motherwell	1	0	
1982–83	Motherwell	1	0	
1983–84	Motherwell	21	0	
1984–85	Motherwell	35	6	
1985–86	Motherwell	1	0	59 6
1985–86	Leicester C	31	7	
1986–87	Leicester C	39	10	
1987–88	Leicester C	42	9	
1988–89	Leicester C	46	11	
1989–90	Leicester C	43	10	201 47
1990–91	Leeds U	38	2	
1991–92	Leeds U	42	5	
1992–93	Leeds U	32	5	
1993–94	Leeds U	42	8	
1994–95	Leeds U	41	6	
1995–96	Leeds U	36	5	231 31
1996–97	Coventry C	38	6	
1997–98	Coventry C	14	0	
1998–99	Coventry C	29	3	
1999–2000	Coventry C	38	11	119 20
2000–01	Liverpool	30	5	30 5

MILES, John (F) 0 0
b.Fazackerley 28-9-81
Source: Trainee.

1998–99	Liverpool	0	0	
1999–2000	Liverpool	0	0	
2000–01	Liverpool	0	0	

MURPHY, Danny (M) 217 35
H: 5 9 W: 12 08 b.Chester 18-3-77
Source: Trainee. *Honours:* England Schools, Youth, Under-21.

1993–94	Crewe Alex	12	2	
1994–95	Crewe Alex	35	5	
1995–96	Crewe Alex	42	10	
1996–97	Crewe Alex	45	10	
1997–98	Liverpool	16	0	
1998–99	Liverpool	1	0	
1998–99	Crewe Alex	16	1	150 28
1999–2000	Liverpool	23	3	
2000–01	Liverpool	27	4	67 7

NAVARRO, Alan (M) 8 1
H: 5 10 W: 11 07 b.Liverpool 31-5-81
Source: Trainee.

1998–99	Liverpool	0	0	
1999–2000	Liverpool	0	0	
2000–01	Liverpool	0	0	
2000–01	Crewe Alex	8	1	8 1

NIELSEN, Jorgen (G) 2 0
H: 6 0 W: 12 11 b.Nykobing 6-5-71

1993–94	Naestved	2	0	
1994–95	Naestved	0	0	2 0
1995–96	Hvidovre	0	0	
1996–97	Liverpool	0	0	
1997–98	Liverpool	0	0	
1998–99	Liverpool	0	0	
1998–99	Wolverhampton W	0	0	
1999–2000	Liverpool	0	0	
2000–01	Liverpool	0	0	

O'BRIEN, Chris (M) 0 0
b.Liverpool 13-1-82
Source: Trainee. *Honours:* England Schools.

1998–99	Liverpool	0	0	
1999–2000	Liverpool	0	0	
2000–01	Liverpool	0	0	

OTSEMOBOR, John (D) 0 0
b.Liverpool 23-3-83
Source: Trainee.

1999–2000	Liverpool	0	0	
2000–01	Liverpool	0	0	

OWEN, Michael (F) 123 64
H: 5 8 W: 10 13 b.Chester 14-12-79
Source: Trainee. *Honours:* England Schools, Youth, Under-21, 29 full caps, 10 goals.

1996–97	Liverpool	2	1	
1997–98	Liverpool	36	18	
1998–99	Liverpool	30	18	
1999–2000	Liverpool	27	11	
2000–01	Liverpool	28	16	123 64

PARTRIDGE, Richie (M) 6 1
H: 5 8 W: 10 07 b.Dublin 12-9-80
Source: Trainee. *Honours:* Eire Under-21.

1998–99	Liverpool	0	0	
1999–2000	Liverpool	0	0	
2000–01	Liverpool	0	0	
2000–01	Bristol R	6	1	6 1

REDKNAPP, Jamie (M) 246 29
H: 6 0 W: 13 04 b.Barton-on-Sea 25-6-73
Source: Tottenham H Schoolboy, Bournemouth Trainee. *Honours:* England Schools, Youth, B, Under-21, 17 full caps, 1 goal.

1989–90	Bournemouth	4	0	
1990–91	Bournemouth	9	0	13 0
1990–91	Liverpool	0	0	
1991–92	Liverpool	6	1	
1992–93	Liverpool	29	2	
1993–94	Liverpool	35	4	
1994–95	Liverpool	41	3	
1995–96	Liverpool	23	3	
1996–97	Liverpool	23	2	
1997–98	Liverpool	20	3	
1998–99	Liverpool	34	8	
1999–2000	Liverpool	22	3	
2000–01	Liverpool	0	0	233 29

SJOLUND, Danny (F) 0 0
H: 5 11 W: 12 00 b.Mariehamn 22-4-83

1999–2000	West Ham U	0	0	
2000–01	West Ham U	0	0	
2000–01	Liverpool	0	0	

SMICER, Vladimir (M) 220 45
H: 5 10 W: 12 02 b.Degin 24-5-73
Honours: Czech Republic 49 full caps, 18 goals.

1992–93	Slavia Prague	21	8	
1993–94	Slavia Prague	17	6	
1994–95	Slavia Prague	15	3	
1995–96	Slavia Prague	28	9	81 26
1996–97	Lens	33	5	
1997–98	Lens	28	7	
1998–99	Lens	30	4	91 16
1999–2000	Liverpool	21	1	
2000–01	Liverpool	27	2	48 3

TORPEY, Steve* (M) 0 0
b.Fazackerley 16-9-81
Source: Trainee. *Honours:* England Youth.

1998–99	Liverpool	0	0	
1999–2000	Liverpool	0	0	
2000–01	Liverpool	0	0	

TRAORE, Djimi (D) 8 0
H: 6 1 W: 12 06 b.Saint-Ouen 1-3-80
Source: Laval.

1998–99	Liverpool	0	0	
1999–2000	Liverpool	0	0	
2000–01	Liverpool	8	0	8 0

VIGNAL, Gregory (D) 6 0
H: 5 11 W: 12 03 b.Montpellier 19-7-81

2000–01	Liverpool	6	0	6 0

WARNOCK, Stephen (M) 0 0
b.Ormskirk 12-12-81
Source: Trainee. *Honours:* England Schools, Youth.

1998–99	Liverpool	0	0	
1999–2000	Liverpool	0	0	
2000–01	Liverpool	0	0	

WELSH, John (D) 0 0
b.Liverpool 10-1-84
Source: Scholar.

2000–01	Liverpool	0	0	

WESTERVELD, Sander (G) 188 0
H: 6 4 W: 13 08 b.Enschede 23-10-74
Source: Tubanters. *Honours:* Holland 6 full caps.

1994–95	Twente	3	0	
1995–96	Twente	11	0	14 0
1996–97	Vitesse	34	0	
1997–98	Vitesse	34	0	
1998–99	Vitesse	32	0	100 0
1999–2000	Liverpool	36	0	
2000–01	Liverpool	38	0	74 0

WRIGHT, Stephen (D) 25 0
H: 6 0 W: 11 11 b.Liverpool 8-2-80
Source: Trainee. *Honours:* England Youth, Under-21.

1997–98	Liverpool	0	0	
1998–99	Liverpool	0	0	
1999–2000	Liverpool	0	0	
1999–2000	Crewe Alex	23	0	23 0
2000–01	Liverpool	2	0	2 0

ZIEGE, Christian (D) 256 52
H: 6 1 W: 12 04 b.Berlin 1-2-72
Honours: Germany 59 full caps, 8 goals.

1990–91	Bayern Munich	13	1	
1991–92	Bayern Munich	26	2	
1992–93	Bayern Munich	28	9	
1993–94	Bayern Munich	29	3	
1994–95	Bayern Munich	29	10	
1995–96	Bayern Munich	20	9	
1996–97	Bayern Munich	27	7	172 41
1997–98	AC Milan	22	2	

1998–99	AC Milan	17	2	**39**	**4**
1999–2000	Middlesbrough	29	6		
2000–01	Middlesbrough	0	0	**29**	**6**
2000–01	Liverpool	16	1	**16**	**1**

Scholars
Cavanagh, Peter J; Chambers, David J; Coupe, Alan E; Culshaw, Paul R; Dawes, Ian; Marsh, Andrew; McIlroy, Brian P; McNulty, Stephen M; Mellor, Neil A; Morton, Anthony P; Nicholas, Andrew P; Noel, Leon RF; Parry, Mathew; Peers, Mark; Prince, Neil M; Thomas, Mark L; Thompson, Christopher M; Whitbread, Zak B

LUTON T

ABBEY, Nathan‡ (G) — **55 0**
H: 6 1 W: 11 13 b.Islington 11-7-78
Source: Trainee.

1995–96	Luton T	0	0		
1996–97	Luton T	0	0		
1997–98	Luton T	0	0		
1998–99	Luton T	2	0		
1999–2000	Luton T	33	0		
2000–01	Luton T	20	0	**55**	**0**

AYRES, James‡ (D) — **0 0**
H: 6 3 W: 13 00 b.Luton 18-9-80
Source: Trainee.

1998–99	Luton T	0	0		
1999–2000	Luton T	0	0		
2000–01	Luton T	0	0		

BAPTISTE, Rocky* (F) — **3 0**
b.Lambeth 8-7-72
Source: Hayes.

| 2000–01 | Luton T | 3 | 0 | **3** | **0** |

BOYCE, Emmerson (D) — **73 4**
H: 5 11 W: 11 02 b.Aylesbury 24-9-79
Source: Trainee.

1997–98	Luton T	0	0		
1998–99	Luton T	1	0		
1999–2000	Luton T	30	1		
2000–01	Luton T	42	3	**73**	**4**

BREITENFELDER, Friedrich‡ (M) — **5 0**
b.Vienna 16-6-80
Source: Rapid Vienna, Bregenz, St Polten.

| 2000–01 | Luton T | 5 | 0 | **5** | **0** |

BRENNAN, Dean (M) — **9 0**
H: 5 9 W: 11 08 b.Dublin 17-6-80

1997–98	Sheffield W	0	0		
1998–99	Sheffield W	0	0		
1999–2000	Sheffield W	0	0		
2000–01	Luton T	9	0	**9**	**0**

BRUCE, Joseph (M) — **0 0**
b.London 5-7-83

| 2000–01 | Luton T | 0 | 0 | | |

CARTER, Tommy‡ (F) — **0 0**
b.Paget 9-7-77
Source: Academia Tahuichi.

| 2000–01 | Luton T | 0 | 0 | | |

DOUGLAS, Stuart (F) — **137 18**
H: 5 8 W: 11 05 b.London 9-4-78
Source: Trainee.

1995–96	Luton T	8	1		
1996–97	Luton T	9	0		
1997–98	Luton T	17	1		
1998–99	Luton T	42	9		
1999–2000	Luton T	40	3		
2000–01	Luton T	21	4	**137**	**18**

DRYDEN, Richard (D) — **282 11**
H: 6 0 W: 13 10 b.Stroud 14-6-69
Source: Trainee.

1986–87	Bristol R	6	0		
1987–88	Bristol R	6	0		
1988–89	Bristol R	1	0	**13**	**0**
1988–89	Exeter C	21	0		
1989–90	Exeter C	30	7	**51**	**7**
1990–91	Manchester C	0	0		
1991–92	Notts Co	29	1		
1992–93	Notts Co	2	0	**31**	**1**
1992–93	Plymouth Arg	5	0	**5**	**0**
1992–93	Birmingham C	11	0		
1993–94	Birmingham C	34	0		
1994–95	Birmingham C	3	0	**48**	**0**
1994–95	Bristol C	19	1		
1995–96	Bristol C	18	1	**37**	**2**
1996–97	Southampton	29	1		
1997–98	Southampton	13	0		
1998–99	Southampton	4	0		
1999–2000	Southampton	1	0		
1999–2000	Stoke C	13	0	**13**	**0**
2000–01	Southampton	0	0	**47**	**1**
2000–01	*Northampton T*	10	0	**10**	**0**

| 2000–01 | *Swindon T* | 7 | 0 | **7** | **0** |
| 2000–01 | Luton T | 20 | 0 | **20** | **0** |

FOTIADIS, Andrew (F) — **98 11**
H: 5 11 W: 11 07 b.Hitchin 6-9-77
Source: School. *Honours:* England Schools.

1996–97	Luton T	17	3		
1997–98	Luton T	15	1		
1998–99	Luton T	21	2		
1999–2000	Luton T	23	2		
2000–01	Luton T	22	3	**98**	**11**

FRASER, Stuart (D) — **44 1**
H: 5 9 W: 10 06 b.Edinburgh 9-1-80
Source: Trainee. *Honours:* Scotland Under-21.

1997–98	Luton T	1	0		
1998–99	Luton T	8	0		
1999–2000	Luton T	20	1		
2000–01	Luton T	15	0	**44**	**1**

GEORGE, Liam (F) — **98 20**
H: 5 9 W: 11 04 b.Luton 2-2-79
Source: Trainee. *Honours:* Eire Under-21.

1996–97	Luton T	1	0		
1997–98	Luton T	1	0		
1998–99	Luton T	12	0		
1999–2000	Luton T	42	13		
2000–01	Luton T	43	7	**98**	**20**

HELIN, Petri (D) — **261 16**
H: 5 10 W: 13 00 b.Helsinki 13-12-69
Honours: Finland 19 full caps, 2 goals.

1988	PPT	12	2	**12**	**2**
1989	HJK Helsinki	18	0		
1990	HJK Helsinki	24	0		
1991	HJK Helsinki	30	4		
1992	HJK Helsinki	30	1		
1992–93	Ikast	0	0		
1993–94	Ikast	28	3		
1994–95	Ikast	18	0		
1995–96	Ikast	2	0	**48**	**3**
1996	HJK Helsinki	12	1		
1997	HJK Helsinki	10	1	**124**	**7**
1998	PK-35	27	2	**27**	**2**
1999	Jokerit	27	1	**27**	**1**
2000–01	Luton T	23	1	**23**	**1**

HOLMES, Peter (M) — **18 1**
H: 5 10 W: 10 00 b.Bishop Auckland 18-11-80
Source: Trainee. *Honours:* England Schools.

1997–98	Sheffield W	0	0		
1998–99	Sheffield W	0	0		
1999–2000	Sheffield W	0	0		
2000–01	Luton T	18	1	**18**	**1**

HOWARD, Steve (F) — **240 48**
H: 6 3 W: 14 06 b.Durham 10-5-76
Source: Tow Law T.

1995–96	Hartlepool U	39	7		
1996–97	Hartlepool U	32	8		
1997–98	Hartlepool U	43	7		
1998–99	Hartlepool U	28	5	**142**	**27**
1998–99	Northampton T	12	0		
1999–2000	Northampton T	41	10		
2000–01	Northampton T	33	8	**86**	**18**
2000–01	Luton T	12	3	**12**	**3**

JOHNSON, Marvin (D) — **355 6**
H: 6 1 W: 13 00 b.Wembley 29-10-68
Source: Apprentice.

1986–87	Luton T	0	0		
1987–88	Luton T	9	0		
1988–89	Luton T	16	0		
1989–90	Luton T	12	0		
1990–91	Luton T	26	0		
1991–92	Luton T	0	0		
1992–93	Luton T	40	3		
1993–94	Luton T	17	0		
1994–95	Luton T	46	1		
1995–96	Luton T	36	0		
1996–97	Luton T	44	0		
1997–98	Luton T	14	2		
1998–99	Luton T	42	0		
1999–2000	Luton T	44	0		
2000–01	Luton T	9	0	**355**	**6**

KANDOL, Tresor* (F) — **21 3**
H: 6 1 W: 11 07 b.Banga 30-8-81
Source: Trainee.

1998–99	Luton T	4	0		
1999–2000	Luton T	4	0		
2000–01	Luton T	13	3	**21**	**3**

KARLSEN, Kent (D) — **68 1**
H: 6 2 W: 13 00 b.Norway 17-2-73

1996	Valerengen	24	0		
1997	Valerengen	0	0		
1998	Valerengen	6	0		
1999	Valerengen	8	0		
2000	Valerengen	3	0	**41**	**0**
2000	Haugesund	21	1	**21**	**1**
2000–01	Luton T	6	0	**6**	**0**

LOCKE, Adam (M) — **280 21**
H: 5 11 W: 12 07 b.Croydon 20-8-70
Source: Trainee.

1988–89	Crystal Palace	0	0		
1989–90	Crystal Palace	0	0		
1990–91	Southend U	28	4		
1991–92	Southend U	10	0		
1992–93	Southend U	27	0		
1993–94	Southend U	8	0	**73**	**4**
1993–94	*Colchester U*	4	0		
1994–95	Colchester U	22	1		
1995–96	Colchester U	25	3		
1996–97	Colchester U	32	4	**83**	**8**
1997–98	Bristol C	37	1		
1998–99	Bristol C	28	3	**65**	**4**
1999–2000	Luton T	34	3		
2000–01	Luton T	25	2	**59**	**5**

MANSELL, Lee (M) — **18 5**
b.Gloucester 23-9-82
Source: Scholar.

| 2000–01 | Luton T | 18 | 5 | **18** | **5** |

McGOWAN, Gavin* (D) — **66 0**
H: 5 10 W: 12 06 b.Blackheath 16-1-76
Source: Trainee. *Honours:* England Schools, Youth.

1992–93	Arsenal	2	0		
1993–94	Arsenal	1	0		
1994–95	Arsenal	1	0		
1995–96	Arsenal	1	0		
1996–97	Arsenal	1	0		
1996–97	*Luton T*	2	0		
1997–98	Arsenal	1	0	**6**	**0**
1997–98	*Luton T*	8	0		
1998–99	Luton T	31	0		
1999–2000	Luton T	13	0		
2000–01	Luton T	6	0	**60**	**0**

McLAREN, Paul* (M) — **167 4**
H: 6 1 W: 13 00 b.High Wycombe 17-11-76
Source: Trainee.

1993–94	Luton T	1	0		
1994–95	Luton T	0	0		
1995–96	Luton T	12	1		
1996–97	Luton T	24	0		
1997–98	Luton T	43	0		
1998–99	Luton T	23	0		
1999–2000	Luton T	29	1		
2000–01	Luton T	35	2	**167**	**4**

MURPHY, Daryl (M) — **0 0**
b.Ireland 15-3-83

| 2000–01 | Luton T | 0 | 0 | | |

OVENDALE, Mark (G) — **121 0**
H: 6 2 W: 13 10 b.Leicester 22-11-73
Source: Wisbech T.

1994–95	Northampton T	6	0	**6**	**0**
From Barry T.					
1997–98	Bournemouth	0	0		
1998–99	Bournemouth	46	0		
1999–2000	Bournemouth	43	0	**89**	**0**
2000–01	Luton T	26	0	**26**	**0**

SCARLETT, Andre* (M) — **18 1**
H: 5 4 W: 9 12 b.Brent 11-1-80
Source: Trainee.

1998–99	Luton T	6	1		
1999–2000	Luton T	3	0		
2000–01	Luton T	9	0	**18**	**1**

SHEPHERD, Paul* (D) — **16 1**
H: 5 11 W: 12 00 b.Leeds 17-11-77
Source: Trainee. *Honours:* England Youth.

1995–96	Leeds U	0	0		
1996–97	Leeds U	1	0		
1997–98	Leeds U	0	0		
1997–98	*Ayr U*	6	1	**6**	**1**
1998–99	Leeds U	0	0		
1998–99	*Tranmere R*	1	0	**1**	**0**
1999–2000	Leeds U	0	0	**1**	**0**
2000–01	Scunthorpe U	1	0	**1**	**0**
2000–01	Luton T	7	0	**7**	**0**

SPRING, Matthew (M) — **143 13**
H: 5 11 W: 11 07 b.Harlow 17-11-79
Source: Trainee.

1997–98	Luton T	12	0		
1998–99	Luton T	45	3		
1999–2000	Luton T	45	6		
2000–01	Luton T	41	4	**143**	**13**

STANDEN, Dean (M) — **0 0**
H: 5 10 W: 11 00 b.Lewisham 23-3-82
Source: Welling U.

| 1999–2000 | Luton T | 0 | 0 | | |
| 2000–01 | Luton T | 0 | 0 | | |

STEIN, Mark* (F) — **453 152**
H: 5 6 W: 11 07 b.Capetown 29-1-66
Honours: England Youth.

| 1983–84 | Luton T | 1 | 0 | | |
| 1984–85 | Luton T | 1 | 0 | | |

1985–86	Luton T	6	0		
1985–86	*Aldershot*	2	1	2	1
1986–87	Luton T	21	8		
1987–88	Luton T	25	11		
1988–89	QPR	31	4		
1989–90	QPR	2	0	33	4
1989–90	Oxford U	41	9		
1990–91	Oxford U	34	8		
1991–92	Oxford U	7	1	82	18
1991–92	Stoke C	36	16		
1992–93	Stoke C	46	26		
1993–94	Stoke C	12	8		
1993–94	Chelsea	18	13		
1994–95	Chelsea	24	8		
1995–96	Chelsea	8	0		
1996–97	Chelsea	0	0		
1996–97	*Stoke C*	11	4	105	54
1997–98	Chelsea	0	0	50	21
1997–98	*Ipswich T*	7	2	7	2
1997–98	*Bournemouth*	11	4		
1998–99	Bournemouth	43	15		
1999–2000	Bournemouth	36	11	90	30
2000–01	Luton T	30	3	84	22

STIRLING, Jude (D)   9   0
H: 6 2   W: 11 12   b.Enfield 29-6-82
Source: Trainee.

1999–2000	Luton T	0	0		
2000–01	Luton T	9	0	9	0

TAYLOR, Matthew (D)   86   5
H: 5 10   W: 11 08   b.Oxford 27-11-81
Source: Trainee.

1998–99	Luton T	0	0		
1999–2000	Luton T	41	4		
2000–01	Luton T	45	1	86	5

THOMSON, Peter (F)   16   2
H: 6 3   W: 13 04   b.Crumpsall 30-6-77
Source: Stand Ath.

1995–96	Bury	0	0		
1996–97	Bury	0	0		
From Lancaster C					
1998–99	NAC Breda	3	0		
1999–2000	NAC Breda	2	0	5	0
2000–01	Luton T	11	2	11	2

WARD, Scott (G)   1   0
H: 6 2   W: 13 00   b.Brent 5-10-81
Source: Trainee.

1998–99	Luton T	0	0		
1999–2000	Luton T	0	0		
2000–01	Luton T	1	0	1	0

WATTS, Julian* (D)   197   12
H: 6 2   W: 13 06   b.Sheffield 17-3-71
Source: Trainee.

1990–91	Rotherham U	10	0		
1991–92	Rotherham U	10	1	20	1
1991–92	Sheffield W	0	0		
1992–93	Sheffield W	4	0		
1992–93	*Shrewsbury T*	9	0	9	0
1993–94	Sheffield W	1	0		
1994–95	Sheffield W	0	0		
1995–96	Sheffield W	11	1	16	1
1995–96	Leicester C	9	0		
1996–97	Leicester C	26	1		
1997–98	Leicester C	3	0	38	1
1997–98	*Crewe Alex*	5	0	5	0
1997–98	*Huddersfield T*	8	0	8	0
1998–99	Bristol C	17	1		
1998–99	*Lincoln C*	2	0	2	0
1998–99	*Blackpool*	9	0	9	0
1999–2000	Bristol C	0	0	17	1
1999–2000	Luton T	45	4		
2000–01	Luton T	28	4	73	8

Scholars
Carroll, John M; Chatfield, Jonathan D; Clarke, Duane L; Deeney, Joseph E; Dillon, Christopher H; Dogbe, Steven YS; Gillman, Robert; James-Barriteau, Rene WJ; Jeffrey, Marcus P; Mortara, Dean P; Osborn, James

MACCLESFIELD T

ABBEY, George (D)   36   0
H: 5 8   W: 10 08   b.Port Harcourt 20-10-78
Source: Sharks.

1999–2000	Macclesfield T	18	0		
2000–01	Macclesfield T	18	0	36	0

ADAMS, Daniel (D)   37   0
b.Manchester 3-1-76
Source: Altrincham.

2000–01	Macclesfield T	37	0	37	0

ASKEY, John* (F)   154   28
H: 6 0   W: 12 02   b.Stoke 4-11-64
Source: Port Vale.

1997–98	Macclesfield T	39	6		
1998–99	Macclesfield T	38	4		
1999–2000	Macclesfield T	40	15		
2000–01	Macclesfield T	37	3	154	28

BAMBER, Michael (D)   6   0
H: 5 7   W: 10 02   b.Preston 1-10-80
Source: Blackpool Trainee.

1999–2000	Macclesfield T	1	0		
2000–01	Macclesfield T	5	0	6	0

BETTNEY, Chris (F)   70   1
H: 5 9   W: 11 02   b.Chesterfield 27-10-77
Source: Trainee.

1995–96	Sheffield U	0	0		
1996–97	Sheffield U	1	0		
1997–98	Sheffield U	0	0		
1997–98	*Hull C*	30	1	30	1
1998–99	Sheffield U	1	0	1	0
1999–2000	Chesterfield	13	0	13	0
1999–2000	Rochdale	24	0	24	0
2000–01	Macclesfield T	2	0	2	0

CAME, Shaun (D)   7   0
H: 6 3   W: 13 00   b.Crewe 15-6-83
Source: Trainee.

2000–01	Macclesfield T	7	0	7	0

COLLINS, Simon* (D)   204   11
H: 6 0   W: 13 00   b.Pontefract 16-12-73
Source: Trainee.

1992–93	Huddersfield T	1	0		
1993–94	Huddersfield T	1	0		
1994–95	Huddersfield T	4	0		
1995–96	Huddersfield T	30	3		
1996–97	Huddersfield T	16	0	52	3
1996–97	Plymouth Arg	12	1		
1997–98	Plymouth Arg	32	2		
1998–99	Plymouth Arg	40	2	84	5
1999–2000	Macclesfield T	39	3		
2000–01	Macclesfield T	17	0	56	3
2000–01	*Shrewsbury T*	12	0	12	0

CONNELL, Darren* (D)   4   0
H: 5 8   W: 10 08   b.Blackpool 3-2-82
Source: Trainee.

1999–2000	Blackpool	3	0		
2000–01	Blackpool	0	0	3	0
2000–01	Macclesfield T	1	0	1	0

DURKAN, Kieron# (M)   224   20
H: 5 10   W: 12 09   b.Chester 1-12-73
Source: Trainee. *Honours:* Eire Under-21.

1991–92	Wrexham	1	0		
1992–93	Wrexham	1	0		
1993–94	Wrexham	10	1		
1994–95	Wrexham	30	2		
1995–96	Wrexham	8	0	50	3
1995–96	Stockport Co	16	0		
1996–97	Stockport Co	41	3		
1997–98	Stockport Co	7	1	64	4
1997–98	Macclesfield T	4	0		
1998–99	Macclesfield T	26	3		
1999–2000	Macclesfield T	42	6		
2000–01	Macclesfield T	31	4	103	13
2000–01	*York C*	7	0	7	0

GLOVER, Lee (F)   275   54
H: 5 11   W: 11 09   b.Kettering 24-4-70
Source: Trainee. *Honours:* Scotland Under-21.

1986–87	Nottingham F	0	0		
1987–88	Nottingham F	20	3		
1988–89	Nottingham F	0	0		
1989–90	Nottingham F	0	0		
1989–90	*Leicester C*	5	1	5	1
1989–90	*Barnsley*	8	0	8	0
1990–91	Nottingham F	8	1		
1991–92	Nottingham F	16	0		
1991–92	*Luton T*	1	0	1	0
1992–93	Nottingham F	14	0		
1993–94	Nottingham F	18	5	76	9
1994–95	Port Vale	28	4		
1995–96	Port Vale	24	3	52	7
1996–97	Rotherham U	22	1		
1996–97	*Huddersfield T*	11	0	11	0
1997–98	Rotherham U	37	17		
1998–99	Rotherham U	19	10		
1999–2000	Rotherham U	7	1	85	29
2000–01	Macclesfield T	37	8	37	8

HITCHEN, Steve (D)   79   0
H: 5 8   W: 11 07   b.Salford 28-11-76
Source: Trainee.

1995–96	Blackburn R	0	0		
1996–97	Blackburn R	0	0		
1997–98	Macclesfield T	2	0		
1998–99	Macclesfield T	35	0		
1999–2000	Macclesfield T	5	0		
2000–01	Macclesfield T	37	0	79	0

INGRAM, Rae# (D)   126   1
H: 5 11   W: 12 09   b.Manchester 6-12-74
Source: Trainee.

1993–94	Manchester C	0	0		
1994–95	Manchester C	0	0		
1995–96	Manchester C	5	0		
1996–97	Manchester C	18	0		
1997–98	Manchester C	0	0	23	0
1997–98	Macclesfield T	5	0		
1998–99	Macclesfield T	29	0		
1999–2000	Macclesfield T	36	0		
2000–01	Macclesfield T	33	1	103	1

KEEN, Kevin (M)   470   40
H: 5 6   W: 10 10   b.Amersham 25-2-67
Source: Wycombe W and Apprentice.
Honours: England Schools, Youth.

1983–84	West Ham U	0	0		
1984–85	West Ham U	0	0		
1985–86	West Ham U	0	0		
1986–87	West Ham U	13	0		
1987–88	West Ham U	23	1		
1988–89	West Ham U	24	3		
1989–90	West Ham U	44	10		
1990–91	West Ham U	40	0		
1991–92	West Ham U	29	0		
1992–93	West Ham U	46	7	219	21
1993–94	Wolverhampton W	41	7		
1994–95	Wolverhampton W	1	0	42	7
1994–95	Stoke C	21	2		
1995–96	Stoke C	33	3		
1996–97	Stoke C	16	1		
1997–98	Stoke C	40	1		
1998–99	Stoke C	44	2		
1999–2000	Stoke C	23	1	177	10
2000–01	Macclesfield T	32	2	32	2

LAMBERT, Ricky† (M)   12   0
H: 6 2   W: 12 01   b.Liverpool 16-2-82
Source: Trainee.

1999–2000	Blackpool	3	0		
2000–01	Blackpool	0	0	3	0
2000–01	Macclesfield T	9	0	9	0

MARTIN, Lee (G)   231   0
H: 6 0   W: 13 07   b.Huddersfield 9-9-68
Source: Trainee. *Honours:* England Schools.

1987–88	Huddersfield T	18	0		
1988–89	Huddersfield T	0	0		
1989–90	Huddersfield T	25	0		
1990–91	Huddersfield T	4	0		
1991–92	Huddersfield T	7	0	54	0
1992–93	Blackpool	24	0		
1993–94	Blackpool	43	0		
1994–95	Blackpool	31	0		
1995–96	Blackpool	0	0		
1995–96	*Bradford C*	0	0		
1996–97	Blackpool	0	0	98	0
1996–97	Rochdale	0	0		
1997–98	Rochdale	0	0		
1998–99	Halifax T	37	0	37	0
1999–2000	Macclesfield T	21	0		
2000–01	Macclesfield T	21	0	42	0

MUNROE, Karl (D)   29   1
H: 6 0   W: 10 08   b.Manchester 23-9-79
Source: Trainee.

1997–98	Swansea C	1	0		
1998–99	Swansea C	0	0		
1999–2000	Swansea C	0	0	1	0
1999–2000	Macclesfield T	5	0		
2000–01	Macclesfield T	23	1	28	1

O'NEILL, Paul (D)   13   0
H: 5 11   W: 11 02   b.Bolton 17-6-82
Source: Trainee.

1999–2000	Macclesfield T	1	0		
2000–01	Macclesfield T	12	0	13	0

PRIEST, Chris (M)   218   34
H: 5 10   W: 12 00   b.Leigh 18-10-73
Source: Trainee.

1992–93	Everton	0	0		
1993–94	Everton	0	0		
1994–95	Everton	0	0		
1994–95	Chester C	24	1		
1995–96	Chester C	39	13		
1996–97	Chester C	32	2		
1997–98	Chester C	37	6		
1998–99	Chester C	35	4	167	26
1999–2000	Macclesfield T	36	4		
2000–01	Macclesfield T	15	4	51	8

TERESKINAS, Andrejus† (D)   142   15
H: 6 3   W: 14 05   b.Lithuania 10-7-70.
Honours: Lithuania 56 full caps, 3 goals.

1992–93	Zalgiris	26	1		
1993–94	Zalgiris	22	4		
1994–95	Zalgiris	18	4		
1995–96	Zalgiris	19	2		
1996–97	Zalgiris	9	0		
1997–98	Zalgiris	8	1		
1998–99	Zalgiris	1	0	103	12
1998	Skonto Riga	7	2		
1999	Skonto Riga	18	1		
2000	Skonto Riga	13	0	38	3
2000–01	Macclesfield T	1	0	1	0

TINSON, Darren (D) 172 4
H: 6 0 W: 13 07 b.Birmingham 15-11-69
Source: Northwich V.
1997–98	Macclesfield T	44	0		
1998–99	Macclesfield T	37	0		
1999–2000	Macclesfield T	46	1		
2000–01	Macclesfield T	45	3	172	4

TRACEY, Richard (F) 69 14
H: 5 11 W: 12 04 b.Muirfield 9-7-79
Source: Trainee.
1997–98	Sheffield U	0	0		
1997–98	Rotherham U	0	0		
1998–99	Rotherham U	3	0	3	0
1998–99	Carlisle U	11	3		
1999–2000	Carlisle U	36	7		
2000–01	Carlisle U	6	1	53	11
2000–01	Macclesfield T	13	3	13	3

TWYNHAM, Gary‡ (M) 9 0
H: 5 11 W: 12 07 b.Manchester 8-2-76
Source: Trainee.
From Hednesford T.
| 2000–01 | Macclesfield T | 9 | 0 | 9 | 0 |

WHITEHEAD, Damien (F) 56 14
H: 5 10 W: 12 00 b.Whiston 24-4-79
Source: Warrington T.
| 1999–2000 | Macclesfield T | 23 | 6 | | |
| 2000–01 | Macclesfield T | 33 | 8 | 56 | 14 |

WHITTAKER, Dan (M) 0 0
H: 5 10 W: 11 00 b.Manchester 14-11-80
| 2000–01 | Macclesfield T | 0 | 0 | | |

WOOD, Steve* (M) 151 19
H: 5 9 W: 10 10 b.Oldham 23-6-63
Source: Ashton U.
1997–98	Macclesfield T	43	13		
1998–99	Macclesfield T	42	4		
1999–2000	Macclesfield T	36	1		
2000–01	Macclesfield T	30	1	151	19

WOOLLEY, Matt (M) 2 0
b.Manchester 22-2-82
| 2000–01 | Macclesfield T | 2 | 0 | 2 | 0 |

Trainees
Booth, Daniel R; Hulse, Paul G; Hutchinson, Neil W; Marsh, Adam R; Morris, Adam S
Scholars
Bayliss, Richard L; Brackenridge, Stephen J; Carr, Michael A; Dolphin, Wesley D; Naylor, Adam R
Non-Contract
Lambert, Rickie L

MANCHESTER C

ALMOND, James (F) 0 0
b.Northallerton 5-10-83
Source: Scholar.
| 2000–01 | Manchester C | 0 | 0 | | |

BISHOP, Ian‡ (M) 532 32
H: 5 10 W: 12 07 b.Liverpool 29-5-65
Source: Apprentice. *Honours:* England B.
1983–84	Everton	0	0		
1983–84	Crewe Alex	4	0	4	0
1984–85	Everton	0	0	1	0
1984–85	Carlisle U	30	2		
1985–86	Carlisle U	36	6		
1986–87	Carlisle U	42	3		
1987–88	Carlisle U	24	3	132	14
1988–89	Bournemouth	44	2	44	2
1989–90	Manchester C	19	2		
1989–90	West Ham U	17	2		
1990–91	West Ham U	40	4		
1991–92	West Ham U	41	1		
1992–93	West Ham U	22	1		
1993–94	West Ham U	36	1		
1994–95	West Ham U	31	1		
1995–96	West Ham U	35	1		
1996–97	West Ham U	29	1		
1997–98	West Ham U	3	0	254	12
1997–98	Manchester C	6	0		
1998–99	Manchester C	25	0		
1999–2000	Manchester C	37	2		
2000–01	Manchester C	10	0	97	4
(Transferred to Miami Fusion, March 2001).

BROWNE, Gary (F) 0 0
b.Ireland 17-1-83
Source: Scholar.
| 2000–01 | Manchester C | 0 | 0 | | |

CHARVET, Laurent (D) 170 22
H: 5 11 W: 12 03 b.Beziers 8-5-73
1994–95	Cannes	19	4		
1995–96	Cannes	31	8		
1996–97	Cannes	38	6		
1997–98	Cannes	11	1	99	19
1997–98	Chelsea	11	2	11	2
1998–99	Newcastle U	31	1		

COOKE, Terry (M) 85 9
H: 5 7 W: 10 08 b.Marston Green 5-8-76
Source: Trainee. *Honours:* England Youth, Under-21.
1994–95	Manchester U	0	0		
1995–96	Manchester U	4	0		
1995–96	Sunderland	6	0	6	0
1996–97	Manchester U	0	0		
1996–97	Birmingham C	4	0	4	0
1997–98	Manchester U	0	0		
1998–99	Manchester U	0	0	4	0
1998–99	Wrexham	10	0	10	0
1998–99	Manchester C	21	7		
1999–2000	Manchester C	13	0		
1999–2000	Wigan Ath	10	1	10	1
2000–01	Manchester C	0	0	34	7
2000–01	Sheffield W	17	1	17	1

DAY, Rhys (D) 0 0
H: 6 2 W: 13 00 b.Bridgend 31-8-82
Source: Scholarship. *Honours:* Wales Under-21.
| 1999–2000 | Manchester C | 0 | 0 | | |
| 2000–01 | Manchester C | 0 | 0 | | |

DICKOV, Paul (F) 193 42
H: 5 6 W: 10 10 b.Glasgow 1-11-72
Source: Trainee. *Honours:* Scotland Under-21, 3 full caps.
1992–93	Arsenal	3	2		
1993–94	Arsenal	1	0		
1993–94	Luton T	15	1	15	1
1993–94	Brighton & HA	8	5	8	5
1994–95	Arsenal	9	0		
1995–96	Arsenal	7	1		
1996–97	Arsenal	1	0	21	3
1996–97	Manchester C	29	5		
1997–98	Manchester C	30	9		
1998–99	Manchester C	35	10		
1999–2000	Manchester C	34	5		
2000–01	Manchester C	21	4	149	33

DUNFIELD, Terry (M) 1 0
H: 5 10 W: 11 03 b.Canada 20-2-82
Source: Trainee.
1998–99	Manchester C	0	0		
1999–2000	Manchester C	0	0		
2000–01	Manchester C	1	0	1	0

DUNNE, Richard (D) 85 0
H: 6 2 W: 14 06 b.Dublin 21-9-79
Source: Trainee. *Honours:* Eire Under-21, 10 full caps, 3 goals.
1996–97	Everton	7	0		
1997–98	Everton	3	0		
1998–99	Everton	16	0		
1999–2000	Everton	31	0		
2000–01	Everton	3	0	60	0
2000–01	Manchester C	25	0	25	0

EDGHILL, Richard (D) 173 1
H: 5 9 W: 12 03 b.Oldham 23-9-74
Source: Trainee. *Honours:* England Under-21.
1992–93	Manchester C	0	0		
1993–94	Manchester C	22	0		
1994–95	Manchester C	14	0		
1995–96	Manchester C	13	0		
1996–97	Manchester C	0	0		
1997–98	Manchester C	36	0		
1998–99	Manchester C	38	0		
1999–2000	Manchester C	41	1		
2000–01	Manchester C	6	0	170	1
2000–01	Birmingham C	3	0	3	0

ELLIOTT, Stephen (F) 0 0
b.Dublin 6-1-84
Source: School.
| 2000–01 | Manchester C | 0 | 0 | | |

ETUHU, Dixon (M) 0 0
H: 6 2 W: 13 00 b.Kano 8-6-82
Source: Scholarship.
| 1999–2000 | Manchester C | 0 | 0 | | |
| 2000–01 | Manchester C | 0 | 0 | | |

GOATER, Shaun (F) 401 159
H: 6 0 W: 12 10 b.Bermuda 25-2-70
Honours: Bermuda 19 full caps.
1988–89	Manchester U	0	0		
1989–90	Manchester U	0	0		
1989–90	Rotherham U	12	2		
1990–91	Rotherham U	22	2		
1991–92	Rotherham U	24	9		
1992–93	Rotherham U	23	7		
1993–94	Rotherham U	39	13		
1993–94	Notts Co	1	0	1	0
1994–95	Rotherham U	45	19		
1995–96	Rotherham U	44	18	209	70
1996–97	Bristol C	42	23		

GRANT, Tony (M) 96 3
H: 5 10 W: 10 10 b.Liverpool 14-11-74
Source: Trainee. *Honours:* England Under-21.
1993–94	Everton	0	0		
1994–95	Everton	5	0		
1995–96	Everton	13	1		
1995–96	Swindon T	3	1	3	1
1996–97	Everton	18	0		
1997–98	Everton	7	1		
1998–99	Everton	16	0		
1999–2000	Everton	0	0	61	2
1999–2000	Tranmere R	9	0	9	0
1999–2000	Manchester C	8	0		
2000–01	Manchester C	10	0	18	0
2000–01	WBA	5	0	5	0

GRANVILLE, Danny (D) 186 9
H: 6 2 W: 12 13 b.Islington 19-1-75
Source: Trainee. *Honours:* England Under-21.
1993–94	Cambridge U	11	5		
1994–95	Cambridge U	16	2		
1995–96	Cambridge U	35	0		
1996–97	Cambridge U	37	0	99	7
1996–97	Chelsea	5	0		
1997–98	Chelsea	13	0	18	0
1998–99	Leeds U	9	0		
1999–2000	Leeds U	0	0	9	0
1999–2000	Manchester C	35	2		
2000–01	Manchester C	19	0	54	2
2000–01	Norwich C	6	0	6	0

HAALAND, Alf-Inge (D) 184 18
H: 6 1 W: 12 06 b.Bryne 23-11-72
Source: Bryne. *Honours:* Norway 34 full caps.
1993–94	Nottingham F	3	0		
1994–95	Nottingham F	20	1		
1995–96	Nottingham F	17	0		
1996–97	Nottingham F	35	6	75	7
1997–98	Leeds U	32	7		
1998–99	Leeds U	29	1		
1999–2000	Leeds U	13	0	74	8
2000–01	Manchester C	35	3	35	3

HODGSON, Steven* (G) 0 0
H: 6 1 W: 12 11 b.Macclesfield 23-12-81
Source: Scholarship. *Honours:* England Youth.
1998–99	Manchester C	0	0		
1999–2000	Manchester C	0	0		
2000–01	Manchester C	0	0		

HOGAN, Barry (M) 0 0
b.Whiston 15-2-83
Source: Scholar.
| 2000–01 | Manchester C | 0 | 0 | | |

HOLMES, Shaun (D) 0 0
H: 5 9 W: 11 03 b.Derry 27-12-80
Source: Trainee. *Honours:* Northern Ireland Under-21.
1997–98	Manchester C	0	0		
1998–99	Manchester C	0	0		
1999–2000	Manchester C	0	0		
2000–01	Manchester C	0	0		

HORLOCK, Kevin (M) 295 52
H: 5 11 W: 12 06 b.Erith 1-11-72
Source: Trainee. *Honours:* Northern Ireland 25 full caps.
1991–92	West Ham U	0	0		
1992–93	West Ham U	0	0		
1992–93	Swindon T	14	1		
1993–94	Swindon T	38	0		
1994–95	Swindon T	38	1		
1995–96	Swindon T	45	12		
1996–97	Swindon T	28	8	163	22
1996–97	Manchester C	18	4		
1997–98	Manchester C	25	5		
1998–99	Manchester C	37	9		
1999–2000	Manchester C	38	10		
2000–01	Manchester C	14	2	132	30

HOWEY, Steve (D) 227 12
H: 6 1 W: 13 10 b.Sunderland 26-10-71
Source: Trainee. *Honours:* England 4 full caps.
1988–89	Newcastle U	1	0		
1989–90	Newcastle U	0	0		
1990–91	Newcastle U	11	0		
1991–92	Newcastle U	21	1		
1992–93	Newcastle U	41	2		
1993–94	Newcastle U	14	0		
1994–95	Newcastle U	30	1		
1995–96	Newcastle U	28	1		
1996–97	Newcastle U	8	1		
1997–98	Newcastle U	14	0		

1998–99	Newcastle U	14	0		
1999–2000	Newcastle U	9	0	191	6
2000–01	Manchester C	36	6	36	6

HUCKERBY, Darren (F)   182   39
H: 5 11　W: 11 04　b.Nottingham 23-4-76
Source: Trainee. *Honours:* England Under-21, B.

1993–94	Lincoln C	6	1		
1994–95	Lincoln C	6	2		
1995–96	Lincoln C	16	2	28	5
1995–96	Newcastle U	1	0		
1996–97	Newcastle U	0	0	1	0
1996–97	*Millwall*	6	3	6	3
1996–97	Coventry C	25	5		
1997–98	Coventry C	34	14		
1998–99	Coventry C	34	9		
1999–2000	Coventry C	1	0	94	28
1999–2000	Leeds U	33	2		
2000–01	Leeds U	7	0	40	2
2000–01	Manchester C	13	1	13	1

JORDAN, Stephen (D)   0   0
H: 6 0　W: 11 05　b.Warrington 6-3-82
Source: Scholarship.

1998–99	Manchester C	0	0		
1999–2000	Manchester C	0	0		
2000–01	Manchester C	0	0		

JOYCE, Damien (M)   0   0
b.Dublin 8-3-83
Source: Scholarship.

1999–2000	Manchester C	0	0		
2000–01	Manchester C	0	0		

KANCHELSKIS, Andrei (F)   319   67
H: 5 10　W: 12 12　b.Kirovograd 23-1-69
Honours: USSR/CIS 23 full caps, 3 goals; Russia 36 full caps, 5 goals.

1988	Dynamo Kiev	7	1		
1989	Dynamo Kiev	15	0	22	1
1990	Donetsk	16	2		
1991	Donetsk	5	1	21	3
1990–91	Manchester U	1	0		
1991–92	Manchester U	34	5		
1992–93	Manchester U	27	3		
1993–94	Manchester U	31	6		
1994–95	Manchester U	30	14	123	28
1995–96	Everton	32	16		
1996–97	Everton	20	4	52	20
1996–97	Fiorentina	9	0		
1997–98	Fiorentina	17	2	26	2
1998–99	Rangers	30	8		
1999–2000	Rangers	28	4		
2000–01	Rangers	7	1	65	13
2000–01	*Manchester C*	10	0	10	0

KENNEDY, Mark (M)   154   19
H: 6 1　W: 12 09　b.Dublin 15-5-76
Source: Belvedere, Trainee. *Honours:* Eire Under-21, 31 full caps, 3 goals.

1992–93	Millwall	1	0		
1993–94	Millwall	12	4		
1994–95	Millwall	30	5	43	9
1994–95	Liverpool	6	0		
1995–96	Liverpool	4	0		
1996–97	Liverpool	5	0		
1997–98	Liverpool	1	0	16	0
1997–98	*QPR*	8	2	8	2
1997–98	Wimbledon	0	0		
1998–99	Wimbledon	17	0	21	0
1999–2000	Manchester C	41	8		
2000–01	Manchester C	25	0	66	8

KILLEN, Chris (F)   12   3
H: 6 0　W: 11 03　b.Wellington 8-10-81
Source: Miramar R.

1998–99	Manchester C	0	0		
1999–2000	Manchester C	0	0		
2000–01	Manchester C	0	0		
2000–01	*Wrexham*	12	3	12	3

LAYCOCK, David‡ (M)   0   0
H: 5 10　W: 10 07　b.Hull 1-10-80
Source: Trainee.

1998–99	Manchester C	0	0		
1999–2000	Manchester C	0	0		
2000–01	Manchester C	0	0		

MASON, Gary‡ (M)   25   0
H: 5 9　W: 10 10　b.Edinburgh 15-10-79
Source: Trainee. *Honours:* Scotland Under-21.

1996–97	Manchester C	0	0		
1997–98	Manchester C	0	0		
1998–99	Manchester C	19	0		
1999–2000	Manchester C	0	0		
1999–2000	*Hartlepool U*	6	0	6	0
2000–01	Manchester C	19	0		

McCARTHY, Patrick (D)   0   0
b.Dublin 31-5-83
Source: Scholar.

2000–01	Manchester C	0	0		

McDOWALL, Ryan (M)   0   0
b.Knowsley 30-3-84
Source: School.

2000–01	Manchester C	0	0		

McKINNEY, Richard* (G)   0   0
H: 6 3　W: 14 00　b.Ballymoney 18-5-79
Source: Ballymena U.

1999–2000	Manchester C	0	0		
2000–01	Manchester C	0	0		

MEARS, Tyrone (D)   0   0
b.Stockport 18-2-83

2000–01	Manchester C	0	0		

MIKE, Leon (F)   10   0
H: 5 10　W: 13 02　b.Manchester 4-9-81
Source: Scholarship. *Honours:* England Schools, Youth.

1998–99	Manchester C	0	0		
1999–2000	Manchester C	0	0		
2000–01	Manchester C	0	0		
2000–01	*Oxford U*	3	0	3	0
2000–01	*Halifax T*	7	0	7	0

MORRISON, Andy (D)   262   16
H: 5 11　W: 12 12　b.Inverness 30-7-70
Source: Trainee.

1987–88	Plymouth Arg	1	0		
1988–89	Plymouth Arg	2	0		
1989–90	Plymouth Arg	19	1		
1990–91	Plymouth Arg	32	2		
1991–92	Plymouth Arg	30	3		
1992–93	Plymouth Arg	29	0	113	6
1993–94	Blackburn R	5	0		
1994–95	Blackburn R	0	0	5	0
1994–95	Blackpool	0	0		
1995–96	Blackpool	29	3		
1996–97	Huddersfield T	10	1		
1997–98	Huddersfield T	23	1		
1998–99	Huddersfield T	12	0	45	2
1998–99	Manchester C	22	4		
1999–2000	Manchester C	12	0		
2000–01	Manchester C	3	0	37	4
2000–01	*Blackpool*	6	1	53	4
2000–01	*Crystal Palace*	5	0	5	0
2000–01	*Sheffield U*	4	0	4	0

MURPHY, Brian (M)   0   0
b.Waterford 7-5-83

2000–01	Manchester C	0	0		

NASH, Carlo (G)   116   0
H: 6 5　W: 14 01　b.Bolton 13-9-73
Source: Clitheroe.

1996–97	Crystal Palace	21	0		
1997–98	Crystal Palace	0	0	21	0
1998–99	Stockport Co	43	0		
1999–2000	Stockport Co	38	0		
2000–01	Stockport Co	8	0	89	0
2000–01	Manchester C	6	0	6	0

PAISLEY, Stephen (D)   0   0
b.Dublin 28-7-83
Source: Scholar.

2000–01	Manchester C	0	0		

PRIOR, Spencer (D)   357   9
H: 6 3　W: 13 09　b.Rochford 22-4-71
Source: Trainee.

1988–89	Southend U	14	1		
1989–90	Southend U	15	1		
1990–91	Southend U	19	0		
1991–92	Southend U	42	1		
1992–93	Southend U	45	0	135	3
1993–94	Norwich C	13	0		
1994–95	Norwich C	17	0		
1995–96	Norwich C	44	1	74	1
1996–97	Leicester C	34	0		
1997–98	Leicester C	30	0	64	0
1998–99	Derby Co	34	1		
1999–2000	Derby Co	20	0	54	1
2000–01	Manchester C	21	1	30	4

RITCHIE, Paul (D)   159   4
H: 5 11　W: 12 06　b.Kirkcaldy 21-8-75
Source: Links U. *Honours:* Scotland Under-21, B, 6 full caps, 1 goal.

1992–93	Hearts	0	0		
1993–94	Hearts	0	0		
1994–95	Hearts	0	0		
1995–96	Hearts	28	1		
1996–97	Hearts	28	1		
1997–98	Hearts	34	0		
1998–99	Hearts	29	1		
1999–2000	Hearts	14	1	133	4
1999–2000	Bolton W	14	0	14	0
2000–01	Manchester C	12	0	12	0

RUSSELL, Craig‡ (F)   212   37
H: 5 10　W: 12 07　b.Jarrow 4-2-74
Source: Trainee.

1991–92	Sunderland	4	0		
1992–93	Sunderland	0	0		
1993–94	Sunderland	35	9		
1994–95	Sunderland	38	5		
1995–96	Sunderland	41	13		
1996–97	Sunderland	29	4		
1997–98	Sunderland	3	0	150	31
1997–98	Manchester C	24	1		
1998–99	Manchester C	7	1		
1998–99	*Tranmere R*	4	0	4	0
1998–99	*Port Vale*	8	1	8	1
1999–2000	Manchester C	0	0		
1999–2000	*Darlington*	12	2	12	2
1999–2000	*Oxford U*	6	0	6	0
1999–2000	*St Johnstone*	1	1	1	1
2000–01	Manchester C	0	0	31	2

SHUKER, Chris (F)   9   1
H: 5 4　W: 9 08　b.Liverpool 9-5-82
Source: Scholarship.

1999–2000	Manchester C	0	0		
2000–01	Manchester C	0	0		
2000–01	*Macclesfield T*	9	1	9	1

TAYLOR, Gareth* (F)   219   56
H: 6 3　W: 14 02　b.Weston-Super-Mare 25-2-73
Source: Southampton Trainee. *Honours:* Wales Under-21, 8 full caps.

1991–92	Bristol R	1	0		
1992–93	Bristol R	0	0		
1993–94	Bristol R	0	0		
1994–95	Bristol R	39	12		
1995–96	Bristol R	7	4	47	16
1995–96	Crystal Palace	20	1	20	1
1995–96	Sheffield U	10	2		
1996–97	Sheffield U	34	12		
1997–98	Sheffield U	28	10		
1998–99	Sheffield U	12	1	84	25
1998–99	Manchester C	26	4		
1999–2000	Manchester C	17	5		
1999–2000	*Port Vale*	4	0	4	0
1999–2000	*QPR*	6	1	6	1
2000–01	Manchester C	0	0	43	9
2000–01	*Burnley*	15	4	15	4

TIATTO, Danny (D)   139   5
H: 5 7　W: 11 03　b.Melbourne 22-5-73
Source: Melbourne Knights 43 apps, 3 goals. *Honours:* Australia 23 full caps, 1 goal.

1994–95	Melbourne Knights	22	2		
1995–96	Melbourne Knights	17	0	39	2
From Baden.					
1997–98	Stoke C	15	1	15	1
1998–99	Manchester C	17	0		
1999–2000	Manchester C	35	0		
2000–01	Manchester C	33	2	85	2

TOPPMOLLER, Dino‡ (M)   12   1
b.Wadern 23-11-80

2000–01	Saarbrucken	12	1	12	1
2000–01	Manchester C	0	0		

TUNNICLIFFE, Andrew (M)   0   0
b.Stockport 25-5-83
Source: Scholar.

2000–01	Manchester C	0	0		

WANCHOPE, Paulo (F)   134   44
H: 6 3　W: 13 08　b.Heredia 31-7-76
Source: Herediano. *Honours:* Costa Rica full caps.

1996–97	Derby Co	5	1		
1997–98	Derby Co	32	13		
1998–99	Derby Co	35	9	72	23
1999–2000	West Ham U	35	12	35	12
2000–01	Manchester C	27	9	27	9

WEAH, George (F)   331   129
H: 6 2　W: 13 02　b.Liberia 1-10-66
Source: Tonnerre. *Honours:* Liberia full caps.

1988–90	Monaco	23	14		
1989–90	Monaco	17	5		
1990–91	Monaco	29	10		
1991–92	Monaco	34	18	103	47
1992–93	Paris St Germain	32	14		
1993–94	Paris St Germain	32	11		
1994–95	Paris St Germain	34	7	96	32
1995–96	AC Milan	26	11		
1996–97	AC Milan	28	13		
1997–98	AC Milan	24	10		
1998–99	AC Milan	26	8		
1999–2000	AC Milan	10	4	114	46
1999–2000	Chelsea	11	3	11	3
2000–01	Manchester C	7	1	7	1

(Transferred to Marseille, October 2000).

WEAVER, Nick (G)   122   0
H: 6 4　W: 14 10　b.Sheffield 2-3-79
Source: Trainee. *Honours:* England Under-21.

1995–96	Mansfield T	1	0		
1996–97	Mansfield T	0	0	1	0
1996–97	Manchester C	0	0		
1997–98	Manchester C	0	0		
1998–99	Manchester C	45	0		

| 1999–2000 | Manchester C | 45 | 0 | | |
| 2000–01 | Manchester C | 31 | 0 | 121 | 0 |

WHELAN, Glenn (M) 0 0
H: 5 8 W: 10 05 b.Dublin 13-1-84
Source: Scholar.

| 2000–01 | Manchester C | 0 | 0 | | |

WHITLEY, Jeff (M) 130 10
H: 5 8 W: 10 05 b.Zambia 28-1-79
Source: Trainee. *Honours:* Northern Ireland Under-21, 7 caps, 1 goal.

1995–96	Manchester C	0	0		
1996–97	Manchester C	23	1		
1997–98	Manchester C	17	1		
1998–99	Manchester C	8	1		
1998–99	*Wrexham*	9	2	9	2
1999–2000	Manchester C	42	4		
2000–01	Manchester C	31	1	121	8

WHITLEY, Jim* (M) 69 1
H: 5 9 W: 10 12 b.Zambia 14-4-75
Source: Trainee. *Honours:* Northern Ireland 3 full caps.

1993–94	Manchester C	0	0		
1994–95	Manchester C	0	0		
1995–96	Manchester C	0	0		
1996–97	Manchester C	0	0		
1997–98	Manchester C	19	0		
1998–99	Manchester C	18	0		
1999–2000	Manchester C	1	0		
1999–2000	*Blackpool*	8	0	8	0
2000–01	Manchester C	0	0	38	0
2000–01	*Norwich C*	8	1	8	1
2000–01	*Swindon T*	2	0	2	0
2000–01	*Northampton T*	13	0	13	0
2000–01	*Nottingham F*	0	0		

WIEKENS, Gerard (D) 180 11
H: 6 0 W: 13 04 b.Tolhuiswyk 25-2-73

1996–97	*Veendam*	33	1	33	1
1997–98	Manchester C	37	5		
1998–99	Manchester C	42	2		
1999–2000	Manchester C	34	1		
2000–01	Manchester C	34	2	147	10

WRIGHT-PHILLIPS, Shaun (F) 19 0
H: 5 4 W: 9 08 b.London 25-10-81

1998–99	Manchester C	0	0		
1999–2000	Manchester C	4	0		
2000–01	Manchester C	15	0	19	0

Scholars
Crawford, Richard E; Egerton, Mark C; Furnival, Gary; Gilder, Phillip G; James, William AA; McTaggart, Daniel A; Orr, Adrian GS
Non-Contract
Barton, Joseph A; Hodgson, David; Kilheeney, Ciaran; Tickle, David

MANCHESTER U

BARTHEZ, Fabien (G) 305 0
H: 5 11 W: 12 08 b.Lavelanet 28-6-71
Honours: France 42 full caps.

1991–92	Toulouse	26	0	26	0
1992–93	Marseille	30	0		
1993–94	Marseille	37	0		
1994–95	Marseille	39	0	106	0
1995–96	Monaco	21	0		
1996–97	Monaco	36	0		
1997–98	Monaco	30	0		
1998–99	Monaco	32	0		
1999–2000	Monaco	24	0	143	0
2000–01	Manchester U	30	0	30	0

BAXTER, Nick (G) 0 0
H: 6 3 W: 13 10 b.Bridlington 25-3-83
Source: Scholar.

| 2000–01 | Manchester U | 0 | 0 | | |

BECKHAM, David (M) 211 46
H: 6 0 W: 11 13 b.Leytonstone 2-5-75
Source: Trainee. *Honours:* England Youth, Under-21, 42 full caps, 4 goals.

1992–93	Manchester U	0	0		
1993–94	Manchester U	0	0		
1994–95	Manchester U	4	0		
1994–95	*Preston NE*	5	2	5	2
1995–96	Manchester U	33	7		
1996–97	Manchester U	36	7		
1997–98	Manchester U	37	9		
1998–99	Manchester U	34	6		
1999–2000	Manchester U	31	6		
2000–01	Manchester U	31	9	206	44

BLOMQVIST, Jesper* (F) 182 30
H: 5 9 W: 11 03 b.Tavelsjo 5-2-74
Honours: Sweden 29 full caps.

1992	Umea	27	6		
1993	Umea	11	2	38	8
1993	IFK Gothenburg	6	1		
1994	IFK Gothenburg	24	8		
1995	IFK Gothenburg	18	3		
1996	IFK Gothenburg	23	7	71	19
1996–97	AC Milan	19	1		
1997–98	AC Milan	11	0	20	1
1997–98	Parma	28	1	28	1
1998–99	Manchester U	25	1		
1999–2000	Manchester U	0	0		
2000–01	Manchester U	0	0	25	1

BROWN, Wes (D) 44 0
H: 6 1 W: 13 11 b.Manchester 13-10-79
Source: Trainee. *Honours:* England Schools, Youth, Under-21, 3 full caps.

1996–97	Manchester U	0	0		
1997–98	Manchester U	2	0		
1998–99	Manchester U	14	0		
1999–2000	Manchester U	0	0		
2000–01	Manchester U	28	0	44	0

BUTT, Nicky (M) 206 19
H: 5 10 W: 11 11 b.Manchester 21-1-75
Source: Trainee. *Honours:* England Schools, Youth, Under-21, 14 full caps.

1992–93	Manchester U	1	0		
1993–94	Manchester U	1	0		
1994–95	Manchester U	22	1		
1995–96	Manchester U	32	2		
1996–97	Manchester U	26	5		
1997–98	Manchester U	33	3		
1998–99	Manchester U	31	2		
1999–2000	Manchester U	32	3		
2000–01	Manchester U	28	3	206	19

CHADWICK, Luke (F) 16 2
H: 5 11 W: 11 08 b.Cambridge 18-11-80
Source: Trainee. *Honours:* England Youth, Under-21.

1998–99	Manchester U	0	0		
1999–2000	Manchester U	0	0		
2000–01	Manchester U	16	2	16	2

CLEGG, George* (F) 10 0
H: 5 10 W: 11 11 b.Manchester 16-11-80
Source: Trainee.

1999–2000	Manchester U	0	0		
2000–01	Manchester U	0	0		
2000–01	*Wycombe W*	10	0	10	0

CLEGG, Michael (D) 18 0
H: 5 8 W: 11 10 b.Ashton-under-Lyne 3-7-77
Source: Trainee. *Honours:* England Under-21.

1995–96	Manchester U	0	0		
1996–97	Manchester U	4	0		
1997–98	Manchester U	3	0		
1998–99	Manchester U	1	0		
1999–2000	Manchester U	2	0		
1999–2000	*Ipswich T*	3	0	3	0
1999–2000	*Wigan Ath*	6	0	6	0
2000–01	Manchester U	0	0	9	0

CLEGG, Steven (D) 0 0
H: 5 9 W: 12 08 b.Ashton-under-Lyne 16-4-82
Source: Scholar.

| 2000–01 | Manchester U | 0 | 0 | | |

COATES, Craig (F) 0 0
H: 5 7 W: 10 11 b.Dryburn 26-10-82
Source: Trainee.

| 1999–2000 | Manchester U | 0 | 0 | | |
| 2000–01 | Manchester U | 0 | 0 | | |

COLE, Andy (F) 309 167
H: 5 11 W: 12 02 b.Nottingham 15-10-71
Source: Trainee. *Honours:* England Schools, Youth, Under-21, B, 13 full caps, 1 goal. Football League.

1989–90	Arsenal	0	0		
1990–91	Arsenal	1	0		
1991–92	Arsenal	0	0	1	0
1991–92	Fulham	13	3	13	3
1991–92	Bristol C	12	8		
1992–93	Bristol C	29	12	41	20
1992–93	Newcastle U	12	12		
1993–94	Newcastle U	40	34		
1994–95	Newcastle U	18	9	70	55
1994–95	Manchester U	18	12		
1995–96	Manchester U	34	11		
1996–97	Manchester U	20	6		
1997–98	Manchester U	33	15		
1998–99	Manchester U	32	17		
1999–2000	Manchester U	28	19		
2000–01	Manchester U	19	9	184	89

COSGROVE, Simon* (M) 0 0
H: 5 9 W: 10 06 b.Glasgow 29-12-80
Source: Trainee.

1998–99	Manchester U	0	0		
1999–2000	Manchester U	0	0		
2000–01	Manchester U	0	0		

CULKIN, Nick (G) 50 0
H: 6 2 W: 13 09 b.York 6-7-78
Source: York C.

1995–96	Manchester U	0	0		
1996–97	Manchester U	0	0		
1997–98	Manchester U	0	0		
1998–99	Manchester U	0	0		
1999–2000	Manchester U	1	0		
1999–2000	*Hull C*	4	0	4	0
2000–01	Manchester U	0	0	1	0
2000–01	*Bristol R*	45	0	45	0

DAVIS, Jimmy (F) 0 0
H: 5 8 W: 11 05 b.Bromsgrove 6-2-82
Source: Trainee. *Honours:* England Youth.

| 1999–2000 | Manchester U | 0 | 0 | | |
| 2000–01 | Manchester U | 0 | 0 | | |

DJORDJIC, Bojan (F) 1 0
H: 5 10 W: 10 10 b.Belgrade 6-2-82
Source: On loan to Brommapojkarna.

1998–99	Manchester U	0	0		
1999–2000	Manchester U	0	0		
2000–01	Manchester U	1	0	1	0

DODD, Ashley* (M) 3 0
H: 5 10 W: 10 02 b.Stafford 7-1-82
Source: Trainee.

1999–2000	Manchester U	0	0		
2000–01	Manchester U	0	0		
2000–01	*Port Vale*	3	0	3	0

EVANS, Wayne‡ (M) 0 0
H: 5 9 W: 9 08 b.Carmarthen 23-10-80
Source: Trainee.

1997–98	Manchester U	0	0		
1998–99	Manchester U	0	0		
1999–2000	Manchester U	0	0		
2000–01	Manchester U	0	0		

FLETCHER, Darren (M) 0 0
H: 6 0 W: 13 01 b.Edinburgh 1-2-84
Source: Scholar.

| 2000–01 | Manchester U | 0 | 0 | | |

FORTUNE, Quinton (F) 88 7
H: 5 9 W: 11 09 b.Cape Town 21-5-77
Source: Kaizer Chiefs, Tottenham H schoolboy. *Honours:* South Africa 25 full caps.

1995–96	Mallorca	8	0	8	0
1995–96	Atletico Madrid	3	0		
1996–97	Atletico Madrid B	30	2		
1996–97	Atletico Madrid	1	0		
1997–98	Atletico Madrid B	31	1		
1997–98	Atletico Madrid	0	0		
1998–99	Atletico Madrid	2	0	6	0
1999–2000	Manchester U	6	2		
2000–01	Manchester U	7	2	13	4

FOX, David (M) 0 0
H: 5 9 W: 12 02 b.Stoke 13-12-83
Source: Scholar.

| 2000–01 | Manchester U | 0 | 0 | | |

GIGGS, Ryan (F) 321 64
H: 5 11 W: 11 00 b.Cardiff 29-11-73
Source: School. *Honours:* England Schools, Wales Youth, Under-21, 32 full caps, 7 goals.

1990–91	Manchester U	2	1		
1991–92	Manchester U	38	4		
1992–93	Manchester U	41	9		
1993–94	Manchester U	38	13		
1994–95	Manchester U	29	1		
1995–96	Manchester U	33	11		
1996–97	Manchester U	26	3		
1997–98	Manchester U	29	8		
1998–99	Manchester U	24	3		
1999–2000	Manchester U	30	6		
2000–01	Manchester U	31	5	321	64

GORAM, Andy‡ (G) 584 1
H: 5 11 W: 11 06 b.Bury 13-4-64
Source: West Bromwich Apprentice. *Honours:* Scotland Under-21, 43 full caps.

1981–82	Oldham Ath	3	0		
1982–83	Oldham Ath	38	0		
1983–84	Oldham Ath	22	0		
1984–85	Oldham Ath	41	0		
1985–86	Oldham Ath	41	0		
1986–87	Oldham Ath	41	0		
1987–88	Oldham Ath	9	0	195	0
1987–88	Hibernian	33	1		
1988–89	Hibernian	36	0		
1989–90	Hibernian	34	0		
1990–91	Hibernian	35	0	138	1
1991–92	Rangers	44	0		
1992–93	Rangers	34	0		
1993–94	Rangers	8	0		
1994–95	Rangers	19	0		
1995–96	Rangers	30	0		
1996–97	Rangers	25	0		
1997–98	Rangers	24	0	184	0
1998–99	Notts Co	1	0	1	0

1998–99	Sheffield U	7	0	7	0
1998–99	Motherwell	13	0		
1999–2000	Motherwell	22	0		
2000–01	Motherwell	22	0	57	0
2000–01	Manchester U	2	0	2	0

GREENING, Jonathan (F)   **39 2**
H: 6 0   W: 11 13   b.Scarborough 2-1-79
Source: Trainee. *Honours:* England Youth, Under-21.

1996–97	York C	5	0		
1997–98	York C	20	2	25	2
1997–98	Manchester U	0	0		
1998–99	Manchester U	3	0		
1999–2000	Manchester U	4	0		
2000–01	Manchester U	7	0	14	0

HEATH, Colin (F)   **0 0**
H: 6 0   W: 13 01   b.Chesterfield 31-12-83
Source: Scholar.

2000–01	Manchester U	0	0		

HILTON, Kirk (D)   **0 0**
H: 5 7   W: 10 01   b.Flixton 2-4-81
Source: Trainee.

1999–2000	Manchester U	0	0		
2000–01	Manchester U	0	0		

IRWIN, Denis* (D)   **595 27**
H: 5 8   W: 10 11   b.Cork 31-10-65
Source: Apprentice. *Honours:* Eire Schools, Youth, Under-21, B, 56 full caps, 4 goals.

1983–84	Leeds U	12	0		
1984–85	Leeds U	41	1		
1985–86	Leeds U	19	0	72	1
1986–87	Oldham Ath	41	0		
1987–88	Oldham Ath	43	0		
1988–89	Oldham Ath	41	2		
1989–90	Oldham Ath	42	1	167	4
1990–91	Manchester U	34	0		
1991–92	Manchester U	38	4		
1992–93	Manchester U	40	5		
1993–94	Manchester U	42	2		
1994–95	Manchester U	40	2		
1995–96	Manchester U	31	1		
1996–97	Manchester U	31	1		
1997–98	Manchester U	25	2		
1998–99	Manchester U	29	2		
1999–2000	Manchester U	25	3		
2000–01	Manchester U	21	0	356	22

JOHNSEN, Ronny (D)   **165 18**
H: 6 3   W: 13 06   b.Sandefjord 10-6-69
Honours: Norway 43 full caps, 2 goals.

1992	Lyn	12	1		
1993	Lyn	19	6	31	7
1994	Lillestrom	10	3		
1995	Lillestrom	13	1	23	4
1995–96	Besiktas	22	1	22	1
1996–97	Manchester U	31	0		
1997–98	Manchester U	22	2		
1998–99	Manchester U	22	3		
1999–2000	Manchester U	3	0		
2000–01	Manchester U	11	1	89	6

JONES, Rhodri* (D)   **0 0**
H: 6 0   W: 12 04   b.Cardiff 19-1-82
Source: Trainee.

1999–2000	Manchester U	0	0		
2000–01	Manchester U	0	0		

JOWSEY, James (G)   **0 0**
H: 6 0   W: 12 04   b.Scarborough 24-11-83
Source: Scholar.

2000–01	Manchester U	0	0		

KEANE, Roy (M)   **327 48**
H: 5 11   W: 11 10   b.Cork 10-8-71
Source: Cobh Ramb. *Honours:* Eire Youth, Under-21, 52 full caps, 8 goals.

1990–91	Nottingham F	35	8		
1991–92	Nottingham F	39	8		
1992–93	Nottingham F	40	6	114	22
1993–94	Manchester U	37	5		
1994–95	Manchester U	25	2		
1995–96	Manchester U	29	6		
1996–97	Manchester U	21	2		
1997–98	Manchester U	9	2		
1998–99	Manchester U	35	2		
1999–2000	Manchester U	29	5		
2000–01	Manchester U	28	2	213	26

LYNCH, Mark (D)   **0 0**
H: 5 11   W: 11 03   b.Manchester 2-9-81
Source: Trainee.

1999–2000	Manchester U	0	0		
2000–01	Manchester U	0	0		

MAY, David (D)   **206 9**
H: 6 0   W: 13 05   b.Oldham 24-6-70
Source: Trainee.

1988–89	Blackburn R	1	0		
1989–90	Blackburn R	17	0		
1990–91	Blackburn R	19	1		
1991–92	Blackburn R	34	1		
1992–93	Blackburn R	40	1	123	3
1994–95	Manchester U	19	2		
1995–96	Manchester U	16	1		
1996–97	Manchester U	29	3		
1997–98	Manchester U	9	0		
1998–99	Manchester U	6	0		
1999–2000	Manchester U	1	0		
1999–2000	Huddersfield T	1	0	1	0
2000–01	Manchester U	2	0	82	6

McDERMOTT, Alan (D)   **0 0**
H: 6 1   W: 11 07   b.Dublin 22-1-82
Source: Trainee.

1998–99	Manchester U	0	0		
1999–2000	Manchester U	0	0		
2000–01	Manchester U	0	0		

MOONIARUCK, Kalam (F)   **0 0**
H: 5 8   W: 11 09   b.Yeovil 22-11-83
Source: Scholar.

2000–01	Manchester U	0	0		

MORAN, David (G)   **0 0**
H: 6 0   W: 14 05   b.Ballinasloe 16-4-82
Source: Trainee.

2000–01	Manchester U	0	0		

MUIRHEAD, Ben (F)   **0 0**
H: 5 9   W: 10 05   b.Doncaster 5-1-83
Source: Trainee.

1999–2000	Manchester U	0	0		
2000–01	Manchester U	0	0		

NARDIELLO, Daniel (F)   **0 0**
H: 5 11   W: 11 04   b.Coventry 22-10-82
Source: Trainee.

1999–2000	Manchester U	0	0		
2000–01	Manchester U	0	0		

NEVILLE, Gary (D)   **203 3**
H: 5 11   W: 12 04   b.Bury 18-2-75
Source: Trainee. *Honours:* England Youth, 44 full caps.

1992–93	Manchester U	0	0		
1993–94	Manchester U	1	0		
1994–95	Manchester U	18	0		
1995–96	Manchester U	31	0		
1996–97	Manchester U	31	1		
1997–98	Manchester U	34	0		
1998–99	Manchester U	34	1		
1999–2000	Manchester U	22	0		
2000–01	Manchester U	32	1	203	3

NEVILLE, Phil (D)   **160 2**
H: 5 11   W: 12 00   b.Bury 21-1-77
Source: Trainee. *Honours:* England Schools, Youth, Under-21, 33 full caps.

1994–95	Manchester U	2	0		
1995–96	Manchester U	24	0		
1996–97	Manchester U	18	0		
1997–98	Manchester U	30	1		
1998–99	Manchester U	28	0		
1999–2000	Manchester U	29	0		
2000–01	Manchester U	29	1	160	2

O'SHEA, John (D)   **10 1**
H: 6 3   W: 12 10   b.Waterford 30-4-81
Source: Waterford. *Honours:* Eire Under-21.

1998–99	Manchester U	0	0		
1999–2000	Manchester U	0	0		
1999–2000	Bournemouth	10	1	10	1
2000–01	Manchester U	0	0		

PUGH, Danny (M)   **0 0**
H: 6 0   W: 12 10   b.Manchester 19-10-82
Source: Scholar.

2000–01	Manchester U	0	0		

RACHUBKA, Paul (G)   **1 0**
H: 6 1   W: 13 01   b.San Luis Opispo 21-5-81
Source: Trainee. *Honours:* England Youth.

1999–2000	Manchester U	0	0		
2000–01	Manchester U	1	0	1	0

RANKIN, John (M)   **0 0**
H: 5 8   W: 12 08   b.Bellshill 27-6-83
Source: Scholar.

2000–01	Manchester U	0	0		

ROCHE, Lee (D)   **41 0**
H: 5 10   W: 10 10   b.Bolton 28-10-80
Source: Trainee. *Honours:* England Youth, Under-21.

1998–99	Manchester U	0	0		
1999–2000	Manchester U	0	0		
2000–01	Manchester U	0	0		
2000–01	Wrexham	41	0	41	0

ROSE, Michael* (M)   **0 0**
H: 5 11   W: 11 01   b.Salford 28-7-82
Source: Trainee.

1999–2000	Manchester U	0	0		
2000–01	Manchester U	0	0		

SAMPSON, Gary (M)   **0 0**
H: 5 9   W: 11 02   b.Manchester 13-9-82
Source: Scholar.

2000–01	Manchester U	0	0		

SCHOLES, Paul (M)   **192 47**
H: 5 7   W: 11 00   b.Salford 16-11-74
Source: Trainee. *Honours:* England Youth, 35 full caps, 13 goals.

1992–93	Manchester U	0	0		
1993–94	Manchester U	0	0		
1994–95	Manchester U	17	5		
1995–96	Manchester U	26	10		
1996–97	Manchester U	24	3		
1997–98	Manchester U	31	8		
1998–99	Manchester U	31	6		
1999–2000	Manchester U	31	9		
2000–01	Manchester U	32	6	192	47

SHERINGHAM, Teddy* (F)   **537 213**
H: 6 0   W: 12 09   b.Highams Park 2-4-66
Source: Apprentice. *Honours:* England Youth, 41 full caps, 10 goals.

1983–84	Millwall	7	1		
1984–85	Millwall	0	0		
1984–85	Aldershot	5	0	5	0
1985–86	Millwall	18	4		
1986–87	Millwall	42	13		
1987–88	Millwall	43	22		
1988–89	Millwall	33	11		
1989–90	Millwall	31	9		
1990–91	Millwall	46	33	220	93
1991–92	Nottingham F	39	13		
1992–93	Nottingham F	3	1	42	14
1992–93	Tottenham H	38	21		
1993–94	Tottenham H	19	13		
1994–95	Tottenham H	42	18		
1995–96	Tottenham H	38	16		
1996–97	Tottenham H	29	7	166	75
1997–98	Manchester U	31	9		
1998–99	Manchester U	17	2		
1999–2000	Manchester U	27	5		
2000–01	Manchester U	29	15	104	31

(Transferred to Tottenahm H, June 2001).

SILVESTRE, Mikael (D)   **128 2**
H: 6 0   W: 13 01   b.Chambray les Tours 9-8-77
Honours: France 6 full caps, 1 goal.

1995–96	Rennes	1	0		
1996–97	Rennes	16	0		
1997–98	Rennes	32	0	49	0
1998–99	Internazionale	18	1	18	1
1999–2000	Manchester U	31	0		
2000–01	Manchester U	30	1	61	1

SOLSKJAER, Ole Gunnar (F)   **175 88**
H: 5 10   W: 11 11   b.Kristiansund 26-2-73
Honours: Norway Under-21, 41 full caps, 16 goals.

1995	Molde	26	20		
1996	Molde	16	11	42	31
1996–97	Manchester U	33	17		
1997–98	Manchester U	22	6		
1998–99	Manchester U	19	12		
1999–2000	Manchester U	28	12		
2000–01	Manchester U	31	10	133	57

STAM, Jaap (D)   **271 18**
H: 6 3   W: 15 00   b.Kampen 17-7-72
Honours: Holland 39 full caps, 3 goals.

1992–93	Zwolle	32	1	32	1
1993–94	Cambuur	33	1		
1994–95	Cambuur	33	2	66	3
1995–96	Willem II	19	1	19	1
1995–96	PSV Eindhoven	14	1		
1996–97	PSV Eindhoven	33	7		
1997–98	PSV Eindhoven	29	4	76	12
1998–99	Manchester U	30	1		
1999–2000	Manchester U	33	0		
2000–01	Manchester U	15	0	78	1

STEWART, Michael (M)   **3 0**
H: 5 11   W: 11 11   b.Edinburgh 26-2-81
Source: Trainee. *Honours:* Scotland Under-21.

1997–98	Manchester U	0	0		
1998–99	Manchester U	0	0		
1999–2000	Manchester U	0	0		
2000–01	Manchester U	3	0	3	0

STRANGE, Gareth* (D)   **0 0**
H: 5 9   W: 10 05   b.Bolton 3-10-81
Source: Trainee. *Honours:* England Schools.

1998–99	Manchester U	0	0		
1999–2000	Manchester U	0	0		
2000–01	Manchester U	0	0		

STUDLEY, Mark* (D) 0 0
H: 5 6 W: 10 00 b.Manchester 27-12-81
Source: Trainee.
1999–2000 Manchester U 0 0
2000–01 Manchester U 0 0

SZMID, Marek* (D) 0 0
H: 5 8 W: 11 06 b.Nuneaton 2-3-82
Source: Trainee.
1999–2000 Manchester U 0 0
2000–01 Manchester U 0 0

TATE, Alan (D) 0 0
H: 6 1 W: 13 05 b.Easington 2-9-82
Source: Scholar.
2000–01 Manchester U 0 0

TAYLOR, Andrew (M) 0 0
H: 5 9 W: 12 10 b.Exeter 17-9-82
Source: Scholar.
2000–01 Manchester U 0 0

TAYLOR, Kris (M) 0 0
H: 5 9 W: 13 05 b.Stafford 12-1-84
Source: Scholar.
2000–01 Manchester U 0 0

TEATHER, Paul‡ (D) 10 0
H: 6 0 W: 11 13 b.Rotherham 26-12-77
Source: Trainee. *Honours:* England Schools, Youth.
1994–95 Manchester U 0 0
1995–96 Manchester U 0 0
1996–97 Manchester U 0 0
1997–98 Manchester U 0 0
1997–98 *Bournemouth* 10 0 **10** **0**
1998–99 Manchester U 0 0
1999–2000 Manchester U 0 0
2000–01 Manchester U 0 0

TIERNEY, Paul (M) 0 0
H: 5 10 W: 12 10 b.Salford 15-9-82
Source: Scholar.
2000–01 Manchester U 0 0

VAN DER GOUW, Raimond* (G) 391 0
H: 6 3 W: 13 09 b.Oldenzaal 24-3-63
1985–86 Go Ahead 28 0
1986–87 Go Ahead 34 0
1987–88 Go Ahead 35 0 **97** **0**
1988–89 Vitesse 36 0
1989–90 Vitesse 34 0
1990–91 Vitesse 31 0
1991–92 Vitesse 34 0
1992–93 Vitesse 34 0
1993–94 Vitesse 34 0
1994–95 Vitesse 34 0
1995–96 Vitesse 21 0 **258** **0**
1996–97 Manchester U 2 0
1997–98 Manchester U 5 0
1998–99 Manchester U 5 0
1999–2000 Manchester U 14 0
2000–01 Manchester U 10 0 **36** **0**

WALKER, Joshua* (M) 0 0
H: 6 1 W: 11 01 b.Birmingham 20-12-81
Source: Trainee.
1999–2000 Manchester U 0 0
2000–01 Manchester U 0 0

WALLWORK, Ronnie (D) 35 1
H: 5 10 W: 13 01 b.Manchester 10-9-77
Source: Trainee. *Honours:* England Youth.
1994–95 Manchester U 0 0
1995–96 Manchester U 0 0
1996–97 Manchester U 0 0
1997–98 Manchester U 1 0
1997–98 *Carlisle U* 10 1 **10** **1**
1997–98 *Stockport Co* 7 0 **7** **0**
1998–99 Manchester U 0 0
1999–2000 Manchester U 5 0
2000–01 Manchester U 12 0 **18** **0**

WEBBER, Danny (F) 0 0
H: 5 9 W: 10 08 b.Manchester 28-12-81
Source: Trainee. *Honours:* England Youth.
1998–99 Manchester U 0 0
1999–2000 Manchester U 0 0
2000–01 Manchester U 0 0

WHITEMAN, Marc (F) 0 0
H: 5 10 W: 13 12 b.St Hellier 1-10-82
Source: Scholar.
2000–01 Manchester U 0 0

WILLIAMS, Matthew (F) 0 0
H: 5 8 W: 9 11 b.St Asaph 5-11-82
Honours: Wales Under-21.
1999–2000 Manchester U 0 0
2000–01 Manchester U 0 0

WILSON, Mark (M) 16 4
H: 6 0 W: 12 07 b.Scunthorpe 9-2-79
Source: Trainee. *Honours:* England Schools, Under-21.
1995–96 Manchester U 0 0
1996–97 Manchester U 0 0
1997–98 Manchester U 0 0
1997–98 *Wrexham* 13 4 **13** **4**
1998–99 Manchester U 0 0
1999–2000 Manchester U 3 0
2000–01 Manchester U 0 0 **3** **0**

WOOD, Neil (F) 0 0
H: 5 10 W: 13 02 b.Manchester 4-1-83
Source: Trainee.
1999–2000 Manchester U 0 0
2000–01 Manchester U 0 0

YORKE, Dwight (F) 317 120
H: 5 10 W: 12 03 b.Canaan 3-11-71
Source: St Clair's, Tobago. *Honours:* Trinidad & Tobago full caps.
1989–90 Aston Villa 2 0
1990–91 Aston Villa 18 2
1991–92 Aston Villa 32 11
1992–93 Aston Villa 27 6
1993–94 Aston Villa 12 2
1994–95 Aston Villa 37 6
1995–96 Aston Villa 35 17
1996–97 Aston Villa 37 17
1997–98 Aston Villa 30 12
1998–99 Aston Villa 1 0 **231** **73**
1998–99 Manchester U 32 18
1999–2000 Manchester U 32 20
2000–01 Manchester U 22 9 **86** **47**

Scholars
Cogger, John S; Humphreys, Christopher N

MANSFIELD T

ANDREWS, John (D) 38 1
H: 6 1 W: 12 08 b.Cork 27-9-78
Source: Shepshed D, Grantham T.
1996–97 Coventry C 0 0
1997–98 Coventry C 0 0
From Shepshd, Grantam
1999–2000 Mansfield T 30 1
2000–01 Mansfield T 8 0 **38** **1**

ASHER, Alistair (D) 63 0
H: 5 11 W: 11 07 b.Leicester 14-10-80
Source: Trainee.
1999–2000 Mansfield T 35 0
2000–01 Mansfield T 28 0 **63** **0**

BACON, Danny (F) 30 3
H: 5 10 W: 10 12 b.Mansfield 20-9-80
Source: Trainee.
1999–2000 Mansfield T 8 2
2000–01 Mansfield T 22 1 **30** **3**

BARRETT, Adam (M) 60 4
H: 5 10 W: 12 00 b.Dagenham 29-11-79
Source: Leyton Orient trainee.
1998–99 Plymouth Arg 1 0
1999–2000 Plymouth Arg 42 3
2000–01 Plymouth Arg 9 0 **52** **3**
2000–01 Mansfield T 8 1 **8** **1**

BLAKE, Mark* (M) 242 20
H: 5 11 W: 13 05 b.Nottingham 16-12-70
Source: Trainee. *Honours:* England Schools, Youth, Under-21.
1989–90 Aston Villa 9 0
1990–91 Aston Villa 7 0
1990–91 *Wolverhampton W* 2 0 **2** **0**
1991–92 Aston Villa 14 2
1992–93 Aston Villa 31 2
1993–94 Portsmouth 15 0 **15** **0**
1993–94 Leicester C 11 1
1994–95 Leicester C 30 3
1995–96 Leicester C 8 0 **49** **4**
1996–97 Walsall 38 4
1997–98 Walsall 23 1 **61** **5**
1999–2000 Mansfield T 43 1
2000–01 Mansfield T 41 8 **84** **9**

BOULDING, Mick# (F) 66 12
H: 5 10 W: 11 03 b.Sheffield 8-2-76
1999–2000 Mansfield T 33 6
2000–01 Mansfield T 33 6 **66** **12**

BRADLEY, Shayne (F) 45 8
H: 5 11 W: 13 13 b.Gloucester 8-12-79
Source: Trainee. *Honours:* England Schools.
1997–98 Southampton 0 0
1998–99 Southampton 3 0
1998–99 *Swindon T* 7 0 **7** **0**
1999–2000 Southampton 1 0

1999–2000 *Exeter C* 8 1 **8** **1**
2000–01 Southampton 0 0 **4** **0**
2000–01 Mansfield T 26 7 **26** **7**

CLARKE, Darrell (M) 161 24
H: 5 10 W: 11 06 b.Mansfield 16-12-77
Source: Trainee.
1995–96 Mansfield T 3 0
1996–97 Mansfield T 19 2
1997–98 Mansfield T 35 4
1998–99 Mansfield T 33 5
1999–2000 Mansfield T 39 7
2000–01 Mansfield T 32 6 **161** **24**

CORDEN, Wayne (M) 100 4
H: 5 10 W: 11 05 b.Leek 1-11-75
Source: Trainee.
1994–95 Port Vale 1 0
1995–96 Port Vale 2 0
1996–97 Port Vale 12 0
1997–98 Port Vale 33 1
1998–99 Port Vale 16 0
1999–2000 Port Vale 2 0 **66** **1**
2000–01 Mansfield T 34 3 **34** **3**

DISLEY, Craig (M) 29 0
H: 5 10 W: 10 12 b.Worksop 24-8-81
Source: Trainee.
1999–2000 Mansfield T 5 0
2000–01 Mansfield T 24 0 **29** **0**

GREENACRE, Chris (F) 112 33
H: 5 11 W: 10 06 b.Halifax 23-12-77
Source: Trainee.
1995–96 Manchester C 0 0
1996–97 Manchester C 4 0
1997–98 Manchester C 3 1
1997–98 *Cardiff C* 11 2 **11** **2**
1997–98 *Blackpool* 4 0 **4** **0**
1998–99 Manchester C 1 0
1998–99 *Scarborough* 12 2 **12** **2**
1999–2000 Manchester C 0 0 **8** **1**
1999–2000 Mansfield T 31 9
2000–01 Mansfield T 46 19 **77** **28**

HASSELL, Bobby (D) 63 2
H: 5 9 W: 12 04 b.Derby 4-6-80
Source: Trainee.
1997–98 Mansfield T 9 0
1998–99 Mansfield T 3 0
1999–2000 Mansfield T 11 1
2000–01 Mansfield T 40 1 **63** **2**

HICKS, Stuart (D) 402 5
H: 6 1 W: 13 03 b.Peterborough 30-5-67
Source: Peterborough U Apprentice, Wisbech T.
1987–88 Colchester U 7 0
1988–89 Colchester U 37 0
1989–90 Colchester U 20 0 **64** **0**
1990–91 Scunthorpe U 46 1
1991–92 Scunthorpe U 21 0 **67** **1**
1992–93 Doncaster R 36 0
1993–94 Doncaster R 0 0 **36** **0**
1993–94 Huddersfield T 22 1 **22** **1**
1993–94 Preston NE 4 0
1994–95 Preston NE 8 0 **12** **0**
1994–95 Scarborough 6 0
1995–96 Scarborough 41 1
1996–97 Scarborough 38 1 **85** **2**
1997–98 Leyton Orient 35 1
1998–99 Leyton Orient 29 0
1999–2000 Leyton Orient 14 0 **78** **1**
1999–2000 *Chester C* 13 0 **13** **0**
2000–01 Mansfield T 25 0 **25** **0**

JERVIS, David (D) 22 0
H: 5 8 W: 10 08 b.Worksop 18-1-82
Source: Trainee.
2000–01 Mansfield T 22 0 **22** **0**

JONES, Adam* (D) 0 0
H: 6 1 W: 13 00 b.Peterborough 18-3-82
Source: Trainee.
2000–01 Mansfield T 0 0

LAWRENCE, Liam (M) 20 4
H: 5 10 W: 11 03 b.Retford 14-12-81
Source: Trainee.
1999–2000 Mansfield T 2 0
2000–01 Mansfield T 18 4 **20** **4**

LOMAS, Jamie‡ (M) 36 0
H: 5 11 W: 10 09 b.Chesterfield 18-10-77
Source: Trainee.
1996–97 Chesterfield 2 0
1997–98 Chesterfield 4 0
1998–99 Chesterfield 7 0
1999–2000 Chesterfield 17 0 **30** **0**
2000–01 Mansfield T 6 0 **6** **0**

MIMMS, Bobby* (G) 477 0
H: 6 3 W: 14 01 b.York 12-10-63
Source: Halifax T Apprentice. *Honours:* England Under-21.

Season	Club				
1981–82	Rotherham U	2	0		
1982–83	Rotherham U	13	0		
1983–84	Rotherham U	22	0		
1984–85	Rotherham U	46	0		
1985–86	Everton	10	0		
1985–86	*Notts Co*	2	0	2	0
1986–87	Everton	11	0		
1986–87	*Sunderland*	4	0	4	0
1986–87	*Blackburn R*	6	0		
1987–88	Everton	8	0	29	0
1987–88	*Manchester C*	3	0	3	0
1987–88	Tottenham H	13	0		
1988–89	Tottenham H	20	0		
1989–90	Tottenham H	4	0		
1989–90	*Aberdeen*	6	0	6	0
1990–91	Tottenham H	0	0	37	0
1990–91	Blackburn R	22	0		
1991–92	Blackburn R	45	0		
1992–93	Blackburn R	42	0		
1993–94	Blackburn R	13	0		
1994–95	Blackburn R	4	0		
1995–96	Blackburn R	2	0	134	0
1996–97	Crystal Palace	1	0	1	0
1996–97	Preston NE	27	0	27	0
1997–98	Rotherham U	43	0		
1998–99	Rotherham U	0	0	126	0
1998–99	York C	35	0		
1999–2000	York C	28	0	63	0
1999–2000	Mansfield T	5	0		
2000–01	Mansfield T	40	0	45	0

MITCHELL, Dean‡ (D) 0 0
H: 5 11 W: 12 00 b.Sutton-in-Ashfield 18-11-81
Source: Trainee.

Season	Club		
2000–01	Mansfield T	0	0

OVERTON, Paul (F) 0 0
H: 5 9 W: 11 00 b.Mansfield 21-9-81
Source: Trainee.

Season	Club		
2000–01	Mansfield T	0	0

PEMBERTON, Martin# (M) 68 3
H: 5 11 W: 11 08 b.Bradford 1-2-76
Source: Trainee.

Season	Club				
1994–95	Oldham Ath	0	0		
1995–96	Oldham Ath	2	0		
1996–97	Oldham Ath	3	0	5	0
1996–97	Doncaster R	9	1		
1997–98	Doncaster R	26	1	35	2
1997–98	Scunthorpe U	6	0	6	0
1998–99	Hartlepool U	4	0		
1999–2000	Hartlepool U	0	0	4	0

From Bradford PA.

Season	Club				
2000–01	Mansfield T	18	1	18	1

PILKINGTON, Kevin (G) 54 0
H: 6 1 W: 13 00 b.Hitchin 8-3-74
Source: Trainee. *Honours:* England Schools.

Season	Club				
1992–93	Manchester U	0	0		
1993–94	Manchester U	0	0		
1994–95	Manchester U	1	0		
1995–96	Manchester U	3	0		
1995–96	*Rochdale*	6	0	6	0
1996–97	Manchester U	0	0		
1996–97	*Rotherham U*	17	0	17	0
1997–98	Manchester U	2	0		
1998–99	Manchester U	0	0	6	0
1998–99	Port Vale	8	0		
1999–2000	Port Vale	15	0	23	0
2000–01	Macclesfield T	0	0		
2000–01	Wigan Ath	0	0		
2000–01	Mansfield T	2	0	2	0

ROBINSON, Les (D) 592 18
H: 5 9 W: 12 02 b.Shirebrook 1-3-67
Source: Local.

Season	Club				
1984–85	Mansfield T	6	0		
1985–86	Mansfield T	7	0		
1986–87	Mansfield T	2	0		
1986–87	Stockport Co	30	1		
1987–88	Stockport Co	37	2	67	3
1987–88	Doncaster R	7	1		
1988–89	Doncaster R	43	3		
1989–90	Doncaster R	32	8	82	12
1989–90	Oxford U	1	0		
1990–91	Oxford U	43	0		
1991–92	Oxford U	27	0		
1992–93	Oxford U	16	0		
1993–94	Oxford U	36	2		
1994–95	Oxford U	46	0		
1995–96	Oxford U	41	0		
1996–97	Oxford U	38	0		
1997–98	Oxford U	46	1		
1998–99	Oxford U	44	0		
1999–2000	Oxford U	46	0	384	3
2000–01	Mansfield T	44	0	59	0

SISSON, Michael (M) 31 2
H: 5 10 W: 11 05 b.Sutton-in-Ashfield 24-11-78
Source: Trainee.

Season	Club				
1997–98	Mansfield T	1	0		
1998–99	Mansfield T	1	0		
1999–2000	Mansfield T	25	2		
2000–01	Mansfield T	4	0	31	2

WHITE, Andy (F) 4 0
H: b.Derby 6-11-81
Source: Hucknall T.

Season	Club				
2000–01	Mansfield T	4	0	4	0

WILLIAMS, Lee (D) 269 10
H: 5 7 W: 11 08 b.Edgbaston 3-2-73
Source: Trainee.

Season	Club				
1991–92	Aston Villa	0	0		
1992–93	Aston Villa	0	0		
1992–93	*Shrewsbury T*	3	0	3	0
1993–94	Aston Villa	0	0		
1993–94	Peterborough U	18	0		
1994–95	Peterborough U	40	1		
1995–96	Peterborough U	33	0	91	1
1996–97	Tranmere R	0	0		
1997–98	Mansfield T	6	0		
1997–98	Mansfield T	38	3		
1998–99	Mansfield T	44	2		
1999–2000	Mansfield T	46	0		
2000–01	Mansfield T	41	4	175	9

WILLIAMSON, Lee (M) 19 0
H: 5 10 W: 10 04 b.Derby 7-6-82
Source: Trainee.

Season	Club				
1999–2000	Mansfield T	4	0		
2000–01	Mansfield T	15	0	19	0

WILLIS, Scott‡ (M) 0 0
b.Liverpool 20-2-82
Source: Wigan Ath Trainee.

Season	Club		
1999–2000	Mansfield T	0	0
2000–01	Mansfield T	0	0

Scholars
Allmark, Dean; Beardsley, Christopher K; Clarke, James W; Elliot, Dominic S; Gaichem, James JF; Gibson, Christopher J; Holyoak, Daniel; Lazarus, Neil P; Murcott, Scott A; Rew, David J; Shaw, James R; Swinscoe, Craig A

MIDDLESBROUGH

BAKER, Steve (D) 25 0
H: 6 0 W: 12 04 b.Pontefract 8-9-78
Source: Trainee. *Honours:* Eire Under-21.

Season	Club				
1997–98	Middlesbrough	6	0		
1998–99	Middlesbrough	2	0		
1999–2000	Middlesbrough	0	0		
1999–2000	*Huddersfield T*	3	0	3	0
1999–2000	*Darlington*	5	0	5	0
2000–01	Middlesbrough	0	0	8	0
2000–01	*Hartlepool U*	9	0	9	0

BENNION, Chris (G) 0 0
H: 6 2 W: 12 00 b.Edinburgh 30-8-80
Source: Trainee.

Season	Club		
1999–2000	Middlesbrough	0	0
2000–01	Middlesbrough	0	0

BERESFORD, Marlon (G) 285 0
H: 6 1 W: 13 00 b.Lincoln 2-9-69
Source: Trainee.

Season	Club				
1987–88	Sheffield W	0	0		
1988–89	Sheffield W	0	0		
1989–90	Sheffield W	0	0		
1989–90	*Bury*	1	0	1	0
1989–90	*Ipswich T*	0	0		
1990–91	Sheffield W	0	0		
1990–91	*Northampton T*	13	0		
1990–91	*Crewe Alex*	3	0	3	0
1991–92	Sheffield W	0	0		
1991–92	*Northampton T*	15	0	28	0
1992–93	Burnley	44	0		
1993–94	Burnley	46	0		
1994–95	Burnley	40	0		
1995–96	Burnley	36	0		
1996–97	Burnley	40	0		
1997–98	Burnley	34	0	240	0
1997–98	Middlesbrough	3	0		
1998–99	Middlesbrough	4	0		
1999–2000	Middlesbrough	1	0		
2000–01	Middlesbrough	1	0	9	0
2000–01	*Sheffield W*	4	0	4	0

BERNHARDT, Arturo (F) 0 0
H: 6 1 W: 12 02 b.Santa Catarina 27-8-82
Source: Hamburg.

Season	Club		
1999–2000	Middlesbrough	0	0
2000–01	Middlesbrough	0	0

BOKSIC, Alen (F) 310 99
H: 6 1 W: 14 01 b.Niakarska 21-1-70

Season	Club				
1987–88	Hajduk Split	13	2		
1988–89	Hajduk Split	26	7		
1989–90	Hajduk Split	27	12		
1990–91	Hajduk Split	29	6	95	27
1991–92	Cannes	1	0	1	0
1992–93	Marseille	37	23		
1993–94	Marseille	12	3	49	26
1993–94	Lazio	21	4		
1994–95	Lazio	23	9		
1995–96	Lazio	23	4		
1996–97	Juventus	22	3	22	3
1997–98	Lazio	26	10		
1998–99	Lazio	3	0		
1999–2000	Lazio	19	4	115	31
2000–01	Middlesbrough	28	12	28	12

BRACKSTONE, Stephen (M) 0 0
H: 5 11 W: 10 08 b.Hartlepool 19-9-82
Source: Scholar. *Honours:* England Youth.

Season	Club		
2000–01	Middlesbrough	0	0

BURTON, Andrew‡ (M) 0 0
b.Stockton 25-8-82
Source: Scholar.

Season	Club		
2000–01	Middlesbrough	0	0

CAMPBELL, Andy (F) 69 7
H: 6 0 W: 12 00 b.Middlesbrough 18-4-79
Source: Trainee. *Honours:* England Youth, Under-21.

Season	Club				
1995–96	Middlesbrough	2	0		
1996–97	Middlesbrough	3	0		
1997–98	Middlesbrough	7	0		
1998–99	Middlesbrough	8	0		
1998–99	*Sheffield U*	11	3	11	3
1999–2000	Middlesbrough	25	4		
2000–01	Middlesbrough	7	0	52	4
2000–01	*Bolton W*	6	0	6	0

CLOSE, Brian (M) 0 0
H: 5 10 W: 11 08 b.Belfast 27-1-82

Season	Club		
1999–2000	Middlesbrough	0	0
2000–01	Middlesbrough	0	0

COOPER, Colin (D) 530 35
H: 5 11 W: 11 09 b.Sedgefield 28-2-67
Honours: England Under-21, 2 full caps.

Season	Club				
1984–85	Middlesbrough	0	0		
1985–86	Middlesbrough	11	0		
1986–87	Middlesbrough	46	0		
1987–88	Middlesbrough	43	2		
1988–89	Middlesbrough	35	2		
1989–90	Middlesbrough	21	2		
1990–91	Middlesbrough	32	0		
1991–92	Millwall	36	2		
1992–93	Millwall	41	4	77	6
1993–94	Nottingham F	37	7		
1994–95	Nottingham F	35	1		
1995–96	Nottingham F	37	5		
1996–97	Nottingham F	36	2		
1997–98	Nottingham F	35	5		
1998–99	Nottingham F	0	0	180	20
1998–99	Middlesbrough	32	1		
1999–2000	Middlesbrough	26	0		
2000–01	Middlesbrough	27	2	273	9

CROSSLEY, Mark (G) 321 0
H: 6 4 W: 15 09 b.Barnsley 16-6-69
Source: Trainee. *Honours:* England Under-21, Wales B, 3 full caps.

Season	Club				
1987–88	Nottingham F	0	0		
1988–89	Nottingham F	2	0		
1989–90	Nottingham F	8	0		
1989–90	*Manchester U*	0	0		
1990–91	Nottingham F	38	0		
1991–92	Nottingham F	36	0		
1992–93	Nottingham F	37	0		
1993–94	Nottingham F	37	0		
1994–95	Nottingham F	42	0		
1995–96	Nottingham F	38	0		
1996–97	Nottingham F	33	0		
1997–98	Nottingham F	0	0		
1997–98	*Millwall*	13	0	13	0
1998–99	Nottingham F	12	0		
1999–2000	Nottingham F	20	0	303	0
2000–01	Middlesbrough	5	0	5	0

DEANE, Brian (F) 505 154
H: 6 3 W: 14 05 b.Leeds 7-2-68
Source: Apprentice. *Honours:* England B, 3 full caps.

Season	Club				
1985–86	Doncaster R	3	0		
1986–87	Doncaster R	20	2		
1987–88	Doncaster R	43	10	66	12
1988–89	Sheffield U	43	22		
1989–90	Sheffield U	45	21		
1990–91	Sheffield U	38	13		
1991–92	Sheffield U	30	12		
1992–93	Sheffield U	41	14		
1993–94	Leeds U	41	11		
1994–95	Leeds U	35	9		

1995–96	Leeds U	34	7		
1996–97	Leeds U	28	5	138	32
1997–98	Sheffield U	24	11	221	93

From Benfica.

1998–99	Middlesbrough	26	6		
1999–2000	Middlesbrough	29	9		
2000–01	Middlesbrough	25	2	80	17

DOVE, Craig (M)   0   0
H: 5 10 W: 10 08 b.Hartlepool 16-8-83
Source: Scholar.

2000–01	Middlesbrough	0	0		

EHIOGU, Ugo (D)   260   15
H: 6 2 W: 14 10 b.Hackney 3-11-72
Source: Trainee. Honours: England Under-21, B, 2 full caps, 1 goal.

1990–91	WBA	2	0	2	0
1991–92	Aston Villa	8	0		
1992–93	Aston Villa	4	0		
1993–94	Aston Villa	17	0		
1994–95	Aston Villa	39	3		
1995–96	Aston Villa	36	1		
1996–97	Aston Villa	38	3		
1997–98	Aston Villa	37	2		
1998–99	Aston Villa	25	2		
1999–2000	Aston Villa	31	1		
2000–01	Aston Villa	2	0	237	12
2000–01	Middlesbrough	21	3	21	3

FESTA, Gianluca (D)   399   15
H: 5 11 W: 13 03 b.Cagliari 15-3-69

1986–87	Cagliari	3	0		
1987–88	*Fersuicis*	26	2	26	2
1988–89	Cagliari	27	0		
1989–90	Cagliari	36	0		
1990–91	Cagliari	28	0		
1991–92	Cagliari	31	0		
1992–93	Cagliari	31	0	156	0
1993–94	Internazionale	4	0		
1993–94	Roma	21	1	21	1
1994–95	Internazionale	26	2		
1995–96	Internazionale	31	1		
1996–97	Internazionale	5	0	66	3
1996–97	Middlesbrough	13	1		
1997–98	Middlesbrough	38	2		
1998–99	Middlesbrough	25	2		
1999–2000	Middlesbrough	29	2		
2000–01	Middlesbrough	25	2	130	9

FLEMING, Curtis (D)   258   3
H: 5 10 W: 12 11 b.Manchester 8-10-68
Source: St Patrick's Ath. Honours: Eire Youth, Under-21, B, 10 full caps.

1991–92	Middlesbrough	28	0		
1992–93	Middlesbrough	24	0		
1993–94	Middlesbrough	40	0		
1994–95	Middlesbrough	21	0		
1995–96	Middlesbrough	13	1		
1996–97	Middlesbrough	30	0		
1997–98	Middlesbrough	31	1		
1998–99	Middlesbrough	14	1		
1999–2000	Middlesbrough	27	0		
2000–01	Middlesbrough	30	0	258	3

GAVIN, Jason (D)   22   0
H: 6 0 W: 12 04 b.Dublin 14-3-80
Source: Trainee. Honours: Eire Under-21.

1996–97	Middlesbrough	0	0		
1997–98	Middlesbrough	0	0		
1998–99	Middlesbrough	2	0		
1999–2000	Middlesbrough	6	0		
2000–01	Middlesbrough	14	0	22	0

GILROY, Keith (M)   0   0
H: 5 10 W: 10 13 b.Sligo 8-7-83

2000–01	Middlesbrough	0	0		

GORDON, Dean (D)   263   24
H: 6 0 W: 14 03 b.Thornton Heath 10-2-73
Source: Trainee. Honours: England Under-21.

1991–92	Crystal Palace	4	0		
1992–93	Crystal Palace	10	0		
1993–94	Crystal Palace	45	5		
1994–95	Crystal Palace	41	2		
1995–96	Crystal Palace	34	8		
1996–97	Crystal Palace	30	3		
1997–98	Crystal Palace	37	2	201	20
1998–99	Middlesbrough	38	3		
1999–2000	Middlesbrough	4	0		
2000–01	Middlesbrough	20	1	62	4

GULLIVER, Philip (D)   0   0
H: 6 2 W: 13 05 b.Bishop Auckland 12-9-82
Source: Scholar.

2000–01	Middlesbrough	0	0		

HANSON, Christian (D)   8   0
H: 6 1 W: 12 11 b.Middlesbrough 3-8-81
Source: Trainee. Honours: England Schools, Youth.

1998–99	Middlesbrough	0	0		
1999–2000	Middlesbrough	0	0		
2000–01	Middlesbrough	0	0		
2000–01	*Cambridge U*	8	0	8	0

HUDSON, Mark (M)   3   0
H: 5 10 W: 11 02 b.Bishop Auckland 24-10-80
Source: Trainee.

1999–2000	Middlesbrough	0	0		
2000–01	Middlesbrough	3	0	3	0

INCE, Paul (M)   459   59
H: 5 10 W: 12 13 b.Ilford 21-10-67
Source: Trainee. Honours: England Youth, Under-21, B, 53 full caps, 2 goals.

1985–86	West Ham U	0	0		
1986–87	West Ham U	10	1		
1987–88	West Ham U	28	3		
1988–89	West Ham U	33	3		
1989–90	West Ham U	1	0	72	7
1989–90	Manchester U	26	0		
1990–91	Manchester U	31	3		
1991–92	Manchester U	33	3		
1992–93	Manchester U	41	5		
1993–94	Manchester U	39	8		
1994–95	Manchester U	36	5	206	24
1995–96	Internazionale	30	3		
1996–97	Internazionale	24	6	54	9
1997–98	Liverpool	31	8		
1998–99	Liverpool	34	6	65	14
1999–2000	Middlesbrough	32	3		
2000–01	Middlesbrough	30	2	62	5

JOB, Joseph-Desire (F)   77   18
H: 5 11 W: 11 02 b.Venissieux 1-12-77
Honours: Cameroon full caps.

1997–98	Lyon	22	5		
1998–99	Lyon	19	6	41	11
1999–2000	Lens	24	4	24	4
2000–01	Middlesbrough	12	3	12	3

JONES, Brad (G)   0   0
H: 6 3 W: 11 07 b.Armadale 19-3-82
Source: Trainee.

1998–99	Middlesbrough	0	0		
1999–2000	Middlesbrough	0	0		
2000–01	Middlesbrough	0	0		

JONES, Tom‡ (F)   0   0
H: 5 10 W: 12 02 b.Middlesbrough 26-3-80
Source: Trainee.

1998–99	Middlesbrough	0	0		
1999–2000	Middlesbrough	0	0		
2000–01	Middlesbrough	0	0		

KAREMBEU, Christian (M)   276   15
H: 6 0 W: 12 06 b.Lifou 3-12-70
Honours: France 50 full caps, 1 goal.

1990–91	Nantes	4	0		
1991–92	Nantes	28	0		
1992–93	Nantes	35	2		
1993–94	Nantes	29	0		
1994–95	Nantes	34	3	130	5
1995–96	Sampdoria	32	5		
1996–97	Sampdoria	30	1		
1997–98	Sampdoria	0	0	62	6
1997–98	Real Madrid	16	0		
1998–99	Real Madrid	20	0		
1999–2000	Real Madrid	15	0	51	0
2000–01	Middlesbrough	33	4	33	4

KILGANNON, Sean (M)   1   0
H: 5 11 W: 12 04 b.Stirling 8-3-81
Source: Trainee.

1999–2000	Middlesbrough	1	0		
2000–01	Middlesbrough	0	0	1	0

MADDISON, Neil* (M)   235   24
H: 5 10 W: 12 02 b.Darlington 2-10-69
Source: Trainee.

1987–88	Southampton	0	0		
1988–89	Southampton	5	2		
1989–90	Southampton	2	0		
1990–91	Southampton	4	0		
1991–92	Southampton	6	0		
1992–93	Southampton	37	4		
1993–94	Southampton	41	7		
1994–95	Southampton	35	3		
1995–96	Southampton	15	1		
1996–97	Southampton	18	1		
1997–98	Southampton	6	1	169	19
1997–98	Middlesbrough	22	4		
1998–99	Middlesbrough	21	0		
1999–2000	Middlesbrough	13	0		
2000–01	Middlesbrough	0	0	56	4
2000–01	Barnsley	3	0	3	0
2000–01	Bristol C	7	1	7	1

MARINELLI, Carlos (M)   15   0
H: 5 8 W: 11 09 b.Buenos Aires 14-3-82
Source: Boca Juniors.

1999–2000	Middlesbrough	2	0		
2000–01	Middlesbrough	13	0	15	0

MOAT, David‡ (D)   0   0
H: 5 8 W: 11 07 b.Gateshead 1-10-81
Source: Trainee.

1999–2000	Middlesbrough	0	0		
2000–01	Middlesbrough	0	0		

MOORE, Alan* (M)   123   14
H: 5 10 W: 12 00 b.Dublin 25-11-74
Source: Rivermount. Honours: Eire Under-21, 8 full caps.

1991–92	Middlesbrough	0	0		
1992–93	Middlesbrough	2	0		
1993–94	Middlesbrough	42	10		
1994–95	Middlesbrough	37	4		
1995–96	Middlesbrough	12	0		
1996–97	Middlesbrough	17	0		
1997–98	Middlesbrough	4	0		
1998–99	Middlesbrough	4	0		
1998–99	*Barnsley*	5	0	5	0
1999–2000	Middlesbrough	0	0		
2000–01	Middlesbrough	0	0	118	14

MUSTOE, Robbie (M)   420   33
H: 6 0 W: 11 13 b.Oxford 28-8-68

1986–87	Oxford U	3	0		
1987–88	Oxford U	17	0		
1988–89	Oxford U	33	3		
1989–90	Oxford U	38	7	91	10
1990–91	Middlesbrough	41	4		
1991–92	Middlesbrough	30	2		
1992–93	Middlesbrough	23	1		
1993–94	Middlesbrough	38	2		
1994–95	Middlesbrough	27	3		
1995–96	Middlesbrough	21	1		
1996–97	Middlesbrough	31	3		
1997–98	Middlesbrough	32	3		
1998–99	Middlesbrough	33	4		
1999–2000	Middlesbrough	28	0		
2000–01	Middlesbrough	25	0	329	23

NELSON, Craig (F)   0   0
H: 5 9 W: 9 12 b.South Shields 14-10-81
Source: Scholar.

2000–01	Middlesbrough	0	0		

O'NEILL, Keith (M)   110   9
H: 6 1 W: 13 03 b.Dublin 16-2-76
Source: Trainee. Honours: Eire 13 full caps, 4 goals.

1994–95	Norwich C	1	0		
1995–96	Norwich C	19	1		
1996–97	Norwich C	26	6		
1997–98	Norwich C	9	1		
1998–99	Norwich C	18	1	73	9
1998–99	Middlesbrough	6	0		
1999–2000	Middlesbrough	16	0		
2000–01	Middlesbrough	15	0	37	0

OKON, Paul (M)   126   1
H: 5 10 W: 13 03 b.Sydney 5-4-72
Source: Marconi Stallions 49 apps, 4 goals.Australia 31 full caps, 1 goal.

1991–92	FC Brugge	0	0		
1992–93	FC Brugge	5	0		
1993–94	FC Brugge	27	0		
1994–95	FC Brugge	26	0		
1995–96	FC Brugge	14	1	72	1
1996–97	Lazio	14	0		
1997–98	Lazio	0	0		
1998–99	Lazio	5	0	19	0
1999–2000	Fiorentina	11	0	11	0
2000–01	Middlesbrough	24	0	24	0

ORMEROD, Anthony (M)   36   3
H: 5 10 W: 11 13 b.Middlesbrough 31-3-79
Source: Trainee. Honours: England Youth.

1995–96	Middlesbrough	0	0		
1996–97	Middlesbrough	0	0		
1997–98	Middlesbrough	18	3		
1998–99	Middlesbrough	0	0		
1998–99	*Carlisle U*	5	0	5	0
1999–2000	Middlesbrough	1	0		
1999–2000	*York C*	12	0	12	0
2000–01	Middlesbrough	0	0	19	3

PALLISTER, Gary* (D)   535   18
H: 6 4 W: 15 02 b.Ramsgate 30-6-65
Source: Billingham T. Honours: England B, 22 full caps.

1984–85	Middlesbrough	0	0		
1985–86	Middlesbrough	28	0		
1985–86	*Darlington*	7	0	7	0
1986–87	Middlesbrough	44	1		
1987–88	Middlesbrough	44	3		
1988–89	Middlesbrough	37	1		
1989–90	Middlesbrough	3	0		
1989–90	Manchester U	35	3		
1990–91	Manchester U	36	0		
1991–92	Manchester U	40	1		
1992–93	Manchester U	41	1		
1993–94	Manchester U	41	1		
1994–95	Manchester U	42	2		
1995–96	Manchester U	21	1		

1996–97	Manchester U	27	3		
1997–98	Manchester U	33	0	317	12
1998–99	Middlesbrough	26	0		
1999–2000	Middlesbrough	21	1		
2000–01	Middlesbrough	8	0	211	6

PARNABY, Stuart (D) 6 0
H: 5 11 W: 11 02 b.Durham City 19-7-82
Source: Trainee. *Honours:* England Youth.

1999–2000	Middlesbrough	0	0		
2000–01	Middlesbrough	0	0		
2000–01	Halifax T	6	0	6	0

RICARD, Hamilton (F) 106 33
H: 6 1 W: 14 05 b.Choco 12-1-74
Source: Deportivo Cali. *Honours:* Colombia 21 full caps, 4 goals.

1997–98	Middlesbrough	9	2		
1998–99	Middlesbrough	36	15		
1999–2000	Middlesbrough	34	12		
2000–01	Middlesbrough	27	4	106	33

ROBINSON, Gerard (F) 0 0
H: 6 0 W: 14 04 b.Dublin 9-6-82
Source: Trainee.

| 1999–2000 | Middlesbrough | 0 | 0 |
| 2000–01 | Middlesbrough | 0 | 0 |

RUSSELL, Sam (G) 0 0
H: 6 0 W: 10 13 b.Middlesbrough 4-10-82
Source: Scholar.

| 2000–01 | Middlesbrough | 0 | 0 |

SCHWARZER, Mark (G) 161 0
H: 6 4 W: 15 01 b.Sydney 6-10-72
Source: Marconi Stallions 58 apps, Dynamo Dresden. *Honours:* Australia 17 full caps.

1995–96	Kaiserslautern	4	0		
1996–97	Kaiserslautern	0	0	4	0
1996–97	Bradford C	13	0	13	0
1996–97	Middlesbrough	7	0		
1997–98	Middlesbrough	35	0		
1998–99	Middlesbrough	34	0		
1999–2000	Middlesbrough	37	0		
2000–01	Middlesbrough	31	0	144	0

STAMP, Phil (M) 110 6
H: 5 11 W: 14 09 b.Middlesbrough 12-12-75
Source: Trainee. *Honours:* England Youth.

1992–93	Middlesbrough	1	0		
1993–94	Middlesbrough	10	0		
1994–95	Middlesbrough	3	0		
1995–96	Middlesbrough	12	2		
1996–97	Middlesbrough	24	1		
1997–98	Middlesbrough	10	0		
1998–99	Middlesbrough	16	2		
1999–2000	Middlesbrough	16	0		
2000–01	Middlesbrough	19	1	110	6

STEPHENSON, Paul (D) 0 0
H: 6 2 W: 11 12 b.Hartlepool 3-1-82
Source: Scholar.

| 2000–01 | Middlesbrough | 0 | 0 |

STOCKDALE, Robbie (D) 37 1
H: 6 0 W: 12 03 b.Redcar 30-11-79
Source: Trainee. *Honours:* England Under-21.

1997–98	Middlesbrough	1	0		
1998–99	Middlesbrough	19	0		
1999–2000	Middlesbrough	11	1		
2000–01	Middlesbrough	0	0	31	1
2000–01	Sheffield W	6	0	6	0

SUMMERBELL, Mark (M) 51 1
H: 5 9 W: 10 07 b.Durham 30-10-76
Source: Trainee.

1995–96	Middlesbrough	1	0		
1996–97	Middlesbrough	2	0		
1997–98	Middlesbrough	11	0		
1998–99	Middlesbrough	11	0		
1999–2000	Middlesbrough	19	0		
2000–01	Middlesbrough	7	1	51	1

TAYLOR, Andrew‡ (D) 0 0
H: 5 11 W: 11 05 b.Middlesbrough 6-9-81
Source: Trainee.

| 1999–2000 | Middlesbrough | 0 | 0 |
| 2000–01 | Middlesbrough | 0 | 0 |

VICKERS, Steve (D) 568 19
H: 6 2 W: 13 01 b.Bishop Auckland 13-10-67
Source: Spennymoor U.

1985–86	Tranmere R	3	0		
1986–87	Tranmere R	36	2		
1987–88	Tranmere R	46	1		
1988–89	Tranmere R	46	3		
1989–90	Tranmere R	42	3		
1990–91	Tranmere R	42	1		
1991–92	Tranmere R	43	1		
1992–93	Tranmere R	42	0		
1993–94	Tranmere R	11	0	311	11
1993–94	Middlesbrough	26	3		
1994–95	Middlesbrough	44	3		
1995–96	Middlesbrough	32	1		
1996–97	Middlesbrough	29	0		
1997–98	Middlesbrough	33	0		
1998–99	Middlesbrough	31	1		
1999–2000	Middlesbrough	32	0		
2000–01	Middlesbrough	30	0	257	8

WHELAN, Noel (F) 209 39
H: 13 05 b.Leeds 30-12-74
Source: Trainee. *Honours:* England Under-21.

1992–93	Leeds U	1	0		
1993–94	Leeds U	16	0		
1994–95	Leeds U	23	7		
1995–96	Leeds U	13	0	48	7
1995–96	Coventry C	21	8		
1996–97	Coventry C	35	6		
1997–98	Coventry C	21	6		
1998–99	Coventry C	31	10		
1999–2000	Coventry C	26	1	134	31
2000–01	Middlesbrough	27	1	27	1

WILFORD, Aaron (D) 0 0
H: 6 3 W: 14 07 b.Scarborough 14-1-82
Source: Harrogate College.

| 1999–2000 | Middlesbrough | 0 | 0 |
| 2000–01 | Middlesbrough | 0 | 0 |

WILKSHIRE, Luke (M) 0 0
H: 5 9 W: 11 05 b.Wollongong 2-10-81
Source: Trainee.

1998–99	Middlesbrough	0	0
1999–2000	Middlesbrough	0	0
2000–01	Middlesbrough	0	0

WINDASS, Dean (F) 364 111
H: 5 10 W: 12 06 b.Hull 1-4-69
Source: N Ferriby U.

1991–92	Hull C	32	6		
1992–93	Hull C	41	7		
1993–94	Hull C	43	23		
1994–95	Hull C	44	17		
1995–96	Hull C	16	4	176	57
1995–96	Aberdeen	20	6		
1996–97	Aberdeen	29	10		
1997–98	Aberdeen	24	5	73	21
1998–99	Oxford U	33	15	33	15
1998–99	Bradford C	12	3		
1999–2000	Bradford C	38	10		
2000–01	Bradford C	24	3	74	16
2000–01	Middlesbrough	8	2	8	2

Scholars
Agbatar, Jonathan T; Cade, Jamie W; Crager, Paul M; Downing, Stewart; Emms, Christopher J; Garbutt, Christopher J; Kelly, Andrew J; Murphy, David P; Ryan, Leon M; Skirving, Richard M; Smith, Gary S; Smith, Liam; Storey, Anthony

MILLWALL

BIRCHAM, Marc (D) 80 3
H: 5 11 W: 12 02 b.Brent 11-5-78
Source: Trainee. *Honours:* Canada 13 full caps, 1 goal.

1996–97	Millwall	6	0		
1997–98	Millwall	4	0		
1998–99	Millwall	28	0		
1999–2000	Millwall	22	1		
2000–01	Millwall	20	2	80	3

BOOTH, Stuart (M) 0 0
b.Roehampton 7-12-83
Source: School.

| 2000–01 | Millwall | 0 | 0 |

BOWRY, Bobby* (M) 190 6
H: 5 9 W: 10 08 b.Croydon 19-5-71

| 1990–91 | QPR | 0 | 0 | | |

From Carshalton Ath.

1991–92	Crystal Palace	0	0		
1992–93	Crystal Palace	11	1		
1993–94	Crystal Palace	21	0		
1994–95	Crystal Palace	18	0	50	1
1995–96	Millwall	38	2		
1996–97	Millwall	28	1		
1997–98	Millwall	43	2		
1998–99	Millwall	25	0		
1999–2000	Millwall	5	0		
2000–01	Millwall	1	0	140	5

BRANIFF, Kevin (F) 5 0
H: 5 11 W: 12 00 b.Belfast 4-3-83
Source: Scholarship.

| 1999–2000 | Millwall | 0 | 0 | | |
| 2000–01 | Millwall | 5 | 0 | 5 | 0 |

BUBB, Byron* (M) 8 0
H: 5 7 W: 10 05 b.Harrow 17-12-81
Source: Scholarship.

1998–99	Millwall	3	0		
1999–2000	Millwall	2	0		
2000–01	Millwall	3	0	8	0

BULL, Ronnie (D) 12 0
H: 5 7 W: 10 11 b.Hackney 27-12-80
Source: Trainee.

1998–99	Millwall	1	0		
1999–2000	Millwall	9	0		
2000–01	Millwall	2	0	12	0

CAHILL, Tim (M) 123 27
H: 5 10 W: 10 10 b.Sydney 6-12-79
Source: Sydney U.

1997–98	Millwall	1	0		
1998–99	Millwall	36	6		
1999–2000	Millwall	45	12		
2000–01	Millwall	41	9	123	27

CONSTANTINE, Leon (F) 1 0
H: 6 2 W: 11 10 b.Hackney 24-2-78
Source: Edgware T.

| 2000–01 | Millwall | 1 | 0 | 1 | 0 |

CORT, Leon* (D) 0 0
H: 6 2 W: 12 13 b.Southwark 11-9-79
Source: Dulwich H.

1997–98	Millwall	0	0
1998–99	Millwall	0	0
1999–2000	Millwall	0	0
2000–01	Millwall	0	0

COTTEE, Tony# (F) 578 225
H: 5 10 W: 12 06 b.West Ham 11-7-65
Source: Apprentice. *Honours:* England Youth, Under-21, 7 full caps.

1982–83	West Ham U	8	5		
1983–84	West Ham U	39	15		
1984–85	West Ham U	41	17		
1985–86	West Ham U	42	20		
1986–87	West Ham U	42	22		
1987–88	West Ham U	40	13		
1988–89	Everton	36	13		
1989–90	Everton	27	13		
1990–91	Everton	29	10		
1991–92	Everton	24	8		
1992–93	Everton	26	12		
1993–94	Everton	39	16		
1994–95	Everton	3	0	184	72
1994–95	West Ham U	31	13		
1995–96	West Ham U	33	10		
1996–97	West Ham U	3	0	279	115

From Selangor.

1997–98	Leicester C	19	4		
1997–98	Birmingham C	5	1	5	1
1998–99	Leicester C	31	10		
1999–2000	Leicester C	33	13		
2000–01	Leicester C	2	0	85	27
2000–01	Norwich C	7	1	7	1
2000–01	Barnet	16	9	16	9
2000–01	Millwall	2	0	2	0

DOLAN, Joe (D) 46 3
H: 6 3 W: 13 05 b.Harrow 27-5-80
Source: Chelsea Trainee. *Honours:* Northern Ireland Under-21.

1998–99	Millwall	9	1		
1999–2000	Millwall	17	1		
2000–01	Millwall	20	1	46	3

DUNNE, Alan (D) 0 0
H: 5 10 W: 11 12 b.Dublin 23-8-82

| 1999–2000 | Millwall | 0 | 0 |
| 2000–01 | Millwall | 0 | 0 |

DYCHE, Sean (D) 296 9
H: 6 0 W: 13 07 b.Kettering 28-6-71
Source: Trainee.

1988–89	Nottingham F	0	0		
1989–90	Nottingham F	0	0		
1989–90	Chesterfield	22	2		
1990–91	Chesterfield	28	2		
1991–92	Chesterfield	42	3		
1992–93	Chesterfield	20	1		
1993–94	Chesterfield	20	0		
1994–95	Chesterfield	22	0		
1995–96	Chesterfield	41	0		
1996–97	Chesterfield	36	0	231	8
1997–98	Bristol C	11	0		
1998–99	Bristol C	6	0	17	0
1998–99	Luton T	14	1	14	1
1999–2000	Millwall	1	0		
2000–01	Millwall	33	0	34	0

GILKES, Michael* (M) 470 46
H: 5 8 W: 10 10 b.Hackney 20-7-65
Source: Leicester C. *Honours:* Barbados full caps.

1984–85	Reading	16	2
1985–86	Reading	9	2
1986–87	Reading	7	0
1987–88	Reading	39	4
1988–89	Reading	46	9
1989–90	Reading	42	2
1990–91	Reading	21	1

Season	Club	Apps	Gls	Total	
1991–92	Reading	20	0		
1991–92	*Chelsea*	1	0	1	0
1991–92	*Southampton*	6	0	6	0
1992–93	Reading	38	12		
1993–94	Reading	39	2		
1994–95	Reading	40	8		
1995–96	Reading	44	0		
1996–97	Reading	32	1	393	43
1996–97	Wolverhampton W	5	1		
1997–98	Wolverhampton W	3	0		
1998–99	Wolverhampton W	30	0	38	1
1999–2000	Millwall	29	2		
2000–01	Millwall	3	0	32	2

GUERET, Willy (G)   11 0
b.Saint Claude 3-8-73

2000–01	Millwall	11	0	11	0

HARRIS, Neil (F)   122 67
H: 5 11   W: 12 04   b.Orsett 12-7-77
Source: Cambridge C.

1997–98	Millwall	3	0		
1998–99	Millwall	39	15		
1999–2000	Millwall	38	25		
2000–01	Millwall	42	27	122	67

HEARN, Charley (M)   0 0
b.Ashford 5-11-83
Source: School.

2000–01	Millwall	0	0		

HICKS, Mark (F)   1 0
H: 5 8   W: 10 04   b.Belfast 24-7-81

1998–99	Millwall	1	0		
1999–2000	Millwall	0	0		
2000–01	Millwall	0	0	1	0

IFILL, Paul (M)   94 18
H: 6 0   W: 12 09   b.Brighton 20-10-79
Source: Trainee.

1998–99	Millwall	15	1		
1999–2000	Millwall	44	11		
2000–01	Millwall	35	6	94	18

KINET, Christophe (M)   95 8
H: 5 8   W: 10 12   b.Huy 31-12-74

1995–96	Ekeren	15	1		
1996–97	Ekeren	23	3	38	4
1997–98	Strasbourg	17	2		
1998–99	Strasbourg	10	0	27	2
1999–2000	Millwall	3	0		
2000–01	Millwall	27	2	30	2

LAWRENCE, Matthew (D)   192 5
H: 6 1   W: 12 12   b.Northampton 19-6-74
Source: Grays Ath. *Honours:* England Schools.

1995–96	Wycombe W	3	0		
1996–97	Wycombe W	13	1		
1996–97	Fulham	15	0		
1997–98	Fulham	43	0		
1998–99	Fulham	1	0	59	0
1998–99	Wycombe W	34	2		
1999–2000	Wycombe W	29	2	79	5
1999–2000	Millwall	9	0		
2000–01	Millwall	45	0	54	0

LIVERMORE, David (M)   71 5
H: 5 11   W: 12 04   b.Edmonton 20-5-80
Source: Trainee.

1998–99	Arsenal	0	0		
1999–2000	Millwall	32	2		
2000–01	Millwall	39	3	71	5

MAY, Ben (M)   0 0
b.Gravesend 10-3-84

2000–01	Millwall	0	0		

MEADE, Darren* (F)   0 0
H: 5 9   W: 11 00   b.Dublin 3-2-82
Source: Belvedere.

1999–2000	Millwall	0	0		
2000–01	Millwall	0	0		

MOODY, Paul (F)   252 93
H: 6 3   W: 14 08   b.Portsmouth 13-6-67
Source: Waterlooville.

1991–92	Southampton	4	0		
1992–93	Southampton	3	0		
1992–93	*Reading*	5	1	5	1
1993–94	Southampton	5	0	12	0
1993–94	Oxford U	15	8		
1994–95	Oxford U	41	20		
1995–96	Oxford U	42	17		
1996–97	Oxford U	38	4	136	49
1997–98	Fulham	33	15		
1998–99	Fulham	7	4	40	19
1999–2000	Millwall	32	11		
2000–01	Millwall	27	13	59	24

NEILL, Lucas (M)   148 12
H: 6 0   W: 12 03   b.Sydney 9-3-78
Source: NSW Soccer Academy. *Honours:* Australia youth, 2 full caps.

1995–96	Millwall	13	0		
1996–97	Millwall	39	3		
1997–98	Millwall	6	0		
1998–99	Millwall	35	6		
1999–2000	Millwall	31	1		
2000–01	Millwall	24	2	148	12

NELSON, Stuart* (G)   0 0
H: 6 1   W: 12 12   b.Stroud 17-9-81

2000–01	Millwall	0	0		

NETHERCOTT, Stuart# (D)   189 5
H: 6 0   W: 13 00   b.Chadwell Heath 21-3-73
Source: Trainee. *Honours:* England Under-21.

1991–92	Tottenham H	0	0		
1991–92	*Maidstone U*	13	1	13	1
1991–92	*Barnet*	3	0	3	0
1992–93	Tottenham H	5	0		
1993–94	Tottenham H	10	0		
1994–95	Tottenham H	17	0		
1995–96	Tottenham H	13	0		
1996–97	Tottenham H	9	0		
1997–98	Tottenham H	0	0	54	0
1997–98	Millwall	10	0		
1998–99	Millwall	37	2		
1999–2000	Millwall	37	0		
2000–01	Millwall	35	2	119	4

ODUNSI, Leke (M)   15 0
H: 5 9   W: 11 07   b.Walworth 5-12-80
Source: Trainee.

1998–99	Millwall	3	0		
1999–2000	Millwall	4	0		
2000–01	Millwall	8	0	15	0

PHILLIPS, Mark (D)   0 0
H: 6 2   W: 13 00   b.Lambeth 27-1-82
Source: Scholarship.

1999–2000	Millwall	0	0		
2000–01	Millwall	0	0		

REES, Matthew (D)   0 0
H: 6 3   W: 13 06   b.Swansea 2-9-82
Source: Trainee.

1999–2000	Millwall	0	0		
2000–01	Millwall	0	0		

REID, Steven (M)   84 7
H: 6 0   W: 12 03   b.Kingston 10-3-81
Source: Trainee. *Honours:* England Youth.

1997–98	Millwall	1	0		
1998–99	Millwall	25	0		
1999–2000	Millwall	21	0		
2000–01	Millwall	37	7	84	7

ROBINSON, Paul (D)   0 0
H: 6 1   W: 11 09   b.Barnet 7-1-82
Source: Scholar.

2000–01	Millwall	0	0		

RYAN, Robbie (D)   133 0
H: 5 10   W: 12 03   b.Dublin 6-5-77
Source: Belvedere. *Honours:* Eire Youth, Under-21.

1994–95	Huddersfield T	0	0		
1995–96	Huddersfield T	0	0		
1996–97	Huddersfield T	5	0		
1997–98	Huddersfield T	10	0	15	0
1997–98	Millwall	16	0		
1998–99	Millwall	26	0		
1999–2000	Millwall	34	0		
2000–01	Millwall	42	0	118	0

SADLIER, Richard (F)   101 19
H: 6 2   W: 13 01   b.Dublin 14-1-79
Source: Belvedere. *Honours:* Eire Youth, Under-21.

1996–97	Millwall	10	0		
1997–98	Millwall	4	3		
1998–99	Millwall	31	5		
1999–2000	Millwall	27	5		
2000–01	Millwall	29	6	101	19

SMITH, Phil* (G)   5 0
H: 6 1   W: 13 11   b.Harrow 14-12-79
Source: Trainee.

1997–98	Millwall	0	0		
1998–99	Millwall	5	0		
1999–2000	Millwall	0	0		
2000–01	Millwall	0	0	5	0

STUART, Jamie* (D)   95 3
H: 5 9   W: 11 10   b.Southwark 15-10-76
Source: Trainee. *Honours:* England Youth, Under-21.

1994–95	Charlton Ath	12	0		
1995–96	Charlton Ath	27	2		
1996–97	Charlton Ath	10	1		
1997–98	Charlton Ath	1	0	50	3
1998–99	Millwall	35	0		
1999–2000	Millwall	9	0		
2000–01	Millwall	1	0	45	0

TUTTLE, David (D)   193 6
H: 6 2   W: 14 02   b.Reading 6-2-72
Source: Trainee. *Honours:* England Youth.

1989–90	Tottenham H				
1990–91	Tottenham H	6	0		
1991–92	Tottenham H	2	0		
1992–93	Tottenham H	5	0	13	0
1992–93	*Peterborough U*	7	0	7	0
1993–94	Sheffield U	31	0		
1994–95	Sheffield U	6	0		
1995–96	Sheffield U	26	1	63	1
1995–96	Crystal Palace	10	1		
1996–97	Crystal Palace	39	2		
1997–98	Crystal Palace	9	0		
1998–99	Crystal Palace	22	2		
1998–99	*Charlton Ath*	0	0		
1999–2000	Crystal Palace	1	0	81	5
1999–2000	Barnsley	12	0	12	0
1999–2000	Millwall	8	0		
2000–01	Millwall	9	0	17	0

TYNE, Tommy* (F)   3 0
H: 6 1   W: 12 05   b.Lambeth 2-3-81

1998–99	Millwall	0	0		
1999–2000	Millwall	0	0		
2000–01	Millwall	3	0	3	0

WARNER, Tony (G)   91 0
H: 6 4   W: 15 01   b.Liverpool 11-5-74
Source: School.

1993–94	Liverpool	0	0		
1994–95	Liverpool	0	0		
1995–96	Liverpool	0	0		
1996–97	Liverpool	0	0		
1997–98	Liverpool	0	0		
1997–98	*Swindon T*	2	0	2	0
1998–99	Liverpool	0	0		
1998–99	*Celtic*	3	0	3	0
1998–99	*Aberdeen*	6	0	6	0
1999–2000	Millwall	45	0		
2000–01	Millwall	35	0	80	0

Scholars
Alderton, Rio; Alimi, Bashiru; Deegan, Darren S; Karaiskos, Andreas; Kevin, Joseph S; McCartney, David J; Simpson, James W; Taylor, William B; Worsfold, Dean C

Non-Contract
Lombardo, Daniel CR; Steele, Daniel; Sweeney, Peter H

NEWCASTLE U

ACUNA, Clarence (M)   197 22
H: 5 10   W: 12 00   b.Rancagua 8-2-75
Honours: Chile 53 full caps, 3 goals.

1994	O'Higgins	28	2		
1995	O'Higgins	26	3		
1996	O'Higgins	27	3	81	8
1997	Univ de Chile	27	3		
1998	Univ de Chile	26	1		
1999	Univ de Chile	36	5	90	11
2000–01	Newcastle U	26	3	26	3

AMEOBI, Foluwashola (F)   20 2
H: 6 3   W: 12 03   b.Zaria 12-10-81
Source: Trainee. *Honours:* England Under-21.

1998–99	Newcastle U	0	0		
1999–2000	Newcastle U	0	0		
2000–01	Newcastle U	20	2	20	2

BARTON, Warren (D)   381 14
H: 6 3   W: 12 09   b.Islington 19-3-69
Source: Leytonstone/Ilford. *Honours:* England B, 3 full caps.

1989–90	Maidstone U	42	0	42	0
1990–91	Wimbledon	37	3		
1991–92	Wimbledon	42	1		
1992–93	Wimbledon	23	2		
1993–94	Wimbledon	39	2		
1994–95	Wimbledon	39	2	180	10
1995–96	Newcastle U	31	0		
1996–97	Newcastle U	18	1		
1997–98	Newcastle U	23	3		
1998–99	Newcastle U	24	0		
1999–2000	Newcastle U	34	0		
2000–01	Newcastle U	29	0	159	4

BASSEDAS, Christian (M)   290 22
H: 5 8   W: 11 9   b.Buenos Aires 16-2-73
Honours: Argentina 18 full caps.

1990–91	Velez Sarsfield	12	1		
1991–92	Velez Sarsfield	36	4		
1992–93	Velez Sarsfield	32	1		
1993–94	Velez Sarsfield	26	1		
1994–95	Velez Sarsfield	21	2		
1995–96	Velez Sarsfield	32	2		
1996–97	Velez Sarsfield	23	4		
1997–98	Velez Sarsfield	31	2		
1998–99	Velez Sarsfield	28	2		
1999–2000	Velez Sarsfield	27	2	268	21
2000–01	Newcastle U	22	1	22	1

BEHARALL, David (D) 6 0
H: 6 2 W: 11 12 b.Newcastle 8-3-79
Source: Trainee.
1997-98	Newcastle U	0	0	
1998-99	Newcastle U	4	0	
1999-2000	Newcastle U	2	0	
2000-01	Newcastle U	0	0	6 0

BERNARD, Olivier (D) 10 2
H: 5 7 W: 10 11 b.Lyon 14-10-79
2000-01	*Darlington*	10	2	10 2

BONVIN, Pablo (F) 0 0
H: 5 10 W: 11 11 b.Concepcion 15-4-81
2000-01	Newcastle U	0	0

BOYD, Mark (M) 0 0
H: 5 10 W: 12 04 b.Carlisle 22-10-81
Source: Trainee.
1998-99	Newcastle U	0	0
1999-2000	Newcastle U	0	0
2000-01	Newcastle U	0	0

BRENNAN, Stephen (D) 0 0
H: 5 8 W: 11 10 b.Dublin 26-3-83
1999-2000	Newcastle U	0	0
2000-01	Newcastle U	0	0

CALDWELL, Gary (D) 0 0
H: 5 11 W: 11 10 b.Stirling 12-4-82
Source: Trainee. Honours: Scotland Under-21.
1998-99	Newcastle U	0	0
1999-2000	Newcastle U	0	0
2000-01	Newcastle U	0	0

CALDWELL, Steven (D) 9 0
H: 6 0 W: 11 05 b.Stirling 12-9-80
Source: Trainee. Honours: Scotland Under-21, 1 full cap.
1997-98	Newcastle U	0	0	
1998-99	Newcastle U	0	0	
1999-2000	Newcastle U	0	0	
2000-01	Newcastle U	9	0	9 0

CHOPRA, Michael (F) 0 0
H: 5 8 W: 9 06 b.Nwcastle 23-12-83
Source: Scholar.
2000-01	Newcastle U	0	0

COPPINGER, James (F) 11 3
H: 5 7 W: 10 03 b.Middlesbrough 18-1-81
Source: Darlington Trainee. Honours: England Youth.
1997-98	Newcastle U	0	0	
1998-99	Newcastle U	0	0	
1999-2000	Newcastle U	0	0	
1999-2000	*Hartlepool U*	10	3	10 3
2000-01	Newcastle U	1	0	1 0

CORDONE, Daniel* (F) 95 19
H: 5 9 W: 11 08 b.Buenos Aires 5-11-74
1993-94	Velez Sarsfield	1	0	
1994-95	Velez Sarsfield	2	0	
1995-96	Velez Sarsfield	3	0	
1996-97	Velez Sarsfield	26	2	
1997-98	Velez Sarsfield	33	13	
1998-99	Velez Sarsfield	9	2	74 17

From Racing.
2000-01	Newcastle U	21	2	21 2

CORT, Carl (F) 92 23
H: 6 4 W: 12 07 b.Southwark 1-11-77
Source: Trainee. Honours: England Under-21.
1996-97	Wimbledon	1	0	
1996-97	*Lincoln C*	6	1	6 1
1997-98	Wimbledon	22	4	
1998-99	Wimbledon	16	3	
1999-2000	Wimbledon	34	9	73 16
2000-01	Newcastle U	13	6	13 6

COWAN, David (D) 0 0
H: 5 11 W: 11 02 b.Whitehaven 5-3-82
Source: Trainee.
1999-2000	Newcastle U	0	0
2000-01	Newcastle U	0	0

DABIZAS, Nikos (D) 183 15
H: 6 1 W: 12 07 b.Amindeo 3-8-73
Honours: Greece 44 full caps.
1994-95	Olympiakos	26	2	
1995-96	Olympiakos	27	1	
1996-97	Olympiakos	31	0	
1997-98	Olympiakos	20	5	104 8
1997-98	Newcastle U	11	1	
1998-99	Newcastle U	30	3	
1999-2000	Newcastle U	29	3	
2000-01	Newcastle U	9	3	79 7

DIMAS, Pedro (M) 0 0
H: 6 0 W: 11 00 b.Dexira 22-4-82
Source: Porto.
2000-01	Newcastle U	0	0

DIXON, Kevin (M) 0 0
H: 5 9 W: 10 11 b.Preston 17-3-83
Source: Scholar.
2000-01	Newcastle U	0	0

DOMI, Didier (D) 103 3
H: 5 10 W: 11 03 b.Sarcelles 2-5-78
1995-96	Paris St Germain	1	0	
1996-97	Paris St Germain	12	0	
1997-98	Paris St Germain	27	0	
1998-99	Paris St Germain	8	0	48 0
1998-99	Newcastle U	14	0	
1999-2000	Newcastle U	27	3	
2000-01	Newcastle U	14	0	55 3

(Transferred to Paris St G, January 2001).

DYER, Kieron (M) 147 17
H: 5 7 W: 9 07 b.Ipswich 29-12-78
Source: Trainee. Honours: England Youth, Under-21, B, 8 full caps.
1996-97	Ipswich T	13	0	
1997-98	Ipswich T	41	4	
1998-99	Ipswich T	37	5	91 9
1999-2000	Newcastle U	30	3	
2000-01	Newcastle U	26	5	56 8

FUMACA, Jose Antunes (M) 9 0
H: 6 0 W: 11 08 b.Belem 15-7-76
Source: Catunese.
1998-99	Birmingham C	0	0	
1998-99	Colchester U	1	0	1 0
1998-99	Barnsley	0	0	
1999-2000	Barnsley	0	0	
1999-2000	Crystal Palace	3	0	3 0
1999-2000	Newcastle U	5	0	
2000-01	Newcastle U	0	0	5 0

GALLACHER, Kevin* (F) 414 105
H: 5 8 W: 10 10 b.Clydebank 23-11-66
Source: Duntocher BC. Honours: Scotland Youth, Under-21, B, 53 full caps, 9 goals.
1983-84	Dundee U	1	0	
1984-85	Dundee U	0	0	
1985-86	Dundee U	20	3	
1986-87	Dundee U	37	10	
1987-88	Dundee U	26	4	
1988-89	Dundee U	31	9	
1989-90	Dundee U	17	1	131 27
1989-90	Coventry C	15	3	
1990-91	Coventry C	32	11	
1991-92	Coventry C	33	8	
1992-93	Coventry C	20	6	100 28
1992-93	Blackburn R	9	5	
1993-94	Blackburn R	30	7	
1994-95	Blackburn R	1	1	
1995-96	Blackburn R	16	2	
1996-97	Blackburn R	34	10	
1997-98	Blackburn R	33	16	
1998-99	Blackburn R	16	5	
1999-2000	Blackburn R	5	0	144 46
1999-2000	Newcastle U	20	2	
2000-01	Newcastle U	19	2	39 4

GAVILAN, Diego (M) 7 1
H: 5 8 W: 10 07 b.Asuncion 1-3-80
Source: Cerro Porteno. Honours: Paraguay 16 full caps.
1999-2000	Newcastle U	6	1	
2000-01	Newcastle U	1	0	7 1

GIVEN, Shay (G) 127 0
H: 6 1 W: 13 00 b.Lifford 20-4-76
Source: Celtic. Honours: Eire Under-21, 31 full caps.
1994-95	Blackburn R	0	0	
1994-95	*Swindon T*	0	0	
1995-96	Blackburn R	0	0	
1995-96	*Swindon T*	5	0	5 0
1995-96	*Sunderland*	17	0	17 0
1996-97	Blackburn R	2	0	2 0
1997-98	Newcastle U	24	0	
1998-99	Newcastle U	31	0	
1999-2000	Newcastle U	14	0	
2000-01	Newcastle U	34	0	103 0

GLASS, Stephen* (M) 149 14
H: 5 9 W: 10 11 b.Dundee 23-5-76
Source: Crombie Sports. Honours: Scotland Under-21, B, 1 full cap.
1994-95	Aberdeen	19	1	
1995-96	Aberdeen	32	3	
1996-97	Aberdeen	24	1	
1997-98	Aberdeen	31	2	106 7
1998-99	Newcastle U	22	3	
1999-2000	Newcastle U	7	1	
2000-01	Newcastle U	14	3	43 7

GREEN, Stuart (M) 0 0
H: 5 10 W: 11 00 b.Carlisle 15-6-81
Source: Trainee.
1999-2000	Newcastle U	0	0
2000-01	Newcastle U	0	0

GRIFFIN, Andy (D) 97 3
H: 5 9 W: 10 10 b.Billinge 7-3-79
Source: Trainee. Honours: England Youth, Under-21.
1996-97	Stoke C	34	1	
1997-98	Stoke C	23	1	57 2
1997-98	Newcastle U	4	0	
1998-99	Newcastle U	14	0	
1999-2000	Newcastle U	3	1	
2000-01	Newcastle U	19	0	40 1

HAMILTON, Des* (M) 129 6
H: 5 11 W: 13 00 b.Bradford 15-8-76
Source: Trainee. Honours: England Under-21.
1993-94	Bradford C	2	1	
1994-95	Bradford C	30	1	
1995-96	Bradford C	24	3	
1996-97	Bradford C	32	0	88 5
1996-97	Newcastle U	0	0	
1997-98	Newcastle U	12	0	
1998-99	Newcastle U	0	0	
1998-99	*Sheffield U*	6	0	6 0
1998-99	*Huddersfield T*	10	1	10 1
1999-2000	Newcastle U	0	0	
1999-2000	*Norwich C*	7	0	7 0
2000-01	Newcastle U	0	0	12 0
2000-01	*Tranmere R*	6	0	6 0

HARPER, Steve (G) 71 0
H: 6 2 W: 13 00 b.Easington 14-3-75
Source: Seaham Red Star.
1993-94	Newcastle U	0	0	
1994-95	Newcastle U	0	0	
1995-96	Newcastle U	0	0	
1995-96	*Bradford C*	1	0	1 0
1996-97	Newcastle U	0	0	
1996-97	*Stockport Co*	0	0	
1997-98	Newcastle U	0	0	
1997-98	*Hartlepool U*	15	0	15 0
1997-98	*Huddersfield T*	24	0	24 0
1998-99	Newcastle U	8	0	
1999-2000	Newcastle U	18	0	
2000-01	Newcastle U	5	0	31 0

HELDER, Rodrigues‡ (D) 171 12
H: 5 11 W: 13 00 b.Luanda 21-3-71
1991-92	Estoril	33	2	33 2
1992-93	Benfica	30	1	
1993-94	Benfica	32	2	
1994-95	Benfica	21	2	
1995-96	Benfica	10	3	93 8
1996-97	La Coruna	22	0	
1997-98	La Coruna	15	1	
1998-99	La Coruna	0	0	
1999-2000	La Coruna	0	0	37 1
1999-2000	Newcastle U	8	1	
2000-01	Newcastle U	0	0	8 1

HUGHES, Aaron (D) 80 2
H: 6 1 W: 11 02 b.Cookstown 8-11-79
Source: Trainee. Honours: Northern Ireland 20 full caps.
1996-97	Newcastle U	0	0	
1997-98	Newcastle U	4	0	
1998-99	Newcastle U	14	0	
1999-2000	Newcastle U	27	2	
2000-01	Newcastle U	35	0	80 2

KARELSE, John (G) 385 0
H: 6 3 W: 13 07 b.Kapelle 17-5-70
1986-87	NAC Breda	8	0	
1987-88	NAC Breda	13	0	
1988-89	NAC Breda	36	0	
1989-90	NAC Breda	34	0	
1990-91	NAC Breda	38	0	
1991-92	NAC Breda	37	0	
1992-93	NAC Breda	33	0	
1993-94	NAC Breda	34	0	
1994-95	NAC Breda	32	0	
1995-96	NAC Breda	29	0	
1996-97	NAC Breda	27	0	
1997-98	NAC Breda	33	0	
1998-99	NAC Breda	28	0	382 0
1999-2000	Newcastle U	3	0	
2000-01	Newcastle U	0	0	3 0

KENDRICK, Joseph (D) 0 0
H: 6 0 W: 11 05 b.Dublin 26-6-83
Source: Scholar.
2000-01	Newcastle U	0	0

KERR, Brian (M) 1 0
H: 5 10 W: 10 11 b.Motherwell 12-10-81
Source: Trainee.
1998-99	Newcastle U	0	0	
1999-2000	Newcastle U	0	0	
2000-01	Newcastle U	1	0	1 0

LEE, Robert (M) **585 102**
H: 5 10 W: 11 13 b.Plaistow 1-2-66
Source: Hornchurch. *Honours:* England Under-21, 21 full caps, 2 goals.

1983–84	Charlton Ath	11	4		
1984–85	Charlton Ath	39	10		
1985–86	Charlton Ath	35	8		
1986–87	Charlton Ath	33	3		
1987–88	Charlton Ath	23	2		
1988–89	Charlton Ath	31	5		
1989–90	Charlton Ath	37	1		
1990–91	Charlton Ath	43	13		
1991–92	Charlton Ath	39	12		
1992–93	Charlton Ath	7	1	**298**	**59**
1992–93	Newcastle U	36	10		
1993–94	Newcastle U	41	7		
1994–95	Newcastle U	35	9		
1995–96	Newcastle U	36	8		
1996–97	Newcastle U	33	5		
1997–98	Newcastle U	28	4		
1998–99	Newcastle U	26	0		
1999–2000	Newcastle U	30	0		
2000–01	Newcastle U	22	0	**287**	**43**

LUA-LUA, Lomano (F) **82 15**
H: 5 8 W: 12 00 b.Kinshasa 28-12-80

1998–99	Colchester U	13	1		
1999–2000	Colchester U	41	12		
2000–01	Colchester U	7	2	**61**	**15**
2000–01	Newcastle U	21	0	**21**	**0**

MANN, Jonathan (F) **0 0**
H: 5 9 W: 10 00 b.Blyth 21-11-82
Source: Scholar.

2000–01	Newcastle U	0	0		

MARCELINO, Elena (D) **134 9**
H: 6 2 W: 13 00 b.Gijon 26-9-71
Honours: Spain 5 full caps.

1993–94	Gijon	2	0		
1994–95	Gijon	8	0		
1995–96	Gijon	4	0	**14**	**0**
1996–97	Mallorca	33	4		
1997–98	Mallorca	36	2		
1998–99	Mallorca	34	3	**103**	**9**
1999–2000	Newcastle U	11	0		
2000–01	Newcastle U	6	0	**17**	**0**

McCLEN, Jamie (M) **10 0**
H: 5 8 W: 10 07 b.Newcastle 13-5-79
Source: Trainee.

1997–98	Newcastle U	0	0		
1998–99	Newcastle U	1	0		
1999–2000	Newcastle U	9	0		
2000–01	Newcastle U	0	0	**10**	**0**

McGUFFIE, Ryan (D) **0 0**
H: 6 0 W: 11 01 b.Dumfries 22-7-80

2000–01	Newcastle U	0	0		

McMAHON, David* (F) **8 1**
H: 6 1 W: 11 05 b.Dublin 17-1-81
Source: Trainee.

1997–98	Newcastle U	0	0		
1998–99	Newcastle U	0	0		
1999–2000	Newcastle U	0	0		
2000–01	Newcastle U	0	0		
2000–01	*Darlington*	8	1	**8**	**1**

McMENAMIN, Colin (F) **0 0**
H: 5 9 W: 10 12 b.Glasgow 12-2-81

2000–01	Newcastle U	0	0		

O'BRIEN, Andy (D) **142 4**
H: 6 3 W: 11 05 b.Harrogate 29-6-79
Source: Trainee. *Honours:* England Youth, Under-21, Eire Under-21, 1 full cap.

1996–97	Bradford C	22	2		
1997–98	Bradford C	26	0		
1998–99	Bradford C	31	0		
1999–2000	Bradford C	36	1		
2000–01	Bradford C	18	0	**133**	**3**
2000–01	Newcastle U	9	1	**9**	**1**

PRINGLE, Philip (G) **0 0**
H: 6 1 W: 14 09 b.Newcastle 1-1-83
Source: Scholar.

2000–01	Newcastle U	0	0		

QUINN, Wayne (D) **154 6**
H: 5 10 W: 11 12 b.Truro 19-11-76
Source: Trainee. *Honours:* England Under-21, B.

1994–95	Sheffield U	0	0		
1995–96	Sheffield U	0	0		
1996–97	Sheffield U	0	0		
1997–98	Sheffield U	28	2		
1998–99	Sheffield U	44	1		
1999–2000	Sheffield U	43	1		
2000–01	Sheffield U	24	2	**139**	**6**
2000–01	Newcastle U	15	0	**15**	**0**

RAYNER, David* (M) **0 0**
H: 5 9 W: 10 11 b.New Zealand 18-3-82

2000–01	Newcastle U	0	0		

ROBSON, Damon (M) **0 0**
H: 5 7 W: 13 06 b.Co Durham 19-9-83
Source: Scholar.

2000–01	Newcastle U	0	0		

SERRANT, Carl* (D) **111 1**
H: 6 0 W: 11 02 b.Bradford 12-9-75
Source: Trainee. *Honours:* England Under-21, B.

1994–95	Oldham Ath	0	0		
1995–96	Oldham Ath	20	1		
1996–97	Oldham Ath	40	0		
1997–98	Oldham Ath	30	0	**90**	**1**
1998–99	Newcastle U	4	0		
1998–99	*Bury*	15	0	**15**	**0**
1999–2000	Newcastle U	2	0		
2000–01	Newcastle U	0	0	**6**	**0**

SHEARER, Alan (F) **390 204**
H: 6 0 W: 12 06 b.Newcastle 13-8-70
Source: Trainee. *Honours:* England Youth, Under-21, B, 63 full caps, 30 goals.

1987–88	Southampton	5	3		
1988–89	Southampton	10	0		
1989–90	Southampton	26	3		
1990–91	Southampton	36	4		
1991–92	Southampton	41	13	**118**	**23**
1992–93	Blackburn R	21	16		
1993–94	Blackburn R	40	31		
1994–95	Blackburn R	42	34		
1995–96	Blackburn R	35	31	**138**	**112**
1996–97	Newcastle U	31	25		
1997–98	Newcastle U	17	2		
1998–99	Newcastle U	30	14		
1999–2000	Newcastle U	37	23		
2000–01	Newcastle U	19	5	**134**	**69**

SOLANO, Nolberto (M) **199 52**
H: 5 9 W: 11 02 b.Callao 12-12-74
Honours: Peru 55 full caps, 1 goal.

1994–95	Sporting Cristal	38	12		
1995–96	Sporting Cristal	26	13		
1996–97	Sporting Cristal	11	7	**75**	**32**
1997–98	Boca Juniors	32	5	**32**	**5**
1998–99	Newcastle U	29	6		
1999–2000	Newcastle U	30	3		
2000–01	Newcastle U	33	6	**92**	**15**

SPEED, Gary (M) **428 74**
H: 5 10 W: 10 12 b.Deeside 8-9-69
Source: Trainee. *Honours:* Wales Under-21, 65 full caps, 4 goals.

1988–89	Leeds U	1	0		
1989–90	Leeds U	25	3		
1990–91	Leeds U	38	7		
1991–92	Leeds U	41	7		
1992–93	Leeds U	39	7		
1993–94	Leeds U	36	10		
1994–95	Leeds U	39	3		
1995–96	Leeds U	29	2	**248**	**39**
1996–97	Everton	37	9		
1997–98	Everton	21	7	**58**	**16**
1997–98	Newcastle U	13	1		
1998–99	Newcastle U	38	4		
1999–2000	Newcastle U	36	9		
2000–01	Newcastle U	35	5	**122**	**19**

Scholars
Bell, Carl W; Brain, Jonathon R; Dunn, Paul J; English, Thomas M; Ferrell, Andrew E; Grindlay, Stephen J; Heiniger, Carl S; Hogg, Ryan; Kent, Robert S; Labonte, Aaron M; Meredith, Christoper A; Moore, James C; Norton, Lee F; Offiong, Richard; Orr, Bradley J; Ramage, Peter I; Wealleans, Kevin; Wright, Peter D
Non-Contract
Robson, Craig

NORTHAMPTON T

CARRUTHERS, Christopher§ (F) **3 0**
b.Kettering 19-8-83
Source: Scholar.

2000–01	Northampton T	3	0	**3**	**0**

DEMPSEY, Paul† (D) **6 0**
H: 5 11 W: 12 00 b.Wirral 3-12-81
Source: Scholar.

2000–01	Sheffield U	0	0		
2000–01	Northampton T	6	0	**6**	**0**

FORRESTER, Jamie (F) **224 67**
H: 5 6 W: 10 12 b.Bradford 1-11-74
Source: Auxerre. *Honours:* England Schools, Youth.

1992–93	Leeds U	6	0		
1993–94	Leeds U	3	0		
1994–95	Leeds U	0	0		
1994–95	*Southend U*	5	0	**5**	**0**
1994–95	*Grimsby T*	9	1		
1995–96	Leeds U	0	0	**9**	**0**
1995–96	Grimsby T	28	5		
1996–97	Grimsby T	13	1	**50**	**7**
1996–97	Scunthorpe U	10	6		
1997–98	Scunthorpe U	45	11		
1998–99	Scunthorpe U	46	20	**101**	**37**
1999–2000	Utrecht	1	0	**1**	**0**
1999–2000	Walsall	5	0	**5**	**0**
1999–2000	*Northampton T*	10	6		
2000–01	Northampton T	43	17	**53**	**23**

FRAIN, John (D) **440 27**
H: 5 10 W: 12 04 b.Birmingham 8-10-68
Source: Apprentice.

1985–86	Birmingham C	3	0		
1986–87	Birmingham C	3	1		
1987–88	Birmingham C	14	2		
1988–89	Birmingham C	28	3		
1989–90	Birmingham C	38	1		
1990–91	Birmingham C	42	3		
1991–92	Birmingham C	44	5		
1992–93	Birmingham C	45	6		
1993–94	Birmingham C	26	2		
1994–95	Birmingham C	7	0		
1995–96	Birmingham C	23	0		
1996–97	Birmingham C	1	0	**274**	**23**
1996–97	Northampton T	13	0		
1997–98	Northampton T	45	1		
1998–99	Northampton T	41	0		
1999–2000	Northampton T	40	2		
2000–01	Northampton T	27	1	**166**	**4**

GABBIADINI, Marco (F) **568 198**
H: 5 10 W: 13 04 b.Nottingham 21-1-68
Source: Apprentice. *Honours:* England Under-21, B.

1984–85	York C	1	0		
1985–86	York C	22	4		
1986–87	York C	29	9		
1987–88	York C	8	1		
1987–88	Sunderland	35	21		
1988–89	Sunderland	36	18		
1989–90	Sunderland	46	21		
1990–91	Sunderland	31	9		
1991–92	Sunderland	9	5	**157**	**74**
1991–92	Crystal Palace	15	5	**15**	**5**
1991–92	Derby Co	20	6		
1992–93	Derby Co	44	9		
1993–94	Derby Co	39	13		
1994–95	Derby Co	32	11		
1995–96	Derby Co	39	11		
1996–97	Derby Co	14	0	**188**	**50**
1996–97	*Birmingham C*	2	0	**2**	**0**
1996–97	*Oxford U*	5	1	**5**	**1**
1997–98	Stoke C	8	0	**8**	**0**
1997–98	York C	7	1	**67**	**15**
1998–99	Darlington	40	23		
1999–2000	Darlington	42	24	**82**	**47**
2000–01	Northampton T	44	6	**44**	**6**

GOULD, James* (M) **1 0**
H: 5 8 W: 10 06 b.Rushden 15-1-82
Source: Trainee.

2000–01	Northampton T	1	0	**1**	**0**

GREEN, Richard* (D) **436 24**
H: 6 1 W: 13 07 b.Wolverhampton 22-11-67
Source: Apprentice.

1986–87	Shrewsbury T	15	0		
1987–88	Shrewsbury T	31	2		
1988–89	Shrewsbury T	39	3		
1989–90	Shrewsbury T	40	0		
1990–91	Shrewsbury T	0	0	**125**	**5**
1990–91	Swindon T	0	0		
1991–92	Swindon T	0	0		
1991–92	Gillingham	12	4		
1992–93	Gillingham	39	3		
1993–94	Gillingham	39	4		
1994–95	Gillingham	37	1		
1995–96	Gillingham	35	2		
1996–97	Gillingham	29	2		
1997–98	Gillingham	25	0		
1998–99	Gillingham	0	0	**216**	**16**
1998–99	Walsall	30	1		
1999–2000	Walsall	0	0	**30**	**1**
1999–2000	*Rochdale*	6	0	**6**	**0**
1999–2000	Northampton T	21	2		
2000–01	Northampton T	38	0	**59**	**2**

HARGREAVES, Chris (M) **272 16**
H: 5 11 W: 12 02 b.Cleethorpes 12-5-72
Source: Trainee.

1989–90	Grimsby T	19	2		
1990–91	Grimsby T	18	3		
1991–92	Grimsby T	10	0		
1992–93	Grimsby T	4	0		
1992–93	*Scarborough*	3	0	**3**	**0**
1993–94	Grimsby T	0	0	**51**	**5**
1993–94	Hull C	28	0		
1994–95	Hull C	21	0	**49**	**0**
1995–96	WBA	1	0	**1**	**0**
1995–96	*Hereford U*	17	2		

| 1996–97 | Hereford U | 44 | 4 | | |
| 1997–98 | Hereford U | 0 | 0 | 61 | 6 |

From Hereford U.

1998–99	Plymouth Arg	32	2		
1999–2000	Plymouth Arg	44	3	76	5
2000–01	Northampton T	31	0	31	0

HODGE, John (F)   343 34
H: 5 7 W: 11 06 b.Skelmersdale 1-4-69
Source: Exmouth.

1991–92	Exeter C	23	1		
1992–93	Exeter C	42	9	65	10
1993–94	Swansea C	27	2		
1994–95	Swansea C	44	7		
1995–96	Swansea C	41	1		
1996–97	Swansea C	0	0	112	10
1996–97	Walsall	37	4		
1997–98	Walsall	39	8	76	12
1998–99	Gillingham	34	1		
1999–2000	Gillingham	15	0	49	1
1999–2000	Northampton T	8	0		
2000–01	Northampton T	33	1	41	1

HOPE, Richard (D)   132 1
H: 6 3 W: 13 05 b.Stockton 22-6-78
Source: Trainee.

1995–96	Blackburn R	0	0		
1996–97	Blackburn R	0	0		
1996–97	Darlington	20	0		
1997–98	Darlington	35	1		
1998–99	Darlington	8	0	63	1
1998–99	Northampton T	19	0		
1999–2000	Northampton T	17	0		
2000–01	Northampton T	33	0	69	0

HOWEY, Lee* (D)   143 14
H: 6 3 W: 14 06 b.Sunderland 1-4-69
Source: AC Hemptinne Eghezee.

1992–93	Sunderland	1	0		
1993–94	Sunderland	14	3		
1994–95	Sunderland	15	2		
1995–96	Sunderland	27	3		
1996–97	Sunderland	12	0	69	8
1997–98	Burnley	23	0		
1998–99	Burnley	3	0	26	0
1998–99	Northampton T	25	6		
1999–2000	Northampton T	20	0		
2000–01	Northampton T	3	0	48	6

HUGHES, Garry* (D)   18 1
H: 6 0 W: 12 00 b.Birmingham 19-11-79
Source: Trainee.

1998–99	Northampton T	0	0		
1999–2000	Northampton T	2	0		
2000–01	Northampton T	16	1	18	1

HUNT, James (M)   153 5
H: 5 11 W: 12 07 b.Derby 17-12-76
Source: Trainee.

1994–95	Notts Co	0	0		
1995–96	Notts Co	10	1		
1996–97	Notts Co	9	0	19	1
1997–98	Northampton T	21	0		
1998–99	Northampton T	35	2		
1999–2000	Northampton T	37	1		
2000–01	Northampton T	41	1	134	4

HUNTER, Roy (M)   146 14
H: 5 10 W: 12 08 b.Saltburn 29-10-73
Source: Trainee.

1991–92	WBA	6	1		
1992–93	WBA	1	0		
1993–94	WBA	2	0		
1994–95	WBA	0	0	9	1
1995–96	Northampton T	34	0		
1996–97	Northampton T	36	6		
1997–98	Northampton T	28	3		
1998–99	Northampton T	18	1		
1999–2000	Northampton T	17	3		
2000–01	Northampton T	4	0	137	13

LOPES, Richard† (M)   6 0
H: 5 7 W: 10 03 b.Waterford 10-8-81
Source: Scholar.

| 2000–01 | Sheffield U | 0 | 0 | | |
| 2000–01 | Northampton T | 6 | 0 | 6 | 0 |

LOWE, Daniel§ (M)   4 0
b.Barnsley 12-1-84
Source: Scholar.

| 2000–01 | Northampton T | 4 | 0 | 4 | 0 |

MORROW, Andrew* (F)   8 0
H: 5 8 W: 9 07 b.Bangor 5-10-80
Source: Trainee. *Honours:* Northern Ireland Under-21.

1998–99	Northampton T	0	0		
1999–2000	Northampton T	4	0		
2000–01	Northampton T	4	0	8	0

SAMPSON, Ian (D)   310 24
H: 6 2 W: 13 05 b.Wakefield 14-11-68
Source: Goole U.

1990–91	Sunderland	0	0		
1991–92	Sunderland	8	0		
1992–93	Sunderland	5	1		
1993–94	Sunderland	4	0	17	1
1993–94	Northampton T	8	0		
1994–95	Northampton T	42	2		
1995–96	Northampton T	33	4		
1996–97	Northampton T	43	5		
1997–98	Northampton T	39	3		
1998–99	Northampton T	42	1		
1999–2000	Northampton T	45	6		
2000–01	Northampton T	41	2	293	23

SAVAGE, Dave# (M)   245 24
H: 6 2 W: 13 00 b.Dublin 30-7-73
Source: Longford T. *Honours:* Eire Under-21, 5 full caps.

1994–95	Millwall	37	2		
1995–96	Millwall	27	0		
1996–97	Millwall	35	3		
1997–98	Millwall	31	1		
1998–99	Millwall	2	0	132	6
1998–99	Northampton T	27	5		
1999–2000	Northampton T	43	5		
2000–01	Northampton T	43	8	113	18

SOLLITT, Adam (G)   6 0
b.Sheffield 22-6-77
Source: Gainsborough Tr, Kettering T.
Honours: England semi-pro.

1995–96	Barnsley	0	0		
1996–97	Barnsley	0	0		
2000–01	Northampton T	6	0	6	0

SPEDDING, Duncan (M)   96 2
H: 6 2 W: 12 01 b.Frimley 7-9-77
Source: Trainee.

1996–97	Southampton	0	0		
1997–98	Southampton	7	0	7	0
1998–99	Northampton T	24	1		
1999–2000	Northampton T	44	1		
2000–01	Northampton T	21	0	89	2

THOMPSON, Ryan* (F)   2 0
H: 5 10 W: 11 10 b.London 24-6-82
Source: Trainee.

| 2000–01 | Northampton T | 2 | 0 | 2 | 0 |

WELCH, Keith (G)   555 0
H: 6 2 W: 13 07 b.Bolton 3-10-68
Source: Trainee.

1986–87	Bolton W	0	0		
1986–87	Rochdale	24	0		
1987–88	Rochdale	46	0		
1988–89	Rochdale	46	0		
1989–90	Rochdale	46	0		
1990–91	Rochdale	43	0	205	0
1991–92	Bristol C	26	0		
1992–93	Bristol C	45	0		
1993–94	Bristol C	45	0		
1994–95	Bristol C	44	0		
1995–96	Bristol C	35	0		
1996–97	Bristol C	11	0		
1997–98	Bristol C	44	0		
1998–99	Bristol C	21	0	271	0
1999–2000	Northampton T	39	0		
2000–01	Northampton T	40	0	79	0

WILSON, Kevin† (F)   602 149
H: 5 8 W: 11 04 b.Banbury 18-4-61
Source: Banbury U. *Honours:* Northern Ireland 42 full caps, 6 goals.

1979–80	Derby Co	4	0		
1980–81	Derby Co	27	7		
1981–82	Derby Co	24	9		
1982–83	Derby Co	22	4		
1983–84	Derby Co	32	2		
1984–85	Derby Co	13	8	122	30
1984–85	Ipswich T	17	7		
1985–86	Ipswich T	39	7		
1986–87	Ipswich T	42	20	98	34
1987–88	Chelsea	25	5		
1988–89	Chelsea	46	13		
1989–90	Chelsea	37	14		
1990–91	Chelsea	22	7		
1991–92	Chelsea	22	3	152	42
1991–92	Notts Co	8	1		
1992–93	Notts Co	32	1		
1993–94	Notts Co	29	1	69	3
1993–94	Bradford C	5	0	5	0
1994–95	Walsall	42	16		
1995–96	Walsall	46	15		
1996–97	Walsall	37	7	125	38
1997–98	Northampton T	9	0		
1998–99	Northampton T	8	1		
1999–2000	Northampton T	8	1		
2000–01	Northampton T	6	0	31	2

Scholars
Carruthers, Christopher P; Cavill, Aaran; Champelovier, Neil M; Colgan, Alan; Daly, Ben AJ; Faulds, Peter J; Georcelin, Justin S; Laws, Michael J; Lowe, Daniel J; Meade, Nathan S; Nash, Ryan M; Spooner, Mark S; Stirling, James S; Taylor, Matthew A; Thompson, Christopher D; White, Robert
Non-Contract
Dempsey, Paul; Lopes, Richard; Wilson, Kevin J

NORWICH C

ABBEY, Zema (F)   42 6
H: 6 1 W: 12 11 b.Luton 17-4-77
Source: Arlesy, Baldock T, Hitchin T.

1999–2000	Cambridge U	8	0		
2000–01	Cambridge U	14	5	22	5
2000–01	Norwich C	20	1	20	1

ANSELIN, Cedric (M)   49 2
H: 5 7 W: 11 02 b.Lens 24-7-77

1995–96	Bordeaux	3	0		
1996–97	Bordeaux	5	0		
1997–98	Lille	14	1	14	1
1998–99	Bordeaux	1	0	9	0
1998–99	Norwich C	7	1		
1999–2000	Norwich C	19	0		
2000–01	Norwich C	0	0	26	1

BLOOMFIELD, Daniel (M)   0 0
b.Ipswich 28-7-82
Source: Felixstowe & Walton U.

| 2000–01 | Norwich C | 0 | 0 | | |

COOTE, Adrian (F)   54 3
H: 6 1 W: 11 11 b.Gt Yarmouth 30-9-78
Source: Trainee. *Honours:* Northern Ireland Under-21, 6 full caps.

1997–98	Norwich C	23	2		
1998–99	Norwich C	6	0		
1999–2000	Norwich C	11	1		
2000–01	Norwich C	14	0	54	3

DALGLISH, Paul (F)   72 3
H: 5 10 W: 11 00 b.Glasgow 18-2-77
Honours: Scotland Under-21.

1995–96	Celtic	0	0		
1996–97	Liverpool	0	0		
1997–98	Liverpool	0	0		
1997–98	Newcastle U	0	0		
1997–98	Bury	12	0	12	0
1998–99	Newcastle U	11	1	11	1
1998–99	Norwich C	5	0		
1999–2000	Norwich C	31	2		
2000–01	Norwich C	7	0	43	2
2000–01	Wigan Ath	6	0	6	0

DE BLASIIS, Yves* (M)   35 0
H: 5 9 W: 11 05 b.Bordeaux 25-9-73
Source: Red Star 93.

| 1999–2000 | Norwich C | 28 | 0 | | |
| 2000–01 | Norwich C | 7 | 0 | 35 | 0 |

DE WAARD, Raymond‡ (F)   124 9
H: 6 1 W: 12 03 b.Rotterdam 23-3-73

1996–97	Excelsior	32	4		
1997–98	Excelsior	28	0		
1998–99	Excelsior	31	5	91	9
1999–2000	Cambuur	23	0	23	0
1999–2000	Norwich C	4	0		
2000–01	Norwich C	6	0	10	0

DERVELD, Fernando (D)   101 2
H: 6 2 W: 13 00 b.Vlissingen 22-10-76

1995–96	Willem II	7	0		
1996–97	Willem II	16	0		
1997–98	Willem II	17	1	40	1
1998–99	Haarlem	23	0		
1999–2000	Haarlem	14	0	37	0
1999–2000	Norwich C	5	0		
2000–01	Norwich C	17	1	22	1
2000–01	WBA	2	0	2	0

DRURY, Adam (D)   154 2
H: 5 10 W: 11 04 b.Cottenham 29-8-78
Source: Trainee.

1995–96	Peterborough U	1	0		
1996–97	Peterborough U	5	1		
1997–98	Peterborough U	31	0		
1998–99	Peterborough U	40	0		
1999–2000	Peterborough U	42	1		
2000–01	Peterborough U	29	0	148	2
2000–01	Norwich C	6	0	6	0

FLEMING, Craig (D)   358 8
H: 5 11 W: 12 10 b.Halifax 6-10-71
Source: Trainee.

1988–89	Halifax T	1	0		
1989–90	Halifax T	10	0		
1990–91	Halifax T	46	0	57	0
1991–92	Oldham Ath	32	1		
1992–93	Oldham Ath	24	0		
1993–94	Oldham Ath	37	0		
1994–95	Oldham Ath	5	0		
1995–96	Oldham Ath	22	0		
1996–97	Oldham Ath	44	0	164	1
1997–98	Norwich C	22	1		
1998–99	Norwich C	37	3		

| 1999–2000 | Norwich C | 39 | 3 | | |
| 2000–01 | Norwich C | 39 | 0 | 137 | 7 |

FORBES, Adrian (F) 112 8
H: 5 7 W: 11 04 b.Greenford 23-1-79
Source: Trainee. *Honours:* England Youth.

1996–97	Norwich C	10	0		
1997–98	Norwich C	33	4		
1998–99	Norwich C	15	0		
1999–2000	Norwich C	25	1		
2000–01	Norwich C	29	3	112	8

GIALLANZA, Gaetano (F) 82 31
H: 5 11 W: 11 09 b.Basle 6-6-74

1996–97	Basle	32	19	32	19
1997–98	Nantes	12	2	12	2
1997–98	Bolton W	3	0	3	0
1998–99	Lugano	21	8	21	8
1999–2000	Norwich C	3	0		
2000–01	Norwich C	11	2	14	2

GREEN, Robert (G) 10 0
H: 6 3 W: 13 00 b.Chertsey 18-1-80
Source: Trainee. *Honours:* England Youth.

1997–98	Norwich C	0	0		
1998–99	Norwich C	2	0		
1999–2000	Norwich C	3	0		
2000–01	Norwich C	5	0	10	0

HOLT, Gary (M) 156 9
H: 6 1 W: 11 11 b.Irvine 9-3-73
Source: Celtic. *Honours:* Scotland 2 full caps.

1994–95	Stoke C	0	0		
1995–96	Kilmarnock	26	0		
1996–97	Kilmarnock	12	1		
1997–98	Kilmarnock	27	2		
1998–99	Kilmarnock	33	3		
1999–2000	Kilmarnock	35	0		
2000–01	Kilmarnock	19	3	152	9
2000–01	Norwich C	4	0	4	0

JACKSON, Matt (D) 337 10
H: 6 0 W: 11 10 b.Leeds 19-10-71
Source: School. *Honours:* England Schools, Under-21.

1990–91	Luton T	0	0		
1990–91	*Preston NE*	4	0	4	0
1991–92	Luton T	9	0	9	0
1991–92	Everton	30	1		
1992–93	Everton	27	3		
1993–94	Everton	38	0		
1994–95	Everton	29	0		
1995–96	Everton	14	0		
1995–96	*Charlton Ath*	8	0	8	0
1996–97	Everton	0	0	138	4
1996–97	*QPR*	7	0	7	0
1996–97	*Birmingham C*	10	0	10	0
1996–97	Norwich C	19	2		
1997–98	Norwich C	41	3		
1998–99	Norwich C	37	1		
1999–2000	Norwich C	38	0		
2000–01	Norwich C	26	0	161	6

KENTON, Darren (D) 88 4
H: 5 11 W: 11 10 b.Wandsworth 13-9-78
Source: Trainee.

1997–98	Norwich C	11	0		
1998–99	Norwich C	22	1		
1999–2000	Norwich C	26	1		
2000–01	Norwich C	29	2	88	4

LLEWELLYN, Chris (F) 124 17
H: 6 0 W: 11 11 b.Merthyr 29-8-79
Source: Trainee. *Honours:* Wales Under-21, B, 2 full caps.

1996–97	Norwich C	0	0		
1997–98	Norwich C	15	4		
1998–99	Norwich C	31	2		
1999–2000	Norwich C	36	3		
2000–01	Norwich C	42	8	124	17

MACKAY, Malky (D) 193 12
H: 6 3 W: 13 03 b.Bellshill 19-2-72
Source: Queen's Park Youth.

1990–91	Queen's Park	10	0		
1991–92	Queen's Park	27	3		
1992–93	Queen's Park	33	3	70	6
1993–94	Celtic	0	0		
1994–95	Celtic	1	0		
1995–96	Celtic	11	1		
1996–97	Celtic	20	1		
1997–98	Celtic	4	1		
1998–99	Celtic	1	1	37	4
1998–99	Norwich C	27	1		
1999–2000	Norwich C	21	0		
2000–01	Norwich C	38	1	86	2

MARSHALL, Andy# (G) 211 0
H: 6 2 W: 13 08 b.Bury 14-4-75
Source: Trainee. *Honours:* England Under-21.

1993–94	Norwich C	0	0		
1994–95	Norwich C	21	0		
1995–96	Norwich C	3	0		

1996–97	Norwich C	7	0		
1996–97	Bournemouth	11	0	11	0
1996–97	Gillingham	5	0	5	0
1997–98	Norwich C	42	0		
1998–99	Norwich C	37	0		
1999–2000	Norwich C	44	0		
2000–01	Norwich C	41	0	195	0

McGOVERN, Brian (D) 18 1
H: 6 3 W: 12 07 b.Dublin 28-4-80
Source: Cherry Orchard. *Honours:* Eire Youth, Under-21.

1997–98	Arsenal	0	0		
1998–99	Arsenal	0	0		
1999–2000	Arsenal	1	0		
1999–2000	*QPR*	5	0	5	0
2000–01	Arsenal	0	0	1	0
2000–01	Norwich C	12	1	12	1

McVEIGH, Paul (F) 15 2
H: 5 6 W: 10 06 b.Belfast 6-12-77
Source: Trainee. *Honours:* Northern Ireland Under-21, 1 full cap.

1995–96	Tottenham H	0	0		
1996–97	Tottenham H	3	1		
1997–98	Tottenham H	0	0		
1998–99	Tottenham H	0	0		
1999–2000	Tottenham H	0	0	3	1
1999–2000	Norwich C	1	0		
2000–01	Norwich C	11	1	12	1

MULRYNE, Phil (M) 45 3
H: 5 9 W: 11 05 b.Belfast 1-1-78
Source: Trainee. *Honours:* Northern Ireland Under-21, 12 full caps, 2 goals.

1994–95	Manchester U	0	0		
1995–96	Manchester U	0	0		
1996–97	Manchester U	0	0		
1997–98	Manchester U	1	0		
1998–99	Manchester U	0	0	1	0
1998–99	Norwich C	7	2		
1999–2000	Norwich C	9	0		
2000–01	Norwich C	28	1	44	3

NEDERGAARD, Steen (M) 215 21
H: 6 1 W: 11 11 b.Denmark 25-2-70

1991–92	Odense	17	0		
1992–93	Odense	30	9		
1993–94	Odense	25	1		
1994–95	Odense	27	1		
1995–96	Odense	30	1		
1996–97	Odense	24	4		
1997–98	Odense	21	2		
1998–99	Odense	0	0		
1999–2000	Odense	26	2	200	20
2000–01	Norwich C	15	1	15	1

NOTMAN, Alex (F) 27 4
H: 5 7 W: 10 11 b.Edinburgh 10-12-79
Source: Trainee. *Honours:* Scotland Under-21.

1996–97	Manchester U	0	0		
1997–98	Manchester U	0	0		
1998–99	Manchester U	0	0		
1998–99	*Aberdeen*	2	0	2	0
1999–2000	Manchester U	0	0		
1999–2000	*Sheffield U*	10	3	10	3
2000–01	Manchester U	0	0		
2000–01	Norwich C	15	1	15	1

ROBERTS, Iwan (F) 502 168
H: 6 3 W: 13 01 b.Bangor 26-6-68
Source: Trainee. *Honours:* Wales Youth, 13 full caps.

1985–86	Watford	4	0		
1986–87	Watford	3	1		
1987–88	Watford	25	2		
1988–89	Watford	22	6		
1989–90	Watford	9	0	63	9
1990–91	Huddersfield T	44	13		
1991–92	Huddersfield T	46	24		
1992–93	Huddersfield T	37	9		
1993–94	Huddersfield T	15	4	142	50
1993–94	Leicester C	26	13		
1994–95	Leicester C	37	9		
1995–96	Leicester C	37	19	100	41
1996–97	Wolverhampton W	33	12	33	12
1997–98	Norwich C	31	5		
1998–99	Norwich C	45	19		
1999–2000	Norwich C	44	17		
2000–01	Norwich C	44	15	164	56

RUSSELL, Darel (M) 88 7
H: 6 0 W: 12 02 b.Mile End 22-10-80
Source: Trainee. *Honours:* England Youth.

1997–98	Norwich C	1	0		
1998–99	Norwich C	13	1		
1999–2000	Norwich C	33	4		
2000–01	Norwich C	41	2	88	7

SUTCH, Daryl (D) 286 9
H: 5 11 W: 12 06 b.Lowestoft 11-9-71
Source: Trainee. *Honours:* England Youth, Under-21.

1989–90	Norwich C	0	0		
1990–91	Norwich C	4	0		
1991–92	Norwich C	9	0		
1992–93	Norwich C	22	2		
1993–94	Norwich C	3	0		
1994–95	Norwich C	30	1		
1995–96	Norwich C	13	0		
1996–97	Norwich C	44	3		
1997–98	Norwich C	40	1		
1998–99	Norwich C	36	0		
1999–2000	Norwich C	45	2		
2000–01	Norwich C	40	0	286	9

WALSH, Steve‡ (D) 499 57
H: 6 3 W: 15 02 b.Fulwood 3-11-64
Source: Local.

1982–83	Wigan Ath	31	0		
1983–84	Wigan Ath	42	1		
1984–85	Wigan Ath	40	2		
1985–86	Wigan Ath	13	1	126	4
1986–87	Leicester C	21	0		
1987–88	Leicester C	32	7		
1988–89	Leicester C	30	2		
1989–90	Leicester C	34	3		
1990–91	Leicester C	35	3		
1991–92	Leicester C	43	7		
1992–93	Leicester C	40	15		
1993–94	Leicester C	10	4		
1994–95	Leicester C	5	0		
1995–96	Leicester C	37	4		
1996–97	Leicester C	22	2		
1997–98	Leicester C	26	3		
1998–99	Leicester C	22	3		
1999–2000	Leicester C	11	0		
2000–01	Leicester C	1	0	369	53
2000–01	Norwich C	4	0	4	0

Scholars
Bilham, Neil; Blois, Lewis P; Davey, Thomas; Dodsworth, Paul; Gay, Daniel K; Gilman, Lee D; Goodchild, Richard I; Hayes, Paul E; Lee-Barrett, Arran; Merrick, Michael T; Ngopwani, Pitshou M; Oxby, Andrew D; Parry, Matthew G; Self, Daniel G; Shackell, Jason; Thompson, Ben; Woodrow, Richard

NOTTINGHAM F

ALLOU, Bernard (M) 47 4
H: 5 8 W: 11 00 b.Cocody 19-6-75

1994–95	Paris St Germain	7	3		
1995–96	Paris St Germain	19	0		
1996–97	Paris St Germain	12	0		
1997–98	Paris St Germain	3	0	41	3

From Grampas 8.

1998–99	Nottingham F	2	0		
1999–2000	Nottingham F	4	1		
2000–01	Nottingham F	0	0	6	1

BART-WILLIAMS, Chris (M) 350 45
H: 5 11 W: 12 07 b.Freetown 16-6-74
Source: Trainee. *Honours:* England Youth, Under-21.

1990–91	Leyton Orient	21	2		
1991–92	Leyton Orient	15	0	36	2
1991–92	Sheffield W	15	0		
1992–93	Sheffield W	34	6		
1993–94	Sheffield W	37	8		
1994–95	Sheffield W	38	2	124	16
1995–96	Nottingham F	33	0		
1996–97	Nottingham F	16	1		
1997–98	Nottingham F	33	4		
1998–99	Nottingham F	24	3		
1999–2000	Nottingham F	38	5		
2000–01	Nottingham F	46	14	190	27

BEASANT, Dave* (G) 730 0
H: 6 4 W: 14 02 b.Willesden 20-3-59
Source: Edgware T. *Honours:* England B, 2 full caps.

1979–80	Wimbledon	2	0		
1980–81	Wimbledon	34	0		
1981–82	Wimbledon	46	0		
1982–83	Wimbledon	46	0		
1983–84	Wimbledon	46	0		
1984–85	Wimbledon	42	0		
1985–86	Wimbledon	42	0		
1986–87	Wimbledon	42	0		
1987–88	Wimbledon	40	0	340	0
1988–89	Newcastle U	20	0	20	0
1988–89	Chelsea	22	0		
1989–90	Chelsea	38	0		
1990–91	Chelsea	35	0		
1991–92	Chelsea	21	0		
1992–93	Chelsea	17	0		
1992–93	*Grimsby T*	6	0	6	0

1992–93	Wolverhampton W	4	0	**4**	**0**
1993–94	Chelsea	0	0	**133**	**0**
1993–94	Southampton	25	0		
1994–95	Southampton	13	0		
1995–96	Southampton	36	0		
1996–97	Southampton	14	0		
1997–98	Southampton	0	0	**88**	**0**
1997–98	Nottingham F	41	0		
1998–99	Nottingham F	26	0		
1999–2000	Nottingham F	27	0		
2000–01	Nottingham F	45	0	**139**	**0**

BOPP, Eugene (M) **0 0**
H: 5 10 W: 12 00 b.Kiev 5-9-83
Source: Bayern Munich.

2000–01	Nottingham F	0	0		

BRENNAN, Jim (D) **94 3**
H: 5 9 W: 11 06 b.Toronto 8-5-77
Source: Sora Lazio. *Honours:* Canada 25 full caps, 2 goals.

1994–95	Bristol C	0	0		
1995–96	Bristol C	0	0		
1996–97	Bristol C	8	0		
1997–98	Bristol C	6	0		
1998–99	Bristol C	29	1		
1999–2000	Bristol C	12	2	**55**	**3**
1999–2000	Nottingham F	25	0		
2000–01	Nottingham F	12	0	**37**	**0**
2000–01	*Huddersfield T*	2	0	**2**	**0**

BYRNE, Michael (M) **0 0**
b.Dublin 14-2-84
Source: Scholar.

2000–01	Nottingham F	0	0		

CALDERWOOD, Colin (D) **632 27**
H: 6 0 W: 13 00 b.Stranraer 20-1-65
Source: Amateur. *Honours:* Scotland 36 full caps, 1 goal. Football League.

1981–82	Mansfield T	1	0		
1982–83	Mansfield T	28	0		
1983–84	Mansfield T	30	1		
1984–85	Mansfield T	41	0	**100**	**1**
1985–86	Swindon T	46	2		
1986–87	Swindon T	46	1		
1987–88	Swindon T	34	1		
1988–89	Swindon T	43	4		
1989–90	Swindon T	46	3		
1990–91	Swindon T	23	2		
1991–92	Swindon T	46	5		
1992–93	Swindon T	46	2	**330**	**20**
1993–94	Tottenham H	26	0		
1994–95	Tottenham H	36	2		
1995–96	Tottenham H	29	0		
1996–97	Tottenham H	34	0		
1997–98	Tottenham H	26	4		
1998–99	Tottenham H	12	0	**163**	**6**
1998–99	Aston Villa	8	0		
1999–2000	Aston Villa	18	0	**26**	**0**
1999–2000	Nottingham F	6	0		
2000–01	Nottingham F	2	0	**8**	**0**
2000–01	*Notts Co*	5	0	**5**	**0**

CASH, Brian (M) **0 0**
H: 5 9 W: 12 00 b.Dublin 24-11-82
Source: Trainee.

1999–2000	Nottingham F	0	0		
2000–01	Nottingham F	0	0		

COLLIS, Stephen* (G) **0 0**
H: 6 1 W: 13 00 b.Barnet 18-3-81

1999–2000	Barnet	0	0		
2000–01	Nottingham F	0	0		

DAWSON, Kevin (D) **13 0**
H: 6 0 W: 10 07 b.Northallerton 18-6-81
Source: Trainee.

1998–99	Nottingham F	0	0		
1999–2000	Nottingham F	7	0		
2000–01	Nottingham F	1	0	**8**	**0**
2000–01	*Barnet*	5	0	**5**	**0**

DAWSON, Michael (D) **0 0**
b.Northallerton 18-11-83
Source: School.

2000–01	Nottingham F	0	0		

DOIG, Chris (D) **28 0**
H: 6 2 W: 12 06 b.Dumfries 13-2-81
Source: Trainee. *Honours:* Scotland Under-21.

1997–98	Nottingham F	0	0		
1998–99	Nottingham F	2	0		
1999–2000	Nottingham F	11	0		
2000–01	Nottingham F	15	0	**28**	**0**

DOYLE, Kevin‡ (D) **0 0**
H: 5 11 W: 12 02 b.Wexford 13-10-80
Source: Trainee.

1997–98	Leeds U	0	0		
1998–99	Leeds U	0	0		
1999–2000	Nottingham F	0	0		

2000–01	Nottingham F	0	0		

EDDS, Gareth (M) **15 1**
H: 5 11 W: 10 12 b.Sydney 3-2-81
Source: Trainee.

1997–98	Nottingham F	0	0		
1998–99	Nottingham F	0	0		
1999–2000	Nottingham F	2	0		
2000–01	Nottingham F	13	1	**15**	**1**

EDWARDS, Christian# (D) **171 8**
H: 6 2 W: 12 03 b.Caerphilly 23-11-75
Source: Trainee. *Honours:* Wales Under-21, B, 1 full cap.

1994–95	Swansea C	9	0		
1995–96	Swansea C	38	2		
1996–97	Swansea C	36	0		
1997–98	Swansea C	32	2	**115**	**4**
1997–98	Nottingham F	0	0		
1998–99	Nottingham F	12	0		
1998–99	*Bristol C*	3	0	**3**	**0**
1999–2000	Nottingham F	0	0		
1999–2000	*Oxford U*	5	1	**5**	**1**
2000–01	Nottingham F	36	3	**48**	**3**

FENTON, Paul (F) **0 0**
H: 5 7 W: 10 10 b.Cork 8-3-83
Source: Scholarship.

1999–2000	Nottingham F	0	0		
2000–01	Nottingham F	0	0		

FORMANN, Pascal (M) **0 0**
b.Werne 16-11-82

2000–01	Nottingham F	0	0		

FOY, Keith (M) **20 0**
H: 5 11 W: 12 03 b.Crumlin 30-12-81
Source: Trainee.

1998–99	Nottingham F	0	0		
1999–2000	Nottingham F	0	0		
2000–01	Nottingham F	20	1	**20**	**1**

FREEMAN, David (F) **11 0**
H: 5 10 W: 11 07 b.Dublin 25-11-79
Source: Cherry Orchard. *Honours:* Eire Under-21.

1996–97	Nottingham F	0	0		
1997–98	Nottingham F	0	0		
1998–99	Nottingham F	0	0		
1999–2000	Nottingham F	3	0		
2000–01	Nottingham F	5	0	**8**	**0**
2000–01	*Port Vale*	3	0	**3**	**0**

GRAY, Andy (M) **85 1**
H: 6 0 W: 13 00 b.Harrogate 15-11-77
Source: Trainee.

1995–96	Leeds U	15	0		
1996–97	Leeds U	7	0		
1997–98	Leeds U	0	0		
1997–98	*Bury*	6	1	**6**	**1**
1998–99	Leeds U	0	0	**22**	**0**
1998–99	Nottingham F	8	0		
1998–99	*Preston NE*	5	0	**5**	**0**
1999–2000	Nottingham F	22	0		
2000–01	Nottingham F	18	0	**48**	**0**

HAIGH, Philip (M) **0 0**
b.Boston 27-9-82

2000–01	Nottingham F	0	0		

HAREWOOD, Marlon (F) **97 9**
H: 6 1 W: 13 03 b.Hampstead 25-8-79
Source: Trainee.

1996–97	Nottingham F	0	0		
1997–98	Nottingham F	1	0		
1998–99	Nottingham F	23	1		
1998–99	*Ipswich T*	6	1	**6**	**1**
1999–2000	Nottingham F	34	4		
2000–01	Nottingham F	33	3	**91**	**8**

HASKINS, Andrew§ (M) **0 0**
b.York 30-4-84
Source: School.

2000–01	Nottingham F	0	0		

HJELDE, Jon Olav (D) **116 3**
H: 6 2 W: 13 05 b.Levanger 30-7-72
Source: Rosenborg.

1994	Rosenborg	1	0		
1995	Rosenborg	7	0		
1996	Rosenborg	16	1		
1997	Rosenborg	3	0	**27**	**1**
1997–98	Nottingham F	28	1		
1998–99	Nottingham F	17	1		
1999–2000	Nottingham F	33	0		
2000–01	Nottingham F	11	2	**89**	**4**

HUDSON, Niall (M) **0 0**
H: 5 10 W: 10 02 b.Ilkeston 7-1-82
Source: Trainee.

1998–99	Nottingham F	0	0		
1999–2000	Nottingham F	0	0		

2000–01	Nottingham F	0	0		

JEFFREY, Richard (F) **0 0**
H: 5 9 W: 11 00 b.Derby 4-11-83
Source: Scholar.

2000–01	Nottingham F	0	0		

JENAS, Jermaine (M) **1 0**
H: 5 10 W: 12 00 b.Nottingham 18-2-83
Source: Scholarship. *Honours:* England Youth.

1999–2000	Nottingham F	0	0		
2000–01	Nottingham F	1	0	**1**	**0**

JOHN, Stern (F) **101 49**
H: 6 1 W: 13 07 b.Trinidad 30-10-76
Honours: Trinidad & Tobago full caps.

1998	Columbus Crew	27	26		
1999	Columbus Crew	28	18	**55**	**44**
1999–2000	Nottingham F	17	3		
2000–01	Nottingham F	29	2	**46**	**5**

JOHNSON, Andy (M) **184 22**
H: 6 1 W: 13 03 b.Bristol 2-5-74
Source: Trainee. *Honours:* Wales 7 full caps.

1991–92	Norwich C	2	0		
1992–93	Norwich C	2	1		
1993–94	Norwich C	2	0		
1994–95	Norwich C	7	0		
1995–96	Norwich C	26	7		
1996–97	Norwich C	27	5	**66**	**13**
1997–98	Nottingham F	34	4		
1998–99	Nottingham F	28	0		
1999–2000	Nottingham F	25	2		
2000–01	Nottingham F	31	3	**118**	**9**

JOHNSON, David (F) **247 75**
H: 5 6 W: 12 00 b.Kingston, Jam 15-8-76
Source: Trainee. *Honours:* England Schools, B. Jamaica full caps.

1994–95	Manchester U	0	0		
1995–96	Bury	36	5		
1996–97	Bury	44	8		
1997–98	Bury	17	5	**97**	**18**
1997–98	Ipswich T	31	20		
1998–99	Ipswich T	42	13		
1999–2000	Ipswich T	44	22		
2000–01	Ipswich T	14	0	**131**	**55**
2000–01	Nottingham F	19	2	**19**	**2**

JONES, Gary (F) **209 29**
H: 6 3 W: 13 05 b.Chester 10-5-75
Source: Trainee.

1993–94	Tranmere R	6	2		
1994–95	Tranmere R	19	3		
1995–96	Tranmere R	23	1		
1996–97	Tranmere R	30	6		
1997–98	Tranmere R	43	8		
1998–99	Tranmere R	26	5		
1999–2000	Tranmere R	31	3	**178**	**28**
2000–01	Nottingham F	31	1	**31**	**1**

KEARNEY, Liam (M) **0 0**
H: 5 7 W: 10 12 b.Dublin 10-1-83
Source: Scholarship.

1999–2000	Nottingham F	0	0		
2000–01	Nottingham F	0	0		

LESTER, Jack (F) **178 27**
H: 5 10 W: 11 10 b.Sheffield 8-10-75
Source: Trainee. *Honours:* England Schools.

1994–95	Grimsby T	7	0		
1995–96	Grimsby T	5	0		
1996–97	Grimsby T	22	5		
1996–97	*Doncaster R*	11	1	**11**	**1**
1997–98	Grimsby T	40	4		
1998–99	Grimsby T	33	4		
1999–2000	Grimsby T	26	4	**133**	**17**
1999–2000	Nottingham F	15	2		
2000–01	Nottingham F	19	7	**34**	**9**

LOUIS-JEAN, Mathieu (D) **134 0**
H: 5 9 W: 10 08 b.Mont-St-Aignan 22-2-76
Source: Le Havre.

1993–94	Le Havre	7	0		
1994–95	Le Havre	9	0		
1995–96	Le Havre	15	0		
1996–97	Le Havre	31	0		
1997–98	Le Havre	16	0	**78**	**0**
1998–99	Nottingham F	16	0		
1999–2000	Nottingham F	27	0		
2000–01	Nottingham F	13	0	**56**	**0**

LOVE, Gordon (F) **0 0**
H: 5 7 W: 10 00 b.Bellshill 17-3-83

1999–2000	Nottingham F	0	0		
2000–01	Nottingham F	0	0		

MATRECANO, Salvatore‡ (D) **256 6**
H: 6 2 W: 14 00 b.Naples 5-10-70

1987–88	Ercolanese	1	0	**1**	**0**
1988–89	V.Lamezia	4	0	**4**	**0**
1989–90	Audax Ravag	20	2	**20**	**2**
1990–91	Turris	33	0	**33**	**0**
1991–92	Foggia	28	0	**28**	**0**

1992–93	Parma	20	1		
1993–94	Parma	16	0	36	1
1994–95	Napoli	16	0		
1995–96	Napoli	1	0	17	0
1995–96	Udinese	19	0	19	0
1996–97	Perugia	26	1		
1997–98	Perugia	32	1		
1998–99	Perugia	29	1	87	3
1999–2000	Nottingham F	11	0		
2000–01	Nottingham F	0	0	11	0

MATTSSON, Jesper‡ (D) 131 11
H: 6 1 W: 13 01 b.Visby 18-4-68

1994	Hacken	24	3	24	3
1995	Halmstad	25	0		
1996	Halmstad	24	1		
1997	Halmstad	26	4		
1998	Halmstad	26	3	101	8
1998–99	Nottingham F	6	0		
1999–2000	Nottingham F	0	0		
2000–01	Nottingham F	0	0	6	0

McNAMARA, Niall* (F) 0 0
H: 5 11 W: 11 09 b.Eire 26-1-82
Source: Trainee.

1998–99	Nottingham F	0	0		
1999–2000	Nottingham F	0	0		
2000–01	Nottingham F	0	0		

OLSEN, Ben‡ (M) 90 12
H: 5 7 W: 10 00 b.USA 3-5-77
Honours: USA 19 full caps, 3 goals.

1998	DC United	31	4		
1999	DC United	28	5		
2000	DC United	13	1	72	10
2000–01	Nottingham F	18	2	18	2

PETRACHI, Gianluca (M) 293 29
H: 5 9 W: 11 05 b.Lecce 14-1-69

1987–88	Lecce	5	0	5	0
1988–89	Nola	29	0	29	0
1989–90	Taranto	0	0		
1990–91	Taranto	0	0		
1990–91	Arezzo	19	1	19	1
1991–92	Fedelis Andria	32	5		
1992–93	Fedelis Andria	33	4	65	9
1993–94	Venezia	34	6	34	6
1994–95	Torino	1	0	1	0
1994–95	Palermo	27	2	27	2
1995–96	Cremonese	26	0		
1996–97	Cremonese	18	1		
1997–98	Cremonese	0	0	44	1
1997–98	Ancona	28	5	28	5
1998–99	Perugia	28	5	28	5
1999–2000	Nottingham F	13	0		
2000–01	Nottingham F	0	0	13	0

PEYTON, Emmet (M) 0 0
b.Castlebar 26-10-83

| 2000–01 | Nottingham F | 0 | 0 | | |

PLATT, David† (M) 448 150
H: 5 10 W: 11 12 b.Chadderton 10-6-66
Source: Chadderton. *Honours:* England Under-21, B, 62 full caps, 27 goals.

1984–85	Manchester U	0	0		
1984–85	Crewe Alex	22	5		
1985–86	Crewe Alex	43	8		
1986–87	Crewe Alex	43	23		
1987–88	Crewe Alex	26	19	134	55
1987–88	Aston Villa	11	5		
1988–89	Aston Villa	38	7		
1989–90	Aston Villa	37	19		
1990–91	Aston Villa	35	19	121	50
1991–92	Bari	29	11	29	11
1992–93	Juventus	16	3	16	3
1993–94	Sampdoria	29	9		
1994–95	Sampdoria	26	8	55	17
1995–96	Arsenal	29	6		
1996–97	Arsenal	28	4		
1997–98	Arsenal	31	3		
1998–99	Arsenal	0	0	88	13
1999–2000	Nottingham F	3	0		
2000–01	Nottingham F	2	1	5	1

PRUTTON, David (D) 76 3
H: 6 1 W: 11 06 b.Hull 12-9-81
Source: Trainee. *Honours:* England Youth, Under-21.

1998–99	Nottingham F	0	0		
1999–2000	Nottingham F	34	2		
2000–01	Nottingham F	42	1	76	3

REID, Andrew (F) 14 2
H: 5 7 W: 11 00 b.Dublin 29-7-82
Source: Trainee.

| 1999–2000 | Nottingham F | 0 | 0 | | |
| 2000–01 | Nottingham F | 14 | 2 | 14 | 2 |

ROBERTSON, Gregor (M) 0 0
b.Edinburgh 19-1-84

| 2000–01 | Nottingham F | 0 | 0 | | |

ROCHE, Barry (G) 2 0
H: 6 4 W: 12 06 b.Dublin 6-4-82
Source: Trainee.

| 1999–2000 | Nottingham F | 0 | 0 | | |
| 2000–01 | Nottingham F | 2 | 0 | 2 | 0 |

ROGERS, Alan (D) 191 18
H: 5 10 W: 12 08 b.Liverpool 3-1-77
Source: Trainee.

1995–96	Tranmere R	26	2		
1996–97	Tranmere R	31	0	57	2
1997–98	Nottingham F	46	1		
1998–99	Nottingham F	34	3		
1999–2000	Nottingham F	37	9		
2000–01	Nottingham F	17	3	134	16

SCIMECA, Riccardo (M) 147 6
H: 6 0 W: 13 11 b.Leamington Spa 13-6-75
Source: Trainee. *Honours:* England Under-21, B.

1993–94	Aston Villa	0	0		
1994–95	Aston Villa	0	0		
1995–96	Aston Villa	17	0		
1996–97	Aston Villa	17	0		
1997–98	Aston Villa	21	0		
1998–99	Aston Villa	18	2	73	2
1999–2000	Nottingham F	38	0		
2000–01	Nottingham F	36	4	74	4

SHEVLIN, Anthony‡ (M) 0 0
b.Dublin 9-12-82
Source: Trainee.

| 1999–2000 | Nottingham F | 0 | 0 | | |
| 2000–01 | Nottingham F | 0 | 0 | | |

THOMPSON, John (D) 0 0
b.Dublin 12-10-81

| 1999–2000 | Nottingham F | 0 | 0 | | |
| 2000–01 | Nottingham F | 0 | 0 | | |

VAUGHAN, Tony (D) 174 6
H: 6 1 W: 12 10 b.Manchester 11-10-75
Source: Trainee. *Honours:* England Schools.

1994–95	Ipswich T	10	0		
1995–96	Ipswich T	25	1		
1996–97	Ipswich T	32	2	67	3
1997–98	Manchester C	19	1		
1998–99	Manchester C	38	1		
1999–2000	Manchester C	1	0	58	2
1999–2000	Cardiff C	14	0	14	0
1999–2000	Nottingham F	10	0		
2000–01	Nottingham F	25	1	35	1

WARD, Darren (G) 332 0
H: 5 11 W: 12 09 b.Worksop 11-5-74
Source: Trainee. *Honours:* Wales Under-21, 1 full cap.

1992–93	Mansfield T	13	0		
1993–94	Mansfield T	33	0		
1994–95	Mansfield T	35	0	81	0
1995–96	Notts Co	46	0		
1996–97	Notts Co	38	0		
1997–98	Notts Co	44	0		
1998–99	Notts Co	43	0		
1999–2000	Notts Co	45	0		
2000–01	Notts Co	35	0	251	0
2000–01	Nottingham F	0	0		

WILLIAMS, Gareth (M) 19 0
H: 5 11 W: 11 08 b.Glasgow 16-12-81
Source: Trainee.

1998–99	Nottingham F	0	0		
1999–2000	Nottingham F	2	0		
2000–01	Nottingham F	17	0	19	0

Scholars
Birch, Jay; Bodkin, Matthew J; Haskins, Andrew E; Jenkins, Ryan M; Myhill, Craig J
Non-Contract
Platt, David A

NOTTS CO

ALLSOPP, Danny (F) 70 22
H: 6 0 W: 14 02 b.Melbourne 10-8-78
Source: South Melbourne, 20 apps, 2 gls; Carlton 16 apps, 2 gls.

1998–99	Manchester C	24	4		
1999–2000	Manchester C	4	0		
1999–2000	Notts Co	3	1		
1999–2000	Wrexham	3	4	3	4
2000–01	Manchester C	1	0	29	4
2000–01	Bristol R	6	0	6	0
2000–01	Notts Co	29	13	32	14

BOLLAND, Paul (M) 57 1
H: 6 0 W: 12 01 b.Bradford 23-12-79
Source: Trainee.

1997–98	Bradford C	10	0		
1998–99	Bradford C	2	0	12	0
1998–99	Notts Co	13	0		
1999–2000	Notts Co	25	1		
2000–01	Notts Co	7	0	45	1

BROUGH, Michael (M) 27 1
H: 6 0 W: 11 07 b.Nottingham 1-8-81
Source: Trainee.

| 1999–2000 | Notts Co | 11 | 0 | | |
| 2000–01 | Notts Co | 16 | 1 | 27 | 1 |

CROSS, David† (M) 1 0
H: 5 10 W: 10 07 b.Bromley 7-9-82
Source: Scholarship.

| 1999–2000 | Notts Co | 1 | 0 | | |
| 2000–01 | Notts Co | 0 | 0 | 1 | 0 |

DEENEY, Saul (G) 0 0
b.Londonderry 12-3-83
Source: Scholar.

| 2000–01 | Notts Co | 0 | 0 | | |

DYER, Alex‡ (M) 465 63
H: 6 1 W: 13 01 b.Forest Gate 14-11-65
Source: Watford Apprentice.

1983–84	Blackpool	9	0		
1984–85	Blackpool	36	8		
1985–86	Blackpool	39	8		
1986–87	Blackpool	24	3	108	19
1986–87	Hull C	17	4		
1987–88	Hull C	28	8		
1988–89	Hull C	15	2	60	14
1988–89	Crystal Palace	7	2		
1989–90	Crystal Palace	10	0	17	2
1990–91	Charlton Ath	35	7		
1991–92	Charlton Ath	13	0		
1992–93	Charlton Ath	30	6	78	13
1993–94	Oxford U	38	5		
1994–95	Oxford U	38	1		
1995–96	Oxford U	0	0	76	6
1995–96	Lincoln C	1	0	1	0
1995–96	Barnet	35	2		
1996–97	Barnet	0	0	35	2
1997–98	Huddersfield T	12	1	12	1
1997–98	Notts Co	0	0		
1998–99	Notts Co	29	0		
1999–2000	Notts Co	30	6		
2000–01	Notts Co	9	0	78	6

FARRELL, Sean* (F) 286 76
H: 6 2 W: 13 01 b.Watford 28-1-69
Source: Apprentice.

1986–87	Luton T	0	0		
1987–88	Luton T	0	0		
1987–88	Colchester U	9	1	9	1
1988–89	Luton T	1	0		
1989–90	Luton T	1	0		
1990–91	Luton T	20	1		
1991–92	Luton T	4	0	25	1
1991–92	Northampton T	4	1	4	1
1991–92	Fulham	25	10		
1992–93	Fulham	35	12		
1993–94	Fulham	34	9	94	31
1994–95	Peterborough U	33	8		
1995–96	Peterborough U	26	9		
1996–97	Peterborough U	7	3	66	20
1996–97	Notts Co	14	0		
1997–98	Notts Co	35	15		
1998–99	Notts Co	11	3		
1999–2000	Notts Co	9	0		
2000–01	Notts Co	19	3	88	22

FENTON, Nick (D) 71 3
H: 6 2 W: 11 10 b.Preston 23-11-79
Source: Trainee. *Honours:* England Youth.

1996–97	Manchester C	0	0		
1997–98	Manchester C	0	0		
1998–99	Manchester C	15	0		
1999–2000	Manchester C	0	0		
1999–2000	Bournemouth	8	0		
2000–01	Manchester C	0	0	15	0
2000–01	Bournemouth	5	0	13	0
2000–01	Notts Co	30	2	43	3

FORD, Ryan (M) 1 0
H: 5 10 W: 10 05 b.Worksop 3-9-78
Source: Trainee.

1997–98	Manchester U	0	0		
1998–99	Manchester U	0	0		
1999–2000	Manchester U	0	0		
1999–2000	Notts Co	1	0		
2000–01	Notts Co	0	0	1	0

GELLERT, Brian* (M) 0 0
b.Kolding 10-5-77
Source: Brescia.

| 2000–01 | Notts Co | 0 | 0 | | |

GIBSON, Paul* (G) 33 0
H: 6 3 W: 13 00 b.Sheffield 1-11-76
Source: Trainee.

| 1995–96 | Manchester U | 0 | 0 | | |
| 1996–97 | Manchester U | 0 | 0 | | |

1997–98	Manchester U	0	0		
1997–98	Mansfield T	13	0	13	0
1998–99	Manchester U	0	0		
1998–99	Hull C	4	0	4	0
1998–99	Notts Co	1	0		
1999–2000	Notts Co	1	0		
1999–2000	Rochdale	5	0	5	0
2000–01	Notts Co	9	0	11	0

HAMILTON, Ian (M)   485 46
H: 5 10   W: 12 07   b.Stevenage 14-12-67
Source: Apprentice.

1985–86	Southampton	0	0		
1986–87	Southampton	0	0		
1987–88	Southampton	0	0		
1987–88	Cambridge U	9	1		
1988–89	Cambridge U	15	0	24	1
1988–89	Scunthorpe U	27	1		
1989–90	Scunthorpe U	43	6		
1990–91	Scunthorpe U	34	2		
1991–92	Scunthorpe U	41	9	145	18
1992–93	WBA	46	7		
1993–94	WBA	42	3		
1994–95	WBA	35	4		
1995–96	WBA	41	3		
1996–97	WBA	39	5		
1997–98	WBA	37	1	240	23
1997–98	Sheffield U	8	1		
1998–99	Sheffield U	30	2		
1999–2000	Sheffield U	7	0		
1999–2000	Grimsby T	6	1	6	1
2000–01	Sheffield U	0	0	45	3
2000–01	Notts Co	25	0	25	0

HEFFERNAN, Paul (F)   3 0
H: 5 10   W: 11 00   b.Dublin 29-12-81
Source: Newton.

| 1999–2000 | Notts Co | 2 | 0 | | |
| 2000–01 | Notts Co | 1 | 0 | 3 | 0 |

HOLMES, Richard (D)   54 0
H: 5 11   W: 10 12   b.Grantham 7-11-80
Source: Trainee.

1998–99	Notts Co	8	0		
1999–2000	Notts Co	41	0		
2000–01	Notts Co	5	0	54	0

HUGHES, Andy (M)   143 18
H: 6 0   W: 12 07   b.Manchester 2-1-78
Source: Trainee.

1995–96	Oldham Ath	15	1		
1996–97	Oldham Ath	8	0		
1997–98	Oldham Ath	10	0	33	1
1997–98	Notts Co	15	2		
1998–99	Notts Co	30	3		
1999–2000	Notts Co	35	7		
2000–01	Notts Co	30	5	110	17

IRELAND, Craig (D)   99 5
H: 6 3   W: 13 09   b.Dundee 29-11-75
Source: Aberdeen Lads.

1994–95	Aberdeen	0	0		
1995–96	Aberdeen	0	0		
1995–96	Dunfermline Ath	10	0		
1996–97	Dunfermline Ath	9	1		
1997–98	Dunfermline Ath	12	1		
1998–99	Dunfermline Ath	23	0		
1999–2000	Dunfermline Ath	3	0	57	2
1999–2000	Dundee	14	1	14	1
2000–01	Airdrieonians	12	2	12	2
2000–01	Notts Co	16	0	16	0

JACOBSEN, Anders* (D)   74 4
H: 6 2   W: 12 09   b.Oslo 18-4-69
Source: Start. Honours: Norway 4 full caps.

1998–99	Sheffield U	12	0	12	0
1999–2000	Stoke C	33	2	33	2
2000–01	Notts Co	29	2	29	2

JORGENSEN, Henrik (D)   5 0
b.Bogense 12-1-79

| 2000–01 | Notts Co | 5 | 0 | 5 | 0 |

JOSEPH, David# (F)   27 4
H: 5 10   W: 11 12   b.Guadeloupe 22-11-76

| 2000–01 | Notts Co | 27 | 4 | 27 | 4 |

LIBURD, Richard (D)   225 9
H: 5 9   W: 11 06   b.Nottingham 26-9-73
Source: Forest Ath.

1992–93	Middlesbrough	0	0		
1993–94	Middlesbrough	41	1	41	1
1994–95	Bradford C	9	1		
1995–96	Bradford C	33	1		
1996–97	Bradford C	36	1		
1997–98	Bradford C	0	0	78	3
1997–98	Carlisle U	9	0	9	0
1998–99	Notts Co	35	1		
1999–2000	Notts Co	31	1		
2000–01	Notts Co	31	3	97	5

LINDLEY, James* (G)   3 0
H: 6 1   W: 13 00   b.Sutton-in-Ashfield 23-7-81
Source: Trainee.

1999–2000	Notts Co	1	0		
2000–01	Notts Co	2	0	3	0
2000–01	Lincoln C	0	0		
2000–01	Mansfield T	0	0		

McCAIG, John (D)   0 0
H: 6 1   W: 12 06   b.Ayr 19-11-82

| 2000–01 | Notts Co | 0 | 0 | | |

McDERMOTT, Andy (D)   83 3
H: 5 9   W: 11 03   b.Sydney 24-3-77
Source: Australian Institute of Sport.

1995–96	QPR	0	0		
1996–97	QPR	6	2	6	2
1996–97	WBA	6	0		
1997–98	WBA	13	0		
1998–99	WBA	20	0		
1999–2000	WBA	13	1	52	1
2000–01	Notts Co	25	0	25	0

MOREAU, Fabrice‡ (M)   38 6
H: 5 9   W: 11 00   b.Paris 7-10-67

1999–2000	Numancia	9	0	9	0
2000–01	Airdrieonians	24	6	24	6
2000–01	Notts Co	5	0	5	0

MURRAY, Shaun* (M)   248 17
H: 5 8   W: 10 12   b.Newcastle 7-10-70
Source: Trainee. Honours: England Schools, Youth.

1987–88	Tottenham H	0	0		
1988–89	Tottenham H	0	0		
1989–90	Portsmouth	0	0		
1990–91	Portsmouth	25	1		
1991–92	Portsmouth	2	0		
1992–93	Portsmouth	7	0		
1993–94	Portsmouth	0	0	34	1
1993–94	Millwall	0	0		
1993–94	Scarborough	29	5	29	5
1994–95	Bradford C	41	5		
1995–96	Bradford C	34	2		
1996–97	Bradford C	17	1		
1997–98	Bradford C	38	0	130	8
1998–99	Notts Co	35	3		
1999–2000	Notts Co	9	0		
2000–01	Notts Co	11	0	55	3

NICHOLSON, Kevin (D)   19 2
H: 5 9   W: 11 07   b.Derby 2-10-80
Source: Trainee. Honours: England Schools.

1997–98	Sheffield W	0	0		
1998–99	Sheffield W	0	0		
1999–2000	Sheffield W	0	0		
2000–01	Sheffield W	1	0	1	0

From Forest Green R

| 2000–01 | Northampton T | 7 | 0 | 7 | 0 |
| 2000–01 | Notts Co | 11 | 2 | 11 | 2 |

OWERS, Gary (M)   518 45
H: 6 0   W: 12 09   b.Newcastle 3-10-68
Source: Apprentice.

1986–87	Sunderland	0	0		
1987–88	Sunderland	37	4		
1988–89	Sunderland	38	3		
1989–90	Sunderland	43	9		
1990–91	Sunderland	38	1		
1991–92	Sunderland	30	4		
1992–93	Sunderland	33	1		
1993–94	Sunderland	30	2		
1994–95	Sunderland	19	1	268	25
1994–95	Bristol C	21	2		
1995–96	Bristol C	37	2		
1996–97	Bristol C	46	4		
1997–98	Bristol C	22	1	126	9
1998–99	Notts Co	39	3		
1999–2000	Notts Co	45	4		
2000–01	Notts Co	40	4	124	11

RAMAGE, Craig* (M)   253 47
H: 5 11   W: 12 10   b.Derby 30-3-70
Source: Trainee. Honours: England Under-21.

1988–89	Derby Co	0	0		
1988–89	Wigan Ath	10	2	10	2
1989–90	Derby Co	12	1		
1990–91	Derby Co	17	1		
1991–92	Derby Co	7	2		
1992–93	Derby Co	1	0		
1993–94	Derby Co	5	0	42	4
1993–94	Watford	13	0		
1994–95	Watford	44	9		
1995–96	Watford	36	15		
1996–97	Watford	11	3	104	27
1996–97	Peterborough U	7	0	7	0
1997–98	Bradford C	32	1		
1998–99	Bradford C	3	0	35	1
1999–2000	Notts Co	40	4		
2000–01	Notts Co	15	3	55	7

RAPLEY, Kevin (F)   124 20
H: 5 10   W: 11 07   b.Reading 21-9-77
Source: Trainee.

1996–97	Brentford	2	0		
1997–98	Brentford	37	9		
1998–99	Brentford	12	3	51	12
1998–99	Southend U	9	4	9	4
1998–99	Notts Co	16	2		
1999–2000	Notts Co	29	2		
2000–01	Notts Co	7	0	52	4
2000–01	Exeter C	7	0	7	0
2000–01	Scunthorpe U	5	0	5	0

RICHARDSON, Ian (D)   152 15
H: 5 10   W: 12 00   b.Barking 22-1-70
Source: Dagenham & Redbridge.

1995–96	Birmingham C	7	0	7	0
1996–97	Notts Co	15	0		
1996–97	Notts Co	19	1		
1997–98	Notts Co	30	2		
1998–99	Notts Co	23	7		
1999–2000	Notts Co	33	4		
2000–01	Notts Co	25	1	145	15

STALLARD, Mark (F)   240 74
H: 6 0   W: 12 13   b.Derby 24-10-74
Source: Trainee.

1991–92	Derby Co	3	0		
1992–93	Derby Co	5	0		
1993–94	Derby Co	0	0		
1994–95	Derby Co	16	2		
1994–95	Fulham	4	3	4	3
1995–96	Derby Co	3	0	27	2
1995–96	Bradford C	21	9		
1996–97	Bradford C	22	1	43	10
1996–97	Preston NE	4	1	4	1
1997–98	Wycombe W	12	4		
1997–98	Wycombe W	43	17		
1998–99	Wycombe W	15	2	70	23
1998–99	Notts Co	14	4		
1999–2000	Notts Co	36	14		
2000–01	Notts Co	42	17	92	35

THOMAS, Geoff* (M)   448 64
H: 6 1   W: 13 03   b.Manchester 5-8-64
Source: Local. Honours: England B, 9 full caps.

1981–82	Rochdale	0	0		
1982–83	Rochdale	1	0		
1983–84	Rochdale	10	1	11	1
1983–84	Crewe Alex	8	1		
1984–85	Crewe Alex	40	4		
1985–86	Crewe Alex	37	6		
1986–87	Crewe Alex	40	9	125	20
1987–88	Crystal Palace	41	6		
1988–89	Crystal Palace	22	5		
1989–90	Crystal Palace	35	1		
1990–91	Crystal Palace	38	6		
1991–92	Crystal Palace	30	6		
1992–93	Crystal Palace	29	2	195	26
1993–94	Wolverhampton W	8	4		
1994–95	Wolverhampton W	14	1		
1995–96	Wolverhampton W	2	0		
1996–97	Wolverhampton W	22	3	46	8
1997–98	Nottingham F	20	3		
1998–99	Nottingham F	5	1	25	4
1999–2000	Barnsley	27	4		
2000–01	Barnsley	11	0	38	4
2000–01	Notts Co	8	1	8	1

WARREN, Mark (D)   223 6
H: 6 0   W: 12 08   b.Clapton 12-11-74
Source: Trainee.

1991–92	Leyton Orient	1	0		
1992–93	Leyton Orient	14	0		
1993–94	Leyton Orient	6	0		
1993–94	West Ham U	0	0		
1994–95	Leyton Orient	31	3		
1995–96	Leyton Orient	22	1		
1996–97	Leyton Orient	27	1		
1997–98	Leyton Orient	41	0		
1998–99	Leyton Orient	10	0	152	5
1998–99	Oxford U	4	0	4	0
1998–99	Notts Co	18	0		
1999–2000	Notts Co	33	1		
2000–01	Notts Co	16	0	67	1

Scholars
Berry, Dean; Briggs, Andrew; Clarke, Ryan A; Cross, David B; Davies, Andrew M; Dunn, Mark A; Housley, Craig; McCaul, Matthew J; Osborne, Calum G; Poznanski, Lee J; Riley, Paul A; Screaton, Iain P; Skevington, Matthew

OLDHAM ATH

ADAMS, Neil* (M)   419 56
H: 5 9   W: 11 04   b.Stoke 23-11-65
Source: Local. Honours: England Under-21.

| 1985–86 | Stoke C | 32 | 4 | 32 | 4 |

1986–87	Everton	12	0		
1987–88	Everton	8	0		
1988–89	Everton	0	0	20	0
1988–89	Oldham Ath	9	0		
1989–90	Oldham Ath	27	4		
1990–91	Oldham Ath	31	6		
1991–92	Oldham Ath	26	4		
1992–93	Oldham Ath	32	9		
1993–94	Oldham Ath	13	0		
1993–94	Norwich C	14	0		
1994–95	Norwich C	33	3		
1995–96	Norwich C	42	2		
1996–97	Norwich C	45	13		
1997–98	Norwich C	30	4		
1998–99	Norwich C	18	3	182	25
1999–2000	Oldham Ath	29	2		
2000–01	Oldham Ath	18	2	185	27

ALLOTT, Mark (F) 139 27
H: 5 11 W: 10 12 b.Middleton 16-3-78
Source: Trainee.

1995–96	Oldham Ath	0	0		
1996–97	Oldham Ath	5	1		
1997–98	Oldham Ath	22	2		
1998–99	Oldham Ath	41	7		
1999–2000	Oldham Ath	32	10		
2000–01	Oldham Ath	39	7	139	27

BOSHELL, Daniel (M) 26 1
H: 5 11 W: 11 10 b.Bradford 30-5-81
Source: Trainee.

1998–99	Oldham Ath	0	0		
1999–2000	Oldham Ath	8	0		
2000–01	Oldham Ath	18	1	26	1

CAMPBELL, Jamie‡ (G) 0 0
H: 6 2 W: 13 00 b.Glasgow 2-12-80
Source: Trainee.

1998–99	Oldham Ath	0	0		
1999–2000	Oldham Ath	0	0		
2000–01	Oldham Ath	0	0		

CARSS, Tony (M) 176 6
H: 5 10 W: 11 08 b.Alnwick 31-3-76
Source: Bradford C Trainee.

1994–95	Blackburn R	0	0		
1995–96	Darlington	28	2		
1996–97	Darlington	29	0	57	2
1997–98	Cardiff C	42	1	42	1
1998–99	Chesterfield	4	0		
1999–2000	Chesterfield	31	1	35	1
2000–01	Carlisle U	7	0	7	0
2000–01	Oldham Ath	35	2	35	2

CORAZZIN, Carlo (F) 295 98
H: 5 10 W: 12 07 b.Canada 25-12-71
Source: Vancouver 86ers. *Honours:* Canada 53 full caps, 10 goals.

1993–94	Cambridge U	28	10		
1994–95	Cambridge U	46	19		
1995–96	Cambridge U	31	10	105	39
1995–96	Plymouth Arg	6	1		
1996–97	Plymouth Arg	30	5		
1997–98	Plymouth Arg	38	16	74	22
1998–99	Northampton T	39	16		
1999–2000	Northampton T	39	14	78	30
2000–01	Oldham Ath	38	7	38	7

DUDLEY, Craig (F) 95 14
H: 5 11 W: 11 02 b.Ollerton 12-9-79
Source: Trainee. *Honours:* England Youth.

1996–97	Notts Co	10	2		
1997–98	Notts Co	17	1		
1997–98	Shrewsbury T	4	0	4	0
1998–99	Notts Co	4	0	31	3
1998–99	Hull C	7	2	7	2
1998–99	Oldham Ath	0	0		
1999–2000	Oldham Ath	25	5		
1999–2000	Chesterfield	2	0	2	0
2000–01	Oldham Ath	26	4	51	9

DUXBURY, Lee (M) 485 58
H: 5 10 W: 10 07 b.Keighley 7-10-69
Source: Trainee.

1988–89	Bradford C	1	0		
1989–90	Bradford C	12	1		
1989–90	Rochdale	10	0	10	0
1990–91	Bradford C	45	5		
1991–92	Bradford C	46	5		
1992–93	Bradford C	42	5		
1993–94	Bradford C	43	9		
1994–95	Bradford C	20	0		
1994–95	Huddersfield T	26	2		
1995–96	Huddersfield T	3	0	29	2
1995–96	Bradford C	30	4		
1996–97	Bradford C	33	3	272	32
1996–97	Oldham Ath	12	1		
1997–98	Oldham Ath	38	5		
1998–99	Oldham Ath	41	6		
1999–2000	Oldham Ath	43	4		
2000–01	Oldham Ath	40	8	174	24

EYRES, David (F) 471 97
H: 5 11 W: 11 06 b.Liverpool 26-2-64
Source: Rhyl.

1989–90	Blackpool	35	7		
1990–91	Blackpool	36	6		
1991–92	Blackpool	41	9		
1992–93	Blackpool	46	16	158	38
1993–94	Burnley	45	19		
1994–95	Burnley	39	8		
1995–96	Burnley	42	6		
1996–97	Burnley	36	3		
1997–98	Burnley	13	1	175	37
1997–98	Preston NE	28	4		
1998–99	Preston NE	34	8		
1999–2000	Preston NE	41	7		
2000–01	Preston NE	5	0	108	19
2000–01	Oldham Ath	30	3	30	3

FUTCHER, Ben (D) 10 0
H: 6 6 W: 12 02 b.Bradford 4-6-81
Source: Trainee.

1999–2000	Oldham Ath	5	0		
2000–01	Oldham Ath	5	0	10	0

GARNETT, Shaun (D) 324 17
H: 6 2 W: 13 01 b.Wallasey 22-11-69
Source: Trainee.

1987–88	Tranmere R	1	0		
1988–89	Tranmere R	4	0		
1989–90	Tranmere R	16	1		
1990–91	Tranmere R	8	0		
1992–93	Tranmere R	5	1		
1992–93	Chester C	9	0	9	0
1992–93	Preston NE	10	2	10	2
1992–93	Wigan Ath	13	1	13	1
1993–94	Tranmere R	26	2		
1994–95	Tranmere R	34	1		
1995–96	Tranmere R	18	0	112	5
1995–96	Swansea C	9	0		
1996–97	Swansea C	6	0	15	0
1996–97	Oldham Ath	23	1		
1997–98	Oldham Ath	34	3		
1998–99	Oldham Ath	37	2		
1999–2000	Oldham Ath	32	2		
2000–01	Oldham Ath	39	1	165	9

HOLT, Andy (D) 134 12
H: 6 1 W: 11 02 b.Manchester 21-5-78
Source: Trainee.

1996–97	Oldham Ath	1	0		
1997–98	Oldham Ath	14	1		
1998–99	Oldham Ath	43	5		
1999–2000	Oldham Ath	46	3		
2000–01	Oldham Ath	20	1	124	10
2000–01	Hull C	10	2	10	2

HOTTE, Mark (M) 65 0
H: 5 11 W: 11 00 b.Bradford 27-9-78
Source: Trainee.

1997–98	Oldham Ath	1	0		
1998–99	Oldham Ath	1	0		
1999–2000	Oldham Ath	35	0		
2000–01	Oldham Ath	28	0	65	0

INNES, Mark (D) 68 1
H: 5 10 W: 12 04 b.Bellshill 27-9-78
Source: Trainee.

1995–96	Oldham Ath	0	0		
1996–97	Oldham Ath	0	0		
1997–98	Oldham Ath	4	0		
1998–99	Oldham Ath	13	1		
1999–2000	Oldham Ath	21	0		
2000–01	Oldham Ath	30	0	68	1

JONES, Paul (D) 28 3
H: 6 1 W: 11 09 b.Liverpool 3-6-78
Source: Trainee.

1995–96	Tranmere R	0	0		
1996–97	Tranmere R	0	0		
1996–97	Blackpool	0	0		
From Barrow, Leigh RMI.					
1999–2000	Oldham Ath	16	1		
2000–01	Oldham Ath	12	2	28	3

KELLY, Gary (G) 496 0
H: 5 11 W: 12 08 b.Fulwood 3-8-66
Source: Apprentice. *Honours:* Eire Under-21, B.

1984–85	Newcastle U	0	0		
1985–86	Newcastle U	0	0		
1986–87	Newcastle U	3	0		
1987–88	Newcastle U	37	0		
1988–89	Newcastle U	9	0		
1988–89	Blackpool	5	0	5	0
1989–90	Newcastle U	4	0	53	0
1989–90	Bury	38	0		
1990–91	Bury	46	0		
1991–92	Bury	46	0		
1992–93	Bury	42	0		
1993–94	Bury	1	0		
1993–94	West Ham U	0	0		
1994–95	Bury	38	0		

1995–96	Bury	25	0	236	0
1996–97	Oldham Ath	42	0		
1997–98	Oldham Ath	26	0		
1998–99	Oldham Ath	45	0		
1999–2000	Oldham Ath	44	0		
2000–01	Oldham Ath	45	0	202	0

McLAUGHLIN, Gerard* (D) 0 0
H: 5 10 W: 12 00 b.Rutherglen 26-9-81
Source: Trainee.

1999–2000	Oldham Ath	0	0		
2000–01	Oldham Ath	0	0		

McNIVEN, Scott (D) 187 3
H: 5 10 W: 10 08 b.Leeds 27-5-78
Source: Trainee. *Honours:* Scotland Under-21.

1994–95	Oldham Ath	1	0		
1995–96	Oldham Ath	15	0		
1996–97	Oldham Ath	12	0		
1997–98	Oldham Ath	32	1		
1998–99	Oldham Ath	37	1		
1999–2000	Oldham Ath	45	1		
2000–01	Oldham Ath	45	0	187	3

MISKELLY, David (G) 5 0
H: 6 0 W: 12 02 b.Ards 3-9-79
Source: Trainee. *Honours:* Northern Ireland Under-21.

1997–98	Oldham Ath	0	0		
1998–99	Oldham Ath	1	0		
1999–2000	Oldham Ath	2	0		
2000–01	Oldham Ath	2	0	5	0

PHILLISKIRK, Tony* (F) 408 110
H: 6 2 W: 12 12 b.Sunderland 10-2-65
Source: Amateur. *Honours:* England Schools.

1983–84	Sheffield U	21	8		
1984–85	Sheffield U	23	2		
1985–86	Sheffield U	4	0		
1986–87	Sheffield U	6	1		
1986–87	Rotherham U	6	1	6	1
1987–88	Sheffield U	26	9	80	20
1988–89	Oldham Ath	10	1		
1988–89	Preston NE	14	6	14	6
1989–90	Bolton W	45	18		
1990–91	Bolton W	43	19		
1991–92	Bolton W	43	12		
1992–93	Bolton W	10	2	141	51
1992–93	Peterborough U	32	11		
1993–94	Peterborough U	11	4	43	15
1993–94	Burnley	19	7		
1994–95	Burnley	13	1		
1995–96	Burnley	8	1	40	9
1995–96	Carlisle U	3	1	3	1
1995–96	Cardiff C	28	4		
1996–97	Cardiff C	33	1		
1997–98	Cardiff C	0	0	61	5
1997–98	Macclesfield T	10	1	10	1
1998–99	Oldham Ath	0	0		
1999–2000	Oldham Ath	0	0		
2000–01	Oldham Ath	0	0	10	1

PRENDERVILLE, Barry# (D) 37 2
H: 6 0 W: 12 08 b.Dublin 16-10-76
Source: Trainee.

1994–95	Coventry C	0	0		
1995–96	Coventry C	0	0		
1996–97	Coventry C	0	0		
1997–98	Coventry C	0	0		
1998–99	Coventry C	0	0		
1998–99	Hibernian	13	2	13	2
1999–2000	St Patrick's Ath	15	0	15	0
2000–01	Oldham Ath	9	0	9	0

RICKERS, Paul (M) 237 18
H: 5 10 W: 11 04 b.Dewsbury 9-5-75
Source: Trainee.

1993–94	Oldham Ath	0	0		
1994–95	Oldham Ath	4	1		
1995–96	Oldham Ath	23	0		
1996–97	Oldham Ath	46	4		
1997–98	Oldham Ath	40	4		
1998–99	Oldham Ath	45	4		
1999–2000	Oldham Ath	41	3		
2000–01	Oldham Ath	38	2	237	18

RITCHIE, Andy* (F) 569 177
H: 5 11 W: 12 04 b.Manchester 28-11-60
Source: Apprentice. *Honours:* England Schools, Youth, Under-21.

1977–78	Manchester U	4	0		
1978–79	Manchester U	17	10		
1979–80	Manchester U	8	3		
1980–81	Manchester U	4	0	33	13
1980–81	Brighton & HA	26	5		
1981–82	Brighton & HA	39	13		
1982–83	Brighton & HA	24	5	89	23
1982–83	Leeds U	10	3		
1983–84	Leeds U	38	7		
1984–85	Leeds U	28	12		
1985–86	Leeds U	29	11		
1986–87	Leeds U	31	7	136	40

1987–88 Oldham Ath 36 19
1988–89 Oldham Ath 31 14
1989–90 Oldham Ath 38 15
1990–91 Oldham Ath 31 15
1991–92 Oldham Ath 14 3
1992–93 Oldham Ath 12 3
1993–94 Oldham Ath 22 1
1994–95 Oldham Ath 33 12
1995–96 Scarborough 37 8
1996–97 Scarborough 31 9 **68 17**
1996–97 Oldham Ath 10 0
1997–98 Oldham Ath 15 2
1998–99 Oldham Ath 1 0
1999–2000 Oldham Ath 0 0
2000–01 Oldham Ath 0 0 **243 84**

ROACH, Neville (F) 33 3
H: 5 11 W: 11 09 b.Reading 29-9-78
Source: Trainee.
1996–97 Reading 3 1
1997–98 Reading 8 0
1998–99 Reading 5 0 **16 1**
1998–99 Southend U 8 1
1999–2000 Southend U 8 1
2000–01 Southend U 0 0 **16 2**
2000–01 Oldham Ath 1 0 **1 0**

SALT, Philip (M) 22 0
H: 5 10 W: 11 02 b.Huddersfield 2-3-79
Source: Trainee.
1997–98 Oldham Ath 2 0
1998–99 Oldham Ath 9 0
1999–2000 Oldham Ath 5 0
2000–01 Oldham Ath 6 0 **22 0**

SHERIDAN, John (M) 552 81
H: 5 10 W: 11 12 b.Stretford 1-10-64
Source: Local. *Honours:* Eire Youth, Under-21, Under-23, B, 34 full caps, 5 goals.
1981–82 Leeds U 0 0
1982–83 Leeds U 27 2
1983–84 Leeds U 11 1
1984–85 Leeds U 42 6
1985–86 Leeds U 32 4
1986–87 Leeds U 40 15
1987–88 Leeds U 38 12
1988–89 Leeds U 40 7 **230 47**
1989–90 Nottingham F 0 0
1989–90 Sheffield W 27 2
1990–91 Sheffield W 46 10
1991–92 Sheffield W 24 6
1992–93 Sheffield W 25 3
1993–94 Sheffield W 20 3
1994–95 Sheffield W 36 1
1995–96 Sheffield W 17 0
1995–96 *Birmingham C* 2 0 **2 0**
1996–97 Sheffield W 2 0 **197 25**
1996–97 Bolton W 20 2
1997–98 Bolton W 12 0 **32 2**
From Doncaster R.
1998–99 Oldham Ath 30 2
1999–2000 Oldham Ath 36 1
2000–01 Oldham Ath 25 4 **91 7**

SUGDEN, Ryan (F) 21 1
H: 6 0 W: 12 07 b.Bradford 26-12-80
1998–99 Oldham Ath 2 0
1999–2000 Oldham Ath 17 1
2000–01 Oldham Ath 2 0 **21 1**

TIPTON, Matthew (F) 90 10
H: 5 10 W: 11 02 b.Bridgend 29-6-80
Source: Trainee. *Honours:* Wales Under-21.
1997–98 Oldham Ath 3 0
1998–99 Oldham Ath 28 2
1999–2000 Oldham Ath 29 3
2000–01 Oldham Ath 30 5 **90 10**

WALSH, Danny* (M) 2 0
H: 5 11 W: 12 03 b.Manchester 16-9-78
Source: Trainee.
1998–99 Oldham Ath 1 0
1999–2000 Oldham Ath 1 0
2000–01 Oldham Ath 0 0 **2 0**

WATSON, Mark‡ (D) 102 0
H: 6 0 W: 12 04 b.Vancouver 8-9-70
Honours: Canada 67 full caps, 3 goals.
1993–94 Watford 17 0
1994–95 Watford 1 0
1995–96 Watford 0 0 **18 0**
1997 Osters 4 0
1998 Osters 20 0 **24 0**
1998–99 Oxford U 23 0
1999–2000 Oxford U 35 0
2000–01 Oxford U 0 0 **58 0**
2000–01 Oldham Ath 2 0 **2 0**

WHITEHALL, Steve‡ (F) 357 112
H: 5 11 W: 11 09 b.Bromborough 8-12-66
Source: Southport.
1991–92 Rochdale 34 8
1992–93 Rochdale 42 14
1993–94 Rochdale 39 14
1994–95 Rochdale 42 10
1995–96 Rochdale 46 20
1996–97 Rochdale 35 9 **238 75**
1997–98 Mansfield T 43 24 **43 24**
1998–99 Oldham Ath 36 4
1999–2000 Oldham Ath 38 9
2000–01 Oldham Ath 2 0 **76 13**

Scholars
Chadderton, Daniel; Clark, Liam J; Davenport, Michael J; Donnelly, Anthony M; Doran, Joseph R; Duncan, Kevin; Griffin, Adam; Haining, William W; Hall, Colin AR; Hall, Daniel A; Lavery, Karl A; Leonoff, Toni J; McLean, Michael J; O'Grady, Paul JO; Oliver, Alun M; Otto, Alastair J; Robertson, Benjamin A; Robinson, Thomas J; Smith, Benjamin; Sutcliffe, Arren; Vernon, Scott M; Wademan, Gareth J; Whittle, Thomas J; Wright, Matthew

OXFORD U

ANTHROBUS, Steve* (F) 247 32
H: 6 2 W: 14 07 b.Lewisham 10-11-68
1986–87 Millwall 0 0
1987–88 Millwall 3 0
1988–89 Millwall 3 0
1989–90 Millwall 15 4 **21 4**
1989–90 *Southend U* 0 0
1989–90 Wimbledon 10 0
1990–91 Wimbledon 3 0
1991–92 Wimbledon 10 0
1992–93 Wimbledon 5 0
1993–94 Wimbledon 0 0
1993–94 *Peterborough U* 2 0 **2 0**
1994–95 Wimbledon 0 0 **28 0**
1994–95 *Chester C* 7 0 **7 0**
1995–96 Shrewsbury T 39 10
1996–97 Shrewsbury T 33 6 **72 16**
1996–97 Crewe Alex 10 0
1997–98 Crewe Alex 30 6
1998–99 Crewe Alex 21 3 **61 9**
1999–2000 Oxford U 36 2
2000–01 Oxford U 20 1 **56 3**

BEAUCHAMP, Joey (M) 409 67
H: 5 10 W: 12 07 b.Oxford 13-3-71
Source: Trainee.
1988–89 Oxford U 1 0
1989–90 Oxford U 3 0
1990–91 Oxford U 4 0
1991–92 Oxford U 27 7
1991–92 *Swansea C* 5 2 **5 2**
1992–93 Oxford U 44 7
1993–94 Oxford U 45 6
1994–95 West Ham U 0 0
1994–95 Swindon T 42 3
1995–96 Swindon T 3 0 **45 3**
1995–96 Oxford U 32 7
1996–97 Oxford U 45 7
1997–98 Oxford U 44 13
1998–99 Oxford U 37 4
1999–2000 Oxford U 34 4
2000–01 Oxford U 43 7 **359 62**

BROOKS, Jamie (M) 4 1
b.Oxford 12-8-83
Source: Scholar.
2000–01 Oxford U 4 1 **4 1**

COOK, Jamie‡ (F) 77 7
H: 5 10 W: 10 10 b.Oxford 2-8-79
Source: Trainee.
1997–98 Oxford U 20 2
1998–99 Oxford U 19 1
1999–2000 Oxford U 29 3
2000–01 Oxford U 9 1 **77 7**

FEAR, Peter* (M) 111 7
H: 5 10 W: 11 10 b.Sutton 10-9-73
Source: Trainee. *Honours:* England Under-21.
1992–93 Wimbledon 4 0
1993–94 Wimbledon 23 1
1994–95 Wimbledon 14 1
1995–96 Wimbledon 4 0
1996–97 Wimbledon 18 0
1997–98 Wimbledon 8 2
1998–99 Wimbledon 2 0 **73 4**
1999–2000 Oxford U 19 1
2000–01 Oxford U 19 2 **38 3**

FOLLAND, Robbie (F) 30 2
H: 5 9 W: 10 07 b.Swansea 16-9-79
Source: Trainee. *Honours:* Wales Under-21.
1997–98 Oxford U 2 0
1998–99 Oxford U 0 0
1999–2000 Oxford U 23 1
2000–01 Oxford U 5 1 **30 2**

FORD, Mike† (D) 486 31
H: 6 0 W: 12 12 b.Bristol 9-2-66
Source: Apprentice.
1983–84 Leicester C 0 0
From Devizes T
1984–85 Cardiff C 20 1
1985–86 Cardiff C 44 4
1986–87 Cardiff C 36 1
1987–88 Cardiff C 45 7
1988–89 Oxford U 10 1
1989–90 Oxford U 31 2
1990–91 Oxford U 28 1
1991–92 Oxford U 9 1
1992–93 Oxford U 44 4
1993–94 Oxford U 41 1
1994–95 Oxford U 18 0
1995–96 Oxford U 44 2
1996–97 Oxford U 42 4
1997–98 Oxford U 22 2
1998–99 Cardiff C 25 0
1999–2000 Cardiff C 26 0
2000–01 Cardiff C 0 0 **196 13**
2000–01 Oxford U 1 0 **290 18**

GLASS, Jimmy‡ (G) 114 1
H: 6 1 W: 13 04 b.Epsom 1-8-73
Source: Trainee.
1991–92 Crystal Palace 0 0
1992–93 Crystal Palace 0 0
1993–94 Crystal Palace 0 0
1994–95 Crystal Palace 0 0
1994–95 *Portsmouth* 3 0 **3 0**
1995–96 Crystal Palace 0 0
1995–96 Bournemouth 13 0
1996–97 Bournemouth 35 0
1997–98 Bournemouth 46 0 **94 0**
1998–99 Swindon T 3 0
1998–99 *Carlisle U* 3 1 **3 1**
1999–2000 Swindon T 8 0 **11 0**
1999–2000 Cambridge U 0 0
1999–2000 Brentford 2 0 **2 0**
2000–01 Oxford U 1 0 **1 0**

GRAY, Phil (F) 326 90
H: 5 9 W: 12 07 b.Belfast 2-10-68
Source: Apprentice. *Honours:* Northern Ireland Schools, Youth, Under-23, 26 full caps, 6 goals.
1986–87 Tottenham H 1 0
1987–88 Tottenham H 1 0
1988–89 Tottenham H 1 0
1989–90 Tottenham H 0 0
1989–90 *Barnsley* 3 0 **3 0**
1990–91 Tottenham H 6 0 **9 0**
1990–91 *Fulham* 3 0 **3 0**
1991–92 Luton T 14 3
1992–93 Luton T 45 19
1993–94 Sunderland 41 14
1994–95 Sunderland 42 12
1995–96 Sunderland 32 8 **115 34**
1996–97 Nancy 16 4 **16 4**
1996–97 Fortuna Sittard 12 1 **12 1**
1997–98 Luton T 17 2
1998–99 Luton T 35 8
1999–2000 Luton T 29 11 **140 43**
2000–01 Burnley 5 1 **5 1**
2000–01 Oxford U 23 7 **23 7**

HACKETT, Christopher (M) 18 2
H: 6 0 W: 11 06 b.Oxford 1-3-83
Source: Scholarship.
1999–2000 Oxford U 2 0
2000–01 Oxford U 16 2 **18 2**

HATSWELL, Wayne (D) 27 0
b.Swindon 8-2-79
Source: Forest Green R.
2000–01 Oxford U 27 0 **27 0**

HOLDER, Jorden§ (M) 2 0
b.Oxford 22-10-82
Source: Scholar.
2000–01 Oxford U 2 0 **2 0**

JARMAN, Lee* (D) 122 2
H: 6 3 W: 14 01 b.Cardiff 16-12-77
Source: Trainee. *Honours:* Wales Under-21.
1995–96 Cardiff C 32 0
1996–97 Cardiff C 32 0
1997–98 Cardiff C 23 0
1998–99 Cardiff C 6 1
1999–2000 Cardiff C 1 0 **94 1**
From Merthyr T.
1999–2000 Exeter C 7 0 **7 0**
2000–01 Oxford U 21 1 **21 1**

KING, Simon (D) 2 0
b.Oxford 11-4-83
Source: Scholar.
2000–01 Oxford U 2 0 **2 0**

KNIGHT, Richard (G)   56   0
H: 6 1   W: 14 00   b.Burton 3-8-79
Source: Burton Alb. *Honours:* England
Youth.

1997–98	Derby Co	0	0		
1998–99	Derby Co	0	0		
1998–99	*Carlisle U*	6	0	6	0
1999–2000	Derby Co	0	0		
1999–2000	*Birmingham C*	0	0		
1999–2000	*Hull C*	1	0	1	0
1999–2000	*Macclesfield T*	3	0	3	0
1999–2000	Oxford U	13	0		
2000–01	Oxford U	33	0	46	0

LILLEY, Derek (F)   273   69
H: 5 9   W: 11 10   b.Paisley 9-2-74
Source: Everton BC.

1991–92	Morton	25	3		
1992–93	Morton	22	4		
1993–94	Morton	38	5		
1994–95	Morton	35	16		
1995–96	Morton	35	14		
1996–97	Morton	25	15	180	57
1996–97	Leeds U	6	0		
1997–98	Leeds U	13	1		
1998–99	Leeds U	2	0	21	1
1998–99	*Bury*	5	1	5	1
1998–99	*Hearts*	4	1	4	1
1999–2000	Oxford U	44	7		
2000–01	Oxford U	19	2	63	9

(Transferred to Dundee U, January 2001).

LINIGHAN, Andy‡ (D)   598   30
H: 6 4   W: 13 10   b.Hartlepool 18-6-62
Source: Smiths BC. *Honours:* England B.

1980–81	Hartlepool U	6	0		
1981–82	Hartlepool U	17	0		
1982–83	Hartlepool U	45	3		
1983–84	Hartlepool U	42	1	110	4
1984–85	Leeds U	42	2		
1985–86	Leeds U	24	1	66	3
1985–86	Oldham Ath	15	1		
1986–87	Oldham Ath	40	3		
1987–88	Oldham Ath	32	2	87	6
1987–88	Norwich C	12	2		
1988–89	Norwich C	37	4		
1989–90	Norwich C	37	2	86	8
1990–91	Arsenal	10	0		
1991–92	Arsenal	17	0		
1992–93	Arsenal	21	2		
1993–94	Arsenal	21	0		
1994–95	Arsenal	20	2		
1995–96	Arsenal	18	0		
1996–97	Arsenal	11	1	118	5
1996–97	Crystal Palace	19	2		
1997–98	Crystal Palace	26	0		
1998–99	Crystal Palace	20	0		
1998–99	*QPR*	7	0	7	0
1999–2000	Crystal Palace	45	2		
2000–01	Crystal Palace	1	0	111	4
2000–01	Oxford U	13	0	13	0

McGOWAN, Neil‡ (D)   97   0
H: 5 8   W: 11 07   b.Glasgow 15-4-77
Source: Bonnyton Th.

1995–96	Stranraer	4	0	4	0
1996–97	Albion R	17	0		
1997–98	Albion R	12	0		
1998–99	Albion R	33	0	62	0
1999–2000	Oxford U	20	0		
2000–01	Oxford U	11	0	31	0

McGUCKIN, Ian (D)   167   0
H: 6 2   W: 14 01   b.Middlesbrough 24-4-73
Source: Trainee.

1991–92	Hartlepool U	7	0		
1992–93	Hartlepool U	14	1		
1993–94	Hartlepool U	35	2		
1994–95	Hartlepool U	34	3		
1995–96	Hartlepool U	40	2		
1996–97	Hartlepool U	22	0		
1997–98	Fulham	0	0		
1998–99	Fulham	0	0		
1998–99	*Hartlepool U*	8	0	160	8
1999–2000	Fulham	0	0		
2000–01	Oxford U	7	0	7	0

MURPHY, Matt# (M)   249   38
H: 6 0   W: 12 02   b.Northampton 20-8-71
Source: Corby T.

1992–93	Oxford U	2	0		
1993–94	Oxford U	0	0		
1994–95	Oxford U	22	7		
1995–96	Oxford U	34	5		
1996–97	Oxford U	30	3		
1997–98	Oxford U	29	2		
1997–98	*Scunthorpe U*	3	0	3	0
1998–99	Oxford U	43	4		
1999–2000	Oxford U	46	11		
2000–01	Oxford U	40	6	246	38

OMOYINMI, Emmanuel (M)   69   10
H: 5 7   W: 10 01   b.Nigeria 28-12-77
Source: Trainee. *Honours:* England Schools.

1994–95	West Ham U	0	0		
1995–96	West Ham U	0	0		
1996–97	West Ham U	1	0		
1996–97	*Bournemouth*	7	0	7	0
1997–98	West Ham U	5	2		
1997–98	*Dundee U*	4	0	4	0
1998–99	West Ham U	3	0		
1998–99	*Leyton Orient*	4	1	4	1
1999–2000	West Ham U	0	0	9	2
1999–2000	*Gillingham*	9	3	9	3
1999–2000	*Scunthorpe U*	6	1	6	1
1999–2000	*Barnet*	6	0	6	0
2000–01	Oxford U	24	3	24	3

PATTERSON, Darren (D)   220   8
H: 6 1   W: 12 10   b.Belfast 15-10-69
Source: Trainee. *Honours:* Northern Ireland
Under-21, 17 full caps, 1 goal.

1988–89	WBA	0	0		
1989–90	Wigan Ath	29	1		
1990–91	Wigan Ath	28	4		
1991–92	Wigan Ath	40	1	97	6
1992–93	Crystal Palace	0	0		
1993–94	Crystal Palace	0	0		
1994–95	Crystal Palace	22	1	22	1
1995–96	Luton T	23	0		
1996–97	Luton T	10	0		
1996–97	*Preston NE*	2	0	2	0
1997–98	Luton T	23	0	56	0
1998–99	Dundee U	19	0		
1999–2000	Dundee U	0	0		
2000–01	Dundee U	0	0	19	0
2000–01	*York C*	0	0		
2000–01	Oxford U	18	1	18	1

POWELL, Paul (M)   128   11
H: 5 8   W: 11 01   b.Wallingford 30-6-78
Source: Trainee.

1995–96	Oxford U	3	0		
1996–97	Oxford U	0	0		
1997–98	Oxford U	21	1		
1998–99	Oxford U	44	3		
1999–2000	Oxford U	40	6		
2000–01	Oxford U	20	1	128	11

QUINN, Robert (D)   145   5
H: 5 11   W: 11 02   b.Sidcup 8-11-76
Source: Trainee.

1994–95	Crystal Palace	0	0		
1995–96	Crystal Palace	1	0		
1996–97	Crystal Palace	21	0		
1997–98	Crystal Palace	1	0	23	1
1998–99	Brentford	43	2		
1999–2000	Brentford	44	0		
2000–01	Brentford	22	0	109	2
2000–01	Oxford U	13	2	13	2

RICHARDSON, Jon (D)   288   10
H: 6 1   W: 12 02   b.Nottingham 29-8-75
Source: Trainee.

1993–94	Exeter C	7	0		
1994–95	Exeter C	38	1		
1995–96	Exeter C	43	1		
1996–97	Exeter C	43	1		
1997–98	Exeter C	41	2		
1998–99	Exeter C	40	2		
1999–2000	Exeter C	35	1	247	8
2000–01	Oxford U	41	2	41	2

RICKETTS, Sam (D)   14   0
H: 6 1   W: 13 00   b.Aylesbury 11-10-81
Source: Trainee.

1999–2000	Oxford U	0	0		
2000–01	Oxford U	14	0	14	0

ROBERTSON, John‡ (D)   191   2
H: 6 0   W: 11 00   b.Irvine 28-3-76

1994–95	Stranraer	3	0		
1995–96	Stranraer	34	1		
1996–97	Stranraer	31	0	68	1
1997–98	Ayr U	31	0		
1998–99	Ayr U	21	1		
1999–2000	Ayr U	31	0	83	1
2000–01	Oxford U	40	0	40	0

SCOTT, Andy (F)   227   42
H: 6 1   W: 11 05   b.Epsom 2-8-72
Source: Sutton U.

1992–93	Sheffield U	2	1		
1993–94	Sheffield U	15	0		
1994–95	Sheffield U	37	4		
1995–96	Sheffield U	7	0		
1996–97	Sheffield U	8	1		
1996–97	*Chesterfield*	5	3	5	3
1996–97	*Bury*	8	0	8	0
1997–98	Sheffield U	6	0	75	6
1997–98	Brentford	26	5		
1998–99	Brentford	34	7		
1999–2000	Brentford	36	3		

SHEPHEARD, Jon (D)   7   0
H: 6 2   W: 12 04   b.Oxford 31-3-81
Source: Trainee.

1999–2000	Oxford U	2	0		
2000–01	Oxford U	5	0	7	0

TAIT, Paul (M)   250   17
H: 5 11   W: 11 10   b.Sutton Coldfield
31-7-71
Source: Trainee.

1987–88	Birmingham C	1	0		
1988–89	Birmingham C	10	0		
1989–90	Birmingham C	14	2		
1990–91	Birmingham C	17	3		
1991–92	Birmingham C	12	0		
1992–93	Birmingham C	28	2		
1993–94	Birmingham C	10	0		
1993–94	*Millwall*	0	0		
1994–95	Birmingham C	25	4		
1995–96	Birmingham C	27	3		
1996–97	Birmingham C	26	0		
1997–98	Birmingham C	0	0		
1997–98	*Northampton T*	3	0	3	0
1998–99	Birmingham C	0	0	170	14
1998–99	Oxford U	17	0		
1999–2000	Oxford U	34	0		
2000–01	Oxford U	26	3	77	3

WEATHERSTONE, Ross‡ (M)   4   0
H: 5 11   W: 11 10   b.Reading 16-5-81
Source: Trainee.

1999–2000	Oxford U	3	0		
2000–01	Oxford U	1	0	4	0

WEATHERSTONE, Simon‡ (F)   52   3
H: 5 10   W: 12 04   b.Reading 26-1-80
Source: Trainee.

1996–97	Oxford U	1	0		
1997–98	Oxford U	11	1		
1998–99	Oxford U	12	1		
1999–2000	Oxford U	21	1		
2000–01	Oxford U	7	0	52	3

WHITEHEAD, Dean (M)   20   0
H: 5 11   W: 12 01   b.Oxford 12-1-82
Source: Trainee.

1999–2000	Oxford U	0	0		
2000–01	Oxford U	20	0	20	0

WILSON, Philip§ (G)   2   0
b.Oxford 17-10-82
Source: Scholar.

2000–01	Oxford U	2	0	2	0

Scholars
Ciampoli, Dwight M; Cruse, Robert P;
Holder, Jorden A; Jones, Brynmor R;
Lovegrove, Robert T; McIntosh, Kelvin R;
Spence, Brynley J; Wilson, Philip J
Non-Contract
Ford, Michael P
**Player who does not hold a current contract
but whose registration has been retained by the
club**
Wickens, Gary J

PETERBOROUGH U

CAMPBELL, James‡ (D)   0   0
H: 6 2   W: 11 12   b.Kent 16-11-79
Source: Trainee.

1998–99	Peterborough U	0	0		
1999–2000	Peterborough U	0	0		
2000–01	Peterborough U	0	0		

CHAPPLE, Phil (D)   346   35
H: 6 2   W: 13 01   b.Norwich 21-11-66
Source: Apprentice.

1984–85	Norwich C	0	0		
1985–86	Norwich C	0	0		
1986–87	Norwich C	0	0		
1987–88	Norwich C	0	0		
1987–88	Cambridge U	6	1		
1988–89	Cambridge U	46	3		
1989–90	Cambridge U	45	5		
1990–91	Cambridge U	43	5		
1991–92	Cambridge U	29	3		
1992–93	Cambridge U	18	2	187	19
1993–94	Charlton Ath	44	5		
1994–95	Charlton Ath	21	2		
1995–96	Charlton Ath	16	2		
1996–97	Charlton Ath	26	2		
1997–98	Charlton Ath	35	4	142	15
1998–99	Peterborough U	1	0		
1999–2000	Peterborough U	16	1		
2000–01	Peterborough U	0	0	17	1

CLARKE, Andy (F) **259 41**
H: 5 10 W: 11 07 b.Islington 22-7-67
Source: Barnet.

1990–91	Wimbledon	12	3		
1991–92	Wimbledon	34	3		
1992–93	Wimbledon	33	5		
1993–94	Wimbledon	23	2		
1994–95	Wimbledon	25	1		
1995–96	Wimbledon	18	2		
1996–97	Wimbledon	11	1		
1997–98	Wimbledon	14	0		
1998–99	Wimbledon	0	0	**170**	**17**
1998–99	*Port Vale*	6	0	**6**	**0**
1998–99	*Northampton T*	4	0	**4**	**0**
1998–99	Peterborough U	0	0		
1999–2000	Peterborough U	37	15		
2000–01	Peterborough U	42	9	**79**	**24**

CONNOR, Dan (G) **3 0**
H: 6 2 W: 13 04 b.Dublin 31-1-81
Source: Trainee.

1997–98	Peterborough U	0	0		
1998–99	Peterborough U	2	0		
1999–2000	Peterborough U	1	0		
2000–01	Peterborough U	0	0	**3**	**0**

CULLEN, Jon (M) **110 22**
H: 6 0 W: 13 00 b.Durham 10-1-73
Source: Trainee.

1990–91	Doncaster R	1	0		
1991–92	Doncaster R	8	0		
1992–93	Doncaster R	0	0		
1993–94	Doncaster R	0	0	**9**	**0**
From Morpeth T					
1996–97	Hartlepool U	6	0		
1997–98	Hartlepool U	28	12	**34**	**12**
1997–98	Sheffield U	2	0		
1998–99	Sheffield U	2	0		
1999–2000	Sheffield U	0	0	**4**	**0**
1999–2000	*Shrewsbury T*	10	1	**10**	**1**
1999–2000	*Halifax T*	11	5	**11**	**5**
1999–2000	Peterborough U	13	3		
2000–01	Peterborough U	18	1	**31**	**4**
2000–01	*Carlisle U*	11	0	**11**	**0**

DANIELSSON, Helgi (M) **6 0**
H: 6 0 W: 12 00 b.Reykjavik 13-7-81
Source: Fylkir.

1998–99	Peterborough U	0	0		
1999–2000	Peterborough U	0	0		
2000–01	Peterborough U	6	0	**6**	**0**

EDWARDS, Andy (D) **386 13**
H: 6 2 W: 12 13 b.Epping 17-9-71
Source: Trainee.

1988–89	Southend U	1	0		
1989–90	Southend U	8	0		
1990–91	Southend U	2	1		
1991–92	Southend U	9	0		
1992–93	Southend U	41	0		
1993–94	Southend U	42	1		
1994–95	Southend U	44	3	**147**	**5**
1995–96	Birmingham C	37	1		
1996–97	Birmingham C	3	0	**40**	**1**
1996–97	Peterborough U	25	0		
1997–98	Peterborough U	46	2		
1998–99	Peterborough U	41	2		
1999–2000	Peterborough U	44	2		
2000–01	Peterborough U	43	1	**199**	**7**

FARRELL, Dave (M) **229 29**
H: 5 11 W: 11 08 b.Birmingham 11-11-71
Source: Redditch U.

1992–93	Aston Villa	2	0		
1992–93	*Scunthorpe U*	5	1	**5**	**1**
1993–94	Aston Villa	4	0		
1994–95	Aston Villa	0	0		
1995–96	Aston Villa	0	0	**6**	**0**
1995–96	Wycombe W	33	7		
1996–97	Wycombe W	27	1	**60**	**8**
1997–98	Peterborough U	42	6		
1998–99	Peterborough U	37	4		
1999–2000	Peterborough U	35	3		
2000–01	Peterborough U	44	7	**158**	**20**

FORINTON, Howard (F) **47 12**
H: 5 11 W: 12 04 b.Boston 18-9-75
Source: Yeovil T.

1997–98	Birmingham C	1	0		
1998–99	Birmingham C	3	1		
1998–99	*Plymouth Arg*	9	3	**9**	**3**
1999–2000	Birmingham C	1	0	**5**	**1**
1999–2000	Peterborough U	25	7		
2000–01	Peterborough U	8	1	**33**	**8**

FORSYTH, Richard (M) **164 21**
H: 5 11 W: 13 00 b.Dudley 3-10-70
Source: Kidderminster H.

1995–96	Birmingham C	26	2	**26**	**2**
1996–97	Stoke C	40	8		
1997–98	Stoke C	37	7		
1998–99	Stoke C	18	2	**95**	**17**
1999–2000	Blackpool	13	0	**13**	**0**
2000–01	Peterborough U	30	2	**30**	**2**

FRENCH, Daniel (M) **8 0**
H: 5 11 W: 11 00 b.Peterborough 25-11-79
Source: Trainee.

1998–99	Peterborough U	0	0		
1999–2000	Peterborough U	6	0		
2000–01	Peterborough U	2	0	**8**	**0**

GILL, Matthew (M) **65 2**
H: 5 11 W: 11 07 b.Cambridge 8-11-80
Source: Trainee.

1997–98	Peterborough U	2	0		
1998–99	Peterborough U	26	0		
1999–2000	Peterborough U	20	1		
2000–01	Peterborough U	17	1	**65**	**2**

GREEN, Francis (F) **63 9**
H: 5 9 W: 11 04 b.Derby 23-4-80
Source: Ilkeston T.

1997–98	Peterborough U	4	1		
1998–99	Peterborough U	7	1		
1999–2000	Peterborough U	20	1		
2000–01	Peterborough U	32	6	**63**	**9**

HALEY, Grant‡ (D) **1 0**
H: 5 8 W: 10 02 b.Bristol 20-9-79
Source: Trainee.

1998–99	Peterborough U	0	0		
1999–2000	Peterborough U	1	0		
2000–01	Peterborough U	0	0	**1**	**0**

HANLON, Ritchie (M) **48 3**
H: 6 1 W: 12 13 b.Kenton 25-5-78
Source: Chelsea Trainee.

1996–97	Southend U	2	0		
1997–98	Southend U	0	0	**2**	**0**
From Rushden & D.					
1998–99	Peterborough U	4	1		
From Welling U.					
1999–2000	Peterborough U	16	1		
2000–01	Peterborough U	26	1	**46**	**3**

HANN, Matthew‡ (F) **4 0**
H: 5 9 W: 10 04 b.Saffron Walden 6-9-80
Source: Trainee.

1998–99	Peterborough U	4	0		
1999–2000	Peterborough U	0	0		
2000–01	Peterborough U	0	0	**4**	**0**

HOOPER, Dean (D) **108 2**
H: 5 11 W: 12 06 b.Harefield 13-4-71
Source: Hayes.

1994–95	Swindon T	4	0		
From Hayes.					
1995–96	Swindon T	0	0		
1995–96	*Peterborough U*	4	0		
1996–97	Swindon T	0	0		
1997–98	Swindon T	0	0	**4**	**0**
From Kingstonian.					
1998–99	Peterborough U	38	2		
1999–2000	Peterborough U	29	0		
2000–01	Peterborough U	33	0	**104**	**2**

INMAN, Niall‡ (M) **12 2**
H: 5 9 W: 11 06 b.Wakefield 6-2-78
Source: Trainee. *Honours:* Eire Youth, Under-21.

1995–96	Peterborough U	1	0		
1996–97	Peterborough U	3	0		
1997–98	Peterborough U	4	1		
1998–99	Peterborough U	3	1		
1999–2000	Peterborough U	1	0		
2000–01	Peterborough U	0	0	**12**	**2**

JELLEYMAN, Gareth (D) **28 0**
H: 5 10 W: 10 03 b.Holywell 14-11-80
Source: Trainee. *Honours:* Wales Under-21.

1998–99	Peterborough U	0	0		
1999–2000	Peterborough U	20	0		
2000–01	Peterborough U	8	0	**28**	**0**

LEE, Jason (F) **329 68**
H: 6 3 W: 13 03 b.Newham 9-5-71
Source: Trainee.

1989–90	Charlton Ath	1	0		
1990–91	Charlton Ath	0	0		
1990–91	*Stockport Co*	2	0	**2**	**0**
1990–91	Lincoln C	17	3		
1991–92	Lincoln C	35	6		
1992–93	Lincoln C	41	12	**93**	**21**
1993–94	Southend U	24	3	**24**	**3**
1993–94	Nottingham F	13	2		
1994–95	Nottingham F	22	3		
1995–96	Nottingham F	28	8		
1996–97	Nottingham F	13	1	**76**	**14**
1996–97	*Charlton Ath*	8	3	**9**	**3**
1996–97	*Grimsby T*	7	1	**7**	**1**
1997–98	Watford	36	10		
1998–99	Watford	1	1	**37**	**11**
1998–99	Chesterfield	22	1		
1999–2000	Chesterfield	6	0	**28**	**1**
1999–2000	Peterborough U	23	6		
2000–01	Peterborough U	30	8	**53**	**14**

LEWIS, Neil (D) **101 1**
H: 5 8 W: 10 05 b.Wolverhampton 28-6-74
Source: Trainee.

1992–93	Leicester C	7	0		
1993–94	Leicester C	24	0		
1994–95	Leicester C	16	0		
1995–96	Leicester C	14	1		
1996–97	Leicester C	6	0	**67**	**1**
1997–98	Peterborough U	34	0		
1998–99	Peterborough U	0	0		
1999–2000	Peterborough U	0	0		
2000–01	Peterborough U	0	0	**34**	**0**

MACDONALD, Gary (M) **1 0**
H: 6 1 W: 12 00 b.Germany 25-10-79

1998–99	Portsmouth	0	0		
1999–2000	Portsmouth	0	0		
2000–01	Portsmouth	0	0		
From Havant & W.					
2000–01	Peterborough U	1	0	**1**	**0**

McKENZIE, Leon (F) **132 28**
H: 5 10 W: 10 03 b.Croydon 17-5-78
Source: Trainee.

1995–96	Crystal Palace	12	0		
1996–97	Crystal Palace	21	2		
1997–98	Crystal Palace	3	0		
1997–98	*Fulham*	3	0	**3**	**0**
1998–99	Crystal Palace	16	1		
1998–99	*Peterborough U*	14	8		
1999–2000	Crystal Palace	25	4		
2000–01	Crystal Palace	8	0	**85**	**7**
2000–01	Peterborough U	30	13	**44**	**21**

MURRAY, Dan (D) **5 0**
H: 6 2 W: 12 12 b.Cambridge 16-5-82
Source: Scholarship.

1999–2000	Peterborough U	2	0		
2000–01	Peterborough U	3	0	**5**	**0**

OLDFIELD, David (M) **490 70**
H: 6 1 W: 13 04 b.Perth (Aus) 30-5-68
Source: Apprentice. *Honours:* England Under-21.

1986–87	Luton T	0	0		
1987–88	Luton T	8	3		
1988–89	Luton T	21	1		
1988–89	Manchester C	11	3		
1989–90	Manchester C	15	3	**26**	**6**
1989–90	Leicester C	20	5		
1990–91	Leicester C	42	7		
1991–92	Leicester C	41	4		
1992–93	Leicester C	44	5		
1993–94	Leicester C	27	4		
1994–95	Leicester C	14	1	**188**	**26**
1994–95	*Millwall*	17	6	**17**	**6**
1995–96	Luton T	34	2		
1996–97	Luton T	38	6		
1997–98	Luton T	45	10	**146**	**22**
1998–99	Stoke C	46	6		
1999–2000	Stoke C	19	1	**65**	**7**
1999–2000	Peterborough U	9	0		
2000–01	Peterborough U	39	3	**48**	**3**

PEARCE, Dennis (D) **127 3**
H: 5 9 W: 11 07 b.Wolverhampton 10-9-74
Source: Trainee.

1993–94	Aston Villa	0	0		
1994–95	Aston Villa	0	0		
1995–96	Wolverhampton W	5	0		
1996–97	Wolverhampton W	4	0	**9**	**0**
1997–98	Notts Co	38	2		
1998–99	Notts Co	33	1		
1999–2000	Notts Co	20	0		
2000–01	Notts Co	27	0	**118**	**3**
2000–01	Peterborough U	0	0		

REA, Simon (D) **51 3**
H: 6 1 W: 13 00 b.Coventry 20-9-76
Source: Trainee.

1994–95	Birmingham C	0	0		
1995–96	Birmingham C	1	0		
1996–97	Birmingham C	0	0		
1997–98	Birmingham C	0	0		
1998–99	Birmingham C	0	0		
1999–2000	Birmingham C	0	0	**1**	**0**
1999–2000	Peterborough U	14	1		
2000–01	Peterborough U	36	2	**50**	**3**

SCOTT, Richard* (M) **198 25**
H: 5 11 W: 12 08 b.Dudley 29-9-74
Source: Trainee.

1992–93	Birmingham C	1	0		
1993–94	Birmingham C	6	0		
1994–95	Birmingham C	5	0	**12**	**0**
1994–95	Shrewsbury T	8	1		
1995–96	Shrewsbury T	36	6		
1996–97	Shrewsbury T	27	1		
1997–98	Shrewsbury T	34	10	**105**	**18**
1998–99	Peterborough U	27	4		
1999–2000	Peterborough U	34	3		
2000–01	Peterborough U	20	0	**81**	**7**

SHIELDS, Tony (M) 67 2
H: 5 8 W: 10 01 b.Derry 4-6-80
Source: Trainee.

Season	Club	App	Gls	Tot	
1997–98	Peterborough U	1	0		
1998–99	Peterborough U	9	0		
1999–2000	Peterborough U	24	1		
2000–01	Peterborough U	33	1	67	2

SHOWLER, Paul* (M) 186 33
H: 5 10 W: 11 00 b.Doncaster 10-10-66
Source: Sheffield W, Sunderland, Colne Dynamoes, Altrincham.

Season	Club	App	Gls	Tot	
1991–92	Barnet	39	7		
1992–93	Barnet	32	5	71	12
1993–94	Bradford C	32	5		
1994–95	Bradford C	23	2		
1995–96	Bradford C	33	8	88	15
1996–97	Luton T	23	6		
1997–98	Luton T	1	0		
1998–99	Luton T	3	0	27	6
1999–2000	Peterborough U	0	0		
2000–01	Peterborough U	0	0		

TYLER, Mark (G) 153 0
H: 5 11 W: 12 00 b.Norwich 2-4-77
Source: Trainee. Honours: England Youth.

Season	Club	App	Gls	Tot	
1994–95	Peterborough U	5	0		
1995–96	Peterborough U	0	0		
1996–97	Peterborough U	3	0		
1997–98	Peterborough U	46	0		
1998–99	Peterborough U	27	0		
1999–2000	Peterborough U	32	0		
2000–01	Peterborough U	40	0	153	0

WILLIAMS, Martin‡ (F) 205 31
H: 5 9 W: 11 12 b.Luton 12-7-73
Source: Leicester C Trainee.

Season	Club	App	Gls	Tot	
1991–92	Luton T	1	0		
1992–93	Luton T	22	1		
1993–94	Luton T	15	1		
1994–95	Luton T	2	0	40	2
1994–95	*Colchester U*	3	0	3	0
1995–96	Reading	15	1		
1996–97	Reading	29	3		
1997–98	Reading	29	6		
1998–99	Reading	26	11		
1999–2000	Reading	29	5		
2000–01	Reading	0	0	128	26
2000–01	Swindon T	19	2	19	2
2000–01	Peterborough U	15	1	15	1

Scholars
Bishop, James; Bowater, Graham J; Brewster, Jorden; Byrne, Matthew J; Cobb, Stuart D; De'ath, Frederick AB; Duncliffe, John P; Evans, Louie; Frew, Michael A; Hardy, Luke; Lang, Adam B; Last, Guy D; Lehtinen, Toni-Pekka; O'Flynn, John; Thomas, Bradley M; Vaughan, Jonathan R
Players who do not hold a current contract but their registrations have been retained by the club
Lewis, Neil A; McCormick, Charles

PLYMOUTH ARG

ADAMS, Steve (D) 18 0
H: 6 0 W: 12 00 b.Plymouth 25-9-80
Source: Trainee.

Season	Club	App	Gls	Tot	
1999–2000	Plymouth Arg	1	0		
2000–01	Plymouth Arg	17	0	18	0

BANCE, Daniel§ (D) 1 0
b.Plymouth 27-9-82
Source: Scholar.

Season	Club	App	Gls	Tot	
2000–01	Plymouth Arg	1	0	1	0

BARLOW, Martin* (M) 329 24
H: 5 7 W: 10 03 b.Barnstable 25-6-71
Source: Trainee.

Season	Club	App	Gls	Tot	
1988–89	Plymouth Arg	1	0		
1989–90	Plymouth Arg	1	0		
1990–91	Plymouth Arg	30	1		
1991–92	Plymouth Arg	28	3		
1992–93	Plymouth Arg	24	1		
1993–94	Plymouth Arg	26	2		
1994–95	Plymouth Arg	42	2		
1995–96	Plymouth Arg	28	5		
1996–97	Plymouth Arg	40	1		
1997–98	Plymouth Arg	42	4		
1998–99	Plymouth Arg	45	5		
1999–2000	Plymouth Arg	2	0		
2000–01	Plymouth Arg	20	0	329	24

BASTOW, Darren (M) 42 3
H: 5 11 W: 12 00 b.Torquay 22-12-81
Source: Trainee.

Season	Club	App	Gls	Tot	
1998–99	Plymouth Arg	29	2		
1999–2000	Plymouth Arg	13	1		
2000–01	Plymouth Arg	0	0	42	3

BESWETHERICK, John (D) 114 0
H: 5 11 W: 11 04 b.Liverpool 15-1-78
Source: Trainee.

Season	Club	App	Gls	Tot	
1996–97	Plymouth Arg	0	0		
1997–98	Plymouth Arg	2	0		
1998–99	Plymouth Arg	22	0		
1999–2000	Plymouth Arg	45	0		
2000–01	Plymouth Arg	45	0	114	0

BROAD, Joseph (M) 0 0
b.Bristol 24-8-82
Source: Trainee.

Season	Club	App	Gls
2000–01	Plymouth Arg	0	0

CONNOLLY, Paul§ (D) 1 0
b.Liverpool 29-9-83
Source: Scholar.

Season	Club	App	Gls	Tot	
2000–01	Plymouth Arg	1	0	1	0

ELLIOTT, Stuart* (D) 73 0
H: 5 8 W: 11 05 b.London 27-8-77
Source: Trainee.

Season	Club	App	Gls	Tot	
1995–96	Newcastle U	0	0		
1996–97	Newcastle U	0	0		
1996–97	Hull C	3	0	3	0
1997–98	Newcastle U	0	0		
1997–98	Swindon T	2	0	2	0
1998–99	Newcastle U	0	0		
1998–99	Gillingham	5	0	5	0
1998–99	Hartlepool U	5	0	5	0
1998–99	Wrexham	9	0	9	0
1999–2000	Newcastle U	0	0		
1999–2000	Bournemouth	8	0	8	0
1999–2000	Stockport Co	5	0	5	0
2000–01	Darlington	24	0	24	0
2000–01	Plymouth Arg	12	0	12	0

EVANS, Micky (F) 279 56
H: 6 0 W: 12 03 b.Plymouth 1-1-73
Source: Trainee. Honours: Eire 1 full cap.

Season	Club	App	Gls	Tot	
1990–91	Plymouth Arg	4	0		
1991–92	Plymouth Arg	13	0		
1992–93	Plymouth Arg	23	1		
1992–93	*Blackburn R*	0	0		
1993–94	Plymouth Arg	22	9		
1994–95	Plymouth Arg	23	4		
1995–96	Plymouth Arg	45	12		
1996–97	Plymouth Arg	33	12		
1996–97	Southampton	12	4		
1997–98	Southampton	10	0	22	4
1997–98	WBA	10	1		
1998–99	WBA	20	2		
1999–2000	WBA	33	3		
2000–01	WBA	0	0	63	6
2000–01	Bristol R	21	4	21	4
2000–01	Plymouth Arg	10	4	173	42

EVERS, Sean (M) 77 6
H: 5 9 W: 9 07 b.Hitchin 10-10-77
Source: Trainee.

Season	Club	App	Gls	Tot	
1995–96	Luton T	1	0		
1996–97	Luton T	1	0		
1997–98	Luton T	23	3		
1998–99	Luton T	27	3	52	6
1998–99	Reading	1	0		
1999–2000	Reading	17	0		
2000–01	Reading	0	0	18	0
2000–01	Plymouth Arg	7	0	7	0

FRIIO, David (M) 26 5
b.Thionville 17-2-73
Source: Epinal, Nimes, ASOA Valence.

Season	Club	App	Gls	Tot	
2000–01	Plymouth Arg	26	5	26	5

GRITTON, Martin (F) 42 7
H: 6 1 W: 12 02 b.Glasgow 1-6-78
Source: Porthleven.

Season	Club	App	Gls	Tot	
1999–2000	Plymouth Arg	2	0		
1999–2000	Plymouth Arg	30	6		
2000–01	Plymouth Arg	10	1	42	7

GUINAN, Stephen (F) 81 14
H: 6 1 W: 13 06 b.Birmingham 24-12-75
Source: Trainee.

Season	Club	App	Gls	Tot	
1992–93	Nottingham F	0	0		
1993–94	Nottingham F	0	0		
1994–95	Nottingham F	0	0		
1995–96	Nottingham F	2	0		
1995–96	*Darlington*	3	1	3	1
1996–97	Nottingham F	2	0		
1996–97	*Burnley*	6	0	6	0
1997–98	Nottingham F	2	0		
1997–98	*Crewe Alex*	3	0	3	0
1998–99	Nottingham F	0	0		
1998–99	*Halifax T*	12	2	12	2
1998–99	*Plymouth Arg*	11	7		
1999–2000	Nottingham F	1	0	7	0
1999–2000	Scunthorpe U	3	1	3	1
1999–2000	Cambridge U	6	0	6	0
1999–2000	Plymouth Arg	8	2		
2000–01	Plymouth Arg	22	1	41	10

HEATHCOTE, Mike* (D) 390 33
H: 6 2 W: 12 08 b.Durham 10-9-65
Source: Middlesbrough, Spennymoor U.

Season	Club	App	Gls	Tot	
1987–88	Sunderland	1	0		
1987–88	Halifax T	7	1	7	1
1988–89	Sunderland	0	0		
1989–90	Sunderland	8	0	9	0
1989–90	York C	3	0	3	0
1990–91	Shrewsbury T	39	6		
1991–92	Shrewsbury T	5	0	44	6
1991–92	Cambridge U	22	5		
1992–93	Cambridge U	42	2		
1993–94	Cambridge U	40	5		
1994–95	Cambridge U	24	1	128	13
1995–96	Plymouth Arg	44	4		
1996–97	Plymouth Arg	42	1		
1997–98	Plymouth Arg	36	4		
1998–99	Plymouth Arg	43	3		
1999–2000	Plymouth Arg	29	1		
2000–01	Plymouth Arg	5	0	199	13

HODGES, John* (G) 2 0
H: 6 0 W: 11 05 b.Leicester 22-1-80
Source: Trainee.

Season	Club	App	Gls	Tot	
1998–99	Leicester C	0	0		
1999–2000	Leicester C	0	0		
2000–01	Plymouth Arg	2	0	2	0

JAVARY, Jean-Philippe (M) 31 0
b.Montpellier 10-1-78

Season	Club	App	Gls	Tot	
1995–96	Montpellier	3	0		
1996–97	Montpellier	7	0		
1997–98	Montpellier	0	0	10	0
1998–99	Espanyol	0	0		
1999–2000	Raith R	11	0	11	0
2000–01	Brentford	6	0	6	0
2000–01	Plymouth Arg	4	0	4	0

LARRIEU, Romain# (G) 15 0
H: 6 4 W: 14 00 b.Mont-de-Marsan 31-8-76
Source: Montpellier, ASOA Valence.

Season	Club	App	Gls	Tot	
2000–01	Plymouth Arg	15	0	15	0

LEADBITTER, Chris* (M) 421 27
H: 5 9 W: 10 06 b.Middlesbrough 17-10-67
Source: Apprentice.

Season	Club	App	Gls	Tot	
1985–86	Grimsby T	0	0		
1986–87	Hereford U	6	0		
1987–88	Hereford U	30	1	36	1
1988–89	Cambridge U	31	6		
1989–90	Cambridge U	43	4		
1990–91	Cambridge U	39	1		
1991–92	Cambridge U	25	1		
1992–93	Cambridge U	38	6	176	18
1993–94	Bournemouth	27	0		
1994–95	Bournemouth	27	3	54	3
1995–96	Plymouth Arg	33	1		
1996–97	Plymouth Arg	26	1		
1997–98	Torquay U	26	1		
1998–99	Torquay U	37	1	63	2
1999–2000	Plymouth Arg	31	2		
2000–01	Plymouth Arg	9	0	92	3

McCALL, Steve† (M) 476 17
H: 5 11 W: 12 10 b.Carlisle 15-10-60
Source: Apprentice. Honours: England Youth, Under-21, B.

Season	Club	App	Gls	Tot	
1978–79	Ipswich T	0	0		
1979–80	Ipswich T	10	0		
1980–81	Ipswich T	31	1		
1981–82	Ipswich T	42	1		
1982–83	Ipswich T	42	4		
1983–84	Ipswich T	42	1		
1984–85	Ipswich T	31	0		
1985–86	Ipswich T	33	0		
1986–87	Ipswich T	26	0	257	7
1987–88	Sheffield W	5	0		
1988–89	Sheffield W	2	0		
1989–90	Sheffield W	3	0		
1989–90	*Carlisle U*	6	0	6	0
1990–91	Sheffield W	19	2		
1991–92	Sheffield W	0	0	29	2
1991–92	Plymouth Arg	9	1		
1992–93	Plymouth Arg	35	1		
1993–94	Plymouth Arg	45	2		
1994–95	Plymouth Arg	7	1		
1995–96	Plymouth Arg	4	0		
1996–97	Torquay U	24	0		
1997–98	Torquay U	27	1	51	2
1998–99	Plymouth Arg	17	0		
1999–2000	Plymouth Arg	16	1		
2000–01	Plymouth Arg	0	0	133	6

McCARTHY, Sean* (F) 521 166
H: 6 1 W: 12 05 b.Bridgend 12-9-67
Source: Bridgend. Honours: Wales B.

Season	Club	App	Gls	Tot	
1985–86	Swansea C	22	3		
1986–87	Swansea C	44	14		
1987–88	Swansea C	25	8	91	25
1988–89	Bradford C	38	8		
1989–90	Bradford C	32	11		
1990–91	Bradford C	42	13		

1991–92	Bradford C	29	16		
1992–93	Bradford C	42	17		
1993–94	Bradford C	18	14	131	60
1993–94	Oldham Ath	20	4		
1994–95	Oldham Ath	39	18		
1995–96	Oldham Ath	35	10		
1996–97	Oldham Ath	21	3		
1997–98	Oldham Ath	25	7	140	42
1997–98	*Bristol C*	7	1	7	1
1998–99	Plymouth Arg	16	3		
1999–2000	Plymouth Arg	29	6		
2000–01	Plymouth Arg	37	10	152	38

McCORMICK, Luke§ (G) 1 0
b.Coventry 15-8-83
Source: Scholar.

| 2000–01 | Plymouth Arg | 1 | 0 | 1 | 0 |

McGLINCHEY, Brian (D) 49 2
H: 5 8 W: 10 05 b.Derry 26-10-77
Source: Trainee. *Honours:* Northern Ireland Under-21.

1995–96	Manchester C	0	0		
1996–97	Manchester C	0	0		
1997–98	Manchester C	0	0		
1998–99	Port Vale	15	1	15	1
1999–2000	Gillingham	13	1		
2000–01	Gillingham	1	0	14	1
2000–01	Plymouth Arg	20	0	20	0

McGREGOR, Paul* (F) 121 25
H: 5 10 W: 11 06 b.Liverpool 17-12-74
Source: Trainee.

1991–92	Nottingham F	0	0		
1992–93	Nottingham F	0	0		
1993–94	Nottingham F	0	0		
1994–95	Nottingham F	11	1		
1995–96	Nottingham F	14	2		
1996–97	Nottingham F	5	0		
1997–98	Nottingham F	0	0		
1998–99	Nottingham F	0	0	30	3
1998–99	*Carlisle U*	10	3	10	3
1998–99	Preston NE	4	0	4	0
1999–2000	Plymouth Arg	44	13		
2000–01	Plymouth Arg	33	6	77	19

MEAKER, Michael* (M) 149 6
H: 5 11 W: 12 12 b.Greenford 18-8-71
Source: Trainee. *Honours:* Wales Under-21.

1989–90	QPR	0	0		
1990–91	QPR	8	0		
1991–92	QPR	1	0		
1991–92	*Plymouth Arg*	4	0		
1992–93	QPR	3	0		
1993–94	QPR	14	1		
1994–95	QPR	8	0	34	1
1995–96	Reading	21	0		
1996–97	Reading	25	1		
1997–98	Reading	21	1	67	2
1998–99	Bristol R	20	2		
1999–2000	Bristol R	2	0		
1999–2000	*Swindon T*	6	0	6	0
2000–01	Bristol R	5	0	27	2
2000–01	Plymouth Arg	11	1	15	1

MORRISON-HILL, Jamie‡ (M) 1 0
H: 5 8 W: 10 04 b.Plymouth 8-6-81
Source: Trainee.

| 1999–2000 | Plymouth Arg | 1 | 0 | | |
| 2000–01 | Plymouth Arg | 0 | 0 | 1 | 0 |

NANCEKIVELL, Kevin‡ (F) 6 1
b.Barnstaple 22-10-71
Source: Tiverton T.

| 2000–01 | Plymouth Arg | 6 | 1 | 6 | 1 |

O'SULLIVAN, Wayne* (M) 259 10
H: 5 7 W: 10 11 b.Akrotiri 25-2-74
Source: Trainee.

1992–93	Swindon T	0	0		
1993–94	Swindon T	0	0		
1994–95	Swindon T	30	0		
1995–96	Swindon T	34	3		
1996–97	Swindon T	25	0		
1997–98	Swindon T	0	0	89	3
1997–98	Cardiff C	43	2		
1998–99	Cardiff C	42	2	85	4
1999–2000	Plymouth Arg	45	2		
2000–01	Plymouth Arg	40	1	85	3

PEAKE, Jason‡ (M) 269 23
H: 5 11 W: 12 13 b.Leicester 29-9-71
Source: Trainee. *Honours:* England Schools, Youth.

1989–90	Leicester C	0	0		
1990–91	Leicester C	8	1		
1991–92	Leicester C	0	0		
1991–92	*Hartlepool U*	6	1	6	1
1992–93	Halifax T	33	1	33	1
1993–94	Rochdale	10	0		
1994–95	Rochdale	39	2		
1995–96	Rochdale	46	4		
1996–97	Brighton & HA	30	1		
1997–98	Brighton & HA	0	0	30	1

1997–98	Bury	6	0	6	0
1998–99	Rochdale	38	5		
1999–2000	Rochdale	43	6	176	17
2000–01	Plymouth Arg	10	2	10	2

PHILLIPS, Lee‡ (F) 50 1
H: 5 10 W: 12 00 b.Penzance 16-9-80
Source: School.

1996–97	Plymouth Arg	2	0		
1997–98	Plymouth Arg	10	0		
1998–99	Plymouth Arg	15	1		
1999–2000	Plymouth Arg	17	0		
2000–01	Plymouth Arg	6	0	50	1

PHILLIPS, Martin (M) 146 7
H: 5 8 W: 10 03 b.Exeter 13-3-76
Source: Trainee.

1992–93	Exeter C	6	0		
1993–94	Exeter C	9	0		
1994–95	Exeter C	24	2		
1995–96	Exeter C	13	3		
1995–96	Manchester C	11	0		
1996–97	Manchester C	4	0		
1997–98	Manchester C	0	0		
1997–98	*Scunthorpe U*	3	0	3	0
1997–98	*Exeter C*	8	0	60	5
1998–99	Manchester C	0	0	15	0
1998–99	Portsmouth	17	1		
1998–99	*Bristol R*	2	0	2	0
1999–2000	Portsmouth	7	0	24	1
2000–01	Plymouth Arg	42	1	42	1

SHEFFIELD, Jon (G) 316 0
H: 5 11 W: 11 06 b.Bedworth 1-2-69
Source: Apprentice.

1986–87	Norwich C	0	0		
1987–88	Norwich C	0	0		
1988–89	Norwich C	1	0		
1989–90	Norwich C	0	0		
1989–90	*Aldershot*	11	0		
1989–90	*Ipswich T*	0	0		
1990–91	Norwich C	0	0	1	0
1990–91	*Aldershot*	15	0	26	0
1990–91	*Cambridge U*	2	0		
1991–92	Cambridge U	13	0		
1992–93	Cambridge U	13	0		
1993–94	Cambridge U	0	0		
1993–94	*Colchester U*	6	0	6	0
1993–94	*Swindon T*	2	0	2	0
1994–95	Cambridge U	28	0	56	0
1994–95	*Hereford U*	8	0	8	0
1995–96	Peterborough U	46	0		
1996–97	Peterborough U	16	0	62	0
1996–97	*Watford*	0	0		
1996–97	*Oldham Ath*	0	0		
1997–98	Plymouth Arg	46	0		
1998–99	Plymouth Arg	39	0		
1999–2000	Plymouth Arg	41	0		
2000–01	Plymouth Arg	29	0	155	0

STONEBRIDGE, Ian (F) 62 20
H: 6 0 W: 11 04 b.Lewisham 30-8-81
Source: Tottenham H Trainee. *Honours:* England Youth.

| 1999–2000 | Plymouth Arg | 31 | 9 | | |
| 2000–01 | Plymouth Arg | 31 | 11 | 62 | 20 |

TAYLOR, Craig (D) 141 9
H: 6 1 W: 12 03 b.Plymouth 24-1-74
Source: Dorchester T.

1996–97	Swindon T	0	0		
1997–98	Swindon T	32	2		
1998–99	Swindon T	21	0		
1998–99	*Plymouth Arg*	6	1		
1999–2000	Swindon T	2	0	55	2
1999–2000	Plymouth Arg	41	3		
2000–01	Plymouth Arg	39	3	86	7

TRUDGIAN, Ryan§ (M) 1 0
b.Truro 15-9-83
Source: Scholar.

| 2000–01 | Plymouth Arg | 1 | 0 | 1 | 0 |

WILKIE, Lee (D) 35 0
H: 6 4 W: 13 00 b.Dundee 20-4-80
Source: Downfield J. *Honours:* Scotland Under-21.

1999–2000	Dundee	24	0		
2000–01	Dundee	9	0	33	0
2000–01	Plymouth Arg	2	0	2	0

WILLS, Kevin (F) 14 1
H: 5 7 W: 10 04 b.Torbay 15-10-80
Source: Trainee.

1998–99	Plymouth Arg	2	0		
1999–2000	Plymouth Arg	2	0		
2000–01	Plymouth Arg	10	1	14	1

WORRELL, David (D) 31 0
H: 5 11 W: 12 04 b.Dublin 12-1-78
Source: Trainee. *Honours:* Eire Youth, Under-21.

| 1994–95 | Blackburn R | 0 | 0 | | |
| 1995–96 | Blackburn R | 0 | 0 | | |

1996–97	Blackburn R	0	0		
1997–98	Blackburn R	0	0		
1998–99	Blackburn R	0	0		
1998–99	Dundee U	4	0		
1999–2000	Dundee U	13	0	17	0
2000–01	Plymouth Arg	14	0	14	0

WOTTON, Paul (D) 152 7
H: 5 11 W: 11 08 b.Plymouth 17-8-77
Source: Trainee.

1994–95	Plymouth Arg	7	0		
1995–96	Plymouth Arg	1	0		
1996–97	Plymouth Arg	9	1		
1997–98	Plymouth Arg	34	1		
1998–99	Plymouth Arg	36	1		
1999–2000	Plymouth Arg	23	0		
2000–01	Plymouth Arg	42	4	152	7

Scholars

Baker, Paul M; Bance, Daniel R; Connolly, Paul; Curtis, Karl G; Edwards, Darren P; McCormick, Luke M; McGowan, Jamie P; McGowan, Matthew J; Sundercombe, Thomas J; Teagle, Robin D; Trudgian, Ryan

PORTSMOUTH

ALLEN, Rory (F) 44 11
H: 5 11 W: 11 10 b.Beckenham 17-10-77
Source: Trainee. *Honours:* England Under-21.

1995–96	Tottenham H	0	0		
1996–97	Tottenham H	12	2		
1997–98	Tottenham H	4	0		
1997–98	*Luton T*	8	6	8	6
1998–99	Tottenham H	5	0	21	2
1999–2000	Portsmouth	15	3		
2000–01	Portsmouth	0	0	15	3

AWFORD, Andy‡ (D) 313 3
H: 5 9 W: 11 09 b.Worcester 14-7-72
Source: Worcester C. *Honours:* England Schools, Youth, Under-21, Football League.

1988–89	Portsmouth	4	0		
1989–90	Portsmouth	0	0		
1990–91	Portsmouth	14	0		
1991–92	Portsmouth	45	0		
1992–93	Portsmouth	44	0		
1993–94	Portsmouth	35	0		
1994–95	Portsmouth	4	0		
1995–96	Portsmouth	18	1		
1996–97	Portsmouth	39	0		
1997–98	Portsmouth	39	0		
1998–99	Portsmouth	35	1		
1999–2000	Portsmouth	34	1		
2000–01	Portsmouth	2	0	313	3

BARNETT, Philip* (M) 0 0
b.Liverpool 2-9-81
Source: Trainee.

| 2000–01 | Portsmouth | 0 | 0 | | |

BRADBURY, Lee (F) 221 56
H: 6 2 W: 13 10 b.Isle of Wight 3-7-75
Source: Cowes. *Honours:* England Under-21.

1995–96	Portsmouth	12	0		
1995–96	*Exeter C*	14	5	14	5
1996–97	Portsmouth	42	15		
1997–98	Manchester C	27	7		
1998–99	Manchester C	13	3	40	10
1998–99	Crystal Palace	22	4		
1998–99	*Birmingham C*	7	0	7	0
1999–2000	Crystal Palace	10	2	32	6
1999–2000	Portsmouth	35	10		
2000–01	Portsmouth	39	10	128	35

BRADY, Garry# (M) 34 0
H: 5 10 W: 11 02 b.Glasgow 7-9-76
Source: Trainee.

1993–94	Tottenham H	0	0		
1994–95	Tottenham H	0	0		
1995–96	Tottenham H	0	0		
1996–97	Tottenham H	0	0		
1997–98	Tottenham H	9	0	9	0
1998–99	Newcastle U	9	0		
1999–2000	Newcastle U	0	0		
1999–2000	*Norwich C*	6	0		
2000–01	Newcastle U	0	0	9	0
2000–01	*Norwich C*	2	0	8	0
2000–01	Portsmouth	8	0	8	0

BUXTON, Lewis (M) 0 0
b.Newport (IW) 10-12-83
Source: School.

| 2000–01 | Portsmouth | 0 | 0 | | |

CLARIDGE, Steve (F) 493 158
H: 5 9 W: 12 09 b.Portsmouth 10-4-66
Source: Portsmouth, Fareham T.

| 1984–85 | Bournemouth | 6 | 1 | | |
| 1985–86 | Bournemouth | 1 | 0 | 7 | 1 |

From Weymouth

1988–89 Crystal Palace 0 0
1988–89 Aldershot 37 9
1989–90 Aldershot 25 10 **62 19**
1989–90 Cambridge U 20 4
1990–91 Cambridge U 30 12
1991–92 Cambridge U 29 12
1992–93 Luton T 16 2 **16 2**
1992–93 Cambridge U 29 7
1993–94 Cambridge U 24 11 **132 46**
1993–94 Birmingham C 18 7
1994–95 Birmingham C 42 20
1995–96 Birmingham C 28 8 **88 35**
1995–96 Leicester C 14 5
1996–97 Leicester C 32 11
1997–98 Leicester C 17 0 **63 16**
1997–98 *Portsmouth* 10 2
1997–98 Wolverhampton W 5 0 **5 0**
1998–99 Portsmouth 39 9
1999–2000 Portsmouth 34 14
2000–01 Portsmouth 31 11 **114 36**
2000–01 *Millwall* 6 3 **6 3**

COOPER, Shaun (M) 0 0
b.Isle of Wight 5-10-83
Source: School.
2000–01 Portsmouth 0 0

CROWE, Jason (D) 65 0
H: 5 9 W: 11 02 b.Sidcup 30-9-78
Source: Trainee. *Honours:* England Schools, Youth.
1995–96 Arsenal 0 0
1996–97 Arsenal 0 0
1997–98 Arsenal 0 0
1998–99 Arsenal 0 0
1998–99 *Crystal Palace* 8 0 **8 0**
1999–2000 Portsmouth 25 0
2000–01 Portsmouth 23 0 **48 0**
2000–01 *Brentford* 9 0 **9 0**

CUNDY, Jason‡ (D) 144 8
H: 6 0 W: 13 11 b.Wimbledon 12-11-69
Source: Trainee. *Honours:* England Under-21.
1988–89 Chelsea 0 0
1989–90 Chelsea 0 0
1990–91 Chelsea 29 0
1991–92 Chelsea 12 1 **41 1**
1991–92 *Tottenham H* 10 0
1992–93 Tottenham H 15 1
1993–94 Tottenham H 0 0
1994–95 Tottenham H 0 0
1995–96 Tottenham H 1 0
1995–96 *Crystal Palace* 4 0 **4 0**
1996–97 Tottenham H 0 0 **26 1**
1996–97 *Bristol C* 6 1 **6 1**
1996–97 Ipswich T 13 2
1997–98 Ipswich T 41 3
1998–99 Ipswich T 4 0 **58 5**
1999–2000 Portsmouth 9 0
2000–01 Portsmouth 0 0 **9 0**

CURTIS, Tom (M) 244 12
H: 5 8 W: 10 08 b.Exeter 1-3-73
Source: School.
1991–92 Derby Co 0 0
1992–93 Derby Co 0 0
1993–94 Chesterfield 36 3
1994–95 Chesterfield 40 2
1995–96 Chesterfield 46 0
1996–97 Chesterfield 40 3
1997–98 Chesterfield 36 1
1998–99 Chesterfield 24 3
1999–2000 Chesterfield 18 0 **240 12**
2000–01 Portsmouth 4 0 **4 0**

DERRY, Shaun (M) 188 5
H: 5 10 W: 13 02 b.Nottingham 6-12-77
Source: Trainee.
1995–96 Notts Co 12 0
1996–97 Notts Co 39 2
1997–98 Notts Co 28 2 **79 4**
1997–98 Sheffield U 12 0
1998–99 Sheffield U 26 0
1999–2000 Sheffield U 34 0 **72 0**
1999–2000 Portsmouth 9 1
2000–01 Portsmouth 28 0 **37 1**

EDINBURGH, Justin (D) 278 1
H: 5 10 W: 12 01 b.Basildon 18-12-69
Source: Trainee.
1988–89 Southend U 15 0
1989–90 Southend U 22 0 **37 0**
1989–90 *Tottenham H* 0 0
1990–91 Tottenham H 16 1
1991–92 Tottenham H 23 0
1992–93 Tottenham H 32 0
1993–94 Tottenham H 25 0
1994–95 Tottenham H 31 0
1995–96 Tottenham H 22 0
1996–97 Tottenham H 24 0
1997–98 Tottenham H 16 0
1998–99 Tottenham H 16 0
1999–2000 Tottenham H 8 0 **213 1**
1999–2000 Portsmouth 11 0
2000–01 Portsmouth 17 0 **28 0**

FLAHAVAN, Aaron (G) 93 0
H: 6 1 W: 11 12 b.Southampton 15-12-75
Source: Trainee.
1993–94 Portsmouth 0 0
1994–95 Portsmouth 0 0
1995–96 Portsmouth 0 0
1996–97 Portsmouth 24 0
1997–98 Portsmouth 26 0
1998–99 Portsmouth 13 0
1999–2000 Portsmouth 10 0
2000–01 Portsmouth 20 0 **93 0**

GRIFFITHS, Ben (D) 0 0
b.Bournemouth 27-11-81
Source: Trainee.
1999–2000 Portsmouth 0 0
2000–01 Portsmouth 0 0

HARPER, Kevin (F) 173 21
H: 5 7 W: 12 00 b.Oldham 15-1-76
Source: Hutcheson Vale BC. *Honours:* Scotland Under-21.
1993–94 Hibernian 2 0
1994–95 Hibernian 23 5
1995–96 Hibernian 16 3
1996–97 Hibernian 26 5
1997–98 Hibernian 27 1
1998–99 Hibernian 2 1 **96 15**
1998–99 Derby Co 27 1
1999–2000 Derby Co 5 0 **32 1**
1999–2000 *Walsall* 9 1 **9 1**
1999–2000 Portsmouth 12 2
2000–01 Portsmouth 24 2 **36 4**

HILEY, Scott# (D) 342 12
H: 5 8 W: 11 08 b.Plymouth 27-9-68
Source: Trainee.
1986–87 Exeter C 0 0
1987–88 Exeter C 15 1
1988–89 Exeter C 37 5
1989–90 Exeter C 46 0
1990–91 Exeter C 46 2
1991–92 Exeter C 33 1
1992–93 Exeter C 33 3 **210 12**
1992–93 Birmingham C 7 0
1993–94 Birmingham C 28 0
1994–95 Birmingham C 9 0
1995–96 Birmingham C 5 0 **49 0**
1995–96 Manchester C 6 0
1996–97 Manchester C 3 0
1997–98 Manchester C 0 0 **9 0**
1998–99 Southampton 29 0
1999–2000 Southampton 3 0 **32 0**
1999–2000 Portsmouth 8 0
2000–01 Portsmouth 34 0 **42 0**

HOLBROOK, Adam‡ (D) 0 0
H: 5 9 W: 11 06 b.Newport (IW) 17-10-80
Source: Trainee.
1998–99 Portsmouth 0 0
1999–2000 Portsmouth 0 0
2000–01 Portsmouth 0 0

HUGHES, Ceri (M) 240 20
H: 5 10 W: 12 07 b.Pontypridd 26-2-71
Source: Trainee. *Honours:* Wales Youth, Under-21, 8 full caps.
1989–90 Luton T 1 0
1990–91 Luton T 17 1
1991–92 Luton T 18 0
1992–93 Luton T 29 2
1993–94 Luton T 42 7
1994–95 Luton T 9 2
1995–96 Luton T 23 1
1996–97 Luton T 36 4 **175 17**
1997–98 Wimbledon 17 1
1998–99 Wimbledon 14 0
1999–2000 Wimbledon 0 0 **31 1**
1999–2000 Portsmouth 15 2
2000–01 Portsmouth 19 0 **34 2**

LOVELL, Stephen (F) 25 2
H: 5 11 W: 11 08 b.Amersham 6-12-80
Source: Trainee.
1998–99 Bournemouth 7 0
1999–2000 Bournemouth 1 0 **8 0**
1999–2000 Portsmouth 3 0
1999–2000 *Exeter C* 5 1 **5 1**
2000–01 Portsmouth 9 1 **12 1**

McNAB, Joe‡ (M) 0 0
H: 5 4 W: 9 00 b.Brighton 29-10-80
Source: Manchester C Trainee.
1998–99 Portsmouth 0 0
1999–2000 Portsmouth 0 0
2000–01 Portsmouth 0 0

McNAB, Neil‡ (M) 0 0
H: 5 6 W: 10 03 b.Brighton 29-10-80
Source: Manchester C Trainee.
1998–99 Portsmouth 0 0
1999–2000 Portsmouth 0 0
2000–01 Portsmouth 0 0

MIGLIORANZI, Stefani (M) 32 2
H: 6 1 W: 12 12 b.Pacos de Caldas 20-9-77
Source: St Johns Univ.
1998–99 Portsmouth 7 0
1999–2000 Portsmouth 13 2
2000–01 Portsmouth 12 0 **32 2**

MILLS, Lee (F) 242 76
H: 6 2 W: 12 09 b.Mexborough 10-7-70
Source: Stocksbridge PS.
1992–93 Wolverhampton W 0 0
1993–94 Wolverhampton W 14 1
1994–95 Wolverhampton W 11 1 **25 2**
1994–95 Derby Co 16 7 **16 7**
1995–96 Port Vale 32 8
1996–97 Port Vale 35 13
1997–98 Port Vale 42 14 **109 35**
1998–99 Bradford C 44 23
1999–2000 Bradford C 21 5 **65 28**
1999–2000 *Manchester C* 3 0 **3 0**
2000–01 Portsmouth 24 4 **24 4**

MOORE, Darren (D) 298 20
H: 6 3 W: 15 08 b.Birmingham 22-4-74
Source: Trainee.
1991–92 Torquay U 5 1
1992–93 Torquay U 31 2
1993–94 Torquay U 37 2
1994–95 Torquay U 30 3 **103 8**
1995–96 Doncaster R 35 2
1996–97 Doncaster R 41 5 **76 7**
1997–98 Bradford C 18 0
1998–99 Bradford C 44 3
1999–2000 Bradford C 0 0 **62 3**
1999–2000 Portsmouth 25 1
2000–01 Portsmouth 32 1 **57 2**

NIGHTINGALE, Luke (F) 45 4
H: 5 11 W: 11 07 b.Portsmouth 22-12-80
Source: Trainee.
1998–99 Portsmouth 19 3
1999–2000 Portsmouth 7 0
2000–01 Portsmouth 19 1 **45 4**

O'NEIL, Gary (M) 11 1
H: 5 10 W: 11 00 b.Beckenham 18-5-83
Source: Scholar.
1999–2000 Portsmouth 1 0
2000–01 Portsmouth 10 1 **11 1**

PANOPOULOS, Mike (M) 74 10
H: 6 1 W: 12 10 b.Melbourne 9-10-76
Source: Heidelberg 8 apps. *Honours:* Australia Youth.
1998–99 Aris Salonika 22 3 **22 3**
1999–2000 Portsmouth 22 1
2000–01 Portsmouth 30 6 **52 7**

PETTEFER, Carl (M) 1 0
H: 5 7 W: 10 02 b.Taplow 22-3-81
Source: Trainee.
1998–99 Portsmouth 0 0
1999–2000 Portsmouth 0 0
2000–01 Portsmouth 1 0 **1 0**

PETTERSON, Andy (G) 145 0
H: 6 2 W: 15 02 b.Fremantle 29-9-69
1988–89 Luton T 0 0
1988–89 *Swindon T* 0 0
1989–90 Luton T 0 0
1990–91 Luton T 0 0
1991–92 Luton T 0 0
1991–92 *Ipswich T* 0 0
1992–93 Luton T 14 0
1992–93 *Ipswich T* 1 0
1993–94 Luton T 5 0 **19 0**
1994–95 Charlton Ath 9 0
1994–95 *Bradford C* 3 0 **3 0**
1995–96 Charlton Ath 9 0
1995–96 *Ipswich T* 1 0 **2 0**
1995–96 *Plymouth Arg* 6 0 **6 0**
1995–96 *Colchester U* 5 0 **5 0**
1996–97 Charlton Ath 21 0
1997–98 Charlton Ath 23 0
1998–99 Charlton Ath 10 0 **72 0**
1998–99 Portsmouth 13 0
1999–2000 Portsmouth 17 0
1999–2000 *Wolverhampton W* 0 0
2000–01 Portsmouth 2 0 **32 0**
2000–01 *Torquay U* 6 0 **6 0**

PRIMUS, Linvoy (D) 249 8
H: 6 0 W: 12 04 b.Forest Gate 14-9-73
Source: Trainee.
1992–93 Charlton Ath 4 0
1993–94 Charlton Ath 0 0 **4 0**
1994–95 Barnet 39 0

1995–96	Barnet	42	4		
1996–97	Barnet	46	3	127	7
1997–98	Reading	36	1		
1998–99	Reading	31	0		
1999–2000	Reading	28	0	95	1
2000–01	Portsmouth	23	0	23	0

QUASHIE, Nigel (M) **132 10**
H: 5 9 W: 12 08 b.Nunhead 20-7-78
Source: Trainee. *Honours:* England Youth, Under-21, B.

1995–96	QPR	11	0		
1996–97	QPR	13	0		
1997–98	QPR	33	3		
1998–99	QPR	0	0	57	3
1998–99	Nottingham F	16	0		
1999–2000	Nottingham F	28	2	44	2
2000–01	Portsmouth	31	5	31	5

RUDONJA, Mladen (F) **217 51**
H: 5 9 W: 11 07 b.Slovenia 26-7-71
Honours: Slovenia 48 full caps.

1992–93	Izola	32	7		
1993–94	Izola	14	9	46	16
1993–94	Zagreb	6	0	6	0
1994–95	Koper	15	3	15	3
1994–95	Olimpija	11	1		
1995–96	Olimpija	15	1	26	2
1995–96	Marsonia	14	1	14	1
1996–97	HIT Gorica	16	4	16	4
From Lugano.					
1997–98	Primoje	9	4	9	4
1997–98	St Truiden	23	6		
1998–99	St Truiden	29	10		
1999–2000	St Truiden	22	5	74	21
2000–01	Portsmouth	11	0	11	0

STONER, Craig* (G) **0 0**
b.Chichester 5-11-81
Source: Trainee.

1999–2000	Portsmouth	0	0
2000–01	Portsmouth	0	0

TARDIF, Chris (G) **4 0**
H: 5 11 W: 12 07 b.Guernsey 19-9-79
Source: Trainee.

1998–99	Portsmouth	0	0		
1999–2000	Portsmouth	0	0		
2000–01	Portsmouth	4	0	4	0

THOGERSEN, Thomas (M) **271 37**
H: 6 2 W: 13 01 b.Copenhagen 2-4-68

1989	Frem	2	0		
1990	Frem	17	0		
1991–92	Frem	20	5		
1992–93	Frem	18	2	57	7
1993–94	Brondby	32	11		
1994–95	Brondby	26	7		
1995–96	Brondby	21	1		
1996–97	Brondby	21	2		
1997–98	Brondby	11	1	111	22
1998–99	Portsmouth	34	0		
1999–2000	Portsmouth	35	5		
2000–01	Portsmouth	34	3	103	8

TILER, Carl (D) **253 11**
H: 6 2 W: 14 03 b.Sheffield 11-2-70
Source: Trainee. *Honours:* England Under-21.

1987–88	Barnsley	1	0		
1988–89	Barnsley	4	0		
1989–90	Barnsley	21	1		
1990–91	Barnsley	45	2	71	3
1991–92	Nottingham F	26	1		
1992–93	Nottingham F	37	0		
1993–94	Nottingham F	3	0		
1994–95	Nottingham F	3	0		
1994–95	*Swindon T*	2	0	2	0
1995–96	Nottingham F	0	0	69	1
1995–96	Aston Villa	1	0		
1996–97	Aston Villa	11	1	12	1
1996–97	Sheffield U	6	1		
1997–98	Sheffield U	17	1	23	2
1997–98	Everton	19	1		
1998–99	Everton	2	0	21	1
1998–99	Charlton Ath	27	1		
1999–2000	Charlton Ath	11	1		
2000–01	Charlton Ath	7	0	45	2
2000–01	*Birmingham C*	1	0	1	0
2000–01	Portsmouth	9	1	9	1

VINCENT, Jamie (D) **211 7**
H: 5 10 W: 11 09 b.London 18-6-75
Source: Trainee.

1993–94	Crystal Palace	0	0		
1994–95	Crystal Palace	0	0		
1994–95	*Bournemouth*	8	0		
1995–96	Crystal Palace	25	0		
1996–97	Crystal Palace	0	0	25	0
1996–97	Bournemouth	29	0		
1997–98	Bournemouth	44	3		
1998–99	Bournemouth	32	2	113	5
1998–99	Huddersfield T	7	0		
1999–2000	Huddersfield T	36	2		
2000–01	Huddersfield T	16	0	59	2
2000–01	Portsmouth	14	0	14	0

VINE, Rowan (F) **2 0**
b.Basingstoke 21-9-82
Source: Scholar.

2000–01	Portsmouth	2	0	2	0

WATERMAN, David# (D) **71 0**
H: 5 10 W: 12 02 b.Guernsey 16-5-77
Source: Trainee. *Honours:* Northern Ireland Under-21.

1995–96	Portsmouth	0	0		
1996–97	Portsmouth	4	0		
1997–98	Portsmouth	15	0		
1998–99	Portsmouth	10	0		
1999–2000	Portsmouth	20	0		
2000–01	Portsmouth	22	0	71	0

WHITBREAD, Adrian* (D) **346 5**
H: 6 0 W: 12 12 b.Epping 22-10-71
Source: Trainee.

1989–90	Leyton Orient	8	0		
1990–91	Leyton Orient	38	0		
1991–92	Leyton Orient	43	1		
1992–93	Leyton Orient	36	1	125	2
1993–94	Swindon T	35	1		
1994–95	Swindon T	1	0	36	1
1994–95	West Ham U	8	0		
1995–96	West Ham U	2	0		
1995–96	*Portsmouth*	13	0		
1996–97	West Ham U	0	0	10	0
1996–97	Portsmouth	24	0		
1997–98	Portsmouth	38	1		
1998–99	Portsmouth	33	0		
1999–2000	Portsmouth	39	1		
2000–01	Portsmouth	0	0	147	2
2000–01	*Luton T*	9	0	9	0
2000–01	*Reading*	19	0	19	0

WHITE, Tom (D) **0 0**
b.Chichester 30-10-81
Source: Trainee.

2000–01	Portsmouth	0	0

Scholars
Bradshaw, Craig RJ; Chin, Gordon R; Clark, Christopher J; Hunt, Warren D; Molyneaux, Lee A; Parker, Terry J; Pook, Robbie J; Pulis, Anthony J

Non-Contract
Knight, Alan E

PORT VALE

BRAMMER, Dave (M) **210 15**
H: 5 11 W: 12 00 b.Bromborough 28-2-75
Source: Trainee.

1992–93	Wrexham	2	0		
1993–94	Wrexham	22	2		
1994–95	Wrexham	14	1		
1995–96	Wrexham	11	2		
1996–97	Wrexham	21	1		
1997–98	Wrexham	33	4		
1998–99	Wrexham	34	2	137	12
1998–99	Port Vale	9	0		
1999–2000	Port Vale	29	0		
2000–01	Port Vale	35	3	73	3

BRIDGE-WILKINSON, Marc (M) **50 9**
H: 5 6 W: 10 08 b.Nuneaton 16-3-79
Source: Trainee.

1996–97	Derby Co	0	0		
1997–98	Derby Co	0	0		
1998–99	Derby Co	1	0		
1998–99	*Carlisle U*	7	0	7	0
1999–2000	Derby Co	0	0	1	0
2000–01	Port Vale	42	9	42	9

BRISCO, Neil (M) **30 1**
H: 5 11 W: 13 01 b.Billinge 26-1-78
Source: Trainee.

1996–97	Manchester C	0	0		
1997–98	Manchester C	0	0		
1998–99	Port Vale	1	0		
1999–2000	Port Vale	12	0		
2000–01	Port Vale	17	1	30	1

BROOKER, Stephen (F) **24 8**
H: 5 10 W: 12 04 b.Newport Pagnell 21-5-81
Source: Trainee.

1999–2000	Watford	1	0		
2000–01	Watford	0	0	1	0
2000–01	Port Vale	23	8	23	8

BURGESS, Richard (F) **1 0**
H: 5 8 W: 11 00 b.Bromsgrove 18-8-78
Source: Trainee.

1996–97	Aston Villa	0	0		
1997–98	Stoke C	0	0		
1998–99	Stoke C	0	0		
1999–2000	Stoke C	0	0		
From Bromsgrove R.					
2000–01	Port Vale	1	0	1	0

BURNS, Liam (D) **42 0**
H: 6 0 W: 13 03 b.Belfast 30-10-78
Source: Trainee. *Honours:* Northern Ireland Under-21.

1997–98	Port Vale	1	0		
1998–99	Port Vale	4	0		
1999–2000	Port Vale	24	0		
2000–01	Port Vale	13	0	42	0

BURTON, Sagi (D) **83 3**
H: 6 2 W: 13 06 b.Birmingham 25-11-77
Source: Trainee.

1995–96	Crystal Palace	0	0		
1996–97	Crystal Palace	0	0		
1997–98	Crystal Palace	2	0		
1998–99	Crystal Palace	23	1	25	1
1999–2000	Colchester U	9	0	9	0
1999–2000	Sheffield U	0	0		
1999–2000	Port Vale	20	2		
2000–01	Port Vale	29	0	49	2

BYRNE, Paul§ (M) **1 0**
b.Natal 26-11-82
Source: Scholar.

2000–01	Port Vale	1	0	1	0

CARRAGHER, Matthew (D) **237 1**
H: 5 9 W: 11 06 b.Liverpool 14-1-76
Source: Trainee.

1993–94	Wigan Ath	32	0		
1994–95	Wigan Ath	41	0		
1995–96	Wigan Ath	28	0		
1996–97	Wigan Ath	18	0	119	0
1997–98	Port Vale	26	0		
1998–99	Port Vale	10	0		
1999–2000	Port Vale	37	1		
2000–01	Port Vale	45	0	118	1

CUMMINS, Michael (M) **59 3**
H: 6 0 W: 12 08 b.Dublin 1-6-78
Source: Trainee. *Honours:* Eire Youth, Under-21.

1995–96	Middlesbrough	0	0		
1996–97	Middlesbrough	0	0		
1997–98	Middlesbrough	0	0		
1998–99	Middlesbrough	1	0		
1999–2000	Middlesbrough	1	0	2	0
1999–2000	Port Vale	12	1		
2000–01	Port Vale	45	2	57	3

DELANY, Dean (G) **8 0**
b.Dublin 15-9-80
Honours: Eire Under-21.

1997–98	Everton	0	0		
1998–99	Everton	0	0		
1999–2000	Everton	0	0		
2000–01	Port Vale	8	0	8	0

DONNELLY, Paul (D) **5 0**
H: 5 7 W: 11 00 b.Newcastle under Lyme 16-2-81
Source: Trainee.

1999–2000	Port Vale	4	0		
2000–01	Port Vale	1	0	5	0

EYRE, Richard* (M) **48 1**
H: 5 8 W: 11 08 b.Poynton 15-9-76
Source: Trainee.

1995–96	Port Vale	0	0		
1996–97	Port Vale	0	0		
1997–98	Port Vale	1	0		
1998–99	Port Vale	11	0		
1999–2000	Port Vale	30	1		
2000–01	Port Vale	6	0	48	1

GOODLAD, Mark (G) **44 0**
H: 6 0 W: 13 02 b.Barnsley 9-9-80
Source: Trainee.

1996–97	Nottingham F	0	0		
1997–98	Nottingham F	0	0		
1998–99	Nottingham F	0	0		
1998–99	*Scarborough*	3	0	3	0
1999–2000	Nottingham F	0	0		
1999–2000	Port Vale	1	0		
2000–01	Port Vale	40	0	41	0

LE GEYT, Sinclair‡ (M) **0 0**
b.Port Elizabeth 10-7-80

1998–99	Derby Co	0	0
1999–2000	Derby Co	0	0
2000–01	Port Vale	0	0

LOWE, Onandi# (F) **5 1**
b.Jamaica 2-12-73
Honours: Jamaica full caps.

2000–01	Port Vale	5	1	5	1

NAYLOR, Tony# (F) **375 116**
H: 5 4 W: 10 07 b.Manchester 29-3-68
Source: Droylsden.

1989–90	Crewe Alex	2	0
1990–91	Crewe Alex	14	1

1991–92	Crewe Alex	34	15		
1992–93	Crewe Alex	35	16		
1993–94	Crewe Alex	37	13	**122**	**45**
1994–95	Port Vale	33	9		
1995–96	Port Vale	39	11		
1996–97	Port Vale	43	17		
1997–98	Port Vale	38	10		
1998–99	Port Vale	22	4		
1999–2000	Port Vale	36	6		
2000–01	Port Vale	42	14	**253**	**71**

O'CALLAGHAN, George (M) **23** **1**
H: 6 1 W: 10 05 b.Cork 5-9-79
Source: Trainee.

1998–99	Port Vale	4	0		
1999–2000	Port Vale	11	0		
2000–01	Port Vale	8	1	**23**	**1**

OLAOYE, Dolapo§ (M) **1** **0**
b.Lagos 17-10-82

2000–01	Port Vale	1	0	**1**	**0**

PAYNTER, Billy§ (F) **1** **0**
b.Liverpool 13-7-84
Source: Schoolboy.

2000–01	Port Vale	1	0	**1**	**0**

SMITH, Alex# (M) **127** **5**
H: 5 8 W: 10 06 b.Liverpool 15-2-76
Source: Trainee.

1994–95	Everton	0	0		
1995–96	Everton	0	0		
1995–96	Swindon T	8	0		
1996–97	Swindon T	18	1		
1997–98	Swindon T	5	0	**31**	**1**
1997–98	Huddersfield T	6	0	**6**	**0**
1998–99	Chester C	32	2	**32**	**2**
1998–99	Port Vale	8	0		
1999–2000	Port Vale	13	0		
2000–01	Port Vale	37	2	**58**	**2**

TANKARD, Allen# (D) **489** **15**
H: 5 10 W: 13 04 b.Fleet 21-5-69
Source: Trainee. *Honours:* England Youth.

1985–86	Southampton	3	0		
1986–87	Southampton	2	0		
1987–88	Southampton	0	0	**5**	**0**
1988–89	Wigan Ath	33	1		
1989–90	Wigan Ath	45	1		
1990–91	Wigan Ath	46	1		
1991–92	Wigan Ath	44	0		
1992–93	Wigan Ath	41	1	**209**	**4**
1993–94	Port Vale	26	0		
1994–95	Port Vale	39	1		
1995–96	Port Vale	29	0		
1996–97	Port Vale	37	1		
1997–98	Port Vale	39	0		
1998–99	Port Vale	37	4		
1999–2000	Port Vale	35	1		
2000–01	Port Vale	33	4	**275**	**11**

TAYLOR, Paul (M) **0** **0**
H: 5 11 W: 12 06 b.Stoke 16-9-80
Source: Trainee.

1999–2000	Port Vale	0	0		
2000–01	Port Vale	0	0		

TWISS, Michael* (M) **30** **4**
H: 5 11 W: 13 03 b.Salford 28-12-77
Source: Trainee.

1996–97	Manchester U	0	0		
1997–98	Manchester U	0	0		
1998–99	*Sheffield U*	12	1	**12**	**1**
1999–2000	Manchester U	0	0		
2000–01	Port Vale	18	3	**18**	**3**

VILJANEN, Ville* (F) **105** **21**
H: 6 2 W: 13 05 b.Helsinki 2-2-71
Honours: Finland 1 full cap.

1996	Hacken	26	7		
1997	Hacken	19	5		
1998	Hacken	26	3	**71**	**15**
1999–2000	Port Vale	15	4		
2000–01	Port Vale	19	2	**34**	**6**

WALSH, Michael (D) **173** **4**
H: 6 0 W: 12 08 b.Rotherham 5-8-77
Source: Trainee.

1994–95	Scunthorpe U	3	0		
1995–96	Scunthorpe U	25	0		
1996–97	Scunthorpe U	36	0		
1997–98	Scunthorpe U	39	1	**103**	**1**
1998–99	Port Vale	19	1		
1999–2000	Port Vale	12	1		
2000–01	Port Vale	39	1	**70**	**3**

WIDDRINGTON, Tommy* (M) **252** **19**
H: 5 9 W: 11 12 b.Newcastle 1-10-71
Source: Trainee.

1989–90	Southampton	0	0		
1990–91	Southampton	0	0		
1991–92	Southampton	3	0		
1991–92	*Wigan Ath*	6	0	**6**	**0**
1992–93	Southampton	12	0		
1993–94	Southampton	11	1		
1994–95	Southampton	28	0		
1995–96	Southampton	21	2	**75**	**3**
1996–97	Grimsby T	42	4		
1997–98	Grimsby T	21	3		
1998–99	Grimsby T	26	1	**89**	**8**
1998–99	*Port Vale*	9	1		
1999–2000	Port Vale	38	5		
2000–01	Port Vale	35	2	**82**	**8**

Scholars
Barker, Philip; Birchall, Christopher; Byrne, Paul; Eldershaw, Simon; Fairbrother, Craig; Fairhurst, Neil A; Farr, David J; Gowan, Christopher J; Kirkham, Shane M; Maye, Daniel P; Olaoye, Dolapo; Paynter, William P; Reid, Levi SJ; Rowland, Stephen J; Rowley, Christopher J; Simpson, Benjamin J; Sneade, Adam V; Stevenson, Matthew JR; Taylor, Andrew

PRESTON NE

ABBOTT, Pawel (F) **0** **0**
b.York 5-5-82
Source: LKS Lodz.

2000–01	Preston NE	0	0		

ALEXANDER, Graham (D) **399** **44**
H: 5 10 W: 12 00 b.Coventry 10-10-71
Source: Trainee.

1989–90	Scunthorpe U	0	0		
1990–91	Scunthorpe U	1	0		
1991–92	Scunthorpe U	36	5		
1992–93	Scunthorpe U	41	5		
1993–94	Scunthorpe U	41	4		
1994–95	Scunthorpe U	40	4	**159**	**18**
1995–96	Luton T	37	1		
1996–97	Luton T	45	2		
1997–98	Luton T	39	8		
1998–99	Luton T	29	4	**150**	**15**
1998–99	Preston NE	10	0		
1999–2000	Preston NE	46	6		
2000–01	Preston NE	34	5	**90**	**11**

ANDERSON, Iain (F) **172** **23**
H: 5 8 W: 9 07 b.Glasgow 23-7-77
Source: X-Form. *Honours:* Scotland Under-21.

1994–95	Dundee	10	1		
1995–96	Dundee	17	0		
1996–97	Dundee	35	5		
1997–98	Dundee	36	6		
1998–99	Dundee	28	3	**126**	**15**
1999–2000	Toulouse	3	0	**3**	**0**
1999–2000	Preston NE	12	2		
2000–01	Preston NE	31	6	**43**	**8**

ANTOINE-CURIER, Mickael* (M) **0** **0**
b.Orsay 5-3-83

2000–01	Preston NE	0	0		

BARRY-MURPHY, Brian (M) **95** **2**
H: 6 0 W: 12 04 b.Cork 27-7-78
Honours: Eire Under-21.

1995–96	Cork City	13	0		
1996–97	Cork City	25	0		
1997–98	Cork City	15	1		
1998–99	Cork City	27	1	**80**	**2**
1999–2000	Preston NE	1	0		
2000–01	Preston NE	14	0	**15**	**0**

BASHAM, Steve (F) **76** **15**
H: 5 11 W: 12 05 b.Southampton 2-12-77
Source: Trainee.

1996–97	Southampton	6	0		
1997–98	Southampton	9	0		
1997–98	*Wrexham*	5	0	**5**	**0**
1998–99	Southampton	4	1	**19**	**1**
1998–99	*Preston NE*	17	10		
1999–2000	Preston NE	24	2		
2000–01	Preston NE	11	2	**52**	**14**

CARTWRIGHT, Lee (F) **327** **21**
H: 5 8 W: 10 07 b.Rossendale 19-9-72
Source: Trainee.

1990–91	Preston NE	14	1		
1991–92	Preston NE	33	4		
1992–93	Preston NE	34	3		
1993–94	Preston NE	39	1		
1994–95	Preston NE	36	1		
1995–96	Preston NE	26	3		
1996–97	Preston NE	14	1		
1997–98	Preston NE	36	2		
1998–99	Preston NE	27	4		
1999–2000	Preston NE	30	1		
2000–01	Preston NE	38	0	**327**	**21**

EATON, Adam (D) **1** **0**
H: 5 10 W: 11 08 b.Wigan 2-5-80
Source: Trainee.

1997–98	Everton	0	0		
1998–99	Everton	0	0		
1999–2000	Preston NE	0	0		
2000–01	Preston NE	1	0	**1**	**0**

EDWARDS, Robert (D) **347** **12**
H: 6 0 W: 12 07 b.Kendal 1-7-73
Source: Trainee. *Honours:* Wales Youth, Under-21, 4 full caps.

1989–90	Carlisle U	12	0		
1990–91	Carlisle U	36	5	**48**	**5**
1990–91	Bristol C	0	0		
1991–92	Bristol C	20	1		
1992–93	Bristol C	18	0		
1993–94	Bristol C	38	2		
1994–95	Bristol C	30	0		
1995–96	Bristol C	19	0		
1996–97	Bristol C	31	0		
1997–98	Bristol C	37	2		
1998–99	Bristol C	23	0	**216**	**5**
1999–2000	Preston NE	41	2		
2000–01	Preston NE	42	0	**83**	**2**

GREGAN, Sean (M) **307** **15**
H: 6 2 W: 12 03 b.Stockton 29-3-74
Source: Trainee.

1991–92	Darlington	17	0		
1992–93	Darlington	17	1		
1993–94	Darlington	23	1		
1994–95	Darlington	25	2		
1995–96	Darlington	38	0		
1996–97	Darlington	16	0	**136**	**4**
1996–97	Preston NE	21	1		
1997–98	Preston NE	35	2		
1998–99	Preston NE	41	3		
1999–2000	Preston NE	33	3		
2000–01	Preston NE	41	2	**171**	**11**

GUNNLAUGSSON, Bjarki (F) **163** **39**
H: 5 9 W: 11 05 b.Iceland 6-3-73
Honours: Iceland 27 full caps, 7 goals.

1990	IA Akranes	7	1		
1991	IA Akranes	0	0		
1992	IA Akranes	17	5		
1992–93	Feyenoord	0	0		
1993–94	Feyenoord	0	0		
1994–95	Nuremberg	27	5	**27**	**5**
1995	IA Akranes	7	3	**31**	**9**
1996–97	Waldhof Mannheim	26	6	**26**	**6**
1997	Molde	10	4		
1998	Molde	8	2	**18**	**6**
1999	KR	16	11	**16**	**11**
1999–2000	Preston NE	26	1		
2000–01	Preston NE	19	1	**45**	**2**

HEALY, David (F) **39** **12**
H: 5 8 W: 11 01 b.Downpatrick 5-8-79
Source: Trainee. *Honours:* Northern Ireland Under-21, 12 full caps, 7 goals.

1997–98	Manchester U	0	0		
1998–99	Manchester U	0	0		
1999–2000	Manchester U	0	0		
1999–2000	*Port Vale*	16	3	**16**	**3**
2000–01	Manchester U	1	0	**1**	**0**
2000–01	Preston NE	22	9	**22**	**9**

JACKSON, Michael (D) **297** **25**
H: 5 11 W: 11 10 b.Chester 4-12-73
Source: Trainee.

1991–92	Crewe Alex	1	0		
1992–93	Crewe Alex	4	0	**5**	**0**
1993–94	Bury	39	0		
1994–95	Bury	24	2		
1995–96	Bury	31	4		
1996–97	Bury	31	3	**125**	**9**
1996–97	Preston NE	7	0		
1997–98	Preston NE	40	2		
1998–99	Preston NE	44	8		
1999–2000	Preston NE	46	5		
2000–01	Preston NE	30	1	**167**	**16**

KEANE, Michael (M) **2** **0**
b.Dublin 29-12-82
Source: Scholar.

2000–01	Preston NE	2	0	**2**	**0**

KIDD, Ryan (D) **254** **9**
H: 5 11 W: 10 10 b.Radcliffe 16-10-71
Source: Trainee.

1990–91	Port Vale	0	0		
1991–92	Port Vale	1	0	**1**	**0**
1992–93	Preston NE	15	0		
1993–94	Preston NE	36	1		
1994–95	Preston NE	32	3		
1995–96	Preston NE	30	0		
1996–97	Preston NE	35	0		
1997–98	Preston NE	33	2		
1998–99	Preston NE	28	3		
1999–2000	Preston NE	29	0		
2000–01	Preston NE	15	0	**253**	**9**

KING, Stuart* (M) **7** **1**
H: 5 11 W: 10 00 b.Derry 20-3-81
Source: Trainee.

1998–99	Preston NE	0	0		
1999–2000	Preston NE	0	0		

2000–01	Ross C	1	0	1	0
2000–01	Q of S	6	1	6	1
2000–01	Preston NE	0	0		

LONERGAN, Andrew (G)   1   0
H: 6 1 b.Preston 19-10-83
Source: Scholar.

2000–01	Preston NE	1	0	1	0

LUCAS, David (G)   94   0
H: 6 1 W: 11 06 b.Preston 23-11-77
Source: Trainee. *Honours:* England Youth.

1995–96	Preston NE	1	0		
1995–96	Darlington	6	0		
1996–97	Preston NE	2	0		
1996–97	Darlington	7	0	13	0
1996–97	Scunthorpe U	6	0	6	0
1997–98	Preston NE	6	0		
1998–99	Preston NE	31	0		
1999–2000	Preston NE	6	0		
2000–01	Preston NE	29	0	75	0

LUDDEN, Dominic* (D)   128   1
H: 5 7 W: 10 09 b.Basildon 30-3-74
Source: Trainee. *Honours:* England Schools.

1992–93	Leyton Orient	24	1		
1993–94	Leyton Orient	34	0	58	1
1994–95	Watford	1	0		
1995–96	Watford	12	0		
1996–97	Watford	20	0		
1997–98	Watford	0	0	33	0
1998–99	Preston NE	32	0		
1999–2000	Preston NE	3	0		
2000–01	Preston NE	2	0	37	0

MACKEN, Jonathan (F)   153   55
H: 5 10 W: 12 00 b.Manchester 7-9-77
Source: Trainee. *Honours:* England Youth.

1996–97	Manchester U	0	0		
1997–98	Preston NE	29	6		
1998–99	Preston NE	42	8		
1999–2000	Preston NE	44	22		
2000–01	Preston NE	38	19	153	55

McBRIDE, Brian‡ (F)   129   46
H: 6 1 W: 12 06 b.USA 17-8-72
Source: St Louis Univ. *Honours:* USA 47 full caps, 10 goals.

1994–95	Wolfsburg	12	1	12	1
1996	Columbus Crew	28	17		
1997	Columbus Crew	13	6		
1998	Columbus Crew	24	10		
1999	Columbus Crew	25	5		
2000	Columbus Crew	18	6	108	44
2000–01	Preston NE	9	1	9	1

McKENNA, Paul (M)   114   8
H: 5 8 W: 11 11 b.Chorley 20-10-77
Source: Trainee.

1995–96	Preston NE	0	0		
1996–97	Preston NE	5	1		
1997–98	Preston NE	5	0		
1998–99	Preston NE	36	0		
1999–2000	Preston NE	24	2		
2000–01	Preston NE	44	5	114	8

MEIJER, Erik‡ (F)   304   85
H: 6 2 W: 13 05 b.Meersen 2-8-69
Honours: Holland 1 full cap.

1988–89	Fortuna Sittard	10	1		
1989–90	Antwerp	0	0		
1989–90	Eindhoven	14	5	14	5
1990–91	Fortuna Sittard	26	5	36	6
1991–92	Maastricht	32	14		
1992–93	Maastricht	34	20	66	34
1993–94	PSV Eindhoven	15	4		
1994–95	PSV Eindhoven	24	9	39	13
1995–96	Uerdingen	32	11	32	11
1996–97	Leverkusen	32	6		
1997–98	Leverkusen	26	6		
1998–99	Leverkusen	26	4	84	16
1999–2000	Liverpool	21	0		
2000–01	Liverpool	3	0	24	0
2000–01	Preston NE	9	0	9	0

(Transferred to Hamburg, December 2000).

MOILANEN, Teuvo (G)   228   0
H: 6 5 W: 12 09 b.Oulu 12-12-73
Honours: Finland Under-21, 3 full caps.

1990	Ilves	3	0		
1991	Ilves	7	0		
1992	Ilves	29	0		
1993	Ilves	5	0		
1994	Ilves	19	0	63	0
1995	Jaro	26	0	26	0
1995–96	Preston NE	2	0		
1996–97	Preston NE	4	0		
1996–97	Scarborough	4	0	4	0
1996–97	Darlington	16	0	16	0
1997–98	Preston NE	40	0		
1998–99	Preston NE	15	0		
1999–2000	Preston NE	41	0		
2000–01	Preston NE	17	0	119	0

MORGAN, Paul (D)   0   0
H: 6 0 W: 11 05 b.Belfast 23-10-78
Source: Trainee. *Honours:* Northern Ireland Under-21.

1997–98	Preston NE	0	0		
1998–99	Preston NE	0	0		
1999–2000	Preston NE	0	0		
2000–01	Preston NE	0	0		

MURDOCK, Colin (D)   130   4
H: 6 1 W: 12 00 b.Ballymena 2-7-75
Source: Trainee. *Honours:* Northern Ireland 12 full caps.

1992–93	Manchester U	0	0		
1993–94	Manchester U	0	0		
1994–95	Manchester U	0	0		
1995–96	Manchester U	0	0		
1996–97	Manchester U	0	0		
1997–98	Preston NE	27	1		
1998–99	Preston NE	33	1		
1999–2000	Preston NE	33	2		
2000–01	Preston NE	37	0	130	4

O'HANLON, Kelham† (G)   485   0
H: 6 1 W: 13 12 b.Saltburn 16-5-62
Source: Apprentice. *Honours:* Eire Under-21, 1 full cap.

1980–81	Middlesbrough	2	0		
1981–82	Middlesbrough	0	0		
1982–83	Middlesbrough	19	0		
1983–84	Middlesbrough	30	0		
1984–85	Middlesbrough	38	0	87	0
1985–86	Rotherham U	46	0		
1986–87	Rotherham U	40	0		
1987–88	Rotherham U	40	0		
1988–89	Rotherham U	46	0		
1989–90	Rotherham U	43	0		
1990–91	Rotherham U	33	0	248	0
1991–92	Carlisle U	42	0		
1992–93	Carlisle U	41	0	83	0
1993–94	Preston NE	23	0		
1994–95	Dundee U	29	0		
1995–96	Dundee U	1	0		
1996–97	Dundee U	0	0	30	0
1996–97	Preston NE	13	0		
1997–98	Preston NE	0	0		
1998–99	Preston NE	0	0		
1999–2000	Preston NE	0	0		
2000–01	Preston NE	1	0	37	0

QUINN, Patrick (M)   0   0
b.Dublin 3-12-81

2000–01	Preston NE	0	0		

RANKINE, Mark (M)   484   29
H: 5 9 W: 11 05 b.Doncaster 30-9-69
Source: Trainee.

1987–88	Doncaster R	18	2		
1988–89	Doncaster R	46	11		
1989–90	Doncaster R	36	2		
1990–91	Doncaster R	40	2		
1991–92	Doncaster R	24	3	164	20
1991–92	Wolverhampton W	15	1		
1992–93	Wolverhampton W	27	0		
1993–94	Wolverhampton W	31	0		
1994–95	Wolverhampton W	27	0		
1995–96	Wolverhampton W	32	0		
1996–97	Wolverhampton W	0	0	132	1
1996–97	Preston NE	23	0		
1997–98	Preston NE	35	1		
1998–99	Preston NE	42	3		
1999–2000	Preston NE	44	0		
2000–01	Preston NE	44	4	188	8

ROBINSON, Steve (F)   264   52
H: 5 9 W: 11 02 b.Crumlin 10-12-74
Source: Trainee. *Honours:* Northern Ireland Under-21, 5 full caps.

1992–93	Tottenham H	0	0		
1993–94	Tottenham H	2	0		
1994–95	Tottenham H	0	0	2	0
1994–95	Leyton Orient	0	0		
1994–95	Bournemouth	32	5		
1995–96	Bournemouth	41	7		
1996–97	Bournemouth	40	7		
1997–98	Bournemouth	45	10		
1998–99	Bournemouth	42	13		
1999–2000	Bournemouth	40	9	240	51
2000–01	Preston NE	22	1	22	1

WRIGHT, Mark (F)   3   0
H: 5 10 W: 11 05 b.Chorley 4-9-81
Source: Schoolboy.

1998–99	Preston NE	1	0		
1999–2000	Preston NE	2	0		
2000–01	Preston NE	0	0	3	0

Scholars
Bailey, John AK; Davies, John M; Douglas, Adam M; Hallam, Anthony T; Lin, Paul; Madin, Lee P; Mercer, Richard M; Nesa, Remo; O'Neill, Joseph; Underwood, Jeffrey H; Wright, Ronnie M

Non-Contract
Moyes, David W; O'Hanlon, Kelham G
Player who does not hold a current contract but his registration has been retained by the club
Wilkinson, Craig

QPR

BARACLOUGH, Ian* (D)   370   28
H: 6 1 W: 12 10 b.Leicester 4-12-70
Source: Trainee.

1988–89	Leicester C	0	0		
1989–90	Leicester C	0	0		
1989–90	Wigan Ath	9	2	9	2
1990–91	Grimsby T	4	0		
1991–92	Grimsby T	0	0		
1992–93	Grimsby T	1	0	5	0
1992–93	Lincoln C	36	5		
1993–94	Lincoln C	37	5	73	10
1994–95	Mansfield T	36	3		
1995–96	Mansfield T	11	2	47	5
1995–96	Notts Co	35	2		
1996–97	Notts Co	38	2		
1997–98	Notts Co	38	6	111	10
1997–98	QPR	8	0		
1998–99	QPR	43	1		
1999–2000	QPR	45	0		
2000–01	QPR	29	0	125	1

BIGNOT, Marcus (D)   130   2
H: 5 9 W: 11 00 b.Birmingham 28-8-74
Source: Kidderminster H.

1997–98	Crewe Alex	42	0		
1998–99	Crewe Alex	26	0		
1999–2000	Crewe Alex	27	0	95	0
2000–01	Bristol R	26	1	26	1
2000–01	QPR	9	1	9	1

BRADY, Richard (F)   0   0
H: 5 8 W: 10 04 b.Dartford 17-9-82
Source: Trainee.

1999–2000	QPR	0	0		
2000–01	QPR	0	0		

BRAYLEY, Albert* (M)   0   0
b.Basildon 5-9-81

2000–01	QPR	0	0		

BREACKER, Tim* (D)   494   13
H: 6 0 W: 13 00 b.Bicester 2-7-65
Source: Apprentice. *Honours:* England Under-21.

1983–84	Luton T	2	0		
1984–85	Luton T	35	0		
1985–86	Luton T	36	0		
1986–87	Luton T	29	1		
1987–88	Luton T	40	1		
1988–89	Luton T	22	0		
1989–90	Luton T	38	1		
1990–91	Luton T	8	0	210	3
1990–91	West Ham U	24	1		
1991–92	West Ham U	34	2		
1992–93	West Ham U	39	2		
1993–94	West Ham U	40	3		
1994–95	West Ham U	33	0		
1995–96	West Ham U	22	0		
1996–97	West Ham U	26	0		
1997–98	West Ham U	19	0		
1998–99	West Ham U	3	0	240	8
1998–99	QPR	18	1		
1999–2000	QPR	16	1		
2000–01	QPR	10	0	44	2

BROWN, Carlos (D)   0   0
H: 6 0 W: 11 07 b.Edmonton 22-4-81
Source: Trainee.

1998–99	QPR	0	0		
1999–2000	QPR	0	0		
2000–01	QPR	0	0		

BROWNE, Rickey (D)   0   0
H: 6 1 W: 12 05 b.Edmonton 19-10-81
Source: Scholarship.

1999–2000	QPR	0	0		
2000–01	QPR	0	0		

BRUCE, Paul* (F)   28   2
H: 5 10 W: 12 06 b.London 18-2-78
Source: Trainee.

1996–97	QPR	0	0		
1997–98	QPR	5	1		
1998–99	QPR	0	0		
1998–99	Cambridge U	4	0	4	0
1999–2000	QPR	12	0		
2000–01	QPR	7	1	24	2

BUBB, Alvin* (F)   1   0
H: 5 4 W: 10 03 b.Paddington 11-10-80
Source: Trainee.

1998–99	QPR	0	0		

| 1999–2000 | QPR | 0 | 0 | | |
| 2000–01 | QPR | 1 | 0 | **1** | **0** |

BULL, Nikki (G) **0 0**
H: 6 1 W: 11 13 b.Hastings 2-10-81
Source: Scholarship.
| 1999–2000 | QPR | 0 | 0 | | |
| 2000–01 | QPR | 0 | 0 | | |

BURGESS, Oliver§ (D) **1 0**
b.Ascot 12-10-81
Source: Scholar.
| 2000–01 | QPR | 1 | 0 | **1** | **0** |

CARLISLE, Clarke (D) **120 10**
H: 6 1 W: 12 07 b.Preston 14-10-79
Source: Trainee. *Honours:* England Under-21.
1997–98	Blackpool	11	2		
1998–99	Blackpool	39	1		
1999–2000	Blackpool	43	4	93	7
2000–01	QPR	27	3	27	3

COCHRANE, Justin (M) **1 0**
H: 5 11 W: 11 01 b.Hackney 26-1-82
Source: Scholarship.
| 1999–2000 | QPR | 0 | 0 | | |
| 2000–01 | QPR | 1 | 0 | **1** | **0** |

CONNOLLY, Karl (F) **381 92**
H: 5 10 W: 11 01 b.Prescot 9-2-70
Source: Napoli (Liverpool Sunday League).
1990–91	Wrexham	0	0		
1991–92	Wrexham	36	8		
1992–93	Wrexham	42	9		
1993–94	Wrexham	39	2		
1994–95	Wrexham	45	10		
1995–96	Wrexham	46	18		
1996–97	Wrexham	30	14		
1997–98	Wrexham	35	7		
1998–99	Wrexham	44	11		
1999–2000	Wrexham	41	9	358	88
2000–01	QPR	23	4	23	4

CROUCH, Peter (F) **42 10**
H: 6 2 W: 11 12 b.Macclesfield 30-1-81
Source: Trainee. *Honours:* England Youth.
1998–99	Tottenham H	0	0		
1999–2000	Tottenham H	0	0		
2000–01	QPR	42	10	**42**	**10**

CURRIE, Michael (F) **0 0**
H: 5 10 W: 11 00 b.Westminster 19-10-79
Source: Trainee.
1997–98	QPR	0	0		
1998–99	QPR	0	0		
1999–2000	QPR	0	0		
2000–01	QPR	0	0		

D'AUSTIN, Ryan (M) **0 0**
H: 5 9 W: 10 13 b.Edgware 29-11-82
Source: Trainee.
| 1999–2000 | QPR | 0 | 0 | | |
| 2000–01 | QPR | 0 | 0 | | |

DARLINGTON, Jermaine (D) **71 2**
H: 5 9 W: 13 00 b.Hackney 11-4-74
Source: Aylesbury U.
1998–99	QPR	4	0		
1999–2000	QPR	34	2		
2000–01	QPR	33	0	**71**	**2**

DICK, Alexander (M) **0 0**
b.Paddington 2-9-82
Source: Scholar.
| 2000–01 | QPR | 0 | 0 | | |

DOWIE, Iain* (F) **323 67**
H: 6 1 W: 14 06 b.Hatfield 9-1-65
Source: Hendon. *Honours:* Northern Ireland Under-21, 59 full caps, 12 goals.
1988–89	Luton T	8	0		
1989–90	Luton T	29	9		
1989–90	*Fulham*	5	1	5	1
1990–91	Luton T	29	7	66	16
1990–91	West Ham U	12	4		
1991–92	West Ham U	0	0		
1991–92	Southampton	30	9		
1992–93	Southampton	36	11		
1993–94	Southampton	39	5		
1994–95	Southampton	17	5	122	30
1994–95	Crystal Palace	15	4		
1995–96	Crystal Palace	4	2	19	6
1995–96	West Ham U	33	8		
1996–97	West Ham U	23	0		
1997–98	West Ham U	12	0	80	12
1997–98	QPR	11	1		
1998–99	QPR	19	1		
1999–2000	QPR	0	0		
2000–01	QPR	1	0	31	2

DUNCAN, Lyndon (D) **0 0**
H: 5 8 W: 11 02 b.Ealing 12-1-83
Source: Trainee.
| 1999–2000 | QPR | 0 | 0 | | |
| 2000–01 | QPR | 0 | 0 | | |

FITZGERALD, Brian (M) **0 0**
b.Perivale 23-10-83
Source: School.
| 2000–01 | QPR | 0 | 0 | | |

GRADLEY, Patrick (M) **0 0**
b.London 1-6-83
Source: Scholar.
| 2000–01 | QPR | 0 | 0 | | |

GRAHAM, Richard (M) **2 0**
H: 5 8 W: 10 06 b.Newry 5-8-79
Source: Trainee. *Honours:* Northern Ireland Youth, Under-21.
1996–97	QPR	0	0		
1997–98	QPR	0	0		
1998–99	QPR	2	0		
1999–2000	QPR	0	0		
2000–01	QPR	0	0	**2**	**0**

GRIEVES, Danny‡ (M) **9 0**
H: 5 11 W: 11 06 b.Watford 21-9-78
Source: Trainee.
1996–97	Watford	0	0		
1997–98	Watford	0	0		
1998–99	Watford	0	0		
1999–2000	Maccabi Herzliya	9	0	**9**	**0**
2000–01	QPR	0	0		

HARPER, Lee* (G) **119 0**
H: 6 1 W: 14 07 b.Chelsea 30-10-71
Source: Sittingbourne.
1994–95	Arsenal	0	0		
1995–96	Arsenal	0	0		
1996–97	Arsenal	1	0	1	0
1997–98	QPR	36	0		
1998–99	QPR	15	0		
1999–2000	QPR	38	0		
2000–01	QPR	29	0	118	0

HEINOLA, Antti‡ (D) **164 8**
H: 5 10 W: 12 03 b.Helsinki 20-3-73
Honours: Finland 5 full caps.
1991–92	HJK Helsinki	18	0		
1992–93	HJK Helsinki	20	0		
1993–94	HJK Helsinki	19	2		
1994–95	HJK Helsinki	23	3	80	5
1995–96	Emmen	10	0		
1996–97	Emmen	9	0	19	0
1996–97	Heracles	13	0		
1997–98	Heracles	18	3	31	3
1997–98	QPR	10	0		
1998–99	QPR	23	0		
1999–2000	QPR	0	0		
2000–01	QPR	1	0	34	0

HIGGINS, Alex (M) **1 0**
H: 5 9 W: 11 04 b.Sheffield 22-7-81
Source: Trainee. *Honours:* England Schools.
1998–99	Sheffield W	0	0		
1999–2000	Sheffield W	0	0		
2000–01	Sheffield W	0	0		
2000–01	QPR	1	0	**1**	**0**

JEANNE, Leon‡ (F) **12 0**
H: 5 8 W: 10 10 b.Cardiff 17-11-80
Source: Trainee. *Honours:* Wales Under-21.
1997–98	QPR	0	0		
1998–99	QPR	10	0		
1999–2000	QPR	2	0		
2000–01	QPR	0	0	**12**	**0**

KIWOMYA, Chris* (F) **332 79**
H: 5 9 W: 10 07 b.Huddersfield 2-12-69
Source: Trainee.
1986–87	Ipswich T	0	0		
1987–88	Ipswich T	0	0		
1988–89	Ipswich T	26	2		
1989–90	Ipswich T	29	5		
1990–91	Ipswich T	37	10		
1991–92	Ipswich T	43	16		
1992–93	Ipswich T	38	10		
1993–94	Ipswich T	37	5		
1994–95	Ipswich T	15	3	225	51
1994–95	Arsenal	14	3		
1995–96	Arsenal	0	0		
1996–97	Arsenal	0	0		
1996–97	*Le Havre*	7	0	7	0
1997–98	Arsenal	0	0	14	3
1998–99	QPR	16	6		
1999–2000	QPR	44	13		
2000–01	QPR	26	6	86	25

KOEJOE, Sammy (F) **113 19**
H: 6 2 W: 14 07 b.Surinam 17-8-74
1997–98	Lustenau	29	7	29	7
1998–99	Salzburg	34	7		
1999–2000	Salzburg	18	2	52	9
1999–2000	QPR	11	1		
2000–01	QPR	21	2	32	3

KULCSAR, George‡ (M) **148 3**
H: 6 1 W: 12 08 b.Budapest 12-8-67
Source: Canberra City 6 apps, Budapest St George 13 apps. *Honours:* Australia 3 full caps.
1992–93	Antwerp	4	0		
1993–94	Antwerp	8	0		
1994–95	Antwerp	25	1		
1995–96	Antwerp	12	0		
1996–97	Antwerp	17	0	66	1
1996–97	Bradford C	9	0		
1997–98	Bradford C	17	1	26	1
1997–98	QPR	12	0		
1998–99	QPR	17	1		
1999–2000	QPR	13	0		
2000–01	QPR	14	0	56	1

LANGLEY, Richard (M) **75 5**
H: 5 10 W: 11 04 b.London 27-12-79
Source: Trainee. *Honours:* England Youth.
1996–97	QPR	0	0		
1997–98	QPR	0	0		
1998–99	QPR	8	1		
1999–2000	QPR	41	3		
2000–01	QPR	26	1	**75**	**5**

LUSARDI, Mario (F) **0 0**
H: 5 9 W: 12 00 b.Islington 27-9-79
Source: Trainee.
1996–97	QPR	0	0		
1997–98	QPR	0	0		
1998–99	QPR	0	0		
1999–2000	QPR	0	0		
2000–01	QPR	0	0		

MADDIX, Danny* (D) **296 13**
H: 5 11 W: 12 00 b.Ashford 11-10-66
Source: Apprentice.
1985–86	Tottenham H	0	0		
1986–87	Tottenham H	0	0		
1986–87	*Southend U*	2	0	2	0
1987–88	QPR	9	0		
1988–89	QPR	33	2		
1989–90	QPR	32	3		
1990–91	QPR	32	1		
1991–92	QPR	19	0		
1992–93	QPR	14	0		
1993–94	QPR	0	0		
1994–95	QPR	27	1		
1995–96	QPR	22	0		
1996–97	QPR	25	0		
1997–98	QPR	25	1		
1998–99	QPR	37	4		
1999–2000	QPR	17	1		
2000–01	QPR	2	0	294	13

McFLYNN, Terry* (M) **2 0**
H: 5 9 W: 11 11 b.Magherafelt 27-3-81
Source: Trainee. *Honours:* Northern Ireland Under-21.
1997–98	QPR	0	0		
1998–99	QPR	0	0		
1999–2000	QPR	0	0		
2000–01	QPR	2	0	**2**	**0**

MIKLOSKO, Ludek* (G) **372 0**
H: 6 5 W: 14 00 b.Protesov 9-12-61
Source: Banik Ostrava. *Honours:* Czech Republic 42 full caps.
1989–90	West Ham U	18	0		
1990–91	West Ham U	46	0		
1991–92	West Ham U	36	0		
1992–93	West Ham U	46	0		
1993–94	West Ham U	42	0		
1994–95	West Ham U	42	0		
1995–96	West Ham U	36	0		
1996–97	West Ham U	36	0		
1997–98	West Ham U	13	0		
1998–99	West Ham U	0	0	315	0
1998–99	QPR	31	0		
1999–2000	QPR	9	0		
2000–01	QPR	17	0	57	0

MILLS, Danny (G) **0 0**
H: 6 0 W: 12 07 b.Sidcup 8-9-82
Source: Trainee.
| 1999–2000 | QPR | 0 | 0 | | |
| 2000–01 | QPR | 0 | 0 | | |

MORROW, Steve* (D) **186 3**
H: 6 0 W: 12 06 b.Bangor 2-7-70
Source: Trainee. *Honours:* Northern Ireland Youth, Under-23, 39 full caps, 1 goal.
1987–88	Arsenal	0	0		
1988–89	Arsenal	0	0		
1989–90	*Reading*	10	0		
1990–91	Arsenal	2	0		
1991–92	Arsenal	0	0		
1991–92	*Watford*	8	0	8	0
1991–92	*Reading*	3	0	13	0
1991–92	*Barnet*	1	0	1	0
1992–93	Arsenal	16	0		
1993–94	Arsenal	11	0		
1994–95	Arsenal	15	1		

1995–96	Arsenal	4	0		
1996–97	Arsenal	14	0	62	1
1996–97	QPR	5	1		
1997–98	QPR	31	1		
1998–99	QPR	24	0		
1999–2000	QPR	7	0		
2000–01	QPR	24	0	91	2
2000–01	*Peterborough U*	11	0	11	0

MURPHY, Danny (D) 0 0
H: 5 6 W: 10 04 b.London 4-12-82
Source: Trainee.
| 1999–2000 | QPR | 0 | 0 | | |
| 2000–01 | QPR | 0 | 0 | | |

MURRAY, Paul# (M) 181 8
H: 5 8 W: 10 05 b.Carlisle 31-8-76
Source: Trainee. *Honours:* England Youth, Under-21, B.
1993–94	Carlisle U	8	0		
1994–95	Carlisle U	5	0		
1995–96	Carlisle U	28	1	41	1
1995–96	QPR	1	0		
1996–97	QPR	32	5		
1997–98	QPR	32	1		
1997–98	QPR	0	0		
1998–99	QPR	39	1		
1999–2000	QPR	30	0		
2000–01	QPR	6	0	140	7

NGONGE, Michel* (F) 174 27
H: 6 0 W: 12 00 b.Huy 10-1-67
Source: Racing Jet, Gent, Seraing, La Louviere. *Honours:* DR Congo full caps.
1995–96	Harelbeke	31	14	31	14
1996–97	Samsunspor	25	0		
1997–98	Samsunspor	27	1	52	1
1998–99	Watford	22	4		
1999–2000	Watford	23	5		
1999–2000	*Huddersfield T*	4	0	4	0
2000–01	Watford	2	0	47	9
2000–01	QPR	13	3	13	3

NUGENT, Marcel (M) 0 0
b.London 10-9-82
Source: Scholar.
| 2000–01 | QPR | 0 | 0 | | |

PACQUETTE, Richard (F) 2 0
H: 6 0 W: 12 07 b.Paddington 28-1-83
Source: Trainee.
| 1999–2000 | QPR | 0 | 0 | | |
| 2000–01 | QPR | 2 | 0 | 2 | 0 |

PEACOCK, Gavin (M) 521 105
H: 5 9 W: 11 08 b.Eltham 18-11-67
Source: Apprentice. *Honours:* England Schools, Youth, Football League.
1984–85	QPR	0	0		
1985–86	QPR	0	0		
1986–87	QPR	12	1		
1987–88	QPR	5	0		
1987–88	Gillingham	26	2		
1988–89	Gillingham	44	9	70	11
1989–90	Bournemouth	41	4		
1990–91	Bournemouth	15	4	56	8
1990–91	Newcastle U	27	7		
1991–92	Newcastle U	46	16		
1992–93	Newcastle U	32	12	105	35
1993–94	Chelsea	37	8		
1994–95	Chelsea	38	4		
1995–96	Chelsea	28	5		
1996–97	Chelsea	0	0	103	17
1996–97	QPR	27	5		
1997–98	QPR	39	9		
1998–99	QPR	42	8		
1999–2000	QPR	30	8		
2000–01	QPR	32	3	187	34

PERRY, Mark (M) 50 1
H: 5 11 W: 13 06 b.Perivale 19-10-78
Source: Trainee. *Honours:* England Schools, Youth.
1995–96	QPR	0	0		
1996–97	QPR	2	1		
1997–98	QPR	8	0		
1998–99	QPR	1	0		
1999–2000	QPR	10	0		
2000–01	QPR	29	0	50	1

PIERCEWRIGHT, Brad‡ (D) 0 0
H: 6 0 W: 12 00 b.Northampton 21-9-80
Source: Northampton T Trainee.
| 1999–2000 | QPR | 0 | 0 | | |
| 2000–01 | QPR | 0 | 0 | | |

PLUMMER, Chris (D) 59 2
H: 6 2 W: 12 12 b.Isleworth 12-10-76
Source: Trainee. *Honours:* England Youth, Under-21.
1994–95	QPR	0	0		
1995–96	QPR	1	0		
1996–97	QPR	5	0		
1997–98	QPR	0	0		

1998–99	QPR	10	0		
1999–2000	QPR	18	0		
2000–01	QPR	25	2	59	2

READY, Karl* (D) 226 10
H: 6 3 W: 13 08 b.Neath 14-8-72
Source: Trainee. *Honours:* Wales Under-21, B, 5 full caps.
1990–91	QPR	0	0		
1991–92	QPR	1	0		
1992–93	QPR	3	0		
1993–94	QPR	22	1		
1994–95	QPR	13	1		
1995–96	QPR	22	1		
1996–97	QPR	29	0		
1997–98	QPR	39	3		
1998–99	QPR	41	2		
1999–2000	QPR	33	2		
2000–01	QPR	23	0	226	10

ROBERTSON, Kristoffer (M) 0 0
b.Paisley 24-9-82
Source: Scholar.
| 2000–01 | QPR | 0 | 0 | | |

ROSE, Matthew* (D) 106 1
H: 5 11 W: 11 09 b.Dartford 24-9-75
Source: Trainee. *Honours:* England Under-21.
1994–95	Arsenal	0	0		
1995–96	Arsenal	4	0		
1996–97	Arsenal	1	0	5	0
1997–98	QPR	16	0		
1998–99	QPR	29	0		
1999–2000	QPR	29	1		
2000–01	QPR	27	0	101	1

ROWLAND, Keith* (M) 222 8
H: 5 10 W: 10 07 b.Portadown 1-9-71
Source: Trainee. *Honours:* Northern Ireland 19 full caps, 1 goal.
1990–91	Bournemouth	0	0		
1991–92	Bournemouth	37	0		
1992–93	Bournemouth	35	2	72	2
1992–93	*Coventry C*	2	0	2	0
1993–94	West Ham U	23	0		
1994–95	West Ham U	12	0		
1995–96	West Ham U	23	0		
1996–97	West Ham U	15	1		
1997–98	West Ham U	7	0	80	1
1997–98	QPR	7	0		
1998–99	QPR	30	3		
1999–2000	QPR	15	0		
2000–01	QPR	4	0	56	3
2000–01	*Luton T*	12	2	12	2

RUSTEM, Adam (F) 0 0
H: 6 0 W: 11 07 b.Whipps Cross 18-9-81
Source: Scholarship.
| 1999–2000 | QPR | 0 | 0 | | |
| 2000–01 | QPR | 0 | 0 | | |

SCULLY, Tony* (M) 83 2
H: 5 7 W: 11 06 b.Dublin 12-6-76
Source: Trainee. *Honours:* Eire Under-21.
1993–94	Crystal Palace	0	0		
1994–95	Crystal Palace	0	0		
1994–95	*Bournemouth*	10	0	10	0
1995–96	Crystal Palace	2	0		
1995–96	*Cardiff C*	14	0	14	0
1996–97	Crystal Palace	1	0		
1997–98	Crystal Palace	0	0	3	0
1997–98	Manchester C	9	0	9	0
1997–98	*Stoke C*	7	0	7	0
1997–98	QPR	7	0		
1998–99	QPR	23	2		
1999–2000	QPR	8	0		
2000–01	QPR	2	0	40	2

SODJE, Iroroakpeyere (M) 0 0
b.Greenwich 31-1-81
| 2000–01 | QPR‡ | 0 | 0 | | |

STEINER, Rob‡ (F) 145 41
H: 6 2 W: 13 05 b.Finsprong 20-6-73
Honours: Sweden 4 full caps, 1 goal.
1995	Norrkoping	16	2		
1996	Norrkoping	25	12		
1997	Norrkoping	6	1	47	15
1997–98	Bradford C	37	10		
1998–99	Bradford C	0	0	52	14
1998–99	*QPR*	12	3		
1998–99	*Walsall*	10	3	10	3
1999–2000	QPR	24	6		
2000–01	QPR	0	0	36	9

THOMSON, Andy (F) 395 146
H: 5 10 W: 11 05 b.Motherwell 14-7-71
Source: Jerviston BC.
1989–90	Q of S	26	6		
1990–91	Q of S	37	11		
1991–92	Q of S	39	26		
1992–93	Q of S	38	21		

1993–94	Q of S	35	29	175	93
1994–95	Southend U	39	11		
1995–96	Southend U	33	6		
1996–97	Southend U	17	5		
1997–98	Southend U	33	6	122	28
1998–99	Oxford U	38	7	38	7
1999–2000	Gillingham	28	9		
2000–01	Gillingham	24	5	52	14
2000–01	QPR	8	4	8	4

WALSHE, Benjamin (M) 1 0
b.London 24-5-83
Source: Scholar.
| 2000–01 | QPR | 1 | 0 | 1 | 0 |

WARDLEY, Stuart (M) 77 14
H: 5 11 W: 12 03 b.Cambridge 10-9-75
Source: Saffron Walden T.
| 1999–2000 | QPR | 43 | 11 | | |
| 2000–01 | QPR | 34 | 3 | 77 | 14 |

WARREN, Christer (M) 147 14
H: 5 10 W: 11 12 b.Poole 10-10-74
Source: Cheltenham T.
1994–95	Southampton	0	0		
1995–96	Southampton	7	0		
1996–97	Southampton	1	0		
1996–97	*Brighton & HA*	3	0	3	0
1996–97	Fulham	11	1	11	1
1997–98	Southampton	0	0	8	0
1997–98	Bournemouth	30	6		
1998–99	Bournemouth	32	5		
1999–2000	Bournemouth	41	2	103	13
2000–01	QPR	22	0	22	0

WATTLEY, David (M) 0 0
b.Enfield 5-9-83
Source: School.
| 2000–01 | QPR | 0 | 0 | | |

WEARE, Ross* (F) 4 0
H: 6 2 W: 13 09 b.Perivale 19-3-77
Source: East Ham U.
1998–99	QPR	0	0		
1999–2000	QPR	4	0		
2000–01	QPR	0	0	4	0

WRIGHT, Danny (M) 0 0
H: 5 7 W: 10 13 b.London 24-9-81
Source: Trainee.
1998–99	QPR	0	0		
1999–2000	QPR	0	0		
2000–01	QPR	0	0		

Scholars
Bean, Marcus T; Burgess, Oliver D; Daly, Wesley JP; Patrick-Heselton, Alistair; Scully, Samuel I

Associated Schoolboy
Egan, Richard L

READING

ALLAWAY, Ricky (D) 0 0
H: 6 2 W: 11 08 b.Reading 16-2-83
Source: Trainee.
| 1999–2000 | Reading | 0 | 0 | | |
| 2000–01 | Reading | 0 | 0 | | |

ASHDOWN, Jamie (G) 1 0
H: 6 3 W: 14 07 b.Wokingham 30-11-80
| 1999–2000 | Reading | 0 | 0 | | |
| 2000–01 | Reading | 1 | 0 | 1 | 0 |

BUTLER, Martin (F) 239 77
H: 6 0 W: 11 07 b.Wordsley 15-9-74
Source: Trainee.
1993–94	Walsall	15	3		
1994–95	Walsall	8	0		
1995–96	Walsall	28	4		
1996–97	Walsall	23	1	74	8
1997–98	Cambridge U	31	10		
1998–99	Cambridge U	46	17		
1999–2000	Cambridge U	26	14	103	41
1999–2000	Reading	17	4		
2000–01	Reading	45	24	62	28

CASKEY, Darren* (M) 240 40
H: 5 8 W: 11 09 b.Basildon 21-8-74
Source: Trainee. *Honours:* England Schools, Youth.
1991–92	Tottenham H	0	0		
1992–93	Tottenham H	0	0		
1993–94	Tottenham H	25	4		
1994–95	Tottenham H	4	0		
1995–96	Tottenham H	3	0	32	4
1995–96	*Watford*	6	1	6	1
1995–96	Reading	15	2		
1996–97	Reading	35	0		
1997–98	Reading	23	0		
1998–99	Reading	42	7		
1999–2000	Reading	44	17		
2000–01	Reading	43	9	202	35

CASPER, Chris (D) 74 2
H: 6 0 W: 11 02 b.Burnley 28-4-75
Source: Trainee. *Honours:* England Youth, Under-21.

1992-93	Manchester U	0	0	
1993-94	Manchester U	0	0	
1994-95	Manchester U	0	0	
1995-96	Manchester U	0	0	
1995-96	*Bournemouth*	16	1	16 1
1996-97	Manchester U	2	0	
1997-98	Manchester U	0	0	
1997-98	*Swindon T*	9	1	9 1
1998-99	Manchester U	0	0	2 0
1998-99	Reading	32	0	
1999-2000	Reading	15	0	
2000-01	Reading	0	0	47 0

CURETON, Jamie (F) 251 104
H: 5 7 W: 11 00 b.Bristol 28-8-75
Source: Trainee. *Honours:* England Youth.

1992-93	Norwich C	0	0	
1993-94	Norwich C	0	0	
1994-95	Norwich C	17	4	
1995-96	Norwich C	12	2	
1995-96	*Bournemouth*	5	0	5 0
1996-97	Norwich C	0	0	29 6
1996-97	Bristol R	38	11	
1997-98	Bristol R	43	13	
1998-99	Bristol R	46	25	
1999-2000	Bristol R	46	22	
2000-01	Bristol R	1	1	174 72
2000-01	Reading	43	26	43 26

FORSTER, Nicky (F) 289 85
H: 5 9 W: 11 01 b.Caterham 8-9-73
Source: Horley T. *Honours:* England Under-21.

1992-93	Gillingham	26	6	
1993-94	Gillingham	41	18	67 24
1994-95	Brentford	46	24	
1995-96	Brentford	38	5	
1996-97	Brentford	25	10	109 39
1996-97	Birmingham C	7	3	
1997-98	Birmingham C	28	3	
1998-99	Birmingham C	33	5	68 11
1999-2000	Reading	36	10	
2000-01	Reading	9	1	45 11

GAMBLE, Joe (M) 1 0
b.Cork 14-1-82
Source: Cork C.

2000-01	Reading	1	0	1 0

GRAY, Stuart‡ (D) 80 3
H: 5 11 W: 12 00 b.Harrogate 18-12-73
Source: Giffnock N. *Honours:* Scotland Under-21.

1992-93	Celtic	1	0	
1993-94	Celtic	0	0	
1994-95	Celtic	11	0	
1995-96	Celtic	5	1	
1996-97	Celtic	11	0	
1997-98	Celtic	0	0	28 1
1997-98	Reading	7	0	
1998-99	Reading	27	2	
1999-2000	Reading	15	0	
2000-01	Reading	3	0	52 2

GURNEY, Andy* (D) 239 22
H: 5 8 W: 10 08 b.Bristol 25-1-74
Source: Trainee.

1992-93	Bristol R	0	0	
1993-94	Bristol R	3	0	
1994-95	Bristol R	38	1	
1995-96	Bristol R	43	6	
1996-97	Bristol R	24	2	108 9
1997-98	Torquay U	44	9	
1998-99	Torquay U	20	1	64 10
1998-99	Reading	8	0	
1999-2000	Reading	38	2	
2000-01	Reading	21	1	67 3

HADDOW, Alex* (M) 3 0
H: 5 8 W: 11 02 b.Fleet 8-1-82
Source: Trainee.

1999-2000	Reading	2	0	
2000-01	Reading	1	0	3 0

HARPER, James (M) 15 1
H: 5 9 W: 11 06 b.Chelmsford 9-11-80
Source: Trainee.

1999-2000	Arsenal	0	0	
2000-01	Arsenal	0	0	
2000-01	*Cardiff C*	3	0	3 0
2000-01	Reading	12	1	12 1

HENDERSON, Darius (F) 10 0
H: 6 1 W: 13 09 b.Doncaster 7-9-81
Source: Trainee.

1999-2000	Reading	6	0	
2000-01	Reading	4	0	10 0

HODGES, Lee* (M) 199 38
H: 5 11 W: 11 06 b.Epping 4-9-73
Source: Trainee.

1991-92	Tottenham H	0	0	
1992-93	Tottenham H	4	0	
1993-94	*Plymouth Arg*	7	2	7 2
1993-94	Tottenham H	0	0	4 0
1993-94	*Wycombe W*	4	0	4 0
1994-95	Barnet	34	4	
1995-96	Barnet	40	17	
1996-97	Barnet	31	5	105 26
1997-98	Reading	24	6	
1998-99	Reading	1	0	
1999-2000	Reading	25	2	
2000-01	Reading	29	2	79 10

HOWIE, Scott* (G) 211 0
H: 6 4 W: 13 07 b.Motherwell 4-1-72
Source: Ferguslie U. *Honours:* Scotland Under-21.

1991-92	Clyde	15	0	
1992-93	Clyde	39	0	
1993-94	Clyde	1	0	55 0
1993-94	Norwich C	2	0	2 0
1994-95	Motherwell	3	0	
1995-96	Motherwell	36	0	
1996-97	Motherwell	30	0	
1997-98	Motherwell	0	0	69 0
1997-98	Reading	7	0	
1998-99	Reading	42	0	
1999-2000	Reading	36	0	
2000-01	Reading	0	0	85 0

HUNTER, Barry (D) 180 10
H: 6 4 W: 12 00 b.Coleraine 18-11-68
Source: Crusaders. *Honours:* Northern Ireland 15 full caps, 1 goal.

1993-94	Wrexham	23	1	
1994-95	Wrexham	37	0	
1995-96	Wrexham	31	3	91 4
1996-97	Reading	27	2	
1997-98	Reading	0	0	
1998-99	Reading	3	0	
1998-99	*Southend U*	5	2	5 2
1999-2000	Reading	31	1	
2000-01	Reading	23	1	84 4

IGOE, Sammy (M) 197 17
H: 5 6 W: 10 08 b.Spelthorne 30-9-75
Source: Trainee.

1993-94	Portsmouth	0	0	
1994-95	Portsmouth	1	0	
1995-96	Portsmouth	22	0	
1996-97	Portsmouth	40	2	
1997-98	Portsmouth	31	3	
1998-99	Portsmouth	40	5	
1999-2000	Portsmouth	26	1	160 11
1999-2000	Reading	6	0	
2000-01	Reading	31	6	37 6

JONES, Keith (M) 492 37
H: 5 9 W: 11 07 b.Dulwich 14-10-65
Source: Apprentice. *Honours:* England Schools, Youth.

1982-83	Chelsea	2	0	
1983-84	Chelsea	0	0	
1984-85	Chelsea	19	2	
1985-86	Chelsea	14	2	
1986-87	Chelsea	17	3	
1987-88	Chelsea	0	0	52 7
1987-88	Brentford	36	1	
1988-89	Brentford	40	3	
1989-90	Brentford	42	2	
1990-91	Brentford	45	6	
1991-92	Brentford	6	1	169 13
1991-92	Southend U	34	5	
1992-93	Southend U	29	1	
1993-94	Southend U	20	5	
1994-95	Southend U	7	0	90 11
1994-95	Charlton Ath	31	1	
1995-96	Charlton Ath	25	0	
1996-97	Charlton Ath	19	0	
1997-98	Charlton Ath	44	3	
1998-99	Charlton Ath	22	1	
1999-2000	Charlton Ath	17	1	158 6
2000-01	Reading	23	0	23 0

LOCKWOOD, Adam (D) 0 0
H: 6 0 W: 12 00 b.Wakefield 26-10-81
Source: Trainee.

1998-99	Reading	0	0	
1999-2000	Reading	0	0	
2000-01	Reading	0	0	

MACKIE, John (D) 10 0
H: 6 0 W: 12 06 b.London 5-7-76
Source: Sutton U.

1999-2000	Reading	0	0	
2000-01	Reading	10	0	10 0

McINTYRE, Jim* (F) 213 36
H: 5 11 W: 11 05 b.Alexandria 24-5-72
Source: Duntocher Boys. *Honours:* Scotland B.

1991-92	Bristol C	1	0	
1992-93	Bristol C	0	0	1 0
1992-93	*Exeter C*	15	3	15 3
1993-94	Airdrieonians	13	0	
1994-95	Airdrieonians	12	1	
1995-96	Airdrieonians	29	9	54 10
1995-96	Kilmarnock	7	2	
1996-97	Kilmarnock	31	6	
1997-98	Kilmarnock	8	1	46 9
1997-98	Reading	6	0	
1998-99	Reading	32	6	
1999-2000	Reading	26	4	
2000-01	Reading	33	4	97 14

McLAREN, Andy (M) 183 13
H: 5 10 W: 10 06 b.Glasgow 5-6-73
Source: Rangers Amateur BC. *Honours:* Scotland Under-21.

1989-90	Dundee U	0	0	
1990-91	Dundee U	0	0	
1991-92	Dundee U	13	0	
1992-93	Dundee U	5	0	
1993-94	Dundee U	27	1	
1994-95	Dundee U	20	0	
1995-96	Dundee U	31	3	
1996-97	Dundee U	34	4	
1997-98	Dundee U	27	4	
1998-99	Dundee U	8	0	165 12
1998-99	Reading	7	1	
1999-2000	Reading	2	0	
1999-2000	*Livingston*	9	0	9 0
2000-01	Reading	0	0	9 1

(Transferred to Kilmarnock, July 2001)

MURTY, Graeme (M) 166 8
H: 5 10 W: 11 10 b.Saltburn 13-11-74
Source: Trainee.

1992-93	York C	0	0	
1993-94	York C	1	0	
1994-95	York C	20	2	
1995-96	York C	35	2	
1996-97	York C	27	2	
1997-98	York C	34	1	117 7
1998-99	Reading	9	0	
1999-2000	Reading	17	0	
2000-01	Reading	23	1	49 1

NEWMAN, Ricky# (M) 254 10
H: 5 10 W: 12 06 b.Guildford 5-8-70
Source: Trainee.

1987-88	Crystal Palace	0	0	
1988-89	Crystal Palace	0	0	
1989-90	Crystal Palace	0	0	
1990-91	Crystal Palace	0	0	
1991-92	Crystal Palace	0	0	
1991-92	*Maidstone U*	10	1	10 1
1992-93	Crystal Palace	2	0	
1993-94	Crystal Palace	11	0	
1994-95	Crystal Palace	35	3	48 3
1995-96	Millwall	36	1	
1996-97	Millwall	41	3	
1997-98	Millwall	35	1	
1998-99	Millwall	24	0	
1999-2000	Millwall	14	0	150 5
1999-2000	*Reading*	7	1	
2000-01	Reading	39	0	46 1

NORBERT, Guilliaume‡ (M) 0 0
b.Chatenoy Malabry 14-10-80
Source: Trainee.

1999-2000	Arsenal	0	0	
2000-01	Reading	0	0	

PARKINSON, Phil# (M) 468 23
H: 6 0 W: 11 06 b.Chorley 1-12-67
Source: Apprentice.

1985-86	Southampton	0	0	
1986-87	Southampton	0	0	
1987-88	Southampton	0	0	
1987-88	Bury	8	1	
1988-89	Bury	39	0	
1989-90	Bury	22	2	
1990-91	Bury	44	2	
1991-92	Bury	32	0	145 5
1992-93	Reading	39	4	
1993-94	Reading	42	3	
1994-95	Reading	31	0	
1995-96	Reading	42	0	
1996-97	Reading	24	1	
1997-98	Reading	37	0	
1998-99	Reading	42	5	
1999-2000	Reading	22	1	
2000-01	Reading	44	4	323 18

POLSTON, John‡ (D) 257 10
H: 5 11 W: 11 12 b.Walthamstow 10-6-68
Source: Apprentice. *Honours:* England Youth.

1985-86	Tottenham H	0	0	

1986–87	Tottenham H	6	0		
1987–88	Tottenham H	2	0		
1988–89	Tottenham H	3	0		
1989–90	Tottenham H	13	1	24	1
1990–91	Norwich C	27	4		
1991–92	Norwich C	19	1		
1992–93	Norwich C	34	1		
1993–94	Norwich C	24	0		
1994–95	Norwich C	38	0		
1995–96	Norwich C	30	0		
1996–97	Norwich C	31	2		
1997–98	Norwich C	12	0	215	8
1998–99	Reading	4	0		
1999–2000	Reading	14	1		
2000–01	Reading	0	0	18	1

ROBINSON, Matt (D) 134 1
H: 5 10 W: 11 02 b.Exeter 23-12-74
Source: Trainee.

1993–94	Southampton	0	0		
1994–95	Southampton	1	0		
1995–96	Southampton	5	0		
1996–97	Southampton	7	0		
1997–98	Southampton	1	0	14	0
1997–98	Portsmouth	15	0		
1998–99	Portsmouth	29	1		
1999–2000	Portsmouth	25	0	69	1
1999–2000	Reading	19	0		
2000–01	Reading	32	0	51	0

ROUGIER, Tony (F) 173 16
H: 5 10 W: 14 07 b.Trinidad 17-7-71
Source: Trinity Pros. *Honours:* Trinidad & Tobago full caps.

1994–95	Raith R	4	0		
1995–96	Raith R	22	1		
1996–97	Raith R	30	1	56	2
1997–98	Hibernian	20	3		
1998–99	Hibernian	15	1	35	4
1998–99	Port Vale	13	0		
1999–2000	Port Vale	38	8	51	8
2000–01	Reading	31	2	31	2

SHOREY, Nicky (D) 15 0
H: 5 9 W: 10 08 b.Romford 19-2-81
Source: Trainee.

1999–2000	Leyton Orient	7	0		
2000–01	Leyton Orient	8	0	15	0
2000–01	Reading	0	0		

SMITH, Christopher* (D) 0 0
H: 5 11 W: 11 01 b.Derby 30-6-81
Source: Trainee.

1999–2000	Reading	0	0		
2000–01	Reading	0	0		

SMITH, Neil (M) 336 13
H: 5 9 W: 12 00 b.Lambeth 30-9-71
Source: Trainee.

1990–91	Tottenham H	0	0		
1991–92	Tottenham H	0	0		
1991–92	Gillingham	26	2		
1992–93	Gillingham	39	3		
1993–94	Gillingham	35	2		
1994–95	Gillingham	33	1		
1995–96	Gillingham	37	1		
1996–97	Gillingham	42	1	212	10
1997–98	Fulham	44	0		
1998–99	Fulham	29	1		
1999–2000	Fulham	0	0	73	1
1999–2000	Reading	36	1		
2000–01	Reading	15	1	51	2

TYSON, Nathan (F) 1 0
H: 6 0 W: 10 01 b.Reading 4-5-82
Source: Trainee.

1999–2000	Reading	1	0		
2000–01	Reading	0	0	1	0

VIVEASH, Adrian (D) 309 18
H: 6 2 W: 12 13 b.Swindon 30-9-69
Source: Trainee.

1988–89	Swindon T	0	0		
1989–90	Swindon T	0	0		
1990–91	Swindon T	25	1		
1991–92	Swindon T	10	0		
1992–93	Swindon T	5	0		
1992–93	*Reading*	5	0		
1993–94	Swindon T	0	0		
1994–95	Swindon T	14	1		
1994–95	*Reading*	6	0		
1995–96	Swindon T	0	0	54	2
1995–96	*Barnsley*	2	1	2	1
1995–96	Walsall	31	0		
1996–97	Walsall	46	9		
1997–98	Walsall	42	3		
1998–99	Walsall	40	0		
1999–2000	Walsall	43	1	202	13
2000–01	Reading	40	2	51	2

WHITEHEAD, Phil (G) 379 0
H: 6 3 W: 13 07 b.Halifax 17-12-69
Source: Trainee.

1986–87	Halifax T	12	0		

1987–88	Halifax T	0	0		
1988–89	Halifax T	11	0		
1989–90	Halifax T	19	0		
1989–90	Barnsley	0	0		
1990–91	Barnsley	0	0		
1990–91	*Halifax T*	9	0	51	0
1991–92	Barnsley	3	0		
1991–92	*Scunthorpe U*	8	0		
1992–93	Barnsley	13	0		
1992–93	*Scunthorpe U*	8	0	16	0
1992–93	*Bradford C*	6	0	6	0
1993–94	Barnsley	0	0	16	0
1993–94	Oxford U	39	0		
1994–95	Oxford U	38	0		
1995–96	Oxford U	34	0		
1996–97	Oxford U	43	0		
1997–98	Oxford U	32	0		
1998–99	Oxford U	21	0	207	0
1998–99	WBA	26	0		
1999–2000	WBA	0	0	26	0
1999–2000	Reading	11	0		
2000–01	Reading	46	0	57	0

WILLIAMS, Adrian (D) 243 15
H: 6 2 W: 12 04 b.Reading 16-8-71
Source: Trainee. *Honours:* Wales 12 full caps, 1 goal.

1988–89	Reading	8	0		
1989–90	Reading	16	2		
1990–91	Reading	7	0		
1991–92	Reading	40	4		
1992–93	Reading	31	4		
1993–94	Reading	41	0		
1994–95	Reading	22	1		
1995–96	Reading	31	3		
1996–97	Wolverhampton W	6	0		
1997–98	Wolverhampton W	20	0		
1998–99	Wolverhampton W	0	0		
1999–2000	Wolverhampton W	1	0	27	0
1999–2000	*Reading*	15	1		
2000–01	Reading	5	0	216	15

Scholars
Alcott, Joseph D; Awbery, Jason S; Birnie, Matthew T; Boddy, Mark S; Brown, Craig; Campion, Adam J; Cox, Simon P; Kurton, Stuart M; Laidler, Stephen T; O'Hara, Declan M; Stamp, Nathan; Stanley, Alex M; Tonna, Michael J; Williams, Scott

ROCHDALE

ATKINSON, Graeme# (D) 306 35
H: 5 7 W: 11 04 b.Hull 11-11-71
Source: Trainee.

1989–90	Hull C	13	1		
1990–91	Hull C	16	0		
1991–92	Hull C	25	8		
1992–93	Hull C	46	6		
1993–94	Hull C	40	7		
1994–95	Hull C	9	1	149	23
1994–95	Preston NE	15	1		
1995–96	Preston NE	44	5		
1996–97	Preston NE	17	0		
1997–98	Preston NE	3	0	79	6
1997–98	*Rochdale*	6	0		
1997–98	Brighton & HA	9	0		
1998–99	Brighton & HA	7	0	16	0
1998–99	Scunthorpe U	1	0	1	0
1998–99	Scarborough	1	1	15	1
1999–2000	Rochdale	40	5		
2000–01	Rochdale	0	0	46	5

BAYLISS, Dave# (D) 177 9
H: 5 11 W: 12 00 b.Liverpool 8-6-76
Source: Trainee.

1994–95	Rochdale	1	0		
1995–96	Rochdale	28	0		
1996–97	Rochdale	24	0		
1997–98	Rochdale	29	2		
1998–99	Rochdale	25	1		
1999–2000	Rochdale	29	3		
2000–01	Rochdale	41	3	177	9

COLEMAN, Simon (D) 379 26
H: 6 1 W: 12 10 b.Mansfield 13-6-68
Source: Apprentice.

1985–86	Mansfield T	0	0		
1986–87	Mansfield T	2	0		
1987–88	Mansfield T	44	2		
1988–89	Mansfield T	45	5		
1989–90	Mansfield T	5	0	96	7
1989–90	Middlesbrough	36	1		
1990–91	Middlesbrough	19	1	55	2
1991–92	Derby Co	43	2		
1992–93	Derby Co	25	0		
1993–94	Derby Co	2	0	70	2
1993–94	Sheffield W	15	1		
1994–95	Sheffield W	1	0	16	1
1994–95	Bolton W	22	4		

1995–96	Bolton W	12	1		
1996–97	Bolton W	0	0		
1997–98	Bolton W	0	0	34	5
1997–98	*Wolverhampton W*	4	0	4	0
1997–98	Southend U	14	0		
1998–99	Southend U	42	4		
1999–2000	Southend U	43	5	99	9
2000–01	Rochdale	5	0	5	0

CONNOR, Paul (F) 68 22
H: 6 2 W: 11 08 b.Bishop Auckland 12-1-79
Source: Trainee.

1996–97	Middlesbrough	0	0		
1997–98	Middlesbrough	0	0		
1997–98	*Hartlepool U*	5	0	5	0
1998–99	Middlesbrough	0	0		
1998–99	Stoke C	3	2		
1999–2000	Stoke C	26	5		
2000–01	Stoke C	7	0	36	7
2000–01	*Cambridge U*	13	5	13	5
2000–01	Rochdale	14	10	14	10

DAVIES, Simon* (M) 102 6
H: 5 11 W: 12 04 b.Davenham 23-4-74
Source: Trainee. *Honours:* Wales 1 full cap.

1992–93	Manchester U	0	0		
1993–94	Manchester U	0	0		
1993–94	*Exeter C*	6	1	6	1
1994–95	Manchester U	5	0		
1995–96	Manchester U	0	0		
1996–97	Manchester U	0	0	11	0
1996–97	*Huddersfield T*	3	0	3	0
1997–98	Luton T	20	1		
1998–99	Luton T	2	0	22	1
1998–99	Macclesfield T	12	2		
1999–2000	Macclesfield T	36	1	48	3
2000–01	Rochdale	12	1	12	1

EDWARDS, Neil (G) 320 0
H: 5 9 W: 11 11 b.Aberdare 5-12-70
Source: Trainee.

1988–89	Leeds U	0	0		
1989–90	Leeds U	0	0		
1990–91	Leeds U	0	0		
1990–91	*Huddersfield T*	0	0		
1991–92	Stockport Co	39	0		
1992–93	Stockport Co	35	0		
1993–94	Stockport Co	26	0		
1994–95	Stockport Co	19	0		
1995–96	Stockport Co	45	0		
1996–97	Stockport Co	0	0		
1997–98	Stockport Co	0	0	164	0
1997–98	Rochdale	27	0		
1998–99	Rochdale	45	0		
1999–2000	Rochdale	40	0		
2000–01	Rochdale	44	0	156	0

ELLIS, Tony* (F) 506 178
H: 5 11 W: 11 00 b.Salford 20-10-64
Source: Horwich RMI, Northwich Vic.

1986–87	Oldham Ath	5	0		
1987–88	Oldham Ath	3	0	8	0
1987–88	Preston NE	24	4		
1988–89	Preston NE	45	19		
1989–90	Preston NE	17	3		
1989–90	Stoke C	24	6		
1990–91	Stoke C	38	9		
1991–92	Stoke C	15	4	77	19
1992–93	Preston NE	35	22		
1993–94	Preston NE	37	26	158	74
1994–95	Blackpool	40	17		
1995–96	Blackpool	43	14		
1996–97	Blackpool	45	15		
1997–98	Blackpool	18	8	146	54
1997–98	Bury	22	6		
1998–99	Bury	16	2	38	8
1998–99	Stockport Co	16	6		
1999–2000	Stockport Co	4	0	20	6
1999–2000	Rochdale	31	11		
2000–01	Rochdale	28	6	59	17

EVANS, Wayne (D) 274 4
H: 5 10 W: 12 03 b.Welshpool 25-8-71
Source: Welshpool.

1993–94	Walsall	41	0		
1994–95	Walsall	36	0		
1995–96	Walsall	24	0		
1996–97	Walsall	28	0		
1997–98	Walsall	43	1		
1998–99	Walsall	11	0	183	1
1999–2000	Rochdale	46	1		
2000–01	Rochdale	45	2	91	3

FLITCROFT, David# (M) 261 22
H: 5 11 W: 13 05 b.Bolton 14-1-74
Source: Trainee.

1991–92	Preston NE	0	0		
1992–93	Preston NE	8	2		
1993–94	Preston NE	0	0	8	2
1993–94	*Lincoln C*	2	0	2	0
1993–94	Chester C	8	1		
1994–95	Chester C	32	0		

1995–96	Chester C	9	1		
1996–97	Chester C	32	6		
1997–98	Chester C	44	4		
1998–99	Chester C	42	6	167	18
1999–2000	Rochdale	43	2		
2000–01	Rochdale	41	0	84	2

FORD, Tony (M) 914 106
H: 5 9 W: 13 00 b.Grimsby 14-5-59
Source: Apprentice. Honours: England B.

1975–76	Grimsby T	15	0		
1976–77	Grimsby T	6	0		
1977–78	Grimsby T	34	2		
1978–79	Grimsby T	45	16		
1979–80	Grimsby T	37	5		
1980–81	Grimsby T	28	4		
1981–82	Grimsby T	35	7		
1982–83	Grimsby T	37	4		
1983–84	Grimsby T	42	8		
1984–85	Grimsby T	42	6		
1985–86	Grimsby T	34	3		
1985–86	*Sunderland*	9	1	9	1
1986–87	Stoke C	41	6		
1987–88	Stoke C	44	7		
1988–89	Stoke C	27	0	112	13
1988–89	WBA	11	1		
1989–90	WBA	42	8		
1990–91	WBA	46	5		
1991–92	WBA	15	0	114	14
1991–92	Grimsby T	22	1		
1992–93	Grimsby T	9	0		
1993–94	Grimsby T	29	0	423	58
1993–94	*Bradford C*	5	0	5	0
1994–95	Scunthorpe U	38	2		
1995–96	Scunthorpe U	38	7	76	9
From Barrow					
1996–97	Mansfield T	27	2		
1997–98	Mansfield T	34	3		
1998–99	Mansfield T	42	2	103	7
1999–2000	Rochdale	34	2		
2000–01	Rochdale	38	2	72	4

GILKS, Matthew§ (G) 3 0
b.Rochdale 4-6-82
Source: Scholar.

2000–01	Rochdale	3	0	3	0

HADLAND, Phil (M) 32 2
H: 5 11 W: 11 11 b.Warrington 20-10-80
Source: Trainee.

1999–2000	Reading	0	0		
2000–01	Rochdale	32	2	32	2

HICKS, Graham (D) 1 0
H: 5 10 W: 13 05 b.Oldham 17-2-81
Source: Trainee.

1998–99	Rochdale	1	0		
1999–2000	Rochdale	0	0		
2000–01	Rochdale	0	0	1	0

HILL, Keith* (D) 395 11
H: 6 1 W: 12 07 b.Bolton 17-5-69
Source: Apprentice.

1986–87	Blackburn R	0	0		
1987–88	Blackburn R	1	0		
1988–89	Blackburn R	15	1		
1989–90	Blackburn R	25	0		
1990–91	Blackburn R	22	2		
1991–92	Blackburn R	32	0		
1992–93	Blackburn R	1	0	96	3
1992–93	Plymouth Arg	36	0		
1993–94	Plymouth Arg	29	1		
1994–95	Plymouth Arg	34	1		
1995–96	Plymouth Arg	24	0	123	2
1996–97	Rochdale	43	3		
1997–98	Rochdale	37	2		
1998–99	Rochdale	33	1		
1999–2000	Rochdale	38	0		
2000–01	Rochdale	25	0	176	6

JONES, Gary (M) 128 17
H: 5 11 W: 11 07 b.Birkenhead 3-6-77

1997–98	Swansea C	8	0	8	0
1997–98	Rochdale	17	2		
1998–99	Rochdale	20	0		
1999–2000	Rochdale	39	7		
2000–01	Rochdale	44	8	120	17

LANCASHIRE, Graham* (F) 180 52
H: 5 9 W: 12 04 b.Blackpool 19-10-72
Source: Trainee.

1990–91	Burnley	1	0		
1991–92	Burnley	25	8		
1992–93	Burnley	3	0		
1992–93	*Halifax T*	2	0	2	0
1993–94	Burnley	1	0		
1993–94	*Chester C*	11	7	11	7
1994–95	Burnley	1	0	31	8
1994–95	Preston NE	17	0		
1995–96	Preston NE	6	2	23	2
1995–96	Wigan Ath	5	3		
1996–97	Wigan Ath	24	9		
1997–98	Wigan Ath	1	0	30	12

1997–98	Rochdale	27	9		
1998–99	Rochdale	11	3		
1999–2000	Rochdale	29	8		
2000–01	Rochdale	16	3	83	23

LANNS, Jason* (D) 0 0
H: 5 8 W: 10 07 b.Birmingham 2-11-81
Source: Birmingham C Trainee.

1998–99	Leeds U	0	0		
1999–2000	Leeds U	0	0		
2000–01	Leeds U	0	0		
2000–01	Rochdale	0	0		

McAULEY, Sean (D) 237 3
H: 5 9 W: 11 13 b.Sheffield 23-6-72
Source: Trainee. Honours: Scotland Under-21.

1991–92	Manchester U	0	0		
1992–93	St Johnstone	26	0		
1993–94	St Johnstone	28	0		
1994–95	St Johnstone	8	0	62	0
1994–95	*Chesterfield*	1	1	1	1
1995–96	Hartlepool U	46	0		
1996–97	Hartlepool U	38	1	84	1
1996–97	Scunthorpe U	9	0		
1997–98	Scunthorpe U	35	1		
1998–99	Scunthorpe U	17	0		
1998–99	*Scarborough*	7	0	7	0
1999–2000	Scunthorpe U	8	0	69	1
1999–2000	Rochdale	13	0		
2000–01	Rochdale	1	0	14	0

MONINGTON, Mark* (D) 258 20
H: 6 1 W: 13 07 b.Mansfield 21-10-70
Source: School.

1988–89	Burnley	8	1		
1989–90	Burnley	13	0		
1990–91	Burnley	0	0		
1991–92	Burnley	12	1		
1992–93	Burnley	31	2		
1993–94	Burnley	20	1		
1994–95	Burnley	0	0	84	5
1994–95	Rotherham U	25	2		
1995–96	Rotherham U	11	0		
1996–97	Rotherham U	28	0		
1997–98	Rotherham U	15	1	79	3
1998–99	Rochdale	37	3		
1999–2000	Rochdale	24	2		
2000–01	Rochdale	34	7	95	12

OLIVER, Michael (M) 211 15
H: 5 10 W: 11 04 b.Middlesbrough 2-8-75
Source: Trainee.

1992–93	Middlesbrough	0	0		
1993–94	Middlesbrough	0	0		
1994–95	Stockport Co	13	0		
1995–96	Stockport Co	9	1	22	1
1996–97	Darlington	39	9		
1997–98	Darlington	39	2		
1998–99	Darlington	36	1		
1999–2000	Darlington	37	2	151	14
2000–01	Rochdale	38	0	38	0

PARKIN, Steve (D) 248 10
H: 5 6 W: 11 01 b.Mansfield 7-11-65
Source: Apprentice. Honours: England Schools, Youth, Under-21.

1982–83	Stoke C	2	0		
1983–84	Stoke C	1	0		
1984–85	Stoke C	13	1		
1985–86	Stoke C	12	1		
1986–87	Stoke C	38	0		
1987–88	Stoke C	43	3		
1988–89	Stoke C	4	0	113	5
1989–90	WBA	14	1		
1990–91	WBA	25	1		
1991–92	WBA	9	0	48	2
1992–93	Mansfield T	16	0		
1993–94	Mansfield T	23	1		
1994–95	Mansfield T	22	1		
1995–96	Mansfield T	26	1		
1996–97	Mansfield T	0	0		
1997–98	Mansfield T	0	0		
1998–99	Mansfield T	0	0		
1999–2000	Mansfield T	0	0	87	3
2000–01	Mansfield T	0	0		

PLATT, Clive (F) 116 21
H: 6 3 W: 12 13 b.Wolverhampton 27-10-77
Source: Trainee.

1995–96	Walsall	4	2		
1996–97	Walsall	1	0		
1997–98	Walsall	20	1		
1998–99	Walsall	7	1		
1999–2000	Walsall	0	0	32	4
1999–2000	Rochdale	41	9		
2000–01	Rochdale	43	8	84	17

PRIESTLEY, Phil* (G) 3 0
H: 6 0 W: 12 09 b.Wigan 30-3-76
Source: Atherton LR.

1998–99	Rochdale	1	0		

1999–2000	Rochdale	2	0		
2000–01	Rochdale	0	0	3	0

TAYLOR, Daniel† (D) 1 0
H: 6 0 W: 11 11 b.Oldham 28-7-82
Source: Scholarship.

1999–2000	Rochdale	1	0		
2000–01	Rochdale	0	0	1	0

TODD, Lee (D) 291 5
H: 5 7 W: 11 01 b.Hartlepool 7-3-72
Source: Hartlepool U Trainee.

1990–91	Stockport Co	14	0		
1991–92	Stockport Co	19	0		
1992–93	Stockport Co	39	0		
1993–94	Stockport Co	33	0		
1994–95	Stockport Co	37	2		
1995–96	Stockport Co	42	0		
1996–97	Stockport Co	41	0	225	2
1997–98	Southampton	10	0	10	0
1998–99	Bradford C	15	0		
1999–2000	Bradford C	0	0	15	0
1999–2000	Walsall	1	0	1	0
2000–01	Rochdale	40	3	40	3

TOWNSON, Kevin (F) 3 0
b.Liverpool 19-4-83

2000–01	Rochdale	3	0	3	0

WARE, Paul (M) 222 18
H: 5 9 W: 11 05 b.Congleton 7-11-70
Source: Trainee.

1987–88	Stoke C	1	0		
1988–89	Stoke C	11	1		
1989–90	Stoke C	16	0		
1990–91	Stoke C	34	2		
1991–92	Stoke C	24	3		
1992–93	Stoke C	28	4		
1993–94	Stoke C	1	0		
1994–95	Stoke C	0	0	115	10
1994–95	Stockport Co	19	1		
1995–96	Stockport Co	27	3		
1996–97	Stockport Co	8	0	54	4
1996–97	*Cardiff C*	5	0	5	0
From Hednesford T.					
1999–2000	Macclesfield T	18	2	18	2
2000–01	Rochdale	30	2	30	2

Scholars
Bell, Colin; Cantello, Stuart L; Crowe, Alex; Duffy, Lee; Duffy, Matthew J; Ford, Joshua MA; Gilks, Matthew; Grand, Simon; Harvey, John D; Hill, Stephen B; McCourt, Patrick J; Murphy, Shane P; Rudd, Paul G; Smith, Steven K; Taylor, Daniel J; Taylor, Warren D; Walsh, David A; Warner, Scott

ROTHERHAM U

ARTELL, David (D) 37 4
H: 6 2 W: 13 00 b.Rotherham 22-11-80
Source: Trainee.

1999–2000	Rotherham U	1	0		
2000–01	Rotherham U	36	4	37	4

BARKER, Richard (F) 143 36
H: 6 1 W: 13 12 b.Sheffield 30-5-75
Source: Trainee. Honours: England Schools.

1993–94	Sheffield W	0	0		
1994–95	Sheffield W	0	0		
1995–96	Sheffield W	0	0		
1995–96	*Doncaster R*	6	0	6	0
1996–97	Sheffield W	0	0		
From Linfield.					
1997–98	Brighton & HA	17	2		
1998–99	Brighton & HA	43	10	60	12
1999–2000	Macclesfield T	35	16		
2000–01	Macclesfield T	23	7	58	23
2000–01	Rotherham U	19	1	19	1

BEECH, Chris# (D) 91 7
H: 5 9 W: 12 09 b.Congleton 5-11-75
Source: Trainee. Honours: England Schools, Youth.

1992–93	Manchester C	0	0		
1993–94	Manchester C	0	0		
1994–95	Manchester C	0	0		
1995–96	Manchester C	0	0		
1996–97	Manchester C	0	0		
1997–98	Cardiff C	46	1	46	1
1998–99	Rotherham U	24	0		
1999–2000	Rotherham U	6	0		
2000–01	Rotherham U	15	0	45	0

BERRY, Trevor (M) 179 21
H: 5 6 W: 11 00 b.Haslemere 1-8-74
Source: Bournemouth.

1991–92	Aston Villa	0	0		
1992–93	Aston Villa	0	0		
1993–94	Aston Villa	0	0		
1994–95	Aston Villa	0	0		
1995–96	Aston Villa	0	0		

1995–96	Rotherham U	36	7		
1996–97	Rotherham U	30	4		
1997–98	Rotherham U	42	3		
1998–99	Rotherham U	18	2		
1999–2000	Rotherham U	36	4		
2000–01	Rotherham U	11	0	173	20
2000–01	*Scunthorpe U*	6	1	6	1

BOLIMA, Cedric† (F)   1 0
b.Kinshasa 26-9-79

| 2000–01 | Rotherham U | 1 | 0 | 1 | 0 |

BRANSTON, Guy (D)   95 12
H: 6 1 W: 13 11 b.Leicester 9-1-79
Source: Trainee.

1997–98	Leicester C	0	0		
1997–98	*Colchester U*	12	1		
1998–99	Leicester C	0	0		
1998–99	*Colchester U*	1	0	13	1
1998–99	*Plymouth Arg*	7	1	7	1
1999–2000	Leicester C	0	0		
1999–2000	*Lincoln C*	4	0	4	0
1999–2000	Rotherham U	30	4		
2000–01	Rotherham U	41	6	71	10

BRYAN, Marvin (D)   224 5
H: 6 0 W: 12 02 b.Paddington 2-8-75
Source: Trainee.

1992–93	QPR	0	0		
1993–94	QPR	0	0		
1994–95	QPR	0	0		
1994–95	*Doncaster R*	5	1	5	1
1995–96	Blackpool	46	1		
1996–97	Blackpool	34	1		
1997–98	Blackpool	43	1		
1998–99	Blackpool	41	1		
1999–2000	Blackpool	18	0	182	4
1999–2000	Bury	9	0	9	0
2000–01	Rotherham U	28	0	28	0

CONNOR, Gareth* (M)   0 0
b.Huddersfield 11-7-82
Source: Scholar.

| 2000–01 | Rotherham U | 0 | 0 | | |

DILLON, Paul‡ (D)   70 2
H: 5 9 W: 10 11 b.Limerick 22-10-78
Source: Trainee.

1996–97	Rotherham U	13	1		
1997–98	Rotherham U	16	0		
1998–99	Rotherham U	26	1		
1999–2000	Rotherham U	15	0		
2000–01	Rotherham U	0	0	70	2

GARNER, Darren (M)   234 21
H: 5 9 W: 12 07 b.Plymouth 10-12-71
Source: Trainee.

1988–89	Plymouth Arg	1	0		
1989–90	Plymouth Arg	1	0		
1990–91	Plymouth Arg	5	1		
1991–92	Plymouth Arg	10	0		
1992–93	Plymouth Arg	10	0		
1993–94	Plymouth Arg	0	0	27	1

From Dorchester T.

1995–96	Rotherham U	31	1		
1996–97	Rotherham U	30	2		
1997–98	Rotherham U	40	3		
1998–99	Rotherham U	40	4		
1999–2000	Rotherham U	35	9		
2000–01	Rotherham U	31	1	207	20

GRAY, Ian (G)   127 0
H: 6 2 W: 13 00 b.Manchester 25-2-75
Source: Trainee.

1993–94	Oldham Ath	0	0		
1994–95	Oldham Ath	0	0		
1994–95	Rochdale	12	0		
1995–96	Rochdale	20	0		
1996–97	Rochdale	46	0	78	0
1997–98	Stockport Co	3	0		
1998–99	Stockport Co	3	0		
1999–2000	Stockport Co	10	0	16	0
2000–01	Rotherham U	33	0	33	0

HUDSON, Danny (M)   48 5
H: 5 8 W: 10 03 b.Mexborough 25-6-79
Source: Trainee.

1997–98	Rotherham U	10	0		
1998–99	Rotherham U	26	4		
1999–2000	Rotherham U	7	1		
2000–01	Rotherham U	5	0	48	5

HURST, Paul (D)   223 11
H: 5 4 W: 9 00 b.Sheffield 25-9-74
Source: Trainee.

1993–94	Rotherham U	4	0		
1994–95	Rotherham U	13	0		
1995–96	Rotherham U	40	1		
1996–97	Rotherham U	30	3		
1997–98	Rotherham U	30	0		
1998–99	Rotherham U	32	2		
1999–2000	Rotherham U	30	2		
2000–01	Rotherham U	44	3	223	11

KNILL, Alan‡ (D)   560 31
H: 6 4 W: 13 00 b.Slough 8-10-64
Source: Apprentice. Honours: Wales Youth, 1 full cap.

1982–83	Southampton	0	0		
1983–84	Southampton	0	0		
1984–85	Halifax T	44	1		
1985–86	Halifax T	33	2		
1986–87	Halifax T	41	3	118	6
1987–88	Swansea C	46	1		
1988–89	Swansea C	43	2	89	3
1989–90	Bury	43	1		
1990–91	Bury	20	1		
1991–92	Bury	35	1		
1992–93	Bury	38	5		
1993–94	Bury	8	0	144	8
1993–94	*Cardiff C*	4	0	4	0
1993–94	Scunthorpe U	25	1		
1994–95	Scunthorpe U	39	4		
1995–96	Scunthorpe U	38	3		
1996–97	Scunthorpe U	29	0	131	8
1997–98	Rotherham U	38	3		
1998–99	Rotherham U	36	3		
1999–2000	Rotherham U	0	0		
2000–01	Rotherham U	0	0	74	6

LEE, Alan (F)   64 17
H: 6 2 W: 13 09 b.Galway 21-8-78
Source: Trainee. Honours: Éire Under-21.

1995–96	Aston Villa	0	0		
1996–97	Aston Villa	0	0		
1997–98	Aston Villa	0	0		
1998–99	Aston Villa	0	0		
1998–99	*Torquay U*	7	2	7	2
1998–99	*Port Vale*	11	2	11	2
1999–2000	Burnley	15	0		
2000–01	Burnley	0	0	15	0
2000–01	Rotherham U	31	13	31	13

LEMARCHAND, Stephane‡ (M)   5 1
b.Saint-Lo 6-8-71
Source: Louhans.

| 2000–01 | Carlisle U | 5 | 1 | 5 | 1 |
| 2000–01 | Rotherham U | 0 | 0 | | |

MINTON, Jeffrey* (F)   221 38
H: 5 10 W: 12 04 b.Hackney 28-12-73
Source: Trainee.

1991–92	Tottenham H	2	1		
1992–93	Tottenham H	0	0		
1993–94	Tottenham H	0	0	2	1
1994–95	Brighton & HA	39	5		
1995–96	Brighton & HA	39	8		
1996–97	Brighton & HA	25	3		
1997–98	Brighton & HA	36	6		
1998–99	Brighton & HA	35	9	174	31
1999–2000	Port Vale	23	3		
2000–01	Port Vale	13	1	36	4
2000–01	Rotherham U	9	2	9	2

MONKHOUSE, Andy (F)   17 1
H: 6 0 W: 13 09 b.Leeds 23-10-80
Source: Trainee.

1998–99	Rotherham U	5	1		
1999–2000	Rotherham U	0	0		
2000–01	Rotherham U	12	0	17	1

PETTINGER, Paul* (G)   20 0
H: 6 0 W: 13 00 b.Sheffield 1-10-75
Source: Barnsley. Honours: England Schools, Youth.

1992–93	Leeds U	0	0		
1993–94	Leeds U	0	0		
1994–95	Leeds U	0	0		
1994–95	*Torquay U*	3	0	3	0
1995–96	Leeds U	0	0		
1995–96	*Rotherham U*	1	0		
1995–96	Gillingham	0	0		
1996–97	Carlisle U	0	0		
1997–98	Rotherham U	3	0		
1998–99	Rotherham U	0	0		
1999–2000	Rotherham U	0	0		
2000–01	Rotherham U	13	0	17	0

ROBINS, Mark (F)   260 73
H: 5 8 W: 11 08 b.Ashton-under-Lyne 22-12-69
Source: Apprentice. Honours: England Under-21.

1986–87	Manchester U	0	0		
1987–88	Manchester U	0	0		
1988–89	Manchester U	10	0		
1989–90	Manchester U	17	7		
1990–91	Manchester U	19	4		
1991–92	Manchester U	2	0	48	11
1992–93	Norwich C	37	15		
1993–94	Norwich C	13	1		
1994–95	Norwich C	17	4	67	20
1994–95	Leicester C	17	5		
1995–96	Leicester C	31	6		
1996–97	Leicester C	8	1		
1997–98	Leicester C	0	0	56	12

| 1997–98 | *Reading* | 5 | 0 | 5 | 0 |

From Panionios.

1998–99	Manchester C	2	0	2	0
1999–2000	Walsall	40	6	40	6
2000–01	Rotherham U	42	24	42	24

SCOTT, Rob (F)   189 28
H: 6 1 W: 12 04 b.Epsom 15-8-73
Source: Sutton U.

1993–94	Sheffield U	0	0		
1994–95	Sheffield U	0	0		
1994–95	*Scarborough*	8	3	8	3
1995–96	Sheffield U	5	1	6	1
1995–96	*Northampton T*	5	0	5	0
1995–96	Fulham	21	5		
1996–97	Fulham	43	9		
1997–98	Fulham	17	3		
1998–99	Fulham	3	0	84	17
1998–99	*Carlisle U*	7	3	7	3
1998–99	Rotherham U	6	1		
1999–2000	Rotherham U	34	1		
2000–01	Rotherham U	39	2	79	4

SEDGWICK, Chris (F)   96 11
H: 5 11 W: 10 10 b.Sheffield 28-4-80
Source: Trainee.

1997–98	Rotherham U	4	0		
1998–99	Rotherham U	33	4		
1999–2000	Rotherham U	38	5		
2000–01	Rotherham U	21	2	96	11

TALBOT, Stuart (M)   175 15
H: 5 11 W: 13 07 b.Birmingham 14-6-73
Source: Doncaster R, Moor Green.

1994–95	Port Vale	2	0		
1995–96	Port Vale	20	0		
1996–97	Port Vale	34	4		
1997–98	Port Vale	42	6		
1998–99	Port Vale	33	0		
1999–2000	Port Vale	6	0	137	10
2000–01	Rotherham U	38	5	38	5

TURNER, Andy* (M)   121 9
H: 5 10 W: 11 10 b.Woolwich 23-3-75
Source: Trainee. Honours: England Schools, Éire Under-21.

1991–92	Tottenham H	0	0		
1992–93	Tottenham H	18	3		
1993–94	Tottenham H	1	0		
1994–95	Tottenham H	1	0		
1994–95	*Wycombe W*	4	0	4	0
1994–95	*Doncaster R*	4	1	4	1
1995–96	Tottenham H	0	0		
1995–96	*Huddersfield T*	5	1	5	1
1995–96	*Southend U*	6	0	6	0
1996–97	Tottenham H	0	0	20	3
1996–97	Portsmouth	24	2		
1997–98	Portsmouth	16	1		
1998–99	Portsmouth	0	0	40	3
1998–99	*Crystal Palace*	2	0	2	0
1998–99	Wolverhampton W	0	0		
1999–2000	Rotherham U	32	1		
2000–01	Rotherham U	4	0	36	1
2000–01	*Rochdale*	4	0	4	0

VARTY, Will* (D)   129 1
H: 6 0 W: 12 00 b.Workington 1-10-76
Source: Trainee.

1995–96	Carlisle U	0	0		
1996–97	Carlisle U	32	0		
1997–98	Carlisle U	44	1		
1998–99	Carlisle U	6	0	82	1
1998–99	*Rotherham U*	14	0		
1999–2000	Rotherham U	27	0		
2000–01	Rotherham U	6	0	47	0

WARNE, Paul (F)   142 28
H: 5 8 W: 11 01 b.Norwich 8-5-73
Source: Wroxham.

1997–98	Wigan Ath	25	2		
1998–99	Wigan Ath	11	1	36	3
1998–99	Rotherham U	19	8		
1999–2000	Rotherham U	43	10		
2000–01	Rotherham U	44	7	106	25

WATSON, Kevin (M)   176 7
H: 5 10 W: 12 08 b.Hackney 3-1-74
Source: Trainee.

1991–92	Tottenham H	0	0		
1992–93	Tottenham H	5	0		
1993–94	Tottenham H	0	0		
1993–94	*Brentford*	3	0	3	0
1994–95	Tottenham H	0	0		
1994–95	*Bristol C*	2	0	2	0
1994–95	*Barnet*	13	0	13	0
1995–96	Tottenham H	0	0	5	0
1996–97	Swindon T	27	1		
1997–98	Swindon T	18	0		
1998–99	Swindon T	18	0	63	1
1999–2000	Rotherham U	44	1		
2000–01	Rotherham U	46	5	90	6

WILLIAMS, Mark‡ (D) 25 1
H: 6 0 W: 11 02 b.Liverpool 10-11-78
Source: Tranmere Trainee.

1998-99	Rochdale	14	1	14 1
1998-99	Rotherham U	11	0	
1999-2000	Rotherham U	0	0	
2000-01	Rotherham U	0	0	11 0

WILSTERMAN, Brian* (D) 94 6
H: 6 1 W: 14 02 b.Surinam 19-11-66
Source: Beerschot.

1996-97	Oxford U	1	0	
1997-98	Oxford U	24	0	
1998-99	Oxford U	17	2	42 2
1999-2000	Rotherham U	42	3	
2000-01	Rotherham U	10	1	52 4

Scholars
Alabi, Stephen; Barker, Shaun; Barraclough, Simon D; Beggs, John A; Bowler, Kris PM; Boyd, Darren; Capill, Stephen L; Clarke, Leon K; Gregory, Benjamin D; Holyer, Ian D; Lees, Scott; Letts, Scott D; McCoy, James TG; Sandland, Guy; Shelton, Lee M; Smith, Thomas; Wright, Mark J

SCUNTHORPE U

BARWICK, Terry† (M) 1 0
H: 5 11 W: 10 12 b.Sheffield 11-1-83
Source: Scholarship.

1999-2000	Scunthorpe U	1	0	
2000-01	Scunthorpe U	0	0	1 0

BROUGH, Scott (M) 4 0
b.Doncaster 10-2-83

2000-01	Scunthorpe U	4	0	4 0

CALVO-GARCIA, Alexander (M) 152 21
H: 5 11 W: 11 10 b.Ordizia 1-1-72
Source: Eibar.

1996-97	Scunthorpe U	13	1	
1997-98	Scunthorpe U	44	6	
1998-99	Scunthorpe U	43	9	
1999-2000	Scunthorpe U	18	1	
2000-01	Scunthorpe U	34	4	152 21

CARRUTHERS, Martin (F) 276 69
H: 5 10 W: 12 02 b.Nottingham 7-8-72
Source: Trainee.

1990-91	Aston Villa	0	0	
1991-92	Aston Villa	3	0	
1992-93	Aston Villa	1	0	4 0
1992-93	Hull C	13	6	13 6
1993-94	Stoke C	34	5	
1994-95	Stoke C	32	5	
1995-96	Stoke C	24	3	
1996-97	Stoke C	1	0	91 13
1996-97	Peterborough U	14	4	
1997-98	Peterborough U	39	15	
1998-99	Peterborough U	14	2	67 21
1998-99	York C	6	0	6 0
1998-99	Darlington	11	2	
1999-2000	Darlington	6	0	17 2
1999-2000	Southend U	38	19	
2000-01	Southend U	32	7	70 26
2000-01	Scunthorpe U	8	1	8 1

COTTERILL, James§ (D) 4 0
H: 6 0 W: 12 04 b.Barnsley 3-8-82
Source: Scholar.

2000-01	Scunthorpe U	4	0	4 0

DAWSON, Andrew (D) 108 6
H: 5 9 W: 11 05 b.Northallerton 20-10-78
Source: Trainee.

1995-96	Nottingham F	0	0	
1996-97	Nottingham F	0	0	
1997-98	Nottingham F	0	0	
1998-99	Nottingham F	0	0	
1998-99	Scunthorpe U	24	0	
1999-2000	Scunthorpe U	43	2	
2000-01	Scunthorpe U	41	4	108 6

EVANS, Tom# (G) 103 0
H: 6 1 W: 13 02 b.Doncaster 31-12-76
Source: Trainee.

1995-96	Sheffield U	0	0	
1996-97	Crystal Palace	0	0	
1996-97	Coventry C	0	0	
1997-98	Scunthorpe U	5	0	
1998-99	Scunthorpe U	24	0	
1999-2000	Scunthorpe U	28	0	
2000-01	Scunthorpe U	46	0	103 0

FICKLING, Ashley* (D) 130 3
H: 5 10 W: 11 08 b.Sheffield 15-11-72
Source: Trainee. *Honours:* England Schools.

1991-92	Sheffield U	0	0
1992-93	Sheffield U	0	0
1992-93	*Darlington*	14	0
1993-94	*Darlington*	1	0
1994-95	Sheffield U	0	0

1994-95	Grimsby T	1	0	
1995-96	Grimsby T	11	0	
1996-97	Grimsby T	27	2	
1997-98	Grimsby T	0	0	39 2
1997-98	*Darlington*	8	0	23 0
1998-99	Scunthorpe U	29	0	
1999-2000	Scunthorpe U	30	1	
2000-01	Scunthorpe U	9	0	68 1

GRAVES, Wayne (M) 56 2
H: 5 8 W: 10 09 b.Scunthorpe 18-9-80
Source: Trainee.

1997-98	Scunthorpe U	3	0	
1998-99	Scunthorpe U	0	0	
1999-2000	Scunthorpe U	19	0	
2000-01	Scunthorpe U	34	2	56 2

HARSLEY, Paul* (M) 128 5
H: 5 10 W: 11 03 b.Scunthorpe 29-5-78
Source: Trainee.

1996-97	Grimsby T	0	0	
1997-98	Scunthorpe U	15	1	
1998-99	Scunthorpe U	34	0	
1999-2000	Scunthorpe U	46	3	
2000-01	Scunthorpe U	33	1	128 5

HODGES, Lee (M) 124 15
H: 5 5 W: 11 00 b.Newham 2-3-78
Source: Trainee. *Honours:* England Schools.

1994-95	West Ham U	0	0	
1995-96	West Ham U	0	0	
1996-97	West Ham U	0	0	
1996-97	Exeter C	17	0	17 0
1996-97	Leyton Orient	3	0	3 0
1997-98	West Ham U	2	0	
1997-98	Plymouth Arg	9	0	9 0
1998-99	West Ham U	1	0	3 0
1998-99	Ipswich T	4	0	4 0
1998-99	*Southend U*	10	1	10 1
1999-2000	Scunthorpe U	40	6	
2000-01	Scunthorpe U	38	8	78 14

HOUSHAM, Steven‡ (M) 115 4
H: 5 10 W: 12 03 b.Gainsborough 24-2-76
Source: Trainee.

1993-94	Scunthorpe U	0	0	
1994-95	Scunthorpe U	4	0	
1995-96	Scunthorpe U	28	0	
1996-97	Scunthorpe U	34	3	
1997-98	Scunthorpe U	24	1	
1998-99	Scunthorpe U	16	0	
1999-2000	Scunthorpe U	9	0	
2000-01	Scunthorpe U	0	0	115 4

JACKSON, Mark (D) 63 1
H: 5 11 W: 12 04 b.Barnsley 30-9-77
Source: Trainee. *Honours:* England Youth.

1995-96	Leeds U	1	0	
1996-97	Leeds U	17	0	
1997-98	Leeds U	1	0	
1998-99	Leeds U	0	0	
1998-99	*Huddersfield T*	5	0	5 0
1999-2000	Leeds U	0	0	19 0
1999-2000	*Barnsley*	1	0	1 0
1999-2000	Scunthorpe U	6	0	
2000-01	Scunthorpe U	32	1	38 1

LARUSSON, Bjarni‡ (M) 159 13
H: 5 10 W: 12 10 b.Iceland 11-3-76

1993	IBV	4	0	
1994	IBV	15	0	
1995	IBV	13	1	
1996	IBV	15	2	
1997	IBV	13	2	60 5
1997-98	Hibernian	7	1	
1998-99	Hibernian	0	0	7 1
1998-99	Walsall	36	3	
1999-2000	Walsall	23	0	59 3
2000-01	Scunthorpe U	33	4	33 4

MAMOUN, Blaise† (F) 2 0
H: 5 9 W: 11 05 b.Cameroon 25-12-79

1997-98	St Etienne	1	0	
1998-99	St Etienne	0	0	1 0

From Red Star Paris

2000-01	Scunthorpe U	1	0	1 0

MORRISON, Peter* (M) 18 0
H: 5 11 W: 10 00 b.Manchester 29-6-80
Source: Trainee.

1998-99	Bolton W	0	0	
1999-2000	Bolton W	0	0	
2000-01	Scunthorpe U	18	0	18 0

PEPPER, Nigel (M) 360 53
H: 5 10 W: 11 13 b.Rotherham 25-4-68
Source: Apprentice.

1985-86	Rotherham U	7	0	
1986-87	Rotherham U	8	0	
1987-88	Rotherham U	15	0	
1988-89	Rotherham U	2	0	
1989-90	Rotherham U	19	1	45 1
1990-91	York C	39	3	
1991-92	York C	35	4	

1992-93	York C	34	8	
1993-94	York C	23	0	
1994-95	York C	35	4	
1995-96	York C	40	8	
1996-97	York C	29	12	235 39
1996-97	Bradford C	11	5	
1997-98	Bradford C	32	5	
1998-99	Bradford C	9	1	52 11
1998-99	Aberdeen	10	0	
1999-2000	Aberdeen	4	0	14 0
1999-2000	Southend U	12	2	12 2
2000-01	Scunthorpe U	2	0	2 0

QUAILEY, Brian (F) 61 10
H: 6 0 W: 13 04 b.Leicester 21-3-78
Source: Nuneaton B.

1997-98	WBA	5	0	
1998-99	WBA	2	0	
1998-99	*Exeter C*	12	2	12 2
1999-2000	WBA	0	0	7 0
1999-2000	*Blackpool*	1	0	1 0
2000-01	Scunthorpe U	14	5	
2000-01	Scunthorpe U	27	3	41 8

RIDLEY, Lee§ (D) 2 0
H: 5 10 W: 12 04 b.Scunthorpe 5-12-81
Source: Scholar.

2000-01	Scunthorpe U	2	0	2 0

ROGERS, Dave† (D) 85 3
H: 6 1 W: 12 00 b.Liverpool 25-8-75
Source: Trainee.

1994-95	Tranmere R	0	0	
1995-96	Chester C	20	1	
1996-97	Chester C	5	0	25 1

From Southport.

1997-98	Dundee	32	1	
1998-99	Dundee	11	0	43 1
1999-2000	Ayr U	16	1	16 1
2000-01	Scunthorpe U	1	0	1 0

SHELDON, Gareth (F) 73 4
H: 5 11 W: 12 06 b.Birmingham 31-1-80
Source: Trainee.

1997-98	Scunthorpe U	1	0	
1998-99	Scunthorpe U	11	1	
1999-2000	Scunthorpe U	22	2	
2000-01	Scunthorpe U	39	1	73 4

SPARROW, Matthew§ (M) 22 4
H: 5 11 W: 10 06 b.Scunthorpe 3-10-83
Source: Scholarship.

1999-2000	Scunthorpe U	11	0	
2000-01	Scunthorpe U	11	4	22 4

STAMP, Darryn‡ (F) 62 6
H: 6 1 W: 11 10 b.Beverley 21-9-78

1997-98	Scunthorpe U	10	1	
1998-99	Scunthorpe U	25	4	
1999-2000	Scunthorpe U	10	0	
1999-2000	*Halifax T*	5	0	5 0
2000-01	Scunthorpe U	12	1	57 6

STANTON, Nathan (D) 77 0
H: 5 9 W: 12 06 b.Nottingham 6-5-81
Source: Trainee. *Honours:* England Youth.

1997-98	Scunthorpe U	1	0	
1998-99	Scunthorpe U	4	0	
1999-2000	Scunthorpe U	34	0	
2000-01	Scunthorpe U	38	0	77 0

THOM, Stuart (D) 60 3
H: 6 3 W: 13 01 b.Dewsbury 27-12-76
Source: Trainee.

1993-94	Nottingham F	0	0	
1994-95	Nottingham F	0	0	
1995-96	Nottingham F	0	0	
1996-97	Nottingham F	0	0	
1997-98	Nottingham F	0	0	
1997-98	*Mansfield T*	5	0	5 0
1998-99	Nottingham F	0	0	
1998-99	Oldham Ath	25	1	
1999-2000	Oldham Ath	9	2	
2000-01	Oldham Ath	0	0	34 3
2000-01	Scunthorpe U	21	0	21 0

TORPEY, Steve (F) 396 91
H: 6 3 W: 13 06 b.Islington 8-12-70
Source: Trainee.

1988-89	Millwall	0	0	
1989-90	Millwall	7	0	
1990-91	Millwall	0	0	7 0
1990-91	Bradford C	29	7	
1991-92	Bradford C	43	10	
1992-93	Bradford C	24	5	96 22
1993-94	Swansea C	40	9	
1994-95	Swansea C	41	11	
1995-96	Swansea C	42	15	
1996-97	Swansea C	39	9	162 44
1997-98	Bristol C	29	8	
1998-99	Bristol C	21	4	
1998-99	*Notts Co*	6	1	6 1
1999-2000	Bristol C	20	1	70 13
1999-2000	Scunthorpe U	15	1	
2000-01	Scunthorpe U	40	10	55 11

WILCOX, Russ# (D) **491 27**
H: 6 0 W: 12 13 b.Hemsworth 25-3-64
Source: Apprentice.
1980–81 Doncaster R 1 0
From Cambridge U, Frickley Ath.
1986–87 Northampton
1987–88 Northampton T 46 4
1988–89 Northampton T 11 1
1989–90 Northampton T 46 3 **138 9**
1990–91 Hull C 31 1
1991–92 Hull C 40 4
1992–93 Hull C 29 2 **100 7**
1993–94 Doncaster R 40 2
1994–95 Doncaster R 37 4
1995–96 Doncaster R 4 0 **82 6**
1995–96 Preston NE 27 1
1996–97 Preston NE 35 0 **62 1**
1997–98 Scunthorpe U 31 2
1998–99 Scunthorpe U 28 1
1999–2000 Scunthorpe U 14 0
2000–01 Scunthorpe U 36 1 **109 4**

Scholars
Anderson, Mark J; Barwick, Terence P; Burraway, David; Butler, Andrew P; Collins, Neil J; Cotterill, James M; Hawcroft, Richard C; Herrick, Leigh; Marsh, Craig; Masson, Daniel P; McCombe, Jamie; Mulchinock, Daniel T; Parton, Andrew; Ridley, Lee; Ridley, Steven; Singh, Sean; Sparrow, Matthew

SHEFFIELD U

ANDERSON, Michael‡ (M) **0 0**
H: 5 10 W: 11 03 b.Leicester 4-10-81
Source: Scholar.
2000–01 Sheffield U 0 0

ASABA, Carl (F) **186 76**
H: 6 2 W: 13 00 b.London 28-1-73
Source: Dulwich Hamlet.
1994–95 Brentford 0 0
1994–95 *Colchester U* 12 2 **12 2**
1995–96 Brentford 10 2
1996–97 Brentford 44 23 **54 25**
1997–98 Reading 32 8
1998–99 Reading 1 0 **33 8**
1998–99 Gillingham 41 20
1999–2000 Gillingham 11 6
2000–01 Gillingham 25 10 **77 36**
2000–01 Sheffield U 10 5 **10 5**

BROWN, Michael R (M) **159 7**
H: 5 9 W: 10 07 b.Hartlepool 25-1-77
Source: Trainee. *Honours:* England Under-21.
1994–95 Manchester C 0 0
1995–96 Manchester C 21 0
1996–97 Manchester C 11 0
1996–97 *Hartlepool U* 6 1 **6 1**
1997–98 Manchester C 26 0
1998–99 Manchester C 31 2
1999–2000 Manchester C 0 0 **89 2**
1999–2000 *Portsmouth* 4 0 **4 0**
1999–2000 Sheffield U 24 3
2000–01 Sheffield U 36 1 **60 4**

BURLEY, Adam (M) **3 1**
H: 5 10 W: 12 06 b.Sheffield 27-11-80
Source: Trainee.
1999–2000 Sheffield U 2 1
2000–01 Sheffield U 1 0 **3 1**

CRYAN, Colin (M) **1 0**
H: 5 10 W: 13 00 b.Dublin 23-3-81
Source: Scholarship.
1999–2000 Sheffield U 0 0
2000–01 Sheffield U 1 0 **1 0**

CURLE, Keith (D) **648 33**
H: 6 0 W: 12 07 b.Bristol 14-11-63
Source: Apprentice. *Honours:* England B, 3 full caps.
1981–82 Bristol R 20 2
1982–83 Bristol R 12 2
1983–84 Bristol R 0 0 **32 4**
1983–84 Torquay U 16 5 **16 5**
1983–84 Bristol C 6 0
1984–85 Bristol C 40 0
1985–86 Bristol C 44 1
1986–87 Bristol C 28 0
1987–88 Bristol C 3 0 **121 1**
1987–88 Reading 30 0
1988–89 Reading 10 0 **40 0**
1988–89 Wimbledon 18 0
1989–90 Wimbledon 38 2
1990–91 Wimbledon 37 1 **93 3**
1991–92 Manchester C 40 5
1992–93 Manchester C 39 3
1993–94 Manchester C 29 1
1994–95 Manchester C 31 2
1995–96 Manchester C 32 0 **171 11**
1996–97 Wolverhampton W 21 2
1997–98 Wolverhampton W 40 1
1998–99 Wolverhampton W 44 4
1999–2000 Wolverhampton W 45 2 **150 9**
2000–01 Sheffield U 25 0 **25 0**

D'JAFFO, Laurent (F) **155 34**
H: 6 0 W: 13 05 b.Aquitane 5-11-70
1991–92 Montpellier 11 2
1992–93 Montpellier 5 0
1993–94 Montpellier 12 1
1994–95 Montpellier 8 0 **36 3**
From Niort.
1997–98 Ayr U 24 10 **24 10**
1998–99 Bury 37 8
1999–2000 Bury 0 0 **37 8**
1999–2000 Stockport Co 21 7 **21 7**
1999–2000 Sheffield U 15 1
2000–01 Sheffield U 22 5 **37 6**

DEVLIN, Paul (F) **350 75**
H: 5 8 W: 11 08 b.Birmingham 14-4-72
Source: Stafford R.
1991–92 Notts Co 2 0
1992–93 Notts Co 32 3
1993–94 Notts Co 41 7
1994–95 Notts Co 40 9
1995–96 Notts Co 26 6
1995–96 Birmingham C 16 7
1996–97 Birmingham C 38 16
1997–98 Birmingham C 22 5 **76 28**
1997–98 Sheffield U 10 1
1998–99 Sheffield U 33 5
1998–99 *Notts Co* 5 0 **146 25**
1999–2000 Sheffield U 44 11
2000–01 Sheffield U 41 5 **128 22**

DOANE, Ben (D) **4 0**
H: 5 10 W: 10 05 b.Sheffield 22-12-79
Source: Trainee.
1998–99 Sheffield U 0 0
1999–2000 Sheffield U 1 0
2000–01 Sheffield U 3 0 **4 0**

EL BANNA, Wassim‡ (F) **12 4**
H: 5 11 W: 12 04 b.Zambia 10-5-79
1997–98 Odense 12 4
1998–99 Odense 0 0 **12 4**
1999–2000 Northampton T 0 0
1999–2000 Oldham Ath 0 0
1999–2000 Sheffield U 0 0
2000–01 Sheffield U 0 0

FORD, Bobby (M) **245 13**
H: 5 8 W: 10 07 b.Bristol 22-9-74
Source: Trainee.
1992–93 Oxford U 0 0
1993–94 Oxford U 14 0
1994–95 Oxford U 23 2
1995–96 Oxford U 28 3
1996–97 Oxford U 33 0
1997–98 Oxford U 18 2 **116 7**
1997–98 Sheffield U 23 1
1998–99 Sheffield U 30 0
1999–2000 Sheffield U 41 2
2000–01 Sheffield U 35 3 **129 6**

GIJSBRECHTS, Davy (D) **245 8**
H: 6 1 W: 13 08 b.Heusden 20-9-72
1990–91 Mechelen 7 0
1991–92 Mechelen 24 1
1992–93 Mechelen 32 3
1993–94 Mechelen 24 0
1994–95 Mechelen 32 2
1995–96 Mechelen 30 2
1996–97 Mechelen 32 0 **181 8**
1997–98 Lokeren 33 0
1998–99 Lokeren 14 0 **47 0**
1999–2000 Sheffield U 17 0
2000–01 Sheffield U 0 0 **17 0**

HAYDEN, John* (D) **0 0**
H: 5 8 W: 10 11 b.Kilkenny 8-9-81
Source: Scholar.
2000–01 Sheffield U 0 0

JAGIELKA, Philip (M) **16 0**
b.Manchester 17-8-82
Source: Scholar. *Honours:* England Youth.
1999–2000 Sheffield U 1 0
2000–01 Sheffield U 15 0 **16 0**

KELLY, David* (F) **564 182**
H: 5 11 W: 11 10 b.Birmingham 25-11-65
Source: Alvechurch. *Honours:* Eire Under-21, Under-23, B, 26 full caps, 9 goals.
1983–84 Walsall 6 3
1984–85 Walsall 32 7
1985–86 Walsall 28 10
1986–87 Walsall 42 23
1987–88 Walsall 39 20 **147 63**
1988–89 West Ham U 25 6
1989–90 West Ham U 16 1 **41 7**
1989–90 Leicester C 10 7
1990–91 Leicester C 44 14
1991–92 Leicester C 12 1 **66 22**
1991–92 Newcastle U 25 11
1992–93 Newcastle U 45 24 **70 35**
1993–94 Wolverhampton W 36 11
1994–95 Wolverhampton W 42 15
1995–96 Wolverhampton W 5 0 **83 26**
1995–96 Sunderland 10 2
1996–97 Sunderland 24 0 **34 2**
1997–98 Tranmere R 29 11
1998–99 Tranmere R 27 4
1999–2000 Tranmere R 32 6 **88 21**
2000–01 Sheffield U 35 6 **35 6**

KOZLUK, Robert (D) **106 0**
H: 5 8 W: 10 07 b.Sutton-in-Ashfield 5-8-77
Source: Trainee. *Honours:* England Under-21.
1995–96 Derby Co 0 0
1996–97 Derby Co 0 0
1997–98 Derby Co 9 0
1998–99 Derby Co 7 0 **16 0**
1998–99 Sheffield U 10 0
1999–2000 Sheffield U 39 0
2000–01 Sheffield U 27 0 **76 0**
2000–01 *Huddersfield T* 14 0 **14 0**

MBOME, Kingsley* (M) **0 0**
H: 6 2 W: 13 06 b.Yaounde 21-11-81
1999–2000 Sheffield U 0 0
2000–01 Sheffield U 0 0

MONTGOMERY, Nick (M) **27 0**
H: 5 9 W: 11 08 b.Leeds 28-10-81
Source: Scholar.
2000–01 Sheffield U 27 0 **27 0**

MURPHY, Shaun (D) **268 20**
H: 6 1 W: 13 10 b.Sydney 5-11-70
Honours: From Blacktown City 10 apps, 1 goal, Heidelberg 9 apps.Australia 17 full caps, 3 goals.
1992–93 Notts Co 8 1
1993–94 Notts Co 11 1
1994–95 Notts Co 35 0
1995–96 Notts Co 39 3
1996–97 Notts Co 16 0 **109 5**
1996–97 WBA 17 2
1997–98 WBA 17 1
1998–99 WBA 37 4 **71 7**
1999–2000 Sheffield U 42 3
2000–01 Sheffield U 46 5 **88 8**

NDLOVU, Peter (F) **305 67**
H: 5 8 W: 10 02 b.Zimbabwe 25-2-73
Source: Highlanders. *Honours:* Zimbabwe full caps.
1991–92 Coventry C 23 2
1992–93 Coventry C 32 7
1993–94 Coventry C 40 11
1994–95 Coventry C 30 11
1995–96 Coventry C 32 5
1996–97 Coventry C 20 1 **177 37**
1997–98 Birmingham C 39 9
1998–99 Birmingham C 43 10
1999–2000 Birmingham C 13 1
2000–01 Birmingham C 12 2 **107 22**
2000–01 *Huddersfield T* 6 4 **6 4**
2000–01 Sheffield U 15 4 **15 4**

QUINN, Gerry (M) **0 0**
b.Dublin 16-9-83
2000–01 Sheffield U 0 0

RIBEIRO, Bruno (M) **106 9**
H: 5 8 W: 12 07 b.Setubal 22-10-75
Honours: Portugal Under-21.
1994–95 Setubal 11 1
1995–96 Setubal 8 2
1996–97 Setubal 20 1 **39 4**
1997–98 Leeds U 29 3
1998–99 Leeds U 13 1
1999–2000 Leeds U 0 0 **42 4**
1999–2000 Sheffield U 20 1
2000–01 Sheffield U 5 0 **25 1**

SANDFORD, Lee (D) **480 13**
H: 6 0 W: 13 06 b.Basingstoke 22-4-68
Source: Apprentice. *Honours:* England Youth.
1985–86 Portsmouth 7 0
1986–87 Portsmouth 0 0
1987–88 Portsmouth 21 1
1988–89 Portsmouth 31 0
1989–90 Portsmouth 13 0 **72 1**
1989–90 Stoke C 23 2
1990–91 Stoke C 32 2
1991–92 Stoke C 38 0
1992–93 Stoke C 42 2
1993–94 Stoke C 42 1
1994–95 Stoke C 35 1

1995–96 Stoke C 46 0 **258 8**
1996–97 Sheffield U 30 2
1997–98 Sheffield U 15 0
1997–98 *Reading* 5 0 **5 0**
1998–99 Sheffield U 35 0
1999–2000 Sheffield U 43 1
2000–01 Sheffield U 22 1 **145 4**

SANTOS, Georges (D) 86 6
H: 6 3 W: 14 08 b.Marseille 15-8-70
Source: Toulon.
1998–99 Tranmere R 37 1
1999–2000 Tranmere R 10 1 **47 2**
1999–2000 WBA 8 0 **8 0**
2000–01 Sheffield U 31 4 **31 4**

SMITH, Andy (F) 8 0
H: 5 11 W: 11 10 b.Lisburn 25-9-80
1999–2000 Sheffield U 0 0
2000–01 Sheffield U 6 0 **6 0**
2000–01 *Bury* 2 0 **2 0**

SPENCER, Steven‡ (D) 0 0
H: 6 0 W: 11 00 b.Manchester 6-10-81
Source: Scholar.
2000–01 Sheffield U 0 0

SUFFO, Patrick (F) 46 5
H: 5 8 W: 12 13 b.Ebolowa 17-1-78
Source: Tonnerre Yaounde. *Honours:* Cameroon full caps.
1995–96 Nantes 0 0
1996–97 Barcelona 0 0
1997–98 Nantes 4 0
1998–99 Nantes 21 4
1999–2000 Nantes 5 0 **30 4**
2000–01 Sheffield U 16 1 **16 1**

TALIA, Frank* (G) 127 0
H: 6 1 W: 13 06 b.Melbourne 20-7-72
Source: Sunshine George Cross 11 apps.
1992–93 Blackburn R 0 0
1992–93 *Hartlepool U* 14 0 **14 0**
1993–94 Blackburn R 0 0
1994–95 Blackburn R 0 0
1995–96 Blackburn R 0 0
1995–96 Swindon T 16 0
1996–97 Swindon T 15 0
1997–98 Swindon T 2 0
1998–99 Swindon T 43 0
1999–2000 Swindon T 31 0 **107 0**
2000–01 Wolverhampton W 0 0
2000–01 Sheffield U 6 0 **6 0**

THETIS, Manuel‡ (D) 201 8
H: 6 3 W: 14 13 b.France 5-11-71
1989–90 Racing Paris 19 1 **19 1**
1990–91 Montpellier 21 0
1991–92 Montpellier 8 1
1992–93 Montpellier 19 0
1993–94 Montpellier 18 1
1994–95 Marseille 22 2 **22 2**
1995–96 Montpellier 23 1
1996–97 Montpellier 8 0 **97 3**
1997–98 Sevilla 12 0 **12 0**
1998–99 Ipswich T 31 2
1999–2000 Ipswich T 16 0
2000–01 Ipswich T 0 0 **47 2**
2000–01 *Wolverhampton W* 3 0 **3 0**
2000–01 Sheffield U 1 0 **1 0**

THOMPSON, Lee (G) 0 0
b.Sheffield 25-3-82
Honours: England Schools.
2000–01 Sheffield U 0 0

THOMPSON, Tyrone (F) 0 0
H: 5 9 W: 11 02 b.Sheffield 8-5-82
Source: Scholar.
2000–01 Sheffield U 0 0

TONGE, Michael (M) 2 0
b.Manchester 7-4-83
Source: Scholar.
2000–01 Sheffield U 2 0 **2 0**

TRACEY, Simon (G) 297 0
H: 6 0 W: 14 00 b.Woolwich 9-12-67
Source: Apprentice.
1985–86 Wimbledon 0 0
1986–87 Wimbledon 0 0
1987–88 Wimbledon 0 0
1988–89 Wimbledon 1 0
1988–89 Sheffield U 7 0
1989–90 Sheffield U 46 0
1990–91 Sheffield U 31 0
1991–92 Sheffield U 29 0
1992–93 Sheffield U 10 0
1993–94 Sheffield U 15 0
1994–95 Sheffield U 5 0
1994–95 *Manchester C* 3 0 **3 0**
1994–95 *Norwich C* 1 0 **1 0**
1995–96 Sheffield U 11 0
1995–96 *Wimbledon* 1 0 **2 0**
1996–97 Sheffield U 7 0
1997–98 Sheffield U 27 0
1998–99 Sheffield U 18 0
1999–2000 Sheffield U 45 0
2000–01 Sheffield U 40 0 **291 0**

TRAVERS, Mervyn (G) 0 0
b.Dublin 22-11-82
Source: Trainee.
1999–2000 Leeds U 0 0
2000–01 Sheffield U 0 0

UHLENBEEK, Gus (D) 222 8
H: 5 9 W: 12 05 b.Paramaribo 20-8-70
1990–91 Ajax 2 0
1991–92 Ajax 0 0 **2 0**
1992–93 Cambuur 24 0
1993–94 Cambuur 15 0 **39 0**
1994–95 TOPS SV 22 3 **22 3**
1995–96 Ipswich T 40 4
1996–97 Ipswich T 38 0
1997–98 Ipswich T 11 0 **89 4**
1998–99 Fulham 23 1
1999–2000 Fulham 16 0 **39 1**
2000–01 Sheffield U 31 0 **31 0**

ULLATHORNE, Robert* (D) 157 8
H: 5 8 W: 10 10 b.Wakefield 11-10-71
Source: Trainee.
1989–90 Norwich C 0 0
1990–91 Norwich C 2 0
1991–92 Norwich C 20 3
1992–93 Norwich C 0 0
1993–94 Norwich C 16 2
1994–95 Norwich C 27 2
1995–96 Norwich C 29 0 **94 7**
1996–97 Osasuna 18 0 **18 0**
1996–97 Leicester C 0 0
1997–98 Leicester C 6 1
1998–99 Leicester C 25 0
1999–2000 Leicester C 0 0 **31 1**
2000–01 Sheffield U 14 0 **14 0**

WARD, Mark (F) 1 0
b.Sheffield 27-1-82
Source: Sheffield Colleges. *Honours:* England Schools.
2000–01 Sheffield U 1 0 **1 0**

WEBER, Nicolas‡ (D) 307 13
H: 6 2 W: 13 00 b.Metz 28-10-70
1990–91 Sochaux 1 0
1991–92 Sochaux 28 1
1992–93 Sochaux 35 1
1993–94 Sochaux 36 1
1994–95 Sochaux 31 0 **131 3**
1995–96 Chateauroux 38 1
1996–97 Chateauroux 40 6
1997–98 Chateauroux 32 1 **110 8**
1998–99 Le Havre 31 1
1999–2000 Le Havre 31 1 **62 2**
2000–01 Sheffield U 4 0 **4 0**

WOODWARD, Andy (D) 150 1
H: 6 0 W: 13 04 b.Stockport 13-9-73
Source: Trainee.
1992–93 Crewe Alex 6 0
1993–94 Crewe Alex 12 0
1994–95 Crewe Alex 2 0 **20 0**
1994–95 Bury 8 0
1995–96 Bury 1 0
1996–97 Bury 23 0
1997–98 Bury 32 0
1998–99 Bury 37 1
1999–2000 Bury 14 0 **115 1**
1999–2000 Sheffield U 3 0
2000–01 Sheffield U 0 0 **3 0**
2000–01 *Scunthorpe U* 12 0 **12 0**

YOHANNA, Buba (M) 0 0
b.Yaounde 16-6-82
1999–2000 Sheffield U 0 0
2000–01 Sheffield U 0 0

Scholars
Adams, Carl; Baum, Adam P; Brown, Thomas P; Crutchley, Steven J; Crutchley, Wayne; Fayenuwo, Victor O; Glarvey, Christopher; Hazell, Robert J; Hurrell, Paul J; Kendrick, Scott; Killeen, Lewis K; Sloane, Daniel; Tansley, Anthony D; Thornley, Carl; Wood, Daniel J
Non-Contract
Blackwell, Kevin P; Featherstone, Lee; Mallon, Ryan; Purkiss, Ben

SHEFFIELD W

BETTNEY, Scott (D) 0 0
H: 5 9 W: 13 00 b.Hull 12-3-80
Source: Trainee.
1998–99 Sheffield W 0 0
1999–2000 Sheffield W 0 0
2000–01 Sheffield W 0 0

BILLINGTON, David‡ (D) 5 0
H: 5 9 W: 10 06 b.Oxford 15-10-80
Source: Trainee. *Honours:* Eire Under-21.
1996–97 Peterborough U 5 0 **5 0**
1996–97 Sheffield W 0 0
1997–98 Sheffield W 0 0
1998–99 Sheffield W 0 0
1999–2000 Sheffield W 0 0
2000–01 Sheffield W 0 0

BROMBY, Leigh (D) 28 1
H: 5 11 W: 11 06 b.Dewsbury 2-6-80
Honours: England Schools.
1998–99 Sheffield W 0 0
1999–2000 Sheffield W 0 0
1999–2000 *Mansfield T* 10 1 **10 1**
2000–01 Sheffield W 18 0 **18 0**

CAWLEY, Alan (M) 0 0
H: 6 2 W: 10 00 b.Sligo 3-1-82
Source: Belvedere.
1998–99 Leeds U 0 0
1999–2000 Leeds U 0 0
2000–01 Leeds U 0 0
2000–01 Sheffield W 0 0

COLLEY, Karl (M) 0 0
b.Sheffield 13-10-83
2000–01 Sheffield W 0 0

CONNOLLY, Calem (M) 0 0
b.Leeds 12-2-82
2000–01 Sheffield W 0 0

CRANE, Anthony (M) 15 2
H: 6 1 W: 12 06 b.Liverpool 8-9-82
Source: Trainee. *Honours:* England Youth.
1999–2000 Sheffield W 0 0
2000–01 Sheffield W 15 2 **15 2**

DE BILDE, Gilles (F) 191 80
H: 5 11 W: 11 04 b.Brussels 9-6-71
Honours: Belgium 25 full caps, 2 goals.
1994–95 Alost 33 21 **33 21**
1995–96 Anderlecht 28 15
1996–97 Anderlecht 18 7 **46 22**
1996–97 PSV Eindhoven 8 7
1997–98 PSV Eindhoven 21 13
1998–99 PSV Eindhoven 20 4 **49 24**
1999–2000 Sheffield W 38 10
2000–01 Sheffield W 21 3 **59 13**
2000–01 *Aston Villa* 4 0 **4 0**

DI PIEDI, Michaelli (F) 25 4
H: 6 6 W: 13 05 b.Palermo 4-12-08
2000–01 Sheffield W 25 4 **25 4**

DONNELLY, Simon (M) 161 32
H: 5 9 W: 10 06 b.Glasgow 1-12-74
Source: Celtic BC. *Honours:* Scotland Under-21, 10 full caps.
1993–94 Celtic 12 5
1994–95 Celtic 17 0
1995–96 Celtic 35 6
1996–97 Celtic 29 4
1997–98 Celtic 30 10
1998–99 Celtic 23 5 **146 30**
1999–2000 Sheffield W 12 1
2000–01 Sheffield W 3 1 **15 2**

EKOKU, Efan* (F) 282 99
H: 6 2 W: 12 00 b.Manchester 8-6-67
Source: Sutton U. *Honours:* Nigeria 4 full caps.
1990–91 Bournemouth 20 3
1991–92 Bournemouth 28 11
1992–93 Bournemouth 14 7 **62 21**
1992–93 Norwich C 4 3
1993–94 Norwich C 27 12
1994–95 Norwich C 6 0 **37 15**
1994–95 Wimbledon 24 9
1995–96 Wimbledon 31 7
1996–97 Wimbledon 30 11
1997–98 Wimbledon 16 4
1998–99 Wimbledon 22 6 **123 37**
1999–2000 Grasshoppers 21 16
2000–01 Grasshoppers 7 3 **28 19**
2000–01 Sheffield W 32 7 **32 7**

GEARY, Derek (D) 5 0
H: 5 6 W: 10 08 b.Dublin 19-6-80
1997–98 Sheffield W 0 0
1998–99 Sheffield W 0 0
1999–2000 Sheffield W 0 0
2000–01 Sheffield W 5 0 **5 0**

GIBSON, Neil (M) 1 0
H: 5 11 W: 11 08 b.St Asaph 10-10-79
Source: Trainee. *Honours:* Wales Under-21.
1997–98 Tranmere R 0 0
1998–99 Tranmere R 1 0
1999–2000 Tranmere R 0 0 **1 0**
From Rhyl.
2000–01 Sheffield W 0 0

HAMSHAW, Matthew (M) 18 0
H:5 9 W:11 09 b.Rotherham 1-1-82
Source: Trainee. *Honours:* England Youth.
1998–99 Sheffield W 0 0
1999–2000 Sheffield W 0 0
2000–01 Sheffield W 18 0 18 0

HARKNESS, Steve (D) 182 3
H:5 9 W:11 09 b.Carlisle 27-8-71
Source: Trainee. *Honours:* England Youth.
1988–89 Carlisle U 13 0 13 0
1989–90 Liverpool 0 0
1990–91 Liverpool 0 0
1991–92 Liverpool 11 0
1992–93 Liverpool 10 0
1993–94 Liverpool 11 0
1993–94 *Huddersfield T* 5 0 5 0
1994–95 Liverpool 8 1
1994–95 *Southend U* 6 0 6 0
1995–96 Liverpool 24 1
1996–97 Liverpool 7 0
1997–98 Liverpool 25 0
1998–99 Liverpool 6 0 102 2
1998–99 Benfica 9 0 9 0
1999–2000 Blackburn R 17 0
2000–01 Blackburn R 0 0 17 0
2000–01 Sheffield W 30 1 30 1

HASLAM, Steven (D) 52 1
H:5 11 W:10 10 b.Sheffield 6-9-79
Source: Trainee. *Honours:* England Schools, Youth.
1996–97 Sheffield W 0 0
1997–98 Sheffield W 0 0
1998–99 Sheffield W 2 0
1999–2000 Sheffield W 23 0
2000–01 Sheffield W 27 1 52 1

HENDON, Ian (D) 328 16
H:6 1 W:13 08 b.Ilford 5-12-71
Source: Trainee. *Honours:* England Youth, Under-21.
1989–90 Tottenham H 0 0
1990–91 Tottenham H 2 0
1991–92 Tottenham H 2 0
1991–92 *Portsmouth* 4 0 4 0
1991–92 *Leyton Orient* 6 0
1992–93 Tottenham H 0 0 4 0
1992–93 *Barnsley* 6 0 6 0
1993–94 Leyton Orient 36 2
1994–95 Leyton Orient 29 0
1994–95 *Birmingham C* 4 0 4 0
1995–96 Leyton Orient 38 2
1996–97 Leyton Orient 28 1 137 5
1996–97 Notts Co 12 0
1997–98 Notts Co 38 0
1998–99 Notts Co 32 6 82 6
1998–99 Northampton T 7 0
1999–2000 Northampton T 44 2
2000–01 Northampton T 9 1 60 3
2000–01 Sheffield W 31 2 31 2

HINCHCLIFFE, Andy (D) 379 22
H:5 10 W:13 07 b.Manchester 5-2-69
Source: Apprentice. *Honours:* England Youth, Under-21, 7 full caps.
1986–87 Manchester C 0 0
1987–88 Manchester C 42 1
1988–89 Manchester C 39 5
1989–90 Manchester C 31 2 112 8
1990–91 Everton 21 1
1991–92 Everton 18 0
1992–93 Everton 25 1
1993–94 Everton 26 0
1994–95 Everton 29 2
1995–96 Everton 28 2
1996–97 Everton 18 1
1997–98 Everton 17 0 182 7
1997–98 Sheffield W 15 1
1998–99 Sheffield W 32 3
1999–2000 Sheffield W 29 1
2000–01 Sheffield W 9 2 85 7

HOULAHAN, Martin (M) 0 0
H:6 0 W:12 13 b.Bishop Auckland 17-9-81
Source: Trainee.
1999–2000 Sheffield W 0 0
2000–01 Sheffield W 0 0

HUTTON, John‡ (F) 0 0
H:5 10 W:11 07 b.Easington 23-9-80
Source: Trainee.
1998–99 Sheffield W 0 0
1999–2000 Sheffield W 0 0
2000–01 Sheffield W 0 0

JONK, Wim* (M) 368 79
H:6 0 W:12 02 b.Volendam 12-10-66
Honours: Holland 49 full caps, 11 goals.
1986–87 Volendam 36 23
1987–88 Volendam 23 5 59 28
1988–89 Ajax 17 6

1989–90 Ajax 13 3
1990–91 Ajax 17 1
1991–92 Ajax 26 5
1992–93 Ajax 23 3 96 18
1993–94 Internazionale 25 6
1994–95 Internazionale 29 2 54 8
1995–96 PSV Eindhoven 29 6
1996–97 PSV Eindhoven 32 9
1997–98 PSV Eindhoven 28 5 89 20
1998–99 Sheffield W 38 2
1999–2000 Sheffield W 30 3
2000–01 Sheffield W 2 0 70 5

LESCOTT, Aaron (M) 35 0
H:5 8 W:10 10 b.Birmingham 2-12-78
Source: Trainee. *Honours:* England Schools.
1996–97 Aston Villa 0 0
1997–98 Aston Villa 0 0
1998–99 Aston Villa 0 0
1999–2000 Aston Villa 0 0
1999–2000 *Lincoln C* 5 0 5 0
2000–01 Lincoln C 0 0
2000–01 Sheffield W 30 0 30 0

MORRISON, Owen (F) 31 6
H:5 8 W:11 12 b.Derry 8-12-81
Source: Trainee. *Honours:* Northern Ireland Under-21.
1998–99 Sheffield W 1 0
1999–2000 Sheffield W 0 0
2000–01 Sheffield W 30 6 31 6

MULLER, Adam (F) 5 0
H:5 11 W:12 02 b.Thackley 17-4-82
1999–2000 Sheffield W 0 0
2000–01 Sheffield W 5 0 5 0

O'DONNELL, Phil (M) 226 30
H:5 10 W:11 07 b.Bellshill 25-3-72
Source: X Form. *Honours:* Scotland Under-21, 1 full cap.
1990–91 Motherwell 12 0
1991–92 Motherwell 42 4
1992–93 Motherwell 32 4
1993–94 Motherwell 35 7
1994–95 Motherwell 3 0 124 15
1994–95 Celtic 27 6
1995–96 Celtic 15 3
1996–97 Celtic 19 2
1997–98 Celtic 14 2
1998–99 Celtic 15 2 90 15
1999–2000 Sheffield W 1 0
2000–01 Sheffield W 11 0 12 0

PRESSMAN, Kevin# (G) 309 0
H:6 1 W:15 05 b.Fareham 6-11-67
Source: Apprentice. *Honours:* England Schools, Youth, Under-21, B.
1985–86 Sheffield W 0 0
1986–87 Sheffield W 0 0
1987–88 Sheffield W 11 0
1988–89 Sheffield W 9 0
1989–90 Sheffield W 15 0
1990–91 Sheffield W 23 0
1991–92 Sheffield W 1 0
1991–92 *Stoke C* 4 0 4 0
1992–93 Sheffield W 3 0
1993–94 Sheffield W 32 0
1994–95 Sheffield W 34 0
1995–96 Sheffield W 30 0
1996–97 Sheffield W 38 0
1997–98 Sheffield W 36 0
1998–99 Sheffield W 15 0
1999–2000 Sheffield W 19 0
2000–01 Sheffield W 39 0 305 0

QUINN, Alan (F) 58 5
H:5 9 W:10 02 b.Dublin 13-6-79
Source: Cherry Orchard. *Honours:* Eire Under-21.
1997–98 Sheffield W 1 0
1998–99 Sheffield W 1 0
1999–2000 Sheffield W 19 3
2000–01 Sheffield W 37 2 58 5

RAND, Craig (M) 0 0
H:6 1 W:11 00 b.Bishop Auckland 24-6-82
Source: Trainee.
1999–2000 Sheffield W 0 0
2000–01 Sheffield W 0 0

RUDI, Petter° (M) 193 15
H:6 2 W:12 00 b.Kristiansund 17-9-73
Honours: Norway 29 full caps, 3 goals.
1991 Molde 12 0
1992 Molde 20 2
1993 Molde 22 3
1994 Molde 0 0
1995 Molde 25 1
1996 Molde 26 0
1997 Molde 11 1 116 7
1997–98 Sheffield W 22 0
1998–99 Sheffield W 34 6

1999–2000 Sheffield W 20 2
2000–01 Sheffield W 1 0 77 8

SCOTT, Philip (M) 143 28
H:5 9 W:11 01 b.Perth 14-11-74
Source: Scone Thistle. *Honours:* Scotland Under-21.
1991–92 St Johnstone 0 0
1992–93 St Johnstone 3 0
1993–94 St Johnstone 24 3
1994–95 St Johnstone 12 1
1995–96 St Johnstone 28 8
1996–97 St Johnstone 29 12
1997–98 St Johnstone 22 1
1998–99 St Johnstone 16 2 134 27
1998–99 Sheffield W 4 1
1999–2000 Sheffield W 5 0
2000–01 Sheffield W 0 0 9 1

SIBON, Gerald (F) 182 69
H:6 3 W:13 04 b.Emmen 19-4-74
1993–94 Twente 3 0 3 0
1994–95 VVV 30 20
1995–96 VVV 23 14 53 34
1996–97 Roda 34 13 34 13
1997–98 Ajax 12 2
1998–99 Ajax 11 2 23 4
1999–2000 Sheffield W 28 5
2000–01 Sheffield W 41 13 69 18

SOLTVEDT, Trond Egil (M) 291 68
H:6 1 W:12 09 b.Voss 15-2-67
Source: Dale, Ny-Krohnborg. *Honours:* Norway 4 full caps.
1988 Viking 21 3
1989 Viking 11 3
1990 Viking 20 3
1991 Viking 13 1 65 10
1992 Brann 22 6
1993 Brann 21 16
1994 Brann 21 12 64 34
1995 Rosenborg 25 4
1996 Rosenborg 26 10
1997 Rosenborg 9 4 60 18
1997–98 Coventry C 30 1
1998–99 Coventry C 27 2
1999–2000 Coventry C 0 0 57 3
1999–2000 Southampton 24 1
2000–01 Southampton 6 1 30 2
2000–01 Sheffield W 15 1 15 1

STANIFORTH, Thomas (D) 0 0
H:5 10 W:13 00 b.Carlisle 15-12-80
Source: Trainee.
1998–99 Sheffield W 0 0
1999–2000 Sheffield W 0 0
2000–01 Sheffield W 0 0

STRINGER, Chris (G) 5 0
H:6 6 W:12 00 b.Grimsby 2-6-83
Source: Scholar.
2000–01 Sheffield W 5 0 5 0

WALKER, Des* (D) 601 1
H:5 11 W:11 13 b.Enfield 26-11-65
Source: Apprentice. *Honours:* England Under-21, 59 full caps.
1983–84 Nottingham F 4 0
1984–85 Nottingham F 3 0
1985–86 Nottingham F 39 0
1986–87 Nottingham F 41 0
1987–88 Nottingham F 35 0
1988–89 Nottingham F 34 0
1989–90 Nottingham F 38 0
1990–91 Nottingham F 37 0
1991–92 Nottingham F 33 1 264 1
1992–93 Sampdoria 30 0 30 0
1993–94 Sheffield W 42 0
1994–95 Sheffield W 38 0
1995–96 Sheffield W 36 0
1996–97 Sheffield W 36 0
1997–98 Sheffield W 38 0
1998–99 Sheffield W 37 0
1999–2000 Sheffield W 37 0
2000–01 Sheffield W 43 0 307 0

WESTWOOD, Ashley (D) 155 13
H:5 11 W:11 02 b.Bridgnorth 31-8-76
Source: Trainee. *Honours:* England Youth.
1994–95 Manchester U 0 0
1995–96 Crewe Alex 33 4
1996–97 Crewe Alex 44 2
1997–98 Crewe Alex 21 3 98 9
1998–99 Bradford C 19 2
1999–2000 Bradford C 5 0
2000–01 Bradford C 0 0 24 2
2000–01 Sheffield W 33 2 33 2

WOODS, Gary‡ (M) 0 0
b.Tullamore 15-8-83
2000–01 Sheffield W 0 0

Scholars
Barrett, Jamie J; Beadsley, Scott M; Byne,

Nicholas F; Callery, Alex J; Cropper, Dene J; Doherty, Michael F; Jubb, Ryan G; Knowles, Alexander S; Quinn, Adam R; Shaw, Jon S; Stevenson, Lee C; Strutt, Luke M; Taylor, Robert J; Tevendale, James R; Wood, Daniel G; Young, Gregory J
Non-Contract
Hodge, Martin J

SHREWSBURY T

AISTON, Sam (M)   **103**   **2**
H: 6 0   W: 13 09   b.Newcastle 21-11-76
Source: Newcastle U Trainee. *Honours:* England Schools.

1995–96	Sunderland	14	0	
1996–97	Sunderland	2	0	
1996–97	*Chester C*	14	0	
1997–98	Sunderland	3	0	
1998–99	Sunderland	1	0	
1998–99	*Chester C*	11	0	25 0
1999–2000	Sunderland	0	0	20 0
1999–2000	*Stoke C*	6	0	6 0
1999–2000	*Shrewsbury T*	10	0	
2000–01	Shrewsbury T	42	2	52 2

BROWN, Mickey* (F)   **472**   **40**
H: 5 9   W: 10 12   b.Birmingham 8-2-68
Source: Apprentice.

1985–86	Shrewsbury T	1	0	
1986–87	Shrewsbury T	22	2	
1987–88	Shrewsbury T	41	5	
1988–89	Shrewsbury T	41	0	
1989–90	Shrewsbury T	43	1	
1990–91	Shrewsbury T	43	1	
1991–92	Bolton W	27	3	
1992–93	Bolton W	6	0	33 3
1992–93	Shrewsbury T	17	1	
1993–94	Shrewsbury T	41	7	
1994–95	Shrewsbury T	9	3	
1994–95	Preston NE	0	0	
1995–96	Preston NE	10	1	
1996–97	Preston NE	6	0	16 1
1996–97	*Rochdale*	5	0	5 0
1996–97	Shrewsbury T	19	1	
1997–98	Shrewsbury T	30	2	
1998–99	Shrewsbury T	34	2	
1999–2000	Shrewsbury T	44	7	
2000–01	Shrewsbury T	34	4	418 36

DAVIDSON, Ross* (D)   **186**   **5**
H: 5 9   W: 12 04   b.Chertsey 13-11-73
Source: Walton & Hersham.

1993–94	Sheffield U	0	0	
1994–95	Sheffield U	1	0	
1995–96	Sheffield U	1	0	2 0
1995–96	Chester C	19	1	
1996–97	Chester C	40	2	
1997–98	Chester C	24	1	
1998–99	Chester C	40	1	
1999–2000	Chester C	9	0	132 5
1999–2000	Barnet	9	0	9 0
1999–2000	Shrewsbury T	10	0	
2000–01	Shrewsbury T	33	0	43 0

DRYSDALE, Leon (D)   **20**   **0**
H: 5 9   W: 10 10   b.Walsall 3-2-81
Source: Trainee.

1998–99	Shrewsbury T	1	0	
1999–2000	Shrewsbury T	0	0	
2000–01	Shrewsbury T	18	0	20 0

DUNBAVIN, Ian (G)   **29**   **0**
H: 6 1   W: 10 10   b.Knowsley 27-5-80
Source: Trainee.

1998–99	Liverpool	0	0	
1999–2000	Liverpool	0	0	
1999–2000	Shrewsbury T	7	0	
2000–01	Shrewsbury T	22	0	29 0

EDWARDS, Paul* (G)   **341**   **0**
H: 6 1   W: 12 05   b.Liverpool 22-2-65
Source: St Helens T.

1988–89	Crewe Alex	10	0	
1989–90	Crewe Alex	8	0	
1990–91	Crewe Alex	9	0	
1991–92	Crewe Alex	2	0	29 0
1992–93	Shrewsbury T	42	0	
1993–94	Shrewsbury T	42	0	
1994–95	Shrewsbury T	31	0	
1995–96	Shrewsbury T	31	0	
1996–97	Shrewsbury T	23	0	
1997–98	Shrewsbury T	34	0	
1998–99	Shrewsbury T	43	0	
1999–2000	Shrewsbury T	40	0	
2000–01	Shrewsbury T	26	0	312 0

FREESTONE, Chris (F)   **133**   **25**
H: 5 11   W: 12 05   b.Nottingham 4-9-71
Source: Arnold T.

1994–95	Middlesbrough	1	0	

1995–96	Middlesbrough	3	1	
1996–97	Middlesbrough	3	0	
1996–97	*Carlisle U*	5	2	5 2
1997–98	Middlesbrough	2	0	9 1
1997–98	Northampton T	25	11	
1998–99	Northampton T	32	2	57 13
1998–99	Hartlepool U	10	3	
1999–2000	Hartlepool U	27	4	37 7
1999–2000	*Cheltenham T*	5	2	5 2
2000–01	Shrewsbury T	20	0	20 0

HANMER, Gary* (D)   **140**
H: 5 6   W: 12 01   b.Shrewsbury 12-10-73
Source: Newtown.

1996–97	WBA	0	0	
1997–98	Shrewsbury T	39	1	
1998–99	Shrewsbury T	46	0	
1999–2000	Shrewsbury T	33	0	
2000–01	Shrewsbury T	22	0	140 1

HOWARTH, Paul* (D)   **0**   **0**
H: 5 6   W: 10 01   b.Nottingham 21-11-80
Source: Trainee.

1997–98	Nottingham F	0	0	
1998–99	Nottingham F	0	0	
1999–2000	Nottingham F	0	0	
2000–01	Shrewsbury T	0	0	

JAGIELKA, Steve (F)   **111**   **9**
H: 5 8   W: 11 03   b.Manchester 10-3-78
Source: Trainee.

1996–97	Stoke C	0	0	
1997–98	Shrewsbury T	16	1	
1998–99	Shrewsbury T	31	1	
1999–2000	Shrewsbury T	33	1	
2000–01	Shrewsbury T	31	6	111 9

JEMSON, Nigel#(F)   **340**   **83**
H: 5 11   W: 13 00   b.Preston 10-8-69
Source: Trainee. *Honours:* England Under-21.

1985–86	Preston NE	1	0	
1986–87	Preston NE	4	3	
1987–88	Preston NE	27	5	
1987–88	Nottingham F	0	0	
1988–89	Nottingham F	0	0	
1988–89	*Bolton W*	5	0	5 0
1988–89	*Preston NE*	9	2	41 10
1989–90	Nottingham F	18	4	
1990–91	Nottingham F	23	8	
1991–92	Nottingham F	6	1	47 13
1991–92	Sheffield W	20	4	
1992–93	Sheffield W	13	0	
1993–94	Sheffield W	18	5	51 9
1993–94	*Grimsby T*	6	2	6 2
1994–95	Notts Co	11	1	
1994–95	*Watford*	4	0	4 0
1994–95	*Coventry C*	0	0	
1995–96	Notts Co	3	0	14 1
1995–96	*Rotherham U*	16	5	16 5
1996–97	Oxford U	44	18	
1997–98	Oxford U	24	9	
1997–98	Bury	15	1	
1998–99	Bury	14	0	
1999–2000	Bury	0	0	29 1
1999–2000	Oxford U	18	0	86 27
2000–01	Shrewsbury T	41	15	41 15

JENKINS, Iain (D)   **200**   **1**
H: 5 9   W: 11 10   b.Whiston 24-12-72
Source: Trainee. *Honours:* Northern Ireland 6 full caps.

1990–91	Everton	1	0	
1991–92	Everton	3	0	
1992–93	Everton	1	0	5 0
1992–93	*Bradford C*	6	0	6 0
1993–94	Chester C	34	0	
1994–95	Chester C	40	0	
1995–96	Chester C	13	0	
1996–97	Chester C	39	0	
1997–98	Chester C	34	1	
1997–98	Dundee U	7	0	
1998–99	Dundee U	6	0	13 0
1999–2000	Chester C	0	0	160 1
2000–01	Shrewsbury T	16	0	16 0

JONES, Matthew* (M)   **7**   **0**
H: 6 1   W: 11 03   b.Shrewsbury 11-10-80
Source: Trainee.

1998–99	Shrewsbury T	1	0	
1999–2000	Shrewsbury T	0	0	
2000–01	Shrewsbury T	6	0	7 0

KEISTER, John‡ (M)   **124**   **2**
H: 5 8   W: 11 00   b.Manchester 11-11-70
Source: Faweh FC. *Honours:* Sierra Leone full caps.

1993–94	Walsall	22	1	
1994–95	Walsall	11	0	
1995–96	Walsall	21	0	
1996–97	Walsall	36	1	
1997–98	Walsall	13	0	
1998–99	Walsall	2	0	

1999–2000	Walsall	1	0	106 2
1999–2000	Chester C	10	0	
2000–01	Chester C	0	0	10 0
2000–01	Shrewsbury T	8	0	8 0

LOWE, Ryan (F)   **30**   **4**
b.Liverpool 18-9-78
Source: Burscough.

2000–01	Shrewsbury T	30	4	30 4

MURPHY, Christopher§ (F)   **1**   **0**
b.Leamington Spa 8-3-83
Source: Scholar.

2000–01	Shrewsbury T	1	0	1 0

MURRAY, Karl (M)   **47**   **1**
H: 5 10   W: 12 00   b.Islington 24-6-82
Source: Trainee.

1999–2000	Shrewsbury T	12	1	
2000–01	Shrewsbury T	35	0	47 1

PEER, Dean* (M)   **359**   **22**
H: 6 2   W: 12 04   b.Stourbridge 8-8-69
Source: Trainee.

1986–87	Birmingham C	2	0	
1987–88	Birmingham C	0	0	
1988–89	Birmingham C	17	1	
1989–90	Birmingham C	27	3	
1990–91	Birmingham C	40	2	
1991–92	Birmingham C	21	1	
1992–93	Birmingham C	13	1	
1992–93	*Mansfield T*	10	0	10 0
1993–94	Birmingham C	0	0	120 8
1993–94	Walsall	33	8	
1994–95	Walsall	12	0	45 8
1995–96	Northampton T	42	1	
1996–97	Northampton T	21	1	
1997–98	Northampton T	30	2	
1998–99	Northampton T	26	1	
1999–2000	Northampton T	9	1	128 6
1999–2000	Shrewsbury T	19	0	
2000–01	Shrewsbury T	37	0	56 0

REDMILE, Matt (D)   **171**   **10**
H: 6 3   W: 15 03   b.Nottingham 12-11-76
Source: Trainee.

1995–96	Notts Co	0	0	
1996–97	Notts Co	23	2	
1997–98	Notts Co	34	3	
1998–99	Notts Co	41	1	
1999–2000	Notts Co	41	1	
2000–01	Notts Co	8	0	147 7
2000–01	Shrewsbury T	24	3	24 3

RIOCH, Greg (D)   **179**   **12**
H: 5 10   W: 12 08   b.Sutton Coldfield 24-6-75
Source: Trainee.

1993–94	Luton T	0	0	
1993–94	*Barnet*	3	0	3 0
1994–95	Luton T	0	0	
1995–96	Peterborough U	18	0	18 0
1996–97	Hull C	39	1	
1997–98	Hull C	39	5	
1998–99	Hull C	13	0	91 6
1999–2000	Macclesfield T	42	5	
2000–01	Macclesfield T	17	1	59 6
2000–01	Shrewsbury T	8	0	8 0

RODGERS, Luke (F)   **32**   **8**
H: 5 6   W: 10 05   b.Birmingham 1-1-82
Source: Trainee.

1999–2000	Shrewsbury T	6	1	
2000–01	Shrewsbury T	26	7	32 8

SEABURY, Kevin (D)   **229**   **7**
H: 5 10   W: 11 06   b.Shrewsbury 24-11-73
Source: Trainee.

1992–93	Shrewsbury T	1	0	
1993–94	Shrewsbury T	0	0	
1994–95	Shrewsbury T	30	0	
1995–96	Shrewsbury T	34	0	
1996–97	Shrewsbury T	38	0	
1997–98	Shrewsbury T	39	2	
1998–99	Shrewsbury T	44	5	
1999–2000	Shrewsbury T	32	0	
2000–01	Shrewsbury T	11	0	229 7

THOMAS, Wayne* (M)   **60**   **1**
H: 5 11   W: 11 10   b.Walsall 28-8-78
Source: Trainee.

1996–97	Walsall	20	0	
1997–98	Walsall	5	0	
1998–99	Walsall	12	0	
1999–2000	*Mansfield T*	5	0	5 0
1999–2000	Walsall	1	0	38 0
1999–2000	Shrewsbury T	13	1	
2000–01	Shrewsbury T	4	0	17 1

TOLLEY, Jamie (M)   **26**   **2**
H: 6 1   W: 10 08   b.Shrewsbury 12-5-83
Source: Scholarship. *Honours:* Wales Under-21.

1999–2000	Shrewsbury T	2	0	
2000–01	Shrewsbury T	24	2	26 2

TRETTON, Andrew (D) 92 6
H: 6 0 W: 12 08 b.Derby 9-10-76
Source: Trainee.

Season	Club				
1993-94	Derby Co	0	0		
1994-95	Derby Co	0	0		
1995-96	Derby Co	0	0		
1996-97	Derby Co	0	0		
1997-98	Chesterfield	0	0		
1997-98	Shrewsbury T	14	1		
1998-99	Shrewsbury T	23	0		
1999-2000	Shrewsbury T	33	3		
2000-01	Shrewsbury T	22	2	92	6

WHELAN, Spencer‡ (D) 240 8
H: 6 2 W: 13 00 b.Liverpool 17-9-71
Source: Liverpool.

Season	Club				
1990-91	Chester C	11	0		
1991-92	Chester C	32	0		
1992-93	Chester C	28	0		
1993-94	Chester C	22	0		
1994-95	Chester C	23	1		
1995-96	Chester C	39	2		
1996-97	Chester C	25	1		
1997-98	Chester C	35	4		
1998-99	Chester C	0	0	215	8
1998-99	Shrewsbury T	9	0		
1999-2000	Shrewsbury T	16	0		
2000-01	Shrewsbury T	0	0	25	0

WILDING, Peter# (D) 138 4
H: 6 1 W: 12 09 b.Shrewsbury 28-11-68
Source: Telford U.

Season	Club				
1997-98	Shrewsbury T	34	1		
1998-99	Shrewsbury T	42	0		
1999-2000	Shrewsbury T	41	2		
2000-01	Shrewsbury T	21	1	138	4

Scholars
Brooks-Courtney, Christian D; Corbett, Mark; Evans, Nicholas J; Hart, Timothy J; Johnson, Mathew T; McCann, Neal; Morgan, Stephen J; Murphy, Christopher P; Rondel, Robert E; Silgram, James; Thompson, Darren M; Tolley, Glenn A; Walker, Richard

SOUTHAMPTON

ASHFORD, Ryan (D) 0 0
b.Honiton 13-10-81
Source: Scholar.

Season	Club		
2000-01	Southampton	0	0

BAIRD, Christopher (D) 0 0
H: 6 1 W: 12 00 b.Ballymena 25-2-82
Source: Scholar.

Season	Club		
2000-01	Southampton	0	0

BEATTIE, James (F) 94 16
H: 6 1 W: 13 08 b.Lancaster 27-2-78
Source: Trainee. *Honours:* England Under-21.

Season	Club				
1994-95	Blackburn R	0	0		
1995-96	Blackburn R	0	0		
1996-97	Blackburn R	1	0		
1997-98	Blackburn R	3	0	4	0
1998-99	Southampton	35	5		
1999-2000	Southampton	18	0		
2000-01	Southampton	37	11	90	16

BENALI, Francis (M) 321 1
H: 5 9 W: 11 00 b.Southampton 30-12-68
Source: Apprentice. *Honours:* England Schools.

Season	Club				
1986-87	Southampton	0	0		
1987-88	Southampton	0	0		
1988-89	Southampton	7	0		
1989-90	Southampton	27	0		
1990-91	Southampton	12	0		
1991-92	Southampton	22	0		
1992-93	Southampton	33	0		
1993-94	Southampton	37	0		
1994-95	Southampton	35	0		
1995-96	Southampton	29	0		
1996-97	Southampton	18	0		
1997-98	Southampton	33	1		
1998-99	Southampton	23	0		
1999-2000	Southampton	26	0		
2000-01	Southampton	4	0	306	1
2000-01	Nottingham F	15	0	15	0

BERESFORD, John‡ (M) 392 16
H: 5 7 W: 11 10 b.Sheffield 4-9-66
Source: Apprentice. *Honours:* England Schools, Youth, B.

Season	Club				
1983-84	Manchester C	0	0		
1984-85	Manchester C	0	0		
1985-86	Manchester C	0	0		
1986-87	Barnsley	27	1		
1987-88	Barnsley	34	3		
1988-89	Barnsley	27	1	88	5
1988-89	Portsmouth	2	0		
1989-90	Portsmouth	28	0		
1990-91	Portsmouth	42	2		
1991-92	Portsmouth	35	6	107	8
1992-93	Newcastle U	42	1		
1993-94	Newcastle U	34	0		
1994-95	Newcastle U	33	0		
1995-96	Newcastle U	33	0		
1996-97	Newcastle U	19	0		
1997-98	Newcastle U	18	2	179	3
1997-98	Southampton	10	0		
1998-99	Southampton	4	0		
1999-2000	Southampton	3	0		
1999-2000	Birmingham C	1	0	1	0
2000-01	Southampton	0	0	17	0

BEVAN, Scott (G) 0 0
H: 6 6 W: 15 06 b.Southampton 16-9-79
Source: Trainee.

Season	Club		
1997-98	Southampton	0	0
1998-99	Southampton	0	0
1999-2000	Southampton	0	0
2000-01	Southampton	0	0

BLEIDELIS, Imants (F) 130 25
H: 5 10 W: 12 01 b.Latvia 16-8-75
Honours: Latvia 51 full caps, 5 goals.

Season	Club				
1994	Interskonto Riga	11	1	11	1
1994	Skonto Riga	11	0		
1995	Skonto Riga	24	1		
1996	Skonto Riga	20	3		
1997	Skonto Riga	20	8		
1998	Skonto Riga	24	8		
1999	Skonto Riga	19	4	118	24
1999-2000	Southampton	0	0		
2000-01	Southampton	1	0	1	0

BOA MORTE, Luis (F) 78 19
H: 5 9 W: 11 11 b.Lisbon 4-8-77
Source: Sporting Lisbon, Lourihanense (loan). *Honours:* Portugal Under-21.

Season	Club				
1997-98	Arsenal	15	0		
1998-99	Arsenal	8	0		
1999-2000	Arsenal	2	0	25	0
1999-2000	Southampton	14	1		
2000-01	Southampton	0	0	14	1
2000-01	Fulham	39	18	39	18

(Transferred to Fulham, July 2001).

BRIDGE, Wayne (F) 80 1
H: 5 10 W: 12 04 b.Southampton 5-8-80
Source: Trainee. *Honours:* England Youth, Under-21.

Season	Club				
1997-98	Southampton	0	0		
1998-99	Southampton	23	0		
1999-2000	Southampton	19	1		
2000-01	Southampton	38	0	80	1

CACERES, Adrian (F) 0 0
H: 5 10 W: 12 05 b.Buenos Aires 10-1-82
Source: Perth SC.

Season	Club		
2000-01	Southampton	0	0

COLLETER, Patrick (D) 410 11
H: 5 9 W: 11 01 b.Brest 6-11-65
Honours: France 2 full caps.

Season	Club				
1986-87	Brest	23	2		
1987-88	Brest	37	2		
1988-89	Brest	32	2		
1989-90	Brest	35	2	127	8
1990-91	Montpellier	31	0	31	0
1991-92	Paris St Germain	28	0		
1992-93	Paris St Germain	36	0		
1993-94	Paris St Germain	32	0		
1994-95	Paris St Germain	28	1		
1995-96	Paris St Germain	33	0	157	1
1996-97	Bordeaux	30	1	30	1
1997-98	Marseille	31	0		
1998-99	Marseille	10	0	41	0
1998-99	Southampton	16	1		
1999-2000	Southampton	8	0		
2000-01	Southampton	0	0	24	1

(Transferred to Cannes, November 2000).

DAVIES, Kevin (F) 227 39
H: 6 0 W: 14 09 b.Sheffield 26-3-77
Source: Trainee. *Honours:* England Youth, Under-21.

Season	Club				
1993-94	Chesterfield	24	4		
1994-95	Chesterfield	41	11		
1995-96	Chesterfield	30	4		
1996-97	Chesterfield	34	3	129	22
1996-97	Southampton	0	0		
1997-98	Southampton	25	9		
1998-99	Blackburn R	21	1		
1999-2000	Blackburn R	2	0	23	1
1999-2000	Southampton	23	6		
2000-01	Southampton	27	1	75	16

DODD, Jason (D) 321 9
H: 5 10 W: 12 05 b.Bath 2-11-70
Source: Bath C. *Honours:* England Under-21.

Season	Club				
1988-89	Southampton	0	0		
1989-90	Southampton	22	0		
1990-91	Southampton	19	0		
1991-92	Southampton	28	0		
1992-93	Southampton	30	1		
1993-94	Southampton	10	0		
1994-95	Southampton	26	2		
1995-96	Southampton	37	2		
1996-97	Southampton	23	1		
1997-98	Southampton	36	1		
1998-99	Southampton	28	1		
1999-2000	Southampton	31	0		
2000-01	Southampton	31	1	321	9

DRAPER, Mark (M) 403 53
H: 5 10 W: 12 04 b.Long Eaton 11-11-70
Source: Trainee. *Honours:* England Under-21.

Season	Club				
1988-89	Notts Co	20	3		
1989-90	Notts Co	34	3		
1990-91	Notts Co	45	9		
1991-92	Notts Co	35	1		
1992-93	Notts Co	44	11		
1993-94	Notts Co	44	13	222	40
1994-95	Leicester C	39	5	39	5
1995-96	Aston Villa	36	2		
1996-97	Aston Villa	29	0		
1997-98	Aston Villa	31	3		
1998-99	Aston Villa	23	2		
1999-2000	Aston Villa	1	0	120	7
2000-01	Southampton	22	1	22	1

EL KHALEJ, Tahar (D) 158 20
H: 6 2 W: 13 06 b.Morocco 16-6-68
Source: KAC Marrakesh. *Honours:* Morocco full caps.

Season	Club				
1994-95	Uniao Leiria	21	5		
1995-96	Uniao Leiria	22	3	43	8
1996-97	Benfica	25	1		
1997-98	Benfica	21	5		
1998-99	Benfica	22	4		
1999-2000	Benfica	4	0	72	10
1999-2000	Southampton	11	1		
2000-01	Southampton	32	1	43	2

GIBBENS, Kevin (M) 11 0
H: 5 10 W: 13 06 b.Southampton 4-11-79
Source: Trainee.

Season	Club				
1997-98	Southampton	2	0		
1998-99	Southampton	4	0		
1999-2000	Southampton	0	0		
1999-2000	Stockport Co	2	0	2	0
2000-01	Southampton	3	0	9	0

GRAY, Steven (M) 0 0
b.Dublin 17-10-81

Season	Club		
1999-2000	Southampton	0	0
2000-01	Southampton	0	0

HOWARD, Brian (M) 0 0
b.Winchester 23-1-83
Source: Trainee.

Season	Club		
1999-2000	Southampton	0	0
2000-01	Southampton	0	0

HUGHES, David‡ (M) 54 3
H: 5 11 W: 11 07 b.St Albans 30-12-72
Source: Trainee. *Honours:* England Schools.

Season	Club				
1991-92	Southampton	0	0		
1992-93	Southampton	0	0		
1993-94	Southampton	2	0		
1994-95	Southampton	12	2		
1995-96	Southampton	11	1		
1996-97	Southampton	6	0		
1997-98	Southampton	14	0		
1998-99	Southampton	9	0		
1999-2000	Southampton	0	0		
2000-01	Southampton	0	0	54	3

HUGHES, Paul‡ (M) 32 3
H: 6 0 W: 12 02 b.Hammersmith 19-4-76
Source: Trainee. *Honours:* England Schools.

Season	Club				
1994-95	Chelsea	0	0		
1995-96	Chelsea	0	0		
1996-97	Chelsea	12	2		
1997-98	Chelsea	9	0		
1998-99	Chelsea	0	0		
1998-99	Stockport Co	7	0	7	0
1998-99	Norwich C	4	1	4	1
1999-2000	Chelsea	0	0	21	2
1999-2000	Crewe Alex	0	0		
2000-01	Southampton	0	0		

JONES, Paul (G) 214 0
H: 6 3 W: 14 08 b.Chirk 18-4-67
Source: Bridgnorth, Kidderminster H. *Honours:* Wales 21 full caps.

Season	Club				
1991-92	Wolverhampton W	0	0		
1992-93	Wolverhampton W	16	0		
1993-94	Wolverhampton W	0	0		
1994-95	Wolverhampton W	0	0		
1995-96	Wolverhampton W	8	0	33	0
1996-97	Stockport Co	46	0	46	0
1997-98	Southampton	38	0		
1998-99	Southampton	31	0		
1999-2000	Southampton	31	0		
2000-01	Southampton	35	0	135	0

KACHLOUL, Hassan (M) 223 46
H: 6 1 W: 12 13 b.Agadir 19-2-73
Honours: Morocco full caps.
1992–93 Nimes 17 1
1993–94 Nimes 37 17
1994–95 Nimes 32 8 **86 26**
1995–96 Dunkerque 28 6 **28 6**
1996–97 Metz 7 0 **7 0**
1997–98 St Etienne 16 0 **16 0**
1998–99 Southampton 22 5
1999–2000 Southampton 32 5
2000–01 Southampton 32 4 **86 14**
(Transferred to Aston Villa, July 2001).

LE TISSIER, Matthew (F) 439 161
H: 6 1 W: 14 01 b.Guernsey 14-10-68
Source: Trainee. *Honours:* England Youth, B, 8 full caps.
1986–87 Southampton 24 6
1987–88 Southampton 19 0
1988–89 Southampton 28 9
1989–90 Southampton 35 20
1990–91 Southampton 35 19
1991–92 Southampton 32 6
1992–93 Southampton 40 15
1993–94 Southampton 38 25
1994–95 Southampton 41 20
1995–96 Southampton 34 7
1996–97 Southampton 31 13
1997–98 Southampton 26 11
1998–99 Southampton 30 6
1999–2000 Southampton 18 3
2000–01 Southampton 8 1 **439 161**

LUNDEKVAM, Claus (D) 211 1
H: 6 3 W: 12 11 b.Austevoll 22-2-73
Honours: Norway 10 full caps.
1993 Brann 3 0
1994 Brann 20 0
1995 Brann 14 0
1996 Brann 16 1 **53 1**
1996–97 Southampton 29 0
1997–98 Southampton 31 0
1998–99 Southampton 33 0
1999–2000 Southampton 27 0
2000–01 Southampton 38 0 **158 0**

MARSDEN, Chris (M) 337 18
H: 5 11 W: 12 03 b.Sheffield 3-1-69
Source: Trainee.
1986–87 Sheffield U 0 0
1987–88 Sheffield U 16 1 **16 1**
1988–89 Huddersfield T 14 1
1989–90 Huddersfield T 32 2
1990–91 Huddersfield T 43 5
1991–92 Huddersfield T 23 1
1992–93 Huddersfield T 7 0
1993–94 Huddersfield T 2 0 **121 9**
1993–94 *Coventry C* 7 0 **7 0**
1993–94 Wolverhampton W 8 0
1994–95 Wolverhampton W 0 0 **8 0**
1994–95 Notts Co 7 0
1995–96 Notts Co 3 0 **10 0**
1995–96 Stockport Co 20 1
1996–97 Stockport Co 35 2
1997–98 Stockport Co 10 0 **65 3**
1997–98 Birmingham C 32 1
1998–99 Birmingham C 20 2 **52 3**
1998–99 Southampton 14 2
1999–2000 Southampton 21 0
2000–01 Southampton 23 0 **58 2**

McDONALD, Scott (F) 0 0
H: 5 8 W: 12 04 b.Melbourne 21-8-83
Source: Eastern Pride 3 apps.
2000–01 Southampton 0 0

MILLS, Jonathan (M) 0 0
b.Swindon 8-9-83
Source: Oxford U.
2000–01 Southampton 0 0

MONK, Garry (D) 26 0
H: 6 0 W: 13 10 b.Bedford 6-3-79
Source: Trainee.
1995–96 Torquay U 5 0
1996–97 Southampton 0 0
1997–98 Southampton 0 0
1998–99 Southampton 4 0
1998–99 *Torquay U* 6 0 **11 0**
1999–2000 Southampton 2 0
1999–2000 *Stockport Co* 2 0 **2 0**
2000–01 Southampton 2 0 **8 0**
2000–01 *Oxford U* 5 0 **5 0**

MOSS, Neil (G) 54 0
H: 6 2 W: 13 12 b.New Milton 10-5-75
Source: Trainee.
1992–93 Bournemouth 1 0
1993–94 Bournemouth 6 0
1994–95 Bournemouth 8 0
1995–96 Bournemouth 7 0 **22 0**
1995–96 Southampton 0 0
1996–97 Southampton 3 0
1997–98 Southampton 0 0
1997–98 *Gillingham* 10 0 **10 0**
1998–99 Southampton 7 0
1999–2000 Southampton 9 0
2000–01 Southampton 3 0 **22 0**

OAKLEY, Matthew (M) 160 10
H: 5 10 W: 12 01 b.Peterborough 17-8-77
Source: Trainee. *Honours:* England Under-21.
1994–95 Southampton 1 0
1995–96 Southampton 10 0
1996–97 Southampton 28 3
1997–98 Southampton 33 1
1998–99 Southampton 22 2
1999–2000 Southampton 31 3
2000–01 Southampton 35 1 **160 10**

PAHARS, Marian (F) 188 76
H: 5 8 W: 10 09 b.Latvia 5-8-76
Honours: Latvia 44 full caps, 10 goals.
1994 Pardaugava Riga 17 3 **17 3**
1995 Skonto/Metals Riga 16 4 **16 4**
1995 Skonto Riga 9 8
1996 Skonto Riga 28 12
1997 Skonto Riga 22 5
1998 Skonto Riga 26 19 **85 44**
1998–99 Southampton 6 3
1999–2000 Southampton 33 13
2000–01 Southampton 31 9 **70 25**

PETERS, Mark (F) 0 0
H: 5 8 W: 10 08 b.Frimley 4-10-83
Source: Scholar.
2000–01 Southampton 0 0

PETRESCU, Dan (M) 411 58
H: 5 10 W: 11 02 b.Bucharest 22-12-67
Honours: Romania 95 full caps, 12 goals.
1985–86 Steaua 2 0
1986–87 *FC Olt* 24 0 **24 0**
1987–88 Steaua 11 0
1988–89 Steaua 28 4
1989–90 Steaua 23 9
1990–91 Steaua 31 13 **95 26**
1991–92 Foggia 25 4
1992–93 Foggia 30 3 **55 7**
1993–94 Genoa 24 1 **24 1**
1994–95 Sheffield W 29 3
1995–96 Sheffield W 8 0 **37 3**
1995–96 Chelsea 24 2
1996–97 Chelsea 34 3
1997–98 Chelsea 31 5
1998–99 Chelsea 32 4
1999–2000 Chelsea 29 4 **150 18**
2000–01 Bradford C 17 1 **17 1**
2000–01 Southampton 9 2 **9 2**

RICHARDS, Dean (D) 271 14
H: 6 2 W: 13 12 b.Bradford 9-6-74
Source: Trainee. *Honours:* England Under-21.
1991–92 Bradford C 7 1
1992–93 Bradford C 3 0
1993–94 Bradford C 46 2
1994–95 Bradford C 30 1 **86 4**
1994–95 *Wolverhampton W* 10 2
1995–96 Wolverhampton W 37 1
1996–97 Wolverhampton W 21 1
1997–98 Wolverhampton W 13 0
1998–99 Wolverhampton W 41 3 **122 7**
1999–2000 Southampton 35 2
2000–01 Southampton 28 1 **63 3**

RIPLEY, Stuart (F) 505 43
H: 6 0 W: 13 06 b.Middlesbrough 20-11-67
Source: Apprentice. *Honours:* England Youth, Under-21, 2 full caps.
1984–85 Middlesbrough 1 0
1985–86 Middlesbrough 8 0
1985–86 *Bolton W* 5 1 **5 1**
1986–87 Middlesbrough 44 4
1987–88 Middlesbrough 43 8
1988–89 Middlesbrough 36 4
1989–90 Middlesbrough 39 1
1990–91 Middlesbrough 39 6
1991–92 Middlesbrough 39 3 **249 26**
1992–93 Blackburn R 40 7
1993–94 Blackburn R 40 4
1994–95 Blackburn R 37 0
1995–96 Blackburn R 28 0
1996–97 Blackburn R 13 0
1997–98 Blackburn R 29 2 **187 13**
1998–99 Southampton 22 0
1999–2000 Southampton 23 1
2000–01 Southampton 3 0 **48 1**
2000–01 *Barnsley* 10 1 **10 1**
2000–01 *Sheffield W* 6 1 **6 1**

RODRIGUES, Danny (F) 11 0
H: 5 11 W: 11 02 b.Madeira 3-3-80
Source: Farense.
1998–99 Bournemouth 5 0 **5 0**
1998–99 Southampton 0 0
1999–2000 Southampton 2 0
2000–01 Southampton 0 0 **2 0**
2000–01 *Bristol C* 4 0 **4 0**

ROSIER, Matthew (M) 0 0
b.Australia 7-1-83
2000–01 Southampton 0 0

ROSLER, Uwe (F) 358 90
H: 6 0 W: 12 09 b.Altenburg 15-11-68
Source: Traktor Starken, Lokomotiv Leipzig, Chemie Leipzig. *Honours:* East Germany 5 full caps.
1988–89 Magdeburg 12 3
1989–90 Magdeburg 24 10
1990–91 Magdeburg 26 9 **62 22**
1991–92 Dynamo Dresden 33 4
1992–93 Nuremberg 28 0 **28 0**
1993–94 Dynamo Dresden 7 0 **40 4**
1993–94 Manchester C 12 5
1994–95 Manchester C 31 15
1995–96 Manchester C 36 9
1996–97 Manchester C 44 15
1997–98 Manchester C 29 6 **152 50**
1998–99 Kaiserslautern 28 8 **28 8**
1999–2000 Tennis Berlin 28 6 **28 6**
2000–01 Southampton 20 0 **20 0**

TEALDI, Daniele* (M) 0 0
b.Italy 15-11-82
Source: Atletico 2000.
1999–2000 Southampton 0 0
2000–01 Southampton 0 0

TESSEM, Jo (M) 158 45
H: 6 2 W: 13 02 b.Norway 28-2-72
Honours: Norway 3 full caps.
1996 Lyn 22 15
1997 Lyn 26 8 **48 23**
1998 Molde 26 8
1999 Molde 26 6 **52 14**
1999–2000 Southampton 25 4
2000–01 Southampton 33 4 **58 8**

WARNER, Phil (D) 20 0
H: 5 10 W: 11 12 b.Southampton 2-2-79
Source: Trainee.
1997–98 Southampton 1 0
1998–99 Southampton 5 0
1999–2000 Southampton 0 0
1999–2000 *Brentford* 14 0 **14 0**
2000–01 Southampton 0 0 **6 0**

Scholars
Blayney, Alan; Broxton, Darren E; Carter, Samuel J; Crowell, Matthew T; Davies, Arron R; Fullam, Craig A; Huxley, Matthew S; McManus, Garry L; Poate, Brett; Robertson, Andrew J; Wallace, Adam J

SOUTHEND U

ABBEY, Ben* (F) 34 8
H: 5 7 W: 11 00 b.London 13-5-78
Source: Crawley T.
1999–2000 Oxford U 10 0
2000–01 Oxford U 0 0 **10 0**
2000–01 Southend U 24 8 **24 8**

ABIODUN, Yemi‡ (F) 3 0
H: 5 10 W: 10 07 b.Clapton 29-12-80
Source: Norwich C Trainee.
1999–2000 Southend U 3 0
2000–01 Southend U 0 0 **3 0**

BLACK, Michael* (M) 50 3
H: 5 8 W: 11 08 b.Chigwell 6-10-76
Source: Trainee. *Honours:* England Schools.
1995–96 Arsenal 0 0
1996–97 Arsenal 0 0
1997–98 Arsenal 0 0
1997–98 *Millwall* 13 2 **13 2**
1998–99 Arsenal 0 0
1999–2000 Tranmere R 22 0
2000–01 Tranmere R 0 0 **22 0**
2000–01 Southend U 15 1 **15 1**

BOOTY, Martyn (D) 245 6
H: 5 8 W: 12 03 b.Kirby Muxloe 30-5-71
Source: Trainee.
1991–92 Coventry C 3 0
1992–93 Coventry C 0 0
1993–94 Coventry C 2 0 **5 0**
1993–94 Crewe Alex 31 1
1994–95 Crewe Alex 44 2
1995–96 Crewe Alex 21 2 **96 5**
1995–96 Reading 17 1
1996–97 Reading 14 0
1997–98 Reading 25 0
1998–99 Reading 8 0 **64 1**
1998–99 Southend U 20 0
1999–2000 Southend U 28 0
2000–01 Southend U 32 0 **80 0**

BRAMBLE, Tesfaye (F) 16 6
b.Ipswich 20-7-80
Source: Cambridge C.
2000–01 Southend U 16 6 16 6

BYRNE, Paul (M) 125 11
H: 5 11 W: 13 00 b.Dublin 30-6-72
Source: Trainee. *Honours:* Eire Youth.
1989–90 Oxford U 3 0
1990–91 Oxford U 2 0
1991–92 Oxford U 1 0 6 0
From Bangor.
1993–94 Celtic 22 2
1994–95 Celtic 6 2 28 4
1994–95 *Brighton & HA* 8 1 8 1
1995–96 Southend U 41 5
1996–97 Southend U 32 1
1997–98 Southend U 10 0
1998–99 Southend U 0 0
1999–2000 Southend U 0 0
2000–01 Southend U 0 0 83 6

CAPLETON, Mel (G) 68 0
H: 6 0 W: 13 00 b.London 24-10-73
Source: Trainee.
1992–93 Southend U 0 0
1993–94 Blackpool 0 0
1994–95 Blackpool 10 0
1995–96 Blackpool 1 0 11 0
1996–97 Leyton Orient 0 0
1997–98 Leyton Orient 0 0
1998–99 Leyton Orient 0 0
From Grays Ath.
1998–99 Southend U 14 0
1999–2000 Southend U 42 0
2000–01 Southend U 1 0 57 0

CROSS, Garry‡ (D) 16 0
H: 5 9 W: 12 00 b.Chelmsford 7-10-80
Source: Trainee.
1999–2000 Southend U 8 0
2000–01 Southend U 8 0 16 0

EDWARDS, Craig§ (M) 1 0
b.London 8-7-82
Source: Scholar.
2000–01 Southend U 1 0 1 0

FITZPATRICK, Trevor‡ (F) 53 8
H: 6 1 W: 13 00 b.Surrey 19-2-80
Source: Trainee.
1997–98 Southend U 3 0
1998–99 Southend U 23 5
1999–2000 Southend U 16 0
2000–01 Southend U 11 3 53 8

FLAHAVAN, Darryl (G) 29 0
H: 5 10 W: 12 01 b.Southampton 28-11-78
Source: Trainee.
From Woking.
2000–01 Southend U 29 0 29 0

FORBES, Scott# (M) 34 3
H: 5 8 W: 11 00 b.Essex 3-12-76
Source: Saffron Walden T.
2000–01 Southend U 34 3 34 3

HUTCHINGS, Carl# (M) 228 0
H: 6 1 W: 12 00 b.Hammersmith 24-9-74
Source: Trainee.
1993–94 Brentford 29 0
1994–95 Brentford 39 0
1995–96 Brentford 23 0
1996–97 Brentford 28 2
1997–98 Brentford 43 5
1998–99 Bristol C 21 2
1999–2000 Bristol C 21 1
1999–2000 *Brentford* 8 0 170 7
2000–01 Bristol C 0 0 42 3
2000–01 *Exeter C* 2 0 2 0
2000–01 Southend U 14 0 14 0

JOHNSON, Leon (M) 20 1
H: 6 0 W: 12 00 b.London 10-5-81
Source: Scholarship.
1999–2000 Southend U 0 0
2000–01 Southend U 20 1 20 1

KERRIGAN, Danny (M) 4 0
H: 5 7 W: 10 04 b.Basildon 4-7-82
Source: Trainee.
1999–2000 Southend U 4 0
2000–01 Southend U 0 0 4 0

LEE, David (M) 42 8
H: 5 11 W: 11 08 b.Basildon 28-3-80
Source: Trainee.
1998–99 Tottenham H 0 0
1999–2000 Tottenham H 0 0
2000–01 Southend U 42 8 42 8

MAHER, Kevin# (M) 117 7
H: 5 11 W: 13 04 b.Ilford 17-10-76
Source: Trainee.
1995–96 Tottenham H 0 0

1996–97 Tottenham H 0 0
1997–98 Tottenham H 0 0
1997–98 Southend U 18 1
1998–99 Southend U 34 4
1999–2000 Southend U 24 0
2000–01 Southend U 41 2 117 7

McDONALD, Tom‡ (D) 4 0
H: 6 2 W: 12 00 b.London 15-9-80
Source: Trainee.
1999–2000 Southend U 3 0
2000–01 Southend U 1 0 4 0

McSWEENEY, Dave (D) 11 0
b.Basildon 28-12-81
Source: Scholar.
2000–01 Southend U 11 0 11 0

NEWMAN, Rob† (D) 679 75
H: 6 1 W: 14 03 b.Bradford-on-Avon
13-12-63
Source: Apprentice.
1981–82 Bristol C 21 3
1982–83 Bristol C 43 3
1983–84 Bristol C 30 1
1984–85 Bristol C 34 3
1985–86 Bristol C 39 3
1986–87 Bristol C 45 6
1987–88 Bristol C 44 11
1988–89 Bristol C 46 6
1989–90 Bristol C 46 8
1990–91 Bristol C 46 8 394 52
1991–92 Norwich C 41 7
1992–93 Norwich C 18 2
1993–94 Norwich C 32 2
1994–95 Norwich C 32 1
1995–96 Norwich C 23 1
1996–97 Norwich C 44 1
1997–98 Norwich C 15 0 205 14
1997–98 *Motherwell* 11 0 11 0
1997–98 *Wigan Ath* 8 0 8 0
1998–99 Southend U 36 7
1999–2000 Southend U 19 0
2000–01 Southend U 6 2 61 9

RAWLE, Mark (F) 14 1
b.Leicester 27-4-79
Source: Boston U.
2000–01 Southend U 14 1 14 1

SEARLE, Damon (M) 401 7
H: 5 10 W: 11 00 b.Cardiff 26-10-71
Source: Trainee. *Honours:* Wales Schools,
Youth, Under-21.
1990–91 Cardiff C 35 0
1991–92 Cardiff C 42 1
1992–93 Cardiff C 42 1
1993–94 Cardiff C 42 0
1994–95 Cardiff C 32 0
1995–96 Cardiff C 41 1 234 3
1996–97 Stockport Co 10 0
1997–98 Stockport Co 31 0 41 0
1998–99 Carlisle U 45 2
1999–2000 Carlisle U 21 1 66 3
1999–2000 *Rochdale* 14 0 14 0
2000–01 Southend U 46 1 46 1

THURGOOD, Stuart (M) 13 1
b.Enfield 4-11-81
From Shimizu S-Pulse
2000–01 Southend U 13 1 13 1

TOLSON, Neil* (F) 199 42
H: 6 2 W: 12 11 b.Wordsley 25-10-73
Source: Trainee.
1991–92 Walsall 9 1 9 1
1991–92 Oldham Ath 0 0
1992–93 Oldham Ath 3 0
1993–94 Oldham Ath 0 0 3 0
1993–94 Bradford C 22 2
1994–95 Bradford C 10 2
1994–95 *Chester C* 4 0 4 0
1995–96 Bradford C 31 8 63 12
1996–97 York C 40 12
1997–98 York C 16 3
1998–99 York C 28 3 84 18
1999–2000 Southend U 31 10
2000–01 Southend U 5 1 36 11

WARDLEY, Shane (M) 2 0
b.Ipswich 26-2-80
Source: Cambridge C.
2000–01 Southend U 2 0 2 0

WEBB, Daniel (F) 15 1
H: 6 0 W: 11 08 b.Poole 2-7-83
2000–01 Southend U 1 1 15 1

WHELAN, Phil (D) 213 10
H: 6 4 W: 14 04 b.Stockport 7-3-72
Honours: England Under-21.
1989–90 Ipswich T 0 0
1990–91 Ipswich T 0 0
1991–92 Ipswich T 8 2
1992–93 Ipswich T 32 0

1993–94 Ipswich T 29 0
1994–95 Ipswich T 13 0 82 2
1994–95 Middlesbrough 0 0
1995–96 Middlesbrough 13 1
1996–97 Middlesbrough 9 0 22 1
1997–98 Oxford U 8 0
1998–99 Oxford U 15 0
1998–99 *Rotherham U* 13 4 13 4
1999–2000 Oxford U 31 2 54 2
2000–01 Southend U 42 1 42 1

WILLIAMSON, Russ* (D) 12 0
H: 5 4 W: 8 10 b.Epping 17-3-80
Source: Trainee.
1998–99 Wimbledon 0 0
1999–2000 Wimbledon 0 0
2000–01 Wimbledon 0 0
2000–01 Southend U 12 0 12 0

Scholars
Boot, Anthony RD; Bourgeois, Daryl TA;
Brown, Jonathan P; Cleverly, Gareth FJ;
Coburn, Sean; Edwards, Craig A; England,
Gerald L; Fisher, James D; Hunter, Leon D;
Ing, Martin P; Lunan, Daniel D; Lunan,
Jamie T; Pitts, Daniel J; Simmons, Michael K;
Smith, Liam K; Window, James S; Wray,
Matthew K
Non-Contract
Newman, Robert N
**Player who does not hold a current contract
but his registration has been retained by the
club**
Byrne, Paul P

STOCKPORT CO

BAILEY, Alan* (F) 28 2
H: 5 11 W: 12 03 b.Macclesfield 1-11-78
Source: Trainee.
1997–98 Manchester C 0 0
1998–99 Manchester C 0 0
1998–99 *Macclesfield T* 10 1 10 1
1999–2000 Stockport Co 14 1
2000–01 Stockport Co 4 0 18 1

BERGERSEN, Kent‡ (M) 205 36
H: 5 10 W: 11 07 b.Oslo 8-2-67
Source: Drobak/Frogn.
1991 Lyn 18 3
1992 Lyn 22 2 40 5
1993 Rosenborg 21 6
1994 Rosenborg 28 8 43 14
1995 Valerengen 24 6
1996 Valerengen 20 4 44 10
1997–98 Panionios 30 1
1998–99 Panionios 12 1 42 2
1999 Stromsgodset 10 4 10 4
1999–2000 Stockport Co 17 0
2000–01 Stockport Co 9 1 26 1

BREBNER, Grant (M) 101 12
H: 5 10 W: 11 11 b.Edinburgh 6-12-77
Source: Trainee. *Honours:* Scotland
Under-21.
1994–95 Manchester U 0 0
1995–96 Manchester U 0 0
1996–97 Manchester U 0 0
1997–98 Manchester U 0 0
1997–98 *Cambridge U* 6 1 6 1
1997–98 *Hibernian* 9 1
1998–99 Reading 39 9
1999–2000 Reading 2 1 41 10
1999–2000 Hibernian 28 0
2000–01 Hibernian 11 0 48 1
2000–01 *Stockport Co* 6 0 6 0

BRIGGS, Keith (D) 7 1
H: 6 0 W: 11 00 b.Glossop 11-12-81
Source: Trainee.
1999–2000 Stockport Co 7 1
2000–01 Stockport Co 0 0 7 1

BRYNGELSSON, Fredrik (D) 75 2
H: 6 2 W: 11 13 b.Sweden 10-4-75
1996 Norrby 13 0
1997 Norrby 23 1 36 1
1998 Hacken 2 0
1999 Hacken 24 1
2000 Hacken 8 0 34 1
2000–01 Stockport Co 5 0 5 0

BYRNE, Chris* (M) 69 11
H: 5 9 W: 10 02 b.Hulme 9-2-75
Source: Crewe Alex, Macclesfield T.
1997–98 Sunderland 8 0 8 0
1997–98 Stockport Co 26 7
1998–99 Stockport Co 11 2
1999–2000 Stockport Co 18 2
1999–2000 *Macclesfield T* 5 0 5 0
2000–01 Stockport Co 1 0 56 11

CARRATT, Philip (F) 2 0
b.Stockport 22-10-81
Source: Scholar.

2000–01	Stockport Co	2	0	2 0

CARRIGAN, Brian (F) 125 26
H: 5 8 W: 10 07 b.Glasgow 26-9-79
Source: Kilsyth R. *Honours:* Scotland Under-21.

1996–97	Clyde	14	1	
1997–98	Clyde	34	3	
1998–99	Clyde	31	3	
1999–2000	Clyde	33	18	112 25
2000–01	Stockport Co	13	1	13 1

CLARE, Robert (M) 22 0
b.Belper 28-2-83
Source: Trainee.

1999–2000	Stockport Co	0	0	
2000–01	Stockport Co	22	0	22 0

CLARK, Peter (D) 116 3
H: 6 1 W: 12 04 b.Romford 10-12-79
Source: Arsenal Trainee.

1998–99	Carlisle U	36	0	
1999–2000	Carlisle U	43	1	79 1
2000–01	Carlisle U	37	2	37 2

CONNELLY, Sean* (D) 308 6
H: 5 10 W: 11 10 b.Sheffield 26-6-70
Source: Hallam.

1991–92	Stockport Co	0	0	
1992–93	Stockport Co	7	0	
1993–94	Stockport Co	32	0	
1994–95	Stockport Co	39	0	
1995–96	Stockport Co	43	0	
1996–97	Stockport Co	45	0	
1997–98	Stockport Co	45	2	
1998–99	Stockport Co	35	1	
1999–2000	Stockport Co	43	3	
2000–01	Stockport Co	13	0	302 6
2000–01	Wolverhampton W	6	0	6 0

DALY, Jon (F) 4 0
H: 6 3 W: 12 00 b.Dublin 8-1-83
Source: Trainee.

1999–2000	Stockport Co	4	0	
2000–01	Stockport Co	0	0	4 0

DIBBLE, Andy# (G) 298 0
H: 6 2 W: 16 07 b.Cwmbran 8-5-65
Source: Apprentice. *Honours:* Wales Schools, Youth, Under-21, 3 full caps.

1981–82	Cardiff C	1	0	
1982–83	Cardiff C	20	0	
1983–84	Cardiff C	41	0	62 0
1984–85	Luton T	13	0	
1985–86	Luton T	7	0	
1985–86	*Sunderland*	12	0	12 0
1986–87	Luton T	1	0	
1986–87	*Huddersfield T*	5	0	5 0
1987–88	Luton T	9	0	
1988–89	Manchester C	38	0	
1989–90	Manchester C	31	0	
1990–91	Manchester C	3	0	
1990–91	*Aberdeen*	5	0	5 0
1990–91	*Middlesbrough*	19	0	
1991–92	Manchester C	2	0	
1991–92	*Bolton W*	13	0	13 0
1991–92	*WBA*	9	0	9 0
1992–93	Manchester C	2	0	
1992–93	*Oldham Ath*	0	0	
1993–94	Manchester C	11	0	
1994–95	Manchester C	15	0	
1995–96	Manchester C	0	0	
1996–97	Manchester C	13	0	115 0
1996–97	*Rangers*	7	0	7 0
1997–98	*Luton T*	31	0	31 0
1997–98	Middlesbrough	2	0	
1998–99	Middlesbrough	0	0	21 0

From Altrincham.

1998–99	Hartlepool U	0	0	
1999–2000	Hartlepool U	6	0	6 0
1999–2000	*Carlisle U*	2	0	2 0
2000–01	Stockport Co	10	0	10 0

EVANS, Lee* (M) 0 0
b.Cardiff 30-11-81

2000–01	Stockport Co	0	0

FLITCROFT, Steven‡ (M) 0 0
H: 5 10 W: 11 01 b.Bolton 17-10-81
Source: Trainee. *Honours:* England Schools.

1998–99	Blackburn R	0	0
1999–2000	Blackburn R	0	0
2000–01	Blackburn R	0	0
2000–01	Stockport Co	0	0

FLYNN, Mike (D) 537 22
H: 6 0 W: 11 02 b.Oldham 23-2-69
Source: Trainee.

1986–87	Oldham Ath	0	0	
1987–88	Oldham Ath	31	1	
1988–89	Oldham Ath	9	0	40 1
1988–89	Norwich C	0	0	
1989–90	Norwich C	0	0	
1989–90	Preston NE	23	1	
1990–91	Preston NE	35	1	
1991–92	Preston NE	43	3	
1992–93	Preston NE	35	2	136 7
1992–93	Stockport Co	10	0	
1993–94	Stockport Co	46	1	
1994–95	Stockport Co	43	2	
1995–96	Stockport Co	46	6	
1996–97	Stockport Co	46	2	
1997–98	Stockport Co	34	1	
1998–99	Stockport Co	46	1	
1999–2000	Stockport Co	46	1	
2000–01	Stockport Co	44	0	361 14

FRADIN, Karim (M) 233 11
H: 5 11 W: 12 00 b.Ste Martin d'Hyeres 2-2-72

1993–94	Niort	36	1	
1994–95	Niort	37	0	
1995–96	Niort	39	1	
1996–97	Niort	37	1	
1997–98	Niort	25	1	174 4
1998–99	Nice	7	0	7 0
1999–2000	Stockport Co	21	1	
2000–01	Stockport Co	31	6	52 7

GIBB, Ali (F) 184 4
H: 5 9 W: 11 07 b.Salisbury 17-2-76
Source: Trainee.

1994–95	Norwich C	0	0	
1995–96	Norwich C	0	0	
1995–96	Northampton T	23	2	
1996–97	Northampton T	18	1	
1997–98	Northampton T	35	1	
1998–99	Northampton T	41	0	
1999–2000	Northampton T	14	0	131 4
1999–2000	Stockport Co	14	0	
2000–01	Stockport Co	39	0	53 0

HANCOCK, Glynn (D) 2 0
H: 6 0 W: 12 02 b.Biddulph 24-5-82
Source: Trainee.

1999–2000	Stockport Co	0	0	
2000–01	Stockport Co	2	0	2 0

HENNESSY, Michael‡ (M) 0 0
b.Dublin 16-10-80

2000–01	Stockport Co	0	0

HURST, Glynn (F) 86 33
H: 5 10 W: 11 06 b.Barnsley 17-1-76
Source: Tottenham H Trainee.

1994–95	Barnsley	2	0	
1995–96	Barnsley	5	0	
1995–96	*Swansea C*	2	1	2 1
1996–97	Barnsley	1	0	8 0
1996–97	*Mansfield T*	6	0	6 0
1998–99	Ayr U	34	18	
1999–2000	Ayr U	25	14	59 32
2000–01	Stockport Co	11	0	11 0

JOHNSON, Ben* (D) 0 0
H: 6 0 W: 12 00 b.Manchester 27-8-80
Source: Trainee.

1999–2000	Stockport Co	0	0
2000–01	Stockport Co	0	0
2000–01	*Carlisle U*	0	0

JONES, Lee (G) 109 0
H: 6 3 W: 14 10 b.Pontypridd 9-8-70
Source: Porth.

1993–94	Swansea C	0	0	
1994–95	Swansea C	2	0	
1995–96	Swansea C	1	0	
1995–96	*Crewe Alex*	0	0	
1996–97	Swansea C	1	0	
1997–98	Swansea C	2	0	6 0
1997–98	Bristol R	8	0	
1998–99	Bristol R	32	0	
1999–2000	Bristol R	36	0	76 0
2000–01	Stockport Co	27	0	27 0

KUQI, Shefki (F) 139 34
H: 6 2 W: 13 13 b.Albania 10-11-76
Source: Trepka, Miki. *Honours:* Albania 8 full caps, 1 goal; Finland 18 full caps, 2 goals.

1995	MP	24	3	
1996	MP	26	7	50 10
1997	HJK Helsinki	25	6	
1998	HJK Helsinki	22	1	
1999	HJK Helsinki	25	11	72 18

From Jokerit.

2000–01	Stockport Co	17	6	17 6

LARSSON, Jonas (M) 0 0
b.Vanersborg 1-4-82
Source: Trainee.

1999–2000	Stockport Co	0	0
2000–01	Stockport Co	0	0

LAWSON, Ian (F) 101 23
H: 5 11 W: 11 00 b.Huddersfield 4-11-77
Source: Trainee.

1994–95	Huddersfield T	0	0	
1995–96	Huddersfield T	0	0	
1996–97	Huddersfield T	18	3	
1997–98	Huddersfield T	18	0	
1998–99	Huddersfield T	6	2	42 5
1998–99	*Blackpool*	9	3	9 3
1999–2000	Bury	25	11	25 11
2000–01	Stockport Co	15	4	
2000–01	Stockport Co	10	0	25 4

NICHOLSON, Shane# (D) 360 10
H: 5 10 W: 11 10 b.Newark 3-6-70
Source: Trainee.

1986–87	Lincoln C	7	0	
1987–88	Lincoln C	0	0	
1988–89	Lincoln C	34	1	
1989–90	Lincoln C	23	0	
1990–91	Lincoln C	40	4	
1991–92	Lincoln C	29	1	133 6
1991–92	Derby Co	0	0	
1992–93	Derby Co	17	0	
1993–94	Derby Co	22	1	
1994–95	Derby Co	15	0	
1995–96	Derby Co	20	0	74 1
1995–96	WBA	18	0	
1996–97	WBA	18	0	
1997–98	WBA	16	0	52 0
1998–99	Chesterfield	24	0	24 0
1999–2000	Stockport Co	42	1	
2000–01	Stockport Co	35	2	77 3

ROGET, Leo (D) 129 7
H: 6 1 W: 12 02 b.Ilford 1-8-77

1995–96	Southend U	8	1	
1996–97	Southend U	25	0	
1997–98	Southend U	11	0	
1998–99	Southend U	14	0	
1999–2000	Southend U	36	2	
2000–01	Southend U	26	4	120 7
2000–01	Stockport Co	9	0	9 0

ROSS, Neil* (F) 2 0
H: 6 1 W: 12 02 b.West Bromwich 10-8-82
Source: Birmingham C Trainee, Leeds U Trainee.

1999–2000	Leeds U	0	0	
1999–2000	Stockport Co	2	0	
2000–01	Stockport Co	0	0	2 0

SMITH, David# (M) 276 5
H: 5 10 W: 12 11 b.Liverpool 26-12-70
Source: Trainee.

1989–90	Norwich C	0	0	
1990–91	Norwich C	3	0	
1991–92	Norwich C	1	0	
1992–93	Norwich C	6	0	
1993–94	Norwich C	7	0	18 0
1994–95	Oxford U	42	0	
1995–96	Oxford U	45	1	
1996–97	Oxford U	45	0	
1997–98	Oxford U	44	1	
1998–99	Oxford U	22	0	198 2
1998–99	Stockport Co	17	1	
1999–2000	Stockport Co	9	1	
2000–01	Stockport Co	34	1	60 3

TOD, Andrew (D) 237 37
H: 6 3 W: 12 00 b.Dunfermline 4-11-71
Source: Kelty Hearts.

1993–94	Dunfermline Ath	22	11	
1994–95	Dunfermline Ath	35	6	
1995–96	Dunfermline Ath	36	5	
1996–97	Dunfermline Ath	35	4	
1997–98	Dunfermline Ath	35	6	
1998–99	Dunfermline Ath	25	1	
1999–2000	Dunfermline Ath	30	1	
2000–01	Dunfermline Ath	8	0	226 34
2000–01	Stockport Co	11	3	11 3

TURNER, Sam (G) 0 0
H: 6 1 W: 12 05 b.Pontypool 9-9-80
Source: Trainee.

1998–99	Charlton Ath	0	0
1999–2000	Charlton Ath	0	0
2000–01	Stockport Co	0	0

WILBRAHAM, Aaron (F) 95 17
H: 6 3 W: 12 04 b.Knutsford 21-10-79
Source: Trainee.

1997–98	Stockport Co	7	1	
1998–99	Stockport Co	26	0	
1999–2000	Stockport Co	26	4	
2000–01	Stockport Co	36	12	95 17

WISS, Jarkko (M) 216 31
H: 6 0 W: 12 08 b.Finland 17-4-72
Honours: Finland 31 full caps, 2 goals.

1993	TPV Tampere	25	0
1994	TPV Tampere	23	3

Year	Club	App	Gls	Tot App	Tot Gls
1995	TPV Tampere	25	3	73	6
1996	Jaro	25	1	25	1
1997	HJK Helsinki	26	5		
1998	HJK Helsinki	26	3	52	8
1999	Molde	3	0	3	0
1999	Lillestrom	16	4	16	4
2000	Moss	17	6	17	6
2000–01	Stockport Co	30	6	30	6

WOODTHORPE, Colin# (D)   365   12
H: 6 0   W: 11 08   b.Ellesmere Pt 13-1-69
Source: Apprentice.

Year	Club	App	Gls	Tot App	Tot Gls
1986–87	Chester C	30	2		
1987–88	Chester C	35	0		
1988–89	Chester C	44	3		
1989–90	Chester C	46	1	155	6
1990–91	Norwich C	1	0		
1991–92	Norwich C	15	1		
1992–93	Norwich C	7	0		
1993–94	Norwich C	20	0	43	1
1994–95	Aberdeen	14	0		
1995–96	Aberdeen	15	1		
1996–97	Aberdeen	19	0	48	1
1997–98	Stockport Co	32	1		
1998–99	Stockport Co	37	2		
1999–2000	Stockport Co	26	0		
2000–01	Stockport Co	24	1	119	4

Trainees
Andrews, Martyn; Budgen, Craig; Eames, Haydn T; Elderton, Ryan; Fenna, Stuart; Johansson, Gustav; Kielty, Anthony; Maguire, Gary J; McLachlan, Fraser M; Myers, John; Norton, Blake A; Ogden, Michael A; Rowley, Paul; Scragg, Jonathan R; Shaw, Matthew A; Stanton, James; Thomas, Andrew; Walsh, Gareth; Welsh, Andrew; Wild, Peter

STOKE C

BULLOCK, Matthew (M)   7   0
H: 5 8   W: 11 00   b.Stoke 1-11-80
Source: Trainee.

Year	Club	App	Gls	Tot App	Tot Gls
1997–98	Stoke C	0	0		
1998–99	Stoke C	0	0		
1999–2000	Stoke C	7	0		
2000–01	Stoke C	0	0	7	0

CLARKE, Clive (D)   65   1
H: 6 1   W: 12 03   b.Dublin 14-1-80
Source: Trainee. *Honours:* Eire Under-21.

Year	Club	App	Gls	Tot App	Tot Gls
1996–97	Stoke C	0	0		
1997–98	Stoke C	0	0		
1998–99	Stoke C	2	0		
1999–2000	Stoke C	42	1		
2000–01	Stoke C	21	0	65	1

COLLINS, Lee‡ (D)   4   0
H: 6 1   W: 12 06   b.Birmingham 10-9-77
Source: Trainee.

Year	Club	App	Gls	Tot App	Tot Gls
1996–97	Aston Villa	0	0		
1997–98	Aston Villa	0	0		
1998–99	Aston Villa	0	0		
1998–99	Stoke C	4	0		
1999–2000	Stoke C	0	0		
2000–01	Stoke C	0	0	4	0
2000–01	Cambridge U	0	0		

COMMONS, Kristian (M)   0   0
b.Nottingham 30-8-83
Source: Scholar.

Year	Club	App	Gls	Tot App	Tot Gls
2000–01	Stoke C	0	0		

COOKE, Andy (F)   193   58
H: 5 11   W: 12 08   b.Stoke 20-1-74
Source: Newtown.

Year	Club	App	Gls	Tot App	Tot Gls
1994–95	Burnley	0	0		
1995–96	Burnley	23	5		
1996–97	Burnley	31	13		
1997–98	Burnley	34	16		
1998–99	Burnley	36	9		
1999–2000	Burnley	36	7		
2000–01	Burnley	11	2	171	52
2000–01	Stoke C	22	6	22	6

CROWE, Dean (F)   76   14
H: 5 5   W: 11 02   b.Stockport 6-6-79
Source: Trainee.

Year	Club	App	Gls	Tot App	Tot Gls
1996–97	Stoke C	0	0		
1997–98	Stoke C	16	4		
1998–99	Stoke C	38	8		
1999–2000	Stoke C	6	0		
1999–2000	Northampton T	5	0	5	0
1999–2000	Bury	4	1		
2000–01	Stoke C	0	0	60	12
2000–01	Bury	7	1	11	2

DADASON, Rikhardur (F)   229   106
H: 6 2   W: 13 04   b.Iceland 26-4-72
Honours: Iceland 38 full caps, 12 goals.

Year	Club	App	Gls	Tot App	Tot Gls
1990	Fram	17	5		
1991	Fram	18	4		
1992	Fram	12	2		
1993	Fram	12	4		
1994	Fram	16	9		
1995	Fram	13	5	88	29
1996	KR	18	14		
1996–97	Kalamata	10	1	10	1
1997	KR	16	7	34	21
1998	Viking	25	15		
1999	Viking	21	17		
2000	Viking	23	17	69	49
2000–01	Stoke C	28	6	28	6

DORIGO, Tony* (D)   535   20
H: 5 9   W: 11 03   b.Adelaide 31-12-65
Source: Apprentice. *Honours:* England Under-21, B, 15 full caps.

Year	Club	App	Gls	Tot App	Tot Gls
1983–84	Aston Villa	1	0		
1984–85	Aston Villa	31	0		
1985–86	Aston Villa	38	1		
1986–87	Aston Villa	41	0	111	1
1987–88	Chelsea	40	6		
1988–89	Chelsea	40	6		
1989–90	Chelsea	35	3		
1990–91	Chelsea	31	2	146	11
1991–92	Leeds U	38	3		
1992–93	Leeds U	33	1		
1993–94	Leeds U	37	0		
1994–95	Leeds U	28	0		
1995–96	Leeds U	17	1		
1996–97	Leeds U	18	0	171	5
1997–98	Torino	30	2	30	2
1998–99	Derby Co	18	1		
1999–2000	Derby Co	23	0	41	1
2000–01	Stoke C	36	0	36	0

FENTON, Graham‡ (F)   114   18
H: 5 10   W: 12 12   b.Wallsend 22-5-74
Source: Trainee. *Honours:* England Under-21.

Year	Club	App	Gls	Tot App	Tot Gls
1991–92	Aston Villa	0	0		
1992–93	Aston Villa	0	0		
1993–94	Aston Villa	12	1		
1993–94	WBA	7	3	7	3
1994–95	Aston Villa	17	2		
1995–96	Aston Villa	3	0	32	3
1995–96	Blackburn R	14	6		
1996–97	Blackburn R	13	1	27	7
1997–98	Leicester C	23	3		
1998–99	Leicester C	9	0		
1999–2000	Leicester C	2	0	34	3
1999–2000	Walsall	9	1	9	1
2000–01	Stoke C	5	1	5	1

FOSTER, Ben (G)   0   0
b.Leamington 3-4-83
Source: Racing Club Warwick.

Year	Club	App	Gls	Tot App	Tot Gls
2000–01	Stoke C	0	0		

GOODFELLOW, Marc (M)   7   0
H: 5 8   W: 10 00   b.Burton 20-9-81

Year	Club	App	Gls	Tot App	Tot Gls
1998–99	Stoke C	0	0		
1999–2000	Stoke C	0	0		
2000–01	Stoke C	7	0	7	0

GUDJONSSON, Bjarni (F)   89   22
H: 5 8   W: 11 02   b.Reykjavik 26-2-79
Honours: Iceland Under-21, 1 full cap.

Year	Club	App	Gls	Tot App	Tot Gls
1995	IA Akranes	2	0		
1996	IA Akranes	17	13		
1997	IA Akranes	6	2	25	15
1997–98	Newcastle U	0	0		
1998–99	Newcastle U	0	0		
1999–2000	Genk	14	0	14	0
1999–2000	Stoke C	0	0		
2000–01	Stoke C	42	6	50	7

GUNNARSSON, Brynjar (M)   123   9
H: 6 1   W: 11 00   b.Reykjavik 16-10-75
Honours: Iceland 28 full caps, 3 goals.

Year	Club	App	Gls	Tot App	Tot Gls
1995	KR	16	1		
1996	KR	18	0		
1997	KR	16	0	50	1
1998	Moss	5	2	5	2
1999–2000	Stoke C	22	1		
2000–01	Stoke C	46	5	68	6

HANSSON, Mikael (D)   309   28
H: 5 8   W: 11 08   b.Norrkoping 15-3-68
Honours: Sweden 1 full cap.

Year	Club	App	Gls	Tot App	Tot Gls
1988	Soderkopings	21	3		
1989	Soderkopings	19	4	40	7
1990	Norrkoping	1	0		
1991	Norrkoping	19	4		
1992	Norrkoping	18	6		
1993	Norrkoping	25	1		
1994	Norrkoping	24	2		
1995	Norrkoping	26	2		
1996	Norrkoping	25	0		
1997	Norrkoping	20	0		
1998	Norrkoping	25	3		
1999	Norrkoping	21	1	204	19
1999–2000	Stoke C	27	0		
2000–01	Stoke C	38	2	65	2

HEATH, Robert (M)   19   0
H: 5 9   W: 10 00   b.Newcastle-Under-Lyme 31-8-78

Year	Club	App	Gls	Tot App	Tot Gls
1996–97	Stoke C	0	0		
1997–98	Stoke C	6	0		
1998–99	Stoke C	10	0		
1999–2000	Stoke C	3	0		
2000–01	Stoke C	0	0	19	0

HENRY, Karl (M)   0   0
H: 6 0   W: 12 00   b.Wolverhampton 26-11-82
Source: Trainee.

Year	Club	App	Gls	Tot App	Tot Gls
1999–2000	Stoke C	0	0		
2000–01	Stoke C	0	0		

IWELUMO, Chris (F)   74   8
H: 6 4   W: 13 00   b.Coatbridge 1-8-78

Year	Club	App	Gls	Tot App	Tot Gls
1996–97	St Mirren	14	0		
1997–98	St Mirren	12	0	26	0
1998–99	Aarhus Fremad	27	4	27	4
1999–2000	Stoke C	3	0		
2000–01	Stoke C	2	1	5	1
2000–01	York C	12	2	12	2
2000–01	*Cheltenham T*	4	1	4	1

KAVANAGH, Graham (M)   246   38
H: 5 10   W: 12 06   b.Dublin 2-12-73
Source: Home Farm. *Honours:* Eire Under-21, 3 full caps.

Year	Club	App	Gls	Tot App	Tot Gls
1991–92	Middlesbrough	0	0		
1992–93	Middlesbrough	10	0		
1993–94	Middlesbrough	11	2		
1993–94	*Darlington*	5	0	5	0
1994–95	Middlesbrough	7	0		
1995–96	Middlesbrough	7	1		
1996–97	Middlesbrough	0	0	35	3
1996–97	Stoke C	38	4		
1997–98	Stoke C	44	5		
1998–99	Stoke C	36	11		
1999–2000	Stoke C	45	7		
2000–01	Stoke C	43	8	206	35

KRISTINSSON, Birkir† (G)   223   0
b.Vestmann 15-8-64
Honours: Iceland 70 full caps.

Year	Club	App	Gls	Tot App	Tot Gls
1987	IA	18	0	18	0
1988	Fram	18	0		
1989	Fram	18	0		
1990	Fram	18	0		
1991	Fram	18	0		
1992	Fram	18	0		
1993	Fram	18	0		
1994	Fram	18	0		
1995	Fram	18	0	144	0
1996	Brann	14	0		
1997	Brann	1	0	15	0
1997	Norrkoping	0	0		
1998	Norrkoping	3	0	3	0
1998–99	Bolton W	0	0		
1998	IBV	0	0		
1999	IBV	18	0	18	0
1999–2000	Lustenau	7	0	7	0
2000–01	Stoke C	18	0	18	0

LIGHTBOURNE, Kyle* (F)   311   91
H: 6 2   W: 12 00   b.Bermuda 29-9-68
Honours: Bermuda full caps.

Year	Club	App	Gls	Tot App	Tot Gls
1992–93	Scarborough	19	3		
1993–94	Scarborough	0	0	19	3
1993–94	Walsall	35	7		
1994–95	Walsall	42	23		
1995–96	Walsall	43	15		
1996–97	Walsall	45	20	165	65
1997–98	Coventry C	7	0	7	0
1997–98	Fulham	4	2	4	2
1997–98	Stoke C	13	2		
1998–99	Stoke C	36	7		
1999–2000	Stoke C	40	7		
2000–01	Stoke C	22	5	111	21
2000–01	*Swindon T*	2	0	2	0
2000–01	*Cardiff C*	3	0	3	0

MOHAN, Nicky (D)   360   17
H: 6 1   W: 14 00   b.Middlesbrough 6-10-70
Source: Trainee.

Year	Club	App	Gls	Tot App	Tot Gls
1987–88	Middlesbrough	0	0		
1988–89	Middlesbrough	6	0		
1989–90	Middlesbrough	22	0		
1990–91	Middlesbrough	0	0		
1991–92	Middlesbrough	27	2		
1992–93	Middlesbrough	18	2		
1992–93	*Hull C*	5	1	5	1
1993–94	Middlesbrough	26	0	99	4
1994–95	Leicester C	23	0	23	0
1995–96	Bradford C	39	4		
1996–97	Bradford C	44	0		
1997–98	Bradford C	0	0	83	4
1997–98	Wycombe W	33	0		
1998–99	Wycombe W	25	2	58	2

1998–99	Stoke C	15	0		
1999–2000	Stoke C	40	5		
2000–01	Stoke C	37	1	**92**	**6**

MUGGLETON, Carl* (G) 271 0
H: 6 2 W: 13 00 b.Leicester 13-9-68
Source: Apprentice. *Honours:* England Under-21.

1986–87	Leicester C	0	0		
1987–88	Leicester C	0	0		
1987–88	*Chesterfield*	17	0		
1987–88	*Blackpool*	2	0	**2**	**0**
1988–89	Leicester C	3	0		
1988–89	*Hartlepool U*	8	0	**8**	**0**
1989–90	Leicester C	0	0		
1989–90	*Stockport Co*	4	0	**4**	**0**
1990–91	Leicester C	22	0		
1990–91	*Liverpool*	0	0		
1991–92	Leicester C	4	0		
1992–93	Leicester C	17	0		
1993–94	Leicester C	0	0	**46**	**0**
1993–94	*Stoke C*	6	0		
1993–94	*Sheffield U*	0	0		
1993–94	Celtic	12	0	**12**	**0**
1994–95	Stoke C	24	0		
1995–96	Stoke C	6	0		
1995–96	*Rotherham U*	6	0	**6**	**0**
1995–96	*Sheffield U*	1	0	**1**	**0**
1996–97	Stoke C	33	0		
1997–98	Stoke C	34	0		
1998–99	Stoke C	40	0		
1999–2000	Stoke C	0	0		
1999–2000	*Mansfield T*	9	0	**9**	**0**
1999–2000	*Chesterfield*	5	0	**22**	**0**
2000–01	Stoke C	12	0	**155**	**0**
2000–01	*Cardiff C*	6	0	**6**	**0**

NEAL, Lewis (M) 1 0
H: 6 0 W: 11 00 b.Leicester 14-7-81

1998–99	Stoke C	0	0		
1999–2000	Stoke C	0	0		
2000–01	Stoke C	1	0	**1**	**0**

O'CONNOR, James (M) 90 14
H: 5 8 W: 11 00 b.Dublin 1-9-79
Source: Trainee. *Honours:* Eire Under-21.

1996–97	Stoke C	0	0		
1997–98	Stoke C	0	0		
1998–99	Stoke C	4	0		
1999–2000	Stoke C	42	6		
2000–01	Stoke C	44	8	**90**	**14**

PETTY, Ben (D) 46 0
H: 6 0 W: 12 05 b.Solihull 22-3-77
Source: Trainee.

1994–95	Aston Villa	0	0		
1995–96	Aston Villa	0	0		
1996–97	Aston Villa	0	0		
1997–98	Aston Villa	0	0		
1998–99	Aston Villa	0	0		
1998–99	Stoke C	11	0		
1999–2000	Stoke C	13	0		
2000–01	Stoke C	22	0	**46**	**0**

RISOM, Henrik* (M) 370 37
H: 5 10 W: 11 06 b.Vildbjerg 24-7-68

1987	Vejle	26	6		
1988	Vejle	25	4		
1989	Vejle	26	0		
1990	Vejle	25	1		
1991	Lyngby	14	0		
1991–92	Lyngby	31	3		
1992–93	Lyngby	31	5		
1993–94	Lyngby	13	3	**89**	**11**
1993–94	Dynamo Dresden	11	0		
1994–95	Dynamo Dresden	4	0	**15**	**0**
1994–95	Odense	12	0		
1995–96	Odense	6	0	**18**	**0**
1995–96	Silkeborg	14	3		
1996–97	Silkeborg	15	2		
1997–98	Silkeborg	15	1	**44**	**6**
1997–98	Vejle	14	0		
1998–99	Vejle	31	4		
1999–2000	Vejle	32	5	**179**	**20**
2000–01	Stoke C	25	0	**25**	**0**

SIGURDSSON, Kris‡ (D) 15 0
H: 5 11 W: 11 11 b.Akureyri 7-10-80

1997	KA	15	0	**15**	**0**
1997–98	Stoke C	0	0		
1998–99	Stoke C	0	0		
1999–2000	Stoke C	0	0		
2000–01	Stoke C	0	0		

TAAFFE, Steven* (F) 8 0
H: 5 7 W: 9 00 b.Stoke 10-9-79
Source: Trainee.

1996–97	Stoke C	0	0		
1997–98	Stoke C	3	0		
1998–99	Stoke C	3	0		
1999–2000	Stoke C	2	0		
2000–01	Stoke C	0	0	**8**	**0**

THOMAS, Wayne (D) 157 5
H: 5 11 W: 11 02 b.Gloucester 17-5-79
Source: Trainee.

1995–96	Torquay U	6	0		
1996–97	Torquay U	12	0		
1997–98	Torquay U	21	1		
1998–99	Torquay U	44	1		
1999–2000	Torquay U	40	3	**123**	**5**
2000–01	Stoke C	34	0	**34**	**0**

THORDARSON, Stefan (F) 30 4
H: 6 1 W: 12 01 b.Akranes 27-3-75
Honours: Iceland 5 full caps, 1 goal.

2000–01	Stoke C	30	4	**30**	**4**

THORNE, Peter (F) 241 88
H: 6 0 W: 13 07 b.Manchester 21-6-73
Source: Trainee.

1991–92	Blackburn R	0	0		
1992–93	Blackburn R	0	0		
1993–94	Blackburn R	0	0		
1993–94	*Wigan Ath*	11	0	**11**	**0**
1994–95	Blackburn R	0	0		
1994–95	Swindon T	20	9		
1995–96	Swindon T	26	10		
1996–97	Swindon T	31	8	**77**	**27**
1997–98	Stoke C	36	12		
1998–99	Stoke C	34	9		
1999–2000	Stoke C	45	24		
2000–01	Stoke C	38	16	**153**	**61**

WARD, Gavin (G) 241 0
H: 6 2 W: 12 02 b.Sutton Coldfield 30-6-70
Source: Aston Villa Trainee.

1988–89	Shrewsbury T	0	0		
1989–90	WBA	0	0		
1989–90	Cardiff C	2	0		
1990–91	Cardiff C	1	0		
1991–92	Cardiff C	24	0		
1992–93	Cardiff C	32	0	**59**	**0**
1993–94	Leicester C	32	0		
1994–95	Leicester C	6	0	**38**	**0**
1995–96	Bradford C	36	0	**36**	**0**
1995–96	Bolton W	5	0		
1996–97	Bolton W	11	0		
1997–98	Bolton W	6	0		
1998–99	Bolton W	0	0	**22**	**0**
1998–99	*Burnley*	17	0	**17**	**0**
1998–99	Stoke C	6	0		
1999–2000	Stoke C	46	0		
2000–01	Stoke C	17	0	**69**	**0**

WOOLISCROFT, Ashley* (D) 1 0
H: 5 10 W: 11 02 b.Stoke 28-12-79
Source: Trainee.

1996–97	Stoke C	0	0		
1997–98	Stoke C	0	0		
1998–99	Stoke C	1	0		
1999–2000	Stoke C	0	0		
2000–01	Stoke C	0	0	**1**	**0**

Scholars
Alcock, Daniel J; Cromie, Mark; Gibson, Alexander J; Hall, Laurence W; Hemmings, Andrew P; Hutchinson, Ryan C; Owen, Gareth D; Rees, Oliver HW; Shaw, Martyn P; Thompson, Neil J; Wilkinson, Andrew G; Wilson, Brian

SUNDERLAND

ARCA, Julio (D) 27 2
H: 6 2 W: 11 00 b.Quilmes 31-1-81
Source: Argentinos Juniors.

2000–01	Sunderland	27	2	**27**	**2**

BLACK, Christopher (M) 0 0
b.Ashington 7-9-82
Source: Scholar.

2000–01	Sunderland	0	0		

BOULD, Steve‡ (D) 500 11
H: 6 4 W: 14 02 b.Stoke 16-11-62
Source: Apprentice. *Honours:* England 2 full caps.

1980–81	Stoke C	0	0		
1981–82	Stoke C	2	0		
1982–83	Stoke C	14	0		
1982–83	*Torquay U*	9	0	**9**	**0**
1983–84	Stoke C	38	2		
1984–85	Stoke C	38	3		
1985–86	Stoke C	33	0		
1986–87	Stoke C	28	1		
1987–88	Stoke C	30	0	**183**	**6**
1988–89	Arsenal	30	2		
1989–90	Arsenal	19	0		
1990–91	Arsenal	38	0		
1991–92	Arsenal	25	1		
1992–93	Arsenal	24	1		
1993–94	Arsenal	25	1		
1994–95	Arsenal	31	0		
1995–96	Arsenal	19	0		
1996–97	Arsenal	33	0		
1997–98	Arsenal	24	0		
1998–99	Arsenal	19	0	**287**	**5**
1999–2000	Sunderland	20	0		
2000–01	Sunderland	1	0	**21**	**0**

BUTLER, Thomas (M) 13 0
H: 5 7 W: 10 06 b.Ballymun 25-4-81
Source: Trainee.

1998–99	Sunderland	0	0		
1999–2000	Sunderland	1	0		
2000–01	Sunderland	4	0	**5**	**0**
2000–01	*Darlington*	8	0	**8**	**0**

BYRNE, Clifford (M) 0 0
b.Dublin 27-4-82

1999–2000	Sunderland	0	0		
2000–01	Sunderland	0	0		

CARTERON, Patrice* (D) 281 15
H: 6 0 W: 12 02 b.St Brieux 30-7-70

1992–93	Laval	26	2		
1993–94	Laval	39	2	**65**	**4**
1994–95	Rennes	34	1		
1995–96	Rennes	35	2		
1996–97	Rennes	35	2	**104**	**5**
1997–98	Lyon	22	2		
1998–99	Lyon	31	1		
1999–2000	Lyon	31	2	**84**	**5**
2000–01	St Etienne	20	0	**20**	**0**
2000–01	Sunderland	8	1	**8**	**1**

CLARK, Ben (D) 0 0
H: 6 2 W: 12 06 b.Shotley Bridge 24-1-83
Source: Manchester U Trainee. *Honours:* England Youth.

2000–01	Sunderland	0	0		

CRADDOCK, Jody (D) 246 4
H: 6 2 W: 12 00 b.Bromsgrove 25-7-75
Source: Christchurch.

1993–94	Cambridge U	20	0		
1994–95	Cambridge U	38	0		
1995–96	Cambridge U	46	3		
1996–97	Cambridge U	41	1	**145**	**4**
1997–98	Sunderland	32	0		
1998–99	Sunderland	6	0		
1999–2000	Sunderland	19	0		
1999–2000	*Sheffield U*	10	0	**10**	**0**
2000–01	Sunderland	34	0	**91**	**0**

DICHIO, Danny (F) 164 34
H: 6 4 W: 13 09 b.Hammersmith 19-10-74
Source: Trainee. *Honours:* England Schools, Under-21.

1993–94	QPR	0	0		
1993–94	*Barnet*	9	2	**9**	**2**
1994–95	QPR	9	3		
1995–96	QPR	29	10		
1996–97	QPR	37	7	**75**	**20**
1997–98	Sampdoria	0	0		
1997–98	Lecce	4	1	**4**	**1**
1997–98	Sunderland	13	0		
1998–99	Sunderland	36	10		
1999–2000	Sunderland	12	0		
2000–01	Sunderland	15	1	**76**	**11**

DICKMAN, Jonjo (D) 0 0
H: 5 8 W: 10 05 b.Hexham 22-9-81

1998–99	Sunderland	0	0		
1999–2000	Sunderland	0	0		
2000–01	Sunderland	0	0		

DOWELL, Adam (G) 0 0
b.Gateshead 6-12-82
Source: Scholar.

2000–01	Sunderland	0	0		

EMERSON (D) 113 2
H: 6 2 W: 13 04 b.Porto Alegre 30-3-72
Source: Benfica.

1997–98	Sheffield W	6	0		
1998–99	Sheffield W	38	1		
1999–2000	Sheffield W	17	0	**61**	**1**
1999–2000	Chelsea	20	0		
2000–01	Chelsea	1	0	**21**	**0**
2000–01	Sunderland	31	1	**31**	**1**

FREDGAARD, Carsten (M) 11 0
H: 6 1 W: 12 01 b.Hillerod 20-5-76
Honours: Denmark 1 full cap.

1999–2000	Sunderland	1	0		
1999–2000	*WBA*	5	0	**5**	**0**
2000–01	Sunderland	0	0	**1**	**0**
2000–01	*Bolton W*	5	0	**5**	**0**

GRAY, Michael (D) 295 15
H: 5 9 W: 10 07 b.Sunderland 3-8-74
Source: Trainee. *Honours:* England 3 full caps.

1992–93	Sunderland	27	2		
1993–94	Sunderland	22	1		
1994–95	Sunderland	16	0		
1995–96	Sunderland	46	4		
1996–97	Sunderland	34	3		

1997–98	Sunderland	44	2		
1998–99	Sunderland	37	2		
1999–2000	Sunderland	33	0		
2000–01	Sunderland	36	1	295	15

GRAYDON, Keith (M)   **0 0**
b.Dublin 10-2-83

1999–2000	Sunderland	0	0		
2000–01	Sunderland	0	0		

HARRISON, Steve (D)   **0 0**
b.Hexham 3-2-82
Source: Scholarship.

1999–2000	Sunderland	0	0		
2000–01	Sunderland	0	0		

HELMER, Thomas‡ (D)   **414 45**
H: 6 1 W: 12 04 b.Herford 21-4-65
Honours: Germany 68 full caps, 5 goals.

1984–85	Arminia Bielefeld	4	0		
1985–86	Arminia Bielefeld	35	5	39	5
1986–87	Borussia Dortmund	34	0		
1987–88	Borussia Dortmund	30	5		
1988–89	Borussia Dortmund	30	3		
1989–90	Borussia Dortmund	34	4		
1990–91	Borussia Dortmund	33	2		
1991–92	Borussia Dortmund	21	2	182	16
1992–93	Bayern Munich	34	7		
1993–94	Bayern Munich	28	2		
1994–95	Bayern Munich	24	4		
1995–96	Bayern Munich	32	4		
1996–97	Bayern Munich	24	4		
1997–98	Bayern Munich	28	1		
1998–99	Bayern Munich	21	2	191	24
1999–2000	Sunderland	2	0		
2000–01	Sunderland	0	0	2	0

HUTCHISON, Don (M)   **289 43**
H: 6 1 W: 12 04 b.Gateshead 9-5-71
Source: Trainee. *Honours:* Scotland 16 full caps, 6 goals.

1989–90	Hartlepool U	13	2		
1990–91	Hartlepool U	11	0	24	2
1990–91	Liverpool	0	0		
1991–92	Liverpool	3	0		
1992–93	Liverpool	31	7		
1993–94	Liverpool	11	0	45	7
1994–95	West Ham U	23	9		
1995–96	West Ham U	12	2	35	11
1995–96	Sheffield U	19	2		
1996–97	Sheffield U	41	3		
1997–98	Sheffield U	18	0	78	5
1997–98	Everton	11	1		
1998–99	Everton	33	3		
1999–2000	Everton	31	6	75	10
2000–01	Sunderland	32	8	32	8

INGHAM, Michael (G)   **25 0**
H: 6 4 W: 13 10 b.Preston 7-9-80
Source: Malachians. *Honours:* Northern Ireland Under-21.

1998–99	Cliftonville	18	0	18	0
1999–2000	Sunderland	0	0		
1999–2000	Carlisle U	7	0	7	0
2000–01	Sunderland	0	0		

JAMES, Craig (D)   **0 0**
b.Middlesbrough 15-11-82
Source: Scholar.

2000–01	Sunderland	0	0		

KENNEDY, Jon (G)   **6 0**
b.Rotherham 30-11-80
Source: Worksop T.

1999–2000	Sunderland	0	0		
2000–01	Sunderland	0	0		
2000–01	Blackpool	6	0	6	0

KILBANE, Kevin (M)   **203 23**
H: 6 0 W: 12 07 b.Preston 1-2-77
Source: Trainee. *Honours:* Eire Under-21, 25 full caps, 3 goals.

1993–94	Preston NE	0	0		
1994–95	Preston NE	0	0		
1995–96	Preston NE	11	1		
1996–97	Preston NE	36	2	47	3
1997–98	WBA	43	4		
1998–99	WBA	44	6		
1999–2000	WBA	19	5	106	15
1999–2000	Sunderland	20	1		
2000–01	Sunderland	30	4	50	5

KYLE, Kevin (F)   **18 1**
H: 6 3 W: 13 00 b.Stranraer 7-6-81

1998–99	Sunderland	0	0		
1999–2000	Sunderland	0	0		
2000–01	Sunderland	3	0	3	0
2000–01	Huddersfield T	4	0	4	0
2000–01	Darlington	5	1	5	1
2000–01	Rochdale	6	0	6	0

LACEY, Glenn (M)   **0 0**
b.Dublin 5-6-83
Source: Scholar.

2000–01	Sunderland	0	0		

LUMSDON, Chris (M)   **24 1**
H: 5 10 W: 10 09 b.Newcastle 15-12-79
Source: Trainee.

1997–98	Sunderland	1	0		
1998–99	Sunderland	0	0		
1999–2000	Sunderland	1	0		
1999–2000	Blackpool	6	1	6	1
2000–01	Sunderland	0	0	2	0
2000–01	Crewe Alex	16	0	16	0

LYNCH, Finbar* (F)   **0 0**
H: 5 8 W: 10 01 b.Dublin 24-1-82

1998–99	Sunderland	0	0		
1999–2000	Sunderland	0	0		
2000–01	Sunderland	0	0		

MACHO, Jurgen (G)   **5 0**
H: 6 4 W: 13 12 b.Vienna 24-8-77
Source: Honda Havelka, First Vienna.

2000–01	Sunderland	5	0	5	0

MALEY, Mark (D)   **4 0**
H: 6 0 W: 13 00 b.Newcastle 26-1-81
Source: Trainee. *Honours:* England Schools, Youth.

1997–98	Sunderland	0	0		
1998–99	Sunderland	0	0		
1999–2000	Sunderland	0	0		
2000–01	Sunderland	0	0		
2000–01	Blackpool	2	0	2	0
2000–01	Northampton T	2	0	2	0

MARCHANT, Ross (M)   **0 0**
b.Bournemouth 6-4-82
Source: Scholar.

2000–01	Sunderland	0	0		

McCANN, Gavin (M)   **68 7**
H: 6 1 W: 12 08 b.Blackpool 10-1-78
Source: Trainee. *Honours:* England 1 full cap.

1995–96	Everton	0	0		
1996–97	Everton	0	0		
1997–98	Everton	11	0		
1998–99	Everton	0	0	11	0
1998–99	Sunderland	11	0		
1999–2000	Sunderland	24	4		
2000–01	Sunderland	22	3	57	7

McCARTNEY, George (D)   **2 0**
H: 5 11 W: 10 10 b.Belfast 29-4-81
Source: Trainee. *Honours:* Northern Ireland Under-21.

1998–99	Sunderland	0	0		
1999–2000	Sunderland	0	0		
2000–01	Sunderland	2	0	2	0

McGHIE, Gareth* (M)   **0 0**
b.Ashington 22-2-82
Source: Scholar.

2000–01	Sunderland	0	0		

McGILL, Brendan (M)   **0 0**
H: 5 8 W: 9 02 b.Dublin 22-3-81

1998–99	Sunderland	0	0		
1999–2000	Sunderland	0	0		
2000–01	Sunderland	0	0		

MORDEY, Gareth (D)   **0 0**
b.Sunderland 28-1-83
Source: Scholar.

2000–01	Sunderland	0	0		

NUNEZ, Milton‡ (F)   **6 0**
H: 5 5 W: 10 08 b.Honduras 30-10-72
Honours: Honduras full caps.

1999–2000	PAOK Salonika	5	0	5	0
1999–2000	Sunderland	1	0		
2000–01	Sunderland	0	0	1	0

OSTER, John (M)   **82 4**
H: 5 9 W: 10 09 b.Boston 8-12-78
Source: Trainee. *Honours:* Wales Under-21, 4 full caps.

1996–97	Grimsby T	24	3	24	3
1997–98	Everton	31	1		
1998–99	Everton	9	0	40	1
1999–2000	Sunderland	10	0		
2000–01	Sunderland	8	0	18	0

PEETERS, Tom (M)   **33 1**
H: 5 10 W: 11 00 b.Bornem 25-9-78
Source: Ekeren.

1999–2000	Mechelen	33	1	33	1
2000–01	Sunderland	0	0		

PHILLIPS, Kevin (F)   **198 120**
H: 5 8 W: 11 05 b.Hitchin 25-7-73
Source: Baldock T. *Honours:* England B, 6 full caps.

1994–95	Watford	16	9		
1995–96	Watford	27	11		
1996–97	Watford	16	4	59	24
1997–98	Sunderland	43	29		
1998–99	Sunderland	26	23		
1999–2000	Sunderland	36	30		
2000–01	Sunderland	34	14	139	96

PROCTOR, Michael (F)   **12 4**
H: 6 0 W: 11 08 b.Sunderland 3-10-80
Source: Trainee.

1997–98	Sunderland	0	0		
1998–99	Sunderland	0	0		
1999–2000	Sunderland	0	0		
2000–01	Sunderland	0	0		
2000–01	Halifax T	12	4	12	4

QUINN, Niall (F)   **427 135**
H: 6 5 W: 14 08 b.Dublin 6-10-66
Honours: Eire Youth, Under-21, Under-23, B, 91 full caps, 20 goals.

1983–84	Arsenal	0	0		
1984–85	Arsenal	0	0		
1985–86	Arsenal	12	1		
1986–87	Arsenal	35	8		
1987–88	Arsenal	11	2		
1988–89	Arsenal	3	1		
1989–90	Arsenal	6	2	67	14
1989–90	Manchester C	9	4		
1990–91	Manchester C	38	20		
1991–92	Manchester C	35	12		
1992–93	Manchester C	39	9		
1993–94	Manchester C	15	5		
1994–95	Manchester C	35	8		
1995–96	Manchester C	32	8	203	66
1996–97	Sunderland	12	2		
1997–98	Sunderland	35	14		
1998–99	Sunderland	39	18		
1999–2000	Sunderland	37	14		
2000–01	Sunderland	34	7	157	55

RAE, Alex (M)   **412 95**
H: 5 10 W: 11 09 b.Glasgow 30-6-69
Source: Bishopbriggs. *Honours:* Scotland Under-21, B.

1987–88	Falkirk	12	0		
1988–89	Falkirk	37	12		
1989–90	Falkirk	34	8	83	20
1990–91	Millwall	39	10		
1991–92	Millwall	38	11		
1992–93	Millwall	30	6		
1993–94	Millwall	36	13		
1994–95	Millwall	38	10		
1995–96	Millwall	37	13	218	63
1996–97	Sunderland	23	2		
1997–98	Sunderland	29	3		
1998–99	Sunderland	15	2		
1999–2000	Sunderland	26	3		
2000–01	Sunderland	18	2	111	12

RAMSDEN, Simon (D)   **0 0**
b.Bishop Auckland 17-12-81
Source: Scholar.

2000–01	Sunderland	0	0		

REDDY, Michael (F)   **28 5**
H: 6 1 W: 11 07 b.Graignamanagh 24-3-80
Source: Kilkenny C. *Honours:* Eire Under-21.

1999–2000	Sunderland	8	1		
2000–01	Sunderland	2	0	10	1
2000–01	Swindon T	18	4	18	4

ROSSITER, Mark (M)   **0 0**
b.Sligo 27-5-83
Source: Scholar.

2000–01	Sunderland	0	0		

ROY, Eric (M)   **345 24**
H: 6 2 W: 13 00 b.Nice 26-9-67

1988–89	Nice	4	0		
1989–90	Nice	19	0		
1990–91	Nice	36	2		
1991–92	Nice	27	2	86	4
1992–93	Toulon	34	2	34	2
1993–94	Lyon	36	3		
1994–95	Lyon	37	3		
1995–96	Lyon	38	3	111	9
1996–97	Marseille	36	5		
1997–98	Marseille	27	1		
1998–99	Marseille	24	3	87	9
1999–2000	Sunderland	24	0		
2000–01	Sunderland	3	0	27	0

(Transferred to Troyes, January 2001).

SCHWARZ, Stefan (M)   **298 17**
H: 6 0 W: 12 00 b.Malmo 18-4-69
Honours: Sweden 69 full caps, 6 goals.

1987	Malmo	0	0		
1988	Malmo	10	0		
1989	Malmo	15	0		
1990	Malmo	7	0	32	0
1990–91	Benfica	9	3		
1991–92	Benfica	16	0		
1992–93	Benfica	29	3		
1993–94	Benfica	23	1	77	7
1994–95	Arsenal	34	2	34	2
1995–96	Fiorentina	32	0		
1996–97	Fiorentina	24	0		
1997–98	Fiorentina	22	2	78	2
1998–99	Valencia	30	4	30	4
1999–2000	Sunderland	27	1		
2000–01	Sunderland	20	1	47	2

SHIELDS, Dene (F) 7 1
H: 5 9 W: 12 00 b.Edinburgh 16-9-82
Source: Granton BC.
1999–2000	Raith R	0	0	
2000–01	Raith R	7	1	7 1
2000–01	Sunderland	0	0	

SORENSEN, Thomas (G) 116 0
H: 6 4 W: 13 08 b.Odense 12-6-76
Source: Odense. *Honours:* Denmark 6 full caps.
1998–99	Sunderland	45	0
1999–2000	Sunderland	37	0
2000–01	Sunderland	34	0	116 0

THIRLWELL, Paul (M) 27 0
H: 5 11 W: 11 04 b.Springwell Village 13-2-79
Source: Trainee. *Honours:* England Under-21.
1996–97	Sunderland	0	0
1997–98	Sunderland	0	0
1998–99	Sunderland	2	0
1999–2000	Sunderland	8	0
1999–2000	*Swindon T*	12	0	12 0
2000–01	Sunderland	5	0	15 0

TURNS, Craig (G) 0 0
b.Easington 4-11-82
Source: Scholar.
2000–01	Sunderland	0	0

VARGA, Stanislav (D) 174 23
H: 6 5 W: 14 09 b.Lipany 8-10-72
Honours: Slovakia 36 full caps.
1993–94	Tatran Presov	12	2
1994–95	Tatran Presov	25	2
1995–96	Tatran Presov	21	2
1996–97	Tatran Presov	22	3
1997–98	Tatran Presov	26	1	106 10
1998–99	Slovan Bratislava	28	3
1999–2000	Slovan Bratislava	28	9	56 12
2000–01	Sunderland	12	1	12 1

WAINWRIGHT, Neil (M) 43 7
H: 6 1 W: 11 07 b.Warrington 4-11-77
Source: Trainee.
1996–97	Wrexham	0	0
1997–98	Wrexham	11	3	11 3
1998–99	Sunderland	2	0
1999–2000	Sunderland	0	0
1999–2000	*Darlington*	17	4	17 4
2000–01	Sunderland	0	0	2 0
2000–01	*Halifax T*	13	0	13 0

WILLIAMS, Darren (D) 145 4
H: 5 11 W: 12 00 b.Middlesbrough 28-4-77
Source: Trainee. *Honours:* England Under-21, B.
1994–95	York C	1	0
1995–96	York C	18	0
1996–97	York C	1	0	20 0
1996–97	Sunderland	11	2
1997–98	Sunderland	36	2
1998–99	Sunderland	25	0
1999–2000	Sunderland	25	0
2000–01	Sunderland	28	0	125 0

Scholars

Atkinson, Mark; Capper, Stephen; Cronin, Christopher; Davidson, Iain; Galloway, Carl W; Hand, Marc; Morgan, David; Rowe, Gerard; Shippen, Carl; Straker, Phillip; Vickers, Thomas A

SWANSEA C

APPLEBY, Ritchie (M) 113 11
H: 5 9 W: 11 04 b.Stockton 18-9-75
Source: Trainee. *Honours:* England Youth.
1993–94	Newcastle U	0	0
1994–95	Newcastle U	0	0
1994–95	*Darlington*	0	0
1995–96	Ipswich T	3	0	3 0
1996–97	Swansea C	11	1
1997–98	Swansea C	35	3
1998–99	Swansea C	39	3
1999–2000	Swansea C	20	4
2000–01	Swansea C	5	0	110 11

BOUND, Matthew (D) 216 13
H: 6 2 W: 14 00 b.Bradford-on-Avon 9-11-72
Source: Trainee.
1990–91	Southampton	1	0
1991–92	Southampton	0	0
1992–93	Southampton	0	0
1993–94	Southampton	1	0
1993–94	*Hull C*	7	1	7 1
1994–95	Southampton	0	0	5 0
1994–95	Stockport Co	14	0
1995–96	Stockport Co	26	5

BOYD, Walter* (F) 44 10
H: 5 11 W: 11 10 b.Kingston 1-1-72
Source: Arnett Gardens. *Honours:* Jamaica full caps.
1999–2000	Swansea C	27	7
2000–01	Swansea C	17	3	44 10

CASEY, Ryan (M) 46 2
H: 6 2 W: 12 05 b.Coventry 3-1-79
Source: Trainee. *Honours:* Eire Under-21.
1996–97	Swansea C	10	0
1997–98	Swansea C	6	1
1998–99	Swansea C	10	1
1999–2000	Swansea C	11	0
2000–01	Swansea C	9	1	46 2

COATES, Jonathan (M) 205 18
H: 5 8 W: 11 04 b.Swansea 27-6-75
Source: Trainee. *Honours:* Wales B, Under-21.
1993–94	Swansea C	4	1
1994–95	Swansea C	5	0
1995–96	Swansea C	18	0
1996–97	Swansea C	40	3
1997–98	Swansea C	44	7
1998–99	Swansea C	33	0
1999–2000	Swansea C	42	6
2000–01	Swansea C	19	1	205 18

CUSACK, Nick (M) 497 68
H: 6 0 W: 12 05 b.Rotherham 24-12-65
Source: Alvechurch.
1987–88	Leicester C	16	1	16 1
1988–89	Peterborough U	44	10	44 10
1989–90	Motherwell	31	11
1990–91	Motherwell	29	4
1991–92	Motherwell	17	2	77 17
1991–92	Darlington	21	6	21 6
1992–93	Oxford U	39	4
1993–94	Oxford U	20	6
1993–94	*Wycombe W*	4	0	4 0
1994–95	Oxford U	2	0	61 10
1994–95	Fulham	27	7
1995–96	Fulham	42	5
1996–97	Fulham	45	2
1997–98	Fulham	2	0	116 14
1997–98	Swansea C	32	0
1998–99	Swansea C	43	1
1999–2000	Swansea C	43	7
2000–01	Swansea C	40	2	158 10

DAVIES, Alex§ (G) 1 0
b.Swansea 2-11-82
Source: Scholar.
2000–01	Swansea C	1	0	1 0

DE-VULGT, Leigh (M) 9 0
H: 5 10 W: 10 07 b.Swansea 17-3-81
Source: Trainee.
1999–2000	Swansea C	2	0
2000–01	Swansea C	7	0	9 0

FABIANO, Nicolas* (M) 16 1
H: 5 11 W: 12 00 b.Paris 8-2-81
Source: Paris St Germain.
2000–01	Swansea C	16	1	16 1

FREESTONE, Roger (G) 516 3
H: 6 2 W: 14 04 b.Newport 19-8-68
Source: Trainee. *Honours:* Wales Under-21, 1 full cap.
1986–87	Newport Co	13	0	13 0
1986–87	Chelsea	6	0
1987–88	Chelsea	15	0
1988–89	Chelsea	21	0
1989–90	Chelsea	0	0
1989–90	*Swansea C*	14	0
1989–90	*Hereford U*	8	0	8 0
1990–91	Chelsea	0	0	42 0
1991–92	Swansea C	42	0
1992–93	Swansea C	46	0
1993–94	Swansea C	46	0
1994–95	Swansea C	45	1
1995–96	Swansea C	45	2
1996–97	Swansea C	45	0
1997–98	Swansea C	43	0
1998–99	Swansea C	38	0
1999–2000	Swansea C	46	0
2000–01	Swansea C	43	0	453 3

GREGSON, Lyndon† (M) 0 0
H: 5 11 W: 12 00 b.Carmarthen 8-2-82
Source: Trainee.
2000–01	Swansea C	0	0

HOWARD, Mike (D) 123 1
H: 5 7 W: 10 07 b.Birkenhead 2-12-78
Source: Tranmere R Trainee.
1997–98	Swansea C	3	0
1998–99	Swansea C	39	1
1999–2000	Swansea C	40	0
2000–01	Swansea C	41	0	123 1

JAMES, Robert (M) 0 0
b.Swansea 5-2-82
Source: Trainee.
2000–01	Swansea C	0	0

JENKINS, Lee (M) 111 2
H: 5 8 W: 11 02 b.Pontypool 28-6-79
Source: Trainee. *Honours:* Wales Under-21.
1996–97	Swansea C	23	2
1997–98	Swansea C	21	0
1998–99	Swansea C	12	0
1999–2000	Swansea C	16	0
2000–01	Swansea C	39	0	111 2

JONES, Jason (G) 7 0
H: 6 2 W: 12 10 b.Wrexham 10-5-79
Source: Liverpool Trainee. *Honours:* Wales Under-21.
1997–98	Swansea C	1	0
1998–99	Swansea C	3	0
1999–2000	Swansea C	0	0
2000–01	Swansea C	3	0	7 0

JONES, Steve* (D) 146 4
H: 5 10 W: 12 09 b.Bristol 25-12-70
Source: Cheltenham T.
1995–96	Swansea C	17	0
1996–97	Swansea C	46	1
1997–98	Swansea C	0	0
1998–99	Swansea C	32	2
1999–2000	Swansea C	38	0
2000–01	Swansea C	13	1	146 4

KEEGAN, Michael (M) 8 0
H: 5 10 W: 11 00 b.Liskeard 12-5-81
Source: Trainee.
1999–2000	Swansea C	4	0
2000–01	Swansea C	4	0	8 0

LACEY, Damien (D) 78 1
H: 5 8 W: 11 10 b.Bridgend 3-8-77
Source: Trainee.
1996–97	Swansea C	10	0
1997–98	Swansea C	22	1
1998–99	Swansea C	12	0
1999–2000	Swansea C	16	0
2000–01	Swansea C	18	0	78 1

MORGAN, Bari* (M) 5 0
H: 5 6 W: 10 08 b.Carmarthen 13-8-80
Source: Trainee.
1999–2000	Swansea C	0	0
2000–01	Swansea C	5	0	5 0

MOUNTY, Carl* (G) 0 0
H: 5 10 W: 12 00 b.Caerphilly 11-12-81
Source: Trainee.
2000–01	Swansea C	0	0

MUMFORD, Andrew* (D) 6 0
b.Neath 18-6-81
Source: Llanelli.
2000–01	Swansea C	6	0	6 0

MUTTON, Tommy‡ (F) 7 0
H: 5 8 W: 10 02 b.Huddersfield 17-1-78
Source: Bangor C.
1999–2000	Swansea C	2	0
2000–01	Swansea C	5	0	7 0

O'LEARY, Kristian (D) 105 5
H: 6 0 W: 13 07 b.Port Talbot 30-8-77
Source: Trainee.
1995–96	Swansea C	1	0
1996–97	Swansea C	12	1
1997–98	Swansea C	29	0
1998–99	Swansea C	19	2
1999–2000	Swansea C	20	0
2000–01	Swansea C	24	2	105 5

PHILLIPS, Gareth (M) 26 0
H: 5 7 W: 11 02 b.Pontypridd 19-8-79
Source: Trainee. *Honours:* Wales Under-21.
1996–97	Swansea C	1	0
1997–98	Swansea C	6	0
1998–99	Swansea C	1	0
1999–2000	Swansea C	3	0
2000–01	Swansea C	15	0	26 0

PRICE, Jason* (D) 144 17
H: 6 2 W: 11 05 b.Aberdare 12-4-77
Source: Aberaman Ath. *Honours:* Wales Under-21.
1995–96	Swansea C	0	0
1996–97	Swansea C	2	0
1997–98	Swansea C	34	3
1998–99	Swansea C	28	4
1999–2000	Swansea C	39	6
2000–01	Swansea C	41	4	144 17

ROBERTS, Stuart (M) 79 9
H: 5 6 W: 9 08 b.Carmarthen 22-7-80
Source: Trainee. *Honours:* Wales Under-21.

1998–99	Swansea C	32	3		
1999–2000	Swansea C	11	1		
2000–01	Swansea C	36	5	79	9

ROMO, David (M) 33 0
b.Nimes 7-8-78
Honours: France Youth.

| 2000–01 | Swansea C | 33 | 0 | 33 | 0 |

SAVARESE, Giovanni* (F) 147 64
b.Caracas 14-7-71
Honours: Venezuela full caps.

1996	New York/ New Jersey M	26	13		
1997	New York/ New Jersey M	29	14		
1998	New York/ New Jersey M	30	15	85	42
1999	New England Rev	27	10	27	10
2000	San Jose Earth	4	0	4	0
2000–01	Swansea C	31	12	31	12

SMITH, Jason (D) 107 5
H: 6 3 W: 14 00 b.Bromsgrove 6-9-74
Source: Tiverton. *Honours:* England Schools.

1993–94	Coventry C	0	0		
1994–95	Coventry C	0	0		
1995–96	Coventry C	0	0		
1996–97	Coventry C	0	0		
1997–98	Coventry C	0	0		
From Tiverton T					
1998–99	Swansea C	42	4		
1999–2000	Swansea C	43	1		
2000–01	Swansea C	22	0	107	5

TODD, Chris (D) 11 1
H: 6 0 W: 13 00 b.Swansea 22-8-81
Source: Trainee.

| 2000–01 | Swansea C | 11 | 1 | 11 | 1 |

VERSCHAVE, Matthias* (F) 12 3
H: 5 9 W: 11 00 b.Paris 24-12-77
Source: Paris St Germain.

| 2000–01 | Swansea C | 12 | 3 | 12 | 3 |

WATKIN, Steve (F) 349 89
H: 5 10 W: 11 12 b.Wrexham 16-6-71
Source: School.

1989–90	Wrexham	0	0		
1990–91	Wrexham	9	1		
1991–92	Wrexham	28	8		
1992–93	Wrexham	33	18		
1993–94	Wrexham	40	9		
1994–95	Wrexham	32	4		
1995–96	Wrexham	29	7		
1996–97	Wrexham	26	7		
1997–98	Wrexham	3	1	200	55
1997–98	Swansea C	32	3		
1998–99	Swansea C	43	17		
1999–2000	Swansea C	39	7		
2000–01	Swansea C	35	7	149	34

Trainees
Berry, James A; Davies, Alex J; Di Battista, Santino P; Draper, Craig JE; Healey, Stephen J; Jenkins, Dean; Middleton, Luke; O'Sullivan, Christopher

Scholars
Cole, Simon D; Davis, Peter B; Eames, Jonathan J; Jones, Stuart J; McLachlan, Lee C; Shannon, Robert

SWINDON T

ALEXANDER, Gary (F) 74 23
H: 6 0 W: 12 00 b.South London 15-8-79
Source: Trainee.

1998–99	West Ham U	0	0		
1999–2000	West Ham U	0	0		
1999–2000	*Exeter C*	37	16	37	16
2000–01	Swindon T	37	7	37	7

BAKALLI, Adrian* (M) 3 0
H: 6 3 W: 13 00 b.Brussels 22-11-76
Source: Molenbeek.

1998–99	Watford	0	0		
1999–2000	Watford	2	0		
2000–01	Watford	0	0	2	0
2000–01	Swindon T	1	0	1	0

CAMPAGNA, Sam* (D) 5 0
H: 6 1 W: 11 07 b.Worcester 19-11-80
Source: Trainee.

1998–99	Swindon T	2	0		
1999–2000	Swindon T	3	0		
2000–01	Swindon T	0	0	5	0

COBIAN, Juan (D) 15 0
H: 5 6 W: 10 10 b.Buenos Aires 11-9-75
Source: Boca Juniors.

1998–99	Sheffield W	9	0	9	0
1999–2000	Charlton Ath	0	0		
1999–2000	Aberdeen	3	0	3	0
2000–01	Swindon T	3	0	3	0

COWE, Steve* (F) 97 11
H: 5 7 W: 10 10 b.Gloucester 29-9-74
Source: Trainee.

1993–94	Aston Villa	0	0		
1994–95	Aston Villa	0	0		
1995–96	Aston Villa	0	0		
1995–96	Swindon T	11	1		
1996–97	Swindon T	38	6		
1997–98	Swindon T	17	2		
1998–99	Swindon T	5	0		
1999–2000	Swindon T	17	1		
2000–01	Swindon T	9	1	97	11

DAVIES, Gareth (D) 170 5
H: 6 1 W: 11 12 b.Hereford 11-12-73
Source: Trainee. *Honours:* Wales Under-21.

1991–92	Hereford U	4	0		
1992–93	Hereford U	32	1		
1993–94	Hereford U	31	0		
1994–95	Hereford U	28	0	95	1
1995–96	Crystal Palace	20	2		
1996–97	Crystal Palace	6	0		
1996–97	*Cardiff C*	6	2	6	2
1997–98	Crystal Palace	1	0	27	2
1997–98	Reading	18	0		
1998–99	Reading	1	0	19	0
1998–99	Swindon T	6	0		
1999–2000	Swindon T	17	0		
2000–01	Swindon T	0	0	23	0

DAVIS, Sol (D) 96 0
H: 5 8 W: 11 00 b.Cheltenham 4-9-79
Source: Trainee.

1997–98	Swindon T	6	0		
1998–99	Swindon T	25	0		
1999–2000	Swindon T	29	0		
2000–01	Swindon T	36	0	96	0

DUKE, David (M) 32 1
H: 5 10 W: 11 01 b.Inverness 7-11-78
Source: Redby CA.

1997–98	Sunderland	0	0		
1998–99	Sunderland	0	0		
1999–2000	Sunderland	0	0		
2000–01	Swindon T	32	1	32	1

GRAZIOLI, Guiliano (F) 88 26
H: 5 11 W: 12 11 b.London 23-3-75
Source: Wembley.

1995–96	Peterborough U	3	1		
1996–97	Peterborough U	4	0		
1997–98	Peterborough U	0	0		
1998–99	Peterborough U	34	15	41	16
1999–2000	Swindon T	19	8		
2000–01	Swindon T	28	2	47	10

GRIEMINK, Bart (G) 107 0
H: 6 3 W: 15 02 b.Holland 29-3-72
Source: WKE.

1995–96	Birmingham C	20	0		
1996–97	Birmingham C	0	0	20	0
1996–97	*Barnsley*	0	0		
1996–97	Peterborough U	27	0		
1997–98	Peterborough U	0	0		
1998–99	Peterborough U	17	0		
1999–2000	Peterborough U	14	0	58	0
1999–2000	*Swindon T*	4	0		
2000–01	Swindon T	25	0	29	0

GRIFFIN, Charlie‡ (F) 28 2
H: 6 0 W: 12 07 b.Bath 25-6-79
Source: Bristol R Schoolboy.

1998–99	Swindon T	5	1		
1999–2000	Swindon T	21	1		
2000–01	Swindon T	2	0	28	2

HALL, Gareth* (D) 279 7
H: 5 8 W: 12 00 b.Croydon 20-3-69
Source: Apprentice. *Honours:* England Schools, Wales Under-21, 9 full caps.

1986–87	Chelsea	1	0		
1987–88	Chelsea	13	0		
1988–89	Chelsea	22	0		
1989–90	Chelsea	13	1		
1990–91	Chelsea	24	0		
1991–92	Chelsea	10	0		
1992–93	Chelsea	37	2		
1993–94	Chelsea	7	0		
1994–95	Chelsea	6	0		
1995–96	Chelsea	5	1	138	4
1995–96	Sunderland	14	0		
1996–97	Sunderland	32	0		
1997–98	Sunderland	2	0	48	0
1997–98	*Brentford*	6	0	6	0
1998–99	Swindon T	41	1		

| 1999–2000 | Swindon T | 39 | 2 | | |
| 2000–01 | Swindon T | 7 | 0 | 87 | 3 |

HEISELBERG, Kim‡ (D) 1 0
b.Denmark 21-9-77

| 2000–01 | Swindon T | 1 | 0 | 1 | 0 |

HEWLETT, Matt (M) 155 9
H: 6 2 W: 12 12 b.Bristol 25-2-76
Source: Trainee. *Honours:* England Youth.

1993–94	Bristol C	12	0		
1994–95	Bristol C	1	0		
1995–96	Bristol C	27	2		
1996–97	Bristol C	36	2		
1997–98	Bristol C	34	4		
1998–99	Bristol C	10	1		
1998–99	*Burnley*	2	0	2	0
1999–2000	Bristol C	7	0	127	9
2000–01	Swindon T	26	0	26	0

HEYWOOD, Matthew (D) 34 2
H: 6 3 W: 14 00 b.Chatham 26-8-79
Source: Trainee.

1998–99	Burnley	13	0		
1999–2000	Burnley	0	0		
2000–01	Burnley	0	0	13	0
2000–01	Swindon T	21	2	21	2

HOWE, Bobby (M) 100 7
H: 5 7 W: 10 04 b.Annisford 6-11-73
Source: Trainee.

1991–92	Nottingham F	0	0		
1992–93	Nottingham F	0	0		
1993–94	Nottingham F	4	0		
1994–95	Nottingham F	9	2		
1996–97	Nottingham F	1	0		
1996–97	*Ipswich T*	3	0	3	0
1997–98	Nottingham F	0	0	14	2
1997–98	Swindon T	10	0		
1998–99	Swindon T	23	3		
1999–2000	Swindon T	31	1		
2000–01	Swindon T	19	1	83	5

INVINCIBLE, Danny (M) 42 9
H: 6 0 W: 12 02 b.Australia 31-3-79
Source: Brisbane Strikers 5 apps, 1 goal, Marconi Stallions 39 apps, 2 goals.

| 2000–01 | Swindon T | 42 | 9 | 42 | 9 |

McAREAVEY, Paul (M) 5 1
H: 5 10 W: 11 00 b.Belfast 3-12-80
Source: Trainee. *Honours:* Northern Ireland Under-21.

1997–98	Swindon T	1	0		
1998–99	Swindon T	1	0		
1999–2000	Swindon T	0	0		
2000–01	Swindon T	3	1	5	1

McHUGH, Frazer* (M) 19 0
H: 5 9 W: 12 05 b.Nottingham 14-7-81
Source: Trainee.

1998–99	Swindon T	1	0		
1999–2000	Swindon T	14	0		
2000–01	Swindon T	4	0	19	0

MILDENHALL, Steve (G) 33 0
H: 6 5 W: 13 05 b.Swindon 13-5-78
Source: Trainee.

1996–97	Swindon T	1	0		
1997–98	Swindon T	4	0		
1998–99	Swindon T	0	0		
1999–2000	Swindon T	5	0		
2000–01	Swindon T	23	0	33	0

MILLS, Jamie* (M) 2 0
H: 5 10 W: 11 00 b.Swindon 31-8-81
Source: Trainee.

| 1999–2000 | Swindon T | 0 | 0 | | |
| 2000–01 | Swindon T | 2 | 0 | 2 | 0 |

O'HALLORAN, Keith (D) 102 7
H: 5 9 W: 11 06 b.Ireland 10-11-75
Source: Cherry Orchard.

1994–95	Middlesbrough	1	0		
1995–96	Middlesbrough	3	0		
1995–96	*Scunthorpe U*	7	0	7	0
1996–97	Middlesbrough	0	0	4	0
1996–97	*Cardiff C*	8	0	8	0
1996–97	St Johnstone	5	0		
1997–98	St Johnstone	22	1		
1998–99	St Johnstone	16	1		
1999–2000	St Johnstone	0	0	43	2
2000–01	Swindon T	40	5	40	5

REEVES, Alan# (D) 347 21
H: 6 0 W: 12 00 b.Birkenhead 19-11-67
Source: Heswall.

1988–89	Norwich C	0	0		
1988–89	*Gillingham*	18	0	18	0
1989–90	Chester C	30	2		
1990–91	Chester C	10	0	40	2
1991–92	Rochdale	34	3		
1992–93	Rochdale	41	3		
1993–94	Rochdale	41	3		

1994–95	Rochdale	5	0	**121**	**9**
1994–95	Wimbledon	31	3		
1995–96	Wimbledon	24	1		
1996–97	Wimbledon	2	0		
1997–98	Wimbledon	0	0	**57**	**4**
1998–99	Swindon T	24	2		
1999–2000	Swindon T	43	1		
2000–01	Swindon T	44	3	**111**	**6**

ROBERTSON, Mark‡ (M) 46 2
H: 5 9 W: 11 09 b.Sydney 6-4-77
Source: Marconi Stallions 23 apps, Wollongong Wolves 12 apps.

1997–98	Burnley	11	0		
1998–99	Burnley	24	1		
1999–2000	Burnley	1	0		
2000–01	Burnley	0	0	**36**	**1**
2000–01	Swindon T	10	1	**10**	**1**

ROBINSON, Mark (D) 425 10
H: 5 9 W: 12 04 b.Rochdale 21-11-68
Source: Trainee.

1985–86	WBA	1	0		
1986–87	WBA	1	0	**2**	**0**
1987–88	Barnsley	3	0		
1988–89	Barnsley	18	2		
1989–90	Barnsley	24	0		
1990–91	Barnsley	22	1		
1991–92	Barnsley	41	2		
1992–93	Barnsley	29	1	**137**	**6**
1992–93	Newcastle U	9	0		
1993–94	Newcastle U	16	0	**25**	**0**
1994–95	Swindon T	40	0		
1995–96	Swindon T	46	1		
1996–97	Swindon T	43	1		
1997–98	Swindon T	27	1		
1998–99	Swindon T	29	0		
1999–2000	Swindon T	42	0		
2000–01	Swindon T	34	1	**261**	**4**

ROBINSON, Steve (M) 104 2
H: 5 9 W: 11 00 b.Nottingham 17-10-75
Source: Trainee.

1993–94	Birmingham C	0	0		
1994–95	Birmingham C	6	0		
1995–96	Birmingham C	0	0		
1995–96	*Peterborough U*	5	0	**5**	**0**
1996–97	Birmingham C	9	0		
1997–98	Birmingham C	25	0		
1998–99	Birmingham C	31	0		
1999–2000	Birmingham C	6	0		
2000–01	Birmingham C	4	0	**81**	**0**
2000–01	Swindon T	18	2	**18**	**2**

SMITH, Bryan† (D) 1 0
H: 6 1 W: 12 00 b.Swindon 26-8-83
Source: Trainee.

1999–2000	Swindon T	1	0		
2000–01	Swindon T	0	0	**1**	**0**

TUOMELA, Marko‡ (D) 151 12
H: 6 4 W: 13 06 b.Finland 3-3-72
Honours: Finland 21 full caps, 2 goals.

1993	Kuusysi	22	1		
1994	Kuusysi	19	4	**41**	**5**
1995	TPV Tampere	23	2		
1996	TPV Tampere	25	2	**48**	**4**
1997	Jaro	25	2	**25**	**2**
1998	Tromso	26	1		
1999	Tromso	4	0		
2000	Tromso	5	0	**35**	**1**
2000–01	Swindon T	2	0	**2**	**0**

VAN DER LINDEN, Antoine* (D) 65 1
H: 6 3 W: 13 03 b.Rotterdam 17-3-76
Source: Nieuwerkerk, SVS, Alexandria 66, Zwervers.

1997–98	Sparta	6	0		
1998–99	Sparta	15	0		
1999–2000	Sparta	11	0	**32**	**0**
2000–01	Swindon T	33	1	**33**	**1**

WILLIAMS, Andy* (M) 65 1
H: 5 10 W: 10 10 b.Bristol 8-10-77
Source: Trainee. *Honours:* Wales Under-21, 2 full caps.

1996–97	Southampton	0	0		
1997–98	Southampton	20	0		
1998–99	Southampton	1	0		
1999–2000	Southampton	0	0	**21**	**0**
1999–2000	Swindon T	36	1		
2000–01	Swindon T	8	0	**44**	**1**

WILLIAMS, James (M) 36 1
H: 5 7 W: 10 08 b.Liverpool 15-7-82
Source: Trainee.

1998–99	Swindon T	3	0		
1999–2000	Swindon T	26	1		
2000–01	Swindon T	7	0	**36**	**1**

WILLIS, Adam (D) 65 0
H: 6 1 W: 12 02 b.Nuneaton 21-9-76
Source: Trainee.

1995–96	Coventry C	0	0		
1996–97	Coventry C	0	0		
1997–98	Coventry C	0	0		
1997–98	Swindon T	0	0		
1998–99	Swindon T	11	0		
1998–99	*Mansfield T*	10	0	**10**	**0**
1999–2000	Swindon T	23	0		
2000–01	Swindon T	21	0	**55**	**0**

WOAN, Ian‡ (F) 246 34
H: 5 10 W: 12 07 b.Wirrall 14-12-67
Source: Runcorn.

1989–90	Nottingham F	0	0		
1990–91	Nottingham F	12	3		
1991–92	Nottingham F	21	5		
1992–93	Nottingham F	28	3		
1993–94	Nottingham F	24	5		
1994–95	Nottingham F	37	5		
1995–96	Nottingham F	33	8		
1996–97	Nottingham F	32	1		
1997–98	Nottingham F	21	1		
1998–99	Nottingham F	2	0		
1999–2000	Nottingham F	11	0	**221**	**31**
2000–01	Barnsley	3	0	**3**	**0**
2000–01	Swindon T	22	3	**22**	**3**

YOUNG, Alan (D) 4 0
b.Swindon 12-8-83
Source: Scholar.

2000–01	Swindon T	4	0	**4**	**0**

Scholars
Andersen, Paul A; Collier, Adam J; Collins, Christopher J; Edwards, Nathan M; Farr, Craig J; Fenwick, Mark T; Halliday, Kevin J; Herring, Ian; Reed, Paul S; Scarlett, Philip J; Smith, Bryan J; Thomas, Joshua O; Walton, Graeme T
Non-Contract
Hughes, Christopher WJ

TORQUAY U

AGGREY, Jimmy (D) 93 2
H: 6 3 W: 13 06 b.London 26-10-78
Source: Chelsea Trainee.

1997–98	Fulham	0	0		
1998–99	Torquay U	25	0		
1999–2000	Torquay U	27	0		
2000–01	Torquay U	41	2	**93**	**2**

ASHINGTON, Ryan§ (M) 14 0
b.Torbay 28-3-83
Source: Scholar.

2000–01	Torquay U	14	0	**14**	**0**

BEDEAU, Anthony (F) 154 36
H: 5 10 W: 11 00 b.Hammersmith 24-3-79
Source: Trainee.

1995–96	Torquay U	4	0		
1996–97	Torquay U	8	1		
1997–98	Torquay U	34	5		
1998–99	Torquay U	36	9		
1999–2000	Torquay U	38	16		
2000–01	Torquay U	34	5	**154**	**36**

BENEFIELD, James§ (M) 1 0
b.Bristol 6-5-83
Source: Scholar.

2000–01	Torquay U	1	0	**1**	**0**

BRANDON, Chris (M) 44 5
H: 5 7 W: 10 00 b.Bradford 7-4-76
Source: Bradford PA.

1999–2000	Torquay U	42	5		
2000–01	Torquay U	2	0	**44**	**5**

CHALQI, Khalid (M) 21 1
b.Oujda 28-4-71

2000–01	Torquay U	21	1	**21**	**1**

DOUGLIN, Troy (D) 3 0
H: 6 2 W: 13 00 b.Coventry 7-5-82
Source: Trainee.

2000–01	Torquay U	3	0	**3**	**0**

GAYLE, John* (F) 249 37
H: 6 3 W: 15 04 b.Bromsgrove 30-7-64
Source: Burton Alb.

1988–89	Wimbledon	2	0		
1989–90	Wimbledon	11	1		
1990–91	Wimbledon	7	1	**20**	**2**
1990–91	Birmingham C	22	6		
1991–92	Birmingham C	3	1		
1992–93	Birmingham C	19	3		
1993–94	Birmingham C	0	0	**44**	**10**
1993–94	*Walsall*	4	1	**4**	**1**
1993–94	Coventry C	3	0		
1994–95	Coventry C	0	0	**3**	**0**
1994–95	Burnley	14	3	**14**	**3**
1994–95	Stoke C	4	0		
1995–96	Stoke C	10	3		
1995–96	*Gillingham*	9	3	**9**	**3**
1996–97	Stoke C	12	1	**26**	**4**
1996–97	Northampton T	13	1		
1997–98	Northampton T	35	6	**48**	**7**
1998–99	Scunthorpe U	37	4		
1999–2000	Scunthorpe U	12	0	**49**	**4**
1999–2000	Shrewsbury T	18	2		
2000–01	Shrewsbury T	1	0	**19**	**2**
2000–01	Torquay U	13	1	**13**	**1**

GRAHAM, David† (F) 29 4
H: 5 10 W: 11 02 b.Edinburgh 6-10-78
Source: Rangers SABC. *Honours:* Scotland Under-21.

1995–96	Rangers	0	0		
1996–97	Rangers	0	0		
1997–98	Rangers	0	0		
1998–99	Rangers	3	0	**3**	**0**
1998–99	Dunfermline Ath	21	2		
1999–2000	Dunfermline Ath	0	0		
2000–01	Dunfermline Ath	0	0	**21**	**2**
2000–01	Torquay U	5	2	**5**	**2**

HEALY, Brian (M) 57 11
H: 6 1 W: 13 02 b.Glasgow 27-12-68
Source: West Auckland, Billingham T, Bishop Auckland, Gateshead, Spennymoor U, Morecambe.

1998–99	Torquay U	19	2		
1999–2000	Torquay U	38	9		
2000–01	Torquay U	0	0	**57**	**11**

HERRERA, Robbie‡ (D) 271 2
H: 5 7 W: 10 06 b.Torbay 12-6-70
Source: Trainee.

1987–88	QPR	0	0		
1988–89	QPR	2	0		
1989–90	QPR	1	0		
1990–91	QPR	3	0		
1991–92	QPR	0	0		
1991–92	*Torquay U*	11	0		
1992–93	QPR	0	0		
1992–93	*Torquay U*	5	0		
1993–94	QPR	0	0	**6**	**0**
1993–94	Fulham	23	1		
1994–95	Fulham	27	0		
1995–96	Fulham	43	0		
1996–97	Fulham	26	0		
1997–98	Fulham	26	0	**145**	**1**
1998–99	Torquay U	40	0		
1999–2000	Torquay U	35	0		
2000–01	Torquay U	29	1	**120**	**1**

HILL, Kevin (M) 159 23
H: 5 8 W: 10 03 b.Exeter 6-3-76
Source: Torrington.

1997–98	Torquay U	37	7		
1998–99	Torquay U	35	5		
1999–2000	Torquay U	43	2		
2000–01	Torquay U	44	9	**159**	**23**

HOCKLEY, Matthew (D) 6 1
H: 5 11 W: 12 00 b.Paignton 5-6-82
Source: Trainee.

2000–01	Torquay U	6	1	**6**	**1**

HOLMES, Paul (D) 383 8
H: 5 10 W: 11 00 b.Stocksbridge 18-2-68
Source: Apprentice.

1985–86	Doncaster R	5	1		
1986–87	Doncaster R	16	0		
1987–88	Doncaster R	26	0	**47**	**1**
1988–89	Torquay U	25	0		
1989–90	Torquay U	44	2		
1990–91	Torquay U	33	1		
1991–92	Torquay U	36	1		
1992–93	Birmingham C	12	0	**12**	**0**
1992–93	Everton	4	0		
1993–94	Everton	15	0		
1994–95	Everton	1	0		
1995–96	Everton	1	0	**21**	**0**
1995–96	WBA	18	0		
1996–97	WBA	38	1		
1997–98	WBA	30	0		
1998–99	WBA	17	0		
1999–2000	WBA	0	0	**103**	**1**
1999–2000	Torquay U	30	0		
2000–01	Torquay U	32	2	**200**	**6**

JONES, Stuart (G) 32 0
H: 6 0 W: 13 07 b.Bristol 24-10-77
Source: Weston-Super-Mare.

1997–98	Sheffield W	0	0		
1998–99	Sheffield W	0	0		
1998–99	*Crewe Alex*	0	0		
1999–2000	Sheffield W	0	0		
1999–2000	Torquay U	16	0		
2000–01	Torquay U	16	0	**32**	**0**

KELL, Richard† (M) 15 3
H: 6 1 W: 11 00 b.Bishop Auckland 15-9-79
Source: Trainee.

1998–99	Middlesbrough	0	0		
1999–2000	Middlesbrough	0	0		
2000–01	Middlesbrough	0	0		
2000–01	Torquay U	15	3	**15**	**3**

LAW, Gareth (F) 10 1
b.Torquay 20-8-82
Source: Scholar.

2000-01	Torquay U	10	1	10	1

LYONS, Simon§ (D) 9 1
b.Watchet 2-12-82
Source: Arsenal Trainee.

2000-01	Torquay U	9	1	9	1

McKINNON, Ray† (M) 166 15
H: 5 10 W: 11 08 b.Dundee 5-8-70
Source: 'S' Form. *Honours:* Scotland Under-21.

1987-88	Dundee U	0	0		
1988-89	Dundee U	1	0		
1989-90	Dundee U	10	0		
1990-91	Dundee U	17	2		
1991-92	Dundee U	25	4		
1992-93	Nottingham F	6	1		
1993-94	Nottingham F	0	0	6	1
1993-94	Aberdeen	5	0		
1994-95	Aberdeen	20	0		
1995-96	Aberdeen	1	0	26	0
1995-96	Dundee U	9	0		
1996-97	Dundee U	26	6		
1997-98	Dundee U	9	0	97	12
1998-99	Luton T	30	2		
1999-2000	Luton T	3	0	33	2
2000-01	East Fife	4	0	4	0
2000-01	Torquay U	0	0		

MENDY, Jules (M) 21 2
b.Pikine 4-9-73

2000-01	Torquay U	21	2	21	2

NEIL, Gary‡ (F) 27 1
H: 6 0 W: 12 10 b.Glasgow 16-8-78
Source: Trainee.

1997-98	Leicester C	0	0		
1998-99	Leicester C	0	0		
1998-99	Torquay U	7	0		
1999-2000	Torquay U	7	0		
2000-01	Torquay U	13	1	27	1

NORTHMORE, Ryan (G) 28 0
H: 6 1 W: 13 00 b.Plymouth 5-9-80
Source: Trainee.

1999-2000	Torquay U	3	0		
2000-01	Torquay U	25	0	28	0

O'BRIEN, Mick (M) 51 5
H: 5 5 W: 10 06 b.Liverpool 25-9-79
Source: Trainee. *Honours:* England Schools.

1997-98	Everton	0	0		
1998-99	Everton	0	0		
1999-2000	Torquay U	30	4		
2000-01	Torquay U	21	1	51	5

PARKER, Kevin (F) 15 2
H: 5 10 W: 11 06 b.Plymouth 20-9-79
Source: Trainee.

1999-2000	Norwich C	0	0		
2000-01	Torquay U	15	2	15	2

PLATTS, Mark‡ (F) 36 1
H: 5 8 W: 11 12 b.Sheffield 23-5-79
Source: Trainee. *Honours:* England Schools, Youth.

1995-96	Sheffield W	2	0		
1996-97	Sheffield W	0	0		
1997-98	Sheffield W	0	0		
1998-99	Sheffield W	0	0	2	0
1998-99	Torquay U	8	0		
1999-2000	Torquay U	22	1		
2000-01	Torquay U	4	0	34	1

REES, Jason† (M) 279 11
H: 5 5 W: 10 05 b.Aberdare 22-12-69
Source: Trainee. *Honours:* Wales Schools, Youth, Under-21, B, 1 full cap.

1988-89	Luton T	0	0		
1989-90	Luton T	14	0		
1990-91	Luton T	21	0		
1991-92	Luton T	5	0		
1992-93	Luton T	32	0		
1993-94	Luton T	10	0	82	0
1993-94	*Mansfield T*	15	1	15	1
1994-95	Portsmouth	19	1		
1995-96	Portsmouth	21	1		
1996-97	Portsmouth	3	1	43	3
1996-97	*Exeter C*	7	0		
1997-98	Cambridge U	20	0	20	0
1998-99	Exeter C	44	1		
1999-2000	Exeter C	43	4		
2000-01	Exeter C	0	0	94	5
2000-01	Torquay U	25	2	25	2

ROWBOTHAM, Jason† (D) 153 3
H: 5 9 W: 11 09 b.Cardiff 3-1-69
Source: Trainee.

1987-88	Plymouth Arg	4	0		
1988-89	Plymouth Arg	5	0		
1989-90	Plymouth Arg	0	0		
1990-91	Plymouth Arg	0	0		
1991-92	Shrewsbury T	0	0		
1992-93	Hereford U	5	1	5	1
1993-94	Raith R	36	1		
1994-95	Raith R	20	0	56	1
1995-96	Wycombe W	27	0		
1996-97	Wycombe W	0	0	27	0
1996-97	Plymouth Arg	15	0		
1997-98	Plymouth Arg	25	0		
1998-99	Plymouth Arg	0	0		
1999-2000	Plymouth Arg	11	1		
2000-01	Plymouth Arg	0	0	60	1
2000-01	Torquay U	5	0	5	0

RUSSELL, Lee (D) 197 3
H: 5 10 W: 11 09 b.Southampton 3-9-69
Source: Trainee.

1988-89	Portsmouth	2	0		
1989-90	Portsmouth	3	0		
1990-91	Portsmouth	19	1		
1991-92	Gillingham	9	0		
1992-93	Portsmouth	14	0		
1993-94	Portsmouth	10	0		
1994-95	Portsmouth	19	0		
1994-95	*Bournemouth*	3	0	3	0
1995-96	Portsmouth	19	0		
1996-97	Portsmouth	20	2		
1997-98	Portsmouth	8	0		
1998-99	Portsmouth	0	0	123	3
1998-99	Torquay U	9	0		
1999-2000	Torquay U	35	0		
2000-01	Torquay U	27	0	71	0

SISSOKO, Habib‡ (F) 21 2
b.Juvisy Orge 24-5-71
Source: Louhans-C.

1997-98	Preston NE	7	0	7	0

From Kapellen.

2000-01	Torquay U	14	2	14	2

STOCCO, Tom§ (F) 10 2
H: 6 2 W: 12 05 b.London 4-1-83
Source: Trainee.

1999-2000	Torquay U	8	2		
2000-01	Torquay U	2	0	10	2

TULLY, Stephen (M) 88 3
H: 5 7 W: 10 04 b.Paignton 10-2-80
Source: Trainee.

1997-98	Torquay U	9	0		
1998-99	Torquay U	37	2		
1999-2000	Torquay U	13	0		
2000-01	Torquay U	29	1	88	3

WATSON, Alex (D) 372 14
H: 6 1 W: 12 00 b.Liverpool 5-4-68
Source: Apprentice. *Honours:* England Youth.

1984-85	Liverpool	0	0		
1985-86	Liverpool	0	0		
1986-87	Liverpool	2	0		
1987-88	Liverpool	2	0		
1988-89	Liverpool	0	0		
1989-90	Liverpool	0	0		
1990-91	Liverpool	0	0	4	0
1990-91	*Derby Co*	5	0	5	0
1990-91	Bournemouth	23	3		
1991-92	Bournemouth	15	0		
1992-93	Bournemouth	46	1		
1993-94	Bournemouth	45	1		
1994-95	Bournemouth	22	0		
1995-96	Bournemouth	0	0	151	5
1995-96	*Gillingham*	10	1	10	1
1995-96	Torquay U	29	2		
1996-97	Torquay U	46	1		
1997-98	Torquay U	46	1		
1998-99	Torquay U	8	0		
1999-2000	Torquay U	43	4		
2000-01	Torquay U	30	0	202	8

WILLIAMS, Eifion (F) 86 23
H: 5 11 W: 11 00 b.Bangor 15-11-75
Source: Barry T.

1998-99	Torquay U	7	5		
1999-2000	Torquay U	42	9		
2000-01	Torquay U	37	9	86	23

Trainees
Ashington, Ryan D; Barwell, Thomas; Benefield, James P; Bevan, Lee W; Dawkins, Luke A; Gibbens, Jonathan D; Griffiths, Kenneth Y; Jones, James P; Lewis, Neil M; Lyons, Simon R; Maguire, Anthony E; O'Donovan, Timothy J; Rosindale, Christopher A; Smith, Robert R; Stephens, Nicholas J; Stocco, Tom L; Williamson, Michael J; Worthington, David M

Non-Contract
Graham, David; Hancox, Richard C; Kell, Richard; Rees, Jason M

TOTTENHAM H

ANDERTON, Darren (M) 286 37
H: 6 1 W: 12 08 b.Southampton 3-3-72
Source: Trainee. *Honours:* England Youth, Under-21, B, 29 full caps, 7 goals.

1989-90	Portsmouth	0	0		
1990-91	Portsmouth	20	0		
1991-92	Portsmouth	42	7	62	7
1992-93	Tottenham H	34	6		
1993-94	Tottenham H	37	6		
1994-95	Tottenham H	37	5		
1995-96	Tottenham H	8	2		
1996-97	Tottenham H	16	3		
1997-98	Tottenham H	15	0		
1998-99	Tottenham H	32	3		
1999-2000	Tottenham H	22	3		
2000-01	Tottenham H	23	2	224	30

ARMSTRONG, Chris (F) 347 111
H: 6 0 W: 13 00 b.Newcastle 19-6-71
Source: Llay Welfare. *Honours:* England B.

1988-89	Wrexham	0	0		
1989-90	Wrexham	22	3		
1990-91	Wrexham	38	10	60	13
1991-92	Millwall	25	4		
1992-93	Millwall	3	1	28	5
1992-93	Crystal Palace	35	15		
1993-94	Crystal Palace	43	22		
1994-95	Crystal Palace	40	8	118	45
1995-96	Tottenham H	36	15		
1996-97	Tottenham H	12	5		
1997-98	Tottenham H	19	5		
1998-99	Tottenham H	34	7		
1999-2000	Tottenham H	31	14		
2000-01	Tottenham H	9	2	141	48

BOWDITCH, Ben (D) 0 0
b.Harlow 19-2-84
Source: Scholar.

2000-01	Tottenham H	0	0		

CAMPBELL, Sol (D) 255 10
H: 6 2 W: 14 02 b.Newham 18-9-74
Source: Trainee. *Honours:* England Youth, Under-21, 40 full caps.

1992-93	Tottenham H	1	1		
1993-94	Tottenham H	34	0		
1994-95	Tottenham H	30	0		
1995-96	Tottenham H	31	1		
1996-97	Tottenham H	38	0		
1997-98	Tottenham H	34	0		
1998-99	Tottenham H	37	6		
1999-2000	Tottenham H	29	0		
2000-01	Tottenham H	21	2	255	10

(Transferred to Arsenal, July 2001).

CARR, Stephen (D) 164 6
H: 5 9 W: 13 00 b.Dublin 29-8-76
Source: Trainee. *Honours:* Eire Under-21, 18 full caps.

1993-94	Tottenham H	1	0		
1994-95	Tottenham H	0	0		
1995-96	Tottenham H	0	0		
1996-97	Tottenham H	26	0		
1997-98	Tottenham H	38	0		
1998-99	Tottenham H	37	0		
1999-2000	Tottenham H	34	3		
2000-01	Tottenham H	28	3	164	6

CLEMENCE, Stephen (M) 84 2
H: 5 11 W: 12 05 b.Liverpool 31-3-78
Source: Trainee. *Honours:* England Schools, Youth, Under-21.

1994-95	Tottenham H	0	0		
1995-96	Tottenham H	0	0		
1996-97	Tottenham H	0	0		
1997-98	Tottenham H	17	0		
1998-99	Tottenham H	18	0		
1999-2000	Tottenham H	20	1		
2000-01	Tottenham H	29	1	84	2

CONSORTI, Maurizio (M) 0 0
b.Rome 6-3-82
Source: Trainee.

1999-2000	Tottenham H	0	0		
2000-01	Tottenham H	0	0		

DAVIES, Simon (M) 81 8
H: 5 10 W: 11 02 b.Haverfordwest 23-10-79
Source: Trainee. *Honours:* Wales Under-21, 2 full caps.

1997-98	Peterborough U	6	0		
1998-99	Peterborough U	43	4		
1999-2000	Peterborough U	16	2	65	6
1999-2000	Tottenham H	3	0		
2000-01	Tottenham H	13	2	16	2

DI GIULANTONIO, Luca* (F) 0 0
b.Rome 30-8-83
Source: Scholar.

2000–01	Tottenham H	0	0		

DOHERTY, Gary (D) 94 15
H: 6 0 W: 12 13 b.Carndonagh 31-1-80
Source: Trainee. *Honours:* Eire Under-21, 8 full caps.

1997–98	Luton T	10	0		
1998–99	Luton T	20	6		
1999–2000	Luton T	40	6	70	12
1999–2000	Tottenham H	2	0		
2000–01	Tottenham H	22	3	24	3

DOMINGUEZ, Jose (F) 142 11
H: 5 3 W: 10 00 b.Lisbon 16-2-74
Source: Benfica. *Honours:* Portugal 3 full caps.

1993–94	Birmingham C	5	0		
1994–95	Birmingham C	30	3	35	3
1995–96	Sporting Lisbon	30	1		
1996–97	Sporting Lisbon	32	3	62	4
1997–98	Tottenham H	18	2		
1998–99	Tottenham H	13	2		
1999–2000	Tottenham H	12	0		
2000–01	Tottenham H	2	0	45	4

(Transferred to Kaiserslautern, November 2000).

ETHERINGTON, Matthew (F) 62 6
H: 5 9 W: 10 11 b.Truro 14-8-81
Source: School. *Honours:* England Youth.

1996–97	Peterborough U	1	0		
1997–98	Peterborough U	2	0		
1998–99	Peterborough U	29	3		
1999–2000	Peterborough U	19	3	51	6
1999–2000	Tottenham H	5	0		
2000–01	Tottenham H	6	0	11	0

FENN, Neale* (F) 26 1
H: 5 11 W: 12 08 b.Edmonton 18-1-77
Source: Trainee. *Honours:* Eire Youth, Under-21.

1995–96	Tottenham H	0	0		
1996–97	Tottenham H	4	0		
1997–98	Tottenham H	4	0		
1997–98	Leyton Orient	3	0	3	0
1997–98	Norwich C	7	1	7	1
1998–99	Tottenham H	0	0		
1998–99	Swindon T	4	0	4	0
1998–99	Lincoln C	4	0	4	0
1999–2000	Tottenham H	0	0		
2000–01	Tottenham H	0	0	8	0

FERDINAND, Les (F) 340 157
H: 6 0 W: 13 08 b.Paddington 8-12-66
Source: Hayes. *Honours:* England B, 17 full caps, 5 goals.

1986–87	QPR	2	0		
1987–88	QPR	1	0		
1987–88	Brentford	3	0	3	0
1988–89	QPR	0	0		
1988–89	Besiktas	24	14	24	14
1989–90	QPR	9	2		
1990–91	QPR	18	8		
1991–92	QPR	23	10		
1992–93	QPR	37	20		
1993–94	QPR	36	16		
1994–95	QPR	37	24	163	80
1995–96	Newcastle U	37	25		
1996–97	Newcastle U	31	16	68	41
1997–98	Tottenham H	21	5		
1998–99	Tottenham H	24	5		
1999–2000	Tottenham H	9	2		
2000–01	Tottenham H	28	10	82	22

FERGUSON, Steven (F) 11 6
H: 5 11 W: 11 00 b.Dunfermline 1-4-82

2000–01	East Fife	11	6	11	6
2000–01	Tottenham H	0	0		

FREUND, Steffen (M) 266 9
H: 5 11 W: 12 04 b.Brandenburg 9-1-70
Source: Motor Sud, Stahl Brandenburg.
Honours: Germany 21 full caps.

1989–90	Brandenburg	9	0		
1990–91	Brandenburg	22	0	31	0
1991–92	Schalke	33	1		
1992–93	Schalke	20	2	53	3
1993–94	Borussia Dortmund	19	0		
1994–95	Borussia Dortmund	28	2		
1995–96	Borussia Dortmund	30	2		
1996–97	Borussia Dortmund	2	0		
1997–98	Borussia Dortmund	25	2		
1998–99	Borussia Dortmund	13	0	117	6
1998–99	Tottenham H	17	0		
1999–2000	Tottenham H	27	0		
2000–01	Tottenham H	21	0	65	0

GARDNER, Anthony (D) 49 4
H: 6 5 W: 12 13 b.Stafford 19-9-80
Source: Trainee.

1998–99	Port Vale	15	1		
1999–2000	Port Vale	26	3	41	4
1999–2000	Tottenham H	0	0		
2000–01	Tottenham H	8	0	8	0

HILLIER, Ian (M) 0 0
H: 6 0 W: 11 07 b.Neath 26-12-79
Source: Trainee. *Honours:* Wales Schools, Youth, Under-21.

1998–99	Tottenham H	0	0		
1999–2000	Tottenham H	0	0		
2000–01	Tottenham H	0	0		

IVERSEN, Steffen (F) 131 40
H: 6 1 W: 12 05 b.Oslo 10-11-76
Honours: Norway 24 full caps, 6 goals.

1996	Rosenborg	25	10	25	10
1996–97	Tottenham H	16	6		
1997–98	Tottenham H	13	0		
1998–99	Tottenham H	27	8		
1999–2000	Tottenham H	36	14		
2000–01	Tottenham H	14	2	106	30

JACKSON, Johnnie (M) 0 0
b.Camden 15-8-82
Source: Trainee. *Honours:* England Youth.

1999–2000	Tottenham H	0	0		
2000–01	Tottenham H	0	0		

JONSSON, Jon (M) 0 0
b.Kristianstad 8-7-83

2000–01	Tottenham H	0	0		

KAMANAN, Yannick (F) 0 0
b.St Pol-sur-Mer 5-10-82
Source: Le Mans.

1999–2000	Tottenham H	0	0		
2000–01	Tottenham H	0	0		

KELLY, Gavin (G) 0 0
H: 6 0 W: 13 05 b.Hammersmith 3-6-81
Source: Trainee.

1999–2000	Tottenham H	0	0		
2000–01	Tottenham H	0	0		

KELLY, Stephen (D) 0 0
b.Dublin 6-9-83

2000–01	Tottenham H	0	0		

KING, Ledley (D) 22 1
H: 6 2 W: 14 02 b.Bow 12-10-80
Source: Trainee. *Honours:* England Youth, Under-21.

1998–99	Tottenham H	1	0		
1999–2000	Tottenham H	3	0		
2000–01	Tottenham H	18	1	22	1

KORSTEN, Willem (M) 105 17
H: 6 4 W: 12 13 b.Boxtel 21-1-75

1992–93	NEC	4	0	4	0
1993–94	Vitesse	22	3		
1994–95	Vitesse	18	6		
1995–96	Vitesse	1	1		
1996–97	Vitesse	12	1		
1997–98	Vitesse	17	1		
1998–99	Vitesse	1	0	71	12
1998–99	Leeds U	7	2	7	2
1999–2000	Tottenham H	9	0		
2000–01	Tottenham H	14	3	23	3

LEONHARDSEN, Oyvind (M) 287 56
H: 5 10 W: 11 02 b.Kristiansund 17-8-70
Source: Clausenengen. *Honours:* Norway 73 full caps, 18 goals.

1989	Molde	22	5		
1990	Molde	21	2		
1991	Molde	21	2	64	9
1992	Rosenborg	22	6		
1993	Rosenborg	19	6		
1994	Rosenborg	22	8	63	20
1994–95	Wimbledon	20	4		
1995–96	Wimbledon	29	4		
1996–97	Wimbledon	27	5	76	13
1997–98	Liverpool	28	6		
1998–99	Liverpool	9	1	37	7
1999–2000	Tottenham H	22	4		
2000–01	Tottenham H	25	3	47	7

McEWEN, Dave* (F) 4 0
H: 6 0 W: 13 00 b.Westminster 2-11-77
Source: Dulwich H.

1999–2000	Tottenham H	1	0		
2000–01	Tottenham H	3	0	4	0

PARTIN, Jonatan‡ (M) 0 0
b.Kungsbacka 24-2-83
Source: Edsbyns.

1999–2000	Tottenham H	0	0		
2000–01	Tottenham H	0	0		

PERRY, Chris (D) 236 4
H: 5 8 W: 10 11 b.Carshalton 26-4-73
Source: Trainee.

1991–92	Wimbledon	0	0		
1992–93	Wimbledon	0	0		
1993–94	Wimbledon	2	0		
1994–95	Wimbledon	22	0		
1995–96	Wimbledon	37	0		
1996–97	Wimbledon	37	1		
1997–98	Wimbledon	35	1		
1998–99	Wimbledon	34	0	167	2
1999–2000	Tottenham H	37	1		
2000–01	Tottenham H	32	1	69	2

PIERCY, John (F) 8 0
H: 5 11 W: 12 04 b.Forest Gate 18-9-79
Source: Trainee. *Honours:* England Youth.

1998–99	Tottenham H	0	0		
1999–2000	Tottenham H	3	0		
2000–01	Tottenham H	5	0	8	0

REBROV, Sergei (F) 226 104
H: 5 7 W: 10 11 b.Gorlovka 3-6-74
Honours: Ukraine 42 full caps, 12 goals.

1991	Shakhtar Donetsk	7	2	7	2
1992–93	Dynamo Kiev	23	5		
1993–94	Dynamo Kiev	10	2		
1994–95	Dynamo Kiev	25	8		
1995–96	Dynamo Kiev	31	9		
1996–97	Dynamo Kiev	30	20		
1997–98	Dynamo Kiev	29	22		
1998–99	Dynamo Kiev	22	9		
1999–2000	Dynamo Kiev	20	18	190	93
2000–01	Tottenham H	29	9	29	9

SHERWOOD, Tim (M) 423 49
H: 6 1 W: 11 04 b.St Albans 2-2-69
Source: Trainee. *Honours:* England Under-21, B, 3 full caps.

1986–87	Watford	0	0		
1987–88	Watford	13	0		
1988–89	Watford	19	2	32	2
1989–90	Norwich C	27	3		
1990–91	Norwich C	37	7		
1991–92	Norwich C	7	0	71	10
1991–92	Blackburn R	11	0		
1992–93	Blackburn R	39	3		
1993–94	Blackburn R	38	2		
1994–95	Blackburn R	38	6		
1995–96	Blackburn R	33	3		
1996–97	Blackburn R	37	3		
1997–98	Blackburn R	31	5		
1998–99	Blackburn R	19	3	246	25
1998–99	Tottenham H	14	2		
1999–2000	Tottenham H	27	8		
2000–01	Tottenham H	33	2	74	12

SNEE, George (F) 0 0
b.Dublin 26-1-83
Source: Scholar.

2000–01	Tottenham H	0	0		

SULLIVAN, Neil (G) 217 0
H: 6 2 W: 14 10 b.Sutton 24-2-70
Source: Trainee. *Honours:* Scotland 22 full caps.

1988–89	Wimbledon	0	0		
1989–90	Wimbledon	0	0		
1990–91	Wimbledon	1	0		
1991–92	Wimbledon	1	0		
1991–92	Crystal Palace	1	0	1	0
1992–93	Wimbledon	1	0		
1993–94	Wimbledon	2	0		
1994–95	Wimbledon	11	0		
1995–96	Wimbledon	16	0		
1996–97	Wimbledon	36	0		
1997–98	Wimbledon	38	0		
1998–99	Wimbledon	38	0		
1999–2000	Wimbledon	37	0	181	0
2000–01	Tottenham H	35	0	35	0

TARICCO, Mauricio (D) 205 4
H: 5 8 W: 10 03 b.Buenos Aires 10-3-73
Honours: Argentina Under-23.

1993–94	Argentinos Juniors	21	1	21	0
1994–95	Ipswich T	0	0		
1995–96	Ipswich T	39	0		
1996–97	Ipswich T	41	3		
1997–98	Ipswich T	41	0		
1998–99	Ipswich T	16	1	137	4
1998–99	Tottenham H	13	0		
1999–2000	Tottenham H	29	0		
2000–01	Tottenham H	5	0	47	0

THATCHER, Ben (D) 188 1
H: 5 11 W: 12 02 b.Swindon 30-11-75
Source: Trainee. *Honours:* England Youth, Under-21.

1992–93	Millwall	0	0		
1993–94	Millwall	8	0		
1994–95	Millwall	40	1		
1995–96	Millwall	42	0	90	1
1996–97	Wimbledon	9	0		
1997–98	Wimbledon	26	0		
1998–99	Wimbledon	31	0		
1999–2000	Wimbledon	20	0	86	0
2000–01	Tottenham H	12	0	12	0

THELWELL, Alton (D) 16 0
H: 6 0 W: 12 05 b.Holloway 5-9-80
Source: Trainee.

1998–99	Tottenham H	0	0		

1999–2000 Tottenham H 0 0
2000–01 Tottenham H 16 0 **16 0**

TONER, Ciaran (M) **0 0**
H: 6 1 W: 12 02 b.Craigavon 30-6-81
Source: Trainee. *Honours:* Northern Ireland Under-21.
1999–2000 Tottenham H 0 0
2000–01 Tottenham H 0 0

VEDEUX, Ghyslain (F) **0 0**
b.Yaounde 23-10-83
2000–01 Tottenham H 0 0

VEGA, Ramon (D) **234 20**
H: 6 3 W: 13 00 b.Olten 14-6-71
Source: Trimbach. *Honours:* Switzerland 22 full caps, 2 goals.
1990–91 Grasshoppers 3 0
1991–92 Grasshoppers 34 2
1992–93 Grasshoppers 20 2
1993–94 Grasshoppers 36 2
1994–95 Grasshoppers 33 3
1995–96 Grasshoppers 30 4 156 13
1996–97 Cagliari 14 0 **14 0**
1996–97 Tottenham H 8 1
1997–98 Tottenham H 25 3
1998–99 Tottenham H 16 2
1999–2000 Tottenham H 5 1
2000–01 Tottenham H 10 0 **64 7**
(Transferred to Celtic, December 2000).

WALKER, Ian (G) **261 0**
H: 6 2 W: 13 08 b.Watford 31-10-71
Source: Trainee. *Honours:* England Youth, Under-21, B, 3 full caps.
1989–90 Tottenham H 0 0
1990–91 Tottenham H 1 0
1990–91 *Oxford U* 2 0 **2 0**
1990–91 *Ipswich T* 0 0
1991–92 Tottenham H 18 0
1992–93 Tottenham H 17 0
1993–94 Tottenham H 11 0
1994–95 Tottenham H 41 0
1995–96 Tottenham H 38 0
1996–97 Tottenham H 37 0
1997–98 Tottenham H 29 0
1998–99 Tottenham H 25 0
1999–2000 Tottenham H 38 0
2000–01 Tottenham H 4 0 **259 0**
(Transferred to Leicester C, July 2001).

YOUNG, Luke (D) **58 0**
H: 6 0 W: 12 04 b.Harlow 19-7-79
Source: Trainee. *Honours:* England Youth, Under-21.
1997–98 Tottenham H 0 0
1998–99 Tottenham H 15 0
1999–2000 Tottenham H 20 0
2000–01 Tottenham H 23 0 **58 0**

Scholars
Attwell, Jamie W; Barnard, Lee J; Burch, Robert K; Galbraith, David J; Gardner, Lee RJ; Henry, Ronnie S; Herron, Christopher J; Hughes, Mark A; Lacy, Neil D; Lee, James M; Marney, Dean E; Norbert, Ludwig; O'Donoghue, Paul M; Quilter, James E; Sutton, John WM; Thomas, Walter A
Non-Contract
Segers, Hans

TRANMERE R

ACHTERBERG, John (G) **116 0**
H: 6 1 W: 13 00 b.Utrecht 8-7-71
Source: VV RUC, Utrecht.
1993–94 NAC 1 0
1994–95 NAC 2 0
1995–96 NAC 6 0 **9 0**
1996–97 Eindhoven 32 0 **32 0**
From Utrecht.
1998–99 Tranmere R 24 0
1999–2000 Tranmere R 26 0
2000–01 Tranmere R 25 0 **75 0**

ALDRIDGE, Paul (F) **6 0**
H: 5 11 W: 11 07 b.Liverpool 2-12-81
Source: Scholarship.
1999–2000 Tranmere R 4 0
2000–01 Tranmere R 2 0 **6 0**

ALLEN, Graham# (D) **93 5**
H: 6 0 W: 12 00 b.Bolton 8-4-77
Source: Trainee. *Honours:* England Youth.
1994–95 Everton 0 0
1995–96 Everton 0 0
1996–97 Everton 1 0
1997–98 Everton 5 0
1998–99 Everton 0 0 **6 0**
1998–99 Tranmere R 41 5
1999–2000 Tranmere R 24 0
2000–01 Tranmere R 22 0 **87 5**

ALLISON, Wayne (F) **537 139**
H: 6 0 W: 14 07 b.Huddersfield 16-10-68
Source: Trainee.
1986–87 Halifax T 8 4
1987–88 Halifax T 35 4
1988–89 Halifax T 41 15 84 23
1989–90 Watford 7 0 **7 0**
1990–91 Bristol C 37 6
1991–92 Bristol C 43 10
1992–93 Bristol C 39 4
1993–94 Bristol C 39 15
1994–95 Bristol C 37 13 195 48
1995–96 Swindon T 44 17
1996–97 Swindon T 41 11
1997–98 Swindon T 16 3 101 31
1997–98 Huddersfield T 27 6
1998–99 Huddersfield T 44 9
1999–2000 Huddersfield T 3 0 **74 15**
1999–2000 Tranmere R 7 0
2000–01 Tranmere R 36 6 **76 22**

BARLOW, Stuart (F) **274 83**
H: 5 10 W: 11 03 b.Liverpool 16-7-68
Source: School.
1990–91 Everton 2 0
1991–92 Everton 7 0
1991–92 *Rotherham U* 0 0
1992–93 Everton 26 5
1993–94 Everton 22 3
1994–95 Everton 11 2
1995–96 Everton 3 0 **71 10**
1995–96 Oldham Ath 26 7
1996–97 Oldham Ath 35 12
1997–98 Oldham Ath 32 12 93 31
1997–98 Wigan Ath 9 3
1998–99 Wigan Ath 41 19
1999–2000 Wigan Ath 33 18 **83 40**
2000–01 Tranmere R 27 2 **27 2**

CHALLINOR, Dave (D) **134 6**
H: 6 1 W: 12 00 b.Chester 2-10-75
Source: Bromborough Pool. *Honours:* England Schools.
1994–95 Tranmere R 0 0
1995–96 Tranmere R 0 0
1996–97 Tranmere R 5 0
1997–98 Tranmere R 32 1
1998–99 Tranmere R 34 2
1999–2000 Tranmere R 41 3
2000–01 Tranmere R 22 0 **134 6**

FLYNN, Sean (M) **305 21**
H: 5 8 W: 11 09 b.Birmingham 13-3-68
Source: Halesowen T.
1991–92 Coventry C 22 2
1992–93 Coventry C 7 0
1993–94 Coventry C 36 3
1994–95 Coventry C 32 4 97 9
1995–96 Derby Co 42 2
1996–97 Derby Co 17 1 59 3
1996–97 Stoke C 5 0 **5 0**
1997–98 WBA 35 2
1998–99 WBA 38 2
1999–2000 WBA 36 4 109 8
2000–01 Tranmere R 35 1 **35 1**

GILL, Wayne (M) **30 9**
H: 5 9 W: 11 00 b.Chorley 28-11-75
Source: Trainee.
1994–95 Blackburn R 0 0
1995–96 Blackburn R 0 0
1996–97 Blackburn R 0 0
1997–98 Blackburn R 0 0
1997–98 Dundee U 2 0 **2 0**
1998–99 Blackburn R 0 0
1999–2000 Blackburn R 0 0
1999–2000 Blackpool 12 7 **12 7**
2000–01 Tranmere R 16 2 **16 2**

HAY, Alexander (F) **0 0**
H: 5 10 W: 11 05 b.Wirral 14-10-81
Source: Scholarship.
1999–2000 Tranmere R 0 0
2000–01 Tranmere R 0 0

HAZELL, Reuben (D) **36 1**
H: 5 11 W: 11 11 b.Birmingham 24-4-79
Source: Trainee.
1996–97 Aston Villa 0 0
1997–98 Aston Villa 0 0
1998–99 Aston Villa 0 0
1999–2000 Tranmere R 23 1
2000–01 Tranmere R 13 0 **36 1**

HENRY, Nick° (M) **347 20**
H: 5 6 W: 10 12 b.Liverpool 21-2-69
Source: Trainee.
1987–88 Oldham Ath 5 0
1988–89 Oldham Ath 18 0
1989–90 Oldham Ath 41 0
1990–91 Oldham Ath 43 4
1991–92 Oldham Ath 42 6
1992–93 Oldham Ath 32 6

1993–94 Oldham Ath 22 0
1994–95 Oldham Ath 34 2
1995–96 Oldham Ath 14 0
1996–97 Oldham Ath 22 1 273 19
1996–97 Sheffield U 9 0
1997–98 Sheffield U 1 0
1998–99 Sheffield U 6 0 **16 0**
1998–99 Walsall 8 0 **8 0**
1999–2000 Tranmere R 30 1
2000–01 Tranmere R 20 0 **50 1**

HILL, Clint (D) **110 14**
H: 6 0 W: 11 06 b.Liverpool 19-10-78
Source: Trainee.
1997–98 Tranmere R 14 0
1998–99 Tranmere R 33 4
1999–2000 Tranmere R 29 5
2000–01 Tranmere R 34 5 **110 14**

HINDS, Richard (D) **37 0**
H: 6 2 W: 12 00 b.Sheffield 22-8-80
Source: Schoolboy.
1998–99 Tranmere R 2 0
1999–2000 Tranmere R 6 0
2000–01 Tranmere R 29 0 **37 0**

HUME, Iain (F) **13 0**
H: 5 7 W: 11 02 b.Edinburgh 31-10-83
1999–2000 Tranmere R 3 0
2000–01 Tranmere R 10 0 **13 0**

JOBSON, Richard (D) **536 37**
H: 6 2 W: 12 10 b.Holderness 9-5-63
Source: Burton Alb. *Honours:* England B.
1982–83 Watford 13 1
1983–84 Watford 13 2
1984–85 Watford 2 1
1984–85 Hull C 8 0
1985–86 Hull C 36 7
1986–87 Hull C 40 5
1987–88 Hull C 44 2
1988–89 Hull C 46 1
1989–90 Hull C 45 2
1990–91 Hull C 2 0 221 17
1990–91 Oldham Ath 44 1
1991–92 Oldham Ath 36 2
1992–93 Oldham Ath 40 2
1993–94 Oldham Ath 37 5
1994–95 Oldham Ath 20 0
1995–96 Oldham Ath 12 0 189 10
1995–96 Leeds U 12 1
1996–97 Leeds U 10 0
1997–98 Leeds U 0 0 **22 1**
1997–98 *Southend U* 8 1 **8 1**
1997–98 Manchester C 6 1
1998–99 Manchester C 1 0
1999–2000 Manchester C 44 3
2000–01 Manchester C 0 0 **50 4**
2000–01 *Watford* 2 0 **30 4**
2000–01 Tranmere R 16 0 **16 0**

KOUMAS, Jason (M) **85 15**
H: 5 10 W: 11 06 b.Wrexham 25-9-79
Source: Trainee. *Honours:* Wales 1 full cap.
1997–98 Tranmere R 0 0
1998–99 Tranmere R 23 3
1999–2000 Tranmere R 23 2
2000–01 Tranmere R 39 10 **85 15**

MELLON, Micky (D) **358 30**
H: 5 10 W: 12 11 b.Paisley 18-3-72
Source: Trainee.
1989–90 Bristol C 9 0
1990–91 Bristol C 0 0
1991–92 Bristol C 16 0
1992–93 Bristol C 10 1 **35 1**
1992–93 WBA 17 3
1993–94 WBA 21 2
1994–95 WBA 7 1 **45 6**
1994–95 Blackpool 26 4
1995–96 Blackpool 45 6
1996–97 Blackpool 43 4
1997–98 Blackpool 10 0 124 14
1997–98 Tranmere R 33 2
1998–99 Tranmere R 24 1
1998–99 Burnley 20 2
1999–2000 Burnley 42 3
2000–01 Burnley 22 0 **84 5**
2000–01 Tranmere R 13 1 **70 4**

MORGAN, Alan (D) **63 1**
H: 5 9 W: 11 00 b.Aberystwyth 2-11-73
Source: Trainee. *Honours:* Wales Under-21.
1991–92 Tranmere R 0 0
1992–93 Tranmere R 0 0
1993–94 Tranmere R 0 0
1994–95 Tranmere R 0 0
1995–96 Tranmere R 4 1
1996–97 Tranmere R 1 0
1997–98 Tranmere R 19 0
1998–99 Tranmere R 6 0
1999–2000 Tranmere R 26 0
2000–01 Tranmere R 7 0 **63 1**

MURPHY, Joe (G)   41   0
H: 6 2   W: 13 06   b.Dublin 21-8-81
Source: Trainee. Honours: Eire Under-21.

| 1999–2000 | Tranmere R | 21 | 0 | | |
| 2000–01 | Tranmere R | 20 | 0 | 41 | 0 |

N'DIAYE, Seyni (F)   76   14
H: 6 2   W: 13 06   b.Dakar 6-1-73

1997–98	Paris St Germain	0	0		
1998–99	Neuchatel Xamax	31	8	31	8
1999–2000	Caen	30	3		
2000–01	Caen	7	1	37	4
2000–01	Tranmere R	8	2	8	2

OLSEN, James (M)   1   0
b.Bootle 23-10-81
Source: Liverpool scholar.

| 2000–01 | Tranmere R | 1 | 0 | 1 | 0 |

OSBORN, Simon* (M)   267   23
H: 5 10   W: 11 04   b.New Addington 9-1-72
Source: Apprentice.

1989–90	Crystal Palace	0	0		
1990–91	Crystal Palace	4	0		
1991–92	Crystal Palace	14	2		
1992–93	Crystal Palace	31	2		
1993–94	Reading	6	1	55	5
1994–95	QPR	32	5	32	5
1995–96	QPR	9	1	9	1
1995–96	Wolverhampton W	21	2		
1996–97	Wolverhampton W	35	5		
1997–98	Wolverhampton W	24	2		
1998–99	Wolverhampton W	37	2		
1999–2000	Wolverhampton W	25	0		
2000–01	Wolverhampton W	20	0	162	11
2000–01	Tranmere R	9	1	9	1

PARKINSON, Andy (F)   123   16
H: 5 8   W: 10 12   b.Liverpool 27-5-79
Source: Liverpool Trainee.

1996–97	Tranmere R	0	0		
1997–98	Tranmere R	18	1		
1998–99	Tranmere R	29	2		
1999–2000	Tranmere R	37	7		
2000–01	Tranmere R	39	6	123	16

RIDEOUT, Paul (F)   498   135
H: 5 11   W: 12 00   b.Bournemouth 14-8-64
Source: Apprentice. Honours: England Schools, Youth, Under-21.

1980–81	Swindon T	16	4		
1981–82	Swindon T	35	14		
1982–83	Swindon T	44	20		
1983–84	Aston Villa	25	5		
1984–85	Aston Villa	29	14	54	19
1985–86	Bari	28	6		
1986–87	Bari	34	10		
1987–88	Bari	37	7	99	23
1988–89	Southampton	24	6		
1989–90	Southampton	31	7		
1990–91	Southampton	16	6		
1990–91	*Swindon T*	9	1	104	39
1991–92	Southampton	4	0	75	19
1991–92	Notts Co	11	3	11	3
1991–92	Rangers	11	1		
1992–93	Rangers	11	1	12	1
1992–93	Everton	24	3		
1993–94	Everton	24	6		
1994–95	Everton	29	14		
1995–96	Everton	25	6		
1996–97	Everton	10	0	112	29

From Shengzhen

| 2000–01 | Tranmere R | 31 | 2 | 31 | 2 |

ROBERTS, Gareth (D)   71   1
H: 5 8   W: 11 00   b.Wrexham 6-2-78
Source: Trainee. Honours: Wales Under-21, B, 4 full caps.

1995–96	Liverpool	0	0		
1996–97	Liverpool	0	0		
1997–98	Liverpool	0	0		
1998–99	Liverpool	0	0		
1999–2000	Tranmere R	37	1		
2000–01	Tranmere R	34	0	71	1

SHARPS, Ian (M)   1   0
H: 6 3   W: 13 05   b.Warrington 23-10-80
Source: Trainee.

1998–99	Tranmere R	1	0		
1999–2000	Tranmere R	0	0		
2000–01	Tranmere R	0	0	1	0

TAYLOR, Perry* (M)   0   0
H: 5 11   W: 12 02   b.Birkenhead 29-1-81
Source: Trainee. Honours: England Schools.

1998–99	Tranmere R	0	0		
1999–2000	Tranmere R	0	0		
2000–01	Tranmere R	0	0		

TAYLOR, Scott* (F)   163   22
H: 5 10   W: 11 06   b.Chertsey 5-5-76
Source: Staines T.

| 1994–95 | Millwall | 6 | 0 | | |
| 1995–96 | Millwall | 22 | 0 | 28 | 0 |

1995–96	Bolton W	1	0		
1996–97	Bolton W	11	1		
1997–98	Bolton W	0	0		
1997–98	Rotherham U	10	3	10	3
1997–98	Blackpool	5	1	5	1
1998–99	Bolton W	0	0	12	1
1998–99	Tranmere R	36	9		
1999–2000	Tranmere R	35	3		
2000–01	Tranmere R	37	5	108	17

YATES, Steve (D)   407   6
H: 5 10   W: 12 02   b.Bristol 29-1-70
Source: Trainee.

1986–87	Bristol R	2	0		
1987–88	Bristol R	0	0		
1988–89	Bristol R	35	0		
1989–90	Bristol R	42	0		
1990–91	Bristol R	34	0		
1991–92	Bristol R	39	0		
1992–93	Bristol R	44	0		
1993–94	Bristol R	1	0	197	0
1993–94	QPR	29	0		
1994–95	QPR	23	1		
1995–96	QPR	30	0		
1996–97	QPR	16	1		
1997–98	QPR	30	0		
1998–99	QPR	6	0	134	2
1999–2000	Tranmere R	33	2		
2000–01	Tranmere R	43	2	76	4

Trainees
Baker, Phillip; Climo, Daniel P; Dreves, Thomas; Dunbar, Karl A; Evans, Dylan T; Farren, Mark J; Garry, Spencer D; Harrison, Daniel R; Linwood, Paul A; McGuire, Jamie A; Ralph, Andrew O; Robinson, Paul; Taylor, Craig; Taylor, Ryan A; Thornton, Sean; Walsham, Paul J
Associated Schoolboy
Roberts, Paul

WALSALL

ANGELL, Brett (F)   412   154
H: 6 2   W: 13 10   b.Marlborough 20-8-68
Source: Portsmouth, Cheltenham T.

1987–88	Derby Co	0	0		
1988–89	Stockport Co	26	5		
1989–90	Stockport Co	44	23		
1990–91	Southend U	42	15		
1991–92	Southend U	43	21		
1992–93	Southend U	13	5		
1993–94	Southend U	5	4		
1993–94	*Everton*	1	0		
1993–94	Southend U	12	2	115	47
1993–94	Everton	15	1		
1994–95	Everton	4	0	20	1
1994–95	Sunderland	28	0		
1995–96	Sunderland	2	0		
1995–96	*Sheffield U*	6	2	6	2
1995–96	WBA	3	0	3	0
1996–97	Sunderland	0	0	10	0
1996–97	Stockport Co	34	15		
1997–98	Stockport Co	45	18		
1998–99	Stockport Co	42	17		
1999–2000	Stockport Co	5	0	196	78
1999–2000	*Notts Co*	6	5	6	5
1999–2000	*Preston NE*	15	8	15	8
2000–01	Walsall	41	13	41	13

ARANALDE, Zigor (D)   45   0
H: 6 0   W: 12 00   b.Ibarra 28-2-73
Source: Logrones.

| 2000–01 | Walsall | 45 | 0 | 45 | 0 |

BARRAS, Tony# (D)   353   23
H: 6 0   W: 13 00   b.Billingham 29-3-71
Source: Trainee.

1988–89	Hartlepool U	3	0		
1989–90	Hartlepool U	9	0	12	0
1990–91	Stockport Co	40	0		
1991–92	Stockport Co	42	5		
1992–93	Stockport Co	14	0		
1993–94	Stockport Co	3	0	99	5
1993–94	*Rotherham U*	5	1	5	1
1994–95	York C	31	1		
1995–96	York C	32	3		
1996–97	York C	46	1		
1997–98	York C	38	6		
1998–99	York C	24	0	171	11
1998–99	*Reading*	6	1	6	1
1999–2000	Walsall	24	4		
2000–01	Walsall	36	1	60	5

BENNETT, Tom (M)   274   15
H: 5 11   W: 11 08   b.Falkirk 12-12-69
Source: Trainee.

1987–88	Aston Villa	0	0		
1988–89	Wolverhampton W	2	0		
1989–90	Wolverhampton W	30	0		
1990–91	Wolverhampton W	26	0		
1991–92	Wolverhampton W	38	2		
1992–93	Wolverhampton W	1	0		
1993–94	Wolverhampton W	10	0		
1994–95	Wolverhampton W	8	0	115	2
1995–96	Stockport Co	24	1		
1996–97	Stockport Co	43	3		
1997–98	Stockport Co	27	1		
1998–99	Stockport Co	7	0		
1999–2000	Stockport Co	9	0	110	5
1999–2000	*Walsall*	11	3		
2000–01	Walsall	38	5	49	8

BIRCH, Gary (F)   9   2
H: 6 0   W: 12 03   b.Birmingham 8-10-81
Source: Trainee.

1998–99	Walsall	0	0		
1999–2000	Walsall	0	0		
2000–01	Walsall	0	0		
2000–01	*Exeter C*	9	2	9	2

BRIGHTWELL, Ian# (M)   375   18
H: 5 9   W: 12 05   b.Lutterworth 9-4-68
Source: Congleton T. Honours: England Schools, Youth, Under-21.

1986–87	Manchester C	16	1		
1987–88	Manchester C	33	5		
1988–89	Manchester C	26	6		
1989–90	Manchester C	28	2		
1990–91	Manchester C	33	0		
1991–92	Manchester C	40	1		
1992–93	Manchester C	21	1		
1993–94	Manchester C	7	0		
1994–95	Manchester C	30	0		
1995–96	Manchester C	29	0		
1996–97	Manchester C	37	2		
1997–98	Manchester C	21	0	321	18
1998–99	Coventry C	0	0		
1999–2000	Coventry C	0	0		
1999–2000	Walsall	0	0		
2000–01	Walsall	44	0	54	0

BUKRAN, Gabby# (M)   73   4
H: 5 11   W: 12 01   b.Eger 16-11-75
Source: Xerxes. Honours: Hungary 1 full cap.

| 1999–2000 | Walsall | 37 | 2 | | |
| 2000–01 | Walsall | 36 | 2 | 73 | 4 |

BYFIELD, Darren‡ (F)   65   11
H: 5 11   W: 11 11   b.Sutton Coldfield 29-9-76
Source: Trainee.

1993–94	Aston Villa	0	0		
1994–95	Aston Villa	0	0		
1995–96	Aston Villa	0	0		
1996–97	Aston Villa	0	0		
1997–98	Aston Villa	7	0		
1998–99	Aston Villa	0	0		
1998–99	*Preston NE*	5	1	5	1
1999–2000	Aston Villa	0	0	7	0
1999–2000	*Northampton T*	6	1	6	1
1999–2000	*Cambridge U*	4	0	4	0
1999–2000	*Blackpool*	3	0	3	0
2000–01	Walsall	40	9	40	9

CARTER, Alfie‡ (F)   3   0
H: 5 10   W: 10 05   b.Birmingham 13-8-80
Source: Trainee.

1998–99	Walsall	1	0		
1999–2000	Walsall	0	0		
2000–01	Walsall	1	0	3	0

EKELUND, Ronnie‡ (M)   104   16
H: 5 10   W: 12 06   b.Glostrup 21-8-72

1993–94	Barcelona	1	0		
1993–94	Barcelona B	29	6	1	0
1994–95	Southampton	17	5	17	5
1995–96	Manchester C	4	0	4	0
1996–97	Coventry C	0	0		
1996–97	Odense	18	1		
1997–98	Odense	26	3	44	4
2000–01	Walsall	9	1	9	1

EMBERSON, Carl* (G)   200   0
H: 6 2   W: 14 07   b.Epsom 13-7-73
Source: Trainee.

1991–92	Millwall	0	0		
1992–93	Millwall	0	0		
1992–93	Colchester U	13	0		
1993–94	Millwall	0	0		
1994–95	Colchester U	20	0		
1995–96	Colchester U	41	0		
1996–97	Colchester U	35	0		
1997–98	Colchester U	46	0		
1998–99	Colchester U	37	0	192	0
1999–2000	Walsall	5	0		
2000–01	Walsall	3	0	8	0

EYJOLFSSON, Siggi‡ (F)   45   12
H: 6 2   W: 12 07   b.Reykjavik 1-12-73
Source: IA Akranes.

1998	IA Akranes	13	7	13	7
1998–99	Walsall	10	1		
1999–2000	Walsall	13	1		
1999–2000	*Chester C*	9	3	9	3
2000–01	Walsall	0	0	23	2

GADSBY, Matthew (D)   15   0
H: 6 1   W: 11 12   b.Sutton Coldfield 6-9-79
Source: Trainee.

1997–98	Walsall	1	0		
1998–99	Walsall	6	0		
1999–2000	Walsall	3	0		
2000–01	Walsall	5	0	15	0

GAUNT, Ian§ (D)   0   0
H: 6 1   W: 12 04   b.Bromsgrove 28-9-81
Source: Scholar.

2000–01	Walsall	0	0		

GOODMAN, Don# (F)   540 158
H: 5 10   W: 12 12   b.Leeds 9-5-66
Source: School.

1983–84	Bradford C	2	0		
1984–85	Bradford C	25	5		
1985–86	Bradford C	20	4		
1986–87	Bradford C	23	5	70	14
1986–87	WBA	10	2		
1987–88	WBA	40	7		
1988–89	WBA	36	15		
1989–90	WBA	39	21		
1990–91	WBA	22	8		
1991–92	WBA	11	7	158	60
1991–92	Sunderland	22	11		
1992–93	Sunderland	41	16		
1993–94	Sunderland	35	10		
1994–95	Sunderland	18	3	116	40
1994–95	Wolverhampton	W24	3		
1995–96	Wolverhampton	W44	16		
1996–97	Wolverhampton	W27	6		
1997–98	Wolverhampton	W30	8	125	33

From Hiroshima.

1998–99	Barnsley	8	0	8	0
1998–99	Motherwell	8	1		
1999–2000	Motherwell	29	7		
2000–01	Motherwell	18	1	55	9
2000–01	Walsall	8	2	8	2

HALL, Paul (F)   358 49
H: 5 8   W: 10 02   b.Manchester 3-7-72
Source: Trainee. Honours: Jamaica full caps.

1989–90	Torquay U	10	0		
1990–91	Torquay U	17	0		
1991–92	Torquay U	38	1		
1992–93	Torquay U	28	0	93	1
1992–93	Portsmouth	0	0		
1993–94	Portsmouth	28	4		
1994–95	Portsmouth	43	5		
1995–96	Portsmouth	46	10		
1996–97	Portsmouth	42	13		
1997–98	Portsmouth	29	5	188	37
1998–99	Coventry C	9	0		
1998–99	Bury	7	0	7	0
1999–2000	Coventry C	1	0	10	0
1999–2000	Sheffield U	4	1	4	1
1999–2000	WBA	4	0	4	0
1999–2000	Walsall	10	4		
2000–01	Walsall	42	6	52	10

HAWLEY, Karl (F)   0   0
H: 5 7   W: 10 06   b.Walsall 6-12-81
Source: Scholar.

2000–01	Walsall	0	0		

HORNE, Barry# (M)   575 35
H: 5 10   W: 12 03   b.St Asaph 18-5-62
Source: Rhyl. Honours: Wales 59 full caps, 2 goals.

1984–85	Wrexham	44	6		
1985–86	Wrexham	46	3		
1986–87	Wrexham	46	8	136	17
1987–88	Portsmouth	39	3		
1988–89	Portsmouth	31	4	70	7
1988–89	Southampton	11	0		
1989–90	Southampton	29	4		
1990–91	Southampton	38	1		
1991–92	Southampton	34	1	112	6
1992–93	Everton	34	1		
1993–94	Everton	32	1		
1994–95	Everton	31	0		
1995–96	Everton	26	1	123	3
1996–97	Birmingham C	33	0		
1997–98	Birmingham C	0	0	33	0
1997–98	Huddersfield T	30	0		
1998–99	Huddersfield T	20	1		
1999–2000	Huddersfield T	14	0	64	1
1999–2000	Sheffield W	7	0	7	0
2000–01	Kidderminster H	27	1	27	1
2000–01	Walsall	3	0	3	0

KEATES, Dean (M)   146   8
H: 5 5   W: 10 06   b.Walsall 30-6-78
Source: Trainee.

1996–97	Walsall	2	0		
1997–98	Walsall	33	1		
1998–99	Walsall	43	2		
1999–2000	Walsall	35	1		
2000–01	Walsall	33	4	146	8

LEITAO, Jorge (F)   44 18
H: 5 11   W: 13 05   b.Oporto 14-1-74
Source: Feirense.

2000–01	Walsall	44	18	44	18

MATIAS, Pedro# (M)   111 17
H: 6 0   W: 12 00   b.Madrid 11-10-73

1998–99	Logrones	12	0	12	0
1998–99	Macclesfield T	22	2	22	2
1999–2000	Tranmere R	4	0	4	0
1999–2000	Walsall	33	6		
2000–01	Walsall	40	9	73	15

ROPER, Ian (D)   128   2
H: 6 3   W: 14 00   b.Nuneaton 20-6-77
Source: Trainee.

1994–95	Walsall	0	0		
1995–96	Walsall	5	0		
1996–97	Walsall	11	0		
1997–98	Walsall	21	0		
1998–99	Walsall	32	1		
1999–2000	Walsall	34	1		
2000–01	Walsall	25	0	128	2

SCOTT, Dion (D)   1   0
H: 5 11   W: 11 00   b.Bearwood 24-12-80
Source: Trainee.

1999–2000	Walsall	0	0		
2000–01	Walsall	1	0	1	0

SIMPSON, Fitzroy (D)   355 24
H: 5 10   W: 11 12   b.Trowbridge 26-2-70
Source: Trainee. Honours: Jamaica full caps.

1988–89	Swindon T	7	0		
1989–90	Swindon T	30	2		
1990–91	Swindon T	38	3		
1991–92	Swindon T	30	4	105	9
1991–92	Manchester C	11	1		
1992–93	Manchester C	29	1		
1993–94	Manchester C	15	0		
1994–95	Manchester C	16	2		
1994–95	Bristol C	4	0	4	0
1995–96	Manchester C	0	0	71	4
1995–96	Portsmouth	30	5		
1996–97	Portsmouth	41	4		
1997–98	Portsmouth	19	0		
1998–99	Portsmouth	41	1		
1999–2000	Portsmouth	17	0	148	10
1999–2000	Hearts	11	0		
2000–01	Hearts	6	0	17	0
2000–01	Walsall	10	1	10	1

SMALL, Bryan# (D)   134   1
H: 5 9   W: 11 09   b.Birmingham 15-11-71
Source: Trainee. Honours: England Under-21.

1989–90	Aston Villa	0	0		
1990–91	Aston Villa	0	0		
1991–92	Aston Villa	8	0		
1992–93	Aston Villa	14	0		
1993–94	Aston Villa	9	0		
1994–95	Aston Villa	5	0		
1994–95	Birmingham C	3	0	3	0
1995–96	Aston Villa	0	0	36	0
1995–96	Bolton W	1	0		
1996–97	Bolton W	11	0		
1997–98	Bolton W	0	0	12	0
1997–98	Luton T	15	0	15	0
1997–98	Bradford C	5	0	5	0
1997–98	Bury	18	1	18	1
1998–99	Stoke C	37	0		
1999–2000	Stoke C	8	0	45	0
2000–01	Walsall	0	0		

TILLSON, Andy (D)   433 19
H: 6 2   W: 13 05   b.Huntingdon 30-6-66
Source: Kettering T.

1988–89	Grimsby T	45	2		
1989–90	Grimsby T	42	3		
1990–91	Grimsby T	18	0		
1990–91	QPR	19	2		
1991–92	QPR	10	0		
1992–93	QPR	0	0	29	2
1992–93	Grimsby T	4	0	109	5
1992–93	Bristol R	29	0		
1993–94	Bristol R	13	0		
1994–95	Bristol R	40	2		
1995–96	Bristol R	38	1		
1996–97	Bristol R	38	2		
1997–98	Bristol R	33	3		
1998–99	Bristol R	19	2		
1999–2000	Bristol R	43	1	253	11
2000–01	Walsall	42	1	42	1

WALKER, James (G)   276   0
H: 5 11   W: 12 13   b.Sutton-in-Ashfield 9-7-73
Source: Trainee.

1991–92	Notts Co	0	0		
1992–93	Notts Co	0	0		
1993–94	Walsall	31	0		
1994–95	Walsall	4	0		
1995–96	Walsall	26	0		
1996–97	Walsall	36	0		
1997–98	Walsall	46	0		
1998–99	Walsall	46	0		
1999–2000	Walsall	43	0		
2000–01	Walsall	44	0	276	0

WRACK, Darren (F)   161 23
H: 5 9   W: 12 02   b.Cleethorpes 5-5-76
Source: Trainee.

1994–95	Derby Co	16	1		
1995–96	Derby Co	10	0	26	1
1996–97	Grimsby T	12	1		
1996–97	Shrewsbury T	4	0	4	0
1997–98	Grimsby T	1	0	13	1
1998–99	Walsall	46	13		
1999–2000	Walsall	44	4		
2000–01	Walsall	28	4	118	21

WRIGHT, Mark (M)   4   0
H: 5 11   W: 12 06   b.Wolverhampton 24-2-82
Source: Scholar.

2000–01	Walsall	4	0	4	0

Scholars
Barrau, Xavier; Bate, Ross; Bishop, Andrew J; Bissell, James; Caines, Gavin L; Fitzpatrick, Andrew J; Gaunt, Ian TF; Hunt, David T; Jones, Craig R; Joseph, Andre P; Paschalis, Eliot D; Smith, Nicholas A; Stanley, Craig; Teesdale, Richard C; Worley, Andrew I

WATFORD

ARMSTRONG, Stephen* (F)   15   1
H: 5 10   W: 10 11   b.Birkenhead 23-7-76

2000	Vastra Frolunda	12	1	12	1
2000–01	Watford	3	0	3	0

BAARDSEN, Espen (G)   50   0
H: 6 5   W: 13 03   b.San Rafael 7-12-77
Source: San Francisco All Blacks. Honours: USA Youth, Norway Under-21, 4 full caps.

1996–97	Tottenham H	2	0		
1997–98	Tottenham H	9	0		
1998–99	Tottenham H	12	0		
1999–2000	Tottenham H	0	0	23	0
2000–01	Watford	27	0	27	0

BONNOT, Alex* (M)   16   0
H: 5 8   W: 11 05   b.Poissy 31-7-73
Source: Angers.

1998–99	Watford	4	0		
1999–2000	Watford	12	0		
2000–01	Watford	0	0	16	0

CHAMBERLAIN, Alec (G)   571   0
H: 6 2   W: 13 10   b.March 20-6-64
Source: Ramsey T.

1981–82	Ipswich T	0	0		
1982–83	Colchester U	0	0		
1983–84	Colchester U	46	0		
1984–85	Colchester U	46	0		
1985–86	Colchester U	46	0		
1986–87	Colchester U	46	0	184	0
1987–88	Everton	0	0		
1987–88	Tranmere R	15	0	15	0
1988–89	Luton T	6	0		
1989–90	Luton T	38	0		
1990–91	Luton T	38	0		
1991–92	Luton T	24	0		
1992–93	Luton T	32	0	138	0
1992–93	Chelsea	0	0		
1993–94	Sunderland	43	0		
1994–95	Sunderland	18	0		
1994–95	Liverpool	0	0		
1995–96	Sunderland	29	0	90	0
1996–97	Watford	4	0		
1997–98	Watford	46	0		
1998–99	Watford	46	0		
1999–2000	Watford	27	0		
2000–01	Watford	21	0	144	0

COOK, Lee (F)
H: 5 9   W: 11 04   b.Hammersmith 3-8-82
Source: Aylesbury U.

1999–2000	Watford	0	0		
2000–01	Watford	4	0	4	0

COX, Neil (D)   310 19
H: 6 0   W: 12 01   b.Scunthorpe 8-10-71
Source: Trainee. Honours: England Under-21.

1989–90	Scunthorpe U	0	0		
1990–91	Scunthorpe U	17	1	17	1
1990–91	Aston Villa	0	0		
1991–92	Aston Villa	7	0		
1992–93	Aston Villa	15	1		
1993–94	Aston Villa	20	2	42	3
1994–95	Middlesbrough	40	1		
1995–96	Middlesbrough	35	2		
1996–97	Middlesbrough	31	0	106	3

1997–98	Bolton W	21	1		
1998–99	Bolton W	44	4		
1999–2000	Watford	15	2	80	7
1999–2000	Watford	21	0		
2000–01	Watford	44	5	65	5

DAY, Chris* (G) 49 0
H: 6 3 W: 13 06 b.Walthamstow 28-7-75
Source: Trainee. *Honours:* England Under-21.

1992–93	Tottenham H	0	0		
1993–94	Tottenham H	0	0		
1994–95	Tottenham H	0	0		
1995–96	Tottenham H	0	0		
1996–97	Crystal Palace	24	0	24	0
1997–98	Watford	0	0		
1998–99	Watford	0	0		
1999–2000	Watford	11	0		
2000–01	Watford	0	0	11	0
2000–01	Lincoln C	14	0	14	0

DOYLEY, Lloyd (M) 0 0
b.London 1-12-82
Source: Scholar.

2000–01	Watford	0	0		

EASTON, Clint (M) 64 1
H: 5 11 W: 10 04 b.Barking 1-11-77
Source: Trainee. *Honours:* England Youth.

1996–97	Watford	17	1		
1997–98	Watford	12	0		
1998–99	Watford	7	0		
1999–2000	Watford	17	0		
2000–01	Watford	11	0	64	1

FISKEN, Gary (M) 0 0
b.Watford 27-10-81
Source: Scholarship.

1999–2000	Watford	0	0		
2000–01	Watford	0	0		

FOLEY, Dominic# (F) 47 6
H: 6 1 W: 12 08 b.Cork 7-7-76
Source: St James Gate. *Honours:* Eire 6 full caps, 2 goals.

1995–96	Wolverhampton W	5	0		
1996–97	Wolverhampton W	5	1		
1997–98	Wolverhampton W	5	0		
1997–98	Watford	8	1		
1998–99	Wolverhampton W	5	2	20	3
1998–99	Notts Co	2	0	2	0
1999–2000	Watford	12	1		
2000–01	Watford	5	1	25	3

FORDE, Fabian (F) 1 0
b.London 26-10-81
Source: Scholar.

2000–01	Watford	1	0	1	0

GIBBS, Nigel (D) 407 5
H: 5 7 W: 11 06 b.St Albans 20-11-65
Source: Apprentice. *Honours:* England Youth, Under-21.

1983–84	Watford	3	0		
1984–85	Watford	12	0		
1985–86	Watford	40	1		
1986–87	Watford	15	0		
1987–88	Watford	30	0		
1988–89	Watford	46	1		
1989–90	Watford	41	0		
1990–91	Watford	34	0		
1991–92	Watford	43	1		
1992–93	Watford	7	0		
1993–94	Watford	0	0		
1994–95	Watford	11	0		
1995–96	Watford	9	0		
1996–97	Watford	45	1		
1997–98	Watford	38	1		
1998–99	Watford	10	0		
1999–2000	Watford	17	0		
2000–01	Watford	6	0	407	5

GODFREY, Elliott (M) 0 0
b.Toronto 22-2-83
Source: Scholar.

2000–01	Watford	0	0		

GUDMUNDSSON, Johann‡ (M) 74 15
H: 6 0 W: 11 07 b.Reykjavik 5-12-77.
Honours: Iceland 3 full caps.

1994	Keflavik	1	0		
1995	Keflavik	14	4		
1996	Keflavik	17	4		
1997	Keflavik	17	5	49	13
1997–98	Watford	0	0		
1998–99	Watford	13	2		
1999–2000	Watford	9	0		
2000–01	Watford	0	0	22	2
2000–01	Cambridge U	3	0	3	0

HELGUSON, Heidar (F) 93 32
H: 5 10 W: 11 00 b.Akureyri 22-8-77
Source: Throttur. *Honours:* Iceland 16 full caps, 1 goal.

1998	Lillestrom	19	2		
1999	Lillestrom	25	16	44	18

1999–2000	Watford	16	6		
2000–01	Watford	33	8	49	14

HYDE, Micah (M) 251 28
H: 5 10 W: 11 07 b.Newham 10-11-74
Source: Trainee.

1993–94	Cambridge U	18	2		
1994–95	Cambridge U	27	0		
1995–96	Cambridge U	24	4		
1996–97	Cambridge U	38	7	107	13
1997–98	Watford	40	4		
1998–99	Watford	44	2		
1999–2000	Watford	34	3		
2000–01	Watford	26	6	144	15

IFIL, Jerel (D) 0 0
H: 6 1 W: 12 11 b.London 27-6-82
Source: Academy.

1999–2000	Watford	0	0		
2000–01	Watford	0	0		

JOHNSON, Richard (M) 230 20
H: 5 10 W: 11 03 b.Kurri Kurri 27-4-74
Source: Trainee. *Honours:* Australia 3 full caps.

1991–92	Watford	2	0		
1992–93	Watford	1	0		
1993–94	Watford	27	0		
1994–95	Watford	35	3		
1995–96	Watford	20	1		
1996–97	Watford	37	2		
1997–98	Watford	42	7		
1998–99	Watford	40	4		
1999–2000	Watford	23	3		
2000–01	Watford	3	0	230	20

KENNEDY, Peter (M) 137 18
H: 5 10 W: 11 11 b.Lisburn 10-9-73
Source: Portadown. *Honours:* Northern Ireland 9 full caps.

1996–97	Notts Co	22	0	22	0
1997–98	Watford	34	11		
1998–99	Watford	46	6		
1999–2000	Watford	18	1		
2000–01	Watford	17	0	115	18

KODRA, Elis* (M) 0 0
b.Pristina 20-5-82
Source: Academy.

1999–2000	Watford	0	0		
2000–01	Watford	0	0		

LANGSTON, Matthew (D) 0 0
H: 6 2 W: 12 04 b.Brighton 2-4-81
Source: Trainee.

1998–99	Watford	0	0		
1999–2000	Watford	0	0		
2000–01	Watford	0	0		

LEE, Richard (M) 0 0
b.Oxford 5-10-82
Source: Scholar.

2000–01	Watford	0	0		

MATTHEWS, Barrie (M) 0 0
b.Forest of Dean 1-2-83
Source: Scholar.

2000–01	Watford	0	0		

MILLER, Charlie (M) 101 10
H: 5 7 W: 12 02 b.Glasgow 18-3-76
Source: Rangers BC. *Honours:* Scotland Under-21.

1992–93	Rangers	0	0		
1993–94	Rangers	3	0		
1994–95	Rangers	21	3		
1995–96	Rangers	23	3		
1996–97	Rangers	13	1		
1997–98	Rangers	7	0		
1998–99	Rangers	16	3		
1998–99	Leicester C	4	0	4	0
1999–2000	Rangers	0	0	83	10
1999–2000	Watford	14	0		
2000–01	Watford	0	0	14	0

(Transferred to Dundee U, November 2000).

MOONEY, Tommy# (F) 371 95
H: 5 11 W: 12 10 b.Teeside North 11-8-71
Source: Trainee.

1989–90	Aston Villa	0	0		
1990–91	Scarborough	27	13		
1991–92	Scarborough	40	8		
1992–93	Scarborough	40	9	107	30
1993–94	Southend U	14	5	14	5
1993–94	Watford	10	2		
1994–95	Watford	29	3		
1995–96	Watford	42	6		
1996–97	Watford	37	13		
1997–98	Watford	45	6		
1998–99	Watford	36	9		
1999–2000	Watford	12	2		
2000–01	Watford	39	19	250	60

NEILL, Thomas (M) 0 0
b.Harrow 13-11-81
Source: Scholar.

2000–01	Watford	0	0		

NIELSEN, Allan (M) 273 47
H: 5 8 W: 11 02 b.Esbjerg 13-3-71
Source: Esbjerg. *Honours:* Denmark Under-21, 41 full caps, 7 goals.

1988–89	Bayern Munich	0	0		
1989–90	Bayern Munich	0	0		
1990–91	Bayern Munich	1	0	1	0
1991–92	Sion	0	0		
1991–92	Odense	8	2		
1992–93	Odense	30	4		
1993–94	Odense	17	3	55	9
1993–94	FC Copenhagen	8	0		
1994–95	FC Copenhagen	18	3	26	3
1994–95	Brondby	10	3		
1995–96	Brondby	28	6		
1996–97	Brondby	4	2	42	11
1996–97	Tottenham H	29	6		
1997–98	Tottenham H	26	3		
1998–99	Tottenham H	28	3		
1999–2000	Tottenham H	14	0	97	12
1999–2000	Wolverhampton W	7	2	7	2
2000–01	Watford	45	10	45	10

NOEL-WILLIAMS, Gifton (F) 124 27
H: 6 1 W: 12 04 b.Islington 21-1-80
Source: Trainee. *Honours:* England Youth.

1996–97	Watford	25	2		
1997–98	Watford	38	7		
1998–99	Watford	26	10		
1999–2000	Watford	3	0		
2000–01	Watford	32	8	124	27

PAGE, Robert (D) 216 2
H: 6 0 W: 12 05 b.Llwynipia 9-9-74
Source: Trainee. *Honours:* Wales Under-21, 20 full caps.

1992–93	Watford	0	0		
1993–94	Watford	4	0		
1994–95	Watford	5	0		
1995–96	Watford	19	0		
1996–97	Watford	36	0		
1997–98	Watford	41	0		
1998–99	Watford	39	0		
1999–2000	Watford	36	1		
2000–01	Watford	36	1	216	2

PALMER, Steve (M) 346 10
H: 6 1 W: 12 03 b.Brighton 31-3-68
Source: Cambridge Univ. *Honours:* England Schools.

1989–90	Ipswich T	5	0		
1990–91	Ipswich T	23	1		
1991–92	Ipswich T	23	0		
1992–93	Ipswich T	7	0		
1993–94	Ipswich T	36	1		
1994–95	Ipswich T	12	0		
1995–96	Ipswich T	5	0	111	2
1995–96	Watford	35	1		
1996–97	Watford	41	2		
1997–98	Watford	41	2		
1998–99	Watford	41	2		
1999–2000	Watford	38	0		
2000–01	Watford	39	1	235	8

PANAYI, James (D) 11 0
H: 6 1 W: 12 06 b.Hammersmith 24-1-80
Source: Trainee.

1998–99	Watford	0	0		
1999–2000	Watford	2	0		
2000–01	Watford	9	0	11	0

PATTERSON, Simon (M) 0 0
b.Northwick 4-9-82
Source: Trainee.

2000–01	Watford	0	0		

PERPETUINI, David (D) 19 1
H: 5 9 W: 10 00 b.Hitchin 26-9-79
Source: Trainee.

1997–98	Watford	0	0		
1998–99	Watford	1	0		
1999–2000	Watford	13	1		
2000–01	Watford	5	0	19	1

ROBINSON, Paul (D) 134 2
H: 5 9 W: 11 11 b.Watford 14-12-78
Source: Trainee. *Honours:* England Under-21.

1996–97	Watford	12	0		
1997–98	Watford	22	2		
1998–99	Watford	29	0		
1999–2000	Watford	32	0		
2000–01	Watford	39	0	134	2

SMART, Allan (F) 131 34
H: 6 2 W: 12 04 b.Perth 8-7-74
Source: Trainee.

1994–95	Caledonian Th	4	0	4	0
1994–95	Preston NE	19	6		
1995–96	Preston NE	2	0		
1995–96	Carlisle U	4	0		
1996–97	Preston NE	0	0	21	6
1996–97	Northampton T	1	0	1	0
1996–97	Carlisle U	28	10		
1997–98	Carlisle U	16	6	48	16

1998–99	Watford	35	7	
1999-2000	Watford	14	5	
2000-01	Watford	8	0	57 12

SMITH, Tommy (F) 74 15
H: 5 9 W: 10 00 b.Hemel Hempstead 22-5-80
Source: Trainee. *Honours:* England Youth, Under-21.

1997-98	Watford	1	0	
1998-99	Watford	8	2	
1999-2000	Watford	22	2	
2000-01	Watford	43	11	74 15

SWONNELL, Sam (M) 0 0
b.Havering 13-9-82
Source: Scholar.

2000-01	Watford	0	0

VERNAZZA, Paulo (M) 37 3
H: 5 10 W: 10 13 b.Islington 1-11-79
Source: Trainee. *Honours:* England Youth, Under-21.

1997-98	Arsenal	1	0	
1998-99	Arsenal	0	0	
1998-99	*Ipswich T*	2	0	2 0
1999-2000	Arsenal	2	0	
1999-2000	*Portsmouth*	7	0	7 0
2000-01	Arsenal	2	1	5 1
2000-01	Watford	23	2	23 2

WARD, Darren (D) 72 2
H: 6 3 W: 12 11 b.Kenton 13-9-78
Source: Trainee.

1995-96	Watford	1	0	
1996-97	Watford	7	0	
1997-98	Watford	0	0	
1998-99	Watford	1	0	
1999-2000	Watford	9	1	
1999-2000	*QPR*	14	0	14 0
2000-01	Watford	40	1	58 2

WARNER, David* (F) 0 0
b.Hillingdon 27-4-81
Source: Brook House.

1999-2000	Watford	0	0
2000-01	Watford	0	0

WILLIAMS, Nicholas (M) 0 0
b.Cheltenham 16-2-83

2000-01	Watford	0	0

WOOTER, Nordin (F) 137 9
H: 5 6 W: 10 08 b.Breda 24-8-76

1994-95	Ajax	5	1	
1995-96	Ajax	25	2	
1996-97	Ajax	28	3	58 6
1997-98	Zaragoza	15	1	
1998-99	Zaragoza	18	0	
1999-2000	Zaragoza	0	0	33 1
1999-2000	Watford	20	1	
2000-01	Watford	26	1	46 2

WRIGHT, Nick (F) 62 11
H: 5 10 W: 11 08 b.Derby 15-10-75
Source: Trainee.

1994-95	Derby Co	0	0	
1995-96	Derby Co	0	0	
1996-97	Derby Co	0	0	
1997-98	Derby Co	0	0	
1997-98	*Carlisle U*	25	5	25 5
1998-99	Watford	33	6	
1999-2000	Watford	4	0	
2000-01	Watford	0	0	37 6

Scholars
Blizzard, Dominic J; Brathwaite, Daniel SC; Buxton, Nicholas J; Deamer, William D; Edghill, Luke P; Hand, Jamie; Hopton, Matthew A; Hughes, Bradley R; McNamee, Anthony; Norville, Jason; Saunders, Neil C; Sinclair, Steve; Smith, Jack D

WBA

ADAMSON, Chris (G) 21 0
H: 6 3 W: 12 00 b.Ashington 4-11-78
Source: Trainee.

1997-98	WBA	3	0	
1998-99	WBA	0	0	
1998-99	*Mansfield T*	2	0	2 0
1999-2000	WBA	9	0	
1999-2000	*Halifax T*	7	0	7 0
2000-01	WBA	0	0	12 0

APPLETON, Michael (M) 144 15
H: 5 8 W: 11 00 b.Salford 4-12-75
Source: Trainee.

1994-95	Manchester U	0	0	
1995-96	Manchester U	0	0	
1995-96	*Lincoln C*	4	0	4 0
1996-97	Manchester U	0	0	
1996-97	*Grimsby T*	10	3	10 3

1997–98	Preston NE	38	2	
1998-99	Preston NE	25	2	
1999-2000	Preston NE	26	3	
2000-01	Preston NE	26	5	115 12
2000-01	WBA	15	0	15 0

BALIS, Igor (M) 143 5
H: 5 11 W: 11 00 b.Czech Republic 5-1-70
Honours: Slovakia 38 full caps, 1 goal.

1995-96	Spartak Trnava	32	0	
1996-97	Spartak Trnava	26	4	
1997-98	Spartak Trnava	28	0	
1998-99	Spartak Trnava	26	1	
1999-2000	Spartak Trnava	24	0	136 5
2000-01	WBA	7	0	7 0

BRIGGS, Mark (M) 0 0
H: 6 1 W: 11 07 b.Wolverhampton 16-2-82
Source: Scholar.

2000-01	WBA	0	0

BURGESS, Daryl* (D) 332 10
H: 5 11 W: 11 04 b.Birmingham 24-1-71
Source: Trainee.

1989-90	WBA	34	0	
1990-91	WBA	25	0	
1991-92	WBA	36	2	
1992-93	WBA	18	1	
1993-94	WBA	43	2	
1994-95	WBA	22	0	
1995-96	WBA	45	2	
1996-97	WBA	33	1	
1997-98	WBA	27	1	
1998-99	WBA	20	0	
1999-2000	WBA	26	1	
2000-01	WBA	3	0	332 10

BUTLER, Tony (D) 317 6
H: 6 2 W: 12 00 b.Stockport 28-9-72
Source: Trainee.

1990-91	Gillingham	6	0	
1991-92	Gillingham	5	0	
1992-93	Gillingham	41	0	
1993-94	Gillingham	27	1	
1994-95	Gillingham	33	2	
1995-96	Gillingham	36	2	148 5
1996-97	Blackpool	42	0	
1997-98	Blackpool	37	0	
1998-99	Blackpool	20	0	99 0
1998-99	Port Vale	4	0	
1999-2000	Port Vale	15	0	19 0
1999-2000	WBA	7	0	
2000-01	WBA	44	1	51 1

CARBON, Matt* (D) 202 15
H: 6 2 W: 12 05 b.Nottingham 8-6-75
Source: Trainee. *Honours:* England Under-21.

1992-93	Lincoln C	1	0	
1993-94	Lincoln C	9	0	
1994-95	Lincoln C	33	7	
1995-96	Lincoln C	26	3	69 10
1995-96	Derby Co	6	0	
1996-97	Derby Co	10	0	
1997-98	Derby Co	4	0	20 0
1997-98	WBA	16	1	
1998-99	WBA	39	2	
1999-2000	WBA	34	2	
2000-01	WBA	24	0	113 5

CHAMBERS, Adam (D) 11 1
H: 5 10 W: 11 08 b.Sandwell 20-11-80
Source: Trainee. *Honours:* England Youth.

1998-99	WBA	0	0	
1999-2000	WBA	0	0	
2000-01	WBA	11	1	11 1

CHAMBERS, James (D) 43 0
H: 5 10 W: 11 08 b.Sandwell 20-11-80
Source: Trainee. *Honours:* England Youth.

1998-99	WBA	0	0	
1999-2000	WBA	12	0	
2000-01	WBA	31	0	43 0

CLEMENT, Neil (D) 77 6
H: 6 0 W: 14 07 b.Reading 3-10-78
Source: Trainee. *Honours:* England Schools, Youth.

1995-96	Chelsea	0	0	
1996-97	Chelsea	1	0	
1997-98	Chelsea	0	0	
1998-99	Chelsea	0	0	
1998-99	*Reading*	11	1	11 1
1998-99	*Preston NE*	4	0	4 0
1999-2000	Chelsea	0	0	1 0
1999-2000	*Brentford*	8	0	8 0
1999-2000	*WBA*	8	0	
2000-01	WBA	45	5	53 5

COLLINS, Matthew (M) 0 0
H: 5 10 W: 10 12 b.Hitchen 10-2-82
Source: Scholar.

2000-01	WBA	0	0

FOX, Ruel (F) 374 48
H: 5 6 W: 10 05 b.Ipswich 14-1-68
Source: Apprentice. *Honours:* England B.

1985-86	Norwich C	0	0	
1986-87	Norwich C	3	0	
1987-88	Norwich C	34	2	
1988-89	Norwich C	4	0	
1989-90	Norwich C	7	3	
1990-91	Norwich C	28	4	
1991-92	Norwich C	37	2	
1992-93	Norwich C	34	4	
1993-94	Norwich C	25	7	172 22
1993-94	Newcastle U	14	2	
1994-95	Newcastle U	40	10	
1995-96	Newcastle U	4	0	58 12
1995-96	Tottenham H	26	6	
1996-97	Tottenham H	25	1	
1997-98	Tottenham H	32	3	
1998-99	Tottenham H	20	3	
1999-2000	Tottenham H	3	0	
2000-01	Tottenham H	0	0	106 13
2000-01	WBA	38	1	38 1

GILCHRIST, Phil (D) 306 11
H: 6 0 W: 13 03 b.Stockton 25-8-73
Source: Trainee.

1990-91	Nottingham F	0	0	
1991-92	Middlesbrough	0	0	
1992-93	Hartlepool U	24	0	
1993-94	Hartlepool U	35	0	
1994-95	Hartlepool U	23	0	82 0
1994-95	Oxford U	18	1	
1995-96	Oxford U	42	3	
1996-97	Oxford U	38	2	
1997-98	Oxford U	39	2	
1998-99	Oxford U	39	2	
1999-2000	Oxford U	1	0	177 10
1999-2000	Leicester C	27	1	
2000-01	Leicester C	12	0	39 1
2000-01	WBA	8	0	8 0

HOULT, Russell (G) 207 0
H: 6 4 W: 14 07 b.Ashby 22-11-72
Source: Trainee.

1990-91	Leicester C	0	0	
1991-92	Leicester C	0	0	
1991-92	*Lincoln C*	2	0	
1991-92	*Blackpool*	0	0	
1992-93	Leicester C	10	0	
1993-94	Leicester C	0	0	
1993-94	*Bolton W*	4	0	4 0
1994-95	Leicester C	0	0	10 0
1994-95	*Lincoln C*	15	0	17 0
1994-95	Derby Co	15	0	
1995-96	Derby Co	41	0	
1996-97	Derby Co	32	0	
1997-98	Derby Co	2	0	
1998-99	Derby Co	23	0	
1999-2000	Derby Co	10	0	123 0
1999-2000	Portsmouth	18	0	
2000-01	Portsmouth	22	0	40 0
2000-01	WBA	13	0	13 0

HUGHES, Lee (F) 156 78
H: 5 10 W: 11 06 b.Birmingham 22-5-76
Source: Kidderminster H.

1997-98	WBA	37	14	
1998-99	WBA	42	31	
1999-2000	WBA	36	12	
2000-01	WBA	41	21	156 78

IEZZI, Massimiliano (M) 0 0
b.Rome 1-2-81

1999-2000	WBA	0	0
2000-01	WBA	0	0

JENSEN, Brian (G) 46 0
H: 6 1 W: 12 04 b.Copenhagen 8-6-75

1997-98	AZ	0	0	
1998-99	AZ	1	0	1 0
1999-2000	WBA	12	0	
2000-01	WBA	33	0	45 0

JORDAO (M) 222 13
b.Malanje 30-8-71

1990-91	Amadora	0	0	
1991-92	Amadora	17	3	
1992-93	Amadora	3	0	
1993-94	Campomaiorense	9	0	9 0
1994-95	Leca	26	3	26 3
1995-96	Amadora	30	1	
1996-97	Amadora	31	3	81 7
1997-98	Benfica	6	0	6 0
1997-98	Braga	14	1	
1998-99	Braga	29	1	
1999-2000	Braga	22	0	65 2
2000-01	WBA	35	1	35 1

LYTTLE, Des (D) 298 5
H: 5 9 W: 11 06 b.Wolverhampton 24-9-71
Source: Worcester C.

1992-93	Swansea C	46	1	46 1
1993-94	Nottingham F	37	1	

1994–95	Nottingham F	38	0		
1995–96	Nottingham F	33	1		
1996–97	Nottingham F	32	1		
1997–98	Nottingham F	35	0		
1998–99	Nottingham F	10	0	185	3
1998–99	*Port Vale*	7	0	7	0
1999–2000	Watford	11	0	11	0
1999–2000	*WBA*	9	0		
2000–01	WBA	40	1	49	1

MARDON, Paul* (D) 270 7
H: 6 0 W: 11 10 b.Bristol 14-9-69
Source: Trainee. Honours: Wales 1 full cap.

1987–88	Bristol C	8	0		
1988–89	Bristol C	20	0		
1989–90	Bristol C	7	0		
1990–91	Bristol C	7	0	42	0
1990–91	Doncaster R	3	0	3	0
1991–92	Birmingham C	35	0		
1992–93	Birmingham C	21	0		
1993–94	Birmingham C	8	0	64	0
1993–94	WBA	22	1		
1994–95	WBA	28	1		
1995–96	WBA	39	0		
1996–97	WBA	14	0		
1997–98	WBA	18	1		
1998–99	WBA	18	0		
1998–99	*Oldham Ath*	12	3	12	3
1999–2000	WBA	0	0		
2000–01	WBA	0	0	139	3
2000–01	*Plymouth Arg*	3	1	3	1
2000–01	*Wrexham*	7	0	7	0

McINNES, Derek (M) 285 21
H: 5 7 W: 11 04 b.Paisley 5-7-71
Source: Gleniffer Th.

1987–88	Greenock Morton	8	0		
1988–89	Greenock Morton	29	1		
1989–90	Greenock Morton	23	1		
1990–91	Greenock Morton	31	3		
1991–92	Greenock Morton	42	7		
1992–93	Greenock Morton	40	2		
1993–94	Greenock Morton	16	1		
1994–95	Greenock Morton	26	3		
1995–96	Greenock Morton	12	1	221	19
1995–96	Rangers	6	0		
1996–97	Rangers	21	1		
1997–98	Rangers	0	0		
1998–99	Rangers	7	0	34	1
1998–99	*Stockport Co*	13	0	13	0
1999–2000	Toulouse	3	0	3	0
2000–01	WBA	14	1	14	1

MORRIS, Elliott (G) 0 0
H: 5 11 W: 11 07 b.Belfast 4-5-81
Source: Trainee.

1999–2000	WBA	0	0	
2000–01	WBA	0	0	

OLIVER, Adam (M) 23 1
H: 5 9 W: 11 02 b.Sandwell 25-10-80
Source: Trainee. Honours: England Youth.

1998–99	WBA	1	0		
1999–2000	WBA	15	1		
2000–01	WBA	7	0	23	1

QUINN, James (F) 263 46
H: 6 1 W: 12 10 b.Coventry 15-12-74
Source: Trainee. Honours: Northern Ireland
Under-21, 24 full caps, 3 goals.

1992–93	Birmingham C	4	0	4	0
1993–94	Blackpool	14	2		
1993–94	*Stockport Co*	1	0	1	0
1994–95	Blackpool	41	9		
1995–96	Blackpool	44	9		
1996–97	Blackpool	38	13		
1997–98	Blackpool	14	4	151	37
1997–98	WBA	13	2		
1998–99	WBA	43	6		
1999–2000	WBA	37	0		
2000–01	WBA	14	1	107	9

ROBERTS, Jason (F) 138 59
H: 6 1 W: 13 06 b.Park Royal 25-1-78
Source: Hayes. Honours: Grenada full caps.

1997–98	Wolverhampton W	0	0		
1997–98	*Torquay U*	14	6	14	6
1997–98	*Bristol C*	3	1	3	1
1998–99	Bristol R	37	16		
1999–2000	Bristol R	41	22	78	38
2000–01	WBA	43	14	43	14

SCOTT, Mark (F) 0 0
H: 6 1 W: 12 02 b.Birmingham 16-7-82
Source: Scholar.

2000–01	WBA	0	0	

SIGURDSSON, Larus (D) 239 7
H: 6 0 W: 13 11 b.Akureyri 4-6-73
Source: Thor. Honours: Iceland 31 full caps, 2
goals.

1994–95	Stoke C	23	1	
1995–96	Stoke C	46	0	
1996–97	Stoke C	45	0	

1997–98	Stoke C	43	1		
1998–99	Stoke C	38	4		
1999–2000	Stoke C	5	1	200	7
1999–2000	WBA	27	0		
2000–01	WBA	12	0	39	0

SNEEKES, Richard* (M) 442 65
H: 5 11 W: 12 03 b.Amsterdam 30-10-68
Honours: Holland Under-21.

1985–86	Ajax	1	0		
1986–87	Ajax	1	0		
1987–88	Ajax	1	0	3	0
1988–89	Volendam	31	7	31	7
1989–90	Fortuna Sittard	32	2		
1990–91	Fortuna Sittard	32	7		
1991–92	Fortuna Sittard	33	5		
1992–93	Fortuna Sittard	29	6	126	20

From Locarno, Fortuna Sittard.

1994–95	Bolton				
1995–96	Bolton W	17	1	55	7
1995–96	WBA	13	10		
1996–97	WBA	45	8		
1997–98	WBA	42	3		
1998–99	WBA	40	4		
1999–2000	WBA	42	3		
2000–01	WBA	45	3	227	31

TAYLOR, Bob (F) 511 186
H: 5 11 W: 13 05 b.Easington 3-2-67
Source: Horden CW.

1985–86	Leeds U	2	0		
1986–87	Leeds U	2	0		
1987–88	Leeds U	32	9		
1988–89	Leeds U	6	0	42	9
1988–89	Bristol C	12	8		
1989–90	Bristol C	37	27		
1990–91	Bristol C	39	11		
1991–92	Bristol C	18	4	106	50
1991–92	WBA	19	8		
1992–93	WBA	46	30		
1993–94	WBA	42	18		
1994–95	WBA	42	11		
1995–96	WBA	42	17		
1996–97	WBA	32	10		
1997–98	WBA	15	2		
1997–98	*Bolton W*	12	3		
1998–99	Bolton W	38	15		
1999–2000	Bolton W	27	3	77	21
1999–2000	WBA	8	5		
2000–01	WBA	40	5	286	106

TURNER, Matthew (F) 0 0
H: 5 9 W: 10 00 b.Nottingham 29-12-81
Source: Trainee. Honours: England Youth.

1998–99	Nottingham F	0	0	
1999–2000	Nottingham F	0	0	
2000–01	Nottingham F	0	0	
2000–01	WBA	0	0	

VAN BLERK, Jason* (D) 201 5
H: 6 1 W: 13 00 b.Sydney 16-3-68
Source: Blacktown City 24 apps, 3 goals,
APIA Leichhardt 39 apps, 5 goals, Go
Ahead. Honours: Australia 33 full caps, 3
goals.

1994–95	Millwall	27	1		
1995–96	Millwall	42	1		
1996–97	Millwall	4	0	73	2
1997–98	Manchester C	19	0	19	0
1997–98	WBA	8	0		
1998–99	WBA	30	0		
1999–2000	WBA	35	1		
2000–01	WBA	36	2	109	3

Scholars

Adams, Richard; Adams, Ross I; Ball, Jamie
C; Briggs, Mark J; Brown, Simon A; Bruce,
Kevin; Carey-Bertram, Daniel P; Crane,
Daniel P; Fox, James E; Gowling, Joshua AI;
McFarlane, Dwaine W; Mkandawire, Tamika
P; Oakey, Paul E; Perry, Joshua; Watson,
Anthony C
**Player who does not hold a current contract
but his registration has been retained by the
club**
Blake, Mosiah N

WEST HAM U

ANGUS, Stevland* (D) 9 0
H: 6 0 W: 12 00 b.Essex 16-9-80
Source: Trainee.

1999–2000	West Ham U	0	0		
2000–01	West Ham U	0	0		
2000–01	*Bournemouth*	9	0	9	0

BASSILA, Christian* (D) 71 3
H: 6 4 W: 13 00 b.Paris 5-10-77
Source: Trainee.

1996–97	Lyon	1	0		
1997–98	Lyon	21	1		
1998–99	Lyon	22	1	44	2

1999–2000	Rennes	23	1		
2000–01	Rennes	1	0	24	1
2000–01	West Ham U	3	0	3	0

BRITTON, Leon (M) 0 0
b.London 16-9-82
Source: Trainee.

1999–2000	West Ham U	0	0	
2000–01	West Ham U	0	0	

BULLARD, Jimmy* (M) 0 0
H: 5 10 W: 11 07 b.Newham 23-10-78
Source: Corinthian, Dartford, Gravesend
& N.

1998–99	West Ham U	0	0	
1999–2000	West Ham U	0	0	
2000–01	West Ham U	0	0	

BYRNE, Shaun (D) 3 0
H: 5 9 W: 11 08 b.Taplow 21-1-81
Source: Trainee.

1999–2000	West Ham U	1	0		
1999–2000	*Bristol R*	2	0	2	0
2000–01	West Ham U	0	0	1	0

BYWATER, Steve (G) 11 0
H: 6 2 W: 12 00 b.Manchester 7-6-81
Source: Trainee. Honours: England Youth,
Under-21.

1997–98	Rochdale	0	0		
1998–99	West Ham U	0	0		
1999–2000	West Ham U	4	0		
1999–2000	*Wycombe W*	2	0	2	0
1999–2000	*Hull C*	4	0	4	0
2000–01	West Ham U	1	0	5	0

CAMARA, Titi (F) 257 47
H: 6 0 W: 13 00 b.Donka 17-11-72
Honours: Guinea full caps.

1990–91	St Etienne	4	0		
1991–92	St Etienne	15	3		
1992–93	St Etienne	16	2		
1993–94	St Etienne	26	4		
1994–95	St Etienne	33	7	94	16
1995–96	Lens	36	8		
1996–97	Lens	27	6	63	14
1997–98	Marseille	31	2		
1998–99	Marseille	30	6	61	8
1999–2000	Liverpool	33	9		
2000–01	Liverpool	0	0	33	9
2000–01	West Ham U	6	0	6	0

CARRICK, Michael (M) 49 4
H: 6 0 W: 11 10 b.Wallsend 28-7-81
Source: Trainee. Honours: England Youth,
Under-21, 1 full cap.

1998–99	West Ham U	0	0		
1999–2000	West Ham U	8	1		
1999–2000	*Swindon T*	6	2	6	2
1999–2000	*Birmingham C*	2	0	2	0
2000–01	West Ham U	33	1	41	2

CASCIONE, Emmanuel (M) 0 0
b.Catanzaro 22-9-83
Source: Lucchese.

2000–01	West Ham U	0	0	

CHARLES, Gary (D) 216 8
H: 5 9 W: 11 08 b.East London 13-4-70
Source: Trainee. Honours: England
Under-21, 2 full caps.

1987–88	Nottingham F	0	0		
1988–89	Nottingham F	1	0		
1988–89	*Leicester C*	8	0	8	0
1989–90	Nottingham F	1	0		
1990–91	Nottingham F	10	0		
1991–92	Nottingham F	30	1		
1992–93	Nottingham F	14	0	56	1
1993–94	Derby Co	43	1		
1994–95	Derby Co	18	2	61	3
1994–95	Aston Villa	16	0		
1995–96	Aston Villa	34	1		
1996–97	Aston Villa	0	0		
1997–98	Aston Villa	18	1		
1998–99	Aston Villa	11	1	79	3
1998–99	Benfica	4	1	4	1
1999–2000	West Ham U	4	0		
2000–01	West Ham U	0	0	5	0
2000–01	*Birmingham C*	3	0	3	0

COLE, Joe (M) 60 6
H: 5 7 W: 9 08 b.Islington 8-11-81
Source: Trainee. Honours: England Schools,
Youth, Under-21, 1 full cap.

1998–99	West Ham U	8	0		
1999–2000	West Ham U	22	1		
2000–01	West Ham U	30	5	60	6

DAILLY, Christian (D) 290 26
H: 6 0 W: 12 00 b.Dundee 23-10-73
Source: 'S' Form. Honours: Scotland B,
Under-21, 27 full caps, 1 goal.

1990–91	Dundee U	18	5	
1991–92	Dundee U	8	0	
1992–93	Dundee U	14	4	

1993–94	Dundee U	38	4		
1994–95	Dundee U	33	4		
1995–96	Dundee U	30	1	**141**	**18**
1996–97	Derby Co	36	3		
1997–98	Derby Co	30	1		
1998–99	Derby Co	1	0	**67**	**4**
1998–99	Blackburn R	17	0		
1999–2000	Blackburn R	43	4		
2000–01	Blackburn R	10	0	**70**	**4**
2000–01	West Ham U	12	0	**12**	**0**

DEFOE, Jermaine (F) **30** **18**
H: 5 7 W: 10 04 b.Beckton 7-10-82
Source: Charlton Ath. *Honours:* England Youth, Under-21.

1999–2000	West Ham U	0	0		
2000–01	West Ham U	1	0	**1**	**0**
2000–01	*Bournemouth*	29	18	**29**	**18**

DI CANIO, Paolo (F) **363** **78**
H: 5 9 W: 11 09 b.Rome 9-7-68
Source: Milan AC.

1985–86	Lazio	0	0		
1986–87	Ternana	27	2	**27**	**2**
1987–88	Lazio	0	0		
1988–89	Lazio	30	1		
1989–90	Lazio	24	3	**54**	**4**
1990–91	Juventus	23	3		
1991–92	Juventus	24	0		
1992–93	Juventus	31	3		
1993–94	Napoli	26	5	**26**	**5**
1994–95	Juventus	0	0	**78**	**6**
1994–95	AC Milan	15	1		
1995–96	AC Milan	22	5	**37**	**6**
1996–97	Celtic	26	12	**26**	**12**
1997–98	Sheffield W	35	12		
1998–99	Sheffield W	6	3	**41**	**15**
1998–99	West Ham U	13	3		
1999–2000	West Ham U	30	16		
2000–01	West Ham U	31	9	**74**	**28**

DIAWARA, Kaba* (F) **126** **17**
H: 5 11 W: 11 08 b.Toulon 16-12-75
Source: Toulon.

1994–95	Bordeaux	0	0		
1995–96	Bordeaux	1	1		
1996–97	Bordeaux	29	7		
1997–98	Bordeaux	13	1		
1997–98	Rennes	12	3	**12**	**3**
1998–99	Bordeaux	17	5	**60**	**14**
1998–99	Arsenal	12	0	**12**	**0**
1999–2000	Marseille	15	0	**15**	**0**
1999–2000	Paris St Germain	10	0		
2000–01	Paris St Germain	1	0	**11**	**0**
2000–01	Blackburn R	5	0	**5**	**0**
2000–01	West Ham U	11	0	**11**	**0**

ETHERINGTON, Craig* (M) **9** **0**
H: 6 0 W: 11 10 b.Basildon 16-9-79
Source: Trainee.

1997–98	West Ham U	0	0		
1998–99	West Ham U	0	0		
1998–99	*Halifax T*	4	0	**4**	**0**
1999–2000	West Ham U	0	0		
1999–2000	*Plymouth Arg*	5	0	**5**	**0**
2000–01	West Ham U	0	0		

FERRANTE, Michael (M) **0** **0**
b.Melbourne 28-4-81
Source: Australia IOS.

1998–99	West Ham U	0	0		
1999–2000	West Ham U	0	0		
2000–01	West Ham U	0	0		

FORBES, Terrell* (D) **3** **0**
H: 6 0 W: 12 05 b.Southwark 17-8-81
Source: Trainee.

1999–2000	West Ham U	0	0		
1999–2000	*Bournemouth*	3	0	**3**	**0**
2000–01	West Ham U	0	0		

FORREST, Craig (G) **307** **0**
H: 6 4 W: 14 04 b.Vancouver 20-9-67
Source: Apprentice. *Honours:* Canada 56 full caps.

1985–86	Ipswich T	0	0		
1986–87	Ipswich T	0	0		
1987–88	Ipswich T	0	0		
1987–88	*Colchester U*	11	0	**11**	**0**
1988–89	Ipswich T	28	0		
1989–90	Ipswich T	45	0		
1990–91	Ipswich T	43	0		
1991–92	Ipswich T	46	0		
1992–93	Ipswich T	11	0		
1993–94	Ipswich T	27	0		
1994–95	Ipswich T	36	0		
1995–96	Ipswich T	21	0		
1996–97	Ipswich T	6	0	**263**	**0**
1996–97	*Chelsea*	3	0	**3**	**0**
1997–98	West Ham U	13	0		
1998–99	West Ham U	2	0		
1999–2000	West Ham U	11	0		
2000–01	West Ham U	4	0	**30**	**0**

FOXE, Hayden (D) **6** **0**
H: 6 3 W: 13 05 b.Sydney 23-6-77
Honours: Australia 14 full caps, 2 goals.

1997–98	Arminia Bielefeld	1	0	**1**	**0**
1998–99	Ajax	0	0		
From Sanfrecce					
2000–01	West Ham U	5	0	**5**	**0**

GARCIA, Richard (F) **18** **4**
b.Perth 4-9-81
Source: Trainee.

1998–99	West Ham U	0	0		
1999–2000	West Ham U	0	0		
2000–01	West Ham U	0	0		
2000–01	*Leyton Orient*	18	4	**18**	**4**

HISLOP, Shaka (G) **250** **0**
H: 6 4 W: 14 04 b.Hackney 22-2-69
Source: Howard Univ, USA. *Honours:* England Under-21. Trinidad & Tobago full caps.

1992–93	Reading	12	0		
1993–94	Reading	46	0		
1994–95	Reading	46	0	**104**	**0**
1995–96	Newcastle U	24	0		
1996–97	Newcastle U	16	0		
1997–98	Newcastle U	13	0	**53**	**0**
1998–99	West Ham U	37	0		
1999–2000	West Ham U	22	0		
2000–01	West Ham U	34	0	**93**	**0**

HOLLIGAN, Gavin* (F) **5** **0**
H: 5 10 W: 13 00 b.Lambeth 13-6-80
Source: Kingstonian.

1998–99	West Ham U	1	0		
1999–2000	West Ham U	0	0		
1999–2000	*Leyton Orient*	1	0	**1**	**0**
2000–01	West Ham U	0	0	**1**	**0**
2000–01	*Exeter C*	3	0	**3**	**0**

IRIEKPEN, Ezomo (D) **0** **0**
H: 6 1 W: 12 02 b.East London 14-5-82
Source: Trainee. *Honours:* England Youth.

1998–99	West Ham U	0	0		
1999–2000	West Ham U	0	0		
2000–01	West Ham U	0	0		

KANOUTE, Frederic (F) **80** **22**
H: 6 3 W: 13 08 b.Ste. Foy-Les-Lyon 2-9-77

1997–98	Lyon	18	6		
1998–99	Lyon	9	2		
1999–2000	Lyon	13	1	**40**	**9**
1999–2000	West Ham U	8	2		
2000–01	West Ham U	32	11	**40**	**13**

KITSON, Paul (F) **257** **68**
H: 5 11 W: 10 12 b.Murton 9-1-71
Source: Trainee. *Honours:* England Under-21.

1988–89	Leicester C	0	0		
1989–90	Leicester C	13	0		
1990–91	Leicester C	7	0		
1991–92	Leicester C	30	6	**50**	**6**
1991–92	Derby Co	12	4		
1992–93	Derby Co	44	17		
1993–94	Derby Co	41	13		
1994–95	Derby Co	8	2	**105**	**36**
1994–95	Newcastle U	26	8		
1995–96	Newcastle U	7	2		
1996–97	Newcastle U	3	0	**36**	**10**
1996–97	West Ham U	14	8		
1997–98	West Ham U	13	4		
1998–99	West Ham U	17	3		
1999–2000	West Ham U	10	0		
1999–2000	*Charlton Ath*	6	1	**6**	**1**
2000–01	West Ham U	2	0	**56**	**15**
2000–01	*Crystal Palace*	4	0	**4**	**0**

LAMPARD, Frank (M) **157** **24**
H: 6 0 W: 11 12 b.Romford 20-6-78
Source: Trainee. *Honours:* England Youth, Under-21, B, 2 full caps.

1994–95	West Ham U	0	0		
1995–96	West Ham U	2	0		
1995–96	*Swansea C*	9	1	**9**	**1**
1996–97	West Ham U	13	0		
1997–98	West Ham U	31	4		
1998–99	West Ham U	38	5		
1999–2000	West Ham U	34	7		
2000–01	West Ham U	30	7	**148**	**23**

(Transferred to Chelsea, July 2001).

LAURIE, Steve (D) **0** **0**
b.Melbourne 30-10-82

1999–2000	West Ham U	0	0		
2000–01	West Ham U	0	0		

LOMAS, Steve (M) **226** **13**
H: 6 0 W: 12 08 b.Hanover 14-3-72
Source: Trainee. *Honours:* Northern Ireland 38 full caps, 2 goals.

1991–92	Manchester C	0	0		
1992–93	Manchester C	0	0		
1993–94	Manchester C	23	0		
1994–95	Manchester C	20	2		
1995–96	Manchester C	33	3		
1996–97	Manchester C	35	3	**111**	**8**
1996–97	West Ham U	7	0		
1997–98	West Ham U	33	2		
1998–99	West Ham U	30	1		
1999–2000	West Ham U	25	1		
2000–01	West Ham U	20	1	**115**	**5**

MARGAS, Javier‡ (D) **51** **4**
H: 6 1 W: 13 00 b.Santiago 10-5-69
Source: Colo-Colo. *Honours:* Chile 65 full caps, 7 goals.

1996–97	America (Mexico)	9	1	**9**	**1**
1997	Univ Catolica	18	2	**18**	**2**
1998–99	West Ham U	3	0		
1999–2000	West Ham U	18	1		
2000–01	West Ham U	3	0	**24**	**1**

McCANN, Grant (M) **33** **3**
b.Belfast 14-4-80
Source: Trainee. *Honours:* Northern Ireland Youth, Under-21.

1998–99	West Ham U	0	0		
1999–2000	West Ham U	0	0		
2000–01	West Ham U	1	0	**1**	**0**
2000–01	*Notts Co*	2	0	**2**	**0**
2000–01	*Cheltenham T*	30	3	**30**	**3**

McMAHON, Daryl (M) **0** **0**
b.Dublin 10-10-83

2000–01	West Ham U	0	0		

MINTO, Scott (D) **309** **11**
H: 5 10 W: 10 00 b.Wirral 6-8-71
Source: Trainee. *Honours:* England Youth, Under-21.

1988–89	Charlton Ath	3	0		
1989–90	Charlton Ath	23	2		
1990–91	Charlton Ath	43	1		
1991–92	Charlton Ath	33	1		
1992–93	Charlton Ath	36	1		
1993–94	Charlton Ath	42	2	**180**	**7**
1994–95	Chelsea	19	0		
1995–96	Chelsea	10	0		
1996–97	Chelsea	25	4	**54**	**4**
1997–98	Benfica	21	0		
1998–99	Benfica	10	0		
1998–99	West Ham U	15	0		
1998–99	Benfica	10	0	**41**	**0**
1999–2000	West Ham U	18	0		
2000–01	West Ham U	1	0	**34**	**0**

MONCUR, John (M) **254** **13**
H: 5 8 W: 9 10 b.Mile End 22-9-66
Source: Apprentice.

1984–85	Tottenham H	0	0		
1985–86	Tottenham H	0	0		
1986–87	Tottenham H	1	0		
1986–87	*Cambridge U*	4	0	**4**	**0**
1986–87	*Doncaster R*	4	0	**4**	**0**
1987–88	Tottenham H	5	0		
1988–89	Tottenham H	1	0		
1988–89	*Portsmouth*	7	0	**7**	**0**
1989–90	Tottenham H	5	1		
1989–90	*Brentford*	5	1	**5**	**1**
1990–91	Tottenham H	9	0	**21**	**1**
1991–92	*Ipswich T*	6	0	**6**	**0**
1991–92	*Nottingham F*	0	0		
1991–92	Swindon T	3	0		
1992–93	Swindon T	14	1		
1993–94	Swindon T	41	4	**58**	**5**
1994–95	West Ham U	30	2		
1995–96	West Ham U	20	0		
1996–97	West Ham U	27	2		
1997–98	West Ham U	20	1		
1998–99	West Ham U	14	0		
1999–2000	West Ham U	22	1		
2000–01	West Ham U	16	0	**149**	**6**

NEWTON, Adam (D) **25** **1**
H: 5 10 W: 11 00 b.Ascot 4-12-80
Source: West Ham U Trainee. *Honours:* England Under-21.

1999–2000	West Ham U	2	0		
1999–2000	*Portsmouth*	3	0	**3**	**0**
2000–01	West Ham U	0	0	**2**	**0**
2000–01	*Notts Co*	20	1	**20**	**1**

PEARCE, Ian (D) **145** **6**
H: 6 3 W: 14 04 b.Bury St Edmunds 7-5-74
Source: School. *Honours:* England Youth, Under-21.

1990–91	Chelsea	1	0		
1991–92	Chelsea	2	0		
1992–93	Chelsea	1	0		
1993–94	Chelsea	0	0	**4**	**0**
1993–94	Blackburn R	5	1		
1994–95	Blackburn R	28	0		
1995–96	Blackburn R	12	1		
1996–97	Blackburn R	12	0		
1997–98	Blackburn R	5	0	**62**	**2**
1997–98	West Ham U	30	1		

1998–99	West Ham U	33	2		
1999–2000	West Ham U	1	0		
2000–01	West Ham U	15	1	79	4

PEARCE, Stuart* (D) — 531 69
H: 5 10 W: 12 06 b.Shepherds Bush 24-4-62
Source: Wealdstone. *Honours:* England Under-21, 78 full caps, 4 goals.

1983–84	Coventry C	23	0		
1984–85	Coventry C	28	4	51	4
1985–86	Nottingham F	30	1		
1986–87	Nottingham F	39	6		
1987–88	Nottingham F	34	5		
1988–89	Nottingham F	36	6		
1989–90	Nottingham F	34	5		
1990–91	Nottingham F	33	11		
1991–92	Nottingham F	30	5		
1992–93	Nottingham F	23	2		
1993–94	Nottingham F	42	6		
1994–95	Nottingham F	36	8		
1995–96	Nottingham F	31	3		
1996–97	Nottingham F	33	5	401	63
1997–98	Newcastle U	25	0		
1998–99	Newcastle U	12	0	37	0
1999–2000	West Ham U	8	0		
2000–01	West Ham U	34	2	42	2

POTTS, Steve (D) — 399 1
H: 5 7 W: 11 6 b.Hartford (USA) 7-5-67
Source: Apprentice. *Honours:* England Youth.

1984–85	West Ham U	1	0		
1985–86	West Ham U	1	0		
1986–87	West Ham U	8	0		
1987–88	West Ham U	8	0		
1988–89	West Ham U	28	0		
1989–90	West Ham U	32	0		
1990–91	West Ham U	37	1		
1991–92	West Ham U	34	0		
1992–93	West Ham U	46	0		
1993–94	West Ham U	41	0		
1994–95	West Ham U	42	0		
1995–96	West Ham U	34	0		
1996–97	West Ham U	20	0		
1997–98	West Ham U	23	0		
1998–99	West Ham U	19	0		
1999–2000	West Ham U	17	0		
2000–01	West Ham U	8	0	399	1

RIZA, Omer (F) — 22 7
b.Edmonton 8-11-79
Source: Trainee.

1998–99	Arsenal	0	0		
1999–2000	Arsenal	0	0		
1999–2000	West Ham U	0	0		
2000–01	West Ham U	0	0		
2000–01	*Barnet*	10	4	10	4
2000–01	*Cambridge U*	12	3	12	3

SCHEMMEL, Sebastian* (D) — 218 3
H: 5 9 W: 11 13 b.Nancy 26-6-75

1993–94	Nancy	6	0		
1994–95	Nancy	35	0		
1995–96	Nancy	33	0		
1996–97	Nancy	32	0		
1997–98	Nancy	40	1	146	1
1998–99	Metz	20	1		
1999–2000	Metz	21	1		
2000–01	Metz	19	0	60	2
2000–01	West Ham U	12	0	12	0

SINCLAIR, Trevor (M) — 384 55
H: 5 10 W: 12 05 b.Dulwich 2-3-73
Source: Trainee. *Honours:* England Youth, Under-21, B.

1989–90	Blackpool	9	0		
1990–91	Blackpool	31	1		
1991–92	Blackpool	27	3		
1992–93	Blackpool	45	11	112	15
1993–94	QPR	32	4		
1994–95	QPR	33	4		
1995–96	QPR	37	2		
1996–97	QPR	39	3		
1997–98	QPR	26	3	167	16
1997–98	West Ham U	14	7		
1998–99	West Ham U	36	7		
1999–2000	West Ham U	36	7		
2000–01	West Ham U	19	3	105	24

SOMA, Ragnvald (D) — 54 5
H: 6 2 W: 12 02 b.Norway 10-11-79

1999	Bryne	25	0		
2000	Bryne	25	5	50	5
2000–01	West Ham U	4	0	4	0

SONG, Rigobert (D) — 180 7
H: 6 0 W: 13 00 b.Nkenlicock 1-7-76
Source: Tonnerre. *Honours:* Cameroon full caps.

1994–95	Metz	24	0		
1995–96	Metz	37	0		
1996–97	Metz	34	0		

1997–98	Metz	28	1	123	3
1998–99	Salernitana	4	1	4	1
1998–99	Liverpool	13	0		
1999–2000	Liverpool	18	0		
2000–01	Liverpool	3	0	34	0
2000–01	West Ham U	19	0	19	0

STIMAC, Igor (D) — 211 10
H: 6 2 W: 13 00 b.Metkovic 6-9-67
Honours: Yugoslavia Youth. Croatia 50 full caps, 2 goals.

1992–93	Hajduk Split	1	0		
1992–93	Cadiz	32	0		
1993–94	Cadiz	30	4	62	4
1994–95	Hajduk Split	21	2	22	2
1995–96	Derby Co	27	1		
1996–97	Derby Co	21	1		
1997–98	Derby Co	22	1		
1998–99	Derby Co	14	0		
1999–2000	Derby Co	0	0	84	3
1999–2000	West Ham U	24	1		
2000–01	West Ham U	19	0	43	1

SUKER, Davor* (F) — 423 197
H: 6 0 W: 12 02 b.Osijek 1-1-68
Honours: Yugoslavia 2 full caps, 1 goal. Croatia 63 caps, 43 goals.

1985–86	Osijek	10	3		
1986–87	Osijek	26	9		
1987–88	Osijek	29	10		
1988–89	Osijek	26	18	91	40
1989–90	Dynamo Zagreb	28	12		
1990–91	Dynamo Zagreb	32	22	60	34
1991–92	Sevilla	22	6		
1992–93	Sevilla	33	13		
1993–94	Sevilla	34	23		
1994–95	Sevilla	32	17		
1995–96	Sevilla	32	16	153	75
1996–97	Real Madrid	38	24		
1997–98	Real Madrid	29	10		
1998–99	Real Madrid	19	4	86	38
1999–2000	Arsenal	22	8	22	8
2000–01	West Ham U	11	2	11	2

TIHINEN, Hannu‡ (D) — 146 21
H: 6 2 W: 13 05 b.Finland 1-7-76
Honours: Finland 20 full caps, 1 goal.

1995	KePS	25	3		
1996	KePS	23	7	48	10
1997	HJK Helsinki	25	2		
1998	HJK Helsinki	13	2		
1999	HJK Helsinki	27	4	65	8
2000	Viking	25	3	25	3
2000–01	West Ham U	8	0	8	0

TODOROV, Svetoslav (F) — 91 40
H: 6 0 W: 11 11 b.Bulgaria 30-8-78
Honours: Bulgaria 23 full caps, 1 goal.

1996–97	Dobrudzha	12	2	12	2
1997–98	Litets Lovech	19	9		
1998–99	Litets Lovech	11	2		
1999–2000	Litets Lovech	26	19		
2000–01	Litets Lovech	15	7	71	37
2000–01	West Ham U	8	1	8	1

WILLIAMS, Tommy (M) — 2 0
b.Carshalton 8-7-80
Source: Walton & Hersham.

1999–2000	West Ham U	0	0		
2000–01	West Ham U	0	0		
2000–01	*Peterborough U*	2	0	2	0

WINTERBURN, Nigel (D) — 638 17
H: 5 8 W: 11 04 b.Coventry 11-12-63
Source: Local. *Honours:* England Youth, Under-21, B, 2 full caps.

1981–82	Birmingham C	0	0		
1982–83	Birmingham C	0	0		
1983–84	Oxford U	0	0		
1983–84	Wimbledon	43	4		
1984–85	Wimbledon	41	4		
1985–86	Wimbledon	39	1		
1986–87	Wimbledon	42	2	165	8
1987–88	Arsenal	17	0		
1988–89	Arsenal	38	3		
1989–90	Arsenal	36	0		
1990–91	Arsenal	36	0		
1991–92	Arsenal	41	1		
1992–93	Arsenal	29	1		
1993–94	Arsenal	34	0		
1994–95	Arsenal	39	0		
1995–96	Arsenal	36	2		
1996–97	Arsenal	38	0		
1997–98	Arsenal	36	1		
1998–99	Arsenal	30	0		
1999–2000	Arsenal	28	0	440	8
2000–01	West Ham U	33	1	33	1

Scholars
Allen, James P; Clark, Steven T; Cleaver, Dean; Dean, Anthony J; Eastwood, Freddy; Foyewa, Amos; Jackson, Glenn G; Johnson, Glen MC; Khan, Terence G; McMahon, William C; Mehmet, Billy O; Metitiri, Kesiena A; Riddle, Louis S; Ritchie, Niall D; Sealey, Joe HJ; Smith, Dean G; Taylor, Sam AJ; Tobolewski, Ross J; Uddin, Anwar
Non-Contract
Sealey, Leslie J

WIGAN ATH

ASHCROFT, Lee (F) — 342 72
H: 5 9 W: 12 07 b.Preston 7-9-72
Source: Trainee. *Honours:* England Under-21.

1990–91	Preston NE	14	1		
1991–92	Preston NE	38	5		
1992–93	Preston NE	39	7		
1993–94	WBA	21	3		
1994–95	WBA	38	10		
1995–96	WBA	26	4		
1995–96	Notts Co	6	0	6	0
1996–97	WBA	5	0	90	17
1996–97	Preston NE	27	8		
1997–98	Preston NE	37	14		
1998–99	Preston NE	0	0	155	35
1998–99	Grimsby T	27	3		
1999–2000	Grimsby T	34	12	61	15
2000–01	Wigan Ath	30	5	30	5

BALMER, Stuart* (D) — 328 12
H: 6 0 W: 13 02 b.Falkirk 20-9-69
Source: Celtic BC.

1987–88	Celtic	0	0		
1988–89	Celtic	0	0		
1989–90	Celtic	0	0		
1990–91	Charlton Ath	24	0		
1991–92	Charlton Ath	18	0		
1992–93	Charlton Ath	45	2		
1993–94	Charlton Ath	31	1		
1994–95	Charlton Ath	29	2		
1995–96	Charlton Ath	32	1		
1996–97	Charlton Ath	32	2		
1997–98	Charlton Ath	16	0		
1998–99	Charlton Ath	0	0	227	8
1998–99	Wigan Ath	36	1		
1999–2000	Wigan Ath	41	2		
2000–01	Wigan Ath	24	1	101	4

BEAGRIE, Peter* (M) — 489 56
H: 5 8 W: 12 00 b.Middlesbrough 28-11-65
Source: Local. *Honours:* England Under-21, B.

1983–84	Middlesbrough	0	0		
1984–85	Middlesbrough	7	1		
1985–86	Middlesbrough	26	1	33	2
1986–87	Sheffield U	41	9		
1987–88	Sheffield U	43	2	84	11
1988–89	Stoke C	41	7		
1989–90	Stoke C	13	0	54	7
1989–90	Everton	19	0		
1990–91	Everton	17	2		
1991–92	Everton	27	3		
1991–92	Sunderland	5	1	5	1
1992–93	Everton	22	3		
1993–94	Everton	29	3		
1993–94	Manchester C	9	1		
1994–95	Manchester C	37	2		
1995–96	Manchester C	5	0		
1996–97	Manchester C	1	0	52	3
1997–98	Bradford C	34	0		
1997–98	Everton	6	0	120	11
1998–99	Bradford C	43	12		
1999–2000	Bradford C	35	7		
2000–01	Bradford C	19	1	131	20
2000–01	Wigan Ath	10	1	10	1

BIDSTRUP, Stefan (D) — 126 15
H: 6 2 W: 13 08 b.Helsinger 24-2-75

1996–97	Lyngby	14	1		
1997–98	Lyngby	30	1		
1998–99	Lyngby	29	1		
1999–2000	Lyngby	24	7		
2000–01	Lyngby	14	3	111	13
2000–01	Wigan Ath	15	2	15	2

BRADSHAW, Carl* (D) — 375 26
H: 5 10 W: 12 00 b.Sheffield 2-10-68
Source: Apprentice. *Honours:* England Youth.

1986–87	Sheffield W	9	2		
1986–87	*Barnsley*	6	1	6	1
1987–88	Sheffield W	20	2		
1988–89	Sheffield W	3	0	32	4
1988–89	Manchester C	5	0		
1989–90	Manchester C	0	0	5	0
1989–90	Sheffield U	30	3		
1990–91	Sheffield U	27	1		
1991–92	Sheffield U	18	2		
1992–93	Sheffield U	32	1		
1993–94	Sheffield U	40	1	147	8
1994–95	Norwich C	26	1		

1995–96	Norwich C	21	1		
1996–97	Norwich C	17	0		
1997–98	Norwich C	1	0	65	2
1997–98	Wigan Ath	28	1		
1998–99	Wigan Ath	39	6		
1999–2000	Wigan Ath	26	1		
2000–01	Wigan Ath	27	3	120	11

BRANNAN, Ged (D) 363 35
H: 6 0 W: 12 05 b.Liverpool 15-1-72
Source: Trainee.

1990–91	Tranmere R	18	1		
1991–92	Tranmere R	18	1		
1992–93	Tranmere R	38	1		
1993–94	Tranmere R	45	9		
1994–95	Tranmere R	41	2		
1995–96	Tranmere R	44	0		
1996–97	Tranmere R	34	6	238	20
1996–97	Manchester C	11	1		
1997–98	Manchester C	32	3		
1998–99	Manchester C	0	0	43	4
1998–99	*Norwich C*	11	1	11	1
1998–99	Motherwell	25	5		
1999–2000	Motherwell	33	5	58	10
2000–01	Wigan Ath	13	0	13	0

CARROLL, Roy (G) 181 0
H: 6 2 W: 13 12 b.Enniskillen 30-9-77
Source: Trainee. Honours: Northern Ireland Under-21, 9 full caps.

1995–96	Hull C	23	0		
1996–97	Hull C	23	0	46	0
1996–97	Wigan Ath	0	0		
1997–98	Wigan Ath	29	0		
1998–99	Wigan Ath	43	0		
1999–2000	Wigan Ath	34	0		
2000–01	Wigan Ath	29	0	135	0

DE ZEEUW, Arjan (D) 324 16
H: 6 3 W: 13 07 b.Castricum 16-4-70
Source: Vitesse 23.

1992–93	Telstar	30	1		
1993–94	Telstar	31	2		
1994–95	Telstar	29	1		
1995–96	Telstar	12	1	102	5
1995–96	Barnsley	31	1		
1996–97	Barnsley	43	2		
1997–98	Barnsley	26	0		
1998–99	Barnsley	38	4	138	7
1999–2000	Wigan Ath	39	3		
2000–01	Wigan Ath	45	1	84	4

DICKSON, Hugh (D) 6 0
b.Down Patrick 28-8-81

| 1999–2000 | Glentoran | 5 | 0 | 5 | 0 |
| 2000–01 | Wigan Ath | 1 | 0 | 1 | 0 |

GREEN, Scott (D) 363 30
H: 5 10 W: 12 09 b.Walsall 15-1-70
Source: Trainee.

1988–89	Derby Co	0	0		
1989–90	Derby Co	0	0		
1989–90	Bolton W	5	2		
1990–91	Bolton W	41	6		
1991–92	Bolton W	37	2		
1992–93	Bolton W	41	6		
1993–94	Bolton W	22	4		
1994–95	Bolton W	31	1		
1995–96	Bolton W	31	3		
1996–97	Bolton W	12	1	220	25
1997–98	Wigan Ath	37	0		
1998–99	Wigan Ath	37	0		
1999–2000	Wigan Ath	33	2		
2000–01	Wigan Ath	35	2	143	5

GREENALL, Colin† (D) 659 39
H: 5 11 W: 12 12 b.Billinge 30-12-63
Source: Apprentice.

1980–81	Blackpool	12	0		
1981–82	Blackpool	18	0		
1982–83	Blackpool	24	1		
1983–84	Blackpool	39	4		
1984–85	Blackpool	44	3		
1985–86	Blackpool	43	1		
1986–87	Blackpool	3	0	183	9
1986–87	Gillingham	37	2		
1987–88	Gillingham	25	2	62	4
1987–88	Oxford U	12	0		
1988–89	Oxford U	40	2		
1989–90	Oxford U	15	0	67	2
1989–90	Bury	3	0		
1990–91	Bury	31	0		
1991–92	Bury	37	5	71	5
1991–92	Preston NE	9	1		
1992–93	Preston NE	20	0	29	1
1993–94	Chester C	42	1	42	1
1994–95	Lincoln C	39	3		
1995–96	Lincoln C	4	0	43	3
1995–96	Wigan Ath	37	2		
1996–97	Wigan Ath	46	2		
1997–98	Wigan Ath	39	4		
1998–99	Wigan Ath	40	6		
1999–2000	Wigan Ath	0	0		
2000–01	Wigan Ath	0	0	162	14

GRIFFITHS, Gareth* (D) 153 6
H: 6 4 W: 14 01 b.Winsford 10-4-70
Source: Rhyl.

1992–93	Port Vale	0	0		
1993–94	Port Vale	4	2		
1994–95	Port Vale	20	0		
1995–96	Port Vale	41	2		
1996–97	Port Vale	26	0		
1997–98	Port Vale	3	0	94	4
1997–98	*Shrewsbury T*	6	0	6	0
1998–99	Wigan Ath	20	0		
1999–2000	Wigan Ath	16	1		
2000–01	Wigan Ath	17	1	53	2

HAWORTH, Simon (F) 138 43
H: 6 1 W: 14 02 b.Cardiff 30-3-77
Source: Trainee. Honours: Wales Under-21, 5 full caps.

1995–96	Cardiff C	13	0		
1996–97	Cardiff C	24	9	37	9
1997–98	Coventry C	10	0		
1998–99	Coventry C	1	0	11	0
1998–99	Wigan Ath	20	10		
1999–2000	Wigan Ath	40	13		
2000–01	Wigan Ath	30	11	90	34

HERNANDEZ, Ferdino‡ (M) 0 0
b.Amersfoort 27-5-71

| 2000–01 | Wigan Ath | 0 | 0 | | |

KILFORD, Ian (M) 202 32
H: 5 10 W: 11 04 b.Bristol 6-10-73
Source: Trainee.

1991–92	Nottingham F	0	0		
1992–93	Nottingham F	0	0		
1993–94	Nottingham F	1	0	1	0
1993–94	*Wigan Ath*	8	3		
1994–95	Wigan Ath	35	5		
1995–96	Wigan Ath	25	3		
1996–97	Wigan Ath	35	8		
1997–98	Wigan Ath	30	10		
1998–99	Wigan Ath	23	0		
1999–2000	Wigan Ath	21	1		
2000–01	Wigan Ath	24	2	201	32

LIDDELL, Andy (F) 304 61
H: 5 8 W: 11 05 b.Leeds 28-6-73
Source: Trainee. Honours: Scotland Under-21.

1990–91	Barnsley	0	0		
1991–92	Barnsley	1	0		
1992–93	Barnsley	21	2		
1993–94	Barnsley	22	1		
1994–95	Barnsley	39	13		
1995–96	Barnsley	43	9		
1996–97	Barnsley	38	8		
1997–98	Barnsley	26	1		
1998–99	Barnsley	8	0	198	34
1998–99	Wigan Ath	28	10		
1999–2000	Wigan Ath	41	8		
2000–01	Wigan Ath	37	9	106	27

MARTINEZ, Roberto* (M) 187 17
H: 5 11 W: 12 03 b.Balaguer 13-7-73
Source: Balaguer.

1995–96	Wigan Ath	42	9		
1996–97	Wigan Ath	43	4		
1997–98	Wigan Ath	33	1		
1998–99	Wigan Ath	10	0		
1999–2000	Wigan Ath	25	3		
2000–01	Wigan Ath	34	0	187	17

McCULLOCH, Lee (M) 132 25
H: 5 11 W: 12 05 b.Bellshill 14-5-78
Source: Cumbernauld U. Honours: Scotland Under-18, Under-21.

1995–96	Motherwell	1	0		
1996–97	Motherwell	15	0		
1997–98	Motherwell	25	2		
1998–99	Motherwell	26	3		
1999–2000	Motherwell	29	9		
2000–01	Motherwell	26	8	122	22
2000–01	Wigan Ath	10	3	10	3

McGIBBON, Pat (D) 156 10
H: 6 2 W: 13 09 b.Lurgan 6-9-73
Source: Portadown. Honours: Northern Ireland Under-21, 7 full caps.

1992–93	Manchester U	0	0		
1993–94	Manchester U	0	0		
1994–95	Manchester U	0	0		
1995–96	Manchester U	0	0		
1996–97	Manchester U	0	0		
1996–97	*Swansea C*	1	0	1	0
1996–97	*Wigan Ath*	10	1		
1997–98	Wigan Ath	35	0		
1998–99	Wigan Ath	36	5		
1999–2000	Wigan Ath	34	2		
2000–01	Wigan Ath	40	2	155	10

McLAUGHLIN, Brian (M) 96 5
H: 5 5 W: 9 02 b.Bellshill 14-5-74
Source: Giffnock N. Honours: Scotland Under-21.

1992–93	Celtic	0	0		
1993–94	Celtic	8	0		
1994–95	Celtic	21	0		
1995–96	Celtic	26	4		
1996–97	Celtic	20	1		
1997–98	Celtic	0	0		
1997–98	*Airdrieonians*	0	0		
1998–99	Celtic	0	0	75	5
1998–99	*Dundee U*	3	0	3	0
1999–2000	Wigan Ath	0	0		
2000–01	Wigan Ath	18	0	18	0

McLOUGHLIN, Alan (M) 482 79
H: 5 8 W: 10 10 b.Manchester 20-4-67
Source: Local. Honours: Eire B, 42 full caps, 2 goals.

1984–85	Manchester U	0	0		
1985–86	Manchester U	0	0		
1986–87	Swindon T	9	0		
1986–87	Torquay U	16	1		
1987–88	Torquay U	8	3	24	4
1987–88	Swindon T	8	0		
1988–89	Swindon T	26	3		
1989–90	Swindon T	46	12		
1990–91	Swindon T	17	4	106	19
1990–91	Southampton	22	1		
1991–92	Southampton	2	0	24	1
1991–92	*Aston Villa*	0	0		
1991–92	Portsmouth	14	2		
1992–93	Portsmouth	46	9		
1993–94	Portsmouth	38	6		
1994–95	Portsmouth	38	6		
1995–96	Portsmouth	40	10		
1996–97	Portsmouth	36	5		
1997–98	Portsmouth	37	4		
1998–99	Portsmouth	41	7		
1999–2000	Portsmouth	19	5	309	54
1999–2000	Wigan Ath	15	1		
2000–01	Wigan Ath	4	0	19	1

McMAHON, Francis* (D) 0 0
H: 6 0 W: 13 05 b.Rainhill 21-12-81
Source: Trainee.

| 2000–01 | Wigan Ath | 0 | 0 | | |

McMILLAN, Stephen (M) 158 6
H: 5 10 W: 11 00 b.Edinburgh 19-1-76
Source: Troon Juniors. Honours: Scotland Under-21.

1993–94	Motherwell	1	0		
1994–95	Motherwell	3	0		
1995–96	Motherwell	12	0		
1996–97	Motherwell	16	0		
1997–98	Motherwell	34	1		
1998–99	Motherwell	30	2		
1999–2000	Motherwell	31	3		
2000–01	Motherwell	25	0	152	6
2000–01	Wigan Ath	6	0	6	0

MITCHELL, Paul (D) 12 0
H: 6 0 W: 12 00 b.Manchester 26-8-81
Source: Trainee.

| 2000–01 | Wigan Ath | 1 | 0 | 1 | 0 |
| 2000–01 | *Halifax T* | 11 | 0 | 11 | 0 |

MORRIS, Andrew* (M) 0 0
H: 5 9 W: 10 11 b.Wigan 18-3-82
Source: Trainee.

| 2000–01 | Wigan Ath | 0 | 0 | | |

NICHOLLS, Kevin (M) 44 2
H: 5 11 W: 12 04 b.Newham 2-1-79
Source: Trainee. Honours: England Youth.

1995–96	Charlton Ath	0	0		
1996–97	Charlton Ath	6	1		
1997–98	Charlton Ath	6	0		
1998–99	Charlton Ath	0	0	12	1
1998–99	*Brighton & HA*	4	1	4	1
1999–2000	Wigan Ath	8	0		
2000–01	Wigan Ath	20	0	28	0

NUZZO, Raffaele# (G) 0 0
H: 6 2 W: 14 00 b.Monza 21-2-73

1999–2000	Coventry C	0	0		
	From Reggiana				
2000–01	Wigan Ath	0	0		

PADULA, Gino* (D) 29 0
H: 5 9 W: 12 01 b.Buenos Aires 11-7-76
Source: Xerex.

1999–2000	Bristol R	0	0		
1999–2000	Walsall	25	0	25	0
2000–01	Wigan Ath	4	0	4	0

PORTER, Andy‡ (M) 399 23
H: 5 9 W: 12 03 b.Holmes Chapel 17-9-68
Source: Trainee.

1986–87	Port Vale	1	0		
1987–88	Port Vale	6	0		
1988–89	Port Vale	14	1		

1989–90	Port Vale	36	1	
1990–91	Port Vale	40	0	
1991–92	Port Vale	32	1	
1992–93	Port Vale	17	1	
1993–94	Port Vale	37	0	
1994–95	Port Vale	44	3	
1995–96	Port Vale	45	10	
1996–97	Port Vale	44	4	
1997–98	Port Vale	41	1	357 22
1998–99	Wigan Ath	16	1	
1999–2000	Wigan Ath	5	0	
1999–2000	*Mansfield T*	5	0	5 0
1999–2000	*Chester C*	16	0	16 0
2000–01	Wigan Ath	0	0	21 1

PRUNTY, Sean‡ (M)   0 0
H: 5 9   W: 10 11   b.Dublin 10-7-80
Source: Belvedere.
1998–99	Middlesbrough	0	0
1999–2000	Middlesbrough	0	0
2000–01	Wigan Ath	0	0

ROBERTS, Neil (F)   118 24
H: 5 10   W: 11 02   b.Wrexham 7-4-78
Source: Trainee. *Honours:* Wales Under-21, 1 full cap.
1996–97	Wrexham	0	0	
1997–98	Wrexham	34	8	
1998–99	Wrexham	22	3	
1999–2000	Wrexham	19	6	75 17
1999–2000	Wigan Ath	9	1	
2000–01	Wigan Ath	34	6	43 7

SHARP, Kevin (D)   193 10
H: 5 9   W: 11 04   b.Ontario 19-9-74
Source: Auxerre. *Honours:* England Schools, Youth.
1992–93	Leeds U	4	0	
1993–94	Leeds U	10	0	
1994–95	Leeds U	2	0	
1995–96	Leeds U	1	0	17 0
1995–96	Wigan Ath	20	6	
1996–97	Wigan Ath	35	2	
1997–98	Wigan Ath	38	0	
1998–99	Wigan Ath	31	2	
1999–2000	Wigan Ath	21	0	
2000–01	Wigan Ath	31	0	176 10

SHERIDAN, Darren* (M)   229 8
H: 5 6   W: 11 04   b.Manchester 8-12-67
Source: Winsford U.
1993–94	Barnsley	3	0	
1994–95	Barnsley	35	2	
1995–96	Barnsley	41	0	
1996–97	Barnsley	41	2	
1997–98	Barnsley	26	0	
1998–99	Barnsley	25	1	171 5
1999–2000	Barnsley	31	3	
2000–01	Wigan Ath	27	0	58 3

STILLIE, Derek (G)   54 0
H: 6 0   W: 12 05   b.Cumnock 3-12-73
Source: Notts Co. *Honours:* Scotland Under-21.
1991–92	Aberdeen	0	0	
1992–93	Aberdeen	0	0	
1993–94	Aberdeen	5	0	
1994–95	Aberdeen	0	0	
1995–96	Aberdeen	0	0	
1996–97	Aberdeen	8	0	
1997–98	Aberdeen	2	0	
1998–99	Aberdeen	8	0	23 0
1999–2000	Wigan Ath	13	0	
2000–01	Wigan Ath	18	0	31 0

Trainees
Charnock, Kieran J; Clarke, Alistair A; Clegg, Michael J; Cunningham, Craig J; Ellis, Lee P; Ishmael, Martin J; Johnson, Ian R; Johnson, Joel; Kay, Stephen B; Lee, Paul K; Pendlebury, Ian D; Pitts, Douglas, J; Rae, Gary J; Robinson, Nigel T; Santus, Paul G; Speakman, Craig A; Spearritt, Thomas J; Tynan, Scott J
Non-Contract
Greenall, Colin A

WIMBLEDON

AGYEMANG, Patrick (F)   41 4
H: 6 1   W: 12 00   b.Walthamstow 29-9-80
Source: Trainee.
1998–99	Wimbledon	0	0	
1999–2000	Wimbledon	0	0	
1999–2000	*Brentford*	12	0	12 0
2000–01	Wimbledon	29	4	29 4

AINSWORTH, Gareth (M)   251 64
H: 5 9   W: 11 00   b.Blackburn 10-5-73
Source: Blackburn R Trainee.
1991–92	Preston NE	5	0	
1992–93	Cambridge U	4	1	4 1

1992–93	Preston NE	26	0	
1993–94	Preston NE	38	11	
1994–95	Preston NE	16	1	
1995–96	Preston NE	2	0	87 12
1995–96	Lincoln C	31	12	
1996–97	Lincoln C	46	22	
1997–98	Lincoln C	6	3	83 37
1997–98	Port Vale	40	5	
1998–99	Port Vale	15	5	55 10
1998–99	Wimbledon	8	0	
1999–2000	Wimbledon	2	2	
2000–01	Wimbledon	12	2	22 4

ANDERSEN, Trond (M)   183 9
H: 6 0   W: 11 06   b.Kristiansund 6-1-75
Source: Clausenengen. *Honours:* Norway 13 full caps.
1995	Molde	18	1	
1996	Molde	21	0	
1997	Molde	25	0	
1998	Molde	24	2	
1999	Molde	17	1	105 4
1999–2000	Wimbledon	36	0	
2000–01	Wimbledon	42	5	78 5

ARDLEY, Neal# (M)   216 15
H: 5 11   W: 11 09   b.Epsom 1-9-72
Source: Trainee. *Honours:* England Under-21.
1990–91	Wimbledon	1	0	
1991–92	Wimbledon	8	0	
1992–93	Wimbledon	26	4	
1993–94	Wimbledon	16	1	
1994–95	Wimbledon	14	1	
1995–96	Wimbledon	6	0	
1996–97	Wimbledon	34	2	
1997–98	Wimbledon	34	2	
1998–99	Wimbledon	23	0	
1999–2000	Wimbledon	17	2	
2000–01	Wimbledon	37	3	216 15

BERNI, Tommaso (G)   0 0
b.Firenze 6-3-83
Source: Internazionale.
2000–01	Wimbledon	0	0

BLACKWELL, Dean (D)   212 1
H: 6 1   W: 12 10   b.Camden 5-12-69
Source: Trainee. *Honours:* England Under-21.
1988–89	Wimbledon	0	0	
1989–90	Wimbledon	3	0	
1989–90	*Plymouth Arg*	7	0	7 0
1990–91	Wimbledon	35	0	
1991–92	Wimbledon	4	1	
1992–93	Wimbledon	24	0	
1993–94	Wimbledon	18	0	
1994–95	Wimbledon	0	0	
1995–96	Wimbledon	8	0	
1996–97	Wimbledon	27	0	
1997–98	Wimbledon	35	0	
1998–99	Wimbledon	28	0	
1999–2000	Wimbledon	17	0	
2000–01	Wimbledon	6	0	205 1

BOLGER, Gavin (M)   0 0
b.Dublin 7-8-82
2000–01	Wimbledon	0	0

BOOTH, Matthew# (D)   0 0
b.Cape Town 14-3-77
Source: Mamoladi Sundowns.
2000–01	Wimbledon	0	0

BYRNE, Des (D)   13 0
H: 6 1   W: 12 07   b.Dublin 10-4-81
Source: Trainee.
1998–99	Stockport Co	2	0	2 0
1999–2000	Sr Patrick's Ath	11	0	11 0
2000–01	Wimbledon	0	0	

COOPER, Kevin (F)   181 24
H: 5 8   W: 10 07   b.Derby 8-2-75
Source: Trainee.
1993–94	Derby Co	0	0	
1994–95	Derby Co	1	0	
1995–96	Derby Co	1	0	
1996–97	Derby Co	0	0	2 0
1996–97	*Stockport Co*	12	3	
1997–98	Stockport Co	38	8	
1998–99	Stockport Co	38	1	
1999–2000	Stockport Co	46	4	
2000–01	Stockport Co	34	5	168 21
2000–01	Wimbledon	11	3	11 3

CUNNINGHAM, Kenny (D)   352 1
H: 5 11   W: 11 04   b.Dublin 28-6-71
Source: Tolka R. *Honours:* Eire Under-21, B, 33 full caps.
1989–90	Millwall	5	0	
1990–91	Millwall	23	0	
1991–92	Millwall	17	0	
1992–93	Millwall	37	0	
1993–94	Millwall	39	1	

1994–95	Millwall	15	0	136 1
1994–95	Wimbledon	28	0	
1995–96	Wimbledon	33	0	
1996–97	Wimbledon	36	0	
1997–98	Wimbledon	32	0	
1998–99	Wimbledon	35	0	
1999–2000	Wimbledon	37	0	
2000–01	Wimbledon	15	0	216 0

DAVIS, Kelvin (G)   141 0
H: 6 1   W: 11 02   b.Bedford 29-9-76
Source: Trainee. *Honours:* England Youth, Under-21.
1993–94	Luton T	1	0	
1994–95	Luton T	9	0	
1994–95	*Torquay U*	2	0	2 0
1995–96	Luton T	6	0	
1996–97	Luton T	0	0	
1997–98	Luton T	32	0	
1997–98	*Hartlepool U*	2	0	2 0
1998–99	Luton T	44	0	92 0
1999–2000	Wimbledon	0	0	
2000–01	Wimbledon	45	0	45 0

EUELL, Jason (F)   141 41
H: 5 11   W: 11 02   b.Lambeth 6-2-77
Source: Trainee. *Honours:* England Youth, Under-21.
1995–96	Wimbledon	9	2	
1996–97	Wimbledon	7	2	
1997–98	Wimbledon	19	4	
1998–99	Wimbledon	33	10	
1999–2000	Wimbledon	37	4	
2000–01	Wimbledon	36	19	141 41

(Transferred to Charlton Ath, July 2001).

FEUER, Ian (G)   161 0
H: 6 6   W: 15 06   b.Las Vegas 20-5-71
Source: Los Angeles Salsa. *Honours:* USA full caps.
1993–94	West Ham U	0	0	
1994–95	West Ham U	0	0	
1994–95	*Peterborough U*	16	0	16 0
1995–96	West Ham U	0	0	
1995–96	Luton T	38	0	
1996–97	Luton T	46	0	
1997–98	Luton T	13	0	97 0
1998	New England Rev	26	0	26 0
1999	Colorado Rapids	19	0	19 0
1999–2000	Cardiff C	0	0	
1999–2000	West Ham U	3	0	3 0
2000–01	Wimbledon	0	0	

FRANCIS, Damien (M)   40 8
H: 6 0   W: 10 10   b.Wandsworth 27-2-79
Source: Trainee.
1996–97	Wimbledon	0	0	
1997–98	Wimbledon	2	0	
1998–99	Wimbledon	0	0	
1999–2000	Wimbledon	9	0	
2000–01	Wimbledon	29	8	40 8

GAYLE, Marcus (F)   392 59
H: 6 1   W: 12 09   b.Hammersmith 27-9-70
Source: Trainee. *Honours:* England Youth. Jamaica full caps.
1988–89	Brentford	3	0	
1989–90	Brentford	9	0	
1990–91	Brentford	33	6	
1991–92	Brentford	38	6	
1992–93	Brentford	38	4	
1993–94	Brentford	35	6	156 22
1993–94	Wimbledon	10	0	
1994–95	Wimbledon	23	2	
1995–96	Wimbledon	34	5	
1996–97	Wimbledon	36	8	
1997–98	Wimbledon	30	2	
1998–99	Wimbledon	35	10	
1999–2000	Wimbledon	36	7	
2000–01	Wimbledon	32	3	236 37

(Transferred to Rangers, March 2001).

GIER, Robert (M)   14 0
H: 5 9   W: 11 07   b.Ascot 6-1-80
Source: Trainee.
1998–99	Wimbledon	0	0	
1999–2000	Wimbledon	0	0	
2000–01	Wimbledon	14	0	14 0

GRAY, Wayne (F)   27 2
H: 5 10   W: 11 10   b.South London 7-11-80
Source: Trainee.
1998–99	Wimbledon	0	0	
1999–2000	Wimbledon	1	0	
1999–2000	*Swindon T*	12	2	12 2
2000–01	Wimbledon	11	0	12 0
2000–01	*Port Vale*	3	0	3 0

HAARA, Heikki (M)   0 0
b.Lahti 20-11-82
2000–01	Wimbledon	0	0

HAWKINS, Peter (D) — 44 0
H: 6 0 W: 11 04 b.Maidstone 19-9-78
Source: Trainee.

Season	Club	App	Gls	Tot App	Tot Gls
1996-97	Wimbledon	0	0		
1997-98	Wimbledon	0	0		
1998-99	Wimbledon	0	0		
1999-2000	Wimbledon	0	0		
1999-2000	York C	14	0	14	0
2000-01	Wimbledon	30	0	30	0

HEALD, Paul (G) — 204 0
H: 6 2 W: 12 05 b.Wath-on-Dearne 20-9-68
Source: Trainee.

Season	Club	App	Gls	Tot App	Tot Gls
1987-88	Sheffield U	0	0		
1988-89	Sheffield U	0	0		
1988-89	Leyton Orient	28	0		
1989-90	Leyton Orient	37	0		
1990-91	Leyton Orient	38	0		
1991-92	Leyton Orient	2	0		
1991-92	Coventry C	2	0	2	0
1992-93	Leyton Orient	26	0		
1992-93	Crystal Palace	0	0		
1993-94	Leyton Orient	0	0		
1993-94	Swindon T	2	0	2	0
1994-95	Leyton Orient	45	0	176	0
1995-96	Wimbledon	18	0		
1996-97	Wimbledon	2	0		
1997-98	Wimbledon	0	0		
1998-99	Wimbledon	0	0		
1999-2000	Wimbledon	1	0		
2000-01	Wimbledon	3	0	24	0

HINDS, Leigh‡ (F) — 0 0
H: 5 9 W: 10 10 b.Beckenham 17-8-78
Source: Trainee.

Season	Club	App	Gls
1996-97	Wimbledon	0	0
1997-98	Wimbledon	0	0
1998-99	Wimbledon	0	0
1999-2000	Wimbledon	0	0
2000-01	Wimbledon	0	0

HOLLOWAY, Darren (D) — 98 0
H: 6 0 W: 12 09 b.Crook 3-10-77
Source: Trainee. Honours: England Under-21.

Season	Club	App	Gls	Tot App	Tot Gls
1995-96	Sunderland	0	0		
1996-97	Sunderland	0	0		
1997-98	Sunderland	32	0		
1997-98	Carlisle U	5	0	5	0
1998-99	Sunderland	6	0		
1999-2000	Sunderland	15	0		
1999-2000	Bolton W	4	0	4	0
2000-01	Sunderland	5	0	58	0
2000-01	Wimbledon	31	0	31	0

HUGHES, Michael (M) — 281 24
H: 5 6 W: 10 08 b.Larne 2-8-71
Source: Carrick R. Honours: Northern Ireland Under-21, 58 full caps, 4 goals.

Season	Club	App	Gls	Tot App	Tot Gls
1988-89	Manchester C	1	0		
1989-90	Manchester C	0	0		
1990-91	Manchester C	1	0		
1991-92	Manchester C	24	1	26	1
1992-93	Strasbourg	36	2		
1993-94	Strasbourg	34	7		
1994-95	Strasbourg	13	0	83	9
1994-95	West Ham U	17	2		
1995-96	West Ham U	28	0		
1996-97	West Ham U	33	3		
1997-98	West Ham U	5	0	83	5
1997-98	Wimbledon	29	4		
1998-99	Wimbledon	30	2		
1999-2000	Wimbledon	20	2		
2000-01	Wimbledon	10	1	89	9

HUNT, Jonathan* (M) — 236 29
H: 5 10 W: 11 71 b.London 2-11-71
Source: Barnet, Slough T.

Season	Club	App	Gls	Tot App	Tot Gls
1991-92	Barnet	14	0		
1992-93	Barnet	19	0	33	0
1993-94	Southend U	42	6		
1994-95	Southend U	7	0	49	6
1994-95	Birmingham C	20	5		
1995-96	Birmingham C	45	11		
1996-97	Birmingham C	12	2	77	18
1997-98	Derby Co	19	1		
1998-99	Derby Co	6	1	25	2
1998-99	Sheffield U	13	2		
1998-99	Ipswich T	6	0	6	0
1999-2000	Sheffield U	14	0		
1999-2000	Cambridge U	7	1	7	1
2000-01	Sheffield U	0	0	27	2
2000-01	Wimbledon	12	0	12	0

JENKINS, Neil (M) — 0 0
b.Carshalton 6-1-82
Source: Scholar. Honours: England Youth.

Season	Club	App	Gls
2000-01	Wimbledon	0	0

JUPP, Duncan (D) — 133 2
H: 6 0 W: 12 11 b.Guildford 25-1-75
Source: Trainee. Honours: Scotland Under-21.

Season	Club	App	Gls	Tot App	Tot Gls
1992-93	Fulham	3	0		
1993-94	Fulham	30	0		
1994-95	Fulham	36	2		
1995-96	Fulham	36	0	105	2
1996-97	Wimbledon	6	0		
1997-98	Wimbledon	3	0		
1998-99	Wimbledon	6	0		
1999-2000	Wimbledon	9	0		
2000-01	Wimbledon	4	0	28	0

KARLSSON, Par (M) — 80 6
H: 5 7 W: 11 01 b.Sweden 29-5-78
Source: Karlskoga.

Season	Club	App	Gls	Tot App	Tot Gls
1997	IFK Gothenburg	10	3		
1998	IFK Gothenburg	13	0		
1999	IFK Gothenburg	25	1		
2000	IFK Gothenburg	16	2	64	6
2000-01	Wimbledon	16	0	16	0

KIMBLE, Alan (D) — 512 24
H: 5 10 W: 12 04 b.Poole 6-8-66
Source: Trainee.

Season	Club	App	Gls	Tot App	Tot Gls
1984-85	Charlton Ath	6	0		
1985-86	Charlton Ath	0	0	6	0
1985-86	Exeter C	1	0	1	0
1986-87	Cambridge U	35	0		
1987-88	Cambridge U	41	2		
1988-89	Cambridge U	45	6		
1989-90	Cambridge U	44	8		
1990-91	Cambridge U	43	4		
1991-92	Cambridge U	45	0		
1992-93	Cambridge U	46	4	299	24
1993-94	Wimbledon	14	0		
1994-95	Wimbledon	26	0		
1995-96	Wimbledon	31	0		
1996-97	Wimbledon	31	0		
1997-98	Wimbledon	25	0		
1998-99	Wimbledon	26	0		
1999-2000	Wimbledon	28	0		
2000-01	Wimbledon	25	0	206	0

LEABURN, Carl* (F) — 390 57
H: 6 3 W: 13 00 b.Lewisham 30-3-69
Source: Apprentice. Honours: England Youth.

Season	Club	App	Gls	Tot App	Tot Gls
1986-87	Charlton Ath	3	1		
1987-88	Charlton Ath	12	0		
1988-89	Charlton Ath	32	2		
1989-90	Charlton Ath	13	0		
1989-90	Northampton T	9	0	9	0
1990-91	Charlton Ath	20	1		
1991-92	Charlton Ath	39	11		
1992-93	Charlton Ath	39	5		
1993-94	Charlton Ath	39	10		
1994-95	Charlton Ath	27	3		
1995-96	Charlton Ath	40	9		
1996-97	Charlton Ath	44	8		
1997-98	Charlton Ath	14	3	322	53
1997-98	Wimbledon	16	4		
1998-99	Wimbledon	22	0		
1999-2000	Wimbledon	18	0		
2000-01	Wimbledon	3	0	59	4

LUND, Andreas (F) — 108 57
H: 6 1 W: 11 04 b.Kristiansand 7-5-75
Honours: Norway 8 full caps, 4 goals.

Season	Club	App	Gls	Tot App	Tot Gls
1995	Start	22	9		
1996	Start	15	4	37	13
1996	Molde	6	3		
1997	Molde	4	2		
1998	Molde	25	16		
1999	Molde	24	21	59	42
1999-2000	Wimbledon	12	2		
2000-01	Wimbledon	0	0	12	2

McANUFF, Joel (M) — 0 0
b.Edmonton 9-11-81
Source: Scholar.

Season	Club	App	Gls
2000-01	Wimbledon	0	0

MENSING, Simon (M) — 0 0
H: 5 10 W: 11 06 b.Woifenbuttel 27-6-82

Season	Club	App	Gls
1999-2000	Wimbledon	0	0
2000-01	Wimbledon	0	0

MORGAN, Lionel (F) — 5 0
b.Enfield 17-2-83
Source: Scholar.

Season	Club	App	Gls	Tot App	Tot Gls
2000-01	Wimbledon	5	0	5	0

NIELSEN, David (F) — 136 43
H: 6 0 W: 11 11 b.Denmark 1-12-76

Season	Club	App	Gls	Tot App	Tot Gls
1996-97	FC Copenhagen	14	1		
1997-98	FC Copenhagen	31	11		
1998-99	FC Copenhagen	30	15		
1999-2000	FC Copenhagen	26	8		
2000-01	FC Copenhagen	7	1	108	36
2000-01	Grimsby T	17	5	17	5
2000-01	Wimbledon	11	2	11	2

ONOCHI, Elliot* (M) — 0 0
b.Nigeria 15-3-82
Honours: England Schools.

Season	Club	App	Gls
2000-01	Wimbledon	0	0

OWUSU, Ansah (M) — 21 0
H: 5 11 W: 11 02 b.Hackney 22-11-79
Source: Trainee.

Season	Club	App	Gls	Tot App	Tot Gls
1998-99	Wimbledon	0	0		
1999-2000	Wimbledon	0	0		
2000-01	Wimbledon	4	0	4	0
2000-01	Bristol R	17	0	17	0

PEDERSEN, Tore‡ (D) — 165 1
H: 6 0 W: 11 00 b.Fredrikstad 29-9-69
Honours: Norway 41 full caps.

Season	Club	App	Gls	Tot App	Tot Gls
1990	IFK Gothenburg	18	0		
1991	IFK Gothenburg	25	0		
1992	IFK Gothenburg	21	0	64	0
1993	Brann	22	0		
1993-94	Oldham Ath	10	0	10	0
1994	Brann	1	0	23	0
	Sanfrecce				
1995-96	St Pauli	12	0		
1996-97	St Pauli	25	0	37	0
1997-98	Blackburn R	5	0	5	0
1998-99	Eintracht Frankfurt	20	1	20	1
1999-2000	Wimbledon	6	0		
2000-01	Wimbledon	0	0	6	0

ROBERTS, Andy (M) — 329 12
H: 5 10 W: 13 00 b.Dartford 20-3-74
Source: Trainee. Honours: England Under-21.

Season	Club	App	Gls	Tot App	Tot Gls
1991-92	Millwall	7	0		
1992-93	Millwall	45	0		
1993-94	Millwall	42	0		
1994-95	Millwall	44	3	138	5
1995-96	Crystal Palace	38	0		
1996-97	Crystal Palace	45	2		
1997-98	Crystal Palace	25	0	108	2
1997-98	Wimbledon	12	1		
1998-99	Wimbledon	28	2		
1999-2000	Wimbledon	16	0		
2000-01	Wimbledon	27	2	83	5

ROBINSON, Paul (F) — 44 3
H: 5 11 W: 12 11 b.Sunderland 20-11-78
Source: Trainee.

Season	Club	App	Gls	Tot App	Tot Gls
1995-96	Darlington	4	0		
1996-97	Darlington	3	0		
1997-98	Darlington	19	3	26	3
1997-98	Newcastle U	0	0		
1998-99	Newcastle U	0	0		
1999-2000	Newcastle U	11	0	11	0
2000-01	Wimbledon	3	0	3	0
2000-01	Burnley	4	0	4	0

SELLEY, Ian (M) — 52 0
H: 5 10 W: 10 09 b.Chertsey 14-6-74
Source: Trainee. Honours: England Youth, Under-21.

Season	Club	App	Gls	Tot App	Tot Gls
1992-93	Arsenal	9	0		
1993-94	Arsenal	18	0		
1994-95	Arsenal	13	0		
1995-96	Arsenal	0	0		
1996-97	Arsenal	1	0		
1996-97	Southend U	4	0	4	0
1997-98	Arsenal	0	0	41	0
1997-98	Fulham	3	0		
1998-99	Fulham	0	0		
1999-2000	Fulham	0	0	3	0
2000-01	Wimbledon	4	0	4	0

TAPP, Alex (M) — 0 0
H: 5 8 W: 11 10 b.Redhill 7-6-82
Source: Trainee.

Season	Club	App	Gls
1999-2000	Wimbledon	0	0
2000-01	Wimbledon	0	0

THOMAS, Michael (M) — 308 33
H: 5 9 W: 12 06 b.Lambeth 24-8-67
Source: Apprentice. Honours: England Schools, Youth, Under-21, B, 2 full caps.

Season	Club	App	Gls	Tot App	Tot Gls
1985-86	Arsenal	0	0		
1986-87	Arsenal	12	0		
1986-87	Portsmouth	3	0	3	0
1987-88	Arsenal	37	9		
1988-89	Arsenal	37	7		
1989-90	Arsenal	36	5		
1990-91	Arsenal	31	2		
1991-92	Arsenal	10	1	163	24
1991-92	Liverpool	17	3		
1992-93	Liverpool	8	1		
1993-94	Liverpool	7	0		
1994-95	Liverpool	23	0		
1995-96	Liverpool	27	1		
1996-97	Liverpool	31	3		
1997-98	Liverpool	11	1		
1997-98	Middlesbrough	10	0	10	0
1998-99	Liverpool	0	0		
1999-2000	Liverpool	0	0	124	9
2000-01	Wimbledon	8	0	8	0

TOWNSEND, Kurtis* (M) 0 0
b.Waltham Forest 28-8-83
2000–01 Wimbledon 0 0

WAEHLER, Kjetil (M) 88 6
H: 5 10 W: 11 00 b.Oslo 16-3-76
1992 Lyn 8 0
1993 Lyn 20 2
1994 Lyn 0 0
1995 Lyn 0 0
1996 Lyn 12 0
1997 Lyn 26 3
1998 Lyn 0 0
1999 Lyn 22 1 **88 6**
1999–2000 Wimbledon 0 0
2000–01 Wimbledon 0 0

WILLIAMS, Mark (D) 334 22
H: 6 0 W: 12 04 b.Stalybridge 28-9-70
Source: Newtown. *Honours:* Northern Ireland 17 full caps, 1 goal.
1991–92 Shrewsbury T 3 0
1992–93 Shrewsbury T 28 1
1993–94 Shrewsbury T 36 1
1994–95 Shrewsbury T 35 1 **102 3**
1995–96 Chesterfield 42 3
1996–97 Chesterfield 42 3
1997–98 Chesterfield 44 3
1998–99 Chesterfield 40 3 **168 12**
1999–2000 Watford 22 1 **22 1**
2000–01 Wimbledon 42 6 **42 6**

WILLMOTT, Chris (D) 35 1
H: 5 11 W: 10 12 b.Bedford 30-9-77
Source: Trainee.
1995–96 Luton T 0 0
1996–97 Luton T 0 0
1997–98 Luton T 0 0
1998–99 Luton T 14 0 **14 0**
1999–2000 Wimbledon 7 0
2000–01 Wimbledon 14 1 **21 1**

Scholars
Cook, Paul T; Gore, Shane S; Hallett, David JN; Innocent, Anton L; Kamara, Malvin G; Leigertwood, Mikele B; Lewington, Craig J; Lewington, Dean S; Maclean-Daley, Kingslee J; Murphy, David C; Nolan, Robert D; O'Flynn, Stephen J; O'Shea, Anthony S; Okikiolu, Samuel K; Reo-Coker, Nigel SA; Shirley, Mark D; Sikora, Christopher J; Sloma, Samuel M; Small, Wade K; Suleymanoglu, Ahmet; Taylor, Glen J; Wallace, Dean; Worgan, Lee J

WOLVERHAMPTON W

AL-JABER, Sami‡ (F) 4 0
H: 5 8 W: 11 02 b.Riyadh 11-12-72
Source: Al-Hilal.
2000–01 Wolverhampton W 4 0 **4 0**

ANDREWS, Keith (M) 28 1
H: 5 10 W: 12 04 b.Dublin 13-9-80
Source: Trainee.
1997–98 Wolverhampton W 0 0
1998–99 Wolverhampton W 0 0
1999–2000 Wolverhampton W 2 0
2000–01 Wolverhampton W 22 0 **24 0**
2000–01 *Oxford U* 4 1 **4 1**

BARRETT, Shane (F) 0 0
H: 5 10 W: 11 00 b.Luton 23-11-81
Source: Trainee.
1999–2000 Wolverhampton W 0 0
2000–01 Wolverhampton W 0 0

BAZELEY, Darren (D) 310 25
H: 5 11 W: 10 09 b.Northampton 5-10-72
Source: Trainee. *Honours:* England Under-21.
1989–90 Watford 1 0
1990–91 Watford 7 0
1991–92 Watford 34 6
1992–93 Watford 22 1
1993–94 Watford 10 1
1994–95 Watford 28 4
1995–96 Watford 41 1
1996–97 Watford 41 3
1997–98 Watford 16 3
1998–99 Watford 40 2 **240 21**
1999–2000 Wolverhampton W 46 3
2000–01 Wolverhampton W 24 1 **70 4**

BRANCH, Michael (F) 110 13
H: 5 10 W: 11 09 b.Liverpool 18-10-78
Source: Trainee. *Honours:* England Schools, Youth, Under-21.
1995–96 Everton 3 0
1996–97 Everton 25 3
1997–98 Everton 6 0
1998–99 Everton 7 0
1998–99 *Manchester C* 4 0 **4 0**
1999–2000 Everton 0 0 **41 3**
2000–01 Wolverhampton W 38 4
1999–2000 Wolverhampton W 27 6 **65 10**

BUTLER, Paul (D) 333 17
H: 6 3 W: 14 09 b.Manchester 2-11-72
Source: Trainee. *Honours:* Eire 1 full cap.
1990–91 Rochdale 2 0
1991–92 Rochdale 25 0
1992–93 Rochdale 16 2
1993–94 Rochdale 38 2
1994–95 Rochdale 39 3
1995–96 Rochdale 38 3 **158 10**
1996–97 Bury 41 2
1997–98 Bury 43 2 **84 4**
1998–99 Sunderland 44 2
1999–2000 Sunderland 32 1
2000–01 Sunderland 3 0 **79 3**
2000–01 Wolverhampton W 12 0 **12 0**

CAMARA, Mohammed (D) 135 2
H: 5 11 W: 11 09 b.Conakry 25-6-75
1993–94 Beauvais 19 0
1994–95 Beauvais 0 0
1995–96 Troyes 13 0 **13 0**
1996–97 Beauvais 35 0 **54 0**
1997–98 Le Havre 14 0
1998–99 Lille 34 2 **34 2**
1999–2000 Le Havre 2 0 **16 0**
2000–01 Wolverhampton W 18 0 **18 0**

COLEMAN, Kenneth (M) 0 0
b.Cork 20-9-82
Source: Scholar.
2000–01 Wolverhampton W 0 0

CROWE, Seamie* (M) 0 0
H: 5 7 W: 11 07 b.Galway 18-11-80
Source: Trainee.
1997–98 Wolverhampton W 0 0
1998–99 Wolverhampton W 0 0
1999–2000 Wolverhampton W 0 0
2000–01 Wolverhampton W 0 0

DICKSON, Andrew (M) 0 0
b.Belfast 3-8-82
Source: Scholar.
2000–01 Wolverhampton W 0 0

DINNING, Tony (M) 222 31
H: 6 0 W: 12 04 b.Wallsend 12-4-75
Source: Trainee.
1993–94 Newcastle U 0 0
1994–95 Stockport Co 40 1
1995–96 Stockport Co 10 1
1996–97 Stockport Co 20 2
1997–98 Stockport Co 30 4
1998–99 Stockport Co 41 5
1999–2000 Stockport Co 44 12
2000–01 Stockport Co 6 0 **191 25**
2000–01 Wolverhampton W 31 6 **31 6**

DOWNES, Lee‡ (M) 0 0
H: 6 0 W: 12 00 b.Wolverhampton 27-2-83
Source: Trainee.
1999–2000 Wolverhampton W 0 0
2000–01 Wolverhampton W 0 0

EMBLEN, Neil (M) 227 16
H: 6 1 W: 13 03 b.Bromley 19-6-71
Source: Tonbridge, Sittingbourne.
1993–94 Millwall 12 0 **12 0**
1994–95 Wolverhampton W 27 7
1995–96 Wolverhampton W 33 2
1996–97 Wolverhampton W 28 0
1997–98 Wolverhampton W 7 0
1997–98 Crystal Palace 13 0 **13 0**
1998–99 Wolverhampton W 33 2
1999–2000 Wolverhampton W 46 5
2000–01 Wolverhampton W 28 0 **202 16**

FLO, Havard* (F) 146 41
H: 6 2 W: 13 08 b.Volda 4-4-70
Source: Stryn, Sogndal. *Honours:* Norway 16 full caps, 3 goals.
1994–95 Aarhus 19 5
1995–96 Aarhus 23 10
1996–97 Aarhus 11 12 **53 27**
1996–97 Werder Bremen 14 0
1997–98 Werder Bremen 25 5
1998–99 Werder Bremen 16 0 **55 5**
1998–99 Wolverhampton W 19 5
1999–2000 Wolverhampton W 19 4
2000–01 Wolverhampton W 0 0 **38 9**

GREEN, Ryan (D) 18 0
H: 5 8 W: 10 10 b.Cardiff 20-10-80
Source: Danes Court. *Honours:* Wales Under-21, 2 full caps.
1997–98 Wolverhampton W 0 0
1998–99 Wolverhampton W 1 0
1999–2000 Wolverhampton W 0 0
2000–01 Wolverhampton W 7 0 **8 0**
2000–01 *Torquay U* 10 0 **10 0**

HAGAN, Conor‡ (D) 0 0
H: 5 10 W: 11 07 b.Belfast 31-3-82
Source: Trainee.
1999–2000 Wolverhampton W 0 0
2000–01 Wolverhampton W 0 0

KETSBAIA, Temuri (F) 314 78
H: 5 8 W: 10 12 b.Gale 18-3-68
Source: Dynamo Sukhumi. *Honours:* Georgia 48 full caps, 17 goals.
1987 Dynamo Tbilisi 14 4
1988 Dynamo Tbilisi 13 0
1989 Dynamo Tbilisi 27 4
1990 Dynamo Tbilisi 0 0 **54 8**
1991–92 Anorthosis 26 13
1992–93 Anorthosis 24 4
1993–94 Anorthosis 26 19 **76 36**
1994–95 AEK Athens 22 5
1995–96 AEK Athens 32 14
1996–97 AEK Athens 30 5 **84 24**
1997–98 Newcastle U 31 3
1998–99 Newcastle U 26 4
1999–2000 Newcastle U 21 0 **78 7**
2000–01 Wolverhampton W 22 3 **22 3**

LARKIN, Colin (F) 3 0
H: 5 9 W: 11 07 b.Dundalk 27-4-82
Source: Trainee.
1998–99 Wolverhampton W 0 0
1999–2000 Wolverhampton W 1 0
2000–01 Wolverhampton W 2 0 **3 0**

LEONARD, Gerard‡ (F) 0 0
H: 5 9 W: 11 04 b.Drogheda 7-7-82
Source: Trainee.
1999–2000 Wolverhampton W 0 0
2000–01 Wolverhampton W 0 0

LESCOTT, Jolean (D) 37 2
H: 6 2 W: 13 00 b.Birmingham 16-8-82
Source: Trainee. *Honours:* England Youth.
1999–2000 Wolverhampton W 0 0
2000–01 Wolverhampton W 37 2 **37 2**

LOUGHLIN, Paul‡ (D) 0 0
H: 5 10 W: 11 00 b.Dublin 5-10-81
Source: Stella Maris.
1998–99 Wolverhampton W 0 0
1999–2000 Wolverhampton W 0 0
2000–01 Wolverhampton W 0 0

McQUADE, Scott (M) 0 0
H: 5 7 W: 10 06 b.Dumfries 7-1-82
Source: Trainee.
2000–01 Wolverhampton W 0 0

MELLIGAN, John (M) 0 0
b.Dublin 11-2-82
Source: Trainee.
2000–01 Wolverhampton W 0 0

MURRAY, Matt (G) 0 0
H: 6 3 W: 13 07 b.Solihull 2-5-81
Source: Trainee. *Honours:* England Youth.
1997–98 Wolverhampton W 0 0
1998–99 Wolverhampton W 0 0
1999–2000 Wolverhampton W 0 0
2000–01 Wolverhampton W 0 0

MUSCAT, Kevin (D) 196 16
H: 5 11 W: 11 07 b.Crawley 7-8-73
Source: From Sunshine George Cross 9 apps, Heidelberg 18 apps, South Melbourne 73 apps, 6 goals. *Honours:* Australia 39 full caps, 9 goals.
1996–97 Crystal Palace 44 2
1997–98 Crystal Palace 9 0 **53 2**
1997–98 Wolverhampton W 24 3
1998–99 Wolverhampton W 37 4
1999–2000 Wolverhampton W 45 4
2000–01 Wolverhampton W 37 3 **143 14**

NAYLOR, Lee (D) 115 4
H: 5 8 W: 12 00 b.Bloxwich 19-3-80
Source: Trainee. *Honours:* England Youth, Under-21.
1997–98 Wolverhampton W 16 0
1998–99 Wolverhampton W 23 1
1999–2000 Wolverhampton W 30 2
2000–01 Wolverhampton W 46 1 **115 4**

NDAH, George (F) 194 30
H: 6 1 W: 11 04 b.Dulwich 23-12-74
Source: Trainee.
1992–93 Crystal Palace 13 0
1993–94 Crystal Palace 1 0
1994–95 Crystal Palace 12 1
1995–96 Crystal Palace 23 4
1995–96 *Bournemouth* 12 2 **12 2**
1996–97 Crystal Palace 26 3
1997–98 Crystal Palace 3 0 **78 8**
1997–98 *Gillingham* 4 0 **4 0**
1997–98 Swindon T 14 2
1998–99 Swindon T 41 11
1999–2000 Swindon T 12 1 **67 14**

1999–2000	Wolverhampton W	4	0		
2000–01	Wolverhampton W	29	6	33	6

NIESTROJ, Robert (M)   6   0
H: 5 10   W: 11 03   b.Oppeln 2-12-74
Source: Fortuna Dusseldorf.

1998–99	Wolverhampton W	5	0		
1999–2000	Wolverhampton W	1	0		
2000–01	Wolverhampton W	0	0	6	0

OAKES, Michael (G)   126   0
H: 6 2   W: 14 07   b.Northwich 30-10-73
Source: Trainee. *Honours:* England Under-21.

1991–92	Aston Villa	0	0		
1992–93	Aston Villa	0	0		
1993–94	Aston Villa	0	0		
1993–94	*Scarborough*	1	0	1	0
1993–94	*Tranmere R*	0	0		
1994–95	Aston Villa	0	0		
1995–96	Aston Villa	0	0		
1996–97	Aston Villa	20	0		
1997–98	Aston Villa	8	0		
1998–99	Aston Villa	23	0		
1999–2000	Aston Villa	0	0	51	0
1999–2000	Wolverhampton W	28	0		
2000–01	Wolverhampton W	46	0	74	0

POLLET, Ludovic (D)   208   10
H: 6 0   W: 12 06   b.Vieux-conde 18-6-70

1991–92	Cannes	9	0		
1992–93	Cannes	6	0		
1993–94	Cannes	8	1		
1994–95	Cannes	15	2	38	3
1995–96	Le Havre	26	0		
1996–97	Le Havre	21	0		
1997–98	Le Havre	34	0		
1998–99	Le Havre	21	0	102	0
1999–2000	Wolverhampton W	39	5		
2000–01	Wolverhampton W	29	2	68	7

PROUDLOCK, Adam (M)   39   12
H: 6 0   W: 12 00   b.Wellington 9-5-81
Source: Trainee.

1999–2000	Wolverhampton W	0	0		
2000–01	*Clyde*	4	4	4	4
2000–01	Wolverhampton W	35	8	35	8

ROBINSON, Carl (M)   145   17
H: 5 10   W: 12 10   b.Llandrindod Wells
13-10-76
Source: Trainee. *Honours:* Wales Under-21, B, 4 full caps.

1995–96	Wolverhampton W	0	0		
1995–96	*Shrewsbury T*	4	0	4	0
1996–97	Wolverhampton W	2	0		
1997–98	Wolverhampton W	32	3		
1998–99	Wolverhampton W	34	8		
1999–2000	Wolverhampton W	33	3		
2000–01	Wolverhampton W	40	3	141	17

ROUSSEL, Cedric (F)   83   19
H: 6 3   W: 13 00   b.Mons 6-1-78
Honours: La Louviere.

1998–99	Gent	31	8		
1999–2000	Gent	4	3	35	11
1999–2000	Coventry C	22	6		
2000–01	Coventry C	17	2	39	8
2000–01	Wolverhampton W	9	0	9	0

SEDGLEY, Steve‡ (D)   459   36
H: 6 1   W: 13 13   b.Enfield 26-5-68
Source: Apprentice. *Honours:* England Under-21.

1986–87	Coventry C	26	0		
1987–88	Coventry C	27	2		
1988–89	Coventry C	31	1	84	3
1989–90	Tottenham H	32	0		
1990–91	Tottenham H	34	0		
1991–92	Tottenham H	34	0		
1992–93	Tottenham H	22	3		
1993–94	Tottenham H	42	6	164	9
1994–95	Ipswich T	26	4		
1995–96	Ipswich T	40	4		
1996–97	Ipswich T	39	7	105	15
1997–98	Wolverhampton W	19	0		
1998–99	Wolverhampton W	44	3		
1999–2000	Wolverhampton W	38	5		
2000–01	Wolverhampton W	5	1	106	9

SINTON, Andy* (M)   610   74
H: 5 7   W: 10 07   b.Newcastle 19-3-66
Source: Apprentice. *Honours:* England Schools, B, 12 full caps.

1982–83	Cambridge U	13	5		
1983–84	Cambridge U	34	6		
1984–85	Cambridge U	26	2		
1985–86	Cambridge U	20	0	93	13
1985–86	Brentford	26	3		
1986–87	Brentford	46	5		
1987–88	Brentford	46	11		
1988–89	Brentford	31	9	149	28
1988–89	QPR	10	3		
1989–90	QPR	38	6		
1990–91	QPR	38	3		
1991–92	QPR	38	3		
1992–93	QPR	36	7	160	22
1993–94	Sheffield W	25	3		
1994–95	Sheffield W	25	0		
1995–96	Sheffield W	10	0	60	3
1995–96	Tottenham H	9	0		
1996–97	Tottenham H	33	6		
1997–98	Tottenham H	19	0		
1998–99	Tottenham H	22	0	83	6
1999–2000	Wolverhampton W	35	0		
2000–01	Wolverhampton W	30	2	65	2

STOWELL, Mike* (G)   428   0
H: 6 2   W: 13 10   b.Portsmouth 19-4-65
Source: Leyland Motors.

1984–85	Preston NE	0	0		
1985–86	Preston NE	0	0		
1985–86	Everton	0	0		
1986–87	Everton	0	0		
1987–88	*Chester C*	14	0	14	0
1987–88	*York C*	6	0	6	0
1987–88	*Manchester C*	14	0	14	0
1988–89	Everton	0	0		
1988–89	*Port Vale*	7	0	7	0
1988–89	Wolverhampton W	7	0		
1989–90	Everton	0	0		
1989–90	*Preston NE*	2	0	2	0
1990–91	Wolverhampton W	39	0		
1991–92	Wolverhampton W	46	0		
1992–93	Wolverhampton W	26	0		
1993–94	Wolverhampton W	46	0		
1994–95	Wolverhampton W	37	0		
1995–96	Wolverhampton W	38	0		
1996–97	Wolverhampton W	46	0		
1997–98	Wolverhampton W	35	0		
1998–99	Wolverhampton W	46	0		
1999–2000	Wolverhampton W	18	0		
2000–01	Wolverhampton W	1	0	385	0

TAYLOR, Robert (F)   332   113
H: 6 1   W: 13 08   b.Norwich 30-4-71
Source: Trainee.

1989–90	Norwich C	0	0		
1990–91	Norwich C	0	0		
1991–92	*Leyton Orient*	3	1		
1991–92	Birmingham C	0	0		
1991–92	Leyton Orient	11	1		
1992–93	Leyton Orient	39	18		
1993–94	Leyton Orient	23	1	76	21
1993–94	Brentford	5	2		
1994–95	Brentford	43	23		
1995–96	Brentford	42	11		
1996–97	Brentford	43	7		
1997–98	Brentford	40	13	173	56
1998–99	Gillingham	43	16		
1999–2000	Gillingham	15	15	58	31
2000–01	Manchester C	16	5	16	5
2000–01	Wolverhampton W	9	0	9	0

TAYLOR, Scott* (M)   303   33
H: 5 9   W: 11 05   b.Portsmouth 23-11-70
Source: Trainee.

1988–89	Reading	3	0		
1989–90	Reading	29	2		
1990–91	Reading	32	1		
1991–92	Reading	29	2		
1992–93	Reading	32	5		
1993–94	Reading	38	6		
1994–95	Reading	44	8	207	24
1995–96	Leicester C	39	6		
1996–97	Leicester C	25	0		
1997–98	Leicester C	0	0		
1998–99	Leicester C	0	0		
1999–2000	Wolverhampton W	28	3		
2000–01	Wolverhampton W	4	0	32	3

TUDOR, Shane (M)   1   0
H: 5 8   W: 11 00   b.Wolverhampton 10-2-82
Source: Trainee.

1999–2000	Wolverhampton W	0	0		
2000–01	Wolverhampton W	1	0	1	0

WARD, Graham (M)   0   0
b.Dublin 25-2-83
Source: Scholar.

2000–01	Wolverhampton W	0	0		

Scholars
Bampfield, Steve D; Clark, Nicholas E; Clingan, Samuel G; Clyde, Mark G; Danks, Mark J; Gilmore, Craig C; Jones, Jimmi L; Kerr, Aaron G; McChrystal, Mark T; McGrane, Ian J; Morrow, Andrew J; Slater, Christopher J; Solly, Lewis A; Tower, Andrew R; Walters, Marlon J; Willis, James R

Associated Schoolboys
Clark, David; Rollins, Mark

Players who do not hold a current contract but their registrations have been retained by the club
Downes, Lee; Mitchell, Patrick J

WREXHAM

BARRETT, Paul (M)   52   2
H: 5 9   W: 11 04   b.Newcastle 13-4-78
Source: Trainee.

1996–97	Newcastle U	0	0		
1997–98	Newcastle U	0	0		
1998–99	Newcastle U	0	0		
1998–99	Wrexham	10	0		
1999–2000	Wrexham	18	2		
2000–01	Wrexham	24	0	52	2

BLACKWOOD, Michael (F)   24   2
H: 5 11   W: 11 10   b.Birmingham 30-9-79
Source: Trainee.

1998–99	Aston Villa	0	0		
1999–2000	Aston Villa	0	0		
1999–2000	Chester C	9	2	9	2
2000–01	Wrexham	15	0	15	0

BOUANANE, Emad* (D)   17   0
H: 6 0   W: 13 00   b.Paris 22-11-76

2000–01	Wrexham	0	0	17	0

CAREY, Brian# (D)   267   9
H: 6 3   W: 13 02   b.Cork 31-5-68
Source: Cork C. *Honours:* Eire 3 full caps.

1989–90	Manchester U	0	0		
1990–91	Manchester U	0	0		
1990–91	*Wrexham*	3	0		
1991–92	Manchester U	0	0		
1991–92	*Wrexham*	13	1		
1992–93	Manchester U	0	0		
1993–94	Leicester C	27	0		
1994–95	Leicester C	12	0		
1995–96	Leicester C	19	1	58	1
1996–97	Wrexham	38	0		
1997–98	Wrexham	43	1		
1998–99	Wrexham	36	2		
1999–2000	Wrexham	43	1		
2000–01	Wrexham	33	3	209	8

CHALK, Martyn# (F)   210   17
H: 5 6   W: 11 03   b.Swindon 30-8-69
Source: Louth U.

1990–91	Derby Co	0	0		
1991–92	Derby Co	7	1		
1992–93	Derby Co	0	0		
1993–94	Derby Co	0	0	7	1
1994–95	Stockport Co	33	6		
1995–96	Stockport Co	10	0	43	6
1995–96	Wrexham	19	4		
1996–97	Wrexham	43	1		
1997–98	Wrexham	26	1		
1998–99	Wrexham	28	0		
1999–2000	Wrexham	20	0		
2000–01	Wrexham	24	4	160	10

DEARDEN, Kevin* (G)   338   0
H: 5 11   W: 12 06   b.Luton 8-3-70
Source: Trainee.

1988–89	Tottenham H	0	0		
1988–89	*Cambridge U*	15	0	15	0
1989–90	Tottenham H	0	0		
1989–90	*Hartlepool U*	10	0	10	0
1989–90	*Oxford U*	0	0		
1989–90	*Swindon T*	1	0	1	0
1990–91	Tottenham H	0	0		
1990–91	*Peterborough U*	7	0	7	0
1990–91	*Hull C*	3	0	3	0
1991–92	Tottenham H	0	0		
1991–92	*Rochdale*	2	0	2	0
1991–92	*Birmingham C*	12	0	12	0
1992–93	Tottenham H	1	0		
1992–93	Portsmouth	0	0		
1993–94	Tottenham H	0	0	1	0
1993–94	Brentford	35	0		
1994–95	Brentford	43	0		
1995–96	Brentford	41	0		
1996–97	Brentford	44	0		
1997–98	Brentford	35	0		
1998–99	Brentford	7	0	205	0
1998–99	*Barnet*	1	0	1	0
1998–99	*Huddersfield T*	0	0		
1999–2000	Wrexham	45	0		
2000–01	Wrexham	36	0	81	0

EDWARDS, Carlos (F)   36   4
H: 5 10   W: 12 00   b.Trinidad 24-10-78
Honours: Trinidad & Tobago full caps.

2000–01	Wrexham	36	4	36	4

FAULCONBRIDGE, Craig (F)   97   19
H: 6 1   W: 13 00   b.Nuneaton 20-4-78
Source: Trainee.

1996–97	Coventry C	0	0		
1997–98	Coventry C	0	0		
1997–98	*Dunfermline Ath*	7	1		
1998–99	*Dunfermline Ath*	6	0	13	1
1998–99	*Hull C*	10	0	10	0
1999–2000	Wrexham	35	8		
2000–01	Wrexham	39	10	74	18

FERGUSON, Darren (M) 224 17
H: 5 10 W: 11 10 b.Glasgow 9-2-72
Source: Trainee. *Honours:* Scotland Under-21.

1990–91	Manchester U	5	0
1991–92	Manchester U	4	0
1992–93	Manchester U	15	0
1993–94	Manchester U	3	0	27	0
1993–94	Wolverhampton W	14	0
1994–95	Wolverhampton W	24	0
1995–96	Wolverhampton W	33	1
1996–97	Wolverhampton W	16	3
1997–98	Wolverhampton W	26	0
1998–99	Wolverhampton W	4	0
1999–2000	Wolverhampton W	0	0	117	4
1999–2000	Wrexham	37	4
2000–01	Wrexham	43	9	80	13

GIBSON, Robin (F) 59 3
H: 5 7 W: 10 07 b.Crewe 15-11-79
Source: Trainee.

1998–99	Wrexham	7	1
1999–2000	Wrexham	24	1
2000–01	Wrexham	28	1	59	3

HANNON, Kevin* (D) 1 0
H: 5 11 W: 11 05 b.Whiston 4-5-80
Source: Trainee.

1999–2000	Wrexham	1	0
2000–01	Wrexham	0	0	1	0

HARDY, Phil* (D) 349 1
H: 5 7 W: 11 08 b.Chester 9-4-73
Source: Trainee. *Honours:* Eire Under-21.

1989–90	Wrexham	1	0
1990–91	Wrexham	32	0
1991–92	Wrexham	42	0
1992–93	Wrexham	32	0
1993–94	Wrexham	25	0
1994–95	Wrexham	44	0
1995–96	Wrexham	42	0
1996–97	Wrexham	13	0
1997–98	Wrexham	34	0
1998–99	Wrexham	33	0
1999–2000	Wrexham	38	1
2000–01	Wrexham	13	0	349	1

LAWRENCE, Dennis (F) 3 0
H: 6 7 W: 14 00 b.Trinidad 1-8-74
Source: Defence Force.

2000–01	Wrexham	3	0	3	0

LOWE, David* (F) 562 133
H: 5 10 W: 11 04 b.Liverpool 30-8-65
Source: Apprentice. *Honours:* England Youth, Under-21.

1982–83	Wigan Ath	28	6
1983–84	Wigan Ath	40	8
1984–85	Wigan Ath	29	5
1985–86	Wigan Ath	46	5
1986–87	Wigan Ath	45	16
1987–88	Ipswich T	41	17
1988–89	Ipswich T	32	6
1989–90	Ipswich T	34	13
1990–91	Ipswich T	13	0
1991–92	Ipswich T	14	1	134	37
1991–92	*Port Vale*	9	2
1992–93	Leicester C	32	11
1993–94	Leicester C	5	0
1993–94	*Port Vale*	19	5	28	7
1994–95	Leicester C	29	8
1995–96	Leicester C	28	3	94	22
1995–96	Wigan Ath	7	3
1996–97	Wigan Ath	42	6
1997–98	Wigan Ath	43	16
1998–99	Wigan Ath	16	1	296	66
1999–2000	Wrexham	10	1
2000–01	Wrexham	0	0	10	1

McGREGOR, Mark# (D) 244 11
H: 5 10 W: 11 05 b.Chester 16-2-77
Source: Trainee.

1994–95	Wrexham	1	0
1995–96	Wrexham	32	1
1996–97	Wrexham	38	1
1997–98	Wrexham	42	2
1998–99	Wrexham	43	1
1999–2000	Wrexham	45	1
2000–01	Wrexham	43	5	244	11

MOODY, Adrian§ (D) 3 0
b.Birkenhead 29-9-82
Source: Scholar.

2000–01	Wrexham	3	0	3	0

MORRELL, Andy (F) 40 4
H: 5 11 W: 11 06 b.Doncaster 28-9-74
Source: Newcastle Blue Star.

1998–99	Wrexham	7	0
1999–2000	Wrexham	13	1
2000–01	Wrexham	20	3	40	4

OWEN, Gareth* (M) 350 36
H: 5 8 W: 12 00 b.Chester 21-10-71
Source: Trainee. *Honours:* Wales Under-21.

1989–90	Wrexham	13	0
1990–91	Wrexham	27	2
1991–92	Wrexham	36	7
1992–93	Wrexham	41	3
1993–94	Wrexham	27	3
1994–95	Wrexham	28	3
1995–96	Wrexham	19	2
1996–97	Wrexham	23	1
1997–98	Wrexham	40	7
1998–99	Wrexham	35	3
1999–2000	Wrexham	39	3
2000–01	Wrexham	22	2	350	36

PEJIC, Shaun§ (D) 1 0
b.Hereford 16-11-82

2000–01	Wrexham	1	0	1	0

PHILLIPS, Wayne (M) 239 17
H: 5 11 W: 11 00 b.Bangor 15-12-70
Source: Trainee. *Honours:* Wales B.

1989–90	Wrexham	5	0
1990–91	Wrexham	28	0
1991–92	Wrexham	30	3
1992–93	Wrexham	15	0
1993–94	Wrexham	21	1
1994–95	Wrexham	18	1
1995–96	Wrexham	44	5
1996–97	Wrexham	26	5
1997–98	Wrexham	20	1
1997–98	Stockport Co	13	0
1998–99	Stockport Co	9	0	22	0
1999–2000	Wrexham	3	0
2000–01	Wrexham	7	1	217	17

RIDLER, Dave* (D) 116 1
H: 6 0 W: 12 02 b.Liverpool 12-3-76
Source: Prescot T.

1996–97	Wrexham	11	0
1997–98	Wrexham	20	0
1998–99	Wrexham	36	1
1999–2000	Wrexham	25	0
2000–01	Wrexham	24	0	116	1

ROBERTS, Steve (D) 26 0
H: 6 2 W: 11 06 b.Wrexham 24-2-80
Source: Trainee. *Honours:* Wales Under-21.

1997–98	Wrexham	0	0
1998–99	Wrexham	0	0
1999–2000	Wrexham	19	0
2000–01	Wrexham	7	0	26	0

ROGERS, Kristian (G) 6 0
H: 6 2 W: 11 07 b.Chester 2-10-80
Honours: England Schools.

1999–2000	Wrexham	1	0
2000–01	Wrexham	5	0	6	0

RUSSELL, Kevin# (M) 445 88
H: 5 9 W: 10 12 b.Portsmouth 6-12-66
Source: Brighton & HA Apprentice. *Honours:* England Youth.

1984–85	Portsmouth	0	0
1985–86	Portsmouth	1	0
1986–87	Portsmouth	3	1	4	1
1987–88	Wrexham	38	21
1988–89	Wrexham	46	22
1989–90	Leicester C	10	0
1990–91	Leicester C	13	5
1990–91	*Peterborough U*	7	3	7	3
1990–91	*Cardiff C*	3	0	3	0
1991–92	Leicester C	20	5	43	10
1991–92	*Hereford U*	3	1	3	1
1991–92	Stoke C	5	1
1992–93	Stoke C	40	5	45	6
1993–94	Burnley	28	6	28	6
1993–94	Bournemouth	17	1
1994–95	Bournemouth	13	0	30	1
1994–95	Notts Co	11	0	11	0
1995–96	Wrexham	40	7
1996–97	Wrexham	41	0
1997–98	Wrexham	16	0
1998–99	Wrexham	31	2
1999–2000	Wrexham	33	4
2000–01	Wrexham	26	4	271	60

SAM, Hector (F) 20 6
H: 5 9 W: 11 04 b.Trinidad 25-2-78
Source: San Juan Jabloteh. *Honours:* Trinidad & Tobago full caps.

2000–01	Wrexham	20	6	20	6

THOMAS, Steve (M) 12 0
H: 5 10 W: 11 07 b.Hartlepool 23-6-79
Source: Trainee. *Honours:* Wales Under-21.

1997–98	Wrexham	0	0
1998–99	Wrexham	4	0
1999–2000	Wrexham	2	0
2000–01	Wrexham	6	0	12	0

TRUNDLE, Lee (F) 14 8
b.Liverpool 10-10-76
Source: Rhyl.

2000–01	Wrexham	14	8	14	8

WALSH, Dave (G) 5 0
H: 6 1 W: 12 05 b.Wrexham 29-4-79
Source: Trainee. *Honours:* Wales Under-21.

1997–98	Wrexham	0	0
1998–99	Wrexham	0	0
1999–2000	Wrexham	0	0
2000–01	Wrexham	5	0	5	0

WARREN, David (M) 1 0
H: 5 10 W: 11 05 b.Cork 28-2-81
Source: Mayfield U.

1999–2000	Wrexham	1	0
2000–01	Wrexham	0	0	1	0

WILLIAMS, Danny* (M) 39 3
H: 6 2 W: 13 01 b.Wrexham 12-7-79
Source: Trainee. *Honours:* Wales Under-21.

1996–97	Liverpool	0	0
1997–98	Liverpool	0	0
1998–99	Liverpool	0	0
1998–99	Liverpool	0	0
1999–2000	Wrexham	24	1
2000–01	Wrexham	15	2	39	3

Scholars
Arkell, Adam N; Campbell, Luke; Cocks, Ian T; Dabbs, Matthew S; Evans, Mark G; Hamill, Christopher D; Jackson, Mark G; Johnson, Darran M; Jones, Darren; Jones, Mark A; Jones, Osian L; Jones, Paul D; Lee, Kenneth; Moody, Adrian JH; Moody, Craig; Pejic, Shaun M; Simpson, Michael S; Stacey, Alec J; Sudlow, Gareth GL; Sweet, David; Watkin, Daniel T; Whitfield, Paul M;
Associated Schoolboys
Bates, Matthew J; Brand, Benjamin J; Cargill, Gary S; Entwistle, Mark R; Graham, Adam; Jones, Adam; O'Toole, Dominic; Taylor, Michael J

WYCOMBE W

BAIRD, Andy (F) 73 13
H: 5 10 W: 11 13 b.East Kilbride 18-1-79
Source: Trainee.

1997–98	Wycombe W	2	0
1998–99	Wycombe W	28	6
1999–2000	Wycombe W	30	4
2000–01	Wycombe W	13	3	73	13

BATES, Jamie (D) 499 22
H: 6 2 W: 14 06 b.Croydon 24-2-68
Source: Trainee.

1986–87	Brentford	24	1
1987–88	Brentford	23	1
1988–89	Brentford	36	1
1989–90	Brentford	15	0
1990–91	Brentford	32	2
1991–92	Brentford	42	1
1992–93	Brentford	24	0
1993–94	Brentford	45	2
1994–95	Brentford	38	2
1995–96	Brentford	36	4
1996–97	Brentford	37	2
1997–98	Brentford	40	1
1998–99	Brentford	27	1	419	18
1998–99	Wycombe W	9	0
1999–2000	Wycombe W	32	1
2000–01	Wycombe W	39	3	80	4

BEETON, Alan‡ (D) 55 0
H: 5 11 W: 11 13 b.Watford 4-10-78
Source: Trainee.

1997–98	Wycombe W	20	0
1998–99	Wycombe W	16	0
1999–2000	Wycombe W	16	0
2000–01	Wycombe W	3	0	55	0

BRADY, Matt* (M) 22 2
H: 5 10 W: 10 04 b.Barnet 27-10-77
Source: Trainee.

1994–95	Barnet	1	0
1995–96	Barnet	2	0
1996–97	Barnet	7	0
1997–98	Barnet	0	0
1998–99	Barnet	0	0	10	0
	From Boreham Wood.		
1999–2000	Wycombe W	7	2
2000–01	Wycombe W	5	0	12	2

BROWN, Steve (M) 428 40
H: 5 10 W: 11 12 b.Northampton 6-7-66
1985–86	Northampton T	0	0
	From Irthlingborough D.		
1989–90	Northampton T	21	1
1990–91	Northampton T	40	2
1991–92	Northampton T	35	3

1992–93	Northampton T	38	9		
1993–94	Northampton T	24	4	158	19
1993–94	Wycombe W	9	2		
1994–95	Wycombe W	40	1		
1995–96	Wycombe W	38	0		
1996–97	Wycombe W	34	5		
1997–98	Wycombe W	40	3		
1998–99	Wycombe W	38	3		
1999–2000	Wycombe W	39	3		
2000–01	Wycombe W	32	4	270	21

BULMAN, Dannie (M) — 76 6
H: 5 9 W: 11 12 b.Ashford 24-1-79
Source: Ashford T.

1998–99	Wycombe W	11	1		
1999–2000	Wycombe W	29	1		
2000–01	Wycombe W	36	4	76	6

CARROLL, Dave# (M) — 290 40
H: 5 10 W: 11 12 b.Paisley 20-9-66
Source: Ruislip Manor. *Honours:* England Schools.

1993–94	Wycombe W	41	6		
1994–95	Wycombe W	41	6		
1995–96	Wycombe W	46	8		
1996–97	Wycombe W	43	9		
1997–98	Wycombe W	39	1		
1998–99	Wycombe W	32	6		
1999–2000	Wycombe W	36	2		
2000–01	Wycombe W	12	2	290	40

CASTLEDINE, Stewart (M) — 52 7
H: 6 1 W: 12 00 b.Wandsworth 22-1-73
Source: Trainee.

1991–92	Wimbledon	2	0		
1992–93	Wimbledon	0	0		
1993–94	Wimbledon	3	1		
1994–95	Wimbledon	6	1		
1995–96	Wimbledon	4	1		
1995–96	*Wycombe W*	7	3	28	4
1996–97	Wimbledon	6	1		
1997–98	Wimbledon	6	0		
1998–99	Wimbledon	1	0		
1999–2000	Wimbledon	0	0	28	4
2000–01	Wycombe W	17	0	24	3

COUSINS, Jason (D) — 298 6
H: 5 10 W: 12 07 b.Hayes 4-10-70
Source: Trainee.

1989–90	Brentford	13	0		
1990–91	Brentford	8	0	21	0
From Wycombe W					
1993–94	Wycombe W	37	1		
1994–95	Wycombe W	41	2		
1995–96	Wycombe W	30	0		
1996–97	Wycombe W	37	0		
1997–98	Wycombe W	29	0		
1998–99	Wycombe W	34	2		
1999–2000	Wycombe W	37	1		
2000–01	Wycombe W	32	0	277	6

DEVINE, Sean (F) — 177 78
H: 5 9 W: 13 00 b.Lewisham 6-9-72
Source: Omonia.

1995–96	Barnet	35	19		
1996–97	Barnet	31	11		
1997–98	Barnet	40	16		
1998–99	Barnet	20	1	126	47
1998–99	Wycombe W	12	8		
1999–2000	Wycombe W	39	23		
2000–01	Wycombe W	0	0	51	31

EMBLEN, Paul# (M) — 70 6
H: 5 9 W: 12 12 b.Bromley 3-4-76
Source: Tonbridge A.

1996–97	Charlton Ath	0	0		
1997–98	Charlton Ath	4	0		
1997–98	*Brighton & HA*	15	4	15	4
1998–99	Charlton Ath	0	0	4	0
1998–99	Wycombe W	35	2		
1999–2000	Wycombe W	16	0		
2000–01	Wycombe W	0	0	51	2

ESSANDOH, Roy* (M) — 43 3
H: 6 0 W: 12 03 b.Belfast 17-2-76
Source: Cumbernauld Juniors.

1994–95	Motherwell	0	0		
1995–96	Motherwell	4	0		
1996–97	Motherwell	1	0	5	0
From St Polten					
1998	Vaasa	4	0		
1999	Vaasa	21	3	25	3
From Rushden & D					
2000–01	Wycombe W	13	0	13	0

HARKIN, Maurice* (M) — 73 2
H: 5 8 W: 11 05 b.Derry 16-8-79
Source: Trainee. *Honours:* Northern Ireland Under-21.

1996–97	Wycombe W	4	0		
1997–98	Wycombe W	35	2		
1998–99	Wycombe W	2	0		
1999–2000	Wycombe W	17	0		
2000–01	Wycombe W	15	0	73	2

HOLSGROVE, Peter* (M) — 0 0
b.Wendover 16-4-82
Source: Scholarship.

| 1999–2000 | Wycombe W | 0 | 0 | | |
| 2000–01 | Wycombe W | 0 | 0 | | |

JOHNSON, Roger§ (D) — 2 0
H: 6 3 W: 11 00 b.Ashford 28-4-83
Source: Trainee.

| 1999–2000 | Wycombe W | 1 | 0 | | |
| 2000–01 | Wycombe W | 1 | 0 | 2 | 0 |

LEE, Martyn (M) — 28 3
H: 5 6 W: 9 00 b.Guilford 10-8-80
Source: Trainee.

1998–99	Wycombe W	3	0		
1999–2000	Wycombe W	4	0		
2000–01	Wycombe W	21	3	28	3

MARSH, Chris (D) — 403 23
H: 5 11 W: 13 02 b.Dudley 14-1-70
Source: Trainee.

1987–88	Walsall	3	0		
1988–89	Walsall	13	0		
1989–90	Walsall	9	0		
1990–91	Walsall	23	2		
1991–92	Walsall	37	1		
1992–93	Walsall	33	3		
1993–94	Walsall	39	4		
1994–95	Walsall	38	9		
1995–96	Walsall	41	2		
1996–97	Walsall	30	0		
1997–98	Walsall	36	0		
1998–99	Walsall	43	2		
1999–2000	Walsall	40	0		
2000–01	Walsall	7	0	392	23
2000–01	Wycombe W	11	0	11	0

McCARTHY, Paul (D) — 341 11
H: 5 10 W: 13 10 b.Cork 4-8-71
Source: Trainee. *Honours:* Eire Youth, Under-21.

1989–90	Brighton & HA	3	0		
1990–91	Brighton & HA	21	0		
1991–92	Brighton & HA	20	0		
1992–93	Brighton & HA	30	0		
1993–94	Brighton & HA	37	3		
1994–95	Brighton & HA	37	2		
1995–96	Brighton & HA	33	1	181	6
1996–97	Wycombe W	40	0		
1997–98	Wycombe W	31	1		
1998–99	Wycombe W	29	1		
1999–2000	Wycombe W	22	1		
2000–01	Wycombe W	38	2	160	5

McSPORRAN, Jermaine (F) — 84 15
H: 5 10 W: 10 12 b.Manchester 1-1-77
Source: Oxford C.

1998–99	Wycombe W	26	4		
1999–2000	Wycombe W	38	9		
2000–01	Wycombe W	20	2	84	15

NUTTER, John‡ (D) — 1 0
b.Taplow 13-6-82
Source: Blackburn R Scholar.

| 2000–01 | Wycombe W | 1 | 0 | 1 | 0 |

OSBORN, Mark (G) — 1 0
H: 6 0 W: 14 01 b.Bletchley 19-6-81
Source: Trainee.

1998–99	Wycombe W	0	0		
1999–2000	Wycombe W	1	0		
2000–01	Wycombe W	0	0	1	0

PHELAN, Leeyon§ (F) — 2 0
b.Hammersmith 6-10-82
Source: Scholar.

| 2000–01 | Wycombe W | 2 | 0 | 2 | 0 |

RAMMELL, Andy (F) — 349 90
H: 6 1 W: 13 12 b.Nuneaton 10-2-67
Source: Atherstone U.

1987–88	Manchester U	0	0		
1989–90	Manchester U	0	0		
1990–91	Barnsley	40	12		
1991–92	Barnsley	37	8		
1992–93	Barnsley	30	7		
1993–94	Barnsley	34	6		
1994–95	Barnsley	24	7		
1995–96	Barnsley	20	4	185	44
1995–96	Southend U	7	2		
1996–97	Southend U	36	9		
1997–98	Southend U	26	2	69	13
1998–99	Walsall	39	18		
1999–2000	Walsall	30	5		
2000–01	Walsall	0	0	69	23
2000–01	Wycombe W	26	10	26	10

ROGERS, Mark (D) — 47 1
H: 5 11 W: 12 12 b.Guelph 3-11-75

1998–99	Wycombe W	0	0		
1999–2000	Wycombe W	25	0		
2000–01	Wycombe W	22	1	47	1

RYAN, Keith (M) — 225 23
H: 5 10 W: 12 06 b.Northampton 25-6-70
Source: Berkhamsted T.

1993–94	Wycombe W	42	1		
1994–95	Wycombe W	24	4		
1995–96	Wycombe W	23	4		
1996–97	Wycombe W	0	0		
1997–98	Wycombe W	40	3		
1998–99	Wycombe W	28	1		
1999–2000	Wycombe W	38	6		
2000–01	Wycombe W	30	4	225	23

SENDA, Danny (F) — 64 3
H: 5 10 W: 10 02 b.Harrow 17-4-81
Source: Southampton Trainee. *Honours:* England Youth.

1998–99	Wycombe W	6	0		
1999–2000	Wycombe W	27	1		
2000–01	Wycombe W	31	2	64	3

SIMPSON, Michael (M) — 223 11
H: 5 8 W: 11 07 b.Nottingham 28-2-74
Source: Trainee.

1992–93	Notts Co	0	0		
1993–94	Notts Co	6	1		
1994–95	Notts Co	19	2		
1995–96	Notts Co	23	0		
1996–97	Notts Co	1	0	49	3
1996–97	*Plymouth Arg*	12	0	12	0
1996–97	Wycombe W	20	1		
1997–98	Wycombe W	21	0		
1998–99	Wycombe W	33	4		
1999–2000	Wycombe W	43	0		
2000–01	Wycombe W	45	3	162	8

TAYLOR, Martin (G) — 302 0
H: 6 0 W: 13 11 b.Tamworth 9-12-66
Source: Mile Oak R.

1986–87	Derby Co	0	0		
1987–88	Derby Co	0	0		
1987–88	*Carlisle U*	10	0	10	0
1987–88	*Scunthorpe U*	8	0	8	0
1988–89	Derby Co	0	0		
1989–90	Derby Co	3	0		
1990–91	Derby Co	7	0		
1991–92	Derby Co	5	0		
1992–93	Derby Co	21	0		
1993–94	Derby Co	46	0		
1994–95	Derby Co	12	0		
1995–96	Derby Co	0	0		
1996–97	Derby Co	3	0	97	0
1996–97	*Crewe Alex*	6	0	6	0
1996–97	*Wycombe W*	4	0		
1997–98	Wycombe W	45	0		
1998–99	Wycombe W	44	0		
1999–2000	Wycombe W	42	0		
2000–01	Wycombe W	46	0	181	0

THOMPSON, Niall‡ (F) — 29 5
H: 5 11 W: 11 00 b.Birmingham 16-4-74
Source: Trainee.

1992–93	Crystal Palace	0	0		
1993–94	Crystal Palace	0	0		
1994–95	Colchester U	13	5	13	5
From Zulte VV.					
1997–98	Brentford	8	0	8	0
From BA Seals					
2000–01	Wycombe W	8	0	8	0

TOWNSEND, Ben (D) — 11 0
H: 5 10 W: 11 03 b.Reading 8-10-81
Source: Scholar.

| 1999–2000 | Wycombe W | 1 | 0 | | |
| 2000–01 | Wycombe W | 10 | 0 | 11 | 0 |

VINNICOMBE, Chris (D) — 275 6
H: 5 9 W: 10 12 b.Exeter 20-10-70
Source: Trainee. *Honours:* England Under-21.

1988–89	Exeter C	25	0		
1989–90	Exeter C	14	1	39	1
1989–90	Rangers	7	0		
1990–91	Rangers	10	1		
1991–92	Rangers	2	0		
1992–93	Rangers	0	0		
1993–94	Rangers	4	0	23	1
1994–95	Burnley	29	1		
1995–96	Burnley	35	2		
1996–97	Burnley	8	0		
1997–98	Burnley	23	0	95	3
1998–99	Wycombe W	41	0		
1999–2000	Wycombe W	35	0		
2000–01	Wycombe W	42	1	118	1

WESTHEAD, Mark* (G) — 4 0
H: 6 1 W: 14 05 b.Blackpool 19-7-75

1996–97	Bolton W	0	0		
1997–98	Bolton W	0	0		
From Telford U.					
1998–99	Wycombe W	2	0		
1999–2000	Wycombe W	2	0		
2000–01	Wycombe W	0	0	4	0

WHITTINGHAM, Guy* (F)   379 138
H: 6 1   W: 12 04   b.Evesham 10-11-64
Source: Yeovil T, Army.

1989-90	Portsmouth	42	23		
1990-91	Portsmouth	37	12		
1991-92	Portsmouth	35	11		
1992-93	Portsmouth	46	42		
1993-94	Aston Villa	18	3		
1993-94	Wolverhampton W	13	8		
1994-95	Aston Villa	7	2	25	5
1994-95	Sheffield W	21	9		
1995-96	Sheffield W	29	6		
1996-97	Sheffield W	33	3		
1997-98	Sheffield W	28	4		
1998-99	Sheffield W	2	0	113	22
1998-99	Wolverhampton W	10	1	23	9
1998-99	Portsmouth	9	7		
1998-99	Watford	5	0	5	0
1999-2000	Portsmouth	25	4		
2000-01	Portsmouth	1	0	195	99
2000-01	Peterborough U	5	1	5	1
2000-01	Oxford U	1	1	1	1
2000-01	Wycombe W	12	1	12	1

Scholars
Cook, Lewis L; Dash, Scott; Dixon, Jonathan J; Johnson, Roger; Leach, Marc T; Lynott, Patrick J; McCullagh, Ryan; Nutter, John RW; Parsons, Ryan D; Phelan, Leeyon; Simpemba, Ian F; Smillie, Jack; Sudheimer, Kai; Williams, Steve

YORK C

AGNEW, Steve* (M)   401 46
H: 5 10   W: 10 06   b.Shipley 9-11-65
Source: Apprentice.

1983-84	Barnsley	1	0		
1984-85	Barnsley	10	1		
1985-86	Barnsley	2	0		
1986-87	Barnsley	33	0		
1987-88	Barnsley	25	6		
1988-89	Barnsley	39	6		
1989-90	Barnsley	46	8		
1990-91	Barnsley	38	8	194	29
1991-92	Blackburn R	2	0		
1992-93	Blackburn R	0	0	2	0
1992-93	Portsmouth	5	0	5	0
1992-93	Leicester C	9	1		
1993-94	Leicester C	36	3		
1994-95	Leicester C	11	0	56	4
1994-95	Sunderland	16	2		
1995-96	Sunderland	29	5		
1996-97	Sunderland	15	2		
1997-98	Sunderland	3	0	63	9
1998-99	York C	20	2		
1999-2000	York C	22	0		
2000-01	York C	39	2	81	4

ALCIDE, Colin (F)   203 37
H: 6 2   W: 13 11   b.Huddersfield 14-4-72
Source: Emley.

1995-96	Lincoln C	27	6		
1996-97	Lincoln C	42	7		
1997-98	Lincoln C	29	12		
1998-99	Lincoln C	23	1	121	26
1998-99	Hull C	17	3		
1999-2000	Hull C	12	1	29	4
1999-2000	York C	15	2		
2000-01	York C	38	5	53	7

BASHAM, Mike# (D)   131 5
H: 6 2   W: 13 09   b.Barking 27-9-73
Source: Trainee. *Honours:* England Schools.

1992-93	West Ham U	0	0		
1993-94	West Ham U	0	0		
1993-94	Colchester U	1	0	1	0
1993-94	Swansea C	5	0		
1994-95	Swansea C	13	0		
1995-96	Swansea C	11	1	29	1
1995-96	Peterborough U	14	1		
1996-97	Peterborough U	5	0	19	1
1997-98	Barnet	20	1		
1998-99	Barnet	32	1		
1999-2000	Barnet	15	0		
2000-01	Barnet	8	0	75	2
2000-01	York C	7	1	7	1

BRASS, Chris (D)   157 2
H: 5 9   W: 12 06   b.Easington 24-7-75
Source: Trainee.

1993-94	Burnley	0	0		
1994-95	Burnley	5	0		
1994-95	Torquay U	7	0	7	0
1995-96	Burnley	9	0		
1996-97	Burnley	39	0		
1997-98	Burnley	40	1		
1998-99	Burnley	34	0		
1999-2000	Burnley	7	0		
2000-01	Burnley	0	0	134	1
2000-01	Halifax T	6	0	6	0
2000-01	York C	10	1	10	1

BULLOCK, Lee (M)   57 3
H: 6 1   W: 12 07   b.Stockton 22-5-81
Source: Trainee.

1999-2000	York C	24	0		
2000-01	York C	33	3	57	3

CONLON, Barry (F)   128 28
H: 6 2   W: 13 07   b.Drogheda 1-12-78
Source: QPR Trainee. *Honours:* Eire Under-21.

1997-98	Manchester C	7	0		
1997-98	Plymouth Arg	13	2	13	2
1998-99	Manchester C	0	0	7	0
1998-99	Southend U	34	7	34	7
1999-2000	York C	40	11		
2000-01	York C	8	0	48	11
2000-01	Colchester U	26	8	26	8

COOPER, Richard (D)   17 0
H: 5 9   W: 10 07   b.Nottingham 27-9-79
Source: Trainee. *Honours:* England Schools, Youth.

1996-97	Nottingham F	0	0		
1997-98	Nottingham F	0	0		
1998-99	Nottingham F	0	0		
1999-2000	Nottingham F	1	0		
2000-01	Nottingham F	2	0	3	0
2000-01	York C	14	0	14	0

DARLOW, Kieran§ (D)   3 0
H: 6 0   W: 13 12   b.Bedford 9-11-82
Source: Trainee.

1999-2000	York C	2	0		
2000-01	York C	1	0	3	0

DUFFIELD, Peter (F)   292 101
H: 5 6   W: 10 04   b.Middlesbrough 4-2-69
Source: Apprentice.

1986-87	Middlesbrough	0	0		
1987-88	Sheffield U	11	1		
1987-88	Halifax T	12	6	12	6
1988-89	Sheffield U	38	11		
1989-90	Sheffield U	5	2		
1990-91	Sheffield U	2	0		
1990-91	Rotherham U	17	4	17	4
1991-92	Sheffield U	2	0		
1992-93	Sheffield U	0	0		
1992-93	Blackpool	5	1	5	1
1992-93	Bournemouth	0	0		
1992-93	Stockport Co	7	4	7	4
1992-93	Crewe Alex	2	0	2	0
1993-94	Sheffield U	0	0	58	14
1993-94	Hamilton A	36	19		
1994-95	Hamilton A	36	20	72	39
1995-96	Airdrieonians	24	6	24	6
1995-96	Raith R	9	5		
1996-97	Raith R	33	5		
1997-98	Raith R	0	0		
1998-99	Raith R	0	0	42	10
1998-99	Darlington	14	2		
1999-2000	Darlington	33	12	47	14
2000-01	York C	6	3	6	3

EDMONDSON, Darren (D)   285 9
H: 6 0   W: 12 10   b.Ulverston 4-11-71
Source: Trainee.

1990-91	Carlisle U	31	0		
1991-92	Carlisle U	27	2		
1992-93	Carlisle U	34	0		
1993-94	Carlisle U	22	3		
1994-95	Carlisle U	38	2		
1995-96	Carlisle U	42	1		
1996-97	Carlisle U	20	1	214	9
1996-97	Huddersfield T	10	0		
1997-98	Huddersfield T	19	0		
1998-99	Huddersfield T	3	0		
1998-99	Plymouth Arg	4	0	4	0
1999-2000	Huddersfield T	5	0	37	0
1999-2000	York C	7	0		
2000-01	York C	23	0	30	0

EMMERSON, Scott§ (F)   8 1
b.Durham 10-10-82
Source: Scholar.

2000-01	York C	8	1	8	1

FAIRCLOUGH, Chris‡ (D)   503 36
H: 5 11   W: 11 07   b.Nottingham 12-4-64
Source: Apprentice. *Honours:* England Under-21, B.

1981-82	Nottingham F	0	0		
1982-83	Nottingham F	15	0		
1983-84	Nottingham F	31	0		
1984-85	Nottingham F	35	0		
1985-86	Nottingham F	0	0		
1986-87	Nottingham F	26	1	107	1
1987-88	Tottenham H	40	4		
1988-89	Tottenham H	20	1	60	5
1988-89	Leeds U	11	0		
1989-90	Leeds U	42	8		
1990-91	Leeds U	34	4		
1991-92	Leeds U	31	2		
1992-93	Leeds U	30	3		
1993-94	Leeds U	40	4		
1994-95	Leeds U	5	0	193	21
1995-96	Bolton W	33	0		
1996-97	Bolton W	46	8		
1997-98	Bolton W	11	0	90	8
1998-99	Notts Co	16	1	16	1
1998-99	York C	11	0		
1999-2000	York C	26	0		
2000-01	York C	0	0	37	0

FETTIS, Alan (G)   212 2
H: 6 2   W: 13 00   b.Newtownards 1-2-71
Source: Ards. *Honours:* Northern Ireland 25 full caps.

1991-92	Hull C	43	0		
1992-93	Hull C	20	0		
1993-94	Hull C	37	0		
1994-95	Hull C	28	2		
1995-96	Hull C	7	0	135	2
1995-96	WBA	3	0	3	0
1996-97	Nottingham F	4	0		
1997-98	Nottingham F	0	0	4	0
1997-98	Blackburn R	8	0		
1998-99	Blackburn R	2	0		
1999-2000	Blackburn R	1	0	11	0
1999-2000	Leicester C	0	0		
1999-2000	York C	13	0		
2000-01	York C	46	0	59	0

FOX, Christian (M)   42 1
H: 5 11   W: 10 00   b.Auchenbrae 11-4-81
Source: Trainee.

1999-2000	York C	34	1		
2000-01	York C	8	0	42	1

HALL, Wayne* (D)   373 9
H: 5 9   W: 10 06   b.Rotherham 25-10-68
Source: Darlington.

1988-89	York C	2	0		
1989-90	York C	27	3		
1990-91	York C	46	1		
1991-92	York C	37	3		
1992-93	York C	42	1		
1993-94	York C	45	0		
1994-95	York C	37	0		
1995-96	York C	23	0		
1996-97	York C	13	0		
1997-98	York C	32	0		
1998-99	York C	27	1		
1999-2000	York C	23	0		
2000-01	York C	19	0	373	9

HOBSON, Gary (D)   271 1
H: 6 2   W: 13 02   b.North Ferriby 12-11-72
Source: Trainee.

1990-91	Hull C	4	0		
1991-92	Hull C	16	0		
1992-93	Hull C	21	0		
1993-94	Hull C	36	0		
1994-95	Hull C	36	0		
1995-96	Hull C	29	0	142	0
1995-96	Brighton & HA	9	0		
1996-97	Brighton & HA	37	1		
1997-98	Brighton & HA	33	0		
1998-99	Brighton & HA	13	0		
1999-2000	Brighton & HA	6	0	98	1
1999-2000	Chester C	20	0	20	0
2000-01	York C	11	0	11	0

HOCKING, Matt (D)   121 4
H: 5 11   W: 12 00   b.Boston 30-1-78
Source: Trainee.

1995-96	Sheffield U	0	0		
1996-97	Sheffield U	0	0		
1997-98	Sheffield U	0	0		
1997-98	Hull C	31	1		
1998-99	Hull C	26	1	57	2
1998-99	York C	6	0		
1999-2000	York C	32	2		
2000-01	York C	26	0	64	2

HOWARTH, Russell§ (G)   6 0
H: 6 1   W: 12 00   b.York 27-3-82
Source: Scholar. *Honours:* England Youth.

1999-2000	York C	6	0		
2000-01	York C	0	0	6	0

HULME, Kevin‡ (M)   253 40
H: 5 10   W: 13 07   b.Farnworth 7-12-67
Source: Radcliffe Borough.

1988-89	Bury	5	0		
1989-90	Bury	19	1		
1989-90	Chester C	4	0	4	0
1990-91	Bury	24	7		
1991-92	Bury	30	4		
1992-93	Bury	32	9		
1993-94	Doncaster R	34	8	34	8
1994-95	Bury	28	0		
1995-96	Bury	1	0	139	21
1995-96	Lincoln C	5	0	5	0

From Macclesfield T.

Season	Club	Apps	Gls	Tot Apps	Tot Gls
1998–99	Halifax T	30	4		
1999–2000	Halifax T	3	0	33	4
1999–2000	York C	23	4		
2000–01	York C	15	3	38	7

JONES, Barry* (D) 329 10
H: 5 10 W: 11 07 b.Prescot 20-6-70
Source: Prescot T.

Season	Club	Apps	Gls	Tot Apps	Tot Gls
1988–89	Liverpool	0	0		
1989–90	Liverpool	0	0		
1990–91	Liverpool	0	0		
1991–92	Liverpool	0	0		
1992–93	Wrexham	42	2		
1993–94	Wrexham	33	2		
1994–95	Wrexham	44	0		
1995–96	Wrexham	40	0		
1996–97	Wrexham	22	0		
1997–98	Wrexham	14	1	195	5
1997–98	York C	23	2		
1998–99	York C	45	2		
1999–2000	York C	37	1		
2000–01	York C	29	0	134	5

JORDAN, Scott‡ (M) 167 12
H: 5 9 W: 11 02 b.Newcastle 19-7-75
Source: Trainee.

Season	Club	Apps	Gls	Tot Apps	Tot Gls
1992–93	York C	1	0		
1993–94	York C	0	0		
1994–95	York C	37	3		
1995–96	York C	26	1		
1996–97	York C	15	1		
1997–98	York C	16	0		
1998–99	York C	32	5		
1999–2000	York C	28	2		
2000–01	York C	12	0	167	12

KEEGAN, John‡ (G) 3 0
H: 5 11 W: 11 09 b.Liverpool 5-8-81
Source: Scholarship.

Season	Club	Apps	Gls	Tot Apps	Tot Gls
1999–2000	York C	3	0		
2000–01	York C	0	0	3	0

MATHIE, Alex (F) 287 80
H: 5 10 W: 11 13 b.Bathgate 20-12-68
Source: Celtic BC.

Season	Club	Apps	Gls	Tot Apps	Tot Gls
1987–88	Celtic	0	0		
1988–89	Celtic	1	0		
1989–90	Celtic	6	0		
1990–91	Celtic	4	0	11	0
1991–92	Morton	42	18		
1992–93	Morton	32	13	74	31
1992–93	*Port Vale*	3	0	3	0
1993–94	Newcastle U	16	3		
1994–95	Newcastle U	9	1	25	4
1994–95	Ipswich T	13	2		
1995–96	Ipswich T	39	18		
1996–97	Ipswich T	12	4		
1997–98	Ipswich T	37	13		
1998–99	Ipswich T	8	1	109	38
1998–99	Dundee U	22	1		
1999–2000	Dundee U	12	3	34	4
1999–2000	Preston NE	12	2	12	2
2000–01	York C	19	1	19	1

McNIVEN, David* (F) 67 10
H: 5 10 W: 12 00 b.Leeds 27-5-78
Source: Trainee.

Season	Club	Apps	Gls	Tot Apps	Tot Gls
1995–96	Oldham Ath	0	0		
1996–97	Oldham Ath	8	0		
1997–98	Oldham Ath	8	1		
1998–99	Oldham Ath	6	0		
1999–2000	Oldham Ath	4	1	26	2
2000–01	York C	41	8	41	8

NOGAN, Lee# (F) 434 88
H: 5 10 W: 11 00 b.Cardiff 21-5-69
Source: Apprentice. *Honours:* Wales Under-21, B, 2 full caps.

Season	Club	Apps	Gls	Tot Apps	Tot Gls
1986–87	Oxford U	0	0		
1986–87	*Brentford*	11	2	11	2
1987–88	Oxford U	3	0		
1987–88	*Southend U*	6	1		
1988–89	Oxford U	3	0		
1989–90	Oxford U	4	0		
1990–91	Oxford U	32	5		
1991–92	Oxford U	22	5	64	10
1991–92	Watford	23	5		
1992–93	Watford	42	11		
1993–94	Watford	26	3		
1993–94	*Southend U*	5	0	11	1
1994–95	Watford	14	7	105	26
1994–95	Reading	20	10		
1995–96	Reading	39	10		
1996–97	Reading	32	6	91	26
1996–97	*Notts Co*	6	0	6	0
1997–98	Grimsby T	36	8		
1998–99	Grimsby T	38	2	74	10
1999–2000	Darlington	31	2		
2000–01	Darlington	18	4	49	6
2000–01	*Luton T*	7	1	7	1
2000–01	York C	16	6	16	6

POTTER, Graham (D) 170 5
H: 6 1 W: 11 12 b.Solihull 20-5-75
Source: Trainee. *Honours:* England Youth, Under-21.

Season	Club	Apps	Gls	Tot Apps	Tot Gls
1992–93	Birmingham C	18	2		
1993–94	Birmingham C	7	0	25	2
1993–94	Wycombe W	3	0	3	0
1993–94	Stoke C	3	0		
1994–95	Stoke C	1	0		
1995–96	Stoke C	41	1	45	1
1996–97	Southampton	8	0	8	0
1996–97	WBA	6	0		
1997–98	WBA	5	0		
1997–98	*Northampton T*	4	0	4	0
1998–99	WBA	22	0		
1999–2000	WBA	10	0	43	0
1999–2000	*Reading*	4	0	4	0
2000–01	York C	38	2	38	2

REED, Martin‡ (D) 46 0
H: 5 11 W: 11 07 b.Scarborough 10-1-78
Source: Trainee.

Season	Club	Apps	Gls	Tot Apps	Tot Gls
1996–97	York C	2	0		
1997–98	York C	22	0		
1998–99	York C	12	0		
1999–2000	York C	8	0		
2000–01	York C	2	0	46	0

RICHARDSON, Nick# (M) 413 45
H: 6 0 W: 12 06 b.Halifax 11-4-67
Source: Local.

Season	Club	Apps	Gls	Tot Apps	Tot Gls
1988–89	Halifax T	7	0		
1989–90	Halifax T	27	6		
1990–91	Halifax T	26	3		
1991–92	Halifax T	41	8	101	17
1992–93	Cardiff C	39	4		
1993–94	Cardiff C	39	5		
1994–95	Cardiff C	33	4	111	13
1994–95	*Wrexham*	4	2	4	2
1994–95	*Chester C*	6	1		
1995–96	Bury	5	0	5	0
1995–96	Chester C	37	4		
1996–97	Chester C	9	0		
1997–98	Chester C	44	2		
1998–99	Chester C	43	3		
1999–2000	Chester C	36	2		
2000–01	Chester C	0	0	175	12
2000–01	York C	17	1	17	1

SKINNER, Craig (M) 166 14
H: 5 8 W: 11 00 b.Bury 21-10-70
Source: Trainee.

Season	Club	Apps	Gls	Tot Apps	Tot Gls
1989–90	Blackburn R	0	0		
1990–91	Blackburn R	7	0		
1991–92	Blackburn R	9	0	16	0
1992–93	Plymouth Arg	13	1		
1993–94	Plymouth Arg	16	0		
1994–95	Plymouth Arg	24	3	53	4
1995–96	Wrexham	23	3		
1996–97	Wrexham	27	4		
1997–98	Wrexham	25	1		
1998–99	Wrexham	12	2	87	10
1998–99	York C	5	0		
1999–2000	York C	5	0		
2000–01	York C	0	0	10	0

STAMP, Neville (D) 14 0
H: 5 11 W: 12 07 b.Reading 7-7-81
Source: Trainee.

Season	Club	Apps	Gls	Tot Apps	Tot Gls
1998–99	Reading	1	0		
1999–2000	Reading	0	0		
2000–01	Reading	0	0	1	0
2000–01	York C	13	0	13	0

SWAN, Peter‡ (D) 383 55
H: 6 2 W: 14 02 b.Leeds 28-9-66
Source: Local.

Season	Club	Apps	Gls	Tot Apps	Tot Gls
1984–85	Leeds U	0	0		
1985–86	Leeds U	16	3		
1986–87	Leeds U	7	0		
1987–88	Leeds U	25	8		
1988–89	Leeds U	1	0	49	11
1988–89	Hull C	11	1		
1989–90	Hull C	31	11		
1990–91	Hull C	38	12	80	24
1991–92	Port Vale	33	3		
1992–93	Port Vale	38	2		
1993–94	Port Vale	40	0	111	5
1994–95	Plymouth Arg	27	2		
1995–96	Plymouth Arg	0	0	27	2
1995–96	Burnley	32	5		
1996–97	Burnley	17	2		
1997–98	Bury	37	6	37	6
1998–99	Burnley	17	0		
1999–2000	Burnley	2	0	68	7
1999–2000	York C	9	0		
2000–01	York C	2	0	11	0

THOMPSON, Marc (D) 22 0
H: 5 10 W: 12 03 b.York 15-1-82
Source: Trainee.

Season	Club	Apps	Gls	Tot Apps	Tot Gls
1999–2000	York C	10	0		
2000–01	York C	12	0	22	0

TURLEY, James* (F) 21 2
H: 5 8 W: 10 07 b.Manchester 24-6-81
Source: Trainee.

Season	Club	Apps	Gls	Tot Apps	Tot Gls
1999–2000	York C	11	2		
2000–01	York C	10	0	21	2

WILLIAMS, Marc‡ (F) 75 16
H: 5 9 W: 11 07 b.Bangor 8-2-73
Source: Bangor C.

Season	Club	Apps	Gls	Tot Apps	Tot Gls
1994–95	Stockport Co	1	0		
1995–96	Stockport Co	17	1		
1996–97	Stockport Co	0	0		
1997–98	Stockport Co	0	0		
1998–99	Stockport Co	0	0	18	1
1998–99	Halifax T	24	6	24	6
1998–99	York C	11	4		
1999–2000	York C	22	5		
2000–01	York C	0	0	33	9

WOOD, Leigh§ (M) 5 0
b.York 21-5-83
Source: Scholar.

Season	Club	Apps	Gls	Tot Apps	Tot Gls
2000–01	York C	5	0	5	0

Scholars
Barry, Daniel; Boyce, Marvin; Collinson, Jonathan E; Darlow, Kieran B; Emmerson, Scott; Fielding, John R; Gowen, Christopher J; Hampshire, Mark; Ibbetson, Luke G; Ormston, Gary; Rhodes, Benjamin; Russell, Adam J; Salvati, Marc R; Vasey, Peter WJ; Wise, Stuart; Wood, Leigh J

TRANSFERS 2000–2001

		From	To	Fee in £
May 2000				
17	Alford, Carl P.	Stevenage Borough	Doncaster Rovers	undisclosed
4	Carlisle, Clarke J.	Blackpool	Queens Park Rangers	500,000
24	Kelly, James	Hednesford Town	Doncaster Rovers	undisclosed
22	Marsh, Michael A.	Kidderminster Harriers	Southport	undisclosed
25	Matthews, Colin E.	Bognor Regis Town	Newport (IW)	undisclosed
9	Morrison, Peter A.	Bolton Wanderers	Scunthorpe United	Free
25	Robinson, Stephen	AFC Bournemouth	Preston North End	375,000
Temporary transfers				
8	Coppinger, James	Newcastle United	Hartlepool United	
5	Gunnlaugsson, Arnar B.	Leicester City	Stoke City	
8	Hendry, Iain	Woking	Kingstonian	
9	Myhre, Thomas	Everton	Birmingham City	
6	Saunders, Edward	Woking	Kingstonian	
7	Simba, Amara S.	Leyton Orient	Kingstonian	
6	Stewart, Jordan B.	Leicester City	Bristol Rovers	
1	Trundle, Lee C.	Southport	Bamber Bridge	
7	Webb, Simon J.	Leyton Orient	Purfleet	
June 2000				
28	Bjornebye, Stig I.	Liverpool	Blackburn Rovers	300,000
9	Bramble, Tesfaye	Chelmsford City	Cambridge City	undisclosed
2	Brooker, Paul	Fulham	Brighton & Hove Albion	25,000
16	Crossley, Matthew	Kingstonian	Aldershot Town	undisclosed
1	Curtis, John C.K.	Manchester United	Blackburn Rovers	1,500,000
21	Darby, Duane	Notts County	Rushden & Diamonds	undisclosed
14	Delaney, Dean	Everton	Port Vale	Free
12	Flitter, Matthew A.H.	Chesham United	Hampton & Richmond Borough	undisclosed
28	Gabbiadini, Marco	Darlington	Northampton Town	Free
16	Haaland, Alf I.R.	Leeds United	Manchester City	2,500,000
16	Jackson, Justin J.	Morecambe	Rushden & Diamonds	undisclosed
28	King, Marlon F.	Barnet	Gillingham	255,000
14	Regan, Carl A.	Everton	Barnsley	20,000
27	Shuttlewood, Justin	Forest Green Rovers	Salisbury City	undisclosed
5	Thomas, Wayne	Torquay United	Stoke City	200,000
8	Walters, Steven P.	Northwich Victoria	Morecambe	undisclosed
15	Warren, Christer	AFC Bournemouth	Queens Park Rangers	Free
July 2000				
21	Aiston, Sam J.	Sunderland	Shrewsbury Town	Free
28	Akinbiyi, Adeola P.	Wolverhampton Wanderers	Leicester City	5,000,000
20	Alexandersson, Niclas	Sheffield Wednesday	Everton	2,500,000
24	Ball, Kevin A.	Fulham	Burnley	Free
19	Barmby, Nicholas J.	Everton	Liverpool	6,000,000
14	Benjamin, Trevor J.	Cambridge United	Leicester City	1,000,000
21	Black, Thomas R.	Arsenal	Crystal Palace	250,000
13	Bothroyd, Jay	Arsenal	Coventry City	1,000,000
11	Cameron, Martin G.W.	Alloa Athletic	Bristol Rovers	100,000
7	Clark, Peter J.	Carlisle United	Stockport County	75,000
7	Clement, Neil	Chelsea	West Bromwich Albion	100,000
21	Collins, John	Everton	Fulham	2,000,000
6	Cort, Carl E.R.	Wimbledon	Newcastle United	7,000,000
19	Cousins, Ian	Burnham Ramblers	Chelmsford City	undisclosed
28	Crouch, Peter J.	Tottenham Hotspur	Queens Park Rangers	60,000
10	Curle, Keith	Wolverhampton Wanderers	Sheffield United	Free
19	Dack, James	Sutton United	Farnborough Town	undisclosed
12	Davidson, Callum I.	Blackburn Rovers	Leicester City	1,700,000
22	Ducros, Andrew J.	Nuneaton Borough	Kidderminster Harriers	100,000
11	Duffield, Peter	Darlington	York City	Free
31	Farrell, Andrew J.	Morecambe	Leigh RMI	undisclosed
14	Forsyth, Richard M.	Blackpool	Peterborough United	Free
24	Frandsen, Per	Blackburn Rovers	Bolton Wanderers	1,600,000
11	Gabbiadini, Marco	Darlington	Northampton Town	Free
21	Gray, Julian R.	Arsenal	Crystal Palace	250,000
12	Gudjohnsen, Eidur S.	Bolton Wanderers	Chelsea	4,000,000
25	Hale, Matthew	Yeovil Town	Weymouth	undisclosed
27	Hicks, Stuart J.	Chester City	Mansfield Town	Free
12	Higginbotham, Daniel J.	Manchester United	Derby County	2,000,000
11	Hignett, Craig J.	Barnsley	Blackburn Rovers	2,250,000
21	Hope, Christopher J.	Scunthorpe United	Gillingham	250,000
12	Hopkin, David	Leeds United	Bradford City	2,500,000
15	Horsfield, Geoffrey M.	Fulham	Birmingham City	2,000,000
21	Hutchinson, Ed	Sutton United	Brentford	75,000
19	Hutchison, Donald	Everton	Sunderland	2,500,000
21	Jensen, Claus W.	Bolton Wanderers	Charlton Athletic	4,000,000
27	Jones, Gary	Hartlepool United	Halifax Town	Free
19	Jones, Lee	Bristol Rovers	Stockport County	50,000
3	King, Marlon F.	Barnet	Gillingham	255,000
27	Lovett, Jay	Crawley Town	Brentford	75,000
18	McCammon, Mark J.	Charlton Athletic	Brentford	100,000
12	McGregor, Marc R.	Forest Green Rovers	Nuneaton Borough	undisclosed
27	Mike, Adrian R.	Southport	Northwich Victoria	undisclosed
11	Neil, Alexander	Airdrieonians	Barnsley	25,000
28	Piper, Leonard H.	St Albans City	Farnborough Town	undisclosed
12	Pistone, Alessandro	Newcastle United	Everton	3,000,000
3	Reed, Ian P.	Nuneaton Borough	Worcester City	undisclosed
5	Reid, Paul M.	Carlisle United	Rangers	200,000
13	Richardson, Leam N.	Blackburn Rovers	Bolton Wanderers	50,000
25	Ricketts, Michael B.	Walsall	Bolton Wanderers	500,000
24	Roberts, Christian J.	Cardiff City	Exeter City	Free
27	Roberts, Jason A.D.	Bristol Rovers	West Bromwich Albion	2,000,000
7	Rowett, Gary	Birmingham City	Leicester City	3,000,000
28	Ruddock, Neil	West Ham United	Crystal Palace	undisclosed
5	Saunders, Edward	Woking	Kingstonian	undisclosed
21	Shaw, Paul	Millwall	Gillingham	450,000
25	Sollitt, Adam J.	Kettering Town	Northampton Town	30,000
14	Strong, G.	Bolton Wanderers	Motherwell	150,000

12 Thatcher, Ben D.	Wimbledon	Tottenham Hotspur	5,000,000
14 Ward, Mitcham D.	Everton	Barnsley	200,000
12 Watson, Stephen C.	Aston Villa	Everton	2,500,000
26 Williams, Mark S.	Watford	Wimbledon	undisclosed
29 Winston, Samuel A.	Sutton United	Kingstonian	undisclosed
5 Winterburn, Nigel	Arsenal	West Ham United	250,000

Temporary transfers

28 Boa Morte, Luis P.	Southampton	Fulham	
4 Culkin, Nicholas J.	Manchester United	Bristol Rovers	
28 Ferguson, Barry	Coventry City	Hartlepool United	
28 Forsell, Mikael K.	Chelsea	Crystal Palace	
21 Jones, Stephen G.	Bristol City	Wycombe Wanderers	
17 Maxwell, Layton J.	Liverpool	Stockport County	
27 McGovern, Brian	Arsenal	Norwich City	
24 Roche, Lee P.	Manchester United	Wrexham	

August 2000

31 Adams, Daniel B.	Altrincham	Macclesfield Town	undisclosed
11 Alexander, Gary G.	West Ham United	Swindon Town	300,000
9 Ashcroft, Lee	Grimsby Town	Wigan Athletic	350,000
3 Baardsen, Espen	Tottenham Hotspur	Watford	1,250,000
14 Beard, Robert	Bedworth United	Rugby United	undisclosed
17 Bellamy, Craig D.	Norwich City	Coventry City	5,000,000
10 Bennett, Thomas M.	Stockport County	Walsall	Free
10 Birch, Mark	Northwich Victoria	Carlisle United	10,000
11 Black, Thomas R.	Arsenal	Crystal Palace	250,000
24 Bradley, Shayne	Southampton	Mansfield Town	undisclosed
31 Constantine, Leon	Edgware Town	Millwall	undisclosed
21 Cureton, Jamie	Bristol Rovers	Reading	250,000
4 Curtis, Thomas D.	Chesterfield	Portsmouth	50,000
10 Duke, David	Sunderland	Swindon Town	Free
19 Ferguson, Duncan	Newcastle United	Everton	3,750,000
11 Foran, Mark J.	Crewe Alexandra	Bristol Rovers	75,000
15 Forbes, Donald	Forest Green Rovers	Basingstoke Town	undisclosed
30 Fox, Ruel A.	Tottenham Hotspur	West Bromwich Albion	200,000
1 Ginola, David D.M.	Tottenham Hotspur	Aston Villa	3,000,000
11 Gray, Julian R.	Arsenal	Crystal Palace	250,000
1 Holmes, Peter J.	Sheffield Wednesday	Luton Town	Free
14 Howey, Stephen N.	Newcastle United	Manchester City	2,000,000
19 Hreidarsson, Hermann	Wimbledon	Ipswich Town	4,000,000
18 Javary, Jean-Phillipe	Raith Rovers	Brentford	undisclosed
11 Jones, Mark A.	Wolverhampton Wanderers	Chesterfield	Free
10 Ketsbaia, Temuri	Newcastle United	Wolverhampton Wanderers	900,000
9 Lormor, Anthony	Mansfield Town	Hartlepool United	30,000
24 Matteo, Dominic	Liverpool	Leeds United	4,750,000
11 McAnespie, Kieran	St Johnstone	Fulham	80,000
22 McGovern, Brian	Arsenal	Norwich City	50,000
11 Mills, Rowan L.	Bradford City	Portsmouth	1,000,000
10 Morley, Dominic A.	Southport	Droylsden	undisclosed
30 Nancekivell, Kevin W.	Tiverton Town	Plymouth Argyle	5000
3 Nielsen, Allan	Tottenham Hotspur	Watford	2,250,000
25 Okita, Jean-Marie	Enfield	Tilbury	undisclosed
10 Ovendale, Mark J.	AFC Bournemouth	Luton Town	425,000
10 Peacock, Lee A.	Manchester City	Bristol City	600,000
4 Pemberton, Martin C.	Bradford Park Avenue	Mansfield Town	10,000
2 Petrescu, Dan V.	Chelsea	Bradford City	1,000,000
11 Phillips, Martin J.	Portsmouth	Plymouth Argyle	25,000
11 Pollock, Jamie	Manchester United	Crystal Palace	750,000
7 Quashie, Nigel F.	Nottingham Forest	Portsmouth	200,000
8 Richardson, Jonathan D.	Exeter City	Oxford United	undisclosed
22 Ritchie, Paul M.	Rangers	Manchester City	500,000
9 Robinson, Paul D.	Newcastle United	Wimbledon	1,500,000
11 Rougier, Anthony L.	Port Vale	Reading	325,000
3 Ruddock, Neil	West Ham United	Crystal Palace	undisclosed
18 Ruffer, Carl J.	Runcorn	Chester City	undisclosed
19 Skelly, Richard B.	Sutton United	Cambridge City	undisclosed
9 Tate, Steven K.	Weymouth	Newport (IW)	undisclosed
15 Taylor, Robert A.	Manchester City	Wolverhampton Wanderers	1,550,000
8 Thompson, David A.	Liverpool	Coventry City	3,000,000
9 Tillson, Andrew	Bristol Rovers	Walsall	10,000
9 Todd, Lee	Bradford City	Rochdale	Free
11 Tutill, Stephen A.	Darlington	Chesterfield	Free
10 Twynham, Gary S.	Hednesford Town	Macclesfield Town	Free
25 Utterson, John	Margate	Ramsgate	undisclosed
16 Wanchope, Watson P.	West Ham United	Manchester City	3,650,000
18 Ward, Ashley S.	Blackburn Rovers	Bradford City	1,500,000
17 Wardley, Shane	Chelmsford City	Cambridge City	undisclosed
4 Whelan, Noel D.	Coventry City	Middlesbrough	2,200,000
2 Williams, Mark S.	Watford	Wimbledon	undisclosed
4 Williams, Stephen J.	Chatham Town	Dartford	undisclosed
3 Windsor, Simon L.	Racing Club Warwick	Stratford Town	undisclosed
19 Wyatt, Nicky	Havant & Waterlooville	Bognor Regis Town	undisclosed
10 Zabek, Lee K.	Bristol Rovers	Exeter City	Free
10 Zamora, Robert L.	Bristol Rovers	Brighton & Hove Albion	100,000
29 Ziege, Christian	Middlesbrough	Liverpool	5,500,000

Temporary transfers

19 Abbey, Benjamin	Oxford United	Aldershot Town	
11 Angus, Stevland D.	West Ham United	AFC Bournemouth	
22 Blake, Robert J.	Bradford City	Nottingham Forest	
22 Bradley, Shayne	Southampton	Mansfield Town	
19 Bridge, Mark	Stevenage Borough	Baldock Town	
10 Cartwright, Mark N.	Wrexham	Brighton & Hove Albion	
11 Collins, Lee D.	Stoke City	Cambridge United	
18 Crompton, Paul A.	Lancaster City	Kendal Town	
11 Crowe, Dean A.	Stoke City	Bury	
12 Dunning, Darren	Blackburn Rovers	Bristol City	
26 Evans, David A.	Barnsley	Chester City	
18 Evans, Michael J.	West Bromwich Albion	Bristol Rovers	
1 Fenton, Nicholas L.	Manchester City	AFC Bournemouth	
27 Ferguson, Barry	Coventry City	Hartlepool United	
31 Fortune, Jonathan J.	Charlton Athletic	Mansfield Town	
26 Fox, Ruel A.	Tottenham Hotspur	West Bromwich Albion	
18 Furlong, Paul A.	Birmingham City	Queens Park Rangers	

10 Gabbidon, Daniel L.	West Bromwich Albion	Cardiff City	
11 Garcia, Richard	West Ham United	Leyton Orient	
11 Gray, Kevin J.	Huddersfield Town	Stockport County	
11 Grayson, Simon N.	Blackburn Rovers	Sheffield Wednesday	
26 Greene, Dennis B.	Windsor & Eton	Harlow Town	
25 Haley, Grant R.	Peterborough United	Bedford Town	
17 Hamilton, Gary I.	Blackburn Rovers	Rochdale	
11 Harrison, Craig	Middlesbrough	Crystal Palace	
18 Hasell, James	Stevenage Borough	Ashford Town	
11 Hawe, Steven J.	Blackburn Rovers	Blackpool	
19 Hayes, Adrian M.	Boston United	Tamworth	
24 Hooper, Nicholas	Farnborough Town	Staines Town	
26 Inman, Niall E.	Peterborough United	Ketteringn Town	
10 Jones, Scott	Barnsley	Bristol Rovers	
25 Keeler, Justin J.	AFC Bournemouth	Dorchester Town	
2 Kendall, Lee M.	Crystal Palace	Barry Town	
26 King, Stuart S.D.	Preston North End	Ross County	
11 Lindley, James E.	Notts County	Lincoln City	
11 McCann, Grant S.	West Ham United	Notts County	
18 McCann, Peter	Barnet	Folkestone Invicta	
19 Meechan, Alexander T.	Bristol City	Forest Green Rovers	
12 Miller, Alan J.	Blackburn Rovers	Bristol City	
25 Nancekivell, Kevin W.	Tiverton Town	Plymouth Argyle	
25 Neal, Jon	Folkestone Invicta	St Leonards	
4 Newby, Jon P.R.	Liverpool	Sheffield United	
21 Okita, Jean-Marie	Enfield	Tilbury	
18 Osborn, Mark	Wycombe Wanderers	Marlow	
18 Pinnock, James E.	Gillingham	Dover Athletic	
1 Proudlock, Adam D.	Wolverhampton Wanderers	Clyde	
11 Rankin, Isaiah	Bradford City	Bolton Wanderers	
19 Rouco, Daniel	Hampton & Richmond Borough	Chertsey Town	
21 Searle, Stuart A.	Aldershot Town	Molesey	
9 Taylor, Stuart J.	Arsenal	Crystal Palace	
25 Thetis, Jean M.	Ipswich Town	Wolverhampton Wanderers	
10 Thom, Stuart P.	Oldham Athletic	Scunthorpe United	
31 Thomas, Anthony	Burton Albion	Kings Lynn	
10 Westwood, Ashley M.	Bradford City	Sheffield Wednesday	
24 Whitley, James	Manchester City	Norwich City	
25 Whittingham, Guy	Portsmouth	Peterborough United	
27 Willmott, Richard	Hitchin Town	Hendon	
8 Woodman, Andrew J.	Brentford	Southend United	

September 2000

14 Cartwright, Mark N.	Wrexham	Brighton & Hove Albion	Free
11 Cottee, Anthony R.	Leicester City	Norwich City	Free
5 Cresswell, Richard P.W.	Sheffield Wednesday	Leicester City	undisclosed
22 Dinning, Tony	Stockport County	Wolverhampton Wanderers	600,000
8 Edwards, Robert	Huddersfield Town	Chesterfield	undisclosed
11 Emerson, Thome A.	Chelsea	Sunderland	undisclosed
11 Evans, Michael J.	West Bromwich Albion	Bristol Rovers	250,000
11 Fortune-West, Leopold O.	Rotherham United	Cardiff City	300,000
1 Foster, Adrian M.	Yeovil Town	Forest Green Rovers	undisclosed
21 Gabbidon, Daniel L.	West Bromwich Albion	Cardiff City	175,000
29 Harkness, Steven	Blackburn Rovers	Sheffield Wednesday	200,000
1 Harrison, Craig	Middlesbrough	Crystal Palace	undisclosed
11 Jones, Scott	Barnsley	Bristol Rovers	200,000
22 Lua-Lua, Lomano T.	Colchester United	Newcastle United	2,250,000
1 McCulloch, Scott A.	Dundee United	Cardiff City	100,000
7 Rammell, Andrew V.	Walsall	Wycombe Wanderers	75,000
18 Thomas, Anthony	Burton Albion	Kings Lynn	undisclosed
11 Thom, Stuart P.	Oldham Athletic	Scunthorpe United	undisclosed
18 Walsh, Steven	Leicester City	Norwich City	Free
12 Westwood, Ashley M.	Bradford City	Sheffield Wednesday	150,000

Temporary transfers

29 Ayres, James M.	Luton Town	Stevenage Borough
28 Baker, Steven R.	Middlesbrough	Hartlepool United
8 Ball, Alex I.	Bristol City	Salisbury City
15 Beresford, David	Huddersfield Town	Port Vale
8 Berg, Henning	Manchester United	Blackburn Rovers
4 Brady, Gary	Newcastle United	Norwich City
22 Brass, Christopher P.	Burnley	Halifax Town
21 Broughton, Drewe O.	Peterborough United	Dagenham & Redbridge
15 Buggie, Lee D.	Bury	Rochdale
22 Burchill, Mark J.	Celtic	Birmingham City
23 Campbell, James R.	Peterborough United	St Albans City
15 Campbell, Stuart P.	Leicester City	Grimsby Town
9 Caton, Sean T.	Heybridge Swifts	Barking
15 Charles, Gary A.	West Ham United	Birmingham City
15 Clarke, Matthew P.	Halifax Town	Gainsborough Trinity
21 Cooke, Terence J.	Manchester City	Sheffield Wednesday
11 Cramb, Colin	Crewe Alexandra	Notts County
1 Cramman, Kenneth W.	Boston United	Slough Town
12 Crowe, Jason W.R.	Portsmouth	Brentford
22 Devenney, Michael P.	Burnley	Leigh RMI
8 Dryden, Richard A.	Southampton	Northampton Town
15 Dudfield, Lawrie G.	Leicester City	Lincoln City
18 Fenton, Nicholas L.	Manchester City	Notts County
29 Fortune, Jonathan J.	Charlton Athletic	Mansfield Town
23 Foster, Martin	Doncaster Rovers	Ilkeston Town
8 Freeman, David B.	Nottingham Forest	Port Vale
12 Garcia, Richard	West Ham United	Leyton Orient
15 Glennon, Matthew W.	Bolton Wanderers	Bristol Rovers
22 Goodyear, Craig	Barnsley	Frickley Athletic
23 Haley, Grant R.	Peterborough United	Bedford Town
22 Hann, Matthew	Peterborough United	Stamford
5 Harvey, Lee	St Albans City	Enfield
21 Hodson, Benjamin M.	Hayes	Sutton United
22 Hollis, Simon	Solihull Borough	Paget Rangers
21 Holmes, David J.	Burton Albion	Ilkeston Town
22 Hooper, Nicholas	Farnborough Town	Staines Town
29 Johnson, Ben	Stockport County	Carlisle United
5 Jones, Daniel	Enfield	St Albans City
22 Jones, Dean	Ilkeston Town	Frickley Athletic

	Player	From	To
26	Keeler, Justin J.	AFC Bournemouth	Dorchester Town
22	Keller, Marc	West Ham United	Portsmouth
8	Killen, Christopher J.	Manchester City	Wrexham
14	Kitson, Paul	West Ham United	Crystal Palace
7	Kozluk, Robert	Sheffield United	Huddersfield Town
8	Kyle, Kevin A.	Sunderland	Huddersfield Town
8	Lambourde, Bernard	Chelsea	Portsmouth
21	Lee, Alan D.	Burnley	Rotherham United
15	Lightfoot, Christopher I.	Crewe Alexandra	Oldham Athletic
11	Lumsdon, Christopher	Sunderland	Crewe Alexandra
21	Mardon, Paul J.	West Bromwich Albion	Plymouth Argyle
1	Marsh, Simon T.	Birmingham City	Brentford
15	Matassa, Vincent	Basingstoke Town	Dorchester Town
27	Mawson, Craig J.	Burnley	Lincoln City
21	McConnell, Barry	Exeter City	Weston-Super-Mare
18	Meechan, Alexander T.	Bristol City	Forest Green Rovers
21	Mike, Leon J.	Manchester City	Oxford United
5	Miller, Alan J.	Bristol City	Blackburn Rovers
29	Miller, Barry S.	Gillingham	Doncaster Rovers
1	Morrison, Andrew C.	Manchester City	Blackpool
22	Morrison-Hill, Jamie S.	Plymouth Argyle	Tiverton Town
20	Murray, Matthew W.	Wolverhampton Wanderers	Slough Town
21	Newell, Paul C.	Billericay Town	Sutton United
20	Osborn, Mark	Wycombe Wanderers	Hampton & Richmond Borough
26	Packham, William J.	Brighton & Hove Albion	Bognor Regis Town
12	Parkin, Sam	Chelsea	Millwall
16	Parsons, David	Leyton Orient	Purfleet
22	Patton, Aaron	Slough Town	Oxford City
4	Peacock, Darren	Blackburn Rovers	West Ham United
18	Pinnock, James	Gillingham	Dover Athletic
20	Randall, Martin J.	St Albans City	Woking
8	Read, David	Stafford Rangers	Sutton Coldfield Town
4	Robertson, Mark W.	Burnley	Swindon Town
13	Robinson, Marvin L.S.	Derby County	Stoke City
22	Scott, Christopher J.	Burnley	Leigh RMI
4	Searle, Stephen	Barnet	Stevenage Borough
21	Searle, Stuart A.	Aldershot Town	Molesey
30	Sills, Timothy	Basingstoke Town	Staines Town
22	Smith, Darren K.	Gravesend & Northfleet	Ashford Town
22	Smith, Ian P.	Burnley	Oldham Athletic
20	Smith, Peter E.	Exeter City	Cambridge City
1	Smith, Philip A.	Millwall	Croydon
21	Speakman, Robert	Exeter City	Bashley
13	Stockdale, Robert K.	Middlesbrough	Sheffield Wednesday
9	Sullivan, Martyn G.	Forest Green Rovers	Weymouth
7	Taylor, Leigh D.	Boston United	Wisbech Town
12	Taylor, Stuart J.	Arsenal	Crystal Palace
15	Walsh, Gary	Bradford City	Middlesbrough
16	Whitehall, Steven C.	Oldham Athletic	Chester City
26	Whitley, James	Manchester City	Norwich City
1	Wicks, Matthew J.	Peterborough United	Brighton & Hove Albion
24	Wilmot, Richard	Hitchin Town	Hendon
8	Wilson, Paul R.	Barnet	Boston United
12	Woodman, Andrew J.	Brentford	Southend United
22	Woodward, Andrew S.	Sheffield United	Scunthorpe United
15	Woozley, David J.	Crystal Palace	AFC Bournemouth
8	Wright, Benjamin	Bristol City	Woking
22	Yeoman, Daniel	Farnborough Town	Northwood

October 2000

	Player	From	To	Fee
26	Charvet, Laurent J.	Newcastle United	Manchester City	1,000,000
27	Collymore, Stanley V.	Leicester City	Bradford City	Free
20	Dunne, Richard P.	Everton	Manchester City	3,000,000
20	Ehiogu, Ugochuku	Aston Villa	Middlesbrough	8,000,000
13	Eyres, David	Preston North End	Oldham Athletic	undisclosed
18	Fitzgerald, Scott B.	Millwall	Colchester United	Free
5	Hayes, Adrian M.	Boston United	Kings Lynn	undisclosed
12	Hendon, Ian M.	Northampton Town	Sheffield Wednesday	40,000
2	Holloway, Darren	Sunderland	Wimbledon	1,200,000
27	Hooper, Nicholas	Farnborough Town	Staines Town	undisclosed
27	Horner, Richard	Farnborough Town	Sutton United	undisclosed
24	Hughes, Leslie M.	Everton	Blackburn Rovers	Free
26	Jordan, Andrew J.	Bristol City	Cardiff City	30,000
3	Lescott, Aaron A.	Aston Villa	Sheffield Wednesday	100,000
19	Matassa, Vincent	Basingstoke Town	Woking	undisclosed
13	McKenzie, Leon M.	Crystal Palace	Peterborough United	Free
19	Miller, Barry S.	Gillingham	Doncaster Rovers	10,000
20	Naysmith, Gary	Heart of Midlothian	Everton	1,750,000
20	O'Connor, Joseph N.	Kingstonian	Stafford Rangers	undisclosed
20	Ormerod, Mark I.	Woking	Dorchester Town	undisclosed
18	Sullivan, Martyn G.	Forest Green Rovers	Dorchester Town	undisclosed
12	Tait, Jordan A.	Oldham Athletic	Darlington	undisclosed
13	Wicks, Matthew J.	Peterborough United	Brighton & Hove Albion	25,000

Temporary transfers

	Player	From	To
12	Allsopp, Daniel	Manchester City	Bristol Rovers
6	Ashdown, Jamie L.	Reading	Bishop's Stortford
27	Austin, Kevin L.	Barnsley	Brentford
30	Baker, Steven R.	Middlesbrough	Hartlepool United
21	Ball, Alex I.	Bristol City	Clevedon Town
6	Bartholomew, Matthew P.	Hendon	Yeading
13	Black, Kingsley T.	Grimsby Town	Lincoln City
25	Blake, Robert J.	Bradford City	Nottingham Forest
25	Broomes, Marlon C.	Blackburn Rovers	Queens Park Rangers
18	Broughton, Drewe O.	Peterborough United	Dagenham & Redbridge
20	Buggie, Lee D.	Bury	Whitby Town
13	Butler, Thomas A.	Sunderland	Darlington
19	Campbell, Stuart P.	Leicester City	Grimsby Town
11	Caton, Sean T.	Heybridge Swifts	Barking
27	Clarke, Matthew P.	Halifax Town	Frickley Athletic
20	Connell, Lee A.	Bury	Whitby Town
23	Cooke, Terence J.	Manchester City	Sheffield Wednesday
18	Cowley, Alan D.	Runcorn	Trafford
18	Cramman, Kenneth W.	Boston United	Farnborough Town

18 Crowe, Jason W.R.	Portsmouth	Brentford	
20 Cummings, Warren	Chelsea	AFC Bournemouth	
6 D'Arcy, Ross	Barnet	Dover Athletic	
13 Deakin, John	Worcester City	Evesham United	
12 De Bilde, Gilles R.G.	Sheffield Wednesday	Aston Villa	
26 Defoe, Jermaine C.	West Ham United	AFC Bournemouth	
6 Denny, Philip M.	Bradford Park Avenue	Bamber Bridge	
18 De Souza, Juan M.	Boston United	Farnborough Town	
20 Druce, Mark A.	Woking	Oxford City	
10 Dryden, Richard A.	Southampton	Northampton Town	
6 Duerden, Ian C.	Doncaster Rovers	Kingstonian	
4 Durkan, Kieron J.	Macclesfield Town	York City	
13 Evers, Sean A.	Reading	St Johnstone	
18 Fenton, Nicholas L.	Manchester City	Notts County	
16 Fitzgerald, Scott B.	Millwall	Colchester United	
30 Fortune, Jonathan J.	Charlton Athletic	Mansfield Town	
30 French, Daniel J.	Peterborough United	Boston United	
16 Garcia, Richard	West Ham United	Leyton Orient	
27 Granville, Daniel P.	Manchester City	Norwich City	
6 Gray, Wayne W.	Wimbledon	Port Vale	
13 Griffin, Charles J.	Swindon Town	Woking	
25 Hamilton, Derrick V.	Newcastle United	Tranmere Rovers	
20 Harley, Jonathan	Chelsea	Wimbledon	
4 Harvey, Lee	St Albans City	Enfield	
3 Hasell, James	Stevenage Borough	Harlow Town	
19 Haworth, Robert J.	Dagenham & Redbridge	Sutton United	
2 Hay, Alexander N.	Tranmere Rovers	Altrincham	
27 Hicks, Graham	Rochdale	Chorley	
17 Holligan, Gavin V.	West Ham United	Exeter City	
26 Holt, Grant	Halifax Town	Workington	
23 Ince, Clayton	Crewe Alexandra	Dundee	
6 Jones, Daniel	Enfield	St Albans City	
30 Keeler, Justin J.	AFC Bournemouth	Dorchester Town	
17 Kennedy, Jon	Sunderland	Blackpool	
13 Kippe, Frode	Liverpool	Stoke City	
7 Kozluk, Robert	Sheffield United	Huddersfield Town	
23 Lee, Alan D.	Burnley	Rotherham United	
20 Lee, Christian	Gillingham	Rochdale	
10 Lumsdon, Christopher	Sunderland	Crewe Alexandra	
13 Maddison, Lee R.	Dundee United	Carlisle United	
6 Maley, Mark	Sunderland	Blackpool	
16 Mardon, Paul J.	West Bromwich Albion	Wrexham	
20 Martin, Jae A.	Woking	Sutton United	
27 Mawson, Craig	Burnley	Lincoln City	
8 Maybury, Alan P.	Leeds United	Crewe Alexandra	
17 McCann, Grant S.	West Ham United	Cheltenham Town	
23 McConnell, Barry	Exeter City	Weston-Super-Mare	
27 McKinlay, William	Blackburn Rovers	Leicester City	
17 Meijer, Erik	Liverpool	Preston North End	
20 Miller, Alan J.	Blackburn Rovers	Coventry City	
19 Morris, Elliott J.	West Bromwich Albion	Doncaster Rovers	
12 Morrison, Andrew C.	Manchester City	Crystal Palace	
20 Mounty, Carl T.	Swansea City	Waterford	
26 Murphy, Peter	Blackburn Rovers	Halifax Town	
20 Murray, Matthew W.	Wolverhampton Wanderers	Kingstonian	
21 Naylor, Dominic J.	Dagenham & Redbridge	Basingstoke Town	
5 Nicholls, Mark	Chelsea	Colchester United	
31 Parker, Scott M.	Charlton Athletic	Norwich City	
11 Parkin, Sam	Chelsea	Millwall	
23 Parnaby, Stuart	Middlesbrough	Halifax Town	
14 Peacock, Darren	Blackburn Rovers	Wolverhampton Wanderers	
27 Prindiville, Steven A.	Nuneaton Borough	Solihull Borough	
2 Rachel, Adam	Blackpool	Northwich Victoria	
28 Read, David	Stafford Rangers	Bilston Town	
6 Reid, Brian R.	Dunfermline Athletic	Blackpool	
20 Riza, Omer K.	West Ham United	Barnet	
10 Robinson, Paul D.	Wimbledon	Burnley	
3 Rodrigues, Daniel F.	Southampton	Bristol City	
6 Rogers, David R.	Ayr United	Peterborough United	
3 Savic, Sinisa	Barnsley	Scarborough	
12 Scott, Keith	Reading	Colchester United	
5 Slater, Carl D.	Burton Albion	Rocester	
20 Smith, Philip A.	Millwall	Walton & Hersham	
6 Souter, Ryan	Bury	AFC Newport	
20 Staunton, Stephen	Liverpool	Crystal Palace	
2 Taaffe, Steven L.	Stoke City	Northwich Victoria	
19 Tarrant, Neil K.	Aston Villa	York City	
6 Tod, Andrew	Dunfermline Athletic	Stockport County	
20 Tunnicliffe, Andrew J.	Manchester City	Macclesfield Town	
5 Turner, Michael C.	Barnsley	Doncaster Rovers	
12 Vanninen, Jukka	Exeter City	Bashley	
17 Wainwright, Neil	Sunderland	Halifax Town	
6 Whittingham, Guy	Portsmouth	Oxford United	
23 Wilmot, Richard	Hitchin Town	Hendon	
26 Woodward, Andrew	Sheffield United	Scunthorpe United	
20 Yeoman, Daniel	Farnborough Town	Northwood	

November 2000

24 Bent, Marcus N.	Sheffield United	Blackburn Rovers	1,300,000
30 Brumwell, Phillip	Hull City	Darlington	Free
23 Collins, Darren	Rushden & Diamonds	Kettering Town	undisclosed
10 Edwards, Robert	Huddersfield Town	Chesterfield	undisclosed
10 Fenton, Nicholas L.	Manchester City	Notts County	150,000
27 Ferdinand, Rio G.	West Ham United	Leeds United	18,000,000
10 Fish, Mark A.	Bolton Wanderers	Charlton Athletic	700,000
7 Friedel, Bradley H.	Liverpool	Blackburn Rovers	undisclosed
10 Hawthorne, Mark D.	Slough Town	Crawley Town	undisclosed
10 Lee, Alan D.	Burnley	Rotherham United	150,000
24 McKinlay, William	Blackburn Rovers	Bradford City	Free
20 Moore, Ian R.	Stockport County	Burnley	1,000,000
16 Morgan, John R.	Enfield	Stevenage Borough	undisclosed
28 Notman, Alexander M.	Manchester United	Norwich City	250,000
24 Nower, Benjamin E.	Kings Lynn	AFC Sudbury	undisclosed
10 Read, David	Stafford Rangers	Bilston Town	undisclosed

24 Richardson, Stephen J.	Basingstoke Town	Salisbury City	undisclosed
17 Samuels, Anthony	St Albans City	Boreham Wood	undisclosed
10 Smith, Jason J.	Stafford Rangers	Bilston Town	undisclosed
29 Song, Bahanag R.	Liverpool	West Ham United	2,500,000
17 Thompson, Paul S.	Devizes Town	Mangotsfield United	undisclosed
21 Weston, Rhys D.	Arsenal	Cardiff City	300,000
17 Wraight, Gary P.	Stevenage Borough	St Albans City	undisclosed

Temporary transfers

4 Adebowale, Andrew	St Albans City	Berkhamsted Town
22 Allsopp, Daniel	Manchester City	Notts County
10 Andrews, Keith J.	Wolverhampton Wanderers	Oxford United
17 Aspinall, Brendan J.	Hyde United	Ossett Town
28 All, Alex	Bristol City	Clevedon Town
3 Banger, Nicholas L.	Dundee	Scunthorpe United
7 Bartholomew, Matthew	Hendon	Yeading
30 Bossu, Bertrand	Barnet	Hayes
30 Bower, Mark	Bradford City	York City
10 Boyce, Robert A.	Wealdstone	Boreham Wood
27 Bradshaw, Mark	Halifax Town	Southport
13 Brennan, Karl A.	Nuneaton Borough	Redditch United
24 Breslan, Geoffrey F.	Exeter City	Tamworth
20 Broughton, Drewe O.	Peterborough United	Dagenham & Redbridge
10 Brown, John K.	Barnsley	Oxford United
17 Butler, Paul J.	Sunderland	Wolverhampton Wanderers
13 Butler, Thomas	Sunderland	Darlington
18 Butterfield, John P.	Chesham United	Dulwich Hamlet
30 Caig, Antony	Blackpool	Charlton Athletic
17 Campbell, James R.	Peterborough United	Spalding United
30 Carr, Darren J.	Brighton & Hove Albion	Rotherham United
10 Caton, Sean T.	Heybridge Swifts	Chelmsford City
24 Clare, Daryl A.	Grimsby Town	Northampton Town
9 Conlon, Barry J.	York City	Colchester United
9 Connor, Paul	Stoke City	Cambridge United
24 Cooper, Michael E.C.	Exeter City	Weston-Super-Mare
15 Cowley, Alan D.	Runcorn	Trafford
20 Cummings, Warren	Chelsea	AFC Bournemouth
8 Darcy, Ross	Barnet	Dover Athletic
11 Deakin, John	Worcester City	Evesham United
26 Defoe, Jermaine C.	West Ham United	AFC Bournemouth
7 Denny, Philip M.	Bradford Park Avenue	Bamber Bridge
23 De Souza, Juan B.	Boston United	Farnborough Town
24 Drewett, Gary P.	Kingstonian	Woking
18 Druce, Mark A.	Woking	Oxford City
24 Dryden, Richard A.	Southampton	Swindon Town
22 Dudgeon, James F.	Barnsley	Lincoln City
14 Edghill, Richard A.	Manchester City	Birmingham City
17 Fredgaard, Carsten	Sunderland	Bolton Wanderers
1 French, Daniel J.	Peterborough United	Boston United
9 Galloway, Michael A.	Chesterfield	Carlisle United
8 Garcia, Richard	West Ham United	Leyton Orient
10 Glennon, Matthew	Bolton Wanderers	Carlisle United
10 Gray, Simon R.	Wivenhoe Town	Witham Town
9 Gudmundsson, Johann B.	Watford	Cambridge United
16 Hann, Matthew	Peterborough United	Bishop's Stortford
24 Hannigan, Al J.	St Albans City	Hayes
10 Harney, Michael	Welling United	Bromley
4 Harvey, Lee	St Albans City	Enfield
3 Hasell, James	Stevenage Borough	Harlow Town
10 Hawe, Steven J.	Blackburn Rovers	Halifax Town
1 Hay, Alexander N.	Tranmere Rovers	Altrincham
3 Henry, Anthony F.	Lincoln City	Northwich Victoria
23 Hicks, Graham	Rochdale	Chorley
10 Holbrook, Adam P.	Portsmouth	Salisbury City
23 Holt, Grant	Halifax Town	Workington
24 Huckerby, Scott	Telford United	Tamworth
30 Hutchings, Carl E.	Bristol City	Exeter City
15 Inman, Niall E.	Peterborough United	Kettering Town
10 Iwellumo, Chris	Stoke City	York City
7 Jobson, Richard I.	Manchester City	Watford
4 Jones, Daniel	Enfield	St Albans City
24 Kadi, Junior	Kingstonian	Woking
14 Kippe, Frode	Liverpool	Stoke City
9 Kozluk, Robert	Sheffield United	Huddersfield Town
1 Kyle, Kevin	Sunderland	Darlington
10 Lumsdon, Christopher	Sunderland	Crewe Alexandra
4 Maddison, Neil S.	Middlesbrough	Barnsley
24 Maley, Mark	Sunderland	Northampton Town
18 Mason, Andrew	Leigh RMI	Leek Town
24 McAreavey, Paul	Swindon Town	Kilkenny City
26 McCann, Grant S.	West Ham United	Cheltenham Town
17 McCann, Peter	Barnet	Folkestone
27 Meechan, Alexander T.	Bristol City	Yeovil Town
20 Meijer, Erik	Liverpool	Preston North End
23 Miller, Alan J.	Blackburn Rovers	Coventry City
20 Morris, Elliott	West Bromwich Albion	Doncaster Rovers
2 Mumford, Andrew O.	Swansea City	Haverfordwest
28 Myhre, Thomas	Everton	Tranmere Rovers
22 Newton, Adam L.	West Ham United	Notts County
10 O'Reilly, Alexander	West Ham United	Wigan Athletic
24 Packham, William J.	Brighton & Hove Albion	Bognor Regis Town
30 Parker, Scott M.	Charlton Athletic	Norwich City
24 Parkin, Sam	Chelsea	Wycombe Wanderers
23 Parnaby, Stuart	Middlesbrough	Halifax Town
17 Patton, Aaron	Slough Town	Hemel Hempstead Town
2 Peschisolido, Paulo P.	Fulham	Queens Park Rangers
18 Pope, Steven A.	Kidderminster Harriers	Moor Green
24 Priestley, Philip A.	Rochdale	Scarborough
24 Prindiville, Steven A.	Nuneaton Borough	Solihull Borough
1 Rapley, Kevin J.	Notts County	Exeter City
3 Redmile, Matthew I.	Notts County	Shrewsbury Town
7 Ripley, Stuart E.	Southampton	Barnsley
27 Riza, Omer K.	West Ham United	Barnet
10 Roberts, Aaron	Basingstoke Town	Leatherhead

10 Roberts, Darren A.	Exeter City	Barrow	
14 Robinson, Paul D.	Wimbledon	Burnley	
17 Simpson, Phillip M.	Slough Town	Boreham Wood	
30 Smith, Andrew W.	Sheffield United	Bury	
9 Smith, Peter E.	Exeter City	Cambridge City	
20 Smith, Philip A.	Millwall	Walton & Hersham	
13 Speakman, Robert	Exeter City	Tiverton Town	
19 Tarrant, Neil K.	Aston Villa	York City	
3 Tate, Christopher D.	Scarborough	Leyton Orient	
17 Taylor, Mark J.	Barnet	Chelmsford City	
24 Thomas, James A.	Blackburn Rovers	Sheffield United	
3 Trees, Robert V.	Bristol Rovers	Leigh RMI	
8 Turner, Andrew P.	Rotherham United	Boston United	
5 Turner, Michael	Barnsley	Doncaster Rovers	
10 Underwood, Steven	Halifax Town	Harrogate Town	
13 Wainwright, Neil	Sunderland	Halifax Town	
10 Westcott, John P.J.	Sutton United	Langney Sports	
23 Whitbread, Adrian R.	Portsmouth	Luton Town	
30 Wolf, Danny	Bishop's Stortford	Leyton Pennant	
10 Woodman, Andrew J.	Brentford	Colchester United	
24 Worrell, David	Dundee United	Plymouth Argyle	

December 2000

15 Abbey, Zema	Cambridge United	Norwich City	350,000
21 Allsopp, Daniel	Manchester City	Notts County	300,000
8 Armstrong, Alun	Middlesbrough	Ipswich Town	500,000
1 Barrett, Adam N.	Plymouth Argyle	Mansfield Town	10,000
15 Berg, Henning	Manchester United	Blackburn Rovers	1,750,000
23 Betts, Simon R.	Scarborough	Yeovil Town	undisclosed
21 Camara, Aboubacar S.	Liverpool	West Ham United	1,500,000
1 Carsley, Lee K.	Blackburn Rovers	Coventry City	2,500,000
1 Cooke, Andrew R.	Burnley	Stoke City	350,000
18 Gordon, Kenyatta G.	Lincoln City	Cardiff City	275,000
1 Hatswell, Wayne	Forest Green Rovers	Oxford United	35,000
1 Hockton, Danny J.	Stevenage Borough	Dover Athletic	undisclosed
29 Huckerby, Darren C.	Leeds United	Manchester City	2,500,000
3 Jones, Matthew G.	Leeds United	Leicester City	3,250,000
22 Kendall, Lee M.	Crystal Palace	Cardiff City	50,000
15 Lilley, Derek	Oxford United	Dundee United	75,000
1 McGlinchey, Brian K.	Gillingham	Plymouth Argyle	Free
15 Mills, Jonathan P.	Oxford United	Southampton	25,000
1 Molenaar, Robert	Leeds United	Bradford City	500,000
20 Moses, Adrian P.	Barnsley	Huddersfield Town	225,000
13 Ngonge, Felix M.	Watford	Queens Park Rangers	50,000
20 Reina, Enrique I.	Ramsgate	Folkestone Invicta	500,000
1 Sjolund, Henrik D.	West Ham United	Liverpool	undisclosed
7 Staunton, Stephen	Liverpool	Aston Villa	Free
14 Vernazza, Paolo	Arsenal	Watford	350,000
16 Wardley, Shane	Cambridge City	Southend United	5000

Temporary transfers

11 Andrews, Keith J.	Wolverhampton Wanderers	Oxford United	
15 Barrett, Graham	Arsenal	Bristol Rovers	
8 Birmingham, David P.	Portsmouth	Bognor Regis Town	
15 Blackford, Gary	Margate	Dulwich Hamlet	
29 Black, Michael J.	Tranmere Rovers	Southend United	
29 Blatsis, Con	Derby County	Sheffield Wednesday	
15 Brennan, Karl A.	Nuneaton Borough	Redditch United	
24 Breslan, Geoff F.	Exeter City	Tamworth	
15 Broughton, Drewe O.	Peterborough United	Stevenage Borough	
29 Burley, Adam G.	Sheffield United	Burton Albion	
3 Caig, Antony	Blackpool	Charlton Athletic	
17 Campbell, James R.	Peterborough United	Spalding United	
12 Caton, Sean T.	Heybridge Swifts	Chelmsford City	
8 Charles, Anthony D.	Crewe Alexandra	Hyde United	
22 Chilvers, Liam C.	Arsenal	Northampton Town	
30 Clare, Daryl A.	Grimsby Town	Cheltenham Town	
10 Conlon, Barry J.	York City	Colchester United	
6 Connor, Paul	Stoke City	Cambridge United	
15 Cooke, Terence J.	Manchester City	Sheffield Wednesday	
15 Cort, Leon T.A.	Millwall	Forest Green Rovers	
29 Craker, Lewis	Walton & Hersham	Maidenhead United	
26 Crooks, Lee R.	Manchester City	Northampton Town	
20 Cummings, Warren	Chelsea	AFC Bournemouth	
15 Cutler, Neil A.	Aston Villa	Oxford United	
15 Davies, Allan A.	Burton Albion	Worcester City	
14 Day, Christopher N.	Watford	Lincoln City	
27 Defoe, Jermaine C.	West Ham United	AFC Bournemouth	
22 Doherty, Gerard	Derby County	Ilkeston Town	
25 Dryden, Richard A.	Southampton	Swindon Town	
9 Duckett, Mark	Stevenage Borough	Aylesbury United	
14 Dudfield, Lawrie G.	Leicester City	Chesterfield	
21 Dudgeon, James F.	Barnsley	Lincoln City	
15 Evans, Lee	Stockport County	Radcliffe Borough	
29 Ferguson, Barry	Coventry City	Northampton Town	
8 Finney, Stephen K.	Chester City	Altrincham	
1 Forrester, Scott	Sutton United	Dulwich Hamlet	
18 Fredgaard, Carsten	Sunderland	Bolton Wanderers	
4 Galloway, Michael A.	Chesterfield	Carlisle United	
1 Gillespie, Keith R.	Blackburn Rovers	Wigan Athletic	
1 Grant, Anthony J.	Manchester City	West Bromwich Albion	
9 Gray, Simon R.	Wivenhoe Town	Witham Town	
7 Greatorex, Mark	Margate	Dartford	
22 Haley, Grant R.	Peterborough United	Bedford Town	
15 Hamsher, John J.	Rushden & Diamonds	Dagenham & Redbridge	
15 Harney, Michael	Welling United	Bromley	
29 Harper, James A.J.	Arsenal	Cardiff City	
29 Healy, David J.	Manchester United	Preston North End	
15 Hendry, Edward C.J.	Coventry City	Bolton Wanderers	
16 Hibbins, John J.	Worksop Town	Lincoln United	
24 Hicks, Graham	Rochdale	Chorley	
23 Holt, Grant	Halifax Town	Workington	
1 Inglethorpe, Alex M.	Exeter City	Canvey Island	
15 Inman, Niall E.	Peterborough United	Kettering Town	

Player	From	To	
10 Iwellumo, Chris	Stoke City	York City	
15 Jenkins, Stephen R.	Huddersfield Town	Birmingham City	
28 Jobson, Richard I.	Manchester City	Tranmere Rovers	
27 Jones, Matthew N.	Shrewsbury Town	Southport	
23 Kadi, Junior	Kingstonian	Woking	
31 Kelly, Gavin R.	Tottenham Hotspur	Kingstonian	
12 Kippe, Frode	Liverpool	Stoke City	
16 Landon, Richard J.	Altrincham	Droylsden	
15 Lindley, James E.	Notts County	Mansfield Town	
8 Ling, Martin	Leyton Orient	Purfleet	
1 Lisbie, Kevin A.	Charlton Athletic	Queens Park Rangers	
12 McDonald, Thomas	Southend United	Slough Town	
15 McMahon, David	Newcastle United	Darlington	
9 Nash, Carlo J.	Stockport County	Wolverhampton Wanderers	
8 Ndlovu, Peter	Birmingham City	Huddersfield Town	
15 Newell, Paul C.	Billericay Town	Hendon	
28 Newton, Adam L.	West Ham United	Notts County	
22 Norris, David M.	Bolton Wanderers	Boston United	
15 Osborn, Mark	Wycombe Wanderers	Carshalton Athletic	
24 Packham, William J.	Brighton & Hove Albion	Bognor Regis Town	
15 Palmer, Carlton L.	Coventry City	Watford	
21 Peake, Jason W.	Plymouth Argyle	Nuneaton Borough	
20 Pearce, Alexander G.	Chesterfield	Worksop Town	
22 Phillips, Lee P.	Plymouth Argyle	Weymouth	
18 Pope, Steven A.	Kidderminster Harriers	Moor Green	
22 Priestley, Philip A.	Rochdale	Scarborough	
3 Rapley, Kevin J.	Notts County	Exeter City	
21 Redmile, Matthew I.	Notts County	Shrewsbury Town	
16 Ricketts, Gary	Hinckley United	Hucknall Town	
13 Ripley, Stuart E.	Southampton	Barnsley	
12 Roberts, Aaron	Basingstoke Town	Leatherhead	
11 Roberts, Darren A.	Exeter City	Barrow	
12 Rogers, Kristian R.	Wrexham	Rushden & Diamonds	
8 Trainer, Philip A.	Crewe Alexandra	Hyde United	
6 Trees, Robert V.	Bristol Rovers	Leigh RMI	
12 Trought, Michael	Bristol Rovers	Clevedon Town	
5 Turner, Michael	Barnsley	Doncaster Rovers	
10 Underwood, Steven	Halifax Town	Harrogate Town	
8 Upson, Matthew J.	Arsenal	Nottingham Forest	
11 Westcott, John P.J.	Sutton United	Langney Sports	
24 Whitbread, Adrian R.	Portsmouth	Luton Town	
15 White, Ben	Gillingham	Dover Athletic	
15 Whitley, James	Manchester City	Swindon Town	
7 Wilkinson, Stephen J.	Kettering Town	Spalding United	
24 Winter, Steven D.	Basingstoke Town	Tiverton Town	
22 Wooding, Timothy D.	Boston United	Cambridge City	
10 Woodman, Andrew J.	Brentford	Colchester United	
22 Woodward, Andrew S.	Sheffield United	Scunthorpe United	

January 2001

Player	From	To	Fee
19 Appleton, Michael A.	Preston North End	West Bromwich Albion	750,000
3 Barker, Richard I.	Macclesfield Town	Rotherham United	60,000
15 Blundell, Gregg	Vauxhall Motors	Northwich Victoria	undisclosed
31 Bradshaw, Darren S.	Rushden & Diamonds	Stevenage Borough	undisclosed
22 Bramble, Tesfaye	Cambridge City	Southend United	undisclosed
29 Brooker, Stephen M.	Watford	Port Vale	nominal
31 Butler, Paul J.	Sunderland	Wolverhampton Wanderers	15,000
9 Caig, Antony	Blackpool	Charlton Athletic	1,000,000
18 Dailly, Christian E.	Blackburn Rovers	West Ham United	Free
25 De Bolla, Mark	Aston Villa	Charlton Athletic	1,750,000
17 De Souza, Juan M.	Boston United	Farnborough Town	nominal
19 Duerden, Ian C.	Doncaster Rovers	Kingstonian	undisclosed
10 Flynn, Lee D.	Hayes	Barnet	undisclosed
9 Forrester, Scott	Sutton United	Dulwich Hamlet	13,500
19 Gower, Mark	Tottenham Hotspur	Barnet	undisclosed
19 Hamsher, John J.	Rushden & Diamonds	Stevenage Borough	32,500
3 Hasell, James	Stevenage Borough	Harlow Town	undisclosed
19 Hayward, Steve L.	Fulham	Barnsley	undisclosed
3 Healy, David J.	Manchester United	Preston North End	25,000
22 Heywood, Matthew S.	Burnley	Swindon Town	1,500,000
5 Hoult, Russell	Portsmouth	West Bromwich Albion	Free
12 Johnson, David A.	Ipswich Town	Nottingham Forest	500,000
25 Kadi, Junior	Kingstonian	Woking	3,000,000
12 Keller, Marc	West Ham United	Blackburn Rovers	undisclosed
5 Lane, Christopher	Hereford United	Southport	Free
25 Maddison, Lee R.	Dundee United	Carlisle United	undisclosed
12 McGleish, Scott	Barnet	Colchester United	Free
4 Mitchell, Richard D.	Nuneaton Borough	Norwich Victoria	15,000
12 Nash, Carlo J.	Stockport County	Manchester City	undisclosed
26 Nwadike, Chukwuemeka	Kings Lynn	Ilkeston Town	100,000
5 Perkins, Christopher P.	Chesterfield	Lincoln City	undisclosed
30 Piper, Christopher C.	St Albans City	Farnborough Town	Free
12 Quinn, Robert J.	Brentford	Oxford United	undisclosed
19 Rankin, Isaiah	Bradford City	Barnsley	75,000
19 Redmile, Matthew I.	Notts County	Shrewsbury Town	350,000
12 Reid, Brian R.	Dunfermline Athletic	Blackpool	30,000
19 Richards, Justin	West Bromwich Albion	Bristol Rovers	Free
2 Rowe, Rodney C.	Gillingham	Hull City	75,000
12 Scott, Andrew	Brentford	Oxford United	Free
4 Shields, Dene	Raith Rovers	Sunderland	75,000
19 Sturridge, Dean	Derby County	Leicester City	undisclosed
4 Summerbee, Nicholas J.	Sunderland	Bolton Wanderers	350,000
25 Worrell, David	Dundee United	Plymouth Argyle	nominal
			nominal

Temporary transfers

Player	From	To	
19 Alford, Carl P.	Doncaster Rovers	Kettering Town	
12 Benali, Francis V.	Southampton	Nottingham Forest	
12 Beresford, Marlon	Middlesbrough	Sheffield Wednesday	
26 Blatsis, Con	Derby County	Sheffield Wednesday	
30 Booth, Andrew D.	Sheffield Wednesday	Tottenham Hotspur	
19 Bramble, Tesfaye	Cambridge City	Southend United	
12 Brennan, Karl A.	Nuneaton Borough	Hinckley United	
5 Brooker, Stephen M.L.	Watford	Port Vale	
22 Broughton, Drewe O.	Peterborough United	Kidderminster Harriers	

2 Caig, Antony	Blackpool	Charlton Athletic
26 Canoville, Lee	Arsenal	Northampton Town
9 Carr, Darren J.	Brighton & Hove Albion	Lincoln City
25 Cartwright, James P.	Telford United	Stafford Rangers
5 Chambers, Leroy D.	Altrincham	Frickley Athletic
6 Charles, Anthony D.	Crewe Alexandra	Hyde United
26 Chudy, Lee	Basingstoke Town	Burnham
26 Coleman, Danny	Farnborough Town	Chalfont St Peter
7 Connor, Paul	Stoke City	Cambridge United
27 Cooper, Kevin	Chertsey Town	Molesey
16 Cort, Leon	Millwall	Forest Green Rovers
3 Crooks, Lee R.	Manchester City	Northampton Town
21 Cutler, Neil	Aston Villa	Oxford United
12 Davies, Allan	Burton Albion	Worcester City
16 Day, Christopher N.	Watford	Lincoln City
20 Denny, Philip M.	Bradford Park Avenue	Guiseley
5 De Souza, Juan M.	Boston United	Farnborough Town
24 Doherty, Gerard	Derby County	Ilkeston Town
6 Duckett, Mark	Stevenage Borough	Aylesbury United
4 Dudfield, Lawrie G.	Leicester City	Chesterfield
9 Ebanks, Michael	Dulwich Hamlet	Croydon Athletic
26 Foster, Martin	Doncaster Rovers	Forest Green Rovers
12 Grayson, Simon N.	Blackburn Rovers	Stockport County
11 Greatorex, Mark	Margate	Dartford
10 Hamilton, Derrik V.	Newcastle United	Tranmere Rovers
12 Harney, Michael	Welling United	Bromley
5 Henry, Anthony F.	Lincoln City	Northwich Victoria
20 Hibbins, John J.	Worksop Town	Lincoln United
5 Hodson, Matthew J.	Hayes	Hampton & Richmond Borough
23 Holsgrove, Lee	Aldershot Town	Boreham Wood
10 Iwelumo, Chris	Stoke City	York City
30 Jobson, Richard I.	Manchester City	Tranmere Rovers
26 Kennerdale, Nick	Eastwood Town	Nuneaton Borough
26 Kirby, Ryan	Stevenage Borough	Aldershot Town
2 Kotylo, Krystof J.	Nuneaton Borough	Eastwood Town
26 Kyle, Kevin A.	Sunderland	Rochdale
17 Landon, Richard J.	Altrincham	Droylsden
19 Lavin, Gerard	Bristol City	Wycombe Wanderers
27 Lenagh, Steven M.	Kettering Town	Kings Lynn
30 Lewis, Karl J.	Gillingham	Leicester City
13 Lightbourne, Kyle L.	Stoke City	Swindon Town
9 Ling, Martin	Leyton Orient	Purfleet
25 Logan, Richard J.	Ipswich Town	Cambridge United
30 Marriott, Andrew	Sunderland	Wigan Athletic
5 Mason, Andrew	Leigh RMI	Chorley
22 McAnespie, Kieran	Fulham	Heart of Midlothian
26 McKenzie, Christy G.	Tamworth	Sutton Coldfield Town
12 Monk, Garry A.	Southampton	Oxford United
26 Morley, David T.	Southend United	Carlisle United
19 Mounty, Carl T.	Swansea City	Bangor
5 Murphy, Brendan F.	Kidderminster Harriers	Redditch United
18 Murray, Jade A.	Leyton Orient	Chelmsford City
5 Mutton, Thomas J.	Swansea City	Merthyr Tydfil
4 Nancekivell, Kevin W.J.	Plymouth Argyle	Tiverton Town
20 Newell, Paul C.	Billericay Town	Grays Athletic
20 Newton, Howard	Hampton & Richmond Borough	Epsom & Ewell
21 Norris, David M.	Bolton Wanderers	Boston United
17 O'Brien, Michael G.	Torquay United	Southport
16 Osborn, Mark	Wycombe Wanderers	Carshalton Athletic
20 Parkin, Sam	Chelsea	Wycombe Wanderers
17 Peake, Jason W.	Plymouth Argyle	Nuneaton Borough
19 Peschisolido, Paolo P.	Fulham	Sheffield United
5 Phillips, Gareth R.	Swansea City	Merthyr Tydfil
22 Phillips, Lee P.	Plymouth Argyle	Weymouth
5 Pearce, Steven	Hereford United	Halesowen Town
19 Pinnock, James E.	Gillingham	Chesham United
20 Pluck, Lee K.	Barnet	Grays Athletic
5 Pope, Steven A.	Kidderminster Harriers	Aberystwyth Town
10 Quinn, Wayne R.	Sheffield United	Newcastle United
27 Reddy, Michael	Sunderland	Swindon Town
5 Robinson, Ian B.	Hednesford Town	Northwich Victoria
19 Ross, Neil J.	Stockport County	Radcliffe Borough
27 Rowland, Keith	Queens Park Rangers	Luton Town
19 Sharpling, Christopher B.	Crystal Palace	Woking
18 Simpson, Phillip M.	Slough Town	Boreham Wood
1 Smith, Andrew W.	Sheffield United	Bury
26 Smith, Darren K.	Gravesend & Northfleet	Aveley
30 Strevens, Benjamin J.	Barnet	St Albans City
4 Summerbee, Nicholas J.	Sunderland	Bolton Wanderers
23 Thompson, Glyn W.	Fulham	Shrewsbury Town
25 Town, David	Rushden & Diamonds	Hayes
6 Trainer, Philip A.	Crewe Alexandra	Hyde United
10 Trought, Michael	Bristol Rovers	Clevedon Town
16 Wakefield, David	Havant & Waterlooville	Salisbury City
5 Walshe, Liam R.	Burton Albion	Shepshed Dynamo
12 Welsby, Kevin J.	Crewe Alexandra	Leek Town
12 Westcott, John P.J.	Sutton United	Langney Sports
12 Wilkie, Lee	Dundee	Plymouth Argyle
23 Williams, Daniel I.L.	Wrexham	Doncaster Rovers
23 Winter, Steven D.	Basingstoke Town	Tiverton Town
4 Wolf, Danny	Bishop's Stortford	Aveley
23 Wooding, Timothy D.	Boston United	Cambridge City
2 Woodward, Andrew	Sheffield United	Scunthorpe United
18 Wright, Thomas J.	Manchester City	Bolton Wanderers

February 2001

16 Beagrie, Peter S.	Bradford City	Wigan Athletic	Free
9 Berkovic, Eyal	Celtic	Blackburn Rovers	undisclosed
16 Brannan, Gerald D.	Motherwell	Wigan Athletic	175,000
15 Brightwell, David J.	Hull City	Darlington	Free
2 Brooker, Stephen M.L.	Watford	Port Vale	undisclosed
21 Broughton, Drewe O.	Peterborough United	Kidderminster Harriers	50,000
9 Clifford, Mark	Ilkeston Town	Boston United	undisclosed
13 Ellison, Kevin	Altrincham	Leicester City	50,000

19 Ford, Mark S.	Torquay United	Darlington	15,000
23 Harper, James	Arsenal	Reading	400,000
15 Harper, Steven J.	Hull City	Darlington	Free
8 Hartson, John	Wimbledon	Coventry City	undisclosed
14 Haydon, Nicky	Heybridge Swifts	Chelmsford City	undisclosed
12 Hendry, Edward C.J.	Coventry City	Bolton Wanderers	250,000
6 Hughes, Robert D.	Shrewsbury Town	Cardiff City	450,000
16 Hurst, Glynn	Ayr United	Stockport County	150,000
9 Jones, Mark A.	Chesterfield	Raith Rovers	Free
22 Kennerdale, Nick	Eastwood Town	Nuneaton Borough	undisclosed
16 Macdonald, Gary	Havant & Waterlooville	Peterborough United	undisclosed
23 Marcelle, Clinton S.	Hull City	Darlington	Free
16 Mawson, Craig J.	Burnley	Halifax Town	Free
15 McIndoe, Michael	Hereford United	Yeovil Town	undisclosed
2 Ndlovu, Peter	Birmingham City	Sheffield United	Free
21 Quinn, Wayne R.	Sheffield United	Newcastle United	750,000
23 Rawle, Mark A.	Boston United	Southend United	60,000
9 Ricketts, Gary	Hinckley United	Hucknall Town	undisclosed
12 Robinson, Steven E.	Birmingham City	Swindon Town	50,000
15 Roussel, Cedric	Coventry City	Wolverhampton Wanderers	1,530,000
16 Sedgemore, Benjamin R.	Macclesfield Town	Lincoln City	undisclosed
9 Shorey, Nicholas	Leyton Orient	Reading	25,000
9 Talbot, Robert T.	Burscough	Morecambe	Free
23 Vincent, Jamie R.	Huddersfield Town	Portsmouth	800,000
2 Woodhouse, Curtis	Sheffield United	Birmingham City	1,000,000

Temporary transfers

17 Abbott, Paul	Stevenage Borough	Arlessey Town
17 Alford, Carl P.	Doncaster Rovers	Kettering Town
15 Atherton, Peter	Bradford City	Birmingham City
10 Barrett, Daniel T.	Chesterfield	Stafford Rangers
16 Beall, Matthew J.	Leyton Orient	Dover Athletic
12 Benali, Francis V.	Southampton	Nottingham Forest
16 Bennett, Frank	Forest Green Rovers	Cinderford Town
9 Berry, Trevor J.	Rotherham United	Scunthorpe United
16 Betts, Robert	Coventry City	Plymouth Argyle
16 Brennan, Karl A.	Nuneaton Borough	Hinckley United
9 Carr, Darren J.	Brighton & Hove Albion	Carlisle United
3 Charles, Anthony D.	Crewe Alexandra	Hyde United
8 Clarke, David L.	Dover Athletic	Chesham United
9 Clark, Richard	Tamworth	Evesham United
16 Collins, Simon J.	Macclesfield Town	Shrewsbury Town
28 Cooper, Kevin	Chertsey Town	Molesey
18 Cort, Leon	Millwall	Forest Green Rovers
16 Cramb, Colin	Crewe Alexandra	Bury
14 Davies, Allan	Burton Albion	Worcester City
14 Day, Christopher N.	Watford	Lincoln City
21 Denny, Philip M.	Bradford Park Avenue	Guiseley
6 Derveld, Fernando	Norwich City	West Bromwich Albion
23 Doherty, Gerard	Derby County	Ilkeston Town
17 Duckett, Mark	Stevenage Borough	Arlessey Town
8 Dudfield, Lawrie G.	Leicester City	Chesterfield
23 Eaton, Jamie	Ilkeston Town	Eastwood Town
9 Ebanks, Michael	Dulwich Hamlet	Croydon Athletic
9 Fewings, Paul J.	Boston United	Kingstonian
24 Forbes, Steven D.	Dagenham & Redbridge	Cambridge City
28 Gittens, Jon	Nuneaton Borough	Dorchester Town
24 Goodridge, Gregory St. C.R.	Bristol City	Cheltenham Town
9 Grant, Gareth M.	Bradford City	Lincoln City
15 Greatorex, Mark	Margate	Dartford
28 Gritton, Martin	Plymouth Argyle	Yeovil Town
2 Hann, Matthew	Peterborough United	Cambridge City
23 Harney, Michael	Welling United	Ashford Town
6 Hodson, Matthew J.	Hayes	Hampton & Richmond Borough
26 Holt, Grant	Halifax Town	Barrow
2 Ireland, Craig	Dundee	Notts County
13 Iwelumo, Chris	Stoke City	Cheltenham Town
21 James, Robert K.	Swansea City	Port Talbot
9 Jefferson, Christopher	Worcester City	Bromsgrove Rovers
8 Kell, Richard	Middlesbrough	Torquay United
1 Kelly, Gavin R.	Tottenham Hotspur	Kingstonian
16 King, Stuart S.E.	Preston North End	Queen of the South
2 Kotylo, Krystof J.	Nuneaton Borough	Eastwood Town
27 Lenagh, Steven M.	Kettering Town	Kings Lynn
20 Lightbourne, Kyle L.	Stoke City	Cardiff City
26 Lindley, James E.	Notts County	Gresley Rovers
9 Matthews, Robert D.	Stockport County	Halifax Town
8 McKeever, Mark A.	Sheffield Wednesday	Bristol Rovers
1 Mensing, Simon R.	Wimbledon	Stenhousemuir
9 Mike, Leon J.	Manchester City	Halifax Town
11 Monk, Garry	Southampton	Oxford United
23 Morris, Elliott J.	West Bromwich Albion	Bromsgrove Rovers
21 Mumford, Andrew O.	Swansea City	Port Talbot
5 Nancekivell, Kevin W.J.	Plymouth Argyle	Tiverton Town
2 Newby, Jon P.R.	Liverpool	Bury
20 Newell, Paul C.	Billericay Town	Grays Athletic
20 Newton, Howard	Hampton & Richmond Borough	Epsom & Ewell
17 O'Brien, Michael G.	Torquay United	Southport
17 Osborn, Mark	Wycombe Wanderers	Carshalton Athletic
9 Ostendstad, Egil	Blackburn Rovers	Manchester City
9 Owusu, Ansah O.	Wimbledon	Bristol Rovers
16 Packham, William J.	Brighton & Hove Albion	Langney Sports
13 Palmer, Carlton L.	Coventry City	Sheffield Wednesday
14 Peake, Jason W.	Plymouth Argyle	Nuneaton Borough
13 Pearce, Alexander G.	Chesterfield	Worksop Town
18 Phillips, Lee P.	Plymouth Argyle	Weymouth
2 Piearce, Steven	Hereford United	Halesowen Town
3 Pinamonte, Lorenzo	Brentford	Leyton Orient
19 Pinnock, James	Gillingham	Chesham United
2 Poland, Lee	Northwich Victoria	Leek Town
27 Priestley, Philip A.	Rochdale	Chester City
27 Reddy, Michael	Sunderland	Swindon Town
9 Robinson, Gerard	Middlesbrough	Scarborough
21 Robinson, Paul D.	Wimbledon	Dundee United

2 Sharpe, Lee S.	Bradford City	Portsmouth	
16 Shittu, Daniel O.	Charlton Athletic	Blackpool	
23 Smith, Darren K.	Gravesend & Northfleet	Aveley	
16 Smith, Peter L.	Crewe Alexandra	Doncaster Rovers	
13 Soltvedt, Trond E.	Southampton	Sheffield Wednesday	
9 Steele, Paul	Yeovil Town	Woking	
16 Stoner, Craig J.	Portsmouth	Bognor Regis Town	
20 Taylor, Gareth K.	Manchester City	Burnley	
15 Taylor, Stuart J.	Arsenal	Peterborough United	
19 Thomas, Nathan	Barking	Grays Athletic	
9 Tiler, Carl	Charlton Athletic	Birmingham City	
3 Trainer, Philip A.	Crewe Alexandra	Hyde United	
16 Trundle, Lee C.	Rhyl	Wrexham	
9 Tyne, Thomas R.	Millwall	Fisher Athletic	
9 Walker, Richard M.	Aston Villa	Blackpool	
23 Walsh, David	Wrexham	Rhyl	
2 Walshe, Liam R.	Burton Albion	Shepshed Dynamo	
8 Wharton, Paul	Farsley Celtic	Bradford Park Avenue	
8 Whitbread, Adrian R.	Portsmouth	Reading	
27 Whitley, James	Manchester City	Northampton Town	
19 Wilkinson, Stephen J.	Kettering Town	Shepshed Dynamo	
24 Willmot, Richard	Hitchin Town	Metropolitan Police	
23 Winter, Steven D.	Basingstoke Town	Tiverton Town	

March 2001

8 Asaba, Carl E.	Gillingham	Sheffield United	92,500
16 Baldacchino, Ryan L.	Blackburn Rovers	Bolton Wanderers	Free
14 Basham, Michael	Barnet	York City	Free
16 Bignot, Marcus	Bristol Rovers	Queens Park Rangers	undisclosed
22 Booth, Andrew D.	Sheffield Wednesday	Huddersfield Town	175,000
15 Brass, Christopher P.	Burnley	York City	Free
16 Brennan, Karl A.	Nuneaton Borough	Hinckley United	undisclosed
22 Carruthers, Martin G.	Southend United	Scunthorpe United	20,000
9 Connor, Paul	Stoke City	Rochdale	100,000
16 Cooper, Kevin L.	Stockport County	Wimbledon	800,000
16 Cooper, Mark N.	Hednesford Town	Forest Green Rovers	undisclosed
2 Crooks, Lee R.	Manchester City	Barnsley	190,000
23 Dixon, Gary J.	Hitchin Town	Boreham Wood	undisclosed
21 Drury, Adam J.	Peterborough United	Norwich City	undisclosed
17 Easter, Jermaine M.	Wolverhampton Wanderers	Hartlepool United	Free
7 Elliott, Stuart T.	Darlington	Plymouth Argyle	Free
22 Epesse-Titi, Steeve	Wolverhampton Wanderers	Exeter City	undisclosed
22 Evans, Michael J.	Bristol Rovers	Plymouth Argyle	undisclosed
8 Evers, Sean A.	Reading	Plymouth Argyle	undisclosed
22 Gall, Kevin A.	Newcastle United	Bristol Rovers	Free
8 Gayle, Marcus A.	Wimbledon	Glasgow Rangers	900,000
23 Gilchrist, Philip A.	Leicester City	West Bromwich Albion	500,000
16 Goma, Alain	Newcastle United	Fulham	4,000,000
22 Greene, David M.	Cardiff City	Cambridge United	Free
20 Holt, Gary J.	Kilmarnock	Norwich City	100,000
16 Hopkin, David	Bradford City	Crystal Palace	1,500,000
22 Howard, Steven J.	Northampton Town	Luton Town	50,000
31 Hoyle, Colin	Boston United	Burton Albion	undisclosed
19 Ipoua, Guy	Scunthorpe United	Gillingham	25,000
1 Jackson, Kirk S.S.	Worksop Town	Darlington	undisclosed
2 Jobson, Richard I.	Manchester City	Tranmere Rovers	Free
16 Kitson, David	Arlesey Town	Cambridge United	undisclosed
22 Lee, Christian	Gillingham	Bristol Rovers	Free
16 Lewis, Karl J.	Gillingham	Leicester City	50,000
7 Makin, Christopher	Sunderland	Ipswich Town	1,250,000
13 Marriott, Andrew	Sunderland	Barnsley	Free
22 Marsh, Christopher J.	Walsall	Wycombe Wanderers	30,000
21 Marshall, Lee	Norwich City	Leicester City	600,000
22 Matthews, Lee J.	Leeds United	Bristol City	100,000
21 Matthews, Robert D.	Stockport County	Hull City	30,000
2 McCulloch, Lee	Motherwell	Wigan Athletic	700,000
15 McKeever, Mark A.	Sheffield Wednesday	Bristol Rovers	Free
2 McMillan, Stephen	Motherwell	Wigan Athletic	550,000
8 Mellon, Michael J.	Burnley	Tranmere Rovers	Free
22 Milligan, Jamie	Everton	Blackpool	Free
22 Newby, Jon P.R.	Liverpool	Bury	100,000
31 Newell, Paul C.	Billericay Town	Grays Athletic	undisclosed
28 O'Brien, Andrew J.	Bradford City	Newcastle United	2,000,000
22 O'Reilly, Alexander	West Ham United	Bristol Rovers	Free
22 Osborn, Simon E.	Wolverhampton Wanderers	Tranmere Rovers	Free
22 Parkinson, Gary A.	Preston North End	Blackpool	undisclosed
22 Prokas, Richard	Carlisle United	Cambridge United	undisclosed
12 Simms, Gordon H.	Wolverhampton Wanderers	Hartlepool United	Free
1 Smith, Craig	Belper Town	Hinckley United	undisclosed
22 Soltvedt, Trond E.	Southampton	Sheffield Wednesday	undisclosed
1 Thomas, Geoffrey R.	Barnsley	Notts County	Free
22 Thomas, Martin R.	Swansea City	Brighton & Hove Albion	Free
9 Thomas, Nathan	Barking	Grays Athletic	undisclosed
22 Thomson, Andrew	Gillingham	Queens Park Rangers	undisclosed
14 Tiler, Carl	Charlton Athletic	Portsmouth	250,000
28 Town, David	Rushden & Diamonds	Boston United	undisclosed
15 Windass, Dean	Bradford City	Middlesbrough	600,000
20 Wright, Thomas J.	Manchester City	Bolton Wanderers	Free

Temporary transfers

9 Ashdown, Jamie L.	Reading	Gravesend & Northfleet
22 Baptiste, Jairzinho R.	Luton Town	Hayes
29 Barlow, Martin D.	Plymouth Argyle	Yeovil Town
30 Barnes, Paul L.	Bury	Nuneaton Borough
11 Barrett, Daniel	Chesterfield	Stafford Rangers
18 Benali, Francis V.	Southampton	Nottingham Forest
2 Bennetts, Scott	Farnborough Town	Boreham Wood
13 Bernard, Olivier	Newcastle United	Darlington
22 Birch, Gary S.	Walsall	Exeter City
22 Boardman, Jonathan G.	Crystal Palace	Woking
15 Bossu, Bertrand	Barnet	Rushden & Diamonds
21 Brennan, James G.	Nottingham Forest	Huddersfield Town
29 Bridgwater, David	Telford United	Bromsgrove Rovers
21 Broad, Stephen	Chelsea	Southend United

22 Brown, Wayne L.	Ipswich Town	Queens Park Rangers
22 Bullock, Darren J.	Bury	Sheffield United
29 Bunce, Nathan	Stevenage Borough	Hayes
13 Calderwood, Colin	Nottingham Forest	Notts County
9 Campbell, Andrew P.	Middlesbrough	Bolton Wanderers
9 Carr, Darren J.	Brighton & Hove Albion	Carlisle United
13 Carr, David	Solihull Borough	Paget Rangers
30 Charles, Anthony D.	Crewe Alexandra	Stalybridge Celtic
30 Chillingworth, Daniel T.	Cambridge United	Cambridge City
21 Claridge, Stephen E.	Portsmouth	Millwall
20 Clarke, Matthew J.	Bradford City	Bolton Wanderers
2 Clegg, George G.	Manchester United	Wycombe Wanderers
28 Cockrill, Dale	Cambridge United	Wisbech Town
22 Collins, Derek	Hibernian	Preston North End
2 Collins, James I.	Crewe Alexandra	Halesowen Town
16 Collins, Simon	Macclesfield Town	Shrewsbury Town
11 Collis, David J.	Charlton Athletic	Barnet
21 Connelly, Sean P.	Stockport County	Wolverhampton Wanderers
22 Dalglish, Paul	Nottingham Forest	York City
2 Cooper, Richard A.	Kidderminster Harriers	Redditch United
5 Corbett, Andrew J.	Fulham	Grimsby Town
13 Cornwall, Lucas C.C.	Millwall	Stevenage Borough
29 Cort, Leon T.A.	Crewe Alexandra	Bury
22 Cramb, Colin	Leicester City	Preston North End
13 Cresswell, Richard P.W.	Wolverhampton Wanderers	Hereford United
22 Crowe, Seamus M.M.	Peterborough United	Carlisle United
16 Cullen, David J.	Chelsea	West Bromwich Albion
21 Cummings, Warren	Norwich City	Wigan Athletic
22 Dalglish, Paul	Nottingham Forest	Barnet
9 Dawson, Kevin E.	Bradford Park Avenue	Guiseley
22 Denny, Philip M.	Manchester United	Port Vale
22 Dodd, Ashley M.	Leeds United	AFC Bournemouth
22 Feeney, Warren J.	Boston United	Farnborough Town
30 Fewings, Paul J.	Stevenage Borough	Hemel Hempstead Town
2 Field, Lewis	Northwich Victoria	Hull City
16 Fletcher, Gary	Arlesey Town	Harrow Borough
5 Fontenelle, Anthony	AFC Bournemouth	Dorchester Town
29 Ford, James A.	Peterborough United	Yeovil Town
23 Forinton, Howard L.	Doncaster Rovers	Forest Green Rovers
1 Foster, Martin	Peterborough United	Bedford Town
5 French, Daniel J.	Reading	Crawley Town
16 Gamble, Joseph F.	Leicester City	West Bromwich Albion
22 Gilchrist, Philip A.	Yeovil Town	Weston Super Mare
8 Giles, Christopher	Bristol City	Cheltenham Town
25 Goodridge, Gregory R.	Crewe Alexandra	Hyde United
19 Grant, John A.C.	Wolverhampton Wanderers	Torquay United
2 Green, Ryan M.	Plymouth Argyle	Yeovil Town
1 Gritton, Martin	Middlesbrough	Cambridge United
22 Hanson, Christian	Hull City	Shrewsbury Town
16 Harris, Jason A.	West Ham United	Kingstonian
29 Holligan, Gavin V.	Burton Albion	Ilkeston Town
29 Holmes, David J.	Oldham Athletic	Hull City
15 Holt, Andrew	Halifax Town	Barrow
26 Holt, Grant	Cheltenham Town	Cinderford Town
24 Hopkins, Gareth	Crewe Alexandra	Rochdale
1 Howell, Dean G.	Coventry City	Grimsby Town
22 Hyldgaard, Morten L.	Charlton Athletic	Colchester United
2 Izzet, Kemal	Ipswich Town	Crystal Palace
2 Karic, Amir	Carlisle United	Darlington
13 Keen, Peter A.	Blackburn Rovers	Tranmere Rovers
20 Kenna, Jeffrey J.	Chelsea	Queens Park Rangers
9 Knight, Leon L.	Nuneaton Borough	Eastwood Town
1 Kotylo, Krystof J.	Gillingham	Leyton Orient
6 Lee, Christian	Notts County	Gresley Rovers
28 Lindley, James E.	Reading	Forest Green Rovers
23 Lockwood, Adam B.	Charlton Athletic	Cheltenham Town
16 Macdonald, Charles L.	Middlesbrough	Bristol City
16 Maddison, Neil S.	Leeds United	Bristol City
16 Matthews, Lee J.	Stockport County	Halifax Town
14 Matthews, Robert	Sheffield Wednesday	Bristol Rovers
9 McKeever, Mark	Burnley	Tranmere Rovers
5 Mellon, Michael J.	Wigan Athletic	Halifax Town
22 Mitchell, Paul A.	Hereford United	Bamber Bridge
2 Moran, Andrew J.	West Bromwich Albion	Bromsgrove Rovers
26 Morris, Elliott	Derby County	Huddersfield Town
8 Morris, Lee	Manchester City	Sheffield United
22 Morrison, Andrew C.	Queens Park Rangers	Peterborough United
22 Morrow, Stephen J.	Runcorn	Vauxhall Motors
26 Moseley, Michael	Swansea City	Bangor City
1 Mounty, Carl T.	Stoke City	Cardiff City
15 Muggleton, Carl D.	Sheffield Wednesday	Worksop Town
1 Muller, Adam P.	Kidderminster Harriers	Solihull Borough
29 Murphy, Brendan F.	Notts County	Kettering Town
22 Murray, Shaun	Liverpool	Crewe Alexandra
22 Navarro, Alan E.	Liverpool	Bury
9 Newby, Jon P.R.	Harrow Borough	Yeading
9 Newby, Keith	Blackburn Rovers	Manchester City
16 Ostenstad, Egil	Wimbledon	Bristol Rovers
12 Owusu, Ansah O.	Chelsea	Oldham Athletic
22 Parkin, Sam	Liverpool	Bristol Rovers
22 Partridge, Richard J.	Chesterfield	Worksop Town
28 Pearce, Alexander G.	Fulham	Norwich City
22 Peschisolido, Paulo P.	Portsmouth	Torquay United
15 Petterson, Andrew K.	Dagenham & Redbridge	Billericay Town
17 Piscopides, Paul	Northwich Victoria	Leek Town
4 Poland, Lee	Crystal Palace	Birmingham City
16 Pollock, Jamie	Rochdale	Chester City
28 Priestley, Philip A.	Sunderland	Halifax Town
14 Proctor, Michael A.	Notts County	Scunthorpe United
17 Rapley, Kevin J.	Chelsea	Mansfield Town
16 Reddington, Stuart	Sunderland	Swindon Town
28 Reddy, Michael	Southampton	Sheffield Wednesday
22 Ripley, Stuart E.	West Ham United	Cambridge United
2 Riza, Omer K.	Southend United	Stockport County
1 Roget, Leo T.E.		

1 Searle, Stuart A.	Aldershot Town	Carshalton Athletic
5 Sharpe, Lee S.	Bradford City	Portsmouth
18 Shittu, Daniel O.	Charlton Athletic	Blackpool
27 Shuker, Christopher A.	Manchester City	Macclesfield Town
1 Simpson, Fitzroy	Heart of Midlothian	Walsall
22 Simpson, Wesley	Northwich Victoria	Winsford United
9 Smith, Mark J.W.	Bristol Rovers	Mangotsfield Town
16 Smith, Peter L.	Crewe Alexandra	Doncaster Rovers
27 Sodje, Akpo	Queens Park Rangers	Stevenage Borough
1 Sodje, Samuel	Stevenage Borough	Grays Athletic
22 Spencer, Damien M.	Bristol City	Exeter City
29 Stamp, Darryn M.	Scunthorpe United	Scarborough
14 Steele, Paul	Yeovil Town	Woking
21 Stoner, Craig J.	Portsmouth	Bognor Regis Town
31 Sugden, Ryan S.	Oldham Athletic	Burton Albion
27 Sykes, Alexander	Nuneaton Borough	Forest Green Rovers
21 Takalogabhashi, Mohammad	Margate	Scunthorpe United
30 Tann, Adam J.	Cambridge United	Cambridge City
22 Taylor, Gareth K.	Manchester City	Burnley
29 Telemaque, Errol	Hayes	Yeading
22 Turner, Andrew P.	Rotherham United	Rochdale
12 Tyne, Thomas R.	Millwall	Fisher Athletic
12 Tyson, Nathan	Reading	Maidenhead United
2 Upson, Matthew J.	Arsenal	Crystal Palace
2 Walker, Richard S.	Crewe Alexandra	Halesowen Town
11 Walker, Richard M.	Aston Villa	Blackpool
27 Wharton, Paul	Farsley Celtic	Bradford Park Avenue
30 Whitley, James	Manchester City	Nottingham Forest
22 Williams, Thomas A.	West Ham United	Peterborough United
22 Wilson, Stephen L.	Hull City	Macclesfield Town
8 Wolleaston, Robert A.	Chelsea	Portsmouth

April 2001

26 Cooper, Richard A.	Nottingham Forest	York City	undisclosed
25 Foster, Benjamin	Racing Club Warwick	Stoke City	undisclosed
11 Izzet, Kemal	Charlton Athletic	Colchester United	undisclosed
28 Ward, Christopher	Lancaster City	Birmingham City	undisclosed

Temporary transfers

13 Bernard, Olivier	Newcastle United	Darlington
23 Birch, Gary S.	Walsall	Exeter City
9 Carr, Darren J.	Brighton & Hove Albion	Carlisle United
3 Clegg, George G.	Manchester United	Wycombe Wanderers
2 Cooper, Richard A.	Nottingham Forest	York City
17 Cornwall, Lucas C.C.	Fulham	Grimsby Town
13 Cullen, David J.	Peterborough United	Carlisle United
23 Dalglish, Paul	Norwich City	Wigan Athletic
4 Field, Lewis	Stevenage Borough	Hemel Hempstead Town
17 Gamble, Joseph	Reading	Crawley Town
9 Giles, Christopher	Yeovil Town	Weston-Super-Mare
13 Grant, John	Crewe Alexandra	Hyde United
2 Green, Ryan M.	Wolverhampton Wanderers	Torquay United
22 Hanson, Christian	Middlesbrough	Cambridge United
26 Holt, Grant	Halifax Town	Barrow
25 Hopkins, Gareth	Cheltenham Town	Cinderford Town
3 Kelly, Alan T.	Blackburn Rovers	Stockport County
17 Macdonald, Charles L.	Charlton Athletic	Cheltenham Town
17 Maddison, Neil S.	Middlesbrough	Bristol City
22 Mitchell, Paul A.	Wigan Athletic	Halifax Town
8 Newby, Keith	Harrow Borough	Yeading
2 Poland, Lee	Northwich Victoria	Leek Town
18 Pollock, Jamie	Crystal Palace	Birmingham City
17 Rapley, Kevin J.	Notts County	Scunthorpe United
17 Reddington, Stuart	Chelsea	Mansfield Town
1 Riza, Omer K.	West Ham United	Cambridge United
3 Roget, Leo T.E.	Southend United	Stockport County
22 Simpson, Wesley	Northwich Victoria	Winsford United
9 Smith, Mark J.W.	Bristol Rovers	Mangotsfield United
1 Sodje, Samuel	Stevenage Borough	Grays Athletic
22 Spencer, Damien M.	Bristol City	Exeter City
25 Stoner, Craig J.	Portsmouth	Bognor Regis Town
26 Taylor, Gareth K.	Manchester City	Burnley
8 Tyne, Thomas R.	Millwall	Fisher Athletic
9 Tyson, Nathan	Reading	Maidenhead United

May 2001

30 Campbell, Stuart P.	Leicester City	Grimsby Town	undisclosed
30 Griffiths, Leroy	Hampton & Richmond Borough	Queens Park Rangers	undisclosed
12 Harford, Paul	Sutton United	Aldershot Town	undisclosed
23 Penny, Andrew J.	Solihull Borough	Hinckley United	undisclosed
3 Roget, Leo T.E.	Southend United	Stockport County	undisclosed
26 Steele, Paul	Yeovil Town	Woking	undisclosed

Temporary transfers

8 Broad, Stephen	Chelsea	Southend United
6 Field, Lewis	Stevenage Borough	Hemel Hempstead Town
8 Holt, Andrew	Oldham Athletic	Hull City
7 Lockwood, Adam B.	Reading	Forest Green Rovers
6 Reddington, Stuart	Chelsea	Mansfield Town

THE THINGS THEY SAID . . .

Coventry boss Gordon Strachan on losing striker Robbie Keane to Inter Milan in £13m deal:
"I'm just hoping Robbie doesn't like the San Siro, doesn't like the wages – and wants to come back here."

Shrewsbury's Kevin Ratcliffe after his side's 8-1 pre-season drubbing by Manchester United:
"We learned a lot from United today – including how to count."

Former World Footballer of the Year, Geoge Weah, after his shock move to Manchester City:
"I will come here and give everything, and I think we will go into Europe."

Emmanuel Petit, after completing his move from Arsenal:
"Two things I promise to do are to learn Spanish quickly, and not to make the same mistake as my international colleague, Fabien Barthez. He signed for Manchester United and then drove to Liverpool by mistake. I promise the Barcelona fans not to turn up in Madrid."

Rangers' Dutch manager Dick Advocaat on speculation linking him with a move away from Ibrox:
"There was a story last week I was leaving in 2002 and had told my friends that. I don't know where it came from. I don't have that many friends."

Kevin Keegan calls for a limit on the number of foreign players in this country:
"I'm not going to sit on the fence on this – I don't want to be called creosote."

Chelsea defender Frank Leboeuf takes a swipe at Blues boss Gianluca Vialli:
"Vialli has problems with everybody, with Albert Ferrer and many others. It's normal for a coach to get along with his lads, but not him."

New Sheffield Wednesday boss Paul Jewell after goalkeeper Kevin Pressman's early red card in the season's opener:
"You expect to change your game plan somewhere along the line, but not after 13 seconds of your first match."

Latvia's English-born manager Gary Johnson ahead of the clash with Scotland:
"In Latvia they have to know you for three years before they smile at you. There is a lot of the old Soviet mentality still there. It has to be a pretty good joke to make them laugh."

Burnley manager Stan Ternent after the 1-1 home draw with Gillingham:
"Gillingham came to make it hard for us and they did. It takes two to tango and Gillingham didn't want to tango."

Paolo di Canio on his decision to stay at Upton Park:
"I had a meeting in the board room with the chairman. We looked into each other's eyes and we decided it was a good marriage. There was no reason for a divorce."

Manchester City boss Joe Royle after Wanchope's goal against Middlesbrough:
"Paulo is dangerous. He does weird and wonderful things and sometimes can't do what mere mortals do."

Andy Cole on his feud with Manchester United's Teddy Sheringham:
"I'm pleased at the way my partnership with Teddy is going on the pitch, but it's fair to say that we don't have Sunday lunch together. We are still not talking."

Ruud Gullit, on Vialli's dismissal from Chelsea. Presumably name calling and hair pulling comes next:
"I can remember just who was ready to whisper in an ear or two for their own ends. Now Vialli has found out that what goes round, comes round."

Concerned Manchester City boss Joe Royle:
"Without naming names, the PFA have got to get involved and start naming and shaming divers."

Rotherham's Ronnie Moore about his striker Leo Fortune-West:
"He may have been upset by one or two comments last weekend . . . on Saturday he's a donkey and then on Monday he's the crown-jewels."

Villa's Luc Nilis excuses Ipswich keeper Richard Wright of any blame after his horrific leg break:
"It was just one of those things."

Arsenal's Arsene Wenger ahead of his side's Champions League clash:
"Lazio are a very strong team. They are missing some players but in their case it's like replacing caviar with caviar."

Palace boss Alan Smith after their defeat at Preston:
"Even if Tom Finney had played at his age he would have had a good game against us."

Villa's John Gregory speaking about the FA appointment of Peter Taylor and Steve McClaren:
"It's brilliant in they are both English, although one has red hair and a slightly Scottish name."

Peter Reid gives his approval to the Taylor–McClaren link-up:
"I think these foreign coaches have been blown up out of proportion. Let's see them at Chester, Darlington and Walsall with no money and see how they get on there."

West Brom's Gary Megson after a home defeat by Norwich:
"If we lose our passion we might as well end up playing netball."

Have-a-go-hero Frank Leboeuf who stopped a burglar outside Harrods in London:
"It's nice to be thought of as a hero, and it's great to be involved in a good story for a change."

Players' Union chief, Gordon Taylor, on the appointment of Sven-Goran Eriksson:
"I think it is a betrayal of our heritage, of our culture and of the structure of the game in this country."

Stoke boss Gudjon Thordarson on his worst English food experience in a Q & A piece:
"The steak we had before the recent Colchester game, I thought they had cooked the sole of my shoe."

Liam Brady speaking about Robbie Keane's problems at Inter Milan:
"Things can change very quickly in Italy. I mean, I won two League titles at Juventus and they were telling me all the time I was surplus to requirements."

Barcelona's Emmanuel Petit on likely away form:
"More and more footballers' wives will cheat on their husbands because they are never at home."

England women's football team coach, Hope Powell:
"We are not going out there to hang on, we are going out there not to lose – and if that means winning, I'll be happy with that."

Harry Redknapp vents his frustration at the difficulty of signing Hayden Foxe:
"I'm not going to let this one die. He's Australian. He's in the Commonwealth. They fought the war with us. I know that this might sound like bollocks to you but we let foreign people in who have no allegiance to the country."

Kaiserslautern coach Andreas Brehme about the Rangers midfielder:
"Claudio Reyna is the best example of diving you need. He was lying on the ground more than he was playing when he was here in the Bundesliga."

Ron Atkinson to an Ipswich steward on being asked to identify himself:
"My goodness! You have been out of the Premiership a long time!"

Former Wolves manager Mark McGhee after his successor Colin Lee was sacked:
"They are a big club that talk a good game."

Newcastle's Bobby Robson after defensive errors led to defeat at Derby:
"If you're careless driving a car you get killed . . . so don't be careless on the football field either."

Upbeat Barry Hearn after Leyton Orient's FA Cup triumph over non-Leaguers Northwich:
"The showbiz side, the circus side and the excitement side of the Premiership is a wonderful show. But it has lost all reality, and without this level of football there's no football in this country."

Arsenal's long serving Lee Dixon:
"They do everything for you. We're treated like babies, really. So much so that there are some players, not necessarily at this club, who wouldn't have a clue how to check in at an airport."

Hammer's Frederic Kanoute on how he views life north of Watford:
"I don't really like the north. It's always raining, it's very cold and I don't like all those little houses."

Former Rangers captain Terry Butcher on the prospect of lining up in an oldies Old Firm clash:
"I haven't had the chance to kick a Celtic player for many years."

Geoffrey Richmond wonders where and what Stan Collymore was doing last week:
"What's Stan doing? It would be fair to say nobody at Bradford City has a clue."

Ken Bates on his resignation as vice-chairman of the company rebuilding Wembley Stadium:
"Even Jesus Christ suffered only one Pontius Pilate. I had a whole team of them. . . ."

Summariser Alan Mullery monitoring the action:
"Nicos the Greek is getting his hands on everything. Except that one. It's now 1-1."

Derby's Jim Smith on the disappearance of God-fearing on-loan Milan defender Taribo West:
"I don't know which church he's in. He's got a mobile phone but it's switched off."

Manchester United's Ferguson answering claims by Leeds' Lucas Radebe that referees favour the Old Trafford club:
"Everyone knows that for us to get a penalty we need a certificate from the Pope and a personal letter from the Queen."

Coventry's Gordon Strachan after a precious win at Leicester:
"The leg is out of the coffin now and if we can get anything at Old Trafford next weekend then we will have two legs out!"

Former Manchester City player Paul Lake about the poor home form:
"Your home ground is supposed to be a fortress but Maine Road is more like Fairyland."

Triumphant Livingston boss Jim Leishman hails Dominic Keane and his bottomless pockets:
"I don't care if people think I'm crawling up the chairman's backside. He has been magnificent."

Hibs boss Ebbe Skovdahl comparing his striker Arild Stavrum's better-efforts-on-target tally than Celtic's goal-snatcher Larsson:
"Statistics are like miniskirts – they give you good ideas but hide the most important things."

Terry Venables on the question of whether he had discussed his Middlesbrough future with chairman Steve Gibson:
"We spoke about it really, and out of it came the fact that we wouldn't speak about it."

Rodney Marsh not altogether certain about Kevin Keegan's long term ambitions:
"We'll have to wait and see if he walks away from the Man City job."

Jean Tigana, totally wrapped up in football-related matters:
"People ask if I enjoy London and I say, yes. But all I have seen of it so far is my house, Craven Cottage and, of course, Harrods. I don't know where Big Ben is or Buckingham Palace and I've never been to a theatre or a museum."

Ray Wilkins on his attempt to get new Watford manager Gianluca Vialli to resume his playing career:
"I have tried already because he is in great physical condition, but he is just smoking a bit too much."

FA CHARITY SHIELD WINNERS 1908–2000

1908	Manchester U v QPR	4-0 after 1-1 draw		1962	Tottenham H v Ipswich T	5-1
1909	Newcastle U v Northampton T	2-0		1963	Everton v Manchester U	4-0
1910	Brighton v Aston Villa	1-0		1964	Liverpool v West Ham U	2-2*
1911	Manchester U v Swindon T	8-4		1965	Manchester U v Liverpool	2-2*
1912	Blackburn R v QPR	2-1		1966	Liverpool v Everton	1-0
1913	Professionals v Amateurs	7-2		1967	Manchester U v Tottenham H	3-3*
1920	WBA v Tottenham H	2-0		1968	Manchester C v WBA	6-1
1921	Tottenham H v Burnley	2-0		1969	Leeds U v Manchester C	2-1
1922	Huddersfield T v Liverpool	1-0		1970	Everton v Chelsea	2-1
1923	Professionals v Amateurs	2-0		1971	Leicester C v Liverpool	1-0
1924	Professionals v Amateurs	3-1		1972	Manchester C v Aston Villa	1-0
1925	Amateurs v Professionals	6-1		1973	Burnley v Manchester C	1-0
1926	Amateurs v Professionals	6-3		1974	Liverpool† v Leeds U	1-1
1927	Cardiff C v Corinthians	2-1		1975	Derby Co v West Ham U	2-0
1928	Everton v Blackburn R	2-1		1976	Liverpool v Southampton	1-0
1929	Professionals v Amateurs	3-0		1977	Liverpool v Manchester U	0-0*
1930	Arsenal v Sheffield W	2-1		1978	Nottingham F v Ipswich T	5-0
1931	Arsenal v WBA	1-0		1979	Liverpool v Arsenal	3-1
1932	Everton v Newcastle U	5-3		1980	Liverpool v West Ham U	1-0
1933	Arsenal v Everton	3-0		1981	Aston Villa v Tottenham H	2-2*
1934	Arsenal v Manchester C	4-0		1982	Liverpool v Tottenham H	1-0
1935	Sheffield W v Arsenal	1-0		1983	Manchester U v Liverpool	2-0
1936	Sunderland v Arsenal	2-1		1984	Everton v Liverpool	1-0
1937	Manchester C v Sunderland	2-0		1985	Everton v Manchester U	2-0
1938	Arsenal v Preston NE	2-1		1986	Everton v Liverpool	1-1*
1948	Arsenal v Manchester U	4-3		1987	Everton v Coventry C	1-0
1949	Portsmouth v Wolverhampton W	1-1*		1988	Liverpool v Wimbledon	2-1
1950	World Cup Team v Canadian Touring Team	4-2		1989	Liverpool v Arsenal	1-0
1951	Tottenham H v Newcastle U	2-1		1990	Liverpool v Manchester U	1-1*
1952	Manchester U v Newcastle U	4-2		1991	Arsenal v Tottenham H	0-0*
1953	Arsenal v Blackpool	3-1		1992	Leeds U v Liverpool	4-3
1954	Wolverhampton W v WBA	4-4*		1993	Manchester U† v Arsenal	1-1
1955	Chelsea v Newcastle U	3-0		1994	Manchester U v Blackburn R	2-0
1956	Manchester U v Manchester C	1-0		1995	Everton v Blackburn R	1-0
1957	Manchester U v Aston Villa	4-0		1996	Manchester U v Newcastle U	4-0
1958	Bolton W v Wolverhampton W	4-1		1997	Manchester U† v Chelsea	1-1
1959	Wolverhampton W v Nottingham F	3-1		1998	Arsenal v Manchester U	3-0
1960	Burnley v Wolverhampton W	2-2*		1999	Arsenal v Manchester U	2-1
1961	Tottenham H v FA XI	3-2				

Each club retained shield for six months.   † Won on penalties.

ONE2ONE CHARITY SHIELD 2000

Chelsea (1) 2, Manchester U (0) 0

At Wembley, 13 August 2000, attendance 65,148

Chelsea: De Goey; Melchiot, Babayaro, Stanic, Leboeuf, Desailly, Poyet (Le Saux), Di Matteo (Morris), Hasselbaink, Zola (Gudjohnsen), Wise.

Scorers: Hasselbaink 22, Melchiot 72.

Manchester U: Barthez; Irwin, Silvestre (Stam), Johnsen, Keane, Neville G, Beckham, Scholes, Solskjaer (Cole), Sheringham (Yorke), Giggs (Fortune).

Referee: M. Riley (Leeds).

ENGLISH LEAGUE HONOURS 1888 to 2001

FA PREMIER LEAGUE
Maximum points: a 126; b 114.

	First	Pts	Second	Pts	Third	Pts
1992–93a	Manchester U	84	Aston Villa	74	Norwich C	72
1993–94a	Manchester U	92	Blackburn R	84	Newcastle U	77
1994–95a	Blackburn R	89	Manchester U	88	Nottingham F	77
1995–96a	Manchester U	82	Newcastle U	78	Liverpool	71
1996–97b	Manchester U	75	Newcastle U*	68	Arsenal*	68
1997–98b	Arsenal	78	Manchester U	77	Liverpool	65
1998–99b	Manchester U	79	Arsenal	78	Chelsea	75
1999–2000b	Manchester U	91	Arsenal	73	Leeds U	69
2000–01	Manchester U	80	Arsenal	70	Liverpool	69

FIRST DIVISION
Maximum points: 138

1992–93	Newcastle U	96	West Ham U*	88	Portsmouth††	88
1993–94	Crystal Palace	90	Nottingham F	83	Millwall††	74
1994–95	Middlesbrough	82	Reading††	79	Bolton W	77
1995–96	Sunderland	83	Derby Co	79	Crystal Palace††	75
1996–97	Bolton W	98	Barnsley	80	Wolverhampton W††	76
1997–98	Nottingham F	94	Middlesbrough	91	Sunderland††	90
1998–99	Sunderland	105	Bradford C	87	Ipswich T††	86
1999–2000	Charlton Ath	91	Manchester C	89	Ipswich T	87
2000–01	Fulham	101	Blackburn R	91	Bolton W	87

SECOND DIVISION
Maximum points: 138

1992–93	Stoke C	93	Bolton W	90	Port Vale††	89
1993–94	Reading	89	Port Vale	88	Plymouth Arg*††	85
1994–95	Birmingham C	89	Brentford††	85	Crewe Alex††	83
1995–96	Swindon T	92	Oxford U	83	Blackpool††	82
1996–97	Bury	84	Stockport Co	82	Luton T††	78
1997–98	Watford	88	Bristol C	85	Grimsby T	72
1998–99	Fulham	101	Walsall	87	Manchester C	82
1999–2000	Preston NE	95	Burnley	88	Gillingham	85
2000–01	Millwall	93	Rotherham U	91	Reading††	86

THIRD DIVISION
Maximum points: a 126; b 138.

1992–93a	Cardiff C	83	Wrexham	80	Barnet	79
1993–94a	Shrewsbury T	79	Chester C	74	Crewe Alex	73
1994–95a	Carlisle U	91	Walsall	83	Chesterfield	81
1995–96b	Preston NE	86	Gillingham	83	Bury	79
1996–97b	Wigan Ath*	87	Fulham	87	Carlisle U	84
1997–98b	Notts Co	99	Macclesfield T	82	Lincoln C	72
1998–99b	Brentford	85	Cambridge U	81	Cardiff C	80
1999–2000b	Swansea C	85	Rotherham U	84	Northampton T	82
2000–01	Brighton & HA	92	Cardiff C	82	Chesterfield¶	80

††Not promoted after play-offs. ¶9pts deducted for irregularities.

FOOTBALL LEAGUE
Maximum points: a 44; b 60

	First	Pts	Second	Pts	Third	Pts
1888–89a	Preston NE	40	Aston Villa	29	Wolverhampton W	28
1889–90a	Preston NE	33	Everton	31	Blackburn R	27
1890–91a	Everton	29	Preston NE	27	Notts Co	26
1891–92b	Sunderland	42	Preston NE	37	Bolton W	36

FIRST DIVISION to 1991–92
Maximum points: a 44; b 52; c 60; d 68; e 76; f 84; g 126; h 120; k 114.

1892–93c	Sunderland	48	Preston NE	37	Everton	36
1893–94c	Aston Villa	44	Sunderland	38	Derby Co	36
1894–95c	Sunderland	47	Everton	42	Aston Villa	39
1895–96c	Aston Villa	45	Derby Co	41	Everton	39
1896–97c	Aston Villa	47	Sheffield U*	36	Derby Co	36
1897–98c	Sheffield U	42	Sunderland	37	Wolverhampton W*	35
1898–99d	Aston Villa	45	Liverpool	43	Burnley	39
1899–1900d	Aston Villa	50	Sheffield U	48	Sunderland	41
1900–01d	Liverpool	45	Sunderland	43	Notts Co	40
1901–02d	Sunderland	44	Everton	41	Newcastle U	37
1902–03d	The Wednesday	42	Aston Villa*	41	Sunderland	41
1903–04d	The Wednesday	47	Manchester C	44	Everton	43
1904–05d	Newcastle U	48	Everton	47	Manchester C	46
1905–06e	Liverpool	51	Preston NE	47	The Wednesday	44
1906–07e	Newcastle U	51	Bristol C	48	Everton*	45
1907–08e	Manchester U	52	Aston Villa*	43	Manchester C	45
1908–09e	Newcastle U	53	Everton	46	Sunderland	44
1909–10e	Aston Villa	53	Liverpool	48	Blackburn R*	45
1910–11e	Manchester U	52	Aston Villa	51	Sunderland*	45
1911–12e	Blackburn R	49	Everton	46	Newcastle U	44
1912–13e	Sunderland	54	Aston Villa	50	Sheffield W	49
1913–14e	Blackburn R	51	Aston Villa	44	Middlesbrough*	43
1914–15e	Everton	46	Oldham Ath	45	Blackburn R*	43

*Won or placed on goal average (ratio), goal difference or most goals scored.

	First	Pts	Second	Pts	Third	Pts
1919–20f	WBA	60	Burnley	51	Chelsea	49
1920–21f	Burnley	59	Manchester C	54	Bolton W	52
1921–22f	Liverpool	57	Tottenham H	51	Burnley	49
1922–23f	Liverpool	60	Sunderland	54	Huddersfield T	53
1923–24f	Huddersfield T*	57	Cardiff C	57	Sunderland	53
1924–25f	Huddersfield T	58	WBA	56	Bolton W	55
1925–26f	Huddersfield T	57	Arsenal	52	Sunderland	48
1926–27f	Newcastle U	56	Huddersfield T	51	Sunderland	49
1927–28f	Everton	53	Huddersfield T	51	Leicester C	48
1928–29f	Sheffield W	52	Leicester C	51	Aston Villa	50
1929–30f	Sheffield W	60	Derby Co	50	Manchester C*	47
1930–31f	Arsenal	66	Aston Villa	59	Sheffield W	52
1931–32f	Everton	56	Arsenal	54	Sheffield W	50
1932–33f	Arsenal	58	Aston Villa	54	Sheffield W	51
1933–34f	Arsenal	59	Huddersfield T	56	Tottenham H	49
1934–35f	Arsenal	58	Sunderland	54	Sheffield W	49
1935–36f	Sunderland	56	Derby Co*	48	Huddersfield T	48
1936–37f	Manchester C	57	Charlton Ath	54	Arsenal	52
1937–38f	Arsenal	52	Wolverhampton W	51	Preston NE	49
1938–39f	Everton	59	Wolverhampton W	55	Charlton Ath	50
1946–47f	Liverpool	57	Manchester U*	56	Wolverhampton W	56
1947–48f	Arsenal	59	Manchester U*	52	Burnley	52
1948–49f	Portsmouth	58	Manchester U*	53	Derby Co	53
1949–50f	Portsmouth*	53	Wolverhampton W	53	Sunderland	53
1950–51f	Tottenham H	60	Manchester U	56	Blackpool	50
1951–52f	Manchester U	57	Tottenham H*	53	Arsenal	53
1952–53f	Arsenal*	54	Preston NE	54	Wolverhampton W	51
1953–54f	Wolverhampton W	57	WBA	53	Huddersfield T	51
1954–55f	Chelsea	52	Wolverhampton W*	48	Portsmouth*	48
1955–56f	Manchester U	60	Blackpool*	49	Wolverhampton W	49
1956–57f	Manchester U	64	Tottenham H*	56	Preston NE	56
1957–58f	Wolverhampton W	64	Preston NE	59	Tottenham H	51
1958–59f	Wolverhampton W	61	Manchester U	55	Arsenal*	50
1959–60f	Burnley	55	Wolverhampton W	54	Tottenham H	53
1960–61f	Tottenham H	66	Sheffield W	58	Wolverhampton W	57
1961–62f	Ipswich T	56	Burnley	53	Tottenham H	52
1962–63f	Everton	61	Tottenham H	55	Burnley	54
1963–64f	Liverpool	57	Manchester U	53	Everton	52
1964–65f	Manchester U*	61	Leeds U	61	Chelsea	56
1965–66f	Liverpool	61	Leeds U*	55	Burnley	55
1966–67f	Manchester U	60	Nottingham F*	56	Tottenham H	56
1967–68f	Manchester C	58	Manchester U	56	Liverpool	55
1968–69f	Leeds U	67	Liverpool	61	Everton	57
1969–70f	Everton	66	Leeds U	57	Chelsea	55
1970–71f	Arsenal	65	Leeds U	64	Tottenham H*	52
1971–72f	Derby Co	58	Leeds U*	57	Liverpool*	57
1972–73f	Liverpool	60	Arsenal	57	Leeds U	53
1973–74f	Leeds U	62	Liverpool	57	Derby Co	48
1974–75f	Derby Co	53	Liverpool*	51	Ipswich T	51
1975–76f	Liverpool	60	QPR	59	Manchester U	56
1976–77f	Liverpool	57	Manchester C	56	Ipswich T	52
1977–78f	Nottingham F	64	Liverpool	57	Everton	55
1978–79f	Liverpool	68	Nottingham F	60	WBA	59
1979–80f	Liverpool	60	Manchester U	58	Ipswich T	52
1980–81f	Aston Villa	60	Ipswich T	56	Arsenal	53
1981–82g	Liverpool	87	Ipswich T	83	Manchester U	78
1982–83g	Liverpool	82	Watford	71	Manchester U	70
1983–84g	Liverpool	80	Southampton	77	Nottingham F*	74
1984–85g	Everton	90	Liverpool*	77	Tottenham H	77
1985–86g	Liverpool	88	Everton	86	West Ham U	84
1986–87g	Everton	86	Liverpool	77	Tottenham H	71
1987–88h	Liverpool	90	Manchester U	81	Nottingham F	73
1988–89k	Arsenal*	76	Liverpool	76	Nottingham F	64
1989–90k	Liverpool	79	Aston Villa	70	Tottenham H	63
1990–91k	Arsenal†	83	Liverpool	76	Crystal Palace	69
1991–92g	Leeds U	82	Manchester U	78	Sheffield W	75

No official competition during 1915–19 and 1939–46; Regional Leagues operated.
†2 pts deducted

SECOND DIVISION to 1991–92

Maximum points: a 44; b 56; c 60; d 68; e 76; f 84; g 126; h 132; k 138.

	First	Pts	Second	Pts	Third	Pts
1892–93a	Small Heath	36	Sheffield U	35	Darwen	30
1893–94b	Liverpool	50	Small Heath	42	Notts Co	39
1894–95c	Bury	48	Notts Co	39	Newton Heath*	38
1895–96c	Liverpool*	46	Manchester C	46	Grimsby T*	42
1896–97c	Notts Co	42	Newton Heath	39	Grimsby T	38
1897–98c	Burnley	48	Newcastle U	45	Manchester C	39
1898–99d	Manchester C	52	Glossop NE	46	Leicester Fosse	45
1899–1900d	The Wednesday	54	Bolton W	52	Small Heath	46
1900–01d	Grimsby T	49	Small Heath	48	Burnley	44
1901–02d	WBA	55	Middlesbrough	51	Preston NE*	42
1902–03d	Manchester C	54	Small Heath	51	Woolwich A	48
1903–04d	Preston NE	50	Woolwich A	49	Manchester U	48

Won or placed on goal average (ratio)/goal difference.

	First	Pts	Second	Pts	Third	Pts
1904–05d	Liverpool	58	Bolton W	56	Manchester U	53
1905–06e	Bristol C	66	Manchester U	62	Chelsea	53
1906–07e	Nottingham F	60	Chelsea	57	Leicester Fosse	48
1907–08e	Bradford C	54	Leicester Fosse	52	Oldham Ath	50
1908–09e	Bolton W	52	Tottenham H*	51	WBA	51
1909–10e	Manchester C	54	Oldham Ath*	53	Hull C*	53
1910–11e	WBA	53	Bolton W	51	Chelsea	49
1911–12e	Derby Co*	54	Chelsea	54	Burnley	52
1912–13e	Preston NE	53	Burnley	50	Birmingham	46
1913–14e	Notts Co	53	Bradford PA*	49	Woolwich A	49
1914–15e	Derby Co	53	Preston NE	50	Barnsley	47
1919–20f	Tottenham H	70	Huddersfield T	64	Birmingham	56
1920–21f	Birmingham*	58	Cardiff C	58	Bristol C	51
1921–22f	Nottingham F	56	Stoke C*	52	Barnsley	52
1922–23f	Notts Co	53	West Ham U*	51	Leicester C	51
1923–24f	Leeds U	54	Bury*	51	Derby Co	51
1924–25f	Leicester C	59	Manchester U	57	Derby Co	55
1925–26f	Sheffield W	60	Derby Co	57	Chelsea	52
1926–27f	Middlesbrough	62	Portsmouth*	54	Manchester C	54
1927–28f	Manchester C	59	Leeds U	57	Chelsea	54
1928–29f	Middlesbrough	55	Grimsby T	53	Bradford PA*	48
1929–30f	Blackpool	58	Chelsea	55	Oldham Ath	53
1930–31f	Everton	61	WBA	54	Tottenham H	51
1931–32f	Wolverhampton W	56	Leeds U	54	Stoke C	52
1932–33f	Stoke C	56	Tottenham H	55	Fulham	50
1933–34f	Grimsby T	59	Preston NE	52	Bolton W*	51
1934–35f	Brentford	61	Bolton W*	56	West Ham U	56
1935–36f	Manchester U	56	Charlton Ath	55	Sheffield U*	52
1936–37f	Leicester C	56	Blackpool	55	Bury	52
1937–38f	Aston Villa	57	Manchester U*	53	Sheffield U	53
1938–39f	Blackburn R	55	Sheffield U	54	Sheffield W	53
1946–47f	Manchester C	62	Burnley	58	Birmingham C	55
1947–48f	Birmingham C	59	Newcastle U	56	Southampton	52
1948–49f	Fulham	57	WBA	56	Southampton	55
1949–50f	Tottenham H	61	Sheffield W*	52	Sheffield U*	52
1950–51f	Preston NE	57	Manchester C	52	Cardiff C	50
1951–52f	Sheffield W	53	Cardiff C*	51	Birmingham C	51
1952–53f	Sheffield U	60	Huddersfield T	58	Luton T	52
1953–54f	Leicester C*	56	Everton	56	Blackburn R	55
1954–55f	Birmingham C*	54	Luton T*	54	Rotherham U	54
1955–56f	Sheffield W	55	Leeds U	52	Liverpool*	48
1956–57f	Leicester C	61	Nottingham F	54	Liverpool	53
1957–58f	West Ham U	57	Blackburn R	56	Charlton Ath	55
1958–59f	Sheffield W	62	Fulham	60	Sheffield U*	53
1959–60f	Aston Villa	59	Cardiff C	58	Liverpool*	50
1960–61f	Ipswich T	59	Sheffield U	58	Liverpool	52
1961–62f	Liverpool	62	Leyton Orient	54	Sunderland	53
1962–63f	Stoke C	53	Chelsea*	52	Sunderland	52
1963–64f	Leeds U	63	Sunderland	61	Preston NE	56
1964–65f	Newcastle U	57	Northampton T	56	Bolton W	50
1965–66f	Manchester C	59	Southampton	54	Coventry C	53
1966–67f	Coventry C	59	Wolverhampton W	58	Carlisle U	52
1967–68f	Ipswich T	59	QPR*	58	Blackpool	58
1968–69f	Derby Co	63	Crystal Palace	56	Charlton Ath	50
1969–70f	Huddersfield T	60	Blackpool	53	Leicester C	51
1970–71f	Leicester C	59	Sheffield U	56	Cardiff C*	53
1971–72f	Norwich C	57	Birmingham C	56	Millwall	55
1972–73f	Burnley	62	QPR	61	Aston Villa	50
1973–74f	Middlesbrough	65	Luton T	50	Carlisle U	49
1974–75f	Manchester U	61	Aston Villa	58	Norwich C	53
1975–76f	Sunderland	56	Bristol C*	53	WBA	53
1976–77f	Wolverhampton W	57	Chelsea	55	Nottingham F	52
1977–78f	Bolton W	58	Southampton	57	Tottenham H*	56
1978–79f	Crystal Palace	57	Brighton & HA*	56	Stoke C	56
1979–80f	Leicester C	55	Sunderland	54	Birmingham C*	53
1980–81f	West Ham U	66	Notts Co	53	Swansea C*	50
1981–82g	Luton T	88	Watford	80	Norwich C	71
1982–83g	QPR	85	Wolverhampton W	75	Leicester C	70
1983–84g	Chelsea*	88	Sheffield W	88	Newcastle U	80
1984–85g	Oxford U	84	Birmingham C	82	Manchester C	74
1985–86g	Norwich C	84	Charlton Ath	77	Wimbledon	76
1986–87g	Derby Co	84	Portsmouth	78	Oldham Ath††	75
1987–88h	Millwall	82	Aston Villa*	78	Middlesbrough	78
1988–89k	Chelsea	99	Manchester C	82	Crystal Palace	81
1989–90k	Leeds U*	85	Sheffield U	85	Newcastle U††	80
1990–91k	Oldham Ath	88	West Ham U	87	Sheffield W	82
1991–92k	Ipswich T	84	Middlesbrough	80	Derby Co	78

No official competition during 1915–19 and 1939–46; Regional Leagues operated.
*Won or placed on goal average (ratio)/goal difference.
††Not promoted after play-offs.

THIRD DIVISION to 1991–92
Maximum points: 92; 138 from 1981–82.

	First	Pts	Second	Pts	Third	Pts
1958–59	Plymouth Arg	62	Hull C	61	Brentford*	57
1959–60	Southampton	61	Norwich C	59	Shrewsbury T*	52
1960–61	Bury	68	Walsall	62	QPR	60
1961–62	Portsmouth	65	Grimsby T	62	Bournemouth*	59
1962–63	Northampton T	62	Swindon T	58	Port Vale	54
1963–64	Coventry C*	60	Crystal Palace	60	Watford	58
1964–65	Carlisle U	60	Bristol C*	59	Mansfield T	59
1965–66	Hull C	69	Millwall	65	QPR	57
1966–67	QPR	67	Middlesbrough	55	Watford	54
1967–68	Oxford U	57	Bury	56	Shrewsbury T	55
1968–69	Watford*	64	Swindon T	64	Luton T	61
1969–70	Orient	62	Luton T	60	Bristol R	56
1970–71	Preston NE	61	Fulham	60	Halifax T	56
1971–72	Aston Villa	70	Brighton & HA	65	Bournemouth*	62
1972–73	Bolton W	61	Notts Co	57	Blackburn R	55
1973–74	Oldham Ath	62	Bristol R*	61	York C	61
1974–75	Blackburn R	60	Plymouth Arg	59	Charlton Ath	55
1975–76	Hereford U	63	Cardiff C	57	Millwall	56
1976–77	Mansfield T	64	Brighton & HA	61	Crystal Palace*	59
1977–78	Wrexham	61	Cambridge U	58	Preston NE*	56
1978–79	Shrewsbury T	61	Watford*	60	Swansea C	60
1979–80	Grimsby T	62	Blackburn R	59	Sheffield W	58
1980–81	Rotherham U	61	Barnsley*	59	Charlton Ath	59
1981–82	Burnley*	80	Carlisle U	80	Fulham	78
1982–83	Portsmouth	91	Cardiff C	86	Huddersfield T	82
1983–84	Oxford U	95	Wimbledon	87	Sheffield U*	83
1984–85	Bradford C	94	Millwall	90	Hull C	87
1985–86	Reading	94	Plymouth Arg	87	Derby Co	84
1986–87	Bournemouth	97	Middlesbrough	94	Swindon T	87
1987–88	Sunderland	93	Brighton & HA	84	Walsall	82
1988–89	Wolverhampton W	92	Sheffield U*	84	Port Vale	84
1989–90	Bristol R	93	Bristol C	91	Notts Co	87
1990–91	Cambridge U	86	Southend U	85	Grimsby T*	83
1991–92	Brentford	82	Birmingham C	81	Huddersfield T	78

FOURTH DIVISION (1958–1992)
Maximum points: 92; 138 from 1981–82.

	First	Pts	Second	Pts	Third	Pts	Fourth	Pts
1958–59	Port Vale	64	Coventry C*	60	York C	60	Shrewsbury T	58
1959–60	Walsall	65	Notts Co*	60	Torquay U	60	Watford	57
1960–61	Peterborough U	66	Crystal Palace	64	Northampton T*	60	Bradford PA	60
1961–62†	Millwall	56	Colchester U	55	Wrexham	53	Carlisle U	52
1962–63	Brentford	62	Oldham Ath*	59	Crewe Alex	59	Mansfield T*	57
1963–64	Gillingham*	60	Carlisle U	60	Workington	59	Exeter C	58
1964–65	Brighton & HA	63	Millwall*	62	York C	62	Oxford U	61
1965–66	Doncaster R*	59	Darlington	59	Torquay U	58	Colchester U*	56
1966–67	Stockport Co	64	Southport*	59	Barrow	59	Tranmere R	58
1967–68	Luton T	66	Barnsley	61	Hartlepools U	60	Crewe Alex	58
1968–69	Doncaster R	59	Halifax T	57	Rochdale*	56	Bradford C	56
1969–70	Chesterfield	64	Wrexham	61	Swansea C	60	Port Vale	59
1970–71	Notts Co	69	Bournemouth	60	Oldham Ath	59	York C	56
1971–72	Grimsby T	63	Southend U	60	Brentford	59	Scunthorpe U	57
1972–73	Southport	62	Hereford U	58	Cambridge U	57	Aldershot*	56
1973–74	Peterborough U	65	Gillingham	62	Colchester U	60	Bury	59
1974–75	Mansfield T	68	Shrewsbury T	62	Rotherham U	59	Chester*	57
1975–76	Lincoln C	74	Northampton T	68	Reading	60	Tranmere R	58
1976–77	Cambridge U	65	Exeter C	62	Colchester U*	59	Bradford C	59
1977–78	Watford	71	Southend U	60	Swansea C*	56	Brentford	56
1978–79	Reading	65	Grimsby T*	61	Wimbledon*	61	Barnsley	61
1979–80	Huddersfield T	66	Walsall	64	Newport Co	61	Portsmouth*	60
1980–81	Southend U	67	Lincoln C	65	Doncaster R	56	Wimbledon	55
1981–82	Sheffield U	96	Bradford C*	91	Wigan Ath	91	Bournemouth	88
1982–83	Wimbledon	98	Hull C	90	Port Vale	88	Scunthorpe U	83
1983–84	York C	101	Doncaster R	85	Reading*	82	Bristol C	82
1984–85	Chesterfield	91	Blackpool	86	Darlington	85	Bury	84
1985–86	Swindon T	102	Chester C*	84	Mansfield T	81	Port Vale	79
1986–87	Northampton T	99	Preston NE	90	Southend U	80	Wolverhampton W††	79
1987–88	Wolverhampton W	90	Cardiff C	85	Bolton W	78	Scunthorpe U††	77
1988–89	Rotherham U	82	Tranmere R	80	Crewe Alex	78	Scunthorpe U††	77
1989–90	Exeter C	89	Grimsby T	79	Southend U	75	Stockport Co††	74
1990–91	Darlington	83	Stockport Co*	82	Hartlepool U	82	Peterborough U	80
1991–92†*	Burnley	83	Rotherham U*	77	Mansfield T	77	Blackpool	76

* Won or placed on goal average (ratio)/goal difference.
†Maximum points: 88 owing to Accrington Stanley's resignation. ††Not promoted after play-offs.
†*Maximum points: 126 owing to Aldershot being expelled (and only 23 teams started the competition).

THIRD DIVISION—SOUTH (1920–1958)
1920–21 season as Third Division.
Maximum points: a 84; b 92.

	First	Pts	Second	Pts	Third	Pts
1920–21a	Crystal Palace	59	Southampton	54	QPR	53
1921–22a	Southampton*	61	Plymouth Arg	61	Portsmouth	53
1922–23a	Bristol C	59	Plymouth Arg*	53	Swansea T	53
1923–24a	Portsmouth	59	Plymouth Arg	55	Millwall	54
1924–25a	Swansea T	57	Plymouth Arg	56	Bristol C	53
1925–26a	Reading	57	Plymouth Arg	56	Millwall	53
1926–27a	Bristol C	62	Plymouth Arg	60	Millwall	56
1927–28a	Millwall	65	Northampton T	55	Plymouth Arg	53
1928–29a	Charlton Ath*	54	Crystal Palace	54	Northampton T*	52
1929–30a	Plymouth Arg	68	Brentford	61	QPR	51
1930–31a	Notts Co	59	Crystal Palace	51	Brentford	50
1931–32a	Fulham	57	Reading	55	Southend U	53
1932–33a	Brentford	62	Exeter C	58	Norwich C	57
1933–34a	Norwich C	61	Coventry C*	54	Reading*	54
1934–35a	Charlton Ath	61	Reading	53	Coventry C	51
1935–36a	Coventry C	57	Luton T	56	Reading	54
1936–37a	Luton T	58	Notts Co	56	Brighton & HA	53
1937–38a	Millwall	56	Bristol C	55	QPR*	53
1938–39a	Newport Co	55	Crystal Palace	52	Brighton & HA	49
1939–46	Competition cancelled owing to war. Regional Leagues operated.					
1946–47a	Cardiff C	66	QPR	57	Bristol C	51
1947–48a	QPR	61	Bournemouth	57	Walsall	51
1948–49a	Swansea T	62	Reading	55	Bournemouth	52
1949–50a	Notts Co	58	Northampton T*	51	Southend U	51
1950–51b	Nottingham F	70	Norwich C	64	Reading*	57
1951–52b	Plymouth Arg	66	Reading*	61	Norwich C	61
1952–53b	Bristol R	64	Millwall*	62	Northampton T	62
1953–54b	Ipswich T	64	Brighton & HA	61	Bristol C*	56
1954–55b	Bristol C	70	Leyton Orient	61	Southampton	59
1955–56b	Leyton Orient	66	Brighton & HA	65	Ipswich T	64
1956–57b	Ipswich T*	59	Torquay U	59	Colchester U	58
1957–58b	Brighton & HA	60	Brentford*	58	Plymouth Arg	58

THIRD DIVISION—NORTH (1921–1958)
Maximum points: a 76; b 84; c 80; d 92.

	First	Pts	Second	Pts	Third	Pts
1921–22a	Stockport Co	56	Darlington*	50	Grimsby T	50
1922–23a	Nelson	51	Bradford PA	47	Walsall	46
1923–24b	Wolverhampton W	63	Rochdale	62	Chesterfield	54
1924–25b	Darlington	58	Nelson*	53	New Brighton	53
1925–26b	Grimsby T	61	Bradford PA	60	Rochdale	59
1926–27b	Stoke C	63	Rochdale	58	Bradford PA	55
1927–28b	Bradford PA	63	Lincoln C	55	Stockport Co	54
1928–29b	Bradford C	63	Stockport Co	62	Wrexham	52
1929–30b	Port Vale	67	Stockport Co	63	Darlington*	50
1930–31b	Chesterfield	58	Lincoln C	57	Wrexham*	54
1931–32c	Lincoln C*	57	Gateshead	57	Chester	50
1932–33b	Hull C	59	Wrexham	57	Stockport Co	54
1933–34b	Barnsley	62	Chesterfield	61	Stockport Co	59
1934–35b	Doncaster R	57	Halifax T	55	Chester	54
1935–36b	Chesterfield	60	Chester*	55	Tranmere R	55
1936–37b	Stockport Co	60	Lincoln C	57	Chester	53
1937–38b	Tranmere R	56	Doncaster R	54	Hull C	53
1938–39b	Barnsley	67	Doncaster R	56	Bradford C	52
1939–46	Competition cancelled owing to war. Regional Leagues operated.					
1946–47b	Doncaster R	72	Rotherham U	60	Chester	56
1947–48b	Lincoln C	60	Rotherham U	59	Wrexham	50
1948–49b	Hull C	65	Rotherham U	62	Doncaster R	50
1949–50b	Doncaster R	55	Gateshead	53	Rochdale*	51
1950–51d	Rotherham U	71	Mansfield T	64	Carlisle U	62
1951–52d	Lincoln C	69	Grimsby T	66	Stockport Co	59
1952–53d	Oldham Ath	59	Port Vale	58	Wrexham	56
1953–54d	Port Vale	69	Barnsley	58	Scunthorpe U	57
1954–55d	Barnsley	65	Accrington S	61	Scunthorpe U*	58
1955–56d	Grimsby T	68	Derby Co	63	Accrington S	59
1956–57d	Derby Co	63	Hartlepools U	59	Accrington S*	58
1957–58d	Scunthorpe U	66	Accrington S	59	Bradford C	57

* *Won or placed on goal average (ratio).*

PROMOTED AFTER PLAY-OFFS
(Not accounted for in previous section)

1986–87	Aldershot to Division 3.
1987–88	Swansea C to Division 3.
1988–89	Leyton Orient to Division 3.
1989–90	Cambridge U to Division 3; Notts Co to Division 2; Sunderland to Division 1.
1990–91	Notts Co to Division 1; Tranmere R to Division 2; Torquay U to Division 3.
1991–92	Blackburn R to Premier League; Peterborough U to Division 1.
1992–93	Swindon T to Premier League; WBA to Division 1; York C to Division 2.
1993–94	Leicester C to Premier League; Burnley to Division 1; Wycombe W to Division 2.
1994–95	Huddersfield T to Division 1.
1995–96	Leicester C to Premier League; Bradford C to Division 1; Plymouth Arg to Division 2.
1996–97	Crystal Palace to Premier League; Crewe Alex to Division 1; Northampton T to Division 2.

1997–98   Charlton Ath to Premier League; Colchester U to Division 2.
1998–99   Watford to Premier League; Scunthorpe U to Division 2.
1999–2000   Peterborough U to Division 2
2000–01   Walsall to Division 1; Blackpool to Division 2

LEAGUE TITLE WINS

FA PREMIER LEAGUE – Manchester U 6, Arsenal 1, Blackburn R 1.

LEAGUE DIVISION 1 – Liverpool 18, Arsenal 10, Everton 9, Sunderland 8, Manchester U 7, Aston Villa 7, Newcastle U 5, Sheffield W 4, Huddersfield T 3, Leeds U 3, Wolverhampton W 3, Blackburn R 2, Portsmouth 2, Preston NE 2, Burnley 2, Manchester C 2, Nottingham F 2, Tottenham H 2, Derby Co 2, Bolton W, Charlton Ath, Chelsea, Crystal Palace, Sheffield U, WBA, Ipswich T, Middlesbrough 1 each.

LEAGUE DIVISION 2 – Leicester C 6, Manchester C 6, Sheffield W 5, Birmingham C (one as Small Heath) 5, Derby Co 4, Liverpool 4, Preston NE 4, Ipswich T 3, Leeds U 3, Notts Co 3, Middlesbrough 3, Stoke C 3, Bury 2, Grimsby T 2, Norwich C 2, Nottingham F 2, Tottenham H 2, WBA 2, Aston Villa 2, Burnley 2, Chelsea 2, Manchester U 2, West Ham U 2, Wolverhampton W 2, Bolton W 2, Fulham 2, Swindon T, Huddersfield T, Bristol C, Brentford, Bradford C, Everton, Sheffield U, Newcastle U, Coventry C, Blackpool, Blackburn R, Sunderland, Crystal Palace, Luton T, QPR, Oxford U, Millwall, Oldham Ath, Reading 1, Watford 1 each.

LEAGUE DIVISION 3 – Portsmouth 2, Oxford U 2, Shrewsbury T 2, Carlisle U 2, Preston NE 2, Brentford 2, Plymouth Arg, Southampton, Bury, Northampton T, Coventry C, Hull C, QPR, Watford, Leyton Orient, Aston Villa, Bolton W, Oldham Ath, Blackburn R, Hereford U, Mansfield T, Wrexham, Grimsby T, Rotherham U, Burnley, Bradford C, Bournemouth, Reading, Sunderland, Wolverhampton W, Bristol R, Cambridge U, Cardiff C, Swansea C, Wigan Ath, Notts Co 1 each.

LEAGUE DIVISION 4 – Chesterfield 2, Doncaster R 2, Peterborough U 2, Port Vale, Walsall, Millwall, Brentford, Gillingham, Brighton & HA, Stockport Co, Luton T, Notts Co, Grimsby T, Southport, Mansfield T, Lincoln C, Cambridge U, Watford, Reading, Huddersfield T, Swindon T, Sheffield U, Wimbledon, York C, Swindon T, Northampton T, Wolverhampton W, Rotherham U, Exeter C, Darlington, Burnley 1 each.

To 1957–58

DIVISION 3 (South) – Bristol C 3; Charlton Ath, Ipswich T, Millwall, Notts Co, Plymouth Arg, Swansea T 2 each; Brentford, Bristol R, Cardiff C, Crystal Palace, Coventry C, Fulham, Leyton Orient, Luton T, Newport Co, Nottingham F, Norwich C, Portsmouth, QPR, Reading, Southampton, Brighton & HA 1 each.

DIVISION 3 (North) – Barnsley, Doncaster R, Lincoln C 3 each; Chesterfield, Grimsby T, Hull C, Port Vale, Stockport Co 2 each; Bradford PA, Bradford C, Darlington, Derby Co, Nelson, Oldham Ath, Rotherham U, Stoke C, Tranmere R, Wolverhampton W, Scunthorpe U 1 each.

RELEGATED CLUBS

1891–92 League extended. Newton Heath, Sheffield W and Nottingham F admitted. *Second Division formed* including Darwen.
1892–93 In Test matches, Sheffield U and Darwen won promotion in place of Notts Co and Accrington S.
1893–94 In Tests, Liverpool and Small Heath won promotion. Newton Heath and Darwen relegated.
1894–95 After Tests, Bury promoted, Liverpool relegated.
1895–96 After Tests, Liverpool promoted, Small Heath relegated.
1896–97 After Tests, Notts Co promoted, Burnley relegated.
1897–98 Test system abolished after success of Stoke C and Burnley. League extended. Blackburn R and Newcastle U elected to First Division. *Automatic promotion and relegation introduced.*

FA PREMIER LEAGUE TO DIVISION 1

1992–93 Crystal Palace, Middlesbrough, Nottingham F	1997–98 Bolton W, Barnsley, Crystal Palace
1993–94 Sheffield U, Oldham Ath, Swindon T	1998–99 Charlton Ath, Blackburn R, Nottingham F
1994–95 Crystal Palace, Norwich C, Leicester C, Ipswich T	1999–2000 Wimbledon, Sheffield W, Watford
1995–96 Manchester C, QPR, Bolton W	2000–01 Manchester C, Coventry C, Bradford C
1996–97 Sunderland, Middlesbrough, Nottingham F	

DIVISION 1 TO DIVISION 2

1898–99 Bolton W and Sheffield W	1929–30 Burnley and Everton
1899–1900 Burnley and Glossop	1930–31 Leeds U and Manchester U
1900–01 Preston NE and WBA	1931–32 Grimsby T and West Ham U
1901–02 Small Heath and Manchester C	1932–33 Bolton W and Blackpool
1902–03 Grimsby T and Bolton W	1933–34 Newcastle U and Sheffield U
1903–04 Liverpool and WBA	1934–35 Leicester C and Tottenham H
1904–05 League extended. Bury and Notts Co, two bottom clubs in First Division, re-elected.	1935–36 Aston Villa and Blackburn R
	1936–37 Manchester U and Sheffield W
1905–06 Nottingham F and Wolverhampton W	1937–38 Manchester C and WBA
1906–07 Derby Co and Stoke C	1938–39 Birmingham C and Leicester C
1907–08 Bolton W and Birmingham C	1946–47 Brentford and Leeds U
1908–09 Manchester C and Leicester Fosse	1947–48 Blackburn R and Grimsby T
1909–10 Bolton W and Chelsea	1948–49 Preston NE and Sheffield U
1910–11 Bristol C and Nottingham F	1949–50 Manchester C and Birmingham C
1911–12 Preston NE and Bury	1950–51 Sheffield W and Everton
1912–13 Notts Co and Woolwich Arsenal	1951–52 Huddersfield T and Fulham
1913–14 Preston NE and Derby Co	1952–53 Stoke C and Derby Co
1914–15 Tottenham H and Chelsea*	1953–54 Middlesbrough and Liverpool
1919–20 Notts Co and Sheffield W	1954–55 Leicester C and Sheffield W
1920–21 Derby Co and Bradford PA	1955–56 Huddersfield T and Sheffield U
1921–22 Bradford C and Manchester U	1956–57 Charlton Ath and Cardiff C
1922–23 Stoke C and Oldham Ath	1957–58 Sheffield W and Sunderland
1923–24 Chelsea and Middlesbrough	1958–59 Portsmouth and Aston Villa
1924–25 Preston NE and Nottingham F	1959–60 Luton T and Leeds U
1925–26 Manchester C and Notts Co	1960–61 Preston NE and Newcastle U
1926–27 Leeds U and WBA	1961–62 Chelsea and Cardiff C
1927–28 Tottenham H and Middlesbrough	1962–63 Manchester C and Leyton Orient
1928–29 Bury and Cardiff C	1963–64 Bolton W and Ipswich T

1964–65 Wolverhampton W and Birmingham C
1965–66 Northampton T and Blackburn R
1966–67 Aston Villa and Blackpool
1967–68 Fulham and Sheffield U
1968–69 Leicester C and QPR
1969–70 Sunderland and Sheffield W
1970–71 Burnley and Blackpool
1971–72 Huddersfield T and Nottingham F
1972–73 Crystal Palace and WBA
1973–74 Southampton, Manchester U, Norwich C
1974–75 Luton T, Chelsea, Carlisle U
1975–76 Wolverhampton W, Burnley, Sheffield U
1976–77 Sunderland, Stoke C, Tottenham H
1977–78 West Ham U, Newcastle U, Leicester C
1978–79 QPR, Birmingham C, Chelsea
1979–80 Bristol C, Derby Co, Bolton W
1980–81 Norwich C, Leicester C, Crystal Palace
1981–82 Leeds U, Wolverhampton W, Middlesbrough
1982–83 Manchester C, Swansea C, Brighton & HA

1983–84 Birmingham C, Notts Co, Wolverhampton W
1984–85 Norwich C, Sunderland, Stoke C
1985–86 Ipswich T, Birmingham C, WBA
1986–87 Leicester C, Manchester C, Aston Villa
1987–88 Chelsea**, Portsmouth, Watford, Oxford U
1988–89 Middlesbrough, West Ham U, Newcastle U
1989–90 Sheffield W, Charlton Ath, Millwall
1990–91 Sunderland and Derby Co
1991–92 Luton T, Notts Co, West Ham U
1992–93 Brentford, Cambridge U, Bristol R
1993–94 Birmingham C, Oxford U, Peterborough U
1994–95 Swindon T, Burnley, Bristol C, Notts Co
1995–96 Millwall, Watford, Luton T
1996–97 Grimsby T, Oldham Ath, Southend U
1997–98 Manchester C, Stoke C, Reading
1998–99 Bury, Oxford U, Bristol C
1999–2000 Walsall, Port Vale, Swindon T
2000–01 Huddersfield T, QPR, Tranmere R

**Relegated after play-offs.*
Subsequently re-elected to Division 1 when League was extended after the War.

DIVISION 2 TO DIVISION 3

1920–21 Stockport Co
1921–22 Bradford PA and Bristol C
1922–23 Rotherham Co and Wolverhampton W
1923–24 Nelson and Bristol C
1924–25 Crystal Palace and Coventry C
1925–26 Stoke C and Stockport Co
1926–27 Darlington and Bradford C
1927–28 Fulham and South Shields
1928–29 Port Vale and Clapton Orient
1929–30 Hull C and Notts Co
1930–31 Reading and Cardiff C
1931–32 Barnsley and Bristol C
1932–33 Chesterfield and Charlton Ath
1933–34 Millwall and Lincoln C
1934–35 Oldham Ath and Notts Co
1935–36 Port Vale and Hull C
1936–37 Doncaster R and Bradford C
1937–38 Barnsley and Stockport Co
1938–39 Norwich C and Tranmere R
1946–47 Swansea T and Newport Co
1947–48 Doncaster R and Millwall
1948–49 Nottingham F and Lincoln C
1949–50 Plymouth Arg and Bradford PA
1950–51 Grimsby T and Chesterfield
1951–52 Coventry C and QPR
1952–53 Southampton and Barnsley
1953–54 Brentford and Oldham Ath
1954–55 Ipswich T and Derby Co
1955–56 Plymouth Arg and Hull C
1956–57 Port Vale and Bury
1957–58 Doncaster R and Notts Co
1958–59 Barnsley and Grimsby T
1959–60 Bristol C and Hull C
1960–61 Lincoln C and Portsmouth
1961–62 Brighton & HA and Bristol R
1962–63 Walsall and Luton T
1963–64 Grimsby T and Scunthorpe U
1964–65 Swindon T and Swansea T
1965–66 Middlesbrough and Leyton Orient
1966–67 Northampton T and Bury

1967–68 Plymouth Arg and Rotherham U
1968–69 Fulham and Bury
1969–70 Preston NE and Aston Villa
1970–71 Blackburn R and Bolton W
1971–72 Charlton Ath and Watford
1972–73 Huddersfield T and Brighton & HA
1973–74 Crystal Palace, Preston NE, Swindon T
1974–75 Millwall, Cardiff C, Sheffield W
1975–76 Oxford U, York C, Portsmouth
1976–77 Carlisle U, Plymouth Arg, Hereford U
1977–78 Blackpool, Mansfield T, Hull C
1978–79 Sheffield U, Millwall, Blackburn R
1979–80 Fulham, Burnley, Charlton Ath
1980–81 Preston NE, Bristol C, Bristol R
1981–82 Cardiff C, Wrexham, Orient
1982–83 Rotherham U, Burnley, Bolton W
1983–84 Derby Co, Swansea C, Cambridge U
1984–85 Notts Co, Cardiff C, Wolverhampton W
1985–86 Carlisle U, Middlesbrough, Fulham
1986–87 Sunderland**, Grimsby T, Brighton & HA
1987–88 Huddersfield T, Reading, Sheffield U**
1988–89 Shrewsbury T, Birmingham C, Walsall
1989–90 Bournemouth, Bradford C, Stoke C
1990–91 WBA and Hull C
1991–92 Plymouth Arg, Brighton & HA, Port Vale
1992–93 Preston NE, Mansfield T, Wigan Ath, Chester C
1993–94 Fulham, Exeter C, Hartlepool T, Barnet
1994–95 Cambridge U, Plymouth Arg, Cardiff C,
        Chester C, Leyton Orient
1995–96 Carlisle U, Swansea C, Brighton & HA, Hull C
1996–97 Peterborough U, Shrewsbury T, Rotherham U,
        Notts Co
1997–98 Brentford, Plymouth Arg, Carlisle U, Southend U
1998–99 York C, Northampton T, Lincoln C,
        Macclesfield T
1999–2000 Cardiff C, Blackpool, Scunthorpe U,
        Chesterfield
2000–01 Bristol R, Luton T, Swansea C, Oxford U

DIVISION 3 TO DIVISION 4

1958–59 Rochdale, Notts Co, Doncaster R, Stockport Co
1959–60 Accrington S, Wrexham, Mansfield T, York C
1960–61 Chesterfield, Colchester U, Bradford C,
        Tranmere R
1961–62 Newport Co, Brentford, Lincoln C, Torquay U
1962–63 Bradford PA, Brighton & HA, Carlisle U,
        Halifax T
1963–64 Millwall, Crewe Alex, Wrexham, Notts Co
1964–65 Luton T, Port Vale, Colchester U, Barnsley
1965–66 Southend U, Exeter C, Brentford, York C
1966–67 Doncaster R, Workington, Darlington, Swansea T
1967–68 Scunthorpe U, Colchester U, Grimsby T,
        Peterborough U (demoted)
1968–69 Oldham Ath, Crewe Alex, Hartlepool,
        Northampton T
1969–70 Bournemouth, Southport, Barrow, Stockport Co
1970–71 Reading, Bury, Doncaster R, Gillingham
1971–72 Mansfield T, Barnsley, Torquay U, Bradford C
1972–73 Rotherham U, Brentford, Swansea C,

        Scunthorpe U
1973–74 Cambridge U, Shrewsbury T, Southport,
        Rochdale
1974–75 Bournemouth, Tranmere R, Watford,
        Huddersfield T
1975–76 Aldershot, Colchester U, Southend U, Halifax T
1976–77 Reading, Northampton T, Grimsby T, York C
1977–78 Port Vale, Bradford C, Hereford U, Portsmouth
1978–79 Peterborough U, Walsall, Tranmere R, Lincoln C
1979–80 Bury, Southend U, Mansfield T, Wimbledon
1980–81 Sheffield U, Colchester U, Blackpool, Hull C
1981–82 Wimbledon, Swindon T, Bristol C, Chester
1982–83 Reading, Wrexham, Doncaster R, Chesterfield
1983–84 Scunthorpe U, Southend U, Port Vale, Exeter C
1984–85 Burnley, Orient, Preston NE, Cambridge U
1985–86 Lincoln C, Cardiff C, Wolverhampton W,
        Swansea C
1986–87 Bolton W**, Carlisle U, Darlington, Newport Co
1987–88 Doncaster R, York C, Grimsby T, Rotherham U**

1988–89 Southend U, Chesterfield, Gillingham, Aldershot 1990–91 Crewe Alex, Rotherham U, Mansfield T
1989–90 Cardiff C, Northampton T, Blackpool, Walsall 1991–92 Bury, Shrewsbury T, Torquay U, Darlington

** Relegated after play-offs. N.B. Relegated clubs not featured in exact order of finishing.

APPLICATIONS FOR RE-ELECTION
FOURTH DIVISION

Eleven: Hartlepool U.
Seven: Crewe Alex.
Six: Barrow (lost League place to Hereford U 1972), Halifax T, Rochdale, Southport (lost League place to Wigan Ath 1978), York C.
Five: Chester C, Darlington, Lincoln C, Stockport Co, Workington (lost League place to Wimbledon 1977).
Four: Bradford PA (lost League place to Cambridge U 1970), Newport Co, Northampton T.
Three: Doncaster R, Hereford U.
Two: Bradford C, Exeter C, Oldham Ath, Scunthorpe U, Torquay U.
One: Aldershot, Colchester U, Gateshead (lost League place to Peterborough U 1960), Grimsby T, Swansea C, Tranmere R, Wrexham, Blackpool, Cambridge U, Preston NE.
Accrington S resigned and Oxford U were elected 1962.
Port Vale were forced to re-apply following expulsion in 1968.
Aldershot expelled March 1992. Maidstone U resigned August 1992.

THIRD DIVISIONS NORTH & SOUTH

Seven: Walsall.
Six: Exeter C, Halifax T, Newport Co.
Five: Accrington S, Barrow, Gillingham, New Brighton, Southport.
Four: Rochdale, Norwich C.
Three: Crystal Palace, Crewe Alex, Darlington, Hartlepool U, Merthyr T, Swindon T.
Two: Aberdare Ath, Aldershot, Ashington, Bournemouth, Brentford, Chester, Colchester U, Durham C, Millwall, Nelson, QPR, Rotherham U, Southend U, Tranmere R, Watford, Workington.
One: Bradford C, Bradford PA, Brighton & HA, Bristol R, Cardiff C, Carlisle U, Charlton Ath, Gateshead, Grimsby T, Mansfield T, Shrewsbury T, Torquay U, York C.

LEAGUE STATUS FROM 1986–87

RELEGATED FROM LEAGUE		PROMOTED TO LEAGUE
1986–87	Lincoln C	Scarborough
1987–88	Newport Co	Lincoln C
1988–89	Darlington	Maidstone U
1989–90	Colchester U	Darlington
1990–91	—	Barnet
1991–92	—	Colchester U
1992–93	Halifax T	Wycombe W
1993–94	—	—
1994–95	—	—
1995–96	—	—
1996–97	Hereford U	Macclesfield T
1997–98	Doncaster R	Halifax T
1998–99	Scarborough	Cheltenham T
1999–2000	Chester C	Kidderminster H
2000–01	Barnet	Rushden & D

Manchester United players celebrate their seventh FA Premier League title and the third in succession.
(Action Images/John Sibley)

LEAGUE ATTENDANCES SINCE 1946–47

Season	Matches	Total	Div. 1	Div. 2	Div. 3 (S)	Div. 3 (N)
1946–47	1848	35,604,606	15,005,316	11,071,572	5,664,004	3,863,714
1947–48	1848	40,259,130	16,732,341	12,286,350	6,653,610	4,586,829
1948–49	1848	41,271,414	17,914,667	11,353,237	6,998,429	5,005,081
1949–50	1848	40,517,865	17,278,625	11,694,158	7,104,155	4,440,927
1950–51	2028	39,584,967	16,679,454	10,780,580	7,367,884	4,757,109
1951–52	2028	39,015,866	16,110,322	11,066,189	6,958,927	4,880,428
1952–53	2028	37,149,966	16,050,278	9,686,654	6,704,299	4,708,735
1953–54	2028	36,174,590	16,154,915	9,510,053	6,311,508	4,198,114
1954–55	2028	34,133,103	15,087,221	8,988,794	5,996,017	4,051,071
1955–56	2028	33,150,809	14,108,961	9,080,002	5,692,479	4,269,367
1956–57	2028	32,744,405	13,803,037	8,718,162	5,622,189	4,601,017
1957–58	2028	33,562,208	14,468,652	8,663,712	6,097,183	4,332,661
					Div. 3	Div. 4
1958–59	2028	33,610,985	14,727,691	8,641,997	5,946,600	4,276,697
1959–60	2028	32,538,611	14,391,227	8,399,627	5,739,707	4,008,050
1960–61	2028	28,619,754	12,926,948	7,033,936	4,784,256	3,874,614
1961–62	2015	27,979,902	12,061,194	7,453,089	5,199,106	3,266,513
1962–63	2028	28,885,852	12,490,239	7,792,770	5,341,362	3,261,481
1963–64	2028	28,535,022	12,486,626	7,594,158	5,419,157	3,035,081
1964–65	2028	27,641,168	12,708,752	6,984,104	4,436,245	3,512,067
1965–66	2028	27,206,980	12,480,644	6,914,757	4,779,150	3,032,429
1966–67	2028	28,902,596	14,242,957	7,253,819	4,421,172	2,984,648
1967–68	2028	30,107,298	15,289,410	7,450,410	4,013,087	3,354,391
1968–69	2028	29,382,172	14,584,851	7,382,390	4,339,656	3,075,275
1969–70	2028	29,600,972	14,868,754	7,581,728	4,223,761	2,926,729
1970–71	2028	28,194,146	13,954,337	7,098,265	4,377,213	2,764,331
1971–72	2028	28,700,729	14,484,603	6,769,308	4,697,392	2,749,426
1972–73	2028	25,448,642	13,998,154	5,631,730	3,737,252	2,081,506
1973–74	2027	24,982,203	13,070,991	6,326,108	3,421,624	2,163,480
1974–75	2028	25,577,977	12,613,178	6,955,970	4,086,145	1,992,684
1975–76	2028	24,896,053	13,089,861	5,798,405	3,948,449	2,059,338
1976–77	2028	26,182,800	13,647,585	6,250,597	4,152,218	2,132,400
1977–78	2028	25,392,872	13,255,677	6,474,763	3,332,042	2,330,390
1978–79	2028	24,540,627	12,704,549	6,153,223	3,374,558	2,308,297
1979–80	2028	24,623,975	12,163,002	6,112,025	3,999,328	2,349,620
1980–81	2028	21,907,569	11,392,894	5,175,442	3,637,854	1,701,379
1981–82	2028	20,006,961	10,420,793	4,750,463	2,836,915	1,998,790
1982–83	2028	18,766,158	9,295,613	4,974,937	2,943,568	1,552,040
1983–84	2028	18,358,631	8,711,448	5,359,757	2,729,942	1,557,484
1984–85	2028	17,849,835	9,761,404	4,030,823	2,667,008	1,390,600
1985–86	2028	16,488,577	9,037,854	3,551,968	2,490,481	1,408,274
1986–87	2028	17,379,218	9,144,676	4,168,131	2,350,970	1,715,441
1987–88	2030	17,959,732	8,094,571	5,341,599	2,751,275	1,772,287
1988–89	2036	18,464,192	7,809,993	5,887,805	3,035,327	1,791,067
1989–90	2036	19,445,442	7,883,039	6,867,674	2,803,551	1,891,178
1990–91	2036	19,508,202	8,618,709	6,285,068	2,835,759	1,768,666
1991–92	2064*	20,487,273	9,989,160	5,809,787	2,993,352	1,694,974
		Total	FA Premier	Div. 1	Div. 2	Div. 3
1992–93	2028	20,657,327	9,759,809	5,874,017	3,483,073	1,540,428
1993–94	2028	21,683,381	10,644,551	6,487,104	2,972,702	1,579,024
1994–95	2028	21,856,020	11,213,168	6,044,293	3,037,752	1,560,807
1995–96	2036	21,844,416	10,469,107	6,566,349	2,843,652	1,965,308
1996–97	2036	22,783,163	10,804,762	6,931,539	3,195,223	1,851,639
1997–98	2036	24,692,608	11,092,106	8,330,018	3,503,264	1,767,220
1998–99	2036	25,435,542	11,620,326	7,543,369	4,169,697	2,102,150
1999–2000	2036	25,341,090	11,668,497	7,810,208	3,700,433	2,161,952
2000–2001	2036	26,030,167	12,472,094	7,909,512	3,488,166	2,160,395

Figures include matches played by Aldershot.
Football League official total for their three divisions in 2000–01 were 13,558,061.

ENGLISH LEAGUE ATTENDANCES 2000–2001

FA CARLING PREMIERSHIP ATTENDANCES

	Average Gate			Season 2000/2001	
	1999/2000	2000/01	+/–%	Highest	Lowest
Arsenal	38,033	37,975	–0.15	38,146	37,318
Aston Villa	31,697	31,597	–0.32	41,366	27,056
Bradford City	18,030	18,511	+2.67	22,057	15,523
Charlton Athletic	19,557	20,020	+2.37	20,043	19,633
Chelsea	34,531	34,698	+0.48	35,196	33,159
Coventry City	20,786	20,535	–1.21	23,063	17,275
Derby County	29,351	28,551	–2.73	33,239	22,310
Everton	34,880	34,130	–2.15	40,260	27,670
Ipswich Town	18,370	22,524	+22.61	24,888	21,767
Leeds United	39,155	39,016	–0.35	40,055	35,552
Leicester City	19,825	20,453	+3.17	22,132	18,084
Liverpool	44,074	43,699	–0.85	44,806	38,474
Manchester City	32,088	34,058	+6.14	34,629	32,053
Manchester United	58,017	67,544	+16.42	67,637	67,447
Middlesbrough	33,263	30,730	–7.61	34,696	27,556
Newcastle United	36,311	51,290	+41.25	52,134	50,159
Southampton	15,132	15,115	–0.11	15,252	14,801
Sunderland	40,495	45,069	+11.29	47,250	43,185
Tottenham Hotspur	34,902	35,216	+0.90	36,096	28,300
West Ham United	25,093	25,697	+2.41	26,048	22,586

TOTAL ATTENDANCES:	12,472,094 (380 games)
	Average 32,821 (+6.89%)
HIGHEST:	67,637 Manchester United v Coventry City
LOWEST:	14,801 Southampton v Coventry City
HIGHEST AVERAGE:	67,544 Manchester United
LOWEST AVERAGE:	15,115 Southampton

NATIONWIDE FOOTBALL LEAGUE: DIVISION ONE ATTENDANCES

	Average Gate			Season 2000/2001	
	1999/2000	2000/01	+/–%	Highest	Lowest
Barnsley	15,412	14,465	-6.1	19,989	12,412
Birmingham City	21,895	21,283	-2.8	29,150	15,579
Blackburn Rovers	19,253	20,740	+7.7	29,426	16,397
Bolton Wanderers	14,244	16,062	+12.8	24,249	10,180
Burnley	12,973	16,234	+25.1	21,369	13,189
Crewe Alexandra	6,222	6,698	+7.7	9,415	5,215
Crystal Palace	15,662	17,061	+8.9	21,133	13,987
Fulham	13,092	14,985	+14.5	19,373	10,437
Gillingham	7,088	9,293	+31.1	10,518	7,810
Grimsby Town	6,157	5,646	-8.3	8,706	3,732
Huddersfield Town	14,029	12,808	-8.7	19,290	7,592
Norwich City	15,539	16,525	+6.3	21,241	13,688
Nottingham Forest	17,196	20,615	+19.9	28,372	17,089
Portsmouth	13,906	13,533	-2.7	19,013	9,235
Preston North End	12,589	14,617	+16.1	17,355	12,632
Queens Park Rangers	13,718	12,013	-12.4	17,608	9,388
Sheffield United	13,718	17,211	+25.5	25,673	10,816
Sheffield Wednesday	24,855	19,268	-22.5	38,433	14,695
Stockport County	7,411	7,031	-5.1	9,782	5,383
Tranmere Rovers	7,273	9,045	+24.4	12,362	7,119
Watford	18,544	13,941	-24.8	18,333	11,166
West Bromwich Albion	14,584	17,657	+21.1	22,301	13,980
Wimbledon	17,156	7,901	-53.9	14,071	4,489
Wolverhampton Wanderers	21,470	19,258	-10.3	26,627	14,853

TOTAL ATTENDANCES:	7,909,512 (552 games)
	Average 14,329 (+1.3%)
HIGHEST:	38,433 Sheffield Wednesday v Sheffield United
LOWEST:	3,732 Grimsby Town v Bolton Wanderers
HIGHEST AVERAGE:	21,283 Birmingham City
LOWEST AVERAGE:	5,646 Grimsby Town

NATIONWIDE FOOTBALL LEAGUE: DIVISION TWO ATTENDANCES

	Average Gate			*Season 2000/2001*	
	1999/2000	2000/01	+/−%	Highest	Lowest
AFC Bournemouth	4,917	4,403	−10.5	6,843	3,004
Brentford	5,742	4,645	−19.1	7,550	3,062
Bristol City	9,803	10,369	+5.8	16,696	7,411
Bristol Rovers	8,402	7,275	−13.4	9,361	5,502
Bury	4,025	3,444	−14.4	4,976	2,274
Cambridge United	4,403	4,403	+0.0	7,505	3,027
Colchester United	3,782	3,555	−6.0	5,010	2,579
Luton Town	5,658	5,754	+1.7	7,405	4,362
Millwall	9,260	11,442	+23.6	18,510	7,064
Northampton Town	5,459	5,654	+3.6	7,079	4,361
Notts County	5,667	5,201	−8.2	9,125	2,860
Oldham Athletic	5,391	4,972	−7.8	9,359	3,011
Oxford United	5,790	5,148	−11.1	7,480	3,676
Peterborough United	6,568	6,252	−4.8	11,274	4,004
Port Vale	5,997	4,458	−25.7	8,948	3,192
Reading	8,985	12,647	+40.8	20,589	7,768
Rotherham United	4,426	5,652	+27.7	9,760	3,545
Stoke City	11,426	13,767	+20.5	22,133	9,350
Swansea City	5,895	4,913	−16.7	8,391	2,002
Swindon Town	6,977	6,187	−11.3	10,031	3,452
Walsall	6,779	5,632	−16.9	7,772	4,437
Wigan Athletic	7,007	6,774	−3.3	10,048	4,798
Wrexham	3,952	3,600	−8.9	6,447	1,584
Wycombe Wanderers	5,101	5,513	+8.1	7,516	4,488

TOTAL ATTENDANCES: 3,488,166 (552 games)
Average 6,319 (−5.7%)
HIGHEST: 22,133 Stoke City v Port Vale
LOWEST: 1,584 Wrexham v Cambridge United
HIGHEST AVERAGE: 13,767 Stoke City
LOWEST AVERAGE: 3,444 Bury

NATIONWIDE FOOTBALL LEAGUE: DIVISION THREE ATTENDANCES

	Average Gate			*Season 2000/2001*	
	1999/2000	2000/01	+/−%	Highest	Lowest
Barnet	2,743	2,406	−12.3	5,523	1,322
Blackpool	4,841	4,457	−7.9	5,862	2,907
Brighton & Hove Albion	5,733	6,603	+15.2	6,995	5,804
Cardiff City	6,895	7,962	+15.5	13,602	4,625
Carlisle United	3,192	3,670	+15.0	8,194	1,309
Cheltenham Town	4,125	3,695	−10.4	5,139	2,368
Chesterfield	2,935	4,846	+65.1	7,014	3,796
Darlington	5,523	3,844	−30.4	6,717	2,689
Exeter City	3,014	3,692	+22.5	5,150	2,470
Halifax Town	2,536	2,214	−12.7	3,979	1,382
Hartlepool United	2,982	3,423	+14.8	5,324	2,130
Hull City	5,736	6,684	+16.5	11,820	4,450
Kidderminster Harriers	2,857	3,422	+19.8	5,122	2,438
Leyton Orient	4,357	4,528	+3.9	7,958	2,200
Lincoln City	3,405	3,273	−3.9	5,487	1,853
Macclesfield Town	2,304	2,064	−10.4	3,045	1,349
Mansfield Town	2,594	2,706	+4.3	7,899	1,623
Plymouth Argyle	5,372	4,945	−7.9	8,671	3,378
Rochdale	2,774	3,249	+17.1	5,008	2,444
Scunthorpe United	4,064	3,446	−15.2	6,101	2,523
Shrewsbury Town	2,832	2,898	+2.3	5,360	2,058
Southend United	4,138	4,322	+4.4	9,950	2,403
Torquay United	2,555	2,556	+0.0	4,505	1,538
York City	3,048	3,026	−0.7	5,493	1,981

TOTAL ATTENDANCES: 2,160,395 (552 games)
Average 3,914 (−0.1%)
HIGHEST: 13,602 Cardiff City v Chesterfield
LOWEST: 1,309 Carlisle United v Cardiff City
HIGHEST AVERAGE: 7,962 Cardiff City
LOWEST AVERAGE: 2,064 Macclesfield Town

LEAGUE CUP FINALISTS 1961–2001

Played as a two-leg final until 1966. All subsequent finals at Wembley.

Year	Winners	Runners-up	Score
1961	Aston Villa	Rotherham U	0-2, 3-0 (aet)
1962	Norwich C	Rochdale	3-0, 1-0
1963	Birmingham C	Aston Villa	3-1, 0-0
1964	Leicester C	Stoke C	1-1, 3-2
1965	Chelsea	Leicester C	3-2, 0-0
1966	WBA	West Ham U	1-2, 4-1
1967	QPR	WBA	3-2
1968	Leeds U	Arsenal	1-0
1969	Swindon T	Arsenal	3-1 (aet)
1970	Manchester C	WBA	2-1 (aet)
1971	Tottenham H	Aston Villa	2-0
1972	Stoke C	Chelsea	2-1
1973	Tottenham H	Norwich C	1-0
1974	Wolverhampton W	Manchester C	2-1
1975	Aston Villa	Norwich C	1-0
1976	Manchester C	Newcastle U	2-1
1977	Aston Villa	Everton	0-0, 1-1 (aet), 3-2 (aet)
1978	Nottingham F	Liverpool	0-0 (aet), 1-0
1979	Nottingham F	Southampton	3-2
1980	Wolverhampton W	Nottingham F	1-0
1981	Liverpool	West Ham U	1-1 (aet), 2-1

MILK CUP

Year	Winners	Runners-up	Score
1982	Liverpool	Tottenham H	3-1 (aet)
1983	Liverpool	Manchester U	2-1 (aet)
1984	Liverpool	Everton	0-0 (aet), 1-0
1985	Norwich C	Sunderland	1-0
1986	Oxford U	QPR	3-0

LITTLEWOODS CUP

Year	Winners	Runners-up	Score
1987	Arsenal	Liverpool	2-1
1988	Luton T	Arsenal	3-2
1989	Nottingham F	Luton T	3-1
1990	Nottingham F	Oldham Ath	1-0

RUMBELOWS LEAGUE CUP

Year	Winners	Runners-up	Score
1991	Sheffield W	Manchester U	1-0
1992	Manchester U	Nottingham F	1-0

COCA-COLA CUP

Year	Winners	Runners-up	Score
1993	Arsenal	Sheffield W	2-1
1994	Aston Villa	Manchester U	3-1
1995	Liverpool	Bolton W	2-1
1996	Aston Villa	Leeds U	3-0
1997	Leicester C	Middlesbrough	1-1 (aet), 1-0 (aet)
1998	Chelsea	Middlesbrough	2-0 (aet)

WORTHINGTON CUP

Year	Winners	Runners-up	Score
1999	Tottenham H	Leicester C	1-0
2000	Leicester C	Tranmere R	2-1
2001	Liverpool	Birmingham C	1-1 (aet)*

*Played at Millennium Stadium. Liverpool won 5-4 on penalties

LEAGUE CUP WINS
Liverpool 6, Aston Villa 5, Nottingham F 4, Leicester C 3, Tottenham H 3, Arsenal 2, Chelsea 2, Manchester C 2, Norwich C 2, Wolverhampton W 2, Birmingham C 1, Leeds U 1, Luton T 1, Manchester U 1, Oxford U 1, QPR 1, Sheffield W 1, Stoke C 1, Swindon T 1, WBA 1.

APPEARANCES IN FINALS
Liverpool 8, Aston Villa 7, Nottingham F 6, Arsenal 5, Leicester C 5, Manchester U 4, Norwich C 4, Tottenham H 4, Chelsea 3, Manchester C 3, WBA 3, Birmingham C 2, Everton 2, Leeds U 2, Luton T 2, Middlesbrough 2, QPR 2, Sheffield W 2, Stoke C 2, West Ham U 2, Wolverhampton W 2, Bolton W 1, Newcastle U 1, Oldham Ath 1, Oxford U 1, Rochdale 1, Rotherham U 1, Southampton 1, Sunderland 1, Swindon T 1, Tranmere R 1.

APPEARANCES IN SEMI-FINALS
Aston Villa 11, Liverpool 11, Arsenal 9, Tottenham H 9, Manchester U 7, West Ham U 7, Chelsea 6, Nottingham F 6, Leeds U 5, Leicester C 5, Manchester C 5, Norwich C 5, Birmingham C 4 Middlesbrough 4, WBA 4, Bolton W 3, Burnley 3, Crystal Palace 3, Everton 3, Ipswich T 3, QPR 3, Sheffield W 3, Sunderland 3, Swindon T 3, Wolverhampton W 3, Blackburn R 2, Bristol C 2, Coventry C 2, Luton T 2, Oxford U 2, Plymouth Arg 2, Southampton 2, Stoke C 2, Tranmere R 2, Wimbledon 2, Blackpool 1, Bury 1, Cardiff C 1, Carlisle U 1, Chester C 1, Derby Co 1, Huddersfield T 1, Newcastle U 1, Oldham Ath 1, Peterborough U 1, Rochdale 1, Rotherham U 1, Shrewsbury T 1, Stockport Co 1, Walsall 1, Watford 1.

WORTHINGTON CUP 2000–2001

FIRST ROUND, FIRST LEG

22 AUG

Barnet (0) 2 *(Doolan 50, McGleish 77)*
Wycombe W (0) 1 *(Rogers 79)*   1741
Barnet: Harrison; Stockley, Sawyers, Newton, Heald, Arber, Currie, Doolan, Strevens (Purser), McGleish, Toms.
Wycombe W: Taylor; Rogers, Vinnicombe, Bulman, Bates, McCarthy, Harkin (Baird), Simpson, McSporran, Jones, Brown.

Bolton W (0) 1 *(Holdsworth 84)*
Macclesfield T (0) 0   4957
Bolton W: Banks; O'Kane, Richardson (Hansen), Warhurst (Bergsson), Barness, Fish, Passi (Frandsen), Norris, Holdsworth, Rankin, Farrelly.
Macclesfield T: Bullock; Hitchen, Ingram, Collins, Tinson, Wood, Munroe (Abbey), Sedgemore, Barker (Askey), Twynham, Durkan.

Brighton & HA (1) 1 *(Watson 44)*
Millwall (1) 2 *(Braniff 39, Livermore 53)*   6039
Brighton & HA: Cartwright; Watson, Mayo, Cullip, Crosby, Carpenter (Rogers), Freeman (Jones), Hart, Zamora, Oatway (Melton), Brooker.
Millwall: Warner; Lawrence, Ryan, Cahill, Tuttle, Dolan, Bircham, Livermore, Harris (Tyne) (Gilkes), Reid, Braniff.

Bristol C (2) 2 *(Thorpe 32 (pen), Peacock 45 (pen))*
Brentford (1) 2 *(Rowlands 45, McCammon 90)*   3471
Bristol C: Malessa; Lavin, Bell, Holland P (Hulbert), Lever (Jordan), Carey, Murray, Testimetanu, Peacock, Thorpe (Spencer), Tinnion.
Brentford: Gottskalksson; Gibbs (Partridge), Scott, Mahon, Quinn, Marshall, Ingimarsson, Evans, Owusu (Rowlands), McCammon, Javary.

Burnley (0) 4 *(Payton 63 (pen), 69, 90, Davis 87)*
Hartlepool U (1) 1 *(Miller 37)*   3319
Burnley: Crichton; Weller, Briscoe, Cox, Davis, Thomas, Little, Cook (Mullin), Cooke (Payton), Gray (Branch), Ball.
Hartlepool U: Hollund; Knowles, Robinson (Shilton), Ferguson, Westwood, Sharp, Fitzpatrick (McAvoy), Miller, Lormor, Henderson (Midgley), Stephenson.

Cambridge U (0) 0
Portsmouth (0) 0   2904
Cambridge U: Perez; Ashbee, Mustoe, Duncan, McAnespie, Dreyer, Wanless, Russell (MacKenzie), Abbey, Hansen (Youngs), Axeldal (Slade).
Portsmouth: Hoult; Derry (Curtis), Edinburgh, Waterman, Primus, Moore, Quashie, Thogersen, Bradbury, Claridge, O'Neil (Rudonja).

Crewe Alex (0) 2 *(Foster 84, Rivers 86)*
Bury (0) 2 *(Bullock 58, Littlejohn 75)*   3199
Crewe Alex: Kearton; Wright D, Smith S, Grant (Smith P), Macauley, Foster, Little (Cramb), Lunt, Jack, Rivers, Sorvel.
Bury: Kenny; Unsworth, Collins, Daws, Swailes C (Swailes D), Redmond, Billy, Bullock (Forrest), Bhutia (Preece), Reid, Littlejohn.

Darlington (1) 2 *(Elliott 15 (pen), Naylor 61)*
Nottingham F (1) 2 *(Bart-Williams 21 (pen), Rogers 73)*   4724
Darlington: Van der Geest; Liddle, Heckingbottom, Reed (Campbell), Aspin, Himsworth, Gray, Elliott, Naylor, Hjorth (Angel), Williamson.
Nottingham F: Beasant; Louis-Jean, Brennan, Bart-Williams, Vaughan, Doig, Prutton, Jones, John, Harewood (Platt), Rogers.

Gillingham (1) 2 *(Asaba 42, Thomson 76)*
Torquay U (0) 0   2743
Gillingham: Bartram; Patterson, Browning, Hope, Ashby, Butters, Lewis, Hessenthaler, Asaba (James), Thomson, Gooden.
Torquay U: Jones; Holmes, Doughlin, Aggrey, Tully, Watson, Ashington (O'Brien), Ford, Parker (Stocco), Williams (Mendy), Hill.

Grimsby T (2) 2 *(Coldicott 36, Allen 37)*
Carlisle U (0) 0   1914
Grimsby T: Coyne; McDermott, Butterfield (Black), Livingstone, Raven, Coldicott, Smith D, Pouton, Allen, Jeffrey (Clare), Groves.
Carlisle U: Weaver; Birch, Darby, Whitehead, Winstanley, Lee, Soley, Stevens (Dobie), Heggs, Hemmings (Tracey), Carss (Pitts).

Hull C (1) 1 *(Eyre 28)*
Notts Co (0) 0   2675
Hull C: Bracey; Brightwell, Whitney, Goodison, Whittle, Brumwell, Swales, Whitmore (Brabin), Wood (Brown), Eyre, Philpott.
Notts Co: Ward; McDermott, Liburd, Warren, Richardson, Dyer, McCann (Rapley), Ramage, Stallard, Joseph, Hamilton.

Leyton Orient (0) 1 *(Brkovic 47)*
Reading (1) 1 *(Cureton 37)*   2316
Leyton Orient: Bayes; Joseph, Lockwood, McGhee, McElholm, Harris, Downer, Martin, Griffiths (Watts), Garcia, Brkovic.
Reading: Whitehead; Gurney, Robinson, Viveash, Mackie, Henderson (Butler), Igoe (Gamble), Evers, Cureton, Newman, Rougier.

Luton T (0) 0
Peterborough U (0) 0   3175
Luton T: Ovendale; Boyce, Taylor, Holmes, Watts, Fraser, George, McLaren, Stein, Fotiadis (Brennan), Spring.
Peterborough U: Tiler; Hooper, Drury, Forsyth, Rea, Edwards, Green, Shields (Scott), Oldfield (Cullen), Forinton, Hanlon (Farrell).

Mansfield T (0) 0
Wrexham (1) 1 *(Ferguson 37)*   1052
Mansfield T: Bowling; Bacon, Andrews, Pemberton (Asher), Hicks, Sisson, Corden (Bradley), Clarke, Williams, Robinson, Greenacre.
Wrexham: Dearden; McGregor, Roche, Owen, Carey, Ridler, Williams, Ferguson, Morrell (Chalk), Edwards, Faulconbridge (Gibson).

Northampton T (1) 1 *(Gabbiadini 24)*
Fulham (0) 0   3847
Northampton T: Welch; Hendon, Frain, Hughes, Green, Hope, Howard, Hunt, Forrester (Hodge), Gabbiadini, Hargreaves.
Fulham: Hahnemann; Neilson, Phelan, Collins W, Symons, Lewis, Fernandes, Betsy (Davis), Hayward, Peschisolido (Cornwall), Boa Morte.

Norwich C (0) 0
Bournemouth (0) 0   12,224
Norwich C: Marshall A; Sutch, De Waard (Coote), Marshall L, Fleming, Kenton, Russell, Giallanza (Forbes), Roberts, Mulryne (McGovern), Llewellyn.
Bournemouth: Menetrier; Young, Purches, Grant, Smith, Tindall, Jorgensen, Fletcher C (Elliott), Eribenne (Huck), Fletcher S, Hughes.

Oldham Ath (1) 1 *(Corazzin 24)*
Huddersfield T (0) 0   4255
Oldham Ath: Kelly; Jones, Holt, Garnett, Rickers, Duxbury, Adams, Boshell (Innes), Allott (Tipton), Corazzin, Hotte.
Huddersfield T: Vaesen; Vincent, Heary, Irons, Lucketti, Armstrong C, Thornley (Baldry), Holland, Hay, Facey, Wijnhard.

Port Vale (1) 1 *(Burton 20)*
Chesterfield (2) 2 *(Breckin 6, Beckett 24)*   3485
Port Vale: Goodlad; Tankard, Carragher, Minton (Smith), Burton, Widdrington, Twiss, Cummins, Viljanen, Naylor, Eyre.
Chesterfield: Armstrong; Breckin, Perkins, Tutill, Blatherwick, Parrish, Ebdon, Williams R, Reeves, Beckett (Howard), Richardson (Willis).

Rochdale (0) 1 *(Ellis 90)*
Blackburn R (0) 1 *(Blake 59)*   4873
Rochdale: Edwards; Evans, Todd, Ware (Jones), Bayliss, Hill, Ford, Flitcroft, Platt, Ellis, Oliver (Davies).
Blackburn R: Filan; Curtis, Harkness, Broomes, Taylor, Dunn, McAteer, Flitcroft, Blake, Jansen, Gillespie (Johnson).

Rotherham U (0) 0
Barnsley (1) 1 *(Barnard 45)*   4940
Rotherham U: Gray; Bryan, Beech, Scott, Garner, Branston, Watson (Hurst), Robins, Fortune-West, Warne, Talbot (Varty).
Barnsley: Miller; Jones, Regan (O'Callaghan), Morgan, Chettle, Barker, Van der Laan, Ward, Sheron, Dyer (Thomas), Barnard (Austin).

Sheffield U (2) 6 *(Bent 34, 65, 90, Devlin 45 (pen), Kelly 52, Brown 58 (og))*
Lincoln C (1) 1 *(Smith 6)*   4152
Sheffield U: Tracey; Uhlenbeek, Weber, Woodhouse (Ford), Murphy, Sandford, Devlin, Ribeiro (Santos), Bent, Kelly (Thompson), Jagielka.
Lincoln C: Marriott; Smith, Mayo, Logan, Holmes, Brown, Walker (Stergiopoulos), Miller, Battersby, Cameron, Finnigan (Gain).

Shrewsbury T (0) 1 *(Freestone 61)*
Preston NE (0) 0   2445
Shrewsbury T: Dunbavin; Jenkins, Hanmer, Tretton, Davidson, Peer (Tolley), Thomas, Jagielka, Freestone (Lowe), Jemson, Aiston.
Preston NE: Lucas; Alexander, Edwards, Murdock, Morgan, Robinson, Cartwright, Basham, Macken, Barry-Murphy, McKenna.

Southend U (0) 0
Birmingham C (3) 5 *(Eaden 5, Marcelo 10, Johnson M 28, Adebola 74, Hughes 85)*   3694
Southend U: Woodman; Booty, Searle, Tinkler, Roget, Morley (Whelan), Lee, Maher (Forbes), Carruthers, Tolson, Houghton (Cross).
Birmingham C: Bennett; Eaden, Johnson M, Hughes, Holdsworth, Gill, O'Connor (Lazaridis), Sonner, Marcelo (Adebola), Ndlovu (Johnson A), Grainger.

Stockport Co (0) 0
Blackpool (1) 1 *(Nowland 45)*   3014
Stockport Co: Jones; Bryngelsson (Woodthorpe), Clark, Flynn, Connelly, Wiss (Smith), Cooper, Moore, Maxwell, Gibb, Daly (Bailey).
Blackpool: Caig; Murphy N, Jaszczun, Bushell, Hughes, Jones, Clarkson, Simpson, Murphy J, Newell (Nowland), Coid.

Swansea C (0) 0
WBA (0) 0   4758
Swansea C: Freestone; Price, Howard, O'Leary, Smith, Bound, Thomas, Jenkins, Boyd, Watkin (Mutton), Roberts (Keegan).
WBA: Jensen; Lyttle, Clement, McInnes, Butler, Carbon, Chambers J, Oliver, Roberts (Sneekes), Hughes, Taylor.

Swindon T (1) 1 *(Howe 36)*
Exeter C (0) 1 *(Ampadu 81)*   5193
Swindon T: Griemink; Cobian, Heiselberg, Van der Linden, Reeves, O'Halloran, Howe, Hewlett, Alexander, Grazioli (Williams A), Duke (Cowe).
Exeter C: Van Heusden; Burrows, Campbell, Roscoe, Curran, Whitworth, Zabek, Ampadu, Flack, Tomlinson (Roberts C), Inglethorpe (Ashton).

Tranmere R (2) 3 *(Allison 16, Rideout 38, Gill 62)*
Halifax T (0) 0   4405
Tranmere R: Achterberg; Yates, Roberts, Henry, Challinor, Hill, Gill (Hinds), Koumas, Rideout (Barlow), Allison, Taylor (Parkinson).
Halifax T: Parks; Wilder, Bradshaw, Mitchell, Stoneman, Jules, Middleton, Kerrigan, Jones, Harrison (Gaughan), Thompson (Fitzpatrick).

Walsall (1) 1 *(Leitao 8)*
Kidderminster H (0) 1 *(Hadley 67)*   5552
Walsall: Walker; Brightwell, Aranalde, Tillson, Roper, Bukran, Wrack, Leitao (Eyjolfsson), Keates, Byfield, Hall.
Kidderminster H: Clarke; Clarkson, Stamps, Bogie (Smith), Hinton, Shail, Bennett, Horne, Hadley, Foster, Bird.

Watford (0) 0
Cheltenham T (0) 0   8289
Watford: Baardsen; Cox, Robinson, Palmer, Page, Ward, Perpetuini (Helguson), Easton, Mooney, Foley, Smith (Gudmundsson) (Miller).
Cheltenham T: Book; Duff, Victory, Banks, Brough, Howarth, Bloomer, Walker, Alsop, McAuley, Yates.

Wigan Ath (0) 1 *(Roberts 72)*
Scunthorpe U (0) 0   2725
Wigan Ath: Carroll; Green, Bradshaw, McGibbon, Mitchell (Kilford), De Zeeuw, McLaughlin, Sheridan (McLoughlin), Ashcroft (Roberts), Liddell, Martinez.
Scunthorpe U: Evans; Harsley, Dawson, Wilcox, Stanton, Dewhurst, Hodges, Graves, Sheldon, Torpey, Morrison (Sparrow).

Wolverhampton W (0) 0
Oxford U (1) 1 *(Murphy 37)*   9399
Wolverhampton W: Oakes; Muscat, Naylor, Lescott, Emblen, Taylor S (Sedgley), Bazeley, Osborn (Robinson), Ketsbaia, Taylor R, Sinton (Ndah).
Oxford U: Knight; Robertson (Folland), Powell, Richardson, Shepheard, Whitehead, Anthrobus, Tait, Murphy (Lilley), Jarman, Omoyimni (Beauchamp).

York C (0) 0 *(Jones 49)*
Stoke C (1) 5 *(Heath 10, Iwelumo 70, Connor 47, 59, O'Connor 80)*   2035
York C: Howarth; Edmondson (Bullock), Potter (Conlon), Sertori, Jones, Hobson, McNiven, Hulme, Duffield, Agnew, Hall.
Stoke C: Muggleton; Petty, Dorigo (Iwelumo), Heath, Gunnarsson, Mohan, Risom, Thordarson (Clarke), Connor, Fenton, O'Connor.

23 AUG

Colchester U (0) 0
QPR (1) 1 *(Kiwomya 27)*   3916
Colchester U: Brown; Dunne, Keith, Skelton, White, Clark, Duguid, McGavin, Lua-Lua, Stockwell (Johnson G), Dozzell.
QPR: Harper; Perry, Baraclough, Carlisle, Morrow, Ready, Langley, Peacock (Heinola), Crouch (Koejoe), Wardley, Kiwomya.

Crystal Palace (2) 2 *(Morrison C 19, Ruddock 34)*
Cardiff C (0) 1 *(Young 55)*   5983
Crystal Palace: Gregg; Black, Harrison, Zhiyi, Carlisle (Gray), Ruddock, Mullins, Rodger, Morrison C (McKenzie), Forssell, Pollock (Fullarton).
Cardiff C: Walton; Gabbidon, Brazier, Bonner, Greene, Young, Low, Boland, Brayson, Nugent, Legg.

Plymouth Arg (0) 1 *(McGregor 72)*
Bristol R (2) 2 *(Bignot 32, Cameron 41)*   3498
Plymouth Arg: Sheffield; O'Sullivan, Beswetherick, Barrett, Wotton (Phillips L), Taylor, Fleming, Barlow, Guinan (McCarthy), Gritton (McGregor).
Bristol R: Culkin; Bignot, Wilson, Thomson (Walters), Foster, Pethick, Astafjevs, Hogg, Ellington (Ellis), Cameron, Bryant.

FIRST ROUND, SECOND LEG

5 SEPT

Barnsley (0) 3 *(Sheron 53, 76, Barnard 82)*
Rotherham U (1) 2 *(Robins 29, Watson 72)*   8088
Barnsley: Miller; Moses (Ward), Barker, Morgan, O'Callaghan, Van der Laan, Appleby, Sheron, Shipperley, Jones (Neil), Woan (Barnard).
Rotherham U: Gray; Bryan (Berry), Hurst, Scott, Wilsterman, Branston (Varty), Watson (Garner), Robins, Fortune-West, Warne, Talbot.
Barnsley won 4-2 on aggregate.

Birmingham C (0) 0
Southend U (0) 0   9507
Birmingham C: Bennett; Gill, Grainger, Hughes, Holdsworth, Johnson M (Purse), Eaden, O'Connor, Marcelo (Williams), Ndlovu (Johnson A), Sonner.
Southend U: Woodman; Booty, Searle, Whelan, Roget, Morley, Lee (Tinkler), Maher, Carruthers, Tolson (Houghton), Connelly (Hunter).
Birmingham C won 5-0 on aggregate.

Blackpool (1) 3 *(Murphy J 17, 85, 90)*
Stockport Co (1) 2 *(Dinning 40, Moore 52)*   3133
Blackpool: Barnes; Wellens, Jaszczun, Bushell, Hughes, Jones, Milligan (Clarkson), Simpson, Murphy J, Newell (Nowland), Coid.
Stockport Co: Jones; Bryngelsson, Clark, Dinning, Flynn, Woodthorpe, Cooper, Moore, Carrigan (Maxwell), Smith, Gibb.
Blackpool won 4-2 on aggregate.

Bournemouth (1) 1 *(Jorgensen 7)*
Norwich C (0) 2 *(Giallanza 59, Russell 84)*   3634
Bournemouth: Menetrier; Young, Purches, Grant (Hayter), Tindall, Smith, Jorgensen, Fletcher C, Eribenne, Fletcher S, Hughes (Huck).
Norwich C: Marshall A; Sutch, Derveld, Marshall L, Fleming, Jackson, McGovern, Giallanza (Coote), Roberts, Russell, Brady (Nedergaard).
Norwich C won 2-1 on aggregate.

Brentford (0) 2 *(Scott 77, 90)*
Bristol C (1) 1 *(Holland P 28)*   2310
Brentford: Gottskalksson; Quinn, Marsh (Partridge), Mahon, Marshall, Rowlands, Ingimarsson, Evans, Javary (Folan), McCammon, Scott.
Bristol C: Phillips; Lavin, Bell, Holland P, Millen, Carey, Murray, Goodridge (Hulbert), Beadle, Hill, Tinnion.
Brentford won 4-3 on aggregate.

Bristol R (0) 1 *(Ellington 48)*
Plymouth Arg (0) 1 *(McCarthy 47)*   5228
Bristol R: Culkin; Bignot, Wilson, Foster, Thomson, Challis (Foran), Astafjevs, Ellis (Walters), Ellington, Hogg, Bryant.
Plymouth Arg: Sheffield; O'Sullivan, Beswetherick, Barrett, Taylor, Fleming, Phillips M, Barlow, McCarthy, Guinan (Gritton), Peake (Nancekivell).
Bristol R won 3-2 on aggregate.

Bury (1) 1 *(Bullock 7 (pen))*
Crewe Alex (1) 2 *(Rivers 14, Little 49)*   2106
Bury: Kenny; Barrass, Collins, Daws, Swailes C, Redmond (Preece), Billy, Reid, Bhutia (James), Bullock (Forrest), Littlejohn.
Crewe Alex: Kearton; Wright, Smith S, Sodje, Macauley, Street, Hulse (Grant), Lunt, Little, Rivers, Sorvel.
Crewe Alex won 4-3 on aggregate.

Cardiff C (0) 0
Crystal Palace (0) 0   4904
Cardiff C: Walton; Gabbidon, McCulloch, Bonner (Thomas), Greene, Jones, Hill, Evans, Nogan (Earnshaw), Nugent, Legg.
Crystal Palace: Gregg; Smith (Austin), Harrison, Black, Zhiyi, Ruddock, Mullins, Gray, Morrison C (McKenzie), Forssell (Harris), Pollock.
Crystal Palace won 2-1 on aggregate.

Carlisle U (1) 1 *(Stevens 17)*
Grimsby T (1) 1 *(Allen 45)*   2228
Carlisle U: Weaver; Birch (Pitts), Squires, Prokas, Winstanley, Darby (Lee), Soley (Thwaites), Stevens, Dobie, Tracey, Carss.
Grimsby T: Coyne; McDermott (Black), Handyside (Bloomer), Livingstone, Raven, Coldicott, Smith D, Pouton, Allen, Jeffrey (Clare), Groves.
Grimsby T won 3-1 on aggregate.

Cheltenham T (0) 0
Watford (2) 3 *(Smith 8, Ward 14, Helguson 76)*   5078
Cheltenham T: Book; Duff, Walker, Banks, Freeman, Howarth, Alsop (Hopkins), Devaney, White, Bloomer (Jackson), Yates.
Watford: Baardsen (Chamberlain); Cox, Gibbs, Palmer, Page, Ward, Helguson, Nielsen, Mooney (Foley), Hyde, Smith (Ngonge).
Watford won 3-0 on aggregate.

Chesterfield (0) 2 *(Beckett 68, Reeves 119)*
Port Vale (0) 2 *(Bridge-Wilkinson 76, Minton 78)*   3480
Chesterfield: Pollitt; Breckin, Perkins, Tutill (Payne), Blatherwick, Parrish, Ebdon, Williams R, Reeves, Beckett (Willis), Richardson (Galloway).
Port Vale: Goodlad; Tankard, Carragher, Minton, Burton, Widdrington, Twiss, Cummins, Viljanen, Naylor, Bridge-Wilkinson.
aet; Chesterfield won 4-3 on aggregate.

Exeter C (0) 1 *(Rawlinson 62)*
Swindon T (2) 2 *(Reeves 14, Invincible 43)*   2825
Exeter C: Fraser; Burrows (Roberts D), Roberts C, Roscoe, Curran, Whitworth, Zabek, Rawlinson, Flack, Tomlinson (Speakman), Inglethorpe.
Swindon T: Griemink; Robinson M, Davis, O'Halloran, Reeves, Willis, Invincible, Hewlett, Howe, Williams M (Grazioli), Duke (Robertson).
Swindon T won 3-2 on aggregate.

Fulham (1) 4 *(Davis 45, Fernandes 56, Saha 71, 90)*
Northampton T (1) 1 *(Sampson 6)*   5302
Fulham: Hahnemann; Collins W, Brevett, Fernandes, Neilson, Lewis (Saha), Davis, Clark, Hayles (Hayward), Knight, Boa Morte.
Northampton T: Welch; Hendon, Spedding, Sampson, Green, Hughes, Savage, Hunt, Forrester, Gabbiadini (Hodge), Howard.
Fulham won 4-2 on aggregate.

Hartlepool U (2) 3 *(Miller 30 (pen), Fitzpatrick 38, Stephenson 90)*
Burnley (1) 2 *(Cooke 18, Payton 82)*   1090
Hartlepool U: Williams; Arnison (Knowles), Shilton, Strodder, Westwood, Sharp, Fitzpatrick (Tennebo), Miller, Sperrevik, Henderson, Stephenson.
Burnley: Crichton; Weller (Maylett), Briscoe, Cox, Davis, Thomas, Ball, Cook, Cooke (Branch), Gray (Payton), Little.
Burnley won 6-4 on aggregate.

Huddersfield T (0) 0
Oldham Ath (1) 2 *(Rickers 40, 65)*   4979
Huddersfield T: Vaesen; Vincent, Heary, Dyson, Lucketti, Beech, Beresford (Baldry), Gorre (Sellars), Smith, Hay (Facey), Thornley.
Oldham Ath: Kelly; Jones, Holt, Garnett, Rickers (Innes), Duxbury, Adams, McNiven, Allott (Tipton), Corazzin (Whitehall), Hotte.
Oldham Ath won 3-0 on aggregate.

Kidderminster H (0) 0
Walsall (0) 1 *(Byfield 83)*   5351
Kidderminster H: Brock; Clarkson, Smith, Bogie, Hinton, Shail, Bennett, Horne, Hadley, Bird, Ducros.
Walsall: Walker; Brightwell, Aranalde, Tillson, Barras, Bukran, Hall, Keates, Angell (Bennett), Leitao (Byfield), Matias.
Walsall won 2-1 on aggregate.

Lincoln C (0) 1 *(Stergiopoulos 58)*
Sheffield U (0) 0   1379
Lincoln C: Marriott; Smith (Peacock), Mayo, Barnett, Holmes, Brown, Finnigan (Walker), Stergiopoulos, Battersby, Cameron (Lewis), Gain.
Sheffield U: Tracey; Jagielka, Weber, Santos, Murphy, Curle, Woodward, Brown (Burley), Bent, Kelly (Smith), Thompson (Ford).
Sheffield U won 6-2 on aggregate.

Macclesfield T (2) 3 *(Sedgemore 31, Munroe 45, Barker 54)*
Bolton W (0) 1 *(Ricketts 78)*   2235
Macclesfield T: Bullock; Hitchen, Abbey, Collins, Tinson, Wood, Askey (Adams), Sedgemore, Barker (Whitehead), Munroe, Durkan.
Bolton W: Banks; O'Kane, Barness, Frandsen, Bergsson, Fish (Richardson), Passi, Rankin (Wheatcroft), Hansen, Holdsworth (Ricketts), Norris.
Macclesfield T won 3-2 on aggregate.

Millwall (1) 1 *(Kinet 45)*
Brighton & HA (0) 0 *(Jones 67)*   5227
Millwall: Warner; Lawrence, Ryan, Cahill, Tuttle, Dolan, Livermore, Odunsi (Bowry), Braniff (Tyne), Reid, Kinet.
Brighton & HA: Cartwright; Watson, Mayo, Cullip, Wicks, Carpenter, Zamora, Rogers (Brooker), Hart (Thomas), Oatway, Jones.
Millwall won 3-2 on aggregate.

Notts Co (0) 2 *(Stallard 59 (pen), 120)*
Hull C (0) 0   1907
Notts Co: Ward; McDermott (Rapley), Liburd, Warren (Hughes), Richardson, Dyer, Owers, Ramage, Stallard, Joseph (Farrell), Hamilton.
Hull C: Bracey; Edwards, Harper, Whitney, Whittle, Greaves, Swales, Brabin, Brown, Marcelle (Brumwell), Brightwell (Wood).
aet; Notts Co won 2-1 on aggregate.

Oxford U (1) 1 *(Shepheard 16)*
Wolverhampton W (0) 3 *(Robinson 51, Taylor R 65, Proudlock 68)*   4679
Oxford U: Knight; Robertson, McGowan (Folland), Whitehead (Murphy), Richardson, Shepheard, Omoyimni, Tait, Anthrobus (Lilley), Jarman, Beauchamp.
Wolverhampton W: Oakes; Green, Naylor, Muscat, Sedgley, Lescott, Bazeley, Robinson, Taylor R, Proudlock (Ketsbaia), Taylor S.
Wolverhampton W won 3-2 on aggregate.

Peterborough U (1) 2 *(Farrell 34, Clarke 69)*
Luton T (1) 2 *(Stein 31, Scarlett 52)*   4286
Peterborough U: Tyler; Hooper (Scott), Drury, Forsyth, Rea, Edwards, Farrell (Hanlon), Green (Shields), Clarke, Whittingham, Oldfield.
Luton T: Ovendale; Boyce, Taylor, Brennan (Holmes), Watts, Fraser, George, McLaren, Stein (Kandol), Scarlett, Spring (Locke).
aet; Luton T won on away goals rule.

Portsmouth (0) 1 *(Mills 57)*
Cambridge U (0) 0   5570
Portsmouth: Hoult; Derry, Edinburgh, Curtis (Waterman), Primus, Moore, Quashie, Thogersen, Claridge, Mills (Bradbury), Hughes (O'Neil).
Cambridge U: Perez; Ashbee, Cowan, Duncan, McAnespie, Dreyer, Wanless, Axeldal (Russell), Youngs (Abbey), Mustoe, MacKenzie (Taylor).
Portsmouth won 1-0 on aggregate.

Preston NE (3) 4 *(Macken 6, 13, 76, Alexander 30)*
Shrewsbury T (0) 1 *(Davidson 55)*   5451
Preston NE: Lucas; Alexander, Edwards, Murdock, Jackson, Gregan (Rankine), Cartwright, Robinson, Macken (Barry-Murphy), Basham, Anderson (Eyres).
Shrewsbury T: Dunbavin; Jenkins (Drysdale), Hanmer, Wilding (Brown), Davidson, Hughes, Murray, Peer, Freestone, Jemson (Lowe), Aiston.
Preston NE won 4-2 on aggregate.

Reading (0) 0
Leyton Orient (0) 2 *(Brkovic 51, Christie 63)*   4337
Reading: Whitehead; Gurney, Robinson, Viveash, Hunter (Mackie), Parkinson (Smith), Hodges, Caskey (McIntyre), Cureton, Butler, Igoe.
Leyton Orient: Bayes; Dorrian (Griffiths), Lockwood, McGhee, Smith, Harris, Walschaerts, Martin (Brissett), Watts, Christie (McElholm), Brkovic.
Leyton Orient won 3-1 on aggregate.

Scunthorpe U (0) 1 *(Torpey 71)*
Wigan Ath (1) 4 *(Sharp 44, Kilford 55, Haworth 60, Liddell 63)*   2062
Scunthorpe U: Evans; Harsley (Quailey), Dawson, Stanton, Wilcox, Fickling, Hodges (Sparrow), Graves, Sheldon (Morrison), Torpey, Calvo-Garcia.
Wigan Ath: Carroll; Green, Sharp (Padula), McGibbon, Mitchell, De Zeeuw, Kilford, McLaughlin, Haworth, Liddell, Martinez.
Wigan Ath won 5-1 on aggregate.

Torquay U (2) 3 *(Bedeau 12, 48, Hill 27)*
Gillingham (1) 2 *(Asaba 24, Aggrey 51 (og))*   1351
Torquay U: Jones; Douglin (Ashington), Herrera, Aggrey, Holmes, Neil, O'Brien, Ford, Parker (Mendy), Bedeau (Platts), Hill.
Gillingham: Bartram; Patterson (Saunders), Edge, Hope, Butters, Lewis, Southall, Browning, Asaba, King (Rowe), Gooden.
Gillingham won 4-3 on aggregate.

Wrexham (0) 0
Mansfield T (2) 3 *(Corden 18, 42, Greenacre 85)*   1447
Wrexham: Rogers; McGregor, Roche (Chalk), Owen, Roberts, Ridler, Williams (Barrett), Ferguson, Sam, Gibson (Edwards), Faulconbridge.
Mansfield T: Mimms; Lomas, Andrews (Asher), Hassell, Hicks, Robinson, Corden, Clarke, Williams (Williamson), Blake, Greenacre.
Mansfield T won 3-1 on aggregate.

Wycombe W (1) 3 *(McSporran 20, Castledine 89, McCarthy 103)*
Barnet (1) 1 *(Richards 24)*   2205
Wycombe W: Taylor; Rogers, Vinnicombe, Bulman, McCarthy, Bates (Cousins), Harkin (Castledine), Simpson, McSporran, Baird, Brown (Senda).
Barnet: Harrison; Stockley, Sawyers (Newton), Basham, Heald, Arber, Currie, Doolan, Richards, Purser (Strevens), Toms (Bell).
aet; Wycombe W won 4-3 on aggregate.

6 SEPT

Blackburn R (2) 6 *(Duff 27, 90, Dunn 45 (pen), 55 (pen), 65 (pen), Diawara 57)*
Rochdale (1) 1 *(Platt 35)*   12,977
Blackburn R: Kelly; Curtis, Bjornebye (Kenna), Carsley, Broomes, Dunn, Taylor, Flitcroft (Johnson), Diawara, Jensen (Ostenstad), Duff.
Rochdale: Edwards; Evans, Todd, Ware, Bayliss, Hill, Ford (Hadland), Jones, Platt (Flitcroft), Oliver (Walsh), Davies.
Blackburn R won 7-2 on aggregate.

Halifax T (1) 1 *(Holt 23)*
Tranmere R (1) 2 *(Rideout 44, Barlow 87)*   612
Halifax T: Shannon; Holt, Bradshaw, Mitchell (Ord), Clarke C, Richards (Herbert), Fitzpatrick, Harrison, Jones (Kerrigan), Reilly, Middleton.
Tranmere R: Achterberg; Allen, Roberts, Flynn, Challinor, Hill, Hinds (Koumas), Gill, Rideout (Allison), Parkinson (Barlow), Taylor S.
Tranmere R won 5-1 on aggregate; at Valley Parade.

Nottingham F (1) 1 *(John 9)*
Darlington (0) 2 *(Campbell 65, Elliott 85)*   6530
Nottingham F: Beasant; Louis-Jean, Brennan, Bart-Williams, Vaughan, Doig, Prutton (Freeman), Johnson, John, Blake, Platt (Jones).
Darlington: Van der Geest; Liddle, Hodgson, Pepper, Reed, Himsworth, Gray, Walklate (Elliott), Hjorth, Williamson (Campbell), Angel (Zeghdane).
Darlington won 4-3 on aggregate.

QPR (1) 1 *(Kiwomya 45)*
Colchester U (2) 4 *(Lua-Lua 11, 18, 86, McGavin 56)* 4042
QPR: Harper; Breacker, Perry, Rose, Morrow (Crouch), Carlisle, Langley, Darlington, Koejoe, Connolly (Bruce), Kiwomya.
Colchester U: Brown; Gregory, Johnson G, Skelton, White, Clark, Duguid, McGavin, Lua-Lua, Stockwell, Dozzell.
Colchester U won 4-2 on aggregate.

Stoke C (0) 0
York C (0) 0 3478
Stoke C: Ward; Hansson, Dorigo (Iwelumo), Clarke, Mohan (Thomas), Gunnarsson, Fenton, Kavanagh, Gudjonsson, Thordarson, O'Connor (Risom).
York C: Fettis; Edmondson, Potter, Hocking, Jones, Thompson (Sertori), Bullock, Hulme, Williams J (McNiven), Alcide (Conlon), Hall.
Stoke C won 5-1 on aggregate.

WBA (0) 2 *(Roberts 63, 88)*
Swansea C (0) 1 *(Bound 74 (pen))* 7328
WBA: Jensen; Lyttle, Clement, McInnes, Butler, Chambers J, Fox (Roberts), Jordao, Taylor (Oliver), Hughes, Van Blerk (Carbon).
Swansea C: Freestone; Price, Howard, Cusack, Bound, O'Leary, Keegan (Roberts), Thomas, Boyd, Watkin (Mutton), Coates.
WBA won 2-1 on aggregate.

SECOND ROUND, FIRST LEG

19 SEPT

Barnsley (1) 4 *(Dyer 41, Van der Laan 57, Sheron 89, 90)*
Crewe Alex (0) 0 5005
Barnsley: Miller; Regan, Corbo, Moses, O'Callaghan, Ward, McClare, Van der Laan, Sheron, Dyer (Jones), Woan (Barker).
Crewe Alex: Kearton; Wright, Smith S, Walton (Hulse), Macauley, Street, Foster (Sodje), Lunt, Jack, Smith P, Sorvel (Collins).

Blackburn R (2) 4 *(Carsley 21, Thomas 23, 60, Ostenstad 53)*
Portsmouth (0) 0 10,360
Blackburn R: Filan; Curtis, Bjornebye (Kenna), Carsley, Berg (Dailly), Taylor, McAteer, Johnson, Ostenstad, Thomas, Duff (Dunn).
Portsmouth: Hoult; Derry, Edinburgh (Birmingham), Waterman, Rudonja (O'Neil), Moore, Quashie (Miglioranzi), Thogersen, Bradbury, Mills, Hughes.

Brentford (0) 0
Tottenham H (0) 0 8580
Brentford: Gottskalksson; Crowe, Marsh, Mahon, Quinn, Marshall, Ingimarsson, Evans, Scott, McCammon, Rowland.
Tottenham H: Sullivan; Carr, Thatcher, Freund, Campbell (Vega), Perry, Leonhardsen, Clemence, Rebrov (Ferdinand), Iversen, Etherington (Walker).

Burnley (0) 2 *(Cooke 68, Payton 83 (pen))*
Crystal Palace (1) 2 *(Forssell 17, Black 47)* 5889
Burnley: Michopoulos; Mullin (Maylett), Briscoe, Cox, Davis, Thomas, Ball, Cook (Mellon), Cooke, Payton, Branch (Jepson).
Crystal Palace: Kolinko; Black, Harrison, Austin, Zhiyi, Linighan, Mullins, Pollock, Morrison C, Forssell (Gray), McKenzie.

Chesterfield (0) 1 *(Parrish 90)*
Fulham (0) 0 3710
Chesterfield: Pollitt; Breckin, Edwards, Payne, Blatherwick, Parrish, Ebdon, Howard, Willis, Beckett, Galloway (Ingledow).
Fulham: Taylor; Neilson, McAnespie, Hudson, Symons, Knight, Hayward, Lewis, Peschisolido, Cornwall (Hammond), Boa Morte.

Darlington (0) 0
Bradford C (1) 1 *(Whalley 45)* 5392
Darlington: Collett; Liddle, Heckingbottom (Himsworth), Reed, Aspin, Gray, Campbell (Kaak), Elliott, Nogan, Naylor, Hjorth (Hodgson).
Bradford C: Clarke; Halle, Nolan (Jacobs), Ward, Atherton, Wetherall, Petrescu, Hopkin (McCall), Windass, Whalley, Sharpe (Grant).

Derby Co (1) 1 *(Burton 33)*
WBA (0) 2 *(Clement 48, Sneekes 83)* 12,183
Derby Co: Poom; Eranio (Sturridge), Higginbotham, Valakari, Carbonari, Bragstad, Jackson, Johnson (Murray), Burton, Kinkladze (Schnoor), Christie.
WBA: Jensen; Lyttle, Clement, McInnes, Butler, Chambers J, Fox, Jordao, Roberts, Chambers A (Sneekes), Van Blerk (Hughes).

Middlesbrough (0) 2 *(Whelan 87, Summerbell 90)*
Macclesfield T (0) 1 *(Barker 59)* 5144
Middlesbrough: Bennion; Parnaby, Gordon (Job), Festa, Gavin, Cooper, Summerbell, Armstrong (O'Neill), Ricard (Boksic), Whelan, Ince.
Macclesfield T: Bullock; Hitchen (Glover), Abbey, Ingram, Tinson, Wood, Askey (Keen), Sedgmore, Barker, Munroe, Durkan.

Millwall (1) 2 *(Ifill 37, Cahill 80)*
Ipswich T (0) 0 8068
Millwall: Warner; Lawrence, Ryan, Cahill, Nethercott, Dolan, Livermore, Braniff (Odunsi), Harris, Ifill (Reid), Kinet (Tyne).
Ipswich T: Wright R; Croft (Wilnis), Clapham, Scales, Hreidarsson, McGreal, Reuser (Holland), Magilton, Johnson (Stewart), Scowcroft, Wright J.

Norwich C (3) 3 *(Roberts 22 (pen), Marshall L 28, Cottee 43)*
Blackpool (2) 3 *(Murphy J 28, 87, Ormerod 44)* 9369
Norwich C: Marshall A; Sutch, Derveld, Walsh (Forbes), Fleming, McGovern, Nedergaard (De Waard), Russell, Roberts, Cottee (Giallanza), Marshall L.
Blackpool: Barnes; Collins, Jaszczun, Bushell, Hughes, Jones, Wellens, Simpson, Ormerod, Murphy J, Coid.

Notts Co (0) 1 *(Stallard 78 (pen))*
Watford (0) 3 *(Mooney 55, 62, Palmer 82)* 2346
Notts Co: Gibson; McDermott, Pearce, Warren, Redmile, Richardson, Owers, Ramage, Stallard, Joseph (Rapley), Hamilton.
Watford: Chamberlain; Cox, Robinson, Palmer, Page, Ward, Foley (Easton), Nielsen, Mooney, Noel-Williams (Ngonge), Smith.

Oldham Ath (1) 1 *(Boshell 20)*
Sheffield W (1) 3 *(Morrison 33, De Bilde 65, Westwood 71)* 3213
Oldham Ath: Kelly; Jones, Holt, Boshell (Salt), Lightfoot (Prenderville), Duxbury, Dudley, McNiven, Tipton (Allott), Corazzin, Innes.
Sheffield W: Pressman; Humphreys, Geary, Quinn, Westwood, Walker, Hamshaw (Sibon), Booth, De Bilde, Crane, Morrison.

Preston NE (0) 1 *(Alexander 48 (pen))*
Coventry C (2) 3 *(Zuniga 4, Hall 45, Strachan 86 (pen))* 10,770
Preston NE: Lucas; Alexander, Edwards, Murdock, Gregan, Appleton, McKenna, Rankine, McBride, Basham, Cartwright.
Coventry C: Hedman; Edworthy, Hall, Williams, Shaw, Chippo (Strachan), Eustace, Palmer, Bellamy (Breen), Hadji, Zuniga (Aloisi).

Sheffield U (1) 3 *(Devlin 18, Clark 80 (og), Kelly 83)*
Colchester U (0) 0 3531
Sheffield U: Tracey; Uhlenbeek, Quinn, Woodhouse (Cryan), Murphy, Sandford, Devlin, Brown, Bent (Smith), Kelly, Ford.
Colchester U: Brown; Dunne, Johnson G, Tanner (Keith), White, Clark, Duguid, Lock, McGavin, Stockwell, Dozzell (Keeble).

Sunderland (0) 3 *(Oster 51, Phillips 61, Thirlwell 87)*
Luton T (0) 0   24,668
Sunderland: Sorensen; Maley (Fredgaard), Peeters, Holloway (McCartney), Butler P, Williams, Roy, Thirlwell, Oster, Phillips, Wainwright.
Luton T: Ovendale; Boyce, Taylor, Fraser, Watts, Holmes, Kandol (Thomson), McLaren, Stein (George), Scarlett, Spring.

Tranmere R (0) 1 *(Hill 49)*
Swindon T (0) 1 *(Hazell 54 (og))*   4289
Tranmere R: Achterberg; Hazell (Hinds), Yates, Flynn, Challinor, Hill, Henry (Gill), Parkinson (Barlow), Rideout, Allison, Taylor S.
Swindon T: Griemink; Cobian (Robinson M), Davis, Robertson (Williams A), Reeves, O'Halloran, Tuomela, Hewlett, Alexander, Williams M, Duke.

Walsall (0) 0
West Ham U (0) 1 *(Defoe 84)*   5435
Walsall: Walker; Brightwell, Aranalde, Tillson, Barras, Bukran, Hall (Angell), Keates, Leitao, Byfield, Matias.
West Ham U: Hislop; Potts, Winterburn, Stimac, Ferdinand, Pearce S, Lomas, Cole, Sinclair, Carrick, Keller (Defoe).

Wimbledon (0) 0
Wigan Ath (0) 0   1941
Wimbledon: Davis; Jupp, Hawkins, Andersen (Morgan), Williams, Willmott, Owusu, Francis, Hartson, Thomas, Robinson.
Wigan Ath: Carroll (Stillie); Green, Sharp, McGibbon, Balmer, De Zeeuw, Kilford (Martinez), Nicholls, Haworth, Liddell, McLaughlin.

Wycombe W (1) 3 *(Rammell 45, Baird 71, Bates 86)*
Birmingham C (3) 4 *(Horsfield 3, 22, Johnson A 24, 87)* 2537
Wycombe W: Taylor; Rogers, Vinnicombe, Bulman (Senda), McCarthy, Bates, Harkin (Baird), Simpson, McSporran, Rammell, Brown (Castledine).
Birmingham C: Bennett; Eaden, Grainger, Hughes, Purse, Holdsworth, O'Connor, Johnson A, Horsfield (Adebola), Ndlovu (Robinson), Sonner.

20 SEPT

Everton (0) 1 *(Campbell 50)*
Bristol R (0) 1 *(Hogg 87)*   25,564
Everton: Gerrard; Watson, Pistone (Hughes S), Unsworth, Weir, Cleland, Nyarko, Alexandersson (Moore), Jeffers, Campbell, Ball (Gascoigne).
Bristol R: Culkin; Bignot, Wilson, Andreasson (Plummer), Foster, Jones, Astafjevs, Evans (Walters), Ellington (Ellis), Hogg, Bryant.

Manchester C (0) 1 *(Weah 83)*
Gillingham (0) 1 *(Smith 62)*   17,408
Manchester C: Weaver; Haaland, Ritchie, Crooks (Granville), Prior, Bishop (Jobson), Kennedy, Jeff Whitley, Weah, Wanchope, Wright-Phillips (Dickov).
Gillingham: Bartram; Southall, Edge, Hope, Ashby, Butters, Smith, Hessenthaler, Asaba (Thomson), King (Lewis), Browning (Saunders).

Newcastle U (1) 2 *(Cort 34, Speed 77)*
Leyton Orient (0) 0   37,284
Newcastle U: Harper; Charvet, Griffin, Goma, Hughes, Solano (Lee), Dyer, Gallacher (Cordone), Shearer, Cort (Gavilan), Speed.
Leyton Orient: Bayes; Joseph, Lockwood, McGhee, Smith, Harris, Walschaerts, Martin (Christie), Griffiths (McElholm), Garcia, Brkovic.

Southampton (1) 2 *(Tessem 36, Le Tissier 67)*
Mansfield T (0) 0   8802
Southampton: Jones; Dodd, Bridge, Marsden (Oakley), Lundekvam, Richards (El Khalej), Tessem, Soltvedt, Beattie (Rosler), Le Tissier, Ripley.
Mansfield T: Mimms; Asher, Andrews (Bacon), Hassell, Hicks (Williamson), Robinson, Corden (Boulding), Clarke, Williams, Blake, Greenacre.

Stoke C (1) 2 *(Thordarson 45 (pen), Goodfellow 86)*
Charlton Ath (1) 1 *(Johansson 41)*   9388
Stoke C: Ward; Hansson, Clarke, Thomas, Mohan, Gunnarsson, Gudjonsson (Risom), Kavanagh, Lightbourne (Goodfellow), Thordarson, O'Connor.
Charlton Ath: Kiely; Kishishev (Konchesky), Powell, Shields, Todd, Parker, Newton, Jensen, Lisbie, Johansson (MacDonald), Robinson (Salako).

SECOND ROUND, SECOND LEG

25 SEPT

Bradford C (4) 7 *(Whalley 3, Windass 8, 47, Carbone 9, 40, Grant 73, Halle 90)*
Darlington (0) 2 *(Elliott 60, Angel 63)*   4751
Bradford C: Davison; Halle, Jacobs, Grant, Atherton, Bower, Lawrence (Hardy), Windass, Ward (Kerr), Carbone, Whalley.
Darlington: Collett; Kilty (Gray), Walklate, Pepper, Reed, Elliott, Hjorth (Zeghdane), Hodgson, Angel, Naylor, Beavers (Kaak).
Bradford C won 8-2 on aggregate.

SECOND ROUND, FIRST LEG

26 SEPT

Grimsby T (1) 3 *(Gallimore 12, Rowan 81, Allen 82)*
Wolverhampton W (2) 2 *(Taylor R 6, 45)*   2396
Grimsby T: Coyne; Butterfield, Gallimore, Groves, Handyside, Coldicott, Donovan (Bloomer), Pouton, Allen, Clare (Rowan), Smith D (Jeffrey).
Wolverhampton W: Stowell; Muscat, Naylor, Robinson, Lescott, Emblen, Bazeley, Al-Jaber (Branch), Taylor R (Proudlock), Ketsbaia, Camara (Sinton).

SECOND ROUND, SECOND LEG

26 SEPT

Birmingham C (0) 1 *(Ndlovu 66)*
Wycombe W (0) 0   8960
Birmingham C: Bennett; Gill, Grainger, Hughes, Purse, Holdsworth, Eaden (Hyde), Burchill (Johnson A), Horsfield (Marcelo), Ndlovu, Sonner.
Wycombe W: Taylor; Rogers, Vinnicombe, Bulman, McCarthy, Bates, Harkin (Baird), Simpson, McSporran (Senda), Rammell, Brown (Castledine).
Birmingham C won 5-3 on aggregate.

Charlton Ath (1) 4 *(Lisbie 25, 111, Johansson 75, 81)*
Stoke C (1) 3 *(O'Connor 36, Gunnarsson 87, Thordarson 107)*   10,037
Charlton Ath: Ilic; Konchesky (Powell), Brown, Shields, Parker, Todd, Newton (MacDonald), Jensen, Lisbie, Johansson (Robinson), Salako.
Stoke C: Ward; Hansson (Kavanagh), Clarke, Thomas, Mohan, Gunnarsson, Gudjonsson, Petty, Lightbourne (Thordarson), Thorne (Connor), O'Connor.
aet; Stoke C won on away goals rule.

Crewe Alex (0) 0
Barnsley (1) 3 *(Shipperley 12, 71, Sheron 48)*   1775
Crewe Alex: Kearton (Bankole); Wright, Smith S, Sodje, Walton, Street, Hulse (Tait), Lunt, Jack, Little, Sorvel (Charnock).
Barnsley: Miller; O'Callaghan, Barker, Morgan, Chettle, McClare, Van der Laan, Sheron (Appleby), Shipperley, Dyer (Jones), Woan.
Barnsley won 7-0 on aggregate.

Crystal Palace (0) 1 *(Linighan 90)*
Burnley (1) 1 *(Cooke 45)*   5720
Crystal Palace: Kolinko; Black, Harrison (Linighan), Austin, Zhiyi, Ruddock, Mullins (Gray), Rodger, Harris (Morrison C), Forssell, Pollock.
Burnley: Michopoulos; Little (Cooke), Armstrong, Cox, Davis, Thomas, Mellon, Cook, Branch (Gray), Payton (Jepson), Ball.
aet; Crystal Palace won on away goals rule.

Gillingham (1) 2 *(Thomson 26, 81)*
Manchester C (0) 4 *(Weah 48, 53, Dickov 113,*
Kennedy 119)   6520
Gillingham: Bartram; Southall, Edge (Patterson), Hope,
Ashby, Butters, Smith, Hessenthaler, Thomson, King,
Browning (Lewis).
Manchester C: Weaver; Crooks, Tiatto, Wiekens
(Granville), Jobson, Ritchie (Kennedy), Haaland
(Bishop), Horlock, Dickov, Weah, Jeff Whitley.
aet; Manchester C won 5-3 on aggregate.

Ipswich T (0) 5 *(Johnson 74, 115, Bramble 88,*
Holland 91, Magilton 105)
Millwall (0) 0   13,008
Ipswich T: Wright R; Wilnis (Wright J), Clapham,
Bramble, Hreidarsson (Karic), McGreal, Holland,
Magilton, Johnson, Scowcroft (Naylor), Reuser.
Millwall: Warner; Lawrence, Ryan, Cahill, Nethercott,
Dolan, Livermore, Reid, Harris (Braniff) (Odunsi), Ifill
(Dyche), Kinet.
aet; Ipswich T won 5-2 on aggregate.

Leyton Orient (1) 1 *(Watts 45)*
Newcastle U (1) 1 *(Gallacher 32)*   9522
Leyton Orient: Bayes; Joseph, Lockwood, McGhee,
Smith, Harris, Walschaerts, Brissett (Ibehre), Watts
(Downer), Garcia, Christie (Murray).
Newcastle U: Given; Griffin, Domi, Charvet, Hughes,
Lee, Dyer, Cort (Cordone), Shearer, Gallacher (Solano),
Speed.
Newcastle U won 3-1 on aggregate.

Luton T (0) 1 *(Kandol 90)*
Sunderland (2) 2 *(Reddy 31, Butler P 39)*   5262
Luton T: Ovendale; Boyce, Taylor, Locke, Watts, Fraser,
George, McLaren, Thomson (Brennan), Kandol, Spring.
Sunderland: Macho; McCartney, Williams (McGill), Roy
(Butler T), Butler P, Clark, Rae, Thirlwell, Dichio, Oster,
Reddy (Nunez).
Sunderland won 5-1 on aggregate.

Macclesfield T (1) 1 *(Sedgemore 38 (pen))*
Middlesbrough (1) 3 *(Ricard 18, 51, 53)*   3153
Macclesfield T: Bullock; Abbey, Adams, Ingram, Tinson,
Wood (Whitehead), Munroe, Sedgemore (Askey),
Barker, Keen, Twynham (Bamber).
Middlesbrough: Crossley; Fleming, Gordon, Ince, Festa,
Cooper, Summerbell, Campbell (Marinelli), Ricard,
Deane (Stamp), Whelan.
Middlesbrough won 5-2 on aggregate.

Mansfield T (0) 1 *(Clarke 55)*
Southampton (2) 3 *(Rosler 32, Soltvedt 44, 65)* 3528
Mansfield T: Mimms; Asher, Andrews (Bacon), Williams
(Williamson), Hicks, Robinson, Corden (Hassell),
Clarke, Boulding, Blake, Greenacre.
Southampton: Jones; Dodd, Ashford (Bridge), Marsden,
El-Khajel (Lundekvam), Richards (Pahars), Le Tissier,
Oakley, Rosler, Soltvedt, Bleidelis.
Southampton won 5-1 on aggregate.

Portsmouth (0) 1 *(Nightingale 77)*
Blackburn R (0) 1 *(Dunn 88)*   2731
Portsmouth: Hoult; Waterman, Hiley, Derry, Primus,
Moore, Quashie, Thogersen, Bradbury (Nightingale),
Mills, Hughes (Rudonja) (Miglioranzi).
Blackburn R: Miller; Kenna, Grayson, Carsley (O'Brien),
Dailly, Taylor, McAteer, Johnson, Burgess, Ostenstad
(Hamilton), Dunn.
Blackburn R won 5-1 on aggregate.

Swindon T (0) 0
Tranmere R (1) 1 *(Taylor S 13)*   4753
Swindon T: Griemink; Robinson M, Davis, O'Halloran,
Reeves, Tuomela (Willis), Robertson (Invincible),
Hewlett, Alexander (Grazioli), Williams M, Duke.
Tranmere R: Achterberg; Yates, Roberts, Flynn,
Challinor, Hill, Gill, Henry (Parkinson), Rideout
(Hinds), Allison, Taylor S.
Tranmere R won 2-1 on aggregate.

Tottenham H (0) 2 *(Leonhardsen 53, Iversen 81)*
Brentford (0) 0   26,909
Tottenham H: Sullivan; Carr, Thatcher, Freund, Vega,
Perry, Sherwood, Iversen, Rebrov, Ferdinand
(Dominguez), Leonhardsen.
Brentford: Gottskalksson; Crowe, Rowlands (Williams),
Mahon, Quinn, Marshall, Ingimarsson, Evans, Folan,
Pinamonte (Dobson), Partridge.
Tottenham H won 2-0 on aggregate.

Watford (0) 0
Notts Co (0) 2 *(McDermott 63, Hughes 90)*   7677
Watford: Chamberlain; Cox, Robinson, Palmer, Page,
Ward, Helguson (Noel-Williams), Nielsen, Mooney,
Gudmundsson (Wooter), Wright (Perpetuini).
Notts Co: Ward (Lindley); McDermott, Liburd
(Hamilton), Fenton, Pearce, Richardson, Owers, Bolland
(Joseph), Stallard, Dyer, Hughes.
aet; Watford won on away goals rule.

WBA (2) 2 *(Jordao 9, Clement 40)*
Derby Co (2) 4 *(Bragstad 3, 78, Riggott 31,*
Burley 59)   19,112
WBA: Jensen; Lyttle, Clement, McInnes, Butler,
Chambers J, Fox, Jordao (Chambers A), Roberts
(Taylor), Hughes, Van Blerk (Sneekes).
Derby Co: Poom; Burley, Higginbotham, Riggott,
Schnoor, Bragstad, Valakari, Burton (Sturridge), Christie
(Morris), Johnson, Powell.
Derby Co won 5-4 on aggregate.

Wigan Ath (0) 1 *(Haworth 62)*
Wimbledon (1) 2 *(Hartson 1, Gayle 62)*   5387
Wigan Ath: Stillie; Green, Sharp, McGibbon, Balmer, De
Zeeuw, Kilford, Nicholls, Haworth, McLaughlin,
Martinez.
Wimbledon: Davis; Jupp (Hunt), Hawkins, Andersen,
Williams, Willmott, Ardley, Roberts, Hartson, Euell
(Robinson), Gayle.
Wimbledon won 2-1 on aggregate.

27 SEPT

Bristol R (0) 1 *(Bignot 58)*
Everton (1) 1 *(Jeffers 14)*   11,045
Bristol R: Culkin; Bignot, Wilson, Foster, Andreasson
(Walters), Jones, Astafjevs, Hogg (Plummer), Ellington,
Ellis, Bryant (Meaker).
Everton: Gerrard; Watson, Unsworth (Ball), Gravesen,
Dunne, Hughes S, Nyarko, Alexandersson, Jeffers
(Cleland), Hughes M (Campbell), Moore.
aet; Bristol R won 4-2 on penalties.

Colchester U (0) 0
Sheffield U (0) 1 *(Devlin 59)*   1981
Colchester U: Brown; Dunne, Johnson G, Skelton
(Tanner), White, Clark (Keith), Keeble, Lock, Dozzell,
Stockwell, Opara (Arnott).
Sheffield U: Tracey; Uhlenbeek, Quinn, Jagielka,
Murphy, Sandford, Devlin, Brown, Bent (Smith),
Ribeiro, Ford (Cryan).
Sheffield U won 4-0 on aggregate.

Coventry C (3) 4 *(Aloisi 6, 26, 56 (pen), Eustace 18)*
Preston NE (0) 1 *(Rankine 47)*   7425
Coventry C: Hedman (Kirkland); Edworthy, Hall,
Williams (Breen), Shaw, Chippo, Telfer, Eustace,
Bellamy, Aloisi (Bothroyd), Hadji.
Preston NE: Lonergan; Alexander, Edwards, Murdock
(Eyres), Jackson, Gregan, Cartwright (Barry-Murphy),
Rankine, Robinson, Basham (Kidd), Anderson.
Coventry C won 7-2 on aggregate.

Fulham (1) 4 *(Hayward 35, Symons 73, Hayles 80,*
Boa Morte 90)
Chesterfield (0) 0   4800
Fulham: Taylor; Hudson, Trollope, Neilson, Symons,
Lewis, Knight (McAnespie), Clark, Boa Morte, Betsy
(Hayles), Hayward (Fernandes).
Chesterfield: Pollitt; Breckin, Edwards, Tutill,
Blatherwick, Parrish, Ebdon, Williams R (Howard),
Willis (Reeves), Beckett, Galloway (Perkins).
Fulham won 4-1 on aggregate.

Sheffield W (1) 5 *(Hamshaw 6, Westwood 68, Di Piedi 70, Sibon 80, Quinn 86)*
Oldham Ath (1) 1 *(Duxbury 25)*   4773
Sheffield W: Pressman (Stringer); Humphreys, Geary, Quinn, Westwood, Walker, Hamshaw, Sibon (Muller), De Bilde (Di Piedi), Crane, Morrison.
Oldham Ath: Kelly; McNiven, Holt, Boshell (Sugden), Watson, Duxbury (Salt), Prenderville (Tipton), Dudley, Allott, Smith, Innes.
Sheffield W won 8-2 on aggregate.

West Ham U (1) 1 *(Lomas 2)*
Walsall (1) 1 *(Leitao 8)*   11,963
West Ham U: Hislop; Lomas, Winterburn, Margas, Stimac, Pearce S, Lampard (Potts), Cole, Kanoute, Di Canio, Carrick.
Walsall: Walker; Brightwell, Aranalde, Tillson, Barras (Roper), Bukran, Hall (Wright), Bennett, Angell (Byfield), Leitao, Matias.
West Ham U won 2-1 on aggregate.

2 OCT

Blackpool (0) 0
Norwich C (2) 5 *(Russell 9, Giallanza 35, 64, Roberts 49, 57)*   4038
Blackpool: Barnes; Murphy N, Jaszczun, Bushell, Jones (Wellens), Hughes, Collins, Simpson (Nowland), Ormerod, Murphy J, Coid.
Norwich C: Marshall A; Sutch, Derveld, Marshall L, Fleming, Kenton, Brady (Nedergaard), Giallanza, Roberts, Russell (Cottee), Llewellyn.
Norwich C won 8-3 on aggregate.

Wolverhampton W (1) 2 *(Proudlock 36, Muscat 73 (pen))*
Grimsby T (0) 0   8058
Wolverhampton W: Oakes; Green, Muscat, Lescott, Naylor, Robinson, Bazeley, Emblen, Branch, Proudlock, Sinton.
Grimsby T: Coyne; McDermott, Gallimore, Butterfield (Rowan), Handyside, Coldicott, Donovan, Pouton, Allen (Clare), Jeffrey, Groves.
Wolverhampton W won 4-3 on aggregate.

THIRD ROUND

31 OCT

Bristol R (0) 1 *(Ellington 63)*
Sunderland (0) 2 *(Hutchison 48, 88)*   11,433
Bristol R: Culkin; Bignot, Wilson, Foster, Foran (Walters), Jones, Astafjevs, Evans, Ellington, Hogg, Bryant.
Sunderland: Sorensen; Makin, Gray, Butler P, Varga, McCartney, Rae (Williams), Reddy (Phillips), Dichio, Oster, Hutchison.

Tottenham H (0) 1 *(Anderton 60 (pen))*
Birmingham C (3) 3 *(Abebola 15, 28, Burchill 45)* 27,096
Tottenham H: Sullivan; Carr, Thatcher, Freund (Davies) (Young), Vega, Perry, Anderton, Sherwood, Ferdinand, Korsten (Dominguez), Clemence.
Birmingham C: Bennett; Gill, Grainger, Hughes, Purse, Johnson M, Eaden, O'Connor, Adebola, Burchill (Ndlovu), Lazaridis (Robinson).

Tranmere R (0) 3 *(Parkinson 52, 120, Yates 76)*
Leeds U (2) 2 *(Huckerby 25, 34)*   11,681
Tranmere R: Murphy; Yates, Roberts, Flynn, Challinor, Hill, Hinds, Barlow (Parkinson), Hamilton (Allison), Koumas, Taylor S (Gill).
Leeds U: Robinson; Kelly, Harte, Woodgate, Hay (Radebe), Bakke, Burns, Jones, Huckerby (Hackworth) (Smith), Viduka, Matteo.
aet.

Watford (0) 0
Manchester U (1) 3 *(Solskjaer 12, 81, Yorke 53)* 18,871
Watford: Chamberlain; Cox, Robinson (Foley), Palmer, Page, Ward, Mooney, Nielsen, Noel-Williams (Helguson), Wooter (Easton), Smith.
Manchester U: Van der Gouw; Clegg, O'Shea, Brown, Neville P, Wallwork (Stewart), Chadwick, Greening, Solskjaer, Yorke, Fortune (Rachubka).

West Ham U (0) 2 *(Suker 67, Di Canio 84)*
Blackburn R (0) 0   21,863
West Ham U: Hislop; Sinclair, Potts, Pearce I, Ferdinand, Pearce S, Lampard, Kanoute (Moncur), Suker, Di Canio, Carrick.
Blackburn R: Kelly; Kenna, Curtis, Taylor (Flitcroft), Dailly, Carsley, McAteer, Dunning, Ostenstad, Richards (Dunn), Johnson (Douglas).

Wimbledon (0) 0 *(Hartson 85 (pen))*
Middlesbrough (0) 0   3666
Wimbledon: Davis; Andersen, Kimble, Roberts, Williams, Gier, Hunt, Francis, Hartson, Gayle (Agyemang), Karlsson.
Middlesbrough: Crossley; Fleming, Gordon, Vickers, Festa, Pallister, Karembeu (Maddison), Job, Ricard, Whelan, Summerbell.

1 NOV

Arsenal (1) 1 *(Stepanovs 44)*
Ipswich T (1) 2 *(Clapham 2, Scowcroft 89)*   26,105
Arsenal: Taylor; Vivas, Cole, Vernazza, Upson, Stepanovs, Weston (Canoville), Voltz (Wreh), Wiltord, Barrett, Pennant (Mendez).
Ipswich T: Wright R; Wilnis, Clapham, Bramble (Reuser) (Karic), Hreidarsson, McGreal, Holland, Magilton, Johnson, Wright J, Stewart (Scowcroft).

Aston Villa (0) 0
Manchester C (0) 1 *(Horlock 89 (pen))*   24,138
Aston Villa: James; Stone (Delaney), Wright, Southgate, Alpay, Barry, Taylor, Boateng, Dublin (Vassell), Joachim, Merson (Hendrie).
Manchester C: Weaver; Haaland, Ritchie, Wiekens, Howey, Prior (Bishop), Horlock, Jeff Whitley, Dickov, Goater (Wright-Phillips), Tiatto (Kennedy).

Derby Co (3) 3 *(Delap 12, Burley 16 (pen), Christie 39)*
Norwich C (0) 0   11,273
Derby Co: Poom; Valakari, Johnson, Riggott, Schnoor (Higginbotham), Delap, Burley, Elliott, Christie (Morris), Kinkladze, Powell.
Norwich C: Marshall A; Sutch, Kenton (De Waard), Russell, Fleming, Mackay, Dalglish (Coote), Forbes (McVeigh), Roberts, Mulryne, Llewellyn.

Fulham (0) 3 *(Boa Morte 67, 83, Saha 85)*
Wolverhampton W (0) 2 *(Ketsbaia 60, Osborn 90)* 6763
Fulham: Taylor; Goldbaek, Trollope (Finnan), Melville, Symons, Collins W, Lewis (Fernandes), Clark, Saha, Davis, Boa Morte.
Wolverhampton W: Oakes; Bazeley, Naylor, Lescott, Peacock, Robinson, Emblen, Osborn, Ketsbaia, Proudlock (Camara), Branch.

Leicester C (0) 0
Crystal Palace (2) 3 *(Morrison C 17, Thomson 23, Rubins 52)*   12,965
Leicester C: Royce; Davidson, Guppy, Rowett, Sinclair, Gilchrist (Elliott), Lennon, McKinlay, Gunnlaugsson, Cresswell (Benjamin), Eadie (Izzet).
Crystal Palace: Kolinko; Smith, Harrison, Black, Austin, Carlisle, Mullins, Rodger, Morrison C, Rubins, Thomson.

Liverpool (1) 2 *(Murphy 11, Fowler 104)*
Chelsea (1) 1 *(Zola 29)*   29,370
Liverpool: Arphexad; Carragher, Traore (Ziege), Hamann, Henchoz, Hyypia, Murphy, Barmby (McAllister), Fowler, Smicer (Heskey), Berger.
Chelsea: De Goey; Bogarde, Babayaro (Gudjohnsen), Melchiot, Terry (Morris), Desailly, Jokanovic, Flo (Poyet), Hasselbaink, Zola, Wise.
aet.

Newcastle U (3) 4 *(Shearer 22, 29, Cordone 27, Caldwell S 71)*
Bradford C (1) 3 *(Nolan 31, Ward 57, 70)* 41,847
Newcastle U: Harper; Griffin (Domi), Caldwell S, Goma, Solano, Lee, Dyer, Acuna, Shearer, Cordone (Bassedas), Speed.
Bradford C: Davison; Petrescu, Nolan, Whalley, Wetherall, Atherton, Lawrence, Windass, Collymore (Saunders), Carbone (Ward), Sharpe (Grant).

Sheffield W (1) 2 *(Ekoku 10, 113)*
Sheffield U (1) 1 *(Brown 33)* 32,283
Sheffield W: Pressman; Haslam, Humphreys (Geary), Lescott, Westwood (Crane), Walker, Hamshaw (Di Piedi), Ekoku, Sibon, Morrison, Quinn.
Sheffield U: Tracey; Uhlenbeek, Quinn, Montgomery (Santos), Murphy, Curle, Devlin, Brown, Bent, Kelly, Ribeiro (Woodhouse).
aet.

Southampton (0) 0
Coventry C (0) 1 *(Eustace 119)* 11,809
Southampton: Jones; Dodd, Bridge, Oakley, Lundekvam, Draper, Tessem (El Khalej), Davies, Beattie, Pahars, Kachloul (Bleidelis).
Coventry C: Kirkland; Breen, Guerrero, Williams, Shaw, Chippo, Hadji, Quinn, Zuniga (Strachan), Eustace, Roussel (Thompson).
aet.

Stoke C (1) 3 *(Gudjonsson 8, 56, Dadason 90)*
Barnsley (1) 2 *(Corbo 33, Jones 85)* 10,480
Stoke C: Muggleton; Petty (Dadason), Clarke, Thomas, Mohan, Gunnarsson, Gudjonsson, Kavanagh, Thorne, Thordarson, O'Connor.
Barnsley: Miller; Regan, Barker, Morgan, Chettle, Ward, McClare (O'Callaghan), Van der Laan, Sheron, Dyer (Thomas), Corbo (Jones).

FOURTH ROUND

28 NOV

Crystal Palace (0) 0
Tranmere R (0) 0 10,271
Crystal Palace: Kolinko; Smith, Harrison, Austin, Zhiyi (Martin), Ruddock, Mullins, Black, Morrison C (Kabba), Forssell, Thomson (Carlisle).
Tranmere R: Myhre; Hazell, Roberts, Flynn, Allen, Hill, Hinds, Koumas, Rideout, Allison (Henry), Taylor S (Parkinson).
aet; Crystal Palace won 6-5 on penalties.

Ipswich T (1) 2 *(Bramble 5, Johnson 65)*
Coventry C (0) 1 *(Bellamy 54 (pen))* 19,563
Ipswich T: Branagan; Wilnis, Clapham, Bramble, Hreidarsson, Scales, Holland (Croft), Reuser (Stewart), Johnson, Scowcroft, Wright J.
Coventry C: Kirkland; Telfer, Breen, Williams, Konjic, Chippo (Hadji), Thompson, Eustace, Bellamy, Aloisi, Quinn.

Sunderland (0) 2 *(Arca 75, Phillips 101 (pen))*
Manchester U (1) 1 *(Yorke 31)* 47,543
Sunderland: Sorensen (Macho); Makin (McCann), Gray, Williams, Craddock, Emerson (Varga), Rae, Arca, Dichio, Phillips, Hutchison.
Manchester U: Van der Gouw; Clegg, Neville P, Johnsen (Stewart), Wallwork (Webber), O'Shea, Chadwick (Healy), Greening, Solskjaer, Yorke, Fortune.
aet.

29 NOV

Birmingham C (1) 2 *(Adebola 31, Johnson M 90)*
Newcastle U (1) 1 *(Dyer 14)* 18,520
Birmingham C: Bennett; Gill, Grainger, Sonner, Purse, Johnson M, Eaden, O'Connor, Horsfield, Adebola (Burchill), Lazaridis (Burrows).
Newcastle U: Harper; Griffin, Barton, Goma, Hughes, Solano, Dyer, Lee, Shearer, Bassidas (Cordone), Speed.

Fulham (2) 3 *(Saha 28, 90, Lewis 39)*
Derby Co (2) 2 *(Christie 13, Powell 45)* 11,761
Fulham: Taylor; Collins W, Trollope, Melville, Symons, Fernandes, Goldbaek, Sahnoun, Saha, Hayles, Lewis.
Derby Co: Poom; Delap, Higginbotham, Riggott, Bragstad, West, Burley, Strupar (Burton), Christie, Johnson, Powell.

Manchester C (1) 2 *(Wanchope 26, Goater 81)*
Wimbledon (1) 1 *(Roberts 11)* 19,513
Manchester C: Weaver; Haaland, Tiatto, Horlock, Howey (Wiekens), Prior, Wright-Phillips, Jeff Whitley, Wanchope, Goater, Bishop (Kennedy).
Wimbledon: Davis; Andersen, Hawkins, Roberts, Williams, Blackwell (Gier), Ardley, Francis, Hartson, Agyemang, Gayle.

Stoke C (0) 0
Liverpool (4) 8 *(Ziege 6, Smicer 26, Babbel 28, Fowler 39, 82, 85 (pen), Hyypia 59, Murphy 65)* 27,109
Stoke C: Muggleton; Hansson (Petty), Dorigo, Clarke, Mohan, Gunnarsson, Risom, Kavanagh, Lightbourne (Thordarson), Thorne (Goodfellow), Gudjonsson.
Liverpool: Arphexad; Babbel (Wright), Ziege, Carragher, Henchoz, Hyypia, Murphy, Smicer (Hamann), Fowler, Partridge (Barmby), McAllister.

West Ham U (0) 1 *(Lampard 72)*
Sheffield W (1) 2 *(Morrison 30, Crane 49)* 20,857
West Ham U: Hislop; Song (Suker), Winterburn, Lomas, Stimac, Pearce S, Lampard, Kanoute, Sinclair, Di Canio, Carrick.
Sheffield W: Pressman; Haslam, Geary, Lescott, Westwood, Walker, Crane, Sibon (Booth), Ekoku, Morrison, Quinn.

FIFTH ROUND

12 DEC

Birmingham C (1) 2 *(Sonner 28, Adebola 57)*
Sheffield W (0) 0 22,911
Birmingham C: Bennett; Gill, Grainger, Sonner, Purse, Johnson M, Eaden, O'Connor (Hughes), Adebola, Burchill (Johnson A), Lazaridis.
Sheffield W: Pressman; Geary (Crane), Quinn, Lescott, Westwood, Walker, Sibon, Booth, Ekoku (Di Piedi), Morrison (O'Donnell), Haslam.

Manchester C 1
Ipswich T 1 23,260
Abandoned 23 minutes; waterlogged pitch.

13 DEC

Liverpool (0) 3 *(Owen 105, Smicer 114, Barmby 120)*
Fulham (0) 0 20,144
Liverpool: Westerveld; Biscan, Carragher, Babbel, Henchoz, Hyypia, Gerrard (McAllister), Smicer, Heskey (Barmby), Fowler (Owen), Murphy.
Fulham: Taylor; Finnan, Brevett, Melville, Coleman, Fernandes (Stolcers), Goldbaek, Clark, Saha, Hayles, Davis.
aet.

19 DEC

Crystal Palace (0) 2 *(Forssell 48, Morrison C 82)*
Sunderland (0) 1 *(Rae 49)* 15,945
Crystal Palace: Kolinko; Smith, Black (Thomson), Austin, Zhiyi, Ruddock, Mullins, Rodger, Morrison C (Carlisle), Forssell, Pollock.
Sunderland: Sorensen; Varga, Gray, Williams, Emerson, Schwarz (Oster), Rae, Arca (McCann), Dichio, Phillips, Kilbane.

Manchester C (1) 1 *(Goater 10)*
Ipswich T (0) 2 *(Holland 60, Venus 109)* 31,252
Manchester C: Weaver; Haaland, Tiatto (Bishop), Wiekens, Prior, Morrison (Kennedy), Wright-Phillips, Jeff Whitley, Wanchope, Goater, Horlock (Granville).
Ipswich T: Wright R; Wilnis, Croft, McGreal, Hreidarsson (Wright J), Venus, Holland, Magilton, Johnson (Reuser), Scowcroft (Bramble), Clapham.
aet.

SEMI-FINAL, FIRST LEG

9 JAN

Ipswich T (1) 1 *(Stewart 45 (pen))*
Birmingham C (0) 0 21,684
Ipswich T: Wright R; Wilnis, Clapham (Reuser), Bramble, Hreidarsson, Venus, Holland, Magilton, Stewart, Scowcroft, Wright J.
Birmingham C: Bennett; Jenkins, Johnson M, Hughes, Purse, Sonner, Eaden (Marcelo), O'Connor, Adebola (Horsfield), Ndlovu (Lazaridis), Grainger.

10 JAN

Crystal Palace (0) 2 *(Rubins 56, Morrison C 77)*
Liverpool (0) 1 *(Smicer 78)* 25,933
Crystal Palace: Kolinko; Smith, Harrison, Austin, Zhiyi, Rubins, Mullins, Rodger, Morrison C, Forssell, Thomson.
Liverpool: Westerveld; Carragher, Biscan, Babbel, Henchoz, Hyypia, Gerrard, Barmby (Hamann), Heskey, Owen (Litmanen), Murphy (Smicer).

SEMI-FINAL, SECOND LEG

24 JAN

Liverpool (3) 5 *(Smicer 13, Murphy 15, 51, Biscan 18, Fowler 89)*
Crystal Palace (0) 0 41,854
Liverpool: Westerveld; Gerrard (Hamann), Carragher (Ziege), Biscan, Henchoz, Hyypia, Murphy, Smicer (Barmby), Fowler, Litmanen, McAllister.
Crystal Palace: Kolinko; Smith, Harrison, Austin, Carlisle (Pollock), Thomson, Black, Rodger, Morrison C, Forssell (Gregg), Rubins (Gray).

31 JAN

Birmingham C (1) 4 *(Grainger 43, Horsfield 56, 103, Johnson A 117)*
Ipswich T (0) 1 *(Scowcroft 57)* 28,624
Birmingham C: Bennett; Gill, Grainger, Sonner, Purse, Johnson M, Eaden (Hughes), O'Connor, Horsfield, Adebola (Johnson A), Lazaridis (Burrows).
Ipswich T: Wright R; Croft (Reuser), Clapham, Venus, Hreidarsson, McGreal, Holland, Magilton (Karic), Stewart, Wright J, Naylor (Scowcroft).
aet.

FINAL (at Millennium Stadium)

25 FEB

Birmingham C (0) 1 *(Purse 90 (pen))*
Liverpool (1) 1 *(Fowler 30)* 73,500
Birmingham C: Bennett; Eaden, Grainger, Sonner (Hughes), Purse, Johnson M, McCarthy, O'Connor, Horsfield (Marcelo), Adebola (Johnson A), Lazaridis.
Liverpool: Westerveld; Babbel, Carragher, Hamann, Henchoz, Hyypia, Gerrard (McAllister), Smicer (Barmby), Heskey, Fowler, Biscan (Ziege).
aet; Liverpool won 5-4 on penalties.
Referee: D. Elleray (Harrow).

The final chance of the 2001 Worthington Cup Final goes begging and Liverpool and Birmingham are forced into a penalty shoot-out. (ASP)

FOOTBALL LEAGUE COMPETITION ATTENDANCES

LEAGUE CUP ATTENDANCES

Season	Attendances	Games	Average
1960/61	1,204,580	112	10,755
1961/62	1,030,534	104	9,909
1962/63	1,029,893	102	10,097
1963/64	945,265	104	9,089
1964/65	962,802	98	9,825
1965/66	1,205,876	106	11,376
1966/67	1,394,553	118	11,818
1967/68	1,671,326	110	15,194
1968/69	2,064,647	118	17,497
1969/70	2,299,819	122	18,851
1970/71	2,035,315	116	17,546
1971/72	2,397,154	123	19,489
1972/73	1,935,474	120	16,129
1973/74	1,722,629	132	13,050
1974/75	1,901,094	127	14,969
1975/76	1,841,735	140	13,155
1976/77	2,236,636	147	15,215
1977/78	2,038,295	148	13,772
1978/79	1,825,643	139	13,134
1979/80	2,322,866	169	13,745
1980/81	2,051,576	161	12,743
1981/82	1,880,682	161	11,681
1982/83	1,679,756	160	10,498
1983/84	1,900,491	168	11,312
1984/85	1,876,429	167	11,236
1985/86	1,579,916	163	9,693
1986/87	1,531,498	157	9,755
1987/88	1,539,253	158	9,742
1988/89	1,552,780	162	9,585
1989/90	1,836,916	168	10,934
1990/91	1,675,496	159	10,538

Season	Attendances	Games	Average
1991/92	1,622,337	164	9,892
1992/93	1,558,031	161	9,677
1993/94	1,744,120	163	10,700
1994/95	1,530,478	157	9,748
1995/96	1,776,060	162	10,963
1996/97	1,529,321	163	9,382
1997/98	1,484,297	153	9,701
1998/99	1,555,856	153	10,169
1999/2000	1,354,233	153	8,851

WORTHINGTON CUP 2000-01

Round	Aggregate	Games	Average
One	293,257	70	4,189
Two	426,160	50	8,616
Three	301,643	16	18,852
Four	175,137	8	21,892
Five	113,512	5	22,702
Semi-finals	118,095	4	29,524
Final	73,500	1	73,500
Total	1,501,304	154	9,749

LDV VANS TROPHY 2000-01

Round	Aggregate	Games	Average
One	38,330	24	1,597
Two	34,335	16	2,146
Area Quarter-finals	20,303	8	2,538
Area Semi-finals	19,422	4	4,856
Area finals	21,619	4	5,405
Final	25,654	1	25,654
Total	159,663	57	2,801

FA CUP ATTENDANCES 1967–2001

	1st Round	2nd Round	3rd Round	4th Round	5th Round	6th Round	Semi-Finals & Final	Total	No. of matches	Average per match
2000-01	171,689	122,061	577,204	398,241	256,899	100,663	177,778	1,804,535	151	11,951
1999-2000	181,485	127,728	514,030	374,795	182,511	105,443	214,921	1,700,913	158	10,765
1998-99	191,954	132,341	609,486	431,613	359,398	181,005	202,150	2,107,947	155	13,599
1997-98	204,803	130,261	629,127	455,557	341,290	192,651	172,007	2,125,696	165	12,883
1996-97	209,521	122,324	651,139	402,293	199,873	67,035	191,813	1,843,998	151	12,211
1995-96	185,538	115,669	748,997	391,218	274,055	174,142	156,500	2,046,199	167	12,252
1994-95	219,511	125,629	640,017	438,596	257,650	159,787	174,059	2,015,249	161	12,517
1993-94	190,683	118,031	691,064	430,234	172,196	134,705	228,233	1,965,146	159	12,359
1992-93	241,968	174,702	612,494	377,211	198,379	149,675	293,241	2,047,670	161	12,718
1991-92	231,940	117,078	586,014	372,576	270,537	155,603	201,592	1,935,340	160	12,095
1990-91	194,195	121,450	594,592	530,279	276,112	124,826	196,434	2,038,518	162	12,583
1989-90	209,542	133,483	683,047	412,483	351,423	123,065	277,420	2,190,463	170	12,885
1988-89	212,775	121,326	690,199	421,255	206,781	176,629	167,353	1,966,318	164	12,173
1987-88	204,411	104,561	720,121	443,133	281,461	119,313	177,585	2,050,585	155	13,229
1986-87	209,290	146,761	593,520	349,342	263,550	119,396	195,533	1,877,400	165	11,378
1985-86	171,142	130,034	486,838	495,526	311,833	184,262	192,316	1,971,951	168	11,738
1984-85	174,604	137,078	616,229	320,772	269,232	148,690	242,754	1,909,359	157	12,162
1983-84	192,276	151,647	625,965	417,298	181,832	185,382	187,000	1,941,400	166	11,695
1982-83	191,312	150,046	670,503	452,688	260,069	193,845	291,162	2,209,625	154	14,348
1981-82	236,220	127,300	513,185	356,987	203,334	124,308	279,621	1,840,955	160	11,506
1980-81	246,824	194,502	832,578	534,402	320,530	288,714	339,250	2,756,800	169	16,312
1979-80	267,121	204,759	804,701	507,725	364,039	157,530	355,541	2,661,416	163	16,328
1978-79	243,773	185,343	880,345	537,748	243,683	263,213	249,897	2,604,002	166	15,687
1977-78	258,248	178,930	881,406	540,164	400,751	137,059	198,020	2,594,578	160	16,216
1976-77	379,230	192,159	942,523	631,265	373,330	205,379	258,216	2,982,102	174	17,139
1975-76	255,533	178,099	867,880	573,843	471,925	206,851	205,810	2,759,941	161	17,142
1974-75	283,596	170,466	914,994	646,434	393,323	268,361	291,369	2,968,903	172	17,261
1973-74	214,236	125,295	840,142	747,909	346,012	233,307	273,051	2,779,952	167	16,646
1972-73	259,432	169,114	938,741	735,825	357,386	241,934	226,543	2,928,975	160	18,306
1971-72	277,726	236,127	986,094	711,399	486,378	230,292	248,546	3,158,562	160	19,741
1970-71	329,687	230,942	956,683	757,852	360,687	304,937	279,644	3,220,432	162	19,879
1969-70	345,229	195,102	925,930	651,374	319,893	198,537	390,700	3,026,765	170	17,805
1968-69	331,858	252,710	1,094,043	883,675	464,915	188,121	216,232	3,431,554	157	21,857
1967-68	322,121	236,195	1,229,519	771,284	563,779	240,095	223,831	3,586,824	160	22,418

LDV VANS TROPHY 2000–2001

FIRST ROUND

28 NOV

Barnet (2) 2 *(Sawyers 22, Purser 29)*
Rushden & D (0) 0   887
Barnet: Harrison; Stockley, Sawyers, Niven, Heald, Arber, Bell, Brown (Berkley), Purser (Strevens), Riza, Gledhill (Pope).
Rushden & D: Naylor; Mustafa, Setchell, Mills, Rodwell, Warburton (Town), Peters, Hamsher, Jackson, Sigere, Burgess.

Lincoln C (1) 3 *(Thorpe 15, 56, 57)*
Morecambe (1) 2 *(Walters 39, Dowe 53)*   1194
Lincoln C: Marriott; Barnett, Bimson (Welsh), Schofield, Holmes, Brown, Peacock, Miller, Battersby (Cameron), Thorpe (Camm), Gain.
Morecambe: Smith; Fensome, Perkins, McKearney, Hardiker, Walters (Knowles), Thompson, Drummond, Dowe (Quayle), Norman, Black (Rigoglioso).

5 DEC

Bournemouth (0) 1 *(Huck 64)*
Dover Ath (1) 1 *(Hockton 29)*   2171
Bournemouth: Menetrier; Howe, Broadhurst, Grant, Day, Huck (Stock), O'Connor, Bernard (Keeler), Eribenne (Hayter), Defoe, Smith.
Dover Ath: Hyde; Carruthers (Nooke), Norman, Pluck, Shearer, Beard, Chapman, Strouts (Clarke), Le Bihan, Vansittart, Hockton.
aet; Bournemouth won 4-2 on penalties.

Brentford (3) 4 *(Lovett 9, Partridge 28, 36, Marshall 89)*
Oxford U (0) 1 *(Anthrobus 54)*   1517
Brentford: Gottskalksson; Theobald, Dobson, Mahon, Quinn, Marshall, Lovett, Evans (Kennedy), Scott (Owusu), Rowlands (O'Connor), Partridge.
Oxford U: Glass; Robertson, Brown, Andrews, Richardson, Hatswell, Omoyimni (Hackett), Gray, Murphy, Ricketts (Anthrobus), Beauchamp.

Brighton & HA (2) 2 *(Johnson 13, Cullip 20)*
Cardiff C (0) 0   2364
Brighton & HA: Kuipers; Watson (Hammond), Mayo, Cullip, Wicks, Crosby, Ramsay (Hart), Melton, Steele, Johnson, Brooker.
Cardiff C: Walton; Low, McCulloch, Collins, Greene, Weston, Thompson, Bonner (Evans), Brayson, Nogan, Hill.

Cambridge U (2) 2 *(Dreyer 3, Axeldal 20)*
Colchester U (0) 0   1555
Cambridge U: Perez; Ashbee, Joseph, Duncan, McAnespie, Dreyer, Mustoe, Axeldal (Taylor), Abbey, Hansen (Preece), Oakes (Guttridge).
Colchester U: Woodman; Dunne, Fitzgerald, Skelton, Keeble (McGavin), Arnott, Duguid, Gregory, Conlon, Stockwell, Dozzell.

Chester C (0) 1 *(Carden 52)*
Hull C (0) 0   770
Chester C: Brown; Fisher, Doughty, Gaunt, Ruffer, Lancaster, Carden, Porter, Ruscoe (Wright), Whitehall, Blackburn (Woods).
Hull C: Musselwhite; Edwards (Morley), Harper, Brightwell, Whitney, Greaves, Swales, Whitmore, Brown (Eyre), Goodison, Wood (Harris).

Doncaster R (1) 3 *(Turner 39, Penney 59 (pen), Campbell 92)*
Rochdale (1) 2 *(Jones 21 (pen), Campbell 90 (og))*   1453
Doncaster R: Richardson; Marples (Hawkins), Shaw, Kelly (Atkins), Miller, Ryan, Cauldwell, Penney, Turner, Whitman (Campbell), McIntyre.
Rochdale: Edwards; Evans, McAuley, Ware (Davies), Bayliss, Monington, Hadland (Flitcroft), Jones, Platt (Lancashire), Ellis, Oliver.
aet; Doncaster R won on sudden death.

Millwall (2) 4 *(Kinet 10, 15, 50 (pen), Sadlier 56)*
Northampton T (0) 1 *(Gould 69)*   2369
Millwall: Gueret; Lawrence, Bull, Bircham, Tuttle, Dolan, Ifill, Odunsi, Harris (Moody), Sadlier (Reid), Kinet (Reid).
Northampton T: Sollitt; Hughes, Spedding, Sampson, Green, Hope, Howard, Morrow (Abbey), Gould, Gabbiadini (Clare), Hargreaves.

Peterborough U (0) 1 *(Green 81)*
Luton T (0) 0   2075
Peterborough U: Connor; Hooper (Forsyth), Rogers, Gill, Murray, Green, Hanlon, Cullen, Clarke (Lee), Forinton (French), Jelleyman.
Luton T: Ovendale; Helin, Taylor, Fraser, Ayres, Karlsen, Locke, McLaren, Thomson (Stein), Fotiadis (Nogan), Spring.

Plymouth Arg (1) 3 *(Stonebridge 26 (pen), Gritton 65, Taylor 74)*
Bristol C (0) 0   1364
Plymouth Arg: Larrieu; Worrell, Beswetherick, Friio (Fleming), Heathcote, Taylor, Phillips M, Wills, Stonebridge (Phillips L), Gritton, McGlinchey.
Bristol C: Malessa; Amankwaah, Burnell, Testimetanu (Jones), Woodman, Coles, Goodridge, Brown A (Clist), Beadle (Spencer), Odejayi, Doherty.

Rotherham U (0) 3 *(Robins 48, Lee 57, Monkhouse 86)*
Chesterfield (3) 4 *(Breckin 8, Jones 22, Hurst 29 (og), Williams R 104)*   3488
Rotherham U: Gray; Bryan, Hurst, Garner, Artell, Scott (Monkhouse), Watson, Robins, Lee, Warne (Berry), Carr.
Chesterfield: Pollitt; Breckin, Edwards (Beaumont), Tutill, Simpkins (Williams R), Parrish, Jones (Dudfield), D'Auria, Howard, Beckett, Perkins.
aet; Chesterfield won on sudden death.

Southend U (2) 2 *(Carruthers 8, Abbey 25)*
Cheltenham T (0) 0   1000
Southend U: Flahavan; McSweeney, Searle, Morley, Newman, Edwards (Williamson), Webb, Maher, Carruthers, Abbey (Fitzpatrick), Forbes.
Cheltenham T: Higgs; Duff, McCann, Banks (Yates), Jackson (McAuley), Hopkins, Bloomer, Milton, White, Devaney, Jones (Griffin).

Wycombe W (0) 1 *(Thompson 88)*
Exeter C (0) 0   1022
Wycombe W: Taylor; Townsend, Rogers, Bulman, Cousins, McCarthy, Harkin (Thompson) (Senda), Simpson, Brown, Rammell, Parkin (McSporran).
Exeter C: Fraser; Ashton (Rawlinson), Power, Buckle, Campbell, Whitworth, Roscoe, Hutchings, Rapley, Francis, Roberts C (Tomlinson).

6 DEC

Stoke C (2) 3 *(Thorne 21, 57, Cooke 25)*
Scarborough (0) 1 *(Brunton 89)*   2336
Stoke C: Kristinsson; Risom, Petty, Kippe, Mohan, Thomas (Hansson), Gudjonsson (Neal), Thordarson, Cooke (Dadason), Thorne, O'Connor.
Scarborough: Priestley; Betts, Thompson (Keegan), Rennison, Ellender, Ingram, Williams, Stoker, Diallo (Jewell), Brodie, Pounder (Brunton).

9 DEC

Bury (1) 2 *(Swailes C 38, Jarrett 50)*
Mansfield T (1) 1 *(Bacon 25)*   1117
Bury: Kenny; Unsworth, Jarrett, Armstrong, Swailes C, Redmond, Smith (James), Reid (Daws), Barnes, Hill, Forrest.
Mansfield T: Pilkington; Asher, Pemberton, Barrett, Williamson, Robinson, Corden, Disley (Greenacre), Bradley, Blake, Bacon (Boulding).

Torquay U (0) 0
Bristol R (0) 2 *(Ellington 52, Evans 90)*   1370
Torquay U: Jones; Tully (Law), Herrera (O'Brien), Aggrey (Neil), Lyons, Watson, Hockley, Ford, Bedeau, Williams, Chalqi.
Bristol R: Culkin; Bignot, Challis, Foster, Foran, Jones, Astafjevs, Evans, Ellington, Hogg (Hillier), Bryant.

Wrexham (0) 0
Halifax T (0) 1 *(Jones 58)*   1545
Wrexham: Walsh; McGregor, Roche (Ridler), Owen, Hardy, Carey, Chalk (Gibson), Ferguson, Sam, Bouanane, Faulconbridge (Russell).
Halifax T: Butler L; Wilder, Murphy, Mitchell, Stoneman, Rezai (Reilly), Thompson, Middleton, Jones, Kerrigan (Clarke M), Wainwright.

11 DEC

Hartlepool U (2) 3 *(Henderson 40, Arnison 45, Miller 51)*
Scunthorpe U (1) 2 *(Sheldon 30, Quailey 86)*   1538
Hartlepool U: Williams; Arnison, Clark, Barron, Westwood, Sharp, Tinkler, Miller, Midgley (Sperrevik), Henderson (Lormor), Stephenson (Fitzpatrick).
Scunthorpe U: Evans; Jackson, Dawson, Stanton, Thom, Larusson, Stamp, Sheldon, Ipoua (Quailey), Graves (Brough), Morrison (Harsley).

12 DEC

Kidderminster H (1) 2 *(Smith 44, Bird 100)*
Carlisle U (0) 1 *(Soley 86)*   777
Kidderminster H: Clarke; Medou-Otye, Stamps (Bogie), Smith, Hinton, Shail, Horne, Hadley, Foster (Bird), Davies, MacKenzie.
Carlisle U: Glennon; Birch, Halliday, Hore, McAughtrie, Prokas, Darby, Thwaites, Heggs (Allan), Thurston (Dawson), Anthony (Soley).
aet; Kidderminster H won on sudden death.

19 DEC

Hereford U (2) 4 *(Williams 40, Snape 42, Clarke 49, Quiggin 87)*
Yeovil T (0) 0 853
Hereford U: Cooksey; Lane, Sturgess, Robinson, Wright, Gardiner, Clarke, Snape (Rodgerson), Giddins, Williams (Quiggin), McIndoe.
Yeovil T: Weale; Piper, Poole, Skiverton (Peters), White, O'Brien, Meechan (Belgrave), Smith, Patmore, Crittenden, Risbridger (Bent).

9 JAN

Oldham Ath (1) 2 *(Salt 36, Tipton 52 (pen))*
Wigan Ath (1) 3 *(McLaughlin 45, McLoughlin 70, 95)* 2551
Oldham Ath: Kelly; McNiven, Holt, Garnett, Rickers, Boshell (Innes), Sugden (Ritchie), Salt, Tipton, Hotte, Eyres.
Wigan Ath: Marriott; Dickson, Padula, Morris (Johnson), Griffiths, Mitchell, Redfearn, Nicholls, Roberts, McLaughlin, McLoughlin.
aet; Wigan Ath won on sudden death.

Port Vale (2) 3 *(Smith 8, Brooker 45, Naylor 59)*
Notts Co (0) 0 1919
Port Vale: Delaney; Tankard, Carragher, Brammer, Walsh, Widdrington, Wilkinson, Cummins, Naylor (Eyre), Brooker (O'Callaghan), Smith (Twiss).
Notts Co: Gibson; Holmes, Gellert, Warren, Jorgensen, Dunn (Heffernan), Murray, Ford, Joseph, Bolland, Hamilton.

York C (0) 0
Darlington (2) 4 *(Elliott 8 (pen), Hodgson 11, McMahon 50, Liddle 69)* 1095
York C: Howarth; Patterson, Thompson (Bower), Sertori, Stamp (Hall), McNiven (Turley), Agnew, Hulme, Mathie, Fox, Alcide.
Darlington: Van der Geest; Elliott, Reed, Brumwell, Liddle, Kilty, Gray, Hodgson, Hjorth, McMahon, Marsh (Williamson).

SECOND ROUND

9 JAN

Bournemouth (0) 0
Swansea C (0) 1 *(Savarese 51)* 3810
Bournemouth: Menetrier; Smith, Stock (Fletcher C), Cummings, Tindall, Huck, Bernard, O'Connor (Elliott), Eribenne (Keeler), Fletcher S, Hughes.
Swansea C: Freestone; Lacey, Howard, O'Leary, Smith, De Vulgt, Jenkins, Romo, Savarese, Boyd (Watkin), Roberts.

Brighton & HA (2) 2 *(Brooker 24, Zamora 27)*
Brentford (1) 2 *(Marshall 35, McCammon 78)* 2482
Brighton & HA: Kuipers; Watson, Mayo, Cullip, Crosby, Carpenter, Zamora, Rogers, Hart (Melton), Brooker (Virgo), Jones (Freeman).
Brentford: Gottskalksson; Gibbs, Dobson, Lovett, Marshall, Rowlands, Ingimarsson, Evans, Owusu, McCammon, Javary (Williams).
aet; Brentford won 4-2 on penalties.

Bristol R (1) 3 *(Astafjevs 8, 82, Evans 87 (pen))*
Plymouth Arg (0) 0 3781
Bristol R: Culkin; Bignot (Pethick), Wilson, Foster, Thomson, Mauge, Astafjevs, Evans, Ellington (Ellis), Meaker, Bryant.
Plymouth Arg: Larrieu; Worrell, Adams, Leadbitter (Fleming), Wotton, Opinel, Phillips M, Gritton, Stonebridge (Guinan), Wills, McGlinchey (McGregor).

Chesterfield (2) 4 *(Ebdon 11, Reeves 42 (pen), 52, Payne 49)*
Macclesfield T (1) 2 *(Glover 25, 85)* 1839
Chesterfield: Pollitt; Breckin, Edwards, Payne, Blatherwick (Beaumont), Ingledow, Ebdon, Williams R, Reeves (Willis), Dudfield, Richardson (Williams D)
Macclesfield T: Bullock; Adams, Hitchen (Bamber), O'Neill, Tinson, Rioch, Munroe, Woolley (Came), Whitehead (Askey), Glover, Priest.

Halifax T (2) 2 *(Kerrigan 14, Jones 27)*
Stoke C (2) 3 *(Dadason 31, Gudjonsson 35, 90)* 1917
Halifax T: Butler L; Clarke C, Murphy, Mitchell, Stoneman (Reilly), Hawe, Wainwright (Painter), Middleton, Jones, Kerrigan (Clarke M), Thompson.
Stoke C: Kristinsson; Petty, Clarke, Thomas (Thordarson), Mohan, Gunnarsson, Gudjonsson, Risom, Cooke (Thorne), Dadason, O'Connor.

Hartlepool U (1) 3 *(Tinkler 29, Clark 51, Miller 54 (pen))*
Doncaster R (0) 1 *(Campbell 49)* 2466
Hartlepool U: Williams; Arnison, Clark (Shilton), Barron, Westwood, Sharp, Tinkler, Miller, Midgley, Henderson (Lormor), Stephenson (Fitzpatrick).
Doncaster R: Richardson; Marples, Shaw, Miller (Cauldwell), Stone, Hawkins, Penney, McIntyre, Paterson, Campbell (Alford), Whitman (Duerden).

Hereford U (0) 1 *(Williams 70)*
Reading (2) 2 *(Cureton 36, McIntyre 39)* 1693
Hereford U: Cooksey; Wall, Sturgess, Robinson, Wright, Gardiner, Rodgerson, Snape, Williams, Elmes (Giddins), McIndoe.
Reading: Howie; Murty, Gray, Viveash, Hunter, Jones, Igoe (Gurney), Caskey, Cureton (Henderson), McIntyre, Rougier.

Leyton Orient (0) 0
Wycombe W (1) 2 *(Brady 21, Parkin 73)* 946
Leyton Orient: Bayes; Joseph, Lockwood, McGhee (Mansley), Smith (Martin), McElholm, Walschaerts, Opara (Hatcher), Beall, Houghton, Brkovic.
Wycombe W: Taylor; Rogers (Senda), Vinnicombe, Bulman, McCarthy, Cousins, Lee, Simpson (Castledine), Brady, Rammell (Baird), Parkin.

Lincoln C (1) 3 *(O'Connor 3 (og), Battersby 56, Thorpe 72)*
Blackpool (0) 1 *(Ormerod 51)* 962
Lincoln C: Day; Smith, Mayo, Barnett, Brown, Garratt (Camm), Finnigan, Walker, Battersby (Schofield), Thorpe (Cameron), Peacock.
Blackpool: Barnes; Coid, Jaszczun (Newell), O'Connor (Hills), Hughes, Thompson, Clarkson, Simpson, Ormerod, Murphy J, Collins (Wellens).

Millwall (0) 0
Swindon T (0) 0 2394
Millwall: Gueret; Lawrence, Bircham, Neill, Nethercott, Dolan, Odunsi (Cahill), Sadlier, Constantine (Harris), Reid, Kinet.
Swindon T: Mildenhall; Hall, Robinson M, Young, Reeves, Van der Linden, Invincible, Williams J (Mills) (Halliday), Alexander, McHugh (Cobian), Duke.
aet; Swindon T won 3-2 on penalties.

Peterborough U (0) 1 *(Cullen 75)*
Barnet (1) 3 *(Rea 28 (og), McGleish 56, Riza 61)* 1891
Peterborough U: Connor; Hooper, Scott, French, Rea (Drury), Murray, Green, Cullen, Hanlon, Forinton, Jelleyman.
Barnet: Harrison; Stockley, Sawyers, Gledhill, Basham, Arber, Berkley (Niven), Bell, McGleish, Riza (Purser), Brown.

Southend U (2) 3 *(Lee 25, 75, Williamson 33)*
Cambridge U (1) 1 *(Wanless 4)* 1694
Southend U: Flahavan; McSweeney, Searle, Williamson, Roget, Whelan, Lee, Maher, Webb, Johnson, Forbes.
Cambridge U: Marshall; Joseph, McNeil, Duncan, McAnespie, Wilson (Perez), Wanless (Guttridge), Axeldal, Russell, Mustoe, Oakes (Traore).

10 JAN

Bury (2) 2 *(Daws 17, 25)*
Kidderminster H (0) 0 1015
Bury: Kenny; Hill, Unsworth, Daws, Swailes D, Redmond, Armstrong, Reid (Peyton), Bhutia, Preece (Littlejohn), James (Buggie).
Kidderminster H: Clarke; Clarkson, Medou-Otye, Webb, Hinton, Shail, Bennett, Horne, Bird, Bogie, MacKenzie.

16 JAN

Darlington (1) 2 *(Liddle 4, Marsh 77)*
Shrewsbury T (0) 0 1502
Darlington: Van der Geest; Elliott (Naylor), Heckingbottom, Liddle, Marsh, Kilty, Brumwell, Gray, Hodgson, Campbell (Hjorth), McMahon (Williamson).
Shrewsbury T: Edwards; Seabury, Jenkins, Peer, Davidson, Hughes, Brown (Freestone), Tolley, Lowe (Rodgers), Jemson, Hanmer.

30 JAN

Port Vale (1) 2 *(Doughty 21 (og), Naylor 65)*
Chester C (0) 0 2507
Port Vale: Goodlad; Tankard (Burns), Carragher, Brammer (Minton), Walsh, Widdrington, Bridge-Wilkinson, Cummins (Brisco), Naylor, Brooker, Smith.
Chester C: Brown; Fisher, Doughty (Ruscoe), Lancaster, Ruffer, Beesley P (Moss), Carden, Woods (Haarhoff), Beesley M, Wright, Blackburn.

Walsall (1) 2 *(Birch 44, Gaunt 90)*
Wigan Ath (1) 1 *(Padula 45)* 3436
Walsall: Emberson; Gaunt, Scott, Small, Barras (Roper), Bukran (Ekelund), Wrack, Gadsby, Birch (Hawley), Byfield, Wright.
Wigan Ath: Marriott; Dickson, Padula, Nicholls, Balmer, Griffiths, Kay, McMahon, Johnson J (Johnson I), McLoughlin, Redfearn (Cunningham).

QUARTER-FINALS

30 JAN

Barnet (0) 1 *(Gower 76)*
Brentford (1) 2 *(Rowlands 45, Evans 75)* 1438
Barnet: Harrison; Stockley, Goodhind, Niven, Heald, Arber, Currie, Bell (Toms), Richards, Gower, Flynn.
Brentford: Gottskalksson; Gibbs, Dobson, Mahon, Lovett, Marshall, Ingimarsson, Evans, Owusu (McCammon), Rowlands, Partridge.

Bury (0) 0
Chesterfield (3) 3 *(Ebdon 5, 45 (pen), Dudfield 11)* 1452
Bury: Kenny; Swailes D, Connell, Armstrong, Swailes C, Jarrett (Hill), Littlejohn, Reid, Preece, Bhutia (Daws), James (Billy).
Chesterfield: Pollitt; Breckin, Edwards (Parrish), Payne, Blatherwick (Beaumont), Ingledow, Ebdon, Williams R, Dudfield (Willis), Beckett, Richardson.

Lincoln C (1) 1 *(Schofield 1)*
Hartlepool U (0) 0 1357
Lincoln C: Day; Smith, Mayo, Welsh, Dudgeon, Holmes, Walker, Schofield, Battersby (Cameron), Thorpe, Finnigan.
Hartlepool U: Williams; Arnison, Shilton, Barron, Westwood (Aspin), Sharp, Tinkler, Miller, Midgley (Fitzpatrick), Henderson, Stephenson (Lormor).

Southend U (1) 1 *(Carruthers 41)*
Bristol R (0) 0 2192
Southend U: Flahavan; McSweeney, Searle, Williamson, Newman, Whelan, Lee, Johnson, Carruthers, Bramble (Maher), Forbes.
Bristol R: Culkin; Bignot, Wilson, Foster, Thomson (Jones), Mauge, Astafjevs, Evans (Richards), Ellington, Meaker, Bryant (Walters).

Swansea C (0) 1 *(Savarese 75)*
Reading (0) 0 2516
Swansea C: Freestone; Lacey, Howard, O'Leary, Smith, Keegan (Casey) (Cusack), Price, Jenkins, Savarese, Romo, Roberts.
Reading: Howie; Murty, Newman, Viveash, Hunter (Mackie), Parkinson, Igoe, Caskey, Cureton, McIntyre (Hodges), Rougier (Butler).

Swindon T (2) 2 *(Alexander 1, 15)*
Wycombe W (1) 1 *(Brown 36)* 3244
Swindon T: Griemink; Robinson M, Duke, O'Halloran, Heywood, Van der Linden, Invincible (Reddy), McHugh (Hall), Alexander, Williams J, Willis.
Wycombe W: Taylor; Lavin, Vinnicombe, Bulman, Bates, Cousins, Brady (Thompson), Simpson, Brown (Lee), Rammell, Baird (Senda).

6 FEB

Port Vale (1) 4 *(Lowe 26, Tankard 59, Naylor 70, 74)*
Darlington (0) 0 2480
Port Vale: Goodlad; Tankard (Burton), Carragher, Brammer (Minton), Walsh, Widdrington, Bridge-Wilkinson, Cummins, Naylor (Viljanen), Lowe, Smith.
Darlington: Van der Geest; Elliott, Heckingbottom, Liddle, Kilty, Brumwell, Convery (Hodgson), Campbell, Hjorth (McMahon), Naylor, Williams.

7 FEB

Stoke C (1) 4 *(Clarke 3, Goodfellow 59, Petty 67, Thordarson 81 (pen))*
Walsall (0) 0 5624
Stoke C: Kristinsson; Hansson, Clarke, Thomas, Kippe, Petty, Risom, Kavanagh (Henry), Goodfellow, Thordarson, Dadason (Neal).
Walsall: Emberson; Gadsby, Wright (Roper), Gaunt, Scott, Small, Ekelund, Keates, Birch (Hawley), Byfield (Wrack), Matias.

NORTHERN SEMI-FINALS

13 FEB

Lincoln C (1) 4 *(Thorpe 32, 75, Grant 54, Walker 90)*
Chesterfield (0) 1 *(Payne 85)* 2540
Lincoln C: Day; Smith, Mayo, Barnett, Dudgeon, Holmes, Walker (Gain), Schofield, Grant (Battersby), Thorpe, Finnigan.
Chesterfield: Pollitt; Breckin, Edwards, Payne, Simpkins, Parrish, Ebdon, Ingledow (Williams D), Reeves, Beckett (Beaumont), Dudfield.

5 MAR

Port Vale (0) 2 *(Cummins 64, Bridge-Wilkinson 105 (pen))*
Stoke C (0) 1 *(Mohan 87)* 11,323
Port Vale: Goodlad; Brisco, Carragher, Burton, Walsh, Brammer, Bridge-Wilkinson, Cummins, Naylor, Brooker, Smith.
Stoke C: Kristinsson; Petty, Clarke, Thomas, Mohan, Kippe, Risom (Gudjonsson), Kavanagh (Gunnarsson), Thorne (Cooke), Thordarson, Goodfellow.
aet; Port Vale won on sudden death.

SOUTHERN SEMI-FINALS

13 FEB

Southend U (0) 2 *(Carruthers 57, Roget 110)*
Swindon T (0) 1 *(Reddy 72)* 3337
Southend U: Flahavan; McSweeney, Searle, Johnson, Roget, Whelan, Lee, Maher, Carruthers, Abbey (Williamson), Webb (Bramble).
Swindon T: Griemink; Robinson M, Davis, O'Halloran, Heywood, Van der Linden, Robinson S (Cobian), Hewlett (McHugh), Reddy, Williams J (Alexander), Duke.
aet; Southend U won on sudden death.

14 FEB

Swansea C (0) 2 *(Lacey 56, Price 66)*
Brentford (1) 3 *(Evans 15 (pen), McCammon 58, Owusu 89)* 2222
Swansea C: Freestone; Lacey, De-Vulgt, O'Leary, Smith (Bound), Keegan (Mounty), Price, Verschave, Savarese, Romo, Roberts.
Brentford: Gottskalksson; Gibbs, Dobson, Mahon, Powell, Marshall, Ingimarsson, Evans, Owusu, McCammon, Partridge.

NORTHERN FINAL, FIRST LEG

13 MAR

Lincoln C (0) 0
Port Vale (0) 2 *(Bridge-Wilkinson 53, Naylor 85)* 4813
Lincoln C: Day; Barnett (Sedgemore), Bimson, Finnigan, Dudgeon, Welsh, Smith, Walker, Battersby, Thorpe, Gain (Cameron).
Port Vale: Goodlad; Carragher, Brisco, Brammer, Walsh, Burton, Twiss, Cummins, Naylor, Bridge-Wilkinson, Smith.

NORTHERN FINAL, SECOND LEG

20 MAR

Port Vale (0) 0
Lincoln C (0) 0 5172
Port Vale: Goodlad; Carragher, Brisco, Brammer, Walsh, Burton, Bridge-Wilkinson, Cummins, Naylor, Brooker, Smith.
Lincoln C: Marriott; Barnett, Bimson, Finnigan, Holmes, Welsh, Walker, Peacock (Miller), Battersby, Thorpe, Gain (Cameron).
Port Vale won 2-0 on aggregate.

SOUTHERN FINAL, FIRST LEG

13 MAR

Southend U (0) 1 *(Whelan 57)*
Brentford (0) 2 *(Dobson 56, 64)* 5055
Southend U: Flahavan; Booty, Searle, Newman, Johnson (Thurgood), Whelan, Lee (Carruthers), Maher, Black, Abbey, Williamson.
Brentford: Gottskalksson; Gibbs (Lovett), Dobson, Mahon, Powell, Theobald, Ingimarsson, Evans, Owusu, Rowlands, Partridge (McCammon).

SOUTHERN FINAL, SECOND LEG

20 MAR

Brentford (1) 2 *(Ingimarsson 13, Owusu 78)*
Southend U (1) 1 *(Searle 26)* 6579
Brentford: Gottskalksson (Smith P); Gibbs, Dobson, Mahon, Powell, Theobald, Ingimarsson, Evans, Owusu (McCammon), Rowlands, Partridge (Lovett).
Southend U: Flahavan; Booty, Searle, Newman, Johnson, Whelan, Lee, Maher, Carruthers (Abbey), Bramble, Forbes (Williamson).
Brentford won 4-2 on aggregate.

FINAL (at Millennium Stadium)

22 APR

Brentford (1) 1 *(Dobson 3)*
Port Vale (0) 2 *(Bridge-Wilkinson 77 (pen), Brooker 84)* 25,654
Brentford: Gottskalksson; Gibbs (Williams), Dobson, Mahon, Powell, Theobald, Ingimarsson, Evans, Owusu, Rowlands (McCammon), Partridge.
Port Vale: Goodlad; Burton, Carragher, Brammer, Walsh, Brisco, Bridge-Wilkinson, Cummins, Naylor, Brooker, Smith.
Referee: W.C. Burns (Scarborough).

FA CUP FINALS 1872–2001

1872 and 1874–92	Kennington Oval	1911	Replay at Old Trafford
1873	Lillie Bridge	1912	Replay at Bramall Lane
1886	Replay at Derby (Racecourse Ground)		
1893	Fallowfield, Manchester	1915	Old Trafford, Manchester
1894	Everton	1920–22	Stamford Bridge
1895–1914	Crystal Palace	1923 to date	Wembley
1901	Replay at Bolton	1970	Replay at Old Trafford
1910	Replay at Everton		

Year	Winners	Runners-up	Score
1872	Wanderers	Royal Engineers	1-0
1873	Wanderers	Oxford University	2-0
1874	Oxford University	Royal Engineers	2-0
1875	Royal Engineers	Old Etonians	2-0 (after 1-1 draw aet)
1876	Wanderers	Old Etonians	3-0 (after 1-1 draw aet)
1877	Wanderers	Oxford University	2-1 (aet)
1878	Wanderers*	Royal Engineers	3-1
1879	Old Etonians	Clapham R	1-0
1880	Clapham R	Oxford University	1-0
1881	Old Carthusians	Old Etonians	3-0
1882	Old Etonians	Blackburn R	1-0
1883	Blackburn Olympic	Old Etonians	2-1 (aet)
1884	Blackburn R	Queen's Park, Glasgow	2-1
1885	Blackburn R	Queen's Park, Glasgow	2-0
1886	Blackburn R†	WBA	2-0 (after 0-0 draw)
1887	Aston Villa	WBA	2-0
1888	WBA	Preston NE	2-1
1889	Preston NE	Wolverhampton W	3-0
1890	Blackburn R	Sheffield W	6-1
1891	Blackburn R	Notts Co	3-1
1892	WBA	Aston Villa	3-0
1893	Wolverhampton W	Everton	1-0
1894	Notts Co	Bolton W	4-1
1895	Aston Villa	WBA	1-0
1896	Sheffield W	Wolverhampton W	2-1
1897	Aston Villa	Everton	3-2
1898	Nottingham F	Derby Co	3-1
1899	Sheffield U	Derby Co	4-1
1900	Bury	Southampton	4-0
1901	Tottenham H	Sheffield U	3-1 (after 2-2 draw)
1902	Sheffield U	Southampton	2-1 (after 1-1 draw)
1903	Bury	Derby Co	6-0
1904	Manchester C	Bolton W	1-0
1905	Aston Villa	Newcastle U	2-0
1906	Everton	Newcastle U	1-0
1907	Sheffield W	Everton	2-1
1908	Wolverhampton W	Newcastle U	3-1
1909	Manchester U	Bristol C	1-0
1910	Newcastle U	Barnsley	2-0 (after 1-1 draw)
1911	Bradford C	Newcastle U	1-0 (after 0-0 draw)
1912	Barnsley	WBA	1-0 (aet, after 0-0 draw)
1913	Aston Villa	Sunderland	1-0
1914	Burnley	Liverpool	1-0
1915	Sheffield U	Chelsea	3-0
1920	Aston Villa	Huddersfield T	1-0 (aet)
1921	Tottenham H	Wolverhampton W	1-0
1922	Huddersfield T	Preston NE	1-0
1923	Bolton W	West Ham U	2-0
1924	Newcastle U	Aston Villa	2-0
1925	Sheffield U	Cardiff C	1-0
1926	Bolton W	Manchester C	1-0
1927	Cardiff C	Arsenal	1-0
1928	Blackburn R	Huddersfield T	3-1
1929	Bolton W	Portsmouth	2-0
1930	Arsenal	Huddersfield T	2-0
1931	WBA	Birmingham	2-1
1932	Newcastle U	Arsenal	2-1
1933	Everton	Manchester C	3-0
1934	Manchester C	Portsmouth	2-1
1935	Sheffield W	WBA	4-2
1936	Arsenal	Sheffield U	1-0
1937	Sunderland	Preston NE	3-1
1938	Preston NE	Huddersfield T	1-0 (aet)
1939	Portsmouth	Wolverhampton W	4-1
1946	Derby Co	Charlton Ath	4-1 (aet)
1947	Charlton Ath	Burnley	1-0 (aet)
1948	Manchester U	Blackpool	4-2
1949	Wolverhampton W	Leicester C	3-1
1950	Arsenal	Liverpool	2-0
1951	Newcastle U	Blackpool	2-0
1952	Newcastle U	Arsenal	1-0

Year	Winners	Runners-up	Score
1953	Blackpool	Bolton W	4-3
1954	WBA	Preston NE	3-2
1955	Newcastle U	Manchester C	3-1
1956	Manchester C	Birmingham C	3-1
1957	Aston Villa	Manchester U	2-1
1958	Bolton W	Manchester U	2-0
1959	Nottingham F	Luton T	2-1
1960	Wolverhampton W	Blackburn R	3-0
1961	Tottenham H	Leicester C	2-0
1962	Tottenham H	Burnley	3-1
1963	Manchester U	Leicester C	3-1
1964	West Ham U	Preston NE	3-2
1965	Liverpool	Leeds U	2-1 (aet)
1966	Everton	Sheffield W	3-2
1967	Tottenham H	Chelsea	2-1
1968	WBA	Everton	1-0 (aet)
1969	Manchester C	Leicester C	1-0
1970	Chelsea	Leeds U	2-1 (aet)
		(after 2-2 draw, after extra time)	
1971	Arsenal	Liverpool	2-1 (aet)
1972	Leeds U	Arsenal	1-0
1973	Sunderland	Leeds U	1-0
1974	Liverpool	Newcastle U	3-0
1975	West Ham U	Fulham	2-0
1976	Southampton	Manchester U	1-0
1977	Manchester U	Liverpool	2-1
1978	Ipswich T	Arsenal	1-0
1979	Arsenal	Manchester U	3-2
1980	West Ham U	Arsenal	1-0
1981	Tottenham H	Manchester C	3-2
		(after 1-1 draw, after extra time)	
1982	Tottenham H	QPR	1-0
		(after 1-1 draw, after extra time)	
1983	Manchester U	Brighton & HA	4-0
		(after 2-2 draw, after extra time)	
1984	Everton	Watford	2-0
1985	Manchester U	Everton	1-0 (aet)
1986	Liverpool	Everton	3-1
1987	Coventry C	Tottenham H	3-2 (aet)
1988	Wimbledon	Liverpool	1-0
1989	Liverpool	Everton	3-2 (aet)
1990	Manchester U	Crystal Palace	1-0
		(after 3-3 draw, after extra time)	
1991	Tottenham H	Nottingham F	2-1 (aet)
1992	Liverpool	Sunderland	2-0
1993	Arsenal	Sheffield W	2-1 (aet)
		(after 1-1 draw, after extra time)	
1994	Manchester U	Chelsea	4-0
1995	Everton	Manchester U	1-0
1996	Manchester U	Liverpool	1-0
1997	Chelsea	Middlesbrough	2-0
1998	Arsenal	Newcastle U	2-0
1999	Manchester U	Newcastle U	2-0
2000	Chelsea	Aston Villa	1-0
2001	Liverpool	Arsenal	2-1

* *Won outright, but restored to the Football Association.*
† *A special trophy was awarded for third consecutive win.*

FA CUP WINS

Manchester U 10, Tottenham H 8, Arsenal 7, Aston Villa 7, Blackburn R 6, Liverpool 6, Newcastle U 6, Everton 5, The Wanderers 5, WBA 5, Bolton W 4, Manchester C 4, Sheffield U 4, Wolverhampton W 4, Chelsea 3, Sheffield W 3, West Ham U 3, Bury 2, Nottingham F 2, Old Etonians 2, Preston NE 2, Sunderland 2, Barnsley 1, Blackburn Olympic 1, Blackpool 1, Bradford C 1, Burnley 1, Cardiff C 1, Charlton Ath 1, Clapham R 1, Coventry C 1, Derby Co 1, Huddersfield T 1, Ipswich T 1, Leeds U 1, Notts Co 1, Old Carthusians 1, Oxford University 1, Portsmouth 1, Royal Engineers 1, Southampton 1, Wimbledon 1.

APPEARANCES IN FINALS

Manchester U 15, Arsenal 14, Newcastle U 13, Everton 12, Liverpool 12, Newcastle U 12, Aston Villa 10, WBA 10, Tottenham H 9, Blackburn R 8, Manchester C 8, Wolverhampton W 8, Bolton W 7, Preston NE 7, Chelsea 6, Old Etonians 6, Sheffield U 6, Sheffield W 6, Huddersfield T 5, *The Wanderers 5, Derby Co 4, Leeds U 4, Leicester C 4, Oxford University 4, Royal Engineers 4, Sunderland 4, West Ham U 4, Blackpool 3, Burnley 3, Nottingham F 3, Portsmouth 3, Southampton 3, Barnsley 2, Birmingham C 2, *Bury 2, Cardiff C 2, Charlton Ath 2, Clapham R 2, Notts Co 2, Queen's Park (Glasgow) 2, *Blackburn Olympic 1, *Bradford C 1, Brighton & HA 1, Bristol C 1, *Coventry C 1, Crystal Palace 1, Fulham 1, *Ipswich T 1, Luton T 4, Middlesbrough 1, *Old Carthusians 1, QPR 1, Watford 1, *Wimbledon 1.
* *Denotes undefeated.*

APPEARANCES IN SEMI-FINALS

Everton 23, Manchester U 22, Arsenal 21, Liverpool 21, Aston Villa 19, WBA 19, Tottenham H 17, Blackburn R 16, Newcastle U 16, Sheffield W 16, Chelsea 14, Wolverhampton W 14, Bolton W 13, Derby Co 13, Nottingham F 12, Sheffield U 12, Sunderland 11, Manchester C 10, Preston NE 10, Southampton 10, Birmingham C 9, Burnley 8, Leeds U 8, Leicester C 8, Huddersfield T 7, Old Etonians 6, Oxford University 6, West Ham U 6, Fulham 5, Notts Co 5, Portsmouth 5, The Wanderers 5, Luton T 4, Queen's Park (Glasgow) 4, Royal Engineers 4, Blackpool 3, Cardiff C 3, Clapham R 3, Ipswich T 3, Millwall 3, Norwich C 3, Old Carthusians 3, Oldham Ath 3, Stoke C 3, The Swifts 3, Watford 3, Barnsley 2, Blackburn Olympic 2, Bristol C 2, Bury 2, Charlton Ath 2, Grimsby T 2, Swindon T 2, Wimbledon 2, Bradford C 1, Brighton & HA 1, Cambridge University 1, Chesterfield 1, Coventry C 1, Crewe Alex 1, Crystal Palace (amateur club) 1, Darwen 1, Derby Junction 1, Glasgow R 1, Hull C 1, Marlow 1, Old Harrovians 1, Middlesbrough 1, Orient 1, Plymouth Arg 1, Port Vale 1, QPR 1, Reading 1, Shropshire W 1, Wycombe W 1, York C 1.

FA CUP 2000–2001
SPONSORED BY AXA

PRELIMINARY AND QUALIFYING ROUNDS

EXTRA PRELIMINARY ROUND

Brigg Town v Willington	3-0
Eccleshill United v Sheffield	2-3
South Shields v Garforth Town	2-1
Tow Law Town v St Helens Town	2-0
Squires Gate v West Auckland Town	1-2
Guisborough Town v Chadderton	1-1, 1-4
Armthorpe Welfare v Penrith	0-1
Pelsall Villa v Kidsgrove Athletic	1-1, 3-1
Holbeach United v Halesowen Harriers	1-0
Royston Town v Newmarket Town	0-5
Harringey Borough v Concord Rangers	4-1
Raunds Town v Soham Town Rangers	2-3
Buckingham Town v Halstead Town	4-1
Lowestoft Town v Fakenham Town	2-3
Yate Town v Brislington	0-3
Melksham Town v Falmouth Town	1-0
Wimbourne Town v Bridport	2-0

PRELIMINARY ROUND

Louth United v North Ferriby United	1-5
Witton Albion v Oldham Town	4-3
Trafford v Flixton	1-0
Marske United v South Shields	3-1
Consett v Hallam	2-1
Yorkshire Amateur v Parkgate	5-0
Workington v Farsley Celtic	0-1
Bradford (Park Avenue) v Brandon United	1-0
Kennek Ryhope CA v Salford City	0-5
Whitley Bay v Ashington	2-1
Gretna v Ramsbottom United	0-0, 2-3
Glasshoughton Welfare v West Auckland Town	0-2
Billingham Synthonia v Brigg Town	1-1, 0-1
Goole v Jarrow Roofing Boldon CA	3-0
Castleton Gabriels v Harrogate Railway	2-3
Tow Law Town v Newcastle Blue Star	2-2, 1-2
Chadderton v Hebburn	2-3
Prescot Cables v Bedlington Terriers	0-2
Maine Road v Easington Colliery	2-2, 2-3
Bacup Borough v Harrogate Town	0-4
Shotton Comrades v Atherton LR	1-2
Clitheroe v Shildon	4-1
Mossley v Hatfield Main	4-1
Winsford United v Selby Town	1-1, 0-2
Durham City v Thackley	4-0
Skelmersdale United v Guiseley	1-1, 0-4
Brodsworth v Blackpool Mechanics	2-2
(Blackpool Mechanics protested – Brodsworth fielded four substitutes)	
Horden CW v Crook Town	2-3
Darwen v Penrith	2-2, 1-0
Dunston FB v Curzon Ashton	2-0
Great Harwood Town v North Allerton Town	2-0
Radcliffe Borough v Rossington Main	3-1
Denaby United v Warrington Town	0-2
Ossett Town v Chorley	0-1
Atherton Collieries v Morpeth Town	2-0
Evenwood Town v Tadcaster Albion	1-2
Woodleigh Sports v Ashton United	0-3
Sheffield v Rossendale United	2-1
Seaham Red Star v Pontefract Collieries	3-1
Peterlee Newtown v Fleetwood Freeport	4-4, 0-3
Thornaby v Esh Winning	4-0
Abbey Hey v Stocksbridge Park Steels	1-2
Liversedge v Chester-Le-Street Town	1-1, 3-0
Billingham Town v Ossett Albion	2-0
Cheadle Town v Bridlington Town	0-1
Kendal Town v Pickering Town	3-1
Boston Town v Leek CSOB	2-3
Spalding United v Glossop North End	4-0
Bilston Town v Sandwell Borough	3-0
Staveley MW v Belper Town	1-2
Gedling Town v Boldmere St Michaels	5-1
Oadby Town v Willenhall Town	2-1
Redditch United v Arnold Town	3-2
Newcastle Town v Buxton	2-0
Stamford v Rushall Olympic	2-0

Holbeach United v Glapwell	2-1
Atherstone United v Pelsall Villa	2-1
Bourne Town v Shepshed Dynamo	1-2
Corby Town v Knypersley Victoria	1-0
Cradley Town v Paget Rangers	1-2
Gresley Rovers v Matlock Town	1-1, 1-4
Racing Club Warwick v Stourport Swifts	1-2
West Midlands Police v Bedworth United	1-1, 0-2
Eastwood Town v Rocester	3-1
Hinckley United v Nantwich Town	7-0
Stapenhill v Bridgnorth Town	1-0
Stratford Town v Stafford Town	1-1, 0-0
Stafford Town won 5-4 on penalties.	
Blakenall v Oldbury United	0-1
Borrowash Victoria v Grantham Town	0-3
Barwell v Lincoln United	0-0, 4-2
Blackstone v Shifnal Town	4-1
Congleton Town v Wednesfield	0-0, 1-0
Solihull Borough v Mickelover Sports	2-1
Stourbridge v Rugby United	0-0, 2-2
Stourbridge won 6-5 on penalties.	
Chasetown v Alfreton Town	0-1
Sutton Coldfield Town v Bromsgrove Rovers	1-1, 2-3
Saffron Walden Town v Histon	1-2
Tiptree United v Buckingham Town	6-2
Flackwell Heath v Bishop's Stortford	0-2
Wroxham v Ford United	0-3
Felixstowe & Walton United v Waltham Abbey	2-3
Edgware Town v Stowmarket Town	2-2, 0-1
Chelmsford City v Sawbridgeworth Town	3-1
Northampton Spencer v Southall	0-0, 2-0
Basildon United withdrew v Yeading w.o.	
Boreham Wood v Great Wakering Rovers	3-0
Bugbrooke St Michaels v Newmarket Town	0-3
Potters Bar Town v Leighton Town	2-1
Coggenhoe United v Desborough Town	4-1
Bowers United v Bedford United	1-1, 1-3
Chalfont St Peter v Harwich & Parkeston	1-1, 1-1
Harwich & Parkeston won 4-3 on penalties.	
Ware v Yaxley	3-2
Romford v Hemel Hempstead Town	1-6
Wingate & Finchley v Wivenhoe Town	2-1
Woodbridge Town v Marlow	3-0
Baldock Town v Ruislip Manor	2-0
Uxbridge v Holmer Green	6-1
Barking v Harringey Borough	2-1
Wotton Blue Cross v London Colney	2-2, 2-2
London Colney won 4-2 on penalties.	
Ilford v Mildenhall Town	1-4
Wellingborough Town v Tring Town	0-0, 1-2
Great Yarmouth Town v Kempston Rovers	4-1
Braintree Town v Banbury United	6-0
Witney Town v Beaconsfield SYCOB	0-3
Harlow Town v Diss Town	2-3
Burnham Ramblers v Burnham	1-0
Hanwell Town v Stotfold	1-2
Hullbridge Sports v Welwyn Garden City	0-1
Witham Town v Bedford Town	0-3
Southend Manor v AFC Sudbury	1-4
St Neots Town v Milton Keynes City	5-0
Tilbury v Fakenham Town	1-0
Rothwell Town v Northwood	0-2
Leyton Pennant v East Thurrock United	2-2, 0-3
Eynesbury Rovers v Stewarts & Lloyds	2-4
Arlesey Town v Aveley	7-1
Brackley Town v Wealdstone	0-3
Long Buckby v Clapton	0-1
Ford Sports Daventry v Hertford Town	1-1, 3-2
Maldon Town v Bury Town	3-3, 2-0
Berkhamsted Town v Hornchurch	4-1
Wembley v Gorleston	1-1
(Wembley protested – Gorleston played an ineligible player; tie awarded to Wembley)	
Potton United v Ely City	0-2
Ipswich Wanderers v Wisbech Town	3-1
Brentford v Staines Town	2-4
Brook House v Kingsbury Town	6-0
Cheshunt v Clacton Town	2-2, 3-2

AFC Wallingford v Worboys Town	2-1
Hoddesdon Town v St Margaretsbury	1-2
Barton Rovers v Soham Town Rangers	0-2
Moneyfields v Epsom & Ewell	0-2
Sandhurst Town v Andover	0-4
Chertsey Town v Abingdon Town	3-1
Thatcham Town v Corinthian Casuals	2-0
Eastbourne Town v Selsey	1-1, 1-3
Camberley Town v Saltdean United	0-1
Bashley v North Leigh	3-0
Littlehampton Town v Peacehaven & Telscombe	2-0
Beckenham Town v Aylesbury United	0-1
Walton & Hersham v Croydon Athletic	3-1
Chichester City United v Abingdon United	2-2, 1-2
Lordswood v Horsham	1-3
Cowes Sports v Cray Wanderers	1-0
Burgess Hill Town v Brockenhurst	4-1
Banstead Athletic v Farnham Town	4-0
St Leonards v Three Bridges	1-1, 3-2
Lewes v Dorking	3-0
Tooting & Mitcham United v Worthing	3-0
Southwick v Langney Sports	0-5
Viking Greenford v Merstham	1-4
Sittingbourne v Godalming & Guildford	2-0
Whitchurch United v AFC Newbury	0-2
Thamesmead Town v Herne Bay	1-2
Greenwich Borough v Hythe United	1-0

(Hythe United protested – Greenwich Borough fielded ineligible players; tie awarded to Hythe United)

Shoreham v Oxford City	1-10
Erith Town v Hassocks	2-2, 1-3
Ashford Town v Walton Casuals	4-1
Wokingham Town v Bedfont	0-3
Dartford v Deal Town	3-1
Chipstead v Ashford Town (Middlesex)	0-1
Fareham Town v Ringmer	1-1, 2-0
Gosport Borough v Slade Green	1-1, 2-1
Windsor & Eton v Whitstable Town	1-0
Portsmouth Royal Navy v Ash United	1-4
Reading Town v Lancing	2-0
Newport (IW) v Arundel	5-2
Metropolitan Police v Leatherhead	2-1
Hungerford Town v Bromley	0-2
East Preston v Redhill	1-0
Tunbridge Wells v VCD Athletic	1-2
Carterton Town v Thame United	1-1, 0-0

Carterton Town 4-1 on penalties.

Hillingdon Borough v Bracknell Town	1-3
Eastbourne United v Egham Town	1-4
Horsham YMCA v Cobham	2-0
Wick v Erith & Belvedere	1-0
Tonbridge Angels v Eastleigh	0-0, 1-0
Lymington & New Milton v Didcot Town	2-1
Hailsham Town v Whyteleafe	1-2
Chatham Town v Molesey	3-1
Chessington & Hook United v Hastings Town	1-6
Bognor Regis Town v Cove	2-3
BAT Sports v Sheppey United	0-0, 2-2

Sheppey United won 5-1 on penalties.

Fleet Town v Ramsgate	1-0
Whitehawk v AFC Totton	0-3
Paulton Rovers v Street	4-0
Westbury United v Bristol Manor Farm	1-3
Downton v Bournemouth	4-0
Bemerton Heath Harlequins v Tiverton Town	0-4
Cinderford Town v Bridgwater Town	0-3
Devizes Town v Melksham Town	1-1, 1-0
Chippenham Town v St Blazey	1-1, 3-0
Tuffley Rovers v Taunton Town	4-1
Brislington v Calne Town	3-2
Weston-Super-Mare v Wimbourne Town	2-1
Welton Rovers v Shortwood United	1-1, 0-1
Elmore v Barnstaple Town	3-4
Frome Town v Bishop Sutton	2-0
Evesham United v Bideford	3-1
Odd Down v Gloucester City	0-2
Cirencester Town v Minehead Town	1-0
Mangotsfield United v Christchurch	4-2
Backwell United v Torrington	5-2

FIRST QUALIFYING ROUND

Warrington Town v Clitheroe	0-2
Tadcaster Albion v Horden CW	0-1
Stocksbridge Park Steels v Darwen	1-0
Harrogate Railway v Bedlington Terriers	1-5
West Auckland Town v Selby Town	3-1
Guiseley v Farsley Celtic	0-1
Thornaby v Marske United	0-1
Seaham Red Star v Great Harwood Town	7-0
Easington Colliery v Yorkshire Amateur	2-1
Blackpool Mechanics v Radcliffe Borough	0-1
Goole v Ramsbottom United	2-1
Durham City v Newcastle Blue Star	3-1
Chorley v Trafford	3-2
North Ferriby United v Ashton United	2-2, 3-4
Witton Albion v Atherton Collieries	1-0
Mossley v Hebburn	2-0
Harrogate Town v Billingham Town	0-2
Dunston FB v Fleetwood Freeport	1-2
Atherton LR v Sheffield	1-5
Whitley Bay v Consett	3-1
Brigg Town v Liversedge	5-1
Bradford (Park Avenue) v Salford City	0-1
Bridlington Town v Kendal Town	3-1
Redditch United v Belper Town	2-3
Hinckley United v Gedling Town	3-0
Bromsgrove Rovers v Oldbury United	1-1, 0-2
Bilston Town v Solihull Borough	1-5
Grantham Town v Bedworth United	3-1
Paget Rangers v Stafford Town	0-2
Atherstone United v Stourport Swifts	0-1
Stourbridge v Stamford	2-3
Leek CSOB v Holbeach United	1-1, 1-3
Stapenhill v Barwell	1-1, 1-5
Shepshed Dynamo v Oadby Town	4-2
Newcastle Town v Corby Town	2-0
Congleton Town v Eastwood Town	4-3
Blackstone v Matlock Town	2-3
Alfreton Town v Spalding United	3-2
Coggenhoe United v Maldon Town	2-3
Northampton Spencer v Mildenhall Town	0-2
Waltham Abbey v St Neots Town	4-2
Wealdstone v Ware	4-0
Stewarts & Lloyds v Baldock Town	1-3
Ford United v Welwyn Garden City	3-0
Tilbury v Chelmsford City	1-3
Stotfold v London Colney	1-1, 3-2
Uxbridge v Potters Bar Town	5-1
Braintree Town v Clapton	5-0
St Margaretsbury v Boreham Wood	1-0
Soham Town Rangers v Ford Sports Daventry	3-1
Ely City v Tring Town	2-2, 2-3
Newmarket Town v Wingate & Finchley	3-3, 1-4
Yeading v Beaconsfield SYCOB	2-3
Arlesey Town v Histon	1-2
Bedford Town v Staines Town	3-1
Woodbridge Town v Burnham Ramblers	3-1
AFC Sudbury v Brook House	5-1
Barking v Berkhamsted Town	2-3
Ipswich Wanderers v Bedford United	1-0
Hemel Hempstead Town v Cheshunt	3-0
Diss Town v Bishop's Stortford	0-5
East Thurrock United v Northwood	1-4
Tiptree United v Stowmarket Town	1-3
Harwich & Parkeston v AFC Wallingford	1-2
Wembley v Great Yarmouth Town	2-0
Cowes Sports v Horsham YMCA	1-1, 0-6
Littlehampton Town v Hythe United	1-1, 1-0
Selsey v Reading Town	4-0
Carterton Town v St Leonards	3-1
East Preston v Merstham	3-3, 1-3
Thatcham Town v Gosport Borough	1-1, 1-1

Thatcham Town won 3-2 on penalties.

Newport (IW) v Bashley	1-1, 2-0
Fareham Town v Herne Bay	0-0, 1-2
Sittingbourne v Horsham	0-3
Ashford Town v Bracknell Town	1-2
Fleet Town v Walton & Hersham	5-1
AFC Totton v Egham Town	0-0, 3-1
Lymington & New Milton v Oxford City	0-1
Abingdon United v Tooting & Mitcham United	4-1
Aylesbury United v Bedfont	4-3
VCD Athletic v Epsom & Ewell	4-4, 0-2
Windsor & Eton v Chatham Town	1-0
Langney Sports v Ashford Town (Middlesex)	3-2
Ash United v Hastings Town	2-4
AFC Newbury v Wick	2-0
Whyteleafe v Burgess Hill Town	4-0
Lewes v Cove	2-2, 2-1
Dartford v Chertsey Town	1-1, 2-0
Bromley v Metropolitan Police	1-2
Andover v Saltdean United	2-3
Banstead Athletic v Sheppey United	3-1
Tonbridge Angels v Hassocks	3-0
Weston-Super-Mare v Shortwood United	0-0, 2-3
Bridgwater Town v Downton	2-1
Tuffley Rovers v Chippenham Town	0-1
Backwell United v Devizes Town	1-2
Gloucester City v Evesham United	2-1

Barnstaple Town v Cirencester Town	1-5
Brislington v Paulton Rovers	2-3
Mangotsfield United v Frome Town	4-2
Tiverton Town v Bristol Manor Farm	1-0
(Tie ordered to be replayed)	4-1

SECOND QUALIFYING ROUND

Emley v Salford City	3-1
Gateshead v Bishop Auckland	2-1
Stalybridge Celtic v Blyth Spartans	2-0
Witton Albion v Fleetwood Freeport	1-1, 2-1
Durham City v Accrington Stanley	2-2, 2-4
Bamber Bridge v Marske United	1-1, 2-0
Spennymoor United v Bedlington Terriers	0-3
Marine v Colwyn Bay	4-3
Sheffield v Farsley Celtic	2-1
Barrow v Droylsden	3-0
Ashton United v Goole	1-1, 3-2
Altrincham v Mossley	0-3
Frickley Athletic v Stocksbridge Park Steels	1-0
Clitheroe v Hyde United	1-2
Horden CW v Gainsborough Trinity	1-3
Bridlington Town v Billingham Town	1-1, 1-3
Whitley Bay v Worksop Town	2-1
Burscough v Runcorn	2-1
Brigg Town v Lancaster City	2-2, 4-3
Radcliffe Borough v West Auckland Town	4-1
Chorley v Whitby Town	0-2
Seaham Red Star v Easington Colliery	0-3
Alfreton Town v Hinckley United	1-1, 1-2
Holbeach United v Belper Town	1-3
Oldbury United v Stourport Swifts	2-3
Stamford v Tamworth	1-1, 1-1
Tamworth won 3-2 on penalties.	
Stafford Town v Moor Green	2-1
Shepshed Dynamo v Ilkeston Town	0-3
Hucknall Town v Congleton Town	4-0
Barwell v Grantham Town	0-3
Matlock Town v Kings Lynn	1-2
Solihull Borough v Stafford Rangers	1-1, 0-0
Stafford Rangers won 4-3 on penalties.	
Halesowen Town v Burton Albion	0-2
Newcastle Town v Leek Town	1-1, 2-3
Histon v Bishop's Stortford	1-2
Hendon v St Margaretsbury	3-2
Ford United v Soham Town Rangers	3-1
Heybridge Swifts v AFC Sudbury	1-1, 2-3
Chesham United v AFC Wallingford	3-2
Hitchin Town v Maidenhead United	1-1, 1-1
Maidenhead United won 7-6 on penalties.	
Cambridge City v Stotfold	3-0
Chelmsford City v Grays Athletic	1-1, 1-2
Purfleet v Ipswich Wanderers	3-1
Canvey Island v Braintree Town	1-1, 3-2
Hemel Hempstead Town v Northwood	3-4
Mildenhall Town v Beaconsfield SYCOB	3-0
Harrow Borough v Tring Town	3-0
Stowmarket Town v Wealdstone	1-2
Woodbridge Town v Wembley	0-0, 4-1
Baldock Town v St Albans City	0-0, 2-1
Uxbridge v Berkhamsted Town	3-2
Waltham Abbey v Maldon Town	1-3
Billericay Town v Wingate & Finchley	5-1
Bedford Town v Enfield	0-0, 1-1
Enfield won 4-3 on penalties.	
Farnborough Town v Oxford City	3-3, 2-1
Fisher Athletic v Newport (IW)	4-2
Dartford v Abingdon United	3-2
Windsor & Eton v Hampton & Richmond Borough	0-3
Carshalton Athletic v Croydon	1-1, 2-2
Croydon won 5-3 on penalties.	
Margate v Banstead Athletic	0-1
Herne Bay v Aylesbury United	0-5
Carterton Town v Havant & Waterlooville	1-4
Saltdean United v AFC Totton	4-2
Tonbridge Angels v Slough Town	2-0
Crawley Town v Aldershot Town	1-2
Gravesend & Northfleet v AFC Newbury	4-0
Lewes v Langney Sports	2-0
Fleet Town v Thatcham Town	1-2
Whyteleafe v Horsham YMCA	2-1
Metropolitan Police v Welling United	1-4
Horsham v Epsom & Ewell	5-1
Folkestone Invicta v Hastings Town	1-1, 0-2
Bracknell Town v Merstham	3-1
Littlehampton Town v Sutton United	0-5
Selsey v Dulwich Hamlet	1-2
Basingstoke Town v Bath City	1-1, 0-2
Gloucester City v Chippenham Town	1-1, 5-3

Mangotsfield United v Paulton Rovers	4-2
Worcester City v Cirencester Town	2-1
Newport County v Merthyr Tydfil	0-4
Clevedon v Salisbury City	2-4
Tiverton Town v Shortwood United	2-0
Weymouth v Dorchester Town	0-1
Devizes Town v Bridgwater Town	2-1

THIRD QUALIFYING ROUND

Sheffield v Ashton United	3-0
Marine v Radcliffe Borough	0-2
Mossley v Frickley Athletic	1-1, 0-3
Stalybridge Celtic v Billingham Town	1-1, 0-3
Hyde United v Brigg Town	2-1
Witton Albion v Burscough	0-0, 1-6
Bamber Bridge v Gateshead	1-1, 1-3
Emley v Barrow	1-2
Bedlington Terriers v Accrington Stanley	5-2
Easington Colliery v Whitby Town	1-0
Gainsborough Trinity v Whitley Bay	0-0, 0-2
AFC Sudbury v Leek Town	1-1, 2-1
Harrow Borough v Stafford Town	0-0, 3-1
Mildenhall Town v Grays Athletic	0-2
Purfleet v Grantham Town	2-2, 0-1
Bishop's Stortford v Billericay Town	1-2
Enfield v Stourport Swifts	3-1
Stafford Rangers v Chesham United	2-0
Wealdstone v Belper Town	2-3
Hendon v Ford United	2-1
Canvey Island v Kings Lynn	2-1
Tamworth v Burton Albion	1-1, 1-3
Ilkeston Town v Baldock Town	3-0
Northwood v Uxbridge	5-1
Cambridge City v Maldon Town	3-2
Hucknall Town v Maidenhead United	3-2
Woodbridge Town v Hinckley United	0-2
Bracknell Town v Banstead Athletic	1-0
Welling United v Tonbridge Angels	1-0
Hastings Town v Horsham	2-3
Saltdean United v Devizes Town	1-2
Bath City v Sutton United	3-0
Tiverton Town v Gloucester City	1-3
Dartford v Havant & Waterlooville	0-4
Fisher Athletic v Aldershot Town	1-2
Merthyr Tydfil v Hampton & Richmond Borough	0-3
Farnborough Town v Aylesbury United	0-2
Worcester City v Thatcham Town	3-1
Gravesend & Northfleet v Croydon	4-1
Dulwich Hamlet v Lewes	1-1, 0-0
Dulwich Hamlet won 3-1 on penalties.	
Dorchester Town v Salisbury City	4-3
Whyteleafe v Mangotsfield United	1-3

FOURTH QUALIFYING ROUND

Gateshead v Billingham Town	4-2
Easington Colliery v Chester City	0-2
Barrow v Whitley Bay	6-1
Burscough v Radcliffe Borough	1-1, 1-2
Sheffield v Northwich Victoria	1-5
Bedlington Terriers v Morecambe	1-3
Scarborough v Leigh RMI	3-4
Doncaster Rovers v Southport	2-2, 0-1
Frickley Athletic v Hyde United	1-0
Boston United v Burton Albion	1-1, 2-3
Hinckley United v Telford United	1-1, 1-4
Nuneaton Borough v Stevenage Borough	1-1, 2-1
Hucknall Town v Ilkeston Town	0-1
Harrow Borough v Enfield	2-1
Hendon v Dagenham & Redbridge	1-3
Rushden & Diamonds v Grantham Town	5-4
Cambridge City v Canvey Island	0-2
Belper Town v AFC Sudbury	2-3
Billericay Town v Hednesford Town	0-0, 1-2
Northwood v Grays Athletic	1-1, 0-1
Chesham United v Kettering Town	0-2
Forest Green Rovers v Bath City	3-1
Havant & Waterlooville v Gloucester City	1-1, 3-2
Aylesbury United v Bracknell Town	0-1
Gravesend & Northfleet v Mangotsfield United	4-0
Dorchester Town v Welling United	1-1, 4-2
Yeovil Town v Horsham	1-1, 2-0
Hayes v Dulwich Hamlet	4-2
Aldershot Town v Dover Athletic	1-0
Kingstonian v Devizes Town	5-2
Hampton & Richmond Borough v Worcester City	5-0
Woking v Hereford United	1-0

FA CUP 2000–2001
SPONSORED BY AXA

COMPETITION PROPER

FIRST ROUND

17 NOV

Luton T (0) 1 *(George 55)*
Rushden & D (0) 0   5771
Luton T: Abbey; Boyce, Taylor, Helin, Watts, Karlsen, George, McLaren, Stein (Thomson), Fraser, Spring.
Rushden & D: Turley; Mustafa, Underwood, Mills (Wormull), Rodwell, Warburton, Peters (Setchell), Brady, Jackson, Sigere, Burgess.

18 NOV

Aldershot T (1) 2 *(Abbott 26 (pen), 88)*
Brighton & HA (2) 6 *(Carpenter 2, Watson 43 (pen), 60 (pen), Oatway 53, Zamora 75, Wicks 77)*   7500
Aldershot T: Pape; Protheroe, Chewins, Crossley (Adedeji), Blake, Ullathorne (Browne), Graham, Pye (Bentley), Abbott, Andrews, Gell.
Brighton & HA: Kuipers; Watson, Mayo, Cullip, Wicks, Carpenter (Melton), Zamora, Rogers (Steele), Hart, Oatway, Jones (Brooker).

Barnet (0) 2 *(Richards 84, Currie 90)*
Hampton & Richmond B (1) 1 *(Maskell 21)*   2340
Barnet: Naisbitt; Stockley, Sawyers (Purser), Niven, Heald, Arber, Currie, Doolan, Richards, Cottee (Gledhill), Toms (Brown).
Hampton & Richmond B: Talbot; Flitter, Wood, Burton (Girvan), Barnsby, Shaw, Manuella, Green, Williams (Russell), Maskell, Griffiths.

Barrow (0) 0
Leyton Orient (0) 2 *(Griffiths 52, Watts 73)*   3608
Barrow: Bishop; Warren, Maxfield, Hume, Waller, Anthony, Housham, Ellison (Roberts D), Peverell, Bullimore, Bennett (Doherty).
Leyton Orient: Bayes; Joseph, Lockwood, McGhee, Smith, Harris, Walschaerts (Castle), Shorey (Downer), Tate (Watts), Griffiths, Brkovic.

Blackpool (2) 3 *(Murphy J 8, Ormerod 45, 66)*
Telford U (0) 1 *(Martindale 65)*   2780
Blackpool: Kennedy; Coid, Hills, O'Connor, Hughes, Reid, Collins, Simpson (Clarkson), Ormerod (Newell), Murphy J, Wellens (Bushell).
Telford U: Price; Travis (Malkin) (Murphy), Davies, Moore, Gale, Bentley, Preece, Jobling, Martindale, Edwards, Palmer.

Bournemouth (0) 2 *(Elliott 54, Hayter 76)*
Swansea C (0) 0   3422
Bournemouth: Stewart; Bernard, Purches, Howe, Day (O'Connor), Tindall, Jorgensen (Eribenne), Elliott, Hayter, Fletcher S, Hughes.
Swansea C: Freestone; Jones S, Howard, Cusack, Smith, Bound, Jenkins (Casey), Thomas, Watkin, Romo (Savarese), Roberts (Keegan).

Brentford (0) 1 *(Pinamonte 90)*
Kingstonian (0) 3 *(Pitcher 46, Winston 62, 77)*   3809
Brentford: Gottskalksson; Gibbs, Rowlands, Mahon, Quinn, Marshall, Ingimarsson, Evans (Pinamonte), Owusu, Scott, Partridge (Williams).
Kingstonian: Farrelly; Beard, Luckett, Allan D, Saunders, Harris, Patterson, Pitcher, Winston (Green), Wingfield (Bass), Akuamoah.

Bury (0) 1 *(Daws 55)*
Northwich Vic (0) 1 *(Fletcher 72)*   2844
Bury: Kenny; Unsworth, Swailes D, Daws, Swailes C, Redmond, Billy, Reid, Barnes, Bhutia (Jarrett), Littlejohn.
Northwich Vic: Key; Bailey, Barnard, Davis, Robertson, Burke, Norris, Simpson, Fletcher, Mike, Devlin.

Cambridge U (1) 2 *(Axeldal 6, Hansen 83)*
Rochdale (1) 1 *(Platt 31)*   3142
Cambridge U: Perez; Joseph, Ashbee, Duncan, McAnespie, Mustoe, Wanless, Taylor, Youngs, Axeldal (Hansen), Russell.
Rochdale: Edwards; Evans, Todd, Ware, Hill, Monington, Ford (Lancashire), Jones, Platt, Oliver (Ellis), Hadland (Davies).

Carlisle U (3) 5 *(Stevens 14, 23, 31, 68, Dobie 69)*
Woking (0) 1 *(West 72)*   2647
Carlisle U: Glennon; Birch, Maddison, Whitehead, Winstanley, Prokas, Connelly, Stevens (Heggs), Dobie, Hemmings (Halliday), Galloway (Thurston).
Woking: Matassa; Wye S, Hollingdale, West, Smith S, Pitman, Hayfield, Roddis, Brown K (Perkins), Randall (Ruggles), Griffin (Teague).

Cheltenham T (1) 4 *(Howells 31, Grayson 79, 84, Alsop 88)*
Shrewsbury T (1) 1 *(Freestone 34)*   3210
Cheltenham T: Book; Duff, McCann, Banks, Freeman (Alsop), Howarth, Howells, Devaney (Milton), Grayson, McAuley (Jackson), Yates.
Shrewsbury T: Dunbavin; Davidson, Jenkins, Hughes, Redmile, Keister (Wilding), Peer, Jagielka, Freestone (Brown), Jemson, Aiston (Lowe).

Chester C (0) 1 *(Wright 78)*
Plymouth Arg (0) 1 *(Peake 87)*   2393
Chester C: Brown; Fisher (Ruscoe) (Gaunt), Doughty, Lancaster, Ruffer, Beesley P, Carden, Blackburn, Beesley M (Wright), Whitehall, Porter.
Plymouth Arg: Hodges; Adams (Wills), Beswetherick, Leadbitter, Wotton, Taylor, Fleming, Barlow, Guinan (Stonebridge), McGregor, Phillips M (Peake).

Chesterfield (0) 0
Bristol C (0) 1 *(Thorpe 55)*   5210
Chesterfield: Pollitt; Simpkins (D'Auria), Edwards, Tutill, Blatherwick, Breckin, Ebdon, Williams R, Willis (Jones), Beckett, Parrish.
Bristol C: Phillips; Hill, Bell, Clist (Burnell), Millen, Carey, Murray, Brown A, Peacock, Thorpe (Beadle), Tinnion.

Dagenham & Redbridge (1) 3 *(Keen 16, Watts 61 (og), Jones 71)*
Hayes (1) 1 *(Boylan 45)*   1150
Dagenham & Redbridge: Roberts; Cole, Vickers, Keen, Matthews, Broome, Janney, Terry (Forbes), Broughton (Shipp), McDougald (Cobb), Jones.
Hayes: Hodgson M; Bezhadi (Barnes), Flynn, Watts, Coppard, Pluck, McKimm, Moore, Stevens (Telemarque), Boylan (Preston), Molesley.

Darlington (1) 6 *(Naylor 31, 64, 76, Hodgson 51, 87, Kyle 55)*
AFC Sudbury (1) 1 *(Claydon 27)*   2462
Darlington: Collett; Reed, Himsworth, Liddle, Aspin (Kilty), Gray, Hodgson, Kyle, Naylor, Butler T, Atkinson (Hjorth).
AFC Sudbury: Walton; Stratton (Smiles), Cornish, Tracey, Sims (Hyde), Rayner, Cheetham, Devereux B, Devereux R, Claydon, Betson (Day).

Forest Green R (0) 0
Morecambe (1) 3 *(Hatswell 40 (og), Norman 65,*
Thompson 81) 1023
Forest Green R: Perrin; Cousins, Hatswell, Norton, Clark,
Burns (Campbell), Daley, Drysdale, Foster (Bailey),
Kilgour (Bennett), Slater.
Morecambe: Smith; Fensome, Lyons, McKearney,
Hardiker, Walters (Knowles), Thompson, Drummond,
Dowe (Quayle), Norman, Black.

Halifax T (0) 0
Gateshead (1) 2 *(Hall 45, Dalton 84)* 1902
Halifax T: Butler L; Wilder, Murphy, Rezai (Middleton),
Stoneman, Hawe, Wainwright, Kerrigan, Jones,
Richards, Thompson (Herbert).
Gateshead: Swan; Pepper, Kitchen S, Watson R, Hall,
Talbot, Proudlock (Bates), Bowey, Dalton, Bean,
McAlindon (Bates), Preen (Edgcumbe).

Havant & Waterlooville (1) 1 *(Wood 4)*
Southport (1) 2 *(Stuart 45, Arnold 74)* 1118
Havant & Waterlooville: Nicholls; Connolly, Cook,
McDonald, Gale, Daish, Wood (Jones), Hambley,
O'Rourke (Blake), Taylor, Anstey (Champion).
Southport: Dickinson; Clark, Stuart, Teale, Guyett,
Bolland, Grayston, Gouck, Arnold, Parke, Furlong
(Elam).

Hednesford T (1) 2 *(Pointon 19, Davis 58)*
Oldham Ath (2) 4 *(Duxbury 4, Dudley 41, Corazzin 46,*
Tipton 90) 2053
Hednesford T: Gayle; Robinson, Pointon, Lake, Bradley,
Cooper (Owen), Bonsall (Colkin), Sedgemore, Davis,
Bagshaw (Norbury), Airdrie.
Oldham Ath: Kelly; McNiven, Innes (Holt), Garnett,
Rickers, Duxbury (Salt), Dudley (Tipton), Carss, Allott,
Corazzin, Eyres.

Kettering T (0) 0
Hull C (0) 0 2831
Kettering T: Bowling; Inman, Adams (Watkins), Perkins,
McNamara, Norman, Codner, Brown, Lenagh, Hudson,
Fisher.
Hull C: Musselwhite; Swales, Harper, Brightwell, Perry,
Greaves, Brabin, Eyre, Brown, Marcelle, Philpott.

Kidderminster H (0) 0
Burton Albion (0) 0 3384
Kidderminster H: Brock; Clarkson, Stamps, Smith,
Hinton, Shail, Bennett (Hadley), Horne, Foster, Bird
(Bogie), Ducros.
Burton Albion: Duke; Kavanagh, Blount, Wassall,
Henshaw, Stride, Clough, Glasser, Starbuck, Webster,
Anderson.

Lincoln C (3) 4 *(Gain 7, Peacock 16, Bere 43 (og),*
Gordon 60)
Bracknell T (0) 0 2387
Lincoln C: Marriott; Smith, Mayo, Barnett J, Brown,
Finnigan, Schofield (Pinkney), Peacock, Gordon
(Cameron), Thorpe (Battersby), Gain.
Bracknell T: Cobby; Edwards, Brown, Pennicott-Bowen
(Page), Bere, Skerritt, Franks (Havermans), Osgood,
Smith, Oliphant, Holzman (Parker).

Macclesfield T (0) 0
Oxford U (0) 1 *(Gray 58)* 2141
Macclesfield T: Martin; Abbey (Durkan), Hitchen,
Adams, Tinson, O'Neill, Askey (Whitehead),
Sedgemore, Barker, Glover, Munroe (Keen).
Oxford U: Knight; Robertson, Brown, Fear, Richardson,
Linighan, Lilley, Gray, Murphy, Jarman, Beauchamp.

Mansfield T (0) 1 *(Greenacre 70 (pen))*
Peterborough U (1) 1 *(Farrell 37)* 3257
Mansfield T: Mimms; Andrews, Jervis (Williamson),
Hassell, Hicks, Robinson, Corden (Bacon), Williams
(Bradley), Boulding, Blake, Greenacre.
Peterborough U: Tiler; Hooper, Drury, Forsyth, Rea,
Edwards, Farrell, Oldfield, Clarke, Lee, McKenzie
(Shields).

Northampton T (1) 4 *(Frain 19, Forrester 56, 81, Hunt 83)*
Frickley Ath (0) 0 3896
Northampton T: Welch; Savage (Hodge) (Gabbiadini),
Frain (Hughes), Sampson, Green, Hope, Howard, Hunt,
Forrester, Hargreaves, Spedding.
Frickley Ath: Mark Wilkinson; Hilton, Jones, West,
Lafferty, Hanby, Morris, Price, Hurst, Duffty (Matt
Wilkinson), Edge (Brookes).

Reading (1) 4 *(Hodges 16, Cureton 60, Butler 72,*
Jones 87)
Grays Ath (0) 0 5643
Reading: Whitehead; Gray, Newman, Viveash, Mackie,
Parkinson, Hodges (McIntyre), Jones, Cureton, Butler,
Igoe (Gamble).
Grays Ath: Desborough; Risley, Taylor, Mosley,
O'Sullivan (Blaney), Dickinson, Feddes, Hazel
(Snowshill), Wright, Wallace (Nestling), Hayzelden.

Scunthorpe U (1) 3 *(Ipoua 38, 77, 88)*
Hartlepool U (1) 1 *(Midgley 13)* 3552
Scunthorpe U: Evans; Jackson, Dawson, Stanton, Wilcox,
Larusson, Hodges (Brough), Sheldon, Ipoua, Torpey,
Calvo-Garcia.
Hartlepool U: Williams; Arnison, Shilton, Strodder,
Westwood, Clark, Barron, Miller, Midgley, Henderson,
Stephenson (Boyd).

Stoke C (0) 0
Nuneaton B (0) 0 8437
Stoke C: Muggleton; Hansson (Clarke), Petty, Thomas,
Mohan, Gunnarsson, Gudjonsson, Kavanagh,
Lightbourne (Dadason), Thorne, Thordarson
(O'Connor).
Nuneaton B: MacKenzie; Sykes, Love, Crowley, Weaver,
Angus, Wray (Taylor), Charles, McGregor (Williams B),
King, Francis.

Swindon T (1) 4 *(Willis 44, Williams M 63, Howe 79,*
Young 88)
Ilkeston T (0) 1 *(Cox 87)* 4406
Swindon T: Mildenhall; Cobian (Duke), Davis,
O'Halloran, Reeves, Willis, Invincible (Young), Howe,
Williams M (Alexander), Van der Linden, Woan.
Ilkeston T: Love; Gould, Whitehead, Timons, Middleton,
Challinor, Knapper, Clifford, Helliwell I (Clark),
Kiwomya (Todd), Eshelby (Cox).

Torquay U (0) 1 *(Ford 59 (pen))*
Southend U (1) 1 *(Williamson 31)* 2171
Torquay U: Jones; Tully, Herrera, Hockley, Watson, Neil
(O'Brien), Chalqi, Ford, Bedeau, Sissoko (Mendy), Hill.
Southend U: Flahavan; Booty, Searle, Williamson
(McSweeney), Roget, Whelan, Lee, Maher, Carruthers,
Abbey, Forbes.

Walsall (2) 4 *(Matias 2, Hall 10, Leitao 61, Barras 90)*
Exeter C (0) 0 4095
Walsall: Walker; Brightwell, Aranalde (Marsh), Tillson,
Barras, Bukran, Hall, Bennett (Keates), Leitao (Angell),
Byfield, Matias.
Exeter C: Van Heusden; Burrows, Campbell, Buckle,
Curran, Whitworth, Roscoe (Tierney), Rawlinson
(Roberts C), Rapley, Francis (Ampadu), Zabek.

Wigan Ath (2) 3 *(Roberts 7, Bidstrup 36, McIvor 80 (og))*
Dorchester T (1) 1 *(Holmes 6)* 3883
Wigan Ath: Stillie; Green, Padula, Bidstrup, Griffiths, De
Zeeuw, Kilford, Hernandez (Ashcroft), Roberts, Liddell,
Martinez.
Dorchester T: Ormerod; Cannie (Groves), Sullivan,
White, McIvor (Radcliffe), Harris, Lonnen, Ferrett,
O'Hagan (Jermyn), Pickard, Holmes.

Wrexham (0) 0
Rotherham U (1) 1 *(Lee 39)* 3887
Wrexham: Dearden; McGregor, Roche, Bouanane
(Russell), Ridler, Barrett (Blackwood), Chalk, Ferguson,
Sam, Edwards, Faulconbridge.
Rotherham U: Gray; Scott, Hurst, Garner, Artell,
Branston, Watson, Robins (Beech), Lee, Warne, Talbot.

Wycombe W (2) 3 *(Bates 8, 68, Simpson 28 (pen))*
Harrow B (0) 0　　　　　　　　　　　　　2681
Wycombe W: Taylor; Townsend, Beeton, Ryan
(Castledine), Cousins, Bates, Harkin (McSporran),
Simpson, Lee (Brown), Rammell, Thompson.
Harrow B: Hook; Rose, Nwaokolo, Lewis (Hurlock),
Cooper, Lyons (Protain), Roberts, Lund, Gavin, Xavier
(Silkman), Payne.

Yeovil T (0) 5 *(Patmore 50, 85, Belgrave 53, Skiverton 57,*
Way 80 (pen))
Colchester U (0) 1 *(Duguid 69)*　　　　　4552
Yeovil T: Pennock; Piper, Tonkin, Skiverton, White,
Way, Belgrave, Smith, Patmore (Bent), Crittenden,
Lindegaard (O'Brien).
Colchester U: Brown; Duguid, Johnson G (Clark),
Skelton (Lock), White, Fitzgerald, Gregory, McGavin,
Conlon, Stockwell, Dozzell (Dunne).

19 NOV

Canvey Island (0) 4 *(Smith 48, Tilson 52 (pen), Jones 89,*
Vaughan 90)
Port Vale (2) 4 *(Minton 7, 76, Brammer 35,*
Bridge-Wilkinson 49)　　　　　　　　　2100
Canvey Island: Harrison; Smith, Davidson (Cooper),
Kennedy, Bodley, Ward, Bennett (Jones), Tilson,
Gregory, Vaughan, Parmenter (Miller).
Port Vale: Goodlad; Tankard, Carragher, Brammer,
Walsh, Minton, Bridge-Wilkinson, Cummins, Viljanen
(Twiss), Naylor, Smith.

Cardiff C (1) 5 *(Evans 15, Earnshaw 50, 78, 81,*
Fortune-West 71)
Bristol R (1) 1 *(Jordan 8 (og))*　　　　　8013
Cardiff C: Walton; Low, Gabbidon, Jordan, Young,
Evans, Earnshaw (Collins), Bonner, Bowen, Fortune-
West (Brayson), Legg (Brazier).
Bristol R: Culkin; Bignot, Wilson, Foster, Thomson,
Jones (Walters), Astafjevs, Hogg, Ellington, Johansen
(Ellis), Bryant.

Leigh RMI (0) 0
Millwall (1) 3 *(Harris 1 (pen), Bircham 67,*
Moody 75)　　　　　　　　　　　　　6907
Leigh RMI: Felgate; Trees, German, Durkin, Farrell, Swan,
Monk (Matthews), Ridings, Kielty (Harris), Black, Jones.
Millwall: Warner; Lawrence, Ryan, Bircham, Nethercott,
Dolan, Livermore, Moody (Braniff), Harris, Reid
(Kinet), Ifill.
at Millwall.

Radcliffe B (0) 1 *(Hardy 69)*
York C (4) 4 *(Potter 3, Bullock 10, McNiven 15,*
Jordan 28)　　　　　　　　　　　　　2495
Radcliffe B: Hurst; Battersby, Bean, Whealing
(Edwards), Kelly S, Dempsey, Wilson (Kelly E), Lunt
(Collins), Carden, Hardy, Price.
York C: Fettis; Edmondson, Potter, Sertori, Hocking,
Iwelumo, Jordan, Bullock, Tarrant (Mathie), McNiven,
Hall (Stamp).
at Bury.

8 DEC

Gravesend & N (0) 1 *(Jackson 75)*
Notts Co (1) 2 *(Stallard 3, Hughes 63)*　　2376
Gravesend & N: Turner; Lee (Hegley), Jackson, Lindsey,
Duku, Wilkins, Smith, Owen, Booth (Restarick),
Stadhart, Spiller (Crawley).
Notts Co: Ward; McDermott (Liburd), Pearce, Fenton,
Richardson, Jacobsen, Owers, Murray (Bolland),
Stallard, Hughes, Hamilton.

FIRST ROUND REPLAYS

21 NOV

Nuneaton B (0) 1 *(McGregor 90)*
Stoke C (0) 0　　　　　　　　　　　　4477
Nuneaton B: MacKenzie; Sykes, Love, Crowley, Weaver,
Angus, Wray, Charles (Taylor), McGregor, King,
Francis.
Stoke C: Muggleton; Hansson (Goodfellow), Dorigo
(Collins), Clarke, Mohan, Risom, Gudjonsson,
Kavanagh, Thorne, Thordarson, Petty.

28 NOV

Burton Albion (0) 2 *(Blount 71, Wassall 84)*
Kidderminster H (3) 4 *(Bogie 22, Hadley 27, 34,*
Bird 90)　　　　　　　　　　　　　　3760
Burton Albion: Duke; Kavanagh, Henshaw, Glasser,
Blount, Wassall, Stride (Moore), Webster (Lyons),
Clough, Starbuck, Anderson.
Kidderminster H: Brock; Clarkson, Stamps, Smith
(Webb), Hinton, Shail, Bogie, Horne, Hadley, Foster
(Bird), Ducros (Bennett).

Hull C (0) 0
Kettering T (0) 1 *(Fisher 57)*　　　　　3858
Hull C: Musselwhite; Edwards, Harper, Brightwell, Perry
(Wood), Greaves, Brabin, Goodison, Brown, Eyre,
Philpott (Whitmore).
Kettering T: Bowling; Codner, Lenagh, Perkins, Norman,
McNamara, Fisher, Brown, Hudson (Shutt), Inman,
Watkins (Diuk).

Northwich Vic (0) 1 *(Mike 72)*
Bury (0) 0　　　　　　　　　　　　　2869
Northwich Vic: Key; Bailey, Barnard, Davis, Robertson,
Burke, Norris, Simpson, Fletcher, Mike, Devlin.
Bury: Kenny; Unsworth, Barrick (Collins), Daws, Swailes
C, Swailes D, Billy, Reid, Barnes, Bullock (Jarrett),
Littlejohn (Preece).

Peterborough U (1) 4 *(Oldfield 30, Edwards 71,*
Clarke 84, Shields 87)
Mansfield T (0) 0　　　　　　　　　　4540
Peterborough U: Tyler; Hooper, Drury (Shields),
Forsyth, Rea, Edwards, Farrell, Oldfield, Clarke, Green,
Lee.
Mansfield T: Mimms; Asher, Andrews, Jervis, Disley,
Robinson, Pemberton (Bradley), Williamson (Williams),
Boulding, Blake, Greenacre.

Plymouth Arg (0) 1 *(McGregor 73)*
Chester C (1) 2 *(Whitehall 42, Ruscoe 107)*　3264
Plymouth Arg: Hodges; Fleming, Beswetherick,
Leadbitter, Wotton, Taylor, Phillips M, Barlow (Gritton),
McGregor, Guinan (Wills), Peake (Stonebridge).
Chester C: Brown; Fisher (Ruscoe), Doughty, Lancaster,
Ruffer, Beesley P, Carden, Blackburn (Woods), Beesley
M, Whitehall (Wright), Porter.
aet.

Port Vale (0) 1 *(Naylor 120)*
Canvey Island (0) 2 *(Gregory 105, Vaughan 119)*　3566
Port Vale: Goodlad; Burns, Carragher (Twiss), Brammer
(O'Callaghan), Burton, Widdrington, Bridge-Wilkinson,
Cummins, Naylor, Minton, Smith.
Canvey Island: Harrison; Smith, Stimson (Clark),
Bennett, Bodley, Ward, Tilson, Kennedy, Gregory
(Miller), Vaughan, Cooper (Jones).
aet.

Southend U (0) 2 *(Williamson 58, Roget 98)*
Torquay U (0) 1 *(Chalqi 79)*　　　　　3877
Southend U: Flahavan; Booty (McSweeney), Searle,
Williamson, Roget, Whelan, Lee, Maher, Carruthers,
Abbey (Fitzpatrick), Forbes (Johnson).
Torquay U: Jones; Tully (Ashington), Lyons, Aggrey,
Hockley, Watson, Chalqi, Ford, Bedeau, Sissoko
(Mendy), Hill (O'Brien).
aet.

SECOND ROUND

8 DEC

Walsall (2) 2 *(Tillson 25, 44)*
Barnet (0) 1 *(Cottee 48)*　　　　　　3699
Walsall: Walker; Brightwell, Aranalde, Tillson, Barras,
Bukran, Hall, Keates, Leitao (Angell), Byfield
(Ekelund), Matias (Wrack).
Barnet: Naisbitt; Stockley, Sawyers, Niven, Heald, Arber,
Currie, Doolan, Cottee, Riza (Purser), Goodhind
(Toms).

9 DEC

Bournemouth (1) 3 *(Hughes 34, Elliott 47, O'Connor 89)*
Nuneaton B (0) 0 5835
Bournemouth: Stewart; Broadhurst, Purches, Howe, Tindall, Elliott, Jorgensen (O'Connor), Fletcher C (Day), Hayter (Eribenne), Fletcher S, Hughes.
Nuneaton B: MacKenzie; Sykes, Love, Crowley, Weaver, Angus, Thackeray (Bacon), Taylor (Williams B), McGregor, King, Francis (Mitchell).

Bristol C (0) 3 *(Peacock 55, Clist 65, Thorpe 83)*
Kettering T (1) 1 *(Collins 29)* 7641
Bristol C: Phillips; Hill, Bell, Clist, Millen, Carey, Murray, Brown A (Burnell), Peacock (Beadle), Thorpe, Tinnion.
Kettering T: Bowling; Perkins, Vowden, Norman, Inman (Shutt), Fisher (Diuk), Codner, Brown, McNamara, Simba (Watkins), Collins.

Cardiff C (2) 3 *(Earnshaw 31, 83 (pen), Evans 37)*
Cheltenham T (1) 1 *(Milton 5)* 9910
Cardiff C: Walton; Gabbidon (Thompson), Legg, Young, McCulloch, Weston, Earnshaw, Bonner (Boland), Bowen (Brayson), Fortune-West, Evans.
Cheltenham T: Book; Duff, McCann, Banks, Freeman, Griffin (Howarth), Howells, McAuley (White), Alsop, Milton (Devaney), Yates.

Chester C (1) 3 *(Beesley P 35, Whitehall 54, 60)*
Oxford U (2) 2 *(Gray 23, Murphy 25)* 2798
Chester C: Brown; Fisher (Wright), Doughty, Lancaster, Ruffer, Beesley P (Ruscoe), Carden, Porter, Beesley M, Whitehall, Blackburn.
Oxford U: Knight; Hackett, Brown, Fear, Richardson, Linighan, Anthrobus (Omoyimni), Gray, Murphy, Jarman (Whitehead), Beauchamp.

Darlington (0) 0
Luton T (0) 0 3641
Darlington: Collett; Reed, Himsworth, Liddle, Aspin, Butler T (Elliott), Gray (Walklate), Hodgson (Brumwell), Naylor, Kyle, Atkinson.
Luton T: Abbey; Fraser, Taylor, Whitbread, Watts, Johnson, George, McLaren, Thomson, Locke, Spring.

Kidderminster H (0) 0
Carlisle U (1) 2 *(Connelly 43, Dobie 56)* 2533
Kidderminster H: Brock; Clarkson (MacKenzie), Stamps, Smith, Hinton, Shail, Bogie (Bennett), Horne, Hadley, Durnin, Ducros.
Carlisle U: Glennon; Birch, Maddison, Whitehead, Winstanley, Prokas, Connelly, Stevens (Heggs), Dobie, Thurston, Galloway.

Lincoln C (0) 0
Dagenham & Redbridge (0) 1 *(Janney 90)* 2823
Lincoln C: Ghent; Smith, Mayo, Finnigan, Holmes (Barnett J), Brown, Walker, Peacock (Battersby), Gordon, Thorpe, Gain (Miller).
Dagenham & Redbridge: Roberts; Cole, Vickers, Goodwin, Matthews, Terry, Janney, Heffer, Shipp (Broughton), McDougald, Broom.

Morecambe (1) 2 *(Hardicker 7, Quayle 74)*
Cambridge U (1) 1 *(Youngs 10)* 3427
Morecambe: Smith; Fensome, Perkins, McKearney, Hardicker, Walters, Thompson (Knowles), Drummond, Dowe (Quayle), Norman, Black (Rigoglioso).
Cambridge U: Perez; Ashbee, Cowan, Duncan, Joseph, Dreyer, Mustoe (Wanless), Russell, Connor (Taylor), Abbey, Youngs (Hansen).

Northwich Vic (0) 3 *(Fletcher 51, 62, Mike 70)*
Leyton Orient (1) 3 *(Griffiths 25, 50, Tate 82)* 2703
Northwich Vic: Key; Robertson, Davis, Burke, Bailey, Norris, Simpson, Devlin, Barnard, Mike, Fletcher.
Leyton Orient: Bayes; Joseph, Lockwood, McGhee, Smith, Harris, Walschaerts, Downer, Watts, Griffiths (Tate), Houghton (Brkovic).

Rotherham U (1) 1 *(Hughes 14 (og))*
Northampton T (0) 0 4964
Rotherham U: Gray; Bryan, Hurst, Garner, Artell, Branston, Watson, Robins (Lemarchand), Lee, Warne, Talbot (Monkhouse).
Northampton T: Sollitt; Savage, Hughes, Sampson, Green, Hope, Howard, Hunt, Forrester, Gabbiadini, Hargreaves.

Scunthorpe U (1) 2 *(Torpey 6, Sheldon 76)*
Brighton & HA (1) 1 *(Zamora 15)* 3879
Scunthorpe U: Evans; Jackson, Dawson, Stanton, Wilcox, Larusson, Hodges, Sheldon (Thom), Torpey, Calvo-Garcia, Morrison (Graves).
Brighton & HA: Kuipers; Watson, Mayo, Cullip, Wicks, Carpenter, Zamora, Rogers (Crosby), Hart (Steele), Oatway, Jones (Brooker).

Southport (1) 1 *(Maamria 39)*
Kingstonian (2) 2 *(Harris 20, Pitcher 33)* 3659
Southport: Dickinson; Guyett, Bolland, Teale, Clark (Elam), Marsh, Gouck, Grayston, Furlong (Whittaker), Arnold, Maamria.
Kingstonian: Kelly; Beard, Allan D, Saunders, Harris, Luckett (Bass), Patterson, Pitcher, Wingfield (Nyamah), Winston, Akuamoah.

Swindon T (1) 5 *(O'Halloran 16, 51, Cowe 84, 89, Howe 87)*
Gateshead (0) 0 3907
Swindon T: Griemink; Robinson M, Davis (Duke), O'Halloran, Reeves, Van der Linden, Invincible (Young), Howe, Alexander, Williams M (Cowe), Woan.
Gateshead: Swan; Watson R, Kitchen D, Hall, Talbot (Bates), Proudlock, Bowey, Pepper (Edgcumbe), Dalton, Preen, McAlindon (Thompson).

York C (0) 2 *(McNiven 56, Mathie 73)*
Reading (0) 2 *(Newman 48, Butler 52)* 2926
York C: Fettis; Edmondson, Potter, Sertori, Bower, Iwelumo (Bullock), Agnew, Hulme, Mathie (Stamp), Alcide, McNiven.
Reading: Whitehead; Newman, Robinson, Viveash, Mackie, Parkinson, Hodges, Jones, Cureton (Rougier), Butler, Igoe (Gurney).

10 DEC

Blackpool (0) 0
Yeovil T (1) 1 *(Crittenden 45)* 3757
Blackpool: Barnes; Hills, Coid (Thompson), O'Connor (Nowland), Hughes, Reid, Collins, Simpson, Ormerod, Murphy J, Bushell (Clarkson).
Yeovil T: Pennock; Piper, White, Skiverton, Tonkin, Lindegaard (O'Brien), Way, Smith, Crittenden, Patmore, Belgrave (Bent).

Canvey Island (0) 1 *(Vaughan 90)*
Southend U (1) 2 *(Forbes 38, Abbey 80)* 11,402
Canvey Island: Harrison; Bennett, Ward, Davidson, Smith (Cooper), Tilson, Kennedy (Jones), Stimson, Gregory, Vaughan, Inglethorpe (Miller).
Southend U: Flahavan; Booty, Searle, Williamson, Roget, Whelan, Lee, Maher, Carruthers, Abbey (Webb), Forbes.
at Southend.

Millwall (0) 0
Wycombe W (0) 0 7819
Millwall: Warner; Lawrence, Bircham, Ifill (Cahill), Dyche, Dolan, Livermore, Moody (Sadlier), Harris, Reid, Kinet.
Wycombe W: Taylor; Rogers, Townsend, Bulman, McCarthy, Bates, Ryan, Brown, McSporran, Rammell, Senda.

Peterborough U (0) 1 *(Lee 90)*
Oldham Ath (0) 1 *(Dudley 62)* 5662
Peterborough U: Tyler; Gill (Forinton), Drury, Forsyth, Edwards, Shields (Hanlon), Farrell, Oldfield, Lee, Cullen (Jelleyman), McKenzie.
Oldham Ath: Kelly; McNiven, Innes, Garnett, Rickers, Prenderville, Carss, Boshell (Sheridan), Dudley (Allott), Corazzin (Holt), Eyres.

12 DEC

Wigan Ath (0) 1 *(Ashcroft 57)*
Notts Co (0) 1 *(Stallard 67)*　　　　　3886
Wigan Ath: Carroll; Green, Sharp, Bidstrup, Griffiths, De Zeeuw, Gillespie, McLaughlin (Sheridan), Ashcroft, Liddell, Martinez (McGibbon).
Notts Co: Ward; Pearce, Liburd, Fenton, Richardson, Jacobsen, Owers, Stallard, Allsopp, Hughes, Hamilton.

SECOND ROUND REPLAYS

19 DEC

Luton T (0) 2 *(Nogan 61, McLaren 79)*
Darlington (0) 0　　　　　3563
Luton T: Abbey; Helin, Taylor, Whitbread, Watts (Boyce), Johnson, George, McLaren, Nogan, Fotiadis, Spring (Locke).
Darlington: Collett; Reed, Heckingbottom, Liddle (Brumwell), Aspin, Himsworth (Hodgson), Gray, Elliott, Naylor, Kyle (Hjorth), Atkinson.

Notts Co (1) 2 *(Liburd 26, 102)*
Wigan Ath (1) 1 *(Kilford 45)*　　　　　3349
Notts Co: Ward; Pearce, Liburd, Fenton, Richardson, Jacobsen, Owers, Stallard, Allsopp, Hughes (Joseph), Murray (Brough).
Wigan Ath: Stillie; Green (Dickson), Padula, Redfearn, Balmer, Griffiths, Kilford (Mitchell), Gillespie, Roberts, Ashcroft, Martinez (McLaughlin).
aet.

Oldham Ath (0) 0
Peterborough U (1) 1 *(Forsyth 5)*　　　　　3404
Oldham Ath: Kelly; McNiven, Innes, Garnett, Rickers (Hotte), Boshell, Carss, Sheridan, Dudley (Allott), Corazzin (Holt), Eyres.
Peterborough U: Tyler; Hooper, Drury, Forsyth, Rea, Edwards, Farrell, Oldfield, Clarke, Lee (McKenzie), Gill.

Reading (1) 1 *(Caskey 24)*
York C (1) 3 *(Agnew 30, Alcide 88, Iwelumo 90)*　　6968
Reading: Whitehead; Newman, Robinson, Viveash, Mackie (Hunter), Parkinson, Hodges (Cureton), Caskey, Butler, Jones (Smith), Rougier.
York C: Fettis; Thompson, Potter, Sertori, Bower, Iwelumo, Patterson, Hulme (Jordan), Mathie, McNiven (Alcide), Agnew.

Wycombe W (2) 2 *(Rammell 18, McCarthy 45)*
Millwall (1) 1 *(Dolan 25)*　　　　　3878
Wycombe W: Taylor; Townsend (Rogers), Vinnicombe, Bulman, Cousins, McCarthy, Harkin (Carroll), Simpson, Brown, Rammell, Thompson (Senda).
Millwall: Warner; Lawrence, Bircham, Ryan (Kinet), Dyche, Dolan, Livermore (Cahill), Sadlier, Harris, Reid, Ifill.

20 DEC

Leyton Orient (0) 3 *(Griffiths 47, Simpson 69 (og), Houghton 116)*
Northwich Vic (2) 2 *(Cooke 10, Mike 11)*　　4028
Leyton Orient: Bayes; Joseph (Mansley), Lockwood, McGhee, Smith, Harris, Walschaerts, Griffiths, Watts (Brkovic), Houghton, Downer (Beall).
Northwich Vic: Key; Bailey, Barnard, Simpson, Robertson, Burke, Norris, Cooke (Walsh), Fletcher (Poland), Mike, Devlin.
aet.

THIRD ROUND

6 JAN

Blackburn R (0) 2 *(Taylor 72, Bent 84)*
Chester C (0) 0　　　　　15,223
Blackburn R: Friedel; Curtis, Bjornebye, Mahon, Taylor, Dunn, McAteer, Dunning (Douglas), Ostenstad (Bent), Jansen, Hignett (Hughes).

Chester C: Brown; Fisher (Woods), Doughty (Moss), Lancaster, Ruffer, Beesley P, Carden, Porter, Beesley M, Whitehall, Blackburn (Wright).

Bolton W (1) 2 *(O'Kane 44, Ricketts 90)*
Yeovil T (1) 1 *(Patmore 25)*　　　　　11,161
Bolton W: Banks; O'Kane, Charlton, Whitlow, Barness, Warhurst, Passi (Nolan), Frandsen, Morini (Ricketts), Marshall (Holdsworth), Gardner.
Yeovil T: Pennock; Piper, White, Skiverton, Tonkin, Lindegaard (O'Brien), Way, Smith, Crittenden, Patmore, Belgrave (Bent).

Bournemouth (1) 2 *(Defoe 21, Fletcher C 55)*
Gillingham (2) 3 *(Hope 17, Hessenthaler 27, Shaw 71)*　　　　　7403
Bournemouth: Stewart; Broadhurst (Smith), Elliott (O'Connor), Howe, Day, Tindall, Jorgensen (Eribenne), Fletcher C, Defoe, Fletcher S, Hayter.
Gillingham: Bartram; Southall, Edge, Hope, Butters (Browning), Pennock, Smith, Hessenthaler (Patterson), Onuora, Shaw (King), Lewis.

Burnley (1) 2 *(Moore 45, Johnrose 90)*
Scunthorpe U (1) 2 *(Hodges 2, Ipoua 47)*　　8054
Burnley: Michopoulos; Weller, Smith, Cox, Davis, Thomas, Mellon (Payton), Cook (Johnrose), Branch (Little), Moore, Mullin.
Scunthorpe U: Evans; Jackson, Dawson, Stanton, Wilcox, Larusson, Hodges (Fickling), Harsley (Graves), Ipoua, Torpey, Calvo-Garcia.

Cardiff C (0) 1 *(Young 62)*
Crewe Alex (1) 1 *(Bowen 18 (og))*　　　　　13,403
Cardiff C: Walton; Gabbidon, Brazier (Low), McCulloch (Boland), Young, Weston, Earnshaw (Nogan), Evans, Bowen, Fortune-West, Legg.
Crewe Alex: Bankole; Wright, Smith S, Lunt, Macauley, Gannon, Foster, Cramb (Hulse), Jack, Rivers, Sorvel.

Carlisle U (0) 0
Arsenal (1) 1 *(Wiltord 22)*　　　　　15,300
Carlisle U: Glennon; Birch, Hemmings (Thwaites), Whitehead, Winstanley, Darby (Heggs), Soley, Prokas, Dobie, Stevens (Halliday), Connelly.
Arsenal: Manninger; Dixon, Cole (Malz), Vieira, Stepanovs, Vivas, Parlour, Pires, Wiltord (Danilevicius), Bergkamp, Ljungberg (Silvinho).

Charlton Ath (0) 1 *(Salako 86)*
Dagenham & Redbridge (1) 1 *(McDougald 42)*　19,059
Charlton Ath: Kiely; Kishishev (Newton), Konchesky, Todd, Rufus, Fish (Salako), Parker, Jensen, Bartlett, Pringle (Svensson), Robinson.
Dagenham & Redbridge: Roberts; Cole, Vickers, Matthews, Terry (Jones), Janney (Hamsher), Goodwin, Heffer, Broom, Shipp, McDougald (Shields).

Chelsea (2) 5 *(Zola 37, 84, Hasselbaink 45, Gudjohnsen 72, Poyet 74)*
Peterborough U (0) 0　　　　　31,912
Chelsea: Cudicini; Ferrer, Babayaro (Le Saux), Jokanovic, Terry, Desailly (Leboeuf), Poyet, Wise, Hasselbaink, Zola, Harley (Gudjohnsen).
Peterborough U: Tyler; Gill, Drury, Forsyth, Edwards, Green (Forinton), Farrell, Oldfield, Clarke, McKenzie (Shields), Jelleyman (Hooper).

Derby Co (1) 3 *(Christie 43, 75, Eranio 53)*
WBA (0) 2 *(Taylor 77, Hughes 80)*　　　　　19,232
Derby Co: Poom; Martin, Higginbotham, Riggott, Carbonari, Mawene, Eranio (Boertien), Burton, Christie, Kinkladze, Murray.
WBA: Adamson; Lyttle (Taylor), Clement, Chambers J, Butler (Balis), Carbon, Jordao, Sneekes, Roberts, Hughes, Fox.

Huddersfield T (0) 0
Bristol C (0) 2 *(Clist 55, Beadle 82)*　　　　　9192
Huddersfield T: Vaesen; Heary (Gorre), Vincent, Dyson, Gray, Armstrong (Sellars), Baldry, Holland, Thornley, Gallen, Facey.
Bristol C: Phillips; Hill, Bell (Burnell), Clist, Millen, Carey, Murray, Brown A, Beadle, Thorpe, Tinnion.

Leeds U (1) 1 *(Viduka 9)*
Barnsley (0) 0   32,386
Leeds U: Robinson; Mills, Matteo, Batty, Radebe,
Ferdinand, Dacourt, Smith, Keane (Wilcox), Viduka,
Bakke.
Barnsley: Miller; Salli, Barker, Morgan (Corbo), Chettle,
Ward (McClare), Appleby (Dyer), Neil, Shipperley,
Sheron, O'Callaghan.

Leicester C (0) 3 *(Rowett 57, Izzet 67 (pen), Cresswell 73)*
York C (0) 0   16,850
Leicester C: Royce; Impey, Guppy, Elliott, Rowett,
Gilchrist (Oakes), Benjamin, Izzet, Akinbiyi (Cresswell),
Jones, Savage (Delaney).
York C: Fettis; Thompson (Hocking), Potter (Mathie),
Patterson, Bower, Iwelumo, Fox (Hall), Hulme, Agnew,
McNiven, Alcide.

Leyton Orient (0) 0
Tottenham H (0) 1 *(Doherty 90)*   12,336
Leyton Orient: Bayes; Joseph, Lockwood, McGhee,
Smith, Harris, Walschaerts, Opara (Tate), Watts,
Houghton, Brkovic (Beall).
Tottenham H: Sullivan; Doherty, Clemence,
Leonhardsen, Campbell, Perry, Anderton, Sherwood,
Rebrov, Ferdinand (Korsten), King.

Liverpool (0) 3 *(Heskey 47, 75, Hamann 73)*
Rotherham U (0) 0   30,689
Liverpool: Westerveld; Biscan, Carragher, Hamann,
Henchoz, Hyypia, Murphy, McAllister, Heskey
(Barmby), Owen (Gerrard), Smicer (Vignal).
Rotherham U: Gray; Scott, Hurst, Garner, Artell,
Branston, Watson, Robins (Sedgwick), Lee (Berry),
Warne (Monkhouse), Talbot.

Luton T (2) 3 *(Fotiadis 27, George 36, Douglas 77)*
QPR (0) 3 *(Crouch 48, 53, Peacock 90 (pen))*   8677
Luton T: Ovendale; Helin (Stirling), Taylor, Whitbread,
Boyce, Fraser, George, Locke, Nogan, Fotiadis
(Douglas), Spring.
QPR: Miklosko; Darlington, Baraclough, Morrow
(Wardley), Plummer, Carlisle, Langley, Koejoe, Crouch,
Kulcsar (Peacock), Connolly.

Manchester C (3) 3 *(Morrison 18, Huckerby 31,
Goater 43 (pen))*
Birmingham C (0) 2 *(Grainger 57, Adebola 61)*   19,380
Manchester C: Weaver; Eghill, Granville, Dunne, Howey
(Prior), Morrison, Haaland, Wiekens (Bishop), Huckerby
(Dickov), Goater, Tiatto.
Birmingham C: Bennett; Gill (Horsfield), Grainger,
Sonner, Purse, Johnson M, Eaden (Marcelo), O'Connor,
Adebola, Ndlovu (Hughes), Lazaridis.

Morecambe (0) 0
Ipswich T (1) 3 *(Stewart 14, Armstrong 65,
Wright J 75)*   5923
Morecambe: Smith; Fensome, Lyons (McGuire),
McKearney, Hardiker, Walters, Thompson, Drummond,
Quayle (Rigoglioso), Norman, Black (Eastwood).
Ipswich T: Wright R; Wilnis, Croft, Bramble,
Hreidarsson, Reuser (Clapham), Holland, Wright J,
Stewart (Logan), Scowcroft (Magilton), Armstrong.

Portsmouth (1) 1 *(Bradbury 8)*
Tranmere R (1) 2 *(Yates 44, Parkinson 69)*   11,058
Portsmouth: Tardif; Crowe, Harper, Derry, Hiley,
Moore, Quashie, Thogersen, Bradbury, Nightingale
(Claridge), Rudonja (Hughes).
Tranmere R: Achterberg; Yates, Roberts, Flynn, Jobson,
Hill, Hinds, Parkinson, Rideout (Gill), Barlow
(Taylor S), Allen.

Preston NE (0) 0
Stockport Co (0) 1 *(Fradin 71)*   9975
Preston NE: Lucas; Parkinson (Cartwright), Eaton, Kidd,
Jackson, Appleton, McKenna, Rankine, McBride
(Macken) Healy, Barry-Murphy.
Stockport Co: Nash; Woodthorpe (Briggs), Clare, Wiss,
Flynn, Clark, Cooper, Matthews (Maxwell), Wilbraham,
Fradin, Smith.

Sheffield W (1) 2 *(Hamshaw 41, Sibon 82)*
Norwich C (0) 1 *(Roberts 74)*   15,971
Sheffield W: Stringer; Hendon, Harkness, Haslam
(Morrison), Blatsis, Walker, Hamshaw (Bromby)
(Crane), Sibon, Ekoku, Lescott, Quinn.
Norwich C: Marshall A; Sutch (Kenton), MacKay,
Marshall L, Fleming, Jackson, Russell, Forbes (Notman),
Roberts, Mulryne (Coote), Llewellyn.

Southampton (0) 1 *(Dodd 73 (pen))*
Sheffield U (0) 0   14,158
Southampton: Jones; Dodd, Bridge, Oakley (Draper),
Lundekvam, El Khalej (Richards), Tessem, Soltvedt
(Kachloul), Beattie, Pahars, Davies.
Sheffield U: Tracey; Uhlenbeek, Kozluk, Santos
(Thomas), Murphy, Sandford, Devlin (Suffo), Ford,
Kelly (D'Jaffo), Woodhouse, Montgomery.

Southend U (0) 0
Kingstonian (1) 1 *(Akuamoah 8)*   7270
Southend U: Flahavan; Booty, Searle, Hutchings, Roget,
Whelan, Webb, Maher, Carruthers, Abbey (Williamson),
Forbes.
Kingstonian: Kelly; Beard, Luckett, Allan, Saunders,
Harris, Patterson, Pitcher, Winston (Bass), Akuamoah
(Green), Wingfield (Stewart).

Sunderland (0) 0
Crystal Palace (0) 0   30,908
Sunderland: Sorensen; Makin, Varga, Williams
(Kilbane), Emerson, McCann, Rae, Schwarz, Dichio
(Quinn), Phillips, Hutchison.
Crystal Palace: Kolinko; Frampton, Harrison, Thomson,
Austin, Carlisle, Mullins, Rodger, Morrison C (Forssell),
Freedman, Rubins.

Swindon T (0) 0
Coventry C (1) 2 *(Bellamy 5, Hadji 64)*   14,445
Swindon T: Griemink; Hall, Davis (Williams J), Whitley
(O'Halloran), Reeves, Dryden, Invincible, Cowe,
Alexander (Young), Woan, Duke.
Coventry C: Kirkland; Edworthy, Quinn, Williams,
Breen, Carsley, Telfer, Thompson, Bellamy, Chippo,
Hadji.

Walsall (1) 2 *(Wrack 33, Angell 87)*
West Ham U (1) 3 *(Lampard 6, Kanoute 57, 81)*   9402
Walsall: Walker; Brightwell (Marsh), Aranalde, Tillson,
Barras, Bukran, Hall (Keates), Bennett, Angell, Leitao
(Byfield), Wrack.
West Ham U: Hislop; Sinclair, Winterburn, Lampard,
Song, Pearce S, Tihinen, Cole, Kanoute, Camara
(Bassila), Carrick.

Watford (1) 1 *(Mooney 21)*
Everton (0) 2 *(Hughes 82, Watson 90)*   15,635
Watford: Chamberlain; Cox, Robinson, Vernazza, Page,
Ward, Kennedy (Palmer S), Nielsen, Mooney, Noel-
Williams (Helguson), Smith.
Everton: Myhre; Watson, Naysmith, Gravesen
(Gemmill), Weir, Ball, Alexandersson, Pembridge (Tal),
Cadamarteri (Moore), Ferguson, Hughes.

Wimbledon (2) 2 *(Ardley 29, Karlsson 42)*
Notts Co (1) 2 *(Hughes 36, Stallard 49)*   4391
Wimbledon: Davis; Holloway (Ainsworth), Kimble,
Andersen (Roberts), Williams, Blackwell, Ardley,
Karlsson, Euell, Francis, Agyemang.
Notts Co: Ward; Fenton, Liburd, Newton (Holmes),
Richardson, Jacobsen, Owers, Stallard, Allsopp, Hughes
(Hamilton), Brough.

Wycombe W (0) 1 *(McCarthy 73)*
Grimsby T (1) 1 *(Nielsen 43)*   5390
Wycombe W: Taylor; Rogers (Senda), Vinnicombe,
Bulman, Cousins, McCarthy, Harkin (Brady), Simpson,
Brown, Rammell, Baird (Ryan).
Grimsby T: Coyne; McDermott, Gallimore, Groves,
Smith R, Butterfield (Coldicott), Donovan, Nielsen,
Livingstone (Handyside), Willens (Burnett), Campbell.

7 JAN

Fulham (1) 1 *(Fernandes 24)*
Manchester U (1) 2 *(Solskjaer 8, Sheringham 89)* 19,178
Fulham: Taylor; Finnan, Brevett, Melville, Symons, Fernandes, Goldbaek, Clark, Saha, Sahnoun, Boa Morte (Stolcers).
Manchester U: Van der Gouw; Neville P, Silvestre, Brown, Keane, Neville G, Beckham (Chadwick), Butt (Wallwork), Solskjaer, Yorke (Sheringham), Giggs.

Newcastle U (0) 1 *(Solano 80)*
Aston Villa (0) 1 *(Stone 55)* 37,862
Newcastle U: Harper; Barton (Glass), Griffin, Goma, Hughes, Solano, Dyer, Acuna, Ameobi (Lua-Lua), Bassedas, Speed (Cordone).
Aston Villa: James; Stone, Wright, Southgate, Staunton, Barry, Merson, Boateng, Dublin, Samuel, Ginola (Vassell).

Nottingham F (0) 0
Wolverhampton W (0) 1 *(Proudlock 87)* 14,601
Nottingham F: Beasant; Edds, Brennan, Bart-Williams, Jenas, Edwards, Gray (Freeman), Harewood (John), Jones, Reid, Williams.
Wolverhampton W: Oakes; Muscat, Naylor, Lescott, Dinning, Andrews, Robinson, Osborn (Emblen), Branch (Green), Proudlock, Sinton.

8 JAN

Bradford C (0) 0
Middlesbrough (0) 1 *(Ricard 67)* 7303
Bradford C: Walsh; Atherton (Beagrie), Jacobs, McCall, Molenaar, O'Brien, McKinlay (Petrescu), Windass, Saunders (Carbone), Blake, Jess.
Middlesbrough: Schwarzer; Fleming, Gordon, Vickers, Ehiogu, Festa, Stamp (Whelan), Okon, Boksic (Mustoe), Ricard (Karembeu), Ince.

THIRD ROUND REPLAYS

16 JAN

Crewe Alex (1) 2 *(Smith S 10 (pen), Rivers 77)*
Cardiff C (1) 1 *(Earnshaw 37)* 5785
Crewe Alex: Bankole; Foster, Smith S, Macauley, Sodje, Gannon, Ashton, Lunt, Jack, Rivers, Sorvel.
Cardiff C: Walton; Gabbidon, Brazier, Weston, Young, McCulloch (Brayson), Earnshaw, Boland (Low), Bowen (Collins), Fortune-West, Legg.

Grimsby T (1) 1 *(Jeffrey 44)*
Wycombe W (2) 3 *(McCarthy 31, Simpson 32, Rogers 66)* 3269
Grimsby T: Coyne; Butterfield, Gallimore, Handyside, Smith R, Coldicott (Nielsen), Donovan, Willems (Burnett), Livingstone, Jeffrey, Campbell.
Wycombe W: Taylor; Rogers (Bates), Vinnicombe, Bulman, Cousins, McCarthy, Brady (Brown), Simpson, Rammell, Baird (Senda), Lee.

17 JAN

Aston Villa (0) 1 *(Vassell 50)*
Newcastle U (0) 0 25,387
Aston Villa: James; Stone, Wright, Southgate (Barry), Alpay, Staunton, Vassell (Walker), Boateng, Dublin, Hendrie, Merson.
Newcastle U: Harper; Griffin, Hughes, Goma, Marcelino, Glass (Lua-Lua), Gallacher (Cordone), Acuna, Ameobi, Bassedas, Speed (Barton).

Crystal Palace (1) 2 *(Morrison C 24, Thomson 89)*
Sunderland (0) 4 *(Quinn 72, Phillips 73, 102, Kilbane 113)* 15,454
Crystal Palace: Kolinko; Smith (Black), Harrison, Austin, Zhiyi (Ruddock), Rubins, Mullins, Rodger, Morrison C, Forssell (Freedman), Thomson.
Sunderland: Sorensen; Williams, Gray, McCann, Varga, Emerson, Schwarz (Kilbane), Rae, Quinn (Dichio), Phillips (Oster), Hutchison.
aet.

QPR (0) 2 *(Kiwomya 90, 112)*
Luton T (1) 1 *(Mansell 1)* 14,395
QPR: Miklosko; Perry, Baraclough, Rose, Carlisle, Plummer (Kiwomya), Langley, Koejoe (Wardley), Crouch, Darlington, Connolly (Ngonge).
Luton T: Ovendale; Fraser (Stirling), McGowan, Holmes, Whitbread, Karlsen, Nogan, Mansell, Douglas (Stein), Fotiadis (Scarlett), Spring.
aet.

23 JAN

Scunthorpe U (0) 1 *(Dawson 84)*
Burnley (0) 1 *(Payton 73)* 4709
Scunthorpe U: Evans; Jackson, Dawson, Stanton, Wilcox, Larusson, Hodges (Morrison), Sheldon, Ipoua, Torpey (Stamp), Calvo-Garcia (Graves).
Burnley: Michopoulos; Weller, Branch (Mullin), Cox, Davis, Thomas, Ball, Cook (Little), Moore, Payton, Johnrose (Armstrong).
aet; Scunthorpe U won 5-4 on penalties.

27 JAN

Dagenham & Redbridge (0) 0
Charlton Ath (0) 1 *(Newton 92)* 5394
Dagenham & Redbridge: Roberts; Goodwin, Vickers, Cole, Matthews, Terry (Jones), Janney, Heffer, Shipp (Cobb), McDougald, Broom (Haworth).
Charlton Ath: Kiely; Brown, Konchesky, Todd, Rufus, Fish, Stuart, Newton (Parker), Lisbie (Robinson), Svensson (MacDonald), Salako.

Notts Co (0) 0
Wimbledon (0) 1 *(Andersen 119)* 9084
Notts Co: Ward; Fenton, Liburd, Newton, Richardson (Brough) (Farrell), Jacobsen, Owers, Stallard, Allsopp, Hughes, Hamilton (Murray).
Wimbledon: Davis; Hawkins, Kimble, Andersen, Willmott, Williams, Ardley, Francis, Euell, Ainsworth (Gayle), Agyemang (Gray) (Cunningham).
aet.

FOURTH ROUND

27 JAN

Aston Villa (0) 1 *(Joachim 76)*
Leicester C (1) 2 *(Akinbiyi 42, Gunnlaugsson 84)* 26,383
Aston Villa: James; Stone, Wright (Joachim), Staunton, Alpay, Barry, Taylor, Boateng, Angel (Dublin), Vassell, Merson.
Leicester C: Royce; Impey, Davidson, Elliott, Rowett, Taggart, Savage, Jones (Gilchrist), Akinbiyi (Gunnlaugsson), Mancini (Cresswell), Delaney.

Blackburn R (0) 0
Derby Co (0) 0 18,858
Blackburn R: Friedel; McAteer (Hignett), Duff, Short, Curtis, Taylor, Flitcroft (Keller), Jansen, Bent (Blake), Mahon, Dunn.
Derby Co: Poom; Martin, Higginbotham, Bragstad, Carbonari, Mawene, Eranio (Boertien), Delap, Christie, O'Neil, Murray.

Bristol C (0) 1 *(Thorpe 90)*
Kingstonian (0) 1 *(Wingfield 57)* 14,787
Bristol C: Phillips; Hill, Bell, Clist (Brown M), Millen, Carey (Amankwaah), Murray, Brown A, Peacock, Beadle (Thorpe), Tinnion.
Kingstonian: Kelly; Beard, Luckett, Allan, Saunders, Harris, Patterson, Pitcher, Duerden (Winston), Akuamoah, Wingfield (Bass).

Crewe Alex (0) 0
Stockport Co (0) 1 *(Wiss 85)* 7318
Crewe Alex: Bankole; Wright, Foster, Gannon (Tait), Macauley, Sodje, Hulse (Ashton), Lunt, Jack, Rivers, Sorvel.
Stockport Co: Jones; Gibb, Nicholson, Wiss, Flynn, Clark, Cooper, Carrigan (Matthews), Wilbraham, Fradin, Smith.

Everton (0) 0
Tranmere R (2) 3 *(Yates 22, 62, Koumas 35)* 39,207
Everton: Myhre; Xavier, Unsworth (Gough), Gravesen, Watson, Ball, Gemmill, Pembridge, Campbell, Cadamarteri (Tal), Hughes (Moore).
Tranmere R: Achterberg; Yates, Allen, Flynn (Henry), Jobson, Hill, Hinds, Parkinson (Taylor S), Rideout (Hume), Hamilton, Koumas.

Leeds U (0) 0
Liverpool (0) 2 *(Barmby 88, Heskey 90)* 37,108
Leeds U: Martyn; Kelly, Harte, Woodgate, Ferdinand, Bakke, Batty, Bowyer, Keane (Smith), Viduka, Matteo.
Liverpool: Westerveld; Babbel (Barmby), Carragher, Hamann, Henchoz, Hyypia, Murphy (Ziege), McAllister, Fowler, Biscan, Smicer (Heskey).

Manchester C (0) 1 *(Goater 90)*
Coventry C (0) 0 24,637
Manchester C: Weaver; Dunne (Wiekens), Ritchie (Charvet), Grant, Morrison, Prior, Haaland, Jeff Whitley, Huckerby, Wanchope (Goater), Granville.
Coventry C: Hedman; Edworthy (Telfer), Quinn, Williams, Shaw, Breen, Carsley, Eustace, Bellamy, Bothroyd, Hall.

QPR (0) 0
Arsenal (2) 6 *(Plummer 32 (og), Wiltord 33, 56, Rose 49 (og), Pires 58, Bergkamp 74)* 19,003
QPR: Miklosko; Darlington, Baraclough, Plummer (Koejoe) (Ngonge), Perry (Connolly), Carlisle, Langley, Peacock, Crouch, Rose, Kiwomya.
Arsenal: Seaman; Dixon, Cole, Vieira (Vivas), Stepanovs, Adams, Parlour, Lauren (Grimandi), Wiltord, Bergkamp, Pires (Malz).

Southampton (1) 3 *(Davies 11, Dodd 80 (pen), Beattie 90)*
Sheffield W (0) 1 *(Booth 66)* 15,251
Southampton: Jones; Dodd, Bridge, Marsden, Lundekvam, Richards, Oakley, Draper (Tessem), Beattie, Pahars, Davies.
Sheffield W: Pressman; Hendon, Harkness, Blatsis, Bromby, Walker, Haslam (Ekoku), Sibon, Booth, Lescott (Crane), Quinn (Morrison).

Sunderland (1) 1 *(Dichio 23)*
Ipswich T (0) 0 33,626
Sunderland: Sorensen; Williams, Gray (Makin), Varga, Craddock, McCann, Rae, Schwarz, Dichio, Phillips (Kilbane), Hutchison.
Ipswich T: Wright R; Wilnis, Hreidarsson, Bramble (Scowcroft), Venus (Clapham), McGreal, Holland, Magilton, Stewart, Wright J, Armstrong (Naylor).

Wycombe W (1) 2 *(Rammell 37, Parkin 85)*
Wolverhampton W (0) 1 *(Robinson 59)* 9617
Wycombe W: Taylor; Rogers, Vinnicombe, Bulman, Cousins, McCarthy (Bates), Brady, Simpson, Baird (Parkin), Rammell, Lee (Brown).
Wolverhampton W: Stowell; Robinson, Naylor, Lescott, Pollet, Andrews (Green), Emblen, Osborn (Ndah), Branch, Proudlock, Sinton (Camara).

28 JAN

Bolton W (2) 5 *(Holdsworth 27, 28, 47, Nolan 51, 74)*
Scunthorpe U (1) 1 *(Calvo-Garcia 30)* 11,737
Bolton W: Banks; Barness, Elliott, Frandsen, Warhurst, Nolan, Summerbee, Marshall (Charlton), Hansen (Wheatcroft), Holdsworth (Ricketts), Farrelly.
Scunthorpe U: Evans; Jackson, Dawson, Stanton, Wilcox, Larusson (Harsley), Hodges, Sheldon (Graves), Ipoua (Stamp), Morrison, Calvo-Garcia.

Gillingham (0) 2 *(Shaw 51, Onuora 67)*
Chelsea (3) 4 *(Gudjohnsen 3, 90, Gronkjaer 14, 24)* 10,419
Gillingham: Bartram; Southall, Edge, Hope, Ashby, Pennock (Patterson), Smith, Lewis (Onuora), King, Shaw (Thomson), Saunders.
Chelsea: Cudicini; Ferrer, Melchiot, Terry, Leboeuf (Le Saux), Morris (Stanic), Gronkjaer, Wise, Gudjohnsen, Zola (Poyet), Harley.

Manchester U (0) 0
West Ham U (0) 1 *(Di Canio 76)* 67,029
Manchester U: Barthez; Irwin (Solskjaer), Silvestre, Neville G, Keane, Stam, Beckham, Butt (Yorke), Cole, Sheringham, Giggs.
West Ham U: Hislop; Schemmel, Winterburn, Tihinen, Dailly, Pearce S, Lampard, Cole (Pearce I), Kanoute, Di Canio (Soma), Carrick.

6 FEB

Middlesbrough (0) 0
Wimbledon (0) 0 20,625
Middlesbrough: Schwarzer; Fleming (Whelan), O'Neill, Festa, Ehiogu, Cooper, Karembeu, Okon, Boksic, Ricard (Campbell), Ince.
Wimbledon: Davis; Hawkins, Kimble, Andersen, Williams, Cunningham, Ainsworth, Karlsson, Euell, Francis, Agyemang (Gayle).

7 FEB

Charlton Ath (1) 2 *(Powell 11, Svensson 49)*
Tottenham H (0) 4 *(Rufus 58 (og), Anderton 62, Leonhardsen 63, Rebrov 82)* 18,101
Charlton Ath: Ilic; Kishishev (Newton), Powell, Todd, Rufus, Fish, Stuart, Jensen, Bartlett (Lisbie), Svensson, Parker (Salako).
Tottenham H: Sullivan; Anderton, Young, Doherty, Campbell, Perry (Carr), Leonhardsen, Sherwood, Rebrov, Freund, King.

FOURTH ROUND REPLAYS

7 FEB

Derby Co (1) 2 *(Riggott 3, Eranio 70)*
Blackburn R (0) 5 *(Flitcroft 48, Bent 57, 71, Dunn 65 (pen), Jansen 77)* 15,203
Derby Co: Oakes; O'Neil, Boertien, Riggott, Carbonari (Morris), West, Eranio (Higginbotham), Burton, Christie, Murray, Burley (Martin).
Blackburn R: Friedel; McAteer (Keller), Duff, Curtis, Berg, Taylor, Flitcroft, Mahon, Bent (Hignett), Hughes (Jansen), Dunn.

Kingstonian (0) 0
Bristol C (0) 1 *(Murray 88)* 3341
Kingstonian: Kelly; Beard, Luckett, Allan D, Saunders, Harris, Patterson, Pitcher, Duerden, Boyce (Winston), Akuamoah.
Bristol C: Phillips; Hill, Bell, Clist, Millen, Carey, Murray, Brown A, Beadle, Thorpe, Tinnion.

13 FEB

Wimbledon (0) 3 *(Ardley 76 (pen), Euell 95, Hunt 112)*
Middlesbrough (0) 1 *(Ricard 45)* 5991
Wimbledon: Davis; Holloway, Hawkins, Andersen, Williams, Cunningham, Ainsworth, Euell, Agyemang (Gray), Karlsson (Hunt), Francis (Ardley).
Middlesbrough: Schwarzer; Fleming, Gordon, Festa, Ehiogu, Cooper, Stamp (Campbell), Mustoe, Ricard (Hudson), Deane (Boksic), Ince.
aet.

FIFTH ROUND

17 FEB

Bolton W (0) 1 *(Ricketts 62)*
Blackburn R (1) 1 *(Dunn 40)*   22,048

Bolton W: Sommer; O'Kane, Charlton, Hendry, Bergsson, Nolan, Summerbee (Wheatcroft), Passi, Ricketts (Hansen), Farrelly (Frandsen), Gardner.
Blackburn R: Friedel; Curtis, Mahon, Short, Berg, Taylor, Flitcroft, Jansen (Hignett), Bent (Hughes), Berkovic (Duff), Dunn.

Leicester C (2) 3 *(Sturridge 10, Hill 15 (og), Izzet 83 (pen))*
Bristol C (0) 0   20,905

Leicester C: Royce; Sinclair, Guppy, Elliott (Oakes), Rowett, Davidson, Savage, Izzet, Akinbiyi (Benjamin), Sturridge (Gunnlaugsson), Jones.
Bristol C: Phillips; Hill, Bell, Clist, Millen, Carey, Murray, Brown A, Peacock, Thorpe, Tinnion.

Southampton (0) 0
Tranmere R (0) 0   15,232

Southampton: Jones; Dodd, Bridge, Oakley (El Khalej), Lundekvam, Richards, Tessem, Draper, Beattie, Pahars, Kachloul (Rosler).
Tranmere R: Achterberg; Hinds, Yates, Hill (Challinor), Jobson, Allen, Flynn, Parkinson (Barlow), Rideout, Hamilton (Henry), Koumas.

Sunderland (0) 0
West Ham U (0) 1 *(Kanoute 76)*   36,005

Sunderland: Sorensen; Williams, Makin, McCann, Varga (McCartney) (Dichio), Emerson, Schwarz, Arca, Quinn, Phillips, Oster.
West Ham U: Hislop; Schemmel, Winterburn, Stimac, Dailly, Pearce S, Lampard, Cole, Kanoute, Di Canio, Carrick.

Tottenham H (3) 4 *(King 5, Davies 30, 50, Flynn 40 (og))*
Stockport Co (0) 0   36,040

Tottenham H: Sullivan; Young, Clemence, Doherty, Campbell, King, Freund, Sherwood, Rebrov (Korsten), Ferdinand (Thelwell), Leonhardsen (Davies).
Stockport Co: Jones; Gibb (Connelly), Clark (Fradin), Grayson, Flynn, Clare, Cooper (Carrigan), Wiss, Wilbraham, Kuqi, Nicholson.

Wycombe W (0) 2 *(Simpson 72, Brown 80)*
Wimbledon (2) 2 *(Williams 32, Agyemang 44)*   9650

Wycombe W: Taylor; Rogers, Vinnicombe, McCarthy, Cousins, Ryan, Carroll (Parkin), Simpson, Rammell (Bulman), Lee (Baird), Brown.
Wimbledon: Davis; Holloway, Hawkins, Andersen, Williams, Cunningham, Ainsworth, Euell, Agyemang (Gayle), Karlsson, Ardley.

18 FEB

Arsenal (0) 3 *(Henry 52 (pen), Wiltord 74, 85)*
Chelsea (0) 1 *(Hasselbaink 62)*   38,096

Arsenal: Seaman; Dixon, Cole, Vieira, Stepanovs, Luzhny, Pires (Wiltord), Lauren, Henry, Bergkamp (Vivas), Ljungberg.
Chelsea: Cudicini; Ferrer (Stanic), Babayaro, Jokanovic, Terry, Desailly, Poyet, Dalla Bona (Gudjohnsen), Hasselbaink, Zola (Gronkjaer), Wise.

Liverpool (2) 4 *(Litmanen 7 (pen), Heskey 13, Smicer 54 (pen), Babbel 85)*
Manchester C (1) 2 *(Kanchelskis 29, Goater 90)*   36,231

Liverpool: Westerveld; Babbel, Carragher, Hamann, Henchoz, Hyypia, Litmanen (Barmby), Smicer (Owen), Heskey (Fowler), Biscan, Ziege.
Manchester C: Weaver; Haaland, Granville, Dunne, Morrison (Grant), Prior, Kanchelskis, Wiekens, Huckerby, Goater, Tiatto.

FIFTH ROUND REPLAYS

20 FEB

Tranmere R (0) 4 *(Rideout 59, 71, 80, Barlow 83)*
Southampton (3) 3 *(Kachloul 12, Tessem 26, Richards 45)*   12,910

Tranmere R: Achterberg; Hinds, Yates, Allen, Jobson, Challinor (Barlow), Flynn, Parkinson, Rideout, Hamilton (Henry), Koumas (Roberts).
Southampton: Jones; Gibbens, Bridge, Marsden, Lundekvam, Richards, Tessem, Draper, Beattie, Pahars (Bleidelis) (Rosler), Kachloul.

Wimbledon (1) 1 *(Ainsworth 12)*
Wycombe W (1) 1 *(Carroll 32)*   9464

Wimbledon: Davis; Holloway, Hawkins, Andersen, Williams, Cunningham, Ainsworth (Hunt), Euell, Agyemang (Gray), Karlsson (Gayle), Ardley.
Wycombe W: Taylor; Bulman, Vinnicombe, McCarthy, Cousins, Bates, Carroll (Townsend), Simpson, Rammell (Baird) (Parkin), Ryan, Brown.
aet; Wycombe W won 8-7 on penalties.

7 MAR

Blackburn R (0) 3 *(Flitcroft 56, Hignett 73 (pen), 80)*
Bolton W (0) 0   20,318

Blackburn R: Friedel; Hignett, Duff (Keller), Short, Taylor, Bjornebye, Flitcroft, Berkovic, Bent (Jansen), Hughes, Mahon (Johnson).
Bolton W: Banks; Richardson, Charlton, Bergsson, Marshall, Elliott, Summerbee (Hansen), Nolan (Frandsen), Ricketts, Holdsworth, Passi (Farrelly).

SIXTH ROUND

10 MAR

Arsenal (3) 3 *(Wiltord 2, Adams 5, Pires 36)*
Blackburn R (0) 0   36,304

Arsenal: Seaman; Dixon, Cole, Grimandi, Adams, Pires (Henry), Lauren, Wiltord, Bergkamp (Vieira), Ljungberg (Silvinho).
Blackburn R: Friedel; McAteer, Mahon (Bjornebye), Curtis, Berg, Taylor, Flitcroft, Berkovic (Duff), Bent, Hughes (Jansen), Dunn.

Leicester C (0) 1 *(Izzet 68)*
Wycombe W (0) 2 *(McCarthy 50, Essendoh 90)*   21,969

Leicester C: Royce; Impey, Guppy, Elliott, Rowett, Taggart, Savage (Eadie), Izzet, Akinbiyi (Gunnlaugsson), Sturridge (Benjamin), Oakes.
Wycombe W: Taylor; Townsend, Vinnicombe (Lee), McCarthy, Cousins, Bates, Bulman, Simpson, Clegg (Essendoh), Ryan (Castledine), Brown.

11 MAR

Tranmere R (0) 2 *(Yates 47, Allison 58)*
Liverpool (2) 4 *(Murphy 12, Owen 27, Gerrard 52, Fowler 82 (pen))*   16,342

Tranmere R: Achterberg; Yates, Roberts, Henry, Jobson (Challinor), Allen, Hinds, Parkinson, Rideout (Allison), Barlow, Koumas.
Liverpool: Westerveld; Babbel, Carragher, McAllister, Wright, Hyypia, Gerrard, Barmby (Biscan), Fowler, Owen (Litmanen), Murphy (Smicer).

West Ham U (1) 2 *(Pearce S 43, Todorov 72)*
Tottenham H (1) 3 *(Rebrov 31, 57, Doherty 62)*   26,048

West Ham U: Hislop; Schemmel (Todorov), Winterburn, Stimac, Dailly, Pearce S, Lampard, Cole, Kanoute, Di Canio, Carrick.
Tottenham H: Sullivan; Young, Clemence, Doherty, Campbell, Perry, Freund, Iversen, Rebrov, Ferdinand (Korsten), King.

SEMI-FINALS

8 APR

Arsenal (1) 2 *(Vieira 33, Pires 74)*
Tottenham H (1) 1 *(Doherty 14)* 63,541

Arsenal: Seaman; Dixon, Silvinho, Vieira, Keown, Adams, Parlour, Lauren, Wiltord (Cole), Henry, Pires (Ljungberg).
Tottenham H: Sullivan; Carr, Young, Doherty, Campbell (King), Perry, Sherwood, Iversen, Rebrov, Ferdinand (Leonhardsen), Clemence (Thelwell).
at Old Trafford.

Wycombe W (0) 1 *(Ryan 88)*
Liverpool (0) 2 *(Heskey 78, Fowler 83)* 40,037

Wycombe W: Taylor; Townsend (Carroll), Vinnicombe, McCarthy, Cousins, Bates, Bulman, Simpson, Rammell (Essendoh), Ryan, Brown (Whittingham).
Liverpool: Westerveld; Babbel, Carragher, Hamann, Henchoz, Hyypia, Barmby (Gerrard), McAllister, Fowler, Owen (Murphy), Ziege (Heskey).
at Villa Park.

FINAL (at Millennium Stadium)

12 MAY

Arsenal (0) 1 *(Ljungberg 72)*
Liverpool (0) 2 *(Owen 83, 88)* 74,200

Arsenal: Seaman; Dixon (Bergkamp), Cole, Vieira, Keown, Adams, Pires, Grimandi, Wiltord (Parlour), Henry, Ljungberg (Kanu).
Liverpool: Westerveld; Babbel, Carragher, Hamann (McAllister), Henchoz, Hyypia, Murphy (Berger), Gerrard, Heskey, Owen, Smicer (Fowler).
Referee: S. Dunn (Bristol).

Thierry Henry (14) the Arsenal striker is challenged by Liverpool's Steve Gerrard (17) during the FA Cup Final.
(Actionimages/John Sibley)

THE SCOTTISH SEASON 2000–2001

There are always plenty of thoughts and expectations at the start of a new season. What is going to happen? Will Rangers still rule the roast? Will Celtic be able to mount a challenge? How will the new set-up in the SPL work? What of the other divisions? Will the new clubs from the Highland League make their presence felt? How will our clubs fare in Europe? Is this new season going to be fun?

The SPL was soon resolved. Celtic and Rangers each started with four straight wins. Celtic then demolished Rangers 6-2 at Parkhead, and many of the pundits at once said that the league was over. They were told not to be silly, but they had interpreted the writing on the wall correctly. Celtic continued on a serene way, and even a heavy loss at Ibrox at the end of November failed to do much more than give a moment's hope to the Rangers' fans. Meantime Hibs had struck a rich patch of form. They topped the league early on, gave way to Celtic in September, but only yielded second place to Rangers in mid-February. They were comfortably esconced in third place when the season ended. There was a flash of public interest as the cut arrived after the 33rd match at the start of April. Whatever anyone may try to say or prove, the league of twelve clubs is ungainly and unwieldy. We know the reason for it of course. Anyway, the division into two groups of six duly took place, and Dundee just managed to beat Dunfermline and Motherwell for the sixth place, and thus a place in the top echelon. And that was the Dens Park season as good as over. It was well for the organisers that there was interest as the last games were played: was it to be Kilmarnock or Hearts for fourth place, and the chance of European football? In the end Killie holed out against a rather weakened Celtic team, and Hearts' final win was to no avail. Craig Levein refused to make capital out of this despite some encouragement, and generously congratulated Killie whilst fully comprehending Celtic's desire to rest some of their not-quite-fit players a week before the Cup Final. In the last weeks the real interest lay in the bottom pair in the table. Dundee United had an abysmal start to their season, which resulted in the resignation of manager Paul Sturrock and subsequently of chairman Jim McLean. These two, who had done so much to put United amongst the top clubs in Scotland – the one as a player, the other as manager – left the club when it was firmly rooted at the foot of the table. Alex Smith, who took over the team, struggled; but with the influx of some useful Scottish players, the tide started to turn. Gradually United began to perform and to gain confidence; but it was not until the end of February that they managed to reach eleventh place – and leave St Mirren in the relegation-facing twelfth place. Both teams showed spirit and determination, but it was not until Dundee United managed to record an unlikely win against St Johnstone after a half-time deficit of two goals, that St Mirren's struggle for survival came to an end. Meantime the crowds at the games of the remainder at the lower level showed that there was not a lot of interest in the final placings, though Aberdeen picked up some of the confidence which had earlier been lacking.

If the SPL had looked all over early on, then the First and Second Divisions also had clubs which were firmly in command by mid-season: Livingston held a substantial lead at the turn of the year. Although, through dropping several games behind, they were temporarily deposed from top spot by Ayr United, it was ephemeral. The Livi Lions swept again into pole position, and were not to be gainsaid. Ayr were comfortably in second place: they had a very sound league season, although this normally difficult-to-beat cup side was dismissed early by lowly opposition in both the Scottish and CIS. Falkirk were rather disappointing and never looked solid; Inverness began with a win, but then lost four in a row to be at the foot of the table; from there they made a steady upward progress, and finished a creditable fourth. Ross County also finished in mid-table after some alarms; the weather was not kind to them, and too many fixtures had to be played in the last few weeks; so perhaps it was as well that they were not challenging for honours. Raith Rovers looked to be slipping towards the Second Division until they won a vital

game against Alloa, who sadly return after one season, accompanied by Morton. Raith, together with Airdrie and Morton and Clydebank, experienced some difficulties off the field, and we can just hope that financial problems will not mean the demise of any league club.

Partick Thistle soon took charge in the Second Division. They really had no business to be there at all, but they showed their class, and swept ahead, led by enthusiastic management on and off the field, and supported by devoted fans. Indeed, it was not unusual for their crowds at home easily to outnumber the total of crowds at all the other games that day in the division. Arbroath took second place, but only after a fascinating struggle with Berwick and Stranraer. At the lower end, Stirling Albion and Queen's Park go down. It is rather sad to see the amateurs descend after such a brief visit, and after they had done so well early in the season; however, Forfar must be congratulated on gritting their teeth, and finishing in a most determined manner when all had seemed almost hopeless. Stirling did not look at all convincing, though at times it seemed very odd that they were at the foot of the table.

There was a group of three looking for the first two places in the Third Division. Early on, Cowdenbeath made the running, and, when their manager was translated to higher spheres, they held on to finish second, whilst Hamilton came through at the tape to win the Division; this left Brechin, who had fought a good fight, a rather disconsolate third. East Fife came next, but never challenged for top spot, whilst Peterhead, fifth, completed a successful inaugural season. Elgin City had their moments, but perhaps need a little more time to adjust to the SFL. Dumbarton looked a better side than their 6th place suggested; perhaps, in their new home, they can look forward to an upward surge soon.

The Tennent's Scottish Cup threw up some new heroes. Buckie Thistle distinguished themselves against league opposition; Berwick lost narrowly in a replay at Tynecastle; Livingston beat Aberdeen. Inverness were within a whisker of defeating Kilmarnock – and there were difficulties with weather in the replay, with their supporters travelling long distances in inclement freezing conditions only for the game to be stopped after a short while. This is a problem which it is not easy to resolve, and it is the referee who usually gets the blame. That is hard. He has to make decisions on the best available advice, and if the conditions change suddenly, as can happen, he is left looking rather stupid. In the later stages of the Cup, Dundee United, now beginning to find some form, dismissed Rangers. For a moment it seemed as if a fairy-tale end might allow Alex Smith to win the trophy with his third different side, but there was an inevitability about Celtic, who went on to add this Cup to the CIS Insurance Cup and the SPL. The Bell's Challenge Cup was won by Airdrieonians – a bright spot in their season; they defeated Livingston in the final after a thrilling penalty shoot-out.

This, then, was Celtic's season. It was inspired by Martin O'Neill, who introduced a discipline and enthusiasm, and a 'togetherness', which have not really been seen since the days of Jock Stein. Celtic can go ahead now with confidence, and hopefully may be able to make an impression in Europe. Rangers had, by their own high standards, a poor season. They lost the place at times, and, though they suffered severe losses through injury, this was not the whole story. It may be hoped that they can regain their challenge in the new season – particularly in Europe, where, after a bright start, they fizzled out.

The vital qualifying games come soon, and Scotland are at least in a challenging position to reach the World Cup finals. 'How,' says Craig Brown, 'can one hope to pick a good team to represent us when so few home players represent their clubs at top level?' He is right. It is not easy, and the fact that he can still produce not-bad teams is a remarkable achievement.

As usual, we are not altogether short of encouraging signs. Can we hope that at last we may glimpse success?

ALAN ELLIOTT

ABERDEEN   Premier League

Year Formed: 1903. *Ground & Address:* Pittodrie Stadium, Pittodrie St, Aberdeen AB24 5QH. *Telephone:* 01224 650400. *Fax:* 01224 644173.
Ground Capacity: all seated: 22,199. *Size of Pitch:* 110yd × 72yd.
Chairman: Stewart Milne. *Secretary:* Roy Johnston. *Operations Manager:* John Morgan.
Manager: Ebbe Skovdahl. *Assistant Manager:* Gardner Speirs. *Physios:* David Wylie, John Sharp.
Managers since 1975: Ally MacLeod, Billy McNeill, Alex Ferguson, Ian Porterfield, Alex Smith and Jocky Scott, Willie Miller, Roy Aitken, Alex Miller, Paul Hegarty. *Club Nicknames(s):* The Dons. *Previous Grounds:* None.
Record Attendance: 45,061 v Hearts, Scottish Cup 4th rd; 13 Mar, 1954.
Record Transfer Fee received: £1.75 million for Eoin Jess to Coventry City (February 1996).
Record Transfer Fee paid: £1m+ for Paul Bernard from Oldham Athletic (September 1995).
Record Victory: 13-0 v Peterhead, Scottish Cup; 9 Feb, 1923.
Record Defeat: 0-8 v Celtic, Division 1; 30 Jan, 1965.
Most Capped Players: Alex McLeish, 77, Scotland.
Most League Appearances: 556: Willie Miller, 1973-90.
Most League Goals in Season (Individual): 38: Benny Yorston, Division I; 1929-30.
Most Goals Overall (Individual): 199: Joe Harper.

ABERDEEN 2000–01 LEAGUE RECORD

Match No.	Date	Venue	Opponents		Result	H/T Score	Lg. Pos.	Goalscorers	Atten-dance
1	Jul 29	A	Dunfermline Ath	D	0-0	0-0	—		7381
2	Aug 5	H	St Mirren	W	2-1	1-1	5	Stavrum [5], Perry [88]	11,996
3	13	H	Hearts	D	1-1	1-1	5	Young Dere [3]	11,139
4	19	H	Hibernian	L	0-2	0-1	7		12,450
5	27	A	Motherwell	D	1-1	1-1	8	Winters [11]	6009
6	Sept 9	H	St Johnstone	D	1-1	0-0	9	Winters [74]	10,464
7	16	A	Kilmarnock	L	0-1	0-1	9		6876
8	23	H	Dundee U	W	5-3	3-0	8	Winters 3 (1 pen) [8, 18, 80 lp], Young Dere [29], Jess [90]	4974
9	Oct 1	H	Celtic	D	1-1	1-0	7	Winters [44]	17,580
10	14	A	Dundee	L	0-2	0-1	7		15,332
11	21	H	Dunfermline Ath	D	0-0	0-0	8		11,195
12	28	A	St Mirren	L	0-2	0-1	9		5763
13	Nov 4	A	Hearts	L	0-3	0-1	10		12,744
14	12	H	Rangers	L	1-2	1-1	10	Stavrum [5]	16,798
15	18	A	Hibernian	W	2-0	0-0	10	Stavrum [61], Mayer [89]	10,995
16	25	H	Motherwell	D	3-3	1-2	10	Stavrum [42], Di Rocco 2 [80, 89]	11,502
17	28	A	St Johnstone	D	0-0	0-0	—		4897
18	Dec 2	H	Kilmarnock	L	1-2	1-2	10	Stavrum [44]	11,584
19	13	A	Rangers	L	1-3	1-1	—	Stavrum [10]	45,285
20	16	A	Celtic	L	0-6	0-2	10		59,677
21	23	A	Dundee	D	2-2	1-0	10	Di Rocco [13], Stavrum (pen) [73]	9093
22	26	A	Dunfermline Ath	L	2-3	2-1	—	Rowson [37], Dow [44]	6880
23	Jan 2	H	Hearts	W	1-0	1-0	—	Rowson [7]	12,760
24	31	A	Rangers	L	0-1	0-1	—		45,621
25	Feb 10	A	Motherwell	W	1-0	0-0	10	Young Dere [88]	6680
26	21	H	St Mirren	W	3-0	1-0	—	Stavrum 3 [43, 69, 82]	9457
27	Mar 3	A	Kilmarnock	D	0-0	0-0	10		6577
28	13	H	Hibernian	W	1-0	1-0	—	Guntweit [2]	8799
29	17	A	Dundee U	D	1-1	1-1	9	Winters [12]	8472
30	27	H	St Johnstone	D	3-3	2-1	—	Young Darr [30], Winters [35], Young Dere [71]	8496
31	Apr 1	H	Celtic	L	0-1	0-0	10		16,064
32	4	H	Dundee U	W	4-1	3-1	—	Stavrum 3 [5, 29, 84], Young Dere [41]	9562
33	7	H	Dundee	L	0-2	0-0	9		12,005
34	21	A	Dunfermline Ath	W	1-0	1-0	8	Stavrum [30]	8613
35	28	A	St Johnstone	W	3-0	2-0	7	Mackie 2 [24, 44], Stavrum [78]	3611
36	May 5	A	Motherwell	W	2-0	1-0	7	Stavrum [30], Winters [56]	3905
37	12	A	St Mirren	L	1-2	1-2	7	Young Dere [14]	5780
38	20	H	Dundee U	L	1-2	0-2	7	Stavrum [72]	11,683

Final League Position: 7

Honours
League Champions: Division I 1954-55. Premier Division 1979-80, 1983-84, 1984-85; *Runners-up:* Division I 1910-11, 1936-37, 1955-56, 1970-71, 1971-72. Premier Division 1977-78, 1980-81, 1981-82, 1988-89, 1989-90, 1990-91, 1992-93, 1993-94.
Scottish Cup Winners: 1947, 1970, 1982, 1983, 1984, 1986, 1990; *Runners-up:* 1937, 1953, 1954, 1959, 1967, 1978, 1993, 2000.
League Cup Winners: 1955-56, 1976-77, 1985-86, 1989-90, (Coca Cola cup) 1995-96; *Runners-up:* 1946-47, 1978-79, 1979-80, 1987-88, 1988-89, 1992-93, 1999-2000.
Drybrough Cup Winners: 1971, 1980.

European: *European Cup:* 12 matches (1980-81, 1984-85, 1985-86); *Cup Winners' Cup:* 39 matches (1967-68, 1970-71, 1978-79, 1982-83 winners, 1983-84 semi-finals, 1986-87, 1990-91, 1993-94); *UEFA Cup:* 44 matches (*Fairs Cup:* 1968-69. *UEFA Cup:* 1971-72, 1972-73, 1973-74, 1977-78, 1979-80, 1981-82, 1987-88, 1988-89, 1989-90, 1991-92, 1994-95, 1996-97, 2000-01).

Club colours: Shirt, Shorts, Stockings: Red with white trim.

Goalscorers: *League* (45): Stavrum 17 (1 pen), Winters 9 (1 pen), Derek Young 6, Di Rocco 3, Mackie 2, Rowson 2, Dow 1, Guntweit 1, Jess 1, Mayer 1, Perry 1, Darren Young 1
Scottish Cup (3): Mackie 1, Rowson 1, Winters 1
CIS Cup (2): Winters 1, Derek Young 1

Esson R 36	Perry M 7+2	McAllister J 21+4	Solberg T 20+2	Dow A 4+11	Young Darr 31	Rowson D 35	Jess E 12+2	Winters R 37	Stavrum A 28+3	Young Dere 27+4	McGuire P 26+3	Zerouali H 2+3	Rutkiewicz K —+3	McNaughton K 30+3	Guntweit C 28+2	Clark C 14+10	Belabed R 5+14	Mackie D 12+10	Whyte D 29	Bernard P 3	Mayer A —+7	Di Rocco A 7+3	Lilley D 2+6	Preece D 2	Bett C —+2	O'Donoghue R —+2	Tiernan F —+2	Michie S —+1	Match No.
1	2	3	4¹	5	6	7	8	9¹	10²	11	12	13	14																1
1	2	3¹	5²		6	7	8	9¹	10				4	11	12	13	14												2
1	2				12	6¹	5	8	9	10¹	11	4	13		3¹	7	14												3
1	2				13	6	5	9	10¹	11	4	12			3	7	8²												4
1				14	6		5	9²	11	2	10¹				3	8	13	12	4		7								5
1				10¹		6²	5	9				2		11	3	8	12	13	4		7								6
1					6²		5	10³	9			2		13	3	8	11	12	4		7¹	14							7
1	14				6		5	8	9²	11		2			3	7	10¹	13	12			4³							8
1					5		8	9	11	2					3	6	10	12	4		7¹								9
1	13				5		8	9	11	2					3	6¹	10	12	4		7²								10
1	2		13		6	5	8	9	12						3	7²	10	11¹	4										11
1	2				6	5	8	9	11						3	7¹	10²		4										12
1	2	3²	7¹		6		8	9	12	11³					5	10	14		4			13							13
1	13	2			6	5		9	10	11					3²	7³	8¹		4			14	12						14
1	14	2			6	12	5	9	10³						3	7	11¹		4			13	8²						15
1		2			6	12	5	9	10	11²					3	7	13		4			8							16
1		12			6	5	8	9²	10²	13		2			3	7	14		4¹			11							17
1	13	4			6¹	5	8	9	10	12		2²			3	7³					14	11							18
1		3	4		13	5		9²	10	11		2			6²	7	8²					12	14						19
1		3²	4		12	5		9²	10	11		2				7	8¹				14		13	6					20
1		3			6	12	5	9	10	11		2				8	13		4		7²								21
1		3²	7³		6	5		9	10	11¹		2			13	12			4		14	8							22
1		3	6		12	7	5	9²	10	11¹		2			13				4			8							23
1	14		6³		7	5		9	13	11		2			3	8²	10¹	12	4						1				24
1		3	2			5		9	10²	12					6	7	8	11¹			4		13		1				25
1	3	4	7¹			5		9	10	11³		2			6²	12	14		8				13						26
1	3²	4		12	6	5		9	10³	11		2				7	14		8¹				13						27
1	3				7	5		9	10¹	11		2		12	6	8			4				13						28
1	3				7	5		9	10	11		2			6²	8¹	12		4				13						29
1	3²				7	5		9	10¹	11		2			6	8	12		4				13						30
1	3	14	7¹			5		9	10	11²		2			6²	12	13	8	4										31
1	3	12	7			5		9²	10	11		2			14	8¹	13		4			6³							32
1	3²	6	14	7²	5			9	10	11		2				8¹	12	13	4										33
1	3	6¹	7		5			9²	10³			2		8	11		13		4				12			14			34
1	3	6	7¹	5²				9	10			2		8	9	14	11³		4							12	13		35
1	3²	5		6				9²	10	12	13	2		8	14	7¹	11		4										36
1	3³	5			7			9	10	11²	14	2		6	12	8			4				13						37
1	3		7²					9	10	11³	2			5	6	8¹			4							12	13	14	38

AIRDRIEONIANS

First Division

Year Formed: 1878. *Ground & Address:* Shyberry Excelsior Stadium, Broomfield Park, Craigneuk Avenue, Airdrie ML6 8QZ. *Telephone:* 01236 622000.
Ground Capacity: all seated: 10,000. *Size of Pitch:* 112yd × 76yd.
Acting Secretary: Ethel Pattenden.
Manager: Ian McCall.
Managers since 1975: I. McMillan, J. Stewart, R. Watson, W. Munro, A. MacLeod, D. Whiteford, G. McQueen, J. Bone, A. MacDonald, Gary Mackay. *Club Nickname(s):* The Diamonds or The Waysiders. *Previous Grounds:* Mavisbank, Broomfield Park.
Record Attendance: 26,000 v Hearts, Scottish Cup; 8 Mar, 1952 (at Broomfield Park). 8762 v Celtic, League Cup 3rd rd, 19 Aug 1998 (at Shyberry Excelsior Stadium).
Record Transfer Fee received: £200,000 for Sandy Clark to West Ham U (May 1982).
Record Transfer Fee paid: £175,000 for Owen Coyle from Clydebank (February 1990).
Record Victory: 15-1 v Dundee Wanderers, Division II; 1 Dec, 1894.
Record Defeat: 1-11 v Hibernian, Division I; 24 Oct, 1959.
Most Capped Player: Jimmy Crapnell, 9, Scotland.
Most League Appearances: 523; Paul Jonquin, 1962-79.
Most League Goals in Season (Individual): 53, Hugh Baird, Division II, 1954-55. *Most Goals Overall (Individual):* —

AIRDRIEONIANS 2000–01 LEAGUE RECORD

Match No.	Date		Venue	Opponents	Result	H/T Score	Lg. Pos.	Goalscorers	Atten- dance
1	Aug	5	A	Inverness CT	L 0-2	0-1	—		2366
2		12	H	Raith R	D 1-1	1-0	8	Sanjuan [18]	2854
3		19	A	Ayr U	L 1-3	1-0	9	Prest [31]	2705
4		26	A	Ross Co	D 1-1	1-1	9	Forrest [44]	2210
5	Sept	9	H	Alloa Ath	D 2-2	1-0	9	Fernandez [28], Sanjuan [58]	1806
6		16	A	Clyde	L 1-4	0-0	10	Prest [72]	1864
7		23	H	Livingston	L 1-2	0-0	10	Prest [47]	1826
8		30	A	Morton	W 5-1	2-1	9	Elliott B [25], Fernandez [44], Moreau [56], Ireland [65], Capin [82]	1377
9	Oct	7	A	Falkirk	L 1-2	1-1	10	Ireland [21]	2879
10		14	H	Inverness CT	L 1-2	0-0	10	Fernandez [58]	1555
11		21	A	Raith R	D 1-1	1-0	10	Elliott J [24]	1930
12		28	H	Ross Co	W 5-1	3-0	9	Fernandez [9], Taylor [11], Calderon [36], Elliott J [54], Prest [72]	1431
13	Nov	4	A	Alloa Ath	L 0-2	0-1	10		1220
14		11	A	Livingston	D 2-2	1-2	9	Taylor [15], Calderon [66]	3915
15		22	H	Clyde	L 1-3	1-0	—	McCann (pen) [37]	1513
16		25	A	Falkirk	W 2-0	1-0	10	Moreau [34], Pilvi [88]	2867
17	Dec	2	H	Morton	D 1-1	0-1	10	Forrest [89]	1643
18		9	H	Ayr U	D 0-0	0-0	9		1572
19		16	A	Inverness CT	L 0-4	0-2	9		1570
20		26	H	Alloa Ath	W 2-1	0-1	—	Sanjuan 2 (2 pens) [53, 78]	1427
21	Jan	2	A	Clyde	D 1-1	0-1	—	Moreau [80]	1769
22		6	H	Livingston	D 1-1	0-1	9	Moreau [76]	2382
23		13	A	Morton	W 3-0	0-0	7	Moreau [70], Pilvi [80], Fernandez [85]	2602
24	Feb	3	A	Ayr U	D 2-2	1-0	8	Moreau [40], Sanjuan [49]	2060
25		10	H	Raith R	W 3-0	1-0	6	Fernandez 2 [24, 49], McGuire [67]	1753
26	Mar	24	H	Falkirk	L 1-2	1-0	7	Taylor [38]	1644
27		27	A	Alloa Ath	L 0-6	0-2	—		632
28		31	H	Clyde	W 1-0	1-0	7	Coyle (pen) [5]	1309
29	Apr	3	A	Ross Co	W 4-3	2-1	—	Coyle 2 [4, 68], Taylor [14], Dunn [77]	1645
30		7	A	Falkirk	D 1-1	0-1	6	Coyle [50]	2040
31		10	H	Ross Co	D 2-2	1-1	—	Bannerman [2], Coyle [37]	1211
32		14	H	Morton	L 0-2	0-1	7		1331
33		21	H	Inverness CT	D 1-1	0-0	6	Coyle (pen) [57]	805
34		28	H	Raith R	L 0-5	0-1	8		2186
35	May	1	A	Livingston	L 0-5	0-4	—		3295
36		5	H	Ayr U	D 1-1	0-1	8	Dunn [65]	8185

Final League Position: 8

Honours
League Champions: Division II 1902-03, 1954-55, 1973-74; *Runners-up:* Division I 1922-23, 1923-24, 1924-25, 1925-26.
First Division 1979-80, 1989-90, 1990-91, 1996-97. Division II 1900-01, 1946-47, 1949-50, 1965-66.
Scottish Cup Winners: 1924; *Runners-up:* 1975, 1992, 1995. *Scottish Spring Cup Winners:* 1976.
League Cup semi-finalists: 1991-92, 1994-95, 1998-99.
B&Q Cup Winners: 1994-95.
Bell's Challenge Cup: 2000-01

European: *Cup Winners' Cup:* 2 matches (1992-93).

Club colours: Shirt: White with red diamond. Shorts: White. Stockings: Red.

Goalscorers: *League* (49): Fernandez 7, Coyle 6 (2 pens), Moreau 6, Sanjuan 5 (2 pens), Prest 4, Taylor 4, Calderon 2, Dunn 2, Elliott J 2, Forrest 2, Ireland 2, Pilvi 2, Bannerman 1, Capin 1, Elliot B 1, McCann 1 (pen), McGuire 1
Scottish Cup (3): Moreau 1, Pilvi 1, Sanjuan 1
CIS Cup (4): Alfonso 1, Elliott J 1, Fernandez 1, McCann 1
Bell's League Cup (10): Prest 3, Calderon 1, Clark 1, Fernandez 1, McGuire 1, McKeown 1, Pacifico 1, Taylor 1

Broto J 23	Alfonso M 11	McAlpine A 7 + 7	Forrest E 25	Struthers W — + 3	Aguilar M 1	Nicolas F 1	Moreau F 21 + 3	Cameron I 9	Capin S 7 + 7	Sanjuan J 21 + 1	Prest M 13 + 5	Wishart F 9	Fernandez D 19 +	Evans G — + 4	Boyce S 13 + 9	McGuire D 2 + 11	Coyle O 9	Taylor S 14 + 5	McCann A 20	Gardner L 9	Brady D 20 + 1	Coulter R 6	Clark P 1 + 2	McWilliams D 6	Elliott J 7 + 8	Elliott B 2 + 1	Wilson S 2 + 2	McKeown S — + 3	Armstrong P 26	Ireland C 12	Phillips T 1 + 1	Ingram S 2 + 3	Pilvi T 4 + 5	Gonzalez R 7 + 1	McManus T 1	Ferguson A 3	McPherson C 7	Sweeney S 10	Bannerman S 9	May E 4 + 2	Dunn R 5 + 6	Zahana-Oni L 1	Davidson S 2 + 3	Match No.
1	2	3²	4	5	6	7	8	9¹	10	11³	12	13	14																															1
1	4		5		6	7	8		10	11	12		9¹		2²	3	13																												2
1		4	2		6		9	10	11²	12			14	3	7	5	13																											3
1	4		5		6		8	12	10	11²	13	2²		3	7		14	9¹																										4
1	4		5		6		8	13	10	11³		2		14	3			9²	7¹	12																								5
	4		5¹		6		8	12	10	11		2		13	3		9¹	7²		1	14																							6
1	4²	3	5		6		8		9³	10³	11			13	7					12		14	2																					7
1		4²			6	12	8		10	11³				13	3	7		14	9		2¹	5																						8
1		4			6	12	8	9	10²	11				3	7²			13		14	2¹	5																						9
1		4			6	13	8	9	10¹	11				7	3			12			2²	5																						10
1³		5			7			9¹	10		3	13	8		4			11²			2	6	15	12																				11
1		5	14	13		12	10	11³		2			8	3	4			9¹			7²	6																					·	12
		5	14		8	9²	10		2¹	13			3	4			11¹			7	6	1	12																				13
1		5	12	7		9	10	11³		2¹	14	8¹		3	4			13			6																							14
1		5		8²	14	12		10¹	11			9		3	4			7²			2	6		13																				15
1		5	11	7²	8		10		13			3	4						2	6		9¹	12																				16
1		5	11³	7¹	8	13	10	14	12			3	4						2	6		9²																					17
1		5	7		8	9²	10	11³	2			3	4¹			13				6			12																					18
1		5	7		8	9¹	10²	11	2	12		3	4	6									13																					19
1⁶		5	7		8	9¹	10³	11		13		3	4						2	6			12	15																				20
1	6	5	10	7²	8	9				12		3	4			13			2			11¹																						21
1	6²	5		7	13	8	9¹	10				12	3	4					2			14		11²																				22
1	6	5	7		8		10²	11				12	3	4			13			2			9¹																					23
1	6	3	5		7		8		10¹	11				12	3	4				2			9																					24
1	6	3	5		7²	13	8		10³	11				12		4				14			9¹																					25
		12		13							2		4			6										1	3	5	7	8	9	10³	11¹											26
		13			5		11³				2¹		6			4					1	7					3		8	10	9		12											27
		14					8³	4		12	6		9		10	11³		2					1			3	5		7¹	13													28
		14					8¹	4		13	6		9		10³	11¹		2				1			3	5	7		12														29
							8¹	4		12	6		9		10	11³		2				1			3	5	7		13														30
							8⁵	4		13	6		9		10	11¹		2				1			3	5	7³	14	12														31
		13					8¹	4		12	6				9	10	11		2				1			3²	5	7³	14	12													32
		3					8⁵	4		13	6		9		10	11¹		2				1			5	7		12															33
		3						4		12	6		9		10			15					2			1⁸		5	7²	8¹	11		13	34
		13	14				8²	4		3			9		6	10			2			1				5	7¹		11³		12	35
		12	13				8			3¹			9		6	10			2			1				5		11		7²		36

ALBION ROVERS

Third Division

Year Formed: 1882. *Ground & Address:* Cliftonhill Stadium, Main St, Coatbridge ML5 3RB. *Telephone/Fax:* 01236 606334.
Ground capacity: total: 2496, seated: 538. *Size of Pitch:* 110yd × 72yd.
Chairman: Andrew Dick, *Company Secretary:* David Shanks BSc. *General Manager:* John Reynolds.
Commercial Managers: Dennis Newall and Chris Fancy.
Manager: John McVeigh. *Assistant Manager:* Andy Smith. *Youth Development:* Jimmy Lindsay. *Physio:* Dan Young.
Managers since 1975: G. Caldwell, S. Goodwin, H. Hood, J. Baker, D. Whiteford, M. Ferguson, W. Wilson, B. Rooney,
A. Ritchie, T. Gemmell, D. Provan, M. Oliver, B. McLaren, T. Gemmell, T Spence, J. Crease, V. Moore, B. McLaren.
Club Nickname(s): The Wee Rovers. *Previous Grounds:* Cowheath Park, Meadow Park, Whifflet.
Record Attendance: 27,381 v Rangers, Scottish Cup 2nd rd; 8 Feb, 1936.
Record Transfer Fee received: £40,000 from Motherwell for Bruce Cleland.
Record Transfer Fee paid: £7000 for Gerry McTeague to Stirling Albion, September 1989.
Record Victory: 12-0 v Airdriehill, Scottish Cup; 3 Sept, 1887.
Record Defeat: 1-11 v Partick T, League Cup, 11 August 1993.
Most Capped Player: Jock White, 1 (2), Scotland.
Most League Appearances: 399, Murdy Walls, 1921-36.
Most League Goals in Season (Individual): 41: Jim Renwick, Division II; 1932-33.
Most Goals Overall (Individual): 105: Bunty Weir, 1928-31.

ALBION ROVERS 2000–01 LEAGUE RECORD

Match No.	Date		Venue	Opponents	Result	H/T Score	Lg. Pos.	Goalscorers	Attendance
1	Aug	5	H	East Fife	L 0-1	0-0	—		465
2		12	A	Cowdenbeath	L 0-5	0-2	10		302
3		19	H	Elgin C	D 1-1	0-1	8	Clyde [76]	412
4		26	H	Dumbarton	L 0-1	0-1	9		343
5	Sept	9	A	Hamilton A	W 2-0	2-0	7	Booth [11], Begue [41]	487
6		16	H	Brechin C	L 1-3	1-1	8	Booth [18]	254
7		23	A	East Stirling	D 1-1	0-0	7	Begue [57]	271
8		30	H	Peterhead	D 0-0	0-0	8		358
9	Oct	7	A	Montrose	W 2-0	1-0	8	Grosset [1], McLees [87]	230
10		14	A	East Fife	D 0-0	0-0	8		445
11		21	H	Cowdenbeath	W 1-0	1-0	6	Shields [25]	429
12		28	A	Dumbarton	W 1-0	1-0	6	Shields [3]	277
13	Nov	4	H	Hamilton A	D 1-1	1-0	6	McKenzie [37]	608
14		11	A	East Stirling	W 2-1	1-1	6	McLees [4], Shields (pen) [82]	334
15		18	A	Brechin C	L 1-2	0-1	6	Diack [72]	337
16		25	H	Montrose	W 3-2	0-0	6	Shields [82], Booth [89], Waldie [90]	311
17	Dec	2	A	Peterhead	W 2-1	0-1	5	Shields [59], Booth [63]	516
18		23	H	East Fife	L 1-2	0-1	6	Smith [66]	372
19	Jan	2	A	Hamilton A	L 1-2	0-1	—	McBride [84], Harty [88]	540
20		27	H	Dumbarton	L 1-3	0-0	6	Smith [48]	369
21	Feb	3	A	Montrose	W 1-0	0-0	5	McKenna [67]	244
22		17	H	Elgin C	L 0-1	0-0	5		287
23		24	A	Cowdenbeath	L 0-1	0-0	5		331
24	Mar	10	A	Dumbarton	W 4-1	1-0	5	Lumsden [29], Harty 2 [60, 79], McMullan [89]	818
25		13	A	East Stirling	L 0-1	0-0	—		196
26		17	H	East Stirling	D 2-2	2-0	6	Stirling [9], McCormick [11]	248
27		20	H	Peterhead	L 0-1	0-0	—		272
28		25	H	Hamilton A	L 0-1	0-0	7		524
29		28	A	Elgin C	W 2-1	1-1	—	McCormick [15], Booth [70]	268
30	Apr	7	H	Montrose	W 2-1	1-0	7	Booth (pen) [37], Harty [52]	213
31		10	H	Brechin C	D 1-1	1-0	—	McCormick [32]	283
32		14	A	Peterhead	D 1-1	0-0	7	Lumsden [78]	526
33		17	A	Brechin C	W 2-1	1-0	—	Easton [43], McCormick [81]	369
34		21	A	East Fife	L 1-2	0-0	7	McCormick [86]	333
35		28	H	Cowdenbeath	D 0-0	0-0	6		405
36	May	5	A	Elgin C	L 0-1	0-0	7		487

Final League Position: 7

Honours
League Champions: Division II 1933-34, Second Division 1988-89; *Runners-up:* Division II 1913-14, 1937-38, 1947-48. *Scottish Cup Runners-up:* 1920. *League Cup:* —.

Club colours: Shirt: Yellow with red/black trim. Shorts: Red. Stockings: Yellow.

Goalscorers: *League* (38): Booth 6 (1 pen) McCormick 5, Shields 5 (1 pen), Harty 4, Begue 2, Lumsden 2, McLees 2, Smith 2, Clyde 1, Diack 1, Easton 1, Grosset 1, McBride 1, McKenna 1, McKenzie 1, McMullan 1, Stirling 1, Waldie 1
Scottish Cup (1): Shields
CIS Cup (0):
Bell's League Cup (0):

Fahey C 34	Smith J 11 + 4	Lumsden T 33	Clyde R 17	Clark S 21 + 1	Booth M 33	Waldie C 35 + 1	McKenzie J 16 + 6	Begue Y 11 + 1	Rankin I 3 + 11	Silvestro C 18 + 3	Diack I 3 + 10	McLees J 9 + 8	Martin A 1 + 1	Tait T 26	McMullan R 22 + 7	Harty M 10 + 9	Grosset W 3 + 3	McBride K 2 + 2	Shields P 11	McCormick S 15 + 1	Easton S 13 + 3	McKenna G 12 + 2	Ingram S 4 + 1	Stirling J 15	Coyne T 1	Rodden P 2 + 5	McMillan A 13	Deegan C — + 1	Carr D — + 1	Shearer S 2 + 1	Match No.
1	2	3	4	5	6	7	8	9¹	10	11	12																				1
1	2	3	4	5	6	7³	8¹	9²	10	11	13	12	14																		2
1	2	3²	4		6	8	13	9¹	12	11	10			5	7																3
1	2¹	3	4		6	12	8	13	11³	10		9²		5	7	14															4
1	2	3	4		6	7³	8	9²	12	11		13		5	10¹	14															5
1	2	3	4		6	7³	8	9²	13	11¹	12			5	10	14															6
1	14	3	4		6	2³	8	9	12	7	10¹			5	11²	13															7
1		3	4	2³	6	7	8	9¹	12	11	13			5	10																8
1		3	4	2	6	7¹	8	13	14	12				5	9	11²	10³														9
1		3	4	2	6	7	12	8		11				5	9¹	10															10
1		3	4	2	6	7		8		11				5	10	9															11
1	14	3	4	2³	6	7	12	8		11²				5	10¹	13	9														12
1	14	3	4	2	6	7	12	13	8	11				5	10¹		9²														13
1		3	4	2		7	8	13	6					5	10²	12	11¹	9													14
1		3	4	2		7	8		6	12	11¹			5	10²	13	9														15
1		3	4	2³	6	7	8		11	12				5	13		9	10²													16
1		3	4	2	6	7	8		11	13				5	12		9¹	10²													17
1	2	3³	4		6	7	10²	14	8¹		11			5	12		9	13													18
1	4	3		6	2		13	10²	11¹					5	7³	14	12		9	8											19
1	4		3	6²	2			12	14	13				5	10	11¹			7	8	9³										20
1	4			6	2	10		14	11²		5	7³	13					3	8	12	9³										21
1	5			6	2	10¹		4	7									8	11	12	3	9									22
1	2	4		6	7			12		5	10				8	11¹	9²	3		13											23
1	2			6	7					5	11	12			10²		8	9¹	3				4	13							24
1	2			6	7					5	11	9			10¹		8		3			12	4								25
1	2			6	7	13				5	11¹	9			10	12	8		3				4								26
1	5			6	2	8¹					7	9			10²	12	11		3			13	4								27
1				4	6	2	8				12	9			10	7	11¹		3			5									28
1	5			2	6	7	8³					14			12		11		10¹	13		3	9²	4							29
1	5			2	6	7¹	13					12	9¹		10	8	11¹		3			14	4								30
1	5			2	6	7					11	9¹			10	8			3			12	4								31
1	5			2³	6	7	13				12				11	9¹			8	14		3	10¹	4							32
1	5			2	6	7						9²				10¹	8	11	3			4	12	13							33
	5			2	6²	7	12				13	14	9³		10	8	11		3			4		1							34
1	2³	13		6	7		9¹	14		5		12			10	8	11³		3			4									35
	14	2		7	6		11	9²		5	13	12			10	8			3³			4¹		1							36

ALLOA ATHLETIC
Second Division

Year Formed: 1878. *Ground & Address:* Recreation Park, Clackmannan Rd, Alloa FK10 1RY. *Telephone:* 01259 722695.
Ground Capacity: total: 3100, seated: 400. *Size of Pitch:* 110yd × 75yd.
Chairman/Secretary: Ewen G. Cameron. *Commercial Director:* Willie McKie.
Manager: Terry Christie. *Assistant Manager:* Graeme Armstrong. *Physio:* Jim Law.
Managers since 1975: H. Wilson, A. Totten, W. Garner, J. Thomson, D. Sullivan, G. Abel, B. Little, H. McCann, W. Lamont, P. McAuley, T. Hendrie. *Club Nickname(s):* The Wasps. *Previous Grounds:* None.
Record Attendance: 13,000 v Dunfermline Athletic, Scottish Cup 3rd rd replay; 26 Feb, 1939.
Record Transfer Fee received: £100,000 for Martin Cameron to Bristol Rovers.
Record Transfer Fee paid: £26,000 for Ross Hamilton from Stenhousemuir.
Record Victory: 9-2 v Forfar Ath, Division II; 18 Mar, 1933.
Record Defeat: 0-10 v Dundee, Division II; 8 Mar, 1947: v Third Lanark, League Cup, 8 Aug, 1953.
Most Capped Player: Jock Hepburn, 1, Scotland.
Most League Appearances: —.
Most League Goals in Season (Individual): 49: 'Wee' Willie Crilley, Division II; 1921-22.
Most Goals Overall (Individual): —.

ALLOA ATHLETIC 2000–01 LEAGUE RECORD

Match No.	Date		Venue	Opponents	Result	H/T Score	Lg. Pos.	Goalscorers	Atten- dance
1	Aug	5	A	Raith R	W 2-1	2-0	—	Clark [24], Gaughan (og) [90]	2123
2		12	H	Ayr U	D 1-1	1-0	3	Irvine [34]	1274
3		19	A	Morton	L 0-2	0-1	5		1267
4		26	H	Livingston	L 0-6	0-1	7		983
5	Sept	9	A	Airdrieonians	D 2-2	0-1	7	Irvine (pen) [53], Wood [89]	1806
6		16	A	Falkirk	D 1-1	1-0	8	Hamilton [8]	2645
7		23	H	Inverness CT	L 1-4	0-2	9	Watson [86]	584
8		30	A	Ross Co	L 0-1	0-0	10		2775
9	Oct	7	H	Clyde	W 3-1	1-0	9	Thomson [31], Conway [50], Hamilton [56]	740
10		14	H	Raith R	L 0-1	0-0	9		987
11		21	A	Ayr U	L 1-3	1-2	9	Irvine [32]	2259
12		28	A	Livingston	L 0-4	0-2	10		3149
13	Nov	4	H	Airdrieonians	W 2-0	1-0	8	Irvine [29], Hamilton [78]	1220
14		11	A	Inverness CT	L 1-2	0-1	8	Johnston [60]	1384
15		18	H	Falkirk	W 3-2	0-1	8	Little [57], Hamilton [60], Conway [88]	1709
16		25	A	Clyde	D 0-0	0-0	8		1012
17	Dec	2	H	Ross Co	D 0-0	0-0	8		620
18		9	H	Morton	W 2-1	1-1	7	Nish 2 [30, 88]	704
19		16	A	Raith R	L 1-2	0-1	8	Nish [69]	1267
20		26	A	Airdrieonians	L 1-2	1-0	—	Hamilton [32]	1427
21	Jan	2	A	Falkirk	D 2-2	1-0	—	Evans [20], French [55]	2627
22		6	H	Inverness CT	D 1-1	0-1	8	Evans [85]	744
23		30	H	Livingston	L 0-2	0-1	—		684
24	Feb	3	A	Morton	D 1-1	1-0	9	Thomson [35]	1179
25		24	A	Livingston	L 0-1	0-0	9		3014
26	Mar	10	H	Clyde	D 0-0	0-0	9		818
27		13	H	Ayr U	L 0-2	0-0	—		539
28		17	A	Inverness CT	L 0-2	0-0	9		1613
29		24	A	Ross Co	W 3-2	1-1	9	Evans [40], Irvine [65], French [79]	2079
30		27	H	Airdrieonians	W 6-0	2-0	9	Hamilton 4 [30, 31, 50, 61], Thomson [64], Wood [85]	632
31		31	H	Falkirk	L 0-1	0-1	9		1186
32	Apr	7	A	Clyde	D 1-1	1-0	9	Wood [33]	1006
33		14	H	Ross Co	D 1-1	0-0	8	Little [82]	647
34		21	H	Raith R	L 1-2	0-1	9	Irvine (pen) [87]	1953
35		28	A	Ayr U	L 1-4	0-1	9	Irvine [66]	2234
36	May	5	H	Morton	L 0-3	0-3	10		770

Final League Position: 10

Honours
League Champions: Division II 1921-22; Third Division 1997-98. *Runners-up:* Division II 1938-39. Second Division 1976-77, 1981-82, 1984-85, 1988-89, 1999-2000.
Bell's League Challenge Cup: Winners 1999-2000.
Scottish Cup: —.
League Cup: —.

Club colours: Shirt: Gold with black trim. Shorts: Black. Stockings: Gold.

Goalscorers: *League* (38): Hamilton 9, Irvine 7 (2 pens), Evans 3, Nish 3, Thomson 3, Wood 3, Conway 2, French 2, Little 2, Clark 1, Johnston 1, Watson 1, own goal 1
Scottish Cup (0):
CIS Cup (2): Wood 2
Bell's League Cup (2): Hamilton 2

Cairns M 22	Huxford R 12+5	Clark D 28+2	Watson G 27+1	Conway F 19+3	Valentine C 28+1	Gardner L 3+4	Thomson S 31+3	Hamilton R 32+1	Irvine W 24+11	Little J 28+6	Wilson M —+5	Wood C 19+11	Beaton D —+1	Brigain C —+2	Davidson S 3	Christie M 25+2	Johnston G 16+8	Evans G 16+6	French H 21+4	McQueen J 1+1	Nish C 10	Murray I 2	Van De Kamp G 13	McQuillan J 11	McManus A 5	Armstrong G —+1	Match No
1	2¹	3	4	5	6		7	8	9	10	11²	12	13														1
1	2	3	4	5	6		7²	8	9	10	11¹	13	12														2
1	2	3¹	4	5¹	6			8	9	10	11					7	12	13									3
1	2¹	3	4	5	6		7²	12	9	10	11					8		13									4
1		3¹	4	5	6	12	7			10	11	9						2	8								5
1		3	4	5	6	12	13	7	10²	11		9						2	8¹								6
1	2	3	4	5¹	6	13	14	9	10	11						7²	8¹	12									7
1	2²	3	4		6	13	5	9	12	11	10					8¹	7										8
1	14	3	4	5	6		2	9³	13	11²	12					8	7	10¹									9
1		3	4	5	6		2	9²	13	11	14					8¹	7³	10	12								10
1²	13	3	2		6		5	7	10	12						8	4²	9¹	11	15							11
1	13	3	4	5¹	6		2	7¹	10	12						8	14	11³	9								12
1	2				6	13		5	12	10	11				3	8		7¹	4²	9							13
1	2				6			5	7	10²	11				3	8¹	12	13	4	9							14
1	2¹	3		12	6			5	7	10	11					8		4	9								15
1	12		2		6			5	7	10²	11	3¹				8	13	4	9								16
1	12		2		6			5	7	13	11	3¹				8²	10	4	9								17
1		3	2		6			5	7	12	11					8²	10¹	13	4	9							18
1		3	2		6			5	7	12	11²	13				8¹	10	14	4²	9							19
1		3	2		6			5	7	10¹	11²	4				8	14	13	12	9							20
1	12	3	2		6			5	7		11²	8				13	10	9¹	4								21
1		3	2		6			5	7	12	11³	13				10²	14	4	9¹	8							22
		2			6		5	7	12	9	11					8	10	4	1				3				23
		2	3		6		5	7	12	11	8¹					10	9	4	1								24
		3	2	4	6		5	10	11	8	9					7			1								25
		3	4	6¹	5		7³	14	11²	13	8					12	9	10	1				2				26
		3	4	13	5		7¹	10	12	11	8					9	6²		1				2				27
		3	4	14	5		7	12	10¹	13	11³	8²	6			9			1				2				28
		11	4	3¹	5		7	10²	13		8	12	9			6			1				2				29
		11	4		5		7	10²	12	14	13	8²	6			9³			1				2	3			30
		11	4		5		7	10	12	14	8²	6¹	9			13			1				2	3³			31
		3	4		5		10	7	11	8¹	9	6							1				2			12	32
		3²	4	13	5		10	11	12	8	9	7¹							1				2	6			33
		14	3¹	4	5		7	10	11	13	8¹	9	12						1				2¹	6			34
	8	3	4²	6	5		9	10	11	14	12	13	7³						1				2¹				35
		3	4	6			9¹	10	8	11	12	7							1				2	5			36

ARBROATH

First Division

Year Formed: 1878. *Ground & Address:* Gayfield Park, Arbroath DD11 1QB. *Telephone and Fax:* 01241 431125.
Ground Capacity: 4020, seated: 715. *Size of Pitch:* 115yd × 71yd.
President: John D. Christison. *Secretary:* Charles Kinnear. *Commercial Manager:* G. Cant.
Manager: John Brownlie. *Assistant Manager:* Steve Kirk. *Physio:* Jim Crosby. *Coach:* Jake Ferrier.
Managers since 1975: A. Henderson, I. J. Stewart, G. Fleming, J. Bone, J. Young, W. Borthwick, M. Lawson,
D. McGrain MBE, J. Scott, J. Brogan, T. Campbell, G. Mackie, D. Baikie.
Club Nickname(s): The Red Lichties. *Previous Grounds:* None.
Record Attendance: 13,510 v Rangers, Scottish Cup 3rd rd; 23 Feb, 1952.
Record Transfer Fee received: £120,000 for Paul Tosh to Dundee (Aug 1993).
Record Transfer Fee paid: £20,000 for Douglas Robb from Montrose (1981).
Record Victory: 36-0 v Bon Accord, Scottish Cup 1st rd; 12 Sept, 1885.
Record Defeat: 1-9 v Celtic, League Cup 3rd rd: 25 Aug 1993.
Most Capped Player: Ned Doig, 2 (5), Scotland.
Most League Appearances: 445: Tom Cargill, 1966-81.
Most League Goals in Season (Individual): 45: Dave Easson, Division II; 1958-59.
Most Goals Overall (Individual): 120: Jimmy Jack; 1966-71.

ARBROATH 2000–01 LEAGUE RECORD

Match No.	Date		Venue	Opponents		Result	H/T Score	Lg. Pos.	Goalscorers	Attendance
1	Aug	5	H	Partick Th	D	1-1	1-1	—	Rowe [42]	1456
2		12	A	Berwick R	L	1-2	1-2	9	Mallan [31]	498
3		19	H	Clydebank	W	1-0	1-0	5	Rowe [5]	691
4		26	A	Stranraer	L	1-2	0-1	7	Mallan [65]	426
5	Sept	9	H	Forfar Ath	L	3-4	0-3	8	McGlashan J [55], McGlashan C [62], Brownlie [70]	876
6		16	H	Stenhousemuir	W	3-0	1-0	5	McGlashan J [7], Mercer [60], McGlashan C [70]	541
7		23	A	Queen's Park	D	0-0	0-0	7		721
8		30	H	Queen of the S	W	2-0	1-0	5	Mallan [30], McGlashan J [75]	667
9	Oct	7	A	Stirling A	D	0-0	0-0	5		576
10		14	A	Partick Th	D	1-1	0-0	5	Fotheringham [82]	2242
11		21	H	Berwick R	L	0-2	0-1	6		648
12		28	H	Stranraer	D	1-1	1-0	7	McGlashan C (pen) [30]	528
13	Nov	4	A	Forfar Ath	W	1-0	0-0	7	Mallan [67]	834
14		11	H	Queen's Park	D	2-2	1-1	7	Brownlie [39], Mallan [67]	573
15		18	A	Stenhousemuir	L	1-3	1-0	8	Fotheringham [20]	369
16		25	H	Stirling A	W	3-2	1-2	7	Gaughan (og) [34], Hinchcliffe [49], Mallan [52]	550
17	Dec	2	A	Queen of the S	D	1-1	0-0	7	McGlashan C (pen) [48]	1087
18		16	H	Partick Th	D	1-1	1-0	7	Rowe [25]	1054
19		23	A	Clydebank	W	2-1	1-0	5	Fotheringham [21], McGlashan J [78]	131
20	Jan	2	H	Forfar Ath	D	1-1	0-0	—	McGlashan C [62]	1061
21		13	H	Stenhousemuir	W	5-0	2-0	3	McGlashan J [4], Rowe [33], McAulay [65], Brownlie [69], Fotheringham [79]	575
22		20	A	Queen's Park	D	1-1	1-1	3	Brownlie [15]	1148
23	Feb	3	A	Stirling A	D	1-1	0-0	3	Heenan [90]	676
24		17	H	Clydebank	W	4-2	2-2	3	McDonald 3 [29,39,79], Brownlie [55]	537
25	Mar	10	A	Stranraer	W	2-1	2-0	2	Mercer [3], McKinnon [40]	670
26		17	H	Queen's Park	W	2-0	1-0	2	Mallan (pen) [18], Webster [84]	605
27		20	H	Queen of the S	W	5-2	1-1	—	Mallan [40], Brownlie 2 [49,77], McKinnon [62], Nixon (og) [68]	698
28		25	A	Stranraer	W	1-0	0-0	2	Rowe [70]	394
29		31	A	Stenhousemuir	W	1-0	0-0	2	Rowe [69]	475
30	Apr	7	H	Stirling A	D	1-1	1-0	2	Mallan [21]	711
31		14	A	Queen of the S	L	0-1	0-0	2		1141
32		17	A	Berwick R	L	0-1	0-0	—		613
33		21	A	Partick Th	W	1-0	0-0	2	McKinnon [49]	3003
34		24	A	Forfar Ath	D	1-1	1-1	—	Mallan [31]	1065
35		28	H	Berwick R	W	2-0	0-0	2	Cusick [78], Mercer [85]	2124
36	May	5	A	Clydebank	L	1-3	0-1	2	Swankie [80]	243

Final League Position: 2

Honours
League Champions Runners-up: Division II 1934-35, 1958-59, 1967-68, 1971-72; Third Division 1997-98.
Scottish Cup: Quarter-finals: 1993.
League Cup: —.

Club colours: Shirt: Maroon with white trim. Shorts: Maroon with white trim. Stockings: Maroon with white hooped tops.

Goalscorers: *League* (54): Mallan 10 (1 pen), Brownlie 7, Rowe 6, McGlashan C 5 (2 pens), McGlashan J 5, Fotheringham 4, McDonald 3, McKinnon 3, Mercer 3, Cusick 1, Heenan 1, McAulay 1, Swankie 1, Webster 1, own goals 3
Scottish Cup (1): Cusick 1
CIS Cup (3): Brownlie 1, McGlashan C 1, Mercer 1
Bell's League Cup(7): McGlashan C 2, Brownlie 1, Mallan 1, Mercer 1, Rowe 1, Webster 1

Hinchcliffe C 29	King T 8	Fotheringham K 19+1	Cusick J 21+8	Rowe G 33	Thomson J 29	Arbuckle D 2	Bryce T 4	McGlashan C 20+7	Mallan S 27+2	Mercer J 34+1	Good I 5+5	Tindal K —+3	Brownlie P 16+4	Florence S 23+1	McGlashan J 23+2	McAulay J 15+14	Crawford J 25	Heenan K 12+12	Webster A 9+4	Henslee G 1+2	Peters S 3+1	Steele K 2+17	Cunningham D 2+4	McInally D 7	Wight C 7+1	McDonald C 4+1	McKinnon C 11	Maughan R 4+2	Graham E 1	Swankie G —+1	Kirk S —+1	Match No.
1	2	3	4	5	6		7[1]	8[2]	9[3]	10	11	12	13	14																		1
1	2[2]	3	7	5	4		8[1]	9	10	11[13]	6	13	14	12																		2
1	2	11	12	5			8[1]	9[13]	13	7	4	10	3	6																		3
1	2	6	4	5			8[1]	9[3]	10	11[13]	12	14	13	3	7																	4
1				5				9	10	11	3		7	2	8	4	6															5
1	2[3]	11	6[2]	5	4			9		7	10[1]	3	8		12	13	14															6
1	2	11	6	5				9	10[1]	7		3	8	12	4																	7
1	2	11	6	5	4			9	10[3]	7[1]		3	8[2]	13	12	14																8
1	2[2]	11[3]	6[1]	5	4			9	10	7	14	3	8	13			12															9
1		11	6[3]	5	4			9	10	14	7[1]	3	8[2]	12	13		2															10
1		11	6	5	4			9	10[3]	7[1]	3	8[2]	12	13		2	14															11
1		11		5				9	10	8	12	3[1]	4	6	7[2]		2	13														12
1		11	12	2	5			9[2]	10	8		7[1]	3	4	6	13																13
1		11	12	2	5			9[2]	10	8[1]	14	7	3	4	6[3]	13																14
1		11		2	5			9		8	3[2]	7[1]	4	6	13	12	10															15
1				2	5			9	10[2]	8[3]	11	4	6[1]	7	14	13	12	3														16
1		12		2	5			9	10	8[2]	11	4	6[3]	7[1]	14	13	3															17
1		11	12	2	5			9	8	10	4	6	7[1]	3																		18
1[3]		11	13	2	5			9	8	10	4	6	12	7[1]	3[2]	15																19
		11	10[1]	2	5			12	9[3]	8	4	6	7[2]	14	13	3	1															20
		11	4[1]	2				8[2]	9	7[3]	10	12	6	14	5	13	3	1														21
		11[3]	4	2	5			14	8	9[2]	7	10[1]	12	6	3	13	1															22
		4[1]	2[3]	5				11	8	9[2]	7	10	13	6	14	3	13	1														23
		4[2]	2	5				8	9	7	10	13	6[1]	12	3	14	1	11[3]														24
		13	2					12	9[3]	8	9[1]	3	10	4[2]	6	14	5						1	11[3]	7							25
1		14	2					9[3]	8	3	10[2]	13	6	7	5	12							11[3]	4								26
1		4[3]	2	3				14	9[2]	8	11	12	6	7[1]	5	13	10															27
1		4[2]	2	3				12	9[3]	8	11	13	6	5	14	7[1]	10															28
1		4	2	3				13	9	8	11[2]	5	6[1]	7	12	10																29
1			2	3				12	9[3]	8	11[1]	13	5[2]	6	7	14	10	4														30
1			2	5				11[1]	9	8	3	13	6	7	12	10	4[2]															31
1		11	2	5				9[2]	8	3	14	4	6	12	13	10[5]	7[1]															32
1		4[2]	2	5				9[1]	8	3	11	13	6	7[3]	12	10	14															33
1		4	2	5				9[2]	8	3	11	12	6	7[1]	13	10																34
1		3[2]	5					14	9[3]	8	12	10	2	6	7	11[1]	4	13														35
		13	5	2				9	8	3	7	11	10[1]		1	10[1]		1										4[3]	6[2]	12	14	36

AYR UNITED

First Division

Year Formed: 1910. *Ground & Address:* Somerset Park, Tryfield Place, Ayr KA8 9NB. *Telephone:* 01292 263435.
Ground Capacity: 10,243, seated: 1549. *Size of Pitch:* 110yd × 72yd.
Chairman: W. J. Barr. *Administrator:* Brian Caldwell. *Secretary:* J. E. Eyley. *Lottery Manager:* Andrew Downie.
Manager: Gordon Dalziel. *Coach:* Frank Connor. *Youth Coach:* Campbell Money. *Physio:* John Kerr.
Managers since 1975: Alex Stuart, Ally MacLeod, Willie McLean, George Caldwell, Ally MacLeod, George Burley,
Simon Stainrod. *Club Nickname(s):* The Honest Men. *Previous Grounds:* None.
Record Attendance: 25,225 v Rangers, Division I; 13 Sept, 1969.
Record Transfer Fee received: £300,000 for Steven Nicol to Liverpool (Oct 1981).
Record Transfer Fee paid: £80,000 for Mark Campbell from Stranraer (March 1999).
Record Victory: 11-1 v Dumbarton, League Cup; 13 Aug, 1952.
Record Defeat: 0-9 in Division I v Rangers (1929); v Hearts (1931); B Division v Third Lanark (1954).
Most Capped Player: Jim Nisbet, 3, Scotland.
Most League Appearances: 459, John Murphy, 1963-78.
Most League League and Cup Goals in Season (Individual): 66, Jimmy Smith, 1927-28.
Most League and Cup Goals Overall (Individual): 213, Peter Price, 1955-61.

AYR UNITED 2000–01 LEAGUE RECORD

Match No.	Date	Venue	Opponents	Result	H/T Score	Lg. Pos.	Goalscorers	Attendance
1	Aug 5	H	Ross Co	W 1-0	1-0	—	Annand (pen) [20]	2740
2	12	A	Alloa Ath	D 1-1	0-1	4	Annand (pen) [66]	1274
3	19	H	Airdrieonians	W 3-1	0-1	3	Hurst [56], McGinlay 2 [73, 81]	2705
4	26	H	Falkirk	W 5-2	1-0	2	Connolly [2], Hurst 3 [65, 79, 82], McGinlay [75]	3213
5	Sept 9	A	Livingston	L 0-2	0-1	2		5271
6	16	A	Morton	D 1-1	0-1	3	Annand [55]	1308
7	23	H	Clyde	W 2-1	0-0	2	Annand (pen) [64], McGinlay [77]	2715
8	30	H	Inverness CT	D 3-3	1-0	3	Hurst 2 [2, 72], Annand [51]	2070
9	Oct 7	A	Raith R	W 3-1	1-0	3	Hurst 2 [5, 47], Connolly [76]	1858
10	14	A	Ross Co	D 1-1	0-0	3	McGinlay [56]	2567
11	21	H	Alloa Ath	W 3-1	2-1	3	Boyack [8], Hurst 2 [23, 76]	2259
12	28	A	Falkirk	L 0-3	0-1	3		3783
13	Nov 4	H	Livingston	D 1-1	1-1	3	Teale [36]	3082
14	11	A	Clyde	W 1-0	1-0	3	Boyack [10]	1318
15	18	H	Morton	D 1-1	0-0	3	McGinlay [52]	2256
16	25	H	Raith R	W 4-2	2-1	3	Robertson [7], Hurst [29], Annand [55], Boyack [89]	2212
17	Dec 2	A	Inverness CT	L 3-7	2-3	3	Annand [10], Robertson [11], Hurst [48]	1513
18	9	A	Airdrieonians	D 0-0	0-0	3		1572
19	16	H	Ross Co	L 0-2	0-1	3		2007
20	Jan 2	A	Morton	W 6-0	4-0	—	Hurst 5 [3, 21, 24, 42, 83], Grady [64]	2866
21	6	H	Clyde	W 2-0	0-0	2	Hughes [79], Grady [88]	2481
22	13	H	Inverness CT	D 1-1	1-1	3	McGinlay [3]	2534
23	Feb 3	H	Airdrieonians	D 2-2	0-1	3	Teale [48], Lovering [56]	2060
24	17	A	Raith R	W 4-1	0-1	2	McGinlay 3 [54, 81, 85], Annand [69]	1217
25	24	A	Falkirk	W 2-1	1-0	2	Bradford [16], Annand [63]	2668
26	Mar 3	H	Livingston	D 1-1	0-1	2	Bradford (pen) [90]	2726
27	6	H	Falkirk	W 6-0	1-0	—	Annand [21], Craig [67], Campbell [70], Sharp [73], Teale [78], Bradford [82]	2041
28	13	A	Alloa Ath	W 2-0	0-0	2	Annand 2 [69, 89]	539
29	17	A	Clyde	D 2-2	2-1	2	Annand [38], Teale [41]	1416
30	20	A	Livingston	W 1-0	1-0	—	Annand [40]	2731
31	31	H	Morton	W 3-0	2-0	1	Annand 2 (2 pens) [21 (p), 44 (p)], Sharp [73]	2111
32	Apr 7	A	Raith R	W 2-0	1-0	2	Grady [11], Annand [84]	2026
33	14	A	Inverness CT	L 0-1	0-0	2		2269
34	21	A	Ross Co	W 1-0	0-0	2	McGinlay [58]	1942
35	28	A	Alloa Ath	W 4-1	1-0	2	McGinlay 2 [41, 88], Sharp [49], Annand [57]	2234
36	May 5	A	Airdrieonians	D 1-1	1-0	2	Teale [28]	8185

Final League Position: 2

Honours
League Champions: Division II 1911-12, 1912-13, 1927-28, 1936-37, 1958-59, 1965-66. Second Division 1987-88, 1996-97;
Runners-up: Division II 1910-11, 1955-56, 1968-69.
Scottish Cup: —.
League Cup: —.
B&Q Cup Runners-up: 1990-91, 1991-92.

Club colours: Shirt: White with black trim. Shorts: Black. Stockings: Black and white.

Goalscorers: *League* (73): Annand 18 (5 pens), Hurst 17, McGinlay 13, Teale 5, Boyack 3, Bradford 3 (1 pen), Grady 3, Sharp 3, Connolly 2, Robertson 2, Campbell 1, Craig 1, Hughes 1, Lovering 1
Scottish Cup (3): Annand 1, Campbell 1, Wilson 1
CIS Cup (0):
Bell's League Cup (1): McGinlay 1

Rovde M 10	Renwick M 13+2	Lovering P 21+8	McGinlay P 34	Hughes J 18	Duffy C 29	Hurst G 19	Wilson M 18+6	Annand E 26+5	Grady J 13+5	Teale G 27+2	Reynolds M 4+14	Scally N 13+10	Crilly M 5+5	Bradford J 10+12	Craig D 30	Connolly P 6	Burns G 1+2	Benharoq M —+1	Campbell M 16+4	Nelson C 26	McEwan C 24+1	Boyack S 10	Robertson H 8	Sharp L 15+2	Kean S —+2	Match No.
1	2	3	4	5	6	7	8^2	9	10^1	11	12	13														1
1	2	3	4	5	6	7	8	9		12	10^2	12				11^1	13									2
1	2	3	11	5	4	9	8				10^3	13	14	7^2	12	6^1										3
1	2	3	11	5	4	9	8					10^1			6	7	12									4
1	2^2	3	11	5^1	4	9	8							14	6	7	10		12^3	13						5
	3	11	4				8^1	9^2		7		12	13		6	10			5	1	2					6
	3	4	5^2			9	8	12		7	14	11^1			6	10			13	1	2^3					7
	3	4	5^2			9	8	12		7^1	11^3	14			6	10			13	1	2					8
	3	11		6		9	8	10^2		12					5	7			4	1	2					9
	3	11		6	9		8	10		12					5				4^1	1	2	7				10
	3	11	5	4	9		8^3	10^2		12	14		13		6				1	2^1	7					11
	3	4	5	2	9		8	10^1	12	11					6				1		7					12
	3	4	5		9		12	10^1	7^3	14	13				6				1	2^2	8	11				13
5	3	4			13	9^2		7^1	12		10				6				1	2	8	11				14
5	3^1	4			13	9		7	12		10^3				6				1	2	8	11				15
5	3	4			9		10^1	7	12						6				1	2	8	11				16
2	3^3	4	5		9		10^1	7^2	13		14				6				1	12	8	11				17
1	2	14	11	5	4	9	8	10^1	13	12					6							7^1	3^3			18
1		4	5	6	9	13	12	10^1	7	11^2										2	8	3				19
1	2	4^1	5	6^3	9	8	10		7	12	13				14							11^{12}	3			20
1	2	3	4	5	6	9	8	10		7	12											11^1				21
1	2	3	4	5	6	9	8^2	12	10^1	7^3	14	13										11				22
	3		5			8	9^1	10^3	7	12	11^2		14	6					4	1	2			13		23
	3^2	10	5	8	14	9^1		7		2	11^1	12		6					4	1				13		24
		10	5		11	9^1		7		12		8	6						4	1	2			3		25
		10	5		11^1	9^2	13	7		12		8	6						4	1	2			3		26
		10	5			9^1	12	7^2		11	13	8	6						4	1	2			3		27
13		10	5			9	12	7		11		8^1	6						4	1	2^2			3		28
14	12		5		9^2	13	7		11^1	10	8^3	6							4	1	2			3		29
		10	5			9^1	8^2	11	13	12	6								4	1	2			3		30
	14	10	5			9^1	8^2	11	13	12	6								4	1	2^3			3		31
	12	10	5			9^2	8	11		7^1	6								4	1	2			3	13	32
	13	10	5			9^1	8	7	11	12	6								4	1	2			3^2		33
	13	10	5		14	9	8^1	7	11	12^3	6								4	1	2^2			3		34
	13	10	5		12	9		7	11^1	8	6								4^2	1	2			3		35
	12	10	4	5^1		9		7	11	8^2	6		14						1	2^3				3	13	36

BERWICK RANGERS　　Second Division

Year Formed: 1881. *Ground & Address:* Shielfield Park, Tweedmouth, Berwick-upon-Tweed TD15 2EF. *Telephone:*
01289 307424. *Fax:* 01289 307424. Club 24 hour hotline 09068 800697. *Ground Capacity:* 4131, seated: 1366. *Size of Pitch:*
110yd × 70yd.
Chairman: Jamie Curle. *Vice-chairman:* Moray McLaren. *Club Secretary:* Dennis McCleary.
Manager: Paul Smith. *Assistant Manager:* David Larter. *Physios:* Rev. Glyn Jones, Ian Smith. *Coaches:* Ian Oliver,
Ian Smith, Greg Shaw, Brian Cordery.
Managers since 1975: H. Melrose, G. Haig, W. Galbraith, D. Smith, F. Connor, J. McSherry, E. Tait, J. Thomson,
J. Jefferies, R. Callachan, J. Anderson, J. Crease, T. Hendrie, I. Ross, J. Thomson.
Club Nickname(s): The Borderers. *Previous Grounds:* Bull Stob Close, Pier Field, Meadow Field, Union Park, Old
Shielfield.
Record Attendance: 13,365 v Rangers, Scottish Cup 1st rd; 28 Jan, 1967.
Record Victory: 8-1 v Forfar Ath. Division II; 25 Dec, 1965: v Vale of Leithen, Scottish Cup; Dec, 1966.
Record Defeat: 1-9 v Hamilton A, First Division; 9 Aug, 1980.
Most Capped Player: —.
Most League Appearances: 435: Eric Tait, 1970-87.
Most League Goals in Season (Individual): 38: Ken Bowron, Division II; 1963-64.
Most Goals Overall (Individual): 115: Eric Tait, 1970-87.

BERWICK RANGERS 2000–01 LEAGUE RECORD

Match No.	Date	Venue	Opponents	Result	H/T Score	Lg. Pos.	Goalscorers	Atten- dance
1	Aug 5	A	Queen's Park	L	0-1	0-0	—	721
2	12	H	Arbroath	W	2-1	2-1	6	Anthony [33], Wood [36]	498
3	19	A	Stranraer	D	2-2	0-0	4	Ritchie [47], Neil M [90]	386
4	26	A	Partick Th	D	1-1	1-0	4	McNicoll [36]	2060
5	Sept 9	H	Clydebank	W	3-1	0-0	3	Anthony [48], Findlay [63], Neil M [89]	482
6	16	H	Queen of the S	L	0-4	0-2	4		572
7	23	A	Stenhousemuir	L	0-2	0-2	9		428
8	30	H	Stirling A	D	2-2	2-0	9	Neil M [29], Wood [44]	604
9	Oct 7	A	Forfar Ath	W	5-3	3-1	6	Forrest [12], Haddow (pen) [33], Smith [38], Ronald 2 [50, 81]	332
10	14	H	Queen's Park	D	1-1	0-1	6	Haddow (pen) [70]	514
11	21	A	Arbroath	W	2-0	1-0	5	Wood [5], Findlay [84]	648
12	28	H	Partick Th	L	1-2	1-0	5	Wood [35]	1240
13	Nov 4	A	Clydebank	W	1-0	0-0	6	Neil A [86]	196
14	11	H	Stenhousemuir	W	4-1	2-0	2	Forrest [23], Ronald 2 [43, 48], Wood [62]	424
15	18	A	Queen of the S	L	1-2	0-2	3	Forrest [55]	1238
16	25	H	Forfar Ath	D	1-1	1-1	4	Wood [25]	430
17	Dec 2	A	Stirling A	D	1-1	0-0	4	Neil M [87]	613
18	16	A	Queen's Park	W	2-0	0-0	3	Elliot [88], Wood [90]	690
19	30	A	Partick Th	D	1-1	0-1	3	Wood [66]	2837
20	Jan 2	H	Clydebank	L	1-2	1-1	—	Wood [1]	572
21	Feb 17	A	Stranraer	D	1-1	1-0	5	Duthie [19]	447
22	Mar 10	H	Partick Th	L	0-1	0-1	8		1405
23	13	A	Stenhousemuir	W	2-0	2-0	—	Duthie [40], Elliot (pen) [43]	345
24	17	A	Stenhousemuir	W	1-0	1-0	5	Walton [9]	402
25	20	H	Stranraer	D	1-1	1-1	—	Ritchie [31]	471
26	25	A	Queen of the S	D	2-2	1-0	5	Ronald [40], Anthony (pen) [60]	608
27	28	H	Stirling A	W	4-1	3-1	—	O'Neil [1], Wood 2 [3, 26], Smith [73]	477
28	31	A	Queen of the S	D	3-3	1-1	3	Anthony [11], Wood 2 [61, 82]	984
29	Apr 3	A	Forfar Ath	W	1-0	0-0	—	Findlay [54]	413
30	7	H	Forfar Ath	W	1-0	0-0	3	Neil M [65]	480
31	10	A	Clydebank	D	2-2	0-1	—	Anthony [73], Wood [80]	167
32	14	A	Stirling A	L	0-1	0-0	3		525
33	17	H	Arbroath	W	1-0	0-0	—	Neil A [59]	613
34	21	H	Queen's Park	W	1-0	1-0	3	Anthony [22]	657
35	28	A	Arbroath	L	0-2	0-0	3		2124
36	May 5	H	Stranraer	L	0-2	0-2	3		545

Final League Position: 3

Honours
League Champions: Second Division 1978-79; *Runners-up:* Second Division 1993-94. Third Division 1999-2000.
Scottish Cup: Quarter-finals: 1953-54, 1979-80.
League Cup: Semi-finals: 1963-64.

Club colours: Shirt: Black with 4 inch gold stripes. Shorts: Black with white trim. Stockings: Gold with black trim.

Goalscorers: *League* (51): Wood 14, Anthony 6 (1 pen), Neil M 5, Ronald 5, Findlay 3, Forrest 3, Duthie 2, Elliot 2 (1 pen), Haddow 2 (2 pens), Neill A 2, Ritchie 2, Smith 2, McNicoll 1, O'Neil 1, Walton 1
Scottish Cup (9): Anthony 2, Elliot 2, Neill A 2, Ronald 1, Watt 1, Wood 1
CIS Cup (0):
Bell's League Cup(2): McMartin 1, Oliver 1

McLean M 11	Whelan J 26 + 4	Haddow L 9 + 1	Ritchie I 36	Neil A 31 + 1	Forrest G 24 + 8	McMartin G 20 + 2	Neil M 29	Wood G 29 + 2	Findlay C 6 + 20	Duthie M 12 + 5	McNicoll G 19 + 2	Ronald P 20 + 9	Smith D 20 + 1	Anthony M 27 + 2	Laidlaw S 1 + 5	McDonald C 4	Gray D 17 + 2	O'Connor G 10	Watt D 4 + 5	Oliver N —- + 1	Magee K 5 + 5	Elliot B 5 + 4	Walton K 4 + 6	McCulloch W 15	O'Neil K 6 + 2	Graham A 6 + 1	Harvey J — + 1	Match No.
1	2	3	4	5	6	7	8	9^3	10^1	11^3	12	13	14															1
1	2	3		5	12	13	8	9	7^2		4	10	11^1	6														2
1	2	3^2	4	13	14		8	9	7^3	5	10^1	11	6	12														3
1	2	3		5	13	14	8	12	7^2		4	11	6	9^1	10^3													4
1	2	3	4		13		8	9	12	7	5		11^2	6		10^1												5
1	2	3^2	4		12		8	9	13	7^1	5		11	6	14	10												6
1	2	3	4	6	8		7	14			5^1	9^3	13	11		10^3	12											7
	12	4	3	7	2^3	8	9^2		13	14	5^1	10^1	11^3	6		1												8
	3	4	5	7	2^3	8	9^2		10	11	6^1	13				1	12	14										9
11^1	3	4	5	7	2	8	9		10^3		6^2			14	1	13	12											10
		4	5	7	2	8	9^1	13	10^2		6	14	3	1	12		11^1											11
		4	5	7	2	8	9	12	10^1		6		3	1		11												12
		4	5	7	2	8	9	13	10^2	12	6^3		3	1	14	11^1												13
14		4	5	7	2	8	9^1	12	10^1	11		13	3	1	6^2													14
14		4	5	7	2^3	8	9	13	10	11^2			3	1	6^1	12												15
13		4	5	7	2	8	9	12	10^1	11^3			3	1	6^2	14												16
		4	5	7	2^1	8	9	14	10	12	13		3	1	6^2	11^1												17
1	6	4	5	7	2		9	10^2			12	8	3						11^1	13								18
1	6	4	5	7	2		9^1				12	11^2	8	3					13	10								19
1	6^1	4	5	7	2		14		10^3		11^2	8	3				12	13										20
1	12	4	5		2	8	9	7^1			11^2	6	3						10	13								21
7		4	5	12	2^1	8	9^2	11^3			6		3						10	14	1	13						22
2		4	5	6	8		9		11^2	12	14	13					3^1				10^3	1		7				23
7		4	5	2	8^3	9		14	3	13		12							11	1	10^2	6^1						24
7^1		4	5	6^2	2		9		11	3	10^1	13	8						12	1								25
6		4	5	7	2			13	14	11^1	3	10^2	12	8						1		9^3						26
6		4	5				9^1	12		3	13	11	8^1						14	7	1	10^2	2					27
6^3		4	5		2^1	8	9			3	14	13	7						11^2	1	10	12						28
7		4	5	14		8	9^1	10^1		3	12	11	6^3						1	13	2							29
7		4	5	12		8	13	14		3	9^1	11	6^1						1	10^3	2							30
7		4	5	2^1		8	9	12		3	14	13	6					11^2	1	10^3								31
7		4	5			8	9	13		3	10^2	11	6^3					12	14	1		2^1						32
7		4	5	2^2		8	9		12	3		11^1	6		10				13	1								33
7		4	5	2		8	9^1	14	13	3	12	11^2	6^3		10					1								34
7		4	5	2^3		8	9	12	13	3	6	11^2			10^1			14		1								35
6		4	5	7		8	9	3^2			10^3	12		2					11^1	13	1		14					36

BRECHIN CITY

Third Division

Year Formed: 1906. *Ground & Address:* Glebe Park, Trinity Rd, Brechin, Angus DD9 6BJ. *Telephone:* 01356 622856. *Fax (to Secretary):* 01356 625524.
Ground Capacity: total: 3980, seated: 1518. *Size of Pitch:* 110yd × 67yd.
Chairman: David Birse. *Vice-Chairman:* Hugh Campbell Adamson. *Secretary:* Ken Ferguson.
Manager: Dick Campbell. *Assistant Manager:* Ian Campbell. *Youth Coach:* Eddie Wolecki. *Physio:* Tom Gilmartin.
Managers since 1975: Charlie Dunn, Ian Stewart, Doug Houston, Ian Fleming, John Ritchie, Ian Redford.
Club Nickname(s): The City. *Previous Grounds:* Nursery Park.
Record Attendance: 8122 v Aberdeen, Scottish Cup 3rd rd; 3 Feb, 1973.
Record Transfer Fee received: £100,000 for Scott Thomson to Aberdeen (1991).
Record Transfer Fee paid: £16,000 for Sandy Ross from Berwick Rangers (1991).
Record Victory: 12-1 v Thornhill, Scottish Cup 1st rd; 28 Jan, 1926.
Record Defeat: 0-10 v Airdrieonians, Albion R and Cowdenbeath, all in Division II; 1937-38.
Most Capped Player: —.
Most League Appearances: 459: David Watt, 1975-89.
Most League Goals in Season (Individual): 26: W. McIntosh, Division II; 1959-60.
Most Goals Overall (Individual): 131: Ian Campbell.

BRECHIN CITY 2000–01 LEAGUE RECORD

Match No.	Date	Venue	Opponents	Result	H/T Score	Lg. Pos.	Goalscorers	Atten-dance
1	Aug 5	H	Elgin C	W 2-1	1-1	—	Bain [34], Grant [67]	509
2	12	A	Dumbarton	W 2-0	0-0	3	Leask [54], Christie [70]	370
3	19	H	Cowdenbeath	D 0-0	0-0	5		337
4	26	A	Peterhead	W 2-1	1-1	4	Grant 2 [1, 84]	563
5	Sept 9	H	Montrose	W 6-1	3-0	2	Leask [20], Smith [38], Coulston [41], Grant [49], Bailey [76], Donachie [88]	465
6	16	A	Albion R	W 3-1	1-1	2	Grant [42], Honeyman [47], Dewar [71]	254
7	23	H	East Fife	W 3-1	2-1	2	Bain [11], Sturrock 2 [30, 61]	403
8	30	H	East Stirling	W 4-1	1-0	2	Honeyman [2], Nairn [59], Coulston [69], Grant [85]	342
9	Oct 7	A	Hamilton A	L 1-4	1-1	2	Grant [44]	422
10	14	A	Elgin C	D 2-2	0-0	2	Grant 2 [83, 88]	835
11	21	H	Dumbarton	W 3-1	0-0	1	Leask [54], Bain [56], Coulston [82]	455
12	28	H	Peterhead	W 3-2	2-1	1	Leask [11], Grant [45], Bailey [88]	469
13	Nov 4	A	Montrose	D 1-1	0-0	2	Grant [89]	622
14	11	A	East Fife	L 0-1	0-0	3		549
15	18	H	Albion R	W 2-1	1-0	2	Bain [9], Leask [50]	337
16	25	H	Hamilton A	D 0-0	0-0	2		483
17	Dec 2	A	East Stirling	W 1-0	0-0	2	Bain [58]	249
18	16	H	Elgin C	W 2-1	1-0	1	Smith D [15], Grant [51]	333
19	23	A	Cowdenbeath	L 1-2	1-0	2	Raynes [37]	434
20	30	A	Peterhead	W 2-0	2-0	1	Coulston [2], Bailey [26]	889
21	Feb 3	A	Hamilton A	L 0-1	0-0	3		521
22	17	H	Cowdenbeath	W 2-0	2-0	2	Grant 2 [13, 15]	545
23	24	A	Dumbarton	L 0-1	0-0	3		722
24	Mar 17	A	East Fife	W 4-1	0-0	3	Campbell [47], Sturrock [58], Fotheringham [66], Grant [84]	416
25	20	A	Montrose	W 3-0	1-0	—	Sturrock 2 [28, 60], Grant [87]	526
26	24	H	East Stirling	W 5-1	3-1	2	Bain (pen) [6], Grant 3 [10, 79, 82], Sturrock [29]	351
27	27	H	Peterhead	D 1-1	0-0	—	Fotheringham [61]	396
28	Apr 3	H	East Fife	W 1-0	0-0	—	Grant [80]	407
29	7	H	Hamilton A	L 3-4	1-2	3	Fotheringham [33], Grant [70], Smith D [72]	586
30	10	A	Albion R	D 1-1	0-1	—	Bain [72]	283
31	14	A	East Stirling	W 2-0	2-0	3	Honeyman [15], Bain [21]	253
32	17	H	Albion R	L 1-2	0-1	—	Bain [88]	369
33	21	A	Elgin C	W 3-0	0-0	3	Bain 2 (2 pens) [18 (p), 38 (p)], Black [21]	570
34	24	A	Montrose	W 3-1	2-0	—	Mackay [28], Coulston [30], Black [85]	544
35	28	H	Dumbarton	W 1-0	1-0	2	Grant [6]	510
36	May 5	A	Cowdenbeath	L 1-2	0-1	3	Smith D [89]	3448

Final League Position: 3

Honours
League Champions: Second Division 1982-83. C Division 1953-54. Second Division 1989-90. *Runners-up:* 1992-93. Third Division Runners-up 1995-96.
Scottish Cup: —.
League Cup: —.

Club colours: Shirt, Shorts, Stockings: Red with white trimmings.

Goalscorers: *League* (71): Grant 22, Bain 11 (3 pens), Sturrock 6, Coulston 5, Leask 5, Smith D 4, Bailey 3, Fotheringham 3, Honeyman 3, Black 2, Campbell 1, Christie 1, Dewar 1, Donachie 1, Mackay 1, Nairn 1, Raynes 1
Scottish Cup (9): Bailey 4, Grant 2, Bain 1, Black 1, Leask 1
CIS Cup (0):
Bell's League Cup (5): Sturrock 2, Grant 1, Leask 1, own goal 1

Soutar D 31	Riley P 18+6	Raynes S 26+1	Bain K 31+1	Smith G 13+6	Nairn J 13+6	Coulston D 32+1	Bailey L 7+10	Grant R 32	Black R 19+4	McKeith J 1+2	Williamson K —+1	Leask M 14+11	Hutcheon A —+1	Honeyman B 12+4	O'Sullivan L 1	Cairney H 32	Sturrock B 20+7	Christie B 1+2	Smith D 14+9	Dewar G 7+5	Campbell P 5+13	Donachie B 9+6	Gardner L 7	Mackay D 16	Miller G 6+6	Fotheringham K 12	Kinnaird P 12+1	Parkyn M 5	Match No.
1	2	3	4	5	6	7	8[2]	9	10[1]	11[3]	12	13	14																1
1	8	6		2	14	12		9	10			7				3[1]	4[2]	5	11[3]	13									2
1	8	3	12		6[2]	11		10[3]	7			14				13	5	9	2	4[1]									3
1	8	3	4		6	11		9[2]	10[1]		12					13	5	7	2										4
1		3	4		6[3]	7	12	9[2]	10					11		5			2		8[1]	13	14						5
1	8	6	4	10	14			9	3[1]			7[2]				5			11[1]		2	12	13						6
1	8	6	4	2		7		9[2]	3[1]			13		11		5	10[3]		12		14								7
1	12	6	4			8		9[3]	3			13		14		11	5		7		2[1]	10[2]							8
1	7	6	4			8[3]	3	14	9		12			11		5	10[2]		13		2[1]								9
1	8[1]	6	5	4	12	3		9						10		7[2]		14	2[3]		13	11							10
1		6	4		14	3	13	9						11[3]		7	5		2[1]	12	10[2]	8							11
1		6	4			7	3	13	9					10[2]		12	5		2[1]	14	11	8[3]							12
1		6	4	14	8	3[1]	13	9	12					10[3]		5			2[2]		11	7							13
1		6		4[1]	8	3	10	9	13					11[3]		5			2[4]	14	12	7							14
1		6	8	4	14	3	9[2]	11[3]						10[1]		5	13		2		12	7							15
1		6	8	4		3	12	9	11[3]					10[1]		5			2[2]	14	13	7							16
1		6[1]	8	4	12	3	13	9[2]	10					11		5			2	14		7[2]							17
1	7		4	6	8[2]	3[1]		9	11					10[3]		5	14		2		12	13							18
1	11[2]	3	4	6	8		12	9	10[1]			7				5	13		2										19
1	7	6	8	4	12	3[3]	9[1]	10[2]					13			5	11		2			14							20
1	4[3]		3			10	7	9						5		11[1]		12	14	13	6[3]			2	8				21
1	4[3]		6			3	11[2]	9	10					5		13			7[1]	12		14		2	8				22
1	7	12	5	6		3	8	9	10[1]					13										4	2²	11			23
1	12	3	4			11[3]	9		13					5	10²		14		8[1]				2		6	7			24
1	13	3	4			7[1]	9		14					5	10		12		8²				2		6	11[3]			25
1	12	3	4			11[3]	9		13					5	10²		14		8[1]				2		6	7			26
1		3[1]	4	12		7²	9		13					5	10							2	8	6	11				27
1		3	4			7²	9	12	13					5	10[1]		14					2	8	6	11[3]				28
		3	4			7[1]	9	13	14					5	10		12					2	8[3]	6	11²	1		29
6	4[3]	3	14			9	8		11²					10[1]	5						2	12	7	13	1			30
	4			11	9	6[3]				10[1]	5	12	13	8²								2	14	3	7	1		31
12	4		7	9	6[3]				10²	5	13						8	14	3			2	14	3[1]	11	1		32
12	4		7		6[3]				10²	5	9	8	14	3						2	13			11[1]	1			33
1	8[3]	4	12	7		6			10²	5	9		14	3[1]						2	13			11				34
1	8	4	13	11	9	6			5	10										2	12	3²	7[1]					35
1	8	4	12	7²	9	6		14	5	10	13									2	3[1]	11²						36

CELTIC   Premier League

Year Formed: 1888. *Ground & Address:* Celtic Park, Glasgow G40 3RE. *Telephone:* 0141 556 2611. *Fax:* 0141 551 8106.
Ground Capacity: all seated: 60,506. *Size of Pitch:* 110m × 68m.
Chairman: Brian Quinn. *Chief Executive:* Ian McLeod. *Secretary:* Robert Howat.
Manager: Martin O'Neill. *Assistant Manager:* John Robertson. *First Team Coach:* Steve Walford. *Youth Development
Manager:* Tommy Burns. *Head Youth Coach:* Willie McStay. *Kit Manager:* John Clark. *Physio:* Brian Scott. *Assistant
Physio:* Neil McLeod.
Managers since 1975: Jock Stein, Billy McNeill, David Hay, Billy McNeill, Liam Brady, Lou Macari, Tommy Burns,
Wim Jansen, Dr Jozef Venglos, John Barnes (Head Coach). *Club Nickname(s):* The Bhoys. *Previous Grounds:* None.
Record Attendance: 92,000 v Rangers, Division I; 1 Jan, 1938.
Record Transfer Fee received: £4,700,000 for Paolo Di Canio to Sheffield W (August 1997).
Record Transfer Fee paid: £6,000,000 for Chris Sutton from Chelsea (July 2000).
Record Victory: 11-0 Dundee, Division I; 26 Oct, 1895.
Record Defeat: 0-8 v Motherwell, Division I; 30 Apr, 1937.
Most Capped Player: Paddy Bonner, 80, Republic of Ireland.
Most League Appearances: 486: Billy McNeill 1957-75.
Most League Goals in Season (Individual): 50: James McGrory, Division I; 1935-36.
Most Goals Overall (Individual): 397: James McGrory; 1922-39.

Honours
League Champions: (37 times) Division I 1892-93, 1893-94, 1895-96, 1897-98, 1904-05, 1905-06, 1906-07, 1907-08, 1908-09,
1909-10, 1913-14, 1914-15, 1915-16, 1916-17, 1918-19, 1921-22, 1925-26, 1935-36, 1937-38, 1953-54, 1965-66, 1966-67,
1967-68, 1968-69, 1969-70, 1970-71, 1971-72, 1972-73, 1973-74. Premier Division 1976-77, 1978-79, 1980-81, 1981-82,
1985-86, 1987-88, 1997-98, 2000-01. *Runners-up:* 26 times.

CELTIC 2000–01 LEAGUE RECORD

Match No.	Date	Venue	Opponents	Result	H/T Score	Lg. Pos.	Goalscorers	Attendance
1	Jul 30	A	Dundee U	W 2-1	1-0	—	Larsson [36], Sutton [67]	5896
2	Aug 5	H	Motherwell	W 1-0	1-0	3	Berkovic [11]	59,057
3	13	H	Kilmarnock	W 2-1	0-1	2	Larsson [49], Johnson [72]	57,258
4	19	A	Hearts	W 4-2	3-0	3	Sutton 2 [23, 27], Larsson [37], Moravcik [62]	16,744
5	27	H	Rangers	W 6-2	3-1	2	Sutton 2 [1, 90], Petrov [8], Lambert [12], Larsson 2 [50, 63]	59,476
6	Sept 9	H	Hibernian	W 3-0	2-0	1	Larsson 2 (1 pen) [17 (p), 47], Burchill [89]	60,040
7	18	A	Dunfermline Ath	W 2-1	0-0	1	Larsson 2 (1 pen) [60 (p), 85]	9493
8	23	H	Dundee	W 1-0	0-0	1	Petrov [89]	59,524
9	Oct 1	A	Aberdeen	D 1-1	0-1	1	Larsson [80]	17,580
10	14	H	St Mirren	W 2-0	1-0	1	Sutton [33], Larsson [86]	59,788
11	17	A	St Johnstone	W 2-0	1-0	—	Valgaeren [41], Larsson [85]	8946
12	21	H	Dundee U	W 2-1	1-0	1	Larsson [34], Thompson [61]	59,323
13	29	A	Motherwell	D 3-3	1-1	1	Mjallby [14], Valgaeren [57], McNamara [71]	12,421
14	Nov 5	H	Kilmarnock	W 1-0	0-0	1	Thompson [60]	13,412
15	12	H	St Johnstone	W 4-1	3-0	1	Sutton [12], Larsson 2 [34, 59], Moravcik [38]	56,952
16	18	H	Hearts	W 6-1	4-1	1	Valgaeren [15], Moravcik [35], Larsson 2 [38, 80], Mjallby [43], Petrov [82]	59,849
17	26	A	Rangers	L 1-5	0-1	1	Larsson [58]	50,083
18	29	A	Hibernian	D 0-0	0-0	—		14,939
19	Dec 2	H	Dunfermline Ath	W 3-1	2-1	1	Moravcik [9], Larsson [26], Johnson [79]	59,196
20	10	A	Dundee	W 2-1	1-0	1	Petrov [4], Agathe [89]	10,763
21	16	H	Aberdeen	W 6-0	2-0	1	Larsson 3 [4, 75, 78], Vega 2 [19, 81], Smith [88]	59,677
22	23	A	St Mirren	W 2-0	1-0	1	Agathe [13], Larsson [62]	9487
23	26	A	Dundee U	W 4-0	3-0	—	Larsson [23], Sutton 2 [34, 41], Petrov [73]	12,306
24	Jan 2	H	Kilmarnock	W 6-0	1-0	—	Sutton 2 [37, 61], Larsson 4 [53, 73, 75, 86]	59,103
25	Feb 4	H	Hearts	W 3-0	1-0	1	Larsson 3 [4, 68, 83]	13,077
26	11	H	Rangers	W 1-0	1-0	1	Thompson [17]	59,496
27	21	H	Motherwell	W 1-0	1-0	—	Moravcik [83]	58,736
28	25	H	Hibernian	D 1-1	0-1	1	Mjallby [22]	59,791
29	Mar 4	A	Dunfermline Ath	W 3-0	2-0	1	Petrov [11], Larsson [26], Lennon [77]	8779
30	14	A	St Johnstone	W 2-1	1-1	—	Johnson [28], Larsson [61]	8993
31	Apr 1	A	Aberdeen	W 1-0	0-0	1	Agathe [72]	16,064
32	4	H	Dundee	W 2-1	1-0	—	Johnson [5], Mjallby [83]	59,190
33	7	H	St Mirren	W 1-0	1-0	1	Johnson [39]	60,102
34	22	H	Hearts	W 1-0	1-0	1	Moravcik [67]	58,708
35	29	A	Rangers	W 3-0	0-0	1	Larsson [86], Moravcik 2 [61, 84]	50,057
36	May 6	A	Hibernian	W 5-2	2-0	1	Thompson [4], McNamara [18], Larsson [61], Stubbs [68], Moravcik [80]	8879
37	13	H	Dundee	L 0-2	0-2	1		58,967
38	20	A	Kilmarnock	L 0-1	0-0	1		12,578

Final League Position: 1

Scottish Cup Winners: (31 times) 1892, 1899, 1900, 1904, 1907, 1908, 1911, 1912, 1914, 1923, 1925, 1927, 1931, 1933, 1937, 1951, 1954, 1965, 1967, 1969, 1971, 1972, 1974, 1975, 1977, 1980, 1985, 1988, 1989, 1995, 2001. *Runners-up:* 17 times.
League Cup Winners: (12 times) 1956-57, 1957-58, 1965-66, 1966-67, 1967-68, 1968-69, 1969-70, 1974-75, 1982-83, 1997-98, 1999-2000, 2000-01. *Runners-up:* 10 times.

European: *European Cup:* 82 matches (1966-67 winners, 1967-68, 1968-69, 1969-70 runners-up, 1970-71, 1971-72 semi-finals, 1972-73, 1973-74 semi-finals, 1974-75, 1977-78, 1979-80, 1981-82, 1982-83, 1986-87, 1988-89, 1998-99). *Cup Winners' Cup:* 39 matches (1963-64 semi-finals, 1975-76, 1980-81, 1984-85, 1985-86, 1989-90, 1995-96). *UEFA Cup:* 54 matches (*Fairs Cup:* 1962-63, 1964-65. *UEFA Cup:* 1976-77, 1983-84, 1987-88, 1991-92, 1992-93, 1993-94, 1996-97, 1997-98, 1998-99, 1999-2000, 2000-01).

Club colours: Shirt: Green and white hoops. Shorts: White. Stockings: White.

Goalscorers: *League* (90): Larsson 35 (2 pens), Sutton 11, Moravcik 9, Petrov 6, Johnson 5, Mjallby 4, Thompson 4, Agathe 3, Valgaeren 3, McNamara 2, Vega 2, Berkovic 1, Burchill 1, Lambert 1, Lennon 1, Smith 1, Stubbs 1
Scottish Cup (17): Larsson 9 (3 pens), McNamara 3, Vega 2, Moravcik 1, Valgaeren 1, own goal 1
CIS Cup (15): Larsson 5, Johnson 2 (1 pen), Sutton 2, Creaney 1, Healy 1, McNamara 1, Moravcik 1, Smith 1, Thompson 1

Gould J 15	Valgaeren J 35	Mahe S 7+3	Boyd T 21+9	Stubbs A 7+4	McNamara J 18+12	Petrov S 27+1	Lambert P 27	Berkovic E 2+2	Larsson H 37	Johnson T 9+7	Tebily O 2+2	Mjallby J 30+5	Petta B 20	Moravcik L 16+11	Thompson A 29+1	Burchill M —+2	Healy C 4+7	Agathe D 26+1	Riseth V —+1	Douglas R 22	Lennon N 17	Vega R 18	Smith J 2+5	Crainey S —+2	Maloney S 1+3	Kharine D 1	Fotheringham M 1+1	Match No.
1	2	3	4	5	6	7	8		9^1	10	11	12																1
1	2	3	4		6	7	8		9^1	10	11			5	12													2
1	2	3	4^1	5		7	8		10		11	12	6	9														3
1	2	3	13	5^1	4	7	8		10	11		12	6	9^2														4
1	2	3	13	5^1	4	7	8^2		10	11		12	6	9		14												5
1	2		3	5^1	4	7	8		10	11		12	6	9^2								13						6
1	2	3^1	4		6	7	8		10	11		5	12	9														7
1	3		4	13	5	7	8	14	10^3	11		2	6^1	9^2			12											8
1	3		12^1	4	5	7	8		10	11		2	6	9^1		14						13						9
1	3		4			7^2	8		10	11		2	6	9^1	5		12					13						10
1	3		4			7^1	8		10	11		2	6	9	5		12											11
1	3		4	12		7	8		10	11		2	6^1	9	5													12
1	3		4	12	5	7	8		10			2^1	6	9	11^2							13						13
1	3		4	5		7^2	8^1		10	11		2	6	9			12					13						14
	3		4			7^1		13	10^2	11^3	14	2	6	9	5		12			1	8							15
	3		4		13	7			10	11^1	14	2^3	6	9^2	5		12			1	8							16
	3		13	4	12	7			10	11^3	14	2^2	6	9^1	5					1	8							17
	3		12	4	5	7			10	11		2	6^1	9^2	5					1	8	13						18
	3		4		12	7			10	11		2	6	9^1	5					1	8							19
	3		4		13	7			10		12	2	6^2	9^1	5			11		1	8							20
	3		12			7			10	11		2	6^1	9^2	5					1	8			4	13			21
	3		12			7			10	11		2	6^1	9	5					1	8			4				22
	3		5			7			10^1	11	12	2	6^1	9						1	8^3	13		4			14	23
	3		5^2			7^3			10	11	12	2	6^1	9						1	8	13		4			14	24
	3^1		12		5		8		10^2	11		2	6^3	9		14				1			7	4	13			25
	3						8		10	11	12	2^1	6	9	5					1			7	4				26
	3^2		13		12		8^3		10	11		2	6	9	5^1	14				1			7	4				27
	3				5		8^1		10	11		2	6	9	12					1			7	4				28
	3				5		8		10	11^1	12	2	6	9						1			7	4	13			29
	3		12		5^1		8		10	11		2	6	9^2						1			7	4	13			30
	3		13				8		10	11^1		2	6	9^2			12			1		5	7	4				31
	3		13		12		8		10	11^1		2	6	9^2						1		5	7	4				32
	3^2		13		12		8		10	11^1		2	6	9^3		14				1		5	7	4				33
	3		14		5		8^3		10	11^2		2	6	9^1			12	7		1				4	13			34
	3		14		13		8^3		10	11^1		2	6	9^2						1		5	7	4	12			35
	3^1		12		5		8^3		10			2	6	9				11					7^2	4	13	1	14	36
1	3^3		12		5		8		10			2	6	9		14						13	7	4^1	11^2			37
	6	3		5		7						2		9						1			10	4	11		8	38

CLYDE

First Division

Year Formed: 1878. *Ground & Address:* Broadwood Stadium, Cumbernauld, G68 9NE. *Telephone:* 01236 451511.
Ground Capacity: all seated: 8200. *Size of Pitch:* 112yd × 76yd.
Chairman: W. B. Carmichael. *Secretary:* John D. Taylor. *Chief Executive:* Ronnie MacDonald.
Manager: Allan Maitland. *First Team Coach:* Denis McDaid. *Physio:* John Watson.
Managers since 1975: S. Anderson, C. Brown, J. Clark, A. Smith, G. Speirs. *Club Nickname(s):* The Bully Wee. *Previous Grounds:* Barrowfield & Shawfield Stadium.
Record Attendance: 52,000 v Rangers, Division I; 21 Nov, 1908.
Record Transfer Fee received: £175,000 for Scott Howie to Norwich City (Aug 1993).
Record Transfer Fee paid: £14,000 for Harry Hood from Sunderland (1966).
Record Victory: 11-1 v Cowdenbeath, Division II; 6 Oct, 1951.
Record Defeat: 0-11 v Dumbarton, Scottish Cup 4th rd, 22 Nov, 1879; v Rangers, Scottish Cup 4th rd, 13 Nov, 1880.
Most Capped Player: Tommy Ring, 12, Scotland.
Most League Appearances: 428: Brian Ahern.
Most League Goals in Season (Individual): 32: Bill Boyd, 1932-33.
Most Goals Overall (Individual): —.

CLYDE 2000–01 LEAGUE RECORD

Match No.	Date	Venue	Opponents	Result	H/T Score	Lg. Pos.	Goalscorers	Attendance
1	Aug 5	H	Falkirk	W 3-1	1-1	—	Proudlock 3 [45, 57, 87]	2706
2	12	A	Ross Co	W 2-0	1-0	1	Proudlock [7], Keogh [66]	2645
3	19	H	Livingston	D 1-1	0-0	1	Kane [70]	1781
4	26	H	Morton	L 0-3	0-1	3		1480
5	Sept 9	A	Inverness CT	W 2-1	0-1	3	Convery 2 (1 pen) [62 (p), 72]	1484
6	16	H	Airdrieonians	W 4-1	0-0	2	Kane [52], McLaughlin [56], Ross [70], Cannie (pen) [90]	1864
7	23	A	Ayr U	L 1-2	0-0	3	Convery [63]	2715
8	30	H	Raith R	D 0-0	0-0	4		1202
9	Oct 7	A	Alloa Ath	L 1-3	0-1	4	McLaughlin [73]	740
10	14	A	Falkirk	L 2-3	2-1	5	Kane [40], Convery [45]	3003
11	21	H	Ross Co	D 2-2	0-1	5	Keogh [52], McLaughlin [69]	987
12	28	A	Morton	D 1-1	0-1	5	Henry [71]	1051
13	Nov 4	H	Inverness CT	D 1-1	0-1	5	Mitchell [73]	935
14	11	H	Ayr U	L 0-1	0-1	7		1318
15	22	A	Airdrieonians	W 3-1	0-1	—	Aitken [56], Boniface [65], Kane [69]	1513
16	25	H	Alloa Ath	D 0-0	0-0	6		1012
17	Dec 2	A	Raith R	W 2-1	1-1	5	Boniface [17], Keogh [62]	1810
18	9	A	Livingston	L 0-2	0-1	5		3230
19	16	H	Falkirk	L 0-3	0-1	6		1629
20	23	A	Inverness CT	D 2-2	0-1	6	Aitken [73], Cannie [76]	1588
21	Jan 2	H	Airdrieonians	D 1-1	1-0	—	Crawford [6]	1769
22	6	A	Ayr U	L 0-2	0-0	6		2481
23	13	H	Raith R	W 3-1	1-0	5	Crawford 2 (1 pen) [6, 69 (p)], Keogh [90]	1305
24	Feb 3	A	Livingston	L 0-3	0-2	5		2506
25	17	H	Morton	D 1-1	0-0	5	Crawford [81]	1609
26	24	A	Morton	W 1-0	0-0	5	Crawford [61]	1221
27	Mar 10	A	Alloa Ath	D 0-0	0-0	5		818
28	17	H	Ayr U	D 2-2	1-2	5	Millen [25], Kane [76]	1416
29	20	A	Ross Co	L 0-2	0-1	—		2115
30	27	H	Inverness CT	D 2-2	2-1	—	Kane [30], Keogh [38]	657
31	31	A	Airdrieonians	L 0-1	0-1	5		1309
32	Apr 7	A	Alloa Ath	D 1-1	0-1	5	Hinds [84]	1006
33	14	A	Raith R	W 1-0	0-0	5	Hinds [58]	1817
34	21	A	Falkirk	D 1-1	1-1	5	Kane [21]	2200
35	28	H	Ross Co	W 2-0	0-0	5	Ross [55], Convery [87]	1313
36	May 5	A	Livingston	W 2-0	1-0	5	Mitchell [30], Hinds [68]	6835

Final League Position: 5

Honours

League Champions: Division II 1904-05, 1951-52, 1956-57, 1961-62, 1972-73. Second Division 1977-78, 1981-82, 1992-93, 1999-2000.
Runners-up: Division II 1903-04, 1905-06, 1925-26, 1963-64.
Scottish Cup Winners: 1939, 1955, 1958: *Runners-up:* 1910, 1912, 1949.
League Cup: —

Club colours: Shirt: White with red and black trim. Shorts: Black. Stockings: Black with red and white tops.

Goalscorers: *League* (44): Kane 7, Convery 5 (1 pen), Crawford 5 (1 pen), Keogh 5, Proudlock 4, Hinds 3, McLaughlin 3, Aitken 2, Boniface 2, Cannie 2 (1 pen), Mitchell 2, Ross 2, Henry 1, Millen 1
Scottish Cup (1): McLaughlin 1
CIS Cup (6): Kane 2, Grant 1, McLaughlin 1, Proudlock 1, Ross 1
Bell's League Cup (1): Cannie 1

Halliwell B 34	Murray D 29 + 2	McLaughlin M 20	Smith B 23 + 2	Cranmer C 16 + 4	Ross J 34	Convery S 18 + 8	Sellars B 5 + 3	Proudlock A 4	Keogh P 28	Grant A 9 + 4	Greer G 22 + 3	Aitken C 7 + 11	Henderson N 3 + 2	McCusker R 4 + 6	Kane A 25 + 8	McPherson C 1 + 2	Mitchell J 25 + 1	Bingham C 10 + 5	Cannie P 4 + 11	Hay P 2 + 1	Dunn D 11 + 7	Hanley D 2 + 1	Henry J 7 + 4	Boniface F 8	McAulay S 2 + 2	Crawford B 11 + 7	McClay A 3 + 2	Millen A 13	McFarlane N 7	Hinds L 4 + 3	Match No.
1	2¹	3	4	5	6²	7	8	9	10	11¹³	12	13	14																		1
1	2	3	4	5	6	7²	8¹	9³	10	11			14		12	13															2
1	2	3	4	5	6	7²	8¹	9	10	11¹³	14				12	13															3
1	2²		4	5	6³			9	10	11	13				8		12	3¹	7	14											4
1		3	4	5	6	12	7¹		8		2				9³	10⁵	11	14	13												5
1	14	3	4	5	6	7³	13		8²		2				9¹		11		10		12										6
1	12	3	4	5¹	6	7	13		8	11	2				14			10³		9²											7
1	2		4¹	5	6	7²	14		8						10	11		3³		9	12	13									8
1⁸	2	3		5	6	7	9		8	13		5			10¹	11²			4	12	15										9
	2	3¹			6	7²			8		5				9	12		11	13	4	10³	1	14								10
	2	3			6³				4		5	14			11			7	13		10¹	1	8²	9	12						11
1	2	3			6²	12			4		5				11		10	7¹						13	9	8					12
1	2	3			6	12			4		5²	13			11		10	7	14						9³	8¹					13
1	2	3			6	7²			4		5	8³			11		10	14	12						9¹	13					14
1		3¹	4	12	6	7²			5		2	8			11		10	14	13						9³						15
1	2		4		6	14			3	12	5	8¹			11²		10	7³		13			9								16
1	5	3	4		6	7			8		2				11		10	12					9¹								17
1	5	3	4		6	7³			8	14	2	13			11²		10	12					9¹								18
1		3	4	5	6	7¹			8	12	2	10			11²								13	14							19
1		3	4	5		7³			8		2	10			11²		9¹	12		14		6	13								20
1		3	4	5	6	7			10		2	8			12		11²	13					9¹								21
1	3		4	5¹	6	7²			10		2	8			12		11	13					9¹								22
1	5	3	4			9	11¹		2			13			6			12					7²	10	8						23
1	2	3¹			6	14			4		5	13			11³		7			12			9	10²	8						24
1	2		4	5	6	7³				11¹					13		10		12	3²			9	14	8						25
1	2				6				3		12				11²		7	13			10		8¹		9		4	5			26
1	2				6				4	3	13				12		7	14			10³		9¹		11		8	5²			27
1	2	12			6				3						13		11²				10		8¹		9		4	5			28
1	2				6	9			3	12					11¹		7				10²		13		8³		4	5	14		29
1	2				6	9²			3	12					11		7				10		8¹		13		4	5			30
1	2	12			6				10	3	13				5¹	11	7				9³		8²		4				14		31
1	2	4	14		6				10¹	3					11		7	8²			12		9					5³	13		32
1	2	4	12		6	13				3					11²		7¹				10		14		8		5	9³			33
1	2	4	3		6	12				5³					14	11	7¹				10		13		8			9²			34
1	2	4	3		6	13				14					11¹		7³	8			10		12		5			9²			35
1	2	4¹	12		6	11¹³				3					13		7²	8			10		14		5			9			36

CLYDEBANK

Second Division

Year Formed: 1965. *Club Address:* c/o West of Scotland RFC, Burnbrae, Milngavie, G62 6HX. *Telephone:* 0141 955 9048.
Fax: 0141 955 9049. *Telephone (Match days only):* 01475 723571. *Ground:* (sharing with Morton) Cappielow Park, Sinclair
St, Greenock PA15 2TY. *Ground Capacity:* total: 14,891, seated: 5741. *Size of Pitch:* 110yd × 71yd.
Chairman: Dr John Hall. *Secretary:* Billy Hall.
Manager: To be appointed.
Club Nickname(s): The Bankies. *Previous Ground:* Kilbowie Park.
Record Attendance: 14,900 v Hibernian, Scottish Cup 1st rd; 10 Feb, 1965.
Record Transfer Fee received: £175,000 for Owen Coyle from Airdrieonians (Feb 1990).
Record Transfer Fee paid: £50,000 for Gerry McCabe from Clyde.
Record Victory: 8-1 Arbroath, First Division; 3 Jan 1977.
Record Defeat: 1-9 v Gala Fairydean, Scottish Cup qual rd; 15 Sept, 1965.
Most Capped Player: —.
Most League Appearances: 620: Jim Fallon; 1968-86.
Most League Goals in Season (Individual): 29: Ken Eadie, First Division, 1990-91.
Most League Goals Overall (Individual): 138, Ken Eadie 1988-95.

CLYDEBANK 2000–01 LEAGUE RECORD

Match No.	Date	Venue	Opponents	Result	H/T Score	Lg. Pos.	Goalscorers	Attendance
1	Aug 5	A	Stirling A	D 2-2	2-1	—	Fal 2 [20, 23]	779
2	12	H	Stenhousemuir	W 1-0	0-0	2	Coyne [79]	236
3	19	A	Arbroath	L 0-1	0-1	6		691
4	26	H	Queen of the S	L 1-2	1-1	8	Coyne [12]	273
5	Sept 9	A	Berwick R	L 1-3	0-0	9	Coyne (pen) [50]	482
6	16	A	Forfar Ath	W 2-0	2-0	8	Jacquel [14], Hamilton [15]	385
7	23	H	Partick Th	W 2-1	0-0	5	Burke [65], Welsh [79]	1379
8	30	A	Stranraer	W 2-0	1-0	3	McKelvie [34], Murray [86]	551
9	Oct 7	H	Queen's Park	W 2-0	1-0	2	McKinstrey [3], Murray [58]	375
10	14	H	Stirling A	W 3-0	2-0	1	Burke 2 [23, 74], Coyne [33]	312
11	21	A	Stenhousemuir	L 1-2	1-0	1	Hamilton [2]	450
12	28	H	Queen of the S	D 1-1	0-1	3	Kaak [57]	1156
13	Nov 4	H	Berwick R	L 0-1	0-0	4		196
14	11	A	Partick Th	L 0-2	0-1	4		3101
15	18	H	Forfar Ath	D 1-1	1-1	6	Glancy [41]	153
16	25	A	Queen's Park	D 1-1	1-1	6	Walker [45]	668
17	Dec 5	H	Stranraer	L 2-3	2-2	—	Paton [2], Glancy [23]	126
18	16	A	Stirling A	D 0-0	0-0	6		534
19	23	H	Arbroath	L 1-2	0-1	7	Murdoch [86]	131
20	Jan 2	A	Berwick R	W 2-1	1-1	—	Glancy [35], Paton (pen) [72]	572
21	27	A	Forfar Ath	W 3-1	2-0	4	Smith [15], Paton (pen) [28], Brannigan [51]	418
22	Feb 13	H	Partick Th	L 0-4	0-0	—		1111
23	17	A	Arbroath	L 2-4	2-2	6	McKinstrey [38], Paton [44]	537
24	Mar 6	A	Stranraer	D 0-0	0-0	—		363
25	10	A	Queen of the S	L 0-1	0-1	6		1022
26	13	H	Queen of the S	L 1-2	1-0	—	Paton (pen) [3]	245
27	17	A	Partick Th	L 0-2	0-0	7		2721
28	20	H	Queen's Park	W 2-1	1-0	—	Burke 2 [13, 88]	209
29	27	H	Stenhousemuir	W 1-0	1-0	—	Burke [44]	256
30	31	H	Forfar Ath	W 2-1	1-0	6	Brannigan [10], Burke [82]	145
31	Apr 7	A	Queen's Park	D 0-0	0-0	6		701
32	10	H	Berwick R	D 2-2	1-0	—	Paton [43], Smith [65]	167
33	14	H	Stranraer	D 0-0	0-0	6		159
34	21	H	Stirling A	D 1-1	0-0	6	Burke [68]	205
35	28	A	Stenhousemuir	D 0-0	0-0	6		404
36	May 5	H	Arbroath	W 3-1	1-0	5	McKelvie 2 [39, 74], Paton [67]	243

Final League Position: 5

Honours

League Champions: Second Division 1975-76; *Runners-up:* 1997-98; *Runners-up:* First Division 1976-77, 1984-85.
Scottish Cup: Semi-finalists 1990. *League Cup:* —.

Club colours: Shirt: Vertical red and white stripes. Shorts: Black. Stockings: Black.

Goalscorers: *League* (42): Burke 8, Paton 7 (3 pens), Coyne 4 (1 pen), Glancy 3, McKelvie 3, Brannigan 2, Fal 2, Hamilton 2, McKinstrey 2, Murray 2, Smith 2, Jacquel 1, Kaak 1, Murdoch 1, Walker 1, Welsh 1
Scottish Cup (0):
CIS Cup (0):
Bell's League Cup (3): Coyne 1, Jacquel 1, McCormick 1

Wyne D 28	McKinstrey J 25 + 5	McKinnon R 31	Wishart F 12 + 2	Brannigan K 34	Taborda E 4	Murray S 17 + 12	Ferguson D 26 + 2	Fal L 3	Coyne T 10 + 5	Hamilton B 14 + 1	Rodden P — + 1	McQuitter R 3	Campbell J 6	Milne D 3	Johnson G 4	McKelvie D 8 + 9	Walker J 16 + 10	Callaghan S 1 + 1	Paton E 21 + 6	Conway C — + 1	Hernandez F 1	Welsh B 7	McCormick S 1 + 2	Jacquel R 2	Racon A — + 2	McVey W 12 + 6	Murdoch S 16 + 3	Burke A 15	Kaak A 1 + 1	Farrell G 20 + 2	Glancy M 17 + 4	Hutchison S 2	Creaney G 3	Gow A — + 3	Smith G 16 + 1	Brown P — + 1	Mooney G 2 + 1	Farrell D 1	Bossy F 14	Match No
1	2	3	4	5	6	7	8	9¹	10	11	12																													1
1	2	3¹		5	6	12	8³	9²	10	11					4	7	13	14																						2
1	2²	3		5	6	4	11		10	8¹					9	12	7³		13	14																				3
1	13	3	2	5	6³	11		9¹	10						4	8²	14	12			7																			4
1	3¹	2		5		12	7	11							4	8	14									6	9²	10³	13											5
1	2			5		7	11²	9³		8					13	6	14	10¹	12							3	4													6
1	2²	3	14	5		7	11			8					9¹	6										12	13	10³		4										7
1	2			5		7	13		10	8					9²		11¹		12							6	3			4										8
1	2			5		7³	12	13		8					9²		11¹	14								6	3	10		4										9
1	2		13	5		7¹	11	9³		8							14		12							6	3	10		4²										10
1	2²	6		5		7	11	9¹		8							12		13	14						3³		10		4										11
1	2	6		5		11	13	9	10	8									7²							3¹	12			4										12
1	6	3		5		12	11	9²	10	8¹					13		7³	14								2				4										13
1	2	6		5		7	11	9		8									12							3¹	10	13		4²										14
	2	3²		5		7	11	9¹		8					12				13							4	10		1											15
1	2	3		5			11			14						7²	8		6¹							12	10³			4					9	13				16
1	14	3¹		5		12	11			13						7³	8		6²							2	10	4							9					17
		3		5		12	11²									13	8		4							2	10³		1		9¹					14			7	18
1	3¹	6		5		7										8²	9		14							4	10			2					13	11	12			19
1	7	3	6	5		12										8	9		4							2	10¹								11					20
1	7	3	6	5		12										14	8²	9	4							2	10³								11		13			21
1	7	3	6	5		12										13	8	9	4¹							2	10²								11					22
	7	3		5		13										12	8²	9								2	10¹								11		4		6	23
	7	3		5						4¹			1				8	9								12	10								11				6	24
	7	3		5						4¹			1				8²	9								13	12			2	10				11				6	25
	7	3		5			8			4¹			1					9								13	12			2	10				11				6	26
	7	3		5		2	4						1				8	9²								11¹	10			13	12								6	27
	7	3		5		8	4						1				9¹									10				2	12				11				6	28
	3			5		7¹	4						1				8²	12								13	2	10		9					11				6²	29
1	2	3		5		13	4										7¹	9								10				8	12				11				6	30
1		3		5			4										7									2	10			8	9				11				6	31
1	12	3		5		13	4²										14	7								2¹	10			8	9³				11				6	32
1	13	3¹		5			4										12	7								2²	10			8	9				11				6	33
1	2	3		5		8	4							9			7										10								11				6	34
1	13	3²		5¹		12								11			9	4	7								10				8				14		2³		6	35
1	2			5		6¹											9	13	7								10				3	12			4²		11			36

COWDENBEATH

Second Division

Year Formed: 1881. *Ground & Address:* Central Park, Cowdenbeath KY4 9EY. *Telephone:* 01383 610166. *Fax:* 01383 512132.
Ground Capacity: total: 5268, seated: 1622. *Size of Pitch:* 107yd × 66yd.
Chairman: Gordon McDougall. *Secretary:* Tom Ogilvie. *General Manager:* Joe McNamara.
Manager: Gary Kirk. *Assistant Manager:* Keith Wright. *Physio:* Wendy McDonald.
Managers since 1975: D. McLindon, F. Connor, P. Wilson, A. Rolland, H. Wilson, W. McCulloch, J. Clark, J. Craig, R. Campbell, J. Blackley, J. Brownlie, A. Harrow, J. Reilly, P Dolan, T. Steven, S. Conn, C. Levein. *Previous Grounds:* North End Park, Cowdenbeath.
Record Attendance: 25,586 v Rangers, League Cup quarter-final; 21 Sept, 1949.
Record Transfer Fee received: £30,000 for Nicky Henderson to Falkirk (March 1994).
Record Transfer Fee paid: —
Record Victory: 12-0 v Johnstone, Scottish Cup 1st rd; 21 Jan, 1928.
Record Defeat: 1-11 v Clyde, Division II; 6 Oct, 1951.
Most Capped Player: Jim Paterson, 3, Scotland.
Most League and Cup Appearances: 491 Ray Allan 1972-75, 1979-89.
Most League Goals in Season (Individual): 54, Rab Walls, Division II, 1938-39.
Most Goals Overall (Individual): 127, Willie Devlin, 1922-26, 1929-30.

COWDENBEATH 2000–01 LEAGUE RECORD

Match No.	Date	Venue	Opponents	Result	H/T Score	Lg. Pos.	Goalscorers	Attendance
1	Aug 5	A	East Stirling	W 2-0	1-0	—	Wright [30], Bradley [66]	297
2	12	H	Albion R	W 5-0	2-0	1	Wright 2 [37, 57], Burns 2 [44, 64], Allan [86]	302
3	19	A	Brechin C	D 0-0	0-0	2		337
4	26	H	Elgin C	W 3-1	0-1	2	White [51], McDowell 2 [77, 88]	354
5	Sept 9	A	East Fife	W 2-0	0-0	1	Wright [63], Winter [87]	735
6	16	H	Hamilton A	W 2-0	2-0	1	Lawrence [18], Nelson (og) [24]	448
7	23	A	Dumbarton	W 4-2	1-1	1	Bradley [40], Winter [62], Wright [84], Burns [88]	348
8	30	H	Montrose	W 2-0	0-0	1	McDowell [72], Bradley [73]	378
9	Oct 7	A	Peterhead	L 0-3	0-2	1		637
10	14	H	East Stirling	W 3-0	2-0	1	White [20], McDowell 2 [30, 73]	289
11	21	A	Albion R	L 0-1	0-1	3		429
12	28	H	Elgin C	W 3-2	2-2	3	Winter [18], Boyle (pen) [21], McDowell [47]	836
13	Nov 4	H	East Fife	W 1-0	1-0	1	Bradley [26]	626
14	11	H	Dumbarton	D 1-1	0-1	1	Burns [83]	341
15	18	A	Hamilton A	D 0-0	0-0	1		598
16	25	H	Peterhead	W 2-0	0-0	1	Burns [61], Smith [80]	404
17	Dec 2	A	Montrose	W 2-1	0-0	1	Allan 2 [72, 81]	311
18	23	H	Brechin C	W 2-1	0-1	1	King [47], McDowell [83]	434
19	Jan 2	A	East Fife	W 2-1	1-1	—	McDowell [14], Brown [90]	1003
20	Feb 17	A	Brechin C	L 0-2	0-2	3		545
21	24	H	Albion R	W 1-0	0-0	2	Wright [85]	331
22	Mar 7	A	Dumbarton	L 0-3	0-1	—		507
23	10	A	Elgin C	W 2-0	0-0	1	Bradley [81], Winter [90]	676
24	13	A	Peterhead	L 0-3	0-2	—		499
25	17	H	Dumbarton	D 2-2	1-2	1	Wright [21], McDowell [85]	369
26	20	H	Hamilton A	D 1-1	1-1	—	King [26]	429
27	25	H	Elgin C	W 1-0	0-0	1	Winter [90]	289
28	31	A	Hamilton A	D 0-0	0-0	2		666
29	Apr 3	A	East Stirling	W 2-0	0-0	—	Bradley [64], White [70]	272
30	7	H	Peterhead	W 4-0	1-0	1	King 2 [4, 74], Brown [56], Lawrence [69]	348
31	10	H	Montrose	W 2-1	0-0	—	Brown [52], Burns [56]	319
32	14	A	Montrose	W 1-0	1-0	1	Bradley (pen) [45]	407
33	17	A	East Fife	W 3-2	3-0	—	Bradley [23], Courts [35], McDowell [38]	531
34	21	H	East Stirling	L 1-3	0-1	1	Brown [84]	488
35	28	A	Albion R	D 0-0	0-0	1		405
36	May 5	H	Brechin C	W 2-1	1-0	2	King [42], Winter [90]	3448

Final League Position: 2

Honours

League Champions: Division II 1913-14, 1914-15, 1938-39; *Runners-up:* Division II 1921-22, 1923-24, 1969-70. Second Division 1991-92. *Runners-up:* Third Division 2000-01.
Scottish Cup: Quarter-finals: 1931.
League Cup: Semi-finals: 1959-60, 1970-71.

Club colours: Shirt: Royal blue with white stripe down shoulder and sleeve; white round neck with one Royal blue stripe. Shorts: White with Royal blue stripe on side. Stockings: Royal blue with one white leg hoop.

Goalscorers: *League* (58): McDowell 10, Bradley 8 (1 pen), Wright 7, Burns 6, Winter 6, King 5, Brown 4, Allan 3, White D 3, Lawrence 2, Boyle 1 (pen), Courts 1, Smith 1, own goal 1
Scottish Cup (3): Bradley 2 (1 pen), Winter 1
CIS Cup (4): Allan 1, Burns 1, McDowell 1, Wright 1
Bell's League Cup (3): Brown 1, Juskowiak 1, McDowell 1

Martin J 36	Boyle J 33	McMillan C 3	White D 35	McCulloch K 10	Lawrence A 27+5	Winter C 34	Bradley M 33+1	McDowell M 23+8	Wright K 20+12	Burns J 22+12	Brown G 21+12	Allan J 6+9	Juskowiak R 2+4	Welsh B 3	Ramsay S 1	Lakie J 2+1	Courts T 23+2	Crabbe G —+1	McDonald I —+4	Neeson C 11+2	Smith A 18	King T 20	Carnie G 1	Simmons S 2+1	Mitchell W 3	Gilfillan F —+3	Hunter M 7+3	Barnes D —+1	Match No.
1	2	3	4	5	6^2	7	8	9^1	10^3	11	12	13	14																1
1	2	3	4	5	6^3	7	8	9^2	10^1	11	12	14	13																2
1	2	3	4		6^1	7	8	9^2		11	10	12	13	5															3
1	2		4			7	8	9	10	11		6			3^1	5	12												4
1	2		4	5	12		8	9	10	11^1		6^2			3				13										5
1	2		4	5	6	7	8	9	10^1	11	12				3														6
1	2		4	5^2	6	7	8	9	10	11		13			3^1		12												7
1	2		4	5	6	7	8	9	10^1	11^2	12	13			3^3		14												8
1	2		4	5^2	6^3	7	8	9	10	11^1	14	12			3		13												9
1	2		4	5	6	7	8	9	10^2	11^1	13	12			3														10
1	2		4	5	6^1	7	8	9	10^3	11	12	14			3^2		13												11
1	2		4		12	7	8	9^2	10	11^1	13	6									3	5							12
1	2	3		5	6^2	7	8	9	10^1	11	12										13	4							13
1	2	3		5	6^2	7	8	9^2	10	11^1	12	13									14	4							14
1	2			5	12	7	8	9	10^1	11	13	6^2									3	4							15
1	2			5	12	7	8	9	10^1	11		6									3	4							16
1	2			5	12	7	8	9	10^1	11		6									3	4	8						17
1	2			5	13	7	8	9	10^2	11	12	6^1									3	4							18
1	2			5	6	7	8	9	10^1	11		12									3	4							19
1	2			5	13	7	8^2	9^3	10		14	6					3^1			12	4	11							20
1	2			5	6	7	12	9	10^2	11^1	13										3	4	8						21
1	2			5	7	8	13	11^1	10	9^2		12									3	4	6						22
1		5		2	7	8	9	12	10^2	11^1							3								6	4	13		23
1		5		2	7	8	9^2	14	12	10^3	11^1						3								6	4	13		24
1	2			5	6^1	7	8	14	9^2	12	13						3				4	11					10^3		25
1	2			5	6^3	7	8	13	9^1	14	12						3				4	11					10^2		26
1	2			5	6^3	7	8	12	9^2	14	13						3				4	11					10^1		27
1	2			5	6^2	7	8	9^1		13	10						3				4	11					12		28
1	2			5	6	7	8	9^1	13		10^2						3				4	11					12		29
1	2			5	6^2	7	8	12	13	9	14						3				4^3	11					10^1		30
1	2			5	6	7	10^2	12	9	4							3					11			13	8^1			31
1	2			5	6^2	8	12	14	13	9^3							3				11	4					10^1		32
1^9		5		2	7	8	9^1	13	6	10^2		4					3					11				12		15	33
1	2			5	6^1	7	8	9^2	13	12	10						4				3	11							34
1	2			5	6^2	7	8	10	12	13	9		4				3					11					10^1		35
1	2			13		7	8	12		6^2	9		4				3				5	11					10^1		36

DUMBARTON
Third Division

Year Formed: 1872. *Ground:* Strathclyde Homes Stadium, Dumbarton G82 1JJ. *Telephone:* 01389 762569/767864. *Fax:* 01389 762629
Ground Capacity: total: 2050. *Size of Pitch:* 110yd × 75yd.
Chairman: D. Dalglish. *Club Secretary:* Colin J. Hosie. *Company Secretary:* John Benn.
Manager: Tom Carson. *Assistant Manager:* Steve Morrison. *Coaches:* George Clark and Ian Lee. *Physio:* Linda McIllwraith.
Managers since 1975: A. Wright, D. Wilson, S. Fallon, W. Lamont, D. Wilson, D. Whiteford, A. Totten, M. Clougherty, R. Auld, J. George, W. Lamont, M. MacLeod, J. Fallon, I. Wallace. *Club Nickname(s):* The Sons. *Previous Grounds:* Broadmeadow, Ropework Lane, Townend Ground, Boghead Park.
Record Attendance: 18,000 v Raith Rovers, Scottish Cup; 2 Mar, 1957.
Record Transfer Fee received: £125,000 for Graeme Sharp to Everton (March 1982).
Record Transfer Fee paid: £50,000 for Charlie Gibson from Stirling Albion (1989).
Record Victory: 13-1 v Kirkintilloch Central. 1st rd; 1 Sept, 1888.
Record Defeat: 1-11 v Albion Rovers, Division II; 30 Jan, 1926: v Ayr United, League Cup; 13 Aug, 1952.
Most Capped Player: James McAulay, 9, Scotland.
Most League Appearances: 297: Andy Jardine, 1957-67.

DUMBARTON 2000–01 LEAGUE RECORD

Match No.	Date		Venue	Opponents	Result		H/T Score	Lg. Pos.	Goalscorers	Atten- dance
1	Aug	5	A	Hamilton A	L	0-2	0-0	—		588
2		12	H	Brechin C	L	0-2	0-0	9		370
3		19	A	Peterhead	L	0-2	0-1	9		630
4		26	A	Albion R	W	1-0	1-0	7	Flannery [31]	343
5	Sept	9	H	East Stirling	L	1-2	1-2	8	Flannery [2]	259
6		16	A	Montrose	D	2-2	1-2	7	Flannery [43], Brown [57]	317
7		23	H	Cowdenbeath	L	2-4	1-1	8	King [35], Brown [83]	348
8		30	A	Elgin C	L	0-2	0-0	9		752
9	Oct	7	A	East Fife	L	2-3	1-2	9	King [35], Dillon [53]	256
10		14	H	Hamilton A	L	2-3	1-1	9	Robertson (pen) [7], Flannery (pen) [88]	368
11		21	A	Brechin C	L	1-3	0-0	10	McCann [50]	455
12		28	H	Albion R	L	0-1	0-1	10		277
13	Nov	4	A	East Stirling	D	1-1	0-1	10	Flannery [80]	246
14		11	A	Cowdenbeath	D	1-1	1-0	10	Bruce [5]	341
15		18	H	Montrose	W	1-0	1-0	9	Grace [42]	238
16		25	A	East Fife	L	0-1	0-1	9		465
17	Dec	2	H	Elgin C	W	3-0	1-0	8	Flannery [24], Brown Andy [59], Brittain [60]	1876
18		16	A	Hamilton A	L	0-2	0-0	8		485
19		23	H	Peterhead	L	1-3	1-2	8	Brown Andy [4]	821
20	Jan	2	H	East Stirling	W	3-0	1-0	—	Hall (og) [28], Flannery [57], Smith [87]	658
21		27	A	Albion R	W	3-1	0-0	7	Flannery 2 [67, 90], Brown Andy [75]	369
22	Feb	3	H	East Fife	W	2-0	1-0	7	Brown Andy [42], Stewart [72]	711
23		24	H	Brechin C	W	1-0	0-0	8	Flannery [89]	722
24	Mar	7	H	Cowdenbeath	W	3-0	1-0	—	Dillon [31], Brown Andy [54], Flannery [68]	507
25		10	H	Albion R	L	1-4	0-1	7	Flannery (pen) [78]	818
26		13	A	Elgin C	W	3-0	3-0	—	Brown Andy [3], Dillon [5], Bruce [32]	424
27		17	A	Cowdenbeath	D	2-2	2-1	7	Flannery 2 (1 pen) [12, 26 (p)]	369
28		20	A	East Stirling	D	0-0	0-0	—		209
29		24	A	Peterhead	W	1-0	1-0	6	Robertson [31]	432
30		27	A	Montrose	W	2-1	0-0	—	Flannery [53], Bonar [64]	165
31		31	H	Montrose	L	1-2	1-1	6	Flannery [44]	751
32	Apr	7	A	East Fife	W	1-0	1-0	6	Lynes [4]	313
33		14	H	Elgin C	W	2-0	1-0	5	Brown Andy [2], O'Neil (pen) [63]	685
34		21	A	Hamilton A	L	1-2	1-1	6	Lynes [3]	864
35		28	A	Brechin C	L	0-1	0-1	7		510
36	May	5	H	Peterhead	D	2-2	1-1	6	Stewart [16], Flannery (pen) [69]	715

Final League Position: 6

Most Goals in Season (Individual): 38: Kenny Wilson, Division II; 1971-72. *(League and Cup):* 46 Hughie Gallacher, 1955-56.
Most Goals Overall (Individual): 169: Hughie Gallacher, 1954-62 (including C Division 1954-55). *(League and Cup):* 202 Hughie Gallacher, 1954-62

Honours
League Champions: Division I 1890-91 (shared with Rangers), 1891-92. Division II 1910-11, 1971-72. Second Division 1991-92; *Runners-up:* First Division 1983-84. Division II 1907-08.
Scottish Cup Winners: 1883; *Runners-up:* 1881, 1882, 1887, 1891, 1897. *League Cup:* —.

Club colours: Shirt: Yellow with black facing. Shorts: Yellow with black facing. Stockings: Yellow.

Goalscorers: *League (46):* Flannery 17 (4 pens), Andy Brown 9, Dillon 3, Bruce 2, King 2, Lynes 2, Robertson 2 (1 pen), Stewart 2, Bonar 1, Brittain 1, Grace 1, McCann 1, O'Neill 1 (pen), Smith 1, own goal 1
Scottish Cup (2): Flannery 1, Robertson 1
CIS Cup (0):
Bell's League Cup (4): Flannery 3, Andy Brown 1

Hillcoat J 27	Dickie M 29 + 1	Dillon J 20 + 5	Bruce J 29	Jack S 25 + 3	Stewart D 32	Wilson W 11	King T 9	Brown Andy 31	Smith C 4 + 9	Robertson J 27 + 6	Bonar S 23 + 6	Melvin M — + 17	McCann K 23 + 4	Dempsey G — + 1	McGinty B — + 1	Brittain C 22 + 6	Flannery P 30 + 1	Grace A 12 + 2	Gentile C 2 + 4	McCormick S 1 + 2	Wight J 9 + 1	Wilson S 1	Brown Alan 1	O'Neill M 15	Robinson R 4 + 1	Ritchie J 1 + 2	Lynes C 8	Match No.
1	2	3	4	5	6	7	8	9	10[2]	11[1]	12	13																1
1	2	3	5[3]	4		7[2]	8	9	10[1]	11	14		6	12	13													2
1	2	11[2]		5		7	6	10		8[1]	12		4			3	9	13										3
1	2[1]			13	4	7	6	10	11[3]		12	14	5			3	9	8[2]										4
1		11[2]		5	8	7	6[1]	10	13	12	2		4			3	9		14									5
1				5	8	7	6	10	13	11	2[1]		4			3	9[2]	12										6
1			8[2]	4	2	6	10		11[2]	12		5				3	13	7[1]	14	9								7
1	2			13	5	7	6	10		11[1]			4			3	9		8[2]	12								8
1	2	7		5	6		8	10		11[2]			4[1]			3	9		12	13								9
	2		5		6			10		11	12		4			3	9	7	8[1]		1							10
	2		5	8	6			10[1]		11	12		4			3	9	7			1							11
	2	14	4	5[1]	6[3]	7		10[2]		11	12	13				3	9	8			1							12
1	12	13		5	4	2		10		11[2]			6			3	9	8[1]			7							13
1	2		5	12	6			10		11	7[1]		4			3	9	8										14
1	2		5		6			10		11	7	12	4			3	9[1]	8										15
1	2		5		6			10[2]	12	11	7	13	4			3	9	8										16
1	2		4		6			10		11	7		5			3	9	8										17
1	2	6	4					10		12	11	7[1]	5			3	9	8										18
1	2	6	4				7[2]	10	13	11[1]		12	5			3	9	8										19
1	2	13	4		6			10		12	11[2]	7[3]	5			3	9[1]	8	14									20
1	2	11	4	5	6			10[1]				7	12			3	9							8				21
1	2	3	4	5	6			10		12		7[1]	13				9							8	11[2]			22
1	2	3[2]	4	5	6			10		12		7[1]	14	13			9							8[2]	11			23
1	2	3[2]	4	5	6			10		12		7	13	14			9							8[3]	11[1]			24
1	2	3[2]	4	5	6			10[1]		11		7	12				9						13	8				25
	2	3	4	5	6			10[2]		13		7	14	12			9[2]				1			8	11[1]			26
	2	3	4	5	6			10[1]		11[3]		7	12	13		14	9				1					8[2]		27
	2	3	4	5	6			10				7	11	12			9				1			8[1]				28
		3	4	5	6			11				7	2	12			9				1			8	10			29
		3[1]	4	5	6			11				7	2	12			9				1			8	10			30
		3[1]	4	5	6		13	11		12			2[2]	7			9				1			8	10			31
1	2	3	4	5	6			10[2]		13		7				11[1]								8	12		9	32
1	2	3[2]	4	5	6			10		14	11[3]	7[1]	12											8	13		9	33
1	2[2]		4	5	6			10		3[1]	11	7	12											8	13		9	34
1	2	14	4	5	6			10		11		7[2]	13	12			9							8[3]	3[1]			35
1	2	13	4	5	6			10		12		7[1]				3[2]	9							8	11			36

DUNDEE

Premier League

Year Formed: 1893. *Ground & Address:* Dens Park Stadium, Sandeman St, Dundee DD3 7JY. *Telephone:* 01382 889966. *Fax:* 01382 832284.
Ground Capacity: all seated: 11,760. *Size of Pitch:* 101m × 66m.
Chairman: Jim Marr. *Chief Executive:* Peter Marr.
Manager: Ivano Bonetti. *Assistant Manager:* Dario Bonetti. *Coach:* Billy Thomson. *Physio:* John McCreadie. *Under 21 Coach:* Ray Farningham. *Under 18 Coach:* Steve Campbell. *Youth Development:* Kenny Cameron.
Managers since 1975: David White, Tommy Gemmell, Donald Mackay, Archie Knox, Jocky Scott, Dave Smith, Gordon Wallace, Iain Munro, Simon Stainrod, Jim Duffy, John McCormack, John Scott. *Club Nickname(s):* The Dark Blues or The Dee. *Previous Grounds:* Carolina Port 1893-98.
Record Attendance: 43,024 v Rangers, Scottish Cup; 1953.
Record Transfer Fee received: £500,000 for Tommy Coyne to Celtic (March 1989).
Record Transfer Fee paid: £200,000 for Jim Leighton (Feb 1992).
Record Victory: 10-0 Division II v Alloa; 9 Mar, 1947 and v Dunfermline Ath; 22 Mar, 1947.
Record Defeat: 0-11 v Celtic, Division I; 26 Oct, 1895.
Most Capped Player: Alex Hamilton, 24, Scotland.
Most League Appearances: 341: Doug Cowie 1945-61.
Most League Goals in Season (Individual): 52: Alan Gilzean, 1963-64.
Most Goals Overall (Individual): 113: Alan Gilzean.

DUNDEE 2000–01 LEAGUE RECORD

Match No.	Date	Venue	Opponents	Result	H/T Score	Lg. Pos.	Goalscorers	Attendance
1	Jul 29	A	Motherwell	W 2-0	1-0	—	Billio [8], Artero [84]	5961
2	Aug 5	H	Dunfermline Ath	W 3-0	1-0	1	Skinner (og) [1], Sara (pen) [54], Caballero (pen) [56]	9507
3	12	A	Hibernian	L 1-5	1-2	4	Caballero [74]	12,730
4	19	A	St Mirren	L 1-2	0-0	4	Sara (pen) [78]	5165
5	27	H	Hearts	D 1-1	0-0	5	Caballero [57]	6779
6	Sept 9	H	Rangers	D 1-1	0-0	5	Sara [75]	10,439
7	16	A	St Johnstone	D 0-0	0-0	5		5055
8	20	H	Dundee U	W 3-0	0-0	—	Sara 2 [47, 87], Nemsadze [70]	9838
9	23	A	Celtic	L 0-1	0-0	5		59,524
10	30	H	Kilmarnock	D 0-0	0-0	6		6170
11	Oct 14	A	Aberdeen	W 2-0	1-0	6	Bonetti [28], Caniggia [89]	15,332
12	21	H	Motherwell	L 1-2	1-2	5	Caniggia [33]	4259
13	28	A	Dunfermline Ath	L 0-1	0-0	6		5925
14	Nov 5	H	Hibernian	L 1-2	1-1	7	Tweed [33]	6602
15	11	A	Dundee U	W 2-0	1-0	6	Caniggia [39], Nemsadze [74]	6667
16	18	H	St Mirren	W 5-0	1-0	5	Caniggia 2 [22, 52], Rae [66], Artero [75], Milne [79]	6393
17	25	A	Hearts	L 1-3	1-0	7	Carranza [24]	11,539
18	Dec 2	H	St Johnstone	D 1-1	1-0	7	Sara [14]	7014
19	10	H	Celtic	L 1-2	0-1	7	Boyd (og) [55]	10,763
20	16	A	Kilmarnock	W 3-2	0-1	7	Bonetti [53], Milne 2 [76, 79]	6573
21	23	H	Aberdeen	D 2-2	0-1	8	Carranza [60], Sara [71]	9093
22	26	A	Motherwell	W 3-0	2-0	—	Sara 2 [4, 69], Rae [35]	6183
23	Jan 2	A	Hibernian	L 0-3	0-2	—		12,381
24	31	H	Dundee U	L 2-3	1-1	—	Caniggia [44], Falconer [88]	6719
25	Feb 3	A	St Mirren	L 1-2	1-1	9	Sara [23]	4085
26	21	H	Dunfermline Ath	L 0-1	0-1	—		6113
27	24	H	Rangers	L 0-1	0-0	9		9778
28	Mar 3	A	St Johnstone	W 3-2	0-1	8	Rae [57], Sara [69], Artero [87]	5065
29	14	A	Rangers	W 2-0	1-0	—	Caniggia [13], Milne [90]	45,035
30	18	H	Hearts	D 0-0	0-0	7		7327
31	31	H	Kilmarnock	D 2-2	1-1	7	Sara [26], Rae [48]	6719
32	Apr 4	A	Celtic	L 1-2	0-1	—	Sara [67]	59,190
33	7	A	Aberdeen	W 2-0	0-0	6	Nemsadze [51], Caballero [63]	12,005
34	21	H	Rangers	L 0-3	0-3	6		10,687
35	29	H	Hibernian	L 0-2	0-0	6		6659
36	May 5	H	Kilmarnock	W 2-1	1-0	6	Sara [35], Carranza (pen) [80]	6261
37	13	A	Celtic	W 2-0	2-0	6	Caballero 2 [29, 42]	58,967
38	20	A	Hearts	L 0-2	0-0	6		13,554

Final League Position: 6

Honours

League Champions: Division I 1961-62. First Division 1978-79, 1991-92, 1997-98. Division II 1946-47; *Runners-up:* Division I 1902-03, 1906-07, 1908-09, 1948-49, 1980-81.
Scottish Cup Winners: 1910; *Runners-up:* 1925, 1952, 1964.
League Cup Winners: 1951-52, 1952-53, 1973-74; *Runners-up:* 1967-68, 1980-81. *(Coca-Cola Cup):* 1995-96.
B&Q (Centenary) Cup Winners: 1990-91; *Runners-up:* 1994-95.

European: *European Cup:* 8 matches (1962-63 semi-finals). *Cup Winners' Cup:* 2 matches: (1964-65).
UEFA Cup: 18 matches: *(Fairs Cup:* 1967-68 semi-finals. *UEFA Cup:* 1971-72, 1973-74, 1974-75).

Club colours: Shirt: Navy with white piping. Shorts: White with navy piping. Stockings: Navy with white hoops on turnover.

Goalscorers: *League* (51): Sara 14 (2 pens), Caniggia 7, Caballero 6 (1 pen), Milne 4, Rae 4, Artero 3, Carranza 3 (1 pen), Nemsadze 3, Bonetti 2, Billio 1, Falconer 1, Tweed 1, own goals 2
Scottish Cup (3): Sara 2, Caniggia 1
CIS Cup (3): Caballero 2, Wilkie 1

Douglas R 11	Smith B 36	Marrocco M 24	de Marchi M 18	Tweed S 32	Bonetti I 15 + 3	Nemsadze G 33 + 2	Artero J 32 + 3	Billio P 8	Caballero F 12 + 3	Sara J 25 + 6	McSkimming S 7 + 5	Falconer W 8 + 6	Robertson H 2 + 1	Yates M — + 6	Milne S 5 + 16	Coyne C 16 + 2	Rae G 31 + 1	Wilkie L 5 + 4	Romano A 14 + 2	Caniggia C 20 + 1	Carranza A 15 + 7	Langfield J 8 + 1	Roccati M 19	del Rio W 7 + 2	Russo M — + 4	Garrido A 8 + 2	Khizanishvili Z 5 + 1	Robertson M 2 + 2	Vargiu M — + 1	Match No.
1	2	3	4	5	6	7	8	9	10²	11¹	12	13																		1
1	2	3	4	5		7³	8	9	10¹	11³		12			6	13	14													2
1	2	3	4	5	6¹	7	8²	9	10	11		12				13														3
1	2	3		5		7¹	8			11					10	6	12	4	9											4
1	2			5	12	7¹	8²	6	10	11	9					13		3	4											5
1	2	3¹	4	5	6¹	7	8		10		12								9	13	11									6
1	2	3¹	4	5	6	7	8²	9	10	13	12					11														7
1	2		4¹	5	6	7	13		10²	11	9						8	12	3											8
1	2			5	6	7¹	8			11²	10	12	14		13		9	3	4³											9
1	2			5		7	8¹	9		11		10²			12	13	6	3	4											10
1	2	3	4	5	6		13	8³		11²					10¹		9				7	12	14							11
	2	3	4		6	12		8²	9¹	11								5			7	10	13	1						12
	2	3	4	5	6¹	7	8²									12				9	11	10	13			1				13
	2	3	4	5		7	8	6				12				11				9		10				1				14
	2	3	4	5	6	7	8²					12				11¹				9		10	13			1				15
	2	3	4	5	6	7	8					13				11²			12	9²	14	10¹				1				16
	2	3	4	5	6		8²					12				11				13	9	10	7¹			1				17
	2	3	4	5¹	6		8²					11³							14		9	12	10	13		1				18
	2	3	4¹	5			8²					11	13						14	12	9	10	6²			1				19
	2	3		5	6¹	7	12					11²	13						10	4	9	8				1				20
	2	3	4	5		7	8¹					11²	12						13	9		10	6			1				21
	2	3		5	12	7	13					11³	9	14					10¹	8			6²	1			4			22
	2			5	6	7	8					11¹	3						12	9		10	6²	1			4			23
	2			5	12²	7	8					3¹	11			4			9	10	6		1			13				24
	2			5		7	8					11				13	4	9¹		3	10	6	1			12²				25
	2	3¹					8					11		13		9²	4	7	12		10	6¹	1		5	14				26
	2		4	5		7	8					11				3	9		10			1			6					27
	2		4¹	5		7	8					11		13		3	9		10²			1		12	6				28
	2	3		5		7²	8					11¹				12	4	9		10			1	13		6				29
	2	3		5		7	8					11²				13	4	9		10	12		1	5		6¹				30
	2	3		5		7	8	12	11							4	9		10	6¹		1								31
	2	3		5		7	8	12	11³							4	9		10¹	13	1				6²	14				32
		3		5		7	8¹	10	11							4	9			6	1				12	2				33
				5		7	8¹	13	11					10²	4³	9		12		6	1		14		3	2				34
	2			5		7	11									9		8	10	1			4		6¹	3	12			35
	2					7	8¹	10²	11							13	4	9	5	6	1				3³	12	14			36
	2						8¹	10²								13	4	9	6		7	1		5		12	3	11		37
	2						7³	10	12							13	4	14	3	6			9²	1		5	8	11¹		38

DUNDEE UNITED   Premier League

Year Formed: 1909 (1923). *Ground & Address:* Tannadice Park, Tannadice St, Dundee DD3 7JW. *Telephone:* 01382
833166. *Fax:* 01382 889398. *Ground Capacity:* total: 14,223 all seated: stands: east 2868, west 2096, south 2201, Fair Play
1601, George Fox 5151, executive boxes 292.
Size of Pitch: 110yd × 72yd.
Chairman: Douglas B. Smith. *Secretary:* Spence Anderson. *Commercial Manager:* Bill Campbell. *Community
Development Officer:* John Holt.
Manager: Alex Smith. *Assistant Manager:* John Blackley. *Coaches:* Maurice Malpas and Paul Hegarty. *Physio:* David Rankine.
Managers since 1975: J. McLean, I. Golac, W. Kirkwood, T. McLean, P. Sturrock. *Club Nickname(s):* The Terrors. *Previous
Grounds:* None.
Record Attendance: 28,000 v Barcelona, Fairs Cup; 16 Nov, 1966.
Record Transfer Fee received: £4,000,000 for Duncan Ferguson from Rangers (July 1993).
Record Transfer Fee paid: £750,000 for Steven Pressley from Coventry C (July 1995).
Record Victory: 14-0 v Nithsdale Wanderers, Scottish Cup 1st rd; 17 Jan, 1931.
Record Defeat: 1-12 v Motherwell, Division II; 23 Jan, 1954.
Most Capped Player: Maurice Malpas, 55, Scotland.
Most League Appearances: 612, Dave Narey; 1973-94.
Most Appearances in European Matches: 76, Dave Narey (record for Scottish player).
Most League Goals in Season (Individual): 41: John Coyle, Division II; 1955-56.
Most Goals Overall (Individual): 158: Peter McKay.

DUNDEE UNITED 2000–01 LEAGUE RECORD

Match No.	Date	Venue	Opponents	Result		H/T Score	Lg. Pos.	Goalscorers	Attendance
1	Jul 30	H	Celtic	L	1-2	0-1	—	McCracken [48]	5896
2	Aug 5	A	Hibernian	L	0-3	0-2	12		9613
3	12	H	Motherwell	D	1-1	0-1	11	Paterson [86]	5598
4	19	H	St Johnstone	L	1-2	0-2	11	Aljofree [63]	5533
5	26	A	Dunfermline Ath	L	0-1	0-1	11		4980
6	Sept 9	A	Kilmarnock	L	0-1	0-1	12		6380
7	16	H	St Mirren	D	0-0	0-0	12		5181
8	20	A	Dundee	L	0-3	0-0	—		9838
9	23	H	Aberdeen	L	3-5	0-3	12	Easton (pen) [64], McConalogue [85], Hannah [89]	4974
10	Oct 1	A	Rangers	L	0-3	0-2	12		44,324
11	14	H	Hearts	L	0-4	0-3	12		7016
12	21	A	Celtic	L	1-2	0-1	12	Lambert (og) [78]	59,323
13	28	H	Hibernian	L	0-1	0-0	12		8042
14	Nov 4	A	Motherwell	L	1-2	0-1	12	Naveda [56]	6864
15	11	H	Dundee	L	0-2	0-1	12		6667
16	18	A	St Johnstone	L	0-1	0-0	12		4295
17	25	H	Dunfermline Ath	W	3-2	2-0	12	O'Connor [7], Easton [43], Miller (pen) [86]	6012
18	28	H	Kilmarnock	L	0-1	0-0	—		5497
19	Dec 5	A	St Mirren	D	1-1	1-0	—	Naveda [35]	4685
20	17	H	Rangers	D	1-1	1-1	12	Lilley [32]	10,750
21	23	A	Hearts	L	1-3	1-2	12	Aljofree [25]	12,128
22	26	H	Celtic	L	0-4	0-3	—		12,306
23	30	A	Hibernian	L	0-1	0-0	12		10,197
24	Jan 2	H	Motherwell	W	2-0	0-0	—	Easton [55], Hamilton [62]	6311
25	31	A	Dundee	W	3-2	1-1	—	Davidson [34], Easton [46], Lauchlan [79]	6719
26	Feb 3	H	St Johnstone	D	1-1	1-0	12	Miller (pen) [42]	6482
27	10	A	Dunfermline Ath	L	1-3	0-0	12	Lilley [55]	4899
28	24	A	Kilmarnock	D	0-0	0-0	11		6289
29	Mar 3	H	St Mirren	W	4-0	2-0	11	Miller [33], Hannah [36], Lilley [80], Hamilton [83]	8334
30	17	H	Aberdeen	D	1-1	1-1	11	Miller (pen) [42]	8472
31	31	A	Rangers	W	2-0	0-0	11	Thompson [70], Lilley [79]	48,382
32	Apr 4	A	Aberdeen	L	1-4	1-3	—	Griffin [12]	9562
33	7	H	Hearts	D	1-1	1-0	11	Thompson [44]	7242
34	23	A	St Mirren	L	1-2	0-0	11	Thompson [53]	6473
35	28	H	Motherwell	W	1-0	1-0	11	Buchan [36]	5928
36	May 6	H	Dunfermline Ath	W	1-0	1-0	11	Thompson [21]	6679
37	12	A	St Johnstone	W	3-2	0-2	11	Miller [65], Easton [82], Lilley [88]	6497
38	20	A	Aberdeen	W	2-1	2-0	11	Venetis [4], Lilley [14]	11,683

Final League Position: 11

Honours
League Champions: Premier Division 1982-83. Division II 1924-25, 1928-29; *Runners-up:* Division II 1930-31, 1959-60. First Division Runners-up 1995-96.
Scottish Cup Winners: 1994; *Runners-up:* 1974, 1981, 1985, 1987, 1988, 1991.
League Cup Winners: 1979-80, 1980-81; *Runners-up:* 1981-82, 1984-85, 1997-98.
Summer Cup Runners-up: 1964-65. *Scottish War Cup Runners-up:* 1939-40.

European: *European Cup:* 8 matches (1983-84, semi-finals). *Cup Winners' Cup:* 10 matches (1974-75, 1988-89, 1994-95). *UEFA Cup:* 84 matches (*Fairs Cup:* 1966-67, 1969-70, 1970-71. *UEFA Cup:* 1975-76, 1977-78, 1978-79, 1979-80, 1980-81, 1981-82, 1982-83, 1984-85, 1985-86, 1986-87 runners-up, 1987-88, 1989-90, 1990-91, 1993-94, 1997-98).

Club colours: Shirts: Tangerine. Shorts: Black. Stockings: Tangerine with black hoop.

Goalscorers: *League* (38): Lilley 6, Easton 5 (1 pen), Miller 5 (3 pens), Thompson 4, Aljofree 2, Hamilton 2, Hannah 2, Naveda 2, Buchan 1, Davidson 1, Griffin 1, Lauchlan 1, McConalogue 1, McCracken 1, O'Connor 1, Paterson 1, Venetis 1, own goal 1
Scottish Cup (6): Lauchlan 2, Easton 1, Hannah 1, Lilley 1 Miller 1
CIS Cup (3): McConalogue 3

Combe A 23	McCracken D 6+3	Buchan J 33+2	De Vos J 33	Aljofree H 24+2	Paterson J 5+1	Easton C 27+6	Hannah D 20+4	Heaney N 7+5	Thompson S 18+13	Mathie A 3+1	Venetis A 3+11	Hamilton J 14+6	McConalogue S 3+8	McQuillan J 12+3	Partridge D 17+2	Fernandez J 6	Davidson H 6+5	Smith A 1+2	Wright S 5	Tchami A 3	Leoni S 5+1	Atangana M 8+3	Licina J 5+2	Gallacher P 15	McDonald K —+1	Robinson P 2+4	Galoppo M 2	Brady D —+1	Fuentes G 3	Marcora C —+1	Ramirez F —+1	Lauchlan J 23	Miller C 24	Naveda A 7+6	O'Connor S 1+1	Fullarton J 3+2	Lilley D 18	Griffin D 18	Winters D —+5	McCunnie J 15	Match No.
1	2	3	4	5	6	7²	8	9¹	10	11²	12	13	14																												1
1	8	4	5	6	7	12	11	10³	13	9¹	14		2²	3																											2
1		7	4	5	6	12	8³	14	10	11²		13	2	9¹																											3
1		6	4	5		7¹	8	9	10	11²			2³	12		13	14																								4
1		7	4	5	6²	14	8	12	13				10³		3			9¹		2	11																				5
1		3	4	5	6¹	7		12	10		14						8³			2	11²	9	13																		6
1		3¹	4	5			13	8	10³								7	14		2	6¹		9¹	11	12																7
1	14	3	4	5¹			12	8²	10							7	9³			6	11	2	13																	8
1	14	3³					12	8	10			13	5			7¹	9²		4	6	11	2																		9
1	3¹		4	5			9	8²	14		13			2						6	11	12				7³	10													10
1		6	4	5				10			13		12	3	7			2¹								8³	11	14													11
1		8	4	5		9			10³		7²				6	3						13	12	2			11¹	14													12
1		8	4	5		9			10		13		12	6	3								11¹	7²									2								13
1		7	4	5		9	12		13					6	3								11¹										2		8³	10²	14				14
1		6		5²		9	8		14				12	4	3								11¹	2									7		10³			13			15
1		2				11²	8	12					13	6¹	3																		4		9	10		7			16
1		3	4	5		7	13	12					11¹²	14																			2		8³	10		9¹	6		17
1		3	4	5			7	9¹²		13		11¹										14											2		8	10		6²			18
1		3	4	5			7	9	13			10³	14	6¹	12																		2		8	11²					19
1	5³		4	6				9			14	12	13		3																		2		8	11¹			10²		20
1	3²	7	4	6			12		9¹				10		13	2			14														8						11	5³	21
1	13	7	4	6			9³		10				11		2¹	3		12															8							5²	14	22
1			4	6			9		10¹				12		3	13																	5	8²				11³	7	14	2	23
			4	6			9		12				10		3																	5	8				11¹	7	2		24
		6	4				9		12				10¹				7							1								3	8	13			11³	5	2		25
		6	4	12			9		13				10²				7¹							1								3	8	14			11³	5	2		26
		6	4	12			9		13				10²				7¹							1								3	8	14			11³	5	2		27
		6	4			9	7		10²									14						1			12					3	8	13			11¹	5	2³		28
		6	4			9	7¹		10²		12													1		14						3	8	13			11³	5	2		29
		2	4			9		14	12	10²							6¹							1		13						3	8				11³	5	7		30
		2	4			9	12		10¹				12					3						1		6						3	8				11	5	7		31
		2	4			9	12		10				12					3						1		6¹						3	8				11	5	7		32
		2	4			9	6		10²	12								3						1		13						3	8¹	14			11³	5	7		33
		6	4			7	8	9				10			2									1								3					11	5			34
		4				9	6	12	13	10¹		2												1								3	8²				11³	5	14	7	35
	13	4				9	6	10³		12		2												1								3	8				11¹	5	14	7²	36
	12	4³				9	6	10²		13		2¹												1								3	8				11	5	14	7	37
	2	6²13		9			4¹	10																1				12				3	8³			14	11	5		7	38

DUNFERMLINE ATHLETIC   Premier League

Year Formed: 1885. *Ground & Address:* East End Park, Halbeath Rd, Dunfermline KY12 7RB. *Telephone:* 01383 724295. *Fax:* 01383 723468. *e-mail:* pars@dunfermline-ath.com
Ground Capacity: all seated: 12,500. *Size of Pitch:* 115yd × 71yd.
Chairman: John Yorkston. *Secretary:* P. A. M. D'Mello. *Commercial Manager:* Miss Audrey Bastianelli.
Manager: Jim Calderwood. *Assistant Manager:* Jimmy Nichol.
Physio: Philip Yeates, MCSP. *Coach and Youth Development Officer:* John Ritchie.
Managers since 1975: G. Miller, H. Melrose, P. Stanton, T. Forsyth, J. Leishman, I. Munro, J. Scott, B. Paton, R. Campbell. *Club Nickname(s):* The Pars. *Previous Grounds:* None.
Record Attendance: 27,816 v Celtic, Division I, 30 April, 1968.
Record Transfer Fee received: £650,000 for Jackie McNamara to Celtic (Oct 1995).
Record Transfer Fee paid: £540,000 for Istvan Kozma from Bordeaux (Sept 1989).
Record Victory: 11-2 v Stenhousemuir, Division II, 27 Sept, 1930.
Record Defeat: 1-11 v Hibernian, Scottish Cup, 3rd rd replay, 26 Oct, 1889.
Most Capped Player: Colin Miller 16(61), Canada.
Most League Appearances: 497: Norrie McCathie, 1981-96.
Most League Goals in Season (Individual): 53: Bobby Skinner, Division II, 1925-26.
Most Goals Overall (Individual): 154: Charles Dickson.

DUNFERMLINE ATHLETIC 2000–01 LEAGUE RECORD

Match No.	Date		Venue	Opponents		Result	H/T Score	Lg. Pos.	Goalscorers	Atten- dance
1	Jul	29	H	Aberdeen	D	0-0	0-0	—		7381
2	Aug	5	A	Dundee	L	0-3	0-1	9		9507
3		12	H	St Johnstone	D	1-1	1-0	9	Crawford (pen) [43]	3477
4		16	A	Motherwell	W	1-0	0-0	—	Moss [55]	5257
5		19	A	Rangers	L	1-4	1-3	8	Boyle [14]	47,452
6		26	H	Dundee U	W	1-0	1-0	4	Crawford [42]	4980
7	Sept	9	A	Hearts	L	0-2	0-1	6		11,811
8		18	H	Celtic	L	1-2	0-0	7	Crawford (pen) [58]	9493
9		23	H	Hibernian	D	1-1	0-1	9	Moss [47]	4017
10		30	A	St Mirren	L	1-2	0-2	9	Dair [64]	5002
11	Oct	14	A	Kilmarnock	L	1-2	1-1	9	Crawford [31]	6454
12		21	A	Aberdeen	D	0-0	0-0	10		11,195
13		28	H	Dundee	W	1-0	0-0	8	Moss [61]	5925
14	Nov	4	A	St Johnstone	W	2-0	0-0	8	Dair [69], Nicholson [76]	4287
15		11	H	Motherwell	L	1-2	1-0	9	Moss [10]	4146
16		18	H	Rangers	D	0-0	0-0	9		10,706
17		25	A	Dundee U	L	2-3	0-2	9	Bullen [61], Moss [64]	6012
18		29	H	Hearts	W	1-0	1-0	—	Dair [41]	5281
19	Dec	2	A	Celtic	L	1-3	1-2	9	Dair [1]	59,196
20		9	A	Hibernian	L	0-3	0-1	9		10,078
21		16	H	St Mirren	W	2-0	1-0	9	Thomson S [38], McGroarty [74]	4538
22		23	H	Kilmarnock	W	1-0	1-0	9	Crawford [23]	5337
23		26	A	Aberdeen	W	3-2	1-2	—	Crawford [13], Rossi [46], Nicholson [51]	6880
24	Jan	2	H	St Johnstone	D	0-0	0-0	—		6117
25		31	A	Motherwell	D	1-1	0-0	—	Bullen [88]	4601
26	Feb	3	A	Rangers	L	0-2	0-1	8		46,302
27		10	H	Dundee U	W	3-1	0-0	6	Hampshire [49], Dijkhuizen [83], Moss [85]	4899
28		21	A	Dundee	W	1-0	1-0	—	Nicholson [12]	6113
29		24	A	Hearts	L	1-7	0-4	6	Dair [50]	11,251
30	Mar	4	A	Celtic	L	0-3	0-2	6		8779
31		17	H	Hibernian	W	2-1	1-0	6	Crawford [28], Hampshire [57]	7154
32		31	A	St Mirren	D	1-1	1-0	6	Crawford [8]	5371
33	Apr	7	A	Kilmarnock	L	1-2	0-1	7	Bullen [61]	6529
34		21	A	Aberdeen	L	0-1	0-1	7		8613
35		28	H	St Mirren	L	1-2	0-2	8	Bullen [90]	4669
36	May	6	A	Dundee U	L	0-1	0-1	8		6679
37		12	H	Motherwell	L	1-2	1-2	9	Crawford (pen) [34]	2437
38		20	H	St Johnstone	D	0-0	0-0	9		4084

Final League Position: 9

Honours
League Champions: First Division 1988-89, 1995-96. Division II 1925-26. Second Division 1985-86; *Runners-up:* First Division 1986-87, 1993-94, 1994-95, 1999-2000. Division II 1912-13, 1933-34, 1954-55, 1957-58, 1972-73. Second Division 1978-79.
Scottish Cup Winners: 1961, 1968; *Runners-up:* 1965.
League Cup Runners-up: 1949-50, 1991-92.

European: *Cup Winners' Cup:* 14 matches (1961-62, 1968-69 semi-finals). *UEFA Cup:* 28 matches (*Fairs Cup:* 1962-63, 1964-65, 1965-66, 1966-67, 1969-70).

Club colours: Shirt: Black and white vertical stripes. Shorts: White with black piping. Stockings: White with black band at top.

Goalscorers: *League* (34): Crawford 9 (3 pens), Moss 6, Dair 5, Bullen 4, Nicholson 3, Hampshire 2, Boyle 1, Dijkhuizen 1, McGroarty 1, Rossi 1, Thomson SM 1
Scottish Cup (6): Thomson SM 2, Dijkhauzen 1, Moss 1, Nicholson 1, Skerla 1
CIS Cup (4): Boyle 1, Moss 1, Nicholson 1, Thomson SM 1

Ruitenbeek M 36	Doesburg M 21 + 6	Thomson S 34	Skinner J 34 + 3	Skerla A 34	Dair J 25 + 8	May E 4 + 3	Ferguson I 28	Mendes J 7 + 6	Crawford S 37	Petrie S 8 + 2	Coyle O 2 + 4	Matthaei R 11 + 6	Nicholson B 36	Nish C — + 4	Moss D 18 + 8	Templeman C — + 1	Reid B 1 + 1	Boyle S 1 + 6	Bullen L 14 + 10	Thomson S 2	Tod A 5 + 3	McGroarty C 19 + 3	Graham D 3 + 1	McGarry M 1 + 3	Hampshire S 11 + 8	Rossi Y 11	Dijkhuizen M 2 + 7	Mason G 8 + 2	Danilevicius T 3	Fotheringham G 2	Match No.
1	2	3	4	5	6	7[1]	8[2]	9	10	11	12	13																			1
1	2[2]	3	4	5	12	7[1]	8	9	10	11			6	13																	2
1	2	3	4[2]	5	6		8	9[1]	10	11[1]	12		7		13	14															3
1	2[1]	3	4		6		8	9[2]	10		14	5[3]	7		11		12	13													4
1		3	4		6	13	8		10		12	5[2]	7		11		2	9[1]													5
1	2	3	4	5	6		8	9[1]	10				7		11							12									6
1	2[2]	3	4	5	6[1]		8	12	10			13	7		11[3]							14	9	1							7
1	2	3	4	5	12		8	11[1]	10		6[2]		7		13			9													8
1	2[3]	3	4	5	12		8[2]		10			6[1]	7	13	11			9			14										9
1	2	3	4	5	12		8	6[1]	10				7	13	11			9[2]													10
1	2	3[3]	4	5	6			14	10				7	9[1]	12							13			8[1]	11					11
1		3	4	5	2			12	10				7	8[1]	11							6	9[3]		13	14					12
1		3	4[1]	5	2		8		10			13	7		11							6	9[2]		12						13
1		3	4	5	2		8		10[2]		9[1]	13	7		11							6			12						14
1		3	4	5	2			12	10		9[1]	8[2]	7		11							6			13						15
1		3	4	5	6			12	10				7		11							9[1]			8[2]		13	2			16
1		3	4	5	6[2]		8[1]		10			9	7		11			13				12						2			17
1		3	4	5	2		9[2]		10			8	7		12			11				6[1]			13						18
1		3	4	5	2[1]			6[2]	10			8[3]	7		11			12							9	14	13				19
1	2[1]	3	4	5	12			8	10			11	13					6			7[2]	9									20
1	13	3	4	5			8		10				7		11[1]			12			6			9[2]			2				21
1	12	3	4	5			8		10				7		11[2]						6			9[1]	2	13					22
1	13	3	4[1]	5			8	14	10				7[3]		11						6			9[2]	2	12					23
1	2	3		5	12		8[2]		10				7		13		14				6			11		4[1]	9[1]				24
1	2[2]	3	4	5	12		8		10				7		11						6[1]			13			9				25
1	2	8	4[2]	5	6				10				7		11[1]						9[3]			12		3	14	13			26
1	2[1]	9	4	5	6		8		10				7[2]		13						12			11[3]		3	14				27
1	13	9	4	5	2		8		10				7		11[1]						12	3	6[2]							28
1	6	11	4[3]	5	2		8[1]		10				7	14								3[2]		9			13				29
1		9	4	5	6		8[3]		10				7		11[2]			14			12			13	2	3[1]					30
1	2[3]	4	12	3	5		8		10	14			7		13						9			6[2]				11[1]			31
1	2	7	4[2]	5[3]	6				10	12		3						14						9		13	8		11[1]		32
1	2[3]	9	4	5	6				10				7		12			13				14		10		3	8		11[2]		33
1	2[1]	12		5	14		8		10				7		11[3]			6			13			9[2]		3	4				34
1	14	4	5[2]	2[3]			8	12	10				7		13			11						9[1]		3	6				35
1	12	4[2]			2		8	14	10				7		11			13						9[3]		3[1]	5	6			36
1	2	13			5		8[2]		10				7		11			14			4[1]			9		3	12	6[3]			37
		3	4				8		10			13	7		11[1]						12			1	5	2	6		9[2]	38

EAST FIFE   Third Division

Year Formed: 1903. *Ground & Address:* Bayview Stadium, Harbour View, Methil, Fife KY8 3RW. *Telephone:* 01333 426323. *Fax:* 01333 426376.
Ground Capacity: all seated: 2000. *Size of Pitch:* 115yd × 75yd.
Chairman: W. Bruce Black. *Secretary:* Kenneth R. MacKay.
Manager: Dave Clarke. *Assistant Manager:* Mike Marshall. *Coach:* Danny Hendry. *Stadium Controller:* Rob Scott. *Physio:* Neil Bryson.
Managers since 1975: Frank Christie, Roy Barry, David Clarke, Gavin Murray, Alex Totten, Steve Archibald, James Bone, Steve Kirk, Rab Shannon. *Club Nickname(s):* The Fifers. *Previous Ground:* Bayview Park.
Record Attendance: 22,515 v Raith Rovers, Division I; 2 Jan, 1950.
Record Transfer Fee received: £150,000 for Paul Hunter from Hull C (March 1990).
Record Transfer Fee paid: £70,000 for John Sludden from Kilmarnock (July 1991).
Record Victory: 13-2 v Edinburgh City, Division II; 11 Dec, 1937.
Record Defeat: 0-9 v Hearts, Division I; 5 Oct, 1957.
Most Capped Player: George Aitken, 5 (8), Scotland.
Most League Appearances: 517: David Clarke, 1968-86.
Most League Goals in Season (Individual): 41: Jock Wood, Division II; 1926-27 and Henry Morris, Division II; 1947-48.
Most Goals Overall (Individual): 225: Phil Weir (215 in League).

EAST FIFE 2000–01 LEAGUE RECORD

Match No.	Date		Venue	Opponents	Result	H/T Score	Lg. Pos.	Goalscorers	Attendance
1	Aug	5	A	Albion R	W 1-0	0-0	—	McKenzie (og) [90]	465
2		12	H	Peterhead	D 1-1	1-0	5	Mackay [28]	619
3		19	A	East Stirling	W 5-2	0-2	3	Mackay [48], Moffat 2 [54, 82], Kerrigan [67], Simpson [86]	310
4		26	A	Montrose	W 1-0	0-0	3	Mackay [53]	355
5	Sept	9	H	Cowdenbeath	L 0-2	0-0	5		735
6		16	H	Elgin C	D 1-1	1-0	3	Wright [16]	444
7		23	A	Brechin C	L 1-3	1-2	4	Moffat [22]	403
8		30	H	Hamilton A	L 1-2	0-0	4	Gallagher (pen) [57]	549
9	Oct	7	A	Dumbarton	W 3-2	2-1	5	Moffat 2 [14, 33], Mortimer [51]	256
10		14	H	Albion R	D 0-0	0-0	5		445
11		21	A	Peterhead	D 0-0	0-0	5		637
12		28	H	Montrose	W 3-1	1-0	4	Kerrigan 2 [14, 54], Ferguson [62]	375
13	Nov	4	A	Cowdenbeath	L 0-1	0-1	5		626
14		11	H	Brechin C	W 1-0	0-0	5	Ferguson [49]	549
15		18	A	Elgin C	W 3-1	1-0	5	Ferguson 2 [10, 52], Mortimer [46]	730
16		25	H	Dumbarton	W 1-0	1-0	4	Ferguson [25]	465
17	Dec	2	A	Hamilton A	D 1-1	1-0	4	Ferguson [4]	518
18		23	A	Albion R	W 2-1	1-0	4	Kerrigan [41], Moffat [76]	372
19		26	H	East Stirling	W 3-1	1-0	—	Hunter [21], Allison [61], Mackay [64]	492
20	Jan	2	H	Cowdenbeath	L 1-2	1-1	—	Mackay [11]	1003
21	Feb	3	A	Dumbarton	L 0-2	0-1	4		711
22		17	A	East Stirling	L 0-1	0-1	4		286
23		24	H	Peterhead	W 2-1	0-1	4	Sharp [68], Gallagher (pen) [77]	380
24	Mar	10	H	Montrose	W 1-0	0-0	4	Wilson [87]	407
25		13	A	Montrose	D 1-1	0-0	4	Mortimer [67]	249
26		17	H	Brechin C	L 1-4	0-0	4	Gibb [88]	416
27		20	H	Elgin C	D 1-1	1-0	—	Kerrigan [36]	223
28		27	H	Hamilton A	L 1-4	1-0	—	Beith [2]	353
29		31	A	Elgin C	W 3-1	3-1	4	Kerrigan [13], Mair [25], Devine (pen) [37]	512
30	Apr	3	A	Brechin C	L 0-1	0-0	—		407
31		7	A	Dumbarton	L 0-1	0-1	5		313
32		14	A	Hamilton A	D 1-1	0-0	4	McManus [51]	507
33		17	A	Cowdenbeath	L 2-3	0-3	—	Mortimer [63], Magee [76]	531
34		21	H	Albion R	W 2-1	0-0	4	Kerrigan [77], Mortimer [83]	333
35		28	A	Peterhead	L 1-2	1-1	4	Kerrigan [3]	511
36	May	5	H	East Stirling	W 4-1	1-1	4	McGhee (og) [39], Mair [48], Mackay 2 [62, 90]	356

Final League Position: 4

Honours
League Champions: Division II 1947-48; *Runners-up:* Division II 1929-30, 1970-71. Second Division 1983-84, 1995-96.
Scottish Cup Winners: 1938; *Runners-up:* 1927, 1950.
League Cup Winners: 1947-48, 1949-50, 1953-54.

Club colours: Shirt: Gold with black shoulders. Shorts: Black. Stockings: Black.

Goalscorers: *League* (49): Kerrigan 8, Mackay 7, Ferguson 6, Moffat 6, Mortimer 5, Gallagher 2 (2 pens), Mair 2, Allison 1, Beith 1, Devine 1 (pen), Gibb 1, Hunter 1, McManus 1, Magee 1, Sharp 1, Simpson 1, Wilson 1, Wright 1, own goals 2
Scottish Cup (5): Ferguson 3, Moffat 2
CIS Cup (1): Moffat 1
Bell's League Cup (0):

Stewart A 22	Munro K 16+3	Gallagher J 22+6	McCloy B 29+2	Sharp R 22+2	Allison J 19	Hunter M 8+7	Mortimer P 28+4	Simpson P 2+4	Kerrigan S 32+2	Mackay S 27+2	Logan R 1+3	Moffat B 22+6	Ferguson S 7+4	Gibb R 16+6	Agostini D 19	Tinley G —+2	O'Neill M 3+1	Wright D 1	Devine C 6+12	McCulloch W 14	Shannon R 4	McWilliams D 2	Bottiglieri E 11+2	McKinnon R 4	McManus P 6+8	Wilson W 11+3	Reid A —+2	Lofting A 1+6	Beith G 15	Wood D 1	Mair L 13	Magee K 8	Nairn J 4+1	Match No.
1	2	3	4	5	6	7	8^1	9^2	10^2	11	12	13	14																					1
1	2	3	4	5	6	7	8^1	9^2	13	11	12	10		14																				2
1	2	3	4		6	14	8	13	9^2	11^1	7^1	10		12	5																			3
1	2	3	4		6		8	13	9^2	7^1	14	10^2		11	5		12																	4
1	2^3	3	4		6	13	8^2	14	9^1	7		10		11	5		12																	5
1	2	11	4		6	5		9				10		3		12	8^2	7^1	13															6
	11^1		4	12	2		8^2		9	7		10		3	5		6		13	1														7
	2	11	4		6		12		13	7^2		10	14	3	5	8^1		9^2		1														8
	2	12	4		6	11	8		9	7^1		10^3	13	3	5					1														9
	2	11^1	4	12	6	7		8^2	14	9^3		10	13	3	5					1														10
	2	13	4		8	12	7		9^3			10^2	11^1	3	5	14				1		6												11
	2	12	4^1	6	8	14		11	10			13	9^2	3	5					1				7^3										12
	2	12		6	8	13	4^2		11^1	10		9		3	5	14				1				7^3										13
	2	8	4	5	6	14	7^1		11	12		10^2	9^2	3					13	1														14
	11	4	3	6		7			10^2	12		13	9^1		5					1			2	8										15
12	3	4		6			7^1		10^3	11		14	9^2		5				13	1			2	8										16
	3	4				8^1	12		10	11		9			5					1	6		2	7										17
12	11				6	8	4		9^1	7		10		3	5					1			2											18
7	11				6	9	4			8		10^1		3	5					1			2		12									19
12	13	2	3	6	11^2	4			9	8		10			5					1				7^1										20
1		4	6^3		8			11		7		10^2		3^1	5				9				2			12	13	14						21
1		4	3		8			9^1		7		10^9			5				12				2			14	13		6	11^2				22
1		11	4	3		9	8		10^2					5^2					14						12	7^1	13		6		2			23
1		3	4	5		8^2		9	6			10^2							14						7^1	12	13		11		2			24
1	9^1	4	3			8		11	7			10														12	2		6		5			25
1		4	5			8		9	7			10^2		3												13	2		11^1		6			26
1		4	3			8		9	7^1			10														12	2		6		5	11		27
1		4^1	3			12		9				13			10				2						7				6		5	11^2	8	28
1		4	3					9				12		7^2	6		2		13							10					5	11^1	8	29
1		4	3			12		9				14		8^2			2		13	7^1						10^3					5	11	6	30
1		4	3			14		9				12		7^2		6^1	2		13							10					5	11	8^3	31
1	12		3			8		9	7			5^5			14				13	10^3	2		6		4	11^2								32
1	3^2		4			8		9	7		12								13	10	2^1		6		5	11								33
1	3	12	4			8		9	7											10	2^1	13	6^2		5	11								34
1	6^2	3	13	4			8		9	7^3										10	2		14^{11}		5		12							35
1	7^3	3	6			4^1		9^2	10		13								14			8	2		12^{11}		5						36

EAST STIRLINGSHIRE

Third Division

Year Formed: 1880. *Ground & Address:* Firs Park, Firs St, Falkirk FK2 7AY. *Telephone:* 01324 623583. *Fax:* 01324 637 862
Ground Capacity: total: 1880, seated: 200. *Size of Pitch:* 112yd × 72yd.
Chairman: A. Mackin. *Vice Chairman:* Tom Kirk. *Secretary:* Leslie G. Thomson.
Manager: Brian Ross. *Coach:* Gordon Russell. *Physio:* Laura Gillogley.
Managers since 1975: I. Ure, D. McLinden, W. P. Lamont, A. Ferguson, W. Little, D. Whiteford, D. Lawson, J. D.
Connell, A. Mackin, D. Sullivan, B. McCulley, B. Little, J. Brownlie, H. McCann, G. Fairley. *Club Nickname(s):* The
Shire. *Previous Grounds:* Burnhouse, Randyford Park, Merchiston Park, New Kilbowie Park.
Record Attendance: 12,000 v Partick T, Scottish Cup 3rd rd; 21 Feb 1921.
Record Transfer Fee received: £35,000 for Jim Docherty to Chelsea (1978).
Record Transfer Fee paid: £6,000 for Colin McKinnon from Falkirk (March 1991).
Record Victory: 11-2 v Vale of Bannock, Scottish Cup 2nd rd; 22 Sept, 1888.
Record Defeat: 1-12 v Dundee United, Division II; 13 Apr, 1936.
Most Capped Player: Humphrey Jones, 5 (14), Wales.
Most League Appearances: 415: Gordon Russell, 1983-2001.
Most League Goals in Season (Individual): 36: Malcolm Morrison, Division II; 1938-39.
Most Goals Overall (Individual): —.

EAST STIRLINGSHIRE 2000–01 LEAGUE RECORD

Match No.	Date		Venue	Opponents	Result		H/T Score	Lg. Pos.	Goalscorers	Attendance
1	Aug	5	H	Cowdenbeath	L	0-2	0-1	—		297
2		12	A	Montrose	W	1-0	1-0	6	McPherson [21]	304
3		19	H	East Fife	L	2-5	2-0	6	McKechnie [32], Hislop [38]	310
4		26	H	Hamilton A	D	0-0	0-0	6		435
5	Sept	9	A	Dumbarton	W	2-1	2-1	6	Hislop [32], Stewart [41]	259
6		16	A	Peterhead	W	4-2	2-0	6	McKechnie [5], Lynes [30], Hislop 2 [44, 90]	614
7		23	H	Albion R	D	1-1	0-0	5	Higgins [78]	271
8		30	A	Brechin C	L	1-4	0-1	6	Hislop (pen) [82]	342
9	Oct	7	H	Elgin C	L	0-2	0-1	6		248
10		14	A	Cowdenbeath	L	0-3	0-2	6		289
11		21	H	Montrose	L	1-2	0-2	7	McKechnie [57]	258
12		24	A	Hamilton A	L	0-4	0-2	—		344
13	Nov	4	H	Dumbarton	D	1-1	1-0	7	Lorimer [33]	246
14		11	A	Albion R	L	1-2	1-1	7	Hislop (pen) [45]	334
15		18	H	Peterhead	L	1-3	0-2	7	Hislop [64]	262
16		25	A	Elgin C	W	2-1	0-0	7	Ferguson 2 [59, 69]	634
17	Dec	2	A	Brechin C	L	0-1	0-0	7		249
18		26	A	East Fife	L	1-3	0-1	—	Hislop [87]	492
19	Jan	2	A	Dumbarton	L	0-3	0-1	—		658
20		13	A	Peterhead	W	2-1	0-0	7	Hislop 2 [50, 70]	606
21		27	H	Hamilton A	L	1-4	1-1	8	Hislop [9]	346
22	Feb	3	H	Elgin C	W	1-0	1-0	8	Hislop [23]	240
23		17	H	East Fife	W	1-0	1-0	7	McKechnie [38]	286
24		24	A	Montrose	D	1-1	0-0	7	McKechnie [84]	305
25	Mar	10	A	Hamilton A	D	2-2	0-1	8	McKechnie 2 [51, 68]	388
26		13	H	Albion R	W	1-0	0-0	—	Hislop [59]	196
27		17	A	Albion R	D	2-2	0-2	8	McKechnie [53], Hislop (pen) [74]	248
28		20	H	Dumbarton	D	0-0	0-0	—		209
29		24	A	Brechin C	L	1-5	1-3	8	Hislop [26]	351
30		31	H	Peterhead	W	1-0	0-0	8	Hislop [55]	190
31	Apr	3	H	Cowdenbeath	L	0-2	0-0	—		272
32		7	A	Elgin C	L	2-4	1-3	8	McKechnie [35], Stewart [72]	405
33		14	H	Brechin C	L	0-2	0-2	8		253
34		21	A	Cowdenbeath	W	3-1	1-0	8	Wood [28], McKechnie 2 [53, 68]	488
35		28	H	Montrose	L	0-1	0-1	8		186
36	May	5	A	East Fife	L	1-4	1-1	8	Lindsay [42]	356

Final League Position: 8

Honours
League Champions: Division II 1931-32; C Division 1947-48. *Runners-up:* Division II 1962-63. Second Division 1979-80. Division Three 1923-24.
Scottish Cup: —.
League Cup: —.

Club colours: Shirt: Black and white stripes. Shorts: Black and white. Stockings: Black with 3 tangerine bands on top.

Goalscorers: *League* (37): Hislop 16 (3 pens), McKechnie 11, Ferguson 2, Stewart 2, Higgins 1, Lindsay 1, Lorimer 1, Lynes 1, McPherson 1, Wood 1
Scottish Cup (1): Hislop 1
CIS Cup (2): Gordon 1, McKechnie 1
Bell's League Cup (11): Hislop 3 (1 pen), Lynes 2, McKechnie 2, Ferguson 1, Gordon 1, Todd D 1, own goal 1

Butter J 36	Russell G 35	McPherson D 13 + 10	Hall M 26 + 2	Quinn C 14 + 1	Todd D 30 + 1	Scott A 13 + 3	Gordon K 21 + 3	Higgins G 4 + 8	Hislop S 36	Stewart S 29 + 4	Lynes C 9 + 7	McKechnie G 23 + 4	Ferguson B 15 + 5	Carlow R 4 + 6	Tortolano J 10 + 1	McKenzie C 2 + 5	Spence J —+1	Clarke J 8	Allison C 8 + 6	McWilliams D 2	McDonald I 20	Lorimer D 9	Wood D 6	McGhee G 13 + 2	Lindsay P 4 + 2	McAuley S 6 + 1	Wilson J —+1	Match No.
1	2	3	4	5	6	7²	8	9¹	10³	11	12	13	14															1
1	4	6¹	3		5		8²	14	9³	7	12	10			2	11	13											2
1	4	6	3	2	5		10	13	9	7	12	8²																3
1	5	6	3	2	4		10³	12	9¹	7²	14	8			13	11												4
1	4	13	3	2	5		10²		8	7	6	9			12	11¹												5
1	4		3	2	5		7²		8	10	6	9¹	13			11	12											6
1	4	12	3	2	5			13	10		7	9²	8			11	6¹											7
1	4	11	3³	2		8			10	5	7¹	9	13	14	6²		12											8
1	4	6	3	2	5¹				9	7		10			8	11	12											9
1	4		3	13	5	12			9	7		10	6¹					2²	8	11								10
1	2	14	5	4	3³	11			9	6		8	10²	13	12			7¹										11
1	4	14	3	2		8			10	7		9²	12	11	5¹			13	6³									12
1	2	12			6	4		11	9	7		13							5		10	3²	8¹					13
1	2	5			6			11	9	7									4		10	3	8					14
1	2	13			5		6²		9	7			12						4		10¹	3	8	11				15
1	2			4	6				10	7¹			12						5		9	3	8	11				16
1	2	14			5	6			10²	7¹		13	12						4		9	3³	8	11				17
1	3	5		2	6	11²	12		9	7		13		14					4		10¹			8³				18
1	6	3		2	5	7³	8²		9	11				14					4¹		13			10	12			19
1	5	6		2	4		10	11¹	9	7							12							8	3			20
1	2	14	5	4	6	11³	12		9	7²		10									13			8¹	3			21
1	4	12	5		6	8¹		11	9²	7		13	10		2						3							22
1	4		6		5			11	9	7		8	10		2						3							23
1	4	6¹	5			8	12		9	7		11	10		2	13					3			5		7¹		24
1	4		6				12	11	9			8	10²		2	13					3			5		7¹		25
1	4		6				12	11	9²			8	10	13	2						3			5		7¹		26
1	4	14	2		6	8	12		9²	11¹		7³	10								13			3	5			27
1	2	7	13		8	11²			9	6¹		10	5								3			4	12			28
1	4	7	6		8	12			9	11		10¹	2								3			5				29
1	4	8	6		7	10		9¹		12			2								3			5		11		30
1	4	6³	8		10	9²		7				2							13		3			5	11¹	12	14	31
1	4	6¹	5		8	11	12		9	13		10	2³						3²					14		7		32
1	5		8		7	10		9		11			4						3					4	6			33
1	4		8		7			9	12	10			2						3				6¹	5	11			34
1	4¹		8	12	11			9		10			2						3				6²	5	13	7		35
1		13	8	12	14			9	4¹	10			2²						3				11	5	7³	6		36

ELGIN CITY

Third Division

Year Formed: 1893. *Ground and Address:* Borough Briggs, Borough Briggs Road, Elgin IV30 1AP.
Telephone: 01343 551114. *Fax:* 01343 547921.
Ground Capacity: 5000, seated 478. *Size of pitch:* 110yd × 75yd.
Chairman: Dennis J. Miller. *Chief Executive:* Martyn Hunter. *General Manager:* Harry McFadden. *Secretary:* John A. Milton.
Manager: Alex Caldwell. *Coach:* Neil MacLennan. *Physio:* Maurice O'Donnell. *Club Nickname(s):* City or Black & Whites. *Previous Grounds:* Association Park 1893-95; Milnfield Park 1895-1909; Station Park 1909-19; Cooper Park 1919-21.
Record Attendance: 12,608 v Arbroath, Scottish Cup, 17 Feb 1968.
Record Victory: 18-1 v Brora Rangers, North of Scotland Cup, 6 Feb 1960.
Record Defeat: 1-14 v Hearts, Scottish Cup, 4 Feb 1939.
Record Transfer Fee received: £32,000 for Michael Teasdale to Dundee, Jan 1994.
Most League Appearances: 36: Jordan MacDonald, 2000-01.
Most League Goals in Season (Individual): 6, Colin Milne & David Ross.

ELGIN CITY 2000–01 LEAGUE RECORD

Match No.	Date	Venue	Opponents	Result	H/T Score	Lg. Pos.	Goalscorers	Attendance
1	Aug 5	A	Brechin C	L 1-2	1-1	—	Slythe [24]	509
2	12	H	Hamilton A	L 0-2	0-1	7		1552
3	19	A	Albion R	D 1-1	1-0	7	Clinton [5]	412
4	26	A	Cowdenbeath	L 1-3	1-0	8	Slythe [23]	354
5	Sept 9	H	Peterhead	L 1-3	1-1	9	Milne CR [8]	1135
6	16	A	East Fife	D 1-1	0-1	9	Morrison [74]	444
7	23	H	Montrose	D 1-1	1-1	9	Morrison [23]	817
8	30	H	Dumbarton	W 2-0	0-0	7	Campbell [67], Clinton [74]	752
9	Oct 7	A	East Stirling	W 2-0	1-0	7	Milne CR [28], Clinton [49]	248
10	14	H	Brechin C	D 2-2	0-0	7	Ross [73], Morrison [90]	835
11	21	A	Hamilton A	L 1-4	0-1	8	Callaghan (og) [60]	414
12	28	H	Cowdenbeath	L 2-3	2-2	8	Edwards [13], Milne C [42]	836
13	Nov 4	A	Peterhead	L 0-1	0-1	8		850
14	11	A	Montrose	D 0-0	0-0	8		459
15	18	H	East Fife	L 1-3	0-1	8	Ross [90]	730
16	25	H	East Stirling	L 1-2	0-0	8	Milne CR [64]	634
17	Dec 2	A	Dumbarton	L 0-3	0-1	9		1876
18	16	A	Brechin C	L 1-2	0-1	9	Ross [78]	333
19	Feb 3	A	East Stirling	L 0-1	0-1	9		240
20	17	A	Albion R	W 1-0	0-0	9	Milne CR [63]	287
21	Mar 6	H	Peterhead	L 0-1	0-0	—		524
22	10	H	Cowdenbeath	L 0-2	0-0	9		676
23	13	H	Dumbarton	L 0-3	0-3	—		424
24	17	A	Montrose	L 1-2	0-2	10	Milne CR (pen) [86]	366
25	20	A	East Fife	D 1-1	0-1	—	Ross [53]	223
26	25	A	Cowdenbeath	L 0-1	0-0	9		289
27	28	H	Albion R	L 1-2	1-1	—	Edwards [44]	268
28	31	H	East Fife	L 1-3	1-3	10	Green R [10]	512
29	Apr 3	H	Montrose	L 0-2	0-1	—		385
30	7	H	East Stirling	W 4-2	3-1	10	Hind [14], Ross 2 (1 pen) [28 (p), 70], Craig [35]	405
31	10	H	Hamilton A	L 0-3	0-0	—		542
32	14	A	Dumbarton	L 0-2	0-1	10		685
33	21	H	Brechin C	L 0-3	0-3	10		570
34	28	A	Hamilton A	L 0-3	0-1	10		773
35	May 1	A	Peterhead	D 1-1	0-0	—	Green R [57]	475
36	5	H	Albion R	W 1-0	0-0	10	Green R [50]	487

Final League Position: 10

Honours
Scottish Cup, Quarter Finals 1968.
Highland League Champions: winners 15 times.
Scottish Qualifying Cup (North): winners 7 times.
North of Scotland Cup: winners 17 times.

Club colours: Shirt: Black and white vertical stripes. Shorts: Black. Stockings: Black.

Goalscorers: *League* (29): Milne CR 6 (1 pen), Ross 6 (1 pen), Clinton 3, Green R 3, Morrison 3, Edwards 2, Slythe 2, Campbell 1, Craig D 1, Hind 1, own goal 1
Scottish Cup (0):
CIS Cup (0):
Bell's League Cup (2): Green R 2

Pirie M 34	Milne CD 26+1	MacDonald J 36	Morris A 4+3	O'Brien L 2+2	Russell G 6+2	Whyte N 28+5	Cameron S 1+3	Milne CR 29+1	Slythe M 5+7	Clinton S 15+4	Noble S —+1	Maguire P —+2	Morrison M 28	Ellis S 5+7	Green R 23+8	Campbell C 21+4	Green M —+1	Peters S 4	Furphy W 17	Craig R 1	Ross D 27	Mackay S 4+1	Edwards S 18+5	Duncan R 6	Irvine D 3+3	Munro G 8	Tully C 15	Craig D 13	Shanks L 1+1	Hind D 8	Rae M 2	McMullan M 6+1	Match No.
1	2	3	4	5	6	7¹	8²	9	10	11	12	13																					1
1	2	3	5	12	4	13		9	10²	11			14	6	7¹	8³																	2
1	2	3	5	14	4	7³	13	9	10³	6					8	11¹	12																3
1	2	3			6¹	12	8	13	9	10			11²		5	7		4															4
1	2²	3	5			13	8	9	12				6	11	10¹	7		4															5
1	2	3					8	7	9	12	6		5		10¹	11		4															6
1	2	3					13	6²	7	9			10¹	12	5	11		8	4														7
1	2	3				13	8¹	12	9				6		5	10		7	4	11²													8
1	2	3				8		9		6			5		10	11			4		7												9
1	2	3				8		9	12	6			5		10	11¹			4		7												10
1	2	3				9¹		9	14	6			5		10³	11²			4		7		12	13									11
1	2	3				12		9		6			5		13			4¹	10²	11	7		8										12
1		3¹				8		9					5	12	11				4		7		6	2	10								13
1		3				8		9	12	6			5		4	11¹					7		10	2									14
1		3²	12²			8		9	11				5	14	4	13					7		10	2¹	6								15
1	2	3				8		9	12	6			5		11¹	7			4		10												16
1	2	3				8		9	13	11²			5		6¹	7			4		2		10	12									17
1	2¹	3				7		9²	14				5	13	11²	8			12		10		6	4									18
1	2	3				13		9		5			8²	6	11¹				4		7		12	10									19
1		3						9					8		10	4¹			7		2	12	5	6	11								20
1		3				12		9					8¹		10	4			7		2²		5	6	11	13							21
1		3				13		12					5		10²	4			7		2		8	6	11	9¹							22
1		3²				10		9					5	13	12	4¹			7		2		8	6	11								23
1	12	3				8		9	14				5		10	13			7		2¹		6	4³	11²								24
1	2	3				8							5		9	10			7		11		6	4									25
1	2	3				8		9					5		12	10			7		11¹		4	6									26
1	2	3				8							5	12	4	10¹			7		9		6	11									27
1	2	3				8							5	13	10				7		9¹	12	4	11²	6								28
1	2	3				8							5	12	10¹				7		9		4	11	6								29
	2	3				8							5		12				4		7			6	11¹			9	1	10			30
	2	3				8		12					5	13	11¹				4		7			6				9	1	10²			31
1	2	3				8		9					5	14	12				4		7		13	6³			11		10²				32
1	2	3²				8		9					5	12	14				7		11³	4¹		10	6			13					33
1	2	3				8		9						13					4		7		12	6	11²			5		10¹			34
1		3				8		9		11									4		7		10	6			5		2				35
1	2	3						9						7	8				4				10	6	11			5					36

FALKIRK

First Division

Year Formed: 1876. *Ground & Address:* Brockville Park, Hope St, Falkirk FK1 5AX. *Telephone:* 01324 624121.
Fax: 01324 612418.
Ground Capacity: total: 9706, seated: 2661. *Size of Pitch:* 110yd × 72yd.
Chairman: Martin Ritchie. *Secretary:* Alex Blackwood. *General Manager:* Crawford Baptie.
Manager: Alex Totten. *Assistant Manager:* Kevin McAllister. *Coach:* Tony Docherty. *Physio:* Alec McQueen.
Managers since 1975: J. Prentice, G. Miller, W. Little, J. Hagart, A. Totten, G. Abel, W. Lamont, D. Clarke, J. Duffy,
W. Lamont, J. Jefferies, J. Lambie E. Bannon, A. Totten. *Club Nickname(s):* The Bairns. *Previous Grounds:* Randyford
1876-81; Blinkbonny Grounds 1881-83; Brockville Park 1883 to present.
Record Attendance: 23,100 v Celtic, Scottish Cup 3rd rd; 21 Feb, 1953.
Record Transfer Fee received: £380,000 for John Hughes to Celtic (Aug 1995).
Record Transfer Fee paid: £225,000 to Chelsea for Kevin McAllister (Aug 1991).
Record Victory: 12-1 v Laurieston, Scottish Cup 2nd rd; 23 Sept, 1893.
Record Defeat: 1-11 v Airdrieonians, Division I; 28 Apr, 1951.
Most Capped Player: Alex Parker, 14 (15), Scotland.
Most League Appearances: (post-war): 353, George Watson, 1975-87.
Most League Goals in Season (Individual): 43: Evelyn Morrison, Division I; 1928-29.
Most Goals Overall (Individual): Dougie Moran, 86, 1957-61 and 1964-67.

FALKIRK 2000–01 LEAGUE RECORD

Match No.	Date	Venue	Opponents	Result	H/T Score	Lg. Pos.	Goalscorers	Atten- dance
1	Aug 5	A	Clyde	L	1-3	1-1	—	Hutchison [36]	2706
2	12	H	Morton	W	1-0	0-0	6	Henry [82]	2563
3	19	A	Inverness CT	W	3-2	2-0	4	Hutchison [5], Kerr [28], McAllister [58]	2132
4	26	A	Ayr U	L	2-5	0-1	5	Roberts (pen) [52], Lawrie [69]	3213
5	Sept 9	H	Raith R	W	2-1	1-0	4	Roberts 2 (1 pen) [24 (p), 51]	2762
6	16	H	Alloa Ath	D	1-1	0-1	5	Kerr [53]	2645
7	23	A	Ross Co	W	2-0	0-0	4	Hutchison [59], Lawrie [85]	3161
8	30	H	Livingston	W	3-2	0-2	2	Nicholls [48], Henry [57], Craig [68]	3547
9	Oct 7	A	Airdrieonians	W	2-1	1-1	2	Roberts [29], Hutchison [66]	2879
10	14	H	Clyde	W	3-2	1-2	2	Hutchison [13], McAllister [53], Greer (og) [65]	3003
11	21	A	Morton	W	4-0	2-0	1	Roberts (pen) [13], Christie [36], Hutchison 2 [53, 55]	1503
12	28	H	Ayr U	W	3-0	1-0	1	Craig [17], Henry [73], McAllister [90]	3783
13	Nov 4	A	Raith R	W	2-0	1-0	1	Roberts [15], Henry [64]	3120
14	11	A	Ross Co	L	2-3	0-1	1	Roberts (pen) [51], Nicholls [78]	2898
15	18	A	Alloa Ath	L	2-3	1-0	1	Nicholls [9], Craig [83]	1709
16	25	H	Airdrieonians	L	0-2	0-1	2		2867
17	Dec 2	A	Livingston	L	1-4	0-3	2	Roberts [90]	4464
18	9	H	Inverness CT	D	2-2	2-0	2	Roberts (pen) [1], Lawrie [20]	2136
19	16	A	Clyde	W	3-0	1-0	2	Henry 2 [26, 64], Nicholls [51]	1629
20	Jan 2	H	Alloa Ath	D	2-2	0-1	—	McAllister [62], Craig [81]	2627
21	13	H	Livingston	W	1-0	0-0	2	Hutchison [78]	4914
22	Feb 3	A	Inverness CT	D	1-1	0-1	2	Lawrie [14]	1913
23	24	H	Ayr U	L	1-2	0-1	3	Craig [48]	2668
24	Mar 6	A	Ayr U	L	0-6	0-1	—		2041
25	10	A	Ross Co	L	1-4	0-3	3	Christie (pen) [90]	2620
26	17	H	Ross Co	D	1-1	1-0	3	Hutchison [33]	1955
27	24	A	Airdrieonians	W	2-1	0-1	3	McAllister (pen) [57], Nicholls [82]	1644
28	27	H	Morton	L	1-3	1-1	—	Nicholls [38]	1276
29	31	A	Alloa Ath	W	1-0	1-0	4	Nicholls (pen) [12]	1186
30	Apr 3	H	Raith R	D	0-0	0-0	—		1586
31	7	H	Airdrieonians	D	1-1	1-0	4	Nicholls [18]	2040
32	10	H	Raith R	W	2-0	0-0	—	Waddell [86], Hutchison [90]	1634
33	21	H	Clyde	D	1-1	1-1	4	Hutchison [44]	2200
34	24	A	Livingston	L	0-3	0-1	—		3659
35	28	A	Morton	L	1-2	0-0	4	Pearson [87]	905
36	May 5	H	Inverness CT	W	2-1	2-0	3	Morris [13], Pearson [31]	2230

Final League Position: 3

Honours
League Champions: Division II 1935-36, 1969-70, 1974-75. First Division 1990-91, 1993-94. Second Division 1979-80;
Runners-up: Division I 1907-08, 1909-10. First Division 1985-86, 1988-89. Division II 1904-05, 1951-52, 1960-61.
Scottish Cup Winners: 1913, 1957; *Runners-up:* 1997. *League Cup Runners-up:* 1947-48. *B&Q Cup Winners:* 1993-94.
League Challenge Cup Winners: 1997-98.

Club colours: Shirt: Navy blue. Shorts: White. Stockings: Navy blue.

Goalscorers: *League* (57): Hutchison 11, Roberts 9 (5 pens), Nicholls 8 (1 pen), Henry 6, Craig 5, McAllister 5 (1 pen), Lawrie 4, Christie 2 (1 pen), Kerr 2, Pearson 2, Morris 1, Waddell 1, own goal 1
Scottish Cup (0):
CIS Cup (4): McAllister 1, McMahon 1, Nicholls 1, Roberts 1
Bell's League Cup (1): Hutchison 1

Hogarth M 36	Lawrie A 36	McQuilken J 34	Rennie S 27 + 1	Christie K 25	Nicholls D 32 + 1	McAllister K 14 + 14	Kerr M 30 + 2	Roberts M 23 + 3	Henry J 27 + 1	Hutchison G 24 + 2	Denham G 24 + 1	Morris I 4 + 12	Avdiu K — + 1	McMahon D 3	Pearson C 1 + 4	Seaton A 4 + 5	Craig S 22 + 5	McStay G 7 + 3	McDonald C — + 1	Burke A 6 + 5	Deuchar K 4 + 8	Waddell R 3 + 2	Match No.
1	2	3	4	5	6	7	8[1]	9	10[2]	11	12	13											1
1	2	3	4	5	6	7[2]	10	9	8	11[1]	13	12											2
1	2	3	4		6		10	9[1]	8	11	5	12											3
1	2	3	4		6		10	9	8	11	5	7											4
1	2	3	5	4	6	12	10	9	8[1]	11		13			7[2]								5
1	2	3	5	4	6		10	9[2]	8	11		12			7[1]	13							6
1	2	3	5	4	6		10	9	8	11		12			7[1]								7
1	2	3	4[4]			7		9	8	11	5	13					10[1]	12					8
1	2	3	4		6	7[3]		9[2]	8	11	5	14					10[3]	12	13				9
1	2	3	4	5	12	6	9[2]	8	11			7[1]			13		10						10
1	2	3[1]	4		6	12	7	9	8[2]	11	5	13	14				10[1]						11
1	2	3	4		6	13	7	9[4]	8	11	5						10[1]			12			12
1	2	3	4		6	13	7	9[2]	8	11	5						10[1]			12			13
1	2	3	4[1]		6	12	7	9	8	13	5						10[2]			11			14
1	2	3	12	4	6	7[2]	10	8	9		5[1]	14					13			11[2]			15
1	2	3	4		12	7	9	8	11[2]	5		10					6[1]	13					16
1	2	3	4		6	13	7	12	8	9	5						10[1]			11[2]			17
1	2	3	8	4	6	7[1]	10	9	11	12	5												18
1	2	3	5	4[2]	6	13	7	9[1]	8	10							12			11			19
1	2	3[1]	6	4	12	7	9[1]	8	10		5	14					13			11[2]			20
1	2	3	5	4	6	7	10	9[1]	8	11										12			21
1	2	3	5	4	6	13	10	9[1]	8[2]	7							12	14		11[2]			22
1	2		5	4	6	7	10		8	11[2]					3	9				12	13		23
1	2	3	5	4		7	12	10	8	11						6	9[1]						24
1	2	3[1]		4	6		7[3]	8[2]		11	5	13			12	9	10			14			25
1	2		4		6	7		9[1]		11	5				3	10	8			12			26
1	2	3	4		6	7	12	9[2]		11	5						10	8[1]		13			27
1	2	3	4		6	7	8	13		11[2]	5						9[1]	12		10			28
1	2	3	4		6	7[3]	13		11	5	8						12	10[1]		9			29
1	2	3	4	8	6				11	5							10	12		9	7[1]		30
1	2	3	4	8	6	7			11	5							10			9[1]	12		31
1	2	3	4	8	6	7		10		5	9[1]									12	11		32
1	2	3	4		12	14	7	8[1]	10	5							9[6]	13		11			33
1	2	3	4		6	7[2]	8	11	5[1]	14	12						9	10[1]		13			34
1	2	3	4		6	7	12	9[3]	11	13	5						10[2]	8[1]		14			35
1	2	3	5		6	14	7	8[2]	13	11	4	9[3]					10[1]	12					36

FORFAR ATHLETIC Second Division

Year Formed: 1885. *Ground & Address:* Station Park, Carseview Road, Forfar. *Telephone:* 01307 463576/462259. *Fax:* 01307 466956.
Ground Capacity: total: 4640, seated: 739. *Size of Pitch:* 115yd × 69yd.
Chairman and Secretary: David McGregor.
Manager: Neil Cooper. *Assistant Manager:* Phil Bonnyman. *Physio:* Jim Peacock. *Coaches:* Jim Moffat, Gordon Wallace.
Managers since 1975: Jerry Kerr, Archie Knox, Alex Rae, Doug Houston, Henry Hall, Bobby Glennie, Paul Hegarty, Tommy Campbell. *Club Nickname(s):* Loons. *Previous Grounds:* None.
Record Attendance: 10,780 v Rangers, Scottish Cup 2nd rd; 2 Feb, 1970.
Record Transfer Fee received: £65,000 for David Bingham to Dunfermline Ath (September 1995).
Record Transfer Fee paid: £50,000 for Ian McPhee from Airdrieonians (1991).
Record Victory: 14-1 v Lindertis, Scottish Cup 1st rd; 1 Sept 1988.
Record Defeat: 2-12 v King's Park, Division II; 2 Jan, 1930.
Most Capped Player: —.
Most League Appearances: 484: Ian McPhee, 1978-88 and 1991-98.
Most League Goals in Season (Individual): 45: Dave Kilgour, Division II; 1929-30.
Most Goals Overall (Individual): 124, John Clark.

FORFAR ATHLETIC 2000–01 LEAGUE RECORD

Match No.	Date		Venue	Opponents	Result	H/T Score	Lg. Pos.	Goalscorers	Attendance
1	Aug	5	A	Stranraer	L	0-2	0-0	—	397
2		12	H	Queen's Park	L	0-1	0-0	10		516
3		19	A	Stirling A	D	3-3	2-2	10	Stewart [19], Ferguson (pen) [35], McPhee [72]	605
4		26	H	Stenhousemuir	D	2-2	1-2	10	Morris [6], Sinclair [89]	381
5	Sept	9	A	Arbroath	W	4-3	3-0	7	Stewart 2 [16, 33], Ferguson 2 [40, 87]	876
6		16	H	Clydebank	L	0-2	0-2	10		385
7		23	A	Queen of the S	W	1-0	1-0	8	Bowman [20]	1167
8		30	H	Partick Th	D	1-1	0-0	8	Ferguson [66]	2218
9	Oct	7	A	Berwick R	L	3-5	1-3	9	Neill A (og) [4], Ferguson (pen) [56], Stewart [89]	332
10		14	H	Stranraer	D	0-0	0-0	10		405
11		21	A	Queen's Park	D	0-0	0-0	10		741
12		28	A	Stenhousemuir	L	0-2	0-1	10		321
13	Nov	4	H	Arbroath	L	0-1	0-1	10		834
14		11	H	Queen of the S	L	0-1	0-0	10		440
15		18	A	Clydebank	D	1-1	1-1	10	Brand [14]	153
16		25	A	Berwick R	D	1-1	1-1	10	Stewart [2]	430
17	Dec	2	H	Partick Th	L	0-1	0-0	10		1052
18		16	A	Stranraer	L	1-3	1-1	10	Stirling (og) [4]	419
19	Jan	2	A	Arbroath	D	1-1	0-0	—	Donaldson [65]	1061
20		6	H	Stenhousemuir	W	7-0	4-0	9	Donaldson [6], Winters 3 [11, 14, 17], Beaton [48], Sellars 2 [51, 81]	441
21		27	H	Clydebank	L	1-3	0-2	9	Beaton [83]	418
22	Feb	10	A	Partick Th	L	0-4	0-0	10		3075
23	Mar	10	A	Stenhousemuir	W	1-0	0-0	9	Christie [78]	376
24		13	H	Queen's Park	W	3-0	0-0	—	Bowman [67], Keogh [84], Beaton [86]	374
25		17	A	Queen of the S	W	3-2	1-1	9	Christie [41], Keogh [75], Beaton [90]	974
26		20	A	Stirling A	L	0-1	0-0	—		515
27		31	A	Clydebank	L	1-2	0-1	9	Donaldson [89]	145
28	Apr	3	H	Berwick R	L	0-1	0-0	—		413
29		7	H	Berwick R	L	0-1	0-0	10		480
30		10	H	Stirling A	W	1-0	0-0	—	Sellars [65]	390
31		14	H	Partick Th	D	2-2	2-1	9	Cargill [8], Ferguson [36]	2081
32		21	H	Stranraer	L	2-3	2-0	10	Sellars [14], Keogh [19]	378
33		24	H	Arbroath	D	1-1	1-1	—	Horn [14]	1065
34		28	A	Queen's Park	W	2-0	0-0	9	Ferguson [81], Stewart [84]	951
35	May	1	H	Queen of the S	W	3-1	0-1	—	Sellars [61], Stewart [79], Ferguson [82]	522
36		5	H	Stirling A	W	3-1	2-0	8	Cargill [11], Stewart 2 [16, 53]	813

Final League Position: 8

Honours

League Champions: Second Division 1983-84. Third Division 1994-95; *Runners-up:* 1996-97. C Division 1948-49.
Scottish Cup: Semi-finals 1982.
League Cup: Semi-finals 1977-78.

Club colours: Shirt: Sky blue with navy piping. Shorts: Navy. Stockings: Sky blue.

Goalscorers: *League* (48): Stewart 9, Ferguson I 8 (2 pens). Sellars 5, Beaton 4, Donaldson 3, Keogh 3, Winters 3, Bowman 2, Cargill 2, Christie 2, Brand 1, Horn 1, McPhee 1, Morris 1, Sinclair 1, own goals 2
Scottish Cup (0):
CIS Cup (1): Taylor 1
Bell's League Cup(1): McPhee 1

Garden S 31	McCheyne G 7+3	Donaldson E 28+2	Horn R 30	Tully C 9	Bowman D 23	McPhee G 9+5	Farnan C 23+5	Ferguson I 24+3	Cargill A 19+5	Taylor S 4+3	Rattray A 23+2	Brand R 7+5	Stewart W 16+12	Morris R 11	Sinclair D —+2	Christie S 14+13	Craig D 7+2	Stirling J 6+2	Beaton D 25+2	Ferrie N 1+1	Farrell G 1+1	McGraw M 4+1	Sellars B 21+2	Good I 12	Winters D 3	Duncan R 16	Dolan J 5	Keogh L 13	Moffat J 4	Match No.
1	2¹	3	4	5	6	7	8²	9	10	11	12	13																		1
1	2	3	5	6	8	7	4	9¹	11	10			12																	2
1	12	3	5	6		8	4	9			2¹	10²	7	11		13														3
1	2²	3	5			8	7	4	9				10	11	6¹	12	13													4
1	2	13	5	6	8	12	4	9								10¹			3	11²										5
1	2	13	5¹	6	8		4	9	12			10¹	7			14			3	11²										6
1	3	4		6	8		11	9²			2	13	7			10¹			12				5							7
1	3	4		6¹	8¹		13	9	11		2		7			10²			12	14			5							8
	3	4²		6	8		11	9	12		2	13	7			10¹				1			5							9
1	12		5		8	10¹		9			2	13	7²	11		14			3			4¹	6							10
1		4	5		8			9			2	10	7	11					3				6							11
1		4	5		8			9			2	10	12	7¹		11			3				6							12
1		4³	5		8			9			2	11	14	7²		13	12		3¹				6							13
1	2	3	4		8	7		9				10	12			11¹	5		6											14
1	3	4	5		8		13				2¹	10	12	11		14			6				9³	7²						15
1	11	4		6	12		13	8			2	9¹	10			14			3¹				5	7²						16
1	11	4		6	8		13	7³			2²		9¹	10		3			12				5	14						17
1	11	4			8			2	9			6²	7			13			12				5	10¹		3				18
1	11	4			8			6	9		2					10¹			12²				5	7		13	3			19
1	12	11	4¹		8²			9			2	6				13			14				5	7		3		10		20
1	11	4			8			9			2¹	6				13			12				5	7²		3		10		21
1		4			8			9			2	6							12				5	7		3¹	10	11		22
1		4			8		13	9¹			2	6				12				14			5	7		3	10²	11³		23
1	11				8		13				2	6							12			4¹	5	7		3	10²	9		24
1	11				8¹		13				2	6							12			4²	5	7		3	10	9		25
1	11				8¹		13				2	6							12			4²	5	7		3	10	9		26
1	11				8		13				2	6¹							12			4	5	7		3	10²	9		27
1	11	4			8		13				2	6¹							12				5	7		3		9		28
1	3	4			8			9				6				12			11¹				5	7	2			10		29
	3	4			8			9				6				12			11¹				5	7	2		10		1	30
	3	4	11		8			9¹				6				12							5	7	2		10		1	31
1	11	4			8			9¹				6				12							5	7	2	3		10		32
1	3	4	11¹		8			9				6³				12				14			5	7²	2			10		33
1	3	4	7		8		11²	9²				6¹				11²			12	14			5		2			10		34
	3	4	11		8			9²				6				13			12				5	7	2		10¹		1	35
	3	4	11		8			9				6				10							5	7	2				1	36

HAMILTON ACADEMICAL   Second Division

Year Formed: 1874. *Ground:* New Douglas Park, Cadzow Avenue, Hamilton ML3 0FT. *Telephone:* 01698 286103. *Fax:* 01698 285422. *Club Address:* Enable Building, Prospect House, New Park St, Hamilton ML3 0BN. *Telephone:* 01698 286103. *Ground Capacity:* total: 14,538, seated: 8397. *Size of Pitch:* 115yd × 75yd.
Secretary: Scott A. Struthers BA. *Commercial Manager:* Chris Norris.
Manager: Ally Dawson. *Assistant Manager:* Robert Prytz. *Physio:* Jim Fallon.
Managers since 1975: J. Eric Smith, Dave McParland, John Blackley, Bertie Auld, John Lambie, Jim Dempsey, John Lambie, Billy McLaren, Iain Munro, Sandy Clark, Colin Miller. *Club Nickname(s):* The Accies. *Previous Grounds:* Bent Farm, South Avenue, South Haugh, Douglas Park, Cliftonhill Stadium, Firhill Stadium.
Record Attendance: 28,690 v Hearts, Scottish Cup 3rd rd; 3 Mar, 1937.
Record Transfer Fee received: £380,000 for Paul Hartley to Millwall (July 1996).
Record Transfer Fee paid: £60,000 for Paul Martin from Kilmarnock (Oct 1988) and for John McQuade from Dumbarton (Aug 1993).
Record Victory: 11-1 v Chryston, Lanarkshire Cup; 28 Nov, 1885.
Record Defeat: 1-11 v Hibernian, Division I; 6 Nov, 1965.
Most Capped Player: Colin Miller, 29, Canada, 1988-94.
Most League Appearances: 452: Rikki Ferguson, 1974-88.
Most League Goals in Season (Individual): 35: David Wilson, Division I; 1936-37.
Most Goals Overall (Individual): 246: David Wilson, 1928-39.

HAMILTON ACADEMICAL 2000–01 LEAGUE RECORD

Match No.	Date	Venue	Opponents	Result	H/T Score	Lg. Pos.	Goalscorers	Atten- dance
1	Aug 5	H	Dumbarton	W 2-0	0-0	—	Eadie [60], Russell [84]	588
2	12	A	Elgin C	W 2-0	1-0	2	Nelson [12], McFarlane D [74]	1552
3	19	H	Montrose	W 6-0	0-0	1	McFarlane D 3 [52, 76, 85], Moore [58], Russell 2 [71, 89]	426
4	26	A	East Stirling	D 0-0	0-0	1		435
5	Sept 9	H	Albion R	L 0-2	0-0	3		487
6	16	A	Cowdenbeath	L 0-2	0-2	4		448
7	23	H	Peterhead	W 3-0	2-0	3	Prytz (pen) [29], Bonnar [30], Nelson [54]	369
8	30	A	East Fife	W 2-1	0-0	3	Gaughan [52], Callaghan (pen) [85]	549
9	Oct 7	H	Brechin C	W 4-1	1-1	3	Moore [37], Callaghan [74], Nelson [79], Russell [88]	422
10	14	A	Dumbarton	W 3-2	1-1	3	Moore [33], Bonnar [55], Clark [90]	368
11	21	H	Elgin C	W 4-1	1-0	3	Moore 3 (1 pen) [14, 89, 90 (p)], Callaghan (pen) [49]	414
12	24	H	East Stirling	W 4-0	2-0	—	Moore 2 [16, 23], Nelson [66], Callaghan (pen) [89]	344
13	Nov 4	H	Albion R	D 1-1	0-1	3	Nelson [83]	608
14	11	A	Peterhead	D 1-1	1-1	2	Prytz [41]	790
15	18	H	Cowdenbeath	D 0-0	0-0	3		598
16	25	A	Brechin C	D 0-0	0-0	3		483
17	Dec 2	H	East Fife	D 1-1	0-1	3	Eadie [64]	518
18	16	H	Dumbarton	W 2-0	0-0	3	McFarlane D 2 [62, 87]	485
19	Jan 2	H	Albion R	W 3-2	1-0	—	Eadie [18], Russell [66], McFarlane D [70]	540
20	20	H	Peterhead	W 3-0	0-0	3	Russell [46], Tindal (og) [80], McFarlane D [69]	645
21	27	A	East Stirling	W 4-1	1-1	1	McFarlane D 3 [37, 69, 71], Callaghan (pen) [58]	346
22	Feb 3	A	Brechin C	W 1-0	0-0	1	Grant (og) [53]	521
23	17	A	Montrose	L 1-3	1-2	1	McFarlane D [4]	411
24	Mar 10	H	East Stirling	D 2-2	1-0	2	Callaghan [24], Moore [74]	388
25	17	A	Peterhead	L 1-2	0-0	2	Clark [83]	710
26	20	A	Cowdenbeath	D 1-1	1-1	—	Callaghan [17]	429
27	25	A	Albion R	W 1-0	0-0	3	Callaghan (pen) [73]	524
28	27	A	East Fife	W 4-1	0-1	—	Kerr [50], Martin [51], MacFarlane [63], McFarlane D [80]	353
29	31	H	Cowdenbeath	D 0-0	0-0	1		666
30	Apr 7	A	Brechin C	W 4-3	2-1	2	Kerr [31], Callaghan [43], McFarlane D 2 [47, 60]	586
31	10	A	Elgin C	W 3-0	0-0	2	Moore 2 [46, 83], McFarlane D [54]	542
32	14	H	East Fife	D 1-1	0-0	2	McFarlane D [89]	507
33	21	A	Dumbarton	W 2-1	1-1	2	McFarlane D [23], Kerr [51]	864
34	28	H	Elgin C	W 3-0	1-0	3	Sherry [33], McFarlane D 2 [61, 62]	773
35	May 1	A	Montrose	W 2-0	1-0	—	McFarlane D [24], MacLaren [53]	495
36	5	A	Montrose	W 4-1	1-0	1	McFarlane D 3 [41, 59, 72], Moore [80]	916

Final League Position: 1

Honours
League Champions: First Division 1985-86, 1987-88; Third Division 2000-01. *Runners-up:* Division II 1903-04, 1952-53, 1964-65; Second Division 1996-97.
Scottish Cup Runners-up: 1911, 1935. *League Cup:* Semi-finalists three times.
B&Q Cup Winners: 1991-92, 1992-93.

Club colours: Shirt: Red and white hoops. Shorts: White. Stockings: White.

Goalscorers: *League* (75): McFarlane D 24, Moore 12 (1 pen), Callaghan 9 (5 pens), Russell 6, Nelson 5, Eadie 3, Kerr 3, Bonnar 2, Clark 2, Prytz 2 (1 pen), Gaughan 1, MacFarlane I 1, MacLaren 1, Martin 1, Sherry 1, own goals 2
Scottish Cup (0):
CIS Cup (1): Russell 1
Bell's League Cup (0):

MacFarlane I 33	Nelson M 23 + 2	Lynn G 6	Davidson W 15 + 4	Gaughan P 36	Vaugh B 3 + 5	Bonnar M 33 + 1	Sherry J 20	Eadie A 11 + 12	McFarlane D 30 + 4	Russell A 22 + 2	Kelly R 7 + 6	Clark G 12 + 8	Grant D 5	Moore M 27 + 4	Hillcoat C 7 + 3	MacLaren R 11 + 1	Martin M 13 + 5	Potter G 3 + 2	Callaghan S 29	Prytz R 9	Renicks S 7 + 2	Hogg K 8 + 2	Thomson S — + 1	Downs R 4 + 5	Oliver N 5	Kerr D 17	Lurinsky A — + 5	Match No.
1	2	3	4	5	6¹	7	8	9	10	11	12																	1
1	3	11	4³	5		8		9¹	12	6	13	2		7²	10	14												2
1	3³	11	4	5		8	6²	13	12	9		2¹	7	10	14													3
1	6	3	4	5		11	8¹		10		7²	12	13	2	9													4
1	6	3	4	5		11	8	10	13	7²		14	2¹	9¹	12													5
1	6	3²		5		11		10	8	7²		13	2¹	9	4	12	14											6
	2²		5	14	11	7¹		10		12			9	4	6		1	3	8³	13								7
1	2		5¹	13	11²	7		10	14				9	4	6			3	8³	12								8
1	2		5		11			12	10	7			9	4	6			3	8¹									9
1	2		5		11		13	10	7		12		9²	4	6			3	8¹									10
1	2		5		11			12	10	7			9	4	6			3	8¹									11
1	2²		5		11			10	7		12		9¹	4	6			3	8	13								12
1	2		5		11		12	10	7²		13		9	6				3	8¹	4								13
1	2		5		11			12	10	7		6	9¹					3	8	4								14
1	2		5	12	11			10		7¹		6			13			3	8²	4								15
1	2	8	5	14	11			10²	13	7²		6	9		12			3		4¹								16
1¹	2	8²	5	14	11			13	10	7		6	9²					3		4	12							17
1	2	7¹	5		11	8	9¹	10	12			6	13					3		4								18
1	2		5		11	8	9¹	10²	7			6	12					3		4	13							19
1			5		11	8		10	7				9		2			3					4	6				20
1		12	5		11	8		10	7¹				9		2			3					4	6				21
1⁸		13	5		11	8	12	10¹	7²				9		2	15		3					4	6				22
1		12	5		11	8	14	10	7¹				9²		2³			3					4	6	13			23
1		12	5	8¹	11			10²	7				9		2			3					4	6	13			24
1	14		4	5		11	8¹			7²		12	9		2³			3					10		6	13		25
1	2		4	5		6		9		8					7	11							10		3			26
1	2¹		4	5		6		9		13	8	12			7	11							10²		3			27
1	2		4	5		6			10	13	8²	9			7¹	11							12		3			28
1	2		4	5		6		13	9		12	8¹			7²	11							10		3			29
1		4	5				8¹	12	10²		6			9		7	11			2³	14		13		3			30
1		4	5	11		8		10		6			9		7¹			2			12		12		3			31
1			5		13	8		10		6²			9		7¹	11			2	4			12		3			32
1			5		6	8	12	10		7			9¹	4		11			2						3			33
1⁸			5		6	8	9¹	10		7				4		15	11		2						3	12		34
	12		5		6	8¹	9¹	10		7³					4	14	1	11	2						3	13		35
			5		6	8	9¹	10		7²				12		4	13	1	11	2						3		36

HEART OF MIDLOTHIAN   Premier League

Year Formed: 1874. *Ground & Address:* Tynecastle Stadium, Gorgie Rd, Edinburgh EH11 2NL. *Telephone:* 0131 200 7200. *Fax:* 0131 200 7222. *Website:* www.heartsfc.co.uk.
Ground Capacity: 18,000. *Size of Pitch:* 108yd × 73yd.
Chairman: Douglas Smith. *Chief Executive:* Christopher Robinson. *Sales and Marketing Manager:* Kenny Wittmann.
Head Coach: Craig Levein. *Assistant Coach:* Peter Houston. *Coach:* John McGlynn.
Physio: Alan Rae.
Managers since 1975: J. Hagart, W. Ormond, R. Moncur, T. Ford, A. MacDonald, A. MacDonald & W. Jardine, A. MacDonald, J. Jordan, S. Clark, T. McLean, J. Jefferies.
Club Nickname(s): Hearts, Jambo's. *Previous Grounds:* The Meadows 1874, Powderhall 1878, Old Tynecastle 1881, (Tynecastle Park, 1886).
Record Attendance: 53,396 v Rangers, Scottish Cup 3rd rd; 13 Feb, 1932.
Record Transfer Fee received: £2,100,000 for Alan McLaren from Rangers (October 1994).
Record of Transfer paid: £750,000 for Derek Ferguson to Rangers (July 1990).
Record Victory: 21-0 v Anchor, EFA Cup 30th October 1880.
Record Defeat: 1-8 v Vale of Leven, Scottish Cup, 1888.
Most Capped Player: Bobby Walker, 29, Scotland.
Most League Appearances: 515: Gary Mackay, 1980-97.
Most League Goals in Season (Individual): 44: Barney Battles.
Most Goals Overall (Individual): 214: John Robertson, 1983-98.

HEART OF MIDLOTHIAN 2000–01 LEAGUE RECORD

Match No.	Date		Venue	Opponents	Result	H/T Score	Lg. Pos.	Goalscorers	Atten- dance
1	Jul	30	H	Hibernian	D 0-0	0-0	—		17,132
2	Aug	6	A	St Johnstone	D 2-2	0-1	7	O'Neil [82], Tomaschek [88]	6165
3		13	A	Aberdeen	D 1-1	1-1	6	McSwegan [30]	11,139
4		19	H	Celtic	L 2-4	0-3	9	Severin [57], Juanjo [66]	16,744
5		27	A	Dundee	D 1-1	0-0	9	Cameron [86]	6779
6	Sept	9	H	Dunfermline Ath	W 2-0	1-0	7	Juanjo [7], McSwegan [63]	11,811
7		17	A	Rangers	L 0-1	0-0	8		47,496
8		20	H	St Mirren	W 2-0	0-0	—	McSwegan [46], Juanjo [67]	10,524
9		24	H	Kilmarnock	L 0-2	0-1	7		10,379
10	Oct	1	H	Motherwell	W 3-0	2-0	5	Durie 2 [12, 58], Kirk [27]	10,460
11		14	A	Dundee U	W 4-0	3-0	5	Tomaschek [8], Kirk 2 [24, 30], James [80]	7016
12		22	A	Hibernian	L 2-6	1-2	6	Kirk [5], Cameron [88]	12,926
13		28	H	St Johnstone	L 0-3	0-0	7		10,883
14	Nov	4	H	Aberdeen	W 3-0	1-0	5	Cameron [25], Severin [75], Kirk [88]	12,744
15		11	A	St Mirren	W 2-1	1-0	5	Cameron (pen) [21], Severin [81]	5234
16		18	A	Celtic	L 1-6	1-4	6	Cameron [13]	59,849
17		25	H	Dundee	W 3-1	0-1	5	McSwegan [52], Cameron 2 (1 pen) [87, 89 (p)]	11,539
18		29	A	Dunfermline Ath	L 0-1	0-1	—		5281
19	Dec	3	A	Rangers	L 0-1	0-1	5		16,710
20		9	A	Kilmarnock	W 3-0	1-0	5	Fulton [44], Kirk 2 [51, 55]	6828
21		16	A	Motherwell	L 0-2	0-0	5		5440
22		23	H	Dundee U	W 3-1	2-1	5	Cameron [3], Heaney (og) [18], McSwegan [73]	12,128
23		26	H	Hibernian	D 1-1	0-1	—	McSwegan [60]	17,619
24		30	A	St Johnstone	D 2-2	1-2	5	Kirk [5], Durie [77]	5173
25	Jan	2	A	Aberdeen	L 0-1	0-1	—		12,760
26		31	H	St Mirren	W 1-0	0-0	—	Cameron [75]	10,164
27	Feb	4	H	Celtic	L 0-3	0-1	5		13,077
28		24	H	Dunfermline Ath	W 7-1	4-0	5	Adam 3 [5, 9, 37], Cameron 2 [30, 46], Kirk [59], Tomaschek [67]	11,251
29	Mar	3	A	Rangers	L 0-2	0-1	5		49,003
30		14	H	Kilmarnock	W 3-0	0-0	—	Flögel [72], Juanjo [76], Severin [89]	9195
31		18	A	Dundee	D 0-0	0-0	5		7327
32		31	H	Motherwell	W 3-0	1-0	4	Tomaschek [15], Kirk 2 [63, 80]	11,581
33	Apr	7	A	Dundee U	D 1-1	0-1	5	Wales [65]	7242
34		22	A	Celtic	L 0-1	0-1	5		58,708
35		27	A	Kilmarnock	D 1-1	0-0	5	Kirk [49]	6867
36	May	5	H	Rangers	L 1-4	0-1	5	Adam [46]	15,315
37		12	A	Hibernian	D 0-0	0-0	5		8512
38		20	H	Dundee	W 2-0	0-0	5	Adam [52], Cameron [70]	13,554

Final League Position: 5

Honours
League Champions: Division I 1894-95, 1896-97, 1957-58, 1959-60. First Division 1979-80; *Runners-up:* Division I 1893-94, 1898-99, 1903-04, 1905-06, 1914-15, 1937-38, 1953-54, 1956-57, 1958-59, 1964-65. Premier Division 1985-86, 1987-88, 1991-92. First Division 1977-78, 1982-83.
Scottish Cup Winners: 1891, 1896, 1901, 1906, 1956, 1998; *Runners-up:* 1903, 1907, 1968, 1976, 1986, 1996.
League Cup Winners: 1954-55, 1958-59, 1959-60, 1962-63; *Runners-up:* 1961-62, 1996-97.

European: *European Cup:* 4 matches (1958-59, 1960-61). *Cup Winners' Cup:* 10 matches (1976-77, 1996-97, 1998-99).
UEFA Cup: 37 matches (*Fairs Cup:* 1961-62, 1963-64, 1965-66. *UEFA Cup:* 1984-85, 1986-87, 1988-89, 1990-91, 1992-93, 1993-94, 2000-01).

Club colours: Shirt: Maroon. Shorts: White. Stockings: Maroon with white tops.

Goalscorers: *League* (56): Cameron 12 (2 pens), Kirk 12, McSwegan 6, Adam 5, Juanjo 4, Severin 4, Tomaschek 4, Durie 3, Flögel 1, Fulton 1, James 1, O'Neil 1, Wales 1, own goal 1
Scottish Cup (4): Juanjo 2, McSwegan 1, Tomaschek 1
CIS Cup (4): Cameron 3 (2 pens), Naysmith 1

Niemi A 37	Pressley S 36	Naysmith G 9	Petric G 19	Flögel T 22 + 3	Severin S 26 + 3	Tomaschek R 22 + 6	Fulton S 23 + 1	Juanjo 23 + 14	Cameron C 37	Kirk A 27 + 4	McSwegan G 13 + 13	Simpson F 3 + 3	Jackson D 6 + 4	Makel L 10 + 3	O'Neil K — + 6	Locke G 7 + 6	Murray J 22 + 3	Neilson R 16 + 2	James K 4	Durie G 12 + 4	Adam S 5 + 1	Milne K 3 + 4	Simmons S — + 3	Goldie D 1	Boyack S 9 + 3	McAnespie K 3 + 2	McKenzie R 1	McCann A 10	Kaczan P — + 1	McKenna K 7 + 1	Wales G 2 + 5	Webster A 3 + 1	Match No.
1	2	3	4	5	6	7		8²	9	10	11¹	12	13																				1
1	2		4¹	3	6	7		8	9	10		12		5¹	11³	13	14																2
1	2	3		4	6	7		8²	9	12		10³		11	5¹	14	13																3
1	2	3		4	6	7		8	9	12		10		11¹	5¹	13																	4
1	2	3		4	6			8	9	11		10			5		7																5
1	2	3		4			7	9	11		10¹	13	8²		12		5	6															6
1	2	3	4	6			8	9	11²			10¹	7	13		12	5																7
1	2	3	4	6			7¹	9	11	13	10²	12	8				5																8
1	2	3	4	6				9	11		10	7²	8³		14	12	5¹	13															9
1	2	3	4	6				9¹	11	8²	14	12					7	5	10³	13													10
1	2		4	12		6	7²	9¹	11	8²	14	13					3	5	10														11
1	2		4³	3		6¹	7	9	11	8²	12	13					14	5	10														12
1	2		12	6	13	7	9²	11³	8					14			4	5	10³		3												13
1	2	4		7	12	8	9	11	10					6¹		5	3																14
1	2	4		7³	12	8	9	11	10²	13				6¹		5	3				14												15
1	2	4	14	7		8	9	11²	10	13				6¹		5	3¹	12															16
1	2	4		6	13	7²	9	11	12	8						5	3	10¹															17
1	2	4		5¹	12	7	9¹¹	11	8²	13						6	3	14	10														18
1	2	4¹		6²	13	7	9	11	8							5	3	10	12														19
1	2		5	6	7²	9	11¹	8	14					12	4	3	10³	13															20
1	2		5	6	7	9	11¹	8	13					14	4	3³	10²	12															21
1	2	4		7¹	6	8	9	12	11²	10					5				3	13													22
1	2	4		7²	6	8	9	13	11³	10					12	5			3¹	14													23
1	2	4			6	7¹	9	11	8	10					5	3		12															24
1	2		12	6	7¹	9	11	13	8²						5	4		10³		14	3												25
1	2	4	5	14	6	9	13	8	10²		12				3				7¹	11³													26
1	2	4	7¹	5	6	9	13	8	14						3			10³			12	11²											27
1	2		3	4	6	9	12	11		8²				5			13	10²			7¹	14											28
1	2		3	5	6	9	12	11		8							10¹				7²	13	1	4									29
1	2		3	6	7¹		10³	11²	13					5	8						12	9		4	14								30
1	2		8	7		9	10¹	11	13		6²			5							12			4	3								31
1	2		10¹		7²	9	13	11		6				3							8			4		5	12						32
1	2		10	13	7	9	14	11³		6¹				3²							8			4		5	12						33
1	2		3	7		9	12	11¹		6²							13				8			4		5¹	10	14					34
1	2		7			9	14	11		6³				5				10²			8³			4		12	13	3					35
1	2		3	7	6		9¹²	11		13							10³				8²			4		5	14						36
1			3	7¹	8		9	14	13					12	2			10³						4		5	11²	6					37
1			7³	6	13	9		11¹						14	2			10			8²			4		5	12	3					38

HIBERNIAN   Premier League

Year Formed: 1875. *Ground & Address:* Easter Road Stadium, Albion Rd, Edinburgh EH7 5QG. *Telephone:* 0131 661 2159. *Fax:* 0131 659 6488.
Ground Capacity: total: 17,500. *Size of Pitch:* 112yd × 74yd.
Managing Director: Rod Petrie. *Commercial Director:* Colin Deas.
Manager: Alex McLeish. *Assistant Manager:* Andrew Watson.
Physio: Malcolm Colquhoun. *Coach:* D. Park.
Managers since 1975: Eddie Turnbull, Willie Ormond, Bertie Auld, Pat Stanton, John Blackley, Alex Miller, Jim Duffy.
Club Nickname(s): Hibees. *Previous Grounds:* Meadows 1875-78, Powderhall 1878-79, Mayfield 1879-80, First Easter Road 1880-92, Second Easter Road 1892-.
Record Attendance: 65,860 v Hearts, Division I; 2 Jan, 1950.
Record Victory: 22-1 v 42nd Highlanders; 3 Sept, 1881.
Record Defeat: 0-10 v Rangers; 24 Dec, 1898.
Most Capped Player: Lawrie Reilly, 38, Scotland.
Most League Appearances: 446: Arthur Duncan.
Most League Goals in Season (Individual): 42: Joe Baker.
Most Goals Overall (Individual): 364: Gordon Smith.

HIBERNIAN 2000–01 LEAGUE RECORD

Match No.	Date		Venue	Opponents		Result	H/T Score	Lg. Pos.	Goalscorers	Atten- dance
1	Jul	30	A	Hearts	D	0-0	0-0	—		17,132
2	Aug	5	H	Dundee U	W	3-0	2-0	4	Agathe 2 [2, 19], McManus [90]	9613
3		12	H	Dundee	W	5-1	2-1	3	Agathe 2 [29, 41], Lehmann 2 [80, 82], Lovell [86]	12,730
4		16	A	Kilmarnock	W	1-0	1-0	—	Paatelainen [37]	8672
5		19	A	Aberdeen	W	2-0	1-0	1	Latapy (pen) [4], Paatelainen [77]	12,450
6		26	H	St Mirren	W	2-0	1-0	1	Lovell 2 [43, 89]	11,814
7	Sept	9	A	Celtic	L	0-3	0-2	2		60,040
8		16	H	Motherwell	W	2-0	0-0	2	Paatelainen 2 [48, 79]	9868
9		23	A	Dunfermline Ath	D	1-1	1-0	2	Latapy (pen) [21]	4017
10		30	A	St Johnstone	W	3-0	2-0	2	Sauzee [15], Zitelli [23], Latapy [73]	5464
11	Oct	14	H	Rangers	W	1-0	1-0	2	Zitelli [22]	14,524
12		22	H	Hearts	W	6-2	2-1	2	Paatelainen 3 [42, 44, 73], Zitelli [50], O'Neil [80], Latapy [83]	12,926
13		28	A	Dundee U	W	1-0	0-0	2	McManus [82]	8042
14	Nov	5	A	Dundee	W	2-1	1-1	2	O'Neil [17], Zitelli [62]	6602
15		11	H	Kilmarnock	D	1-1	1-0	2	Paatelainen [32]	12,588
16		18	H	Aberdeen	L	0-2	0-0	2		10,995
17		25	A	St Mirren	D	1-1	1-0	2	O'Neil [7]	5225
18		29	H	Celtic	D	0-0	0-0	—		14,939
19	Dec	3	A	Motherwell	W	3-1	1-0	2	Zitelli 2 [38, 55], Townsley (og) [49]	5715
20		9	H	Dunfermline Ath	W	3-0	1-0	2	Laursen [4], Zitelli [54], Paatelainen [69]	10,078
21		16	H	St Johnstone	W	2-0	1-0	2	Lovell [39], Paatelainen [73]	10,374
22		23	A	Rangers	L	0-1	0-0	2		49,993
23		26	A	Hearts	D	1-1	1-0	—	Lovell [41]	17,619
24		30	H	Dundee U	W	1-0	0-0	2	Latapy (pen) [90]	10,197
25	Jan	2	H	Dundee	W	3-0	2-0	—	Paatelainen [7], Fenwick [41], O'Neil [70]	12,381
26		30	A	Kilmarnock	D	1-1	0-0	—	Laursen [87]	6385
27	Feb	10	H	St Mirren	W	4-2	1-1	2	Sauzee [17], Zitelli 2 [59, 61], Latapy [80]	8799
28		25	A	Celtic	D	1-1	1-0	3	Murray [84]	59,791
29	Mar	4	A	Motherwell	D	1-1	0-0	3	Latapy [81]	8225
30		13	A	Aberdeen	L	0-1	0-1	—		8799
31		17	A	Dunfermline Ath	L	1-2	0-1	3	Murray [87]	7154
32	Apr	1	A	St Johnstone	L	0-2	0-0	3		4346
33		8	H	Rangers	D	0-0	0-0	3		9704
34		21	H	Kilmarnock	D	1-1	1-1	3	Libbra [34]	8113
35		29	A	Dundee	W	2-0	0-0	3	Libbra [54], Zitelli [66]	6659
36	May	6	H	Celtic	L	2-5	0-2	3	Libbra 2 [84, 87]	8879
37		12	H	Hearts	D	0-0	0-0	3		8512
38		20	A	Rangers	L	0-4	0-2	3		47,023

Final League Position: 3

Honours
League Champions: Division I 1902-03, 1947-48, 1950-51, 1951-52. First Division 1980-81, 1998-99. Division II 1893-94, 1894-95, 1932-33; *Runners-up:* Division I 1896-97, 1946-47, 1949-50, 1952-53, 1973-74, 1974-75.
Scottish Cup Winners: 1887, 1902; *Runners-up:* 1896, 1914, 1923, 1924, 1947, 1958, 1972, 1979, 2001.
League Cup Winners: 1972-73, 1991-92; *Runners-up:* 1950-51, 1968-69, 1974-75, 1993-94.

European: *European Cup:* 6 matches (1955-56 semi-finals). *Cup Winners' Cup:* 6 matches (1972-73). *UEFA Cup:* 59 matches (*Fairs Cup:* 1960-61 semi-finals, 1961-62, 1962-63, 1965-66, 1967-68, 1968-69, 1970-71. *UEFA Cup:* 1973-74, 1974-75, 1975-76, 1976-77, 1978-79, 1989-90, 1992-93).

Club colours: Shirt: Green with white sleeves. Shorts: White. Stockings: Green with white trim.

Goalscorers: *League* (57): Paatelainen 11, Zitelli 10, Latapy 7 (3 pens), Lovell 5, Agathe 4, Libbra 4, O'Neil 4, Laursen 2, Lehmann 2, McManus 2, Murray 2, Sauzee 2, Fenwick 1, own goal 1
Scottish Cup (13): O'Neil 3, Lehmann 2, McManus 2, Sauzee 2, Jack 1, Laursen 1, Paatelainen 1, Zitelli 1
CIS Cup (5): Latapy 3, Lehmann 1, McManus 1

Colgan N 37	Laursen U 29	Smith T 8	Smith G 37	Fenwick P 31	Jack M 37	Sauzee F 33	Latapy R 31 + 2	O'Neil J 33	Paatelainen M 32 + 4	Agathe D 5	McManus T 3 + 14	Lehmann D 9 + 21	Murray I 11 + 10	Lovell S 30 + 1	McIntosh M 4	Bannerman S — + 2	Zitelli D 24 + 7	Brebner G 5 + 6	Sar-Temsoury H — + 1	Andrews L 4 + 7	Franks M 1 + 1	Libbra M 7 + 3	Dempsie M 1	Arpinen F 6 + 1	O'Connor G — + 1	Match No.
1	2	3	4	5	6	7	8	9	10	11[1]	12															1
1	2[3]	3	4	5	6	7	8	9	10[1]	11[3]	14	12	13													2
1	2[3]	3	4	5	6[1]	7	8	9	10[2]	11		13	14	12												3
1	2	3	4		6	7	8	9	10	11[1]	12				5											4
1	2[1]	5	3		6[2]	7	8	9	10	11[3]	14				4	12	13									5
1	2	3	4	5		7	8	9	10		12			11[1]	6											6
1	5		3	2	6		8	9	10		12			7[2]			11[1]	13								7
1	5		3	2	6	4	8	9[1]	10			11		7			12									8
1	5[1]		3	2	6	4	8	9	10[2]			11	12	7			13									9
1	5		3	2	6[2]	4	8	9	10[1]			13	14	7			11[3]			12						10
1	5		3	2	6	4	8	9	10			12		7			11[1]									11
1	5		3	2	6[1]	4	8	9	10					7			11			12						12
1	5		3	2	6	4	8	9	10[1]			13	12	7			11[2]									13
1	5		3	2	6	4	8	9	10			12		7			11[1]									14
1	5		3	2	6	4[1]	8	9	10[2]			13	12	7			11									15
1	5[1]		3	2	6	4	8	9	10[2]				13	7			11			12						16
1	4		3	2	5		8	9	10[2]		12	13	6	7			11[1]									17
1[1]	5		3	2	6	4	8	9	10			12		7			11[1]				15					18
	5[1]		3	2	6	4	8	9	10[3]		14	13	12	7			11[2]		1							19
1	5		3	2	6	4	8[3]	9	10[1]		12	13		7			11[2]			14						20
1	5		3	2	6[1]	4	8	9	10					7			11			12						21
1	5[2]		3	2	6	4	8[3]	9	10		12	13		7			11[1]			14						22
1	5[1]		3	2	6	4	8		10			12		7			11	9								23
1	5		3	2	6	4	8	9	10[1]		12	13		7			11[2]									24
1	5		3	2	6[2]	4	8[1]	9	10[3]		14	13		7			11			12						25
1	5		3	2		4	8		10					7	13	12	11[1]	6		9[5]						26
1	5		3	2	6	4	8	9	10			12		7			11[1]									27
1	5		3[1]	2	6	4		9	10		13	12		7[2]			11	8								28
1	5		3	2		4[2]	8	9	10[1]		14		6	7			11[3]	13		12						29
1		3		2	12		9	10				13	14	5	7		4[3]	8		6[5]		11[2]				30
1		3		2			9	10				11[2]		5	7		13	8	6[1]			12	4			31
1	5		3	2	6[2]	4	8	12	10[1]		14						11	13				9		7[3]		32
1	5		3	2	6[1]	4	8		10			13		7			11[3]	12				14		9[2]		33
1			3	5	4		9	12	10[1]			13	6	7[2]	14		11[3]	8								34
1			3	5	4		12	13	10				2	7[1]			11[2]	8				9[2]		6	14	35
1			3	5[2]	4		8	9	10[1]				2	7			11	12				13		6		36
1			3	5	4		9		10			11	2	7			13	12				8[2]		6[1]		37
1	5		3[3]	4			9		13		14		6	7			11	12				10[2]		8[1]		38

INVERNESS CALEDONIAN THISTLE
First Division

Year Formed: 1994. *Ground & Address:* Caledonian Stadium, East Longman, Inverness IV1 1FF. *Telephone:* 01463 222880.
Ground Capacity: 6500, seated: 2200. *Size of Pitch:* 115yd × 75yd.
Chairman: David Sutherland. *Hon. Presidents:* John S. McDonald and Norman Miller. *Secretary:* Jim Falconer.
Manager: Steven W. Paterson. *Assistant Manager:* Duncan Shearer. *Coach:* John Docherty. *Physio:* Ian Manning.
Record Attendance: 6290 v Aberdeen, Scottish Cup, 20 February 2000.
Record Victory: 8-1, v Annan Ath, Scottish Cup 3rd rd, 24 January 1998.
Record Defeat: 1-5, v Morton, First Division, 12 November 1999 and v Airdrieonians, First Division, 15 April 2000.
Most League Appearances: 231, Charlie Christie, 1995-2001.
Most League Goals in Season: 27, Ian Stewart, 1996-97.
Most Goals Overall (Individual): 70, Ian Stewart, 1995-2001.

INVERNESS CALEDONIAN THISTLE 2000–01 LEAGUE RECORD

Match No.	Date	Venue	Opponents	Result	H/T Score	Lg. Pos.	Goalscorers	Attendance
1	Aug 5	H	Airdrieonians	W 2-0	1-0	—	Tokely [14], Xausa [83]	2366
2	12	A	Livingston	L 1-3	0-1	5	Stewart [75]	3838
3	19	H	Falkirk	L 2-3	0-2	6	Bavidge 2 [53, 79]	2132
4	26	A	Raith R	L 1-4	0-1	8	Stewart [59]	1615
5	Sept 9	H	Clyde	L 1-2	1-0	10	Bagan [16]	1484
6	16	H	Ross Co	L 0-1	0-0	9		4823
7	23	A	Alloa Ath	W 4-1	2-0	8	Robson [14], Sheerin [39], Xausa [74], Bavidge [84]	584
8	30	A	Ayr U	D 3-3	0-1	8	Xausa [62], Sheerin [85], Mann [89]	2070
9	Oct 7	H	Morton	W 4-0	2-0	6	McBain [32], Bavidge 2 [44, 77], Bagan [81]	1439
10	14	A	Airdrieonians	W 2-1	0-0	6	Sheerin [61], Xausa [86]	1555
11	21	H	Livingston	D 2-2	0-1	6	McBain [54], Sheerin [83]	2147
12	28	A	Raith R	L 1-2	0-2	6	Sheerin [79]	1723
13	Nov 4	A	Clyde	D 1-1	1-0	6	Wyness [6]	935
14	11	H	Alloa Ath	W 2-1	1-0	5	Teasdale [32], Sheerin [79]	1384
15	18	A	Ross Co	W 3-0	1-0	5	Wyness 2 [36, 72], Teasdale [56]	5761
16	25	A	Morton	L 0-2	0-2	5		708
17	Dec 2	H	Ayr U	W 7-3	3-2	4	Teasdale [8], Sheerin (pen) [17], Wyness 3 [42, 79, 86], Bagan 2 [58, 73]	1513
18	9	A	Falkirk	D 2-2	0-2	4	Wyness [66], Sheerin [82]	2136
19	16	H	Airdrieonians	W 4-0	2-0	4	Bagan [7], Christie [42], Xausa [62], Wyness [72]	1570
20	23	H	Clyde	D 2-2	1-0	4	Bagan [45], Xausa [79]	1588
21	Jan 2	H	Ross Co	D 3-3	1-3	—	Sheerin [12], Wyness 2 [89, 90]	5291
22	6	A	Alloa Ath	D 1-1	1-0	4	Xausa [25]	744
23	13	A	Ayr U	D 1-1	1-1	4	Wyness [21]	2534
24	Feb 3	H	Falkirk	D 1-1	1-0	4	Wyness [67]	1913
25	Mar 10	A	Raith R	D 1-1	0-0	4	Wyness [51]	1342
26	13	H	Morton	W 4-2	2-1	—	Wyness 3 [3, 50, 56], Bagan [28]	1016
27	17	H	Alloa Ath	W 2-0	0-0	4	Wyness [51], Robson [86]	1613
28	23	H	Raith R	W 2-0	0-0	4	Wyness 2 [53, 80]	1299
29	27	A	Clyde	D 2-2	1-2	—	Bagan [11], Wyness [53]	657
30	31	A	Ross Co	W 1-0	1-0	3	McBain [39]	5876
31	Apr 3	A	Livingston	L 1-4	0-1	—	Wyness [78]	2136
32	7	A	Morton	W 3-0	1-0	3	Christie [17], Wyness [77], MacDonald [88]	931
33	14	H	Ayr U	W 1-0	0-0	3	Mann [81]	2269
34	21	A	Airdrieonians	D 1-1	0-0	3	Wyness [71]	805
35	28	H	Livingston	L 2-3	1-2	3	Sheerin 2 (2 pens) [17 (p), 90 (p)]	2824
36	May 5	A	Falkirk	L 1-2	0-2	4	Wyness [71]	2230

Final League Position: 4

Honours
Scottish Cup: Quarter-finals 1996.
League Champions: Third Division 1996-97; *Runners-up:* Second Division 1998-99.
Bell's League Challenge Cup runners-up: 1999-2000.

Club colours: Shirts: Royal blue with red stripes. Shorts: Blue. Stockings: Blue.

Goalscorers: *League* (71): Wyness 24, Sheerin 11 (3 pens), Bagan 8, Xausa 7, Bavidge 5, McBain 3, Teasdale 3, Christie 2, Mann 2, Robson 2, Stewart 2, McDonald 1, Tokely 1
Scottish Cup (6): Xausa 2, Mann 1, Robson 1, Sheerin 1, Wyness 1
CIS Cup (3): Mann 1, Stewart 1, Xausa 1
Bell's League Cup (4): Bavidge 2, Stewart 2

Fridge L 8	Tokely R 25+5	Golabek S 16	Mann R 33	Hastings R 21	Byers K 4+9	Bagan D 29+5	Xausa D 16+6	Stewart I 4+2	Christie C 31+4	Wyness D 28+3	Bavidge M 23+7	Sheerin P 33	Robson B 13+12	McBain R 30+3	Calder J 28	McCaffrey S 31	Teasdale M 17+8	Munro G 4	Graham D —+2	MacDonald N 1+4	Stewart G 1+1	Match No.
1	2	3	4	5	6	7	8	9^{1}	10	11	12											1
1	2	3	4	5	7^{2}		8	12	10	11	9^{1}	6	13									2
1	2	3	4	5	13	12		9	10^{2}	7^{1}	8	6^{1}	11	14								3
1	2	3	4	5	7			8	9	10		6^{1}	12	11								4
	2	3	4		14	7^{1}	8^{2}	13	10	9^{2}	12	6	11		1	5						5
	7			13	14	8	9^{2}		10		12	6^{1}	11	3	1	4	2^{3}	5				6
	7^{1}	3		5		12	8		13	9		6	11	10	1	4	2					7
	2	3	5			7	8		12		9	6	11	10^{1}	1	4						8
	2	3	4			7			10		9	6	11	8	1	5						9
	2	3	5			7^{1}	12		10	9		6	11	8	1	4						10
	2	3	4			7^{2}	8^{3}	12	14	9		6	11^{1}	10	1	5	13					11
		3	2			7	8^{1}		10	12	9	6		11	1	5	4					12
		3	5		12	7			10^{1}	8	9	6		11	1	4	2					13
	12	3	5			7	8^{1}		10	9		6		11	1	4	2					14
	13	3	5^{2}			7	12		10^{1}	8	9	6		11	1	4	2					15
	4	5	3		14	7^{2}		12	10	8	9^{1}	6	13	11^{2}	1		2					16
	13	5	3			7		12	10	8	9^{1}	6	14	11^{3}	1	4	2^{2}					17
	13	5	3			7		12	10	8	9^{1}	6		11	1	4	2^{2}					18
		5	3			7	9^{1}		10	8	12	6		11	1	4	2					19
	13	5	3			7	9		10	8		6^{1}	12	11	1	4	2^{2}					20
1	3	5				7			10	9	8^{1}	6	12	11		4	2					21
1		5	3			7	8^{1}		10	9	12	6		11		4	2					22
1		5	3			7	8^{1}		10	9		6^{2}	13	11		4	2		12			23
1	2	5	3			7	8^{1}		10	9		6		11		4			12			24
	2	5	3			7^{1}		13	10	9	8^{2}	6	12	11	1	4						25
	2^{2}	5	3			7	8		10	9		6	12	11^{1}	1	4	13					26
	2^{3}	5	3		13	7^{2}			10	9	8	6	12	11^{1}	1	4	14					27
	2	5	3		13	7^{2}			10	9	8^{3}	6	12	11	1	4	14					28
	2	5	3^{1}			7		13		9	8^{2}	6	10	11	1	4	12					29
	2	5	3			7			10	9^{2}	8^{1}	6	12	11	1	4	13					30
	2	5	3			7^{2}			10	9	13	6^{1}	8	11	1	4	12					31
	2	6	5			12			10	9^{2}	8^{1}		11	14	1	4	7^{3}	3		13		32
	2	5	3			7		13		9^{2}	8^{1}	6	10	11	1	4	12					33
	11	5		14					10^{1}	9	13	6	12		1	4	2	3		8^{2}	7^{3}	34
	3	5	12			7^{2}			10^{1}	9	8^{2}	6		11	1	4	2			14	13	35
	2	5		14		7			10	9	8^{2}	6^{3}		11	1	4	12		3^{1}	13		36

KILMARNOCK

Premier League

Year Formed: 1869. *Ground & Address:* Rugby Park, Kilmarnock KA1 2DP. *Telephone:* 01563 545300. *Fax:* 01563 522181. *Website:* www.kilmarnockfc.co.uk.
Ground Capacity: all seated: 18,128. *Size of Pitch:* 114yd × 72yd.
Chairman: J. Orr. *Secretary:* Kevin Collins. *Commercial Manager:* J. McSherry. *Stadium Manager:* Bobby Williamson.
Assistant Managers: Jim Clark, Gerry McCabe. *Physio:* A. MacFie.
Managers since 1975: W. Fernie, D. Sneddon, J. Clunie, E. Morrison, J. Fleeting, T. Burns, A. Totten. *Club Nickname(s):* Killie. *Previous Grounds:* Rugby Park (Dundonald Road); The Grange; Holm Quarry; Present ground since 1899.
Record Attendance: 35,995 v Rangers, Scottish Cup; 10 March, 1962.
Record Transfer Fee received: £300,000 for Shaun McSkimming to Motherwell (1995).
Record Transfer Fee paid: £300,000 for Paul Wright from St Johnstone (1995).
Record Victory: 11-1 v Paisley Academical, Scottish Cup; 18 Jan, 1930 (15-0 v Lanemark, Ayrshire Cup; 15 Nov, 1890).
Record Defeat: 1-9 v Celtic, Division I; 13 Aug, 1938.
Most Capped Player: Joe Nibloe, 11, Scotland.
Most League Appearances: 481: Alan Robertson, 1972-88.
Most League Goals in Season (Individual): 34: Harry 'Peerie' Cunningham 1927-28 and Andy Kerr 1960-61.
Most Goals Overall (Individual): 148: W. Culley; 1912-23.

KILMARNOCK 2000–01 LEAGUE RECORD

Match No.	Date		Venue	Opponents	Result		H/T Score	Lg. Pos.	Goalscorers	Attendance
1	Jul	29	A	St Mirren	W	1-0	0-0	—	Holt [71]	7388
2	Aug	5	H	Rangers	L	2-4	2-1	6	McLaren 2 (1 pen) [3 (pl. 9)]	14,680
3		13	A	Celtic	L	1-2	1-0	7	McLaren [17]	57,258
4		16	H	Hibernian	L	0-1	0-1	—		8672
5		19	H	Motherwell	W	3-2	1-1	5	Dargo [25], Wright (pen) [77], Dindeleux [80]	6533
6		26	A	St Johnstone	D	1-1	1-1	6	McLaren [14]	3773
7	Sept	9	H	Dundee U	W	1-0	1-0	4	Mitchell [30]	6380
8		16	H	Aberdeen	W	1-0	1-0	4	Mitchell [26]	6876
9		24	A	Hearts	W	2-0	1-0	4	Wright [5], Dindeleux [47]	10,379
10		30	A	Dundee	D	0-0	0-0	4		6170
11	Oct	14	H	Dunfermline Ath	W	2-1	1-1	4	Wright (pen) [39], Holt [84]	6454
12		21	H	St Mirren	W	2-1	0-1	3	McLaren [47], Mahood [58]	7839
13		28	A	Rangers	W	3-0	2-0	3	Cocard [5], Holt [32], Numan (og) [67]	49,659
14	Nov	5	H	Celtic	L	0-1	0-0	3		13,412
15		11	A	Hibernian	D	1-1	0-1	4	Wright [85]	12,588
16		18	H	Motherwell	W	2-1	1-1	3	Wright [37], Cocard [87]	6571
17		25	H	St Johnstone	L	0-2	0-0	4		6330
18		28	A	Dundee U	W	1-0	0-0	—	de Vos (og) [77]	5497
19	Dec	2	A	Aberdeen	W	2-1	2-1	3	McLaren [38], Fowler [39]	11,584
20		9	H	Hearts	L	0-3	0-1	4		6828
21		16	H	Dundee	L	2-3	1-0	4	Cocard [4], Baker [46]	6573
22		23	A	Dunfermline Ath	L	0-1	0-1	4		5337
23		26	H	St Mirren	W	3-1	0-1	—	Wright 3 [66, 85, 90]	8142
24	Jan	2	A	Celtic	L	0-6	0-1	—		59,103
25		30	H	Hibernian	D	1-1	0-0	—	Hay [67]	6385
26	Feb	3	H	Motherwell	L	1-2	0-1	4	Dargo [90]	6018
27		11	A	St Johnstone	W	2-1	0-0	4	Dargo [69], Canero [90]	6627
28		24	H	Dundee U	D	0-0	0-0	4		6289
29	Mar	3	A	Aberdeen	D	0-0	0-0	4		6577
30		14	A	Hearts	L	0-3	0-0	—		9195
31		31	A	Dundee	D	2-2	1-1	5	Dargo [7], Mahood [74]	6719
32	Apr	7	H	Dunfermline Ath	W	2-1	1-0	4	McCoist [44], MacPherson [68]	6529
33		11	A	Rangers	L	1-2	0-2	—	Hay [74]	14,585
34		21	A	Hibernian	D	1-1	1-1	4	Cocard [11]	8113
35		27	H	Hearts	D	1-1	0-0	4	McGowne [53]	6867
36	May	5	A	Dundee	L	1-2	0-1	4	Dargo [88]	6261
37		12	A	Rangers	L	1-5	0-1	4	Dargo [69]	46,577
38		20	H	Celtic	W	1-0	0-0	4	Mahood [78]	12,578

Final League Position: 4

Honours
League Champions: Division I 1964-65. Division II 1897-98, 1898-99; *Runners-up:* Division I 1959-60, 1960-61, 1962-63, 1963-64. First Division 1975-76, 1978-79, 1981-82, 1992-93. Division II 1953-54, 1973-74. Second Division 1989-90.
Scottish Cup Winners: 1920, 1929, 1997; *Runners-up:* 1898, 1932, 1938, 1957, 1960.
League Cup Runners-up: 1952-53, 1960-61, 1962-63, 2000-01.

European: *European Cup:* 4 matches (1965-66). *Cup Winners' Cup:* 4 matches (1997-98). *UEFA Cup:* 20 matches (*Fairs Cup:* 1964-65, 1966-67, 1969-70, 1970-71, *UEFA Cup:* 1998-99, 1999-2000).

Club colours: Shirt: Blue and white vertical stripes. Shorts: Blue. Stockings: Blue.

Goalscorers: *League* (44): Wright 8 (2 pen), Dargo 6, McLaren 6 (1 pen), Cocard 4, Holt 3, Mahood 3, Dindeleux 2, Hay 2, Mitchell 2, Baker 1, Canero 1, Fowler 1, McCoist 1, McGowne 1, MacPherson 1, own goals 2
Scottish Cup (4): Hay 1, McGowne 1, Mitchell 1, Wright 1
CIS Cup (6): Dargo 2, McLaren 2, Canero 1, McCoist 1

Marshall G 31	MacPherson A 32	Baker M 14	McGowne K 20	Dindeleux F 35	Mahood A 33 + 1	Holt G 19	Durrant I 12 + 2	McLaren A 30 + 2	Cocard C 16 + 17	Varelile J 2 + 7	Canero P 16 + 12	Wright P 15 + 10	Di Giacomo P 2 + 7	Hay G 27 + 4	McCoist A 11 + 7	Hessey S 6	Fowler J 3 + 11	Mitchell A 25 + 1	Dargo C 16 + 9	Innes C 23 + 1	Reilly M 11 + 3	Davidson S 2	Meldrum C 7 + 1	Sanjuan J 3	Canning M — + 1	Calderon A 7	Boyd K — + 1	Match No.
1	2	3	4	5	6^1	7	8	9^3	10^2	11	12	13	14															1
1	2	3	4	5	6	7		9^3	10^1	11^2	8			14	12	13												2
1	2	3		5	6^3	7		11	14	12	9	13			10^2	4	8^1											3
1	2^3		4	5	12	7		11			9	6	13		10^2	3	8^1	14										4
1	2	3		5	6	7		9^3		13	8	12			10^1	4	14	11^2										5
1	2^3			5	6	7	12	9		13	11^1			3	10		8	4										6
1	2			5	6	7^1	14	9	13		12	11^2		3	10^3		8	4										7
1	2			5	6		8^3	9	12	14	11^2			3	10^1	13	7	4										8
1	2			5	6	7^3	8	11^2	12		10^1			3	14	9	13	4										9
1	2			5	6	7	8^2		13		11^1			3	10	9	12	4										10
1	2			5	6	7	8^2	11^3	13		14	10^1		3	9		12	4										11
1	2			5	6	7	8^3	11^2	13		14	10^1		3	9		12	4										12
1	2			5	6	7	8^2	11^3	10^1	12				3	13	9	14	4										13
1	2			5	6		8	11^3	10^2	12	14			3	7^1	9	13	4										14
1	2			5	6		8	11	10^2	7^1	13			3	9	12	4										15
1	2	4		5	6		8	9	13	12	10^1			3	7	11^2												16
1	2	4		5	6		8	9^3	13	14	10^2			3	12	7^1	11											17
1	2	4			6		8^1	9	13	14	10^2			3	5	12	7	11^3										18
1	2				6			9	10	13	8			3	4	12	7^1	11^2	5									19
1	2	5			6			9	10^1	13	12	14		3	4	8^2	11^3	7										20
1	3	2	5	6				9^2	12	8	10^1			14	13	11	4	7^3										21
1	3^1	2	5	6				11	10^2		8	14	12		13	4	7^3	9										22
1		2	4	6	7			9	12	8	10			3	11			5^1										23
1		2	4^2	6	7			9	8	5	10^1			3	12			11^3	13	14								24
1	2	3		5	6^1	7		11^2		8	13	12		9	10		4											25
1	2	6	5^2		7			11	13		8^3	14	3^1		12	9	10	4										26
1	2	3	4	5		7		9	12		6	10^1			8	11												27
1	2	3	4	5	6^1				12		9	10^1			8	11		6										28
1	2	3	4	5	6^1			10		9	13	12			8	11^2		7										29
1	2^1		5	8	7			11^3	13		6	10^2	14	3				4	9	12	1		9^1	13				30
	2		4	5	7			14						3	10^3			8^2	11	6	12		1	9^1	13			31
	2		4	5	7			11^3	14		12		13	3	10^2				6	8		1				9^1		32
	2		4	5	7			11	12			14	3	10^3		13			6^1	8		1				9^2		33
	2		4	5	7			11	10^1				3	12	13	8			6			1				9^2		34
	2		4	5	7^2			11	10^1				3	12		8			6	13		1				9		35
	2		4	5				11	10^1				3	13		8	12		6^1	7		1				9		36
	2			5	7			12					13	3		8^1	10	4	6			1		11		9^2		37
1	2^2		4	5	7			12				11^3	3	10^1		13			6				8		9	14		38

LIVINGSTON

Premier League

Year Formed: 1974. *Ground:* West Lothian Courier Stadium, Alderton Road, Livingston EH54 7DN. *Telephone:* 01506 417000. *Fax:* 01506 418888. *Email:* livingstonfc@btinternet.com.
Ground Capacity: 10,004 (all seated). *Size of Pitch:* 105yd × 72yd.
Chairman: Dominic Keane. *Secretary:* J. R. S. Renton.
Team Manager: Jim Leishman. *Head Coach:* David Hay. *First Team Coach:* John Robertson. *Physios:* Michael McBride and Arthur Duncan.
Managers since 1975: John Bain, Alec Ness, Willie MacFarlane, Terry Christie, Michael Lawson. *Club Nickname:* Livi Lions. *Previous Grounds:* None.
Record Attendance: 6289 v Aberdeen, Scottish Cup; 17 Feb, 2001.
Record Transfer Fee received: £115,000 for John Inglis to St Johnstone (1990).
Record Transfer Fee paid: £28,000 for Victor Kasule from Albion Rovers (1987).
Record Victory: 7-0 v Queen of the South, Scottish Cup; 29 Jan, 2000.
Record Defeat: 0-8 v Hamilton A. Division II; 14 Dec, 1974.
Most Capped Player (under 18): I. Little.
Most League Appearances: 446: Walter Boyd, 1979-89.
Most League Goals in Season (Individual): 21: John McGachie, 1986-87. *(Team):* 69; Second Division, 1986-87.
Most Goals Overall (Individual): 64: David Roseburgh, 1986-93.

LIVINGSTON 2000–01 LEAGUE RECORD

Match No.	Date	Venue	Opponents	Result		H/T Score	Lg. Pos.	Goalscorers	Attendance
1	Aug 5	A	Morton	W	2-0	0-0	—	McCulloch [59], Bingham [84]	1729
2	12	H	Inverness CT	W	3-1	1-0	2	Deas [24], Crabbe [49], Wilson [85]	3838
3	19	A	Clyde	D	1-1	0-0	2	Anderson [73]	1781
4	26	A	Alloa Ath	W	6-0	1-0	1	Bingham [35], McCulloch 2 [53, 79], Hagen [62], Fleming [74], McCormick [84]	983
5	Sept 9	H	Ayr U	W	2-0	1-0	1	Wilson [4], Bingham [49]	5271
6	16	H	Raith R	L	0-4	0-3	1		3961
7	23	A	Airdrieonians	W	2-1	0-0	1	Anderson [48], Bingham (pen) [57]	1826
8	30	A	Falkirk	L	2-3	2-0	1	Coughlan [18], Burns [26]	3547
9	Oct 7	H	Ross Co	W	3-1	1-0	1	Keith 2 [40, 54], Bingham (pen) [70]	3466
10	14	H	Morton	W	1-0	1-0	1	Bingham (pen) [44]	3468
11	21	A	Inverness CT	D	2-2	1-0	2	McCulloch 2 [31, 58]	2147
12	28	H	Alloa Ath	W	4-0	2-0	2	Andrews [29], Bingham 2 (2 pens) [42 (p), 84 (p)], Burns [75]	3149
13	Nov 4	A	Ayr U	D	1-1	1-1	2	Fleming [34]	3082
14	11	H	Airdrieonians	D	2-2	2-1	2	Keith [10], Burns [12]	3915
15	25	A	Ross Co	W	2-0	1-0	1	Burns [14], Bingham [79]	2723
16	Dec 2	H	Falkirk	W	4-1	3-0	1	Wilson [9], Coughlan [24], Burns [40], Bingham [80]	4464
17	5	A	Raith R	W	2-1	2-0	—	Bingham 2 [18, 38]	1626
18	9	H	Clyde	W	2-0	1-0	1	Crabbe [17], Tosh [63]	3230
19	16	A	Morton	W	2-1	0-1	1	Britton [72], Burns [96]	888
20	Jan 2	H	Raith R	W	2-0	2-0	—	Bingham [7], Burns [24]	3305
21	6	A	Airdrieonians	D	1-1	1-0	1	Crabbe [44]	2382
22	13	A	Falkirk	L	0-1	0-1	1		4914
23	30	A	Alloa Ath	W	2-0	1-0	—	Wilson [21], Anderson [52]	684
24	Feb 3	A	Clyde	W	3-0	2-0	1	McPhee [18], Wilson 2 (1 pen) [44 (p), 83]	2506
25	24	H	Alloa Ath	W	1-0	0-0	1	Bingham [63]	3014
26	Mar 3	A	Ayr U	D	1-1	1-0	1	Wilson (pen) [16]	2726
27	20	H	Ayr U	L	0-1	0-1	—		2731
28	27	H	Ross Co	D	1-1	1-1	—	Wilson [32]	1736
29	31	A	Raith R	L	0-2	0-1	2		1794
30	Apr 3	H	Inverness CT	W	4-1	1-0	—	Xausa 2 [20, 75], Wilson 2 [60, 86]	2136
31	7	A	Ross Co	W	1-0	0-0	1	Wilson [53]	2549
32	21	H	Morton	W	2-0	1-0	1	Xausa [27], Fleming [83]	2727
33	24	H	Falkirk	W	3-0	1-0	—	Fernandez [20], Wilson [42], Jackson [74]	3659
34	28	A	Inverness CT	W	3-2	2-1	1	Fernandez 2 [30, 52], Wilson (pen) [42]	2824
35	May 1	A	Airdrieonians	W	5-0	4-0	—	Britton 3 [5, 11, 68], McPhee [20], Crabbe [44]	3295
36	5	A	Clyde	L	0-2	0-1	1		6835

Final League Position: 1

Honours

League Champions: First Division: Champions: 2000-01. Second Division 1986-87, 1998-99. Third Division 1995-96; *Runners-up:* Second Division 1982-83. First Division 1987-88.
Scottish Cup: —. *League Cup:* Semi-finals 1984-85. *B&Q Cup:* Semi-finals 1992-93, 1993-94, 2001.
Bell's Challenge Cup Runners-up: 2000-01.

Club colours: Shirt: Gold, black and white trim, black band. Shorts: Black, gold and white trim. Stockings: Gold.

Goalscorers: *League* (72): Bingham 14 (5 pens), Wilson B 13 (3 pens), Burns 7, McCulloch 5, Britton 4, Crabbe 4, Anderson 3, Fernandez 3, Fleming 3, Keith 3, Xausa 3, Coughlan 2, McPhee 2, Andrews 1, Deas 1, Hagan 1, Jackson 1, McCormick 1, Tosh 1
Scottish Cup (8): Anderson 2, Bingham 2, Wilson B 2, Britton 1, Crabbe 1
CIS Cup (4): Bingham 2, Hagan 2
Bell's League Cup (12): Britton 4, Anderson 2, Bingham 2 (1 pen), Crabbe 1, Keith 1, McCormick 1, Wilson B 1

Alexander N 26	McManus A 11+1	Deas P 19+5	Dolan J 6+2	Coughlan G 21	Anderson J 30	Wilson B 34+1	Keith M 7+4	Crabbe S 17+11	McCulloch M 35	Bingham D 33	McPhee B 7+16	Fleming D 24+4	Hagan D 8+12	Britton G 3+9	McCormick M —+5	Sweeney S 1	Smith G —+2	Burns A 20+4	Hart M 16+6	Tosh S 24	Andrews M 13	McCaldon I 5+1	Jackson D 8+1	Madsen J —+1	Brinquin P 11	Fernandez D 6+2	Broto F 5+1	McEwan D —+1	Ormiston D —+1	Match No.
1	2	3	4	5	6	7^1	8^2	9	10	11	12	13																		1
1	2	3	4	5	6	7^1		9^1	8	10		11	12	13																2
1	2		4	5	6	7^1		9^2	8	10	12	3	11^3	13	14															3
1	2		4	5		9^2		8	10^1	7	3	11^1	13	12	6	14														4
1	2			5	6	7^2	13		4	10	8	3	11^1	9	12															5
1	2			5	6	7^3	12	13	4	10	8^1	3	11	9^2	14															6
1	2^1	12		5	6	7^1	8	9	4	10	13	3	11^{12}				14													7
1	2^3		4	5	6	7		9^2	13	8	10^1		3	12				11	14											8
1		3	12		6	7^1	11^{12}	13	8	10								9	2	4	5									9
1		3			6	7^3	11^2	12	8	10	13							9	2	4	5									10
1^8		3			6	9	11^1	12	8	10								7	2	4	5	15								11
1		14			6	7	13	9^2	4^1	11		3	12					10	2	8^3	5									12
1					6	7^2	12	9^1	4	11		3	13					10	2	8	5									13
1	13		5		6	7	9		4^1	11		3	12					10	2	8										14
1	4		5	6	12		9^1	8	11	13	3							10^2	2	7										15
1	14		5	6	7^1		9^1	4	11	12	3	13						10^3	2	8										16
1	12		5	6	7		9^2	4	11^1	13	3							10	2	8										17
1				5	6	7		9^1	4	11^{12}	12	3	13					10	2	8										18
1	3^1		5	6	7^3		9^2	4			14	11	12	13				10	2	8										19
1					5	7		9^1	8	11		3		12				10	2	6	4									20
1					5	7^3		9^1	8	11	13	3	12	14				10^2	2	6	4									21
1	13			6	7^3		9^1	4	11	12	3	14					10	2	5		8^2								22
1	2	3			6		9^1		4	10	7^2	12	11	13				14		5		8^1								23
1	13	3			6		9		12	4^3	10	7	11^1					2^2		5		8	14							24
1	4	3			6		9^2			5	11	12						10	13	8			7^1			2				25
1	3				6		9^2	13	4	11	7^1							10	12	8		5				2				26
	3				6	9		7^3	4^3	11								10^1	14	8		5			1	2	13			27
	3^3	5		6	9			7^1	4	11			14									12	8	1	10^2	2	13			28
	3	5^2		6	9			4	11				13	14				10^1	7			1			2	8^2	12			29
		6		5				7		4	11^2	3	12						14	8		1	13		2	9^1	10^3			30
		6		5	7			4^1	11			3	12					13	8			1^1			2	9	10	15		31
		6		5				9^2		14	4	12	3					13	7			10^1			2	8^1	11	1		32
		6		5^1				9^1	13	4	11	12	3	14					7			10			2	8^2	1			33
		6		5				9^2	14	4	11	13	3						7			10^1			2	12	8^3	1		34
	4			6				9			7	3	11^2					10	2	5		8^2	12		1^8	15	13			35
		6		5				9^1	14	4	11	12	3					13	7^3			2	10^2	8	1					36

MONTROSE

Third Division

Year Formed: 1879. *Ground & Address:* Links Park, Wellington St, Montrose DD10 8QD. *Telephone:* 01674 673200.
Ground Capacity: total: 3292, seated: 1338. *Size of Pitch:* 113yd × 70yd.
Chairman: John F. Paton. *Secretary:* Malcolm J. Watters.
Manager: John Sheran. *Assistant Manager:* Malcolm Lowe. *Physio:* Allan Borthwick.
Managers since 1975: A. Stuart, K. Cameron, R. Livingstone, S. Murray, D. D'Arcy, I. Stewart, C. McLelland, D. Rougvie, J. Leishman, J Holt, A. Dornan, D. Smith, T. Campbell, K. Drinkell.
Club Nickname(s): The Gable Endies. *Previous Grounds:* None.
Record Attendance: 8983 v Dundee, Scottish Cup 3rd rd; 17 Mar, 1973.
Record Transfer Fee received: £50,000 for Gary Murray to Hibernian (Dec 1980).
Record Transfer Fee paid: £17,500 for Jim Smith from Airdrieonians (Feb 1992).
Record Victory: 12-0 v Vale of Leithen, Scottish Cup 2nd rd; 4 Jan, 1975.
Record Defeat: 0-13 v Aberdeen; 17 Mar, 1951.
Most Capped Player: Alexander Keillor, 2 (6), Scotland.
Most League Appearances: 426: David Larter, 1987-98.
Most League Goals in Season (Individual): 28: Brian Third, Division II; 1972-73.

MONTROSE 2000–01 LEAGUE RECORD

Match No.	Date	Venue	Opponents		Result	H/T Score	Lg. Pos.	Goalscorers	Atten- dance
1	Aug 5	A	Peterhead	L	0-2	0-1	—		745
2	12	H	East Stirling	L	0-1	0-1	8		304
3	19	A	Hamilton A	L	0-6	0-0	10		426
4	26	H	East Fife	L	0-1	0-0	10		355
5	Sept 9	A	Brechin C	L	1-6	0-3	10	McKenzie [62]	465
6	16	H	Dumbarton	D	2-2	2-1	10	McKenzie [10], O'Driscoll [11]	317
7	23	A	Elgin C	D	1-1	1-1	10	McKenzie [36]	817
8	30	A	Cowdenbeath	L	0-2	0-0	10		378
9	Oct 7	H	Albion R	L	0-2	0-1	10		230
10	14	H	Peterhead	L	0-2	0-1	10		409
11	21	A	East Stirling	W	2-1	2-0	9	Mitchell 2 [2, 19]	258
12	28	A	East Fife	L	1-3	0-1	9	Mailer [66]	375
13	Nov 4	H	Brechin C	D	1-1	0-0	9	McKenzie (pen) [90]	622
14	11	H	Elgin C	D	0-0	0-0	9		459
15	18	A	Dumbarton	L	0-1	0-1	10		238
16	25	A	Albion R	L	2-3	0-0	10	Marwick [54], McKenzie (pen) [71]	311
17	Dec 2	H	Cowdenbeath	L	1-2	0-0	10	Mitchell [85]	311
18	Feb 3	H	Albion R	L	0-1	0-0	10		244
19	17	A	Hamilton A	W	3-1	2-1	10	Laidlaw 3 [9, 45, 49]	411
20	24	A	East Stirling	D	1-1	0-0	10	Joy [55]	305
21	Mar 10	A	East Fife	L	0-1	0-0	10		407
22	13	H	East Fife	D	1-1	0-0	—	Craig [75]	249
23	17	H	Elgin C	W	2-1	2-0	9	Tully (og) [12], McIlravey [17]	366
24	20	A	Brechin C	L	0-3	0-1	—		526
25	27	H	Dumbarton	L	1-2	0-0	—	Hutcheon [84]	165
26	31	A	Dumbarton	W	2-1	1-1	9	Hutcheon [30], Mitchell [77]	751
27	Apr 3	A	Elgin C	W	2-0	1-0	9	Joy [21], Ferguson [53]	385
28	7	A	Albion R	L	1-2	0-1	9	Mitchell [47]	213
29	10	A	Cowdenbeath	L	1-2	0-0	—	Hutcheon [57]	319
30	14	H	Cowdenbeath	L	0-1	0-1	9		407
31	17	A	Peterhead	D	1-1	1-1	—	Harrison [44]	325
32	21	H	Peterhead	D	2-2	2-0	9	Mitchell [4], McKenzie [39]	369
33	24	H	Brechin C	L	1-3	0-2	—	Mailer [70]	544
34	28	A	East Stirling	W	1-0	1-0	9	Mitchell [3]	186
35	May 1	H	Hamilton A	L	0-2	0-1	—		495
36	5	H	Hamilton A	L	1-4	0-1	9	Hutcheon [65]	916

Final League Position: 9

Honours
League Champions: Second Division 1984-85; *Runners-up:* 1990-91. Third Division, *Runners-up:* 1994-95.
Scottish Cup: Quarter-finals 1973, 1976.
League Cup: Semi-finals 1975-76.
B&Q Cup: Semi-finals 1992-93.
League Challenge Cup: Semi-finals: 1996-97.

Club colours: Shirt: Royal blue. Shorts: Royal blue. Stockings: White.

Goalscorers: *League* (31): Mitchell 7, McKenzie 6 (2 pens), Hutcheon 4, Laidlaw 3, Joy 2, Mailer 2, Craig 1, Ferguson 1, Harrison 1, McIlravey 1, Marwick 1, O'Driscoll 1, own goal 1
Scottish Cup (4): McKenzie 2, Harrison 1, Mitchell 1
CIS Cup (1): Dailly 1
Bell's League Cup (0):

McGlynn G 33	Young J 8	Black M 4	Marwick S 19+1	Niddrie K 1	Craib M 35	Robertson S 8	Harrison T 24+3	McIlravey P 7+5	McKenzie M 22+11	Dailly G 5+5	Mailer C 28+4	Mitchell J 12+18	McWilliam R 3+10	Ferguson S 23+2	McKellar J 17+6	O'Driscoll J 8+2	Sneddon S 2	Ogboke C 1+5	Lowe B 11+4	Muirhead D 22	Scott W 1	Gilfillan F 2+2	Thompson B 3	Joy I 24+1	Zahana-Oni L 2	Catto P 8+1	Christie G 23	Shand M —+1	Hutcheon A 14+4	Laidlaw S 7	Byers K 2	Craig D 14	Fox R 3+1	Match No.
1	2	3	4	5¹	6	7²	8	9¹	10	11	12	13	14																					1
1	2		4		6		10	11²	9³	3¹	8	13	7	5	12	14																		2
1	2		4		6		8²		9		7	13	10¹	3	11		5	12																3
1	2				6	7³	8	13		4		10²	3	11	12	5¹	14																	4
1	2		7		6		8		9		12		13	3¹	11²	10²		14		4	5													5
1	2		7		6		8		9		5			3	11	10¹				4		12												6
1	2		7		6		8²		9		5	13	12	3	11³	10¹				4		14												7
		3	4		6	2			9		5							12	7					8¹	1	10	11							8
	5	7			6	2	14		9		4	13				8³								10²	1	3	11¹¹	12						9
1	5¹	4			6	2		14	9²		7	13		3		10¹		11	12					8										10
1		14			6		8		13		2	9²	12		7¹	10²				4				3		11	5							11
1		7²			6		8³		12		2	9			13	10¹				4				3		11	5	14						12
1		7¹			6		8		13		2	9			12	10²				4				3		11	5							13
1		7			6		8		10		2	9¹		13						4²				3		11	5	12						14
1		7		6	4	8		13		2	12				10¹					4				3²		11	5	9						15
1		7		6	4	8		9		2		11							4					3		5	10							16
1		7¹			6	2			9	8		13		3					12	4				11²		5	10							17
					6		8³				2	13	12	3	7¹					14	4		1			5	10²	9	11					18
	2				6			13	10¹		8	12								4						11	5		9²	7	3			19
1	2				6		13	10¹		8	12								4	7²					11	5		9		3			20
1					6			8¹	10²		2	12			13					7	4				11	5	14	9¹		3			21
1					6			8¹	10²		2	12		13						7	4				11²	5	14	9		3			22
1					6			8¹	10³		2			13	12					7	4				11²	5	14	9		3			23
1					6			8	12	14		13		11	7					4						2¹	5	10	9¹	3			24
1					6				9³		2	12	14	11²	7¹					4				13		8	5	10		3			25
1					6		8¹				2	9²	13	7						4					11		5	10			3	12	26
1					6		8		12		2	9¹	13	7						4					11			10²			3	5	27
1					6		8²	14	13		2	9²	12	7						4					11			10			3	5¹	28
1	2				6			8	12	10¹		13		3	7					4					11²		5	9					29
1	2				6		8³		12	10²	13	14		3	7					4					11		5	9¹					30
1					6		4		9	12		10		8	7					2					11¹		5			3			31
1					6		4	12	9		13	10		8	7¹					2					11²		5			3			32
1					6		4	10¹	9²	12	8	13	14	11	7					2							5			3¹			33
1					8				13	6	10²			3	7¹			12		4					11		5	9			2		34
1					6¹		8		13	12	2	10		3	7					4					11²		5	9					35
1	2				6			13	12		5	10³		4	7			14		8					11²			9			3¹		36

MORTON

Second Division

Year Formed: 1874. *Ground & Address:* Cappielow Park, Sinclair St, Greenock. *Telephone:* 01475 723571. *Fax:* 01475 781084
Ground Capacity: total: 14,891, seated: 5741. *Size of Pitch:* 110yd × 71yd.
Managers since 1975: Joe Gilroy, Benny Rooney, Alex Miller, Tommy McLean, Willie McLean, Allan McGraw, Billy Stark, Ian McCall, Allan Evans. *Club Nickname(s):* The Ton. *Previous Grounds:* Grant Street 1874, Garvel Park 1875, Cappielow Park 1879, Ladyburn Park 1882, (Cappielow Park 1883).
Record Attendance: 23,500 v Celtic; 29 April, 1922.
Record Transfer Fee received: £350,000 for Neil Orr to West Ham U.
Record Transfer Fee paid: £150,000 for Allan Mahood from Nottingham Forest.
Record Victory: 11-0 v Carfin Shamrock, Scottish Cup 1st rd; 13 Nov, 1886.
Record Defeat: 1-10 v Port Glasgow Ath, Division II; 5 May, 1894 and v St Bernards, Division II; 14 Oct, 1933.
Most Capped Player: Jimmy Cowan, 25, Scotland.
Most League Appearances: 358: David Hayes, 1969-84.
Most League Goals in Season (Individual): 58: Allan McGraw, Division II; 1963-64.

MORTON 2000–01 LEAGUE RECORD

Match No.	Date	Venue	Opponents	Result		H/T Score	Lg. Pos.	Goalscorers	Atten- dance
1	Aug 5	H	Livingston	L	0-2	0-0	—		1729
2	12	A	Falkirk	L	0-1	0-0	9		2563
3	19	H	Alloa Ath	W	2-0	1-0	7	Whalen [45], McDonald P [71]	1267
4	26	A	Clyde	W	3-0	1-0	4	Whalen 2 [2, 55], Matheson [90]	1480
5	Sept 9	H	Ross Co	L	0-1	0-1	6		1187
6	16	H	Ayr U	D	1-1	1-0	6	Whalen (pen) [31]	1308
7	23	A	Raith R	W	1-0	0-0	6	Whalen [71]	2078
8	30	A	Airdrieonians	L	1-5	1-2	6	Boukraa [23]	1377
9	Oct 7	A	Inverness CT	L	0-4	0-2	7		1439
10	14	A	Livingston	L	0-1	0-1	8		3468
11	21	H	Falkirk	L	0-4	0-2	8		1503
12	28	H	Clyde	D	1-1	1-0	8	Raeside [33]	1051
13	Nov 4	A	Ross Co	L	1-3	1-2	9	Matheson [41]	2048
14	11	H	Raith R	L	1-2	0-2	10	Matheson [90]	742
15	18	A	Ayr U	D	1-1	0-0	9	Curran [55]	2256
16	25	H	Inverness CT	W	2-0	2-0	9	Anderson [3], Aitken [19]	708
17	Dec 2	A	Airdrieonians	D	1-1	1-0	9	Aitken [10]	1643
18	9	A	Alloa Ath	L	1-2	1-1	10	Anderson [39]	704
19	16	H	Livingston	L	1-2	1-0	10	Matheson [12]	888
20	Jan 2	H	Ayr U	L	0-6	0-4	—		2866
21	6	A	Raith R	D	0-0	0-0	10		1721
22	13	H	Airdrieonians	L	0-3	0-0	10		2602
23	Feb 3	H	Alloa Ath	D	1-1	0-1	10	Whalen [56]	1179
24	17	A	Clyde	D	1-1	0-0	10	Whalen [55]	1609
25	24	H	Clyde	L	0-1	0-0	10		1221
26	Mar 13	A	Inverness CT	L	2-4	1-2	—	McDonald P [42], Matheson [81]	1016
27	17	H	Raith R	D	1-1	1-0	10	Matheson [22]	947
28	27	A	Falkirk	W	3-1	1-1	—	James 2 [7, 53], Denham (og) [57]	1276
29	31	A	Ayr U	L	0-3	0-2	10		2111
30	Apr 7	H	Inverness CT	L	0-3	0-1	10		931
31	14	A	Airdrieonians	W	2-0	1-0	10	Anderson [35], Kerr [80]	1331
32	17	A	Ross Co	W	2-0	2-0	—	Matheson 2 [16, 26]	1894
33	21	A	Livingston	L	0-2	0-1	10		2727
34	24	H	Ross Co	L	0-3	0-3	—		812
35	28	H	Falkirk	W	2-1	0-0	10	Redmond [55], Matheson [64]	905
36	May 5	A	Alloa Ath	W	3-0	3-0	9	McDonald P [2], Aitken [15], Murie [45]	770

Final League Position: 9

Honours
League Champions: First Division 1977-78, 1983-84, 1986-87. Division II 1949-50, 1963-64, 1966-67. Second Division 1994-95. *Runners-up:* Division 1 1916-17, Division II 1899-1900, 1928-29, 1936-37.
Scottish Cup Winners: 1922; *Runners-up:* 1948. *League Cup Runners-up:* 1963-64.
B&Q Cup Runners-up: 1992-93.

European: *UEFA Cup:* 2 matches (*Fairs Cup:* 1968-69).

Club colours: Shirt: Royal blue and white 4" Hoops. Shorts: White with royal blue panel down side. Stockings: Royal blue and white hoops.

Goalscorers: *League* (34): Matheson 9, Whalen 7 (1 pen), Aitken 3, Anderson 3, McDonald P 3, James 2, Boukraa 1, Curran 1, Kerr 1, Murie 1, Raeside 1, Redmond 1, own goal 1
Scottish Cup (1): Matheson 1
CIS Cup (1): Anderson 1
Bell's League Cup (6): Matheson 2, Whalen 2, Boukraa 1, Kerr 1

Boswell M 9	Naylor M 4+4	Davies D 20+2	Anderson D 29+1	Raeside R 33	Medou Otye P 10	Brownrigg A 1	Millen A 15+1	Whalen S 21+2	Boukraa K 11+7	Curran H 21	Matheson R 27+5	McDonald P 23+5	Murie D 27+3	Aitken S 27+4	Kerr B 5+6	Macdonald S 24+2	Tweedie G 11+10	Carin A 20	Robb R 5	Easton S 1	McGregor D 15+2	Wingate D 1	Beattie D 1	James K 9	McDonald K 2	McConaligue S 4	Patterson S 11	Redmond G 2+6	Maxwell A 1+1	Webster S 6+1	Broadfield G —+3	Match No.
1	2	3	4	5	6	7^2	8	9	10^1	11	12	13																				1
1	2	3	4	5	6		8	12	10^1	7	9	11																				2
1	13	3^2	5	4			8	9	12	6	10^5	11	2	7																		3
1		3	5	4			8	9^1	12	6	10	11^2	2	7																		4
1		3	5	4			8	9	12	6^1	10	11^2	2	7	13																	5
1		3	5	4			8	9	10^2	6		11	2	12	13	7^1																6
1	13	3	5	4			8	9	10	6	12	11	2^2			7^1																7
1		3^2	13	5	4^3		8	9	10	6	7^1	11	2	12		14																8
1		3		5			8	9	10	6^2	12	11^1	2	7	4	13																9
	2		4	5			8	9^1	10	6	12		3	7	11			1														10
	12	3	4	5			8	9	10^2	6	13		2	7	11^1			1														11
		3		5	6		8	9	10		7	11	2		4			1														12
		3		5	8			9	10	6		11	2	7	4			1														13
		3	4	5	6^2			9	10^1	8	7	11	2	12	13			1														14
	13	3	4	5				9	12	6	10	11^2	2	7		8^1		1														15
		3	4	5	12			9^1	14	6	10	11	13	7^2	2	8^1		1														16
		3	4	5	6^1			9^1	13		10	11	12	7	2	8		1														17
		3	4	5	6			9	13		10	11^2	12	7	2	8^1		1														18
		3		5				9		11		7			2	8		1	4		6	10										19
	2	3						8	9	11		7				6		1	4		12					5^1	10					20
		3						8	10	11	7^1		2					1	4		7^2					5	6	9				21
		3	11					13		8	10		2^3	12			4	14	1		7^2					5	6^1	9				22
		3		5				9	8		11		2^1	7	12			1	4					10^4		6	13					23
		3		5				9	8^2		2		7^1	11	12			1			10			4		6	13					24
	13	3		5				9	8^3		2		7^1	11				1	12		10			4		10	6	14				25
		3		5				9			7	11	2^1	12	6	13		1			10^2			4			8					26
	14	3		5^2				9^1		7	11^1		2	13	12	6		10						4			8	1				27
	11	3		5				9			2		7		6			1			10			4			8					28
	11^2	3		5				9			2	7	13		6	12		1			10			4			8^1					29
		4	3	5				9			2	7	11	6	8^1	1^3					10			12							15	30
		4	3	5				9	12		2	7	11^3	6							10			8^2			14	1		13		31
		4	3	5				9	12		2	7^2	11^1	6							10			8				1		13		32
		4^1	3	5				9	12		2	7	11^2	6							10			8			14	1		13		33
		4^2	3	5				9	13		2	7	11	6	12						10			8^1				1				34
		3^1		5				9	11		2	7		6	12	4					10			8				1				35
				5				9	11		2	7	12	6	6^1	3					4			10			8^2	13		1		36

MOTHERWELL

Premier League

Year Formed: 1886. *Ground & Address:* Fir Park Stadium, Motherwell ML1 2QN. *Telephone:* 01698 333333. *Fax:* 01698 338001.
Ground Capacity: all seated: 13,742. *Size of Pitch:* 110yd × 75yd.
Chairman: John Boyle. *General Manager/Secretary:* Alisdair Barron. *Commercial Manager:* Karen Paterson. *Director of Football:* Pat Nevin.
Manager: Billy Davies. *First Team Coach:* Miodrag Krivokapic. *Physio:* John Porteous.
Managers since 1975: Ian St. John, Willie McLean, Rodger Hynd, Ally MacLeod, David Hay, Jock Wallace, Bobby Watson, Tommy McLean, Alex McLeish, Harri Kampman.
Club Nickname(s): The Well. *Previous Grounds:* Roman Road, Dalziel Park.
Record Attendance: 35,632 v Rangers, Scottish Cup 4th rd replay; 12 Mar, 1952.
Record Transfer Fee received: £1,750,000 for Phil O'Donnell to Celtic (September 1994).
Record Transfer Fee paid: £500,000 for John Spencer from Everton (Jan 1999).
Record Victory: 12-1 v Dundee U, Division II; 23 Jan, 1954.
Record Defeat: 0-8 v Aberdeen, Premier Division; 26 Mar, 1979.
Most Capped Player: Tommy Coyne, 13, Republic of Ireland.
Most League Appearances: 626: Bobby Ferrier, 1918-37.

MOTHERWELL 2000–01 LEAGUE RECORD

Match No.	Date	Venue	Opponents	Result	H/T Score	Lg. Pos.	Goalscorers	Atten- dance
1	Jul 29	H	Dundee	L 0-2	0-1	—		5961
2	Aug 5	A	Celtic	L 0-1	0-1	11		59,057
3	12	A	Dundee U	D 1-1	1-0	10	Spencer [12]	5598
4	16	H	Dunfermline Ath	L 0-1	0-0	—		5257
5	19	A	Kilmarnock	L 2-3	1-1	12	Elliott 2 [6, 64]	6533
6	27	H	Aberdeen	D 1-1	1-1	11	McCulloch [33]	6009
7	Sept 9	A	St Mirren	W 1-0	0-0	10	McCulloch [53]	5264
8	16	H	Hibernian	L 0-2	0-0	10		9868
9	23	H	Rangers	L 0-1	0-1	10		11,275
10	Oct 1	A	Hearts	L 0-3	0-2	11		10,460
11	14	H	St Johnstone	W 4-0	2-0	10	Dods (og) [21], McCulloch [25], Brannan [59], Elliott [71]	7118
12	21	A	Dundee	W 2-1	2-1	9	Elliott [1], McCulloch [5]	4259
13	29	H	Celtic	D 3-3	1-1	10	Adams [23], McCulloch [53], Brannan [78]	12,421
14	Nov 4	H	Dundee U	W 2-1	1-0	9	Brannan (pen) [45], Elliott [51]	6864
15	11	A	Dunfermline Ath	W 2-1	0-1	7	Townsley [85], Brannan (pen) [89]	4146
16	18	H	Kilmarnock	L 1-2	1-1	8	Brannan [3]	6571
17	25	A	Aberdeen	D 3-3	2-1	8	Townsley [14], McCulloch 2 [44, 70]	11,502
18	29	H	St Mirren	W 2-0	0-0	—	Twaddle [74], Nicholas [90]	5312
19	Dec 3	H	Hibernian	L 1-3	0-1	8	Elliott [84]	5715
20	10	A	Rangers	L 0-2	0-1	8		46,058
21	16	H	Hearts	W 2-0	0-0	8	Townsley [57], Adams [88]	5440
22	23	A	St Johnstone	W 3-2	3-0	6	Spencer [5], Adams [40], Townsley [43]	3489
23	26	H	Dundee	L 0-3	0-2	—		6183
24	Jan 2	A	Dundee U	L 0-2	0-0	—		6311
25	31	H	Dunfermline Ath	D 1-1	0-0	—	McCulloch [69]	4601
26	Feb 3	A	Kilmarnock	W 2-1	1-0	6	Brannan (pen) [30], Twaddle [83]	6018
27	10	H	Aberdeen	L 0-1	0-0	7		6680
28	21	A	Celtic	L 0-1	0-1	—		58,736
29	24	A	St Mirren	W 1-0	0-0	7	Townsley [75]	3704
30	Mar 4	A	Hibernian	D 1-1	0-0	7	Strong [80]	8225
31	17	H	Rangers	L 1-2	1-0	8	Goodman [2]	11,208
32	31	A	Hearts	L 0-3	0-1	8		11,581
33	Apr 7	H	St Johnstone	W 1-0	1-0	8	Elliott [24]	4600
34	21	H	St Johnstone	L 0-1	0-0	9		3195
35	28	A	Dundee U	L 0-1	0-1	9		5928
36	May 5	H	Aberdeen	L 0-2	0-1	10		3905
37	12	A	Dunfermline Ath	W 2-1	2-1	8	Elliott 2 [8, 16]	2437
38	20	H	St Mirren	D 3-3	1-1	8	Lasley [3], Elliott [74], Townsley [79]	4158

Final League Position: 8

Most League Goals in Season (Individual): 52: Willie McFadyen, Division I; 1931-32.
Most Goals Overall (Individual): 283: Hugh Ferguson, 1916-25.

Honours
League Champions: Division I 1931-32. First Division 1981-82, 1984-85. Division II 1953-54, 1968-69; *Runners-up:* Premier Division 1994-95. Division I 1926-27, 1929-30, 1932-33, 1933-34. Division II 1894-95, 1902-03. *Scottish Cup:* 1952, 1991; *Runners-up:* 1931, 1933, 1939, 1951.
League Cup: 1950-51. *Runners-up:* 1954-55. *Scottish Summer Cup:* 1944, 1965.

Club colours: Shirt: Amber with claret hoop and trimmings. Shorts: White. Stockings: Claret.

European: *Cup Winners' Cup:* 2 matches (1991-92). *UEFA Cup:* 6 matches (1994-95, 1995-96).

Goalscorers: *League* (42): Elliott 10, McCulloch 8, Brannan 6 (3 pens), Townsley 6, Adams 3, Spencer 2, Twaddle 2, Goodman 1, Lasley 1, Nicholas 1, Strong 1, own goal 1
Scottish Cup (2): McCulloch 1, Spencer 1
CIS Cup (3): Harvey 1, McCulloch 1, Strong 1

Goram A 22	Corrigan M 31+4	McMillan S 25	Kemble B 23	Strong G 31+1	Davies J 2	Brannan G 23	Townsley D 22+8	Harvey P 10+1	Twaddle K 20+5	Nicholas S 5+13	Wood M 3+5	Elliott S 20+13	Queifio A 14+3	Hammell S 32+2	McCulloch L 26	Spencer J 20+2	Goodman D 6+12	Leitch S 23+3	Adams D 17+9	Ramsay D 3+8	Woods S 14	McClen J 1+2	Lasley K 6+6	McFadden J 1+5	Pearson S 3+3	Okoli J 6	Chiba S 7	Connolly J 2	Match No.
1	2³	3	4	5	6	7	8	9	10¹	11²	12	13	14																1
1	2³	3	4	5	8	7	12	9¹		13	11²	14		6	10														2
1	2	3		5		7	8¹	9²				6	4	10	11	12	13												3
1	2	3²		5			12	9	8¹			6	4	10³	11	14		7	13										4
1	6	7	4¹	5		8	13					9²	2	3	11	10	12												5
1	2	3		5		7	12		14	13		9	4	10³	11²		8	6¹											6
1	14	3	4			7	13		8²			9	2	5	10	11¹	12	6³											7
1	14	3	4	12		7	6²	8				9²	2	5	10	11	13												8
1		3	4²			6		8³	12			2	5	10	14	13	9	11¹											9
12		3	5			7	13	6¹				9	2	4	10³	11	14	8²	1										10
	2	3	5			7²	6		14			9	4	10	11³	12	8³				1	13							11
	2	6	5			7	12		14			9	3	4	10²	11³	13	8¹			1								12
	2	6²	3	5		7	14					9	4	10	11	12	13	8³			1								13
	2	6	3	5		7	12					9	4²	10³	11	14	13	8¹			1								14
	2	3	5			7	12		13			9	4	10²	11			6¹	8		1								15
	2	3	5			7	8¹	12	14			9	4	10	11³			6²	13		1								16
1	2	6	3	5		7²		9	14	12		4	10³	11¹	8	13													17
	2	3	5			7	9	8¹	12	11²		4	10			6		13			1								18
	2	6	3	5		7	9	11²	13	12		4¹	10³			8		14			1								19
1	2	3¹	5			7	8³	11	12			4	10	14	9²	13				6									20
1	2	3	5			7	9	8¹	13			4	10	11²		6	12												21
1	2	3	5		6		8²	13	14			4	10³	11¹	7	9		12											22
1	2	6	3	5²		9	10		4		11	7		8¹	12	13													23
1	2	3	5			7	9	8²	13			4	10³	11	14	6¹	12												24
1	2	3	4	5¹		7	8	12				10²	11	13	6	9													25
1	2	3	5			7	8	13				4	12	10	11²	6¹	9³		14										26
1	2	3²	5			7	8³	12	14			4¹	13	10	11	6	9												27
1	2	6	3	5			8	13				4	10²	11	7¹	9³	14	12											28
	2¹	6	3	5			8	9	14	12		4	10³	11	13	7²													29
1	2		5				8	9	12			10¹	13	6	11	3²		7³	14										30
1	2		5						12	13	11²	10	6	3¹		9³		7	14				4	8					31
	2		5			7¹		9²	13	11		4³		6	10	14			12		1				3	8			32
	2		5				8³	9	12	11		4		7²	10¹		1				13	14			3	6			33
			5				9¹	8	10²	11		2	4	7	13		1		12				3	6					34
12			5				9	10		11¹	14	2	4	13				7	8²				3	6²	1				35
			5			7¹	9²	8		10³	11	2	4	12	14	13			3	6	1								36
	2		5			3³	9²	10	7	14	11	4		13			1				12	6	8¹						37
	2		5			7	9¹	10	12	11		4		3²			1		6	13	8								38

PARTICK THISTLE

First Division

Year Formed: 1876. *Ground & Address:* Firhill Stadium, 80 Firhill Rd, Glasgow G20 7AL. *Telephone:* 0141 579 1971. *Fax:* 0141 945 1525
Ground Capacity: total: 14,538, seated: 8397. *Size of Pitch:* 110yd × 75yd.
Chairman: T. Brown McMaster. *Chief Executive Secretary:* Alan C. Dick. *Commercial Manager:* Amanda Stark.
Manager: John Lambie. *Assistant Manager:* Gerry Collins. *Physio:* Walter Cannon.
Managers since 1975: R. Auld, P. Cormack, B. Rooney, R. Auld, D. Johnstone, W. Lamont, S. Clark, J. Lambie, M. MacLeod, J. McVeigh, T. Bryce. *Club Nickname(s):* The Jags. *Previous Grounds:* Jordanvale Park; Muirpark; Inchview; Meadowside Park.
Record Attendance: 49,838 v Rangers, Division I; 18 Feb, 1922. *Ground Record:* 54,728, Scotland v Ireland, 25 Feb 1928.
Record Transfer Fee received: £200,000 for Mo Johnston to Watford.
Record Transfer Fee paid: £85,000 for Andy Murdoch from Celtic (Feb 1991).
Record Victory: 16-0 v Royal Albert, Scottish Cup 1st rd; 17 Jan, 1931.
Record Defeat: 0-10 v Queen's Park, Scottish Cup; 3 Dec, 1881.
Most Capped Player: Alan Rough, 51 (53), Scotland.
Most League Appearances: 410: Alan Rough, 1969-82.
Most League Goals in Season (Individual): 41: Alec Hair, Division I; 1926-27.

PARTICK THISTLE 2000–01 LEAGUE RECORD

Match No.	Date	Venue	Opponents	Result	H/T Score	Lg. Pos.	Goalscorers	Attendance
1	Aug 5	A	Arbroath	D 1-1	1-1	—	McLean [37]	1456
2	12	H	Stranraer	W 2-1	1-0	3	Hardie [35], Lindau [66]	2357
3	19	A	Stenhousemuir	L 0-4	0-3	7		1130
4	26	H	Berwick R	D 1-1	0-1	5	Hardie [85]	2060
5	Sept 9	A	Queen's Park	W 1-0	0-0	4	Lennon [61]	4019
6	16	H	Stirling A	W 3-1	1-0	4	Lindau [17], Lennon [53], McLean [60]	2251
7	23	A	Clydebank	L 1-2	0-0	3	McLean [53]	1379
8	30	H	Forfar Ath	D 1-1	1-0	4	McLean (pen) [52]	2218
9	Oct 7	A	Queen of the S	W 2-1	1-0	4	McLean [26], McGrillen [87]	1499
10	14	H	Arbroath	D 1-1	0-0	4	McLean [58]	2242
11	21	A	Stranraer	W 3-0	1-0	2	Moore [36], Lindau [53], McLean [72]	1101
12	28	A	Berwick R	W 2-1	0-1	1	McLean 2 (1 pen) [42, 79 (p)]	1240
13	Nov 4	H	Queen's Park	W 2-1	2-1	1	Hardie [13], McLean [36]	4035
14	11	H	Clydebank	W 2-0	1-0	1	Hardie [24], Lindau [53]	3101
15	18	A	Stirling A	D 1-1	1-0	1	Hardie [37]	1753
16	25	H	Queen of the S	W 2-1	2-1	1	McLean [26], McCallum [43]	2610
17	Dec 2	A	Forfar Ath	W 1-0	0-0	1	Hardie [59]	1052
18	16	A	Arbroath	D 1-1	0-1	1	Lennon [59]	1054
19	26	H	Stenhousemuir	W 3-0	0-0	—	Hardie 2 [57, 80], Archibald [64]	2635
20	30	H	Berwick R	D 1-1	1-0	1	Shaw [5]	2837
21	Jan 2	A	Queen's Park	W 2-0	2-0	—	Hardie [5], Shaw [36]	3938
22	13	H	Stirling A	D 1-1	0-1	1	Lennon [64]	3113
23	Feb 3	A	Queen of the S	W 3-1	1-1	1	Hardie 2 [19, 58], McLean [83]	2432
24	10	H	Forfar Ath	W 4-0	0-0	1	Collins [54], Archibald [72], McLean [80], Lindau [81]	3075
25	13	A	Clydebank	W 4-0	0-0	—	Hardie [53], McLean [56], Lindau [86], Shaw [87]	1111
26	17	A	Stenhousemuir	L 0-2	0-1	1		1343
27	24	H	Stranraer	W 3-0	2-0	1	Hardie [22], Smith [36], Lennon [78]	2959
28	Mar 3	H	Queen's Park	W 2-1	1-1	1	McLean [11], Smith [50]	2852
29	10	A	Berwick R	W 1-0	1-0	1	Hardie [50]	1405
30	17	A	Clydebank	W 2-0	0-0	1	Lennon [49], Lindau [59]	2721
31	31	A	Stirling A	W 3-0	3-0	1	Lindau 3 [4, 61, 79]	2748
32	Apr 7	H	Queen of the S	L 0-2	0-1	1		3810
33	14	A	Forfar Ath	D 2-2	1-2	1	Elliot [2], McGrillen [77]	2081
34	21	H	Arbroath	L 0-1	0-0	1		3003
35	28	A	Stranraer	W 4-3	1-3	1	McLean [63], McNally [26], Elliot [52], McGrillen [87]	928
36	May 5	H	Stenhousemuir	W 4-0	0-0	1	McGrillen 2 [48, 70], Elliot [56], Craigan [69]	4624

Final League Position: 1

Honours

League Champions: First Division 1975-76. Division II 1896-97, 1899-1900, 1970-71; Second Division 2000-01;
Runners-up: First Division 1991-92. Division II 1901-02.
Scottish Cup Winners: 1921; *Runners-up:* 1930.
League Cup Winners: 1971-72; *Runners-up:* 1953-54, 1956-57, 1958-59.

European: *Fairs Cup:* 4 matches (1963-64). *UEFA Cup:* 2 matches (1972-73). *Inter Toto Cup:* 4 matches 1995-96.

Club colours: Shirt: Red and yellow hoops. Shorts: Black. Stockings: Red and yellow hoops.

Goalscorers: *League* (66): McLean 16 (2 pens), Hardie 14, Lindau 10, Lennon 6, McGrillen 5, Elliot 3, Shaw 3, Archibald 2, Smith 2, Collins 1, Creagan 1, McCallum 1, McNally 1, Moore 1
Scottish Cup (3): Hardie 2, Collins 1
CIS Cup (1): McLean 1
Bell's League Cup (0):

Arthur K 34	McCallum D 18 + 8	Stirling J 4	Lennon D 33	Smith J 30 + 1	Archibald A 34	McWilliams D 2 + 1	Cameron I 3 + 10	McLean S 32 + 1	McGrillen P 11 + 9	McKeown D 6 + 3	Hardie M 27 + 3	Lyle D 1 + 12	Moore A 12 + 7	Bottiglieri E 2	Craigan S 35	Lindau P 29 + 2	Howie W 2 + 10	Docherty S 12	Brown M 2	Stewart A 12 + 10	Legat G 1	Dunn R — + 3	McNally M 22	Shaw G 4 + 9	Hamilton B 12 + 4	Collins D 12	Elliot B 4 + 2	Match No.
1	2	3	4	5	6	7¹	8	9²	10²	11	12	13	14															1
1	3	5	6				8	9²	11	12	10¹	13			2	4	7³	14										2
1	14		11	12	6		8³	9	10	3	4²	7¹			5			13	2									3
1	3	5					12	9²	10³	11	13	14		2¹	6	7	8	4	1									4
1	8	5	6	3¹	13			9	11		10	12²			4	7³				2			14					5
1	8	5	6	3	13			9	11		10³		14		4	7¹				2²			12					6
1	8	5	6	3			12	9	11¹	13	10³		14		4	7²				2								7
1	8		6	3			12	9	11³		10¹	7²			5	14			2	4	10¹	13						8
1	11²				8			13	9	12	3				5	7¹	14	10		2³		4						9
1	11²				8			13	9	12	3		14		4	7¹		10		2³		5						10
1	12			8¹	5	3		9²				10³	13	7	4	11		2		14		6						11
1	2			8²	5	3		9			10	12	7	4	11¹					13		6						12
1	2²			8	5	3	14	9¹			10	12	7	4	11³					13		6						13
1	2²			8	5	3		9			10		7¹	4	11³	13				12	14	6						14
1	2			8	5	3		9		14	10³	12	7²	4	11¹					13		6						15
1	2³			8	5	3	12	9			10¹		7	4	11²	14				6			13					16
1	2			8	5	3		9²			10¹		7	4	11					12		6	13					17
1	2			8	5	3		9			10³		7²	4	11					12		6¹	13	14				18
1	12			8¹	5	3	14	9²	13		10			4						6				11	2²	7		19
1	14			8	5	3	13				10³	12		4	9¹					6				11	2²	7		20
1				8	5	3			12		10			4	11³					6				9	2	7		21
1				8	5	3	12	9²	13		10			4						6	11			2¹	7			22
1				8	5	3		9	11¹		10			4	12					6					2	7		23
1				8	5	3		9²			10		12	4	11¹	14				13	6				2³	7		24
1	14			8	5	3		9²			10³		12	4	11¹					6	13			2	7			25
1	13			8	5			9	14		10			4	11¹		3³			6	12			2²	7			26
1	2			8	5	3		9			10²	12		4	11¹	13				6					7			27
1	2			8	5	3		9			10	12		4	11¹			6							7			28
1	2			8	5	3		9			10			4	11¹					6	12				7			29
1	2³			8	5	3		9	13		10¹		14	4	11²					6			12	7			30
1	2²			8	5	3		9¹			10		14	4	11³	13				6			7			10³		31
1				8	5	3		9²			10			4	11¹		2			6	13		7			12		32
1	2			8	5	3		9²	13			10		4	12	11¹					14	7			10³			33
	12			8		3			11³				13	4	7²		2	1	5	6	14	9¹			10			34
1	11³			8	5	3		9²	13					4	7	2¹		12		6			14			10		35
1	6			8		3		12	11³		14		7	4	10¹					2			5		13	9²		36

PETERHEAD   Third Division

Year Formed: 1891. *Ground and Address:* Balmoor Stadium, Lord Catto Park, Peterhead AB42 1EU.
Telephone: 01779 478256. *Fax:* 01779 490682. *Ground Capacity:* 3250, seated 1000.
Chairman: Roger Taylor. *General Manager:* Dave Watson. *Secretary:* George Moore.
Team Manager: Ian Wilson. *Assistant Manager:* Alan Lyons. *Physio:* Jennifer Johnson.
Managers since 1975: C. Grant, D. Darcy, I. Taylor, J. Harper, D. Smith, J. Hamilton, G. Adams, J. Guyan, I. Wilson, D. Watson, R. Brown, D. Watson, I. Wilson. *Club Nickname(s):* Blue Toon. *Previous Ground:* Recreation Park.
Record Attendance: 6310 friendly v Celtic, 1948.
Record Victory: 17-0 v Fort William, 1998-99 (in Highland League).
Record Defeat: 0-13 v Aberdeen, Scottish Cup 1923-24.
Most League Appearances: 35: S. King, I. Pirie, 2000-01.
Most League Goals in Season (Individual): 11, C. Yeats.
Most Goals Overall (Individual): 11, C. Yeats.

PETERHEAD 2000–01 LEAGUE RECORD

Match No.	Date	Venue	Opponents	Result	H/T Score	Lg. Pos.	Goalscorers	Attendance
1	Aug 5	H	Montrose	W 2-0	1-0	—	Herd [26], Johnston [75]	745
2	12	A	East Fife	D 1-1	0-1	4	Paterson [82]	619
3	19	A	Dumbarton	W 2-0	1-0	4	Cooper (pen) [35], Johnston [55]	630
4	26	H	Brechin C	L 1-2	1-1	5	Smith [22]	563
5	Sept 9	A	Elgin C	W 3-1	1-1	4	Peters (og) [40], Yeats (pen) [80], O'Connor [86]	1135
6	16	H	East Stirling	L 2-4	0-2	5	Cooper (pen) [58], Yeats [75]	614
7	23	A	Hamilton A	L 0-3	0-2	6		369
8	30	A	Albion R	D 0-0	0-0	5		358
9	Oct 7	H	Cowdenbeath	W 3-0	2-0	4	Yeats [2], McCulloch (og) [27], Smith [78]	637
10	14	A	Montrose	W 2-0	1-0	4	Stewart 2 [5, 85]	409
11	21	A	East Fife	D 0-0	0-0	4		637
12	28	A	Brechin C	L 2-3	1-2	5	Smith [7], Stewart [86]	469
13	Nov 4	H	Elgin C	W 1-0	1-0	4	Simpson [8]	850
14	11	H	Hamilton A	D 1-1	1-1	4	Yeats [32]	790
15	18	A	East Stirling	W 3-1	2-0	4	Yeats [41], Bett [44], Johnston [53]	262
16	25	A	Cowdenbeath	L 0-2	0-0	5		404
17	Dec 2	H	Albion R	L 1-2	1-0	6	Yeats [27]	516
18	23	A	Dumbarton	W 3-1	2-1	5	Stewart [17], Yeats [20], Cooper [89]	821
19	30	H	Brechin C	L 0-2	0-2	5		889
20	Jan 13	A	East Stirling	L 1-2	0-0	5	Smith [85]	606
21	20	A	Hamilton A	L 0-3	0-0	4		645
22	Feb 24	A	East Fife	L 1-2	1-0	6	Stewart [10]	380
23	Mar 6	A	Elgin C	W 1-0	0-0	—	Cooper [75]	524
24	13	A	Cowdenbeath	W 3-0	2-0	—	Yeats [35], Johnston [43], Stewart [77]	499
25	17	A	Hamilton A	W 2-1	0-0	—	Stewart [60], Yeats [83]	710
26	20	A	Albion R	W 1-0	0-0	—	Stewart [55]	272
27	24	H	Dumbarton	L 0-1	0-1	5		432
28	27	A	Brechin C	D 1-1	0-0	—	Johnston [75]	396
29	31	A	East Stirling	L 0-1	0-0	5		190
30	Apr 7	A	Cowdenbeath	L 0-4	0-1	5		348
31	14	H	Albion R	D 1-1	0-0	6	Smith D [50]	526
32	17	H	Montrose	D 1-1	1-1	—	Johnston [34]	325
33	21	A	Montrose	D 2-2	0-2	5	Smith G [55], Yeats [85]	369
34	28	H	East Fife	W 2-1	1-1	5	Gibson [5], Johnston [50]	511
35	May 1	H	Elgin C	D 1-1	0-0	—	Yeats [85]	475
36	5	A	Dumbarton	D 2-2	1-1	5	Cooper [4], Johnston [64]	715

Final League Position: 5

Honours
Scottish Cup: Quarter Finals 2001.
Highland League Champions: winners 5 times.
Scottish Qualifying Cup (North): winners 6 times.
North of Scotland Cup: winners 5 times.
Aberdeenshire Cup: winners 20 times.

Club colours: Shirt: Blue and White; Shorts: White; Stockings: Blue.

Goalscorers: *League* (46): Yeats 11 (1 pen), Johnston 8, Stewart 8, Cooper 5 (2 pens), Smith D 5, Bett 1, Gibson 1, Herd 1, O'Connor 1, Paterson 1, Simpson 1, Smith G 1, own goals 2
Scottish Cup (11): Johnston 2, Cooper 1, Herd 1, King 1, Livingstone 1, Simpson 1, Smith D 1, Stewart 1, Tindal 1, own goal 1
CIS Cup (2): Cooper 2 (2 pens)
Bell's League Cup (1): Clark G 1

Pirie J 35	Craig D 7+1	King S 35	Herd W 25+1	Simpson M 31	Paterson S 8+2	Cooper C 16+7	Johnston M 30+5	Clark G 2	Brown S 6+2	Livingstone R 25+4	De Barros M 4+8	Smith D 17+11	Gibson A 16+10	Kiddie J —+2	Clark S 24+5	O'Connor G 4	Yeats C 27+5	Tindal K 25+2	Stewart J 22+2	Watson C 3+8	Bett B 4+2	Murray J 11+5	Buchanan R 1+1	Smith G 4+2	Huggon R 3+5	Clark P —+1	Duffy J 11	Match No.
1	2	3	4	5	6	7	8	9	10	11[1]	12																	1
1	2	3	4	5	6	7[2]	8[1]	9	10	11	13	12																2
1	2	3	4	5	6	7[1]	8			11	12	10[3]	9[2]	13	14													3
1	2	3	4	5	6	7[1]	8			11	12	10		13			9[2]											4
1	2	3	4				8			10[2]	11	6	7	12	5		9	13										5
1	2	3	4	5	6	7[2]	8			10	11			13			9[2]	12										6
1	2	3	4[1]	5	6	7[2]	8			11		13		12			9	10										7
1			4	5	6		8[1]			11	12	13	7		2		9[2]	10	3									8
1	12	3	4	5	6[1]					11	7[2]	10		13	2		9	8										9
1		3		5	12	13	14			11		10[3]	7[2]	6[1]	4		8	2	9									10
1		3	4	5	14	13	12			11		10[1]	7[2]		2		8[3]	6	9									11
1		3	4[1]	5		7				11		13	10[2]		2		8	6	9	12								12
1		3	4	5		7[2]	11					10[2]	14	13	2		8[1]	6	9		12							13
1		3	4	5		7[2]	8[2]					10[1]	14	12	2		9	6				13	11					14
1		3	4	5			8			11		13	10	12	2		9[2]					6	7[1]					15
1		3	4	5			8[2]			11		10[2]	14		2		9[2]	13				6	7	12				16
1		3	4	5			8			11[2]		10[2]	14		2		9	12	13	1		6[1]	7					17
1		3								12	11	10[2]	14		6		9[3]	2	5	8	4	13	7[1]					18
1	3[1]			5						11	14	12	10	13			9	2	6	8[2]	4		7[3]					19
1		3	4			7	10			11[3]	12		13		2[2]		9[1]	6	8	5		14						20
1		3[3]	4			13	10[1]			11		6			2		12	5	8	14			7[3]	9				21
1		3	4	5		13				11[3]		10[2]	14		2	7		8		12				9	6[1]			22
1		3	4	5						11		10	14		2[1]		12	6	8					9[2]	7[3]	13		23
1		3		5		7[2]	10			11	12	6					9[3]	2	8			13			14		4[1]	24
1		3		5		7[1]	10			11[2]	12	6					9	2[1]	8						14	13	4	25
1		3		5		7	10			11[1]		6		12			9	2	8								4	26
1		3	12	5		7[2]				11[3]	6	10[1]					9	2[1]	8						14		4	27
1		3	6	5		7[2]				11		10					9	2[1]	8			13			12		4	28
1		3	6	5		7				11[2]		10		14			9[3]	2[1]	8			13			12		4	29
1		3	4	5						11[3]	6	10[2]		14			9	2	8			12		13	7[1]		4	30
1		3	4	5		7				11	6	10		12			9	2[1]	8									31
1		3		5						11[3]	6	10	9[1]		2	4			8				14	12	7[1]		13	32
1		3	4	5						11	12	10	9	13			6[2]	2	8						7[1]			33
1		3	4	5[1]		7[2]				11	12	10	9	14			6[3]		8			13					2	34
1		3		5[1]						11	12	10	9	13		14	6[2]	4	8[1]						7		2	35
1		3				8				11[3]	12	10	9[3]	14	2		6		5					13	7[1]		4	36

QUEEN OF THE SOUTH Second Division

Year Formed: 1919. *Ground & Address:* Palmerston Park, Dumfries DG2 9BA. *Telephone and Fax:* 01387 254853.
Ground Capacity: total: 8352, seated: 3549. *Size of Pitch:* 112yd × 73yd.
Chairman: Ronald Bradford. *Secretary:* Richard Shaw MBE. *Commercial Manager:* Margaret Heuchan.
Manager: John Connolly. *Assistant Manager:* Ian Scott.
Managers since 1975: M. Jackson, W. Hunter, B. Little, G. Herd, H. Hood, A. Busby, R. Clark, M. Jackson, D. Wilson,
W. McLaren, F. McGarvey, A. MacLeod, D. Frye, W. McLaren, M. Shanks, R. Alexander. *Club Nickname(s):* The
Doonhamers. *Previous Grounds:* None.
Record Attendance: 24,500 v Hearts, Scottish Cup 3rd rd; 23 Feb, 1952.
Record Transfer Fee received: £250,000 for Andy Thomson to Southend U (1994).
Record Transfer Fee paid: £30,000 for Jim Butter from Alloa Athletic (1995).
Record Victory: 11-1 v Stranraer, Scottish Cup 1st rd; 16 Jan, 1932.
Record Defeat: 2-10 v Dundee, Division I; 1 Dec, 1962.
Most Capped Player: Billy Houliston, 3, Scotland.
Most League Appearances: 731: Allan Ball, 1963-82.
Most League Goals in Season (Individual): 37: Jimmy Gray, Division II; 1927-28.

QUEEN OF THE SOUTH 2000–01 LEAGUE RECORD

Match No.	Date	Venue	Opponents	Result	H/T Score	Lg. Pos.	Goalscorers	Atten- dance
1	Aug 5	A	Stenhousemuir	L 3-4	0-3	—	Sunderland [68], Martin [75], Aitken [86]	520
2	12	H	Stirling A	D 0-0	0-0	8		1168
3	19	A	Queen's Park	L 0-1	0-1	9		839
4	26	A	Clydebank	W 2-1	1-1	6	Weatherson (pen) [43], Martin [67]	273
5	Sept 9	A	Stranraer	L 1-4	0-1	10	Caldwell [76]	1630
6	16	A	Berwick R	W 4-0	2-0	6	Hawke [33], Preen [36], Weatherson [88], Muir [90]	572
7	23	H	Forfar Ath	L 0-1	0-1	10		1167
8	30	A	Arbroath	L 0-2	0-1	10		667
9	Oct 7	H	Partick Th	L 1-2	0-1	10	Atkinson P [72]	1499
10	14	A	Stenhousemuir	W 4-2	3-0	8	Pittman (og) [9], Weatherson 3 [28, 57, 90]	1013
11	21	A	Stirling A	W 1-0	0-0	7	Hawke [70]	748
12	28	H	Clydebank	D 1-1	1-0	8	Weatherson [6]	1156
13	Nov 4	A	Stranraer	L 2-3	2-2	8	Johnstone (og) [15], Suddick [41]	767
14	11	A	Forfar Ath	W 1-0	0-0	8	Caldwell [88]	440
15	18	H	Berwick R	W 2-1	2-0	7	Weatherson 2 (1 pen) [13 (p), 41]	1238
16	25	A	Partick Th	L 1-2	1-2	8	Hawke [33]	2610
17	Dec 2	H	Arbroath	D 1-1	0-0	8	Caldwell [60]	1087
18	23	H	Queen's Park	D 1-1	1-1	8	Weatherson [8]	1288
19	Jan 2	H	Stranraer	L 2-3	1-2	—	Johnstone (og) [7], Atkinson P [65]	1643
20	Feb 3	A	Partick Th	L 1-3	1-1	8	O'Neil [41]	2432
21	17	A	Queen's Park	W 2-1	0-1	8	King [66], Weatherson [75]	711
22	24	H	Stirling A	W 2-1	2-0	8	Connell [20], Gaughan (og) [32]	1157
23	Mar 6	A	Stenhousemuir	W 2-1	0-0	—	Weatherson [61], O'Neil [83]	250
24	10	H	Clydebank	W 1-0	1-0	4	O'Neil [37]	1022
25	13	A	Clydebank	W 2-1	0-1	—	Connell [75], O'Neil [77]	245
26	17	H	Forfar Ath	L 2-3	1-1	4	Weatherson [36], O'Neil (pen) [67]	974
27	20	A	Arbroath	L 2-5	1-1	—	Angell [2], Hogg [90]	698
28	25	A	Berwick R	D 2-2	0-1	4	Weatherson [72], O'Neil [83]	608
29	31	H	Berwick R	D 3-3	1-1	5	Weatherson [14], Armstrong [47], O'Neil (pen) [50]	984
30	Apr 3	A	Stranraer	L 0-2	0-1	—		600
31	7	A	Partick Th	W 2-0	1-0	5	O'Neil 2 (1 pen) [23 (p), 55]	3810
32	14	A	Arbroath	W 1-0	0-0	5	Muir [90]	1141
33	21	H	Stenhousemuir	L 1-3	1-1	5	O'Neil (pen) [30]	1111
34	28	A	Stirling A	D 1-1	1-0	—	Weatherson [23]	587
35	May 1	H	Forfar Ath	L 1-3	1-0	—	Weatherson [31]	522
36	5	H	Queen's Park	L 0-1	0-1	6		1176

Final League Position: 6

Most Goals in Season: 41: Jimmy Rutherford, 1931-32.
Most Goals Overall (Individual): 250: Jim Patterson, 1949-63.

Honours
League Champions: Division II 1950-51; *Runners-up:* Division II 1932-33, 1961-62, 1974-75. Second Division 1980-81, 1985-86.
Scottish Cup: semi-finalists 1949-50.
League Cup: semi-finalists 1950-51, 1960-61.
B&Q Cup: semi-finalists 1991-92. *League Challenge Cup:* runners-up 1997-98.

Club colours: Shirt: Royal blue. Shorts: White. Stockings: Royal blue with white tops.

Goalscorers: *League* (52): Weatherson 16 (2 pens), O'Neil 10 (4 pens), Caldwell 3, Hawke 3, Atkinson P 2, Connell 2, Martin 2, Muir 2, Aitken 1, Angell 1, Armstrong 1, Hogg 1, King 1, Preen 1, Suddick 1, Sunderland 1, own goals 4
Scottish Cup (4): Weatherson 3, Hawke 1
CIS Cup (3): Hawke 1, Hodge 1, Weatherson 1
Bell's League Cup (1): Atkinson P 1

Matheson D 25	Atkinson P 29	Hodge A 7 + 1	Aitken A 35	Martin A 7	Sunderland J 26 + 5	Boyle D 4 + 3	Nelson A 4 + 3	Weatherson P 31 + 3	Hawke W 29 + 3	Weir M 4 + 1	Nixon P 12 + 7	Muir D 7 + 11	Caldwell B 5 + 5	Pickering S 20 + 7	Young K 1 + 2	Atkinson R 3 + 1	Preen S 4	Patterson G 3	Greacan S 3	Gibson W — + 1	Patterson D 7 + 2	Davidson S 9	Suddick J 9 + 2	McQuilter R 24	Skinner S 1 + 5	Kinnaird P 5 + 1	Creaney G — + 1	McKeown D 16 + 2	Milne D — + 1	O'Neil J 17 + 1	Connell G 16	Hogg A 2 + 6	Angell M 4 + 1	Scott C 3	King S 6	Hughes M 3 + 5	Walklate S 6 + 1	Campbell J 8	Armstrong G 1 + 1	Match No.
1	2	3	4	5	6²	7¹	8	9	10³	11	12	13	14																												1
1	7	3	4	6	8¹	13	12	9	14	11²	5	2	10³																												2
1	8³	3	6	5	7¹			9	10	11²	4		13	2	12	14																								3
1	8	3	6	5	14		12	9³	11		4	2²		13		7	10																							4
1	3³	13	5	6			8	9³	7		4	12	14	2²		11	10																							5
1	3	11	5	4			8³	12	10		7²	6	14	2	13		9¹																							6
1	3³	11		5	12		8²	14	10	13	7¹	6		2			9	4																						7
1		3	5		12		13	9	8	11²			10	2	7¹	6²		4	14																					8
1	11		5		6			9	8		12	10²	2			4¹	3	7	13																					9
1	11		4		6²			10	13		8	12		2			3	7¹	9	5																				10
1	11		5		6²			10	12		8¹	13		2			3	7	9	4																				11
1	11¹		5		6²	12		10	8			13		2			3	7	9²	4	14																			12
1	11		5		6			10	8			12		2			3¹	7²	9	4	13																			13
1	3		5		6			10	8					12	2			7	9¹	4		11																		14
1	3³		5		6¹			10	8		12	14		2				7	9²	4		11	13																	15
1			5		12			10	8		14	6¹		2³				7	9²	4	13	11		3																16
1			5		6			10	8					11	2			3	7	9¹	4	12																		17
1	2		5		6			9	8		12	7¹						14		13	4	10²	11³	3																18
1	2		5		6			7				10²							3³		9¹	4	13	11		8	12	14												19
1	2		5		6			10				13									4		12	3		7	8	9⁴	11¹											20
	2		5		6¹			10²	9					12							4			3		7	8			1	11	13								21
	2		5		6¹			10	9					12							4			3		7	8			1	11									22
1	2		5					10¹	9					6							4			3		7	8		11				12							23
1	2		5		6	3		10²	9³					12							4					7	8	14	11¹				13							24
1	2		5		6¹	11		13	9					12							4					7	8						10²							25
1	2¹		5		6	13		10	9					12							4³			3		7	8					11³	14							26
1			5		11¹			10	9	12				2²							4			3		7	8	14	6³		13									27
			5					10	9					6¹							4			3		7	8	12		1	11		2							28
	2		5		6			9		13											4			3		7	8	10¹			11			3	1	12²				29
	2		5		6²			9				13									4			12		7	8				11¹	10	3	1						30
	2		5		10			9	11¹			6	12								4			3		7	8							1						31
	2		5		10			9	11			6	13								4			12		7²	8						3¹	1						32
	2		5		10				11			6	9²	12							4					7	8	13				8¹		1						33
			5		6²			10³	9			4			2			11¹						3		7	8	14	12					13	1					34
			5		6			9	10						2		11							3		7	8						4	1						35
	2		5		12			9						4³			11¹		14					3		7	8	13					6	1	10²					36

QUEEN'S PARK

Third Division

Year Formed: 1867. *Ground & Address:* Hampden Park, Mount Florida, Glasgow G42 9BA. *Telephone:* 0141 632 1275.
Fax: 0141 636 1612.
Ground Capacity: all seated: 52,000. *Size of Pitch:* 115yd × 75yd.
President: Kenneth Harvey. *Secretary:* Alistair Mackay. *Commercial Director:* Garry Templeman.
Coach: John McCormack. *Physio:* R.C.Findlay.
Coaches since 1975: D. McParland, J. Gilroy, E. Hunter, H. McCann. *Club Nickname(s):* The Spiders. *Previous Grounds:* 1st Hampden (Recreation Ground); (Titwood Park was used as an interim measure between 1st & 2nd Hampdens); 2nd Hampden (Cathkin); 3rd Hampden.
Record Attendance: 95,772 v Rangers, Scottish Cup, 18 Jan, 1930.
Record for Ground: 149,547 Scotland v England, 1937.
Record Transfer Fee received: Not applicable due to amateur status.
Record Transfer Fee paid: Not applicable due to amateur status.
Record Victory: 16-0 v St. Peters, Scottish Cup 1st rd; 29 Aug, 1885.
Record Defeat: 0-9 v Motherwell, Division I; 26 Apr, 1930.
Most Capped Player: Walter Arnott, 14, Scotland.
Most League Appearances: 516: Ross Caven.

QUEEN'S PARK 2000–01 LEAGUE RECORD

Match No.	Date		Venue	Opponents	Result		H/T Score	Lg. Pos.	Goalscorers	Atten- dance
1	Aug	5	H	Berwick R	W	1-0	0-0	—	Marshall [48]	721
2		12	A	Forfar Ath	W	1-0	0-0	1	Carroll [69]	516
3		19	H	Queen of the S	W	1-0	1-0	1	Finlayson [30]	839
4		26	A	Stirling A	W	1-0	1-0	1	Carroll [30]	753
5	Sept	9	H	Partick Th	L	0-1	0-0	1		4019
6		16	A	Stranraer	L	0-3	0-0	—		587
7		23	H	Arbroath	D	0-0	0-0	2		721
8		30	H	Stenhousemuir	W	2-0	0-0	1	Caven (pen) [72], Borland [89]	793
9	Oct	7	A	Clydebank	L	0-2	0-1	3		375
10		14	A	Berwick R	D	1-1	1-0	3	Finlayson [29]	514
11		21	H	Forfar Ath	D	0-0	0-0	3		741
12		28	A	Stirling A	W	3-0	0-0	2	Finlayson [47], Gallagher [58], Miller [71]	920
13	Nov	4	A	Partick Th	L	1-2	1-2	3	Gallagher [25]	4035
14		11	A	Arbroath	D	2-2	1-1	4	Crawford (og) [3], Gallagher [50]	573
15		18	H	Stranraer	L	1-2	1-0	4	Gallagher [24]	753
16		25	H	Clydebank	D	1-1	1-1	5	Travers [43]	668
17	Dec	2	A	Stenhousemuir	D	1-1	0-1	5	Caven (pen) [87]	492
18		16	H	Berwick R	L	0-2	0-0	5		690
19		23	A	Queen of the S	D	1-1	1-1	6	Finlayson [9]	1288
20	Jan	2	H	Partick Th	L	0-2	0-2	—		3938
21		13	A	Stranraer	W	1-0	0-0	5	Caven (pen) [77]	556
22		20	H	Arbroath	D	1-1	1-1	4	Borland [12]	1148
23	Feb	10	H	Stenhousemuir	L	1-2	0-0	6	Brown [88]	704
24		17	H	Queen of the S	L	1-2	1-0	7	Canning [25]	711
25	Mar	3	A	Partick Th	L	1-2	1-1	7	Marshall [37]	2852
26		10	H	Stirling A	D	1-1	0-0	7	Gaughan (og) [78]	822
27		13	A	Forfar Ath	L	0-3	0-0	—		374
28		17	A	Arbroath	L	0-2	0-1	8		605
29		20	A	Clydebank	L	1-2	0-1	—	Orr (pen) [60]	209
30		24	A	Stirling A	W	2-0	1-0	8	Gallagher [13], Orr [46]	568
31		31	H	Stranraer	W	1-0	0-0	7	Gallagher [50]	619
32	Apr	7	H	Clydebank	D	0-0	0-0	7		701
33		14	A	Stenhousemuir	L	0-2	0-0	8		519
34		21	A	Berwick R	L	0-1	0-1	8		657
35		28	H	Forfar Ath	L	0-2	0-0	8		951
36	May	5	A	Queen of the S	W	1-0	1-0	9	Gallagher [22]	1176

Final League Position: 9

Most League Goals in Season (Individual): 30: William Martin, Division I; 1937-38.
Most Goals Overall (Individual): 163: J. B. McAlpine.

Honours
League Champions: Division II 1922-23. B Division 1955-56. Second Division 1980-81. Third Division 1999-2000.
Scottish Cup Winners: 1874, 1875, 1876, 1880, 1881, 1882, 1884, 1886, 1890, 1893; *Runners-up:* 1892, 1900.
League Cup: —.
FA Cup runners-up: 1884, 1885.

Club colours: Shirt: White and black hoops. Shorts: White. Stockings: Black with white tops.

Goalscorers: *League* (28): Gallagher 7, Finlayson 4, Caven 3 (3 pens), Borland 2, Carroll 2, Marshall 2, Orr 2 (1 pen), Brown 1, Canning 1, Miller 1, Travers 1, own goals 2
Scottish Cup (0):
CIS Cup (2): Brown 1, Gallagher 1
Bell's League Cup (3): Gallagher 2, Finlayson 1

Stewart C 13	Ferry D 28+1	Marshall S 31	Duncan G 16+1	Connaghan D 33	Sinclair R 17+3	Finlayson K 32	Connell G 12+1	Gallagher M 26+2	Brown J 12+7	Carroll F 13+15	Miller G 26+7	Kwick-Ajet W —+2	Flannigan C 3+2	Martin P —+1	Scobie R 4+9	Orr S 12+11	Caven R 21+3	Borland P 16+2	Smith A 4	Christie F —+2	Fisher C —+3	Travers M 9+1	Bruce G 7	MacFarlane N 8	Jackson R 5+7	Cunningham J 11	Canning S 16+2	Martin H 2+3	Corr B 12	Martin W 5+6	Clarke R —+4	Collins N 2+3	Match No.
1	2	3	4	5	6	7	8	9	10	11																							1
1	2	3	4	5	6	7	8	9^3	10^1	11^3	12	13	14																				2
1	2	3	4	5	6	7^2	8	9^2	12	11	10^1	14	13																				3
1	2	3	4	5	6^1	7	8	9	10^3	11^2						12	13	14															4
1	2	3	4	5	6^3	7		9	10	11^1	8^2					12	13	14															5
1	2	3	4^3	5		7		9^1	12	11	10^2					14	8	6	13														6
	2^1	3^2	4^3	5		7		9		11	10	13	14			12	8	6					1										7
1	2	10		4	5	7		9		11							8	6	3														8
	2	10	4^1	5	12	7	14	9	13	11^3							8^5	6				3	1										9
1	2	10	4	5^2	6	7	8	9	12	11^3	14	13						3^1															10
	2	10	4	5	6	7	8	9	13	11^2	12							3^1				1											11
	2	6	4	5		7^1	8^3	9^2	11	10	14						13	12	3	1													12
	2	6	4	5		7	8^2	9	11	10						12	13					3	1										13
	2	8^1	4	5	13	7		9	14	12	10^3					11^3	12	6				14	3	1									14
	2^2	8	4	5	13	7		9	14	12	10^3					11^1		6				3	1										15
	10	4^2	5	6	7^3	8	9		13	12						14		11^1				3		2									16
	10		5	6	7^1	8	9		11^2	14						4	12	1				3^3		2	13								17
1	10	12	5	2	7	8	9^3		13	14						6	3					4^1	11^2										18
1	10		5	2^1	7	8	13	9^2		12						6	3								11^3	4	14						19
1	10		5		7	12	9^1	13	2							6	3								8^1	11^2	4	14					20
1	10		5	6		9	7	11^3	8							14	12	3^3				4	13			2^1							21
1	10		5	6	7			9^2	11^1	13	8						3					4	12			2							22
12	10		5	4				13		8	7			14				1	3			3^3		6	11^2	2^1	9^3						23
3			5		7			11^1	12	8						10	6						1		4	13	2	3^2					24
	2	10		5	4^1	7^3				8						14	12	6	3							11	13	1	9^2				25
	2	4		5	7				12	8	10^1					13	6	3^2							14	11	1	9^3					26
	2	4		5	7				12	8	10^1					13	6	3^2							11	14	1	9^3					27
	2	4^1		5					11^3	8	7					12	6								13	3	10	14	1	9^3			28
	2			5				9^2		12	8					13	10					3^3			7^1	4	6	1	11	14			29
	2			5	7^1			9		8	10^2						6	3^3							4	11	1	12	13	14			30
	2			5	7^3			9^1	13	8	10^2						6	3							4	11	1	12	14				31
	2			5	7^3			9	14	8	10^2						6	3^1							4	11	1	12	13				32
	2	11		5	7^1			9^4	12	8	10						6								4	3^2	1	13			14		33
	2^3	11		5	7^2			9	10^1	8							12	6							4	3	1	13			14		34
	2	3		4^3	7			9^2	12	8						10^1	14								13	5	11	1			6		35
	2	10			7^3			9^1	13	14	8						6	3^2							5	11	1	12			4		36

RAITH ROVERS   First Division

Year Formed: 1883. *Ground & Address:* Stark's Park, Pratt St, Kirkcaldy KY1 1SA. *Telephone:* 01592 263514. *Fax:* 01592 642833.
Ground Capacity: all seated: 10,104. *Size of Pitch:* 113yd × 70yd.
Chairman: Danny Smith. *Office Manager:* Billy McPhee.
Manager: Peter Hetherston. *Assistant Manager:* Kenny Black. *Physio:* Paul Green.
Managers since 1975: R. Paton, A. Matthew, W. McLean, G. Wallace, R. Wilson, F. Connor, J. Nicholl, J. Thomson, T. McLean, I. Munro, J. Nicholl, J. McVeigh. *Club Nickname:* Rovers. *Previous Grounds:* Robbie's Park.
Record Attendance: 31,306 v Hearts, Scottish Cup 2nd rd; 7 Feb, 1953.
Record Transfer Fee received: £900,000 for S. McAnespie to Bolton Wanderers (Sept 1995).
Record Transfer Fee paid: £225,000 for Paul Harvey from Airdrieonians (1996).
Record Victory: 10-1 v Coldstream, Scottish Cup 2nd rd; 13 Feb, 1954.
Record Defeat: 2-11 v Morton, Division II; 18 Mar, 1936.
Most Capped Player: David Morris, 6, Scotland.
Most League Appearances: 430: Willie McNaught.
Most League Goals in Season (Individual): 38: Norman Haywood, Division II; 1937-38.
Most Goals Overall (Individual): 154: Gordon Dalziel (League), 1987-94.

RAITH ROVERS 2000–01 LEAGUE RECORD

Match No.	Date		Venue	Opponents	Result		H/T Score	Lg. Pos.	Goalscorers	Attendance
1	Aug	5	H	Alloa Ath	L	1-2	0-2	—	Mballa [61]	2123
2		12	A	Airdrieonians	D	1-1	0-1	7	Burns [72]	2854
3		26	H	Inverness CT	W	4-1	1-0	6	McKinnon [10], Tosh P [50], Burns [54], Creaney [82]	1615
4	Sept	2	A	Ross Co	W	4-1	1-0	3	Tosh P [7], Stein [53], Burns [63], Mballa [89]	1759
5		9	A	Falkirk	L	1-2	0-1	5	Andrews [67]	2762
6		16	A	Livingston	W	4-0	3-0	4	Andrews 2 [4, 68], Burns [15], Tosh P [39]	3961
7		23	H	Morton	L	0-1	0-0	5		2078
8		30	A	Clyde	D	0-0	0-0	5		1202
9	Oct	7	H	Ayr U	L	1-3	0-1	5	Mballa [90]	1858
10		14	A	Alloa Ath	W	1-0	0-0	4	Mballa [90]	987
11		21	H	Airdrieonians	D	1-1	0-1	4	Shields [46]	1930
12		28	A	Inverness CT	W	2-1	2-0	4	Stein [16], Mballa [21]	1723
13	Nov	4	H	Falkirk	L	0-2	0-1	4		3120
14		11	A	Morton	W	2-1	2-0	4	Mballa [14], Nicol [31]	742
15		25	A	Ayr U	L	2-4	1-2	4	Ellis [36], Mballa [87]	2212
16	Dec	2	H	Clyde	L	1-2	1-1	6	Bayne [36]	1810
17		5	H	Livingston	L	1-2	0-2	—	Stein [90]	1626
18		9	A	Ross Co	D	0-0	0-0	6		2578
19		16	H	Alloa Ath	W	2-1	1-0	5	Mballa [37], Tosh P [75]	1267
20	Jan	2	A	Livingston	L	0-2	0-2	—		3305
21		6	H	Morton	D	0-0	0-0	5		1721
22		13	A	Clyde	L	1-3	0-1	6	Tosh P (pen) [61]	1305
23	Feb	3	H	Ross Co	L	0-4	0-1	7		1380
24		10	A	Airdrieonians	L	0-3	0-1	8		1753
25		17	A	Ayr U	L	1-4	0-1	8	Jones [40]	1217
26	Mar	10	H	Inverness CT	D	1-1	0-0	8	Jones [63]	1342
27		17	A	Morton	D	1-1	0-1	8	Tosh P [68]	947
28		23	A	Inverness CT	L	0-2	0-0	8		1299
29		31	H	Livingston	W	2-0	1-0	8	Jones 2 [19, 74]	1794
30	Apr	3	H	Falkirk	D	0-0	0-0	2		1586
31		7	A	Ayr U	L	0-2	0-1	8		2026
32		10	A	Falkirk	L	0-2	0-0	—		1634
33		14	H	Clyde	L	0-1	0-0	9		1817
34		21	A	Alloa Ath	W	2-1	1-0	8	Smith [22], Tosh P [61]	1953
35		28	H	Airdrieonians	W	5-0	1-0	7	Tosh P 2 [21, 70], Stein 3 [52, 55, 79]	2186
36	May	5	A	Ross Co	L	0-4	0-0	7		3004

Final League Position: 7

Honours
League Champions: First Division: 1992-93, 1994-95. Division II 1907-08, 1909-10 (shared), 1937-38, 1948-49;
Runners-up: Division II 1908-09, 1926-27, 1966-67. Second Division 1975-76, 1977-78, 1986-87.
Scottish Cup Runners-up: 1913. *League Cup Winners: (Coca-Cola Cup):* 1994-95. *Runners-up:* 1948-49.

European: *UEFA Cup:* 6 matches (1995-96).

Club colours: Shirt: Navy blue, white trim. Shorts: White with navy blue edges. Stockings: Navy blue with white turnover.

Goalscorers: *League* (41): Tosh P 9 (1 pen), Mballa 8, Stein 6, Burns 4, Jones 4, Andrews 3, Bayne 1, Creaney 1, Ellis 1, McKinnon 1, Nicol 1, Shields 1, Smith 1
Scottish Cup (0):
CIS Cup (4): Burns 2 (1 pen), Stein 1, Tosh P 1
Bell's League Cup (0):

Van De Kamp G 22	McCulloch G 24	Opinel S 6+1	Gaughan K 3	Browne P 32	McEwan C 1+1	Javary J 1	Tosh S 7	Clark A 14+12	Burns A 7	Stein J 33+2	Mballa I 12+19	Andrews M 3+1	Ellis L 24+4	Black K 27+3	Tosh P 19+10	Creaney G 1+5	McKinnon R 3	Dennis S 21	Hetherston B 13+6	Hamilton S 15+3	Nicol K 17+5	Shields D 1+6	Hampshire P 15+3	Agnew P —+1	Dempsie M 2	Bayne G 8	Coyle C 3	Inglis J 12	McInally D —+2	Niven D —+1	Jones M 8	Kelly P 7	Monin S 11	Nanou W 4+3	Alfonsolobez M 5+1	Capin S 7	Smith A 8	Match No.
1	2	3	4	5	6²	7	8	9¹	10	11	12	13																										1
1	2		4	5	14		8	13	10	11	9¹		3²	6	7³	12																						2
1	2	3	4	5			7	13	10	11	14		6²	9¹	12	8³																						3
1	2	3		5			7	14	10	11	12		6³	9¹	13	8²	4																					4
	2²	11		5³			7	12	10	13	14	4	6	9¹		8	3																					5
1	2	8³		5			7	13	10²	11		4	14	6	9¹	12	3																					6
	2³	8		5			7	13	10	11¹	12	4	6	9²		3	14																					7
1	2			5				10		11			8	6	9²			3	7¹	4	12	13																8
1	2			5				10		11³	13		8	6	9²			3	14	4¹	7	12																9
1	2			5				10²		11	9		8	6				3	7¹	4	12	13																10
1	2			5				10		11			8	6	12			3	7	4¹	9																	11
1	2			5				10¹		11	9		8	6¹				3	7²	4	13	12	14															12
1	2			5				10³		11	9		8²	6	12			3	7	4¹	14	13																13
1	2	12		5				10		11	9²		8¹		13			3	7	4	6																	14
1	2			5				10		11	9		8	14	12			3	7³	4¹	6²	13																15
1	2			5				7¹		11	9		3²	6	12			8							13			4	10									16
1	2			5						11	13		3	6	9²			7	8	12								4¹	10									17
1	2			5				13		11	12		4	6	9¹			8	7				3					10²										18
1	2			5				13		11	9²		4	6	12			8	7²				3					10										19
1	2			5				13		11	9¹		4²		12			8	7	6			3					10										20
1	4			5				9		11			3		7		12	2	8		6¹							10										21
1	2			5				9		11	12		3	6²	4				13	7			3					10¹										22
	2			5				7			9¹		6²					11	8				3			10	1	4	12	13								23
				5				10²		11³	13		12	6				7	8				3				1	4¹	14		9							24
				5				14		11	12		4	7¹	10³			13	8				3				1	6¹			9	2						25
				5¹						11	9²		12	14	13			6	7				3					4			10	2	1	8³				26
				5²				13		11	9¹		6	14	12			4	7³				3								10	2	1	8				27
				13				11		14	6		10		5			12	7				3					4¹			9²	2³	1	8				28
								11					3¹	6²	14			4	12	7			5					10		1	13	2	8		9³			29
								11		14			6	12				4		7²			3					5¹			10³	1	13	2	8	9		30
		5						12		13			14	6	11¹				7				3					4			10²	8	1	2³		9		31
		5						11²		13			6	10				4	7¹				3					2				1	12	8	9		32
		5						11		12			3	6	10			4					2¹				7	1					8	9			33
		5						11³		13			3²	6	10			4	12				2				7	1			14	8	9²			34
		5						11³		13			3	6³	10			4		14	12		2					1				7	8	9²			35
	4²							11		12			3		10					13	6		8¹						1		7	5	2	9				36

RANGERS

Premier League

Year Formed: 1873. *Ground & Address:* Ibrox Stadium, 150 Edmiston Drive, Glasgow G51 2XD.
Telephone: 0870 600 1972. *Fax:* 0870 600 1978. *Website:* www.rangers.co.uk
Ground Capacity: all seated: 50,444. *Size of Pitch:* 114.5m × 81.5m.
Chairman: David Murray. *Secretary:* R. C. Ogilvie. *Commercial & Marketing Manager:* Martin Bain.
Manager: Dick Advocaat. *Assistant Manager:* Bert Van Lingen. *First Team Coach:* Jan Wouters. *Physio:* Grant Downie.
Reserve team coaches: John McGregor, John Brown.
Managers since 1975: Jock Wallace, John Greig, Jock Wallace, Graeme Souness, Walter Smith. *Club Nickname(s):* The
Gers. *Previous Grounds:* Flesher's Haugh, Burnbank, Kinning Park, Old Ibrox.
Record Attendance: 118,567 v Celtic, Division I; 2 Jan, 1939.
Record Transfer Fee received: £5,580,000 for Trevor Steven to Marseille (Aug 1991).
Record Transfer Fee paid: £12 million for Tore Andre Flo from Chelsea (November 2000).
Record Victory: 14-2 v Blairgowrie, Scottish Cup 1st rd; 20 Jan, 1934.
Record Defeat: 2-10 v Airdrieonians; 1886.
Most Capped Player: Ally McCoist, 60, Scotland.
Most League Appearances: 496: John Greig, 1962-78.
Most League Goals in Season (Individual): 44: Sam English, Division I; 1931-32.
Most Goals Overall (Individual): 355: Ally McCoist; 1985-98.

Honours

League Champions: (49 times) Division I 1890-91 (shared), 1898-99, 1899-1900, 1900-01, 1901-02, 1910-11, 1911-12,
1912-13, 1917-18, 1919-20, 1920-21, 1922-23, 1923-24, 1924-25, 1926-27, 1927-28, 1928-29, 1929-30, 1930-31, 1932-33,

RANGERS 2000–01 LEAGUE RECORD

Match No.	Date	Venue	Opponents	Result	H/T Score	Lg. Pos.	Goalscorers	Attendance
1	Jul 29	H	St Johnstone	W 2-1	0-1	—	Dodds 2 [55, 57]	48,062
2	Aug 5	A	Kilmarnock	W 4-2	1-2	2	Dodds 2 (1 pen) [36 (p), 74], Miller [77], Tugay [84]	14,680
3	13	A	St Mirren	W 3-1	1-0	1	Albertz 2 [28, 65], Dodds [50]	9251
4	19	H	Dunfermline Ath	W 4-1	3-1	2	Albertz (pen) [10], Van Bronckhorst [22], Dodds [30], Wallace [49]	47,452
5	27	A	Celtic	L 2-6	1-3	3	Reyna [40], Dodds (pen) [53]	59,476
6	Sept 9	A	Dundee	D 1-1	0-0	3	McCann [56]	10,439
7	17	H	Hearts	W 1-0	0-0	3	de Boer [58]	47,496
8	23	H	Motherwell	W 1-0	1-0	3	Mols [14]	11,275
9	Oct 1	A	Dundee U	W 3-0	2-0	3	Kanchelskis [32], Albertz [42], Van Bronckhorst [72]	44,324
10	14	A	Hibernian	L 0-1	0-1	3		14,524
11	22	H	St Johnstone	L 1-2	0-1	4	Miller [55]	7763
12	28	H	Kilmarnock	L 0-3	0-2	4		49,659
13	Nov 4	H	St Mirren	W 7-1	4-1	4	Miller 5 [1, 23, 24, 31, 78], Dodds [76], McCann [89]	48,795
14	12	A	Aberdeen	W 2-1	1-1	3	Miller [41], Mols [50]	16,798
15	18	A	Dunfermline Ath	D 0-0	0-0	4		10,706
16	26	H	Celtic	W 5-1	1-0	3	Ferguson [35], Flo [60], de Boer [68], Amoruso [76], Mols [87]	50,083
17	Dec 3	H	Hearts	W 1-0	1-0	4	Albertz (pen) [12]	16,710
18	10	H	Motherwell	W 2-0	1-0	3	Konterman [37], Ferguson [78]	46,058
19	13	A	Aberdeen	W 3-1	1-1	—	Mols [25], Dodds [59], Albertz [88]	45,285
20	17	A	Dundee U	D 1-1	1-1	3	Reyna [18]	10,750
21	23	H	Hibernian	W 1-0	0-0	3	de Boer [49]	49,993
22	26	H	St Johnstone	W 3-0	1-0	—	McCann [32], Ricksen [55], Flo [88]	46,180
23	Jan 2	A	St Mirren	W 3-1	2-1	—	Flo 2 [12, 44], Konterman [60]	8142
24	31	H	Aberdeen	W 1-0	1-0	—	Tugay [34]	45,621
25	Feb 3	H	Dunfermline Ath	W 2-0	1-0	2	Tugay [28], Mols [88]	46,302
26	11	A	Celtic	L 0-1	0-1	3		59,496
27	24	A	Dundee	W 1-0	0-0	2	Konterman [75]	9778
28	Mar 3	H	Hearts	W 2-0	1-0	2	Flo 2 [35, 57]	49,003
29	14	H	Dundee	L 0-2	0-1	—		45,035
30	17	A	Motherwell	W 2-1	0-1	2	Fernandes [59], Malcolm [89]	11,208
31	31	H	Dundee U	L 0-2	0-0	2		48,382
32	Apr 8	A	Hibernian	D 0-0	0-0	2		9704
33	11	A	Kilmarnock	W 2-0	2-0	—	Flo 2 [1, 44]	14,585
34	21	A	Dundee	W 3-0	3-0	2	Wallace [4], Flo [22], Albertz [27]	10,687
35	29	H	Celtic	L 0-3	0-0	2		50,057
36	May 5	A	Hearts	W 4-1	1-0	2	Albertz 2 [29, 78], Wallace [49], Flo [85]	15,315
37	12	H	Kilmarnock	W 5-1	1-0	2	de Boer [19], Wallace 2 [65, 78], Amoruso [68], Flo [87]	46,577
38	20	H	Hibernian	W 4-0	2-0	2	Albertz [13], de Boer 2 [34, 56], Vidmar [90]	47,023

Final League Position: 2

1933-34, 1934-35, 1936-37, 1938-39, 1946-47, 1948-49, 1949-50, 1952-53, 1955-56, 1956-57, 1958-59, 1960-61, 1962-63, 1963-64, 1974-75. Premier Division: 1975-76, 1977-78, 1986-87, 1988-89, 1989-90, 1990-91, 1991-92, 1992-93, 1993-94, 1994-95, 1995-96, 1996-97, 1998-99, 1999-2000 *Runners-up:* 24 times.
Scottish Cup Winners: (29 times) 1894, 1897, 1898, 1903, 1928, 1930, 1932, 1934, 1935, 1936, 1948, 1949, 1950, 1953, 1960, 1962, 1963, 1964, 1966, 1973, 1976, 1978, 1979, 1981, 1992, 1993, 1996, 1999, 2000; *Runners-up:* 17 times.
League Cup Winners: (21 times) 1946-47, 1948-49, 1960-61, 1961-62, 1963-64, 1964-65, 1970-71, 1975-76, 1977-78, 1978-79, 1981-82, 1983-84, 1984-85, 1986-87, 1987-88, 1988-89, 1990-91, 1992-93, 1993-94, 1996-97, 1998-99; *Runners-up:* 7 times.

European: *European Cup:* 109 matches (1956-57, 1957-58, 1959-60 semi-finals, 1961-62, 1963-64, 1964-65, 1975-76, 1976-77, 1978-79, 1987-88, 1989-90, 1990-91, 1991-92, 1992-93 final pool, 1993-94, 1994-95, 1995-96; 1996-97, 1997-98, 1999-2000, 2000-01).
Cup Winners' Cup: 54 matches (1960-61 runners-up, 1962-63, 1966-67 runners-up, 1969-70, 1971-72 winners, 1973-74, 1977-78, 1979-80, 1981-82, 1983-84). *UEFA Cup:* 54 matches (*Fairs Cup:* 1967-68, 1968-69 semi-finals, 1970-71. *UEFA Cup:* 1982-83, 1984-85, 1985-86, 1986-87, 1988-89, 1997-98, 1998-99, 1999-2000, 2000-01).

Club colours: Shirt: Royal blue with white trim and red panels. Shorts: White with blue trim. Stockings: Black with red tops.

Goalscorers: *League* (76): Flo 11, Albertz 10 (2 pens), Dodds 9 (2 pens), Miller 8, de Boer 6, Mols 5, Wallace 5, Konterman 3, McCann 3, Tugay 3, Amoruso 2, Ferguson 2, Reyna 2, Van Bronckhorst 2, Fernandes 1, Kanchelskis 1, Malcolm 1, Ricksen 1, Vidmar 1
Scottish Cup (5): Flo 2, Ferguson 1, Johnston 1, Miller 1
CIS Cup (7): Albertz 1, Amoruso 1, Dodds 1, Ferguson 1, Miller 1, Van Bronckhorst 1, Wallace 1

Klos S 32	Ricksen F 26 + 1	Amoruso L 29	Konterman B 36 + 1	Vidmar T 11 + 4	Kanchelskis A 3 + 4	Ferguson B 30	Van Bronckhorst G 10 + 1	Albertz J 20 + 4	Dodds W 16 + 14	Wallace R 14 + 1	McCann N 16 + 5	Reyna C 16 + 2	Miller K 12 + 15	Porrini S 12	Tugay17 + 9	Lovenkrands P 1 + 7	Wilson S 19 + 1	Numan A 22	de Boer R 17	Mols M 10 + 3	Johnston A 9 + 4	Brown M 3	Negri M 1	Adamczuk D 1 + 2	Christiansen J 3	Flo T 18 + 1	Carson S 1 + 1	Ross M — + 1	Malcolm R 3 + 3	Hughes S — + 1	Moore C 5	Kauppila J 1 + 3	Gayle M 4	Fernandes F — + 4	Match No.
1	2	3	4	5¹	6²	7	8	9	10	11³	12	13	14																						1
1	2¹	3	4		12	7	8		10	11³	9	6	14	5²	13																				2
1	2	3	4	12		7	5	9	10	11	8¹		6																					3
1	2	3	4		12	7	5	8¹	10	11¹	9³	13		6	14																			4
1	2¹	3	4	5²	13	7	8		10	11	9²	6		12	14																			5
1	14	3				8		10		9¹	2²	13		7	12	4	5	6²	11															6
1	2	3	4	13		8	9¹	10²		12		14		7			5	11³		6														7
	3	4	14			8		11			2²	13		7	12		5		10¹	6²														8
	2	3¹	4	12	6	8	9²	13				14		7			5	11³			1	10												9
	3	4	5	12	8		9	10			13	2¹	7	11				6²	1															10
	3	4			6		10¹	13	8		11	2	7	12		9			1	5²														11
6	3	4		9¹			12	11³	8		13	2²	7		5	10						14	1											12
2	3	14			8	9	12		13		11		7³		4	5	6¹	10²				1												13
6	3	4	2		7	9	12			11¹			5²		8	10				13	1													14
1		3	4	2	7	8		12		11			5	6	9	10¹																		15
1		3	4		7	8		14	2	11¹	13		5	6	9²	12						10³												16
1		3	4		7	8	13		2	11²		12	5	6	9							10¹												17
1	2		3	5	6		9³	13	7			12	4			11	8³					10¹	14											18
1	2		3		6		12	13	8	7	10²		4	5	9¹	11						11												19
1	2	3	4	5³	6		14	10¹	8	7	12			9²	11	13																		20
1	2	3	4		6		9	14	8	7	13	5¹	12		10³	11²																		21
1	2	3	4		6			8³	7	12		9		5	10²	11¹	14				13													22
1	2¹	3	4		6		12		8	7	11²			5	9¹	13					10	14												23
1	7		6	4				9		10¹	2²	8		3	5			12			11		13											24
1	2		6	4¹					7	10²		8		3	5	12	9				11			13										25
1	7		4		6	9²			8		10¹	12		3	5		13				11		2											26
1		3	7		6			12		10²	13	2	8		5		9¹				11		4											27
1		3	7		6	8¹		10			13	2			5		9				11		14			4³	12²							28
1	4¹		7		6		12				2			5			9²				11	8¹	13			3	14	10						29
1		4			6		13			10²	2¹			5		9					11		3			7	8	12						30
1			4	5		6¹		9	13	10		2			7		3					11						8²	12					31
1	7		4		6			12	11	10		8			2			3	5				9¹											32
1	7		4		6			11¹	10		8	12	2			3	5					9												33
1	2	3	7			6²		8	11¹	10			14		13		4	5					9³										12	34
1	2	3²	7¹			6		8	11³	10				12	13		5						9					4				14		35
1	2	3	7			6		8		10	9					5							11					4						36
1	2	3	7					8³	13	10					6	12			5	9²									11			4¹	14		37
1	2	3	7	4			13	8	14	10¹					6	12				5²	9³												11	38

ROSS COUNTY

First Division

Year Formed: 1929. *Ground & Address:* Victoria Park, Dingwall IV15 9QW. *Telephone:* 01349 860860. *Fax:* 01349 866277. *Website:* www.rosscountyfootballclub.co.uk
Ground Capacity: total 5500, seated 2700. *Size of Ground:* 110×75yd.
Chairman: Roy McGregor. *Secretary:* Donnie MacBean. *Facilities Manager:* Brian Campbell.
Manager: Neale Cooper. *Assistant Manager:* Gordon Chisholm. *Physio:* Douglas Sim. *Record Attendance:* 6600, benefit match v Celtic, 31 August 1970.
Record Transfer Fee Received: £200,000 for Neil Tarrant to Aston Villa (April 1999).
Record Transfer Fee Paid: £25,000 for Barry Wilson from Southampton (Oct. 1992).
Record Victory: 11-0 v St Cuthbert Wanderers, Scottish Cup, Dec. 1993.
Record Defeat: 1-10 v Inverness Thistle, Highland League.
Most League Appearances: 124: W. Herd, 1995-98.
Most League Goals in Season: 22: D. Adams, 1996-97.
Most League Goals (Overall): 38: D. Adams, 1996-98.

ROSS COUNTY 2000–01 LEAGUE RECORD

Match No.	Date		Venue	Opponents	Result		H/T Score	Lg. Pos.	Goalscorers	Attendance
1	Aug	5	A	Ayr U	L	0-1	0-1	—		2740
2		12	H	Clyde	L	0-2	0-1	10		2645
3		26	H	Airdrieonians	D	1-1	1-1	10	Shaw (pen) [17]	2210
4	Sept	2	A	Raith R	L	1-4	0-1	10	Bone [74]	1759
5		9	A	Morton	W	1-0	1-0	8	Bone [15]	1187
6		16	A	Inverness CT	W	1-0	0-0	7	Bone (pen) [54]	4823
7		23	H	Falkirk	L	0-2	0-0	7		3161
8		30	H	Alloa Ath	W	1-0	0-0	7	Bone [71]	2775
9	Oct	7	A	Livingston	L	1-3	0-1	8	Bone [53]	3466
10		14	H	Ayr U	D	1-1	0-0	7	Holmes [81]	2567
11		21	A	Clyde	D	2-2	1-0	7	Taggart [25], Henderson [58]	987
12		28	A	Airdrieonians	L	1-5	0-3	7	Armstrong (og) [64]	1431
13	Nov	4	H	Morton	W	3-1	2-1	7	Bone [3], Holmes [22], Taggart [46]	2048
14		11	A	Falkirk	W	3-2	1-0	6	Ferguson [28], Irvine [53], Holmes [83]	2898
15		18	H	Inverness CT	L	0-3	0-1	6		5761
16		25	H	Livingston	L	0-2	0-1	7		2723
17	Dec	2	A	Alloa Ath	D	0-0	0-0	7		620
18		9	H	Raith R	D	0-0	0-0	8		2578
19		16	A	Ayr U	W	2-0	1-0	7	Coyle [7], McCormick [49]	2007
20	Jan	2	A	Inverness CT	D	3-3	3-1	—	Coyle [15], Ferguson [35], Irvine [40]	5291
21	Feb	3	A	Raith R	W	4-0	1-0	6	Henderson [34], Maxwell [59], Bone 2 [76, 89]	1380
22	Mar	10	H	Falkirk	W	4-1	3-0	6	Perry [8], Henderson [23], Bone [44], Ferguson [62]	2620
23		17	A	Falkirk	D	1-1	0-1	6	Henderson [56]	1955
24		20	H	Clyde	W	2-0	1-0	—	Henderson [25], Holmes [57]	2115
25		24	H	Alloa Ath	L	2-3	1-1	6	Henderson [15], Bone [61]	2079
26		27	A	Livingston	D	1-1	1-1	—	Robertson [19]	1736
27		31	H	Inverness CT	L	0-1	0-1	6		5876
28	Apr	3	H	Airdrieonians	L	3-4	1-2	—	Holmes 2 [12, 54], McQuade [53]	1645
29		7	H	Livingston	L	0-1	0-0	7		2549
30		10	A	Airdrieonians	D	2-2	1-1	—	Bone [7], Ferguson [88]	1211
31		14	A	Alloa Ath	D	1-1	0-0	6	Bone [74]	647
32		17	H	Morton	L	0-2	0-2	—		1894
33		21	H	Ayr U	L	0-1	0-0	7		1942
34		24	A	Morton	W	3-0	3-0	—	Bone 2 [34, 45], Canning [40]	812
35		28	A	Clyde	L	0-2	0-0	6		1313
36	May	5	H	Raith R	W	4-0	0-0	6	Prest 3 [48, 58, 63], Ferguson [66]	3004

Final League Position: 6

Honours
League Champions: Third Division: 1998-99.

Club colours: Navy blue, white and red.

Goalscorers: *League* (48): Bone 14 (1 pen), Henderson 6, Holmes 6, Ferguson S 5, Prest 3, Coyle 2, Irvine 2, Taggart 2, Canning 1, McCormick 1, McQuade 1, Maxwell 1, Perry 1, Robertson 1, Shaw 1 (1 pen), own goal 1
Scottish Cup (4): Bone 2, Cunnington 1, Henderson 1
CIS Cup (2): Holmes 1, Shaw 1
Bell's League Cup (2): Bone 1, Henderson 1

Walker J 30	Gilbert K 11+2	Mackay D 23+4	Maxwell I 32	Irvine B 25+2	Taggart C 13+1	Shaw G 3+2	Fraser J 13+12	Bone A 28+1	Millar M 12	Henderson D 21+3	Miller S —+1	Escalon F 10+4	Holmes D 17+12	Cunnington E 22+2	Ross D —+1	Ferguson S 27+6	McQuade J 17+8	Kinnaird P 5+4	King S —+1	Canning M 3+3	Smith A 3	Campbell C —+1	Zahani-Oni L —+6	O'Neill J —+3	Mackay S 2+1	Perry M 20	McCormick M 14+3	Coyle O 5	Boukraa K 14	Hamilton G 6	Robertson H 16	Prest M 3+5	Cowie D 1	Disgonski B —+1	Match No.
1	2	3	4	5	6²	7¹	8	9	10	11³	12	13	14																						1
1	2	5	4		6¹		8	9	10		12					7³	11²	3	13	14															2
1	2		4	5		7	14	9	10				12	11¹	3	8¹	6²		13																3
1	2	6	4	5			7	9							3	8²	10	11¹	12	13															4
1	2	5	4	14			8	9³	10	11			13		3	6²	7¹	12																	5
1	2	5	4				6	9	10	11			13	8¹	3	7²	12																		6
1	3	5	4				12	13		9	10	8				2	6²	7¹	11																7
1	12	5	4					9	10	6		2¹	13		3	14	7	11³				8²													8
1	2	5	4				14	9	10	6²				11¹	3	13	7³	12				8													9
1	3	2	4	5				9	10	6¹		7	13			12	11					8²													10
1	14	2	4	5	6²			9	10³			7	8		3	12	13	11¹																	11
1		2	4	5	6		8	12	10	3		9				7¹	11²						13												12
1	2	13	4	5	6		10¹	9		8²				11	3	7	12																		13
1	2	14	4	5	6		12	9		10				11²		7³	8¹								13										14
1			4	5	6		12	9		10		2¹	11³	3		7	8²									14	13								15
1	2		4	5	6²	7	10¹	9				3³				8	11									14	12	13							16
1			4	5	6²		12	9¹		3						8	11³									14	13	2	7	10					17
1			4	5	6¹		12	9²		3						8	11										13	2	7	10					18
1	13		4	5	6					11						12	3	8²										2	7	9	10¹				19
		3	4	5	6¹		12			11						8			13						14			2	7²	9	10³	1			20
1			4	5			6	12		11						8												2	7	9	10¹	3			21
1	13		4	5			12	9		11		6²				8												2	7		10¹	3			22
1			4	5				9		11		6				8												2	7		10	3			23
1			4	5			14	9		11¹		6³	12	13		8												2	7		10²	3			24
1			4	5			8	9		11¹		6	12															2	7		10	3			25
1		5				7		9				2²	12	13		6¹	8			14						4					10	3	11²		26
1	6¹		4	5				9		11			13			8				14								2	7³		10²	3	12		27
		5	4		13			9		11²		6³				8	12											2	7¹		10	3	14		28
1			4	5			8	9		11²		6	12			7												2			10	3¹	13		29
1			4	5			8²	9		12		6	14			7											13	2			10	3²	11¹		30
			4	5			14	9		12		6				8	7³										13	2		10¹		3	11²		31
1			4	5				9		11		6				8	7²										12	2		10		3¹	13		32
1	10		4	14				9		12		11¹	6³			8	13						5				2	7			3²			33
1	10		4				6²	9				12	3			8	13						5				2	7¹		11				34
1	10		4				6²	9				13	12			8	14				2		11			5	7³			3¹				35
1	6¹		4	5			13	9								8	7³	11²									2			3	12	10	14	36

ST JOHNSTONE Premier League

Year Formed: 1884. *Ground & Address:* McDiarmid Park, Crieff Road, Perth PH1 2SJ. *Telephone:* 01738 459090. *Fax:* 01738 625 771. *Clubcall:* 0898 121559. *Website:* www.stjohnstonefc.co.uk
Ground Capacity: all seated: 10,673. *Size of Pitch:* 115yd × 75yd.
Chairman: G.S.Brown. *Secretary and Managing Director:* Stewart Duff.
Manager: Sandy Clark. *Sales Executive:* Helen Harcus. *Physio:* Nick Summersgill. *Coach:* Billy Kirkwood. *Youth Development Officer:* Alistair Stevenson.
Managers since 1975: J. Stewart, J. Storrie, A. Stuart, A. Rennie, I. Gibson, A. Totten, J. McClelland, P. Sturrock. *Club Nickname(s):* Saints. *Previous Grounds:* Recreation Grounds, Muirton Park.
Record Attendance: (McDiarmid Park): 10,545 v Dundee, Premier Division; 23 May, 1999.
Record Transfer Fee received: £1,750,000 for Calum Davidson to Blackburn R (March 1998).
Record Transfer Fee paid: £300,000 for Billy Dodds from Dundee (1994).
Record Victory: 9-0 v Albion R, League Cup; 9 March, 1946.
Record Defeat: 1-10 v Third Lanark, Scottish Cup; 24 January, 1903.
Most Capped Player: Nick Dasovic, 17, Canada.
Most League Appearances: 298: Drew Rutherford.

ST JOHNSTONE 2000–01 LEAGUE RECORD

Match No.	Date	Venue	Opponents	Result	H/T Score	Lg. Pos.	Goalscorers	Attendance
1	Jul 29	A	Rangers	L 1-2	1-0	—	Kernaghan [14]	48,062
2	Aug 6	H	Hearts	D 2-2	1-0	8	Weir [31], Jones [73]	6165
3	12	A	Dunfermline Ath	D 1-1	0-1	8	Jones (pen) [50]	3477
4	19	A	Dundee U	W 2-1	2-0	6	Jones [12], Parker [24]	5533
5	26	H	Kilmarnock	D 1-1	1-1	7	Lovenkrands [13]	3773
6	Sept 9	A	Aberdeen	D 1-1	0-0	8	Sylla [66]	10,464
7	16	H	Dundee	D 0-0	0-0	6		5055
8	23	A	St Mirren	W 1-0	1-0	6	Parker [10]	4119
9	30	H	Hibernian	L 0-3	0-2	8		5464
10	Oct 14	A	Motherwell	L 0-4	0-2	8		7118
11	17	H	Celtic	L 0-2	0-1	—		8946
12	22	H	Rangers	W 2-1	1-0	7	Parker [17], Sylla [66]	7763
13	28	A	Hearts	W 3-0	0-0	5	Parker (pen) [49], Connolly 2 [62, 88]	10,883
14	Nov 4	H	Dunfermline Ath	L 0-2	0-0	6		4287
15	12	A	Celtic	L 1-4	0-3	8	Russell [82]	56,952
16	18	H	Dundee U	W 1-0	0-0	7	Parker [80]	4295
17	25	A	Kilmarnock	W 2-0	0-0	6	Parker 2 (1 pen) [51 (p), 60]	6330
18	28	H	Aberdeen	D 0-0	0-0	—		4897
19	Dec 2	A	Dundee	D 1-1	0-1	6	Sylla [89]	7014
20	9	H	St Mirren	W 2-0	1-0	6	McBride [42], Parker [77]	4434
21	16	A	Hibernian	L 0-2	0-1	6		10,374
22	23	H	Motherwell	L 2-3	0-3	7	Parker [52], Sylla [72]	3489
23	26	A	Rangers	L 0-3	0-1	—		46,180
24	30	A	Hearts	D 2-2	2-1	8	Sylla [24], Connolly [35]	5173
25	Jan 2	A	Dunfermline Ath	D 0-0	0-0	—		6117
26	Feb 3	A	Dundee U	D 1-1	0-1	7	Lowndes [60]	6482
27	11	H	Kilmarnock	L 1-2	0-0	8	Connolly [87]	6627
28	Mar 3	H	Dundee	L 2-3	1-0	9	Bollan [13], Kane (pen) [78]	5065
29	14	H	Celtic	L 1-2	1-1	—	McCluskey [41]	8993
30	17	A	St Mirren	L 0-1	0-1	10		4563
31	27	A	Aberdeen	D 3-3	1-2	—	McBride 2 [25, 70], Lowndes [88]	8496
32	Apr 1	H	Hibernian	W 2-0	0-0	9	Lovenkrands 2 [70, 72]	4346
33	7	A	Motherwell	L 0-1	0-1	10		4600
34	21	A	Motherwell	W 1-0	0-0	10	Sylla [65]	3195
35	28	H	Aberdeen	L 0-3	0-2	10		3611
36	May 5	H	St Mirren	D 2-2	1-2	9	Dods [29], Hartley [67]	4122
37	12	H	Dundee U	L 2-3	2-0	10	McClune [5], Hartley [40]	6497
38	20	A	Dunfermline Ath	D 0-0	0-0	10		4084

Final League Position: 10

Most League Goals in Season (Individual): 36: Jimmy Benson, Division II; 1931-32.
Most Goals Overall (Individual): 140: John Brogan, 1977-83.

Honours
League Champions: First Division 1982-83, 1989-90, 1996-97. Division II 1923-24, 1959-60, 1962-63; *Runners-up:* Division II 1931-32. Second Division 1987-88.
Scottish Cup: Semi-finals 1934, 1968, 1989, 1991.
League Cup Runners-up: 1969, 1998.
League Challenge Cup Runners-up: 1996-97.

European: *UEFA Cup:* 10 matches (1971-72, 1999-2000).

Club colours: Shirt: Royal blue with white trim. Shorts: White. Stockings: Royal blue with white hoops.

Goalscorers: *League* (40): Parker 9 (2 pens), Sylla 6, Connolly 4, Jones 3 (1 pen), Lovenkrands 3, McBride 3, Hartley 2, Lowndes 2, Bollan 1, Dods 1, Kane 1 (pen), Kernaghan 1, McClune 1, McCluskey 1, Russell 1, Weir 1
Scottish Cup (2): Lowndes 1, Russell 1
CIS Cup (3): Bollan 1, Dasovic 1, Hartley 1

Main A 38	Sylla M 34	Bollan G 28	Weir J 33	Kernaghan A 17+1	McBride J 20+6	Dasovic N 35+1	Kane P 27+1	Parker K 30+7	Lovenkrands T 16+7	Jones G 9	Russell C 6+8	Connolly P 15+6	Dods D 26+3	O'Neill M 7+3	Hartley P 16+7	McCulloch M 13+9	Forsyth R 9+2	Evers S 5+1	Lauchlan M —+1	Malcolm S —+1	McCluskey S 18+1	Lowndes N 2+8	Frail S 6	Crozier B 3+1	Ferry M —+1	McClune D 5	Fotheringham M —+2	Match No.
1	2	3	4	5	6	7	8	9¹	10²	11	12	13																1
1	2	3	4	5¹	6	7	8	9²	10	11		13	12															2
1	2	3	4		6	7	8¹	9	10²	11	12	13	5															3
1	2	3	4			7		9	10²	11		13	5	6¹	8	12												4
1	2	3	4		14	7		12	10²	11	9¹		5	6¹	8	13												5
1	2	3	4	5		7	8	9¹		11	12		10	6														6
1	2	3		5	6²		8	13	10¹	11	12		4	9														7
1	2	3	4	5		7	8	9	12	11¹	6		10															8
1	2	3	4	5		7	8	9³	13	11²	6		12	10¹		14												9
1	2	3		5	6²		8	12	10¹		11	4	9³		13	14												10
1	6¹	3	4	5		7	8	10		11²	2	13			9		12											11
1	6	3	4	5	13	7	8	10	12	11¹	2				9²													12
1	6	3	4	5		7	8	10¹	12	11	2				9													13
1	6	3		5	12	7	8	10²		11	2	13			9¹		4											14
1	6	3		5³	12	7	8	10	13	11²	2				9¹	14	4											15
1	6	3	4		9¹	7	8	10	11²	13	2		5		12													16
1	9	3	4			7	8	10	11¹	2	12	6									5							17
1	9	3	4			7	8	10	11¹	12	2	6									5							18
1	6		4	12		7	8	10	11	2	9¹	3									5							19
1	9		4	6		7	8	10	11	2	3										5							20
1		3	4	9		7	8	10	11	2²	13	12	6¹								5							21
1	9	3	4	6	7¹	8	10	12	13	11²	2										5							22
1	9	3	4	7	12	8¹	10	11³	2	6	13	14									5²							23
1	9	3	4	8	7	10¹	11	2	6	5					12													24
1	9	3	4	8¹	7	10²	11	2	6	12					13	5												25
1	9	3	4	6	7	8	10²	11	2	13					12	5												26
1	9	3	4	6	7²	8	10¹	11	2	13					12	5												27
1	9	3	4	5	7	8	10	14	11³	6¹	13	12								2¹								28
1	9		4	5		7	8	11	12	13	10										2	3²	6¹					29
1			4	5		7	11	12	8¹	10	14	9									2	3²	6³	13				30
1		4		12	9	7³	8	11	6¹	10³	13	5									2	14	3					31
1	8	4	5	6¹	7	13	9	10	12	3											11¹²					2		32
1	8³	4	5	7	13	12	9	10¹	3²	6											14	11				2		33
1	9	4		8¹	11	7	12	10²	3	6											5	13				2		34
1	8²	3	4	14	7	11	9	5	10¹	6²											2	12					13	35
1	9	4		8	7	12	11²	5	10	3¹	6										2	13						36
1	9	4		8¹	7	12	11	5	10	3	6											13				2¹		37
1		3		10	7	11	12	4	5	8²	2	9¹	6								2					6	13	38

ST MIRREN

First Division

Year Formed: 1877. *Ground & Address:* St Mirren Park, Love St, Paisley PA3 2EJ. *Telephone:* 0141 889 2558/0141 840 1337. *Fax:* 0141 848 6444.
Ground Capacity: 10,866 (all seated). *Size of Pitch:* 112yd × 73yd.
Chairman: Stewart Gilmour. *Vice-Chairman:* George Campbell. *Secretary:* Allan Marshall.
Manager: Tom Hendrie. *Physio:* Colin Brow. *Youth Development Officer:* Joe Hughes.
Managers since 1975: Alex Ferguson, Jim Clunie, Rikki MacFarlane, Alex Miller, Alex Smith, Tony Fitzpatrick, David Hay, Jimmy Bone, Tony Fitzpatrick. *Club Nickname(s):* The Buddies. *Previous Grounds:* Short Roods 1877-79, Thistle Park Greenhill 1879-83, Westmarch 1883-94.
Record Attendance: 47,438 v Celtic, League Cup, 20 Aug, 1949.
Record Transfer Fee received: £850,000 for Ian Ferguson to Rangers (1988).
Record Transfer Fee paid: £400,000 for Thomas Stickroth from Bayer Uerdingen (1990).
Record Victory: 15-0 v Glasgow University, Scottish Cup 1st rd; 30 Jan, 1960.
Record Defeat: 0-9 v Rangers, Division I; 4 Dec, 1897.
Most Capped Player: Godmundor Torfason, 29, Iceland.
Most League Appearances: 351: Tony Fitzpatrick, 1973-88.

ST MIRREN 2000–01 LEAGUE RECORD

Match No.	Date		Venue	Opponents		Result	H/T Score	Lg. Pos.	Goalscorers	Atten- dance
1	Jul	29	H	Kilmarnock	L	0-1	0-0	1		7388
2	Aug	5	A	Aberdeen	L	1-2	1-1	10	Gillies [38]	11,996
3		13	H	Rangers	L	1-3	0-1	12	Paeslack [62]	9251
4		19	H	Dundee	W	2-1	0-0	10	Gillies [70], McGarry [77]	5165
5		26	A	Hibernian	L	0-2	0-1	10		11,814
6	Sept	9	H	Motherwell	L	0-1	0-0	11		5264
7		16	A	Dundee U	D	0-0	0-0	11		5181
8		20	A	Hearts	L	0-2	0-0	—		10,524
9		23	H	St Johnstone	L	0-1	0-1	11		4119
10		30	H	Dunfermline Ath	W	2-1	2-0	10	McGowan [22], Yardley [32]	5002
11	Oct	14	A	Celtic	L	0-2	0-1	11		59,788
12		21	A	Kilmarnock	L	1-2	1-0	11	Yardley [29]	7839
13		28	H	Aberdeen	W	2-0	1-0	11	Walker [24], Gillies [54]	5763
14	Nov	4	A	Rangers	L	1-7	1-4	11	Gillies [44]	48,795
15		11	H	Hearts	L	1-2	0-1	11	Gillies [90]	5234
16		18	A	Dundee	L	0-5	0-1	11		6393
17		25	H	Hibernian	D	1-1	0-1	11	McGarry [89]	5225
18		29	A	Motherwell	L	0-2	0-0	—		5312
19	Dec	5	H	Dundee U	D	1-1	0-1	—	Renfurm [71]	4685
20		9	A	St Johnstone	L	0-2	0-1	11		4434
21		16	A	Dunfermline Ath	L	0-2	0-1	11		4538
22		23	H	Celtic	L	0-2	0-1	11		9487
23		26	H	Kilmarnock	L	1-3	1-0	—	Fenton [13]	8142
24	Jan	2	H	Rangers	L	1-3	1-2	—	Gillies (pen) [35]	8142
25		31	A	Hearts	L	0-1	0-0	—		10,164
26	Feb	3	H	Dundee	W	2-1	1-1	11	Rudden [41], Dagnogo [84]	4085
27		10	A	Hibernian	L	2-4	1-1	11	Gillies 2 (1 pen) [44 (p), 55]	8799
28		21	A	Aberdeen	L	0-3	0-1	—		9457
29		24	H	Motherwell	L	0-1	0-0	12		3704
30	Mar	3	A	Dundee U	L	0-4	0-2	12		8334
31		17	H	St Johnstone	W	1-0	1-0	12	McGarry [28]	4563
32		31	H	Dunfermline Ath	D	1-1	0-1	12	McGowan [82]	5371
33	Apr	7	A	Celtic	L	0-1	0-1	12		60,102
34		23	H	Dundee U	W	2-1	0-0	12	Gillies 2 [70, 89]	6473
35		28	A	Dunfermline Ath	W	2-1	2-0	12	McGowan [31], Yardley [41]	4669
36	May	5	A	St Johnstone	D	2-2	2-1	12	Dods (og) [14], Yardley [22]	4122
37		12	H	Aberdeen	W	2-1	2-1	12	Walker [41], McGarry [44]	5780
38		20	A	Motherwell	D	3-3	1-1	12	Quitongo 2 [32, 57], Fenton [49]	4158

Final League Position: 12

Most League Goals in Season (Individual): 45: Dunky Walker, Division I; 1921-22.
Most Goals Overall (Individual): 221: David McCrae, 1923-34.

Honours
League Champions: First Division 1976-77, 1999-2000. Division II 1967-68; *Runners-up:* 1935-36.
Scottish Cup Winners: 1926, 1959, 1987. *Runners-up:* 1908, 1934, 1962.
League Cup Runners-up: 1955-56.
B&Q Cup Runners-up: 1993-94. *Victory Cup:* 1919-20. *Summer Cup:* 1943-44. *Anglo-Scottish Cup:* 1979-80.

European: *Cup Winners' Cup:* 4 matches (1987-88). *UEFA Cup:* 10 matches (1980-81, 1983-84, 1985-86).

Club colours: Shirt: Black and white vertical stripes. Shorts: Black. Stockings: Black with white trim. Change colours: Predominantly red.

Goalscorers: *League* (32): Gillies 10 (2 pens), McGarry 4, Yardley 4, McGowan 3, Fenton 2, Quitongo 2, Walker 2, Dagnogo 1, Paeslack 1, Renfurm 1, Rudden 1, own goal 1
Scottish Cup (1): Quitongo 1
CIS Cup (8): Brown 2, Walker 2, Gillies 1, McGarry 1, Murray 1, Paeslack 1

Roy L 28	McLaughlin B 29	McGowan J 23	Turner T 32	Nicolson I 21+7	Ross I 4	Murray H 22+1	Gillies R 34+2	Paeslack J 9+6	McGarry S 17+16	Yardley M 20+13	Quitongo J 12+11	McKnight P —+4	Drew C 1+1	Rudden P 10+4	Mackenzie S 22+6	Brown T 7+5	Walker S 30	Bowman G 12+5	Baltacha S 17+3	Sharp L 4+2	Fenton G 26	Renfurm M 8+8	Scrimgour D 6+1	Robinson R —+2	McCaldon I 4+1	Kerr C 12+2	Dagnogo M 2+3	McPhee S 6+1	Match No.
1	2	3	4	5	6	7	8	9²	10	11¹	12	13																	1
1	2	3		12	6		8	14	10²	11³	9	13	4	5¹															2
1	2		4	3²	6	7	8		10	12	11¹	9³			5	13	14												3
1	2	3	4	5	6²	7	8	11¹	10	12	9		13																4
1	2	3	4	6		7	8	11¹	10¹	13	9³				14	12	5												5
1	2	3	4	6³		7	8	11¹	10²	13	9					12	5	14											6
1	2	3³	4			7¹	8	11²	10	13	9					12	5		14										7
1	2		4	6		7	8	11	10²	13	9						5		12										8
1	2		4	3		7	13	10¹	12	11	9				8²		5	6											9
1	2	3	4	6		7	8	14	10²	11³	12						5					9¹	13						10
	2		4	3		7	8	14	13	11³							5	12	6¹			9¹	10						11
1	2		4	3		7¹	8	14	13	11					12		5	6				9²	10³						12
1⁶	2	3	4	6²		7	8	10	12	11¹					13		5					9		15					13
	2	3	4	6¹			8	13	10³			14			9		5			7	11²			1	12				14
	2	3	4				8	14	10¹	11					7	12	5	13			6²	9³		1					15
	2	3	4			7²	8		10	11					6	13	5¹	12				9	1						16
	2	3	4			7³	8		13	14				12	6	10		9	5¹		11²		1						17
	2	3¹	4			7	8³		14	13					6²	10		9	5	12	11	1							18
1	2						8		12	11¹			3	6	10	5	7	4			9²	13	1⁶	15					19
	2		4	14			8		12	13				6¹		5	9	3³			11²	10		1					20
	2						8		13	12	14			6	11	5	7	3¹			9²	10³		1					21
	2		4	12		7	8		14		13			3¹	11²	5					9	10³		1		6			22
1	2¹		4	3		7	8		13				12		11	5	6				9²	10³				14			23
1			4	3¹		7	8		12	13				14	11¹	5		6			9	10²			2				24
1			4			7³	8		10²	12	13		3	9		5	14	6			11¹				2				25
1			4	6			12	13		11	10⁵		3¹	9²		5	8	7							2	14			26
1		4³	6				8			11¹	14		3	9		5	13	7		10					2²	12			27
1			4			7¹	8			11²	13		3	9		5		6		10					2	12			28
1		6	4	12			8		14	13	11²		3	9		5				10³					2	7			29
1	2	6	4	14			8		13	12			3	9²		5		7		10					3³	11¹			30
1	2	5	4				8		10	11²	12			7			6			9¹	13				3				31
1	2	5	4				8		10²	11¹	12			7			5			9¹	14				3	13			32
1	2	5		12			8		14		11³			7	4		6¹			10²	13				3	9			33
1	2	3	4				8			11	12			7		5	6			10¹						9			34
1	2	3	4				8			11²	13			7		5	6	12		10¹	14					9³			35
1		4	2²				8		10¹	11²			12	7		5	6	3			14					13	9		36
1	2	4	12						10³	11			13	7		5	6	3²		9¹	14						8		37
1		4	6						10		11	13			5	7				9²		12			2	8¹			38

STENHOUSEMUIR　　　　　Second Division

Year Formed: 1884. *Ground & Address:* Ochilview Park, Gladstone Rd, Stenhousemuir FK5 5QL. *Telephone:* 01324 562992. *Fax:* 01324 562980.
Ground Capacity: total: 2374, seated: 626. *Size of Pitch:* 110yd × 72yd.
Chairman: A Terry Bulloch. *Secretary:* David O. Reid.
Manager: Brian Fairley. *Assistant Manager:* Alan McGonigal. *Physio:* Lee Campbell.
Managers since 1975: H. Glasgow, J. Black, A. Rose, W. Henderson, A. Rennie, J. Meakin, D. Lawson, T. Christie, G. Armstrong. *Club Nickname(s):* The Warriors. *Previous Grounds:* Tryst Ground 1884-86, Goschen Park 1886-90.
Record Attendance: 12,500 v East Fife, Scottish Cup 4th rd; 11 Mar, 1950.
Record Transfer Fee received: £70,000 for Euan Donaldson to St Johnstone (May 1995).
Record Transfer Fee paid: £20,000 to Livingston for Ian Little (June 1995).
Record Victory: 9-2 v Dundee U, Division II; 19 Apr, 1937.
Record Defeat: 2-11 v Dunfermline Ath. Division II; 27 Sept, 1930.
Most Capped Player: —.
Most League Appearances: 360: Archie Rose.
Most League Goals in Season (Individual): 32: Robert Taylor, Division II; 1925-26.
Most Goals Overall (Individual): —.

STENHOUSEMUIR 2000–01 LEAGUE RECORD

Match No.	Date	Venue	Opponents	Result		H/T Score	Lg. Pos.	Goalscorers	Attendance
1	Aug 5	H	Queen of the S	W	4-3	3-0	—	Wood [19], English [26], Menelaws 2 [43, 90]	520
2	12	A	Clydebank	L	0-1	0-0	5		236
3	19	H	Partick Th	W	4-0	3-0	2	McKinnon [30], English [33], Cormack [39], Gibson L [75]	1130
4	26	A	Forfar Ath	D	2-2	2-1	2	McKinnon [6], English [9]	381
5	Sept 9	H	Stirling A	L	0-2	0-0	5		594
6	16	A	Arbroath	L	0-3	0-1	7		541
7	23	H	Berwick R	W	2-0	2-0	4	McKinnon [18], Mooney (pen) [26]	428
8	30	A	Queen's Park	L	0-2	0-0	7		793
9	Oct 7	H	Stranraer	L	1-2	0-0	8	Lorimer [82]	277
10	14	A	Queen of the S	L	2-4	0-3	9	Blaikie [60], Miller [68]	1013
11	21	A	Clydebank	W	2-0	0-1	8	English 2 [76, 86]	450
12	28	H	Forfar Ath	W	2-0	1-0	6	English [28], Miller [70]	321
13	Nov 4	A	Stirling A	W	3-2	0-1	5	Blaikie [68], English 2 [70, 75]	645
14	11	A	Berwick R	L	1-4	0-2	6	English [78]	424
15	18	A	Arbroath	W	3-1	0-1	5	Miller [52], English 2 [55, 62]	369
16	25	A	Stranraer	W	4-1	1-0	2	English 2 [28, 70], Miller [49], McAneny [77]	454
17	Dec 2	H	Queen's Park	D	1-1	1-0	2	Miller [35]	492
18	26	A	Partick Th	L	0-3	0-0	—		2635
19	Jan 2	H	Stirling A	D	1-1	0-1	—	McKinnon [87]	573
20	6	A	Forfar Ath	L	0-7	0-4	—		441
21	13	A	Arbroath	L	0-5	0-2	6		575
22	Feb 3	H	Stranraer	D	2-2	0-1	7	Miller (pen) [60], Henderson [78]	351
23	10	A	Queen's Park	W	2-1	0-0	4	Miller [60], English [65]	704
24	17	H	Partick Th	W	2-0	1-0	4	English [15], McKinnon [70]	1343
25	Mar 6	A	Queen of the S	L	1-2	0-0	—	McColligan [70]	250
26	10	H	Forfar Ath	L	0-1	0-0	5		376
27	13	H	Berwick R	L	0-2	0-2	—		345
28	17	A	Berwick R	L	0-1	0-1	6		402
29	27	A	Clydebank	L	0-1	0-1	—		256
30	31	H	Arbroath	L	0-1	0-0	8		475
31	Apr 3	A	Stirling A	D	0-0	0-0	—		390
32	7	A	Stranraer	L	1-2	0-0	8	English [79]	365
33	14	H	Queen's Park	W	2-0	1-0	7	Mensing (pen) [19], Miller [75]	519
34	21	A	Queen of the S	W	3-1	1-1	7	Davidson [9], English 2 [46, 60]	1111
35	28	H	Clydebank	D	0-0	0-0	7		404
36	May 5	A	Partick Th	L	0-4	0-0	7		4624

Final League Position: 7

Honours
League Champions: Third Division runners-up: 1998-99. *Scottish Cup:* Semi-finals 1902-03. Quarter-finals 1948-49, 1949-50, 1994-95. *League Cup:* Quarter-finals 1947-48, 1960-61, 1975-76. *League Challenge Cup:* Winners 1995-96.

Club colours: Shirt: Maroon. Shorts: White. Stockings: Maroon.

Goalscorers: *League* (45): English 18, Miller 8 (1 pen), McKinnon 5, Blaikie 2, Menelaws 2, Cormack 1, Davidson 1, Gibson 1, Henderson 1, Lorimer 1, McAneny 1, McColligan 1, Mensing 1 (pen), Mooney 1 (pen), Wood 1
Scottish Cup (1): Menelaws 1
CIS Cup (2): McKinnon 1, McLauchlan 1
Bell's League Cup (2): Gibson 1, Menelaws 1

Gow G 34	Davidson G 27	Fishar J 11 + 3	McAneny P 19 + 1	Cormack P 19 + 2	Ferguson P 9 + 4	Mooney M 9 + 5	McKinnon C 19 + 3	English I 28 + 5	Menelaws D 11 + 14	Wood D 8 + 1	McLauchlan M 2 + 3	Gibson L 2 + 7	Lorimer D — + 3	Donald B 26 + 2	Storrar A 20 + 5	Pitman S 3	Duncan G 16 + 5	Miller S 30 + 1	Graham T 15 + 1	Gibson J 6	Smith G 1 + 2	Henderson N 14 + 9	Blaikie A 3 + 7	Fallon S 3	Mensing S 15	Sandison J 15	McColligan B 11 + 1	Jackson C 10 + 3	Abbott G 5 + 5	Henry J 3	McGurk R 2	Murphy S — + 1	Match No.
1	2	3	4	5	6	7^2	8	9^1	10	11^1	12	13	14																				1
1	2	3	4	5		8^2	13	9^1	10	11	12	14		6	7^3																		2
1	2	3	4	5		7^3	8	9	10^1	11^2	13	12		6	14																		3
1	2		4	5		14	8	11	10	13		9^2	12	6^2	7	3^1																	4
1			4	5		7^2	8	9	12	11^1			13	6^2	3		2	10	14														5
1	2			5			8	9	12	11^2			13	14	3		7^1	10	4	6^3													6
1		2	5		6		8	12	9^1	11			7	13				10^2	4	3^1	14												7
1		2	5		6^2		8	13	9	11^2			7	12				10	4	3^1	14												8
1			4	5		7^1	8^2		12	11^2	9		14	6	3		2	10				13											9
1			4	14	12		8	13						6	3^2		2	10	5			9^3	7^1	11									10
1	6		4		13		8	12						10			2	9	5	3		7^2	11^1										11
1	6		4				8	11	12					10			2	9	5	3^1		7^2	13										12
1	6		4	3	12		8^1	11^3	14					10			2	9	5			7^2	13										13
1			4	3	6^2		8	11	13					10^1	14		2	9	5			7^3	12										14
1	6		4	3	7^2		8	10^3	14					13			2	9	5			12	11^1										15
1	6		4	3	7		8	11^3	12					10			2	9	5														16
1	6		4	3	7		8	11						10			2	9	5														17
1	6		4	3	7^2		8^1	11	12					10			2	9	5^3			13	14										18
1	6	11^2	4	3	7^3		8^1		14					10			2	9	5			12	13										19
1	6	11^1	4^2	3	12		8		14					10	13		2	9	5			7^3											20
1	11	13	6			7^1	12	8	10	14							2	4	9^3	5^2						3							21
1	4^1			12				13	11^3	14				8	2		9					7^2			5	6	3						22
1	4							11^1	12					8	2			9^3	10			7^2			5	6	3	13					23
1	4						8	11^1	12						2		13	9	10^2						5	6	3	7					24
1	4^2							11^1	12					8	2		13	9	10^3						5	6	3	7	14				25
1	4							11	13					8^1	2			9	10^3			14			5	6	3	12	7^3				26
1	4							11^2	12					8	2^2			9	10						5	6	3	7	13				27
1	4^1							11	14					8	2			9^2	10^3			13			5	6	3	7	12				28
1	11^3		4						12					8^2	2			9^1	13			14			5	6	3	7	10				29
1	4							11	13					8	2				12						5	6	3^2	7	9^1	10			30
1	6	3^1						11						8	2			9^2				13			5	4	12	7	10				31
1	4							11	13					8	2			9	12			14			5	6^3	3	7^2	10^1				32
1	4	3						11	12					8	2			9	10^1						5	6		7					33
1	4	3						11^2	12					8	2			9	10^1						5	6		7	13				34
1	4^2	3						11^2	12						2			9	10^1						5	6	8	7	13		1	14	35
1	4							11^2	13					8	2			9	10^1			12			5	6	3	7			1		36

STIRLING ALBION Third Division

Year Formed: 1945. *Ground & Address:* Forthbank Stadium, Springkerse Industrial Estate, Stirling FK7 7UJ.
Telephone: 01786 450399. *Fax:* 01786 448592.
Ground Capacity: 3808, seated: 2508. *Size of Pitch:* 110yd × 74yd.
Chairman: Peter McKenzie. *Secretary:* Mrs Marlyn Hallam.
Manager: Ray Stewart. *Assistant Manager:* Ian Miller. *Physio:* George Cameron.
Managers since 1975: A. Smith, G. Peebles, J. Fleeting, J. Brogan, K. Drinkell, J. Philliben. *Club Nickname(s):* The Binos.
Previous Grounds: Annfield 1945-92.
Record Attendance: 26,400 (at Annfield) v Celtic, Scottish Cup 4th rd; 14 Mar, 1959. 3808 v Aberdeen, Scottish Cup
4th rd, 15 February 1996 (Forthbank).
Record Transfer Fee received: £70,000 for John Philliben to Doncaster R (Mar 1984).
Record Transfer Fee paid: £25,000 for Craig Taggart from Falkirk (Aug 1994).
Record Victory: 20-0 v Selkirk, Scottish Cup 1st rd; 8 Dec, 1984.
Record Defeat: 0-9 v Dundee U, Division I; 30 Dec, 1967.
Most Capped Player: —.
Most League Appearances: 504: Matt McPhee, 1967-81.

STIRLING ALBION 2000–01 LEAGUE RECORD

Match No.	Date	Venue	Opponents	Result	H/T Score	Lg. Pos.	Goalscorers	Attendance
1	Aug 5	H	Clydebank	D 2-2	1-2	—	Graham [15], Feroz [70]	779
2	12	A	Queen of the S	D 0-0	0-0	7		1168
3	19	H	Forfar Ath	D 3-3	2-2	8	Graham [14], Gardner [22], Feroz [88]	605
4	26	H	Queen's Park	L 0-1	0-1	9		753
5	Sept 9	A	Stenhousemuir	W 2-0	0-0	6	Millar [57], Donald [60]	594
6	16	H	Partick Th	L 1-3	0-1	9	Feroz [70]	2251
7	23	H	Stranraer	W 2-0	2-0	6	Donald [16], King [20]	763
8	30	A	Berwick R	D 2-2	0-2	6	Donald [64], Graham [66]	604
9	Oct 7	H	Arbroath	D 0-0	0-0	7		576
10	14	A	Clydebank	L 0-3	0-2	7		312
11	21	H	Queen of the S	L 0-1	0-0	9		748
12	28	A	Queen's Park	L 0-3	0-0	9		920
13	Nov 4	H	Stenhousemuir	L 2-3	1-0	9	Millar [1], Templeman [46]	645
14	11	A	Stranraer	D 1-1	1-0	9	Gaughan [11]	441
15	18	A	Partick Th	D 1-1	0-1	9	Feroz [66]	1753
16	25	A	Arbroath	L 2-3	2-1	9	King [13], Donald [45]	550
17	Dec 2	H	Berwick R	D 1-1	0-0	9	Templeman [47]	613
18	16	H	Clydebank	D 0-0	0-0	9		534
19	Jan 2	A	Stenhousemuir	D 1-1	1-0	—	Millar [10]	573
20	13	A	Partick Th	D 1-1	1-0	10	Graham [21]	3113
21	Feb 3	H	Arbroath	D 1-1	0-0	9	Graham [70]	676
22	24	A	Queen of the S	L 1-2	0-2	9	Williams [78]	1157
23	Mar 10	A	Queen's Park	D 1-1	0-0	10	McAulay (pen) [85]	822
24	13	H	Stranraer	L 0-1	0-0	—		448
25	17	A	Stranraer	W 3-0	1-0	10	Bennett [24], Templeman [75], Williams [89]	446
26	20	H	Forfar Ath	W 1-0	0-0	—	Gardner [48]	515
27	24	H	Queen's Park	L 0-2	0-1	10		568
28	28	A	Berwick R	L 1-4	1-3	—	Martin [9]	477
29	31	H	Partick Th	L 0-3	0-3	10		2748
30	Apr 3	H	Stenhousemuir	D 0-0	0-0	—		390
31	7	A	Arbroath	D 1-1	0-1	9	McCallion [69]	711
32	10	A	Forfar Ath	L 0-1	0-0	—		390
33	14	H	Berwick R	W 1-0	0-0	10	Millar [73]	525
34	21	A	Clydebank	D 1-1	0-0	9	Williams [78]	205
35	28	H	Queen of the S	D 1-1	0-1	10	Feroz [52]	587
36	May 5	A	Forfar Ath	L 1-3	0-2	10	Williams [85]	813

Final League Position: 10

Most League Goals in Season (Individual): 27: Joe Hughes, Division II; 1969-70.
Most Goals Overall (Individual): 129: Billy Steele, 1971-83.

Honours
League Champions: Division II 1952-53, 1957-58, 1960-61, 1964-65. Second Division 1976-77, 1990-91, 1995-96; *Runners-up:* Division II 1948-49, 1950-51.
Scottish Cup: —. *League Cup:* —.

Club colours: Shirt: Red and white halves. Shorts: Red and white halves. Stockings: Red.

Goalscorers: *League* (34): Feroz 5, Graham 5, Donald 4, Millar 4, Williams 4, Templeman 3, Gardner 2, King 2, Bennett 1, Gaughan 1, McAulay 1 (1 pen), McCallion 1, Martin 1
Scottish Cup (7): Graham 3 (1 pen), Templeman 2, Donald 1, Williams 1
CIS Cup (0):
Bell's League Cup (2): McAulay 1, O'Neill 1

Reid C 36	McStea A 10	Bennett N 21	Milne K 27	Millar J 28 + 4	Donald G 33 + 1	King C 16	McAulay I 23 + 2	Graham A 17 + 1	Feroz C 23 + 7	Gardiner J 11 + 8	Hunter G 4 + 1	O'Neill M — + 3	McCallion K 6 + 8	Whiteford A 10	Joy I — + 2	McGraw M — + 3	Munro G — + 3	Love G 17 + 1	Kelly G 11 + 10	Gaughan K 26	Williams A 11 + 18	Templeman C 20 + 1	McKinnon R 1	Aitken A 3 + 7	Reilly S 2	Devine S 7 + 1	Martin C 14 + 1	Stuart W — + 6	Hay P 12	Bailey L 7 + 2	McLellan K — + 1	Match No.
1	2	3³	4	5	6	7	8²	9	10	11¹	12	13	14																			1
1		3¹	4	6	8²	7	11	9³	10		5	13		2	12	14																2
1		3	5		8²	7	6	9	10	11¹	4³	14	12	2			13															3
1		3	4	11		7	8³	10	9²	12			2		13	14	5	6¹														4
1	2	3	5	6	8	7	14	9³	10¹	11²			13					4	12													5
1	2	3	5¹	6	8	7	12	9³	10	11²							14	4	13													6
1	2	3³		10	8	7		9¹	13			14	4					6	12	5	11²											7
1	2¹		3³	10	8	7		9	12	13			4					6	14	5	11³											8
1	2¹		3	6	8	7	11	9	10²				4						12	5	13											9
1	2		3	6	8	7	11		10²	12			4¹		13			14	5	9³												10
1	2		3	6	8	7		12	9	13	5	11²							4	10¹												11
1	2		6	8¹	7				11³			13	4					3	5	12	9	10										12
1	2³		8	13	7	6²		14					4					3	10	5	12	9		11¹								13
1		5	10	6	7	8		13				2¹						3	12		9			11²								14
1		3	11	8	7	6		10²			2¹							4	12	5		9		13								15
1		3	8	2	7¹	6		10	12									4	11²	5	13	9										16
1		4	6	11		8		10	7¹									3	2	5	12	9										17
1		4	13	6		8	9	7²	11									3¹		5	12	10			2							18
1		3	11	8		6	9	7¹					13							5	12	10				2²	4					19
1		3	11	8		6³	9	7				12						14		5	13	10³				4¹	2					20
1		3	4	8			9	7				13						2¹	5	6²	10			12			11					21
1		3		8			9	7³				4¹						6	2²	5	14	10		12			11	13				22
1	3	5	8	7³	6	11		13											4	9²	10¹	12			2	14						23
1	3	5²	8	7		6¹													4	9	10		11		13	2	12					24
1	3	5		6				9²	11¹										4	13	10		12		8	2		7				25
1	3	5	13	6				9¹	11²										4	12	10				8	2		7				26
1	3	5	12	6				9³	11										4	14	10				8¹	2²		7	13			27
1		8	4³	14			6		11¹								13			5	12	9				3	7		2²	10		28
1		8²		6	4			9		11³			13					3	12	5	14						7¹		2	10		29
1		10³		6			8	9	13				12					5		4	11²		14		3¹			2	7		30
1		3		8	6		7			4¹		11³						5	14	13	9						12		2	10⁸		31
1		3	6	8	4		11	12										5		13	9²						7		2	10¹		32
1		10	3¹	8	6				12									5	11³		7		13				4	14	2	9²		33
1		3		6	5¹		8		12				11						7		9						4	13	2	10⁸		34
1		3		8	4		6		7²	12			11¹					5	10		9								2	13		35
1		3		10	8		6		11³									5²	7¹		9	13					4	12	2		14	36

STRANRAER

Second Division

Year Formed: 1870. *Ground & Address:* Stair Park, London Rd, Stranraer DG9 8BS. *Telephone:* 01776 703271.
Ground Capacity: total: 6100, seated: 1800. *Size of Pitch:* 110yd × 70yd.
Chairman/Secretary: Graham Rodgers. *Commercial Manager:* T. L. Sutherland.
Manager: Billy McLaren.
Managers since 1975: J. Hughes, N. Hood, G. Hamilton, D. Sneddon, J. Clark, R. Clark, A. McAnespie, C. Money.
Club Nickname(s): The Blues. *Previous Grounds:* None.
Record Attendance: 6500 v Rangers, Scottish Cup 1st rd; 24 Jan, 1948.
Record Transfer Fee received: £30,000 for Mark Campbell to Ayr Utd, 1999.
Record Transfer Fee paid: £15,000 for Colin Harkness from Kilmarnock (Aug 1989).
Record Victory: 7-0 v Brechin C, Division II; 6 Feb, 1965.
Record Defeat: 1-11 v Queen of the South, Scottish Cup 1st rd; 16 Jan, 1932.
Most Capped Player: —.
Most League Appearances: 256: Danny McDonald.
Most League Goals in Season (Individual): 27: Derek Frye, Second Division; 1977-78.
Most Goals Overall (Individual): —.

STRANRAER 2000–01 LEAGUE RECORD

Match No.	Date	Venue	Opponents	Result	H/T Score	Lg. Pos.	Goalscorers	Attendance
1	Aug 5	H	Forfar Ath	W 2-0	0-0	—	Harty [48], Geraghty [72]	397
2	12	A	Partick Th	L 1-2	0-1	4	Harty [49]	2357
3	19	A	Berwick R	D 2-2	0-0	3	George [71], Walker [90]	386
4	26	H	Arbroath	W 2-1	1-0	3	Walker [33], Harty [67]	426
5	Sept 9	A	Queen of the S	W 4-1	1-0	2	Geraghty [13], Walker 2 [57, 88], Blaikie [67]	1630
6	16	H	Queen's Park	W 3-0	0-0	1	Walker 2 [62, 74], George [79]	587
7	23	A	Stirling A	L 0-2	0-2	1		763
8	30	H	Clydebank	L 0-2	0-1	2		551
9	Oct 7	A	Stenhousemuir	W 2-1	0-0	1	Harty [53], Walker [69]	277
10	14	A	Forfar Ath	D 0-0	0-0	2		405
11	21	A	Partick Th	L 0-3	0-1	4		1101
12	28	A	Arbroath	D 1-1	0-1	4	Harty [80]	528
13	Nov 4	H	Queen of the S	W 3-2	2-2	2	Macdonald W [23], Knox [45], Walker [59]	767
14	11	H	Stirling A	D 1-1	0-1	3	George [85]	441
15	18	A	Queen's Park	W 2-1	0-1	2	Stirling 2 [47, 58]	753
16	25	H	Stenhousemuir	L 1-4	0-1	3	Macdonald W [51]	454
17	Dec 5	A	Clydebank	W 3-2	2-2	—	Knox [6], George [12], Geraghty [90]	126
18	16	H	Forfar Ath	W 3-1	1-1	2	Rae [39], Walker [56], Blair [66]	419
19	Jan 2	A	Queen of the S	W 3-2	2-1	—	Harty 2 [26, 50], Walker [37]	1643
20	13	H	Queen's Park	L 0-1	0-0	2		556
21	Feb 3	A	Stenhousemuir	D 2-2	1-0	2	Jenkins 2 [43, 65]	351
22	17	H	Berwick R	D 1-1	0-1	2	Jenkins [57]	447
23	24	A	Partick Th	L 0-3	0-2	2		2959
24	Mar 6	A	Clydebank	D 0-0	0-0	—		363
25	10	A	Arbroath	L 1-2	0-2	3	Knox [70]	670
26	13	A	Stirling A	W 1-0	0-0	—	Harty [58]	448
27	17	H	Stirling A	L 0-3	0-1	3		446
28	20	H	Berwick R	D 1-1	1-1	—	Harty [5]	471
29	25	H	Arbroath	L 0-1	0-0	3		394
30	31	A	Queen's Park	L 0-1	0-0	4		619
31	Apr 3	H	Queen of the S	W 2-0	1-0	—	Harty 2 [6, 83]	600
32	7	A	Stenhousemuir	W 2-1	0-0	4	Jenkins [46], Farrell [53]	365
33	14	A	Clydebank	D 0-0	0-0	4		159
34	21	A	Forfar Ath	W 3-2	0-2	4	Wright [78], McGowan [89], Farrell [90]	378
35	28	H	Partick Th	L 3-4	3-1	4	Harty [23], Walker 2 [33, 42]	928
36	May 5	A	Berwick R	W 2-0	2-0	4	Harty [5], Wright [27]	545

Final League Position: 4

Honours
League Champions: Second Division 1993-94, 1997-98.
Scottish Cup: —.
League Cup: —.
Qualifying Cup Winners: 1937.
League Challenge Cup Winners: 1996-97.

Club colours: Shirt: Blue with white side panels. Shorts: Blue with white side panels. Stockings: Blue with two white hoops.

Goalscorers: *League* (51): Harty 13, Walker 12, George 4, Jenkins 4, Geraghty 3, Knox 3, Farrell 2, Macdonald W 2, Stirling 2, Wright 2, Blaikie 1, Blair 1, McGowan 1, Rae 1
Scottish Cup (3): Harty 2 (1 pen), Walker 1
CIS Cup (0):
Bell's League Cup (9): Harty 4, Geraghty 2, Rae 1, Walker 1, Wright 1

McGeown M 28	Paterson A 11	Johnstone D 23	Knox K 34	McDonald G 15 + 1	George D 32	Walker P 27 + 4	Macdonald W 29	Harty J 35	Geraghty M 13 + 10	Blaikie A 2 + 5	Blair P 18 + 3	Wright F 35	McCormick S 1 + 1	Hughes M — + 2	Rae D 8 + 8	Bryce T 6 + 9	McMillan A 1 + 2	Edgar S — + 2	McQuilter R 1	McLauchlan M 5 + 5	Stewart P — + 3	Hodge A 8	Stirling J 7	Jenkins A 11 + 4	O'Neill S 8 + 1	Weir M 8 + 4	Grace A 10 + 2	Farrell D 13	McGowan N 7	Match No.
1	2	3	4	5	6	7	8	9	10¹	11	12																			1
1		2	5	4	7	6	9	8	12	11²	3	10¹	13																	2
1	2¹		4	3	6	11	8	9	10	13	7	5	12²																	3
1	2		5	4	6	11	8	9		12	7	3¹			10															4
1	11	2	4	3¹	8	7		9	10	12	6	5																		5
1	3	2	4	5¹	6	7	10²	9	11³		12	8					13	14												6
1		2	4	5	6	7²	9	10²	13	11¹	3	8					12	14												7
1			5	4	6		8³	9	10	11²	7	3¹	12	14			2	13												8
1		2	3		8	10	5¹	9	11		7	6			12				4											9
1		2	4		5	7	6	9	8		3				12	10²				11¹	13									10
1		2	3		5¹	6	8	4²	9	10	7	11			12					13										11
1		2	4	5	8	6	9	11²	7³		3	13			10¹					12	14									12
1		2	5	4	6	11	7	9	10		3				8															13
1	3	2	5		8	6	9	12	7		4		10¹			13				11²										14
1		2	5		10¹	8	9	12	7		4		6			3				11										15
1		2	5		7	6	9	10¹	4		8		12			3				11										16
1		2	5¹		10	8³	9	12	4		7		6¹	14		3				11	13									17
1		5	3	4	10	6	9	12	7²	2	8¹		13			11														18
1	6	2	3		11	8	9	5	10¹		4		7	12																19
	4	2		5	6		9	10²	7	3			13			11¹	8	1	12											20
1	4	2		5		8	9¹	7	3			12				11	6		13	10²										21
1		2	5	7	6	9	12		3							4¹	10		11	8										22
1	4¹	2	5²	13	8	9	10		3			12	14			7	11	6¹												23
1	7	2	5	12	6	9		3	10¹							8	11		4											24
1	7¹	2	5	8	13	6	9	3	10							12²	11²	14	4											25
1		2	5	8	10	6²	9	13	3							11	12	7	4											26
1		2	4	8	10	9²		13	3							11	7¹	6	5											27
1	2	5		8	7	6	9	3								11¹	10	12	4											28
1	7	2	5	6		8	9¹	12	3			13				10	11²	4												29
7¹	3	2		6	12	9	13	5	10²					1	14	8	4³	11												30
	2		5	8	7	9		3	12					10¹		1	6	4	11											31
	2		5	7	8	9		3	13					10¹	12	1	6¹	4	11											32
	2		5	7¹	10	9	12	3						8	1	11	4	6												33
	2	6	3	7	8²	14	5	12	9¹					1	10²	13	4	11												34
	3¹	2		7	9	8	5	12	13					1	6	10¹	4	11												35
	3	2		10	9	7	5	12						1	8	6¹	4	11												36

SCOTTISH LEAGUE TABLES 2000–2001

Premier Division

	P	W	D	L	F	A	W	D	L	F	A	GD	Pts
		Home			*Goals*		*Away*			*Goals*			
Celtic	38	17	1	1	49	11	14	3	2	41	18	61	97
Rangers	38	15	0	4	45	16	11	4	4	31	20	40	82
Hibernian	38	11	6	2	37	15	7	6	6	20	20	22	66
Kilmarnock	38	7	4	8	20	25	8	5	6	24	28	–9	54
Hearts	38	11	2	6	36	21	3	8	8	20	20	6	52
Dundee	38	4	7	8	25	24	9	1	9	26	25	2	47
Aberdeen	38	6	6	7	24	24	5	6	8	21	28	–7	45
Motherwell	38	5	4	10	22	27	7	3	9	20	29	–14	43
Dunfermline Ath	38	8	6	5	20	17	3	3	13	14	37	–20	42
St Johnstone	38	4	6	9	22	31	5	7	7	18	25	–16	40
Dundee U	38	5	6	8	21	28	4	2	13	17	35	–25	35
St Mirren	38	7	3	9	20	25	1	3	15	12	47	–40	30

First Division

	P	W	D	L	F	A	W	D	L	F	A	GD	Pts
		Home			*Goals*		*Away*			*Goals*			
Livingston	36	13	2	3	39	14	10	5	3	33	17	41	76
Ayr U	36	11	6	1	44	19	8	6	4	29	22	32	69
Falkirk	36	8	6	4	29	24	8	2	8	28	35	–2	56
Inverness CT	36	9	4	5	42	25	5	8	5	29	29	17	54
Clyde	36	4	10	4	23	24	7	4	7	21	22	–2	47
Ross Co	36	5	3	10	21	25	6	7	5	27	27	–4	43
Raith R	36	5	4	9	24	26	5	4	9	17	29	–14	38
Airdrieonians	36	4	8	6	25	24	4	6	8	24	43	–18	38
Morton	36	3	4	11	13	37	6	4	8	21	24	–27	35
Alloa Ath	36	5	5	8	21	28	2	6	10	17	33	–23	32

Second Division

	P	W	D	L	F	A	W	D	L	F	A	GD	Pts
		Home			*Goals*		*Away*			*Goals*			
Partick T	36	11	5	2	34	13	11	4	3	32	19	34	75
Arbroath	36	10	6	2	39	20	5	7	6	15	18	16	58
Berwick R	36	8	5	5	26	22	6	7	5	25	22	7	54
Stranraer	36	7	4	7	25	27	8	5	5	26	23	1	54
Clydebank	36	8	4	6	25	22	4	7	7	17	21	–1	47
Queen of the S	36	5	5	8	24	30	8	2	8	28	29	–7	46
Stenhousemuir	36	8	4	6	27	19	4	2	12	18	44	–18	42
Forfar Ath	36	5	4	9	28	25	5	6	7	20	27	–4	40
Queen's Park	36	5	6	7	14	16	5	4	9	14	24	–12	40
Stirling Albion	36	3	9	6	15	20	2	8	8	19	30	–16	32

Third Division

	P	W	D	L	F	A	W	D	L	F	A	GD	Pts
		Home			*Goals*		*Away*			*Goals*			
Hamilton A	36	11	5	2	40	13	11	5	2	35	17	45	76
Cowdenbeath	36	14	3	1	38	13	9	4	5	20	18	27	76
Brechin C	36	13	3	2	42	17	9	3	6	29	19	35	72
East Fife	36	8	4	6	24	23	7	4	7	25	23	3	53
Peterhead	36	7	5	6	24	19	6	5	7	22	27	0	49
Dumbarton	36	7	1	10	28	28	6	5	7	18	21	–3	45
Albion R	36	4	6	8	16	22	8	3	7	22	21	–5	45
East Stirlingshire	36	4	4	10	11	26	6	3	9	26	43	–32	37
Montrose	36	1	6	11	13	29	5	2	11	18	36	–34	26
Elgin C	36	3	2	13	17	37	2	5	11	12	28	–36	22

SCOTTISH LEAGUE HONOURS 1890 to 2001

*On goal average (ratio)/difference. †Held jointly after indecisive play-off. ‡Won on deciding match.
††Held jointly. ¶Two points deducted for fielding ineligible player.
Competition suspended 1940–45 during war; Regional Leagues operating. ‡‡Two points deducted for registration
irregularities.

PREMIER LEAGUE
Maximum points: 108

	First	Pts	Second	Pts	Third	Pts
1998–99	Rangers	77	Celtic	71	St Johnstone	57
1999–2000	Rangers	90	Celtic	69	Hearts	54
2000–01	Celtic	97	Rangers	82	Hibernian	66

PREMIER DIVISION
Maximum points: 72

	First	Pts	Second	Pts	Third	Pts
1975–76	Rangers	54	Celtic	48	Hibernian	43
1976–77	Celtic	55	Rangers	46	Aberdeen	43
1977–78	Rangers	55	Aberdeen	53	Dundee U	40
1978–79	Celtic	48	Rangers	45	Dundee U	44
1979–80	Aberdeen	48	Celtic	47	St Mirren	42
1980–81	Celtic	56	Aberdeen	49	Rangers*	44
1981–82	Celtic	55	Aberdeen	53	Rangers	43
1982–83	Dundee U	56	Celtic*	55	Aberdeen	55
1983–84	Aberdeen	57	Celtic	50	Dundee U	47
1984–85	Aberdeen	59	Celtic	52	Dundee U	47
1985–86	Celtic*	50	Hearts	50	Dundee U	47

Maximum points: 88

	First	Pts	Second	Pts	Third	Pts
1986–87	Rangers	69	Celtic	63	Dundee U	60
1987–88	Celtic	72	Hearts	62	Rangers	60

Maximum points: 72

	First	Pts	Second	Pts	Third	Pts
1988–89	Rangers	56	Aberdeen	50	Celtic	46
1989–90	Rangers	51	Aberdeen*	44	Hearts	44
1990–91	Rangers	55	Aberdeen	53	Celtic*	41

Maximum points: 88

	First	Pts	Second	Pts	Third	Pts
1991–92	Rangers	72	Hearts	63	Celtic	62
1992–93	Rangers	73	Aberdeen	64	Celtic	60
1993–94	Rangers	58	Aberdeen	55	Motherwell	54

Maximum points: 108

	First	Pts	Second	Pts	Third	Pts
1994–95	Rangers	69	Motherwell	54	Hibernian	53
1995–96	Rangers	87	Celtic	83	Aberdeen*	55
1996–97	Rangers	80	Celtic	75	Dundee U	60
1997–98	Celtic	74	Rangers	72	Hearts	67

FIRST DIVISION
Maximum points: 52

	First	Pts	Second	Pts	Third	Pts
1975–76	Partick T	41	Kilmarnock	35	Montrose	30

Maximum points: 78

	First	Pts	Second	Pts	Third	Pts
1976–77	St Mirren	62	Clydebank	58	Dundee	51
1977–78	Morton*	58	Hearts	58	Dundee	57
1978–79	Dundee	55	Kilmarnock*	54	Clydebank	54
1979–80	Hearts	53	Airdrieonians	51	Ayr U*	44
1980–81	Hibernian	57	Dundee	52	St Johnstone	51
1981–82	Motherwell	61	Kilmarnock	51	Hearts	50
1982–83	St Johnstone	55	Hearts	54	Clydebank	50
1983–84	Morton	54	Dumbarton	51	Partick T	46
1984–85	Motherwell	50	Clydebank	48	Falkirk	45
1985–86	Hamilton A	56	Falkirk	45	Kilmarnock	44

Maximum points: 88

	First	Pts	Second	Pts	Third	Pts
1986–87	Morton	57	Dunfermline Ath	56	Dumbarton	53
1987–88	Hamilton A	56	Meadowbank T	52	Clydebank	49

Maximum points: 78

	First	Pts	Second	Pts	Third	Pts
1988–89	Dunfermline Ath	54	Falkirk	52	Clydebank	48
1989–90	St Johnstone	58	Airdrieonians	54	Clydebank	44
1990–91	Falkirk	54	Airdrieonians	53	Dundee	52

Maximum points: 88

	First	Pts	Second	Pts	Third	Pts
1991–92	Dundee	58	Partick T*	57	Hamilton A	57
1992–93	Raith R	65	Kilmarnock	54	Dunfermline Ath	52
1993–94	Falkirk	66	Dunfermline Ath	65	Airdrieonians	54

Maximum points: 108

	First	Pts	Second	Pts	Third	Pts
1994–95	Raith R	69	Dunfermline Ath*	68	Dundee	68
1995–96	Dunfermline Ath	71	Dundee U*	67	Morton	67
1996–97	St Johnstone	80	Airdieonians	60	Dundee*	58
1997–98	Dundee	70	Falkirk	65	Raith R*	60
1998–99	Hibernian	89	Falkirk	66	Ayr U	62
1999–2000	St Mirren	76	Dunfermline Ath	71	Falkirk	68
2000–01	Livingston	76	Ayr U	69	Falkirk	56

SECOND DIVISION

Maximum points: 52

	First	Pts	Second	Pts	Third	Pts
1975–76	Clydebank*	40	Raith R	40	Alloa	35

Maximum points: 78

	First	Pts	Second	Pts	Third	Pts
1976–77	Stirling A	55	Alloa	51	Dunfermline Ath	50
1977–78	Clyde*	53	Raith R	53	Dunfermline Ath	48
1978–79	Berwick R	54	Dunfermline Ath	52	Falkirk	50
1979–80	Falkirk	50	East Stirling	49	Forfar Ath	46
1980–81	Queen's Park	50	Queen of the S	46	Cowdenbeath	45
1981–82	Clyde	59	Alloa*	50	Arbroath	50
1982–83	Brechin C	55	Meadowbank T	54	Arbroath	49
1983–84	Forfar Ath	63	East Fife	47	Berwick R	43
1984–85	Montrose	53	Alloa	50	Dunfermline Ath	49
1985–86	Dunfermline Ath	57	Queen of the S	55	Meadowbank T	49
1986–87	Meadowbank T	55	Raith R*	52	Stirling A*	52
1987–88	Ayr U	61	St Johnstone	59	Queen's Park	51
1988–89	Albion R	50	Alloa	45	Brechin C	43
1989–90	Brechin C	49	Kilmarnock	48	Stirling A	47
1990–91	Stirling A	54	Montrose	46	Cowdenbeath	45
1991–92	Dumbarton	52	Cowdenbeath	51	Alloa	50
1992–93	Clyde	54	Brechin C*	53	Stranraer	53
1993–94	Stranraer	56	Berwick R	48	Stenhousemuir*	47

Maximum points: 108

	First	Pts	Second	Pts	Third	Pts
1994–95	Morton	64	Dumbarton	60	Stirling A	58
1995–96	Stirling A	81	East Fife	67	Berwick R	60
1996–97	Ayr U	77	Hamilton A	74	Livingston	64
1997–98	Stranraer	61	Clydebank	60	Livingston	59
1998–99	Livingston	77	Inverness CT	72	Clyde	53
1999–2000	Clyde	65	Alloa Ath	64	Ross Co	62
2000–01	Partick T	75	Arbroath	58	Berwick R*	54

THIRD DIVISION

Maximum points: 108

	First	Pts	Second	Pts	Third	Pts
1994–95	Forfar Ath	80	Montrose	67	Ross Co	60
1995–96	Livingston	72	Brechin C	63	Caledonian T	57
1996–97	Inverness CT	76	Forfar Ath*	67	Ross Co	67
1997–98	Alloa Ath	76	Arbroath	68	Ross Co	67
1998–99	Ross Co	77	Stenhousemuir	64	Brechin C	59
1999–2000	Queen's Park	69	Berwick R	66	Forfar Ath	61
2000–01	Hamilton A*	76	Cowdenbeath	76	Brechin C	72

FIRST DIVISION to 1974–75

Maximum points: a 36; b 44; c 40; d 52; e 60; f 68; g 76; h 84.

	First	Pts	Second	Pts	Third	Pts
1890–91*a*	Dumbarton††	29	Rangers††	29	Celtic	21
1891–92*b*	Dumbarton	37	Celtic	35	Hearts	34
1892–93*a*	Celtic	29	Rangers	28	St Mirren	20
1893–94*a*	Celtic	29	Hearts	26	St Bernard's	23
1894–95*a*	Hearts	31	Celtic	26	Rangers	22
1895–96*a*	Celtic	30	Rangers	26	Hibernian	24
1896–97*a*	Hearts	28	Hibernian	26	Rangers	25
1897–98*a*	Celtic	33	Rangers	29	Hibernian	22
1898–99*a*	Rangers	36	Hearts	26	Celtic	24
1899–1900*a*	Rangers	32	Celtic	25	Hibernian	24
1900–01*c*	Rangers	35	Celtic	29	Hibernian	25
1901–02*a*	Rangers	28	Celtic	26	Hearts	22
1902–03*b*	Hibernian	37	Dundee	31	Rangers	29
1903–04*d*	Third Lanark	43	Hearts	39	Celtic*	38
1904–05*d*	Celtic‡	41	Rangers	41	Third Lanark	35
1905–06*e*	Celtic	49	Hearts	43	Airdrieonians	38
1906–07*f*	Celtic	55	Dundee	48	Rangers	45
1907–08*f*	Celtic	55	Falkirk	51	Rangers	50
1908–09*f*	Celtic	51	Dundee	50	Clyde	48
1909–10*f*	Celtic	54	Falkirk	52	Rangers	46
1910–11*f*	Rangers	52	Aberdeen	48	Falkirk	44
1911–12*f*	Rangers	51	Celtic	45	Clyde	42
1912–13*f*	Rangers	53	Celtic	49	Hearts*	41
1913–14*g*	Celtic	65	Rangers	59	Hearts*	54
1914–15*g*	Celtic	65	Hearts	61	Rangers	50
1915–16*g*	Celtic	67	Rangers	56	Morton	51
1916–17*g*	Celtic	64	Morton	54	Rangers	53
1917–18*f*	Rangers	56	Celtic	55	Kilmarnock*	43
1918–19*f*	Celtic	58	Rangers	57	Morton	47
1919–20*h*	Rangers	71	Celtic	68	Motherwell	57
1920–21*h*	Rangers	76	Celtic	66	Hearts	50
1921–22*h*	Celtic	67	Rangers	66	Raith R	51
1922–23*g*	Rangers	55	Airdrieonians	50	Celtic	46
1923–24*g*	Rangers	59	Airdrieonians	50	Celtic	46
1924–25*g*	Rangers	60	Airdrieonians	57	Hibernian	52
1925–26*g*	Celtic	58	Airdrieonians*	50	Hearts	50

	First	Pts	Second	Pts	Third	Pts
1926–27g	Rangers	56	Motherwell	51	Celtic	49
1927–28g	Rangers	60	Celtic*	55	Motherwell	55
1928–29g	Rangers	67	Celtic	51	Motherwell	50
1929–30g	Rangers	60	Motherwell	55	Aberdeen	53
1930–31g	Rangers	60	Celtic	58	Motherwell	56
1931–32g	Motherwell	66	Rangers	61	Celtic	48
1932–33g	Rangers	62	Motherwell	59	Hearts	50
1933–34g	Rangers	66	Motherwell	62	Celtic	47
1934–35g	Rangers	55	Celtic	52	Hearts	50
1935–36g	Celtic	66	Rangers*	61	Aberdeen	61
1936–37g	Rangers	61	Aberdeen	54	Celtic	52
1937–38g	Celtic	61	Hearts	58	Rangers	49
1938–39g	Rangers	59	Celtic	48	Aberdeen	46
1946–47e	Rangers	46	Hibernian	44	Aberdeen	39
1947–48e	Hibernian	48	Rangers	46	Partick T	36
1948–49e	Rangers	46	Dundee	45	Hibernian	39
1949–50e	Rangers	50	Hibernian	49	Hearts	43
1950–51e	Hibernian	48	Rangers*	38	Dundee	38
1951–52e	Hibernian	45	Rangers	41	East Fife	37
1952–53e	Rangers*	43	Hibernian	43	East Fife	39
1953–54e	Celtic	43	Hearts	38	Partick T	35
1954–55e	Aberdeen	49	Celtic	46	Rangers	41
1955–56f	Rangers	52	Aberdeen	46	Hearts*	45
1956–57f	Rangers	55	Hearts	53	Kilmarnock	42
1957–58f	Hearts	62	Rangers	49	Celtic	46
1958–59f	Rangers	50	Hearts	48	Motherwell	44
1959–60f	Hearts	54	Kilmarnock	50	Rangers*	42
1960–61f	Rangers	51	Kilmarnock	50	Third Lanark	42
1961–62f	Dundee	54	Rangers	51	Celtic	46
1962–63f	Rangers	57	Kilmarnock	48	Partick T	46
1963–64f	Rangers	55	Kilmarnock	49	Celtic*	47
1964–65f	Kilmarnock*	50	Hearts	50	Dunfermline Ath	49
1965–66f	Celtic	57	Rangers	55	Kilmarnock	45
1966–67f	Celtic	58	Rangers	55	Clyde	46
1967–68f	Celtic	63	Rangers	61	Hibernian	45
1968–69f	Celtic	54	Rangers	49	Dunfermline Ath	45
1969–70f	Celtic	57	Rangers	45	Hibernian	44
1970–71f	Celtic	56	Aberdeen	54	St Johnstone	44
1971–72f	Celtic	60	Aberdeen	50	Rangers	44
1972–73f	Celtic	57	Rangers	56	Hibernian	45
1973–74f	Celtic	53	Hibernian	49	Rangers	48
1974–75f	Rangers	56	Hibernian	49	Celtic	45

SECOND DIVISION to 1974–75

Maximum points: a 76; b 72; c 68; d 52; e 60; f 36; g 44.

	First	Pts	Second	Pts	Third	Pts
1893–94f	Hibernian	29	Cowlairs	27	Clyde	24
1894–95f	Hibernian	30	Motherwell	22	Port Glasgow	20
1895–96f	Abercorn	27	Leith Ath	23	Renton	21
1896–97f	Partick T	31	Leith Ath	27	Kilmarnock*	21
1897–98f	Kilmarnock	29	Port Glasgow	25	Morton	22
1898–99f	Kilmarnock	32	Leith Ath	27	Port Glasgow	25
1899–1900f	Partick T	29	Morton	28	Port Glasgow	20
1900–01f	St Bernard's	25	Airdrieonians	23	Abercorn	21
1901–02g	Port Glasgow	32	Partick T	31	Motherwell	26
1902–03g	Airdrieonians	35	Motherwell	28	Ayr U*	27
1903–04g	Hamilton A	37	Clyde	29	Ayr U	27
1904–05g	Clyde	32	Falkirk	28	Hamilton A	27
1905–06g	Leith Ath	34	Clyde	31	Albion R	27
1906–07g	St Bernard's	32	Vale of Leven*	27	Arthurlie	27
1907–08g	Raith R	30	Dumbarton*‡‡	27	Ayr U	27
1908–09g	Abercorn	31	Raith R*	28	Vale of Leven	28
1909–10g	Leith Ath‡	33	Raith R	33	St Bernard's	27
1910–11g	Dumbarton	31	Ayr U	27	Albion R	25
1911–12g	Ayr U	35	Abercorn	30	Dumbarton	27
1912–13d	Ayr U	34	Dunfermline Ath	33	East Stirling	32
1913–14g	Cowdenbeath	31	Albion R	27	Dunfermline Ath*	26
1914–15d	Cowdenbeath*	37	St Bernard's*	37	Leith Ath	37
1921–22a	Alloa	60	Cowdenbeath	47	Armadale	45
1922–23a	Queen's Park	57	Clydebank¶	50	St Johnstone¶	45
1923–24a	St Johnstone	56	Cowdenbeath	55	Bathgate	44
1924–25a	Dundee U	50	Clydebank	48	Clyde	47
1925–26a	Dunfermline Ath	59	Clyde	53	Ayr U	52
1926–27a	Bo'ness	56	Raith R	49	Clydebank	45
1927–28a	Ayr U	54	Third Lanark	45	King's Park	44
1928–29b	Dundee U	51	Morton	50	Arbroath	47
1929–30a	Leith Ath*	57	East Fife	57	Albion R	54
1930–31a	Third Lanark	61	Dundee U	50	Dunfermline Ath	47
1931–32a	East Stirling*	55	St Johnstone	55	Raith R*	46
1932–33c	Hibernian	54	Queen of the S	49	Dunfermline Ath	47

	First	Pts	Second	Pts	Third	Pts
1933–34c	Albion R	45	Dunfermline Ath*	44	Arbroath	44
1934–35c	Third Lanark	52	Arbroath	50	St Bernard's	47
1935–36c	Falkirk	59	St Mirren	52	Morton	48
1936–37c	Ayr U	54	Morton	51	St Bernard's	48
1937–38c	Raith R	59	Albion R	48	Airdrieonians	47
1938–39c	Cowdenbeath	60	Alloa*	48	East Fife	48
1946–47d	Dundee	45	Airdrieonians	42	East Fife	31
1947–48e	East Fife	53	Albion R	42	Hamilton A	40
1948–49e	Raith R*	42	Stirling A	42	Airdrieonians*	41
1949–50e	Morton	47	Airdrieonians	44	Dunfermline Ath*	36
1950–51e	Queen of the S*	45	Stirling A	45	Ayr U*	36
1951–52e	Clyde	44	Falkirk	43	Ayr U	39
1952–53e	Stirling A	44	Hamilton A	43	Queen's Park	37
1953–54e	Motherwell	45	Kilmarnock	42	Third Lanark*	36
1954–55e	Airdrieonians	46	Dunfermline Ath	42	Hamilton A	39
1955–56b	Queen's Park	54	Ayr U	51	St Johnstone	49
1956–57b	Clyde	64	Third Lanark	51	Cowdenbeath	45
1957–58b	Stirling A	55	Dunfermline Ath	53	Arbroath	47
1958–59b	Ayr U	60	Arbroath	51	Stenhousemuir	46
1959–60b	St Johnstone	53	Dundee U	50	Queen of the S	49
1960–61b	Stirling A	55	Falkirk	54	Stenhousemuir	50
1961–62b	Clyde	54	Queen of the S	53	Morton	44
1962–63b	St Johnstone	55	East Stirling	49	Morton	48
1963–64b	Morton	67	Clyde	53	Arbroath	46
1964–65b	Stirling A	59	Hamilton A	50	Queen of the S	45
1965–66b	Ayr U	53	Airdrieonians	50	Queen of the S	47
1966–67a	Morton	69	Raith R	58	Arbroath	57
1967–68b	St Mirren	62	Arbroath	53	East Fife	49
1968–69b	Motherwell	64	Ayr U	53	East Fife*	48
1969–70b	Falkirk	56	Cowdenbeath	55	Queen of the S	50
1970–71b	Partick T	56	East Fife	51	Arbroath	46
1971–72b	Dumbarton*	52	Arbroath	52	Stirling A	50
1972–73b	Clyde	56	Dumfermline Ath	52	Raith R*	47
1973–74b	Airdrieonians	60	Kilmarnock	58	Hamilton A	55
1974–75a	Falkirk	54	Queen of the S*	53	Montrose	53

Elected to First Division: 1894 Clyde; 1895 Hibernian; 1896 Abercorn; 1897 Partick T; 1899 Kilmarnock; 1900 Morton and Partick T; 1902 Port Glasgow and Partick T; 1903 Airdrieonians and Motherwell; 1905 Falkirk and Aberdeen; 1906 Clyde and Hamilton A; 1910 Raith R; 1913 Ayr U and Dumbarton.

RELEGATED FROM PREMIER LEAGUE

1998–99 Dunfermline Ath
1999–2000 *No relegation due to League reorganization*
2000–01 St Mirren

RELEGATED FROM PREMIER DIVISION

1974–75 *No relegation due to League reorganization*
1975–76 Dundee, St Johnstone
1976–77 Hearts, Kilmarnock
1977–78 Ayr U, Clydebank
1978–79 Hearts, Motherwell
1979–80 Dundee, Hibernian
1980–81 Kilmarnock, Hearts
1981–82 Partick T, Airdrieonians
1982–83 Morton, Kilmarnock
1983–84 St Johnstone, Motherwell
1984–85 Dumbarton, Morton
1985–86 *No relegation due to League reorganization*
1986–87 Clydebank, Hamilton A
1987–88 Falkirk, Dunfermline Ath, Morton
1988–89 Hamilton A
1989–90 Dundee
1990–91 *None*
1991–92 St Mirren, Dunfermline Ath
1992–93 Falkirk, Airdrieonians
1993–94 *See footnote*
1994–95 Dundee U
1995–96 Partick T, Falkirk
1996–97 Raith R
1997–98 Hibernian

RELEGATED FROM DIVISION 1

1974–75 *No relegation due to League reorganization*
1975–76 Dunfermline Ath, Clyde
1976–77 Raith R, Falkirk
1977–78 Alloa Ath, East Fife
1978–79 Montrose, Queen of the S
1979–80 Arbroath, Clyde
1980–81 Stirling A, Berwick R
1981–82 East Stirling, Queen of the S
1982–83 Dunfermline Ath, Queen's Park
1983–84 Raith R, Alloa
1984–85 Meadowbank T, St Johnstone
1985–86 Ayr U, Alloa
1986–87 Brechin C, Montrose
1987–88 East Fife, Dumbarton
1988–89 Kilmarnock, Queen of the S
1989–90 Albion R, Alloa
1990–91 Clyde, Brechin C
1991–92 Montrose, Forfar Ath
1992–93 Meadowbank T, Cowdenbeath
1993–94 *See footnote*
1994–95 Ayr U, Stranraer
1995–96 Hamilton A, Dumbarton
1996–97 Clydebank, East Fife
1997–98 Partick T, Stirling A
1998–99 Hamilton A, Stranraer
1999–2000 Clydebank
2000–01 Morton, Alloa

RELEGATED FROM DIVISION 2

1994–95 Meadowbank T, Brechin C
1995–96 Forfar Ath, Montrose
1996–97 Dumbarton, Berwick R

1997–98 Stenhousemuir, Brechin C
1998–99 East Fife, Forfar Ath
1999–2000 Hamilton A**

RELEGATED FROM DIVISION 1 (TO 1973–74)

1921–22	*Queen's Park, Dumbarton, Clydebank
1922–23	Albion R, Alloa Ath
1923–24	Clyde, Clydebank
1924–25	Third Lanark, Ayr U
1925–26	Raith R, Clydebank
1926–27	Morton, Dundee U
1927–28	Dunfermline Ath, Bo'ness
1928–29	Third Lanark, Raith R
1929–30	St Johnstone, Dundee U
1930–31	Hibernian, East Fife
1931–32	Dundee U, Leith Ath
1932–33	Morton, East Stirling
1933–34	Third Lanark, Cowdenbeath
1934–35	St Mirren, Falkirk
1935–36	Airdrieonians, Ayr U
1936–37	Dunfermline Ath, Albion R
1937–38	Dundee, Morton
1938–39	Queen's Park, Raith R
1946–47	Kilmarnock, Hamilton A
1947–48	Airdrieonians, Queen's Park
1948–49	Morton, Albion R
1949–50	Queen of the S, Stirling A
1950–51	Clyde, Falkirk
1951–52	Morton, Stirling A
1952–53	Motherwell, Third Lanark
1953–54	Airdrieonians, Hamilton A
1954–55	*No clubs relegated*
1955–56	Stirling A, Clyde
1956–57	Dunfermline Ath, Ayr U
1957–58	East Fife, Queen's Park
1958–59	Queen of the S, Falkirk
1959–60	Arbroath, Stirling A
1960–61	Ayr U, Clyde
1961–62	St Johnstone, Stirling A
1962–63	Clyde, Raith R
1963–64	Queen of the S, East Stirling
1964–65	Airdrieonians, Third Lanark
1965–66	Morton, Hamilton A
1966–67	St Mirren, Ayr U
1967–68	Motherwell, Stirling A
1968–69	Falkirk, Arbroath
1969–70	Raith R, Partick T
1970–71	St Mirren, Cowdenbeath
1971–72	Clyde, Dunfermline Ath
1972–73	Kilmarnock, Airdrieonians
1973–74	East Fife, Falkirk

*Season 1921–22 – only 1 club promoted, 3 clubs relegated. **15pts deducted for failing to field a team.*

Scottish League championship wins: Rangers 49, Celtic 37, Aberdeen 4, Hearts 4, Hibernian 4, Dumbarton 2, Dundee 1, Dundee U 1, Kilmarnock 1, Motherwell 1, Third Lanark 1.

At the end of the 1993–94 season four divisions were created assisted by the admission of two new clubs Ross County and Caledonian Thistle. Only one club was promoted from Division 1 and Division 2. The three relegated from the Premier joined with teams finishing second to seventh in Division 1 to form the new Division 1. Five relegated from Division 1 combined with those who finished second to sixth to form a new Division 2 and the bottom eight in Division 2 linked with the two newcomers to form a new Division 3. At the end of the 1997–98 season the nine clubs remaining in the Premier Division plus the promoted team from Division 1 formed a breakaway Premier League. At the end of the 1999–2000 season two teams were added to the Scottish League. There was no relegation from the Premier League but two promoted from the First Division and three from each of the Second and Third Divisions. One team was relegated from the First Division and one from the Second Division, leaving 12 teams in each division.

Celtic's Henrik Larsson rounds Rangers goalkeeper Stefan Klos for his third goal of the game and his 50th of the season. (Actionimages/Aidan Ellis)

SCOTTISH LEAGUE CUP FINALS 1946–2001

Season	Winners	Runners-up	Score
1946–47	Rangers	Aberdeen	4-0
1947–48	East Fife	Falkirk	4-1 after 0-0 draw
1948–49	Rangers	Raith R	2-0
1949–50	East Fife	Dunfermline Ath	3-0
1950–51	Motherwell	Hibernian	3-0
1951–52	Dundee	Rangers	3-2
1952–53	Dundee	Kilmarnock	2-0
1953–54	East Fife	Partick T	3-2
1954–55	Hearts	Motherwell	4-2
1955–56	Aberdeen	St Mirren	2-1
1956–57	Celtic	Partick T	3-0 after 0-0 draw
1957–58	Celtic	Rangers	7-1
1958–59	Hearts	Partick T	5-1
1959–60	Hearts	Third Lanark	2-1
1960–61	Rangers	Kilmarnock	2-0
1961–62	Rangers	Hearts	3-1 after 1-1 draw
1962–63	Hearts	Kilmarnock	1-0
1963–64	Rangers	Morton	5-0
1964–65	Rangers	Celtic	2-1
1965–66	Celtic	Rangers	2-1
1966–67	Celtic	Rangers	1-0
1967–68	Celtic	Dundee	5-3
1968–69	Celtic	Hibernian	6-2
1969–70	Celtic	St Johnstone	1-0
1970–71	Rangers	Celtic	1-0
1971–72	Partick T	Celtic	4-1
1972–73	Hibernian	Celtic	2-1
1973–74	Dundee	Celtic	1-0
1974–75	Celtic	Hibernian	6-3
1975–76	Rangers	Celtic	1-0
1976–77	Aberdeen	Celtic	2-1
1977–78	Rangers	Celtic	2-1
1978–79	Rangers	Aberdeen	2-1
1979–80	Dundee U	Aberdeen	3-0 after 0-0 draw
1980–81	Dundee U	Dundee	3-0
1981–82	Rangers	Dundee U	2-1
1982–83	Celtic	Rangers	2-1
1983–84	Rangers	Celtic	3-2
1984–85	Rangers	Dundee U	1-0
1985–86	Aberdeen	Hibernian	3-0
1986–87	Rangers	Celtic	2-1
1987–88	Rangers	Aberdeen	3-3
		(Rangers won 5-3 on penalties)	
1988–89	Rangers	Aberdeen	3-2
1989–90	Aberdeen	Rangers	2-1
1990–91	Rangers	Celtic	2-1
1991–92	Hibernian	Dunfermline Ath	2-0
1992–93	Rangers	Aberdeen	2-1
1993–94	Rangers	Hibernian	2-1
1994–95	Raith R	Celtic	2-2
		(Raith R won 6-5 on penalties)	
1995–96	Aberdeen	Dundee	2-0
1996–97	Rangers	Hearts	4-3
1997–98	Celtic	Dundee U	3-0
1998–99	Rangers	St Johnstone	2-1
1999–2000	Celtic	Aberdeen	2-0
2000–01	Celtic	Kilmarnock	3-0

SCOTTISH LEAGUE CUP WINS

Rangers 21, Celtic 12, Aberdeen 5, Hearts 4, Dundee 3, East Fife 3, Dundee U 2, Hibernian 2, Motherwell 1, Partick T 1, Raith R 1.

APPEARANCES IN FINALS

Rangers 27, Celtic 24, Aberdeen 12, Hibernian 7, Dundee 6, Hearts 6, Dundee U 5, Kilmarnock 4, Partick T 4, East Fife 3, Dunfermline Ath 2, Motherwell 2, Raith R 2, St Johnstone 2, Falkirk 1, Morton 1, St Mirren 1, Third Lanark 1.

CIS SCOTTISH LEAGUE CUP 2000–2001

FIRST ROUND

8 AUG

Arbroath (0) 2 *(Mercer 79, McGlashan C 84)*
Brechin C (0) 0 686
Arbroath: Hinchcliffe; King, Fotheringham (Tindal), Thomson, Rowe, Good, Cusick, Bryce (Florence), McGlashan C, Mallan, Mercer (Brownlie).
Brechin C: Soutar; Smith, Raynes, Bain, Cairney, Nairn, McKeith (Leask), Riley P, Bailey (Williamson), Grant, Coulston (Honeyman).

Clyde (2) 5 *(Proudlock 14, Ross 33, Grant 66, McLaughlin 78, Kane 85)*
Morton (0) 1 *(Anderson 56)* 1048
Clyde: Halliwell; Murray, McLaughlin, Smith, Cranmer, Ross (Henderson), Convery (McCusker), Sellars, Proudlock (Kane), Keogh, Grant.
Morton: Boswell; Naylor, Davies, Anderson, Raeside, Medou Otye, Brownrigg (McDonald P), Millen, Matheson, Boukraa, Curran.

Clydebank (0) 0
Alloa Ath (0) 2 *(Wood 55, 88)* 216
Clydebank: Wylie; McKinstrey, McKinnon, Wishart, Brannigan, Taborda, Murray (Rodden), Ferguson, Fal, Coyne, Hamilton (Johnson).
Alloa Ath: Cairns; Huxford (Farrell), Clark, Watson, Conway, Valentine, Gardner, Thomson, Hamilton, Irvine (Wilson), Little (Wood).

Cowdenbeath (2) 3 *(McDowell 38, Wright 41, Burns 84)*
Elgin C (0) 0 234
Cowdenbeath: Martin; Boyle, McMillan, White, Lakie, Lawrence (Allan), Winter, Bradley, McDowell (Brown), Wright (Juskowiak), Burns.
Elgin C: Pirie; Milne CD, MacDonald, Morris, O'Brien, Russell, Whyte (Green M), Green R, Milne CR, Slythe (Maguire), Clinton.

East Fife (0) 1 *(Moffat 69)*
Raith R (0) 2 *(Tosh P 54, Stein 83)* 1540
East Fife: Stewart; Munro, Gallacher, McCloy, Sharp, Allison, Hunter, Logan, Simpson (Ferguson), Moffat (Kerrigan), Mackay.
Raith R: Van De Kamp; McCulloch, Ellis, Andrews, Browne, Black, Tosh P (Clark), Tosh S, Mballa (Shields), Burns, Stein.

East Stirling (0) 2 *(McKechnie 82, Gordon 86)*
Hamilton A (0) 1 *(Russell 67)* 504
East Stirling: Butter; Quinn, Hall, Russell, Todd D, McPherson, Stewart, Gordon, Hislop, Higgins (McKechnie), Tortolano.
Hamilton A: Macfarlane I; Nelson, Lynn, Davidson, Gaughan, Vaugh (Moore), Bonnar, Sherry, Eadie, McFarlane D (Kelly), Russell.

Montrose (0) 1 *(Dailly 73)*
Berwick R (0) 0 282
Montrose: McGlynn; Young, Dailly, Marwick, Ferguson, Craib, McWilliam, Mailer, McKenzie (Mitchell J), Harrison (McKellar), McIlravey.
Berwick R: McLean; Whelan (Findlay), Haddow, Ritchie, McNicoll, Anthony, McMartin (Duthie), Neil M, Ronald, Wood (Laidlaw), Smith.

Partick T (0) 1 *(McLean 66)*
Airdrieonians (1) 2 *(Alfonso 28, McCann 112)* 2652
Partick T: Brown; Smith, Stirling, Lennon, Craigan, Archibald (McKeown), McCallum (Moore), Cameron, McLean, Lindau (McGrillen), Hardie.
Airdrieonians: Wilson; Boyce (Capin), McCann, Alfonso (Coulter), Forrest, Moreau, Evans, Sanjuan, McGuire, Fernandez (Brady), Taylor.
aet

Peterhead (0) 2 *(Cooper 65 (pen), 71 (pen))*
Inverness CT (2) 3 *(Stewart 16, Xausa 43, Mann 77)* 1001
Peterhead: Pirie; Craig, King, Herd, Simpson, Paterson, Cooper, Johnston, Clark G, Brown, Livingstone.
Inverness CT: Fridge; Tokely, Golabek (McBain), Mann, Hastings, Byers, Bagan (Sheerin), Xausa, Stewart (Bavidge), Christie, Wyness.

Queen of the S (1) 2 *(Hodge 35, Weatherson 51)*
Forfar Ath (0) 1 *(Taylor S 85)* 1187
Queen of the S: Mathieson; Muir (Pickering), Hodge, Aitken, Martin, Nixon, Atkinson P, Sunderland (Boyle), Weatherson, Caldwell (Hawke), Weir.
Forfar Ath: Garden; Ramsay, Donaldson, Bowman (Farnan), Horn, Tully, McPhee, Cargill, Ferguson, Brand, Taylor S.

Queen's Park (1) 2 *(Brown 19, Gallagher 61)*
Stranraer (0) 0 566
Queen's Park: Smith; Ferry, Marshall (Travers), Duncan, Connaghan, Sinclair, Finlayson, Connell, Gallagher (Flannigan), Brown (Miller), Carroll.
Stranraer: McGeown; Paterson, Johnstone, Knox, McDonald G (Hughes), George, Walker, Macdonald W, Harty, Geraghty (Wright), Blaikie (Edgar).

Ross Co (0) 1 *(Holmes 64)*
Albion R (0) 0 777
Ross Co: Walker; Gilbert, Cunnington, Maxwell, Irvine, Taggart, Shaw, Henderson (Holmes), Bone, Millar (Escalon), Kinnaird (Ross).
Albion R: Fahey; Smith, Lumsden, Clyde, Clark, Booth, Waldie (Martin), McKenzie, Begue (Diack), Rankin (Harty), Silvestro.

Stirling Albion (0) 0
Stenhousemuir (0) 1 *(McLauchlan 51)* 605
Stirling Albion: Reid; McStea (McGraw), Bennett (Jack), Milne, Hunter, Millar, King, Donald, Graham, Feroz, McAulay (Gardner).
Stenhousemuir: Gow; Davidson, Fisher, McAneny, Graham, Donald, Gibson L, Lorimer (Ferguson), McLauchlan, Menelaws (English), Wood (Cormack).

9 AUG

Dumbarton (0) 0
Ayr U (0) 0 421
Dumbarton: Hillcoat; Dickie, Dillon, Bruce, Jack, McCann, Wilson, King, Andrew Brown (Grace), Smith (Flannery), Robertson.
Ayr U: Nelson (Rovde); Renwick, Lovering, McGinlay, Hughes, Duffy, Hurst, Wilson, Annand, Teale (Scally), Reynolds.
aet; Dumbarton won 5-4 on penalties.

SECOND ROUND

22 AUG

Alloa Ath (0) 0
Dundee U (2) 3 *(McConalogue 36, 40, 55)* 1088
Alloa Ath: Cairns; Huxford, Clark, Watson, Conway, Valentine, Gardner, Thomson (Wood), Hamilton, Irvine (Brigain), Little.
Dundee U: Combe; Wright (McQuillan), Partridge, de Vos, Aljofree, Buchan (Fernandez), Davidson, Hannah, McConalogue (Smith), Mathie, Hamilton.

Clyde (0) 1 *(Kane 109)*
Kilmarnock (0) 2 *(Dindeleux 113, McCoist 114)* 2018
Clyde: Halliwell; Murray, McLaughlin, Smith, Cranmer (Green), Ross, Mitchell (Kane), Henderson (Sellars), Proudlock, Keogh, Grant.

Kilmarnock: Meldrum; MacPherson, Baker, Dindeleux, Hessey, Mahood, Holt, Mitchell, Vareille (Fowler), McLaren, Wright (McCoist).
aet

Dumbarton (0) 0
Livingston (4) 4 *(Hagen 5, 6, Bingham 7, 44)*		357
Dumbarton: Hillcoat; Dickie, Brittain, McCann, Jack, King, Wilson, Grace (Gentile), Flannery (Smith), Brown, Robertson (Stewart).
Livingston: Alexander; McManus, Fleming, Dolan (Kelly), Coughlan (Sweeney), Anderson, McPhee (McCormick), Grant Smith, Bingham, Britton, Hagen.

Dunfermline Ath (0) 1 *(Boyle 82)*
East Stirling (0) 0		2691
Dunfermline Ath: Ruitenbeek; Dair, Thomson SM, Skinner, Skerla, Mendes (May), Ferguson, Crawford, Boyle, Moss, Nicholson.
East Stirling: Butter; Quinn, Tortolano, Stewart (Lynes), Russell, Hall, Gordon, Carlow, Hislop, McPherson, McKechnie (Higgins).

Falkirk (3) 3 *(Roberts 14, Nicholls 27, McAllister 45)*
Queen of the S (0) 1 *(Hawke 47)*		1696
Falkirk: Hogarth; Lawrie, McQuilken, Christie, Denham, Nicholls, McAllister, Henry, Roberts, Kerr, Hutchison.
Queen of the S: Mathieson; Robison, Hodge, Atkinson R, Martin, Aitken, Pickering (Caldwell), Sunderland, Weatherson (Preen), Hawke, Weir (Nelson).

Inverness CT (0) 0
Airdrieonians (0) 2 *(Fernandez 48, Elliott 51)*		867
Inverness CT: Fridge; Tokely, Golabek, Mann, Hastings (Byers), Sheerin, Bagan, Bavidge (Xausa), Stewart, Christie, Robson (McBain).
Airdrieonians: Broto; Boyce, McCann, Coulter, Forrest, Moreau, Brady, Sanjuan, Elliott (Prest), Calderon, Fernandez (Evans).

Queen's Park (0) 0
Motherwell (1) 3 *(Strong 13, Harvey 71, McCulloch 86)*		1845
Queen's Park: Smith; Ferry, Marshall, Duncan, Connaghan, Sinclair, Finlayson, Connell, Gallagher (Ajet), Brown (Flannigan), Carroll (Miller).
Motherwell: Goram; Corrigan, McMillan, Strong, Hammell, Oueifio (Wood), Townsley, Goodman, Adams (Davies), McCulloch, Elliott (Harvey).

Raith R (0) 2 *(Burns 63, 90 (pen))*
Arbroath (1) 1 *(Brownlie 6)*		1354
Raith R: Van De Kamp; McCulloch, Opinel, Andrews (Gaughan), Browne, Black, Tosh S (Clark), McKinnon, Tosh P (Creaney), Burns, Stein.
Arbroath: Hinchcliffe; King (McGlashan C), Good, Thomson, Rowe, Florence, Cusick (Mercer), McGlashan J, Mallan, Brownlie, Fotheringham.

Ross Co (0) 1 *(Shaw 83)*
St Mirren (0) 3 *(Murray 85, Walker 112, Brown 118)*		1115
Ross Co: Walker; Gilbert, Cunnington, Maxwell, Irvine, Taggart (McQuade), Shaw, Ferguson (Escalon), Bone, Millar (Fraser), Holmes.
St Mirren: Roy; Drew, McGowan, Rudden, Walker, Murray, Nicolson (Mackenzie), Gillies, Paeslack (Yardley), McGarry (Brown), Quitongo.
aet

St Johnstone (3) 3 *(Hartley 5, Dasovic 17, Bollan 22)*
Cowdenbeath (0) 1 *(Allan 57)*		2139
St Johnstone: Main; Sylla, Bollan, Dods, Weir, O'Neill (McCulloch), Dasovic, Hartley, Parker (Russell), Lovenkrands, Jones.
Cowdenbeath: Martin; Boyle, McMillan (Ramsay), White, Lakie, Lawrence (Allan), Winter, Bradley, McDowell, Brown (Wright), Burns.

Stenhousemuir (1) 1 *(McKinnon 19)*
Hibernian (1) 2 *(McManus 23 (pen), Lehmann 62)*		1723
Stenhousemuir: Gow; Davidson, Pittman, McAneny, Cormack, Fisher (Donald), Gibson L, McKinnon, English (Storrar), Mooney (Menelaws), Wood.

Hibernian: Colgan; Smith T, Smith G, Fenwick, McIntosh, Brebner, Lovell, Collins, Andrews (Sar-Temsoury), Lehmann, McManus (Agathe).

23 AUG

Dundee (1) 3 *(Wilkie 7, Caballero 50, 60)*
Montrose (0) 0		2635
Dundee: Douglas; Smith, Marrocco (McSkimming), Wilkie, Tweed (Coyne), Yates, Nemsadze, Rae, Billio, Caballero (Sara), Falconer.
Montrose: McGlynn; Young, Ferguson, Mailer, Snedden, Craib, Marwick, Harrison, McKenzie (McIlravey P), Robertson (McWilliam), McKellar (O'Driscoll).

THIRD ROUND

5 SEPT

Celtic (2) 4 *(Sutton 42, Johnson 44 (pen), 54, Thompson 68)*
Raith R (0) 0		30,753
Celtic: Kerr; Boyd, Mahe, Valgaeren, McNamara, Petta (Tebily) (Rafael), Healy, Thompson, Burchill, Johnson, Sutton (Berkovic).
Raith R: Van De Kamp; McCulloch, Dennis, Andrews, Browne, Black, Tosh S, McKinnon (Clark), Tosh P (Mballa), Burns, Stein (Creaney).

Dundee U (0) 0
Airdrieonians (0) 0		5018
Dundee U: Combe; Wright, Partridge, McQuillan, Aljofree, Buchan, Paterson (Thompson), McDonald (de Vos), Heaney (Hannah), Tchami, McConalogue.
Airdrieonians: Broto; Boyce (Taylor), McCann, Alfonso, Forrest, Moreau, Elliott J (Pacifico), Sanjuan, Elliot B (Clark), Calderon, Fernandez.
aet; Dundee U won 4-3 on penalties.

St Johnstone (0) 0
Kilmarnock (0) 1 *(McCoist 68)*		3231
St Johnstone: Main; Sylla, Bollan, Weir, Kernaghan, McCulloch, McBride, Kane, Hartley (Parker), Lovenkrands (Russell), Jones.
Kilmarnock: Marshall; MacPherson, Hay, Dindeleux, Innes, Mahood, Holt, Mitchell, McLaren (Fowler), McCoist (Cocard), Wright (Durrant).

St Mirren (0) 3 *(Walker 47, Brown 62, Paeslack 88)*
Dundee (0) 0		3571
St Mirren: Roy; McLaughlin, McGowan (Rudden (McKenzie)), Turner, Walker, Murray, Nicolson, Gillies, Paeslack, McGarry (Brown), Quitongo.
Dundee: Douglas; Smith, Marrocco, Wilkie, Tweed, Bonetti, Romano (Coyne), Artero, Billio, Sara (Rae), Caballero (Nemsadze).

6 SEPT

Dunfermline Ath (1) 2 *(Thomson SM 12, Moss 70)*
Motherwell (0) 0		3428
Dunfermline Ath: Ruitenbeek; Doesburg, Dair, Skinner, Skerla, Thomson SM (Matthaei), Mendes (Bullen), Ferguson, Crawford, Moss, Nicholson.
Motherwell: Goram; Corrigan, McMillan, Oueifio, Hammell, Leitch, Davies (Brannan), Townsley, Goodman, McCulloch (Elliott), Spencer.

Falkirk (0) 1 *(McMahon 74)*
Hibernian (0) 2 *(Latapy 80, 116)*		4344
Falkirk: Hogarth; Lawrie, McQuilken, Christie, Denham, Nicholls, McMahon (McAllister), Henry, Roberts, Kerr (Morris), Hutchison.
Hibernian: Colgan; Smith T, Fenwick, Jack, McIntosh, Collins, Sauzee, Brebner (Latapy), O'Neil, Lehmann (Sar-Temsoury), Zitelli (Paatelainen).
aet

Livingston (0) 0
Hearts (1) 2 *(Cameron 15, Naysmith 54)* 5549
Livingston: Alexander; McManus, Fleming, Anderson, Coughlan (Britton), Sweeney, Wilson (Keith), McCulloch, McPhee (McCormick), Bingham, Hagen.
Hearts: Niemi; Pressley, Naysmith, Locke (O'Neil), Murray, Makel (Jackson), Flögel, Fulton, Juanjo, Cameron, McSwegan (Kirk).

Rangers (1) 4 *(Van Bronckhorst 26, Wallace 74, Dodds 81, Amoruso 85)*
Aberdeen (0) 2 *(Winters 52, Derek Young 59)* 37,026
Rangers: Klos; Ricksen, Amoruso, Wilson (Tugay), Numan, Van Bronckhorst, Ferguson, de Boer, McCann (Johnston), Dodds, Wallace.
Aberdeen: Esson; McGuire, McNaughton (Clark), Whyte, Rowson, Darren Young, Guntweit, Mackie, Belabed, Winters, Derek Young (McAllister).

QUARTER-FINALS
31 OCT

Kilmarnock (0) 2 *(McLaren 48, Dargo 73)*
Hibernian (1) 1 *(Latapy 2)* 7879
Kilmarnock: Marshall; MacPherson, Hay, Dindeleux, Innes, Mahood, Holt (Dargo), Durrant, McLaren, Cocard (Wright), Mitchell.
Hibernian: Colgan; Laursen, Smith G, Fenwick (Collins), McIntosh, Jack, Lovell, Latapy, Andrews (Smith T), Paatelainen (Lehmann), O'Neil.

Rangers (2) 2 *(Miller 11, Ferguson 30)*
Dundee U (0) 0 30,966
Rangers: Christiansen; Porrini, Amoruso, Wilson, Numan, Ricksen, Tugay, Ferguson, McCann, Dodds, Miller (Lovenkrands).
Dundee U: Combe; Licina, Partridge (Atangana), de Vos, Aljofree, McQuillan, Lauchlan, Buchan, Venetis (Leoni), Easton, Thompson (McConalogue).

St Mirren (2) 2 *(McGarry 26, Gillies 42)*
Dunfermline Ath (1) 1 *(Nicholson 29)* 4045
St Mirren: Scrimgour; McLaughlin, McGowan, Turner, Walker, Nicolson, Murray (McKenzie), Gillies, Fenton (Sharp), McGarry, Yardley.
Dunfermline Ath: Ruitenbeek; McGroarty, Dair, Skinner, Skerla, Thomson SM, Nicholson, Ferguson, Moss, Crawford, Coyle (Hampshire).

1 NOV

Hearts (1) 2 *(Cameron 35 (pen), 70 (pen))*
Celtic (1) 5 *(Crainey 41, Smith 60, Healy 100, Moravcik 117, McNamara 118)* 13,076
Hearts: Niemi; Pressley, Severin, Petric, Locke (Neilson), Murray, Tomaschek, Fulton (Milne), Flögel (Juanjo), Cameron, Kirk.
Celtic: Gould; Riseth, Crainey (Petta), Valgaeren, Stubbs, McNamara, Smith (Petrov), Thompson, Moravcik, Johnson (Boyd), Healy.
aet

SEMI-FINALS
6 FEB

Kilmarnock (1) 3 *(McLaren 39, Dargo 68, Canero 78)*
St Mirren (0) 0 9213
Kilmarnock: Marshall; MacPherson, Baker, McGowne, Dindeleux, Canero, Holt, Mitchell (Reilly), McLaren, Wright (Cocard), Dargo (Fowler).
St Mirren: Roy; Baltacha, Rudden, Turner, Walker, Bowman (Murray), Kerr, Gillies, McKenzie (Quitongo), Fenton (McGarry), Yardley.

7 FEB

Celtic (2) 3 *(Sutton 7, Larsson 16, 69)*
Rangers (1) 1 *(Albertz 36 (pen))* 50,000
Celtic: Gould; Mjallby, Vega, Boyd, McNamara (Petta), Lennon, Petrov, Lambert, Thompson, Larsson (Moravcik), Sutton (Johnson).
Rangers: Klos; Reyna, Wilson, Konterman, Numan, Malcolm, Tugay (Johnston), Ferguson, Albertz, Flo, McCann (Mols).

FINAL (at Hampden Park)
18 MAR

Celtic 3 (0) *(Larsson 47, 74, 80)*
Kilmarnock 0 (0) 48,830
Celtic: Gould; Mjallby, Valgaeren, Vega, Petta (Crainey) (Boyd), Healy, Lennon, Lambert, Moravcik (Smith), Larsson, Sutton.
Kilmarnock: Marshall; MacPherson, McGowne, Dindeleux (Canero), Innes, Hay, Holt, Durrant (Reilly), Mahood, Cocard (McLaren), Dargo.
Referee: Hugh Dallas

Martin O'Neill completed a hat-trick of honours in his first season as manager of Celtic, beginning with the League Cup. (Pool/Actionimages)

BELL'S CHALLENGE CUP 2000–2001

FIRST ROUND

15 AUG

Airdrieonians (0) 2 *(Calderon 67, Clark 92)*
Queen of the S (0) 1 *(Atkinson P 47)*   1936
Airdrieonians: Broto; Brady, McCann (McAlpine), Alfonso, Coulter, Moreau, Capin, Sanjuan, Prest (Clark), Calderon (Taylor), Evans.
Queen of the S: Mathieson; Muir (Pickering), Hodge, Nixon, Martin, Aitken, Atkinson P, Sunderland, Weatherson, Caldwell (Hawke), Weir (Nelson).
aet

Albion R (0) 0
Clydebank (1) 1 *(Coyne 34)*   212
Albion R: Fahey; Waldie, Lumsden, Smith, Clyde, Booth, McMullan, Silvestro, Diack, Rankin (Begue), McLees (McKenzie).
Clydebank: Wylie; McKinstrey, Wishart, McQuilter (Murdoch), Brannigan, Taborda, Johnson, Hamilton, McKelvie (Fal), Coyne, Ferguson.

Alloa (2) 2 *(Hamilton 1, 7)*
Inverness CT (0) 3 *(Stewart 53, 82, Bavidge 85)*   597
Alloa: Cairns; Farrell (Brigain), Clark, Watson, Conway, Valentine, Gardner, Thomson, Hamilton, Wilson (Huxford), Wood (Irvine).
Inverness CT: Fridge; Tokely, Golabek, Mann, Munro, Sheerin, Wyness (Christie), Bavidge, Stewart, McBain (Hind), Robson.

Brechin C (2) 3 *(Duffy (og) 23, Sturrock 44, Grant 81)*
Ayr U (0) 1 *(McGinlay 50)*   276
Brechin C: Soutar; Christie, Raynes, Nairn, Cairney, Riley (Donachie), McKeith (Honeyman), Black, Sturrock, Leask (Fal), Coulston.
Ayr U: Rovde; Renwick, Lovering (Reynolds), McGinlay (Crilly), Hughes, Duffy, Scally, Wilson, Annand (Hurst), Teale, Bradford.

Cowdenbeath (1) 2 *(Brown 18, Juskowiak 112)*
Falkirk (1) 1 *(Hutchison 5)*   544
Cowdenbeath: Martin; Boyle, McMillan, White, McCulloch (Lakie), Lawrence (McDonald), Winter, Bradley, McDowell (Juskowiak), Brown, Allan.
Falkirk: Hogarth; Lawrie, Seaton (McQuilken), Christie, Denham, Nicholls, Morris, Hutchison, McDonald, Avdiu (Roberts), Waddell (Kerr).
aet

East Stirling (1) 3 *(Hislop 24, McKechnie 71, Lynes 83)*
East Fife (0) 0   201
East Stirling: Butter; Quinn, Hall, Russell, Todd D (Lynes), McPherson, Stewart, McKechnie, Hislop (Higgins), McKenzie (Gordon), Tortolano.
East Fife: Stewart; Munro, Gallagher, Logan, Agostini, Sharp (Mackay), Ferguson (Allison), Mortimer, Kerrigan, Moffat, Hunter.

Elgin C (0) 2 *(Green 62, 63)*
Dumbarton (1) 4 *(Flannery 44, 51, 65, Brown 78)*   828
Elgin C: Pirie; Milne D, MacDonald, Russell, O'Brien, Green M, Ellis (Morrison), Green R, Milne CR, Slythe, Clinton (Cameron).
Dumbarton: Hillcoat; Dickie, Bonar, McCann, Jack, Stewart (Brittain), Grace (Wilson), King, Flannery, Andrew Brown (Gentile), Robertson.

Forfar Ath (0) 1 *(McPhee 50)*
Peterhead (1) 1 *(Clark G 14)*   407
Forfar Ath: Garden; Bowman (Morris), Donaldson, Farnan, Horn, Tully, Stewart, McPhee, Ferguson I (Brand), Taylor S, Cargill (McCheyne).
Peterhead: Pirie; Craig, King, Herd, Simpson, Paterson, De-Barros (Clark S) (Gibson), Johnston, Clark G (Smith), Brown, Livingstone.
aet; Peterhead won 4-2 on penalties

Partick T (0) 0
Livingston (0) 2 *(Britton 83, Wilson 89)*   1805
Partick T: Brown; Docherty (Smith), McKeown, Howie (Cameron), Craigan, Archibald, Moore, Lyle, Dunn (Lindau), McCallum, Stirling.
Livingston: Alexander; McManus, Fleming, Dolan (Grant Smith), Coughlan, Anderson, Wilson, McCulloch, Crabbe (Britton), Bingham, Hagen (McCormick).

Queen's Park (2) 2 *(Gallagher 8, 40 (pen))*
Montrose (0) 0   482
Queen's Park: Stewart; Miller, Marshall, Duncan, Martin P (Travers), Sinclair, Finlayson, Connell (Canning), Gallagher, Brown, Carroll (Ajet).
Montrose: McGlynn; Young, Ferguson, Marwick (Robertson), Snedden, Craib, McKellar, Harrison (Mailer), McKenzie, McIlravey (Mitchell J), McWilliam.

Raith R (0) 0
Morton (3) 4 *(Matheson 21, Whalen 25, 28, Kerr 90)* 1160
Raith R: Van De Kamp; McCulloch, Ellis (Stein), Gaughan, Browne, Black (Hetherston), McEwan, Tosh S, Clark, Burns, Creaney (Mballa).
Morton: Boswell; Murie, Anderson, Medou-Otye, Raeside, Curran, Aitken, Millen (Brownrigg), Whalen, Matheson (Kerr), McDonald P.

Ross Co (1) 2 *(Bone 17, Henderson 62)*
Clyde (0) 1 *(Cannie 80)*   521
Ross Co: Walker; Mackay D, Cunnington, Maxwell, Irvine, Escalon (Ferguson), Shaw, Fraser (Henderson), Bone, Millar, Holmes.
Clyde: Hanley; Greer, McPherson, Hay, McGhee, Henry (Aitken), Bingham, Dunn (Sean McAuley), Barrett (Stephen McAulay), McCusker, Cannie.

Stirling Albion (1) 2 *(O'Neill 20, McAulay 79)*
Arbroath (1) 3 *(Rowe 15, McGlashan C 50, 56 (pen))* 424
Stirling Albion: Reid; Whiteford, Joy, Hunter, Milne, Millar, King, McAulay, McGraw (Aitken), Feroz (Graham), Donald (O'Neill).
Arbroath: Hinchcliffe; King, Florence, Webster (Cusick), Rowe, Good, Brownlie (Mallan), McGlashan J, McGlashan C, Mercer (Tindal), Fotheringham.

Stranraer (2) 4 *(Wright 2, Walker 44, Geraghty 49, Harty 56)*
Berwick R (0) 2 *(McMartin 64, Oliver 66)*   285
Stranraer: O'Neill; Paterson, Wright, Knox, McDonald G (Abbott), George, Walker, Macdonald W, Harty, Blair (Blaikie), Geraghty.
Berwick R: O'Connor; Oliver, Duthie (Anderson), McNicoll, Neill A, Rafferty, McMartin, Forrest, Laidlaw, Findlay (Harvey), Smith (Magee).

SECOND ROUND

29 AUG

Brechin C (1) 1 *(Sturrock 27)*
Queen's Park (1) 1 *(Finlayson 20)*   328
Brechin C: Soutar; Riley (Williamson), Donachie (Leask), Bain, Cairney, Nairn, Smith, McKeith (Honeyman), Grant, Sturrock, Coulston.
Queen's Park: Stewart; Caven, Marshall, Duncan, Connaghan, Martin P, Finlayson, Connell, Gallagher (Scobie), Brown (Orr), Carroll (Flannigan).
aet; Brechin C won 4-2 on penalties.

Cowdenbeath (0) 1 *(McDowell 68)*
Stenhousemuir (0) 2 *(Gibson L 68, Menelaws 73)*   223
Cowdenbeath: Martin; Boyle, Courts, White, Lakie, Allan (McDonald), Winter, Bradley, McDowell, Wright, Burns.
Stenhousemuir: Gow; Duncan, Gibson L, Graham, Cormack, Ferguson (McKinnon), Storrar, Lorimer, McLauchlan (English), Mooney (Menelaws), Wood.

East Stirling (0) 3 *(Gordon 48, Lynes 62, Todd D 80)*
Morton (1) 2 *(Boukraa 13, Matheson 81)* 427
East Stirling: Butter; Quinn, Hall, Lynes, Russell, Todd D, Stewart, Higgins (Hislop), McKechnie, Gordon, Tortolano.
Morton: Boswell; Murie, Anderson, Medou-Otye, Raeside, Curran, Aitken, Millen, Boukraa (Kerr), Matheson, McDonald (Davies).

Ross Co (0) 0
Livingston (0) 3 *(Bingham 51, Britton 56, 79)* 825
Ross Co: Walker; Gilbert, Cunnington, Maxwell, Irvine, Escalon (Bone), Shaw, Fraser, Ferguson, Millar, Kinnaird (King).
Livingston: Alexander; McManus, Fleming, Grant Smith (Britton), Coughlan, Anderson, McPhee (McCormick), McCulloch, Wilson (Kelly), Bingham, Hagen.

2 SEPT

Arbroath (0) 2 *(Mallan 85, Brownlie 89 (pen))*
Dumbarton (0) 0 459
Arbroath: Hinchcliffe; Florence, Fotheringham, McAulay, Rowe, Webster, Cusick (Tindal), Bryce (Mercer), McGlashan C (Mallan), Brownlie, McGlashan J.
Dumbarton: Hillcoat; Bonar, Brittain, McCann, Jack, King, Wilson, Stewart, Flannery, Andrew Brown, Dillon.

Clydebank (1) 1 *(McCormick 9)*
Peterhead (0) 0 202
Clydebank: Wylie; McKinstrey, McKinnon, McQuilter, Brannigan, Welsh, Rodden (Coyne), Paton, McCormick (McKelvie), Jacquel, Walker (Johnston).
Peterhead: Pirie; Craig (De-Barros), King, Herd, Simpson, Paterson (Gibson), Cooper, Johnston, O'Connor, Smith (Clark), Livingstone.

Hamilton A (0) 0
Airdrieonians (0) 1 *(Pacifico 98)* 1108
Hamilton A: Macfarlane I; Grant, Lynn, Davidson (Hillcoat), Gaughan, Nelson, Russell (Eadie), Sherry, Moore, McFarlane D, Bonnar (Prytz).
Airdrieonians: Broto; Boyce, McCann, Alfonso, Forrest, Moreau, Brady (Taylor), Sanjuan, Elliott J (Pacifico), Calderon, Fernandez (Prest).
aet

Inverness CT (0) 1 *(Bavidge 57)*
Stranraer (1) 2 *(Rae 35, Harty 48 (pen))* 664
Inverness CT: Calder; Hind (Byers), McBain, Mann, Tokely, Sheerin, Bagan, Bavidge, Stewart, Christie, Robson (Wyness).
Stranraer: McGeown; Paterson, Wright, Knox, McDonald G, George, Blair, Macdonald W (Johnstone), Harty, Rae (Hughes) (Blaikie), Walker.

QUARTER-FINALS

12 SEPT

East Stirling (2) 4 *(Hislop 7 (pen), 62, Davidson (og) 27, Ferguson 46)*
Stenhousemuir (0) 0 251
East Stirling: Butter; Ferguson (Carlow), Hall, Russell, Todd D, Gordon, Stewart, Lynes (McPherson), McKechnie (McKenzie), Hislop, Tortolano.
Stenhousemuir: Gow; Duncan, Storrar, McAneny (Graham), Cormack, Davidson, Gibson L (Donald), McKinnon, English, Menelaws, Wood (Lorimer).

Livingston (0) 3 *(McCormick 48, Britton 70, Keith 85)*
Brechin C (1) 1 *(Leask 23)* 873
Livingston: Alexander; McManus (Greacen), Fleming, McCulloch, Coughlan, Sweeney, Wilson, McPhee (Keith), Britton (Hagen), Bingham, McCormick.
Brechin C: Soutar; Donachie (Smith G), Coulston, Bain, Cairney, Raynes, Smith D, Nairn (Dewar), Grant, Leask (Sturrock), Honeyman.

Stranraer (3) 3 *(Harty 10, 36, Geraghty 16)*
Arbroath (1) 2 *(Mercer 45, McGlashan C 53)* 230
Stranraer: McGeown; Johnstone, Wright, McDonald G, Knox, Macdonald W (Blair), Paterson, George, Harty, Geraghty (Blaikie), Walker.
Arbroath: Hinchcliffe; King, Florence, McAulay (Heenan), Rowe, Good, Mercer, McGlashan J, McGlashan C, Brownlie (Bryce), Fotheringham.

19 SEPT

Airdrieonians (0) 1 *(Prest 55)*
Clydebank (0) 1 *(Jacquel 65)* 979
Airdrieonians: Broto; Boyce, McAlpine (McCann), Alfonso, Forrest, Moreau, Brady, Sanjuan, Prest, Calderon (Elliott), Fernandez (McKeown).
Clydebank: Smith; McKinstrey, McVey, Murdoch (Walker), Brannigan, Wishart, Murray, Hamilton (Paton), Coyne, Jacquel (McCormick), Burke.
aet; Airdrieonians won 4-3 on penalties.

SEMI-FINALS

26 SEPT

Livingston (2) 2 *(Bingham 22 (pen), Anderson 44)*
East Stirling (1) 1 *(McKechnie 9)* 789
Livingston: Alexander; Hart (McManus), Fleming, Dolan, Anderson, Deas, Wilson (McPhee), McCulloch, Crabbe (Hagen), Bingham, Keith.
East Stirling: Butter; Quinn, Hall, Russell, Todd D (Ferguson), Lynes, Stewart, Higgins (McPherson), Hislop, McKechnie, Tortolano.

Stranraer (2) 2 *(Harty 8, George 20)*
Airdrieonians (2) 4 *(Prest 3, Fernandez 10, Taylor 101, McKeown 110)* 528
Stranraer: McGeown; Johnstone (Edgar), McMillan, Knox, Wright, Paterson (McDonald G), Blair, George, Harty, Macdonald W (Blaikie), Geraghty.
Airdrieonians: Broto; Armstrong, McAlpine (McKeown), Taylor, Forrest, Moreau, Brady, Sanjuan, Prest (Pacifico), Elliott J (Elliot B), Fernandez.
aet

FINAL (at Broadwood Stadium)

19 NOV

Airdrieonians (1) 2 *(Prest 28, McGuire 78)*
Livingston (1) 2 *(Crabbe 17, Anderson 50)* 5623
Airdrieonians: Broto; Armstrong (Capin), McCann, Brady, Forrest, Ireland, Elliott J (McGuire), Moreau, Prest, Calderon (Sanjuan), Fernandez.
Livingston: Alexander; McManus, Fleming, Anderson, Coughlan, Deas, Wilson (Hart), McCulloch, Keith (McPhee), Crabbe, Bingham (Hagen).
aet; Airdrieonians won 4-3 on penalties.
Referee: John Rowbotham.

SCOTTISH CUP FINALS 1874–2001

Year	Winners	Runners-up	Score
1874	Queen's Park	Clydesdale	2-0
1875	Queen's Park	Renton	3-0
1876	Queen's Park	Third Lanark	2-0 after 1-1 draw
1877	Vale of Leven	Rangers	3-2 after 0-0 and 1-1 draws
1878	Vale of Leven	Third Lanark	1-0
1879	Vale of Leven*	Rangers	
1880	Queen's Park	Thornlibank	3-0
1881	Queen's Park†	Dumbarton	3-1
1882	Queen's Park	Dumbarton	4-1 after 2-2 draw
1883	Dumbarton	Vale of Leven	2-1 after 2-2 draw
1884	Queen's Park‡	Vale of Leven	
1885	Renton	Vale of Leven	3-1 after 0-0 draw
1886	Queen's Park	Renton	3-1
1887	Hibernian	Dumbarton	2-1
1888	Renton	Cambuslang	6-1
1889	Third Lanark§	Celtic	2-1
1890	Queen's Park	Vale of Leven	2-1 after 1-1 draw
1891	Hearts	Dumbarton	1-0
1892	Celtic¶	Queen's Park	5-1
1893	Queen's Park	Celtic	2-1
1894	Rangers	Celtic	3-1
1895	St Bernard's	Renton	2-1
1896	Hearts	Hibernian	3-1
1897	Rangers	Dumbarton	5-1
1898	Rangers	Kilmarnock	2-0
1899	Celtic	Rangers	2-0
1900	Celtic	Queen's Park	4-3
1901	Hearts	Celtic	4-3
1902	Hibernian	Celtic	1-0
1903	Rangers	Hearts	2-0 after 1-1 and 0-0 draws
1904	Celtic	Rangers	3-2
1905	Third Lanark	Rangers	3-1 after 0-0 draw
1906	Hearts	Third Lanark	1-0
1907	Celtic	Hearts	3-0
1908	Celtic	St Mirren	5-1
1909	••		
1910	Dundee	Clyde	2-1 after 2-2 and 0-0 draws
1911	Celtic	Hamilton A	2-0 after 0-0 draw
1912	Celtic	Clyde	2-0
1913	Falkirk	Raith R	2-0
1914	Celtic	Hibernian	4-1 after 0-0 draw
1920	Kilmarnock	Albion R	3-2
1921	Partick T	Rangers	1-0
1922	Morton	Rangers	1-0
1923	Celtic	Hibernian	1-0
1924	Airdrieonians	Hibernian	2-0
1925	Celtic	Dundee	2-1
1926	St Mirren	Celtic	2-0
1927	Celtic	East Fife	3-1
1928	Rangers	Celtic	4-0
1929	Kilmarnock	Rangers	2-0
1930	Rangers	Partick T	2-1 after 0-0 draw
1931	Celtic	Motherwell	4-2 after 2-2 draw
1932	Rangers	Kilmarnock	3-0 after 1-1 draw
1933	Celtic	Motherwell	1-0
1934	Rangers	St Mirren	5-0
1935	Rangers	Hamilton A	2-1
1936	Rangers	Third Lanark	1-0
1937	Celtic	Aberdeen	2-1
1938	East Fife	Kilmarnock	4-2 after 1-1 draw
1939	Clyde	Motherwell	4-0
1947	Aberdeen	Hibernian	2-1
1948	Rangers	Morton	1-0 after 1-1 draw
1949	Rangers	Clyde	4-1
1950	Rangers	East Fife	3-0
1951	Celtic	Motherwell	1-0
1952	Motherwell	Dundee	4-0
1953	Rangers	Aberdeen	1-0 after 1-1 draw
1954	Celtic	Aberdeen	2-1
1955	Clyde	Celtic	1-0 after 1-1 draw
1956	Hearts	Celtic	3-1
1957	Falkirk	Kilmarnock	2-1 after 1-1 draw
1958	Clyde	Hibernian	1-0
1959	St Mirren	Aberdeen	3-1
1960	Rangers	Kilmarnock	2-0
1961	Dunfermline Ath	Celtic	2-0 after 0-0 draw
1962	Rangers	St Mirren	2-0
1963	Rangers	Celtic	3-0 after 1-1 draw
1964	Rangers	Dundee	3-1
1965	Celtic	Dunfermline Ath	3-2
1966	Rangers	Celtic	1-0 after 0-0 draw
1967	Celtic	Aberdeen	2-0
1968	Dunfermline Ath	Hearts	3-1
1969	Celtic	Rangers	4-0
1970	Aberdeen	Celtic	3-1

Year	Winners	Runners-up	Score
1971	Celtic	Rangers	2-1 after 1-1 draw
1972	Celtic	Hibernian	6-1
1973	Rangers	Celtic	3-2
1974	Celtic	Dundee U	3-0
1975	Celtic	Airdrieonians	3-1
1976	Rangers	Hearts	3-1
1977	Celtic	Rangers	1-0
1978	Rangers	Aberdeen	2-1
1979	Rangers	Hibernian	3-2 after 0-0 and 0-0 draws
1980	Celtic	Rangers	1-0
1981	Rangers	Dundee U	4-1 after 0-0 draw
1982	Aberdeen	Rangers	4-1 (aet)
1983	Aberdeen	Rangers	1-0 (aet)
1984	Aberdeen	Celtic	2-1 (aet)
1985	Celtic	Dundee U	2-1
1986	Aberdeen	Hearts	3-0
1987	St Mirren	Dundee U	1-0 (aet)
1988	Celtic	Dundee U	2-1
1989	Celtic	Rangers	1-0
1990	Aberdeen	Celtic	0-0 (aet)
		(Aberdeen won 9-8 on penalties)	
1991	Motherwell	Dundee U	4-3 (aet)
1992	Rangers	Airdrieonians	2-1
1993	Rangers	Aberdeen	2-1
1994	Dundee U	Rangers	1-0
1995	Celtic	Airdrieonians	1-0
1996	Rangers	Hearts	5-1
1997	Kilmarnock	Falkirk	1-0
1998	Hearts	Rangers	2-1
1999	Rangers	Celtic	1-0
2000	Rangers	Aberdeen	4-0
2001	Celtic	Hibernian	3-0

*Vale of Leven awarded cup, Rangers failing to appear for replay after 1-1 draw.
†After Dumbarton protested the first game, which Queen's Park won 2-1.
‡Queen's Park awarded cup, Vale of Leven failing to appear.
§Replay by order of Scottish FA because of playing conditions in first match, won 3-0 by Third Lanark.
¶After mutually protested game which Celtic won 1-0.
••Owing to riot, the cup was withheld after two drawn games – between Celtic and Rangers 2-2 and 1-1.

SCOTTISH CUP WINS

Celtic 31, Rangers 29, Queen's Park 10, Aberdeen 7, Hearts 6, Clyde 3, Kilmarnock 3, St Mirren 3, Vale of Leven 3, Dunfermline Ath 2, Falkirk 2, Hibernian 2, Motherwell 2, Renton 2, Third Lanark 2, Airdrieonians 1, Dumbarton 1, Dundee 1, Dundee U 1, East Fife 1, Morton 1, Partick T 1, St Bernard's 1.

APPEARANCES IN FINAL

Celtic 49, Rangers 46, Aberdeen 15, Queen's Park 12, Hearts 12, Hibernian 11, Kilmarnock 8, Vale of Leven 7, Clyde 6, Dumbarton 6, Dundee U 7, Motherwell 6, St Mirren 6, Third Lanark 6, Renton 5, Airdrieonians 4, Dundee 4, Dunfermline Ath 3, East Fife 3, Falkirk 3, Hamilton A 2, Morton 2, Partick T 2, Albion R 1, Cambuslang 1, Clydesdale 1, Raith R 1, St Bernard's 1, Thornliebank 1.

Tom Boyd and Paul Lambert lift the Tennent's Scottish Cup Trophy following the 3-0 win over Hibernian.
(Actionimages/Darren Walsh)

TENNENT'S SCOTTISH CUP 2000–2001

FIRST ROUND

9 DEC

Albion R (1) 1 *(Shields 24)*
East Fife (0) 1 *(Ferguson 60)*   360
Albion R: Fahey; Clark, Lumsden, Clyde, Tait, Booth, Waldie, McKenzie, Shields (Diack), McMullan (Rankin), Silvestro (McLees).
East Fife: McCulloch; Bottiglieri, Sharp (Gibb), McCloy, Agostini, Allison, McKinnon, Mackay, Ferguson (Devine), Kerrigan, Hunter.

Dumbarton (1) 1 *(Flannery 40)*
East Stirling (0) 1 *(Hislop 63)*   834
Dumbarton: Hillcoat (Wight); Dickie, Brittain, Bruce, McCann, Stewart, Bonar (Dillon), Grace, Flannery (Smith), Brown, Robertson.
East Stirling: Butter; Ferguson, Russell, Clarke, Hall, Scott, Stewart, Lorimer (Todd D), Allison, Hislop (McKechnie), Wood.

Montrose (0) 0
Arbroath (0) 1   1038
SFA ordered game to be replayed as Arbroath fielded ineligible player.

Stenhousemuir (0) 1 *(Menelaws 75)*   303
Berwick R (3) 4 *(Watt 38, Anthony 41, Wood 45, Ronald 55)*
Stenhousemuir: Gow; Duncan, Cormack, McAneny, Graham (Menelaws), Davidson, Ferguson (Blaikie), McKinnon (Henderson), Miller, Donald, English.
Berwick R: McLean; McMartin, Gray, Ritchie, Neill A, Anthony, Forrest, Watt, Wood (Whelan), Ronald (Findlay), Magee (Smith).

12 DEC

Brechin C (1) 3 *(Leask 32, Black 72, Bain 83)*
Forfar Ath (0) 0   447
Brechin C: Soutar; Smith D, Coulston, Bain, Cairney, Smith G, Leask (Bailey), Nairn, Grant (Sturrock), Riley (Donachie), Black.
Forfar Ath: Garden; Morris, Tully (McGraw), Horn, Beaton, Farnan, Taylor, Bowman (Cargill), Ferguson (Brand), Stewart, Donaldson.

16 DEC

Whitehill Welfare (0) 0
Peterhead (0) 0   237
Whitehill Welfare: Cantley; McLaren, Gowrie, Martin, Steel (Cunningham), Bennett, Jardine, Samuel, Bird, Hope (Black), Manson (Baillie).
Peterhead: Pirie; Clark S, King, Herd, Simpson, Tindal, Murray, Yeats, Stewart, Smith D, Livingstone.

18 DEC

Queen of the S (2) 2 *(Weatherson 7, 22)*
Clydebank (0) 0   1017
Queen of the S: Mathieson; Atkinson P, McKeown, McQuilter, Aitken, Sunderland (Nixon), Muir, Hawke, Weatherson (Suddick), Skinner (Caldwell), Kinnaird.
Clydebank: Hutchison; Mackay, McKinstrey, Murdoch, Brannigan, Wishart, Murray, Paton, Coyne, Glancy, McVey (Morrison).

20 DEC

Edinburgh C (0) 0
Buckie T (1) 1 *(Rowley 4)*   246
Edinburgh C: Mackintosh; Burrell, Ferry, Scott, Foster, Edgar (Rennie), Salton (Blair), Summerville, O'Donnell, Hartley, Seeley.
Buckie T: Rae; Grant, Lamberton, Anderson, McPherson, Rattray, Rowley, Stephen, Thompson (Reid), Bruce (Stewart), Craik (Milne).

6 JAN

Montrose (0) 0
Arbroath (0) 0   1250
Montrose: McGlynn; Marwick, Ferguson, Lowe, Christie, Craib, Muirhead, Mailer, McKenzie, McIlravey (Hutcheon) (McWilliam), Joy (Catto).
Arbroath: Hinchcliffe; Rowe, McInally, Cusick (Heenan), Thomson, Webster, Steele, Mercer, McGlashan C (Brownlie), McGlashan J (Cunningham), Florence.

FIRST ROUND REPLAYS

12 DEC

East Fife (0) 2 *(Ferguson 53, 70)*
Albion R (0) 0   398
East Fife: McCulloch; Bottiglieri, Gibb, McCloy, Agostini, Allison, McKinnon, Mackay, Ferguson (Moffat), Kerrigan, Hunter (Mortimer).
Albion R: Fahey; Clark, Lumsden, Smith, Tait, Booth, Waldie, McKenzie J, Shields, Begue (Diack), Silvestro (McMullan).

East Stirling (0) 0
Dumbarton (0) 1 *(Robertson 55)*   170
East Stirling: Rutter; Ferguson, Russell, Clarke, Hall, Scott (Todd D), Stewart (McPherson), Lorimer, Hislop, Allison, Wood.
Dumbarton: Hillcoat; Dickie, Brittain (Dillon), Bruce, McCann, Stewart, Bonar, Jack, Flannery, Brown, Robertson.

18 DEC

Peterhead (1) 3 *(King 34, Livingstone 66, Tindal 85)*
Whitehill Welfare (0) 0   465
Peterhead: Pirie; Clark S, King, Herd, Simpson, Tindal, Murray (Bett), Stewart (De-Barros), Yeats (Gibson), Johnston, Livingstone.
Whitehill Welfare: Cantley; McLaren (Temple), Gowrie, Malcolm, Martin (Steele), Bennett, Jardine, Samuel, Bird, Baillie (Black), Manson.

9 JAN

Arbroath (1) 1 *(Cusick 7)*
Montrose (1) 2 *(McKenzie 27, 47)*   1225
Arbroath: Hinchcliffe; Rowe, McInally (Steele), Florence (Cunningham), Webster, Cusick, Heenan (Brownlie), Mercer, McGlashan C, McGlashan J, Fotheringham.
Montrose: McGlynn; Mailer, Ferguson, Lowe (Harrison), Christie, Craib, McWilliam (Joy), Muirhead, McIlravey (Mitchell J), McKenzie, Catto.

SECOND ROUND

6 JAN

Berwick R (2) 3 *(Neill A 4, 41, Anthony 70)*
Cowdenbeath (0) 3 *(Bradley 51, 75 (pen), Winter 79)*   505
Berwick R: McLean; McMartin, Gray, Ritchie, Neill A, Watt, Forrest, Anthony, Wood, Elliot (Findlay), Smith.
Cowdenbeath: Martin; Boyle, Courts (Neeson), Smith, White, Lawrence, Winter, Bradley, McDowell, Brown, King (Allan).

Buckie T (0) 2 *(Stephen 46, Stewart 62)*
Hamilton A (0) 0   1028
Buckie T: Rae; Grant, Lamberton, Anderson, McPherson, Rattray, Rowley, Stephen, Thomson (Reid), Bruce (Craik), Stewart (Milne).
Hamilton A: Macfarlane I; Nelson (Downs), Callaghan, Hogg, Gaughan, Clark, Russell, Sherry, Eadie (Moore), McFarlane D, Bonnar.

Coldstream (0) 2 *(Hutchison 60, Dishington 77)*
Brechin C (3) 6 *(Grant 8, 18, Bailey 36, 69, 71, 87)* 393
Coldstream: Weir; Hutchison, Finlay, O'Connor, Wilson, Keenan (Dishington), Evans, Cummings (McLeod), Shennan (Cowie), Cockburn, Tait.
Brechin C: Soutar; Smith G, Coulston (Smith D), Bain, Cairney, Raynes (Nairn), Dewar (Black), Bailey, Grant, Riley, Sturrock.

East Fife (1) 1 *(Moffat 27)*
Queen's Park (0) 0 759
East Fife: McCulloch; Bottiglieri, Sharp, McCloy, Agostini, Allison, Munro (Stewart), Mortimer (Gibb), Kerrigan, Moffat (Hunter), Mackay.
Queen's Park: Smith; Canning, Travers, Duncan (Jackson), Connaghan, Sinclair, Finlayson, Miller, Gallagher, Brown, Carroll (Scobie).

Partick T (0) 3 *(Hardie 50, 57, Collins 89)*
Deveronvale (0) 0 3160
Partick T: Arthur; Hamilton, Archibald (McCallum), Creagan, Smith, McNally (Stewart), Collins, Lennon, Shaw, Hardie, Lindau (McGrillen).
Deveronvale: Speirs; Dolan, Kinghorn, Chisholm, Henderson, Montgomery, More (Singer), Brown (McAllister), Cadger, Watt (Nicol), Urquhart.

Peterhead (0) 3 *(Johnston 56, Herd 70, Stewart 75)*
Cove R (0) 0 1425
Peterhead: Pirie; Clark S, King, Herd, Simpson, Tindal, Cooper (Murray), Stewart (Gibson), Yeats (Smith), Johnston, Livingstone.
Cove R: Coull M; Mullen, McGinlay, Alexander, Murphy, Baxter, Adam (Summers), Yule, Coutts (Taylor), Beattie, Brown.

Spartans (1) 1 *(Hughes 25)*
Stirling Albion (1) 3 *(Donald 36, Graham 59, Williams 77)* 709
Spartans: Brown; Robertson (Quinn B), Rae, Hughes, Thomson M, McKeating, Watson (Wilson), Thomson S, Hoggins, McGovern, Quinn M (Ford).
Stirling Albion: Reid; Kelly, Milne, Devine, Gaughan, McAulay, Feroz, Donald, Graham (Williams), Templeman (McCallion), Millar.

Stranraer (0) 2 *(Walker 54, Harty 87)*
Dumbarton (0) 0 595
Stranraer: McGeown; Knox, Wright, Johnstone, George, Macdonald, Blair, Walker, Harty, Rae (Geraghty), Stirling.
Dumbarton: Hillcoat; Dickie, Brittain (Melvin), Bruce, Jack, Stewart (Smith), Bonar, Grace, Flannery, Brown, Dillon.

13 JAN

Montrose (0) 1 *(Harrison 87)*
Keith (0) 1 *(Still 65)* 1150
Montrose: Thompson; Marwick (McKellar), Ferguson, Mailer, Muirhead, Craib, Byers, Harrison, McKenzie, Laidlaw, Catto (McWilliam).
Keith: Rodd; Darcy (Hendry), Simmers, Maver, Watt, Gibson, Still, Presslie, Robertson (Stewart), Nicol, McPherson (Brown).

27 JAN

Elgin C (0) 0
Queen of the S (1) 1 *(Weatherson 38)* 1035
Elgin C: Pirie; Milne CD, MacDonald (Green), Furphy, Morrison, Munro, Campbell, Whyte (Clinton), Milne CR, Edwards (Irvine), Ross.
Queen of the S: Mathieson; Atkinson P, McKeown, McQuilter, Aitken, Sunderland, Muir (Nixon), Boyle, Skinner (Hogg), Weatherson, Paterson (Kinnaird).

SECOND ROUND REPLAYS

24 JAN

Cowdenbeath (0) 0
Berwick R (0) 1 *(Elliot 89)* 544
Cowdenbeath: Martin; Boyle, Courts, White, Smith, Lawrence, Winter, Bradley, McDowell, Brown, Neeson (Burns).
Berwick R: McLean; McMartin (Elliot), Gray, Ritchie, Neill A, Anthony, Forrest, Neil M, Wood, Ronald, Smith (Duthie).

Keith (0) 0
Montrose (0) 1 *(Mitchell 96)* 489
Keith: Thain; Darcy, Simmers, Maver, Watt, Gibson, Stewart (Hendry), Presslie (Green), Robertson, Nicol, McPherson (McKenzie).
Montrose: McGlynn; McWilliam (McKellar), Ferguson, Mailer, Christie, Craib, Byers, Muirhead, McKenzie (Harrison), Laidlaw (Mitchell J), Joy.
aet

THIRD ROUND

27 JAN

Alloa Ath (0) 0
Aberdeen (1) 3 *(Rowson 12, Winters 85, Mackie 88)* 2877
Alloa Ath: Cairns (McQueen); Huxford (Watson), Clark D, French, Thomson, Valentine, Hamilton, Christie, Little (Evans), Irvine, Wood.
Aberdeen: Preece; McNaughton, McGuire, Whyte, Solberg, Rowson, Darren Young, Belabed, Winters (Derek Young), Stavrum (Mackie), Dow.

Berwick R (0) 0
Hearts (0) 0 3139
Berwick R: McLean; McMartin, Gray, Ritchie, Neill A, Anthony, Forrest, Neil M, Wood (Whelan), Elliot (Findlay), Smith (Duthie).
Hearts: Niemi; Pressley, Flögel, Petric, Murray, Tomaschek (Makel), Boyack, Fulton (Juanjo), Cameron, Durie (McSwegan), Kirk.

Dundee (0) 0
Falkirk (0) 0 6395
Dundee: Roccati; Smith, Marrocco, Coyne, Tweed (McSkimming), Milne (Falconer), Nemsadze, Artero (Romano), Rae, Caniggia, Carranza.
Falkirk: Hogarth; Lawrie, McQuilken, Christie, Rennie, Nicholls, McAllister (Burke), Henry, Roberts, Kerr, Hutchison (Craig).

East Fife (1) 1 *(Moffat 7)* 1819
Livingston (2) 4 *(Bingham 33, Wilson 44, 75, Britton 78)*
East Fife: Stewart; Bottiglieri, Sharp, McCloy, Agostini, Allison, Mackay (Gallagher), Mortimer, Kerrigan, Moffat, Devine (McManus).
Livingston: Alexander; McManus, Deas, McCulloch, Andrews, Anderson, McPhee (Crabbe), Tosh, Wilson (Britton), Bingham, Hagen (Fleming).

Hibernian (3) 6 *(Laursen 22, Jack 28, Sauzee 45, Paatelainen 47, Lehmann 59, 64)*
Clyde (0) 1 *(McLaughlin 84)* 9494
Hibernian: Colgan; Fenwick, Smith, Sauzee, Jack (Brebner), Laursen, Lovell (Zitelli), Latapy (Andrews), O'Neil, Paatelainen, Lehmann.
Clyde: Halliwell; Murray, McLaughlin, Smith, Greer, Ross, Crawford (Cranmer), Millen, Keogh, McClay (Henry), Grant (Kane).

Inverness CT (0) 4 *(Sheerin 54, Mann 60, Xausa 68, Wyness 72)*
Ayr U (3) 3 *(Annand 7, Campbell 17, Wilson 33)* 2257
Inverness CT: Fridge; Teasdale (Tokely), Hastings, McCaffray, Mann, Sheerin, Bagan, Xausa (Graham), Wyness, Christie, McBain.
Ayr U: Rovde; Renwick (Reynolds), Lovering, McGinlay, Hughes, Campbell, Teale (Craig), Wilson, Hurst, Annand (Grady), Scally.

Kilmarnock (1) 1 *(Mitchell 27)*
Partick T (0) 0   3836
Kilmarnock: Marshall; Dindeleux, Baker, Innes, Mahood, Canero, Holt, Mitchell, McLaren (Hay), Cocard (Vareille), Dargo (Wright).
Partick T: Arthur; Hamilton, Archibald, Craigan, Docherty (Stewart), McNally, Collins, Lennon, McLean (McGrillen), Hardie, Shaw.

Montrose (0) 0
Dundee U (2) 2 *(Lauchlan 8, 18)*   2592
Montrose: McGlynn; Mailer, Joy, Muirhead, Christie, Craib, McKellar (Lowe), Harrison (McWilliam), McKenzie (Mitchell J), Laidlaw, Byers.
Dundee U: Gallacher; McCunnie, Partridge, de Vos, Lauchlan, Griffin, Aljofree (Buchan), Miller (Heaney), Easton, Hamilton (Thompson), Lilley.

Peterhead (1) 4 *(Smith G 10, Carlin (og) 53, Cooper 61, Simpson 80)*
Morton (1) 1 *(Matheson 27)*   1647
Peterhead: Pirie; Tindal, King, Herd, Simpson, Gibson, Murray (Clark S), Stewart (Smith D), Smith G, Yeats, Cooper (Livingstone).
Morton: Carlin; Murie (McGregor), Davies (McDonald K), MacDonald S, James, Aitken (Raeside), Matheson, Curran, Whalen, Anderson, McDonald P.

Rangers (2) 2 *(Johnston 9, Miller 37)*
Brechin C (0) 0   22,606
Rangers: Klos; Ricksen, Vidmar, Konterman, Numan, Ferguson, Reyna (Wallace), Johnston, Albertz (Tugay), de Boer (Mols), Miller.
Brechin C: Soutar; Smith D (Campbell), Coulston (Sturrock), Bain, Cairney, Raynes, Bailey, Riley P, Grant, Black (Donachie), Smith G.

Ross Co (1) 2 *(Henderson 2, Cunnington 71)*
Buckie T (0) 1 *(Rowley 66)*   2461
Ross Co: Walker; Perry, Cunnington, Maxwell, Irvine, Fraser, McCormick (Bone), Ferguson, Coyle, Boukraa, Henderson.
Buckie T: Rae; Grant, Lamberton, Anderson, McPherson, Rattray (Milne), Rowley (Reid), Stephen, Thomson, Bruce, Craik (Stewart).

St Johnstone (0) 0
Dunfermline Ath (0) 0   5026
St Johnstone: Main; Dods, Bollan, Weir, Frail, McBride (Lovenkrands), Dasovic, O'Neill (Kane), Sylla, Parker, Connolly (Lowndes).
Dunfermline Ath: Ruitenbeek; Doesburg, Thomson SM, Skinner, Skerla, McGroarty, Nicholson (Mason), Ferguson, Hampshire (Dair), Crawford, Moss (Dijkhuizen).

St Mirren (0) 1 *(Quitongo 80)*
Motherwell (1) 2 *(McCulloch 32, Spencer 64)*   5002
St Mirren: Roy; Kerr, Rudden, Turner, Walker, Baltacha, Murray, Gillies, Mackenzie (Yardley), Fenton (Quitongo), Renfurm (McGarry).
Motherwell: Goram; Corrigan, Kemble, Hammell, Strong, Leitch, Brannan, Townsley, Adams (Spencer), McCulloch (Twaddle), Goodman.

Stirling Albion (0) 2 *(Graham 57, Templeman 81)*
Raith R (0) 0   1389
Stirling Albion: Reid; Kelly (McCallion), Milne, Devine (Aitken), Gaughan, McAulay (Williams), Feroz, Donald, Graham, Templeman, Martin.
Raith R: Van De Kamp; McCulloch, Hampshire, Ellis (Hetherston), Browne, Black, Tosh S, Nicol, Bayne (Mdala), Clark, Stein.

28 JAN
Stranraer (0) 1 *(Harty 84)*
Celtic (1) 4 *(Valgaeren 24, McNamara 51, Knox (og) 56, Moravcik 87)*   5660
Stranraer: McGeown; Johnstone, Wright, Knox, George, Hodge, Blair, Macdonald, Harty, Jenkins (Bryce), Walker.
Celtic: Douglas; Boyd, Valgaeren (Mjallby), Vega, Thompson, McNamara, Lennon, Petta (Lambert), Agathe, Larsson (Moravcik), Sutton.

12 FEB
Queen of the S (1) 1 *(Hawke 18)*   2216
Airdrieonians (1) 3 *(Moreau 14, Pilvi 50, Sanjuan 89)*
Queen of the S: Scott; Atkinson P, McKeown, McQuilter, Aitken, Sunderland, O'Neil, Connell, Hawke, Weatherson, Patterson (Hogg).
Airdrieonians: Broto; Armstrong, McAlpine, Brady, Catin, Alfonso, Moreau, Sanjuan, Pilvi (McGuire), Calderon, Fernandez.

THIRD ROUND REPLAYS

7 FEB
Hearts (0) 2 *(McSwegan 69, Juanjo 71)*
Berwick R (1) 1 *(Elliot 18)*   7502
Hearts: Niemi; Pressley, Flögel, Petric, Murray (Neilson), Tomaschek, Boyack (Severin), Juanjo, Cameron, McSwegan, Kirk (Adam).
Berwick R: McLean; McMartin, Gray, Ritchie, Neill A, Anthony, Forrest (Whelan), Neil M, Wood (Findlay), Elliot, Duthie (Smith).

12 FEB
Falkirk (0) 0
Dundee (0) 2 *(Sara 71, Caniggia 88)*   5156
Falkirk: Hogarth; Lawrie, McQuilken (Craig), Christie, Rennie, Nicholls, McAllister, Henry, Roberts (Burke), Kerr, Hutchison.
Dundee: Roccati; Smith, Romano, Coyne, Tweed, Carranza (Russo), Nemsadze, Artero, Rae, Caniggia (Milne), Sara (Falconer).

13 FEB
Dunfermline Ath (0) 3 *(Thomson 61, Dijkhuizen 77, Moss 82)*
St Johnstone (2) 2 *(Russell 13, Lowndes 43)*   4748
Dunfermline Ath: Ruitenbeek; Dair, Thomson SM, Skinner (Mason), Skerla, Nicholson, Rossi, Dijkhuizen (Matthaei), Moss, Bullen, Petrie (Tod).
St Johnstone: Main; Dods, Bollan, Weir, Frail, McBride, Dasovic, Kane, Russell (Parker), Sylla (Lovenkrands), Lowndes.

FOURTH ROUND

17 FEB
Dunfermline Ath (0) 2 *(Skerla 83, Nicholson 90)*
Celtic (0) 2 *(Larsson 66, 88)*   11,222
Dunfermline Ath: Ruitenbeek; Tod, Thomson SM, Skinner, Skerla, Mason (Dair), Nicholson, Ferguson, Rossi, Dijkhuizen (Bullen), Moss (McGroarty).
Celtic: Douglas; Boyd, Valgaeren (Tebily), Vega, Thompson, Petta (Petrov), Lennon, Lambert, Agathe, Larsson, Sutton.

Hearts (0) 1 *(Juanjo 81)*
Dundee (1) 1 *(Sara 30)*   9970
Hearts: Niemi; Pressley, Flögel, McCann, Severin, Tomaschek (McAnespie), Boyack, Juanjo, Cameron, McSwegan (Wales)(Murray), Adam.
Dundee: Roccati; Smith, Marrocco, Coyne, Tweed, Carranza, Nemsadze, Artero, Rae, Caniggia, Sara (Milne).

Inverness CT (0) 1 *(Robson 89)*
Kilmarnock (0) 1 *(Hay 90)*   5294
Inverness CT: Calder; Mann, McCaffrey, Hastings, Tokely, Christie, Sheerin, Bagan (Robson), McBain, Xausa, Wyness (Graham).
Kilmarnock: Marshall; MacPherson, Baker, McGowne (Fowler), Dindeleux, Canero, Holt, Mitchell, McLaren, Wright (Cocard), Dargo (Hay).

Livingston (0) 0
Aberdeen (0) 0 6288

Livingston: Alexander; Brinquin (McManus), Deas, Andrews, Anderson, McCulloch, Jackson (Britton), McPhee (Fleming), Wilson, Burns, Bingham.
Aberdeen: Preece; McNaughton (Derek Young), McAllister (Darren Young), Whyte (McGuire), Rowson, Solberg, Guntweit, Belabed, Winters, Stavrum, Mackie.

Motherwell (0) 0
Dundee U (2) 2 *(Miller 3, Easton 38)* 6186

Motherwell: Goram; Corrigan (Dempsie), Oueifio, Townsley, Hammell, Leitch, Lasley, Adams (McFadden), Twaddle (Nicholas), Spencer, Elliott.
Dundee U: Gallacher; McCunnie, Lauchlan, de Vos, Aljofree, Griffin, Hannah (Smith), Miller, Easton, Hamilton (Thompson), Lilley (Naveda).

Peterhead (0) 0
Airdrieonians (0) 0

Peterhead were awarded a walk-over as Airdrieonians could not produce a team.

Stirling Albion (1) 2 *(Templeman 4, Graham 53 (pen))*
Hibernian (2) 3 *(Sauzee 10, O'Neil 26, McManus 78)* 3673

Stirling Albion: Reid; Kelly (Stuart), Milne, Gaughan, Martin, McCallion (Gardner), Donald, Templeman, Millar, Feroz (Aitken), Graham.
Hibernian: Colgan; Fenwick, Smith, Sauzee, Jack, Laursen, Murray (McManus), Latapy, O'Neil, Paatelainen, Zitelli.

18 FEB

Ross Co (1) 2 *(Bone 20, 54)*
Rangers (2) 3 *(Flo 4, 17, Ferguson 63)* 5972

Ross Co: Walker; Perry, Robertson, Maxwell, Irvine, Ferguson, McCormick (Fraser), Coyle, Bone, Boukraa (Holmes), Henderson (Mackay).
Rangers: Klos; Ricksen, Malcolm, Konterman, Wilson, Ferguson, Reyna, Tugay, McCann, Miller (Johnston), Flo.

FOURTH ROUND REPLAYS

6 MAR

Aberdeen (0) 0
Livingston (0) 1 *(Crabbe 83)* 9959

Aberdeen: Esson; McGuire, McAllister, Solberg (Lilley), Rowson, Darren Young (Clark), Guntweit, Belabed, Winters, Stavrum, Dow (Derek Young).
Livingston: Alexander; Brinquin, Deas, Andrews, Anderson, McCulloch, Tosh, Jackson (McPhee), Burns (Crabbe), Wilson, Bingham.

Kilmarnock (0) 2 *(McGowne 60, Wright 68 (pen))*
Inverness CT (0) 1 *(Xausa 51)* 6528

Kilmarnock: Marshall; MacPherson, Baker, McGowne, Dindeleux, Canero, Holt, Mahood (Hay), Reilly, Cocard, Wright (McCoist).
Inverness CT: Calder; Tokely, Hastings, Mann, McCaffrey, Bagan (Robson), Sheerin (Bavidge), Christie, McBain, Xausa, Wyness.

7 MAR

Celtic (1) 4 *(Vega 26,49, Larsson 61 (pen), 73 (pen))*
Dunfermline Ath (1) 1 *(Thomson 30)* 33,900

Celtic: Douglas; Mjallby, Valgaeren, Vega, Thompson, McNamara (Petrov), Lennon, Agathe, Moravcik, Larsson (Crainey), Johnson (Lambert).
Dunfermline Ath: Ruitenbeek; Doesburg (Bullen), Thomson SM, McGroarty, Skerla, Dair (Dijkhuizen), Nicholson, Ferguson, Rossi, Crawford, Hampshire.

Dundee (0) 0
Hearts (0) 1 *(Tomaschek 72)* 6947

Dundee: Roccati; Smith, Marrocco (Carrenza), Coyne, Tweed, De Marchi, Nemsadze, Artero, Rae, Caniggia, Sara.
Hearts: Niemi; Pressley, Flögel, McCann, Severin (Juanjo), Tomaschek, Makel, Boyack (Neilson), Cameron, Durie, Kirk.

QUARTER-FINALS

10 MAR

Kilmarnock (0) 0
Hibernian (0) 1 *(McManus 89)* 8288

Kilmarnock: Marshall; MacPherson (Canero), Baker, McGowne (McCoist), Innes, Dindeleux, Holt, Mahood, Reilly, Cocard, Wright (McLaren).
Hibernian: Colgan; Fenwick, Smith, Sauzee (Murray), Laursen (Paatelainen), Brebner, Lovell, Latapy, O'Neil, Libbra, Zitelli (McManus).

Livingston (2) 3 *(Anderson 21, 34, Bingham 61)*
Peterhead (1) 1 *(Johnston 8)* 3552

Livingston: McCaldon; Brinquin, Deas, McCulloch, Andrews (Fleming), Anderson, Crabbe (McPhee), Tosh, Wilson, Jackson (Burns), Bingham.
Peterhead: Pirie; Tindal, King, Herd (Clark S), Simpson, Gibson, Cooper (Murray), Stewart (Livingstone), Yeats, Johnston, Smith.

11 MAR

Celtic (1) 1 *(Larsson 40)*
Hearts (0) 0 34,529

Celtic: Douglas; Mjallby (Boyd), Valgaeren, Vega, Thompson, Petrov, Lennon, Lambert, Moravcik (Johnson), Larsson, Agathe.
Hearts: Niemi; Pressley, Flögel, McCann, Makel (McSwegan), Tomaschek, Severin, Boyack (Murray), Cameron, Juanjo, Kirk.

Dundee U (0) 1 *(Hannah 62)*
Rangers (0) 0 11,793

Dundee U: Gallacher; McCunnie, Lauchlan, de Vos, Buchan, Griffin, Hannah, Miller, Easton, Hamilton (Thompson), Lilley.
Rangers: Klos; Porrini, Moore (Malcolm), Amoruso, Wilson, Ferguson, Konterman, Ricksen (Carson), Johnston (Miller), Dodds, Flo.

SEMI-FINALS (at Hampden Park)

14 APR

Hibernian (1) 3 *(O'Neil 1, 76, Zitelli 69)*
Livingston (0) 0 24,658

Hibernian: Colgan; Fenwick, Smith, Sauzee, Laursen, Jack (Brebner), Murray, Latapy, O'Neil, Paatelainen (Libbra), Zitelli (McManus).
Livingston: McCaldon; Brinquin, Fleming, Andrews, Anderson, Deas (Jackson), Tosh, McCulloch (Hagen), Wilson, Burns (Britton), Bingham.

15 APR

Celtic (1) 3 *(Larsson 32, 78, McNamara 80)*
Dundee U (0) 1 *(Lilley 84)* 38,699

Celtic: Douglas; Mjallby (Boyd), Valgaeren, Vega, Thompson, Agathe, Lennon, Lambert, Moravcik (McNamara), Larsson, Sutton (Johnson).
Dundee U: Gallacher; McCunnie (Partridge), Lauchlan, de Vos, Buchan, Griffin, Hannah, Miller, Easton (Hamilton), Thompson, Lilley.

FINAL (at Hampden Park)

26 MAY

Celtic (1) 3 *(McNamara 38, Larsson 47, 79 (pen))*
Hibernian (0) 0 51,284

Celtic: Douglas; Mjallby, Valgaeren, Vega, Thompson (Johnson), Agathe, Lennon, Lambert (Boyd), Moravcik (McNamara), Larsson, Sutton.
Hibernian: Colgan; Fenwick, Smith, Sauzee, Jack, Laursen, Murray, Brebner (Arpinon) (Lovell), O'Neil, Paatelainen (Zitelli), Libbra.
Referee: Kenny Clark.

WELSH FOOTBALL 2000–2001

To paraphrase T. S. Eliot, it began with a whimper and ended with a bang.

A wretched opening defeat in Belarus did not bode well. We prepared ourselves for the same old story: Wales would lose the plot and with it, the chance of reaching the finals of a major competition for the first time in 44 years. But four successive draws – two of which should have been wins – steadied the World Cup qualifying ship and it was only a home defeat by Poland at the Millennium Stadium in early June that finally put paid to Welsh hopes of reaching Japan and Korea. In that sense, we had seen it all before but, just as the prophets of doom were clearing their throats, Wales produced a breathtaking second-half performance in Ukraine to lift the gloom. They picked up a point – and it could easily have been three – as well as the spirits of their long-suffering supporters.

Welsh football is definitely on the way back but there is no miracle cure. Progress is being made under Mark Hughes because his team are well-organised and play to a pattern with which all squad members are comfortable. The trouble is … so are the opposition. Regular defensive lapses are costing Wales dear as they seem unable to hang onto a lead. Norway, Ukraine and Armenia all fought back for a point while Poland took all three. Hughes has succeeded in making his team difficult to beat but they seem to lack the confidence to win. But the spirited display in Kiev, as this time Wales came from behind, has raised hopes that the corner may have at last been turned. The next World Cup has come too soon for this gradually maturing team but by blending the experience of Paul Jones, Robert Page, Andrew Melville, Gary Speed, John Hartson and Ryan Giggs with the potential of Matthew Jones, Craig Bellamy, Simon Davies and the recently recruited Jason Koumas, Hughes might just take Wales to Euro 2004.

The green shoots are starting to appear too down at Ninian Park where Sam Hammam's big-spending Cardiff City finally sealed promotion to Division Two. The Lebanese businessman has certainly put his money where his mouth is. After buying the club for £3 million, he has regularly dipped into his seemingly bottomless pockets to strengthen the squad in pursuit of his dream of propelling the Bluebirds into the Premiership. But his most significant decision was to replace Bobby Gould as manager with another member of the former Wimbledon Crazy Gang. Under Alan Cork – Cardiff's third manager after Gould and the sacked Billy Ayre – the team broke a 54-year-old scoring record but leaked like a sieve – largely because City's admirable policy of planning for the future led to young and inexperienced players making costly mistakes. Cork took Cardiff from 13th position in mid-October to third at season's end and, with Hammam brandishing his cheque book over the summer, the next planned stop is Division One. The new arrivals include Cardiff's first million pound player in Stoke's Graham Kavanagh, the Republic of Ireland international midfielder.

Trading places was the name of the game for the two South Wales clubs. Just a year after Swansea had won the Third Division championship and replaced relegated Cardiff, they found themselves passing their arch-rivals on the way down. Having broken a clutch of records – including the number of clean sheets in a league season – the Swans slunk back to Division Three with another, but this time unwanted, statistic – for the first time ever, they lost 30 of their 46 league games. A power struggle, an abandoned stock market flotation and little or no money to spend meant manager John Hollins was on a hiding to nothing and it's to be hoped that the proposed takeover of the club will bring some much-needed stability to the Vetch Field.

It was business as usual for Wrexham as they completed another solid if unspectacular season but the Racecourse too was shaken by boardroom unrest. Their much-respected managing director, David Rhodes, bade a not very fond and reluctant farewell after eleven successful years at the helm. Manager Brian Flynn freshened up his side with a number of new signings with £50,000 striker Lee Trundle making an immediate impact as the club moved up one place from 11th to fourth in Division Two.

In the English pyramid, Newport slipped slightly to tenth in the Dr Martens League while both Merthyr and Colwyn Bay again narrowly avoided relegation in the Dr Martens and Unibond Leagues respectively.

Once again, the four League of Wales clubs failed to make progress in Europe. Cwmbran lost 2-0 to Nistru-Unisport Otaci in the Intertoto Cup while Barry were beaten 5-0 on aggregate by Boavista and Bangor were hammered 11-0 over two legs by Halmstad in the UEFA Cup. TNS Llansantffraid at least managed a 2-2 draw at home against Levadia Maardu in the Champions League before losing 4-0 in the second leg.

Hats off to Barry Town and new manager Peter Nicholas, the former Welsh captain, who bounced back to regain the League of Wales title in completing the 'double'. They are the Welsh representatives in the Champions League, Cwmbran play in the UEFA Cup as league runners-up along with TNS who were beaten 2-0 by Barry in the Welsh Cup Final. Carmarthen Town qualified for the first time for Europe through the Intertoto Cup while Wrexham retained the F.A.W. Premier Cup by beating Swansea 2-0 at the Vetch Field.

The highlight of the season was undoubtedly the hosting of the first FA Cup Final away from Wembley. With the future of the Twin Towers still unresolved, the world's greatest knockout competition came to Cardiff's new Millennium Stadium. The teething troubles thrown up by the Worthington Cup Final had been resolved, fears about traffic congestion and the state of the pitch proved unfounded and Liverpool and Arsenal produced an absorbing and ultimately breathtaking final. A successfully staged event silenced the critics and Cardiff's new status as the capital of English football was confirmed when the Nationwide League play-off finals were held at the stadium in late May.

The FA Cup has put Wales well and truly on the football map but Welsh teams need to play their part in raising the profile of the sport. Although there has been little or no change domestically – although Barry once again hold out most hopes of success – there are signs that the national team could be on the verge of achieving that long-awaited appearance at the finals of a major tournament. The Welsh public will have to remain patient – but, hopefully, not for too much longer.

GRAHAME LLOYD

LEAGUE OF WALES 2000–2001

	Aberystwyth Town	Afan Lido	Bangor City	Barry Town	Caersws	Carmarthen Town	Connah's Quay Nomads	Cwmbran Town	Flexsys Cefn Druids	Haverfordwest County	Llanelli	Newtown	Oswestry Town	Port Talbot Athletic	Rhayader Town	Rhyl	Total Network Solutions	UWIC Inter Cardiff
Aberystwyth Town	—	1-1	0-2	3-2	2-2	2-2	1-1	2-0	3-0	0-2	6-0	3-0	6-0	1-0	2-2	2-2	2-0	5-0
Afan Lido	4-3	—	3-1	1-0	3-1	0-0	2-2	0-1	1-1	3-1	1-0	1-2	3-1	0-1	3-0	0-0	2-2	1-0
Bangor City	1-1	3-1	—	2-3	2-2	1-3	0-1	1-3	3-1	3-2	3-2	0-2	0-1	3-5	3-3	0-3	0-4	3-0
Barry Town	4-0	1-0	6-1	—	3-3	2-0	4-0	3-1	2-0	3-2	7-1	0-2	6-0	2-0	2-1	0-0	1-0	8-0
Caersws	1-1	1-0	5-0	2-2	—	2-2	0-0	1-4	1-2	0-1	4-0	1-0	1-0	7-1	2-2	2-1	0-1	6-1
Carmarthen Town	1-1	0-1	4-0	1-4	0-0	—	3-0	1-0	2-0	0-4	5-1	1-2	0-1	1-1	2-0	3-0	4-3	9-1
Connah's Quay Nomads	1-2	2-0	1-1	0-1	0-3	2-1	—	1-0	2-0	0-0	2-1	0-0	0-2	1-3	5-0	1-2	1-2	2-0
Cwmbran Town	1-0	1-0	5-2	3-0	1-2	0-2	2-1	—	1-0	0-0	3-2	2-0	3-0	2-0	4-2	3-2	2-2	3-1
Flexsys Cefn Druids	4-1	3-0	2-0	1-2	1-4	3-4	1-2	0-3	—	3-3	5-1	0-1	3-7	3-2	3-2	2-1	2-1	3-0
Haverfordwest County	1-3	2-3	0-1	2-0	2-1	3-1	2-0	0-2	2-0	—	3-3	0-3	2-1	2-3	0-4	2-4	0-2	3-1
Llanelli	2-4	0-0	2-4	1-6	2-1	1-0	2-3	2-0	1-3	3-2	—	1-2	11-0	1-2	2-3	3-1	3-3	1-0
Newtown	1-2	1-0	3-2	2-4	0-2	2-1	1-2	2-0	2-1	0-1	4-1	—	1-0	2-1	1-2	2-0	3-1	3-0
Oswestry Town	1-2	1-0	3-3	0-1	0-1	0-0	2-3	2-3	0-0	2-5	5-2	1-0	—	2-2	2-2	0-3	0-3	1-0
Port Talbot Athletic	0-2	1-0	2-2	0-0	1-3	0-2	1-3	0-1	2-1	2-2	1-0	2-3	0-2	—	1-3	1-6	0-6	2-1
Rhayader Town	0-0	2-0	2-4	0-1	0-2	0-1	1-2	2-5	1-1	1-2	4-2	2-0	3-2	3-2	—	0-2	2-2	2-0
Rhyl	1-0	2-0	6-1	1-2	2-1	2-1	1-1	1-0	5-3	3-0	7-0	0-0	1-1	2-1	5-1	—	2-0	1-2
Total Network Solutions	1-0	0-2	2-2	0-1	1-3	1-5	3-4	0-3	3-3	0-1	3-1	0-0	4-1	2-1	3-3	3-0	—	2-1
UWIC Inter Cardiff	2-1	1-1	1-2	2-1	0-6	0-4	3-3	0-3	2-6	1-4	1-2	1-1	1-2	1-3	1-1	2-2	0-3	—

LEAGUE OF WALES

		Home			Goals		Away			Goals			
	P	W	D	L	F	A	W	D	L	F	A	GD	Pts
Barry Town	34	14	2	1	54	11	10	3	4	30	19	54	77
Cwmbran Town	34	13	2	2	38	16	11	0	6	33	18	37	74
Carmarthen Town	34	10	3	4	39	18	7	4	6	29	21	29	58
Newtown	34	10	0	7	30	22	8	4	5	18	15	11	58
Caersws	34	7	5	5	35	19	9	4	4	37	20	33	57
Aberystwyth Town	34	9	6	2	41	16	6	4	7	23	26	22	55
Rhyl	34	10	2	5	45	26	6	4	7	29	26	22	54
Total Network Solutions	34	8	5	4	29	23	7	4	6	35	24	17	54
Connah's Quay Nomads	34	7	3	7	20	18	7	5	5	25	29	–2	50
Haverfordwest County	34	6	3	8	24	31	8	4	5	32	24	1	49
Afan Lido	34	9	5	3	28	16	4	3	10	14	21	5	47
Rhayader Town	34	6	4	7	23	24	4	6	7	31	41	–11	40
Flexsys Cefn Druids	34	8	1	8	38	37	3	4	10	22	33	–10	38
Bangor City	34	5	3	9	28	37	5	4	8	28	47	–28	37
Oswestry Town	34	4	5	8	19	28	6	1	10	21	46	–34	36
Port Talbot Athletic	34	4	3	10	19	40	6	2	9	30	37	–28	35
Llanelli	34	8	1	8	38	33	1	1	15	19	64	–40	29
UWIC Inter Cardiff	34	2	4	11	18	49	1	0	16	8	55	–78	13

WELSH CUP 2000–2001

First Round (played Saturday 16th September 2000)

Ammanford Town v Severn Sisters	3-1
Blaenrhondda v Taffs Well	3-1
Bridgend Town v Pontyclun	2-0
Briton Ferry Athletic v Cardiff Civil Service	0-1
Caerleon v Chepstow Town	2-0
Caernarfon Town v Cemaes Bay	5-1
Caldicot Town v Risca United	2-0
Cardiff Corries v Pontypridd Town	2-1
(aet)	
Dinas Powys v Pontlottyn BF	1-3
(aet + pens)	
Fields Park v Abergavenny Thursdays	7-0
Garw v Ely Rangers	1-3
Glan Conwy v Llandyrnog United	6-2
Halkyn United v Bethesda Athletic	0-1
Holyhead Hotspur v Porthmadog	2-3
Lex XI v Buckley Town	3-5
Llandidloes Town v Meifod	4-0
Merthyr Saints v Penrhiwceiber Rangers	0-5
Mold Alex v Llangefni Town	1-3
Newport YMCA v Tredegar	2-0
Penrhyncoch v Newcastle Emlyn	3-1
(aet)	
Rhostyllen United v Brickfield Rangers	2-6
Rhydymwyn v Welshpool Town	0-3
Ruthin Town v Flint Town United	3-1
Skewen Athletic v Porth Tywyn Sub	3-2
Ton Pentre v AFC Llwydcoed	5-1

First Round (played Saturday 23rd September 2000)

Abercynon Athletic v Neath	0-2
AFC Rhondda v Maesteg Park Athletic	3-6
Airbus U.K. v Brymbo Broughton	2-3
(aet)	
Caerau v Aberaman Athletic	6-8
(aet + pens)	
Chirk A.A.A. v Bala Town	0-3
Conwy United v Glantraeth	0-4
Corwen Amateurs v Rhos Aelwyd	4-7
(aet + pens)	
Gresford Athletic v Penycae	2-0
Guilsfield v Presteigne St. Andrews	1-0
Gwynfi United v Goytre United	7-6
(aet + pens)	
Llandudno v Denbigh Town	2-3
Llanfairpwll v Holywell Town	2-1
Llanwern v Treowen Stars	1-2
Pontardawe Town v Garden Village	2-0
Portos Grange Harlequins v Porthcawl Town	3-2

Second Round

Aberaman Athletic v Fields Park Pontllanfraith	1-3
Ammanford Town v Maesteg Park Athletic	2-4
Bethesda Athletic v Bala Town	2-3
Blaenrhondda v Penrhiwceiber Rangers	4-1

Bridgend Town v Ton Pentre	0-2
Caersws v Brymbo Broughton	6-2
Cardiff Civil Service v Caerleon	4-2
(aet + pens)	
Cardiff Corinthians v Llanelli	1-2
Connah's Quay Nomads v Gresford Athletic	3-0
Guilsfield v Buckley Town	0-4
Gwynfi United v Treowen Stars	2-3
Haverfordwest County v Skewen Athletic	8-0
Llangefni Town v Glan Conwy	10-2
Newport YMCA v Caldicot Town	0-2
Oswestry Town v Caernarfon Town	0-2
Penrhyncoch v Glantraeth	1-0
Pontardwe Town v Ely Rangers	3-1
Pontlottyn Blast Furnace v Neath	3-5
(aet + pens)	
Porthmadog v Newtown	1-2
Portos Grange Harlequins v Port Talbot Athletic	3-6
(aet)	
Rhayader Town v Llanidloes Town	4-2
Rhos Aelwyd v Llanfairpwll	2-3
Rhyl v Flexsys Cefn Druids	2-1
(aet)	
Ruthin Town v Denbigh Town	3-2
UWIC Inter Cardiff v Aberystwyth Town	1-2
Welshpool Town v Brickfield Rangers	5-1

Third Round

Blaenrhondda v Bala Town	1-0
Caerleon v Carmarthen Town	0-4
Caernarfon Town v Cwmbran Town	2-4
Connah's Quay Nomads v Maesteg Park Athletic	1-2
Fields Park Pontllanfraith v Caersws	0-2
Haverfordwest County v Afan Lido	1-2
Llanelli v Ruthin Town	4-1
Llanfairpwll v Caldicot Town	2-1
Llangefni Town v Aberystwyth Town	1-3
Neath v Welshpool Town	1-2
Newtown v Rhyl	2-1
Penrhyncoch v Barry Town	1-2
Port Talbot Athletic v Total Network Solutions	1-2
Rhayader Town v Buckley Town	3-1
Ton Pentre v Pontardawe Town	1-0
Treowen Stars v Bangor City	0-3

Fourth Round

Bangor City v Newtown	3-2
(aet)	
Blaenrhondda v Llanelli	0-5
Caersws v Afan Lido	3-0
Llanfairpwll v Barry Town	0-4
Maesteg Park Athletic v Ton Pentre	1-0
Rhayader Town v Carmarthen Town	2-1
Total Network Solutions v Cwmbran Town	2-1
(aet)	
Welshpool Town v Aberystwyth Town	2-4

Fifth Round

Barry Town v Bangor City	3-0
Llanelli v Aberystwyth Town	0-4
Maesteg Park Athletic v Caersws	3-1
Total Network Solutions v Rhayader Town	2-1

Semi Final

Aberystwyth Town v Barry Town	1-2
Maesteg Park Athletic v Total Network Solutions	1-2

Final

Barry Town (0) 2 Total Network Solutions (0) 0

(At the Racecourse, Wrexham 25 May 2001)

Barry Town: Digby; Evans, Lloyd, Kennedy, Yorke, Sharpe, Phillips, French, Moralee, Davies (Flynn 62), Staton (Jenkins 62).
Scorers: Moralee 77, Lloyd 86.
Total Network Solutions: Deegan; Holmes, Coathup, Morgan, Edwards, Alexander (McKenna 78), Powell, Wright, Toner (Welton 67), Evans (Edge 53).
Referee: R. A. Jones (Caernarfon).
Attendance: 1019

Scores in earlier rounds include penalties from shoot-outs.

FAW PREMIER CUP

Group A	P	W	D	L	F	A	GD	Pts
Wrexham	6	5	1	0	19	1	+18	16
Aberystwyth T	6	3	1	2	9	9	0	10
Carmarthen T	6	2	1	3	4	7	−3	7
Bangor City	6	0	1	5	3	18	−15	1

Group B	P	W	D	L	F	A	GD	Pts
Cardiff City	6	6	0	0	12	4	+8	18
Merthyr Tydfil	6	3	0	3	10	11	−1	9
Llanelli	6	2	0	4	13	14	−1	6
Cwmbran T	6	1	0	5	7	13	−6	3

Group C	P	W	D	L	F	A	GD	Pts
Barry Town	6	5	1	0	13	5	+8	16
Swansea City	6	3	2	1	12	8	+4	11
Total Network S	6	2	1	3	9	8	+1	7
Connah's Quay N	6	0	0	6	2	15	−13	0

Quarter-finals

Swansea City v Carmarthen Town	1-0
Wrexham v Aberystwyth Town	3-0
Cardiff City v Merthyr Tydfil	0-1
Barry Town v Total Network Solutions	3-2 *(aet)*

Semi-finals (two legs)

Barry Town v Wrexham	1-3
Merthyr Tydfil v Swansea City	0-2
Wrexham v Barry Town	4-2
Swansea City v Merthyr Tydfil	2-0

Final

Swansea City v Wrexham	0-2

C.C. SPORTS WELSH LEAGUE

Division One

	P	W	D	L	F	A	Pts
Ton Pentre	34	20	11	3	81	28	71
Maesteg Park Athletic	34	21	8	5	61	28	71
FP Pontllanfraith	34	21	5	8	77	39	68
Goytre United	34	21	5	8	72	52	68
Caerleon	34	17	12	5	55	37	63
Pontardawe Town	34	13	9	12	64	50	48
Cardiff Corries	34	12	8	14	50	49	44
AFC Rhondda	34	11	10	13	47	54	43
Ammanford	34	11	8	15	45	56	41
Neath	34	10	10	14	49	53	40
Penrhiwceiber Rangers	34	11	7	16	62	73	40
Gwynfi United	34	12	3	19	47	73	39
Milford United	34	10	8	16	44	58	38
Bridgend Town	34	10	8	16	47	65	38
Cardiff Civil Service	34	8	13	13	47	51	37
Porth Tywyn Suburbs	34	10	7	17	35	63	37
Briton Ferry Athletic	34	9	8	17	49	66	35
Treowen Stars	34	6	6	22	35	72	24

HUWS GRAY – FITLOCK CYMRU ALLIANCE LEAGUE

	P	W	D	L	F	A	Pts
Caernarfon Town	32	24	4	4	105	29	76
Llangefni Town	30	20	5	5	67	34	65
Welshpool Town	32	19	7	6	96	35	64
Cemaes Bay	32	17	8	6	64	38	60
Buckley Town	31	17	7	7	66	29	58
Porthmadog	31	16	6	9	62	37	54
Llandudno	32	14	6	12	45	52	48
Lex XI	31	12	4	15	68	84	40
Halkyn United	30	11	6	13	47	55	39
Holywell Town	32	11	6	15	47	69	39
Airbus UK	31	10	7	14	54	63	37
Ruthin Town	32	10	7	15	48	60	37
Holyhead Hotspur	31	10	6	15	59	76	36
Glantraeth	25	7	5	13	40	60	26
Denbigh Town	32	5	5	22	32	84	20
Brymbo Broughton	30	5	4	21	34	78	19
Flint Town United***	32	6	4	22	43	85	13

*** 9 Points deducted for fielding ineligable players for three games

NORTHERN IRISH FOOTBALL 2000–2001

Northern Ireland's season can be described as a stop-start one – interrupted first by Christmas, early January by severe weather then the foot and mouth crisis which caused a fixture backlog. Add to that the financial plight of some clubs, and it made for a difficult 12 months to say the least.

Michael McGimpsey, Northern Ireland Minster of Sport and a lover of football, created a task force to examine all aspects of the problems, especially those affecting Irish League teams. His final report, scheduled for December – an interim one may be issued earlier – should make interesting reading. Although recommendations will be made, it is the football authorities who will either implement or reject them and some painful decisions may have to be taken.

Unless there is a huge financial injection from the Government, and this seems most unlikely except for structural work at stadia, one just cannot envisage any vast reorganisation. The bullet has, however, to be bitten.

The Government has already allocated several million pounds for the first and long delayed phase of upgrading Premier club grounds to meet with Health and Safety regulations. Further grants will shortly be available for First Division clubs.

There has been a hue and cry for a new line up in the Premier and First Divisions which currently consist of 10 teams in each, but this format will continue in the coming season; a sub-committee is examining a series of changes which could be operative from season 2002–2003 with promotion and relegation included.

Many clubs have been forced to embark on cost cutting exercises, players forced to take pay reductions and signing on fees abolished while there is a possibility the Professional Players Association may be re-established, a likely recommendation of the Task Force, to protect players' rights, to re-assess insurance cover for injuries and loss of work, new signing-on rules and registrations.

Clubs will insist, and rightly so, any agreement will work both ways but the bottom line is many of them just don't possess the financial resources to cope with further demands.

Linfield again proved Smirnoff Premiership pacesetters, winning the title for the second successive year, while Glentoran, knock-out competition specialists, collected the Nationwide Irish Cup – setting an amazing record of wins in their last eleven Cup Final appearances.

Glenavon, Coleraine and Glentoran provided a championship challenge but Linfield's lead, at one stage almost 20 points, was unassailable. Indeed, at their peak the Blues were a class above the rest, backed with excellent cover for virtually every position.

The Cup Final, watched by almost 15,000, was a day when football won – a wonderful sporting and joyous finale to a troublesome season.

Internationally, it was disappointing for manager Sammy McIlroy whose contract will be extended for another two seasons taking him to the end of the next European championship qualifying series. Bad luck, conceding late goals, elementary defensive blunders, injuries and suspensions were the main cause of the downfall.

For instance, he was without 10 players for the World Cup qualifying match against the Czech Republic in Prague last June yet his makeshift team held the score to 1-1 until the final two minutes when the Czechs struck twice. Luck once more had deserted the Irish.

Then in Bulgaria they lost 4-3, the highest number of away goals scored for years, but bad defending ruined the script. So far in Qualifying Group Three they have one win (Malta), one draw (Denmark) and five defeats – Bulgaria (twice), Czech Republic (twice) and Iceland. They occupy second bottom place just above Malta, slipping so far down the FIFA list they are in danger of becoming fourth seeds in future World Cup and European championship draws.

Yet it is not all gloom and doom. There are a number of quality youngsters in the side but, frankly, none who potentially measures up to world-class, essential if a national side is to make an impact. Nevertheless, they are gradually gaining experience, and, by the next European championships, will be much more mature but, such is the limitation of supply that, if hit by major withdrawals, as happened in Prague, then the reserve strength in depth just doesn't exist.

The blunt fact has to be faced that Northern Ireland will hover on the periphery creating the odd shock result but always battling against the odds. With the ever changing face of football, especially the growth in Third World countries, few can envisage a return to those heady days of Sweden '58, Spain '82 and Mexico '86.

The 4-0 defeat by Norway in a friendly international at Windsor Park last February proved disastrous in more ways than one. Glasgow Celtic midfielder Neil Lennon was booed by a small number of fans every time he moved on to the ball – their protest at affiliation with the Parkhead club following his transfer from Leicester City.

Lennon, who came off at half-time, pondered over his international future but, given full support by his team-mates, opted to continue. The action of this minority was totally condemned by the entire Northern Ireland sporting public and the Irish FA who immediately drew up a Code of Conduct which operates now at all games. It has been an outstanding success and, hopefully, will eliminate what Irish FA general secretary David Bowen called a "cancer in the game". The IFA, who over two years revealed a loss of £1m, due primarily to the lack of large-scale revenue from the World Cup – only Germany, France, Italy and Spain generate worthwhile revenue – has a youth development and mini-soccer programme the envy of many other better endowed countries. Northern Ireland schoolboys team this year won the Victory Shield.

Women's football has gained a foothold and, for the first time, a woman, Maureen Muldoon, chairman of the NIWFA, has been elected on to the IFA Council. Like Lord's, the feminine barrier has been broken.

Football is passing through a transitional phase in Northern Ireland. Care must be taken over the next 12 months to ensure it goes down the correct road otherwise some clubs and organisations could find themselves in dire trouble. That is not being ultra-pessimistic – just pragmatic.

MALCOLM BRODIE

CALOR COUNTY ANTRIM SHIELD FINAL

Glentoran 1 Linfield 2

(at Windsor Park)

Glentoran: Gouch; Nixon, Kennedy, Walker, McCombe (Rainey), Smyth, McCann, Lockhart (Halliday), Hamill, Leeman, McBride. Sub not used: Fitzgerald.
Linfield: Robinson; Shaw (Morgan), Beatty, Marks, Murphy, Gorman, Larmour, Arthur (Scates), Ferguson, Kelly N, Bailie. Sub not used: Hunter.
Referee: M. Ross (Carrickfergus).
Scorers: Glentoran – Nixon; *Linfield* – Ferguson 2.
Man of the Match: Glenn Ferguson (Linfield).
Attendance: 5,200. *Receipts:* £31,459.
Note: Venue selected by toss of coin.
Final year of sponsorship.

SMIRNOFF IFL PREMIERSHIP

	P	W	D	L	F	A	GD	Pts
Linfield	36	22	9	5	75	31	44	75
Glenavon	36	18	8	10	56	42	14	62
Glentoran	36	15	12	9	52	37	15	57
Coleraine	36	14	11	11	48	44	4	53
Cliftonville	36	12	11	13	53	57	–4	47
Newry Town	36	12	8	16	42	55	–13	44
Omagh Town	36	11	10	15	48	54	–6	43
Portadown	36	10	11	15	48	60	–12	41
Crusaders	36	8	11	17	44	59	–15	35
Ballymena United	36	9	7	20	41	68	–27	34

Relegated – Ballymena United.

Promotion and Relegation Play-Offs
First Leg: Lisburn Distillery 2 Crusaders 1 (*at New Grosvenor Stadium*)
Second Leg: Crusaders 3 Lisburn Distillery 1 (*aggregate 4-3*)

First Division

	P	W	D	L	F	A	GD	Pts
Ards	36	21	10	5	69	31	38	73
Lisburn Distillery	36	20	11	5	66	37	29	71
Armagh City	36	19	9	8	74	52	22	66
Bangor	36	18	9	9	56	42	14	63
Institute	36	16	7	13	58	48	10	55
Larne	36	12	9	15	53	62	–9	45
Dungannon Swifts	36	10	11	15	45	48	–3	41
Limavady United	36	9	10	17	37	51	–14	37
Ballyclare Comrades	36	5	8	23	35	69	–34	23
Carrick Rangers	36	6	4	26	34	87	–53	22

Promoted – Ards   Re-elected – Carrick Rangers

Second Division

	P	W	D	L	F	A	GD	Pts
Dundela	26	19	4	3	67	27	40	61
Moyola Park	26	18	4	4	74	29	45	58
Loughgall	26	17	2	7	53	33	20	53
RUC	26	16	2	8	52	40	12	50
H&W Welders	26	13	5	8	61	51	10	44
Coagh United	26	12	4	10	36	36	0	40
Banbridge Town	26	11	5	10	48	38	10	38
Brantwood	26	7	7	12	32	39	–7	28
Ballymoney United	26	7	5	14	36	47	–11	26
Tobermore United	26	7	5	14	36	53	–17	26
Portstewart	26	7	5	14	35	55	–20	26
Ballinamallard United	26	6	5	15	34	53	–19	23
Cookstown United	26	5	7	14	42	68	–26	22
Chimney Corner	26	4	6	16	31	67	–36	18

IFL Youth League

	P	W	D	L	F	A	GD	Pts
Glentoran Colts	22	18	3	1	53	12	41	57
Cliftonville Strollers	22	14	4	4	71	34	37	46
Glenavon III	22	12	3	7	55	31	24	39
Linfield Rangers	22	10	6	6	48	41	7	36
Lisburn Distillery III	22	10	5	7	47	42	5	35
Ballyclare Com Colts	22	10	2	10	38	48	–10	32
Crusaders Colts	22	8	5	9	35	42	–7	29
Ballymena United III	22	7	5	10	50	50	0	26
Coleraine Colts	22	7	5	10	44	55	–11	26
Institute Academy	22	6	1	15	38	64	–26	19
Portadown III	22	4	3	15	26	50	–24	15
Ards Colts	22	3	4	15	34	70	–36	13

IFL Reserve League North

	P	W	D	L	F	A	GD	Pts
Cliftonville Olympic	24	18	4	2	68	17	51	58
Crusaders Res	24	14	3	7	65	29	36	45
Coleraine Res	24	13	6	5	42	25	17	45
Ballymena Utd Res	24	9	9	6	42	29	13	36
Institute Res	24	10	5	9	52	43	9	35
Limavady Utd Res	24	8	3	13	31	43	–12	27
Ballyclare Utd Res	24	6	7	11	34	46	–12	25
Carrick Rangers Res	24	7	2	15	21	81	–60	23
Larne Olympic	24	2	5	17	31	73	–42	11

IFL Reserve League South

	P	W	D	L	F	A	GD	Pts
Linfield Swifts	27	23	2	2	60	21	39	71
Glentoran II	27	21	2	4	94	34	60	65
Dungannon Sw Res	27	13	6	8	44	39	5	45
Glenavon Res	27	11	4	12	51	52	–1	37
Newry Town Res	27	11	4	12	44	51	–7	37
Portadown Res	27	10	3	14	45	48	–3	33
Ards II	27	7	7	13	38	53	–15	28
Lisburn Distillery II	27	7	5	15	41	54	–13	26
Bangor Res	27	5	7	15	30	49	–19	22
Armagh City Res	27	4	6	17	33	79	–46	18

SECTIONAL PLAY OFF
Cliftonville Olympic 1 Linfield Swifts 0
(*at Dixon Park, Ballyclare*)

IRISH LEAGUE CHAMPIONSHIP WINNERS

1891	Linfield	1911	Linfield	1936	Belfast Celtic	1964	Glentoran	1985	Linfield
1892	Linfield	1912	Glentoran	1937	Belfast Celtic	1965	Derry City	1986	Linfield
1893	Linfield	1913	Glentoran	1938	Belfast Celtic	1966	Linfield	1987	Linfield
1894	Glentoran	1914	Linfield	1939	Belfast Celtic	1967	Glentoran	1988	Glentoran
1895	Linfield	1915	Belfast Celtic	1940	Belfast Celtic	1968	Glentoran	1989	Linfield
1896	Distillery	1920	Belfast Celtic	1948	Belfast Celtic	1969	Linfield	1990	Portadown
1897	Glentoran	1921	Glentoran	1949	Linfield	1970	Glentoran	1991	Portadown
1898	Linfield	1922	Linfield	1950	Linfield	1971	Linfield	1992	Glentoran
1899	Distillery	1923	Linfield	1951	Glentoran	1972	Glentoran	1993	Linfield
1900	Belfast Celtic	1924	Queen's Island	1952	Glenavon	1973	Crusaders	1994	Linfield
1901	Distillery	1925	Glentoran	1953	Glentoran	1974	Coleraine	1995	Crusaders
1902	Linfield	1926	Belfast Celtic	1954	Linfield	1975	Linfield	1996	Portadown
1903	Distillery	1927	Belfast Celtic	1955	Linfield	1976	Crusaders	1997	Crusaders
1904	Linfield	1928	Belfast Celtic	1956	Linfield	1977	Glentoran	1998	Cliftonville
1905	Glentoran	1929	Belfast Celtic	1957	Glentoran	1978	Linfield	1999	Glentoran
1906	Cliftonville	1930	Linfield	1958	Ards	1979	Linfield	2000	Linfield
	Distillery	1931	Glentoran	1959	Linfield	1980	Linfield	2001	Linfield
1907	Linfield	1932	Linfield	1960	Glenavon	1981	Glentoran		
1908	Linfield	1933	Belfast Celtic	1961	Linfield	1982	Linfield		
1909	Linfield	1934	Linfield	1962	Linfield	1983	Linfield		
1910	Cliftonville	1935	Linfield	1963	Distillery	1984	Linfield		

FIRST DIVISION

1996	Coleraine	1999	Distillery
1997	Ballymena United	2000	Omagh Town
1998	Newry Town	2001	Ards

ULSTER CUP WINNERS

1949	Linfield	1960	Linfield	1971	Linfield	1981	Glentoran	1991	Bangor
1950	Larne	1961	Ballymena U	1972	Coleraine	1982	Glentoran	1992	Linfield
1951	Glentoran	1962	Linfield	1973	Ards	1983	Glentoran	1993	Crusaders
1952		1963	Crusaders	1974	Linfield	1984	Linfield	1994	Bangor
1953	Glentoran	1964	Linfield	1975	Coleraine	1985	Coleraine	1995	Portadown
1954	Crusaders	1965	Coleraine	1976	Glentoran	1986	Coleraine	1996	Portadown
1955	Glenavon	1966	Glentoran	1977	Linfield	1987	Larne	1997	Coleraine
1956	Linfield	1967	Linfield	1978	Linfield	1988	Glentoran	1998	Ballyclare Comrades
1957	Linfield	1968	Coleraine	1979	Linfield	1989	Glentoran	1999	Distillery
1958	Distillery	1969	Coleraine	1980	Ballymena U	1990	Portadown	2000	*No competition*
1959	Glenavon	1970	Linfield						

NATIONWIDE IRISH CUP 2000–2001

Sixth Round

Institute v Portstewart	2-2, 3-1
Dungannon Swifts v Cliftonville	2-2, 1-4
Glenavon v Killyleagh YC	1-1, 4-0
Armagh City v Glentoran	0-3
Moyola Park v Crumlin United	2-1
Linfield v Larne	4-2
Ballyclare Comrades v H&W Welders	3-1
Ards v RUC	1-0
Omagh Town v Malachians	2-0
Tobermore United v Bangor	0-2
Portadown v Ards Rangers	3-1
Carrick Rangers v Knockbreda Parish	1-3
Ballymena United v Lurgan Celtic Bhoys	4-2
Limavady United v Newry Town	2-5
Loughgall v Coleraine	2-2, 3-0

Seventh Round

Ballymena United v Glenavon	1-1, 1-2
Omagh Town v Lisburn Distillery	1-1, 1-2
Loughgall v Bangor	0-1
Glentoran v Moyola Park	4-0
Institute v Knockbreda Parish	4-1
Linfield v Ards	0-0, 5-0
Ballyclare Comrades v Cliftonville	2-0
Newry Town v Portadown	1-1, 1-2

Quarter-finals

Glentoran v Institute	2-1
Linfield v Bangor	1-0
Portadown v Lisburn Distillery	0-1
Glenavon v Ballyclare Comrades	2-1

Semi-finals

Linfield v Glenavon	3-1 *(at The Oval)*
Glentoran v Lisburn Distillery	2-1 *(at Windsor Park)*

Final

Glentoran 1 Linfield 0 *(aet) (at Windsor Park)*

Glentoran: Gough; Nixon, Ferguson, Young, Leeman, Smyth, McCann, Halliday, Fitzgerald, Batey, Lockhart (McBride). Subs not used: Hunter, Walker.

Linfield: Robinson; McDonald (Collier), Easton (Morgan), Marks, Murphy, Arthur, Larmour, Scates, Ferguson, Kelly N (Beatty), Bailie.

Referee: L. Irvine (Limavady).

Attendance: 14,190.

Scorer: Halliday

Note: This was Glentoran's eleventh successive winning appearance. Linfield have not defeated Glentoran in a cup final since 1945.

Glentoran midfielder Rory Hamill was banned until October 4 by FIFA on the eve of the cup final on a drugs offence. A test after the August UEFA Cup tie against a Norwegian side proved positive with traces of cannabis in the urine.

Linfield midfielders Tony Gorman and Russell Kelly and full-back Johnny Shaw were ruled out of the final by Irish FA disciplinary committee suspensions.

IRISH CUP FINALS (from 1946–47)

1946–47	Belfast Celtic 1, Glentoran 0		1975–76	Carrick Rangers 2, Linfield 1
1947–48	Linfield 3, Coleraine 0		1976–77	Coleraine 4, Linfield 1
1948–49	Derry City 3, Glentoran 1		1977–78	Linfield 3, Ballymena U 1
1949–50	Linfield 2, Distillery 1		1978–79	Cliftonville 3, Portadown 2
1950–51	Glentoran 3, Ballymena U 1		1979–80	Linfield 2, Crusaders 0
1951–52	Ards 1, Glentoran 0		1980–81	Ballymena U 1, Glenavon 0
1952–53	Linfield 5, Coleraine 0		1981–82	Linfield 2, Coleraine 1
1953–54	Derry City 1, Glentoran 0		1982–83	Glentoran 1:2, Linfield 1:1
1954–55	Dundela 3, Glenavon 0		1983–84	Ballymena U 4, Carrick Rangers 1
1955–56	Distillery 1, Glentoran 0		1984–85	Glentoran 1:1, Linfield 1:0
1956–57	Glenavon 2, Derry City 0		1985–86	Glentoran 2, Coleraine 1
1957–58	Ballymena U 2, Linfield 0		1986–87	Glentoran 1, Larne 0
1958–59	Glenavon 2, Ballymena U 0		1987–88	Glentoran 1, Glenavon 0
1959–60	Linfield 5, Ards 1		1988–89	Ballymena U 1, Larne 0
1960–61	Glenavon 5, Linfield 1		1989–90	Glentoran 3, Portadown 0
1961–62	Linfield 4, Portadown 0		1990–91	Portadown 2, Glenavon 1
1962–63	Linfield 2, Distillery 1		1991–92	Glenavon 2, Linfield 1
1963–64	Derry City 2, Glentoran 0		1992–93	Bangor 1:1:1, Ards 1:1:0
1964–65	Coleraine 2, Glenavon 1		1993–94	Linfield 2, Bangor 0
1965–66	Glentoran 2, Linfield 0		1994–95	Linfield 3, Carrick Rangers 1
1966–67	Crusaders 3, Glentoran 1		1995–96	Glentoran 1, Glenavon 0
1967–68	Crusaders 2, Linfield 0		1996–97	Glenavon 1, Cliftonville 0
1968–69	Ards 4, Distillery 2		1997–98	Glentoran 1, Glenavon 0
1969–70	Linfield 2, Ballymena U 1		1998–99	*Portadown awarded trophy after*
1970–71	Distillery 3, Derry City 0			*Cliftonville were eliminated for using an*
1971–72	Coleraine 2, Portadown 1			*ineligible player in semi-final.*
1972–73	Glentoran 3, Linfield 2		1999–2000	Glentoran 1, Portadown 0
1973–74	Ards 2, Ballymena U 1		2000–01	Glentoran 1, Linfield 0
1974–75	Coleraine 1:0:1, Linfield 1:0:0			

NATIONWIDE GOLD CUP

Preliminary Round

Lisburn Distillery v Larne	2-0
Armagh City v Limavady United	3-1
Institute v Bangor	5-4
Dungannon Swifts v Ards	2-1

First Round

Linfield v Carrick Rangers	1-0
Newry Town v Armagh City	5-4
Lisburn Distillery v Coleraine	3-4
Glenavon v Ballyclare Comrades	2-0
Dungannon Swifts v Ballymena United	2-1
Portadown v Crusaders	1-0
Cliftonville v Glentoran	0-1
Institute v Omagh Town	0-3

Quarter-finals

Linfield v Glenavon	4-3
Newry Town v Omagh Town	3-2
Glentoran v Portadown	2-1
Dungannon Swifts v Coleraine	1-2

Semi-finals first leg

Glentoran v Newry Town	0-1
Linfield v Coleraine	1-3

Semi-finals second leg

Newry Town v Glentoran	1-3 (aggregate 2-3)
Coleraine v Linfield	3-3 (aggregate 6-4)

Final

Glentoran 4 Coleraine 3 *(at Windsor Park, Belfast)*

Glentoran: Gough; Nixon, Ferguson, Leeman, McCombe, Smyth, McCann, Lockhart, Fitzgerald, Batey (Halliday), McBride. Subs not used: Armstrong, Rainey.

Coleraine: McKeown (McCann); Clanachan, McDonald (Gaston), McLaughlin, Devine, Beavers (Loughery), Picking, McCoosh, Tolan, McAllister, Keegan.

Referee: L. Irvine (Limavady).

Attendance: 3,000.

Scorers: Glentoran: Ferguson, Lockhart, Smyth, McCann. *Coleraine:* Devine (pen), Loughery, Tolan.

COCA-COLA IRISH LEAGUE CUP

Preliminary Round

Carrick Rangers v Ballyclare Comrades	1-0
Ards v Lisburn Distillery	2-0
Dungannon Swifts v Limavady United	0-3
Larne v Bangor	2-0

First Round

Carrick Rangers v Glenavon	0-2
Larne v Portadown	0-1
Glentoran v Limavady United	2-1
Armagh City v Coleraine	0-0
(aet – Armagh City won 4-3 on penalties)	
Crusaders v Linfield	1-2
Cliftonville v Omagh Town	2-3
Institute v Newry Town	2-2
(aet – Newry Town won 3-1 on penalties)	
Ards v Ballymena United	2-1

Quarter-finals

Armagh City v Glentoran	0-1
Ards v Omagh Town	0-2 *(aet)*

Newry v Linfield	0-0
(aet – Linfield won 4-3 on penalties)	
Glenavon v Portadown	3-0

Semi-finals

Omagh Town v Glentoran	0-2
Linfield v Glenavon	0-1

Final

Glentoran 1 Glenavon 0 *(at Windsor Park)*

Glentoran: Gough; Nixon, Leeman, Smyth, Ferguson, McCann T, Young, Batey, Lockhart, Hamill (Fitzgerald), Halliday (McBride). Sub not used: Walker.

Glenavon: Addis; Wright, Rafferty, Montgomery, Glendinning, Collins, Murphy, McCann M, McMahon (McAree), Haylock (Hill), Smith (Divin).

Referee: H. Barr (Bangor).

Scorer: Young (pen).

Attendance: 2,515.

Note: Coca-Cola sponsorship ended with this match after an agreed six year period.

WHERE THE TROPHIES WENT

Smirnoff Irish League	*Winners*	*Runners-up*
Premier Division	Linfield	Glenavon
First Division	Ards	Lisburn Distillery
Irish League Second Division	Dundela	Moyola Park
Irish Reserve League North	Cliftonville	Crusaders
Irish Reserve League South	Linfield Swifts	Glentoran
Play-Off	Cliftonville 1	Linfield Swifts 0
Smirnoff Knock-Out Cup	H&W Welders	Dundela
Irish League Youth Cup	Cliftonville Strollers	Lisburn Distillery II
Nationwide Irish Cup	Glentoran	Linfield
Coca-Cola Irish League Cup	Glentoran	Glenavon
Calor County Antrim Shield	Linfield	Glentoran
Calor Steel & Sons Cup	Glentoran II	Cliftonville Olympic
Calor County Antrim Junior Shield	Ballywalter	Holywood Rec
Belfast Telegraph Intermediate Cup	Dundela	Moyola Park
Sunday Mirror Irish Junior Cup Final	Irvinestown Wanderers	Dergview
Mid Ulster Cup	Armagh City	Newry Town
North West Senior Cup	Omagh Town	Limavady United
Harry Cavan Youth Cup	Cliftonville Strollers	Coleraine Colts
George Wilson Memorial Cup	Glentoran II	Ballymena United Reserves
Wilkinson Sword Charity Shield	Linfield	Glentoran

Ulster Footballer of Year (Castlereagh Glentoran Supporters)	Glenn Ferguson (Linfield)
Northern Ireland Play of Year (NIFWA)	Glenn Ferguson (Linfield)
Young Footballer of Year Award	Marc McCann (Glenavon)
Premier Division Manager of Year	David Jeffrey (Linfield)
Irish League First Division Manager of Year	Paul Kirk (Lisburn Distillery)
Outstanding Non Senior Team	Neil Lennon (Glasgow Celtic)
Irish League First Division Player of Year	Gary McKinstry (Armagh City)
Merit Award	Mickey Keenan (Portadown)

Leading Scorers:

Premier Division	Glenn Ferguson (Linfield)	30 goals
First Division	Gary McKinstry (Armagh City)	32 goals

EUROPEAN CUP

EUROPEAN CUP FINALS 1956–2001

Year	Winners		Runners-up		Venue	Attendance	Referee
1956	Real Madrid	4	Reims	3	Paris	38,000	Ellis (E)
1957	Real Madrid	2	Fiorentina	0	Madrid	124,000	Horn (Ho)
1958	Real Madrid	3	AC Milan	2 *(aet)*	Brussels	67,000	Alsteen (Bel)
1959	Real Madrid	2	Reims	0	Stuttgart	80,000	Dutsch (WG)
1960	Real Madrid	7	Eintracht Frankfurt	3	Glasgow	135,000	Mowat (S)
1961	Benfica	3	Barcelona	2	Berne	28,000	Dienst (Sw)
1962	Benfica	5	Real Madrid	3	Amsterdam	65,000	Horn (Ho)
1963	AC Milan	2	Benfica	1	Wembley	45,000	Holland (E)
1964	Internazionale	3	Real Madrid	1	Vienna	74,000	Stoll (A)
1965	Internazionale	1	Benfica	0	Milan	80,000	Dienst (Sw)
1966	Real Madrid	2	Partizan Belgrade	1	Brussels	55,000	Kreitlein (WG)
1967	Celtic	2	Internazionale	1	Lisbon	56,000	Tschenscher (WG)
1968	Manchester U	4	Benfica	1 *(aet)*	Wembley	100,000	Lo Bello (I)
1969	AC Milan	4	Ajax	1	Madrid	50,000	Ortiz (Sp)
1970	Feyenoord	2	Celtic	1 *(aet)*	Milan	50,000	Lo Bello (I)
1971	Ajax	2	Panathinaikos	0	Wembley	90,000	Taylor (E)
1972	Ajax	2	Internazionale	0	Rotterdam	67,000	Helies (F)
1973	Ajax	1	Juventus	0	Belgrade	93,500	Guglovic (Y)
1974	Bayern Munich	1	Atletico Madrid	1	Brussels	49,000	Loraux (Bel)
Replay	Bayern Munich	4	Atletico Madrid	0	Brussels	23,000	Delcourt (Bel)
1975	Bayern Munich	2	Leeds U	0	Paris	50,000	Kitabdjian (F)
1976	Bayern Munich	1	St Etienne	0	Glasgow	54,864	Palotai (H)
1977	Liverpool	3	Moenchengladbach	1	Rome	57,000	Wurtz (F)
1978	Liverpool	1	FC Brugge	0	Wembley	92,000	Corver (Ho)
1979	Nottingham F	1	Malmo	0	Munich	57,500	Linemayr (A)
1980	Nottingham F	1	Hamburg	0	Madrid	50,000	Garrido (P)
1981	Liverpool	1	Real Madrid	0	Paris	48,360	Palotai (H)
1982	Aston Villa	1	Bayern Munich	0	Rotterdam	46,000	Konrath (F)
1983	Hamburg	1	Juventus	0	Athens	80,000	Rainea (R)
1984	Liverpool	1	Roma	1	Rome	69,693	Fredriksson (Se)
	(aet; Liverpool won 4–2 on penalties)						
1985	Juventus	1	Liverpool	0	Brussels	58,000	Daina (Sw)
1986	Steaua Bucharest	0	Barcelona	0	Seville	70,000	Vautrot (F)
	(aet; Steaua won 2–0 on penalties)						
1987	Porto	2	Bayern Munich	1	Vienna	59,000	Ponnet (Bel)
1988	PSV Eindhoven	0	Benfica	0	Stuttgart	70,000	Agnolin (I)
	(aet; PSV won 6–5 on penalties)						
1989	AC Milan	4	Steaua Bucharest	0	Barcelona	97,000	Tritschler (WG)
1990	AC Milan	1	Benfica	0	Vienna	57,500	Kohl (A)
1991	Red Star Belgrade	0	Marseille	0	Bari	56,000	Lanese (I)
	(aet; Red Star won 5–3 on penalties)						
1992	Barcelona	1	Sampdoria	0 *(aet)*	Wembley	70,827	Schmidhuber (G)
1993	Marseille*	1	AC Milan	0	Munich	64,400	Rothlisberger (Sw)
1994	AC Milan	4	Barcelona	0	Athens	70,000	Don (E)
1995	Ajax	1	AC Milan	0	Vienna	49,730	Craciunescu (Ro)
1996	Juventus	1	Ajax	1	Rome	67,000	Vega (Sp)
	(aet; Juventus won 4–2 on penalties)						
1997	Borussia Dortmund	3	Juventus	1	Munich	59,000	Puhl (H)
1998	Real Madrid	1	Juventus	0	Amsterdam	47,500	Krug (G)
1999	Manchester U	2	Bayern Munich	1	Barcelona	90,000	Collina (I)
2000	Real Madrid	3	Valencia	0	Paris	78,759	Braschi (I)
2001	Bayern Munich	1	Valencia	1	Milan	71,500	Jol (Ho)
	(aet; Bayern Munich won 5-4 on penalties)						

Subsequently stripped of title.

EUROPEAN CUP 2000–2001

FIRST QUALIFYING ROUND, FIRST LEG

Birkirkara (1) 1 *(Nwoko 28)*, KR Reykjavik (0) 2 *(Sigthorsson 46, Juliusson 57)*	2000
F91 Dudelange (0) 0, Levski Sofia (2) 4 *(Ivanov G 12, 87, Ivankov 17 (pen), Isykhmeistruk 69)*	1200
Haka (0) 1 *(Wilson 56)*, Linfield (0) 0	1799
KI (0) 0, Red Star Belgrade (1) 3 *(Ilic 45, Stevanovic 65, Mirkovic 90)*	1000
Shirak (1) 1 *(Takmadyan 31)*, BATE Borisov (1) 1 *(Kutuzov 24)*	2500
Skonto Riga (0) 2 *(Kolesnicenko 52, 90 (pen))*, Shamkir (0) 1 *(Kulikov 82)*	3200
Sloga (0) 0, Shelbourne (0) 1 *(Baker 85)*	6000
SK Tirana (2) 2 *(Dede 13, Fortuzi 16)*, Zimbru Chisinau (2) 3 *(Berco 29, 50, Boret 45)*	4000
TNS (0) 2 *(Wright 62, Toner 89)*, Levadia (0) 2 *(Bragin 50, Krasnopjorov 88)*	1432
Zalgiris Kaunas (3) 4 *(Ksanavicius 13, 37, Zuta 19, Tuotkalis 87)*, Brotnjo (0) 0	2000

FIRST QUALIFYING ROUND, SECOND LEG

BATE Borisov (1) 2 *(Rogozhkin 17, Loshenkov 58)*, Shirak (0) 1 *(Takmadyan 73)*	5000
Brotnjo (3) 3 *(Katic 32, 41 (pen), Juricic 39)*, Zalgiris Kaunas (0) 0	6000
KR Reykjavik (2) 4 *(Winnie 11, Benediktsson 45, Sigurdsson 60, Marteisson 66)*, Birkirkara (0) 1 *(Spiteri 56)*	2000
Levadia (1) 4 *(Krom 49, Fenin 58, Tselnokov 60, Edwards 64 (og))*, TNS (0) 0	550
Levski Sofia (1) 2 *(Ivanov G 35, Ivankov 53 (pen))*, F91 Dudelange (0) 0	3000
Linfield (1) 2 *(Ferguson 22 (pen), 72)*, Haka (0) 1 *(Kovacs 85 (pen))*	3587
Red Star Belgrade (2) 2 *(Boskovic 10 (pen), Drulic 16)*, KI (0) 0	10,000
Shamkir (1) 4 *(Kvaratskhelia 2, 90, 100, Kulikov 110)*, Skonto Riga (1) 1 *(Samusevas 30)*	15,000
Shelbourne (0) 1 *(Haylock 67)*, Sloga (0) 1 *(Nuhiji 81 (pen))*	6511
Zimbru Chisinau (2) 3 *(Oprea 7, 31, Boret 85)*, SK Tirana (2) 2 *(Rrezart 10, Kenesei 23)*	3500

SECOND QUALIFYING ROUND, FIRST LEG

Anderlecht (3) 4 *(Baseggio 4, Koller 14, 27, 58)*, Anorthosis (1) 2 *(Pavlovits 9, Papavasiliou 89)*	17,000
Besiktas (0) 1 *(Nouma 82)*, Levski Sofia (0) 0	17,000
Brondby (1) 3 *(Bagger 14, Lindrup 86, Madsen 84)*, KR Reykjavik (1) 1 *(Danielsson 17)*	8567
Dinamo Bucharest (2) 3 *(Lupu 7 (pen), Mihalcea 45, Niculae 63)*, Polonia (2) 4 *(Wyeszczycki 25, 60, Olisadebe 35, Golaszewski 90)*	5000
Hajduk Split (0) 0, Dunaferr (0) 2 *(Tokoli 57, Lengyel 90)*	25,000
Haka (0) 0, Inter Bratislava (0) 0	1785
Helsingborg (0) 0, BATE Borisov (0) 0	4417
Rangers (1) 4 *(Johnston 14, Albertz 62 (pen), Dodds 89, 90)*, Zalgiris Kaunas (1) 1 *(Zuta 26)*	45,974
Red Star Belgrade (3) 4 *(Drulic 24, 90, Boskovic 37, Pjanovic 39)*, Torpedo Kutaisi (0) 0	25,000
Shakhtjor Donetsk (2) 4 *(Atelkin 4, 16, 57, Belik 72)*, Levadia (0) 1 *(Rychkov 79)*	25,000
Shelbourne (0) 1 *(Foran 62)*, Rosenborg (2) 3 *(Berg 2, Winsnes 14, Belsvik 89)*	8642
Slavia Prague (1) 1 *(Zelenka 38)*, Shamkir (0) 0	2819
Sturm Graz (1) 3 *(Vastic 13, Reinmayr 73, Neukirchner 90)*, Hapoel Tel Aviv (0) 0	10,300
Zimbru Chisinau (0) 2 *(Kulik 50 (pen), Epureanu 67)*, Maribor (0) 0	4000

SECOND QUALIFYING ROUND, SECOND LEG

Anorthosis (0) 0, Anderlecht (0) 0	5000
BATE Borisov (0) 0, Helsingborg (2) 3 *(Santos 11, Andersson 24, Wahlstedt 84)*	7500
Dunaferr (1) 2 *(Zavadszki 20, Tekely 88)*, Hajduk Split (2) 2 *(Bilic 9, 29)*	5500
Hapoel Tel Aviv (0) 1 *(Balili 80)*, Sturm Graz (0) 2 *(Korsos 70, Kocian 85)*	12,000
Inter Bratislava (0) 1 *(Nemeth 108)*, Haka (0) 0	4000

KR Reykjavik (0) 0, Brondby (0) 0	500
Levadia (0) 1 *(Bragin 48)*, Shakhtjor Donetsk (2) 5 *(Vorobei 26, 31, 80 (pen), Atelkin 89, Zubov 90)*	7000
Levski Sofia (0) 1 *(Markov 64)*, Besiktas (1) 1 *(Tayfur 34)*	5000
Maribor (1) 1 *(Ceh 3)*, Zimbru Chisinau (0) 0	6500
Polonia (0) 3 *(Olisadebe 60, 62, Golaszewski 66)*, Dinamo Bucharest (1) 1 *(Tames 42)*	9000
Rosenborg (0) 1 *(Berg 80)*, Shelbourne (0) 1 *(Foran 64)*	5470
Shamkir (1) 1 *(Kvaratshkelia 51)*, Slavia Prague (1) 4 *(Dostalek 36, Dosek 56, 60, Svankera 72)*	7000
Torpedo Kutaisi (1) 2 *(Imedadze 42, Janashia 90)*, Red Star Belgrade (0) 0	11,000
Zalgiris Kaunas (0) 0, Rangers (0) 0	4000

THIRD QUALIFYING ROUND, FIRST LEG

Anderlecht (1) 1 *(Koller 37)*, Porto (0) 0	24,000
Besiktas (1) 3 *(Nihat 11, Nouma 80, Karhan 89)*, Lokomotiv Moscow (0) 0	20,000
Brondby (0) 0, Hamburg (0) 2 *(Barbarez 83, Mahdavikia 85)*	11,682
Dunaferr (0) 2 *(Lengyel 80, Tokoli 88)*, Rosenborg (0) 2 *(Johnsen 52, Knudsen 87)*	19,000
Helsingborg (0) 1 *(Hansson 82)*, Internazionale (0) 0	12,617
Herfolge (0) 0, Rangers (2) 3 *(Albertz 28, Wallace 31, Amoruso 60)*	3523
Inter Bratislava (1) 1 *(Nemeth 75)*, Lyon (0) 2 *(Anderson 50, Delmotte 89)*	3000
Dynamo Kiev (0) 0, Red Star Belgrade (0) 0	20,000
Leeds United (1) 2 *(Smith 39, Harte 71 (pen))*, 1860 Munich (0) 1 *(Agostino 90)*	33,769
AC Milan (1) 3 *(Shevchenko 22, 60, Comandini 90)*, Dynamo Zagreb (1) 1 *(Pilipovic 20)*	25,000
Polonia (1) 2 *(Klelbowicz 45, Kaliszan 68)*, Panathinaikos (2) 2 *(Warzycha 9, Fissas 38)*	8000
St Gallen (1) 1 *(Amoah 14)*, Galatasaray (1) 2 *(Jardel 39, 78)*	16,000
Shakhtjor Donetsk (0) 0, Slavia Prague (0) 1 *(Dosek 87)*	32,000
Sturm Graz (1) 2 *(Schopp 22 (pen), 90 (pen))*, Feyenoord (1) 1 *(Korneev 7)*	15,400
Tirol Innsbruck (0) 0, Valencia (0) 0	6500
Zimbru Chisinau (0) 0, Sparta Prague (0) 1 *(Obajdin 61)*	6000

THIRD QUALIFYING ROUND, SECOND LEG

Dynamo Zagreb (0) 0, AC Milan (2) 3 *(Shevchenko 23, 43, Jose Mari 57)*	18,000
Feyenoord (0) 1 *(Jochemsen 87)*, Sturm Graz (0) 1 *(Reinmayr 56)*	35,000
Galatasaray (2) 2 *(Zellweger 23 (og), Jardel 29 (pen))*, St Gallen (1) 2 *(Gane 30, Amoah 85)*	22,000
Hamburg (0) 0, Brondby (0) 0	18,000
Internazionale (0) 0, Helsingborg (0) 0	50,000
Lokomotiv Moscow (0) 1 *(Cherevchenko 51)*, Besiktas (1) 3 *(Nouma 28, Nihat 72, Tayfur 87)*	8000
Lyon (0) 2 *(Marlet 56, Malbranque 90)*, Inter Bratislava (1) 1 *(Pinte 38)*	15,000
1860 Munich (0) 0, Leeds United (0) 1 *(Smith 46)*	45,000
Panathinaikos (1) 2 *(Limberopoulos 30, Pflipsen 61 (pen))*, Polonia (0) 1 *(Bak 86)*	44,312
Porto (0) 0, Anderlecht (0) 0	32,000
Rangers (0) 3 *(Wallace 48, Johnston 78, Kanchelskis 89)*, Herfolge	34,141
Red Star Belgrade (1) 1 *(Boskovic 22)*, Dynamo Kiev (1) 1 *(Bialkevich 33)*	53,000
Rosenborg (1) 2 *(Berg 4, Belsvik 48)*, Dunaferr (1) 1 *(Tokoli 17)*	10,000
Slavia Prague (0) 0, Shakhtjor Donetsk (0) 2 *(Vorobiev 90, Atelkin 97)*	6000
Sparta Prague (0) 1 *(Obajdin 57)*, Zimbru Chisinau (0) 0	8588
Valencia (2) 4 *(Mendieta 22, 53 (pen), Diego Alonso 44, 63)*, Tirol Innsbruck (0) 1 *(Gilewicz 69)*	50,000

CHAMPIONS LEAGUE

GROUP A

Spartak Moscow (0) 2 *(Titov 51, Bezrodny 89)*,
   Leverkusen (0) 0   48,000
Sporting Lisbon (2) 2 *(Sa Pinto 39, Cruz 42)*,
   Real Madrid (0) 2 *(Roberto Carlos 50, Rui Jorge 70
   (og))*   42,000
Leverkusen (0) 3 *(Ramelow 65, Brdaric 72,
   Neuville 77)*, Sporting Lisbon (1) 2 *(Cruz 12,
   Sa Pinto 79 (pen))*   22,500
Real Madrid (0) 1 *(Helguera 50)*, Spartak
   Moscow (0) 0   25,000
Spartak Moscow (1) 3 *(Robson 43, Marcao 67, 81)*,
   Sporting Lisbon (1) 1 *(Sa Pinto 24)*   70,000
Leverkusen (2) 2 *(Schneider 27, Ballack 44)*,
   Real Madrid (1) 3 *(Roberto Carlos 32, 75,
   Guti 69)*   22,500
Real Madrid (2) 5 *(Guti 3, 65, Helguera 24, Raul
   75, Figo 88 (pen))*, Leverkusen (1) 3 *(Brdaric
   19, Kirsten 55, Rink 78)*   60,000
Sporting Lisbon (0) 0, Spartak Moscow (1) 3
   (Dimas 16 (og), Titov 52, 67)   30,000
Leverkusen (0) 1 *(Ballack 52)*, Spartak
   Moscow (0) 0   20,000
Real Madrid (2) 4 *(Guti 11, Savio 41, Morientes
   61, 69)*, Sporting Lisbon (0) 0   55,000
Spartak Moscow (0) 1 *(Geremi 46 (og))*, Real
   Madrid (0) 0   77,000
Sporting Lisbon (0) 0, Leverkusen (0) 0   10,000

FINAL TABLE	P	W	D	L	F	A	Pts
Real Madrid	6	4	1	1	15	8	13
Spartak Moscow	6	4	0	2	9	3	12
Leverkusen	6	2	1	3	9	12	7
Sporting Lisbon	6	0	2	4	5	15	2

GROUP B

Shakhtjor Donetsk (0) 0, Lazio (1) 3 *(Claudio Lopez
   27, Nedved 70, Inzaghi 80)*   31,000
Sparta Prague (0) 0, Arsenal (1) 1 *(Silvinho 33)*   17,656
Arsenal (1) 3 *(Wiltord 45, Keown 85, 90)*, Shakhtjor
   Donetsk (2) 2 *(Bakharev 26, Vorobei 29)*   33,922
Lazio (1) 3 *(Inzaghi 35, 70, Simeone 58)*,
   Sparta Prague (0) 0   45,000
Arsenal (1) 2 *(Ljungberg 43, 56)*, Lazio (0) 0   34,521
Sparta Prague (0) 3 *(Rosicky 54, Hornak 73,
   Jarosik 82)*, Shakhtjor Donetsk (0) 2 *(Zubov 56,
   Abramov 84)*   7931
Lazio (1) 1 *(Nedved 24)*, Arsenal (0) 1 *(Pires 88)*   42,500
Shakhtjor Donetsk (1) 2 *(Gleveckas 35, Zubov
   87 (pen))*, Sparta Prague (1) 1 *(Jarosik 16)*   20,000
Arsenal (3) 4 *(Parlour 5, Lauren 7, Dixon 35,
   Kanu 52)*, Sparta Prague (1) 2 *(Labant 41 (pen),
   Rosicky 90)*   34,497
Lazio (0) 5 *(Lopez 48, 68, 90, Favalli 54, Veron 57)*,
   Shakhtjor Donetsk (1) 1 *(Vorobei 42)*   30,000
Shakhtjor Donetsk (1) 3 *(Atelkin 35, Vorobei 57,
   Bielik 66)*, Arsenal (0) 0   30,000
Sparta Prague (0) 0, Lazio (1) 1 *(Ravanelli 43)*   19,414

FINAL TABLE	P	W	D	L	F	A	Pts
Arsenal	6	4	1	1	11	8	13
Lazio	6	4	1	1	13	4	13
Shakhtjor Donetsk	6	2	0	4	10	15	6
Sparta Prague	6	1	0	5	6	13	3

GROUP C

Lyon (2) 3 *(Anderson 2, Houttuin 10 (og), Marlet
   58)*, Heerenveen (1) 1 *(Talan 35)*   30,000
Valencia (2) 2 *(Baraja 36, Diego Alonso 44)*,
   Olympiakos (0) 1 *(Djordjevic 73)*   44,000
Heerenveen (0) 0, Valencia (1) 1 *(Kily Gonzalez
   38)* 14,000
Olympiakos (2) 2 *(Ofori-Quaye 19, Giovanni 34)*,
   Lyon (0) 1 *(Foe 88)*   70,000
Olympiakos (0) 2 *(Giovanni 52, 69)*, Heerenveen (0) 0
        52,000
Valencia (0) 1 *(Zahovic 78)*, Lyon (0) 0   34,000
Heerenveen (0) 1 *(Jensen 82)*, Olympiakos (0) 0   12,000
Lyon (1) 3 *(Marlet 90)*, Valencia (1) 2 *(Sanchez 45,
   Baraja 85)*   38,959
Heerenveen (0) 0, Lyon (0) 2 *(Malbranque 68,
   Marlet 78)*   14,000

Olympiakos (0) 1 *(Djordjevic 65 (pen))*,
   Valencia (0) 0 58,000
Lyon (1) 1 *(Laigle 2)*, Olympiakos (0) 0   42,000
Valencia (1) 1 *(Alonso 10)*, Heerenveen (1) 1
   (Venema 37)   28,000

FINAL TABLE	P	W	D	L	F	A	Pts
Valencia	6	4	1	1	7	4	13
Lyon	6	3	0	3	8	6	9
Olympiakos	6	3	0	3	6	5	9
Heerenveen	6	1	1	4	3	9	4

GROUP D

Galatasaray (2) 3 *(Jardel 16, Hagi 29, Capone 80)*,
   Monaco (0) 2 *(Nonda 50, Simone 62 (pen))*   22,000
Rangers (3) 5 *(Mols 9, De Boer 19, Albertz 29, Van
   Bronckhorst 71, Dodds 85)*, Sturm Graz (0) 0   49,317
Monaco (0) 0, Rangers (1) 1 *(Van Bronckhorst 8)* 18,000
Sturm Graz (1) 3 *(Yuran 31, Schopp 64, Schupp 82)*,
   Galatasaray (0) 0   15,400
Galatasaray (0) 3 *(Bulent A 52, Hakan Unsal 57,
   Jardel 70)*, Rangers (0) 2 *(Kanchelskis 72, Van
   Bronckhorst 90)*   22,000
Monaco (3) 5 *(Simone 13, 38, 41, Farnerud 76,
   Nonda 84)*, Sturm Graz (0) 0   8000
Rangers (0) 0, Galatasaray (0) 0   49,603
Sturm Graz (1) 2 *(Schopp 40, 88)*, Monaco (0) 0 15,400
Monaco (4) 4 *(Contreras 6, Bonnal 19, Simone 22,
   Nonda 26)*, Galatasaray (1) 2 *(Hakan Unsal 24,
   Bulent K 63)* 18,000
Sturm Graz (1) 2 *(Yuran 20, Prilasnig 90)*,
   Rangers (0) 0   15,400
Galatasaray (1) 2 *(Ergun 30 (pen), Jardel 75)*,
   Sturm Graz (0) 2 *(Yuran 64, Hakan
   Unsal 80 (og))* 22,000
Rangers (1) 2 *(Miller 3, Mols 51)*, Monaco (1) 2
   (Costinha 38, Simone 78)   50,228

FINAL TABLE	P	W	D	L	F	A	Pts
Sturm Graz	6	3	1	2	9	12	10
Galatasaray	6	2	2	2	10	13	8
Rangers	6	2	2	2	10	7	8
Monaco	6	2	1	3	13	10	7

GROUP E

Hamburg (1) 4 *(Yeboah 17, Mahdavikia 65, Butt 72
   (pen), Kovac 82)*, Juventus (2) 4 *(Tudor 5,
   Inzaghi 36, 53, 88 (pen))*   48,600
Panathinaikos (1) 1 *(Warzycha 29)*, La Coruna (0) 1
   (Naybet 84)   52,000
Juventus (1) 2 *(Tacchinardi 35, Trezeguet 83)*,
   Panathinaikos (1) 1 *(Goumas 45)*   35,422
La Coruna (1) 2 *(Pandiani 43, Scaloni 89)*,
   Hamburg (0) 1 *(Barbarez 53)*   15,000
Hamburg (0) 0, Panathinaikos (1) 1
   (Nassiopoulos 37)   46,000
Juventus (0) 0, La Coruna (0) 0   25,000
La Coruna (1) 1 *(Victor 12)*, Juventus (1) 1
   (Inzaghi 10)   25,000
Panathinaikos (0) 0, Hamburg (0) 0   32,000
La Coruna (0) 1 *(Pandiani 82)*, Panathinaikos (0) 0
        20,000
Juventus (0) 1 *(Kovacevic 56)*, Hamburg (1) 3
   (Prager 24, Yeboah 48, Panadic 62)   35,209
Hamburg (1) 1 *(Mahdavikia 10)*, La Coruna (0) 1
   (Makaay 58)   48,500
Panathinaikos (1) 3 *(Paulo Sousa 6, Basinas 58 (pen),
   Warzycha 66)*, Juventus (1) 1 *(Inzaghi 23)*   67,000

FINAL TABLE	P	W	D	L	F	A	Pts
La Coruna	6	2	4	0	6	4	10
Panathinaikos	6	2	2	2	6	5	8
Hamburg	6	1	3	2	9	9	6
Juventus	6	1	3	2	9	12	6

GROUP F

Helsingborg (0) 1 *(Bjorn Johansen 90)*, Bayern Munich
   (1) 3 *(Scholl 7, Salihamidzic 48, Jancker 54)*   12,623
Rosenborg (1) 3 *(Berg 17, Frode Johnsen 62,
   Skammelsrud 90 (pen))*, Paris St Germain (1) 1
   (Christian 7)   13,921
Bayern Munich (0) 3 *(Jancker 73, Elber 77, Linke 80)*,
   Rosenborg (1) 1 *(Sorensen 38)*   20,000

Paris St Germain (1) 4 *(Anelka 24, Robert 63,
 Christian 80, El Karkouri 89)*, Helsingborg (1) 1
 (Bjorn Johansen 45) 28,303
Paris St Germain (0) 1 *(Leroy 90)*, Bayern Munich (0) 0
 45,000

Rosenborg (2) 6 *(Frode Johnsen 20, 29, 78, Strand
 50, 51, Stig Johansen 64 (og))*, Helsingborg (0) 1
 (Prica 90) 13,702
Bayern Munich (1) 2 *(Salihamidzic 4, Sergio 88)*,
 Paris St Germain (0) 0 33,000
Helsingborg (1) 2 *(Jansson 32, Santos 77)*,
 Rosenborg (0) 0 12,587
Bayern Munich (0) 0, Helsingborg (0) 0 20,000
Paris St Germain (4) 7 *(Dehu 16, Christian 25,
 Anelka 35, 90, Luccin 45, Leroy 76, Robert 86 (pen))*,
 Rosenborg (2) 2 *(George 36, 38)* 39,536
Helsingborg (0) 1 *(Persson 70)*, Paris St Germain (1) 1
 (Anelka 34) 12,583
Rosenborg (1) 1 *(Johnsen 27)*, Bayern Munich (0) 1
 (Jeremies 86) 13,965

FINAL TABLE	P	W	D	L	F	A	Pts
Bayern Munich	6	3	2	1	9	4	11
Paris St Germain	6	3	1	2	14	9	10
Rosenborg	6	2	1	3	13	15	7
Helsingborg	6	1	2	3	6	14	5

GROUP G
Manchester United (3) 5 *(Cole 15, 49, 71, Irwin 30 (pen),
 Sheringham 41)*, Anderlecht (0) 1 *(Koller 54)* 62,739
PSV Eindhoven (1) 2 *(Lucius 39, Bruggink 52)*,
 Dynamo Kiev (1) 1 *(Shatskikh 6)* 28,000
Anderlecht (0) 1 *(Dheedene 81)*, PSV Eindhoven (0) 0
 28,000
Dynamo Kiev (0) 0, Manchester United (0) 0 48,432
Dynamo Kiev (0) 4 *(Gusin 52, Shatskikh 80,
 Demetradze 89, 90)*, Andelecht (0) 0 35,000
PSV Eindhoven (2) 3 *(Bouma 17, Van Bommel 38,
 Kezman 64)*, Manchester United (1) 1 *(Scholes 2
 (pen))* 33,500
Anderlecht (4) 4 *(Vashchuk 10 (og), Radzinski 37,
 41, Stoica 45)*, Dynamo Kiev (1) 2 *(Kaladze 1,
 Bialkevich 88)* 25,000
Manchester United (1) 3 *(Sheringham 9, Scholes 82,
 Yorke 87)*, PSV Eindhoven (0) 1 *(Van Bommel 76)*
 66,313
Anderlecht (0) 2 *(Radzinski 15, 34)*, Manchester United
 (1) 1 *(Irwin 36 (pen))* 27,500
Dynamo Kiev (0) 0, PSV Eindhoven (1) 1 *(Ooijer 45)*
 40,000
Manchester United (1) 1 *(Sheringham 18)*, Dynamo
 Kiev (0) 0 66,776
PSV Eindhoven (1) 2 *(Ramzi 45, 47)*, Anderlecht (2) 3
 (Crasson 9, Koller 37, Youla 90) 30,000

FINAL TABLE	P	W	D	L	F	A	Pts
Anderlecht	6	4	0	2	11	14	12
Manchester United	6	3	1	2	11	7	10
PSV Eindhoven	6	3	0	3	9	9	9
Dynamo Kiev	6	1	1	4	7	8	4

GROUP H
Barcelona (2) 4 *(Rivaldo 10, De Boer 20,
 Kluivert 75, 84)*, Leeds United (0) 0 85,000
AC Milan (3) 4 *(Coco 36, Bierhoff 44, Shevchenko 45
 (pen), 77)*, Besiktas (1) 1 *(Tayfur 20 (pen))* 53,436
Besiktas (1) 3 *(Ahmet 37, 74, Nouma 87)*,
 Barcelona (0) 0 20,000
Leeds United (0) 1 *(Bowyer 89)*, AC Milan (0) 0 35,398
Barcelona (0) 0, AC Milan (1) 2 *(Coco 45, Bierhoff 71)*
 90,000
Leeds United (3) 6 *(Bowyer 7, 90, Viduka 11, Matteo
 22, Bakke 65, Huckerby 90)*, Besiktas (0) 0 34,485
Besiktas (0) 0, Leeds United (0) 0 20,000
AC Milan (3) 3 *(Albertini 25, 39, Jose Mari 45)*,
 Barcelona (2) 3 *(Rivaldo 19, 43, 68)* 79,000
Besiktas (0) 0, AC Milan (2) 2 *(Shevchenko 39,
 Jose Mari 43)* 18,000
Leeds United (1) 1 *(Bowyer 5)*, Barcelona (0) 1
 (Rivaldo 90) 36,721
Barcelona (2) 5 *(Cocu 11, Luis Enrique 17, 49,
 Rivaldo 80 (pen), Gabri 88)*, Besiktas (0) 0 55,000
AC Milan (0) 1 *(Serginho 68)*, Leeds United (1) 1
 (Matteo 45) 52,289

FINAL TABLE	P	W	D	L	F	A	Pts
AC Milan	6	3	2	1	12	6	11
Leeds United	6	2	3	1	9	6	9
Barcelona	6	2	2	2	13	9	8
Besiktas	6	1	1	4	4	17	4

SECOND STAGE
GROUP A
Manchester United (0) 3 *(Sheringham 48, Scholes 81, 90)*,
 Panathinaikos (0) 1 *(Karagounis 64)* 65,024
Valencia (1) 2 *(Carew 45, Sanchez 47)*, Sturm
 Graz (0) 0 27,000
Panathinaikos (0) 0, Valencia (0) 0 48,000
Sturm Graz (0) 0, Manchester United (1) 2
 (Scholes 17, Giggs 89) 16,500
Sturm Graz (0) 2 *(Haas 60, Kocijan 85)*,
 Panathinaikos (0) 0 16,500
Valencia (0) 0, Manchester United (0) 0 49,451
Manchester United (1) 1 *(Cole 12)*, Valencia (0) 1
 (Brown 88 (og)) 66,715
Panathinaikos (0) 1 *(Goumas 73)*, Sturm Graz (2) 2
 (Schopp 25, Haas 42) 20,000
Panathinaikos (1) 1 *(Seitaridis 25)*, Manchester United
 (0) 1 *(Scholes 90)* 27,230
Sturm Graz (0) 0, Valencia (1) 5 *(Ayala 5, Carew 50,
 Gonzalez 60, Alonso 87, 90)* 16,000
Manchester United (2) 3 *(Butt 5, Sheringham 20,
 Keane 87)*, Sturm Graz (0) 0 66,404
Valencia (1) 2 *(Sanchez 39, Angloma 74)*,
 Panathinaikos (1) 1 *(Basinas 27 (pen))* 40,000

FINAL TABLE	P	W	D	L	F	A	Pts
Valencia	6	3	3	0	10	2	12
Manchester United	6	3	3	0	10	2	12
Sturm Graz	6	2	0	4	4	13	6
Panathinaikos	6	0	2	4	4	10	2

GROUP B
AC Milan (0) 2 *(Jose Mari 48, Shevchenko 73 (pen))*,
 Galatasaray (2) 2 *(Jardel 39, Hasan Sas 41)* 46,324
Paris St Germain (1) 1 *(Algerino 38)*, La Coruna (0) 3
 (Naybet 63, Turu Flores 70, Makaay 90) 31,890
La Coruna (0) 0, AC Milan (1) 1 *(Helveg 45)* 23,000
Galatasaray (0) 1 *(Umit 51 (pen))*, Paris St
 Germain (0) 0 35,000
Galatasaray (1) 1 *(Suat 10)*, La Coruna (0) 0 19,000
AC Milan (1) 1 *(Leonardo 26)*, Paris St Germain (1) 1
 (Anelka 30) 50,043
La Coruna (1) 2 *(Victor 39, Djalminha 72 (pen))*,
 Galatasaray (0) 0 30,000
Paris St Germain (0) 1 *(Robert 75)*, AC Milan (0) 1
 (Jose Mari 90) 41,450
Galatasaray (1) 2 *(Hagi 20, Jardel 86)*, AC Milan (0) 0
 22,000
La Coruna (0) 4 *(Pandiani 56, 75, 83, Tristan 59)*,
 Paris St Germain (2) 3 *(Okocha 29, Leroy 42, 54)*
 28,000
AC Milan (0) 1 *(Shevchenko 85 (pen))*, La Coruna (0) 1
 (Djalminha 74 (pen)) 70,000
Paris St Germain (2) 2 *(Christian 2, 26)*,
 Galatasaray (0) 0 31,254

FINAL TABLE	P	W	D	L	F	A	Pts
La Coruna	6	3	1	2	10	7	10
Galatasaray	6	3	1	2	6	6	10
AC Milan	6	1	4	1	6	7	7
Paris St Germain	6	1	2	3	8	10	5

GROUP C
Bayern Munich (0) 1 *(Jeremies 55)*, Lyon (0) 0 18,000
Spartak Moscow (1) 4 *(Marcao 29, 51, Titov 77,
 Robson 82)*, Arsenal (1) 1 *(Silvinho 2)* 75,000
Arsenal (1) 2 *(Henry 4, Kanu 55)*, Bayern Munich (0) 2
 (Tarnat 56, Scholl 66) 35,318
Lyon (3) 3 *(Marlet 2, Anderson 30, 42)*, Spartak
 Moscow (0) 0 38,404
Bayern Munich (0) 1 *(Elber 79)*, Spartak
 Moscow (0) 0 31,000
Lyon (1) 1 *(Marlet 50)*, Arsenal (0) 1 *(Henry 58)* 39,541
Arsenal (1) 1 *(Bergkamp 33)*, Lyon (0) 1
 (Edmilson 90) 34,303
Spartak Moscow (0) 0, Bayern Munich (1) 3 *(Scholl 17,
 75 (pen), Sergio 87)* 65,000
Arsenal (0) 1 *(Henry 82)*, Spartak Moscow (0) 0 35,196

Lyon (2) 3 *(Govou 12, 20, Laigle 71)*, Bayern
   Munich (0) 0   39,460
Bayern Munich (1) 1 *(Elber 10)*, Arsenal (0) 0   58,000
Spartak Moscow (1) 1 *(Parfenov 4 (pen))*, Lyon (0) 1
   (Anderson 68 (pen))   10,000

FINAL TABLE	P	W	D	L	F	A	Pts
Bayern Munich	6	4	1	1	8	5	13
Arsenal	6	2	2	2	6	8	8
Lyon	6	2	2	2	8	4	8
Spartak Moscow	6	1	1	4	5	10	4

GROUP D

Anderlecht (0) 1 *(Radzinski 83)*, Lazio (0) 0   21,631
Leeds United (0) 0, Real Madrid (0) 2 *(Hierro 66,*
   Raul 68)   36,794
Lazio (0) 0, Leeds United (0) 1 *(Smith 80)*   42,450
Real Madrid (3) 4 *(Morientes 12, Figo 23 (pen),*
   Helguera 44, Roberto Carlos 73), Anderlecht (0) 1
   (Stoica 89)   55,000
Leeds United (0) 2 *(Harte 74, Bowyer 86)*,
   Anderlecht (0) 1 *(Stoica 65)*   36,064
Real Madrid (1) 3 *(Morientes 32, Helguera 82, Figo 89*
   (pen)), Lazio (1) 2 *(Crespo 4, Gottardi 83)*   75,000
Anderlecht (0) 1 *(Koller 76)*, Leeds United (3) 4
   (Smith 13, 38, Viduka 35, Harte 81 (pen))   28,000
Lazio (1) 2 *(Nedved 3, Crespo 52)*, Real Madrid (1) 2
   (Solari 32, Raul 73)   60,000
Lazio (1) 2 *(Lopez 39, Baronio 76)*, Anderlecht (0) 1
   (Stoica 50)   10,000
Real Madrid (2) 3 *(Raul 7, 59, Figo 41)*, Leeds
   United (1) 2 *(Smith 6, Viduka 54)*   40,000
Anderlecht (0) 2 *(Dindane 85, Goor 90)*, Real
   Madrid (0) 0   22,000
Leeds United (2) 3 *(Bowyer 28, Wilcox 43, Viduka*
   62), Lazio (2) 3 *(Ravanelli 21, Mihajlovic 29 (pen), 90)*
    36,741

FINAL TABLE	P	W	D	L	F	A	Pts
Real Madrid	6	4	1	1	14	9	13
Leeds United	6	3	1	2	12	10	10
Anderlecht	6	2	0	4	7	12	6
Lazio	6	1	2	3	9	11	5

QUARTER-FINALS, FIRST LEG

Arsenal (0) 2 *(Henry 58, Parlour 60)*, Valencia (1) 1
   (Ayala 41)   35,104
Galatasaray (0) 3 *(Davala 47 (pen), Sas 66, Jardel 75)*,
   Real Madrid (2) 2 *(Helguera 33, Makelele 43)*   19,000
Leeds United (1) 3 *(Harte 27, Smith 51, Ferdinand 66)*,
   La Coruna (0) 0   35,508
Manchester United (0) 0, Bayern Munich (0) 1
   (Sergio 86)   66,584

QUARTER-FINALS, SECOND LEG

Bayern Munich (2) 2 *(Elber 5, Scholl 40)*,
   Manchester United (0) 1 *(Giggs 49)*   60,000
La Coruna (1) 2 *(Djalminha 9 (pen), Tristan 73)*,
   Leeds United (0) 0   35,600
Real Madrid (3) 3 *(Raul 15, 37, Helguera 28)*,
   Galatasaray (0) 0   76,300
Valencia (0) 1 *(Carew 75)*, Arsenal (0) 0   47,700
   (Valencia won on away goals).

SEMI-FINALS, FIRST LEG

Leeds United (0) 0, Valencia (0) 0   36,437
Real Madrid (0) 0, Bayern Munich (0) 1 *(Elber 55)*
    75,000

SEMI-FINALS, SECOND LEG

Bayern Munich (2) 2 *(Elber 8, Jeremies 35)*,
   Real Madrid (1) 1 *(Figo 18)*   60,000
Valencia (1) 3 *(Sanchez 15, 46, Mendieta 52)*,
   Leeds United (0) 0   53,000

FINAL

Bayern Munich (0) 1, Valencia (1) 1
(aet; Bayern Munich won 5-4 on penalties).

(in Milan, 23 May 2001, 71,500)

Bayern Munich: Kahn; Sagnol, Lizarazu, Kuffour, Andersson, Linke, Scholl (Sergio 108), Salihamidzic (Jancker 46), Elber (Zickler 102), Hargreaves, Effenberg.
Scorer: Effenberg 51 (pen).
Valencia: Canizares; Angloma, Carboni, Ayala (Djukic 89), Pellegrino, Baraja, Aimar (Albelda 46), Gonzalez, Sanchez (Zahovic 65), Carew, Mendieta.
Scorer: Mendieta 3 (pen).
Referee: Jol (Holland).

Bayern Munich goalkeeper Oliver Kahn is mobbed by delighted team mates after his penalty save in the European Cup Final against Valencia. (ASP)

EUROPEAN CUP 2000–2001 – BRITISH AND IRISH CLUBS

FIRST QUALIFYING ROUND, FIRST LEG

12 JULY

Haka (0) 1 *(Wilson 56)*
Linfield (0) 0   1799
Haka: Vilnrotter; Salli, Ivanov, Reynders, Nyyssonen (Torkkeli 65), Ruhanen (Bajic 78), Kovacs, Wilson, Pasanen (Hyokyvaara 71), Okkonen, Koskinen.
Linfield: Mathers; Collier, Easton, McShane (Young 83), Bailie, Murphy, Gorman, Kelly, Beatty, Arthur, Larmour (Ferguson 63).

Sloga (0) 0
Shelbourne (0) 1 *(Baker 85)*   6000
Sloga: Nikoloski; Jovanovski (I), Sterjovski, Zdravevski, Jovanovski (II), Ramadan (Ramadani 75), Mustafi, Maznov, Bajram (Janevski 46), Beciri, Presilski (Nuhiji 46).
Shelbourne: Williams; Heary, McCarthy, Doolin (Haylock 46), Geoghegan (Foran 77), Baker, Raeside (Scully 46), Fenlon, Hutchison, Keddy.

TNS (0) 2 *(Wright 62, Toner 89)*
Levadia (0) 2 *(Bragin 50, Krasnopjorov 88)*   1432
TNS: Williams; Parry, Coathup, Edwards, Alexander, Roberts, Toner, Wright (Ward 78), Edge (Webster 83), Powell (Maloney 58).
Levadia: Pareiko; Staleliunas, Prins, Vinogradov, Kolbasenko, Rotskov, Olumets, Leitan (Tselnokov 70), Fenin (Krom 63), Bragin, Krasnopjorov.

FIRST QUALIFYING ROUND, SECOND LEG

19 JULY

Levadia (1) 4 *(Krom 49, Fenin 58, Tselnokov 60, Edwards 64 (og))*
TNS (0) 0   550
Levadia: Pareiko; Leitan, Staleliunas, Prins, Kolbasenko (Kirilov 76), Rotskov, Olumets (Leitan V 65), Fenin, Bragin, Krasnopjorov, Krom (Tselnokov 57).
TNS: Williams; Parry, Coathup (Ward 46), Evans S (McKenna 68), Edwards, Alexander, Roberts, Toner, Wright, Edge (Evans G 68), Maloney.

Linfield (1) 2 *(Ferguson 22 (pen), 72)*
Haka (0) 1 *(Kovacs 85 (pen))*   3587
Linfield: Mathers; Collier, Easton (McCracken 85), Marks, Murphy, Beatty, Morgan, Gorman, Ferguson (McShane 81), Kelly, Bailie.
Haka: Vilnrotter; Karjalainen, Salli, Nyyssonen (Pogioli 86), Ruhanen, Torkkeli (Reynders 77), Kovacs, Wilson, Okkonen, Kangaskorpi, Koskinen (Savolainen 76).

Shelbourne (0) 1 *(Haylock 67)*
Sloga (0) 1 *(Nuhiji 81 (pen))*   6511
Shelbourne: Williams; Heary, McCarthy, Scully, Baker D, Doolin (Prizeman 88), Haylock, Baker R, Fenlon, Hutchison, Keddy.
Sloga: Nikoloski; Jovanovski (I), Sterjovski, Zdravevski, Jovanovski (II), Ramadan (Bajram 78), Mustafi (Ramadani 79), Maznov, Beciri, Janevski (Presilski 58), Nuhiji.

SECOND QUALIFYING ROUND, FIRST LEG

26 JULY

Rangers (1) 4 *(Johnston 14, Albertz 62 (pen), Dodds 89, 90)*
Zalgiris Kaunas (1) 1 *(Zuta 26)*   45,974
Rangers: Klos; Ricksen, Vidmar (Miller 72), Ferguson B, Moore, Wilson (Dodds 46), Wallis, Reyna, Johnston, Johansson (McCann 46), Albertz.
Zalgiris Kaunas: Poskus; Dedura, Barasa, Juodeikis, Zelmikas, Kancelskis, Petrenko, Bezykornovas (Gelgota 71), Zuta (Danilicevas 65), Ksanavicius, Regelskis (Mika 54).

Shelbourne (0) 1 *(Foran 62)*   8642
Rosenborg (2) 3 *(Berg 2, Winsnes 14, Belsvik 89)*
Shelbourne: Williams; Heary, McCarthy, Scully, Baker D (Gilzean 77), Haylock (Byrne 46), Geoghegan (Foran 46), Baker R, Fenlon, Hutchison, Keddy.
Rosenborg: Arason; Hoftun, Basma, Strand (Hernes 80), Berg, Sorensen (Knutsen 90), Frode Johnsen (Belsvik 71), Skammelsrud, Winsnes, Bent Johnsen, Stensaas.

SECOND QUALIFYING ROUND, SECOND LEG

2 AUG

Rosenborg (0) 1 *(Berg 80)*
Shelbourne (0) 1 *(Foran 64)*   5470
Rosenborg: Arason; Hoftun, Basma, Strand (Svenning 88), Berg, Frode Johnsen (Belsvik 78), Skammelsrud, Knutsen (Hernes 64), Winsnes, Bent Johnsen, Stensaas.
Shelbourne: Williams; Heary, McCarthy, Scully, Baker D, Geoghegan (Foran 62), Baker R, Fenlon, Hutchison, Keddy, Byrne (Doolin 65).

Zalgiris Kaunas (0) 0
Rangers (0) 0   4000
Zalgiris Kaunas: Padimanskas; Kancelskis, Danilicevas (Velicka 62), Juodeikis, Bezykornovas (Puotkalis 82), Zuta, Mika, Regelskis (Gelgota 46), Ksanavicius, Dedura, Zelmikas.
Rangers: Klos; Ricksen (Kanchelskiks 75), Vidmar (Porrini 46), Ferguson B, Konterman, Amoruso, Wallis (Johnston 70), Reyna, Dodds, Kerimoglu, Van Bronckhorst.

THIRD QUALIFYING ROUND, FIRST LEG

9 AUG

Herfolge (0) 0   3523
Rangers (2) 3 *(Albertz 28, Wallace 31, Amoruso 60)*
Herfolge: Mikkelsen; Kastrup, Lykke, Lustu, Thomsen, Jacobsen, Hoyer, Schram (Heyde 80), Falck, Hermansen, Jensen.
Rangers: Klos; Porrini, Van Bronckhorst, Ferguson B, Konterman, Amoruso, Wallace (Miller 63), Reyna, Dodds (Kanchelskis 78), McCann (Johnston 60), Albertz.

Leeds United (1) 2 *(Smith 39, Harte 71 (pen))*
1860 Munich (0) 1 *(Agostino 90)*   33,769
Leeds United: Martyn; Kelly, Harte, Duberry, Radebe, Bakke, Dacourt, Smith, Bridges (Mills 79), Viduka, Bowyer.
1860 Munich: Hofmann; Cerny, Stranzl (Winkler 72), Mykland, Kurz, Zelic, Hassler, Votava, Max, Agostino, Bieroska (Passlack 46).

THIRD QUALIFYING ROUND, SECOND LEG

23 AUG

1860 Munich (0) 0
Leeds United (0) 1 *(Smith 46)*   45,000
1860 Munich: Hofmann; Cerny, Bieroska (Tyce 73), Mykland, Kurz, Stranzl, Borimirov (Beierle 75), Hassler, Max, Agostino, Passlack (Winkler 62).
Leeds United: Martyn; Kelly, Harte, Duberry, Woodgate, Mills, Jones (Evans 73), Radebe, Smith, Viduka, Bowyer (Huckerby 86).

Rangers (0) 3 *(Wallace 48, Johnston 78, Kanchelskis 89)*
Herfolge (0) 0   34,141
Rangers: Klos; Ricksen (Kanchelskis 46), Van Bronckhorst, Ferguson B, Konterman, Amoruso, Wallace, Reyna, Dodds (Johnston 73), McCann, Albertz (Vidmar 73).
Herfolge: Mikkelsen; Lustu, Jacobsen (Knudsen 62), Lykke, Hoyer, Falck, Jakobsen (Hermansen 70), Kastrup, Lubbes, Schramm (Jensen 79), Heyde.

CHAMPIONS LEAGUE

GROUP B

12 SEPT

Sparta Prague (0) 0
Arsenal (1) 1 *(Silvinho 33)* 17,656
Sparta Prague: Postulka; Mynar (Flachbart 85), Grygera, Obajdin, Bolf, Novotny J, Papousek (Prohaszka 79), Kincl (Siegl 61), Rosicky, Svoboda, Novotny P.
Arsenal: Seaman; Dixon, Silvinho, Vieira, Keown, Luzhny, Ljungberg (Vivas 80), Grimandi, Kanu, Henry (Wiltord 76), Pires.

20 SEPT

Arsenal (1) 3 *(Wiltord 45, Keown 85, 90)*
Shakhtjor Donetsk (2) 2 *(Bakharev 26, Vorobei 29)* 33,922
Arsenal: Seaman; Dixon, Silvinho, Vieira, Keown, Luzhny, Ljungberg (Bergkamp 65), Grimandi, Kanu, Henry, Pires (Wiltord 32).
Shakhtjor Donetsk: Virt; Starostyak, Gleveckas, Popov, Shevchuk, Zubov, Tymoschuk, Bakharev (Byelik 68), Abramov (Kriventsov 57), Atelkin (Kovalyov 77), Vorobei.

27 SEPT

Arsenal (1) 2 *(Ljungberg 43, 56)*
Lazio (0) 0 34,521
Arsenal: Seaman; Luzhny, Silvinho, Vieira, Keown, Adams, Parlour, Kanu, Henry (Wiltord 84), Bergkamp (Vivas 78), Ljungberg.
Lazio: Marchegiani; Negro, Nesta, Mihajlovic, Pancaro, Stankovic (Lombardo 46) (Ravanelli 73), Veron, Simeone, Nedved, Claudio Lopez, Inzaghi (Salas 57).

17 OCT

Lazio (1) 1 *(Nedved 24)*
Arsenal (0) 1 *(Pires 88)* 42,500
Lazio: Peruzzi; Negro, Nesta, Mihajlovic, Pancaro, Stankovic (Claudio Lopez 46), Veron, Simeone, Nedved, Inzaghi (Crespo 68), Salas.
Arsenal: Lukic; Dixon, Silvinho, Vieira, Keown, Luzhny, Parlour (Pires 60), Grimandi (Lauren 69), Kanu, Henry, Ljungberg (Wiltord 74).

25 OCT

Arsenal (3) 4 *(Parlour 5, Lauren 7, Dixon 35, Kanu 52)*
Sparta Prague (1) 2 *(Labant 41 (pen), Rosicky 90)* 34,497
Arsenal: Seaman; Dixon, Silvinho (Cole 46), Vieira, Luzhny, Vivas, Parlour, Lauren, Kanu, Henry (Wiltord 70), Pires (Bergkamp 63).
Sparta Prague: Postulka; Hornak, Labant, Sionko (Papousek 85), Novotny, Bolf, Hasek, Jarosik, Kinci, Jun (Mynar 46), Rosicky.

7 NOV

Shakhtjor Donetsk (1) 3 *(Atelkin 35, Vorobei 57, Bielik 66)*
Arsenal (0) 0 30,000
Shakhtjor Donetsk: Starostyak; Okoronkyo, Gleveckas, Popov, Zubov, Bakharev, Tymoschuk, Abramov (Aliuta 77), Atelkin (Bielik 51), Vorobei (Savu 86).
Arsenal: Taylor; Dixon, Cole, Vivas, Keown, Upson, Parlour (Vernazza 72), Lauren, Kanu, Henry (Ljungberg 62), Wiltord.

GROUP D

12 SEPT

Rangers (3) 5 *(Mols 9, De Boer 19, Albertz 29, Van Bronckhorst 71, Dodds 85)*
Sturm Graz (0) 0 49,317
Rangers: Klos; Reyna, Numan, Ferguson B, Konterman, Amoruso, de Boer (McCann 73), Mols (Dodds 59), Johnston (Kanchelskis 76), Albertz, Van Bronckhorst.
Sturm Graz: Schicklgruber; Strafner, Foda, Mamedov, Schopp, Schupp, Fleurquin, Prilasnig, Yuran (Szabics 79), Reinmayr (Mahlich 79), Korsos.

20 SEPT

Monaco (0) 0
Rangers (1) 1 *(Van Bronckhorst 8)* 18,000
Monaco: Porato; Irles, Rodriguez, Marquez, Abidal, Bonnal (Gravelaine 68), Giuly, Djetou, Riise (Prso 46), Nonda (Courville 83), Simone.
Rangers: Klos; Reyna (Vidmar 80), Numan, Tugay, Konterman, Amoruso, de Boer, Ferguson B, Johnston, Mols (McCann 57), Van Bronckhorst.

27 SEPT

Galatasaray (0) 3 *(Bulent A 51, Hakan Unsal 57, Jardel 70)*
Rangers (0) 2 *(Kanchelskis 72, Van Bronckhorst 90)* 22,000
Galatasaray: Taffarel; Fatih, Bulent A, Popescu, Hakan Unsal, Umit, Akin, Ergun, Sas (Ahmet 90), Belozoglu (Faruk 75), Jardel.
Rangers: Klos; Reyna, Numan, Tugay, Konterman, Amoruso, de Boer, Ferguson B, Johnston (Kanchelskis 59), Mols (Dodds 66), Van Bronckhorst.

17 OCT

Rangers (0) 0
Galatasaray (0) 0 49,603
Rangers: Klos; Reyna, Vidmar (Wilson 71), Tugay, Konterman, Porrini, Kanchelskis, Ferguson B, Lovenkrands (McCann 55), Albertz, de Boer.
Galatasaray: Taffarel; Fatih, Bulent, Popescu, Hakan Unsal, Umit, Akin, Ergun, Hagi (Okan 71), Sas, Jardel (Marcio 86).

25 OCT

Sturm Graz (1) 2 *(Yuran 20, Prilasnig 90)*
Rangers (0) 0 15,400
Sturm Graz: Schiklgruber; Neukirchner, Popovic, Korsos, Mamedov, Schupp, Fleurquin, Prilasnig, Reinmayr (Minavand 46), Kocijan, Yuran (Strafner 64).
Rangers: Christiansen; Kanchelskis, Numan, Amoruso, Porrini (Negri 78), Konterman, Ferguson B, Tugay, de Boer, Wallace (Dodds 73), Van Bronckhorst (McCann 55).

7 NOV

Rangers (1) 2 *(Miller 3, Mols 51)*
Monaco (1) 2 *(Costinha 38, Simone 78)* 50,228
Rangers: Christiansen; Ricksen, Numan, Amoruso, Wilson, Vidmar, Ferguson B, Miller, Mols (Tugay 55), Albertz (McCann 88), de Boer (Wallace 77).
Monaco: Porato; Costinha, Christanval, Irles, Contreras, Giuly (Eloi 68), Dabo, Bonnal, Gallardo (Gravelaine 25), Simone, Nonda (Prso 57).

GROUP G

13 SEPT

Manchester United (3) 5 *(Cole 15, 49, 71, Irwin 30 (pen), Sheringham 41)*
Anderlecht (0) 1 *(Koller 54)* 62,739
Manchester United: Barthez; Irwin (Neville P 69), Silvestre, Johnsen, Keane, Neville G, Beckham, Scholes, Cole (Yorke 73), Sheringham, Giggs (Solskjaer 59).
Anderlecht: De Wilde; Crasson, Dheedene, Van Diemen, Staelens, De Boeck, Vanderhaeghe, Baseggio, Koller, Radzinski (Youla 59), Goor (Ilic 59).

19 SEPT

Dynamo Kiev (0) 0
Manchester United (0) 0 48,432
Dynamo Kiev: Shovkovskyi; Dmitrulin (Bodnar 83), Vashchuk, Golovko, Nesmachnyi, Khatskevich, Bialkevich, Gusin (Fedorov 86), Kaladze, Shatskikh, Demetradze (Kuzmichev 68).
Manchester United: Van der Gouw; Irwin, Silvestre, Johnsen, Keane, Neville G, Beckham, Butt, Cole (Solskjaer 78), Yorke (Sheringham 67), Giggs.

26 SEPT

PSV Eindhoven (2) 3 *(Bouma 17, Van Bommel 38, Kezman 64)*
Manchester United (1) 1 *(Scholes 2 (pen))*   33,500
PSV Eindhoven: Waterreus; Van der Weerden, Nikiforov, Hofland, Heintze, Van der Doelen (Lucius 77), Vogel, Van Bommel, Bouma (Rommedahl 79), Kezman (Kolkka 83), Bruggink.
Manchester United: Van der Gouw; Neville P, Silvestre (Wallwork 71), Brown, Keane, Neville G, Greening (Giggs 71), Butt, Solskjaer, Yorke, Scholes (Beckham 71).

18 OCT

Manchester United (1) 3 *(Sheringham 9, Scholes 82, Yorke 87)*
PSV Eindhoven (0) 1 *(Van Bommel 76)*   66,313
Manchester United: Barthez; Irwin (Brown 79), Silvestre, Johnsen, Keane, Neville G, Beckham (Butt 87), Scholes, Cole, Sheringham (Yorke 73), Giggs.
PSV Eindhoven: Waterreus; Van der Weerden, Nikiforov, Hofland, Heintze, Van der Doelen (De Jong 73), Vogel, Van Bommel, Ramzi (Kolkka 65), Kezman, Bruggink (Lucius 28).

24 OCT

Anderlecht (2) 2 *(Radzinski 15, 34)*
Manchester United (1) 1 *(Irwin 36 pen)*   27,500
Anderlecht: De Wilde; Crasson, Dheedene, Vanderhaeghe, Staelens, De Boeck, Stoica (Oyen 80), Koller, Radzinski (Dindane 90), Baseggio, Goor.
Manchester United: Barthez; Irwin (Solskjaer 78), Silvestre (Brown 62), Neville G, Scholes, Johnsen, Beckham, Butt, Cole, Yorke, Giggs.

8 NOV

Manchester United (1) 1 *(Sheringham 18)*
Dynamo Kiev (0) 0   66,776
Manchester United: Barthez; Neville P, Irwin, Brown, Keane, Neville G, Beckham, Butt, Cole, Sheringham (Yorke 74), Giggs (Fortune 34) (Silvestre 88).
Dynamo Kiev: Shovkovskyi; Bodnar, Gerasimenko (Kuzmichev 62), Golovko (Fedorov 76), Vaskuk, Nesmachnyi, Khatskevich, Kaladze, Lysytsky, Shatskikh (Demetradze 67), Bialkevich.

GROUP H

13 SEPT

Barcelona (2) 4 *(Rivaldo 10, De Boer 20, Kluivert 75, 84)*
Leeds United (0) 0   85,000
Barcelona: Dutruel; Abelardo, Frank de Boer, Sergi, Gerard, Cocu (Petit 50), Simao, Rivaldo (Alfonso 73), Kluivert, Dani (De La Pena 64), Overmars.
Leeds United: Martyn; Kelly, Harte, Duberry, Radebe (Hay 89), Mills, Dacourt, Bowyer, Smith, Bridges, McPhail (Hackworth 73), Matteo.

19 SEPT

Leeds United (0) 1 *(Bowyer 89)*
AC Milan (0) 0   35,398
Leeds United: Martyn; Kelly, Harte, Duberry, Mills, Bakke, Dacourt, Smith, Bridges, Bowyer, Matteo.
AC Milan: Dida; Chamot, Costacurta, Maldini, Helveg, Albertini, Coco, Giunti (Saudati 90), Guglielminpietro (De Ascentis 58), Bierhoff, Shevchenko.

26 SEPT

Leeds United (3) 6 *(Bowyer 7, 90, Viduka 11, Matteo 22, Bakke 65, Huckerby 90)*
Besiktas (0) 0   34,485
Leeds United: Martyn; Kelly, Harte, Mills, Radebe, Bakke, Dacourt (McPhail 74), Smith (Huckerby 79), Viduka, Bowyer.
Besiktas: Shorunmu; Karhan, Erman (Rahim 81), Khlestov, Ibrahim (Mehmet 72), Tayfur, Munch, Umit, Nihat, Ahmet, Nouma (Fazli 71).

18 OCT

Besiktas (0) 0
Leeds United (0) 0   20,000
Besiktas: Shorunmu; Ali Eren (Murat 62), Umit, Tayfur, Khlestov, Karhan, Mehmet (Ibrahim 80), Yasin, Munch, Ahmet (Ayhan 80), Nihat.
Leeds United: Robinson; Kelly, Harte, Woodgate, Mills, Bakke, Burns, Bowyer, Bridges (Huckerby 27) (McPhail 85), Viduka, Matteo.

24 OCT

Leeds United (1) 1 *(Bowyer 5)*
Barcelona (0) 1 *(Rivaldo 90)*   36,721
Leeds United: Robinson; Kelly, Harte, Woodgate, Mills, Bakke, Dacourt (Burns 74), Bowyer, Smith, Viduka, Matteo.
Barcelona: Dutruel; Puyol, Abelardo, Reiziger (Gerard 67), Zavi, Cocu, Simao, Alfonso, Rivaldo, Sergi, Luis Enrique (Dani 67).

8 NOV

AC Milan (0) 1 *(Serginho 68)*
Leeds United (1) 1 *(Matteo 45)*   52,289
AC Milan: Dida; Roque Junior, Chamot, Maldini, Helveg, Gattuso, Albertini, Serginho, Leonardo (Boban 53), Bierhoff, Shevchenko.
Leeds United: Robinson; Kelly, Harte, Mills, Radebe, Bakke, Dacourt, Bowyer, Smith, Viduka, Matteo.

SECOND STAGE

21 NOV

GROUP A

Manchester United (0) 3 *(Sheringham 48, Scholes 81, 90)*
Panathinaikos (0) 1 *(Karagounis 64)*   65,024
Manchester United: Barthez; Neville P, Silvestre, Brown, Keane, Neville G, Beckham, Butt, Yorke, Sheringham, Scholes.
Panathinaikos: Nikopolidis; Henriksen, Goumas, Vokolos, Fyssas, Basinas, Galetto, Liberopoulos, Karagounis (Vlaovic 67), Warzycha (Kiassos 75), Sypniewski (Olivares 78).

6 DEC

Sturm Graz (0) 0   16,500
Manchester United (1) 2 *(Scholes 17, Giggs 89)*
Sturm Graz: Sidorczuk; Neukirchner (Strafner 82), Mamedov (Mahlich 85), Popovic, Schopp, Korsos (Reinmayr 70), Prilasnig, Fleurquin, Minavand, Vastic, Kocijan.
Manchester United: Barthez; Irwin (Neville P 88), Silvestre, Brown, Keane, Neville G, Beckham, Butt (Giggs 80), Yorke (Solskjaer 88), Sheringham, Scholes.

14 FEB

Valencia (0) 0
Manchester United (0) 0   49,451
Valencia: Canizares; Angloma, Ayala, Pellegrino, Carboni, Angulo, Mendieta, Baraja, Gonzalez, Carew (Alonzo 75), Aimar.
Manchester United: Barthez; Neville G, Silvestre, Brown, Keane, Stam, Beckham (Butt 75), Scholes, Cole (Solskjaer 85), Sheringham, Giggs.

20 FEB

Manchester United (1) 1 *(Cole 12)*
Valencia (0) 1 *(Brown 88 (og))*   66,715
Manchester United: Barthez; Neville G, Silvestre, Brown, Keane, Stam, Beckham, Scholes, Cole, Sheringham (Solskjaer 63), Giggs (Butt 18).
Valencia: Canizares; Angloma, Ayala, Pellegrino, Carboni, Angulo (Sanchez 65), Mendieta, Baraja, Gonzalez (Vicente 75), Aimar (Albelda 89), Carew.

7 MAR

Panathinaikos (1) 1 *(Seitaridis 25)*

Manchester United (0) 1 *(Scholes 90)*   27,230

Panathinaikos: Nikopolidis; Seitaridis, Goumas, Henriksen, Fyssas, Basinas (Pflipsen 84), Boateng, Karagounis, Olivares, Vlaovic (Galetto 58), Liberopoulos (Warzycha 66).
Manchester United: Barthez; Neville G, Silvestre (Chadwick 64), Brown, Keane, Stam, Beckham, Neville P (Sheringham 78), Cole (Solskjaer 78), Yorke, Scholes.

13 MAR

Manchester United (2) 3 *(Butt 5, Sheringham 20, Keane 87)*

Sturm Graz (0) 0   66,404

Manchester United: Barthez; Irwin, Silvestre, Neville G, Keane, Stam, Chadwick, Butt, Solskjaer, Sheringham, Scholes (Greening 74).
Sturm Graz: Sidorczuk; Neukirchner, Ibertsberger, Korsos, Schopp, Schupp (Martens 64), Mahlich (Hlinka 46), Fleurquin, Minavand (Szabics 46), Vastic, Haas.

22 NOV

GROUP C

Spartak Moscow (1) 4 *(Marcao 29, 51, Titov 77, Robson 82)*

Arsenal (1) 1 *(Silvinho 2)*   75,000

Spartak Moscow: Filimonov; Tchuise, Ananko (Bushmanov 87), Parfenov, Kovtun, Baranov, Bulatov, Titov, Bezrodni, Robson, Marcao.
Arsenal: Manninger; Luzhny, Silvinho, Vivas, Keown, Adams, Parlour, Ljungberg, Kanu (Wiltord 66), Henry, Pires (Lauren 70).

5 DEC

Arsenal (1) 2 *(Henry 4, Kanu 55)*

Bayern Munich (0) 2 *(Tarnat 56, Scholl 66)*   35,318

Arsenal: Manninger; Luzhny (Lauren 82), Cole, Vieira, Keown, Adams, Ljungberg, Grimandi, Kanu, Henry, Pires (Wiltord 77).
Bayern Munich: Kahn; Linke, Sforza, Kuffour, Sagnol (Sergio 46), Jeremies, Effenberg, Tarnat, Salihamidzic, Elber, Scholl (Zickler 83).

13 FEB

Lyon (0) 0

Arsenal (0) 1 *(Henry 58)*   39,541

Lyon: Coupet; Deflandre, Edmilson, Muller, Brechet, Dhorasoo (Govou 75), Violeau (Malbranque 75), Foe, Laigle (Delmotte 83), Anderson, Marlet.
Arsenal: Seaman; Dixon, Cole, Vieira, Grimandi, Adams, Parlour, Lauren, Kanu (Vivas 89), Henry, Pires (Ljungberg 68).

21 FEB

Arsenal (1) 1 *(Bergkamp 33)*

Lyon (0) 1 *(Edmilson 90)*   34,303

Arsenal: Seaman; Dixon, Cole, Vieira, Grimandi, Luzhny, Parlour, Ljungberg, Henry (Kanu 83), Bergkamp (Wiltord 71), Pires (Lauren 80).
Lyon: Coupet; Deflandre, Edmilson, Muller, Brechet, Govou (Loko 78), Foe (Linares 66), Violeau, Laigle (Dhorasoo 66), Anderson, Marlet.

6 MAR

Arsenal (0) 1 *(Henry 82)*

Spartak Moscow (0) 0   35,196

Arsenal: Seaman; Dixon, Cole, Vieira, Grimandi, Adams, Pires (Wiltord 71), Lauren, Henry (Vivas 90), Bergkamp (Kanu 71), Ljungberg.
Spartak Moscow: Filimonov; Tchuise, Parfenov, Mitreski, Kovtun, Baranov, Bulatov, Titov (Pisarev 58), Kalynychenko, Riismetov, Robson.

14 MAR

Bayern Munich (1) 1 *(Elber 10)*

Arsenal (0) 0   58,000

Bayern Munich: Kahn; Kuffour, Andersson, Linke, Lizarazu, Salihamidzic, Jeremies, Fink, Scholl (Wiesinger 90), Elber (Tarnat 90), Jancker.
Arsenal: Seaman; Dixon, Cole, Vieira, Grimandi, Adams, Pires (Silvinho 76), Lauren, Kanu (Wiltord 61), Henry, Ljungberg (Parlour 61).

22 NOV

GROUP D

Leeds United (0) 0

Real Madrid (0) 2 *(Hierro 66, Raul 68)*   36,794

Leeds United: Robinson; Mills, Harte, Woodgate, Radebe, Burns (Wilcox), Kelly, Bowyer, Smith, Viduka, Matteo.
Real Madrid: Casillas; Geremi, Campo, Hierro, Roberto Carlos, Makelele, Helguera, Figo (Savio 83), Guti (Munitis 88), McManaman, Raul.

5 DEC

Lazio (0) 0

Leeds United (0) 1 *(Smith 80)*   42,450

Lazio: Peruzzi; Pancaro, Nesta, Fernando Couto, Favalli, Lombardo (Gottardi 81), Veron (Ravanelli 71), Simeone, Nedved, Crespo, Salas.
Leeds United: Robinson; Kelly, Matteo, Woodgate, Radebe, Bakke, Dacourt, Bowyer, Smith, Viduka, Wilcox (Kewell 76).

13 FEB

Leeds United (0) 2 *(Harte 74, Bowyer 86)*

Anderlecht (0) 1 *(Stoica 65)*   36,064

Leeds United: Martyn; Mills, Harte, Batty, Radebe, Ferdinand, Dacourt (Bakke 73), Bowyer, Smith, Viduka, Matteo (Kewell 53).
Anderlecht: Milojevic; Crasson, De Boeck, Ilic, Dheedene, Stoica, Baseggio, Vanderhaeghe, Goor, Koller, Radzinski.

21 FEB

Anderlecht (0) 1 *(Koller 76)*

Leeds United (3) 4 *(Smith 13, 38, Viduka 35, Harte 81 (pen))*   28,000

Anderlecht: Milojevic; Crasson, De Boeck, Ilic (Dindane 38), Dheedene, Stoica, Baseggio, Vanderhaeghe, Goor, Koller, Radzinski.
Leeds United: Martyn; Mills, Harte, Ferdinand, Radebe, Bakke, Dacourt, Batty, Smith, Viduka (Kewell 83), Matteo.

6 MAR

Real Madrid (2) 3 *(Raul 7, 59, Figo 41)*

Leeds United (1) 2 *(Smith 6, Viduka 54)*   40,000

Real Madrid: Cesar; Geremi, Hierro, Karanka, Solari, Figo (Rivera 90), Makelele (Savio 86), Celades, McManaman, Raul, Morientes (Munitis 76).
Leeds United: Martyn; Harte, Matteo, Ferdinand, Radebe (Kelly 65), Bakke (Wilcox 85), Dacourt, Batty, Smith, Viduka, Kewell.

14 MAR

Leeds United (2) 3 *(Bowyer 28, Wilcox 43, Viduka 62)*

Lazio (2) 3 *(Ravanelli 21, Mihajlovic 29 (pen), 90)* 36,741

Leeds United: Robinson; Kelly, Harte, Burns, Mills, Matteo, Maybury (Batty 90), Bowyer, Viduka (Hackworth 63), Kewell, Wilcox.
Lazio: Marchegiani; Colonnese, Fernando Couto, Mihajlovic, Pesaresi, Castroman (Ruggiu 88), Baronio, Stankovic, Nedved, Lopez (Salas 72), Ravanelli.

QUARTER-FINALS, FIRST LEG

3 APR

Manchester United (0) 0
Bayern Munich (0) 1 *(Sergio 86)*   66,584
Manchester United: Barthez; Neville G, Silvestre, Brown, Keane, Stam, Beckham (Yorke 86), Scholes, Cole, Solskjaer, Giggs.
Bayern Munich: Kahn; Kuffour, Andersson, Linke, Salihamidzic, Jeremies, Effenberg, Lizarazu, Scholl (Sergio 76), Jancker (Zickler 68), Elber.

4 APR

Arsenal (0) 2 *(Henry 58, Parlour 60)*
Valencia (1) 1 *(Ayala 41)*   35,104
Arsenal: Seaman; Dixon, Cole, Vieira, Keown, Adams, Parlour, Ljungberg (Wiltord 46), Kanu (Lauren 84), Henry, Pires.
Valencia: Canizares; Angloma, Ayala, Pellegrino, Carboni, Mendieta (Bicente 89), Baraja, Aimar (Angulo 68), Gonzalez, Sanchez, Carew.

Leeds United (1) 3 *(Harte 27, Smith 51, Ferdinand 66)*
La Coruna (0) 0   35,508
Leeds United: Martyn; Mills, Harte, Batty, Ferdinand, Matteo, Dacourt, Bowyer, Smith, Viduka, Kewell (Wilcox 83).
La Coruna: Molina; Pablo, Naybet, Cesar, Romero, Scaloni (Tristan 71), Emerson, Duscher (Valeron 54), Fran (Pandiani 71), Djalminha, Makaay.

QUARTER-FINALS, SECOND LEG

17 APR

La Coruna (1) 2 *(Djalminha 9 (pen), Tristan 73)*
Leeds United (0) 0   35,600
La Coruna: Molina; Pablo, Donato, Naybet, Romeo, Victor (Tristan 62), Djalminha (Valeron 69), Silva, Fran, Pandiani (Flores 79), Makaay.
Leeds United: Martyn; Mills, Harte, Batty, Ferdinand, Matteo, Dacourt, Bowyer, Smith, Viduka, Kewell (Bakke 77).

Valencia (0) 1 *(Carew 75)*
Arsenal (0) 0   47,700
Valencia: Canizares; Angloma, Ayala (Djukic 49), Pellegrino, Carboni, Angulo (Aimar 66), Mendieta, Baraja, Vicente, Sanchez (Zahovic 72), Carew.
Arsenal: Seaman; Dixon, Cole, Vieira, Keown, Adams, Parlour (Ljungberg 46), Lauren, Wiltord, Henry, Pires (Kanu 76).

18 APR

Bayern Munich (2) 2 *(Elber 5, Scholl 40)*
Manchester United (0) 1 *(Giggs 49)*   60,000
Bayern Munich: Kahn; Kuffour, Andersson, Linke, Sagnol, Jeremies, Effenberg, Tarnat, Scholl (Sergio 88), Jancker (Zickler 35), Elber (Santa Cruz 63).
Manchester United: Barthez; Neville G, Silvestre, Brown (Chadwick 84), Keane, Stam, Scholes, Butt (Solskjaer 77), Cole, Yorke (Sheringham 65), Giggs.

SEMI-FINALS, FIRST LEG

2 MAY

Leeds United (0) 0
Valencia (0) 0   36,437
Leeds United: Martyn; Mills, Harte, Batty, Ferdinand, Matteo, Dacourt, Bowyer, Smith, Viduka, Kewell.
Valencia: Canizares; Angloma, Ayala, Pellegrino, Carboni, Mendieta, Baraja, Albelda, Gonzalez (Vicente 89), Carew, Sanchez (Zahovic 66).

SEMI-FINALS, SECOND LEG

8 MAY

Valencia (1) 3 *(Sanchez 15, 46, Mendieta 52)*
Leeds United (0) 0   53,000
Valencia: Canizares; Angloma, Aurelio, Albelda, Ayala, Pellegrino, Mendieta (Angulo 73), Aimar (Deschamps 69), Carew, Sanchez, Gonzalez (Vicente 64).
Leeds United: Martyn; Mills, Harte, Bakke, Ferdinand, Matteo, Dacourt, Batty, Smith, Viduka, Kewell.

Leeds United's valiant European Cup venture eventually failed against Valencia, but here Mark Viduka (white shirt) gets ahead of Mauricio Pellegrino. (ASP)

EUROPEAN CUP-WINNERS' CUP

EUROPEAN CUP-WINNERS' CUP FINALS 1961–99

Year	Winners		Runners-up		Venue	Attendance	Referee
1961	Fiorentina	2	Rangers	0 *(1st Leg)*	Glasgow	80,000	Steiner (A)
	Fiorentina	2	Rangers	1 *(2nd Leg)*	Florence	50,000	Hernadi (H)
1962	Atletico Madrid	1	Fiorentina	1	Glasgow	27,389	Wharton (S)
Replay	Atletico Madrid	3	Fiorentina	0	Stuttgart	38,000	Tschenscher (WG)
1963	Tottenham Hotspur	5	Atletico Madrid	1	Rotterdam	49,000	Van Leuwen (Ho)
1964	Sporting Lisbon	3	MTK Budapest	3 *(aet)*	Brussels	3000	Van Nuffel (Bel)
Replay	Sporting Lisbon	1	MTK Budapest	0	Antwerp	19,000	Versyp (Bel)
1965	West Ham U	2	Munich 1860	0	Wembley	100,000	Szolt (H)
1966	Borussia Dortmund	2	Liverpool	1 *(aet)*	Glasgow	41,657	Schwinte (F)
1967	Bayern Munich	1	Rangers	0 *(aet)*	Nuremberg	69,480	Lo Bello (I)
1968	AC Milan	2	Hamburg	0	Rotterdam	53,000	Ortiz (Sp)
1969	Slovan Bratislava	3	Barcelona	2	Basle	19,000	Van Ravens (Ho)
1970	Manchester C	2	Gornik Zabrze	1	Vienna	8,000	Schiller (A)
1971	Chelsea	1	Real Madrid	1 *(aet)*	Athens	42,000	Scheurer (Sw)
Replay	Chelsea	2	Real Madrid	1 *(aet)*	Athens	35,000	Bucheli (Sw)
1972	Rangers	3	Moscow Dynamo	2	Barcelona	24,000	Ortiz (Sp)
1973	AC Milan	1	Leeds U	0	Salonika	45,000	Mihas (Gr)
1974	Magdeburg	2	AC Milan	0	Rotterdam	4000	Van Gemert (Ho)
1975	Dynamo Kiev	3	Ferencvaros	0	Basle	13,000	Davidson (S)
1976	Anderlecht	4	West Ham U	2	Brussels	58,000	Wurtz (F)
1977	Hamburg	2	Anderlecht	0	Amsterdam	65,000	Partridge (E)
1978	Anderlecht	4	Austria/WAC	0	Paris	48,679	Adlinger (WG)
1979	Barcelona	4	Fortuna Dusseldorf	3 *(aet)*	Basle	58,000	Palotai (H)
1980	Valencia	0	Arsenal	0	Brussels	36,000	Christov (Cz)
	(aet; Valencia won 5-4 on penalties)						
1981	Dynamo Tbilisi	2	Carl Zeiss Jena	1	Dusseldorf	9000	Lattanzi (I)
1982	Barcelona	2	Standard Liege	1	Barcelona	100,000	Eschweiler (WG)
1983	Aberdeen	2	Real Madrid	1 *(aet)*	Gothenburg	17,804	Menegali (I)
1984	Juventus	2	Porto	1	Basle	60,000	Prokop (EG)
1985	Everton	3	Rapid Vienna	1	Rotterdam	50,000	Casarin (I)
1986	Dynamo Kiev	3	Atletico Madrid	0	Lyon	39,300	Wohrer (A)
1987	Ajax	1	Lokomotiv Leipzig	0	Athens	35,000	Agnolin (I)
1988	Mechelen	1	Ajax	0	Strasbourg	39,446	Pauly (WG)
1989	Barcelona	2	Sampdoria	0	Berne	45,000	Courtney (E)
1990	Sampdoria	2	Anderlecht	0	Gothenburg	20,103	Galler (Sw)
1991	Manchester U	2	Barcelona	1	Rotterdam	42,000	Karlsson (Se)
1992	Werder Bremen	2	Monaco	0	Lisbon	16,000	D'Elia (I)
1993	Parma	3	Antwerp	1	Wembley	37,393	Assenmacher (G)
1994	Arsenal	1	Parma	0	Copenhagen	33,765	Krondl (Czr)
1995	Zaragoza	2	Arsenal	1	Paris	42,424	Ceccarini (I)
1996	Paris St Germain	1	Rapid Vienna	0	Brussels	37,500	Pairetto (I)
1997	Barcelona	1	Paris St Germain	0	Rotterdam	45,000	Merk (G)
1998	Chelsea	1	Stuttgart	0	Stockholm	30,216	Braschi (I)
1999	Lazio	2	Mallorca	1	Villa Park	33,021	Benko (A)

INTER-CITIES FAIRS & UEFA CUP

FAIRS CUP FINALS 1958–71
(Winners in italics)

Year	First Leg	Attendance	Second Leg	Attendance
1958	London 2 Barcelona 2	45,466	*Barcelona* 6 London 0	62,000
1960	Birmingham C 0 Barcelona 0	40,500	*Barcelona* 4 Birmingham C 1	70,000
1961	Birmingham C 2 Roma 2	21,005	*Roma* 2 Birmingham C 0	60,000
1962	Valencia 6 Barcelona 2	65,000	Barcelona 1 *Valencia* 1	60,000
1963	Dynamo Zagreb 1 Valencia 2	40,000	*Valencia* 2 Dynamo Zagreb 0	55,000
1964	*Zaragoza* 2 Valencia 1	50,000	(in Barcelona)	
1965	*Ferencvaros* 1 Juventus 0	25,000	(in Turin)	
1966	Barcelona 0 Zaragoza 1	70,000	Zaragoza 2 *Barcelona* 4	70,000
1967	Dynamo Zagreb 2 Leeds U 0	40,000	Leeds U 0 *Dynamo Zagreb* 0	35,604
1968	Leeds U 1 Ferencvaros 0	25,368	Ferencvaros 0 *Leeds U* 0	70,000
1969	Newcastle U 3 Ujpest Dozsa 0	60,000	Ujpest Dozsa 2 *Newcastle U* 3	37,000
1970	Anderlecht 3 Arsenal 1	37,000	*Arsenal* 3 Anderlecht 0	51,612
1971	Juventus 0 Leeds U 0 *(abandoned 51 minutes)*	42,000		
	Juventus 2 Leeds U 2	42,000	*Leeds U* 1* Juventus 1	42,483

UEFA CUP FINALS 1972–97
(Winners in italics)

Year	First Leg	Attendance	Second Leg	Attendance
1972	Wolverhampton W 1 Tottenham H 2	45,000	*Tottenham H* 1 Wolverhampton W 1	48,000
1973	Liverpool 0 Moenchengladbach 0			
	(abandoned 27 minutes)	44,967		
	Liverpool 3 Moenchengladbach 0	41,169	Moenchengladbach 2 *Liverpool* 0	35,000
1974	Tottenham H 2 Feyenoord 2	46,281	*Feyenoord* 2 Tottenham H 0	68,000
1975	Moenchengladbach 0 Twente 0	45,000	Twente 1 *Moenchengladbach* 5	24,500
1976	Liverpool 3 FC Brugge 2	56,000	FC Brugge 1 *Liverpool* 1	32,000
1977	Juventus 1 Athletic Bilbao 0	75,000	Athletic Bilbao 2 *Juventus* 1*	43,000
1978	Bastia 0 PSV Eindhoven 0	15,000	*PSV Eindhoven* 3 Bastia 0	27,000
1979	Red Star Belgrade 1 Moenchengladbach 1	87,500	*Moenchengladbach* 1 Red Star Belgrade 0	45,000
1980	Moenchengladbach 3 Eintracht Frankfurt 2	25,000	*Eintracht Frankfurt* 1* Moenchengladbach 0	60,000
1981	Ipswich T 3 AZ 67 Alkmaar 0	27,532	AZ 67 Alkmaar 4 *Ipswich T* 2	28,500
1982	Gothenburg 1 Hamburg 0	42,548	Hamburg 0 *Gothenburg* 3	60,000
1983	Anderlecht 1 Benfica 0	45,000	Benfica 1 *Anderlecht* 1	80,000
1984	Anderlecht 1 Tottenham H 1	40,000	*Tottenham H* 1[1] Anderlecht 1	46,258
1985	Videoton 0 Real Madrid 3	30,000	*Real Madrid* 0 Videoton 1	98,300
1986	Real Madrid 5 Cologne 1	80,000	Cologne 2 *Real Madrid* 0	15,000
1987	Gothenburg 1 Dundee U 0	50,023	Dundee U 1 *Gothenburg* 1	20,911
1988	Espanol 3 Bayer Leverkusen 0	42,000	*Bayer Leverkusen* 3[2] Espanol 0	22,000
1989	Napoli 2 Stuttgart 1	83,000	Stuttgart 3 *Napoli* 3	67,000
1990	Juventus 3 Fiorentina 1	45,000	Fiorentina 0 *Juventus* 0	32,000
1991	Internazionale 2 Roma 0	68,887	Roma 1 *Internazionale* 0	70,901
1992	Torino 2 Ajax 2	65,377	*Ajax* 0* Torino 0	40,000
1993	Borussia Dortmund 1 Juventus 3	37,000	*Juventus* 3 Borussia Dortmund 0	62,781
1994	Salzburg 0 Internazionale 1	47,500	*Internazionale* 1 Salzburg 0	80,326
1995	Parma 1 Juventus 0	23,000	Juventus 1 *Parma* 1	80,750
1996	Bayern Munich 2 Bordeaux 0	62,000	Bordeaux 1 *Bayern Munich* 3	36,000
1997	Schalke 1 Internazionale 0	56,824	Internazionale 1 *Schalke* 0[3]	81,670

UEFA CUP FINALS 1998–2001

Year	Winners	Runners-up	Venue	Attendance	Referee
1998	Internazionale 3	Lazio 0	Paris	42,938	Nieto (Sp)
1999	Parma 3	Marseille 0	Moscow	61,000	Dallas (S)
2000	Galatasaray 0	Arsenal 0	Copenhagen	38,919	Nieto (Sp)
(aet; Galatasaray won 4-1 on penalties)					
2001	Liverpool 5¶	Alaves 4	Dortmund	65,000	Veissiere (F)

*won on away goals   [1]*Tottenham H won 4-3 on penalties aet*   [2]*Bayer Leverkusen won 3-2 on penalties aet*
[3]*Schalke won 4-1 on penalties aet*   ¶*won on sudden death*

UEFA CUP 2000–2001

QUALIFYING ROUND, FIRST LEG

AB Copenhagen (2) 8 *(Michaelsen 32, 69, Johansen M 45, Daugaard 47, Sule 57, 58, Rasmussen 67, Bjur 68)*, B36 Torshavn (0) 0   4098
Aberdeen (0) 1 *(Winters 62)*, Bohemians (0) 2 *(Maher 82, Molloy 90 (pen))*   13,638
AIK Stockholm (1) 1 *(Tjernstrom 27)*, Gomel (0) 0   7746
Amica (1) 3 *(Krysztalovicz 33, Davidovski 79, Krol 87)*, Vaduz (0) 0   2000
Ararat Erevan (0) 2 *(Migoyan 53 (pen), Mesropyan 90)*, Kosice (1) 3 *(Barsegyan 15 (og), Lubarski 54, Oravec 84)*   2500
Bangor City (0) 0, Halmstad (3) 7 *(Andersson R 29, Svensson 31, Arvidsson 44, Selakovic 49, 81, Karlsson 86, Bertilsson 90)*   761 *(at Wrexham)*.
Boavista (2) 2 *(Silva 22, Rogerio 40)*, Barry Town (0) 0   3039
Coleraine (0) 1 *(McLaughlin 59)*, Orgryte (1) 2 *(Hemberg 8, Johansson 82)*   780
Constelacio (0) 0, Rayo Vallecano (6) 10 *(Michel 12, 66, Cembranos 27, Bolic 31, 39, 60, 67, Bolo 35, 42, Sanz 72)*   750
Constructorul (1) 2 *(Druce 30, Zabolotny 83)*, CSKA Sofia (2) 3 *(Berbanov 10, 25, Mirchev 89)*   3000
Ekranas (0) 0, Lierse (2) 3 *(Claeys 5, Van Meir 10 (pen), Cavens 79)*   4000
FC Brugge (1) 4 *(Fadiga 41 (pen), 53 (pen), Mendoza 79, Verheyen 83)*, Flora Tallinn (1) 1 *(Saviauk 21 (pen))*   3500
Folgore (0) 1 *(Zanotti 81)*, Basle (3) 5 *(Tchouga 10, 20, Muff 38, Aziawonou 60, Magro 80)*   1584
GI Gotu (0) 0, Norrkoping (0) 2 *(Bjurstrom 55, Bergstrom 86)*   700
Glentoran (0) 0, Lillestrom (2) 3 *(Powell 20, Berntsen 37 (pen), Sundgot 53)*   1293
HJK Helsinki (2) 4 *(Rafael 3, Roiha 17, Jeremenko 78, Haarala 83)*, Grevenmacher (0) 1 *(Huss 56)*   850
IA Akranes (0) 0, Gent (0) 3 *(Schepens 50, Pedersen 78, Olcese 90)*   1000
IBV (0) 0, Hearts (0) 2 *(Severin 49, Jackson 67)*   500
Jeunesse Esch (0) 0, Celtic (1) 4 *(Moravcik 37, 58, Larsson 61, Petta 81)*   3587
Kapaz (0) 0, Antalya (1) 2 *(Khinali 37, Anjelovic 52)*   12,000
Lausanne (0) 1 *(Horjak 89)*, Cork City (0) 0   3800
Metalurgs (0) 1 *(Solonicin 80 (pen))*, Brann (1) 1 *(Karadas 5)*   2500
MTK Budapest (1) 1 *(Illes 7)*, Jokerit (0) 0   1500
Napredak (4) 5 *(Kojicic 23, 45, 82 (pen), Belic 4, 21)*, Tulevik (0) 1 *(Ustritski 47)*   8500
Neftchi (1) 1 *(Guseinov 1)*, Gorica (0) 0   17,000
Omonia (0) 0, Neftochimik (0) 0   17,000
Petra Drnovice (0) 3 *(Zavadil 47, Cupak 65, 72)*, Buducnost (0) 0   4256
Rapid Bucharest (2) 3 *(Lencsi 37, Maldarasanu 40, Constantin 88)*, Mika (0) 0   5000
Rapid Vienna (0) 2 *(Wagner 51, Schottel 77)*, Teuta (0) 0   5500
Rijeka (1) 2 *(Mijatovic 29, 54, Hasancic 89)*, Valletta (1) 2 *(Giglio 19, Oretan 87)*   4730
Serif (0) 0, Olimpija (0) 0   8000
Slavia Mozyr (0) 1 *(Shutov 50)*, Maccabi Haifa (1) 1 *(Katan 47)*   5300
Sliema Wanderers (1) 2 *(Sylla 10, Busuttil 73)*, Partizan Belgrade (1) 1 *(Ilic 34)*   2500
Slovan Bratislava (1) 2 *(Jancula 38, Hrncar 70 (pen))*, Lokomotiv Tbilisi (0) 0   4321
Tomori (0) 2 *(Lako 62, Fani 90)*, Apoel (3) 3 *(Obiku 23, Skoric 25, Yiasoumis 37 (pen))*   2000
Uni Craiova (1) 1 *(Papura 31)*, Pobeda (0) 1 *(Zdraveski 88)*   5000
Ventspils (2) 2 *(Landriev 17, 43)*, Vasas (0) 1 *(Szili 88)*   3200
Vorskla (1) 2 *(Kobzar 34, Melashchenko 65)*, Rabotnicki (0) 0   7500
WIT (0) 0, Beitar Jerusalem (1) 3 *(Mizrahi 32, Ganon 61, Rosso 90)*   3000
Zalgiris (1) 2 *(Saulenas 32, Viliniskis 55)*, Ruch (1) 1 *(Pawlak 13)*   4000
Zeljeznicar (0) 0, Wisla (0) 0   10,000

QUALIFYING ROUND, SECOND LEG

Antalya (1) 5 *(Khinali 4, Music 51, 88, Cakir 67, Kariklar 74)*, Kapaz (0) 0   9500
Apoel (2) 2 *(Yiasoumis 23, Obiku 30)*, Tomori (0) 0   2400
B36 Torshavn (0) 0, AB Copenhagen (0) 1 *(Nielsen 70)*   400
Barry Town (0) 0, Boavista (1) 3 *(Rogerio 13, Brown 55 (og), Sanchez 60)*   1372
Basle (5) 7 *(Muff 7, Magro 19, 21, Cantaluppi 31, Tholot 39, 85, Koumantarakis 81)*, Folgore (0) 0   2113
Beitar Jerusalem (0) 1 *(Sandor 47)*, WIT (0) 1 *(Mekhadze 66)*   7000
Bohemians (0) 0, Aberdeen (0) 1 *(Morrison 69 (og))*   7450
Brann (0) 1 *(Razanuskas 68 (pen))*, Metalurgs (0) 0   2276
Buducnost (0) 0, Petra Drnovice (0) 1 *(Gomes 69)*   4000
Celtic (4) 7 *(Burchill 12, 14, 15, Berkovic 22, 46, Riseth 52, Petrov 71)*, Jeunesse Esch (0) 0   40,282
Cork City (0) 0, Lausanne (0) 1 *(Gobet 61)*   6000
CSKA Sofia (5) 8 *(Yanchev 16 (pen), Petrov S 18 (pen), Berbatov 36, 40, 43, 55, 78, Yanev 83)*, Constructorul (0) 0   9000
Flora Tallin (0) 0, FC Brugge (1) 2 *(Vermant 24, Martens 82)*   850
Gent (1) 3 *(Kaklamanos 16, 72, Cipi 63)*, IA Akranes (2) 2 *(Hinriksson 8, Reynisson 43)*   3000
Gomel (0) 0, AIK Stockholm (0) 2 *(Alm 76, Mattiasson 87 (pen))*   9000
Gorica (1) 3 *(Zlogar 11, 88, Gutalj 90)*, Neftchi (0) 1 *(Musayev 62)*   1500
Grevenmacher (0) 2 *(Rodrigues 57, Thill 90)*, HJK Helsinki (0) 0   800
Halmstad (3) 4 *(Arvidsson 5, 26, Bertilsson 34 (pen), Selakovic 76)*, Bangor City (0) 0   646
Hearts (3) 3 *(McSwegan 6, Tomaschek 19, O'Neil 39)*, IBV (0) 0   8720
Jokerit (0) 2 *(Hyrylainen 63, Sumiala 83)*, MTK Budapest (1) 4 *(Ferenczi 20, 89, Illes 60 (pen), Kuttor 75)*   2476
Kosice (0) 1 *(Lubarski 66)*, Ararat Erevan (0) 1 *(Nigoyan 75 (pen))*   1168
Lierse (1) 4 *(Claeys 7, Snoeckx 47, 89, Spiteri 58)*, Ekranas (0) 0   2000
Lillestrom (0) 1 *(Powell 60)*, Glentoran (0) 0   1046
Lokomotiv Tbilisi (0) 0, Slovan Bratislava (1) 2 *(Mesaros 37, Gog 80)*   7000
Maccabi Haifa (0) 0, Slavia Mozyr (0) 0   5000
Mika (0) 1 *(Nikolyan 84)*, Rapid Bucharest (0) 0   500
Neftochimik (2) 2 *(Timnev 15, 44)*, Omonia (1) 1 *(Mihajlovic 36)*   8000
Norrkoping (1) 2 *(Flodstrom 41, Andersson P 57)*, GI Gotu (0) 1 *(Olsen 50)*   5771
Olimpija (1) 3 *(Oslaj 30, 70, Cimerotic 90)*, Serif (0) 0   2500
Orgryte (1) 1 *(Kuhn 44)*, Coleraine (0) 0   2350
Partizan Belgrade (3) 4 *(Ilic 4 (pen), 32, 45 (pen), Rankovic 59)*, Sliema Wanderers (0) 1 *(Turner 90)*   10,000
Pobeda (0) 1 *(Zdraveski 77)*, Uni Craiova (0) 0   9000
Rabotnicki (0) 0, Vorskla (1) 2 *(Melashchenko 10, Kobzar 48)*   9000
Rayo Vallecano (2) 6 *(Cembranos 20, Bolo 41, 54, Sanz 56, Michel 72, Bolic 90)*, Constelacio (0) 0   7000
Ruch (4) 6 *(Paluch 15, Bizacki 36, Jikia 44, 45, Surma 78, Mizia 88)*, Zalgiris (0) 0   1300
Teuta (0) 0, Rapid Vienna (2) 4 *(Lagonikakis 20, Wagner 25, 65, Wetl 78)*   2000
Tulevik (1) 1 *(Ustritski 37)*, Napredak (1) 1 *(Belic 45)* 400
Vaduz (2) 3 *(Wegmann 8, Viadotas 42, Polverino 75 (pen))*, Amica (2) 3 *(Zak 13, Krol 23, Zienczuk 83)* 550
Valletta (1) 5 *(Hasancic 32, 119, Milicic 64, Brajkovic 94, Bonnici 103 (og))*, Rijeka (1) 5 *(Hasancic 32, 119, Milicic 64, Brajkovic 94, Bonnici 103 (og))*   3932
Vasas (1) 3 *(Kabad 15, Beto 75, 120)*, Ventspils (1) 1 *(Bezdorodov 6)*   1000
Wisla (1) 3 *(Frankowski 25, 53, 60)*, Zeljeznicar (1) 1 *(Muharemovic 34)*   7000

FIRST ROUND, FIRST LEG

AIK Stockholm (0) 0, Herfolge (1) 1 *(Falck 25)*   7159
Alaves (0) 0, Gaziantep (0) 0   11,446
Antalya (1) 2 *(Gaudino 43, Birlik 68)*, Werder Bremen (0) 0   3300

Basle (1) 3 *(Magro 7, Tchouga 53, Kreuzer 86)*,
Brann (0) 2 *(Ludvigsen 47, Helstad 72)* 3215
Bohemians (0) 1 *(Crowe 90 (pen))*, Kaiserslautern
(0) 3 *(Reich 73, Hristov 76, Tare 79)* 5750
Brondby (1) 1 *(Jonsson 39)*, Osijek (1) 2 *(Gaspar 32, Mitu 56)* 7679
Celta Vigo (0) 0, Rijeka (0) 0 8300
Celtic (2) 2 *(Larsson 14, 25)*, HJK Helsinki (0) 0 40,544
Chelsea (1) 1 *(Panucci 24)*, St Gallen (0) 0 18,196
CSKA Moscow (0) 0, Viborg (0) 0 9500
CSKA Sofia (1) 1 *(Yanev 6)*, MTK Budapest (0) 2
(Ferenczi 50, Kuttor 69) 20,010
Dunaferr (0) 0, Feyenoord (0) 1 *(Molnar 60 (og))* 13,000
FC Brugge (2) 4 *(Simons 37, Mendoza 62)*,
Apoel (0) 0 6000
Gent (0) 0, Ajax (2) 6 *(Arveladze 16, Knopper 40, 69, Gronkjaer 74, Van der Vaar 82, Van der Gun 84)* 5309
Gorica (1) 1 *(Zlogar 29)*, Roma (3) 4 *(Delvecchio 17, 19, 49, Samuel 41)* 2200
Gueugnon (0) 0, Iraklis (0) 0 5569
Halmstad (1) 2 *(Svensson 36, Selakovic 57)*,
Benfica (1) 1 *(Van Hooijdonk 40)* 3796
Kosice (0) 2 *(Zvara 53, Jambor 75)*, Graz (0) 3
(Akwuegbu 57, Standfest 83, Pamic 90) 1817
Krivbas (0) 0, Nantes (0) 1 *(Ziani 81)* 16,000
Lausanne (1) 3 *(Kuzba 22, 48, Mazzoni 51)*,
Torpedo Moscow (2) 2 *(Gashkin 13, Litvinov 33)* 3100
Leicester City (1) 1 *(Taggart 43)*, Red Star
Belgrade (1) 1 *(Acimovic 1)* 21,198
Lierse (0) 0, Bordeaux (0) 0 4151
Lillestrom (2) 3 *(Kristinsson 8, 13, Kihlberg 68)*,
Dynamo Moscow (1) 1 *(Romashchenko 42)* 1172
Lokomotiv Moscow (2) 4 *(Sarkisian 20, Tsymbalar 32, Janashia 63, Pimenov 65)*, Neftochimik (1) 2
(Petrov R 9, Timnev 56) 4900
Molde (0) 1, Rayo Vallecano (1) 1 *(Bolo 16)* 3000
Napredak (0) 0, Ofi Crete (0) 0 7723
Norrkoping (1) 2 *(Flodstrom 33, Andersson P 79)*,
Slovan Liberec (0) 2 *(Leandro 70, Nezmar 77)* 3714
Olimpija (2) 2 *(Jukic 14, Rakovic 44)*, Espanyol (1) 1
(Galca 43) 4400
PAOK Salonika (1) 3 *(Camps 44, Cohen 48 (og), Nalitzis 55)*, Beitar Jerusalem (1) 1 *(Hamar 39)* 17,584
Partizan Belgrade (1) 1 *(Rankovic 24)*, Porto (1)
(Pena 89) 23,427
Petra Drnovice (0) 0, 1860 Munich (0) 0 6040
Pobeda (0) 0, Parma (1) 2 *(Conceicao 23, Di Vaio 74)* 9500
Polonia (0) 0, Udinese (0) 1 *(Warley 56)* 2000
Rapid Bucharest (0) 0, Liverpool (1) 1 *(Barmby 29)* 9782
Rapid Vienna (2) 3 *(Wagner 20, Savicevic 27, Ratajczyk 79)*, Orgryte (0) 0 4017
Roda (0) 2 *(Peto 89, Inter Bratislava (1) 2 (Nemeth 21, Babnic 68)* 7950
Ruch (0) 0, Internazionale (0) 3 *(Seedorf 62, Recoba 66, Keane 71)* 13,000
Slavia Prague (1) 3 *(Kuchar 29, 73, Dosek T 84)*,
AB Copenhagen (0) 0 4274
Slovan Bratislava (0) 0, Dynamo Zagreb (1) 3
(Mujcin 38, Cvitanovic 61, Pilipovic 90) 6500
Stuttgart (1) 1 *(Balakov 35)*, Hearts (0) 0 9845
Tirol Innsbruck (2) 3 *(Gilewicz 28, 49, Baur 45)*,
Fiorentina (0) 1 *(Mijatovic 54)* 13,190
Vasas (0) 2 *(Peto 89, Komodi 90)*, AEK Athens (0) 2
(Peto 47 (og), Nikolaidis 50) 2500
Vitesse (1) 3 *(Martel 19, Peeters 63, Amoah 90)*,
Maccabi Haifa (0) 0 12,350
Vladikavkaz (0) 0, Amica (1) 3 *(Kryszalowicz 44, Krol 49, Zienczuk 90)* 16,200
Vorskla (1) 1 *(Melashchenko 38)*, Boavista (0) 2
(Couto 50, Silva 89) 9000
Zaragoza (1) 4 *(Acuna 30, Saenz 54, Gonzalez 63, 68)*, Wisla (1) 1 *(Kaluzny 12)* 20,500
Zimbru Chisinau (1) 1 *(Epureanu 1)*, Hertha
Berlin (1) 2 *(Preetz 25, Daei 64)* 7000
Zurich (0) 1 *(Bartlett 65)*, Genk (0) 2 *(Paas 53, Ban 89)* 4561

FIRST ROUND, SECOND LEG

AB Copenhagen (0) 0, Slavia Prague (0) 2
(Dostalek 46, Dosek 90) 1470
AEK Athens (2) 2 *(Maladenis 28, Nikolaidis 30)*,
Vasas (0) 0 11,200
Ajax (1) 3 *(Van der Gun 27, 58, Van der Vaar 85)*,
Gent (0) 0 26,000

Amica (1) 2 *(Kryszalowicz 39, Sobocinski 73)*,
Vladikavkaz (0) 0 1500
Apoel (0) 0, FC Brugge (1) 1 *(Mendoza 21)* 1241
Beitar Jerusalem (1) 3 *(Sivila 45, 61, Abukasis 54)*,
PAOK Salonika (2) 3 *(Katsampis 5, Nalitzis 43, Konstantinidis 90)* 5120
Benfica (1) 2 *(Van Hooijdonk 24, Monteiro 90)*,
Halmstad (1) 2 *(Gustafsson 32, Selakovic 88)* 33,000
Boavista (2) 2 *(Freking 28, Melo 38)*, Vorskla (0) 1
(Onopko 47) 1500
Bordeaux (1) 5 *(Pauleta 24, 46, 90, Feindouno 58, 73)*,
Lierse (0) 1 *(Cavens 60)* 8883
Brann (4) 4 *(Karadas 3, 40, Brendesaether 8, Terehov 30)*, Basle (1) 4 *(Tchouga 19, Wassberg 58, Kreuzer 60, Muff 90)* 4176
Dynamo Moscow (2) 2 *(Romashchenko 26, Shtaniuk 44)*, Lillestrom (0) 1 *(Sundgot 70)* 4048
Dynamo Zagreb (0) 1 *(Mujcin 70)*, Slovan
Bratislava (1) 1 *(Sedlak 5)* 5780
Espanyol (2) 2 *(Posse 15, Martinez 25)*, Olimpija (0) 0 10,200
Feyenoord (1) 3 *(De Haan 16, Korneev 47, Van Vossen 83)*, Dunaferr (0) 1 *(Tokoli 87)* 24,000
Fiorentina (1) 2 *(Mijatovic 25, Leandro 62)*, Tirol
Innsbruck (1) 2 *(Mair 18, Gilewicz 88)* 22,215
Gaziantep (2) 3 *(Yigit 13, Polat 35, Erhan 90)*,
Alaves (1) 4 *(Alonso 30, Tomic 55, 79, Moreno 72)* 9901
Genk (1) 2 *(Daerden 31, Hendrikx 90)*, Zurich (0) 0 12,000
Graz (0) 0, Kosice (0) 0 2368
Hearts (1) 3 *(Pressley 17, Petric 62, Cameron 84 (pen))*,
Stuttgart (1) 2 *(Dundee 37, Bordon 58)* 14,488
Herfolge (0) 1 *(Jensen 97)*, AIK Stockholm (0) 1
(Novakovic 51) 1659
Hertha Berlin (2) 2 *(Hartmann 23, Daei 36)*,
Zimbru Chisinau (0) 0 23,400
HJK Helsinki (1) 2 *(Roiha 41, 75)*, Celtic (0) 1
(Sutton 108) 6530
Inter Bratislava (2) 2 *(Babnic 37, Nemeth 42)*,
Roda (0) 1 *(Tchoutang 53)* 3050
Internazionale (2) 4 *(Recoba 6, Seedorf 41, 87, Colombo 89)*, Ruch (0) 1 *(Skwara 85)* 4771
Iraklis (0) 1 *(Konstantinou 77)*, Gueugnon (0) 0 5000
Kaiserslautern (0) 0, Bohemians (1) 1 *(Crowe 45)* 12,379
Liverpool (0) 0, Rapid Bucharest (0) 0 37,954
Maccabi Haifa (0) 2 *(Zano 68, Atar 87)*, Vitesse (0) 1
(Amoah 89) 2036
MTK Budapest (0) 0, CSKA Sofia (0) 1
(Mirchev 86) 1850
1860 Munich (0) 1 *(Kurz 72)*, Petra Drnovice (0) 0 18,200
Nantes (3) 5 *(Moldovan 8, 34, 55, Da Rocha 35, Gillet 66)*, Krivbas (0) 0 16,334
Neftochimik (0) 0, Lokomotiv Moscow (0) 0 7440
Ofi Crete (5) 6 *(Silva 12, 45, Iordanidis 20, Gomez 23, 50, Dingozis 35)*, Napredak (0) 0 1420
Orgryte (0) 1 *(Johansson 72)*, Rapid Vienna (1) 1
(Wagner 20) 1701
Osijek (0) 0, Brondby (0) 0 8712
Parma (1) 4 *(Montano 39, Bonazzoli 53, 80, Di Vaio 88)*,
Pobeda (0) 0 6169
Porto (0) 1 *(Drulovic 88)*, Partizan Belgrade (0) 0 15,610
Rayo Vallecano (1) 1 *(Sanchez 38)*, Molde (0) 1
(Hulsker 74) 5290
Red Star Belgrade (1) 3 *(Drulic 22, 71, Gvozdenovic 47)*,
Leicester City (1) 1 *(Izzet 41)* 12,700
Rijeka (0) 0, Celta Vigo (0) 1 *(Djorovic 112)* 4691
Roma (5) 7 *(Samuel 8, Montella 11, 19, Delvecchio 23, Totti 41, 47, Batistuta 66)*, Gorica (0) 0 5000
Slovan Liberec (0) 2 *(Jun 62, Nezmar 63)*,
Norrkoping (0) 1 *(Bergstrom 54)* 6480
St Gallen (2) 2 *(Muller 19, Amoah 35)*, Chelsea (0) 0 15,620
Torpedo Moscow (0) 0, Lausanne (1) 2 *(Kuzba 29, Puce 62)* 5500
Udinese (1) 2 *(Walem 32, Muzzi 89)*, Polonia (0) 0 11,159
Viborg (0) 1 *(Kaergaard 100)*, CSKA Moscow (0) 0 3196
Werder Bremen (2) 6 *(Wicky 3, Bode 41, Stalteri 51, Ailton 55, 58, 64)*, Antalya (0) 0 25,600
Wisla (0) 4 *(Kelech 51, Frankowski 53, 88, Moskal 60)*, Zaragoza (1) 1 *(Baszczinski 5 (og))* 4500
Wisla won 4-3 on penalties.

SECOND ROUND, FIRST LEG

AEK Athens (0) 5 *(Nikolaidis 48, 53, 64, 75, Zikos 61)*,
Herfolge (0) 0   9075
Basle (0) 1 *(Tchouga 62)*, Feyenoord (0) 2 *(Kalou 60, Bosvelt 84)*   9700
Boavista (0) 0, Roma (0) 1 *(Montella 74)*   6000
Bordeaux (1) 1 *(Dugarry 23)*, Celtic (1) 1
(Larsson 25 (pen))   21,318
FC Brugge (0) 2 *(Lembi 53 (pen), Vermant 76 (pen))*,
St Gallen (1) 1 *(Amoah 28)*   10,000
Espanyol (4) 4 *(Tamudo 15, Galca 20 (pen), Sergio 30, 45)*, Graz (0) 0   11,000
Halmstad (2) 3 *(Svensson M 13, Selakovic 34, Andersson R 56)*, 1860 Munich (2) 2 *(Max 35, Hassler 37 (pen))*   3145
Hertha Berlin (1) 3 *(Preetz 8, Beinlich 46, Reiss 65)*,
Amica (0) 1 *(Piskula 88)*   13,157
Internazionale (0) 0, Vitesse (0) 0   9093
Iraklis (0) 1 *(Konstantinou M 47 (pen))*, Kaiserslautern
(2) 3 *(Klose 7, Hristov 35, Taviardis 64 (og))*   6958
Lausanne (1) 1 *(Mazzoni 38)*, Ajax (0) 0   11,500
Lillestrom (0) 1 *(Helland 84)*, Alaves (2) 3 *(Begona 2, Tellez 22, Contra 47)*   1120
Liverpool (0) 1 *(Heskey 88)*, Slovan Liberec (0) 0   29,662
Lokomotiv Moscow (1) 1 *(Loskov 38 (pen))*,
Inter Bratislava (0) 0   2850
Nantes (0) 2 *(Ziani 63, Gillet 73)*, MTK Budapest (1) 1
(Illes 28)   13,925
Ofi Crete (1) 2 *(Kolitsidakis 42, Mauro Silva 78)*,
Slavia Prague (1) 2 *(Nicas 30, Rada 70)*   3600
Osijek (1) 2 *(Bjelica 27, 90 (pen))*, Rapid Vienna (1) 1
(Radovic 37)   12,000
Parma (0) 2 *(Amoroso 61, 78)*, Dinamo Zagreb (0) 0   4822
Rayo Vallecano (1) 1 *(Quevedo 18)*, Viborg (0) 0   6599
Red Star Belgrade (0) 1 *(Drulic 62)*, Celta Vigo (0) 0   43,328
Tirol Innsbruck (0) 1 *(Mair 54)*, Stuttgart (0) 0   16,500
Udinese (0) 1 *(Margiotta 90)*, PAOK Salonika (0) 0   14,258
Werder Bremen (2) 4 *(Ernst 16, Herzog 28, Baumann 56, Bode 72)*, Genk (1) 1 *(Sonck 35)*   14,150
Wisla (0) 0, Porto (0) 0   8200

SECOND ROUND, SECOND LEG

Ajax (1) 2 *(Arveladze 17, Van der Gun 78)*,
Lausanne (1) 2 *(Mazzoni 38, Kuzba 77 (pen))*   40,000
Alaves (1) 2 *(Mocelin 1, Epitie 70)*, Lillestrom (1) 2
(Strand 4, Sogard 50)   13,000
Amica (0) 1 *(Krol 54)*, Hertha Berlin (0) 1 *(Veit 63)*   9000
Celta Vigo (0) 5 *(Catanha 22, 70, McCarthy 55, Lopez G 49 (pen), 65 (pen))*, Red Star Belgrade (2) 3
(Drulic 14, 38, 90)   19,000
(Match awarded 3-0 to Celta Vigo; Red Star Belgrade fielded two suspended players).
Celtic (0) 1 *(Moravcik 54)*, Bordeaux (0) 2
(Laslandes 78, 114)   51,242
Dinamo Zagreb (1) 1 *(Sokota 32)*, Parma (0) 0   20,000
Feyenoord (1) 1 *(Kalou 3)*, Basle (0) 0   24,000
Genk (1) 2 *(Thijs 26, Zokora 57)*, Werder Bremen
(3) 5 *(Pizarro 24, 27 (pen), 44, Stalteri 73, Maximov 80)*   8000
Graz (0) 1 *(Ehmann 65)*, Espanyol (0) 0   2918
Herfolge (1) 2 *(Jakobsen 1, Hermansen 46 (pen))*,
AEK Athens (1) 1 *(Petkov 34)*   1684
Inter Bratislava (0) 1 *(Cisovsky 47)*, Lokomotiv
Moscow (1) 2 *(Chugainov 31, Janashia 69)*   3280
1860 Munich (2) 3 *(Max 6, 84, Agostino 45)*,
Halmstad (1) 1 *(Andersson R 25)*   10,000
Kaiserslautern (2) 2 *(Koch H 25 (pen), Djorkaeff 29)*, Iraklis (0) 3 *(Konstantinou M 54, 89, Fofonka 90)*   14,500
MTK Budapest (0) 0, Nantes (0) 1 *(Monterrubio 84)*   1500
PAOK Salonika (0) 3 *(Camps 72, 102, Froussos 108)*,
Udinese (0) 0   29,745
Porto (1) 3 *(Pena 4, 61, Alenichev 90)*, Wisla (0) 0   13,000
Rapid Vienna (0) 0, Osijek (1) 2 *(Bjelica 14, Jukic 90)*   12,000
Roma (1) 1 *(Nakata 74)*, Boavista (0) 1 *(Silva 53)*   10,831
St Gallen (1) 1 *(Amoah 20)*, FC Brugge (0) 1
(Mendoza 90)   14,500
Slavia Prague (0) 4 *(Kuchar 62, Zelenka 70, 78, 89)*,
Ofi Crete (0) 1 *(Munoz 60)*   3200
Slovan Liberec (1) 2 *(Stajner 9, Breda 85)*,
Liverpool (1) 3 *(Barmby 30, Heskey 76, Owen 82)*   6808

Stuttgart (3) 3 *(Schneider 7, Ganea 18, 45)*,
Tirol Innsbruck (0) 1 *(Brzeczek 62)*   10,000
Viborg (1) 2 *(Fernandez 29, 85)*, Rayo
Vallecano (0) 1 *(Michel 77)*   10,000
Vitesse (1) 1 *(Peeters 14)*, Internazionale (0) 1
(Simic 80)   8500

THIRD ROUND, FIRST LEG

Alaves (0) 1 *(Moreno 56)*, Rosenborg (0) 1
(Johnsen 80)   12,000
Bordeaux (2) 4 *(Dugarry 20, Batiles 40, Wilmots 66, 76)*, Werder Bremen (1) 1 *(Pizarro 15)*   28,000
FC Brugge (0) 0, Barcelona (2) 2 *(Rivaldo 24, Kluivert 31)*   29,500
Espanyol (0) 0, Porto (0) 2 *(Drulovic 47, Pena 72)*   15,000
Feyenoord (2) 2 *(Tomasson 10, Leonardo 45)*,
Stuttgart (1) 2 *(Dundee 36, Ganea 75)*   30,000
Hertha Berlin (0) 0, Internazionale (0) 0   39,000
Leverkusen (2) 4 *(Kirsten 25, 42, Kovac 48, Ramelow 90)*, AEK Athens (1) 4 *(Lakis 5, Navas 46, 79, Tsartas 55 (pen))*   22,550
Lokomotiv Moscow (0) 0, Rayo Vallecano (0) 0   5500
Nantes (2) 4 *(Moldovan 18, Monterrubio 43, Puce 73 (og), Gillet 86)*, Lausanne (1) 3 *(Kuzba 40 (pen), 69, Mazzoni 53)*   22,000
Olympiakos (0) 2 *(Alexandris 65, 90)*,
Liverpool (1) 2 *(Barmby 38, Gerrard 67)*   43,855
Osijek (1) 2 *(Turkovic 33, Neretljak 82)*,
Slavia Prague (0) 0   12,000
Parma (2) 2 *(Appiah 2, Micoud 11)*, 1860 Munich (0) 2
(Tyce 79, Beierle 90)   22,000
PSV Eindhoven (3) 3 *(Bruggink 4, Kezman 15, 44)*,
PAOK Salonika (0) 0   28,000
Rangers (0) 1 *(Albertz 88)*, Kaiserslautern (0) 0   47,279
Roma (1) 1 *(Guigou 33)*, Hamburg (0) 0   42,705
Shakhtjor Donetsk (0) 0, Celta Vigo (0) 0   32,000

THIRD ROUND, SECOND LEG

AEK Athens (1) 2 *(Navas 17, Tsartas 49)*,
Leverkusen (0) 0   32,200
Barcelona (1) 1 *(Rivaldo 17 (pen))*,
FC Brugge (1) 1 *(Verheyen 27)*   35,000
Celta Vigo (1) 1 *(Catanha 28)*, Shakhtjor
Donetsk (0) 0   9917
Hamburg (0) 0, Roma (1) 3 *(Aldair 29, Delvecchio 58, Samuel 60)*   48,000
Internazionale (1) 2 *(Recoba 6, Hakan Sukur 89)*,
Hertha Berlin (0) 1 *(Tretschok 54)*   12,693
1860 Munich (0) 0, Parma (2) 2 *(Amoroso 74 (pen), Conceicao 86)*   28,600
Kaiserslautern (1) 3 *(Klose 8, Buck 65, Lokvenc 79)*,
Rangers (0) 0   28,757
Lausanne (0) 1 *(Lombardo 51)*, Nantes (1) 3
(Ziani 25, Moldovan 60, Carriere 90)   14,200
Liverpool (0) 2 *(Heskey 28, Barmby 60)*,
Olympiakos (0) 0   35,484
PAOK Salonika (0) 0, PSV Eindhoven (1) 1
(Bruggink 44)   34,300
Porto (0) 0, Espanyol (0) 0   7360
Rayo Vallecano (0) 2 *(Bolic 65, Alcazar 68)*,
Lokomotiv Moscow (0) 0   7844
Rosenborg (0) 1 *(Skammelsrud 89 (pen))*,
Alaves (2) 3 *(Johnsen 18 (og), Vucko 37, Moreno 62)*   9556
Slavia Prague (2) 5 *(Dosek T 15, 53, Zelenka 28, Svancara 89, Kuchar 90)*, Osijek (1) 1
(Turkovic 45)   4215
Stuttgart (1) 2 *(Meissner 29, Balakov 90 (pen))*,
Feyenoord (0) 1 *(Paauwe 71)*   10,000
Werder Bremen (0) 0, Bordeaux (0) 0   16,166

FOURTH ROUND, FIRST LEG

AEK Athens (0) 0, Barcelona (1) 1 *(Luis Enrique 42)*   24,000
Alaves (1) 3 *(Moreno 43, Tellez 71, Alonso 73)*,
Internazionale (1) 3 *(Recoba 45, 50, Vieri 65)*   17,307
Porto (1) 3 *(Esguerdinha 17 (pen), Gillet 59 (og), Secretario 87)*, Nantes (1) 1 *(Ahamada 14)*   25,000
PSV Eindhoven (1) 2 *(Ooijer 23, Rommedahl 72)*,
Parma (0) 1 *(Mboma 67)*   31,000
Rayo Vallecano (1) 4 *(De Quintana 19, Bolic 74, Quevedo 84, Michel 90)*, Bordeaux (1) 1
(Laslandes 2)   7500

Roma (0) 0, Liverpool (0) 2 *(Owen 46, 72)*   60,000
Slavia Prague (0) 0, Kaiserslautern (0) 0   17,840
Stuttgart (0) 0, Celta Vigo (0) 0   20,000

FOURTH ROUND, SECOND LEG
Barcelona (2) 5 *(Luis Enrique 19, 29, 58, Rivaldo 56, Gerard 87 (pen))*, AEK Athens (0) 0   40,000
Bordeaux (1) 1 *(Ballesteros 23 (og))*, Rayo Vallecano (1) 2 *(Cembranos 19 (pen), Bolo 48)*   22,000
Celta Vigo (1) 2 *(Karpin 6, Mostovoi 85)*, Stuttgart (1) 1 *(Blank 45)*   20,000
Internazionale (0) 0, Alaves (0) 2 *(Cruyff 77, Tomic 83)*   9845
Kaiserslautern (0) 1 *(Lokvenc 59)*, Slavia Prague (0) 0   28,000
Liverpool (0) 0, Roma (0) 1 *(Guigou 70)*   43,688
Nantes (0) 2 *(Vahirua 68, Armand 75)*, Porto (1) 1 *(Pena 35)*   29,000
Parma (0) 3 *(Milosevic 64 (pen), 69, Montano 90)*, PSV Eindhoven (2) 2 *(Rommedahl 32, Kezman 45)*   11,883

QUARTER-FINALS, FIRST LEG
Alaves (1) 3 *(Azkoitia 30, Eggen 79, Vucko 80)*, Rayo Vallecano (0) 0   17,500
Barcelona (1) 2 *(Kluivert 13, 55)*, Celta Vigo (0) 1 *(Coira 68)*   33,000

Kaiserslautern (1) 1 *(Koch 31 (pen))*, PSV Eindhoven (0) 0   23,850
Porto (0) 0, Liverpool (0) 0   22,000

QUARTER-FINALS, SECOND LEG
Celta Vigo (1) 3 *(Catanha 33, Lopez 63 (pen), Mostovoi 90)*, Barcelona (2) 2 *(Rivaldo 28, 42)*   29,000
Liverpool (2) 2 *(Murphy 33, Owen 38)*, Porto (0) 0   40,502
PSV Eindhoven (0) 0, Kaiserslautern (0) 1 *(Basler 71 (pen))*   31,500
Rayo Vallecano (1) 2 *(Quevedo 41, Cembranos 79 (pen))*, Alaves (1) 1 *(Cruyff 19)*   9500

SEMI-FINALS, FIRST LEG
Alaves (3) 5 *(Contra 20 (pen), 31 (pen), Cruyff 42, Alonso 58 (pen), Magno 81)*, Kaiserslautern (0) 1 *(Koch H 67 (pen))*   17,000
Barcelona (0) 0, Liverpool (0) 0   90,000

SEMI-FINALS, SECOND LEG
Kaiserslautern (1) 1 *(Djorkaeff 7)*, Alaves (1) 4 *(Alonso 22, Vucko 64, 85, Ganan 88)*   31,000
Liverpool (1) 1 *(McAllister 45 (pen))*, Barcelona (0) 0   44,203

FINAL

Liverpool (3) 5, Alaves (1) 4
(aet; Liverpool won in sudden death.)
(in Dortmund, 16 May 2001, 65,000)

Liverpool: Westerveld; Babbel, Carragher, Hamann, Henchoz (Smicer 56), Hyypia, Gerrard, McAllister, Heskey (Fowler 65), Owen (Berger 79), Murphy.
Scorers: Babbel 4, Gerrard 16, McAllister 41 (pen), Fowler 73, Geli 117 (og).
Alaves: Herrera; Eggen (Alonso 23), Karmona, Tellez, Contra, Tomic, Desio, Astudillo (Magno 46), Geli, Cruyff, Javi Moreno (Pablo 65).
Scorers: Alonso 27, Javi Moreno 48, 51, Cruyff 89.
Referee: Veissiere (France).

Michael Owen is brought down by Alaves goalkeeper Martin Herrera and Liverpool go ahead 3-1 from the penalty spot during their nine-goal UEFA Cup Final thriller. (Actionimages/Michael Regan).

UEFA CUP 2000–2001 – BRITISH AND IRISH CLUBS

QUALIFYING ROUND, FIRST LEG

10 AUG

Aberdeen (0) 1 *(Winters 62)*
Bohemians (0) 2 *(Maher 82, Molloy 90 (pen))*   13,638
Aberdeen: Esson; McGuire, McNaughton, Jess, Winters, Stavrum (Clark 78), Dow (Belabed 86), Rowson, Darren Young, Zerouali (Derek Young 65), Perry.
Bohemians: Russell; Bowman, Webb, Hunt, Maher, Hill, Morrison (O'Connor 51), O'Brien (Crowe 67), Molloy, O'Keeffe, Dempsey.

Bangor City (0) 0   761*(at Wrexham)*
Halmstad (3) 7 *(Andersson R 29, Svensson 31, Arvidsson 44, Selakovic 49, 81, Karlsson 86, Bertilsson 90)*
Bangor City: Mulliner; Johnson, Foster (Owen 82), Jardine, Williams S, Williams R, Rowlands, Hughes (Comley-Exceli 78), Roberts, Coady (Williams E 67), Bird.
Halmstad: Svensson H; Gustavsson, Arvidsson (Hansson 72), Jonsson, Gustafson, Andersson F, Lennartsson (Nilsson 56), Selakovic, Karlsson, Andersson R (Bertilsson 46), Svensson M.

Boavista (2) 2 *(Silva 22, Rogerio 40)*
Barry Town (0) 0   3039
Boavista: Andem; Viana, Rui Bento, Jorge Silva, Rui Lima, Ventura, Silva (Whelliton 69), Oliveira, Magalhaes, Santos (Sanchez 46), Rogerio (Martelinho 80).
Barry Town: Kendall; Brown, Lloyd, Phillips, York, Ince (Jenkins 29), Jones, Moralee, Holsgrove (MacLean 84), Lambert, Staton (French 74).

Coleraine (0) 1 *(McLaughlin 59)*
Orgryte (1) 2 *(Hemberg 8, Johansson 82)*   780
Coleraine: McKeown; Clanachan, Smyth, Gaston, Devine, McCoosh, McAllister, Gray (Keegan 46), McLaughlin, Loughery (Picking 46), Tolan (Kerr 86).
Orgryte: Last; Owusu, Karlsson (Allback 66), Nilsson, Kallander, Lohm (Sjostedt 74), Tomaz, Ulander, Anegrund, Elmander (Johansson 23), Hemberg.

Glentoran (0) 0
Lillestrom (2) 3 *(Powell 20, Berntsen 37 (pen), Sundgot 53)*   1293
Glentoran: Gough; Leeman, Kennedy, Walker, McCombe, Young, McCann, Hamill, Russell (Armstrong 75), Lockhart (Ferguson 29), McBride (Fitzgerald 55).
Lillestrom: Baron; Bjarmann, Hansen, Strand, Kihlberg (Sogard 83), Kristinsson, Helland, Berget, Powell, Sundgot, Berntsen.

IBV (0) 0
Hearts (0) 2 *(Severin 49, Jackson 67)*   500
IBV: Kristinsson; Gudmundsson, Aleksic, Stefansson, Sigurdsson I (Thorvaldsson 36), Bragason, Johannesson, Vidarsson (Sigurdsson M 69), Jonsson (Moller 78), Mileta, Almarsson.
Hearts: Niemi; Pressley, Naysmith, Flogel, Severin, Tomaschek, Makel (Locke 80), Fulton, McSwegan (O'Neil 80), Jackson (Kirk 84).

Jeunesse Esch (0) 0
Celtic (1) 4 *(Moravcik 37, 58, Larsson 61, Petta 81)* 3587
Jeunesse Esch: Van Rijswijck; Thill, Schaack, Lamborelle, Scuto, Amodio, Schauls, Betis (Dillmann 67), Kurtz (Neis 65), Borbiconi, Wagner (Meylender 73).
Celtic: Gould; Riseth, Mahe, McNamara (Healy), Valgaeren, Moravcik, Larsson (Johnson 63), Sutton, Mjallby, Lambert (Scheidt 67), Petta.

Lausanne (0) 1 *(Horjak 89)*
Cork City (0) 0   3800
Lausanne: Rapo; Meyer (Horjak 55), Lombardo, Mazzoni (Gomes 31), Baudry, Santini (Lutsenko 77), Kuzba, Puce, Karlen, Hellebuyck, Gobet.
Cork City: Mooney; O'Halloran, Delaney, Daly, Napier, Freyne (Caulfield 59), Cahill, Flanagan, Herrick, Morley (Cotter 82), O'Brien.

QUALIFYING ROUND, SECOND LEG

24 AUG

Barry Town (0) 0   1372
Boavista (1) 3 *(Rogerio 13, Brown 55 (og), Sanchez 60)*
Barry Town: Kendall; Brown (Evans 83), Lloyd, Phillips, York, Jones, French, Moralee, Holsgrove (Staton 58), Lambert (Ince 63), Jenkins.
Boavista: Andem; Viana, Rui Bento, Pedro Emanuel, Rui Lima, Jorge Silva, Ventura (Teixeira 81), Silva (Whelliton 75), Magalhaes, Rogerio (Jorge Couto 67), Sanchez.

Bohemians (0) 0
Aberdeen (0) 1 *(Morrison 69 (og))*   7450
Bohemians: Russell; Bowman (O'Connor 46), Webb, Hunt, Maher, Hill, Morrison, Caffrey, Molloy, O'Keeffe, Dempsey.
Aberdeen: Esson; Whyte, Guntveit, Winters, Zerouali, Dow (Rutkiewicz 83), Bernard (Mackie 56), Rowson, Young, McGuire, McNaughton.

Celtic (4) 7 *(Burchill 12, 14, 15, Berkovic 22, 46, Riseth 52, Petrov 71)*
Jeunesse Esch (0) 0   40,282
Celtic: Gould; Rafael, Tebily, Riseth, Lynch (Petrov 60), Healy, Lambert (Boyd 46), Mjallby, Burchill (Miller 46), Berkovic, Petta.
Jeunesse Esch: Van Rijswijck; Lamborelle, Schauls, Wagner (Phill 71), Schaack, Meylender, Kurtz (Nies 64), Borbiconi, Amodio, Sabotic, Betis (Felgin 68).

Cork City (0) 0
Lausanne (0) 1 *(Gobet 61)*   6000
Cork City: Mooney; Horgan, Delaney (O'Halloran 66), Daly, Napier, Freyne, Cahill, Cotter (Caulfield 59), Herrick, Morley, O'Brien (Flanagan 82).
Lausanne: Rapo; Meyer, Lombardo (Horjak 85), Mazzoni (Simon 90), Santini, Kuzba (Lutsenko 78), Puce, Karlen, Hellebuyck, Gomes, Gobet.

Halmstad (3) 4 *(Arvidsson 5, 26, Bertilsson 34 (pen), Selakovic 76)*
Bangor City (0) 0   646
Halmstad: Johansson; Arvidsson, Gustafson (Karlsson 68), Vennberg, Bertilsson, Nilsson (Jensen 53), Hansson, Aubynn Obeng (Gustavsson 63), Bjorklund, Klaesson, Selakovic.
Bangor City: Mulliner; Johnson, Foster, Williams E, Williams S, Williams R (Coady 51), Rowlands, Hughes, Owen (Comley-Exceli 78), Hazelden (Bird 78), Cross.

Hearts (3) 3 *(McSwegan 6, Tomaschek 19, O'Neil 39)*
IBV (0) 0   8720
Hearts: Niemi; Pressley, Naysmith, Locke (Murray 60), Severin, Tomaschek (Flogel 46), Juanjo, Fulton, McSwegan (Kirk 64), Makel, O'Neil.
IBV: Kristinsson; Gudmundsson, Aleksic, Stefansson, Sigurdsson I (Moller 69), Bragason, Johanesson, Jonsson, Sigurdsson M (Johannson 80), Almarsson, Mileta (Vidarsson 69).

Lillestrom (0) 1 *(Powell 60)*
Glentoran (0) 0 1046

Lillestrom: Baron; Bjarmann, Hansen, Kihlberg, Fjeldstad (Sigurdsson 53), Kristinsson, Helland, Powell (Hjartarson 73), Sundgot (Eriksen 83), Berntsen, Nilsen.
Glentoran: Gough; Leeman, Kennedy, Walker, McCombe (Ferguson 90), Young, McCann, Hamill, Fitzgerald (Armstrong 62), Batey, Lockhart.

Orgryte (1) 1 *(Kuhn 44)*
Coleraine (0) 0 2350

Orgryte: Last; Lindqvist, Sjostedt, Kuhn, Owusu, Allback (Karlsson 78), Kallander, Lohm (Nilsson 78), Tomaz, Elmander (Johansson 75), Hemberg.
Coleraine: McKeown; Smyth, Devine, Stewart, Picking, McCoosh, McAllister, Gray, Keegan (McAuley 78), McLaughlin, Tolan.

FIRST ROUND, FIRST LEG
11 SEPT

Bohemians (0) 1 *(Crowe 90 (pen))*
Kaiserslautern (0) 3 *(Reich 73, Hristov 76, Tare 79)* 5750

Bohemians: Russell; O'Connor (Shelly 90), Maher, Hill, Morrison (Williamson 66), O'Brien (O'Neill 58), Webb, Caffrey, Hunt, Crowe, Molloy.
Kaiserslautern: Koch G; Komljenovic, Koch H, Ramzy, Basler (Reich 20), Grammozis (Klose 46), Strasser, Pettersson (Tare 70), Hristov, Lokvenc, Djorkaeff.

14 SEPT

Celtic (2) 2 *(Larsson 14, 25)*
HJK Helsinki (0) 0 40,544

Celtic: Gould; McNamara, Mahe (Healy 51), Valgaeren, Mjallby, Boyd, Petrov, Lambert, Sutton, Larsson, Moravcik (Berkovic 76).
HJK Helsinki: Viander; Turpeinen, Heikkenen, Quivasto, Saarinen, Jeremenko (Haraala 81), Nylund, Hakapaa, Jussila (Paulus 90), Kallio, Rafael (Antonio 76).

Chelsea (1) 1 *(Panucci 24)*
St Gallen (0) 0 18,196

Chelsea: Cudicini; Panucci, Le Saux, Dalla Bona (Morris 73), Leboeuf, Desailly, Wise, Di Matteo, Hasselbaink, Flo (Gudjohnsen 73), Zola.
St Gallen: Stiel; Zellweger, Imhof, Zwyssig, Dal Santo, Winkler, Muller, Guido, Nixon, Amoah, Jairo.

Leicester C (1) 1 *(Taggart 43)*
Red Star Belgrade (1) 1 *(Acimovic 1)* 21,198

Leicester C: Flowers; Impey (Collymore 46), Guppy, Elliott, Rowett, Taggart, Lennon, Izzet, Akinbiyi (Cresswell 65), Eadie, Savage.
Red Star Belgrade: Kocic; Bunjevcevic, Glogovac, Lalatovic, Markovic, Lerinc, Boskovic (Gvozdenovic 87), Vitakic, Acimovic (Bajcetic 8), Drulic (Stevanovic 75), Pjanovic.

Rapid Bucharest (0) 0
Liverpool (1) 1 *(Barmby 29)* 9782

Rapid Bucharest: Lucescu; Stanciu, Mutica, Lencsi, Buta (Schumacher 46), Maldarasanu, Isaila, Iftodi (Buga 73), Frasineanu, Pancu, Constantin (Radu 60).
Liverpool: Westerveld; Song, Ziege (Traore 85), Hamann, Henchoz, Babbel, Carragher, Diomede, Heskey (Murphy 38), Owen (Fowler 80), Barmby.

Stuttgart (1) 1 *(Balakov 35)*
Hearts (0) 0 9845

Stuttgart: Hildebrand; Meissner, Thiam, Balakov, Carnell, Seitz (Pinto 62), Soldo, Endress (Schneider 38), Lisztes, Hosny, Dundee (Ganea 80).
Hearts: Niemi; Pressley, Naysmith, Severin (Makel 46), Murray, Petric, Carricondo-Perez, Flogel, Jackson (McSwegan 78), Cameron (Nielson 90), Simpson.

FIRST ROUND, SECOND LEG
21 SEPT

Kaiserslautern (0) 0
Bohemians (1) 1 *(Crowe 45)* 12,379

Kaiserslautern: Koch G; Ramzy, Hristov, Koch H, Grammozis, Komljenovic, Tare (Klose 46), Petterson, Reich, Strasser, Lokvenc.
Bohemians: Russell; Hopper (O'Connor 58), Webb, Hunt, Bowman, Hill, Morrison, Caffrey, O'Keeffe, Crowe, Williamson (O'Neill 62).

28 SEPT

HJK Helsinki (1) 2 *(Roiha 41, 75)*
Celtic (0) 1 *(Sutton 108)* aet 6530

HJK Helsinki: Viander; Turpeinen, Heikkinen, Quivasto, Nylund, Jeremenko (Antonio 78), Kallio, Hakkanpaa (Yla-Jussila 46), Saarinen, Kopteff (Haarala 65), Roiha.
Celtic: Gould; McNamara (Moravcik 90), Petta, Mjallby, Boyd (Riseth 35), Valgaeren, Lambert, Petrov, Sutton, Larsson, Berkovic (Healy 69).

Hearts (1) 3 *(Pressley 17, Petric 62, Cameron 84 (pen))*
Stuttgart (1) 2 *(Dundee 37, Bordon 58)* 14,488

Hearts: Niemi; Pressley, Naysmith, Murray, James, Petric, Carricondo-Perez, Flogel, Kirk (McSwegan 76), Cameron, Locke (Nielson 27).
Stuttgart: Hildebrand; Meissner, Bordon, Thiam, Balakov (Blank 87), Schneider, Carnell, Seitz (Pinto 68), Lisztes (Todt 72), Hosny, Dundee.

Liverpool (0) 0
Rapid Bucharest (0) 0 37,954

Liverpool: Westerveld; Heggem, Traore (Ziege 50), Hamann, Babbel, Hyypia, Gerrard, Diomede (Barmby 60), Fowler, Owen, Berger.
Rapid Bucharest: Lucescu; Stanciu, Constantinovici, Lencsi, Chirita, Maldarasanu, Isaila, Frasineanu, Schumacher (Radu 66), Iftodi (Bundea 56), Pancu (Constantin 74).

Red Star Belgrade (1) 3 *(Drulic 22, 71, Gvozdenovic 47)*
Leicester City (1) 1 *(Izzet 41)* 12,700

Red Star Belgrade: Kocic; Lalatovic, Bunjevcevic, Vitakic, Markovic, Ilic (Bajcetic 43), Lerinc (Boskovic 60), Gvozdenovic, Acimovic (Zoric 81), Drulic, Pjanovic.
Leicester City: Flowers; Impey, Guppy (Davidson 78), Elliott, Rowett, Taggart, Lennon, Izzet, Akinbiyi (Gunnlaugsson 78), Eadie (Cresswell 57), Savage.

St Gallen (2) 2 *(Muller 19, Amoah 35)*
Chelsea (0) 0 15,620

St Gallen: Zellweger; Imhof, Zwyssig, Dal Santo, Muller (Contini 78), Guido, Gairo, Nixon (Colacino 73), Amoah, Gane (Berger 68).
Chelsea: Cudicini; Panucci (Aleksidze 46), Le Saux, Melchiot, Leboeuf, Bogarde, Morris, Di Matteo (Dalla Bona 31), Hasselbaink, Flo (Gudjohnsen 57), Zola.

SECOND ROUND, FIRST LEG
26 OCT

Bordeaux (1) 1 *(Dugarry 23)*
Celtic (1) 2 *(Larsson 25 (pen))* 21,318

Bordeaux: Rame; Grenet, Roche (Saveljic 82), Somneil, Basto, Feindouno, Legwinski (Batiles 82), Diabate, Laslandes (Bugnet 90), Pauleta, Dugarry.
Celtic: Gould; Agathe, Petta (Healy 90), Mjallby, Boyd, Valgaeren, McNamara, Petrov, Moravcik, Larsson, Lambert.

Liverpool (0) 1 *(Heskey 88)*
Slovan Liberec (0) 0 29,662

Liverpool: Westerveld; Carragher, Ziege, Hamann, Babbel, Henchoz, Murphy (McAllister 69), Smicer (Barmby 69), Heskey, Fowler, Berger.
Slovan Liberec: Hauzr; Lexa, Pilny, Johana, Capek, Neumann, Janu, Michalik, Kozuch (Bakes 83), Stajner (Jun 71), Liuni (Nezmar 79).

SECOND ROUND, SECOND LEG

9 NOV

Celtic (0) 1 *(Moravcik 54)*
Bordeaux (0) 2 *(Laslandes 78, 114)*   *aet* 51,242
Celtic: Gould; Agathe, Petta (Berkovic 105), Mjallby, Boyd, Valgaeren, McNamara (Healy 40), Petrov, Sutton, Larsson, Moravcik (Johnson 78).
Bordeaux: Rame; Jemmali (Saveljic 101), Roche, Sommeil, Bonnisel, Diabate (Afanou 56), Batiles (Basto 81), Legwinski, Dugarry, Laslandes, Pauleta.

Slovan Liberec (1) 2 *(Stajner 9, Breda 85)*
Liverpool (1) 3 *(Barmby 30, Heskey 76, Owen 82)*   6808
Slovan Liberec: Hauzr; Lexa, Pilny, Johana, Capek, Neumann, Janu, Michalik (Breda 84), Jun (Nezmar 81), Stajner, Liuni (Kozuch 73).
Liverpool: Westerveld; Carragher (Murphy 55), Ziege, Hamann (Owen 81), Babbel, Hyypia, Gerrard, Smicer, Heskey, Fowler (McAllister 63), Barmby.

THIRD ROUND, FIRST LEG

23 NOV

Olympiakos (0) 2 *(Alexandris 65, 90)*
Liverpool (0) 1 *(Barmby 38, Gerrard 67)*   43,855
Olympiakos: Eleftheropoulos; Amanatidis, Kontis, Anatolakis, Mavrogenidis (Giannakopoulos 58), Patsatzoglou, Poursanidis (Luciano 45), Zetterberg (Georgatos 72), Djordjevic, Giovanni, Alexandris.
Liverpool: Westerveld; Carragher, Traore (Staunton 46), Hamann, Babbel, Hyypia, Gerrard, Barmby, Heskey, Owen (Smicer 66), Murphy (McAllister 90).

30 NOV

Rangers (0) 1 *(Albertz 88)*
Kaiserslautern (0) 0   47,279
Rangers: Klos; Wilson, Numan, Ferguson B, Amoruso, Konterman, de Boer (McCann 69), Reyna, Mols (Wallace 85), Miller, Albertz.
Kaiserslautern: Koch G; Koch H, Yakin, Ramzy, Buck (Reich 90), Pettersson, Komljenovic, Hristov, Grammozis, Djorkaeff (Strasser 82), Lokvenc (Klose 56).

THIRD ROUND, SECOND LEG

7 DEC

Kaiserslautern (1) 3 *(Klose 8, Buck 65, Lokvenc 79)*
Rangers (0) 0   28,757
Kaiserslautern: Koch G; Koch H, Yakin, Ramzy, Buck, Komljenovic (Strasser 4), Hristov (Basler 88), Grammozis, Djorkaeff, Lokvenc, Klose (Marschall 70).
Rangers: Klos; Wilson, Numan, Ricksen (McCann 46), Amoruso, Konterman, Reyna, Tugay (Dodds 77), Wallace, Miller (Mols 46), Albertz.

Liverpool (1) 2 *(Heskey 28, Barmby 60)*
Olympiakos (0) 0   35,484
Liverpool: Westerveld; Babbel, Carragher, Hamann, Henchoz, Hyypia, Gerrard (McAllister 90), Smicer, Heskey, Barmby, Murphy (Ziege 78).
Olympiakos: Eleftheropoulos; Poursanidis, Amanatidis, Anatolakis, Georgatos, Mavrogenidis (Luciano 54), Patsatzoglou, Zetterberg (Niniadis 64), Djordjevic, Giovanni, Alexandris (Oforiquaye 64).

FOURTH ROUND, FIRST LEG

15 FEB

Roma (0) 0
Liverpool (0) 2 *(Owen 46, 72)*   60,000
Roma: Antonioli; Rinaldi, Samuel, Mangone, Cafu, Emerson, Tomassi (Batistuta 66), Candela, Nakata (Assuncao 51), Montella, Delvecchio (Guigou 82).
Liverpool: Westerveld; Babbel, Carragher, Hamann, Henchoz, Hyypia, Barmby, McAllister, Fowler, Owen (Litmanen 80), Ziege (Smicer 74).

FOURTH ROUND, SECOND LEG

22 FEB

Liverpool (0) 0
Roma (0) 1 *(Guigou 70)*   43,688
Liverpool: Westerveld; Babbel, Carragher, Hamann, Henchoz, Hyypia, Barmby (Fowler 81), McAllister, Heskey, Owen (Smicer 67), Ziege.
Roma: Antonioli; Zebina, Samuel, Zago, Rinaldi (Guigou 59), Tomassi, Assuncao, Nakata, Candela, Montella (Balbo 78), Delvecchio (Batistuta 59).

Gallant Alaves cruelly succumb to an own goal conceded by Delfiin Geli in the Final with Liverpool. (Colorsport)

QUARTER-FINALS, FIRST LEG

8 MAR

Porto (0) 0
Liverpool (0) 0   22,000
Porto: Ovchinnikov; Secretario, Jorge Costa (Aloisio 59), Andrade, Nelson, Deco, Paredes, Chainho, Capucho, Pena, Drulovic (Candido Costa 74).
Liverpool: Westerveld; Babbel, Carragher, Hamann, Henchoz, Hyypia, Gerrard, Smicer, Fowler (Heskey 70), Owen (Barmby 79), Ziege (Murphy 55).

QUARTER-FINALS, SECOND LEG

15 MAR

Liverpool (2) 2 *(Murphy 33, Owen 38)*
Porto (0) 0   40,502
Liverpool: Westerveld; Babbel, Carragher, Hamann, Henchoz, Hyypia, Gerrard, Smicer (Litmanen 74), Fowler (Heskey 74), Owen, Murphy (Ziege 89).
Porto: Espinha; Secretario (Capucho 46), Silva, Andrade, Nelson, Alenichev, Paulinho Santos (Maric 80), Paredes, Candido Costa (Deco 46).

SEMI-FINALS, FIRST LEG

5 APR

Barcelona (0) 0
Liverpool (0) 0   90,000
Barcelona: Reina; Gabri, Puyol, Frank de Boer, Sergi, Guardiola, Cocu, Luis Enrique (Xavi 72), Rivaldo, Overmars (Zenden 72), Kluivert.
Liverpool: Westerveld; Babbel, Carragher, Hamann, Henchoz, Hyypia, Gerrard, Murphy (Smicer 59), Heskey, Owen (Fowler 73), Berger (McAllister 84).

SEMI-FINALS, SECOND LEG

19 APR

Liverpool (1) 1 *(McAllister 45 (pen))*
Barcelona (0) 0   44,203
Liverpool: Westerveld; Babbel, Carragher, Hamann, Henchoz, Hyypia, Gerrard (Murphy 78), Smicer (Fowler 81), Heskey, Owen (Berger 63), McAllister.
Barcelona: Reina; Puyol, Reiziger (Simao 58), Frank de Boer, Cocu, Guardiola, Petit, Luis Enrique, Rivaldo, Overmars (Dani 74), Kluivert.

FINAL

(in Dortmund, 16 May 2001, 65,000)

Liverpool (3) 5 *(Babbel 4, Gerrard 16, McAllister 41 (pen), Fowler 73, Geli 117 (og))*
Alaves (1) 4 *(Alonso 27, Javi Moreno 48, 51, Cruyff 89)*
aet; Liverpool won in sudden death.
Liverpool: Westerveld; Babbel, Carragher, Hamann, Henchoz (Smicer 56), Hyypia, Gerrard, McAllister, Heskey (Fowler 65), Owen (Berger 79), Murphy.
Alaves: Herrera; Eggen (Alonso 23), Karmona, Tellez, Contra, Tomic, Desio, Astudillo (Magno 46), Geli, Cruyff, Javi Moreno (Pablo 65).
Referee: Veissiere (France).

Liverpool manager Gerard Houllier beams with justified delight, holding the UEFA Cup, his third trophy of the season. (ASP)

SUMMARY OF APPEARANCES

EUROPEAN CUP (1955–2001)

English clubs
12 Liverpool, Manchester U
5 Arsenal
4 Leeds U
3 Nottingham F
2 Derby Co, Wolverhampton W, Everton, Aston Villa
1 Burnley, Tottenham H, Ipswich T, Manchester C,
   Blackburn R, Newcastle U, Chelsea

Scottish clubs
21 Rangers
16 Celtic
3 Aberdeen
2 Hearts
1 Dundee, Dundee U, Kilmarnock, Hibernian

Welsh clubs
3 Barry T
1 Cwmbran T, TNS

Northern Ireland clubs
19 Linfield
9 Glentoran
3 Crusaders
2 Portadown
1 Glenavon, Ards, Distillery, Derry C, Coleraine,
   Cliftonville

Eire clubs
7 Shamrock R, Dundalk
6 Waterford
3 Drumcondra, St Patrick's Ath, Shelbourne
2 Bohemians, Limerick, Athlone T, Derry C*
1 Cork Celtic, Cork City, Sligo R

**Winners: Celtic 1966–67; Manchester U 1967–68,
1998–99; Liverpool 1976–77, 1977–78, 1980–81, 1983–84;
Nottingham F 1978–79, 1979–80; Aston Villa 1981–82**

**Finalists: Celtic 1969–70; Leeds U 1974–75; Liverpool
1984–85**

EUROPEAN CUP-WINNERS' CUP (1960–1999)

English clubs
6 Tottenham H
5 Manchester U, Liverpool, Chelsea
4 West Ham U
3 Arsenal, Everton
2 Manchester C
1 Wolverhampton W, Leicester C, WBA, Leeds U,
   Sunderland, Southampton, Ipswich T, Newcastle U

Scottish clubs
10 Rangers
8 Aberdeen, Celtic
3 Hearts
2 Dunfermline Ath, Dundee U
1 Dundee, Hibernian, St Mirren, Motherwell,
   Airdrieonians, Kilmarnock

Welsh clubs
14 Cardiff C
8 Wrexham
7 Swansea C
3 Bangor C
1 Borough U, Newport Co, Merthyr Tydfil, Barry T,
   Llansantfraid, Cwmbran T

Northern Ireland clubs
9 Glentoran
5 Glenavon
4 Ballymena U, Coleraine
3 Crusaders, Linfield
2 Ards, Bangor
1 Derry C, Distillery, Portadown, Carrick Rangers,
   Cliftonville

Eire clubs
6 Shamrock R
4 Shelbourne
3 Limerick, Waterford, Dundalk, Bohemians
2 Cork Hibs, Galway U, Sligo R, Derry C*, Cork City
1 Cork Celtic, St Patrick's Ath, Finn Harps, Home
   Farm, University College Dublin, Bray W

**Winners: Tottenham H 1962–63; West Ham U 1964–65;
Manchester C 1969–70; Chelsea 1970–71, 1997–98;
Rangers 1971–72; Aberdeen 1982–83; Everton 1984–85;
Manchester U 1990-91; Arsenal 1993–94**

**Finalists: Rangers 1960–61, 1966–67; Liverpool 1965–66;
Leeds U 1972–73; West Ham U 1975–76; Arsenal
1979–80, 1994–95**

EUROPEAN FAIRS CUP & UEFA CUP (1955–2001)

English clubs
11 Leeds U
10 Liverpool
9 Aston Villa, Arsenal
8 Ipswich T
7 Manchester U, Newcastle U
6 Everton, Tottenham H
5 Southampton, Nottingham F
4 Manchester C, Birmingham C, Wolverhampton W,
   WBA, Chelsea
3 Sheffield W
2 Stoke C, Derby Co, QPR, Blackburn R, Leicester C
1 Burnley, Coventry C, Norwich C, London Rep XI,
   Watford, West Ham U

Scottish clubs
18 Dundee U
14 Hibernian, Aberdeen, Celtic
11 Rangers
10 Hearts
6 Kilmarnock
5 Dunfermline Ath
4 Dundee
3 St Mirren
2 Partick T, Motherwell, St Johnstone
1 Morton, Raith R

Welsh Clubs
3 Inter Cardiff (formerly Inter Cable-Tel), Bangor C
2 Newtown, Barry T
1 Afan Lido, Cwmbran

Northern Ireland clubs
12 Glentoran
8 Coleraine
7 Linfield
5 Portadown
4 Glenavon
3 Crusaders
1 Ards, Ballymena U, Bangor

Eire clubs
11 Bohemians
5 Dundalk
4 Shamrock R, Shelbourne, Cork City
3 Finn Harps, St Patrick's Ath
2 Drumcondra, Derry C*
1 Cork Hibs, Athlone T, Limerick, Drogheda U,
   Galway U, Bray Wanderers

**Winners: Leeds U 1967–68, 1970–71; Newcastle U
1968–69; Arsenal 1969–70; Tottenham H 1971–72,
1983–84; Liverpool 1972–73, 1975–76; Ipswich T 1980–81**

**Finalists: London 1955–58, Birmingham C 1958–60,
1960–61; Leeds U 1966–67; Wolverhampton W 1971–72;
Tottenham H 1973–74; Dundee U 1986–87**

* Now play in League of Ireland

INTERTOTO CUP 2000

FIRST ROUND
Cwmbran Town v Otaci 0-1, 0-1
Araks v Olomouc 1-2, 0-1
Dynamo Tbilisi v Standard Liege 2-2, 1-1
Dnepr v Silkeborg 2-1, 2-1
Trencin v Dinaburg 0-3, 0-1
Pelister v Hobscheid 3-1, 1-0
Floriana v Stabaek 1-1, 0-2
Glenavon v Belupo 1-1, 0-3
HB Torshavn v Tatabanya 0-4, 0-3
Cibalia v Obilic 3-1, 1-1
Trans v Ceahlaul 2-5, 2-4
Kocaeli v Atlantas 0-1, 1-0
Atlantas won 5-3 on penalties.
LASK v Hapoel Petah Tikva 3-0, 1-1
Leiftur v Lucerne 2-2, 4-4
MyPa v Neuchatel Xamax 1-2, 3-3
Nea v Vllaznia 4-1, 2-1
Primorje v Westerlo 5-0, 6-0
UCD v Velbazhd 3-3, 0-0
Vastra Frolunda v Zrinjski 1-0, 1-2
Lubin v Vllash 4-0, 3-1

SECOND ROUND
Perugia v Standard Liege 1-2, 1-1
Sedan v Leiftur 3-0, 3-2
Dinaburg v Aalborg 0-0, 0-1
Otaci v Salzburg 2-6, 1-1
Velbazhd v Olomouc 2-0, 0-8
Zenit v Primorje 3-0, 3-1
Atlantas v Bradford City 1-3, 1-4
Chmel v Dnepr 6-2, 2-0
Pelister v Vastra Frolunda 3-1, 0-0
LASK v Pribram 1-1, 2-3
Tatabanya v Cibalia 3-2, 0-0
Nea v FK Austria 1-0, 0-3
Neuchatel Xamax v Stuttgart 1-6, 1-4
Mallorca v Ceahlaul 2-1, 1-3
Stabaek v Auxerre 0-2, 0-3
Lubin v Belupo 1-1, 0-0

THIRD ROUND
Aalborg v Udinese 0-2, 2-1
Bradford City v RKC 2-0, 1-0
Celta Vigo v Pelister 3-0, 2-1
Sedan v Wolfsburg 0-0, 1-2
Ceahlaul v FK Austria 2-2, 0-3
Pribram v Aston Villa 0-0, 1-3
Rostelmash v Auxerre 0-2, 1-3
Zenit v Tatabanya 2-1, 2-1
Chmel v Kalamata 5-0, 3-0
Belupo v Olomouc 1-1, 0-2
Standard Liege v Salzburg 3-1, 1-1
Lens v Stuttgart 2-1, 0-1

SEMI-FINALS
Auxerre v Wolfsburg 1-1, 2-1
Celta Vigo v Aston Villa 1-0, 2-1
Zenit v Bradford City 1-0, 3-0
FK Austria v Udinese 0-1, 0-2
Olomouc v Chmel 3-1, 0-0
Stuttgart v Standard Liege 1-1, 1-0

FINALS
Auxerre v Stuttgart 0-2, 1-1
Celta Vigo v Zenit 2-1, 2-2
Olomouc v Udinese 2-2, 2-4
Stuttgart, Celta Vigo and Udinese qualified for the UEFA Cup.

Atlantas (1) 1 *(Lukosevicius 26 (pen))*   3174
Bradford City (2) 3 *(Rankin 9, Windass 38, Blake 74 (pen))*
Bradford City: Davison; Todd, Jacobs, Myers, Westwood, Bower, Kerr, Blake, Windass, Rankin, Whalley.

Bradford City (2) 4 *(Mills 12, 36, Blake 70 (pen), Grant 85)*
Atlantas (0) 1 *(Karalius 90)*   10,012
Bradford City: Clarke; Todd, Jacobs (Myers 75), McCall, Wetherall, O'Brien, Windass, Blake, Mills (Rankin 83), Saunders (Grant 70), Whalley.

Bradford City (0) 2 *(Windass 50, 73 (pen))*
RKC (0) 0   8343
Bradford City: Clarke (Davison 46); Nolan, Myers, McCall, Wetherall, Atherton, Windass, Whalley (Hopkin 67), Mills, Saunders, Sharpe (Grant 80).

RKC (0) 0
Bradford City (0) 1 *(Mills 81)*   3700
Bradford City: Walsh; Halle, Nolan, O'Brien, Wetherall (Westwood 85), Atherton, Hopkin (Lawrence 75), Windass (Blake 85), Mills, Whalley, Sharpe.

Pribram (0) 0
Aston Villa (0) 0   7852
Aston Villa: James; Delaney, Wright, Barry, Ehiogu, Samuel, Taylor, Boateng, Dublin, Merson, Stone (Vassell 71).

Aston Villa (1) 3 *(Dublin 8, Taylor 56, Nilis 61)*
Pribram (1) 1 *(Kulic 21)*   8200
Aston Villa: James; Barry, Wright, Southgate, Ehiogu, Taylor, Stone, Boateng (Hendrie 56), Dublin (Vassell 65), Nilis (Joachim 75), Merson.

Zenit (1) 1 *(Tarasov 16)*
Bradford City (0) 0   18,500
Bradford City: Davison; Nolan, Myers, McCall, Atherton, O'Brien, Hopkin (Whalley 85), Windass, Mills, Saunders, Sharpe.

Bradford City (0) 0   9572
Zenit (0) 3 *(Ugarov 68, Gorovoy 75, Tarasov 85)*
Bradford City: Clarke; Halle, Nolan, McCall, Atherton, O'Brien, Hopkin, Windass, Mills, Blake (Beagrie 73), Whalley (Lawrence 82).

Celta Vigo (0) 1 *(McCarthy 89)*
Aston Villa (0) 0   9550
Aston Villa: James; Stone, Wright, Barry, Samuel, Taylor, Thompson, Boateng, Dublin, Hendrie, Nilis (Vassell 19) (Joachim 90).

Aston Villa (1) 1 *(Barry 45 (pen))*
Celta Vigo (1) 2 *(McCarthy 11, 58)*   11,909
Aston Villa: James; Stone (Thompson 48), Wright, Southgate, Barry, Samuel (Hendrie 33), Taylor, Boateng, Joachim (Cooke 74), Walker, Merson.

EUROPEAN CUP DRAWS 2001–2002

EUROPEAN CUP
FIRST QUALIFYING ROUND
1. Levski Sofia v Zeljeznicar
2. Linfield v Kutaisi
3. KR v Vllaznia
4. Jugo v Kaunas
5. VB v Slavia Mozyr
6. Bohemians v Levadia
7. Barry Town v Shamkir
8. Valletta v Haka
9. Dudelange v Skonto Riga
10. Araks v Serif

SECOND QUALIFYING ROUND
Anderlecht v Winners of 10
Shakhtjor Donetsk v Lugano
Dunaferr or Ferencvaros v Hajduk Split
Winners of 6 v Halmstad
Winners of 2 v FC Copenhagen
Omonia v Red Star Belgrade
Winners of 8 v Maccabi Haifa
Winners of 1 v Brann
Galatasaray v Winners of 3
Porto v Winners of 7
Steaua v Winners of 4

Winners of 9 v Wisla
Winners of 5 v Inter Bratislava
Maribor v Glasgow Rangers

UEFA CUP
QUALIFYING ROUND
Cosmos v Rapid Vienna
Pelister v St Gallen
Dinamo Bucharest v Dynamo Tirana
Olimpija v Baku
Midtjylland v Glentoran
Trans v Elfsborg
FC Brugge v IA Akranes
GI Gotu v Obilic
Brasov v Mika
Viking v Brotnjo
CSKA Kiev v Jokerit
Vardar v Standard Liege
HJK Helsinki v Ventspils
Cwmbran Town v Slovan Bratislava
Maritimo v Sarajevo
Pogon v Fylkir
Dynamo Zagreb v Flora
Glenavon v Kilmarnock

AEL v SK Tirana
Hapoel Tel Aviv v Ararat Erevan
Etzella v Legia
Zimbru Chisinau v Gaziantep
Dinaburg v Osijek
Neftchi v Gorica
HB v Graz
Atlantas v Rapid Bucharest
Pouchov v Sliema Wanderers
Longford Town v Litets
Brondby v Shelbourne
Santa Coloma v Partizan Belgrade
Maccabi Tel Aviv v Zalgiris
Shakhter v CSKA Sofia
MyPa v Helsingborg
Dynamo Tbilisi v BATE Borisov
Debrecen v Otaci
Polonia v TNS
Lokomotiv Tbilisi v Birkirkara
Grevenmacher v AEK Athens
Ruzomberok v Belshina
Olympiakos Nicosia v Dunaferr,
Ferencvaros or Hajduk Split
Vaduz v Varteks

WORLD CLUB CHAMPIONSHIP

Played annually up to 1974 and intermittently since then between the winners of the European Cup and the winners of the South American Champions Cup — known as the Copa Libertadores. In 1980 the winners were decided by one match arranged in Tokyo in February 1981 and the venue has been the same since. AC Milan replaced Marseille who had been stripped of their European Cup title in 1993.

1960 Real Madrid beat Penarol 0-0, 5-1	1981 Flamengo beat Liverpool 3-0
1961 Penarol beat Benfica 0-1, 5-0, 2-1	1982 Penarol beat Aston Villa 2-0
1962 Santos beat Benfica 3-2, 5-2	1983 Gremio Porto Alegre beat SV Hamburg 2-1
1963 Santos beat AC Milan 2-4, 4-2, 1-0	1984 Independiente beat Liverpool 1-0
1964 Inter-Milan beat Independiente 0-1, 2-0, 1-0	1985 Juventus beat Argentinos Juniors 4-2 on penalties
1965 Inter-Milan beat Independiente 3-0, 0-0	after a 2-2 draw
1966 Penarol beat Real Madrid 2-0, 2-0	1986 River Plate beat Steaua Bucharest 1-0
1967 Racing Club beat Celtic 0-1, 2-1, 1-0	1987 FC Porto beat Penarol 2-1 after extra time
1968 Estudiantes beat Manchester United 1-0, 1-1	1988 Nacional (Uru) beat PSV Eindhoven 7-6 on
1969 AC Milan beat Estudiantes 3-0, 1-2	penalties after 1-1 draw
1970 Feyenoord beat Estudiantes 2-2, 1-0	1989 AC Milan beat Atletico Nacional (Col) 1-0 after
1971 Nacional beat Panathinaikos* 1-1, 2-1	extra time
1972 Ajax beat Independiente 1-1, 3-0	1990 AC Milan beat Olimpia 3-0
1973 Independiente beat Juventus* 1-0	1991 Red Star Belgrade beat Colo Colo 3-0
1974 Atlético Madrid* beat Independiente 0-1, 2-0	1992 Sao Paulo beat Barcelona 2-1
1975 Independiente and Bayern Munich could not	1993 Sao Paulo beat AC Milan 3-2
agree dates; no matches.	1994 Velez Sarsfield beat AC Milan 2-0
1976 Bayern Munich beat Cruzeiro 2-0, 0-0	1995 Ajax beat Gremio Porto Alegre 4-3 on penalties
1977 Boca Juniors beat Borussia Moenchengladbach*	after 0-0 draw
2-2, 3-0	1996 Juventus beat River Plate 1-0
1978 Not contested	1997 Borussia Dortmund beat Cruzeiro 2-0
1979 Olimpia beat Malmö* 1-0, 2-1	1998 Real Madrid beat Vasco da Gama 2-1
1980 Nacional beat Nottingham Forest 1-0	1999 Manchester U beat Palmeiras 1-0

*European Cup runners-up; winners declined to take part.

2000

28 November, Tokyo

Boca Juniors (2) 2 *(Palermo 3, 6)*

Real Madrid (1) 1 *(Roberto Carlos 11)*   51,000

Boca Juniors: Cordoba; Bermudez, Matellan, Serna, Traverso, Ibarra, Basualdo, Battaglia (Burdisso 88), Delgardo (Schelotto 85), Palermo, Riquelme.
Real Madrid: Casillas; McManaman (Savio 66), Geremi, Karanka, Hierro, Roberto Carlos, Figo, Makelele (Morientes 75), Raul, Guti, Helguera.
Referee: Acosta (Colombia).

EUROPEAN SUPER CUP

Played annually between the winners of the European Champions' Cup and the European Cup-Winners' Cup. AC Milan replaced Marseille in 1993–94.

1972 Ajax beat Rangers 3-1, 3-2	1986 Steaua Bucharest beat Dynamo Kiev 1-0
1973 Ajax beat AC Milan 0-1, 6-0	1987 FC Porto beat Ajax 1-0, 1-0
1974 Not contested	1988 KV Mechelen beat PSV Eindhoven 3-0, 0-1
1975 Dynamo Kiev beat Bayern Munich 1-0, 2-0	1989 AC Milan beat Barcelona 1-1, 1-0
1976 Anderlecht beat Bayern Munich 4-1, 1-2	1990 AC Milan beat Sampdoria 1-1, 2-0
1977 Liverpool beat Hamburg 1-1, 6-0	1991 Manchester U beat Red Star Belgrade 1-0
1978 Anderlecht beat Liverpool 3-1, 1-2	1992 Barcelona beat Werder Bremen 1-1, 2-1
1979 Nottingham F beat Barcelona 1-0, 1-1	1993 Parma beat AC Milan 0-1, 2-0
1980 Valencia beat Nottingham F 1-0, 1-2	1994 AC Milan beat Arsenal 0-0, 2-0
1981 Not contested	1995 Ajax beat Zaragoza 1-1, 4-0
1982 Aston Villa beat Barcelona 0-1, 3-0	1996 Juventus beat Paris St. Germain 6-1, 3-1
1983 Aberdeen beat Hamburg 0-0, 2-0	1997 Barcelona beat Borussia Dortmund 2-0, 1-1
1984 Juventus beat Liverpool 2-0	1998 Chelsea beat Real Madrid 1-0
1985 Juventus v Everton not contested due to UEFA	1999 Lazio beat Manchester U 1-0
ban on English clubs	

2000

25 August, Monaco

Galatasaray (1) 2 *(Jardel 40 (pen), 102)*

Real Madrid (0) 1 *(Raul 78 (pen))*   14,000

Galatasaray: Taffarel; Capone (Fatih 85), Unsal, Emre, Popescu, Bulent K, Okan (Hasan Sas 81), Suat, Jardel, Hagi (Bulent A 72), Umit.
Real Madrid: Casillas; Geremi, Helguera, Roberto Carlos, Celades (Michel Salgado 100), Campo (Conceicao 66), Guti (Munitis 53), Figo, Raul, Savio, Makelele.
aet; Galatasaray won on sudden death.
Referee: Benko (Austria).

INTERNATIONAL DIRECTORY

The latest available information has been given regarding numbers of clubs and players registered with FIFA, the world governing body. Where known, official colours are listed. With European countries, League tables show a number of signs. * indicates relegated teams, + play-offs, *+ relegated after play-offs, ++ promoted.

There are 197 member associations and one provisional member, Palestine. The four home countries, England, Scotland, Northern Ireland and Wales, are dealt with elsewhere in the Yearbook; but basic details appear in this directory.

EUROPE

ALBANIA

The Football Association of Albania, Rruga Dervish Hima Nr. 31, Tirana.
Founded: 1930; *Number of Clubs:* 49; *Number of Players:* 5,192; *National Colours:* All red.
Telephone: 00-355-42 27 877; *Cable:* ALBSPORT TIRANA; *Telex:* 2228 bfssh ab. *Fax:* 00 355-42 50 275.

International matches 2000
Andorra (h) 3-0, Azerbaijan (h) 1-0, Malta (a) 1-0, Macedonia (a) 0-1, Cyprus (h) 0-0, Finland (a) 1-2, Greece (h) 2-0, Malta (h) 3-0.

League Championship wins (1930-37; 1945-2001)
SK Tirana 19 (including 17 Nentori 8); Dinamo Tirana 15; Partizani Tirana 9; Vllaznia 9; Flamurtari 1; Elbasan 2 (including Labinoti 1); Skenderbeu 1, Teuta 1.

Cup wins (1948-2001)
Partizani Tirana 14; Dinamo Tirana 12; SK Tirana 9 (including 17 Nentori 6); Vllaznia 5; Teuta 3; Elbasan 3 (including Labintoti 1); Flamurtari 2; Apolonia 1.

Final League Table 2000-01
	P	W	D	L	F	A	Pts
Vllaznia	26	17	5	4	51	22	56
SK Tirana	26	16	6	4	56	13	54
Dinamo	26	15	7	4	43	21	52
Bylis	26	12	6	8	31	28	42
Shkumbini	26	12	5	9	40	36	41
Teuta	26	9	6	11	28	30	33
Beselidhja	26	9	6	11	34	41	33
Luftetari	26	9	5	12	31	33	32
Lushnja	26	8	8	10	33	36	32
Apolonia	26	8	6	12	28	42	30
Flamurtari	26	8	5	13	26	33	29
Tomori	26	8	4	14	33	48	28
Besa*	26	6	6	14	16	37	24
Skenderbeu*	26	5	5	16	25	55	20

Top scorer: Fortuzi (SK Tirana) 31.
Cup Final: Teuta 0, SK Tirana 0.
Teuta won 5-4 on penalties.

ANDORRA

Federacio Andorrana de Futbol, C/Sant Salvador, 10-2-5, Edifici Galerias Plaza, Andorra la Vella, Principat d'Andorra.
Founded: 1994; *Number of Clubs:* 12; *Number of Players:* 300; *National Colours:* Yellow shirts, red shorts, yellow stockings.
Telephone: 00376 862003; *Fax:* 00376 862006.

International matches 2000
Albania (a) 0-3, Malta (a) 1-1, Azerbaijan (a) 0-0, Belarus (h) 2-0, Estonia (a) 0-1, Cyprus (h) 2-3, Estonia (h) 1-2, Cyprus (a) 0-5.

League Championship wins (1996-2001)
Principat 3; Dicoansa 1; Constelacio 1; St Julia 1.

Cup wins (1996-2000)
Principat 4; Constelacio 1.

Final League Table 2000-01
	P	W	D	L	F	A	Pts
St Julia	14	12	0	2	47	16	36
Santa Coloma	14	9	4	1	29	14	31
Inter	14	5	4	5	25	22	19
Principat	14	5	4	5	20	24	19
Encamp	14	5	3	6	25	29	18
Lusitanos	14	3	3	8	21	37	12
Deportivo LM	14	2	5	7	17	30	11
Sporting	14	1	5	8	21	33	8

ARMENIA

Football Federation of Armenia, 9, Abovian Str. 375001 Erevan, Armenia.
Founded: 1992; *Number of Clubs:* 32; *Number of Players:* 15,000; *National Colours:* Red shirts, blue shorts, orange stockings.
Telephone: 00374 2/589480; *Telex:* 243337 minor su; *Fax:* 00374 2/151573.

International matches 2000
Guatemala (a) 1-1, Moldova (h) 2-1, Cyprus (a) 2-3, Georgia (a) 1-2, Georgia (h) 0-0, Lithuania (a) 2-1, Norway (a) 0-0, Ukraine (h) 2-3, Belarus (a) 1-2.

League Championship wins (1992-2000)
Shirak Gyumri 4*; Pyunik 2; Ararat Erevan 2*; Homenmen 1; FC Erevan 1; Tsement 1; Araks 1.
*Includes one unofficial title.

Cup wins (1992-2001)
Ararat Erevan 5; Tsement 2; Banants 1; Pyunik 1; Mika 1.

Final League Table 2000
	P	W	D	L	F	A	Pts
Araks (ex-Tsement)	28	19	4	5	65	33	61
Ararat	28	18	5	5	50	23	59
Shirak	28	17	7	4	64	21	58
Mika	28	15	4	9	45	31	49
Zvartnorts#	28	11	8	9	44	41	41
Kilikia	28	9	3	16	49	56	30
Lemagorts	28	3	3	22	29	82	12
Dinamo	28	1	4	23	19	78	7

excluded from competition; refusing to complete programme.
Top scorer: Hakobian (Araks) 21.
Cup Final: Ararat 1, Mika 1.
Ararat won 4-3 on penalties.

AUSTRIA

Oesterreichischer Fussball-Bund, Ernst-Happel Stadion, Postfach 340, Meierestrasse, A-1021 Wien.
Founded: 1904; *Number of Clubs:* 2,081; *Number of Players:* 253,576; *National Colours:* White shirts, black shorts, white stockings.
Telephone: 0043 1 727 180; *Cable:* FOOTBALL WIEN; *Telex:* 111919 oefb a; *Fax:* 0043 1 728 1632.

International matches 2000
Greece (a) 1-4, Sweden (h) 1-1, Croatia (h) 1-2, Hungary (a) 1-1, Iran (h) 5-1, Liechtenstein (a) 1-0, Spain (h) 1-1.

League Championship wins (1912-2001)
Rapid Vienna 30; FK Austria 22; Admira-Energie-Wacker 9; Tirol-Svarowski-Innsbruck 9; First Vienna 6; Wiener Sportklub 3; Austria Salzburg 3; Sturm Graz 2; FAC 1; Hakoah 1; Linz ASK 1; WAF 1; Voest Linz 1.

Cup wins (1919-2001)
FK Austria 25; Rapid Vienna 14; TS Innsbruck (prev. Wacker Innsbruck) 7; Admira-Energie-Wacker (prev. Sportklub Admira & Admira-Energie) 5; First Vienna 3; Sturm Graz 3; Graz 2; Linz ASK 1; Wacker Vienna 1; WAF 1; Wiener Sportklub 1; Stockerau 1; Ried 1; Karnten 1.

Final League Table 2000-01

	P	W	D	L	F	A	Pts
Innsbruck	36	20	8	8	63	31	68
Rapid	36	16	12	8	62	36	60
Graz	36	16	9	11	49	40	57
Sturm Graz	36	16	7	13	58	44	55
FK Austria	36	14	8	14	47	43	50
Austria Salzburg	36	13	10	13	49	45	49
Ried	36	13	9	14	51	52	48
Bregenz	36	10	8	18	40	67	38
Modling	36	8	12	16	29	63	36
Linz ASK*	36	8	9	19	43	70	33

Top scorer: Gilewicz (Innsbruck) 22.
Cup Final: Karnten 2, Innsbruck 1.

AZERBAIJAN

Association of Football Federations of Azerbaijan, Husu Haciyev kuc., 42, 370009 Baku, Azerbaijan.
Founded: 1992; *Number of Clubs:* 1,500;. *Number of Players:* 95,000; *National Colours:* White shirts with blue stripes, blue shorts, white stockings.
Telephone: 00994 12 94 49 16; *Cable:* FOOTBALL ASSOCIATION, AZ; *Fax:* 00994 12 98 93 93.

International matches 2000
Malta (a) 0-3, Albania (a) 0-1, Andorra (h) 0-0, Georgia (h) 0-0, Sweden (a) 0-1, Macedonia (a) 0-3, Turkey (h) 0-1.

League Championship wins (1992-2001)
Kopaz 3; Karabach 2; Neftchi 2; Shamkir 2; Turan 1.

Cup wins (1992-2001)
Kopaz 4; Neftchi 3; Karabach 1; Inshatchi 1; Shafa 1.

Final League Table 2000-01

	P	W	D	L	F	A	Pts
Shamkir	20	16	3	1	60	14	51
Neftchi	20	16	3	1	57	11	51
Vilash	20	11	5	4	24	11	38
Shafa	20	10	1	9	27	26	31
Turan	20	9	3	8	42	28	30
Dinamo Baku	20	9	2	9	30	29	29
Khazar Universitesi	20	9	2	9	26	38	29
Kopaz	20	8	1	11	34	29	25
Karabach	20	5	3	12	21	38	18
Araz*	20	4	2	14	16	56	15
Shahdagh*	20	0	1	19	5	63	1

Play-Off
Shamkir 1, Neftchi 0.
Top scorer: Aliyev (Dinamo Baku) 12.
Cup Final: Shafa 2, Neftchi 1.

BELARUS

Belarus Football Association, 8–2 Kyrov Str. 220600 Minsk, Belarus.
Founded: 1989; *Number of Clubs:* 455; *Number of Players:* 120,000; *National Colours:* All green.
Telephone: 007 0172 375 272325; *Telex:*252175 athlet su; *Fax:* 007 0172 27 29 20.

International matches 2000
Bulgaria (a) 1-4, Andorra (a) 0-2, Estonia (a) 0-2, Latvia (a) 1-0, Wales (h) 2-1, Poland (a) 1-3, Armenia (h) 2-1.

League Championship wins (1992-2000)
Dynamo Minsk 6; Slavia Mozyr (formerly MPKC Mozyr) 2; Dnepr Mogilev 1; BATE Borisov 1.

Cup wins (1992-2001)
Belshina 3; Dynamo Minsk 2; Slavia Mozyr (formerly MPKC Mozyr) 2; Neman 1; Dynamo 93 Minsk 1; Lokomotiv 96 1.

Final League Table 2000

	P	W	D	L	F	A	Pts
Slavia	30	23	5	2	78	25	74
BATE Borisov	30	20	4	6	68	26	64
Dynamo Minsk	30	19	5	6	49	21	62
Neman	30	17	6	7	56	29	57
Shakhter	30	15	9	6	47	29	54
Gomel	30	17	2	11	50	41	53
Dnepr Mogilev	30	14	7	9	55	33	49
Torpedo Minsk	30	13	10	7	43	28	49
Belshina	30	11	5	14	42	38	38
Dynamo Brest	30	10	4	16	37	51	34
Lokomotiv 96	30	8	7	15	34	50	31
Vedrich 97	30	6	11	13	23	36	29
Naftan	30	5	7	18	25	69	22
Lida	30	3	10	17	16	60	19
Torpedo Kadino	30	5	2	23	31	71	17
Kommunalnik	30	3	8	19	19	66	17

Top scorer: Vasiliuk (Slavia) 31.
Cup Final: Belshina 1, Slavia 0.

BELGIUM

Union Royale Belge Des Societes De Football Association, 145 Avenue Houba de Strooper, B-1020 Bruxelles.
Founded: 1895; *Number of Clubs:* 2,120; *Number of Players:* 390,468; *National Colours:* All red.
Telephone: 0032 2 477 12 11; *Cable:* URBSFA BRUX-ELLES; *Telex:* 23257 bvbfbf b; *Fax:* 0032 2 478 23 91.

International matches 2000
Portugal (h) 1-1, Holland (h) 2-2, Norway (a) 2-0, Denmark (a) 2-2, Sweden (h) 2-1, Italy (h) 0-2, Turkey (h) 0-2, Bulgaria (a) 3-1, Croatia (h) 0-0, Latvia (a) 4-0.

League Championship wins (1896-2001)
Anderlecht 26; Union St Gilloise 11; FC Brugge 11; Standard Liege 8; Beerschot 7; RC Brussels 6; FC Liege 5; Daring Brussels 5; Antwerp 4; Mechelen 4; Lierse SK 4; SV Brugge 3; Beveren 2; RWD Molenbeek 1; Genk 1.

Cup wins (1954-2001)
Anderlecht 8; FC Brugge 7; Standard Liege 5; Beerschot 2; Waterschei 2; Beveren 2; Gent 2; Antwerp 2; Lierse SK 2; Genk 2; Racing Doornik 1; Waregem 1; SV Brugge 1; Mechelen 1; FC Liege 1; Ekeren 1; Westerlo 1.

Final League Table 2000-01

	P	W	D	L	F	A	Pts
Anderlecht	34	25	8	1	88	25	83
FC Brugge	34	23	9	2	83	24	78
Standard Liege	34	16	12	6	72	42	60
Lokeren	34	16	9	9	56	42	57
Gent	34	16	9	9	61	49	57
Beerschot	34	17	3	14	62	53	54
Mouscron	34	15	8	11	63	49	53
Westerlo	34	15	8	11	61	53	53
Charleroi	34	14	5	15	51	65	47
Lierse	34	12	7	15	44	51	43
Genk	34	11	9	14	45	51	42
Royal Antwerp	34	11	7	16	38	45	40
St Truiden	34	9	8	17	44	54	35
Beveren	34	9	8	17	30	64	35
La Louviere	34	6	12	16	32	56	30
Aalst	34	7	8	19	33	65	29
Harelbeke*	34	8	4	22	36	79	28
Mechelen*	34	4	10	20	40	72	22

Top scorer: Radzinski (Anderlecht) 23.
Cup Final: Westerlo 1, Lommel 0.

BOSNIA HERZEGOVINA

Bosnia & Herzegovina Football Federation, Sime Milutinovico, 12/1 71000 Sarajevo.
Founded: 1992; *National Colours:* White shirts, blue shorts, white stockings.
Telephone: 00387 71/213881; *Fax:* 00387 71/444332.

International matches 2000
Qatar (a) 0-2, Macedonia (h) 1-0, FIFA XI (h) 0-1, Turkey (h) 2-0, Spain (h) 1-2, Israel (a) 1-3.

League Championship wins (1996-2000)
Celik 2; Zeljeznicar 1; Sarajevo 1; Brotnjo 1.
Cup wins (1996-2001)
Sarajevo 2; Zeljeznicar 2; Bosna 1; Celik 1.

Muslim Final League Table 2000-01

	P	W	D	L	F	A	Pts
Zeljeznicar	42	28	7	7	113	38	91
Brotnjo	42	26	6	10	82	28	84
Sarajevo	42	24	9	9	81	35	81
Celik	42	21	10	11	75	40	73
Velez	42	22	3	17	86	54	69
Jedinstvo	42	20	8	14	67	40	68
Siroki	42	18	11	13	72	43	65
Posusje	42	20	5	17	59	43	65
Iskra	42	17	14	11	56	49	65
Troglav	42	19	8	15	59	57	65
Sloboda	42	17	13	12	50	41	64
Orasje	42	19	6	17	66	54	63
Zrinjski	42	19	6	17	53	54	63
Olimpik	42	18	8	16	61	47	62
Travnik*	42	18	7	17	65	72	61
Buducnost*	42	17	7	18	68	63	58
Kiseljak*	42	18	4	20	59	65	58
Rudar*	42	17	5	20	72	62	56
Capljina*	42	15	6	21	53	71	51
Ljubuski*	42	8	5	29	41	86	29
Krajina*	42	3	5	34	23	147	14
Zenica*	42	1	1	40	10	196	4

Cup Final: Zeljeznicar 3, Sarajevo 2.

Croatian Final League Table 2000-01

	P	W	D	L	F	A	Pts
Borac	30	20	3	7	66	22	63
Sloboda	30	15	6	9	50	39	51
Rudar Ugljevik	30	15	5	10	45	32	50
Boksit	30	15	3	12	55	36	48
BSK	30	14	6	10	40	28	48
Leotar	30	13	8	9	58	37	47
Mladost	30	14	3	13	46	31	45
Modrica	30	14	3	13	41	44	45
Kozara	30	14	1	15	48	46	43
Radnik	30	12	5	13	34	37	41
Ljubic	30	11	7	12	35	39	40
Slavija	30	12	3	15	38	51	39
Glasinac	30	10	7	13	26	41	37
Polet	30	12	0	18	43	49	36
Rudar Prijedor	30	8	7	15	38	60	31
Lijebce	30	6	3	21	28	99	21

There are three separate leagues in Bosnia, Muslim, Serbian and Croatian. An agreement was reached on play-offs for an overall winner between Muslim and Croatian League in 2000.

BULGARIA

Bulgarian Football Union, Karnigradska 19, BG-1000 Sofia.
Founded: 1923; *Number of Clubs:* 376; *Number of Players:* 48,240; *National Colours:* White shirts, green shorts, white stockings.
Telephone: 00359 2 987 74 90; *Cable:* BULFUTBOL SOFIA; *Telex:* 23145 bfs bg; *Fax:* 00359 2 986 2538.

International matches 2000
Slovakia (h) 1-0, Chile (a) 2-3, Australia (a) 1-1, Belarus (h) 4-1, Ukraine (h) 0-1, Belgium (h) 1-3, Czech Republic (h) 0-1, Malta (h) 3-0, Denmark (a) 1-1, Algeria (a) 2-1.

League Championship wins (1925-2001)
CSKA Sofia 28; Levski Sofia 21; Slavia Sofia 7; Vladislav Varna 3; Lokomotiv Sofia 3; Litets 2; Trakia Plovdiv 2; AC 23 Sofia 1; Botev Plovdiv 1; SC Sofia 1; Sokol Varna 1; Spartak Plovdiv 1; Tichka Varna 1; JSZ Sofia 1; Beroe Stara Zagora 1; Etur 1.

Cup wins (1946-2001)
Levski Sofia 20; CSKA Sofia 16; Slavia Sofia 7; Lokomotiv Sofia 4; Botev Plovdiv 1; Spartak Plovdiv 1; Spartak Sofia 1; Marek Stanke 1; Trakia Plovdiv 1; Spartak Varna 1; Sliven 1; Litets 1.

Final League Table 2000-01

	P	W	D	L	F	A	Pts
Levski Sofia	26	22	3	1	63	13	69
CSKA Sofia	26	19	5	2	65	16	62
Kustendil	26	18	3	5	48	29	57
Litets	26	17	4	5	70	23	55
Neftochimik	26	12	6	8	47	34	42
Slavia Sofia	26	10	5	11	35	35	35
Spartak Varna	26	10	4	12	38	40	34
Lokomotiv Sofia	26	9	6	11	37	37	33
Hebar	26	7	5	14	39	55	26
Chemo Varna	26	7	5	14	20	49	26
Chernomorets	26	6	4	16	22	48	22
Beroe+	26	6	4	16	21	47	22
Botev Plovdiv*	26	6	2	18	28	55	20
Mineur*	26	3	4	19	19	71	13

Top scorer: Ivanov G (Levski Sofia) 22.
Cup Final: Litets 1, Kustendil 0.

CROATIA

Croatian Football Federation, Illica 31, CRO-10000 Zagreb, Croatia.
Founded: 1912; *Number of Clubs:* 1,221; *Number of Players:* 78,127; *National Colours:* Red/white shirts, white shorts, blue stockings.
Telephone: 00385 1/4554100. *Fax:* 00385 1 42 46 39.

International matches 2000
Spain (h) 0-0, Germany (h) 1-1, Austria (a) 2-1, France (h) 0-2, Slovakia (a) 1-1, Belgium (a) 0-0, Scotland (h) 1-1.

League Championship wins (1941-44; 1992-2001)
Dynamo Zagreb (Formerly Croatia Zagreb) 6; Hajduk Split 4; Gradanski 3; Concordia 1.

Cup wins (1993-2001)
Dynamo Zagreb (Formerly Croatia Zagreb) 5, Hajduk Split 3, Osijek 1.

Championship Table 2000-01

	P	W	D	L	F	A	Pts
Hajduk Split	32	20	6	6	66	23	66
Dynamo Zagreb	32	19	8	5	70	36	65
Osijek	32	17	6	9	61	47	57
Varteks	32	12	9	11	56	56	45
Slaven	32	11	11	10	39	37	44
Zagreb	32	11	5	16	51	58	38

Promotion/Relegation Table 2000-01

	P	W	D	L	F	A	Pts
Sibenik	32	12	7	13	40	40	43
Cakovec	32	10	9	13	28	37	39
Rijeka	32	9	6	17	30	44	33
Cibalia	32	5	18	9	31	45	33
Dragovoljac	32	9	6	15	35	57	33
Marsonia+	32	7	8	17	41	68	29

Top scorer: Sokota (Dynamo Zagreb) 18.
Cup Final: Dynamo Zagreb 2, 1, Hajduk Split 0, 0.

CYPRUS

Cyprus Football Association, 1 Stasinos Str., Engomi, P.O. Box 5071, CY-2404 Nicosia.
Founded: 1934; *Number of Clubs:* 85; *Number of Players:* 6,000; *National Colours:* Blue shirts, white shorts, blue stockings.
Telephone: 00357 2 /352341; *Cable:* FOOTBALL CYPRUS; *Telex:* 3880 football cy; *Fax:* 00357 2/590544.

International matches 2000
Lithuania (h) 2-1, Armenia (h) 3-2, Romania (h) 3-2, Iran (h) 0-0, Romania (a) 0-2, Albania (a) 0-0, Andorra (a) 3-2, Holland (h) 0-4, Andorra (h) 5-0.

League Championship wins (1935-2001)
Omonia 18; Apoel 16; Anorthosis 11; AEL 5; EPA 3; Olympiakos 3; Apollon 2; Pezoporikos 2; Chetin Kayal 1; Trast 1.

Cup wins (1935-2001)
Apoel 17; Omonia 11; AEL 6; EPA 5; Anorthosis 5; Apollon 5; Trast 3; Chetin Kayal 2; Olympiakos 1; Pezoporikos 1; Salamina 1.

Final League Table 2000-01

	P	W	D	L	F	A	Pts
Omonia	26	17	6	3	60	27	57
Olympiakos	26	16	6	4	58	30	54
AEL	26	15	7	4	48	28	52
Anorthosis	26	15	6	5	60	32	51
Apoel	26	12	8	6	58	37	44
Apollon	26	12	8	6	56	40	44
AEK	26	9	9	8	52	47	36
APOP	26	8	9	9	45	53	33
ENP	26	8	6	12	42	53	30
Doxa	26	7	8	11	26	37	29
Ethnikos	26	6	10	10	44	49	28
Salamina*	26	7	6	13	41	47	27
Digenis*	26	3	2	21	28	78	11
Aris*	26	1	1	24	28	88	4

Top scorer: Rauffmann (Omonia) 30.
Cup Final: Apollon 1, Salamina 0.

CZECH REPUBLIC

Football Association of Czech Republic, Diskarska 100, 169 00 Prague 6 - Strahov, Czech Republic.
Founded: 1901; *Number of Clubs:* 3,836; *Number of Players:* 319,500; *National Colours:* Red shirts, white shorts, blue stockings.
Telephone: 00422 20513575; *Cable:* SPORTSVAZ PRAHA; *Telex:* 122650 cstv c; *Fax:* 004202 3335 3107.

International matches 2000
Mexico (h) 2-1, Republic of Ireland (a) 2-3, Australia (h) 3-1, Israel (h) 4-1, Germany (a) 2-3, Holland (a) 0-1, France (n) 1-2, Denmark (n) 2-0, Slovenia (h) 0-1, Bulgaria (a) 1-0, Iceland (h) 4-0, Malta (a) 0-0.

League Championship wins (1926-93)
Sparta Prague 20; Slavia Prague 12; Dukla Prague (prev. UDA) 11; Slovan Bratislava 7; Spartak Trnava 5; Banik Ostrava 3; Inter-Bratislava 1; Spartak Hradec Kralove 1; Viktoria Zizkov 1; Zbrojovka Brno 1; Bohemians 1; Vitkovice 1.

Cup wins (1961-93)
Dukla Prague 8; Sparta Prague 8; Slovan Bratislava 5; Spartak Trnava 4; Banik Ostrava 3; Lokomotiv Kosice 3; TJ Gottwaldov 1; Dunajska Streda 1.
From 1993-94, there were two separate countries; the Czech Republic and Slovakia.

League Championship wins (1993-2001)
Sparta Prague 8; Slavia Prague 1.

Cup wins (1994-2001)
Slavia Prague 2; Viktoria Zizkov 2; Spartak Hradec Kralove 1; Sparta Prague 1; Jablonec 1, Slovan Liberec 1.

Final League Table 2000-01

	P	W	D	L	F	A	Pts
Sparta Prague	30	21	5	4	71	31	68
Sigma Olomouc	30	14	10	6	47	33	52
Slavia Prague	30	14	10	6	46	32	52
Marila Pribran	30	14	9	7	40	26	51
Viktoria Zizkov	30	12	10	8	45	40	46
Slovan Liberec	30	12	9	9	39	31	45
Petra Drnovice	30	11	8	11	35	36	41
Teplice	30	12	4	14	45	39	40
Chmel Blsany	30	10	10	10	35	35	40
Bohemians	30	10	10	10	33	34	40
Synot	30	9	10	11	37	35	37
Jablonec	30	8	8	14	26	40	32
Artikel Brno	30	7	9	14	24	35	30
Banik Ostrava	30	7	9	14	28	45	30
Ceske Budejovice*	30	6	8	16	32	56	26
Victoria Plsen*	30	4	9	17	30	65	21

Top scorer: Tuma (Drnovice) 15.
Cup Final: Viktoria Zizkov 2, Sparta Prague 1.

DENMARK

Danish Football Association, Idraettens Hus, Brondby Stadion 20, DK-2605, Brondby.
Founded: 1889; *Number of Clubs:* 1,555; *Number of Players:* 268,517; *National Colours:* Red shirts, white shorts, red stockings.
Telephone: 0045 43/262222; *Cable:* DANSKBOLDSPIL COPENHAGEN; *Telex:* 15545 dbu dk; *Fax:* 0045 43/262245.

International matches 2000
Sweden (a) 0-1, Norway (a) 2-4, Finland (h) 1-2, Portugal (a) 1-2, Sweden (h) 0-1, Belgium (h) 2-2, France (n) 0-3, Holland (n) 0-3, Czech Republic (n) 0-2, Faeroes (a) 2-0, Iceland (a) 2-1, Northern Ireland (a) 1-1, Bulgaria (h) 1-1, Germany (h) 2-1.

League Championship wins (1913-2000)
KB Copenhagen 15; B 93 Copenhagen 10; AB (Akademisk) 9; Brondby 8; B 1903 Copenhagen 7; Frem 6; Esbjerg BK 5; Vejle BK 5; AGF Aarhus 5; Hvidovre 3; Odense BK 3; AaB Aalborg 2; B 1909 Odense 2; Koge BK 2; Lyngby 2; FC Copenhagen 1; Silkeborg 1; Herfolge 1.

Cup wins (1955-2001)
Aarhus GF 9; Vejle BK 6; Randers Freja 3; Lyngby 3; OB Odense 3; Brondby 3; B1909 Odense 2; Aalborg BK 2; Esbjerg BK 2; Frem 2; B 1903 Copenhagen 2; FC Copenhagen 2; B 93 Copenhagen 1; KB Copenhagen 1; Vanlose 1; Hvidovre 1; B1913 Odense 1; AB Copenhagen 1, Viborg 1; Silkeborg 1.

Final League Table 2000-01

	P	W	D	L	F	A	Pts
FC Copenhagen	33	17	12	4	55	27	63
Brondby	33	17	7	9	71	42	58
Silkeborg	33	15	11	7	49	36	56
Midtjylland	33	13	12	8	53	43	51
Aalborg	33	13	11	9	51	47	50
Viborg	33	13	7	13	51	42	46
Odense	33	13	7	13	49	44	46
Aarhus	33	13	5	15	53	58	44
Lyngby	33	12	8	13	40	53	33
AB Copenhagen	33	8	15	10	43	41	39
Herfolge*	33	7	9	17	41	65	30
Sonderjylland*	33	1	8	24	30	88	11

Top scorer: Graulund (Brondby) 21.
Cup Final: Silkeborg 4, AB Copenhagen 1.

ENGLAND

The Football Association, 16 Lancaster Gate, London W2 3LW.
Founded: 1863; *Number of Clubs:* 42,000; *Number of Players:* 2,250,000; *National Colours:* White shirts with navy blue collar, navy blue shorts, white stockings with light blue top.
Telephone: 020 7262 4542, 020 7402 7151; *Cable:* FOOTBALL ASSOCIATION LONDON W2; *Telex:* 261110 faldn g; *Fax:* 020 7402 0486.

ESTONIA

Estonian Football Association, Voidu 16, Tallinn EE 0012.
Founded: 1921; *Number of Clubs:* 40; *Number of Players:* 12,000; *National Colours:* Blue shirts, black shorts, white stockings.
Telephone: 00372 6/542715, 542716, 542717; *Fax:* 00372 6/542719.

International matches 2000
Finland (h) 2-4, Thailand (a) 1-2, Luxembourg (a) 1-1, Belarus (h) 2-0, Georgia (h) 1-0, Andorra (h) 1-0, Portugal (h) 1-3, Andorra (a) 2-1, Republic of Ireland (a) 0-2, Krygyzstan (h) 2-1, Hong Kong (a) 2-1.

League Championship wins (1922-40; 1992-2001)
Sport 8; Estonia 5; Flora Tallinn 4; Norma Tallinn 2; Tallinn JK 2; Kalev 2; Levadia 2; LFLS 1; Olimpia 1; Lantana 1.

Cup wins (1992-2001)
Levadia 4 (merged with Sadam); VMV Tallinn 1; Nikol Tallinn 1; Norma Tallinn 1, Lantana 1; Flora Tallinn 1; Trans 1.

Final League Table 2000

	P	W	D	L	F	A	Pts
Levadia	28	23	5	0	88	20	74
Flora	28	16	7	5	51	25	55
VMK	28	14	6	8	54	29	48
Tulevik	28	12	9	7	45	35	45
Trans	28	12	7	9	65	40	43
Lootus	28	6	4	18	26	54	22
Kuressaare	28	5	4	19	25	68	19
Valga*	28	2	2	24	11	94	8

Top scorers: Juska (VMK) 24, Krom (Levadia) 24.
Cup Final: Trans 1, Flora 0.

FAEROE ISLANDS

Fotboltssamband Foroya, The Faeroes' Football Assn., Gundalur, P.O. Box 3028, FR-110, Torshavn.
Founded: 1979; *Number of Clubs:* 16; *Number of Players:* 1,014; *National Colours:* White shirts, blue shorts, white stockings.
Telephone: 00298 31 6707/457607; *Telex:* 81328 nspkkl fa; *Fax:* 00298 31 9079.

International matches 2000
Finland (h) 0-1, Iceland (h) 2-3, Liechtenstein (a) 1-0, Denmark (h) 0-2, Slovenia (h) 2-2, Switzerland (a) 1-5.

League Championship wins (1942-2000)
KI Klaksvik 16; HB Torshavn 15; TB Tvoroyri 7; GI Gotu 7; B36 Torshavn 6; B68 Toftir 3; SI Sorvag 1; IF Fuglafjordur 1; B71 Sandur 1; VB 1.

Cup wins (1955-2000)
HB Torshavn 25; KI Klaksvik 5; GI Gotu 5; TB Tvoroyri 4; B36 Torshavn 1; VB Vagur 1; NSI Runavik 1; B71 Sandur 1.

Final League Table 2000

	P	W	D	L	F	A	Pts
VB	18	12	4	2	40	22	40
HB	18	11	5	2	40	21	38
B68	18	10	1	7	43	38	31
NSI	18	9	3	6	43	29	30
KI	18	9	3	6	42	28	30
B36	18	9	1	8	49	27	28
GI	18	8	2	8	41	38	26
B71	18	4	2	12	25	33	14
Vagar+	18	3	2	13	22	54	11
Sumba*	18	3	1	14	16	71	10

Cup Final: GI 1, HB 0.

FINLAND

Suomen Palloliitto Finlands Bollfoerbund, Lantinen Brahenkatu 2, P.O. Box 179, SF-00511 Helsinki.
Founded: 1907; *Number of Clubs:* 1,135; *Number of Players:* 66,100; *National Colours:* White shirts, blue shorts, white stockings.
Telephone: 00358 0 9701 01 01; *Cable:* SUOMIFOT-BOLL HELSINKI; *Telex:* 126033 spl sf; *Fax:* 00358 0 9701 01 099.

International matches 2000
Faeroes (a) 1-0, Iceland (h) 0-1, Denmark (a) 2-1, Thailand (a) 0-0, Estonia (a) 4-2, Thailand (a) 1-5, Wales (a) 2-1, Poland (a) 0-0, Latvia (a) 0-1, Norway (h) 3-1, Albania (h) 2-1, Greece (a) 0-1, England (h) 0-0, Republic of Ireland (a) 0-3.

League Championship wins (1949-2000)
HJK Helsinki 10; Valkeakosken Haka 8; Turun Palloseura 5; Kuopion Palloseura 5; Kuusysi 4; Lahden Reipas 3; IF Kamraterna 3; Ilves-Kissat 2; Jazz Pori 2; Kotkan TP 2; OPS Oulu 2; Torun Pyrkiva 1; IF Kronohagens 1; Helsinki PS 1; Kokkolan PV 1; Vasa 1; TPV Tampere 1.

Cup wins (1955-2000)
Valkeakosken Haka 10; Lahden Reipas 7; HJK Helsinki 7; Kotkan TP 4; Mikkeli 2; Kuusysi 2; Kuopion Palloseura 2; Ilves Tampere 2; TPS Turku 2; ; MyPa 2; IFK Abo 1; Drott 1; Helsinki PS 1; Pallo-Peikot 1; Rovaniemi PS 1, Jokerit 1 (formerly PK-35).

Final League Table 2000

	P	W	D	L	F	A	Pts
Haka	33	20	6	7	56	20	66
Jokerit	33	16	14	3	56	26	62
MyPa	33	18	7	8	50	34	61
HJK Helsinki	33	16	9	8	51	33	57
Jazz Pori	33	14	11	8	41	32	53
Tampere U	33	12	10	11	48	52	46
Inter	33	11	7	15	47	54	40
Lahti	33	10	9	14	36	35	39
RoPS Rovaniemi	33	10	6	17	35	50	36
VPS	33	8	10	15	38	42	34
TPS Turku	33	7	6	20	30	75	27
KTP Kotka	33	5	7	21	29	64	22

Final Pool:- Haka 67; HKJ Helsinki 65; MyPa 47; Jokerit 40; Inter 39; Jazz Pori 37; KTP Kotka 34; RoPS Rovaniemi 31.

Promotion/Relegation Pool:- TPS Turku 39; Lahti 30; VPS 29; TPV Tampere* 12.
Top scorer: Kuqi (Jokerit) 19.
Cup Final: HJK Helsinki 1, KTP Kotka 0.

FRANCE

Federation Francaise De Football, 60 Bis Avenue D'Iena, F-75783 Paris, Cedex 16.
Founded: 1919; *Number of Clubs:* 21,629; *Number of Players:* 1,692,205; *National Colours:* Blue shirts, white shorts, red stockings.
Telephone: 0033 1 44 31 73 00; *Cable:* CEFI PARIS 034; *Telex:* 640000 fedfoot f; *Fax:* 0033 1 47 20 82 96.

International matches 2000
Poland (h) 1-0, Scotland (a) 2-0, Slovenia (h) 3-2, Croatia (a) 2-0, Japan (h) 2-2, Morocco (a) 5-1, Denmark (n) 3-0, Czech Republic (n) 2-1, Holland (n) 2-3, Spain (n) 2-1, Portugal (n) 2-1, Italy (n) 2-1, FIFA XI (h) 5-1, England (h) 1-1, Cameroon (h) 1-1, South Africa (a) 0-0, Turkey (a) 4-0.

League Championship wins (1933-2001)
Saint Etienne 10; Olympique Marseille 8; Nantes 8; AS Monaco 7; Stade de Reims 6; Girondins Bordeaux 5; OGC Nice 4; Lille OSC 3; Paris St Germain 2; FC Sete 2; Sochaux 2; Racing Club Paris 1; Roubaix-Tourcoing 1; Strasbourg 1; Auxerre 1; Lens 1.

Cup wins (1918-2001)
Olympique Marseille 10; Saint Etienne 6; AS Monaco 6; Lille OSC 5; Racing Club Paris 5; Red Star 5; Olympique Lyon 4; Paris St Germain 4; Girondins Bordeaux 3; OGC Nice 3; Nantes 3; CAS Genereaux 2; Nancy 2; Racing Club Strasbourg 2; Sedan 2; FC Sete 2; Stade de Reims 2; SO Montpellier 2; Stade Rennes 2; Auxerre 2; AS Cannes 1; Club Français 1; Excelsior Roubaix 1; Le Havre 1; Olympique de Pantin 1; CA Paris 1; Sochaux 1; Toulouse 1; Bastia 1; Metz 1.

Final League Table 2000-01

	P	W	D	L	F	A	Pts
Nantes	34	21	5	8	58	36	68
Lyon	34	17	13	4	57	30	64
Lille	34	16	11	7	43	27	59
Bordeaux	34	15	12	7	48	33	57
Sedan	34	14	10	10	47	40	52
Rennes	34	14	6	14	46	39	48
Troyes	34	11	13	10	45	47	46
Bastia	34	13	6	15	45	41	45
Paris St Germain	34	12	8	14	44	45	44
Guingamp	34	11	11	12	40	48	44
Monaco	34	12	7	15	53	50	43
Metz	34	11	10	13	37	44	43
Auxerre	34	11	8	15	41	41	41
Lens	34	9	13	12	37	39	40
Marseille	34	11	7	16	31	40	40
St Etienne*	34	9	10	15	43	56	37
Toulouse*	34	8	10	16	34	50	34
Strasbourg*	34	7	8	19	28	61	29

Top scorer: Anderson (Lyon) 22.
Cup Final: Monaco 0, Nantes 0.
Monaco won 6-5 on penalties.

GEORGIA

Georgian Football Federation, 5 Shota Iamanidze Str, Tbilisi 380012, Georgia.
Founded: 1990; *Number of Clubs:* 4050. *Number of Players:* 115,000; *National Colours:* White shirts, black shorts, cherry stockings.
Telephone: 00995 32/960750; *Fax:* 00995 32/001128.

International matches 2000
Slovakia (a) 2-0, Romania (a) 1-1, Armenia (h) 2-1, Israel (a) 1-1, Armenia (a) 0-0, Azerbaijan (a) 0-0, Estonia (a) 0-1, Iran (a) 1-2, Lithuania (a) 4-0, Italy (a) 0-2.

League Championship wins (1990-2001)
Dynamo Tbilisi 10; Torpedo Kutaisi 2.

Cup wins (1992-2001)
Dynamo Tbilisi 7; Torpedo Kutaisi 2; Dynamo Batumi 1; Lokomotivi 1.

Championship Table 2000-01

	P	W	D	L	F	A	Pts
Torpedo Kutaisi	10	6	2	2	15	7	44
Lokomotivi	10	3	4	3	8	9	41
Dynamo Tbilisi	10	3	5	2	13	9	38
WIT	10	4	4	2	14	9	35
Kolkheti	10	3	2	5	14	18	24
Merani 91	10	1	3	6	4	16	19

Promotion/Relegation Table

	P	W	D	L	F	A	Pts
Dynamo Batumi	10	5	3	2	13	7	32
Sioni	10	5	2	3	16	15	27
Gorda	10	6	2	2	19	15	26
Dila Gori+	10	5	1	4	19	11	25
Armazi*	10	4	1	5	11	17	23
Samtredia*	10	0	1	9	7	26	3

Top scorer: Zirakishvili (Dynamo Tbilisi) 21.
Cup Final: Torpedo Kutaisi 0, Lokomotivi 0.
Torpedo Kutaisi won 4-3 on penalties.

GERMANY

Deutsche Fussball-Bund, Postfach 710265, D-60492, Frankfurt Am Main.
Founded: 1900; *Number of Clubs:* 26,760; *Number of Players:* 5,260,320; *National Colours:* White shirts, black shorts, white stockings.
Telephone: 0049 69 678 80; *Telex:* 416815 dfb d; *Fax:* 0049 69 678 82 66.

International matches 2000
Holland (a) 1-2, Croatia (a) 1-1, Switzerland (h) 1-1, Czech Republic (h) 3-2, Liechtenstein (h) 8-2, Romania (n) 1-1, England (n) 0-1, Portugal (n) 0-3, Spain (h) 4-1, Greece (h) 2-0, England (a) 1-0, Denmark (a) 1-2.

League Championship wins (1903-2001)
Bayern Munich 17; 1FC Nuremberg 9; Schalke 04 7; SV Hamburg 6; Borussia Moenchengladbach 5; Borussia Dortmund 5; VfB Stuttgart 4; 1FC Kaiserslautern 4; VfB Leipzig 3; Sp Vgg Furth 3; 1FC Cologne 3; Werder Bremen 3; Viktoria Berlin 2; Hertha Berlin 2; Hanover 96 2; Dresden SC 2; Munich 1860 1; Union Berlin 1; FC Freiburg 1; Phoenix Karlsruhe 1; Karlsruher FV 1; Holsten Kiel 1; Fortuna Dusseldorf 1; Rapid Vienna 1; VfB Mannheim 1; Rot-Weiss Essen 1; Eintracht Frankfurt 1; Eintracht Brunswick 1.

Cup wins (1935-2001)
Bayern Munich 10; 1FC Cologne 4; Eintracht Frankfurt 4; Werder Bremen 4; 1FC Nuremberg 3; SV Hamburg 3; Moenchengladbach 3; VfB Stuttgart 3; Schalke 04 3; Dresden SC 2; Fortuna Dusseldorf 2; Karlsruhe SC 2; Munich 1860 2; Borussia Dortmund 2; Kaiserslautern 2; First Vienna 1; VfB Leipzig 1; Kickers Offenbach 1; Rapid Vienna 1; Rot-Weiss Essen 1; SW Essen 1; Bayer Uerdingen 1; Hannover 96 1; Leverkusen 1.

Final League Table 2000-01

	P	W	D	L	F	A	Pts
Bayern Munich	34	19	6	9	62	37	63
Schalke	34	18	8	8	65	35	62
Borussia Dortmund	34	16	10	8	62	42	58
Leverkusen	34	17	6	11	54	40	57
Hertha	34	18	2	14	58	52	56
Freiburg	34	15	10	9	54	37	55
Werder Bremen	34	15	8	11	53	48	53
Kaiserslautern	34	15	5	14	49	54	50
Wolfsburg	34	12	11	11	60	45	47
Cologne	34	12	10	12	59	52	46
Munich 1860	34	12	8	14	43	55	44
Hansa Rostock	34	12	7	15	34	47	43
Hamburg	34	10	11	13	58	58	41
Cottbus	34	12	3	19	38	52	39
Stuttgart	34	9	11	14	42	49	38
Unterhaching*	34	8	11	15	35	59	35
Eintracht Frankfurt*	34	10	5	19	41	68	35
Bochum*	34	7	6	21	30	67	27

Top scorers: Barbarez (Hamburg) 22, Sand (Schalke) 22.
Cup Final: Schalke 2, Union Berlin 0.

GREECE

Federation Hellenique De Football, Singrou Avenue 137, 17121 Athens.
Founded: 1926; *Number of Clubs:* 4,050; *Number of Players:* 180,000; *National Colours:* White shirts, blue shorts, white stockings.
Telephone: 0030 1 933 88 50; *Cable:* FOOTBALL ATHENS; *Telex:* 215328 epo gr; *Fax:* 0030 1 935 96 66.

International matches 2000
Austria (h) 4-1, Romania (h) 2-0, Republic of Ireland (a) 1-0, Romania (a) 1-2, Switzerland (a) 2-2, Germany (a) 0-2, Finland (h) 1-0, Albania (a) 0-2, Slovakia (h) 0-2, Yugoslavia (h) 1-1.

League Championship wins (1928-2001)
Olympiakos 30; Panathinaikos 18; AEK Athens 11; Aris Salonika 3; PAOK Salonika 2; Larissa 1.

Cup wins (1932-2001)
Olympiakos 21; Panathinaikos 16; AEK Athens 12; PAOK Salonika 3; Panionios 2; Aris Salonika 1; Ethnikos 1; Iraklis 1; Kastoria 1; Larissa 1; Ofi Crete 1.

Final League Table 2000-01

	P	W	D	L	F	A	Pts
Olympiakos	30	25	3	2	84	22	78
Panathinaikos	30	20	6	4	61	20	66
AEK Athens	30	19	4	7	61	34	61
PAOK Salonika	30	14	9	7	66	48	51
Iraklis	30	14	4	12	45	40	46
Ionikos	30	12	8	10	46	46	44
Aris	30	13	5	12	37	41	44
Xanthi	30	11	5	14	24	37	38
Panionios	30	9	9	12	39	43	36
Ethnikos	30	9	7	14	34	52	34
Ofi Crete	30	9	6	15	39	49	33
Yiannina	30	8	9	13	40	53	33
Panachaiki	30	9	6	15	40	56	33
Paniliakos	30	7	8	15	26	46	29
Kalamata*	30	4	9	17	39	66	21
Athinaikos*	30	5	5	20	37	65	20

Top scorer: Alexandris (Olympiakos) 20.
Cup Final: PAOK Salonika 4, Olympiakos 2.

HOLLAND

Koninklijke Nederlandsche Voetbalbond, Woudenbergseweg 56-58, Postbus 515, NL-3700 AM, Zeist.
Founded: 1889; *Number of Clubs:* 3,097; *Number of Players:* 962,397; *National Colours:* Orange shirts, white shorts, orange stockings.
Telephone: 0031343 499211; *Cable:* VOETBAL ZEIST; *Telex:* 40497 knvb nl; *Fax:* 0031343 499189.

International matches 2000
Germany (h) 2-1, Belgium (a) 2-2, Scotland (h) 0-0, Romania (h) 2-1, Poland (h) 3-1, Czech Republic (h) 1-0, Denmark (h) 3-0, France (h) 3-2, Yugoslavia (h) 6-1, Italy (h) 0-0, Republic of Ireland (h) 2-2, Cyprus (h) 4-0, Portugal (h) 0-2, Spain (a) 2-1.

League Championship wins (1898-2001)
Ajax Amsterdam 27; PSV Eindhoven 16; Feyenoord 15; HVV The Hague 8; Sparta Rotterdam 6; Go Ahead Deventer 4; HBS The Hague 3; Willem II Tilburg 3; RCH Haarlem 2; RAP 2; Heracles 2; ADO The Hague 2; Quick The Hague 1; BVV Den Bosch 1; NAC Breda 1; Eindhoven 1; Enschede 1; Volewijckers Amsterdam 1; Limburgia 1; Rapid JC Heerlen 1; DOS Utrecht 1; DWS Amsterdam 1; Haarlem 1; Be Quick Groningen 1; SVV Schiedam 1; AZ 67 Alkmaar 1.

Cup wins (1899-2001)
Ajax Amsterdam 14; Feyenoord 10; PSV Eindhoven 8; Quick The Hague 4; AZ 67 Alkmaar 3; Rotterdam 3; DFC 2; Fortuna Geleen 2; Haarlem 2; HBS The Hague 2; RCH 2; Roda 2; VOC 2; Wageningen 2; Willem II Tilburg 2; FC Den Haag 2; Twente Enschede 2; Concordia Rotterdam 1; CVV 1; Eindhoven 1; HVV The Hague 1; Longa 1; Quick Nijmegen 1; RAP 1; Roermond 1; Schoten 1; Velocitas Breda 1; Velocitas Groningen 1; VSV 1; VUC 1; VVV Groningen 1; ZFC 1; NAC Breda 1; Utrecht 1.

Final League Table 2000-01

	P	W	D	L	F	A	Pts
PSV Eindhoven	34	25	8	1	73	23	83
Feyenoord	34	21	3	10	67	37	66
Ajax	34	18	7	9	85	43	61
Roda JC	34	17	8	9	59	41	59
Utrecht	34	17	8	9	58	43	59
Vitesse	34	16	11	7	56	43	59
RKC Waalwijk	34	16	11	7	48	36	59
Willem II	34	14	9	11	60	50	51
NAC Breda	34	13	10	11	41	40	49
Heerenveen	34	11	14	9	51	42	47
Twente	34	10	11	13	47	60	41
NEC Nijmegen	34	9	13	12	42	53	40
AZ	34	9	8	17	45	63	35
Groningen	34	8	9	17	36	56	33
De Graafschap	34	9	4	21	44	66	31
Fortuna Sittard+	34	8	7	19	31	64	31
Sparta+	34	6	7	21	42	72	25
Roosendaal*	34	4	2	28	37	90	14

Top scorer: Kezman (PSV Eindhoven) 24.
Cup Final: Twente 0, PSV Eindoven 0.
Twente won 4-3 on penalties.

HUNGARY

Hungarian Football Federation, Magyar Labdarugo Szovetseg, Istvanmezei ut. 3-5, Nepstadion (Toronyepulet), H-1146 Budapest. For correspondence: Pf. 106H-1581 Budapest.
Founded: 1901; *Number of Clubs:* 1944; *Number of Players* 95,986; *National Colours:* Red shirts, white shorts, green stockings.
Telephone: 0036 1 222 0343; *Telex:* 225782 misz h; *Fax:* 0036 1 222 0324/222 0344.

International matches 2000
Australia (h) 0-3, Poland (h) 0-0, Northern Ireland (a) 1-0, Saudi Arabia (h) 2-2, Israel (h) 2-1, Austria (h) 1-1, Italy (h) 2-2, Lithuania (a) 6-1, Macedonia (a) 1-0.

League Championship wins (1901-2000)
Ferencvaros 26; MTK-VM Budapest 21; Ujpest Dozsa 20; Honved 13; Vasas Budapest 6; Csepel 4; Raba Gyor 3; BTC 2; Nagyvarad 1; Vac 1; Dunaferr 1.

Cup wins (1910-2001)
Ferencvaros 17; MTK-VM Budapest 12; Ujpest Dozsa 8; Raba Gyor 4; Kispest Honved 4; Vasas Budapest 3; Diösgyör 2; ; Debrecen 2; Bocskai 1; III Ker 1; Kispesti AC 1; Soroksar 1; Szolnoki MAV 1; Siofok Banyasz 1; Bekescsaba 1; Pecs 1.
Cup not regularly held until 1964.

Qualifying League Table 2000-01
Group A

	P	W	D	L	F	A	Pts
Dunaferr	14	8	5	1	37	20	29
Tatabanya	14	8	5	1	29	18	29
Ferencvaros	14	6	3	5	23	21	21
Matav	14	6	2	6	21	23	20
Gyori	14	5	3	6	21	23	18
Kispest Honved	14	3	6	5	18	20	15
Haladas	14	3	4	7	14	24	13
Nyiregyhaza	14	3	0	11	10	24	9

Group B

	P	W	D	L	F	A	Pts
MTK	14	8	3	3	32	13	27
Ujpest	14	7	4	3	33	19	25
Vasas	14	7	4	3	24	11	25
Debrecen	14	7	2	5	27	20	23
Videoton	14	6	3	5	21	22	21
Zalaegerszeg	14	3	7	4	12	22	16
Pecs	14	2	3	9	13	24	9
Nagykanizsa	14	2	2	10	12	43	8

Final League Table 2000-01

	P	W	D	L	F	A	Pts
Ferencvaros	22	12	8	2	36	14	48
Dunaferr	22	13	2	7	40	35	46
Vasas	22	10	6	6	42	33	40
Ujpest	22	10	5	7	40	37	40
Gyori	22	11	5	6	34	32	40
MTK	22	8	5	9	31	22	35
Kispest Honved	22	9	6	7	33	31	34
Videoton	22	9	2	11	37	34	31
Matav	22	7	6	9	26	30	30
Zalaegerszeg	22	7	7	8	33	36	29
Debrecen*	22	6	3	13	31	44	24
Tatabanya*	22	1	3	18	20	55	12

Szeged (excluded).
Top scorer: Kabat (Vasas) 24.
Cup Final: Debrecen 5, Videoton 2.

ICELAND

Knattspyrnusamband Island, Laugardal, 104 Reykjavik.
Founded: 1929; *Number of Clubs:* 73; *Number of Players:* 23,673; *National Colours;* All blue.
Telephone: 00354 5102900; *Cable* KSI REYKJAVIK; *Telex:* 2314 isi is; *Fax:* 00354 75689793.

International matches 2000
Norway (a) 0-0, Finland (a) 1-0, Faeroes (a) 3-2, Malta (h) 5-0, Sweden (h) 2-1, Denmark (h) 1-2, Czech Republic (a) 0-4, Northern Ireland (h) 1-0, Poland (a) 0-1.

League Championship wins (1912-2000)
KR 22; Valur 19; Fram 18; IA Akranes 17; Vikingur 5; IBV Vestmann 4; IBK Keflavik 3; KA Akureyri 1.

Cup wins (1960-2000)
KR 10; Valur 8; Fram 7; IA Akranes 7; IBV Vestmann 4; IBK Keflavik 2; IBA Akureyri 1; Vikingur 1.

Final League Table 2000

	P	W	D	L	F	A	Pts
KR	18	11	4	3	27	14	37
Fylkir	18	10	5	3	39	16	35
Grindavik	18	8	6	4	25	18	30
IBV	18	8	5	5	29	17	29
IA	18	7	5	6	21	17	26
Keflavik	18	4	7	7	21	35	19
Breidablik	18	5	3	10	29	35	18
Fram	18	4	5	9	22	33	17
Stjarnan	18	4	5	9	18	31	17
Leiftur	18	3	7	8	24	39	18

Top scorers: Sigthorsson (KR) 14, Steinarsson (Keflavik) 14.
Cup Final: IA 2, IBV 1.

REPUBLIC OF IRELAND

The Football Association of Ireland, (Cumann Peile Na H-Eireann), 80 Merrion Square, South Dublin 2.
Founded: 1921; *Number of Clubs:* 3,190; *Number of Players:* 124,615; *National Colours:* Green shirts, white shorts, green and white stockings.
Telephone: 00353 1 676 68 64; *Telex:* 91397 fai ei; *Fax:* 00353 1 661 09 31.

International matches 2000
Czech Republic (h) 3-2, Greece (h) 0-1, Scotland (h) 1-2, Mexico (a) 2-2, USA (a) 1-1, South Africa (h) 2-1, Holland (a) 2-2, Portugal (h) 1-1, Estonia (h) 2-0, Finland (h) 3-0.

League Championship wins (1922-2001)
Shamrock Rovers 15; Dundalk 9; Shelbourne 9; St Patrick's Athletic 8; Bohemians 8; Waterford 6; Cork United 5; Drumcondra 5; St James's Gate 2; Cork Athletic 2; Sligo Rovers 2; Limerick 2; Athlone Town 2; Derry City 2; Dolphin 1; Cork Hibernians 1; Cork Celtic 1; Cork City 1.

Cup wins (1922-2001)
Shamrock Rovers 24; Dundalk 8; Shelbourne 6; Bohemians 6; Drumcondra 5; Cork Athletic 2; Cork United 2; St James's Gate 2; St Patrick's Athletic 2; Cork Hibernians 2; Limerick 2; Waterford 2; Derry

City 2; Athlone Town 2; Sligo 2; Bray Wanderers 2; Alton United 1; Cork 1; Fordsons 1; Transport 1; Finn Harps 1; Home Farm 1; UCD 1; Galway United 1; Cork City 1.

Final League Table 2000-01

	P	W	D	L	F	A	Pts
Bohemians	33	18	8	7	66	35	62
Shelbourne	33	17	9	7	53	37	60
Cork City	33	15	11	7	36	29	56
Bray Wanderers	33	15	10	8	52	35	55
St Patrick's Ath	33	14	11	8	54	41	53
Derry City	33	12	9	12	31	28	45
Shamrock Rovers	33	10	12	11	50	47	42
Longford Town	33	12	6	15	40	47	42
Galway United	33	10	10	13	34	47	40
UCD+	33	9	10	14	36	44	37
Finn Harps*	33	8	12	13	36	46	36
Kilkenny City*	33	1	6	26	14	66	9

Top scorer: Crowe (Bohemians) 25.
Cup Final: Bohemians 1, Longford Town 0.

ISRAEL

Israel Football Association, Ramat-Gan Stadium, 299 Aba Hilell Street, Ramat-Gan 52594.
Founded: 1948; *Number of Clubs:* 544; *Number of Players:* 30,449; *National Colours:* Blue shirts, white shorts, blue stockings.
Telephone: 00972 3 570 59 99; *Cable:* CADUREGEL RAMAT-GAN; *Telex:* 361353 fa; *Fax:* 00972 3 570 20 44.

International matches 2000
Russia (h) 4-1, Georgia (h) 1-1, Czech Republic (a) 1-4, Hungary (a) 1-2, Russia (a) 0-1, Liechtenstein (h) 2-0, Spain (a) 0-2, Bosnia (h) 3-1, Portugal (a) 1-2.

League Championship wins (1932-2001)
Maccabi Tel Aviv 18; Hapoel Tel Aviv 13; Hapoel Petah Tikva 6; Maccabi Haifa 6; Maccabi Netanya 5; Beitar Jerusalem 4; Hakoah Ramat Gan 2; Hapoel Beersheba 2; Bnei Yehouda 1; British Police 1; Hapoel Kfar Sava 1; Hapoel Ramat Gan 1; Hapoel Haifa 1.

Cup wins (1928-2001)
Maccabi Tel Aviv 20; Hapoel Tel Aviv 11; Beitar Jerusalem 5; Maccabi Haifa 5; Hapoel Haifa 3; Hapoel Kfar Sava 3; Beitar Tel Aviv 2; Bnei Yehouda 2; Hakoah Ramat Gan 2; Hapoel Petah Tikva 2; Maccabi Petah Tikva 2; British Police 1; Hapoel Jerusalem 1; Hapoel Lod 1; Maccabi Netanya 1; Hapoel Beersheba 1.

Final League Table 2000-01

	P	W	D	L	F	A	Pts
Maccabi Haifa	33	22	10	1	61	22	76
Hapoel Tel Aviv	33	19	10	4	51	25	67
Beitar Jerusalem	33	18	8	7	45	27	62
Hapoel Haifa	33	16	11	6	50	32	59
Maccabi Tel Aviv	33	15	10	8	57	32	55
Hapoel Petah Tikva	33	12	8	13	52	52	44
Maccabi Petah Tikva	33	10	8	15	35	40	38
Maccabi Netanya	33	10	8	15	46	52	38
Ironi Rishon	33	9	6	18	33	56	33
Ironi Ashdod	33	8	7	18	36	49	31
Bnei Yehuda*	33	6	9	18	34	58	27
Zafirim Holon*	33	4	3	26	22	77	15

Championship Pool: Maccabi Haifa 82 pts; Hapoel Tel Aviv 75; Hapoel Haifa 71; Maccabi Tel Aviv 65; Beitar Jerusalem 62*; Hapoel Petah Tikva 46.
Beitar Jerusalem one point deducted for player contract irregularity.

Promotion/Relegation Pool: Maccabi Netanya 49 pts; Maccabi Petah Tikva 45; Ironi Rishon 41; Ironi Ashdod 38; Bnei Yehouda 34; Zafirim Holon 16.
Cup Final: Maccabi Tel Aviv 3, Maccabi Petah Tikva 0.

ITALY

Federazione Italiana Giuoco Calcio, Via Gregorio Allegri 14, C.P. 2450, 1-0198, Roma.
Founded: 1898; *Number of Clubs:* 20,961; *Number of Players:* 1,420,160; *National Colours:* Blue shirts, white shorts, blue stockings with white trim.
Telephone: 0039 6 849 11; *Cable:* FEDERCALCIO ROMA; *Telex:* 624132 calcio i; *Fax:* 0039 6 849 12 526.

International matches 2000
Sweden (h) 1-0, Spain (a) 0-2, Portugal (h) 2-0, Norway (a) 0-1, Turkey (n) 2-1, Belgium (n) 2-0, Sweden (n) 2-1, Romania (n) 2-0, Holland (n) 0-0, France (n) 1-2, Hungary (a) 2-2, Romania (h) 3-0, Georgia (h) 2-0, England (h) 1-0.

League Championship wins (1898-2001)
Juventus 25; AC Milan 16; Inter-Milan 13; Genoa 9; Torino 8; Pro Vercelli 7; Bologna 7; AS Roma 3; Fiorentina 2; Lazio 2; Napoli 2; Casale 1; Novese 1; Cagliari 1; Verona 1; Sampdoria 1.

Cup wins (1922-2001)
Juventus 9; AS Roma 8; Fiorentina 6; Torino 4; AC Milan 4; Sampdoria 4; Lazio 3; Inter-Milan 3; Napoli 3; Bologna 2; Parma 2; Atalanta 1; Genoa 1; Vado 1; Venezia 1; Vicenza 1.

Final League Table 2000-01

	P	W	D	L	F	A	Pts
Roma	34	22	9	3	68	33	75
Juventus	34	21	10	3	61	27	73
Lazio	34	21	6	7	65	36	69
Parma	34	16	8	10	51	31	56
Internazionale	34	14	9	11	47	47	51
AC Milan	34	12	13	9	56	46	49
Atalanta	34	10	14	10	38	34	44
Brescia	34	10	14	10	44	42	44
Fiorentina	34	10	13	11	53	52	43
Bologna	34	11	10	13	49	53	43
Perugia	34	10	12	12	49	53	42
Udinese	34	11	5	18	49	59	38
Lecce	34	8	13	13	40	54	37
Reggina+	34	10	7	17	32	49	37
Verona+	34	10	7	17	40	59	37
Vicenza*	34	9	9	16	37	51	36
Napoli*	34	8	12	14	35	51	36
Bari*	34	5	5	24	31	68	20

Top scorer: Crespo (Lazio) 26.
Cup Final: Fiorentina 1, 1, Parma 0, 1.

LATVIA

Latvian Football Federation, Augsiela, 1, LV-1009, Riga.
Founded: 1921; *Number of Clubs:* 50; *Number of Players:*12,000; *National Colours:* Carmine red shirts, white shorts, carmine red stockings.
Telephone: 00371 2 29 29 88; *Fax:* 00371 7828331.

International matches 2000
Romania (a) 0-2, Slovakia (a) 1-3, Lithuania (a) 1-2, Lithuania (a) 1-2, Finland (h) 1-0, Belarus (h) 0-1, Scotland (h) 0-1, Belgium (h) 0-4, San Marino (a) 2-2.

League Championship wins (1922-2000)
Skonto Riga 10; ASK Riga 9; RFK Riga 8; Olympia Liepaya 7; Sarkanais Metalurgs Liepaya 7; VEF Riga 6; Energija Riga 4; Elektrons Riga 3; Torpedo Riga 3; Daugava Liepaya 2; ODO Riga 2; Khimikis Daugavpils 2; RAF Yelgava 2; Keisermezhs Riga 2; Dinamo Riga 1; Zhmilyeva Team 1; Darba Rezervi 1; REZ Riga 1; Start Brotseni 1; Venta Ventspils 1; Yurnieks Riga 1; Alfa Riga 1; Gauya Valmiera 1.

Cup wins (1937-2001)
Elektrons Riga 7; Skonto Riga 6; Sarkanais Metalurgs Liepaya 5; ODO Riga 3; VEF Riga 3; ASK Riga 3; Tseltnieks Riga 3; RAF Yelgava 3; RFK Riga 2; Daugava Liepaya 2; Start Brotseni 2; Selmash Liepaya 2; Yurnieks Riga 2; Khimikis Daugavpils 2; Rigas Vilki 1; Dinamo Liepaya 1; Dinamo Riga 1; REZ Riga 1; Voulkan Kouldiga 1; Baltija Liepaya 1; Venta Ventspils 1; Pilot Riga 1; Lielupe Yurmala 1; Energija Riga 1; Torpedo Riga 1; Daugava SKIF Riga 1; Tseltnieks Riga 1; Olympia Riga 1; FK Riga 1.

Final League Table 2000

	P	W	D	L	F	A	Pts
Skonto Riga	28	24	3	1	86	10	75
FK Ventspils	28	19	8	1	55	20	65
Metalurgs Liepaya	28	16	7	5	51	25	55
Dinaburg Daugavpils	28	10	5	13	32	32	35
FK Riga	28	9	4	15	35	47	31
FK Valmiera	28	5	9	14	25	48	24
Police FK	28	4	4	20	13	62	16
LU Daugava Riga	28	2	6	20	21	74	12

Top scorer: Kolesnichenko (Skonto Riga) 17.
Cup Final: Skonto Riga 2, Dinaburg Daugavpils 0.

LIECHTENSTEIN

Liechtensteiner Fussball-Verband, Malbuner Huus Altenbach 11, Postfach 165, 9490 Vaduz.
Founded: 1934; *Number of Clubs:* 7; *Number of Players:* 1,247; *National Colours:* Blue shirts, red shorts, blue stockings.
Telephone: 004175 237 4747; *Cable:* FUSSBALL-VERBAND VADUZ; *Fax:* 004175 237 4748.

International matches 2000
Faeroes (h) 0-1, Germany (a) 2-8, Israel (a) 0-2, Austria (h) 0-1.
Liechtenstein has no national league. Teams compete in Swiss regional leagues.

Cup wins (1946-2001)
Vaduz 30; Balzers 11; Triesen 8; Eschen/Mauren 4; Schaan 3.
Cup Final: Vaduz 9, Ruggell 0.

LITHUANIA

Lithuanian Football Federation, Seimyniskiu str. 15, 2005 Vilnius.
Founded: 1922; *Number of Clubs:* 152; *Number of Players:* 16,600; *National Colours:* Yellow shirts, green shorts, yellow stockings.
Telephone: 00370 2/723654; *Fax:* 00370 2/723651.

International matches 2000
Cyprus (a) 1-2, Moldova (a) 1-2, Latvia (h) 2-1, Latvia (h) 2-1, Armenia (h) 1-2, Portugal (a) 1-5, Romania (a) 0-1, Georgia (h) 0-4, Hungary (h) 1-6.

League Championship wins (1922-2001)
Kovas Kaunas 6; KSS Klaipeda 6; LFLS Kaunas 4; Zalgiris Vilnius 4; LGSF Kaunas 2; Kareda 2; FBK Kaunas 2; MSK Kaunas 1; Ekranas Panevezys 1; Romar Mazeikiai 1; Inkaras Grifas 1.

Cup wins (1992-2001)
Zalgiris Vilnius 3; Kareda 2; Ekranas 2; Inkaras 1; Atlantas 1.

Final League Table 2000
	P	W	D	L	F	A	Pts
Kaunas	36	26	8	2	115	24	86
Zalgiris	36	25	8	3	108	28	83
Atlantas	36	21	4	11	70	45	67
Ekranas	36	18	8	10	59	31	62
Kareda	36	17	9	10	56	49	60
Nevezis	36	11	13	12	30	44	46
Dainava	36	9	8	19	34	65	35
Polonija	36	6	7	23	27	82	25
Inkaras	36	5	6	25	28	95	21
Banga*	36	3	7	26	19	83	16

Promotion/Relegation Play-Offs
Atletas 2, 1, Silute 1, 0
Polonija 1, 3, Siauliai 0, 3.
Top scorer: Velicka (Kaunas) 26.
Cup Final: Atlantas 1, Zalgiris 0.

LUXEMBOURG

Federation Luxembourgeoise De Football, (F.L.F.), 50, Rue De Strasbourg, L-2560, Luxembourg.
Founded: 1908; *Number of Clubs:* 126; *Number of Players:* 21,684; *National Colours:* All red.
Telephone: 00352 48 86 65; *Cable:* FOOTBALL LUXEMBOURG; *Telex:* 2426 flf l; *Fax:* 00352 40 02 01.

International matches 2000
Northern Ireland (h) 1-3, Estonia (h) 1-1, Spain (h) 0-1, Yugoslavia (h) 0-2, Slovenia (h) 1-2, Russia (a) 0-3.

League Championship wins (1910-2001)
Jeunesse Esch 26; Spora Luxembourg 11; Stade Dudelange 10; Avenir Beggen 7; Red Boys Differdange 6; US Hollerich-Bonnevoie 5; Fola Esch 5; US Luxembourg 5; Aris Bonnevoie 3; Progres Niedercorn 3; F91 Dudelange 2.

Cup wins (1922-2001)
Red Boys Differdange 16; Jeunesse Esch 12; US Luxembourg 10; Spora Luxembourg 8; Avenir Beggen 6; Stade Dudelange 4; Progres Niedercorn 4; Fola Esch 3; Alliance Dudelange 2; US Rumelange 2; Grevenmacher 2; Aris Bonnevoie 1; US Dudelange 1; Jeunesse

Hautcharage 1; National Schiffige 1; Racing Luxembourg 1; SC Tetange 1; Hesperange 1; Etzella 1.

Championship Table 2000-01
	P	W	D	L	F	A	Pts
F91 Dudelange	28	19	6	3	57	26	63
Grevenmacher	28	18	5	5	59	19	59
Hobscheid	28	14	4	10	53	44	46
Etzella	28	12	7	9	51	48	43

Promotion/Relegation Table 2000-01
Group 1
	P	W	D	L	F	A	Pts
Sporting Mertzig	28	12	6	10	72	50	42
Union	28	7	12	9	35	37	33
Mondercange	28	8	5	15	32	54	29
Rodange*	28	4	16	36	67	28	28

Group 2
	P	W	D	L	F	A	Pts
Jeunesse Esch	28	14	3	11	52	35	45
Avenir Beggen	28	10	6	12	45	55	36
Rumelange	28	6	8	14	31	56	26
FC Wiltz 71*	28	4	4	20	34	68	16

Top scorer: Zaritski (Sporting Mertzig) 23.
Cup Final: Etzella 5, FC Wiltz 71 3.

MACEDONIA

Football Association of the Former Yugoslav Republic of Macedonia, VIII-ma Udarna Brigada 31A, PO Box 84, MAC-91000 Skopje.
Founded: 1948; *Number of Clubs:* 598; *Number of Players:* 15,165; *National Colours:* All red.
Telephone: 00389 1 22 90 42; *Fax:* 00389 1 23 54 48.

International matches 2000
Yugoslavia (h) 1-2, Bosnia (a) 0-1, Albania (h) 1-0, South Korea (a) 1-2, Iran (a) 1-3, Slovakia (a) 0-2, Azerbaijan (h) 3-0, Moldova (a) 0-0.

League Championship wins (1993-2001)
Vardar 3; Sileks 3; Sloga 3.

Cup wins (1993-2001)
Vardar 4; Sileks 1; Sloga 1; Pellister 1.

Final Table 2000-01
	P	W	D	L	F	A	Pts
Sloga	26	20	3	3	61	15	63
Vardar	26	20	3	3	52	15	63
Pobeda	26	18	2	6	64	27	56
Belasica	26	17	4	5	56	22	55
Sileks	26	14	1	11	52	40	43
Rabotnicki	26	12	3	11	43	36	39
Cement	26	11	3	12	38	31	36
Pelister	26	10	4	12	41	38	34
Osogovo	26	10	4	12	39	42	34
Makedonia	26	9	4	13	44	42	31
Sasa*	26	8	5	13	39	47	29
Shkendija*	26	9	1	16	34	48	28
Borec*	26	4	1	21	18	80	13
Tikves*	26	1	0	25	12	110	3

Top scorer: Bekiri (Sloga) 27.
Cup Final: Sloga 1, Pellister 2.

MALTA

Malta Football Association, 280 St. Paul Street, Valletta VLT07.
Founded: 1900; *Number of Clubs:* 252; *Number of Players:* 5,544; *National Colours:* Red shirts, white shorts, red stockings.
Telephone: 00356 22 26 97; *Cable:* FOOTBALL MALTA VALLETTA; *Fax:* 00356 24 51 36.

International matches 2000
Qatar (h) 2-0, Azerbaijan (h) 3-0, Andorra (h) 1-1, Albania (h) 0-1, Northern Ireland (h) 0-3, South Africa (h) 0-1, England (h) 1-2, Iceland (a) 0-5, Moldova (a) 0-4, Northern Ireland (a) 0-1, Bulgaria (a) 0-3, Czech Republic (h) 0-0, Albania (a) 0-3.

League Championship wins (1910-2001)
Floriana 25; Sliema Wanderers 23; Valletta 18; Hibernians 8; Hamrun Spartans 7; Rabat Ajax 2; St George's 1; KOMR 1; Birkirkara 1.

Cup wins (1935-2001)
Floriana 18; Sliema Wanderers 18; Valletta 10; Hamrun Spartans 6; Hibernians 6; Gzira United 1; Melita 1; Zurrieq 1; Rabat Ajax 1.

Championship Table 2000-01

	P	W	D	L	F	A	Pts
Valletta	28	21	4	3	76	38	46
Sliema Wanderers	28	18	5	5	95	37	40
Birkirkara	28	16	6	6	50	27	36
Hibernians	28	14	7	7	60	40	32
Floriana	28	13	4	11	54	48	27
Hamrun Spartans	28	8	4	16	28	56	13

Promotion/Relegation Table 2000-01

	P	W	D	L	F	A	Pts
Pieta Hotspurs	24	7	7	10	56	49	20
Naxxar Lions	24	6	5	13	40	55	17
Rabat Ajax*	24	5	6	13	35	63	16
Xghajra Tornados*	24	0	2	22	11	93	1

Top scorer: Mifsud (Sliema Wanderers) 30.
Cup Final: Valletta 3, Birkirkara 0.

MOLDOVA

Moldavian Football Federation, 39 Tricolorului Str, 2012, Chisinau.
Founded: 1990; *Number of Clubs:* 143; *Number of Players:* 75,000; *National Colours:* Blue shirts, red shorts, yellow stockings.
Telephone: 00373 2 247878. *Fax:* 00373 2 247890.

International matches 2000
Armenia (a) 2-2, Lithuania (h) 2-1, Slovakia (h) 2-0, San Marino (a) 1-0, Russia (h) 0-1, Malta (h) 4-0, Turkey (a) 0-2, Slovakia (h) 0-1, Macedonia (h) 0-0.

League Championship wins (1992-2001)
Zimbru Chisinau 8; Constructorul 1; Serif 1.

Cup wins (1992-2001)
Tiligul 4; Zimbru Chisinau 2; Serif 2; Combat 1; Constructorul 1.

Final League Table 2000-01

	P	W	D	L	F	A	Pts
Serif	28	21	4	3	58	18	67
Zimbru Chisinau	28	20	6	2	46	15	66
Tiligul	28	11	8	9	36	34	41
Constructorul	28	10	9	9	30	30	39
Otaci	28	9	6	13	31	39	33
Haiduc-Sporting	28	6	7	15	34	45	25
Agro	28	6	7	15	29	50	25
Olimpia	28	3	5	20	19	52	14

Top scorers: Mujiri (Serif) 17, Barburos (Haiduc-Sporting/Agro/Serif) 17.
Cup Final: Serif 0, Otaci 0.
Serif won 5-4 on penalties.

NORTHERN IRELAND

Irish Football Association Ltd, 20 Windsor Avenue, Belfast BT9 6EG.
Founded: 1880; *Number of Clubs:* 1,555; *Number of Players:* 24,558; *National Colours:* Green shirts, white shorts, green stockings.
Telephone: 01232 66 94 58; *Cable:* FOOTBALL BELFAST; *Telex:* 747317 ifa ni g; *Fax:* 01232 66 76 20.

NORWAY

Norges Fotballforbund Ulleval Stadion, Postboks 3823, Ulleval Hageby, 0805 Oslo 8.
Founded: 1902; *Number of Clubs:* 1,810; *Number of Players:* 300,000; *National Colours:* Red shirts, white shorts, blue stockings.
Telephone: 0047 22/024500 ; *Cable* FOTBALLFORBUND OSLO; *Telex:* 71722 nff n; *Fax:* 0047 22 95 10 10.

International matches 2000
Iceland (h) 0-0, Denmark (h) 4-2, Sweden (h) 1-1, Turkey (a) 2-0, Switzerland (a) 2-2, Belgium (h) 0-2, Slovakia (h) 2-0, Italy (h) 1-0, Spain (n) 1-0, Yugoslavia (n) 0-1, Slovenia (n) 0-0, Finland (a) 1-3, Armenia (h) 0-0, Wales (a) 1-1, Ukraine (h) 0-1.

League Championship wins (1938-2000)
Rosenborg Trondheim 14; Fredrikstad 9; Viking Stavanger 8; Lillestroem 6; Valerengen 4; Larvik Turn 3; Brann Bergen 2; Lyn Oslo 2; IK Start 1; Friedig 1; Fram 1; Skeid Oslo 1; Strömsgodset Drammen 1; Moss 1.

Cup wins (1902-2000)
Odds Bk Skien 11; Fredrikstad 10; Lyn Oslo 8; Skeid Oslo 8; Rosenborg Trondheim 7; Sarpsborg FK 6; Brann Bergen 5; Orn F Horten 4; Lillestroem 4; Viking

Stavanger 4; Strömsgodset Drammen 4; Frigg 3; Mjondalens F 3; Bodo-Glimt 2; Mercantile 2; Tromso 2; Valerengen 2; Grane Nordstrand 1; Kvik Halden 1; Sparta 1; Gjovik 1; Moss 1; Byrne 1; Molde 1; Stabaek 1; Odd Grenland 1.
(Known as the Norwegian Championship for HM The King's Trophy).

Final League Table 2000

	P	W	D	L	F	A	Pts
Rosenborg	26	16	6	4	61	26	54
Brann	26	14	5	7	53	40	47
Viking	26	13	6	7	51	39	45
Tromso	26	13	5	8	51	46	44
Stabaek	26	12	6	8	59	33	42
Lillestrom	26	11	7	8	42	29	40
Molde	26	11	7	8	46	47	40
Odd	26	11	5	10	40	31	38
Moss	26	8	8	10	38	44	32
Bodo-Glimt	26	6	10	10	48	59	28
Bryne	26	7	6	13	32	60	27
Valerengen*	26	5	9	12	32	44	24
Start*	26	5	6	15	40	66	21
Haugesund*	26	5	4	17	33	62	19

Top scorer: Helstad (Brann) 18.
Cup Final: Odd 2, Viking 1.

POLAND

Federation Polonaise De Foot-Ball, Al. Ujazdowskie 22, 00-478 Warszawa.
Founded: 1919; *Number of Clubs:* 5,881; *Number of Players:* 317,442; *National Colours:* White shirts, red shorts, white & red stockings.
Telephone: 0048 22 6223398; *Cable:* PEZETPEEN WARSZAWA; *Telex:* 825320 pzpn pl; *Fax:* 0048 22 629 24 89.

International matches 2000
Spain (a) 0-3, France (a) 0-1, Hungary (a) 0-0, Finland (h) 0-0, Holland (a) 1-3, Romania (a) 1-1, Ukraine (a) 3-1, Belarus (h) 3-1, Wales (h) 0-0, Iceland (h) 1-0.

League Championship wins (1921-2001)
Gornik Zabrze 14; Ruch Chorzow 13; Wisla Krakow 8; Legia Warsaw 6; Widzew Lodz 6; Lech Poznan 5; Pogon Lwow 4; Cracovia 3; Warta Poznan 2; Polonia Bytom 2; Stal Mielec 2; LKS Lodz 2; Polonia Warsaw 2; Garbarnia Krakow 1; Slask Wroclaw 1; Szombierki Bytom 1; Zaglebie Lubin 1.

Cup wins (1951-2001)
Legia Warsaw 12; Gornik Zabrze 6; Zaglebie Sosnowiec 4; Lech Poznan 3; GKS Katowice 3; Ruch Chorzow 3; Amica Wronki 3; Slask Wroclaw 2; Polonia Warsaw 2; Gwardia Warsaw 1; LKS Lodz 1; Wisla Krakow 1; Stal Rzeszow 1; Arka Gdynia 1; Lechia Gdansk 1; Widzew Lodz 1; Miedz Legnica 1.

Final League Table 2000-01

	P	W	D	L	F	A	Pts
Wisla	30	19	5	6	66	27	62
Pogon	30	16	5	9	43	33	53
Legia	30	14	8	8	45	29	50
Polonia	30	13	7	10	38	30	46
Zaglebie Lubin	30	14	4	12	43	40	46
Amica	30	13	5	12	48	44	44
Ruch	30	13	5	12	50	48	44
Katowice	30	9	15	6	27	21	42
Odra	30	10	9	11	38	45	39
Groclin	30	9	10	11	35	38	37
Slask	30	9	9	12	32	38	36
Widzew	30	9	9	12	33	40	36
Gornik Zabrze	30	9	7	14	29	35	34
Stomil+	30	10	4	16	22	41	34
Orlen Plock*	30	9	4	17	37	55	31
Radzionkow*	30	9	4	17	29	51	31

Top scorer: Frankowski (Wisla) 18.
Cup Final: Gornik Zabrze 1, 2, Polonia 2, 2.

PORTUGAL

Federacao Portuguesa De Futebol, Praca De Alegria N.25, Apartado 21.100, P-1127, Lisboa Codex.
Founded: 1914; *Number of Clubs:* 204; *Number of Players:* 79,235; *National Colours:* Red shirts, green shorts, red stockings.
Telephone: 00351 1 342 8207/8/9/0; *Cable:* FUTEBOL LISBOA; *Telex:* 13489 fpf p; *Fax:* 00351 1 346 72 31.

International matches 2000
Belgium (a) 1-1, Denmark (h) 2-1, Italy (a) 0-2, Wales (h) 3-0, England (n) 3-2, Romania (n) 1-0, Germany (n) 3-0, Turkey (n) 2-0, France (n) 1-2, Lithuania (h) 5-1, Estonia (a) 3-1, Republic of Ireland (h) 1-1, Holland (a) 2-0, Israel (h) 2-1.

League Championship wins (1935-2001)
Benfica 30; FC Porto 18; Sporting Lisbon 17; Belenenses 1; Boavista 1.

Cup wins (1939-2001)
Benfica 23; Sporting Lisbon 12; FC Porto 11; Boavista 5; Belenenses 3; Vitoria Setubal 2; Academica Coimbra 1; Leixoes Porto 1; Sporting Braga 1; Amadora 1; Beira Mar 1.

Final League Table 2000-01

	P	W	D	L	F	A	Pts
Boavista	34	23	8	3	63	22	77
Porto	34	24	4	6	73	27	76
Sporting Lisbon	34	19	5	10	56	37	62
Braga	34	16	9	9	58	48	57
Uniao Leiria	34	15	11	8	46	41	56
Benfica	34	15	9	10	54	44	54
Belenenses	34	14	10	10	43	36	52
Beira Mar	34	14	7	13	45	49	49
Pacos	34	12	12	10	47	39	48
Maritimo	34	12	7	15	34	37	43
Alverca	34	12	7	15	45	52	43
Salgueiros	34	13	4	17	41	55	43
Farense	34	10	9	15	37	47	39
Gil Vicente	34	10	7	17	34	41	37
Guimaraes	34	9	9	16	41	49	36
Campomaiorense+	34	7	11	16	29	58	32
Aves*	34	4	10	20	31	68	22
Amadora*	34	4	7	23	30	57	19

Top scorer: Pena (Porto) 22.
Cup Final: Maritimo 0, Porto 2.

ROMANIA

Federatia Romana De Fotbal, Str. Poligrafiei 3, Sector 1, 71556 Bucharest.
Founded: 1909; *Number of Clubs:* 414; *Number of Players:* 22,920; *National Colours:* All yellow.
Telephone: 0040 1 224 1993/224 2983; *Cable:* SPORTROM BUCURESTI-FOTBAL; *Telex:* 10097 frf r; *Fax:* 0040 1 224 0661.

International matches 2000
Mexico (a) 1-3, Latvia (h) 2-0, Georgia (h) 1-1, Cyprus (a) 2-3, Greece (a) 0-2, Cyprus (h) 2-0, Holland (a) 1-2, Greece (h) 2-1, Germany (n) 1-1, Portugal (n) 0-1, England (n) 3-2, Italy (n) 0-2, Poland (n) 1-1, Lithuania (h) 1-0, Italy (a) 0-3, Yugoslavia (h) 2-1, Algeria (a) 2-3, Algeria (a) 3-2.

League Championship wins (1910-2001)
Steaua Bucharest 21; Dinamo Bucharest 15; Venus Bucharest 8; Chinezul Timisoara 6; UT Arad 6; Ripensia Temesvar 4; Uni Craiova 4; Petrolul Ploesti 3; Olimpia Bucharest 2; Colentina Bucharest 2; Arges Pitesti 2; ICO Oradea 2; ; Rapid Bucharest 2; Soc RA Bucharest 1; Prahova Ploesti 1; Coltea Brasov 1; Juventus Bucharest 1; Metalochimia Resita 1; Ploesti United 1; Unirea Tricolor 1.

Cup wins (1934-2001)
Steaua Bucharest 20; Rapid Bucharest 10; Dinamo Bucharest 9; Uni Craiova 6; UT Arad 2; Ripensia Temesvar 2; Politehnica Timisoara 2; Petrolul Ploesti 2; ICO Oradeo 1; Metalochimia Resita 1; Stinta Cluj 1; CFR Turnu Severin 1; Chimia Ramnicu Vilcea 1; Jiul Petroseni 1; Progresul Bucharest 1; Progresul Oradea 1; Gloria Bistrita 1.

Final League Table 2000-01

	P	W	D	L	F	A	Pts
Steaua	30	17	9	4	55	32	60
Dinamo	30	15	6	9	56	44	51
Brasov	30	15	5	10	33	25	50
Rapid	30	13	10	7	38	25	49
Arges	30	12	10	8	42	42	46
Gloria	30	13	4	13	44	42	43
National	30	13	4	13	40	40	43

Uni Craiova	30	11	8	11	34	38	41
Astra	30	11	7	12	41	36	40
Petrolul	30	12	4	14	34	36	40
Ceahlaul	30	9	11	10	36	40	38
Otelul	30	10	8	12	32	39	38
Foresta+	30	8	12	10	39	43	36
Bacau+	30	9	7	14	38	45	34
Rocar*	30	10	4	16	41	56	34
Gaz*	30	3	9	18	21	41	18

Top scorer: Niculae (Dinamo) 20.
Cup Final: Dinamo 4, Rocar 2.

RUSSIA

Football Union of Russia; Luzhnetskaya Naberezhnaja, 8. SU-119871 Moscow.
Founded: 1912; *Number of Clubs:* 43,700; *Number of Players:*785,000; *National Colours:* White shirts, blue shorts, red stockings.
Telephone: 0070 95 2011637; *Telex:* 411287 priz su; *Fax:* 0070 95 2011303.

International matches 2000
Israel (a) 1-4, USA (h) 2-0, Slovakia (h) 1-1, Moldova (a) 1-0, Israel (h) 1-0, Switzerland (a) 1-0, Luxembourg (h) 3-0.

League Championship wins (1945-2000)
Spartak Moscow 19; Dynamo Kiev 13; Dynamo Moscow 11; CSKA Moscow 7; Torpedo Moscow 3; Dynamo Tbilisi 2; Dnepr Dnepropetrovsk 2; Saria Voroshilovgrad 1; Ararat Erevan 1; Dynamo Minsk 1; Zenit Leningrad 1; Spartak Vladikavkaz 1.

Cup wins (1936-2001)
Spartak Moscow 12; Dynamo Kiev 10; Torpedo Moscow 7; Dynamo Moscow 7; Lokomotiv Moscow 6; CSKA Moscow 5; Donetsk Shaktyor 4; Dynamo Tbilisi 2; Ararat Erevan 2; Zenit Leningrad 2; Karpaty Lvov 1; SKA Rostov 1; Metallist Kharkov 1; Dnepr 1.

Final League Table 2000

	P	W	D	L	F	A	Pts
Spartak Moscow	30	23	1	6	69	30	70
Lokomotiv Moscow	30	18	8	4	50	20	62
Torpedo Moscow	30	16	7	7	42	29	55
Anzhi	30	15	7	8	41	30	52
Dynamo Moscow	30	14	8	8	45	35	50
Chernomorets	30	13	10	7	46	28	49
Zenit	30	13	8	9	38	26	47
CSKA Moscow	30	12	5	13	45	39	41
Saturn	30	10	10	10	26	29	40
Vladikavkaz	30	10	8	12	32	36	38
Rostelmash	30	6	14	10	24	27	32
Volgograd	30	8	8	14	35	54	32
Fakel	30	6	12	12	25	45	30
Krylia Sovekov	30	8	5	17	25	45	29
Lokomotiv Nizhniy*	30	3	9	18	16	44	18
Uralan*	30	2	6	22	16	58	12

Top scorer: Loskov (Lokomotiv Moscow) 15.
Cup Final: Lokomotiv Moscow 1, Anzhi 1.
Lokomotiv Moscow won 4-3 on penalties.

SAN MARINO

Federazione Sammarinese Giuoco Calcio, Viale Campo dei Giudei, 14; 47031-Rep. San Marino.
Founded: 1931; *Number of Clubs:* 17; *Number of Players:* 1,033; *National Colours:* All light blue.
Telephone: 00378 9990515; *Telex:* 0505284 cosmar so; *Fax:* 00378 9992348.

International matches 2000
Moldova (h) 0-1, Scotland (h) 0-2, Latvia (h) 0-1.

League Championship wins (1986-2000)
Tre Fiori 4; Faetano 3; Folgore 3; Fiorita 2; Domagnano 1; Montevito 1, Libertas 1.

Cup wins (1986-2000)
Domagnano 4; Libertas 3; Faetano 3; Cosmos 2; Fiorita 1; Tre Penne 1; Murata 1.

Final League Table 2000-01
Group A

	P	W	D	L	F	A	Pts
Cosmos	21	12	4	5	38	18	40
Faetano	21	10	6	5	38	26	36
Tre Penne	21	10	5	6	36	27	35
Domagnano	21	8	8	5	36	27	32
Cailungo	21	7	5	9	34	27	26
Libertas	21	7	5	9	46	47	26
Montevito	21	7	5	9	21	38	26
Fiorita	21	2	6	13	24	51	12

Group B

	P	W	D	L	F	A	Pts
Virtus	20	12	6	2	45	23	42
Murata	20	10	5	5	25	22	35
Folgore	20	9	6	5	34	19	33
Pennarossa	20	9	4	7	39	30	31
San Giovanni	20	7	7	6	27	32	28
Tre Fiori	20	2	4	14	25	50	10
Juvenes/Dogana	20	2	4	14	15	46	10

SCOTLAND

The Scottish Football Association Ltd, 6 Park Gardens, Glasgow G3 7YF.
Founded: 1873; *Number of Clubs:* 6,148; *Number of Players:* 135,474; *National Colours:* Dark blue shirts, white shorts, red stockings with dark blue tops.
Telephone: 0141 332 6372; *Cable:* EXECUTIVE GLASGOW; *Telex:* 778904 sfa g; *Fax:* 0141 332 7559.

SLOVAKIA

Slovak Football Association, Junacka 6, 83280 Bratislava, Slovakia.
Founded: 1993; *Number of Clubs:* 2,140; *Number of Players:* 141,000; *National Colours:* All blue.
Telephone: 00421 75049151/5; *Fax:* 00421 75 049554.

International matches 2000
Georgia (h) 0-2, Latvia (h) 3-1, Moldova (a) 0-2, Bulgaria (a) 0-1, Australia (h) 0-0, Chile (a) 2-0, Saudi Arabia (h) 1-1, Norway (a) 0-2, Russia (a) 1-1, Japan (a) 1-1, Bolivia (a) 2-0, Croatia (h) 1-1, Macedonia (h) 2-0, Moldova (a) 1-0, Sweden (h) 0-0, Greece (a) 2-0.

League Championship wins (1939-44; 1994-2001)
Slovan Bratislava 8; Kosice 2; Inter 2; Bystrica 1; OAP Bratislava 1.

Cup wins (1994-2001)
Inter 3; Slovan Bratislava 2; Tatran Presov 1; Humenne 1; Spartak Trnava 1.

Final League Table 2000-01

	P	W	D	L	F	A	Pts
Inter	36	25	5	6	72	27	80
Slovan Bratislava	36	21	8	7	83	48	71
Ruzomberok	36	15	10	11	50	48	55
Petrzalka	36	15	9	12	59	55	54
Zilina	36	11	12	13	41	46	45
Matador	36	9	13	14	45	51	40
Kosice	36	11	7	18	44	58	40
Odu Trencin	36	11	6	19	37	60	39
Tatran Presov	36	9	10	17	42	58	36
Spartak Trnava*	36	8	10	18	38	60	34

Top scorer: Nemeth S (Inter Bratislava) 22.
Cup Final: Inter 1, Ruzomberok 0.

SLOVENIA

Football Association of Slovenia, P.P. 3986, 1001 Ljubljana, Slovenia.
Founded: 1920; *Number of Clubs:* 375; *Number of Players:* 20,117; *National Colours:* White shirts, green shorts, white stockings.
Telephone: 00386 1 5300400; *Fax:* 00386 1 5300410.

International matches 2000
UAE (a) 1-1, Oman (a) 4-0, France (a) 2-3, Saudi Arabia (h) 2-0, Yugoslavia (n) 3-3, Spain (n) 1-2, Norway (n) 0-0, Czech Republic (a) 1-0, Faeroes (a) 2-2, Luxembourg (a) 2-1, Switzerland (h) 2-2.

League Championship wins (1992-2001)
Maribor 5; SCT Olimpija 4; Gorica 1.

Cup wins (1992-2001)
Maribor 4; SCT Olimpija 3; Mura 1; Rudar 1; Gorica 1.

Final League Table 2000-01

	P	W	D	L	F	A	Pts
Maribor Teatanic	33	18	8	7	61	36	62
Olimpija	33	18	6	9	73	46	60
Primorje	33	16	8	9	47	34	56
Mura	33	14	9	10	43	39	51
Publikum	33	15	5	13	59	52	50
Koper	33	12	10	11	43	43	46
Gorica	33	13	4	16	52	46	43
Rudar	33	12	7	14	43	44	43
Korotan	33	12	7	14	44	51	43
Domzale	33	11	4	18	44	64	37
Dravograd*	33	10	5	18	48	62	35
Tabor*	33	7	7	19	34	74	28

Top scorer: Pekic (Publikum) 23.
Cup Final: Olimpija 1, 2, Gorica 0, 4.

SPAIN

Real Federacion Espanola De Futbol, Calle Alberto Bosch 13, Apartado Postal 347, E-28014 Madrid.
Founded: 1913; *Number of Clubs:* 10,240; *Number of Players:* 408,135; *National Colours:* Red shirts, blue shorts, blue stockings with red, blue & yellow border.
Telephone: 0034 91 420 1362; *Cable:* FUTBOL MADRID; *Fax:* 0034 91 420 2094.

International matches 2000
Poland (h) 3-0, Croatia (a) 0-0, Sweden (a) 1-1, Luxembourg (a) 1-0, Norway (n) 0-1, Slovenia (n) 2-1, Yugoslavia (n) 4-3, France (n) 1-2, Germany (a) 1-4, Italy (h) 2-0, Bosnia (a) 2-1, Israel (h) 2-0, Austria (a) 1-1, Holland (h) 1-2.

League Championship wins (1929-36; 1940-2001)
Real Madrid 28; Barcelona 16; Atletico Madrid 9; Athletic Bilbao 8; Valencia 4; Real Sociedad 2; Real Betis 1; Seville 1; La Coruna 1.

Cup wins (1902-2001)
Barcelona 24; Athletic Bilbao 23; Real Madrid 17; Atletico Madrid 9; Valencia 6; Real Zaragoza 5; Real Union de Irun 3; Seville 3; Espanyol 3; Arenas 1; Ciclista Sebastian 1; Racing de Irun 1; Vizcaya Bilbao 1; Real Betis 1; Real Sociedad 1, La Coruna 1.

Final League Table 2000-01

	P	W	D	L	F	A	Pts
Real Madrid	38	24	8	6	81	40	80
La Coruna	38	22	7	9	73	44	73
Mallorca	38	20	11	7	61	43	71
Barcelona	38	17	12	9	80	57	63
Valencia	38	18	9	11	55	34	63
Celta	38	16	11	11	51	49	59
Villarreal	38	16	9	13	58	52	57
Malaga	38	16	8	14	60	61	56
Espanyol	38	14	8	16	46	44	50
Alaves	38	14	7	17	58	57	49
Las Palmas	38	13	7	18	42	62	46
Rayo Vallecano	38	10	13	15	56	68	43
Real Sociedad	38	11	10	17	52	68	43
Athletic Bilbao	38	11	10	17	44	60	43
Zaragoza	38	9	15	14	54	57	42
Valladolid	38	9	15	14	42	50	42
Osasuna	38	10	12	16	43	54	42
Oviedo*	38	11	8	19	51	67	41
Santander*	38	10	9	19	48	62	39
Numancia*	38	10	9	19	40	64	39

Top scorer: Raul (Real Madrid) 24.
Cup Final: Zaragoza 3, Celta 1.

SWEDEN

Svenska Fotbollfoerbundet, Box 1216, S-17123 Solna.
Founded: 1904; *Number of Clubs:* 3,250; *Number of Players:* 485,000; *National Colours:* Yellow shirts, blue shorts, yellow stockings.
Telephone: 0046 8 735 09 00; *Cable:* FOOTBALL-S; *Fax:* 0046 8 27 51 47.

International matches 2000
Denmark (h) 1-0, Norway (a) 1-1, Italy (a) 0-1, Austria (a) 1-1, Denmark (a) 1-0, Spain (h) 1-1, Belgium (n) 1-2, Turkey (n) 0-0, Italy (n) 1-2, Iceland (a) 1-2, Azerbaijan (a) 1-0, Turkey (h) 1-1, Slovakia (a) 0-0.

League Championship wins (1896-2000)
IFK Gothenburg 18; Oergryte IS Gothenburg 14; Malmo FF 14; IFK Norrköping 11; AIK Stockholm 10; Djurgaarden 8; GAIS Gothenburg 6; IF Helsingborg 6; Boras IF Elfsborg 4; Oster Vaxjo 4; Halmstad 4; Atvidaberg 2; IFK Ekilstune 1; IF Gavic Brynas 1; IF Gothenburg 1; Fassbergs 1; Norrköping IK Sleipner 1.

Cup wins (1941-2001)
Malmo FF 13; AIK Stockholm 8; IFK Norrköping 6; IFK Gothenburg 4; Atvidaberg 2; Kalmar 2; Helsingborg 2; GAIS Gothenburg 1; IF Raa 1; Landskrona 1; Oster Vaxjo 1; Djurgaarden 1; Degerfors 1, Halmstad 1, Orgryte 1.

Final League Table 2000

	P	W	D	L	F	A	Pts
Halmstad	26	16	4	6	47	24	52
Helsingborg	26	14	4	8	51	30	46
AIK	26	13	6	7	38	30	45
IFK Gothenburg	26	12	8	6	46	33	44
Elfsborg	26	13	4	9	43	37	43
Trelleborg	26	10	8	8	30	28	38
Orgryte	26	11	4	11	32	32	37
Hammarby	26	10	6	10	34	38	36
Norrköping	26	8	11	7	40	31	35
Orebro	26	9	6	11	44	40	33
Sundsvall	26	7	8	11	34	42	29
Hacken	26	4	13	9	40	52	25
GAIS*	26	4	8	14	26	43	20
Vastra*	26	3	6	17	17	62	15

Top scorer: Berglund (Elfsborg) 18.
Cup Final: AIK Stockholm 1, Elfsborg 1
AIK Stockholm won 10-9 on penalties..

SWITZERLAND

Schweizerisher Fussballverband, Postfach 3000 Berne 15.
Founded: 1895; *Number of Clubs:* 1,473; *Number of Players:* 185,286; *National Colours:* Red shirts, white shorts, red stockings.
Telephone: 0041 31 950 81 11; *Cable:* SWISSFOOT BERNE; *Fax:* 0041 31 950 81 81.

International matches 2000
Oman (a) 4-1, UAE (a) 0-1, Norway (h) 2-2, Germany (a) 1-1, Greece (h) 2-2, Russia (h) 0-1, Faeroes (h) 5-1, Slovenia (h) 2-2, Tunisia (a) 1-1.

League Championship wins (1898-2001)
Grasshoppers 25; Servette 17; Young Boys Berne 11; FC Zurich 9; FC Basle 8; Lausanne 7; La Chaux-des-Fonds 3; FC Lugano 3; Winterthur 3; FX Aarau 3; Neuchatel Xamax 3; Sion 2; St Gallen 2; FC Anglo-American 1; FC Brühl 1; Cantonal-Neuchatel 1; Biel 1; Bellinzona 1; Etoile Le Chaux-de-Fonds 1; Lucerne 1.

Cup wins (1926-2001)
Grasshoppers 18; FC Sion 9; Lausanne 9; Servette 7; La Chaux-de-Fonds 6; Young Boys Berne 6; FC Zurich 6; FC Basle 5; Lucerne 2; FC Lugano 2; FC Granges 1; St Gallen 1; Urania Geneva 1; Young Fellows Zurich 1; Aarau 1.

Qualifying Table 2000-2001

	P	W	D	L	F	A	Pts
Lugano	22	12	6	4	33	16	42
St Gallen	22	11	7	4	43	18	40
Grasshoppers	22	11	3	8	46	25	36
Lausanne	22	11	2	9	37	34	35
Basle	22	10	4	8	42	36	34
Servette	22	9	6	7	34	26	33
Sion	22	9	5	8	27	31	32
Zurich	22	8	7	7	36	29	31
Aarau	22	6	6	10	31	43	24
Yverdon	22	5	6	11	27	43	21
Neuchatel Xamax	22	6	2	14	21	53	20
Lucerne	22	5	4	13	27	50	19

Top scorer: Kuzba (Lausanne) 15.

Final Table 2000-01

	P	W	D	L	F	A	Pts
Grasshoppers	14	8	4	2	29	14	46
Lugano	14	5	5	4	24	19	41
St Gallen	14	6	2	6	23	28	40
Basle	14	4	8	2	18	16	37
Servette	14	5	5	4	26	19	37
Lausanne	14	4	3	7	15	27	33
Sion	14	4	4	6	16	22	32
Zurich	14	3	3	8	12	18	28

Teams take half points from qualifying table.

Promotion/Relegation Table 2000-01

	P	W	D	L	F	A	Pts
Neuchatel Xamax	14	7	6	1	24	16	27
Aarau	14	7	3	4	23	15	24
Lucerne	14	7	3	4	24	18	24
Young Boys	14	7	3	4	17	14	24
Yverdon	14	4	7	3	23	20	19
Winterthur	14	5	2	7	18	21	17
Wil	14	2	5	7	17	22	11
Bellinzona	14	1	3	10	8	28	6

Top scorers: Gimenez (Lugano) 21, Chapuisat (Grasshoppers) 21.
Cup Final: Servette 3, Yverdon 0.

TURKEY

Turkiye Futbol Federasyonu, Konaklar Mah. Ihlamurlu Sok. 9, 80620 4 Levent, Istanbul.
Founded: 1923; *Number of Clubs:* 230; *Number of Players:* 64,521; *National Colours:* White shirts, white shorts, red and white stockings.
Telephone: 0090 212 282 70 10; *Cable:* ISTANBUL FUTBOL SPOR; *Telex:* 46308 btff tr; *Fax:* 0090 212 282 70 15.

International matches 2000
Norway (h) 0-2, Italy (n) 1-2, Sweden (n) 0-0, Belgium (n) 2-0, Portugal (n) 0-2, Bosnia (a) 0-2, Moldova (h) 2-0, Sweden (a) 1-1, Azerbaijan (a) 1-0, France (h) 0-4.

League Championship wins (1960-2001)
Galatasaray 14; Fenerbahce 14; Besiktas 10; Trabzonspor 6.

Cup wins (1963-2001)
Galatasaray 13; Besiktas 6; Trabzonspor 5; Fenerbahce 4; Goztepe Izmir 2; Altay Izmir 2; Ankaragucu 2; Genclerbirligi 2; Eskisehirspor 1; Bursapor 1; Sakaryaspor 1; Kocaeli 1.

Final League Table 2000-01

	P	W	D	L	F	A	Pts
Fenerbahce	34	24	4	6	82	39	76
Galatasaray	34	23	4	7	77	35	73
Gaziantep	34	20	8	6	67	40	68
Besiktas	34	19	7	8	68	48	64
Trabzonspor	34	17	7	10	69	52	58
Ankaragucu	34	16	8	10	65	59	56
Yozgat	34	13	10	11	55	46	49
Samsun	34	13	9	12	55	52	48
Rize	34	13	7	14	45	43	46
Genclerbirligi	34	14	4	16	44	53	46
Denizli	34	12	9	13	53	56	45
Istanbul	34	12	8	14	47	58	44
Kocaeli	34	10	11	13	56	60	41
Bursa	34	11	7	16	55	60	40
Antalya	34	9	9	16	45	64	36
Siirt*	34	6	6	22	47	81	24
Erzurum*	34	5	6	23	36	80	21
Adana*	34	2	10	22	51	91	16

Top scorer: Okan (Bursa) 23.
Cup Final: Genclerbirligi 2, Fenerbahce 2.
Genclerbirligi won 4-1 on penalties.

UKRAINE

Football Federation of Ukraine, Ulianovyh Street 1, P.O. Box 503, 252150 Kiev, Ukraine.
Founded: 1991; *Number of Clubs:* 1500; *Number of Players:* 759,500; *National Colours:* Yellow and blue shirts, blue shorts, yellow stockings.
Telephone: 00380 44 2528498; *Fax:* 00380 44 2528513 (or) 2692550; *Telex:* 631461 uff ux.

International matches 2000
Bulgaria (a) 1-0, England (a) 0-2, Poland (h) 1-3, Armenia (a) 3-2, Norway (a) 1-0.

League Championship wins (1992-2001)
Dynamo Kiev 8; Tavria Simferopol 1.

Cup wins (1992-2001)
Dynamo Kiev 5; Shakhtjor Donetsk 3; Chernomorets 2.

Final League Table 2000-01

	P	W	D	L	F	A	Pts
Dynamo Kiev	26	20	4	2	58	17	64
Shakhtjor Donetsk	26	19	6	1	71	21	63
Dnepr	26	17	4	5	37	18	55
Metalurg Donetsk	26	11	9	6	30	24	42
Metalurg Mariupol	26	12	4	10	34	27	40
CSKA	26	10	10	6	30	23	40
Metalurg Zapor	26	9	8	9	28	31	35
Tavriya	26	8	9	9	24	31	33
Metallist Charkov	26	8	7	11	27	37	31
Karpaty	26	9	3	14	33	42	30
Krivbas	26	6	7	13	23	37	25
Vorskla	26	5	6	15	17	30	21
Stal*	26	3	6	17	19	48	15
Ternopol*	26	2	3	21	20	65	9

Top scorer: Vorobei (Shakhtjor Donetsk) 21.
Cup Final: Shakhtjor Donetsk 2, CSKA 1.

WALES

The Football Association of Wales Limited, Plymouth Chambers, 3 Westgate Street, Cardiff, South Glamorgan CF1 1DD.
Founded: 1876; *Number of Clubs:* 2,326; *Number of Players:* 53,926; *National Colours:* All red.
Telephone: 01222 372325; *Telex:* 497 363 faw g; *Cable:* WELSOCCER CARDIFF; *Fax:* 01222 343961.

YUGOSLAVIA

Yugoslav Football Association, P.O. Box 263, Terazije 35, 11000 Beograd.
Founded: 1919; *Number of Clubs:* 6,532; *Number of Players:* 229,024; *National Colours:* Blue shirts, white shorts, red stockings.
Telephone: 00381 11 323 3447; *Cable:* JUGOFUDBAL BEOGRAD; *Telex:* 11666 fsj yu; *Fax:* 00381 11 323 3433.

International matches 2000
Macedonia (a) 2-1, China (h) 1-0, China (a) 2-0, South Korea (a) 0-0, South Korea (a) 0-0, Slovenia (n) 3-3, Norway (n) 1-0, Spain (n) 3-4, Holland (n) 1-6, Northern Ireland (a) 2-1, Luxembourg (a) 2-0, Romania (a) 1-2, Greece (a) 1-1.

League Championship wins (1923-2001)
Red Star Belgrade 22; Partizan Belgrade 16; Hajduk Split 9; Gradjanski Zagreb 5; BSK Belgrade 5; Dynamo Zagreb 4; Jugoslavija Belgrade 2; Concordia Zagreb 2; FC Sarajevo 2; Vojvodina Novi Sad 2; HASK Zagreb 1; Zeljeznicar 1; Obilic 1.

Cup wins (1947-2001)
Red Star Belgrade 18; Hajduk Split 9; Partizan Belgrade 9; Dynamo Zagreb 8; BSK Belgrade 2; OFK Belgrade 2; Rijeka 2; Velez Mostar 2; Vardar Skopje 1; Borac Banjaluka 1.

Final League Table 2000-01

	P	W	D	L	F	A	Pts
Red Star Belgrade	34	28	4	2	93	20	88
Partizan Belgrade	34	28	2	4	94	36	86
Obilic	34	19	6	9	53	37	63
Sartid 1913	34	17	3	14	49	47	54
OFK Belgrade	34	15	5	14	52	46	50
Vojvodina	34	13	8	13	51	36	47
Sutjeska	34	14	4	16	52	64	46
Zeleznik	34	12	8	14	49	56	44
Radnicki Kragujevac	34	13	5	16	39	51	44
Cukaricki	34	13	4	17	42	50	43
Hajduk Kula	34	12	6	16	45	51	42
Zemun	34	11	9	14	37	46	42
Zeta	34	11	9	14	38	50	42
Rad	34	12	5	17	48	58	41
Buducnost*	34	11	5	18	29	48	38
Napredak*	34	8	10	16	38	63	34
Radnicki Nis*	34	9	5	20	30	59	32
Milicionar*	34	8	6	20	29	50	30

Top scorer: Divic (OFK Belgrade) 27.
Cup Final: Partizan Belgrade 1, Red Star Belgrade 0.

SOUTH AMERICA

ARGENTINA

Asociacion Del Futbol Argentina, Viamonte 1366/76, 1053 Buenos Aires.
Founded: 1893; *Number of Clubs:* 3,035; *Number of Players:* 306,365; *National Colours:* Light blue & white striped shirts, black shorts, white stockings.
Telephone: 00541 371 4276; *Cable:* FUTBOL BUENOS AIRES; *Telex:* 17848 AFA AR; *Fax:* 00541 375 4410.

International matches 2000
England (a) 0-0, Chile (h) 4-1, Venezuela (a) 4-0, Bolivia (h) 1-0, Colombia (a) 3-1, Ecuador (h) 2-0, Brazil (a) 1-3, Paraguay (h) 1-1, Peru (a) 2-1, Uruguay (h) 2-1, Chile (a) 2-0, Mexico (a) 2-0.

BOLIVIA

Federacion Boliviana De Futbol, Av. Libertador Bolivar No. 1168, Casilla de Correo 484, Cochabamba, Bolivia.
Founded: 1925; *Number of Clubs:* 305; *Number of Players:* 15,290; *National Colours:* Green shirts with white borders, white shorts with green borders, green stockings.
Telephone: 0059142 44982; *Cable:* FEDFUTBOL COCHABAMBA; *Telex:* 6239 FEDBOL; *Fax:* 0059142 82132.

International matches 2000
Haiti (h) 9-2, Venezuela (a) 0-0, Uruguay (a) 0-1, Colombia (h) 1-1, Argentina (a) 0-1, Slovakia (a) 0-2, Japan (a) 0-2, Venezuela (a) 2-4, Chile (h) 1-0, Paraguay (h) 0-0, Ecuador (a) 0-2, Brazil (a) 0-5, Mexico (a) 0-1, Peru (h) 1-0, Uruguay (h) 0-0.

BRAZIL

Confederacao Brasileira De Futebol, Rua Da Alfandega, 70, P.O. Box 1078, 20.070 Rio De Janeiro.
Founded: 1914; *Number of Clubs:* 12,987; *Number of Players:* 551,358; *National Colours:* Yellow shirts with green collar/cuffs, blue shorts, white stockings with green-yellow border.
Telephone: 005521 509 5937; *Cable:* DESPORTOS RIO DE JANEIRO; *Telex:* 21509 CBDS BR; *Fax:* 005521 252 9294.

International matches 2000
Thailand (a) 7-0, Colombia (a) 0-0, Ecuador (h) 3-2, Wales (a) 3-0, England (a) 1-1, Peru (a) 1-0, Uruguay (h) 1-1, Paraguay (a) 1-2, Argentina (h) 3-1, Chile (a) 0-3, Bolivia (h) 5-0, Venezuela (a) 6-0, Colombia (h) 1-0.

CHILE

Federacion De Futbol De Chile, Avda. Quillin No. 5635, Casilla postal 3733, Correo Central, Santiago de Chile.
Founded: 1895; *Number of Clubs:* 4,598; *Number of Players:* 609,724; *National Colours:* Red shirts with white collar & cuffs, blue shorts, white stockings.
Telephone: 00562 2849000; *Cable:* FEDFUTBOL SANTIAGO DE CHILE; *Fax:* 00562 2843510.

International matches 2000
USA (h) 2-1, Costa Rica (a) 0-1, Guatemala (a) 1-2, Australia (h) 2-1, Bulgaria (h) 3-2, Slovakia (h) 0-2, Honduras (h) 5-2, Argentina (a) 1-4, Peru (h) 1-1, Uruguay (a) 1-2, Paraguay (h) 3-1, Bolivia (a) 0-1, Venezuela (a) 2-0, Brazil (h) 3-0, Colombia (h) 0-1, Ecuador (a) 0-1, Argentina (h) 0-2.

COLOMBIA

Federacion Colombiana De Futbol, Avenida 32, No. 16-22 piso 40. Apartado Aereo 17602, Santafe de Bogota.
Founded: 1924; *Number of Clubs:* 3,685; *Number of Players:* 188,050; *National Colours:* Yellow shirts with tricolour borders, blue shorts, Red stockings with tricolour borders.
Telephone: 00571 2853320; *Cable:* COLFUTBOL BOGOTA; *Fax:* 00571 2889740.

International matches 2000
Jamaica (n) 1-0, Honduras (n) 0-2, USA (n) 2-2, Peru (n) 2-1, Canada (n) 0-2, Brazil (h) 0-0, Bolivia (a) 1-1, Jamaica (h) 3-0, Venezuela (h) 3-0, Argentina (h) 1-3, Peru (a) 1-0, Ecuador (a) 0-0, Uruguay (h) 1-0, Chile (a) 1-0, Paraguay (h) 0-2, Brazil (a) 0-1.

ECUADOR

Federacion Ecuatoriana del Futbol, km 4 via a la Costa (Avda. del Bombero), Guayaquil.
Founded: 1925; *Number of Clubs:* 170; *Number of Players:* 15,700; *National Colours:* Yellow shirts with blue and red fringes, blue shorts, red stockings.
Telephone: 005934 352 372/3; *Cable:* ECUAFUTBOL GUAYAQUIL; *Fax:* 005934 352 116.

International matches 2000
Honduras (a) 1-1, Honduras (h) 1-3, Venezuela (h) 2-0, Brazil (a) 2-3, Paraguay (a) 1-3, Panama (h) 5-0, Peru (h) 2-1, Argentina (a) 0-2, Colombia (h) 0-0, Panama (a) 0-0, Bolivia (h) 2-0, Uruguay (a) 0-4, Mexico (a) 0-2, Chile (h) 1-0, Venezuela (a) 2-1.

PARAGUAY

Asociacion Paraguaya de Futbol, Estadio De Sajonia, Calles Mayor Martinez Y Alejo Garcia, Asuncion.
Founded: 1906; *Number of Clubs:* 1,500; *Number of Players:* 140,000; *National Colours:* Red & white shirts, blue shorts, blue stockings.
Telephone: 0059521 480120; *Telex:* 38009 PY FUTBOL; *Fax:* 0059521 480124.

International matches 2000
Hungary (h) 1-1, Peru (a) 0-2, Uruguay (h) 1-0, Ecuador (h) 3-1, Australia (a) 0-0, Australia (a) 0-0, Australia (a) 1-2, Costa Rica (h) 1-0, Chile (a) 1-3, Brazil (h) 2-1, Bolivia (a) 0-0, Argentina (a) 1-1, Venezuela (h) 3-0, Colombia (a) 2-0, Peru (h) 5-1.

PERU

Federacion Peruana De Futbol, Av. Aviacion Cdra. 20 s/n, San Luis, Lima.
Founded: 1922; *Number of Clubs:* 10,000; *Number of Players:* 325,650; *National Colours:* White shirts with red stripe, white shorts with red lines, white stockings with red line.
Telephone: 00511 2258236-9; *Cable* FEPEFUTBOL LIMA; *Fax:* 00511 2258240; *Telex:* 20066 FEPEFUT PE.

International matches 2000
Haiti (n) 1-1, USA (n) 0-1, Honduras (n) 5-3, Colombia (n) 1-2, Paraguay (h) 2-0, Chile (a) 1-1, Brazil (h) 0-1, Ecuador (a) 1-2, Colombia (h) 0-1, Uruguay (a) 0-0, Venezuela (h) 1-0, Argentina (h) 1-2, Bolivia (a) 0-1, Paraguay (a) 1-5.

URUGUAY

Asociacion Uruguaya De Futbol, Guayabo 1531, 11200 Montevideo.
Founded: 1900; *Number of Clubs:* 1,091; *Number of Players:* 134,310; *National Colours:* Sky blue shirts with white collar/cuffs, black shorts, black stockings with sky blue borders.
Telephone: 005982 4007101/06; *Cable:* FOOTBALL MONTEVIDEO; *Fax:* 005982 4090550; *Telex:* AUF UY 22607.

International matches 2000
Hungary (h) 2-0, Bolivia (h) 1-0, Paraguay (a) 0-1, Chile (h) 2-1, Brazil (a) 1-1, Venezuela (h) 3-1, Peru (h) 0-0, Colombia (a) 0-1, Ecuador (h) 4-0, Argentina (a) 1-2, Bolivia (a) 0-0.

VENEZUELA

Federacion Venezolana De Futbol, Avda S. Erminy, Torre Mega II Pent House B, e/Sabana Gr. y la Solano, Parroquia el Recreo, Caracas.
Founded: 1926; *Number of Clubs:* 1,753; *Number of Players:* 63,175; *National Colours:* Dark red shirts, white shorts, white stockings with black border.
Telephone: 00582 7620362; *Cable:* FEVEFUTBOL CARACAS; *Telex:* 26140 FVFCS VC; *Fax:* 00582 7620596.

International matches 2000
Bolivia (h) 0-0, Ecuador (a) 0-2, Argentina (h) 0-4, Panama (h) 3-1, Colombia (a) 0-3, Panama (a) 0-2, Bolivia (h) 4-2, Mexico (a) 1-2, Uruguay (a) 1-3, Chile (h) 0-2, Costa Rica (a) 5-1, Peru (a) 0-1, Paraguay (a) 0-3, Brazil (h) 0-6, Ecuador (h) 1-2.

ASIA

AFGHANISTAN

Afghanistan Football Federation, c/o Afghanistan Olympic Committee, P.O. Box 1824, Kabul.
Founded: 1933; Number of Clubs: 30; Number of Players: 3,300; National Colours: All white with red lines.
Telephone: 0093 11420579; *Cable:* OLYMPIC KABUL.

BAHRAIN

Bahrain Football Association, P.O. Box 5464, Manama.
Founded: 1957; *Number of Clubs:* 25; *Number of Players:* 2,030; *National Colours:* All red.
Telephone: 00973 252929; *Cable:* BAHKORA BAHRAIN; *Telex:* 9040 FAB BN; *Fax:* 00973 255560.

BANGLADESH

Bangladesh Football Federation, National Stadium-1, Dhaka 1000.
Founded: 1972; *Number of Clubs:* 1,265; *Number of Players:* 30,385; *National Colours:* Orange shirts, white shorts, green stockings.
Telephone: 008802 9556072; *Cable:* FOOTBALFED DHAKA; *Fax:* 008802 9563419.

BHUTAN

Bhutan Football Federation, P.O. Box 365, Thimphu.
Telephone: 009752 322350; *Fax:* 009752 321131.

BRUNEI

The Football Association of Brunei Darussalam, P.O. Box 2010, 1920 Bandar Seri Begawan.
Founded: 1959; *Number of Clubs:* 22; *Number of Players:* 830; *National Colours:* Yellow shirts, black shorts, yellow stockings.
Telephone: 006732 383883; *Cable:* BAFA BRUNEI; *Telex:* BU 2575 Attn: BAFA; *Fax:* 006732 382900.

CAMBODIA

Cambodian Football Federation, PO Box 2327 PTT, Phnom-Penh 3.
Founded: 1933; *Number of Clubs:* 30; *Number of Players:* 650; *National Colours:* Blue, red and white shirts, white and blue shorts, red, white and blue stockings.
Telephone: 0085523 364889; *Cable:* CFF PHNOM PENH; *Fax:* 0088523 367191.

CHINA PR

Football Association of The People's Republic of China, 9 Tiyuguan Road, Beijing 100763.
Founded: 1924; *Number of Clubs:* 1,045; *Number of Players:* 2,250,000; *National Colours:* All white.
Telephone: 008610 67117019; *Cable:* SPORTSCHINE BEIJING; *Telex:* 22034 ACSF CN; *Fax:* 008610 67142533.

CHINA TAIPEI

Chinese Taipei Football Association, 100, Kuang-Fu South Road, Taipei, Taiwan.
Founded: 1936; *Number of Players:* 17,000; *National Colours:* Blue shirts, white shorts, red stockings.
Telephone: 008862 27117710; *Cable:* CTFA Taipei; *Fax:* 008862 27117713.

GUAM

Guam Soccer Association, P.O.Box 5093, Agana, Guam 96932.
Founded: 1975; *National Colours:* Blue shirts, white shorts, blue stockings.
Telephone: 00671 472 1824, 646 9609; *Fax:* 00671 4775424.

HONG KONG

The Hong Kong Football Association Ltd, 55 Fat Kwong Street, Homantin, Kowloon, Hong Kong.
Founded: 1914; *Number of Clubs:* 69; *Number of Players:* 3,274; *National Colours:* All Red.
Telephone: 00852 27129122; *Cable:* FOOTBALL HONG KONG; *Telex:* 40518 FAHKG HX; *Fax:* 00852 27604303.

INDIA

All India Football Federation , Mr KN Mour, Gen. Secretary, Youth Hostel Complex, Paltan Bazar, Guwahati - 781 008, Assam.
Founded: 1937; *Number of Clubs:* 2,000; *Number of Players:* 56,000; *National Colours:* Orange shirts, white shorts, green stockings.
Telephone: 0091361 525109; *Fax:* 0091 361525110.

INDONESIA

All Indonesia Football Federation, Wisma Karsa Pemuda, Jl.Gerbang Pemuda No. 3, PO Box 2305, Jakarta 10023.
Founded: 1930; *Number of Clubs:* 2,880; *Number of Players:* 97,000; *National Colours:* Red shirts, white shorts, red and white stockings.
Telephone: 006221 5722948; *Cable:* PSSI JAKARTA; *Telex:* 65739 PSSI IA; *Fax:* 006221 5734386.

IRAN

IR Iran Football Federation, Shahid Keshvari Sports Complex, Mirdamad Ave., Razan Jonoobi Str., PO Box 15875-6967 Tehran 15875.
Founded: 1920; *Number of Clubs:* 6,326; *Number of Players:* 306,000; *National Colours:* All white.
Telephone: 009821 2258116; *Cable:* FOOTBALL IRAN - TEHRAN; *Telex:* 212691 NOC IR; *Fax:* 009821 2258123.

IRAQ

Iraqi Football Association, Olympic Committee Building, Palestine Street, PO Box 484, Baghdad.
Founded: 1948; *Number of Clubs:* 155; *Number of Players:* 4,400; *National Colours:* All black.
Telephone: 009641 7729990; *Cable:* BALL BAGHDAD; *Telex:* 213409 IRFA IK; *Fax:* 009641 7744475.

JAPAN

Japan Football Association, 2nd Floor, Gotoh Ikueikai Bldg, 1-10-7 Dogenzaka, Shibuya-Ku, Tokyo 150, Japan.
Founded: 1921; *Number of Clubs:* 13,047; *Number of Players:* 358,989; *National Colours:* Blue shirts, white shorts, blue stockings.
Telephone: 00813 34762011; *Cable:* SOCCERJAPAN TOKYO; *Telex:* 2422975 FOTJPN J; *Fax:* 00813 34762291.

JORDAN

Jordan Football Association, P.O. Box 962024 Al. Hussein Sports City, 11196 Amman.
Founded: 1949; *Number of Clubs:* 98; *Number of Players:* 4,305; *National Colours:* All white and red.
Telephone: 009626 5657662/3/4/5; *Cable:* JORDAN FOOTBALL ASSN AMMAN; *Fax:* 009626 5657660.

KAZAKHSTAN

The Football Association of the Republic of Kazakhstan, 44 Abai Street, 480072 Almaty, Kazakhstan.
Founded: 1914; *Number of Clubs:* 5,793; *Number of Players:* 260,000.

Telephone: 0073272 671885; *Telex:* 251347 TREK SU; *Fax:* 0073272 671885.

KOREA, NORTH

Football Association of The Democratic People's Rep. of Korea, Kumsong-dong 2, Mangyongdae Distr, Pyongyang.
Founded: 1945; *Number of Clubs:* 90; *Number of Players:* 3,420; *National Colours:* All white.
Telephone: 008502 3814164; *Cable:* DPR KOREA FOOTBALL PYONGYANG; *Telex:* 5472 KP; *Fax:* 008502 3814403.

KOREA, SOUTH

Korea Football Association, 110-39, Kyeonji-Dong, Chongro-Ku, Seoul.
Founded: 1928; *Number of Clubs:* 476; *Number of Players:* 2,047; *National Colours:* Red shirts, black shorts, red stockings.
Telephone: 00822 7336764; *Cable:* FOOTBALLKOREA SEOUL; *Telex:* KFASEL K 25373; *Fax:* 00822 7352755.

KUWAIT

Kuwait Football Association, P.O. Box 2029 Safat, 13021 Safat.
Founded: 1952; *Number of Clubs:* 14 (senior); *Number of Players:* 1,526; *National Colours:* Blue shirts, white shorts, blue stockings.
Telephone: 00965 2555851; *Cable:* FOOT KUWAIT; *Fax:* 00965 2549955.

KYRGYZSTAN

Football Association of Kyrgyz Republic, Frunze Street, 503 Bishkek 720040, Kyrgyzstan.
Founded: 1992; *Number of Players:* 20,000; *National Colours:* Red shirts, white shorts, red stockings.
Telephone: 00331 2223507; *Fax:* 00331 2225492.

LAOS

Federation Lao de Football, National Stadium, Vientiane, Laos.
Founded: 1951; *Number of Clubs:* 76; *Number of Players:* 2,060; *National Colours:* Red shirts, white shorts, blue stockings.
Telephone: 0085621 216008/9; *Cable:* FOOTBALL VIENTIANE; *Fax:* 0085621 216008.

LEBANON

Federation Libanaise De Football-Association, P.O. Box 4732, Verdun Street, Bristol, Radwan Centre Building, Beirut.
Founded: 1933; *Number of Clubs:* 105; *Number of Players:* 8,125; *National Colours:* Red shirts, white shorts, red stockings.
Telephone: 009611 347157; *Cable:* FOOTBALL BEIRUT; *Telex:* 21404 LIBALL; *Fax:* 009611 349529; *Internet:* http://www.lebanon-online.com/lfa; *E-mail:* lfa@lebanon-online.com.lb.

MACAO

Associacao De Futebol De Macau (AFM), P.O. Box 920, Macau.
Founded: 1939; *Number of Clubs:* 52; *Number of Players:* 800; *National Colours:* Green shirts, black shorts, green stockings.
Telephone: 00853 71996; *Cable:* FOOTBALL MACAU; *Fax:* 00853 260148.

MALAYSIA

Football Association of Malaysia, Wisma Fam, Tingkat 3, Jalan SS5A/9, Kelana Jaya, 47301 Petaling Jaya, Selangor.
Founded: 1933; *Number of Clubs:* 450; *Number of Players:* 11,250; *National Colours:* All yellow and black.
Telephone: 00603 7763766; *Cable:* FOOTB. PETALING JAYA SELANGO; *Telex:* FAM PJ MA 36701; *Fax:* 00603 7757984.

MALDIVES REPUBLIC

Football Association of Maldives, National Stadium Ghalolhu, Male 20-04.
Founded: 1982; *Number of Clubs: Number of Players: National Colours:* Green shirts, white shorts, red stockings.
Telephone: 0096031 7006; *Fax:* 0096031 7005.

MONGOLIA

Mongolia Football Federation, R413, Mongolia Youth Association Building, Baga Toiruu 10, Ulaanbaatar 10.
Telephone & fax: 009761 313145.

MYANMAR

Myanmar Football Federation, Attn Maj. Naw Tawng, Gen. Secr. Youth Training Centre, Thuwunna, Yangon.
Founded: 1947; *Number of Clubs:* 600; *Number of Players:* 21,000; *National Colours:* Red shirts, white shorts, red stockings.
Telephone: 00951 577366; *Cable:* FOOTBALL YANGON; *Telex:* 21253 SPED BM; *Fax:* 00951 571253.

NEPAL

All-Nepal Football Association, Dasharath Rangashala, Tripureshwor, PO Box 2090, Kathmandu.
Founded: 1951; *Number of Clubs:* 85; *Number of Players:* 2,550; *National Colours:* All red.
Telephone: 009771 241367; *Cable:* ANFA KATHMANDU; *Telex:* 2390 NSC NP; *Fax:* 009771 241365.

OMAN

Oman Football Association, P.O. Box 3462, Ruwi Postal Code 112.
Founded: 1978; *Number of Clubs:* 47; *Number of Players:* 2,340; *National Colours:* Red shirts with white sleeves, red/white shorts and stockings.
Telephone: 00968 787638/9; *Cable:* FOOTBALL MUSCAT; *Telex:* FOOTBALL 3223 ON; *Fax:* 00968 787632/33.

PAKISTAN

Pakistan Football Federation, 183, Abu Bakar Block, New Garden Town, Lahore, Pakistan.
Founded: 1948; *Number of Clubs:* 882; *Number of Players:* 21,000; *National Colours:* Green shirts, white shorts, green stockings.
Telephone: 009242 5832786; *Cable:* FOOTBALL LAHORE; *Telex:* 47643 PFF PK; *Fax:* 009242 7281541.

PALESTINE

Palestinian Football Federation, Al-Yarmouk, Gaza.
Telephone: 009727 829433; *Fax:* 009727 857020.

PHILIPPINES

Philippine Football Federation, Room 207 PSC, Administration Building, Rizal Memorial Sports Complex, P. Ocampo Street, Manila.
Founded: 1907; *Number of Clubs:* 650; *Number of Players:* 45,000; *National Colours:* Blue and red shirts, blue shorts, white stockings.
Telephone: 00632 5256502; *Cable:* FOOTBALL MANILA; *Telex:* 65014 POC PACA PN; *Fax:* 00632 5233741.

QATAR

Qatar Football Association, P.O. Box 5333, Doha.
Founded: 1960; *Number of Clubs:* 8 (senior); *Number of Players:* 1,380; *National Colours:* All white.
Telephone: 00974 434455; *Cable:* FOOTQATAR DOHA; *Telex:* 4749 QATFOT DH; *Fax:* 00974 411660.

SAUDI ARABIA

Saudi Arabian Football Federation, Al Mather Quarter (Olympic Complex), P.O. Box 5844, Riyadh 11432.
Founded: 1959; *Number of Clubs:* 120; *Number of Players:* 9,600; *National Colours:* White shirts, green shorts, white stockings.
Telephone: 009661 4822240; *Cable:* KURA RIYADH; *Telex:* 404300 SAFOTB SJ; *Fax:* 009661 4821215.

SINGAPORE

Football Association of Singapore, Jalan Besar Stadium, Tyrwhitt Road, Singapore 207542.
Founded: 1892; *Number of Clubs:* 250; *Number of Players:* 8,000; *National Colours:* All red.
Telephone: 0065 2931477; *Fax:* 0065 2933728.

SRI LANKA

Football Federation of Sri Lanka, No. 2, Old Grand Stand, Race Course, Reid Avenue, Colombo 7.
Founded: 1939; *Number of Clubs:* 600; *Number of Players:* 18,825; *National Colours:* Maroon and gold shirts, white shorts and stockings.
Telephone: 00941 696179; *Cable:* SOCCER COLOMBO; *Telex:* 21537 METALIX CE; *Fax:* 00941 682471.

SYRIA

Syrian Football Federation, Maysaloon St., PO Box 421, Damascus.
Founded: 1936; *Number of Clubs:* 102; *Number of Players:* 30,600; *National Colours:* All white.
Telephone: 0096311 3335866; *Cable:* FOOTBALL DAMASCUS; *Telex:* 411578 SPOFED SY; *Fax:* 0096311 3331511.

TAJIKISTAN

Tajikistan National Football Federation, 44, Rudaki Ave., PO Box 26, 734025 Dushanbe, Tajikistan.
Founded: 1991; *Number of Clubs:* 1,804; *Number of Players:* 71,400; *National Colours:* Green shirts, white shorts, green stockings.
Telephone: 0073772 212363; *Telex:* 116286 SHAKH; *Fax:* 00992 372212447 (or) 212953.

THAILAND

The Football Association of Thailand, National Stadium, Rama I Road, Bangkok.
Founded: 1916; *Number of Clubs:* 168; *Number of Players:* 15,000; *National Colours:* All red.
Telephone: 00662 2141058; *Cable:* FOOTBALL BANGKOK; *Telex:* 20211 FAT TH; *Fax:* 00662 2154494.

TURKMENISTAN

Turkmenistan Football Federation, 10 Turkmenbashi Avenue, 744005 Ashgabat, Turkmenistan.
Founded: 1992; *Number of Players:* 75,000; *National Colours:* Green shirts, white shorts, green stockings.
Telephone: 00363 2353739; *Fax:* 00363 2355327; *Telex:* 116175 TINTO SU.

UNITED ARAB EMIRATES

United Arab Emirates Football Association, P.O. Box 916, Abu Dhabi.
Founded: 1971; *Number of Clubs:* 23 (senior); *Number of Players:* 1,787; *National Colours:* All white.
Telephone: 00971 2444 5600; *Cable:* FOOTBALL EMIRATES ABU DHABI; *Telex:* 22121 UAEFA EM; *Fax:* 00971 2444 8558.

UZBEKISTAN

Uzbekistan Football Federation, Massiv Almazar Furkat Street 15/1, 700003 Tashkent, Uzbekistan.
Founded: 1946; *Number of Clubs:* 15,000; *Number of Players:* 217,000; *National Colours:* Blue shirts, white shorts, green stockings.
Telephone: 0073712 457106; *Telex:* 116108 PTB SU; *Fax:* 0073712 454948.

VIETNAM

Vietnam Football Federation, 141 Nguyen Thai Hoc Str., Dis Dongda, Hanoi.
Founded: 1962; *Number of Clubs:* 55 (senior); *Number of Players:* 16,000; *National Colours:* All red.
Telephone: 008448 452480; *Cable:* AFBVN, 141 NGUYEN THAI HOC STR.; *Fax:* 008448 233119.

YEMEN

Yemen Football Association, P.O. Box 908, Sana'a.
Founded: 1962; *Number of Clubs:* 26; *Number of Players:* 1750; *National Colours:* All green.
Telephone: 009671 269066. *Cable:* SANA'A FOOTBALL; *Telex:* 2710 YOUTH YE; *Fax:* 009671 276067.

CONCACAF

ANGUILLA

Anguilla Football Association, P.O. Box 608, The Valley, Anguilla, BWI.
National Colours: All blue.
Telephone: 001264 4975214/4972416; *Fax:* 001264 4972326.

ANTIGUA & BARBUDA

The Antigua Football Association, P.O. Box 773, St. John's.
Founded: 1928; *Number of Clubs:* 60; *Number of Players:* 1,008; *National Colours:* Gold shirts, black shorts and stockings.
Telephone: 001268 4624863; *Cable:* AFA ANTIGUA; *Fax:* 001268 4624864.

ARUBA

Arubaanse Voetbal Bond, PO Box 376, Oranjestad, Aruba.
Founded: 1932; *Number of Clubs:* 50; *Number of Players:* 1,000; *National Colours:* Yellow shirts, blue shorts, yellow and blue stockings.
Telephone: 00297 829550; *Cable:* AVB ARUBA; *Fax:* 00297 820624.

BAHAMAS

Bahamas Football Association, P.O. Box N 8434, Nassau, N.P.
Founded: 1967; *Number of Clubs:* 14; *Number of Players:* 700; *National Colours:* Yellow shirts, black shorts, yellow stockings.
Telephone: 001809 3233426; *Cable:* BAHSOCA NASSAU; *Fax:* 001809 3288006.

BARBADOS

Barbados Football Association, P.OI. Box 1362, Bridgetown, Barbados.
Physical address: Hadley Court, Upper Collymore Rock, St. Michael.
Founded: 1910; *Number of Clubs:* 92; *Number of Players:* 1,100; *National Colours;* Royal blue and gold shirts, gold shorts, white, gold and blue stockings.
Tel: 001246 2281707; *Cable:* FOOTBALL BRIDGETOWN; *Fax:* 001246 2286484.

BELIZE

Belize National Football Association, P.O. Box 1742, Belize City.
Founded: 1980; *National Colours:* Red, white and blue shirts and shorts, red stockings.
Telephone: 005012 36563; *Fax:* 005012 36564.

BERMUDA

The Bermuda Football Association, P.O. Box HM 745, Hamilton HM CX.
Founded: 1928; *Number of Clubs:* 30; *Number of Players:* 1,947; *National Colours:* Royal blue shirts, white shorts and stockings.
Telephone: 001809 2952199; *Cable:* FOOTBALL BERMUDA; *Telex:* 3441 BFA BA; *Fax:* 001809 2950773.

BRITISH VIRGIN ISLANDS

British Virgin Islands Football Association, P.O. Box 29, Road Town, Tortola, BVI.
Telephone: 001284 4945655; *Fax:* 001284 4948968.

US VIRGIN ISLANDS

V.I. Soccer Federation, P.O. Box 2618, Kingshill, St. Croix, US.V.I. 00851-2618.
Telephone: 001 340 7737216; *Fax:* 001 340 7739686.

CANADA

The Canadian Soccer Association, Place Soccer Canada, 237 Metcalfe Street, Ottawa, ONT K2P 1R2.
Founded: 1912; *Number of Clubs:* 1,600; *Number of Players:* 224,290; *National Colours:* All red.
Telephone: 001613 2377678; *Cable:* SOCCANADA OTTAWA; *Fax:* 001613 2371516.

CAYMAN ISLANDS

Cayman Islands Football Association, PO Box 178 GT, George Town, Grand Cayman, Cayman Islands W1.
Founded: 1966; *Number of Clubs:* 25; *Number of Players:* 875; *National Colours:* Red shirts, blue shorts, white stockings.
Telephone: 001345 9497822328. *Fax:* 001345 945 7673.

COSTA RICA

Federacion Costarricense De Futbol, Apartado 670-1000, Calle 40, Avda CTL & I, San Jose.
Founded: 1921; *Number of Clubs:* 431; *Number of Players:* 12,429; *National Colours:* Red and white shirts, blue shorts, white stockings.
Telephone: 00506 2221544; *Cable:* FEDEFUTBOL SAN JOSE; *Telex:* 3394 DIDER CR; *Fax:* 00506 2552674.

CUBA

Federacion Cubana De Futbol, c/o Comite Olimpico Cubano, Calle 13 No. 601, Esq. C. Vedado, La Habana, ZP 4.
Founded: 1924; *Number of Clubs:* 70; *Number of Players:* 12,900; *National Colours:* White shirts with red collar & cuffs, dark blue shorts, white and red stockings.
Telephone: 00537 403581; *Cable:* FOOTBALL HABANA; *Telex:* 511332 INDER CU; *Fax:* 00537 409037.

DOMINICA

Dominica Football Association, P.O. Box 372, Roseau, Commonwealth of Dominica.
Founded: 1970; *Number of Clubs:* 30; *Number of Players:* 500; *National Colours:* Emerald green shirts, green shorts, yellow stockings.
Telephone & fax: 001767 4492173.

DOMINICAN REPUBLIC

Federacion Dominicana De Futbol, Apartado De Correos No. 1953, Santo Domingo.
Founded: 1953; *Number of Clubs:* 128; *Number of Players:* 10,706; *National Colours:* Navy blue shirts, white shorts, red stockings.
Telephone: 001809542 6923. *Cable:* FEDOFUTBOL SANTO DOMINGO; *Telex:* 817240; *Fax:* 001809547 5363.

EL SALVADOR

Federacion Salvadorena De Futbol, Av. J.M. Delgado, Col. Escalon, Frente Ctro Espanol, Apartado 1029, San Salvador.
Founded: 1935; *Number of Clubs:* 944; *Number of Players:* 21,294; *National Colours:* Blue shirts, white shorts, blue stockings.
Telephone: 00503 2637525/6; *Cable:* FESFUT SAN SALVADOR; *Fax:* 00503 2637583.

GRENADA

Grenada Football Association, P.O. Box 326, St. Juilles Street, St George's, Grenada, West Indies.
Founded: 1924; *Number of Clubs:* 15; *Number of Players:* 200; *National Colours:* Green & yellow striped shirts, red shorts, yellow stockings.
Telephone & fax: 001473 4404850; *Cable:* GRENBALL GRENADA; *Telex:* 3431 CW BUR.

GUATEMALA

Federacion Nacional de Futbol de Guatemala, 7a Avenida 12-23 Zona 9, Edificio Etisa 6. Nivel, Guatemala City.
Founded: 1946; *Number of Clubs:* 1,611; *Number of Players:* 43,516; *National Colours:* Blue shirts, white shorts, blue stockings.
Telephone: 005023 322424; *Cable:* FEDFUTBOL GUATEMALA C.A.; *Fax:* 005023 320406.

GUYANA

Guyana Football Association, Lot 65 King Street, P.O. Box 10727 Georgetown.
Founded: 1902; *Number of Clubs:* 103; *Number of*

Players: 1,665; *National Colours:* Green shirts and shorts, yellow stockings.
Telephone: 0059222 78758, 63226;*Telex:* 2266 RICEBRD GY; *Fax:* 0059222 52096, 62641.

HAITI
Federation Haitienne De Football, P.O. Box 2258, Port-Au-Prince.
Founded: 1904; *Number of Clubs:* 40; *Number of Players:* 4,000; *National Colours:* Blue and red shirts, blue shorts, blue and red stockings.
Telephone: 00509 464509; *Cable:* FEDHAFOOB PORT-AU-PRINCE; *Fax:* 00509 573001.

HONDURAS
Federacion Nacional Autonoma De Futbol De Honduras, Apartado Postal 827, Costa Oeste Del Est. Nac, Tegucigalpa, D. C.
Founded: 1951; *Number of Clubs:* 1,050; *Number of Players:* 15,300; *National Colours:* Blue shirts, white shorts, blue stockings.
Telephone: 00504 235 4236 (or) 235 4246; *Cable* FENA-FUTH TEGUCIGALPA; *Fax:* 00504 235 4237.

JAMAICA
Jamaica Football Federation, General Secretariat, Room 8, Nat. Arena, Institue of Sports, Independence Park, Kingston 6.
Founded: 1910; *Number of Clubs:* 266; *Number of Players:* 45,200; *National Colours:* Gold shirts, black shorts, gold stockings.
Telephone: 001809 9290484; *Cable:* FOOTBALL JAMAICA KINGSTON; *Telex:* 2224 FEDLASCO JA; *Fax:* 001809 9290483.

MEXICO
Federacion Mexicana De Futbol Asociacion, A.C., Abraham Gonzales 74, Col. Juarez, C.P. 06600, Mexico 6, D.F.
Founded: 1927; *Number of Clubs:* 77 (senior); *Number of Players:* 1,402,270; *National Colours:* Green shirts with white collar, white shorts, red stockings.
Telephone: 00525 5662155; *Cable:* MEXFUTBOL MEX-ICO; *Fax:* 00525 5667580.

MONSERRAT
Monserrat Football Association, P.O. Box 46, Church Road, Plymouth, Monserrat.
Telephone: 001664 4912346; *Fax:* 001664 4912719.

NETHERLANDS ANTILLES
Nederlands Antiliaanse Voetbal Unie, P.O. Box 341, Curacao, N.A.
Founded: 1921; *Number of Clubs:* 85; *Number of Players:* 4,500; *National Colours:* white shirts with red and blue strips, white shorts, red, white and blue stockings.
Telephone: 005999 4627222/4343862; *Cable:* NAVU CURACAO; *Telex:* 1046 ENNIA NA; *Fax:* 005999 4627087/4343837.

NICARAGUA
Federacion Nicaraguense De Futbol, Estadio Futbol Camilo Ortega (Cranshaw), Apdo Postal 976, Managua.
Founded: 1931; *Number of Clubs:* 31; *Number of Players:* 160 (senior); *National Colours:* Blue and white striped shirts, blue shorts, blue and white striped stockings.
Telephone: 005052 680006/7/8; *Cable:* FENIFUT MAN-AGUA; *Fax:* 005052 664134.

PANAMA
Federacion Panamena De Futbol, Apartado Postal 8-391, Zona 8, Panama.

Founded: 1937; *Number of Clubs:* 65; *Number of Players:* 4,225; *National Colours:* Red shirts, blue shorts, white stockings.
Telephone & fax: 00507 2282238.

PUERTO RICO
Federacion Puertorriquena De Futbol, Coliseo Roberto Clemente, P.O. Box 1944355, Hato Rey, P.R. 00919-4355.
Founded: 1940; *Number of Clubs:* 175; *Number of Players:* 4,200; *National Colours:* Blue shirts, blue and white shorts and stockings.
Telephone & fax: 001787 7642025.

SAINT LUCIA
St Lucia National Football Association, PO Box 255, Castries, St Lucia.
Founded: 1979; *Number of Clubs:* 100; *Number of Players:* 4,000; *National Colours:* Blue and white shirts, black shorts, blue stockings.
Telephone: 001758 0689; *Cable:* NFU ST. LUCIA; *Telex:* 6394 FOR AFF LC; *Fax:* 001758 2506.

SAINT KITTS & NEVIS
St Kitts-Nevis Football Association, P.O. Box 465, Basseterre, St Kitts, W.I.
Founded: 1932; *Number of Clubs:* 36; *Number of Players:* 600; *National Colours:* Green and yellow shirts, red shorts, yellow stockings.
Telephone: 001869 465 6809; *Cable:* HORSFORD ST. KITTS; *Telex:* 6822 HORSFDSKB KC; *Fax:* 001869 465 1190; *Internet:* www.skbee.com/sknfa; *E-mail:* sknfa@skbee.com.

SAINT VINCENT & THE GRENADINES
St Vincent & The Grenadines Football Federation, PO Box 1278, Kingstown, St Vincent, W.I.
Founded: 1979; *Number of Clubs:* 500; *Number of Players:* 5,000; *National Colours:* Green shirts with yellow border, blue shorts, yellow stockings.
Telephone: 001784 4561659; *Fax:* 001784 4571659.

SURINAM
Surinaamse Voetbal Bond, Letitia Vriesde Laan 7, P.O. Box 1223, Paramaribo.
Founded: 1920; *Number of Clubs:* 168; *Number of Players:* 4,430; *National Colours:* Red green and white shirts, white or green shorts and stockings.
Telephone: 00597 473112; *Cable:* SVB Paramaribo; *Fax:* 00597 479718.

TRINIDAD AND TOBAGO
Trinidad & Tobago Football Federation, Petrotrin Savannah Building, 9 Queen's Park West, P.O. Box 400, Port of Spain.
Founded: 1908; *Number of Clubs:* 124; *Number of Players:* 5,050; *National Colours:* Red shirts, black shorts, white stockings.
Telephone: 001809 6271011; *Fax:* 001809 6271007.

TURKS & CAICOS
Turks & Caicos Football Association, P.O. Box 180, Providenciales, Turks & Caicos Islands, BWI.
Telephone: 001649 9464650; *Fax:* 001649 9464663.

USA
US Soccer, Soccer House, 1801-1811 S. Prairie Avenue, Chicago, Illinois 60616.
Founded: 1913; *Number of Clubs:* 7,000; *Number of Players:* 1,411,500; *National Colours:* All white.
Telephone: 001312 8081300; *Telex:* 450024 US SOCCER FED; *Fax:* 001312 8081301.

OCEANIA

AMERICAN SAMOA
American Samoa Football Association, P.O. Box 282, Pago Pago.
Telephone: 00684 6882290; *Fax:* 00684 6882291.

AUSTRALIA
Soccer Australia, Sydney Football Stadium, Driver Avenue, P.O. Box 175, Paddington NSW 2021.
Founded: 1961; *Number of Clubs:* 6,816; *Number of Players:* 433,957; *National Colours:* Gold shirts with green trim, gold shorts, gold and green stockings.

Telephone: 0061 293806099; *Cable:* FOOTBALL SYD-NEY; *Fax:* 0061 293806155.

COOK ISLANDS
Cook Islands Football Federation, P.O. Box 29, Avarua, Rarotonga, Cook Islands.
Founded: 1971; *Number of Clubs:* 9; *National Colours:* Green shirts and shorts with golden stripes, gold and green stockings.
Telephone: 00682 21231; *Fax:* 00682 25912.

FIJI

Fiji Football Association, Bob S. Kumar, Hon. Secretary, Government Bldgs, P.O.Box 2514, Suva.
Founded: 1938; *Number of Clubs;* 140: *Number of Players:* 21,300; *National Colours:* White shirts, blue shorts and stockings.
Telephone: 00679 300453; *Fax:* 00679 304642.

NEW ZEALAND

Soccer New Zealand, 51 O'Rorke Road, Penrose, Auckland, New Zealand.
Founded: 1891; *Number of Clubs:* 312; *Number of Players:* 52,969; *National Colours:* White shirts with black trim, white shorts and stockings.
Telephone: 00649 5256120; *Fax:* 00649 5256123.

PAPUA NEW GUINEA

Papua New Guinea Football (Soccer) Association, c/o National Sports Institute, P.O. Box 337, Goroka, EHP 441.
Founded: 1962; *Number of Clubs:* 350; *Number of Players:* 8,250; *National Colours:* Red shirts, black shorts, red stockings.
Telephone: 00675 7321699; *Telex:* TOTOTRA NE 23436; *Fax:* 00675 7321941.

SOLOMAN ISLANDS

Soloman Islands Football Federation, PO Box 854, Honiara, Soloman Islands.
Founded: 1978; *Number of Players:* 4,000; *National Colours:* Green, yellow and blue shirts and shorts, white stockings.
Telephone: 00677 26496; *Telex:* HQ 66349; *Fax:* 00677 26497.

TAHITI

Federation Tahitienne de Football (F.T.F.), B.P.50 358, Pirae, Tahiti, French Polynesia.
Founded: 1989; *National Colours:* White shirts, red shorts, white stockings.
Telephone: 00689 540954; *Cable:* FOOTBALL TAHITI; *Fax:* 00689 419629.

TONGA

Tonga Football Association, P.O. Box 852, Nuku'Alofa, Tonga.
Founded: 1965; *Number of Clubs:* 23; *Number of Players:* 350; *National Colours:* Red shirts, white shorts, red and white stockings.
Telephone: 00676 24442; *Cable:* SOCCER NUKU' ALOFA; *Fax:* 00676 23340; *E-mail:* tfa@kalianet.to.

VANUATU

Vanuatu Football Federation, P.O. Box 226, Port Vila, Vanuatu.
Founded: 1934; *National Colours:* Gold and black shirts, black shorts, gold and black stockings.
Telephone: 00678 25236; *Cable:* FUTBOL BLONG VANUATU; *Fax:* 00678 25236.

WESTERN SAMOA

Samoa Football (Soccer) Association, P.O. Box 960, Apia.
Founded: 1968; *National Colours:* Royal blue shirts, white shorts, royal blue and white stockings.
Telephone: 00685 22822; *Telex:* 233 TREASURY SX; *Fax:* 00685 21312.

AFRICA

ALGERIA

Federation Algerienne De Foot-ball, Chemin Ahmed Ouaked, Boite Postale No. 39, Dely-Ibrahim-Alger.
Founded: 1962; *Number of Clubs:* 780; *Number of Players:* 58,567; *National Colours:* Green shirts, white shorts, green stockings.
Telephone: 002132 365938; *Cable:* FAFOOT ALGER; *Telex:* 61378. *Fax:* 002132 365949.

ANGOLA

Federation Angolaise De Football, Compl. da Cidadela Desportiva, B.P. 3449, Luanda.
Founded: 1979; *Number of Clubs:* 276; *Number of Players:* 4,269; *National Colours:* Red shirts, black shorts, red stockings.
Telephone: 002442 261331, 264948, 265936; *Cable:* FUTANGOLA; *Telex:* 2580 PALANCA AN; *Fax:* 002442 260566.

BENIN

Federation Beninoise De Football, B.P. 965, Cotonou.
Founded: 1962; *Number of Clubs:* 117; *Number of Players:* 6,700; *National Colours:* Yellow shirts, green shorts, red stockings.
Telephone & fax: 00229 330537; *Cable:* FEBEFOOT COTONOU; *Telex:* 5245 SONACOP COTONOU.

BOTSWANA

Botswana Football Association, P.O. Box 1396, Gaborone.
Founded: 1970; *National Colours:* Blue and white shirts, blue, white and black shorts, blue, white and black striped stockings.
Telephone: 00267 300279; *Cable:* BOTSBALL GABARONE; *Telex:* 2977 BD; *Fax:* 00267 300280.

BURKINA FASO

Federation Burkinabe De Foot-Ball, 01 B.P. 57, Ouagadougou 01.
Founded: 1960; *Number of Clubs:* 57; *Number of Players:* 4,672; *National Colours:* Red shirts, green shorts with yellow star, red stockings.
Telephone: 00226 318815; *Cable:* FEDEFOOT OUA-GADOUGOU; *Fax:* 00226 318843.

BURUNDI

Federation De Football Du Burundi, B.P. 3426, Bujumbura.
Founded: 1948; *Number of Clubs:* 132; *Number of Players:* 3,930; *National Colours:* Red shirts, white shorts, green stockings.
Telephone & fax: 00257 212891; *Cable:* FFB BUJA.

CAMEROON

Federation Camerounaise De Football, B.P. 1116, Yaounde.
Founded: 1959; *Number of Clubs:* 200; *Number of Players:* 9,328; *National Colours:* Green shirts, red shorts, yellow stockings.
Telephone: 00237 216662; *Cable:* FECAFOOT YAOUNDE; *Telex:* 8568 JEUNESPO KN; *Fax:* 00237 210012.

CAPE VERDE ISLANDS

Federacao Cabo-Verdiana De Futebol, P.O. Box 234, Praia.
Founded: 1982; *National Colours:* All green.
Telephone & fax: 00238 611362; *Cable:* FUTEBOL PRAIA CV; *Telex:* 6005 ACAS CV.

CENTRAL AFRICAN REPUBLIC

Federation Centrafricaine De Football Amateur, B.P. 344, Bangui.
Founded: 1937; *Number of Clubs:* 256; *Number of Players:* 7,200; *National Colours:* Grey & blue shirts with Nat. emblem and star, white shorts, red stockings with yellow trim.
Telephone: 00236 612433; *Cable:* FOOTBANGUI BANGUI; *Fax:* 00236 615660.

CHAD

Federation Tchadienne de Football, B.P. 886, N'Djamena.
Founded: 1962; *National Colours:* Blue shirts, yellow shorts, red stockings.
Telephone: 00235/519204; *Telex:* 5248 kd; *Fax:* 00235/518648.

CONGO

Federation Congolaise De Football, B.P. 4041, Brazzaville.
Founded: 1962; *Number of Clubs:* 250; *Number of Players:* 5,940; *National Colours:* All red.
Telephone: 00242 834885; *Cable:* FECOFOOT BRAZZAVILLE; *Telex:* 5210 KG; *Fax:* 00242 836199.

CONGO DR

Federation Congolaise De Football-Association (FECOFA), P.O. Box 1284, Av. De L'Enseignem. 210, Z/Kasa-Vubu, Kinshasa 1.
Founded: 1919; *Number of Clubs:* 3,800; *Number of Players:* 64,627; *National Colours:* Green shirts, yellow shorts, red stockings.
Telephone & fax: 001212 3769411; *Cable:* FECOFA KINSHASA.

DJIBOUTI

Federation Djiboutienne de Football, B.P. 2694, Djibouti.
Founded: 1977; *Number of Players:* 2,000; *National Colours:* Green shirts, white shorts, blue stockings.
Telephone: 00253 342049; *Fax:* 00253 356793.

EGYPT

Egyptian Football Association, 5, Shareh Gabalaya, Guezira, Al Borg Post Office, Cairo.
Founded: 1921; *Number of Clubs:* 247; *Number of Players:* 19,735; *National Colours:* Red shirts, white shorts, black stockings.
Telephone: 00202 3401793; *Cable:* KORA CAIRO; *Telex:* 93506 KORA UN; *Fax:* 00202 3417817.

ERITREA

The Eritrean National Football Federation, P.O. Box 3665, Asmara.
Telephone & fax: 002911 126821.

ETHIOPIA

Ethiopia Football Federation, Addis Ababa Stadium, P.O. Box 1080, Addis Ababa.
Founded: 1943; *Number of Clubs:* 767; *Number of Players:* 20,594; *National Colours:* Green shirts, yellow shorts, red stockings.
Telephone: 002511 514453; *Cable:* FOOTBALL ADDIS ABABA; *Telex:* 21377 NESCO ET; *Fax:* 002511 513345.

GABON

Federation Gabonaise De Football, B.P. 181, Libreville.
Founded: 1962; *Number of Clubs:* 320; *Number of Players:* 10,000; *National Colours:* Green, yellow and blue shirts, blue and yellow shorts, white stockings with tri-colour trims.
Telephone: 00241 730460; *Cable:* FEGAFOOT LIBREVILLE; *Telex:* 5526 GO; *Fax:* 00241 746047.

GAMBIA

Gambia Football Association, Independence Stadium, Bakau, P.O. Box 523, Banjul.
Founded: 1952; *Number of Clubs:* 30; *Number of Players:* 860; *National Colours:* White shirts with striped band, white shorts, white stockings with red tops.
Telephone: 00220 496980; *Cable:* SPORTS GAMBIA BANJUL; *Telex:* 2262 FISCO GV.

GHANA

Ghana Football Association, P.O. Box 1272, Accra.
Founded: 1957; *Number of Clubs:* 347; *Number of Players:* 11,275; *National Colours:* All yellow.
Telephone: 0023321 666697; *Cable:* GFA ACCRA; *Telex:* 2519 SPORTS GH; *Fax:* 0023321 668590.

GUINEA

Federation Guineenne De Football, P.O. Box 3645, Conakry.
Founded: 1959; *Number of Clubs:* 351; *Number of Players:* 10,000; *National Colours:* Red shirts, yellow shorts, green stockings.
Telephone: 00224 461159; *Cable:* GUINEFOOT CONAKRY; *Telex:* 22302 MJ GE; Fax: 00224 411926.

GUINEA-BISSAU

Federacao De Football Da Guinea-Bissau, Rua 4 No. 10-C, Apartado 375, 1035 Bissau- Codex.
Founded: 1974; *National Colours:* All red.
Telephone & fax: 00245 201918; *Cable:* FUTEBOL BISSAU.

GUINEA, EQUATORIAL

Federacion Ecuatoguineana De Futbol, Malabo.
Founded: 1986; *National Colours:* All red.
Telephone: 002409 2392; *Cable:* FEGUIFUT MALABO; *Telex:* 9991111 EG; *Fax:* 002409 3353.

IVORY COAST

Federation Ivoirienne De Football, Av. 1 Treichville, 01 B.P. 1202, Abidjan 01.
Founded: 1960; *Number of Clubs:* 84 (senior); *Number of Players:* 3,655; *National Colours:* Orange shirts, white shorts, green stockings.
Telephone: 00225 242301; *Cable:* FIF ABIDJAN; *Telex:* 42344 FIF CI; *Fax:* 00225 257111.

KENYA

Kenya Football Federation, Nyayo National Stadium, P.O. Box 40234, Nairobi.
Founded: 1960; *Number of Clubs:* 351; *Number of Players:* 8,880; *National Colours:* Red, green and white shirts, red, green and black shorts and stockings.
Telephone: 002542 501825/35; *Cable:* KEFF NAIROBI; *Telex:* 24069 SPICERS KE; *Fax:* 002542 501120.

LESOTHO

Lesotho Football Association, P.O. Box 756, Maseru-100, Lesotho.
Founded: 1932; *Number of Clubs:* 88; *Number of Players:* 2,076; *National Colours:* Blue shirts, green shorts, white stockings.
Telephone: 00266 311879; *Cable:* LEFA MASERU; *Telex:* 4493, 4228; *Fax:* 00266 310586.

LIBERIA

Liberia Football Association, 110 Camp Johnson Road, P.O. Box 10-1066, 1000 Monrovia 10.
Founded: 1936; *National Colours:* Red shirts, white shorts, blue stockings.
Telephone: 00231 226284; *Cable:* LIBFOTASS MONROVIA; *Telex:* 44220 EXM IBR. *Fax:* 00231 225217.

LIBYA

Libyan Arab Football Federation, 7th October Stadium, P.O. Box 5137, Tripoli.
Founded: 1963; *Number of Clubs:* 89; *Number of Players:* 2,941; *National Colours:* Green shirts, white shorts, green stockings.
Telephone & fax: 0021821 4446610/3339150; *Telex:* 20896 LY.

MADAGASCAR

Federation Malagasy de Football, Immeuble Preservatrice Vie-Lot IBF-9B, Rue Rabearivelo-Antsahavola, Antananarivo 101.
Founded: 1961; *Number of Clubs:* 775; *Number of Players:* 23,536; *National Colours:* Red shirts, white shorts, green stockings.
Telephone: 0026120 2268374; *Telex:* 22265 AROSUR MG; *Fax:* 0026120 2268373.

MALAWI

Football Association of Malawi, P.O. Box 865, Blantyre.
Founded: 1966; *Number of Clubs:* 465; *Number of Players:* 12,500; *National Colours:* Red shirts, red and green shorts, green stockings.
Telephone & fax: 00265 674290; *Cable:* FOOTBALL BLANTYRE; *Telex:* 4526 SPORTS MI.

MALI

Federation Malienne De Football, Stade Mamdou Konate, B.P. 1020, Bamako.
Founded: 1960; *Number of Clubs:* 128; *Number of Players:* 5,480; *National Colours:* Green shirts, yellow shorts, red stockings.
Telephone: 00223 224254; *Cable:* MALIFOOT BAMAKO; Telex: 0985 1200 MJ; *Fax:* 00356 245136.

MAURITANIA

Federation De Foot-Ball De La Rep. Islamique. De Mauritanie, B.P. 566, Nouakchott.
Founded: 1961; *Number of Clubs:* 59; *Number of Players:* 1,930; *National Colours:* Green and yellow shirts, yellow shorts, green stockings.
Telephone: 00222 291032 (or) 50424; *Cable:* FOOTRIM NOUAKCHOTT; *Telex:* 577 MTN NKTT RIM; *Fax:* 00222 291031 (or) 250424 (or) 291077.

MAURITIUS

Mauritius Football Association, Chancery House, 2nd Floor Nos. 303-305, 14 Lislet Geoffroy Street, Port Louis.
Founded: 1952; *Number of Clubs:* 397; *Number of Players:* 29,375; *National Colours:* Red shirts, white shorts, red stockings with white tops.

Telephone: 00230 2121418; *Cable:* MFA PORT LOUIS; *Fax:* 00230 2084100.

MOROCCO

Federation Royale Marocaine De Football, Av. Ibn Sina, C.N.S. Bellevue, B.P. 51, Rabat.
Founded: 1955; *Number of Clubs:* 350; *Number of Players:* 19,768; *National Colours:* All red.
Telephone: 002127 672706/08; *Cable:* FERMAFOOT RABAT; *Telex:* 32940 FERMFOOT M. *Fax:* 002127 671070.

MOZAMBIQUE

Federacao Mocambicana De Futebol, Av. Samora Machel, 11-2, Caixa Postal 1467, Maputo.
Founded: 1978; *Number of Clubs:* 144; *National Colours:* Red shirts, black shorts, black and red stockings.
Telephone: 002581 300366; *Cable:* MOCAMBOLA MAPUTO; *Telex:* 6-747 MCID MO; *Fax:* 002581 300367.

NAMIBIA

Namibia Football Federation, Abraham Mashego Street 8521, Katurua Council of Churches in Namibia, PO Box 1345, Windhoek, Namibia.
Founded: 1990; *Number of Clubs:* 244; *Number of Players:* 7320; *National Colours:* All blue, red, green, yellow and white.
Telephone: 0026461 217621; *Fax:* 0026461 265693.

NIGER

Federation Nigerienne De Football (Fenifoot), Stade du 29 Juillet, B.P. 10299, Niamey.
Founded: 1967; *Number of Clubs:* 64; *Number of Players:* 1,525; *National Colours:* Orange shirts, white shorts, green stockings.
Telephone: 00227 725127/722147; *Cable:* FEDERFOOT NIGER NIAMEY; *Telex:* 5527; *Fax:* 00227 722147/ 734694.

NIGERIA

Nigeria Football Association, Plot 2033, Olusegun Obasanjo Way, Wuse Zone 7, Abuja, Nigeria.
Founded: 1945; *Number of Clubs:* 326; *Number of Players:* 80,190; *National Colours:* Green shirts, white shorts, green stockings.
Telephone: 002349 5237326; *Cable:* FOOTBALL ABUJA; *Telex:* 26570 NFA NG; *Fax:* 002349 5237327.

RWANDA

Federation Rwandaise De Football Amateur, B.P. 2000, Kigali.
Founded: 1972; *Number of Clubs:* 167; *National Colours:* Red, green and yellow shirts, green shorts, red stockings.
Telephone: 00250 84999; *Cable:* FERWAFA KIGALI; *Telex:* 22504 PUBLIC RW; *Fax:* 00250 76574.

SENEGAL

Federation Senegalaise De Football, Stade L.S. Senghor, Route De L'Aeroport De Yoff, B.P. 130 21, Dakar.
Founded: 1960; *Number of Clubs:* 75 (senior); *Number of Players:* 3,977; *National Colours:* Green shirts, yellow shorts, red stockings.
Telephone & fax: 00221 8273524; *Cable:* SENEFOOT DAKAR ; *Telex:* 13048 PUBLIDK SG.

SEYCHELLES

Seychelles Football Federation, P.O. Box 843, People's Stadium, Victoria-Mahe, Seychelles.
Founded: 1979; *National Colours:* Red and blue shirts, blue and red shorts, white stockings.
Telephone: 00248 323908 ext. 244; *Fax:* 00248 225468.

ST. THOMAS AND PRINCIPE

Federation Santomense De Futebol, P.O. Box 42, Sao Tome.
Founded: 1975; *National Colours:* All green and yellow.
Telephone: 0023912 23431; *Telex:* 213 PUBLICO STP; *Fax:* 0023912 21365.

SIERRA LEONE

Sierra Leone Football Association, P.O. Box 672, National Stadium, Brookfields, Freetown.
Founded: 1967; *Number of Clubs:* 104; *Number of Players:* 8,120; *National Colours:* Green, white and blue shirts, white shorts, blue stockings with white tops.
Telephone: 00232 2224 1872; *Fax:* 00232 22227771.

SOMALIA

Somali Football Federation, c/o Conf. Afric. de Football, 5 Gabalaya Street, 11567, El Borg, Cairo, Egypt.
Founded: 1951; *Number of Clubs:* 46 (senior); *Number of Players:* 1,150; *National Colours:* All sky blue and white.
Telephone: 0020 2/3412497; *Cable:* SOMALIA FOOTBALL CAIRO; *Telex:* 93162 CAF UN; *Fax:* 0020 2/3420114 (CAF).

SOUTH AFRICA

South African Football Association, First National Bank Stadium, Nasrec/ PO Box 910, Johannesburg 2000; South Africa.
Founded: 1991; *Number of Teams:* 51,944; *Number of Players:* 1,039,880; *National Colours:* Gold and black shirts, green shorts, white stockings.
Telephone: 002711 4943522; *Fax:* 002711 4943013.

SUDAN

Sudan Football Association, P.O. Box 437, Khartoum.
Founded: 1936; *Number of Clubs:* 750; *Number of Players:* 42,200; *National Colours:* Green shirts, white shorts, green stockings.
Telephone & fax: 0024911 776633; *Cable:* ALKOURA KHARTOUM; *Telex:* 23007 KORA SD.

SWAZILAND

National Football Association of Swaziland, P.O. Box 641, Mbabane.
Founded: 1968; *Number of Clubs:* 136; *National Colours:* Blue shirts, gold shorts, white stockings.
Telephone: 00268 46852; *Telex:* 2245 EXP WD; *Fax:* 00268 46206.

TANZANIA

Football Association of Tanzania, Uhuru/Shaurimoyo Road, Karume Memorial Stadium, P.O. Box 1574, Ilala/Dar Es Salaam.
Founded: 1930; *Number of Clubs:* 51; *National Colours:* Yellow shirts with black stripes, yellow shorts, yellow and black stockings with horiz. stripe.
Telephone: 0025551 117931; *Cable:* FAT DAR- ES-SALAAM; *Telex:* 41873 TZ; *Fax:* 0025551 117930.

TOGO

Federation Togolaise De Football, C.P. 5, Lome.
Founded: 1960; *Number of Clubs:* 144; *Number of Players:* 4,346; *National Colours:* White shirts, green shorts, red and yellow stockings with green stripes.
Telephone: 00228 221412; *Cable:* TOGOFOOT LOME; *Telex:* 5015 CNOT TG. *Fax:* 00228 221413.

TUNISIA

Federation Tunisienne De Football, 16 Rue de la Ligue Arabe, El-Menzah VI, Tunis 1004.
Founded: 1956; *Number of Clubs:* 215; *Number of Players:* 18,300; *National Colours:* Red shirts, white shorts, red stockings.
Telephone: 002161 233303; *Cable:* FOOTBALL TUNIS; *Telex:* 14783 FTFOOT TN; *Fax:* 002161 767929.

UGANDA

Federation of Uganda Football Associations, P.O. Box 22518, Kampala, Uganda.
Founded: 1924; *Number of Clubs:* 400; *Number of Players:* 1,518; *National Colours:* Yellow shirts with black stripes, black shorts with yellow stripes, yellow and red stockings.
Telephone: 0025641 342731; *Cable:* FUFA LUGOGO STADIUM, KAMPALA; *Telex:* 61605; *Fax:* 0025641 342731.

ZAMBIA

Football Association of Zambia, P.O. Box 34751, Lusaka.
Founded: 1929; *Number of Clubs:* 20 (senior); *Number of Players:* 4,100; *National Colours:* Copper shirts, black shorts, copper stockings.
Telephone: 002601 750254; *Cable:* FOOTBALL LUSAKA; *Fax:* 002601 225046.

ZIMBABWE

Zimbabwe Football Association, P.O. Box CY 114, Causeway, Harare.
Founded: 1965; *National Colours:* Green shirts, gold shorts, green and gold stockings.
Telephone: 002634 731262; *Cable:* SOCCER HARARE; *Telex:* 22299 SOCCER ZW; *Fax:* 002634 731265.

THE WORLD CUP 1930–98

Year	Winners		Runners-up		Venue	Attendance	Referee
1930	Uruguay	4	Argentina	2	Montevideo	90,000	Langenus (B)
1934	Italy	2	Czechoslovakia	1	Rome	50,000	Eklind (Se)
	(after extra time)						
1938	Italy	4	Hungary	2	Paris	45,000	Capdeville (F)
1950	Uruguay	2	Brazil	1	Rio de Janeiro	199,854	Reader (E)
1954	West Germany	3	Hungary	2	Berne	60,000	Ling (E)
1958	Brazil	5	Sweden	2	Stockholm	49,737	Guigue (F)
1962	Brazil	3	Czechoslovakia	1	Santiago	68,679	Latychev (USSR)
1966	England	4	West Germany	2	Wembley	93,802	Dienst (Sw)
	(after extra time)						
1970	Brazil	4	Italy	1	Mexico City	107,412	Glockner (EG)
1974	West Germany	2	Holland	1	Munich	77,833	Taylor (E)
1978	Argentina	3	Holland	1	Buenos Aires	77,000	Gonella (I)
	(after extra time)						
1982	Italy	3	West Germany	1	Madrid	90,080	Coelho (Br)
1986	Argentina	3	West Germany	2	Mexico City	114,580	Filho (Br)
1990	West Germany	1	Argentina	0	Rome	73,603	Codesal (Mex)
1994	Brazil	0	Italy	0	Los Angeles	94,194	Puhl (H)
	(Brazil won 3-2 on penalties aet)						
1998	France	3	Brazil	0	St-Denis	75,000	Belqola (Mor)

GOALSCORING AND ATTENDANCES IN WORLD CUP FINAL ROUNDS

Venue	Matches	Goals (av)	Attendance (av)
1930, Uruguay	18	70 (3.9)	434,500 (24,138)
1934, Italy	17	70 (4.1)	395,000 (23,235)
1938, France	18	84 (4.6)	483,000 (26,833)
1950, Brazil	22	88 (4.0)	1,337,000 (60,772)
1954, Switzerland	26	140 (5.4)	943,000 (36,270)
1958, Sweden	35	126 (3.6)	868,000 (24,800)
1962, Chile	32	89 (2.8)	776,000 (24,250)
1966, England	32	89 (2.8)	1,614,677 (50,458)
1970, Mexico	32	95 (2.9)	1,673,975 (52,311)
1974, West Germany	38	97 (2.5)	1,774,022 (46,684)
1978, Argentina	38	102 (2.7)	1,610,215 (42,374)
1982, Spain	52	146 (2.8)	2,064,364 (38,816)
1986, Mexico	52	132 (2.5)	2,441,731 (46,956)
1990, Italy	52	115 (2.2)	2,515,168 (48,368)
1994, USA	52	141 (2.7)	3,567,415 (68,604)
1998, France	64	171 (2.6)	2,775,400 (43,366)

LEADING GOALSCORERS

Year	Player	Goals
1930	Guillermo Stabile (Argentina)	8
1934	Angelo Schiavio (Italy)	
	Oldrich Nejedly (Czechoslovakia)	
	Edmund Conen (Germany)	4
1938	Leonidas da Silva (Brazil)	8
1950	Ademir (Brazil)	9
1954	Sandor Kocsis (Hungary)	11
1958	Just Fontaine (France)	13
1962	Valentin Ivanov (USSR), Leonel Sanchez (Chile), Garrincha, Vava (both Brazil), Florian Albert (Hungary), Drazen Jerkovic (Yugoslavia)	4
1966	Eusebio (Portugal)	9
1970	Gerd Muller (West Germany)	10
1974	Grzegorz Lato (Poland)	7
1978	Mario Kempes (Argentina)	6
1982	Paolo Rossi (Italy)	6
1986	Gary Lineker (England)	6
1990	Salvatore Schillaci (Italy)	6
1994	Oleg Salenko (Russia)	
	Hristo Stoichkov (Bulgaria)	6
1998	Davor Suker (Croatia)	6

EUROPEAN FOOTBALL CHAMPIONSHIP
(formerly EUROPEAN NATIONS' CUP)

Year	Winners		Runners-up		Venue	Attendance
1960	USSR	2	Yugoslavia	1	Paris	17,966
1964	Spain	2	USSR	1	Madrid	120,000
1968	Italy	2	Yugoslavia	0	Rome	60,000
	After 1-1 draw					75,000
1972	West Germany	3	USSR	0	Brussels	43,437
1976	Czechoslovakia	2	West Germany	2	Belgrade	45,000
	(Czechoslovakia won on penalties)					
1980	West Germany	2	Belgium	1	Rome	47,864
1984	France	2	Spain	0	Paris	48,000
1988	Holland	2	USSR	0	Munich	72,308
1992	Denmark	2	Germany	0	Gothenburg	37,800
1996	Germany	2	Czech Republic	1	Wembley	73,611
	(Germany won on sudden death)					
2000	France	2	Italy	1	Rotterdam	50,000
	(France won on sudden death)					

FIFA WORLD CUP 2002 RESULTS

EUROPE
(Members 51, Entries 51)

Fourteen or fifteen teams qualify including France as world champions and play-offs between UEFA and Asia.

GROUP 1

Zurich, 2 September 2000, 14,500

Switzerland (0) 0
Russia (0) 1 *(Bestchastnykh 74)*

Switzerland: Pascolo; Lubamba, Henchoz, Muller P, Mazarelli (Buhlmann 72), Cantaluppi (Wicky 64), Vogel, Sforza, Comisetti, Rey, Yakin H (N'Kufo 64).
Russia: Nigmatullin; Khlestov, Chugainov, Smertin, Gusev (Alenichev 52), Drozdov, Onopko, Karpin, Titov (Panov 46) (Semak 88), Mostovoi, Bestchastnykh.
Referee: Nielsen (Denmark).

Toftir, 3 September 2000, 3200

Faeroes (0) 2 *(Arge 87, Hansen O 90)*
Slovenia (1) 2 *(Udovic 25, Osterc 86)*

Faeroes: Mikkelsen; Hansen H, Johannesen O, Hansen JK, Morkore A, Joensen S, Petersen (Joensen J 78), Johnsson, Hansen O, Arge, Jonsson T (Morkore K 57).
Slovenia: Simeunovic; Bulajic, Vugdalic, Milinovic, Novak, Karic, Ceh, Pavlin, Zahovic, Rudonja (Zlogar 89), Udovic (Osterc 71).
Referee: Vuorela (Finland).

Luxembourg, 3 September 2000, 3305

Luxembourg (0) 0
Yugoslavia (2) 2 *(Milosevic 4, Jokanovic 26)*

Luxembourg: Besic; Vanek, Schauls, Funck, Strasser, Deville L, Saibene, Alverdi (Theis 84), Holtz (Ferron 89), Schneider, Zaritski (Huss 62).
Yugoslavia: Cicovic; Mirkovic, Dudic (Sakic 62), Jokanovic, Bunjevcevic, Djordjevic, Lazetic, Stankovic D (Ilic 73), Drulovic, Mijatovic (Kovacevic 70), Milosevic.
Referee: Smolik (Belarus).

Luxembourg, 7 October 2000, 1788

Luxembourg (0) 1 *(Strasser 46)*
Slovenia (2) 2 *(Zahovic 39, Milinovic 41)*

Luxembourg: Besic; Vanek, Schauls, Funck, Strasser (Posing 88), Saibene, Peters, Holtz, Schneider, Cardoni (Zaritski 80), Huss (Braun 73).
Slovenia: Dabanovic; Milinovic, Vugdalic, Karic, Knavs, Novak, Ceh, Siljak (Udovic 80), Zahovic, Pavlin (Pavlovic 67), Acimovic.
Referee: Benes (Czech Republic).

Zurich, 7 October 2000, 9500

Switzerland (4) 5 *(Zwyssig 26, Fournier 35, Turkyilmaz 43 (pen), 45 (pen), 53 (pen))*
Faeroes (1) 1 *(Petersen 4)*

Switzerland: Zuberbuhler; Lubamba (Wicky 66), Henchoz, Zwyssig, Fournier, Sesa, Vogel (Celestini 66), Sforza, Comisetti, Chapuisat, Turkyilmaz (Cantaluppi 76).
Faeroes: Mikkelsen; Morkore A, Johannesen O, Hansen JK, Hansen H, Petersen (Jacobsen 63), Joensen S (Joensen J 63), Johnsson, Hansen O, Hansen JB, Arge.
Referee: Kapitanis (Cyprus).

Moscow, 11 October 2000, 12,000

Russia (1) 3 *(Buznikin 19, Khokhlov 57, Titov 90)*
Luxembourg (0) 0

Russia: Nigmatullin; Khlestov, Khokhlov, Smertin, Tetradze, Buznikin, Onopko, Karpin, Titov, Mostovoi, Bestchastnykh.
Luxembourg: Gillet; Funck (Ferron 86), Schauls, Vanek, Strasser, Saibene, Peters, Holtz, Schneider (Posing 77), Cardoni, Huss (Zaritsky 61).
Referee: Ferry (Northern Ireland).

Ljubljana, 11 October 2000, 7000

Slovenia (1) 2 *(Siljak 44, Acimovic 78)*
Switzerland (1) 2 *(Turkyilmaz 20, 66)*

Slovenia: Dabanovic; Milinovic, Vugdalic, Knavs, Novak, Ceh, Pavlin (Acimovic 69), Karic, Udovic (Tavcar 46), Zahovic, Siljak (Osterc 59).
Switzerland: Zuberbuhler; Zellweger, Mazzarelli, Zwyssig, Fournier (Magnin 64) (Muller P 72), Wicky (Cantaluppi 46), Comisetti, Vogel, Chapuisat, Sforza, Turkyilmaz.
Referee: Durkin (England).

Luxembourg, 24 March 2001, 2380

Luxembourg (0) 0
Faeroes (0) 2 *(Jacobsen C 75, Morkore K 82)*

Luxembourg: Besic; Deville L, Schauls, Posing, Strasser, Saibene, Peters (Huss 46), Holtz, Zaritski, Cardoni, Schneider (Braun 77).
Faeroes: Mikkelsen; Johannesen O, Hansen JB, Borg (Olsen 84), Hansen HF, Hansen O, Benjaminsen (Jacobsen R 73), Johnsson J, Morkore K, Jonsson T (Jacobsen C 20), Petersen.
Referee: Hanacsek (Hungary).

Moscow, 24 March 2001, 35,000

Russia (1) 1 *(Khlestov 8)*
Slovenia (1) 1 *(Knavs 22)*

Russia: Nigmatullin; Khlestov, Nikiforov, Kovtun, Tetradze, Karpin, Smertin (Bestchastnykh 46), Onopko, Alenichev (Semak 66), Titov, Buznikin.
Slovenia: Simeunovic; Gajser, Milinovic, Knavs, Bulajic, Novak, Ceh, Pavlin, Rudonja (Pavlovic 88), Zahovic, Osterc (Cimerotic 66).
Referee: Dallas (Scotland).

Belgrade, 24 March 2001, 36,000

Yugoslavia (0) 1 *(Mihajlovic 68)*
Switzerland (0) 1 *(Chapuisat 84)*

Yugoslavia: Kocic; Duljaj, Djukic, Mihajlovic, Obradovic, Lazetic (Stefanovic 78), Jugovic, Stankovic D (Ivic 56), Djordjevic (Kovacevic 64), Kezman, Milosevic.
Switzerland: Pascolo; Zellweger, Henchoz, Muller P, Quentin, Lombardo (Buhlmann 72), Vogel, Fournier, Lonfat, Yakin H (Frei 58), Chapuisat (Vega 86).
Referee: Nilsson (Sweden).

Moscow, 28 March 2001, 10,500

Russia (1) 1 *(Mostovoi 19)*
Faeroes (0) 0

Russia: Nigmatullin; Tetradze (Alenichev 46), Nikiforov, Kovtun, Karpin, Gusev (Drozdov 46), Onopko, Khokhlov, Mostovoi, Titov, Buznikin (Bestchastnykh 67).
Faeroes: Mikkelsen; Johannesen O, Thorsteinsson, Borg, Hansen BH, Hansen HF, Benjaminsen, Johnsson J, Morkore K (Joensen 75), Jacobsen C, Petersen.
Referee: Irvine (Republic of Ireland).

Ljubljana, 28 March 2001, 10,000

Slovenia (0) 1 *(Zahovic 90)*
Yugoslavia (1) 1 *(Milosevic 32)*

Slovenia: Simeunovic; Gajser (Acimovic 37), Vugdalic, Bulajic, Knavs, Novak, Ceh, Osterc (Cimerotic 46), Pavlin (Pavlovic 62), Zahovic, Rudonja.
Yugoslavia: Kocic; Obradovic, Djukic, Mihajlovic, Krstajic, Stefanovic, Jokanovic (Duljaja 68), Lazetic, Djordjevic, Milosevic (Ivic 79), Kezman (Drulic 57).
Referee: Jol (Holland).

Zurich, 28 March 2001, 8600

Switzerland (2) 5 *(Frei 9, 31, 90, Lonfat 64, Chapuisat 72)*
Luxembourg (0) 0

Switzerland: Pascolo; Zellweger, Henchoz, Muller P, Quentin, Lonfat (Buhlmann 74), Vogel, Fournier, Lombardo (Muller S 86), Frei, Chapuisat (Yakin H 79).
Luxembourg: Besic; Schauls, Saibene, Deville L, Peters (Reimer 77), Cardoni, Strasser, Posing, Holtz, Schneider (Schaak 53), Huss (Zaritski 68).
Referee: Larsen (Denmark).

Belgrade, 25 April 2001, 48,000

Yugoslavia (0) 0
Russia (0) 1 *(Bestchastnykh 72)*

Yugoslavia: Ilic; Dudic, Djukic, Bunjevcevic, Krstajic (Stefanovic 84), Jokanovic, Mihajlovic, Lazetic, Tomic, Drulic (Stankovic 73), Kezman (Djordjevic 63).
Russia: Nigmatullin; Tugaynov, Onopko, Drozdov (Tetradze 47), Kovtun, Alenichev, Mostovoi, Khokhlov, Gusev (Semak 87), Titov, Fedkov (Bestchastnykh 46).
Referee: Plautz (Austria).

Toftir, 2 June 2001, 4000

Faeroes (0) 0
Switzerland (0) 1 *(Frei 81)*

Faeroes: Mikkelsen; Hansen HF, Johannesen O, Hansen JB, Borg, Benjaminsen, Petersen J (Petersen H 87), Johnsson, Hansen O, Arge (Jacobsen J 78), Jacobsen C.
Switzerland: Pascolo; Zellweger, Henchoz, Muller P, Quentin, Wicky, Vogel, Sforza (Lonfat 69), Lombardo, Sesa (N'Kufo 58), Frei (Magnin 87).
Referee: McDonald (Scotland).

Moscow, 2 June 2001, 70,000

Russia (1) 1 *(Kovtun 25)*
Yugoslavia (1) 1 *(Mijatovic 38)*

Russia: Nigmatullin; Smertin, Chugainov, Onopko, Kovtun, Karpin, Titov, Mostovoi, Khokhlov, Alenichev, Bestchastnykh (Buznikin 71).
Yugoslavia: Radakovic; Obradovic, Djukic, Mihajlovic, Djorovic, Mirkovic (Bunjevcevic 85), Lazetic (Drulovic 71), Dmitrovic, Tomic, Mijatovic (Kezman 65), Milosevic.
Referee: Fandel (Germany).

Ljubljana, 2 June 2001, 5000

Slovenia (1) 2 *(Zahovic 35, 65 (pen))*
Luxembourg (0) 0

Slovenia: Simeunovic; Galic, Milinovic, Knavs, Novak, Ceh, Pavlin, Cimerotic (Osterc 80), Karic (Rudonja 46), Zahovic, Acimovic (Pavlovic 62).
Luxembourg: Gillet; Deville L, Schauls, Theis, Strasser, Saibene, Peters, Holtz, Huss, Cardoni (Braun 82), Schneider.
Referee: Brugger (Austria).

Toftir, 6 June 2001, 4371

Faeroes (0) 0
Yugoslavia (2) 6 *(Stankovic D 20, 55, Kezman 29, 87, 90, Milosevic 68)*

Faeroes: Mikkelsen; Hansen HF, Benjaminsen, Hansen JB, Borg, Hansen O, Joensen S (Jacobsen R 88), Johnsson (Morkore A 75), Jacobsen C (Petersen H 75), Arge, Petersen J.
Yugoslavia: Radakovic; Mirkovic (Bunjevcevic 46), Mihajlovic, Djorovic, Dmitrovic, Lazetic (Obradovic 46), Stankovic D, Drulovic (Ilic 74), Mijatovic, Milosevic, Kezman.
Referee: Jara (Czech Republic).

Luxembourg, 6 June 2001, 2200

Luxembourg (0) 1 *(Schneider 48)*
Russia (1) 2 *(Alenichev 16, Semak 76)*

Luxembourg: Gillet; Schauls, Deville L, Theis, Strasser, Peters (Reiter 89), Saibene, Holtz, Cardoni, Schneider (Braun 83), Huss (Christophe 64).
Russia: Nigmatullin; Smertin (Popov 52), Nikiforov, Onopko, Kovtun, Karpin, Titov, Mostovoi, Khokhlov, Alenichev (Semak 61), Bestchastnykh (Fedkov 66).
Referee: Skjervold (Norway).

Basle, 6 June 2001, 26,000

Switzerland (0) 0
Slovenia (0) 1 *(Cimerotic 83)*

Switzerland: Pascolo; Zellweger, Henchoz, Muller P, Quentin, Wicky (Lonfat 66), Vogel, Fournier, Lombardo (Sforza 56), N'Kufo, Frei (Sesa 79).
Slovenia: Simeunovic; Galic, Milinovic, Knavs, Novak, Ceh, Pavlin, Rudonja, Karic (Cimerotic 32), Zahovic, Osterc (Acimovic 46).
Referee: Granat (Poland).

Group 1 Table	P	W	D	L	F	A	Pts
Russia	7	5	2	0	10	3	17
Slovenia	7	3	4	0	11	7	13
Switzerland	7	3	2	2	14	6	11
Yugoslavia	6	2	3	1	11	4	9
Faeroes	6	1	1	4	5	15	4
Luxembourg	7	0	0	7	2	18	0

GROUP 2

Tallinn, 16 August 2000, 1695

Estonia (0) 1 *(Reim 64 (pen))*
Andorra (0) 0

Estonia: Tohver; Allas, Lemsalu, Stepanovs, Rooba U, Piiroja (Jurisson 73), Reim, Alonen (Anniste 67), Terehov, Oper, Zelinski (Ustritski 87).
Andorra: Koldo; Alvarez F (Forla 71), Jonas, Garcia T, Lima I, Escura, Sonejee, Gonzalez E (Pujol 74), Manolo, Ruiz, Sanchez J.
Referee: Arsic (Yugoslavia).

La Vella, 2 September 2000, 1000

Andorra (1) 2 *(Gonzalez E 45, Lima I 51)*
Cyprus (1) 3 *(Constantinou M 25 (pen), 90, Agathocleous 77)*

Andorra: Koldo; Ramirez, Garcia T, Jonas, Sonejee, Lima I, Gonzalez E (Lucendo 89), Escura, Ruiz, Jimenez, Sanchez J.
Cyprus: Panayiotou N; Theodotou, Charalambous Z (Agathocleous 54), Ioannou D, Charalambous M, Ioakim, Engomitis, Aristocleous (Yiasonmi 71), Christodolou M, Okkas (Kotsonis 85), Constantinou M.
Referee: Yarmenchuk (Ukraine).

Amsterdam, 2 September 2000, 50,000

Holland (0) 2 *(Talan 71, Van Bronckhorst 84)*
Republic of Ireland (1) 2 *(Robbie Keane 21, McAteer 65)*

Holland: Van der Sar; Reiziger (Seedorf 46), Konterman (Talan 66), Frank de Boer, Van Bronckhorst, Witschge (Bruggnik 59), Ronald de Boer, Bosvelt, Cocu, Bouma, Kluivert.
Republic of Ireland: Kelly A; Carr, Harte, Dunne, Breen, Roy Keane, McAteer (Kelly G 75), Kinsella, Quinn (Connolly 71), Robbie Keane, Kilbane (Staunton 79).
Referee: Michel (Slovakia).

Tallinn, 3 September 2000, 4700

Estonia (0) 1 *(Oper 84)*
Portugal (1) 3 *(Rui Costa 15, Figo 49, Sa Pinto 57)*

Estonia: Poom; Allas, Stepanovs, Lemsalu, Rooba U, Jurisson (Haavistu 71), Alonen (Anniste 36), Reim, Terehov, Zelinski (Viikmae 67), Oper.
Portugal: Quim; Nelson (Costinho 64), Fernando Couto, Jorge Costa, Rui Jorge, Figo, Rui Costa, Paulo Sousa, Simao (Vidigal 71), Sa Pinto, Joao Pinto (Pauleta 74).
Referee: Agius (Malta).

La Vella, 7 October 2000, 800

Andorra (0) 1 *(Ruiz 90 (pen))*
Estonia (0) 2 *(Reim 54, Oper 65)*

Andorra: Koldo; Ramirez, Garcia T, Jonas, Lima T, Lima I, Gonzalez E, Sonejee (Lucendo 60), Sanchez J, Jimenez (Soria 83), Ruiz.
Estonia: Poom; Allas, Rooba U, Lemsalu, Stepanovs, Viikmae (Haavistu 80), Terehov, Oper, Kristal (Anniste 58), Reim, Zelinski (Ustritski 46).
Referee: Koren (Israel).

Nicosia, 7 October 2000, 12,000

Cyprus (0) 0

Holland (0) 4 *(Seedorf 69, 78, Overmars 81, Kluivert 90)*

Cyprus: Panayiotou N; Theodotou, Charalambous C, Ioannou D, Charalambous M (Poyiatzis 62), Pounas (Dziouref 80), Melanarkitis, Spoljaric, Ioakim, Malekkos (Okkas 77), Agathocleous.

Holland: Van der Sar; Bosvelt (Van Bommel 75), Reiziger, Frank de Boer, Van Bronckhorst, Cocu, Talan (Seedorf 58), Davids, Kluivert, Ronald de Boer (Bouma 80), Overmars.

Referee: Cesari (Italy).

Lisbon, 7 October 2000, 65,000

Portugal (0) 1 *(Conceicao 57)*

Republic of Ireland (0) 1 *(Holland 72)*

Portugal: Quim; Beto, Fernando Couto, Jorge Costa, Dimas (Capucho 88), Conceicao, Rui Costa, Vidigal, Figo, Sa Pinto (Pauleta 76), Joao Pinto (Simao 76).

Republic of Ireland: Kelly A; Carr, Harte, Dunne, Breen, Roy Keane, McAteer (Duff 69), Kinsella, Quinn (Holland 46), Robbie Keane (Finnan 83), Kilbane.

Referee: Ouzounov (Bulgaria).

Rotterdam, 11 October 2000, 48,000

Holland (0) 0

Portugal (2) 2 *(Conceicao 11, Pauleta 44)*

Holland: Van der Sar; Melchiot, Frank de Boer, Cocu, Reiziger, Van Bommel (Bosvelt 72), Overmars (Talan 46), Davids, Kluivert (Vennegoor of Hesselink 65), Seedorf, Bouma.

Portugal: Quim; Jorge Costa, Dimas, Secretario, Fernando Couto, Vidigal (Fernando Meira 90), Figo, Bino, Pauleta (Simao 90), Rui Costa (Sa Pinto 87), Conceicao.

Referee: Poll (England).

Dublin, 11 October 2000, 34,562

Republic of Ireland (1) 2 *(Kinsella 25, Dunne 50)*

Estonia (0) 0

Republic of Ireland: Kelly A; Carr, Harte, Dunne, Breen, Roy Keane, McAteer (Duff 46), Kinsella, Quinn, Robbie Keane (Foley 87), Kilbane (Finnan 87).

Estonia: Poom; Allas, Stepanovs, Lemsalu, Saviauk, Viikmae (Haavistu 68), Reim, Anniste, Terehov, Oper, Zelinski (Ustritski 68).

Referee: Hauge (Norway).

Nicosia, 15 November 2000, 8000

Cyprus (3) 5 *(Okkas 10, 18, Agathocleous 42, Christodoulou M 74, Spoljaric 90 (pen))*

Andorra (0) 0

Cyprus: Panayiotou N; Konnafis, Charalambous Z, Ioannou D (Nicolaou 82), Charalambous M, Pounas, Ioakim, Spoljaric, Okkas, Agathocleous (Neophytou 74), Constantinou M (Christodoulou M 46).

Andorra: Koldo; Garcia T, Bernaus, Alonso, Sonejee, Lima I (Jonas 88), Gonzalez E (Ramirez 59), Sanchez J, Lucendo, Jimenez, Ruiz (Escura 78).

Referee: Johansson (Sweden).

Madeira, 28 February 2001, 12,000

Portugal (2) 3 *(Figo 1, 48, Pauleta 36)*

Andorra (0) 0

Portugal: Quim; Xavier, Rui Jorge, Fernando Couto (Capucho 46), Beto, Paulo Bento (Joao Pinto 63), Rui Costa, Conceicao, Figo, Nuno Gomes (Tomas 75), Pauleta.

Andorra: Koldo; Pol, Ramirez, Jonas, Lucendo (Soria 89), Txema, Gonzalez E (Escura 61), Sonejee, Ruiz, Dernaus, Sanchez J (Garcia 89).

Referee: Allaerts (Belgium).

Barcelona, 24 March 2001, 1000

Andorra (0) 0

Holland (2) 5 *(Kluivert 9, Hasselbaink 36, Van Hooijdonk 60, 71, Van Bommel 85)*

Andorra: Sanchez A; Pol, Jonas, Sonejee, Lima I, Ramirez, Emiliano (Escura 85), Txema, Lucendo (Jimenez 64), Ruiz (Fernandez 90), Sanchez J.

Holland: Van der Sar; Bosvelt, Stam (Bouma 72), Frank de Boer, Cocu, Van Bommel, Davids (Paauwe 46), Zenden, Hasselbaink, Kluivert (Van Hooijdonk 58), Overmars.

Referee: Trivkovic (Croatia).

Nicosia, 24 March 2001, 13,000

Cyprus (0) 0

Republic of Ireland (2) 4 *(Roy Keane 32, 89, Harte 42 (pen), Kelly 81)*

Cyprus: Panayiotou N; Melanarkitis (Filippou 56), Konnafis, Charalambous M, Christodolou M, Theodotou, Pounnas (Malekkos 43), Ioachim, Spoljaric, Constantinou M, Okkas (Agathocleous 75).

Republic of Ireland: Given; Kelly G, Harte, Roy Keane, Breen, Cunningham, McAteer (Holland 78), Kinsella, Connolly, Robbie Keane (Doherty 89), Kilbane (Duff 82).

Referee: De Bleeckere (Belgium).

Barcelona, 28 March 2001, 5000

Andorra (0) 0

Republic of Ireland (1) 3 *(Harte 33 (pen), Kilbane 76, Holland 80)*

Andorra: Sanchez A; Pol, Jonas (Soria 90), Lima T, Lucendo, Lima I, Sonejee, Txema, Sanchez J (Jimenez 87), Emiliano (Escura 80), Ruiz.

Republic of Ireland: Given; Kelly G, Harte, Roy Keane, Breen, Cunningham, Holland, Kilbane (Finnan 84), Connolly (Doherty 25), Robbie Keane, Duff.

Referee: Ishchenko (Ukraine).

Limassol, 28 March 2001, 5000

Cyprus (0) 2 *(Constantinou M 48, Okkas 66)*

Estonia (0) 2 *(Kristal 77, Piiroja 79)*

Cyprus: Panayiotou N; Ioachim, Germanou, Charalambous M, Theodotou, Kunnafis, Agathocleous (Christodolou M 63), Engomitis (Melanarkitis 69), Malekkos (Spoljaric 46), Okkas, Constantinou M.

Estonia: Kaalma; Rooba M, Stepanov, Piiroja, Rooba U, Novikov (Alonen 81), Reim, Kristal, Haavistu (Terehov 54), Zelinski (Viikmae 59), Oper.

Referee: Mikulski (Poland).

Oporto, 28 March 2001, 45,000

Portugal (0) 2 *(Pauleta 83, Figo 90 (pen))*

Holland (1) 2 *(Hasselbaink 17 (pen), Kluivert 47)*

Portugal: Quim; Secretario, Litos, Fernando Couto, Rui Jorge, Da Costa, Paulo Bento (Chapucho 32), Conceicao (Nuno Gomes 57), Figo, Rui Costa, Pauleta.

Holland: Van der Sar; Reiziger, Frank de Boer, Stam, Cocu, Zenden (Makaay 72), Davids, Van Bommel (Bosvelt 68), Overmars, Kluivert, Hasselbaink (Van Hooijdonk 80).

Referee: Meier (Switzerland).

Eindhoven, 25 April 2001, 30,000

Holland (3) 4 *(Hasselbaink 29, Overmars 35, Kluivert 44, Van Nistelrooy 82)*

Cyprus (0) 0

Holland: Van der Sar; Melchiot, Hofland, Frank de Boer, Cocu, Zenden, Seedorf (Van Nistelrooy 71), Van Bommel, Overmars (Sikora 83), Kluivert, Hasselbaink (Van Hooijdonk 71).

Cyprus: Morphis; Konnafis, Filippou, Charalambous, Germanou, Melanarkitis, Engomitis (Kaiafas 89), Christodolou M (Yiasoumi 76), Satsias, Okkas (Agathocleous 84), Constantinou M.

Referee: Baskakov (Russia).

Dublin, 25 April 2001, 34,000

Republic of Ireland (2) 3 *(Kilbane 34, Kinsella 36, Breen 76)*

Andorra (1) 1 *(Lima I 32)*

Republic of Ireland: Given; Kelly G, Harte, Breen (Staunton 84), Dunne, Holland, Kennedy (Carr 66), Kinsella (Finnan 79), Connolly, Doherty, Kilbane.

Andorra: Sanchez A; Escura, Lima I, Lima A, Jonas, Txema, Emiliano (Soria 86), Ruiz, Oscar, Jimenez (Pujol 81), Sanchez J (Fernandez 90).

Referee: Jakobsson (Iceland).

Tallinn, 2 June 2001, 9500

Estonia (0) 2 *(Oper 65, Zelinski 78)*

Holland (0) 4 *(Frank de Boer 68, Van Nistelrooy 82, 90, Kluivert 89)*

Estonia: Kaalma; Saviauk, Stepanovs, Piiroja, Rooba U, Viikmae (Zelinski 29), Reim, Haavistu (Rahn 70), Novikov, Kristal, Oper.
Holland: Van der Sar; Reiziger, Melchiot, Frank de Boer, Cocu, Paauwe (Landzaat 60), Zenden, Makaay (Van Hooijdonk 69), Hasselbaink (Van Nistelrooy 60), Kluivert, Overmars.
Referee: Richards (Wales).

Dublin, 2 June 2001, 34,000

Republic of Ireland (0) 1 *(Roy Keane 65)*

Portugal (0) 1 *(Figo 79)*

Republic of Ireland: Given; Carr, Harte, Kelly G, Dunne, Staunton, Kinsella (Doherty 79), Roy Keane, Quinn (Holland 75), Robbie Keane (Duff 60), Kilbane.
Portugal: Ricardo; Frechaut, Litos (Boa Morte 87), Jorge Costa, Rui Jorge (Joao Pinto 74), Beto, Petit, Barbosa (Capucho 71), Figo, Rui Costa, Pauleta.
Referee: Fisker (Denmark).

Tallinn, 6 June 2001, 9000

Estonia (0) 0

Republic of Ireland (2) 2 *(Dunne 9, Holland 39)*

Estonia: Kaalma; Saviauk, Stepanovs, Piiroja, Rooba U (Allas 69), Reim, Novikov (Ustritski 72), Haavistu (Terehov 49), Kristal, Oper, Zelinski.
Republic of Ireland: Given; Carr, Harte, Kelly G, Dunne, Staunton, Kinsella, Holland, Quinn (Doherty 37), Kilbane, Duff (O'Brien 89).
Referee: Mircea (Romania).

Lisbon, 6 June 2001, 35,000

Portugal (1) 6 *(Pauleta 36, 71, Barbosa 55, 59, Joao Pinto 76, 81)*

Cyprus (0) 0

Portugal: Ricardo; Frechaut, Jorge Costa (Nuno Gomes 82), Beto, Rui Jorge, Petit (Paulo Bento 87), Rui Costa, Barbosa (Sa Pinto 72), Capucho, Pauleta, Joao Pinto.
Cyprus: Morphis; Theodotou, Filippou, Charalambous, Ioakim, Satsias, Engomitis (Yiasoumi 69), Christodoulou M (Melanarkitis 61), Germanou, Okkas (Stavrou 83), Constantinou M.
Referee: Farina (Italy).

Group 2 Table	P	W	D	L	F	A	Pts
Republic of Ireland	8	5	3	0	18	5	18
Portugal	7	4	3	0	18	5	15
Holland	7	4	2	1	21	8	14
Estonia	7	2	1	4	8	14	7
Cyprus	7	2	1	4	10	22	7
Andorra	8	0	0	8	4	25	0

GROUP 3

Sofia, 2 September 2000, 15,000

Bulgaria (0) 0

Czech Republic (0) 1 *(Poborsky 73 (pen))*

Bulgaria: Zdravkov; Peev, Markov, Ivanov B, Kirilov (Topuzakov 76), Petrov S, Todorov (Ivanov G 63), Stoyanov, Yovov (Petrov M 33), Balakov, Iliev.
Czech Republic: Srnicek; Repka, Rada, Nedved, Fukal, Horvath (Rosicky 77), Tyce, Poborsky, Koller (Lokvenc 63), Smicer (Vicek 90), Bejbl.
Referee: Marin (Spain).

Reykjavik, 2 September 2000, 7072

Iceland (1) 1 *(Sverrisson E 12)*

Denmark (1) 2 *(Tomasson 26, Bisgaard 49)*

Iceland: Arason; Helgason A (Gunnarsson B 29), Hreidarsson, Marteinsson, Kolvidsson, Kristinsson R, Gudmundsson (Helguson 70), Sverrisson E, Gudjohnsen E, Gudjonsson T (Sigurdsson I 70), Dadason.
Denmark: Schmeichel; Goldbaek (Nielsen A 76), Henriksen, Gravesen, Heintze, Helveg, Steen-Nielsen, Rommedahl (Michaelsen 81), Tomasson, Bisgaard (Jensen C 70), Sand.
Referee: Bre (France).

Belfast, 2 September 2000, 8227

Northern Ireland (0) 1 *(Gray 70)*

Malta (0) 0

Northern Ireland: Carroll; Nolan, Hughes, Murdock, Taggart, Horlock, Johnson, Magilton, Healy, Elliott (Gray 61), Lomas.
Malta: Barry; Dimech, Debono, Said, Carabott, Sylla (Brincat 46), Thuma, Camilleri (Veselji 78), Chetcuti, Busuttil, Mallia (Turner 58).
Referee: Bezubiak (Russia).

Sofia, 7 October 2000, 4000

Bulgaria (1) 3 *(Ivanov G 39, 65, Todorov 90)*

Malta (0) 0

Bulgaria: Zdravkov; Markov, Pazjin, Petrov S, Hristov, Stoyanov (Petkov M 59), Ivanov G (Todorov 88), Balakov, Iliev (Petkov I 70), Peev, Petrov M.
Malta: Barry; Carabott, Chetcuti, Said, Debono, Dimech (Holland 67), Busuttil (Mallia 60), Giglio, Nwoko, Brincat (Agius 75), Zahra.
Referee: Caljia (Bosnia).

Teplice, 7 October 2000, 9843

Czech Republic (3) 4 *(Koller 17, 41, Nedved 44, 90)*

Iceland (0) 0

Czech Republic: Srnicek; Repka, Rada, Nedved, Fukal, Horvath (Rosicky 79), Tyce, Poborsky (Latal 68), Koller (Lokvenc 75), Sionko, Bejbl.
Iceland: Kristinsson B; Helgason A, Hreidarsson, Marteinsson (Gudmundsson T 46), Kolvidsson, Kristinsson R (Gretarsson 85), Jonsson S, Sverrisson E, Gudjohnsen E, Helguson, Dadason (Gudjonsson T 46).
Referee: Vassaros (Greece).

Belfast, 7 October 2000, 11,823

Northern Ireland (1) 1 *(Healy 38)*

Denmark (0) 1 *(Rommedahl 60)*

Northern Ireland: Carroll; Lomas, Hughes, Murdock, Taggart, Horlock, Magilton, Jeff Whitley (Mulryne 72), Healy, Elliott (Gray 84), Lennon.
Denmark: Schmeichel; Helveg, Henriksen, Gravesen, Heintze, Steen-Nielsen, Tofting, Rommedahl, Tomasson, Sand (Jensen C 82), Gronkjaer (Bisgaard 63).
Referee: Pereira (Portugal).

Copenhagen, 11 October 2000, 39,847

Denmark (0) 1 *(Sand 73)*

Bulgaria (0) 1 *(Berbatov 82)*

Denmark: Schmeichel; Helveg, Henriksen, Gravesen, Heintze, Rommedahl, Tofting, Steen-Nielsen (Jensen C 46), Gronkjaer (Mikaelsen 55), Tomasson (Nielsen A 79), Sand.
Bulgaria: Zdravkov; Kishishev, Petkov M (Todorov 77), Kirilov, Pazjin, Petrov S, Hristov (Peev 68), Ivanov B, Balakov, Ivanov G (Berbatov 64), Petrov M.
Referee: Sarvan (Turkey).

Reykjavik, 11 October 2000, 5415

Iceland (0) 1 *(Gudjonsson T 89)*

Northern Ireland (0) 0

Iceland: Kristinsson B; Helgason A, Hreidarsson, Sverrisson E, Vidarsson, Helguson, Gunnarsson, Kristinsson R (Gretarsson 46), Gudjonsson T, Gudjohnsen E, Dadason (Sigurdsson H 64).
Northern Ireland: Carroll; Lomas, Hughes, Murdock, Taggart (Williams 46), Horlock, Lennon, Johnson, Healy, Magilton, Elliott (Gray 82).
Referee: Merk (Germany).

Valletta, 11 October 2000, 4000

Malta (0) 0

Czech Republic (0) 0

Malta: Muscat; Said, Chetcuti (Camilleri 61), Spiteri, Debono, Agius, Busuttil, Giglio (Turner 75), Brincat (Theuma 63), Nwoko, Zahra.
Czech Republic: Srnicek; Fukal (Latal 46), Rada, Repka, Tyce, Poborsky, Nedved, Bejbl, Horvath (Vicek 65), Koller, Sionko (Lokvenc 82).
Referee: Siric (Croatia).

Sofia, 24 March 2001, 20,000
Bulgaria (1) 2 *(Chamokov 36, Berbatov 78)*
Iceland (1) 1 *(Hreidarsson 24)*

Bulgaria: Zdravkov; Kishishev (Pejev 63), Pazjin, Chomakov, Markov, Kirilov (Todorov 77), Petkov M, Balakov, Hristov, Ivanov G (Berbatov 63), Petrov M.
Iceland: Arason; Sigurdsson, Hreidarsson, Vidarsson, Gunnarsson, Kristinsson R, Helguson, Sverrisson, Gudjonsson T (Gretarsson 59), Gudjohnsen E (Highorsson 61), Dadason.
Referee: Riley (England).

Valletta, 24 March 2001, 2500
Malta (0) 0
Denmark (1) 5 *(Sand 8, 65, 80, Heintze 50, Jensen C 76)*

Malta: Muscat; Turner (Okoh 46), Carabott, Dimech (Holland 65), Zahra, Debono, Giglio (Camilleri 65), Busuttil, Saliba, Nwoko, Brincat.
Denmark: Sorensen; Tofting, Henriksen, Laursen, Heintze, Helveg (Goldbaek 68), Gravesen (Steen-Nielsen 63), Gronkjaer, Rommedahl, Sand, Jorgensen (Jensen C 75).
Referee: McCurry (Scotland).

Belfast, 24 March 2001, 10,368
Northern Ireland (0) 0
Czech Republic (0) 1 *(Nedved 11)*

Northern Ireland: Carroll; Griffin, Hughes A, Elliott (Gray 78), Williams, Murdock, Gillespie, Lennon, Healy (Ferguson 78), Magilton, Hughes M.
Czech Republic: Srnicek; Fukal, Votava, Ujfalusi, Tyce, Poborsky, Bejbl, Rosicky (Jarosik 81), Nedved, Smicer (Nemec 90), Koller (Lokvenc 73).
Referee: Gonzalez (Spain).

Sofia, 28 March 2001, 20,000
Bulgaria (2) 4 *(Balakov 10, Petrov M 17, 78, Chomakov 72)*
Northern Ireland (1) 3 *(Williams 14, Healy 83, 90 (pen))*

Bulgaria: Zdravkov; Kishishev, Petkov M (Stoilov 58), Markov, Chomakov, Pazjin, Ivanov B, Hristov (Petrov S 67), Berbatov (Ivanov G 81), Balakov, Petrov M.
Northern Ireland: Carroll; Griffin, Nolan (McCarthy 90), Elliott, Williams, Murdock, Gillespie (Johnson 85), Lennon (Kennedy 85), Healy, Magilton, Hughes M.
Referee: Hrinak (Slovakia).

Prague, 28 March 2001, 16,354
Czech Republic (0) 0
Denmark (0) 0

Czech Republic: Srnicek; Fukal, Votava, Ujfalusi, Poborsky, Rosicky (Jarosik 86), Bejbl, Nedved, Nemec, Smicer (Kuka 67), Koller (Lokvenc 89).
Denmark: Sorensen; Helveg, Henriksen, Laursen, Heintze (Nygaard 88), Rommedahl (Jensen C 78), Tofting, Gravesen, Gronkjaer (Jorgensen 46), Tomasson, Sand.
Referee: Barber (England).

Valletta, 25 April 2001, 1500
Malta (1) 1 *(Mifsud 14)*
Iceland (2) 4 *(Gudmundsson 42, Sigurdsson 45, Gudjohnsen 83, Gudjonsson T 90)*

Malta: Muscat; Debono, Said, Carabott, Spiteri, Giglio (Theuma 63), Busuttil, Mifsud, Zahra (Mallia 70), Nwoko, Brincat (Turner 56).
Iceland: Arason; Vidarsson, Sverrisson (Marteinsson 67), Hreidarsson, Kristinsson R, Gudmundsson, Gretarsson, Gunnarsson, Sigurdsson, Gudjohnsen, Sigthorsson (Gudjonsson T 80).
Referee: Zotta (Romania).

Copenhagen, 2 June 2001, 41,669
Denmark (1) 2 *(Sand 6, Tomasson 82)*
Czech Republic (1) 1 *(Tyce 40)*

Denmark: Sorensen; Helveg, Henriksen, Laursen, Heintze, Tofting, Tomasson, Steen-Nielsen (Jensen C 58), Rommedahl (Gronkjaer 74), Sand, Jorgensen (Nielsen A 87).
Czech Republic: Srnicek; Johana, Ujfalusi, Votava, Tyce (Rada 60), Poborsky (Kuka 85), Nedved, Galasek, Berger, Lokvenc (Koller 68), Smicer.
Referee: Merk (Germany).

Reykjavik, 2 June 2001, 3554
Iceland (2) 3 *(Gudmundsson 7, Dadason 38, Gudjohnsen E 68)*
Malta (0) 0

Iceland: Arason; Helgason, Vidarsson, Gretarsson, Gunnarsson, Kristinsson R (Kolvidsson 74), Gudmundsson, Sverrisson E (Marteinsson 74), Gudjohnsen E, Sigurdsson, Dadason (Helguson 74).
Malta: Muscat; Said, Turner, Spiteri, Theuma, Dimech, Agius, Ciglio (Suda 74), Mifsud, Brincat (Camilleri 46), Mallia (Nwoko 69).
Referee: Lajuks (Latvia).

Was Keith Gillespie attempting to head the ball off Milen Petkov's foot in this World Cup qualifier between Northern Ireland and Bulgaria? (Actionimages/David Slater)

Belfast, 2 June 2001, 7663
Northern Ireland (0) 0
Bulgaria (0) 1 *(Ivanov G 52)*
Northern Ireland: Taylor; Nolan (Quinn 86), Griffin,
Murdock, Hughes A, Lennon (Mulryne 79), Gillespie,
Johnson, Healy, Elliott (Ferguson 79), Hughes M.
Bulgaria: Zdravkov; Ivanov B, Markov, Pazjin, Kishishev
(Peev 23), Hristov (Stoilov 87), Petrov M (Kirilov 77),
Balakov, Chomokov, Petkov M, Ivanov G.
Referee: Busacca (Switzerland).

Teplice, 6 June 2001, 14,850
Czech Republic (1) 3 *(Kuka 40, 88, Baros 90)*
Northern Ireland (1) 1 *(Mulryne 45)*
Czech Republic: Srnicek; Repka, Votava (Bejbl 46),
Tyce, Poborsky (Lokvenc 83), Nedved, Galasek, Rosicky,
Berger, Koller (Baros 65), Kuka.
Northern Ireland: Taylor; Nolan, Hughes A, Murdock,
Williams, Griffin, Johnson (Ferguson 76), Mulryne
(Kennedy 81), Healy, Elliott (Quinn 65), Hughes M.
Referee: Sundell (Sweden).

Copenhagen, 6 June 2001, 38,499
Denmark (1) 2 *(Sand 43, 83)*
Malta (1) 1 *(Mallia 8)*
Denmark: Sorensen; Helveg, Henriksen, Heintze, Tofting
(Nielsen A 75), Tomasson (Nygaard 68), Gravesen,
Jensen C, Rommedahl (Gronkjaer 55), Sand, Jorgensen.
Malta: Barry; Debono, Said, Theuma, Camilleri, Turner,
Brincat (Holland 73), Mallia (Nwoko 65), Dimech, Agius
(Okoh 78), Mifsud.
Referee: Shmolik (Belarus).

Reykjavik, 6 June 2001, 4316
Iceland (1) 1 *(Dadason 43)*
Bulgaria (0) 1 *(Berbatov 81)*
Iceland: Arason; Helgason, Vidarsson, Gretarsson,
Gunnarsson, Kristinsson R, Hreidarsson, Sverrisson E,
Gudjohnsen E, Sigurdsson, Dadason (Helguson 46).
Bulgaria: Zdravkov; Pazjin (Petrov S 54), Markov,
Ivanov B, Stoilov, Chomakov (Petrov M 65), Balakov
(Todorov 73), Kirilov, Peev, Ivanov G, Berbatov.
Referee: Gallagher (England).

Group 3 Table	P	W	D	L	F	A	Pts
Denmark	7	4	3	0	13	5	15
Czech Republic	7	4	2	1	10	3	14
Bulgaria	7	4	2	1	12	7	14
Iceland	7	3	1	3	11	10	10
Northern Ireland	7	1	1	5	6	11	4
Malta	7	0	1	6	2	18	1

GROUP 4

Baku, 2 September 2000, 20,000
Azerbaijan (0) 0
Sweden (1) 1 *(Svensson A 10)*
Azerbaijan: Kramarenko; Kuliyev E, Agayev, Akhmedov,
Yadullayev, Kuliyev S, Mamedov R (Aliev 86), Tagizade,
Musayev (Kurbanov 65), Vasilyev, Kvaratshelia.
Sweden: Hedman; Nilsson R, Andersson P, Bjorklund,
Mellberg, Mjallby, Alexandersson, Svensson A (Mild 75),
Ljungberg, Andersson K, Larsson.
Referee: Luinge (Holland).

Istanbul, 2 September 2000, 22,000
Turkey (1) 2 *(Okan 45, Emre 70)*
Moldova (0) 0
Turkey: Rustu; Umit D, Ogun, Fatih, Emre, Bulent K,
Okan (Tayfur 60), Suat (Tayfun 65), Hakan Sukur, Cenk
(Umit K 84), Unsal.
Moldova: Dinov; Kovalenko, Sosnovski, Testimitanu,
Rebeja, Stroenco, Curtianu (Sischin 46), Oprea (Tanurkov
77), Catansus, Epureanu (Stratulat 34), Rogaciov.
Referee: Benko (Austria).

Bratislava, 3 September 2000, 4011
Slovakia (1) 2 *(Lazarevski 3 (og), Demo 74)*
Macedonia (0) 0
Slovakia: Konig; Dzurik, Karhan, Timko, Leitner, Balis,
Kratochvil, Moravcik (Nemeth P 46), Ujlaky (Demo 46),
Jancula (Meszaros 76), Nemeth S.

Macedonia: Filevski; Veselinovski, Stojanoski
(Lazarevski 64), Sedloski, Nikolovski, Stavrevski,
Serafimovski, Micevski (Gerasimovski 69), Hristov, Ciric
(Bekiri 77), Savevski.
Referee: Hamer (Luxembourg).

Skopje, 6 October 2000, 4000
Macedonia (2) 3 *(Hristov 35, 42, Bekiri 75)*
Azerbaijan (0) 0
Macedonia: Filevski; Lazarevski (Veselinovski 70),
Stavrevski, Sedloski, Nikolovski (Gerasimovski 20),
Serafimovski, Sainovski, Micevski, Hristov, Sakiri, Bekiri
(Miserdovski 80).
Azerbaijan: Kramarenko; Asadov, Yadullayev,
Akhmedov, Agayev, Kuliyev E (Garaselia 55),
Kurbanov, Tagizade, Musayev, Vasiliev, Rzayev (Loesjki
80).
Referee: Fisker (Denmark).

Chisinau, 7 October 2000, 5000
Moldova (0) 0
Slovakia (0) 1 *(Nemeth S 79)*
Moldova: Dinov; Kovalenko, Catinsus, Testimitanu,
Rebeja, Stroenco, Curtianu, Sischin (Rogaciov 60),
Sosnovski (Epureanu 82), Gaidamasciuc (Stratulat 72),
Clescenco.
Slovakia: Konig; Dzurik, Sobona, Sucanchak, Karhan,
Demo (Nemeth P 74), Valachovic, Leitner, Pinte,
Nemeth S (Prohaszka 88), Moravcik (Meszaros 53).
Referee: Stuchlik (Austria).

Gothenburg, 7 October 2000, 42,152
Sweden (0) 1 *(Larsson 68)*
Turkey (0) 1 *(Tayfur 90 (pen))*
Sweden: Hedman; Nilsson R, Andersson P, Bjorklund,
Alexandersson (Corneliusson 55), Jonsson (Svensson A
63), Mjallby, Ljungberg, Mild, Andersson K, Larsson
(Osmanovski 90).
Turkey: Rustu; Ogun, Fatih, Bulent K, Arif, Ergun
(Abdullah 80), Suat (Tayfur 64), Hakan Sukur, Nihat,
Izzet (Hasan Sas 75), Unsal.
Referee: Krug (Germany).

Baku, 11 October 2000, 40,000
Azerbaijan (0) 0
Turkey (0) 1 *(Hakan Sukur 72)*
Azerbaijan: Kramarenko; Agayev, Yadullayev,
Akhmedov, Lichkin (Mamedov 85), Kuliyev S,
Kurbanov, Tagizade (Kambarov 72), Musayev
(Charimov 58), Vasiliev, Kuliyev E.
Turkey: Rustu; Nihat (Fatih 46), Ogun, Bulent K, Alpay,
Arif (Tayfur 90), Ergun, Suat, Hakan Sukur, Izzet
(Hasan Sas 62), Unsal.
Referee: Snoddy (Northern Ireland).

Chisinau, 11 October 2000, 4000
Moldova (0) 0
Macedonia (0) 0
Moldova: Khmaruk; Stratulat, Catinsus, Testimitanu,
Rebeja (Epureanu 46), Stroenco, Curtianu (Borets 65),
Sischin (Rogaciov 56), Sosnovski, Gaidamasciuc,
Clescenco.
Macedonia: Filevski; Stavrevski, Lazarevski, Sedloski,
Gerasimovski, Serafimovski (Veselinovski 70), Sainovski
(Karanfilovski 76), Micevski, Hristov, Ciric (Miserdovski
85), Sakiri.
Referee: Ibanez (Spain).

Bratislava, 11 October 2000, 11,227
Slovakia (0) 0
Sweden (0) 0
Slovakia: Konig; Dzurik, Sobona, Timko, Karhan,
Sucanchak, Balis, Leitner, Meszaros (Prohaszka 86),
Nemeth S, Moravcik (Gresko 58).
Sweden: Hedman; Nilsson R, Andersson P, Bjorklund,
Mellberg, Mjallby, Svensson A (Osmanovski 70), Jonsson
(Mild 47), Ljungberg, Andersson K (Andersson D 82),
Larsson.
Referee: Dallas (Scotland).

Baku, 24 March 2001, 20,000
Azerbaijan (0) 0
Moldova (0) 0
Azerbaijan: Kramarenko; Agayev, Akhmedov, Kuliyev E
(Getman 68), Yadullayev, Niftalijev (Ismailov 46),
Kuliyev K, Tagizade, Rzayev, Lichkin (Kuliyev R 80),
Vasiliev.
Moldova: Khmaruk; Kovalenko, Rebeja, Testimitanu
(Romanenco 13), Sosnovschi, Catinsus, Epureanu,
Gaidamasciuc, Sischin, Rogaciov (Oprea 46), Clescenco
(Pogreban 61).
Referee: Stark (Germany).

Gothenburg, 24 March 2001, 22,106
Sweden (1) 1 *(Svensson A 43)*
Macedonia (0) 0
Sweden: Hedman; Mellberg, Andersson P, Matovac,
Corneliusson, Linderoth (Andersson D 64), Schwarz
(Selakovic 80), Svensson A (Mild 66), Ljungberg,
Osmanovski, Larsson.
Macedonia: Milosevski; Mitrevski, Stavrevski, Sedloski,
Zdravevski (Krstev 68), Veselinovski, Serafimovski,
Micevski, Lazarevski, Sakiri, Bekiri (Sainoski 82).
Referee: Wegereef (Holland).

Istanbul, 24 March 2001, 23,000
Turkey (0) 1 *(Hakan Sukur 53 (pen))*
Slovakia (0) 1 *(Tomaschek 68)*
Turkey: Rustu; Bulent K, Ogun, Fatih, Alpay, Okan
(Arif 77) (Tayfun 83), Umit, Emre (Ergun 1), Abdullah,
Hakan Sukur, Sas.
Slovakia: Konig; Karhan, Valachovic, Varga, Dzurik,
Dimo (Nemeth P 89), Labant, Tomaschek, Gresko,
Nemeth S, Pinte.
Referee: Wojcik (Poland).

Chisinau, 28 March 2001, 8000
Macedonia (1) 1 *(Micevski 20)*
Turkey (0) 2 *(Mitrevski 68 (og), Umit D 69)*
Macedonia: Milosevski; Stavrevski, Zdravevski (Krstev
82), Sedloski, Mitrevski, Serafimovski (Georgievski 75),
Micevski (Krsevski 75), Hristov, Bekiri, Sakiri,
Lazarevski.
Turkey: Rustu; Fatih, Alpay, Tayfur, Okan (Tayfun 82),
Umit D, Ogun (Umit O 37), Ergun (Ozer 59), Abdullah,
Hakan Sukur, Sas.
Referee: Colombo (France).

Skopje, 28 March 2001, 7000
Moldova (0) 0
Sweden (0) 2 *(Allback 89, 90)*
Moldova: Romanenko; Kovalenco, Rebeja, Catinsus,
Sosnovski, Gaidamasciuc, Rogaciov (Pogreban 67),
Oprea (Berco 72), Cebotari (Lungu 55), Sischin,
Clescenco.
Sweden: Hedman; Mellberg, Andersson P, Matovac,
Corneliusson, Selakovic (Andersson D 55), Schwarz,
Mild (Jonson 44), Ljungberg, Larsson, Svensson A
(Allback 78).
Referee: Duhamel (France).

Trnava, 28 March 2001, 10,000
Slovakia (2) 3 *(Nemeth S 1, 10, Meszaros 57)*
Azerbaijan (1) 1 *(Vasiliev 3 (pen))*
Slovakia: Konig; Varga, Karhan, Meszaros, Tomaschek,
Labant, Pinte, Dzurik (Ujlaky 64), Demo (Jancula 78),
Gresko, Nemeth S (Valachovic 68).
Azerbaijan: Kramarenko; Agayev, Yadullayev,
Akhmedov, Kuliyev E, Kuliyev K, Kurbanov, Aliev I,
Niftalijev, Vasiliev (Musayev 82), Lichkin (Aliev S 46).
Referee: Kapitanis (Cyprus).

Skopje, 2 June 2001, 3000
Macedonia (1) 2 *(Sakiri 20 (pen), Krstev M 65)*
Moldova (1) 2 *(Pogreban 10, Barbaros 72)*
Macedonia: Zekir; Stavrevski, Stojanov, Guzelov,
Nikolovski (Trajanov 46), Jovanovski Z, Serafimovski
(Jovanovski G 70), Krstev M, Krstev S, Sakiri, Bekiri
(Nacevski 46).

Moldova: Romanenko; Kovalenko, Rebeja, Testimitanu
(Osipenco 65), Sosnovski, Stroenco, Sischin (Barbaros
70), Catinsus, Pogreban (Epureanu 46), Gaidamasciuc,
Clescenco.
Referee: Van Hulten (Holland).

Stockholm, 2 June 2001, 34,327
Sweden (1) 2 *(Allback 45, 51)*
Slovakia (0) 0
Sweden: Hedman; Mellberg, Andersson P, Saarenpaa,
Lucic, Alexandersson (Jonson 73), Linderoth (Svensson
A 90), Svensson M, Allback (Andersson D 88), Larsson,
Ljungberg.
Slovakia: Konig; Karhan, Timko, Varga, Dzurik,
Tomaschek, Demo (Janocko 58), Nemeth S (Vittek 58),
Gresko (Babnik 82), Labant, Pinte.
Referee: Aranda (Spain).

Istanbul, 2 June 2001, 25,000
Turkey (3) 3 *(Tayfun 2, Oktay 29, Hakan Sukur 33)*
Azerbaijan (0) 0
Turkey: Rustu; Umit D, Alpay, Bulent K, Abdullah,
Tayfun, Okan, Tugay, Emre (Ergun 80), Hakan Sukur,
Oktay (Sas 37).
Azerbaijan: Gasanadze; Yunusov, Mamedov A
(Niftalijev 68), Akhmedov, Mamedov R, Berbanov,
Kuliyev K, Tagizade (Kuliyev R 80), Rzayev (Oruov 50),
Kurbanov, Mardanov.
Referee: Roca (Spain).

Baku, 6 June 2001, 20,000
Azerbaijan (1) 2 *(Vasiliev 26, Tagizade 55)*
Slovakia (0) 0
Azerbaijan: Gasanzade; Yemosov, Akhmedov, Mamedov
R, Niftalijev, Kurbanov M, Yadullayev, Tagizade
(Kuliyev R 82), Kurbanov G (Ismailov 89), Getman,
Vasiliev (Rzayev 75).
Slovakia: Konig; Dzurik, Vittek (Bencik 69), Varga,
Karhan, Tomaschek, Janocko, Nemeth S, Labant,
Gresko, Pinte (Babnic 62).
Referee: Vollquartz (Denmark).

Gothenburg, 6 June 2001, 30,233
Sweden (1) 6 *(Larsson 38 (pen), 58, 68 (pen), 79 (pen),*
Alexandersson 74, Allback 77)
Moldova (0) 0
Sweden: Hedman; Mellberg, Andersson P, Saarenpaa
(Andersson C 34), Lucic, Alexandersson, Linderoth,
Magnus Svensson (Mathias Svensson 83), Svensson A
(Andersson D 71), Allback, Larsson.
Moldova: Romanenko; Kovalenko, Stroenco, Rebeja
(Osipenco 63), Catinsus, Gaidamasciuc, Epureanu,
Testimitanu, Oprea, Pogreban (Barburos 46), Clescenco
(Sischin 78).
Referee: Dunn (England).

Bursa, 6 June 2001, 20,000
Turkey (1) 3 *(Alpay 43, 58, 70)*
Macedonia (2) 3 *(Sakiri 7, Serafimovski 20,*
Nikolovski 62)
Turkey: Rustu; Umit O, Bulent K, Alpay, Abdullah,
Tayfun (Fatih 84), Okan (Basturk 69), Tugay, Emre,
Hakan Sukur, Oktay (Ozer 46).
Macedonia: Filevski; Stavrevski, Nikolovski, Mitreveski,
Stojanov, Serafimovski (Trajanov 72), Krstev M,
Guzelov, Sakiri, Nacevski (Lazarevski 48), Bekiri
(Pandev 66).
Referee: Rodomonti (Italy).

Group 4 Table	P	W	D	L	F	A	Pts
Sweden	7	5	2	0	13	1	17
Turkey	7	4	3	0	13	6	15
Slovakia	7	3	2	2	7	6	11
Macedonia	7	1	3	3	9	10	6
Azerbaijan	7	1	1	5	3	11	4
Moldova	7	0	3	4	2	13	3

GROUP 5

Minsk, 2 September 2000, 35,000

Belarus (1) 2 *(Khatskevich 40, Belkevich 56)*
Wales (0) 1 *(Speed 89)*

Belarus: Tumilovich; Lukhvich, Yakhimovic, Shtanyuk, Gurenko, Khatskevich, Yaskovich (Shuneiko 71), Orlovski (Skripchenko 85), Vasilyuk, Romashchenko M (Ryndyuk 28), Belkevich.
Wales: Jones P; Page, Roberts G, Savage, Coleman, Melville, Robinson, Speed, Bellamy, Roberts I (Blake 73), Giggs.
Referee: Trentalange (Italy).

Oslo, 2 September 2000, 19,201

Norway (0) 0
Armenia (0) 0

Norway: Olsen F; Bergdolmo, Hoftun, Berg, Riseth (Basma 49), Mykland, Leonhardsen, Iversen, Flo T (Helstad 85), Solskjaer, Skammelsrud (Strand 70).
Armenia: Berezovski; Soukiassian, Hovsepian, Khodgoyan, Vardanian, Khachatrian, Art Petrossian (Minasian 90), Voskanian, Dokhoyan, Shahgeldian (Demirchian 65), Movsissian (Karamian 85).
Referee: Young (Scotland).

Kiev, 2 September 2000, 50,000

Ukraine (1) 1 *(Shevchenko 13)*
Poland (2) 3 *(Olisadebe 3, 33, Kaluzny 57)*

Ukraine: Kernozenko; Luzhny, Tymoshchuk (Zubov 46), Golovko, Vashchuk, Dmitrulin, Gusin, Popov (Kossovski V 75), Vorobei (Yashkin 61), Shevchenko, Rebrov.
Poland: Dudek; Klos (Hajto 85), Zielinski, Michal Zewlakow, Waldoch, Kozminski (Krzynowek 89), Czereszewski, Iwan, Juskowiak (Gilewicz 70), Kaluzny, Olisadebe.
Referee: Aranda (Spain).

Erevan, 7 October 2000, 14,000

Armenia (2) 2 *(Art Petrossian 17, 44)*
Ukraine (1) 3 *(Shevchenko 45, 59, Gusin 55)*

Armenia: Berezovski; Soukiassian, Khodgoyan (Arm Karamian 63), Hovsepian, Vardanian, Khachatrian, Art Petrossian, Voskanian, Dokhoyan, Shahgeldian (Akopian 77), Movsissian (Art Karamian 63).
Ukraine: Shovkovskyi; Luzhny, Nesmachni, Golovko, Vashchuk, Dmitrulin, Shevchenko, Gusin, Vorobei (Mikhailenko 67), Tymoshchuk (Yashkin 46), Rebrov.
Referee: Larsen (Denmark).

Lodz, 7 October 2000, 7000

Poland (1) 3 *(Kaluzny 24, 62, 73)*
Belarus (1) 1 *(Ryndyuk 37)*

Poland: Dudek; Klos, Zielinksi, Michal Zewlakow, Waldoch, Krzynowek, Swierczewski P, Karwan (Iwan 81), Juskowiak (Kryszalowicz 46), Kaluzny, Olisadebe.
Belarus: Varivonchik; Yakhimovic, Ostrovski, Lukhvich, Shtanyuk, Gurenko, Baranov (Lavrik 74), Belkevich, Romashchenko, Vasilyuk (Ryndyuk 30), Skripchenko (Orlovski 68).
Referee: Frisk (Sweden).

Cardiff, 7 October 2000, 51,000

Wales (0) 1 *(Blake 60)*
Norway (0) 1 *(Helstad 80)*

Wales: Jones P; Delaney, Savage, Page, Coleman, Melville, Robinson, Speed, Hartson (Roberts I 86), Blake, Giggs.
Norway: Olsen F; Basma, Bjornebye, Leonhardsen, Berg, Johnsen, Bakke (Helstad 78), Mykland, Iversen (Flo T 59), Solskjaer, Strand.
Referee: Strampe (Germany).

Minsk, 11 October 2000, 20,000

Belarus (2) 2 *(Khatskevich 23, Ryndyuk 34)*
Armenia (0) 1 *(Khodgoyan 50)*

Belarus: Tumilovich; Yakhimovic, Ostrovski, Lukhvich, Lavrik, Gurenko, Khatskevich, Belkevich, Romashchenko (Skripchenko 89), Vasilyuk (Shumeiko 60), Ryndyuk.

Armenia: Abramian; Soukiassian, Khodgoyan (Art Karamian 61), Hovsepian, Vardanian, Khachatrian, Art Petrossian (Arm Karamian 85), Voskanian, Dokhoyan, Shakhgeldian, Movsissian.
Referee: Corpodean (Romania).

Oslo, 11 October 2000, 23,612

Norway (0) 0
Ukraine (0) 1 *(Shevchenko 49)*

Norway: Olsen F; Basma, Johnsen, Berg, Bergdolmo, Bakke (Helstad 75), Mykland, Iversen, Solskjaer, Leonhardsen (Flo T 54), Strand.
Ukraine: Shovkovskyi; Luzhny (Federov 80), Nesmachni, Golovko, Vashchuk, Dmitrulin, Shevchenko, Gusin, Vorobei, Popov (Yashkin 50), Rebrov.
Referee: Meier (Switzerland).

Warsaw, 11 October 2000, 14,000

Poland (0) 0
Wales (0) 0

Poland: Dudek; Klos, Zielinski, Waldoch, Michal Zewlakow, Karwan, Kaluzny, Czereszewski, Krzynowek (Rzasa 70), Gilewicz (Kryszalowicz 56), Juskowiak (Olisadebe 75).
Wales: Jones P; Delaney, Savage, Page, Coleman, Melville, Robinson, Speed, Hartson (Jones N 75), Blake, Giggs.
Referee: Cortez (Portugal).

Erevan, 24 March 2001, 12,000

Armenia (1) 2 *(Minasian 32, Movsissian 71)*
Wales (1) 2 *(Hartson 41, 48)*

Armenia: Abramian; Vardanian, Hovsepian, Khodgoyan (Art Karamian 58), Sargsyan, Art Petrossian, Voskanian (Hakobian 70), Dokhoyan, Minasian (Demirchian 39), Shakhgeldian, Movsissian.
Wales: Jones P; Delaney, Legg, Melville, Page, Pembridge (Jones M 46), Saunders (Robinson C 70), Speed, Bellamy, Hartson (Roberts I 79), Robinson J.
Referee: Kasnaferis (Greece).

Oslo, 24 March 2001, 15,077

Norway (0) 2 *(Carew 58, Solskjaer 66)*
Poland (2) 3 *(Olisadebe 23, 29, Karwan 80)*

Norway: Myhre; Bergdolmo, Berg, Lundekvam, Stensaas (Flo T 84), Winsnes, Larsen T, Tessem, Solskjaer, Carew, Helstad (Iversen 60).
Poland: Matysek (Dudek 64); Klos, Hajto, Zielinski, Michal Zewlakow, Iwan (Karwan 64), Kaluzny, Swierzcewski P (Zdebel 88), Kozminski, Kryszalowicz, Olisadebe.
Referee: Dougal (Scotland).

Kiev, 24 March 2001, 75,000

Ukraine (0) 0
Belarus (0) 0

Ukraine: Shovkovskyi; Luzhny, Golovko, Vashchuk, Nesmachni, Popov (Vorobei 61), Dmitrulin (Tymoshchuk 78), Cardash, Yashkin, Shevchenko, Rebrov.
Belarus: Tumilovich; Shuneiko, Ostrovski, Shtanyuk, Yaskovich, Gurenko, Khatskevich, Belkevich, Vasilyuk, Milevski, Romashchenko (Lavrik 73).
Referee: Marin (Spain).

Minsk, 28 March 2001, 39,000

Belarus (1) 2 *(Khatskevich 19, Vasilyuk 90)*
Norway (0) 1 *(Solskjaer 68)*

Belarus: Tumilovich; Shumeiko, Yakhimovic, Shtanyuk, Lukhvich, Gurenko, Khatskevich, Belkevich, Vasilyuk, Milevski (Lavrik 46), Romashchenko.
Norway: Myhre; Riseth, Berg, Eggen, Bergdolmo, Tessem (Stensaas 87), Larsen, Winsnes, Solskjaer, Carew, Iversen S (Flo T 46).
Referee: Vassaras (Greece).

Warsaw, 28 March 2001, 11,000

Poland (2) 4 *(Michal Zewlakow 15 (pen), Olisadebe 41, Marcin Zewlakow 81, Karwan 88)*

Armenia (0) 0

Poland: Dudec; Klos, Zielinski, Hajto, Michal Zewlakow (Krzynowek 76), Swierczewski P, Iwan (Karwan 67), Kaluzny, Kozminsky, Kryszalowicz (Marcin Zewlakow 79), Olisadebe.

Armenia: Abramian; Mkrchian, Demirchian, Hovsepian, Vardanian, Khachatrian, Art Petrossian, Voskanian (Art Karamian 66), Dokhoyan, Shakhgeldian (Arm Karamian 73), Movsissian

Referee: Poulat (France).

Cardiff, 28 March 2001, 46,750

Wales (1) 1 *(Hartson 12)*

Ukraine (0) 1 *(Shevchenko 52)*

Wales: Jones P; Delaney, Barnard, Melville, Page, Jones M (Davies 55), Robinson C, Speed, Bellamy, Hartson (Saunders 70), Giggs.

Ukraine: Shovkovskyi; Luzhny, Golovko, Vashchuk, Nesmachni, Tymoshchuk, Popov (Melashchenko 70), Yashkin, Rebrov (Kardash 46), Vorobei, Shevchenko.

Referee: Romain (Belgium).

Erevan, 2 June 2001, 10,000

Armenia (0) 0

Belarus (0) 0

Armenia: Abramian; Soukiassian, Khodgoyan, Demirchian (Dokhoyan A 65), Vardanian A, Khachatrian, Art Petrossian, Minasian (Art Karamian 36), Sarkissian, Arm Karamian (Gevorgian 69), Dokhoyan K.

Belarus: Tumilovic; Yakhimovic, Ostrovski, Lukavic, Shtanyuk (Kulchi 84), Gurenko, Khatskevich, Belkevich, Shuneiko (Romashchenko 80), Vasilyuk, Milevski (Yaskovich 72).

Referee: Guenov (Bulgaria).

Kiev, 2 June 2001, 42,000

Ukraine (0) 0

Norway (0) 0

Ukraine: Shovkovskyi; Starostyak, Golovko, Vashchuk, Dmitrulin, Parfionov, Tymoshchuk, Zoubov, Vorobei (Spivak 68), Shevchenko, Yashkin (Rebrov 46).

Norway: Myhre; Basma, Hoftun, Berg, Riseth, Rudi, Leonhardsen, Andersen T, Bakke, Strand (Helstad 78), Carew.

Referee: Maric (Croatia).

Cardiff, 2 June 2001, 48,500

Wales (1) 1 *(Blake 13)*

Poland (1) 2 *(Olisadebe 32, Kryszalowicz 72)*

Wales: Jones P; Page (Jenkins 84), Barnard (Jones M 79), Melville, Symons, Pembridge, Savage, Speed, Hartson, Blake, Giggs.

Poland: Dudek; Klos, Bak J, Hajto, Michal Zewlakow, Iwan, Zdebel (Krynowek 62), Bak A, Kozminski, Juskowiak (Kryszalowicz 54), Olisadebe (Marcin Zewlakow 90).

Referee: Ersoy (Turkey).

Erevan, 6 June 2001, 10,000

Armenia (1) 1 *(Art Petrossian 11)*

Poland (1) 1 *(Kaluzny 4)*

Armenia: Abramian; Soukiassian, Khodgoyan, Hovsepian, Vardanian (Demirchian 41), Khachatrian, Art Petrossian, Dokhoyan A (Okopian 33) (Gevorgian 66), Dokhoyan K, Sarkissian, Art Karamian.

Poland: Dudek; Kukielka, Hajto, Bak J, Michal Zewlakow, Swierczewski P, Bak A, Kaluzny (Krzynowek 36), Kozminsky (Zdebel 84), Juskowiak (Marcin Zewlakow 64), Kryszalowicz.

Referee: Romain (Belgium).

Oslo, 6 June 2001, 17,164

Norway (0) 1 *(Carew 80)*

Belarus (1) 1 *(Belkevich 23)*

Norway: Myhre; Basma (Aas 90), Hoftun, Berg, Riseth, Johnsen F, Leonhardsen, Andersen T, Bakke (Rudi 69), Strand (Nevland 69), Carew.

Belarus: Tumilovic; Yakhimovic, Ostrovski (Tarlovski 85), Lukavic, Shtanyuk, Gurenko, Khatskevich, Belkevich, Shuneiko, Vasilyuk (Khomutovsky 81), Milevski (Yaskovich 50).

Referee: Radoman (Yugoslavia).

Kiev, 6 June 2001, 33,000

Ukraine (1) 1 *(Zoubov 44)*

Wales (0) 1 *(Pembridge 74)*

Ukraine: Shovkovskyi (Levytsky 90); Starostiak (Luzhny 46), Golovko, Vashchuk, Dmitrulin (Nesmachni 46), Parfionov, Tymoshchuk, Zoubov, Vorobei, Shevchenko, Rebrov.

Wales: Jones P; Delaney (Jenkins 38), Barnard, Page, Melville, Pembridge, Davies, Speed, Hartson, Blake (Koumas 73), Giggs.

Referee: Gomes (Portugal).

Group 5 Table	P	W	D	L	F	A	Pts
Poland	7	5	2	0	16	6	17
Belarus	7	3	3	1	8	7	12
Ukraine	7	2	4	1	7	7	10
Wales	7	0	5	2	7	9	5
Norway	7	0	4	3	5	8	4
Armenia	7	0	4	3	6	12	4

GROUP 6

Brussels, 2 September 2000, 40,000

Belgium (0) 0

Croatia (0) 0

Belgium: De Vlieger; Deflandre, Valgaeren, Van Meir, Van Kerckhoven, Vanderhaeghe, Wilmots, Goor (Henrikx 88), Mpenza E (Mpenza M 74), Strupar (Peeters 60), Verheyen.

Croatia: Pletikosa; Kovac R, Jarni, Soldo, Stimac, Simic, Vugrinec (Biscan 46), Jurcic, Suker, Kovac N, Balaban (Tudor 90).

Referee: Levnikov (Russia).

Riga, 2 September 2000, 9500

Latvia (0) 0

Scotland (0) 1 *(McCann 89)*

Latvia: Kolinko; Laizans, Lobanyov, Stepanovs, Blagonadezhdin, Bleidelis, Ivanov, Astafjevs, Rubins, Pahars, Stolcers.

Scotland: Sullivan; Boyd, Davidson (Naysmith 46), Weir (Cameron 46), Hendry, Dailly, Ferguson B, Elliott, Dodds (Holt 90), Hutchison, McCann.

Referee: Schluchter (Switzerland).

Riga, 7 October 2000, 9000

Latvia (0) 0

Belgium (2) 4 *(Wilmots 5, Peeters 13, Cavens 82, Verheyen 90)*

Latvia: Kolinko; Stepanovs, Laizans, Lobanyov (Zemlinsky 75), Blagonadezhdin (Polyakov 63), Astafjevs, Bleidelis, Ivanov, Pahars, Rubins, Stolcers (Peltsis 68).

Belgium: De Vlieger; Deflandre, Valgaeren, Van Meir, Van Kerckhoven, Vanderhaeghe, Wilmots (Goossens 88), Goor, Peeters (Cavens 80), Walem (Boffin 85), Verheyen.

Referee: Irvine (Northern Ireland).

Serravalle, 7 October 2000, 4377

San Marino (0) 0

Scotland (0) 2 *(Elliott 71, Hutchison 73)*

San Marino: Gasperoni F; Gennari, Gobbi, Matteoni (Valentini V 74), Bacciocchi S, Marani, Gasperoni B, Zonzini (Della Valle 80), Manzaroli, Muccioli R, Montagna (De Luigi 60).

Scotland: Sullivan; McNamara, Naysmith, Elliott, Hendry, Dailly (Weir 36), Cameron, Gallacher (Dickov 65), Dodds, Hutchison, McCann (Johnston 46).

Referee: Orrason (Iceland).

Zagreb, 11 October 2000, 30,000
Croatia (1) 1 *(Boksic 16)*
Scotland (1) 1 *(Gallacher 24)*
Croatia: Pavalovic; Kovac R, Stimac, Simic D, Saric, Kovac N, Soldo (Biscan 46), Jarni (Zivkovic 46), Prosinecki, Balaban, Boksic (Vugrinec 75).
Scotland: Sullivan; Boyd, Naysmith, Elliott, Hendry, Weir, Cameron, Burley, Gallacher, Hutchison, Johnston (Dickov 46) (Holt 90).
Referee: Veissiere (France).

Serravalle, 15 November 2000, 537
San Marino (0) 0
Latvia (1) 1 *(Yeliseyev 9)*
San Marino: Gasperoni F; Gennari, Marani, Valentini V, Matteoni, Bacciocchi, Muccioli, Zonzoni (Selva R 84), Montagna (De Luigi 78), Manzaroli (Bugli 74), Selva A.
Latvia: Kolinko; Stepanovs, Laizans, Zemlinsky, Blagonadezhdin, Bleidelis, Troitsky, Astafjevs, Pahars, Rubins (Verpakovsky 66), Yeliseyev (Ivanov 84).
Referee: Cheferin (Slovakia).

Brussels, 28 February 2001, 40,104
Belgium (3) 10 *(Vanderhaeghe 10, 50, Mpenza E 13, Goor 26, 60, Baseggio 64, Wilmots 72, Peeters 76, 84, 88)*
San Marino (0) 1 *(Selva 90)*
Belgium: De Vlieger; Deflandre (Crasson 67), Van Meir, Van Buyton, Dheedene, Englebert (Peeters 59), Vanderhaeghe, Baseggio (Vermant 75), Goor, Mpenza E, Wilmots.
San Marino: Gasperoni F; Gennari, Gobbi, Della Balda, Marani, Matteoni, Muccioli, Selva, Valentini, Zonzini (Vannucci 78), De Luigi (Bugli 87).
Referee: Kaldma (Estonia).

Osijek, 24 March 2001, 18,000
Croatia (3) 4 *(Balaban 8, 43, 45, Vugrinec 89)*
Latvia (0) 1 *(Stolcers 60)*
Croatia: Pletikosa; Simic D, Tudor, Kovac (Vranjes 77), Jarni, Zivkovic, Stanic (Citanovic 46), Prosinecki (Bjelica 63), Balaban, Suker, Vugrinec.
Latvia: Kolinko; Troitsky, Stepanovs, Zemlinsky, Blagonadezhdin, Bleidelis (Verpakovsky 39), Astafjevs, Laizans, Rubins (Rimkus 73), Pahars, Yeliseyev (Stolcers 54).
Referee: Ingvarsson (Sweden).

Glasgow, 24 March 2001, 37,480
Scotland (2) 2 *(Dodds 1, 28 (pen))*
Belgium (0) 2 *(Wilmots 58, Van Buyten 90)*
Scotland: Sullivan; Weir, Boyd, Elliott, Hendry, Ferguson B, Burley, Lambert, Dodds (Gallacher 88), Hutchison, Matteo.
Belgium: De Vlieger (Vermant 79); Mpenza M, Wilmots, Goor, Vanderhaege, Baseggio, Hendrikx (Peeters 46), Dheedene, De Boeck, Valgaeren (Van Buyten 57), Deflandre.
Referee: Nielsen (Denmark).

Glasgow, 28 March 2001, 27,313
Scotland (3) 4 *(Hendry 22, 33, Dodds 34, Cameron 65)*
San Marino (0) 0
Scotland: Sullivan; Johnston, Matteo (Gallacher 64), Elliott (Boyd 46), Hendry, Weir, Burley, Lambert, Dodds, Hutchison, Cameron (Gemmill 82).
San Marino: Gasperoni F; Della Balda (Albani 90), Marani, Gobbi, Matteoni, Bacciocchi, Manzaroli (Selva R 80), Zonzini, Muccioli, Vannucci (Bugli 69), Selva A.
Referee: Kari (Finland).

Riga, 25 April 2001, 4000
Latvia (1) 1 *(Pahars 1)*
San Marino (0) 1 *(Albani 59)*
Latvia: Kolinko; Astafjevs, Stepanovs, Zemlinsky, Kolesnichenko (Mikholap 46), Ivanov (Zakreshevski 77), Blagonadezhdin, Rubins, Rimkus (Yeliseyev 66), Pahars, Stolcers.
San Marino: Gasperoni F; Albani, Vannucci, Della Balda, Matteoni, Bugli (Selva R 80), Bacciocchi, Muccioli, Zonzini, Manzaroli (Nanni 90), Selva A (Montagna P 83).
Referee: Nalbandian (Albania).

Brussels, 2 June 2001, 30,000
Belgium (2) 3 *(Wilmots 2, Mpenza E 12, Zemlinsky 49 (og))*
Latvia (0) 1 *(Pahars 51)*
Belgium: De Vlieger; Crasson, Valgaeren, Van Meir, Van der Heyden, Simons, Wilmots (Vermant 83), Goor (Boffin 68), Mpenza E (Sonck 78), Walem, Verheyen.
Latvia: Kolinko; Stepanovs, Astafjevs (Stolcers 67), Zemlinsky, Laizans, Blagonadezhdin (Zakreshevsky 68), Ivanov, Bleidelis, Pahars (Mikholap 71), Rubins, Isakov.
Referee: Dobrinov (Bulgaria).

Varazdin, 2 June 2001, 15,000
Croatia (2) 4 *(Vlaovic 3, Balaban 29, Suker 54 (pen), Vugrinec 61)*
San Marino (0) 0
Croatia: Pletikosa; Saric, Tudor, Simic D, Jarni, Kovac R, Kovac N (Agic 64), Prosinecki, Vugrinec (Vucko 76), Vlaovic, Balaban (Suker 46).
San Marino: Gasperoni F; Albani, Della Balda, Matteoni (Manzaroli 26), Bacciocchi, Marani, Gennari, Vannucci, Gasperoni B (Ugolini 86), Zonzini (Selva R 76), Selva A.
Referee: Timofejev (Estonia).

Riga, 6 June 2001, 5000
Latvia (0) 0
Croatia (1) 1 *(Balaban 40)*
Latvia: Kolinko; Stepanovs, Astafjevs (Mikholap 71), Zemlinsky, Laizans, Blagonadezhdin, Zakreshevsky, Bleidelis (Dobretsov 88), Isakov, Rubins (Verpakovsky 61), Stolcers.
Croatia: Pletikosa; Saric, Jarni, Tomas, Tudor, Simic D, Rapaic (Vugrinec 75), Prosinecki, Suker, Kovac (Agic 90), Balaban (Vlaovic 65).
Referee: McDermott (Republic of Ireland).

Serraville, 6 June 2001, 1000
San Marino (1) 1 *(Selva A 11)*
Belgium (1) 4 *(Wilmots 10, 89 (pen), Verheyen 60, Sonck 68)*
San Marino: Gasperoni F; Albani (Selva R 69), Della Balda, Bacciocchi, Marani, Gennari, Muccioli, Vannucci, Zonzini (Ugolini 82), Selva A, Gasperoni B (Bugli 74).
Belgium: De Vlieger; Deflandre, Van Meir, Valgaeren, Van Kerckhoven (Boffin 79), Verheyen, Vanderhaeghe, Walem, Goor (Vermant 75), Peeters (Sonck 52), Wilmots.
Referee: Yakov (Israel).

Group 6 Table	P	W	D	L	F	A	Pts
Belgium	6	4	2	0	23	5	14
Croatia	5	3	2	0	10	2	11
Scotland	5	3	2	0	10	3	11
Latvia	7	1	1	5	4	14	4
San Marino	7	0	1	6	3	26	1

GROUP 7

Sarajevo, 2 September 2000, 35,000
Bosnia (1) 1 *(Baljic 41)*
Spain (1) 2 *(Gerard 39, Etxeberria 72)*
Bosnia: Guso; Akrapovic, Hujdurovic, Mujcin (Topic 79), Varesanovic, Hibic, Bolic, Sabic (Muratovic 86), Barbarez, Salihamidzic, Baljic.
Spain: Casillas; Manuel Pablo, Sergi, Paco, Abelardo, Mendieta, Helguera, Gerard (Guerrero 85), Urzaiz (Celades 70), Raul, Munitis (Etxeberria 58).
Referee: Fandel (Germany).

Ramat Gan, 3 September 2000, 14,000
Israel (1) 2 *(Mizrahi A 1, Balili 79)*
Liechtenstein (0) 0
Israel: Davidovich; Talkar (Benayoun 66), Shelach, Gershon, Harazi A, Keissi, Berkovic (Zohar 82), Tal (Balili 77), Nimny, Mizrahi A, Banin.
Liechtenstein: Jehle; Ospelt, Zech, Hasler D, Frick C (Gigon 76), Martin Stocklasa (Hanselmann 85), Michael Stocklasa (Burgmeier 85), Hefti, Telser, Frick M, Beck T.
Referee: O'Hanlon (Republic of Ireland).

Vaduz, 7 October 2000, 3500
Liechtenstein (0) 0
Austria (1) 1 *(Flogel 20)*
Liechtenstein: Jehle; Ospelt, Hasler D, Telser, Martin Stocklasa, Hanselmann, Hefti, Michael Stocklasa (Nigg 74), Gigon, Beck T, Frick M.

Austria: Wohlfahrt; Hiden, Baur, Stranzi, Schopp (Hortnagl 67), Kuhbauer, Herzog, Flogel, Kirchler, Brunmayr (Kitzbichler 46), Mayrleb.
Referee: Rowbotham (Scotland).

Madrid, 7 October 2000, 80,000

Spain (1) 2 *(Gerard 22, Hierro 53)*
Israel (0) 0

Spain: Casillas; Hierro, Manuel Pablo, Abelardo, Sergi, Helguera, Gerard (Baraja 31), Mendieta, Munitis, Raul (Guerrero 85), Urzaiz (Catanha 75).
Israel: Davidovich; Alfon, Talkar, Shelach, Benado, Keissi, Tal, Nimny (Benayoun 65), Badir (Berkovic 75), Revivo, Mizrahi A.
Referee: Colombo (France).

Vienna, 11 October 2000, 48,000

Austria (1) 1 *(Baur 21)*
Spain (1) 1 *(Baraja 27)*

Austria: Wohlfahrt; Hatz, Baur, Hiden, Stranzi (Hortnagl 46), Flogel, Cerny, Kuhbauer (Schopp 75), Mayrleb, Herzog, Kocijan (Kirchler 54).
Spain: Casillas; Hierro, Abelardo, Sergi, Baraja, Helguera, Mendieta, Urzaiz (Catanha 60), Raul (Guerrero 88), Victor Sanchez (Rufete 46), Luis Enrique.
Referee: Ivanov (Russia).

Tel Aviv, 11 October 2000, 30,000

Israel (1) 3 *(Berkovic 12, Abuksis 62, Katan 76)*
Bosnia (0) 1 *(Akrapovic 48)*

Israel: Davidovich; Benado, Talkar, Shelach, Gershon, Keissi (Ben-Dayan 86), Tal, Revivo, Abuksis, Berkovic (Benayoun 60), Mizrahi A (Katan 73).
Bosnia: Guso; Akrapovic, Music, Hujdurovic (Krupinac 79), Varesanovic, Hibic, Bolic, Demirovich (Juldic 73), Barbarez, Salihamidzic, Baljic.
Referee: Jol (Holland).

Sarajevo, 24 March 2001, 25,000

Bosnia (1) 1 *(Barbarez 42)*
Austria (0) 1 *(Baur 61)*

Bosnia: Piplica; Varesanovic, Hujdorovic, Hibic, Rizvic (Hota 70), Sabic, Akrapovic, Barbarez, Music, Bolic, Baljic (Topic 83).
Austria: Wohlfahrt; Baur, Hiden, Neukirchner (Prilasnig 54), Cerny (Schopp 46), Kuhbauer, Stranzl, Herzog (Haas 71), Flogel, Vastic, Mayrleb.
Referee: Ovrebo (Norway).

Alicante, 24 March 2001, 29,900

Spain (2) 5 *(Helguera 20, Mendieta 36, 81, Hierro 54 (pen), Raul 68)*
Liechtenstein (0) 0

Spain: Casillas; Manuel Pablo, Hierro, Nadal, Romero, Mendieta, Guardiola (Sergio 82), Helguera (Baraja 67), Raul, Moreno, Munitis (Etxeberria 39).
Liechtenstein: Jehle; Ospelt, Zech, Hefti, Hasler D, Gigon, Beck (Buchel 88), Martin Stocklasa (Gerster 90), Telser, Michael Stocklasa, Frick M.
Referee: Ceferin (Slovakia).

Vienna, 28 March 2001, 21,000

Austria (2) 2 *(Baur 9, Herzog 41 (pen))*
Israel (1) 1 *(Baur 6 (og))*

Austria: Wohlfahrt; Baur, Hiden, Prilasnig, Schopp, Kuhbauer, Herzog (Kitzbichler 90) Stranzl, Flogel, Vastic (Hortnagl 57), Mayrleb (Haas 63).
Israel: Davidovich; Benado (Mizrahi A 57), Talkar, Shelach (Brumer 46), Gershon, Banin (Tal 72), Keissi, Nimni, Berkovic, Zeituni, Benayoun.
Referee: Trentalange (Italy).

Vaduz, 28 March 2001, 3400

Liechtenstein (0) 0
Bosnia (1) 3 *(Barbarez 10, 72, Hota 89)*

Liechtenstein: Jehle; Ospelt, Hefti, Zech, Martin Stocklasa, Hasler D, Beck (Nigg 73), Telser M (Buchel 46), Michael Stocklasa (Rither 90), Gigon, Frick M.
Bosnia: Piplica; Varesanovic, Hujdorovic, Hibic, Music, Salihamidzic, Akrapovic, Sabic (Rivzic 90), Barbarez, Bolic (Topic 63), Baljic (Hota 81).
Referee: Sipailo (Latvia).

Innsbruck, 25 April 2001, 13,000

Austria (1) 2 *(Glieder 43, Flogel 75)*
Liechtenstein (0) 0

Austria: Manninger; Prilasnig, Baur, Hiden, Kitzbichler (Ibertsberger 75), Kirchler, Flogel, Herzog (Wallner 89), Hortnagel, Vastic (Weissenberger 61), Glieder.
Liechtenstein: Jehle; Ospelt (Buchel 66), Hefti, Ritter, Zech, Beck T (D'Elia 52), Hasler, Telser, Martin Stocklasa, Gigon, Frick (Michael Stocklasa 81).
Referee: Malcolm (Northern Ireland).

Vaduz, 2 June 2001, 1500

Liechtenstein (0) 0
Israel (3) 3 *(Revivo 2, Tal 6, Nimni 17)*

Liechtenstein: Jehle; Ospelt J, Ritter, Zech, Martin Stocklasa, Michael Stocklasa, Beck T (Gerster 85), Buchel (Beck M 71), Telser, Gigon, Hasler D (D'Elia 65).
Israel: Davidovich; Ben-Dayan (Badir 65), Talkar, Benado, Gershon, Keisi, Zeituni, Revivo (Mizrahi A 74), Nimni, Berkovic (Banayoun 65), Tal.
Referee: Isaksen (Faeroes).

Oviedo, 2 June 2001, 27,000

Spain (1) 4 *(Hierro 26, Javi Moreno 75, Raul 88, Diego Tristan 90)*
Bosnia (1) 1 *(Beslija 41)*

Spain: Canizares; Manuel Pablo, Hierro, Nadal, Juanfran, Mendieta (Munitis 55) Guardiola, Helguera (Valeron 46), Luis Enrique (Javi Moreno 75), Raul, Diego Tristan.
Bosnia: Piplica; Hujdurovic, Varesanovic, Hibic, Beslija, Akrapovic, Mujcin, Barbarez, Music (Hota 70), Baljic, Bolic (Demirovic 82).
Referee: Olsen (Norway).

Tel Aviv, 6 June 2001, 25,000

Israel (1) 1 *(Revivo 4)*
Spain (0) 1 *(Raul 63)*

Israel: Davidovich (Awat 46); Brumer G, Talkar, Benado, Gershon, Keisi, Zeituni, Berkovic (Benayoun 87), Tal, Nimni, Revivo (Banin 70).
Spain: Canizares; Manuel Pablo, Hierro, Nadal, Sergi, Valeron (Helguera 76), Guardiola (Diego Tristan 60), Baraja, Luis Enrique (Puyol 83), Javi Moreno, Raul.
Referee: Frisk (Sweden).

Group 7 Table	P	W	D	L	F	A	Pts
Spain	6	4	2	0	15	4	14
Austria	5	3	2	0	7	3	11
Israel	6	3	1	2	10	6	10
Bosnia	5	1	1	3	7	10	4
Liechtenstein	6	0	0	6	0	16	0

GROUP 8

Budapest, 3 September 2000, 57,000

Hungary (1) 2 *(Horvath 29, 78)*
Italy (1) 2 *(Inzaghi F 26, 35)*

Hungary: Kiraly; Korsos G, Sebok V, Matyus (Peto 46), Feher C, Halmai, Hamar (Lendvai 89), Illes, Lisztes, Horvath, Tokoli (Dombi 75).
Italy: Toldo; Cannavaro, Nesta, Iuliano, Zambrotta, Albertini, Maldini, Fiore (Gattuso 80), Totti, Inzaghi F, Del Piero (Delvecchio 73).
Referee: Barber (England).

Bucharest, 3 September 2000, 4500

Romania (0) 1 *(Ganea 89)*
Lithuania (0) 0

Romania: Stelea; Ciobotariu (Mutu 49), Filipescu, Belodedici, Contra (Petre 58), Petrescu, Munteanu C, Munteanu D, Chivu, Moldovan (Ganea 67), Vladoiu.
Lithuania: Padimanskas; Kanchelskis, Gleveckas, Skerla, Zvrigzdauskas, Zutautas, Danilevicius, Semberas, Preiksaitis (Butkus 46), Maciulevicius (Mikalajunas 46), Fomenka (Radzius 80).
Referee: Norman (Sweden).

Milan, 7 October 2000, 54,297

Italy (3) 3 *(Inzaghi F 13, Delvecchio 17, Totti 42)*
Romania (0) 0

Italy: Toldo; Cannavaro, Nesta, Maldini, Di Livio, Albertini, Fiore (Pancaro 55), Coco, Totti, Inzaghi F (Del Piero 81), Delvecchio (Gattuso 71).

Romania: Stelea; Petrescu (Contra 46), Belodedici, Filipescu, Chivu, Rosu, Galca, Lupescu, Munteanu D (Munteanu C 62), Moldovan (Mutu 58), Ganea.
Referee: Wegereef (Holland).

Vilnius, 7 October 2000, 5000

Lithuania (0) 0
Georgia (2) 4 *(Ketsbaia 18, 33, Kinkladze 46, Arveladze A 84)*

Lithuania: Padimanskas; Skerla, Gleveckas, Graziunas (Maciulevicius 39), Zutautas, Butkus, Zemberas, Ivanauskas (Morinas 46), Fomenka (Zvinglas 55), Danilevicius, Jankauskas.
Georgia: Gvaramadze; Silagadze, Kobiashvili, Rekhviashvili, Khizanishvili, Kaladze, Nemsadze, Kavelashvili, Ketsbaia (Menteshashvili 67), Kinkladze (Jamarauli 70), Demetradze (Arveladze A 56).
Referee: Wojcik (Poland).

Ancona, 11 October 2000, 26,000

Italy (0) 2 *(Del Piero 47 (pen), 88 (pen))*
Georgia (0) 0

Italy: Toldo; Cannavaro, Nesta, Bertotto, Di Livio, Albertini, Fiore (Pancaro 76), Coco, Totti (Montella 83), Delvecchio (Gattuso 52), Del Piero.
Georgia: Gvaramadze; Silagadze, Kobiashvili, Rekhviashvili, Khizanishvili, Kaladze, Nemsadze, Kavelashvili, Ketsbaia (Menteshashvili 68), Kinkladze (Jamarauli 61), Arveladze A (Demetradze 61).
Referee: Nilsson (Sweden).

Vilnius, 11 October 2000, 2000

Lithuania (0) 1 *(Butkus 71)*
Hungary (2) 6 *(Illes 24, Feher M 36, 62, 72, Horvath 66, Lisztes 84 (pen))*

Lithuania: Padimanskas; Skerla, Gleveckas, Radzius, Kanchelskis (Graziunas 69), Butkus, Semberas, Ivanauskas, Preiksaitis, Morinas (Danilevicius 83), Jankauskas.
Hungary: Kiraly; Korsos G (Bodnar 84), Feher C (Juhar 78), Matyus (Dombi 73), Sebok V, Peto, Feher M, Lisztes, Horvath, Illes, Hamar.
Referee: Erdemir (Turkey).

Budapest, 24 March 2001, 20,000

Hungary (0) 1 *(Sebok V 70 (pen))*
Lithuania (0) 1 *(Razanauskas 74)*

Hungary: Kiraly; Feher C, Sebok V, Korsos G, Juhar, Miriuta, Dardai, Illes, Hamar (Egressy 46), Horvath, Feher M (Dombi 64).
Lithuania: Stauce; Skarbalius, Dedura (Dziaukstas 35), Gleveckas, Zvirgzdauskas, Razanauskas (Joksas 89), Zutautas, Poskus, Morinas, Semberas, Mikalajunas.
Referee: Melnischuk (Ukraine).

Bucharest, 24 March 2001, 24,500

Romania (0) 0
Italy (2) 2 *(Inzaghi F 29, 32)*

Romania: Stelea; Rodai (Serban 71), Filipescu, Prodan, Contra, Codrea, Galca (Munteanu C 59), Munteanu D, Moldovan (Ganea 78), Niculae, Ilie A.
Italy: Buffon; Cannavaro, Nesta, Maldini, Zambrotta, Tommasi, Fiore (Tacchinardi 62), Albertini, Pancaro, Inzaghi F (Montella 86), Del Piero.
Referee: Fandel (Germany).

Tbilisi, 28 March 2001, 27,000

Georgia (0) 0
Romania (0) 2 *(Munteanu D 68, Contra 81)*

Georgia: Gvaramadze; Silagadze, Rekhviashvili (Lashvili 73), Kobiashvili, Khizanishvili, Nemsadze, Kaladze, Kavelashvili (Dzhavashia 52), Ketsbaia (Kemoklidze 62), Arveladze S, Kinkladze.
Romania: Stelea; Contra, Filipescu, Prodan, Radoi (Galca 58), Munteanu C, Codrea, Chivu, Munteanu D, Moldovan (Stoica 82), Ilie A (Niculae 21).
Referee: Pedersen (Norway).

Trieste, 28 March 2001, 14,800

Italy (1) 4 *(Inzaghi F 17, 63, Del Piero 49, 79)*
Lithuania (0) 0

Italy: Buffon; Cannavaro, Nesta, Maldini, Zambrotta, Tommasi, Tacchinardi, Coco, Totti (Fiore 75), Inzaghi F (Montella 69), Del Piero (Di Livio 83).
Lithuania: Stauce; Zvirgzdauskas, Skarbalius, Joksas, Dziaukstas, Razanauskas (Danilevicius 50), Zutautas, Semberas, Morinas, Poskus (Stankevicius 77), Mikalajunas (Jankauskas 65).
Referee: Shmolik (Belarus).

Tbilisi, 2 June 2001, 28,000

Georgia (0) 1 *(Gakhokidze 80)*
Italy (1) 2 *(Delvecchio 45, Totti 66)*

Georgia: Zoidze; Silagadze, Abramidze, Kaladze, Kobiashvili, Khizanishvili (Gakhokidze 79), Nemsadze (Arveladze S 80), Rekhviashvili, Menteshashvili (Arveladze A 60), Ketsbaia, Kavelashvili.
Italy: Buffon; Cannavaro, Nesta (Materazzi 74), Maldini, Zambrotta, Tommasi, Tacchinardi, Pancaro, Totti, Delvecchio (Montella 79), Del Piero (Di Livio 58).
Referee: Iturralde (Spain).

Bucharest, 2 June 2001, 22,000

Romania (1) 2 *(Niculae 4, 54)*
Hungary (0) 0

Romania: Stelea; Contra, Radoi (Prodan 64), Ciobotariu, Chivu, Munteanu D, Codrea, Ilie A (Munteanu C 75), Dumitru, Moldovan (Ganea 72), Niculae.
Hungary: Kiraly; Feher C, Korsos G, Sebok V, Matyus, Peto, Lisztes, Sowunmi (Kabat 73), Dardai, Horvath (Korsos A 46), Hamar (Dombi 41).
Referee: Poulat (France).

Budapest, 6 June 2001, 10,000

Hungary (2) 4 *(Matyus 40, Sebok V 45 (pen), Korsos A 55, 62)*
Georgia (0) 1 *(Kobiashvili 77)*

Hungary: Kiraly; Korsos G, Sebok V, Peto, Matyus, Lisztes (Lendvai 80), Halmai (Dardai 70), Illes, Korsos A (Dombi 77), Horvath, Hamar.
Georgia: Zoidze; Abramidze, Kaladze (Todua 67), Arveladze A, Kobiashvili, Nemsadze (Kemoklidze 67), Rekhviashvili, Khizanishvili, Ketsbaia, Arveladze S, Kavelashvili (Kinkladze 53).
Referee: Strampe (Germany).

Kaunas, 6 June 2001, 7000

Lithuania (0) 1 *(Fomenko 87)*
Romania (1) 2 *(Ilie A 31, Moldovan 49)*

Lithuania: Stauce; Zvirgzdauskas, Dedura, Skarbalius, Graziunas, Morinas (Fomenko 46), Zutautas, Mikalajunas, Semberas, Razanauskas (Butkis 73), Poskus.
Romania: Stelea; Contra (Ganea 54), Radoi, Filipescu, Chivu, Dumutru, Niculae, Kodrea, Munteanu D, Moldovan (Prodan 57), Ilie A (Mutu 63).
Referee: Stredak (Slovakia).

Group 8 Table	P	W	D	L	F	A	Pts
Italy	6	5	1	0	15	3	16
Romania	6	4	0	2	7	6	12
Hungary	5	2	2	1	13	7	8
Georgia	5	1	0	4	6	10	3
Lithuania	6	0	1	5	3	18	1

GROUP 9

Helsinki, 2 September 2000, 10,770

Finland (1) 2 *(Litmanen 45, Riihilahti 67)*
Albania (0) 1 *(Murati 63)*

Finland: Jaaskelainen; Saarinen, Turpeinen, Hyypia, Tihinen, Nurmela (Johansson 57), Koppinen (Riihilahti 46), Valakari, Forssell (Ylonen 77), Litmanen, Kolkka.
Albania: Strakosha; Lala, Cipi, Xhumba, Vata R, Murati (Bushi 76), Haxhi, Muka (Skela 46), Kola, Rraklli, Tare.
Referee: Timmink (Holland).

Hamburg, 2 September 2000, 48,500

Germany (1) 2 *(Deisler 17, Ouzounidis 75 (og))*
Greece (0) 0

Germany: Kahn; Rehmer, Nowotny, Heinrich (Linke 46), Deisler, Ramelow, Ballack, Bode, Scholl, Jancker, Zickler (Rink 71).
Greece: Eleftheropoulos; Ouzounidis, Goumas, Amanatidis, Georgatos, Poursanidis (Choutos 66), Mavrogenidis (Patsatzoglou 23), Tsartas, Zagorakis, Limberopoulos, Georgiadis (Lakis 76).
Referee: Nieto (Spain).

Wembley, 7 October 2000, 76,377

England (0) 0
Germany (1) 1 *(Hamann 14)*

England: Seaman; Neville G (Dyer 46), Le Saux (Barry 77), Southgate, Keown, Adams, Beckham (Parlour 82), Barmby, Andy Cole, Owen, Scholes.
Germany: Kahn; Rehmer, Nowotny, Linke, Deisler, Ramelow, Hamann, Ballack, Bode (Ziege 86), Scholl, Bierhoff.
Referee: Braschi (Italy).

Athens, 7 October 2000, 14,800

Greece (0) 1 *(Limberopoulos 59)*
Finland (0) 0

Greece: Nikopolidis; Georgatos (Venetidis 72), Patsatzoglou, Amanatidis, Ouzounidis, Karagounis (Lakis 76), Zagorakis, Basinas, Limberopoulos, Georgiadis, Choutos (Antzas 83).
Finland: Niemi; Reini, Helin, Hyypia, Tihinen, Nurmela, Jarkko (Kottila 81), Valakari, Johansson (Kuqi 64), Litmanen, Kolkka (Forssell 46).
Referee: Collina (Italy).

Tirana, 11 October 2000, 11,000

Albania (0) 2 *(Bushi 50, Fakaj 90)*
Greece (0) 0

Albania: Strakosha; Muka, Cipi, Xhumba (Fakaj 75), Vata R, Vata F (Basha 78), Skela, Kola, Haxhi, Bushi, Tare (Bogdani 86).
Greece: Nikopolidis; Bassinas, Venetidis (Kyparissis 72), Patsatzoglou, Ouzounidis, Zagorakis (Lakis 70), Georgiadis, Karagounis, Choutos, Limberopoulos, Zikos (Poursanidis 70).
Referee: Pedersen (Norway).

Helsinki, 11 October 2000, 36,210

Finland (0) 0
England (0) 0

Finland: Niemi; Helin (Reini 36), Tihinen, Hyypia, Saarinen (Salli 66), Nurmela, Wiss, Valakari, Johansson, Litmanen, Forssell (Kuqi 76).
England: Seaman; Neville P, Barry (Brown 69), Southgate, Keown, Wise, Parlour, Scholes, Andy Cole, Sheringham (McManaman 69), Heskey.
Referee: Sars (France).

Liverpool, 24 March 2001, 44,262

England (1) 2 *(Owen 43, Beckham 50)*
Finland (1) 1 *(Neville G 26 (og))*

England: Seaman; Neville G, Powell, Ferdinand R, Campbell, Scholes, Beckham, Gerrard, Andy Cole (Fowler 82), Owen (Butt 90), McManaman (Heskey 72).
Finland: Niemi; Pasanen, Hyypia, Tihinen, Ylonen (Helin 89), Wiss, Nurmela (Forssell 63), Riihilahti, Litmanen, Kolka (Kuqi 63), Johansson.
Referee: Ivanov (Russia).

Leverkusen, 24 March 2001, 22,500

Germany (0) 2 *(Deisler 50, Klose 88)*
Albania (0) 1 *(Kola 65)*

Germany: Kahn; Nowotny, Worns, Jeremies, Ramelow, Deisler, Hamann (Rehmer 46), Bode, Neuville (Klose 73), Bierhoff (Jancker 46), Scholl.
Albania: Strakosha; Cipi, Vata R, Lala, Xhumba, Vata F (Skela 79), Hasi (Fakaj 86), Kola, Murati, Tare, Bushi (Rraklli 67).
Referee: Cesari (Italy).

Tirana, 28 March 2001, 18,000

Albania (0) 1 *(Rraklli 90)*
England (0) 3 *(Owen 73, Scholes 85, Andy Cole 90)*

Albania: Strakosha; Cipi, Fakaj, Lala, Xhumba, Hasi, Vata F (Rraklli 88), Kola (Beqaj 82), Bellai (Skela 90), Tare, Bushi.
England: Seaman; Neville G, Ashley Cole, Ferdinand R, Campbell (Brown 29), Butt, Beckham, Scholes, Andy Cole, Owen (Sheringham 84), McManaman (Heskey 46).
Referee: Hamer (Luxembourg).

Germany inflicted a crucial 1-0 defeat on England in the World Cup. Here Mehmet Scholl and Martin Keown dispute possession. (Colorsport)

Athens, 28 March 2001, 53,000

Greece (2) 2 *(Haristeas 21, Georgiadis 44)*
Germany (2) 4 *(Rehmer 6, Ballack 25 (pen), Klose 82, Bode 90)*

Greece: Eleftheropoulos; Patsatzoglou, Kostoulas (Mavrogenidis 35), Goumas, Basinas, Karagounis (Niniadis 75), Zagorakis, Georgiadis, Haristeas (Alexandris 84), Liberopoulos, Georgatos.
Germany: Kahn; Worns, Nowotny, Heinrich, Rehmer, Jeremies (Ramelow 90), Deisler, Ballack, Ziege, Jancker (Bode 78), Neuville (Klose 67).
Referee: Pereira (Portugal).

Helsinki, 2 June 2001, 35,774

Finland (2) 2 *(Forssell 28, 43)*
Germany (0) 2 *(Ballack 68 (pen), Jancker 72)*

Finland: Niemi; Pasanen, Nylund, Hyypia, Tihinen, Nurmela (Johansson 71), Riihilati (Gronlund 80), Litmanen, Rantanen, Forssell, Kolka (Kuqi 85).
Germany: Kahn; Rehmer, Nowotny, Linke, Asamoah, Ramelow, Ballack, Bode (Ziege 69), Ricken, Neuville (Klose 62), Jancker (Bierhoff 83).
Referee: Jol (Holland).

Iraklion, 2 June 2001, 4000

Greece (1) 1 *(Mahlas 72)*
Albania (0) 0

Greece: Nikopolidis; Patsatzoglou, Dabizas, Venetidis, Zagorakis, Goumas, Ouzounidis, Georgiadis (Basinas 85), Karagounis, Alexandris (Charisteas 62), Liberopoulos (Mahlas 46).
Albania: Strakosha; Cipi, Vata R, Lala, Xhumba, Hasi, Haxhi (Skela 76), Bushi, Vata F, Murati, Tare (Bogdani 71).
Referee: Levnikov (Russia).

Tirana, 6 June 2001, 18,000

Albania (0) 0
Germany (1) 2 *(Rehmer 28, Ballack 68)*

Albania: Strakosha; Vata R, Cipi, Xhumba (Bellai 46), Lala, Vata F, Murati, Hasi (Skela 61), Haxhi (Muka 81), Bushi, Tare.
Germany: Kahn; Rehmer, Nowotny, Linke, Asamoah (Ricken 70), Ramelow, Ballack, Ziege, Deisler (Baumann 84), Jancker, Neuville (Zickler 46).
Referee: Veissiere (France).

Athens, 6 June 2001, 46,000

Greece (0) 0
England (0) 2 *(Scholes 64, Beckham 87)*

Greece: Nikopolidis; Goumas, Ouzounidis, Dabizas, Mavrogenidis (Giannakopoulos 70), Basinas, Zagorakis, Fyssas, Karagounis (Limberopoulos 24), Mahlas (Alexandris 64), Vryzas.
England: Seaman; Neville P, Ashley Cole, Gerrard, Keown, Ferdinand, Beckham, Scholes (Butt 88), Fowler (Smith 79), Owen, Heskey (McManaman 74).
Referee: Pedersen (Norway).

Group 9 Table	P	W	D	L	F	A	Pts
Germany	6	5	1	0	13	5	16
England	5	3	1	1	7	3	10
Greece	6	2	0	4	4	10	6
Finland	5	1	2	2	5	6	5
Albania	6	1	0	5	5	10	3

SOUTH AMERICA
(Members 10, Entries 10)

Four or five teams qualify including play-offs with Oceania.

Bogota, 28 March 2000, 42,493

Colombia (0) 0
Brazil (0) 0

Colombia: Cordoba O; Bermudez, Cordoba I, Yepes, Martinez, Viveros, Dinas, Rincon, Oviedo (Moreno 74), Angel, Ricard (Maturana 60).
Brazil: Dida; Evanilson, Aldair, Antonio Carlos, Roberto Carlos, Emerson, Ze Roberto, Vampeta, Alex (Ricardinho 46), Elber (Ronaldinho Gaucho 68), Jardel (Edilson 46).
Referee: Mendez (Uruguay).

Buenos Aires, 29 March 2000, 50,000

Argentina (2) 4 *(Batistuta 9, Veron 33, 71 (pen), Lopez C 88)*
Chile (1) 1 *(Tello 29)*

Argentina: Bonano; Pochettino, Roberto Ayala, Samuel, Zanetti, Simeone, Kily Gonzalez, Veron, Ortega (Sensini 85), Batistuta (Crespo 89), Lopez C (Lopez D 89).
Chile: Ramirez; Maldonado, Reyes, Margas, Contreras, Ormazabal (Aros 83), Acuna, Tello, Pizarro (Sierra 70), Zamorano, Salas.
Referee: Moreno (Ecuador).

Quito, 29 March 2000, 50,000

Ecuador (1) 2 *(Delgado 17, Aguinaga 51)*
Venezuela (0) 0

Ecuador: Cevallos; De La Cruz, Jacome, Montano, Cagua (Ayovi 49), Blandon, Tenorio (Chala 73), Aguinaga, Obregon, Graziani (Porozo 38), Delgado.
Venezuela: Dudamel; Alvarez, Villafraz (Mea Vitali 62), Becerra, Rey, Urdaneta, Rojas (Arango 55), Bidoglio, Jesus Vera, Casseres, Garcia (Ochoa 55).
Referee: Gamboa (Chile).

Lima, 29 March 2000, 45,000

Peru (0) 2 *(Solano 55 (pen), Palacios 60)*
Paraguay (0) 0

Peru: Ibanez; Soto J, Rebosio, Pajuelo, Percy Olivares (Huaman 72), Jayo, Palacios, Del Solar, Solano, Pizarro (Ciurlizza 81), Zuniga (Holsen 59).

Paraguay: Chilavert; Arce, Ayala, Gamarra, Caniza, Enciso (Struway 68), Paredes (Gavilan 74), Acuna, Jorge Campos, Santa Cruz, Cardozo (Gonzales 68).
Referee: Elizondo (Argentina).

Montevideo, 29 March 2000, 55,000

Uruguay (1) 1 *(Pablo Garcia 26)*
Bolivia (0) 0

Uruguay: Carini; Mendez, Diego Lopez, Montero, Rodriguez, Coelho, Pablo Garcia, O'Neill, Cedres (Olivera 58), Alonso (Zalayeta 76), Recoba (Poyet 89).
Bolivia: Fernandez; Rivera, Pena, Oscar Sanchez, Sandy (Rimba 75), Ivan Castillo, Cristaldo, Justiniano, Erwin Sanchez, Gutierrez (Suarez 59), Moreno (Botero 70).
Referee: Pereira (Argentina).

La Paz, 26 April 2000, 20,000

Bolivia (1) 1 *(Sanchez 16)*
Colombia (1) 1 *(Castillo 32)*

Bolivia: Fernandez; Ribeiro, Pena, Sandy (Rimba 33), Ivan Castillo, Cristaldo, Soria, Gutierrez (Galindo 63), Sanchez, Antelo (Suarez 46), Moreno.
Colombia: Cordoba O; Cordoba I, Bermudez, Yepes, Viveros, Martinez (Cardona 79), Dinas, Oviedo (Ortegon 82), Rincon, Ricard (Angel 74), Castillo.
Referee: Arana (Peru).

Sao Paulo, 26 April 2000, 65,000

Brazil (2) 3 *(Rivaldo 18, 51, Antonio Carlos 42)*
Ecuador (1) 2 *(Aguinaga 12, De La Cruz 76)*

Brazil: Dida; Cafu, Antonio Carlos, Aldair, Roberto Carlos (Athirson 68), Cesar Sampaio, Vampeta, Rivaldo, Ze Roberto (Alex 68), Amoroso, Edilson.
Ecuador: Cevallos; De La Cruz, Poroso, Capurro, Hurtado I, Tenorio, Obregon, Aguinaga (Ayovi 40) (Kaviedes 88), Blandon, Delgado, Graziani (Hurtado E 66).
Referee: Cervantes (Colombia).

Santiago, 26 April 2000, 45,000

Chile (1) 1 *(Margas 42)*
Peru (1) 1 *(Jayo 38)*

Chile: Tapia N; Vargas, Reyes, Margas, Maldonado (Nunez C 70), Acuna, Rojas (Nunez R 70), Pizarro (Sierra 58), Tello, Zamorano, Salas.

Peru: Ibanez; Soto, Rebosio, Pajuelo, Olivares, Jayo, Soria (Zuniga 58), Del Solar, Palacios, Solano, Pizarro.
Referee: Rojas (Paraguay).

Asuncion, 26 April 2000, 15,000

Paraguay (1) 1 *(Ayala 35)*

Uruguay (0) 0

Paraguay: Chilavert; Espinola, Gamarra, Ayala, Caniza, Quintana (Gonzalez 59), Paredes, Struway, Acuna (Enciso 68), Santa Cruz, Baez (Benitez 82).
Uruguay: Carini; Mendez, Ramos, Lembo, Tabare Silva (Guigou 67), Coelho, Pablo Garcia, De Los Santos, Poyet (Olivera 63), Recoba, Dario Silva (Alvez 75).
Referee: Sanchez (Argentina).

Maracaibo, 26 April 2000, 27,000

Venezuela (0) 0

Argentina (2) 4 *(Ayala 7, Ortega 23, 76, Crespo 88)*

Venezuela: Dudamel; Rojas, Rey, Villafraz (Luzardo 46), Gonzalez, Mea, Bidoglio, Urdaneta, Vera, Juan Garcia (Martinez 70), Castellin.
Argentina: Bonano; Ayala, Samuel, Sensini, Kily Gonzalez, Zanetti, Simeone, Veron, Ortega (Gallardo 78), Lopez C (Lopez G 68), Crespo.
Referee: Amarilla (Paraguay).

Ascunion, 3 June 2000, 22,000

Paraguay (2) 3 *(Toledo 11, Brizuela 43, 64)*

Ecuador (0) 1 *(Graziani 87)*

Paraguay: Chilavert; Caniza, Gamarra, Ayala, Toledo, Paredes, Struway (Enciso 82), Quintana, Acuna, Brizuela (Gonzalez 76), Baez (Benitez 66).
Ecuador: Ceballos; De La Cruz, Poroso (Kaviedes 66), Montano, Capurro, Blandon, Hurtado I, Tenorio (Chala 46), Aguinaga, Juarez, Delgado (Graziani 61).
Referee: Gallesio (Uruguay).

Montevideo, 3 June 2000, 60,000

Uruguay (2) 2 *(Dario Silva 35, Montero 41)*

Chile (1) 1 *(Zamorano 39 (pen))*

Uruguay: Carini; Mendez, Montero, Lembo, Rodriguez, Pablo Garcia, Guigou, O'Neill, Olivera, Recoba (Giacomazzi 89), Dario Silva (Alonso 81).
Chile: Tapia N; Rojas, Vargas, Reyes, Olarra (Rozental 68), Galdames, Estay (Nunez C 87), Vallaseca, Tello, Zamorano, Salas.
Referee: Troxler (Paraguay).

Buenos Aires, 4 June 2000, 50,669

Argentina (0) 1 *(Lopez G 83)*

Bolivia (0) 0

Argentina: Bonano; Sensini, Ayala, Samuel, Zanetti (Lopez G 71), Simeone, Kily Gonzalez, Veron, Ortega (Aimar 83), Batistuta, Lopez C (Almeyda 88).
Bolivia: Fernandez; Carballo, Pena, Sandy, Ivan Castillo, Ribera, Baldivieso, Cristaldo, Etcheverry (Galindo 78), Suarez (Garcia 65), Botero (Coimbra 83).
Referee: Rezende (Brazil).

Bogota, 4 June 2000, 22,000

Colombia (2) 3 *(Viveros 27, Cordoba I 42 (pen), Valenciano 88)*

Venezuela (0) 0

Colombia: Cordoba O; Martinez, Cordoba I, Ortegon, Bedoya, Rincon, Bolano, Oviedo (Candelo 70), Viveros (Dinas 77), Angel, Castillo (Valenciano 81).
Venezuela: Dudamel; Filosa, Gonzalez, Alvarado, Echenausi, Arango, Vera (Farias 55), Mea, Bidoglio (De Ornelas 67), Castellin (Savarese 52), Moran.
Referee: Godoi (Brazil).

Lima, 4 June 2000, 45,000

Peru (0) 0

Brazil (1) 1 *(Antonio Carlos 35)*

Peru: Miranda; Soto, Pajuelo, Olivares, Rebosio, Palacios, Del Solar, Jayo (Searrano 49), Zuniga, Holsen (Ciurlizza 46), Huaman (Maldonado 46).
Brazil: Dida; Cafu, Roberto Carlos, Aldair, Antonio Carlos, Cesar Sampaio, Alex (Denilson 65), Emerson, Edmundo, Rivaldo (Vampeta 90), Franca (Ze Roberto 77).
Referee: Giminez (Argentina).

Rio, 28 June 2000, 47,715

Brazil (0) 1 *(Rivaldo 85 (pen))*

Uruguay (1) 1 *(Dario Silva 6)*

Brazil: Dida; Cafu, Antonio Carlos, Aldair, Roberto Carlos, Emerson, Vampeta (Ze Roberto 70), Rivaldo, Ronaldinho (Guilherme 46), Franca, Savio (Alex 46).
Uruguay: Carini; Tais, Lembo, Montero, Rodriguez, Garcia, O'Neill (Giacomazzi 82), Recoba (Coelho 59), Olivera, Dario Silva, Guigou.
Referee: Acosta (Colombia).

Santiago, 28 June 2000, 60,000

Chile (2) 3 *(Caniza 18 (og), Salas 35, Zamorano 78 (pen))*

Paraguay (0) 1 *(Cardoso 71)*

Chile: Tapia N; Fuentes, Rojas, Reyes, Villarroel, Maldonado, Tello, Estay, Nunez (Pizarro 68), Zamorano, Salas.
Paraguay: Chilavert; Caniza, Zelaya, Ayala, Toledo, Quintana, Struway (Gonzalez 46), Paredes, Acuna (Gabilan 37), Santa Cruz (Cardoso 76), Brizuela.
Referee: Martin (Argentina).

Bogota, 28 June 2000, 50,000

Colombia (1) 1 *(Oviedo 27)*

Argentina (2) 3 *(Batistuta 24, 45, Crespo 75)*

Colombia: Cordoba O; Cordoba I, Bermudez, Yepes, Bolano, Oviedo, Rincon, Dinas (Grisales 51) (Candelo 85), Viveros, Angel, Castillo (Valenciano 58).
Argentina: Bonano; Sensini, Ayala, Samuel, Zanetti, Veron (Lopez G 70), Kily Gonzalez, Ortega (Sorin 86), Simeone, Lopez C, Batistuta (Crespo 70).
Referee: Larrionda (Uruguay).

San Cristobal, 28 June 2000, 7000

Venezuela (2) 4 *(Vitali 23, Moran 38, Savaresse 61, Tortolero 67 (pen))*

Bolivia (0) 2 *(Moreno 49, Baldivieso 59)*

Venezuela: Angelucci; Gimenez, Gonzalez, Alvarado, Martinez, Urdaneta (Echenausi 90), Farias, Tortolero, Vitali, Moran, Savaresse (Galan 72).
Bolivia: Fernandez; Ribera, Etcheverry (Galindo 80), Pena, Sandy, Ivan Castillo, Cristaldo, Sanchez, Baldivieso, Suarez (Garcia 73), Botero (Moreno 46).
Referee: Zambrano (Ecuador).

Quito, 29 June 2000, 45,000

Ecuador (1) 2 *(Chala 16, Hurtado E 51)*

Peru (0) 1 *(Pajuelo 76)*

Ecuador: Cevallos; De La Cruz, Hurtado I, Poroso, Ayovi, Abregon, Blandon, Chala, Aguinaga (Burbano 70), Delgado (Graziani 70), Hurtado E (Kaviedes 74).
Peru: Ibanez; Soto, Rebosio, Pajuelo, Olivares (Zuniga 75), Solano, Del Solar, Jayo (Ciurlizza 75), Serrano (Soria 20), Palacios, Pizarro.
Referee: Simon (Brazil).

Asuncion, 18 July 2000, 36,000

Paraguay (1) 2 *(Paredes 6, Campos 84)*

Brazil (0) 1 *(Rivaldo 75)*

Paraguay: Chilavert; Sarabia, Ayala, Gamarra, Caniza, Gavilan (Quintana 72), Enciso, Acuna, Paredes (Campos 63), Cardozo, Santa Cruz (Avalos 79).
Brazil: Dida; Cafu, Roque Junior, Edmilson, Roberto Carlos, Cesar Sampaio, Flavio Conceicao, Rivaldo, Ze Roberto (Marques 70), Djalminha (Vampeta 60), Franca (Guilherme 46).
Referee: Larrionda (Uruguay).

Montevideo, 18 July 2000, 62,000

Uruguay (1) 3 *(Olivera 29, 89, Rodriguez 52)*

Venezuela (1) 1 *(Noriega 23)*

Uruguay: Carini; Tais, Lembo, Montero (Ramos 81), Rodriguez, O'Neill, Garcia, Olivera, Guigou, Recoba, Dario Silva.
Venezuela: Angelucci; Jimenez, Gonzalez, Alvarado, Martinez, Urdaneta, Farias (Vera 63), Tortolero, Vitali, Savarese (Perez 73), Noriega (Alvarez 63).
Referee: Ortube (Bolivia).

Buenos Aires, 19 July 2000, 50,000
Argentina (1) 2 *(Crespo 23, Lopez C 50)*
Ecuador (0) 0

Argentina: Bonano; Ayala, Sensini, Samuel, Zanetti, Simeone, Kily Gonzalez (Sorin 76), Veron, Ortega, Crespo (Aimar 76), Lopez C.
Ecuador: Cevallos; De La Cruz, Hurtado I, Poroso, Ayovi, Tenorio E, Blandon, Obregon, Aguinaga (Chala 88), Hurtado E, Delgado (Graziani 73).
Referee: Bello (Uruguay).

La Paz, 19 July 2000, 35,000
Bolivia (0) 1 *(Suarez 84)*
Chile (0) 0

Bolivia: Soria; Ribeiro, Pena, Sandy, Carballo (Rimba 38), Galindo (Colque 65), Garcia, Calustro, Baldivieso, Botero (Gutierrez 55), Suarez.
Chile: Tapia N; Villarroel, Reyes, Fuentes, Rojas R, Maldonado, Cornejo, Tello, Estay (Tapia H 69), Zamorano (Navia 84), Rozental (Pizarro 69).
Referee: Toro (Colombia).

Lima, 19 July 2000, 45,000
Peru (0) 0
Colombia (0) 1 *(Angel 48)*

Peru: Vegas; Jorge Soto (Carlos Flores 57), Rebosio, Pajuela, Olivares, Jayo, Solano, Del Solar, Palacios, Pizarro, Zuniga (Lobaton 57).
Colombia: Cordoba O; Martinez, Cordoba I, Yepes, Bolano, Candelo (Hernandez 66), Viveros, Luis Garcia (Dinas 77), Bedoya, Angel, Valenciano (Restrepo 46).
Referee: Sanchez (Chile).

Quito, 25 July 2000, 43,000
Ecuador (0) 0
Colombia (0) 0

Ecuador: Cevallos; De La Cruz, Hurtado I, Poroso, Ayovi, Obregon, Chala (Herrera 68), Aguinaga, Hurtado Ed, Graziani (Delgado 68), Hurtado E (Juarez 76).
Colombia: Cordoba O; Martinez, Cordoba I, Yepes, Bolano, Candelo (Hurtado 46), Viveros, Luis Garcia, Bedoya, Moreno (Restrepo 46), Preciado (Dinas 78).
Referee: Aquino (Paraguay).

San Cristobal, 25 July 2000, 23,000
Venezuela (0) 0
Chile (0) 2 *(Tapia H 69, Zamorano 90)*

Venezuela: Angelucci; Alvarez, Alvarado, Ornella, Martinez, Vitali (Urango 72), Farias, Tortolero, Urdaneta, Moran, Savarese (Perez 85).
Chile: Tapia N; Fuentes, Rojas R, Margas, Rojas F, Maldonado, Tello, Estay (Cornejo 72), Sierra (Pizarro 65), Zamorano, Rozental (Tapia H 46).
Referee: Baldassi (Argentina).

Sao Paulo, 26 July 2000, 80,000
Brazil (2) 3 *(Alex 4, Vampeta 44, 50)*
Argentina (1) 1 *(Almeyda 45)*

Brazil: Dida; Evanilson, Antonio Carlos, Roque Junior, Roberto Carlos, Emerson, Vampeta, Ze Roberto (Marques 60), Alex (Cesar Sampaio 75), Ronaldinho, Rivaldo.
Argentina: Bonano; Sensini, Ayala, Samuel, Zanetti (Almeyda 39), Simeone, Veron, Kily Gonzalez (Sorin 73), Ortega (Lopez G 73), Crespo, Lopez C.
Referee: Mendez (Uruguay).

Montevideo, 26 July 2000, 60,000
Uruguay (0) 0
Peru (0) 0

Uruguay: Carini; Tais, Lembo, Montero, Rodriguez, O'Neill, Garcia, Olivera, Guigou (Zalayeta 56), Recoba (Coelho 69), Magallanes.
Peru: Vegas; Jorge Soto, Rebosio, Pajuelo, Olivares, Serrano (Torres 81), Jayo, Ciurlizza, Solano, Palacios, Pizarro.
Referee: Godoi (Brazil).

La Paz, 27 July 2000, 40,000
Bolivia (0) 0
Paraguay (0) 0

Bolivia: Soria; Ribeiro, Pena, Sandy, Rimba (Paz Garcia 38), Calustro (Cardenas 71), Garcia, Colque, Baldivieso, Botero (Gutierrez 52), Suarez.
Paraguay: Chilavert; Caballero, Ayala, Gamarra, Da Silva, Esteche, Enciso, Acuna (Ortiz 85), Paredes (Struway 55), Gonzalez (Benitez 58), Cardozo.
Referee: Almeida (Brazil).

Santiago, 15 August 2000, 65,000
Chile (2) 3 *(Estay 26, Zamorano 43, Salas 75)*
Brazil (0) 0

Chile: Tapia N; Fuentes, Rojas R, Reyes, Villaseca (Pizarro 13), Rojas F, Galdames, Tello, Estay, Salas (Villarroel 80), Zamorano (Tapia H 87).
Brazil: Dida; Evanilson, Edmilson, Antonio Carlos, Roberto Carlos, Assuncao (Djalminha 46), Emerson, Alex (Marques 61), Ricardinho, Rivaldo, Amoroso (Luizao 46).
Referee: Gonzalez (Paraguay).

Bogota, 15 August 2000, 32,000
Colombia (0) 1 *(Castillo 72)*
Uruguay (0) 0

Colombia: Cordoba O; Martinez, Cordoba I, Yepes, Bedoya, Luis Garcia (Morantes 64), Bolano, Oviedo, Aristizabal (Dinas 88), Angel, Castillo (Restrepo 90).
Uruguay: Carini; Mendez, Lembo, Sorondo, Rodriguez, O'Neill, Garcia, Guigou (Giacomazzi 56), Olivera, Otero (Ruben Da Silva 51), Dario Silva (Magallanes 85).
Referee: Gimenez (Argentina).

Buenos Aires, 16 August 2000, 55,000
Argentina (0) 1 *(Aimar 67)*
Paraguay (0) 1 *(Acuna 61)*

Argentina: Bonano; Sensini, Ayala, Samuel, Veron, Simeone (Vivas 71), Kily Gonzalez (Sorin 46), Aimar, Ortega, Crespo, Lopez C (Saviola 75).
Paraguay: Tavarelli; Sarabia, Ayala, Gamarra, Caniza, Esteche, Struway (Quintana 78), Enciso, Acuna, Santa Cruz (Campos 55), Cardozo (Benitez 85).
Referee: Pereira (Brazil).

Quito, 16 August 2000, 25,000
Ecuador (1) 2 *(Delgado 17, 59)*
Bolivia (0) 0

Ecuador: Ibarra; De La Cruz, Hurtado I, Poroso, Ayovi (Reascos 46), Obregon, Chala, Aguinaga, Ed Hurtado, Graziani (Juarez 62), Delgado.
Bolivia: Soria; Paz, Ribera, Sandy, Arana, Garcia, Calustro (Vaca 76), Castillo S, Galindo, Baldivieso (Coimbra 46), Suarez.
Referee: Solorzano (Venezuela).

Lima, 16 August 2000, 40,000
Peru (0) 1 *(Palacios 70)*
Venezuela (0) 0

Peru: Ibanez; Jorge Soto, Jose Soto, Pajuelo (Marengo 40), Soria, Solano (Maldonado 67), Jayo, Palacios, Del Solar, Pizarro, Zuniga.
Venezuela: Angelucci; Jimenez, Alvarado, Gonzalez, Martinez, Vitali (De Ornelas 82), Farias, Tortolero, Urdaneta, Moran, Savarese (Caceres 71).
Referee; Moreno (Ecuador).

Santiago, 2 September 2000, 60,000
Chile (0) 0
Colombia (0) 1 *(Castillo 66)*

Chile: Tapia N; Fuentes, Rojas R (Contreras 30), Reyes, Rojas F, Galdames, Tello, Estay (Cornejo 63), Sierra (Valencia 63), Zamorano, Salas.
Colombia: Cordoba O; Martinez, Cordoba I, Yepes, Mazziri, Luis Garcia (Viveros 46), Bolano, Grisales, Aristizabal, Castillo (Dinas 86), Angel.
Referee: Gallesio (Uruguay).

Asuncion, 2 September 2000, 40,000

Paraguay (3) 3 *(Gonzalez 30, Cardozo 35, Paredes 44)*
Venezuela (0) 0

Paraguay: Chilavert; Gamarra (Gonzalez 21), Sarabia, Arce, Ayala, Caniza, Enciso, Paredes, Santa Cruz (Caceres 87), Cardozo (Campos 77).
Venezuela: Angelucci; Jimenez, Alvarado, Gonzalez (Rey 46), Martinez, Vitali (Garcia 55), Tortolero (Paez 67), Farias, Urdaneta, De Ornelas, Moran.
Referee: Arandia (Bolivia).

Rio de Janeiro, 3 September 2000, 55,000

Brazil (1) 5 *(Romario 11 (pen), 78, 81, Rivaldo 46, Marques 88)*
Bolivia (0) 0

Brazil: Rogerio; Cafu, Antonio Carlos, Emerson Carvalho, Junior (Athirson 64), Vampeta, Flavio Conceicao, Alex (Juninho 59), Rivaldo, Ronaldinho (Marques 80), Romario.
Bolivia: Soria; Ribeiro, Sanchez O, Paz Garcia (Gutierrez 73), Sandy, Garcia, Baldivieso, Alvarez, Cristaldo, Etcheverry, Moreno (Lider Paz 28).
Referee: Aros (Chile).

Lima, 3 September 2000, 45,000

Peru (0) 1 *(Samuel 69 (og))*
Argentina (2) 2 *(Crespo 25, Veron 38)*

Peru: Vegas; Solano, Pajuelo, Jose Soto, Olivares (Zuniga 78), Pereda, Jayo, Del Solar (Tempone 46), Palacios, Mendoza, Pizarro.
Argentina: Bonano; Sensini, Ayala, Samuel, Veron, Simeone (Vivas 80), Sorin, Aimar, Ortega (Husain 73), Crespo, Lopez C (Lopez G 84).
Referee: Ruiz (Colombia).

Montevideo, 3 September 2000, 60,000

Uruguay (2) 4 *(Magallanes 14, Dario Silva 37, Olivera 55, Cedras 87)*
Ecuador (0) 0

Uruguay: Carini; Tais, Lembo, Rodriguez, Mendez, Garcia (Fleurquin 68), Cedras, Olivera, Guigou, Dario Silva (Recoba 73), Magallanes (Abreu 63).
Ecuador: Cevallos; De La Cruz, Poroso, Hurtado I, Capurro, Tenorio (Burbano 56), Obregon, Chala (Candelario 46), Aguinaga, Juarez, Graziani.
Referee: Jimenez (Colombia).

Bogota, 7 October 2000, 46,000

Colombia (0) 0
Paraguay (1) 2 *(Santa Cruz 4, Chilavert 90)*

Colombia: Cordoba O; Cordoba I, Yepes, Mazziri (Grisales 46), Martinez, Dinas, Bolano, Oviedo (Morantes 59), Aristizabal, Bonilla (Castro 67), Angel.
Paraguay: Chilavert; Arce, Sarabia, Ayala, Da Silva, Struway, Quintana (Alvarengo 66), Paredes, Acuna, Santa Cruz (Yegros 66) (Esteche 90), Cardozo.
Referee: Gallesio (Uruguay).

Buenos Aires, 8 October 2000, 60,000

Argentina (2) 2 *(Gallardo 28, Batistuta 42)*
Uruguay (0) 1 *(Magallanes 48)*

Argentina: Burgos; Vivas, Ayala, Samuel, Sorin, Simeone, Husain, Gallardo (Delgado 80), Kily Gonzalez, Lopez C (Lopez G 73), Batistuta.
Uruguay: Carini; Garcia, Tais, Lembo, Rodriguez, Sorondo, Cedres (Regueiro 65), Olivera, Guigou, Recoba (Abreu 70), Magallanes (Alonso 87).
Referee: Rezende (Brazil).

La Paz, 8 October 2000, 25,000

Bolivia (1) 1 *(Suarez 4)*
Peru (0) 0

Bolivia: Soria; Ribeiro, Sanchez O, Pena, Paz Garcia, Colque, Calustro, Garcia, Vaca (Gutierrez 66), Lider Paz (Moreno 46), Suarez (Galindo 80).
Peru: Ibanez; Zeballos, Rebosio, Pajuelo, Soria, Jayo, Solano (Carmona 46), Bernales, Palacios, Pizarro (Lobaton 57), Zuniga (Alba 57).
Referee: Guevara (Ecuador).

Quito, 8 October 2000, 45,000

Ecuador (0) 1 *(Delgado 76)*
Chile (0) 0

Ecuador: Cevallos; De La Cruz, Espinoza, Hurtado I, Guerron, Obregon, Tenorio (Fernandez 63), Aguinaga, Chala (Sanchez 59), Kaviedes (Ordonez 76), Delgado.
Chile: Tapia N; Alvarez, Contreras, Vargas, Olarra, Pizarro (Valencia 85), Maldonado, Tello, Estay (Rozental 78), Navia (Nunez 46), Zamorano.
Referee: Rendon (Colombia).

San Cristobal, 8 October 2000, 20,000

Venezuela (0) 0
Brazil (5) 6 *(Euller 21, Paulista 29, Romario 31, 36 (pen), 39, 64)*

Venezuela: Angelucci; Gonzalez, Martinez, Rey, Alvarado, Farias, De Ornelas, Jimenez, Echenausi (Arango 46), Moran (Paz 66), Garcia (Savarese 77).
Brazil: Rogerio; Cafu, Antonio Carlos, Cleber, Silvinho, Donizete, Vampeta, Juninho (Ze Roberto 66), Paulista (Ricardinho 81), Euller (Marquez 70), Romario.
Referee: Aquino (Paraguay).

La Paz, 15 November 2000, 29,112

Bolivia (0) 0
Uruguay (0) 0

Bolivia: Soria; Sanchez O, Sandy, Paz Garcia (Vaca 80), Ribeiro, Calustro, Garcia, Sanchez E, Colque, Menacho, Suarez (Lider Paz 66).
Uruguay: Carini; Varela, Lembo, Sorondo, Rodriguez, Garcia, Romero, Coelho (Callejas 64), Regueiro, Magallanes (Dario Silva 56), Franco (Cedres 76).
Referee: Elizondo (Argentina).

Sao Paulo, 15 November 2000, 56,213

Brazil (0) 1 *(Roque Junior 90)*
Colombia (0) 0

Brazil: Rogerio; Cafu, Lucio, Roque Junior, Junior, Cesar Sampaio, Vampeta (Permanbucano 71), Rivaldo, Paulista, Franca (Adriano 79), Edmundo (Marques 67).
Colombia: Calero; Martinez, Dinas, Yepes, Bedoya, Bolano, Serna, Viveros, Aristizabal, Angel (Bonilla 67), Castillo.
Referee: Larrionda (Uruguay).

Santiago, 15 November 2000, 56,529

Chile (0) 0
Argentina (1) 2 *(Ortega 26, Husain 90)*

Chile: Tapia N; Reyes, Rojas R, Contreras (Navia 79), Galdames, Maldonado (Villarroel 74), Rojas F, Pizarro, Estay (Valencia 64), Salas, Zamorano.
Argentina: Burgos (Bonano 74); Vivas, Ayala, Samuel, Almeyda, Husain, Sorin, Veron (Aimar 52), Kily Gonzalez, Cruz (Berizzo 84), Ortega.
Referee: Amarilla (Paraguay).

Asuncion, 15 November 2000, 30,000

Paraguay (3) 5 *(Santa Cruz 15, Del Solar 25 (og), Cardozo 44, Paredes 65, Chilavert 84 (pen))*
Peru (0) 1 *(Garcia 78)*

Paraguay: Chilavert; Arce, Sarabia, Ayala, Caniza, Paredes, Enciso, Acuna, Cardozo (Brizuela 76), Alvarenga (Campos 86), Santa Cruz (Ferreira 70).
Peru: Ibanez; Zevallos (Garcia 60), Pajuelo (Velasquez 16), Rebosio, Soria, Bernales, Del Solar, Pereda (Lobaton 46), Palacios, Muchotrigo, Alva.
Referee: Gimenez (Argentina).

Maracaibo, 15 November 2000, 11,000

Venezuela (0) 1 *(Arango 65)*
Ecuador (2) 2 *(Kaviedes 4, Sanchez 21)*

Venezuela: Angelucci; De Ornelas, Alvarado, Gonzalez, Vallenilla (Perez J 86), Vitali (Luzardo 46), Farias, Urdaneta, Arango, Castellin (Perez G 64), Garcia.
Ecuador: Ceballos; De La Cruz, Poroso, Hurtado I, Guerron, Burbano, Chala, Mendez (Zamora 72), Sanchez, Kaviedes (Fernandez 67), Delgado.
Referee: Betancourt (Peru).

Bogota, 27 March 2001, 45,000

Colombia (0) 2 *(Angel 53, 73 (pen))*

Bolivia (0) 0

Colombia: Cordoba O; Gonzalez, Dinas, Yepes, Bedoya, Serna, Grisales, Aristizabal (Viveros 46), Asprilla, Bonilla (Ferreira 46), Angel (Quintana 84).
Bolivia: Fernandez; Ribeiro, Pena, Sandy, Arana, Colque, Justiniano, Rojas, Vaca, Coimbra (Lider Paz 79), Cardenas (Suarez 57).
Referee: Souza (Brazil).

Lima, 27 March 2001, 45,000

Peru (0) 3 *(Maestri 54, Mendoza 73, Pizarro 81)*

Chile (0) 1 *(Navia 62)*

Peru: Miranda; Solano, Rebosio, Pajuela, Olivares (Hidalgo 42), Jayo, Palacios, Del Solar (Maestri 46), Muchotrigo (Ciurlizza 75), Mendoza, Pizarro.
Chile: Tapia N; Vargas, Rojas, Ramirez, Ponce, Parraguez (Mirosevic 25) (Reyes 65), Maldonado, Osorio, Tello (Tapia H 46), Zamorano, Navia.
Referee: Sanchez (Argentina).

Buenos Aires, 28 March 2001, 32,000

Argentina (2) 5 *(Crespo 13, Sorin 31, Veron 51, Gallardo 60, Samuel 85)*

Venezuela (0) 0

Argentina: Burgos; Vivas, Pochettino, Samuel, Sorin (Zanetti 61), Simeone, Veron, Ortega (Lopez G 70), Kily Gonzalez, Gallardo (Lopez C 76), Crespo.
Venezuela: Dudamel; Alvarado, Rey, Vallenilla (Perez R 86), De Ornelas (Perez G 51), Urdaneta, Vera J (Vitali 74), Vera L, Rojas (Martinez 65), Noriega, Paez.
Referee: Zamora (Peru).

Quito, 28 March 2001, 40,800

Ecuador (0) 1 *(Delgado 49)*

Brazil (0) 0

Ecuador: Cevallos; De La Cruz, Hurtado I, Poroso, Gueron, Tenorio (Sanchez W 69), Burbano, Mendes, Aguinaga, Kaviedes (Obregon 90), Delgado.
Brazil: Rogerio; Belletti, Lucio, Roque Junior, Silvinho (Cesar 59), Emerson, Vampeta, Paulista, Rivaldo (Luizao 64), Ronaldinho (Euller 46), Romario.
Referee: Rizo (Mexico).

Montevideo, 28 March 2001, 60,000

Uruguay (0) 0

Paraguay (0) 1 *(Alvarenga 64)*

Uruguay: Carini; Varela, Sorondo, Montero, Rodriguez, De Los Santos, Fleurquin (O'Neill 69), Olivera, Guigou (Pandiani 49), Dario Silva (Zalayeta 76), Recoba.
Paraguay: Chilavert; Ayala, Gamarra, Sarabia, Quintana (Alvarenga 46), Struway, Paredes, Acuna, Caniza, Caceres (Cuevas 83), Cardozo (Esteche 88).
Referee: Aranda (Spain).

Santiago, 24 April 2001, 51,000

Chile (0) 0

Uruguay (1) 1 *(Diaz 12 (og))*

Chile: Vargas S; Diaz (Valdes 57), Reyes, Contreras, Tello, Maldonado, Galdames, Osorio (Gomez 74), Estay, Tapia H (Nunez 46), Zamorano.
Uruguay: Carini; Mendez, Lembo, Sorondo, Rodriguez, Garcia, Guigou, Olivera (Regueiro 84), Magallanes, Recoba (Romero 72), Dario Silva (Varela 76).
Referee: Elizondo (Argentina).

Quito, 24 April 2001, 40,000

Ecuador (1) 2 *(Delgado 45, 54)*

Paraguay (1) 1 *(Cardozo 26)*

Ecuador: Cevallos; De la Cruz, Hurtado I, Poroso, Guerron, Burbano (Espinoza 46), Chala (Sanchez 68), Aguinaga (Mendez 46), Tenorio, Kaviedes, Delgado.
Paraguay: Tavarelli; Espinola, Gamarra, Ayala, Da Silva (Quintana 73), Esteche, Struway, Paredes, Alvarenga (Gonzalez 62), Quevas (Brizuela 46), Cardozo.
Referee: Sanchez (Argentina).

San Cristobal, 24 April 2001, 35,000

Venezuela (1) 2 *(Rondon 22, Arango 81)*

Colombia (0) 2 *(Bedoya 83, Bonilla 88)*

Venezuela: Dudamel; Valenilla, Vitali RM, Rey, Rojas J, Vera L, Arango, Vitali MM (De Ornelas 61), Urdaneta (Paez 70), Savarese (Vera J 55), Rondon.
Colombia: Calera; Martinez, Bermudez, Dinas, Bedoya, Grisales, Viveros (Quintana 70), Bolano (Gonzalez 61), Restrepo (Ferreira 46), Bonilla, Angel.
Referee: Alvaredo (Chile).

La Paz, 25 April 2001, 35,000

Bolivia (1) 3 *(Lider Paz 41, Colque 55, Botero 81)*

Argentina (1) 3 *(Crespo 44, 89, Sorin 90)*

Bolivia: Fernandez; Ribeiro, Pena, Garcia, Sandy, Colque, Justiniano, Baldivieso, Vaca (Rojas R 59), Lider Paz (Cardenas 74), Botero.
Argentina: Burgos; Vivas, Ayala, Samuel, Zanetti (Ortega 62), Simeone, Veron, Sorin, Aimar (Gallardo 57), Crespo, Lopez G (Lopez C 46).
Referee: Ruiz (Colombia).

Sao Paolo, 25 April 2001, 40,000

Brazil (0) 1 *(Romario 66)*

Peru (0) 1 *(Pajuelo 79)*

Brazil: Rogerio; Alessandro, Edmilson, Lucio, Cesar, Leomar, Vampeta (Washington 80), Ricardinho (Mineiro 77), Marcelinho Carioca (Paulista 46), Ewerthon, Romario.
Peru: Miranda; Rebosio, Pajuelo, Hidalgo, Solano, Jayo, Ciurlizza, Muchotrigo (Mendoza 46), Palacios, Olivares (Tempone 75), Maestri (Pizarro 46).
Referee: Al-Zaid (Saudi Arabia).

Asuncion, 2 June 2001, 45,000

Paraguay (0) 1 *(Paredes 90)*

Chile (0) 0

Paraguay: Chilavert; Arce, Sarabia, Ayala, Caniza, Quintana (Amarilla 77), Paredes, Acuna, Alvarenga, Santa Cruz (Cuevas 66), Brizuela (Julio Gonzalez 46).
Chile: Vargas S; Reyes, Vargas J, Contreras, Pozo, Osorio, Villaseca, Perez (Valenzuela 78), Tello, Montecinos, Navia (Neira 63).
Referee: Badilla (Costa Rica).

Lima, 2 June 2001, 60,000

Peru (1) 1 *(Pizarro 2)*

Ecuador (1) 2 *(Mendez 12, Delgado 90)*

Peru: Miranda; Pajuelo, Rebosio, Olivares (Hidalgo 62), Solano, Jayo, Palacios, Ciurlizza, Mendoza (Muchotrigo 74), Pizarro, Maestri (Roberto Silva 46).
Ecuador: Cevallos; De la Cruz, Hurtado I, Espinosa, Guerron, Obregon (Guagua 71), Tenorio E, Chala (Aguinaga 86), Mendez, Delgado, Kaviedes (Fernandez 81).
Referee: Marrufo (Mexico).

Buenos Aires, 3 June 2001, 40,000

Argentina (3) 3 *(Kily Gonzalez 23, Lopez C 35, Crespo 38)*

Colombia (0) 0

Argentina: Cavallero; Vivas, Ayala, Pochettino, Simeone, Zanetti, Veron (Gallardo 84), Zorin, Kily Gonzalez, Lopez C (Aimar 82), Crespo (Delgado 48).
Colombia: Cordoba O; Martinez, Dinas, Yepes, Bedoya, Serna, Rincon, Viveros (Gonzalez 46), Asprilla F (Ferreira 46), Castillo, Angel (Murillo 77).
Referee: Sanchez (Chile).

La Paz, 3 June 2001, 20,000

Bolivia (3) 5 *(Baldivieso 32, 68, Botero 35, 51, Justiniano 38)*

Venezuela (0) 0

Bolivia: Arias; Raldes, Pena J, Paz Garcia, Ribeiro (Rojas R 85), Justiniano, Baldivieso (Pena D 90), Calustro, Colque, Lider Paz (Cardenas 73), Botero.
Venezuela: Sanhouse; Valenilla, Rey, Vitali RM, Martinez, Vera, Vitali MM, Arango (Casseres 67), Gonzalez (Alvarado 54), Paez (Jimenez 42), Rondon.
Referee: Carpio (Ecuador).

Montevideo, 1 July 2001, 62,000

Uruguay (1) 1 *(Magallanes 32 (pen))*

Brazil (0) 0

Uruguay: Carini; Mendez, Montero, Sorondo, Guigou, De Los Santos, Garcia, Romero, Recoba (Lembo 76), Dario Silva (Reguero 62), Magallanes.

Brazil: Marcos; Cris, Antonio Carlos (Jardel 76), Roque Junior, Cafu, Emerson, Rivaldo, Paulista, Roberto Carlos, Elber (Euller 60), Romario.

Referee: Dallas (Scotland)

Table	P	W	D	L	F	A	Pts
Argentina	13	10	2	1	33	11	32
Paraguay	13	8	2	3	21	11	26
Ecuador	13	8	1	4	17	16	25
Brazil	13	6	3	4	22	12	21
Uruguay	13	6	3	4	14	8	21
Colombia	13	5	4	4	12	12	19
Bolivia	13	3	4	6	13	19	13
Peru	13	3	3	7	12	17	12
Chile	13	3	1	9	12	18	10
Venezuela	13	1	1	11	8	40	4

OCEANIA
(Members 11, Entries 10)

Either one or no team qualifies, play-offs with South America.

Group 1: Australia, Tonga, Fiji, American Samoa, Samoa.

Samoa 0, Tonga 1; Fiji 13, American Samoa 0; Tonga 0, Australia 22; American Samoa 0, Samoa 8; Samoa 1, Fiji 6; Australia 31, American Samoa 0; Fiji 0, Australia 2; American Samoa 0, Tonga 5; Australia 11, Samoa 0; Tonga 1, Fiji 8.

Group 2: New Zealand, Tahiti, Solomon Islands, Vanuatu, Cook Islands.

Vanuatu 1, Tahiti 6; Solomon Islands 9, Cook Islands 1; Tahiti 0, New Zealand 5; Cook Islands 1, Vanuatu 8; Vanuatu 2, Soloman Islands 7; New Zealand 2, Cook Islands 0; Soloman Islands 1, New Zealand 5; Cook Islands 0, Tahiti 6; New Zealand 7, Vanuatu 0; Tahiti 1, Soloman Islands 0.

Final Round, First Leg: New Zealand 0, Australia 2.

Final Round, Second Leg: Australia 4, New Zealand 1.

ASIA
(Members 44, Entries 42)

Four or five teams qualify, including hosts South Korea and Japan plus play-offs with UEFA.

Group 1: Laos, Oman, Philippines, Syria.

Oman 12, Laos 0; Syria 12, Philippines 0; Philippines 1, Syria 5; Laos 0, Oman 7; Oman 7, Philippines 0; Syria 11, Laos 0; Philippines 0, Oman 2; Laos 0, Syria 9; Syria 3, Oman 3; Laos 2, Philippines 0; Oman 2, Syria 0; Philippines 1, Laos 1.

Group 2: Guam, Iran, Tajikistan.

Iran 19, Guam 0; Tajikistan 16, Guam 0; Iran 2, Tajikistan 0.

(all ties played in Iran)

Group 3: Hong Kong, Malaysia, Palestine, Qatar.

Qatar 5, Malaysia 1; Hong Kong 1, Palestine 1; Palestine 1, Qatar 2; Malaysia 2, Hong Kong 0; Palestine 1, Malaysia 0; Qatar 2, Hong Kong 0; Palestine 1, Hong Kong 0; Malaysia 0, Qatar 0; Qatar 2, Palestine 1; Hong Kong 2, Malaysia 1; Hong Kong 0, Qatar 3; Malaysia 4, Palestine 3.

Group 4: Bahrain, Kuwait, Kyrgyzstan, Singapore.

Bahrain 1, Kuwait 2; Singapore 0, Kyrgyzstan 1; Bahrain 1, Kyrgyzstan 0; Kuwait 1, Singapore 1; Kyrgyzstan 0, Kuwait 3; Singapore 1, Bahrain 2; Kyrgyzstan 1, Bahrain 2; Singapore 0, Kuwait 1, Kuwait 1, Kyrgyzstan 0; Bahrain 2, Singapore 0; Kyrgyzstan 1, Singapore 1; Kuwait 0, Bahrain 1.

Group 5: Lebanon, Pakistan, Sri Lanka, Thailand.

Thailand 4, Sri Lanka 2; Lebanon 6, Pakistan 0; Thailand 3, Pakistan 0; Lebanon 4, Sri Lanka 0; Pakistan 3, Sri Lanka 3; Lebanon 1, Thailand 2; Pakistan 1, Lebanon 8; Sri Lanka 0, Thailand 3; Sri Lanka 0, Lebanon 5; Pakistan 0, Thailand 6; Sri Lanka 3, Pakistan 1; Thailand 2, Lebanon 2.

Group 6: Iraq, Kazakhstan, Macao, Nepal.

Nepal 0, Kazakhstan 6; Iraq 8, Macao 0; Kazakhstan 3, Macao 0; Nepal 1, Iraq 9; Nepal 4, Macao 3; Kazakhstan 1, Iraq 1;

Kazakhstan 4, Nepal 0; Macao 0, Iraq 5; Macao 0, Kazakhstan 5; Iraq 4, Nepal 2; Macao 1, Nepal 6; Iraq 1, Kazakhstan 1.

Group 7: Uzbekistan, Jordan, Turkmenistan, Taiwan.

Turkmenistan 2, Jordan 0; Uzbekistan 7, Taiwan 0; Taiwan 0, Jordan 2; Uzbekistan 1, Turkmenistan 0; Taiwan 0, Turkmenistan 5; Uzbekistan 2, Jordan 2; Jordan 6, Taiwan 0; Turkmenistan 0, Uzbekistan 5; Taiwan 0, Uzbekistan 4; Jordan 1, Turkmenistan 2; Turkmenistan 1, Taiwan 0; Jordan 1, Uzbekistan 1.

Group 8: Brunei, India, UAE, Yemen.

Brunei 0, Yemen 5; India 1, UAE 0; Brunei 0, UAE 12; India 1, Yemen 1; UAE 1, India 0; Yemen 1, Brunei 0; Yemen 3, India 3; UAE 4, Brunei 0; Yemen 2, UAE 1; Brunei 0, India 0; UAE 3, Yemen 2; India 5, Brunei 0.

Group 9: Cambodia, China, Indonesia, Maldives.

Maldives 6, Cambodia 0; Indonesia 5, Maldives 0; Cambodia 1, Maldives 1; China 10, Indonesia 6, Cambodia 0; Maldives 0, China 1; Cambodia 0, Indonesia 2; Cambodia 0, China 4; Maldives 0, Indonesia 2; China 5, Indonesia 1; China 3, Cambodia 1; Indonesia 0, China 2.

Group 10: Bangladesh, Mongolia, Saudi Arabia, Vietnam.

Vietnam 0, Bangladesh 0; Saudi Arabia 6, Mongolia 0; Mongolia 0, Vietnam 4; Bangladesh 0, Saudi Arabia 3, Mongolia 0; Bangladesh 3, Saudi Arabia 5, Vietnam 0; Mongolia 0, Saudi Arabia 6; Bangladesh 0, Vietnam 4; Vietnam 4, Mongolia 0; Saudi Arabia 6, Bangladesh 0; Bangladesh 2, Mongolia 2; Vietnam 0, Saudi Arabia 4.

Second Round

Group A: Saudi Arabia, Bahrain, Iraq, Thailand, Iran.

Group B: UAE, Uzbekistan, Qatar, Oman, China.

CONCACAF
(Members 35, Entries 35)

Three teams qualify

Caribbean Zone

First Round

Group 1: Barbados 2, Grenada 2; Grenada 2, Barbados 3; Cuba 4, Cayman Islands 0; Cayman Islands 0, Cuba 0; St Lucia 1, Surinam 0; Surinam 1, St Lucia 0 (Surinam won 3-1 on penalties); Aruba 4, Puerto Rico 2; Puerto Rico 1, Aruba 2.

Group 2: St Vincent & Grenadines 9, US Virgin Islands 0; US Virgin Islands 1, St Vincent & Grenadines 5; British Virgin Islands 1, Bermuda 5; Bermuda 9, British Virgin Islands 0; St Kitts & Nevis 8, Turks & Caicos

Islands 0; Turks & Caicos Islands 0, St Kitts & Nevis 6; Guyana suspended, Antigua and Barbuda w.o.

Group 3: Trinidad & Tobago 5, Netherlands Antilles 0; Netherlands Antilles 1, Trinidad & Tobago 1; Anguilla 1, Bahamas 3; Bahamas 2, Anguilla 1; Dominican Republic 3, Montserrat 0; Montserrat 1, Dominican Republic 3; Haiti 4, Dominica 0; Dominica 1, Haiti 3.

Caribbean Zone

Second Round

Group 1: Cuba 1, Surinam 0; Surinam 0, Cuba 0; Aruba 1, Barbados 3; Barbados 4, Aruba 0.

Group 2: St Vincent & the Grenadines 1, St Kitts &

Nevis 0; St Kitts & Nevis 1, St Vincent & the Grenadines 2; Antigua & Barbuda 0, Bermuda 0; Bermuda 1, Antigua & Barbuda 1.

Group 3: Trinidad & Tobago 3, Dominican Republic 0; Dominican Republic 0, Trinidad & Tobago 1; Haiti 9, Bahamas 0; Bahamas 0, Haiti 4.

Caribbean Zone Finals

Group 1: Cuba 1, Barbados 1, Barbados 1, Cuba 1 *(Barbados won 5-4 on penalties).*

Group 2: Antigua & Barbuda 2, St Vincent & the Grenadines 1; St Vincent & the Grenadines 4, Antigua & Barbuda 0.

Group 3: Trinidad & Tobago 3, Haiti 1; Haiti 1, Trinidad & Tobago 1.

Central American Zone

Group A: El Salvador 5, Belize 0; Belize 1, Guatemala 2; Guatemala 0, El Salvador 1; Belize 1, El Salvador 3; El Salvador 1, Guatemala 1; Guatemala 0, Belize 0.

Group B: Honduras 3, Nicaragua 0; Nicaragua 0, Panama 2; Panama 1, Honduras 0; Nicaragua 0, Honduras 1; Honduras 3, Panama 1; Panama 4, Nicaragua 0

Inter zone round

Group 1: Cuba 0, Canada 1; Canada 0, Cuba 0.

Group 2: Antigua & Barbuda 0, Guatemala 1; Guatemala 8, Antigua & Barbuda 1.

Group 3: Honduras 4, Haiti 0; Haiti 1, Honduras 3.

Semi-Final Round

Costa Rica, Jamaica, Mexico and USA qualified.

Group C: Canada, Mexico, Panama, Trinidad & Tobago. Canada 0, Trinidad & Tobago 2; Panama 0, Mexico 1;

Panama 0, Canada 0; Trinidad & Tobago 1, Mexico 0; Mexico 2, Canada 0; Trinidad & Tobago 6, Panama 0; Mexico 7, Panama 1; Trinidad & Tobago 4, Canada 0; Mexico 7, Trinidad & Tobago 0; Canada 1, Panama 0; Canada 0, Mexico 0; Panama 0, Trinidad & Tobago 1.

Group D: El Salvador, Honduras, Jamaica, St Vincent & the Grenadines.
El Salvador 2, Honduras 5; St Vincent & the Grenadines 0, Jamaica 1; El Salvador 7, St Vincent & the Grenadines 1; Jamaica 3, Honduras 1; Honduras 6, St Vincent & the Grenadines 0; Jamaica 1, El Salvador 0; Honduras 5, El Salvador 0; Jamaica 2, St Vincent & the Grenadines 0; Honduras 1, Jamaica 0; St Vincent & the Grenadines 1, El Salvador 2; St Vincent & the Grenadines 0, Honduras 7; El Salvador 2, Jamaica 0.

Group E: Barbados, Costa Rica, Guatemala, USA.
Barbados 2, Costa Rica 1; Guatemala 1, USA 1; Guatemala 2, Barbados 0; Costa Rica 2, USA 1; Costa Rica 2, Guatemala 1; USA 7, Barbados 0; Costa Rica 3, Barbados 0; USA 1, Guatemala 0; Barbados 1, Guatemala 3; USA 0, Costa Rica 0; Barbados 0, USA 4; Guatemala 2, Costa Rica 1.

Play-Off: Costa Rica 5, Guatemala 0.

Final Round: Costa Rica, Honduras, Jamaica, Mexico, Trinidad & Tobago, USA.
USA 2, Mexico 0; Jamaica 1, Trinidad & Tobago 0; Costa Rica 2, Honduras 2; Mexico 4, Jamaica 0; Costa Rica 3, Trinidad & Tobago 0; Honduras 1, USA 2; Jamaica 1, Honduras 1; Trinidad & Tobago 1, Mexico 1; USA 1, Costa Rica 0; Mexico 1, Costa Rica 2; Trinidad & Tobago 2, Honduras 4; Jamaica 0, USA 0; USA 2, Trinidad & Tobago 0; Honduras 3, Mexico 1; Costa Rica 2, Jamaica 1; Trinidad & Tobago 1, Jamaica 2; Mexico 1, USA 0; Honduras 2, Costa Rica 3.

AFRICA
(Members 52, Entries 50)

Five teams qualify

First Round

Group A: Mauritania 1, Tunisia 2; Tunisia 3, Mauritania 0; Guinea Bissau 0, Togo 0; Togo 3, Guinea Bissau 0; Benin 1, Senegal 1; Senegal 1, Benin 0; Cape Verde Islands 0, Algeria 0; Algeria 2, Cape Verde Islands 0; Gambia 0, Morocco 1; Morocco 2, Gambia 0.

Group B: Botswana 0, Zambia 1; Zambia 1, Botswana 0; Madagascar 2, Gabon 0; Gabon 1, Madagascar 0; Lesotho 0, South Africa 2; South Africa 1, Lesotho 0; Sudan 1, Mozambique 0; Mozambique 2, Sudan 1; Swaziland 0, Angola 1; Angola 7, Swaziland 1.

Group C: Sao Tome e Principe 2, Sierra Leone 0; Sierra Leone 4, Sao Tome e Principe 0; Central African Republic 0, Zimbabwe 1; Zimbabwe 3, Central African Republic 1; Equatorial Guinea 1, Congo 3; Congo 2, Equatorial Guinea 1; Libya 3, Mali 0; Mali 3, Libya 1; Rwanda 2, Ivory Coast 2; Ivory Coast 2, Rwanda 0.

Group D: Djibouti 0, Congo DR 1; Congo DR 9, Djibouti 1; Seychelles 1, Namibia 1; Namibia 3, Seychelles 0; Eritrea 0, Nigeria 0; Nigeria 4, Eritrea 0; Mauritius 0, Egypt 2; Egypt 4, Mauritius 0; Somalia 0, Cameroon 3; Cameroon 3, Somalia 0.

Group E: Malawi 2, Kenya 0; Kenya v Malawi abandoned 0-0 after 88 minutes; result stands; Tanzania 0, Ghana 1; Ghana 3, Tanzania 2; Uganda 4, Guinea 4; Guinea 3, Uganda 0; Chad 0, Liberia 1; Liberia 0, Chad 0; Ethiopia 2, Burkina Faso 1; Burkina Faso 3, Ethiopia 0.

Second Round

Group A: Angola, Cameroon, Libya, Togo, Zambia.
Angola 2, Zambia 1; Libya 0, Cameroon 3; Zambia 2, Togo 0; Cameroon 3, Angola 0; Angola 3, Libya 1; Togo 0, Cameroon 2; Libya 3, Togo 3; Zambia 0; Zambia 2, Libya 0; Togo 1, Angola 1; Zambia 1, Angola 1; Cameroon 1, Libya 0; Togo 3, Zambia 2; Angola 2,

Cameroon 0; Libya 1, Angola 1; Cameroon 2, Togo 0.

Group B: Ghana, Liberia, Nigeria, Sierra Leone, Sudan.
Nigeria 2, Sierra Leone 0; Sudan 2, Liberia 0; Ghana 5, Sierra Leone 0; Liberia 2, Nigeria 1; Nigeria 3, Sudan 0; Ghana 1, Liberia 3; Sudan 1, Ghana 0; Liberia 1, Sierra Leone 0; Sierra Leone 0, Sudan 2; Ghana 0, Nigeria 0; Sierra Leone 1, Nigeria 0; Liberia 2, Sudan 0; Sierra Leone 1, Ghana 1; Nigeria 2, Liberia 0; Sudan 0, Nigeria 4; Liberia 1, Ghana 2.

Group C: Algeria, Egypt, Morocco, Namibia, Senegal.
Algeria 1, Senegal 1; Namibia 0, Morocco 0; Algeria 1; Senegal 0, Egypt 0; Algeria 1, Namibia 0; Egypt 0, Morocco 0; Namibia 1, Egypt 1; Morocco 0, Senegal 0; Senegal 4, Namibia 0; Egypt 5, Algeria 2; Senegal 3, Algeria 0; Morocco 3, Namibia 0; Algeria 1, Morocco 2; Egypt 1, Senegal 0; Morocco 1, Egypt 0; Namibia 0, Algeria 4.

Group D: Congo, Congo DR, Ivory Coast, Madagascar, Tunisia.
Ivory Coast 2, Tunisia 2; Madagascar 3, Congo DR 0; Tunisia 1, Madagascar 0; Congo DR 2, Congo 0; Congo 1, Tunisia 2; Madagascar 1, Ivory Coast 3; Tunisia 6, Congo DR 0; Congo DR 1, Ivory Coast 2; Congo DR 1, Madagascar 0; Ivory Coast 2, Congo 0; Congo 2, Madagascar 0; Madagascar 0, Tunisia 2; Congo 1, Congo DR 1; Tunisia 1, Ivory Coast 1; Tunisia 6, Cogo 0; Ivory Coast 6, Madagascar 0.

Group E: Burkina Faso, Guinea*, Malawi, South Africa, Zimbabwe.
Malawi 1, Burkina Faso 1; Guinea 3, Zimbabwe 0; Burkina Faso 2, Guinea 3; Zimbabwe 0, South Africa 2 (abandoned 82 minutes; result stands); South Africa 1, Burkina Faso 0; Guinea 1, Malawi 1; Burkina Faso 1, Zimbabwe 2; Malawi 1, South Africa 2; Zimbabwe 2, Malawi 0; Burkina Faso 4, Malawi 2; South Africa 2, Zimbabwe 1; Burkina Faso 1, South Africa 1.
*Guinea subsequently suspended.

FIFA WORLD CUP 2002 REMAINING FIXTURES

EUROPE

Group 1
Yugoslavia v Faeroes
01.09.01 Faeroes v Luxembourg
01.09.01 Switzerland v Yugoslavia
01.09.01 Slovenia v Russia
05.09.01 Yugoslavia v Slovenia
05.09.01 Faeroes v Russia
05.09.01 Luxembourg v Switzerland
06.10.01 Russia v Switzerland
06.10.01 Slovenia v Faeroes
06.10.01 Yugoslavia v Luxembourg

Group 2
15.08.01 Estonia v Cyprus
01.09.01 Republic of Ireland v Holland
01.09.01 Andorra v Portugal
05.09.01 Holland v Estonia
05.09.01 Cyprus v Portugal
06.10.01 Republic of Ireland v Cyprus
06.10.01 Holland v Andorra
06.10.01 Portugal v Estonia

Group 3
01.09.01 Denmark v Northern Ireland
01.09.01 Malta v Bulgaria
01.09.01 Iceland v Czech Republic
05.09.01 Northern Ireland v Iceland
05.09.01 Czech Republic v Malta
05.09.01 Bulgaria v Denmark
06.10.01 Czech Republic v Bulgaria
06.10.01 Malta v Northern Ireland
06.10.01 Denmark v Iceland

Group 4
01.09.01 Moldova v Azerbaijan
01.09.01 Slovakia v Turkey
01.09.01 Macedonia v Sweden
05.09.01 Turkey v Sweden
05.09.01 Azerbaijan v Macedonia
05.09.01 Slovakia v Moldova
07.10.01 Sweden v Azerbaijan
07.10.01 Moldova v Turkey
07.10.01 Macedonia v Slovakia

Group 5
01.09.01 Wales v Armenia
01.09.01 Belarus v Ukraine
01.09.01 Poland v Norway
04.09.01 Norway v Wales
04.09.01 Belarus v Poland
04.09.01 Ukraine v Armenia
06.10.01 Armenia v Norway
06.10.01 Poland v Ukraine
06.10.01 Wales v Belarus

Group 6
01.09.01 Scotland v Croatia
05.09.01 Belgium v Scotland
05.09.01 San Marino v Croatia
06.10.01 Scotland v Latvia
06.10.01 Croatia v Belgium

Group 7
01.09.01 Spain v Austria
01.09.01 Bosnia v Israel
05.09.01 Liechtenstein v Spain
05.09.01 Austria v Bosnia
07.10.01 Bosnia v Liechtenstein
07.10.01 Israel v Austria

Group 8
01.09.01 Lithuania v Italy
01.09.01 Georgia v Hungary
05.09.01 Georgia v Lithuania
05.09.01 Hungary v Romania
06.10.01 Romania v Georgia
06.10.01 Italy v Hungary

Group 9
01.09.01 Albania v Finland
01.09.01 Germany v England
05.09.01 Finland v Greece
05.09.01 England v Albania
06.10.01 Germany v Finland
06.10.01 England v Greece

SOUTH AMERICA

14.08.01 Venezuela v Uruguay
14.08.01 Chile v Bolivia
15.08.01 Colombia v Peru
15.08.01 Brazil v Paraguay
15.08.01 Ecuador v Argentina
04.09.01 Peru v Uruguay
04.09.01 Chile v Venezuela
05.09.01 Argentina v Brazil
05.09.01 Colombia v Ecuador
05.09.01 Paraguay v Bolivia
06.10.01 Venezuela v Peru
06.10.01 Brazil v Chile
06.10.01 Paraguay v Argentina

06.10.01 Bolivia v Ecuador
06.10.01 Uruguay v Colombia
07.11.01 Venezuela v Paraguay
07.11.01 Colombia v Chile
07.11.01 Ecuador v Uruguay
07.11.01 Argentina v Peru
07.11.01 Bolivia v Brazil
14.11.01 Chile v Ecuador
14.11.01 Peru v Bolivia
14.11.01 Uruguay v Argentina
14.11.01 Paraguay v Colombia
14.11.01 Brazil v Venezuela

BRITISH AND IRISH INTERNATIONAL RESULTS 1872–2001

Note: In the results that follow, WC=World Cup, EC=European Championship, UI=Umbro International Trophy. TF = Tournoi de France. For Ireland, read Northern Ireland from 1921.

ENGLAND v SCOTLAND

Played: 110; England won 45, Scotland won 41, Drawn 24. *Goals:* England 192, Scotland 169.

Year	Date	Venue	E	S	Year	Date	Venue	E	S
1872	30 Nov	Glasgow	0	0	1932	9 Apr	Wembley	3	0
1873	8 Mar	Kennington Oval	4	2	1933	1 Apr	Glasgow	1	2
1874	7 Mar	Glasgow	1	2	1934	14 Apr	Wembley	3	0
1875	6 Mar	Kennington Oval	2	2	1935	6 Apr	Glasgow	0	2
1876	4 Mar	Glasgow	0	3	1936	4 Apr	Wembley	1	1
1877	3 Mar	Kennington Oval	1	3	1937	17 Apr	Glasgow	1	3
1878	2 Mar	Glasgow	2	7	1938	9 Apr	Wembley	0	1
1879	5 Apr	Kennington Oval	5	4	1939	15 Apr	Glasgow	2	1
1880	13 Mar	Glasgow	4	5	1947	12 Apr	Wembley	1	1
1881	12 Mar	Kennington Oval	1	6	1948	10 Apr	Glasgow	2	0
1882	11 Mar	Glasgow	1	5	1949	9 Apr	Wembley	1	3
1883	10 Mar	Sheffield	2	3	WC1950	15 Apr	Glasgow	1	0
1884	15 Mar	Glasgow	0	1	1951	14 Apr	Wembley	2	3
1885	21 Mar	Kennington Oval	1	1	1952	5 Apr	Glasgow	2	1
1886	31 Mar	Glasgow	1	1	1953	18 Apr	Wembley	2	2
1887	19 Mar	Blackburn	2	3	WC1954	3 Apr	Glasgow	4	2
1888	17 Mar	Glasgow	5	0	1955	2 Apr	Wembley	7	2
1889	13 Apr	Kennington Oval	2	3	1956	14 Apr	Glasgow	1	1
1890	5 Apr	Glasgow	1	1	1957	6 Apr	Wembley	2	1
1891	6 Apr	Blackburn	2	1	1958	19 Apr	Glasgow	4	0
1892	2 Apr	Glasgow	4	1	1959	11 Apr	Wembley	1	0
1893	1 Apr	Richmond	5	2	1960	9 Apr	Glasgow	1	1
1894	7 Apr	Glasgow	2	2	1961	15 Apr	Wembley	9	3
1895	6 Apr	Everton	3	0	1962	14 Apr	Glasgow	0	2
1896	4 Apr	Glasgow	1	2	1963	6 Apr	Wembley	1	2
1897	3 Apr	Crystal Palace	1	2	1964	11 Apr	Glasgow	0	1
1898	2 Apr	Glasgow	3	1	1965	10 Apr	Wembley	2	2
1899	8 Apr	Birmingham	2	1	1966	2 Apr	Glasgow	4	3
1900	7 Apr	Glasgow	1	4	EC1967	15 Apr	Wembley	2	3
1901	30 Mar	Crystal Palace	2	2	EC1968	24 Jan	Glasgow	1	1
1902	3 Mar	Birmingham	2	2	1969	10 May	Wembley	4	1
1903	4 Apr	Sheffield	1	2	1970	25 Apr	Glasgow	0	0
1904	9 Apr	Glasgow	1	0	1971	22 May	Wembley	3	1
1905	1 Apr	Crystal Palace	1	0	1972	27 May	Glasgow	1	0
1906	7 Apr	Glasgow	1	2	1973	14 Feb	Glasgow	5	0
1907	6 Apr	Newcastle	1	1	1973	19 May	Wembley	1	0
1908	4 Apr	Glasgow	1	1	1974	18 May	Glasgow	0	2
1909	3 Apr	Crystal Palace	2	0	1975	24 May	Wembley	5	1
1910	2 Apr	Glasgow	0	2	1976	15 May	Glasgow	1	2
1911	1 Apr	Everton	1	1	1977	4 June	Wembley	1	2
1912	23 Mar	Glasgow	1	1	1978	20 May	Glasgow	1	0
1913	5 Apr	Chelsea	1	0	1979	26 May	Wembley	3	1
1914	14 Apr	Glasgow	1	3	1980	24 May	Glasgow	2	0
1920	10 Apr	Sheffield	5	4	1981	23 May	Wembley	0	1
1921	9 Apr	Glasgow	0	3	1982	29 May	Glasgow	1	0
1922	8 Apr	Aston Villa	0	1	1983	1 June	Wembley	2	0
1923	14 Apr	Glasgow	2	2	1984	26 May	Glasgow	1	1
1924	12 Apr	Wembley	1	1	1985	25 May	Glasgow	0	1
1925	4 Apr	Glasgow	0	2	1986	23 Apr	Wembley	2	1
1926	17 Apr	Manchester	0	1	1987	23 May	Glasgow	0	0
1927	2 Apr	Glasgow	2	1	1988	21 May	Wembley	1	0
1928	31 Mar	Wembley	1	5	1989	27 May	Glasgow	2	0
1929	13 Apr	Glasgow	0	1	EC1996	15 June	Wembley	2	0
1930	5 Apr	Wembley	5	2	EC1999	13 Nov	Glasgow	2	0
1931	28 Mar	Glasgow	0	2	EC1999	17 Nov	Wembley	0	1

ENGLAND v WALES

Played: 97; England won 62, Wales won 14, Drawn 21. *Goals:* England 239, Wales 90.

Year	Date	Venue	E	W	Year	Date	Venue	E	W
1879	18 Jan	Kennington Oval	2	1	1882	13 Mar	Wrexham	3	5
1880	15 Mar	Wrexham	3	2	1883	3 Feb	Kennington Oval	5	0
1881	26 Feb	Blackburn	0	1	1884	17 Mar	Wrexham	4	0

			E	W
1885	14 Mar	Blackburn	1	1
1886	29 Mar	Wrexham	3	1
1887	26 Feb	Kennington Oval	4	0
1888	4 Feb	Crewe	5	1
1889	23 Feb	Stoke	4	1
1890	15 Mar	Wrexham	3	1
1891	7 May	Sunderland	4	1
1892	5 Mar	Wrexham	2	0
1893	13 Mar	Stoke	6	0
1894	12 Mar	Wrexham	5	1
1895	18 Mar	Queen's Club, Kensington	1	1
1896	16 Mar	Cardiff	9	1
1897	29 Mar	Sheffield	4	0
1898	28 Mar	Wrexham	3	0
1899	20 Mar	Bristol	4	0
1900	26 Mar	Cardiff	1	1
1901	18 Mar	Newcastle	6	0
1902	3 Mar	Wrexham	0	0
1903	2 Mar	Portsmouth	2	1
1904	29 Feb	Wrexham	2	2
1905	27 Mar	Liverpool	3	1
1906	19 Mar	Cardiff	1	0
1907	18 Mar	Fulham	1	1
1908	16 Mar	Wrexham	7	1
1909	15 Mar	Nottingham	2	0
1910	14 Mar	Cardiff	1	0
1911	13 Mar	Millwall	3	0
1912	11 Mar	Wrexham	2	0
1913	17 Mar	Bristol	4	3
1914	16 Mar	Cardiff	2	0
1920	15 Mar	Highbury	1	2
1921	14 Mar	Cardiff	0	0
1922	13 Mar	Liverpool	1	0
1923	5 Mar	Cardiff	2	2
1924	3 Mar	Blackburn	1	2
1925	28 Feb	Swansea	2	1
1926	1 Mar	Crystal Palace	1	3
1927	12 Feb	Wrexham	3	3
1927	28 Nov	Burnley	1	2
1928	17 Nov	Swansea	3	2
1929	20 Nov	Chelsea	6	0
1930	22 Nov	Wrexham	4	0
1931	18 Nov	Liverpool	3	1
1932	16 Nov	Wrexham	0	0
1933	15 Nov	Newcastle	1	2
1934	29 Sept	Cardiff	4	0
1936	5 Feb	Wolverhampton	1	2
1936	17 Oct	Cardiff	1	2
1937	17 Nov	Middlesbrough	2	1
1938	22 Oct	Cardiff	2	4
1946	13 Nov	Manchester	3	0
1947	18 Oct	Cardiff	3	0
1948	10 Nov	Aston Villa	1	0
wc1949	15 Oct	Cardiff	4	1
1950	15 Nov	Sunderland	4	2
1951	20 Oct	Cardiff	1	1
1952	12 Nov	Wembley	5	2
wc1953	10 Oct	Cardiff	4	1
1954	10 Nov	Wembley	3	2
1955	27 Oct	Cardiff	1	2
1956	14 Nov	Wembley	3	1
1957	19 Oct	Cardiff	4	0
1958	26 Nov	Aston Villa	2	2
1959	17 Oct	Cardiff	1	1
1960	23 Nov	Wembley	5	1
1961	14 Oct	Cardiff	1	1
1962	21 Oct	Wembley	4	0
1963	12 Oct	Cardiff	4	0
1964	18 Nov	Wembley	2	1
1965	2 Oct	Cardiff	0	0
EC1966	16 Nov	Wembley	5	1
EC1967	21 Oct	Cardiff	3	0
1969	7 May	Wembley	2	1
1970	18 Apr	Cardiff	1	1
1971	19 May	Wembley	0	0
1972	20 May	Cardiff	3	0
wc1972	15 Nov	Cardiff	1	0
wc1973	24 Jan	Wembley	1	1
1973	15 May	Wembley	3	0
1974	11 May	Cardiff	2	0
1975	21 May	Wembley	2	2
1976	24 Mar	Wrexham	2	1
1976	8 May	Cardiff	1	0
1977	31 May	Wembley	0	1
1978	3 May	Cardiff	3	1
1979	23 May	Wembley	0	0
1980	17 May	Wrexham	1	4
1981	20 May	Wembley	0	0
1982	27 Apr	Cardiff	1	0
1983	23 Feb	Wembley	2	1
1984	2 May	Wrexham	0	1

ENGLAND v IRELAND

Played: 96; England won 74, Ireland won 6, Drawn 16. *Goals:* England 319, Ireland 80.

			E	I
1882	18 Feb	Belfast	13	0
1883	24 Feb	Liverpool	7	0
1884	23 Feb	Belfast	8	1
1885	28 Feb	Manchester	4	0
1886	13 Mar	Belfast	6	1
1887	5 Feb	Sheffield	7	0
1888	31 Mar	Belfast	5	1
1889	2 Mar	Everton	6	1
1890	15 Mar	Belfast	9	1
1891	7 Mar	Wolverhampton	6	1
1892	5 Mar	Belfast	2	0
1893	25 Feb	Birmingham	6	1
1894	3 Mar	Belfast	2	2
1895	9 Mar	Derby	9	0
1896	7 Mar	Belfast	2	0
1897	20 Feb	Nottingham	6	0
1898	5 Mar	Belfast	3	2
1899	18 Feb	Sunderland	13	2
1900	17 Mar	Dublin	2	0
1901	9 Mar	Southampton	3	0
1902	22 Mar	Belfast	1	0
1903	14 Feb	Wolverhampton	4	0
1904	12 Mar	Belfast	3	1
1905	25 Feb	Middlesbrough	1	1
1906	17 Feb	Belfast	5	0
1907	16 Feb	Everton	1	0
1908	15 Feb	Belfast	3	1
1909	13 Feb	Bradford	4	0
1910	12 Feb	Belfast	1	1
1911	11 Feb	Derby	2	1
1912	10 Feb	Dublin	6	1
1913	15 Feb	Belfast	1	2
1914	14 Feb	Middlesbrough	0	3
1919	25 Oct	Belfast	1	1
1920	23 Oct	Sunderland	2	0
1921	22 Oct	Belfast	1	1
1922	21 Oct	West Bromwich	2	0
1923	20 Oct	Belfast	1	2
1924	22 Oct	Everton	3	1
1925	24 Oct	Belfast	0	0
1926	20 Oct	Liverpool	3	3
1927	22 Oct	Belfast	0	2

			E	I					E	I
1928	22 Oct	Everton	2	1		1962	20 Oct	Belfast	3	1
1929	19 Oct	Belfast	3	0		1963	20 Nov	Wembley	8	3
1930	20 Oct	Sheffield	5	1		1964	3 Oct	Belfast	4	3
1931	17 Oct	Belfast	6	2		1965	10 Nov	Wembley	2	1
1932	17 Oct	Blackpool	1	0		EC1966	20 Oct	Belfast	2	0
1933	14 Oct	Belfast	3	0		EC1967	22 Nov	Wembley	2	0
1935	6 Feb	Everton	2	1		1969	3 May	Belfast	3	1
1935	19 Oct	Belfast	3	1		1970	21 Apr	Wembley	3	1
1936	18 Nov	Stoke	3	1		1971	15 May	Belfast	1	0
1937	23 Oct	Belfast	5	1		1972	23 May	Wembley	0	1
1938	16 Nov	Manchester	7	0		1973	12 May	Everton	2	1
1946	28 Sept	Belfast	7	2		1974	15 May	Wembley	1	0
1947	5 Nov	Everton	2	2		1975	17 May	Belfast	0	0
1948	9 Oct	Belfast	6	2		1976	11 May	Wembley	4	0
wc1949	16 Nov	Manchester	9	2		1977	28 May	Belfast	2	1
1950	7 Oct	Belfast	4	1		1978	16 May	Wembley	1	0
1951	14 Nov	Aston Villa	2	0		EC1979	7 Feb	Wembley	4	0
1952	4 Oct	Belfast	2	2		1979	19 May	Belfast	2	0
wc1953	11 Nov	Everton	3	1		EC1979	17 Oct	Belfast	5	1
1954	2 Oct	Belfast	2	0		1980	20 May	Wembley	1	1
1955	2 Nov	Wembley	3	0		1982	23 Feb	Wembley	4	0
1956	10 Oct	Belfast	1	1		1983	28 May	Belfast	0	0
1957	6 Nov	Wembley	2	3		1984	24 Apr	Wembley	1	0
1958	4 Oct	Belfast	3	3		wc1985	27 Feb	Belfast	1	0
1959	18 Nov	Wembley	2	1		wc1985	13 Nov	Wembley	0	0
1960	8 Oct	Belfast	5	2		EC1986	15 Oct	Wembley	3	0
1961	22 Nov	Wembley	1	1		EC1987	1 Apr	Belfast	2	0

SCOTLAND v WALES

Played: 102; Scotland won 60, Wales won 19, Drawn 23. *Goals:* Scotland 238, Wales 112.

			S	W					S	W
1876	25 Mar	Glasgow	4	0		1921	12 Feb	Aberdeen	2	1
1877	5 Mar	Wrexham	2	0		1922	4 Feb	Wrexham	1	2
1878	23 Mar	Glasgow	9	0		1923	17 Mar	Paisley	2	0
1879	7 Apr	Wrexham	3	0		1924	16 Feb	Cardiff	0	2
1880	3 Apr	Glasgow	5	1		1925	14 Feb	Tynecastle	3	1
1881	14 Mar	Wrexham	5	1		1925	31 Oct	Cardiff	3	0
1882	25 Mar	Glasgow	5	0		1926	30 Oct	Glasgow	3	0
1883	12 Mar	Wrexham	3	0		1927	29 Oct	Wrexham	2	2
1884	29 Mar	Glasgow	4	1		1928	27 Oct	Glasgow	4	2
1885	23 Mar	Wrexham	8	1		1929	26 Oct	Cardiff	4	2
1886	10 Apr	Glasgow	4	1		1930	25 Oct	Glasgow	1	1
1887	21 Mar	Wrexham	2	0		1931	31 Oct	Wrexham	3	2
1888	10 Mar	Edinburgh	5	1		1932	26 Oct	Edinburgh	2	5
1889	15 Apr	Wrexham	0	0		1933	4 Oct	Cardiff	2	3
1890	22 Mar	Paisley	5	0		1934	21 Nov	Aberdeen	3	2
1891	21 Mar	Wrexham	4	3		1935	5 Oct	Cardiff	1	1
1892	26 Mar	Edinburgh	6	1		1936	2 Dec	Dundee	1	2
1893	18 Mar	Wrexham	8	0		1937	30 Oct	Cardiff	1	2
1894	24 Mar	Kilmarnock	5	2		1938	9 Nov	Edinburgh	3	2
1895	23 Mar	Wrexham	2	2		1946	19 Oct	Wrexham	1	3
1896	21 Mar	Dundee	4	0		1947	12 Nov	Glasgow	1	2
1897	20 Mar	Wrexham	2	2		wc1948	23 Oct	Cardiff	3	1
1898	19 Mar	Motherwell	5	2		1949	9 Nov	Glasgow	2	0
1899	18 Mar	Wrexham	6	0		1950	21 Oct	Cardiff	3	1
1900	3 Feb	Aberdeen	5	2		1951	14 Nov	Glasgow	0	1
1901	2 Mar	Wrexham	1	1		wc1952	18 Oct	Cardiff	2	1
1902	15 Mar	Greenock	5	1		1953	4 Nov	Glasgow	3	3
1903	9 Mar	Cardiff	1	0		1954	16 Oct	Cardiff	1	0
1904	12 Mar	Dundee	1	1		1955	9 Nov	Glasgow	2	0
1905	6 Mar	Wrexham	1	3		1956	20 Oct	Cardiff	2	2
1906	3 Mar	Edinburgh	0	2		1957	13 Nov	Glasgow	1	1
1907	4 Mar	Wrexham	0	1		1958	18 Oct	Cardiff	3	0
1908	7 Mar	Dundee	2	1		1959	4 Nov	Glasgow	1	1
1909	1 Mar	Wrexham	2	3		1960	20 Oct	Cardiff	0	2
1910	5 Mar	Kilmarnock	1	0		1961	8 Nov	Cardiff	2	0
1911	6 Mar	Cardiff	2	2		1962	20 Oct	Cardiff	3	2
1912	2 Mar	Tynecastle	1	0		1963	20 Nov	Glasgow	2	1
1913	3 Mar	Wrexham	0	0		1964	3 Oct	Cardiff	2	3
1914	28 Feb	Glasgow	0	0		EC1965	24 Nov	Glasgow	4	1
1920	26 Feb	Cardiff	1	1		EC1966	22 Oct	Cardiff	1	1

Year	Date	Venue	S	W		Year	Date	Venue	S	W
1967	22 Nov	Glasgow	3	2		wc1977	12 Oct	Liverpool	2	0
1969	3 May	Wrexham	5	3		1978	17 May	Glasgow	1	1
1970	22 Apr	Glasgow	0	0		1979	19 May	Cardiff	0	3
1971	15 May	Cardiff	0	0		1980	21 May	Glasgow	1	0
1972	24 May	Glasgow	1	0		1981	16 May	Swansea	0	2
1973	12 May	Wrexham	2	0		1982	24 May	Glasgow	1	0
1974	14 May	Glasgow	2	0		1983	28 May	Cardiff	2	0
1975	17 May	Cardiff	2	2		1984	28 Feb	Glasgow	2	1
1976	6 May	Glasgow	3	1		wc1985	27 Mar	Glasgow	0	1
wc1976	17 Nov	Glasgow	1	0		wc1985	10 Sept	Cardiff	1	1
1977	28 May	Wrexham	0	0		1997	27 May	Kilmarnock	0	1

SCOTLAND v IRELAND

Played: 92; Scotland won 61, Ireland won 15, Drawn 16. *Goals:* Scotland 254, Ireland 81.

Year	Date	Venue	S	I		Year	Date	Venue	S	I
1884	26 Jan	Belfast	5	0		1934	20 Oct	Belfast	1	2
1885	14 Mar	Glasgow	8	2		1935	13 Nov	Edinburgh	2	1
1886	20 Mar	Belfast	7	2		1936	31 Oct	Belfast	3	1
1887	19 Feb	Glasgow	4	1		1937	10 Nov	Aberdeen	1	1
1888	24 Mar	Belfast	10	2		1938	8 Oct	Belfast	2	0
1889	9 Mar	Glasgow	7	0		1946	27 Nov	Glasgow	0	0
1890	29 Mar	Belfast	4	1		1947	4 Oct	Belfast	0	2
1891	28 Mar	Glasgow	2	1		1948	17 Nov	Glasgow	3	2
1892	19 Mar	Belfast	3	2		1949	1 Oct	Belfast	8	2
1893	25 Mar	Glasgow	6	1		1950	1 Nov	Glasgow	6	1
1894	31 Mar	Belfast	2	1		1951	6 Oct	Belfast	3	0
1895	30 Mar	Glasgow	3	1		1952	5 Nov	Glasgow	1	1
1896	28 Mar	Belfast	3	3		1953	3 Oct	Belfast	3	1
1897	27 Mar	Glasgow	5	1		1954	3 Nov	Glasgow	2	2
1898	26 Mar	Belfast	3	0		1955	8 Oct	Belfast	1	2
1899	25 Mar	Glasgow	9	1		1956	7 Nov	Glasgow	1	0
1900	3 Mar	Belfast	3	0		1957	5 Oct	Belfast	1	1
1901	23 Feb	Glasgow	11	0		1958	5 Nov	Glasgow	2	2
1902	1 Mar	Belfast	5	1		1959	3 Oct	Belfast	4	0
1903	21 Mar	Glasgow	0	2		1960	9 Nov	Glasgow	5	2
1904	26 Mar	Dublin	1	1		1961	7 Oct	Belfast	6	1
1905	18 Mar	Glasgow	4	0		1962	7 Nov	Glasgow	5	1
1906	17 Mar	Dublin	1	0		1963	12 Oct	Belfast	1	2
1907	16 Mar	Glasgow	3	0		1964	25 Nov	Glasgow	3	2
1908	14 Mar	Dublin	5	0		1965	2 Oct	Belfast	2	3
1909	15 Mar	Glasgow	5	0		1966	16 Nov	Glasgow	2	1
1910	19 Mar	Belfast	0	1		1967	21 Oct	Belfast	0	1
1911	18 Mar	Glasgow	2	0		1969	6 May	Glasgow	1	1
1912	16 Mar	Belfast	4	1		1970	18 Apr	Belfast	1	0
1913	15 Mar	Dublin	2	1		1971	18 May	Glasgow	0	1
1914	14 Mar	Belfast	1	1		1972	20 May	Glasgow	2	0
1920	13 Mar	Glasgow	3	0		1973	16 May	Glasgow	1	2
1921	26 Feb	Belfast	2	0		1974	11 May	Glasgow	0	1
1922	4 Mar	Glasgow	2	1		1975	20 May	Glasgow	3	0
1923	3 Mar	Belfast	1	0		1976	8 May	Glasgow	3	0
1924	1 Mar	Glasgow	2	0		1977	1 June	Glasgow	3	0
1925	28 Feb	Belfast	3	0		1978	13 May	Glasgow	1	1
1926	27 Feb	Glasgow	4	0		1979	22 May	Glasgow	1	0
1927	26 Feb	Belfast	2	0		1980	17 May	Belfast	0	1
1928	25 Feb	Glasgow	0	1		wc1981	25 Mar	Glasgow	1	1
1929	23 Feb	Belfast	7	3		1981	19 May	Glasgow	2	0
1930	22 Feb	Glasgow	3	1		wc1981	14 Oct	Belfast	0	0
1931	21 Feb	Belfast	0	0		1982	28 Apr	Belfast	1	1
1931	19 Sept	Glasgow	3	1		1983	24 May	Glasgow	0	0
1932	12 Sept	Belfast	4	0		1983	13 Dec	Belfast	0	2
1933	16 Sept	Glasgow	1	2		1992	19 Feb	Glasgow	1	0

WALES v IRELAND

Played: 90; Wales won 42, Ireland won 27, Drawn 21. *Goals:* Wales 181, Ireland 127.

Year	Date	Venue	W	I		Year	Date	Venue	W	I
1882	25 Feb	Wrexham	7	1		1886	27 Feb	Wrexham	5	0
1883	17 Mar	Belfast	1	1		1887	12 Mar	Belfast	1	4
1884	9 Feb	Wrexham	6	0		1888	3 Mar	Wrexham	11	0
1885	11 Apr	Belfast	8	2		1889	27 Apr	Belfast	3	1

			W	I
1890	8 Feb	Shrewsbury	5	2
1891	7 Feb	Belfast	2	7
1892	27 Feb	Bangor	1	1
1893	8 Apr	Belfast	3	4
1894	24 Feb	Swansea	4	1
1895	16 Mar	Belfast	2	2
1896	29 Feb	Wrexham	6	1
1897	6 Mar	Belfast	3	4
1898	19 Feb	Llandudno	0	1
1899	4 Mar	Belfast	0	1
1900	24 Feb	Llandudno	2	0
1901	23 Mar	Belfast	1	0
1902	22 Mar	Cardiff	0	3
1903	28 Mar	Belfast	0	2
1904	21 Mar	Bangor	0	1
1905	18 Apr	Belfast	2	2
1906	2 Apr	Wrexham	4	4
1907	23 Feb	Belfast	3	2
1908	11 Apr	Aberdare	0	1
1909	20 Mar	Belfast	3	2
1910	11 Apr	Wrexham	4	1
1911	28 Jan	Belfast	2	1
1912	13 Apr	Cardiff	2	3
1913	18 Jan	Belfast	1	0
1914	19 Jan	Wrexham	1	2
1920	14 Feb	Belfast	2	2
1921	9 Apr	Swansea	2	1
1922	4 Feb	Belfast	1	1
1923	14 Apr	Wrexham	0	3
1924	15 Mar	Belfast	1	0
1925	18 Apr	Wrexham	0	0
1926	13 Feb	Belfast	0	3
1927	9 Apr	Cardiff	2	2
1928	4 Feb	Belfast	2	1
1929	2 Feb	Wrexham	2	2
1930	1 Feb	Belfast	0	7
1931	22 Apr	Wrexham	3	2
1931	5 Dec	Belfast	0	4
1932	7 Dec	Wrexham	4	1
1933	4 Nov	Belfast	1	1
1935	27 Mar	Wrexham	3	1

			W	I
1936	11 Mar	Belfast	2	3
1937	17 Mar	Wrexham	4	1
1938	16 Mar	Belfast	0	1
1939	15 Mar	Wrexham	3	1
1947	16 Apr	Belfast	1	2
1948	10 Mar	Wrexham	2	0
1949	9 Mar	Belfast	2	0
wc1950	8 Mar	Wrexham	0	0
1951	7 Mar	Belfast	2	1
1952	19 Mar	Swansea	3	0
1953	15 Apr	Belfast	3	2
wc1954	31 Mar	Wrexham	1	2
1955	20 Apr	Belfast	3	2
1956	11 Apr	Cardiff	1	1
1957	10 Apr	Belfast	0	0
1958	16 Apr	Cardiff	1	1
1959	22 Apr	Belfast	1	4
1960	6 Apr	Wrexham	3	2
1961	12 Apr	Belfast	5	1
1962	11 Apr	Cardiff	4	0
1963	3 Apr	Belfast	4	1
1964	15 Apr	Cardiff	2	3
1965	31 Mar	Belfast	5	0
1966	30 Mar	Cardiff	1	4
EC1967	12 Apr	Belfast	0	0
EC1968	28 Feb	Wrexham	2	0
1969	10 May	Belfast	0	0
1970	25 Apr	Swansea	1	0
1971	22 May	Belfast	0	1
1972	27 May	Wrexham	0	0
1973	19 May	Everton	0	1
1974	18 May	Wrexham	1	0
1975	23 May	Belfast	0	1
1976	14 May	Swansea	1	0
1977	3 June	Belfast	1	1
1978	19 May	Wrexham	1	0
1979	25 May	Belfast	1	1
1980	23 May	Cardiff	0	1
1982	27 May	Wrexham	3	0
1983	31 May	Belfast	1	0
1984	22 May	Swansea	1	1

OTHER BRITISH INTERNATIONAL RESULTS 1908–2001

ENGLAND

		v ALBANIA	E	A
wc1989	8 Mar	Tirana	2	0
wc1989	26 Apr	Wembley	5	0
wc2001	28 Mar	Tirana	3	1

		v ARGENTINA	E	A
1951	9 May	Wembley	2	1
1953	17 May	Buenos Aires	0	0
(abandoned after 21 mins)				
wc1962	2 June	Rancagua	3	1
1964	6 June	Rio de Janeiro	0	1
wc1966	23 July	Wembley	1	0
1974	22 May	Wembley	2	2
1977	12 June	Buenos Aires	1	1
1980	13 May	Wembley	3	1
wc1986	22 June	Mexico City	1	2
1991	25 May	Wembley	2	2
wc1998	30 June	St Etienne	2	2
2000	23 Feb	Wembley	0	0

		v AUSTRALIA	E	A
1980	31 May	Sydney	2	1
1983	11 June	Sydney	0	0
1983	15 June	Brisbane	1	0
1983	18 June	Melbourne	1	1
1991	1 June	Sydney	1	0

		v AUSTRIA	E	A
1908	6 June	Vienna	6	1
1908	8 June	Vienna	11	1

			E	A
1909	1 June	Vienna	8	1
1930	14 May	Vienna	0	0
1932	7 Dec	Chelsea	4	3
1936	6 May	Vienna	1	2
1951	28 Nov	Wembley	2	2
1952	25 May	Vienna	3	2
wc1958	15 June	Boras	2	2
1961	27 May	Vienna	1	3
1962	4 Apr	Wembley	3	1
1965	20 Oct	Wembley	2	3
1967	27 May	Vienna	1	0
1973	26 Sept	Wembley	7	0
1979	13 June	Vienna	3	4

		v BELGIUM	E	B
1921	21 May	Brussels	2	0
1923	19 Mar	Highbury	6	1
1923	1 Nov	Antwerp	2	2
1924	8 Dec	West Bromwich	4	0
1926	24 May	Antwerp	5	3
1927	11 May	Brussels	9	1
1928	19 May	Antwerp	3	1
1929	11 May	Brussels	5	1
1931	16 May	Brussels	4	1
1936	9 May	Brussels	2	3
1947	21 Sept	Brussels	5	2

			E	B
1950	18 May	Brussels	4	1
1952	26 Nov	Wembley	5	0
wc1954	17 June	Basle	4	4*
1964	21 Oct	Wembley	2	2
1970	25 Feb	Brussels	3	1
EC1980	12 June	Turin	1	1
wc1990	27 June	Bologna	1	0*
1998	29 May	Casablanca	0	0
1999	10 Oct	Sunderland	2	1

*After extra time

		v BOHEMIA	E	B
1908	13 June	Prague	4	0

		v BRAZIL	E	B
1956	9 May	Wembley	4	2
wc1958	11 June	Gothenburg	0	0
1959	13 May	Rio de Janeiro	0	2
wc1962	10 June	Vina del Mar	1	3
1963	8 May	Wembley	1	1
1964	30 May	Rio de Janeiro	1	5
1969	12 June	Rio de Janeiro	1	2
wc1970	7 June	Guadalajara	0	1
1976	23 May	Los Angeles	0	1
1977	8 June	Rio de Janeiro	0	0
1978	19 Apr	Wembley	1	1
1981	12 May	Wembley	0	1
1984	10 June	Rio de Janeiro	2	0
1987	19 May	Wembley	1	1
1990	28 Mar	Wembley	1	0
1992	17 May	Wembley	1	1
1993	13 June	Washington	1	1
UI1995	11 June	Wembley	1	3
TF1997	10 June	Paris	0	1
2000	27 May	Wembley	1	1

		v BULGARIA	E	B
wc1962	7 June	Rancagua	0	0
1968	11 Dec	Wembley	1	1
1974	1 June	Sofia	1	0
EC1979	6 June	Sofia	3	0
EC1979	22 Nov	Wembley	2	0
1996	27 Mar	Wembley	1	0
EC1998	10 Oct	Wembley	0	0
EC1999	9 June	Sofia	1	1

		v CAMEROON	E	C
wc1990	1 July	Naples	3	2*
1991	6 Feb	Wembley	2	0
1997	15 Nov	Wembley	2	0

*After extra time

		v CANADA	E	C
1986	24 May	Burnaby	1	0

		v CHILE	E	C
wc1950	25 June	Rio de Janeiro	2	0
1953	24 May	Santiago	2	1
1984	17 June	Santiago	0	0
1989	23 May	Wembley	0	0
1998	11 Feb	Wembley	0	2

		v CHINA	E	C
1996	23 May	Beijing	3	0

		v CIS	E	C
1992	29 Apr	Moscow	2	2

		v COLOMBIA	E	C
1970	20 May	Bogota	4	0
1988	24 May	Wembley	1	1
1995	6 Sept	Wembley	0	0
wc1998	26 June	Lens	2	0

		v CROATIA	E	C
1996	24 Apr	Wembley	0	0

		v CYPRUS	E	C
EC1975	16 Apr	Wembley	5	0
EC1975	11 May	Limassol	1	0

		v CZECHOSLOVAKIA	E	C
1934	16 May	Prague	1	2
1937	1 Dec	Tottenham	5	4
1963	29 May	Bratislava	4	2
1966	2 Nov	Wembley	0	0
wc1970	11 June	Guadalajara	1	0
1973	27 May	Prague	1	1
EC1974	30 Oct	Wembley	3	0
EC1975	30 Oct	Bratislava	1	2
1978	29 Nov	Wembley	1	0
wc1982	20 June	Bilbao	2	0
1990	25 Apr	Wembley	4	2
1992	25 Mar	Prague	2	2

		v CZECH REPUBLIC	E	C
1998	18 Nov	Wembley	2	0

		v DENMARK	E	D
1948	26 Sept	Copenhagen	0	0
1955	2 Oct	Copenhagen	5	1
wc1956	5 Dec	Wolverhampton	5	2
wc1957	15 May	Copenhagen	4	1
1966	3 July	Copenhagen	2	0
EC1978	20 Sept	Copenhagen	4	3
EC1979	12 Sept	Wembley	1	0
EC1982	22 Sept	Copenhagen	2	2
EC1983	21 Sept	Wembley	0	1
1988	14 Sept	Wembley	1	0
1989	7 June	Copenhagen	1	1
1990	15 May	Wembley	1	0
EC1992	11 June	Malmo	0	0
1994	9 Mar	Wembley	1	0

		v ECUADOR	E	Ec
1970	24 May	Quito	2	0

		v EGYPT	E	Eg
1986	29 Jan	Cairo	4	0
wc1990	21 June	Cagliari	1	0

		v FIFA	E	FIFA
1938	26 Oct	Highbury	3	0
1953	21 Oct	Wembley	4	4
1963	23 Oct	Wembley	2	1

		v FINLAND	E	F
1937	20 May	Helsinki	8	0
1956	20 May	Helsinki	5	1
1966	26 June	Helsinki	3	0
wc1976	13 June	Helsinki	4	1
wc1976	13 Oct	Wembley	2	1
1982	3 June	Helsinki	4	1
wc1984	17 Oct	Wembley	5	0
wc1985	22 May	Helsinki	1	1
1992	3 June	Helsinki	2	1
wc2000	11 Oct	Helsinki	0	0
wc2001	24 Mar	Liverpool	2	1

		v FRANCE	E	F
1923	10 May	Paris	4	1
1924	17 May	Paris	3	1
1925	21 May	Paris	3	2
1927	26 May	Paris	6	0
1928	17 May	Paris	5	1
1929	9 May	Paris	4	1
1931	14 May	Paris	2	5
1933	6 Dec	Tottenham	4	1
1938	26 May	Paris	4	2
1947	3 May	Highbury	3	0
1949	22 May	Paris	3	1
1951	3 Oct	Highbury	2	2

			E	F
1955	15 May	Paris	0	1
1957	27 Nov	Wembley	4	0
EC1962	3 Oct	Sheffield	1	1
EC1963	27 Feb	Paris	2	5
WC1966	20 July	Wembley	2	0
1969	12 Mar	Wembley	5	0
WC1982	16 June	Bilbao	3	1
1984	29 Feb	Paris	0	2
1992	19 Feb	Wembley	2	0
EC1992	14 June	Malmo	0	0
TF1997	7 June	Montpellier	1	0
1999	10 Feb	Wembley	0	2
2000	2 Sept	Paris	1	1

v GEORGIA			E	G
WC1996	9 Nov	Tbilisi	2	0
WC1997	30 Apr	Wembley	2	0

v GERMANY			E	G
1930	10 May	Berlin	3	3
1935	4 Dec	Tottenham	3	0
1938	14 May	Berlin	6	3
1991	11 Sept	Wembley	0	1
1993	19 June	Detroit	1	2
EC1996	26 June	Wembley	1	1*
EC2000	17 June	Charleroi	1	0
WC2000	7 Oct	Wembley	0	1

v EAST GERMANY			E	EG
1963	2 June	Leipzig	2	1
1970	25 Nov	Wembley	3	1
1974	29 May	Leipzig	1	1
1984	12 Sept	Wembley	1	0

v WEST GERMANY			E	WG
1954	1 Dec	Wembley	3	1
1956	26 May	Berlin	3	1
1965	12 May	Nuremberg	1	0
1966	23 Feb	Wembley	1	0
WC1966	30 July	Wembley	4	2*
1968	1 June	Hanover	0	1
WC1970	14 June	Leon	2	3*
EC1972	29 Apr	Wembley	1	3
EC1972	13 May	Berlin	0	0
1975	12 Mar	Wembley	2	0
1978	22 Feb	Munich	1	2
WC1982	29 June	Madrid	0	0
1982	13 Oct	Wembley	1	2
1985	12 June	Mexico City	3	0
1987	9 Sept	Dusseldorf	1	3
WC1990	4 July	Turin	1	1*

*After extra time

v GREECE			E	G
EC1971	21 Apr	Wembley	3	0
EC1971	1 Dec	Piraeus	2	0
EC1982	17 Nov	Salonika	3	0
EC1983	30 Mar	Wembley	0	0
1989	8 Feb	Athens	2	1
1994	17 May	Wembley	5	0
WC2001	6 June	Athens	2	0

v HOLLAND			E	H
1935	18 May	Amsterdam	1	0
1946	27 Nov	Huddersfield	8	2
1964	9 Dec	Amsterdam	1	1
1969	5 Nov	Amsterdam	1	0
1970	14 Jun	Wembley	0	0
1977	9 Feb	Wembley	0	2
1982	25 May	Wembley	2	0
1988	23 Mar	Wembley	2	2
EC1988	15 June	Dusseldorf	1	3
WC1990	16 June	Cagliari	0	0
WC1993	28 Apr	Wembley	2	2
WC1993	13 Oct	Rotterdam	0	2
EC1996	18 June	Wembley	4	1

v HUNGARY			E	H
1908	10 June	Budapest	7	0
1909	29 May	Budapest	4	2
1909	31 May	Budapest	8	2
1934	10 May	Budapest	1	2
1936	2 Dec	Highbury	6	2
1953	25 Nov	Wembley	3	6
1954	23 May	Budapest	1	7
1960	22 May	Budapest	0	2
WC1962	31 May	Rancagua	1	2
1965	5 May	Wembley	1	0
1978	24 May	Wembley	4	1
WC1981	6 June	Budapest	3	1
WC1982	18 Nov	Wembley	1	0
EC1983	27 Apr	Wembley	2	0
EC1983	12 Oct	Budapest	3	0
1988	27 Apr	Budapest	0	0
1990	12 Sept	Wembley	1	0
1992	12 May	Budapest	1	0
1996	18 May	Wembley	3	0
1999	28 Apr	Budapest	1	1

v ICELAND			E	I
1982	2 June	Reykjavik	1	1

v REPUBLIC OF IRELAND			E	RI
1946	30 Sept	Dublin	1	0
1949	21 Sept	Everton	0	2
WC1957	8 May	Wembley	5	1
WC1957	19 May	Dublin	1	1
1964	24 May	Dublin	3	1
1976	8 Sept	Wembley	1	1
EC1978	25 Oct	Dublin	1	1
EC1980	6 Feb	Wembley	2	0
1985	26 Mar	Wembley	2	1
EC1988	12 June	Stuttgart	0	1
WC1990	11 June	Cagliari	1	1
EC1990	14 Nov	Dublin	1	1
EC1991	27 Mar	Wembley	1	1
1995	15 Feb	Dublin	0	1
(abandoned after 27 mins)				

v ISRAEL			E	I
1986	26 Feb	Ramat Gan	2	1
1988	17 Feb	Tel Aviv	0	0

v ITALY			E	I
1933	13 May	Rome	1	1
1934	14 Nov	Highbury	3	2
1939	13 May	Milan	2	2
1948	16 May	Turin	4	0
1949	30 Nov	Tottenham	2	0
1952	18 May	Florence	1	1
1959	6 May	Wembley	2	2
1961	24 May	Rome	3	2
1973	14 June	Turin	0	2
1973	14 Nov	Wembley	0	1
1976	28 May	New York	3	2
WC1976	17 Nov	Rome	0	2
WC1977	16 Nov	Wembley	2	0
EC1980	15 June	Turin	0	1
1985	6 June	Mexico City	1	2
1989	15 Nov	Wembley	0	0
WC1990	7 July	Bari	1	2
WC1997	12 Feb	Wembley	0	1
TF1997	4 June	Nantes	2	0
WC1997	11 Oct	Rome	0	0
2000	15 Nov	Turin	0	1

v JAPAN			E	J
UI1995	3 June	Wembley	2	1

v KUWAIT			E	K
WC1982	25 June	Bilbao	1	0

v LUXEMBOURG			E	L
1927	21 May	Esch-sur-Alzette	5	2
wc1960	19 Oct	Luxembourg	9	0
wc1961	28 Sept	Highbury	4	1
EC1977	30 Mar	Wembley	5	0
EC1977	12 Oct	Luxembourg	2	0
EC1982	15 Dec	Wembley	9	0
EC1983	16 Nov	Luxembourg	4	0
EC1998	14 Oct	Luxembourg	3	0
EC1999	4 Sept	Wembley	6	0

v MALAYSIA			E	M
1991	12 June	Kuala Lumpur	4	2

v MALTA			E	M
EC1971	3 Feb	Valletta	1	0
EC1971	12 May	Wembley	5	0
2000	3 June	Valletta	2	1

v MEXICO			E	M
1959	24 May	Mexico City	1	2
1961	10 May	Wembley	8	0
wc1966	16 July	Wembley	2	0
1969	1 June	Mexico City	0	0
1985	9 June	Mexico City	0	1
1986	17 May	Los Angeles	3	0
1997	29 Mar	Wembley	2	0
2001	25 May	Derby	4	0

v MOLDOVA			E	M
wc1996	1 Sept	Chisinau	3	0
wc1997	10 Sept	Wembley	4	0

v MOROCCO			E	M
wc1986	6 June	Monterrey	0	0
1998	27 May	Casablanca	1	0

v NEW ZEALAND			E	NZ
1991	3 June	Auckland	1	0
1991	8 June	Wellington	2	0

v NIGERIA			E	N
1994	16 Nov	Wembley	1	0

v NORWAY			E	N
1937	14 May	Oslo	6	0
1938	9 Nov	Newcastle	4	0
1949	18 May	Oslo	4	1
1966	29 June	Oslo	6	1
wc1980	10 Sept	Wembley	4	0
wc1981	9 Sept	Oslo	1	2
wc1992	14 Oct	Wembley	1	1
wc1993	2 June	Oslo	0	2
1994	22 May	Wembley	0	0
1995	11 Oct	Oslo	0	0

v PARAGUAY			E	P
wc1986	18 June	Mexico City	3	0

v PERU			E	P
1959	17 May	Lima	1	4
1962	20 May	Lima	4	0

v POLAND			E	P
1966	5 Jan	Everton	1	1
1966	5 July	Chorzow	1	0
wc1973	6 June	Chorzow	0	2
wc1973	17 Oct	Wembley	1	1
wc1986	11 June	Monterrey	3	0
wc1989	3 June	Wembley	3	0
wc1989	11 Oct	Katowice	0	0
EC1990	17 Oct	Wembley	2	0
EC1991	13 Nov	Poznan	1	1
wc1993	29 May	Katowice	1	1
wc1993	8 Sept	Wembley	3	0
wc1996	9 Oct	Wembley	2	1
wc1997	31 May	Katowice	2	0
EC1999	27 Mar	Wembley	3	1
EC1999	8 Sept	Warsaw	0	0

v PORTUGAL			E	P
1947	25 May	Lisbon	10	0
1950	14 May	Lisbon	5	3
1951	19 May	Everton	5	2
1955	22 May	Oporto	1	3
1958	7 May	Wembley	2	1
wc1961	21 May	Lisbon	1	1
wc1961	25 Oct	Wembley	2	0
1964	17 May	Lisbon	4	3
1964	4 June	São Paulo	1	1
wc1966	26 July	Wembley	2	1
1969	10 Dec	Wembley	1	0
1974	3 Apr	Lisbon	0	0
EC1974	20 Nov	Wembley	0	0
EC1975	19 Nov	Lisbon	1	1
wc1986	3 June	Monterrey	0	1
1995	12 Dec	Wembley	1	1
1998	22 Apr	Wembley	3	0
EC2000	12 June	Eindhoven	2	3

v ROMANIA			E	R
1939	24 May	Bucharest	2	0
1968	6 Nov	Bucharest	0	0
1969	15 Jan	Wembley	1	1
wc1970	2 June	Guadalajara	1	0
wc1980	15 Oct	Bucharest	1	2
wc1981	29 April	Wembley	0	0
wc1985	1 May	Bucharest	0	0
wc1985	11 Sept	Wembley	1	1
1994	12 Oct	Wembley	1	1
wc1998	22 June	Toulouse	1	2
EC2000	20 June	Charleroi	2	3

v SAN MARINO			E	SM
wc1992	17 Feb	Wembley	6	0
wc1993	17 Nov	Bologna	7	1

v SAUDI ARABIA			E	SA
1988	16 Nov	Riyadh	1	1
1998	23 May	Wembley	0	0

v SOUTH AFRICA			E	SA
1997	24 May	Old Trafford	2	1

v SPAIN			E	S
1929	15 May	Madrid	3	4
1931	9 Dec	Highbury	7	1
wc1950	2 July	Rio de Janeiro	0	1
1955	18 May	Madrid	1	1
1955	30 Nov	Wembley	4	1
1960	15 May	Madrid	0	3
1960	26 Oct	Wembley	4	2
1965	8 Dec	Madrid	2	0
1967	24 May	Wembley	2	0
EC1968	3 Apr	Wembley	1	0
EC1968	8 May	Madrid	2	1
1980	26 Mar	Barcelona	2	0
EC1980	18 June	Naples	2	1
1981	25 Mar	Wembley	1	2
wc1982	5 July	Madrid	0	0
1987	18 Feb	Madrid	4	2
1992	9 Sept	Santander	0	1
EC 1996	22 June	Wembley	0	0
2001	28 Feb	Villa Park	3	0

v SWEDEN			E	S
1923	21 May	Stockholm	4	2
1923	24 May	Stockholm	3	1
1937	17 May	Stockholm	4	0
1947	19 Nov	Highbury	4	2
1949	13 May	Stockholm	1	3
1956	16 May	Stockholm	0	0
1959	28 Oct	Wembley	2	3
1965	16 May	Gothenburg	2	1
1968	22 May	Wembley	3	1
1979	10 June	Stockholm	0	0
1986	10 Sept	Stockholm	0	1
wc1988	19 Oct	Wembley	0	0
wc1989	6 Sept	Stockholm	0	0
EC1992	17 June	Stockholm	1	2
UI1995	8 June	Leeds	3	3
EC1998	5 Sept	Stockholm	1	2
EC1999	5 June	Wembley	0	0

v SWITZERLAND

			E	S
1933	20 May	Berne	4	0
1938	21 May	Zurich	1	2
1947	18 May	Zurich	0	1
1948	2 Dec	Highbury	6	0
1952	28 May	Zurich	3	0
wc1954	20 June	Berne	2	0
1962	9 May	Wembley	3	1
1963	5 June	Basle	8	1
EC1971	13 Oct	Basle	3	2
EC1971	10 Nov	Wembley	1	1
1975	3 Sept	Basle	2	1
1977	7 Sept	Wembley	0	0
wc1980	19 Nov	Wembley	2	1
wc1981	30 May	Basle	1	2
1988	28 May	Lausanne	1	0
1995	15 Nov	Wembley	3	1
EC1996	8 June	Wembley	1	1
1998	25 Mar	Berne	1	1

v TUNISIA

			E	T
1990	2 June	Tunis	1	1
wc1998	15 June	Marseilles	2	0

v TURKEY

			E	T
wc1984	14 Nov	Istanbul	8	0
wc1985	16 Oct	Wembley	5	0
EC1987	29 Apr	Izmir	0	0
EC1987	14 Oct	Wembley	8	0
EC1991	1 May	Izmir	1	0
EC1991	16 Oct	Wembley	1	0
wc1992	18 Nov	Wembley	4	0
wc1993	31 Mar	Izmir	2	0

v UKRAINE

			E	U
2000	31 May	Wembley	2	0

v URUGUAY

			E	U
1953	31 May	Montevideo	1	2
wc1954	26 June	Basle	2	4
1964	6 May	Wembley	2	1
wc1966	11 July	Wembley	0	0
1969	8 June	Montevideo	2	1
1977	15 June	Montevideo	0	0

			E	U
1984	13 June	Montevideo	0	2
1990	22 May	Wembley	1	2
1995	29 Mar	Wembley	0	0

v USA

			E	USA
wc1950	29 June	Belo Horizonte	0	1
1953	8 June	New York	6	3
1959	28 May	Los Angeles	8	1
1964	27 May	New York	10	0
1985	16 June	Los Angeles	5	0
1993	9 June	Foxboro	0	2
1994	7 Sept	Wembley	2	0

v USSR

			E	USSR
1958	18 May	Moscow	1	1
wc1958	8 June	Gothenburg	2	2
wc1958	17 June	Gothenburg	0	1
1958	22 Oct	Wembley	5	0
1967	6 Dec	Wembley	2	2
EC1968	8 June	Rome	2	0
1973	10 June	Moscow	2	1
1984	2 June	Wembley	0	2
1986	26 Mar	Tbilisi	1	0
EC1988	18 June	Frankfurt	1	3
1991	21 May	Wembley	3	1

v YUGOSLAVIA

			E	Y
1939	18 May	Belgrade	1	2
1950	22 Nov	Highbury	2	2
1954	16 May	Belgrade	0	1
1956	28 Nov	Wembley	3	0
1958	11 May	Belgrade	0	5
1960	11 May	Wembley	3	3
1965	9 May	Belgrade	1	1
1966	4 May	Wembley	2	0
EC1968	5 June	Florence	0	1
1972	11 Oct	Wembley	1	1
1974	5 June	Belgrade	2	2
EC1986	12 Nov	Wembley	2	0
EC1987	11 Nov	Belgrade	4	1
1989	13 Dec	Wembley	2	1

SCOTLAND

v ARGENTINA

			S	A
1977	18 June	Buenos Aires	1	1
1979	2 June	Glasgow	1	3
1990	28 Mar	Glasgow	1	0

v AUSTRALIA

			S	A
wc1985	20 Nov	Glasgow	2	0
wc1985	4 Dec	Melbourne	0	0
1996	27 Mar	Glasgow	1	0
2000	15 Nov	Glasgow	0	2

v AUSTRIA

			S	A
1931	16 May	Vienna	0	5
1933	29 Nov	Glasgow	2	2
1937	9 May	Vienna	1	1
1950	13 Dec	Glasgow	0	1
1951	27 May	Vienna	0	4
wc1954	16 June	Zurich	0	1
1955	19 May	Vienna	4	1
1956	2 May	Glasgow	1	1
1960	29 May	Vienna	1	4
1963	8 May	Glasgow	4	1
(abandoned after 79 mins)				
wc1968	6 Nov	Glasgow	2	1
wc1969	5 Nov	Vienna	0	2
EC1978	20 Sept	Vienna	2	3
EC1979	17 Oct	Glasgow	1	1
1994	20 Apr	Vienna	2	1
wc1996	31 Aug	Vienna	0	0
wc1997	2 Apr	Celtic Park	2	0

v BELARUS

			S	B
wc1997	8 June	Minsk	1	0
wc1997	7 Sept	Aberdeen	4	1

v BELGIUM

			S	B
1947	18 May	Brussels	1	2
1948	28 Apr	Glasgow	2	0
1951	20 May	Brussels	5	0
EC1971	3 Feb	Liège	0	3
EC1971	10 Nov	Aberdeen	1	0
1974	2 June	Brussels	1	2
EC1979	21 Nov	Brussels	0	2
EC1979	19 Dec	Glasgow	1	3
EC1982	15 Dec	Brussels	2	3
EC1983	12 Oct	Glasgow	1	1
EC1987	1 Apr	Brussels	1	4
EC1987	14 Oct	Glasgow	2	0
wc2001	24 Mar	Glasgow	2	2

v BOSNIA

			S	B
EC1999	4 Sept	Sarajevo	2	1
EC1999	5 Oct	Glasgow	1	0

v BRAZIL

			S	B
1966	25 June	Glasgow	1	1
1972	5 July	Rio de Janeiro	0	1
1973	30 June	Glasgow	0	1
wc1974	18 June	Frankfurt	0	0
1977	23 June	Rio de Janeiro	0	2
wc1982	18 June	Seville	1	4
1987	26 May	Glasgow	0	2
wc1990	20 June	Turin	0	1
wc1998	10 June	Sant-Denis	1	2

v BULGARIA

			S	B
1978	22 Feb	Glasgow	2	1
EC1986	10 Sept	Glasgow	0	0
EC1987	11 Nov	Sofia	1	0
EC1990	14 Nov	Sofia	1	1
EC1991	27 Mar	Glasgow	1	1

v CANADA			S	C
1983	12 June	Vancouver	2	0
1983	16 June	Edmonton	3	0
1983	20 June	Toronto	2	0
1992	21 May	Toronto	3	1

v CHILE			S	C
1977	15 June	Santiago	4	2
1989	30 May	Glasgow	2	0

v CIS			S	C
EC1992	18 June	Norrkoping	3	0

v COLOMBIA			S	C
1988	17 May	Glasgow	0	0
1996	30 May	Miami	0	1
1998	23 May	New York	2	2

v COSTA RICA			S	CR
wc1990	11 June	Genoa	0	1

v CROATIA			S	C
wc2000	11 Oct	Zagreb	1	1

v CYPRUS			S	C
wc1968	17 Dec	Nicosia	5	0
wc1969	11 May	Glasgow	8	0
wc1989	8 Feb	Limassol	3	2
wc1989	26 Apr	Glasgow	2	1

v CZECHOSLOVAKIA			S	C
1937	22 May	Prague	3	1
1937	8 Dec	Glasgow	5	0
wc1961	14 May	Bratislava	0	4
wc1961	26 Sept	Glasgow	3	2
wc1961	29 Nov	Brussels	2	4*
1972	2 July	Porto Alegre	0	0
wc1973	26 Sept	Glasgow	2	1
wc1973	17 Oct	Prague	0	1
wc1976	13 Oct	Prague	0	2
wc1977	21 Sept	Glasgow	3	1

*After extra time

v CZECH REPUBLIC			S	C
EC1999	31 Mar	Glasgow	1	2
EC1999	9 June	Prague	2	3

v DENMARK			S	D
1951	12 May	Glasgow	3	1
1952	25 May	Copenhagen	2	1
1968	16 Oct	Copenhagen	1	0
EC1970	11 Nov	Glasgow	1	0
EC1971	9 June	Copenhagen	0	1
wc1972	18 Oct	Copenhagen	4	1
wc1972	15 Nov	Glasgow	2	0
EC1975	3 Sept	Copenhagen	1	0
EC1975	29 Oct	Glasgow	3	1
wc1986	4 June	Nezahualcayotl	0	1
1996	24 Apr	Copenhagen	0	2
1998	25 Mar	Glasgow	0	1

v ECUADOR			S	E
1995	24 May	Toyama	2	1

v EGYPT			S	E
1990	16 May	Aberdeen	1	3

v ESTONIA			S	E
wc1993	19 May	Tallinn	3	0
wc1993	2 June	Aberdeen	3	1
wc1997	11 Feb	Monaco	0	0
wc1997	29 Mar	Kilmarnock	2	0
EC1998	10 Oct	Edinburgh	3	2
EC1999	8 Sept	Tallinn	0	0

v FAEROES			S	F
EC1994	12 Oct	Glasgow	5	1
EC1995	7 June	Toftir	2	0
EC1998	14 Oct	Aberdeen	2	1
EC1999	5 June	Toftir	1	1

v FINLAND			S	F
1954	25 May	Helsinki	2	1
wc1964	21 Oct	Glasgow	3	1
wc1965	27 May	Helsinki	2	1
1976	8 Sept	Glasgow	6	0
1992	25 Mar	Glasgow	1	1
EC1994	7 Sept	Helsinki	2	0
EC1995	6 Sept	Glasgow	1	0
1998	22 Apr	Edinburgh	1	1

v FRANCE			S	F
1930	18 May	Paris	2	0
1932	8 May	Paris	3	1
1948	23 May	Paris	0	3
1949	27 Apr	Glasgow	2	0
1950	27 May	Paris	1	0
1951	16 May	Glasgow	1	0
wc1958	15 June	Orebro	1	2
1984	1 June	Marseilles	0	2
wc1989	8 Mar	Glasgow	2	0
wc1989	11 Oct	Paris	0	3
1997	12 Nov	St Etienne	1	2
2000	29 Mar	Glasgow	0	2

v GERMANY			S	G
1929	1 June	Berlin	1	1
1936	14 Oct	Glasgow	2	0
EC1992	15 June	Norrkoping	0	2
1993	24 Mar	Glasgow	0	1
1998	28 Apr	Bremen	1	0

v EAST GERMANY			S	EG
1974	30 Oct	Glasgow	3	0
1977	7 Sept	East Berlin	0	1
EC1982	13 Oct	Glasgow	2	0
EC1983	16 Nov	Halle	1	2
1985	16 Oct	Glasgow	0	0
1990	25 Apr	Glasgow	0	1

v WEST GERMANY			S	WG
1957	22 May	Stuttgart	3	1
1959	6 May	Glasgow	3	2
1964	12 May	Hanover	2	2
wc1969	16 Apr	Glasgow	1	1
wc1969	22 Oct	Hamburg	2	3
1973	14 Nov	Glasgow	1	1
1974	27 Mar	Frankfurt	1	2
wc1986	8 June	Queretaro	1	2

v GREECE			S	G
EC1994	18 Dec	Athens	0	1
EC1995	16 Aug	Glasgow	1	0

v HOLLAND			S	H
1929	4 June	Amsterdam	2	0
1938	21 May	Amsterdam	3	1
1959	27 May	Amsterdam	2	1
1966	11 May	Glasgow	0	3
1968	30 May	Amsterdam	0	0
1971	1 Dec	Rotterdam	1	2
wc1978	11 June	Mendoza	3	2
1982	23 Mar	Glasgow	2	1
1986	29 Apr	Eindhoven	0	0
EC1992	12 June	Gothenburg	0	1
1994	23 Mar	Glasgow	0	1
1994	27 May	Utrecht	1	3
EC1996	10 June	Birmingham	0	0
2000	26 Apr	Arnhem	0	0

v HUNGARY			S	H
1938	7 Dec	Glasgow	3	1
1954	8 Dec	Glasgow	2	4
1955	29 May	Budapest	1	3
1958	7 May	Glasgow	1	1
1960	5 June	Budapest	3	3
1980	31 May	Budapest	1	3
1987	9 Sept	Glasgow	2	0

v ICELAND			S	I
wc1984	17 Oct	Glasgow	3	0
wc1985	28 May	Reykjavik	1	0

		v IRAN	S	I
wc1978	7 June	Cordoba	1	1

		v REPUBLIC OF IRELAND	S	RI
wc1961	3 May	Glasgow	4	1
wc1961	7 May	Dublin	3	0
1963	9 June	Dublin	0	1
1969	21 Sept	Dublin	1	1
EC1986	15 Oct	Dublin	0	0
EC1987	18 Feb	Glasgow	0	1
2000	30 May	Dublin	2	1

		v ISRAEL	S	I
wc1981	25 Feb	Tel Aviv	1	0
wc1981	28 Apr	Glasgow	3	1
1986	28 Jan	Tel Aviv	1	0

		v ITALY	S	I
1931	20 May	Rome	0	3
wc1965	9 Nov	Glasgow	1	0
wc1965	7 Dec	Naples	0	3
1988	22 Dec	Perugia	0	2
wc1992	18 Nov	Glasgow	0	0
wc1993	13 Oct	Rome	1	3

		v JAPAN	S	J
1995	21 May	Hiroshima	0	0

		v LATVIA	S	L
wc1996	5 Oct	Riga	2	0
wc1997	11 Oct	Glasgow	2	0
wc2000	2 Sept	Riga	1	0

		v LITHUANIA	S	L
EC1998	5 Sept	Vilnius	0	0
EC1999	9 Oct	Glasgow	3	0

		v LUXEMBOURG	S	L
1947	24 May	Luxembourg	6	0
EC1986	12 Nov	Glasgow	3	0
EC1987	2 Dec	Esch	0	0

		v MALTA	S	M
1988	22 Mar	Valletta	1	1
1990	28 May	Valletta	2	1
wc1993	17 Feb	Glasgow	3	0
wc1993	17 Nov	Valletta	2	0
1997	1 June	Valletta	3	2

		v MOROCCO	S	M
wc1998	23 June	St Etienne	0	3

		v NEW ZEALAND	S	NZ
wc1982	15 June	Malaga	5	2

		v NORWAY	S	N
1929	28 May	Oslo	7	3
1954	5 May	Glasgow	1	0
1954	19 May	Oslo	1	1
1963	4 June	Bergen	3	4
1963	7 Nov	Glasgow	6	1
1974	6 June	Oslo	2	1
EC1978	25 Oct	Glasgow	3	2
EC1979	7 June	Oslo	4	0
wc1988	14 Sept	Oslo	2	1
wc1989	15 Nov	Glasgow	1	1
1992	3 June	Oslo	0	0
wc1998	16 June	Bordeaux	1	1

		v PARAGUAY	S	P
wc1958	11 June	Norrkoping	2	3

		v PERU	S	P
1972	26 Apr	Glasgow	2	0
wc1978	3 June	Cordoba	1	3
1979	12 Sept	Glasgow	1	1

		v POLAND	S	P
1958	1 June	Warsaw	2	1
1960	4 June	Glasgow	2	3
wc1965	23 May	Chorzow	1	1
wc1965	13 Oct	Glasgow	1	2
1980	28 May	Poznan	0	1
1990	19 May	Glasgow	1	1
wc2001	25 Apr	Bydgoszcz	1	1

		v PORTUGAL	S	P
1950	21 May	Lisbon	2	2
1955	4 May	Glasgow	3	0
1959	3 June	Lisbon	0	1
1966	18 June	Glasgow	0	1
EC1971	21 Apr	Lisbon	0	2
EC1971	13 Oct	Glasgow	2	1
1975	13 May	Glasgow	1	0
EC1978	29 Nov	Lisbon	0	1
EC1980	26 Mar	Glasgow	4	1
wc1980	15 Oct	Glasgow	0	0
wc1981	18 Nov	Lisbon	1	2
wc1992	14 Oct	Glasgow	0	0
wc1993	28 Apr	Lisbon	0	5

		v ROMANIA	S	R
EC1975	1 June	Bucharest	1	1
EC1975	17 Dec	Glasgow	1	1
1986	26 Mar	Glasgow	3	0
EC1990	12 Sept	Glasgow	2	1
EC1991	16 Oct	Bucharest	0	1

		v RUSSIA	S	R
EC1994	16 Nov	Glasgow	1	1
EC1995	29 Mar	Moscow	0	0

		v SAN MARINO	S	SM
EC1991	1 May	Serravalle	2	0
EC1991	13 Nov	Glasgow	4	0
EC1995	26 Apr	Serravalle	2	0
EC1995	15 Nov	Glasgow	5	0
wc2000	7 Oct	Serravalle	2	0
wc2001	28 Mar	Glasgow	4	0

		v SAUDI ARABIA	S	SA
1988	17 Feb	Riyadh	2	2

		v SPAIN	S	Sp
wc1957	8 May	Glasgow	4	2
wc1957	26 May	Madrid	1	4
1963	13 June	Madrid	6	2
1965	8 May	Glasgow	0	0
EC1974	20 Nov	Glasgow	1	2
EC1975	5 Feb	Valencia	1	1
1982	24 Feb	Valencia	0	3
wc1984	14 Nov	Glasgow	3	1
wc1985	27 Feb	Seville	0	1
1988	27 Apr	Madrid	0	0

		v SWEDEN	S	Sw
1952	30 May	Stockholm	1	3
1953	6 May	Glasgow	1	2
1975	16 Apr	Gothenburg	1	1
1977	27 Apr	Glasgow	3	1
wc1980	10 Sept	Stockholm	1	0
wc1981	9 Sept	Glasgow	2	0
wc1990	16 June	Genoa	2	1
1995	11 Oct	Stockholm	0	2
wc1996	10 Nov	Glasgow	1	0
wc1997	30 Apr	Gothenburg	1	2

		v SWITZERLAND	S	Sw
1931	24 May	Geneva	3	2
1948	17 May	Berne	1	2
1950	26 Apr	Glasgow	3	1
wc1957	19 May	Basle	2	1
wc1957	6 Nov	Glasgow	3	2
1973	22 June	Berne	0	1

			S	Sw
1976	7 Apr	Glasgow	1	0
EC1982	17 Nov	Berne	0	2
EC1983	30 May	Glasgow	2	2
EC1990	17 Oct	Glasgow	2	1
EC1991	11 Sept	Berne	2	2
wc1992	9 Sept	Berne	1	3
wc1993	8 Sept	Aberdeen	1	1
EC1996	18 June	Birmingham	1	0

v TURKEY			S	T
1960	8 June	Ankara	2	4

v URUGUAY			S	U
wc1954	19 June	Basle	0	7
1962	2 May	Glasgow	2	3
1983	21 Sept	Glasgow	2	0
wc1986	13 June	Nezahualcoyotl	0	0

v USA			S	USA
1952	30 Apr	Glasgow	6	0
1992	17 May	Denver	1	0

			S	USA
1996	26 May	New Britain	1	2
1998	30 May	Washington	0	0

v USSR			S	USSR
1967	10 May	Glasgow	0	2
1971	14 June	Moscow	0	1
wc1982	22 June	Malaga	2	2
1991	6 Feb	Glasgow	0	1

v YUGOSLAVIA			S	Y
1955	15 May	Belgrade	2	2
1956	21 Nov	Glasgow	2	0
wc1958	8 June	Vasteras	1	1
1972	29 June	Belo Horizonte	2	2
wc1974	22 June	Frankfurt	1	1
1984	12 Sept	Glasgow	6	1
wc1988	19 Oct	Glasgow	1	1
wc1989	6 Sept	Zagreb	1	3

v ZAIRE			S	Z
wc1974	14 June	Dortmund	2	0

WALES

v ALBANIA			W	A
EC1994	7 Sept	Cardiff	2	0
EC1995	15 Nov	Tirana	1	1

v ARGENTINA			W	A
1992	3 June	Tokyo	0	1

v ARMENIA			W	A
wc2001	24 Mar	Erevan	2	2

v AUSTRIA			W	A
1954	9 May	Vienna	0	2
EC1955	23 Nov	Wrexham	1	2
EC1974	4 Sept	Vienna	1	2
1975	19 Nov	Wrexham	1	0
1992	29 Apr	Vienna	1	1

v BELARUS			W	B
EC1998	14 Oct	Cardiff	3	2
EC1999	4 Sept	Minsk	2	2
wc2000	2 Sept	Minsk	1	2

v BELGIUM			W	B
1949	22 May	Liège	1	3
1949	23 Nov	Cardiff	5	1
EC1990	17 Oct	Cardiff	3	1
EC1991	27 Mar	Brussels	1	1
wc1992	18 Nov	Brussels	0	2
wc1993	31 Mar	Cardiff	2	0
wc1997	29 Mar	Cardiff	1	2
wc1997	11 Oct	Brussels	2	3

v BRAZIL			W	B
wc1958	19 June	Gothenburg	0	1
1962	12 May	Rio de Janeiro	1	3
1962	16 May	São Paulo	1	3
1966	14 May	Rio de Janeiro	1	3
1966	18 May	Belo Horizonte	0	1
1983	12 June	Cardiff	1	1
1991	11 Sept	Cardiff	1	0
1997	12 Nov	Brasilia	0	3
2000	23 May	Cardiff	0	3

v BULGARIA			W	B
EC1983	27 Apr	Wrexham	1	0
EC1983	16 Nov	Sofia	0	1
EC1994	14 Dec	Cardiff	0	3
EC1995	29 Mar	Sofia	1	3

v CANADA			W	C
1986	10 May	Toronto	0	2
1986	20 May	Vancouver	3	0

v CHILE			W	C
1966	22 May	Santiago	0	2

v COSTA RICA			W	CR
1990	20 May	Cardiff	1	0

v CYPRUS			W	C
wc1992	14 Oct	Limassol	1	0
wc1993	13 Oct	Cardiff	2	0

v CZECHOSLOVAKIA			W	C
wc1957	1 May	Cardiff	1	0
wc1957	26 May	Prague	0	2
EC1971	21 Apr	Swansea	1	3
EC1971	27 Oct	Prague	0	1
wc1977	30 Mar	Wrexham	3	0
wc1977	16 Nov	Prague	0	1
wc1980	19 Nov	Cardiff	1	0
wc1981	9 Sept	Prague	0	2
EC1987	29 Apr	Wrexham	1	1
EC1987	11 Nov	Prague	0	2
wc1993	28 Apr	Ostrava†	1	1
wc1993	8 Sept	Cardiff†	2	2

†Czechoslovakia played as RCS (Republic of Czechs and Slovaks).

v DENMARK			W	D
wc1964	21 Oct	Copenhagen	0	1
wc1965	1 Dec	Wrexham	4	2
EC1987	9 Sept	Cardiff	1	0
EC1987	14 Oct	Copenhagen	0	1
1990	11 Sept	Copenhagen	0	1
EC1998	10 Oct	Copenhagen	2	1
EC1999	9 June	Liverpool	0	2

v ESTONIA			W	E
1994	23 May	Tallinn	2	1

v FINLAND			W	F
EC1971	26 May	Helsinki	1	0
EC1971	13 Oct	Swansea	3	0
EC1987	10 Sept	Helsinki	1	1
EC1987	1 Apr	Wrexham	4	0
wc1988	19 Oct	Swansea	2	2
wc1989	6 Sept	Helsinki	0	1
2000	29 Mar	Cardiff	1	2

v FAEROES			W	F
wc1992	9 Sept	Cardiff	6	0
wc1993	6 June	Toftir	3	0

v FRANCE			W	F
1933	25 May	Paris	1	1
1939	20 May	Paris	1	2
1953	14 May	Paris	1	6
1982	2 June	Toulouse	1	0

v GEORGIA

			W	G
EC1994	16 Nov	Tbilisi	0	5
EC1995	7 June	Cardiff	0	1

v GERMANY

			W	G
EC1995	26 Apr	Dusseldorf	1	1
EC1995	11 Oct	Cardiff	1	2

v EAST GERMANY

			W	EG
wc1957	19 May	Leipzig	1	2
wc1957	25 Sept	Cardiff	4	1
wc1969	16 Apr	Dresden	1	2
wc1969	22 Oct	Cardiff	1	3

v WEST GERMANY

			W	WG
1968	8 May	Cardiff	1	1
1969	26 Mar	Frankfurt	1	1
1976	6 Oct	Cardiff	0	2
1977	14 Dec	Dortmund	1	1
EC1979	2 May	Wrexham	0	2
EC1979	17 Oct	Cologne	1	5
wc1989	31 May	Cardiff	0	0
wc1989	15 Nov	Cologne	1	2
EC1991	5 June	Cardiff	1	0
EC1991	16 Oct	Nuremberg	1	4

v GREECE

			W	G
wc1964	9 Dec	Athens	0	2
wc1965	17 Mar	Cardiff	4	1

v HOLLAND

			W	H
wc1988	14 Sept	Amsterdam	0	1
wc1989	11 Oct	Wrexham	1	2
1992	30 May	Utrecht	0	4
wc1996	5 Oct	Cardiff	1	3
wc1996	9 Nov	Eindhoven	1	7

v HUNGARY

			W	H
wc1958	8 June	Sanviken	1	1
wc1958	17 June	Stockholm	2	1
1961	28 May	Budapest	2	3
EC1962	7 Nov	Budapest	1	3
EC1963	20 Mar	Cardiff	1	1
EC1974	30 Oct	Cardiff	2	0
EC1975	16 Apr	Budapest	2	1
1985	16 Oct	Cardiff	0	3

v ICELAND

			W	I
wc1980	2 June	Reykjavik	4	0
wc1981	14 Oct	Swansea	2	2
wc1984	12 Sept	Reykjavik	0	1
wc1984	14 Nov	Cardiff	2	1
1991	1 May	Cardiff	1	0

v IRAN

			W	I
1978	18 Apr	Teheran	1	0

v REPUBLIC OF IRELAND

			W	RI
1960	28 Sept	Dublin	3	2
1979	11 Sept	Swansea	2	1
1981	24 Feb	Dublin	3	1
1986	26 Mar	Dublin	1	0
1990	28 Mar	Dublin	0	1
1991	6 Feb	Wrexham	0	3
1992	19 Feb	Dublin	1	0
1993	17 Feb	Dublin	1	2
1997	11 Feb	Cardiff	0	0

v ISRAEL

			W	I
wc1958	15 Jan	Tel Aviv	2	0
wc1958	5 Feb	Cardiff	2	0
1984	10 June	Tel Aviv	0	0
1989	8 Feb	Tel Aviv	3	3

v ITALY

			W	I
1965	1 May	Florence	1	4
wc1968	23 Oct	Cardiff	0	1
wc1969	4 Nov	Rome	1	4
1988	4 June	Brescia	1	0
1996	24 Jan	Terni	0	3
EC1998	5 Sept	Liverpool	0	2
EC1999	5 June	Bologna	0	4

v JAMAICA

			W	J
1998	25 Mar	Cardiff	0	0

v JAPAN

			W	J
1992	7 June	Matsuyama	1	0

v KUWAIT

			W	K
1977	6 Sept	Wrexham	0	0
1977	20 Sept	Kuwait	0	0

v LUXEMBOURG

			W	L
EC1974	20 Nov	Swansea	5	0
EC1975	1 May	Luxembourg	3	1
EC1990	14 Nov	Luxembourg	1	0
EC1991	13 Nov	Cardiff	1	0

v MALTA

			W	M
EC1978	25 Oct	Wrexham	7	0
EC1979	2 June	Valletta	2	0
1988	1 June	Valletta	3	2
1998	3 June	Valletta	3	0

v MEXICO

			W	M
wc1958	11 June	Stockholm	1	1
1962	22 May	Mexico City	1	2

v MOLDOVA

			W	M
EC1994	12 Oct	Kishinev	2	3
EC1995	6 Sept	Cardiff	1	0

v NORWAY

			W	N
EC1982	22 Sept	Swansea	1	0
EC1983	21 Sept	Oslo	0	0
1984	6 June	Trondheim	0	1
1985	26 Feb	Wrexham	1	1
1985	5 June	Bergen	2	4
1994	9 Mar	Cardiff	1	3
wc2000	7 Oct	Cardiff	1	1

v POLAND

			W	P
wc1973	28 Mar	Cardiff	2	0
wc1973	26 Sept	Katowice	0	3
1991	29 May	Radom	0	0
wc2000	11 Oct	Warsaw	0	0
wc2001	2 June	Cardiff	1	2

v PORTUGAL

			W	P
1949	15 May	Lisbon	2	3
1951	12 May	Cardiff	2	1
2000	2 June	Chaves	0	3

v QATAR

			W	Q
2000	23 Feb	Doha	1	0

v ROMANIA

			W	R
EC1970	11 Nov	Cardiff	0	0
EC1971	24 Nov	Bucharest	0	2
1983	12 Oct	Wrexham	5	0
wc1992	20 May	Bucharest	1	5
wc1993	17 Nov	Cardiff	1	2

v SAN MARINO

			W	SM
wc1996	2 June	Serravalle	5	0
wc1996	31 Aug	Cardiff	6	0

v SAUDI ARABIA

			W	SA
1986	25 Feb	Dahran	2	1

v SPAIN

			W	S
wc1961	19 Apr	Cardiff	1	2
wc1961	18 May	Madrid	1	1
1982	24 Mar	Valencia	1	1
wc1984	17 Oct	Seville	0	3
wc1985	30 Apr	Wrexham	3	0

v SWEDEN			W	S
wc1958	15 June	Stockholm	0	0
1988	27 Apr	Stockholm	1	4
1989	26 Apr	Wrexham	0	2
1990	25 Apr	Stockholm	2	4
1994	20 Apr	Wrexham	0	2

v SWITZERLAND			W	S
1949	26 May	Berne	0	4
1951	16 May	Wrexham	3	2
1996	24 Apr	Lugano	0	2
EC1999	31 Mar	Zurich	0	2
EC1999	9 Oct	Wrexham	0	2

v TUNISIA			W	T
1998	6 June	Tunis	0	4

v TURKEY			W	T
EC1978	29 Nov	Wrexham	1	0
EC1979	21 Nov	Izmir	0	1
wc1980	15 Oct	Cardiff	4	0
wc1981	25 Mar	Ankara	1	0
wc1996	14 Dec	Cardiff	0	0
wc1997	20 Aug	Istanbul	4	6

v REST OF UNITED KINGDOM			W	UK
1951	5 Dec	Cardiff	3	2
1969	28 July	Cardiff	0	1

v UKRAINE			W	U
wc2001	28 Mar	Cardiff	1	1
wc2001	6 June	Kiev	1	1

v URUGUAY			W	U
1986	21 Apr	Wrexham	0	0

v USSR			W	USSR
wc1965	30 May	Moscow	1	2
wc1965	27 Oct	Cardiff	2	1
wc1981	30 May	Wrexham	0	0
wc1981	18 Nov	Tbilisi	0	3
1987	18 Feb	Swansea	0	0

v YUGOSLAVIA			W	Y
1953	21 May	Belgrade	2	5
1954	22 Nov	Cardiff	1	3
EC1976	24 Apr	Zagreb	0	2
EC1976	22 May	Cardiff	1	1
EC1982	15 Dec	Titograd	4	4
EC1983	14 Dec	Cardiff	1	1
1988	23 Mar	Swansea	1	2

NORTHERN IRELAND

v ALBANIA			NI	A
wc1965	7 May	Belfast	4	1
wc1965	24 Nov	Tirana	1	1
EC1982	15 Dec	Tirana	0	0
EC1983	27 Apr	Belfast	1	0
wc1992	9 Sept	Belfast	3	0
wc1993	17 Feb	Tirana	2	1
wc1996	14 Dec	Belfast	2	0
wc1997	10 Sept	Zurich	0	1

v ALGERIA			NI	A
wc1986	3 June	Guadalajara	1	1

v ARGENTINA			NI	A
wc1958	11 June	Halmstad	1	3

v ARMENIA			NI	A
wc1996	5 Oct	Belfast	1	1
wc1997	30 Apr	Erevan	0	0

v AUSTRALIA			NI	A
1980	11 June	Sydney	2	1
1980	15 June	Melbourne	1	1
1980	18 June	Adelaide	2	1

v AUSTRIA			NI	A
wc1982	1 July	Madrid	2	2
EC1982	13 Oct	Vienna	0	2
EC1983	21 Sept	Belfast	3	1
EC1990	14 Nov	Vienna	0	0
EC1991	16 Oct	Belfast	2	1
EC1994	12 Oct	Vienna	2	1
EC1995	15 Nov	Belfast	5	3

v BELGIUM			NI	B
wc1976	10 Nov	Liège	0	2
wc1977	16 Nov	Belfast	3	0
1997	11 Feb	Belfast	3	0

v BRAZIL			NI	B
wc1986	12 June	Guadalajara	0	3

v BULGARIA			NI	B
wc1972	18 Oct	Sofia	0	3
wc1973	26 Sept	Sheffield	0	0
EC1978	29 Nov	Sofia	2	0
EC1979	2 May	Belfast	2	0
wc2001	28 Mar	Sofia	3	4
wc2001	2 June	Belfast	0	1

v CANADA			NI	C
1995	22 May	Edmonton	0	2
1999	27 Apr	Belfast	1	1

v CHILE			NI	C
1989	26 May	Belfast	0	1
1995	25 May	Edmonton	1	2

v COLOMBIA			NI	C
1994	4 June	Boston	0	2

v CYPRUS			NI	C
EC1971	3 Feb	Nicosia	3	0
EC1971	21 Apr	Belfast	5	0
wc1973	14 Feb	Nicosia	0	1
wc1973	8 May	London	3	0

v CZECHOSLOVAKIA			NI	C
wc1958	8 June	Halmstad	1	0
wc1958	17 June	Malmo	2	1*

*After extra time

v CZECH REPUBLIC			NI	C
wc2001	24 Mar	Belfast	0	1
wc2001	6 June	Teplice	1	3

v DENMARK			NI	D
EC1978	25 Oct	Belfast	2	1
EC1979	6 June	Copenhagen	0	4
1986	26 Mar	Belfast	1	1
EC1990	17 Oct	Belfast	1	1
EC1991	13 Nov	Odense	1	2
wc1992	18 Nov	Belfast	0	1
wc1993	13 Oct	Copenhagen	0	1
wc2000	7 Oct	Belfast	1	1

v FAEROES			NI	F
EC1991	1 May	Belfast	1	1
EC1991	11 Sept	Landskrona	5	0

v FINLAND			NI	F
wc1984	27 May	Pori	0	1
wc1984	14 Nov	Belfast	2	1
EC1998	10 Oct	Belfast	1	0
EC1998	9 Oct	Helsinki	1	4

v FRANCE			NI	F
1951	12 May	Belfast	2	2
1952	11 Nov	Paris	1	3
wc1958	19 June	Norrkoping	0	4
1982	24 Mar	Paris	0	4
wc1982	4 July	Madrid	1	4
1986	26 Feb	Paris	0	0
1988	27 Apr	Belfast	0	0
1999	18 Aug	Belfast	0	1

v GERMANY

			NI	G
1992	2 June	Bremen	1	1
1996	29 May	Belfast	1	1
wc1996	9 Nov	Nuremberg	1	1
wc1997	20 Aug	Belfast	1	3
EC1999	27 Mar	Belfast	0	3
EC1999	8 Sept	Dortmund	0	4

v WEST GERMANY

			NI	WG
wc1958	15 June	Malmo	2	2
wc1960	26 Oct	Belfast	3	4
wc1961	10 May	Hamburg	1	2
1966	7 May	Belfast	0	2
1977	27 Apr	Cologne	0	5
EC1982	17 Nov	Belfast	1	0
EC1983	16 Nov	Hamburg	1	0

v GREECE

			NI	G
wc1961	3 May	Athens	1	2
wc1961	17 Oct	Belfast	2	0
1988	17 Feb	Athens	2	3

v HOLLAND

			NI	H
1962	9 May	Rotterdam	0	4
wc1965	17 Mar	Belfast	2	1
wc1965	7 Apr	Rotterdam	0	0
wc1976	13 Oct	Rotterdam	2	2
wc1977	12 Oct	Belfast	0	1

v HONDURAS

			NI	H
wc1982	21 June	Zaragoza	1	1

v HUNGARY

			NI	H
wc1988	19 Oct	Budapest	0	1
wc1989	6 Sept	Belfast	1	2
2000	26 Apr	Belfast	0	1

v ICELAND

			NI	I
wc1977	11 June	Reykjavik	0	1
wc1977	21 Sept	Belfast	2	0
wc2000	11 Oct	Reykjavik	0	1

v REPUBLIC OF IRELAND

			NI	RI
EC1978	20 Sept	Dublin	0	0
EC1979	21 Nov	Belfast	1	0
wc1988	14 Sept	Belfast	0	0
wc1989	11 Oct	Dublin	0	3
wc1993	31 Mar	Dublin	0	3
wc1993	17 Nov	Belfast	1	1
EC1994	16 Nov	Belfast	0	4
EC1995	29 Mar	Dublin	1	1
1999	29 May	Dublin	1	0

v ISRAEL

			NI	I
1968	10 Sept	Jaffa	3	2
1976	3 Mar	Tel Aviv	1	1
wc1980	26 Mar	Tel Aviv	0	0
wc1981	18 Nov	Belfast	1	0
1984	16 Oct	Belfast	3	0
1987	18 Feb	Tel Aviv	1	1

v ITALY

			NI	I
wc1957	25 Apr	Rome	0	1
1957	4 Dec	Belfast	2	2
wc1958	15 Jan	Belfast	2	1
1961	25 Apr	Bologna	2	3
1997	22 Jan	Palermo	0	2

v LATVIA

			NI	L
wc1993	2 June	Riga	2	1
wc1993	8 Sept	Belfast	2	0
EC1995	26 Apr	Riga	1	0
EC1995	7 June	Belfast	1	2

v LIECHTENSTEIN

			NI	L
EC1994	20 Apr	Belfast	4	1
EC1995	11 Oct	Eschen	4	0

v LITHUANIA

			NI	L
wc1992	28 Apr	Belfast	2	2
wc1993	25 May	Vilnius	1	0

v LUXEMBOURG

			NI	L
2000	23 Feb	Luxembourg	3	1
wc2000	2 Sept	Belfast	1	0

v MALTA

			NI	M
wc1988	21 May	Belfast	3	0
wc1989	26 Apr	Valletta	2	0
2000	28 Mar	Valletta	3	0
wc2000	2 Sept	Belfast	1	0

v MEXICO

			NI	M
1966	22 June	Belfast	4	1
1994	11 June	Miami	0	3

v MOLDOVA

			NI	M
EC1998	18 Nov	Belfast	2	2
EC1999	31 Mar	Chisinau	0	0

v MOROCCO

			NI	M
1986	23 Apr	Belfast	2	1

v NORWAY

			NI	N
EC1974	4 Sept	Oslo	1	2
EC1975	29 Oct	Belfast	3	0
1990	27 Mar	Belfast	2	3
1996	27 Mar	Belfast	0	2
2001	28 Feb	Belfast	0	4

v POLAND

			NI	P
EC1962	10 Oct	Katowice	2	0
EC1962	28 Nov	Belfast	2	0
1988	23 Mar	Belfast	1	1
1991	5 Feb	Belfast	3	1

v PORTUGAL

			NI	P
wc1957	16 Jan	Lisbon	1	1
wc1957	1 May	Belfast	3	0
wc1973	28 Mar	Coventry	1	1
wc1973	14 Nov	Lisbon	1	1
wc1980	19 Nov	Lisbon	0	1
wc1981	29 Apr	Belfast	1	0
EC1994	7 Sept	Belfast	1	2
EC1995	3 Sept	Lisbon	1	1
wc1997	29 Mar	Belfast	0	0
wc1997	11 Oct	Lisbon	0	1

v ROMANIA

			NI	R
wc1984	12 Sept	Belfast	3	2
wc1985	16 Oct	Bucharest	1	0
1994	23 Mar	Belfast	2	0

v SLOVAKIA

			NI	S
1998	25 Mar	Belfast	1	0

v SPAIN

			NI	S
1958	15 Oct	Madrid	2	6
1963	30 May	Bilbao	1	1
1963	30 Oct	Belfast	0	1
EC1970	11 Nov	Seville	0	3
EC1972	16 Feb	Hull	1	1
wc1982	25 June	Valencia	1	0
1985	27 Mar	Palma	0	0
wc1986	7 June	Guadalajara	1	2
wc1988	21 Dec	Seville	0	4
wc1989	8 Feb	Belfast	0	2
wc1992	14 Oct	Belfast	0	0
wc1993	28 Apr	Seville	1	3
1998	2 June	Santander	1	4

v SWEDEN

			NI	S
EC1974	30 Oct	Solna	2	0
EC1975	3 Sept	Belfast	1	2
wc1980	15 Oct	Belfast	3	0
wc1981	3 June	Solna	0	1
1996	24 Apr	Belfast	1	2

v SWITZERLAND

			NI	S
wc1964	14 Oct	Belfast	1	0
wc1964	14 Nov	Lausanne	1	2
1998	22 Apr	Belfast	1	0

v THAILAND

			NI	T
1997	21 May	Bangkok	0	0

v TURKEY

			NI	T
wc1968	23 Oct	Belfast	4	1
wc1968	11 Dec	Istanbul	3	0
EC1983	30 Mar	Belfast	2	1
EC1983	12 Oct	Ankara	0	1

			NI	T
wc1985	1 May	Belfast	2	0
wc1985	11 Sept	Izmir	0	0
EC1986	12 Nov	Izmir	0	0
EC1987	11 Nov	Belfast	1	0
EC1998	5 Sept	Istanbul	0	3
EC1999	4 Sept	Belfast	0	3

		v UKRAINE	NI	U
wc1996	31 Aug	Belfast	0	1
wc1997	2 Apr	Kiev	1	2

		v URUGUAY	NI	U
1964	29 Apr	Belfast	3	0
1990	18 May	Belfast	1	0

		v USSR	NI	USSR
wc1969	19 Sept	Belfast	0	0
wc1969	22 Oct	Moscow	0	2
EC1971	22 Sept	Moscow	0	1
EC1971	13 Oct	Belfast	1	1

		v YUGOSLAVIA	NI	Y
EC1975	16 Mar	Belfast	1	0
EC1975	19 Nov	Belgrade	0	1
wc1982	17 June	Zaragoza	0	0
EC1987	29 Apr	Belfast	1	2
EC1987	14 Oct	Sarajevo	0	3
EC1990	12 Sept	Belfast	0	2
EC1991	27 Mar	Belgrade	1	4
2000	16 Aug	Belfast	1	2

REPUBLIC OF IRELAND

		v ALBANIA	RI	A
wc1992	26 May	Dublin	2	0
wc1993	26 May	Tirana	2	1

		v ALGERIA	RI	A
1982	28 Apr	Algiers	0	2

		v ANDORRA	RI	A
wc2001	28 Mar	Barcelona	3	0
wc2001	25 Apr	Dublin	3	1

		v ARGENTINA	RI	A
1951	13 May	Dublin	0	1
1979	29 May	Dublin	0	0*
1980	16 May	Dublin	0	1
1998	22 Apr	Dublin	0	2

* Not considered a full international

		v AUSTRIA	RI	A
1952	7 May	Vienna	0	6
1953	25 Mar	Dublin	4	0
1958	14 Mar	Vienna	1	3
1962	8 Apr	Dublin	2	3
EC1963	25 Sept	Vienna	0	0
EC1963	13 Oct	Dublin	3	2
1966	22 May	Vienna	0	1
1968	10 Nov	Dublin	2	2
EC1971	30 May	Dublin	1	4
EC1971	10 Oct	Linz	0	6
EC1995	11 June	Dublin	1	3
EC1995	6 Sept	Vienna	1	3

		v BELGIUM	RI	B
1928	12 Feb	Liège	4	2
1929	30 Apr	Dublin	4	0
1930	11 May	Brussels	3	1
wc1934	25 Feb	Dublin	4	4
1949	24 Apr	Dublin	0	2
1950	10 May	Brussels	1	5
1965	24 Mar	Dublin	0	2
1966	25 May	Liège	3	2
wc1980	15 Oct	Dublin	1	1
wc1981	25 Mar	Brussels	0	1
EC1986	10 Sept	Brussels	2	2
EC1987	29 Apr	Dublin	0	0
wc1997	29 Oct	Dublin	1	1
wc1997	16 Nov	Brussels	1	2

		v BOLIVIA	RI	B
1994	24 May	Dublin	1	0
1996	15 June	New Jersey	3	0

		v BRAZIL	RI	B
1974	5 May	Rio de Janeiro	1	2
1982	27 May	Uberlandia	0	7
1987	23 May	Dublin	1	0

		v BULGARIA	RI	B
wc1977	1 June	Sofia	1	2
wc1977	12 Oct	Dublin	0	0
EC1979	19 May	Sofia	0	1
EC1979	17 Oct	Dublin	3	0

			RI	B
wc1987	1 Apr	Sofia	1	2
wc1987	14 Oct	Dublin	2	0

		v CHILE	RI	C
1960	30 Mar	Dublin	2	0
1972	21 June	Recife	1	2
1974	12 May	Santiago	2	1
1982	22 May	Santiago	0	1
1991	22 May	Dublin	1	1

		v CHINA	RI	C
1984	3 June	Sapporo	1	0

		v CROATIA	RI	C
1996	2 June	Dublin	2	2
EC1998	5 Sept	Dublin	2	0
EC1999	4 Sept	Zagreb	0	1

		v CYPRUS	RI	C
wc1980	26 Mar	Nicosia	3	2
wc1980	19 Nov	Dublin	6	0
wc2001	24 Mar	Nicosia	4	0

		v CZECHOSLOVAKIA	RI	C
1938	18 May	Prague	2	2
EC1959	5 Apr	Dublin	2	0
EC1959	10 May	Bratislava	0	4
wc1961	8 Oct	Dublin	1	3
wc1961	29 Oct	Prague	1	7
EC1967	21 May	Dublin	0	2
EC1967	22 Nov	Prague	2	1
wc1969	4 May	Dublin	1	2
wc1969	7 Oct	Prague	0	3
1979	26 Sept	Prague	1	4
1981	29 Apr	Dublin	3	1
1986	27 May	Reykjavik	1	0

		v CZECH REPUBLIC	RI	C
1994	5 June	Dublin	1	3
1996	24 Apr	Prague	0	2
1998	25 Mar	Olomouc	1	2
2000	23 Feb	Dublin	3	2

		v DENMARK	RI	D
wc1956	3 Oct	Dublin	2	1
wc1957	2 Oct	Copenhagen	2	0
wc1968	4 Dec	Dublin	1	1
(*abandoned after 51 mins*)				
wc1969	27 May	Copenhagen	0	2
wc1969	15 Oct	Dublin	1	1
EC1978	24 May	Copenhagen	3	3
EC1979	2 May	Dublin	2	0
wc1984	14 Nov	Copenhagen	0	3
wc1985	13 Nov	Dublin	1	4
wc1992	14 Oct	Copenhagen	0	0
wc1993	28 Apr	Dublin	1	1

		v ECUADOR	RI	E
1972	19 June	Natal	3	2

v EGYPT

			RI	E
wc1990	17 June	Palermo	0	0

v ENGLAND

			RI	E
1946	30 Sept	Dublin	0	1
1949	21 Sept	Everton	2	0
wc1957	8 May	Wembley	1	5
wc1957	19 May	Dublin	1	1
1964	24 May	Dublin	1	3
1976	8 Sept	Wembley	1	1
EC1978	25 Oct	Dublin	1	1
EC1980	6 Feb	Wembley	0	2
1985	26 Mar	Wembley	1	2
EC1988	12 June	Stuttgart	1	0
wc1990	11 June	Cagliari	1	1
EC1990	14 Nov	Dublin	1	1
EC1991	27 Mar	Wembley	1	1
1995	15 Feb	Dublin	1	0

(abandoned after 27 mins)

v ESTONIA

			RI	E
wc2000	11 Oct	Dublin	2	0
wc2001	6 June	Tallinn	2	0

v FINLAND

			RI	F
wc1949	8 Sept	Dublin	3	0
wc1949	9 Oct	Helsinki	1	1
1990	16 May	Dublin	1	1
2000	15 Nov	Dublin	3	0

v FRANCE

			RI	F
1937	23 May	Paris	2	0
1952	16 Nov	Dublin	1	1
wc1953	4 Oct	Dublin	3	5
wc1953	25 Nov	Paris	0	1
wc1972	15 Nov	Dublin	2	1
wc1973	19 May	Paris	1	1
wc1976	17 Nov	Paris	0	2
wc1977	30 Mar	Dublin	1	0
wc1980	28 Oct	Paris	0	2
wc1981	14 Oct	Dublin	3	2
1989	7 Feb	Dublin	0	0

v GERMANY

			RI	G
1935	8 May	Dortmund	1	3
1936	17 Oct	Dublin	5	2
1939	23 May	Bremen	1	1
1994	29 May	Hanover	2	0

v WEST GERMANY

			RI	WG
1951	17 Oct	Dublin	3	2
1952	4 May	Cologne	0	3
1955	28 May	Hamburg	1	2
1956	25 Nov	Dublin	3	0
1960	11 May	Dusseldorf	1	0
1966	4 May	Dublin	0	4
1970	9 May	Berlin	1	2
1975	1 Mar	Dublin	1	0†
1979	22 May	Dublin	1	3
1981	21 May	Bremen	0	3†
1989	6 Sept	Dublin	1	1

†v West Germany 'B'

v GREECE

			RI	G
2000	26 Apr	Dublin	0	1

v HOLLAND

			RI	N
1932	8 May	Amsterdam	2	0
1934	8 Apr	Amsterdam	2	5
1935	8 Dec	Dublin	3	5
1955	1 May	Dublin	1	0
1956	10 May	Rotterdam	4	1
wc1980	10 Sept	Dublin	2	1
wc1981	9 Sept	Rotterdam	2	2
EC1982	22 Sept	Rotterdam	1	2
EC1983	12 Oct	Dublin	2	3
EC1988	18 June	Gelsenkirchen	0	1
wc1990	21 June	Palermo	1	1
1994	20 Apr	Tilburg	1	0
wc1994	4 July	Orlando	0	2
EC1995	13 Dec	Liverpool	0	2
1996	4 June	Rotterdam	1	3
wc2000	2 Sept	Amsterdam	2	2

v HUNGARY

			RI	H
1934	15 Dec	Dublin	2	4
1936	3 May	Budapest	3	3
1936	6 Dec	Dublin	2	3
1939	19 May	Cork	2	2
1939	18 May	Budapest	2	2
wc1969	8 June	Dublin	1	2
wc1969	5 Nov	Budapest	0	4
wc1989	8 Mar	Budapest	0	0
wc1989	4 June	Dublin	2	0
1991	11 Sept	Gyor	2	1

v ICELAND

			RI	I
EC1962	12 Aug	Dublin	4	2
EC1962	2 Sept	Reykjavik	1	1
EC1982	13 Oct	Dublin	2	0
EC1983	21 Sept	Reykjavik	3	0
1986	25 May	Reykjavik	2	1
wc1996	10 Nov	Dublin	0	0
wc1997	6 Sept	Reykjavik	4	2

v IRAN

			RI	I
1972	18 June	Recife	2	1

v N. IRELAND

			RI	NI
EC1978	20 Sept	Dublin	0	0
EC1979	21 Nov	Belfast	0	1
wc1988	14 Sept	Belfast	0	0
wc1989	11 Oct	Dublin	3	0
wc1993	31 Mar	Dublin	3	0
wc1993	17 Nov	Belfast	1	1
EC1994	16 Nov	Belfast	4	0
EC1995	29 Mar	Dublin	1	1
1999	29 May	Dublin	0	1

v ISRAEL

			RI	I
1984	4 Apr	Tel Aviv	0	3
1985	27 May	Tel Aviv	0	0
1987	10 Nov	Dublin	5	0

v ITALY

			RI	I
1926	21 Mar	Turin	0	3
1927	23 Apr	Dublin	1	2
EC1970	8 Dec	Rome	0	3
EC1971	10 May	Dublin	1	2
1985	5 Feb	Dublin	1	2
wc1990	30 June	Rome	0	1
1992	4 June	Foxboro	0	2
wc1994	18 June	New York	1	0

v LATVIA

			RI	L
wc1992	9 Sept	Dublin	4	0
wc1993	2 June	Riga	2	1
EC1994	7 Sept	Riga	3	0
EC1995	11 Oct	Dublin	2	1

v LIECHTENSTEIN

			RI	L
EC1994	12 Oct	Dublin	4	0
EC1995	3 June	Eschen	0	0
wc1996	31 Aug	Eschen	5	0
wc1997	21 May	Dublin	5	0

v LITHUANIA

			RI	L
wc1993	16 June	Vilnius	1	0
wc1993	8 Sept	Dublin	2	0
wc1997	20 Aug	Dublin	0	0
wc1997	10 Sept	Vilnius	2	1

v LUXEMBOURG

			RI	I
1936	9 May	Luxembourg	5	1
wc1953	28 Oct	Dublin	4	0
wc1954	7 Mar	Luxembourg	1	0
EC1987	28 May	Luxembourg	2	0
EC1987	9 Sept	Dublin	2	1

v MACEDONIA

			RI	M
wc1996	9 Oct	Dublin	3	0
wc1997	2 Apr	Skopje	2	3
EC1999	9 June	Dublin	1	0
EC1999	9 Oct	Skopje	1	1

v MALTA

			RI	M
EC1983	30 Mar	Valletta	1	0
EC1983	16 Nov	Dublin	8	0
wc1989	28 May	Dublin	2	0
wc1989	15 Nov	Valletta	2	0
1990	2 June	Valletta	3	0
EC1998	14 Oct	Dublin	5	0
EC1999	8 Sept	Valletta	3	2

v MEXICO

			RI	M
1984	8 Aug	Dublin	0	0
wc1994	24 June	Orlando	1	2
1996	13 June	New Jersey	2	2
1998	23 May	Dublin	0	0
2000	4 June	Chicago	2	2

v MOROCCO

			RI	M
1990	12 Sept	Dublin	1	0

v NORWAY

			RI	N
wc1937	10 Oct	Oslo	2	3
wc1937	7 Nov	Dublin	3	3
1950	26 Nov	Dublin	2	2
1951	30 May	Oslo	3	2
1954	8 Nov	Dublin	2	1
1955	25 May	Oslo	3	1
1960	6 Nov	Dublin	3	1
1964	13 May	Oslo	4	1
1973	6 June	Oslo	1	1
1976	24 Mar	Dublin	3	0
1978	21 May	Oslo	0	0
wc1984	17 Oct	Oslo	0	1
wc1985	1 May	Dublin	0	0
1988	1 June	Oslo	0	0
wc1994	28 June	New York	0	0

v PARAGUAY

			RI	P
1999	10 Feb	Dublin	2	0

v POLAND

			RI	P
1938	22 May	Warsaw	0	6
1938	13 Nov	Dublin	3	2
1958	11 May	Katowice	2	2
1958	5 Oct	Dublin	2	2
1964	10 May	Kracow	1	3
1964	25 Oct	Dublin	3	2
1968	15 May	Dublin	2	2
1968	30 Oct	Katowice	0	1
1970	6 May	Dublin	1	2
1970	23 Sept	Dublin	0	2
1973	16 May	Wroclaw	0	2
1973	21 Oct	Dublin	1	0
1976	26 May	Poznan	2	0
1977	24 Apr	Dublin	0	0
1978	12 Apr	Lodz	0	3
1981	23 May	Bydgoszcz	0	3
1984	23 May	Dublin	0	0
1986	12 Nov	Warsaw	0	1
1988	22 May	Dublin	3	1
EC1991	1 May	Dublin	0	0
EC1991	16 Oct	Poznan	3	3

v PORTUGAL

			RI	P
1946	16 June	Lisbon	1	3
1947	4 May	Dublin	0	2
1948	23 May	Lisbon	0	2
1949	22 May	Dublin	1	0
1972	25 June	Recife	1	2
1992	7 June	Boston	2	0
EC1995	26 Apr	Dublin	1	0
EC1995	15 Nov	Lisbon	0	3
1996	29 May	Dublin	0	1
wc2000	7 Oct	Lisbon	1	1
wc2001	2 June	Dublin	1	1

v ROMANIA

			RI	R
1988	23 Mar	Dublin	2	0
wc1990	25 June	Genoa	0	0*
wc1997	30 Apr	Bucharest	0	1
wc1997	11 Oct	Dublin	1	1

After extra time

v RUSSIA

			RI	R
1994	23 Mar	Dublin	0	0
1996	27 Mar	Dublin	0	2

v SCOTLAND

			RI	S
wc1961	3 May	Glasgow	1	4
wc1961	7 May	Dublin	0	3
1963	9 June	Dublin	1	0
1969	21 Sept	Dublin	1	1
EC1986	15 Oct	Dublin	0	0
EC1987	18 Feb	Glasgow	1	0

v SOUTH AFRICA

			RI	SA
2000	11 June	New Jersey	2	1
2000	30 May	Dublin	1	2

v SPAIN

			RI	S
1931	26 Apr	Barcelona	1	1
1931	13 Dec	Dublin	0	5
1946	23 June	Madrid	1	0
1947	2 Mar	Dublin	3	2
1948	30 May	Barcelona	1	2
1949	12 June	Dublin	1	4
1952	1 June	Madrid	0	6
1955	27 Nov	Dublin	2	2
EC1964	11 Mar	Seville	1	5
EC1964	8 Apr	Dublin	0	2
wc1965	5 May	Dublin	1	0
wc1965	27 Oct	Seville	1	4
wc1965	10 Nov	Paris	0	1
EC1966	23 Oct	Dublin	0	0
EC1966	7 Dec	Valencia	0	2
1977	9 Feb	Dublin	0	1
EC1982	17 Nov	Dublin	3	3
EC1983	27 Apr	Zaragoza	0	2
1985	26 May	Cork	0	0
wc1988	16 Nov	Seville	0	2
wc1989	26 Apr	Dublin	1	0
wc1992	18 Nov	Seville	0	0
wc1993	13 Oct	Dublin	1	3

v SWEDEN

			RI	S
wc1949	2 June	Stockholm	1	3
wc1949	13 Nov	Dublin	1	3
1959	1 Nov	Dublin	3	2
1960	18 May	Malmo	1	4
EC1970	14 Oct	Dublin	1	1
EC1970	28 Oct	Malmo	0	1
1999	28 Apr	Dublin	2	0

v SWITZERLAND			RI	S
1935	5 May	Basle	0	1
1936	17 Mar	Dublin	1	0
1937	17 May	Berne	1	0
1938	18 Sept	Dublin	4	0
1948	5 Dec	Dublin	0	1
EC1975	11 May	Dublin	2	1
EC1975	21 May	Berne	0	1
1980	30 Apr	Dublin	2	0
wc1985	2 June	Dublin	3	0
wc1985	11 Sept	Berne	0	0
1992	25 Mar	Dublin	2	1

v TRINIDAD & TOBAGO			RI	TT
1982	30 May	Port of Spain	1	2

v TUNISIA			RI	T
1988	19 Oct	Dublin	4	0

v TURKEY			RI	T
EC1966	16 Nov	Dublin	2	1
EC1967	22 Feb	Ankara	1	2
EC1974	20 Nov	Izmir	1	1
EC1975	29 Oct	Dublin	4	0
1976	13 Oct	Ankara	3	3
1978	5 Apr	Dublin	4	2
1990	26 May	Izmir	0	0
EC1990	17 Oct	Dublin	5	0
EC1991	13 Nov	Istanbul	3	1
EC2000	13 Nov	Dublin	1	1
EC2000	17 Nov	Bursa	0	0

v URUGUAY			RI	U
1974	8 May	Montevideo	0	2
1986	23 Apr	Dublin	1	1

v USA			RI	USA
1979	29 Oct	Dublin	3	2
1991	1 June	Boston	1	1
1992	29 Apr	Dublin	4	1
1992	30 May	Washington	1	3
1996	9 June	Boston	1	2
2000	6 June	Boston	1	1

v USSR			RI	USSR
wc1972	18 Oct	Dublin	1	2
wc1973	13 May	Moscow	0	1
EC1974	30 Oct	Dublin	3	0
EC1975	18 May	Kiev	1	2
wc1984	12 Sept	Dublin	1	0
wc1985	16 Oct	Moscow	0	2
EC1988	15 June	Hanover	1	1
1990	25 Apr	Dublin	1	0

v WALES			RI	W
1960	28 Sept	Dublin	2	3
1979	11 Sept	Swansea	1	2
1981	24 Feb	Dublin	1	3
1986	26 Mar	Dublin	0	1
1990	28 Mar	Dublin	1	0
1991	6 Feb	Wrexham	3	0
1992	19 Feb	Dublin	0	1
1993	17 Feb	Dublin	2	1
1997	11 Feb	Cardiff	0	0

v YUGOSLAVIA			RI	Y
1955	19 Sept	Dublin	1	4
1988	27 Apr	Dublin	2	0
EC1998	18 Nov	Belgrade	0	1
EC1999	1 Sept	Dublin	2	1

Qualification for the World Cup proved a struggle for Wales. However, Ryan Giggs caused the Polish defence many problems during their two matches. (ASP)

OTHER BRITISH AND IRISH INTERNATIONAL MATCHES 2000–2001

FRIENDLIES

Stade de France, 2 September 2000, 70,000

France (0) 1 *(Petit 64)*
England (0) 1 *(Owen 86)*
France: Lama; Thuram (Candela 80), Lizarazu, Deschamps (Vieira 59), Blanc (Leboeuf 59), Desailly, Djorkaeff, Anelka (Wiltord 46), Zidane (Pires 64), Henry (Trezeguet 73), Petit.
England: Seaman; Anderton (Dyer 69), Barry, Campbell, Keown, Adams (Southgate 46), Beckham, Barmby (McManaman 83), Andy Cole, Scholes (Owen 79), Wise.
Referee: Roca (Spain).

Turin, 15 November 2000, 22,000

Italy (0) 1 *(Gattuso 57)*
England (0) 0
Italy: Buffon; Di Livio (Di Biagio 52), Maldini (Bertotto 74), Cannavaro (Adani 66), Nesta, Albertini (Zenoni 52), Gattuso, Coco, Inzaghi F (Del Piero 72), Delvecchio (Inzaghi S 61), Fiore.
England: James; Parlour (Anderton 78), Barry (Johnson 72), Neville, Ferdinand, Southgate, Beckham, Butt (Carragher 25), Dyer (Fowler 80), Barmby, Heskey (Phillips 72).
Referee: Puhl (Hungary).

Villa Park, 28 February 2001, 42,129

England (1) 3 *(Barmby 38, Heskey 53, Ehiogu 70)*
Spain (0) 0
England: James (Martyn 46); Neville P (Neville G 77), Powell (Ball 46), Butt (McCann 46), Campbell, Ferdinand (Ehiogu 46), Beckham (Heskey 46), Scholes (Lampard 46), Andy Cole, Owen, Barmby.
Spain: Casillas (Canizares 64); Pablo, Romero, Guardiola (Baraja 80), Abelardo (Sanchez 64), Unal, Helguera (Paco 80), Mendieta, Raul (Etxeberria J 80), Luis Enrique (Sergi 64), Urzaiz (Javi Moreno 46).
Referee: Vassaras (Greece).

Pride Park, 25 May 2001, 33,597

England (3) 4 *(Scholes 3, Fowler 14, Beckham 29, Sheringham 74)*
Mexico (0) 0
England: Martyn (James 46); Neville P, Ashley Cole (Powell 46), Gerrard (Carrick 46), Keown (Southgate 46), Ferdinand (Carragher 46), Beckham (Cole J 46), Scholes (Butt 46), Fowler (Sheringham 54), Owen (Smith 46), Heskey (Mills 66).
Mexico: Sanchez; Beltran (Davino 46), Suarez, Oteo, Chavez (Pardo 46), Ruiz V (Osomo 58), Rodriguez (Perez 82), Coyote (Rangel 77), Ruiz M, de Nigris, Abundis.
Referee: Batista (Portugal).

Hampden Park, 15 November 2000, 30,985

Scotland (0) 0
Australia (1) 2 *(Emerton 12, Zdrilic 66)*
Scotland: Gould; Boyd, Matteo, O'Neil B (Hendry 57), Dailly, Weir (Elliott 46), Burley (Dickov 63), Ferguson B, Dodds, Hutchison, Cameron (McCann 46).
Australia: Schwarzer; Muscat, Lazaridis, Popovic, Murphy, Okon, Emerton, Skoko (Wehrman 73), Agostino (Sterjovski 46), Zdrilic (Zane 90), Tiatto (Burns 67).
Referee: Garibian (France).

Bydgoszcz, 25 April 2001, 20,000

Poland (0) 1 *(Kaluzny 49)*
Scotland (0) 1 *(Booth 69 (pen))*
Poland: Dudek; Klos, Michal Zewlakow (Mieciel 64), Iwan, Kozminski (Kaluzny 46), Waldoch, Zielinski, Zdebel (Swierczewski 59), Hajto (Krzynuwek 46), Krysalowicz (Zurawski 75), Marcin Zewlakow.
Scotland: Sullivan; Nicholson, O'Neil J (Gemmill 74), Dailly, Boyd, Davidson (Weir 73), Miller C (Caldwell 56), Rae, Dodds (Crawford 46), Booth (Miller K 80), Cameron (McLaren 46).
Referee: Roca (Spain).

Belfast, 16 August 2000, 6095

Northern Ireland (1) 1 *(Healy 45)*
Yugoslavia (0) 2 *(Kezman 63, Mijatovic 78)*
Northern Ireland: Taylor; Nolan, Hughes A, Murdock (Griffin 81), Williams, Horlock (Gillespie 72), Johnson, Mulryne (Quinn 68), Healy, Jeff Whitley, Magilton.
Yugoslavia: Cicovic; Grujic (Obradovic 71), Bunjevcevic, Sakic, Dudic, Stankovic, Lazertic, Grozdic (Ilic 67), Djordevic, Milosevic (Kezman 55), Mijatovic.
Referee: Young (Scotland).

Belfast, 28 February 2001 7502

Northern Ireland (0) 0
Norway (3) 4 *(Helstad 20, 49, Carew 30, Stensaas 37)*
Northern Ireland: Taylor; McCarthy (Johnson 62), Kennedy (Griffin 46), Murdock, Taggart (Williams 46), Hughes A, Lennon (Elliott 46), Ferguson (Gray 69), Healy (Kirk 69), Jeff Whitley (Sonner 66), Magilton.
Norway: Myhre; Bergdolmo, Stensaas, Berg (Eggen 36), Lundekvam, Bakke (Aarsheim 78), Tessem, Larsen, Solskjaer (Berre 46), Carew (Johnsen F 62), Helstad (Andersen T 78).
Referee: Clark (Scotland).

Dublin, 15 November 2000, 22,368

Republic of Ireland (1) 3 *(Finnan 14, Kilbane 84, Staunton 90)*
Finland (0) 0
Republic of Ireland: Given; Kelly G (McAteer 46), Harte (Staunton 46), Finnan, Breen, Dunne, Kinsella, Holland, Robbie Keane (Connolly 90), Foley (Carsley 46), Kilbane.
Finland: Jaaskelainen; Nylund, Pasanen (Nurmela 78), Tihinen, Saarinen, Johansson (Kuqi 46), Tainio (Kuivasto 66), Riihilahti, Kolkka (Kottila 85), Litmanen, Forssell (Gronlund 46).
Referee: Durkin (England).

5th UEFA WOMEN'S EUROPEAN CHAMPIONSHIP

(Finals in Germany)

GROUP A
Germany 3, Sweden 1
Russia 1, England 1
Germany 5, Russia 0
Sweden 4, England 0
England 0, Germany 3
Sweden 1, Russia 0

GROUP B
Italy 2, Denmark 1
Norway 3, France 0
France 3, Denmark 4
Norway 1, Italy 1

Denmark 1, Norway 0
France 2, Italy 0

SEMI-FINALS
Germany 1, Norway 0
Sweden 1, Denmark 0

FINAL
Sweden 0, Germany 1 aet

ENGLAND'S WOMEN'S RECORD

Year	Date	Venue	Opponents	Score	Scorers
1993	25 Sept	Ljubljana	Slovenia	10-0	Spacey 4, Walker 3, Taylor, Borman, Davis
1993	6 Nov	Koksijde	Belgium	3-0	Powell 2, Sempare
1993	19 Dec	Osasuna	Spain	0-0	
1994	20 Feb	Bradford	Spain	0-0	
1994	13 Mar	Nottingham	Belgium	6-0	Spacey 2, Walker 2, Davis, Coultard
1994	17 Apr	Brentford	Slovenia	10-0	Taylor 2, Walker 2, Britton 2, Coultard, Powell, Borman, Spacey
1994	8 Oct	Reykjavik	Iceland	2-1	Coultard, Davis
1994	30 Oct	Brighton	Iceland	2-1	Coultard, Spacey
1994	11 Dec	Watford	Germany	1-4	Farley
1995	25 Jan	Florence	Italy	1-1	Farley
1995	23 Feb	Bochum	Germany	1-2	Farley
1995	13 May	Halmstad	Sweden	0-4	
1995	6 June	Helsingborg	Canada	3-2	Coultard 2, Spacey
1995	8 June	Karlstad	Norway	0-2	
1995	10 June	Karlstad	Nigeria	3-2	Farley 2, Walker
1995	13 June	Vasteras	Germany	0-3	
1995	1 Nov	Sunderland	Italy	1-1	Coultard
1995	19 Nov	Charlton	Croatia	5-0	Farley 2, Walker 2, Smith
1996	11 Feb	Benavente	Portugal	5-0	Powell, Farley, Coultard, Catterall, Burke
1996	16 Mar	Calabria	Italy	1-2	Smith
1996	18 Apr	Osijek	Croatia	2-0	Smith, Exley
1996	19 May	Brentford	Portugal	3-0	Davies 2, Smith
1996	8 Sept	Montilla	Spain	1-2	Powell
1996	29 Sept	Tranmere	Spain	1-1	Harper
1997	27 Feb	Preston	Germany	4-6	Broadhurst 2, Powell, Smith
1997	9 Mar	Sheffield	Scotland	6-0	Broadhurst 3, Coultard 2, Marley
1997	23 Apr	Turin	Italy	0-2	
1997	9 May	San Jose	USA	0-5	
1997	11 May	Portland	USA	0-6	
1997	8 June	Lillestrom	Norway	0-4	
1997	23 Aug	Livingston	Scotland	4-0	Davis 2, Britton, Yankey
1997	25 Sept	Dessau	Germany	0-3	
1997	30 Oct	West Ham	Holland	1-0	Smith
1998	15 Feb	Alencon	France	2-3	Burke, Davis
1998	8 Mar	Millwall	Germany	0-1	
1998	21 Apr	West Bromwich	Italy	1-2	White
1998	14 May	Oldham	Norway	1-2	White
1998	23 May	Waalwijk	Holland	1-2	Walker
1998	26 July	Dagenham	Sweden	0-1	
1998	15 Aug	Lillestrom	Norway	0-2	
1998	12 Sept	Campina	Romania	4-1	Yankey, Smith S, Walker 2
1998	11 Oct	Wycombe	Romania	2-1	Walker, Broadhurst
1999	26 May	Bologna	Italy	1-4	Walker
1999	22 Aug	Odense	Denmark	1-0	Walker
1999	15 Sept	Yeovil	France	0-1	
1999	16 Oct	Zofingen	Switzerland	3-0	Walker, Burke, Smith S
2000	20 Feb	Barnsley	Portugal	2-0	Walker, Smith S
2000	7 Mar	Norwich	Norway	0-3	
2000	22 Apr	Sacavem	Portugal	2-2	Burke, Smith S
2000	13 May	Bristol	Switzerland	1-0	Smith S
2000	4 June	Moss	Norway	0-8	
2000	16 Aug	Marseilles	France	0-1	
2000	28 Sept	Leyton Orient	Finland	2-1	Burke, Banks
2000	30 Oct	Kiev	Ukraine	2-1	Smith K, Walker
2000	28 Nov	Leyton Orient	Ukraine	2-0	Smith S, Yankey
2001	22 Mar	Luton	Spain	4-2	Smith K, Smith S 3
2001	27 May	Bolton	Scotland	1-0	Banks

INTERNATIONAL APPEARANCES 1872–2001

This is a list of full international appearances by Englishmen, Irishmen, Scotsmen and Welshmen in matches against the Home Countries and against foreign nations. It does not include unofficial matches against Commonwealth and Empire countries. The year indicated refers to the season; ie 2001 is the 2000-01 season.

Explanatory code for matches played by all five countries: A represents Austria; Alb, Albania; Alg, Algeria; An, Angola; And, Andorra; Arg, Argentina; Arm, Armenia; Aus, Australia; B, Bohemia; Bel, Belgium; Bl, Belarus; Bol, Bolivia; Bos, Bosnia; Br, Brazil; Bul, Bulgaria; C,CIS; Ca, Canada; Cam, Cameroon; Ch, Chile; Chn, China; Co, Colombia; Cr, Costa Rica; Cro, Croatia; Cy, Cyprus; Cz, Czechoslovakia; CzR, Czech Republic; D, Denmark; E, England; Ec, Ecuador; Ei, Republic of Ireland; EG, East Germany; Eg, Egypt; Es, Estonia; F, France; Fa, Faeroes; Fi, Finland; G, Germany; Ge, Georgia; Gr, Greece; H, Hungary; Ho, Holland; Hon, Honduras; I, Italy; Ic, Iceland; Ir, Iran; Is, Israel; J, Japan; Jam, Jamaica; K, Kuwait; L, Luxembourg; La, Latvia; Li, Lithuania; Lie, Liechtenstein; M, Belarus; Ma, Malta; Mac, Macedonia; Mal, Malaysia; Mol, Moldova; Mor, Morocco; N, Norway; Ni, Ng, Nigeria; Ni, Northern Ireland; Nz, New Zealand; P, Portugal; Para, Paraguay; Pe, Peru; Pol, Poland; R, Romania; RCS, Republic of Czechs and Slovaks; R of E, Rest of Europe; R of UK, Rest of United Kingdom; R of W, Rest of World; Ru, Russia; S.Af, South Africa; S.Ar, Saudi Arabia; S, Scotland; Se, Sweden; Slo, Slovakia; Sm, San Marino; Sp, Spain; Sw, Switzerland; T, Turkey; Th, Thailand; Tr, Trinidad & Tobago; Tun, Tunisia; U, Uruguay; Uk, Ukraine; US, United States of America; USSR, Soviet Union; W, Wales; WG, West Germany; Y, Yugoslavia; Z, Zaire.

As at July 2001.

ENGLAND

Abbott, W. (Everton), 1902 v W (1)

A'Court, A. (Liverpool), 1958 v Ni, Br, A, USSR; 1959 v W (5)

Adams, T. A. (Arsenal), 1987 v Sp, T, Br; 1988 v WG, T, Y, Ho, H, S, Co, Sw, Ei, Ho, USSR; 1989 v D, Se, S.Ar.; 1991 v Ei (2); 1993 v N, T, Sm, T, Ho, Pol, N; 1994 v Pol, Ho, D, Gr, N; 1995 v US, R, Ei, U; 1996 v Co, N, Sw, P, Chn, Sw, S, Ho, Sp, G; 1997 v Ge (2); 1998 v I, Ch, P, S.Ar, Tun, R, Co, Arg; 1999 v Se, F; 2000 v L, Pol, Bel, S (2), Uk, P; 2001 v F, G (66)

Adcock, H. (Leicester C), 1929 v F, Bel, Sp; 1930 v Ni, W (5)

Alcock, C. W. (Wanderers), 1875 v S (1)

Alderson, J. T. (C Palace), 1923 v F (1)

Aldridge, A. (WBA), 1888 v Ni; (with Walsall Town Swifts), 1889 v Ni (2)

Allen, A. (Stoke C) 1960 v Se, W, Ni (3)

Allen, A. (Aston Villa), 1888 v Ni (1)

Allen, C. (QPR), 1984 v Br (sub), U, Ch; (with Tottenham H), 1987 v T; 1988 v Is (5)

Allen, H. (Wolverhampton W), 1888 v S, W, Ni; 1889 v S; 1890 v S (5)

Allen, J. P. (Portsmouth), 1934 v Ni, W (2)

Allen, R. (WBA), 1952 v Sw; 1954 v Y, S; 1955 v WG, W (5)

Alsford, W. J. (Tottenham H), 1935 v S (1)

Amos, A. (Old Carthusians), 1885 v S; 1886 v W (2)

Anderson, R. D. (Old Etonians), 1879 v W (1)

Anderson, S. (Sunderland), 1962 v A, S (2)

Anderson, V. (Nottingham F), 1979 v Cz, Se; 1980 v Bul, Sp; 1981 v N, R, W, S; 1982 v Ni, Ic; 1984 v Ni; (with Arsenal), 1985 v T, Ni, Ei, R, Fi, S, M, US; 1986 v USSR, M; 1987 v Se, Ni (2), Y, Sp, T; (with Manchester U), 1988 v WG, H, Co (30)

Anderton, D. R. (Tottenham H), 1994 v D, Gr, N; 1995 v US, Ei, U, J, Se, Br; 1996 v H, Chn, Sw, S, Ho, Sp, G; 1998 v S.Ar, Mor, Tun, R, Co, Arg; 1999 v Se, Bul, L, CzR, P; 2001 v F, I (sub) (29)

Angus, J. (Burnley), 1961 v A (1)

Armfield, J. C. (Blackpool), 1959 v Br, Pe, M, US; 1960 v Y, Sp, H, S; 1961 v L, P, Sp, M, I, A, W, Ni, S; 1962 v A, Sw, Pe, W, Ni, S, L, P, H, Arg, Bul, Br; 1963 v F (2), Br, EG, Sw, Ni, W, S; 1964 v R of W, W, Ni, S; 1966 v Y, Fi (43)

Armitage, G. H. (Charlton Ath), 1926 v Ni (1)

Armstrong, D. (Middlesbrough), 1980 v Aus; (with Southampton), 1983 v WG; 1984 v W (3)

Armstrong, K. (Chelsea), 1955 v S (1)

Arnold, J. (Fulham), 1933 v S (1)

Arthur, J. W. H. (Blackburn R), 1885 v S, W, Ni; 1886 v S, W; 1887 v W, Ni (7)

Ashcroft, J. (Woolwich Arsenal), 1906 v Ni, W, S (3)

Ashmore, G. S. (WBA), 1926 v Bel (1)

Ashton, C. T. (Corinthians), 1926 v Ni (1)

Ashurst, W. (Notts Co), 1923 v Se (2); 1925 v S, W, Bel (5)

Astall, G. (Birmingham C), 1956 v Fi, WG (2)

Astle, J. (WBA), 1969 v W; 1970 v S, P, Br (sub), Cz (5)

Aston, J. (Manchester U), 1949 v S, W, D, Sw, Se, N, F; 1950 v S, W, Ni, Ei, I, P, Bel, Ch, US; 1951 v Ni (17)

Athersmith, W. C. (Aston Villa), 1892 v Ni, 1897 v S, W, Ni; 1898 v S, W, Ni; 1899 v S, W, Ni; 1900 v S, W (12)

Atyeo, P. J. W. (Bristol C), 1956 v Br, Se, Sp; 1957 v D, Ei (2) (6)

Austin, S. W. (Manchester C), 1926 v Ni (1)

Bach, P. (Sunderland), 1899 v Ni (1)

Bache, J. W. (Aston Villa), 1903 v W; 1904 v W, Ni; 1905 v S; 1907 v Ni; 1910 v Ni; 1911 v S (7)

Baddeley, T. (Wolverhampton W), 1903 v S, Ni; 1904 v S, W, Ni (5)

Bagshaw, J. J. (Derby Co), 1920 v Ni (1)

Bailey, G. R. (Manchester U), 1985 v Ei, M (2)

Bailey, H. P. (Leicester Fosse), 1908 v W, A (2), H, B (5)

Bailey, M. A. (Charlton Ath), 1964 v US; 1965 v W (2)

Bailey, N. C. (Clapham Rovers), 1878 v S; 1879 v S, W; 1880 v S; 1881 v S; 1882 v S, W; 1883 v S, W; 1884 v S, W, Ni; 1885 v S, W, Ni; 1886 v S, W; 1887 v S, W (19)

Baily, E. F. (Tottenham H), 1950 v Sp; 1951 v Y, Ni, W; 1952 v A (2), Sw, W; 1953 v Ni (9)

Bain, J. (Oxford University), 1887 v S (1)

Baker, A. (Arsenal), 1928 v W (1)

Baker, B. H. (Everton), 1921 v Bel; (with Chelsea), 1926 v Ni (2)

Baker, J. H. (Hibernian), 1960 v Y, Sp, H, Ni, S; (with Arsenal) 1966 v Sp, Pol, Ni (8)

Ball, A. J. (Blackpool), 1965 v Y, WG, Se; 1966 v S, Sp, Fi, D, U, Arg, P, WG (2), Pol (2); (with Everton), 1967 v W, S, Ni, A, Cz, Sp; 1968 v W, S, USSR, Sp (2), Y, WG; 1969 v Ni, W, S, R (2), M, Br, U; 1970 v P, Co, Ec, R, Br, Cz (sub), WG, W, S, Bel; 1971 v Ma, EG, Gr, Ma (sub), Ni, S; 1972 v Sw, Gr; (with Arsenal) WG (2), S; 1973 v W (3), Y, S (2), Cz, Ni, Pol; 1974 v P (sub); 1975 v WG, Cy (2), Ni, W, S (72)

Ball, J. (Bury), 1928 v Ni (1)

Ball, M. J. (Everton), 2001 v Sp (sub) (1)

Balmer, W. (Everton), 1905 v Ni (1)

Bamber, J. (Liverpool), 1921 v W (1)

Bambridge, A. L. (Swifts), 1881 v W; 1883 v W; 1884 v Ni (3)

Bambridge, E. C. (Swifts), 1879 v S; 1880 v S; 1881 v S; 1882 v S, W, Ni; 1883 v W; 1884 v S, W, Ni; 1885 v S, W, Ni; 1886 v S, W; 1887 v S, W, Ni (18)

Bambridge, E. H. (Swifts), 1876 v S (1)

Banks, G. (Leicester C), 1963 v S, Br, Cz, EG; 1964 v W, Ni, S, R of W, U, P (2), US, Arg; 1965 v Ni, S, H, Y, WG, Se; 1966 v Ni, S, Sp, Pol (2), WG (2), Y, Fi, U, M, F, Arg, P; 1967 v Ni, W, S, Cz; (with Stoke C), 1968 v W, Ni, S, USSR (2), Sp, WG, Y; 1969 v Ni, S, R (2), F, U, Br; 1970 v W, Ni, S, Ho, Bel, Co, Ec, R, Br, Cz; 1971 v Gr, Ma (2), Ni, S; 1972 v Sw, Gr, WG (2), W, S (73)

Banks, H. E. (Millwall), 1901 v Ni (1)

Banks, T. (Bolton W), 1958 v USSR (3), Br, A; 1959 v Ni (6)

Bannister, W. (Burnley), 1901 v W; (with Bolton W), 1902 v Ni (2)

Barclay, R. (Sheffield U), 1932 v S; 1933 v Ni; 1936 v S (3)

Bardsley, D. J. (QPR), 1993 v Sp (sub), Pol (2)

Barham, M. (Norwich C), 1983 v Aus (2) (2)

Barkas, S. (Manchester C), 1936 v Bel; 1937 v S; 1938 v W, Ni, Cz (5)

Barker, J. (Derby Co), 1935 v I, Ho, S, W, Ni; 1936 v G, A, S, W, Ni; 1937 v W (11)

Barker, R. (Herts Rangers), 1872 v S (1)

Barker, R. R. (Casuals), 1895 v W (1)

Barlow, R. J. (WBA), 1955 v Ni (1)

Barmby, N.J. (Tottenham H), 1995 v U (sub), Se (sub); (with Middlesbrough), 1996 v Co, N, P, Chn, Sw (sub), Ho (sub), Sp (sub); 1997 v Mol; (with Everton), 2000 v Br (sub), Uk (sub), Ma, G (sub), R (sub); (with Liverpool), 2001 v F, G, I, Sp (19)

Barnes, J. (Watford), 1983 v Ni (sub), Aus (sub), Aus (2); 1984 v D, L (sub), F (sub), S, USSR, Br, U, Ch; 1985 v EG, Fi, T, Ni, R, Fi, S, I (sub), M, WG (sub), US (sub); 1986 v R (sub), Is (sub), M (sub), Ca (sub), Arg (sub); 1987 v Se, T (sub), Br; (with Liverpool), 1988 v WG, T, Y, Is, Ho, S, Co, Sw, Ei, Ho, USSR; 1989 v Se, Gr, Alb, Pol, D; 1990 v Se, I, Br, D, U, Tun, Ei, Ho, Eg, Bel, Cam; 1991 v H, Pol, Cam, Ei, T, USSR, Arg; 1992 v Cz, Fi; 1993 v Sm, T, Ho, Pol, US, G; 1995 v US, R, Ng, U, Se; 1996 v Co (sub) (79)

Barnes, P. S. (Manchester C), 1978 v I, WG, Br, W, S, H; 1979 v D, Ei, Cz, Ni (2), S, Bul, A; (with WBA), 1980 v D, W; 1981 v Sp (sub), Br, W, Sw (sub); (with Leeds U), 1982 v N (sub), Ho (sub) (22)

Barnet, H. H. (Royal Engineers), 1882 v Ni (1)

Barrass, M. W. (Bolton W), 1952 v W, Ni; 1953 v S (3)

Barrett, A. F. (Fulham), 1930 v Ni (1)

Barrett, E. D. (Oldham Ath), 1991 v Nz; 1993 v Br, G (3)

Barrett, J. W. (West Ham U), 1929 v Ni (1)

Barry, G. (Aston Villa), 2000 v Uk (sub), Ma (sub); 2001 v F, G (sub), Fi, I (6)

Barry, L. (Leicester C), 1928 v F, Bel; 1929 v F, Bel, Sp (5)

Barson, F. (Aston Villa), 1920 v W (1)

Barton, J. (Blackburn R), 1890 v Ni (1)

Barton, P. H. (Birmingham), 1921 v Bel; 1922 v Ni; 1923 v F; 1924 v Bel, S, W; 1925 v Ni (7)

Barton, W. D. (Wimbledon), 1995 v Ei; (with Newcastle U), Se, Br (sub) (3)

Bassett, W. I. (WBA), 1888 v Ni, 1889 v S, W; 1890 v S, W; 1891 v S, Ni; 1892 v S; 1893 v S, W; 1894 v S; 1895 v S, Ni; 1896 v S, W, Ni (16)

Bastard, S. R. (Upton Park), 1880 v S (1)

Bastin, C. S. (Arsenal), 1932 v W; 1933 v I, Sw; 1934 v S, Ni, W, H, Cz; 1935 v S, Ni, I; 1936 v S, W, G, A; 1937 v W, Ni; 1938 v S, G, Sw, F (21)

Batty, D. (Leeds U), 1991 v USSR (sub), Arg, Aus, Nz, Mal; 1992 v G, T, H (sub), F, Se; 1993 v N, Sm, US, Br; (with Blackburn R), 1994 v D (sub); 1995 v J, Br; (with Newcastle U), 1997 v Mol (sub), Ge, I, M, Ge, S.Af (sub), Pol (sub), F; 1998 v Mol, I, Ch, Sw (sub), P, S.Ar, Tun, R, Co (sub), Arg (sub); 1999 v Bul (sub), L; (with Leeds U), H, Se, Bul; 2000 v L, Pol (42)

Baugh, R. (Stafford Road), 1886 v Ni; (with Wolverhampton W) 1890 v Ni (2)

Bayliss, A. E. J. M. (WBA), 1891 v Ni (1)

Baynham, R. L. (Luton T), 1956 v Ni, D, Sp (3)

Beardsley, P. A. (Newcastle U), 1986 v Eg (sub), Is, USSR, M, Ca (sub), P (sub), Pol, Para, Arg; 1987 v Ni (2), Y, Sp, Br, S; (with Liverpool), 1988 v WG, T, Y, Is, Ho, H, S, Co, Sw, Ei, Ho; 1989 v D, Se, S.Ar, Gr (sub), Alb (sub+1), Pol, D; 1990 v Se, Pol, I, Br, U (sub), Tun (sub), Ei, Eg (sub), Cam (sub), WG, I; 1991 v Pol (sub), Ei (2), USSR (sub); (with Newcastle U), 1994 v D, Gr, N; 1995 v Ng, Ei, U, J, Se; 1996 v P (sub), Chn (sub) (59)

Beasant, D. J. (Chelsea), 1990 v I (sub), Y (sub) (2)

Beasley, A. (Huddersfield T), 1939 v S (1)

Beats, W. E. (Wolverhampton W), 1901 v W; 1902 v S (2)

Beattie, T. K. (Ipswich T), 1975 v Cy (2), S; 1976 v Sw, P; 1977 v Fi, I (sub), Ho; 1978 v L (sub) (9)

Beckham, D. R. J. (Manchester U), 1997 v Mol, Pol, Ge, I, Ge, S.Af (sub), Pol, I, F; 1998 v Mol, I, Cam, P, S.Ar, Bel (sub), R (sub), Co, Arg; 1999 v L, CzR, F, Pol, Se; 2000 v L, Pol, S(2), Arg, Br, Uk, Ma, P, G, R; 2001 v F, G, I, Sp, Fi, Alb, M, Gr (42)

Becton, F. (Preston NE), 1895 v Ni; (with Liverpool), 1897 v W (2)

Bedford, H. (Blackpool), 1923 v Se; 1925 v Ni (2)

Bell, C. (Manchester C), 1968 v Se, WG; 1969 v W, Bul, F, U, Br; 1970 v Ni (sub), Ho (2), P, Br (sub), Cz, WG (sub); 1972 v Gr, WG (2), W, Ni, S; 1973 v W (3), Y, S (2), Ni, Cz, Pol; 1974 v A, Pol, I, W, Ni, S, Arg, EG, Bul, Y; 1975 v Cz, P, WG, Cy (2), Ni, S; 1976 v Sw, Cz (48)

Bennett, W. (Sheffield U), 1901 v S, W (2)

Benson, R. W. (Sheffield U), 1913 v Ni (1)

Bentley, R. T. F. (Chelsea), 1949 v Se; 1950 v S, P, Bel, Ch, USA; 1953 v W, Bel; 1955 v WG, S, Sp, P (12)

Beresford, J. (Aston Villa), 1934 v Cz (1)

Berry, A. (Oxford University), 1909 v Ni (1)

Berry, J. J. (Manchester U), 1953 v Arg, Ch, U; 1956 v Se (4)

Bestall, J. G. (Grimsby T), 1935 v Ni (1)

Betmead, H. A. (Grimsby T), 1937 v Fi (1)

Betts, M. P. (Old Harrovians), 1877 v S (1)

Betts, W. (Sheffield W), 1889 v W (1)

Beverley, J. (Blackburn R), 1884 v S, W, Ni (3)

Birkett, R. H. (Clapham Rovers), 1879 v S (1)

Birkett, R. J. E. (Middlesbrough), 1936 v Ni (1)

Birley, F. H. (Oxford University), 1874 v S; (with Wanderers), 1875 v S (2)

Birtles, G. (Nottingham F), 1980 v Arg (sub), I; 1981 v R (3)

Bishop, S. M. (Leicester C), 1927 v S, Bel, L, F (4)

Blackburn, F. (Blackburn R), 1901 v S; 1902 v Ni; 1904 v S (3)

Blackburn, G. F. (Aston Villa), 1924 v F (1)

Blenkinsop, E. (Sheffield W), 1928 v F, Bel; 1929 v S, W, Ni, F, Bel, Sp; 1930 v S, W, Ni, G, A; 1931 v S, W, Ni, F, Bel; 1932 v S, W, Ni, Sp; 1933 v S, W, Ni, A (26)

Bliss, H. (Tottenham H), 1921 v S (1)

Blissett, L. (Watford), 1983 v WG (sub), L, W, Gr (sub), H, Ni, S (sub), Aus (1+1 sub); (with AC Milan), 1984 v D (sub), H, W (sub), S, USSR (14)

Blockley, J. P. (Arsenal), 1973 v Y (1)

Bloomer, S. (Derby Co), 1895 v S, Ni; 1896 v W, Ni; 1897 v S, W, Ni; 1898 v S; 1899 v S, W, Ni; 1900 v S; 1901 v S, W; 1902 v S, W, Ni; 1904 v S; 1905 v S, W, Ni; (with Middlesbrough), 1907 v W (23)

Blunstone, F. (Chelsea), 1955 v W, S, F, P; 1957 v Y (5)

Bond, R. (Preston NE), 1905 v Ni, W; 1906 v S, W, Ni; (with Bradford C), 1910 v S, W, Ni (8)

Bonetti, P. P. (Chelsea), 1966 v D; 1967 v Sp, A; 1968 v Sp; 1970 v Ho, P, WG (7)

Bonsor, A. G. (Wanderers), 1873 v S; 1875 v S (2)

Booth, F. (Manchester C), 1905 v Ni (1)

Booth, T. (Blackburn R), 1898 v W; (with Everton), 1903 v S (2)

Bould, S. A. (Arsenal), 1994 v Gr, N (2)

Bowden, E. R. (Arsenal), 1935 v W, I; 1936 v W, Ni, A; 1937 v H (6)

Bower, A. G. (Corinthians), 1924 v Ni, Bel; 1925 v W, Bel; 1927 v W (5)

Bowers, J. W. (Derby Co), 1934 v S, Ni, W (3)

Bowles, S. (QPR), 1974 v P, W, Ni; 1977 v I, Ho (5)

Bowser, S. (WBA), 1920 v Ni (1)

Boyer, P. J. (Norwich C), 1976 v W (1)

Boyes, W. (WBA), 1935 v Ho; (with Everton), 1939 v W, R of É (3)

Boyle, T. W. (Burnley), 1913 v Ni (1)

Brabrook, P. (Chelsea), 1958 v USSR; 1959 v Ni; 1960 v Sp (3)

Bracewell, P. W. (Everton), 1985 v WG (sub), US; 1986 v Ni (3)

Bradford, G. R. W. (Bristol R), 1956 v D (1)

Bradford, J. (Birmingham), 1924 v Ni; 1925 v Bel; 1928 v S; 1929 v Ni, W, F, Sp; 1930 v S, Ni, G, A; 1931 v W (12)

Bradley, W. (Manchester U), 1959 v I, US, M (sub) (3)

Bradshaw, F. (Sheffield W), 1908 v A (1)

Bradshaw, T. H. (Liverpool), 1897 v Ni (1)

Bradshaw, W. (Blackburn R), 1910 v W, Ni; 1912 v Ni; 1913 v W (4)

Brann, G. (Swifts), 1886 v S, W; 1891 v W (3)

Brawn, W. F. (Aston Villa), 1904 v W, Ni (2)

Bray, J. (Manchester C), 1935 v W; 1936 v S, W, Ni, G; 1937 v S (6)

Brayshaw, E. (Sheffield W), 1887 v Ni (1)

Bridges, B. J. (Chelsea), 1965 v S, H, Y; 1966 v A (4)

Bridgett, A. (Sunderland), 1905 v S; 1908 v S, A (2), H, B; 1909 v Ni, W, H (2), A (11)

Brindle, T. (Darwen), 1880 v S, W (2)

Brittleton, J. T. (Sheffield W), 1912 v S, W, Ni; 1913 v S; 1914 v W (5)

Britton, C. S. (Everton), 1935 v S, W, Ni, I; 1937 v S, Ni, H, N, Se (9)

Broadbent, P. F. (Wolverhampton W), 1958 v USSR; 1959 v W, Ni, I, Br; 1960 v S (7)

Broadis, I. A. (Manchester C), 1952 v S, A, I; 1953 v S, Arg, Ch, U, US; (with Newcastle U), 1954 v S, H, Y, Bel, Sw, U (14)

Brockbank, J. (Cambridge University), 1872 v S (1)

Brodie, J. B. (Wolverhampton W), 1889 v S, Ni; 1891 v Ni (3)

Bromilow, T. G. (Liverpool), 1921 v W; 1922 v S, W; 1923 v Bel; 1926 v Ni (5)

Bromley-Davenport, W. E. (Oxford University), 1884 v S, W (2)

Brook, E. F. (Manchester C), 1930 v Ni; 1933 v Sw; 1934 v S, W, H, F, H, Cz; 1935 v S, W, Ni, I; 1936 v S, W, Ni; 1937 v H; 1938 v W, Ni (18)

Brooking, T. D. (West Ham U), 1974 v P, Arg, EG, Bul, Y; 1975 v Cz (sub), P; 1976 v P, W, Br, I, Fi; 1977 v Ei, Fi, I, Ho, Ni, W; 1978 v I, WG, W, S (sub), H; 1979 v D, Ei, Ni, W (sub), S, Bul, Se (sub), A; 1980 v D, Ni, Arg (sub), W, Ni, S, Bel, Sp; 1981 v Sw, Sp, R, H; 1982 v H, I, S, Fi, Sp (sub) (47)

Brooks, J. (Tottenham H), 1957 v W, Y, D (3)

Broome, F. H. (Aston Villa), 1938 v G, Sw, F; 1939 v N, I, R, Y (7)

Brown, A. (Aston Villa), 1882 v S, W, Ni (3)

Brown, A. S. (Sheffield U), 1904 v W; 1906 v Ni (2)

Brown, A. (WBA), 1971 v W (1)

Brown, G. (Huddersfield T), 1927 v S, W, Ni, Bel, L, F; 1928 v W; 1929 v S; (with Aston Villa), 1933 v W (9)
Brown, J. (Blackburn R), 1881 v W; 1882 v Ni; 1885 v S, W, Ni (5)
Brown, J. H. (Sheffield W), 1927 v S, W, Bel, L, F; 1930 v Ni (6)
Brown, K. (West Ham U), 1960 v Ni (1)
Brown, W. (West Ham U), 1924 v Bel (1)
Brown, W. M. (Manchester U), 1999 v H; 2001 v Fi (sub), Alb (sub) (3)
Bruton, J. (Burnley), 1928 v F, Bel; 1929 v S (3)
Bryant, W. I. (Clapton), 1925 v F (1)
Buchan, C. M. (Sunderland), 1913 v Ni; 1920 v W; 1921 v W, Bel; 1923 v F; 1924 v S (6)
Buchanan, W. S. (Clapham R), 1876 v S (1)
Buckley, F. C. (Derby Co), 1914 v Ni (1)
Bull, S. G. (Wolverhampton W), 1989 v S (sub), D (sub); 1990 v Y, Cz, D (sub), U (sub), Tun (sub), Ei (sub), Ho (sub), Eg, Bel (sub); 1991 v H, Pol (13)
Bullock, F. E. (Huddersfield T), 1921 v Ni (1)
Bullock, N. (Bury), 1923 v Bel; 1926 v W; 1927 v Ni (3)
Burgess, H. (Manchester C), 1904 v S, W, Ni; 1906 v S (4)
Burgess, H. (Sheffield W), 1931 v S, Ni, F, Bel (4)
Burnup, C. J. (Cambridge University), 1896 v S (1)
Burrows, H. (Sheffield W), 1934 v H, Cz; 1935 v Ho (3)
Burton, F. E. (Nottingham F), 1889 v Ni (1)
Bury, L. (Cambridge University), 1877 v S; (with Old Etonians), 1879 v W (2)
Butcher, T. (Ipswich T), 1980 v Aus; 1981 v Sp; 1982 v W, S, F, Cz, WG, Sp; 1983 v D, WG, L, W, Gr, H, Ni, S, Aus (3); 1984 v D, H, L, F, Ni; 1985 v EG, Fi, T, Ni, Ei, R, Fi, S, I, WG, US; 1986 v Is, USSR, S, M, Ca, P, Mor, Pol, Para, Arg; (with Rangers), 1987 v Se, Ni (2), Y, Sp, Br, S; 1988 v T, Y; 1989 v D, Se, Gr, Alb (2), Ch, S, Pol, D; 1990 v Se, Pol, I, Y, Br, Cz, D, U, Tun, Ei, Ho, Bel, Cam, WG (77)
Butler, J. D. (Arsenal), 1925 v Bel (1)
Butler, W. (Bolton W), 1924 v S (1)
Butt, N. (Manchester U), 1997 v M (sub), S.Af (sub); 1998 v Mol (sub), I (sub), Ch, Bel, CzR; 1999 v H; 2001 v I, Sp, Fi (sub), Alb, M (sub), Gr (sub) (14)
Byrne, G. (Liverpool), 1963 v S; 1966 v N (2)
Byrne, J. J. (C Palace), 1962 v Ni; (with West Ham U), 1963 v Sw; 1964 v S, U, P (2), Ei, Br, Arg; 1965 v W, S (11)
Byrne, R. W. (Manchester U), 1954 v S, H, Y, Bel, Sw, U; 1955 v S, W, Ni, WG, F, Sp, P; 1956 v S, W, Ni, Br, Se, Fi, WG, D, Sp; 1957 v S, W, Ni, Y, D (2), Ei (2); 1958 v W, Ni, F (33)

Callaghan, I. R. (Liverpool), 1966 v Fi, F; 1978 v Sw, L (4)
Calvey, J. (Nottingham F), 1902 v S (1)
Campbell, A. F. (Blackburn R), 1929 v W, Ni; (with Huddersfield T), 1931 v W, S, Ni; 1932 v W, Ni, Sp (8)
Campbell, S. (Tottenham H), 1996 v H (sub), S (sub); 1997 v Ge, I, Ge, S.Af (sub), Pol, F, Br; 1998 v Mol, I, Cam, Ch, P, Mor, Bel, Tun, R, Co, Arg; 1999 v Se, Bul, L, CzR, Pol, Se, Bul; 2000 v S (2), Arg, Br, Uk, Ma, P, G, R; 2001 v F, Sp, Fi, Alb (40)
Camsell, G. H. (Middlesbrough), 1929 v F, Bel; 1930 v Ni, W; 1934 v F; 1936 v S, G, A, Bel (9)
Capes, A. J. (Stoke C), 1903 v S (1)
Carr, J. (Middlesbrough), 1920 v Ni; 1923 v W (2)
Carr, J. (Newcastle U), 1905 v Ni; 1907 v Ni (2)
Carr, W. H. (Owlerton, Sheffield), 1875 v S (1)
Carragher, J. L. (Liverpool), 1999 v H (sub); 2001 v I (sub), M (sub) (3)
Carrick, M. (West Ham U), 2001 v M (sub) (1)
Carter, H. S. (Sunderland), 1934 v S, H; 1936 v G; 1937 v S, Ni, H; (with Derby Co), 1947 v S, W, Ni, Ei, Ho, F, Sw (13)
Carter, J. H. (WBA), 1926 v Bel; 1929 v Bel, Sp (3)
Catlin, A. E. (Sheffield W), 1937 v W, Ni, H, N, Se (5)
Chadwick, A. (Southampton), 1900 v S, W (2)
Chadwick, E. (Everton), 1891 v S, W; 1892 v S; 1893 v S; 1894 v S; 1896 v Ni; 1897 v S (7)
Chamberlain, M (Stoke C), 1983 v L (sub); 1984 v D (sub), S, USSR, Br, U, Ch; 1985 v Fi (sub) (8)
Chambers, H. (Liverpool), 1921 v S, W, Bel; 1923 v S, W, Ni, Bel; 1924 v Ni (8)
Channon, M. R. (Southampton), 1973 v Y, S (2), Ni, W, Cz, USSR, I; 1974 v A, Pol, I, P, W, Ni, S, Arg, EG, Bul, Y; 1975 v Cz, P, WG, Cy (2), Ni (sub), W, S; 1976 v Sw, Cz, P, W, Ni, S, Br, I, Fi; 1977 v Fi, I, L, Ni, W, S, Br (sub), Arg, U; (with Manchester C), 1978 v Sw (46)
Charles, G. A. (Nottingham F), 1991 v Nz, Mal (2)
Charlton, J. (Leeds U), 1965 v S, H, Y, WG, Se; 1966 v W, Ni, S, A, Sp, Pol (2), WG (2), Y, Fi, D, U, M, F, Arg, P; 1967 v W, S, Ni, Cz; 1968 v W, Sp; 1969 v W, R, F; 1970 v Ho (2), P, Cz (35)

Charlton, R. (Manchester U), 1958 v S, P, Y; 1959 v S, W, Ni, USSR, I, Br, Pe, M, US; 1960 v W, S, Se, Y, Sp, H; 1961 v Ni, W, S, L, P, Sp, M, I, A; 1962 v W, Ni, S, A, Sw, Pe, L, P, H, Arg, Bul, Br; 1963 v S, F, Br, Cz, EG, Sw; 1964 v S, W, Ni, R of W, U, P, Ei, Br, Arg, US (sub); 1965 v Ni, S, Ho; 1966 v W, Ni, S, A, Sp, WG (2), Y, Fi, N, Pol, U, M, F, Arg, P; 1967 v W, S, Ni, Cz; 1968 v W, Ni, S, USSR (2), Sp (2), Se, Y; 1969 v S, W, Ni, R (2), Bul, M, Br; 1970 v W, Ni, Ho (2), P, Co, Ec, Cz, R, Br, WG (106)
Charnley, R. O. (Blackpool), 1963 v F (1)
Charsley, C. C. (Small Heath), 1893 v Ni (1)
Chedgzoy, S. (Everton), 1920 v W; 1921 v W, S, Ni; 1922 v Ni; 1923 v S; 1924 v W; 1925 v Ni (8)
Chenery, C. J. (C Palace), 1872 v S; 1873 v S; 1874 v S (3)
Cherry, T. J. (Leeds U), 1976 v W, S (sub), Br, Fi; 1977 v Ei, I, L, Ni, S (sub), Br, Arg, U; 1978 v Sw, L, I, Br, W; 1979 v Cz, W, Se; 1980 v Ei, Arg (sub), W, Ni, S, Aus, Sp (sub) (27)
Chilton, A. (Manchester U), 1951 v Ni; 1952 v F (2)
Chippendale, H. (Blackburn R), 1894 v Ni (1)
Chivers, M. (Tottenham H), 1971 v Ma (2), Gr, Ni, S; 1972 v Sw (1+1 sub), Gr, WG (2), Ni (sub), S; 1973 v W (3), S (2), Ni, Cz, Pol, USSR, I; 1974 v A, Pol (24)
Christian, E. (Old Etonians), 1879 v S (1)
Clamp, E. (Wolverhampton W), 1958 v USSR (2), Br, A (4)
Clapton, D. R. (Arsenal), 1959 v W (1)
Clare, T. (Stoke C), 1889 v Ni; 1892 v Ni; 1893 v W; 1894 v S (4)
Clarke, A. J. (Leeds U), 1970 v Cz; 1971 v EG, Ma, Ni, W (sub), S (sub); 1973 v S (2), W, Cz, Pol, USSR, I; 1974 v A, Pol, I; 1975 v P; 1976 v Cz, P (sub) (19)
Clarke, H. A. (Tottenham H), 1954 v S (1)
Clay, T. (Tottenham H), 1920 v W; 1922 v W, S, Ni (4)
Clayton, R. (Blackburn R), 1956 v Ni, Br, Se, Fi, WG, Sp; 1957 v S, W, Ni, Y, D (2), Ei (2); 1958 v S, W, Ni, F, P, Y, USSR; 1959 v S, W, Ni, USSR, I, Br, Pe, M, US; 1960 v W, Ni, S, Se, Y (35)
Clegg, J. C. (Sheffield W), 1872 v S (1)
Clegg, R. E. (Sheffield W), 1873 v S; (with Sheffield Albion), 1879 v W (2)
Clemence, R. N. (Liverpool), 1973 v W (2); 1974 v EG, Bul, Y; 1975 v Cz, P, WG, Cy, Ni, W, S; 1976 v Sw, Cz, P, W (2), Ni, S, Br, Fi; 1977 v Ei, Fi, I, Ho, L, S, Br, Arg, U; 1978 v Sw, L, I, WG, Ni, S; 1979 v D, Ei, Ni (2), S, Bul, A (sub); 1980 v D, Bul, Ei, Arg, W, S, Bel, Sp; 1981 v R, Sp, Br, Sw, H; (with Tottenham H), 1982 v N, Ni, Fi; 1983 v L; 1984 v L (61)
Clement, D. T. (QPR), 1976 v W (sub+1), I; 1977 v I, Ho (5)
Clough, B. H. (Middlesbrough), 1960 v W, Se (2)
Clough, N. H. (Nottingham F), 1989 v Ch; 1991 v Arg (sub), Aus, Mal; 1992 v F, Cz, C; 1993 v Sp, T (sub), Pol (sub), N (sub), US, Br, G (14)
Coates, R. (Burnley), 1970 v Ni; 1971 v Gr (sub); (with Tottenham H), Ma, W (4)
Cobbold, W. N. (Cambridge University), 1883 v S, Ni; 1885 v S, Ni; 1886 v S, W; (with Old Carthusians), 1887 v S, W, Ni (9)
Cock, J. G. (Huddersfield T), 1920 v Ni; (with Chelsea), v S (2)
Cockburn, H. (Manchester U), 1947 v W, Ni, Ei; 1948 v S, I; 1949 v S, Ni, D, Sw, Se; 1951 v Arg, P; 1952 v F (13)
Cohen, G. R. (Fulham), 1964 v U, P, Ei, US, Br; 1965 v W, S, Ni, Bel, H, Ho, Y, WG, Se; 1966 v W, S, Ni, A, Sp, Pol (2), WG (2), N, D, U, M, F, Arg, P; 1967 v W, S, Ni, Cz, Sp; 1968 v W, Ni (37)
Cole, A. (Manchester U), 1995 v U (sub); 1997 v I (sub); 1999 v F (sub), Pol, Se; 2000 v S (sub), Arg (sub); 2001 v F, G, Fi, Sp, Fi, Alb (13)
Cole, A. (Arsenal), 2001 v Alb, M, Gr (3)
Cole, J. J. (West Ham U), 2001 v M (sub) (1)
Colclough, H. (C Palace), 1914 v W (1)
Coleman, E. H. (Dulwich Hamlet), 1921 v W (1)
Coleman, J. (Woolwich Arsenal), 1907 v Ni (1)
Collymore, S. V. (Nottingham F), 1995 v J, Br (sub); (with Aston Villa), 1998 v Mol (sub) (3)
Common, A. (Sheffield U), 1904 v W, Ni; (with Middlesbrough), 1906 v W (3)
Compton, L. H. (Arsenal), 1951 v W, Y (2)
Conlin, J. (Bradford C), 1906 v S (1)
Connelly, J. M. (Burnley), 1960 v W, N, S, Se; 1962 v W, A, Sw, P; 1963 v W, F; (with Manchester U), 1965 v H, Y, Se; 1966 v W, Ni, S, A, N, D, U (20)
Cook, T. E. R. (Brighton), 1925 v W (1)
Cooper, C. T. (Nottingham F), 1995 v Se, Br (2)
Cooper, N. C. (Cambridge University), 1893 v Ni (1)
Cooper, T. (Derby Co), 1928 v Ni; 1929 v W, Ni, S, F, Bel, Sp; 1931 v F; 1932 v W, Sp; 1933 v S; 1934 v S, H, Cz; 1935 v W (15)

Cooper, T. (Leeds U), 1969 v W, S, F, M; 1970 v Ho, Bel, Co, Ec, R, Cz, Br, WG; 1971 v EG, Ma, Ni, W, S; 1972 v Sw (2); 1975 v P (20)

Coppell, S. J. (Manchester U), 1978 v I, WG, Br, W, Ni, S, H; 1979 v D, Ei, Cz, Ni (2), W (sub), S, Bul, A; 1980 v D, Ni, Ei (sub), Sp, Arg, W, S, Bel, I; 1981 v R (sub), Sw, R, Br, W, S, Sw, H; 1982 v H, S, Fi, F, Cz, K, WG; 1983 v L, Gr (42)

Copping, W. (Leeds U), 1933 v I, Sw; 1934 v S, Ni, W, F; (with Arsenal), 1935 v Ni, I; 1936 v A, Bel; 1937 v N, Se, Fi; 1938 v S, W, Ni, Cz; 1939 v W, R of E; (with Leeds U), R (20)

Corbett, B. O. (Corinthians), 1901 v W (1)

Corbett, R. (Old Malvernians), 1903 v W (1)

Corbett, W. S. (Birmingham), 1908 v A, H, B (3)

Corrigan, J. T. (Manchester C), 1978 v I (sub), Br; 1979 v W; 1980 v Ni, Aus; 1981 v W, S; 1982 v W, Ic (9)

Cottee, A. R. (West Ham U), 1987 v Se (sub), Ni (sub); 1988 v H (sub); (with Everton) 1989 v D (sub), Se (sub), Ch (sub), S (7)

Cotterill, G. H. (Cambridge University), 1891 v Ni; (with Old Brightonians), 1892 v W; 1893 v S, Ni (4)

Cottle, J. R. (Bristol C), 1909 v Ni (1)

Cowan, S. (Manchester C), 1926 v Bel; 1930 v A; 1931 v Bel (3)

Cowans, G. (Aston Villa), 1983 v W, H, Ni, S, Aus (3); (with Bari), 1986 v Eg, USSR; (with Aston Villa), 1991 v Ei (10)

Cowell, A. (Blackburn R), 1910 v Ni (1)

Cox, J. (Liverpool), 1901 v Ni; 1902 v S; 1903 v S (3)

Cox, J. D. (Derby Co), 1892 v Ni (1)

Crabtree, J. W. (Burnley), 1894 v Ni; 1895 v Ni, S; (with Aston Villa), 1896 v W, S, Ni; 1899 v S, W, Ni; 1900 v S, W, Ni; 1901 v W; 1902 v W (14)

Crawford, J. F. (Chelsea), 1931 v S (1)

Crawford, R. (Ipswich T), 1962 v Ni, A (2)

Crawshaw, T. H. (Sheffield W), 1895 v Ni; 1896 v S, W, Ni; 1897 v S, W, Ni; 1901 v W; 1904 v W, Ni (10)

Crayston, W. J. (Arsenal), 1936 v S, W, G, A, Bel; 1938 v W, Ni, Cz (8)

Creek, F. N. S. (Corinthians), 1923 v F (1)

Cresswell, W. (South Shields), 1921 v W; (with Sunderland), 1923 v F; 1924 v Bel; 1925 v Ni; 1926 v W; 1927 v Ni; (with Everton), 1930 v Ni (7)

Crompton, R. (Blackburn R), 1902 v S, W, Ni; 1903 v S, W; 1904 v S, W, Ni; 1906 v S, W, Ni; 1907 v S, W, Ni; 1908 v S, W, Ni, A (2), H, B; 1909 v S, W, Ni H (2), A; 1910 v S, W; 1911 v S, W, Ni; 1912 v S, W, Ni; 1913 v S, W, Ni; 1914 v S, W, Ni (41)

Crooks, S. D. (Derby Co), 1930 v S, G, A; 1931 v S, W, Ni, F, Bel; 1932 v S, W, Ni, Sp; 1933 v Ni, W, A; 1934 v S, Ni, W, F, H, Cz; 1935 v Ni; 1936 v S, W; 1937 v W, H (26)

Crowe, C. (Wolverhampton W), 1963 v F (1)

Cuggy, F. (Sunderland), 1913 v Ni; 1914 v Ni (2)

Cullis, S. (Wolverhampton W), 1938 v S, W, Ni, F, Cz; 1939 v S, Ni, R of E, N, I, R, Y (12)

Cunliffe, A. (Blackburn R), 1933 v Ni, W (2)

Cunliffe, D. (Portsmouth), 1900 v Ni (1)

Cunliffe, J. N. (Everton), 1936 v Bel (1)

Cunningham, L. (WBA), 1979 v W, Se, A (sub); (with Real Madrid), 1980 v Ei (sub), Sp (sub); 1981 v R (sub) (6)

Curle, K. (Manchester C), 1992 v C (sub), H, D (3)

Currey, E. S. (Oxford University), 1890 v S, W (2)

Currie, A. W. (Sheffield U), 1972 v Ni; 1973 v USSR, I; 1974 v A, Pol, I; 1976 v Sw; (with Leeds U), 1978 v Br, W (sub), Ni, S, H (sub); 1979 v Cz, Ni (2), W, Se (17)

Cursham, A. W. (Notts Co), 1876 v S; 1877 v S; 1878 v S; 1879 v W; 1883 v S, W (6)

Cursham, H. A. (Notts Co), 1880 v W; 1882 v S, W, Ni; 1883 v S, W, Ni (8)

Daft, H. B. (Notts Co), 1889 v Ni; 1890 v S, W; 1891 v Ni; 1892 v Ni (5)

Daley, A. M. (Aston Villa), 1992 v Pol (sub), C, H, Br, Fi (sub), D (sub), Se (7)

Danks, T. (Nottingham F), 1885 v S (1)

Davenport, P. (Nottingham F), 1985 v Ei (sub) (1)

Davenport, J. K. (Bolton W), 1885 v W; 1890 v Ni (2)

Davis, G. (Derby Co), 1904 v W, Ni (2)

Davis, H. (Sheffield W), 1903 v S, W, Ni (3)

Davison, J. E. (Sheffield W), 1922 v W (1)

Dawson, J. (Burnley), 1922 v S, Ni (2)

Day, S. H. (Old Malvernians), 1906 v Ni, W, S (3)

Dean, W. R. (Everton), 1927 v S, W, F, Bel, L; 1928 v S, W, Ni, F, Bel; 1929 v S, W, Ni; 1931 v S; 1932 v Sp; 1933 v Ni (16)

Deane, B. C. (Sheffield U), 1991 v Nz (sub + 1); 1993 v Sp (sub) (3)

Deeley, N. V. (Wolverhampton W), 1959 v Br, Pe (2)

Devey, J. H. G. (Aston Villa), 1892 v Ni; 1894 v Ni (2)

Devonshire, A. (West Ham U), 1980 v Aus (sub), Ni; 1982 v Ho, Ic; 1983 v WG, W, Gr; 1984 v L (8)

Dewhurst, F. (Preston NE), 1886 v W, Ni; 1887 v S, W, Ni; 1888 v S, W, Ni; 1889 v W (9)

Dewhurst, G. P. (Liverpool Ramblers), 1895 v W (1)

Dickinson, J. W. (Portsmouth), 1949 v N, F; 1950 v S, W, Ei, P, Bel, Ch, US, Sp; 1951 v Ni, W, Y; 1952 v W, Ni, S, A (2), I, Sw; 1953 v W, Ni, S, Bel, Arg, Ch, U, US; 1954 v W, Ni, S, R of E, H (2), Y, Bel, Sw, U; 1955 v Sp, P; 1956 v W, Ni, S, D, Sp; 1957 v W, Y, D (48)

Dimmock, J. H. (Tottenham H), 1921 v S; 1926 v W, Bel (3)

Ditchburn, E. G. (Tottenham H), 1949 v Sw, Se; 1953 v US; 1957 v W, Y, D (6)

Dix, R. W. (Derby Co), 1939 v N (1)

Dixon, J. A. (Notts Co), 1885 v W (1)

Dixon, K. M. (Chelsea), 1985 v M (sub), WG, US; 1986 v Ni, Is, M (sub), Pol (sub); 1987 v Se (8)

Dixon, L. M. (Arsenal), 1990 v Cz; 1991 v H, Pol, Ei (2), Cam, T, Arg; 1992 v G, T, Pol, Cz (sub); 1993 v Sp, N, T, Sm, T, Ho, N, US; 1994 v Sm; 1999 v F (22)

Dobson, A. T. C. (Notts Co), 1882 v Ni; 1884 v S, W, Ni (4)

Dobson, C. F. (Notts Co), 1886 v Ni (1)

Dobson, J. M. (Burnley), 1974 v P, EG, Bul, Y; (with Everton), 1975 v Cz (5)

Doggart, A. G. (Corinthians), 1924 v Bel (1)

Dorigo, A. R. (Chelsea), 1990 v Y (sub), Cz (sub), D (sub), I; 1991 v H (sub), USSR; (with Leeds U), 1992 v G, Cz (sub), H, Br; 1993 v Sm, Pol, US, Br; 1994 v H (15)

Dorrell, A. R. (Aston Villa), 1925 v W, Bel, F; 1926 v Ni (4)

Douglas, B. (Blackburn R), 1958 v S, W, Ni, F, P, Y, USSR (2), Br, A; 1959 v S, USSR; 1960 v Y, H; 1961 v Ni, W, S, L, P, Sp, M, I, A; 1962 v W, Ni, S, Pe, L, P, H, Arg, Bul, Br; 1963 v S, Br, Sw (36)

Downs, R. W. (Everton), 1921 v Ni (1)

Doyle, M. (Manchester C), 1976 v W, S (sub), Br, I; 1977 v Ho (5)

Drake, E. J. (Arsenal), 1935 v Ni, I; 1936 v W; 1937 v H; 1938 v F (5)

Dublin, D. (Coventry C), 1998 v Ch, Mor, Bel (sub); (with Aston Villa), 1999 v CzR (4)

Ducat, A. (Woolwich Arsenal), 1910 v S, W, Ni; (with Aston Villa), 1920 v S, W; 1921 v Ni (6)

Dunn, A. T. B. (Cambridge University), 1883 v Ni; 1884 v Ni; (with Old Etonians), 1892 v S, W (4)

Duxbury, M. (Manchester U), 1984 v L, F, W, S, USSR, Br, U, Ch; 1985 v EG, Fi (10)

Dyer, K. C. (Newcastle U), 2000 v L, Pol (sub), Bel, Arg, Uk (sub); 2001 v F (sub), G (sub), I (8)

Earle, S. G. J. (Clapton), 1924 v F; (with West Ham U), 1928 v Ni (2)

Eastham, G. (Arsenal), 1963 v Br, Cz, EG; 1964 v W, Ni, S, R of W, U, P, Ei, US, Br, Arg; 1965 v H, WG, Se; 1966 v Sp, Pol, D (19)

Eastham, G. R. (Bolton W), 1935 v Ho (1)

Eckersley, W. (Blackburn R), 1950 v Sp; 1951 v S, Y, Arg, P; 1952 v A (2), Sw; 1953 v Ni, Arg, Ch, U, US; 1954 v W, Ni, R of E, H (17)

Edwards, D. (Manchester U), 1955 v S, F, Sp, P; 1956 v S, Br, Se, Fi, WG; 1957 v S, Ni, Ei (2), D (2); 1958 v W, Ni, F (18)

Edwards, J. H. (Shropshire Wanderers), 1874 v S (1)

Edwards, J. (Leeds U), 1926 v S, W; 1927 v W, Ni, S, F, Bel, L; 1928 v S, F, Bel; 1929 v S, W, Ni; 1930 v W, Ni (16)

Ehiogu, U. (Aston Villa), 1996 v Chn (sub); (with Middlesbrough), 2001 v Sp (sub) (2)

Ellerington, W. (Southampton), 1949 v N, F (2)

Elliott, G. W. (Middlesbrough), 1913 v Ni; 1914 v Ni; 1920 v W (3)

Elliott, W. H. (Burnley), 1952 v I, A; 1953 v Ni, W, Bel (5)

Evans, R. E. (Sheffield U), 1911 v S, W, Ni; 1912 v W (4)

Ewer, F. H. (Casuals), 1924 v F; 1925 v Bel (2)

Fairclough, P. (Old Foresters), 1878 v S (1)

Fairhurst, D. (Newcastle U), 1934 v F (1)

Fantham, J. (Sheffield W), 1962 v L (1)

Fashanu, J. (Wimbledon), 1989 v Ch, S (2)

Felton, W. (Sheffield W), 1925 v F (1)

Fenton, M. (Middlesbrough), 1938 v S (1)

Fenwick, T. (QPR), 1984 v W (sub), S, USSR, Br, U, Ch; 1985 v Fi, S, M, US; 1986 v R, T, Ni, Eg, M, P, Mor, Pol, Arg; (with Tottenham H), 1988 v Is (sub) (20)

Ferdinand, L. (QPR), 1993 v Sm, Ho, N, US; 1994 v Pol, Sm; 1995 v US (sub); (with Newcastle U), 1996 v P, Bul, H; 1997 v Pol, Ge, I (sub); (with Tottenham H), 1998 v Mol, S.Ar (sub), Mor (sub), Bel (17)

Ferdinand, R. G. (West Ham U), 1998 v Cam (sub), Sw, Bel (sub); 1999 v L, CzR, F (sub), H, Se (sub); 2000 v Arg (sub); 2001 v I; (with Leeds U), Sp, Fi, Alb, M, Gr (15)
Field, E. (Clapham Rovers), 1876 v S; 1881 v S (2)
Finney, T. (Preston NE), 1947 v W, Ni, Ei, Ho, F, P; 1948 v S, W, Ni, Bel, Se, I; 1949 v S, W, Ni, Se, N, F; 1950 v S, W, Ni, Ei, I, P, Bel, Ch, US, Sp; 1951 v W, S, Arg, P; 1952 v W, Ni, S, F, I, Sw, A; 1953 v W, Ni, S, Bel, Arg, Ch, U, US; 1954 v W, S, Bel, Sw, U, H, Y; 1955 v WG; 1956 v S, W, Ni, D, Sp; 1957 v S, W, Y, D (2), Ei (2); 1958 v W, S, F, P, Y, USSR (2); 1959 v Ni, USSR (76)
Fleming, H. J. (Swindon T), 1909 v S, H (2); 1910 v W, Ni; 1911 v W, Ni; 1912 v Ni; 1913 v S, W; 1914 v S (11)
Fletcher, A. (Wolverhampton W), 1889 v W; 1890 v W (2)
Flowers, R. (Wolverhampton W), 1955 v F; 1959 v S, W, I, Br, Pe, US, M (sub); 1960 v W, Ni, S, Se, Y, Sp, H; 1961 v Ni, W, S, L, P, Sp, M, I, A; 1962 v W, Ni, S, A, Sw, Pe, L, P, H, Arg, Bul, Br; 1963 v Ni, W, S, F (2), Sw; 1964 v Ei, US, P; 1965 v W, Ho, WG; 1966 v N (49)
Flowers, T. D. (Southampton), 1993 v Br; (with Blackburn R), 1994 v Gr; 1995 v Ng, U, J, Se, Br; 1996 v Chn; 1997 v I; 1998 v Sw, Mor (11)
Forman, Frank (Nottingham F), 1898 v S, Ni; 1899 v S, W, Ni; 1901 v S; 1902 v S, Ni; 1903 v W (9)
Forman, F. R. (Nottingham F), 1899 v S, W, Ni (3)
Forrest, J. H. (Blackburn R), 1884 v W; 1885 v S, W, Ni; 1886 v S, W; 1887 v S, W, Ni; 1889 v S; 1890 v Ni (11)
Fort, J. (Millwall), 1921 v Bel (1)
Foster, R. E. (Oxford University), 1900 v W; (with Corinthians), 1901 v W, Ni, S; 1902 v W (5)
Foster, S. (Brighton & HA), 1982 v Ni, Ho, K (3)
Foulke, W. J. (Sheffield U), 1897 v W (1)
Foulkes, W. A. (Manchester U), 1955 v Ni (1)
Fowler, R. B. (Liverpool), 1996 v Bul (sub), Cro, Chn (sub), Ho (sub), Sp (sub); 1997 v M; 1998 v Cam; 1999 v CzR (sub); 2000 v L, Pol, Br (sub), Uk, Ma (sub); 2001 v I (sub), Fi (sub), M, Gr (18)
Fox, F. S. (Millwall), 1925 v F (1)
Francis, G. C. J. (QPR), 1975 v Cz, P, W, S; 1976 v Sw, Cz, P, W, Ni, S, Br, Fi (12)
Francis, T. (Birmingham C), 1977 v Ho, L, S, Br; 1978 v Sw, L, I (sub), WG (sub), Br, W, S, H; (with Nottingham F), 1979 v Bul (sub), Se, A (sub); 1980 v Ni, Bul, Sp; 1981 v Sp, R, S (sub), Sw; (with Manchester C), 1982 v N, Ni, W, S (sub), Fi (sub), F, Cz, K, WG, Sp; (with Sampdoria), 1983 v D, Gr, H, Ni, S, Aus (3); 1984 v D, Ni, USSR; 1985 v EG (sub), T (sub), Ni (sub), R, Fi, S, I, M; 1986 v S (52)
Franklin, C. F. (Stoke C), 1947 v S, W, Ni, Ei, Ho, F, Sw, P; 1948 v S, W, Ni, Bel, Se, I; 1949 v S, W, Ni, D, Sw, N, F, Se; 1950 v W, S, Ni, Ei, I (27)
Freeman, B. C. (Everton), 1909 v S, W; (with Burnley), 1912 v S, W, Ni (5)
Froggatt, J. (Portsmouth), 1950 v Ni, I; 1951 v S; 1952 v S, A (2), I, Sw; 1953 v Ni, W, S, Bel, US (13)
Froggatt, R. (Sheffield W), 1953 v W, S, Bel, US (4)
Fry, C. B. (Corinthians), 1901 v Ni (1)
Furness, W. I. (Leeds U), 1933 v I (1)

Galley, T. (Wolverhampton W), 1937 v N, Se (2)
Gardner, T. (Aston Villa), 1934 v Cz; 1935 v Ho (2)
Garfield, B. (WBA), 1898 v Ni (1)
Garratty, W. (Aston Villa), 1903 v W (1)
Garrett, T. (Blackpool), 1952 v S, I; 1954 v W (3)
Gascoigne, P. J. (Tottenham H), 1989 v D (sub), S.Ar (sub), Alb (sub), Ch, S (sub); 1990 v Se (sub), Br (sub), Cz, D, U, Tun, Ei, Ho, Eg, Bel, Cam, WG; 1991 v H, Pol, Cam; (with Lazio), 1993 v N, T, Sm, T, Ho, Pol, N; 1994 v Pol, D; 1995 v J (sub), Se (sub), Br (sub); (with Rangers), 1996 v Co, Sw, P, Bul, Cro, Chn, Sw, S, Ho, Sp, G; 1997 v Mol, Pol, Ge, S.Af, Pol, I (sub), F, Br; 1998 v Mol, I, Cam; (with Middlesbrough), S.Ar (sub), Mor, Bel (57)
Gates, E. (Ipswich T), 1981 v N, R (2)
Gay, L. H. (Cambridge University), 1893 v S; (with Old Brightonians), 1894 v S, W (3)
Geary, F. (Everton), 1890 v Ni; 1891 v S (2)
Geaves, R. L. (Clapham Rovers), 1875 v S (1)
Gee, C. W. (Everton), 1932 v W, Sp; 1937 v Ni (3)
Geldard, A. (Everton), 1933 v I, Sw; 1935 v S; 1938 v Ni (4)
George, C. (Derby Co), 1977 v Ei (1)
George, W. (Aston Villa), 1902 v S, W, Ni (3)
Gerrard, S. G. (Liverpool), 2000 v Uk, G (sub); 2001 v Fi, M, Gr (5)
Gibbins, W. V. T. (Clapton), 1924 v F; 1925 v F (2)
Gidman, J. (Aston Villa), 1977 v L (1)
Gillard, I. T. (QPR), 1975 v WG, W; 1976 v Cz (3)
Gilliat, W. E. (Old Carthusians), 1893 v Ni (1)
Goddard, P. (West Ham U), 1982 v Ic (sub) (1)

Goodall, F. R. (Huddersfield T), 1926 v S; 1927 v S, F, Bel, L; 1928 v S, W, F, Bel; 1930 v S, G, A; 1931 v S, W, Ni, Bel; 1932 v Ni; 1933 v W, Ni, A, I, Sw; 1934 v W, Ni, F (25)
Goodall, J. (Preston NE), 1888 v S, W; 1889 v S, W; (with Derby Co), 1891 v S, W; 1892 v S; 1893 v W; 1894 v S; 1895 v S, Ni; 1896 v S, W; 1898 v W (14)
Goodhart, H. C. (Old Etonians), 1883 v S, W, Ni (3)
Goodwyn, A. G. (Royal Engineers), 1873 v S (1)
Goodyer, A. C. (Nottingham F), 1879 v S (1)
Gosling, R. C. (Old Etonians), 1892 v W; 1893 v S; 1894 v W; 1895 v W, S (5)
Gosnell, A. A. (Newcastle U), 1906 v Ni (1)
Gough, H. C. (Sheffield U), 1921 v S (1)
Goulden, L. A. (West Ham U), 1937 v Se, N; 1938 v W, Ni, Cz, G, Sw, F; 1939 v S, W, R of E, I, R, Y (14)
Graham, L. (Millwall), 1925 v S, W (2)
Graham, T. (Nottingham F), 1931 v F; 1932 v Ni (2)
Grainger, C. (Sheffield U), 1956 v Br, Se, Fi, WG; 1957 v W, Ni; (with Sunderland), 1957 v S (7)
Gray, A. A. (C Palace), 1992 v Pol (1)
Gray, M. (Sunderland), 1999 v H (sub), Se (sub), Bul (3)
Greaves, J. (Chelsea), 1959 v Pe, M, US; 1960 v W, Se, Y, Sp; 1961 v Ni, W, S, L, P, Sp, I, A; (with Tottenham H), 1962 v S, Sw, Pe, H, Arg, Bul, Br; 1963 v Ni, W, S, F (2), Br, Cz, Sw; 1964 v W, Ni, R of W, P (2), Ei, Br, U, Arg; 1965 v Ni, S, Bel, Ho, H, Y; 1966 v W, A, Y, N, D, Pol, U, M, F; 1967 v S, Sp, A (57)
Green, F. T. (Wanderers), 1876 v S (1)
Green, G. H. (Sheffield U), 1925 v F; 1926 v S, Bel, W; 1927 v W, Ni; 1928 v F, Bel (8)
Greenhalgh, E. H. (Notts Co), 1872 v S; 1873 v S (2)
Greenhoff, B. (Manchester U), 1976 v W, Ni; 1977 v Ei, Fi, I, Ho, Ni, W, S, Br, Arg, U; 1978 v Br, W, Ni, S (sub), H (sub); (with Leeds U), 1980 v Aus (sub) (18)
Greenwood, D. H. (Blackburn R), 1882 v S, Ni (2)
Gregory, J. (QPR), 1983 v Aus (3); 1984 v D, H, W (6)
Grimsdell, A. (Tottenham H), 1920 v S, W; 1921 v S, Ni; 1923 v W, Ni (6)
Grosvenor, A. T. (Birmingham), 1934 v Ni, W, F (3)
Gunn, W. (Notts Co), 1884 v S, W (2)
Guppy, S. (Leicester C), 2000 v Bel (1)
Gurney, R. (Sunderland), 1935 v S (1)

Hacking, J. (Oldham Ath), 1929 v S, W, Ni (3)
Hadley, N. (WBA), 1903 v Ni (1)
Hagan, J. (Sheffield U), 1949 v D (1)
Haines, J. T. W. (WBA), 1949 v Sw (1)
Hall, A. E. (Aston Villa), 1910 v Ni (1)
Hall, G. W. (Tottenham H), 1934 v F; 1938 v S, W, Ni, Cz; 1939 v S, Ni, R of E, I, Y (10)
Hall, J. (Birmingham C), 1956 v S, W, Ni, Br, Se, Fi, WG, D, Sp; 1957 v S, W, Ni, Y, D (2), Ei (2) (17)
Halse, H. J. (Manchester U), 1909 v A (1)
Hammond, H. E. D. (Oxford University), 1889 v S (1)
Hampson, J. (Blackpool), 1931 v Ni, W; 1933 v A (3)
Hampton, H. (Aston Villa), 1913 v S, W; 1914 v S, W (4)
Hancocks, J. (Wolverhampton W), 1949 v Sw; 1950 v W; 1951 v Y (3)
Hapgood, E. (Arsenal), 1933 v I, Sw; 1934 v S, Ni, W, H, Cz; 1935 v S, Ni, W, I, Ho; 1936 v S, Ni, W, G, A, Bel; 1937 v Fi; 1938 v S, G, Sw, F; 1939 v S, W, Ni, R of E, N, I, Y (30)
Hardinge, H. T. W. (Sheffield U), 1910 v S (1)
Hardman, H. P. (Everton), 1905 v W; 1907 v S, Ni; 1908 v W (4)
Hardwick, G. F. M. (Middlesbrough), 1947 v S, W, Ni, Ei, Ho, F, Sw, P; 1948 v S, W, Ni, Bel, Se (13)
Hardy, H. (Stockport Co), 1925 v Bel (1)
Hardy, S. (Liverpool), 1907 v S, W, Ni; 1908 v S; 1909 v S, W, Ni, H (2), A; 1910 v S, W, Ni; 1912 v Ni; (with Aston Villa), 1913 v S; 1914 v Ni, W, S; 1920 v S, W, Ni (21)
Harford, M. G. (Luton T), 1988 v Is (sub); 1989 v D (2)
Hargreaves, F. W. (Blackburn R), 1880 v W; 1881 v W; 1882 v Ni (3)
Hargreaves, J. (Blackburn R), 1881 v S, W (2)
Harper, E. C. (Blackburn R), 1926 v S (1)
Harris, G. (Burnley), 1966 v Pol (1)
Harris, P. P. (Portsmouth), 1950 v Ei; 1954 v H (2)
Harris, S. S. (Cambridge University), 1904 v S; (with Old Westminsters), 1905 v Ni, W; 1906 v S, W, Ni (6)
Harrison, A. H. (Old Westminsters), 1893 v S, Ni (2)
Harrison, G. (Everton), 1921 v Bel; 1922 v Ni (2)
Harrow, J. H. (Chelsea), 1923 v Ni, Se (2)
Hart, E. (Leeds U), 1929 v W; 1930 v W, Ni; 1933 v S, A; 1934 v S, H, Cz (8)
Hartley, F. (Oxford C), 1923 v F (1)
Harvey, A. (Wednesbury Strollers), 1881 v W (1)
Harvey, J. C. (Everton), 1971 v Ma (1)

Jones, A. (Walsall Swifts), 1882 v S, W; (with Great Lever), 1883 v S (3)
Jones, H. (Blackburn R), 1927 v S, Bel, L, F; 1928 v S, Ni (6)
Jones, H. (Nottingham F), 1923 v F (1)
Jones, M. D. (Sheffield U), 1965 v WG, Se; (with Leeds U), 1970 v Ho (3)
Jones, R. (Liverpool), 1992 v F; 1994 v Pol, Gr, N; 1995 v US, R, Ng, U (8)
Jones, W. (Bristol C), 1901 v Ni (1)
Jones, W. H. (Liverpool), 1950 v P, Bel (2)
Joy, B. (Casuals), 1936 v Bel (1)

Kail, E. I. L. (Dulwich Hamlet), 1929 v F, Bel, Sp (3)
Kay, A. H. (Everton), 1963 v Sw (1)
Kean, F. W. (Sheffield W), 1923 v S, Bel; 1924 v W; 1925 v Ni; 1926 v Ni, Bel; 1927 v L; (with Bolton W), 1929 v F, Sp (9)
Keegan, J. K. (Liverpool), 1973 v W (2); 1974 v W, Ni, Arg, EG, Bul, Y; 1975 v Cz, WG, Cy (2), Ni, S; 1976 v Sw, Cz, P, W (2), Ni, S, Br, Fi; 1977 v Ei, Fi, I, Ho, L; (with SV Hamburg), W, Br, Arg, U; 1978 v Sw, I, WG, Br, H; 1979 v D, Ei, Cz, Ni, W, S, Bul, Se, A; 1980 v D, Ni, Ei, Sp (2), Arg, Bel, I; (with Southampton), 1981 v Sp, Sw, H; 1982 v N, H, Ni, S, Fi, Sp (sub) (63)
Keen, E. R. L. (Derby Co), 1933 v A; 1937 v W, Ni, H (4)
Kelly, R. (Burnley), 1920 v S; 1921 v S, W, Ni; 1922 v S, W; 1923 v S; 1924 v Ni; 1925 v W, Ni, S; (with Sunderland), 1926 v W; (with Huddersfield T), 1927 v L; 1928 v S (14)
Kennedy, A. (Liverpool), 1984 v Ni (1)
Kennedy, R. (Liverpool), 1976 v W (2), Ni, S; 1977 v L, W, S, Br (sub), Arg (sub); 1978 v Sw, L; 1980 v Bul, Sp, Arg, W, Bel (sub), I (17)
Kenyon-Slaney, W. S. (Wanderers), 1873 v S (1)
Keown, M. R. (Everton), 1992 v F, Cz, C, H, Br, Fi, D, Fe, Se; (with Arsenal), 1993 v Ho, G (sub); 1997 v M, S.Af, I, Br; 1998 v Sw, Mor, Bel; 1999 v CzR, F, Pol, H, Se; 2000 v L, Pol, Bel, S, Arg, Br, Ma, P (sub), G, R; 2001 v F, G, Fi, M, Gr (38)
Kevan, D. T. (WBA), 1957 v S; 1958 v W, Ni, S, P, Y, USSR (3), Br, A; 1959 v M, US; 1961 v M (14)
Kidd, B. (Manchester U), 1970 v Ni, Ec (sub) (2)
King, R. S. (Oxford University), 1882 v Ni (1)
Kingsford, R. K. (Wanderers), 1874 v S (1)
Kingsley, M. (Newcastle U), 1901 v W (1)
Kinsey, G. (Wolverhampton W), 1892 v W; 1893 v S; (with Derby Co), 1896 v W, Ni (4)
Kirchen, A. J. (Arsenal), 1937 v N, Se, Fi (3)
Kirton, W. J. (Aston Villa), 1922 v Ni (1)
Knight, A. E. (Portsmouth), 1920 v Ni (1)
Knowles, C. (Tottenham H), 1968 v USSR, Sp, Se, WG (4)

Labone, B. L. (Everton), 1963 v Ni, W, F; 1967 v Sp, A; 1968 v S, Sp, Se, Y, USSR, WG; 1969 v Ni, S, R, Bul, M, U, Br; 1970 v W, Bel, Co, Ec, R, Br, WG (26)
Lampard, F. J. (West Ham U), 2000 v Bel; 2001 v Sp (sub) (2)
Lampard, F. R. G. (West Ham U), 1973 v Y; 1980 v Aus (2)
Langley, E. J. (Fulham), 1958 v S, P, Y (3)
Langton, R. (Blackburn R), 1947 v W, Ni, Ei, Ho, F, Sw; 1948 v Se; (with Preston NE), 1949 v D, Se; (with Bolton W), 1950 v S; 1951 v Ni (11)
Latchford, R. D. (Everton), 1978 v I, Br, W; 1979 v D, Ei, Cz (sub), Ni (2), W, S, Bul, A (12)
Latheron, E. G. (Blackburn R), 1913 v W; 1914 v Ni (2)
Lawler, C. (Liverpool), 1971 v Ma, W, S; 1972 v Sw (4)
Lawton, T. (Everton), 1939 v S, W, Ni, R of E, N, I, R, Y; (with Chelsea), 1947 v S, W, Ni, Ei, Ho, F, Sw, P; 1948 v W, Ni, Bel; (with Notts Co), 1948 v S, Se, I; 1949 v D (23)
Leach, T. (Sheffield W), 1931 v W, Ni (2)
Leake, A. (Aston Villa), 1904 v S, Ni; 1905 v S, W, Ni (5)
Lee, E. A. (Southampton), 1904 v W (1)
Lee, F. H. (Manchester C), 1969 v Ni, W, S, Bul, F, M, U; 1970 v W, Ho (2), P, Bel, Co, Ec, R, Br, WG; 1971 v EG, Gr, Ma, Ni, W, S; 1972 v Sw (2), Gr, WG (27)
Lee, J. (Derby Co), 1951 v Ni (1)
Lee, R. M. (Newcastle U), 1995 v R, Ng; 1996 v Co (sub), N, Sw, Bul (sub), H; 1997 v M, Ge, S.Af, Pol, F (sub), Br (sub); 1998 v Cam (sub), Ch, Sw, Bel, Co (sub); 1999 v Se (sub), Bul, L (sub) (21)
Lee, S. (Liverpool), 1983 v Gr, L, W, Gr, H, S, Aus; 1984 v D, H, L, F, Ni, W, Ch (sub) (14)
Leighton, J. E. (Nottingham F), 1886 v Ni (1)
Le Saux, G. P. (Blackburn R), 1994 v D, Gr, N; 1995 v US, R, Ng, Ei, U, Se, Br; 1996 v Co, P (sub); 1997 v I, M, Ge, S.Af, Pol, I, F, Br; (with Chelsea), 1998 v I, Ch (sub), P, Mor, Bel, Tun, R, Co, Arg; 1999 v Se, Bul (sub), CzR, F, Pol, Se; 2001 v G (36)
Le Tissier, M. P. (Southampton), 1994 v D (sub), Gr (sub), N (sub); 1995 v R, Ng (sub), Ei; 1997 v Mol (sub), I (8)

Lilley, H. E. (Sheffield U), 1892 v W (1)
Linacre, H. J. (Nottingham F), 1905 v W, S (2)
Lindley, T. (Cambridge University), 1886 v S, W, Ni; 1887 v S, W, Ni; 1888 v S, W, Ni; (with Nottingham F), 1889 v S; 1890 v S, W; 1891 v Ni (13)
Lindsay, A. (Liverpool), 1974 v Arg, EG, Bul, Y (4)
Lindsay, W. (Wanderers), 1877 v S (1)
Lineker, G. (Leicester C), 1984 v S (sub); 1985 v Ei, R (sub), S (sub), I (sub), WG, US; (with Everton), 1986 v R, T, Ni, Eg, USSR, Ca, P, Mor, Pol, Para, Arg; (with Barcelona), 1987 v Ni (2), Y, Sp, T, Br; 1988 v WG, T, Y, Ho, H, S, Co, Sw, Ei, Ho, USSR; 1989 v Se, S.Ar, Gr, Alb (2), Pol, D; (with Tottenham H) 1990 v Se, Pol, I, Y, Br, Cz, D, U, Tun, Ei, Ho, Eg, Bel, Cam, WG, I; 1991 v H, Pol, Ei (2), Cam, T, Arg, Aus, Nz, Mal; 1992 v G, T, Pol, F (sub), Cz (sub), C, H, Br, Fi, D, F, Se (80)
Lintott, E. H. (QPR), 1908 v S, W, Ni; (with Bradford C), 1909 v S, Ni, H (2) (7)
Lipsham, H. B. (Sheffield U), 1902 v W (1)
Little, B. (Aston Villa), 1975 v W (sub) (1)
Lloyd, L. V. (Liverpool), 1971 v W; 1972 v Sw, Ni; (with Nottingham F), 1980 v W (4)
Lockett, A. (Stoke C), 1903 v Ni (1)
Lodge, L. V. (Cambridge University), 1894 v W; 1895 v S, W; (with Corinthians), 1896 v S, Ni (5)
Lofthouse, J. M. (Blackburn R), 1885 v S, W, Ni; 1887 v S, W; (with Accrington), 1889 v Ni; (with Blackburn R), 1890 v Ni (7)
Lofthouse, N. (Bolton W), 1951 v Y; 1952 v W, Ni, S, A (2), I, Sw; 1953 v W, Ni, S, Bel, Arg, Ch, U, US; 1954 v W, Ni, R of E, Bel, U; 1955 v Ni, S, F, Sp, P; 1956 v W, S, Sp, D, Fi (sub); 1959 v W, USSR (33)
Longworth, E. (Liverpool), 1920 v S; 1921 v Bel; 1923 v S, W, Bel (5)
Lowder, A. (Wolverhampton W), 1889 v W (1)
Lowe, E. (Aston Villa), 1947 v F, Sw, P (3)
Lucas, T. (Liverpool), 1922 v Ni; 1924 v F; 1926 v Bel (3)
Luntley, E. (Nottingham F), 1880 v S, W (2)
Lyttelton, Hon. A. (Cambridge University), 1877 v S (1)
Lyttelton, Hon. E. (Cambridge University), 1878 v S (1)

McCall, J. (Preston NE), 1913 v S, W; 1914 v S; 1920 v S; 1921 v Ni (5)
McCann, G. P. (Sunderland), 2001 v Sp (sub) (1)
McDermott, T. (Liverpool), 1978 v Sw, L; 1979 v Ni, W, Se; 1980 v D, Ni (sub), Ei, Ni, S, Bel (sub), Sp; 1981 v N, R, Sw, R (sub), Br, Sw (sub), H; 1982 v N, H, W (sub), Ho, S (sub), Ic (25)
McDonald, C. A. (Burnley), 1958 v USSR (3), Br, A; 1959 v W, Ni, USSR (8)
McFarland, R. L. (Derby Co), 1971 v Gr, Ma (2), Ni, S; 1972 v Sw, Gr, WG, W, S; 1973 v W (3), Ni, S, Cz, Pol, USSR, I; 1974 v A, Pol, I, W, Ni; 1976 v Cz, S; 1977 v Ei, I (28)
McGarry, W. H. (Huddersfield T), 1954 v Sw, U; 1956 v W, D (4)
McGuinness, W. (Manchester U), 1959 v Ni, M (2)
McInroy, A. (Sunderland), 1927 v Ni (1)
McMahon, S. (Liverpool), 1988 v Is, H, Co, USSR; 1989 v D (sub); 1990 v Se, Pol, I, Y (sub), Br, Cz (sub), D, Ei (sub), Eg, Bel, I; 1991 v Ei (17)
McManaman, S. (Liverpool), 1995 v Ng (sub), U (sub), J (sub); 1996 v Co, N, Sw, P (sub), Bul, Cro, Chn, Sw, S, Ho, Sp, G; 1997 v Pol, I, M; 1998 v Cam, Sw, Mor, Co (sub); 1999 v Pol, H; (with Real Madrid), 2000 v L, Pol, Uk, Ma (sub), P; 2001 v F (sub), Fi (sub+1), Alb, Gr (sub) (34)
McNab, R. (Arsenal), 1969 v Ni, Bul, R (1+1 sub) (4)
McNeal, R. (WBA), 1914 v S, W (2)
McNeil, M. (Middlesbrough), 1961 v W, Ni, S, L, P, Sp, M, I; 1962 v L (9)
Mabbutt, G. (Tottenham H), 1983 v WG, Gr, L, W, Gr, H, Ni, S (sub); 1984 v H; 1987 v Y, Ni, T; 1988 v WG; 1992 v T, Pol, Cz (16)
Macaulay, R. H. (Cambridge University), 1881 v S (1)
Macdonald, M. (Newcastle U), 1972 v W, Ni, S (sub); 1973 v USSR (sub); 1974 v P, S (sub), Y (sub); 1975 v WG, Cy (2), Ni; 1976 v Sw (sub), Cz, P (14)
Macrae, S. (Notts Co), 1883 v S, W, Ni; 1884 v S, Ni (5)
Maddison, F. B. (Oxford University), 1872 v S (1)
Madeley, P. E. (Leeds U), 1971 v Ni; 1972 v Sw (2), Gr, WG (2), W, S; 1973 v S, Cz, Pol, USSR, I; 1974 v A, Pol, I; 1975 v Cz, P, Cy; 1976 v Cz, Fi; 1977 v Ei, Ho (24)
Magee, T. P. (WBA), 1923 v W, Se; 1925 v S, Bel, F (5)
Makepeace, H. (Everton), 1906 v S; 1910 v S; 1912 v S, W (4)
Male, C. G. (Arsenal), 1935 v S, Ni, I, Ho; 1936 v S, W, Ni, G, A, Bel; 1937 v S, Ni, H, N, Se, Fi; 1939 v I, R, Y (19)

Mannion, W. J. (Middlesbrough), 1947 v S, W, Ni, Ei, Ho, F, Sw, P; 1948 v W, Ni, Bel, Se, I; 1949 v N, F; 1950 v S, Ei, P, Bel, Ch, US; 1951 v Ni, W, S, Y; 1952 v F (26)

Mariner, P. (Ipswich T), 1977 v L; 1978 v L, W (sub), S; 1980 v W, Ni (sub), S, Aus, I (sub), Sp (sub); 1981 v N, Sw, Sp, Sw, H; 1982 v N, H, Ho, S, Fi, F, Cz, K, WG, Sp; 1983 v D, WG, Gr, W; 1984 v D, H, L; (with Arsenal), 1985 v EG, R (35)

Marsden, J. T. (Darwen), 1891 v Ni (1)

Marsden, W. (Sheffield W), 1930 v W, S, G (3)

Marsh, R. W. (QPR), 1972 v Sw (sub); (with Manchester C), WG (sub+1), W, Ni, S; 1973 v W (2), Y (9)

Marshall, T. (Darwen), 1880 v W; 1881 v W (2)

Martin, A. (West Ham U), 1981 v Br, S (sub); 1982 v H, Fi; 1983 v Gr, L, W, Gr, H; 1984 v H, L, W; 1985 v Ni; 1986 v Is, Ca, Para; 1987 v Se (17)

Martin, H. (Sunderland), 1914 v Ni (1)

Martyn, A. N. C (Palace), 1992 v C (sub), H; 1993 v G; (with Leeds U), 1997 v S.Af; 1998 v Cam, Ch, Bel; 1999 v CzR, F (sub); 2000 v L, Pol, Bel (sub), Uk, R; 2001 v Sp (sub), M (16)

Marwood, B. (Arsenal), 1989 v S.Ar (sub) (1)

Maskrey, H. M. (Derby Co), 1908 v Ni (1)

Mason, C. (Wolverhampton W), 1887 v Ni; 1888 v W; 1890 v Ni (3)

Matthews, R. D. (Coventry C), 1956 v S, Br, Se, WG; 1957 v Ni (5)

Matthews, S. (Stoke C), 1935 v W, I; 1936 v G; 1937 v S; 1938 v S, W, Cz, G, Sw, F; 1939 v S, W, Ni, R of E, N, I, Y; 1947 v S; (with Blackpool), 1947 v Sw, P; 1948 v S, W, Ni, Bel, I; 1949 v S, W, Ni, D, Sw; 1950 v Sp; 1951 v Ni, S; 1954 v Ni, R of E, H, Bel, U; 1955 v Ni, W, S, F, WG, Sp, P; 1956 v W, Br; 1957 v S, W, Ni, Y, D (2), Ei (54)

Matthews, V. (Sheffield U), 1928 v F, Bel (2)

Maynard, W. J. (1st Surrey Rifles), 1872 v S; 1876 v S (2)

Meadows, J. (Manchester C), 1955 v S (1)

Medley, L. D. (Tottenham H), 1951 v Y, W; 1952 v F, A, W, Ni (6)

Meehan, T. (Chelsea), 1924 v Ni (1)

Melia, J. (Liverpool), 1963 v S, Sw (2)

Mercer, D. W. (Sheffield U), 1923 v Ni, Bel (2)

Mercer, J. (Everton), 1939 v S, Ni, I, R, Y (5)

Merrick, G. H. (Birmingham C), 1952 v Ni, S, A (2), I, Sw; 1953 v N, S, Bel, Arg, Ch, U; 1954 v W, Ni, S, R of E, H (2), Y, Bel, Sw, U (23)

Merson, P. C. (Arsenal), 1992 v G (sub), Cz, H, Br (sub), Fi (sub), D, Se (sub); 1993 v Sp (sub), N (sub), Ho (sub), Br (sub); G; 1994 v Ho, Gr; 1997 v I (sub); (with Middlesbrough), 1998 v Sw, P (sub), Bel, Arg (sub); 1999 v Se (sub); (with Aston Villa), CzR (21)

Metcalfe, V. (Huddersfield T), 1951 v Arg, P (2)

Mew, J. W. (Manchester U), 1921 v Ni (1)

Middleditch, B. (Corinthians), 1897 v Ni (1)

Milburn, J. E. T. (Newcastle U), 1949 v S, W, Ni, Sw; 1950 v W, P, Bel, Sp; 1951 v W, Arg, P; 1952 v F; 1956 v D (13)

Miller, B. G. (Burnley), 1961 v A (1)

Miller, H. S. (Charlton Ath), 1923 v Se (1)

Mills, D. J. (Leeds U), 2001 v M (sub) (1)

Mills, G. R. (Chelsea), 1938 v W, Ni, Cz (3)

Mills, M. D. (Ipswich T), 1973 v Y; 1976 v W (2), Ni, S, Br, I (sub), Fi; 1977 v Fi (sub), I, Ni, W, S; 1978 v WG, Br, W, Ni, S, H; 1979 v D, Ei, Ni (2), S, Bul, A; 1980 v D, Ni, Sp (2); 1981 v Sw (2), H; 1982 v N, H, S, Fi, F, Cz, K, WG, Sp (42)

Milne, G. (Liverpool), 1963 v Br, Cz, EG; 1964 v W, Ni, S, R of W, U, P, Ei, Br, Arg; 1965 v Ni, Bel (14)

Milton, C. A. (Arsenal), 1952 v A (1)

Milward, A. (Everton), 1891 v S, W; 1897 v S, W (4)

Mitchell, C. (Upton Park), 1880 v W; 1881 v S; 1883 v S, W; 1885 v W (5)

Mitchell, J. F. (Manchester C), 1925 v Ni (1)

Moffat, H. (Oldham Ath), 1913 v W (1)

Molyneux, G. (Southampton), 1902 v S; 1903 v S, W, Ni (4)

Moon, W. R. (Old Westminsters), 1888 v S, W; 1889 v S, W; 1890 v S, W; 1891 v S (7)

Moore, H. T. (Notts Co), 1883 v Ni; 1885 v W (2)

Moore, J. (Derby Co), 1923 v Se (1)

Moore, R. F. (West Ham U), 1962 v Pe, H, Arg, Bul, Br; 1963 v W, Ni, S, F (2), Br, Cz, EG, Sw; 1964 v W, Ni, S, R of W, U, P (2), Ei, Br, Arg; 1965 v Ni, S, Bel, H, Y, WG, Se; 1966 v W, Ni, S, A, Sp, Pol (2), WG (2), N, D, U, M, F, Arg, P; 1967 v W, Ni, S, Cz, Sp, A; 1968 v W, Ni, S, USSR (2), Sp (2), Se, Y, WG; 1969 v Ni, W, S, R, Bul, F, M, U, Br; 1970 v W, Ni, S, Ho, P, Bel, Co, Ec, R, Br, Cz, WG; 1971 v EG, Gr, Ma, Ni, S; 1972 v Sw (2), G, W, S; 1973 v W (3), Y, S (2), Ni, Cz, Pol, USSR, I; 1974 v I (108)

Moore, W. G. B. (West Ham U), 1923 v Se (1)

Mordue, J. (Sunderland), 1912 v Ni; 1913 v Ni (2)

Morice, C. J. (Barnes), 1872 v S (1)

Morley, A. (Aston Villa), 1982 v H (sub), Ni, W, Ic; 1983 v D, Gr (6)

Morley, H. (Notts Co), 1910 v Ni (1)

Morren, T. (Sheffield U), 1898 v Ni (1)

Morris, F. (WBA), 1920 v S; 1921 v Ni (2)

Morris, J. (Derby Co), 1949 v N, F; 1950 v Ei (3)

Morris, W. W. (Wolverhampton W), 1939 v S, Ni, R (3)

Morse, H. (Notts Co), 1879 v S (1)

Mort, T. (Aston Villa), 1924 v W, F; 1926 v S (3)

Morten, A. (C Palace), 1873 v S (1)

Mortensen, S. H. (Blackpool), 1947 v P; 1948 v W, S, Ni, Bel, Se, I; 1949 v S, W, Ni, Se, N; 1950 v S, W, Ni, I, P, Bel, Ch, US, Sp; 1951 v S, Arg; 1954 v R of E, H (25)

Morton, J. R. (West Ham U), 1938 v Cz (1)

Mosforth, W. (Sheffield W), 1877 v S; (with Sheffield Albion), 1878 v S; 1879 v S, W; 1880 v S, W; (with Sheffield W), 1881 v W; 1882 v S, W (9)

Moss, F. (Arsenal), 1934 v S, H, Cz; 1935 v I (4)

Moss, F. (Aston Villa), 1922 v S, Ni; 1923 v Ni; 1924 v S, Bel (5)

Mosscrop, E. (Burnley), 1914 v S, W (2)

Mozley, B. (Derby Co), 1950 v W, Ni, Ei (3)

Mullen, J. (Wolverhampton W), 1947 v S; 1949 v N, F; 1950 v Bel (sub), Ch, US; 1954 v W, Ni, S, R of E, Y, Sw (12)

Mullery, A. P. (Tottenham H), 1965 v Ho; 1967 v Sp, A; 1968 v W, Ni, S, USSR, Sp (2), Se, Y; 1969 v Ni, S, R, Bul, F, M, U, Br; 1970 v W, Ni, S (sub), Ho (sub), Bel, P, Co, Ec, R, Cz, WG, Br; 1971 v Ma, EG, Gr; 1972 v Sw (35)

Neal, P. G. (Liverpool), 1976 v W, I; 1977 v W, S, Br, Arg, U; 1978 v Sw, I, WG, Ni, S, H; 1979 v D, Ei, Ni (2), S, Bul, A; 1980 v D, Ni, Sp, Arg, W, Bel, I; 1981 v R, Sw, Sp, Br, H; 1982 v N, H, W, Ho, Ic, F (sub), K; 1983 v D, Gr, L, W, Gr, H, Ni, S, Aus (2); 1984 v D (50)

Needham, E. (Sheffield U), 1894 v S; 1895 v S; 1897 v S, W, Ni; 1898 v S, W; 1899 v S, W, Ni; 1900 v S, Ni; 1901 v S, W, Ni; 1902 v W (16)

Neville, G. A. (Manchester U), 1995 v J, Br; 1996 v Co, N, Sw, P, Bul, Cro, H, Chn, Sw, S, Ho, Sp; 1997 v Mol, Pol, I, Ge, Pol, I (sub), F, Br (sub); 1998 v Mol, Ch, P, S.Ar, Bel, R, Co, Arg; 1999 v Bul, Pol; 2000 v L (sub), Pol, Br, Ma, P, G, R; 2001 v G, I, Sp (sub), Fi, Alb (44)

Neville, P. J. (Manchester U), 1996 v Chn; 1997 v S.Af, Pol (sub), I, F, Br; 1998 v Mol, Cam, Ch, P (sub), S.Ar (sub), Bel; 1999 v L, Pol (sub), H, Se, Bul; 2000 v L (sub), Pol (sub), Bel (sub), S (2), Arg (sub), Br, Uk, Ma, P, G, R; 2001 v Fi, Sp, M, Gr (33)

Newton, K. R. (Blackburn R), 1966 v S, WG; 1967 v Sp, A; 1968 v W, S, Sp, Se, Y, WG; 1969 v Ni, W, S, R, Bul, M, U, Br, F; (with Everton), 1970 v Ni, S, Ho, Co, Ec, R, Cz, WG (27)

Nicholls, J. (WBA), 1954 v S, Y (2)

Nicholson, W. E. (Tottenham H), 1951 v P (1)

Nish, D. J. (Derby Co), 1973 v Ni; 1974 v P, W, Ni, S (5)

Norman, M. (Tottenham H), 1962 v Pe, H, Arg, Bul, Br; 1963 v S, F, Br, Cz, EG; 1964 v W, Ni, S, R of W, U, P (2), US, Br, Arg; 1965 v Ni, Bel, Ho (23)

Nuttall, H. (Bolton W), 1928 v W, Ni; 1929 v S (3)

Oakley, W. J. (Oxford University), 1895 v W; 1896 v S, W, Ni; (with Corinthians), 1897 v S, W, Ni; 1898 v S, W, Ni; 1900 v S, W, Ni; 1901 v S, W, Ni (16)

O'Dowd, J. P. (Chelsea), 1932 v S; 1933 v Ni, Sw (3)

O'Grady, M. (Huddersfield T), 1963 v Ni; (with Leeds U), 1969 v F (2)

Ogilvie, R. A. M. M. (Clapham R), 1874 v S (1)

Oliver, L. F. (Fulham), 1929 v Bel (1)

Olney, B. A. (Aston Villa), 1928 v F, Bel (2)

Osborne, F. R. (Fulham), 1923 v Ni, F; (with Tottenham H), 1925 v Bel; 1926 v Bel (4)

Osborne, R. (Leicester C), 1928 v W (1)

Osgood, P. L. (Chelsea), 1970 v Bel, R (sub), Cz (sub); 1974 v I (4)

Osman, R. (Ipswich T), 1980 v Aus; 1981 v Sp, R, Sw; 1982 v N, Ic; 1983 v D, Aus (3); 1984 v D (11)

Ottaway, C. J. (Oxford University), 1872 v S; 1874 v S (2)

Owen, J. R. B. (Sheffield), 1874 v S (1)

Owen, M. J. (Liverpool), 1998 v Ch, Sw, P (sub), Mor (sub), Bel (sub), Tun (sub), R (sub), Co, Arg; 1999 v Se, Bul, L, F; 2000 v L (sub), Pol (sub), Bel (sub), S (2), Br, P, G, R; 2001 v F (sub), G, Sp, Fi, Alb, M, Gr (29)

Owen, S. W. (Luton T), 1954 v H, Y, Bel (3)

Page, L. A. (Burnley), 1927 v S, W, Bel, L, F; 1928 v W, Ni (7)

Paine, T. L. (Southampton), 1963 v Cz, EG; 1964 v W, Ni, S, R of W, U, US, P; 1965 v Ni, H, Y, WG, Se; 1966 v W, A, Y, N, M (19)

Pallister, G. A. (Middlesbrough), 1988 v H; 1989 v S.Ar; (with Manchester U), 1991 v Cam (sub), T; 1992 v G; 1993 v N, US, Br, G; 1994 v Pol, Ho, Sm, D; 1995 v US, R, Ei, U, Se; 1996 v N, Sw; 1997 v Mol, Pol (sub) (22)

Palmer, C. L. (Sheffield W), 1992 v C, H, Br, Fi (sub), D, F, Se; 1993 v Sp (sub), N (sub), T, Sm, T, Ho, Pol, N, US, Br (sub); 1994 v Ho (18)

Pantling, H. H. (Sheffield U), 1924 v Ni (1)

Paravacini, P. J. de (Cambridge University), 1883 v S, W, Ni (3)

Parker, P. A. (QPR), 1989 v Alb (sub), Ch, D; 1990 v Y, U, Ho, Eg, Bel, Cam, WG, I; 1991 v H, Pol, USSR, Aus, Nz; (with Manchester U), 1992 v G; 1994 v Ho, D (19)

Parker, T. R. (Southampton), 1925 v F (1)

Parkes, P. B. (QPR), 1974 v P (1)

Parkinson, J. (Liverpool), 1910 v S, W (2)

Parlour, R. (Arsenal), 1999 v Pol (sub), Se (sub), Bul (sub); 2000 v L, S (sub), Arg (sub), Br (sub); 2001 v G (sub), Fi, I (10)

Parr, P. C. (Oxford University), 1882 v W (1)

Parry, E. H. (Old Carthusians), 1879 v W; 1882 v W, S (3)

Parry, R. A. (Bolton W), 1960 v Ni, S (2)

Patchitt, B. C. A. (Corinthians), 1923 v Se (2) (2)

Pawson, F. W. (Cambridge University), 1883 v Ni; (with Swifts), 1885 v Ni (2)

Payne, J. (Luton T), 1937 v Fi (1)

Peacock, A. (Middlesbrough), 1962 v Arg, Bul; 1963 v Ni, W; (with Leeds U), 1966 v W, Ni (6)

Peacock, J (Middlesbrough), 1929 v F, Bel, Sp (3)

Pearce, S. (Nottingham F), 1987 v Br, S; 1988 v WG (sub), Is, H; 1989 v D, Se, S.Ar, Gr, Alb (2), Ch, S, Pol, D; 1990 v Se, Pol, I, Y, Br, Cz, D, U, Tun, Ei, Ho, Eg, Bel, Cam, WG; 1991 v H, Pol, Ei (2), Cam, T, Arg, Aus, Nz (2), Mal; 1992 v T, Pol, F, Cz, Br (sub), Fi, D, F, Se; 1993 v Sp, N, T; 1994 v Pol, Sm, Gr (sub); 1995 v R (sub), J, Br; 1996 v N, Sw, P, Bul, Cro, H, Sw, S, Ho, Sp, G; 1997 v Mol, Pol, I, M, S.Af, I; (with West Ham U), 2000 v L, Pol (78)

Pearson, H. F. (WBA), 1932 v S (1)

Pearson, J. H. (Crewe Alex), 1892 v Ni (1)

Pearson, J. S. (Manchester U), 1976 v W, Ni, S, Br, Fi; 1977 v Ei, Ho (sub), W, S, Br, Arg, U; 1978 v I (sub), WG, Ni (15)

Pearson, S. C. (Manchester U), 1948 v S; 1949 v S, Ni; 1950 v Ni, I; 1951 v P; 1952 v S, I (8)

Pease, W. H. (Middlesbrough), 1927 v W (1)

Pegg, D. (Manchester U), 1957 v Ei (1)

Pejic, M. (Stoke C), 1974 v P, W, Ni, S (4)

Pelly, F. R. (Old Foresters), 1893 v Ni; 1894 v S, W (3)

Pennington, J. (WBA), 1907 v S, W; 1908 v S, W, Ni, A; 1909 v S, W, H (2), A; 1910 v S, W; 1911 v S, W, Ni; 1912 v S, W, Ni; 1913 v S, W; 1914 v S, Ni; 1920 v S, W (25)

Pentland, F. B. (Middlesbrough), 1909 v S, W, H (2), A (5)

Perry, C. (WBA), 1890 v Ni; 1891 v Ni; 1893 v W (3)

Perry, T. (WBA), 1898 v W (1)

Perry, W. (Blackpool), 1956 v Ni, S, Sp (3)

Perryman, S. (Tottenham H), 1982 v Ic (sub) (1)

Peters, M. (West Ham U), 1966 v Y, Fi, Pol, M, F, Arg, P, WG; 1967 v Ni, W, S, Cz; 1968 v W, Ni, S, USSR (2), Sp (2), Se, Y; 1969 v Ni, S, Bul, F, M, U, Br; 1970 v Ho (2), P (sub), Bel; (with Tottenham H), W, Ni, S, Co, Ec, R, Br, Cz, WG; 1971 v EG, Gr, Ma (2), Ni, W, S; 1972 v Sw, Gr, WG (1+1 sub), Ni; 1973 v S (2), Ni, W, Cz, Pol, USSR, I; 1974 v A, Pol, I, P, S (67)

Phelan, M. C. (Manchester U), 1990 v I (sub) (1)

Phillips, K. (Sunderland), 1999 v H; 2000 v Bel, Arg (sub), Br (sub), Ma; 2001 v I (sub) (6)

Phillips, L. H. (Portsmouth), 1952 v Ni; 1955 v W, WG (3)

Pickering, F. (Everton), 1964 v US; 1965 v Ni, Bel (3)

Pickering, J. (Sheffield U), 1933 v S (1)

Pickering, N. (Sunderland), 1983 v Aus (1)

Pike, T. M. (Cambridge University), 1886 v Ni (1)

Pilkington, B. (Burnley), 1955 v Ni (1)

Plant, J. (Bury), 1900 v S (1)

Platt, D. (Aston Villa), 1990 v I (sub), Y (sub), Br, D (sub), Tun (sub), Ho (sub), Eg (sub), Bel (sub), Cam, WG, I; 1991 v H, Pol, Ei (2), T, USSR, Arg, Aus, Nz (2), Mal; (with Bari), 1992 v G, T, Pol, Cz, C, Br, Fi, D, F, Se; (with Juventus), 1993 v Sp, N, T, Sm, T, Ho, Pol, N, Br (sub), G; (with Sampdoria), 1994 v Pol, Ho, Sm, D, Gr, N; 1995 v US, Ng, Ei, U, J, Se, Br; (with Arsenal), 1996 v Bul (sub), Cro, H, Sw (sub), Ho (sub), Sp, G (62)

Plum, S. L. (Charlton Ath), 1923 v F (1)

Pointer, R. (Burnley), 1962 v W, L, P (3)

Porteous, T. S. (Sunderland), 1891 v W (1)

Powell, C. G. (Charlton Ath), 2001 v Sp, Fi, M (sub) (3)

Priest, A. E. (Sheffield U), 1900 v Ni (1)

Prinsep, J. F. M. (Clapham Rovers), 1879 v S (1)

Puddefoot, S. C. (Blackburn R), 1926 v S, Ni (2)

Pye, J. (Wolverhampton W), 1950 v Ei (1)

Pym, R. H. (Bolton W), 1925 v S, W; 1926 v W (3)

Quantrill, A. (Derby Co), 1920 v S, W; 1921 v W, Ni (4)

Quixall, A. (Sheffield W), 1954 v W, Ni, R of E; 1955 v Sp, P (sub) (5)

Radford, J. (Arsenal), 1969 v R; 1972 v Sw (sub) (2)

Raikes, G. B. (Oxford University), 1895 v W; 1896 v W, Ni, S (4)

Ramsey, A. E. (Southampton), 1949 v Sw; (with Tottenham H), 1950 v S, I, P, Bel, Ch, US, Sp; 1951 v S, Ni, W, Y, Arg, P; 1952 v S, W, Ni, F, A (2), I, Sw; 1953 v Ni, W, S, Bel, Arg, Ch, U, US; 1954 v R of E, H (32)

Rawlings, A. (Preston NE), 1921 v Bel (1)

Rawlings, W. E. (Southampton), 1922 v S, W (2)

Rawlinson, J. F. P. (Cambridge University), 1882 v Ni (1)

Rawson, H. E. (Royal Engineers), 1875 v S (1)

Rawson, W. S. (Oxford University), 1875 v S; 1877 v S (2)

Read, A. (Tufnell Park), 1921 v Bel (1)

Reader, J. (WBA), 1894 v Ni (1)

Reaney, P. (Leeds U), 1969 v Bul (sub); 1970 v P; 1971 v Ma (3)

Redknapp, J. F. (Liverpool), 1996 v Co, N, Sw, Chn, S (sub); 1997 v M (sub), Ge (sub), S.Af; 1999 v Se, Bul, F, Pol (sub), H (sub), Bul; 2000 v Bel, S (2) (17)

Reeves, K. (Norwich C), 1980 v Bul; (with Manchester C), Ni (2)

Regis, C. (WBA), 1982 v Ni (sub), W (sub), Ic; 1983 v WG; (with Coventry C), 1988 v T (sub) (5)

Reid, P. (Everton), 1985 v M (sub), WG, US (sub); 1986 v R, S (sub), Ca (sub), Pol, Para, Arg; 1987 v Br; 1988 v WG, Y (sub), Sw (sub) (13)

Revie, D. G. (Manchester C), 1955 v Ni, S, F; 1956 v W, D; 1957 v Ni (6)

Reynolds, J. (WBA), 1892 v S; 1893 v S, W; (with Aston Villa), 1894 v S, Ni; 1895 v S; 1897 v S, W (8)

Richards, C. H. (Nottingham F), 1898 v Ni (1)

Richards, G. H. (Derby Co), 1909 v A (1)

Richards, J. P. (Wolverhampton W), 1973 v Ni (1)

Richardson, J. R. (Newcastle U), 1933 v I, Sw (2)

Richardson, K. (Aston Villa), 1994 v Gr (1)

Richardson, W. G. (WBA), 1935 v Ho (1)

Rickaby, S. (WBA), 1954 v Ni (1)

Rigby, A. (Blackburn R), 1927 v S, Bel, L, F; 1928 v W (5)

Rimmer, E. J. (Sheffield W), 1930 v S, G, A; 1932 v Sp (4)

Rimmer, J. J. (Arsenal), 1976 v I (1)

Ripley, S. E. (Blackburn R), 1994 v Sm; 1998 v Mol (sub) (2)

Rix, G. (Arsenal), 1981 v Ni, Sw (sub), Br, W, S; 1982 v Ho (sub), Fi (sub), F, Cz, K, WG, Sp; 1983 v D, WG (sub), Gr (sub); 1984 v Ni (17)

Robb, G. (Tottenham H), 1954 v H (1)

Roberts, C. (Manchester U), 1905 v Ni, W, S (3)

Roberts, F. (Manchester C), 1925 v S, W, Bel, F (4)

Roberts, G. (Tottenham H), 1983 v Ni, S; 1984 v F, Ni, S, USSR (6)

Roberts, H. (Arsenal), 1931 v S (1)

Roberts, H. (Millwall), 1931 v Bel (1)

Roberts, R. (WBA), 1887 v S; 1888 v Ni; 1890 v Ni (3)

Roberts, W. T. (Preston NE), 1924 v W, Bel (2)

Robinson, J. (Sheffield W), 1937 v Fi; 1938 v G, Sw; 1939 v W (4)

Robinson, J. W. (Derby Co), 1897 v S, Ni; (with New Brighton Tower), 1898 v S, W, Ni; (with Southampton), 1899 v W, S; 1900 v S, W, Ni; 1901 v Ni (11)

Robson, B. (WBA), 1980 v Ei, Aus; 1981 v N, R, Sw, Sp, R, Br, W, S, Sw, H; 1982 v N; (with Manchester U), H, Ni, W, Ho, S, Fi, F, Cz, WG, Sp; 1983 v D, Gr, L, S; 1984 v H, L, F, Ni, S, USSR, Br, U, Ch; 1985 v EG, Fi, T, Ei, R, Fi, S, M, I, WG, US; 1986 v R, T, Is, M, P, Mor; 1987 v Ni (2), Sp, T, Br, S; 1988 v T, Y, Ho, H, S, Co, Sw, Ei, Ho, USSR; 1989 v S, Se, S.Ar, Gr, Alb (2), Ch, S, Pol, D; 1990 v Pol, I, Y, Cz, U, Tun, Ei, Ho; 1991 v Cam, Ei; 1992 v T (90)

Robson, R. (WBA), 1958 v F, USSR (2), Br, A; 1960 v Sp, H; 1961 v Ni, W, S, L, P, Sp, M, I; 1962 v W, Ni, Sw, L, P (20)

Rocastle, D. (Arsenal), 1989 v D, S.Ar, Gr, Alb (2), Pol (sub), D; 1990 v Se (sub), Pol, Y, D (sub); 1992 v Pol, Cz, Br (sub) (14)

Rose, W. C. (Wolverhampton W), 1884 v S, W, Ni; (with Preston NE), 1886 v Ni; (with Wolverhampton W), 1891 v Ni (5)

Rostron, T. (Darwen), 1881 v S, W (2)

Rowe, A. (Tottenham H), 1934 v F (1)

Rowley, J. F. (Manchester U), 1949 v Sw, Se, F; 1950 v Ni, I; 1952 v S (6)

Rowley, W. (Stoke C), 1889 v Ni; 1892 v Ni (2)

Royle, J. (Everton), 1971 v Ma; 1973 v Y; (with Manchester C), 1976 v Ni (sub), I; 1977 v Fi, L (6)
Ruddlesdin, H. (Sheffield W), 1904 v W, Ni; 1905 v S (3)
Ruddock, N. (Liverpool), 1995 v Ng (1)
Ruffell, J. W. (West Ham U), 1926 v S; 1927 v Ni; 1929 v S, W, Ni; 1930 v W (6)
Russell, B. B. (Royal Engineers), 1883 v W (1)
Rutherford, J. (Newcastle U), 1904 v S; 1907 v S, Ni, W; 1908 v S, Ni, W, A (2), H, B (11)

Sadler, D. (Manchester U), 1968 v Ni, USSR; 1970 v Ec (sub); 1971 v EG (4)
Sagar, C. (Bury), 1900 v Ni; 1902 v W (2)
Sagar, E. (Everton), 1936 v S, Ni, A, Bel (4)
Salako, J. A. (C Palace), 1991 v Aus (sub), Nz (sub + 1), Mal; 1992 v G (5)
Sandford, E. A. (WBA), 1933 v W (1)
Sandilands, R. R. (Old Westminsters), 1892 v W; 1893 v Ni; 1894 v W; 1895 v W; 1896 v W (5)
Sands, J. (Nottingham F), 1880 v W (1)
Sansom, K. (C Palace), 1979 v W; 1980 v Bul, Ei, Arg, W (sub), Ni, S, Bel, I; (with Arsenal), 1981 v N, R, Sw, Sp, R, Br, W, S, Sw; 1982 v Ni, W, Ho, S, Fi, F, Cz, WG, Sp; 1983 v D, WG, Gr, L, Gr, H, Ni, S; 1984 v D, H, L, F, S, USSR, Br, U, Ch; 1985 v EG, Fi, T, Ni, Ei, R, Fi, S, I, M, WG, US; 1986 v R, T, Ni, Eg, Is, USSR, S, M, Ca, P, Mor, Pol, Para, Arg; 1987 v Se, Ni (2), Y, Sp, T; 1988 v WG, T, Y, Ho, S, Co, Sw, Ei, Ho, USSR (86)
Saunders, F. E. (Swifts), 1888 v W (1)
Savage, A. H. (C Palace), 1876 v S (1)
Sayer, J. (Stoke C), 1887 v Ni (1)
Scales, J. R. (Liverpool), 1995 v J, Se (sub), Br (3)
Scattergood, E. (Derby Co), 1913 v W (1)
Schofield, J. (Stoke C), 1892 v W; 1893 v W; 1895 v Ni (3)
Scholes, P. (Manchester U), 1997 v S.Af (sub), I, Br; 1998 v Mol, Cam, P, S.Ar, Tun, R, Co, Arg; 1999 v Se, Bul, L, F (sub), Pol, Se; 2000 v Pol, S (2), Arg, Br, Uk, Ma, P, G, R; 2001 v F, G, Fi, Sp, Fi, Alb, M, Gr (35)
Scott, L. (Arsenal), 1947 v S, W, Ni, Ei, Ho, F, Sw, P; 1948 v S, W, Ni, Bel, Se, I; 1949 v W, Ni, D (17)
Scott, W. R. (Brentford), 1937 v W (1)
Seaman, D. A. (QPR), 1989 v S.Ar, D (sub); 1990 v Cz (sub); (with Arsenal), 1991 v Cam, Ei, T, Arg; 1992 v Cz, H (sub); 1994 v Pol, Ho, Sm, D, N; 1995 v US, R, Ei; 1996 v Co, N, Sw, P, Bul, Cro, H, Sw, S, Ho, Sp, G; 1997 v Mol, Pol, Ge (2), Pol, F, Br; 1998 v Mol, I, P, S.Ar, Tun, R, Co, Arg; 1999 v Se, Bul, L, F, Pol, H, Se, Bul; 2000 v Bel, S (2), Arg, Br, P, G; 2001 v F, G, Fi (2), Alb, Gr (65)
Seddon, J. (Bolton W), 1923 v F, Se (2); 1924 v Bel; 1927 v W; 1929 v S (6)
Seed, J. M. (Tottenham H), 1921 v Bel: 1923 v W, Ni, Bel; 1925 v S (5)
Settle, J. (Bury), 1899 v S, W, Ni; (with Everton), 1902 v S, Ni; 1903 v Ni (6)
Sewell, J. (Sheffield W), 1952 v Ni, A, Sw; 1953 v Ni; 1954 v H (2) (6)
Sewell, W. R. (Blackburn R), 1924 v W (1)
Shackleton, L. F. (Sunderland), 1949 v W, D; 1950 v W; 1955 v W, WG (5)
Sharp, J. (Everton), 1903 v Ni; 1905 v S (2)
Sharpe, L. S. (Manchester U), 1991 v Ei (sub); 1993 v T (sub), N, US, Br; 1994 v Pol, Ho (8)
Shaw, G. E. (WBA), 1932 v S (1)
Shaw, G. L. (Sheffield U), 1959 v S, W, USSR, I; 1963 v W (5)
Shea, D. (Blackburn R), 1914 v W, Ni (2)
Shearer, A. (Southampton), 1992 v F, C, F; (with Blackburn R), 1993 v Sp, N, T; 1994 v Ho, D, Gr, N; 1995 v US, R, Ng, Ei, J, Se, Br; 1996 v Co, N, Sw, P, H (sub), Chn, Sw, S, Ho, Sp, G; (with Newcastle U), 1997 v Mol, Pol, I, Ge, Pol, F, Br; 1998 v Ch (sub), Sw, P, S.Ar, Tun, R, Co, Arg; 1999 v Se, Bul, L, F, Pol, H, Se, Bul; 2000 v Bel, S (2), Arg, Br, Uk, Ma, P, G, R (63)
Shellito, K. J. (Chelsea), 1963 v Cz (1)
Shelton A. (Notts Co), 1889 v Ni; 1890 v S, W; 1891 v S, W; 1892 v S (6)
Shelton, C. (Notts Rangers), 1888 v Ni (1)
Shepherd, A. (Bolton W), 1906 v S; (with Newcastle U), 1911 v Ni (2)
Sherwood, T. A. (Tottenham H), 1999 v Pol, H, Se (3)
Sheringham, E. P. (Tottenham H), 1993 v Pol, N; 1995 v US, R (sub), Ng (sub), U, J (sub); Se, Br; 1996 v Co (sub), N (sub), Sw, Bul, Cro, H, Sw, S, Ho, Sp, G; 1997 v Ge, M, Ge, S.Af, Pol, I, F (sub), Br; (with Manchester U), 1998 v I, Ch, Sw (sub), P, S.Ar, Tun, R; 1999 v Se (sub), Bul (sub), Bul; 2001 v Fi, Alb (sub), M (sub) (41)

S, Arg; (with Stoke C), 1975 v Cy; 1977 v Ni, W; (with Nottingham F), 1978 v W, H; 1979 v Cz, Se, A; 1980 v Ni, Sp, I; 1981 v N, Sw, R; 1982 v H, Ho, S, F, Cz, K, WG, Sp; (with Southampton), 1983 v D, WG, Gr, W, Gr, H, Ni, S, Aus (3); 1984 v D, H, F, Ni, W, S, USSR, Br, U, Ch; 1985 v EG, Fi, T, Ni, R, Fi, S, I, WG; 1986 v R, T, Ni, Eg, Is, USSR, S, M, Ca, P, Mor, Pol, Para, Arg; 1987 v Se, Ni (2), Sp, Br; (with Derby Co), 1988 v WG, T, Y, Ho, S, Co, Sw, Ei, Ho; 1989 v D, Se, Gr, Alb (2), Ch, S, Pol, D; 1990 v Se, Pol, I, Y, Br, Cz, D, U, Tun, Ei, Ho, Eg, Bel, Cam, WG, I (125)
Shimwell, E. (Blackpool), 1949 v Se (1)
Shutt, G. (Stoke C), 1886 v Ni (1)
Silcock, J. (Manchester U), 1921 v S, W; 1923 v Se (3)
Sillett, R. P. (Chelsea), 1955 v F, Sp, P (3)
Simms, E. (Luton T), 1922 v Ni (1)
Simpson, J. (Blackburn R), 1911 v S, W, Ni; 1912 v S, W, Ni; 1913 v S; 1914 v W (8)
Sinton, A. (QPR), 1992 v Pol, C, H (sub), Br, F, Se; 1993 v Sp, T, Br, G; (with Sheffield W), 1994 v Ho (sub), Sm (12)
Slater, W. J. (Wolverhampton W), 1955 v W, WG; 1958 v S, P, Y, USSR (3), Br, A; 1959 v USSR; 1960 v S (12)
Smalley, T. (Wolverhampton W), 1937 v W (1)
Smart, T. (Aston Villa), 1921 v S; 1924 v S, W; 1926 v Ni; 1930 v W (5)
Smith, A. (Nottingham F), 1891 v S, W; 1893 v Ni (3)
Smith, A. (Leeds U), 2001 v M (sub), Gr (sub) (2)
Smith, A. K. (Oxford University), 1872 v S (1)
Smith, A. M. (Arsenal), 1989 v S.Ar (sub), Gr, Alb (sub), Pol (sub); 1991 v T, USSR, Arg; 1992 v G, T, Pol (sub), H (sub), D, Se (sub) (13)
Smith, B. (Tottenham H), 1921 v S; 1922 v W (2)
Smith, C. E. (C Palace), 1876 v S (1)
Smith, G. O. (Oxford University), 1893 v Ni; 1894 v W, S; 1895 v W; 1896 v W, S; (with Old Carthusians), 1897 v Ni, W, S; 1898 v Ni, W, S; (with Corinthians), 1899 v Ni, W, S; 1899 v Ni, W, S; 1901 v S (20)
Smith, H. (Reading), 1905 v W, S; 1906 v W, Ni (4)
Smith, J. (WBA), 1920 v Ni; 1923 v Ni (2)
Smith, Joe (Bolton W), 1913 v Ni; 1914 v S, W; 1920 v W, Ni (5)
Smith, J. C. R. (Millwall), 1939 v Ni, N (2)
Smith, J. W. (Portsmouth), 1932 v Ni, W, Sp (3)
Smith, Leslie (Brentford), 1939 v R (1)
Smith, Lionel (Arsenal), 1951 v W; 1952 v W, Ni; 1953 v W, S, Bel (6)
Smith, R. A. (Tottenham H), 1961 v Ni, W, S, L, P, Sp; 1962 v S; 1963 v S, F, Br, Cz, EG; 1964 v W, Ni, R of W (15)
Smith, S. (Aston Villa), 1895 v S (1)
Smith, S. C. (Leicester C), 1936 v Ni (1)
Smith, T. (Birmingham C), 1960 v W, Se (2)
Smith, T. (Liverpool), 1971 v W (1)
Smith, W. H. (Huddersfield T), 1922 v W, S; 1928 v S (3)
Sorby, T. H. (Thursday Wanderers, Sheffield), 1879 v W (1)
Southgate, G. (Aston Villa), 1996 v P (sub), Bul, H (sub), Chn, Sw, S, Ho, Sp, G; 1997 v Mol, Pol, Ge, M, Ge (sub), S.Af, Pol, I, F, Br; 1998 v Mol, I, Cam, Sw, S.Ar, Mor, Tun, Arg (sub); 1999 v Se, Bul, L, Bul; 2000 v Bel, S, Arg, Uk, Ma (sub), R (sub); 2001 v F (sub), G, Fi, I, M (sub) (42)
Southworth, J. (Blackburn R), 1889 v Ni; 1891 v W; 1892 v S (3)
Sparks, F. J. (Herts Rangers), 1879 v S; (with Clapham Rovers), 1880 v S, W (3)
Spence, J. W. (Manchester U), 1926 v Bel; 1927 v Ni (2)
Spence, R. (Chelsea), 1936 v A, Bel (2)
Spencer, C. W. (Newcastle U), 1924 v S; 1925 v W (2)
Spencer, H. (Aston Villa), 1897 v S, W; 1900 v W; 1903 v Ni; 1905 v W, S (6)
Spiksley, F. (Sheffield W), 1893 v S, W; 1894 v S, Ni; 1896 v Ni; 1898 v S, W (7)
Spilsbury, B. W. (Cambridge University), 1885 v Ni; 1886 v Ni, S (3)
Spink, N. (Aston Villa), 1983 v Aus (sub) (1)
Spouncer, W. A. (Nottingham F), 1900 v W (1)
Springett, R. D. G. (Sheffield W), 1960 v Ni, S, Y, Sp, H; 1961 v Ni, S, L, P, Sp, M, I, A; 1962 v W, Ni, S, A, Sw, Pe, L, P, H, Arg, Bul, Br; 1963 v Ni, W, F (2), Sw; 1966 v W, A, N (33)
Sproston, B. (Leeds U), 1937 v W; 1938 v S, W, Ni, Cz, G, Sw, F; (with Tottenham H), 1939 v W, R of E; (with Manchester C), N (11)
Squire, R. T. (Cambridge University), 1886 v S, W, Ni (3)
Stanbrough, M. H. (Old Carthusians), 1895 v W (1)
Staniforth, R. (Huddersfield T), 1954 v S, H, Y, Bel, Sw, U; 1955 v W, WG (8)
Starling, R. W. (Sheffield W), 1933 v S; (with Aston Villa), 1937 v S (2)
Statham, D. (WBA), 1983 v W, Aus (2) (3)

Steele, F. C. (Stoke C), 1937 v S, W, Ni, N, Se, Fi (6)
Stein, B. (Luton T), 1984 v F (1)
Stephenson, C. (Huddersfield T), 1924 v W (1)
Stephenson, G. T. (Derby Co), 1928 v F, Bel; (with Sheffield W), 1931 v F (3)
Stephenson, J. E. (Leeds U), 1938 v S; 1939 v Ni (2)
Stepney, A. C. (Manchester U), 1968 v Se (1)
Sterland, M. (Sheffield W), 1989 v S.Ar (1)
Steven, T. M. (Everton), 1985 v Ni, Ei, R, Fi, I, US (sub); 1986 v T (sub), Eg, USSR (sub), M (sub), Pol, Para, Arg; 1987 v Se, Y (sub), Sp (sub); 1988 v T, Y, Ho, H, S, Sw, Ho, USSR; 1989 v S; (with Rangers), 1990 v Cz, Cam (sub), WG (sub), I; 1991 v Cam; (with Marseille), 1992 v G, C, Br, Fi, D, F (36)
Stevens, S. A. (Tottenham H), 1985 v Fi (sub), T (sub), Ni; 1986 v S (sub), M (sub), Mor (sub), Para (sub) (7)
Stevens, M. G. (Everton), 1985 v I, WG; 1986 v R, T, Ni, Eg, Is, S, Ca, P, Mor, Pol, Para, Arg; 1987 v Br, S; 1988 v T, Y, Is, Ho, H (sub), S, Sw, Ei, Ho, USSR; (with Rangers), 1989 v D, Se, Gr, Alb (2), S, Pol; 1990 v Se, Pol, I, Br, D, Tun, Ei, I; 1991 v USSR; 1992 v C, H, Br, Fi (46)
Stewart, J. (Sheffield W), 1907 v S, W; (with Newcastle U), 1911 v S (3)
Stewart, P. A. (Tottenham H), 1992 v G (sub), Cz (sub), C (sub) (3)
Stiles, N. P. (Manchester U), 1965 v S, H, Y, Se; 1966 v W, Ni, S, A, Sp, Pol (2), WG (2), N, D, U, M, F, Arg, P; 1967 v Ni, W, S, Cz; 1968 v USSR; 1969 v S; 1970 v Ni, S (28)
Stoker, J. (Birmingham), 1933 v W; 1934 v S, H (3)
Stone, S. B. (Nottingham F), 1996 v N (sub), Sw (sub), P, Bul, Cro, Chn (sub), Sw (sub), S (sub), Sp (sub) (9)
Storer, H. (Derby Co), 1924 v F; 1928 v Ni (2)
Storey, P. E. (Arsenal), 1971 v Gr, Ni, S; 1972 v Sw, WG, W, Ni, S; 1973 v W (3), Y, S (2), Ni, Cz, Pol, USSR, I (19)
Storey-Moore, I. (Nottingham F), 1970 v Ho (1)
Strange, A. H. (Sheffield W), 1930 v S, A, G; 1931 v S, W, Ni, F, Bel; 1932 v S, W, Ni, Sp; 1933 v S, Ni, A, I, Sw; 1934 v Ni, W, F (20)
Stratford, A. H. (Wanderers), 1874 v S (1)
Streten, B. (Luton T), 1950 v Ni (1)
Sturgess, A. (Sheffield U), 1911 v Ni; 1914 v S (2)
Summerbee, M. G. (Manchester C), 1968 v S, Sp, WG; 1972 v Sw, WG (sub), W, Ni; 1973 v USSR (sub) (8)
Sunderland, A. (Arsenal), 1980 v Aus (1)
Sutcliffe, J. W. (Bolton W), 1893 v W; 1895 v S, Ni; 1901 v S; (with Millwall), 1903 v W (5)
Sutton, C. R. (Blackburn R), 1998 v Cam (sub) (1)
Swan, P. (Sheffield W), 1960 v Y, Sp, H; 1961 v Ni, W, S, L, P, Sp, M, I, A; 1962 v W, Ni, S, A, Sw, L, P (19)
Swepstone, H. A. (Pilgrims), 1880 v S; 1882 v S, W; 1883 v S, W, Ni (6)
Swift, F. V. (Manchester C), 1947 v S, W, Ni, Ei, Ho, F, Sw, P; 1948 v S, W, Ni, Bel, Se, I; 1949 v S, W, Ni, D, N (19)

Tait, G. (Birmingham Excelsior), 1881 v W (1)
Talbot, B. (Ipswich T), 1977 v Ni (sub), S, Br, Arg, U; (with Arsenal), 1980 v Aus (6)
Tambling, R. V. (Chelsea), 1963 v W, F; 1966 v Y (3)
Tate, J. T. (Aston Villa), 1931 v F, Bel; 1933 v W (3)
Taylor, E. (Blackpool), 1954 v H (1)
Taylor, E. H. (Huddersfield T), 1923 v S, W, Ni, Bel; 1924 v S, Ni, F; 1926 v S (8)
Taylor, J. G. (Fulham), 1951 v Arg, P (2)
Taylor, P. H. (Liverpool), 1947 v W, Ni, Se (3)
Taylor, P. J. (C Palace), 1976 v W (sub+1), Ni, S (4)
Taylor, T. (Manchester U), 1953 v Arg, Ch, U; 1954 v Bel, Sw; 1956 v S, Br, Se, Fi, WG; 1957 v Ni, Y (sub), D (2), Ei (2); 1958 v W, Ni, F (19)
Temple, D. W. (Everton), 1965 v WG (1)
Thickett, H. (Sheffield U), 1899 v S, W (2)
Thomas, D. (Coventry C), 1983 v Aus (1+1 sub) (2)
Thomas, D. (QPR), 1975 v Cz (sub), P, Cy (sub+1), W, S (sub); 1976 v Cz (sub), P (sub) (8)
Thomas, G. R. (C Palace), 1991 v T, USSR, Arg, Aus, Nz (2), Mal; 1992 v Pol, F (9)
Thomas, M. L. (Arsenal), 1989 v S.Ar; 1990 v Y (2)
Thompson, P. (Liverpool), 1964 v P (2), Ei, US, Br, Arg; 1965 v Ni, W, S, Bel, Ho; 1966 v Ni; 1968 v Ni, WG; 1970 v S, Ho (sub) (16)
Thompson, P. B. (Liverpool), 1976 v W (2), Ni, S, Br, I, Fi; 1977 v Fi; 1979 v Ei (sub), Cz, Ni, S, Bul, Se (sub), A; 1980 v D, Ni, Bul, Ei, Sp (2), Arg, W, S, Bel, I; 1981 v N, R, H; 1982 v N, H, W, Ho, S, Fi, F, Cz, K, WG, Sp; 1983 v WG, Gr (42)
Thompson T. (Aston Villa), 1952 v W; (with Preston NE), 1957 v S (2)

Thomson, R. A. (Wolverhampton W), 1964 v Ni, US, P, Arg; 1965 v Bel, Ho, Ni, W (8)
Thornewell, G. (Derby Co), 1923 v Se (2); 1924 v F; 1925 v F (4)
Thornley, I. (Manchester C), 1907 v W (1)
Tilson, S. F. (Manchester C), 1934 v H, Cz; 1935 v W; 1936 v Ni (4)
Titmuss, F. (Southampton), 1922 v W; 1923 v W (2)
Todd, C. (Derby Co), 1972 v Ni; 1974 v P, W, Ni, S, Arg, EG, Bul, Y; 1975 v P (sub), WG, Cy (2), Ni, W, S; 1976 v Sw, Cz, P, Ni, S, Br, Fi; 1977 v Ei, Fi, Ho (sub), Ni (27)
Toone, G. (Notts Co), 1892 v S, W (2)
Topham, A. G. (Casuals), 1894 v W (1)
Topham, R. (Wolverhampton W), 1893 v Ni; (with Casuals) 1894 v W (2)
Towers, M. A. (Sunderland), 1976 v W, Ni (sub), I (3)
Townley, W. J. (Blackburn R), 1889 v W; 1890 v Ni (2)
Townrow, J. E. (Clapton Orient), 1925 v S; 1926 v W (2)
Tremelling, D. R. (Birmingham), 1928 v W (1)
Tresadern, J. (West Ham U), 1923 v S, Se (2)
Tueart, D. (Manchester C), 1975 v Cy (sub), Ni; 1977 v Fi, Ni, W (sub), S (sub) (6)
Tunstall, F. E. (Sheffield U), 1923 v S; 1924 v S, W, Ni, F; 1925 v Ni, S (7)
Turnbull, R. J. (Bradford), 1920 v Ni (1)
Turner, A. (Southampton), 1900 v Ni; 1901 v Ni (2)
Turner, H. (Huddersfield T), 1931 v F, Bel (2)
Turner, J. A. (Bolton W), 1893 v W; (with Stoke C) 1895 v Ni; (with Derby Co) 1898 v Ni (3)
Tweedy, G. J. (Grimsby T), 1937 v H (1)

Ufton, D. G. (Charlton Ath), 1954 v R of E (1)
Underwood A. (Stoke C), 1891 v Ni; 1892 v Ni (2)
Unsworth, D. G. (Everton), 1995 v J (1)
Urwin, T. (Middlesbrough), 1923 v Se (2); 1924 v Bel; (with Newcastle U), 1926 v W (4)
Utley, G. (Barnsley), 1913 v Ni (1)

Vaughton, O. H. (Aston Villa), 1882 v S, W, Ni; 1884 v S, W (5)
Veitch, C. C. M. (Newcastle U), 1906 v S, W, Ni; 1907 v S, W; 1909 v W (6)
Veitch, J. G. (Old Westminsters), 1894 v W (1)
Venables, T. F. (Chelsea), 1965 v Ho, Bel (2)
Venison, B. (Newcastle U), 1995 v US, U (2)
Vidal, R. W. S. (Oxford University), 1873 v S (1)
Viljoen, C. (Ipswich T), 1975 v Ni, W (2)
Viollet, D. S. (Manchester U), 1960 v H; 1962 v L (2)
Von Donop (Royal Engineers), 1873 v S; 1875 v S (2)

Wace, H. (Wanderers), 1878 v S; 1879 v S, W (3)
Waddle, C. R. (Newcastle U), 1985 v Ei, R (sub), Fi (sub), S (sub), I, M (sub), WG, US; (with Tottenham H), 1986 v R, T, Ni, Is, USSR, S, M, Ca, P, Mor, Pol (sub), Arg (sub); 1987 v Se (sub), Ni (2), Y, Sp, T, Br, S; 1988 v WG, Is, H (sub), Co, Sw (sub), Ei, Ho (sub); 1989 v Se, S.Ar, Alb (2), Ch, S, Pol, D (sub); (with Marseille), 1990 v Se, Pol, I, Y, Br, D, U, Tun, Ei, Ho, Eg, Bel, Cam, WG, I (sub); 1991 v H, Pol, Ei (2), Cam, T, Arg, Aus, Nz (2), Mal; 1992 v T, Pol, F, Cz, C, H, Br, Fi, D, F, Se; (with Sampdoria), 1993 v Sp, N, T, Sm, T, Ho, Pol, N, US (sub), Br, G; (with Sheffield W), 1994 v Sm (59)
Walker, I. M. (Tottenham H), 1996 v H (sub), Chn (sub); 1997 v I (3)
Walker, W. H. (Aston Villa), 1921 v Ni; 1922 v Ni, W, S; 1923 v Se (2); 1924 v S; 1925 v Ni, W, S, Bel, F; 1926 v Ni, W, S; 1927 v Ni, W; 1933 v A (18)
Wall, G. (Manchester U), 1907 v W; 1908 v Ni; 1909 v S; 1910 v W, S; 1912 v S; 1913 v Ni (7)
Wallace, C. W. (Aston Villa), 1913 v W; 1914 v Ni; 1920 v S (3)
Wallace, D. L. (Southampton), 1986 v Eg (1)
Walsh, P. (Luton T), 1983 v Aus (2 + 1 sub); 1984 v F, W (5)
Walters, A. M. (Cambridge University), 1885 v S, N; 1886 v S; 1887 v S, W; (with Old Carthusians), 1889 v S, W; 1890 v S, W (9)
Walters, K. M. (Rangers), 1991 v Nz (1)
Walters, P. M. (Oxford University), 1885 v S, Ni; (with Old Carthusians), 1886 v S, W, Ni; 1887 v S, W; 1888 v S, Ni; 1889 v S, W; 1890 v S, W (13)

Wadsworth, S. J. (Huddersfield T), 1922 v S; 1923 v S, Bel; 1924 v S, Ni; 1925 v S, Ni; 1926 v W; 1927 v Ni (9)
Wainscoat, W. R. (Leeds U), 1929 v S (1)
Waiters, A. K. (Blackpool), 1964 v Ei, Br; 1965 v W, Bel, Ho (5)
Walden, F. I. (Tottenham H), 1914 v S; 1922 v W (2)
Walker, D. S. (Nottingham F), 1989 v D (sub), Se (sub), Gr, Alb (2), Ch, S, Pol, D; 1990 v Se, Pol, I, Y, Br, Cz, D, U, Tun, Ei, Ho, Eg, Bel, Cam, WG, I; 1991 v H, Pol, Ei (2), Cam, T, Arg, Aus, Nz (2), Mal; 1992 v T, Pol, F, Cz, C, H, Br, Fi, D, F, Se; (with Sampdoria), 1993 v Sp, N, T, Sm, T, Ho, Pol, N, US (sub), Br, G; (with Sheffield W), 1994 v Sm (59)

R. E. Evans also played for Wales against E, Ni, S; J. Reynolds also played for Ireland against E, W, S.

NORTHERN IRELAND

Addis, D. J. (Cliftonville), 1922 v N (1)

Aherne, T. (Belfast C), 1947 v E; 1948 v S; 1949 v W; (with Luton T), 1950 v W (4)

Alexander, T. E. (Cliftonville), 1895 v S (1)

Allan, C. (Cliftonville), 1936 v E (1)

Allen, J. (Limavady), 1887 v E (1)

Anderson, J. (Distillery), 1925 v S.Af (1)

Anderson, T. (Manchester U), 1973 v Cy, E, S, W; 1974 v Bul, P; (with Swindon T), 1975 v S (sub); 1976 v Is; 1977 v Ho, Bel, WG, E, S, W, Ic; 1978 v Ic, Ho, Bel; (with Peterborough U), S, E, W; 1979 v D (sub) (22)

Anderson, W. (Linfield), 1898 v W, E, S; (with Cliftonville), 1899 v S (4)

Andrews, W. (Glentoran), 1908 v S; (with Grimsby T), 1913 v E, S (3)

Armstrong, G. J. (Tottenham H), 1977 v WG, E, W (sub), Ic (sub); 1978 v Bel, S, E, W; 1979 v Ei, D, Bul, E, Bul, E, S, W, D; 1980 v E, Ei, Is, S, E, W, Aus (3); 1981 v Se; (with Watford), P, S, P, S, Se; 1982 v Is, E, F, W, Y, Hon, Sp, A, F; 1983 v A, T, Alb, S, E, W; (with Real Mallorca), 1984 v A, WG, E, W, Fi; 1985 v R, Fi, E, Sp; (with WBA), 1986 v T, R (sub), E (sub), F (sub); (with Chesterfield), D (sub), Br (sub) (63)

Baird, G. (Distillery), 1896 v S, E, W (3)

Baird, H. C. (Huddersfield T), 1939 v E (1)

Balfe, J. (Shelbourne), 1909 v E; 1910 v W (2)

Bambrick, J. (Linfield), 1929 v W, S, E; 1930 v W, S, E; 1932 v W; (with Chelsea), 1935 v W; 1936 v E, S; 1938 v W (11)

Banks, S. J. (Cliftonville), 1937 v W (1)

Barr, H. H. (Linfield), 1962 v E; (with Coventry C), 1963 v E, Pol (3)

Barron, J. H. (Cliftonville), 1894 v E, W, S; 1895 v S; 1896 v S; 1897 v E, W (7)

Barry, J. (Cliftonville), 1888 v W, S; 1889 v E (3)

Barry, J. (Bohemians), 1900 v S (1)

Baxter, R. A. (Distillery), 1887 v S (1)

Baxter, S. N. (Cliftonville), 1887 v W (1)

Bennett, L. V. (Dublin University), 1889 v W (1)

Best, G. (Manchester U), 1964 v W, U; 1965 v E, Ho (2), S, Sw (2), Alb; 1966 v S, E, Alb; 1967 v E; 1968 v S; 1969 v E, S, W, T; 1970 v S, E, W, USSR; 1971 v Cy (2), Sp, E, S, W; 1972 v USSR, Sp; 1973 v Bul; 1974 v P; (with Fulham), 1977 v Ho, Bel, WG; 1978 v Ic, Ho (37)

Bingham, W. L. (Sunderland), 1951 v F; 1952 v E, S, W; 1953 v E, S, F, W; 1954 v E, S, W; 1955 v E, S, W; 1956 v E, S, W; 1957 v E, S, W, P (2), I; 1958 v S, E, W, I (2), Arg, Cz (2), WG, F; (with Luton T), 1959 v E, S, W, Sp; 1960 v S, E, W; (with Everton), 1961 v E, S, WG (2), Gr, I; 1962 v E, Gr; 1963 v E, S, Pol (2), Sp; (with Port Vale), 1964 v S, E, Sp (56)

Black, K. T. (Luton T), 1988 v Fr (sub), Ma (sub); 1989 v Ei, H, Sp (2), Ch (sub); 1990 v H, N, U; 1991 v Y (2), D, A, Pol, Fa; (with Nottingham F), 1992 v Fa, A, D, S, Li, G; 1993 v Sp, D (sub), Alb, Ei (sub), Sp; 1994 v D (sub), Ei (sub), R (sub) (30)

Black, T. (Glentoran), 1901 v E (1)

Blair, H. (Portadown), 1928 v F; 1931 v S; 1932 v S; (with Swansea), 1934 v S (4)

Blair, J. (Cliftonville), 1907 v W, E, S; 1908 v E, S (5)

Blair, R. V. (Oldham Ath), 1975 v Se (sub), S (sub), W; 1976 v Se, Is (5)

Blanchflower, J. (Manchester U), 1954 v W; 1955 v E, S; 1956 v S, W; 1957 v S, E, P; 1958 v S, E, I (2) (12)

Blanchflower, R. D. (Barnsley), 1950 v S, W; 1951 v E, S; (with Aston Villa), F; 1952 v W; 1953 v E, S, W, F; 1954 v E, S, W; 1955 v E, S (with Tottenham H), W; 1956 v E, S, W; 1957 v E, S, W, I, P (2); 1958 v E, S, W, I (2), Cz (2), Arg, F, WG; 1959 v E, S, W, Sp; 1960 v S, W; 1961 v E, S, W, WG (2); 1962 v E, S, W, Gr, Ho; 1963 v E, S, Pol (2) (56)

Bookman, L. J. O. (Bradford C), 1914 v W; (with Luton T), 1921 v S, W; 1922 v E (4)

Bothwell, A. W. (Ards), 1926 v S, E, W; 1927 v E, W (5)

Bowler, G. C. (Hull C), 1950 v E, S, W (3)

Boyle, P. (Sheffield U), 1901 v E; 1902 v E; 1903 v S, W; 1904 v E (5)

Braithwaite, R. M. (Linfield), 1962 v W; 1963 v P, Sp; (with Middlesbrough), 1964 v W, U; 1965 v E, S, Sw (2), Ho (10)

Breen, T. (Belfast C), 1935 v E, W; 1937 v E, S; (with Manchester U), 1937 v W; 1938 v E, S; 1939 v W, S (9)

Brennan, B. (Bohemians), 1912 v W (1)

Brennan, R. A. (Luton T), 1949 v W; (with Birmingham C), 1950 v E, S, W; (with Fulham), 1951 v E (5)

Briggs, W. R. (Manchester U), 1962 v W; (with Swansea T), 1965 v Ho (2)

Brisby, D. (Distillery), 1891 v S (1)

Brolly, T. H. (Millwall), 1937 v W; 1938 v W; 1939 v E, W (4)

Brookes, E. A. (Shelbourne), 1920 v S (1)

Brotherston, N. (Blackburn R), 1980 v S, E, W, Aus (3); 1981 v Se, P; 1982 v S, Is, E, F, S, W, Hon (sub), A (sub); 1983 v A (sub), WG, Alb, T, Alb, S (sub), E (sub), W; 1984 v T; 1985 v Is (sub), T (27)

Brown, J. (Glenavon), 1921 v W; (with Tranmere R), 1924 v E, W (3)

Brown, J. (Wolverhampton W), 1935 v E, W; 1936 v E; (with Coventry C), 1937 v E, W; 1938 v S, W; (with Birmingham C), 1939 v E, S, W (10)

Brown, N. M. (Limavady), 1887 v E (1)

Brown, W. G. (Glenavon), 1926 v W (1)

Browne, F. (Cliftonville), 1887 v E, S, W; 1888 v E, S (5)

Browne, R. J. (Leeds U), 1936 v E, W; 1938 v E, W; 1939 v E, S (6)

Bruce, A. (Belfast C), 1925 v S.Af (1)

Bruce, W. (Glentoran), 1961 v S; 1967 v W (2)

Buckle, H. R. (Cliftonville), 1903 v S; (with Sunderland), 1904 v E; (with Bristol R), 1908 v W (3)

Buckle, J. (Cliftonville), 1882 v E (1)

Burnett, J. (Distillery), 1894 v E, W, S; (with Glentoran), 1895 v E, W (5)

Burnison, J. (Distillery), 1901 v E, W (2)

Burnison, S. (Distillery), 1908 v E; 1910 v E, S; (with Bradford), 1911 v E, S, W; (with Distillery), 1912 v E; 1913 v W (8)

Burns, J. (Glenavon), 1923 v E (1)

Burns, W. (Glentoran), 1925 v S.Af (1)

Butler, M. P. (Blackpool), 1939 v W (1)

Campbell, A. C. (Crusaders), 1963 v W; 1965 v Sw (2)

Campbell, D. A. (Nottingham F), 1986 v Mor (sub), Br; 1987 v E (2), T, Y; (with Charlton Ath), 1988 v Y, T (sub), Gr (sub), Pol (sub) (10)

Campbell, James (Cliftonville), 1897 v E, S, W; 1898 v E, S, W; 1899 v E; 1900 v E, S; 1901 v S, W; 1902 v S; 1903 v E; 1904 v S (14)

Campbell, John (Cliftonville), 1896 v W (1)

Campbell, J. P. (Fulham), 1951 v E, S (2)

Campbell, R. M. (Bradford C), 1982 v S, W (sub) (2)

Campbell, W. G. (Dundee), 1968 v S, E; 1969 v T; 1970 v S, W, USSR (6)

Carey, J. J. (Manchester U), 1947 v E, S, W; 1948 v E; 1949 v E, S, W (7)

Carroll, E. (Glenavon), 1925 v S (1)

Carroll, R. E. (Wigan Ath), 1997 v Th (sub); 1999 v Ei (sub); 2000 v L, Ma; 2001 v Ma, D, Ic, CzR, Bul (9)

Casey, T. (Newcastle U), 1955 v W; 1956 v W; 1957 v E, S, W, I, P (2); 1958 v WG, F; (with Portsmouth), 1959 v E, Sp (12)

Caskey, W. (Derby Co), 1979 v Bul, E, Bul, E, S (sub), D (sub); 1980 v E (sub); (with Tulsa R), 1982 v F (sub) (8)

Cassidy, T. (Newcastle U), 1971 v E (sub); 1972 v USSR (sub); 1974 v Bul (sub), S, E, W; 1975 v N; 1976 v S, E, W; 1977 v WG (sub); 1980 v E, Ei (sub), Is, S, E, W, Aus (3); (with Burnley), 1981 v Se, P; 1982 v Is, Sp (sub) (24)

Caughey, M. (Linfield), 1986 v F (sub), D (sub) (2)

Chambers, R. J. (Distillery), 1921 v W; (with Bury), 1928 v E, S, W; 1929 v E, S, W; 1930 v S, W; (with Nottingham F), 1932 v E, S, W (12)

Chatton, H. A. (Partick T), 1925 v E, S; 1926 v E (3)

Christian, J. (Linfield), 1889 v S (1)

Clarke, C. J. (Bournemouth), 1986 v F, D, Mor, Alg (sub), Sp, Br; (with Southampton), 1987 v E, T, Y; 1988 v Y, T, Gr, Pol, F, Ma; 1989 v Ei, H, Sp (1+1 sub); (with QPR), Ma, Ch; 1990 v H, Ei, N; (with Portsmouth), 1991 v Y (sub), D, A, Pol, Y (sub), Fa; 1992 v Fa, D, S, G; 1993 v Alb, Sp, D (38)

Clarke, R. (Belfast C), 1901 v E, S (2)

Cleary, J. (Glentoran), 1982 v S, W; 1983 v W (sub); 1984 v T (sub); 1985 v Is (5)

Clements, D. (Coventry C), 1965 v W, Ho; 1966 v M; 1967 v S, W; 1968 v S, E; 1969 v T (2), S, W; 1970 v S, W, USSR (2); 1971 v Sp, E, S, W, Cy; (with Sheffield W), 1972 v USSR, Sp, E, S, W; 1973 v Bul, Cy (2), P, E, S, W; (with Everton), 1974 v Bul, P, S, E, W; 1975 v N, Y, E, S, W; 1976 v Se, Y; (with New York Cosmos), E, W (48)

Clugston, J. (Cliftonville), 1888 v W; 1889 v W, S, E; 1890 v E, S; 1891 v W; 1892 v E, S, W; 1893 v E, S, W (14)

Cochrane, D. (Leeds U), 1939 v E, W; 1947 v E, S, W; 1948 v E, S, W; 1949 v S, W; 1950 v S, E (12)

Cochrane, G. (Cliftonville), 1903 v S (1)

Cochrane, G. T. (Coleraine), 1976 v N (sub); (with Burnley), 1978 v S (sub), E (sub), W (sub); 1979 v Ei (sub); (with Middlesbrough), D, Bul, E, Bul, E; 1980 v Is, E (sub), W

(sub), Aus (1+2 sub); 1981 v Se (sub), P (sub), S, P, S, Se; 1982 v E (sub), F; (with Gillingham), 1984 v S, Fi (sub) (26)

Cochrane, M. (Distillery), 1898 v S, W, E; 1899 v E; 1900 v E, S, W; (with Leicester Fosse), 1901 v S (8)

Collins, F. (Celtic), 1922 v S (1)

Collins, R. (Cliftonville), 1922 v N (1)

Condy, J. (Distillery), 1882 v W; 1886 v E, S (3)

Connell, T. E. (Coleraine), 1978 v W (sub) (1)

Connor, J. (Glentoran), 1901 v S, E; (with Belfast C), 1905 v E, S, W; 1907 v E, S; 1908 v E, S; 1909 v W; 1911 v S, E, W (13)

Connor, M. J. (Brentford), 1903 v S, W; (with Fulham), 1904 v E (3)

Cook, W. (Celtic), 1933 v E, W, S; (with Everton), 1935 v E; 1936 v S, W; 1937 v E, S, W; 1938 v E, S, W; 1939 v E, S, W (15)

Cooke, S. (Belfast YMCA), 1889 v E; (with Cliftonville), 1890 v E, S (3)

Coote, A. (Norwich C), 1999 v Ca (sub), Ei (sub); 2000 v Fi (sub), L (sub), Ma (sub), H (sub) (6)

Coulter, J. (Belfast C), 1934 v E, S, W; (with Everton), 1935 v E, S, W; 1937 v S, W; (with Grimsby T), 1938 v S, W; (with Chelmsford C), 1939 v S (11)

Cowan, J. (Newcastle U), 1970 v E (sub) (1)

Cowan, T. S. (Queen's Island), 1925 v W (1)

Coyle, F. (Coleraine), 1956 v E, S; 1957 v P; (with Nottingham F), 1958 v Arg (4)

Coyle, L. (Derry C), 1989 v Ch (sub) (1)

Coyle, R. I. (Sheffield W), 1973 v P, Cy (sub), W (sub); 1974 v Bul (sub), P (sub) (5)

Craig, A. B. (Rangers), 1908 v E, S, W; 1909 v S; (with Morton), 1912 v S, W; 1914 v E, S, W (9)

Craig, D. J. (Newcastle U), 1967 v W; 1968 v W; 1969 v T (2), E, S, W; 1970 v E, S, W, USSR; 1971 v Cy (2), Sp, S (sub); 1972 v USSR, S (sub); 1973 v Cy (2), E, S, W; 1974 v Bul, P; 1975 v N (25)

Crawford, A. (Distillery), 1889 v E, W; (with Cliftonville), 1891 v E, S, W; 1893 v E, W (7)

Croft, T. (Queen's Island), 1922 v N; 1924 v E; 1925 v S.Af (3)

Crone, R. (Distillery), 1889 v S; 1890 v E, S, W (4)

Crone, W. (Distillery), 1882 v W; 1884 v E, S, W; 1886 v E, S, W; 1887 v E; 1888 v E, W; 1889 v S; 1890 v W (12)

Crooks, W. J. (Manchester U), 1922 v W (1)

Crossan, E. (Blackburn R), 1950 v S; 1951 v E; 1955 v W (3)

Crossan, J. A. (Sparta-Rotterdam), 1960 v E; (with Sunderland), 1963 v W, P, Sp; 1964 v E, S, W, U, Sp; 1965 v E, S, Sw (2); (with Manchester C), W, Ho (2), Alb; 1966 v S, E, Alb, WG; 1967 v E, S; (with Middlesbrough), 1968 v S (24)

Crothers, C. (Distillery), 1907 v W (1)

Cumming, L. (Huddersfield T), 1929 v W, S; (with Oldham Ath), 1930 v E (3)

Cunningham, W. (Ulster), 1892 v S, E, W; 1893 v E (4)

Cunningham, W. E. (St Mirren), 1951 v W; 1953 v E; 1954 v S; 1955 v S; (with Leicester C), 1956 v E, S, W; 1957 v E, S, W, I, P (2); 1958 v S, W, I, Cz (2), Arg, WG, F; 1959 v E, S, W; 1960 v E, S, W; (with Dunfermline Ath), 1961 v W, Ho (30)

Curran, S. (Belfast C), 1926 v S, W; 1928 v F, S (4)

Curran, J. J. (Glenavon), 1922 v W, N; (with Pontypridd), 1923 v E, S; (with Glenavon), 1924 v E (5)

Cush, W. W. (Glenavon), 1951 v E, S; 1954 v S, E; 1957 v W, I, P (2); (with Leeds U), 1958 v I (2), W, Cz (2), Arg, WG, F; 1959 v S, W, Sp; 1960 v E, S, W; (with Portadown), 1961 v WG, Gr; 1962 v Gr (26)

Dalrymple, J. (Distillery), 1922 v N (1)

Dalton, W. (YMCA), 1888 v S; (with Linfield), 1890 v S, W; 1891 v S, W; 1892 v E, S, W; 1894 v E, S, W (11)

D'Arcy, S. D. (Chelsea), 1952 v W; 1953 v E; (with Brentford), 1953 v S, W, F (5)

Darling, J. (Linfield), 1897 v E, S; 1900 v S; 1902 v E, S, W; 1903 v E, S (2), W; 1905 v E, S, W; 1906 v E, S, W; 1908 v W; 1909 v E; 1910 v E, S, W; 1912 v S (22)

Davey, H. H. (Reading), 1926 v E; 1927 v E, S; 1928 v E; (with Portsmouth), 1928 v W (5)

Davis, T. L. (Oldham Ath), 1937 v E (1)

Davison, A. J. (Bolton W), 1996 v Se; (with Bradford C), 1997 v Th; (with Grimsby T), 1998 v G (3)

Davison, J. R. (Cliftonville), 1882 v E, W; 1883 v E, W; 1884 v E, W, S; 1885 v E (8)

Dennison, R. (Wolverhampton W), 1988 v F, Ma; 1989 v H, Sp Ch (2); 1990 v Ei, U; 1991 v Y (2), A, Pol, Fa (sub); 1992 v Fa, A, D (sub); 1993 v Sp (sub); 1994 v Co (sub); 1997 v I (sub) (18)

Devine, A. O. (Limavady), 1886 v E, W; 1887 v W; 1888 v W (4)

Devine, J. (Glentoran), 1990 v U (sub) (1)

Dickson, D. (Coleraine), 1970 v S (sub), W; 1973 v Cy, P (4)

Dickson, T. A. (Linfield), 1957 v S (1)

Dickson, W. (Chelsea), 1951 v W, F; 1952 v E, S, W; 1953 v E, S, W, F; (with Arsenal), 1954 v E, W; 1955 v E (12)

Diffin, W. J. (Belfast C), 1931 v W (1)

Dill, A. H. (Knock), 1882 v E, W; (with Down Ath), 1883 v W; (with Cliftonville), 1884 v E, S, W; 1885 v E, S, W (9)

Doherty, I. (Belfast C), 1901 v E (1)

Doherty, J. (Portadown), 1928 v F (1)

Doherty, J. (Cliftonville), 1933 v E, W (2)

Doherty, L. (Linfield), 1985 v Is; 1988 v T (sub) (2)

Doherty, M. (Derry C), 1938 v S (1)

Doherty, P. D. (Blackpool), 1935 v E, W; 1936 v E, S; (with Manchester C), 1937 v E, W; 1938 v E, S; 1939 v E, W; (with Derby Co), 1947 v E; (with Huddersfield T), 1947 v W; 1948 v E, W; 1949 v S; (with Doncaster R), 1951 v S (16)

Donaghey, B. (Belfast C), 1903 v S (1)

Donaghy, M. M. (Luton T), 1980 v S, E, W; 1981 v Se, P, S (sub); 1982 v S, Is, E, F, S, W, Y, Hon, Sp, F; 1983 v A, WG, Alb, T, Alb, S, E, W; 1984 v A, T, WG, S, E, W, Fi; 1985 v R, Fi, E, Sp, T; 1986 v T, R, E, F, D, Mor, Alg, Sp, Br; 1987 v E (2), T, Is, Y; 1988 v Y, T, Gr, Pol, F, Ma; 1989 v Ei, H; (with Manchester U), Sp (2), Ma, Ch; 1990 v Ei, N; 1991 v Y (2), D, A, Pol, Fa; 1992 v Fa, A, D, S, Li, G; (with Chelsea), 1993 v Alb, Sp, D, Alb, Ei, Sp, Li, La; 1994 v La, D, Ei, R, Lie, Co, M (91)

Donnelly, L. (Distillery), 1913 v W (1)

Doran, J. F. (Brighton), 1921 v E; 1922 v E, W (3)

Dougan, A. D. (Portsmouth), 1958 v Cz; (with Blackburn R), 1960 v S; 1961 v E, S, W, I, Gr; (with Aston Villa), 1963 v S, Pol (2); (with Leicester C), 1966 v S, E, W, M, Alb, WG; 1967 v E, S; (with Wolverhampton W), 1967 v W; 1968 v S, W.; 1969 v Is, T (2), E, S, W; 1970 v S, E, USSR (2); 1971 v Cy (2), Sp, E, S, W; 1972 v USSR (2), E, S, W; 1973 v Bul, Cy (43)

Douglas, J. P. (Belfast C), 1947 v E (1)

Dowd, H. O. (Glenavon), 1974 v W; (with Sheffield W), 1975 v N (sub), Se (3)

Dowie, I. (Luton T), 1990 v N (sub), U; 1991 v Y, D, A (sub), (with West Ham U), Y, Fa; (with Southampton) 1992 v Fa, A, D (sub), S (sub), Li; 1993 v Alb (2), Ei, Sp (sub), Li, La; 1994 v La, D, Ei (sub), R (sub), Lie, Co, M (sub); 1995 v A, Ei; (with C Palace) Ei, La, Ca, Ch, La; 1996 v P; (with West Ham U), A, N, G; 1997 v Uk, Arm, G, Alb, P, Uk, Arm, Th; 1998 v Alb, P; (with QPR), Slo, Sw, Sp; 1999 v T, Fi, Mol. G, Mol. Ca, Ei; 2000 v F, T, G (59)

Duggan, H. A. (Leeds U), 1930 v E; 1931 v E, W; 1933 v E; 1934 v E; 1935 v S, W; 1936 v S (8)

Dunlop, G. (Linfield), 1985 v Is; 1987 v E, Y; 1990 v Ei (4)

Dunne, J. (Sheffield U), 1928 v W; 1931 v W, E; 1932 v E, S; 1933 v E, W (7)

Eames, W. L. E. (Dublin U), 1885 v E, S, W (3)

Eglington, T. J. (Everton), 1947 v S, W; 1948 v E, S, W; 1949 v E (6)

Elder, A. R. (Burnley), 1960 v W; 1961 v S, E, W, WG (2), Gr; 1962 v S, Gr; 1963 v E, S, W, Pol (2), Sp; 1964 v W, U; 1965 v E, S, W, Sw (2), Ho (2), Alb; 1966 v E, S, W, M, Alb; 1967 v E, S, W; (with Stoke C), 1968 v E, W; 1969 v E (sub), S, W; 1970 v USSR (40)

Elleman, A. R. (Cliftonville), 1889 v W; 1890 v E (2)

Elliott, S. (Motherwell), 2001 v Ma, D, Ic, N (sub), CzR, Bul (2), CzR (8)

Elwood, J. H. (Bradford), 1929 v W; 1930 v E (2)

Emerson, W. (Glentoran), 1920 v E, S, W; 1921 v E; 1922 v E, S; (with Burnley), 1922 v W; 1923 v E, S, W; 1924 v E (11)

English, S. (Rangers), 1933 v W, S (2)

Enright, J. (Leeds C), 1912 v S (1)

Falloon, E. (Aberdeen), 1931 v S; 1933 v S (2)

Farquharson, T. G. (Cardiff C), 1923 v S, W; 1924 v E, S, W; 1925 v E, S (7)

Farrell, P. (Distillery), 1901 v S, W (2)

Farrell, P. (Hibernian), 1938 v W (1)

Farrell, P. D. (Everton), 1947 v S, W; 1948 v E, S, W; 1949 v E, W (7)

Feeney, J. M. (Linfield), 1947 v S; (with Swansea T), 1950 v E (2)

Feeney, W. (Glentoran), 1976 v Is (1)

Ferguson, G. (Linfield), 1999 v Ca (sub); 2001 v N, CzR (sub), Bul (sub), CzR (sub) (5)

Ferguson, W. (Linfield), 1966 v M; 1967 v E (2)

Ferris, J. (Belfast C), 1920 v E, W; (with Chelsea), 1921 v S, E; (with Belfast C), 1928 v F, S (6)

Ferris, R. O. (Birmingham C), 1950 v S; 1951 v F; 1952 v S (3)

Fettis, A. W. (Hull C), 1992 v D, Li; 1993 v D; 1994 v M; 1995 v P, Ei, La, Ca, Ch, La; 1996 v P, Lie, A; (with Nottingham F), v N, G; 1997 v Uk, Arm (2); (with Blackburn R), 1998 v P, Slo, Sw, Sp; 1999 v T, Fi, Mol (25)

Finney, T. (Sunderland), 1975 v N, E (sub), S, W; 1976 v N, Y, S; (with Cambridge U), 1980 v E, Is, S, E, W, Aus (2) (14)

Fitzpatrick, J. C. (Bohemians), 1896 v E, S (2)

Flack, H. (Burnley), 1929 v S (1)

Fleming, J. G. (Nottingham F), 1987 v E (2), Is, Y; 1988 v T, Gr, Pol; 1989 v Ma, Ch; (with Manchester C), 1990 v H, Ei; (with Barnsley), 1991 v Y; 1992 v Li (sub), G; 1993 v Alb, Sp, D, Alb, Sp, Li, La; 1994 v La, D, Ei, R, Lie, Co, M; 1995 v P, A, Ei (31)

Forbes, G. (Limavady), 1888 v W; (with Distillery), 1891 v E, S (3)

Forde, J. T. (Ards), 1959 v Sp; 1961 v E, S, WG (4)

Foreman, T. A. (Cliftonville), 1899 v S (1)

Forsyth, J. (YMCA), 1888 v E, S (2)

Fox, W. T. (Ulster), 1887 v E, S (2)

Frame, T. (Linfield), 1925 v S.Af (1)

Fulton, R. P. (Larne), 1928 v F; (Belfast C), 1930 v W; 1931 v E, S, W; 1932 v W, E; 1933 v E, S; 1934 v E, S, W; 1935 v E, W, S; 1936 v S, W; 1937 v E, S, W; 1938 v W (21)

Gaffikin, G. (Linfield Ath), 1890 v S, W; 1891 v S, W; 1892 v E, S, W; 1893 v E, S, W; 1894 v E, S, W; 1895 v E, W (15)

Galbraith, W. (Distillery), 1890 v W (1)

Gallagher, P. (Celtic), 1920 v E, S; 1922 v S; 1923 v S, W; 1924 v S, W; 1925 v S, W, E; (with Falkirk), 1927 v S (11)

Gallogly, C. (Huddersfield T), 1951 v E, S (2)

Gara, A. (Preston NE), 1902 v E, S, W (3)

Gardiner, A. (Cliftonville), 1930 v S, W; 1931 v S; 1932 v E, S (5)

Garrett, J. (Distillery), 1925 v W (1)

Gaston, R. (Oxford U), 1969 v Is (sub) (1)

Gaukrodger, G. (Linfield), 1895 v W (1)

Gaussen, A. D. (Moyola Park), 1884 v E, S; (with Magherafelt), 1888 v E, W; 1889 v E, W (6)

Geary, J. (Glentoran), 1931 v S; 1932 v S (2)

Gibb, J. T. (Wellington Park) 1884 v S, W; 1885 v S, E, W; 1886 v S; 1887 v S, E, W; (with Cliftonville), 1889 v S (10)

Gibb, T. J. (Cliftonville), 1936 v W (1)

Gibson W. K. (Cliftonville), 1894 v S, W, E; 1895 v S; 1897 v W; 1898 v S, W, E; 1901 v S, W, E; 1902 v S, W; 1903 v S (14)

Gillespie, K. R. (Manchester U), 1995 v P, A, Ei; (with Newcastle U) Ei, La, Ca, Ch (sub), La (sub); 1996 v P, A, N, G; 1997 v Uk, Arm, Bel, P, Uk; 1998 v G, Alb, Slo, Sw; 1999 v T, Fi, Mol; (with Blackburn R), G, Mol; 2000 v F (sub), T (sub), G (sub), L, Ma, H; 2001 v Y (sub), CzR, Bul (2) (36)

Gillespie, S. (Hertford), 1886 v S, W; 1887 v E, S, W (6)

Gillespie, W. (Sheffield U), 1913 v E, S; 1914 v E, W; 1920 v S, W; 1921 v E; 1922 v E, S, W; 1923 v E, S, W; 1924 v E, S, W; 1925 v E, S; 1926 v S, W; 1927 v E, W; 1928 v E; 1929 v E; 1931 v E (25)

Gillespie, W. (West Down), 1889 v W (1)

Goodall, A. L. (Derby Co), 1899 v S, W; 1900 v E, W; 1901 v E; 1902 v S; 1903 v E, W; (with Glossop), 1904 v E, W (10)

Goodbody, M. F. (Dublin University), 1889 v E; 1891 v W (2)

Gordon, H. (Linfield), 1895 v E; 1896 v E, S (3)

Gordon R. W. (Linfield), 1891 v S; 1892 v W, E, S; 1893 v E, S, W (7)

Gordon, T. (Linfield), 1894 v W; 1895 v E (2)

Gorman, W. C. (Brentford), 1947 v E, S, W; 1948 v W (4)

Gough, J. (Queen's Island), 1925 v S.Af (1)

Gowdy, J. (Glentoran), 1920 v E; (with Queen's Island), 1924 v W; (with Falkirk), 1926 v E, S; 1927 v E, S (6)

Gowdy, W. A. (Hull C), 1932 v S; (with Sheffield W), 1933 v S; (with Linfield), 1935 v E, S, W; (with Hibernian), 1936 v W (6)

Graham, W. G. L. (Doncaster R), 1951 v W, F; 1952 v E, S, W; 1953 v S, F; 1954 v E, W; 1955 v S, W; 1956 v E, S; 1959 v E (14)

Gray, P. (Luton T), 1993 v D (sub), Alb, Ei, Sp; (with Sunderland), 1994 v La, D, Ei, R, Lie (sub); 1995 v P, A, Ei, Ca, Ch (sub); 1996 v P (sub), Lie, A; (with Nancy), 1997 v Uk, Arm, G (sub); (with Luton T), 1999 v Mol (sub); (with Burnley), 2001 v Ma (sub), D (sub), Ic (sub); (with Oxford U), N (sub), CzR (sub) (26)

Greer, W. (QPR), 1909 v E, S, W (3)

Gregg, H. (Doncaster R), 1954 v W; 1957 v E, S, W, I, P (2); 1958 v E, I; (with Manchester U), 1958 v Cz, Arg, WG, F, W; 1959 v E, W; 1960 v S, E, W; 1961 v E, S; 1962 v S, Gr; 1964 v S, E (25)

Griffin, D. J. (St Johnstone), 1996 v G; 1997 v Uk, I, Bel (sub), Th; 1998 v G (sub), Alb; 1999 v Mol, Ei (sub); 2000 v L, Ma,

H; (with Dundee U), 2001 v Y (sub), N (sub), CzR, Bul (2), CzR (18)

Hall, G. (Distillery), 1897 v E (1)

Halligan, W. (Derby Co), 1911 v W; (with Wolverhampton W), 1912 v E (2)

Hamill, M. (Manchester U), 1912 v E; 1914 v E, S; (with Belfast C), 1920 v E, S, W; (with Manchester C), 1921 v S (7)

Hamill, R. (Glentoran), 1999 v Ca (sub) (1)

Hamilton, B. (Linfield), 1969 v T; 1971 v Cy (2), E, S, W; (with Ipswich T), 1972 v USSR (1+1 sub), Sp; 1973 v Bul, Cy (2), P, E, S, W; 1974 v Bul, S, E, W; 1975 v N, Se, Y, E; 1976 v Se, N, Y; (with Everton), Is, S, E, W; 1977 v Ho, Bel, WG, E, S, W, Ic; (with Millwall), 1978 v S, E, W; 1979 v Ei (sub); (with Swindon T), Bul (2), E, S, W, D; 1980 v Aus (2 sub) (50)

Hamilton, J. (Knock), 1882 v E, W (2)

Hamilton, R. (Rangers), 1928 v S; 1929 v E; 1930 v S, E; 1932 v S (5)

Hamilton, W. D. (Dublin Association), 1885 v W (1)

Hamilton, W. J. (Distillery), 1908 v W (1)

Hamilton, W. J. (Dublin Association), 1885 v W (1)

Hamilton, W. R. (QPR), 1978 v S (sub); (with Burnley), 1980 v S, E, W, Aus (2); 1981 v Se, P, S, P, S, Se; 1982 v S, Is, E, W, Y, Hon, Sp, A, F; 1983 v A, WG, Alb (2), S, E, W; 1984 v A, T, WG, S, E, W, Fi; (with Oxford U), 1985 v R, Sp; 1986 v Mor (sub), Alg, Sp (sub), Br (sub) (41)

Hampton, H. (Bradford C), 1911 v E, S, W; 1912 v E, W; 1913 v E, S, W; 1914 v E (9)

Hanna, J. (Nottingham F), 1912 v S, W (2)

Hanna, J. D. (Royal Artillery, Portsmouth), 1899 v W (1)

Hannon, D. J. (Bohemians), 1908 v E, S; 1911 v E, S; 1912 v W; 1913 v E (6)

Harkin, J. T. (Southport), 1968 v W; 1969 v T; (with Shrewsbury T), W (sub); 1970 v USSR; 1971 v Sp (5)

Harland, A. I. (Linfield), 1922 v N; 1923 v E (2)

Harris, J. (Cliftonville), 1921 v W; (with Glenavon), 1925 v S.Af (2)

Harris, V. (Shelbourne), 1906 v E; 1907 v E, W; 1908 v E, W, S; (with Everton), 1909 v E, W, S; 1910 v E, S, W; 1911 v E, S, W; 1912 v E; 1913 v E, S; 1914 v S, W (20)

Harvey, M. (Sunderland), 1961 v I; 1962 v Ho; 1963 v W, Sp; 1964 v S, E, W, U, Sp; 1965 v E, S, W, Sw (2), Ho (2), Alb; 1966 v S, E, W, M, Alb, WG; 1967 v E, S; 1968 v E, W; 1969 v Is, T (2), E; 1970 v USSR; 1971 v Cy, W (sub) (34)

Hastings, J. (Knock), 1882 v E, W; (with Ulster), 1883 v W; 1884 v E, S; 1886 v E, S (7)

Hatton, S. (Linfield), 1963 v S, Pol (2)

Hayes, W. E. (Huddersfield T), 1938 v E, S; 1939 v E, S (4)

Healy, D. J. (Manchester U), 2000 v L, Ma, H; 2001 v Y, Ma, D, Ic; (with Preston NE), N, CzR, Bul (2), CzR (12)

Healy, P. J. (Coleraine), 1982 v S, W, Hon (sub); (with Glentoran), 1983 v A (sub) (4)

Hegan, D. (WBA), 1970 v USSR; (with Wolverhampton W), 1972 v USSR, E, S, W; 1973 v Bul, Cy (7)

Henderson, J. (Ulster), 1885 v S, W (3)

Hewison, G. (Moyola Park), 1885 v E, S (2)

Hill, C. F. (Sheffield U), 1990 v N, U; 1991 v Pol, Y; 1992 v A, D; (with Leicester C) 1995 v Ei, La; 1996 v P, Lie, A, N, Se, G; 1997 v Uk, Arm, G, Alb, P, Uk, Arm, Th; (with Trelleborg), 1998 v G, Alb, P; (with Northampton T), Slo; 1999 v T (27)

Hill, M. J. (Norwich C), 1959 v W; 1960 v W; 1961 v WG; 1962 v S; (with Everton), 1964 v S, E, Sp (7)

Hinton, E. (Fulham), 1947 v S, W; 1948 v S, E, W; (with Millwall), 1951 v W, F (7)

Hopkins, J. (Brighton), 1926 v E (1)

Horlock, K. (Swindon T), 1995 v La, Ca; 1997 v G, Alb, I; (with Manchester C), v Bel, Uk, Arm, Th; 1998 v G, Alb, P; 1999 v T, Fi, G, Mol, Ca; 2000 v F, T, G, Ma (sub); 2001 v Y, Ma, D, Ic (25)

Houston, J. (Linfield), 1912 v S, W; 1913 v W; (with Everton), 1913 v E, S; 1914 v S (6)

Houston, W. (Linfield), 1933 v W (1)

Houston, W. J. (Moyola Park), 1885 v E, S (2)

Hughes, A. W. (Newcastle U), 1998 v Slo, Sw, Sp (sub); 1999 v T, Fi, Mol (sub), Ca, Ei; 2000 v F, T, L, H; 2001 v Y, Ma, D, Ic, N, CzR, Bul, CzR (20)

Hughes, M. E. (Manchester C), 1992 v D, S, Li, G; (with Strasbourg), 1993 v Alb, Sp, D, Ei, Sp, Li, La; 1994 v La, D, Ei, R, Lie, Co, M; 1995 v P, A, Ei (2) La, Ca, Ch, La; 1996 v P, Lie, A, N, G; (with West Ham U), 1997 v Uk, Arm, G, Alb, I, Uk; 1998 v G; (with Wimbledon), P, Slo, Sw, Sp; 1999 v T, Fi, Mol, G, Mol; 2000 v F, T, G, Fi, L (sub), Ma, H; 2001 v CzR, Bul (2), CzR (58)

Hughes, P. A. (Bury), 1987 v E, T, Is (3)

Hughes, W. (Bolton W), 1951 v W (1)

Humphries, W. M. (Ards), 1962 v W; (with Coventry C), 1962 v Ho; 1963 v E, S, W, Pol, Sp; 1964 v S, E, Sp; 1965 v S, Ho; (with Swansea T), 1965 v W, Alb (14)

Hunter, A. (Distillery), 1905 v W; 1906 v W, E, S; (with Belfast C), 1908 v W; 1909 v W, E, S (8)

Hunter, A. (Blackburn R), 1970 v USSR; 1971 v Cy (2), E, S, W; (with Ipswich T), 1972 v USSR (2), Sp, E, S, W; 1973 v Bul, Cy (2), P, E, S, W; 1974 v Bul, S, E, W; 1975 v N, Se, Y, E, S, W; 1976 v Se, N, Y, Is, S, E, W; 1977 v Ho, Bel, WG, E, S, W, Ic; 1978 v Ic, Ho, Bel; 1979 v Ei, D, S, W, D; 1980 v E, Ei (53)

Hunter, B. V. (Wrexham), 1995 v La; 1996 v P, Lie, A, Se, G; (with Reading), 1997 v Arm, G, Alb, I, Bel; 1999 v Ca, Ei; 2000 v F, T (15)

Hunter, R. J. (Cliftonville), 1884 v E, S, W (3)

Hunter, V. (Coleraine), 1962 v E; 1964 v Sp (2)

Irvine, R. J. (Linfield), 1962 v Ho; 1963 v E, S, W, Pol (2), Sp; (with Stoke C), 1965 v W (8)

Irvine, R. W. (Everton), 1922 v S; 1923 v E, W; 1924 v E, S; 1925 v E; 1926 v E; 1927 v E, W; 1928 v E, S; (with Portsmouth), 1929 v E; 1930 v S; (with Connah's Quay), 1931 v E; (with Derry C), 1932 v W (15)

Irvine, W. J. (Burnley), 1963 v W, Sp; 1965 v S, W, Sw, Ho (2), Alb; 1966 v S, E, W, M, Alb; 1967 v E, S; 1968 v E, W; (with Preston NE), 1969 v Is, T, E; (with Brighton), 1972 v E, S, W (23)

Irving, S. J. (Dundee), 1923 v S, W; 1924 v S, E, W; 1925 v S, E, W; 1926 v S, W; (with Cardiff C), 1927 v S, E, W; 1928 v S, E, W; (with Chelsea) 1929 v E; 1931 v W (18)

Jackson, T. A. (Everton), 1969 v Is, E, S, W; 1970 v USSR (1+1 sub); (with Nottingham F), 1971 v Sp; 1972 v E, S, W; 1973 v Cy, E, S, W; 1974 v Bul, P, S (sub), E (sub), W (sub); 1975 v N (sub), Se, Y, E, S, W; (with Manchester U); 1976 v Se, N, Y; 1977 v Ho, Bel, WG, E, S, W, Ic (35)

Jamison, J. (Glentoran), 1976 v N (1)

Jenkins, I. (Chester C), 1997 v Arm, Th; 1998 v Slo; (with Dundee U), Sw, Sp; 2000 v Fi (6)

Jennings, P. A. (Watford), 1964 v W, U; (with Tottenham H), 1965 v E, S, Sw (2), Ho, Alb; 1966 v S, E, W, Alb, WG; 1967 v E, S; 1968 v S, E, W; 1969 v Is, T (2), E, S, W; 1970 v S, E, USSR (2); 1971 v Cy (2), E, S, W; 1972 v USSR, Sp, S, E, W; 1973 v Bul, Cy, P, E, S, W; 1974 v P, S, E, W; 1975 v N, Se, Y, E, W; 1976 v Se, N, Y, Is, S, E, W; 1977 v Ho, Bel, WG, E, S, W, Ic; (with Arsenal), 1978 v Ic, Ho, Bel; 1979 v Ei, D, Bul, E, Bul, E, S, W, D; 1980 v E, Ei, Is; 1981 v S, P, S, Se; 1982 v S, Is, E, W, Y, Hon, Sp, F; 1983 v Alb, S, E, W; 1984 v A, T, WG, S, W, Fi; 1985 v R, Fi, E, Sp, T; (with Tottenham H), 1986 v T, R, E, F, D, (with Everton), Mor; (with Tottenham H), Alg, Sp, Br (119)

Johnson, D. M. (Blackburn R), 1999 v Ei (sub); 2000 v Fi (sub), L, Ma (sub), H (sub); 2001 v Y, Ma, Ic, N (sub), Bul (sub+1), CzR (12)

Johnston, H. (Portadown), 1927 v W (1)

Johnston, R. S. (Distillery), 1882 v W; 1884 v E; 1886 v E, S (4)

Johnston, R. S. (Distillery), 1905 v W (1)

Johnston, S. (Linfield), 1890 v W; 1893 v S, W; 1894 v E (4)

Johnston, W. (Oldpark), 1885 v S, W (2)

Johnston, W. C. (Glenavon), 1962 v W; (with Oldham Ath), 1966 v M (sub) (2)

Jones, J. (Linfield), 1930 v S, W; 1931 v S, W, E; 1932 v S, E; 1933 v S, E, W; 1934 v S, E, W; 1935 v S, E, W; 1936 v E, S; (with Hibernian), 1936 v W; 1937 v E, W, S; (with Glenavon), 1938 v E (23)

Jones, J. (Glenavon), 1956 v W; 1957 v E, W (3)

Jones, S. (Distillery), 1934 v E; (with Blackpool), 1934 v W (2)

Jordan, T. (Linfield), 1895 v E, W (2)

Kavanagh, P. J. (Celtic), 1930 v E (1)

Keane, T. R. (Swansea T), 1949 v S (1)

Kearns, A. (Distillery), 1900 v E, S, W; 1902 v E, S, W (6)

Kee, P. V. (Oxford U), 1990 v N; 1991 v Y (2), D, A, Pol, Fa; (with Ards), 1995 v A, Ei (9)

Keith, R. M. (Newcastle U), 1958 v E, W, Cz (2), Arg, I, WG, F; 1959 v E, S, W, Sp; 1960 v S, E; 1961 v S, E, W, I, WG (2), Gr; 1962 v W, Ho (23)

Kelly, H. R. (Fulham), 1950 v E, W; (with Southampton), 1951 v E, S (4)

Kelly, J. (Glentoran), 1896 v E (1)

Kelly, J. (Derry C), 1932 v E, W; 1933 v E, W, S; 1934 v W; 1936 v E, S, W; 1937 v S, E (11)

Kelly, P. J. (Manchester C), 1921 v E (1)

Kelly, P. M. (Barnsley), 1950 v S (1)

Kennedy, A. L. (Arsenal), 1923 v W; 1925 v E (2)

Kennedy, P. H. (Watford), 1999 v Mol, G (sub); 2000 v F, T, G, Fi; 2001 v N, Bul (sub), CzR (sub) (9)

Kernaghan, N. (Belfast C), 1936 v W; 1937 v S; 1938 v E (3)

Kirk, A. (Hearts), 2000 v H; 2001 v N (sub) (2)

Kirkwood, H. (Cliftonville), 1904 v W (1)

Kirwan, J. (Tottenham H), 1900 v W; 1902 v E, W; 1903 v E, S, W; 1904 v E, S, W; 1905 v E, S, W; (with Chelsea), 1906 v E, S, W; 1907 v W; (with Clyde), 1909 v S (17)

Lacey, W. (Everton), 1909 v E, S, W; 1910 v E, S, W; 1911 v E, S, W; 1912 v E; (with Liverpool), 1913 v W; 1914 v E, S, W; 1920 v E, S, W; 1921 v E, S, W; 1922 v E, S; (with New Brighton), 1925 v E (23)

Lawther, R. (Glentoran), 1888 v E, S (2)

Lawther, W. I. (Sunderland), 1960 v W; 1961 v I; (with Blackburn R), 1962 v S, Ho (4)

Leatham, J. (Belfast C), 1939 v W (1)

Ledwidge, J. J. (Shelbourne), 1906 v S, W (2)

Lemon, J. (Glentoran), 1886 v W; (with Belfast YMCA), 1888 v S; 1889 v W (3)

Lennon, N. F. (Crewe Alex), 1994 v M (sub); 1995 v Ch; 1996 v P, Lie, A; (with Leicester C), v N; 1997 v Uk, Arm, G, Alb, Bel, P, Uk, Arm, Th; 1998 v G, Alb, P, Slo, Sw, Sp; 1999 v T, Fi, Mol, G, Mol, Ei; 2000 v F, T, G, Fi, Ma, H; 2001 v D, Ic; (with Celtic), N, CzR, Bul (2) (39)

Leslie, W. (YMCA), 1887 v E (1)

Lewis, J. (Glentoran), 1899 v S, E, W; (with Distillery), 1900 v S (4)

Lockhart, H. (Russell School), 1884 v W (1)

Lockhart, N. H. (Linfield), 1947 v E; (with Coventry C), 1950 v W; 1951 v W; 1952 v W; (with Aston Villa), 1954 v S, E; 1955 v W; 1956 v W (8)

Lomas, S. M. (Manchester C), 1994 v R, Lie, Co (sub), M; 1995 v P, A; 1996 v P, Lie, A, N, Se, G; 1997 v Uk, Arm, G, Alb, I, Bel; (with West Ham U), P, Uk, Arm, Th; 1998 v Alb, P, Slo, Sw; 1999 v Mol, G, Mol, Ca; 2000 v F, T, G, L, Ma; 2001 v Ma, D, Ic (38)

Loyal, J. (Clarence), 1891 v S (1)

Lutton, R. J. (Wolverhampton W), 1970 v S, E; (with West Ham U), 1973 v Cy (sub), S (sub), W (sub); 1974 v P (6)

Lynas, R. (Cliftonville), 1925 v S.Af (1)

Lyner, D. R. (Glentoran), 1920 v E, W; 1922 v S, W; (with Manchester U), 1923 v E; (with Kilmarnock), 1923 v W (6)

Lytle, J. (Glentoran), 1898 v W (1)

McAdams, W. J. (Manchester C), 1954 v W; 1955 v S; 1957 v E; 1958 v S, I; (with Bolton W), 1961 v E, S, W, I, WG (2), Gr; 1962 v E, Gr; (with Leeds U), Ho (15)

McAlery, J. M. (Cliftonville), 1882 v E, W (2)

McAlinden, J. (Belfast C), 1938 v S; 1939 v S; (with Portsmouth), 1947 v E; (with Southend U), 1949 v E (4)

McAllen, J. (Linfield), 1898 v E; 1899 v E, S, W; 1900 v E, S, W; 1901 v W; 1902 v S (9)

McAlpine, S. (Cliftonville), 1901 v S (1)

McArthur, A. (Distillery), 1886 v W (1)

McAuley, J. L. (Huddersfield T), 1911 v E, W; 1912 v E, S; 1913 v E, S (6)

McAuley, P. (Belfast C), 1900 v S (1)

McBride, S. D.(Glenavon), 1991 v D (sub), Pol (sub); 1992 v Fa (sub), D (4)

McCabe, J. J. (Leeds U), 1949 v S, W; 1950 v E; 1951 v W; 1953 v W; 1954 v S (6)

McCabe, W. (Ulster), 1891 v E (1)

McCambridge, J. (Ballymena), 1930 v S, W; (with Cardiff C), 1931 v W; 1932 v E (4)

McCandless, J. (Bradford), 1912 v W; 1913 v W; 1920 v W, S; 1921 v E (5)

McCandless, W. (Linfield), 1920 v E, W; 1921 v E; (with Rangers), 1921 v W; 1922 v S; 1924 v W, S; 1925 v S; 1929 v W (9)

McCann, P. (Belfast C), 1910 v E, S, W; 1911 v E; (with Glentoran), 1911 v S; 1912 v E; 1913 v W (7)

McCarthy, J. D. (Port Vale), 1996 v Se; 1997 v I, Arm, Th; (with Birmingham C), 1998 v P (sub), Slo (sub), Sp; 1999 v Fi (sub), Mol (sub), G (sub), Ca, Ei; 2000 v F, T, G, Fi; 2001 v N, Bul (sub) (18)

McCartney, A. (Ulster), 1903 v S, W; (with Linfield), 1904 v S, W; (with Everton), 1905 v E, S; (with Belfast C), 1907 v E, S, W; 1908 v E, S, W; (with Glentoran), 1909 v E, S, W (15)

McCashin, J. W. (Cliftonville), 1896 v W; 1898 v S, W; 1899 v S; 1903 v S (5)

McCavana, W. T. (Coleraine), 1955 v S; 1956 v E, S (3)

McCaw, D. (Malone), 1882 v E (1)

McCaw, J. H. (Linfield), 1927 v W; 1928 v F; 1930 v S; 1931 v E, S, W (6)

McClatchey, J. (Distillery), 1886 v E, S, W (3)

McClatchey, T. (Distillery), 1895 v S (1)

Martin, C. J. (Glentoran), 1947 v S; (with Leeds U), 1948 v E, S, W; (with Aston Villa), 1949 v E; 1950 v W (6)

Martin, D. K. (Belfast C), 1934 v E, S, W; 1935 v S; (with Wolverhampton W), 1935 v E; 1936 v W; (with Nottingham F), 1937 v S; 1938 v E, S; 1939 v S (10)

Mathieson, A. (Luton T), 1921 v W; 1922 v E (2)

Maxwell, J. (Linfield), 1902 v W; 1903 v W, E; (with Glentoran), 1905 v W, S; (with Belfast C), 1906 v W; 1907 v S (7)

Meek, H. L. (Glentoran), 1925 v W (1)

Mehaffy, J. A. C. (Queen's Island), 1922 v W (1)

Meldon, P. A. (Dublin Freebooters), 1899 v S, W (2)

Mercer, H. V. A. (Linfield), 1908 v E (1)

Mercer, J. T. (Distillery), 1898 v E, S, W; 1899 v E; (with Linfield), 1902 v E, W; (with Distillery), 1903 v S (2), W; (with Derby Co), 1904 v E, W; 1905 v S (12)

Millar, W. (Barrow), 1932 v W; 1933 v S (2)

Miller, J. (Middlesbrough), 1929 v W, S; 1930 v E (3)

Milligan, D. (Chesterfield), 1939 v W (1)

Milne, R. G. (Linfield), 1894 v E, S, W; 1895 v E, W; 1896 v E, S, W; 1897 v E, S; 1898 v E, S, W; 1899 v E; 1901 v W; 1902 v E, S, W; 1903 v E, S (2); 1904 v E, S, W; 1906 v E, S, W (28)

Mitchell, E. J. (Cliftonville), 1933 v S; (with Glentoran), 1934 v W (2)

Mitchell, W. (Distillery), 1932 v E, W; 1933 v E, W; (with Chelsea), 1934 v W, S; 1935 v S, E; 1936 v S, E; 1937 v E, S, W; 1938 v E, S (15)

Molyneux, T. B. (Ligoniel), 1883 v E, W; (with Cliftonville), 1884 v E, W, S; 1885 v E, W; 1886 v E, W, S; 1888 v S (11)

Montgomery, F. J. (Coleraine), 1955 v E (1)

Moore, C. (Glentoran), 1949 v W (1)

Moore, P. (Aberdeen), 1933 v E (1)

Moore, R. (Linfield Ath), 1891 v E, S, W (3)

Moore, R. L. (Ulster), 1887 v S, W (2)

Moore, W. (Falkirk), 1923 v S (1)

Moorhead, F. W. (Dublin University), 1885 v E (1)

Moorhead, G. (Linfield), 1923 v S; 1928 v F, S; 1929 v S (4)

Moran, J. (Leeds C), 1912 v S (1)

Moreland, V. (Derby Co), 1979 v Bul (2 sub), S; 1980 v E, Ei (6)

Morgan, G. F. (Linfield), 1922 v N; 1923 v E; (with Nottingham F), 1924 v S; 1927 v E; 1928 v E, S, W; 1929 v E (8)

Morgan, S. (Port Vale), 1972 v Sp; 1973 v Bul (sub), P, Cy, E, S, W; (with Aston Villa), 1974 v Bul, P, S, E; 1975 v Se; 1976 v Se (sub), N, Y; (with Brighton & HA), S, W (sub); (with Sparta Rotterdam), 1979 v D (18)

Morrison, R. (Linfield Ath), 1891 v E, W (2)

Morrison, T. (Glentoran), 1895 v E, S, W; (with Burnley), 1899 v W; 1900 v W; 1902 v E, S (7)

Morrogh, D. (Bohemians), 1896 v S (1)

Morrow, S. J. (Arsenal), 1990 v U (sub); 1991 v A (sub), Pol, Y; 1992 v Fa, S (sub), G (sub); 1993 v Sp (sub), Alb, Ei; 1994 v R, Co, M (sub); 1995 v P, Ei (2), La; 1996 v P, Se; 1997 v Uk, G, Alb, I, Bel; (with QPR), P, Uk, Arm; 1998 v G, P, Slo, Sw, Sp; 1999 v T, Fi, Mol, G, Mol; 2000 v G, Fi (39)

Morrow, W. J. (Moyola Park), 1883 v E, W; 1884 v S (3)

Muir, R. (Oldpark), 1885 v S, W (2)

Mulholland, S. (Celtic), 1906 v S, E (2)

Mullan, G. (Glentoran), 1983 v S, E, W, Alb (sub) (4)

Mulligan, J. (Manchester C), 1921 v S (1)

Mulryne, P. P. (Manchester U), 1997 v Bel (sub), Arm (sub), Th; 1998 v Alb (sub), Sp (sub); 1999 v T, Fi; (with Norwich C), Ca; 2001 v Y, D (sub), Bul (sub), CzR (12)

Murdock, C. J. (Preston NE), 2000 v L (sub), Ma, H (sub); 2001 v Y, Ma, D, Ic, N, CzR, Bul (2), CzR (12)

Murphy, J. (Bradford C), 1910 v E, S, W (3)

Murphy, N. (QPR), 1905 v E, S, W (3)

Murray, J. M. (Motherwell), 1910 v E, S; (with Sheffield W), 1910 v W (3)

Napier, R. J. (Bolton W), 1966 v WG (1)

Neill, W. J. T. (Arsenal), 1961 v I, Gr, WG; 1962 v E, S, W, Gr; 1963 v E, W, Pol, Sp; 1964 v S, E, W, U, Sp; 1965 v E, S, W, Sw, Ho (2); 1966 v S, E, W, Alb, WG, M; 1967 v S, W; 1968 v S, E; 1969 v E, S, W, Is, T (2); 1970 v E, W, USSR (2); (with Hull C), 1971 v Cy, Sp; 1972 v USSR (2), Sp, S, E, W; 1973 v Bul, Cy (2), P, E, S, W (59)

Nelis, P. (Nottingham F), 1923 v E (1)

Nelson, S. (Arsenal), 1970 v W, E (sub); 1971 v Cy, Sp, E, S, W; 1972 v USSR (2), Sp, E, S, W; 1973 v Bul, Cy, P; 1974 v S, E; 1975 v Se, Y; 1976 v Se, N, Is, E; 1977 v Bel (sub), WG, W, Ic; 1978 v Ic, Ho, Bel; 1979 v Ei D, Bul, E, Bul, E, S, W, D; 1980 v E, Ei, Is; 1981 v S, P, S, Se; (with Brighton & HA), 1982 v E, S, Sp (sub), A (51)

Nicholl, C. J. (Aston Villa), 1975 v Se, Y, E, S, W; 1976 v Se, N, Y, S, E, W; 1977 v W; (with Southampton), 1978 v Bel (sub), S, E, W; 1979 v Ei, Bul, E, Bul, E, W; 1980 v Ei, Is, S, E, W, Aus (3); 1981 v Se, P, S, P, S, Se; 1982 v S, Is, E, F, W, Y, Hon, Sp, A, F; 1983 v S (sub), E, W; (with Grimsby T), 1984 v A, T (51)

Nicholl, H. (Belfast C), 1902 v W; 1905 v E (3)

Nicholl, J. M. (Manchester U), 1976 v Is, W (sub); 1977 v Ho, Bel, E, S, W, Ic; 1978 v Ic, Ho, Bel, S, E, W; 1979 v Ei, D, Bul, E, Bul, E, S, W, D; 1980 v E, Ei, Is, S, E, W, Aus (3); 1981 v Se, P, S, P, S, Se; 1982 v S, Is, E; (with Toronto B), F, W, Y, Hon, Sp, A, F; (with Sunderland), 1983 v A, WG, Alb, T, Alb; (with Toronto B), S, E, W; 1984 v T; (with Rangers), WG, S, E; (with Toronto B), F; 1985 v R; (with WBA), Fi, E, Sp, T; 1986 v T, R, E, F, Alg, Sp, Br (73)

Nicholson, J. J. (Manchester U), 1961 v S, W; 1962 v E, W, Gr, Ho; 1963 v E, S, Pol (2); (with Huddersfield T), 1965 v W, Ho (2), Alb; 1966 v S, E, W, Alb, M; 1967 v S, W; 1968 v S, E, W; 1969 v S, E, W, T (2); 1970 v S, E, W, USSR (2); 1971 v Cy (2), E, S, W; 1972 v USSR (2) (41)

Nixon, R. (Linfield), 1914 v S (1)

Nolan, I. R. (Sheffield W), 1997 v Arm, G, Alb, P, Uk; 1998 v G, P; 2000 v G, Fi, L, Ma, H; (with Bradford C), 2001 v Y, Ma, Bul (2), CzR (17)

Nolan-Whelan, J. V. (Dublin Freebooters), 1901 v E, W; 1902 v S, W; 1903 v S (5)

O'Boyle, G. (Dunfermline Ath), 1994 v Co (sub), M; (with St Johnstone), 1995 v P (sub), La (sub), Ca (sub), Ch (sub); 1996 v Se (sub), G (sub); 1997 v I (sub), Bel (sub); 1998 v Slo (sub), Sw (sub); 1999 v Fi (sub) (13)

O'Brien, M. T. (QPR), 1921 v S; (with Leicester C), 1922 v S, W; 1924 v S, W; (with Hull C), 1925 v S, E, W; 1926 v W; (with Derby Co), 1927 v W (10)

O'Connell, P. (Sheffield W), 1912 v E, S; (with Hull C), 1914 v E, S, W (5)

O'Doherty, A. (Coleraine), 1970 v E, W (sub) (2)

O'Driscoll, J. F. (Swansea T), 1949 v E, S, W (3)

O'Hagan, C. (Tottenham H), 1905 v S, W; 1906 v S, W, E; (with Aberdeen), 1907 v E, S, W; 1908 v S, W; 1909 v E (11)

O'Hagan, W. (St Mirren), 1920 v E, W (2)

O'Hehir, J. C. (Bohemians), 1910 v W (1)

O'Kane, J. (Nottingham F), 1970 v E, W, S (sub); 1971 v Sp, E, S, W; 1972 v USSR (2); 1973 v P, Cy; 1974 v Bul, P, S, E, W; 1975 v N, Se, E, S (20)

O'Mahoney, M. T. (Bristol R), 1939 v S (1)

O'Neill, C. (Motherwell), 1989 v Ch (sub); 1990 v Ei (sub); 1991 v D (3)

O'Neill, J. (Sunderland), 1962 v W (1)

O'Neill, J. P. (Leicester C), 1980 v Is, S, E, W, Aus (3); 1981 v P, S, P, S, Se; 1982 v S, Is, E, F, S, F (sub); 1983 v A, WG, Alb, T, Alb, S; 1984 v S (sub); 1985 v Is, Fi, E, Sp, T; 1986 v T, R, E, F, D, Mor, Alg, Sp, Br (39)

O'Neill, M. A. M. (Newcastle U), 1988 v Gr, Pol, F, Ma; 1989 v Ei, H, Sp (sub), Sp (sub), Ma (sub), Ch; (with Dundee U), 1990 v H (sub), Ei; 1991 v Pol; 1992 v Fa (sub), S (sub); 1993 v Alb (sub + 1), Ei, Sp, Li, La; (with Hibernian), 1994 v Lie (sub); 1995 v A (sub), Ei; 1996 v Lie, A, N, Se; (with Coventry C), 1997 v Uk (sub), Arm (sub) (31)

O'Neill, M. H. M. (Distillery), 1972 v USSR (sub), (with Nottingham F), Sp (sub), W (sub); 1973 v P, Cy, E, S, W; 1974 v Bul, P, E (sub), W; 1975 v Se, Y, E, S; 1976 v Y (sub); 1977 v E (sub), S; 1978 v Ic, Ho, S, E, W; 1979 v Ei, D, Bul, E, Bul, D; 1980 v Ei, Is, Aus (3); 1981 v Se, P; (with Norwich C), P, S, Se; (with Manchester C), 1982 v S; (with Norwich C), E, F, S, Y, Hon, Sp, A, F; 1983 v A, WG, Alb, T, Alb, S, E; (with Notts Co), 1984 v A, T, WG, E, W, Fi; 1985 v R, Fi (64)

O'Reilly, H. (Dublin Freebooters), 1901 v S, W; 1904 v S (3)

Parke, J. (Linfield), 1964 v S; (with Hibernian), 1964 v E, Sp; (with Sunderland), 1965 v Sw, S, W, Ho (2), Alb; 1966 v WG; 1967 v E, S; 1968 v S, E (14)

Patterson, D. J. (C Palace), 1994 v Co (sub), M (sub); 1995 v Ei (sub+1), La, Ca, Ch (sub), La (sub); (with Luton T), 1996 v N (sub), Se; 1998 v Sw, Sp; (with Dundee U), 1999 v Fi, Mol, G, Mol, Ei (17)

Peacock, R. (Celtic), 1952 v S; 1953 v F; 1954 v W; 1955 v E, S; 1956 v E, S; 1957 v W, I, P; 1958 v S, E, W, I (2), Arg, Cz (2), WG; 1959 v E, S, W; 1960 v S, E; 1961 v E, S, I, WG (2), Gr; (with Coleraine), 1962 v S (31)

Peden, J. (Distillery), 1887 v S, W; 1888 v W, E; 1889 v S, E; 1890 v W, S; 1891 v W, E; 1892 v W, E; 1893 v E, S, W; 1896 v W, E, S; 1897 v W, S; 1898 v W, E, S; 1899 v W (24)

Penney, S. (Brighton & HA), 1985 v Is; 1986 v T, R, E, F, D, Mor, Alg, Sp; 1987 v E, T, Is; 1988 v Pol, F, Ma; 1989 v Ei, Sp (17)

Percy, J. C. (Belfast YMCA), 1889 v W (1)
Platt, J. A. (Middlesbrough), 1976 v Is (sub); 1978 v S, E, W; 1980 v S, E, W, Aus (3); 1981 v Se, P; 1982 v F, S, W (sub), A; 1983 v A, WG, Alb, T; (with Ballymena U), 1984 v E, W (sub); (with Coleraine), 1986 v Mor (sub) (23)
Pollock, W. (Belfast C), 1928 v F (1)
Ponsonby, J. (Distillery), 1895 v S, W; 1896 v E, S, W; 1897 v E, S, W; 1899 v E (9)
Potts, R. M. C. (Cliftonville), 1883 v E, W (2)
Priestley, T. J. M. (Coleraine), 1933 v S; (with Chelsea), 1934 v E (2)
Pyper, Jas. (Cliftonville), 1897 v S, W; 1898 v S, E, W; 1899 v S; 1900 v E (7)
Pyper, John (Cliftonville), 1897 v E, S, W; 1899 v E, W; 1900 v E, W, S; 1902 v S (9)
Pyper, M. (Linfield), 1932 v W (1)

Quinn, J. M. (Blackburn R), 1985 v Is, Fi, E, Sp, T; 1986 v T, R, E, F, D (sub), Mor (sub); 1987 v E (sub), T; (with Swindon T), 1988 v Y (sub), T, Gr, Pol, F (sub), Ma; (with Leicester C), 1989 v Ei, H (sub), Sp (sub+1); (with Bradford C), Ma, Ch; 1990 v H, (with West Ham U), N; 1991 v Y (sub); (with Bournemouth), 1992 v Li; (with Reading), 1993 v Sp, D, Alb (sub), Ei (sub), La (sub); 1994 v La, D (sub), Ei, R, Lie, Co, M; 1995 v P, A (sub), La (sub); 1996 v Lie, A (sub) (46)
Quinn, S. J. (Blackpool), 1996 v Se (sub); 1997 v Alb (sub), I, Bel, P, Uk (sub), Arm, Th (sub); 1998 v G, Alb; (with WBA), Slo, Sw; 1999 v T (sub), Fi (sub), Ei; 2000 v F (sub), T (sub), G (sub), Fi, L, Ma; 2001 v Y (sub), Bul (sub), CzR (sub) (24)

Rafferty, P. (Linfield), 1980 v E (sub) (1)
Ramsey, P. C. (Leicester C), 1984 v A, WG, S; 1985 v Is, E, Sp, T; 1986 v T, Mor; 1987 v Is, E, Y (sub); 1988 v Y; 1989 v Sp (14)
Rankine, J. (Alexander), 1883 v E, W (2)
Rattray, D. (Avoniel), 1882 v E; 1883 v E, W (3)
Rea, R. (Glentoran), 1901 v E (1)
Redmond, R. (Cliftonville), 1884 v W (1)
Reid, G. H. (Cardiff C), 1923 v S (1)
Reid, J. (Ulster), 1883 v E; 1884 v W; 1887 v S; 1889 v W; 1890 v S, W (6)
Reid, S. E. (Derby Co), 1934 v E, W; 1936 v E (3)
Reid, W. (Hearts), 1931 v E (1)
Reilly, M. M. (Portsmouth), 1900 v E; 1902 v E (2)
Renneville, W. T. J. (Leyton), 1910 v S, E, W; (with Aston Villa), 1911 v W (4)
Reynolds, J. (Distillery), 1890 v E, W; (with Ulster), 1891 v E, S, W (5)
Reynolds, R. (Bohemians), 1905 v W (1)
Rice, P. J. (Arsenal), 1969 v Is; 1970 v USSR; 1971 v E, S, W; 1972 v USSR, Sp, E, S, W; 1973 v Bul, Cy, E, S, W; 1974 v Bul, P, S, E, W; 1975 v N, Y, E, S, W; 1976 v Se, N, Y, Is, S, E, W; 1977 v Ho, Bel, WG, E, S, Ic; 1978 v Ic, Ho, Bel; 1979 v Ei, D, E (2), S, W, D; 1980 v E (49)
Roberts, F. C. (Glentoran), 1931 v S (1)
Robinson, P. (Distillery), 1920 v S; (with Blackburn R), 1921 v W (2)
Robinson, S. (Bournemouth), 1997 v Th (sub); 1999 v Mol, Ei; 2000 v L (sub), H (sub) (5)
Rogan, A. (Celtic), 1988 v Y (sub), Gr, Pol (sub); 1989 v Ei (sub), H, Sp (2), Ma (sub), Ch; 1990 v H, N (sub), U; 1991 v Y (2), D, A; (with Sunderland), 1992 v Li (sub); (with Millwall), 1997 v G (sub) (18)
Rollo, D. (Linfield), 1912 v W; 1913 v W; 1914 v W, E; (with Blackburn R), 1920 v S, W; 1921 v E, S, W; 1922 v E; 1923 v E; 1924 v S, W; 1925 v W; 1926 v E; 1927 v E (16)
Roper, E. O. (Dublin University), 1886 v W (1)
Rosbotham, A. (Cliftonville), 1887 v E, S, W; 1888 v E, S, W; 1889 v E (7)
Ross, W. E. (Newcastle U), 1969 v Is (1)
Rowland, K. (West Ham U), 1994 v La (sub); 1995 v Ca, Ch, La; 1996 v P (sub), Lie (sub), N (sub), Se, G (sub); 1997 v Uk, Arm, I (sub); 1998 v Alb; (with QPR), 1999 v T, Fi, Mol, G, Ca, Ei (19)
Rowley, R. W. M. (Southampton), 1929 v S, W; 1930 v W, E; (with Tottenham H), 1931 v W; 1932 v S (6)
Rushe, F. (Distillery), 1925 v S.Af (1)
Russell, A. (Linfield), 1947 v E (1)
Russell, S. R. (Bradford C), 1930 v E, S; (with Derry C), 1932 v E (3)
Ryan, R. A. (WBA), 1950 v W (1)

Sanchez, L. P. (Wimbledon), 1987 v T (sub); 1989 v Sp, Ma (3)
Scott, E. (Liverpool), 1920 v S; 1921 v E, S, W; 1922 v E; 1925 v W; 1926 v E, S, W; 1927 v E, S, W; 1928 v E, S, W; 1929 v E, S, W; 1930 v E; 1931 v E; 1932 v W; 1933 v E, S, W; 1934 v E, S, W; (with Belfast C), 1935 v S; 1936 v E, S, W (31)
Scott, J. (Grimsby), 1958 v Cz, F (2)
Scott, J. E. (Cliftonville), 1901 v S (1)
Scott, L. J. (Dublin University), 1895 v S, W (2)
Scott, P. W. (Everton), 1975 v W; 1976 v Y; (with York C), Is, S, E (sub); W; 1978 v S, E, W; (with Aldershot), 1979 v S (sub) (10)
Scott, T. (Cliftonville), 1894 v E, S; 1895 v S, W; 1896 v S, E, W; 1897 v E, W; 1898 v E, S, W; 1900 v W (13)
Scott, W. (Linfield), 1903 v E, S, W; 1904 v E, S, W; (with Everton), 1905 v E, S; 1907 v E, S; 1908 v E, S; 1909 v E, S, W; 1910 v E, S, W; 1912 v E; (with Leeds City), 1913 v E, S, W (25)
Scraggs, M. J. (Glentoran), 1921 v W; 1922 v E (2)
Seymour, H. C. (Bohemians), 1914 v W (1)
Seymour, J. (Cliftonville), 1907 v W; 1909 v W (2)
Shanks, T. (Woolwich Arsenal), 1903 v S; 1904 v W; (with Brentford), 1905 v E (3)
Sharkey, P. G. (Ipswich T), 1976 v S (1)
Sheehan, Dr G. (Bohemians), 1899 v S; 1900 v E, W (3)
Sheridan, J. (Everton), 1903 v W, E, S; 1904 v E, S; (with Stoke C), 1905 v E (6)
Sherrard, J. (Limavady), 1885 v S; 1887 v W; 1888 v W (3)
Sherrard, W. C. (Cliftonville), 1895 v E, W, S (3)
Sherry, J. J. (Bohemians), 1906 v E; 1907 v W (2)
Shields, R. J. (Southampton), 1957 v S (1)
Silo, M. (Belfast YMCA), 1888 v E (1)
Simpson, W. J. (Rangers), 1951 v W, F; 1954 v E, S; 1955 v E; 1957 v I, P; 1958 v S, E, W, I; 1959 v S (12)
Sinclair, J. (Knock), 1882 v E, W (2)
Slemin, J. C. (Bohemians), 1909 v W (1)
Sloan, A. S. (London Caledonians), 1925 v W (1)
Sloan, D. (Oxford U), 1969 v S; 1971 v Sp (2)
Sloan, H. A. de B. (Bohemians), 1903 v E; 1904 v S; 1905 v E; 1906 v W; 1907 v E, W; 1908 v W; 1909 v S (8)
Sloan, J. W. (Arsenal), 1947 v W (1)
Sloan, T. (Cardiff C), 1926 v S, W, E; 1927 v W, S; 1928 v E, W; 1929 v E; (with Linfield), 1930 v W, S; 1931 v S (11)
Sloan, T. (Manchester U), 1979 v S, W (sub), D (sub) (3)
Small, J. M. (Clarence), 1887 v E; (with Cliftonville), 1893 v E, S, W (4)
Smith, E. E. (Cardiff C), 1921 v S; 1923 v W, E; 1924 v E (4)
Smith, J. E. (Distillery), 1901 v S, W (2)
Smyth, R. H. (Dublin University), 1886 v W (1)
Smyth, S. (Wolverhampton W), 1948 v E, S, W; 1949 v S, W; 1950 v E, S, W; (with Stoke C), 1952 v E (9)
Smyth, W. (Distillery), 1949 v E, S; 1954 v S, E (4)
Snape, A. (Airdrie), 1920 v E (1)
Sonner, D. J. (Ipswich T), 1998 v Alb (sub); (with Sheffield W), 1999 v Ei (sub), Ca (sub); 2000 v L (sub), Ma (sub), H; (with Birmingham C), 2001 v N (sub) (7)
Spence, D. W. (Bury), 1975 v Y, E, S, W; 1976 v Se, Is, E, W, S (sub); (with Blackpool), 1977 v Ho (sub), WG (sub), E (sub), S (sub), W (sub), Ic (sub); 1979 v Ei, D (sub), E (sub), Bul (sub), E (sub), S, W, D; 1980 v Ei; (with Southend U), Is (sub), Aus (sub); 1981 v S (sub), Se (sub); 1982 v F (sub) (29)
Spencer, S. (Distillery), 1890 v E, S; 1892 v E, S, W; 1893 v E (6)
Spiller, E. A. (Cliftonville), 1883 v E, W; 1884 v E, W, S (5)
Stanfield, O. M. (Distillery), 1887 v E, S, W; 1888 v E, S, W; 1889 v E, S; 1890 v E, S; 1891 v E, S, W; 1892 v E, S, W; 1893 v E, W; 1894 v E, S, W; 1895 v E, S; 1896 v E, S, W; 1897 v E, S, W (30)
Steele, A. (Charlton Ath), 1926 v W, S; (with Fulham), 1929 v W, S (4)
Stevenson, A. E. (Rangers), 1934 v E, S, W; (with Everton), 1935 v E, S; 1936 v S, W; 1937 v E, W; 1938 v E, W; 1939 v E, S, W; 1947 v S, W; 1948 v S (17)
Stewart, A. (Glentoran), 1967 v W; 1968 v S, E; (with Derby Co), 1968 v W; 1969 v Is, T (1+1 sub) (7)
Stewart, D. C. (Hull C), 1978 v Bel (1)
Stewart, I. (QPR), 1982 v F (sub); 1983 v A, WG, Alb, T, Alb, S, E, W; 1984 v A, T, WG, S, E, W, Fi; 1985 v R, Fi, Is, E, Sp, T; (with Newcastle U), 1986 v R, E, D, Mor, Alg (sub), Sp (sub), Br; 1987 v E, Is (sub) (31)
Stewart, R. K. (St Columb's Court), 1890 v E, S, W; (with Cliftonville), 1892 v E, S, W; 1893 v E, W; 1894 v E, S, W (11)
Stewart, T. C. (Linfield), 1961 v W (1)
Swan, S. (Linfield), 1899 v S (1)

Taggart, G. P. (Barnsley), 1990 v N, U; 1991 v Y, D, A, Pol, Fa; 1992 v Fa, A, D, S, Li, G; 1993 v Alb, Sp, D, Alb, Ei, Sp, Li, La; 1994 v La, D, Ei, R, Lie, Co, M; 1995 v P (sub), A, Ei (2), Ca, Ch, La; (with Bolton U), 1997 v G, Alb, I, Bel, P,

Uk, Arm; 1998 v G, P, Sp; (with Leicester C), 2000 v H; 2001 v Ma, D, Ic, N (50)

Taggart, J. (Walsall), 1899 v W (1)

Taylor, M. S. (Fulham), 1999 v G, Mol, Ca, Ei; 2000 v F, T, G, Fi, L (sub), Ma (sub), H; 2001 v Y, N, Bul, CzR (15)

Thompson, F. W. (Cliftonville), 1910 v E, S, W; (with Linfield), 1911 v W; (with Bradford C), 1911 v E; 1912 v E, W; 1913 v E, S, W; (with Clyde), 1914 v E, S (12)

Thompson, J. (Distillery), 1897 v S (1)

Thompson, R. (Queen's Island), 1928 v F (1)

Thompson, W. (Belfast Ath), 1889 v S (1)

Thunder, P. J. (Bohemians), 1911 v W (1)

Todd, S. J. (Burnley), 1966 v M (sub); 1967 v E; 1968 v W; 1969 v E, S, W; 1970 v S, USSR; (with Sheffield W), 1971 v Cy (2), Sp (sub) (11)

Toner, J. (Arsenal), 1922 v W; 1923 v W; 1924 v W, E; 1925 v E, S; (with St Johnstone), 1927 v E, S (8)

Torrans, R. (Linfield), 1893 v S (1)

Torrans, S. (Linfield), 1889 v S; 1890 v S, W; 1891 v S, W; 1892 v E, S, W; 1893 v E, S; 1894 v E, S, W; 1895 v E; 1896 v E, S, W; 1897 v E, S, W; 1898 v E, S; 1899 v E, W; 1901 v S, W (26)

Trainor, D. (Crusaders), 1967 v W (1)

Tully, C. P. (Celtic), 1949 v E; 1950 v E; 1952 v S; 1953 v E, S, W, F; 1954 v S; 1956 v E; 1959 v Sp (10)

Turner, A. (Cliftonville), 1896 v W (1)

Turner, E. (Cliftonville), 1896 v E (1)

Turner, W. (Cliftonville), 1886 v E, S; 1888 v S (3)

Twoomey, J. F. (Leeds U), 1938 v W; 1939 v E (2)

Uprichard, W. N. M. C. (Swindon T), 1952 v E, S, W; 1953 v E, S; (with Portsmouth), 1953 v W, F; 1955 v E, S, W; 1956 v E, S, W; 1958 v S, I, Cz; 1959 v S, Sp (18)

Vernon, J. (Belfast C), 1947 v E, S; (with WBA), 1947 v W; 1948 v E, S, W; 1949 v E, S, W; 1950 v E, S; 1951 v E, S, W, F; 1952 v S, E (17)

Waddell, T. M. R. (Cliftonville), 1906 v S (1)

Walker, J. (Doncaster R), 1955 v W (1)

Walker, T. (Bury), 1911 v S (1)

Walsh, D. J. (WBA), 1947 v S, W; 1948 v E, S, W; 1949 v E, S, W; 1950 v W (9)

Walsh, W. (Manchester C), 1948 v E, S, W; 1949 v E, S (5)

Waring, J. (Cliftonville), 1899 v E (1)

Warren, P. (Shelbourne), 1913 v E, S (2)

Watson, J. (Ulster), 1883 v E, W; 1886 v E, S, W; 1887 v S, W; 1889 v E, W (9)

Watson, P. (Distillery), 1971 v Cy (sub) (1)

Watson, T. (Cardiff C), 1926 v S (1)

Wattie, J. (Distillery), 1899 v E (1)

Webb, C. G. (Brighton), 1909 v S, W; 1911 v S (3)

Weir, E. (Clyde), 1939 v W (1)

Welsh, E. (Carlisle U), 1966 v W, WG, M; 1967 v W (4)

Whiteside, N. (Manchester U), 1982 v Y, Hon, Sp, A, F; 1983 v WG, Alb, T; 1984 v A, T, WG, S, E, W, Fi; 1985 v R, Fi, Is, E, Sp, T; 1986 v R, E, F, D, Mor, Alg, Sp, Br; 1987 v E (2), Is, Y; 1988 v T, Pol, F; (with Everton), 1990 v H, Ei (38)

Whiteside, T. (Distillery), 1891 v E (1)

Whitfield, E. R. (Dublin University), 1886 v W (1)

Whitley, Jeff (Manchester C), 1997 v Bel (sub), Th (sub); 1998 v Sp (sub); 2000 v Fi; 2001 v Y, D, N (7)

Whitley, Jim (Manchester C), 1998 v Sp; 1999 v T (sub); 2000 v Fi (sub) (3)

Williams, J. R. (Ulster), 1886 v E, S (2)

Williams, M. S. (Chesterfield), 1999 v G, Mol, Ca, Ei; (with Watford), 2000 v F, T, G, Fi, L, Ma, H (sub); 2001 v Y, Ic (sub), N (sub), CzR, Bul, CzR (17)

Williams, P. A. (WBA), 1991 v Fa (sub) (1)

Williamson, J. (Cliftonville), 1890 v E; 1892 v S; 1893 v S (3)

Willighan, T. (Burnley), 1933 v W; 1934 v S (2)

Willis, G. (Linfield), 1906 v S, W; 1907 v S; 1912 v S (4)

Wilson, D. J. (Brighton & HA), 1987 v T, Is, E (sub); (with Luton C), 1988 v Y, T, Gr, Pol, F, Ma; 1989 v Ei, H, Sp, Ma, Ch; 1990 v H, Ei, N, U; (with Sheffield W), 1991 v Y, D, A, Fa; 1992 v A (sub), S (24)

Wilson, H. (Linfield), 1925 v W, S.Af (2)

Wilson, K. J. (Ipswich T), 1987 v Is, E, Y; (with Chelsea), 1988 v Y, T, Gr (sub), Pol (sub), F (sub); 1989 v H (sub), Sp (2), Ma, Ch; 1990 v Ei (sub), N, U; 1991 v Y (2), A, Pol, Fa; 1992 v Fa, D, S; (with Notts Co), Li, G; 1993 v Alb, Sp, D, Sp, Li, La; 1994 v La, D, Ei, R, Lie, Co, M; (with Walsall), 1995 v Ei (sub), La (42)

Wilson, M. (Distillery), 1884 v E, S, W (3)

Wilson, R. (Cliftonville), 1888 v S (1)

Wilson, S. J. (Glenavon), 1962 v S; 1964 v S; (with Falkirk), 1964 v E, W, U; Sp; 1965 v E, Sw; (with Dundee), 1966 v W, WG; 1967 v S; 1968 v E (12)

Wilton, J. M. (St Columb's Court), 1888 v E, W; 1889 v S, E; (with Cliftonville), 1890 v E; (with St Columb's Court); 1893 v W, S (7)

Wood, T. J. (Walsall), 1996 v Lie (sub) (1)

Worthington, N. (Sheffield W), 1984 v W, Fi (sub); 1985 v Is, Sp (sub); 1986 v T, R (sub), E (sub), D, Alg, Sp; 1987 v E (2), T, Is, Y; 1988 v Y, T, Gr, Pol, F, Ma; 1989 v Ei, H, Sp, Ma; 1990 v H, Ei, U; 1991 v Y, D, A, Fa; 1992 v A, D, S, Li, G; 1993 v Alb, Sp, D, Ei, Sp, Li, La; 1994 v La, D, Ei, Lie, Co, M; (with Leeds U), 1995 v P, A, Ei (2), La, Ca (sub), Ch, La; 1996 v P, Lie, A, N, Se, G; (with Stoke C), 1997 v I, Bel (sub) (66)

Wright, J. (Cliftonville), 1906 v E, S, W; 1907 v E, S, W (6)

Wright, T. J. (Newcastle U), 1989 v Ma, Ch; 1990 v H, U; 1992 v Fa, A, S, G; 1993 v Alb, Sp, Alb, Ei, Sp, Li, La; 1994 v La; (with Nottingham F), D, Ei, R, Lie, Co, M (sub); 1997 v G, Alb, I, Bel; (with Manchester C), P, Uk; 1998 v Alb; 1999 v Ca (sub); 2000 v F (sub) (31)

Young, S. (Linfield), 1907 v E, S; 1908 v E, S; (with Airdrie), 1909 v E; 1912 v S; (with Linfield), 1914 v E, S, W (9)

SCOTLAND

Adams, J. (Hearts), 1889 v Ni; 1892 v W; 1893 v Ni (3)

Agnew, W. B. (Kilmarnock), 1907 v Ni; 1908 v W, Ni (3)

Aird, A. S. (Burnley), 1954 v N (2), A, U (4)

Aitken, A. (Newcastle U), 1901 v E; 1902 v E; 1903 v E, W; 1904 v E; 1905 v E, W; 1906 v E; (with Middlesbrough), 1907 v E, W; 1908 v E; (with Leicester Fosse), 1910 v E; 1911 v E, Ni (14)

Aitken, G. G. (East Fife), 1949 v E, F; 1950 v W, Ni, Sw; (with Sunderland), 1953 v W, Ni; 1954 v E (8)

Aitken, R. (Dumbarton), 1886 v E; 1888 v Ni (2)

Aitken, R. (Celtic), 1980 v Pe (sub), Bel, W (sub), E, Pol; 1983 v Bel, Ca (1+1 sub); 1984 v Bel (sub), Ni, W (sub); 1985 v E, Ic; 1986 v W, EG, Aus (2), Is, R, E, D, WG, U; 1987 v Bul, Ei (2), L, Bel, E, Br; 1988 v H, Bel, Bul, L, S.Arr, Ma, Sp, Co, E; 1989 v N, Y, I, Cy, F, Cy, E, Ch; 1990 v Y, F, N; (with Newcastle U), Arg (sub), Pol, Ma, Cr, Se, Br; (with St Mirren), 1992 v R (sub) (57)

Aitkenhead, W. A. C. (Blackburn R), 1912 v Ni (1)

Albiston, A. (Manchester U), 1982 v Ni; 1984 v U, Bel, EG, W, E; 1985 v Y, Ic, Sp (2), W; 1986 v EG, Ho, U (14)

Alexander, D. (East Stirlingshire), 1894 v W, Ni (2)

Allan, D. S. (Queen's Park), 1885 v E, W; 1886 v W (3)

Allan, G. (Liverpool), 1897 v E (1)

Allan, H. (Hearts), 1902 v W (1)

Allan, J. (Queen's Park), 1887 v E, W (2)

Allan, T. (Dundee), 1974 v WG, N (2)

Ancell, R. F. D. (Newcastle U), 1937 v W, Ni (2)

Anderson, A. (Hearts), 1933 v E; 1934 v A, E, W, Ni; 1935 v E, W, Ni; 1936 v E, W, Ni; 1937 v G, E, W, Ni, A; 1938 v E, W, Ni, Cz, Ho; 1939 v W, H (23)

Anderson, F. (Clydesdale), 1874 v E (1)

Anderson, G. (Kilmarnock), 1901 v Ni (1)

Anderson, H. A. (Raith R), 1914 v W (1)

Anderson, J. (Leicester C), 1954 v Fi (1)

Anderson, K. (Queen's Park), 1896 v Ni; 1898 v S, Ni (3)

Anderson, W. (Queen's Park), 1882 v E; 1883 v E, W; 1884 v E; 1885 v E, W (6)

Andrews, P. (Eastern), 1875 v E (1)

Archibald, A. (Rangers), 1921 v W; 1922 v W, E; 1923 v Ni; 1924 v E, W; 1931 v E; 1932 v E (8)

Archibald, S. (Aberdeen), 1980 v P (sub); (with Tottenham H), Ni, Pol, H; 1981 v Se (sub), Is, Ni, Is, Ni, E; 1982 v Ni, P, Sp (sub), Ho, Nz (sub), Br, USSR; 1983 v EG, Sw (sub); 1984 v EG, E, F; (with Barcelona), 1985 v Sp, E, Ic (sub); 1986 v WG (27)

Armstrong, M. W. (Aberdeen), 1936 v W, Ni; 1937 v G (3)

Arnott, W. (Queen's Park), 1883 v W; 1884 v E, Ni; 1885 v E, W; 1886 v E; 1887 v E, W; 1888 v E; 1889 v E; 1890 v E; 1891 v E; 1892 v E; 1893 v E (14)

Auld, J. R. (Third Lanark), 1887 v E, W; 1889 v W (3)

Auld, R. (Celtic), 1959 v H, P; 1960 v W (3)

Baird, A. (Queen's Park), 1892 v Ni; 1894 v W (2)

Baird, D. (Hearts), 1890 v Ni; 1891 v W (2); 1892 v W (3)

Baird, H. (Airdrieonians), 1956 v A (1)

Baird, J. C. (Vale of Leven), 1876 v E; 1878 v W; 1880 v E (3)

Baird, S. (Rangers), 1957 v Y, Sp (2), Sw, WG; 1958 v F, N, Ni (7)

Baird, W. U. (St Bernard), 1897 v Ni (1)

Bannon, E. (Dundee U), 1980 v Bel; 1983 v Ni, W, E, Ca; 1984 v EG; 1986 v Is, R, E, D (sub), WG (11)

Barbour, A. (Renton), 1885 v Ni (1)
Barker, J. B. (Rangers), 1893 v W; 1894 v W (2)
Barrett, F. (Dundee), 1894 v Ni; 1895 v W (2)
Battles, B. (Celtic), 1901 v E, W, Ni (3)
Battles, B. jun. (Hearts), 1931 v W (1)
Bauld, W. (Hearts), 1950 v E, Sw, P (3)
Baxter, J. C. (Rangers), 1961 v Ni, Ei (2), Cz; 1962 v Ni, W, E, Cz (2), U; 1963 v W, Ni, E, A, N, Ei, Sp; 1964 v W, E, N, WG; 1965 v W, Ni, Fi; (with Sunderland), 1966 v P, Br, Ni, W, E, I; 1967 v W, E, USSR; 1968 v W (34)
Baxter, R. D. (Middlesbrough), 1939 v E, W, H (3)
Beattie, A. (Preston NE), 1937 v E, A, Cz; 1938 v E; 1939 v W, Ni, H (7)
Beattie, R. (Preston NE), 1939 v W (1)
Begbie, I. (Hearts), 1890 v Ni; 1891 v E; 1892 v W; 1894 v E (4)
Bell, A. (Manchester U), 1912 v Ni (1)
Bell, J. (Dumbarton), 1890 v Ni; 1892 v E; (with Everton), 1896 v E; 1897 v E; 1898 v E; (with Celtic), 1899 v E, W, Ni; 1900 v E, W (10)
Bell, M. (Hearts), 1901 v W (1)
Bell, W. J. (Leeds U), 1966 v P, Br (2)
Bennett, A. (Celtic), 1904 v W; 1907 v Ni; 1908 v W; (with Rangers), 1909 v W, Ni, E; 1910 v E, W; 1911 v E, W; 1913 v Ni (11)
Bennie, R. (Airdrieonians), 1925 v W, Ni; 1926 v Ni (3)
Bernard, P. R. J. (Oldham Ath), 1995 v J (sub), Ec (2)
Berry, D. (Queen's Park), 1894 v W; 1899 v W, Ni (3)
Berry, W. H. (Queen's Park), 1888 v E; 1889 v E; 1890 v E; 1891 v E (4)
Bett, J. (Rangers), 1982 v Ho; 1983 v Bel; (with Lokeren), 1984 v Bel, W, E, F; 1985 v Y, Ic, Sp (2), W, E, Ic; (with Aberdeen), 1986 v W, Is, Ho; 1987 v Bel; 1988 v H (sub); 1989 v Y; 1990 v F (sub), N, Arg, Eg, Ma, Cr (25)
Beveridge, W. W. (Glasgow University), 1879 v E, W; 1880 v W (3)
Black, A. (Hearts), 1938 v Cz, Ho; 1939 v H (3)
Black, D. (Hurlford), 1889 v Ni (1)
Black, E. (Metz), 1988 v H (sub), L (sub) (2)
Black, I. H. (Southampton), 1948 v E (1)
Blackburn, J. E. (Royal Engineers), 1873 v E (1)
Blacklaw, A. S. (Burnley), 1963 v N, Sp; 1966 v I (3)
Blackley, J. (Hibernian), 1974 v Cz, E, Bel, Z; 1976 v Sw; 1977 v W, Se (7)
Blair, D. (Clyde), 1929 v W, Ni; 1931 v E, A, I; 1932 v W, Ni; (with Aston Villa), 1933 v W (8)
Blair, J. (Sheffield W), 1920 v E, Ni; (with Cardiff C), 1921 v E; 1922 v E; 1923 v E, W, Ni; 1924 v W (8)
Blair, J. (Motherwell), 1934 v W (1)
Blair, J. A. (Blackpool), 1947 v W (1)
Blair, W. (Third Lanark), 1896 v W (1)
Blessington, J. (Celtic), 1894 v E, Ni; 1896 v E, Ni (4)
Blyth, J. A. (Coventry C), 1978 v Bul, W (2)
Bone, J. (Norwich C), 1972 v Y (sub); 1973 v D (2)
Booth, S. (Aberdeen), 1993 v G (sub), Es (2 subs); 1994 v Sw, Ma (sub); 1995 v Fa, Ru; 1996 v Fi, Sm, Aus (sub), US, Ho, Sw (sub); (with Borussia Dortmund), 1998 v D, Fi, Co (sub), Mor (sub); (with Twente), 2001 v Pol (18)
Bowie, J. (Rangers), 1920 v E, Ni (2)
Bowie, W. (Linthouse), 1891 v Ni (1)
Bowman, D. (Dundee U), 1992 v Fi, US (sub); 1993 v G, Es; 1994 v Sw, I (6)
Bowman, G. A. (Montrose), 1892 v Ni (1)
Boyd, J. M. (Newcastle U), 1934 v Ni (1)
Boyd, R. (Mossend Swifts), 1889 v Ni; 1891 v W (2)
Boyd, T. (Motherwell), 1991 v R (sub), Sw, Bul, USSR; (with Chelsea), 1992 v Sw, R; (with Celtic), Fi, Ca, N, C; 1993 v Sw, P, I, Ma, G, Es (2); 1994 v I, Ma (sub), Ho (sub), A; 1995 v Fi, Fa, Ru, Gr, Ru, Sm; 1996 v Gr, Fi, Se, Aus, D, US, Co, Ho, E, Sw; 1997 v A, La, Se, Es (2), A, Se, W, Ma, Bl; 1998 v Bl, La, F, D, Fi (sub), Co, US, Br, N, Mor; 1999 v Li, Es, Fa, CzR, Fa, CzR; 2001 v La, Cro, Aus, Bel, Sm (sub), Pol (71)
Boyd, W. G. (Clyde), 1931 v I, Sw (2)
Brackenbridge, T. (Hearts), 1888 v Ni (1)
Bradshaw, T. (Bury), 1928 v E (1)
Brand, R. (Rangers), 1961 v Ni, Cz, Ei (2); 1962 v Ni, W, Cz, U (8)
Branden, T. (Blackburn R), 1896 v E (1)
Brazil, A. (Ipswich T), 1980 v Pol (sub), H; 1982 v Sp, Ho (sub), Ni, W, E, Nz, USSR (sub); 1983 v EG, Sw, (with Tottenham H), W, E (sub) (13)
Bremner, D. (Hibernian), 1976 v Sw (sub) (1)
Bremner, W. J. (Leeds U), 1965 v Sp; 1966 v E, Pol, P, Br, I (2); 1967 v W, Ni, E; 1968 v W, E; 1969 v W, E, Ni, D, A, WG, Cy (2); 1970 v Ei, WG, A; 1971 v W, E; 1972 v P, Bel, Ho, Ni, W, E, Y, Cz, Br; 1973 v D (2), E (2), Ni (sub), Sw,

Br; 1974 v Cz, WG, Ni, W, E, Bel, N, Z, Br, Y; 1975 v Sp (2); 1976 v D (54)
Brennan, F. (Newcastle U), 1947 v W, Ni; 1953 v W, Ni, E; 1954 v Ni, E (7)
Breslin, B. (Hibernian), 1897 v W (1)
Brewster, G. (Everton), 1921 v E (1)
Brogan, J. (Celtic), 1971 v W, Ni, P, E (4)
Brown, A. (Middlesbrough), 1904 v E (1)
Brown, A. (St Mirren), 1890 v W; 1891 v W (2)
Brown, A. D. (East Fife), 1950 v Sw, P, F; (with Blackpool), 1952 v USA, D, Se; 1953 v W; 1954 v W, E, N (2), Fi, A, U (14)
Brown, G. C. P. (Rangers), 1931 v W; 1932 v E, W, Ni; 1933 v E; 1934 v A; 1935 v E, W; 1936 v E, W; 1937 v G, E, W, Ni, Cz; 1938 v E, W, Cz, Ho (19)
Brown, H. (Partick T), 1947 v W, Bel, L (3)
Brown, J. (Cambuslang), 1890 v W (1)
Brown, J. B. (Clyde), 1939 v W (1)
Brown, J. G. (Sheffield U), 1975 v R (1)
Brown, R. (Dumbarton), 1884 v W, Ni (2)
Brown, R. (Rangers), 1947 v Ni; 1949 v Ni; 1952 v E (3)
Brown, R. jun. (Dumbarton), 1885 v W (1)
Brown, W. D. F. (Dundee), 1958 v F; 1959 v E, W, Ni; (with Tottenham H), 1960 v W, Ni, Pol, A, H, T; 1962 v Ni, W, E, Cz; 1963 v W, Ni, E, A; 1964 v Ni, W, N; 1965 v E, Fi, Pol, Sp; 1966 v Ni, Pol, I (28)
Browning, J. (Celtic), 1914 v W (1)
Brownlie, J. (Hibernian), 1971 v USSR; 1972 v Pe, Ni, E; 1973 v D (2); 1976 v R (7)
Brownlie, J. (Third Lanark), 1909 v E, Ni; 1910 v E, W, Ni; 1911 v W, Ni; 1912 v W, Ni, E; 1913 v W, Ni, E; 1914 v W, Ni, E (16)
Bruce, D. (Vale of Leven), 1890 v W (1)
Bruce, R. F. (Middlesbrough), 1934 v A (1)
Buchan, M. M. (Aberdeen), 1972 v P (sub), Bel; (with Manchester U), W, Y, Cz, Br; 1973 v D (2), E; 1974 v WG, Ni, W, N, Br, Y; 1975 v EG, Sp, P; 1976 v D, R; 1977 v Fi, Cz, Ch, Arg, Br; 1978 v EG, W (sub), Ni, Pe, Ir, Ho; 1979 v A, N, P (34)
Buchanan, J. (Cambuslang), 1889 v Ni (1)
Buchanan, J. (Rangers), 1929 v E; 1930 v E (2)
Buchanan, P. S. (Chelsea), 1938 v Cz (1)
Buchanan, R. (Abercorn), 1891 v W (1)
Buckley, P. (Aberdeen), 1954 v N; 1955 v W, Ni (3)
Buick, A. (Hearts), 1902 v W, Ni (2)
Burchill, M. J. (Celtic), 2000 v Bos (sub), Li, E (sub + sub), F (sub), Ho (sub) (6)
Burley, C. W. (Chelsea), 1995 v J, Ec, Fa; 1996 v Gr, Se, Aus, D, US, Co (sub), Ho (sub), E (sub), Sw; 1997 v A, La, Se, Es, A, Se, Ma, Bl; (with Celtic), 1998 v Bl, La, F, Co, US (sub), Br, N, Mor; 1999 v Fa, CzR; 2000 v Bos, Es, Bos, Li, E (2); (with Derby Co), Ho, Ei; 2001 v Cro, Aus, Bel, Sm (42)
Burley, G. (Ipswich T), 1979 v W, Ni, E, Arg, N; 1980 v P, Ni, E (sub), Pol; 1982 v W (sub), E (11)
Burns, F. (Manchester U), 1970 v A (1)
Burns, K. (Birmingham C), 1974 v WG; 1975 v EG (sub), Sp (2); 1977 v Cz (sub), W, Se, W (sub); (with Nottingham F), 1978 v Ni (sub), W, E, Pe, Ir; 1979 v N; 1980 v Pe, A, Bel; 1981 v Is, Ni, W (20)
Burns, T. (Celtic), 1981 v Ni; 1982 v Ho (sub), W; 1983 v Bel (sub), Ni, Ca (1 + 1 sub); 1988 v E (sub) (8)
Busby, M. W. (Manchester C), 1934 v W (1)

Cairns, T. (Rangers), 1920 v W; 1922 v E; 1923 v E, W; 1924 v Ni; 1925 v W, E, Ni (8)
Calderhead, D. (Queen of the South), 1889 v Ni (1)
Calderwood, C. (Tottenham H), 1995 v Ru, Sm, J, Ec, Fa; 1996 v Gr, Fi, Se, Sm, US, Co, Ho, E, Sw; 1997 v A, La, Se, Es (2), A, Se; 1998 v Bl, La, F, D, Fi, Co, US, Br, N; 1999 v Li, Es; (with Aston Villa) Fa, CzR; 2000 v Bos (1 + sub) (36)
Calderwood, R. (Cartvale), 1885 v Ni, E, W (3)
Caldow, E. (Rangers), 1957 v Sp (2), Sw, WG, E; 1958 v Ni, W, Sw, Par, H, Pol, Y, F; 1959 v E, W, Ni, WG, Ho, P; 1960 v E, W, Ni, A, H, T; 1961 v E, W, Ni, Ei (2), Cz; 1962 v Ni, W, E, Cz (2), U; 1963 v W, Ni, E (40)
Caldwell, S. (Newcastle U), 2001 v Pol (sub) (1)
Callaghan, P. (Hibernian), 1900 v Ni (1)
Callaghan, W. (Dunfermline Ath), 1970 v Ei (sub), W (2)
Cameron, C. (Hearts), 1999 v G (sub), Fa (sub); 2000 v Li (sub), F, Ei (sub); 2001 v La (sub), Sm, Cro, Aus, Sm, Pol (11)
Cameron, J. (Rangers), 1886 v Ni (1)
Cameron, J. (Queen's Park), 1896 v Ni (1)
Cameron, J. (St Mirren), 1904 v Ni; (with Chelsea), 1909 v E (2)

Campbell, C. (Queen's Park), 1874 v E; 1876 v W; 1877 v E, W; 1878 v E; 1879 v E; 1880 v E; 1881 v E; 1882 v E, W; 1884 v E; 1885 v E; 1886 v E (13)

Campbell, H. (Renton), 1889 v W (1)

Campbell, Jas (Sheffield W), 1913 v W (1)

Campbell, J. (South Western), 1880 v W (1)

Campbell, J. (Kilmarnock), 1891 v Ni; 1892 v W (2)

Campbell, John (Celtic), 1893 v E, Ni; 1898 v E, Ni; 1900 v E, Ni; 1901 v E, W, Ni; 1902 v W, Ni; 1903 v W (12)

Campbell, John (Rangers), 1899 v E, W, Ni; 1901 v Ni (4)

Campbell, K. (Liverpool), 1920 v E, W, Ni; (with Partick T), 1921 v W, Ni; 1922 v W, Ni, E (8)

Campbell, P. (Rangers), 1878 v W; 1879 v W (2)

Campbell, P. (Morton), 1898 v W (1)

Campbell, R. (Falkirk), 1947 v Bel, L; (with Chelsea), 1950 v Sw, P, F (5)

Campbell, W. (Morton), 1947 v Ni; 1948 v E, Bel, Sw, F (5)

Carabine, J. (Third Lanark), 1938 v Ho; 1939 v E, Ni (3)

Carr, W. M. (Coventry C), 1970 v Ni, W, E; 1971 v D; 1972 v Pe; 1973 v D (sub) (6)

Cassidy, J. (Celtic), 1921 v W, Ni; 1923 v Ni; 1924 v W (4)

Chalmers, S. (Celtic), 1965 v W, Fi; 1966 v P (sub), Br; 1967 v Ni (5)

Chalmers, W. (Rangers), 1885 v Ni (1)

Chalmers, W. S. (Queen's Park), 1929 v Ni (1)

Chambers, T. (Hearts), 1894 v W (1)

Chaplin, G. D. (Dundee), 1908 v W (1)

Cheyne, A. G. (Aberdeen), 1929 v E, N, G, Ho; 1930 v F (5)

Christie, A. J. (Queen's Park), 1898 v W; 1899 v E, Ni (3)

Christie, R. M. (Queen's Park), 1884 v E (1)

Clark, J. (Celtic), 1966 v Br; 1967 v W, Ni, USSR (4)

Clark, R. B. (Aberdeen), 1968 v W, Ho; 1970 v Ni; 1971 v W, Ni, E, D, P, USSR; 1972 v Bel, Ni, W, E, Cz, Br; 1973 v D, E (17)

Clarke, S. (Chelsea), 1988 v H, Bel, Bul, S.Ar, Ma; 1994 v Ho (6)

Cleland, J. (Royal Albert), 1891 v Ni (1)

Clements, R. (Leith Ath), 1891 v Ni (1)

Clunas, W. L. (Sunderland), 1924 v E; 1926 v W (2)

Collier, W. (Raith R), 1922 v W (1)

Collins, J. (Hibernian), 1988 v S.Ar; 1990 v EG, Pol (sub), Ma (sub); (with Celtic), 1991 v Sw (sub), Bul (sub); 1992 v Ni (sub), Fi; 1993 v P, Ma, G, P, Es (2); 1994 v Sw, Ho (sub), A, Ho; 1995 v Fi, Fa, Ru, Gr, Ru, Sm, Fa; 1996 v Gr, Fi, Se, Sm, Aus, D, US (sub), Co, Ho, E, Sw; (with Monaco), 1997 v A, La, Se, Es, A, Se, Ma; 1998 v Bl, La, F, Fi, Co, US, Br, N, Mor; (with Everton), 1999 v Li; 2000 v Bos, Es, Bos, E (2) (58)

Collins, R. Y. (Celtic), 1951 v W, Ni, A; 1955 v Y, A, H; 1956 v Ni, W; 1957 v E, W, Sp (2), Sw, WG; 1958 v Ni, W, Sw, H, Pol, Y, F, Par; (with Everton), 1959 v E, W, Ni, WG, Ho, P; (with Leeds U), 1965 v E, Pol, Sp (31)

Collins, T. (Hearts), 1909 v W (1)

Colman, D. (Aberdeen), 1911 v E, W, Ni; 1913 v Ni (4)

Colquhoun, E. P. (Sheffield U), 1972 v P, Ho, Pe, Y, Cz, Br; 1973 v D (2), E (9)

Colquhoun, J. (Hearts), 1988 v S.Ar (sub), Ma (sub) (2)

Combe, J. R. (Hibernian), 1948 v E, Bel, Sw (3)

Conn, A. (Hearts), 1956 v A (1)

Conn, A. (Tottenham H), 1975 v Ni (sub), E (2)

Connachan, E. D. (Dunfermline Ath), 1962 v Cz, U (2)

Connelly, G. (Celtic), 1974 v Cz, WG (2)

Connolly, J. (Everton), 1973 v Sw (1)

Connor, J. (Airdrieonians), 1886 v Ni (1)

Connor, J. (Sunderland), 1930 v F; 1932 v Ni; 1934 v E; 1935 v Ni (4)

Connor, R. (Dundee), 1986 v Ho; (with Aberdeen), 1988 v S.Ar (sub); 1989 v E; 1991 v R (4)

Cook, W. L. (Bolton W), 1934 v E; 1935 v W, Ni (3)

Cooke, C. (Dundee), 1966 v W, I; (with Chelsea), P, Br; 1968 v E, Ho; 1969 v W, Ni, A, WG (sub), Cy (2); 1970 v A; 1971 v Bel; 1975 v Sp, P (16)

Cooper, D. (Rangers), 1980 v Pe, A (sub); 1984 v W, E; 1985 v Y, Ic, Sp (2), W; 1986 v W (sub), EG, Aus (2), Ho, WG (sub), U (sub); 1987 v Bul, L, Ei, Br; (with Motherwell), 1990 v W, Eg (22)

Cormack, P. B. (Hibernian), 1966 v Br; 1969 v D (sub); 1970 v Ei, WG; (with Nottingham F), 1971 v D (sub), W, P, E; 1972 v Ho (sub) (9)

Cowan, J. (Aston Villa), 1896 v E; 1897 v E; 1898 v E (3)

Cowan, J. (Morton), 1948 v Bel, Sw, F; 1949 v E, W, F; 1950 v E, W, Ni, Sw, P, F; 1951 v E, W, Ni, A (2), D, F, Bel; 1952 v Ni, W, USA, D, Se (25)

Cowan, W. D. (Newcastle U), 1924 v E (1)

Cowie, D. (Dundee), 1953 v E, Se; 1954 v Ni, W, Fi, N, A, U; 1955 v W, Ni, A, H; 1956 v W, A; 1957 v Ni; 1958 v H, Pol, Y, Par (20)

Cox, C. J. (Hearts), 1948 v F (1)

Cox, S. (Rangers), 1949 v E, F; 1950 v E, F, W, Ni, Sw, P; 1951 v E, D, F, Bel, A; 1952 v Ni, W, USA, D, Se; 1953 v W, Ni, E; 1954 v W, Ni, E (24)

Craig, A. (Motherwell), 1929 v N, Ho; 1932 v E (3)

Craig, J. (Celtic), 1977 v Se (sub) (1)

Craig, J. P. (Celtic), 1968 v W (1)

Craig, T. (Rangers), 1927 v Ni; 1928 v Ni; 1929 v N, G, Ho; 1930 v Ni, E, W (8)

Craig, T. B. (Newcastle U), 1976 v Sw (1)

Crapnell, J. (Airdrieonians), 1929 v E, N, G; 1930 v F; 1931 v Ni, Sw; 1932 v E, F; 1933 v Ni (9)

Crawford, D. (St Mirren), 1894 v W, Ni; 1900 v W (3)

Crawford, J. (Queen's Park), 1932 v F, Ni; 1933 v E, W, Ni (5)

Crawford, S. (Raith R), 1995 v Ec (sub); (with Dunfermline Ath), 2001 v Pol (sub) (2)

Crerand, P. T. (Celtic), 1961 v Ei (2), Cz; 1962 v Ni, W, E, Cz (2), U; 1963 v W, Ni; (with Manchester U), 1964 v Ni; 1965 v E, Pol, Fi; 1966 v Pol (16)

Cringan, W. (Celtic), 1920 v W; 1922 v E, Ni; 1923 v W, E (5)

Crosbie, J. A. (Ayr U), 1920 v W; (with Birmingham), 1922 v E (2)

Croal, J. A. (Falkirk), 1913 v Ni; 1914 v E, W (3)

Cropley, A. J. (Hibernian), 1972 v P, Bel (2)

Cross, J. H. (Third Lanark), 1903 v Ni (1)

Cruickshank, J. (Hearts), 1964 v WG; 1970 v W, E; 1971 v D, Bel; 1976 v R (6)

Crum, J. (Celtic), 1936 v E; 1939 v Ni (2)

Cullen, M. J. (Luton T), 1956 v A (1)

Cumming, D. S. (Middlesbrough), 1938 v E (1)

Cumming, J. (Hearts), 1955 v E, H, P, Y; 1960 v E, Pol, A, H, T (9)

Cummings, G. (Partick T), 1935 v E; 1936 v W, Ni; (with Aston Villa), E; 1937 v G; 1938 v W, Ni, Cz; 1939 v E (9)

Cunningham, A. N. (Rangers), 1920 v Ni; 1921 v W, E; 1922 v Ni; 1923 v E, W; 1924 v E, Ni; 1926 v E, Ni; 1927 v E, W (12)

Cunningham, W. C. (Preston NE), 1954 v N (2), U, Fi, A; 1955 v W, E, H (8)

Curran, H. P. (Wolverhampton W), 1970 v A; 1971 v Ni, E, D, USSR (sub) (5)

Dailly, C. (Derby Co), 1997 v W, Ma, Bl; 1998 v Bl, La, F, D, Fi, Co, US, Br, N, Mor; (with Blackburn R), 1999 v Li; 2000 v Bos (sub), Es, Bos, Li, E (2), F, Ho, Ei; 2001 v La, Sm, Aus; (with West Ham U), Pol (27)

Dalglish, K. (Celtic), 1972 v Bel (sub), Ho; 1973 v D (1+1 sub), E (2), W, Ni, Sw, Br; 1974 v Cz (2), WG (2), Ni, W, E, Bel, N (sub), Z, Br, Y; 1975 v EG, Sp (sub+1), Se, P, W, Ni, E, R; 1976 v D (2), R, Sw, Ni, E; 1977 v Fi, Cz, W (2), Se, Ni, E, Ch, Arg, Br; (with Liverpool), 1978 v EG, Cz, W, Bul, Ni (sub), W, E, Pe, Ir, Ho; 1979 v A, N, P, W, Ni, E, Arg, N; 1980 v Pe, A, Bel (2), P, Ni, W, E, Pol, H; 1981 v Se, P, Is; 1982 v Se, Ni, P (sub), Sp, Ho, Ni, W, E, Nz, Br (sub); 1983 v Bel, Sw; 1984 v U, Bel, EG; 1985 v Y, Ic, Sp, W; 1986 v EG, Aus, R; 1987 v Bul (sub), L (102)

Davidson, C. I. (Blackburn R), 1999 v Li (sub), Es, Fa, CzR, G, Fa, CzR; 2000 v Es, Bos, Li, E, F; (with Leicester C), 2001 v La, Pol (14)

Davidson, D. (Queen's Park), 1878 v W; 1879 v W; 1880 v W; 1881 v E, W (5)

Davidson, J. A. (Partick T), 1954 v N (2), A, U; 1955 v Ni, E, H (8)

Davidson, S. (Middlesbrough), 1921 v E (1)

Dawson, A. (Rangers), 1980 v Pol (sub), H; 1983 v Ni, Ca (2) (5)

Dawson, J. (Rangers), 1935 v Ni; 1936 v E; 1937 v G, E, W, Ni, A, Cz; 1938 v W, Ho, Ni; 1939 v E, Ni, H (14)

Deans, J. (Celtic), 1975 v EG, Sp (2)

Delaney, J. (Celtic), 1936 v W, Ni; 1937 v G, E, A, Cz; 1938 v Ni; 1939 v W, Ni; (with Manchester U), 1947 v E; 1948 v E, W, Ni (13)

Divine, A. (Falkirk), 1910 v W (1)

Dewar, G. (Dumbarton), 1888 v Ni; 1889 v E (2)

Dewar, N. (Third Lanark), 1932 v E, F; 1933 v W (3)

Dick, J. (West Ham U), 1959 v E (1)

Dickie, M. (Rangers), 1897 v Ni; 1899 v Ni; 1900 v W (3)

Dickov, P. (Manchester C), 2001 v Sm (sub), Cro (sub), Aus (sub) (3)

Dickson, W. (Dumbarton), 1888 v Ni (1)

Dickson, W. (Kilmarnock), 1970 v Ni, W, E; 1971 v D, USSR (5)

Divers, J. (Celtic), 1895 v W (1)

Divers, J. (Celtic), 1939 v Ni (1)

Docherty, T. H. (Preston NE), 1952 v W; 1953 v E, Se; 1954 v N (2), A, U; 1955 v W, E, H (2), A; 1957 v E, Y, Sp (2), Sw, WG; 1958 v Ni, W, E, Sw; (with Arsenal), 1959 v W, E, Ni (25)

Dodds, D. (Dundee U), 1984 v U (sub), Ni (2)

Dodds, J. (Celtic), 1914 v E, W, Ni (3)

Dodds, W. (Aberdeen), 1997 v La (sub), W, Bl (sub); 1998 v Bl (sub); (with Dundee U), 1999 v Es (sub), Fa, G, Fa, CzR; 2000 v Bos, Es, Bos, Li (sub), E (2); (with Rangers), F, Ho, Ei; 2001 v La, Sm, Aus, Bel, Sm, Pol (24)

Doig, J. E. (Arbroath), 1887 v Ni; 1889 v Ni; (with Sunderland), 1896 v E; 1899 v E; 1903 v E (5)

Donachie, W. (Manchester C), 1972 v Pe, Ni, E, Y, Cz, Br; 1973 v D, E, W, Ni; 1974 v Ni; 1976 v R, Ni, W, E; 1977 v Fi, Cz, W (2), Se, Ni, E, Ch, Arg, Br; 1978 v EG, W, Bul, W, E, Ir, Ho; 1979 v A, N, P (sub) (35)

Donaldson, A. (Bolton W), 1914 v E, Ni, W; 1920 v E, Ni; 1922 v Ni (6)

Donnachie, J. (Oldham Ath), 1913 v E; 1914 v E, Ni (3)

Donnelly, S. (Celtic), 1997 v W (sub), Ma (sub); 1998 v La (sub), F (sub), D (sub), Fi (sub), Co (sub), US (sub); 1999 v Es (sub), Fa (10)

Dougall, C. (Birmingham C), 1947 v W (1)

Dougall, J. (Preston NE), 1939 v E (1)

Dougan, R. (Hearts), 1950 v Sw (1)

Douglas, A. (Chelsea), 1911 v Ni (1)

Douglas, J. (Renfrew), 1880 v W (1)

Dowds, P. (Celtic), 1892 v Ni (1)

Downie, R. (Third Lanark), 1892 v W (1)

Doyle, D. (Celtic), 1892 v E; 1893 v W; 1894 v E; 1895 v E, Ni; 1897 v E; 1898 v E, Ni (8)

Doyle, J. (Ayr U), 1976 v R (1)

Drummond, J. (Falkirk), 1892 v Ni; (with Rangers), 1894 v Ni; 1895 v Ni, E; 1896 v E, Ni; 1897 v Ni; 1898 v E; 1900 v E; 1901 v E; 1902 v E, W, Ni; 1903 v Ni (14)

Dunbar, M. (Cartvale), 1886 v Ni (1)

Duncan, A. (Hibernian), 1975 v P (sub), W, Ni, E, R; 1976 v D (sub) (6)

Duncan, D. (Derby Co), 1933 v E, W; 1934 v A, W; 1935 v E, W; 1936 v E, W, Ni; 1937 v G, E, W, Ni; 1938 v W (14)

Duncan, D. M. (East Fife), 1948 v Bel, Sw, F (3)

Duncan, J. (Alexandra Ath), 1878 v W; 1882 v W (2)

Duncan, J. (Leicester C), 1926 v W (1)

Duncanson, J. (Rangers), 1947 v Ni (1)

Dunlop, J. (St Mirren), 1890 v W (1)

Dunlop, W. (Liverpool), 1906 v E (1)

Dunn, J. (Hibernian), 1925 v W, Ni; 1927 v Ni; 1928 v Ni, E; (with Everton), 1929 v W (6)

Durie, G. S. (Chelsea), 1988 v Bul (sub); 1989 v I (sub), Cy; 1990 v Y, EG, Eg, Se; 1991 v Sw (sub), Bul (2), USSR (sub), Sm; (with Tottenham H), 1992 v Sw, R, Sm, Ni (sub), Fi, Ca, N (sub), Ho, G; 1993 v Sw, I; 1994 v Sw, I; (with Rangers), Ho (2); 1996 v US, Ho, E, Sw; 1997 v A (sub), Se (sub), Ma (sub), Bl; 1998 v Bl, La, F, Fi (sub), Co, Br, N, Mor (43)

Durrant, I. (Rangers), 1988 v H, Bel, Ma, Sp; 1989 v N (sub); 1993 v Sw (sub), P (sub), I, P (sub); 1994 v I (sub), Ma; (with Kilmarnock), 1999 v Es, Fa (sub), G, Fa, CzR; 2000 v Bos (sub), Es, Ho (sub), Ei (sub) (20)

Dykes, J. (Hearts), 1938 v Ho; 1939 v Ni (2)

Easson, J. F. (Portsmouth), 1931 v A, Sw; 1934 v W (3)

Elliott, M. S. (Leicester C), 1998 v F (sub), D, Fi; 1999 v Li, Fa, CzR Fa; 2000 v Ho, Ei; 2001 v La, Sm, Cro, Aus (sub), Bel, Sm (15)

Ellis, J. (Mossend Swifts), 1892 v Ni (1)

Evans, A. (Aston Villa), 1982 v Ho, Ni, E, Nz (4)

Evans, R. (Celtic), 1949 v E, W, Ni, F; 1950 v W, Ni, Sw, P; 1951 v E, A; 1952 v Ni; 1953 v Se; 1954 v Ni, W, E, N, Fi; 1955 v Ni, P, Y, A, H; 1956 v E, Ni, W, A; 1957 v WG, Sp; 1958 v E, Ni, W, E, Sw, H, Pol, Y, Par, F; 1959 v E, WG, Ho, P; 1960 v E, Ni, W, Pol; (with Chelsea), 1960 v A, H, T (48)

Ewart, J. (Bradford C), 1921 v E (1)

Ewing, T. (Partick T), 1958 v W, E (2)

Farm, G. N. (Blackpool), 1953 v W, Ni, E, Se; 1954 v Ni, W, E; 1959 v WG, Ho, P (10)

Ferguson, B. (Rangers), 1999 v Li; 2000 v Bos, Es (sub), E (2), F, Ei; 2001 v La, Aus, Bel (10)

Ferguson, D. (Rangers), 1988 v Ma, Co (sub) (2)

Ferguson, D. (Dundee U), 1992 v US (sub), Ca, Ho (sub); 1993 v G; (with Everton) 1995 v Gr; 1997 v A, Es (7)

Ferguson, I. (Rangers), 1989 v I, Cy (sub), F; 1993 v Ma (sub), Es; 1994 v Ma, A (sub), Ho (sub); 1997 v Es (sub) (9)

Ferguson, J. (Vale of Leven), 1874 v E; 1876 v E, W; 1877 v E, W; 1878 v W (6)

Ferguson, R. (Kilmarnock), 1966 v W, E, Ho, P, Br; 1967 v W, Ni (7)

Fernie, W. (Celtic), 1954 v Fi, A, U; 1955 v W, Ni; 1957 v E, Ni, W, Y; 1958 v W, Sw, Par (12)

Findlay, R. (Kilmarnock), 1898 v W (1)

Fitchie, T. T. (Woolwich Arsenal), 1905 v W; 1906 v W, Ni; (with Queen's Park), 1907 v W (4)

Flavell, R. (Airdrieonians), 1947 v Bel, L (2)

Fleck, R. (Norwich C), 1990 v Arg, Se, Br (sub); 1991 v USSR (4)

Fleming, C. (East Fife), 1954 v Ni (1)

Fleming, J. W. (Rangers), 1929 v G, Ho; 1930 v E (3)

Fleming, R. (Morton), 1886 v Ni (1)

Forbes, A. R. (Sheffield U), 1947 v Bel, L, E; 1948 v W, Ni; (with Arsenal), 1950 v E, P, F; 1951 v W, Ni, A; 1952 v W, D, Se (14)

Forbes, J. (Vale of Leven), 1884 v E, W, Ni; 1887 v W, E (5)

Ford, D. (Hearts), 1974 v Cz (sub), WG (sub), W (3)

Forrest, J. (Rangers), 1966 v W, I; (with Aberdeen), 1971 v Bel (sub), D, USSR (5)

Forrest, J. (Motherwell), 1958 v E (1)

Forsyth, A. (Partick T), 1972 v Y, Cz, Br; 1973 v D; (with Manchester U), E; 1975 v Sp, Ni (sub), R, EG; 1976 v D (10)

Forsyth, C. (Kilmarnock), 1964 v E; 1965 v W, Ni, Fi (4)

Forsyth, T. (Motherwell), 1971 v D; (with Rangers), 1974 v Cz; 1976 v Sw, Ni, W, E; 1977 v Fi, Se, W, Ni, E, Ch, Arg, Br; 1978 v Cz. W, Ni, W (sub), E, Pe, Ir (sub); Ho (22)

Foyers, R. (St Bernards), 1893 v W; 1894 v W (2)

Fraser, D. M. (WBA), 1968 v Ho; 1969 v Cy (2)

Fraser, J. (Moffat), 1891 v Ni (1)

Fraser, M. J. E. (Queen's Park), 1880 v W; 1882 v W, E; 1883 v W, E (5)

Fraser, J. (Dundee), 1907 v Ni (1)

Fraser, W. (Sunderland), 1955 v W, Ni (2)

Fulton, W. (Abercorn), 1884 v Ni (1)

Fyfe, J. H. (Third Lanark), 1895 v W (1)

Gabriel, J. (Everton), 1961 v W; 1964 v N (sub) (2)

Gallacher, H. K. (Airdrieonians), 1924 v Ni; 1925 v E, W, Ni; 1926 v W; (with Newcastle U), 1926 v E, Ni; 1927 v E, W, Ni; 1928 v E, W; 1929 v E, W, Ni; 1930 v W, Ni, F; (with Chelsea), 1934 v E; (with Derby Co), 1935 v E (20)

Gallacher, K. W. (Dundee U), 1988 v Co, E; 1989 v N, I; (with Coventry C), 1991 v Sm; 1992 v R (sub), Sm (sub), Ni (sub), N (sub), Ho (sub), G (sub), C; 1993 v Sw (sub), P; (with Blackburn R), P, Es (2); 1994 v I, Ma; 1996 v Aus (sub), D, Co (sub), Ho; 1997 v Se (sub), Es (2), A, Se, W, Ma, Bl; 1998 v Bl, La, F, Fi (sub), US, Br, N, Mor; 1999 v Li, Es, Fa, CzR; 2000 v Bos (sub); (with Newcastle U), Bos, Li (sub), E, F, Ei (sub); 2001 v Sm, Cro, Bel, Sm (sub) (53)

Gallacher, P. (Sunderland), 1935 v Ni (1)

Galloway, M. (Celtic), 1992 v R (1)

Galt, J. H. (Rangers), 1908 v W, Ni (2)

Gardiner, I. (Motherwell), 1958 v W (1)

Gardner, D. R. (Third Lanark), 1897 v W (1)

Gardner, R. (Queen's Park), 1872 v E; 1873 v E; (with Clydesdale), 1874 v E; 1875 v E; 1878 v E (5)

Gemmell, T. (St Mirren), 1955 v P, Y (2)

Gemmell, T. (Celtic), 1966 v E; 1967 v W, Ni, E, USSR; 1968 v Ni, E; 1969 v W, Ni, E, D, A, WG, Cy; 1970 v E, Ei, WG; 1971 v Bel (18)

Gemmill, A. (Derby Co), 1971 v Bel; 1972 v P, Ho, Pe, Ni, W, E; 1976 v D, R, Ni, W, E; 1977 v Fi, Cz, W (2), Ni (sub), E (sub), Ch (sub), Arg, Br; 1978 v EG (sub); (with Nottingham F), Bul, Ni, W, E (sub), Pe (sub), Ir, Ho; 1979 v A, N, P, N; (with Birmingham C), 1980 v A, P, Ni, W, E, H; 1981 v Se, P, Is, Ni (43)

Gemmill, S. (Nottingham F), 1995 v J, Ec, Fa (sub); 1996 v Sm, D (sub), US; 1997 v Es, Se (sub), W, Ma (sub), Bl (sub); 1998 v D, Fi; (with Everton), 1999 v G, Fa (sub); 2001 v Sm (sub), Pol (sub) (17)

Gibb, W. (Clydesdale), 1873 v E (1)

Gibson, D. W. (Leicester C), 1963 v A, N, Ei, Sp; 1964 v Ni; 1965 v W, Fi (7)

Gibson, J. D. (Partick T), 1926 v E; 1927 v E, W, Ni; (with Aston Villa), 1928 v E, W; 1930 v W, Ni (8)

Gibson, N. (Rangers), 1895 v E, Ni; 1896 v E, Ni; 1897 v E, Ni; 1898 v E; 1899 v E, W, Ni; 1900 v E, Ni; 1901 v W; (with Partick T), 1905 v Ni (14)

Gilchrist, J. E. (Celtic), 1922 v E (1)

Gilhooley, M. (Hull C), 1922 v W (1)

Gillespie, G. (Rangers), 1880 v W; 1881 v E; 1882 v E; (with Queen's Park), 1886 v W; 1890 v W; 1891 v Ni (7)

Gillespie, G. T. (Liverpool), 1988 v Bel, Bul, Sp; 1989 v N, F, Ch; 1990 v Y, EG, Eg, Pol, Ma, Br (sub); 1991 v Bul (13)

Gillespie, Jas (Third Lanark), 1898 v W (1)

Gillespie, John (Queen's Park), 1896 v W (1)

Gillespie, R. (Queen's Park), 1927 v W; 1931 v W; 1932 v F; 1933 v E (4)

Gillick, T. (Everton), 1937 v A, Cz; 1939 v W, Ni, H (5)

Gilmour, J. (Dundee), 1931 v W (1)
Gilzean, A. J. (Dundee), 1964 v W, E, N, WG; 1965 v Ni, (with Tottenham H), Sp; 1966 v Ni, W, Pol, I; 1968 v W; 1969 v W, E, WG, Cy (2), A (sub); 1970 v Ni, E (sub), WG, A; 1971 v P (22)
Glass, S. (Newcastle U), 1999 v Fa (sub) (1)
Glavin, R. (Celtic), 1977 v Se (1)
Glen, A. (Aberdeen), 1956 v E, Ni (2)
Glen, R. (Renton), 1895 v W; 1896 v W; (with Hibernian), 1900 v Ni (3)
Goram, A. L. (Oldham Ath), 1986 v EG (sub), R, Ho; 1987 v Br; (with Hibernian) 1989 v Y, I; 1990 v EG, Pol, Ma; 1991 v R, Sw, Bul (2), USSR, Sm; (with Rangers), 1992 v Sw, R, Sm, Fi, N, Ho, G, C; 1993 v Sw, P, I, Ma, P; 1994 v Ho; 1995 v Fi, Fa, Ru, Gr; 1996 v Se (sub), D (sub), Co, Ho, E, Sw; 1997 v A, La, Es; 1998 v D (sub) (43)
Gordon, J. E. (Rangers), 1912 v E, Ni; 1913 v E, Ni, W; 1914 v E, Ni; 1920 v E, Ni (10)
Gossland, J. (Rangers), 1884 v Ni (1)
Goudie, J. (Abercorn), 1884 v Ni (1)
Gough, C. R. (Dundee U), 1983 v Sw, Ni, W, E, Ca (3); 1984 v U, Bel, EG, Ni, W, E, F; 1985 v Sp, E, Ic; 1986 v W, EG, Aus, Is, R, E, D, WG, U; (with Tottenham H), 1987 v Bul, L, Ei (2), Bel, E, Br; 1988 v H; (with Rangers), S.Ar, Sp, Co, E; 1989 v Y, I, Cy, F, Cy; 1990 v F, Arg, EG, Eg, Pol, Ma, Cr; 1991 v USSR, Bul; 1992 v Sm, Ni, Ca, N, Ho, G, C; 1993 v Sw, P (61)
Gould, J. (Celtic), 2000 v Li; 2001 v Aus (2)
Gourlay, J. (Cambuslang), 1886 v Ni; 1888 v W (2)
Govan, J. (Hibernian), 1948 v E, W, Bel, Sw, F; 1949 v Ni (6)
Gow, D. R. (Rangers), 1888 v E (1)
Gow, J. J. (Queen's Park), 1885 v E (1)
Gow, J. R. (Rangers), 1888 v Ni (1)
Graham, A. (Leeds U), 1978 v EG (sub); 1979 v A (sub), N, W, Ni, E, Arg, N; 1980 v A; 1981 v W (10)
Graham, G. (Arsenal), 1972 v P, Ho, Ni, Y, Cz, Br; 1973 v D (2); (with Manchester U), E, W, Ni, Br (sub) (12)
Graham, J. (Annbank), 1884 v Ni (1)
Graham, J. A. (Arsenal), 1921 v Ni (1)
Grant, J. (Hibernian), 1959 v W, Ni (2)
Grant, P. (Celtic), 1989 v E (sub), Ch (2)
Gray, A. (Hibernian), 1903 v Ni (1)
Gray, A. M. (Aston Villa), 1976 v R, Sw; 1977 v Fi, Cz; 1979 v A, N; (with Wolverhampton W), 1980 v P, E (sub); 1981 v Se, P, Is (sub), Ni; 1982 v Se (sub), Ni (sub); 1983 v Ni, W, E, Ca (1+1 sub); (with Everton), 1985 v Ic (20)
Gray, D. (Rangers), 1929 v W, Ni, G, Ho; 1930 v W, E, Ni; 1931 v W; 1933 v Ni (10)
Gray, E. (Leeds U), 1969 v E, Cy; 1970 v WG, A; 1971 v W, Ni; 1972 v Bel, Ho; 1976 v W, E; 1977 v Fi, W (12)
Gray, F. T. (Leeds U), 1976 v Sw; 1979 v N, P, W, Ni, E, Arg (sub); (with Nottingham F), 1980 v Bel (sub); 1981 v Se, P, Is, Ni, Is, W; (with Leeds U), Ni, E; 1982 v Se, Ni, P, Sp, Ho, W, Nz, Br, USSR; 1983 v EG, Sw, Bel, Sw, W, E, Ca (32)
Gray, W. (Pollokshields Ath), 1886 v E (1)
Green, A. (Blackpool), 1971 v Bel (sub), P (sub), Ni, E; (with Newcastle U), 1972 v W, E (sub) (6)
Greig, J. (Rangers), 1964 v E, WG; 1965 v W, Ni, E, Fi (2), Sp, Pol; 1966 v Ni, W, E, Pol, I (2), P, Ho, Br; 1967 v W, Ni, E; 1968 v Ni, W, E, Ho; 1969 v W, Ni, E, D, A, WG, Cy (2); 1970 v W, E, Ei, WG, A; 1971 v D, Bel, W (sub), Ni, E; 1976 v D (44)
Groves, W. (Hibernian), 1888 v W; (with Celtic), 1889 v Ni; 1890 v E (3)
Guilliland, W. (Queen's Park), 1891 v W; 1892 v Ni; 1894 v E; 1895 v E (4)
Gunn, B. (Norwich C), 1990 v Eg; 1993 v Es (2); 1994 v Sw, I, Ho (sub) (6)

Haddock, H. (Clyde), 1955 v E, H (2), P, Y; 1958 v E (6)
Haddow, D. (Rangers), 1894 v E (1)
Haffey, F. (Celtic), 1960 v E; 1961 v E (2)
Hamilton, A. (Queen's Park), 1885 v E, W; 1886 v E; 1888 v E (4)
Hamilton, A. W. (Dundee), 1962 v Cz, U, W, E; 1963 v W, Ni, E, A, N, Ei; 1964 v Ni, W, E, N, WG; 1965 v Ni, W, E, Fi (2), Pol, Sp; 1966 v Pol, Ni (24)
Hamilton, G. (Aberdeen), 1947 v Ni; 1951 v Bel, A; 1954 v N (2) (5)
Hamilton, G. (Port Glasgow Ath), 1906 v Ni (1)
Hamilton, J. (Queen's Park), 1892 v W; 1893 v E, Ni (3)
Hamilton, J. (St Mirren), 1924 v Ni (1)
Hamilton, R. C. (Rangers), 1899 v E, W, Ni; 1900 v W; 1901 v E, Ni; 1902 v W, Ni; 1903 v E; 1904 v Ni; (with Dundee), 1911 v W (11)
Hamilton, T. (Hurlford), 1891 v Ni (1)
Hamilton, T. (Rangers), 1932 v E (1)

Hamilton, W. M. (Hibernian), 1965 v Fi (1)
Hannah, A. B. (Renton), 1888 v W (1)
Hannah, J. (Third Lanark), 1889 v W (1)
Hansen, A. D. (Liverpool), 1979 v W, Arg; 1980 v Bel, P; 1981 v Se, P, Is; 1982 v Se, Ni, P, Sp, Ni (sub), W, E, Nz, Br, USSR; 1983 v EG, Sw, Bel, Sw; 1985 v W (sub); 1986 v R (sub); 1987 v Ei (2), L (26)
Hansen, J. (Partick T), 1972 v Bel (sub), Y (sub) (2)
Harkness, J. D. (Queen's Park), 1927 v E, Ni; 1928 v E; (with Hearts), 1929 v W, E, Ni; 1930 v E, W; 1932 v W, F; 1934 v Ni (11)
Harper, J. M. (Aberdeen), 1973 v D (1+1 sub); (with Hibernian), 1976 v D; (with Aberdeen), 1978 v Ir (sub) (4)
Harper, W. (Hibernian), 1923 v E, Ni, W; 1924 v E, Ni, W; 1925 v E, Ni, W; (with Arsenal), 1926 v E, Ni (11)
Harris, J. (Partick T), 1921 v W, Ni (2)
Harris, N. (Newcastle U), 1924 v E (1)
Harrower, W. (Queen's Park), 1882 v E; 1884 v Ni; 1886 v W (3)
Hartford, R. A. (WBA), 1972 v Pe, W (sub), E, Y, Cz, Br; (with Manchester C), 1976 v D, R, Ni (sub); 1977 v Cz (sub), W (sub), Se, W, Ni, E, Ch, Arg, Br; 1978 v EG, Cz, W, Bul, W, E, Pe, Ir, Ho; 1979 v A, N, P, W, Ni, E, Arg, N; (with Everton), 1980 v Pe, Bel; 1981 v Ni (sub), Is, W, Ni, E; 1982 v Se; (with Manchester C), Ni, P, Sp, Ni, W, E, Br (50)
Harvey, D. (Leeds U), 1973 v D; 1974 v Cz, WG, Ni, W, E, Bel, Z, Br, Y; 1975 v EG, Sp (2); 1976 v D (2); 1977 v Fi (sub) (16)
Hastings, A. C. (Sunderland), 1936 v Ni; 1938 v Ni (2)
Haughney, M. (Celtic), 1954 v E (1)
Hay, D. (Celtic), 1970 v Ni, W, E; 1971 v D, Bel, W, P, Ni; 1972 v P, Bel, Ho; 1973 v W, Ni, E, Sw, Br; 1974 v Cz (2), WG, Ni, W, E, Bel, N, Z, Br, Y (27)
Hay, J. (Celtic), 1905 v Ni; 1909 v Ni; 1910 v W, Ni, E; 1911 v Ni, E; (with Newcastle U), 1912 v E, W; 1914 v E, Ni (11)
Hegarty, P. (Dundee U), 1979 v W, Ni, E, Arg, N (sub); 1980 v W, E; 1983 v Ni (8)
Heggie, C. (Rangers), 1886 v Ni (1)
Henderson, G. H. (Rangers), 1904 v Ni (1)
Henderson, J. G. (Portsmouth), 1953 v Se; 1954 v Ni, E, N; 1956 v W; (with Arsenal), 1959 v W, Ni (7)
Henderson, W. (Rangers), 1963 v W, Ni, E, A, N, Ei, Sp; 1964 v W, Ni, E, N, WG; 1965 v Fi, Pol, E, Sp; 1966 v Ni, W, Pol, I, Ho; 1967 v W, Ni; 1968 v Ho; 1969 v Ni, E, Cy; 1970 v Ei; 1971 v P (29)
Hendry, E. C. J. (Blackburn R), 1993 v Es (2); 1994 v Ma, Ho, A, Ho; 1995 v Fi, Fa, Gr, Ru, Sm; 1996 v Fi, Se, Sm, Aus, D, US, Co, Ho, E, Sw; 1997 v A, Se, Es (2), A, Se; 1998 v La, D, Fi, Co, US, Br, N, Mor; (with Rangers), 1999 v Li, Es, Fa, G; 2000 v Bos, Es, Bos, E (2); (with Coventry C), F; 2001 v La, Sm, Cro, Aus (sub); (with Bolton W), Bel, Sm (51)
Hepburn, J. (Alloa Ath), 1891 v W (1)
Hepburn, R. (Ayr U), 1932 v Ni (1)
Herd, A. C. (Hearts), 1935 v Ni (1)
Herd, D. G. (Arsenal), 1959 v E, W, Ni; 1961 v Ei, Cz (5)
Herd, G. (Clyde), 1958 v E; 1960 v H, T; 1961 v W, Ni (5)
Herriot, J. (Birmingham C), 1969 v Ni, E, D, Cy (2), W (sub); 1970 v Ei (sub), WG (8)
Hewie, J. D. (Charlton Ath), 1956 v E, A; 1957 v E, Ni, W, Y, Sp (2), Sw, WG; 1958 v H, Pol, Y, F; 1959 v Ho, P; 1960 v Ni, W, Pol (19)
Higgins, A. (Kilmarnock), 1885 v Ni (1)
Higgins, A. (Newcastle U), 1910 v E, Ni; 1911 v E, Ni (4)
Highet, T. C. (Queen's Park), 1875 v E; 1876 v E, W; 1878 v E (4)
Hill, D. (Rangers), 1881 v E, W; 1882 v W (3)
Hill, D. A. (Third Lanark), 1906 v Ni (1)
Hill, F. R. (Aberdeen), 1930 v F; 1931 v W, Ni (3)
Hill, J. (Hearts), 1891 v E; 1892 v W (2)
Hogg, G (Hearts), 1896 v E, Ni (2)
Hogg, J. (Ayr U), 1922 v Ni (1)
Hogg, R. M. (Celtic), 1937 v Cz (1)
Holm, A. H. (Queen's Park), 1882 v W; 1883 v E, W (3)
Holt, D. D. (Hearts), 1963 v A, N, Ei, Sp; 1964 v WG (sub) (5)
Holt, G. J. (Kilmarnock), 2001 v La (sub), Cro (sub) (2)
Holton, J. A. (Manchester U), 1973 v W, Ni, E, Sw, Br; 1974 v Cz, WG, Ni, W, E, N, Z, Br, Y; 1975 v EG (15)
Hope, R. (WBA), 1968 v Ho; 1969 v D (2)
Hopkin, D. (Crystal Palace), 1997 v Ma, Bl; (with Leeds U), 1998 v Bl (sub), F (sub); 1999 v CzR; 2000 v Bos (2) (7)
Houliston, W. (Queen of the South), 1949 v E, Ni, F (3)
Houston, S. M. (Manchester U), 1976 v D (1)
Howden, W. (Partick T), 1905 v Ni (1)
Howe, R. (Hamilton A), 1929 v N, Ho (2)
Howie, H. (Hibernian), 1949 v W (1)
Howie, J. (Newcastle U), 1905 v E; 1906 v E; 1908 v E (3)

Howieson, J. (St Mirren), 1927 v Ni (1)
Hughes, J. (Celtic), 1965 v Pol, Sp; 1966 v Ni, I (2); 1968 v E; 1969 v A; 1970 v Ei (8)
Hughes, W. (Sunderland), 1975 v Se (sub) (1)
Humphries, W. (Motherwell), 1952 v Se (1)
Hunter, A. (Kilmarnock), 1972 v Pe, Y; (with Celtic), 1973 v E; 1974 v Cz (4)
Hunter, J. (Dundee), 1909 v W (1)
Hunter, J. (Third Lanark), 1874 v E; (with Eastern), 1875 v E; (with Third Lanark), 1876 v E; 1877 v W (4)
Hunter, R. (St Mirren), 1890 v Ni (1)
Hunter, W. (Motherwell), 1960 v H, T; 1961 v W (3)
Husband, J. (Partick T), 1947 v W (1)
Hutchison, D. (Everton), 1999 v CzR (sub), G; 2000 v Bos, Es, Li, E (2), F, Ho, Ei; (with Sunderland), 2001 v La, Sm, Cro, Aus, Bel, Sm (16)
Hutchison, T. (Coventry C), 1974 v Cz (2), WG (2), Ni, W, Bel (sub), N, Z (sub), Y (sub); 1975 v EG, Sp (2), P, E (sub), R (sub); 1976 v D (17)
Hutton, J. (Aberdeen), 1923 v E, W, Ni; 1924 v Ni; 1926 v W, E, Ni; (with Blackburn R), 1927 v Ni; 1928 v W, Ni (10)
Hutton, J. (St Bernards), 1887 v Ni (1)
Hyslop, T. (Stoke C), 1896 v E; (with Rangers), 1897 v E (2)

Imlach, J. J. S. (Nottingham F), 1958 v H, Pol, Y, F (4)
Imrie, W. N. (St Johnstone), 1929 v N, G (2)
Inglis, J. (Kilmarnock Ath), 1884 v Ni (1)
Inglis, J. (Rangers), 1883 v E, W (2)
Irons, J. H. (Queen's Park), 1900 v W (1)
Irvine, B. (Aberdeen), 1991 v R; 1993 v G, Es (2); 1994 v Sw, I, Ma, A, Ho (9)

Jackson, A. (Cambuslang), 1886 v W; 1888 v Ni (2)
Jackson, A. (Aberdeen), 1925 v E, W, Ni; (with Huddersfield T), 1926 v E, W, Ni; 1927 v W, Ni; 1928 v E, W; 1929 v E, W, Ni; 1930 v E, W, Ni, F (17)
Jackson, C. (Rangers), 1975 v Se, P (sub), W; 1976 v D, R, Ni, W, E (8)
Jackson, D. (Hibernian), 1995 v Ru, Sm, J, Ec, Fa; 1996 v Gr, Fi (sub), Se (sub), Sm (sub), Aus (sub), D (sub), US; 1997 v La, Se, Es, A, Se, W, Ma, Bl; (with Celtic), 1998 v D, Fi, Co, US, Br, N; 1999 v Li, Es (sub) (28)
Jackson, J. (Partick T), 1931 v A, I, Sw; 1933 v E; (with Chelsea), 1934 v E; 1935 v E; 1936 v W, Ni (8)
Jackson, T. A. (St Mirren), 1904 v W, E, Ni; 1905 v W; 1907 v W, Ni (6)
James, A. W. (Preston NE), 1926 v W; 1928 v E; 1929 v E, Ni; (with Arsenal), 1930 v E, W, Ni; 1933 v W (8)
Jardine, A. (Rangers), 1971 v D (sub); 1972 v P, Bel, Ho; 1973 v E, Sw, Br; 1974 v Cz (2), WG (2), Ni, W, E, Bel, N, Z, Br, Y; 1975 v EG, Sp (2), Se, P, W, Ni, E; 1977 v Se (sub), Ch (sub), Br (sub); 1978 v Cz, W, Ni, Ir; 1980 v Pe, A, Bel (2) (38)
Jarvie, A. (Airdrieonians), 1971 v P (sub), Ni (sub), E (sub) (3)
Jenkinson, T. (Hearts), 1887 v Ni (1)
Jess, E. (Aberdeen), 1993 v I (sub); Ma; 1994 v Sw (sub), I, Ho (sub), A, Ho (sub); 1995 v Fi (sub); 1996 v Se (sub), Sm; (with Coventry C), US, Co (sub); E (sub); (with Aberdeen), 1998 v D (sub); 1999 v CzR (sub), G (sub), Fa (sub), CzR (sub) (18)
Johnston, A. (Sunderland), 1999 v Es, Fa, CzR (sub), G, Fa, CzR; 2000 v Es, F (sub), Ei (sub); (with Rangers), 2001 v Sm (sub), Cro, Sm (12)
Johnston, L. H. (Clyde), 1948 v Bel, Sw (2)
Johnston, M. (Watford), 1984 v W (sub), E (sub), F; 1985 v Y; (with Celtic), Ic, Sp (2), W; 1986 v EG; 1987 v Bul, Ei (2), L; (with Nantes), 1988 v H, Bel, L, S.Ar, Sp, Co, E; 1989 v N, Y, I, Cy, F, Cy, E, Ch (sub); (with Rangers), 1990 v F, N, EG, Pol, Ma, Cr, Se, Br; 1992 v Sw, Sm (sub) (38)
Johnston, R. (Sunderland), 1938 v Cz (1)
Johnston, W. (Rangers), 1966 v W, E, Pol, Ho; 1968 v W, E; 1969 v Ni (sub); 1970 v Ni; 1971 v D; (with WBA), 1977 v Se, W (sub), Ni, E, Ch, Arg, Br; 1978 v EG, Cz, W (2), E, Pe (22)
Johnston, D. (Rangers), 1973 v W, Ni, E, Sw, Br; 1975 v EG (sub), Se (sub); 1976 v Sw, Ni (sub), E (sub); 1978 v Bul (sub), Ni, W; 1980 v Bel (14)
Johnstone, J. (Abercorn), 1888 v W (1)
Johnstone, J. (Celtic), 1965 v W, Fi; 1966 v E; 1967 v W, USSR; 1968 v W; 1969 v A, WG; 1970 v E, WG; 1971 v D, E; 1972 v P, Bel, Ho, Ni, E (sub); 1974 v W, E, Bel, N; 1975 v EG, Sp (23)
Johnstone, Jas (Kilmarnock), 1894 v W (1)
Johnstone, J. A. (Hearts), 1930 v W; 1933 v W, Ni (3)

Johnstone, R. (Hibernian), 1951 v E, D, F; 1952 v Ni, E; 1953 v E, Se; 1954 v W, E, N, Fi; 1955 v Ni, H; (with Manchester C), 1955 v E; 1956 v E, Ni, W (17)
Johnstone, W. (Third Lanark), 1887 v Ni; 1889 v W; 1890 v E (3)
Jordan, J. (Leeds U), 1973 v E (sub), Sw (sub), Br; 1974 v Cz (sub+1), WG (sub), Ni (sub), W, E, Bel, N, Z, Br, Y; 1975 v EG, Sp (2); 1976 v Ni, W, E; 1977 v Cz, W, Ni, E; 1978 v EG, Cz, W; (with Manchester U), Bul, Ni, E, Pe, Ir, Ho; 1979 v A, P, W (sub), Ni, E, N; 1980 v Bel, Ni (sub), W, E, Pol; 1981 v Is, W, E; (with AC Milan), 1982 v Se, Ho, W, E, USSR (52)

Kay, J. L. (Queen's Park), 1880 v E; 1882 v E, W; 1883 v E, W; 1884 v W (6)
Keillor, A. (Montrose), 1891 v W; 1892 v Ni; (with Dundee), 1894 v Ni; 1895 v W; 1896 v W; 1897 v W (6)
Keir, L. (Dumbarton), 1885 v W; 1886 v Ni; 1887 v E, W; 1888 v E (5)
Kelly, H. T. (Blackpool), 1952 v USA (1)
Kelly, J. (Renton), 1888 v E; (with Celtic), 1889 v E; 1890 v E; 1892 v E; 1893 v E, Ni; 1894 v W; 1896 v Ni (8)
Kelly, J. C. (Barnsley), 1949 v W, Ni (2)
Kelso, R. (Renton), 1885 v W, Ni; 1886 v W; 1887 v E, W; 1888 v E, Ni; (with Dundee), 1898 v Ni (8)
Kelso, T. (Dundee), 1914 v W (1)
Kennaway, J. (Celtic), 1934 v W, A (2)
Kennedy, A. (Eastern), 1875 v E; 1876 v E, W; (with Third Lanark), 1878 v E; 1882 v W; 1884 v W (6)
Kennedy, J. (Celtic), 1964 v W, E, WG; 1965 v W, Ni, Fi (6)
Kennedy, J. (Hibernian), 1897 v W (1)
Kennedy, S. (Aberdeen), 1978 v Bul, W, E, Pe, Ho; 1979 v A, P; 1982 v P (sub) (8)
Kennedy, S. (Partick T), 1905 v W (1)
Kennedy, S. (Rangers), 1975 v Se, P, W, Ni, E (5)
Ker, G. (Queen's Park), 1880 v E; 1881 v E, W; 1882 v W, E (5)
Ker, W. (Granville), 1872 v E; (with Queen's Park), 1873 v E (2)
Kerr, A. (Partick T), 1955 v A, H (2)
Kerr, P. (Hibernian), 1924 v Ni (1)
Key, G. (Hearts), 1902 v Ni (1)
Key, W. (Queen's Park), 1907 v Ni (1)
King, A. (Hearts), 1896 v E, W; (with Celtic), 1897 v Ni; 1898 v Ni; 1899 v Ni, W (6)
King, J. (Hamilton A), 1933 v Ni; 1934 v Ni (2)
King, W. S. (Queen's Park), 1929 v W (1)
Kinloch, J. D. (Partick T), 1922 v Ni (1)
Kinnaird, A. F. (Wanderers), 1873 v E (1)
Kinnear, D. (Rangers), 1938 v Cz (1)

Lambert, P. (Motherwell), 1995 v J, Ec (sub); (with Borussia Dortmund), 1997 v La (sub), Se (sub), A, Se, Bl; 1998 v Bl, La; (with Celtic), Fi (sub), Co, US, Br, N, Mor; 1999 v Li, CzR, G, Fa, CzR; 2000 v Bos, Li, Ho, Ei; 2001 v Bel, Sm (26)
Lambie, J. A. (Queen's Park), 1886 v Ni; 1887 v Ni; 1888 v E (3)
Lambie, W. A. (Queen's Park), 1892 v Ni; 1893 v W; 1894 v E; 1895 v E, Ni; 1896 v E, Ni; 1897 v E, Ni (9)
Lamont, D. (Pilgrims), 1885 v Ni (1)
Lang, A. (Dumbarton), 1880 v W (1)
Lang, J. J. (Clydesdale), 1876 v W; (with Third Lanark), 1878 v W (2)
Latta, A. (Dumbarton), 1888 v W; 1889 v E (2)
Law, D. (Huddersfield T), 1959 v W, Ni, Ho, P; 1960 v Ni, W; (with Manchester C), 1960 v E, Pol, A; 1961 v E, Ni; (with Torino), 1962 v Cz (2), E; (with Manchester U), 1963 v W, Ni, E, A, N, Ei, Sp; 1964 v W, E, N, WG; 1965 v W, Ni, E, Fi (2), Pol, Sp; 1966 v Ni, E, Pol; 1967 v W, E, USSR; 1968 v Ni; 1969 v Ni, A, WG; 1972 v Pe, Ni, W, E, Y, Cz, Br; (with Manchester C), 1974 v Cz (2), WG (2), Ni, Z (55)
Law, G. (Rangers), 1910 v E, Ni, W (3)
Law, T. (Chelsea), 1928 v E; 1930 v E (2)
Lawrence, J. (Newcastle U), 1911 v E (1)
Lawrence, T. (Liverpool), 1963 v Ei; 1969 v W, WG (3)
Lawson, D. (St Mirren), 1923 v E (1)
Leckie, R. (Queen's Park), 1872 v E (1)
Leggat, G. (Aberdeen), 1956 v E; 1957 v W; 1958 v Ni, H, Pol, Y, Par; (with Fulham), 1959 v E, W, Ni, WG, Ho; 1960 v E, Ni, W, Pol, A, H (18)
Leighton, J. (Aberdeen), 1983 v EG, Sw, Bel, Sw, W, E, Ca (2); 1984 v U, Bel, Ni, W, E, F; 1985 v Y, Ic, Sp (2), W, E, Ic; 1986 v W, EG, Aus (2), Is, D, WG, U; 1987 v Bul, Ei (2), L, Bel, E; 1988 v H, Bel, Bul, L, S.Ar, Ma, Sp; (with Manchester U), Co, E; 1989 v N, Cy, F, Cy, E, Ch; 1990 v Y, F, N, Arg, Ma (sub, Cr, Se, Br; (with Hibernian), 1994 v Ma,

A, Ho; 1995 v Gr (sub), Ru, Sm, J, Ec, Fa; 1996 v Gr, Fi, Se, Sm, Aus, D, US; 1997 v Se, Es, A, Se, W (sub), Ma, Bl; (with Aberdeen), 1998 v Bl, La, D, Fi, US, Br, N, Mor; 1999 v Li, Es (91)

Lennie, W. (Aberdeen), 1908 v W, Ni (2)

Lennox, R. (Celtic), 1967 v Ni, E, USSR; 1968 v W, L; 1969 v D, A, WG, Cy (sub); 1970 v W (sub) (10)

Leslie, L. G. (Airdrieonians), 1961 v W, Ni, Ei (2), Cz (5)

Levein, C. (Hearts), 1990 v Arg, EG, Eg (sub), Pol, Ma (sub), Se; 1992 v R, Sm; 1993 v P, G, P; 1994 v Sw, Ho; 1995 v Fi, Fa, Ru (16)

Liddell, W. (Liverpool), 1947 v W, Ni; 1948 v E, W, Ni; 1950 v E, W, P, F; 1951 v W, Ni, E, A; 1952 v W, Ni, E, USA, D, Se; 1953 v W, Ni, E; 1954 v W; 1955 v P, Y, A, H; 1956 v Ni (28)

Liddle, D. (East Fife), 1931 v A, I, Sw (3)

Lindsay, D. (St Mirren), 1903 v Ni (1)

Lindsay, J. (Dumbarton), 1880 v W; 1881 v W, E; 1884 v W, E; 1885 v W, E; 1886 v E (8)

Lindsay, J. (Renton), 1888 v E; 1893 v E, Ni (3)

Linwood, A. B. (Clyde), 1950 v W (1)

Little, R. J. (Rangers), 1953 v Se (1)

Livingstone, G. T. (Manchester C), 1906 v E; (with Rangers), 1907 v W (2)

Lochhead, A. (Third Lanark), 1889 v W (1)

Logan, J. (Ayr U), 1891 v W (1)

Logan, T. (Falkirk), 1913 v Ni (1)

Logie, J. T. (Arsenal), 1953 v Ni (1)

Loney, W. (Celtic), 1910 v W, Ni (2)

Long, H. (Clyde), 1947 v Ni (1)

Longair, W. (Dundee), 1894 v Ni (1)

Lorimer, P. (Leeds U), 1970 v A (sub); 1971 v W, Ni; 1972 v Ni (sub), W, E; 1973 v D (2), E (2); 1974 v WG (sub), E, Bel, N, Z, Br, Y; 1975 v Sp (sub); 1976 v D (2), R (sub) (21)

Love, A. (Aberdeen), 1931 v A, I, Sw (3)

Low, A. (Falkirk), 1934 v Ni (1)

Low, T. P. (Rangers), 1897 v Ni (1)

Low, W. L. (Newcastle U), 1911 v E, W; 1912 v Ni; 1920 v E, Ni (5)

Lowe, J. (Cambuslang), 1891 v Ni (1)

Lowe, J. (St Bernards), 1887 v Ni (1)

Lundie, J. (Hibernian), 1886 v W (1)

Lyall, J. (Sheffield W), 1905 v E (1)

McAdam, J. (Third Lanark), 1880 v W (1)

McAllister, B. (Wimbledon), 1997 v W, Ma, Bl (sub) (3)

McAllister, G. (Leicester C), 1990 v EG, Pol, Ma (sub); (with Leeds U), 1991 v R, Sw, Bul, USSR, Sm; 1992 v Sw (sub), Sm, Ni, Fi (sub), US, Ca, N, Ho, G, C; 1993 v P, I, Ma; 1994 v Sw, I, Ma, Ho, A, Ho; 1995 v Fi, Ru, Gr, Ru, Sm; 1996 v Gr, Fi, Se, Sm, Aus, D, US (sub), Co, Ho, E, Sw; (with Coventry C), 1997 v A, La, Es (2), A, Se, W, Ma, Bl; 1998 v Bl, La, F; 1999 v CzR (57)

McArthur, D. (Celtic), 1895 v E, Ni; 1899 v W (3)

McAtee, A. (Celtic), 1913 v W (1)

McAulay, J. (Arthurlie), 1884 v Ni (1)

McAulay, J. D. (Dumbarton), 1882 v W; 1883 v E, W; 1884 v E; 1885 v E, W; 1886 v E; 1887 v E, W (9)

McAuley, R. (Rangers), 1932 v Ni, W (2)

McAvennie, F. (West Ham U), 1986 v Aus (2), D (sub), WG (sub); (with Celtic), 1988 v S.Ar (5)

McBain, E. (St Mirren), 1894 v W (1)

McBain, N. (Manchester U), 1922 v E; (with Everton), 1923 v Ni; 1924 v W (3)

McBride, J. (Celtic), 1967 v W, Ni (2)

McBride, P. (Preston NE), 1904 v E; 1906 v E; 1907 v E, W; 1908 v E; 1909 v W (6)

McCall, J. (Renton), 1886 v W; 1887 v E, W; 1888 v E; 1890 v E (5)

McCall, S. M. (Everton), 1990 v Arg, EG, Eg (sub), Pol, Ma, Cr, Se, Br; 1991 v Sw, USSR, Sm; (with Rangers), 1992 v Sw, R, Sm, US, Ca, N, Ho, G, C; 1993 v Sw, P (2); 1994 v I, Ho, A (sub), Ho; 1995 v Fi (sub), Ru, Gr; 1996 v Gr, D, US (sub), Co, Ho, E, Sw; 1997 v A, La; 1998 v D (sub) (40)

McCalliog, J. (Sheffield W), 1967 v E, USSR; 1968 v Ni; 1969 v D; (with Wolverhampton W), 1971 v P (5)

McCallum, N. (Renton), 1888 v Ni (1)

McCann, N. (Hearts), 1999 v Li (sub); (with Rangers), CzR; 2000 v Bos, Es (sub), E, F (sub), Ho, Ei; 2001 v La, Sm, Aus (sub) (11)

McCann, R. J. (Motherwell), 1959 v WG; 1960 v E, Ni, W; 1961 v E (5)

McCartney, W. (Hibernian), 1902 v Ni (1)

McClair, B. (Celtic), 1987 v L, Ei, E, Br (sub); (with Manchester U), 1988 v Bul, Ma (sub), Sp (sub); 1989 v N, Y, I (sub), Cy, F (sub); 1990 v N (sub), Arg (sub); 1991 v Bul (2), Sm; 1992 v Sw (sub), R, Ni, US, Ca (sub), N, Ho, G, C; 1993 v Sw, P (sub), Es (2) (30)

McClory, A. (Motherwell), 1927 v W; 1928 v Ni; 1935 v W (3)

McCloy, P. (Ayr U), 1924 v E; 1925 v E (2)

McCloy, P. (Rangers), 1973 v W, Ni, Sw, Br (4)

McCoist, A. (Rangers), 1986 v Ho; 1987 v L (sub), Ei (sub), Bel, E, Br; 1988 v H, Bel, Ma, Sp, Co, E; 1989 v Y (sub), F, Cy, E; 1990 v Y, F, N, EG (sub), Eg, Pol, Ma (sub), Cr (sub), Se (sub), Br; 1991 v R, Sw, Bul (2), USSR; 1992 v Sw, Sm, Ni, Fi (sub), US, Ca, N, Ho, G, C; 1993 v Sw, P, I, Ma, P; 1996 v Gr (sub), Fi (sub), Sm (sub), Aus (sub), Co, E (sub), Sw; 1997 v A, Se (sub), Es (sub), A (sub); 1998 v Bl (sub); (with Kilmarnock), 1999 v Li, Es (61)

McColl, A. (Renton), 1888 v Ni (1)

McColl, I. M. (Rangers), 1950 v E, F; 1951 v W, Ni, Bel; 1957 v E, Ni, W, Y, Sp, Sw, WG; 1958 v Ni, E (14)

McColl, R. S. (Queen's Park), 1896 v W, Ni; 1897 v Ni; 1898 v Ni; 1899 v Ni, E, W; 1900 v E, W; 1901 v E, W; (with Newcastle U), 1902 v E; (with Queen's Park), 1908 v Ni (13)

McColl, W. (Renton), 1895 v W (1)

McCombie, A. (Sunderland), 1903 v E, W; (with Newcastle U), 1905 v E, W (4)

McCorkindale, J. (Partick T), 1891 v W (1)

McCormick, R. (Abercorn), 1886 v W (1)

McCrae, D. (St Mirren), 1929 v N, G (2)

McCredie, A. (Rangers), 1893 v W; 1894 v E (2)

McCreadie, E. G. (Chelsea), 1965 v E, Sp, Fi, Pol; 1966 v P, Ni, W, Pol, I; 1967 v E, USSR; 1968 v Ni, W, E, Ho; 1969 v W, Ni, E, D, A, WG, Cy (2) (23)

McCulloch, D. (Hearts), 1935 v W; (with Brentford), 1936 v E; 1937 v W, Ni; 1938 v Cz; (with Derby Co), 1939 v H, W (7)

MacDonald, A. (Rangers), 1976 v Sw (1)

McDonald, J. (Edinburgh University), 1886 v E (1)

McDonald, J. (Sunderland), 1956 v W, Ni (2)

MacDougall, E. J. (Norwich C) 1975 v Se, P, W, Ni, E; 1976 v D, R (sub) (7)

McDougall, J. (Liverpool), 1931 v I, A (2)

McDougall, J. (Airdrieonians), 1926 v Ni (1)

McDougall, J. (Vale of Leven), 1877 v E, W; 1878 v E; 1879 v E, W (5)

McFadyen, W. (Motherwell), 1934 v A, W (2)

Macfarlane, A. (Dundee), 1904 v W; 1906 v W; 1908 v W; 1909 v Ni; 1911 v W (5)

Macfarlane, W. (Hearts), 1947 v L (1)

McFarlane, R. (Greenock Morton), 1896 v W (1)

McGarr, E. (Aberdeen), 1970 v Ei, A (2)

McGarvey, F. P. (Liverpool), 1979 v Ni (sub), Arg; (with Celtic), 1984 v U, Bel (sub), EG (sub), Ni, W (7)

McGeoch, A. (Dumbreck), 1876 v E; 1877 v E, W (4)

McGhee, J. (Hibernian), 1886 v W (1)

McGhee, M. (Aberdeen), 1983 v Ca (1+1 sub); 1984 v Ni (sub), E (4)

McGinlay, J. (Bolton W), 1994 v A, Ho; 1995 v Fa, Ru, Gr, Ru, Sm, Fa; 1996 v Se; 1997 v Se, Es (1 + sub), A (sub) (13)

McGonagle, W. (Celtic), 1933 v E; 1934 v A, E, Ni; 1935 v Ni, W (6)

McGrain, D. (Celtic), 1973 v W, Ni, E, Sw, Br; 1974 v Cz (2), WG, W (sub), E, Bel, N, Z, Br, Y; 1975 v Sp, Se, P, W, Ni, E, R; 1976 v D (2), Sw, Ni, W, E; 1977 v Fi, Cz, W (2), Se, Ni, E, Ch, Arg, Br; 1978 v EG, Cz; 1980 v Bel, P, Ni, W, E, Pol, H; 1981 v Se, P, Is, Ni, Is, W (sub), Ni, E; 1982 v Se, Sp, Ho, Ni, E, Nz, USSR (sub) (62)

McGregor, J. C. (Vale of Leven), 1877 v E, W; 1878 v E; 1880 v E (4)

McGrory, J. E. (Kilmarnock), 1965 v Ni, Fi; 1966 v P (3)

McGrory, J. (Celtic), 1928 v Ni; 1931 v E; 1932 v Ni, W; 1933 v E, Ni; 1934 v Ni (7)

McGuire, W. (Beith), 1881 v E, W (2)

McGurk, F. (Birmingham), 1934 v W (1)

McHardy, H. (Rangers), 1885 v Ni (1)

McInally, A. (Aston Villa), 1989 v Cy (sub), Ch; (with Bayern Munich), 1990 v Y (sub), F (sub), Arg, Pol (sub), Ma, Cr (8)

McInally, J. (Dundee U), 1987 v Bel, Br; 1988 v Ma (sub); 1991 v Bul (2); 1992 v US (sub), N (sub), C (sub); 1993 v G, P (10)

McInally, T. B. (Celtic), 1926 v Ni; 1927 v W (2)

McInnes, T. (Cowlairs), 1889 v Ni (1)

McIntosh, W. (Third Lanark), 1905 v Ni (1)

McIntyre, A. (Vale of Leven), 1878 v E; 1882 v E (2)

McIntyre, H. (Rangers), 1880 v W (1)

McIntyre, J. (Rangers), 1884 v W (1)

MacKay, D. (Celtic), 1959 v E, WG, Ho, P; 1960 v E, Pol, A, H, T; 1961 v W, Ni; 1962 v Ni, Cz, U (sub) (14)

Mackay, D. C. (Hearts), 1957 v Sp; 1958 v F; 1959 v W, Ni; (with Tottenham H), 1959 v WG, E; 1960 v W, Ni, A, Pol, H, T; 1961 v W, Ni, E; 1963 v E, A, N; 1964 v Ni, W, N; 1966 v Ni (22)

Mackay, G. (Hearts), 1988 v Bul (sub), L (sub), S.Ar (sub), Ma (4)

McKay, J. (Blackburn R), 1924 v W (1)

McKay, R. (Newcastle U), 1928 v W (1)

McKean, R. (Rangers), 1976 v Sw (sub) (1)

McKenzie, D. (Brentford), 1938 v Ni (1)

Mackenzie, J. A. (Partick T), 1954 v W, E, N, Fi, A, U; 1955 v E, H; 1956 v A (9)

McKeown, M. (Celtic), 1889 v Ni; 1890 v E (2)

McKie, J. (East Stirling), 1898 v W (1)

McKillop, T. R. (Rangers), 1938 v Ho (1)

McKimmie, S. (Aberdeen), 1989 v E, Ch; 1990 v Arg, Eg, Cr (sub), Br; 1991 v R, Sw, Bul, Sm; 1992 v Sw, R, Ni, Fi, US, Ca (sub), N (sub), Ho, G, C; 1993 v P, Es (sub); 1994 v Sw, I, Ho, A, Ho; 1995 v Fi, Fa, Ru, Gr, Ru, Fa; 1996 v Gr, Fi, Se, D, Co, Ho, E (40)

McKinlay, D. (Liverpool), 1922 v W, Ni (2)

McKinlay, T. (Celtic), 1996 v Gr, Fi, D, Co, E, Sw; 1997 v A, La, Se, Es (sub + 1), A, Se, W, Ma, Bl; 1998 v Bl, La (sub), F (sub), US, Br (sub), Mor (sub) (22)

McKinlay, W. (Dundee U), 1994 v Ma, Ho (sub), A, Ho; 1995 v Fa (sub), Ru, Gr, Ru (sub), Sm (sub), J, Ec, Fa; 1996 v Fi (sub), Se (sub); (with Blackburn R), Sm (sub), Aus, D (sub), Ho (sub); 1997 v Se, Es (sub); 1998 v La (sub), F, D, Fi, Co (sub), US, Br (sub); 1999 v Es, Fa (29)

McKinnon, A. (Queen's Park), 1874 v E (1)

McKinnon, R. (Rangers), 1966 v W, E, I (2), Ho, Br; 1967 v W, Ni, E; 1968 v Ni, W, E, Ho; 1969 v D, A, WG, Cy; 1970 v Ni, W, E, Ei, WG, A; 1971 v D, Bel, P, USSR, D (28)

McKinnon, R. (Motherwell), 1994 v Ma; 1995 v J, Fa (3)

MacKinnon, D. (Dumbarton), 1883 v E, W; 1884 v E, W (4)

MacKinnon, W. W. (Queen's Park), 1872 v E; 1873 v E; 1874 v E; 1875 v E; 1876 v E, W; 1877 v E; 1878 v E; 1879 v E (9)

McLaren, A. (St Johnstone), 1929 v N, G, Ho; 1933 v W, Ni (5)

McLaren, A. (Preston NE), 1947 v E, Bel, L; 1948 v W (4)

McLaren, A. (Hearts), 1992 v US, Ca, N; 1993 v I, Ma, G, Es (sub + 1); 1994 v I, Ma, Ho, A; 1995 v Fi, Fa; (with Rangers), Ru, Gr, Ru, Sm, J, Ec, Fa; 1996 v Fi, Se, Sm (24)

McLaren, A. (Kilmarnock), 2001 v Pol (sub) (1)

McLaren, J. (Hibernian), 1888 v W; (with Celtic), 1889 v E; 1890 v E (3)

McLean, A. (Celtic), 1926 v W, Ni; 1927 v W, E (4)

McLean, D. (St Bernards), 1896 v W; 1897 v Ni (2)

McLean, D. (Sheffield W), 1912 v E (1)

McLean, G. (Dundee), 1968 v Ho (1)

McLean, T. (Kilmarnock), 1969 v D, Cy, W; 1970 v Ni, W; 1971 v D (6)

McLeish, A. (Aberdeen), 1980 v P, Ni, W, E, Pol, H; 1981 v Se, Is, Ni, Is, Ni, E; 1982 v Se, Sp, Ni, Br (sub); 1983 v Bel, Sw (sub), W, E, Ca (3); 1984 v U, Bel, EG, Ni, W, E, F; 1985 v Y, Ic, Sp (2), W, E, Ic; 1986 v W, EG, Aus (2), E, Ho, D; 1987 v Bel, E, Br; 1988 v Bel, Bul, L, S.Ar (sub), Ma, Sp, Co, E; 1989 v N, Y, I, Cy, F, Cy, E, Ch; 1990 v Y, F, N, Arg, EG, Eg, Cr, Se, Br; 1991 v R, Sw, USSR, Bul; 1993 v Ma (77)

McLeod, D. (Celtic), 1905 v Ni; 1906 v E, W, Ni (4)

McLeod, J. (Dumbarton), 1888 v Ni; 1889 v W; 1890 v Ni; 1892 v E; 1893 v W (5)

MacLeod, J. M. (Hibernian), 1961 v E, Ei (2), Cz (4)

MacLeod, M. (Celtic), 1985 v E (sub); 1987 v Ei, L, E, Br; (with Borussia Dortmund), 1988 v Co, E; 1989 v I, Ch; 1990 v Y, F, N (sub), Arg, EG, Pol, Se Br; (with Hibernian) 1991 v R, Sw, USSR (sub) (20)

McLeod, W. (Cowlairs), 1886 v Ni (1)

McLintock, A. (Vale of Leven), 1875 v E; 1876 v E; 1880 v E (3)

McLintock, F. (Leicester C), 1963 v N (sub), Ei, Sp; (with Arsenal), 1965 v Ni; 1967 v USSR; 1970 v Ni; 1971 v W, Ni, E (9)

McLuckie, J. S. (Manchester C), 1934 v W (1)

McMahon, A. (Celtic), 1892 v E; 1893 v E, Ni; 1894 v E; 1901 v Ni; 1902 v W (6)

McMenemy, J. (Celtic), 1905 v Ni; 1909 v Ni; 1910 v E, W; 1911 v Ni, W, E; 1912 v W; 1914 v W, Ni, E; 1920 v Ni (12)

McMenemy, J. (Motherwell), 1934 v W (1)

McMillan, I. L. (Airdrieonians), 1952 v E, USA, D; 1955 v E; 1956 v E; (with Rangers), 1961 v Cz (6)

McMillan, J. (St Bernards), 1897 v W (1)

McMillan, T. (Dumbarton), 1887 v Ni (1)

McMullan, J. (Partick T), 1920 v W; 1921 v W, Ni, E; 1924 v E, Ni; 1925 v E; 1926 v W; (with Manchester C), 1926 v E; 1927 v E, W; 1928 v E, W; 1929 v E, W, Ni (16)

McNab, A. (Morton), 1921 v E, Ni (2)

McNab, A. (Sunderland), 1937 v A; (with WBA), 1939 v E (2)

McNab, C. D. (Dundee), 1931 v E, W, A, I, Sw; 1932 v E (6)

McNab, J. S. (Liverpool), 1923 v W (1)

McNair, A. (Celtic), 1906 v W; 1907 v Ni; 1908 v E, W; 1909 v E; 1910 v W; 1912 v E, W, Ni; 1913 v E; 1914 v E, Ni; 1920 v E, W, Ni (15)

McNamara, J. (Celtic), 1997 v La (sub), Se, Es, W (sub); 1998 v D, Co, US (sub), N (sub), Mor; 2000 v Ho; 2001 v Sm (11)

McNaught, W. (Raith R), 1951 v A, W, Ni; 1952 v E; 1955 v Ni (5)

McNiel, H. (Queen's Park), 1874 v E; 1875 v E; 1876 v E, W; 1877 v W; 1878 v E; 1879 v E, W; 1881 v E, W (10)

McNiel, M. (Rangers), 1876 v W; 1880 v E (2)

McNeill, W. (Celtic), 1961 v E, Ei (2), Cz; 1962 v Ni, E, Cz, U; 1963 v Ei, Sp; 1964 v W, E, WG; 1965 v E, Fi, Pol, Sp; 1966 v Ni, Pol; 1967 v USSR; 1968 v E; 1969 v Cy, W, E, Cy (sub); 1970 v WG; 1972 v Ni, W, E (29)

McPhail, J. (Celtic), 1950 v W; 1951 v W, Ni, A; 1954 v Ni (5)

McPhail, R. (Airdrieonians), 1927 v E; (with Rangers), 1929 v W; 1931 v E, Ni; 1932 v W, Ni, F; 1933 v E, Ni; 1934 v A, Ni; 1935 v E; 1937 v G, E, Cz; 1938 v W, Ni (17)

McPherson, D. (Kilmarnock), 1892 v Ni (1)

McPherson, D. (Hearts), 1989 v Cy, E; 1990 v N, Ma, Cr, Se, Br; 1991 v Sw, Bul (2), USSR (sub), Sm; 1992 v Sw, R, Sm, Ni, Fi, US, Ca, N, Ho, G, C; (with Rangers), 1993 v Sw, I, Ma, P (27)

McPherson, J. (Clydesdale), 1875 v E (1)

McPherson, J. (Vale of Leven), 1879 v E, W; 1880 v E; 1881 v W; 1883 v E, W; 1884 v E; 1885 v Ni (8)

McPherson, J. (Kilmarnock), 1888 v W; (with Cowlairs), 1889 v E; 1890 v Ni, E; (with Rangers), 1892 v W; 1894 v E; 1895 v E, Ni; 1897 v Ni (9)

McPherson, J. (Hearts), 1891 v E (1)

McPherson, R. (Arthurlie), 1882 v E (1)

McQueen, G. (Leeds U), 1974 v Bel; 1975 v Sp (2), P, W, Ni, E, R; 1976 v D; 1977 v Cz, W (2), Ni, E; 1978 v EG, Cz, W; (with Manchester U), Bul, Ni, W; 1979 v A, N, P, Ni, E, N; 1980 v Pe, A, Bel; 1981 v W (30)

McQueen, M. (Leith Ath), 1890 v W; 1891 v W (2)

McRorie, D. M. (Morton), 1931 v W (1)

McSpadyen, A. (Partick T), 1939 v E, H (2)

McStay, P. (Celtic), 1984 v U, Bel, EG, Ni, W, E (sub); 1985 v Y, Ic, Sp (2), W; 1986 v EG (sub), Aus, Is, U; 1987 v Bul, Ei (1+1 sub), L (sub), Bel, E, Br; 1988 v H, Bel, Bul, L, S.Ar, Sp, Co, E; 1989 v N, Y, I, Cy, F, Cy, E, Ch; 1990 v Y, F, N, Arg, EG (sub), Eg, Pol (sub), Ma, Cr, Se (sub), Br; 1991 v R, USSR, Bul; 1992 v Sm, Fi, US, Ca, N, Ho, G, C; 1993 v Sw, P, I, Ma, P, Es (2); 1994 v I (sub), Ho; 1995 v Fi, Fa, Ru; 1996 v Aus; 1997 v Es (2), A (sub) (76)

McStay, W. (Celtic), 1921 v W, Ni; 1925 v E, Ni, W; 1926 v E, Ni, W; 1927 v E, Ni, W; 1928 v W, Ni (13)

McSwegan, G. (Hearts), 2000 v Bos (sub), Li (2)

McTavish, J. (Falkirk), 1910 v Ni (1)

McWattie, G. C. (Queen's Park), 1901 v W, Ni (2)

McWilliam, P. (Newcastle U), 1905 v E; 1906 v E; 1907 v E, W; 1909 v E, W; 1910 v E; 1911 v W (8)

Macari, L. (Celtic), 1972 v W (sub), E, Y, Cz, Br; 1973 v D; (with Manchester U), E (2), W (sub), Ni (sub); 1975 v Se, P (sub), W, E (sub), R; 1977 v Ni (sub), E (sub), Ch, Arg; 1978 v EG, W, Bul, Pe (sub), Ir (24)

Macauley, A. R. (Brentford), 1947 v E; (with Arsenal), 1948 v E, W, Ni, Bel, Sw, F (7)

Madden, J. (Celtic), 1893 v W; 1895 v W (2)

Main, F. R. (Rangers), 1938 v W (1)

Main, J. (Hibernian), 1909 v Ni (1)

Maley, W. (Celtic), 1893 v E, Ni (2)

Malpas, M. (Dundee U), 1984 v F; 1985 v E, Ic; 1986 v W, Aus (2), Is, R, E, Ho, D, WG; 1987 v Bul, Ei, Bel; 1988 v Bel, Bul, L, S.Ar, Ma; 1989 v N, Y, I, Cy, F, Cy, E, Ch; 1990 v Y, F, N, Eg, Pol, Ma, Cr, Se, Br; 1991 v R, Bul (2), USSR, Sm; 1992 v Sw, R, Sm, Ni, Fi, US, Ca (sub), N, Ho, G; 1993 v Sw, P, I (55)

Marshall, G. (Celtic), 1992 v US (1)

Marshall, H. (Celtic), 1899 v W; 1900 v Ni (2)

Marshall, J. (Middlesbrough), 1921 v E, W, Ni; 1922 v E, W, Ni; (with Llanelly), 1924 v W (7)

Marshall, J. (Third Lanark), 1885 v Ni; 1886 v W; 1887 v E, W (4)

Marshall, J. (Rangers), 1932 v E; 1933 v E; 1934 v E (3)

Marshall, R. W. (Rangers), 1892 v Ni; 1894 v Ni (2)

Martin, B. (Motherwell), 1995 v J, Ec (2)

Martin, F. (Aberdeen), 1954 v N (2), A, U; 1955 v E, H (6)

Martin, N. (Hibernian), 1965 v Fi, Pol; (with Sunderland), 1966 v I (3)

Martis, J. (Motherwell), 1961 v W (1)

Mason, J. (Third Lanark), 1949 v E, W, Ni; 1950 v Ni; 1951 v Ni, Bel, A (7)

Massie, A. (Hearts), 1932 v Ni, W, F; 1933 v Ni; 1934 v E, Ni; 1935 v E, Ni, W; 1936 v W, Ni; (with Aston Villa), 1936 v E; 1937 v G, E, W, Ni, A; 1938 v W (18)

Masson, D. S. (QPR), 1976 v Ni, W, E; 1977 v Fi, Cz, W, Ni, E, Ch, Arg, Br; 1978 v EG, Cz, W; (with Derby Co), Ni, E, Pe (17)

Mathers, D. (Partick T), 1954 v Fi (1)

Matteo, D. (Leeds U), 2001 v Aus, Bel, Sm (3)

Maxwell, W. S. (Stoke C), 1898 v E (1)

May, J. (Rangers), 1906 v W, Ni; 1908 v E, Ni; 1909 v W (5)

Meechan, P. (Celtic), 1896 v Ni (1)

Meiklejohn, D. D. (Rangers), 1922 v W; 1924 v W; 1925 v W, Ni, E; 1928 v W, Ni; 1929 v E, Ni; 1930 v E, Ni; 1931 v E; 1932 v W, Ni; 1934 v A (15)

Menzies, A. (Hearts), 1906 v E (1)

Mercer, R. (Hearts), 1912 v W; 1913 v Ni (2)

Middleton, R. (Cowdenbeath), 1930 v Ni (1)

Millar, A. (Hearts), 1939 v W (1)

Millar, J. (Rangers), 1897 v E; 1898 v E, W (3)

Millar, J. (Rangers), 1963 v A, Ei (2)

Miller, C. (Dundee U), 2001 v Pol (1)

Miller, J. (St Mirren), 1931 v E, I, Sw; 1932 v F; 1934 v E (5)

Miller, K. (Rangers), 2001 v Pol (sub) (1)

Miller, P. (Dumbarton), 1882 v E; 1883 v E, W (3)

Miller, T. (Liverpool), 1920 v E; (with Manchester U), 1921 v E, Ni (3)

Miller, W. (Third Lanark), 1876 v E (1)

Miller, W. (Celtic), 1947 v E, W, Bel, L; 1948 v W, Ni (6)

Miller, W. (Aberdeen), 1975 v R; 1978 v Bul; 1980 v Bel, W, E, Pol, H; 1981 v Se, P, Is (sub), Ni, W, Ni, E; 1982 v Ni, P, Ho, Br, USSR; 1983 v EG, Sw (2), W, E, Ca (3); 1984 v U, Bel, EG, W, E, F; 1985 v Y, Ic, Sp (2), W, E, Ic; 1986 v W, EG, Aus (2), Is, R, E, Ho, D, WG, U; 1987 v Bul, E, Br; 1988 v H, L, S.Ar, Ma, Sp, Co, E; 1989 v N, Y; 1990 v Y, N (65)

Mills, W. (Aberdeen), 1936 v W, Ni; 1937 v W (3)

Milne, J. V. (Middlesbrough), 1938 v E; 1939 v E (2)

Mitchell, D. (Rangers), 1890 v Ni; 1892 v E; 1893 v E, Ni; 1894 v E (5)

Mitchell, J. (Kilmarnock), 1908 v Ni; 1910 v Ni, W (3)

Mitchell, R. C. (Newcastle U), 1951 v D, F (2)

Mochan, N. (Celtic), 1954 v N, A, U (3)

Moir, W. (Bolton W), 1950 v E (1)

Moncur, R. (Newcastle U), 1968 v Ho; 1970 v Ni, W, E, Ei; 1971 v D, Bel, W, P, Ni, E, D; 1972 v Pe, Ni, W, E (16)

Morgan, H. (St Mirren), 1898 v W; (with Liverpool), 1899 v E (2)

Morgan, W. (Burnley), 1968 v Ni; (with Manchester U), 1972 v Pe, Y, Cz, Br; 1973 v D (2), E (2), W, Ni, Sw, Br; 1974 v Cz (2), WG (2), Ni, Bel (sub), Br, Y (21)

Morris, D. (Raith R), 1923 v Ni; 1924 v E, Ni; 1925 v E, W, Ni (6)

Morris, H. (East Fife), 1950 v Ni (1)

Morrison, T. (St Mirren), 1927 v E (1)

Morton, A. L. (Queen's Park), 1920 v W, Ni; (with Rangers), 1921 v E; 1922 v E, W; 1923 v E, W, Ni; 1924 v E, W, Ni; 1925 v E, W, Ni; 1927 v E, Ni; 1928 v E, W, Ni; 1929 v E, W, Ni; 1930 v E, W, Ni; 1931 v E, W, Ni; 1932 v E, W, F (31)

Morton, H. A. (Kilmarnock), 1929 v G, Ho (2)

Mudie, J. K. (Blackpool), 1957 v W, Ni, E, Y, Sw, Sp (2), WG; 1958 v Ni, E, W, Sw, H, Pol, Y, Par, F (17)

Muir, W. (Dundee), 1907 v Ni (1)

Muirhead, T. A. (Rangers), 1922 v Ni; 1923 v E; 1924 v W; 1927 v Ni; 1928 v Ni; 1929 v W, Ni; 1930 v W (8)

Mulhall, G. (Aberdeen), 1960 v Ni; (with Sunderland), 1963 v Ni; 1964 v Ni (3)

Munro, A. D. (Hearts), 1937 v W, Ni; (with Blackpool), 1938 v Ho (3)

Munro, F. M. (Wolverhampton W), 1971 v Ni (sub), E (sub), D, USSR; 1975 v Se, W (sub), Ni, E, R (9)

Munro, I. (St Mirren), 1979 v Arg, N; 1980 v Pe, A, Bel, W, E (7)

Munro, N. (Abercorn), 1888 v W; 1889 v E (2)

Murdoch, J. (Motherwell), 1931 v Ni (1)

Murdoch, R. (Celtic), 1966 v W, E, I (2); 1967 v Ni; 1968 v Ni; 1969 v W, Ni, E, WG, Cy; 1970 v A (12)

Murphy, F. (Celtic), 1938 v Ho (1)

Murray, J. (Renton), 1895 v W (1)

Murray, J. (Hearts), 1958 v E, H, Pol, Y, F (5)

Murray, J. W. (Vale of Leven), 1890 v W (1)

Murray, P. (Hibernian), 1896 v Ni; 1897 v W (2)

Murray, S. (Aberdeen), 1972 v Bel (1)

Mutch, G. (Preston NE), 1938 v E (1)

Napier, C. E. (Celtic), 1932 v E; 1935 v E, W; (with Derby Co), 1937 v Ni, A (5)

Narey, D. (Dundee U), 1977 v Se (sub); 1979 v P, Ni (sub), Arg; 1980 v P, Ni, Pol, H; 1981 v W, E (sub); 1982 v Ho, W, E, Nz (sub), Br, USSR; 1983 v EG, Sw, Bel, Ni, W, E, Ca (3); 1986 v Is, R, Ho, WG, U; 1987 v Bul, E, Bel; 1989 v I, Cy (35)

Naysmith, G. A. (Hearts), 2000 v Ei; 2001 v La (sub), Sm, Cro (4)

Neil, R. G. (Hibernian), 1896 v W; (with Rangers), 1900 v W (2)

Neill, R. W. (Queen's Park), 1876 v W; 1877 v E, W; 1878 v W; 1880 v E (5)

Nellies, P. (Hearts), 1913 v Ni; 1914 v W (2)

Nelson, J. (Cardiff C), 1925 v W, Ni; 1928 v E; 1930 v F (4)

Nevin, P. K. F. (Chelsea), 1986 v R (sub), E (sub); 1987 v L, Ei, Bel (sub); 1988 v L; (with Everton), 1989 v Cy, E; 1991 v R (sub), Bul (sub), Sm (sub); 1992 v US, G (sub), C (sub); (with Tranmere R), 1993 v Ma, P (sub), Es; 1994 v Sw, Ma, Ho, A (sub), Ho; 1995 v Fa, Ru (sub), Sm; 1996 v Se (sub), Sm, Aus (sub) (28)

Niblo, T. D. (Aston Villa), 1904 v E (1)

Nibloe, J. (Kilmarnock), 1929 v E, N, Ho; 1930 v W; 1931 v E, Ni, A, I, Sw; 1932 v E, F (11)

Nicholas, C. (Celtic), 1983 v Sw, Ni, E, Ca (3); (with Arsenal), 1984 v Bel, F (sub); 1985 v Y (sub), Ic (sub), Sp (sub), W (sub); 1986 v Is, R (sub), E, D, U (sub); 1987 v Bul, E (sub); (with Aberdeen), 1989 v Cy (sub) (20)

Nicholson, B. (Dunfermline Ath), 2001 v Pol (1)

Nicol, S. (Liverpool), 1985 v Y, Ic, Sp, W; 1986 v W, EG, Aus, E, D, WG, U; 1988 v H, Bul, S.Ar, Sp, Co, E; 1989 v N, Y, Cy, F; 1990 v Y, F; 1991 v Sw, USSR, Sm; 1992 v Sw (27)

Nisbet, J. (Ayr U), 1929 v N, G, Ho (3)

Niven, J. B. (Moffatt), 1885 v Ni (1)

O'Donnell, F. (Preston NE), 1937 v E, A, Cz; 1938 v W; (with Blackpool), E, Ho (6)

O'Donnell, P. (Motherwell), 1994 v Sw (sub) (1)

Ogilvie, D. H. (Motherwell), 1934 v A (1)

O'Hare, J. (Derby Co), 1970 v W, Ni, E; 1971 v D, Bel, W, Ni; 1972 v P, Bel, Ho (sub), Pe, Ni, W (13)

O'Neil, B. (Celtic), 1996 v Aus; (with Wolfsburg), 1999 v G (sub); 2000 v Li, Ho (sub), Ei; (with Derby Co), 2001 v Aus (6)

O'Neil, J. (Hibernian), 2001 v Pol (1)

Ormond, W. E. (Hibernian), 1954 v E, N, Fi, A, U; 1959 v E (6)

O'Rourke, F. (Airdrieonians), 1907 v Ni (1)

Orr, J. (Kilmarnock), 1892 v W (1)

Orr, R. (Newcastle U), 1902 v E; 1904 v E (2)

Orr, T. (Morton), 1952 v Ni, W (2)

Orr, W. (Celtic), 1900 v Ni; 1903 v Ni; 1904 v W (3)

Orrock, R. (Falkirk), 1913 v W (1)

Oswald, J. (Third Lanark), 1889 v E; (with St Bernards), 1895 v E; (with Rangers), 1897 v W (3)

Parker, A. H. (Falkirk), 1955 v P, Y, A; 1956 v E, Ni, W, A; 1957 v Ni, W, Y; 1958 v Ni, W, E, Sw; (with Everton), Par (15)

Parlane, D. (Rangers), 1973 v W, Sw, Br; 1975 v Sp (sub), Se, P, W, Ni, E, R; 1976 v D (sub); 1977 v W (12)

Parlane, R. (Vale of Leven), 1878 v W; 1879 v E, W (3)

Paterson, G. D. (Celtic), 1939 v Ni (1)

Paterson, J. (Leicester C), 1920 v E (1)

Paterson, J. (Cowdenbeath), 1931 v A, I, Sw (3)

Paton, A. (Motherwell), 1952 v D, Se (2)

Paton, D. (St Bernards), 1896 v W (1)

Paton, M. (Dumbarton), 1883 v E; 1884 v W; 1885 v W, E; 1886 v E (5)

Paton, R. (Vale of Leven), 1879 v E, W (2)

Patrick, J. (St Mirren), 1897 v E, W (2)

Paul, H. McD. (Queen's Park), 1909 v E, W, Ni (3)

Paul, J. (Partick T), 1888 v W; 1889 v W; 1890 v W (3)

Paul, W. (Dykebar), 1891 v Ni (1)

Pearson, T. (Newcastle U), 1947 v E, Bel (2)

Penman, A. (Dundee), 1966 v Ho (1)

Pettigrew, W. (Motherwell), 1976 v Sw, Ni, W; 1977 v W (sub), Se (5)

Phillips, J. (Queen's Park), 1877 v E, W; 1878 v W (3)

Plenderleith, J. B. (Manchester C), 1961 v Ni (1)

Porteous, W. (Hearts), 1903 v Ni (1)

Pressley, S. J. (Hearts), 2000 v F (sub), Ei (sub) (2)

Pringle, C. (St Mirren), 1921 v W (1)

Provan, D. (Rangers), 1964 v Ni, N; 1966 v I (2), Ho (5)

Provan, D. (Celtic), 1980 v Bel (2 sub), P (sub), Ni (sub); 1981 v Is, W, E; 1982 v Se, P, Ni (10)

Pursell, P. (Queen's Park), 1914 v W (1)

Quinn, J. (Celtic), 1905 v Ni; 1906 v Ni, W; 1908 v Ni, E; 1909 v E; 1910 v E, Ni, W; 1912 v E, W (11)

Quinn, P. (Motherwell), 1961 v E, Ei (2); 1962 v U (4)

Rae, G. (Dundee), 2001 v Pol (1)

Rae, J. (Third Lanark), 1889 v W; 1890 v Ni (2)

Raeside, J. S. (Third Lanark), 1906 v W (1)
Raisbeck, A. G. (Liverpool), 1900 v E; 1901 v E; 1902 v E; 1903 v E, W; 1904 v E; 1906 v E; 1907 v E (8)
Rankin, G. (Vale of Leven), 1890 v Ni; 1891 v E (2)
Rankin, R. (St Mirren), 1929 v N, G, Ho (3)
Redpath, W. (Motherwell), 1949 v W, Ni; 1951 v E, D, F, Bel, A; 1952 v Ni, E (9)
Reid, J. G. (Airdrieonians), 1914 v W; 1920 v W; 1924 v Ni (3)
Reid, R. (Brentford), 1938 v E, Ni (2)
Reid, W. (Rangers), 1911 v E, W, Ni; 1912 v Ni; 1913 v E, W, Ni; 1914 v E, Ni (9)
Reilly, L. (Hibernian), 1949 v E, W, F; 1950 v W, Ni, Sw, F; 1951 v W, E, D, F, Bel, A; 1952 v Ni, W, E, USA, D, Se; 1953 v Ni, W, E, Se; 1954 v W; 1955 v H (2), P, Y, A, E; 1956 v E, W, Ni, A; 1957 v E, Ni, W, Y (38)
Rennie, H. G. (Hearts), 1900 v E, Ni; (with Hibernian), 1901 v E; 1902 v E, Ni, W; 1903 v Ni, W; 1904 v Ni; 1905 v W; 1906 v Ni; 1908 v Ni, W (13)
Renny-Tailyour, H. W. (Royal Engineers), 1873 v E (1)
Rhind, A. (Queen's Park), 1872 v E (1)
Richmond, A. (Queen's Park), 1906 v W (1)
Richmond, J. T. (Clydesdale), 1877 v E; (with Queen's Park), 1878 v E; 1882 v W (3)
Ring, T. (Clyde), 1953 v Se; 1955 v W, Ni, E, H; 1957 v E, Sp (2), Sw, WG; 1958 v Ni, Sw (12)
Rioch, B. D. (Derby Co), 1975 v P, W, Ni, E, R; 1976 v D (2), R, Ni, W, E; 1977 v Fi, Cz, W; (with Everton), W, Ni, E, Ch, Br; 1978 v Cz; (with Derby Co), Ni, E, Pe, Ho (24)
Ritchie, A. (East Stirlingshire), 1891 v W (1)
Ritchie, H. (Hibernian), 1923 v W; 1928 v Ni (2)
Ritchie, J. (Queen's Park), 1897 v W (1)
Ritchie, P. S. (Hearts), 1999 v G (sub), CzR; 2000 v Li, E; (with Bolton W), F, Ho (6)
Ritchie, W. (Rangers), 1962 v U (sub) (1)
Robb, D. T. (Aberdeen), 1971 v W, E, P, D (sub), USSR (5)
Robb, W. (Rangers), 1926 v W; (with Hibernian), 1928 v W (2)
Robertson, A. (Clyde), 1955 v P, A, H; 1958 v Sw, Par (5)
Robertson, D. (Rangers), 1992 v Ni; 1994 v Sw, Ho (3)
Robertson, G. (Motherwell), 1910 v W; (with Sheffield W), 1912 v W; 1913 v E, Ni (4)
Robertson, G. (Kilmarnock), 1938 v Cz (1)
Robertson, H. (Dundee), 1962 v Cz (1)
Robertson, J. (Dundee), 1931 v A, I (2)
Robertson, J. (Hearts), 1991 v R, Sw, Bul (sub), Sm (sub); 1992 v Sm, Ni (sub), Fi; 1993 v I (sub), Ma (sub), G, Es; 1995 v J (sub), Ec, Fa (sub); 1996 v Gr (sub), Se (16)
Robertson, J. N. (Nottingham F), 1978 v Ni, W (sub), Ir; 1979 v P, N; 1980 v Pe, A, Bel (2), P; 1981 v Se, P, Is, Ni, Is, Ni, E; 1982 v Se, Ni (2), E (sub), Nz, Br, USSR; 1983 v EG, Sw; (with Derby Co), 1984 v U, Bel (28)
Robertson, J. G. (Tottenham H), 1965 v W (1)
Robertson, J. T. (Everton), 1898 v E; (with Southampton), 1899 v E; (with Rangers), 1900 v E, W; 1901 v W, Ni, E; 1902 v W, Ni, E; 1903 v E, W; 1904 v E, W, Ni; 1905 v W (16)
Robertson, P. (Dundee), 1903 v Ni (1)
Robertson, T. (Queen's Park), 1889 v Ni; 1890 v E; 1891 v W; 1892 v Ni (4)
Robertson, T. (Hearts), 1898 v Ni (1)
Robertson, W. (Dumbarton), 1887 v E, W (2)
Robinson, R. (Dundee), 1974 v WG (sub); 1975 v Se, Ni, R (sub) (4)
Rough, A. (Partick T), 1976 v Sw, Ni, W, E; 1977 v Fi, Cz, W (2), Se, Ni, E, Ch, Arg, Br; 1978 v Cz, W, Ni, E, Pe, Ir, Ho; 1979 v A, P, W, Arg, N; 1980 v Pe, A, Bel (2), P, W, E, Pol, H; 1981 v Se, P, Is, Ni, Is, W, E; 1982 v Se, Ni, Sp, Ho, W, E, Nz, Br, USSR; (with Hibernian), 1986 v W (sub), E (53)
Rougvie, D. (Aberdeen), 1984 v Ni (1)
Rowan, A. (Caledonian), 1880 v E; (with Queen's Park), 1882 v W (2)
Russell, D. (Hearts), 1895 v E, Ni; (with Celtic), 1897 v W; 1898 v Ni; 1901 v W, Ni (6)
Russell, J. (Cambuslang), 1890 v Ni (1)
Russell, W. F. (Airdrieonians), 1924 v W; 1925 v E (2)
Rutherford, E. (Rangers), 1948 v F (1)

St John, I. (Motherwell), 1959 v WG; 1960 v E, Ni, W, Pol, A; 1961 v E; (with Liverpool), 1962 v Ni, W, E, Cz (2), U; 1963 v W, Ni, E, N, Ei (sub), Sp; 1964 v Ni; 1965 v E (21)
Sawers, W. (Dundee), 1895 v W (1)
Scarff, P. (Celtic), 1931 v Ni (1)
Schaedler, E. (Hibernian), 1974 v WG (1)
Scott, A. S. (Rangers), 1957 v Ni, Y, WG; 1958 v W, Sw; 1959 v P; 1962 v Ni, W, E, Cz, U; (with Everton), 1964 v W, N; 1965 v Fi; 1966 v P, Br (16)
Scott, J. (Hibernian), 1966 v Ho (1)

Scott, J. (Dundee), 1971 v D (sub), USSR (2)
Scott, M. (Airdrieonians), 1898 v W (1)
Scott, R. (Airdrieonians), 1894 v Ni (1)
Scoular, J. (Portsmouth), 1951 v D, F, A; 1952 v E, USA, D, Se; 1953 v W, Ni (9)
Sellar, W. (Battlefield), 1885 v E; 1886 v E; 1887 v E, W; 1888 v E; (with Queen's Park), 1891 v E; 1892 v E; 1893 v E, Ni (9)
Semple, W. (Cambuslang), 1886 v W (1)
Shankly, W. (Preston NE), 1938 v E; 1939 v E, W, Ni, H (5)
Sharp, G. M. (Everton), 1985 v Ic; 1986 v W, Aus (2 sub), Is, R, U; 1987 v Ei; 1988 v Bel (sub), Bul, L, Ma (12)
Sharp, J. (Dundee), 1904 v W; (with Woolwich Arsenal), 1907 v W, E; 1908 v E; (with Fulham), 1909 v W (5)
Shaw, D. (Hibernian), 1947 v W, Ni; 1948 v E, Bel, Sw, F; 1949 v W, Ni (8)
Shaw, F. W. (Pollokshields Ath), 1884 v E, W (2)
Shaw, J. (Rangers), 1947 v E, Bel, L; 1948 v Ni (4)
Shearer, D. (Aberdeen), 1994 v A (sub), Ho (sub); 1995 v Fi, Ru (sub), Sm, Fa; 1996 v Gr (7)
Shearer, R. (Rangers), 1961 v E, Ei (2), Cz (4)
Sillars, D. C. (Queen's Park), 1891 v Ni; 1892 v E; 1893 v W; 1894 v E; 1895 v W (5)
Simpson, J. (Third Lanark), 1895 v E, W, Ni (3)
Simpson, J. (Rangers), 1935 v E, W, Ni; 1936 v E, W, Ni; 1937 v G, E, W, Ni, A, Cz; 1938 v W, Ni (14)
Simpson, N. (Aberdeen), 1983 v Ni; 1984 v U (sub), F (sub); 1987 v E; 1988 v E (5)
Simpson, R. C. (Celtic), 1967 v E, USSR; 1968 v Ni, E; 1969 v A (5)
Sinclair, G. L. (Hearts), 1910 v Ni; 1912 v W, Ni (3)
Sinclair, J. W. E. (Leicester C), 1966 v P (1)
Skene, L. H. (Queen's Park), 1904 v W (1)
Sloan, T. (Third Lanark), 1904 v W (1)
Smellie, R. (Queen's Park), 1887 v Ni; 1888 v W; 1889 v E; 1891 v E; 1893 v E, Ni (6)
Smith, A. (Rangers), 1898 v E; 1900 v E, Ni, W; 1901 v E, Ni, W; 1902 v E, Ni, W; 1903 v E, Ni, W; 1904 v Ni; 1905 v W; 1906 v E, Ni; 1907 v W; 1911 v E, Ni (20)
Smith, D. (Aberdeen), 1966 v Ho; (with Rangers), 1968 v Ho (2)
Smith, G. (Hibernian), 1947 v E, Ni; 1948 v W, Bel, Sw, F; 1952 v E, USA; 1955 v P, Y, A, H; 1956 v E, Ni, W; 1957 v Sp (2), Sw (18)
Smith, H. G. (Hearts), 1988 v S.Ar (sub); 1992 v Ni, Ca (3)
Smith, J. (Rangers), 1935 v Ni; 1938 v Ni (2)
Smith, J. (Ayr U), 1924 v E (1)
Smith, J. (Aberdeen), 1968 v Ho (sub); (with Newcastle U), 1974 v WG, Ni (sub), W (sub) (4)
Smith, J. E. (Celtic), 1959 v H, P (2)
Smith, Jas (Queen's Park), 1872 v E (1)
Smith, John (Mauchline), 1877 v E, W; 1879 v E, W; (with Edinburgh University), 1880 v E; (with Queen's Park), 1881 v W, E; 1883 v E, W; 1884 v E (10)
Smith, N. (Rangers), 1897 v E; 1898 v W; 1899 v E, W, Ni; 1900 v E, W, Ni; 1901 v Ni, W; 1902 v E, Ni (12)
Smith, R. (Queen's Park), 1872 v E; 1873 v E (2)
Smith, T. M. (Kilmarnock), 1934 v E; (with Preston NE), 1938 v E (2)
Somers, P. (Celtic), 1905 v E, Ni; 1907 v Ni; 1909 v W (4)
Somers, W. S. (Third Lanark), 1879 v E, W; (with Queen's Park), 1880 v W (3)
Somerville, G. (Queen's Park), 1886 v E (1)
Souness, G. J. (Middlesbrough), 1975 v EG, Sp, Se; (with Liverpool), 1978 v Bul, W, E (sub), Ho; 1979 v A, N, W, Ni, E; 1980 v Pe, A, Bel, P, Ni; 1981 v P, Is (2); 1982 v Ni, P, Sp, W, E, Nz, Br, USSR; 1983 v EG, Sw, Bel, Sw, W, E, Ca (2 + 1 sub); 1984 v U, Ni, W; (with Sampdoria), 1985 v Y, Ic, Sp (2), W, E, Ic; 1986 v EG, Aus (2), R, E, D, WG (54)
Speedie, D. R. (Chelsea), 1985 v E; 1986 v W, EG (sub), Aus, E; (with Coventry C), 1989 v Y (sub), I (sub), Cy (1+1 sub), Ch (10)
Speedie, F. (Rangers), 1903 v E, W, Ni (3)
Speirs, J. H. (Rangers), 1908 v W (1)
Spencer, J. (Chelsea), 1995 v Ru (sub), Gr (sub), Sm (sub), J; 1996 v Fi, Aus, D, US (sub), Co, Ho (sub), E, Sw (sub); 1997 v La; (with QPR), W (sub) (14)
Stanton, P. (Hibernian), 1966 v Ho; 1969 v Ni; 1970 v Ei, A; 1971 v D, Bel, P, USSR, D; 1972 v P, Bel, Ho, W; 1973 v W, Ni; 1974 v WG (16)
Stark, J. (Rangers), 1909 v E, Ni (2)
Steel, W. (Morton), 1947 v E, Bel, L; (with Derby Co), 1948 v F, E, W, Ni; 1949 v E, W, Ni, F; 1950 v E, W, Ni, Sw, P, F; (with Dundee), 1951 v W, Ni, E, A (2), D, F, Bel; 1952 v W; 1953 v W, E, Ni, Se (30)
Steele, D. M. (Huddersfield), 1923 v E, W, Ni (3)

Stein, C. (Rangers), 1969 v W, Ni, D, E, Cy (2); 1970 v A (sub), Ni (sub), W, E, Ei, WG; 1971 v D, USSR, Bel, D; 1972 v Cz (sub); (with Coventry C), 1973 v E (2 sub), W (sub), Ni (21)

Stephen, J. F. (Bradford), 1947 v W; 1948 v W (2)

Stevenson, G. (Motherwell), 1928 v W, Ni; 1930 v Ni, E, F; 1931 v E, W; 1932 v W, Ni; 1933 v Ni; 1934 v E; 1935 v Ni (12)

Stewart, A. (Queen's Park), 1888 v Ni; 1889 v W (2)

Stewart, A. (Third Lanark), 1894 v W (1)

Stewart, D. (Dumbarton), 1888 v Ni (1)

Stewart, D. (Queen's Park), 1893 v W; 1894 v Ni; 1897 v Ni (3)

Stewart, D. S. (Leeds U), 1978 v EG (1)

Stewart, G. (Hibernian), 1906 v W, E; (with Manchester C), 1907 v E, W (4)

Stewart, J. (Kilmarnock), 1977 v Ch (sub); (with Middlesbrough), 1979 v N (2)

Stewart, R. (West Ham U), 1981 v W, Ni, E; 1982 v Ni, P, W; 1984 v F; 1987 v Ei (2), L (10)

Stewart, W. E. (Queen's Park), 1898 v Ni; 1900 v Ni (2)

Storrier, D. (Celtic), 1899 v E, W, Ni (3)

Strachan, G. (Aberdeen), 1980 v Ni, W, E, Pol, H (sub); 1981 v Se, P; 1982 v Ni, P, Sp, Ho (sub), Nz, Br, USSR; 1983 v Sw, Bel, Sw, Ni (sub), W, E, Ca (2 + 1 sub); 1984 v EG, Ni, E, F; (with Manchester U), 1985 v Sp (sub), E, Ic; 1986 v W, Aus, R, D, WG, U; 1987 v Bul, Ei (2); 1988 v H; 1989 v F (sub); (with Leeds U), 1990 v F; 1991 v USSR, Bul, Sm; 1992 v Sw, R, Ni, Fi (50)

Sturrock, P. (Dundee U), 1981 v W (sub), Ni, E (sub); 1982 v P, Ni (sub), W (sub), E (sub); 1983 v EG (sub), Sw, Bel (sub), Ca (3); 1984 v W; 1985 v Y (sub); 1986 v Is (sub), Ho, D, U; 1987 v Bel (20)

Sullivan, N. (Wimbledon), 1997 v W; 1998 v F, Co; 1999 v Fa, CzR, G, Fa, CzR; 2000 v Bos, Es, Bos, E (2), F, Ho, Ei; (with Tottenham H), 2001 v La, Sm, Cro, Bel, Sm, Pol (22)

Summers, W. (St Mirren), 1926 v E (1)

Symon, J. S. (Rangers), 1939 v H (1)

Tait, T. S. (Sunderland), 1911 v W (1)

Taylor, J. (Queen's Park), 1872 v E; 1873 v E; 1874 v E; 1875 v E; 1876 v E, W (6)

Taylor, J. D. (Dumbarton), 1892 v W; 1893 v W; 1894 v Ni; (with St Mirren), 1895 v Ni (4)

Taylor, W. (Hearts), 1892 v E (1)

Telfer, P. N. (Coventry C), 2000 v F (1)

Telfer, W. (Motherwell), 1933 v Ni; 1934 v Ni (2)

Telfer, W. D. (St Mirren), 1954 v W (1)

Templeton, R. (Aston Villa), 1902 v E; (with Newcastle U), 1903 v E, W; 1904 v E; (with Woolwich Arsenal), 1905 v W; (with Kilmarnock), 1908 v Ni; 1910 v E, Ni; 1912 v E, Ni; 1913 v W (11)

Thomson, A. (Arthurlie), 1886 v Ni (1)

Thomson, A. (Third Lanark), 1889 v W (1)

Thomson, A. (Airdrieonians), 1909 v Ni (1)

Thomson, A. (Celtic), 1926 v E; 1932 v F; 1933 v W (3)

Thomson, C. (Hearts), 1904 v Ni; 1905 v E, Ni, W; 1906 v W, Ni; 1907 v E, W, Ni; 1908 v E, W, Ni; (with Sunderland), 1909 v W; 1910 v E; 1911 v Ni; 1912 v E, W; 1913 v E, W; 1914 v E, Ni (21)

Thomson, C. (Sunderland), 1937 v Cz (1)

Thomson, D. (Dundee), 1920 v W (1)

Thomson, J. (Celtic), 1930 v F; 1931 v E, W, Ni (4)

Thomson, J. J. (Queen's Park), 1872 v E; 1873 v E; 1874 v E (3)

Thomson, J. R. (Everton), 1933 v W (1)

Thomson, R. (Celtic), 1932 v W (1)

Thomson, R. W. (Falkirk), 1927 v E (1)

Thomson, S. (Rangers), 1884 v W, Ni (2)

Thomson, W. (Dumbarton), 1892 v W; 1893 v W; 1898 v Ni, W (4)

Thomson, W. (Dundee), 1896 v W (1)

Thornton, W. (Rangers), 1947 v W, Ni; 1948 v E, Ni; 1949 v F; 1952 v D, Se (7)

Thomson, W. (St Mirren), 1980 v Ni; 1981 v Ni (sub+1) 1982 v P; 1983 v Ni, Ca; 1984 v EG (7)

Toner, W. (Kilmarnock), 1959 v W, Ni (2)

Townsley, T. (Falkirk), 1926 v W (1)

Troup, A. (Dundee), 1920 v E; 1921 v W, Ni; 1922 v Ni; (with Everton), 1926 v E (5)

Turnbull, E. (Hibernian), 1948 v Bel, Sw; 1951 v A; 1958 v H, Pol, Y, Par, F (8)

Turner, T. (Arthurlie), 1884 v W (1)

Turner, W. (Pollokshields Ath), 1885 v Ni; 1886 v Ni (2)

Ure, J. F. (Dundee), 1962 v W, Cz; 1963 v W, Ni, E, A, N, Sp; (with Arsenal), 1964 v Ni, N; 1968 v Ni (11)

Urquhart, D. (Hibernian), 1934 v W (1)

Vallance, T. (Rangers), 1877 v E, W; 1878 v E; 1879 v E, W; 1881 v E, W (7)

Venters, A. (Cowdenbeath), 1934 v Ni; (with Rangers), 1936 v E; 1939 v E (3)

Waddell, T. S. (Queen's Park), 1891 v Ni; 1892 v E; 1893 v E, Ni; 1895 v E, Ni (6)

Waddell, W. (Rangers), 1947 v W; 1949 v E, W, Ni, F; 1950 v E, Ni; 1951 v E, D, F, Bel, A; 1952 v Ni, W; 1954 v Ni; 1955 v W, Ni (17)

Wales, H. M. (Motherwell), 1933 v W (1)

Walker, A. (Celtic), 1988 v Co (sub); 1995 v Fi, Fa (sub) (3)

Walker, F. (Third Lanark), 1922 v W (1)

Walker, G. (St Mirren), 1930 v F; 1931 v Ni, A, Sw (4)

Walker, J. (Hearts), 1895 v Ni; 1897 v W; 1898 v Ni; (with Rangers), 1904 v W, Ni (5)

Walker, J. (Swindon T), 1911 v E, W, Ni; 1912 v E, W, Ni; 1913 v E, W, Ni (9)

Walker, J. N. (Hearts), 1993 v G; (with Partick T), 1996 v US (sub) (2)

Walker, R. (Hearts), 1900 v E, Ni; 1901 v E, W; 1902 v E, W, Ni; 1903 v E, W, Ni; 1904 v E, W, Ni; 1905 v E, W, Ni; 1906 v Ni; 1907 v E, Ni; 1908 v E, W, Ni; 1909 v E, W; 1912 v E, W, Ni; 1913 v E, W (29)

Walker, T. (Hearts), 1935 v E, W; 1936 v E, W, Ni; 1937 v G, E, W, Ni, A, Cz; 1938 v E, W, Ni, Cz, Ho; 1939 v E, W, Ni, H (20)

Walker, W. (Clyde), 1909 v Ni; 1910 v Ni (2)

Wallace, I. A. (Coventry C), 1978 v Bul (sub); 1979 v P (sub), W (3)

Wallace, W. S. B. (Hearts), 1965 v Ni; 1966 v E, Ho; (with Celtic), 1967 v E, USSR (sub); 1968 v Ni; 1969 v E (sub) (7)

Wardhaugh, J. (Hearts), 1955 v H; 1957 v Ni (2)

Wark, J. (Ipswich T), 1979 v W, Ni, E, Arg, N (sub); 1980 v Pe, A, Bel (2); 1981 v Is, Ni; 1982 v Se, Sp, Ho, Ni, Nz, Br, USSR; 1983 v EG, Sw (2), Ni, E (sub); 1984 v U, Bel, EG; (with Liverpool), E, F; 1985 v Y (29)

Watson, A. (Queen's Park), 1881 v E, W; 1882 v E (3)

Watson, J. (Sunderland), 1903 v E, W; 1904 v E; 1905 v E; (with Middlesbrough), 1909 v E, Ni (6)

Watson, J. (Motherwell), 1948 v Ni; (with Huddersfield T), 1954 v Ni (2)

Watson, J. A. K. (Rangers), 1878 v W (1)

Watson, P. R. (Blackpool), 1934 v A (1)

Watson, R. (Motherwell), 1971 v USSR (1)

Watson, W. (Falkirk), 1898 v W (1)

Watt, F. (Kilbirnie), 1889 v W, Ni; 1890 v W; 1891 v E (4)

Watt, W. W. (Queen's Park), 1887 v Ni (1)

Waugh, W. (Hearts), 1938 v Cz (1)

Weir, A. (Motherwell), 1959 v WG; 1960 v E, P, A, H, T (6)

Weir, D. G. (Hearts), 1997 v W, Ma (sub); 1998 v F, D (sub), Fi (sub), N (sub), Mor; 1999 v Es, Fa; (with Everton) CzR, G, Fa, CzR; 2000 v Bos, Es, Bos, Li, E (2), Ho; 2001 v La, Sm (sub), Cro, Aus, Bel, Sm, Pol (sub) (27)

Weir, J. (Third Lanark), 1887 v Ni (1)

Weir, J. B. (Queen's Park), 1872 v E; 1874 v E; 1875 v E; 1878 v W (4)

Weir, P. (St Mirren), 1980 v Ni, W, Pol (sub), H; (with Aberdeen), 1983 v Sw; 1984 v Ni (6)

White, John (Albion R), 1922 v W; (with Hearts), 1923 v Ni (2)

White, J. A. (Falkirk), 1959 v WG, Ho, P; 1960 v Ni; (with Tottenham H), 1960 v W, Pol, A, T; 1961 v W; 1962 v Ni, W, E, Cz (2); 1963 v W, Ni, E; 1964 v Ni, W, E, N, WG (22)

White, W. (Bolton W), 1907 v E; 1908 v E (2)

Whitelaw, A. (Vale of Leven), 1887 v Ni; 1890 v W (2)

Whyte, D. (Celtic), 1988 v Bel (sub), L; 1989 v Ch (sub); 1992 v US (sub); (with Middlesbrough), 1993 v P, I; 1995 v J (sub), Ec; 1996 v US; 1997 v La; (with Aberdeen), 1998 v Fi; 1999 v G (sub) (12)

Wilson, A. (Sheffield W), 1907 v E; 1908 v E; 1912 v E; 1913 v E, W; 1914 v Ni (6)

Wilson, A. (Portsmouth), 1954 v Fi (1)

Wilson, A. N. (Dunfermline), 1920 v E, W, Ni; 1921 v E, W, Ni; (with Middlesbrough), 1922 v E, W, Ni; 1923 v E, W, Ni (12)

Wilson, D. (Queen's Park), 1900 v W (1)

Wilson, D. (Oldham Ath), 1913 v E (1)

Wilson, D. (Rangers), 1961 v E, W, Ni, Ei (2), Cz; 1962 v Ni, W, E, Cz, U; 1963 v W, E, A, N, Ei, Sp; 1964 v E, WG; 1965 v Ni, E, Fi (22)

Wilson, G. W. (Hearts), 1904 v W; 1905 v E, Ni; 1906 v W; (with Everton) 1907 v E; (with Newcastle U), 1909 v E (6)

Wilson, Hugh, (Newmilns), 1890 v W; (with Sunderland), 1897 v E; (with Third Lanark), 1902 v W; 1904 v Ni (4)

Wilson, I. A. (Leicester C), 1987 v E, Br; (with Everton), 1988 v Bel, Bul, L (5)

Wilson, J. (Vale of Leven), 1888 v W; 1889 v E; 1890 v E; 1891 v E (4)
Wilson, P. (Celtic), 1926 v Ni; 1930 v F; 1931 v Ni; 1933 v E (4)
Wilson, P. (Celtic), 1975 v Sp (sub) (1)
Wilson, R. P. (Arsenal), 1972 v P, Ho (2)
Winters, R. (Aberdeen), 1999 v G (sub) (1)
Wiseman, W. (Queen's Park), 1927 v W; 1930 v Ni (2)
Wood, G. (Everton), 1979 v Ni, E, Arg (sub); (with Arsenal), 1982 v Ni (4)
Woodburn, W. A. (Rangers), 1947 v E, Bel, L; 1948 v W, Ni; 1949 v E, F; 1950 v E, W, Ni, P, F; 1951 v E, W, Ni, A (2), D, F, Bel; 1952 v E, W, Ni, USA (24)
Wotherspoon, D. N. (Queen's Park), 1872 v E; 1873 v E (2)
Wright, K. (Hibernian), 1992 v Ni (1)
Wright, S. (Aberdeen), 1993 v G, Es (2)
Wright, T. (Sunderland). 1953 v W, Ni, E (3)
Wylie, T. G. (Rangers), 1890 v Ni (1)

Yeats, R. (Liverpool), 1965 v W; 1966 v I (2)
Yorston, B. C. (Aberdeen), 1931 v Ni (1)
Yorston, H. (Aberdeen), 1955 v W (1)
Young, A. (Hearts), 1960 v E, A (sub), H, T; 1961 v W, Ni; (with Everton), Ei; 1966 v P (8)
Young, A. (Everton), 1905 v E; 1907 v W (2)
Young, G. L. (Rangers), 1947 v E, Ni, Bel, L; 1948 v E, Ni, Bel, Sw, F; 1949 v E, W, Ni, F; 1950 v E, W, Ni, Sw, P, F; 1951 v E, W, Ni, A (2), D, F, Bel; 1952 v E, W, Ni, USA, D, Se; 1953 v W, E, Ni, Se; 1954 v Ni, W; 1955 v W, Ni, P, Y; 1956 v Ni, W, E, A; 1957 v E, Ni, W, Y, Sp, Sw (53)
Young, J. (Celtic), 1906 v Ni (1)
Younger, T. (Hibernian), 1955 v P, Y, A, H; 1956 v E, Ni, W, A; (with Liverpool), 1957 v E, Ni, W, Y, Sp (2), Sw, WG; 1958 v Ni, W, E, Sw, H, Pol, Y, Par (24)

WALES

Adams, H. (Berwyn R), 1882 v Ni, E; (with Druids), 1883 v Ni, E (4)
Aizlewood, M. (Charlton Ath), 1986 v S.Ar, Ca (2); 1987 v Fi; (with Leeds U), USSR, Fi (sub); 1988 v D (sub), Se, Ma, I; 1989 v Ho, Se (sub), WG; (with Bradford C), 1990 v Fi, WG, Ei, Cr; (with Bristol C), 1991 v D, Bel (2), L, Ei, Ic, Pol, WG; 1992 v Br, L, Ei, A, R, Ho, Arg, J; 1993 v Ei, Bel, Fa; 1994 v RCS, Cy; (with Cardiff C) 1995v Bul (39)
Allchurch, I. J. (Swansea T), 1951 v E, Ni, P, Sw; 1952 v E, S, Ni, R of UK; 1953 v E, Ni, F, Y; 1954 v S, E, Ni, A; 1955 v S, E, Ni, Y; 1956 v E, S, Ni, A; 1957 v E, S; 1958 v Ni, Is (2), H (2), M, Sw, Br; (with Newcastle U), 1959 v E, S, Ni; 1960 v E, S; 1961 v Ni, H, Sp (2); 1962 v E, S, Br (2), M; (with Cardiff C), 1963 v S, E, Ni, H (2); 1964 v E; 1965 v S, E, Ni, Gr, I, USSR; (with Swansea T), 1966 v USSR, E, S, D, Br (2), Ch (68)
Allchurch, L. (Swansea T), 1955 v Ni; 1956 v A; 1958 v S, Ni, EG, Is; 1959 v S; (with Sheffield U), 1962 v S, Ni, Br; 1964 v E (11)
Allen, B. W. (Coventry C), 1951 v S, E (2)
Allen, M. (Watford), 1986 v S.Ar (sub), Ca (1 + 1 sub); (with Norwich C), 1989 v Is (sub); 1990 v Ho, WG; (with Millwall), Ei, Se, Cr (sub); 1991 v L (sub), Ei (sub); 1992 v A; 1993 v Ei (sub); (with Newcastle U), 1994 v R (sub) (14)
Arridge, S. (Bootle), 1892 v S, Ni; (with Everton), 1894 v Ni; 1895 v Ni; 1896 v E; (with New Brighton Tower), 1898 v E, Ni; 1899 v E (8)
Astley, D. J. (Charlton Ath), 1931 v Ni; (with Aston Villa), 1932 v E; 1933 v E, S, Ni; 1934 v E, S; 1935 v S; 1936 v E, Ni; (with Derby Co), 1939 v E, S; (with Blackpool), F (13)
Atherton, R. W. (Hibernian), 1899 v E, Ni; 1903 v E, S, Ni; (with Middlesbrough), 1904 v E, S, Ni; 1905 v Ni (9)

Bailiff, W. E. (Llanelly), 1913 v E, S, Ni; 1920 v Ni (4)
Baker, C. W. (Cardiff C), 1958 v M; 1960 v S, Ni; 1961 v S, E, Ei; 1962 v S (7)
Baker, W. G. (Cardiff C), 1948 v Ni (1)
Bamford, T. (Wrexham), 1931 v E, S, Ni; 1932 v Ni; 1933 v F (5)
Barnard, D. S. (Barnsley), 1998 v Jam; 1999 v I, D, Bl, I, D; 2000 v Bl, Sw, Q, Fi, Br (sub), P; 2001 v Uk, Pol, Uk (15)
Barnes, W. (Arsenal), 1948 v E, S, Ni; 1949 v E, S, Ni; 1950 v E, S, Ni, Bel; 1951 v E, S, Ni, P; 1952 v E, S, Ni, R of UK; 1954 v E, S; 1955 v S, Y (22)
Bartley, T. (Glossop NE), 1898 v E (1)
Bastock, A. M. (Shrewsbury), 1892 v Ni (1)
Beadles, G. H. (Cardiff C), 1925 v E, S (2)
Bell, W. S. (Shrewsbury Engineers), 1881 v E, S; (with Crewe Alex), 1886 v E, S, Ni (5)
Bellamy, C. D. (Norwich C), 1998 v Jam (sub), Ma, Tun; 1999 v D (sub), Sw (sub), I, D (sub); 2000 v Br (sub), P; (with Coventry C), 2001 v Bl, Arm, Uk (12)
Bennion, S. R. (Manchester U), 1926 v S; 1927 v S; 1928 v S, E, Ni; 1929 v S, E, Ni; 1930 v S; 1932 v Ni (10)
Berry, G. F. (Wolverhampton W), 1979 v WG; 1980 v Ei, WG (sub), T; (with Stoke C), 1983 v E (sub) (5)
Blackmore, C. G. (Manchester U), 1985 v N (sub); 1986 v S (sub), H (sub), S.Ar, Ei, U; 1987 v Fi (2), USSR, Cz; 1988 v D (2), Cz, Y, Se, Ma, I; 1989 v Ho, Fi, Is, WG; 1990 v F; Ho, WG, Cr; 1991 v Bel, L; 1992 v Ei (sub), A, R (sub), Ho, Arg, J; 1993 v Fa, Cy, Bel, RCS; 1994 v Se (sub); (with Middlesbrough), 1997 v Bel (39)
Blake, N. A. (Sheffield U), 1994 v N, Se (sub); 1995 v Alb, Mol; 1996 v G (with Bolton W), I (sub); 1998 v T; 1999 v I, D, Bl; (with Blackburn R) Sw; 2000 v Bl, Sw, Q, Fi; 2001 v Bl (sub), N, Pol (2), Uk (20)

Blew, H. (Wrexham), 1899 v E, S, Ni; 1902 v S, Ni; 1903 v E, S; 1904 v E, S, Ni; 1905 v S, Ni; 1906 v E, S, Ni; 1907 v S; 1908 v E, S, Ni; 1909 v E, S; 1910 v E (22)
Boden, T. (Wrexham), 1880 v E (1)
Bodin, P. J. (Swindon T), 1990 v Cr; 1991 v D, Bel, L, Ei; (with C Palace), Bel, Ic, Pol, WG; 1992 v Br, G, L (sub); (with Swindon T), Ei (sub), Ho, Arg; 1993 v Ei, Bel, RCS, Fa; 1994 v R, Se, Es (sub); 1995 v Alb (23)
Boulter, L. M. (Brentford), 1939 v Ni (1)
Bowdler, H. E. (Shrewsbury), 1893 v S (1)
Bowdler, J. C. H. (Shrewsbury), 1890 v Ni; (with Wolverhampton W), 1891 v S; 1892 v Ni; (with Shrewsbury), 1894 v E (4)
Bowen, D. L. (Arsenal), 1955 v S, Y; 1957 v Ni, Cz, EG; 1958 v E, S, Ni, EG, Is (2), H (2), M, Se, Br; 1959 v E, S, Ni (19)
Bowen, E. (Druids), 1880 v S; 1883 v S (2)
Bowen, J. P. (Swansea C), 1994 v Es; (with Birmingham C), 1997 v Ho (2)
Bowen, M. R. (Tottenham H), 1986 v Ca (2 sub); (with Norwich C), 1988 v Y (sub); 1989 v Fi (sub), Is, Se, WG (sub); 1990 v Fi (sub), Ho, WG, Se; 1992 v Br (sub), G, L, Ei, A, R, Ho (sub), J; 1993 v Fa, Cy, Bel (1 + sub), RCS (sub); 1994 v RCS, Se; 1995 v Mol, Ge, Bul (2), G, Ge; 1996 v Mol, G, Alb, Sw, Sm; (with West Ham U), 1997 v Sm, Ho (2), Ei (sub) (41)
Bowsher, S. J. (Burnley), 1929 v Ni (1)
Boyle, T. (C Palace), 1981 v Ei, S (sub) (2)
Britten, T. J. (Parkgrove), 1878 v S; (with Presteigne), 1880 v S (2)
Brookes, S. J. (Llandudno), 1900 v E, Ni (2)
Brown, A. I. (Aberdare Ath), 1926 v Ni (1)
Browning, M. T. (Bristol R), 1996 v I (sub), Sm; 1997 v Sm, Ho (with Huddersfield T), S (sub) (5)
Bryan, T. (Oswestry), 1886 v E, Ni (2)
Buckland, T. (Bangor), 1899 v E (1)
Burgess, W. A. R. (Tottenham H), 1947 v E, S, Ni; 1948 v E, S; 1949 v E, S, Ni, P, Bel, Sw; 1950 v E, S, Ni, Bel; 1951 v S, Ni, P, Sw; 1952 v E, S, Ni, R of UK; 1953 v S, E, Ni, F, Y; 1954 v S, E, Ni, A (32)
Burke, T. (Wrexham), 1883 v E; 1884 v S; 1885 v E, S, Ni; (with Newton Heath), 1887 v E, S; 1888 v S (8)
Burnett, T. B. (Ruabon), 1887 v S (1)
Burton, A. D. (Norwich C), 1963 v Ni, H; (with Newcastle U), 1964 v E; 1969 v S, E, Ni, I, EG; 1972 v Cz (9)
Butler, J. (Chirk), 1893 v E, S, Ni (3)
Butler, W. T. (Druids), 1900 v S, Ni (2)

Cartwright, L. (Coventry C), 1974 v E (sub), S, Ni; 1976 v S (sub); 1977 v WG (sub); (with Wrexham), 1978 v Ir (sub); 1979 v Ma (7)
Carty, T. [s] See McCarthy [s] (Wrexham).
Challen, J. B. (Corinthians), 1887 v E, S; 1888 v E; (with Wellingborough GS), 1890 v E (4)
Chapman, T. (Newtown), 1894 v E, S, Ni; 1895 v S, Ni; (with Manchester C), 1896 v E; 1897 v E (7)
Charles, J. M. (Swansea C), 1981 v Cz, T (sub), S (sub), USSR (sub); 1982 v Ic; 1983 v N (sub), Y (sub), Bul (sub), S, Ni, Br; 1984 v Bul (sub); (with QPR), Y (sub), S; (with Oxford U), 1985 v Ic (sub), Sp, Ic; 1986 v Ei; 1987 v Fi (19)
Charles, M. (Swansea T), 1955 v Ni; 1956 v E, S, A; 1957 v E, Ni, Cz (2); 1958 v E, S, EG, Is (2), H (2), M, Se, Br; 1959 v E, S; (with Arsenal), 1961 v Ni, H, Sp (2); 1962 v E, S; (with Cardiff C), 1962 v Br, Ni; 1963 v S, H (31)
Charles, W. J. (Leeds U), 1950 v Ni; 1951 v Sw; 1953 v Ni, F, Y; 1954 v E, S, Ni, A; 1955 v S, E, Ni, Y; 1956 v E, S, A, Ni; 1957 v E, S, Ni, Cz (2), EG; (with Juventus), 1958 v Is (2), H

(2) M, Se; 1960 v S; 1962 v E, Br (2), M; (with Leeds U), 1963 v S; (with Cardiff C), 1964 v S; 1965 v S, USSR (38)

Clarke, R. J. (Manchester C), 1949 v E; 1950 v S, Ni, Bel; 1951 v E, S, Ni, P, Sw; 1952 v S, E, Ni, R of UK; 1953 v S, E; 1954 v E, S, Ni; 1955 v Y, S, E; 1956 v Ni (22)

Coleman, C. (C Palace), 1992 v A (sub); 1993 v Ei (sub); 1994 v N, Es; 1995 v Alb, Mol, Ge, Bul (2), G; 1996 v Mol; (with Blackburn R), I, Sw, Sm; 1997 v Sm; 1998 v Br; (with Fulham), Jam, Ma, Tun; 1999 v I, D, Bl, Sw, D; 2000 v Bl, Sw, Q, Fi; 2001 v Bl, N, Pol (31)

Collier, D. J. (Grimsby T), 1921 v S (1)

Collins, W. S. (Llanelly), 1931 v S (1)

Conde, C. (Chirk), 1884 v E, S, Ni (3)

Cook, F. C. (Newport Co), 1925 v E, S; (with Portsmouth), 1928 v E, S; 1930 v E, S, Ni; 1932 v E (8)

Cornforth, J.M. (Swansea C), 1995 v Bul (sub), Ge (2)

Coyne, D. (Tranmere R), 1996 v Sw (1)

Crompton, W. (Wrexham), 1931 v E, S, Ni (3)

Cross, E. A. (Wrexham), 1876 v S; 1877 v S (2)

Crosse, K. (Druids), 1879 v S; 1881 v E, S (3)

Crossley, M. G. (Nottingham F), 1997 v Ei; 1999 v Sw (sub); 2000 v Fi (3)

Crowe, V. H. (Aston Villa), 1959 v E, Ni; 1960 v E, Ni; 1961 v S, E, Ni, Ei, H, Sp (2); 1962 v E, S, Br, M; 1963 v H (16)

Cumner, R. H. (Arsenal), 1939 v E, S, Ni (3)

Curtis, A. (Swansea C), 1976 v E, Y (sub), S, Ni, Y (sub); E; 1977 v WG, S (sub), Ni (sub); 1978 v WG, E, S; 1979 v WG, S; (with Leeds U), E, Ni, Ma; 1980 v Ei, WG, T; (with Swansea C), 1982 v Cz, Ic, USSR, Sp, E, S, Ni; 1983 v N; 1984 v R (sub); (with Southampton), S; 1985 v Sp, N (1 + 1 sub); 1986 v H; (with Cardiff C), 1987 v USSR (35)

Curtis, E. R. (Cardiff C), 1928 v S; (with Birmingham), 1932 v S; 1934 v Ni (3)

Daniel, R. W. (Arsenal), 1951 v E, Ni, P; 1952 v E, S, Ni, R of UK; 1953 v S, E, Ni, F, Y; (with Sunderland), 1954 v E, S, Ni; 1955 v E, Ni; 1957 v S, E, Ni, Cz (21)

Darvell, S. (Oxford University), 1897 v S, Ni (2)

Davies, A. (Manchester U), 1983 v Ni, Br; 1984 v E, Ni; 1985 v Ic (2), N; (with Newcastle U), 1986 v H; (with Swansea C), 1988 v Ma. I; 1989 v Ho; (with Bradford C), 1990 v Fi, Ei (13)

Davies, A. (Wrexham), 1876 v S; 1877 v S (2)

Davies, A. (Druids), 1904 v S; (with Middlesbrough), 1905 v S (2)

Davies, A. O. (Barmouth), 1885 v Ni; 1886 v E, S; (with Swifts), 1887 v E, S; 1888 v E, Ni; (with Wrexham), 1889 v S; (with Crewe Alex), 1890 v E (9)

Davies, A. T. (Shrewsbury), 1891 v Ni (1)

Davies, C. (Charlton Ath), 1972 v R (sub) (1)

Davies, D. (Bolton W), 1904 v S, Ni; 1908 v E (sub) (3)

Davies, D. C. (Brecon), 1899 v Ni; (with Hereford), 1900 v Ni (2)

Davies, D. W. (Treharris), 1912 v Ni; (with Oldham Ath), 1913 v Ni (2)

Davies, E. Lloyd (Stoke C), 1904 v E; 1907 v E, S, Ni; (with Northampton T), 1908 v S; 1909 v Ni; 1910 v Ni; 1911 v E, S; 1912 v E, S; 1913 v E, S; 1914 v Ni, E, S (16)

Davies, E. R. (Newcastle U), 1953 v S, E; 1954 v E, S; 1958 v E, EG (6)

Davies, G. (Fulham), 1980 v T, Ic; 1982 v Sp (sub), F (sub); 1983 v E, Bul, S, Ni, Br; 1984 v R (sub), S (sub), E, Ni; 1985 v Ic; (with Manchester C), 1986 v S.Ar, Ei (16)

Davies, Rev. H. (Wrexham), 1928 v Ni (1)

Davies, Idwal (Liverpool Marine), 1923 v S (1)

Davies, J. E. (Oswestry), 1885 v E (1)

Davies, Jas (Wrexham), 1878 v S (1)

Davies, John (Wrexham), 1879 v S (1)

Davies, Jos (Newton Heath), 1888 v E, S, Ni; 1889 v S; 1890 v E; (with Wolverhampton W), 1892 v E; 1893 v E (7)

Davies, Jos (Everton), 1889 v S, Ni; (with Chirk), 1891 v Ni; (with Ardwick), v E, S; (with Sheffield U), 1895 v E, S, Ni; (with Manchester C), 1896 v E; (with Millwall), 1897 v E; (with Reading), 1900 v E (11)

Davies, J. P. (Druids), 1883 v E, Ni (2)

Davies, Ll. (Wrexham), 1907 v Ni; 1910 v Ni, S, E; (with Everton), 1911 v S, Ni; (with Wrexham), 1912 v Ni, S, E; 1913 v Ni, S; E; 1914 v Ni (13)

Davies, L. S. (Cardiff C), 1922 v E, S, Ni; 1923 v E, S, Ni; 1924 v E, S, Ni; 1925 v S, Ni; 1926 v E, Ni; 1927 v E, Ni; 1928 v S, Ni, E; 1929 v S, Ni, E; 1930 v E, S (23)

Davies, O. (Wrexham), 1890 v S (1)

Davies, R. (Wrexham), 1883 v Ni; 1884 v Ni; 1885 v Ni (3)

Davies, R. (Druids), 1885 v E (1)

Davies, R. O. (Wrexham), 1892 v Ni, E (2)

Davies, R. T. (Norwich C), 1964 v Ni; 1965 v E; 1966 v Br (2), Ch; (with Southampton), 1967 v S, E, Ni; 1968 v S, Ni, WG;

1969 v S, E, Ni, I, WG, R of UK; 1970 v E, S, Ni; 1971 v Cz, S, E, Ni; 1972 v R, E, S, N; (with Portsmouth), 1974 v E (29)

Davies, R. W. (Bolton W), 1964 v E; 1965 v E, S, Ni, D, Gr, USSR; 1966 v E, S, Ni, USSR, D, Br (2), Ch (sub); 1967 v S; (with Newcastle U), E; 1968 v S, Ni, WG; 1969 v S, E, Ni, I; 1970 v EG; 1971 v R, Cz; (with Manchester C), 1972 v E, S, Ni; (with Manchester U), 1973 v E, S (sub), Ni; (with Blackpool), 1974 v Pol (34)

Davies, S. (Tottenham H), 2001 v Uk (sub+1) (2)

Davies, S. I. (Manchester U), 1996 v Sw (sub) (1)

Davies, Stanley (Preston NE), 1920 v E, S, Ni; (with Everton), 1921 v E, S, Ni; (with WBA), 1922 v E, S, Ni; 1923 v S; 1925 v S, Ni; 1926 v S, E, Ni; 1927 v S; 1928 v S; (with Rotherham U), 1930 v Ni (18)

Davies, T. (Oswestry), 1886 v E (1)

Davies, T. (Druids), 1903 v E, Ni, S; 1904 v S (4)

Davies, W. (Wrexham), 1884 v Ni (1)

Davies, W. (Swansea T), 1924 v E, S, Ni; (with Cardiff C), 1925 v E, S, Ni; 1926 v E, S, Ni; 1927 v S; 1928 v Ni; (with Notts Co), 1929 v E, S, Ni; 1930 v E, S, Ni (17)

Davies, William (Wrexham), 1903 v Ni; 1905 v Ni; (with Blackburn R), 1908 v E, S; 1909 v E, S, Ni; 1911 v E, S, Ni; 1912 v Ni (11)

Davies, W. C. (C Palace), 1908 v S; (with WBA), 1909 v E; 1910 v S; (with C Palace), 1914 v E (4)

Davies, W. D. (Everton), 1975 v H, L, S, E, Ni; 1976 v Y (2), E, Ni; 1977 v WG, S (2), Cz, E, Ni; 1978 v K; (with Wrexham), S, Cz, WG, Ir, E, S, Ni; 1979 v Ma, T, WG, S, E, Ni, Ma; 1980 v Ei, WG, T, E, S, Ni, Ic; 1981 v T, Cz, Ei, T, S, E, USSR; (with Swansea C), 1982 v Cz, Ic, USSR, Sp, E, S, F; 1983 v Y (52)

Davies, W. H. (Oswestry), 1876 v S; 1877 v S; 1879 v E; 1880 v E (4)

Davies, W. O. (Millwall Ath), 1913 v E, S, Ni; 1914 v S, Ni (5)

Davis, G. (Wrexham), 1978 v Ir, E (sub), Ni (3)

Day, A. (Tottenham H), 1934 v Ni (1)

Deacy, N. (PSV Eindhoven), 1977 v Cz, S, E, Ni; 1978 v K (sub), S (sub), Cz (sub), WG, Ir, S (sub), Ni; (with Beringen), 1979 v T (12)

Dearson, D. J. (Birmingham), 1939 v S, Ni, F (3)

Delaney, M. A. (Aston Villa), 2000 v Sw, Q, Br, P; 2001 v N, Pol, Arm, Uk (2) (9)

Derrett, S. C. (Cardiff C), 1969 v S, WG; 1970 v I; 1971 v Fi (4)

Dewey, F. T. (Cardiff Corinthians), 1931 v E, S (2)

Dibble, A. (Luton T), 1986 v Ca (1+1 sub); (with Manchester C), 1989 v Is (3)

Doughty, J. (Druids), 1886 v S; (with Newton Heath), 1887 v S, Ni; 1888 v E, S, Ni; 1889 v S; 1890 v E (8)

Doughty, R. (Newton Heath and Druids), 1888 v S, Ni (2)

Durban, A. (Derby Co), 1966 v Br (sub); 1967 v Ni; 1968 v E, S, Ni, WG; 1969 v EG, S, E, Ni, WG; 1970 v E, S, Ni, EG, I; 1971 v R, S, E, Ni, Cz, Fi; 1972 v Fi, Cz, E, S, Ni (27)

Dwyer, P. (Cardiff C), 1978 v Ir, E, S, Ni; 1979 v T, S, E, Ni, Ma (sub); 1980 v WG (10)

Edwards, C. (Wrexham), 1878 v S (1)

Edwards, C. N. H. (Swansea C), 1996 v Sw (sub) (1)

Edwards, G. (Birmingham C), 1947 v E, S, Ni; 1948 v E, S, Ni; (with Cardiff C), 1949 v Ni, P, Bel, Sw; 1950 v E, S (12)

Edwards, H. (Wrexham Civil Service), 1878 v S; 1880 v E, S; 1882 v E, S; 1883 v S; 1884 v Ni; 1887 v Ni (8)

Edwards, J. H. (Wanderers), 1876 v S (1)

Edwards, J. H. (Oswestry), 1895 v Ni; 1897 v E, Ni (3)

Edwards, J. H. (Aberystwyth), 1898 v Ni (1)

Edwards, L. T. (Charlton Ath), 1957 v Ni, EG (2)

Edwards, R. I. (Chester), 1978 v K (sub); 1979 v Ma, WG; (with Wrexham), 1980 v T (sub) (4)

Edwards, R. W. (Bristol C), 1998 v T (sub), Bel, Ma (sub), Tun (sub) (4)

Edwards, T. (Linfield), 1932 v S (1)

Egan, W. (Chirk), 1892 v S (1)

Ellis, B. (Motherwell), 1932 v E; 1933 v E, S; 1934 v S; 1936 v E; 1937 v S (6)

Ellis, E. (Nunhead), 1931 v S; (with Oswestry), E; 1932 v Ni (3)

Emanuel, W. J. (Bristol C), 1973 v E (sub), Ni (sub) (2)

England, H. M. (Blackburn R), 1962 v Ni, Br, M; 1963 v Ni, H; 1964 v E, S, Ni; 1965 v E, D, Gr (2), USSR, Ni, I; 1966 v E, S, Ni, USSR, D; (with Tottenham H), 1967 v S, E; 1968 v E, Ni, WG; 1969 v EG; 1970 v R of UK, EG, E, S, Ni, I; 1971 v R; 1972 v Fi, E, S, Ni; 1973 v E (3), S; 1974 v Pol; 1975 v H, L (44)

Evans, B. C. (Swansea C), 1972 v Fi, Cz; 1973 v E (2), Pol, S; (with Hereford U), 1974 v Pol (7)

Evans, D. G. (Reading), 1926 v Ni; 1927 v Ni, E; (with Huddersfield T), 1929 v S (4)

Evans, H. P. (Cardiff C), 1922 v E, S, Ni; 1924 v E, S, Ni (6)

Evans, I. (C Palace), 1976 v A, E, Y (2), E, Ni; 1977 v WG, S (2), Cz, E, Ni; 1978 v K (13)

Evans, J. (Oswestry), 1893 v Ni; 1894 v E, Ni (3)

Evans, J. (Cardiff C), 1912 v Ni; 1913 v Ni; 1914 v S; 1920 v S, Ni; 1922 v Ni; 1923 v E, Ni (8)

Evans, J. H. (Southend U), 1922 v E, S, Ni; 1923 v S (4)

Evans, Len (Aberdare Ath), 1927 v Ni; (with Cardiff C), 1931 v E, S; (with Birmingham), 1934 v Ni (4)

Evans, M. (Oswestry), 1884 v E (1)

Evans, R. (Clapton), 1902 v Ni (1)

Evans, R. E. (Wrexham), 1906 v E, S; (with Aston Villa), Ni; 1907 v E; 1908 v E, S; (with Sheffield U), 1909 v S; 1910 v E, S, Ni (10)

Evans, R. O. (Wrexham), 1902 v Ni; 1903 v E, S, Ni; (with Blackburn R), 1908 v Ni; (with Coventry C), 1911 v E, Ni; 1912 v E, S, Ni (10)

Evans, R. S. (Swansea T), 1964 v Ni (1)

Evans, T. J. (Clapton Orient), 1927 v S; 1928 v E, S; (with Newcastle U), Ni (4)

Evans, W. (Tottenham H), 1933 v Ni; 1934 v E, S; 1935 v E; 1936 v E, Ni (6)

Evans, W. A. W. (Oxford University), 1876 v S; 1877 v S (2)

Evans, W. G. (Bootle), 1890 v E; 1891 v E; (with Aston Villa), 1892 v E (3)

Evelyn, E. C. (Crusaders), 1887 v E (1)

Eyton-Jones, J. A. (Wrexham), 1883 v Ni; 1884 v Ni, E, S (4)

Farmer, G. (Oswestry), 1885 v E, S (2)

Felgate, D. (Lincoln C), 1984 v R (sub) (1)

Finnigan, R. J. (Wrexham), 1930 v Ni (1)

Flynn, B. (Burnley), 1975 v L (2 sub), H (sub), S, E, Ni; 1976 v A, E, Y (2), E, Ni; 1977 v WG (sub), S (2), Cz, E, Ni; 1978 v K (2), S; (with Leeds U), Cz, WG, Ir (sub), E, S, Ni; 1979 v Ma, T, S, E, Ni, Ma; 1980 v Ei, WG, E, S, Ni, Ic; 1981 v T, Cz, Ei, T, S, E, USSR; 1982 v Cz, USSR, E, S, Ni, F; 1983 v N; (with Burnley), Y, E, Bul, S, Ni, R; 1984 v N, R, Bul, Y, S, N, Is (66)

Ford, T. (Swansea T), 1947 v S; (with Aston Villa), 1947 v Ni; 1948 v S, Ni; 1949 v E, S, Ni, P, Bel, Sw; 1950 v E, S, Ni, Bel; 1951 v S; (with Sunderland), 1951 v E, Ni, P, Sw; 1952 v E, S, Ni, R of UK; 1953 v S, E, Ni, F, Y; (with Cardiff C), 1954 v A; 1955 v S, E, Ni, Y; 1956 v S, Ni, E, A; 1957 v S (38)

Foulkes, H. E. (WBA), 1932 v Ni (1)

Foulkes, W. I. (Newcastle U), 1952 v E, S, Ni, R of UK; 1953 v E, S, F, Y; 1954 v E, S, Ni (11)

Foulkes, W. T. (Oswestry), 1884 v Ni; 1885 v S (2)

Fowler, J. (Swansea T), 1925 v E; 1926 v E, Ni; 1927 v S; 1928 v S; 1929 v E (6)

Freestone, R. (Swansea C), 2000 v Br (1)

Garner, J. (Aberystwyth), 1896 v S (1)

Giggs, R. J. (Manchester U), 1992 v G (sub), L (sub), R (sub); 1993 v Fa (sub), Bel (sub + 1), RCS, Fa; 1994 v RCS, Cy, R; 1995 v Alb, Bul; 1996 v G, Alb, Sm; 1997 v Sm, T, Bel; 1998 v T, Bel; 1999 v I (2), D; 2000 v Bl, Fi; 2001 v Bl, N, Pol, Uk, Pol, Uk (32)

Giles, D. (Swansea C), 1980 v E, S, Ni, Ic; 1981 v T, Cz, T (sub), E (sub), USSR (sub); (with C Palace), 1982 v Sp (sub); 1983 v Ni (sub), Br (12)

Gillam, S. G. (Wrexham), 1889 v S (sub), Ni; (with Shrewsbury), 1890 v E, Ni; (with Clapton), 1894 v S (5)

Glascodine, G. (Wrexham), 1879 v E (1)

Glover, E. M. (Grimsby T), 1932 v S; 1934 v Ni; 1936 v S; 1937 v E, S, Ni; 1939 v Ni (7)

Godding, G. (Wrexham), 1923 v S, Ni (2)

Godfrey, B. C. (Preston NE), 1964 v Ni; 1965 v D, I (3)

Goodwin, U. (Ruthin), 1881 v E (1)

Goss, J. (Norwich C), 1991 v Ic, Pol (sub); 1992 v A; 1994 v Cy (sub), R (sub), Se; 1995 v Alb; 1996 v Sw (sub), Sm (sub) (9)

Gough, R. T. (Oswestry White Star), 1883 v S (1)

Gray, A. (Oldham Ath), 1924 v E, S, Ni; 1925 v E, S, Ni; 1926 v E, S; 1927 v S; (with Manchester C), 1928 v E, S; 1929 v E, S, Ni; (with Manchester Central), 1930 v S; (with Tranmere R), 1932 v E, S, Ni; (with Chester), 1937 v E, S, Ni; 1938 v E, S, Ni (24)

Green, A. W. (Aston Villa), 1901 v Ni; (with Notts Co), 1903 v E; 1904 v S, Ni; 1906 v Ni, E; (with Nottingham F), 1907 v E; 1908 v S (8)

Green, C. R. (Birmingham C), 1965 v USSR, I; 1966 v E, S, USSR, Br (2); 1967 v E; 1968 v E, S, Ni, WG; 1969 v S, I, Ni (sub) (15)

Green, G. H. (Charlton Ath), 1938 v Ni; 1939 v E, Ni, F (4)

Green, R. M. (Wolverhampton W), 1998 v Ma, Tun (2)

Grey, Dr W. (Druids), 1876 v S; 1878 v S (2)

Griffiths, A. T. (Wrexham), 1971 v Cz (sub); 1975 v A, H (2), L (2), E, Ni; 1976 v A, E, S, E (sub), Ni, Y (2); 1977 v WG, S (17)

Griffiths, F. J. (Blackpool), 1900 v E, S (2)

Griffiths, G. (Chirk), 1887 v Ni (1)

Griffiths, J. H. (Swansea T), 1953 v Ni (1)

Griffiths, L. (Wrexham), 1902 v S (1)

Griffiths, M. W. (Leicester C), 1947 v Ni; 1949 v P, Bel; 1950 v E, S, Bel; 1951 v E, Ni, P, Sw; 1954 v A (11)

Griffiths, P. (Chirk), 1884 v E, Ni; 1888 v E; 1890 v S, Ni; 1891 v Ni (6)

Griffiths, P. H. (Everton), 1932 v S (1)

Griffiths, T. P. (Everton), 1927 v E, Ni; 1929 v E; 1930 v E; 1931 v Ni; 1932 v Ni, S, E; (with Bolton W), 1933 v E, S, Ni; (with Middlesbrough), F; 1934 v E, S; 1935 v E, Ni; 1936 v S; (with Aston Villa), Ni; 1937 v E, S, Ni (21)

Hall, G. D. (Chelsea), 1988 v Y (sub), Ma, I; 1989 v Ho, Fi, Is; 1990 v Ei; 1991 v Ei; 1992 v A (sub) (9)

Hallam, J. (Oswestry), 1889 v E (1)

Hanford, H. (Swansea T), 1934 v Ni; 1935 v S; 1936 v E; (with Sheffield W), 1936 v Ni; 1938 v E, S; 1939 v F (7)

Harrington, A. C. (Cardiff C), 1956 v Ni; 1957 v E, S; 1958 v S, Ni, Is (2); 1961 v S, E; 1962 v E, S (11)

Harris, C. S. (Leeds U), 1976 v E, S; 1978 v WG, Ir, E, S, Ni; 1979 v Ma, T, WG, E (sub), Ma; 1980 v Ni (sub), Ic (sub); 1981 v T, Cz (sub), Ei, T, S, E, USSR; 1982 v Cz, Ic, E (sub) (24)

Harris, W. C. (Middlesbrough), 1954 v A; 1957 v EG, Cz; 1958 v E, S, EG (6)

Harrison, W. C. (Wrexham), 1899 v E; 1900 v E, S, Ni; 1901 v Ni (5)

Hartson, J. (Arsenal), 1995 v Bul, G (sub), Ge (sub); 1996 v Mol (sub), Sw; 1997 v Ho, T (sub). Ei; (with West Ham U), Bel (sub), S; 1998 v Bel, Jam, Ma, Tun; (with Wimbledon), 1999 v Sw (sub), I (sub); D; 2000 v Sw (sub); 2001 v N, Pol; (with Coventry C), Arm, Uk, Pol, Uk (24)

Haworth, S. O. (Cardiff C), 1997 v S (sub); (with Coventry C), 1998 v Br, Jam (sub), Ma (sub), Tun (sub) (5)

Hayes, A. (Wrexham), 1890 v Ni; 1894 v Ni (2)

Hennessey, W. T. (Birmingham C), 1962 v Ni, Br (2); 1963 v S, E, H (2); 1964 v E, S; 1965 v S, E, D, Gr, USSR; 1966 v E, USSR; (with Nottingham F), 1966 v S, Ni, D, Br (2), Ch; 1967 v S, E; 1968 v E, S, Ni; 1969 v WG, EG, R of UK; 1970 v EG; (with Derby Co), E, S, Ni; 1972 v Fi, Cz, E, S; 1973 v E (39)

Hersee, A. M. (Bangor), 1886 v S, Ni (2)

Hersee, R. (Llandudno), 1886 v Ni (1)

Hewitt, R. (Cardiff C), 1958 v Ni, Is, Se, H, Br (5)

Hewitt, T. J. (Wrexham), 1911 v E, S, Ni; (with Chelsea), 1913 v E, S, Ni; (with South Liverpool), 1914 v E, S (8)

Heywood, D. (Druids), 1879 v E (1)

Hibbott, H. (Newtown Excelsior), 1880 v E, S; (with Newtown), 1885 v S (3)

Higham, G. G. (Oswestry), 1878 v S; 1879 v E (2)

Hill, M. R. (Ipswich T), 1972 v Cz, E (2)

Hockey, T. (Sheffield U), 1972 v Fi, R; 1973 v E (2); (with Norwich C), Pol, S, E, Ni; (with Aston Villa), 1974 v Pol (9)

Hoddinott, T. F. (Watford), 1921 v E, S (2)

Hodges, G. (Wimbledon), 1984 v N (sub), Is (sub); 1987 v USSR, Fi, Cz; (with Newcastle U), 1988 v D; (with Watford), D (sub), Cz (sub), Se, Ma (sub), I (sub); 1990 v Se, Cr; (with Sheffield U), 1992 v Br (sub), Ei (sub), A; 1996 v G (sub), I (18)

Hodgkinson, A. V. (Southampton), 1908 v Ni (1)

Holden, A. (Chester C), 1984 v Is (sub) (1)

Hole, B. G. (Cardiff C), 1963 v Ni; 1964 v Ni; 1965 v S, E, Ni, D, Gr (2), USSR, I; 1966 v E, S, Ni, USSR, D, Br (2), Ch; (with Blackburn R), 1967 v S, E, Ni; 1968 v E, S, Ni, WG; (with Aston Villa), 1969 v I, WG, EG; 1970 v I; (with Swansea C), 1971 v R (30)

Hole, W. J. (Swansea T), 1921 v Ni; 1922 v E; 1923 v E, Ni; 1928 v E, S, Ni; 1929 v E, S (9)

Hollins, D. M. (Newcastle U), 1962 v Br (sub), M; 1963 v Ni, H; 1964 v E; 1965 v Ni, Gr, I; 1966 v S, D, Br (11)

Hopkins, I. J. (Brentford), 1935 v S, Ni; 1936 v E, Ni; 1937 v E, S, Ni; 1938 v E, Ni; 1939 v E, S, Ni (12)

Hopkins, J. (Fulham), 1983 v Ni, Br; 1984 v N, R, Bul, Y, S, E, Ni, N, Is; 1985 v Ic (1 + 1 sub), N; (with C Palace), 1990 v Ho, Cr (16)

Hopkins, M. (Tottenham H), 1956 v Ni; 1957 v Ni, S, E, Cz (2), EG; 1958 v E, S, Ni, EG, Is (2), H (2), M, Se, Br; 1959 v E, S, Ni; 1960 v E, S; 1961 v Ni, H, Sp (2); 1962 v Ni, Br (2), M; 1963 v S, Ni, H (34)

Horne, B. (Portsmouth), 1988 v D (sub), Y, Se (sub), Ma, I; 1989 v Ho, Fi, Is; (with Southampton), Se, WG; 1990 v WG (sub), Ei, Se, Cr; 1991 v D, Bel (2), L, Ei, Ic, Pol, WG; 1992 v Br, G, L, Ei, A, R, Ho, Arg, J; (with Everton), 1993 v Fa, Cy, Bel, Ei, Bel, RCS, Fa; 1994 v RCS, Cy, R, N, Se, Es;

1995 v Mol, Ge, Bul, G, Ge; 1996 v Mol, G, I, Sw, Sm; (with Birmingham C), 1997 v Sm, Ho, T, Ei, Bel (59)
Howell, E. G. (Builth), 1888 v Ni; 1890 v E; 1891 v E (3)
Howells, R. G. (Cardiff C), 1954 v E, S (2)
Hugh, A. R. (Newport Co), 1930 v Ni (1)
Hughes, A. (Rhos), 1894 v E, S (2)
Hughes, A. (Chirk), 1907 v Ni (1)
Hughes, C. M. (Luton T), 1992 v Ho (sub); 1994 v N (sub), Se (sub), Es; 1996 v Alb; 1997 v Ei (sub); (with Wimbledon), 1998 v T, Bel (8)
Hughes, E. (Everton), 1899 v S, Ni; (with Tottenham H), 1901 v E, S; 1902 v Ni; 1904 v E, Ni, S; 1905 v E, Ni, S; 1906 v E, Ni; 1907 v E (14)
Hughes, E. (Wrexham), 1906 v S; (with Nottingham F), 1906 v Ni; 1908 v S, E; 1910 v Ni, E, S; 1911 v Ni, E, S; (with Wrexham), 1912 v Ni, E, S; (with Manchester C), 1913 v E, S; 1914 v N (16)
Hughes, F. W. (Northwich Victoria), 1882 v E, Ni; 1883 v E, Ni, S; 1884 v S (6)
Hughes, I. (Luton T), 1951 v E, Ni, P, Sw (4)
Hughes, J. (Cambridge University), 1877 v S; (with Aberystwyth), 1879 v S (2)
Hughes, J. (Liverpool), 1905 v E, S, Ni (3)
Hughes, J. I. (Blackburn R), 1935 v Ni (1)
Hughes, L. M. (Manchester U), 1984 v E, Ni; 1985 v Ic, Sp, Ic, N, S, Sp, N; 1986 v S, H, U; (with Barcelona), 1987 v USSR, Cz; 1988 v D (2), Cz, Se, Ma, I; (with Manchester U), 1989 v Ho, Fi, Is, Se, WG; 1990 v Fi, WG, Cr; 1991 v D, Bel (2), L, Ic, Pol, WG; 1992 v Br, G, L, Ei, R, Ho, Arg, J; 1993 v Fa, Cy, Bel, Ei, Bel, RCS, Fa; 1994 v RCS, Cy, N; 1995 v Ge, Bul, G, Ge; (with Chelsea), 1996 v Mol, I, Sm; 1997 v Sm, Ho, T, Ei, Bel; 1998 v T; (with Southampton), 1999 v I, D, Bl, Sw, I, D (72)
Hughes, P. W. (Bangor), 1887 v Ni; 1889 v Ni, E (3)
Hughes, W. (Bootle), 1891 v E; 1892 v S, Ni (3)
Hughes, W. A. (Blackburn R), 1949 v E, Ni, P, Bel, Sw (5)
Hughes, W. M. (Birmingham), 1938 v E, Ni, S; 1939 v E, Ni, S, F; 1947 v E, S, Ni (10)
Humphreys, J. V. (Everton), 1947 v Ni (1)
Humphreys, R. (Druids), 1888 v Ni (1)
Hunter, A. H. (FA of Wales Secretary), 1887 v Ni (1)

Jackett, K. (Watford), 1983 v N, Y, E, Bul, S; 1984 v N, R, Y, S, Ni, N, Is; 1985 v Ic, Sp, Ic, N, S, Sp, N; 1986 v S, H, S.Ar, Ei, Ca (2); 1987 v Fi (2); 1988 v D, Cz, Y, Se (31)
Jackson, W. (St Helens Rec), 1899 v Ni (1)
James, E. (Chirk), 1893 v E, Ni; 1894 v E, S, Ni; 1898 v S, E; 1899 v Ni (8)
James, E. G. (Blackpool), 1966 v Br (2), Ch; 1967 v Ni; 1968 v S; 1971 v Cz, S, E, Ni (9)
James, L. (Burnley), 1972 v Cz, R, S (sub); 1973 v E (3), Pol, S, Ni; 1974 v Pol, E, S, Ni; 1975 v A, H (2), L (2), S, E, Ni; 1976 v A; (with Derby Co), S, E, Y (2), Ni; 1977 v WG, S (2), Cz, E, Ni; 1978 v K (2); (with QPR); (with Burnley), 1979 v T; (with Swansea C), 1980 v E, S, Ni, Ic; 1981 v T, Ei, T, S, E; 1982 v Cz, Ic, USSR, E (sub), S, Ni, F; (with Sunderland), 1983 v E (sub) (54)
James, R. M. (Swansea C), 1979 v Ma, WG (sub), S, E, Ni, Ma; 1980 v WG; 1982 v Cz (sub), Ic, Sp, E, S, Ni, F; 1983 v N, Y, E, Bul; (with Stoke C), 1984 v N, R, Bul, Y, S, E, Ni, N, Is; 1985 v Ic, Sp, Ic; (with QPR), N, S, Sp, N; 1986 v S, S.Ar, Ei, U, Ca (2); 1987 v Fi (2), USSR, Cz; (with Leicester C), 1988 v D (2); (with Swansea C), Y (47)
James, W. (West Ham U), 1931 v Ni; 1932 v Ni (2)
Jarrett, R. H. (Ruthin), 1889 v Ni; 1890 v S (2)
Jarvis, A. L. (Hull C), 1967 v S, E, Ni (3)
Jenkins, E. (Lovell's Ath), 1925 v E (1)
Jenkins, J. (Brighton), 1924 v Ni, E, S; 1925 v S, Ni; 1926 v E, S; 1927 v S (8)
Jenkins, R. W. (Rhyl), 1902 v Ni (1)
Jenkins, S. R. (Swansea C), 1996 v G; (with Huddersfield T), Alb, I; 1997 v Ho (sub), T, S; 1998 v T, Bel, Br, Jam; 1999 v I (sub), D; 2001 v Pol (sub), Uk (sub) (14)
Jenkyns, C. A. L. (Small Heath), 1892 v E, S, Ni; 1895 v E; (with Woolwich Arsenal), 1896 v S; (with Newton Heath), 1897 v Ni; (with Walsall), 1898 v S, E (8)
Jennings, W. (Bolton W), 1914 v E, S; 1920 v S; 1923 v Ni, E; 1924 v E, S, Ni; 1927 v S, Ni; 1929 v S (11)
John, R. F. (Arsenal), 1923 v S, Ni; 1925 v Ni; 1926 v E; 1927 v E; 1928 v E, Ni; 1930 v E, S; 1932 v E; 1933 v F, Ni; 1935 v Ni; 1936 v S; 1937 v E (15)
John, W. R. (Walsall), 1931 v Ni; (with Stoke C), 1933 v E, S, Ni, F; 1934 v E, S; (with Preston NE), 1935 v E, S; (with Sheffield U), 1936 v E, S, Ni; (with Swansea T), 1939 v E, S (14)
Johnson, A. J. (Nottingham F), 1999 v I, D, Bl, Sw; 2000 v Fi (sub), Br (sub), P (sub) (7)

Johnson, M. G. (Swansea T), 1964 v Ni (1)
Jones, A. (Port Vale), 1987 v Fi, Cz (sub); 1988 v D, (with Charlton Ath), D (sub), Cz (sub); 1990 v Hol (sub) (6)
Jones, A. F. (Oxford University), 1877 v S (1)
Jones, A. T. (Nottingham F), 1905 v E; (with Notts Co), 1906 v E (2)
Jones, Bryn (Wolverhampton W), 1935 v Ni; 1936 v E, S, Ni; 1937 v E, S, Ni; 1938 v E, S, Ni; (with Arsenal), 1939 v E, S, Ni; 1947 v S, Ni; 1948 v E; 1949 v S (17)
Jones, B. S. (Swansea T), 1963 v S, E, Ni, H (2); 1964 v S, Ni; (with Plymouth Arg), 1965 v D; (with Cardiff C), 1969 v S, E, Ni, I (sub), WG, EG, R of UK (15)
Jones, Charlie (Nottingham F), 1926 v E; 1927 v S, Ni; 1928 v E; (with Arsenal), 1930 v E, S; 1932 v E; 1933 v F (8)
Jones, Cliff (Swansea T), 1954 v A; 1956 v E, Ni, S, A; 1957 v E, S, Ni, Cz (2), EG; 1958 v EG, E, S, Is (2); (with Tottenham H), 1958 v Ni, H (2), M, Se, Br; 1959 v Ni; 1960 v E, S, Ni; 1961 v S, E, Ni, Sp, H, Ei; 1962 v E, Ni, S, Br (2), M; 1963 v S, Ni, H; 1964 v E, S, Ni; 1965 v E, S, Ni, D, Gr (2), USSR, I; 1967 v S, E; 1968 v E, S, WG; (with Fulham), 1969 v I, R of UK (59)
Jones, C. W. (Birmingham), 1935 v Ni; 1939 v F (2)
Jones, D. (Chirk), 1888 v S, Ni; (with Bolton W), 1889 v E, S, Ni; 1890 v E; 1891 v S; 1892 v Ni; 1893 v E; 1894 v E; 1895 v E; 1898 v S; (with Manchester C), 1900 v E, Ni (14)
Jones, D. E. (Norwich C), 1976 v S, E (sub); 1978 v S, Cz, WG, Ir, E; 1980 v E (8)
Jones, D. O. (Leicester C), 1934 v E, Ni; 1935 v E, S; 1936 v E, Ni; 1937 v Ni (7)
Jones, Evan (Chelsea), 1910 v S, Ni; (with Oldham Ath), 1911 v E, S; 1912 v E, S; (with Bolton W), 1914 v Ni (7)
Jones, F. R. (Bangor), 1885 v E, Ni; 1886 v S (3)
Jones, F. W. (Small Heath), 1893 v S (1)
Jones, G. P. (Wrexham), 1907 v S, Ni (2)
Jones, H. (Aberaman), 1902 v Ni (1)
Jones, Humphrey (Bangor), 1885 v E, Ni, S; 1886 v E, Ni, S; (with Queen's Park), 1887 v E; (with East Stirlingshire), 1889 v E, Ni; 1890 v E, S, Ni; (with Queen's Park), 1891 v E, S (14)
Jones, Ivor (Swansea T), 1920 v S, Ni; 1921 v Ni, E; 1922 v S, Ni; (with WBA), 1923 v E, Ni; 1924 v S; 1926 v Ni (10)
Jones, Jeffrey (Llandrindod Wells), 1908 v Ni; 1909 v Ni; 1910 v S (3)
Jones, J. (Druids), 1876 v S (1)
Jones, J. (Berwyn Rangers), 1883 v S, Ni; 1884 v S (3)
Jones, J. (Wrexham), 1925 v Ni (1)
Jones, J. L. (Sheffield U), 1895 v E, S, Ni; 1896 v Ni, S, E; 1897 v Ni, S, E; (with Tottenham H), 1898 v Ni, E, S; 1899 v S, Ni; 1900 v S; 1902 v E, S, Ni; 1904 v E, S, Ni (21)
Jones, J. Love (Stoke C), 1906 v S; (with Middlesbrough), 1910 v Ni (2)
Jones, J. O. (Bangor), 1901 v S, Ni (2)
Jones, J. P. (Liverpool), 1976 v A, E; 1977 v WG, S (2), Cz, E, Ni; 1978 v K (2), S, Cz, WG, Ir, E, S, Ni; (with Wrexham), 1979 v Ma, T, WG, S, E, Ni, Ma; 1980 v Ei, WG, T, E, S, Ni, Ic; 1981 v T, Ei, T, S, E, USSR; 1982 v Cz, Ic, USSR, Sp, E, S, Ni, F; 1983 v N; (with Chelsea), Y, E, Bul, S, Ni, Br; 1984 v N, R, Bul, Y, S, E, Ni, N, Is; 1985 v Ic, N, S, N; (with Huddersfield T), 1986 v S, H, Ei, U, Ca (2) (72)
Jones, J. T. (Stoke C), 1912 v E, S, Ni; 1913 v E, Ni; 1914 v S, Ni; 1920 v E, S, Ni; (with C Palace), 1921 v E, S; 1922 v E, S, Ni (15)
Jones, K. (Aston Villa), 1950 v S (1)
Jones, Leslie J. (Cardiff C), 1933 v F; (with Coventry C), 1935 v Ni; 1936 v S; 1937 v E, S, Ni; (with Arsenal), 1938 v E, S, Ni; 1939 v E, S (11)
Jones, M. G. (Leeds U), 2000 v Sw (sub), Q, Br, P; 2001 v Pol (sub); (with Leicester C), Arm (sub), Uk, Pol (sub) (8)
Jones, P. L. (Liverpool), 1997 v S (sub); (with Tranmere R), 1998 v T (sub) (2)
Jones, P. S. (Stockport Co), 1997 v S (sub); (with Southampton), 1998 v T (sub), Br, Jam, Ma; 1999 v I, D, Bl, Sw, I, D; 2000 v Bl, Sw, Q; 2001 v Bl, N, Pol, Arm, Uk, Pol, Uk (21)
Jones, P. W. (Bristol R), 1971 v Fi (1)
Jones, R. (Bangor), 1887 v S; 1889 v E; (with Crewe Alex), 1890 v E (3)
Jones, R. (Leicester Fosse), 1898 v S (1)
Jones, R. (Druids), 1899 v S (1)
Jones, R. (Bangor), 1900 v S, Ni (2)
Jones, R. (Millwall), 1906 v S, Ni (2)
Jones, R. A. (Druids), 1884 v E, Ni, S; 1885 v S (4)
Jones, R. A. (Sheffield W), 1994 v Es (1)
Jones, R. S. (Everton), 1894 v Ni (1)
Jones, S. (Wrexham), 1887 v Ni; (with Chester), 1890 v S (2)
Jones, S. (Wrexham), 1893 v S, Ni; (with Burton Swifts), 1895 v S; 1896 v E, Ni; (with Druids), 1899 v E (6)

Jones, T. (Manchester U), 1926 v Ni; 1927 v E, Ni; 1930 v Ni (4)

Jones, T. D. (Aberdare), 1908 v Ni (1)

Jones, T. G. (Everton), 1938 v Ni; 1939 v E, S, Ni; 1947 v E, S; 1948 v E, S, Ni; 1949 v E, Ni, P, Bel, Sw; 1950 v E, S, Bel (17)

Jones, T. J. (Sheffield W), 1932 v Ni; 1933 v F (2)

Jones, V. P. (Wimbledon), 1995 v Bul (2), G, Ge; 1996 v Sw; 1997 v Ho, T, Ei, Bel (9)

Jones, W. E. A. (Swansea T), 1947 v E, S; (with Tottenham H), 1949 v E, S (4)

Jones, W. J. (Aberdare), 1901 v E, S; (with West Ham U), 1902 v E, S (4)

Jones, W. Lot (Manchester C), 1905 v E, Ni; 1906 v E, S, Ni; 1907 v E, S, Ni; 1908 v S; 1909 v E, S, Ni; 1910 v E; 1911 v E; 1913 v E, S; 1914 v S, Ni; (with Southend U), 1920 v E, Ni (20)

Jones, W. P. (Druids), 1889 v E, Ni; (with Wynstay), 1890 v S. Ni (4)

Jones, W. R. (Aberystwyth), 1897 v S (1)

Keenor, F. C. (Cardiff C), 1920 v E, Ni; 1921 v E, Ni, S; 1922 v Ni; 1923 v E, Ni, S; 1924 v E, Ni, S; 1925 v E, Ni, S; 1926 v S; 1927 v E, Ni, S; 1928 v E, Ni, S; 1929 v E, Ni, S; 1930 v E, Ni, S; 1931 v E, Ni, S; (with Crewe Alex), 1933 v S (32)

Kelly, F. C. (Wrexham), 1899 v S, Ni; (with Druids), 1902 v Ni (3)

Kelsey, A. J. (Arsenal), 1954 v Ni, A; 1955 v S, Ni, Y; 1956 v E, Ni, S, A; 1957 v E, Ni, S, Cz (2), EG; 1958 v E, S, Ni, Is (2), H (2), M, Se, Br; 1959 v E, S; 1960 v E, Ni, S; 1961 v E, Ni, S, H, Sp (2); 1962 v E, S, Ni, Br (2) (41)

Kenrick, S. L. (Druids), 1876 v S; 1877 v S; (with Oswestry), 1879 v E, S; (with Shropshire Wanderers), 1881 v E (5)

Ketley, C. F. (Druids), 1882 v Ni (1)

King, J. (Swansea T), 1955 v E (1)

Kinsey, N. (Norwich C), 1951 v Ni, P, Sw; 1952 v E; (with Birmingham C), 1954 v Ni; 1956 v E, S (7)

Knill, A. R. (Swansea C), 1989 v Ho (1)

Koumas, J. (Tranmere R), 2001 v Uk (sub) (1)

Krzywicki, R. L. (WBA), 1970 v EG, I; (with Huddersfield T), Ni, E, S; 1971 v R, Fi; 1972 v Cz (sub) (8)

Lambert, R. (Liverpool), 1947 v S; 1948 v E; 1949 v P, Bel, Sw (5)

Latham, G. (Liverpool), 1905 v E, S; 1906 v S; 1907 v E, S, Ni; 1908 v E; 1909 v Ni; (with Southport Central), 1910 v E; (with Cardiff C), 1913 v Ni (10)

Law, B. J. (QPR), 1990 v Se (1)

Lawrence, E. (Clapton Orient), 1930 v Ni; (with Notts Co), 1932 v S (2)

Lawrence, S. (Swansea T), 1932 v Ni; 1933 v F; 1934 v S, E, Ni; 1935 v E, S; 1936 v S (8)

Lea, A. (Wrexham), 1889 v E; 1891 v S, Ni; 1893 v Ni (4)

Lea, C. (Ipswich T), 1965 v Ni, I (2)

Leary, P. (Bangor), 1889 v Ni (1)

Leek, K. (Leicester C), 1961 v S, E, Ni, H, Sp (2); (with Newcastle U), 1962 v S; (with Birmingham C), v Br (sub), M; 1963 v E; 1965 v S, Gr; (with Northampton T), 1965 v Gr (13)

Legg, A. (Birmingham C), 1996 v Sw, Sm (sub); 1997 v Ho (sub), Ei; (with Cardiff C), 1999 v D (sub); 2001 v Arm (6)

Lever, A. R. (Leicester C), 1953 v S (1)

Lewis, B. (Chester), 1891 v Ni; (with Wrexham), 1892 v S, E, Ni; (with Middlesbrough), 1893 v S, E; (with Wrexham), 1894 v S, E, Ni; 1895 v S (10)

Lewis, D. (Arsenal), 1927 v E; 1928 v Ni; 1930 v E (3)

Lewis, D. (Swansea C), 1983 v Br (sub) (1)

Lewis, D. J. (Swansea T), 1933 v E, S (2)

Lewis, D. M. (Bangor), 1890 v Ni, S (2)

Lewis, J. (Bristol R), 1906 v E (1)

Lewis, J. (Cardiff C), 1926 v S (1)

Lewis, T. (Wrexham), 1881 v E, S (2)

Lewis, W. (Bangor), 1885 v E; 1886 v E, S; 1887 v E, S; 1888 v E; 1889 v E, Ni, S; (with Crewe Alex), 1890 v E; 1891 v E, S; 1892 v E, S, Ni; 1894 v E, S, Ni; (with Chester), 1895 v S, Ni, E; 1896 v E, S, Ni; (with Manchester C), 1897 v E, S; (with Chester), 1898 v Ni (27)

Lewis, W. L. (Swansea T), 1927 v E, Ni; 1928 v E, Ni; 1929 v S; (with Huddersfield T), 1930 v E (6)

Llewellyn, C. M. (Norwich C), 1998 v Ma (sub), Tun (sub) (2)

Lloyd, B. W. (Wrexham), 1976 v A, E, S (3)

Lloyd, J. W. (Wrexham), 1879 v S; (with Newtown), 1885 v S (2)

Lloyd, R. A. (Ruthin), 1891 v Ni; 1895 v S (2)

Lockley, A. (Chirk), 1898 v Ni (1)

Lovell, S. (C Palace), 1982 v USSR (sub); (with Millwall), 1985 v N; 1986 v S (sub), H (sub), Ca (1+1 sub) (6)

Lowrie, G. (Coventry C), 1948 v E, S, Ni; (with Newcastle U), 1949 v P (4)

Lowndes, S. (Newport Co), 1983 v S (sub), Br (sub); (with Millwall), 1985 v N (sub); 1986 v S.Ar (sub), Ei, U, Ca (2); (with Barnsley), 1987 v Fi (sub); 1988 v Se (sub) (10)

Lucas, P. M. (Leyton Orient), 1962 v Ni, M; 1963 v S, E (4)

Lucas, W. H. (Swansea T), 1949 v S, Ni, P, Bel, Sw; 1950 v E; 1951 v E (7)

Lumberg, A. (Wrexham), 1929 v Ni; 1930 v E, S; (with Wolverhampton W), 1932 v S (4)

McCarthy, T. P. (Wrexham), 1899 v Ni (1)

McMillan, R. (Shrewsbury Engineers), 1881 v E, S (2)

Maguire, G. T. (Portsmouth), 1990 v Fi (sub), Ho, WG, Ei, Se; 1992 v Br (sub), G (7)

Mahoney, J. F. (Stoke C), 1968 v E; 1969 v EG; 1971 v Cz; 1973 v E (3), Pol; 1974 v Pol, E, S, Ni; 1975 v A, H (2), L (2), S, E, Ni; 1976 v A, Y (2), E, Ni; 1977 v WG, Cz, S, E, Ni; (with Middlesbrough), 1978 v K (2), S, Cz, Ir, E (sub), S, Ni; 1979 v WG, S, E, Ni, Ma; (with Swansea C), 1980 v Ei, WG, T (sub); 1982 v Ic, USSR; 1983 v Y, E (51)

Mardon, P. J. (WBA), 1996 v G (sub) (1)

Marriott, A. (Wrexham), 1996 v Sw (sub); 1997 v S; 1998 v Bel, Br (sub), Tun (5)

Martin, T. J. (Newport Co), 1930 v Ni (1)

Marustik, C. (Swansea C), 1982 v Sp, E, S, Ni, F; 1983 v N (6)

Mates, J. (Chirk), 1891 v Ni; 1897 v E, S (3)

Mathews, R. W. (Liverpool), 1921 v Ni; (with Bristol C), 1923 v E; (with Bradford), 1926 v Ni (3)

Matthews, W. (Chester), 1905 v Ni; 1908 v E (2)

Matthias, J. S. (Brymbo), 1896 v S, Ni; (with Shrewsbury), 1897 v E, S; (with Wolverhampton W), 1899 v S (5)

Matthias, T. J. (Wrexham), 1914 v S, E; 1920 v Ni, S, E; 1921 v S, E, Ni; 1922 v S, E, Ni; 1923 v S (12)

Mays, A. W. (Wrexham), 1929 v Ni (1)

Medwin, T. C. (Swansea T), 1953 v Ni, F, Y; (with Tottenham H), 1957 v E, S, Ni, Cz (2), EG; 1958 v E, S, Ni, Is (2), H (2), M, Br; 1959 v E, S, Ni; 1960 v E, S, Ni; 1961 v S, Ei, E, Sp; 1963 v E, H (30)

Melville, A. K. (Swansea C), 1990 v WG, Ei, Se, Cr (sub); (with Oxford U), 1991 v Ic, Pol, WG; 1992 v Br, G, L, R, Ho, J (sub); 1993 v RCS, Fa (sub); (with Sunderland), 1994 v RCS (sub), R, N, Se, Es; 1995 v Alb, Mol (sub), Ge, Bul; 1996 v G, Alb, Sm; 1997 v Sm, Ho (2), T; 1998 v T; (with Fulham), 1999 v I, D; 2000 v Bl, Q, Fi, Br, P; 2001 v Bl, N, Pol, Arm, Uk, Pol, Uk (46)

Meredith, S. (Chirk), 1900 v S; 1901 v S, E, Ni; (with Stoke C), 1902 v E; 1903 v Ni; 1904 v E; (with Leyton), 1907 v E (8)

Meredith, W. H. (Manchester C), 1895 v E, Ni; 1896 v E, Ni; 1897 v S, Ni; 1898 v E, Ni; 1899 v E; 1900 v E, Ni; 1901 v E, Ni; 1902 v E, S; 1903 v E, S, Ni; 1904 v E; 1905 v E, S; (with Manchester U), 1907 v E, S, Ni; 1908 v E, Ni; 1909 v E, S, Ni; 1910 v E, S, Ni; 1911 v E, S, Ni; 1912 v E, S, Ni; 1913 v E, S, Ni; 1914 v E, S, Ni; 1920 v E, S, Ni (48)

Mielczarek, R. (Rotherham U), 1971 v Fi (1)

Millership, H. (Rotherham Co), 1920 v E, S, Ni; 1921 v E, S, Ni (6)

Millington, A. H. (WBA), 1963 v S, E, H; (with C Palace), 1965 v E, USSR; (with Peterborough U), 1966 v Ch, Br; 1967 v E, Ni; 1968 v Ni, WG; 1969 v I, EG; (with Swansea T), 1970 v E, S, Ni; 1971 v Cz, Fi; 1972 v Fi (sub), Cz, R (21)

Mills, T. J. (Clapton Orient), 1934 v E, Ni; (with Leicester C), 1935 v E, S (4)

Mills-Roberts, R. H. (St Thomas' Hospital), 1885 v E, S, Ni; 1886 v E; 1887 v E; (with Preston NE), 1888 v E, Ni; (with Llanberis), 1892 v E (8)

Moore, G. (Cardiff C), 1960 v E, S, Ni; 1961 v Ei, Sp; (with Chelsea), 1962 v Br; 1963 v Ni, H; (with Manchester U), 1964 v S, Ni; (with Northampton T), 1966 v Ni, Ch; (with Charlton Ath), 1969 v S, E, Ni, R of UK; 1970 v E, S, Ni, I; 1971 v R (21)

Morgan, J. R. (Cambridge University), 1877 v S; (with Swansea T), 1879 v S; (with Derby School Staff), 1880 v E, S; 1881 v E, S; 1882 v E, S, Ni; (with Swansea T), 1883 v E (10)

Morgan, J. T. (Wrexham), 1905 v Ni (1)

Morgan-Owen, H. (Oxford University), 1902 v S; 1906 v E, Ni; (with Welshpool), 1907 v S (5)

Morgan-Owen, M. M. (Oxford University), 1897 v S, Ni; 1898 v E, S; 1899 v S; 1900 v E; (with Corinthians), 1901 v S, E; 1903 v S; 1906 v S, E, Ni; 1907 v E (13)

Morley, E. J. (Swansea T), 1925 v E; (with Clapton Orient), 1929 v E, S, Ni (4)

Morris, A. G. (Aberystwyth), 1896 v E, Ni, S; (with Swindon T), 1897 v E; 1898 v S; (with Nottingham F), 1899 v E, S; 1903 v E, S; 1905 v E, S; 1907 v E, S; 1908 v E; 1910 v E, S, Ni; 1911 v E, S, Ni; 1912 v E (21)

Morris, C. (Chirk), 1900 v E, S, Ni; (with Derby Co), 1901 v E, S, Ni; 1902 v E; 1903 v E, S, Ni; 1904 v Ni; 1905 v E, S, Ni; 1906 v S; 1907 v S; 1908 v E, S; 1909 v E, S, Ni; 1910 v E, S, Ni; (with Huddersfield T), 1911 v E, S, Ni (27)

Morris, E. (Chirk), 1893 v E, S, Ni (3)

Morris, H. (Sheffield U), 1894 v S; (with Manchester C), 1896 v E; (with Grimsby T), 1897 v E (3)

Morris, J. (Oswestry), 1887 v S (1)

Morris, J. (Chirk), 1898 v Ni (1)

Morris, R. (Chirk), 1900 v E, Ni; 1901 v Ni; 1902 v S; (with Shrewsbury T), 1903 v E, Ni (6)

Morris, R. (Druids), 1902 v E, S; (with Newtown), Ni; (with Liverpool), 1903 v S, Ni; 1904 v E, S, Ni; (with Leeds C), 1906 v S; (with Grimsby T), 1907 v Ni; (with Plymouth Arg), 1908 v Ni (11)

Morris, S. (Birmingham), 1937 v E, S; 1938 v E, S; 1939 v F (5)

Morris, W. (Burnley), 1947 v Ni; 1949 v E; 1952 v S, Ni, R of UK (5)

Moulsdale, J. R. B. (Corinthians), 1925 v Ni (1)

Murphy, J. P. (WBA), 1933 v F, E, Ni; 1934 v E, S; 1935 v E, S, Ni; 1936 v E, S, Ni; 1937 v S, Ni; 1938 v E, S (15)

Nardiello, D. (Coventry C), 1978 v Cz, WG (sub) (2)

Neal, J. E. (Colwyn Bay), 1931 v E, S (2)

Neilson, A. B. (Newcastle U), 1992 v Ei; 1994 v Se, Es; 1995 v Ge; (with Southampton), 1997 v Ho (5)

Newnes, J. (Nelson), 1926 v Ni (1)

Newton, L. F. (Cardiff Corinthians), 1912 v Ni (1)

Nicholas, D. S. (Stoke C), 1923 v S; (with Swansea T), 1927 v E, Ni (3)

Nicholas, P. (C Palace), 1979 v S (sub), Ni (sub), Ma; 1980 v Ei, WG, T, E, S, Ni, Ic; 1981 v T, Cz, E; (with Arsenal), T, S, E, USSR; 1982 v Cz, Ic, USSR, Sp, E, S, Ni, F; 1983 v Y, Bul, S, Ni; 1984 v N, Bul, N, Is; (with C Palace), 1985 v Sp; (with Luton T), N, S, Sp, N; 1986 v S, H, S.Ar, Ei, U, Ca (2); 1987 v Fi (2) USSR, Cz; (with Aberdeen), 1988 v D (2), Cz, Y, Se; (with Chelsea), 1989 v Ho, Fi, Is, Se, WG; 1990 v Fi, Ho, WG, Ei, Se, Cr; 1991 v D (sub), Bel, L, Ei; (with Watford), Bel, Pol, WG; 1992 v L (73)

Nicholls, J. (Newport Co), 1924 v E, Ni; (with Cardiff C), 1925 v E, S (4)

Niedzwiecki, E. A. (Chelsea), 1985 v N (sub); 1988 v D (2)

Nock, W. (Newtown), 1897 v S, Ni (2)

Nogan, L. M. (Watford), 1992 v A (sub); (with Reading), 1996 v Mol (2)

Norman, A. J. (Hull C), 1986 v Ei (sub), U, Ca; 1988 v Ma, I (5)

Nurse, M. T. G. (Swansea T), 1960 v E, Ni; 1961 v S, E, H, Ni, Ei, Sp (2); (with Middlesbrough), 1963 v E, H; 1964 v S (12)

O'Callaghan, E. (Tottenham H), 1929 v Ni; 1930 v S; 1932 v S, E; 1933 v Ni, S, E; 1934 v Ni, S, E; 1935 v E (11)

Oliver, A. (Blackburn R), 1905 v E; (with Bangor), S (2)

Oster, J. M. (Everton), 1998 v Bel (sub), Br, Jam; (with Sunderland), 2000 v Sw (4)

O'Sullivan, P. A. (Brighton), 1973 v S (sub); 1976 v S; 1979 v Ma (sub) (3)

Owen, D. (Oswestry), 1879 v E (1)

Owen, E. (Ruthin Grammar School), 1884 v E, Ni, S (3)

Owen, G. (Chirk), 1888 v S; (with Newton Heath), 1889 v S, Ni; 1893 v Ni (4)

Owen, J. (Newton Heath), 1892 v E (1)

Owen, Trevor (Crewe Alex), 1899 v E, S (2)

Owen, T. (Oswestry), 1879 v E (1)

Owen, W. (Chirk), 1884 v E; 1885 v Ni; 1887 v E; 1888 v E; 1889 v E, Ni, S; 1890 v S, Ni; 1891 v E, S, Ni; 1892 v E, S; 1893 v S, Ni (16)

Owen, W. P. (Ruthin), 1880 v E, S; 1881 v E, S; 1882 v E, S; 1883 v E, S; 1884 v E, S, Ni (12)

Owens, J. (Wrexham), 1902 v S (1)

Page, M. E. (Birmingham C), 1971 v Fi; 1972 v S, Ni; 1973 v E (1+1 sub), Ni; 1974 v S, Ni; 1975 v H, L, S, E, Ni; 1976 v E, Y (2), E, Ni; 1977 v WG, S; 1978 v K (sub+1), WG, Ir, E, S; 1979 v Ma, WG (28)

Page, R. J. (Watford), 1997 v T, Bel, S; 1998 v T, Bel (sub), Br, I; 2000 v Bl, Sw, Q, Fi, Br, P; 2001 v Bl, N, Pol, Arm, Uk, Pol, Uk (20)

Palmer, D. (Swansea T), 1957 v Cz; 1958 v E, EG (3)

Parris, J. E. (Bradford), 1932 v Ni (1)

Parry, B. J. (Swansea T), 1951 v S (1)

Parry, C. (Everton), 1891 v E, S; 1893 v E; 1894 v E; 1895 v E, S; (with Newtown), 1896 v E, S, Ni; 1897 v Ni; 1898 v E, S, Ni (13)

Parry, E. (Liverpool), 1922 v S; 1923 v E, Ni; 1925 v Ni; 1926 v Ni (5)

Parry, M. (Liverpool), 1901 v E, S, Ni; 1902 v E, S, Ni; 1903 v E, S; 1904 v E, Ni; 1906 v E; 1908 v E, S, Ni; 1909 v E, S (16)

Parry, T. D. (Oswestry), 1900 v E, S, Ni; 1901 v E, S, Ni; 1902 v E (7)

Parry, W. (Newtown), 1895 v Ni (1)

Pascoe, C. (Swansea C), 1984 v N, Is; (with Sunderland), 1989 v Fi, Is, WG (sub); 1990 v Ho (sub), WG (sub); 1991 v Ei, Ic (sub); 1992 v Br (10)

Paul, R. (Swansea T), 1949 v E, S, Ni, P, Sw; 1950 v E, S, Ni, Bel; (with Manchester C), 1951 v S, E, Ni, P, Sw; 1952 v E, S, Ni, R of UK; 1953 v S, E, Ni, F, Y; 1954 v E, S, Ni; 1955 v S, E, Y; 1956 v E, Ni, S, A (33)

Peake, E. (Aberystwyth), 1908 v Ni; (with Liverpool), 1909 v Ni, S, E; 1910 v S, Ni; 1911 v Ni; 1912 v E; 1913 v E, Ni; 1914 v Ni (11)

Peers, E. J. (Wolverhampton W), 1914 v Ni, S, E; 1920 v E, S; 1921 v S, Ni, E; (with Port Vale), 1922 v E, S, Ni; 1923 v E (12)

Pembridge, M. A. (Luton T), 1992 v Br, Ei, R (with Derby Co), Ho, J (sub); 1993 v Bel (sub), Ei; 1994 v N (sub); 1995 v Alb (sub), Mol, Ge (sub); (with Sheffield W), 1996 v Mol, G, Alb, Sw, Sm; 1997 v Sm, Ho (2), T, Ei, Bel, S; 1998 v Bel, Br, Jam, Ma, Tun; (with Benfica), 1999 v D (sub), Bl, Sw, I (sub), D (sub); (with Everton), 2000 v Bl, Q, Fi; 2001 v Arm, Pol, Uk (39)

Perry, E. (Doncaster R), 1938 v E, S, Ni (3)

Perry, J. (Cardiff C), 1994 v N (1)

Phennah, E. (Civil Service), 1878 v S (1)

Phillips, C. (Wolverhampton W), 1931 v Ni; 1932 v E; 1933 v S; 1934 v E, S, Ni; 1935 v E, S, Ni; 1936 v S; (with Aston Villa), 1936 v E, Ni; 1938 v S (13)

Phillips, D. (Plymouth Arg), 1984 v E, Ni, N; (with Manchester C), 1985 v Sp, Ic, S, Sp, N; 1986 v S, H, S.Ar, Ei, U; (with Coventry C), 1987 v Fi, Cz; 1988 v D (2), Cz, Y, Se; 1989 v Se, WG; (with Norwich C), 1990 v Fi, Ho, WG, Ei, Se; 1991 v D, Bel, Ic, Pol, WG; 1992 v L, Ei, A, R, Ho (sub), Arg, J; 1993 v Fa, Cy, Bel, Ei, Bel, RCS, Fa; (with Nottingham F), 1994 v RCS, Cy, R, N, Se, Es; 1995 v Alb, Mol, Ge, Bul (2), G, Ge; 1996 v Mol (sub), Alb, I (62)

Phillips, L. (Cardiff C), 1971 v Cz, S, E, Ni; 1972 v Cz, R, S, Ni; 1973 v E; 1974 v Pol (sub), Ni; 1975 v A; (with Aston Villa), H (2), L (2), S, E, Ni; 1976 v A, E, Y (2), E, Ni; 1977 v WG, S (2), Cz, E; 1978 v K (2), S, Cz, WG, E, S; 1979 v Ma; (with Swansea C), T, WG, S, E, Ni, Ma; 1980 v Ei, WG, T, S (sub), Ni, Ic; 1981 v T, Cz, T, S, E, USSR; (with Charlton Ath), 1982 v Cz, USSR (58)

Phillips, T. J. S. (Chelsea), 1973 v E; 1974 v E; 1975 v H (sub); 1978 v K (4)

Phoenix, H. (Wrexham), 1882 v S (1)

Poland, G. (Wrexham), 1939 v Ni, F (2)

Pontin, K. (Cardiff C), 1980 v E (sub), S (2)

Powell, A. (Leeds U), 1947 v E, S; 1948 v E, S, Ni; (with Everton), 1949 v E; 1950 v Bel; (with Birmingham C), 1951 v S (8)

Powell, D. (Wrexham), 1968 v WG; (with Sheffield U), 1969 v S, E, Ni, I, WG; 1970 v E, S, Ni, EG; 1971 v R (11)

Powell, D. (Wrexham), 1968 v WG; (with Sheffield U), 1969 v S, E, Ni, I, WG; 1970 v E, S, Ni, EG; 1971 v R (11)

Powell, I. V. (QPR), 1947 v E; 1948 v E, S, Ni; (with Aston Villa), 1949 v Bel; 1950 v S, Bel; 1951 v S (8)

Powell, J. (Druids), 1878 v S; 1880 v E, S; 1882 v E, S, Ni; 1883 v E, S, Ni; (with Bolton W), 1884 v E; (with Newton Heath), 1887 v E, S; 1888 v E, S, Ni (15)

Powell, Seth (WBA), 1885 v S; 1886 v E, Ni; 1891 v E, S; 1892 v E, S (7)

Price, H. (Aston Villa), 1907 v S; (with Burton U), 1908 v Ni; (with Wrexham), 1909 v S, E, Ni (5)

Price, J. (Wrexham), 1877 v S; 1878 v S; 1879 v E; 1880 v E, S; 1881 v E, S; (with Druids), 1882 v S, E, Ni; 1883 v S, Ni (12)

Price, P. (Luton T), 1980 v E, S, Ni, Ic; 1981 v T, Cz, S, T, E, USSR; (with Tottenham H), 1982 v USSR, Sp, F; 1983 v N, Y, E, Bul, S, Ni; 1984 v N, R, Bul, Y, S (sub) (25)

Pring, K. D. (Rotherham U), 1966 v Ch, D; 1967 v Ni (3)

Pritchard, H. K. (Bristol C), 1985 v N (sub) (1)

Pryce-Jones, A. W. (Newtown), 1895 v E (1)

Pryce-Jones, M. E. (Cambridge University), 1887 v S; 1888 v S, E, Ni; 1890 v Ni (5)

Pugh, A. (Rhostyllen), 1889 v S (sub) (1)

Pugh, D. H. (Wrexham), 1896 v S, Ni; 1897 v S, Ni; (with Lincoln C), 1900 v S; 1901 v S, E (7)

Pugsley, J. (Charlton Ath), 1930 v Ni (1)

Pullen, W. J. (Plymouth Arg), 1926 v E (1)

Rankmore, F. E. J. (Peterborough), 1966 v Ch (sub) (1)

Ratcliffe, K. (Everton), 1981 v Cz, Ei, T, S, E, USSR; 1982 v Cz, Ic, USSR, Sp, E; 1983 v Y, E, Bul, S, Ni, Br; 1984 v N, R, Bul, Y, S, E, Ni, N, Is; 1985 v Ic, Sp, Ic, N, S, Sp; 1986 v S, H, S.Ar, U; 1987 v Fi (2), USSR, Cz; 1988 v D (2), Cz; 1989

v Fi, Is, Se, WG; 1990 v Fi; 1991 v D, Bel (2), L, Ei, Ic, Pol, WG; 1992 v Br, G; (with Cardiff C), 1993 v Bel (59)

Rea, J. C. (Aberystwyth), 1894 v Ni, S, E; 1895 v S; 1896 v S, Ni; 1897 v S, Ni; 1898 v Ni (9)

Ready, K. (QPR), 1997 v Ei; 1998 v Bel, Br, Ma, Tun (5)

Reece, G. I. (Sheffield U), 1966 v E, S, Ni, USSR; 1967 v S; 1969 v R of UK (sub); 1970 v I (sub); 1971 v S, E, Ni, Fi; 1972 v Fi, R, E (subs), S, Ni; (with Cardiff C), 1973 v E (sub), Ni; 1974 v Pol (sub), E, S, Ni; 1975 v A, H (2), L (2), S, Ni (29)

Reed, W. G. (Ipswich T), 1955 v S, Y (2)

Rees, A. (Birmingham C), 1984 v N (sub) (1)

Rees, J. M. (Luton T), 1992 v A (sub) (1)

Rees, R. R. (Coventry C), 1965 v S, E, Ni, D, Gr (2), I, R; 1966 v E, S, Ni, R, D, Br (2), Ch; 1967 v E, Ni; 1968 v E, S, Ni; (with WBA), WG; 1969 v I; (with Nottingham F), 1969 v WG, EG, S (sub), R of UK; 1970 v E, S, Ni, EG, I; 1971 v Cz, R, E (sub), Ni (sub), Fi; 1972 v Cz (sub), R (39)

Rees, W. (Cardiff C), 1949 v Ni, Bel, Sw; (with Tottenham H), 1950 v Ni (4)

Richards, A. (Barnsley), 1932 v S (1)

Richards, D. (Wolverhampton W), 1931 v Ni; 1933 v E, S, Ni; 1934 v E, S, Ni; 1935 v E, S, Ni; 1936 v S; (with Brentford), 1936 v E, Ni; 1937 v S, E; (with Birmingham), Ni; 1938 v E, S, Ni; 1939 v E, S (21)

Richards, G. (Druids), 1899 v E, S, Ni; (with Oswestry), 1903 v Ni; (with Shrewsbury), 1904 v S; 1905 v Ni (6)

Richards, R. W. (Wolverhampton W), 1920 v E, S; 1921 v Ni; 1922 v E, S; (with West Ham U), 1924 v E, S, Ni; (with Mold), 1926 v S (9)

Richards, S. V. (Cardiff C), 1947 v E (1)

Richards, W. E. (Fulham), 1933 v Ni (1)

Roach, J. (Oswestry), 1885 v Ni (1)

Robbins, W. W. (Cardiff C), 1931 v E, S; 1932 v Ni, E, S; (with WBA), 1933 v F, E, S, Ni; 1934 v S; 1936 v S (11)

Roberts, A. M. (QPR), 1993 v Ei (sub); 1997 v Sm (sub) (2)

Roberts, D. F. (Oxford U), 1973 v Pol, E (sub), Ni; 1974 v E, S; 1975 v A; (with Hull C), L, Ni; 1976 v S, Ni, Y; 1977 v E (sub), Ni; 1978 v K (1+1 sub), S, Ni (17)

Roberts, G. W. (Tranmere R), 2000 v Fi (sub), Br, P; 2001 v Bl (4)

Roberts, I. W. (Watford), 1990 v Ho; (with Huddersfield T), 1992 v A, Arg, J; (with Leicester C), 1994 v Se; 1995 v Alb (sub), Mol; (with Norwich C), 2000 v Fi (sub), Br, P; 2001 v Bl, N (sub), Arm (sub) (13)

Roberts, Jas (Wrexham), 1913 v S, Ni (2)

Roberts, J. (Corwen), 1879 v S; 1880 v E, S; 1882 v E, S, Ni; (with Berwyn R), 1883 v E (7)

Roberts, J. (Ruthin), 1881 v S; 1882 v S (2)

Roberts, J. (Bradford C), 1906 v Ni; 1907 v Ni (2)

Roberts, J. G. (Arsenal), 1971 v S, E, Ni, Fi; 1972 v Fi, E, Ni; (with Birmingham C), 1973 v E (2), Pol, S, Ni; 1974 v Pol, E, S, Ni; 1975 v A, H, S, E; 1976 v E, S (22)

Roberts, J. H. (Bolton), 1949 v Bel (1)

Roberts, N. W. (Wrexham), 2000 v Sw (sub) (1)

Roberts, P. S. (Portsmouth), 1974 v E; 1975 v A, H, L (4)

Roberts, R. (Druids), 1884 v S; (with Bolton W), 1887 v S; 1888 v S, E; 1889 v S, E; 1890 v S; 1892 v Ni; (with Preston NE), S (9)

Roberts, R. (Wrexham), 1886 v Ni; 1887 v Ni; 1891 v Ni (3)

Roberts, R. (Rhos), 1891 v Ni; (with Crewe Alex), 1893 v E (2)

Roberts, R. L. (Chester), 1890 v Ni (1)

Roberts, W. (Llangollen), 1879 v E, S; 1880 v E, S; (with Berwyn R), 1881 v S; 1883 v S (6)

Roberts, W. (Wrexham), 1886 v E, S, Ni; 1887 v Ni (4)

Roberts, W. H. (Ruthin), 1882 v E, S; 1883 v E, S, Ni; (with Rhyl), 1884 v S (6)

Robinson, C. P. (Wolverhampton W), 2000 v Bl (sub), P (sub); 2001 v Arm (sub), Uk (4)

Robinson, J. R. C. (Charlton Ath), 1996 v Alb (sub), Sw, Sm; 1997 v Sm, Ho (1 + sub), Ei, S; 1998 v Bel, Br; 1999 v I, D (sub), Bl, Sw, I, D; 2000 v Bl, Sw, Q, Fi, Br, P; 2001 v Bl, N, Pol, Arm (26)

Rodrigues, P. J. (Cardiff C), 1965 v Ni, Gr (2); 1966 v USSR, E, S, D; (with Leicester C), Ni, Br (2), Ch; 1967 v S; 1968 v E, S, Ni; 1969 v E, Ni, EG, R of UK; 1970 v E, S, Ni, EG; (with Sheffield W), 1971 v R, E, S, Cz, Ni; 1972 v Fi, Cz, R, E, Ni (sub); 1973 v E (3), Pol, S, Ni; 1974 v Pol (40)

Rogers, J. P. (Wrexham), 1896 v E, S, Ni (3)

Rogers, W. (Wrexham), 1931 v E, S (2)

Roose, L. R. (Aberystwyth), 1900 v Ni; (with London Welsh), 1901 v E, S, Ni; (with Stoke C), 1902 v E, S; 1904 v E; (with Everton), 1905 v S, E; (with Stoke C), 1906 v E, S, Ni; 1907 v E, S, Ni; (with Sunderland), 1908 v S, E; 1909 v E, S, Ni; 1910 v E, S; 1911 v S (24)

Rouse, R. V. (C Palace), 1959 v Ni (1)

Rowlands, A. C. (Tranmere R), 1914 v E (1)

Rowley, T. (Tranmere R), 1959 v Ni (1)

Rush, I. (Liverpool), 1980 v S (sub), Ni; 1981 v E (sub); 1982 v Ic (sub), USSR, E, S, Ni, F; 1983 v N, Y, E, Bul; 1984 v N, R, Bul, Y, S, E, Ni; 1985 v Ic, N, S, Sp; 1986 v S, S.Ar, Ei, U; 1987 v Fi (2), USSR, Cz; (with Juventus), 1988 v D, Cz, Y, Se, Ma, I; (with Liverpool), 1989 v Ho, Fi, Se, WG; 1990 v Fi, Ei; 1991 v D, Bel (2), L, Ei, Pol, WG; 1992 v G, L, R; 1993 v Fa, Cy, Bel (2), RCS, Fa; 1994 v RCS, Cy, R, N, Se, Es; 1995 v Alb, Ge, Bul, G, Ge; 1996 v Mol, I (73)

Russell, M. R. (Merthyr T), 1912 v S, Ni; 1914 v E; (with Plymouth Arg), 1920 v E, S, Ni; 1921 v E, S, Ni; 1922 v E, Ni; 1923 v E, S, Ni; 1924 v E, S, Ni; 1925 v E, S; 1926 v E, S; 1928 v S; 1929 v E (23)

Sabine, H. W. (Oswestry), 1887 v Ni (1)

Saunders, D. (Brighton & HA), 1986 v Ei (sub), Ca (2); 1987 v Fi, USSR (sub); (with Oxford U), 1988 v Y, Se, Ma, I (sub); 1989 v Ho (sub), Fi; (with Derby Co), Is, Se, WG; 1990 v Fi, Ho, WG, Se, Cr; 1991 v D, Bel (2), L, Ei, Ic, Pol, WG; (with Liverpool), 1992 v Br, G, Ei, R, Ho, Arg, J; 1993 v Fa; (with Aston Villa), Cy, Bel (2), RCS, Fa; 1994 v RCS, Cy, R, N (sub); 1995 v Ge, Bul (2), G, Ge; (with Galatasaray), 1996 v G, Alb, Sm; (with Nottingham F), 1997 v Sm, Ho (2), T, Bel, S; 1998 v T, Bel, Br; (with Sheffield U), Ma, Tun; 1999 v I (sub), D, Bl; (with Benfica) Sw, I, D; (with Bradford C), 2000 v Bl, Sw, Fi (sub), Br; 2001 v Arm, Uk (sub) (75)

Savage, R. W. (Crewe Alex), 1996 v Alb (sub), Sw (sub), Sm (sub); 1997 v Ei (sub), S; (with Leicester C), 1998 v T, Bel, Jam, Tun; 1999 v I (sub), D, Bl, Sw; 2000 v Sw, Fi, Br; 2001 v Bl, N, Pol (2) (20)

Savin, G. (Oswestry), 1878 v S (1)

Sayer, P. (Cardiff C), 1977 v Cz, S, E, Ni; 1978 v K (2), S (7)

Scrine, F. H. (Swansea T), 1950 v E, Ni (2)

Sear, C. R. (Manchester C), 1963 v E (1)

Shaw, E. G. (Oswestry), 1882 v Ni; 1884 v S, Ni (3)

Sherwood, A. T. (Cardiff C), 1947 v E, Ni; 1948 v S, Ni; 1949 v E, S, Ni, P, Sw; 1950 v E, S, Ni, Bel; 1951 v E, S, Ni, P, Sw; 1952 v E, S, Ni, R of UK; 1953 v S, E, Ni, F, Y; 1954 v E, S, Ni, A; 1955 v S, E, Y, Ni; 1956 v E, S, Ni, A; (with Newport Co), 1957 v E, S (41)

Shone, W. W. (Oswestry), 1879 v E (1)

Shortt, W. W. (Plymouth Arg), 1947 v Ni; 1950 v Ni, Bel; 1952 v E, S, Ni, R of UK; 1953 v S, E, Ni, F, Y (12)

Showers, D. (Cardiff C), 1975 v E (sub), Ni (2)

Sidlow, C. (Liverpool), 1947 v E, S; 1948 v E, S, Ni; 1949 v S; 1950 v E (7)

Sisson, H. (Wrexham Olympic), 1885 v Ni; 1886 v S, Ni (3)

Slatter, N. (Bristol R), 1983 v S; 1984 v N (sub), Is; 1985 v Ic, Sp, Ic, N, S, Sp, N; (with Oxford U), 1986 v H (sub), S.Ar, Ca (2); 1987 v Fi (sub), Cz; 1988 v D (2), Cz, Ma, I; 1989 v Is (sub) (22)

Smallman, D. P. (Wrexham), 1974 v E (sub), S (sub), Ni; (with Everton), 1975 v H (sub), E, Ni (sub); 1976 v A (7)

Southall, N. (Everton), 1982 v Ni; 1983 v N, E, Bul, S, Ni, Br; 1984 v N, R, Bul, Y, S, E, Ni, N, Is; 1985 v Ic, Sp, N, S, Sp, N; 1986 v S, H, S.Ar, Ei; 1987 v USSR, Fi, Cz; 1988 v D, Cz, Y, Se; 1989 v Ho, Fi, Se, WG; 1990 v Fi, Ho, WG, Ei, Se, Cr; 1991 v D, Bel (2), L, Ei, Ic, Pol, WG; 1992 v Br, G, L, Ei, A, R, Ho, Arg, J; 1993 v Fa, Cy, Bel, Ei, Bel, RCS, Fa; 1994 v RCS, Cy, R, N, Se, Es; 1995 v Alb, Mol, Ge, Bul (2), G, Ge; 1996 v Mol, G, Alb, I, Sm; 1997 v Sm, Ho (2), T, Bel; 1998 v T (92)

Speed, G. A. (Leeds U), 1990 v Cr (sub); 1991 v D, L (sub), Ei (sub), Ic, WG (sub); 1992 v Br, G (sub), L, Ei, R, Ho.Arg,J; 1993 v Cy, Bel, Ei, Bel, Fa (sub); 1994 v RCS (sub), Cy, R, N, Se; 1995 v Alb, Mol, Ge, Bul (2), G; 1996 v Mol, G, I, Sw (sub); (with Everton), 1997 v Sm (sub), Ho (2), T, Ei, Bel, S; 1998 v T, Br; (with Newcastle U), Jam, Ma, Tun; 1999 v I, D, Sw, I, D; 2000 v Bl, Sw, Q, Fi, Br, P; 2001 v Bl, N, Pol, Arm, Uk, Pol, Uk (65)

Sprake, G. (Leeds U), 1964 v S, Ni; 1965 v S, D, Gr; 1966 v E, Ni, USSR; 1967 v S; 1968 v E, S; 1969 v S, E, Ni, WG, R of UK; 1970 v EG, I; 1971 v R, S, E, Ni; 1972 v Fi, E, S, Ni; 1973 v E (2), Pol, S, Ni; 1974 v Pol; (with Birmingham C), S, Ni; 1975 v A, H, L (37)

Stansfield, F. (Cardiff C), 1949 v S (1)

Stevenson, B. (Leeds U), 1978 v Ni; 1979 v Ma, T, S, E, Ni, Ma; 1980 v WG, T, Ic (sub); 1982 v Cz; (with Birmingham C), Sp, S, Ni, F (15)

Stevenson, N. (Swansea C), 1982 v E, S, Ni; 1983 v N (4)

Stitfall, R. F. (Cardiff C), 1953 v E; 1957 v Cz (2)

Sullivan, D. (Cardiff C), 1953 v Ni, F, Y; 1954 v Ni; 1955 v E, Ni; 1957 v E, S; 1958 v Ni, H (2), Se, Br; 1959 v S, Ni; 1960 v E, S (17)

Symons, C. J. (Portsmouth), 1992 v Ei, Ho, Arg, J; 1993 v Fa, Cy, Bel, Ei, RCS, Fa; 1994 v RCS, Cy, R; 1995 v Mol, Ge

(sub), Bul, G, Ge; (with Manchester C), 1996 v Mol, G, I, Sw; 1997 v Ho (2), Ei, Bel, S; (with Fulham), 1999 v I, D, Bl, Sw; 2000 v Q (sub); 2001 v Pol (33)

Tapscott, D. R. (Arsenal), 1954 v A; 1955 v S, E, Ni, Y; 1956 v E, Ni, S, A; 1957 v Ni, Cz, EG; (with Cardiff C), 1959 v E, Ni (14)

Taylor, G. K. (C Palace), 1996 v Alb, I (sub); (with Sheffield U), Sw; 1997 v Sm (sub), Ho (sub), Ei (sub); 1998 v Bel (sub), Jam (8)

Taylor, J. (Wrexham), 1898 v E (1)

Taylor, O. D. S. (Newtown), 1893 v S, Ni; 1894 v S, Ni (4)

Thomas, C. (Druids), 1899 v Ni; 1900 v S (2)

Thomas, D. A. (Swansea T), 1957 v Cz; 1958 v EG (2)

Thomas, D. S. (Fulham), 1948 v E, S, Ni; 1949 v S (4)

Thomas, E. (Cardiff Corinthians), 1925 v E (1)

Thomas, G. (Wrexham), 1885 v E, S (2)

Thomas, H. (Manchester U), 1927 v E (1)

Thomas, M. (Wrexham), 1977 v WG, S (1+1 sub), Ni (sub); 1978 v K (sub), S, Cz, Ir, E, Ni (sub); 1979 v Ma; (with Manchester U), T, WG, Ma (sub); 1980 v Ei, WG (sub), T, E, S, Ni; 1981 v Cz, S, E, USSR; (with Everton), 1982 v Cz; (with Brighton & HA), USSR (sub), Sp, E, S (sub), Ni (sub); 1983 (with Stoke C), v N, Y, E, Bul, S, Ni, Br; 1984 v R, Bul, Y; (with Chelsea), S, E; 1985 v Ic, Sp, Ic, S, Sp, N; 1986 v S; (with WBA), H, S.Ar (sub) (51)

Thomas, M. R. (Newcastle U), 1987 v Fi (1)

Thomas, R. J. (Swindon T), 1967 v Ni; 1968 v WG; 1969 v E, Ni, I, WG, R of UK; 1970 v E, S, Ni, EG, I; 1971 v S, E, Ni, R, Cz; 1972 v Fi, Cz, R, E, S, Ni; 1973 v E (3), Pol, S, Ni; 1974 v Pol; (with Derby Co), E, S, Ni; 1975 v H (2), L (2), S, E, Ni; 1976 v A, Y, E; 1977 v Cz, S, E, Ni; 1978 v K, S; (with Cardiff C), Cz (50)

Thomas, T. (Bangor), 1898 v S, Ni (2)

Thomas, W. R. (Newport Co), 1931 v E, S (2)

Thomson, D. (Druids), 1876 v S (1)

Thomson, G. F. (Druids), 1876 v S; 1877 v S (2)

Toshack, J. B. (Cardiff C), 1969 v S, E, Ni, WG, EG, R of UK; 1970 v EG, I; (with Liverpool), 1971 v S, E, Ni, Fi; 1972 v Fi, E; 1973 v E (3), Pol, S; 1975 v A, H (2), L (2), S, E; 1976 v Y (2), E; 1977 v S; 1978 v K (2), S, Cz; (with Swansea C), 1979 v WG (sub), S, E, Ni, Ma; 1980 v WG (40)

Townsend, W. (Newtown), 1887 v Ni; 1893 v Ni (2)

Trainer, H. (Wrexham), 1895 v E, S, Ni (3)

Trainer, J. (Bolton W), 1887 v S; (with Preston NE), 1888 v S; 1889 v E; 1890 v S; 1891 v S; 1892 v Ni, S; 1893 v E; 1894 v Ni, E; 1895 v Ni, E; 1896 v S; 1897 v Ni, S, E; 1898 v S, E; 1899 v Ni, S (20)

Trollope, P. J. (Derby Co), 1997 v S; 1998 v Br (sub); (with Fulham), Jam (sub), Ma, Tun (5)

Turner, H. G. (Charlton Ath), 1937 v E, S, Ni; 1938 v E, S, Ni; 1939 v Ni, F (8)

Turner, J. (Wrexham), 1892 v E (1)

Turner, R. E. (Wrexham), 1891 v E, Ni (2)

Turner, W. H. (Wrexham), 1887 v E, Ni; 1890 v S; 1891 v E, S (5)

Van Den Hauwe, P. W. R. (Everton), 1985 v Sp; 1986 v S, H; 1987 v USSR, Fi, Cz; 1988 v D (2), Cz, Y, I; 1989 v Fi, Se (13)

Vaughan, Jas (Druids), 1893 v E, S, Ni; 1899 v E (4)

Vaughan, John (Oswestry), 1879 v S; 1880 v S; 1881 v E, S; 1882 v E, S, Ni; 1883 v E, S, Ni; (with Bolton W), 1884 v E (11)

Vaughan, J. O. (Rhyl), 1885 v Ni; 1886 v Ni, E, S (4)

Vaughan, N. (Newport Co), 1983 v Y (sub), Br; 1984 v N; (with Cardiff C), R, Bul, Y, Ni (sub), N, Is; 1985 v Sp (sub) (10)

Vaughan, T. (Rhyl), 1885 v E (1)

Vearncombe, G. (Cardiff C), 1958 v EG; 1961 v Ei (2)

Vernon, T. R. (Blackburn R), 1957 v Ni, Cz (2), EG; 1958 v E, S, EG, Se; 1959 v S; (with Everton), 1960 v Ni; 1961 v S, E, Ei; 1962 v Ni, Br (2), M; 1963 v S, E, H; 1964 v E, S; (with Stoke C), 1965 v Ni, Gr, I; 1966 v E, S, Ni, USSR, D; 1967 v Ni; 1968 v E (32)

Villars, A. K. (Cardiff C), 1974 v E, S, Ni (sub) (3)

Vizard, E. T. (Bolton W), 1911 v E, S, Ni; 1912 v E, S; 1913 v S; 1914 v E, Ni; 1920 v E; 1921 v E, S, Ni; 1922 v E, S; 1923 v E, Ni; 1924 v E, S, Ni; 1926 v E, S; 1927 v S (22)

Walley, J. T. (Watford), 1971 v Cz (1)

Walsh, I. (C Palace), 1980 v Ei, T, E, S, Ic; 1981 v T, Cz, Ei, T, S, E, USSR; 1982 v Cz (sub), Ic; (with Swansea C), Sp, S (sub), Ni (sub), F (18)

Ward, D. (Bristol R), 1959 v E; (with Cardiff C), 1962 v E (2)

Ward, D. (Notts Co), 2000 v P (1)

Warner, J. (Swansea T), 1937 v E; (with Manchester U), 1939 v F (2)

Warren, F. W. (Cardiff C), 1929 v Ni; (with Middlesbrough), 1931 v Ni; 1933 v F, E; (with Hearts), 1937 v Ni; 1938 v Ni (6)

Watkins, A. E. (Leicester Fosse), 1898 v E, S; (with Aston Villa), 1900 v E, S; (with Millwall), 1904 v Ni (5)

Watkins, W. M. (Stoke C), 1902 v E; 1903 v E, S; (with Aston Villa), 1904 v E, S, Ni; (with Sunderland), 1905 v E, S, Ni; (with Stoke C), 1908 v Ni (10)

Webster, C. (Manchester U), 1957 v Cz; 1958 v H, M, Br (4)

Weston, R. D. (Arsenal), 2000 v P (sub) (1)

Whatley, W. J. (Tottenham H), 1939 v E, S (2)

White, P. F. (London Welsh), 1896 v Ni (1)

Wilcock, A. R. (Oswestry), 1890 v Ni (1)

Wilding, J. (Wrexham Olympians), 1885 v E, S, Ni; 1886 v E, Ni; (with Bootle), 1887 v E; 1888 v S, Ni; (with Wrexham), 1892 v S (9)

Williams, A. (Reading), 1994 v Es; 1995 v Alb, Mol, G (sub), Ge; 1996 v Mol, I; (with Wolverhampton W), 1998 v Br (sub), Jam; 1999 v I, D, I (12)

Williams, A. L. (Wrexham), 1931 v E (1)

Williams, A. P. (Southampton), 1998 v Br (sub), Ma (2)

Williams, B. (Bristol C), 1930 v Ni (1)

Williams, B. D. (Swansea T), 1928 v Ni, E; 1930 v E, S; (with Everton), 1931 v Ni; 1932 v E; 1933 v E, S, Ni; 1935 v Ni (10)

Williams, D. G. (Derby Co), 1988 v Cz, Y, Se, Ma, I; 1989 v Ho, Is, Se, WG; 1990 v Fi, Ho; (with Ipswich T), 1993 v Ei; 1996 v G (sub) (13)

Williams, D. M. (Norwich C), 1986 v S.Ar (sub), U, Ca (2); 1987 v Fi (5)

Williams, D. R. (Merthyr T), 1921 v E, S; (with Sheffield W), 1923 v S; 1926 v S; 1927 v E, Ni; (with Manchester U), 1929 v E, S (8)

Williams, E. (Crewe Alex), 1893 v E, S (2)

Williams, E. (Druids), 1901 v E, Ni, S; 1902 v E, Ni (5)

Williams, G. (Chirk), 1893 v S; 1894 v S; 1895 v E, S, Ni; 1898 v Ni (6)

Williams, G. E. (WBA), 1960 v Ni; 1961 v S, E, Ei; 1963 v Ni, H; 1964 v S, Ei; 1965 v S, E, Ni, D, Gr (2), USSR, I; 1966 v Ni, Br (2), Ch; 1967 v S, E, Ni; 1968 v Ni; 1969 v I (26)

Williams, G. G. (Swansea T), 1961 v Ni, H, Sp (2); 1962 v E (5)

Williams, G. J. J. (Cardiff C), 1951 v Sw (1)

Williams, G. O. (Wrexham), 1907 v Ni (1)

Williams, H. J. (Swansea), 1965 v Gr (2); 1972 v R (3)

Williams, H. T. (Newport Co), 1949 v Ni, Sw; (with Leeds U), 1950 v Ni; 1951 v S (4)

Williams, J. H. (Oswestry), 1884 v E (1)

Williams, J. J. (Wrexham), 1939 v F (1)

Williams, J. T. (Middlesbrough), 1925 v Ni (1)

Williams, J. W. (C Palace), 1912 v S, Ni (2)

Williams, R. (Newcastle U), 1935 v S, E (2)

Williams, R. P. (Caernarvon), 1886 v S (1)

Williams, S. G. (WBA), 1954 v A; 1955 v E, Ni; 1956 v E, S, A; 1958 v E, S, Ni, Is (2), H (2), M, Se, Br; 1959 v E, S, Ni; 1960 v E, S, Ni; 1961 v Ni, Ei, H, Sp (2); 1962 v E, S, Ni, Br (2), M; (with Southampton), 1963 v E, S, E, H (2); 1964 v E, S; 1965 v S, E, D; 1966 v D (43)

Williams, W. (Druids), 1876 v S; 1878 v S; (with Oswestry), 1879 v E, S; (with Druids), 1880 v E; 1881 v E, S; 1882 v E, S, Ni; 1883 v Ni (11)

Williams, W. (Northampton T), 1925 v S (1)

Witcomb, D. F. (WBA), 1947 v E, S; (with Sheffield W), 1947 v Ni (3)

Woosnam, A. P. (Leyton Orient), 1959 v S; (with West Ham U), E; 1960 v E, S, Ni; 1961 v S, E, Ni, Ei, Sp, H; 1962 v E, S, Ni, Br; (with Aston Villa), 1963 v Ni, H (17)

Woosnam, G. (Newton White Star), 1879 v S (1)

Worthington, T. (Newtown), 1894 v S (1)

Wynn, G. A. (Wrexham), 1909 v E, S, Ni; (with Manchester C), 1910 v E; 1911 v Ni; 1912 v E, S; 1913 v E, S; 1914 v E, S (11)

Wynn, W. (Chirk), 1903 v Ni (1)

Yorath, T. C. (Leeds U), 1970 v I; 1971 v S, E, Ni; 1972 v Cz, E, S, Ni; 1973 v E, Pol, S; 1974 v Pol, E, S, Ni; 1975 v A, H (2), L (2), S; 1976 v A, E, S, Y (2), E, Ni; (with Coventry C), 1977 v WG, S (2), Cz, E, Ni; 1978 v K (2), S, Cz, WG, Ir, E, S, Ni; 1979 v T, WG, S, E, Ni; (with Tottenham H), 1980 v Ei, T, E, S, Ni, Ic; 1981 v T, Cz; (with Vancouver W), Ei, T, USSR (59)

Young, E. (Wimbledon), 1990 v Cr; (with C Palace), 1991 v D, Bel (2), L, Ei; 1992 v G, L, Ei, A; 1993 v Fa, Cy, Bel, Ei, Bel, Fa; 1994 v RCS, Cy, R, N; (with Wolverhampton W) 1996 v Alb (21)

REPUBLIC OF IRELAND

Aherne, T. (Belfast C), 1946 v P, Sp; (with Luton T), 1950 v Fi, E, Fi, Se, Bel; 1951 v N, Arg, N; 1952 v WG (2), A, Sp; 1953 v F; 1954 v F (16)

Aldridge, J. W. (Oxford U), 1986 v W, U, Ic, Cz; 1987 v Bel, S, Pol; (with Liverpool), S, Bul, Bel, Br, L; 1988 v Bul, Pol, N, E, USSR, Ho; 1989 v Ni, Tun, Sp, F (sub), H, Ma (sub), H; 1990 v WG; (with Real Sociedad), Ni, Ma, Fi (sub), T, E, Eg, Ho, R, I; 1991 v T, E (2), Pol; (with Tranmere R), 1992 v H (sub), T, W (sub), Sw (sub), US (sub), Alb, I, P (sub); 1993 v La, D, Sp, D, Alb, La, Li; 1994 v Li, Ni, CzR, I (sub), M (sub), N; 1995 v La, Ni, P, Lie; 1996 v La, P, Ho, Ru; 1997 v Mac (sub) (69)

Ambrose, P. (Shamrock R), 1955 v N, Ho; 1964 v Pol, N, E (5)

Anderson, J. (Preston NE), 1980 v Cz (sub), US (sub); 1982 v Ch. Br, Tr; (with Newcastle U), 1984 v Chn; 1986 v W, Ic, Cz; 1987 v Bul, Bel, Br, L; 1988 v R (sub), Y (sub); 1989 v Tun (16)

Andrews, P. (Bohemians), 1936 v Ho (1)

Arrigan, T. (Waterford), 1938 v N (1)

Babb, P. A. (Coventry C), 1994 v Ru, Ho, Bol, G, CzR (sub), I, M, N, Ho; (with Liverpool), 1995 v La, Lie, Ni (2), P, Lie, A; 1996 v La, P, Ho, CzR; 1997 v Ic; 1998 v Li (sub), R, Arg (sub), M; 1999 v Cro, Para (sub), Se (sub), Ni; 2000 v CzR (sub), S, M (sub), US, S.Af (34)

Bailham, E. (Shamrock R), 1964 v E (1)

Barber, E. (Shelbourne), 1966 v Sp; (with Birmingham C), 1966 v Bel (2)

Barry, P. (Fordsons), 1928 v Bel; 1929 v Bel (2)

Beglin, J. (Liverpool), 1984 v Chn; 1985 v M, D, I, Is, E, N, Sw; 1986 v Sw, USSR, D, W; 1987 v Bel (sub), S, Pol (15)

Bermingham, J. (Bohemians), 1929 v Bel (1)

Bermingham, P. (St James' Gate), 1935 v H (1)

Braddish, S. (Dundalk), 1978 v T (sub), Pol (2)

Bonner, P. (Celtic), 1981 v Pol; 1982 v Alg; 1984 v Ma, Is, Chn; 1985 v I, Is, E, N; 1986 v U, Ic; 1987 v Bel (2), S (2), Pol, Bul, Br, L; 1988 v Bul, R, Y, N, E, USSR, Ho; 1989 v Sp, F, H, Sp, Ma, H; 1990 v WG, Ni, Ma, W, Fi, T, E, Eg, Ho, R, I; 1991 v Mor, T, E (2), W, Pol, US; 1992 v H, Pol, T, W, Sw, Alb, I; 1993 v La, D, Sp, W, Ni, D, Alb, La, Li; 1994 v Li, Sp, Ni, Ru, Ho, Bol, CzR, I, M, N, Ho; 1995 v Lie; 1996 v M, Bol (sub) (80)

Bradshaw, P. (St James' Gate), 1939 v Sw, Pol, H (2), G (5)

Brady, F. (Fordsons), 1926 v I; 1927 v I (2)

Brady, T. R. (QPR), 1964 v A (2), Sp (2), Pol, N (6)

Brady, W. L. (Arsenal), 1975 v USSR, T, Sw, USSR, Sw, WG; 1976 v T, N, Pol; 1977 v E, T, F (2), Sp, Bul; 1978 v Bul, N; 1979 v Ni, E, D, Bul, WG; 1980 v W, Bul, E, Cy; (with Juventus), 1981 v Ho, Bel, F, Cy, Bel; 1982 v Ho, F, Ch, Br, Tr; (with Sampdoria), 1983 v Ho, Sp, Ic, Ma; 1984 v Ic, Ho, Ma, Pol, Is; (with Internazionale), 1985 v USSR, N, D, I, E, N, Sp, Sw; 1986 v Sw, USSR, D, W; (with Ascoli), 1987 v Bel, S (2), Pol; (with West Ham U), Bul, Bel, Br, L; 1988 v L, Bul; 1989 v F, H (sub), H (sub); 1990 v WG, Fi (72)

Branagan, K. G. (Bolton W), 1997 v W (1)

Breen, G. (Birmingham C), 1996 v P (sub), Cro, Ho, US, M, Bol (sub); 1997 v Lie, Mac, Ic; (with Coventry C), v Mac; 1998 v Li (sub), R, CzR, Arg, M; 1999 v Ma, Y, Para, Se, Mac; 2000 v Y, Cro, Ma, Mac, T (2), Gr, S, M, US, S.Af; 2001 v Ho, P, Es, Fi, Cy, And (2) (38)

Breen, T. (Manchester U), 1937 v Sw, F; (with Shamrock R), 1947 v E, Sp, P (5)

Brennan, F. (Drumcondra), 1965 v Bel (1)

Brennan, S. A. (Manchester U), 1965 v Sp; 1966 v Sp, A, Bel; 1967 v Sp, T, Sp; 1969 v Cz, D, H; 1970 v S, Cz, D, H, Pol (sub), WG; (with Waterford), 1971 v Pol, Se, I (19)

Brown, J. (Coventry C), 1937 v Sw, F (2)

Browne, W. (Bohemians), 1964 v A, Sp, E (3)

Buckley, L. (Shamrock R), 1984 v Pol (sub); (with Waregem), 1985 v M (2)

Burke, F. (Cork Ath), 1952 v WG (1)

Burke, J. (Cork), 1934 v Bel (1)

Burke, J. (Shamrock R), 1929 v Bel (1)

Butler, P. J. (Sunderland), 2000 v CzR (1)

Byrne, A. B. (Southampton), 1970 v D, Pol, WG; 1971 v Pol, Se (2), I (2), A; 1973 v F, USSR (sub), F, N; 1974 v Pol (14)

Byrne, D. (Shelbourne), 1929 v Bel; (with Shamrock R), 1932 v Sp; (with Coleraine), 1934 v Bel (3)

Byrne, J. (Bray Unknowns), 1928 v Bel (1)

Byrne, J. (QPR), 1985 v I, Is (sub), E (sub), Sp (sub); 1987 v S (sub), Bel (sub), Br, L (sub); 1988 v L, Bul (sub), Is, R, Y (sub), Pol (sub); (with Le Havre), 1990 v WG (sub), W, Fi, T (sub), Ma; (with Brighton & HA), 1991 v W; (with Sunderland), 1992 v T, W; (with Millwall), 1993 v W (23)

Byrne, P. (Shamrock R), 1984 v Pol, Chn; 1985 v M; 1986 v D (sub), W (sub), U (sub), Ic (sub), Cz (8)

Byrne, P. (Dolphin), 1931 v Sp; 1932 v Ho; (with Drumcondra), 1934 v Ho (3)

Byrne, S. (Bohemians), 1931 v Sp (1)

Campbell, A. (Santander), 1985 v I (sub), Is, Sp (3)

Campbell, N. (St Patrick's Ath), 1971 v A (sub); (with Fortuna, Cologne), 1972 v Ir, Ec, Ch, P; 1973 v USSR, F (sub); 1975 v WG; 1976 v N; 1977 v Sp, Bul (sub) (11)

Cannon, H. (Bohemians), 1926 v I; 1928 v Bel (2)

Cantwell, N. (West Ham U), 1954 v L; 1956 v Sp, Ho; 1957 v D, WG, E (2); 1958 v D, Pol, A; 1959 v Pol, Cz (2); 1960 v Se, Ch, Se; 1961 v N; (with Manchester U), S (2); 1962 v Cz (2), A; 1963 v Ic (2), S; 1964 v A, Sp, E; 1965 v Pol, Sp; 1966 v Sp (2), A, Bel; 1967 v Sp, T (36)

Carey, B. P. (Manchester U), 1992 v US (sub); 1993 v W; (with Leicester C), 1994 v Ru (3)

Carey, J. J. (Manchester U), 1938 v N, Cz, Pol; 1939 v Sw, Pol, H (2), G; 1946 v P, Sp; 1947 v E, Sp, P; 1948 v P, Sp; 1949 v Sw, Bel, P, Se, Sp; 1950 v Fi, E, Fi, Se; 1951 v N, Arg, N; 1953 v F, A (29)

Carolan, J. (Manchester U), 1960 v Se, Ch (2)

Carr, S. (Tottenham H), 1999 v Se, Ni, Mac; 2000 v Y (sub), Cro, Ma, T (2), S, M, US, S.Af; 2001 v Ho, P, Es, And (sub), P, Es (18)

Carroll, B. (Shelbourne), 1949 v Bel; 1950 v Fi (2)

Carroll, T. R. (Ipswich T), 1968 v Pol; 1969 v Pol, A, D; 1970 v Cz, Pol, WG; 1971 v Se; (with Birmingham C), 1972 v Ir, Ec, Ch, P; 1973 v USSR (2), Pol, F, N (17)

Carsley, L. K. (Derby Co), 1998 v R, Bel (1 + sub), CzR, Arg, M; 1999 v Cro (sub), Ma (sub), Para (sub); (with Blackburn R) Ni, Mac; 2000 v Y (sub), Cro, Ma, T; 2001 v Fi (sub) (16)

Cascarino, A. G. (Gillingham), 1986 v Sw, USSR, D; (with Millwall), 1988 v Pol, N (sub), USSR (sub), Ho (sub); 1989 v Ni, Tun, Sp, F, H, Sp, Ma, H; 1990 v WG (sub), Ni, Ma; (with Aston Villa), W, Fi, T, E, Eg, Ho (sub), R (sub), I (sub); 1991 v Mor (sub),T(sub), E (2 sub), Pol (sub), Ch (sub), US; (with Celtic), 1992 v Pol, T; (with Chelsea), W, Sw, US (sub); 1993 v W, Ni (sub), D (sub), Alb (sub), La (sub); 1994 v Li (sub), Sp (sub), Ni (sub), Ru, Bol (sub), G, CzR, Ho (sub); (with Marseille), 1995 v La (sub), Ni (sub), P (sub), Lie (sub), A (sub); 1996 v A (sub), P (sub), Ho, Ru (sub), P, Cro (sub), Ho; 1997 v Lie (sub), Mac, Ic; (with Nancy), v W, Mac, R (sub), Lie (sub); 1998 v Li (sub), Ic (sub), Li, R, Bel (2); 1999 v Cro (sub), Ma (sub), Y (sub), Para (sub), Se (sub), Ni (sub), Mac (sub); 2000 v Y (sub), Cro, Mac (sub), T (1 + sub) (88)

Chandler, J. (Leeds U), 1980 v Cz (sub), US (2)

Chatton, H. A. (Shelbourne), 1931 v Sp; (with Dumbarton), 1932 v Sp; (with Cork), 1934 v Ho (3)

Clarke, J. (Drogheda U), 1978 v Pol (sub) (1)

Clarke, K. (Drumcondra), 1948 v P, Sp (2)

Clarke, M. (Shamrock R), 1950 v Bel (1)

Clinton, T. J. (Everton), 1951 v N; 1954 v F, L (3)

Coad, P. (Shamrock R), 1947 v E, Sp, P; 1948 v P, Sp; 1949 v Sw, Bel, P, Se; 1951 v N (sub); 1952 v Sp (11)

Coffey, T. (Drumcondra), 1950 v Fi (1)

Colfer, M. D. (Shelbourne), 1950 v Bel; 1951 v N (2)

Collins, F. (Jacobs), 1927 v I (1)

Conmy, O. M. (Peterborough U), 1965 v Bel; 1967 v Cz; 1968 v Cz, Pol; 1970 v Cz (5)

Connolly, D. J. (Watford), 1996 v P, Ho, US, M; 1997 v R, Lie; (with Feyenoord), 1998 v Li, Ic, Li, Bel (1 + sub), CzR, M; (with Wolverhampton W), 1999 v Y, Para (sub), Se, Ni (sub), Mac (sub); (with Excelsior), 2000 v T (1 + sub), CzR (sub), Gr; 2001 v Ho (sub), Fi (sub), Cy, And; (with Feyenoord), And (27)

Connolly, H. (Cork), 1937 v G (1)

Connolly, J. (Fordsons), 1926 v I (1)

Conroy, G. A. (Stoke C), 1970 v Cz, D, H, Pol, WG; 1971 v Pol, Se (2), I; 1973 v USSR, F, USSR, N; 1974 v Pol, Br, U, Ch; 1975 v T, Sw, USSR, Sw, WG (sub); 1976 v T (sub), Pol; 1977 v E, T, Pol (27)

Conway, J. P. (Fulham), 1967 v Sp, T, Sp; 1968 v Cz; 1969 v A (sub), H; 1970 v S, Cz, D, H, Pol, WG; 1971 v I, A; 1974 v U, Ch; 1975 v WG (sub); 1976 v N, Pol; (with Manchester C), 1977 v Pol (20)

Corr, P. J. (Everton), 1949 v P, Sp; 1950 v E, Se (4)

Courtney, E. (Cork U), 1946 v P (1)

Coyle, O. C. (Bolton W), 1994 v Ho (sub) (1)

Coyne, T. (Celtic), 1992 v Sw, US, Alb (sub), US (sub), I (sub), P (sub); 1993 v W (sub), La (sub); (with Tranmere R), Ni; (with Motherwell), 1994 v Ru (sub), Ho, Bol, G

(sub), CzR (sub), I, M, Ho; 1995 v Lie, Ni (sub), A; 1996 v Ru (sub); 1998 v Bel (sub) (22)

Cummins, G. P. (Luton T), 1954 v L (2); 1955 v N (2), WG; 1956 v Y, Sp; 1958 v D, Pol, A; 1959 v Pol, Cz (2); 1960 v Se, Ch, WG, Se; 1961 v S (2) (19)

Cuneen, T. (Limerick), 1951 v N (1)

Cunningham, K. (Wimbledon), 1996 v CzR, P, Cro, Ho (sub), US, Bol; 1997 v Ic (sub), W, R, Lie; 1998 v Li, Ic, Li, Bel (2), CzR; 1999 v Cro, Ma, Y, Para, Se, Ni, Mac; 2000 v Y, Cro, Ma, Mac, T (2), CzR, Gr; 2001 v Cy, And (33)

Curtis, D. P. (Shelbourne), 1957 v D, WG; (with Bristol C), 1957 v E (2); 1958 v D, Pol, A; (with Ipswich T), 1959 v Pol; 1960 v Se, Ch, WG, Se; 1961 v N, S; 1962 v A; 1963 v Ic; (with Exeter C), 1964 v A (17)

Cusack, S. (Limerick), 1953 v F (1)

Daish, L. S. (Cambridge U), 1992 v W, Sw (sub); (with Coventry C), 1996 v CzR (sub), Cro, M (5)

Daly, G. A. (Manchester U), 1973 v Pol (sub), N; 1974 v Br (sub), U (sub); 1975 v Sw (sub), WG; 1977 v E, T, F; (with Derby Co), F, Bul; 1978 v Bul, T, D; 1979 v Ni, E, D, Bul; 1980 v Ni, E, Cy, Sw, Arg; (with Coventry C), 1981 v WG 'B', Ho, Bel, Cy, W, Bel, Cz, Pol (sub); 1982 v Alg, Ch, Br, Tr; 1983 v Ho, Sp (sub); 1984 v Is (sub), Ma; (with Birmingham C), 1985 v M (sub), N, Sp, Sw; 1986 v Sw; (with Shrewsbury T), U, Ic (sub), Cz (sub); 1987 v S (sub) (48)

Daly, J. (Shamrock R), 1932 v Ho; 1935 v Ho (2)

Daly, M. (Wolverhampton W), 1978 v T, Pol (2)

Daly, P. (Shamrock R), 1950 v Fi (sub) (1)

Davis, T. L. (Oldham Ath), 1937 v G, H; (with Tranmere R), 1938 v Cz, Pol (4)

Deacy, E. (Aston Villa), 1982 v Alg (sub), Ch, Br, Tr (4)

Delap, R. J. (Derby Co), 1998 v CzR (sub), Arg (sub), M (sub); 2000 v T (2), Gr (sub) (6)

De Mange, K. J. P. P. (Liverpool), 1987 v Br (sub); (with Hull C), 1989 v Tun (sub) (2)

Dempsey, J. T. (Fulham), 1967 v Sp, Cz; 1968 v Cz, Pol; 1969 v Pol, A, D; (with Chelsea), 1969 v Cz, D; 1970 v H, WG; 1971 v Pol, Se (2), I; 1972 v Ir, Ec, Ch, P (19)

Dennehy, J. (Cork Hibernians), 1972 v Ec (sub), Ch; (with Nottingham F), 1973 v USSR (sub), Pol, F, N; 1974 v Pol (sub); 1975 v T (sub), WG (sub); (with Walsall), 1976 v Pol (sub); 1977 v Pol (sub) (11)

Desmond, P. (Middlesbrough), 1950 v Fi, E, Fi, Se (4)

Devine, J. (Arsenal), 1980 v Cz, Ni; 1981 v WG 'B', Cz; 1982 v Ho, Alg; 1983 v Sp, Ma; (with Norwich C), 1984 v Ic, Ho, Is; 1985 v USSR, N (13)

Doherty, G. M. T. (Luton T), 2000 v Gr (sub); (with Tottenham H), US, S.Af (sub); 2001 v Cy (sub), And (sub+1), P (sub), Es (sub) (8)

Donnelly, J. (Dundalk), 1935 v H, Sw, G; 1936 v Ho, Sw, H, L; 1937 v G, H; 1938 v N (10)

Donnelly, T. (Drumcondra), 1938 v N; (Shamrock R), 1939 v Sw (2)

Donovan, D. C. (Everton), 1955 v N, Ho, N, WG; 1957 v E (5)

Donovan, T. (Aston Villa), 1980 v Cz; 1981 v WG 'B'(sub) (2)

Dowdall, C. (Fordsons), 1928 v Bel; (with Barnsley), 1929 v Bel; (with Cork), 1931 v Sp (3)

Doyle, C. (Shelbourne), 1959 v Cz (1)

Doyle, D. (Shamrock R), 1926 v I (1)

Doyle, L. (Dolphin), 1932 v Sp (1)

Duff, D. A. (Blackburn R), 1998 v CzR, M; 1999 v Cro, Ma, Y, Para, Se (sub), Ni, Mac; 2000 v Cro, Ma (sub), T (sub + sub), S (sub); 2001 v P (sub), Es (sub), Cy (sub), And, P (sub), Es (20)

Duffy, B. (Shamrock R), 1950 v Bel (1)

Duggan, H. A. (Leeds U), 1927 v I; 1930 v Bel; 1936 v H, L; (with Newport Co), 1938 v N (5)

Dunne, A. P. (Manchester U), 1962 v A; 1963 v Ic, S; 1964 v A, Sp, Pol, N, E; 1965 v Pol, Sp; 1966 v Sp (2), A, Bel; 1967 v Sp, T, Sp; 1969 v Pol, D, H; 1970 v H; 1971 v Se, I, A; (with Bolton W), 1974 v Br (sub), U, Ch; 1975 v T, Sw, USSR, Sw, WG; 1976 v T (33)

Dunne, J. (Sheffield U), 1930 v Bel; (with Arsenal), 1936 v Sw, H, L; (with Southampton), 1937 v Sw, F; (with Shamrock R), 1938 v N (2), Cz, Pol; 1939 v Sw, Pol, H (2), G (15)

Dunne, J. C. (Fulham), 1971 v A (1)

Dunne, L. (Manchester U), 1935 v Sw, G (2)

Dunne, P. A. J. (Manchester U), 1965 v Sp; 1966 v Sp (2), WG; 1967 v T (5)

Dunne, R. P. (Everton), 2000 v Gr, S (sub), M; 2001 v Ho, P, Es; (with Manchester C), Fi, And, P, Es (10)

Dunne, S. (Luton T), 1953 v F, A; 1954 v F, L; 1956 v Sp, Ho; 1957 v D, WG, E; 1958 v D, Pol, A; 1959 v Pol; 1960 v WG, Se (15)

Dunne, T. (St Patrick's Ath), 1956 v Ho; 1957 v D, WG (3)

Dunning, P. (Shelbourne), 1971 v Se, I (2)

Dunphy, E. M. (York C), 1966 v Sp; (with Millwall), 1966 v WG; 1967 v T, Sp, T, Cz; 1968 v Cz, Pol; 1969 v Pol, A, D (2), H; 1970 v D, H, Pol, WG (sub); 1971 v Pol, Se (2), I (2), A (23)

Dwyer, N. M. (West Ham U), 1960 v Se, Ch, WG, Se; (with Swansea T), 1961 v W, N, S (2); 1962 v Cz (2); 1964 v Pol (sub), N, E; 1965 v Pol (14)

Eccles, P. (Shamrock R), 1986 v U (sub) (1)

Egan, R. (Dundalk), 1929 v Bel (1)

Eglington, T. J. (Shamrock R), 1946 v P, Sp; (with Everton), 1947 v E, Sp, P; 1948 v P; 1949 v Sw, P, Se; 1951 v N, Arg; 1952 v WG (2), A, Sp; 1953 v F, A; 1954 v F, L, F; 1955 v N, Ho, WG; 1956 v Sp (24)

Ellis, P. (Bohemians), 1935 v Sw, G; 1936 v Ho, Sw, L; 1937 v G, H (7)

Evans, M. J. (Southampton), 1998 v R (sub) (1)

Fagan, E. (Shamrock R), 1973 v N (sub) (1)

Fagan, F. (Manchester C), 1955 v N; 1960 v Se; (with Derby Co), 1960 v Ch, WG, Se; 1961 v W, N, S (8)

Fagan, J. (Shamrock R), 1926 v I (1)

Fairclough, M. (Dundalk), 1982 v Ch (sub), Tr (sub) (2)

Fallon, S. (Celtic), 1951 v N; 1952 v WG (2), A, Sp; 1953 v F; 1955 v N, WG (8)

Fallon, W. J. (Notts Co), 1935 v H; 1936 v H; 1937 v H, Sw, F; 1939 v Sw, Pol; (with Sheffield W), 1939 v H, G (9)

Farquharson, T. G. (Cardiff C), 1929 v Bel; 1930 v Bel; 1931 v Sp; 1932 v Sp (4)

Farrell, P. (Hibernian), 1937 v Sw, F (2)

Farrell, P. D. (Shamrock R), 1946 v P, Sp; (with Everton), 1947 v P; 1948 v P, Sp; 1949 v Sw, P (sub), Sp; 1950 v E, Fi, Se; 1951 v Arg, N; 1952 v WG (2), A, Sp; 1953 v F, A; 1954 v F (2); 1955 v N, Ho, WG; 1956 v Y, Sp; 1957 v E (28)

Farrelly, G. (Aston Villa), 1996 v P, US, Bol; (with Everton), 1998 v CzR, M; (with Bolton W), 2000 v US (6)

Feenan, J. J. (Sunderland), 1937 v Sw, F (2)

Finnan, S. (Fulham), 2000 v Gr, S; 2001 v P (sub), Es (sub), Fi, And (sub+sub) (7)

Finucane, A. (Limerick), 1967 v T, Cz; 1969 v Cz, D, H; 1970 v S, Cz; 1971 v Se, I (1+sub); 1972 v A (11)

Fitzgerald, F. J. (Waterford), 1955 v Ho; 1956 v Ho (2)

Fitzgerald, P. J. (Leeds U), 1961 v W, N, S; (with Chester), 1962 v Cz (2) (5)

Fitzpatrick, K. (Limerick), 1970 v Cz (1)

Fitzsimons, A. G. (Middlesbrough), 1950 v Fi, Bel; 1952 v WG (2), A, Sp; 1953 v F, A; 1954 v F, L, F; 1955 v Ho, N, WG; 1956 v Y, Sp, Ho; 1957 v D, WG, E (2); 1958 v D, Pol, A; 1959 v Pol; (with Lincoln C), 1959 v Cz (26)

Fleming, C. (Middlesbrough), 1996 v CzR (sub), P, Cro (sub), Ho (sub), US (sub), M, Bol; 1997 v Lie (sub); 1998 v R (sub), M (10)

Flood, J. J. (Shamrock R), 1926 v I; 1929 v Bel; 1930 v Bel; 1931 v Sp; 1932 v Sp (5)

Fogarty, A. (Sunderland), 1960 v WG, Se; 1961 v S; 1962 v Cz (2); 1963 v Ic (2), S (sub); 1964 v A (2); (with Hartlepools U), Sp (11)

Foley, D. J. (Watford), 2000 v S (sub), M (sub), US, S.Af; 2001 v Es (sub), Fi (6)

Foley, J. (Cork), 1934 v Bel, Ho; (with Celtic), 1935 v H, Sw, G; 1937 v G, H (7)

Foley, M. (Shelbourne), 1926 v I (1)

Foley, T. C. (Northampton T), 1964 v Sp, Pol, N; 1965 v Pol, Bel; 1966 v Sp (2), WG; 1967 v Cz (9)

Foy, T. (Shamrock R), 1938 v N; 1939 v H (2)

Fullam, J. (Preston NE), 1961 v N; (with Shamrock R), 1964 v Sp, Pol, N; 1966 v A, Bel; 1968 v Pol; 1969 v Pol, A, D; 1970 v Cz (sub) (11)

Fullam, R. (Shamrock R), 1926 v I; 1927 v I (2)

Gallagher, C. (Celtic), 1967 v T, Cz (2)

Gallagher, M. (Hibernian), 1954 v L (1)

Gallagher, P. (Falkirk), 1932 v Sp (1)

Galvin, A. (Tottenham H), 1983 v Ho, Ma; 1984 v Ho (sub), Is (sub); 1985 v M, USSR, N, D, I, N, Sp; 1986 v U, Ic, Cz; 1987 v Bel (2), S, Bul, L; (with Sheffield W), 1988 v L, Bul, R, Pol, N, E, USSR, Ho; 1989 v Sp; (with Swindon T), 1990 v WG (29)

Gannon, E. (Notts Co), 1949 v Sw; (with Sheffield W), 1949 v Bel, P, Se, Sp; 1950 v Fi; 1951 v N; 1952 v WG, A; 1954 v L, F; 1955 v N; (with Shelbourne), 1955 v N, WG (14)

Gannon, M. (Shelbourne), 1972 v A (1)

Gaskins, P. (Shamrock R), 1934 v Bel, Ho; 1935 v H, Sw, G; (with St James' Gate), 1938 v Cz, Pol (7)

Gavin, J. T. (Norwich C), 1950 v Fi (2); 1953 v F; 1954 v L; (with Tottenham H), 1955 v Ho, WG; (with Norwich C), 1957 v D (7)

Geoghegan, M. (St James' Gate), 1937 v G; 1938 v N (2)

Gibbons, A. (St Patrick's Ath), 1952 v WG; 1954 v L; 1956 v Y, Sp (4)

Gilbert, R. (Shamrock R), 1966 v WG (1)

Giles, C. (Doncaster R), 1951 v N (1)

Giles, M. J. (Manchester U), 1960 v Se, Ch; 1961 v W, N, S (2); 1962 v Cz (2), A; 1963 v Ic, S; (with Leeds U), 1964 v A (2), Sp (2), Pol, N, E; 1965 v Sp; 1966 v Sp (2), A, Bel; 1967 v Sp, T (2); 1969 v A, D, Cz; 1970 v S, Pol, WG; 1971 v I; 1973 v F, USSR; 1974 v Br, U, Ch; 1975 v USSR, T, Sw, USSR, Sw; (with WBA), 1976 v T; 1977 v E, T, F (2), Pol, Bul; (with Shamrock R), 1978 v Bul, T, Pol, N, D; 1979 v Ni, D, Bul, WG (59)

Given, S. J. J. (Blackburn R), 1996 v Ru, CzR, P, Cro, Ho, US, Bol; 1997 v Lie (2); (with Newcastle U), 1998 v Li, Ic, Li, Bel (2), CzR, Arg, M; 1999 v Cro, Ma, Y, Para, Se, Ni; 2000 v Gr, S.Af; 2001 v Fi, Cy, And (2), P, Es (31)

Givens, D. J. (Manchester U), 1969 v D, H; 1970 v S, Cz, D, H; (with Luton T), 1970 v Pol, WG; 1971 v Se, I (2), A; 1972 v Ir, Ec, P; (with QPR), 1973 v F, USSR, Pol, F, N; 1974 v Pol, Br, U, Ch; 1975 v USSR, T, Sw, USSR, Sw, WG; 1976 v T, N, Pol; 1977 v E, T, F (2), Sp, Bul; 1978 v Bul, N, D; (with Birmingham C), 1979 v Ni (sub), E, D, Bul, WG; 1980 v US (sub), Ni (sub), Sw, Arg; 1981 v Ho, Bel, Cy (sub), W; (with Neuchatel X), 1982 v F (sub) (56)

Glen, W. (Shamrock R), 1927 v I; 1929 v Bel; 1930 v Bel; 1932 v Sp; 1936 v Ho, Sw, H, L (8)

Glynn, D. (Drumcondra), 1952 v WG; 1955 v N (2)

Godwin, T. F. (Shamrock R), 1949 v P, Se, Sp; 1950 v Fi, E; (with Leicester C), 1950 v Fi, Se, Bel; 1951 v N; (with Bournemouth), 1956 v Ho; 1957 v E; 1958 v D, Pol (13)

Golding, J. (Shamrock R), 1928 v Bel; 1930 v Bel (2)

Goodman, J. (Wimbledon), 1997 v W, Mac, R (sub), Lie (sub) (4)

Gorman, W. C. (Bury), 1936 v Sw, H, L; 1937 v G, H; 1938 v N, Cz, Pol; 1939 v Sw, Pol (with Brentford) H; 1947 v E, P (13)

Grace, J. (Drumcondra), 1926 v I (1)

Grealish, A. (Orient), 1976 v N, Pol; 1978 v N, D; 1979 v Ni, E, WG; (with Luton T), 1980 v W, Cz, Bul, US, Ni, E, Cy, Sw, Arg; 1981 v WG 'B', Ho, Bel, F, Cy, W, Bel, Pol; (with Brighton & HA), 1982 v Ho, Alg, Ch, Br, Tr; 1983 v Ho, Sp, Ic, Sp; 1984 v Ic, Ho; (with WBA), 1985 v M, USSR, N, D, Sp (sub), Sw; 1986 v USSR, D (45)

Gregg, E. (Bohemians), 1978 v Pol, D (sub); 1979 v E (sub), D, Bul, WG; 1980 v W, Cz (8)

Griffith, R. (Walsall), 1935 v H (1)

Grimes, A. A. (Manchester U), 1978 v T, Pol, N (sub); 1980 v Bul, US, Ni, E, Cy; 1981 v WG 'B' (sub), Cz, Pol; 1982 v Alg; 1983 v Sp (2); (with Coventry C), 1984 v Pol, Is; (with Luton T), 1988 v L, R (18)

Hale, A. (Aston Villa), 1962 v A; (with Doncaster R), 1963 v Ic; 1964 v Sp (2); (with Waterford), 1967 v Sp; 1968 v Pol (sub); 1969 v Pol, A, D; 1970 v S, Cz; 1971 v Pol (sub); 1972 v A (sub); 1974 v Pol (sub) (14)

Hamilton, T. (Shamrock R), 1959 v Cz (2) (2)

Hand, E. K. (Portsmouth), 1969 v Cz (sub); 1970 v Pol, WG; 1971 v Pol, A; 1973 v USSR, F, USSR, Pol, F; 1974 v Pol, Br, U, Ch; 1975 v T, Sw, USSR, Sw, WG; 1976 v T (20)

Harrington, W. (Cork), 1936 v Ho, Sw, H, L; 1938 v Pol (sub) (5)

Harte, I.P. (Leeds U), 1996 v Cro (sub), Ho, M, Bol; 1997 v Lie, Mac, Ic (sub), W, Mac (sub), R, Lie; 1998 v Li, Ic, Li, Bel (2), Arg, M; 1999 v Para; 2000 v Cro (sub), Ma (sub), CzR; 2001 v Ho, P, Es, Fi, Cy, And (2), P, Es (31)

Hartnett, J. B. (Middlesbrough), 1949 v Sp; 1954 v L (2)

Haverty, J. (Arsenal), 1956 v Ho; 1957 v D, WG, E (2); 1958 v D, Pol, A; 1959 v Pol; 1960 v Se, Ch; 1961 v W, N, S (2); (with Blackburn R), 1962 v Cz (2); (with Millwall), 1963 v S; 1964 v A, Sp, Pol, N, E; (with Celtic), 1965 v Pol; (with Bristol R), 1965 v Sp; (with Shelbourne), 1966 v Sp (2), WG, A, Bel; 1967 v T, Sp (32)

Hayes, A. W. P. (Southampton), 1979 v D (1)

Hayes, W. E. (Huddersfield T), 1947 v E, P (2)

Hayes, W. J. (Limerick), 1949 v Bel (1)

Healey, R. (Cardiff C), 1977 v Pol; 1980 v E (sub) (2)

Heighway, S. D. (Liverpool), 1971 v Pol, Se (2), I, A; 1973 v USSR; 1975 v USSR, T, USSR, WG; 1976 v T, N; 1977 v E, F (2), Bul; 1978 v Bul, N, D; 1979 v Ni, Bul; 1980 v Bul, US, Ni, E, Cy, Arg; 1981 v Bel, F, Cy, W, Bel; (with Minnesota K), 1982 v Ho (34)

Henderson, B. (Drumcondra), 1948 v P, Sp (2)

Hennessy, J. (Shelbourne), 1965 v Pol, Bel, Sp; 1966 v WG; (with St Patrick's Ath), 1969 v A (5)

Herrick, J. (Cork Hibernians), 1972 v A, Ch (sub); (with Shamrock R), 1973 v F (sub) (3)

Higgins, J. (Birmingham C), 1951 v Arg (1)

Holland, M. R. (Ipswich T), 2000 v Mac (sub), M, US, S.Af; 2001 v P (sub), Fi, Cy (sub), And (2), P (sub), Es (11)

Holmes, J. (Coventry C), 1971 v A (sub); 1973 v F, USSR, Pol, F, N; 1974 v Pol, Br; 1975 v USSR, Sw; 1976 v T, N, Pol; 1977 v E, T, F, Sp; (with Tottenham H), F, Pol, Bul; 1978 v Bul, T, Pol, N, D; 1979 v Ni, E, D, Bul; (with Vancouver W), 1981 v W (30)

Horlacher, A. F. (Bohemians), 1930 v Bel; 1932 v Sp, Ho; 1934 v Ho (sub); 1935 v H;1936 v Ho, Sw (7)

Houghton, R. J. (Oxford U), 1986 v W, U, Ic, Cz; 1987 v Bel (2), S (2), Pol, L; 1988 v L, Bul; (with Liverpool), Is, Y, N, E, USSR, Ho; 1989 v Ni, Tun, Sp, F, H, Sp, Ma, H; 1990 v Ni, Ma, Fi, E, Eg, Ho, R, I; 1991 v Mor, T, E (2), Pol, Ch, US; 1992 v H, Alb, US, I, P; (with Aston Villa), 1993 v D, Sp, Ni, D, Alb, La, Li; 1994 v Li, Sp, Ni, Bol, G (sub), I, M, N, Ho; (with C Palace), 1995 v P, A; 1996 v A, CzR; 1997 v Lie, R, Lie; (with Reading), 1998 v Li, R, Bel (1 + sub) (73)

Howlett, G. (Brighton & HA), 1984 v Chn (sub) (1)

Hoy, M. (Dundalk), 1938 v N; 1939 v Sw, Pol, H (2), G (6)

Hughton, C. (Tottenham H), 1980 v US, E, Sw, Arg; 1981 v Ho, Bel, F, Cy, W, Bel, Pol; 1982 v F; 1983 v Ho, Sp, Ma, Sp; 1984 v Ic, Ho, Ma; 1985 v M (sub), USSR, N, I, Is, E, Sp; 1986 v Sw, USSR, U, Ic; 1987 v Bel, Bul; 1988 v Is, Y, Pol, N, E, USSR, Ho; 1989 v Ni, F, H, Sp, Ma, H; 1990 v W (sub), USSR (sub), Fi, T (sub), Ma; 1991 v T; (with West Ham U); Ch; 1992 v T (53)

Hurley, C. J. (Millwall), 1957 v E; (with Sunderland), 1958 v D, Pol, A; 1959 v Cz (2); 1960 v Se, Ch, WG, Se; 1961 v W, N, S (2); 1962 v Cz (2), A; 1963 v Ic (2), S; 1964 v A (2), Sp (2), Pol, N; 1965 v Sp; 1966 v WG, A, Bel; 1967 v T, Sp, T, Cz; 1968 v Cz, Pol; 1969 v Pol, D, Cz, (with Bolton W), H (40)

Hutchinson, F. (Drumcondra), 1935 v Sw, G (2)

Irwin, D. J. (Manchester U), 1991 v Mor, T, W, E, Pol, US; 1992 v H, Pol, W, US, Alb, US (sub). I; 1993 v La, D, Sp, Ni, D, Alb, La, Li; 1994 v Li, Sp, Ni, Bol, G, I, M; 1995 v La, Lie, Ni, E, Ni, P, Lie, A; 1996 v A, P, Ho, CzR; 1997 v Lie, Mac, Ic, Mac, R; 1998 v Li, Bel, Arg (sub); 1999 v Cro, Y, Para, Mac; 2000 v Y, Mac, T (2) (56)

Jordan, D. (Wolverhampton W), 1937 v Sw, F (2)

Jordan, W. (Bohemians), 1934 v Ho; 1938 v N (2)

Kavanagh, G. A. (Stoke C), 1998 v CzR (sub); 1999 v Se (sub), Ni (sub) (3)

Kavanagh, P. J. (Celtic), 1931 v Sp; 1932 v Sp (2)

Keane, R. D. (Wolverhampton W), 1998 v CzR (sub), Arg, M; 1999 v Cro, Ma, Para, Se (sub), Ni, Mac; (with Coventry C), 2000 v Y, Ma, Mac, T, CzR, Gr, S, M, S.Af (sub); (with Internazionale), 2001 v Ho, P, Es, Fi, Cy, And, P (25)

Keane, R. M. (Nottingham F), 1991 v Ch; 1992 v H, Pol, W, Sw, Alb, US; 1993 v La, D, Sp, W, Ni, D, Alb, La, Li; (with Manchester U), 1994 v Li, Sp, Ni, Bol, G, CzR (sub), I, M, N, Ho; 1995 v Ni (2); 1996 v A, Ru; 1997 v Ic, W, Mac, R, Lie; 1998 v Li, Ic, Li; 1999 v Cro, Ma, Y, Para; 2000 v Y, T (2), CzR; 2001 v Ho, P, Es, Cy, And, P (52)

Keane, T. R. (Swansea T), 1949 v Sw, P, Se, Sp (4)

Kearin, M. (Shamrock R), 1972 v A (1)

Kearns, F. T. (West Ham U), 1954 v L (1)

Kearns, M. (Oxford U), 1971 v Pol (sub); (with Walsall), 1974 v Pol (sub), U, Ch; 1976 v N, Pol; 1977 v E, T, F (2), Sp, Bul; 1978 v N, D; 1979 v Ni, E; (with Wolverhampton W), 1980 v US, Ni (18)

Kelly, A. T. (Sheffield U), 1993 v W (sub); 1994 v Ru (sub), G; 1995 v La, Ni, E, Ni, P, Lie, A; 1996 v A, La, P, Ho; 1997 v Mac, Ic, Mac, R; 1998 v R, Arg (sub); 1999 v Para (sub), Mac; (with Blackburn R), 2000 v Y, Cro, Ma, Mac, T, CzR, S, US; 2001 v Ho, P, Es (33)

Kelly, D. T. (Walsall), 1988 v Is, R, Y; (with West Ham U), 1989 v Tun (sub); (with Leicester C), 1990 v USSR, Ma; 1991 v Mor, W (sub), Ch, US; 1992 v H; (with Newcastle U), I (sub); P; 1993 v Sp (sub), Ni; (with Wolverhampton W), 1994 v Ru, N (sub); 1995 v E, Ni; (with Sunderland), 1996 v La (sub); 1997 v Ic, W (sub), Mac (sub); (with Tranmere R), 1998 v Li (sub), R (sub), Bel (sub) (26)

Kelly, G. (Leeds U), 1994 v Ru, Ho, Bol (sub), G (sub), CzR, N, Ho; 1995 v La, Lie, Ni (2), P, Lie, A; 1996 v A, La, P, Ho; 1997 v W (sub), R, Lie; 1998 v Li, Ic, Li, Bel (2), CzR, Arg, M; 2000 v Cro, Mac, CzR; 2001 v Ho (sub), Fi, Cy, And (2), P, Es (38)

Kelly, J. (Derry C), 1932 v Ho; 1934 v Bel; 1936 v Sw, L (4)

Kelly, J. A. (Drumcondra), 1957 v WG, E; (with Preston NE), 1962 v A; 1963 v Ic (2), S; 1964 v A (2), Sp (2), Pol; 1965 v Bel; 1966 v A, Bel; 1967 v Sp (2), T, Cz; 1968 v Pol, Cz; 1969 v Pol, A, D, Cz, D, H; 1970 v S, D, H, Pol, WG; 1971 v Pol,

Se (2), I (2), A; 1972 v Ir, Ec, Ch, P; 1973 v USSR, F, USSR, Pol, F, N (47)

Kelly, J. P. V. (Wolverhampton W), 1961 v W, N, S; 1962 v Cz (2) (5)

Kelly, M. J. (Portsmouth), 1988 v Y, Pol (sub); 1989 v Tun; 1991 v Mor (4)

Kelly, N. (Nottingham F), 1954 v L (1)

Kendrick, J. (Everton), 1927 v I; (with Dolphin) 1934 v Bel, Ho; 1936 v Ho (4)

Kenna, J. J. (Blackburn R), 1995 v P (sub), Lie (sub), A (sub); 1996 v La, P, Ho, Ru (sub), CzR, P, Cro, Ho, US; 1997 v Lie, Mac, Ic, R (sub), Lie; 1998 v Li, Ic, R, Bel (1 + sub), CzR, Arg; 1999 v Cro (sub), Ma; 2000 v T (sub) (27)

Kennedy, M. J. (Liverpool), 1996 v A, La (sub), P, Ru, CzR, Cro, Ho (sub), US (sub), M, Bol (sub); 1997 v R, Lie; 1998 v Li, Ic (sub), R, Bel (2), (with Wimbledon), M (sub); 1999 v Ma (sub), Se, Ni, Mac; (with Manchester C), 2000 v Y, Ma, Mac, CzR, S, M, US (sub), S.Af (sub); 2001 v And (31)

Kennedy, M. F. (Portsmouth), 1986 v Ic, Cz (sub) (2)

Kennedy, W. (St James' Gate), 1934 v Bel, Ho (3)

Keogh, J. (Shamrock R), 1966 v WG (sub) (1)

Keogh, S. (Shamrock R), 1959 v Pol (1)

Kernaghan, A. N. (Middlesbrough), 1993 v La, D (2), Alb, La, Li; 1994 v Li; (with Manchester C), Sp, Ni, Bol (sub), CzR; 1995 v Lie, E; 1996 v A, P (sub), Ho (sub), Ru, P, Cro (sub), Ho, US, Bol (22)

Kiely, D. L. (Charlton Ath), 2000 v T (sub + 1), Gr (sub), M (4)

Kiernan, F. W. (Shamrock R), 1951 v Arg, N; (with Southampton), 1952 v WG (2), A (5)

Kilbane, K. D. (WBA), 1998 v Ic, CzR (sub), Arg; 1999 v Se (sub), Mac (sub); 2000 v Y, Cro (sub), Ma, T (2); (with Sunderland), CzR, Gr, S, M (sub), US, S.Af (sub); 2001 v Ho, P, Es, Fi, Cy, And (2), P, Es (25)

Kinnear, J. P. (Tottenham H), 1967 v T; 1968 v Cz, Pol; 1969 v A; 1970 v Cz, D, H, Pol; 1971 v Se (sub), I; 1972 v Ir, Ec, Ch, P; 1973 v USSR, F; 1974 v Pol, Br, U, Ch; 1975 v USSR, T, Sw, USSR, WG; (with Brighton & HA), 1976 v T (sub) (26)

Kinsella, J. (Shelbourne), 1928 v Bel (1)

Kinsella, M. A. (Charlton Ath), 1998 v CzR, Arg; 1999 v Cro, Ma, Y, Para, Se, Ni, Mac; 2000 v Y, Cro, Ma, Mac, T, CzR, Gr; 2001 v Ho, P, Es, Fi, Cy, And, P, Es (24)

Kinsella, O. (Shamrock R), 1932 v Ho; 1938 v N (2)

Kirkland, A. (Shamrock R), 1927 v I (1)

Lacey, W. (Shelbourne), 1927 v I; 1928 v Bel; 1930 v Bel (3)

Langan, D. (Derby Co), 1978 v T, N; 1980 v Sw, Arg; (with Birmingham C), 1981 v WG 'B', Ho, Bel, F, Cy, W, Bel, Cz, Pol; 1982 v Ho, F; (with Oxford U), 1985 v N, Sp, Sw; 1986 v W, U; 1987 v Bel, S, Pol, Br (sub), L (sub); 1988 v L (26)

Lawler, J. F. (Fulham), 1953 v A; 1954 v L, F; 1955 v N, H, N, WG; 1956 v Y (8)

Lawlor, J. C. (Drumcondra), 1949 v Bel; (with Doncaster R), 1951 v N, Arg (3)

Lawlor, M. (Shamrock R), 1971 v Pol, Se (2), I (sub); 1973 v Pol (5)

Lawrenson, M. (Preston NE), 1977 v Pol; (with Brighton), 1978 v Bul, Pol, N (sub); 1979 v Ni, E; 1980 v E, Cy, Sw; 1981 v Ho, Bel, F, Cy, Pol; (with Liverpool), 1982 v Ho, F; 1983 v Ho, Sp, Ic, Ma, Sp; 1984 v Ic, Ho, Ma, Is; 1985 v USSR, N, D, I, E, N; 1986 v Sw, USSR, D; 1987 v Bel, S; 1988 v Bul, Is (38)

Leech, M. (Shamrock R), 1969 v Cz, D, H; 1972 v A, Ir, Ec, P; 1973 v USSR (sub) (8)

Lennon, C. (St James' Gate), 1935 v H, Sw, G (3)

Lennox, G. (Dolphin), 1931 v Sp; 1932 v Sp (2)

Lowry, D. (St Patrick's Ath), 1962 v A (sub) (1)

Lunn, R. (Dundalk), 1939 v Sw, Pol (2)

Lynch, J. (Cork Bohemians), 1934 v Bel (1)

McAlinden, J. (Portsmouth), 1946 v P, Sp (2)

McAteer, J. W. (Bolton W), 1994 v Ru, Ho (sub), Bol (sub), G, CzR (sub), I (sub), M (sub), N, Ho (sub); 1995 v La, Lie, Ni (2 sub), Lie; (with Liverpool), 1996 v La, P, Ho (sub), Ru; 1997 v Mac, Ic, W, Mac; 1998 v Ic (sub), Li, R; 1999 v Cro, Ma, Y; (with Blackburn R), Para, Se; 2000 v CzR (sub), S, M, US (sub), S.Af; 2001 v Ho, P, Es, Fi (sub), Cy (40)

McCann, J. (Shamrock R), 1957 v WG (1)

McCarthy, J. (Bohemians), 1926 v I; 1928 v Bel; 1930 v Bel (3)

McCarthy, M. (Manchester C), 1984 v Pol, Chn; 1985 v M, D, I, Is, E, Sp, Sw; 1986 v USSR, W (sub), U, Ic, Cz; 1987 v S (2), Pol, Bul, Bel (with Celtic), Br, L; 1988 v Bul, Is, R, Y, N, E, USSR, Ho; 1989 v Ni, Tun, Sp, F, H, Sp; (with Lyon), 1990 v WG, Ni (with Millwall), W, USSR, Fi, T, E, Eg, Ho, R, I; 1991 v Mor, T, E, US; 1992 v H, T, Alb (sub), US, I, P (57)

McCarthy, M. (Shamrock R), 1932 v Ho (1)

McConville, T. (Dundalk), 1972 v A; (with Waterford), 1973 v USSR, F, USSR, Pol, F (6)

McDonagh, Jacko (Shamrock R), 1984 v Pol (sub), Ma (sub); 1985 v M (sub) (3)

McDonagh, J. (Everton), 1981 v WG 'B', W, Bel, Cz; (with Bolton W), 1982 v Ho, F, Ch, Br; 1983 v Ho, Sp, Ic, Ma, Sp; (with Notts Co), 1984 v Ic, Ho, Pol; 1985 v M, USSR, N, D, Sp, Sw; 1986 v Sw, USSR; (with Wichita Wings) D (25)

McEvoy, M. A. (Blackburn R), 1961 v S (2); 1963 v S; 1964 v A, Sp (2), Pol, N, E; 1965 v Pol, Bel, Sp; 1966 v Sp (2); 1967 v Sp, T, Cz (17)

McGee, P. (QPR), 1978 v T, N (sub), D (sub); 1979 v Ni, E, D (sub), Bul (sub); 1980 v Cz, Bul; (with Preston NE), US, Ni, Cy, Sw, Arg; 1981 v Bel (sub) (15)

McGoldrick, E. J. (C Palace), 1992 v Sw, US, I, P (sub); 1993 v D, W, Ni (sub), D; (with Arsenal), 1994 v Ni, Ru, Ho, CzR; 1995 v La (sub), Lie, E (15)

McGowan, D. (West Ham U), 1949 v P, Se, Sp (3)

McGowan, J. (Cork U), 1947 v Sp (1)

McGrath, M. (Blackburn R), 1958 v A; 1959 v Pol, Cz (2); 1960 v Se, WG, Se; 1961 v W; 1962 v Cz (2); 1963 v S; 1964 v A (2), E; 1965 v Pol, Bel, Sp; 1966 v Sp; (with Bradford), 1966 v WG, A, Bel; 1967 v T (22)

McGrath, P. (Manchester U), 1985 v I (sub), Is, E, N (sub), Sw (sub); 1986 v Sw (sub), D, W, Ic, Cz; 1987 v Bel (2), S (2), Pol, Bul, Br, L; 1988 v L, Bul, Y, Pol, N, E, Ho; 1989 v Ni, F, H, Sp, Ma, H; (with Aston Villa), 1990 v WG, Ma, USSR, Fi, T, E, Eg, Ho, R, I; 1991 v E (2), W, Pol, Ch (sub), US; 1992 v Pol, T, Sw, US, Alb, US, I, P; 1993 v La, Sp, Ni, D, La, Li; 1994 v Sp, Ni, G, CzR, I, M, N, Ho; 1995 v La, Ni, E, Ni, P, Lie, A; 1996 v A, La, P, Ho, Ru, CzR; (with Derby Co), 1997 v W (83)

McGuire, W. (Bohemians), 1936 v Ho (1)

McKenzie, G. (Southend U), 1938 v N (2), Cz, Pol; 1939 v Sw, Pol, H (2), G (9)

Mackey, G. (Shamrock R), 1957 v D, WG, E (3)

McLoughlin, A. F. (Swindon T), 1990 v Ma, E (sub), Eg (sub); 1991 v Mor (sub), E (sub); (with Southampton), W, Ch (sub); 1992 v H (sub), W (sub); (with Portsmouth), US (1 + sub), I (sub), P; 1993 v W; 1994 v Ni (sub), Ru, Ho (sub); 1995 v Lie (sub); 1996 v P, Cro, Ho, US, M, Bol (sub); 1997 v Lie, Mac, Ic, W, Mac; 1998 v Li (sub), Ic, Li, R, Bel, CzR (sub); 1999 v Y, Para (sub), Se, Ni (sub); 2000 v Cro, Ma (sub), Mac (42)

McLoughlin, F. (Fordsons), 1930 v Bel; (with Cork), 1932 v Sp (2)

McMillan, W. (Belfast Celtic), 1946 v P, Sp (2)

McNally, J. B. (Luton T), 1959 v Cz; 1961 v S; 1963 v Ic (3)

McPhail, S. (Leeds U), 2000 v S, US, S.Af (3)

Macken, A. (Derby Co), 1977 v Sp (1)

Madden, O. (Cork), 1936 v H (1)

Maguire, J. (Shamrock R), 1929 v Bel (1)

Mahon, A. J. (Tranmere R), 2000 v Gr (sub), S.Af (2)

Malone, G. (Shelbourne), 1949 v Bel (1)

Mancini, T. J. (QPR), 1974 v Pol, Br, U, Ch; (with Arsenal), 1975 v USSR (5)

Martin, C. (Bo'ness), 1927 v I (1)

Martin, C. J. (Glentoran), 1946 v P (sub), Sp; 1947 v E; (with Leeds U), 1947 v Sp; 1948 v P, Sp; (with Aston Villa), 1949 v Sw, Bel, P, Se, Sp; 1950 v Fi, E, Fi, Se, Bel; 1951 v Arg; 1952 v WG, A, Sp; 1954 v F (2), L; 1955 v N, Ho, N, WG; 1956 v Y, Sp, Ho (30)

Martin, M. P. (Bohemians), 1972 v A, Ir, Ec, Ch, P; 1973 v USSR; (with Manchester U), 1973 v USSR, Pol, F, N; 1974 v Pol, Br, U, Ch; 1975 v USSR, T, Sw, USSR, Sw, WG; (with WBA), 1976 v T, N, Pol; 1977 v E, T, F (2), Sp, Pol, Bul; (with Newcastle U), 1979 v D, Bul, WG; 1980 v W, Cz, Bul, US, Ni; 1981 v WG 'B', F, Bel, Cz; 1982 v Ho, F, Alg, Ch, Br, Tr; 1983 v Ho, Sp, Ma, Sp (52)

Maybury, A. (Leeds U), 1998 v CzR; 1999 v Ni (2)

Meagan, M. K. (Everton), 1961 v S; 1962 v A; 1963 v Ic; 1964 v Sp; (with Huddersfield T), 1965 v Bel; 1966 v Sp (2), A, Bel; 1967 v Sp, T, Sp, T, Cz; 1968 v Cz, Pol; (with Drogheda), 1970 v S (17)

Meehan, P. (Drumcondra), 1934 v Ho (1)

Milligan, M. J. (Oldham Ath), 1992 v US (sub) (1)

Monahan, P. (Sligo R), 1935 v Sw, G (2)

Mooney, J. (Shamrock R), 1965 v Pol, Bel (2)

Moore, A. (Middlesbrough), 1996 v CzR, Cro (sub), Ho, M, Bol; 1997 v Lie (sub), Mac (sub), Ic (sub) (8)

Moore, P. (Shamrock R), 1931 v Sp; 1932 v Ho; (with Aberdeen), 1934 v Bel, Ho; 1935 v H, G; (with Shamrock R), 1936 v Ho; 1937 v G, H (9)

Moran, K. (Manchester U), 1980 v Sw, Arg; 1981 v WG 'B', Bel, F, Cy, W (sub), Bel, Cz, Pol; 1982 v F, Alg; 1983 v Ic; 1984 v Ic, Ho, Ma, Is; 1985 v M; 1986 v D, Ic, Cz; 1987 v Bel

(2), S (2), Pol, Bul, Br, L; 1988 v L, Bul, Is, R, Y, Pol, N, E, USSR, Ho; (with Sporting Gijon), 1989 v Ni, Sp, H, Sp, Ma, H; 1990 v Ni, Ma; (with Blackburn R), W, USSR (sub), Ma, E, Eg, Ho, R, I; 1991 v T (sub), W, E, Pol, Ch, US; 1992 v Pol, US; 1993 v D, Sp, Ni, Alb; 1994 v Li, Sp, Ho, Bol (71)

Moroney, T. (West Ham U), 1948 v Sp; 1949 v P, Se, Sp; 1950 v Fi, E, Fi, Bel; 1951 v N (2); 1952 v WG; (with Evergreen U), 1954 v F (12)

Morris, C. B. (Celtic), 1988 v Is, R, Y, Pol, N, E, USSR, Ho; 1989 v Ni, Tun, Sp, F, H (1+sub); 1990 v WG, Ni, Ma (sub), W, USSR, Fi (sub), T, E, Eg, Ho, R, I; 1991 v E; 1992 v H (sub), Pol, W, Sw, US (2), P; (with Middlesbrough), 1993 v W (35)

Moulson, C. (Lincoln C), 1936 v H, L; (with Notts Co), 1937 v H, Sw, F (5)

Moulson, G. B. (Lincoln C), 1948 v P, Sp; 1949 v Sw (3)

Mucklan, C. (Drogheda U), 1978 v Pol (1)

Muldoon, T. (Aston Villa), 1927 v I (1)

Mulligan, P. M. (Shamrock R), 1969 v Cz, D, H; 1970 v S, Cz, D; (with Chelsea), 1970 v H, Pol, WG; 1971 v Pol, Se, I; 1972 v A, Ir, Ec, Ch, P; (with C Palace), 1973 v F, USSR, Pol, F, N; 1974 v Pol, Br, U, Ch; 1975 v USSR, T, Sw, USSR, Sw; (with WBA), 1976 v T, Pol; 1977 v E, T, F (2), Pol, Bul; 1978 v Bul, N, D; 1979 v E, D, Bul (sub), WG; (with Shamrock R), 1980 v W, Cz, Bul, US (sub) (50)

Munroe, L. (Shamrock R), 1954 v L (1)

Murphy, A. (Clyde), 1956 v Y (1)

Murphy, B. (Bohemians), 1986 v U (1)

Murphy, J. (C Palace), 1980 v W, US, Cy (3)

Murray, T. (Dundalk), 1950 v Bel (1)

Newman, W. (Shelbourne), 1969 v D (1)

Nolan, R. (Shamrock R), 1957 v D, WG, E; 1958 v Pol; 1960 v Ch, WG, Se; 1962 v Cz (2); 1963 v Ic (10)

O'Brien, A. J. (Newcastle U), 2001 v Es (sub) (1)

O'Brien, F. (Philadelphia F), 1980 v Cz, E, Cy (sub) (3)

O'Brien, L. (Shamrock R), 1986 v U; (with Manchester U), 1987 v Br; 1988 v Is (sub), R (sub), Y (sub), Pol (sub); 1989 v Tun; (with Newcastle U), Sp (sub); 1992 v Sw (sub); 1993 v W; (with Tranmere R), 1994 v Ru; 1996 v Cro, Ho, US, Bol; 1997 v Mac (sub) (16)

O'Brien, M. T. (Derby Co), 1927 v I; (with Walsall), 1929 v Bel; (with Norwich C), 1930 v Bel; (with Watford), 1932 v Ho (4)

O'Brien, R. (Notts Co), 1976 v N, Pol; 1977 v Sp, Pol; 1980 v Arg (sub) (5)

O'Byrne, L. B. (Shamrock R), 1949 v Bel (1)

O'Callaghan, B. R. (Stoke C), 1979 v WG (sub); 1980 v W, US; 1981 v W; 1982 v Br, Tr (6)

O'Callaghan, K. (Ipswich T), 1981 v WG 'B', Cz, Pol; 1982 v Alg, Ch, Br, Tr (sub); 1983 v Sp, Ic (sub), Ma (sub), Sp (sub); 1984 v Ic, Ho, Ma; 1985 v M (sub), N (sub), D (sub), (with Portsmouth) E (sub); 1986 v Sw (sub), USSR (sub); 1987 v Br (21)

O'Connell, A. (Dundalk), 1967 v Sp; (with Bohemians), 1971 v Pol (sub) (2)

O'Connor, T. (Shamrock R), 1950 v Fi, E, Fi, Se (4)

O'Connor, T. (Fulham), 1968 v Cz; (with Dundalk), 1972 v A, Ir, Ec (sub), Ch; (with Bohemians), 1973 v F (sub), Pol (sub) (7)

O'Driscoll, J. F. (Swansea T), 1949 v Sw, Bel, Se (3)

O'Driscoll, S. (Fulham), 1982 v Ch, Br, Tr (sub) (3)

O'Farrell, F. (West Ham U), 1952 v A; 1953 v A; 1954 v F; 1955 v Ho, N; 1956 v Y, Ho; (with Preston NE), 1958 v D; 1959 v Cz (9)

O'Flanagan, K. P. (Bohemians), 1938 v N, Cz, Pol; 1939 v Pol, H (2), G; (with Arsenal), 1947 v E, Sp, P (10)

O'Flanagan, M. (Bohemians), 1947 v E (1)

O'Hanlon, K. G. (Rotherham U), 1988 v Is (1)

O'Kane, P. (Bohemians), 1935 v H, Sw, G (3)

O'Keefe, E. (Everton), 1981 v W; (with Port Vale), 1984 v Chn; 1985 v M, USSR (sub), E (5)

O'Keefe, T. (Cork), 1934 v Bel; (with Waterford), 1938 v Cz, Pol (3)

O'Leary, D. (Arsenal), 1977 v E, F (2), Sp, Bul; 1978 v Bul, N, D; 1979 v E, Bul, WG; 1980 v W, Bul, Ni, E, Cy; 1981 v WG 'B',Ho, Cz, Pol; 1982 v Ho, F; 1983 v Ho, Ic, Sp; 1984 v Pol, Is, Chn; 1985 v USSR, N, D, Is, E (sub), N, Sp, Sw; 1986 v Sw, USSR, D, W; 1989 v Sp, Ma, H; 1990 v WG, Ni (sub), Ma, W (sub), USSR, Fi, T, Ma, R (sub); 1991 v Mor, T, E (2), Pol, Ch; 1992 v H, Pol, T, W, Sw, US, Alb, I, P; 1993 v W (68)

O'Leary, P. (Shamrock R), 1980 v Bul, US, Ni, E (sub), Cz, Arg; 1981 v Ho (7)

O'Mahoney, M. T. (Bristol R), 1938 v Cz, Pol; 1939 v Sw, Pol, H, G (6)

O'Neill, F. S. (Shamrock R), 1962 v Cz (2); 1965 v Pol, Bel, Sp; 1966 v Sp (2), WG, A; 1967 v Sp, T, Sp, T; 1969 v Pol, A, D, Cz, D (sub), H (sub); 1972 v A (20)

O'Neill, J. (Everton), 1952 v Sp; 1953 v F, A; 1954 v F, L, F; 1955 v N, Ho, N, WG; 1956 v Y, Sp; 1957 v D; 1958 v A; 1959 v Pol, Cz (2) (17)

O'Neill, J. (Preston NE), 1961 v W (1)

O'Neill, K. P. (Norwich C), 1996 v P (sub), Cro, Ho (sub), US (sub), M, Bol; 1997 v Lie, Mac (1 + sub); 1999 v Cro, Y (sub); (with Middlesbrough), Ni (sub); 2000 v Mac (sub) (13)

O'Neill, W. (Dundalk), 1936 v Ho, Sw, H, L; 1937 v G, H, Sw, F; 1938 v N; 1939 v H, G (11)

O'Regan, K. (Brighton & HA), 1984 v Ma, Pol; 1985 v M, Sp (sub) (4)

O'Reilly, J. (Brideville), 1932 v Ho; (with Aberdeen), 1934 v Bel, Ho; (with Brideville), 1936 v Ho; Sw, H, L; (with St James' Gate), 1937 v H, Sw, F; 1938 v N (2), Cz, Pol; 1939 v Sw, Pol, H (2), G (20)

O'Reilly, J. (Cork U), 1946 v P, Sp (2)

Peyton, G. (Fulham), 1977 v Sp (sub); 1978 v Bul, T, Pol; 1979 v D, Bul, WG; 1980 v W, Cz, Bul, E, Cy, Sw, Arg; 1981 v Ho, Bel, F, Cy; 1982 v Tr; 1985 v M (sub); 1986 v W, Cz; (with Bournemouth), 1988 v L, Pol; 1989 v Ni, Tun; 1990 v USSR, Ma; 1991 v Ch; (with Everton) 1992 v US (2), I (sub), P (33)

Peyton, N. (Shamrock R), 1957 v WG; (with Leeds U), 1960 v WG, Se (sub); 1961 v W; 1963 v Ic, S (6)

Phelan, T. (Wimbledon), 1992 v H, Pol (sub), T, W, Sw, US, I (sub), P; (with Manchester C), 1993 v La (sub), D, Sp, Ni, Alb, La, Li; 1994 v Li, Sp, Ni, Ho, Bol, G, CzR, I, M, Ho; 1995 v E; 1996 v La; (with Chelsea), Ho, Ru, P, Cro, Ho, US, M (sub), Bol; (with Everton), 1997 v W, Mac; 1998 v R; (with Fulham), 2000 v S (sub), M, US, S.Af (42)

Quinn, B. S. (Coventry C), 2000 v Gr, M, US (sub), S.Af (sub) (4)

Quinn, N. J. (Arsenal), 1986 v Ic (sub), Cz; 1987 v Bul (sub), Br (sub); 1988 v L (sub), Bul (sub), Is, R (sub), Pol (sub), E (sub); 1989 v Tun (sub), Sp (sub), H (sub); (with Manchester C), 1990 v USSR, Ma, Eg (sub), Ho, R, I; 1991 v Mor, T, E(2) W, Pol; 1992 v H, W (sub), US, Alb, US, I (sub), P; 1993 v La, D, Sp, Ni, D, Alb, La, Li; 1994 v Li, Sp, Ni; 1995 v La, Lie, Ni, E, Ni, P, Lie, A; 1996 v A, La, P, Ru, CzR, P (sub), Cro, Ho (sub), US; (with Sunderland), 1997 v Lie; 1998 v Li, Arg; 1999 v Ma, Y, Para, Se, Ni, Mac; 2000 v Y, Cro (sub), Ma, Mac, T, CzR, S, M, US (sub), S.Af; 2001 v Ho, P, Es, P, Es (84)

Reid, C. (Brideville), 1931 v Sp (1)

Richardson, D. J. (Shamrock R), 1972 v A (sub); (with Gillingham), 1973 v N (sub); 1980 v Cz (3)

Rigby, A. (St James' Gate), 1935 v H, Sw, G (3)

Ringstead, A. (Sheffield U), 1951 v Arg, N; 1952 v WG (2), A, Sp; 1953 v A; 1954 v F; 1955 v N; 1956 v Y, Sp, Ho; 1957 v E (2); 1958 v D, Pol, A; 1959 v Pol, Cz (2) (20)

Robinson, J. (Bohemians), 1928 v Bel; (with Dolphin), 1931 v Sp (2)

Robinson, M. (Brighton & HA), 1981 v WG 'B', F, Cy, Bel, Pol; 1982 v Ho, F, Alg, Ch; 1983 v Ho, Sp, Ic, Ma; (with Liverpool), 1984 v Ic, Ho, Is; 1985 v USSR, N; (with QPR), N, Sp, Sw; 1986 v D (sub), W, Cz (24)

Roche, P. J. (Shelbourne), 1972 v A; (with Manchester U), 1975 v USSR, T, Sw, USSR, Sw, WG; 1976 v T (8)

Rogers, E. (Blackburn R), 1968 v Cz, Pol; 1969 v Pol, A, D, Cz, D, H; 1970 v S, D, H; 1971 v I (2), A; (with Charlton Ath), 1972 v Ir, Ec, Ch, P; 1973 v USSR (19)

Ryan, G. (Derby Co), 1978 v T; (with Brighton & HA), 1979 v E, WG; 1980 v W, Cy (sub), Sw, Arg (sub); 1981 v WG 'B' (sub), F (sub), Pol (sub); 1982 v Br (sub), Ho (sub), Alg (sub), Ch (sub), Tr; 1984 v Pol, Chn; 1985 v M (18)

Ryan, R. A. (WBA), 1950 v Se, Bel; 1951 v N, Arg, N; 1952 v WG (2), A, Sp; 1953 v F, A; 1954 v F, L, F; 1955 v N; (with Derby Co), 1956 v Sp (16)

Savage, D. P. T. (Millwall), 1996 v P (sub), Cro (sub), US (sub), M, Bol (5)

Saward, P. (Millwall), 1954 v L; (with Aston Villa), 1957 v E (2); 1958 v D, Pol, A; 1959 v Pol; 1960 v Se, Ch, WG, Se; 1961 v W, N; (with Huddersfield T), 1961 v S; 1962 v A; 1963 v Ic (2) (18)

Scannell, T. (Southend U), 1954 v L (1)

Scully, P. J. (Arsenal), 1989 v Tun (sub) (1)

Sheedy, K. (Everton), 1984 v Ho (sub), Ma; 1985 v D, I, Is, Sw; 1986 v Sw, D; 1987 v S, Pol; 1988 v Is, R, Pol, E (sub), USSR; 1989 v Ni, Tun, H, Sp, Ma, H; 1990 v Ni, Ma, W

(sub), USSR, Fi (sub), T, E, Eg, Ho, R, I; 1991 v W, E, Pol, Ch, US; 1992 v H, Pol, T, W; (with Newcastle U), Sw (sub), Alb; 1993 v La, W (sub) (45)

Sheridan, J. J. (Leeds U), 1988 v R, Y, Pol, N (sub); 1989 v Sp; (with Sheffield W), 1990 v W, T (sub), Ma, I (sub); 1991 v Mor (sub), T, Ch, US (sub); 1992 v H; 1993 v La; 1994 v Sp (sub), Ho, Bol, G, CzR, I, M, N, Ho; 1995 v La, Lie, Ni, E, Ni, P, Lie, A; 1996 v A, Ho (34)

Slaven, B. (Middlesbrough), 1990 v W, Fi, T (sub). Ma; 1991 v W, Pol (sub); 1993 v W (7)

Sloan, J. W. (Arsenal), 1946 v P, Sp (2)

Smyth, M. (Shamrock R), 1969 v Pol (sub) (1)

Squires, J. (Shelbourne), 1934 v Ho (1)

Stapleton, F. (Arsenal), 1977 v T, F, Sp, Bul; 1978 v Bul, N, D; 1979 v Ni, E (sub), D, WG; 1980 v W, Bul, Ni, E, Cy; 1981 v WG 'B', Ho, Bel, F, Cy, Bel, Cz, Pol; (with Manchester U), 1982 v Ho, F, Alg; 1983 v Ho, Sp, Ic, Ma, Sp; 1984 v Ic, Ho, Ma, Pol, Is, Chn; 1985 v N, D, I, Is, E, N, Sw; 1986 v Sw, USSR, D, U, Ic, Cz (sub); 1987 v Bel (2), S (2), Pol, Bul, L; (with Ajax), 1988 v L, Bul, R, Y, N, E, USSR, Ho; (with Le Havre), 1989 v F, Sp, Ma; (with Blackburn R), 1990 v WG, Ma (sub) (71)

Staunton, S. (Liverpool), 1989 v Tun, Sp (2), Ma, H; 1990 v WG, Ni, Ma, W, USSR, Fi, T, Ma, E, Eg, Ho, R, I; 1991 v Mor, T, E (2), W, Pol, Ch, US; (with Aston Villa), 1992 v Pol, T, Sw, US, Alb, US, I, P; 1993 v Sp, Ni, D, Alb, La, Li; 1994 v Li, Sp, Ho, Bol, G, CzR, I, M, N, Ho; 1995 v La, Lie, Ni, E, Ni, P, Lie, A; 1996 v La, P, Ru; 1997 v Lie, Mac (2), W, R, Lie; 1998 v Li, Ic, Li, Bel (2), Arg; (with Liverpool), 1999 v Cro, Ma, Y, Se; 2000 v Y, Cro, Ma, Mac, CzR (sub); Gr; 2001 v Ho (sub), Fi (sub); (with Aston Villa), And (sub), P, Es (89)

Stevenson, A. E. (Dolphin), 1932 v Ho; (with Everton), 1947 v E, Sp, P; 1948 v P, Sp; 1949 v Sw (7)

Strahan, F. (Shelbourne), 1964 v Pol, N, E; 1965 v Pol; 1966 v WG (5)

Sullivan, J. (Fordsons), 1928 v Bel (1)

Swan, M. M. G. (Drumcondra), 1960 v Se (sub) (1)

Synnott, N. (Shamrock R), 1978 v T, Pol; 1979 v Ni (3)

Taylor, T. (Waterford), 1959 v Pol (sub) (1)

Thomas, P. (Waterford), 1974 v Pol, Br (2)

Townsend, A. D. (Norwich C), 1989 v F, Sp (sub), Ma (sub), H; 1990 v WG (sub), Ni, Ma, W, USSR, Fi (sub), T, Ma (sub), E, Eg, Ho, R, I; (with Chelsea), 1991 v Mor, T, E (2), W, Pol, Ch, US; 1992 v Pol, W, US, Alb, US, I; 1993 v La, D, Sp, Ni, D, Alb, La, Li; (with Aston Villa), 1994 v Li, Ni, Ho, Bol, G, CzR, I, M, N, Ho; 1995 v La, Ni, E, Ni, P; 1996 v A, La, Ho, Ru, CzR, P; 1997 v Lie, Mac (2), Ic, R, Lie; 1998 v Li; (with Middlesbrough), Ic, Bel (2) (70)

Traynor, T. J. (Southampton), 1954 v L; 1962 v A; 1963 v Ic (2), S; 1964 v A (2), Sp (8)

Treacy, R. C. P. (WBA), 1966 v WG; 1967 v Sp, Cz; 1968 v Cz; (with Charlton Ath), 1968 v Pol; 1969 v Pol, Cz, D; 1970 v S, D, H (sub), Pol (sub), WG (sub); 1971 v Pol, Se (sub+1), I, A; (with Swindon T), 1972 v Ir, Ec, Ch, P; 1973 v USSR, F, USSR, Pol, F, N; 1974 v Pol; (with Preston NE), Br; 1975 v USSR, Sw (2), WG; 1976 v T, N (sub), Pol (sub); (with WBA), 1977 v F, Pol; (with Shamrock R), 1978 v T, Pol; 1980 v Cz (sub) (42)

Tuohy, L. (Shamrock R), 1956 v Y; 1959 v Cz (2); (with Newcastle U), 1962 v A; 1963 v Ic (2); (with Shamrock R), 1964 v A; 1965 v Bel (8)

Turner, C. J. (Southend U), 1936 v Sw; 1937 v G, H, Sw, F; 1938 v N (2), (with West Ham U) Cz, Pol; 1939 v H (10)

Turner, P. (Celtic), 1963 v S; 1964 v Sp (2)

Vernon, J. (Belfast C), 1946 v P, Sp (2)

Waddock, G. (QPR), 1980 v Sw, Arg; 1981 v W, Pol (sub); 1982 v Alg; 1983 v Ic, Ma, Sp, Ho (sub); 1984 v Ma (sub), Ic, Ho, Is; 1985 v I, Is, E, N, Sp; 1986 v USSR; (with Millwall), 1990 v USSR, T (21)

Walsh, D. J. (Linfield), 1946 v P, Sp; (with WBA), 1947 v Sp, P; 1948 v P, Sp; 1949 v Sw, P, Se, Sp; 1950 v E, Fi, Se; 1951 v N; (with Aston Villa), Arg, N; 1952 v Sp; 1953 v A; 1954 v F (2) (20)

Walsh, J. (Limerick), 1982 v Tr (1)

Walsh, M. (Blackpool), 1976 v N, Pol; 1977 v F (sub), Pol; (with Everton), 1979 v Ni (sub); (with QPR), D (sub), Bul, WG (sub); (with Porto), 1981 v Bel (sub), Cz; 1982 v Alg (sub); 1983 v Sp, Ho (sub), Sp (sub); 1984 v Ic (sub), Ma, Pol, Chn; 1985 v USSR, N (sub), D (21)

Walsh, M. (Everton), 1982 v Ch, Br, Tr; 1983 v Ic (4)

Walsh, W. (Manchester C), 1947 v E, Sp, P; 1948 v P, Sp; 1949 v Bel; 1950 v E, Se, Bel (9)

Waters, J. (Grimsby T), 1977 v T; 1980 v Ni (sub) (2)

Watters, F. (Shelbourne), 1926 v I (1)

Weir, E. (Clyde), 1939 v H (2), G (3)

Whelan, R. (St Patrick's Ath), 1964 v A, E (sub) (2)

Whelan, R. (Liverpool), 1981 v Cz (sub); 1982 v Ho (sub), F; 1983 v Ic, Ma, Sp; 1984 v Is; 1985 v USSR, N, I (sub), Is, E, N (sub), Sw (sub); 1986 v USSR (sub), W; 1987 v Bel (sub), S, Bul, Bel, Br, L; 1988 v L, Bul, Pol, N, E, USSR, Ho; 1989 v Ni, F, H, Sp, Ma; 1990 v WG, Ni, Ma, W, Ho (sub); 1991 v Mor, E; 1992 v Sw; 1993 v La, W (sub), Li (sub); 1994 v Li (sub), Sp, Ru, Ho, G (sub), N (sub); (with Southend U), 1995 v Lie, A (53)

Whelan, W. (Manchester U), 1956 v Ho; 1957 v D, E (2) (4)

White, J. J. (Bohemians), 1928 v Bel (1)

Whittaker, R. (Chelsea), 1959 v Cz (1)

Williams, J. (Shamrock R), 1938 v N (1)

Scotland's Colin Hendry is given a lesson by Croatia's Robert Prosinecki on how to trap the ball during this World Cup qualifier. (Actionimages/John Sibley)

BRITISH AND IRISH INTERNATIONAL GOALSCORERS SINCE 1872

Where two players with the same surname and initials have appeared for the same country, and one or both have scored, they have been distinguished by reference to the club which appears *first* against their name in the international appearances section.

ENGLAND

A'Court, A.	1
Adams, T. A.	5
Adcock, H.	1
Alcock, C. W.	1
Allen, A.	3
Allen, R.	2
Amos, A.	1
Anderson, V.	2
Anderton, D. R.	7
Astall, G.	1
Athersmith, W. C.	3
Atyeo, P. J. W.	5
Bache, J. W.	4
Bailey, N. C.	2
Baily, E. F.	5
Baker, J. H.	3
Ball, A. J.	8
Bambridge, A. L.	1
Bambridge, E. C.	11
Barclay, R.	2
Barmby, N. J.	4
Barnes, J.	11
Barnes, P. S.	4
Barton, J.	1
Bassett, W. I.	8
Bastin, C. S.	12
Beardsley, P. A.	9
Beasley, A.	1
Beattie, T. K.	1
Beckham, D. R. J.	4
Becton, F.	2
Bedford, H.	1
Bell, C.	9
Bentley, R. T. F.	9
Bishop, S. M.	1
Blackburn, F.	1
Blissett, L.	3
Bloomer, S.	28
Bond, R.	2
Bonsor, A. G.	1
Bowden, E. R.	1
Bowers, J. W.	2
Bowles, S.	1
Bradford, G. R. W.	1
Bradford, J.	7
Bradley, W.	2
Bradshaw, F.	3
Brann, G.	1
Bridges, B. J.	1
Bridgett, A.	3
Brindle, T.	1
Britton, C. S.	1
Broadbent, P. F.	2
Broadis, I. A.	8
Brodie, J. B.	1
Bromley-Davenport, W.	2
Brook, E. F.	10
Brooking, T. D.	5
Brooks, J.	2
Broome, F. H.	3
Brown, A.	4
Brown, A. S.	1
Brown, G.	5
Brown, J.	3
Brown, W.	1
Buchan, C. M.	4
Bull, S. G.	4
Bullock, N.	2
Burgess, H.	4
Butcher, T.	3
Byrne, J. J.	8
Camsell, G. H.	18
Carter, H. S.	7
Carter, J. H.	4
Chadwick, E.	3
Chamberlain, M.	1
Chambers, H.	5
Channon, M. R.	21
Charlton, J.	6
Charlton, R.	49
Chenery, C. J.	1
Chivers, M.	13
Clarke, A. J.	10
Cobbold, W. N.	6
Cock, J. G.	2
Cole, A.	1
Common, A.	2
Connelly, J. M.	7
Coppell, S. J.	7
Cotterill, G. H.	2
Cowans, G.	2
Crawford, R.	1
Crawshaw, T. H.	1
Crayston, W. J.	1
Creek, F. N. S.	1
Crooks, S. D.	7
Currey, E. S.	2
Currie, A. W.	3
Cursham, A. W.	2
Cursham, H. A.	5
Daft, H. B.	3
Davenport, J. K.	2
Davis, G.	1
Davis, H.	1
Day, S. H.	2
Dean, W. R.	18
Devey, J. H. G.	1
Dewhurst, F.	11
Dix, W. R.	1
Dixon, K. M.	4
Dixon, L. M.	1
Dorrell, A. R.	1
Douglas, B.	11
Drake, E. J.	6
Ducat, A.	1
Dunn, A. T. B.	2
Eastham, G.	2
Edwards, D.	5
Ehiogu, U.	1
Elliott, W. H.	3
Evans, R. E.	1
Ferdinand, L.	5
Finney, T.	30
Fleming, H. J.	9
Flowers, R.	10
Forman, Frank	1
Forman, Fred	3
Foster, R. E.	3
Fowler, R. B.	4
Francis, G. C. J.	3
Francis, T.	12
Freeman, B. C.	3
Froggatt, J.	2
Froggatt, R.	2
Galley, T.	1
Gascoigne, P. J.	10
Geary, F.	3
Gibbins, W. V. T.	3
Gilliatt, W. E.	3
Goddard, P.	1
Goodall, J.	12
Goodyer, A. C.	1
Gosling, R. C.	2
Goulden, L. A.	4
Grainger, C.	3
Greaves, J.	44
Grosvenor, A. T.	2
Gunn, W.	1
Haines, J. T. W.	2
Hall, G. W.	9
Halse, H. J.	2
Hampson, J.	5
Hampton, H.	2
Hancocks, J.	2
Hardman, H. P.	1
Harris, S. S.	2
Hassall, H. W.	4
Hateley, M.	9
Haynes, J. N.	18
Hegan, K. E.	4
Henfrey, A. G.	2
Heskey, E. W.	2
Hilsdon, G. R.	14
Hine, E. W.	4
Hinton, A. T.	1
Hirst, D. E.	1
Hitchens, G. A.	5
Hobbis, H. H. F.	1
Hoddle, G.	8
Hodgetts, D.	1
Hodgson, G.	1
Holley, G. H.	8
Houghton, W. E.	5
Howell, R.	1
Hughes, E. W.	1
Hulme, J. H. A.	4
Hunt, G. S.	1
Hunt, R.	18
Hunter, N.	2
Hurst, G. C.	24
Ince, P. E. C.	2
Jack, D. N. B.	3
Johnson, D. E.	6
Johnson, E.	2
Johnson, J. A.	2
Johnson, T. C. F.	5
Johnson, W. H.	1
Kail, E. I. L.	2
Kay, A. H.	1
Keegan, J. K.	21
Kelly, R.	8
Kennedy, R.	1
Kenyon-Slaney, W. S.	2
Keown, M. R.	1
Kevan, D. T.	8
Kidd, B.	1
Kingsford, R. K.	1
Kirchen, A. J.	2
Kirton, W. J.	1
Langton, R.	1
Latchford, R. D.	5
Latherton, E. G.	1
Lawler, C.	1
Lawton, T.	22
Lee, F.	10
Lee, J.	1
Lee, R. M.	2
Lee, S.	2
Le Saux, G. P.	1
Lindley, T.	14
Lineker, G.	48
Lofthouse, J. M.	3
Lofthouse, N.	30
Hon. A. Lyttelton	1
Mabbutt, G.	1
Macdonald, M.	6
Mannion, W. J.	11
Mariner, P.	13
Marsh, R. W.	1
Matthews, S.	11
Matthews, V.	1
McCall, J.	1
McDermott, T.	3
McManaman, S.	3
Medley, L. D.	1
Melia, J.	1
Mercer, D. W.	1
Merson, P. C.	3
Milburn, J. E. T.	10
Miller, H. S.	1
Mills, G. R.	3
Milward, A.	3
Mitchell, C.	5
Moore, J.	1
Moore, R. F.	2
Moore, W. G. B.	2
Morren, T.	1
Morris, F.	1
Morris, J.	3
Mortensen, S. H.	23
Morton, J. R.	1
Mosforth, W.	3
Mullen, J.	6
Mullery, A. P.	1
Neal, P. G.	5
Needham, E.	3
Nicholls, J.	1
Nicholson, W. E.	1
O'Grady, M.	3
Osborne, F. R.	3
Owen, M. J.	10
Own goals	23
Page, L. A.	1
Paine, T. L.	7
Palmer, C. L.	1
Parry, E. H.	1
Parry, R. A.	1
Pawson, F. W.	1
Payne, J.	2
Peacock, A.	3
Pearce, S.	5
Pearson, J. S.	5
Pearson, S. C.	5
Perry, W.	2
Peters, M.	20

Hughton, C.	1	McAteer, J. W.	1	O'Farrell, F.	2	Sheridan, J.	5
Hurley, C.	2	McCann, J.	1	O'Flanagan, K.	3	Slaven, B.	1
		McCarthy, M.	2	O'Keefe, E.	1	Sloan, W.	1
Irwin, D.	4	McEvoy, A.	6	O'Leary, D. A.	1	Squires, J.	1
		McGee, P.	4	O'Neill, F.	1	Stapleton, F.	20
Jordan, D.	1	McGrath, P.	8	O'Neill, K. P.	4	Staunton, S.	7
		McLoughlin, A. F.	2	O'Reilly, J. (*Brideville*)	2	Strahan, J.	1
Kavanagh, G. A.	1	McPhail, S. J. P.	1	O'Reilly, J. (*Cork*)	1	Sullivan, J.	1
Keane, R. D.	7	Mancini, T.	1	Own goals	8		
Keane, R. M.	8	Martin, C.	6			Townsend, A. D.	7
Kelly, D.	9	Martin, M.	4	Quinn, N.	20	Treacy, R.	5
Kelly, G.	1	Mooney, J.	1			Touhy, L.	4
Kelly, J.	2	Moore, P.	7	Ringstead, A.	7		
Kennedy, M.	3	Moran, K.	6	Robinson, M.	4	Waddock, G.	3
Kernaghan, A. N.	1	Moroney, T.	1	Rogers, E.	5	Walsh, D.	5
		Mulligan, P.	1	Ryan, G.	1	Walsh, M.	3
Lacey, W.	1			Ryan, R.	3	Waters, J.	1
Lawrenson, M.	5	O'Callaghan, K.	1			White, J. J.	2
Leech, M.	2	O'Connor, T.	2	Sheedy, K.	9	Whelan, R.	3

BRITISH & IRISH INTERNATIONAL MANAGERS

England
Walter Winterbottom 1946–1962 (after period as coach); Alf Ramsey 1963–1974; Joe Mercer (caretaker) 1974; Don Revie 1974–1977; Ron Greenwood 1977–1982; Bobby Robson 1982–1990; Graham Taylor 1990–1993; Terry Venables (coach) 1994–1996; Glenn Hoddle 1996–1999; Kevin Keegan 1999–2000; Sven-Goran Eriksson from January 2001.

Northern Ireland
Peter Doherty 1951–1952; Bertie Peacock 1962–1967; Billy Bingham 1967–1971; Terry Neill 1971–1975; Dave Clements (player-manager) 1975–1976; Danny Blanchflower 1976–1979; Billy Bingham 1980–1994; Bryan Hamilton 1994–1998; Lawrie McMenemy 1998–1999; Sammy McIlroy from January 2000.

Scotland (since 1967)
Bobby Brown 1967–1971; Tommy Docherty 1971–1972; Willie Ormond 1973–1977; Ally MacLeod 1977–1978; Jock Stein 1978–1985; Alex Ferguson (caretaker) 1985–1986 Andy Roxburgh (coach) 1986–1993; Craig Brown from September 1993.

Wales (since 1974)
Mike Smith 1974–1979; Mike England 1980–1988; David Williams (caretaker) 1988; Terry Yorath 1988–1993; John Toshack 1994 for one match; Mike Smith 1994–1995; Bobby Gould 1995–1999; Mark Hughes from November 1999.

Republic of Ireland
Liam Tuohy 1971–1972; Johnny Giles 1973–1980 (after period as player-manager); Eoin Hand 1980–1985; Jack Charlton 1986–1996; Mick McCarthy from February 1996.

Sven-Goran Eriksson and his immediate caretaker/predecessor Peter Taylor are either applauding or about to offer a lengthy prayer. (Actionimages/Darren Walsh)

SOUTH AMERICA

COPA LIBERTADORES 2001

QUALIFYING GROUP

	P	W	D	L	F	A	Pts
Cruz Azul	6	4	0	2	15	8	12
Dep Tachira	6	4	0	2	7	8	12
Ital-Chacao	6	3	0	3	9	10	9
Atlante	6	1	0	5	8	13	3

GROUP 1

	P	W	D	L	F	A	Pts
Rosario Central	6	4	1	1	13	4	13
At Junior	6	3	1	2	10	6	10
Velez Sarsfield	6	3	0	3	5	8	9
Universitario	6	0	2	4	3	13	2

GROUP 2

	P	W	D	L	F	A	Pts
Palmeiras	6	5	1	0	16	5	16
Cerro Porteno	6	4	1	1	17	6	13
Univ de Chile	6	1	1	4	5	13	4
Sport Boys	6	0	1	5	3	17	1

GROUP 3

	P	W	D	L	F	A	Pts
Nacional (Uru)	6	4	2	0	9	2	14
Concepcion	6	2	1	3	8	8	7
San Lorenzo	6	2	1	3	9	10	7
Wilstermann	6	2	0	4	7	13	6

GROUP 4

	P	W	D	L	F	A	Pts
Cruzeiro	6	5	1	0	15	4	16
Emelec	6	2	3	1	7	6	9
Olimpia	6	1	2	3	10	13	5
Sporting Cristal	6	1	0	5	4	13	3

GROUP 5

	P	W	D	L	F	A	Pts
River Plate	6	4	0	2	13	6	12
El Nacional	6	3	0	3	8	9	9
Guarani	6	2	1	3	9	11	7
The Strongest	6	2	1	3	10	14	7

GROUP 6

	P	W	D	L	F	A	Pts
Vasco da Gama	6	6	0	0	16	5	18
America (Col)	6	4	0	2	10	9	12
Penarol	6	1	1	4	7	10	4
Dep Tachira	6	0	1	5	3	12	1

GROUP 7

	P	W	D	L	F	A	Pts
Cruz Azul	6	4	1	1	12	7	13
Sao Caetano	6	2	2	2	6	4	8
Defensor	6	2	1	3	8	11	7
Olmedo	6	2	0	4	11	15	6

GROUP 8

	P	W	D	L	F	A	Pts
Boca Juniors	6	5	0	1	7	5	15
Cobreloa	6	3	1	2	8	7	10
Dep Cali	6	3	0	3	13	8	9
Oriente	6	0	1	5	6	14	1

SECOND ROUND, FIRST LEG

Cobreloa 2, Rosario Central 3
El Nacional 1, Cruzeiro 2
America (Col) 2, Nacional (Uru) 0
Concepcion 1, Vasco da Gama 3
Emelec 2, River Plate 0
Sao Caetano 1, Palmeiras 0
At Junior 2, Boca Juniors 3
Cerro Porteno 2, Cruz Azul 1

SECOND ROUND, SECOND LEG

Cruzeiro 4, El Nacional 1
Rosario Central 1, Cobreloa 1
Boca Juniors 1, At Junior 1
Cruz Azul 3, Cerro Porteno 1
Palmeiras 1, Sao Caetano 0
(Palmeiras won 5-3 on penalties).
Vasco da Gama 1, Concepcion 0
Nacional (Uru) 1, America (Col) 3
River Plate 5, Emelec 0

QUARTER-FINALS, FIRST LEG

Rosario Central 1, America (Col) 0
River Plate 0, Cruz Azul 0
Palmeiras 3, Cruzeiro 3
Vasco da Gama 0, Boca Juniors 1

QUARTER-FINALS, SECOND LEG

Cruz Azul 3, River Plate 0
Boca Juniors 3, Vasco da Gama 0
Cruzeiro 2, Palmeiras 2
America (Col) 3, Rosario Central 2

SEMI-FINALS, FIRST LEG

Boca Juniors 2, Palmeiras 2
Cruz Azul 2, Rosario Central 0

SEMI-FINALS, SECOND LEG

Palmeiras 2, Boca Juniors 2
(Boca Juniors won 3-2 on penalties).
Rosario Central 3, Cruz Azul 3

FINAL, FIRST LEG

Cruz Azul 0, Boca Juniors 1

FINAL, SECOND LEG

Boca Juniors 0, Cruz Azul 1
Boca Juniors won 3-1 on penalties.

MERCONORTE CUP

GROUP A

	P	W	D	L	F	A	Pts
Guadalajara	6	3	2	1	12	7	11
El Nacional	6	2	3	1	7	6	9
Merida	6	2	1	3	9	11	7
America Cali	6	1	2	3	3	7	5

GROUP B

	P	W	D	L	F	A	Pts
Atl Nacional	6	3	1	2	10	8	10
Alajuelense	6	2	3	1	9	7	9
Necaxa	6	1	4	1	5	5	7
Alianza	6	1	2	3	6	10	5

GROUP C

	P	W	D	L	F	A	Pts
Millonarios	6	3	3	0	11	6	12
Toluca	6	2	2	2	15	11	8
Barcelona	6	1	3	2	6	10	6
Universitario	6	1	2	3	7	12	5

GROUP D

	P	W	D	L	F	A	Pts
Emelec	6	3	1	2	6	5	10
Sporting Cristal	6	2	3	1	10	6	9
Pachuca	6	3	0	3	6	7	9
Oriente	6	1	2	3	7	11	5

SEMI-FINALS, FIRST LEG

Guadalajara 1, Atl Nacional 1
Emelec 3, Millonarios 3

SEMI-FINALS, SECOND LEG

Atl Nacional 3, Guadalajara 3
Atl Nacional won 4-2 on penalties.
Millonarios 2, Emelec 0

FINAL, FIRST LEG

Millonarios 0, Atl Nacional 0

FINAL, SECOND LEG

Atl Nacional 2, Millonarios 1

MERCOSUR CUP

GROUP A	P	W	D	L	F	A	Pts
River Plate	6	4	2	0	10	5	14
Flamengo	6	3	2	1	10	3	11
Velez Sarsfield	6	1	3	2	7	8	6
Univ de Chile	6	0	1	5	4	15	1

GROUP B	P	W	D	L	F	A	Pts
Cruzeiro	6	4	1	1	12	4	13
Palmeiras	6	3	2	1	8	5	11
Independiente	6	2	1	3	9	10	7
Univ Catolica	6	0	2	4	7	17	2

GROUP C	P	W	D	L	F	A	Pts
Rosario	6	4	1	1	9	4	13
Sao Paulo	6	2	1	3	13	13	7
Cerro Porteno	6	2	1	3	13	15	7
Colo Colo	6	2	1	3	6	9	7

GROUP D	P	W	D	L	F	A	Pts
Boca Juniors	6	3	3	0	15	8	12
Nacional	6	2	3	1	8	8	9
Olimpia	6	3	0	3	9	10	9
Corinthians	6	0	2	4	7	13	2

GROUP E	P	W	D	L	F	A	Pts
Atl Mineiro	6	4	1	1	13	10	13
Vasco da Gama	6	3	1	2	11	7	10
Penarol	6	2	2	2	11	11	8
San Lorenzo	6	1	0	5	8	15	3

QUARTER-FINALS, FIRST LEG
Flamengo 1, River Plate 2
Vasco da Gama 1, Rosario 0
Palmeiras 3, Cruzeiro 2
Atl Mineiro 2, Boca Juniors 0

QUARTER-FINALS, SECOND LEG
Boca Juniors 2, Atl Mineiro 2
Rosario 1, Vasco da Gama 0
Vasco da Gama won 5-4 on penalties.
River Plate 4, Flamengo 3
Cruzeiro 1, Palmeiras 2

SEMI-FINALS, FIRST LEG
River Plate 1, Vasco da Gama 4
Palmeiras 4, Atl Mineiro 1

SEMI-FINALS, SECOND LEG
Atl Mineiro 0, Palmeiras 2
Vasco da Gama 1, River Plate 0

FINAL, FIRST LEG
Vasco da Gama 2, Palmeiras 0

FINAL, SECOND LEG
Palmeiras 1, Vasco da Gama 0

PLAY-OFF
Palmeiras 3, Vasco da Gama 4

FIFA CONFEDERATIONS CUP (in South Korea & Japan)

GROUP A
Australia 1, France 0
South Korea 2, Mexico 1
France 4, Mexico 0
South Korea 1, Australia 0

	P	W	D	L	F	A	Pts
France	3	2	0	1	9	1	6
Australia	3	2	0	1	3	1	6
South Korea	3	2	0	1	3	6	6
Mexico	3	0	0	3	1	8	0

GROUP B
Brazil 2, Cameroon 0
Japan 3, Canada 0
Canada 0, Brazil 0
Japan 2, Cameroon 0

	P	W	D	L	F	A	Pts
Japan	3	2	1	0	5	0	7
Brazil	3	1	2	0	2	0	5
Cameroon	3	1	0	2	2	4	3
Canada	3	0	1	2	0	5	1

SEMI-FINALS
Japan 1, Australia 0
France 2, Brazil 1

THIRD/FOURTH PLACE
Australia 1, Brazil 0

FINAL
France 1, Japan 0

ASIA

ASIAN NATIONS' CUP 2001
(Finals in Libya)

GROUP A
Iraq 2, Thailand 0
Libya 0, Iran 4
Iran 1, Thailand 1
Libya 2, Iraq 2
Iran 1, Iraq 0
Libya 1, Thailand 1

GROUP B
South Korea 2, China 2
Kuwait 0, Indonesia 0
China 4, Indonesia 0
Kuwait 1, South Korea 0
China 0, Kuwait 0
South Korea 3, Indonesia 0

GROUP C
Japan 4, Saudi Arabia 1
Qatar 1, Uzbekistan 1
Japan 8, Uzbekistan 0
Saudi Arabia 0, Qatar 0
Saudi Arabia 5, Uzbekistan 0
Japan 1, Qatar 1

QUARTER-FINALS
South Korea 2, Iran 1
China 3, Qatar 1
Japan 4, Iraq 1
Saudi Arabia 3, Kuwait 2

SEMI-FINALS
South Korea 1, Saudi Arabia 2
China 2, Japan 3

MATCH FOR 3RD PLACE
South Korea 1, China 0

FINAL
Japan 1, Saudi Arabia 0

UEFA UNDER-21 CHAMPIONSHIP 2000–2002

GROUP 1
Switzerland 3, Russia 1
Luxembourg 0, Yugoslavia 3
Luxembourg 1, Slovenia 5
Slovenia 0, Switzerland 0
Russia 2, Luxembourg 0
Yugoslavia 3, Switzerland 3
Russia 0, Slovenia 1
Slovenia 1, Yugoslavia 2
Switzerland 6, Luxembourg 0
Yugoslavia 2, Russia 2
Slovenia 1, Luxembourg 0
Russia 2, Yugoslavia 0
Switzerland 2, Slovenia 1
Luxembourg 0, Russia 10

GROUP 2
Holland 2, Republic of Ireland 0
Estonia 1, Portugal 3
Portugal 3, Republic of Ireland 1
Cyprus 0, Holland 1
Holland 1, Portugal 1
Republic of Ireland 1, Estonia 0
Cyprus 0, Republic of Ireland 1
Cyprus 3, Estonia 1
Portugal 3, Holland 0
Holland 4, Cyprus 2
Estonia 0, Holland 5
Republic of Ireland 0, Portugal 1
Estonia 0, Republic of Ireland 3
Portugal 7, Cyprus 0

GROUP 3
Bulgaria 1, Czech Republic 0
Iceland 0, Denmark 0
N Ireland 3, Malta 0
Czech Republic 2, Iceland 1
N Ireland 0, Denmark 3
Bulgaria 2, Malta 0
Iceland 2, N Ireland 5
Malta 0, Czech Republic 1
Denmark 2, Bulgaria 2
Bulgaria 1, Iceland 0
Malta 0, Denmark 0
N Ireland 0, Czech Republic 2
Bulgaria 2, N Ireland 0
Czech Republic 3, Denmark 0
Malta 1, Iceland 1
Iceland 3, Malta 0
Denmark 3, Czech Republic 4
N Ireland 1, Bulgaria 1
Denmark 3, Malta 0

Iceland 3, Bulgaria 2
Czech Republic 4, N Ireland 0

GROUP 4
Turkey 1, Moldova 0
Azerbaijan 0, Sweden 5
Slovakia 2, Macedonia 0
Sweden 0, Turkey 0
Macedonia 1, Azerbaijan 2
Moldova 0, Slovakia 3
Slovakia 1, Sweden 1
Moldova 3, Macedonia 0
Azerbaijan 1, Turkey 2
Sweden 2, Macedonia 0
Turkey 0, Slovakia 1
Azerbaijan 0, Moldova 0
Macedonia 1, Turkey 4
Slovakia 5, Azerbaijan 0
Moldova 0, Sweden 2
Sweden 4, Slovakia 0
Turkey 3, Azerbaijan 0
Macedonia 2, Moldova 0
Azerbaijan 0, Slovakia 0
Sweden 3, Moldova 0
Turkey 2, Macedonia 0

GROUP 5
Belarus 4, Wales 1
Norway 5, Armenia 1
Ukraine 0, Belarus 2
Armenia 1, Ukraine 2
Poland 0, Belarus 4
Wales 0, Norway 2
Belarus 5, Armenia 0
Poland 2, Wales 1
Norway 3, Ukraine 1
Armenia 1, Wales 0
Ukraine 1, Belarus 0
Norway 1, Poland 2
Belarus 1, Norway 0
Poland 1, Armenia 1
Wales 0, Ukraine 3
Armenia 1, Belarus 0
Ukraine 1, Norway 3
Wales 0, Poland 4
Armenia 2, Poland 0
Ukraine 1, Wales 0
Norway 5, Belarus 1

GROUP 6
Latvia 1, Scotland 3
Belgium 2, Croatia 1

Latvia 0, Belgium 2
Croatia 3, Scotland 1
Croatia 2, Latvia 1
Scotland 0, Belgium 1
Belgium 3, Latvia 0
Latvia 1, Croatia 1

GROUP 7
France 3, Israel 0
Bosnia 0, Spain 2
France 2, Austria 1
Spain 1, Israel 0
Austria 2, Spain 1
Israel 2, Bosnia 1
Bosnia 0, France 1
Israel 3, France 4
Bosnia 0, Austria 0
Spain 1, France 1
Austria 0, Israel 2
Austria 1, France 1
Spain 5, Bosnia 1
Israel 0, Spain 1

GROUP 8
Romania 3, Lithuania 0
Hungary 0, Italy 3
Lithuania 2, Georgia 1
Italy 1, Romania 1
Lithuania 0, Hungary 1
Italy 3, Georgia 2
Hungary 4, Lithuania 1
Romania 0, Italy 1
Georgia 0, Romania 3
Italy 1, Lithuania 0
Romania 1, Hungary 0
Georgia 0, Italy 2
Lithuania 0, Romania 1
Hungary 2, Georgia 1

GROUP 9
Finland 3, Albania 0
Germany 2, Greece 1
Greece 3, Finland 1
England 1, Germany 1
Albania 0, Greece 1
Finland 2, England 2
Germany 8, Albania 0
England 4, Finland 0
Albania 0, England 1
Greece 2, Germany 0
Finland 1, Germany 3
Greece 0, Albania 0
Greece 3, England 1

OLYMPIC FOOTBALL

Previous medallists

1896 Athens*	1 Denmark 2 Greece	1948 London	1 Sweden 2 Yugoslavia 3 Denmark	1980 Moscow	1 Czechoslovakia 2 East Germany 3 USSR
1900 Paris*	1 Great Britain 2 France	1952 Helsinki	1 Hungary 2 Yugoslavia 3 Sweden	1984 Los Angeles	1 France 2 Brazil 3 Yugoslavia
1904 St Louis**	1 Canada 2 USA	1956 Melbourne	1 USSR 2 Yugoslavia 3 Bulgaria	1988 Seoul	1 USSR 2 Brazil 3 West Germany
1908 London	1 Great Britain 2 Denmark 3 Holland	1960 Rome	1 Yugoslavia 2 Denmark 3 Hungary	1992 Barcelona	1 Spain 2 Poland 3 Ghana
1912 Stockholm	1 England 2 Denmark 3 Holland	1964 Tokyo	1 Hungary 2 Czechoslovakia 3 East Germany	1996 Atlanta	1 Nigeria 2 Argentina 3 Brazil
1920 Antwerp	1 Belgium 2 Spain 3 Holland	1968 Mexico City	1 Hungary 2 Bulgaria 3 Japan	2000 Sydney	1. Cameroon 2. Spain 3. Chile
1924 Paris	1 Uruguay 2 Switzerland 3 Sweden	1972 Munich	1 Poland 2 Hungary 3 E Germany/USSR		
1928 Amsterdam	1 Uruguay 2 Argentina 3 Italy	1976 Montreal	1 East Germany 2 Poland 3 USSR		
1932 Los Angeles	no tournament				
1936 Berlin	1 Italy 2 Austria 3 Norway				

* No official tournament
** No official tournament but gold medal later awarded by IOC

19TH UEFA UNDER-16 CHAMPIONSHIP

(Finals in England)

GROUP A
Romania 0, Spain 3
Germany 1, Belgium 2
Romania 2, Germany 8
Spain 5, Belgium 0
Belgium 2, Romania 0
Spain 0, Germany 2

GROUP B
Holland 0, Turkey 1
Poland 0, Russia 0
Holland 2, Poland 0
Turkey 0, Russia 1
Russia 0, Holland 0
Turkey 2, Poland 1

GROUP C
Switzerland 2, Hungary 1
England 1, Italy 3
England 2, Switzerland 0
Italy 3, Hungary 4
Hungary 0, England 1
Italy 1, Switzerland 1

GROUP D
Croatia 2, Finland 0
France 3, Scotland 0
France 3, Croatia 0
Scotland 3, Finland 1
Finland 0, France 5
Scotland 0, Croatia 1

QUARTER-FINALS
Spain 1, Italy 1
(Spain won 4-3 on penalties)
England 1, Germany 1
(England won 5-4 on penalties)
France 2, Russia 0
Turkey 0, Croatia 2

SEMI-FINALS
England 0, France 4
Spain 3, Croatia 0

MATCH FOR THIRD PLACE
Croatia 4, England 1

FINAL
France 0, Spain 1
(at Stadium of Light)

17TH UEFA UNDER-18 CHAMPIONSHIP

(Finals in Germany)

GROUP A
Germany 0, Ukraine 1
Holland 3, Croatia 0
Ukraine 2, Croatia 1
Germany 3, Holland 0
Germany 3, Croatia 2
Holland 0, Ukraine 0

GROUP B
France 1, Finland 2
Czech Republic 1, Russia 1

Russia 1, Finland 1
Czech Republic 0, France 1
France 2, Russia 0
Czech Republic 3, Finland 2

MATCH FOR 3RD PLACE
Czech Republic 1, Germany 3

FINAL
France 1, Ukraine 0

FIFA WORLD YOUTH UNDER-20 CHAMPIONSHIP

(Finals in Argentina)

GROUP A
Argentina 2, Finland 0
Egypt 0, Jamaica 0
Jamaica 0, Finland 1
Egypt 1, Argentina 7
Argentina 5, Jamaica 1
Egypt 2, Finland 1

GROUP B
Brazil 2, Germany 0
Iraq 3, Canada 0
Canada 0, Germany 4
Iraq 1, Brazil 6
Brazil 2, Canada 0
Germany 3, Iraq 1

GROUP C
USA 0, China 1
Chile 2, Ukraine 4
Ukraine 0, China 0
Chile 1, USA 4
USA 1, Ukraine 1
Chile 1, China 0

GROUP D
Angola 0, Czech Republic 0
Australia 2, Japan 0
Australia 0, Czech Republic 3
Japan 1, Angola 2
Angola 1, Australia 1
Czech Republic 0, Japan 3

GROUP E
Ecuador 2, Ethiopia 1
Costa Rica 3, Holland 1
Costa Rica 3, Ethiopia 1
Holland 1, Ecuador 1
Ecuador 0, Costa Rica 1
Ethiopia 2, Holland 3

GROUP F
Ghana 2, Paraguay 1
France 5, Iran 0
France 2, Paraguay 2
Iran 0, Ghana 1
Ghana 0, France 0
Paraguay 2, Iran 0

SECOND ROUND
USA 0, Egypt 2
Argentina 2, China 1
France 3, Germany 2
Brazil 4, Australia 0
Ukraine 1, Paraguay 2
Costa Rica 1, Czech Republic 2
Angola 0, Holland 2
Ghana 1, Ecuador 0

QUARTER-FINALS
Argentina 3, France 1
Czech Republic 0, Paraguay 1
Holland 1, Egypt 2
Ghana 2, Brazil 1

SEMI-FINALS
Egypt 0, Ghana 2
Argentina 5, Paraguay 0

MATCH FOR 3RD PLACE
Paraguay 0, Egypt 1

FINAL
Argentina 3, Ghana 0

ENGLAND UNDER-21 RESULTS 1976–2001

EC UEFA Competition for Under-21 Teams

Year	Date		Venue	Eng	Alb
			v ALBANIA	Eng	Alb
EC1989	Mar	7	Shkroda	2	1
EC1989	April	25	Ipswich	2	0
EC2001	Mar	27	Tirana	1	0
			v ANGOLA	Eng	Ang
1995	June	10	Toulon	1	0
1996	May	28	Toulon	0	2
			v ARGENTINA	Eng	Arg
1998	May	18	Toulon	0	2
2000	Feb	22	Fulham	1	0
			v AUSTRIA	Eng	Aus
1994	Oct	11	Kapfenberg	3	1
1995	Nov	14	Middlesbrough	2	1
			v BELGIUM	Eng	Bel
1994	June	5	Marseille	2	1
1996	May	24	Toulon	1	0
			v BRAZIL	Eng	B
1993	June	11	Toulon	0	0
1995	June	6	Toulon	0	2
1996	June	1	Toulon	1	2
			v BULGARIA	Eng	Bul
EC1979	June	5	Pernik	3	1
EC1979	Nov	20	Leicester	5	0
1989	June	5	Toulon	2	3
EC1998	Oct	9	West Ham	1	0
EC1999	June	8	Vratsa	1	0
			v CROATIA	Eng	Cro
1996	Apr	23	Sunderland	0	1
			v CZECHOSLOVAKIA	Eng	Cz
1990	May	28	Toulon	2	1
1992	May	26	Toulon	1	2
1993	June	9	Toulon	1	1
			v CZECH REPUBLIC	Eng	CzR
1998	Nov	17	Ipswich	0	1
			v DENMARK	Eng	Den
EC1978	Sept	19	Hvidovre	2	1
EC1979	Sept	11	Watford	1	0
EC1982	Sept	21	Hvidovre	4	1
EC1983	Sept	20	Norwich	4	1
EC1986	Mar	12	Copenhagen	1	0
EC1986	Mar	26	Manchester	1	1
1988	Sept	13	Watford	0	0
1994	Mar	8	Brentford	1	0
1999	Oct	8	Bradford	4	1
			v EAST GERMANY	Eng	EG
EC1980	April	16	Sheffield	1	2
EC1980	April	23	Jena	0	1
			v FINLAND	Eng	Fin
EC1977	May	26	Helsinki	1	0
EC1977	Oct	12	Hull	8	1
EC1984	Oct	16	Southampton	2	0
EC1985	May	21	Mikkeli	1	3
EC2000	Oct	10	Valkeakoski	2	2
EC2001	Mar	23	Barnsley	4	0
			v FRANCE	Eng	Fra
EC1984	Feb	28	Sheffield	6	1
EC1984	Mar	28	Rouen	1	0
1987	June	11	Toulon	0	2
EC1988	April	13	Besancon	2	4
EC1988	April	27	Highbury	2	2
1988	June	12	Toulon	2	4
1990	May	23	Toulon	7	3
1991	June	3	Toulon	1	0
1992	May	28	Toulon	0	0
1993	June	15	Toulon	1	0
1994	May	31	Aubagne	0	3
1995	June	10	Toulon	0	2
1998	May	14	Toulon	1	1
1999	Feb	9	Derby	2	1
			v GEORGIA	Eng	Geo
EC1996	Nov	8	Batumi	1	0
EC1997	April	29	Charlton	0	0
2000	Aug	31	Middlesbrough	6	1
			v GERMANY	Eng	Ger
1991	Sept	10	Scunthorpe	2	1
EC2000	Oct	6	Derby	1	1
			v GREECE	Eng	Gre
EC1982	Nov	16	Piraeus	0	1
EC1983	Mar	29	Portsmouth	2	1
1989	Feb	7	Patras	0	1
EC1997	Nov	13	Heraklion	0	2
EC1997	Dec	17	Norwich	4	2
EC2001	June	5	Athens	1	3
			v HOLLAND	Eng	H
EC1993	April	27	Portsmouth	3	0
EC1993	Oct	12	Utrecht	1	1
			v HUNGARY	Eng	Hun
EC1981	June	5	Keszthely	2	1
EC1981	Nov	17	Nottingham	2	0
EC1983	April	26	Newcastle	1	0
EC1983	Oct	11	Nyiregyhaza	2	0
1990	Sept	11	Southampton	3	1
1992	May	12	Budapest	2	2
1999	April	27	Budapest	2	2
			v ITALY	Eng	Italy
EC1978	Mar	8	Manchester	2	1
EC1978	April	5	Rome	0	0
EC1984	April	18	Manchester	3	1
EC1984	May	2	Florence	0	1
EC1986	April	9	Pisa	0	2
EC1986	April	23	Swindon	1	1
EC1997	Feb	12	Bristol	1	0
EC1997	Oct	10	Rieti	1	0
EC2000	May	27	Bratislava	0	2
2000	Nov	14	Monza*	0	0

*Abandoned 11 mins; fog.

				Eng	
			v ISRAEL	Eng	Isr
1985	Feb	27	Tel Aviv	2	1
			v LATVIA	Eng	Lat
1995	April	25	Riga	1	0
1995	June	7	Burnley	4	0
			v LUXEMBOURG	Eng	Lux
EC1998	Oct	13	Greven Macher	5	0
EC1999	Sept	3	Reading	5	0
			v MALAYSIA	Eng	Mal
1995	June	8	Toulon	2	0
			v MEXICO	Eng	Mex
1988	June	5	Toulon	2	1
1991	May	29	Toulon	6	0
1992	May	25	Toulon	1	1
2001	May	24	Leicester	3	0
			v MOLDOVA	Eng	Mol
EC1996	Aug	31	Chisinau	2	0
EC1997	Sept	9	Wycombe	1	0
			v MOROCCO	Eng	Mor
1987	June	7	Toulon	2	0
1988	June	9	Toulon	1	0
			v NORWAY	Eng	Nor
EC1977	June	1	Bergen	2	1
EC1977	Sept	6	Brighton	6	0
1980	Sept	9	Southampton	3	0
1981	Sept	8	Drammen	0	0
EC1992	Oct	13	Peterborough	0	2
EC1993	June	1	Stavanger	1	1
1995	Oct	10	Stavanger	2	2
			v POLAND	Eng	Pol
EC1982	Mar	17	Warsaw	2	1
EC1982	April	7	West Ham	2	2
EC1989	June	2	Plymouth	2	1
EC1989	Oct	10	Jastrzebie	3	1
EC1990	Oct	16	Tottenham	1	1
EC1991	Nov	12	Pila	1	2
EC1993	May	28	Zdroj	4	1
EC1993	Sept	7	Millwall	1	2
EC1996	Oct	8	Wolverhampton	0	0
EC1997	May	30	Katowice	1	1
EC1999	Mar	26	Southampton	5	0
EC1999	Sept	7	Plock	1	3
			v PORTUGAL	Eng	Por
1987	June	13	Toulon	0	0
1990	May	21	Toulon	0	1
1993	June	7	Toulon	2	0
1994	June	7	Toulon	0	0
EC1994	Sept	6	Leicester	0	0
1995	Sept	2	Lisbon	0	2
1996	May	30	Toulon	1	3

v REPUBLIC OF IRELAND

				Eng	RoI
1981	Feb	25	Liverpool	1	0
1985	Mar	25	Portsmouth	3	2
1989	June	9	Toulon	0	0
EC1990	Nov	13	Cork	3	0
EC1991	Mar	26	Brentford	3	0
1994	Nov	15	Newcastle	1	0
1995	Mar	27	Dublin	2	0

v ROMANIA

				Eng	Rom
EC1980	Oct	14	Ploesti	0	4
EC1981	April	28	Swindon	3	0
EC1985	April	30	Brasov	0	0
EC1985	Sept	10	Ipswich	3	0

v RUSSIA

				Eng	Rus
1994	May	30	Bandol	2	0

v SAN MARINO

				Eng	SM
EC1993	Feb	16	Luton	6	0
EC1993	Nov	17	San Marino	4	0

v SENEGAL

				Eng	Sen
1989	June	7	Toulon	6	1
1991	May	27	Toulon	2	1

v SCOTLAND

				Eng	Sco
1977	April	27	Sheffield	1	0
EC1980	Feb	12	Coventry	2	1
EC1980	Mar	4	Aberdeen	0	0
EC1982	April	19	Glasgow	1	0
EC1982	April	28	Manchester	1	1
EC1988	Feb	16	Aberdeen	1	0
EC1988	Mar	22	Nottingham	1	0
1993	June	13	Toulon	1	0

v SLOVAKIA

				Eng	Slo
EC2000	June	1	Bratislava	0	2

v SOUTH AFRICA

				Eng	SA
1998	May	16	Toulon	3	1

v SPAIN

				Eng	Spa
EC1984	May	17	Seville	1	0
EC1984	May	24	Sheffield	2	0
1987	Feb	18	Burgos	2	1
1992	Sept	8	Burgos	1	0
2001	Feb	27	Birmingham	0	4

v SWEDEN

				Eng	Swe
1979	June	9	Vasteras	2	1
1986	Sept	9	Ostersund	1	1
EC1988	Oct	18	Coventry	1	1
EC1989	Sept	5	Uppsala	0	1
EC1998	Sept	4	Sundvall	2	0
EC1999	June	4	Huddersfield	3	0

v SWITZERLAND

				Eng	Swit
EC1980	Nov	18	Ipswich	5	0
EC1981	May	31	Neuenburg	0	0
1988	May	28	Lausanne	1	1
1996	April	1	Swindon	0	0
1998	Mar	24	Brugglifeld	0	2

v USA

				Eng	USA
1989	June	11	Toulon	0	2
1994	June	2	Toulon	3	0

v TURKEY

				Eng	Tur
EC1984	Nov	13	Bursa	0	0
EC1985	Oct	15	Bristol	3	0
EC1987	April	28	Izmir	0	0
EC1987	Oct	13	Sheffield	1	1
EC1991	April	30	Izmir	2	2
1991	Oct	15	Reading	2	0
EC1992	Nov	17	Orient	0	1
EC1993	Mar	30	Izmir	0	0
EC2000	May	29	Bratislava	6	0

v USSR

				Eng	USSR
1987	June	9	Toulon	0	0
1988	June	7	Toulon	1	0
1990	May	25	Toulon	2	1
1991	May	31	Toulon	2	1

v WALES

				Eng	Wales
1976	Dec	15	Wolverhampton	0	0
1979	Feb	6	Swansea	1	0
1990	Dec	5	Tranmere	0	0

v WEST GERMANY

				Eng	WG
EC1982	Sept	21	Sheffield	3	1
EC1982	Oct	12	Bremen	2	3
1987	Sept	8	Ludenscheid	0	2

v YUGOSLAVIA

				Eng	Yugo
EC1978	April	19	Novi Sad	1	2
EC1978	May	2	Manchester	1	1
EC1986	Nov	11	Peterborough	1	1
EC1987	Nov	10	Zemun	5	1
EC2000	Mar	29	Barcelona	3	0

ENGLAND B RESULTS 1949–2001

Year	Date		Venue		

v ALGERIA

				Eng	Alg
1990	Dec	11	Algiers	0	0

v AUSTRALIA

				Eng	Aust
1980	Nov	17	Birmingham	1	0

v AUSTRIA

				Eng	Aus
1979†	June	12	Klagenfurt	1	0

†Abandoned 60 mins; waterlogged pitch.

v CHILE

				Eng	Ch
1998	Feb	10	West Bromwich	1	2

v CIS

				Eng	CIS
1992	April	28	Moscow	1	1

v CZECHOSLOVAKIA

				Eng	Cz
1978	Nov	28	Prague	1	0
1990	April	24	Sunderland	2	0
1992	Mar	24	Budejovice	1	0

v FINLAND

				Eng	Fin
1949	May	15	Helsinki	4	0

v FRANCE

				Eng	Fra
1952	May	22	Le Havre	1	7
1992	Feb	18	Loftus Road	3	0

v WEST GERMANY

				Eng	WG
1954	Mar	24	Gelsenkirchen	4	0
1955	Mar	23	Sheffield	1	1
1978	Feb	21	Augsburg	2	1

v HOLLAND

				Eng	Hol
1949	May	18	Amsterdam	4	0
1950	Feb	22	Newcastle	1	0
1952	Mar	26	Amsterdam	1	0

v ICELAND

				Eng	Ice
1989	May	19	Reykjavik	2	0
1991	April	27	Watford	1	0

v ITALY

				Eng	Italy
1950	May	11	Milan	0	5
1989	Nov	14	Brighton	1	1

v LUXEMBOURG

				Eng	Lux
1950	May	21	Luxembourg	2	1

v MALAYSIA

				Eng	Mal
1978	May	30	Kuala Lumpur	1	1

v MALTA

				Eng	Mal
1987	Oct	14	Ta'Qali	2	0

v NEW ZEALAND

				Eng	NZ
1978	June	7	Christchurch	4	0
1978	June	11	Wellington	3	1
1978	June	14	Auckland	4	0
1979	Oct	15	Leyton	4	1
1984	Nov	13	Nottingham	2	0

v NORTHERN IRELAND

				Eng	NI
1994	May	10	Sheffield	4	2

v NORWAY

				Eng	Nor
1989	May	22	Stavanger	1	0

v REPUBLIC OF IRELAND

				Eng	RoI
1990	Mar	27	Cork	1	4
1994	Dec	13	Liverpool	2	0

v RUSSIA

				Eng	Rus
1998	Apr	21	Loftus Road	4	1

			v SCOTLAND	Eng	Sco
1953	Mar	11	Edinburgh	2	2
1954	Mar	3	Sunderland	1	1
1956	Feb	29	Dundee	2	2
1957	Feb	6	Birmingham	4	1

			v SINGAPORE	Eng	Sin
1978	June	18	Singapore	8	0

			v SPAIN	Eng	Sp
1980	Mar	26	Sunderland	1	0
1981	Mar	25	Granada	2	3
1991*	Dec	18	Castellon	1	0

*Spanish Olympic XI

			v SWITZERLAND	Eng	Swit
1950	Jan	18	Sheffield	5	0
1954	May	22	Basle	0	2
1956	Mar	21	Southampton	4	1
1989	May	16	Winterthur	2	0
1991	May	20	Walsall	2	1

			v USA	Eng	USA
1980	Oct	14	Manchester	1	0

			v WALES	Eng	Wales
1991	Feb	5	Swansea	1	0

			v YUGOSLAVIA	Eng	Yugo
1954	May	16	Ljubljana	1	2
1955	Oct	19	Manchester	5	1
1989	Dec	12	Millwall	2	1

BRITISH AND IRISH UNDER-21 TEAMS 2000–2001

ENGLAND UNDER-21 INTERNATIONALS

31 Aug

England (4) 6 *(Young 18, Ashley Cole 37, Jeffers 44, Dunn 45, Greening 61, Smith 90)*
Georgia (1) 1 *(Tskitishvili 30)*   5103
England: Robinson; Newton (Stockdale 79), Ashley Cole (Smith T 74), Bramble (Wright 46), Young (Carlisle 46), Dunn (Prutton 46), Greening (Campbell 63), Jeffers (Chadwick 63), Vassell (Thirlwell 74), Cole J (Parker 74), Carrick (Hargreaves 63).

6 Oct

England (1) 1 *(Bramble 45)*
Germany (0) 1 *(Ernst 88)*   30,155
England: Robinson; Wright, Ashley Cole, Bramble, Brown, Dunn (Vernazza 83), Parker (Prutton 41), Vassell (Carlisle 66), Smith A, Greening, Carrick.

10 Oct

Finland (1) 2 *(Sjolund 15, 76)*
England (1) 2 *(Dunn 31, Smith A 48)*   1426
England: Robinson; Roche, Ashley Cole, Bramble (Carlisle 46), Terry, Dunn (Parker 90), Prutton, Vassell (Christie 87), Smith A, Greening, Carrick.

14 Nov

Italy (0) 0
England (0) 0
Abandoned 11 minutes; fog.
England: Weaver; Griffin, Ashley Cole, Upson, King, Dunn, Chadwick, Hargreaves, Vassell, Greening, Carrick.

27 Feb

England (0) 0
Spain (2) 4 *(Gonzalez 14, 21, Colsa 64, Xisco 86)*   13,761
England: Robinson; Griffin (Thelwell 59), Bridge, Barry (Riggott 46), Terry (Upson 46), Dunn (King 46), Chadwick (Greening 46), Hargreaves (Prutton 71), Christie (Ameobi 46), Smith A, Wilson.

23 Mar

England (1) 4 *(Vassell 28, Terry 75, Ameobi 82, 90)*
Finland (0) 0   17,176
England: Weaver; Young, Barry, King (Riggott 46), Terry, Davis, Chadwick, Vassell, Christie (Ameobi 71), Johnson (Wilson 61), Greening.

27 Mar

Albania (0) 0
England (0) 1 *(Greening 69 (pen))*   2000
England: Weaver; Young, Barry, Riggott (Bramble 25), Terry, Davis, Chadwick, Vassell, Christie (Ameobi 59), Wilson (Parker 59), Greening.

24 May

England (0) 3 *(Christie 49, Defoe 74, Bothroyd 85)*
Mexico (0) 0   10,000
England: Kirkland (Bywater 46); Young (Wright 46), Naylor (Upson 46), Bramble (Riggott 60), Terry (Taylor 46), Dunn (Wilson 46), Prutton (Cadamarteri 87), Defoe (Bothroyd 76), Christie (Benjamin 63), Ameobi (Pennant 46), Davis (Vernazza 78).

5 June

Greece (2) 3 *(Papadopoulos 27, Vakouftsis 42, Terry 60 (og))*
England (0) 1 *(Carrick 85)*   1500
England: Bywater; Young, Naylor, Upson, Terry, Dunn, Defoe (Pennant 46), Cole J, Christie (Ameobi 72), Davis (Prutton 74), Carrick.

SCOTLAND UNDER-21 INTERNATIONALS

1 Sept
Lativa 1
Scotland 3 *(Hughes 24, Burchill 57, Easton 87)*
Scotland: Esson; Wilkie, Caldwell S, Doig, Fraser, Severin (Canero), Stewart (Easton), Hughes, Cummings, Notman (Kyle), Burchill.

10 Oct
Croatia 3
Scotland 1 *(Notman 36 (pen))*
Scotland: Esson; Fraser, Wilkie, Caldwell S, Cummings, Hughes, Stewart, Easton, Doig (Canero), Miller K (Kyle), Notman (Young).

23 Mar
Scotland 0
Belgium 1
Scotland: Esson; Canero, Caldwell G, Caldwell S, Cummings, Easton, Stewart (Young), Severin (Murray), Hughes, Miller K, Burchill (McManus).

24 Apr
Poland 1
Scotland 0
Scotland: Esson; McCunnie, Cummings (Kyle), Malcolm, Doig, Murray, Canero (Kerr), Caldwell G, Burchill (Hammell), Young (Parker), Stewart (McManus).

WALES UNDER-21 INTERNATIONALS

1 Sept
Belarus (2) 4 *(Kutuzau 25, 90, Ledzianiou 44, Tarashchuk 57)*
Wales (0) 1 *(Earnshaw 85)*   8000
Wales: Walsh; Green, Evans S, Steve Roberts, Weston, Williams D (Earnshaw 55), Slatter, Jeanne (Stuart Roberts 65), Thomas J, Davies, Maxwell.

6 Oct

Wales (0) 0
Norway (1) 2 *(Ludvigsen 9, 64)* 1900
Wales: Kendall; Green (Steve Roberts 77), Gabbidon, Weston, Llewellyn, Jenkins (Slatter 69), Stuart Roberts, Davies, Thomas J, Earnshaw (Evans K 90).

10 Oct

Poland (0) 2 *(Glowacki 66, Rasiak 89)*
Wales (1) 1 *(Thomas 15)* 1100
Wales: Kendall; Green (Slatter 34), Gabbidon, Weston, Llewellyn, Jenkins, Stuart Roberts, Davies, Thomas J (Evans K 44), Earnshaw, Maxwell.

23 Mar

Armenia (0) 1 *(Ara 84)*
Wales (0) 0 1000
Wales: Walsh; Green, Evans S (Tipton 85), Weston, Gabbidon, Jenkins, Stuart Roberts, Davies, Thomas J, Llewellyn, Maxwell.

27 Mar

Wales (0) 0
Ukraine (3) 3 *(Monarov 12, 20, Zapoyaska 16)* 1277
Wales: Walsh; Green, Price, Day, Gabbidon, Jenkins (Hillier 77), Stuart Roberts (Tipton 82), Maxwell (Phillips 46), Thomas J, Llewellyn, Gibson.

1 June

Wales (0) 0
Poland (2) 4 *(Smolarek 16, 54, Gorawski 32, 60)* 1367
Wales: Jones; Gabbidon, Green (Hillier 68), Valentine, Day, Gibson, Thomas S (Price 68), Tolley, Thomas J (Williams M 80), Earnshaw, Maxwell.

5 June

Ukraine (0) 1
Wales (0) 0 3214
Wales: Jones; Hillier, Price, Gabbidon, Day, Valentine (Tolley 63), Thomas S, Gibson, Thomas J (Slatter 63), Earnshaw, Maxwell (Williams M 75).

NORTHERN IRELAND UNDER-21 INTERNATIONALS

1 Sept

Northern Ireland (0) 1 *(Hamilton 62)*
Malta (1) 1 *(Galea 22)* 1032
Northern Ireland awarded 3-0 win; Malta fielded an ineligible player.
Northern Ireland: Miskelly; Kelly, Holmes, Whitley, Dolan, Friars, Carlisle, McAreavey (McFlynn 69), Kirk (Harkin 80), Hamilton, Graham.

6 Oct

Northern Ireland (0) 0 1434
Denmark (1) 3 *(Christensen 20, Loevenkrands 62, 71)*
Northern Ireland: Miskelly; Convery, Holmes, Toner, Dolan, Friars, Graham (Harkin 62), McAreavey, Kirk (Morrow 75), Hamilton, McCartney (McCann 58).

10 Oct

Iceland (0) 2 *(Gunnarsson 84, Gudjonsson 90)* 400
Northern Ireland (3) 5 *(Hamilton 7, Friars 11, Harkin 32, 63, McCann 77)*
Northern Ireland: Miskelly; Convery, Holmes, Whitley (Scates 65), Dolan (Kelly 82), Friars, Carlisle, Toner, Harkin, Hamilton (Kirk 85), McCann.

23 Mar

Northern Ireland (0) 0
Czech Republic (0) 2 *(Baros 47, Posposil 87)* 1411
Northern Ireland: Ingham; Howe, McCartney, Toner, Kelly, Holmes, Scates (Graham 65), Friars, Harkin (Boyle 75), Hamilton, McCann (McFlynn).

27 Mar

Bulgaria (2) 2 *(Genchev 4, Yanev 27)*
Northern Ireland (0) 0 3400
Nothern Ireland: Ingham; Simms, McCartney, Toner, Kelly, Holmes, Carlisle, McCann (McFlynn 46), Boyle (Morrison 54), Hamilton (Harkin 65), Friars.

1 June

Northern Ireland (1) 1 *(Carlisle 3)*
Bulgaria (1) 1 *(Bukarev 5)* 769
Northern Ireland: Ingham; Kelly, McCartney (McFlynn 64), Toner, Simms, Holmes, Carlisle (Graham 85), Friars, Harkin (Boyle 75), Hamilton, McCann.

5 June

Czech Republic (1) 4 *(Kaufmann 23, 48, Kobylik 54, Vachousek 59)*
Northern Ireland (0) 0
Northern Ireland: Ingham; Kelly, McCann, Toner (Scates 63), Simms, Holmes (Howe 75), Carlisle, McFlynn, Boyle (Graham 78), Hamilton, Friars.

REPUBLIC OF IRELAND UNDER-21 INTERNATIONALS

2 Sept

Holland (0) 2 *(Van der Gun 50, Ax 84)*
Republic of Ireland (0) 0
Republic of Ireland: Delaney; Healy, O'Shea, Gavin, Clarke, O'Connor, Quinn B, McGrath, Quinn A (Partridge 80), Doherty (Barrett 76), Reddy.

6 Oct

Portugal (0) 3 *(Costa 64, Miguel 81, Edmilson 72)*
Republic of Ireland (1) 1 *(Reddy 44)* 6100
Republic of Ireland: Delaney; Healy, Clarke, O'Shea, Gavin, Quinn B, O'Connor, Quinn A (Lynch 69), Reddy, Doherty, Barrett.

10 Oct

Republic of Ireland (0) 1 *(Quinn B 57)*
Estonia (0) 0 3800
Republic of Ireland: Murphy; Healy, Gavin, O'Shea, Clarke (McGrath 80), Quinn B, Lynch, O'Connor, Barrett (Partridge 71), Doherty (Hunt 90), Reddy.

23 Mar

Cyprus (0) 0
Republic of Ireland (1) 1 *(O'Brien 18)* 3200
Republic of Ireland: Murphy; Gavin (Byrne 83), O'Shea, O'Brien, Clarke, Healy, O'Connor, Quinn B (Quinn A 64), Reid, Reddy, Foran (George 68).

1 June

Republic of Ireland (0) 0
Portugal (1) 1 *(Simao 39)*
Republic of Ireland: Murphy; Quinn B, O'Brien, O'Shea, Clarke, Byrne (Butler 63), Healy, O'Connor (Reddy 78), Reid, Barrett, Morrison (Foran 75).

5 June

Estonia (0) 0
Republic of Ireland (1) 3 *(Barrett 7, 58, Goodwin 88)* 908
Republic of Ireland: Murphy; Gavin (Goodwin 82), O'Shea, Delaney, Foy, Butler, Healy, Byrne, Reid, Barrett, Morrison.

BRITISH UNDER-21 APPEARANCES 1976–2001

ENGLAND

Ablett, G. (Liverpool), 1988 v F (1)
Adams, A. (Arsenal), 1985 v Ei, Fi; 1986 v D; 1987 v Se, Y (5)
Adams, N. (Everton), 1987 v Se (1)
Allen, B. (QPR), 1992 v H, M, Cz, F; 1993 v N (sub), T, P, Cz (sub) (8)
Allen, C. A. (Oxford U), 1995 v Br (sub), F (sub) (2)
Allen, C. (QPR), 1980 v EG (sub): (with C Palace), 1981 v N, R (3)
Allen, M. (QPR), 1987 v Se (sub); 1988 v Y (sub) (2)
Allen, P. (West Ham U), 1985 v Ei, R: (with Tottenham H, 1986 v R (3)
Allen, R. W. (Tottenham H), 1998 v F (sub), S.Af, Arg (sub) (3)
Ameobi, F. (Newcastle U), 2001 v Sp (sub), Fi (sub), Alb (sub), M, Gr (sub) (5)
Anderson, V. A. (Nottingham F), 1978 v I (1)
Anderton, D. R. (Tottenham H), 1993 v Sp, Sm, Ho, Pol, N, P, Cz, Br, S, F; 1994 v Pol, Sm (12)
Andrews, I. (Leicester C), 1987 v Se (1)
Ardley, N. C. (Wimbledon), 1993 v Pol, N, P, Cz, Br, S, F, 1994 v Pol (sub), Ho, Sm (10)
Ashcroft, L. (Preston NE), 1992 v H (sub) (1)
Atherton, P. (Coventry C), 1992 v T (1)
Atkinson, B. (Sunderland), 1991 v W (sub), Sen, M, USSR (sub), F; 1992 v Pol (sub) (6)
Awford, A. T. (Portsmouth), 1993 v Sp, N, T, P, Cz, Br, S, F; 1994 v Ho (9)

Bailey, G. R. (Manchester U), 1979 v W, Bul; 1980 v D, S (2), EG; 1982 v N; 1983 v D, Gr; 1984 v H, F (2), I, Sp (14)
Baker, G. E. (Southampton), 1981 v N, R (2)
Ball, M. J. (Everton), 1999 v Se, Bul, L, CzR, Pol; 2000 v L, D (sub) (7)
Barker, S. (Blackburn R), 1985 v Is (sub), Ei, R; 1986 v I (4)
Barmby, N. J. (Tottenham H), 1994 v D; 1995 v P, A (sub); (with Everton), 1998 v Sw (4)
Bannister, G. (Sheffield W), 1982 v Pol (1)
Barnes, J. (Watford), 1983 v D, Gr (2)
Barnes, P. S. (Manchester C), 1977 v W (sub), S, Fi, N; 1978 v N, Fi, I (2), Y (9)
Barrett, E. D. (Oldham Ath), 1990 v P, F, USSR, Cz (4)
Barry, G. (Aston Villa), 1999 v CzR, F, H; 2000 v Y; 2001 v Sp, Fi, Alb (7)
Bart-Williams, C. G. (Sheffield W), 1993 v Sp, N, T; 1994 v D, Ru, F, Bel, P; 1995 v P, A, Ei (2), La (2): (with Nottingham F) 1996 v P (sub), A (16)
Batty, D. (Leeds U), 1988 v Sw (sub); 1989 v Gr (sub), Bul, Sen, Ei, US; 1990 v Pol (7)
Bazeley, D. S. (Watford), 1992 v H (sub) (1)
Beagrie, P. (Sheffield U), 1988 v WG, T (2)
Beardsmore, R. (Manchester U), 1989 v Gr, Alb (sub), Pol, Bul, USA (5)
Beattie, J. S. (Southampton), 1999 v CzR (sub), F (sub), Pol, H; 2000 v Pol (5)
Beckham, D. R. J. (Manchester U), 1995 v Br, Mal, An, F; 1996 v P, A (sub), Bel, An, P (9)
Bent, M. N. (Crystal Palace), 1998 v S.Af (sub), Arg (2)
Beeston, C (Stoke C), 1988 v USSR (1)
Benjamin, T. J. (Leicester C), 2001 v M (sub) (1)
Bertschin, K. E. (Birmingham C), 1977 v S; 1978 v Y (2) (3)
Birtles, G. (Nottingham F), 1980 v Bul, EG (sub) (2)
Blackwell, D. R. (Wimbledon), 1991 v W, T, Sen (sub), M, USSR, F (6)
Blake, M. A. (Aston Villa), 1991 v D, Gr (1 + 1 sub), H; 1984 v H, Pol, Ei (2), W; 1992 v Pol (8)
Blissett, L. L. (Watford), 1979 v W, Bul, Se; 1980 v D (4)
Booth, A. D. (Huddersfield T), 1995 v La (2 subs); 1996 v N (3)
Bothroyd, J. (Coventry C), 2001 v M (sub) (1)
Bowyer, L. D. (Charlton Ath), 1996 v N (sub), Bel, P, Br; (with Leeds U), 1997 v Mol, I, Sw, Ge; 1998 v Mol; 1999 v F, Pol; 2000 v D, Arg (13)
Bracewell, P. (Stoke C), 1983 v D, Gr (1 + 1 sub), H; 1984 v D, H, F (2), I (2), Sp (2); 1985 v T (13)
Bradbury, L. M. (Portsmouth), 1997 v Pol: (with Manchester C), 1998 v Mol (sub), I (sub) (3)

Bramble, T. M. (Ipswich T), 2001 v Ge, G, Fi, Alb (sub), M (5)
Branch, P. M. (Everton), 1997 v Pol (sub) (1)
Bradshaw, P. W. (Wolverhampton W), 1977 v W, S; 1978 v Fi, Y (4)
Breacker, T. (Luton T), 1986 v I (2) (2)
Brennan, M. (Ipswich T), 1987 v Y, Sp, T, Mor, F (5)
Bridge, W. M. (Southampton), 1999 v H (sub); 2001 v Sp (2)
Bridges, M. (Sunderland), 1997 v Sw (sub); 1999 v F; (with Leeds U), 2000 v D (3)
Brightwell, I. (Manchester C), 1989 v D, Alb; 1990 v Se (sub), Pol (4)
Briscoe, L. S. (Sheffield W), 1996 v Cro, Bel (sub), An, Br; 1997 v Sw (sub) (5)
Brock, K. (Oxford U), 1984 v I, Sp (2); 1986 v I (4)
Broomes, M. C. (Blackburn R), 1997 v Sw, Ge (2)
Brown, M. R. (Manchester C), 1996 v Cro, Bel, An, P (4)
Brown, W. M. (Manchester U), 1999 v Se, Bul, L, CzR, Pol, Se, Bul; 2001 v G (8)
Bull, S. G. (Wolverhampton W), 1989 v Alb (2) Pol; 1990 v Se, Pol (5)
Bullock, M. J. (Barnsley), 1998 v Gr (sub) (1)
Burrows, D. (WBA), 1989 v Se (sub); (with Liverpool), Gr, Alb (2), Pol; 1990 v Se, Pol (7)
Butcher, T. I. (Ipswich T), 1979 v Se; 1980 v D, Bul, S (2), EG (2) (7)
Butt, N. (Manchester U), 1995 v Ei (2), La; 1996 v P, A; 1997 v Ge, Pol (7)
Butters, G. (Tottenham H), 1989 v Bul, Sen (sub), Ei (sub) (3)
Butterworth, I. (Coventry C), 1985 v T, R: (with Nottingham F), 1986 v R, T, D (2), I (2) (8)
Bywater, S. (West Ham U), 2001 v M (sub), Gr (2)

Cadamarteri, D. L. (Everton), 1999 v CzR (sub); 2000 v Y (sub); 2001 v M (sub) (3)
Caesar, G. (Arsenal), 1987 v Mor, USSR (sub), F (3)
Callaghan, N. (Watford), 1983 v D, Gr (sub), H (sub); 1984 v D, H, F (2), I, Sp (9)
Campbell, A. P. (Middlesbrough), 2000 v Y, T (sub), Slo (sub); 2001 v Ge (sub) (4)
Campbell, K. J. (Arsenal), 1991 v H, T (sub); 1992 v G, T (4)
Campbell, S. (Tottenham), 1994 v D, Ru, F, US, Bel, P; 1995 v P, A, Ei; 1996 v N, A (11)
Carbon, M. P. (Derby Co), 1996 v Cro (sub); 1997 v Ge, I, Sw (4)
Carr, C. (Fulham), 1985 v Ei (sub) (1)
Carr, F. (Nottingham F), 1987 v Se, Y, Sp (sub), Mor, USSR; 1988 v WG (sub), T, Y, F (9)
Carragher, J. L. (Liverpool), 1997 v I (sub), Sw, Ge, Pol; 1998 v Mol (sub), I, Gr, Sw (sub), F, S.Af, Arg; 1999 v Se, Bul, L, CzR, F, Pol, Se, Bul; 2000 v L, Pol, D, Arg, Y, I, T, Slo (27)
Carlisle, C. J. (QPR), 2001 v Ge (sub), G (sub), Fi (sub) (3)
Carrick, M. (West Ham U), 2001 v Ge, G, Fi, I, Gr (5)
Casper, C. M. (Manchester U), 1995 v Mal (1)
Caton, T. (Manchester C), 1982 v N, H (sub), Pol (2), S; 1983 v WG (2), Gr; 1984 v D, H, F (2), I (2) (14)
Chadwick, L. H. (Manchester U), 2000 v D, Arg, I (sub), Slo (sub); 2001 v Ge (sub), I, Sp, Fi, Alb (10)
Challis, T. M. (QPR), 1996 v An, P (2)
Chamberlain, M. (Stoke C), 1983 v Gr; 1984 v F (sub), I, Sp (4)
Chapman, L. (Stoke C), 1981 v Ei (1)
Charles, G. A. (Nottingham F), 1991 v H, W (sub), Ei; 1992 v T (4)
Chettle, S. (Nottingham F), 1988 v M, USSR, Mor, F; 1989 v D, Se, Gr, Alb (2), Bul; 1990 v Se, Pol (12)
Clark, L. R. (Newcastle U), 1992 v Cz, F; 1993 v Sp, N, T, Ho (sub), Pol (sub), Cz, Br, S; 1994 v Ho (11)
Christie, M. N. (Derby Co), 2001 v Fi (sub), Sp, Fi, Alb, M, Gr (6)
Clegg, M. J. (Manchester U), 1998 v Fr (sub), S.Af (sub) (2)
Clemence, S. N. (Tottenham H), 1999 v Se (sub) (1)
Clough, N. (Nottingham F), 1986 v D (sub); 1987 v Se, Y, T, USSR, F (sub), P; 1988 v WG, T, Y, S (2), M, Mor, F (15)

Cole, A. A. (Arsenal), 1992 v H, Cz (sub), F (sub); (with Bristol C), 1993 v Sm; (with Newcastle U), Pol, N; 1994 v Pol, Ho (8)

Cole, A. (Arsenal), 2001 v Ge, G, Fi, I (4)

Cole, J. J. (West Ham U), 2000 v Arg (sub); 2001 v Ge, Gr (3)

Coney, D. (Fulham), 1985 v T (sub); 1986 v R; 1988 v T, WG (4)

Connor, T. (Brighton & HA), 1987 v Y (1)

Cooke, R. (Tottenham H), 1986 v D (sub) (1)

Cooke, T. J. (Manchester U), 1996 v Cro, Bel, An (sub), P (4)

Cooper, C. (Middlesbrough), 1988 v F (2), M, USSR, Mor; 1989 v D, Se, Gr (8)

Corrigan, J. T. (Manchester C), 1978 v I (2), Y (3)

Cort, C. E. R. (Wimbledon), 1999 v L (sub), CzR, H (sub), Se, Bul; 2000 v L (sub), Pol, D (sub), Arg, I, T, Slo (12)

Cottee, A. (West Ham U), 1985 v Fi (sub), Is (sub), Ei, R, Fi; 1987 v Sp, P; 1988 v WG (8)

Couzens, A. J. (Leeds U), 1995 v Mal (sub), An, F (sub) (3)

Cowans, G. S. (Aston Villa), 1979 v W, Se; 1980 v Bul, EG; 1981 v R (5)

Cox, N. J. (Aston Villa), 1993 v T, Ho, Pol, N; 1994 v Pol, Sm (6)

Cranson, I. (Ipswich T), 1985 v Fi, Is, R; 1986 v R, I (5)

Cresswell, R. P. W. (York C), 1999 v F (sub); (with Sheffield W) H (sub), Se, Bul (4)

Croft, G. (Grimsby T), 1995 v Br, Mal, An, F (4)

Crooks, G. (Stoke C), 1980 v Bul, S (2), EG (sub) (4)

Crossley, M. G. (Nottingham F), 1990 v P, USSR, Cz (3)

Cundy, J. V. (Chelsea), 1991 v Ei (2); 1992 v Pol (3)

Cunningham, L. (WBA), 1977 v S, Fi, N (sub); 1978 v N, Fi, I (6)

Curbishley, L. C. (Birmingham C), 1981 v Sw (1)

Curtis, J. C. K. (Manchester U), 1998 v I (sub), Gr, Sw, F, S.Af, Arg; 1999 v Se (sub), Bul, L, CzR, F, Pol (sub), H, Se (sub), Bul; 2000 v Pol (16)

Daniel, P. W. (Hull C), 1977 v S, Fi, N; 1978 v Fi, I, Y (2) (7)

Davies, K. C. (Southampton), 1998 v Gr (sub); (with Blackburn R), 1999 v CzR; (with Southampton), 2000 v Y (sub) (3)

Davis, K. G. (Luton T), 1995 v An; 1996 v Cro (sub), P (3)

Davis, P. (Arsenal), 1982 v Pol, S; 1983 v D, Gr (1 + 1 sub), H (sub); 1987 v T; 1988 v WG, T, Y, Fr (11)

Davis, S. (Fulham), 2001 v Fi, Alb, M, Gr (4)

Day, C. N. (Tottenham H), 1996 v Cro, Bel, Br; (with Crystal Palace), 1997 v Mol, Ge, Sw (6)

D'Avray, M. (Ipswich T), 1984 v I, Sp (sub) (2)

Deehan, J. M. (Aston Villa), 1977 v N; 1978 v N, Fi, I; 1979 v Bul, Se (sub); 1980 v D (7)

Defoe, J. C. (West Ham U), 2001 v M, Gr (2)

Dennis, M. E. (Birmingham C), 1980 v Bul; 1981 v N, R (3)

Dichio, D. S. E. (QPR), 1996 v N (sub) (1)

Dickens, A. (West Ham U), 1985 v Fi (sub) (1)

Dicks, J. (West Ham U), 1988 v Sw (sub), M, Mor, F (4)

Digby, F. (Swindon T), 1987 v Sp (sub), USSR, P; 1988 v T; 1990 v Pol (5)

Dillon, K. P. (Birmingham C), 1981 v R (1)

Dixon, K. (Chelsea), 1985 v Fi (1)

Dobson, A. (Coventry C), 1989 v Bul, Sen, Ei, US (4)

Dodd, J. R. (Southampton), 1991 v Pol, Ei, T, Sen, M, F; 1992 v G, Pol (8)

Donowa, L. (Norwich C), 1985 v Is, R (sub), Fi (sub) (3)

Dorigo, A. (Aston Villa), 1987 v Se, Sp, T, Mor, USSR, F, P; 1988 v WG, Y, S (2) (11)

Dozzell, J. (Ipswich T), 1987 v Se, Y (sub), Sp, USSR, F, P; 1989 v Se, Gr (sub); 1990 v Se (sub) (9)

Draper, M. A. (Notts Co), 1991 v Ei (sub); 1992 v G, Pol (3)

Duberry, M. W. (Chelsea), 1997 v Mol, Pol, Ge; 1998 v Mol, Gr (5)

Dunn, D. J. I. (Blackburn R), 1999 v CzR (sub); 2000 v I (sub), T, Slo; 2001 v Ge, G, Fi, I, Sp, M, Gr (11)

Duxbury, M. (Manchester U), 1981 v Sw (sub), Ei (sub), R (sub), Sw; 1982 v N; 1983 v WG (2) (7)

Dyer, B. A. (Crystal Palace), 1994 v Ru, F, US, Bel, P; 1995 v P (sub); 1996 v Cro; 1997 v Mol, Ge; 1998 v Mol, Gr (10)

Dyer, K. C. (Ipswich T), 1998 v Mol, I, Gr, Sw, S.Af, Arg; 1999 v Se, Bul, CzR, Se; (with Newcastle U), 2000 v Y (11)

Dyson, P. I. (Coventry C), 1981 v N, R, Sw, Ei (4)

Eadie, D. M. (Norwich C), 1994 v F (sub), US; 1997 v Mol, Ge (2); 1998 v I (7)

Ebbrell, J. (Everton), 1989 v Sen, Ei, US (sub); 1990 v P, F, USSR, Cz; 1991 v H, Pol, Ei, W, T; 1992 v G, T (14)

Edghill, R. A. (Manchester C), 1994 v D, Ru; 1995 v A (3)

Ehiogu, U. (Aston Villa), 1992 v H, M, Cz, F; 1993 v Sp, N, T, Sm, T, Ho, Pol, N; 1994 v Pol, Ho, Sm (15)

Elliott, P. (Luton T), 1985 v Fi; 1986 v T, D (3)

Elliott, R. J. (Newcastle U), 1996 v P, A (2)

Elliott, S. W. (Derby Co), 1998 v F, Arg (sub) (2)

Euell, J. J. (Wimbledon), 1998 v F, Arg (sub); 1999 v Se (sub), Bul (se), Pol (sub), H (6)

Fairclough, C. (Nottingham F), 1985 v T, Is, Ei; 1987 v Sp, T; (with Tottenham H), 1988 v Y, F (7)

Fairclough, D. (Liverpool), 1977 v W (1)

Fashanu, J. (Norwich C), 1980 v EG; 1981 v N (sub), R, Sw, Ei (sub), H; (with Nottingham F), 1982 v N, H, Pol, S; 1983 v WG (sub) (11)

Fear, P. (Wimbledon), 1994 v Ru, F, US (sub) (3)

Fenton, G. A. (Aston Villa), 1995 v Ei (1)

Fenwick, T. W. (C Palace), 1981 v N, R, Sw, Ei; (with QPR); R; 1982 v N, H, S (2); 1983 v WG (2) (11)

Ferdinand, R. G. (West Ham U), 1997 v Sw, Ge; 1998 v I, Gr; 2000 v Y (5)

Fereday, W. (QPR), 1985 v T, Ei (sub). Fi; 1986 v T (sub), I (5)

Flitcroft, G. W. (Manchester C), 1993 v Sm, Hol, N, P, Cz, Br, S, F; 1994 v Pol, Ho (10)

Flowers, T. (Southampton), 1987 v Mor, F; 1988 v WG (sub) (3)

Ford, M. (Leeds U), 1996 v Cro; 1997 v Mol (2)

Forster, N. M. (Brentford), 1995 v Br, Mal, An, F (4)

Forsyth, M. (Derby Co), 1988 v Sw (1)

Foster, S. (Brighton & HA), 1980 v EG (sub) (1)

Fowler, R. B. (Liverpool), 1994 v Sm, Ru (sub), F, US; 1995 v P, A; 1996 v P, A (8)

Froggatt, S. J. (Aston Villa), 1993 v Sp, Sm (sub) (2)

Futcher, P. (Luton T), 1977 v W, S, Fi, N; (with Manchester C), 1978 v N, Fi, I (2), Y (2); 1979 v D (11)

Gabbiadini, M. (Sunderland), 1989 v Bul, USA (2)

Gale, A. (Fulham), 1982 v Pol (1)

Gallen, K. A. (QPR), 1995 v Ei, La (2); 1996 v Cro (4)

Gascoigne, P. (Newcastle U), 1987 v Mo, USSR, P; 1988 v WG, Y, S (2), F (2), Sw, M, USSR, Mor (13)

Gayle, H. (Birmingham C), 1984 v I, Sp (2) (3)

Gernon, T. (Ipswich T), 1983 v Gr (1)

Gerrard, P. W. (Oldham Ath), 1993 v T, Ho, Pol, N, P, Cz, Br, S, F; 1994 v D, Ru; 1995 v P, A, Ei (2), La (2); 1996 v P (18)

Gerrard, S. G. (Liverpool), 2000 v L, Pol, D, Y (4)

Gibbs, N. (Watford), 1987 v Mor, USSR, F, P; 1988 v T (5)

Gibson, C. (Aston Villa), 1982 v N (1)

Gilbert, W. A. (C Palace), 1979 v W, Bul; 1980 v Bul; 1981 v N, R, Sw, R, Sw, H; 1982 v N (sub), H (11)

Goddard, P. (West Ham U), 1981 v N, Sw, Ei (sub); 1982 v N (sub), Pol, S; 1983 v WG (2) (8)

Gordon, D. (Norwich C), 1987 v T (sub), Mor (sub), F, P (4)

Gordon, D. D. (Crystal Palace), 1994 v Ru, F, US, Bel, P; 1995 v P, A, Ei (2), La (2); 1996 v P, N (13)

Grant, A. J. (Everton), 1996 v An (sub) (1)

Granville, D. P. (Chelsea), 1997 v Ge (sub), Pol; 1998 v Mol (3)

Gray, A. (Aston Villa), 1988 v S, F (2)

Greening, J. (Manchester U), 1999 v H, Se (sub), Bul; 2000 v Pol; 2001 v Ge, G, Fi, I, Sp (sub), Fi, Alb (11)

Griffin, A. (Newcastle U), 1999 v H; 2001 v I, Sp (3)

Guppy, S. A. (Leicester C), 1998 v Sw (1)

Haigh, P. (Hull C), 1977 v N (sub) (1)

Hall, M. T. J. (Coventry C), 1997 v Pol (2), I, Sw, Ge; 1998 v Mol, Gr (2) (8)

Hall, R. A. (Southampton), 1992 v H (sub), F; 1993 v Sm, T, Ho, Pol, P, Cz, Br, S, F (11)

Hamilton, D. V. (Newcastle U), 1997 v Pol (1)

Hardyman, P. (Portsmouth), 1985 v Ei; 1986 v D (2)

Murphy, D. B. (Liverpool), 1998 v Mol, Gr (sub); 2000 v T, Slo (4)

Murray, P. (QPR), 1997 v I, Pol; 1998 v I, Gr (4)

Mutch, A. (Wolverhampton W), 1989 v Pol (1)

Myers. A. (Chelsea), 1995 v Br, Mal, An (sub), F (4)

Naylor, L. M. (Wolverhampton W), 2000 v Arg; 2001 v M, Gr (3)

Nethercott, S. (Tottenham), 1994 v D, Ru, F, US, Bel, P; 1995 v La (2) (8)

Neville, P. J. (Manchester U), 1995 v Br, Mal, An, F; 1996 v P, N (sub); 1997 v Ge (7)

Newell, M. (Luton T), 1986 v D (1 + 1 sub), I (1 + 1 sub) (4)

Newton, A. L. (West Ham U), 2001 v Ge (1)

Newton, E. J. I. (Chelsea), 1993 v T (sub); 1994 v Sm (2)

Newton, S. O. (Charlton Ath), 1997 v Mol, Pol, Ge (3)

Nicholls, A. (Plymouth Arg), 1994 v F (1)

Oakes, M. C. (Aston Villa), 1994 v D (sub), F (sub), US, Bel, P; 1996 v A (6)

Oakes, S. J. (Luton T), 1993 v Br (sub) (1)

Oakley, M. (Southampton), 1997 v Ge; 1998 v F, S.Af, Arg (4)

O'Brien, A. J. (Bradford C), 1999 v F (1)

O'Connor, J. (Everton), 1996 v Cro, An, Br (3)

Oldfield, D. (Luton T), 1989 v Se (1)

Olney, I. A. (Aston Villa), 1990 v P, F, USSR, Cz; 1991 v H, Pol, Ei (2), T; 1992 v Pol (sub) (10)

Ord, R. J. (Sunderland), 1991 v W, M, USSR (3)

Osman, R. C. (Ipswich T), 1979 v W (sub), Se; 1980 v D, S (2), EG (2) (7)

Owen, G. A. (Manchester C), 1977 v S, Fi, N; 1978 v N, Fi, I (2), Y; 1979 v D, W; (with WBA), Bul, Se (sub); 1980 v D, S (2), EG; 1981 v Sw, R; 1982 v N (sub), H; 1983 v WG (2) (22)

Owen, M. J. (Liverpool), 1998 v Gr (1)

Painter, I. (Stoke C), 1986 v I (1)

Palmer, C. (Sheffield W), 1989 v Bul, Sen, Ei, US (4)

Parker, G. (Hull C), 1986 v I (2); (with Nottingham F), F; 1987 v Se, Y (sub), Sp (6)

Parker, P. (Fulham), 1985 v Fi, T, Is (sub), Ei, R, Fi; 1986 v T, D (8)

Parker, S. M. (Charlton Ath), 2001 v Ge (sub), G, Fi (sub), Alb (sub) (4)

Parkes, P. B. F. (QPR), 1979 v D (1)

Parkin, S. (Stoke C), 1987 v Sp (sub); 1988 v WG (sub), T, S (sub), F (5)

Parlour, R. (Arsenal), 1992 v H, M, Cz, F; 1993 v Sp, N, T; 1994 v D, Ru, Bel, P; 1995 v A (12)

Peach, D. S. (Southampton), 1977 v S, Fi, N; 1978 v N, I (2) (6)

Peake, A. (Leicester C), 1982 v Pol (1)

Pearce, I. A. (Blackburn R), 1995 v Ei, La; 1996 v N (3)

Pearce, S. (Nottingham F), 1987 v Y (1)

Pennant, J. (Arsenal), 2001 v M (sub), Gr (sub) (2)

Pickering N. (Sunderland), 1983 v D (sub), Gr, H; 1984 v F (sub + 1), I (2), Sp; 1985 v Is, R, Fi; 1986 v R, T; (with Coventry C), D, I (15)

Platt, D. (Aston Villa), 1988 v M, Mor, F (3)

Plummer, C. S. (QPR), 1996 v Cro (sub), Bel, An, P (sub), Br (5)

Pollock, J. (Middlesbrough), 1995 v Ei (sub); 1996 v N, A (3)

Porter, G. (Watford), 1987 v Sp (sub), T, Mor, USSR, F, P (sub); 1988 v T (sub), Y, S (2), F, Sw (12)

Potter, G. S. (Southampton), 1997 v Mol (1)

Pressman, K. (Sheffield W), 1989 v D (sub) (1)

Proctor, M. (Middlesbrough), 1981 v Ei (sub), Sw; (with Nottingham F) 1982 v N, Pol (4)

Prutton, D. T. (Nottingham F), 2001 v Ge (sub), G (sub), Fi, Sp (sub), M, Gr (sub) (6)

Purse, D. J. (Birmingham C), 1998 v F. S.Af (2)

Quashie, N. F. (QPR), 1997 v Pol; 1998 v Mol, Gr, Sw (4)

Quinn, W. R. (Sheffield U), 1998 v Mol (sub), I (2)

Ramage, C. D. (Derby Co), 1991 v Pol (sub), W; 1992 v Fr (sub) (3)

Ranson, R. (Manchester C), 1980 v Bul, EG; 1981 v R (sub), R, Sw (1 + 1 sub), H, Pol (2), S (10)

Redknapp, J. F. (Liverpool), 1993 v Sm, Pol, N, P, Cz, Br, S, F; 1994 v Pol, Ho (sub), D, Ru, F, US, Bel, P; 1995 v P, A; 1998 v Sw (19)

Redmond, S. (Manchester C), 1988 v F (2), M, USSR, Mor, F; 1989 v D, Se, Gr, Alb (2), Pol; 1990 v Se, Pol (14)

Reeves, K. P. (Norwich C), 1978 v I, Y (2); 1979 v N, W, Bul. Sw; 1980 v D, S; (with Manchester C), EG (10)

Regis, C. (WBA), 1979 v D, Bul, Se; 1980 v S, EG; 1983 v D (6)

Reid, N. S. (Manchester C), 1981 v H (sub); 1982 v H, Pol (2), S (2) (6)

Reid, P. (Bolton W), 1977 v S, Fi, N; 1978 v Fi, I, Y (6)

Richards, D. I. (Wolverhampton W), 1995 v Br, Mal, An, F (4)

Richards, J. P. (Wolverhampton W), 1977 v Fi, N (2)

Rideout, P. (Aston Villa), 1985 v Fi, Is, Ei (sub), R; (with Bari), 1986 v D (5)

Riggott, C. M. (Derby Co), 2001 v Sp (sub), Fi (sub), Alb, M (sub) (4)

Ripley, S. (Middlesbrough), 1988 v USSR, F (sub); 1989 v D (sub), Se, Gr, Alb (2); 1990 v Se (8)

Ritchie, A. (Brighton & HA), 1982 v Pol (1)

Rix, G. (Arsenal), 1978 v Fi (sub), Y; 1979 v D, Se; 1980 v D (sub), Bul, S (7)

Roberts, A. J. (Millwall), 1995 v Ei, La (2); (with C Palace), 1996 v N, A (5)

Roberts, B. J. (Middlesbrough), 1997 v Sw (sub) (1)

Robins, M. G. (Manchester U), 1990 v P, F, USSR, Cz; 1991 v H (sub), Pol (6)

Robinson, P. P. (Watford), 1999 v Se, Bul; 2000 v Pol (3)

Robinson, P. W. (Leeds U), 2000 v D; 2001 v Ge, G, Fi, Sp (5)

Robson, B. (WBA), 1979 v W, Bul (sub), Se; 1980 v D, Bul, S (2) (7)

Robson, S. (Arsenal), 1984 v I; 1985 v Fi, Is, Fi; 1986 v R, I (with West Ham U); 1988 v S, Sw (8)

Rocastle, D. (Arsenal), 1987 v Se, Y, Sp, T; 1988 v WG, T, Y, S (2), F (2 subs), M, USSR, Mor (14)

Roche, L. P. (Manchester U), 2001 v Fi (1)

Rodger, G. (Coventry C), 1987 v USSR, F, P; 1988 v WG (4)

Rogers, A. (Nottingham F), 1998 v F, S.Af, Arg (3)

Rosario, R. (Norwich C), 1987 v T (sub), Mor, F, P (sub) (4)

Rose, M. (Arsenal), 1997 v Ge (sub), I (2)

Rowell, G. (Sunderland), 1977 v Fi (1)

Ruddock, N. (Southampton), 1989 v Bul (sub), Sen, Ei, US (4)

Rufus, R. R. (Charlton Ath), 1996 v Cro, Bel, An, P, Br; 1997 v I (6)

Ryan, J. (Oldham Ath), 1983 v H (1)

Ryder, S.H. (Walsall), 1995 v Br, An, F (3)

Samways, V. (Tottenham H), 1988 v Sw (sub), USSR, F; 1989 v D, Se (5)

Sansom, K. G. (C Palace), 1979 v D, W, Bul, Se; 1980 v S (2), EG (2) (8)

Scimeca, R. (Aston Villa), 1996 v P; 1997 v Mol, Pol, Ge, I; 1998 v Mol, I, Gr (2) (9)

Scowcroft, J. B. (Ipswich T), 1997 v Pol, Ge (2), I (sub); 1998 v Gr (sub) (5)

Seaman, D. (Birmingham C), 1985 v Fi, T, Is, Ei, R, Fi; 1986 v R, F, D, I (10)

Sedgley, S. (Coventry C), 1987 v USSR, F (sub), P; 1988 v F; 1989 v D (sub), Se, Gr, Alb (2), Pol; (with Tottenham H), 1990 v Se (11)

Sellars, S. (Blackburn R), 1988 v S (sub), F, Sw (3)

Selley, I. (Arsenal), 1994 v Ru (sub), F (sub), US (3)

Serrant, C. (Oldham Ath), 1998 v Gr (2) (2)

Sharpe, L. (Manchester U), 1989 v Gr; 1990 v P (sub), F, USSR, Cz; 1991 v H, Pol (sub), Ei (8)

Shaw, G. R. (Aston Villa), 1981 v Ei, Sw, H; 1982 v H, S; 1983 v WG (2) (7)

Shearer, A. (Southampton), 1991 v Ei (2), W, T, Sen, M, USSR, F; 1992 v G, T, Pol (11)

Shelton, G. (Sheffield W), 1985 v Fi (1)

Sheringham, T. (Millwall), 1988 v Sw (1)

Sheron, M. N. (Manchester C), 1992 v H, F; 1993 v N (sub), T (sub), Sm, Ho, Pol, N, P, Cz, Br, S, F; 1994 v Pol (sub), Ho, Sm (16)

Sherwood, T. A. (Norwich C), 1990 v P, F, USSR, Cz (4)

Shipperley, N. J. (Chelsea), 1994 v Sm (sub); (with Southampton) 1995 v Ei, La (2); 1996 v P, N, A (7)

Simonsen, S. P. A. (Tranmere R), 1998 v F; (with Everton), 1999 v CzR, F, Bul (4)

Simpson, P. (Manchester C), 1986 v D (sub); 1987 v Y, Mor, F, P (5)

Sims, S. (Leicester C), 1977 v W, S, Fi, N; 1978 v N, Fi, I (2), Y (2) (10)

Sinclair, T. (QPR), 1994 v Ho, Sm, D, Ru, F, US, Bel, P; 1995 v P, Ei (2), La: 1996 v P: (with West Ham U), 1998 v Sw (5)

Sinnott, L. (Watford), 1985 v Is (sub) (1)

Slade, S. A. (Tottenham H), 1996 v Bel, An, P, Br (4)

Slater, S. I. (West Ham U), 1990 v P, USSR (sub), Cz (sub) (3)

Small, B. (Aston Villa), 1993 v Sm, T, Ho, Pol, N, P, Cz, Br, S, F; 1994 v Pol, Sm (12)

Smith, A. (Leeds U), 2000 v D, Arg (sub): 2001 v G, Fi, Sp (5)

Smith, D. (Coventry C), 1988 v M, USSR (sub), Mor; 1989 v D, Se, Alb (2), Pol; 1990 v Se, Pol (10)

Smith, M. (Sheffield W), 1981 v Ei, R, Sw, H; 1982 v Pol (sub) (5)

Smith, M. (Sunderland), 1995 v Ei (sub) (1)

Smith, T. W. (Watford), 2001 v Ge (sub) (1)

Snodin, I. (Doncaster R), 1985 v T, Is, R, Fi (4)

Statham, B. (Tottenham H), 1988 v Sw; 1989 v D (sub), Se (3)

Statham, D. J. (WBA), 1978 v Fi, 1979 v W, Bul, Se; 1980 v D; 1983 v D (6)

Stein, B. (Luton T), 1984 v D, H, I (3)

Sterland, M. (Sheffield W), 1984 v D, H, F (2), I, Sp (2) (7)

Steven, T. (Everton), 1985 v Fi, T (2)

Stevens, G. (Brighton & HA), 1983 v H: (with Tottenham H), 1984 v H, F (1+1 sub), I (sub), Sp (1+1 sub): 1986 v I (8)

Stewart, P. (Manchester C), 1988 v F (1)

Stockdale, R. K. (Middlesbrough), 2001 v Ge (sub) (1)

Stuart, G. C. (Chelsea), 1990 v P (sub), F, USSR, Cz: 1991 v T (sub) (5)

Stuart, J. C. (Charlton Ath), 1996 v Bel, An, P, Br (4)

Suckling, P. (Coventry C), 1986 v D: (with Manchester C), 1987 v Se (sub), Y, Sp, T: (with C Palace), 1988 v S (2), F (2), Sw (10)

Summerbee, N.J. (Swindon T), 1993 v P (sub), S (sub), F (3)

Sunderland, A. (Wolverhampton W), 1977 v W (1)

Sutton, C. R. (Norwich), 1993 v Sp (sub), T (sub + 1),Ho, P (sub), Cz, Br, S, F; 1994 v Pol, Ho, Sm, D (13)

Swindlehurst, D. (C Palace), 1977 v W (1)

Sutch, D. (Norwich C), 1992 v H, M, Cz; 1993 v T (4)

Talbot, B. (Ipswich T), 1977 v W (1)

Taylor, M. (Blackburn R), 2001 v M (sub) (1)

Terry, J. G. (Chelsea), 2001 v Fi, Sp, Fi, Alb, M, Gr (6)

Thatcher, B. D. (Millwall), 1996 v Cro: (with Wimbledon), 1997 v Mol, Pol: 1998 v I (4)

Thirlwell, P. (Sunderland), 2001 v Ge (sub), Sp (sub) (2)

Thomas, D. (Coventry C), 1981 v Ei; 1983 v WG (2), Gr, H: (with Tottenham H), I, Sp (7)

Thomas, M. (Luton T), 1986 v T, D, I (3)

Thomas, M. (Arsenal), 1988 v Y, S, F (2), M, USSR, Mor; 1989 v Gr, Alb, Pol; 1990 v Se (12)

Thomas, R. E. (Watford), 1990 v P (1)

Thompson, A. (Bolton W), 1995 v La; 1996 v P (2)

Thompson, D. A. (Liverpool), 1997 v Pol (sub), Ge: 2000 v L (sub), Pol (sub), D (sub), I, T (sub) (7)

Thompson, G. L. (Coventry C), 1981 v R, Sw, H: 1982 v N, H, S (6)

Thorn, A. (Wimbledon), 1988 v WG (sub). Y, S, F, Sw (5)

Thornley, B. L. (Manchester U), 1996 v Bel, P, Br (3)

Tiler, C. (Barnsley), 1990 v P, USSR, Cz; 1991 v H, Pol, Ei (2), T, Sen, USSR, F: (with Nottingham F), 1992 v G, T (13)

Unsworth, D. G. (Everton), 1995 v A, Ei (2), La: 1996 v N, A (6)

Upson, M. J. (Arsenal), 1999 v Se, Bul, L, F: 2000 v L, Pol, D; 2001 v I, Sp (sub), M (sub), Gr (11)

Vassell, D. (Aston Villa), 1999 v H (sub): 2000 v Pol (sub); 2001 v Ge, G, Fi, I, Fi, Alb (8)

Venison, B. (Sunderland), 1983 v D, Gr; 1985 v Fi, T, Is, Fi; 1986 v R, T, D (2) (10)

Vernazza, P. A. P. (Arsenal), 2001 v G (sub): (with Watford), M (sub) (2)

Vinnicombe, C. (Rangers), 1991 v H (sub), Pol, Ei (2), T, Sen, M, USSR (sub), F: 1992 v G, T, Pol (12)

Waddle, C. (Newcastle U), 1985 v Fi (1)

Wallace, D. (Southampton), 1983 v Gr, H: 1984 v D, H, F (2), I, Sp (sub): 1985 v Fi, T, Is: 1986 v R, D, I (14)

Wallace, Ray (Southampton), 1989 v Bul, Sen (sub), Ei: 1990 v Se (4)

Wallace, Rod (Southampton), 1989 v Bul, Ei (sub), US: 1991 v H, Pol, Ei, T, Sen, M, USSR, F (11)

Walker, D. (Nottingham F), 1985 v Fi: 1987 v Se, T: 1988 v WG, T, S (2) (7)

Walker, I. M. (Tottenham H), 1991 v W: 1992 v H, Cz, F: 1993 v Sp, N, T, Sm; 1994 v Pol (9)

Walsh, G. (Manchester U), 1988 v WG, Y (2)

Walsh, P. M. (Luton T), 1983 v D (sub), Gr (2), H (4)

Walters, K. (Aston Villa), 1984 v D (sub), H (sub); 1985 v Is, Ei, R: 1986 v R, T, D, I (sub) (9)

Ward, P. D. (Brighton & HA), 1978 v N; 1980 v EG (2)

Warhurst, P. (Oldham Ath), 1991 v H, Pol, W, Sen, M (sub), USSR, F (sub): (with Sheffield W), 1992 v G (8)

Watson, D. (Norwich C), 1984 v D, F (2), I (2), Sp (2) (7)

Watson, D. N. (Barnsley), 1994 v Ho, Sm; 1995 v Br, F: 1996 v N (5)

Watson, G. (Sheffield W), 1991 v Sen, USSR (2)

Watson, S. C. (Newcastle U), 1993 v Sp (sub), N: 1994 v Sm (sub), D: 1995 v P, A, Ei (2), La (2): 1996 v N, A (12)

Weaver, N. J. (Manchester C), 2000 v L, Pol, Arg, I, T, Slo: 2001 v I, Fi, Alb (9)

Webb, N. (Portsmouth), 1985 v Ei: (with Nottingham F), 1986 v D (2) (3)

Whelan, P. J. (Ipswich T), 1993 v Sp, T (sub), P (3)

Whelan, N. (Leeds U), 1995 v A (sub), Ei (2)

Wilson, M. A. (Manchester U), 2001 v Sp, Fi (sub), Alb, M (sub) (4)

White, D. (Manchester C), 1988 v S (2), F, USSR; 1989 v Se: 1990 v Pol (6)

Whyte, C. (Arsenal), 1982 v S (1+1 sub): 1983 v D, Gr (4)

Wicks, S. (QPR), 1982 v S (1)

Wilkins, R. C. (Chelsea), 1977 v W (1)

Wilkinson, P. (Grimsby T), 1985 v Ei, R (sub): (with Everton), 1986 v R (sub), I (4)

Williams, D. (Sunderland), 1998 v Sw (sub): 1999 v F (2)

Williams, P. (Charlton Ath), 1989 v Bul, Sen, Ei, US (sub) (4)

Williams, P. D. (Derby Co), 1991 v Sen, M, USSR: 1992 v G, T, Pol (6)

Williams, S. C. (Southampton), 1977 v S, Fi, N: 1978 v N, I (1 + 1 sub), Y (2); 1979 v D, Bul, Se (sub): 1980 v D, EG (2) (14)

Winterburn, N. (Wimbledon), 1986 v I (1)

Wise, D. (Wimbledon), 1988 v Sw (1)

Woodcock, A. S. (Nottingham F), 1978 v Fi, I (2)

Woodgate, J. S. (Leeds U), 2000 v Arg (1)

Woodhouse, C. (Sheffield U), 1999 v H, Se, Bul; 2000 v Pol (sub) (4)

Woods, C. C. E. (Nottingham F), 1979 v W (sub), Se: (with QPR), Mol, Bul, EG: 1981 v Sw: (with Norwich C), 1984 v D (6)

Wright, A. G. (Blackburn), 1993 v Sp, N (2)

Wright, M. (Southampton), 1983 v Gr, H: 1984 v D, H (4)

Wright, R. I. (Ipswich T), 1997 v Ge, Pol: 1998 v Mol, I, Gr (2), S,Af, Arg: 1999 v Se, Bul, L, Pol, H, Se; 2000 v Y (15)

Wright, S. J. (Liverpool), 2001 v Ge (sub), G, M (sub) (3)

Wright, W. (Everton), 1979 v D, W, Bul: 1980 v D, S (2) (6)

Yates, D. (Notts Co), 1989 v D (sub), Bul, Sen, Ei, US (5)

Young, L. P. (Tottenham H), 1999 v H: 2000 v D (sub), Arg (sub), T, Slo (5)

SCOTLAND

Aitken, R. (Celtic), 1977 v Cz, W, Sw: 1978 v Cz, W: 1979 v P, N (2): 1980 v Bel, E: 1984 v EG, Y (2): 1985 v WG, Ic, Sp (16)

Albiston, A. (Manchester U), 1977 v Cz, W, Sw: 1978 v Sw, Cz (5)

Alexander, N. (Stenhousemuir), 1997 v P (sub): 1998 v Bl, Ei, I: (with Livingston), 1999 v Li, Es, Bel (2), CzR, G (10)

Anderson, I. (Dundee), 1997 v Co (sub), US, CzR, P: 1998 v Bl, La, Fi, D (sub), Ei (sub), Ni; 1999 v G (sub), Ei, Ni, CzR: (with Toulouse), 2000 v Bos (15)

Anderson, R. (Aberdeen), 1997 v Es, A, Se: 1998 v La (sub), Fi, Ei, I: 1999 v Es, Bel, G, Ei, Ni, CzR: 2000 v Bos, Es (15)

Anthony, M. (Celtic), 1997 v La (sub), Es (sub), Col (3)

Archdeacon, O. (Celtic), 1987 v WG (sub) (1)

Archibald, A. (Partick T), 1998 v Fi, Ei, Ni, I; 1999 v Li (5)
Archibald, S. (Aberdeen), 1980 v B, E (2), WG; (with Tottenham H), 1981 v D (5)

Bagen, D. (Kilmarnock), 1997 v Es, A (sub), Se (sub), Bl (4)
Bain, K. (Dundee), 1993 v P, I, Ma, P (4)
Baker, M. (St. Mirren), 1993 v F, M, E; 1994 v Ma, A; 1995 v Gr, M, F (sub), Sk (sub); 1996 v H (sub) (10)
Baltacha, S. S. (St Mirren), 2000 v Bos, Li (sub), F (sub) (3)
Bannon, E. J. P. (Hearts), 1979 v US; (with Chelsea), P, N (2); (with Dundee U), 1980 v Bel, WG, E (7)
Beattie, J. (St Mirren), 1992 v D, US, P, Y (4)
Beaumont, D. (Dundee U), 1985 v Ic (1)
Bell, D. (Aberdeen), 1981 v D; 1984 v Y (2)
Bernard, P. R. J. (Oldham Ath), 1992 v R (sub), D, Se (sub), US; 1993 v Sw, P, I, Ma, P, F, Bul, M, E; 1994 v I, Ma (15)
Bett, J. (Rangers), 1981 v Se, D; 1982 v Se, D, I, E (2) (7)
Black, E. (Aberdeen), 1983 v EG, Sw (2), Bel; 1985 v Ic, Sp (2), Ic (8)
Blair, A. (Coventry C), 1980 v E; 1981 v Se; (with Aston Villa), 1982 v Se, D, I (5)
Bollan, G. (Dundee U), 1992 v D, G (sub), US, P, Y; 1993 v Sw, P, I, P, F, Bul, M, E; 1994 v Sw; 1995 v Gr; (with Rangers) v Ru, Sm (17)
Bonar, P. (Raith R), 1997 v A, La, Es (sub), Se (4)
Booth, S. (Aberdeen), 1991 v R (sub), Bul (sub + 1), Pol, F (sub); 1992 v Sw, R, D, Se, US, P, Y; 1993 v Ma, P (14)
Bowes, M. J. (Dunfermline Ath), 1992 v D (sub) (1)
Bowman, D. (Hearts), 1985 v WG (sub) (1)
Boyack, S. (Rangers), 1997 v Se (1)
Boyd, T. (Motherwell), 1987 v WG, Ei (2), Bel; 1988 v Bel (5)
Brazil, A. (Hibernian), 1978 v W (1)
Brazil, A. (Ipswich T), 1979 v N; 1980 v Bel (2), E (2), WG; 1981 v Se; 1982 v Se (8)
Brebner, G. I. (Manchester U), 1997 v Col, CzR (sub), US (sub), P; 1998 v Bl, La, Fi, D; (with Reading), 1999 v Li, Es, Bel (2), CzR, G, Ei, Ni, CzR; (with Hibernian), 2000 v Bos (18)
Brough, J. (Hearts), 1981 v D (1)
Browne, P. (Raith R), 1997 v A (1)
Buchan, J. (Aberdeen), 1997 v Se, Col, CzR, P; 1998 v Bl, La, Fi; 1999 v Li, Es, Bel, CzR, G, Ei (13)
Burchill, M. (Celtic), 1998 v Fi, D (sub); 1999 v Li, Es (sub), Bel (2), CzR, Ei, Ni, CzR; 2000 v Bos, Es; 2001 v La, Bel, Pol (15)
Burke, A. (Kilmarnock), 1997 v Es, A, Bl (sub); 1998 v Ei (sub) (4)
Burley, G. E. (Ipswich T), 1977 v Cz, W, Sw; 1978 v Sw, Cz (5)
Burley, C. (Chelsea), 1992 v D; 1993 v Sw, P, I, P; 1994 v Sw, I (sub) (7)
Burns, H. (Rangers), 1985 v Sp, Ic (sub) (2)
Burns, T. (Celtic), 1977 v Cz, W, E; 1978 v Sw; 1982 v E (5)

Caldwell, G. (Newcastle U), 2000 v F, Ni, W (3)
Caldwell, S. (Newcastle U), 2001 v La, Cro, Bel (3)
Campbell, S. (Dundee), 1989 v N (sub), Y, F (3)
Campbell, S. P. (Leicester C), 1998 v Fi (sub), D, Ei, Ni (sub), I; 1999 v Li, Es, Bel (2), CzR, G, Ei, Ni, CzR (sub); 2000 v Bos (sub) (15)
Canero, P. (Kilmarnock), 2000 v F; 2001 v La (sub), Cro (sub), Bel, Pol (5)
Carey, L. A. (Bristol C), 1998 v D (1)
Casey, J. (Celtic), 1978 v W (1)
Christie, M. (Dundee), 1992 v D, P (sub), Y (3)
Clark, R. (Aberdeen), 1977 v Cz, W, Sw (3)
Clarke, S. (St Mirren), 1984 v Bel, EG, Y; 1985 v WG, Ic, Sp (2), Ic (8)
Cleland, A. (Dundee U), 1990 v F, N (2); 1991 v R, Sw, Bul; 1992 v Sw, R, G, Se (2) (11)
Collins, J. (Hibernian), 1988 v Bel, E; 1989 v N, Y, F; 1990 v Y, F, N (8)
Connolly, P. (Dundee U), 1991 v R (sub), Sw, Bul (3)
Connor, R. (Ayr U), 1981 v Se; 1982 v Se (2)
Cooper, D. (Clydebank), 1977 v Cz, W, Sw, E; (with Rangers), 1978 v Sw, Cz (6)
Cooper, N. (Aberdeen), 1982 v D, E (2); 1983 v Bel, EG, Sw (2); 1984 v Bel, EG, Y; 1985 v Ic, Sp, Ic (13)
Crabbe, S. (Hearts), 1990 v Y (sub), F (2)
Craig, M. (Aberdeen), 1998 v Bl, La (2)

Craig, T. (Newcastle U), 1977 v E (1)
Crainey, S. D. (Celtic), 2000 v F (sub) (1)
Crainie, D. (Celtic), 1983 v Sw (sub) (1)
Crawford, S. (Raith R), 1994 v A, Eg, P, Bel; 1995 v Fi, Ru,Gr, Ru, Sm, M, F (sub), Sk (sub), Br (sub); 1996 v Gr, Fi (sub), H (1 + sub), Sp (sub), F (sub) (19)
Creaney, G. (Celtic), 1991 v Sw, Bul (2), Pol, F; 1992 v Sw, R, G (2), Se (2) (11)
Cummings, W. (Chelsea), 2000 v F, Ni; 2001 v La, Cro, Bel, Pol (6)

Dailly, C. (Dundee U), 1991 v R; 1992 v US, R; 1993 v Sw, P, I, Ic, P, F, Bul, M, E; 1994 v Sw, I, Ma, A, Eg, P, Bel; 1995 v Fi, Ru, Gr, Ru, Sm, M, F, Sk, Br; 1996 v Fi, Sm, H (2), Sp, F (34)
Dalglish, P. (Newcastle U), 1999 v Es, Bel, CzR; (with Norwich C), 2000 v Es (sub), Bos, Li (sub) (6)
Dargo, C. (Raith R), 1998 v Fi, Ei, Ni (sub), I; 1999 v Es, Bel (1+sub), CzR (sub), G, Ni (sub) (10)
Davidson, C. (St Johnstone), 1997 v Se, Bl (2)
Davidson, H. N. (Dundee U), 2000 v Es (sub), Li, F (3)
Dawson, A. (Rangers), 1979 v P, N (2); 1980 v B (2), E (2), WG (8)
Deas, P. A. (St Johnstone), 1992 v D (sub); 1993 v Ma (2)
Dennis, S. (Raith R), 1992 v Sw (1)
Dickov, P. (Arsenal), 1992 v Y; 1993 v F, M, E (4)
Dodds, D. (Dundee U), 1978 v W (1)
Dods, D. (Hibernian), 1997 v La, Es, Se (2), Bl (5)
Doig, C. R. (Nottingham F), 2000 v Ni, W; 2001 v La, Cro, Pol (5)
Donald, G. S. (Hibernian), 1992 v US (sub), P, Y (sub) (3)
Donnelly, S. (Celtic), 1994 v Eg, P, Bel; 1995 v Fi, Gr (sub); 1996 v Gr (sub), Sm, H (2), Sp, F (11)
Dow, A. (Dundee), 1993 v Ma, Ic; (with Chelsea) 1994 v I (3)
Duffy, J. (Dundee), 1987 v Ei (1)
Durie, G. S. (Chelsea), 1987 v WG, Ei, Bel; 1988 v Bel (4)
Durrant, I. (Rangers), 1987 v WG, Ei, Bel; 1988 v E (4)
Doyle, J. (Partick Th), 1981 v D, I (sub) (2)

Easton, C. (Dundee U), 1997 v Col, US, CzR, P; 1998 v Bl, Fi, D, Ei, Ni, I; 1999 v Li, Es, Bel (1+sub); 2000 v Li, F; 2001 v La (sub), Cro, Bel (19)
Elliot, B. (Celtic), 1998 v Ni; 1999 v Li (sub) (2)
Esson, R. (Aberdeen), 2000 v Li, Ni; 2001 v La, Cro, Bel, Pol (6)

Ferguson, B. (Rangers), 1997 v Col (sub), US, CzR, P; 1998 v Bl, La, Fi, D (sub), Ei, Ni, I; 1999 v Bel (12)
Ferguson, D. (Rangers), 1987 v WG, Ei, Bel; 1988 v E; 1990 v Y (5)
Ferguson, D. (Dundee U), 1992 v D, G, Se (2); 1993 v Sw, I, Ma (7)
Ferguson, D. (Manchester U), 1992 v US, P (sub), Y; 1993 v Sw, Ma (5)
Ferguson, I. (Dundee), 1983 v EG (sub), Sw (sub); 1984 v Bel (sub), EG (4)
Ferguson, I. (Clyde), 1987 v WG (sub), Ei; (with St Mirren), Ei, Bel; 1988 v Bel; (with Rangers), E (sub) (6)
Ferguson, R. (Hamilton A), 1977 v E (1)
Findlay, W. (Hibernian), 1991 v R, Pol, Bul (2), Pol (5)
Fitzpatrick, A. (St Mirren), 1977 v W (sub), Sw (sub), E; 1978 v Sw, Cz (5)
Flannigan, C. (Clydebank), 1993 v Ic (sub) (1)
Fleck, R. (Rangers), 1987 v WG (sub), Ei, Bel; (with Norwich C), 1988 v E (2); 1989 v Y (6)
Fraser, S. T. (Luton T), 2000 v Ni (sub), W; 2001 v La, Cro (4)
Freedman, D. A. (Barnet), 1995 v Ru (sub + 1), Sm, M, F, Sk, Br; (with C Palace) 1996 v Sm (sub) (8)
Fridge, L. (St Mirren), 1989 v F; 1990 v Y (2)
Fullarton, J. (St. Mirren), 1993 v F, Bul; 1994 v Ma, A, Eg, P, Bel; 1995 v M, F, Sk, Br; 1996 v Gr, Fi, H (sub + 1), Sp (sub), F (17)
Fulton, M. (St Mirren), 1980 v Bel, WG, E; 1981 v Se, D (sub) (5)
Fulton, S. (Celtic), 1991 v R, Sw, Bul, Pol, F; 1992 v G (2) (7)

Gallacher, K. (Dundee U), 1987 v WG, Ei (2), Bel (sub); 1988 v E (2); 1990 v Y (7)
Gallacher, P. (Dundee U), 1999 v Ei, Ni, CzR; 2000 v Bos, Es, Bos, F (7)

McManus, T. (Hibernian), 2001 v Bel (sub), Pol (sub) (2)
McMillan, S. (Motherwell), 1997 v A (sub + sub), Se, Bl (4)
McNab, N. (Tottenham H), 1978 v W (1)
McNally, M. (Celtic), 1991 v Bul: 1993 v Ic (2)
McNamara, J. (Dunfermline Ath), 1994 v A, Bel; 1995 v Gr, Ru, Sm; 1996 v Gr, Fi: (with Celtic), Sm, H (2), Sp, F (12)
McNichol, J. (Brentford), 1979 v P, N (2); 1980 v Bel (2), WG, E (7)
McNiven, D. (Leeds U), 1977 v Cz, W (sub), Sw (sub) (3)
McNiven, S. A. (Oldham Ath), 1996 v Sm (sub) (1)
McPherson, D. (Rangers), 1984 v Bel; 1985 v Sp: (with Hearts), 1989 v N, Y (4)
McQuilken, J. (Celtic), 1993 v Bul, E (2)
McStay, P. (Celtic), 1983 v EG, Sw (2); 1984 v Y (2) (5)
McWhirter, N. (St Mirren), 1991 v Bul (sub) (1)
Main, A. (Dundee U), 1988 v E: 1989 v Y; 1990 v N (3)
Malcolm, R. (Rangers), 2001 v Pol (1)
Malpas, M. (Dundee U), 1983 v Bel, Sw (1+1 sub); 1984 v Bel, EG, Y (2); 1985 v Sp (8)
Marshall, S. R. (Arsenal), 1995 v Ru, Gr; 1996 v H, Sp, F (5)
Mason, G. R. (Manchester C), 1999 v Li (sub) (1)
Mathieson, D. (Queen of the South), 1997 v Col; 1998 v La: 1999 v G (sub) (3)
May, E. (Hibernian), 1989 v Y (sub), F (2)
Meldrum, C. (Kilmarnock), 1996 v F (sub); 1997 v A (2), La, Es, Se (6)
Melrose, J. (Partick Th), 1977 v Sw; 1979 v US, P, N (2): 1980 v Bel (sub), WG, E (8)
Miller, C. (Rangers), 1995 v Gr, Ru; 1996 v Gr, Sp, F; 1997 v A, La, Es (8)
Miller, J. (Aberdeen), 1987 v Ei (sub); 1988 v Bel: (with Celtic), E; 1989 v N, Y; 1990 v F, N (7)
Miller, K. (Hibernian), 2000 v F, Ni, W: (with Rangers), 2001 v Cro, Bel (5)
Miller, W. (Aberdeen), 1978 v Sw, Cz (2)
Miller, W. (Hibernian), 1991 v R, Sw, Bul, Pol, F; 1992 v R, G (sub) (7)
Milne, K. (Hearts), 2000 v F (1)
Milne, R. (Dundee U), 1982 v Se (sub); 1984 v Bel, EG (3)
Money, I. C. (St Mirren), 1987 v Ei; 1988 v Bel; 1989 v N (3)
Muir, L. (Hibernian), 1977 v Cz (sub) (1)
Murray, H. (St Mirren), 2000 v F (sub), Ni (sub), W (sub) (3)
Murray, I. (Hibernian), 2001 v Bel (sub), Pol (2)
Murray, N. (Rangers), 1993 v P (sub), Ma, Ic, P; 1994 v Sw, I; 1995 v Fi, Ru, Gr, Sm; 1996 v Gr (sub), Fi, Sm, H (2), F (16)
Murray, R. (Bournemouth), 1993 v Ic (sub) (1)

Narey, D. (Dundee U), 1977 v Cz, Sw; 1978 v Sw, Cz (4)
Naysmith, G. (Hearts), 1997 v La, Es (1 + sub), Se, A, Col, US, CzR, P; 1998 v La, D; 1999 v Es, Bel (2), CzR, G, Ei, CzR; 2000 v Bos, Es, Bos, Li (22)
Neilson, R. (Hearts), 2000 v Ni (1)
Nevin, P. (Chelsea), 1985 v WG, Ic, Sp (2), Ic (5)
Nicholas, C. (Celtic), 1981 v Se; 1982 v Se; 1983 v EG, Sw, Bel: (with Arsenal), 1984 v Y (6)
Nicholson, B. (Rangers), 1999 v G, Ni, CzR (sub): 2000 v Bos (sub), Es, Bos, Li (7)
Nicol, S. (Ayr U), 1981 v Se: 1982 v Se, D: (with Liverpool), I (2), E (2); 1983 v EG, Sw (2), Bel: 1984 v Bel, EG, Y (14)
Nisbet, S. (Rangers), 1989 v N, Y, F; 1990 v Y, F (5)
Notman, A. M. (Manchester U), 1999 v Li (sub), Es, Bel (sub+sub); 2000 v Li, F (sub), Ni, W; 2001 v La, Cro (10)

O'Brien, B. (Blackburn R), 1999 v Ei (sub), Ni (sub), CzR (sub): 2000 v Bos (sub) (4)
O'Donnell, P. (Motherwell), 1992 v Sw (sub), R, D, G (2), Se (1 + 1 sub); 1993 v P (8)
O'Neil, B. (Celtic), 1992 v D, G, Se (2): 1993 v Sw, P, I (7)
O'Neil, J. (Dundee U), 1991 v Bul (sub) (1)
O'Neill, M. (Clyde), 1995 v Ru (sub), F, Sk, Br: 1997 v Se (sub), Bl (sub) (6)
Orr, N. (Morton), 1978 v W (sub); 1979 v US, P, N (2): 1980 v Bel, E (7)

Parker, K. (St Johnstone), 2001 v Pol (sub) (1)
Parlane, D. (Rangers), 1977 v W (1)
Paterson, C. (Hibernian), 1981 v Se: 1982 v I (2)
Paterson, J. (Dundee U), 1997 v Col, US, CzR; 1999 v Bel (sub+sub): 2000 v Es, Bos, Li (8)

Payne, G. (Dundee U), 1978 v Sw, Cz, W (3)
Peacock, L. A. (Carlisle U), 1997 v Bl (1)
Pressley, S. (Rangers), 1993 v Ic, F, Bul, M, E: 1994 v Sw, I, M, A, Eg, P, Bel; 1995 v Fi: (with Coventry C), Ru (2), Sm, M, F, Sk, Br: (with Dundee U), 1996 v Gr, Sm, H (2), Sp, F (26)
Provan, D. (Kilmarnock), 1977 v Cz (sub) (1)

Rae, A. (Millwall), 1991 v Bul (sub + 1), F (sub): 1992 v Sw, R, G (sub), Se (2) (8)
Rae, G. (Dundee), 1999 v Ei (sub), Ni, CzR: 2000 v Bos, Es, Bos (6)
Redford, I. (Rangers), 1981 v Se (sub): 1982 v Se, D, I (2), E (6)
Reid, B. (Rangers), 1991 v F; 1992 v D, US, P (4)
Reid, C. (Hibernian), 1993 v Sw, P, I (3)
Reid, M. (Celtic), 1982 v E: 1984 v Y (2)
Reid, R. (St Mirren), 1977 v W, Sw, E (3)
Renicks, S. (Hamilton A), 1997 v Bl (1)
Rice, B. (Hibernian), 1985 v WG (1)
Richardson, L. (St Mirren), 1980 v WG, E (sub) (2)
Ritchie, A. (Morton), 1980 v Bel (1)
Ritchie, P. R. (Hearts), 1996 v H: 1997 v A (2), La, Es (2), Se (7)
Robertson, A. (Rangers) 1991 v F (1)
Robertson, C. (Rangers), 1977 v E (sub) (1)
Robertson, D. (Aberdeen), 1987 v Ei (sub); 1988 v E (2); 1989 v N, Y; 1990 v Y, N (7)
Robertson, H. (Aberdeen), 1994 v Eg; 1995 v Fi (2)
Robertson, J. (Hearts), 1985 v WG, Ic (sub) (2)
Robertson, L. (Rangers), 1993 v F, M (sub), E (sub) (3)
Robertson, S. (St Johnstone), 1998 v Fi, Ni (2)
Roddie, A. (Aberdeen), 1992 v US, P; 1993 v Sw (sub), P, Ic (5)
Ross, T. W. (Arsenal), 1977 v W (1)
Rowson, D. (Aberdeen), 1997 v La, Es, Se (2), Bl (5)
Russell, R. (Rangers), 1978 v W; 1980 v Bel; 1984 v Y (3)

Salton, D. B. (Luton T), 1992 v D, US, P, Y; 1993 v Sw, I (6)
Scott, P. (St Johnstone), 1994 v A (sub), Eg (sub), P, Bel (4)
Scrimgour, D. (St Mirren), 1997 v US, CzR; 1998 v D (3)
Seaton, A. (Falkirk), 1998 v Bl (sub) (1)
Severin, S. D. (Hearts), 2000 v Es, Bos, Li (sub), F, Ni, W: 2001 v La, Bel (8)
Shannon, R. (Dundee), 1987 v WG, Ei (2), Bel; 1988 v Bel, E (2) (7)
Sharp, G. (Everton), 1982 v E (1)
Sharp, R. (Dunfermline Ath), 1990 v N (sub): 1991 v R, Sw, Bul (4)
Sheerin, P. (Southampton), 1996 v Sm (1)
Shields, G. (Rangers), 1997 v A, La (2)
Simpson, N. (Aberdeen), 1982 v I (2), E: 1983 v EG, Sw (2), Bel: 1984 v Bel, EG, Y; 1985 v Sp (11)
Sinclair, D. (Dumbarton), 1977 v E (1)
Skilling, M. (Kilmarnock), 1993 v Ic (sub): 1994 v I (2)
Smith, B. M. (Celtic), 1992 v G (2), US, P, Y (5)
Smith, G. (Rangers), 1978 v W (1)
Smith, H. G. (Hearts), 1987 v WG, Bel (2)
Sneddon, A. (Celtic), 1979 v US (1)
Speedie, D. (Chelsea), 1985 v Sp (1)
Spencer, J. (Rangers), 1991 v Sw (sub), F; 1992 v Sw (3)
Stanton, P. (Hibernian), 1977 v Cz (1)
Stark, W. (Aberdeen), 1985 v Ic (1)
Stephen, R. (Dundee), 1983 v Bel (sub) (1)
Stevens, G. (Motherwell), 1977 v E (1)
Stewart, J. (Kilmarnock), 1978 v Sw, Cz; (with Middlesbrough), 1979 v P (3)
Stewart, M. J. (Manchester U), 2000 v Ni: 2001 v La, Cro, Bel, Pol (5)
Stewart, R. (Dundee U), 1979 v P, N (2): (with West Ham U), 1980 v Bel (2), E (2), WG; 1981 v D; 1982 v I (2), E (12)
Stillie, D. (Aberdeen), 1995 v Ru (2), Sm, M, F, Sk, Br: 1996 v Gr, Fi, Sm, H (2), Sp, F (14)
Strachan, D. (Aberdeen), 1980 v Bel (1)
Strachan, G. D. (Coventry C), 1998 v D, Ei: 1999 v Li, Es, Bel (2); 2000 v Li (7)
Sturrock, P. (Dundee U), 1977 v Cz, W, Sw, E: 1978 v Sw, Cz: 1982 v Se, I, E (9)
Sweeney, S. (Clydebank), 1991 v R, Sw (sub), Bul (2), Pol: 1992 v Sw, R (7)

Tarrant, N. K. (Aston Villa), 1999 v Ni (sub): 2000 v Es (sub), Bos (sub), Li, Ni (sub) (5)

Teale, G. (Clydebank), 1997 v La (sub), Es, Bl; (with Ayr U), 1999 v CzR (sub), G (sub), Ei (sub) (6)
Telfer, P. (Luton T), 1993 v Ma, P; 1994 v Sw (3)
Thomas, K. (Hearts), 1993 v F (sub), Bul, M, E; 1994 v Sw, Ma; 1995 v Gr; 1997 v A (8)
Thompson, S. (Dundee U), 1997 v US, CzR, P; 1998 v Bl, La; 1999 v G (sub), Ei, Ni, CzR; 2000 v Bos, Es, Bos (12)
Thomson, W. (Partick Th), 1977 v E (sub); 1978 v W; (with St Mirren), 1979 v US, N (2); 1980 v Bel (2), E (2), WG (10)
Tolmie, J. (Morton), 1980 v Bel (sub) (1)
Tortolano, J. (Hibernian), 1987 v WG, Ei (2)
Tweed, S. (Hibernian), 1993 v Ic; 1994 v Sw, I (3)

Wales, G. (Hearts), 2000 v F (1)
Walker, A. (Celtic), 1988 v Bel (1)
Wallace, I. (Coventry C), 1978 v Sw (1)
Walsh, C. (Nottingham F), 1984 v EG, Sw (2), Bel; 1984 v EG (5)
Wark, J. (Ipswich T), 1977 v Cz, W, Sw; 1978 v W; 1979 v P; 1980 v E (2), WG (8)
Watson, A. (Aberdeen), 1981 v Se, D; 1982 v D, I (sub) (4)
Watson, K. (Rangers), 1977 v E; 1978 v Sw (sub) (2)
Watt, M. (Aberdeen), 1991 v R, Sw, Bul (2), Pol, F; 1992 v Sw, R, G (2), Se (2) (12)
Whiteford, A. (St Johnstone), 1997 v US (1)
Whyte, D. (Celtic), 1987 v Ei (2), Bel; 1988 v E (2); 1989 v N, Y; 1990 v Y, N (9)
Wilkie, L. (Dundee), 2000 v Bos, F, Ni, W; 2001 v La, Cro (6)
Will, J. A. (Arsenal), 1992 v D (sub), Y; 1993 v Ic (sub) (3)
Wilson, S. (Rangers), 1999 v Es, Bel (2), G, Ei, CzR; 2000 v Bos (7)
Wilson, T. (St Mirren), 1983 v Sw (sub) (1)
Wilson, T. (Nottingham F), 1988 v E; 1989 v N, Y; 1990 v F (4)
Winnie, D. (St Mirren), 1988 v Bel (1)
Wright, P. (Aberdeen), 1989 v Y, F; (with QPR), 1990 v Y (sub) (3)
Wright, S. (Aberdeen), 1991 v Bul, Pol, F; 1992 v Sw, G (2); 1993 v Sw, P, I, Ma; 1994 v I, Ma (14)
Wright, T. (Oldham Ath), 1987 v Bel (sub) (1)

Young, D. (Aberdeen), 1997 v Es (sub), Se, Col, CzR (sub), P; 1998 v La (sub); 1999 v CzR (sub), G (sub); 2000 v W; 2001 v Cro (sub), Bel (sub), Pol (12)

WALES
Aizlewood, M. (Luton T), 1979 v E; 1981 v Ho (2)

Baddeley, L. M. (Cardiff C), 1996 v Mol (sub), G (sub) (2)
Balcombe, S. (Leeds U), 1982 v F (sub) (1)
Barnhouse, D. J. (Swansea), 1995 v Mol; 1996 v Mol, Sm (3)
Bater, P. T. (Bristol R), 1977 v E, S (2)
Bellamy, C. D. (Norwich C), 1996 v Sm (sub); 1997 v Sm, T, Bel; 1998 v T, Bel, I; 1999 v I (8)
Bird, A. (Cardiff C), 1993 v Cy (sub); 1994 v Cy (sub); 1995 v Mol, Ge (sub), Bul; 1996 v G (sub) (6)
Blackmore, C. (Manchester U), 1984 v N, Bul, Y (3)
Blake, N. (Cardiff C), 1991 v Pol (sub); 1993 v Cy, Bel, RCS; 1994 v RCS (5)
Blaney, S. D. (West Ham U), 1997 v Sm, Ho, T (3)
Bodin, P. (Cardiff C), 1983 v Y (1)
Bowen, J. P. (Swansea C), 1993 v Cy, Bel (2); 1994 v RCS, R (sub) (5)
Bowen, M. (Tottenham H), 1983 v N; 1984 v Bul, Y (3)
Boyle, T. (C Palace), 1982 v F (1)
Brace, D. P. (Wrexham), 1995 v Ge, Bul (2); 1997 v Sm Ho; 1998 v T (6)

Cegielski, W. (Wrexham), 1977 v E (sub), S (2)
Chapple, S. R. (Swansea C), 1992 v R; 1993 v Cy, Bel (2), RCS; 1994 v RCS; Bul (2) (8)
Charles, J. M. (Swansea C), 1979 v E; 1981 v Ho (2)
Clark, J. (Manchester U), 1978 v S; (with Derby Co), 1979 v E (2)
Coates, J. S. (Swansea C), 1996 v Mol, G; 1997 v Ho, T (sub); 1998 v T (sub) (5)
Coleman, C. (Swansea C), 1990 v Pol; 1991 v E, Pol (3)
Coyne, D. (Tranmere R), 1992 v R; 1994 v Cy (sub), R; 1995 v Mol, Ge, Bul (2) (7)
Curtis, A. T. (Swansea C), 1977 v E (1)

Davies, A. (Manchester U), 1982 v F (2), Ho; 1983 v N, Y, Bul (6)

Davies, D. (Barry T), 1999 v D (sub) (1)
Davies, G. M. (Hereford U), 1993 v Bel, RCS; 1995 v Mol (sub), Ge, Bul (2); (with C Palace) 1996 v Mol (7)
Davies, I. C. (Norwich C), 1978 v S (sub) (1)
Davies, S. (Peterborough U), 1999 v D, Bl, Sw, I, D; (with Tottenham H), 2000 v S; 2001 v Bl, N, Pol, Arm (10)
Day, R. (Manchester C), 2000 v S (sub), Ni; 2001 v Uk, Pol, Uk (3)
Deacy, N. (PSV Eindhoven), 1977 v S (1)
Dibble, A. (Cardiff C), 1983 v Bul; 1984 v N, Bul (3)
Doyle, S. C. (Preston NE), 1979 v E (sub); (with Huddersfield T), 1984 v N (2)
Dwyer, P. J. (Cardiff C), 1979 v E (1)

Earnshaw, R. (Cardiff C), 1999 v P (sub), I, D; 2000 v S, Ni; 2001 v Bl (sub), N, Pol (2), Uk (10)
Ebdon, M. (Everton), 1990 v Pol; 1991 v E (2)
Edwards, C. N. H. (Swansea C), 1996 v G; 1997 v Sm, Ho (2), T, Bel; 1998 v T (7)
Edwards, R. I. (Chester), 1977 v S; 1978 v W (2)
Edwards, R. W. (Bristol C), 1991 v Pol; 1992 v R; 1993 v Cy, Bel (2), RCS; 1994 v RCS, Cy, R; 1995 v Ge, Bul; 1996 v Mol, G (13)
Evans, A. (Bristol R), 1977 v E (1)
Evans, K. (Leeds U), 1999 v I (sub), D; (with Cardiff C), 2001 v N (sub), Pol (sub) (4)
Evans, P. S. (Shrewsbury T), 1996 v G (1)
Evans, S. J. (Crystal Palace), 2001 v Bl, Arm (2)
Evans, T. (Cardiff C), 1995 v Bul (sub); 1996 v Mol, G (3)

Folland, R. W. (Oxford U), 2000 v Ni (sub) (1)
Foster, M. G. (Tranmere R), 1993 v RCS (1)
Freestone, R. (Chelsea), 1990 v Pol (1)

Gabbidon, D. L. (WBA), 1999 v D, P, Sw, I (sub), D; 2000 v Bl, Sw, S, Ni; (with Cardiff C), 2001 v N, Pol, Arm, Uk, Pol, Uk (15)
Gale, D. (Swansea C), 1983 v Bul; 1984 v N (sub) (2)
Gibson, N. D. (Tranmere R), 1999 v D (sub), Bl (sub), P; 2000 v S (sub), Ni; (with Sheffield W), 2001 v Uk, Pol, Uk (8)
Giggs, R. (Manchester U), 1991 v Pol (1)
Giles, D. C. (Cardiff C), 1977 v S; 1978 v S; (with Swansea C), 1981 v Ho; (with C Palace), 1983 v Y (4)
Giles, P. (Cardiff C), 1982 v F (2), Ho (3)
Graham, D. (Manchester U), 1991 v E (1)
Green, R. M. (Wolverhampton W), 1998 v I; 1999 v I, D, Bl, Sw, I, D; 2000 v Bl, S, Ni; 2001 v Bl, N, Pol, Arm, Uk, Pol (16)
Griffith, C. (Cardiff C), 1990 v Pol (1)
Griffiths, C. (Shrewsbury T), 1991 v Pol (sub) (1)

Hall, G. D. (Chelsea), 1990 v Pol (1)
Hartson, J. (Luton T), 1994 v Cy, R; 1995 v Mol, Ge, Bul; (with Arsenal), 1996 v G, Sm; 1997 v Sm, Ho (9)
Haworth, S. O. (Cardiff C), 1997 v Ho, T, Bel; (with Coventry C), 1998 v T, Bel; I; 1999 v I, D; (with Wigan Ath) Bl, Sw; 2000 v Bl, Sw (12)
Hillier, I. M. (Tottenham H), 2001 v Uk (sub), Pol (sub), Uk (3)
Hodges, G. (Wimbledon), 1983 v Y (sub), Bul (sub); 1984 v N, Bul, Y (5)
Holden, A. (Chester C), 1984 v Y (sub) (1)
Holloway, C. D. (Exeter C), 1999 v P, D (2)
Hopkins, J. (Fulham), 1982 v F (sub), Ho; 1983 v N, Y, Bul (5)
Hopkins, S. A. (Wrexham), 1999 v P (sub) (1)
Huggins, D. S. (Bristol C), 1996 v Sm (1)
Hughes, D. R. (Southampton), 1994 v R (1)
Hughes, R. D. (Aston Villa), 1996 v Sm; 1997 v Sm (sub), Ho (2), T, Bel; 1998 v T, Bel, I; 1999 v I, Sw, I; (with Shrewsbury T), 2000 v Sw (13)
Hughes, I. (Bury), 1992 v R; 1993 v Cy, Bel (sub), RCS; 1994 v Cy, R; 1995 v Mol, Ge, Bul; 1996 v Mol (sub), G (11)
Hughes, L. M. (Manchester U), 1983 v N, Y; 1984 v N, Bul, Y (5)
Hughes, W. (WBA), 1977 v E, S; 1978 v S (3)

Jackett, K. (Watford), 1981 v Ho; 1982 v F (2)
James, R. M. (Swansea C), 1977 v E, S; 1978 v S (3)
Jarman, L. (Cardiff C), 1997 v Sm, Ho (2), Bel; 1998 v T, Bel; 1999 v I, P; 2000 v Bl (10)
Jeanne, L. C. (QPR), 1999 v P (sub), Sw, I; 2000 v Bl, Sw, S, Ni; 2001 v Bl (8)

Jelleyman, G. A. (Peterborough U), 1999 v D (sub) (1)
Jenkins, L. D. (Swansea C), 1998 v T (sub); 2000 v Bl, Sw, S, Ni; 2001 v N, Pol, Arm, Uk (9)
Jenkins, S. R. (Swansea C), 1993 v Cy (sub), Bel (2)
Jones, E. P. (Blackpool), 2000 v Ni (sub) (1)
Jones, F. (Wrexham), 1981 v Ho (1)
Jones, J. A. (Swansea C); 2001 v Pol, Uk (2)
Jones, L. (Cardiff C), 1982 v F (2), Ho (3)
Jones, M. G. (Leeds U), 1998 v Bel; 1999 v I, D, Bl, Sw, I; 2000 v Sw (7)
Jones, P. L. (Liverpool), 1992 v R; 1993 v Cy, Bel (2), RCS; 1994 v RCS (sub), Cy, R; 1995 v Mol, Ge; 1996 v Mol, G (12)
Jones, R. (Sheffield W), 1994 v R; 1995 v Bul (2) (3)
Jones, V. (Bristol R), 1979 v E; 1981 v Ho (2)

Kendall, L. M. (Crystal Palace), 2001 v N, Pol (2)
Kendall, M. (Tottenham H), 1978 v S (1)
Kenworthy, J. R. (Tranmere R), 1994 v Cy; 1995 v Mol, Bul (3)
Knott, G. R. (Tottenham H), 1996 v Sm (1)

Law, B. J. (QPR), 1990 v Pol; 1991 v E (2)
Letheran, G. (Leeds U), 1977 v E, S (2)
Lewis, D. (Swansea C), 1982 v F (2), Ho; 1983 v N, Y, Bul; 1984 v N, Bul, Y (9)
Lewis, J. (Cardiff C), 1983 v N (1)
Llewellyn, C. M. (Norwich C), 1998 v T (sub), Bel (sub), I; 1999 v I, D, Bl, I; 2000 v Bl, Sw, S; 2001 v N, Pol, Arm, Uk (14)
Loveridge, J. (Swansea C), 1982 v Ho; 1983 v N, Bul (3)
Low, J. D. (Bristol R), 1999 v P (1)
Lowndes, S. R. (Newport Co), 1979 v E; 1981 v Ho; (with Millwall), 1984 v Bul, Y (4)

McCarthy, A. J. (QPR), 1994 v RCS, Cy, R (3)
Maddy, P. (Cardiff C), 1982 v Ho; 1983 v N (sub) (2)
Margetson, M. W. (Manchester C), 1992 v R; 1993 v Cy, Bel (2), RCS; 1994 v RCS, Cy (7)
Martin, A. P. (Crystal Palace), 1999 v D (1)
Marustik, C. (Swansea C), 1982 v F (2); 1983 v Y, Bul; 1984 v N, Bul, Y (7)
Maxwell, L. J. (Liverpool), 1999 v Sw (sub), I; 2000 v Sw (sub), S, Ni; 2001 v Bl, Pol, Arm, Uk, Pol, Uk (11)
Meaker, M. J. (QPR), 1994 v RCS (sub), R (sub) (2)
Melville, A. K. (Swansea C), 1990 v Pol; (with Oxford U), 1991 v E (2)
Micallef, C. (Cardiff C), 1982 v F, Ho; 1983 v N (3)
Morgan, A. M. (Tranmere R), 1995 v Mol, Bul; 1996 v Mol, G (4)
Mountain, P. D. (Cardiff C), 1997 v Ho, T (2)

Nardiello, D. (Coventry C), 1978 v S (1)
Neilson, A. B. (Newcastle U), 1993 v Cy, Bel (2), RCS; 1994 v RCS, Cy, R (7)
Nicholas, P. (C Palace), 1978 v S; 1979 v E; (with Arsenal), 1982 v F (3)
Nogan, K. (Luton T), 1990 v Pol; 1991 v E (2)
Nogan, L. (Oxford U) 1991 v E (1)

Oster, J. M. (Grimsby T), 1997 v Sm (sub), Ho (sub), T, Bel; (with Everton), 1998 v T, Bel, I; 1999 v I, Sw (9)
Owen, G. (Wrexham), 1991 v E (sub), Pol; 1992 v R; 1993 v Cy, Bel (2); 1994 v Cy, R (8)

Page, R. J. (Watford), 1995 v Mol, Ge, Bul; 1996 v Mol (4)
Partridge, D. W. (West Ham U), 1997 v T (1)
Pascoe, C. (Swansea C), 1983 v Bul (sub); 1984 v N (sub), Bul, Y (4)
Pembridge, M. (Luton T), 1991 v Pol (1)
Perry, J. (Cardiff C), 1990 v Pol; 1991 v E, Pol (3)
Peters, M. (Manchester C), 1992 v R; (with Norwich C), 1993 v Cy, RCS (3)
Phillips, D. (Plymouth Arg), 1984 v N, Bul, Y (3)
Phillips, G. R. (Swansea C), 2001 v Uk (sub) (1)
Phillips, L. (Swansea C), 1979 v E; (with Charlton Ath), 1983 v N (2)
Pontin, K. (Cardiff C), 1978 v S (1)
Powell, L. (Southampton), 1991 v Pol (sub); 1992 v R (sub); 1993 v Bel (sub); 1994 v RCS (4)
Price, J. J. (Swansea C), 1998 v I (sub); 1999 v I (sub), D, Bl, P; 2000 v Bl, Sw (7)
Price, M. D. (Everton), 2001 v Uk. Pol (sub), Uk (3)
Price, P. (Luton T), 1981 v Ho (1)
Pugh, D. (Doncaster R), 1982 v F (2) (2)

Pugh, S. (Wrexham), 1993 v Bel (2 subs) (2)

Ramasut, M. W. T. (Bristol R), 1997 v Ho, Bel; 1998 v T, I (4)
Ratcliffe, K. (Everton), 1981 v Ho; 1982 v F (2)
Ready, K. (QPR), 1992 v R; 1993 v Bel (2); 1994 v RCS, Cy (5)
Rees, A. (Birmingham C), 1984 v N (1)
Rees, J. (Luton T), 1990 v Pol; 1991 v E, Pol (3)
Roberts, A. (QPR), 1991 v E, Pol (2)
Roberts, C. J. (Cardiff C), 1999 v D (sub) (1)
Roberts, G. (Hull C), 1983 v Bul (1)
Roberts, G. W. (Liverpool), 1997 v Ho, T, Bel; 1998 v T, I; 1999 v I, D, Bl, P; (with Panionios) D; (with Tranmere R), 2000 v Sw (11)
Roberts, J. G. (Wrexham), 1977 v E (1)
Roberts, N. W. (Wrexham), 1999 v I (sub), P; 2000 v Sw (sub) (3)
Roberts, P. (Porthmadog), 1997 v Ho (sub) (1)
Roberts, S. I. (Swansea C), 1999 v Sw, I (sub), D; 2000 v Bl (sub), Ni; 2001 v Bl (sub), N, Pol, Arm, Uk (10)
Roberts, S. W. (Wrexham), 2000 v S; 2001 v Bl, N (sub) (3)
Robinson, C. P. (Wolverhampton W), 1996 v Sm; 1997 v Sm, Ho (2), T, Bel (6)
Robinson, J. (Brighton & HA), 1992 v R; (with Charlton Ath), 1993 v Bel; 1994 v RCS, Cy, R (5)
Rowlands, A. J. R. (Manchester C), 1996 v Sm; 1997 v Sm, Ho (1 + sub), T (sub) (5)
Rush, I. (Liverpool), 1981 v Ho; 1982 v F (2)

Savage, R. W. (Crewe Alex), 1995 v Bul; 1996 v Mol, G (3)
Sayer, P. A. (Cardiff C), 1977 v E, S (2)
Searle, D. (Cardiff C), 1991 v Pol (sub); 1992 v R; 1993 v Cy, Bel (2), RCS; 1994 v RCS (6)
Slatter, D. (Chelsea), 2000 v Sw (sub), S; 2001 v Bl, N (sub), Pol (sub), Uk (sub) (6)
Slatter, N. (Bristol R), 1983 v N, Y, Bul; 1984 v N, Bul, Y (6)
Speed, G. A. (Leeds U), 1990 v Pol; 1991 v E, Pol (3)
Stevenson, N. (Swansea C), 1982 v F, Ho (2)
Stevenson, W. B. (Leeds U), 1977 v E, S; 1978 v S (3)
Symons, K. (Portsmouth), 1991 v E, Pol (2)

Taylor, G. K. (Bristol R), 1995 v Ge, Bul (2); 1996 v Mol (4)
Thomas, D. J. (Watford), 1998 v T, Bel (2)
Thomas, J. A. (Blackburn R), 1996 v Sm; 1997 v Sm, Ho (2), T, Bel; 1998 v Bel; 1999 v D, Bl, P; 2000 v Bl (sub); 2001 v Bl, N, Pol, Arm, Uk, Pol, Uk (18)
Thomas, Martin R. (Bristol R), 1979 v E; 1981 v Ho (2)
Thomas, Mickey R. (Wrexham), 1977 v E; 1978 v S (2)
Thomas, S. (Wrexham), 2001 v Pol, Uk (2)
Thomas, D. G. (Leeds U), 1977 v E; 1979 v E; 1984 v N (3)
Tibbott, L. (Ipswich T), 1977 v E, S (2)
Tipton, M. J. (Oldham Ath), 1998 v I (sub); 1999 v P, Sw (sub); 2000 v Ni; 2001 v Arm (sub), Uk (sub) (6)
Tolley, J. C. (Shrewsbury T), 2001 v Pol, Uk (sub) (2)
Twiddy, C. (Plymouth Arg), 1995 v Mol, Ge; 1996 v G (sub) (3)

Vaughan, N. (Newport Co), 1982 v F, Ho (2)
Valentine, R. D. (Everton), 2001 v Pol, Uk (2)

Walsh, D. (Wrexham), 2000 v S, Ni; 2001 v Bl, Arm, Uk (5)
Walsh, I. P. (C Palace), 1979 v E; (with Swansea C), 1983 v Bul (2)
Walton, M. (Norwich C.), 1991 v Pol (sub) (1)
Ward, D. (Notts Co), 1996 v Mol, G (2)
Weston, R. D. (Arsenal), 2001 v Bl, N, Pol; (with Cardiff C), Arm (4)
Williams, A. P. (Southampton), 1998 v Bel, I; 1999 v I, D (sub), Bl, Sw, I; 2000 v Bl, Sw (9)
Williams, A. S. (Blackburn R), 1996 v Sm; 1997 v Sm, Ho, Bel; 1998 v T, Bel, I; 1999 v I, D, Bl, P, Sw, I, D; 2000 v Bl, Sw (16)
Williams, D. (Bristol R), 1983 v Y (1)
Williams, D. I. L. (Liverpool), 1998 v I; 1999 v D, Bl; (with Wrexham) I, D; 2000 v Bl, S, Ni; 2001 v Bl (9)
Williams, E. (Caernarfon T), 1997 v Ho (sub), T (sub) (2)
Williams, G. (Bristol R), 1983 v Y, Bul (2)
Williams, M. (Manchester U), 2001 v Pol (sub), Uk (sub) (2)

Williams, S. J. (Wrexham), 1995 v Mol, Ge, Bul (2) (4)
Wilmot, R. (Arsenal), 1982 v F (2), Ho; 1983 v N, Y; 1984 v Y (6)
Wright, A. A. (Oxford U), 1998 v Bel, I (sub); 1999 v D (sub) (3)

Young, S. (Cardiff C), 1996 v Sm; 1997 v Sm, Ho (2), Bel (sub) (5)

NORTHERN IRELAND

Bailie, N. (Linfield), 1990 v Is; 1994 v R (sub) (2)
Beatty, S. (Chelsea), 1990 v Is; (with Linfield), 1994 v R (2)
Black, K. T. (Luton T), 1990 v Is (1)
Blackledge, G. (Portadown), 1978 v Ei (1)
Boyle, W. S. (Leeds U), 1998 v Sw (sub), S (sub); 2001 v CzR (sub), Bul (1+sub), CzR (6)
Brotherston, N. (Blackburn R), 1978 v Ei (sub) (1)
Burns, L. (Port Vale), 1998 v Sw, S, Ei; 1999 v T, Fi, Mol, G, Mol, Ei; 2000 v F, T, G, Fi (13)

Carlisle, W. T. (Crystal Palace), 2000 v Fi (sub); 2001 v Ma, Ic, Bul (1+sub), CzR (6)
Carroll, R. E. (Wigan Ath), 1998 v S, Ei; 1999 v T, Fi, Mol, G, Mol, Ei; 2000 v T, G, Fi (11)
Carson, S. (Rangers), 2000 v Ma (1)
Clarke, R. D. J. (Portadown), 1999 v Ei (sub), S; 2000 v F (sub), S, W (sub) (5)
Connell, T. E. (Coleraine), 1978 v Ei (sub) (1)
Coote, A. (Norwich C), 1998 v Sw (sub), S, Ei; 1999 v T, Fi, Mol, G, Mol, Ei; 2000 v F, T, G (12)
Convery, J. (Celtic), 2000 v S, W; 2001 v D, Ic (4)

Devine, D. (Omagh T), 1994 v R (1)
Devine, J. (Glentoran), 1990 v Is (1)
Dolan, J. (Millwall), 2000 v Fi, Ma, S; 2001 v Ma, D, Ic (6)
Donaghy, M. M. (Larne), 1978 v Ei (1)
Dowie, I. (Luton T), 1990 v Is (1)

Elliott, S. (Glentoran), 1999 v Fi (sub), Ei, S (sub) (3)

Feeney, L. (Linfield), 1998 v Ei (sub); 1999 v T, Fi, Mol; (with Rangers), G (sub), Ei, S; 2000 v Fi (8)
Ferguson, M. (Glentoran), 2000 v T (sub), Ma (sub) (2)
Fitzgerald, D. (Rangers), 1998 v Sw, S; 1999 v T (sub), Fi (4)
Friars, S. M. (Liverpool), 1998 v Sw, S, Ei; (with Ipswich T), 1999 v T, Fi, Mol, G, Mol; 2000 v F, T, G, Ma, S, W; 2001 v Ma, D, Ic, CzR, Bul (2), CzR (21)

Gillespie, K. R. (Manchester U), 1994 v R (1)
Glendinning, M. (Bangor), 1994 v R (1)
Graham, G. L. (Crystal Palace), 1999 v S; 2000 v F, T, G, Fi (5)
Graham, R. S. (QPR), 1999 v Fi (sub), Mol, Ei (sub); 2000 v F (sub), T (sub), G (sub), Fi (sub), Ma, S, W; 2001 v Ma, D, CzR (sub), Bul (sub), CzR (sub) (15)
Gray, P. (Luton T), 1990 v Is (sub) (1)
Griffin, D. J. (St Johnstone), 1998 v S (sub), Ei; 1999 v T, Fi, G, Mol, Ei, S; 2000 v F, T (10)

Hamilton, G. (Blackburn R), 2000 v Ma (sub), S, W (sub); 2001 v Ma, D, Ic, CzR, Bul (2), CzR (10)
Hamilton, W. R. (Linfield), 1978 v Ei (1)
Harkin, M. P. (Wycombe W), Ma (sub), S (sub), W; 2001 v Ma (sub), D (sub), Ic, CzR, Bul (sub+1) (9)
Harvey, J. (Arsenal), 1978 v Ei (1)
Hawe, S. (Blackburn R), 2001 v Cz (1+sub) (2)
Hayes, T. (Luton T), 1978 v Ei (1)
Healy, D. J. (Manchester U), 1999 v Mol (sub), G (sub), Ei (sub), S; 2000 v F (sub), T, G, Fi (8)
Holmes, S. (Manchester C), Ma, S, W; 2001 v Ma, D, Ic, CzR, Bul (2), CzR (10)
Hughes, M. E. (Manchester C), 1990 v Is (sub)

Ingham, M. (Sunderland), 2001 v CzR, Bul (2), CzR (4)

Johnson, D. M. (Blackburn R), 1998 v Sw, S, Ei; 1999 v T, Fi, G, Mol, Ei; 2000 v F, T, G (11)
Johnston, B. (Cliftonville), 1978 v Ei (1)

Kee, P. V. (Oxford U), 1990 v Is (1)
Kelly, D. (Derry C), 2000 v Ma, W; 2001 v Ma, Ic (sub), CzR, Bul (2), CzR (8)
Kelly, N. (Oldham Ath), 1990 v Is (sub) (1)
Kirk, A. (Hearts), 1999 v S; 2000 v Ma, S, W; 2001 v Ma, D, Ic (sub) (7)

Lennon, N. F. (Manchester C), 1990 v Is; (with Crewe Alex), 1994 v R (2)
Lyttle, G. (Celtic), 1998 v Sw, S; (with Peterborough U), 1999 v T (sub), Mol (2), S; 2000 v G, Fi (8)

Magee, J. (Bangor), 1994 v R (sub) (1)
Magilton, J. (Liverpool), 1990 v Is (1)
Matthews, N. P. (Blackpool), 1990 v Is (1)
McAreavey, P. (Swindon T), 2000 v Ma, S; 2001 v Ma, D (4)
McBride, J. (Glentoran), 1994 v R (sub) (1)
McCallion, E. (Coleraine), 1998 v Sw (sub) (1)
McCann, G. S. (West Ham U), 2000 v S (sub), W; 2001 v D (sub), Ic, CzR, Bul (2), CzR (8)
McCartney, G. (Sunderland), 2001 v D, CzR, Bul (2) (4)
McCoy, R. K. (Coleraine), 1990 v Is (1)
McCreery, D. (Manchester U), 1978 v Ei (1)
McGibbon, P. C. G. (Manchester U), 1994 v R (1)
McGlinchey, B. (Manchester C), 1998 v Sw, S, Ei; (with Port Vale), 1999 v T, Fi, Mol, G, Mol, Ei, S; (with Gillingham), 2000 v F, G, T, Fi (14)
McIlroy, T. (Linfield), 1994 v R (sub) (1)
McKnight, P. (Rangers), 1998 v Sw; 1999 v T (sub), Mol (sub) (3)
McFlynn, T. (QPR), 2000 v Ma (sub), W (sub); 2001 v Ma (sub), CzR (sub), Bul (sub+sub), CzR (7)
McMahon, G. J. (Tottenham H),1994 v R (sub) (1)
McVeigh, P. F. (Tottenham H), 1998 v S (sub), Ei; 1999 v T, Mol, G, Mol, Ei; 2000 v F, T (sub), G (sub), Fi (11)
Millar, W. P. (Port Vale), 1990 v Is (1)
Miskelly, D. T. (Oldham Ath), 2000 v F, Ma, S, W; 2001 v Ma, D, Ic (7)
Moreland, V. (Glentoran), 1978 v Ei (sub) (1)
Morgan, M, P. T. (Preston NE), 1999 v S (1)
Morrison, O. (Sheffield W), 2001 v Bul (sub) (1)
Morrow, A. (Northampton T), 2001 v D (sub) (1)
Mulryne, P. P. (Manchester U), Sw, S, Ei; (with Norwich C), 1999 v G, Mol (5)
Murray, W. (Linfield), 1978 v Ei (sub) (1)

Nicholl, J. M. (Manchester U), 1978 v Ei (1)
Nixon, C. (Glentoran), 2000 v Fi (sub) (1)

O'Hara, G. (Leeds U), 1994 v R (1)
O'Neill, M. A. M. (Hibernian), 1994 v R (1)
O'Neill, J. P. (Leicester C), 1978 v Ei (1)

Patterson, D. J. (Crystal Palace), 1994 v R (1)

Quinn, S. J. (Blackpool), 1994 v R (1)

Robinson, S. (Tottenham H), 1994 v R (1)

Simms, G. (Hartlepool U), 2001 v Bul (2), CzR (3)
Skates, G. (Blackburn R), 2000 v Ma; 2001 v Ic (sub), CzR (2) (4)
Sloan, T. (Ballymena U), 1978 v Ei (1)

Taylor, M. S. (Fulham), 1998 v Sw (1)
Toner, C. (Tottenham H), 2000 v Ma (sub), S (sub), W; 2001 v D, Ic, CzR, Bul (2), CzR (9)

Waterman, D. G. (Portsmouth), 1998 v Sw, S, Ei; 1999 v T, Fi, Mol, G, Mol, Ei, S (sub); 2000 v F, T, G, Fi (14)
Wells, D. P. (Barry T), 1999 v S (1)
Whitley, Jeff (Manchester C), 1998 v Sw, S, Ei; 1999 v T, Fi, Mol, G, Ei, S; 2000 v F, G, T, Ma, S, W; 2001 v Ma, Ic (17)

FA SCHOOLS & YOUTH GAMES 2000–2001

ENGLAND UNDER-18

1 Sept+

Israel 1 England 3 *(Clarke 13, Richardson 28, Davis 39)*
England: Evans (Chelsea); Richardson (Leeds U), Jenkins (Wimbledon), Jackson (Tottenham H), Clarke (Everton), Parnaby (Middlesbrough), Hamshaw (Sheffield W) [Noble (Arsenal)], McMaster (Leeds U), Fallon (Barnsley) [Richards (Blackburn R)], Davis (Manchester U) [Knight (Chelsea)], Defoe (West Ham U) [Ricketts (Arsenal)].

7 Oct**

Andorra 0 England 4 *(Hamshaw 2, Jackson 28, Defoe 37, Ricketts 54)*
England: Evans (Chelsea); Halls (Arsenal), Jenkins (Wimbledon), Jackson (Tottenham H), Clarke (Everton), Parnaby (Middlesbrough), Hamshaw (Sheffield W) [Pennant (Arsenal)], McMaster (Leeds U) [Ricketts (Arsenal)], Fallon (Barnsley), Davis (Manchester U), Defoe (West Ham U) [Knight (Chelsea)].

9 Oct**

Faeroes 0 England 5 *(Jackson 8, Richards 11, Hamshaw 27, og 46, Knight 58)*
England: Howarth (York C); Richardson (Leeds U), Ricketts (Arsenal), Jackson (Tottenham H), Clarke (Everton), Parnaby (Middlesbrough), Knight (Chelsea), Bryant (Bristol R) [Davis (Manchester U)], Richards (Blackburn R) [Fallon (Barnsley)], McMaster (Leeds U), Hamshaw (Sheffield W) [Pennant (Arsenal)].

11 Oct**

Italy 1 England 2 *(Hamshaw 89, Parnaby 90)*
England: Evans (Chelsea); Halls (Arsenal), Jenkins (Wimbledon), Jackson (Tottenham H), Clarke (Everton), Parnaby (Middlesbrough), Hamshaw (Sheffield W), Ricketts (Arsenal) [Knight (Chelsea)], Fallon (Barnsley) [Davis (Manchester U)], McMaster (Leeds U) [Pennant (Arsenal)], Defoe (West Ham U).

16 Nov+

England 3 *(Jackson 40, Nolan 67, Clarke 74)* **Belgium 2**
England: Howarth (York C); Halls (Arsenal), Jenkins (Wimbledon), Jackson (Tottenham H), Clarke (Everton), Parnaby (Middlesbrough) [Clark (Sunderland)], Pennant (Arsenal) [Bothroyd (Coventry C)], Nolan (Bolton W), Defoe (West Ham U) [Fallon (Barnsley)], Davis (Manchester U) [Ricketts (Arsenal)], Hamshaw (Sheffield W) [Knight (Chelsea)].

1 Mar+

England 1 *(Defoe 59)* **Holland 1**
England: Evans (Chelsea); Richardson (Leeds U), Stewart (Leicester C), Jackson (Tottenham H), Clarke (Everton), Pennant (Arsenal), Jenas (Nottingham F), Defoe (West Ham U), Ricketts (Arsenal), Knight (Chelsea) [Fallon (Barnsley)].

22 Mar**

England 0 Poland 1
England: Evans (Chelsea); Richardson (Leeds U), Stewart (Leicester C), Jackson (Tottenham H), Clarke (Everton), Lescott (Wolverhampton W), Pennant (Arsenal), Nolan (Bolton W) [Jenas (Nottingham F)], Richards (Blackburn R), Ricketts (Arsenal) [Knight (Chelsea)], Hamshaw (Sheffield W) [Bothroyd (Coventry C)].

26 Apr**

Poland 0 England 0
England: Evans (Chelsea); Richardson (Leeds U)], Jackson (Tottenham H), Clarke (Everton), Parnaby (Middlesbrough), Pennant (Arsenal) [Knight (Chelsea)], Jenas (Nottingham F), Defoe (West Ham U), Keenan (Chelsea), Bothroyd (Coventry C) [Richards (Blackburn R)].

30 May+

Switzerland 1 England 0
England: Howath (Myhill); Richardson, Stewart, Henry, Clarke (Reid), Parnaby, Knight, Ricketts (Kay), Richards (Jagielka), Keenan, Logan (Britton).

ENGLAND UNDER-17

5 Sept*

Czech Republic 2 England 2 *(Howard 5, 15)*
England: Allaway (Leeds U); Clark (Sunderland), Otsemobor (Liverpool), Thomas (Arsenal), Cooke (Aston Villa) [Johnson (Leeds U)], Moore (Aston Villa) [Mooniaruck (Manchester U)], Chopra (Newcastle U), Howard (Southampton), Sherman (Leeds U) [Austin (Barnsley), Fox (Manchester U), Willetts (Aston Villa) [Duncan (QPR)].

6 Sept*

Sweden 0 England 0
England: Lonergan (Preston NE); Austin (Barnsley), Bowditch (Tottenham H) [Fox (Manchester U)], Clark (Sunderland), Cooke (Aston Villa), Chopra (Newcastle U), Howard (Southampton), Sherman (Leeds U) [Thomas (Arsenal)], Willetts (Aston Villa) [Otsemobor (Liverpool)], Mooniaruck (Manchester U), Johnson (Leeds U).

8 Sept*

Poland 2 England 1 *(Howard 79)*
England: Allaway (Leeds U); Duncan (QPR), Austin (Barnsley), Bowditch (Tottenham H) [Clark (Sunderland)], Otsemobor (Liverpool), Howard (Southampton), Fox (Manchester U), Willetts (Aston Villa) [Chopra (Newcastle U)], Mooniaruck (Manchester U) [Cooke (Aston Villa)], Johnson (Leeds U), O'Hanlon (Everton).

6 Dec+

England 1 *(Chopra 77)* **France 0**
England: Grant (Derby Co) [Allaway (Leeds U)]; Bowditch (Tottenham H), Clark (Sunderland), Otsemobor (Liverpool), Hylton (Aston Villa) [Willetts (Aston Villa)], Brown (Bristol C) [Martin (Charlton)], Cooke (Aston Villa) [Fox (Manchester U)], Jenas (Nottingham F) [O'Hanlon (Everton)], Pennant (Arsenal) [Mooniaruck (Manchester U)], Moore (Aston Villa), Chopra (Newcastle U).

1 Mar+

England 1 *(Cooke 53)* **Holland 1**
England: Lonergan (Preston NE) [Myhill (Aston Villa)]; Austin (Barnsley), Garry (Arsenal) [Willetts (Aston Villa)], Clark (Sunderland) [Fox (Manchester U)], Otsemobor (Liverpool), O'Hanlon (Everton) [Dawson (Nottingham F)], Muirhead (Manchester U) [Offiong (Newcastle U)], Cooke (Aston Villa) [Robson (Newcastle U)], Chopra (Newcastle U), Mooniaruck (Manchester U) [Dove (Middlesbrough)], Howard (Southampton) [Prince (Liverpool)].

14 June +

Italy 4 England 1 *(Ashton)*
England: Grant (Derby Co); Austin (Barnsley), Willets (Aston Villa) [Duncan (QPR)], Mooniaruck (Manchester U [O'Neil (Portsmouth)], Rehman (Fulham) [O'Hannlon (Everton), Clark (Sunderland), Moore (Aston Villa) [Howard (Southampton)], Cooke (Aston Villa), Ashton (Crewe Alex [Townson (Rochdale)], Chopra (Newcastle U), Morgan (Wimbledon) [Bloomfield (Ipswich T)].

ENGLAND UNDER-16

11 July~

England 3 *(Westcarr 49, Donnelly 61, Schumacher 72)* **Thailand 0**
England: Camp (Derby Co); Welsh (Liverpool), Moogan (Everton) [McKie (Tottenham H)], Schumacher (Everton), Johnson (West Ham U), Taylor (Manchester U), Lambu (Millwall), Beck (Everton) [Cade (Middlesbrough)], Bell (Blackburn R), Donnelly (Blackburn R), Poole (Manchester U) [Westcarr (Nottingham F)].

16 July~

England 1 *(Donnelly 69)* **Brazil 2**
England: Pidgeley (Chelsea); Welsh (Liverpool), McKie (Tottenham H) [Bell (Blackburn R)], Schumacher (Everton), Johnson (West Ham U), Taylor (Manchester U), Westcarr (Nottingham F), Beck (Everton), Samba (Millwall), Donnelly (Blackburn R), Lambu (Millwall).

31 July+*

Finland 1   England 2 *(Peers 35, Harding 54)*
England: Stevenson (Blackburn R); Donnelly (Blackburn R), McKie (Tottenham H), Johnson (West Ham U), Hand (Watford) [Bent (Ipswich T)], Cade (Middlesbrough) [Haskins (Nottingham F)], Bell (Blackburn R) [Hopton (Watford)], Kamara (Arsenal), Lawrence (Manchester U), Danks (Wolverhampton W), Peers (Liverpool) [Harding (Wimbledon)].

1 Aug+*

Denmark 0   England 0
(England won 3-2 on penalties)
England: Pidgeley (Chelsea); Donnelly (Blackburn R), McKie (Tottenham H), Johnson (West Ham U), Kilgallon (Leeds U), Bell (Blackburn R), Bent (Ipswich T), Harding (Wimbledon), Kamara (Arsenal) [Hand (Watford)], Lawrence (Manchester U), Danks (Wolverhampton W) [Haskins (Nottingham F)].

3 Aug+*

Faeroes 0   England 3 *(Bent 52, Donnelly 62, Bell 78)*
England: Pidgeley (Chelsea); McKie (Tottenham H) [Peers (Liverpool)], Fowler (Arsenal), Johnson (West Ham U), Kilgallon (Leeds U), Bell (Blackburn R), Harding (Wimbledon) [Lawrence (Manchester U)], Hopton (Watford) [Donnelly (Blackburn R)], Kamara (Arsenal), Danks (Wolverhampton W) [Bent (Ipswich T)], Haskins (Nottingham F).

4 Aug+*

Sweden 3   England 0
England: Stevenson (Blackburn R); Donnelly (Blackburn R), Fowler (Arsenal) [Danks (Wolverhampton W)], Johnson (West Ham U), Kilgallon (Leeds U), Hand (Watford), Bell (Blackburn R) [Hopton (Watford)], Bent (Ipswich T), Lawrence (Manchester U), Peers (Liverpool), Haskins (Nottingham F) [Cade (Middlesbrough)].

22 Sept+

England 3 *(Bent 24, 60, Peers 70)* **Republic of Ireland 1**
England: Pidgeley (Chelsea); Arndale (Bristol R), McKie (Tottenham H) [Moogan (Everton)], Schumacher (Everton) [Beck (Everton)], Johnson (West Ham U), Taylor (Manchester U) [Murphy (Middlesbrough)], Westcarr (Nottingham F) [Lambu (Millwall)], Welsh (Liverpool), Bent (Ipswich T) [Samba (Millwall)], Donnelly (Blackburn R) [Fowler (Arsenal)], Peers (Liverpool).

16 Nov+

England 6 *(Poole 27, 31, 36, Bentley 57, Hoyte 66, Watt 69)*
Wales 0
England: Camp (Derby Co) [Holloway (Arsenal)]; Hoyte (Arsenal), Lawrence (Manchester U) [Fowler (Arsenal)], Watt (Blackburn R) [Buari (Fulham)], Foster (Tottenham H) [Kitamirike (Chelsea)], Murphy (Middlesbrough) [Kamara (Arsenal)], Buari (Fulham) [Lambu (Millwall)], Cade (Middlesbrough), Poole (Manchester U) [Bell (Blackburn R)], Bentley (Arsenal), Bailey (Preston NE) [Massie (Liverpool)].

6 Dec+

England 0   France 2
England: Camp (Derby Co); Hoyte (Arsenal) [Kitamirike (Chelsea)], McKie (Tottenham H), Schumacher (Everton), Johnson (West Ham U), Taylor (Manchester U) [Beck (Everton)], Lambu (Millwall) [Peers (Liverpool)], Welsh (Liverpool), Samba (Millwall), Donnelly (Blackburn R) [Watt (Blackburn R)].

6 Jan@

Uruguay 1   England 0
England: Camp (Derby Co); Hoyte (Arsenal), McKie (Tottenham H), Schumacher (Everton) [Watt (Blackburn R)], Johnson (West Ham U), Taylor (Manchester U) [Cade (Middlesbrough)], Peers (Liverpool), Bentley (Arsenal) [Westcarr (Nottingham F)], Bent (Ipswich T), Donnelly (Blackburn R), Bailey (Preston NE) [Samba (Millwall)].

8 Jan@

France 2   England 0
England: Pidgeley (Chelsea); Hoyte (Arsenal) [Bentley (Arsenal)], McKie (Tottenham H) [Bailey (Preston NE)], Schumacher (Everton), Johnson (West Ham U), Taylor (Manchester U), Donnelly (Blackburn R), Cade (Middlesbrough), Westcarr (Nottingham F), Watt (Blackburn R) [Peers (Liverpool)].

10 Jan@

England 1 *(Bailey 7)*   **Mexico 3**
England: Camp (Derby Co); Hoyte (Arsenal), Schumacher (Everton) [Johnson (West Ham U)], Taylor (Manchester U), Peers (Liverpool), Bentley (Arsenal), Bent (Ipswich T), Bailey (Preston NE) [McKie (Tottenham H)], Cade (Middlesbrough), Westcarr (Nottingham F) [Samba (Millwall)], Watt (Blackburn R) [Donnelly (Blackburn R)].

12 Jan@

England 0   Korea 4
England: Pidgeley (Chelsea); McKie (Tottenham H), Johnson (West Ham U), Bentley (Arsenal), Bent (Ipswich T) [Samba (Millwall)], Donnelly (Blackburn R), Bailey (Preston NE) [Peers (Liverpool)], Bowditch (Tottenham H) [Schumacher (Everton)], Westcarr (Nottingham F), Murphy (Middlesbrough) [Hoyte (Arsenal)], Watt (Blackburn R) [Cade (Middlesbrough)].

14 Jan@

Brazil 5   England 0
England: Camp (Derby Co); Hoyte (Arsenal), McKie (Tottenham H) [Taylor (Manchester U)], Schumacher (Everton), Johnson (West Ham U), Peers (Liverpool), Donnelly (Blackburn R) [Bentley (Arsenal)], Bowditch (Tottenham H) [Murphy (Middlesbrough)], Cade (Middlesbrough), Westcarr (Nottingham F) [Watt (Blackburn R)] [Bailey (Preston NE)], Samba (Millwall).

24 Feb<

Spain 2   England 1 *(Downing 10)*
England: Camp (Derby Co); Arndale (Bristol R), McKie (Tottenham H) [Mills (Derby Co)], Schumacher (Everton), Hoyte (Arsenal), Bowditch (Tottenham H), Cade (Middlesbrough) [Watt (Blackburn R)], Beck (Everton) [Bent (Ipswich T)], Samba (Millwall) [Poole (Manchester U)], Donnelly (Blackburn R), Downing (Middlesbrough).

25 Feb<

Portugal 0   England 0
England: Camp (Derby Co); Arndale (Bristol R), Schumacher (Everton), Hoyte (Arsenal), Bowditch (Tottenham H), Cade (Middlesbrough), Samba (Millwall), Donnelly (Blackburn R) [Bent (Ipswich T)], Kitamirike (Chelsea), Poole (Manchester U), Watt (Blackburn R) [Beck (Everton)].

27 Feb<

Finland 0   England 2 *(Samba 22, 26)*
England: Pidgeley (Chelsea); Schumacher (Everton), Hoyte (Arsenal), Bowditch (Tottenham H), Beck (Everton), Samba (Millwall) [Poole (Manchester U)], Downing (Middlesbrough) [Cade (Middlesbrough)] [Bent (Ipswich T)], Kitamirike (Chelsea), Ambrose (Ipswich T), Mills (Derby Co), Watt (Blackburn R).

30 Mar+

Hungary 1   England 3 *(Peers 29, 55, Taylor 76)*
England: Pidgeley (Chelsea) [Stevenson (Blackburn R)]; Hoyte (Arsenal) [Arndale (Bristol R)], Murphy (Middlesbrough) [Carr (Newcastle U)], Bowditch (Tottenham H) [Ambrose (Ipswich T)], Mills (Derby Co), Taylor (Manchester U), Westcarr (Nottingham F) [Watt (Blackburn R)], Welsh (Liverpool), Johnson (Manchester U), Beck (Everton) [Samba (Millwall)], Peers (Liverpool) [Cade (Middlesbrough)].

22 Apr#

England 1 *(Welsh 21)*   **Italy 3**
England: Camp (Derby Co); Hoyte (Arsenal), Schumacher (Everton), Johnson (West Ham U), Bowditch (Tottenham H), Westcarr (Nottingham F) [Johnson (Manchester U)], Welsh (Liverpool), Samba (Millwall), Donnelly (Blackburn R), Peers (Liverpool) [Caig (Middlesbrough)], Murphy (Middlesbrough) [Taylor (Manchester U)].

24 Apr#

England 2 *(Schumacher 56, Johnson E 80)*   **Switzerland 0**
England: Pidgeley (Chelsea); Hoyte (Arsenal) [Arndale (Bristol R)]. Taylor (Manchester U). Schumacher (Everton). Johnson G (West Ham U). Bowditch (Tottenham H). Welsh (Liverpool), Samba (Millwall), Cade (Middlesbrough)   [Donnelly   (Blackburn   R)]. Beck (Everton) [Watt (Blackburn R)], Johnson E (Manchester U).

26 Apr#

England 1 *(Johnson G 22)*   **Hungary 0**
England: Pidgeley (Chelsea); Hoyte (Arsenal), Taylor (Manchester U), Schumacher (Everton), Johnson G (West Ham U), Bowditch (Tottenham H), Welsh (Liverpool), Samba (Millwall), Watt (Blackburn R) [Cade (Middlesbrough)], Beck (Everton), Johnson E (Manchester U) [Westcarr (Nottingham F)] [Arndale (Bristol R)].

29 Apr#

England 1 *(Samba 67)*   **Germany 1**
(England won 5-4 on penalties)
England: Pidgeley (Chelsea); Hoyte (Arsenal), Taylor (Manchester U) [Peers (Liverpool)], Schumacher (Everton), Johnson G (West Ham U), Bowditch (Tottenham H), Westcarr (Nottingham F), Welsh (Liverpool), Samba (Millwall), Donnelly (Blackburn R), Arndale (Bristol R).

3 May#

England 0   France 4
England: Pidgeley (Chelsea); Hoyte (Arsenal), Taylor (Manchester U) [Beck (Everton)], Schumacher (Everton), Johnson G (West Ham U), Bowditch (Tottenham H) [Murphy (Middlesbrough)], Westcarr (Nottingham F), Welsh (Liverpool), Samba (Millwall), Donnelly (Blackburn R), Arndale (Bristol R) [Watt (Blackburn R)].

6 May#

Croatia 4   England 1 *(Johnson G 53)*
England: Pidgeley (Chelsea); Hoyte (Arsenal), Schumacher (Everton), Johnson G (West Ham U), Bowditch (Tottenham H) [Taylor (Manchester U)], Westcarr (Nottingham F), Samba (Millwall), Arndale (Bristol R), Cade (Middlesbrough), Murphy (Middlesbrough) [Peers (Liverpool)], Beck (Everton) [Watt (Blackburn R)].

ENGLAND UNDER-15

20 Oct##

Northern Ireland 1   England 0
England: Eyre (Tottenham H); Vaughan (Liverpool), Chick (Norwich C), Mannix (Liverpool) [Small (Arsenal)], Hogg (York C), Bridges (Aston Villa), Frempong (Fulham) [Malcolm (Tottenham H)], Brown (Everton) [Taylor (Swindon T)], Oldham (Barnsley), Long (Charlton Ath) [Gardner (Newcastle U)], Doherty (Everton).

3 Nov##

Wales 1   England 1 *(Guy 78)*
England: Turnbull (Middlesbrough); Biggins (Nottingham F), Tillen (Chelsea) [Sadler (Birmingham C)], Groves (Nottingham F), Raven (Liverpool), Hammond (Cambridge U) [Sankofa (Charlton Ath)], Price (Tottenham H) [Rooney (Everton)], Jeffreys (Chelsea), Guy (Newcastle U), Gobern (Wolverhampton W) [McDermott (Newcastle U)], Smyth (Liverpool).

1 Dec##

England 5 *(Rooney 25, Croft 40, Proffitt 43, Doherty 70, 76)*
Scotland 0
England: Yeomans (Manchester U); Bridges (Aston Villa), Sadler (Birmingham C), Howell (Reading), Raven (Liverpool), Cartwright (Manchester C) [Hogg (York C)], Rooney (Everton) [Mannix (Liverpool)], Croft (Manchester C), Oldham (Barnsley) [Proffitt (Manchester C)], Gardner (Newcastle U) [Pratley (Arsenal)], Doherty (Everton).

9 Feb++

England 1 *(Doherty 40)*   **Spain 1**
England: Turnbull (Middlesbrough); Biggins (Nottingham F), Sadler (Birmingham C), Groves (Nottingham F), Raven (Liverpool), Hogg (York C), Rooney (Everton) [Malcolm (Tottenham H)], Croft (Manchester C) [Sankofa (Charlton Ath)], Proffitt (Manchester C) [Guy (Newcastle U)], Gardner (Newcastle U) [McDermott (Newcastle U)], Doherty (Everton) [Oldham (Barnsley)].

22 Feb++

England 0   Holland 0
England: Eyre (Tottenham H) [Yeomans (Manchester U)]; Bridges (Aston Villa) [Vaughan (Liverpool)], Sadler (Birmingham C), Mannix (Liverpool), Hogg (York C), Sankofa (Charlton Ath), Oldham (Barnsley), Croft (Manchester C) [Price (Tottenham H)], Guy (Newcastle U) [Proffitt (Manchester C)], Brown (Everton) [Gardner (Newcastle U)], Doherty (Everton).

24 Feb++

England 1 *(Doherty 51)*   **Germany 2**
England: Turnbull (Middlesbrough); Vaughan (Liverpool), Sadler (Birmingham C), Howell (Reading) [Mannix (Liverpool)], Hogg (York C), Cartwright (Manchester C) [Sankofa (Charlton Ath)], Oldham (Barnsley) [Price (Tottenham H)], Croft (Manchester C), Proffitt (Manchester C), Gardner (Newcastle U) [Brown (Everton)], Doherty (Everton) [Forte (Sheffield U)].

11 Apr=

Czech Republic 1   England 3 *(Proffitt 5, 78, Croft 70)*
England: Turnbull (Middlesbrough); Sadler (Birmingham C), Hogg (York C), Oldham (Barnsley) [Malcolm (Tottenham H)], Croft (Manchester C) [Tolley (Peterborough U)], Proffitt (Manchester C) [Bridges (Aston Villa)], Gardner (Newcastle U) [Groves (Nottingham F)], Doherty (Everton), Biggins (Nottingham F), Small (Arsenal), McDermott (Newcastle U) [Long (Charlton Ath)].

12 Apr=

Peru 0   England 1 *(Malcolm 4)*
England: Drench (Blackburn R); Bridges (Aston Villa), Sadler (Birmingham C), Hogg (York C), Raven (Liverpool), Croft (Manchester C) [Oldham (Barnsley)], Gardner (Newcastle U), McDermott (Newcastle U) [Biggins (Nottingham F)], Malcolm (Tottenham H) [Proffitt (Manchester C)], Long (Charlton Ath), Tolley (Peterborough U) [Doherty (Everton)].

14 Apr=

Morocco 0   England 2 *(Oldham 72, Malcolm 73)*
England: Drench (Blackburn R); Bridges (Aston Villa), Raven (Liverpool), Hogg (York C) [Sadler (Birmingham C)] [McDermott (Newcastle U)], Oldham (Barnsley) [Proffitt (Manchester C)], Doherty (Everton), Biggins (Nottingham F), Small (Arsenal), Malcolm (Tottenham H), Long (Charlton Ath), Tolley (Peterborough U) [Gardner (Newcastle U)].

16 Apr=

France 1   England 0
England: Turnbull (Middlesbrough); Bridges (Aston Villa) [Biggins (Nottingham F)], Sadler (Birmingham C), Raven (Liverpool), Hogg (York C), Proffitt (Manchester C), Gardner (Newcastle U) [Small (Arsenal)], Doherty (Everton), McDermott (Newcastle U) [Groves (Nottingham F)], Malcolm (Tottenham H), Long (Charlton Ath) [Oldham (Barnsley)].

3 May+

England 3 *(Rooney 12, Guy 26, Brown 69)*   **Canada 0**
England: Eyre (Tottenham H) [Cronin (Crystal Palace)], Harbon (Barnsley [Borrowdale (Crystal Palace)], Tillen (Chelsea), Howell (Reading), Nowacki (Fulham), Cartwright (Manchester C), Rooney (Everton), Brown (Everton), Guy (Newcastle U) [Moore L (Aston Villa)], Taylor (Swindon T) [Pratley (Arsenal)], Forte (Sheffield U) [Cole M (West Ham U)].

** Under-17 Tournament; + Friendly; ** UEFA Under-18; #
UEFA Under-16; ## Adidas Victory Shield; = Montaigu
Tournament; ~ Nationwide Under-16 Tournament; +*
Nordic Tournament; @ Mundialito Tournament; < Algarve
Tournament; ++ Walkers Under-15 Tournament.*

WOMEN'S FOOTBALL 2000–2001

Although professional football came to English Women's soccer for the first time last season, in the shape of Fulham LFC, it was still Arsenal who commanded the Ladies' scene. The two sides met in the Women's FA Cup (also sponsored by AXA) with the Gunners defeating the team that Mohammed Al Fayed funded (to the reported tune of five million pounds) by 1-0 thanks to a strike by Angela Banks, the match played at Selhurst Park produced the best post (last war) crowd of 13,824. With the score 0-0, Emma Byrne saved a penalty from Margunn Haugenes who won silver medals for Norway in Women's World Cup and European Championships and whose husband helps to coach her team.

Arsenal completed what would have been an unprecedented "treble" but for the fact they are the only team to have already done so back in the 1992/93 season. Their Premier League Cup success was at the expense of Tranmere Rovers whom they easily beat 3-0. The Premier League National Championship was the result of a long and rain protracted season, achieving 52 points from 18 games; 7 more than runners up Doncaster Belles, their greatest rivals. The Gunners scored 88 and conceded a mere 9, creating an amazing goal difference of plus seventy-nine. Liverpool finished bottom without a point having lost all their 18 games; with a goal difference of minus seventy-six. They are relegated along with Millwall Lionesses. The Northern Division of the League was won by Leeds United, who are promoted. In the Southern Division Brighton and Hove Albion, who are also promoted, were narrow winners of the League by one point from Chelsea. In the Women's Premier League Reserve section Midlands/North, Everton were the winners and Southampton Saints won the incompleted South Division.

Hope Powell, the Women's and Girl's National Team Coach produced a fine achievement in taking her Ladies to the European Championships in June/July 2001 which were held in Germany. Unfortunately, England, who played all their matches in Jena, were eliminated in the opening group phase with only one point gained, that in their first match, when drawing 1-1 with Russia. Defeats thereafter by a strong Sweden team by 4-0 and an even stronger Germany (who prior to the tournament had won three out the last four Finals) by 3-0 meant an early return for the English girls.

Nonetheless the spread of the Women's game is enormous having created some fascinating side issues such as the re-launch of a monthly women's football magazine entitled "She Kicks". Moreover the London Football Coaches Association has also started bringing in top class Coaches for their monthly sessions at Highbury, to demonstrate coaching methods utilising the Arsenal Ladies Under 15 side.

There are now three sections dealing with Women's Football at the FA's Headquarters at Soho Square, being the domestic, the international and the competitions sections, which show every likelihood of expanding further as the game remains the fastest growing sport in the Country.

KEN GOLDMAN

The F.A. Women's Football Awards were won by the following

AXA PLAYER'S PLAYER OF THE YEAR
National Division   Jayne Ludlow   Arsenal
Northern Division   Stacey Daniel   Leeds U
Southern Division   Kristy Moore   Barnet

NATIONWIDE INTERNATIONAL PLAYER OF THE YEAR
Sue Smith – Tranmere R

AXA SPECIAL ACHIVEMENT AWARD
Maureen Marley – Everton, England

WALKERS YOUNG PLAYER OF THE YEAR
Katie Chapman – Fulham, England

AXA MANAGER OF THE YEAR
Vic Akers – Arsenal

UMBRO TOP GOALSCORERS
National Division   Angela Banks   Arsenal
Northern Division   Kelly Dean   Oldham Curzon
Southern Division   Kristy Moore   Barnet

SHE KICKS MEDIA AWARD
Gravesend Messenger

RESULTS 2000-2001
National Division

	Arsenal	Barry Town	Charlton Athletic	Doncaster Belles	Everton	Liverpool	Millwall Lionesses	Southampton Saints	Sunderland	Tranmere Rovers
Arsenal	—	2-1	5-0	2-1	2-1	11-0	10-0	7-1	6-0	5-0
Barry Town	1-3	—	0-4	1-3	1-5	2-1	2-1	2-0	1-0	1-4
Charlton Athletic	1-1	1-1	—	2-0	1-0	6-1	5-0	0-0	6-0	2-1
Doncaster Belles	0-1	5-0	1-0	—	4-1	3-1	8-0	3-1	4-0	6-1
Everton	1-2	4-1	1-0	1-5	—	5-0	2-0	3-0	5-2	3-1
Liverpool	0-10	2-3	0-7	0-5	1-2	—	0-1	2-4	1-4	2-4
Millwall Lionesses	0-5	0-1	0-4	1-2	2-2	7-1	—	1-2	0-3	2-1
Southampton Saints	1-9	1-1	0-0	0-2	1-1	6-1	1-1	—	2-5	3-6
Sunderland	1-3	0-2	0-4	0-4	1-3	4-0	3-0	2-2	—	4-5
Tranmere Rovers	0-4	3-1	0-0	0-2	0-2	5-0	3-1	6-1	2-0	—

National Division	P	W	D	L	F	A	GD	Pts
Arsenal LFC	18	17	1	0	88	9	+79	52
Doncaster Belles LFC	18	15	0	3	58	13	+45	45
Charlton Athletic WFC	18	10	5	3	43	11	+32	35
Everton LFC	18	11	2	5	42	24	+18	35
Tranmere Rovers LFC	18	9	1	8	42	39	+3	28
Barry Town LFC	18	7	2	9	22	39	−17	23
Sunderland AFC Women	18	5	1	12	29	50	−21	16
Southampton Saints LFC	18	3	6	9	27	52	−25	15
Millwall Lionesses LFC	18	3	2	13	17	55	−38	11
Liverpool LFC	18	0	0	18	13	89	−76	0

RESULTS 2000-2001

Northern Division

	Aston Villa	Bangor City	Birmingham City	Coventry City	Garswood Saints	Huddersfield Town	Ilkeston Town	Leeds United	Newcastle Town	Oldham Curzon	Sheffield Weds	Wolverhampton
Aston Villa	—	1-3	2-2	1-1	4-0	4-1	3-2	0-3	1-1	3-2	1-1	8-1
Bangor City	0-0	—	4-2	3-2	2-0	1-0	3-3	0-2	7-0	0-0	4-0	2-0
Birmingham City	6-1	2-2	—	1-1	3-4	1-0	0-3	0-1	5-3	0-1	2-0	1-0
Coventry City	1-4	1-2	1-1	—	3-4	1-0	0-2	0-4	2-1	0-3	0-0	3-2
Garswood Saints	5-2	2-2	1-4	3-2	—	1-0	2-1	2-3	4-3	0-1	4-1	1-4
Huddersfield Town	0-4	0-2	0-3	2-1	2-1	—	0-1	0-3	2-1	1-4	2-3	0-5
Ilkeston Town	1-2	1-1	3-3	4-0	3-1	3-1	—	1-2	2-1	2-2	0-0	1-4
Leeds United	1-2	2-2	7-1	3-0	6-1	2-1	4-0	—	6-1	5-2	7-0	1-1
Newcastle Town	0-1	3-1	1-10	1-1	5-2	0-0	1-0	1-4	—	3-1	1-2	0-3
Oldham Curzon	4-2	2-1	2-0	4-0	1-0	2-0	6-2	2-1	4-0	—	5-0	6-4
Sheffield Weds	1-3	2-1	1-2	0-2	6-2	5-1	1-3	1-3	2-1	1-5	—	2-1
Wolverhampton	1-3	2-0	4-1	3-1	2-1	3-2	2-1	0-5	2-0	0-2	3-1	—

Northern Division	P	W	D	L	F	A	GD	Pts
Leeds United	22	18	2	2	75	18	+57	56
Oldham Curzon LFC	22	17	2	3	61	25	+36	53
Aston Villa LFC	22	12	5	5	52	37	+15	41
Bangor City LFC	22	10	7	5	43	27	+16	37
Wolverhampton Wanderers	22	12	1	9	47	42	+5	37
Birmingham City LFC	22	9	5	8	50	42	+8	32
Ilkeston Town LFC	22	8	5	9	39	39	0	29
Garswood Saints WFC	22	8	1	13	41	60	−19	25
Sheffield Wednesday LFC	22	7	3	12	30	53	−23	24
Coventry City LFC	22	4	5	13	23	48	−25	17
Newcastle Town LFC	22	4	3	15	28	62	−34	15
Huddersfield Town LFC	22	3	1	18	15	51	−36	10

RESULTS 2000-2001

Southern Division

	Barking	Barnet	Berkhamsted Town	Brighton & Hove A	Cardiff City	Chelsea	Ipswich Town	Langford	Newport County	Reading Royals	Wembley Mill Hill	Wimbledon
Barking	—	6-3	3-1	0-2	2-1	2-4	5-1	2-3	3-2	12-0	1-2	1-3
Barnet	7-2	—	2-2	0-1	3-2	4-2	6-1	1-1	1-1	3-1	4-1	2-1
Berkhamsted Town	2-1	0-4	—	1-4	4-3	1-2	4-3	0-2	0-1	5-1	6-3	2-4
Brighton & Hove A	5-1	1-0	1-0	—	2-1	0-0	2-2	2-0	2-0	3-0	4-0	2-1
Cardiff City	2-4	1-7	0-1	1-3	—	1-3	1-6	3-0	2-1	4-2	4-1	1-2
Chelsea	3-0	2-1	2-1	1-0	5-0	—	2-2	1-0	4-2	2-0	3-3	3-1
Ipswich Town	4-0	1-7	2-3	2-5	3-0	1-6	—	2-2	1-3	4-1	3-0	0-3
Langford	1-0	1-0	2-0	1-5	5-1	1-4	0-1	—	1-1	5-2	5-0	1-2
Newport County	2-1	1-2	1-3	1-3	2-0	1-2	0-3	1-3	—	3-2	3-0	1-4
Reading Royals	1-3	1-4	3-1	0-4	1-2	1-9	3-0	0-7	2-4	—	2-2	2-2
Wembley Mill Hill	3-2	0-3	5-3	1-4	3-1	0-4	0-3	0-3	2-0	7-0	—	2-3
Wimbledon	2-1	4-2	2-0	2-1	0-1	2-2	4-2	2-3	3-2	6-0	3-0	—

Southern Division	P	W	D	L	F	A	GD	Pts
Brighton & Hove Albion	22	18	2	2	56	15	+41	56
Chelsea LFC	22	17	4	1	66	24	+42	55
Wimbledon LFC	22	15	2	5	56	31	+25	47
Barnet LFC	22	13	3	6	66	33	+33	42
Langford LFC	22	12	3	7	47	30	+17	39
Ipswich Town LFC	22	8	3	11	47	57	−10	27
Berkhamsted Town LFC	22	8	1	13	40	51	−11	25
Barking LFC	22	8	0	14	52	54	−2	24
Newport County LFC	22	7	2	13	33	44	−11	23
Wembley Mill Hill LFC	22	6	2	14	35	64	−29	20
Cardiff City LFC	22	6	0	16	32	60	−28	18
Reading Royals LFC	22	2	2	18	25	92	−67	8

AXA FA WOMEN'S CUP 2000–2001

EXTRA PRELIMINARY ROUND

Chorley v Barnsley	0-3
Morley Spurs v Billingham	3-3
Billingham won 4-1 on penalties.	
Hull City v Killingworth YPC	2-4
Stockport County v Newton Aycliffe	13-1
Real Maghull v Chester City	0-12
Trafford v Bury Girls & Ladies	5-3
Ambassadors in Sport v Preston North End	1-2
Newsham PH v Bolton Wanderers (Supp)	4-3
Penrith Sapphires v Corwen	5-0
Deans v Windscale	0-4
Carlisle Wanderers v Stockport Celtic	0-1
AFC Preston Ladies v Scunthorpe United	1-6

Witton Albion v Greyhound Gunners	9-0
Warrington Grange v Wigan	6-4
Thorpe United v Broughton Aerospace	5-2

Broughton Aerospace awarded tie; Thorpe United fielded 2 ineligible players.

Lichfield Diamonds v ES Barwell	11-0
Willenhall Town v Steel City Wanderers	1-4
Belper Town v Worksop Town	6-0
Crewe Alexandra v Kettering Amazons	2-6
Great Wyrley v Nettleham	4-4

Great Wyrley won 3-2 on penalties.

Tamworth v Kidderminster Harriers	2-3
Gresley Rovers v Atherstone United	4-4

Atherstone United won 4-3 on penalties.

Lincoln City v North Staffs	6-0
Chaffoteaux v Billesley United	2-0
Loughborough Dynamo v Leicester City	0-8
Loughborough Students v Wem Town Raiders	6-1

Wem Town Raiders awarded tie; Loughborough Students fielded 12 ineligible players.

Tipton Town v Grantham Town	1-2
West Ham United v Tring	7-0
Wycombe Wanderers v Malling	1-3
Kings Lynn v Romford	4-0
Leighton Linslade v Slough	0-3
Haywards Heath v Abbey Rangers	3-2
Luton v Chesham United	0-6
Aldershot Town v Northampton Town & County	0-2
Tottenham Hotspur v Colney Heath	5-1
Royston Town v Redbridge Raiders	0-6
Newport Pagnell Town v Woodham Radars	4-1
Wisbech Town v Bishop's Stortford	0-7
Cambridge United v Crystal Palace (Bromley)	0-4
Barnet Copthall v Maidstone United	8-0
Harringey Borough v London Ladies	5-3
Croydon Postal v Hackney	7-1
Caversham v Woodbridge Town	9-3
Viking v Hastings Town	6-6

Hastings Town won 3-1 on penalties.

Billericay Town v Basingstoke Town	2-0
Gravesend & Northfleet v Gillingham	1-11
Haverhill Rovers v Thame United	9-0
Launceston Ladies v Keynsham Town	1-10
Hereford United v Bristol United	3-1
Elmore Eagles v Dorchester	4-2
Wendron v Penzance	0-8
Wimbourne Town v Swindon Spitfires	4-1
Exeter Rangers v Cogan Coronation	1-3
Marjons v Madron	20-1
Warminster Town v Okeford United	0-11
Corfe Hills United v North Malton Sports	3-0

PRELIMINARY ROUND

Preston North End v Stockport Celtic	2-0

(abandoned 79 minutes; waterlogged pitch)

	7-0
Stockport County v Billingham	2-7
Barnsley v Windscale	1-0
Trafford v Newsham PH	5-2
Warrington Grange v Killingworth YPC	1-3
Mond Rangers v Chester City	1-3
Silsden Ladies v Witton Albion	4-5
Penrith Sapphires v Scunthorpe United	2-5
Broughton Aerospace v Wakefield	1-1

Wakefield won 4-3 on penalties.

Lichfield Diamonds v Leicester City	6-1
Wem Town Raiders v Atherstone United	3-4
Grantham Town v Belper Town	2-4
Kidderminster Harriers v Lincoln City	0-4
Steel City Wanderers v Kettering Amazons	2-4
Great Wyrley v Chaffoteaux	1-3
Barnet Copthall v Chesham United	2-6
Redbridge Wanderers v Gillingham	0-12
Malling v Woking	3-2
Haywards Heath v Newport Pagnell Town	1-0
Tottenham Hotspur v Hastings Town	2-1
Haverhill Rovers v Bishop's Stortford	2-1
Redbridge Raiders v West Ham United	0-1
Harringey Borough v Billericay Town	4-1
Slough v Kings Lynn	4-0
Croydon Postal v Crystal Palace (Bromley)	1-2
Caversham v Launton	5-2
Brentford v Northampton Town & County	2-13
Penzance v Cogan Coronation	2-1
Wimbourne Town v Hereford United	5-2
Elburton Villa v Corfe Hills United	0-2

Marjons v Okeford United	0-5
Elmore Eagles v Keynsham Town	6-1

FIRST ROUND

Darlington v Billingham	2-4
Blackpool (Wren) Rovers v Newcastle	6-0
Witton Albion v Stockport Hatters	1-2
Doncaster Rovers v Bradford City	3-4
Middlesbrough v Leeds City Vixens	2-3
Killingworth YPC v Blackburn Rovers	1-2

Trafford removed from competition for fielding an ineligible player; Wakefield w.o.

Preston North End v Barnsley	4-2
Manchester City v Manchester United	4-1
Chester City v Scunthorpe United	4-1
Chesterfield v Kettering Amazons	8-2
Mansfield Town v Chaffoteaux	3-3

Mansfield Town won 4-3 on penalties.

Atherstone United v Walsall	0-3
Highfield Rangers v Lichfield Diamonds	5-1
Telford United v Belper Town	1-0
Peterborough United v Derby County	0-2
Stafford Rangers v Arnold Town	5-3
Shrewsbury Town v Lincoln City	3-2
Ilkeston v Parkgate	1-2
Racers v Chesham United	1-1

(abandoned extra time)

	1-7
Crowborough Athletic v West Ham United	0-7
Whitehawk v Haywards Heath	3-2
Gillingham v Bedford Town Bells	5-1
Rushden & Diamonds (Formerly Northampton Town & County) v Watford	3-0
Slough v Chelmsford	0-4
Enfield v Caversham	4-0
Fulham v Crystal Palace (Bromley)	14-0
Harringey Borough v Tottenham Hotspur	1-7
Haverhill Rovers v Charlton	1-3
Stowmarket v Hampton	2-1
Denham United v Malling	1-5
Swindon Town v Wimbourne Town	9-0
Clevedon v Bristol Rovers	0-9
Southampton v Penzance	3-1
Portsmouth v Okeford United	9-2
Saltash Pilgrims v Cheltenham Town	1-4
Oxford United v Bristol United	1-6
Corfe Hills United v Elmore Eagles	3-0
Reading v Yeovil Town	2-2

Reading won 8-7 on penalties.

Bye: Chester-Le-Street.

SECOND ROUND

Chester-Le-Street v Billingham	5-3
Blackburn Rovers v Parkgate	3-5
Preston North End v Blackpool (Wren) Rovers	2-3
Bradford City v Leeds City Vixens	1-4
Chester City v Wakefield	7-1
Stockport Hatters v Manchester City	0-3
Shrewsbury Town v Derby County	1-4
Mansfield Town v Chesterfield	5-3
Telford United v Rushden & Diamonds	0-2
Walsall v Stafford Rangers	1-1

Walsall won 3-2 on penalties.

Gillingham v Tottenham Hotspur	6-2
Stowmarket v Chelmsford	3-0
Whitehawk v West Ham United	0-6
Enfield v Malling	15-0
Bristol City v Bristol Rovers	0-4
Chesham United v Highfield Rangers	6-5
Charlton v Fulham	1-19
Swindon Town v Southampton	3-0
Corfe Hills United v Reading	3-3

Reading won 2-0 on penalties.

Cheltenham Town v Portsmouth	3-2

THIRD ROUND

Blackpool (Wren) Rovers v Newcastle Town	3-0
Derby County v Telford United	1-0
Ilkeston Town v Leeds City Vixens	1-0
Chester-Le-Street v Sheffield Wednesday	2-0
Birmingham City v Oldham Curzon	2-0
Aston Villa v Bangor City	1-0
Wolverhampton Wanderers v Garswood Saints	4-0
Mansfield Town v Parkgate	2-2

Mansfield Town won 4-3 on penalties.

Leeds United v Huddersfield Town	8-0
Coventry City v Chester City	0-3

Manchester City v Walsall	2-1
Chesham United v Newport County	2-4
Bristol Rovers v Cheltenham Town	7-0
Ipswich Town v Fulham	0-10
West Ham United v Wembley Mill Hill	3-0
Berkhamsted Town v Reading Royals	2-0
Barking v Barnet	0-11
Wimbledon v Cardiff City	6-0
Reading v Enfield	0-2
Langford v Chelsea	0-3
Brighton & Hove Albion v Gillingham	3-1
Stowmarket v Swindon Town	1-2

FOURTH ROUND

Blackpool (Wren) Rovers v Barnet	1-7
Birmingham City v Aston Villa	1-2
Chelsea v Barry Town	5-3
Millwall Lionesses v Everton	1-4
Arsenal v Leeds United	5-3
Wimbledon v Southampton Saints	0-4
Liverpool v Chester City	3-0
Berkhamsted Town v Brighton & Hove Albion	0-1
West Ham United v Ilkeston Town	1-4
Bristol Rovers v Mansfield Town	1-0
Sunderland v Charlton Athletic	1-3
Swindon Town v Enfield	1-2
Newport County v Chester-Le-Street	3-3
Chester-Le-Street won 4-2 on penalties.	
Fulham v Manchester City	8-0
Derby County v Wolverhampton Wanderers	0-8
Tranmere Rovers v Doncaster Belles	2-3

FIFTH ROUND

Liverpool v Fulham	0-8
Doncaster Belles v Wolverhampton Wanderers	8-0
Everton v Charlton Athletic	1-2
Bristol Rovers v Chester-Le-Street	4-3
Barnet v Enfield	3-0
Chelsea v Arsenal	0-10
Brighton & Hove Albion v Aston Villa	1-3
Ilkeston Town v Southampton Saints	1-4

SIXTH ROUND

Fulham v Barnet	5-0
Arsenal v Doncaster Belles	1-0
Southampton Saints v Charlton Athletic	3-2
Bristol Rovers v Aston Villa	1-0

SEMI-FINALS

| Fulham v Southampton Saints | 5-0 |
| Bristol Rovers v Arsenal | 0-3 |

FINAL (at Selhurst Park)

7 MAY

Arsenal (0) 1 *(Banks 52)*

Fulham (0) 0   13,824

Arsenal: Byrne; Pealling, Wheatley, Harwood, White, Stoney, Ludlow, Williams, Spacey (Maggs 82), Banks, Grant.
Fulham: Bowry; Gibbons, Jerray-Silver, Petersen, Phillip, Duncan (Mork 77), Chapman, McArthur (Rahman 81), Haugenes, Pettersen, Yankey.
Referee: T. Parkes (Birmingham).

AXA FA WOMEN'S PREMIER LEAGUE CUP 2000–2001

PRELIMINARY ROUND

| Langford v Ilkeston Town | 1-3 |
| Wolverhampton Wanderers v Birmingham City | 0-3 |

FIRST ROUND

Aston Villa v Liverpool	2-3
Barnet v Ipswich Town	7-1
Berkhamsted Town v Barking	4-3
Brighton & Hove Albion v Newport County	4-0
Cardiff City v Coventry City	5-1
Doncaster Belles v Garswood Saints	7-2
Everton v Huddersfield Town	7-0
Leeds United v Ilkeston Town	6-0
Millwall Lionesses v Barry Town	3-2
Newcastle Town v Charlton Athletic	0-14
Oldham Curzon v Wimbledon	2-1
(abandoned waterlogged pitch)	
Reading Royals v Birmingham City	4-5
Southampton Saints v Sheffield Wednesday	0-6
Sunderland v Arsenal	5-0
Tranmere Rovers v Chelsea	0-7
Wembley Mill Hill v Bangor City	7-1
	0-3

SECOND ROUND

Millwall Lionesses v Berkhamsted Town	3-0
Bangor City v Charlton Athletic	3-5
Liverpool v Doncaster Belles	1-6
Birmingham City v Everton	0-4
Brighton & Hove Albion v Tranmere Rovers	0-1
Cardiff City v Barnet	0-5
Arsenal v Southampton Saints	5-1
Wimbledon v Leeds United	0-1

THIRD ROUND

Tranmere Rovers v Everton	4-2
Barnet v Charlton Athletic	0-2
Doncaster Belles v Arsenal	1-2
Millwall Lionesses v Leeds United	2-1

SEMI-FINALS

| Tranmere Rovers v Millwall Lionesses | 3-2 |
| Charlton Athletic v Arsenal | 0-3 |

FINAL

| Tranmere Rovers v Arsenal | 0-3 |

The Women's FA Cup Final produced a trophy for Arsenal and Angela Banks settles it against Fulham Ladies. (Colorsport)

FA PREMIER RESERVE LEAGUE 2000–2001

FA PREMIER RESERVE LEAGUE NORTH SECTION

FINAL TABLE

	P	W	D	L	F	A	W	D	L	F	A	GD	Pts
Everton	22	7	1	3	14	9	7	1	3	21	13	13	44
Sunderland	22	6	4	1	20	9	6	2	3	18	12	17	42
Leeds U	22	6	2	3	19	7	5	2	4	21	17	16	37
Blackburn R	22	5	5	1	17	10	4	5	2	14	13	8	37
Manchester U	22	7	2	2	22	13	4	0	7	17	23	3	35
Manchester C	22	4	3	4	21	20	5	3	3	21	13	9	33
Middlesbrough	22	6	1	4	26	23	3	5	3	13	15	1	33
Liverpool	22	5	3	3	23	11	4	2	5	20	21	11	32
Aston Villa	22	4	2	5	16	18	4	4	3	17	16	−1	30
Newcastle U	22	4	2	5	15	15	4	2	5	19	20	−1	28
Bradford C	22	2	2	7	18	25	1	0	10	12	38	−33	11
Sheffield W	22	1	1	9	16	42	0	2	9	9	26	−43	6

HIGHEST ATTENDANCE
Sunderland v Manchester U — 8060

LEADING APPEARANCES
Hackworth (Leeds U)	22
Melaugh (Aston Villa)	22
O'Brien (Blackburn R)	22
Kerr (Bradford C)	21
Clegg M (Manchester U)	21
Djordjic (Manchester U)	21
Southern K (Everton)	21
McLeod (Everton)	20
Standing (Aston Villa)	20
Evans (Leeds U)	20

LEADING GOALSCORERS
Taylor (Manchester C)	9
Huckerby (Manchester C)	9
Including 8 for Leeds U	
Hackworth (Leeds U)	9
Jevons (Everton)	7
Moore (Aston Villa)	7
Fowler (Liverpool)	6
Grant (Bradford C)	6
Lua-Lua (Newcastle U)	6
Marinelli (Middlesbrough)	6
Kyle (Sunderland)	6
Chadwick (Everton)	6
Wilson (Manchester U)	6
Richards (Manchester U)	6

FA PREMIER RESERVE LEAGUE SOUTH SECTION

FINAL TABLE

	P	W	D	L	F	A	W	D	L	F	A	GD	Pts
Derby Co	24	11	0	1	31	6	4	4	4	19	17	27	49
Coventry C	24	8	2	2	22	11	5	1	6	23	20	14	42
Watford	24	8	1	3	28	15	4	3	5	20	22	11	40
Tottenham H	24	6	4	2	19	6	5	1	6	13	30	−4	38
Chelsea	24	6	2	4	20	19	5	2	5	13	21	−7	37
Ipswich T	24	6	1	5	21	20	4	5	3	18	21	−2	36
Arsenal	24	5	2	5	25	24	5	1	6	24	16	9	33
Charlton Ath	24	3	3	6	18	30	5	3	4	17	14	−9	30
Southampton	24	4	3	5	27	20	4	1	7	13	21	−1	28
Leicester C	24	2	4	6	17	18	5	3	4	20	26	−7	28
Nottingham F	24	3	5	4	24	26	4	2	6	19	25	−8	28
Wimbledon	24	5	3	4	17	14	2	3	7	17	30	−10	27
West Ham U	24	2	2	8	15	22	3	3	6	15	21	−13	20

HIGHEST ATTENDANCE
Leicester C v Chelsea — 4731

LEADING APPEARANCES
Bolder (Derby Co)	24
Nicholls (Ipswich T)	24
Miller (Ipswich T)	23
Gibbens (Southampton)	23
Abidallah (Ipswich T)	23
Osei-Kuffour (Arsenal)	23
Etherington (Tottenham H)	22
Hillier (Tottenham H)	22
Hunt (Derby Co)	22
Forde (Watford)	22

LEADING GOALSCORERS
Harewood (Nottingham F)	14
Osei-Kuffour (Arsenal)	11
Korsten (Tottenham H)	11
Smart (Watford)	10
Logan (Ipswich T)	10
Morris (Derby Co)	9
Benjamin (Leicester C)	9
Sturridge (Derby Co)	8
Forde (Watford)	7
Dudfield (Leicester C)	7
Caceres (Southampton)	7

RESULTS 2000–2001 Season:

North Section

	Aston Villa	Blackburn R	Bradford C	Everton	Leeds U	Liverpool	Manchester C	Manchester U	Middlesbrough	Newcastle U	Sheffield W	Sunderland
Aston Villa	—	2-1	2-0	2-4	2-1	3-4	1-2	0-1	0-0	1-3	2-1	1-1
Blackburn R	1-1	—	1-0	3-1	2-2	0-1	1-1	2-0	3-1	1-0	2-2	1-1
Bradford C	2-3	1-2	—	0-1	0-2	4-2	1-1	2-3	4-1	1-5	2-2	1-3
Everton	1-0	0-0	3-1	—	0-2	2-1	1-0	0-3	2-0	3-1	2-0	0-1
Leeds U	0-1	4-0	4-1	0-1	—	1-1	0-2	2-0	0-0	4-1	2-0	2-0
Liverpool	1-1	0-0	8-0	1-0	1-2	—	0-1	4-2	2-3	1-1	2-0	3-1
Manchester C	4-1	1-1	3-0	2-4	0-5	1-2	—	2-1	0-0	2-2	4-1	2-3
Manchester U	4-2	0-0	3-2	2-3	3-0	2-2	2-1	—	0-3	4-0	1-0	1-0
Middlesbrough	1-1	1-3	3-1	1-3	4-1	3-2	4-3	4-3	—	0-3	4-1	1-2
Newcastle U	0-1	2-3	1-2	1-0	1-3	2-0	1-1	2-1	2-2	—	3-1	0-1
Sheffield W	1-5	2-4	6-4	0-3	3-3	1-4	1-7	1-3	1-2	0-2	—	0-5
Sunderland	1-1	0-0	4-1	1-1	1-0	2-1	1-2	4-0	1-1	3-1	2-1	—

League winners Everton League appearances:
Alexandersson 1; Ball 1; Berhalter 1; Cadamarteri 8; Caires 1; Chadwick 7+7; Clarke 13; Cleland 4; Curran +2; Degn 4+1; Dunne 1; Eaton +6; Gascoigne 2; Gemmill 5; Hibbert 19; Hughes S 6; Jevons 17; Kearney 1+2; McKay 10+1; McLeod 20; Milligan 12+1; Moore 5; Myhre 2; Naysmith 1; Nyarko 2; O'Hanlon 10+1; Osman 16+2; Pilkington 9+2; Pistone 2; Seddon 2; Simonsen 20; Southern K 18+3; Tal 6; Unsworth 8; Valentine 6+1; Zampereni 2.

Goals: Jevons 9, Chadwick 7, McKay 3, Osman 3, Cadamarteri 2, Eaton 2, McLeod 2, Southern K 2, Alexandersson 1, Hughes S 1, Milligan 1, Moore 1, O'Hanlon 1.

RESULTS 2000–2001 Season:

South Section

	Arsenal	Charlton Ath	Chelsea	Coventry C	Derby Co	Ipswich T	Leicester C	Nottingham F	Southampton	Tottenham H	Watford	West Ham U	Wimbledon
Arsenal	—	1-0	1-1	0-2	3-2	2-2	2-6	3-4	2-1	4-0	0-2	1-2	6-2
Charlton Ath	1-6	—	2-0	0-4	0-0	1-1	1-3	0-6	2-1	5-0	2-2	2-4	2-3
Chelsea	1-0	1-1	—	3-2	0-2	2-1	0-1	1-4	3-1	4-2	2-3	2-2	1-0
Coventry C	3-2	2-1	0-1	—	2-0	3-3	0-0	2-0	0-1	3-0	2-1	3-1	2-1
Derby Co	1-0	0-2	5-1	3-2	—	6-1	3-0	3-0	3-0	3-0	1-0	2-0	1-0
Ipswich T	0-3	3-6	2-0	2-1	2-1	—	1-2	4-0	1-1	0-2	0-2	2-0	4-2
Leicester C	1-2	1-2	1-2	2-2	0-0	0-1	—	1-1	0-2	1-2	4-0	4-2	2-2
Nottingham F	2-1	3-0	2-2	2-5	4-4	2-2	2-2	—	2-3	1-3	3-2	0-1	1-1
Southampton	2-2	0-0	0-1	4-2	1-2	2-4	5-1	1-2	—	7-0	2-2	1-0	2-4
Tottenham H	1-0	0-0	1-2	1-2	0-0	2-0	6-0	1-1	2-0	—	2-1	0-0	3-0
Watford	2-1	2-1	4-0	1-0	2-3	1-2	3-1	2-1	3-1	1-2	—	2-2	5-1
West Ham United	1-2	1-3	1-2	2-0	1-5	0-1	1-2	3-0	1-2	1-2	2-2	—	1-1
Wimbledon	1-5	0-1	2-1	0-1	2-0	0-0	2-2	4-0	2-2	0-3	2-1	—	—

League winners Derby County League appearances:
Bannister 1; Blatsis 8; Boertien 18; Bohinen 8; Bolder 22+2; Bragstad 10; Brayley 1; Brown K 1+1; Burley 1; Burton 3; Carbonari 1; Christie 3; Donnelly +1; Elliott 8; Evatt 18+2; Frederickson 1; Grant 18; Gudjonsson 4; Higginbotham 3; Holmes 1; Hunt 16+6; Isik 2; Jackson 16+1; Kinkladze 2; Martin 8; Mawene 10; McArdle 3+3; McKeown 2+2; Mills 3+1; Molloy +3; Morris 18; Moukoko 2; Murray 11; Oakes 5; O'Halloran 1+10; O'Neil 1; Riggott 4; Robinson 3; Schnoor 3; Strupar 2; Sturridge 6; Tudgay 13+4; Twigg 4+4; Valakari 1; Weckstrom +2.

Goals: Morris 9, Sturridge 8, Burton 6, Gudjonsson 6, Bolder 5, O'Halloran 3, Twigg 3, Tudgay 2, Blatsis 1, Evatt 1, Hunt 1, Isik 1, Kinkladze 1, Murray 1, Strupar 1, own goal 1.

NATIONWIDE CONFERENCE 2000–2001

At the turn of the year Yeovil Town had looked home and dry. Seven points clear of Rushden & Diamonds, with two games in hand and Colin Addison installed successfully as manager in place of Southend United-bound Dave Webb, everything seemed to be going Somerset way.

Though this margin was eroded in the next month or so, Yeovil still had the advantage of their games in hand and having won at Rushden should have been confident of the return fixture. But by the beginning of March, Rushden had caught them and were two points ahead, though with the two-match disadvantage.

In a month, Rushden had stretched the points lead to five as Yeovil began to show signs of erratic form. Then on 14 April it seemed fortunes might be swinging back to Yeovil as Rushden lost 3-1 at Hereford United, while their rivals were hammering Leigh RMI 6-1. Again Yeovil's inconsistent streak revealed itself two days later on Easter Monday when they lost 2-0 at Dagenham & Redbridge, who enjoyed a fine season throughout. Rushden's goalless home draw with Doncaster Rovers gave them a three point lead and Yeovil had only one game in hand.

The following Saturday was the crunch. Yeovil at home to Rushden. But the Somerset team could only draw 0-0 and lost the psychological advantage. Their final distress call went out on May day in the outstanding game with Hereford who won 3-2 at Yeovil to virtually hand the title to Rushden. Yeovil even failed to win their last home game to Scarborough and Rushden's margin was ultimately six points.

At the bottom of the table, Hednesford Town's plight had long been known, but Kingstonian's FA Cup run merely masked their problems and the third relegated club proved to be Kettering Town after a strenuous battle at the foot of the table involving themselves, Morecambe, Hayes, Northwich Victoria and Forest Green Rovers who reached the Umbro Trophy Final.

Despite the success of both Rushden and Yeovil in terms of support, aggregated attendances fell to 719,733 compared with 748,008 in the 1999–2000 season.

Disappointment came to the Nationwide Conference in the summer when the Football League turned down the idea of two clubs being promoted into the Conference on the grounds of finance.

NATIONWIDE CONFERENCE 2000–2001 FINAL LEAGUE TABLE

		Home			Goals		Away			Goals		
	P	W	D	L	F	A	W	D	L	F	A	Pts
Rushden & Diamonds	42	14	6	1	41	13	11	5	5	37	23	86
Yeovil Town	42	14	3	4	41	17	10	5	6	32	33	80
Dagenham & Redbridge	42	13	4	4	39	19	10	4	7	32	35	77
Southport	42	9	5	7	33	24	11	4	6	25	22	69
Leigh RMI	42	11	5	5	38	24	8	6	7	25	33	68
Telford United	42	13	1	7	33	23	6	7	8	18	28	65
Stevenage Borough	42	8	7	6	36	33	7	11	3	35	28	63
Chester City	42	9	8	4	29	19	7	6	8	20	24	62
Doncaster Rovers	42	11	5	5	28	17	4	8	9	19	26	58
Scarborough	42	7	9	5	29	25	7	7	7	27	29	58
Hereford United	42	6	12	3	27	19	8	3	10	33	27	57
Boston United	42	10	7	4	43	28	3	10	8	31	35	56
Nuneaton Borough	42	9	5	7	35	26	4	10	7	25	34	54
Woking	42	5	10	6	30	30	8	5	8	22	27	54
Dover Athletic	42	9	6	6	32	22	5	5	11	22	34	53
Forest Green Rovers	42	6	9	6	28	28	5	6	10	15	26	48
Northwich Victoria	42	8	7	6	31	24	3	6	12	18	43	46
Hayes	42	5	6	10	22	31	7	4	10	22	40	46
Morecambe	42	8	5	8	35	29	3	7	11	29	37	45
Kettering Town	42	5	5	11	23	31	6	5	10	23	31	43
Kingstonian	42	3	5	13	19	40	5	5	11	28	33	34
Hednesford Town	42	2	6	13	24	38	3	7	11	22	48	28

NATIONWIDE CONFERENCE LEADING GOALSCORERS 2000–2001

Conf.		NVCT	FAC	UT
24	Duane Darby (Rushden & Diamonds) +	–	–	3
19	Steve Jones (Leigh RMI) +	1	1	–
18	Warren Patmore (Yeovil Town) +	1	3	–
18	Justin Jackson (Rushden & Diamonds) +	–	1	1
15	Darran Hay (Stevenage Borough) +	–	–	1
14	Rob Elmes (Hereford United) +	–	–	4
13	Alex Meechan (Forest Green Rovers) +	–	–	5
13	Ken Charlery (Boston United) +	–	3	1
13	Marc McGregor (Nuneaton Borough) +	2	1	–
13	Ian Arnold (Southport) +	–	1	1
13	Dave Ridings (Leigh RMI) +	1	–	–
13	Simon Parke (Southport) +	–	–	–
13	Charlie Griffin (Woking) +	–	–	–
12	Mark Beesley (Chester City) +	3	1	1
12	Tony Black (Leigh RMI) +	1	3	1
12	Darren Collins (Kettering Town) +	–	2	–
12	Gary Paterson (Doncaster Rovers) +	–	1	–
12	Jeff Vansittart (Dover Athletic) +	–	–	–
11	Neil Illman (Stevenage Borough) +	2	–	4
11	Rocky Baptiste (Hayes) +	–	–	–
11	Dale Watkins (Kettering Town) +	–	–	–
11	Jon Brady (Rushden & Diamonds) +	–	–	–

NVCT: National Variety Club Trophy; FAC: FA Cup; UT: Umbro Trophy.

NATIONWIDE CONFERENCE RESULTS 2000–2001

	Boston United	Chester City	Dagenham & Redbridge	Doncaster Rovers	Dover Athletic	Forest Green Rovers	Hayes	Hednesford Town	Hereford United	Kettering Town	Kingstonian	Leigh RMI	Morecambe	Northwich Victoria	Nuneaton Borough	Rushden & Diamonds	Scarborough	Southport	Stevenage Borough	Telford United	Woking	Yeovil Town
Boston United	—	0-0	2-1	4-2	0-0	0-3	1-1	2-4	1-1	2-2	0-0	2-2	2-0	0-3	4-1	1-1	2-2	1-0	3-3	2-1	0-0	4-1
Chester City	2-2	—	1-1	3-0	1-0	1-1	0-0	1-1	2-0	2-1	0-0	1-1	1-0	1-1	4-0	1-2	3-2	0-1	1-1	1-0	3-3	2-1
Dagenham & Redbridge	2-1	1-1	—	2-1	1-1	3-1	2-0	1-1	0-3	0-0	0-0	2-1	3-2	1-0	1-1	0-2	1-0	0-1	3-0	0-0	1-2	2-0
Doncaster Rovers	4-2	1-0	1-0	—	1-1	3-0	2-0	6-1	2-1	5-1	1-2	4-0	1-0	1-0	1-1	3-2	1-0	0-1	3-0	0-0	0-1	2-0
Dover Athletic	0-0	1-1	3-1	1-1	—	3-0	4-1	4-0	1-0	1-0	0-2	4-0	2-2	3-0	2-1	4-1	0-2	2-0	1-0	1-3	0-0	1-1
Forest Green Rovers	0-3	1-1	4-4	2-2	1-2	—	1-0	0-2	1-1	3-2	2-1	3-1	0-0	1-0	0-0	0-3	2-3	2-0	1-0	1-1	0-0	2-3
Hayes	0-1	0-0	2-0	3-0	4-1	1-2	—	1-3	3-2	0-2	0-1	4-0	3-4	4-0	2-0	2-0	2-0	3-3	2-0	1-2	3-0	3-0
Hednesford Town	3-4	0-1	6-1	3-1	4-0	0-2	1-1	—	1-1	0-0	3-1	2-2	0-0	5-1	0-0	2-0	2-0	4-1	2-1	1-1	1-1	4-2
Hereford United	5-3	2-1	2-1	2-1	1-0	1-1	0-2	0-3	—	0-0	0-3	2-1	1-1	1-0	2-4	1-0	2-4	1-1	1-1	1-0	0-3	2-3
Kettering Town	4-3	2-1	5-1	1-0	0-3	1-0	3-2	2-1	0-0	—	0-1	1-0	0-2	1-0	1-2	1-1	2-3	2-0	2-0	2-1	2-0	2-0
Kingstonian	2-1	0-0	1-2	0-2	4-0	1-3	1-1	3-2	0-0	3-1	—	2-1	2-1	2-1	2-1	2-1	1-0	2-2	2-5	0-1	0-0	3-1
Leigh RMI	0-1	1-1	2-1	4-0	1-2	3-1	1-2	1-2	1-1	0-1	0-2	—	1-2	1-1	2-1	1-1	1-1	1-2	3-0	2-1	1-1	6-1
Morecambe	2-1	1-0	3-2	1-0	0-2	2-2	0-0	1-1	0-0	2-2	1-5	1-6	—	1-0	1-0	5-1	4-1	2-2	1-2	1-1	2-0	3-1
Northwich Victoria	1-1	1-1	0-2	1-0	3-0	1-0	2-2	7-1	0-0	2-3	1-0	3-0	4-0	—	3-1	3-1	4-0	1-1	3-1	2-3	1-1	1-0
Nuneaton Borough	4-1	4-0	1-1	1-1	2-1	0-0	0-0	0-3	1-1	1-2	2-2	6-2	4-2	2-2	—	2-1	1-0	1-2	1-1	2-1	0-2	0-0
Rushden & Diamonds	1-1	1-2	0-2	3-2	4-1	0-0	0-3	2-3	3-1	0-2	2-4	1-0	2-1	0-0	1-1	—	0-3	1-3	0-2	1-2	1-4	0-0
Scarborough	2-2	3-2	1-0	0-2	0-2	2-3	0-1	0-1	1-1	1-1	2-2	2-0	4-4	3-0	1-0	1-0	—	3-1	1-1	1-0	1-1	0-1
Southport	1-0	0-1	0-1	0-1	0-1	2-0	1-0	0-1	0-0	1-1	3-1	2-2	1-3	0-2	1-2	4-0	1-1	—	1-3	2-3	1-2	0-1
Stevenage Borough	3-3	1-1	3-0	0-0	1-0	2-3	0-1	1-1	1-1	1-2	0-2	1-4	1-2	0-3	2-2	1-0	3-1	1-3	—	2-2	0-1	2-2
Telford United	2-1	1-0	0-0	1-2	1-3	1-1	0-1	1-1	2-0	0-1	0-1	1-1	0-0	0-1	3-0	3-0	1-1	3-0	1-1	—	5-3	3-0
Woking	0-0	3-3	1-2	0-1	0-0	1-1	1-2	1-2	0-1	2-0	0-3	2-0	3-0	4-0	1-1	1-1	3-2	0-1	3-2	3-1	—	1-0
Yeovil Town	4-1	2-1	2-0	2-0	1-1	0-1	2-3	1-2	2-2	2-1	3-4	2-3	0-0	1-2	0-2	1-2	2-2	3-0	0-0	1-2	1-0	—

CONFERENCE SEQUENCES

	NC	UT	NVCT	FAC	Sw	Sd	Wd	Ws
Boston United	12	4	1	4q	3	2	6	9
Chester City	8	Sf	F	3	2	2	11	7
Dagenham & Redbridge	3	3	1	3	9	2	9	4
Doncaster Rovers	9	3	2	4q	2	3	5	5
Dover Athletic	15	3	1	4q	2	4	6	10
Forest Green Rovers	16	F	1	1	2	4	9	7
Hayes	18	3	1	1	3	7	6	7
Hednesford Town	22	3	2	1	1	3	5	15
Hereford United	11	Sf	2	4q	3	3	8	7
Kettering Town	20	3	Qf	2	3	5	4	11
Kingstonian	21	4	F	4	2	3	2	13
Leigh RMI	5	4	2	1	6	3	8	7
Morecambe	19	5	2	3	4	5	8	8
Northwich Victoria	17	3	1	2	3	6	6	7
Nuneaton Borough	13	3	Sf	2	2	2	5	6
Rushden & Diamonds	1	5	Qf	1	5	3	16	3
Scarborough	10	4	2	4q	4	3	10	8
Southport	4	Qf	Qf	2	5	2	7	5
Stevenage Borough	7	5	2	4q	4	2	10	6
Telford United	6	Qf	1	1	3	3	6	3
Woking	14	3	2	1	2	2	9	6
Yeovil Town	2	5	Sf	3	4	2	14	5

Columns represent finishing position for Conference, round reached in Umbro Trophy, National Variety Club Trophy and FA Cup; Sw straight wins; Sd straight defeats; Wd without defeat; Ws without success.

ATTENDANCES BY CLUB 2000–2001

	Aggregate 2000–2001	Average 2000–2001	Highest Attendance 2000–2001
Rushden & Diamonds	81,408	3,876	5,482 v Dover Athletic
Yeovil Town	71,726	3,415	8,868 v Rushden & Diamonds
Doncaster Rovers	47,901	2,281	3,648 v Nuneaton Borough
Hereford United	41,847	1,902	3,393 v Yeovil Town
Boston United	41,650	1,983	3,434 v Rushden & Diamonds
Chester City	38,473	1,832	4,040 v Rushden & Diamonds
Stevenage Borough	38,091	1,813	3,327 v Rushden & Diamonds
Woking	36,600	1,742	2,319 v Dagenham & Redbridge
Kettering Town	33,703	1,604	4,750 v Rushden & Diamonds
Southport	29,879	1,422	2,255 v Rushden & Diamonds
Nuneaton Borough	29,802	1,419	2,614 v Rushden & Diamonds
Dagenham & Redbridge	26,201	1,247	2,136 v Yeovil Town
Morecambe	26,094	1,242	2,023 v Scarborough
Scarborough	23,409	1,114	2,381 v Doncaster Rovers
Northwich Victoria	23,118	1,100	2,651 v Chester City
Telford United	22,157	1,055	2,371 v Dagenham & Redbridge
Dover Athletic	21,883	1,042	1,604 v Doncaster Rovers
Kingstonian	20,379	970	1,717 v Woking
Hednesford Town	19,164	926	1,516 v Rushden & Diamonds
Forest Green Rovers	18,109	862	1,756 v Yeovil Town
Hayes	15,151	721	1,044 v Rushden & Diamonds
Leigh RMI	12,688	604	1,405 v Rushden & Diamonds

THE CONFERENCE NEWS AWARDS

MANAGER OF THE YEAR
Brian Talbot   (Rushden & Diamonds)

MANAGER OF THE MONTH AWARDS

August	Brian Talbot (Rushden & Diamonds)
September	Brian Talbot/Dave Webb (Rushden & Diamonds/Yeovil Town)
October	Jim Harvey (Morecambe)
November	Keith Alexander (Northwich Victoria)
December	Colin Addison (Yeovil Town)
January	Brian Talbot (Rushden & Diamonds)
February	Gerry Hill/Colin Lippiatt (Dagenham & Redbridge/Woking)
March	Gerry Hill (Dagenham & Redbridge)
April/May	Steve Evans (Boston United)

GOALSCORER OF THE YEAR
Duane Darby   (Rushden & Diamonds)

GOALSCORER OF THE MONTH AWARDS

August	Duane Darby (Rushden & Diamonds)
September	Marc McGregor (Nuneaton Borough)
October	Ken Charlery/Tony Black (Boston United/Leigh RMI)
November	Marc McGregor (Nuneaton Borough)
December	Mark Quayle (Morecambe)
January	Warren Patmore/Duane Darby (Yeovil Town/Rushden & Diamonds)
February	John Norman (Morecambe)
March	Steve Jones (Leigh RMI)

April/May   Darren Collins (Kettering Town)

PLAYER OF THE YEAR
Duane Darby   (Rushden & Diamonds)

TEAM OF THE YEAR

Goalkeeper	Wayne Brown (Chester City)
Right-back	Tarkan Mustafa (Rushden & Diamonds)
Centre-backs	Terry Skiverton (Yeovil Town)
	Scott Guyett (Southport)
Left-back	Paul Underwood (Rushden & Diamonds)
Midfield	Darren Way (Yeovil Town)
	Geoff Pitcher (Kingstonian)
	Nick Crittenden (Yeovil Town)
Forwards	Duane Darby (Rushden & Diamonds)
	Justin Jackson (Rushden & Diamonds)
	Steve Jones (Leigh RMI)

PERFORMANCE OF THE MONTH AWARDS

August	Dover Athletic
September	Hednesford Town
October	Leigh RMI
November	Kingstonian
December	Dover Athletic
January	Southport
February	Dagenham & Redbridge
March	Hayes
April/May	Hereford United

PROGRAMME OF THE YEAR AWARD
Doncaster Rovers

NATIONWIDE CONFERENCE 2000–2001
APPEARANCES AND GOALSCORERS

Boston United
Appearances: Bastock, 42; Charlery, 30+1; Clifford, 11; Conroy, 0+2; Cook, 11+2; Costello, 13+5; Cramman, 1; Curtis, 4; De Souza, 7+2; Diaf, 3+1; Dick, 26+1; Elding, 1+8; Fewings, 15+9; French, 2+4; Gowshall, 35+2; Howarth, 30; Hoyle, 26+3; Livett, 2+4; Lodge, 17+5; Lucas, 29+5; Mills, 5+2; Minett, 4+5; Norris, 5; Nuttell, 11+6; Rawle, 13+13; Raynor, 31+1; Rusk, 6+2; Stanhope, 17+5; Town, 6+1; Turner, 4; Weatherstone R, 6+1; Weatherstone S, 13; Wilson, 18; Wooding, 12.
Goals (74): Charlery 13, Rawle 10, Costello 7, Wilson 7, Weatherstone S, 5, Fewings 4, Norris 4, Howarth 3, Raynor 3, Town 3, Cook 2, Rusk 2, Stanhope 2, De Souza 1, Diaf 1, Dick 1, Hoyle 1, Minett 1, own goals 4.

Chester City
Appearances: Beesley M, 36+4; Beesley P, 32; Berry, 0+1; Blackburn, 33; Brown, 34; Carden, 36; Doughty, 35+5; Evans, 5+3; Finney, 4+5; Fisher, 32+5; Gaunt, 22+3; Greygoose, 3; Haarhoff, 5+6; Kerr, 4+5; Lancaster, 37+2; Moss, 14+5; Porter, 9+2; Priestly, 5+1; Richardson, 1+4; Ruffer, 16+4; Ruscoe, 20+8; Shelton, 0+3; Whitehall, 25+3; Woods, 34+3; Woodyatt, 7+6; Wright, 13+16.
Goals (49): Beesley M, 11 (1 pen), Whitehall 9 (1 pen), Woods 5 (1 pen), Fisher 4, Wright 4 (1 pen), Blackburn 3, Evans 2, Porter 2 (1 pen), Carden 1, Doughty 1, Gaunt 1, Haarhoff 1, Lancaster 1, Ruscoe 1, own goals 3.

Dagenham & Redbridge
Appearances: Ayres, 1; Brennan, 17+7; Broom, 25+2; Browne, 0+3; Broughton, 8+1; Cobb, 10+17; Cole, 35; Forbes, 8+4; Gallagher, 3+3; Goodwin, 27+1; Hamsher, 4; Haworth, 3+5; Heffer, 35+2; Hayzelden, 6+3; Honey, 2; Janney, 28+5; Jones, 32+5; Keen, 7+16; Lock, 6+1; McDougald, 34+3; Matthews, 35; Naylor, 1; Opara, 1+4; Payne, 2+4; Roberts, 40; Rooney, 6; Shipp, 21+9; Terry, 35+3; Vickers, 28+1; Wignall, 2+3.
Goals (71): McDougald 9 (2 pens), Shipp 9, Goodwin 7, Cobb 6, Cole 5 (1 pen), Broughton 4 (1 pen), Terry 4, Brennan 3, Broom 3, Keen 3, Matthews 3, Hayzelden 2, Janney 2, Jones 2, Lock 2, Opara 2, Browne 1, Gallagher 1, Haworth 1, Heffer 1, own goal 1.

Doncaster Rovers
Appearances: Alford, 12+6; Atkins, 20+2; Barnard, 14; Barrick, 11; Campbell, 27+5; Cauldwell, 17+9; Duerden, 0+7; Foster, 2; Halliday, 8+4; Hawkins, 22+5; Kelly, 23+6; McIntyre, 37+1; Marples, 29+3; Miller, 29+1; Paterson, 30+5; Penney, 23+4; Ryam. 27; Richardson, 30; Shaw, 26+3; Smith, 1; Stone, 2; Tierney, 7+2; Turner, 17+7; Walling, 5; Warrington, 12; Watson, 6+16; Whitman, 19+5; Williams, 6.
Goals (47): Paterson 11 (6 pens), Campbell 7, Whitman 5, Cauldwell 4, Tyrner 4, Barnard 3, Penney 3 (1 pen), Kelly 2, Tierney 2, Atkins 1, Barrick 1, Hawkins 1, McIntyre 1, Shaw 1, own goal 1.

Dover Athletic
Appearances: Beard, 32+2; Beale, 3+1; Briggs, 1+1; Brown, 18+10; Browne, 17+5; Carruthers, 32+8; Chapman, 24; Clarke, 0+1; Darcy, 5; Godden, 0+1; Hockton, 12+4; Hogg, 3+7; Hyde, 42; Lebert, 27+1; Le Bihan, 29+1; McRobert, 15+18; Moore, 0+4; Munday, 30; Norman, 41; Okafor, 3+1; Pinnock, 7+6; Pluck, 8+4; Shearer, 41; Strouts, 34+3; Vansittart, 36+2; White, 2+1.
Goals (54): Vansittart 13, Hockton 9 (3 pens), Shearer 7 (2 pens), Brown 5 (1 pen), Carruthers 4, Strouts 4, Le Bihan 3, McRobert 3, Beard 2, Pinnock 2, own goals 2.

Forest Green Rovers
Appearances: Danny Bailey 2+2; Dennis Bailey 13+8; Bennett, 11+7; Birkby, 0+3; Burns, 32; Campbell, 1+5; Clark, 38; Clarke, 1; Cooper, 11; Cort, 12; Cousins, 40+1; Daley, 23+7; Dobson, 0+2; Drysdale, 30; Eaton, 11+1; Foster A, 27+5; Foster M, 15+1; Ghent, 2; Hatswell, 19; Hedges, 14+7; Hunt, 0+2; Kilgour, 1; Lightbody, 9+7; Lockwood, 10; Meechan, 31; Middleton, 4+3; Nicholson, 1; Norton, 25; Olney, 0+2; Perrin, 26; Prince, 4+3; Shaw, 5+1; Slater, 20+1; Spink, 14; Sullivan, 3+1; Sykes, 6+1; Thomas, 2+6.
Goals (43): Meechan 13, Foster A 8, Hatswell 5, Clark 3, Daley 2, Eaton 2, Sykes 2, Bennett 1, Cooper 1, Foster M 1, Lightbody 1, Lockwood 1, Norton 1, Sullivan 1, own goal 1.

Hayes
Appearances: Baptiste, 20+1; Barnes, 15+4; Bezhardi, 8+6; Bossu, 1; Boylan, 10+2; Bryson 1+1; Bunce, 6; Coppard,

24+11; Dyer, 1; Everitt, 8; Flynn, 25; Gallen, 12+4; Goodliffe, 17; Gothard, 25; Hannigan, 3; Herbert, 1; Hodson B, 10+10. Hodson M, 16+2; McKimm, 40+1; Molesley, 16+7; Moore, 40+1; Newton, 6; Nyamah, 6+1; Pluck, 4; Preston, 17+10; Quinn, 6; Spencer, 25; Sterling, 36+2; Stevens, 26+5; Telemarque, 1+16; Town, 3+1; Tucker, 2+2; Watts, 21+1; White, 5+4.
Goals (44): Baptiste 11, Quinn 6, Stevens 5, Hodson B 4, Moore 4 (1 pen), Boylan 3, Coppard 2, Barnes 1, Bunce 1, Everitt 1, Gallen 1, McKimm 1, Molesley 1, Preston 1, Town 1, Watts 1.

Hednesford Town
Appearances: Airdrie, 12+10; Bagshaw, 31+5; Bonsail. 11+11; Bradley, 31+3; Brown, 6+8; Carney, 0+1; Carter, 0+1; Colkin, 20+2; Cooper, 23+1; Craven, 5; Davis, 31+4; Evans, 14; Ford, 4; Garratt, 1+1; Gayle, 38; Goodwin, 21+3; Griffiths, 13+1; Haran, 33+1; Lake, 27+1; Leadbeater, 4+1; Meechan, 0+1; Norbury, 27+3; Owen, 28+1; Pointon, 20+2; Rhodes, 0+1; Robinson, 25+1; Russell, 5+7; Sedgemore, 23+8; Shakespeare, 8+3.
Goals (46): Davis 10 (1 pen), Norbury 8, Bagshaw 6, Cooper 4 (2 pens), Bonsail 3, Owen 3, Goodwin 2, Robinson 2, Sedgemore 2 (1 pen), Brown 1, Haran 1, Lake 1, Russell 1, own goals 1.

Hereford United
Appearances: Baker, 2; Bull, 0+7; Clarke, 36+2; Cooksey, 40; Crowe, 4; Elmes, 29+9; Gardener, 7+6; Giddings, 12+13; Hanson, 2+4; James, 31+2; Lane, 24; McIndoe, 27; Moran, 0+1; Parry, 11+7; Piearce, 0+8; Plotnick, 0+1; Quiggin, 13+2; Quinn, 2; Rodgerson, 29+1; Robinson, 40; Shirley, 10+1; Snape, 39+2; Sturgess, 22; Wall, 9+1; Williams, 39; Wright, 34.
Goals (60): Elmes 14, Williams 8, Giddings 5, Lane 5 (4 pens), Rodgerson 5, Clarke 3, Wright 3, Bull 2, McIndoe 2, Gardener 1, Hanson 1, Parry 1, Piearce 2 (1 pen), Robinson 2, Snape 2, Quiggin 1, own goals 3.

Kettering Town
Appearances: Adams, 16+2; Alford, 2+3; Ayres, 0+1; Bowling, 25; Brown, 30+2; Codner, 22; Collins, 25+7; Cowling, 25+7; Cox, 2+2; Diuk, 24+5; Fisher, 31; Fothergil, 0+6; Hudson, 5+15; Inman, 24+4; Lee, 0+2; Lenagh, 11+8; McNamara, 28+11; Matthews, 22+2; Murray, 3+2; Norman, 26+1; Perkins, 27+4; Ridgeway, 8; Shutt, 17+4; Simba, 2; Vowden, 38; Watkins, 32+8; Wilkinson, 3+6; Wilson, 17.
Goals (46): Collins 12, Watkins 11 (1 pen), Inman 4, Hudson 3, Norman 3 (1 pen), Brown 2, Diuk 2, Fisher 2, Lenagh 2, McNamara 2, Adams 1, Codner 1, own goal 1.

Kingstonian
Appearances: Akuamoah, 31+8; Allan, 30; Allen, 2+1; Basford, 1; Bass, 22+7; Beard, 23+1; Blake, 5; Boyce, 26+3; Duerden, 14+1; Farrelly, 6; Fewings, 2; Glass, 14; Green, 12+23; Harriott, 4+1; Harris, 33; Holligan, 9; Hurst 9+1; Jones, 7+6; Kadi, 2+4; Kelly, 7; Luckett, 40; Mean, 2; Murray, 1; Patterson, 34+1; Pitcher, 34+1; Saunders, 26+3; Simba, 7+2; Stewart, 20+3; Thurgood, 1; Wall. 0+1; Wingfield, 12+3; Winston, 27+9.
Goals (47): Luckett 7 (5 pens), Pitcher 7, Duerden 5, Green 4, Winston 4, Akuamoah 3, Allan 3, Simba 3, Holligan 2, Bass 1, Boyce 1, Harris 1, Jones 1, Kadi 1, Patterson 1, Stewart 1, Wingfield 1, own goal 1.

Leigh RMI
Appearances: Black, 36+1; Blackmore, 1; Critchley, 0+2; Cumiskey, 7+2; Devenney, 3+1; Dootson, 19+1; Durkin, 20+4; Farrell, 42; Felgate, 23+1; Gardner, 1+5; German, 26+8; Harris, 15+6; Hayder, 2+8; Jones, 41+1; Kielty, 39+1; Mason, 1+10; Matthews, 3+9; Monk, 28+2; Morrell, 5+3; Murphy, 1+1; Reid, 0+1; Ridings, 40; Scott, 16; Spooner, 21+1; Swan, 39; Trees, 18+5; Udall, 15; Walker, 0+1.
Goals (63): Jones 19 (3 pens), Black 12 (6 pens), Riding 11, Kielty 5, Monk 4, Harris 2, Mason 2, Matthews 2, Cumiskey 1, Hayder 1, Swan 1, own goals 2.

Morecambe
Appearances: Alty 0+2; Banks, 6+1; Black, 20+13; Brown, 8+3; Dowe, 7; Drummond, 40; Eastwood, 18+12; Fensome, 39; Hardiker, 31; Heald, 2+8; Hunter, 6+7; Keeling 1; Knowles, 1+3; Lee, 12; Lyons, 2+7; McGuire, 4+9; McKearney, 42; Murphy J, 22+6; Norman, 29+7; Perkins, 4; Potts 1; Price, 2+1; Quayle, 15+3; Rigoglioso, 19+10; Smith L, 5; Smith M, 36; Stringfellow, 6+3; Swanick, 3+2; Talbot,

10+10; Takano, 10+7; Thompson, 11+8; Uberschar, 2+1; Walters, 20+2; Wright, 3+2.
Goals (64): Norman 10, Eastwood 9 (3 pens), Quayle 8, Drummond 7, Talbot 7, Black 5, McKearney 4, Thompson 4, Heald 2, Rigoglioso 2, Hunter 1, Lyons 1, Murphy 1, Walters 1, own goals 2.

Nuneaton Borough

Appearances: Angus, 35+1; Bacon, 12+1; Barnes, 9; Brennan, 8+4; Charles, 34+5; Crowley, 30+5; Francis, 15+10; Gittens, 11+2; Hanney 0+3; King, 15+8; Kotylo, 3+2; Love, 35+4; McGregor, 25; MacKenzie, 33; Mitchell, 1+3; Peake, 21+1; Prindiville, 1; Simpson, 30+5; Sykes, 10+15; Taylor, 19+1; Thackeray, 21+2; Weaver, 27+1; White, 0+3; Williams B, 22+7; Williams J, 19+4; Wray, 17+1; Young, 9+1.
Goals (60): McGregor 13, Barnes 10, Charles 5, Francis 5, Angus 4, King 4 (1 pen), Peake 4, Sykes 4, Williams B 3, Wray 3, Thackeray 2, Williams J 2, own goals 2.

Northwich Victoria

Appearances: Bailey, 26+7; Barnard, 23; Bates, 21+2; Blundell, 14+1; Burke, 29+5; Challender, 3+4; Cooke, 1+7; Davis, 18; Devlin, 41; Ellis, 8+3; Fletcher, 21+3; Halcroft, 10+7; Henry, 3+1; Houghton, 0+1; Key, 33; Kimmins, 4+3; Laurie, 1+8; Lewis, 8+4; McDermott, 1+2; Mike, 31+4; Mitchell, 4+12; Newhouse, 0+1; Norris, 38+1; Poland, 3+7; Quigley, 0+2; Quinn, 7; Rachel, 1; Rigby, 8; Robertson, 34+1; Robinson, 2; Rose, 8+3; Simpson, 16+1; Taaffe, 1; Talbot, 19; Vicary, 14+4; Walling, 8+6; Walsh, 3+10.
Goals (49): Mike 9, Devlin 8, Fletcher 8, Blundell 4, Quinn 4, Bailey 3, Barnard 2 (1 pen), Lewis 2, Mitchell 2, Burke 1, Cooke 1, Halcroft 1, Norris 1, Simpson 1, Talbot 1, Vicary 1.

Rushden & Diamonds

Appearances: Bradshaw, 0+1; Brady, 39+2; Burgess, 37+3; Butterworth, 40+1; Carey, 32+1; Collins, 0+1; Darby 38; Essandoh, 0+2; Gray, 4+2; Iga, 0+1; Jackson 40; Mills, 12+9; Mustafa, 41; Naylor, 0+1; Peters 20+2; Rogers, 1; Rodwell, 28+2; Sale, 0+2; Setchell, 19+10; Sigere, 5+15; Solkhon, 1; Town, 1+2; Turley, 41; Underwood, 23+2; Warburton, 37; Wormull, 3+5.
Goals (78): Darby 24 (3 pens), Jackson 18 (1 pen), Brady 11, Burgess 7, Sigere 6, Underwood 3 (2 pens), Peters 2, Butterworth 1, Carey 1, Setchell 1, Town 1, Warburton 1, Wormull 1, own goal 1.

Scarborough

Appearances: Atkinson, 15+1; Betts, 21; Blunt, 10; Brodie, 28+2; Brunton, 30; Burt, 10+4; Diallo, 15+6; Di Lella, 3+1; Dowson, 1+5; Ellender, 36; Faure, 12+4; Gildea, 0+3; Ingram 25; Jewell, 1; Jones, 15+1; Jordan, 5+3; Keegan, 2; Lyth, 5+1; Morris, 1+14; Newton, 0+1; Piercewright, 1+3; Pounder, 33+6; Priestley, 6; Reed, 2+1; Rennison, 32+2; Robinson, 4; Russell, 18+1; Savic, 2; Shuttleworth, 2; Stamp, 1; Stoker, 31+7; Tate, 8+3; Thompson, 18; Toone, 0+1; Williams, 32+2; Windross, 1+3; Woods, 36.
Goals (56): Brodie 10, Pounder 9, Diallo 8, Williams 7, Ellender 6, Betts 4 (3 pens), Burt 2, Jordan 2, Rennison 2, Thompson 2, Ingram 1, Stoker 1, Tate 1, own goal 1.

Southport

Appearances: Arnold, 33+4; Bolland, 33+1; Bradshaw, 2; Burke, 0+1; Clark, 34+2; Dickinson, 42; Elam, 14+14; Furlong, 13+11; Gouck, 26; Grayston, 39+2; Guyett, 36; Jones 2; Lane, 18; Linighan, 15+4; Macauley, C, 12+1; McAuley, S, 1; Maamria, 15+10; Marsh, 35; Obong, 2+3; O'Brien, 2+1; Parke, 29+5; Pell, 0+2; Stuart, 19+4; Teale, 26+7; Underwood, 1; Whittaker, 13+15.

Goals (58): Arnold 13 (2 pens), Parke 13, Marsh 7 (5 pens), Whittaker 5, Maamria 3, Clark 2, Guyett 2, Lane 2, Linighan 2, Obong 2, Stuart 2, Elam 1, Furlong 1, Gouck 1, Grayston 1, Jones 1.

Stevenage Borough

Appearances: Abbot, 2+3, Armstrong, 25+16; Ayres, 2; Boylan, 1; Bradshaw, 7; Bridge, 0+3; Brissett, 1+1; Broughton, 4; Brown, 0+1; Bunce, 24+1; Clarke, 34+2; Cort, 8+1; Duckett, 0+1; Dyer, 2+2; Graham, 9+1; Hampshire, 18; Hay, 24+4; Hockton, 0+1; Illman, 24+10; Kirby, 18+4; Leadbeater, 5+1; McMahon, 27; Martin, 28+2; Metcalfe, 6+2; Miller, 24+8; Morgan, 12+6; Nyamah, 5+4; Pearson, 0+4; Phillips, 18+2; Searle, 5; Sodje, 8+1; Smith 35; Taylor 15; Trott, 28+1; Walters, 7; Wilkerson, 27; Worrell, 1; Wraight, 8.
Goals (71): Hay 15, Illman 11, Clarke 9 (2 pens), Armstrong 8, Martin 4, Broughton 3, Leadbeater 3, McMahon 2, Morgan 2, Pearson 2, Trott 2, Walters 2, Bunce 1, Graham 1, Hampshire 1 (pen), Kirby 1, Phillips 1, Sodje 1, Wraight 1, own goals 2.

Telford United

Appearances: Albrighton, 25+1; Bentley, 23; Bridgewater, 1+3; Cartwright, 3+4; Davies, 31+1; Edwards J, 23+9; Edwards S, 0+1; Fitzpatrick, 5+5; Fowler, 21; Gale, 18; Huckerby, 4+12; Jobling, 41; McGorry, 35; Malkin, 14+7; Martindale, 28+4; Moore, 37; Murphy, 17+12; Palmer, 38; Preece, 9+5; Price, 21; Sandwith, 13+3; Travis, 34+2; Williams, 21+1.
Goals (51): Edwards J 10; Martindale 7 (2 pens), Murphy 7, Palmer 5, Jobling 4, Malkin 4, Moore 3, Albrighton 2, Bentley 2, Huckerby 2, Travis 2, Davies 1, Preece 1, own goal 1.

Woking

Appearances: Alighien, 1+5; Basford, 3; Baverstock, 1; Boardman, 9; Brown, 9+3; Da Costa, 0+3; Davies, 1; Drewett, 0+1; Druce, 4+4; Edghill, 1+1; Flahavan, 6; Fowler, 0+1; Griffin, 25+3; Hayfield, 27+4; Hollingdale, 35+1; Kadi, 9+11; Martin J, 5; Martin, 1; Matassa, 26; Metcalfe, 5+2; O'Donnell, 1; Ormerod, 8; Panter, 0+3; Perkins, 35+5; Pitman, 27+2; Randall, 22+7; Reeks, 5+3; Roddis, 36+1; Ruggles, 0+2; Sharpling, 14; Smith 33; Steele P, 6; Steele S, 36+4; Taylor, 4+3; Teague, 1+14; Watson, 8+5; West, 38+2; Wilkinson, 2+1; Woodcock, 0+1; Wright, 3; Wye, 15.
Goals (52): Griffin 13 (1 pen), Sharpling 9, Steele S 9 (4 pens), Randall 7, West 3, Hayfield 2 (1 pen), Kadi 2, Perkins 2, Pitman 1, Steele P 1, Watson 1, own goals 2.

Yeovil Town

Appearances: Barlow, 0+1; Belgrave, 36+3; Bent, 15+11; Betts, 14+3; Crittenden, 42; Forinton, 1+1; Foster, 0+2; Giles, 0+1; Gritton, 3+1; Jones, 10+2; Lindegard, 13+14; McIndoe, 13+3; Meechan 0+1; O'Brien, 15+11; Patmore, 35+1; Pennock, 40; Peters, 4+2; Piper, 35+1; Poole, 2+4; Risbridger, 0+1; Skiverton, 39; Smith, 29+3; Steele, 9+6; Thompson, 0+2; Tonkin, 37; Way, 40+1; Weale, 2+2; White, 28+2.
Goals (73): Patmore 18, Belgrave 9, Way 9 (5 pens), Bent 6, Crittenden 6, Smith 4, Steele 4, McIndoe 3, Skiverton 3, Tonkin 3, Betts 1, Forinton 1, O'Brien 1, Piper 1, White 1, own goals 4.

NATIONWIDE VARIETY CLUB TROPHY

First Round
Boston United 1, Nuneaton Borough 5
Dagenham & Redbridge 1, Stevenage Borough 2
Hayes 3, Woking 5
Hednesford Town 1, Telford United 0
Kettering Town 3, Forest Green Rovers 0
Northwich Victoria 3, Leigh RMI 3
Replay: Leigh RMI 1, Northwich Victoria 0

Second Round
Chester City 2, Hednesford Town 2
Replay: Hednesford Town 1, Chester City 1
Dover Athletic 0, Kingstonian 1
Hereford United 0, Kettering Town 1
Morecambe 5, Leigh RMI 2
Nuneaton Borough 2, Scarborough 0
Rushden & Diamonds 2, Stevenage Borough 1

Southport 1, Doncaster Rovers 0
Woking 0, Yeovil Town 1

Quarter-Finals
Kingstonian 1, Rushden & Diamonds 0
Nuneaton Borough 2, Morecambe 0
Southport 0, Chester City 3
Yeovil Town 2, Kettering Town 0

Semi-Finals
Chester City 2, Nuneaton Borough 1
Yeovil Town 0, Kingstonian 5

Final
Kingstonian 0, Chester City 0
Chester City won 4-2 on penalties.

UNIBOND LEAGUE 2000–2001

Premier Division

	P	W	D	L	F	A	W	D	L	F	A	Pts
			Home		*Goals*			*Away*		*Goals*		
Stalybridge Celtic	44	19	1	2	57	15	12	8	2	39	17	102
Emley	44	16	5	1	44	19	15	3	4	43	23	101
Bishop Auckland	44	15	2	5	45	24	11	5	6	43	29	85
Lancaster City	44	15	4	3	48	27	9	5	8	36	33	81
Worksop Town	44	10	8	4	60	30	10	5	7	42	30	73
Barrow	44	14	3	5	49	26	7	6	9	34	37	72
Altrincham	44	13	4	5	45	24	7	6	9	35	34	70
Gainsborough Trinity	44	13	6	3	35	19	4	8	10	24	37	65
Accrington Stanley	44	12	4	6	44	34	6	6	10	28	33	64
Hucknall Town	44	11	4	7	34	30	6	8	8	23	33	63
Gateshead	44	9	7	6	39	26	7	5	10	29	35	60
Bamber Bridge	44	9	3	10	34	31	8	5	9	29	34	59
Runcorn	44	12	5	5	35	27	3	5	14	21	43	55
Blyth Spartans	44	10	6	6	28	17	5	3	14	33	47	54
Burscough	44	8	6	8	32	27	6	4	12	27	41	52
Hyde United	44	9	8	5	48	36	4	4	14	24	43	51
Whitby Town	44	4	8	10	27	35	9	3	10	33	41	50
Marine	44	8	7	7	30	31	4	6	12	32	47	49
Colwyn Bay	44	9	6	7	42	45	3	4	15	26	57	46
Frickley Athletic	44	6	8	8	31	34	4	7	11	19	45	45
Droylsden	44	7	3	12	29	40	6	3	13	21	40	45
Leek Town	44	8	5	9	26	30	4	3	15	19	40	44
Spennymoor United*	44	3	2	17	17	48	1	3	18	15	60	16

* 1 point deducted for breach of rule

First Division

	P	W	D	L	F	A	W	D	L	F	A	Pts
			Home		*Goals*			*Away*		*Goals*		
Bradford Park Avenue	42	14	2	5	43	19	14	3	4	40	21	89
Vauxhall Motors	42	13	5	3	53	20	10	5	6	42	30	79
Ashton United	42	12	6	3	53	22	11	3	7	38	27	78
Stocksbridge Park Steels	42	10	6	5	47	35	9	7	5	33	25	70
Trafford*	42	12	5	4	36	25	8	4	9	34	37	68
Belper Town	42	8	7	6	37	32	10	4	7	34	30	65
Witton Albion	42	10	7	4	29	20	5	9	7	22	30	61
Ossett Town	42	10	6	5	34	27	6	6	9	32	31	60
Radcliffe Borough	42	10	4	7	38	27	7	4	10	34	44	59
Chorley	42	7	9	5	40	34	8	5	8	31	36	59
Harrogate Town	42	9	6	6	39	30	6	4	11	21	40	55
Matlock Town	42	8	5	8	40	42	6	5	10	30	32	52
North Ferriby United	42	10	2	9	33	37	4	8	9	31	36	52
Workington	42	8	5	8	26	27	5	7	9	27	33	51
Lincoln United	42	11	5	5	35	25	2	7	12	25	50	51
Gretna	42	8	5	8	42	33	4	7	10	30	49	48
Guiseley	42	6	8	7	19	22	5	7	9	18	28	48
Kendal Town*	42	9	7	5	35	24	3	5	13	25	45	47
Farsley Celtic	42	7	3	11	26	31	5	8	8	27	40	47
Eastwood Town	42	7	5	9	21	29	6	3	12	19	34	47
Winsford United**	42	6	8	7	35	33	7	3	11	26	37	44
Congleton Town	42	6	2	13	24	44	2	4	15	19	50	30

* 1 point deducted for breach of rule
** 6 points deducted for breach of rule

LEADING GOALSCORERS
(In order of League Goals)
Premier Division

Lge	Cup	Tot	
29	14	43	Chris Ward (Lancaster City)
28	12	40	Kirk Jackson (Worksop Town)
24	9	33	Nicky Peverill (Barrow)
23	8	31	Simeon Bambrook (Emley)
22	10	32	Simon Yeo (Hyde United)
22	9	31	Andy Shaw (Bishop Auckland)
22	7	29	Glen Robson (Blyth Spartans)
22	7	29	Andy Whittaker (Bamber Bridge)
22	5	27	Rod Thornley (Altrincham)
			(13 + 5 for Congleton Town)

First Division

Lge	Cup	Tot	
28	3	31	Mark Dobie (Gretna)
25	4	29	Nicky Young (Vauxhall Motors)
24	3	27	Andy Haward (Bradford Park Avenue)
			(2 for Frickley Athletic)
22	8	30	Steve Taylor (Matlock Town)
22	6	28	Gary Hurlstone (Stocksbridge Park Steels)
22	4	26	Danny Mills (Chorley)
21	1	22	Danny Worthington (Winsford United)
20	6	26	Darren Emmett (Trafford)

UNIBOND CLUB OF THE MONTH AWARD

August	Stalybridge Celtic
September	Emley
October	Barrow
November	Gainsborough Trinity
December	Hucknall Town
January	Emley
February	Stalybridge Celtic
March	Lancaster City
April	Stalybridge Celtic

UNIBOND CLUB OF THE MONTH AWARD

August	Ashton United
September	Vauxhall Motors
October	Belper Town
November	Belper Town
December	Chorley
January	Vauxhall Motors
February	Bradford Park Avenue
March	Trafford
April	Bradford Park Avenue

ATTENDANCES
Premier Division
Premier Division
Highest Attendance: 3708 Emley v Stalybridge Celtic

ATTENDANCES
Division One
Highest Attendance: 538 Matlock Town v Belper Town

UNIBOND LEAGUE — PREMIER DIVISION RESULTS 2000–2001

	Accrington Stanley	Altrincham	Bamber Bridge	Barrow	Bishop Auckland	Blyth Spartans	Burscough	Colwyn Bay	Droylsden	Emley	Frickley Athletic	Gainsborough Trinity	Gateshead	Hucknall Town	Hyde United	Lancaster City	Leek Town	Marine	Runcorn	Spennymoor United	Stalybridge Celtic	Whitby Town	Worksop Town
Accrington Stanley	—	2-1	1-3	2-1	3-1	3-3	2-0	2-2	3-0	3-1	1-1	1-1	3-1	1-2	4-1	1-2	2-1	3-2	2-1	1-0	1-4	0-2	3-4
Altrincham	5-2	—	1-2	1-1	0-2	3-1	2-2	3-0	3-0	0-2	3-1	0-2	3-2	1-0	2-0	3-1	1-1	3-1	2-1	5-0	0-0	3-1	1-2
Bamber Bridge	3-0	1-1	—	1-2	0-2	1-3	0-1	3-4	2-1	1-1	0-1	2-0	4-2	1-3	2-1	1-4	1-0	2-0	3-1	0-0	0-2	5-0	1-2
Barrow	3-0	2-3	3-1	—	1-4	2-0	2-2	3-2	2-0	1-3	2-0	3-2	3-1	5-0	1-0	2-2	3-0	1-0	1-2	5-0	0-0	2-3	2-1
Bishop Auckland	2-1	2-0	5-2	2-2	—	1-0	4-0	5-1	2-1	1-3	2-0	3-1	0-1	2-0	3-1	1-3	3-1	1-1	0-2	2-0	0-2	2-1	2-1
Blyth Spartans	1-0	1-1	0-0	1-1	1-2	—	1-0	5-2	0-1	2-1	3-0	1-0	2-1	1-1	0-0	0-1	0-0	4-1	3-0	0-1	1-2	0-2	1-0
Burscough	0-0	1-1	3-0	1-2	2-1	3-1	—	1-2	3-1	0-1	1-2	1-1	0-1	2-1	2-1	2-3	1-0	1-3	0-0	4-1	1-1	2-3	2-2
Colwyn Bay	2-4	1-2	1-1	2-1	3-3	1-0	4-1	—	3-2	0-4	0-0	3-3	2-2	0-2	2-4	1-2	4-1	2-3	0-2	3-2	1-7	2-3	3-2
Droylsden	0-4	2-1	0-1	2-1	0-3	1-2	1-2	1-0	—	1-3	3-2	4-0	0-0	1-1	3-1	3-2	1-0	2-3	2-1	4-1	0-1	1-3	2-5
Emley	1-0	3-1	1-0	0-0	3-1	1-0	2-1	4-1	2-1	—	1-3	1-0	2-0	0-0	1-1	1-0	1-1	3-2	1-1	3-3	2-3	4-0	5-3
Frickley Athletic	0-2	3-3	1-2	3-2	0-1	4-2	1-0	6-2	1-1	1-3	—	2-2	1-0	1-2	2-1	0-0	1-3	0-1	1-1	2-0	0-0	1-1	1-5
Gainsborough Trinity	2-0	1-0	2-0	2-0	0-0	4-2	2-1	1-0	0-1	1-0	2-2	—	0-2	1-1	3-0	1-1	4-1	2-0	5-1	2-1	0-0	1-3	1-1
Gateshead	0-0	2-1	0-2	1-2	0-3	2-5	1-1	4-2	1-1	2-0	5-0	1-0	—	1-2	1-2	1-0	2-1	3-0	1-0	4-0	2-2	1-1	0-0
Hucknall Town	2-0	1-3	1-0	1-4	2-5	4-1	3-2	1-0	1-2	1-2	3-1	0-1	2-2	—	1-2	3-1	2-0	1-1	1-1	1-0	2-2	0-1	1-1
Hyde United	3-3	4-2	1-4	4-4	1-1	6-2	1-1	1-1	3-2	0-2	0-0	2-1	3-1	5-1	—	1-1	2-1	2-1	3-1	4-0	1-2	3-2	1-3
Lancaster City	1-1	4-1	3-2	1-1	1-0	1-1	5-2	1-0	1-0	1-2	2-1	2-1	2-0	4-1	1-4	—	3-2	3-1	2-1	2-0	3-2	3-1	2-0
Leek Town	0-2	0-0	1-1	2-1	3-1	0-4	4-0	2-4	1-1	2-1	2-1	2-2	1-2	0-0	2-0	0-2	—	2-2	4-1	3-1	0-2	0-1	0-3
Marine	1-1	0-4	2-1	1-2	1-3	1-1	3-5	2-0	1-0	0-1	1-0	1-1	1-1	1-1	1-4	1-1	2-0	—	4-1	2-2	0-3	4-1	0-1
Runcorn	2-0	0-2	2-3	3-1	4-4	1-0	2-0	1-1	3-1	1-1	0-5	0-3	1-2	2-1	1-1	1-0	0-1	2-2	—	2-0	2-1	1-2	0-1
Spennymoor United	1-6	0-4	1-2	2-3	0-3	1-2	1-1	3-2	0-1	0-2	3-0	7-1	1-4	0-1	4-0	0-3	2-0	2-2	2-0	—	0-1	1-1	0-4
Stalybridge Celtic	4-0	1-0	3-0	1-3	2-0	2-0	0-2	4-0	4-1	0-1	2-2	0-1	2-1	1-0	1-2	5-0	1-2	2-1	3-1	3-2	—	1-0	0-1
Whitby Town	0-0	2-2	1-1	0-2	1-1	1-0	0-2	5-1	0-1	1-1	2-2	1-1	0-1	2-2	3-2	1-5	1-2	3-2	3-1	3-3	1-1	—	1-0
Worksop Town	0-2	1-2	1-1	4-2	1-2	4-3	1-0	1-1	5-0	1-2	12-0	1-1	2-2	1-1	1-3	4-2	3-1	3-3	1-1	6-0	1-1	3-2	—

UNIBOND LEAGUE — FIRST DIVISION RESULTS 2000–2001

	Ashton United	Belper Town	Bradford Park Avenue	Chorley	Congleton Town	Eastwood Town	Farsley Celtic	Gretna	Guiseley	Harrogate Town	Kendal Town	Lincoln United	Matlock Town	North Ferriby United	Ossett Town	Radcliffe Borough	Stocksbridge Park Steels	Trafford	Vauxhall Motors	Winsford United	Witton Albion	Workington
Ashton United	—	3-4	0-2	2-1	4-1	0-2	1-0	9-2	0-0	4-1	8-1	3-1	2-2	0-0	1-1	3-0	3-2	0-0	2-0	1-0	0-0	2-1
Belper Town	0-4	—	0-2	1-1	3-1	4-0	2-2	0-0	1-1	1-1	3-2	3-1	3-1	2-2	0-1	4-6	1-2	0-2	1-1	4-1	2-1	2-0
Bradford Park Avenue	1-2	2-1	—	2-1	1-2	4-1	3-0	2-2	3-0	4-2	4-0	2-0	0-2	2-1	3-2	0-1	1-0	1-0	0-1	4-0	4-1	1-0
Chorley	2-1	1-1	1-1	—	1-1	3-1	1-4	2-2	1-1	1-0	2-2	8-1	1-1	3-2	1-1	3-3	0-1	0-3	5-5	2-0	0-1	1-2
Congleton Town	0-1	1-4	0-2	1-1	—	2-0	1-3	1-1	3-1	1-3	2-0	0-0	2-1	1-4	2-1	0-1	0-3	2-6	0-2	1-2	2-2	0-3
Eastwood Town	2-1	0-0	0-1	3-1	1-0	—	1-1	4-1	0-1	0-2	2-0	0-0	0-4	3-1	0-2	2-1	0-2	2-2	0-4	1-0	2-2	2-2
Farsley Celtic	0-3	2-3	0-3	1-1	1-0	0-0	—	2-0	0-1	1-1	1-2	3-1	1-2	1-1	3-2	1-3	1-2	1-0	1-2	2-3	3-0	2-1
Gretna	1-1	1-2	0-1	2-2	5-1	0-1	3-3	—	1-1	2-0	4-3	2-3	2-0	5-4	1-0	3-2	1-1	7-1	1-2	1-1	1-2	1-2
Guiseley	1-2	1-1	0-0	1-1	0-1	0-2	1-1	0-0	—	1-0	0-0	3-2	0-4	1-1	0-3	4-1	1-1	0-1	1-1	3-0	1-0	1-0
Harrogate Town	3-2	3-1	1-2	3-1	5-1	3-0	0-3	2-2	1-1	—	0-3	5-0	2-1	1-0	0-4	2-2	1-1	4-1	1-2	2-2	0-2	0-0
Kendal Town	4-3	1-0	0-1	2-2	4-0	1-1	1-2	0-1	1-1	0-0	—	1-0	2-0	2-2	2-2	1-0	3-2	1-2	3-1	1-2	2-2	2-0
Lincoln United	1-2	3-2	2-2	1-1	2-1	1-0	2-0	3-1	3-1	0-1	1-0	—	0-1	2-1	1-0	2-0	1-2	2-2	4-4	1-1	3-0	2-2
Matlock Town	0-1	2-1	1-4	2-1	4-2	0-4	1-2	7-0	2-0	3-1	3-3	2-1	—	2-2	2-0	3-2	1-2	1-4	0-3	1-2	2-2	2-2
North Ferriby United	1-3	3-0	2-1	3-2	2-1	2-0	2-1	2-6	1-0	4-1	2-2	3-1	2-2	—	2-0	1-2	2-2	1-3	3-2	0-3	0-2	0-1
Ossett Town	0-3	1-2	1-1	1-1	1-1	2-0	0-1	0-0	0-1	3-0	2-1	1-2	1-0	0-3	—	5-2	1-1	3-1	1-3	3-2	0-1	2-1
Radcliffe Borough	2-3	0-4	1-2	0-1	3-1	1-0	6-0	4-1	4-2	3-0	1-0	2-2	1-1	4-0	5-2	—	1-1	2-0	1-0	1-2	0-0	4-2
Stocksbridge Park Steels	2-2	2-2	1-2	2-2	3-1	4-1	2-2	4-1	1-1	4-1	1-0	3-3	1-0	0-1	3-3	1-2	—	1-2	1-0	2-1	5-2	1-1
Trafford	3-1	1-0	1-3	0-3	2-0	0-1	5-0	1-0	1-1	8-1	2-2	1-0	1-4	0-1	2-1	2-2	3-1	—	2-1	3-1	2-1	1-4
Vauxhall Motors	0-2	3-1	2-0	0-2	3-0	1-1	0-0	3-2	3-0	2-0	1-0	2-2	0-3	0-3	2-2	1-1	1-2	4-2	—	2-0	1-1	4-0
Winsford United	1-0	1-2	1-2	1-0	2-2	2-3	2-2	3-3	0-3	2-2	1-3	2-2	1-2	1-1	0-0	1-2	0-3	3-2	2-2	—	0-0	2-2
Witton Albion	1-1	0-1	2-2	1-1	0-0	3-1	3-0	1-4	1-0	0-3	1-0	3-0	2-2	0-2	2-0	3-1	5-2	2-0	1-4	0-0	—	1-1
Workington	2-0	0-1	2-5	2-0	3-2	1-0	2-1	0-1	0-1	0-3	2-0	2-2	2-2	4-2	0-1	2-0	2-1	0-0	0-2	1-3	1-1	—

UNIBOND LEAGUE CHALLENGE CUP 2000–2001

GROUP 1

	P	W	D	L	F	A	Pts
Bishop Auckland	4	3	0	1	11	8	9
Blyth Spartans	4	2	1	1	7	7	7
Gateshead	4	1	2	1	6	4	5
Whitby Town	4	0	3	1	4	6	3
Spennymoor United	4	0	2	2	4	7	2

GROUP 2

	P	W	D	L	F	A	Pts
Lancaster City	4	4	0	0	9	2	12
Workington	4	3	0	1	9	4	9
Barrow	4	2	0	2	6	6	6
Gretna	4	0	1	3	5	10	1
Kendal Town	4	0	1	3	2	9	1

GROUP 3

	P	W	D	L	F	A	Pts
Farsley Celtic	4	2	1	1	5	3	7
Harrogate Town	4	1	3	0	5	4	6
Emley	4	2	0	2	5	5	6
Bradford Park Avenue	4	1	2	1	7	8	5
Frickley Athletic	4	0	2	2	5	7	2

GROUP 4

	P	W	D	L	F	A	Pts
Hyde United	4	3	1	0	15	7	10
Ashton United	4	2	1	1	12	8	7
Altrincham	4	1	2	1	8	6	5
Stocksbridge Park Steels	4	1	1	2	10	14	4
Ossett Town	4	0	1	3	6	16	1

GROUP 5

	P	W	D	L	F	A	Pts
Bamber Bridge	4	4	0	0	9	2	12
Accrington Stanley	4	2	1	1	12	6	7
Runcorn	4	2	1	1	9	4	7
Trafford	4	1	0	3	7	15	3
Winsford United	4	0	0	4	3	13	0

GROUP 6

	P	W	D	L	F	A	Pts
Marine	4	3	0	1	9	6	9
Vauxhall Motors	4	3	0	1	6	3	9
Burscough	4	2	1	1	9	6	7
Witton Albion	4	1	1	2	5	8	4
Colwyn Bay	4	0	0	4	3	9	0

GROUP 7

	P	W	D	L	F	A	Pts
Droylsden	4	3	1	0	9	6	10
Stalybridge Celtic	4	3	0	1	11	6	9
Chorley	4	2	0	2	11	9	6
Radcliffe Borough	4	1	1	2	5	7	4
Congleton Town	4	0	0	4	3	11	0

GROUP 8

	P	W	D	L	F	A	Pts
Gainsborough Trinity*	4	4	0	0	9	2	9
Worksop Town	4	1	2	1	9	9	5
Guiseley	4	1	2	1	5	6	5
Lincoln United	4	1	1	2	5	6	4
North Ferriby United	4	0	1	3	2	7	1

Gainsborough Trinity deducted 3 points for breach of rules.

GROUP 9

	P	W	D	L	F	A	Pts
Belper Town	4	4	0	0	15	3	12
Hucknall Town	4	3	0	1	7	4	9
Leek Town	4	2	0	2	6	8	6
Matlock Town	4	1	0	3	5	11	3
Eastwood Town	4	0	0	4	2	9	0

Top 8 group winners qualified for Quarter-finals.

Top 7 runners-up qualified for President's Cup along with Farsley Celtic.

Harrogate Town and Worksop Town qualified for the Chairman's Cup.

Top 6 Third placed teams qualified for the Chairman's Cup with Harrogate Town and Worksop Town.

QUARTER-FINALS
Belper Town 1, Droylsden 0
Hyde United 0, Bishop Auckland 2
Lancaster City 1, Bamber Bridge 0
Marine 2, Gainsborough Trinity 1

SEMI-FINALS
Lancaster City 6, Belper Town 1
Marine 0, Bishop Auckland 3

FINAL
Lancaster City 2, Bishop Auckland 2
Lancaster City won 4-3 on penalties.

PRESIDENT'S CUP

QUARTER-FINALS
Ashton United 1, Stalybridge Celtic 2
Blyth Spartans 1, Workington 0
Farsley Celtic 0, Accrington Stanley 3
Hucknall Town 2, Vauxhall Motors 4

FINAL
Blyth Spartans 3, Stalybridge Celtic 3
Stalybridge Celtic won 3-2 on penalties.

SEMI-FINALS
Blyth Spartans 2, Accrington Stanley 1
Stalybridge Celtic 2, Vauxhall Motors 1

CHAIRMAN'S CUP

QUARTER-FINALS
Barrow 4, Emley 2
Burscough 0, Worksop Town 1
Chorley 2, Leek Town 0
Harrogate Town 1, Runcorn 0

FINAL
Harrogate Town 1, Barrow 1
Barrow won 3-0 on penalties.

SEMI-FINALS
Chorley 0, Barrow 2
Harrogate Town 1, Worksop Town 0

DR MARTENS LEAGUE 2000–2001

Premier Division	P	W	D	L	F	A	GD	Pts
Margate	42	28	7	7	75	27	48	91
Burton Albion	42	25	13	4	76	36	40	88
King's Lynn	42	18	11	13	67	58	9	65
Welling United	42	17	13	12	59	55	4	64
Weymouth	42	17	12	13	69	51	18	63
Havant & Waterlooville	42	18	9	15	66	54	12	63
Stafford Rangers	42	18	9	15	76	59	11	63
Worcester City	42	18	8	16	52	53	–1	62
Moor Green	42	18	8	16	50	53	–3	62
Newport County	42	17	10	15	70	61	9	61
Crawley Town	42	17	10	15	61	54	7	61
Tamworth	42	18	8	17	58	55	3	59
Salisbury City	42	17	8	17	64	69	–5	59
Ilkeston Town	42	16	11	15	51	61	–10	59
Bath City*	42	15	13	14	67	68	–1	55
Cambridge City	42	13	11	18	56	59	–3	50
Folkestone Invicta	42	14	6	22	49	74	–25	48
Merthyr Tydfil	42	11	13	18	49	62	–13	46
Clevedon Town	42	11	7	24	61	74	–13	40
Fisher Athletic Lon*	42	12	6	24	51	85	–34	39
Dorchester Town	42	10	8	24	40	71	–31	38
Halesowen Town	42	8	13	21	47	69	–22	37

(*Bath City & Fisher Athletic London, 3 points deducted – ineligible player)

Eastern Division	P	W	D	L	F	A	GD	Pts
Newport (IW)	42	28	10	4	91	30	61	94
Chelmsford City	42	27	9	6	102	45	57	90
Grantham Town	42	25	11	6	100	47	53	86
Histon	42	23	11	8	84	53	31	80
Baldock Town	42	23	10	9	81	44	37	79
Hastings Town	42	22	10	10	72	50	22	76
Stamford	42	20	11	11	69	59	10	71
Tonbridge Angels	42	18	11	13	79	58	21	65
Langney Sports	42	19	8	15	75	55	20	65
Rothwell Town**	42	20	5	17	86	74	12	62
Corby Town	42	14	10	18	64	92	–28	52
Ashford Town	42	15	4	23	53	83	–30	49
Banbury United	42	12	11	19	57	54	3	47
Witney Town	42	12	11	19	55	71	–16	47
Bashley	42	10	14	18	57	71	–14	44
Dartford	42	11	11	20	49	67	–18	44
Burnham*	42	10	14	18	39	65	–26	43
Wisbech Town	42	10	9	23	45	89	–44	39
St Leonards	42	9	10	23	55	87	–32	37
Erith & Belvedere	42	10	7	25	49	92	–43	37
Sittingbourne	42	8	9	25	41	79	–38	33
Spalding	42	7	12	23	35	73	–38	33

(*Burnham 1 point deducted, **Rothwell Town 3 points deducted – ineligible players)

Western Division	P	W	D	L	F	A	GD	Pts
Hinckley United	42	30	8	4	102	38	64	98
Tiverton Town	42	28	7	7	97	36	61	91
Bilston Town	42	27	9	6	88	48	40	90
Evesham United	42	27	5	10	86	46	40	86
Mangotsfield United	42	25	9	8	91	45	46	84
Solihull Borough	42	22	12	8	73	43	30	78
Redditch United	42	17	13	12	76	69	7	64
Weston-Super-Mare	42	17	10	15	68	58	10	61
Atherstone United	42	16	11	15	64	58	6	59
Rocester	42	18	5	19	57	77	–20	59
Cirencester Town	42	14	15	13	65	74	–9	57
Rugby United	42	13	10	19	51	68	–17	49
Gloucester City	42	12	11	19	76	86	–10	47
Blakenall*	42	13	10	19	54	64	–10	46
Shepshed Dynamo	42	12	9	21	56	73	–17	45
Bedworth United	42	12	9	21	38	60	–22	45
Racing Club Warwick	42	13	6	23	46	77	–31	45
Gresley Rovers	42	11	8	23	46	65	–19	41
Cinderford Town	42	11	8	23	56	84	–28	41
Sutton Coldfield Town	42	7	14	21	45	66	–21	35
Paget Rangers	42	9	4	29	38	93	–55	31
Bromsgrove Rovers	42	7	9	26	47	92	–45	30

(*Blakenall 3 points deducted – ineligible player)

LEADING GOALSCORERS
(League and Cup)
(up to and including Saturday 5 May 2001

Premier Division

Philip Collins (Margate)	31
Gary Shepherd (Newport County)	26
Mark Owen (Worcester City)	22
Darren Rowbotham (Weymouth)	19
Warren Haughton (Tamworth)	18
Lyndon Rowland (King's Lynn)	18
Paul Sales (Salisbury City)	18
Scott Dundas (Stafford Rangers)	17
Andrew Mainwaring (Clevedon Town)	17
Martin Paul (Bath City)	17
Mark Hallam (Tamworth)	16
Paul Chambers (Folkestone Invicta)	15
Mark Hynes (Crawley Town)	15
Darren Stride (Burton Albion)	15
Kevin Wilkin (Cambridge City)	15
Robert Gould (Ilkeston Town)	14
David Leworthy (Havant & Waterlooville)	14
John Palmer (King's Lynn)	14
Samuel Bowen (Halesowen Town)	13
David Laws (Weymouth)	13
Dean Wordsworth (Crawley Town)	13
Christian Moore (Burton Albion)	12
Mark Munday (Margate)	12
Joseph O'Connor (Stafford Rangers)	12

Eastern Division

Stephen Portway (Chelmsford City)	38
Gary Bull (Grantham Town)	31
Ashley Warner (Corby Town)	31
Wade Falana (Tonbridge Angels)	25
Neil Kennedy (Histon)	25
Malcolm Ndekwe (Stamford)	22
David Arter (Tonbridge Angels)	19
Dominic Barclay (St Leonards)	18
Gary Bennett (Chelmsford City)	18
Daniel Gibbons (Newport IW)	18
Matthew Gooderick (Banbury United)	17
Shaun Keeble (Stamford)	17
Christopher Arnold (Dartford)	16
Dean Foley (Rothwell Town)	16
Liam Morris (Rothwell Town)	15
Richard Ranshaw (Grantham Town)	15
Michael Bignall (Baldock Town)	14
Daniel Simmonds (Hastings Town)	14
Shaun Harrington (Histon)	13
Paul Jones (Hastings Town)	13
John Snelgrove (Langney Sports)	13
Matthew Allen (Langney Sports)	12
Gary Harrison (Banbury United)	12
Stuart Myall (Hastings Town)	12
Stephen White (Erith & Belvedere)	12

Western Division

Scott Voice (Bilston Town)	36
Christopher Smith (Solihull Borough)	25
David Sadler (Hinckley United)	23
Darren Edwards (Mangotsfield United)	22
Jody Bevan (Weston-Super-Mare)	21
Simon Tucker (Gresley Rovers)	21
James Cox (Gloucester City)	19
Karl Bayliss (Gloucester City)	18
Stephen Ovens (Tiverton Town)	18
Andrew Lucas (Hinckley United)	17
Lee McGlinchey (Shepshed Dynamo)	17
Ian Bennett (Redditch United)	15
Jamie Lenton (Hinckley United)	15
Leon Mitchell (Sutton Coldfield)	15
David Seal (Mangotsfield United)	15
Robert Claridge (Mangotsfield United)	14
Giles Harris (Cirencester Town)	14
Paul Hunter (Hinckley United)	14
Leon Jackson (Bilston Town)	14
Stuart Payne (Evesham United)	14
Philip Everrett (Tiverton Town)	13
Lee Rollason (Bilston Town)	13
David Toomey (Tiverton Town)	13

DR MARTENS LEAGUE CUP

PRELIMINARY ROUND
Evesham United 1, Bilston Town 2
Merthyr Tydfil 1, Cirencester Town 0

FIRST ROUND
Worcester City 4, Blakenall 0
Cambridge City 1, Kings Lynn 2
Banbury United 0, Ilkeston Town 1
Bilston Town 2, Redditch United 1
Bromsgrove Rovers 0, Halesowen Town 2
Dorchester Town 2, Bashley 3
Fisher Athletic 0, Burnham 2
Gloucester City 2, Clevedon Town 1
Grantham Town 5, Wisbech Town 1
Margate 4, Tonbridge Angels 0
Salisbury City 2, Havant & Waterlooville 2
    Havant & Waterlooville won 3-2 on penalties.
Shepshed Dynamo 0, Moor Green 1
Sittingbourne 2, Ashford Town 2
    Ashford Town won 4-3 on penalties.
Stafford Rangers 1, Rocester 2
Tamworth 2, Burton Albion 1
Weston-Super-Mare 1, Tiverton Town 3
Solihull Borough 7, Paget Rangers 1
Stamford 2, Spalding United 0
Cinderford Town 0, Mangotsfield United 3
Gresley Rovers 2, Hinckley United 2
    Gresley Rovers won 3-2 on penalties.
Langney Sports 3, Welling United 0
Newport County 1, Merthyr Tydfil 0
Corby Town 0, Rothwell Town 7
Dartford 0, Crawley Town 1
Bath City 3, Witney Town 1
Sutton Coldfield Town 4, Bedworth United 0
Chelmsford City 1, Hastings Town 6
Folkestone Invicta 4, St Leonards 6
Racing Club Warwick 1, Atherstone United 2
Baldock Town 3, Erith & Belvedere 3
    Baldock Town won 9-8 on penalties.
Histon 2, Rugby United 0
Newport (IW) 2, Weymouth 1

SECOND ROUND
Newport County 5, Bath City 0
Tiverton Town 4, Havant & Waterlooville 0
Ashford Town 4, Burnham 1

Rocester 1, Bilston Town 4
Sutton Coldfield Town 1, Gresley Rovers 4
Tamworth 0, Worcester City 0
    Worcester City won 5-4 on penalties.
Histon 3, Stamford 4
Halesowen Town 0, Moor Green 1
Kings Lynn 2, Ilkeston Town 0
St Leonards 4, Langney Sports 2
Baldock Town 1, Margate 0
Crawley Town 1, Hastings Town 0
Rothwell Town 2, Grantham Town 1
Atherstone United 3, Solihull Borough 3
    Atherstone United won 4-2 on penalties.
Bashley 3, Newport (IW) 2
Mangotsfield United 1, Gloucester City 0

THIRD ROUND
Bilston Town 1, Moor Green 0
Stamford 1, Gresley Rovers 0
Worcester City 3, Atherstone United 2
Newport County 2, Mangotsfield United 0
Bashley 2, Tiverton Town 2
    Bashley won 5-4 on penalties.
Kings Lynn 4, Rothwell Town 1
Crawley Town 3, Baldock Town 0
St Leonards 1, Ashford Town 0

FOURTH ROUND
Stamford 2, Kings Lynn 3
Newport County 2, Bashley 0
Worcester City 3, Bilston Town 2
Crawley Town 3, St Leonards 0

SEMI-FINALS
Crawley Town 3, Kings Lynn 2
Newport County 3, Worcester City 5

FINAL FIRST LEG
Worcester City 4, Crawley Town 0

FINAL SECOND LEG
Crawley Town 1, Worcester City 0

DR MARTENS LEAGUE — PREMIER DIVISION RESULTS 2000–2001

	Bath City	Burton Albion	Cambridge City	Clevedon Town	Crawley Town	Dorchester Town	Fisher Athletic	Folkestone Invicta	Halesowen Town	Havant & Waterlooville	Ilkeston Town	King's Lynn	Margate	Merthyr Tydfil	Moor Green	Newport County	Salisbury City	Stafford Rangers	Tamworth	Welling United	Weymouth	Worcester City
Bath City	—	3-1	0-0	4-1	3-2	3-0	4-3	2-1	4-0	3-2	1-0	2-1	1-1	1-1	3-1	2-0	0-1	2-2	2-1	0-2	0-0	3-2
Burton Albion	2-2	—	2-2	1-0	1-0	1-1	3-0	0-2	1-0	4-0	0-0	1-2	2-0	1-0	2-0	2-1	5-0	0-0	3-1	1-1	1-0	1-0
Cambridge City	2-0	1-1	—	2-0	1-2	0-1	0-3	0-2	3-0	1-0	2-3	1-2	0-2	0-1	1-2	5-6	1-2	1-1	1-2	4-1	2-2	2-3
Clevedon Town	0-1	1-2	3-0	—	1-2	4-1	8-1	0-1	1-4	0-1	1-1	1-0	1-2	2-2	1-0	2-3	3-1	2-1	1-1	2-3	2-1	0-1
Crawley Town	1-2	2-2	1-2	1-0	—	1-0	4-3	4-1	2-1	2-0	1-2	3-0	0-0	3-1	0-3	1-2	5-1	2-2	0-2	2-1	2-1	1-0
Dorchester Town	4-3	1-3	1-0	1-0	2-2	—	2-2	1-0	1-2	0-1	1-1	0-1	0-1	4-0	0-3	0-3	2-1	0-2	1-1	0-3	1-1	0-1
Fisher Athletic	1-0	0-4	1-2	1-1	3-2	1-0	—	1-2	0-0	0-3	1-2	2-3	1-0	0-2	3-0	1-3	1-2	2-3	2-1	1-1	1-2	1-0
Folkestone Invicta	0-2	0-2	4-3	0-3	2-1	2-0	2-1	—	2-1	0-4	1-3	1-2	2-2	3-1	1-2	3-1	2-1	0-3	1-0	0-1	1-2	1-2
Halesowen Town	2-0	1-2	3-0	1-1	2-2	1-1	0-2	4-4	—	2-2	0-1	0-4	0-0	1-1	0-2	1-3	3-0	0-1	1-0	2-2	0-2	1-3
Havant & Waterlooville	2-0	1-1	4-2	1-0	0-0	2-1	3-2	1-4	0-0	—	0-1	4-1	2-3	1-0	0-0	3-0	3-1	2-0	3-2	0-1	5-1	2-0
Ilkeston Town	3-0	2-1	0-2	3-1	1-1	1-0	1-0	3-0	1-0	2-1	—	1-1	0-3	2-1	1-0	0-1	1-1	1-1	2-1	0-1	1-6	2-4
King's Lynn	1-1	1-1	0-4	3-1	2-0	2-0	0-1	0-0	2-2	2-2	2-0	—	1-4	1-0	0-1	2-3	2-1	3-2	6-0	2-0	2-1	0-0
Margate	2-0	1-3	2-1	2-0	3-0	3-2	5-0	3-2	1-0	1-0	2-0	3-1	—	3-2	0-1	0-0	1-1	3-1	1-0	5-0	3-0	3-0
Merthyr Tydfil	3-3	1-5	2-2	2-0	0-2	1-2	5-0	2-0	0-0	2-1	4-4	1-0	0-2	—	2-0	2-1	1-0	3-0	0-1	0-1	0-1	4-1
Moor Green	3-2	1-2	0-0	3-3	1-0	2-1	3-1	1-2	3-2	4-1	1-0	2-1	0-4	1-1	—	1-1	0-2	1-2	0-1	1-1	1-1	1-0
Newport County	3-0	1-1	3-0	5-2	3-1	5-0	0-4	5-0	0-2	2-2	3-1	1-3	0-0	2-0	0-1	—	1-3	1-0	0-1	1-1	0-0	0-1
Salisbury City	4-4	1-0	2-1	4-1	1-1	0-2	3-0	0-0	2-1	0-0	2-0	1-4	0-1	2-2	3-1	4-0	—	4-1	1-3	1-1	3-2	2-0
Stafford Rangers	6-2	0-2	1-1	4-1	1-2	1-0	3-0	3-0	0-1	3-2	4-2	0-1	0-2	1-0	0-2	1-1	4-2	—	1-1	5-2	3-2	1-2
Tamworth	3-1	2-3	0-0	0-2	0-2	2-2	2-0	1-0	3-2	2-2	3-0	2-0	1-0	4-0	0-1	1-0	4-1	2-0	—	3-3	2-3	1-2
Welling United	1-0	1-2	0-2	2-3	1-1	1-1	4-0	1-1	2-2	2-1	1-2	1-4	1-0	1-0	0-0	3-1	2-1	0-0	4-0	—	2-0	0-1
Weymouth	1-1	1-1	1-1	0-1	1-0	4-1	3-0	1-1	4-1	1-2	4-1	4-1	1-0	1-1	5-1	0-0	3-1	0-2	0-2	2-1	—	4-0
Worcester City	0-0	1-1	2-0	3-3	2-0	1-2	1-2	2-0	4-1	1-0	1-0	1-1	0-1	1-1	1-0	4-4	0-1	2-4	1-0	1-2	0-0	—

DR MARTENS LEAGUE — WESTERN DIVISION RESULTS 2000–2001

	Atherstone United	Bedworth United	Bilston Town	Blakenall	Bromsgrove Rovers	Cinderford Town	Cirencester Town	Evesham United	Gloucester City	Gresley Rovers	Hinckley United	Mangotsfield United	Paget Rangers	Racing Club Warwick	Redditch United	Rocester	Rugby United	Shepshed Dynamo	Solihull Borough	Sutton Coldfield Town	Tiverton Town	Weston super Mare
Atherstone United	—	1-0	0-3	2-0	3-2	3-0	2-2	1-2	2-3	1-1	1-2	0-5	3-1	2-0	3-1	0-2	0-1	2-0	0-3	1-1	2-1	0-0
Bedworth United	0-0	—	0-2	2-2	4-0	1-3	1-2	0-2	1-2	2-0	0-3	0-1	2-0	1-3	1-2	0-0	1-0	0-1	0-2	1-0	0-1	0-1
Bilston Town	2-1	4-1	—	2-0	5-5	2-1	1-1	1-0	3-0	3-1	0-2	2-4	2-0	5-2	0-0	3-3	1-1	1-0	3-3	4-0	1-0	3-1
Blakenall	0-2	0-0	2-3	—	3-1	3-0	1-0	0-1	3-3	0-1	1-2	1-2	4-1	0-1	1-1	3-2	0-3	2-2	1-2	2-2	0-3	0-4
Bromsgrove Rovers	0-2	1-2	0-2	3-1	—	1-0	1-1	1-3	0-1	1-1	0-1	1-3	2-1	1-3	0-4	2-1	1-3	3-3	0-3	3-0	0-1	0-4
Cinderford Town	2-5	3-3	0-3	1-2	0-1	—	5-1	0-1	2-3	1-0	2-3	0-2	2-2	0-2	2-0	0-4	4-0	1-2	1-3	1-3	1-3	5-2
Cirencester Town	1-1	0-3	2-0	1-0	3-1	0-2	—	1-2	4-2	0-0	1-2	2-2	0-1	2-1	3-3	1-0	4-0	1-0	1-3	3-3	2-2	1-0
Evesham United	1-1	2-2	0-1	2-1	3-3	3-1	1-1	—	3-2	2-1	0-1	4-0	4-2	5-1	2-3	4-1	3-2	4-2	3-2	2-1	1-2	2-0
Gloucester City	3-4	2-2	1-3	1-3	2-2	2-2	5-0	3-2	—	2-2	0-2	0-4	4-1	0-1	0-0	0-1	2-1	3-1	2-2	3-3	2-3	2-0
Gresley Rovers	1-1	1-2	3-5	0-3	1-0	4-0	2-2	1-3	1-3	—	0-1	0-1	2-0	1-0	1-1	1-2	2-1	5-0	0-2	3-2	0-1	1-2
Hinckley United	2-0	3-1	0-0	5-2	4-2	5-0	2-2	1-1	1-1	3-0	—	1-0	4-1	1-1	4-2	3-0	3-0	3-0	2-1	2-1	3-1	1-2
Mangotsfield United	1-3	2-0	2-1	3-0	1-3	2-2	1-1	1-2	2-1	0-3	2-2	—	8-0	0-0	2-0	7-0	1-1	1-3	0-3	4-0	2-0	4-2
Paget Rangers	1-4	0-0	0-2	1-2	2-1	1-1	3-2	0-4	3-0	2-1	0-2	1-0	—	2-1	1-2	0-2	2-2	1-0	0-1	1-2	0-1	1-2
Racing Club Warwick	3-1	4-0	0-2	0-2	1-0	0-2	2-3	2-1	1-5	2-2	1-3	1-3	1-2	—	3-1	2-2	0-1	2-0	0-0	0-0	2-1	2-4
Redditch United	1-5	3-1	2-3	1-2	1-1	1-1	2-2	1-0	2-1	3-4	2-1	2-2	2-1	7-0	—	2-2	2-0	2-2	2-2	4-2	0-5	4-2
Rocester	2-1	1-0	0-2	0-0	3-2	0-1	0-3	0-3	4-3	1-0	1-9	1-2	1-0	2-0	0-3	—	1-3	2-1	1-2	1-2	2-1	1-5
Rugby United	1-2	0-0	0-1	1-1	4-0	1-1	3-0	1-3	3-2	0-1	1-3	1-4	2-0	1-2	0-0	1-0	—	1-2	2-0	1-1	3-3	1-2
Shepshed Dynamo	2-0	0-1	1-0	2-2	3-3	1-2	1-3	0-3	1-0	2-0	3-2	0-2	2-0	2-1	1-2	3-5	1-1	—	2-2	1-1	0-1	1-1
Solihull Borough	0-0	4-0	2-2	1-0	2-0	3-1	0-1	1-0	2-2	1-0	0-3	3-1	5-0	1-0	0-1	1-2	2-1	2-2	—	1-0	0-1	1-2
Sutton Coldfield Town	1-0	3-0	1-2	0-1	0-1	0-0	2-2	1-3	1-2	1-0	2-2	1-2	0-1	1-2	3-1	1-2	1-1	1-1	0-0	—	0-0	1-1
Tiverton Town	2-1	0-1	2-1	1-0	5-0	5-1	7-1	2-0	2-0	4-0	2-0	0-0	4-1	7-2	5-1	1-0	6-0	6-2	0-1	1-0	—	1-1
Weston super Mare	2-2	0-1	1-2	0-1	0-0	2-1	1-2	2-1	2-2	1-0	1-1	2-2	2-0	4-0	2-2	0-2	3-1	0-1	1-1	2-0	1-2	—

DR MARTENS LEAGUE — EASTERN DIVISION RESULTS 2000–2001

	Ashford Town	Baldock Town	Banbury United	Bashley	Burnham	Chelmsford City	Corby Town	Dartford	Erith & Belvedere	Grantham Town	Hastings Town	Histon	Langney Sports	Newport IoW	Rothwell Town	Sittingbourne	Spalding	St Leonards	Stamford	Tonbridge Angels	Wisbech Town	Witney Town
Ashford Town	—	1-4	1-0	3-2	1-1	0-6	1-3	1-0	4-0	1-2	0-2	2-1	3-1	1-3	2-3	4-1	2-1	1-0	0-1	0-0	1-2	1-1
Baldock Town	2-1	—	1-0	1-0	0-1	1-1	3-0	0-0	3-1	2-1	1-1	3-2	1-0	2-0	2-0	2-1	5-0	4-1	3-1	1-1	1-1	1-2
Banbury United	4-0	0-1	—	3-3	1-1	2-3	1-2	1-1	2-2	2-3	0-2	1-1	0-2	1-1	1-0	1-1	2-0	4-1	3-0	1-2	2-3	1-1
Bashley	2-0	1-0	3-3	—	2-0	1-1	4-4	3-0	1-2	1-1	2-2	0-2	1-0	1-1	3-2	0-2	6-1	0-2	0-1	2-5	0-2	3-0
Burnham	0-2	0-3	0-1	2-2	—	1-5	1-0	3-1	1-0	2-1	0-2	1-3	1-1	0-1	1-0	0-0	0-0	2-2	1-1	0-5	2-0	1-0
Chelmsford City	3-1	4-3	3-2	3-1	5-0	—	3-1	1-0	2-0	1-2	2-2	4-2	3-1	2-3	0-0	1-0	1-0	2-1	4-1	4-1	6-0	2-2
Corby Town	1-5	1-6	2-1	2-2	2-0	3-1	—	3-4	4-2	0-2	2-1	0-3	0-2	1-1	6-0	0-2	1-1	2-1	0-1	2-2	0-4	1-0
Dartford	1-2	2-4	1-0	1-1	1-1	0-1	2-2	—	1-1	2-2	1-0	1-2	1-0	1-3	3-2	1-1	0-1	3-0	0-4	0-1	3-2	0-3
Erith & Belvedere	3-0	0-2	0-5	0-1	2-1	0-3	2-4	1-2	—	1-1	1-5	0-1	1-5	1-3	2-3	3-0	0-2	1-1	2-2	4-3	3-1	1-2
Grantham Town	6-1	1-3	1-0	6-0	2-1	2-0	5-1	4-2	1-1	—	5-0	1-2	5-0	3-0	1-0	4-2	1-1	2-1	0-1	1-0	2-0	0-0
Hastings Town	3-1	1-1	1-0	0-1	2-0	2-2	1-1	2-1	3-0	0-5	—	0-0	1-0	1-2	4-3	1-1	3-2	0-0	3-0	0-4	2-0	3-1
Histon	2-0	2-2	2-0	0-1	2-0	1-3	2-2	1-1	4-1	1-1	0-0	—	2-1	3-1	3-0	0-0	4-2	3-1	2-2	3-1	5-1	3-0
Langney Sports	1-0	4-1	1-1	1-1	2-1	4-1	3-1	1-2	2-0	1-1	0-1	1-3	—	0-1	0-1	4-2	2-0	3-1	2-2	1-1	5-1	4-2
Newport IoW	5-0	1-0	1-1	3-2	0-0	0-0	3-0	2-0	2-0	6-0	2-0	0-0	1-0	—	1-1	4-0	1-0	4-1	3-1	1-0	7-1	6-0
Rothwell Town	3-0	2-0	3-2	1-2	5-0	3-1	2-2	2-1	7-2	2-1	0-1	1-4	3-1	3-1	—	2-2	1-0	10-2	3-1	2-3	7-0	1-0
Sittingbourne	2-1	2-3	1-0	0-1	0-2	0-3	0-0	2-5	1-2	0-5	1-5	1-2	0-4	1-2	1-2	—	1-0	3-0	1-2	1-0	3-1	0-2
Spalding	0-0	0-3	0-1	0-0	0-4	1-1	0-1	1-0	1-1	3-3	0-3	0-4	0-2	3-2	2-0	2-1	—	1-1	0-4	1-3	1-1	0-0
St Leonards	2-1	1-0	0-1	3-3	4-1	1-3	8-2	1-2	3-1	0-2	0-1	0-1	2-1	0-3	4-1	1-1	3-1	—	2-0	3-3	0-4	1-3
Stamford	1-2	3-2	1-1	3-1	1-0	1-0	2-2	1-1	2-1	2-2	0-2	3-3	1-2	0-0	4-1	2-0	3-2	2-0	—	3-2	1-1	3-2
Tonbridge Angels	5-0	0-0	0-2	2-1	2-3	1-1	1-2	2-0	1-0	1-1	2-4	1-1	2-5	1-1	4-0	2-1	2-1	1-0	6-2	—	2-1	1-0
Wisbech Town	2-3	1-4	1-2	0-0	1-0	0-3	0-1	1-2	2-3	0-1	2-1	3-1	2-3	0-2	1-0	2-1	0-0	1-1	0-5	1-1	—	0-0
Witney Town	1-3	1-1	1-2	3-1	2-2	1-1	1-3	2-0	3-0	0-3	3-3	3-1	2-1	0-5	2-1	1-1	2-3	4-1	0-2	1-0	0-0	—

RYMAN FOOTBALL LEAGUE 2000–2001

Premier Division

	P	W	D	L	F	A	W	D	L	F	A	Pts
			Home						*Away*			
Farnborough Town	42	14	5	2	43	13	17	1	3	43	14	99
Canvey Island	42	16	4	1	46	17	11	4	6	33	24	89
Basingstoke Town	42	13	6	2	40	19	9	7	5	33	21	79
Aldershot Town	41	15	4	1	41	11	6	7	8	32	28	74
Chesham United	42	13	3	5	42	22	9	3	9	36	30	72
Gravesend & Northfleet	42	12	3	6	32	21	10	2	9	31	25	71
Heybridge Swifts	42	11	7	3	47	29	7	6	8	27	31	67
Billericay Town	41	10	8	3	34	22	8	5	7	28	32	67
Hampton & Richmond Borough	42	14	3	4	43	22	4	9	8	30	38	66
Hitchin Town	42	10	2	9	40	32	8	3	10	32	37	59
Purfleet	42	8	8	5	31	21	6	5	10	24	34	55
Hendon	40	9	2	9	32	28	7	4	9	30	34	54
Sutton United	41	7	6	7	40	35	7	5	9	34	35	53
St Albans City	42	7	2	12	25	33	8	3	10	25	36	50
Grays Athletic	42	9	6	6	32	28	5	2	14	17	40	50
Maidenhead United	42	10	1	10	28	27	5	1	15	19	36	47
Croydon	42	9	6	6	34	24	3	4	14	21	53	46
Enfield	42	9	5	7	31	32	3	4	14	17	42	45
Harrow Borough	41	6	4	11	32	48	4	7	9	30	43	41
Slough Town	42	8	4	9	26	29	2	5	14	14	33	39
Carshalton Athletic	42	9	3	9	26	36	1	3	17	14	49	36
Dulwich Hamlet	42	4	4	13	18	36	0	6	15	15	48	22

NB. The following games were not played:
Aldershot Town v Billericay Town, Hendon v Harrow Borough, Sutton United v Hendon.

Division One

	P	W	D	L	F	A	W	D	L	F	A	Pts
			Home						*Away*			
Boreham Wood	42	15	2	4	48	27	11	5	5	34	22	85
Bedford Town	42	14	6	1	50	19	8	10	3	31	21	82
Braintree Town	42	15	3	3	64	24	10	3	8	48	36	81
Bishop's Stortford	42	13	2	6	58	37	11	4	6	45	39	78
Thame United	42	13	3	5	50	27	9	5	7	36	27	74
Ford United	42	9	6	6	30	26	10	6	5	40	32	69
Uxbridge	42	12	2	7	44	24	9	3	9	29	31	68
Northwood	42	11	4	6	50	39	9	4	8	39	42	68
Whyteleafe	42	11	2	8	33	32	9	4	8	29	37	66
Oxford City	42	8	7	6	37	25	8	6	7	27	24	61
Harlow Town	42	10	9	2	34	22	5	7	9	36	44	61
Worthing	42	7	6	8	35	32	9	3	9	34	37	57
Staines Town	42	7	6	8	30	30	9	2	10	30	36	56
Aylesbury United	42	8	3	10	34	29	9	1	11	31	26	55
Yeading	42	8	5	8	38	34	7	4	10	34	40	54
Bognor Regis Town	42	9	4	8	40	31	4	7	10	31	40	50
Walton & Hersham	42	6	5	10	22	35	8	3	10	37	45	50
Bromley	42	7	3	11	28	40	7	3	11	35	46	48
Wealdstone	42	5	6	10	30	34	7	3	11	24	39	45
Leatherhead	42	8	3	10	30	38	4	1	16	7	49	40
Romford	42	6	2	13	33	54	3	2	16	20	59	31
Barton Rovers	42	1	3	17	10	38	1	6	14	20	56	15

Division Two

	P	W	D	L	F	A	W	D	L	F	A	Pts
			Home						*Away*			
Tooting & Mitcham United	42	14	6	1	48	15	12	5	4	44	20	89
Windsor & Eton	42	11	5	5	33	22	13	5	3	37	18	82
Barking	42	15	4	2	43	25	8	9	4	39	29	82
Berkhamsted Town	42	13	4	4	52	20	11	4	6	47	29	80
Wivenhoe Town	42	11	7	3	39	22	12	4	5	39	30	80
Hemel Hempstead Town	42	10	5	6	35	28	12	5	4	39	16	76
Horsham	42	12	4	5	47	30	7	5	9	37	31	66
Chertsey Town	42	10	6	5	33	21	8	3	10	26	38	63
Great Wakering Rovers	42	11	8	2	45	22	5	5	11	24	37	61
Tilbury	42	11	4	6	36	28	7	2	12	25	39	60
Banstead Athletic	42	10	2	9	37	27	7	6	8	32	31	59
East Thurrock United	42	10	5	6	37	28	6	6	9	35	36	59
Metropolitan Police	42	10	1	10	32	43	8	3	10	32	34	58
Marlow	42	7	7	7	29	30	8	4	9	33	31	56
Molesey	42	8	5	8	31	30	6	4	11	22	31	51
Wembley	42	6	5	10	18	35	6	5	10	21	28	46
Hungerford Town	42	4	4	13	17	44	7	5	9	23	29	42
Leyton Pennant	42	5	5	11	21	36	5	6	10	26	38	41
Cheshunt	42	6	3	12	24	38	5	3	13	24	39	39
Edgware Town	42	5	4	12	24	37	4	5	12	17	40	36
Leighton Town	42	4	7	10	21	38	4	3	14	23	49	34
Wokingham Town*	42	3	4	14	20	45	0	8	13	19	49	20

* Wokingham Town deducted 1 point for breach of rule.

Division Three

	P	W	D	L	F	A	W	D	L	F	A	Pts
			Home						Away			
Arlesey Town	42	17	3	1	75	22	17	3	1	63	15	108
Lewes	41	12	6	2	63	18	13	5	3	41	16	86
Ashford Town (Middlesex)	42	10	4	7	50	27	16	3	2	52	22	85
Flackwell Heath	42	14	5	2	47	18	10	5	6	46	33	82
Corinthian Casuals	42	12	5	4	43	24	12	5	4	40	26	82
Aveley	42	13	2	6	44	26	11	1	9	41	35	75
Epsom & Ewell	42	9	2	10	40	29	14	2	5	36	23	73
Witham Town	42	12	6	3	44	23	9	3	9	32	34	72
Bracknell Town	41	11	5	5	50	37	8	5	7	40	33	67
Croydon Athletic	41	10	5	5	45	20	5	7	9	33	43	57
Ware	42	8	4	9	33	33	9	2	10	42	43	57
Tring Town	42	5	6	10	26	31	11	3	7	34	40	57
Egham Town	42	7	5	9	33	28	8	6	7	27	32	56
Hornchurch	42	7	5	9	35	29	7	8	6	38	31	55
Wingate & Finchley	42	9	5	7	43	32	6	2	13	32	43	52
Kingsbury Town	42	6	5	10	40	46	5	3	13	34	54	41
Abingdon Town*	42	6	4	11	28	49	6	3	12	25	53	40
Dorking	42	8	2	11	37	56	2	7	12	22	43	39
Hertford Town	41	6	1	14	29	44	3	7	10	28	53	35
Camberley Town	42	4	4	13	28	57	4	4	13	25	50	32
Clapton	42	3	4	14	25	63	2	5	14	23	58	24
Chalfont St Peter	42	3	1	17	18	54	1	0	20	12	96	13

NB. The following games were not played:
Croydon Athletic v Bracknell Town, Lewes v Hertford Town.
*Abingdon Town deducted 3 points for breach of rule.

LEADING GOALSCORERS

Premier Division		Lge	RLC	FMC
29	Gary Abbott (Aldershot Town)	29		
26	Kris Lee (Heybridge Swifts)	22	4	
26	Simon Parker (Heybridge Swifts)	22	4	
24	Craig Maskell (Hampton & Richmond B)	16	8	
23	Danny Bolt (Sutton United)	20		3
23	Tim Sills (Basingstoke Town)	19	3	1
	(includes while at Staines Town)	7		1
21	Lenny Piper (Farnborough Town)	19	2	

Division One				
37	Robbie Reinelt (Braintree Town)	36		1
36	Lawrence Yaku (Northwood)	30	4	2
34	Vinnie John (Bishop's Stortford)	34		
29	Steve Hale (Northwood)	20	8	1
28	John Lawford (Boreham Wood)	27	1	
28	Trevor Paul (Bishop's Stortford)	27	1	

Divison Two				AMC
37	Nigel Webb (Tooting & Mitcham United)	37		
28	Gavin Geddes (Horsham)	24	3	1
22	Ben Smith (Berkhamsted Town)	22		
21	Marcel Dennis (Banstead Athletic)	20		1
21	Jean-Marie Okita (Tilbury)	21		

Division Three				
31	Glen Driver (Witham Town)	31		
27	Warren Bagnall (Lewes)	25	2	
26	Ricci Crace (Ware)	24		2
26	John Fowler (Croydon Athletic)	25		1
25	Jamie Charles (Flackwell Heath)	23	1	1

Lge: Ryman League; RLC: Ryman League Cup; FMC: Full Members Cup; AMC: Associate Members Cup.

ATTENDANCES

Premier Divison Highest Individual crowd: 3478 Farnborough Town v Aldershot Town 26.12.2000 Aggregate: 203,698

Division One Highest Individual crowd: 1004 Aylesbury United v Staines Town 5.5.2001 Aggregate: 103,034

Division Two Highest Individual crowd: 405 Horsham v Tilbury 4.11.2000 Aggregate: 48,431

PREVIOUS SEASONS

SEASON	CLUBS	GAMES	AGG	AVE
1988–1989	86	1764	323,197	183
1989–1990	87	1806	387,441	215
1990–1991	88	1848	404,703	219
1991–1992	86	1764	397,553	225
1992–1993	85	1724	430,518	247
1993–1994	87	1806	423,306	234
1994–1995	87	1806	433,703	240
1995–1996	86	1764	440,285	250
1996–1997	83	1658	461,944	278
1997–1998	86	1766	456,454	258
1998–1999	86	1766	446,637	253
1999–2000	87	1806	435,700	241

RYMAN FOOTBALL LEAGUE—PREMIER DIVISION RESULTS 2000–2001

	Aldershot Town	Basingstoke Town	Billericay Town	Canvey Island	Carshalton Athletic	Chesham United	Croydon	Dulwich Hamlet	Enfield	Farnborough Town	Gravesend & Northfleet	Grays Athletic	Hampton & Richmond	Harrow Borough	Hendon	Heybridge Swifts	Hitchin Town	Maidenhead United	Purfleet	Slough Town	St Albans City	Sutton United
Aldershot Town	—	1-0	NP	1-0	4-0	1-0	4-0	1-0	2-1	1-1	1-0	6-0	2-2	3-0	1-1	2-1	2-0	2-1	3-0	1-0	2-3	1-1
Basingstoke Town	2-1	—	1-1	0-0	1-1	2-1	1-1	2-2	4-0	0-1	4-0	1-0	1-0	2-2	5-0	3-2	2-1	2-1	1-2	3-2	2-1	1-0
Billericay Town	2-2	2-2	—	2-1	0-0	1-1	0-0	3-0	0-2	1-2	1-0	3-1	3-1	1-1	2-0	5-1	3-1	2-0	1-1	0-0	2-1	0-5
Canvey Island	1-1	0-0	2-1	—	3-2	2-1	5-0	3-2	4-1	0-1	1-1	1-0	1-0	3-0	3-2	3-0	2-2	1-0	1-0	1-0	3-1	6-2
Carshalton Athletic	2-1	1-0	5-0	1-4	—	0-4	4-2	3-1	2-1	0-5	1-3	1-0	0-3	1-1	1-2	1-1	0-5	1-0	1-0	0-1	1-1	0-1
Chesham United	0-3	1-2	2-0	1-1	3-1	—	4-1	2-0	0-0	1-4	3-0	3-1	1-0	1-1	4-1	2-3	3-0	2-1	5-0	2-0	2-0	0-3
Croydon	2-2	0-1	0-0	4-1	3-0	2-1	—	2-0	2-2	0-1	1-2	1-0	1-1	0-1	2-0	1-2	5-1	0-2	0-0	4-1	0-2	2-1
Dulwich Hamlet	2-4	1-4	0-1	2-3	1-0	0-1	1-4	—	1-1	0-2	0-1	1-2	1-1	0-1	0-3	1-0	0-2	2-3	1-1	2-2	1-0	2-1
Enfield	1-0	1-4	1-0	3-0	2-1	3-1	1-0	1-1	—	0-3	0-2	2-1	2-2	0-1	0-2	1-1	2-5	3-1	2-1	1-1	2-3	2-2
Farnborough Town	1-0	1-1	3-0	1-2	3-0	0-0	3-1	3-0	1-1	—	1-0	3-0	1-1	3-1	0-2	0-1	3-0	4-1	3-2	1-1	4-0	2-2
Gravesend & Northfleet	2-0	0-2	1-2	0-3	3-0	3-2	2-0	2-1	1-0	2-1	—	0-1	2-0	3-6	3-3	0-2	2-1	0-2	1-0	1-2	1-0	1-2
Grays Athletic	1-1	0-0	2-3	0-3	3-1	3-1	2-2	1-1	2-0	0-3	2-1	—	1-3	1-1	0-2	1-0	2-1	2-1	1-1	1-0	6-0	3-1
Hampton & Richmond	1-0	3-2	1-2	2-2	4-2	3-1	3-0	4-0	4-0	1-0	1-0	0-0	—	3-3	0-2	2-1	2-4	1-0	1-2	2-0	1-2	2-1
Harrow Borough	0-5	1-4	4-2	0-2	2-2	3-2	4-0	2-1	2-1	2-3	0-6	1-1	4-5	—	1-4	1-1	4-0	2-1	1-2	1-0	2-2	2-1
Hendon	2-1	1-1	2-2	2-1	1-0	3-1	1-2	4-0	3-0	2-3	1-2	1-1	2-0	NP	—	1-4	0-0	4-0	4-3	2-1	0-1	0-1
Heybridge Swifts	2-1	1-1	2-2	1-1	2-1	3-1	1-2	3-1	2-0	2-3	3-2	4-0	3-2	4-2	2-2	—	0-0	0-2	4-3	3-2	0-1	2-2
Hitchin Town	2-5	0-1	2-1	4-1	3-0	1-2	7-3	1-0	2-1	1-2	2-0	2-0	2-0	3-6	0-0	0-2	—	0-2	0-1	3-0	0-0	3-0
Maidenhead United	3-0	3-2	2-1	0-2	2-0	1-2	3-1	3-1	2-1	0-1	1-3	3-2	0-0	4-1	1-2	1-3	0-1	—	1-2	1-0	1-0	0-2
Purfleet	2-2	0-0	1-1	3-0	3-0	1-2	3-0	1-1	3-0	0-2	1-0	3-1	2-2	4-2	0-0	1-1	0-3	1-1	—	2-0	1-3	2-1
Slough Town	0-1	0-2	0-2	0-1	3-1	0-2	1-0	1-1	3-1	0-2	1-0	1-0	1-0	1-2	1-0	1-1	0-3	1-0	3-2	—	1-2	2-1
St Albans City	0-1	0-3	0-0	1-4	0-1	0-1	2-2	0-2	0-1	2-4	0-2	1-2	5-0	1-0	1-3	3-0	2-0	3-1	0-2	1-0	—	0-1
Sutton United	1-1	2-0	1-4	0-1	3-1	2-3	2-1	7-1	2-3	1-0	1-4	2-3	2-2	3-3	NP	1-2	1-1	2-0	2-2	1-0	4-2	—

NP indicates match not played

RYMAN FOOTBALL LEAGUE—DIVISION ONE RESULTS 2000–2001

	Aylesbury United	Barton Rovers	Bedford Town	Bishop's Stortford	Bognor Regis Town	Boreham Wood	Braintree Town	Bromley	Ford United	Harlow Town	Leatherhead	Northwood	Oxford City	Romford	Staines Town	Thame United	Uxbridge	Walton & Hersham	Wealdstone	Whyteleafe	Worthing	Yeading
Aylesbury United	—	0-0	3-0	1-2	2-0	2-2	1-2	1-4	1-1	1-3	1-0	5-1	1-0	0-1	0-4	1-2	3-0	0-1	0-2	5-1	1-2	5-1
Barton Rovers	0-4	—	0-1	0-1	2-2	0-2	0-3	1-2	0-1	1-3	0-1	0-1	0-0	2-1	0-1	1-2	1-3	0-0	0-1	0-2	2-4	0-3
Bedford Town	1-0	1-1	—	3-1	1-1	1-0	2-2	3-0	2-3	4-0	3-0	6-1	2-1	3-1	4-4	1-0	0-0	2-1	4-1	1-1	1-0	5-1
Bishop's Stortford	2-3	2-2	2-3	—	2-4	4-0	5-3	0-1	4-0	4-3	4-0	1-3	1-2	3-2	2-1	1-0	2-1	4-3	2-2	4-1	4-2	5-1
Bognor Regis Town	2-1	0-1	2-3	2-5	—	0-2	2-0	1-2	2-3	1-1	5-0	2-0	1-2	5-0	4-5	1-0	1-0	2-3	2-3	1-1	1-0	2-1
Boreham Wood	3-2	2-0	3-0	0-3	0-2	—	1-4	1-0	2-3	1-1	2-1	2-0	1-1	3-0	2-0	1-0	2-3	3-0	1-1	0-3	4-2	6-2
Braintree Town	3-2	2-1	2-1	1-1	3-1	0-3	—	5-0	2-4	6-3	4-0	1-2	3-1	10-0	4-1	4-1	3-0	5-1	4-0	5-0	2-2	3-1
Bromley	3-2	0-2	1-1	3-0	0-1	2-4	0-6	—	1-3	1-1	1-0	0-4	2-3	1-0	0-1	1-1	3-2	1-3	4-0	2-3	0-3	2-0
Ford United	2-0	4-2	0-0	0-0	0-0	1-1	0-6	3-1	—	0-3	2-1	2-0	0-0	1-0	3-0	1-3	2-2	0-2	2-1	5-1	1-2	0-3
Harlow Town	0-0	3-0	0-2	2-2	0-0	1-1	0-3	3-1	3-2	—	3-0	3-2	0-2	1-0	3-0	0-0	1-1	3-2	3-1	5-1	3-2	0-3
Leatherhead	2-0	3-0	0-0	3-0	2-1	0-2	0-0	1-0	2-1	1-1	—	1-5	1-0	2-2	3-0	2-1	5-0	5-1	1-0	1-3	1-2	0-6
Northwood	1-3	1-0	2-2	7-3	2-2	1-1	1-2	3-3	0-2	4-2	4-1	—	1-1	4-1	1-0	1-5	0-1	5-3	3-1	4-1	3-1	0-1
Oxford City	0-2	5-1	0-0	2-2	2-1	2-2	3-2	2-3	2-3	1-1	3-0	2-5	—	2-0	5-0	0-0	0-1	2-2	3-0	1-2	0-2	0-1
Romford	0-1	2-2	0-6	1-2	1-4	0-4	1-0	1-0	1-1	5-2	2-0	3-1	0-1	—	1-0	2-4	2-6	1-1	0-2	0-3	2-0	0-1
Staines Town	0-3	3-1	1-5	2-3	4-5	1-2	2-4	0-1	1-3	0-1	3-0	3-1	0-2	0-1	—	2-1	5-0	4-0	4-1	1-0	0-1	1-1
Thame United	1-0	11-3	0-0	3-2	2-1	1-0	2-2	1-1	0-1	2-2	4-0	3-0	1-1	3-1	0-4	—	4-1	1-3	4-0	0-1	3-1	2-1
Uxbridge	2-0	8-2	2-2	1-0	3-0	1-0	3-0	3-2	2-2	2-1	3-0	0-2	4-0	3-1	0-4	5-0	—	1-2	4-0	0-0	1-2	0-2
Walton & Hersham	0-2	1-0	1-1	2-4	5-2	2-3	5-1	1-3	0-2	3-2	0-0	2-2	1-1	2-4	0-1	4-1	1-2	—	0-2	2-3	2-1	3-2
Wealdstone	1-3	2-0	1-1	1-2	2-0	0-1	0-4	4-0	1-1	2-2	0-1	1-2	0-1	1-0	4-0	4-0	4-0	0-2	—	1-2	0-1	2-2
Whyteleafe	1-0	4-1	1-2	5-4	2-4	1-2	2-1	3-1	1-0	0-0	5-0	1-1	0-2	3-3	1-0	0-1	0-0	1-0	1-2	—	0-3	3-1
Worthing	0-3	1-1	1-2	2-3	3-3	1-2	0-3	2-2	3-3	4-1	5-0	1-1	1-5	2-0	0-1	3-0	3-1	1-0	0-1	0-0	—	3-1
Yeading	1-0	0-0	1-1	0-3	1-0	1-2	5-2	2-4	3-2	0-3	0-1	2-2	0-2	7-2	1-2	2-2	0-1	3-2	2-2	3-1	3-1	—

RYMAN FOOTBALL LEAGUE—DIVISION TWO RESULTS 2000–2001

	Banstead Athletic	Barking	Berkhamsted Town	Chertsey Town	Cheshunt	East Thurrock United	Edgware Town	Great Wakering Rovers	Hemel Hempstead Town	Horsham	Hungerford Town	Leighton Town	Leyton Pennant	Marlow	Metropolitan Police	Molesey	Tilbury	Tooting & Mitcham United	Wembley	Windsor & Eton	Wivenhoe Town	Wokingham Town
Banstead Athletic	—	1-1	6-3	4-0	1-4	0-2	1-2	1-0	0-1	2-0	2-0	2-0	0-1	2-2	6-1	0-1	3-0	0-3	3-1	0-2	1-2	2-1
Barking	2-0	—	1-6	2-1	2-1	2-2	4-1	2-0	1-0	2-1	2-0	1-1	3-2	2-1	2-0	0-0	3-5	3-1	2-0	2-1	2-2	3-0
Berkhamsted Town	1-1	0-0	—	2-0	5-0	4-0	5-0	5-2	2-2	2-1	0-1	4-2	1-1	4-1	3-0	4-1	2-0	2-0	0-1	0-3	1-2	5-2
Chertsey Town	3-1	2-4	2-3	—	2-2	0-0	1-0	1-0	1-1	0-0	4-2	4-1	3-0	2-1	2-1	1-0	3-0	1-1	0-2	0-1	0-0	2-0
Cheshunt	2-1	1-2	1-1	1-0	—	2-4	3-1	1-2	0-3	1-0	0-0	1-4	2-1	2-3	0-4	0-3	3-1	1-2	0-1	1-2	1-2	1-1
East Thurrock United	1-1	2-1	0-0	3-1	3-1	—	2-1	1-1	1-2	1-1	2-1	4-2	1-2	3-2	4-2	0-1	0-1	0-1	2-1	2-2	1-3	4-1
Edgware Town	2-1	0-0	1-3	1-2	2-1	3-1	—	2-1	1-2	0-1	1-2	1-1	2-1	0-2	0-1	1-1	2-4	2-2	0-2	1-2	1-5	2-1
Great Wakering Rovers	1-1	1-1	1-4	2-1	2-1	4-2	1-1	—	0-0	1-1	4-0	3-0	3-1	2-1	3-3	0-0	3-0	2-2	3-1	0-1	2-1	7-0
Hemel Hempstead Town	2-1	0-1	0-2	0-1	1-3	3-3	2-0	3-0	—	1-1	2-0	3-1	3-1	0-2	2-2	3-1	1-0	0-3	2-1	2-1	2-1	4-0
Horsham	1-4	4-0	1-6	6-0	4-0	2-1	1-1	1-1	0-2	—	2-0	3-1	3-1	3-2	1-1	2-2	2-2	3-2	0-1	0-3	3-1	3-3
Hungerford Town	0-3	0-3	1-4	1-0	3-1	2-1	1-1	1-1	1-4	0-4	—	0-2	0-1	0-2	0-3	2-0	0-3	0-4	0-0	1-2	1-4	2-2
Leighton Town	2-0	0-3	1-3	2-2	1-1	4-3	0-1	1-5	0-0	1-5	1-0	—	1-1	0-1	0-2	1-3	1-2	0-3	0-0	0-0	4-1	1-1
Leyton Pennant	1-3	1-3	0-2	0-0	0-2	1-3	2-0	2-0	1-6	1-1	0-1	4-0	—	0-0	1-0	2-1	3-3	0-3	0-0	0-2	2-4	1-0
Marlow	3-4	2-2	2-0	1-3	1-1	3-0	2-1	1-2	0-4	4-1	1-3	1-1	1-1	—	2-1	1-0	2-1	1-2	0-0	1-3	0-0	1-1
Metropolitan Police	0-1	2-0	1-4	1-2	2-1	0-1	3-2	5-3	1-0	1-6	1-1	2-1	4-2	0-4	—	1-3	3-0	0-5	1-0	1-2	0-3	3-2
Molesey	1-1	1-2	0-0	1-0	2-0	1-5	3-0	1-2	1-3	4-2	1-3	0-1	0-0	2-2	4-3	—	1-0	0-2	1-2	3-3	4-1	2-0
Tilbury	3-2	2-1	1-1	1-2	1-2	1-1	2-3	3-0	2-0	2-1	0-0	3-2	2-1	0-1	2-0	2-1	—	1-1	3-2	0-1	0-1	3-2
Tooting & Mitcham United	3-0	2-2	3-0	1-1	2-0	1-0	1-1	1-1	2-0	2-3	2-1	4-0	3-3	1-0	1-4	4-0	4-0	—	2-1	1-0	5-0	2-1
Wembley	1-2	2-2	3-2	2-4	2-1	0-0	1-1	1-0	0-1	2-1	0-0	2-1	0-3	2-1	1-0	1-0	0-1	0-3	—	0-3	0-2	0-0
Windsor & Eton	0-3	2-2	1-2	5-0	2-1	1-0	0-0	4-0	1-2	0-4	2-3	3-0	2-2	2-2	0-1	4-2	1-0	1-1	2-0	—	0-2	0-0
Wivenhoe Town	2-2	2-2	1-0	1-3	1-0	1-5	4-0	0-0	1-1	4-0	2-0	3-0	3-0	2-3	0-2	1-0	1-0	3-1	4-2	2-2	—	1-1
Wokingham Town	0-0	2-7	2-1	1-2	1-0	0-0	0-1	3-2	0-5	0-3	1-4	2-3	1-2	2-3	0-2	1-2	1-2	0-2	2-2	1-1	0-1	—

RYMAN FOOTBALL LEAGUE—DIVISION THREE RESULTS 2000–2001

	Abingdon Town	Arlesey Town	Ashford Town (Middlesex)	Aveley	Bracknell Town	Camberley Town	Chalfont St Peter	Clapton	Corinthian Casuals	Croydon Athletic	Dorking	Egham Town	Epsom & Ewell	Flackwell Heath	Hertford Town	Hornchurch	Kingsbury Town	Lewes	Tring Town	Ware	Wingate & Finchley	Witham Town
Abingdon Town	—	0-5	0-3	1-6	3-1	2-1	1-0	1-1	0-4	3-2	3-1	0-1	2-1	1-4	2-2	2-3	1-3	1-1	1-1	1-2	1-3	2-4
Arlesey Town	5-0	—	2-0	2-1	2-1	4-1	9-1	3-0	4-0	2-1	3-3	3-0	2-1	2-3	8-1	3-3	5-1	1-1	6-0	4-3	3-1	2-0
Ashford Town (Middlesex)	1-2	1-2	—	2-1	2-2	3-0	8-0	3-2	2-0	2-2	5-1	1-1	0-1	0-1	1-1	3-0	5-1	1-3	3-4	3-0	1-2	3-1
Aveley	4-0	1-1	0-4	—	6-1	1-0	3-1	3-1	1-3	2-0	3-1	2-0	0-1	0-3	5-2	2-1	5-2	0-1	4-2	1-0	1-1	0-1
Bracknell Town	4-1	0-3	2-2	2-2	—	2-1	3-0	2-1	2-2	3-3	0-3	3-3	2-3	3-2	2-0	0-1	3-1	3-1	0-2	3-2	5-1	6-3
Camberley Town	2-1	1-3	0-4	2-2	1-5	—	4-2	0-3	2-4	2-2	2-2	1-1	0-4	1-2	1-3	0-5	1-2	0-5	0-2	0-3	5-2	1-1
Chalfont St Peter	1-2	0-5	2-3	1-5	0-6	0-2	—	3-0	0-1	1-2	2-1	1-1	1-2	2-6	1-2	0-3	0-2	0-3	0-2	1-4	0-5	1-2
Clapton	1-1	2-8	0-4	2-4	1-0	1-3	2-0	—	1-1	1-3	3-1	1-1	0-4	2-0	2-1	2-2	0-2	0-1	2-4	1-5	2-1	1-2
Corinthian Casuals	4-0	0-6	0-1	2-4	1-0	3-2	8-1	8-1	—	3-2	3-1	1-2	0-1	2-6	2-2	2-2	0-2	0-0	2-2	1-5	2-1	1-5
Croydon Athletic	0-1	0-2	0-2	4-1	1-0	3-2	3-1	3-1	0-0	—	4-0	2-2	0-1	2-0	1-1	2-2	4-1	3-0	2-2	5-0	0-2	2-1
Dorking	3-2	2-3	1-3	1-2	0-5	3-2	4-0	1-0	0-2	0-3	—	2-1	0-2	4-3	4-3	0-4	4-4	2-7	1-3	4-4	3-2	0-3
Egham Town	2-1	3-2	1-2	2-1	1-2	0-1	7-0	1-1	1-1	4-2	1-1	—	1-2	0-1	4-0	0-4	0-1	1-1	1-2	0-0	2-1	1-2
Epsom & Ewell	1-2	0-2	1-2	3-1	0-2	4-0	1-2	5-0	1-2	0-1	3-0	1-2	—	1-1	3-1	2-2	2-1	1-2	3-1	2-1	0-4	4-0
Flackwell Heath	2-2	1-1	2-3	1-2	4-0	2-1	4-0	2-2	2-0	2-2	2-2	2-1	3-0	—	3-1	1-0	2-1	1-0	4-0	2-0	3-0	2-0
Hertford Town	1-3	0-3	0-3	2-3	0-3	3-3	6-1	2-1	0-1	1-3	3-1	1-2	2-3	2-0	—	0-3	3-2	0-1	0-1	1-4	1-0	1-3
Hornchurch	5-1	4-0	0-3	0-2	2-0	1-2	4-1	1-3	0-3	2-2	0-0	4-0	2-2	2-2	0-1	—	3-2	0-1	0-1	1-2	1-0	1-3
Kingsbury Town	6-2	2-3	0-5	0-2	0-3	1-1	5-2	1-1	1-5	5-0	0-0	4-0	2-2	2-2	1-1	3-2	—	0-4	0-1	2-3	3-0	1-1
Lewes	3-0	1-1	4-4	0-1	3-0	6-0	13-0	1-1	1-1	5-0	4-2	3-0	0-1	1-0	NP	3-3	4-2	—	2-2	4-0	2-0	0-0
Tring Town	2-3	0-3	1-2	0-2	1-2	1-1	1-0	2-1	2-4	2-0	1-1	0-1	1-1	1-2	5-1	1-1	1-0	0-1	—	2-2	2-2	0-0
Ware	1-0	1-5	1-3	0-3	2-2	4-0	2-1	1-1	2-3	3-3	0-1	0-2	1-2	1-1	3-1	2-0	1-0	1-3	1-2	—	3-0	3-0
Wingate & Finchley	4-0	0-1	1-3	1-2	1-1	4-3	8-0	5-1	2-3	0-0	1-0	1-3	1-0	1-2	2-2	1-1	5-3	1-1	2-1	1-6	—	2-1
Witham Town	1-1	0-1	1-1	3-1	2-2	0-0	5-0	6-1	2-0	1-0	1-0	1-2	4-2	5-4	2-2	1-1	1-0	0-4	2-0	4-0	2-1	—

NP indicates match not played

RYMAN LEAGUE CUP 2000–2001

Preliminary Round
Ashford Town (Middlesex) 5, Croydon Athletic 3
Aveley 4, Tooting & Mitcham United 2
Banstead Athletic 4, Bracknell Town 2
Barking 0, Arlesey Town 0
Arlesey Town 3, Barking 1
Berkhamsted Town 2, Flackwell Heath 3
Chalfont St Peter 2, Northwood 4
Chertsey Town 0, East Thurrock United 3
Clapton 0, Corinthian Casuals 1
Dorking 1, Hungerford Town 2
Edgware Town 0, Metropolitan Police 0
Metropolitan Police 0, Edgware Town 1
Egham Town 2, Hemel Hempstead Town 2
Hemel Hempstead Town 3, Egham Town 1
Ford United 1, Hornchurch 0
Great Wakering Rovers 2, Tilbury 0
Hertford Town 4, Witham Town 0
Leatherhead 1, Romford 0
Leighton Town 1, Espom & Ewell 2
Lewes 5, Kingsbury Town 0
Leyton Pennant 2, Abingdon Town 1
Marlow 1, Wivenhoe Town 0
Molesey 0, Cheshunt 0
Cheshunt 1, Molesey 2
Tring Town 0, Wingate & Finchley 2
Ware 2, Windsor & Eton 1
Wembley 4, Camberley Town 0
Wokingham Town 1, Horsham 3

First Round
Bognor Regis Town 5, Harlow Town 3
Gravesend & Northfleet 6, Hungerford Town 1
Molesey 2, Ware 4
Arlesey Town 3, Hendon 4
Banstead Athletic 0, Horsham 2
Harrow Borough 2, Croydon 3
Thame United 4, Wealdstone 3
Lewes 0, Aylesbury United 0
Aylesbury United 2, Lewes 1
Edgware Town 0, Basingstoke Town 1
Hemel Hempstead Town 2, Great Wakering Rovers 0
Walton & Hersham 2, Aldershot Town 1
Ashford Town (Middlesex) 1, Bromley 3
Bedford Town 1, Epsom & Ewell 2
Billericay Town 3, Barton Rovers 1
Bishop's Stortford 3, Canvey Island 5
Carshalton Athletic 1, Hitchin Town 0
Corinthian Casuals 1, Sutton United 0
Dulwich Hamlet 5, Aveley 2
East Thurrock United 1, Braintree Town 2
Farnborough Town 2, Enfield 1
Flackwell Heath 1, Slough Town 3
Ford United 0, Heybridge Swifts 2
Grays Athletic 0, Northwood 4
Hertford Town 2, Oxford City 3
Leyton Pennant 0, Hampton & Richmond Borough 4
Maidenhead United 1, Leatherhead 3
St Albans City 1, Boreham Wood 1

Boreham Wood 2, St Albans City 3
Uxbridge 2, Purfleet 3
Wembley 2, Staines Town 1
Whyteleafe 2, Worthing 3
Wingate & Finchley 1, Chesham United 3
Yeading 0, Marlow 1

Second Round
Hampton & Richmond Borough 3, Bognor Regis Town 2
Croydon 3, Wembley 0
Billericay Town 4, Corinthian Casuals 0
Bromley 1, Chesham United 3
Dulwich Hamlet 1, Carshalton Athletic 2
Marlow 0, Slough Town 2
Slough Town removed from competition.
Thame United 0, Basingstoke Town 4
Walton & Hersham 0, Bedford Town 5
Farnborough Town 5, Hemel Hempstead Town 1
St Albans City 3, Leatherhead 1
Purfleet 4, Horsham 0
Heybridge Swifts 3, Oxford City 0
Worthing 0, Northwood 2
Canvey Island 2, Gravesend & Northfleet 0
Aylesbury United 4, Ware 0
Hendon 3, Braintree Town 2

Third Round
Carshalton Athletic 0, Hampton & Richmond Borough 3
St Albans City 3, Marlow 1
Farnborough Town 1, Basingstoke Town 3
Heybridge Swifts 3, Bedford Town 0
Hendon 2, Chesham United 3
Aylesbury United 0, Purfleet 1
Croydon 5, Canvey Island 0
Northwood 4, Billericay Town 3

Fourth Round
St Albans City 3, Hampton & Richmond Borough 3
Hampton & Richmond Borough 3, St Albans City 0
Basingstoke Town 0, Croydon 2
Northwood 4, Purfleet 1
Heybridge Swifts 3, Chesham United 1

Semi-Finals, First Leg
Hampton & Richmond Borough 2, Croydon 3
Heybridge Swifts 4, Northwood 1

Semi-Finals, Second Leg
Croydon 3, Hampton & Richmond Borough 2
Northwood 1, Heybridge Swifts 2

Final
Croydon 0, Heybridge Swifts 3

FULL MEMBERS CUP

First Round
Purfleet 3, Boreham Wood 1
Aylesbury United 1, Thame United 2
Braintree Town 5, Enfield 0
Carshalton Athletic 3, Basingstoke Town 3
Basingstoke Town won 4-2 on penalties.
Harrow Borough 1, Romford 2
Heybridge Swifts 2, Billericay Town 0
Slough Town 4, Aldershot Town 3
Staines Town 4, Sutton United 4
Sutton United won 6-5 on penalties.
Walton & Hersham 1, Farnborough Town 0
Worthing 2, Hampton & Richmond Borough 0
Harlow Town 0, Hendon 2
Hitchin Town 2, Bedford Town 1

Second Round
Yeading 1, Uxbridge 4
Bromley 1, Slough Town 0
Grays Athletic 4, Bishop's Stortford 2
Northwood 3, St Albans City 4
Sutton United 2, Croydon 2
Sutton United won 4-3 on penalties.
Thame United 2, Oxford City 3
Dulwich Hamlet 2, Walton & Hersham 1
Worthing 2, Bognor Regis Town 4
Romford 0, Barton Rovers 2
Basingstoke Town 2, Whyteleafe 1
Chesham United 3, Braintree Town 2
Gravesend & Northfleet 4, Ford United 0
Heybridge Swifts 6, Hendon 5

Maidenhead United 2, Leatherhead 1
Purfleet 1, Canvey Island 0
Wealdstone 0, Hitchin Town 3

Third Round
Oxford City 2, Bromley 0
Chesham United 0, St Albans City 2
Dulwich Hamlet 0, Basingstoke Town 2
Heybridge Swifts 1, Purfleet 3
Barton Rovers 2, Grays Athletic 0
Bognor Regis Town 2, Maidenhead United 1
Gravesend & Northfleet 7, Hitchin Town 1
Uxbridge 2, Sutton United 0

Fourth Round
Basingstoke Town 1, Bognor Regis Town 3
Gravesend & Northfleet 1, St Albans City 1
Gravesend & Northfleet won 4-3 on penalties.
Barton Rovers 0, Purfleet 1
Oxford City 4, Uxbridge 1

Semi-Finals
Bognor Regis Town 0, Gravesend & Northfleet 2
Oxford City 1, Purfleet 3

Final
Gravesend & Northfleet 3, Purfleet 1

ASSOCIATE MEMBERS TROPHY

First Round
Abingdon Town 2, Hungerford Town 2
Hungerford Town won 5-4 on penalties.
Arlesey Town 4, Tring Town 0
Dorking 2, Croydon Athletic 1
Berkhamsted Town 1, Edgware Town 3
East Thurrock United 3, Clapton 1
Flackwell Heath 3, Chalfont St Peter 0
Hertford Town 2, Cheshunt 3
Windsor & Eton 4, Ashford Town (Middlesex) 1
Witham Town 0, Tilbury 2
Molesey 1, Tooting & Mitcham United 1
Molesey won 3-0 on penalties.
Leyton Pennant 2, Wembley 1
Bracknell Town 1, Wokingham Town 1
Bracknell Town won 6-5 on penalties.

Second Round
East Thurrock United 4, Aveley 0
Lewes 2, Epsom & Ewell 1
Marlow 4, Camberley Town 2
Tilbury 1, Wivenhoe Town 4
Chertsey Town 1, Bracknell Town 2
Hungerford Town 0, Banstead Athletic 5
Molesey 0, Windsor & Eton 1
Edgware Town 2, Cheshunt 1
Great Wakering Rovers 1, Barking 2
Horsham 5, Flackwell Heath 2
Metropolitan Police 1, Egham Town 1
Egham Town won 3-2 on penalties.
Ware 2, Arlesey Town 1

Dorking 3, Corinthian Casuals 2
Kingsbury Town 2, Leighton Town 0
Hemel Hempstead Town 4, Wingate & Finchley 1
Leyton Pennant 2, Hornchurch 3

Third Round
Windsor & Eton 0, Lewes 5
Egham Town 0, Horsham 1
Barking 4, Kingsbury Town 0
Dorking 1, Bracknell Town 0
Edgware Town 1, Hornchurch 0
Marlow 2, Banstead Athletic 1
Ware 0, East Thurrock United 4
Wivenhoe Town 2, Hemel Hempstead Town 4

Fourth Round
Barking 0, Hemel Hempstead Town 1
Edgware Town 1, East Thurrock United 2
Horsham 3, Lewes 1
Marlow 3, Dorking 3
Marlow won 3-1 on penalties.

Semi-Finals
East Thurrock United 1, Marlow 4
Hemel Hempstead Town 5, Horsham 2

CUP ATTENDANCES

Ryman League Cup	11,190
Full Members Cup	6,200
Associate Members Trophy	2,768

FA UMBRO TROPHY 2000–2001

FIRST ROUND

Belper Town v Blakenall	4-1
North Ferriby United v Gresley Rovers	2-3
Gainsborough Trinity v Bradford (Park Avenue)	3-2
Droylsden v Bromsgrove Rovers	0-0, 0-1
Kendal Town v Stamford	2-2, 1-1
Stamford won 3-2 on penalties.	
Bishop Auckland v Whitby Town	1-1, 2-2
Bishop Auckland won 5-4 on penalties.	
Guiseley v Eastwood Town	4-1
Stalybridge Celtic v Bedworth United	4-1
Harrogate Town v Witton Albion	3-3, 2-3
Ilkeston Town v Altrincham	1-1, 3-4
Bamber Bridge v Atherstone United	1-3
Corby Town v Matlock Town	3-5
Winsford United v Congleton Town	2-4
Shepshed Dynamo v Burscough	2-3
Halesowen Town v Bilston Town	1-3
Colwyn Bay v Tamworth	3-3, 1-2
Blyth Spartans v Hinckley United	2-0
Stafford Rangers v Ossett Town	3-1
Spennymoor United v Frickley Athletic	3-1
Barrow v Runcorn	0-1
Trafford v Farsley Celtic	5-1
Spalding United v Sutton Coldfield Town	2-0
Rocester v Stocksbridge Park Steels	3-1
Chorley v Accrington Stanley	1-1, 1-2
Paget Rangers v Worksop Town	1-2
Ashton United v Solihull Borough	5-0
Moor Green v Hucknall Town	0-1
Vauxhall Motors v Lincoln United	4-0
Racing Club Warwick v Lancaster City	0-4
Leek Town v Radcliffe Borough	2-2, 1-2
Gretna v Workington	2-1
Redditch United v Grantham Town	3-1
Romford v Braintree Town	2-2, 0-2
Ford United v St Leonards	4-2
Grays Athletic v Ashford Town	3-4
Tiverton Town v Sittingbourne	3-0
Welling United v Uxbridge	0-2
Billericay Town v Farnborough Town	2-0
Yeading v Bromley	2-1
Chelmsford City v St Albans City	0-2
Baldock Town v Staines Town	1-1, 1-2
Langney Sports v Histon	0-1
Cirencester Town v Clevedon Town	0-1
Newport (IW) v Hitchin Town	2-2, 1-4
Worthing v Thame United	2-2, 0-0
Worthing won 4-2 on penalties.	
Aylesbury United v Rugby United	1-1, 3-1
Barton Rovers v Banbury United	2-1
Crawley Town v Heybridge Swifts	2-1
Worcester City v Mangotsfield United	3-0
Folkestone Invicta v Oxford City	2-2, 4-3
Bashley v Salisbury City	1-0
Harlow Town v Basingstoke Town	2-1
Hampton & Richmond Borough v	
Maidenhead United	1-4
Hendon v Tonbridge Angels	2-0
Weymouth v Sutton United	2-1
Fisher Athletic v Burnham	3-2
Dorchester Town v Boreham Wood	2-1
Leatherhead v Evesham United	1-2
Bognor Regis Town v Whyteleafe	0-0, 1-0
Gravesend & Northfleet v Hastings Town	0-1
Slough Town v Bishop's Stortford	5-0
Wisbech Town v Carshalton Athletic	1-2
Cinderford Town v Dulwich Hamlet	1-1, 2-1
Rothwell Town v Merthyr Tydfil	2-1
Havant & Waterlooville v Croydon	2-1
Cambridge City v Gloucester City	1-0
Dartford v Northwood	0-3
Bedford Town v Newport County	1-2
Witney Town v Harrow Borough	2-3
Wealdstone v Weston-Super-Mare	3-3, 0-2
Enfield v Erith & Belvedere	4-2
Bye: Walton & Hersham.	

SECOND ROUND

Gresley Rovers v Rocester	4-0
Hyde United v Spalding United	1-0

Matlock Town v Gretna	3-1
Marine v Gateshead	2-1
Ashton United v Bilston Town	2-2, 1-3
Altrincham v Bishop Auckland	2-2, 1-3
Stalybridge Celtic v Witton Albion	2-0
Blyth Spartans v Stafford Rangers	3-0
Hucknall Town v Redditch United	1-0
Runcorn v Guiseley	2-1
Emley v Vauxhall Motors	5-3
Radcliffe Borough v Accrington Stanley	0-3
Burscough v Gainsborough Trinity	1-0
Congleton Town v Stamford	3-1
Tamworth v Belper Town	1-1, 5-0
Worksop Town v Atherstone United	4-2
Lancaster City v Bromsgrove Rovers	0-1
Trafford v Spennymoor United	2-0
Bashley v St Albans City	1-7
Kings Lynn v Chesham United	2-0
Hendon v Worcester City	1-1, 3-2
Maidenhead United v Enfield	1-0
Carshalton Athletic v Histon	3-4
Braintree Town v Rothwell Town	1-1, 2-2
Braintree Town won 4-3 on penalties.	
Folkestone Invicta v Worthing	4-0
Staines Town v Walton & Hersham	1-1, 3-2
Tiverton Town v Aylesbury United	2-1
Barton Rovers v Uxbridge	3-2
Aldershot Town v Havant & Waterlooville	1-0
Burton Albion v Yeading	4-1
Northwood v Purfleet	3-1
Ashford Town v Weston-Super-Mare	4-2
Cinderford Town v Evesham United	0-2
Newport County v Slough Town	2-1
Harlow Town v Canvey Island	2-2, 0-2
Cambridge City v Bath City	1-1, 0-1
Billericay Town v Hastings Town	2-2, 2-1
Ford United v Bognor Regis Town	1-3
Fisher Athletic v Crawley Town	2-3
Harrow Borough v Dorchester Town	3-0
Margate v Clevedon Town	2-1
Weymouth v Hitchin Town	2-0

THIRD ROUND

Matlock Town v Northwich Victoria	2-0
Runcorn v Scarborough	0-4
Congleton Town v Gresley Rovers	2-0
Trafford v Telford United	1-1, 1-7
Bilston Town v Nuneaton Borough	3-2
Leigh RMI v Hucknall Town	1-0
Emley v Accrington Stanley	3-0
Marine v Stalybridge Celtic	2-0
Southport v Hednesford Town	3-0
Worksop Town v Bromsgrove Rovers	3-3, 0-3
Burscough v Morecambe	0-3
Tamworth v Boston United	0-3
Burton Albion v Bishop Auckland	0-0, 1-2
Hyde United v Blyth Spartans	2-0
Chester City v Doncaster Rovers	1-2
Hendon v Tiverton Town	1-3
Folkestone Invicta v Kings Lynn	1-2
Woking v Margate	1-2
Crawley Town v Ashford Town	0-2
Bognor Regis Town v Billericay Town	1-5
Aldershot Town v Stevenage Borough	1-0
St Albans City v Newport County	6-1
Forest Green Rovers v Barton Rovers	5-1
Canvey Island v Northwood	3-0
Histon v Kettering Town	2-1
Yeovil Town v Bath City	1-2
Braintree Town v Maidenhead United	4-2
Evesham United v Harrow Borough	0-1
Hayes v Rushden & Diamonds	2-2, 0-2
Staines Town v Kingstonian	0-1
Dagenham & Redbridge v Weymouth	1-0
Hereford United v Dover Athletic	

FOURTH ROUND

Worksop Town v Congleton Town	6-2
Blyth Spartans v Maidenhead United	2-1
Scarborough v Burton Albion	0-1

Histon v Billericay Town 0-3
Bilston Town v Canvey Island 0-1
Chester City v St Albans City 3-2
Kingstonian v Southport 0-1
Hereford United v Leigh RMI 0-0, 2-1
Weymouth v Ashford Town 3-1
Tiverton Town v Boston United 2-1
Stevenage Borough v Margate 2-1
Kings Lynn v Telford United 1-2
Emley v Yeovil Town 2-4
Matlock Town v Forest Green Rovers . 2-2, 1-3
Evesham United v Morecambe 0-0, 1-4
Marine v Rushden & Diamonds 0-6

FIFTH ROUND

Burton Albion v Yeovil Town 2-1
Weymouth v Southport 1-2
Morecambe v Hereford United 0-0, 1-1
  Hereford United won 3-1 on penalties.
Canvey Island v Stevenage Borough .. 1-1, 0-0
  Canvey Island won 4-2 on penalties.
Billericay Town v Telford United 2-3
Tiverton Town v Worksop Town 1-2
Chester City v Blyth Spartans 4-2
Forest Green Rovers v Rushden & Diamonds . 2-0

SIXTH ROUND

Hereford United v Burton Albion 1-0
Canvey Island v Telford United 1-0
Forest Green Rovers v Worksop Town 2-1
Chester City v Southport 1-0

SEMI-FINAL (two legs)

Forest Green Rovers v Hereford United . 2-2, 4-1
Canvey Island v Chester City 2-0, 2-0

FINAL (at Villa Park)

13 MAY

Canvey Island (1) 1 *(Chenery 16)*
Forest Green Rovers (0) 0 10,007

Canvey Island: Harrison; Ward, Bodley, Chenery, Kennedy, Parmenter, Stimson (Tanner 84), Tilson, Duffy, Gregory, Vaughan (Jones 75).
Forest Green Rovers: Perrin; Lockwood, Cousins, Clark, Daley, Drysdale (Bennett F 46), Foster M, Slater, Burns, Foster A (Hunt 74), Meechan.
Referee: A. Wiley (Burntwood).

Stephen Perrin, the Forest Green goalkeeper, seems not to be intimidated by Canvey Island's John Kennedy.
(Actionimages/Andrew Couldridge)

FA CARLSBERG VASE 2000–2001

FIRST QUALIFYING ROUND

Dunston FB v Denaby United	3-0
Willington v Hallam	0-3
Evenwood Town v Ramsbottom United	2-5
Squires Gate v Bacup Borough	5-0
Chadderton v Rossendale United	1-3
Guisborough Town v Prescot Cables	0-1
West Allotment Celtic v Northallerton Town	0-1
Thornaby v Blackpool Mechanics	1-1, 3-2
Worsbrough Bridge MW v Maltby Main	2-1
Darwen v Louth United	3-2
Morpeth Town v Brandon United	2-3
Prudhoe Town v Glasshoughton Welfare	1-5
Hatfield Main v Harrogate Railway	1-0
Fleetwood Freeport v Washington Ikeda Hoover	2-1
Billingham Synthonia v Peterlee Newtown	3-1
Borrowash Victoria v Marconi	3-2
Ludlow Town v Selston	3-1
St Andrews v Wolverhampton Casuals	1-0
Blackstone v Highgate United	5-4
Cheslyn Hay v Shifnal Town	2-4
Highfield Rangers v Studley BKL	1-1, 1-0
Boldmere St Michaels v Downes Sports	4-0
Staveley MW v Holwell Sports	3-1
Meir KA v Stafford Town	2-0
Arnold Town v Kirby Muxloe	2-1
Witham Town v Brackley Town	2-4
Swaffham Town v Bedford United	1-1, 2-3
Sawbridgeworth Town v Haverhill Rovers	1-2
Hoddesdon Town v Burnham Ramblers	2-0
AFC Wallingford v Ipswich Wanderers	3-2
Brentwood v Brach Sparta	1-2
Tiptree United v Royston Town	3-1
Long Buckby v Derham Town	1-6
Worboys Town v Thetford Town	3-0
Hadleigh United v Southend Manor	2-1
St Margaretsbury v Dunstable Town	2-2, 1-4
Bicester Town v Edgware Town	1-0
Potton United v Holmer Green	2-3
Harwich & Parkeston v Brook House	4-0
Southall v Chalfont St Peter	5-3
Downham Town v Harpenden Town	2-1
Langford v Kempston Rovers	1-2
Ware v Leverstock Green	2-0
Northampton Spencer v Harringey Borough	3-3, 1-1
Harringey Borough won 3-2 on penalties.	
Wellingborough Town v Desborough Town	1-0
Wokingham Town v Whitehawk	1-0
Wick v Lancing	5-0
Blackfield & Langley v Whitstable Town	1-1, 0-3
Southwick v Crowborough Athletic	3-2
Tie awarded to Crowborough Athletic; Southwick	
fielded ineligible players.	
Camberley Town v Bracknell Town	0-3
Reading Town v Three Bridges	3-2
Horsham v Pagham	4-0
Hailsham Town v Carterton Town	1-2
Portsmouth Royal Navy v Moneyfields	0-1
VCD Athletic v Tonbridge Wells	2-1
Windsor & Eton v Ash United	3-2
Whitchurch United v Peacehaven & Telscombe	1-0
Gosport Borough v Ashford Town (Middlesex)	0-4
Brockenhurst v Chatham Town	3-1
Brislington v Odd Down	3-2
Frome Town v Westbury United	1-0
Bemerton Heath Harlequins v Almondsbury Town	2-0
Wellington Town v Hallen	1-2
Fairford Town v Keynsham Town	1-3
Devizes Town v Backwell United	1-2
Bridport v Christchurch	2-2, 5-2

SECOND QUALIFYING ROUND

Garforth Town v Jarrow Roofing Boldon CA	1-3
Easington Colliery v Shotton Comrades	1-0
Maine Road v Newcastle Benfield Saints	3-4
Hatfield Main v Atherton LR	1-2
Newcastle Blue Star v Castleton Gabriels	1-1, 1-1
Castleton Gabriels won 4-2 on penalties.	
Squires Gate v Tadcaster Albion	4-1
Poulton Victoria v Cheadle Town	1-2
Northallerton Town v Holker Old Boys	0-2

Selby Town v Atherton Collieries	2-0
Woodleigh Sports v Dunston FB	2-3
Hebburn v Glasshoughton Welfare	1-4
Bridlington Town v Goole	1-2
Durham City v West Auckland Town	1-2
Brandon United v Horden CW	4-0
Sheffield v Pontefract Collieries	2-0
Kennek Ryhope CA v Hall Road Rangers	1-2
Curzon Ashton v Darwen	4-1
Ramsbottom United v Thackley	4-3
Billingham Synthonia v Salford City	3-0
Rossington Main v Marske United	0-2
Rossendale United v Parkgate	1-0
Yorkshire Amateur v St Helens Town	3-6
Ashington v Billingham Town	1-3
Oldham Town v Thornaby	1-2
Great Harwood Town v Armthorpe Welfare	3-2
Chester-Le-Street Town v Hallam	2-0
South Shields v Penrith	2-1
Esh Winning v Prescot Cables	0-2
Worsbrough Bridge MW v Fleetwood Freeport	1-3
Winterton Rangers v Shildon	5-2
Liversedge v Nelson	4-2
Brodsworth v Pickering Town	0-4
Abbey Hey v Wickham	2-1
Barwell v Staveley MW	2-0
Shirebrook Town v Pelsall Villa	2-1
Dudley Town v Rainworth MW	3-0
Buxton v Boston Town	3-2
Lye Town v Southam United	2-0
Westfields v Sandwell Borough	1-0
Barrow Town v Blackstone	5-2
Bolehall Swifts v Anstey Nomads	1-0
Cradley Town v Pegasus Juniors	1-3
Handrahan Timbers v Dunkirk	2-0
Heath Hayes v Bourne Town	3-0
Arnold Town v Malvern Town	1-0
West Midlands Police v Halesowen Harriers	1-6
Gornal Athletic v Bridgnorth Town	0-4
Causeway United v Meir KA	3-0
Boldmere St Michaels v Bloxwich Town	1-0
Nettleham v Kidsgrove Athletic	0-5
Highfield Rangers v Birstal United	7-0
Knypersley Victoria v Holbeach United	0-4
Stapenhill v St Andrews	1-1, 1-3
Long Eaton United v Alvechurch	1-1, 2-1
Gedling Town v Ludlow Town	3-1
Shifnal Town v Ibstock Welfare	0-2
Tivedale v Kington Town	4-4, 1-2
Stourport Swifts v Kings Heath	8-1
Wednesfield v Borrowash Victoria	0-4
Quorn v Kimberley Town	2-1
Leek CSOB v Friar Lane OB	3-0
Sutton Town v Star	1-1, 3-0
Rushall Olympic v Sandiacre Town	9-0
Glapwell v Willenhall Town	1-1, 1-2
Tring Town v Arlesey Town	1-4
Holmer Green v Somersett Ambury V&E	1-5
Lowestoft Town v Leyton	10-1
Waltham Abbey v Hoddesdon Town	2-1
Cheshunt v Yaxley	3-2
Kempston Rovers v Wotton Blue Cross	1-1, 3-4
Milton Keynes City v Kingsbury Town	4-1
Marlow v Clacton Town	1-0
Great Yarmouth Town v Cockfosters	1-0
Beaconsfield SYCOB v Bicester Town	0-2
Haverhill Rovers v Hornchurch	1-1, 0-2
Cornard United v Leighton Town	0-7
St Neots Town v Flackwell Heath	1-1, 0-6
Southall v AFC Wallingford	1-2
Clapton v Brach Sparta	2-4
Eynesbury Rovers v Harringey Borough	0-1
Derham Town v Halstead Town	0-1
Welwyn Garden City v Somersham Town	2-0
Harefield United v Stowmarket Town	1-2
Barking v Wingate & Finchley	3-0
March Town United v Concord Rangers	1-2
Stewarts & Lloyds v Ely City	5-2
Ilford v Aveley	0-1
Basildon United withdrew v Maldon Town w.o.	
Saffron Walden Town v East Ham United	5-2
Tiptree United v Hadleigh United	3-0

Bedford United v Newmarket Town — 3-2
Worboys Town v Potters Bar Town — 2-5
Soham Town Rangers v Gorleston — 1-3
Needham Market v Brightlingsea United — 2-0
Felixstowe & Walton United v Wivenhoe Town — 1-2
Buckingham Town v Stanway Rovers — 3-1
Wellingborough Town v Dunstable Town — 0-1
Downham Town v Norwich United — 7-1
Bury Town v Bowers United — 2-3
Ruislip Manor v East Thurrock United — 0-5
Ware v Chatteris Town — 3-4
Bugbrooke St Michaels v Hullbridge Sports — 1-2
Biggleswade Town v Hertford Town — 2-0
Brackley Town v AFC Sudbury — 0-4
Stansted v Hanwell Town — 1-6
  *Hanwell Town removed from competition after fielding
  a suspended player; Stansted Town reinstated.*
Witton United v Dunstable Town — 0-2
Harwich & Parkeston v Brimsdown Rovers — 2-1
Dorking v Erith Town — 2-3
Croydon Athletic v Ringmer — 5-2
Godalming & Guildford v Herne Bay — 1-3
Ashford Town (Middlesex) v Beckenham Town — 2-1
Hillingdon Borough v Chipstead — 2-0
Crowborough Athletic v Sheppey United — 0-2
Merstham v Cobham — 0-1
Horsham v Egham Town — 3-1
North Leigh v BAT Sports — 0-2
Viking Greenford v Wokingham Town — 0-4
Eastleigh v Whitchurch United — 4-1
Chessington United v East Preston — 0-0, 1-3
Cray Wanderers v Sidley United — 2-3
Windsor & Eton v Epsom & Ewell — 0-1
Oakwood v Lordswood — 0-2
Fareham Town v Eastbourne United — 1-3
Cove v VCD Athletic — 4-2
Whitstable Town v Shoreham — 2-0
Abingdon Town v Molesey — 1-4
Milton United v Greenwich Borough — 2-4
Bracknell Town v Hythe United — 1-2
Walton Casuals v Selsey — 5-3
Arundel v Chessington & Hook United — 8-5
Hungerford Town v Carterton Town — 0-2
Eastbourne Town v Andover — 5-1
Corinthian Casuals v Wick — 1-2
Sandhurst Town v Lewes — 0-4
Didcot Town v Reading Town — 3-0
Moneyfields v Brockenhurst — 1-2
Thatcham Town v Redhill — 1-2
Farnham Town v Hassocks — 0-4
Chichester City United v Littlehampton Town — 1-0
Abingdon United v Slade Green — 1-0
Westfield v Wantage Town — 3-1
Melksham Town v Keynsham Town — 3-0
Shepton Mallet v Pershore Town — 0-2
Bishop Sutton v St Blazey — 0-6
Elmore v Dawlish Town — 4-1
Swindon Super Marine v Ross Town — 4-1
Bemerton Heath Harlequins v Falmouth Town — 0-2
Downton v Cirencester Academy — 2-5
Harrow Hill v Barnstaple Town — 3-0
Backwell United v Warminster Town — 0-1
Willand Rovers v Welton Rovers — 1-0
Bournemouth v Calne Town — 1-1, 1-1
  Bournemouth won 6-5 on penalties.
Brislington v Frome Town — 3-2
Bridgwater Town v Bridport — 1-0
Clevedon United v Bristol Manor Farm — 4-1
Bideford v Cullompton Rangers — 3-0
Chard Town v Street — 1-2
Hallen v Shortwood United — 1-0
Minehead Town v Torrington — 1-2
Ilfracombe Town v Tuffley Rovers — 0-3

FIRST ROUND

Winterton Rangers v St Helens Town — 2-3
Castleton Gabriels v Tow Law Town — 0-1
Dunston FB v Liversedge — 2-1
Glasshoughton Welfare v Goole — 1-0
Seaham Red Star v Hall Road Rangers — 5-3
Ramsbottom United v Easington Colliery — 1-3
South Shields v Jarrow Roofing Boldon CA — 1-2
Squires Gate v Flixton — 4-0
Thornaby v Whitley Bay — 0-3
Abbey Hey v Warrington Town — 0-4

Marske United v Atherton LR — 6-1
Billingham Synthonia v West Auckland Town — 0-3
Fleetwood Freeport v Cheadle Town — 2-0
Great Harwood Town v Brigg Town — 1-1, 2-3
Selby Town v Rossendale United — 0-0, 0-2
Chester-Le-Street Town v Pickering Town — 0-1
Prescot Cables v Brandon United — 3-2
Clitheroe v Holker Old Boys — 2-0
Newcastle Benfield Saints v Sheffield — 3-2
Curzon Ashton v Billingham Town — 2-3
Holbeach United v Bolehall Swifts — 4-2
St Andrews v Rushall Olympic — 0-3
Kidsgrove Athletic v Shirebrook Town — 1-2
Ibstock Welfare v Bridgnorth Town — 3-4
Handrahan Timbers v Westfields — 1-0
Stratford Town v Stourbridge — 0-0, 2-0
Sutton Town v Arnold Town — 0-3
Pegasus Juniors v Dudley Town — 2-1
Kington Town v Boldmere St Michaels — 0-1
Willenhall Town v Borrowash Victoria — 0-2
Quorn v Gedling Town — 0-2
Heath Hayes v Barrow Town — 3-3, 2-3
Halesowen Harriers v Oadby Town — 0-3
Nantwich Town v Long Eaton United — 2-0
Oldbury United v Stourport Swifts — 1-2
Highfield Rangers v Lye Town — 4-3
Leek CSOB v Causeway United — 1-1, 2-1
Barwell v Buxton — 1-0
Stotfold v Brach Sparta — 5-1
Bowers United v Coggenhoe United — 4-2
Biggleswade Town v Great Yarmouth Town — 4-2
Hornchurch v Bicester Town — 2-0
AFC Sudbury v Wotton Blue Cross — 5-2
Maldon Town v Somersett Ambury V&E — 2-1
Chatteris Town v Diss Town — 0-2
Stansted Town v Bedford United — 1-3
East Thurrock United v Wivenhoe Town — 3-0
Marlow v Flackwell Heath — 5-1
Harwich & Parkeston v Dunstable Town — 3-4
Mildenhall Town v Saffron Walden Town — 3-2
Lowestoft Town v Potters Bar Town — 2-1
Stewarts & Lloyds v Welwyn Garden City — 2-3
Barking v Concord Rangers — 3-1
Fakenham Town v Aveley — 1-3
Stowmarket Town v Harringey Borough — 4-0
Ford Sports Daventry v Needham Market — 1-0
Waltham Abbey v Raunds Town — 4-3
  *Waltham Abbey removed from competition; fielding
  suspended player under another name.*
Arlesey Town v Leyton Pennant — 4-0
Hullbridge Sports v Wembley — 1-4
Hemel Hempstead Town v AFC Wallingford — 2-0
Leighton Town v Downham Town — 7-2
Cheshunt v Tiptree United — 2-1
Gorleston v Halstead Town — 5-1
Milton Keynes City v Buckingham Town — 2-1
Tooting & Mitcham United v Bedfont — 5-2
Hythe United v Eastbourne Town — 1-0
Chichester City United v Eastbourne United — 5-2
Redhill v Greenwich Borough — 1-3
Sheppey United v Herne Bay — 0-3
Croydon Athletic v BAT Sports — 4-1
Fleet Town v Epsom & Ewell — 1-2
Chertsey Town v Banstead Athletic — 2-2, 0-2
Cobham v Thamesmead Town — 0-1
Abingdon United v East Preston — 1-0
Erith Town v Whitstable Town — 1-2
Arundel v Molesey — 2-3
Ashford Town (Middlesex) v Hillingdon Borough — 1-0
Walton Casuals v Cove — 2-2, 0-2
Hassocks v Horsham — 2-2, 1-2
Wokingham Town v Lordswood — 3-2
Lewes v Wick — 2-1
Westfield v Sidley United — 1-0
Melksham Town v Eastleigh — 3-0
Highworth Town v Brislington — 1-2
Warminster Town v Elmore — 4-1
Carterton Town v Cirencester Academy — 2-0
Brockenhurst v Didcot Town — 4-3
Clevedon United v Torrington — 3-1
Hallen v Harrow Hill — 4-1
Street v Pershore Town — 3-1
Tuffley Rovers v Lymington & New Milton — 0-2
Wimbourne Town v AFC Newbury — 2-0
Swindon Super Marine v Yate Town — 0-3
Falmouth Town v Willand Rovers — 4-1

Bideford v Bridgwater Town — 1-3
St Blazey v Bournemouth — 4-1

SECOND ROUND
Squires Gate v Glossop North End — 3-2
Glasshoughton Welfare v Billingham Town — 0-2
Ossett Albion v Bedlington Terriers — 3-4
Crook Town v Rossendale United — 0-3
Prescot Cables v Seaham Red Star — 5-2
Skelmersdale United v St Helens Town — 1-2
Mossley v Consett — 2-3
Easington Colliery v Clitheroe — 0-1
Brigg Town v Jarrow Roofing Boldon CA — 2-1
West Auckland Town v Dunston FB — 1-4
Warrington Town v Fleetwood Freeport — 0-3
Eccleshill United v Newcastle Benfield Saints — 3-1
Tow Law Town v Whitley Bay — 1-0
Marske United v Pickering Town — 2-1
Barrow Town v Barwell — 1-2
Shirebrook Town v Newcastle Town — 0-1
Handrahan Timbers v Bridgnorth Town — 2-3
Holbeach United v Heanor Town — 1-2
Oadby Town v Boldmere St Michaels — 2-1
Highfield Rangers v Rushall Olympic — 1-3
Alfreton Town v Arnold Town — 3-4
Stourport Swifts v Chasetown — 3-2
Gedling Town v Leek CSOB — 2-2, 1-0
Pegasus Juniors v Nantwich Town — 2-2, 2-4
Stratford Town v Mickelover Sports — 1-2
Borrowash Victoria v Milton Keynes City — 4-1
Biggleswade Town v Gorleston — 4-2
Arlesey Town v Aveley — 2-0
Hornchurch v Letchworth — 1-0
Mildenhall Town v Stowmarket Town — 3-3, 1-0
Woodbridge Town v Barking — 2-2, 0-3
Stotfold v Great Wakering Rovers — 3-2
Welwyn Garden City v Dunstable Town — 1-3
Raunds Town v AFC Sudbury — 3-2
Bowers United v Wroxham — 3-0
Cheshunt v Maldon Town — 0-4
Wembley v London Colney — 1-2
Hemel Hempsted Town v Tilbury — 1-1
(Abandoned 90 minutes; waterlogged pitch), — 2-1
Ford Sports Daventry v East Thurrock United — 0-3
Leighton Town v Berkhamsted Town — 2-5
Bedford United v Diss Town — 0-1
Marlow v Lowestoft Town — 1-0
Whitstable Town v Hythe United — 0-1
Epsom & Ewell v Banstead Athletic — 2-1
AFC Totton v Molesey — 4-0
Cowes Sports v Horsham YMCA — 4-0
Lewes v Westfield — 0-1
Greenwich Borough v Cove — 3-3, 1-2
Saltdean United v Chichester City United — 4-1
Metropolitan Police v Croydon Athletic — 1-2
Ramsgate v Ashford Town (Middlesex) — 0-2
Horsham v Herne Bay — 5-2
Abingdon United v Burgess Hill Town — 0-0, 1-2
Deal Town v Tooting & Mitcham United — 0-2
Wokingham Town v Thamesmead Town — 0-4
Lymington & New Milton v Bridgwater Town — 1-1
(Abandoned 65 minutes; waterlogged pitch), — 2-0
Brockenhurst v Paulton Rovers — 3-2
Clevedon United v Hallen — 0-2
Melksham Town v Porthleven — 1-2
Warminster Town v Falmouth Town — 1-3
Brislington v Wimbourne Town — 1-2
St Blazey v Carterton Town — 4-4, 1-3
Taunton Town v Street — 9-0
Chippenham Town v Yate Town — 2-0

THIRD ROUND
Fleetwood Freeport v Clitheroe — 2-3
Stourport Swifts v Dunston FB — 1-0
Prescot Cables v Oadby Town — 1-1, 1-3
Mickelover Sports v Newcastle Town — 3-1
Borrowash Victoria v Eccleshill United — 3-1
Billingham Town v Tow Law Town — 2-1
Squires Gate v St Helens Town — 0-3
Arnold Town v Gedling Town — 3-1
Bridgnorth Town v Rushall Olympic — 0-3
Rossendale United v Brigg Town — 2-3
Consett v Heanor Town — 3-0

Bedlington Terriers v Nantwich Town — 0-0, 1-0
Barwell v Marske United — 1-2
Berkhamsted Town v Hythe United — 2-0
Cove v London Colney — 6-1
Mildenhall Town v Porthleven — 0-0, 1-2
Maldon Town v Hallen — 1-2
Biggleswade Town v Brockenhurst — 2-5
Thamesmead Town v Raunds Town — 2-1
Ashford Town (Middlesex) v Saltdean United — 2-0
Westfield v Bowers United — 3-0
Lymington & New Milton v Stotfold — 3-4
Hemel Hempstead Town v Croydon Athletic — 1-2
Wimbourne Town v East Thurrock United — 3-2
Diss Town v Taunton Town — 2-3
Barking v Chippenham Town — 1-2
AFC Totton v Horsham — 3-1
Epsom & Ewell v Marlow — 1-1, 1-2
Tooting & Mitcham United v Dunstable Town — 1-0
Arlesey Town v Burgess Hill Town — 4-1
Cowes Sports v Hornchurch — 0-1
Falmouth Town v Carterton Town — 3-0

FOURTH ROUND
Hallen v Borrowash Victoria — 2-1
Consett v St Helens Town — 0-1
Stourport Swifts v Mickelover Sports — 5-2
Arnold Town v Tooting & Mitcham United — 0-3
Berkhamsted Town v Hornchurch — 1-1, 2-1
Ashford Town (Middlesex) v Oadby Town — 0-1
Brigg Town v Billingham Town — 3-2
AFC Totton v Chippenham Town — 0-2
Thamesmead Town v Rushall Olympic — 0-0
(abandoned after 90 mins) — 0-1
Marske United v Porthleven — 2-1
Wimbourne Town v Clitheroe — 2-4
Marlow v Stotfold — 1-0
Brockenhurst v Taunton Town — 1-4
Cove v Croydon Athletic — 5-1
Arlesey Town v Westfield — 6-0
Bedlington Terriers v Falmouth Town — 4-1

FIFTH ROUND
Marlow v Marske United — 0-1
Cove v Chippenham Town — 2-3
Clitheroe v Rushall Olympic — 3-1
Taunton Town v Arlesey Town — 2-1
Berkhamsted Town v St Helens Town — 3-1
Oadby Town v Bedlington Terriers — 2-4
Tooting & Mitcham United v Stourport Swifts — 4-1
Brigg Town v Hallen — 6-5

SIXTH ROUND
Marske United v Bedlington Terriers — 1-1, 0-4
Chippenham Town v Clitheroe — 0-2
Brigg Town v Berkhamsted Town — 1-2
Taunton Town v Tooting & Mitcham United — 3-0

SEMI-FINALS (two legs)
Bedlington Terriers v Berkhamsted Town — 0-3, 1-2
Taunton Town v Clitheroe — 5-0, 3-4

FINAL (at Villa Park)

6 MAY

Berkhamsted Town (0) 1 *(Lowe 73 (pen))*
Taunton Town (2) 2 *(Fields 31, Laight 45)* — 8439
Berkhamsted Town: O'Connor; Mullins, Nightingale, Aldridge, Coleman, Lowe, Yates, Brockett, Richardson, Smith B, Adebowale.
Taunton Town: Draper; Down, Chapman, Cann (Tallon), West, Hawkings, Fields (Groves), Kelly, Laight, Lynch (Hapgood), Bastow.
Referee: E. Wolstenholme (Lancs).

THE AXA FA YOUTH CUP 2000–2001

(in association with *The Times*)

FIRST QUALIFYING ROUND

Chadderton v Gretna	4-1
Doncaster Rovers v Chester City	2-2, 2-1
Ashton United v Selby Town	4-1
Pontefract Collieries v Worksop Town	2-2, 4-3
Burscough v Northwich Victoria	1-0
Guiseley w.o. v Louth United withdrew	
Clitheroe v Consett	1-4
Warrington Town v Kendal Town	2-1
Scarborough v Farsley Celtic	1-0
Salford City v Runcorn	2-1

Match awarded to Runcorn; Salford City fielded an ineligible player.

Emley v Stocksbridge Park Steels	1-0
Rossendale United v Workington	2-5
Crook Town v Morecambe	0-0, 5-3
Frickley Athletic w.o. v Stalybridge Celtic withdrew	
Harrogate Town v Lancaster City	0-2
Holwell Sports v Pegasus Juniors	2-0
Redditch United v Malvern Town	2-1
Alvechurch v Mickelover Sports	2-0
Kettering Town v Bridgnorth Town	3-1
Congleton Town v Racing Club Warwick	1-2
Ilkeston Town v Boldmere St Michaels	1-1, 0-4
Lincoln United v Gresley Rovers	9-1
Leek Town v Telford United	1-2
Sutton Coldfield Town v Bloxwich Town	1-2
Handrahan Timbers v Willenhall Town	0-4
Hednesford Town v Glossop North End	6-1
Birstall United v Burton Albion	1-3
Paget Rangers v Arnold Town	2-0
Grantham Town v Rugby United	2-0
Bromsgrove Rovers v Bedworth United	1-1, 3-5
Tamworth v Hinckley United	4-6
Atherstone United v Dudley Sports	3-1
Newcastle Town v Matlock Town	5-1
Nuneaton Borough v Belper Town	3-1
Stevenage Borough v Witham Town	5-1
Hemel Hempstead Town v Leyton Pennant	6-0
Bury Town v Burnham Ramblers	2-0
Southall v Tring Town	2-0
Ilford v Cambridge City	0-10
Hornchurch v Banbury United	0-1
Wellingborough Town v Braintree Town	3-3, 3-0
Brook House v Beaconsfield SYCOB withdrew	
Enfield v Bugbrooke St Michaels	1-0
Wingate & Finchley v Harlow Town	1-0
Potters Bar Town v Leyton	9-1
Clacton Town v Romford	1-7
Wroxham v Bowers United	5-0
Concord Rangers v Long Buckby	1-2
Chesham United v Maldon Town	2-2, 2-2

Maldon Town won 4-3 on penalties.

Bedford Town v Welwyn Garden City	6-0
Wisbech Town v Ware	3-1
Southend Manor v Waltham Abbey	1-1

Southend Manor won 5-3 on penalties.

Great Wakering Rovers v Uxbridge	1-1, 0-1
Heybridge Swifts v Northwood	3-1
Wembley v Flackwell Heath	6-1
Tilbury v Ruislip Manor	0-1
Ipswich Wanderers v St Neots Town	8-0
Rushden & Diamonds v Northampton Spencer	4-0
Canvey Island v Bishop's Stortford	2-3
Histon v Soham Town Rangers	3-0
Sawbridgeworth Town withdrew v Coggenhoe United w.o.	
St Albans City v Ely City	2-1
Marlow v Milton Keynes City	7-1
Leighton Town v Hitchin Town	0-1
Staines Town v Royston Town	3-1
Aylesbury United v Clapton	4-0

Match awarded to Clapton; Aylesbury United fielded two ineligible players.

Eynesbury Rovers v Haverhill Rovers	3-1
Cheshunt v Brentwood	1-2
Tiptree United v Chelmsford City	5-0
Moneyfields v Bashley	2-1
Littlehampton Town v Hillingdon Borough	3-3

Match abandoned; floodlight failure 0-4

Folkestone Invicta v Erith Town	3-1
BAT Sports v North Leigh	2-5
Whyteleafe v Westfield	4-1
Deal Town withdrew v Eastbourne Town w.o.	
AFC Lewisham v Sandhurst Town	3-2
Didcot Town w.o. v Maidenhead United withdrew	
Kingstonian v Lewes	1-4
Margate v Whitstable Town	1-3
Tonbridge Angels v Banstead Athletic	0-0, 6-2
Oxford City v Dartford	6-0
Saltdean United v Godalming & Guildford	4-1
Sutton United v Aldershot Town	2-2, 2-4
Burgess Hill Town v Ashford Town (Middlesex)	2-2, 2-6
Basingstoke Town v Abingdon United	7-1
Lordswood v Molesey	2-1
Crowborough Athletic v Camberley Town	8-2
Three Bridges v Walton & Hersham	1-2
Welling United v Tooting & Mitcham United	0-4
Chatham Town v Dover Athletic	1-0
Bedfont v Chipstead	0-3
Farnborough Town v Chichester City United	0-4
Eastleigh v Thamesmead Town	0-3
Ramsgate v Reading Town	0-4
Herne Bay v Croydon	3-2
Sittingbourne v Leatherhead	2-0
Havant & Waterlooville v Bracknell Town	3-1
Cobham v Gosport Borough	1-0
Thame United v Fleet United	6-0
AFC Newbury v Paulton Rovers	1-1

AFC Newbury won 4-1 on penalties.

Cirencester Town v Thatcham Town	3-2
Brislington v Street	2-1
Salisbury City v Newport County	1-4
Evesham United v Worcester City	3-5
Mangotsfield United v Yeovil Town	2-0
Chippenham Town v Gloucester City	2-4

SECOND QUALIFYING ROUND

Scarborough v Oldham Town	5-2
Crook Town v Chadderton	5-2
Ashton United v Lancaster City	3-1
Runcorn v Pontefract Collieries	4-2
Guiseley v Emley	2-1
Burscough w.o. v Frickley Athletic withdrew	
Warrington Town v Consett	2-2

Warrington Town won 4-2 on penalties.

Workington v Doncaster Rovers	1-4
Boldmere St Michaels v Bloxwich Town	1-3
Atherstone United v Redditch United	0-1
Nuneaton Borough v Hednesford Town	1-1, 2-1
Kettering Town v Bedworth United	3-2
Willenhall Town v Hinckley United	0-5
Telford United v Lincoln United	0-3
Racing Club Warwick v Corby Town	1-0
Stourbridge v Newcastle Town	4-1
Paget Rangers v Cradley Town	0-4
Alvechurch v Marconi	1-4
Grantham Town v Holwell Sports	0-0

Holwell Sports won 5-3 on penalties.

Burton Albion v Chasetown	4-1
Ipswich Wanderers v Tiptree United	1-0
Hayes v St Albans City	1-0
Stevenage Borough v Staines Town	8-0
Bishop's Stortford v Enfield	2-0
Wroxham w.o. v Kingsbury Town withdrew	
Rushden & Diamonds v Brook House	5-2
Coggenhoe United v Uxbridge	0-3
Long Buckby v Newmarket Town	1-0
Histon v Wealdstone	4-2
Ford United v Wellingborough Town	4-1
Heybridge Swifts v Kempston Rovers	1-0
Wembley v Wisbech Town	2-1
Banbury United v Potters Bar Town	1-5
Brentwood v Hemel Hempstead Town	1-3
Southend Manor v Lowestoft Town	3-1
Wingate & Finchley v Southall	5-1
AFC Wallingford v Ruislip Manor	2-1
Bury Town v Bedford Town	3-1
Clapton v Hitchin Town	1-0

Eynesbury Rovers v Cambridge City	0-4
Romford v Purfleet	5-2
Marlow v Maldon Town	1-2
Moneyfields v Crowborough Athletic	1-2
Walton & Hersham v Chatham Town	2-0
Whitstable Town v Hillingdon Borough	2-3
Thame United v Tooting & Mitcham United	0-1
Woking v Cobham	5-0
Herne Bay v Chichester City United	0-4
Havant & Waterlooville v Ashford Town (Middlesex)	3-1
Eastbourne Town v AFC Lewisham	1-5
North Leigh v Lordswood	0-1
Chipstead v Saltdean United	3-1
Oxford City v Reading Town	3-0
Carshalton Athletic v Thamesmead Town	0-4
Lewes v Sittingbourne	2-4
Whyteleafe v Aldershot Town	0-3
Folkestone Invicta v Tonbridge Angels	1-5
Basingstoke Town v Didcot Town	3-2
Newport County v Cinderford Town	2-1
Forest Green Rovers v Bath City	2-3
Cirencester Town v AFC Newbury	3-0
Worcester City v Mangotsfield United	2-0
Brislington v Gloucester City	2-0
Pershore Town withdrew v Hereford United w.o.	

THIRD QUALIFYING ROUND

Warrington Town v Burscough	0-2
Runcorn v Guiseley	3-2
Ashton United v Crook Town	0-2
Scarborough v Doncaster Rovers	1-3
Kettering Town v Burton Albion	0-2
Cradley Town v Holwell Sports	3-0
Redditch United v Bloxwich Town	1-1, 0-1
Hinckley United v Lincoln United	1-4
Nuneaton Borough v Racing Club Warwick	3-1
Marconi v Stourbridge	7-0
Rushden & Diamonds v Ipswich Wanderers	5-1
Wembley v Bishop's Stortford	1-0
Bury Town v Clapton	1-0
Hemel Hempstead Town v Stevenage Borough	2-2, 1-3
Wingate & Finchley v Maldon Town	5-0
Ford United v Cambridge City	3-1
Long Buckby v Potters Bar Town	0-2
AFC Wallingford v Uxbridge	2-3
Wroxham v St Albans City	0-1
Romford v Kempston Rovers	3-1
Southend Manor v Histon	0-4
Lordswood v Basingstoke Town	0-2
Sittingbourne v Crowborough Athletic	2-1
Hillingdon Borough v Tonbridge Angels	5-10
Chipstead v Tooting & Mitcham United	1-0
Chichester City United v Oxford City	3-1
Woking v Aldershot Town	3-2
AFC Lewisham v Havant & Waterlooville	6-4
AFC Lewisham submitted incorrect teamsheet.	5-1
Thamesmead Town v Walton & Hersham	1-3
Worcester City v Newport County	2-4
Cirencester Town v Brislington	1-0
Bath City v Hereford United	1-6

FIRST ROUND

Oldham Athletic v Crook Town	5-2
Doncaster Rovers v Hull City	1-4
Lincoln City v Wrexham	0-1
Burscough v Stoke City	1-3
Walsall v Notts County	2-0
Rochdale v Halifax Town	1-1
Halifax Town won 4-3 on penalties.	
Shrewsbury Town v Wigan Athletic	0-2
Bury v Runcorn	1-3
Mansfield Town v York City	0-4
Darlington v Hartlepool United	1-1, 4-1
Blackpool v Port Vale	1-2
Chesterfield v Scunthorpe United	1-4
Rotherham United v Carlisle United	1-4
Cambridge United v Bloxwich Town	7-1
Southend United v Potters Bar Town	1-0
Wembley v Cradley Town	1-2
Histon v Marconi	1-3
Colchester United v Ford United	2-2, 2-1
Lincoln United v Luton Town	2-2, 1-2
St Albans City v Romford	1-2
Hullbridge Sports v Oxford United	0-7
Burton Albion v Kidderminster Harriers	0-1
Peterborough United v Northampton Town	2-3

Stevenage Borough v Nuneaton Borough	1-0
Barnet v Wingate & Finchley	2-1
Bury Town v Uxbridge	3-3, 5-2
Rushden & Diamonds v Leyton Orient	1-0
Bristol Rovers v Tonbridge Angels	4-0
Chipstead v AFC Bournemouth	0-2
Brentford v Torquay United	4-0
Basingstoke Town v Reading	1-3
Swansea City v Bristol City	1-0
Cheltenham Town v Cirencester Town	0-4
Plymouth Argyle v Swindon Town	0-4
Woking v Sittingbourne	1-1, 3-1
Brighton & Hove Albion v Wycombe Wanderers	1-1, 2-0
Newport County v Hereford United	2-2, 5-1
Chichester City United v Cardiff City	2-2, 0-4
Walton & Hersham v Millwall	0-6
Exeter City v AFC Lewisham	4-2

SECOND ROUND

Carlisle United v Wigan Athletic	0-1
Halifax Town v Hull City	1-3
Darlington v York City	0-0, 1-1
York City won 5-4 on penalties.	
Stoke City v Wrexham	2-1
Oldham Athletic v Port Vale	4-1
Scunthorpe United v Runcorn	3-2
Southend United v Cambridge United	3-0
Luton Town v Walsall	4-1
Northampton Town v Cradley Town	3-0
Oxford United v Bury Town	6-0
Marconi v Stevenage Borough	1-3
Colchester United v Rushden & Diamonds	6-2
Romford v Kidderminster Harriers	0-3
Cirencester Town v Swansea City	2-5
Barnet v Millwall	0-2
Bristol Rovers v Reading	0-6
AFC Bournemouth v Cardiff City	2-1
Brighton & Hove Albion v Brentford	2-2, 3-1
Newport County v Exeter City	4-1
Swindon Town v Woking	4-1

THIRD ROUND

Millwall v Leeds United	1-3
Newcastle United v Crystal Palace	2-2, 1-4
Stevenage Borough v Colchester United	2-2, 1-4
West Ham United v Southend United	3-0
Aston Villa v Gillingham	0-0, 2-2
Aston Villa won 4-3 on penalties.	
Everton v Nottingham Forest	1-1, 2-3
Newport County v Crewe Alexandra	1-3
Norwich City v Scunthorpe United	0-2
York City v Huddersfield Town	1-1, 1-0
Arsenal v Sunderland	1-0
Brighton & Hove Albion v Oldham Athletic	0-1
Tranmere Rovers v Wigan Athletic	2-0
Stoke City v Wolverhampton Wanderers	0-0, 0-2
Liverpool v Chelsea	1-1, 7-1
Ipswich Town v Leicester City	3-2
Bolton Wanderers v Swindon Town	2-1
Manchester City v Fulham	1-1, 5-1
Swansea City v Sheffield United	2-2, 0-2
Queens Park Rangers v Wimbledon	1-1, 1-1
Wimbledon won 4-2 on penalties.	
West Bromwich Albion v Derby County	0-4
Tottenham Hotspur v Bradford City	4-2
Southampton v Birmingham City	1-0
Coventry City v Oxford United	3-1
Stockport County v Watford	1-1, 2-1
Northampton Town v Blackburn Rovers	0-0
Blackburn Rovers won 5-3 on penalties.	
Reading v Manchester United	0-1
Luton Town v AFC Bournemouth	4-0
Burnley v Sheffield Wednesday	0-6
Middlesbrough v Kidderminster Harriers	4-1
Preston North End v Charlton Athletic	1-5
Hull City v Barnsley	0-3
Grimsby Town v Portsmouth	0-2

FOURTH ROUND

Leeds United v Southampton	3-0
Blackburn Rovers v Colchester United	2-2, 4-0
Manchester United v Scunthorpe United	8-0
Aston Villa v Barnsley	2-0
Ipswich Town v Crystal Palace	3-1
Arsenal v Middlesbrough	3-1
Tranmere Rovers v Sheffield United	1-2

Coventry City v Crewe Alexandra — 3-3, 2-1
Liverpool v Charlton Athletic — 4-0
West Ham United v Oldham Athletic — 0-0, 2-4
Nottingham Forest v Portsmouth — 2-1
Bolton Wanderers v Sheffield Wednesday — 1-1, 2-2
Bolton Wanderers won 4-2 on penalties.
Stockport County v Tottenham Hotspur — 2-1
Wimbledon v Derby County — 0-0
Wimbledon won 5-3 on penalties.
Luton Town v Manchester City — 2-3
Wolverhampton Wanderers v York City — 2-1

FIFTH ROUND

Manchester United v Nottingham Forest — 1-2
Wolverhampton Wanderers v Wimbledon — 0-3
Liverpool v Stockport County — 3-1
Aston Villa v Leeds United — 1-0
Manchester City v Coventry City — 1-2
Blackburn Rovers v Bolton Wanderers — 3-0
Ipswich Town v Sheffield United — 1-1, 4-2
Oldham Athletic v Arsenal — 1-3

SIXTH ROUND

Liverpool v Wimbledon — 2-1
Ipswich Town v Nottingham Forest — 2-1
Coventry City v Blackburn Rovers — 1-2
Arsenal v Aston Villa — 2-0

SEMI-FINALS (TWO LEGS)

Arsenal v Ipswich Town — 3-4, 4-2
Liverpool v Blackburn Rovers — 1-1, 1-1
Blackburn R won 4-3 on penalties.

FINAL FIRST LEG

18 MAY

Arsenal (2) 5 *(Aliadiere 13, 66, Thomas 14, Sidwell 56, Volz 72)*
Blackburn Rovers (0) 0 — 4056
Arsenal: Holloway; Bailey, Svard, Garry, Nicolau, Volz, Sidwell, Ricketts (Santry 84), Thomas, Pennant (Itonga 80), Aliadiere (Brown 88).
Blackburn Rovers: Robinson; Stone, Hockenhull, Woodhead, Cole, Blakeman, Watt, Danns, Morgan, Hevicon (Black 51) (Donnelly 80), Walters.
Referee: J. Winter (Stockton).

FINAL SECOND LEG

22 MAY

Blackburn Rovers (2) 3 *(Walters 13, Morgan 25, Danns 59)*
Arsenal (1) 1 *(Chorley 45)* — 2411
Blackburn Rovers: Robinson; Stone, Hockenhull, Woodhead, Cole, Blakeman (Watt 85), Nelson, Donnelly, Morgan, Danns (Bell 89), Walters.
Arsenal: Holloway; Bailey, Svard, Chorley, Garry, Volz (Santry 87), Sidwell, Ricketts, Thomas, Aliadiere, Itonga (Brown 69).
Referee: J. Winter (Stockton).

SEMI-PROFESSIONAL INTERNATIONALS

13 Feb

England 0
Wales 0

England: Brown (Chester C); Mustafa (Rushden & D), Underwood (Rushden & D), Skiverton (Yeovil T), Goodliffe (Hayes), Ryan (Doncaster R), Drummond (Morecambe), Pitcher (Kingstonian), Patmore (Yeovil T), Jackson (Rushden & D), Patterson (Kingstonian).
Subs: McGregor (Nuneaton B) for Patmore; Ellender (Scarborough) for Ryan; McIntyre (Doncaster R) for Underwood; West (Woking) for Skiverton; Cooksey (Hereford U) for Brown.
Attendance: 1181 at Rushden & D.

22 Mar

Holland 0
England 3 *(Roddis, Charlery, McDougald)*

England: Cooksey (Hereford U); Mustafa (Rushden & D), McIntyre (Doncaster R), Guyett (Southport), Ryan (Doncaster R), Roddis (Woking), Pitcher (Kingstonian), Drummond (Morecambe), Patmore (Yeovil T), Patterson (Kingstonian), Jones (Leigh RMI).
Subs: McDougald (Dagenham & R) for Jones; Brown (Chester C) for Cooksey; Ruffer (Chester C) for Roddis; Beesley (Chester C) for Pitcher; Charlery (Boston U) for Patmore.
At Wilhelmina 08 FC.

FA UMBRO SUNDAY CUP 2000–2001

FIRST ROUND

Ship Inn v Allerton	0-2
Northwood v East Bowling Unity	2-1
Cramlington Benedictine CSC v Hartlepool Lion Hillcarter	1-4
Littlewoods Athletic withdrew v Seymour w.o.	
Fantail v Lobster	3-0
Britannia v A3 (Canada)	3-1
Taxi Club v Hessle Rangers	0-1
Salerno v Canon	3-0
Tithebarn v Shankhouse United	1-5
Mainstay v Clubmoor Nalgo	2-4
Sandon v Oakenshaw AFC	2-0
Edwards Birmingham Celtic v Lucas Sports & Social	1-4
Rangers v Wyrley Club	4-2
Lodge Cottrell v North Road	5-2
Readflex GI's v Wedgewood	0-1
Leicester City Bus v Mackadown Lane S&S	1-3
Melton Youth Old Boys v Standens Barn	3-0
Gedling United v Little Paxton	3-0
Park Inn v Schofields	1-6
Slade Celtic v Broseley Town	1-0
Rolls Royce Celtic v Duke of York	1-0
Gossoms End v Lebeq Tavern Courage	3-5
Rainham Sports v Theale	2-0
Kingsclere Sunday v Peacock	6-3
Real Surveyor v Wishing Well	1-9
Bradley Stoke Sports v Celtic SC (Luton)	1-1
Bradley Stoke Sports won 4-3 on penalties.	
Oakwood Sports withdrew v Santos w.o.	
Branksome Railway Hotel v FC Houghton Centre	0-6
Foresters v Toby	3-0
Bretforton Sports Vic v Hexton	6-2
Heybridge Social v Percival	0-1
Continental withdrew v Hanham Sunday w.o.	
Luton Old Boys v Pioneer	2-4
Hammer v Hawkins Insulation	3-4
Longfleet St Marys v Ouzavich	0-1
Courage v Belstone	4-0
St Joseph's (South Oxhey) v Old Moat House	1-3

SECOND ROUND

Queensbury v Nicosia	1-3
Shankhouse United v Freehouse	2-3
Hartlepool Lion Hillcarter v Prestige Brighams	2-1
Albion Sports v Seymour	3-2
Orchard Park v Northwood	1-0
Salerno v Fantail	0-3
Hessle Rangers v Sandon	2-2
Sandon won 5-4 on penalties.	
Clubmoor Nalgo v Allerton	2-1
Caldway v Stanley Road	1-1
Caldway won 5-4 on penalties.	
Britannia v Frames	1-3
Dudley & Weetslade v Bolton Woods	1-3
Queens Park v Cheadle United	2-3
Melton Youth Old Boys v Lodge Cottrell	1-2
Caple Plough v Slade Celtic	1-2
Bretforton Sports Vic v Schofields	2-3
Lucas Sports & Social v Gedling United	2-1
Azaad Sports v Mackadown Lane S&S	4-0
Wedgewood v Rangers	5-1

Rolls Royce Celtic w.o. v Bishops Frome withdrew	
Grosvenor Park v Clifton Albion	5-1
Global v Bournemouth Electric	1-2
Courage v Percival	2-3
Lebeq Tavern Courage v Cavaliers	5-0
St Joseph's (Luton) v Kingsclere Sunday	3-0
Santos v Pioneer	1-0
Concord Rangers v Ouzavich	0-1
Old Oak v Rainham Sports	0-1
Balmoral v Foresters	2-3
Hanham Sunday v Bradley Stoke Sports	1-3
Biggleswade v Hawkins Insulation	4-0
Old Moat House v Wishing Well	2-3
FC Houghton Centre v Aidan Rangers	2-2
FC Houghton Centre won 4-3 on penalties.	

THIRD ROUND

Freehouse v Fantail	2-5
Nicosia v Albion Sports	0-1
Hartlepool Lion Hillcarter v Bolton Woods	2-1
Azaad Sports v Clubmoor Nalgo	2-0
Cheadle United v Frames	2-0
Lucas Sports & Social v Orchard Park	1-2
Sandon v Caldway	4-0
Lebeq Tavern Courage v Grosvenor Park	0-1
Rolls Royce Celtic v Foresters	2-1
St Joseph's (Luton) v Wishing Well	3-0
Biggleswade v Bournemouth Electric	1-0
FC Houghton Centre v Rainham Sports	3-0
Wedgewood v Lodge Cottrell	2-1
Bradley Stoke Sports v Santos	2-0
Percival v Schofields	2-1
Slade Celtic v Ouzavich	3-1

FOURTH ROUND

Grosvenor Park v Percival	3-1
St Joseph's (Luton) v FC Houghton Centre	1-3
Azaad Sports v Orchard Park	4-1
Bradley Stoke Sports v Albion Sports	0-4
Hartlepool Lion Hillcarter v Sandon	2-0
Rolls Royce Celtic v Cheadle United	3-1
Fantail v Slade Celtic	1-0
Biggleswade v Wedgewood	1-0

FIFTH ROUND

Grosvenor Park v Hartlepool Lion Hillcarter	0-1
Azaad Sports v FC Houghton Centre	1-2
Biggleswade v Rolls Royce Celtic	0-3
Fantail v Albion Sports	2-1

SEMI-FINALS

Hartlepool Lion Hillcarter v Fantail	1-0
FC Houghton Centre v Rolls Royce Celtic	0-0
FC Houghton Centre won 4-2 on penalties.	

FINAL

Hartlepool Lion Hillcarter v FC Houghton Centre	3-2

FA COUNTY YOUTH CHALLENGE CUP 2000–2001

FIRST ROUND

Northumberland v North Riding	4-0
Westmorland v East Riding	0-3
Leicestershire & Rutland v Liverpool	4-3
Staffordshire v Manchester	7-1
Isle of Man v Cumberland	3-1
Wiltshire v Kent	3-3, 2-3
Devon v Suffolk	2-0
Bedfordshire v Huntingdonshire	4-0
Norfolk v Herefordshire	1-3
Sussex v Somerset	1-0
Jersey v Middlesex	3-4
London v Berks & Bucks	3-1
Northamptonshire v Worcestershire	2-0
Army v Hertfordshire	0-1

Sussex v Cornwall	1-3
Hertfordshire v Herefordshire	1-2
Oxfordshire v Hampshire	2-4

THIRD ROUND

Herefordshire v Northamptonshire	1-2
Durham v Devon	4-2
Birmingham v East Riding	4-1
Sheffield & Hallamshire v Isle of Man	5-2
Cornwall v Lincolnshire	0-1
Hampshire v Middlesex	2-1
Tie replayed: Hampshire fielded over age player	0-4
Cambridgeshire v Gloucestershire	3-5
Surrey v Lancashire	3-1

SECOND ROUND

Northumberland v Birmingham	0-0, 2-4
Cheshire v East Riding	2-3
Isle of Man v Leicestershire & Rutland	2-2, 2-1
Sheffield & Hallamshire v Staffordshire	4-3
Durham v West Riding	4-2
Nottinghamshire v Lincolnshire	1-2
Shropshire v Lancashire	1-2
Middlesex v Essex	5-5, 2-1
Surrey v London	1-0
Kent v Cambridgeshire	2-4
Northamptonshire v Dorset	3-1
Gloucestershire v Guernsey	2-1
Devon v Bedfordshire	2-0

FOURTH ROUND

Durham v Middlesex	1-2
Gloucestershire v Sheffield & Hallamshire	1-2
Birmingham v Surrey	2-2, 3-1
Northamptonshire v Lincolnshire	1-0

SEMI-FINALS

Northamptonshire v Middlesex	1-0
Sheffield & Hallamshire v Birmingham	2-3

FINAL

Birmingham v Northamptonshire	0-3

FA XI REPRESENTATIVE MATCHES

20 Nov

FA XI 4 *(Brodie 2, Campbell, Arnold)*

Northern Premier League 0

FA XI: Brown (Chester C); Marples (Doncaster R), McIntyre (Doncaster R), Guyett (Southport), Beesley (Chester C), Ryan (Doncaster R), Carden (Chester C), Blackburn (Chester C), Campbell (Doncaster R), Brodie (Scarborough), Hawes (Altrincham).
Subs: Miller (Doncaster R) for Guyett; Woods (Scarborough) for Brown; Doughty (Chester C) for Hawes; Jones (Leigh RMI) for Carden; Arnold (Southport) for Campbell.
Attendance: 209 at Lancaster City FC.

22 Nov

FA XI 3 *(Charlery, Stevens, Burns)*

Isthmian League 1

FA XI: Bastock (Boston U); Mustafa (Rushden & D), Flynn (Hayes), Hoyle (Boston U), West (Woking), Matthews (Dagenham & R), Fisher (Kettering T), Cousins (Forest Green R), Charlery (Boston U), Watkins (Kettering T), Slater (Forest Green R).
Subs: Burns (Forest Green R) for Cousins; Stevens (Hayes) for Watkins.
Attendance: 135 at Boreham Wood.

8 Jan

FA XI 3 *(Martindale, Palmer, Barnard)*

British Universities 2

FA XI: McKenzie (Nuneaton B); Bailey (Northwich Vic), Barnard (Northwich Vic), Angus (Nuneaton B), Smith G (Worksop T), Moore (Telford U), Brunskill (Droylsden), Bambrook (Emley), Martindale (Telford U), Davis (Hednesford T), Palmer (Telford U).
Subs: Haran (Hednesford T) for Bailey; Nicholson (Emley) for Moore; Francis (Nuneaton B) for Brunskill; Wray (Nuneaton B) for Davis; Young (Nuneaton B) for McKenzie.
Attendance: 120 at Burton Albion.

30 Jan

FA XI 6 *(Roddis, Braithwaite, Perkins, Moore, Collins, Shearer)*

Combined Services 1

FA XI: Hyde (Dover Ath); Cole (Dagenham & R), Vickers (Dagenham & R), Roddis (Woking), Shearer (Dover Ath), Ward (Canvey Island), Pitman (Woking), Perkins (Woking), Vansittart (Dover Ath), Gregory (Canvey Island), Bentley (Aldershot T).
Subs: Moore (Hayes) for Bentley; Matassa (Woking) for Hyde; Collins (Margate) for Vansittart; Braithwaite (Margate) for Gregory.
Attendance: 150 at Bishop's Stortford.

15 May

FA XI 3 *(Ryan, Pitcher, Jones)*

Highland League 0

FA XI: Bastock (Boston U); Travis (Telford U), Ryan (Doncaster R), Goodliffe (Hayes), Moore (Telford U), Drummond (Morecambe), Pitcher (Kingstonian), Patterson (Kingstonian), Charlery (Boston U), Brodie (Scarborough), Jones (Leigh RMI).
Subs: Brown (Chester C) for Bastock; Roddis (Woking) for Brodie; McDougald (Dagenham & R) for Charlery.
Attendance: 350 at Clachnacuddin.

UNIVERSITY FOOTBALL 2000–2001

117th UNIVERSITY MATCH

(at Manor Ground, Oxford, May 4th 2001)

Oxford 1, Cambridge 3

Oxford: Casarella; Addley (Elliott), Stevenson, Redmaine, Adamson, Akkaya, Richards, Studin, Davis, Costello, Ratcliffe. *Subs:* Ross, McGurke, Taylor.
Scorer: Akkaya.
Cambridge: Madden; Smith (Hall), Challis, Hepburn, Drayhura, Betts (Lockwood), Harding (Maluza), Baxton, Dimmock, Glamocak, Kelly.
Scorers: Kelly 2 (1 pen), Harding.
Cambridge won for the first time in thirteen years to lead Oxford 46 wins to 45 with 26 drawn. The original fixture at Craven Cottage was postponed due to a waterlogged pitch.

UNIVERSITY OF LONDON MEN'S COMPETITIONS

(Limited to one game against each member)

Premier Division

	P	W	D	L	F	A	Pts
King's College	11	11	0	0	36	7	33
London School of Economics	11	7	3	1	29	10	24
University College	11	8	0	3	28	11	24
Royal Holloway College	11	6	2	3	14	11	20
R Free, UC & Middx Hospitals M S	11	6	1	4	35	26	19
Queen Mary Westfield College	11	6	0	5	32	25	18
Imperial College School of Medicine	11	5	2	4	35	29	17
Guy's, King's & St Thomas's M S	11	4	2	5	16	25	14
Imperial College School of Medicine	11	3	2	6	10	23	11
Goldsmiths' College	11	3	0	8	22	38	9
St Barts & R. London Hospitals M C	11	1	0	10	15	33	3
R. School of Mines (Imperial College)	11	0	0	11	9	43	0

Division 1

	P	W	D	L	F	A	Pts
University College 3rd	11	8	2	1	34	13	26
London School of Economics Res	11	8	2	1	20	11	26
Imperial College Res	11	6	2	3	30	17	20
University College Res	11	6	1	4	27	15	19
St George's Hospital M S	11	6	1	4	33	22	19
Imperial College Sch Med Res	11	5	3	3	23	16	18
Royal Holloway College Res	11	5	2	4	19	13	17
Queen Mary Westfield College Res	11	3	2	6	16	19	11
King's College 3rd	11	3	1	7	25	33	10
King' College 3rd	11	3	1	7	14	44	10
Goldsmiths' College Res	11	3	0	8	11	30	9
Royal Veterinary College	11	0	3	8	8	27	3

Division 2

	P	W	D	L	F	A	Pts
London School of Economics 3rd	10	8	0	2	26	18	24
King's College 4th	11	7	2	2	36	22	23
Imperial College 3rd	11	6	2	3	33	16	20
University College 4th	11	5	3	3	37	26	18
Guy's, King's, St Thomas's M S Res	11	5	2	4	24	20	17
Royal Holloway College 3rd	10	5	2	3	26	25	17
Queen Mary Westfield College 4th	11	5	1	5	36	29	16
R Free, UC & Middx Hosp M S Res	11	4	1	6	26	37	13
Wye College	10	3	3	4	21	21	12
Imperial College 4th	11	3	2	6	26	31	11
Queen Mary Westfield College 3rd	10	2	1	7	26	37	7
London School of Economics 4th	11	1	1	9	17	52	4

Division 3

	P	W	D	L	F	A	Pts
Royal Holloway College 4th	11	10	1	0	42	9	31
Goldsmiths' College 3rd	10	8	0	2	47	17	24
Imperial College Sch Med Res 3rd	11	6	2	3	31	16	20
R Free, UC & Middx Hosp M S 3rd	10	6	1	3	18	13	19
Goldsmiths' College 4th	11	5	2	4	23	27	17
Guy's, King's, St Thomas's M S 4th	11	3	3	5	18	27	12
St George's Hospital M S Res	9	3	2	4	13	9	11
St Barts & R. London Hosps M C Res	9	3	1	5	29	22	10
Guy's, King's, St Thomas's M S 3rd	10	3	1	6	21	30	10
Imperial College Sch Med 4th	11	3	1	7	17	44	10
St George's Hospital M S 3rd	10	2	2	6	15	29	8
St Barts & R. London Hosps M C 3rd	11	2	0	9	12	43	6

Division 4–13 teams
Won by School of Oriental & African Studies

Division 5–13 teams
Won by Imperial College 6th

BRITISH UNIVERSITIES SPORTS ASSOCIATION CHAMPIONSHIP

Men's Championship
Bath 2, Luton 1

Men's Shield
Liverpool 1, St Mark and St John 0

Men's Trophy (2nd teams and below)
Loughborough 2nds 6, Brunel WL 2nds 1

English Unis 3, Prison Service 0

British University Games, Glamorgan
England 1, Welsh 0
Scottish 1, English 1
Scottish 3, Welsh 0

Women's Championship
Loughborough 1, Crewe & Alsager 0
held at Burton Albion FC

Women's Shield
Liverpool 4, UC Chichester 1
held at Oxford Uni

English Unis 0, Fulham 2
English Unis 1, Arsenal 2

British University Games, Glamorgan
English Unis 5, Welsh Unis 0
English Unis 4, Scottish Unis 0
Scottish Unis 6, Welsh Unis 2

UNIVERSITY OF LONDON WOMEN'S LEAGUES

Premier Division

	P	W	D	L	F	A	Pts
Queen Mary Westfield College	10	7	1	2	50	16	22
Imperial College	10	7	1	2	30	33	22
Guy's, King's & St Thomas's M S	10	5	1	4	43	23	16
London School of Economics	10	3	2	5	20	31	11
University College	10	2	2	6	23	39	8
Royal Holloway College	10	1	1	7	18	42	7

Division 1

	P	W	D	L	F	A	Pts
School of Oriental & African Studies	8	8	0	0	46	1	24
King's College	8	6	0	2	22	11	18
R Free, UC & Middx Hosp M S	8	3	1	4	4	11	10
Goldsmiths' College	8	1	1	6	2	31	4
St George's Hospital M S	8	1	0	7	3	20	3

Division 2

	P	W	D	L	F	A	Pts
Royal Veterinary College	8	4	1	3	7	4	13
Royal Holloway College Res	8	4	0	4	8	3	12
R Free, UC & Middx Hosp M S Res	8	4	0	4	16	18	12
Wye College	8	3	2	3	19	16	11
Guy's, King's, St Thomas's M S Res	8	2	3	3	5	14	9

LONDON UNIVERSITY REPRESENTATIVE XI

v Ulysses	Won	4-1
v London Legal League	Won	4-1
v Oxford University	Lost	1-4
v Cambridge University	Lost	0-6
v Army Crusaders	Won	8-0
v Amateur Football Alliance	Canc'd	Rain
v Southern Olympian League	Canc'd	Rain

SCHOOLS FOOTBALL 2000–2001

BOODLE & DUNTHORNE INDEPENDENT SCHOOLS FA CUP 2000-01

FIRST ROUND
Aldenham 3, Forest 3 *(aet; Aldenham won 5-4 on penalties)*; Batley GS 0, Bury GS 5; Brentwood 3, Shrewsbury 0; Kimbolton 0, Charterhouse 1; KES, Witley 1, Manchester GS 6; King's, Chester 0, QEGS, Blackburn 2; Latymer Upper 2, City of London 0; Malvern 3, Wellingborough 0; St Bede's (Manchester) 3, John Lyon 0; St Edmund's, Canterbury 2, Ardingly 5

SECOND ROUND
Aldenham 1, Winchester 0; Alleyn's 0, Charterhouse 2; Ardingly 1, Repton 1 *(aet; Ardingly won 5-3 on penalties)*; Emanuel 0, Brentwood 4; Eton 6, Grange 0; Haileybury 2, Millfield 3; Hampton 2, St Mary's, Crosby 0; Hulme GS 1, Highgate 0; Latymer Upper 2, Victoria College, Jersey 0; Malvern 0, Bolton 2; Oswestry 0, Bradfield 4; QEGS, Blackburn 2, Lancing 0; St Bede's (Hailsham) 1, Bury GS 2; St Bede's (Manchester) 3, Dover College 1; Westminster 0, Manchester GS 3; Wolverhampton GS 2, Chigwell 0

THIRD ROUND
Charterhouse 3, Brentwood 4; Eton 2, Hulme GS 0; Latymer Upper 1, Hampton 1 *(aet; Latymer Upper won 4-2 on penalties)*; Manchester GS 1, Bury GS 2; Millfield 4, Bradfield 4 *(aet; Bradfield won 4-2 on penalties)*; St Bede's (Manchester) 4, Aldenham 0; QEGS, Blackburn 1, Ardingly 1 *(aet; QEGS, Blackburn won 7-6 on penalties)*; Wolverhampton GS 3, Bolton 1

FOURTH ROUND
Bradfield 1, Brentwood 3; Bury GS 2, Latymer Upper 0; QEGS, Blackburn 8, Eton 0; Wolverhampton GS 1, St Bede's (Manchester) 2

SEMI-FINALS
Brentwood 2, St Bede's (Manchester) 0; QEGS, Blackburn 0, Bury GS 0 *(aet; QEGS, Blackburn won 4-2 on penalties)*.

FINAL (at Leicester City)
QEGS, Blackburn 2 *(Hedley, Porter)*
Brentwood 1 *(Selby (pen))* 989
QEGS, Blackburn: A Guy; J Mohammad, A Beardsworth, R Coar, M Hedley, P MacMahon (M Naqvi), J Nicol, J West, S Maclean, C Porter, J Tootell (J Holden).
Brentwood: T Karim; C Bond, B Allen, P Harlow, D Ward, J Harrison (A Smith), E Bowler, D Paterek, P Barker, D Selby, T Winothai.
Referee: P. Jones (Loughborough).

CENTENARY SHIELD 2000–2001

UNDER-18	P	W	D	L	F	A	Pts
Scotland	3	1	2	0	2	0	5
England	3	1	2	0	2	1	5
Wales	3	1	1	1	2	3	4
Northern Ireland	3	0	1	2	0	2	1

CENTENARY SHIELD RESULTS
Wales 0, Scotland 2 – Wrexham
Scotland 0, England 0 – Kilmarnock
Grainger; Jolly, Kitchen, Pell, Stanford, Hockless, Honey, Thompson, McGill (Kennedy), Porter, Thornby (Broxup).
Subs not used: Griffin, Bull, Mortimer.

Wales 1, Northern Ireland 0 – Haverfordwest
Northern Ireland 0, Scotland 0 – Ballyclare
England 1, Northern Ireland 0 – Gillingham
England 1, Wales 1 – Swindon

UNDER-18 INVITATION INTERNATIONALS
Malaysia 0, England 0 – Malaysia
Grainger; Jolly, Kitchen, Pell, Stanford, Hockless, Honey, Griffin (Thompson), McGill (Kennedy), Thornby (Broxup), Porter.
Sub not used: Mortimer.

Singapore 0, England 2 (Thornby, Hockless (pen)) – Singapore
Bull; Mortimer (McGill), Kitchen, Pell, Kennedy (Stanford), Jolly, Honey (Griffin), Thompson, Hockless, Broxup (Porter), Thornby.
Sub not used: Grainger.

Hungary 2, England 0 – Budapest
Bull; Jolly, Kitchen, Pell, Stanford, Griffin (Thornby), Honey (Mortimer), Thompson, Hockless, Broxup, Porter.
Subs not used: Grainger, Kennedy.

ESFA WAGONWHEELS 5-A-SIDE COMPETITION
U.12 FINALS
Staged at Aston Villa Sports Centre.

BOYS FINAL:
George Stephenson School (North Tyneside) 1, Springfield School (Portsmouth) 2

GIRLS FINAL:
All Hallows RC High School (Macclesfield) 1, All Saints RC High School (Kirkby-Knowsley)

ESFA U.11 ADIDAS PREDATOR FINAL 6-A-SIDE TROPHY
FINAL:
Cranborne School (Hertfordshire) 1, Talbot Primary School (West Yorkshire) 1
Trophy Shared.
Played at JJB Stadium, Wigan Athletic FC.

ESFA PREMIER LEAGUE U.19 INTER-COUNTY TROPHY
FINAL:
Humberside CSFA 1, Gwent CSFA 0
Played at Baseball Ground, Derby County FC.

ESFA GENIE U.19 INDIVIDUAL SCHOOLS TROPHY
FINAL:
Southend High School for Boys (Essex) 0, St Cuthbert's High School (Northumberland) 1
Played at The Hawthorns, West Bromwich Albion FC.

ESFA GENIE U.19 SCHOOLS & COLLEGES TROPHY
FINAL:
Ridge Danyers College (Greater Manchester) 1, West Suffolk College (Suffolk) 2
Played at The Hawthorns, West Bromwich Albion FC.

ESFA SCHOOLSNET U.16 INDIVIDUAL SCHOOLS CUP
FINAL:
Cardinal Heenan RC High School (Merseyside) 1, Kingsdown School (Wiltshire) 4
Played at Coventry City FC.

ESFA U.16 UNITED NORWEST CO-OP TROPHY
BOYS FINAL:
Merseyside 1, Oxfordshire 0
Played at Baseball Ground, Derby County FC.

GIRLS FINAL:
Shropshire CSFA 3, Hampshire CSFA 1
Played at Blackburn Rovers FC.

ESFA U.16 UNITED NORWEST CO-OP CUP
GIRLS FINAL:
Bridgnorth Endowed School (Shropshire) 2, Castle Manor Upper School (Suffolk) CSFA 1
Played at Shrewsbury Town FC.

ESFA U.15 HEINZ KETCHUP INTER ASSOCIATION TROPHY
FINAL (two legs):
Bradford Metropolitan (West Yorkshire) 1, Swindon (Wiltshire) 1
Played at Bradford City FC.
Swindon 1, Bradford Metropolitan 1
Trophy Shared.
Played at Swindon Town FC.

ESFA U.14 HEINZ KETCHUP CUP
FINAL:
Barlow RC High School (Greater Manchester) 2, Forest Hill School (Inner London) 1
Played at Chelsea FC.

AVON INSURANCE COMBINATION 2000–2001

Fulham deservedly won the Avon Insurance Combination, narrowly seeing off the challenge of Norwich City and Reading. A 6-2 win over Brighton in their last game of the season confirmed Fulham's first ever Combination title.

Norwich City, Reading and QPR were always in the running but Fulham finally triumphed by a three point margin in what was a close and exciting title race.

Steve Kean's Fulham's squad was an eclectic and exotic mix of talented youngsters such as Zat Knight, Elvis Hammond and the precociously talented Calum Willock, scorer of hat-tricks against both Bristol Rovers and Bournemouth, a feat matched by Eddie Lewis against Swindon and Oxford, foreign imports, Nicolas Sahnoun, Andrejs Stolcers, Peter Moller and Karl Heinz Riedle. Experienced professionals such as Wayne Collins, Paul Trollope and Alan Neilson steadied the ship and Luke Cornwall and Kevin Betsy were also regular goalscorers.

Norwich scored an amazing 73 goals in their 24 League matches with Adrian Coote, winner of the Avon Insurance Top Scorer Award, and Paul McVeigh particularly deadly in front of goal.

The main purpose of the Combination is to encourage the development of young talent and many players emerged last season who are likely to make their names in the near future.

The aforementioned Calum Willock, Warren Feeney of Bournemouth, Jay Tabb of Brentford, Daniel Chillingworth of Cambridge United, Richard Kear of Cheltenham, Ben White of Gillingham, Jabo Ibehre of Leyton Orient, and Lee Mansell of Luton amongst many others, are all names to make note of.

Congratulations are due to Norwich City, winners of the League Cup in a penalty shoot-out over Reading and Fulham who also won the Avon Insurance Fair Play Award.

Norwich City capped a successful season by winning the Avon Insurance Enterprise Award for their successful Family Night Football scheme.

Avon Insurance are about to enter the eighth season of their sponsorship which has been extended to the end of the 2002–03 season by which time it will be one of the longest lasting sponsorships in English football.

Avon also concluded a successful first year of their sponsorship of the Avon Insurance League, which covers Reserve Team football in the Midlands and the North of England, thus providing the company with national UK sponsorship of Reserve Team football.

The long-awaited news from the Football Association that disciplinary points incurred in Reserve Team football will with the exception of violent conduct be counted only in the competition in which they were incurred will be a major fillip to Reserve Team football and Avon Insurance look forward with anticipation to the new season.

2000–01 SEASON SUMMARY
Champions – Fulham
League Cup Winners – Norwich City
Top Scorer – Adrian Coote – Norwich City
Fair Play Award – Fulham
Avon Insurance Enterprise Award – Norwich City
Avon Insurance Programme Award – Reading

Division One	P	W	D	L	F	A	GD	Pts
Fulham	24	18	3	3	66	17	49	57
Norwich C	24	16	6	2	73	27	46	54
Reading	24	17	2	5	43	22	21	53
QPR	24	15	2	7	36	22	14	47
Cambridge U	24	13	4	7	37	30	7	43
Millwall	24	12	5	7	33	18	15	41
Crystal Palace	24	11	6	7	42	35	7	39
Luton T	24	9	9	6	27	21	6	36
Brighton & HA	24	10	6	8	45	40	5	36
Gillingham	24	10	6	8	32	32	0	36
Portsmouth	24	9	7	8	31	29	2	34
Brentford	24	8	10	6	28	33	−5	34
Oxford U	24	9	5	10	37	40	−3	32
Swindon T	24	8	7	9	33	31	2	31
Peterborough U	24	8	5	11	32	32	0	29
Bristol R	24	7	7	10	24	34	−10	28
Bristol C	24	6	9	9	26	30	−4	27
Southend U	24	7	6	11	36	42	−6	27
Barnet	24	7	5	12	29	40	−11	26
Colchester U	24	6	6	12	25	38	−13	24
Cheltenham T	24	5	9	10	28	44	−16	24
AFC Bournemouth	24	5	6	13	27	51	−24	21
Northampton T	24	5	5	14	20	40	−20	20
Wycombe W	24	4	5	15	21	55	−34	17
Leyton O	24	2	5	17	22	50	−28	11

This table assumes that the following 18 games did not take place, and are counted as 0-0 draws:: Barnet v Colchester U, Barnet v Peterborough U, Brighton & HA v Barnet, Bristol R v Crystal Palace, Bristol R v Northampton T, Cheltenham T v Northampton T, Gillingham v Brighton & HA, Gillingham v Bristol R, Leyton O v Bristol C, Luton T v Brighton & HA, Luton T v Bristol R, Luton T v Cheltenham T, Northampton T v Luton T, Northampton T v Gillingham, Peterborough U v Luton T, Portsmouth v Crystal P (the two teams did however play a 2-2 draw in the League Cup before certain fixtures started counting for both competitions), Swindon T v Bristol C, Swindon T v Gillingham.

AVON INSURANCE LEAGUE 2000–2001

Avon Insurance's first year of sponsoring the Avon Insurance League, the reserve team league for clubs in the Midlands and North of England saw a series of exciting tussles for the titles of all three divisions.

Tranmere Rovers narrowly saw off the challenge of Huddersfield Town to win the Premier Division with Sheffield United and Bury triumphing in Divisions One and Two over Wrexham and Doncaster Rovers respectively.

Sheffield United defeated Stoke City in the Avon Insurance League Cup and the Divisional Top Scorer Awards were won by Chris Hay of Huddersfield Town, Andy Morrell of Wrexham and Mansfield's Danny Bacon.

Burnley won the Avon Insurance Enterprise Award and Wolverhampton Wanderers the Avon Insurance Programme Award.

Premier Division	P	W	D	L	F	A	GD	Pts
Tranmere R	24	16	4	4	46	25	21	52
Huddersfield T	24	16	3	5	57	28	29	51
Birmingham C	24	10	3	11	30	29	7	39
Burnley	24	12	3	9	44	43	1	39
WBA	24	11	4	9	34	25	9	37
Barnsley	24	11	4	9	36	54	−1	37
Oldham Ath	24	10	4	10	38	44	−6	34
Preston NE	24	9	3	12	44	41	3	30
Port Vale	24	9	3	12	38	42	−4	27
Rotherham U	24	6	8	10	25	34	−9	26
Bolton W	24	7	4	13	25	44	−19	25
Wolverhampton W	24	6	6	12	31	37	−6	24
Stockport Co	24	4	5	15	26	51	−25	17

Division One	P	W	D	L	F	A	GD	Pts
Sheffield U	22	13	2	7	34	20	14	41
Wrexham	22	12	2	8	41	32	9	38
Walsall	22	10	6	6	30	26	4	36
Lincoln C	22	10	3	9	42	43	−1	33
Stoke C	22	9	5	8	35	32	3	32
Scunthorpe U	22	8	6	8	37	34	3	30
Grimsby T	22	8	6	8	31	30	1	30
Blackpool	22	8	5	9	32	41	−9	29
York C	22	8	4	10	31	32	−1	28
Shrewsbury T	22	8	3	11	35	40	−5	27
Darlington	22	7	4	11	29	38	−9	25
Wigan Ath	22	7	2	13	29	38	−9	23

Division Two	P	W	D	L	F	A	Pts
Bury	20	14	3	3	51	21	45
Doncaster R	20	12	4	4	40	19	40
Mansfield T	20	11	3	6	40	27	36
Notts Co	20	9	6	5	42	32	33
Hull C	20	8	4	8	31	35	28
Scarborough	20	7	4	9	27	31	25
Halifax T	20	6	6	8	23	27	24
Hartlepool U	20	6	5	9	23	33	23
Chesterfield	20	6	4	10	22	33	22
Macclesfield T	20	5	4	11	18	31	19
Rochdale	20	4	1	15	17	45	13

FA ACADEMY UNDER-19 LEAGUE 2000–2001

Group A	P	W	D	L	F	A	GD	Pts
Nottingham F	28	16	9	3	67	34	33	57
Derby Co	28	14	8	6	38	24	14	50
Middlesbrough	28	13	7	8	46	33	13	46
Sheffield W	28	13	3	12	47	49	−2	42
Huddersfield T	28	12	4	12	43	47	−4	40
Leicester C	28	11	5	12	35	34	1	38
Leeds U	28	11	5	12	39	47	−8	38
Sunderland	29	9	8	11	28	32	−4	35
Barnsley	28	10	4	14	34	44	−10	34
Newcastle U	28	5	6	17	32	54	−22	21

Group B	P	W	D	L	F	A	GD	Pts
Everton	28	19	4	5	50	16	34	61
Manchester C	28	16	4	8	50	27	23	52
Blackburn R	28	13	9	6	46	34	12	48
Crewe Alex	28	15	3	10	56	46	10	48
Manchester U	28	13	5	10	43	32	11	44
Liverpool	28	12	5	11	47	35	12	41
Wolverhampton W	28	11	4	13	38	39	−1	37
Stoke C	28	6	7	15	37	59	−22	25
Bolton W	28	5	3	20	31	61	−30	18
Wrexham	28	2	4	22	24	77	−53	10

Group C	P	W	D	L	F	A	GD	Pts
Arsenal	28	21	4	3	75	24	51	67
Watford	28	19	3	6	53	22	31	60
Aston Villa	28	16	5	7	54	37	17	53
Millwall	28	14	7	7	51	37	14	49
Birmingham C	28	14	5	9	42	37	5	47
Coventry C	27	12	7	8	64	40	24	43
Ipswich T	28	9	6	13	40	52	−12	33
Norwich C	28	6	7	15	30	54	−24	25
Charlton Ath	28	5	7	16	36	69	−33	22
Peterborough U	28	4	2	22	18	75	−57	14

Group D	P	W	D	L	F	A	GD	Pts
QPR	28	16	7	5	47	27	20	55
Chelsea	28	12	8	8	57	36	21	44
Tottenham H	27	13	5	9	37	37	0	44
Fulham	27	10	8	9	39	42	−3	38
Wimbledon	27	9	9	9	38	26	12	36
West Ham U	27	11	3	13	47	51	−4	36
Crystal Palace	28	9	6	13	39	48	−9	33
Reading	26	8	4	14	45	57	−12	28
Southampton	28	7	5	16	52	65	−13	26
Bristol C	27	6	3	18	36	71	−35	21

UNDER-19 PLAY-OFFS

SEMI-FINALS
Nottingham F 2, Everton 0
QPR 1, Arsenal 1 (*aet*)
(*QPR won 4-3 on penalties*)

FINAL (two legs)
QPR 1, Nottingham F 0
Nottingham F 4 QPR 2 (*aet*)

FA ACADEMY UNDER-17 LEAGUE 2000–2001

Group A	P	W	D	L	F	A	GD	Pts
Derby Co	24	20	2	2	68	28	40	62
Middlesbrough	24	13	7	4	50	23	27	46
Blackburn R	24	14	3	7	55	30	25	45
Newcastle U	24	14	1	9	64	43	21	43
Leeds U	24	8	7	9	36	44	−8	31
Nottingham F	24	8	5	11	42	60	−18	29
Sunderland	24	5	5	14	17	31	−14	20
Sheffield W	24	3	3	18	29	75	−46	12

Group B	P	W	D	L	F	A	GD	Pts
Manchester U	24	13	6	5	50	36	14	45
Aston Villa	24	12	7	5	57	33	24	43
Manchester C	24	13	3	8	48	34	14	42
Wolverhampton W	24	10	4	10	36	44	−8	34
Liverpool	24	7	10	7	45	41	4	31
Everton	24	7	6	11	42	42	0	27
Bolton W	24	7	2	15	30	44	−14	23
Crewe Alex	24	6	4	14	23	49	−26	22

Group C	P	W	D	L	F	A	GD	Pts
Ipswich T	24	14	4	6	51	29	22	46
Tottenham H	24	12	6	6	57	37	20	42
Coventry C	24	13	3	8	52	40	12	42
Watford	24	8	6	10	40	39	1	30
Millwall	24	7	6	11	42	51	−9	27
Charlton Ath	24	6	5	13	31	60	−29	23
Birmingham C	24	6	3	15	28	61	−33	21
QPR	24	3	4	17	28	67	−39	13

Group D	P	W	D	L	F	A	GD	Pts
West Ham U	23	16	3	4	63	29	34	51
Arsenal	24	15	2	7	54	22	32	47
Wimbledon	22	12	1	9	28	19	9	37
Southampton	23	10	4	9	52	43	9	34
Fulham	23	10	4	9	49	48	1	34
Crystal Palace	23	9	6	8	40	46	−6	33
Reading	22	6	1	15	20	51	−31	19
Bristol C	24	4	5	15	33	61	−28	17

UNDER-17 PLAY-OFFS

Group 1	P	W	D	L	F	A	Pts
Derby Co	3	2	1	0	9	3	7
Manchester C	3	1	2	0	7	5	5
Bolton W	3	1	0	2	4	6	3
Leeds U	3	0	1	2	3	9	1

Group 2	P	W	D	L	F	A	Pts
Blackburn R	3	2	1	0	8	4	7
Manchester U	3	1	2	0	3	2	5
Liverpool	3	1	0	2	5	6	3
Sunderland	3	0	1	2	1	5	1

Group 3	P	W	D	L	F	A	Pts
Middlesbrough	3	3	0	0	8	1	9
Nottingham F	3	2	0	1	6	3	6
Wolverhampton W	3	1	0	2	2	6	3
Crewe Alex	3	0	0	3	0	6	0

Group 4	P	W	D	L	F	A	Pts
Newcastle U	3	3	0	0	13	6	9
Everton	3	2	0	1	6	4	6
Aston Villa	3	0	1	2	6	8	1
Sheffield W	3	0	1	3	3	10	1

Group 5	P	W	D	L	F	A	Pts
Ipswich T	3	2	0	1	15	4	6
Reading	3	1	1	1	4	4	4
Millwall	3	1	1	1	2	8	4
Wimbledon	3	1	0	2	4	9	3

Group 6	P	W	D	L	F	A	Pts
West Ham U	3	2	0	1	12	4	6
Coventry C	3	1	2	0	6	5	5
Birmingham C	3	1	1	1	6	4	4
Fulham	3	0	1	2	2	13	1

Group 7	P	W	D	L	F	A	Pts
Tottenham H	3	2	1	0	7	1	7
Charlton Ath	3	1	1	1	2	3	4
Bristol C	3	1	1	1	3	5	4
Southampton	3	0	1	2	1	4	1

Group 8	P	W	D	L	F	A	Pts
Watford	3	1	2	0	5	4	5
QPR	3	1	2	0	1	0	5
Arsenal	3	1	1	1	7	5	4
Crystal Palace	3	1	1	2	2	6	1

QUARTER-FINALS
Blackburn R 1, Middlesbrough 2
Derby Co 1, Newcastle U 6
Ipswich T 3, Watford 1
West Ham U 2, Tottenham H 1

SEMI-FINALS
Newcastle U 3, Middlesbrough 1
West Ham U 0 Ipswich T 2

FINAL (two legs)
Ipswich T 5, Newcastle U 0
Newcastle U 2, Ipswich T 0

NON-LEAGUE TABLES 2000–2001

JEWSON EASTERN COUNTIES

Premier Division

	P	W	D	L	F	A	Pts
AFC Sudbury	42	32	7	3	134	37	103
Gorleston	42	29	8	5	99	41	95
Lowestoft Town	42	26	10	6	99	41	88
Maldon Town	42	20	10	12	68	52	70
Clacton Town	42	19	11	12	79	58	68
Wroxham	42	18	9	15	88	66	63
Woodbridge Town	42	17	12	13	62	67	63
Great Yarmouth Town	42	18	8	16	64	59	62
Soham Town Rangers	42	18	6	18	68	70	60
Stowmarket Town	42	16	12	14	55	58	60
Diss Town	42	16	10	16	69	66	58
Ipswich Wanderers	42	16	8	18	54	52	56
Fakenham Town	42	17	5	20	60	68	56
Tiptree United	42	15	10	17	70	64	55
Mildenhall Town	42	15	9	18	58	58	54
Bury Town	42	15	9	18	56	73	54
Ely City	42	12	10	20	61	74	46
Felixstowe & Walton U	42	12	9	21	45	75	45
Harwich & Parkeston	42	11	6	25	51	98	39
Newmarket Town	42	9	9	24	50	83	36
Warboys Town	42	7	9	26	38	104	30
Halstead Town	42	7	7	28	42	106	28

First Division

	P	W	D	L	F	A	Pts
Swaffham Town	32	24	5	3	83	27	77
Dereham Town	32	22	5	5	83	23	71
Stanway Rovers	32	22	5	5	86	29	71
Needham Market	32	20	5	7	70	33	65
Chatteris Town	32	17	6	9	73	46	57
Hadleigh United	32	16	5	11	51	46	53
Haverhill Rovers	32	15	7	10	67	39	52
Cambridge City Reserves	32	14	9	9	62	47	51
Downham Town	32	14	7	11	71	60	49
Norwich United	32	12	5	15	53	46	41
Cornard United	32	10	3	19	37	85	33
Whitton United	32	8	6	18	41	64	30
Somersham Town	32	7	8	17	42	69	29
Wisbech Town Reserves	32	8	4	20	42	72	28
Thetford Town	32	7	4	21	37	81	25
Brightlingsea United	32	4	7	21	32	88	19
March Town United (–1)	32	3	7	22	18	93	15

EVERARDS BREWERY LEICESTERSHIRE SENIOR FOOTBALL LEAGUE

Premier Division

	P	W	D	L	F	A	Pts
Quorn	34	25	7	2	86	22	82
Holwell Sports	34	22	10	2	79	38	76
Highfield Rangers	34	19	10	5	78	38	67
St Andrews	34	20	6	8	72	38	66
Thringstone	34	20	5	9	73	50	65
Downes Sports	34	19	6	9	69	40	63
Coalville Town	34	18	3	13	69	56	57
Ibstock Welfare	34	15	5	14	50	44	50
Barrow Town	34	14	5	15	45	58	47
Anstey Nomads	34	14	3	17	68	65	45
Leicester YMCA	34	11	9	14	47	50	42
Thurmaston Town	34	12	6	16	49	57	42
Kirby Muxloe	32	12	5	15	54	50	41
Friar Lane OB	33	9	6	18	55	65	33
Blaby Whetstone	34	7	8	19	38	72	29
Birstall United	34	8	4	22	55	81	28
Aylestone Park	34	6	5	23	30	84	23
Cottesmore*	33	1	1	31	24	133	0
*6 points deducted							

Division One

	P	W	D	L	F	A	Pts
Thurnby Rangers	32	20	7	5	92	42	67
Ellistown	32	21	4	7	79	33	67
Ratby Sports	32	20	6	6	85	43	66
Earl Shilton Albion	32	19	5	8	61	33	62
Sileby Town	31	16	9	6	67	35	57
Huncote S&S	31	14	8	9	63	45	50
Stoney Stanton	32	14	4	14	67	50	46
Bardon Hill	29	13	7	9	72	61	46
Asfordby Amateurs*	31	15	4	12	55	52	46
Lutterworth Town	32	13	6	13	64	50	45

	P	W	D	L	F	A	Pts
Fosse Imps	31	11	10	10	60	47	43
Leics Constabulary	32	11	3	18	47	61	36
Narborough*	27	9	6	12	31	50	30
Saffron Dynamo	30	9	2	19	53	77	29
North Kilworth	32	7	2	23	45	128	23
Anstey Town	32	5	3	24	38	88	18
Loughborogh Dynamo	30	3	2	25	32	116	11
Harborough Town**	0	0	0	0	0	0	0

*3 points deducted, **resigned after 6 games – record expunged*

NORTHERN COUNTIES EAST

Premier Division

	P	W	D	L	F	A	Pts
Brigg Town	38	29	5	4	87	36	92
Ossett Albion	38	25	7	6	84	33	82
Alfreton Town	38	23	4	11	71	44	73
Goole	38	19	9	10	65	46	66
Hallam	38	19	7	12	61	51	64
Arnold Town	38	16	14	8	67	46	62
Sheffield	38	15	15	8	59	38	60
Thackley	38	16	9	13	59	57	57
Selby Town	38	16	7	15	71	71	55
Glapwell	38	13	11	14	62	58	50
Denaby United	38	15	4	19	54	63	49
Buxton	38	12	9	17	38	57	45
Harrogate Railway	38	11	9	18	59	65	42
Ecclesfield United	38	9	13	16	48	58	40
Liversedge	38	9	13	16	50	63	40
Glasshoughton Welfare	38	9	11	18	57	64	38
Garforth Town	38	9	10	19	56	75	37
Brodsworth MW*	38	11	7	20	41	86	37
Armthorpe Welfare	38	9	7	22	53	81	34
Staveley MW	38	6	7	25	42	92	25
*3 points deducted							

Division One

	P	W	D	L	F	A	Pts
Borrowash Victoria	30	22	4	4	74	28	70
Pickering Town	30	21	6	3	67	24	69
Mickleover Sports	30	18	5	7	65	39	59
Bridlington Town	30	15	7	8	48	41	52
Gedling Town	30	14	7	9	47	37	49
Hall Road Rangers	30	14	6	10	43	37	48
Parkgate	30	13	6	11	60	52	45
Hatfield Main	30	13	4	13	54	49	43
Maltby Main	30	11	6	13	36	48	39
Yorkshire Amateur	30	9	5	16	33	53	32
Worsborough Bridge MW	30	9	4	17	31	54	31
Louth United	30	8	6	16	48	58	30
Pontefract Collieries	30	6	9	15	37	56	27
Winterton Rangers*	30	8	6	16	30	53	27
Rossington Main	30	7	5	18	39	54	26
Tadcaster Albion	30	6	6	18	29	58	24
*3 points deducted							

EAGLE BITTER UNITED COUNTIES

Premier Division

	P	W	D	L	F	A	Pts
Boston Town	40	26	8	6	89	46	86
Cogenhoe United	40	27	4	9	97	51	85
Raunds Town	40	25	4	11	100	48	79
Ford Sports Daventry	40	24	4	12	78	61	76
St Neots Town	40	22	9	9	97	56	75
Wootton Blue Cross	40	21	12	7	85	48	75
Desborough Town	40	19	10	11	72	48	67
Northampton Spencer	40	19	7	14	76	60	64
Kempston Rovers	40	16	13	11	68	52	61
Yaxley	40	18	7	15	69	58	61
Stewart & Lloyds Corby	40	17	9	14	64	56	60
Blackstone FC	40	15	10	15	93	71	55
Bourne Town	40	15	9	16	72	84	54
Holbeach United	40	15	8	17	69	65	53
Stotfold	40	12	10	18	74	66	46
Bugbrooke St Michael	40	9	15	16	43	63	42
Buckingham Town	40	10	9	21	72	108	39
Wellingborough Town	40	8	9	23	57	90	33
Long Buckby AFC	40	6	6	28	57	150	24
Potton United	40	4	7	29	38	111	19
Eynesbury Rovers	40	4	6	30	40	118	18

Division One

	P	W	D	L	F	A	Pts
Daventry Town	34	23	6	5	104	30	75
Deeping Rangers	34	22	9	3	82	30	75
Thrapston Town	34	21	8	5	91	41	71
Blisworth	34	21	7	6	71	43	70
Cottingham	34	18	9	7	70	43	63
Newport Pagnell Town	34	15	5	14	59	64	50
Rothwell Corinthians	34	13	11	10	55	47	50
Woodford United	34	13	8	13	70	63	47
Harrowby United	34	12	10	12	55	43	46
Northampton ON Chs	34	11	8	15	65	71	41
Wellingborough Whits	34	10	10	14	56	68	40
Higham Town	34	9	12	13	40	49	39
St Ives Town	34	8	14	12	51	59	38
Burton Park Wanderers	34	9	8	17	53	68	35
Olney Town	34	9	6	19	44	58	33
Northampton Sileby R	34	6	11	17	52	70	29
Irchester United	34	5	8	21	30	86	23
Sharnbrook AFC	34	4	4	26	32	167	16

CHERRY RED RECORDS HELLENIC FOOTBALL LEAGUE

Premier Division

	P	W	D	L	F	A	Pts
Swindon Supermarine	38	29	4	5	86	29	91
Brackley Town	38	25	8	5	84	45	83
Yate Town	38	21	9	8	92	38	72
Didcot Town	38	20	12	6	57	27	72
Abingdon United	38	21	6	11	80	53	69
North Leigh	38	20	6	12	77	51	66
Cirencester Academy	38	18	5	15	70	54	59
Highworth Town	38	19	2	17	74	68	59
Fairford Town	38	17	7	14	54	45	58
Carterton Town	38	16	9	13	64	57	57
Shortwood United	38	15	11	12	62	58	56
Tuffley Rovers	38	16	6	16	54	58	54
Wootton Bassett Town	38	14	10	14	54	60	52
Bicester Town	38	14	7	17	59	67	49
Pegasus Juniors	38	12	4	22	67	96	40
Wantage Town	38	11	4	23	49	83	37
Cheltenham Saracens	38	9	5	24	31	76	32
Harrow Hill	38	5	10	23	36	80	25
Almondsbury Town	38	7	3	28	36	76	24
Milton United	38	5	4	29	31	96	19

Division One (West)

	P	W	D	L	F	A	Pts
Gloucester United	30	26	3	1	119	15	81
Bishops Cleeve	30	22	3	5	70	36	69
Ardley United	30	21	3	6	81	34	66
Malmesbury Victoria	30	15	5	10	65	59	50
Headington Amateurs	30	15	5	10	54	50	50
Easington Sports	30	12	6	12	55	61	42
Cirencester United	30	11	6	13	50	59	39
Middle Barton	30	9	11	10	45	47	38
Clanfield FC	30	8	8	14	45	58	32
Ross Town*	30	9	6	15	48	54	30
Kidlington	30	7	9	14	39	50	30
Letcombe FC	30	7	9	14	38	61	30
Purton FC	30	7	9	14	46	73	30
Witney Academy	30	8	6	16	37	82	30
Old Woodstock Town	30	6	8	16	36	61	26
Worcester College OB	30	5	7	18	41	69	22

*3 points deducted

Division One (East)

	P	W	D	L	F	A	Pts
Henley Town	32	25	4	3	105	33	79
RS Basingstoke	32	17	8	7	63	37	59
Southall Town	32	15	10	7	63	44	55
Quarry Nomads	32	16	7	9	66	56	55
Eton Wick	32	16	6	10	71	50	54
Rayners Lane	32	15	7	10	77	58	52
Finchampstead	32	14	8	10	75	58	50
Harrow Hill Rovers	32	15	4	13	72	71	49
Englefield Green Rovers	32	13	6	13	75	71	45
Binfield	32	13	6	13	56	55	45
Prestwood	32	12	9	11	60	65	45
Peppard	32	9	12	11	58	65	39
Chalfont Wasps	32	11	4	17	58	75	37
Martin Baker Sports	32	7	11	14	49	61	32
Penn & Tylers Green	32	10	2	20	47	75	32
Drayton Wanderers	32	7	3	22	44	90	24
Aston Clinton	32	3	1	28	40	115	10

BANKS'S WEST MIDLANDS LEAGUE

Premier Division

	P	W	D	L	F	A	Pts
Ludlow Town	44	34	9	1	100	35	111
Warley Rangers	44	29	7	8	129	54	94
Little Drayton Rangers	44	27	7	10	91	53	88
Darlaston Town	44	24	7	13	111	76	79
Causeway United	44	22	11	11	78	47	77
Shawbury United	44	22	6	16	77	59	72
Malvern Town (−1)	44	19	16	9	83	67	72
Kington Town	44	19	9	16	92	78	66
Lye Town	44	18	12	14	68	63	66
Wolverhampton Casuals	44	17	12	15	80	65	63
Wellington	44	19	6	19	67	73	63
Tividale	44	16	11	17	72	74	59
Star	44	15	12	17	77	69	57
Westfields	44	14	14	16	60	63	56
Heath Hayes	44	15	8	21	63	74	53
Bustleholme	44	15	6	23	79	91	51
Ettingshall Holy Trinity	44	14	9	21	58	80	51
Dudley Town	44	13	8	23	48	72	47
Bromyard Town	44	10	10	24	51	97	40
Walsall Wood	44	9	10	25	56	80	37
Gornal Athletic	44	10	7	27	59	105	37
Brierley Hill Town	44	10	7	27	50	127	37
Tipton Town	44	10	6	28	61	108	36

RICH CITY SUSSEX COUNTY LEAGUE

Division One

	P	W	D	L	F	A	Pts
Sidley United	38	25	8	5	65	31	83
Burgess Hill Town	38	23	9	6	77	46	78
Wick	38	19	10	9	78	51	67
Selsey	38	20	5	13	68	48	65
Horsham YMCA	38	19	6	13	74	54	63
Pagham	38	17	11	10	78	56	62
Chichester	38	17	6	15	82	67	57
Three Bridges	38	16	9	13	61	59	57
Sidlesham	38	17	6	15	64	64	57
Ringmer	38	17	5	16	55	67	56
Eastbourne United	38	14	10	14	60	53	52
Hassocks	38	15	5	18	57	58	50
Arundel	38	14	8	16	52	68	50
Redhill	38	13	8	17	62	65	47
Littlehampton Town	38	11	10	17	57	61	43
Saltdean United	38	11	8	19	54	73	41
Whitehawk	38	9	11	18	53	73	38
Lancing	38	9	10	19	58	77	37
Eastbourne Town	38	9	8	21	47	66	35
East Preston	38	7	3	28	40	105	24

Division Two

	P	W	D	L	F	A	Pts
Southwick	34	23	3	8	76	32	72
Peacehaven & Telscombe	34	22	5	7	66	36	71
Hailsham Town	34	20	6	8	81	43	66
East Grinstead	34	19	6	9	58	37	63
Broadbridge Heath	34	18	7	9	80	43	61
Worthing United	34	18	6	10	77	46	60
Oving SC	34	16	6	12	64	50	54
Westfield	34	13	9	12	49	52	48
Oakwood	34	12	10	12	55	50	46
Bosham	34	13	6	15	49	73	45
Wealden	34	12	8	14	61	59	44
Storrington	34	12	5	17	54	75	41
Shoreham	34	12	4	18	67	84	40
Shinewater Association	34	12	4	18	57	78	40
Mile Oak	34	11	6	17	66	69	39
Crawley Down	34	10	7	17	50	68	37
Crowborough	34	6	7	21	49	79	25
Lingfield	34	3	3	28	26	110	12

*Lingfield withdrawn

Division Three

	P	W	D	L	F	A	Pts
Rye United	28	21	3	4	89	38	66
Seaford Town	28	20	2	6	70	33	62
Haywards Heath	28	19	5	4	62	30	62
Steyning Town	28	15	5	8	51	43	50
Franklands Village	28	12	7	9	62	38	43
Ifield	28	12	5	11	58	57	41
TSC	28	10	8	10	58	53	38
St Francis	28	9	9	10	49	53	36
Uckfield Town	28	11	2	15	45	60	35
Ansty Rangers	28	10	4	14	51	63	34
Bexhill Town	28	8	5	15	37	51	29
Forest	28	6	10	12	39	45	28
Hurstpierpoint	28	6	6	16	37	64	24
Newhaven	28	7	3	18	39	69	24
Royal & Sun Alliance	28	4	6	18	26	76	18

MANCHESTER LEAGUE
(sponsored by Finnair)

Premier Division	P	W	D	L	F	A	Pts
Stand Athletic	28	21	0	7	91	25	63
Wythenshawe Amateurs	28	17	8	3	57	32	59
Atherton Town	28	16	6	6	46	27	54
Mitchell Shackleton	28	13	7	8	56	37	46
East Manchester	28	13	6	9	58	48	45
Failsworth Town	28	14	2	12	51	44	44
Willows	28	11	8	9	57	63	41
Dukinfield Town	28	12	4	12	39	40	40
Prestwich Heys	28	10	8	10	56	57	38
Sacred Heart	28	10	7	11	44	46	37
Monton Amateurs	28	9	5	14	51	61	32
Elton Fold	28	7	10	11	32	43	31
Springhead	28	5	12	11	46	57	27
Stockport Georgians	28	4	4	20	38	77	16
Pennington	28	3	3	22	29	94	12

MIDLAND ALLIANCE

	P	W	D	L	F	A	Pts
Stourport Swifts	42	28	9	5	109	38	93
Rushall Olympic	42	28	9	5	98	28	93
Barwell	42	26	11	5	74	35	89
Oadby Town (–3)	42	26	7	9	89	45	82
Stourbridge	42	23	10	9	93	52	79
Stratford Town	42	20	10	12	96	58	70
Boldmere St Michaels	42	19	13	10	73	59	70
Willenhall Town	42	19	8	15	76	62	65
Bridgnorth Town	42	17	8	17	79	66	59
Chasetown	42	15	10	17	55	78	55
Oldbury United	42	14	11	17	70	71	53
Cradley Town	42	15	4	23	52	80	49
Stafford Town	42	12	12	18	68	83	48
Bloxwich Town	42	14	6	22	54	80	48
Wednesfield	42	14	6	22	60	91	48
Shifnal Town	42	12	11	19	56	75	47
Halesowen Harriers	42	13	7	22	55	73	46
Stapenhill	42	12	8	22	58	91	44
Pelsall Villa	42	12	6	24	60	90	42
Knypersley Victoria (–3)	42	10	10	22	64	100	37
West Midlands Police	42	9	7	26	67	112	34
Sandwell Borough	42	9	7	26	62	111	34

REDFERN REMOVERS CENTRAL MIDLANDS LEAGUE

Supreme Division	P	W	D	L	F	A	Pts
Shirebrook Town	38	27	8	3	96	29	89
Lincoln Moorlands	38	27	8	3	78	28	89
Sneinton	38	22	4	12	79	54	70
South Normanton Ath	38	20	8	10	95	57	68
Collingham	38	19	7	12	76	52	64
Clipstone Welfare	38	18	8	12	77	52	62
Long Eaton United	38	19	5	14	73	56	62
Graham Street Prims	38	19	4	15	77	58	61
Selston	38	17	10	11	68	59	61
Dunkirk	38	17	8	13	71	69	59
Holbrook	38	18	3	17	65	62	57
Hucknall Rolls Royce	38	17	6	15	64	65	57
Welbeck CW	38	12	9	17	56	65	45
Kimberley Town	38	13	4	21	65	78	43
Nettleham	38	11	9	18	58	65	42
Heanor Town	38	12	6	20	59	89	42
Sandiacre Town	38	11	4	23	72	87	37
Mickleover RBL	38	7	5	26	50	103	26
Blackwell MW	38	6	6	26	55	102	24
Harworth CI	38	4	6	28	34	138	18

Premier Division	P	W	D	L	F	A	Pts
North Notts	32	22	4	6	96	33	70
Greenwood Meadows	32	21	5	6	75	31	68
Bottesford Town	32	20	5	7	89	49	65
Askern Welfare	32	19	6	7	75	39	63
Teversal	32	18	8	6	84	47	62
Dinnington Town	32	15	8	9	61	52	53
Ripley Town	32	15	5	12	90	61	50
Thorne Colliery	32	14	6	12	58	57	48
Radford	32	12	8	12	51	49	44
Shardlow St James	32	13	5	14	63	64	44
Ollerton Town	32	10	8	14	51	55	38
Forest Town	32	9	7	16	46	77	34
Blidworth Welfare	32	9	6	17	46	71	33
Kiveton Park	32	8	8	16	54	84	32
Stanton Ilkeston	32	8	6	18	46	67	30
Yorkshire Main	32	6	4	22	42	104	22
Mexborough Town Ath	32	2	3	27	31	118	9

JEWSON SOUTH WESTERN LEAGUE

	P	W	D	L	F	A	Pts
St Blazey	36	27	6	3	124	33	87
Porthleven	36	25	8	3	90	26	83
Liskeard Athletic	36	24	7	5	97	55	79
Holsworthy	36	24	3	9	84	44	75
Millbrook	36	22	6	8	94	45	72
Saltash United	36	21	8	7	85	43	71
Falmouth Town	36	18	10	8	72	46	64
Penzance	36	16	9	11	65	59	57
Tavistock	36	14	8	14	50	52	50
Torpoint Athletic	36	14	7	15	56	60	49
Plymouth Parkway	36	12	4	20	53	77	40
Callington Town	36	11	6	19	63	93	39
Newquay	36	10	8	18	58	81	38
Truro City	36	11	4	21	58	81	37
Penryn Athletic	36	10	5	21	49	80	35
St Austell	36	7	6	23	41	76	27
Launceston	36	8	3	25	39	92	27
Wadebridge Town	36	6	4	26	51	115	22
Bodmin Town	36	5	2	29	39	110	17

MINERVA SPARTAN SOUTH MIDLANDS

Premier Division	P	W	D	L	F	A	Pts
Beaconsfield SYCOB	36	28	4	4	80	36	88
London Colney	36	25	6	5	91	36	81
Potters Bar Town (–3)	36	25	6	5	82	39	78
Brook House	36	22	6	8	64	36	72
Somersett Ambury V&E	36	17	9	10	67	47	60
Holmer Green	36	18	2	16	58	58	56
Hanwell Town	36	16	6	14	67	52	54
Hillingdon Borough	36	14	12	10	63	61	54
Brache Sparta	36	14	7	15	70	78	49
New Bradwell St Peter	36	11	12	13	49	52	45
Hoddesdon Town	36	13	5	18	54	60	44
Bedford United	36	11	10	15	49	50	43
St Margaretsbury (+3)	36	9	8	19	45	68	38
Biggleswade Town	36	9	9	18	40	55	36
Ruislip Manor	36	10	6	20	44	60	36
Milton Keynes City	36	9	7	20	50	79	34
Royston Town	36	8	9	19	31	60	33
Haringey Borough	36	6	11	19	33	78	29
Welwyn Garden City	36	6	7	23	25	57	25

Waltham Abbey withdrew – record expunged

Senior Division	P	W	D	L	F	A	Pts
Letchworth	36	28	5	3	94	32	89
Dunstable Town	36	27	6	3	94	25	87
Biggleswade United	36	21	6	9	82	46	69
Tring Athletic	36	19	10	7	74	27	67
Colney Heath	36	19	7	10	86	44	64
Cockfosters	36	18	8	10	67	62	62
Langford	36	17	7	12	72	57	58
Ampthill Town	36	17	5	14	76	54	56
Stony Stratford	36	14	8	14	65	68	50
Leverstock Green	36	14	4	18	38	57	46
Risborough Rangers	36	12	6	18	57	73	42
Letchworth Bridger (+3)	36	11	6	19	59	82	42
Greenacres (–1)	36	10	12	14	46	66	41
Brimsdown Rovers	36	12	4	20	53	64	40
Harefield United	36	10	9	17	53	59	39
Amersham Town	36	10	8	18	34	55	38
Harpenden Town	36	7	10	19	51	76	31
Luton Old Boys	36	6	8	22	38	77	26
Totternhoe	36	3	5	28	25	140	14

Division One	P	W	D	L	F	A	Pts
Pitstone & Ivinghoe	34	26	4	4	91	34	82
Flamstead	34	22	5	7	96	46	71
The 61 FC	34	19	8	7	79	54	65
Winslow United (–3)	34	20	7	7	81	41	64
Kent Athletic	34	18	9	7	83	54	63
Old Dunstablians	34	17	7	10	88	58	58
Mursley United	34	16	8	10	93	46	56
Scot	34	15	7	12	98	76	52
Haywood United	34	13	8	13	75	50	47
Buckingham Athletic	34	11	11	12	61	58	44
Milcutt Rovers	34	12	8	14	62	73	44
Crawley Green	34	12	7	15	58	48	43
Abbey National (+3)	34	12	4	18	54	58	43
Shillington	34	11	4	19	54	74	37
Caddington	34	10	5	19	44	90	35
Markyate	34	6	8	20	36	78	26
Old Bradwell United	34	6	6	22	37	95	24
North Crawley United	34	2	0	32	21	178	6

BASS BREWERS KENT LEAGUE

	P	W	D	L	F	A	Pts
Chatham Town	32	23	7	2	76	28	76
Herne Bay	32	23	5	4	93	43	74
VCD Athletic	32	21	4	7	74	32	67
Thamesmead Town	32	18	8	6	63	29	62
Ramsgate	32	15	10	7	83	36	55
Tunbridge Wells	32	13	11	8	52	41	50
Beckenham Town	32	13	9	10	48	58	48
Whitstable Town	32	12	9	11	43	44	45
Greenwich Borough	32	12	8	12	46	40	44
Lordswood	32	12	7	13	57	55	43
Erith Town	32	13	4	15	42	49	43
Cray Wanderers	32	10	5	17	39	46	35
Slade Green	32	9	3	20	33	75	30
Hythe United	32	6	11	15	41	46	29
Deal Town	32	7	8	17	41	60	29
Faversham Town	32	6	5	21	33	68	23
Canterbury City	32	0	4	28	15	129	4

CARLSBERG WEST CHESHIRE LEAGUE

Division One

	P	W	D	L	F	A	Pts
Cammell Laird	30	24	5	1	82	27	77
Christleton	30	17	5	8	61	33	56
Poulton Victoria	30	15	6	9	73	59	51
Maghull	30	13	8	9	41	37	47
Mersey Royal	30	12	9	9	53	39	45
Helsby	30	13	5	12	59	61	44
Vauxhall Motors	30	10	11	9	57	41	41
Heswall	30	11	7	12	45	46	40
General Chemicals	30	10	6	14	45	50	36
Ashville	30	9	9	12	40	52	36
Shell Tessuti	30	10	5	15	46	56	35
Stork	30	9	8	13	44	58	35
Newton	30	10	4	16	42	75	34
Mond Rangers	30	9	6	15	39	57	33
Capenhurst Villa	30	8	8	14	47	61	32
Blacon Youth Club	30	6	6	18	48	70	24

JEWSON WESSEX LEAGUE

	P	W	D	L	F	A	Pts
Andover	44	37	5	2	153	33	116
Lymington & New Milton	44	34	6	4	106	29	108
Wimborne Town	44	28	9	7	111	52	93
Fleet Town	44	29	3	12	91	56	90
Totton	44	26	9	9	87	47	87
Thatcham Town	44	24	9	11	81	58	81
Eastleigh	44	23	10	11	87	48	79
Gosport Borough	44	23	8	13	74	44	77
Brockenhurst	44	23	7	14	93	72	76
Cowes Sports	44	22	4	18	80	70	70
Bemerton Heath H	44	15	9	20	63	70	54
Newbury	44	15	8	21	71	78	53
BAT Sports	44	14	10	20	52	75	52
Bournemouth	44	13	12	19	51	65	51
Fareham Town	44	12	10	22	48	74	46
Moneyfields	44	12	9	23	52	76	45
Christchurch	44	11	12	21	55	80	45
Hamble ASSC	44	10	14	20	39	70	44
Whitchurch United	44	8	13	23	37	72	37
Swanage T & H	44	11	4	29	52	123	37
Blackfield & Langley	44	7	8	29	32	95	29
Downton	44	6	8	30	45	103	26
Portsmouth Royal Navy	44	4	11	29	37	107	23

WADE ASSOCIATES NORTHERN ALLIANCE

Premier Division

	P	W	D	L	F	A	Pts
Walker Central	30	23	5	2	83	27	74
West Allotment Celtic	30	21	5	4	91	36	68
Shankhouse	30	18	3	9	64	32	57
Northbank	30	17	4	9	84	58	55
Seaton Delaval Amateurs	30	14	7	9	56	46	49
Ponteland United	30	14	6	10	56	46	48
Benfield Saints (–3)	30	14	4	12	69	59	43
Carlisle City	30	11	6	13	47	51	39
Coxlodge SC	30	12	2	16	53	75	38
Percy Main Amateurs	30	9	10	11	39	51	37
Newcastle University (–3)	30	12	3	15	70	67	36
Spittal Rovers	30	10	4	16	60	71	34
Winlaton	30	11	1	18	41	62	34
Ryton	30	9	4	17	39	59	31
Heaton Stannington	30	8	4	18	34	82	28
Hebburn Reyrolle	30	2	2	26	34	98	8

SCREWFIX DIRECT WESTERN LEAGUE

	P	W	D	L	F	A	Pts
Taunton Town	38	31	4	3	133	41	97
Chippenham Town	38	30	5	3	109	27	95
Paulton Rovers	38	22	11	5	91	44	77
Yeovil Town Reserves	38	21	8	9	84	46	71
Bideford	38	19	10	9	71	45	67
Backwell United	38	19	7	12	59	37	64
Devizes Town	38	19	5	14	88	62	62
Brislington	38	17	10	11	67	48	61
Melksham Town	38	16	7	15	56	55	55
Welton Rovers	38	15	8	15	63	53	53
Dawlish Town	38	14	6	18	50	68	48
Elmore	38	14	4	20	67	80	46
Bridport	38	10	13	15	51	63	43
Barnstaple Town	38	12	7	19	45	79	43
Bridgwater Town (–3)	38	11	11	16	45	58	41
Bishop Sutton	38	10	11	17	59	84	41
Odd Down	38	10	8	20	34	57	38
Bristol Manor Farm	38	8	8	22	37	66	32
Westbury United	38	3	5	30	27	101	14
Minehead Town (–3)	38	5	0	33	34	156	12

Division One

	P	W	D	L	F	A	Pts
Team Bath	36	26	6	4	108	22	84
Keynsham Town	36	25	7	4	79	35	82
Frome Town	36	21	4	11	77	45	67
Hallen	36	20	6	10	81	52	66
Bitton	36	19	7	10	66	49	64
Bath City Reserves	36	17	6	13	74	70	57
Exmouth Town	36	15	7	14	76	54	52
Warminster Town	36	14	10	12	48	53	52
Corsham Town	36	16	4	16	60	67	52
Torrington	36	14	8	14	69	72	50
Chard Town	36	11	9	16	52	75	42
Pewsey Vale	36	12	6	18	47	79	42
Street	36	10	9	17	40	63	39
Wellington	36	11	5	20	40	63	38
Larkhall Athletic	36	11	5	20	46	73	38
Ilfracombe	36	9	10	17	48	64	37
Cadbury Heath	36	10	5	21	48	68	35
Worle St Johns	36	10	5	21	64	87	35
Calne Town	36	8	7	21	35	67	31

ALBANY NORTHERN LEAGUE

Division One

	P	W	D	L	F	A	Pts
Bedlington Terriers	40	28	5	7	108	31	89
Dunston Federation	40	26	7	7	93	49	85
Marske United	40	24	7	9	82	35	79
Durham City	40	24	6	10	95	42	78
Brandon United	40	23	8	9	86	53	77
Peterlee Newtown	40	22	9	9	75	55	75
Tow Law Town	40	20	7	13	90	64	67
Billingham Synthonia	40	18	11	11	81	58	65
Billingham Town	40	19	7	14	74	59	64
Consett	40	17	8	15	63	60	59
Whitley Bay	40	15	10	15	69	61	55
West Auckland Town	40	16	7	17	65	68	55
Jarrow Roofing BCA	40	12	12	16	63	71	48
Guisborough Town	40	13	8	19	53	60	47
Chester-le-Street	40	13	5	22	61	64	44
Newcastle Blue Star	40	12	8	20	53	83	44
Seaham Red Star	40	14	2	24	59	111	44
Morpeth Town	40	12	6	22	63	78	36
Easington Colliery	40	10	6	24	57	86	36
Hebburn Town	40	5	7	28	33	113	22
Crook Town	40	2	4	34	33	155	10

ASDA LOGIC WEST LANCS LEAGUE

Premier Division

	P	W	D	L	F	A	Pts
Kirkham & Wesham	28	22	5	1	90	24	71
Dalton United	28	20	2	6	79	34	62
Blackrod Town	28	18	5	5	72	38	59
Fulwood Amateurs	28	14	8	6	62	36	50
Norcross & Warbreck	28	13	5	10	70	62	44
Springfields	28	13	5	10	56	48	44
Charnock Richard	28	11	8	9	44	50	41
Garstang	28	11	5	12	43	59	38
Leyland Motors Athletic	28	9	5	14	41	53	32
Freckleton	28	8	6	14	34	53	30
Barnoldswick United	28	7	7	14	44	60	28
Vickers SC	28	6	9	13	39	69	27
Eagley	28	7	4	17	45	58	25
Wyre Villa	28	6	5	17	41	65	23
Burnley United	28	4	3	21	43	94	15

NORTH WEST COUNTIES LEAGUE

Division One	P	W	D	L	F	A	Pts
Rossendale United	42	29	5	8	114	44	92
Clitheroe	42	27	8	7	105	47	89
Ramsbottom United	42	28	4	10	85	44	88
St Helens Town	42	26	9	7	98	40	87
Fleetwood Freeport	42	26	4	12	90	50	82
Kidsgrove Athletic	42	24	10	8	81	46	82
Salford City	42	23	10	9	87	41	79
Prescot Cables	42	24	5	13	94	54	77
Newcastle Town	42	20	7	15	69	45	67
Mossley	42	19	7	16	73	56	64
Curzon Ashton	42	18	9	15	67	66	63
Skelmersdale United	42	17	8	17	69	69	59
Woodley Sports	42	16	9	17	69	69	57
Abbey Hey	42	15	6	21	76	92	51
Maine Road	42	15	3	24	75	102	48
Nantwich Town	42	10	9	23	46	79	39
Atherton Collieries	42	11	6	25	43	88	39
Glossop North End	42	9	4	29	41	111	31
Great Harwood Town	42	7	9	26	44	93	30
Flixton	42	5	13	24	47	100	28
Leek CSOB	42	5	12	25	39	89	27
Cheadle Town	42	5	9	28	42	129	24

COMBINED COUNTIES LEAGUE

	P	W	D	L	F	A	Pts
Cove	40	35	2	3	146	28	107
Wallingford	40	30	6	4	128	39	96
Ash United	40	28	4	8	121	53	88
Bedfont	40	24	4	12	96	64	76
Chipstead	40	23	5	12	92	48	74
Westfield	40	19	6	15	66	56	63
Walton Casuals	40	19	5	16	73	68	62
Merstham (+2)	40	16	8	16	85	64	58
Feltham	40	17	7	16	74	75	58
Sandhurst Town	39	17	6	16	75	61	57
Southall	40	17	8	15	84	70	56
Godalming & Guildford	40	15	10	15	73	80	55
Chessington & Hook (+3)	40	15	7	18	83	92	55
Cobham	40	16	6	18	69	72	54
Chessington United (−4)	40	14	13	13	67	57	51
Raynes Park Vale	40	15	5	20	63	78	50
Hartley Wintney	40	12	4	24	73	99	40
Viking Greenford	40	9	7	24	58	100	34
Reading Town (+3)	40	6	9	25	43	97	30
Farnham Town	39	4	3	32	30	145	15
Cranleigh	40	4	3	33	28	181	15

(Farnham v Sandhurst is subject to a Berks & Bucks FA disciplinary hearing. The game was abandoned at 1-0 to Sandhurst when the visiting manager was sent-off but refused to leave the pitch perimeter.)

MIDLAND COMBINATION

Premier Division	P	W	D	L	F	A	Pts
Nuneaton Griff	40	31	4	5	93	34	97
Studley BKL	40	30	6	4	98	32	96
Romulus	40	27	7	6	79	34	88
Pershore Town	40	22	8	10	82	62	74
Coventry Sphinx	39	20	6	13	63	38	66
Meir KA	39	20	6	13	67	53	66
Alvechurch	40	21	3	16	77	64	66
Coventry Marconi	40	19	8	13	87	61	65
Kings Heath	40	15	12	13	61	53	57
Sutton Town	40	16	7	17	67	57	55
Bolehall Swifts	40	15	9	16	77	76	54
Massey-Ferguson	40	15	8	17	81	81	53
Handrahan Timbers	40	12	7	21	51	69	43
Cheslyn Hay	40	11	9	20	53	71	42
Alveston	40	11	9	20	53	87	42
Feckenham	40	9	11	20	49	80	38
Blackheath Inv	40	10	7	23	51	91	37
Highgate United	40	11	4	25	49	96	37
Northfield Town	40	8	12	20	44	83	36
Southam United (−3)	40	10	5	25	53	79	32
Continental Star (−3)	40	10	4	26	64	98	31

SCHWEPPES ESSEX SENIOR LEAGUE

	P	W	D	L	F	A	Pts
Brentwood	30	21	3	6	68	26	66
Saffron Walden Town	30	18	3	9	53	24	57
Barkingside	30	17	5	8	55	34	56
Southend Manor	30	17	4	9	71	40	55
Concord Rangers	30	17	3	10	57	38	54
Ilford	30	15	5	10	64	48	50
Bowers United	30	13	8	9	53	47	47
Basildon United	30	13	6	11	66	48	45
Stansted	30	12	8	10	45	47	44
Leyton	30	12	7	11	50	43	43
East Ham United	30	12	3	15	52	73	39
Hullbridge Sports	30	11	4	15	60	59	37
Sawbridgeworth Town	30	10	6	14	41	46	36
Burnham Ramblers	30	8	6	16	47	59	30
Eton Manor	30	3	5	22	38	92	14
Woodford Town	30	2	2	26	23	119	8

WEARSIDE LEAGUE

	P	W	D	L	F	A	Pts
Washington Nissan	38	31	3	4	120	29	96
North Shields	38	29	6	3	143	24	93
Wolviston	38	24	6	8	107	58	78
Windscale	38	23	6	9	102	49	75
Harton & Westoe	38	23	4	11	118	67	73
Boldon CA (−3)	38	24	4	10	104	63	73
Redcar Town (−3)	38	21	8	9	103	61	68
New Marske SC	38	19	7	12	90	58	64
Stokesley SC	38	19	6	13	116	67	63
Whitehaven Amateurs	38	19	5	14	82	78	62
Ferryhill Athletic	38	16	4	18	92	89	52
Stanley United	38	12	12	14	77	76	48
Thornaby	38	14	6	18	86	101	48
Birtley Town (−6)	38	15	4	19	79	101	43
Annfield Plain (−3)	38	13	3	22	87	96	39
Cleadon SC	38	7	4	27	49	113	25
Ryhope CW	38	6	5	27	46	102	23
Simonside SC	38	7	2	−29	33	195	23
Jarrow	38	5	6	27	50	117	21
Whitburn	38	2	1	35	38	178	7

HIGHLAND LEAGUE

		Home			Away			Goals			
	P	W	D	L	W	D	L	F	A	Pts	GD
Cove Rangers	26	12	1	0	8	2	3	74	32	63	42
Huntly	26	11	0	2	8	2	3	61	28	59	33
Buckie Thistle	26	8	3	2	5	4	4	46	33	46	13
Clachnacuddin	26	9	2	2	4	3	6	47	34	44	13
Keith	26	8	3	2	6	4	4	54	43	42	11
Deveronvale	26	5	5	3	6	3	4	39	32	41	7
Forres Mechanics	26	7	2	4	3	8	2	44	39	40	5
Fraserburgh	26	6	3	4	6	0	7	47	38	39	9
Nairn County	26	5	4	4	3	3	7	44	58	31	−14
Wick Academy	26	6	3	4	2	2	9	39	43	29	−4
Rothes	26	4	3	6	2	2	9	30	45	23	−15
Lossiemouth	26	4	4	5	2	0	11	27	60	22	−33
Brora Rangers	26	4	3	6	0	0	13	41	78	15	−37
Fort William	26	3	2	8	0	3	10	27	57	14	−30

AMATEUR FOOTBALL ALLIANCE 2000–2001

AFA SENIOR CUP

1st Round Proper
Old Manorians 0 Glyn Old Boys 6
Parkfield w/o Old Malvernians w/d
Hon. Artillery Company 2 Crouch End Vampires 1
Old Esthameians 1 UCL Academicals 2
Old Tenisonians 1 Old Finchleians 6
West Wickham 6 Southgate Olympic 0
Old Vaughanians 4 Cardinal Manning Old Boys 2
Old Lyonians 0 Nottsborough 2
Old Salesians 6 Old Salopians 4
Old Wokingians 6 Rugby Clubs 0
Old Woodhouseians 6 Wood Green Old Boys 0
Lensbury 8 Ealing Association 2
Shene Old Grammarians 0 Merton 2
Bank of England 3 Barclays Bank 0
Old Kingsburians 0 Southgate County 3
Carshalton 6 Old Dorkinian 1
Duncombe Sports 4 Kings Old Boys 1
Old Suttonians 3 Old Danes 2
Queen Mary College Old Boys 0 Winchmore Hill 5
University of Hertfordshire 0 Alleyn Old Boys 5
Civil Service 2 Albanian 1
Old Foresters 2 HSBC 1
Old Stationers 4 Old Westminster Citizens 2
Latymer Old Boys 1 E. Barnet Old Grammarians 0
National Westminster Bank 0 Old Actonians Assn 6
Old Meadonians 2 Old Elizabethans 0
Old Aloysians 3 Old Bromleians 1
Polytechnic 5 Old Buckwellians 1
Old Salvatorians 2 Kew Association 1
Old Owens 4 Old Bealonians 2
Chertsey Old Salesians 3 Mill Hill Village 4

2nd Round Proper
Glyn Old Boys 1 Parkfield 0
Norsemen 1 Hon. Artillery Company 2

UCL Academicals 3 Old Finchleians 1
West Wickham 1* Old Vaughanians 3*
Nottsborough 0 Old Salesians 2
Old Wokingians 3 Old Woodhouseians 2
Lensbury 6 Merton 0
Bank of England 2 Southgate County 3
Carshalton 5 Duncombe Sports 2
Old Suttonians 2 Winchmore Hill 0
Alleyn Old Boys 1 Civil Service 3
Old Foresters 1 Old Stationers 0
Latymer Old Boys 0 Old Actonians Assn 2
Old Meadonians 2 Old Aloysians 1
Polytechnic 6 Old Salvatorians 1
Old Owens 3 Mill Hill Village 4

3rd Round Proper
Glyn Old Boys 0 Honourable Artillery Co 5
UCL Academicals 1 Old Vaughanians 0
Old Salesians 3 Old Wokingians 2
Old Meadonians 2 Old Aloysians 1
Lensbury 7 Southgate County 4
Carshalton 3 Old Suttonians 2
Civil Service 1*:3p Old Foresters 1*:2p
Old Actonians Assn 0 Old Meadonians 3
Polytechnic 2 Mill Hill Village 0

4th Round Proper
Hon Artillery Company 0 UCL Academicals 1
Old Salesians 5 Lensbury 3
Carshalton 2 Civil Service 3
Old Meadonians 1 Polytechnic 5

Semi-Finals
UCL Academicals 4 Old Salesians 1
Civil Service 1 Polytechnic 2

Final
UCL Academicals 2 Civil Service 1
* *(after extra time; p – penalty kicks)*

OTHER AFA CUP RESULTS

Essex Senior
Old Bealonians 2 Old Brentwoods 5
Middlesex Senior
Old Ignatians 1 Old Actonians Assn 0
Surrey Senior
HSBC 2 Old Wokingians 3
Intermediate
Crouch End Vampires 3*:7p Old Parmiterians Res 3*:6p
Junior
Old Owens 3rd 0 Old Challoners Res 1
Minor
Mill Hill Village 4th 2 Albanian 4th 1
Youth
Old Parmiterians 2 Norsemen 8
Veterans
Old Parmitarians A 7 Old Buckwellians 1
Open Veterans
Police (Chigwell) 1 Port of London Authority 2
Greenland
Old Actonians Assn 2*:1p Old Ignatians 2*:4p

Essex Intermediate
Davenant Wanderers O B 1st 2 Mt Pleasant P O 1st 1
Kent Intermediate
Morgan Guaranty 1st 0 West Wickham Res 6
Middlesex Intermediate
Civil Service Res 0 Alexandra Park Res 2
Surrey Intermediate
Royal Sun Alliance 4 Carshalton Res 0
Senior Novets
O. Finchleians 5th 2*:2p O. Actonians Assn 5th 2*:4p
Intermediate Novets
Old Aloysians 6th 3 Phoenix Old Boys 6th 1
Junior Novets
Old Actonians Assn 8th 2 Old Actonians 7th 1

ARTHUR DUNN CUP FINAL

Old Carthusians 4 Old Bradfieldians 1

ARTHURIAN LEAGUE

Often dependent on use of their School grounds the competition decided it could not complete but issued these final tables to indicate the effect of the unusual winter rains. All AFA leagues were similarly affected but rearranged programmes to ensure that games determining promotion or relegation were played and 0-0 draws were awarded for the rest.

PREMIER DIVISION	P	W	D	L	F	A	Pts
Old Etonians	9	6	3	0	29	16	15
Old Carthusians	13	5	4	4	33	31	14
Old Cholmeleians	8	3	4	1	18	14	10
Old Brentwoods	8	3	3	2	15	15	9
Old Reptonians	9	3	3	3	18	18	9
Old Chigwellians	10	3	2	5	16	19	8
Old Harrovians	6	3	1	2	15	12	7
Old Salopians	9	1	4	4	17	20	6
Lancing Old Boys	10	1	2	7	10	26	4

DIVISION 1	P	W	D	L	F	A	Pts
Old Bradfieldians	10	7	3	1	37	9	16
Old Foresters	8	7	3	1	30	11	14
Old Malvernians	8	5	2	2	26	17	11
Old Haberdashers	9	4	2	3	24	26	10
Old Wellingburians	12	4	2	7	27	37	9
Old Witleians	12	3	1	7	26	38	8
Old Aldenhamians	12	4	2	8	27	44	8
Old Wykehamists	11	2	3	7	25	40	6

DIVISION 2	P	W	D	L	F	A	Pts
Old Carthusians Res	12	8	1	3	52	18	17
Old Westminsters	9	8	0	1	31	8	16
Old Chigwellians Res	10	8	0	2	29	12	16
Old Etonians Res	11	4	2	5	22	26	10
Lancing Old Boys Res	10	4	1	5	16	31	9
Old Brentwoods Res	9	4	0	5	26	37	8
Old Etonians 3rd	13	3	2	8	15	39	8
Old Haberdashers Res	7	0	1	6	11	28	1
Old Salopians Res	5	0	1	4	4	22	1

DIVISION 3

	P	W	D	L	F	A	Pts
Old Carthusians 3rd	13	9	0	4	31	19	18
Old Bradfieldians Res	12	7	1	4	32	17	15
Old Cholmeleians Res	8	5	1	2	28	17	11
Old Foresters Res	10	4	2	4	27	21	10
Old Foresters 3rd	10	3	2	5	23	36	8
Old Aldenhamians Res	11	3	1	7	27	51	7
Old Millhillians	7	3	0	4	20	19	6
Old Harrovians Res	9	2	1	6	17	25	5

	Teams:	Leading at abandonment:
DIVISION 4	8	Old Haileyburians
DIVISION 5	6	Old Chigwellians 3rd

JUNIOR LEAGUE CUP
Old Westminsters 2 Old Chigwellians Res 1

DERRIK MOORE VETERANS' CUP
Old Brentwoods 2 Old Cholmeleians 1

JIM DIXSON 6-a-S
Won by Old Foresters

LONDON FINANCIAL FA

DIVISION ONE

	P	W	D	L	F	A	Pts
Coutts & Co.	16	13	1	2	55	22	40
Morgan Guaranty	16	10	4	2	40	22	31 *
Bank of America	16	8	2	6	30	34	26
Dresdner Kleinwort Benson	16	6	5	5	35	22	23
Granby	16	4	6	6	27	24	18
Mount Pleasant Post Office	16	2	10	4	11	15	16
Royal Sun Alliance	16	2	9	5	18	29	15
Foreign & Commonwealth Office	16	2	5	9	17	34	11
Citibank	16	3	2	11	22	53	11

DIVISION TWO

	P	W	D	L	F	A	Pts
Chase Manhattan Bank	12	12	0	0	63	12	36
Chelsea Exiles	12	8	0	4	47	25	24
Royal Sun Alliance Res	12	7	1	4	34	23	22
Eagle Star	12	5	1	6	34	29	16
Marsh	12	3	2	7	25	31	11
Temple Bar	12	1	4	7	10	46	7
GEFC	12	1	2	9	11	58	5

DIVISION THREE

	P	W	D	L	F	A	Pts
Granby Res	18	14	1	3	57	23	43
C Hoare & Co	18	13	2	3	73	29	41
Coutts & Co Res	18	13	2	3	60	14	29*
Marsh Res	18	6	8	4	38	28	26
Royal Bank of Scotland	18	7	2	9	29	32	23
Salomon Smith Barney	18	6	4	8	32	36	22
Customs & Excise	18	6	3	9	26	51	21
ANZ Banking	18	5	3	10	31	51	18
Eagle Star Res	18	4	2	12	19	59	14
UCB Home Loans	18	2	1	15	19	61	7

DIVISION FOUR

	P	W	D	L	F	A	Pts
Citibank Res	18	14	2	2	50	14	44
Royal Sun Alliance 3rd	18	13	2	3	79	26	41
Credit Suisse First Boston	18	11	3	4	52	29	36
Bank of Ireland	18	8	6	4	42	22	30
Granby 3rd	18	8	3	7	29	35	27
Marsh 3rd	18	7	3	8	52	57	24
CGU Cuaco 5th	18	4	7	7	44	69	19
Standard Chartered Bank	18	4	2	12	29	50	14
Temple Bar Res	18	2	6	10	16	49	12
Royal Bank of Scotland Res	18	1	2	15	25	67	5

* – Pts deducted: Breach of Rule

SENIOR CUP
Dresdner Kleinwort Benson 2 R. Sun Alliance 4

JUNIOR CUP
Customs & Excise 1 Bank of Ireland 0

VETERANS' CUP
Granby 1 HSBC 2

The prolonged winter rainfall prevented playing 39 games in the competition which are entered as 0-0 draws. Some League Cup competitions also were abandoned.

LONDON LEGAL LEAGUE

DIVISION I

	P	W	D	L	F	A	Pts
Linklaters & Alliance	18	12	3	3	46	18	39
Gray's Inn	18	11	5	2	44	22	38
Denton Wilde Sapte (A)	18	11	2	5	26	20	35
Clifford Chance	18	10	4	4	46	24	34
Slaughter & May	18	8	3	7	26	25	27
Lovells	18	8	0	10	33	48	24
Nabarro Nathanson	18	7	2	9	29	27	23
KPMG ICE	18	7	2	9	38	38	23
CMS Cameron McKenna	18	2	2	14	24	59	8
Norton Rose	18	2	1	15	24	55	7

DIVISION II

	P	W	D	L	F	A	Pts
Eversheds	18	12	4	2	50	25	40
Rosling King	18	12	3	3	51	17	39
Watson Farley & Williams	18	11	4	3	32	17	37
Nicholson Graham & Jones	18	7	5	6	43	43	26
Baker & McKenzie	18	6	4	8	45	38	22
Herbert Smith	18	6	4	8	38	42	22
Simmons & Simmons	18	6	3	9	35	41	21
Taylor Joynson Garrett	18	6	1	11	33	65	19
Pegasus (Inner Temple)	18	5	3	10	28	46	18
Freshfields	18	2	3	13	25	46	9

DIVISION III

	P	W	D	L	F	A	Pts
Allen & Overy	18	13	3	2	78	31	42
Barlow Lyde & Gilbert	18	13	3	2	54	21	42
Titmuss Sainer Dechert	18	11	2	5	45	33	35
S J Berwin & Co	18	9	5	4	53	35	32
London Stock Exchange	18	8	1	9	42	30	25
Richards Butler	18	7	2	9	36	45	23
Denton Wilde Sapte (B)	18	5	4	9	43	46	19
Stephenson Harwood	18	4	3	11	32	64	15
Hammonds Suddards Edge	18	4	2	11	32	63	14
Macfarlanes	18	3	1	14	27	74	10

LEAGUE CHALLENGE CUP
Denton Wilde Sapte (A) 2 Gray's Inn 0

WEAVERS ARMS CHALLENGE CUP
Lovells 3 Dechert 1

LONDON OLD BOYS' CUP

Senior
Old Ignatians 1 Old Vaughanians 0
Intermediate
Albanian Res 0 Old Parmiterians Res 1
Junior
Latymer Old Boys 3rd 0 Old Actonians Assn 3rd 3
Minor
Sinjuns 4th 0 Old Tenisonians 4th 6
Novets
Mill Hill County Old Boys 4th 0*:2p Old Actonians Assn 5th 0*:4p
Drummond
Old Meadonians 6th 0 Old Aloysians 6th 1
Nemean
Old Actonians Assn 9th 0 Old Aloysians 7th 6

MIDLAND AMATEUR ALLIANCE

PREMIER DIVISION

	P	W	D	L	F	A	Pts
Nottingham Trent University	26	19	6	1	79	33	63
Lady Bay	26	16	5	5	91	64	53
Old Elizabethans	26	15	5	6	70	31	50
Woodborough United	26	15	5	6	91	55	50
Caribbean Cavaliers	26	14	8	4	75	50	50
Nottinghamshire	26	14	5	7	64	35	47
ASC Dayncourt Res	26	13	1	12	53	55	40
Square Form Stealers	26	10	3	13	70	79	33
Bassingfield	26	8	7	11	48	58	31
Ashland Rovers	26	6	8	12	51	68	26
Wollaton 3rd	26	6	6	14	41	65	24
Horse & Jockey	26	6	4	16	46	90	22
Beeston Old Boys Assn	26	4	2	20	40	88	14
Old Bemrosians	26	3	1	22	52	100	10

DIVISION 1	P	W	D	L	F	A	Pts
Magdala Amateurs Res	24	18	0	6	99	36	54
Old Elizabethans Res	24	17	2	5	68	39	53
Smithys	24	16	3	5	81	35	51
County NALGO	24	13	2	9	76	53	41
Wollaton 4th	24	10	5	9	59	53	35
Brunts Old Boys	24	11	2	11	52	52	35
Nottinghamshire Res	24	9	7	8	62	49	34
Bassingfield Res	24	9	5	10	55	58	32
Ilkeston Rangers	24	9	5	10	66	82	32
Chilwell	24	7	5	12	53	71	26
Southwell Arms	24	7	3	14	47	74	24
Derbyshire Amateurs Res	24	6	2	16	56	88	20
Dynamo	24	2	3	19	25	109	9

DIVISION 2	P	W	D	L	F	A	Pts
Pakistan Centre	28	21	4	3	109	36	67
Sherwood Forest	28	19	5	4	87	48	62
FLL Aerospace	28	18	1	9	95	47	55
Old Elizabethans 3rd	28	16	5	7	82	41	53
West Bridgford United	28	12	9	7	58	42	45
ASC Dayncourt 3rd	28	13	6	9	59	48	45
Magdala Arms 3rd	28	11	7	10	75	69	40
Edwinstowe FC	28	11	6	11	75	70	39
Tibshelf Old Boys	28	11	4	13	44	65	37
Nottinghamshire 3rd	28	11	3	14	57	53	36
EMTEC	28	10	4	14	65	96	34
Beeston O B Assn 3rd	28	8	5	15	49	79	29
Wollaton 5th	28	9	2	17	65	96	29
Derbyshire Amateurs 3rd	28	5	4	19	62	99	19
Old Bemrosians Res	28	2	1	25	29	122	7

LEAGUE SENIOR CUP
Won by Nottinghamshire

LEAGUE INTERMEDIATE CUP
Won by: Old Elizabethans Res

LEAGUE MINOR CUP
Won by: FLL Aerospace

OLD BOYS' AMATEUR FOOTBALL LEAGUE

PREMIER DIVISION	P	W	D	L	F	A	Pts
Old Meadonians	20	17	0	3	50	19	51
Old Aloysians	20	11	5	4	42	24	38
Old Vaughanians	20	10	4	6	36	32	34
Old Wilsonians	20	9	4	7	34	27	31
Shene Old Grammarians	20	9	4	7	48	46	31
Old Ignatians	20	6	8	6	33	33	26
Phoenix Old Boys	20	6	6	8	36	31	24
Cardinal Manning Old Boys	20	7	2	11	28	51	23
Old Hamptonians	20	5	6	9	31	33	21
Glyn Old Boys	20	5	3	12	22	42	16*
Old Tenisonians	20	2	4	14	16	38	10

SENIOR DIVISION 1	P	W	D	L	F	A	Pts
Old Salvatorians	20	16	3	1	50	9	51
Old Danes	20	15	3	2	65	18	48
Latymer Old Boys	20	15	2	3	64	21	47
Old Dorkinia	20	9	2	9	25	30	29
Old Isleworthians	20	8	2	10	33	44	26
Enfield Old Grammarians	20	8	1	11	33	41	25
Old Suttonians	20	7	2	11	25	39	23
Old Manorians	20	6	3	11	40	42	21
Old Minchendenians	20	4	4	12	40	61	16
Old Buckwellians	20	4	4	12	26	50	16
Sinjuns	20	3	4	13	19	65	6*

SENIOR DIVISION 2	P	W	D	L	F	A	Pts
Old Tiffinians	20	15	2	3	52	17	47
Chertsey Old Salesians	20	13	1	6	50	28	40
Phoenix Old Boys Res	20	11	5	4	51	35	38
Old Kingsburians	20	9	5	6	59	38	32
John Fisher Old Boys	20	8	3	9	31	36	27
Latymer Old Boys Res	19	8	4	7	38	33	28
Queen Mary College Old Boys	20	7	4	9	42	44	25
Old Sedcopians	20	5	6	9	31	50	21
Old Reigatian	20	4	8	8	24	32	20
Old Vaughanians Res	19	3	5	11	20	49	12*
Clapham Old Xaverians	20	2	5	13	20	56	11

SENIOR DIVISION 3	P	W	D	L	F	A	Pts
Old Wokingians	22	21	0	1	81	13	63
Wood Green Old Boys	22	14	4	4	70	31	46
Old Salvatorians Res	22	11	6	5	25	17	39
Old Aloysians Res	22	12	1	9	49	33	37
Old Meadonians Res	22	11	4	7	51	38	37
Old St Marys	22	9	5	8	47	43	32
Old Wilsonians Res	22	8	6	8	34	31	30
Old Hamptonians Res	22	9	3	10	39	40	30
Old Manorians Res	22	7	6	9	40	46	27
Old Tenisonians Res	22	4	3	15	32	60	15
Old Isleworthians Res	22	4	0	18	28	84	12
Phoenix Old Boys 3rd	22	0	6	16	13	73	6

* – *Points deducted : Breach of Rule*

Intermediate Division North–10 teams
Won by Old Egbertians

Intermediate Division South–10 teams
Won by Fitzwilliam Old Boys

NORTHERN

Division 1–11 teams
Won by Old Egbertians Res

Division 2–10 teams
Won by Old Camdenians

Division 3–11 teams
Won by Old Edmontonians 3rd

Division 4–10 teams
Won by The Royal London Hospital Old Boys Res

Division 5–9 teams
Won by Old Aloysians 7th

Division 6–10 teams
Won by Old Edmontonians 6th

SOUTHERN

Division 1–11 teams
Won by Old Tenisonians 4th

Division 2–10 teams
Won by Old Tiffinians Res

Division 3–11 teams
Won by Old Josephians Res

Division 4–10 teams
Won by Old Thorntonians Res

Division 5–12 teams
Won by Chertsey Old Salesians 3rd

Division 6–10 teams
Won by Chertsey Old Salesians 4th

Division 7–10 teams
Won by Old Wilsonians 7th

Division 8–9 teams
Won by Old Reigatian 7th

WESTERN

Division 1–10 teams
Won by Old Hendonians

Division 2–11 teams
Won by Old Challoners Res

Division 3–11 teams
Won by Mill Hill County Old Boys 3rd

Division 4–10 teams
Won by Holland Park Old Boys Res

Division 5–9 teams
Won by Old Salvatorians 8th

Division 6–6 teams
Won by Old Kolsassians

SOUTHERN AMATEUR LEAGUE

SENIOR SECTION:

DIVISION 1	P	W	D	L	F	A	Pts
Old Actonians Association	22	16	1	5	57	14	49
Old Owens	22	14	4	4	59	21	46
Old Esthameians	22	11	7	4	47	36	40
Polytechnic	22	11	6	5	57	27	39
Barclays Bank	22	10	4	8	46	32	34
Alleyn Old Boys	22	8	5	9	42	42	29

	P	W	D	L	F	A	Pts
Norsemen	22	8	5	9	32	38	29
East Barnet Old Grammarians	22	7	7	8	35	40	28
Carshalton	22	7	7	8	31	38	28
Crouch End Vampires	22	7	4	11	31	39	25
Old Bromleians	22	2	3	17	23	66	7*
National Westminster Bank	22	4	1	17	27	94	7*

DIVISION 2

	P	W	D	L	F	A	Pts
Broomfield	22	15	4	3	42	20	49
Civil Service	22	13	3	6	38	26	42
Winchmore Hill	22	11	4	7	25	20	37
Old Salesians	22	10	5	7	33	29	35
HSBC	22	10	4	8	41	28	34
Old Stationers	22	7	8	7	44	39	29
West Wickham	22	8	4	10	36	38	28
Lensbury	22	7	6	9	28	30	27
Lloyds TSB Bank	22	7	6	9	44	47	27
Old Finchleians	22	8	1	13	56	62	25
Alexandra Park	22	5	5	12	25	49	20
Old Parmiterians	22	4	4	14	27	51	16

DIVISION 3

	P	W	D	L	F	A	Pts
Old Lyonians	22	17	4	1	63	17	55
Old Parkonians	22	14	3	5	57	24	45
Bank of England	22	14	2	6	61	21	44
Kew Association	22	13	4	5	66	30	43
Old Westminster Citizens	22	9	4	9	45	52	31
Ibis	22	8	5	9	27	32	29
CGU Cuaco	22	8	4	10	47	42	28
Old Latymerians	22	8	4	10	39	46	28
Merton	22	5	8	9	22	28	23
Southgate Olympic	22	6	1	15	31	65	19
South Bank	22	4	3	15	21	63	15
Brentham	22	2	6	14	24	83	12

* – Points deducted: Breach of Rule

RESERVE TEAM SECTION

Division 1–12 teams
Won by HSBC Res

Division 2–12 teams
Won by Old Parmiterians Res

Division 3–11 teams
Won by Old Esthameians Res

THIRD TEAM SECTION

Division 1–12 teams
Won by Old Owens 3rd

Division 2–12 teams
Won by Old Esthameians 3rd

Division 3–11 teams
Won by Old Latymerians 3rd

FOURTH TEAM SECTION

Division 1–12 teams
Won by Old Actonians Association 4th

Division 2–12 teams
Won by Carshalton 4th

Division 3–9 teams
Won by Ibis 4th

FIFTH TEAM SECTION

Division 1–11 teams
Won by Old Actonians Association 5th

Division 2–10 teams
Won by Crouch End Vampires 5th

Division 3–8 teams
Won by Old Latymerians 5th

SIXTH TEAM SECTION:

Division 1–12 teams
Won by Old Actonians Association 6th

Division 2–11 teams
Won by Civil Service 6th

MINOR SECTION:

Division 1–10 teams
Won by Old Actonians Association 7th

Division 2–9 teams
Won by Old Actonians Association 9th

Division 3–8 teams
Won by Kew Association 7th

Division 4–7 teams
Won by Old Parmiterians 9th

SOUTHERN OLYMPIAN LEAGUE

SENIOR SECTION:

PREMIER DIVISION

	P	W	D	L	F	A	Pts
UCL Academicals	18	13	4	1	45	17	43
Hale End Athletic	18	11	4	3	45	22	37
Mill Hill Village	18	10	5	3	44	28	32*
Albanian	15	8	6	1	33	16	30
Nottsborough	16	7	3	6	31	35	24
Old Woodhouseans	18	7	1	10	30	32	22
Old Grammarians	16	5	4	7	22	22	19
Ulysses	18	5	1	12	23	38	16
Honourable Artillery Company	17	3	2	12	27	41	11
Wandsworth Borough	18	1	2	15	18	67	5

DIVISION 2

	P	W	D	L	F	A	Pts
Southgate County	16	10	5	1	37	16	35
Parkfield	15	9	4	2	26	10	31
Pegasus	15	6	7	2	25	21	25
Old Bealonians	15	5	5	5	26	21	20
St Mary's College	15	6	2	7	28	29	20
University of Hertford	15	3	6	6	20	24	15
Kings Old Boys	15	3	6	6	31	47	15
BBC	15	2	5	8	20	28	11
Old Colfeians	15	2	4	9	12	29	10
Duncombe Sports	Record expunged						
City of London	Record expunged						

DIVISION 3

	P	W	D	L	F	A	Pts
Economicals	19	17	1	1	54	18	52
Brent	20	11	4	5	48	28	37
Ealing Association	20	10	2	8	59	37	32
Centymca	20	9	2	9	48	41	29
The Rugby Clubs	19	9	1	9	48	60	28
Hampsted Heathens	18	8	3	7	48	31	27
Fulham Compton	14	8	1	5	37	30	25
Witan	17	5	5	7	28	32	20
London Welsh	19	6	2	11	32	53	20
The Comets	19	5	1	13	26	41	16
Inland Revenue	19	2	2	15	27	84	8

* – Points deducted: Breach of Rule

INTERMEDIATE SECTION:
Division 1–10 teams
Won by St Mary's College Res
Division 2–11 teams
Won by Pegasus Res
Division 3–10 teams
Won by Kings Old Boys Res
JUNIOR NORTH SECTION:
Division 1–10 teams
Won by University of Hertfordshire Res
Division 2–11 teams
Won by Albanian 6th
Division 3–10 teams
Won by Old Bealonians 6th
JUNIOR SOUTH-WEST SECTION:
Division 1–10 teams
Won by Nottsborough 3rd
Division 2–8 teams
Won by Old Grammarians 4th
Division 3–9 teams
Won by Witan 4th
Veterans' Cup
Won by UCL Academicals

Other League Cups were not completed

IMPORTANT ADDRESSES

The Football Association: A. Crozier, 25 Soho Square, London W1D 4FA. *020 7745 4545*

Scotland: David Taylor, Hampden Park, Glasgow G42 9AY. *0141 616 6000*
Northern Ireland (Irish FA): D. I. Bowen, 20 Windsor Avenue, Belfast BT9 6EG. *028 9066 9458*
Wales: A. Evans, 3 Westgate Street, Cardiff, South Glamorgan CF1 1DD. *029 2037 2325*
Republic of Ireland (FA of Ireland): 80 Merrion Square South, Dublin 2. *00353 16766864*

International Federation (FIFA): M. Zen-Ruffinen, P. O. Box 85 8030 Zurich, Switzerland. *00 411 384 9595. Fax: 00 411 384 9696*
Union of European Football Associations: G. Aigner, Route de Geneve 46, Case Postale CH-1260 Nyon, Switzerland. *0041 22 994 44 44. Fax: 0041 22 994 44 88*

THE LEAGUES

The Premier League: R. Scudamore, 11 Connaught Place, London W2 2ET. *020 7298 1651*
The Football League: D. Burns, The Football League, Unit 5, Edward VII Quay, Navigation Way, Preston, Lancashire PR2 2YF. *01772 325800. Fax 01772 325801*
Scottish Premier League: R. Mitchell, Hampden Park, Somerville Drive, Glasgow G42 9BA. *0141 646 6962*
The Scottish League: P. Donald, Hampden Park, Glasgow G42 9AY. *0141 616 6000*
The Irish League: H. Wallace, 96 University Street, Belfast BT7 1HE. *028 9024 2888*
Football League of Ireland: D. Crowther, 80 Merrion Square, Dublin 2. *00353 16765120*
Nationwide Conference: J. A. Moules, Chief Executive, Riverside House, 14b High Street, Crayford, DA1 4HG. *01322 411021*
Central League: A. Williamson, The Football League, Unit 5, Edward VII Quay, Navigation Way, Preston, Lancashire PR2 2YF. *01772 325800. Fax 01772 325801*
Eastern Counties League: B. A. Badcock, 41 The Copse, Southwood, Farnborough, Hampshire GU14 0QD. *01252 387588*
Football Combination: N. Chamberlain, 2 Vicarage Close, Old Costessey, Norwich NR8 5DL. *01603 743998*
Hellenic League: B. King, 83 Queens Road, Carterton, Oxon OX18 3YF. *01993 212738*
Kent League: R. Vinter, Bakery House, The Street, Chilham, Canterbury, Kent CT4 8BX. *01227 730457*
Leicestershire Senior League: R. J. Holmes, 8 Huntsman Close, Markfield, Leics LE67 9XE. *01530 243093*
Manchester League: J. Hall, 31 Sunhill Close, Rochdale, OL16 4RU. *01706 719829*
Midland Combination: N. Harvey, 115 Millfield Road, Handsworth Wood, Birmingham B20 1ED. *0121 357 4172*
Northern Premier: R. D. Bayley, 22 Woburn Drive, Hale, Altrincham, Cheshire WA15 8LZ. *0161 980 7007*
Northern League: T. Golightly, 85 Park Road North, Chester-le-Street, Co Durham DH3 3SA. *0191 3882056*

Isthmian League: N. Robinson, 226 Rye Lane, Peckham SE15 4NL. *020 8409 1978. Fax: 020 7639 5726*
Southern League: D. J. Strudwick, P. O. Box 90, Worcester, WR3 8RX. *01905 757509*
Spartan South Midlands League: M. Mitchell, 26 Leighton Court, Dunstable, Beds LU6 1EW. *01582 667291*
United Counties League: R. Gamble, 8 Bostock Avenue, Northampton NN1 4LW. *01604 637766*
Western League: K. A. Clarke, 32 Westmead Lane, Chippenham, Wilts SN15 3HZ. *01249 464467*
West Midlands Regional League: N. R. Juggins, 14 Badger Way, Blackwell, Bromsgrove, Worcs B60 1EX. *0121 445 2953*
Northern Counties (East): B. Wood, 6 Restmore Avenue, Guiseley, Leeds LS20 9DG. *01943 874558*
Central Midlands Football League: Frank Harwood, 103 Vestry Road, Oakwood, Derby, Derbyshire DE21 2BN. *01332 832372*
Combined Counties League: Clive R. Tidey, 22 Silo Road, Farncombe, Godalming, Surrey GU7 3PA. *01483 428453*
Essex Senior League: David Walls, Bramley Cottage, 2 Birch Street, Colchester CO2 0NW. *0207 587 4139*
Lancashire Football League: Barbara Howarth, 86 Windsor Road, Great Harwood, Blackburn, Lancs BB6 7RR. *01254 886267*
Midland Football Alliance: Peter Dagger, 32 Drysdale Close, Wickhamford, Worcs WR11 6RZ. *01386 831763*
North West Counties Football League: G. J. Wilkinson, 46 Oaklands Drive, Penwortham, Preston, Lancs PR1 0XY. *01772 762172*
Wessex League: Tom Lindon, 63 Downs Road, South Wonston, Winchester, Hants SO21 3EW. *01962 884760*
South Western League: R. Rowe, 5 Alverton Gardens, Truro, Cornwall TR1 1JA. *01872 242190*

COUNTY FOOTBALL ASSOCIATIONS

Bedfordshire: P. D. Brown, Century House, Skimpot Road, Dunstable, Beds LU5 4JU. *01582 565111*
Berks and Bucks: B. G. Moore, 15a London Street, Faringdon, Oxon SN7 7HD. *01367 242099*
Birmingham County: M. Pennick, County FA Offices, Rayhall Lane, Great Barr, Birmingham B43 6JF. *0121 357 4278*
Cambridgeshire: R. K. Pawley, City Ground, Milton Road, Cambridge CB4 1FA. *01223 576770*
Cheshire: Mrs M. Dunford, The Cottage, Hartford Moss Rec Centre, Winnington, Northwich CW8 4BG. *01606 871166*
Cornwall: B. Cudmore, 1 High Cross Street, St. Austell, Cornwall PL25 4AB. *01726 74080*
Cumberland: G. Turrell, 17 Oxford Street, Workington, Cumbria CA14 2AL. *01900 872310*
Derbyshire: K. Compton, The Grandstand, Moorways Stadium, Moor Lane, Derby DE24 9HY. *01332 362411*
Devon County: C. Davidson, County HQ, Coach Road, Newton Abbot, Devon TQ12 1EJ. *01626 332077*
Dorset County: P. Hough, County Ground, Blandford Close, Hamworthy, Poole, Dorset BH15 4BF. *01202 682375*

Durham: J. Topping, 'Codeslaw', Ferens Park, Durham DH1 1JZ. *0191 3848653*
East Riding County: D. R. Johnson, 50 Boulevard, Hull HU3 2TB. *01482 221158*
Essex County: P. Sammons, 31 Mildmay Road, Chelmsford, Essex CM2 0DN. *01245 357727*
Gloucestershire: P. Britton, Oaklands Park, Almondsbury, Bristol BS12 4AG. *01454 615888*
Guernsey: D. Dorey, Haut Regard, St. Clair Hill, St. Sampson's, Guernsey, GY2 4DT, CI. *01481 246231*
Hampshire: L. Jones, William Pickford House, 8 Ashwood Gardens, off Winchester Road, Southampton SO16 7PW. *023 8079 1110*
Herefordshire: J. S. Lambert, 1 Muirfield Close, Holmer, Hereford HR1 1QB. *01432 270308*
Hertfordshire: R. G. Kibble, County Ground, Baldock Road, Letchworth, Herts SG6 2EN. *01462 677622*
Huntingdonshire: M. M. Armstrong, Cromwell Chambers, 8 St Johns Street, Huntingdon, Cambs PE29 6DD. *01480 414422*
Isle of Man: Mrs A. Garrett, P.O. Box 53, The Bowl, Douglas IOM IM99 1GY. *01624 615576*
Jersey: S. Monks, Rocqueberg View, Rue De Samares, St. Clement, Jersey JE2 6LS. *01534 852642*

Kent County: K. T. Masters, 69 Maidstone Road, Chatham, Kent ME4 6DT. *01634 843824*

Lancashire: J. Kenyon, The County Ground, Thurston Road, Leyland, Preston, Lancs PR5 1LF. *01772 624000*

Leicestershire and Rutland: P. Morrison, Holmes Park, Dog and Gun Lane, Whetstone, Leicester LE8 3LJ. *0116 2867828*

Lincolnshire: J. Griffin, PO Box 26, 12 Dean Road, Lincoln LN2 4DP. *01522 524917*

Liverpool County: F. L. J. Hunter, Liverpool Soccer Centre, Walton Hall Park, Walton Hall Avenue, Liverpool L4 9XP. *0151 523 4488*

London: D. Fowkes, 6 Aldworth Grove, London SE13 6HY. *020 8690 9626*

Manchester County: John Dutton, Brantingham Road, Chorlton, Manchester M21 0TT. *0161 881 0299*

Middlesex County: P. J. Clayton, 39 Roxborough Road, Harrow, Middx HA1 1NS. *020 8424 8524*

Norfolk County: R. J. Howlett, Plantation Park, Blofield, Norwich, Norfolk, NR13 4PL. *01603 717177*

Northamptonshire: B. Walden, 2 Duncan Close, Moulton Park, Northampton NN3 6WL. *01604 670741*

North Riding County: M. Jarvis, Southlands Centre, Ormesby Road, Middlesbrough TS3 0HB. *01642 318603*

Northumberland: R. E. Maughan, Seymour House, 10 Brenkley Way, Blezard Bus Park, Seaton Burn, Newcastle upon Tyne NE13 6DT. *0191 236 8020*

Nottinghamshire: M. Kilbee, 7 Clarendon Street, Nottingham NG1 5HS. *0115 9418954*

Oxfordshire: I. Mason, 20 Wychwood Drive, Milton under Wychwood, Chipping Norton, Oxon OX7 6JA

Sheffield and Hallamshire: J. Hope-Gill, Clegg House, 5 Onslow Road, Sheffield S11 7AF. *01142 670068*

Shropshire: D. Rowe, Gay Meadow, Abbey Foregate, Shrewsbury SY2 6AB. *01743 362769*

Somerset & Avon (South): Mrs H. Marchment, 30 North Road, Midsomer Norton, Radstock BA3 2QD. *01761 410280*

Staffordshire: B. J. Adshead, County Showground, Weston Road, Stafford ST18 0BD. *01785 256994*

Suffolk County: W. M. Steward, Felaw Maltings, 44 Felaw Street, Ipswich IP2 8SJ. *01473 407290*

Surrey County: R. Ward, 321 Kingston Road, Leatherhead, Surrey KT22 7TU. *01372 373543*

Sussex County: Ken Benham, County Office, Culver Road, Lancing, West Sussex BN15 9AX. *01903 753547*

Westmorland: P. G. Ducksbury, Unit 1, Angel Court, 21 Highgate, Kendal, Cumbria LA9 4DA. *01539 730946*

West Riding County: R. Carter, Fleet Lane, Woodlesford, Leeds LS26 8NX. *0113 2821222*

Wiltshire: M. G. Benson, 16 Robins Green, Covingham, Swindon SN3 5AY. *01793 525245*

Worcestershire: M. R. Leggett Fermain, 12 Worcester Road, Evesham, Worcs WR11 4JU. *01386 443215*

OTHER USEFUL ADDRESSES

Amateur Football Alliance: M. L. Brown, 55 Islington Park Street, London N1 1QB. *020 7359 3493*

English Schools FA: Ms A. Pritchard, 1/2 Eastgate Street, Stafford ST16 2NN. *01785 51142*

Oxford University: Ann Harvey, University College, Oxford OX1 4BH. *01865 276555*

Cambridge University: Dr J. A. Little, St Catherine's College, Cambridge CB2 1RL. *01223 334376*

Army: B. Le Breton ASCB (MOD), Clayton Barracks, Thornhill Road, Aldershot, Hants GU11 2BG. *01252 348571/4*

Royal Air Force: Sqn Ldr R. Moorehouse, OC PACS, RAF Coltishall, Norwich. *01603 737361 ext 7306*

Royal Navy: Lt-Cdr S. Vasey, RN Sports Office, HMS Temeraire, Portsmouth, Hants PO1 2HB. *023 9272 2671*

British Universities Sports Association: G. Gregory-Jones, Chief Executive: BUSA, 8 Union Street, London SE1 1SZ. *020 7357 8555*

British Olympic Association: 6 John Prince's Street, London W1M 0DH. *020 7408 2029*

National Federation of Football Supporters' Clubs: Chairman: Ian D. Todd MBE, 8 Wyke Close, Wyke Gardens, Isleworth, Middlesex TW7 5PE. *020 8847 2905 (and fax)*. Mobile: *0961 558908*. National Secretary: Mark Agate, "The Stadium", 14 Coombe Close, Lordswood, Chatham, Kent ME5 8NU. *01634 319461 (and fax)*

National Playing Fields Association: Col. R. Satterthwaite, O.B.E., 578b Catherine Place, London, SW1.

The Scottish Football Commercial Managers Association: J. E. Hillier (Chairman), c/o Keith FC Promotions Office, 60 Union Street, Keith, Banffshire, Scotland.

Professional Footballers' Association: G. Taylor, 2 Oxford Court, Bishopsgate, Off Lower Mosley Street, Manchester M2 3WQ. *0161 236 0575*

Referees' Association: A. Smith, 1 Westhill Road, Coundon, Coventry CV6 2AD. *024 7660 1701*

Women's Football Alliance: Miss K. Simmons, The Football Association, 25 Soho Square, London W1D 4FA. *020 7745 4545*

Institute of Football Management and Administration: 44 Holy Walk, Leamington Spa, Warwickshire, CV32 4YS. *01926 882313. Fax: 01926 886829*

Football Administrators Association: as above.

Commercial and Marketing Managers Association: as above.

Management Stats Association: as above.

League Managers Association: as above.

The Association of Football Statisticians: R. J. Spiller, PO Box 5828, Basildon, Essex SS15 5GQ. *01268 416020 (and fax 01268-543559)*

The Football Programme Directory: David Stacey, 'The Beeches', 66 Southend Road, Wickford, Essex SS11 8EN. *01268 732041 (and fax)*

England Football Supporters Association: Publicity Officer, David Stacey, 'The Beeches', 66 Southend Road, Wickford, Essex SS11 8EN. *01268 732041 (and fax)*

World Cup (1966) Association: as above.

The Ninety-Two Club: 104 Gilda Crescent, Whitchurch, Bristol BS14 9LD.

Scottish 38 Club: Mark Byatt, 6 Greenfields Close, Loughton, Essex IG10 3HG. *0181 508 6088*

The Football Trust: Second Floor, Walkden House, 10 Melton Street, London NW1 2EJ. *020 7388 4504*

Association of Provincial Football Supporters Clubs in London: Stephen Moon, 32 Westminster Gardens, Barking, Essex IG11 0BJ. *020 8594 2367*

World Association of Friends of English Football: Carlisle Hill, Gluck, Habichthof 2, D24939 Flensburg, Germany. *0049 461 4700222*

Football Postcard Collectors Club: PRO: Bryan Horsnell, 275 Overdown Road, Tilehurst, Reading RG31 6NX. *0118 9424448 (and fax)*

UK Programme Collectors Club: Secretary, John Litster, 46 Milton Road, Kirkcaldy, Fife KY1 1TL. *01592 268718. Fax: 01592 595069*

Programme Monthly: as above.

Scottish Football Historians Association: as above.

Phil Gould (Licensed Football Agent), c/o Whoppit Management Ltd, P. O. Box 27204, London N11 2WS. *07071 732 468. Fax: 07070 732 469*

The Scandinavian Union of Supporters of British Football: Postboks, 15 Stovner, N-0913 Oslo, Norway.

REFEREEING AND THE REFEREES

For the first time in many seasons FIFA has not made substantive changes to any of the Laws of the Game. Instead the International Board has taken the opportunity to clarify and re-work several, where ambiguities and anomalies had crept in or where innovations had taken place without close enough reference being made to the existing Laws or their sub-rules. Now there is imported formal reference to the 'golden goal' procedures; the right for a Fourth Official if he/she exists to expedite the return of an injured player to the field; and the relaxing of the rule requiring Referees to caution celebrating players who remove their shirts. If the celebrations are provocative, inciting, or ridiculing of opponents or spectators or just simply time wasting the player will still be cautioned for unsporting behaviour.

A great cause of confusion has always occurred with what to do about bad behaviour by Coaches and Club Officials. Frequently Referees have utilised the red or yellow cards towards the transgressor. It has now been made clear that the use of the cards are for players and substitutes only, whilst all other wrongdoers will be treated as before **without** the use of the cards. A player who has been sent off, is now required to leave the vicinity of the field of play, which is another major clarification.

There appears to be a new air of caring and sharing expressed in these interpretations, so that it is appreciated that not all holding and pulling is necessarily intended; but where it is so and especially when blatant, Referees are instructed to caution for unsporting behaviour. In this respect some might think a dismissal more appropriate but at least we can hope for consistency. Further appreciation of the practical playing aspects comes in the form of recognition that Managers and Coaches need to convey tactical instructions during the game. This is now permitted but the Coach must return to the Technical Area, if there is one, after imparting information.

Turning to the experiments currently in use – the '10 yard rule' which allows the ball to be moved forwards 9.15 metres for certain offences will be continued for another season. However it now ends at the penalty area line and not beyond. Many have said this is to pacify the free-kick experts, but hopefully it was because it was realised how nonsensical it was to have a direct free kick in the penalty area which was not a penalty and which itself brings the Law into disrepute. Unfortunately the experiment using a two-Referee system has been abandoned. Those of us who feel that the game is getting faster and needs a Referee in each half will be disappointed particularly as FIFA is propounding the use of professional Referees which would have aided both to its cause and hopefully effect. Instead they appear to have been persuaded to employ an unofficial experiment promoted by Michel Platini that there be two extra Assistant Referees, one behind each goal. Arguably of little value the experiment would have become better by externally dividing the pitch into quarters with an Assistant in each.

The year 2001 has become a totally revolutionary one for Referees in that a reclassification has taken place from the rank and file to the top of the ladder and for the first time in this Country an elite band of top Officials are being offered professional contracts. The old classification of the starting point from Class 3 moving up to Class 1 is being replaced by a revision importing levels which run from 1 to 10 in descending order with a further higher level which is termed 'International'. Level 1 covers Referees on the National List and Level 2 those on the panel list; Levels 3–6 inclusive are for various senior Referees and Level 7 is for Referees in Junior football. Those in '8' are for Youth Referees; those in '9' will be trainee Referees whilst Level 10 is for declared non-active Referees. The minimum age for the taking of the initial examination is now 14 and if successful the candidate moves to Level 8, thereafter automatically rising to 7 on his/her sixteenth birthday. Subsequently promotion is on performance and by achieving the relevant markings.

The move that is likely to most improve the art of refereeing is the one announced by the English FA on the 13th of June 2001. Thus the professional game is now to have 'professional' Officials initially comprising 24 Referees and 48 Assistant Referees, the former of whom will receive an 'annual retainer' of £33,000 plus match fees. These Officials will undertake the care of the Premier League and other specified competitions. The structure at this level is also altered with the National Review Board being replaced by a stand-alone organisation entitled 'The Professional Game Match Officials Board'. The input for this organisation will come from the FA; the Football League; the Premier League and the FA's Head of Refereeing John Baker. The Referees on the elite list will be the responsibility of Referees' Manager Philip Don. A further National group consisting of 50 Referees and 188 Assistant Referees will officiate in the Football League and will be supervised by their Referees' Manager Jim Ashworth.

KEN GOLDMAN

NATIONAL LIST OF REFEREES FOR SEASON 2001–2002

Alcock, P.E. (Paul) Kent
Armstrong, P. (Paul) Berkshire
Baines, S.J. (Steve) Chesterfield
Barber, G.P. (Graham) Hertfordshire
Barry, N.S. (Neale) N. Lincolnshire
Bates, A. (Tony) Stoke-on-Trent
Beeby, R.J. (Richard) Northampton
Bennett, S.G. (Steve) Kent
Brandwood, M.J. (John) Staffordshire
Butler, A.N. (Alan) Notts
Cable, L.E. (Lee) Woking
Cain, G. (George) Merseyside
Clattenburg, M. (Mark) Chester-le-Street
Cooper, M.A. (Mark) Walsall
Cowburn, M.G. (Mark) Blackpool
Crick, D.R. (David) Surrey
Curson, B. (Brian) Leicestershire
Danson, P.S. (Paul) Leicester
Dean, M.L. (Mike) Wirral
Dowd, P. (Phil) Stoke-on-Trent
Dunn, S.W. (Steve) Bristol
Durkin, P.A. (Paul) Dorset
D'Urso, A.P. (Andy) Essex
Elleray, D.R. (David) Harrow-on-the-Hill

Fletcher, M. (Mick) Worcestershire
Foy, C.J. (Chris) Merseyside
Frankland, G.B. (Graham) Middlesbrough
Furnandiz, R.D. (Roger) Doncaster
Gallagher, D.J. (Dermot) Oxfordshire
Hall, A.R. (Andy) Birmingham
Halsey, M.R. (Mark) Welwyn Garden City
Harris, R.J. (Rob) Isle of Wight
Hegley, G.K. (Grant) Bishops Stortford
Hill, K.D. (Keith) Hertfordshire
Jones, M.J. (Michael) Chester
Jones, P. (Peter) Loughborough
Jones, T. (Trevor) Cumbria
Jordan, W.M. (Bill) Hertfordshire
Joslin, P.J. (Phil) Nottinghamshire
Kaye, A. (Alan) Wakefield
Knight, B. (Barry) Kent
Laws, D. (David) Whitley Bay
Laws, G. (Graham) Whitley Bay
Leake, A.R. (Tony) Lancashire
Mathieson, S.W. (Scott) Stockport
Messias, M.D. (Matt) York
Olivier, R.J. (Ray) Sutton Coldfield
Parkes, T.A. (Trevor) Birmingham

Pearson, R. (Roy) Durham
Penton, C. (Clive) Sussex
Pike, M.S. (Mike) Barrow-in-Furness
Poll, G. (Graham) Hertfordshire
Prosser, P.J. (Phil) Tewkesbury
Pugh, D. (David) Merseyside
Rejer, P. (Paul) Worcestershire
Rennie, U.D. (Uriah) Sheffield
Richards, P.R. (Phil) Lancashire
Riley, M.A. (Mike) Leeds
Robinson, J.P. (Paul) Hull
Ross, J.J. (Joe) London
Ryan, M. (Michael) Preston
Salisbury, G. (Graham) Preston
Stretton, F.G. (Frazer) Nottingham
Styles, R. (Rob) Hampshire
Taylor, P. (Paul) Hertfordshire
Tomlin, S.G. (Steve) East Sussex
Walton, P. (Peter) Northants
Warren, M.R. (Mark) Walsall
Webb, H.M. (Howard) Rotherham
Webster, C.H. (Colin) Durham
Wiley, A.G. (Alan) Burntwood
Wilkes, C.R. (Clive) Gloucester
Winter, J.T. (Jeff) Stockton-on-Tees
Wolstenholme, E.K. (Eddie) Blackburn

ASSISTANT REFEREES

Artis, S.G. (Stephen)
Aston, G.A. (Glenn)
Atkins, G. (Graeme)
Atkinson, M. (Martin)
Babski, D.S. (Dave)
Baker, B.D. (Bernard)
Bannister, N. (Nigel)
Barker, C. (Craig)
Barnes, K.G. (Kevin)
Barnes, P.W. (Paul)
Barston, P.S. (Phil)
Bassindale, C. (Carl)
Beadle, J. (Jon)
Beale, G.A. (Guy)
Bentley, I.F. (Ian)
Birkett, D.J. (Dave)
Bishop, M.E. (Martin)
Bone, R. (Ralph)
Booth, R.J. (Russell)
Boyeson, C. (Carl)
Brand, S.R. (Steve)
Bratt, S.J. (Steve)
Brayne, R.E. (Robert)
Brittain, G.M. (Gary)
Brown, A.R. (Adrian)
Bryan, D.S. (Dave)
Buller, K.R. (Keith)
Burton, R. (Roy)
Butler, A.N. (Andrew)
Cairns, M.J. (Mike)
Canadine, P. (Paul)
Cann, D.J. (Darren)
Carter, J.E. (John)
Castle, S. (Steve)
Catterall, S.A. (Steven)
Chapman, G.J. (Gary)
Chittenden, S. (Steve)
Clingo, S.G. (Steve)
Clyde, A.L. (Alex)
Cockwill, N.R. (Nigel)
Coffey, S. (Stephen)
Conn, A. (Tony)
Cooke, D.G. (Dave)
Cordy, J.N. (John)
Crossley, P.T. (Phil)
Deadman, D. (Darren)
Denniff, A.P. (Andy)
Desmond, R.P. (Bob)
Devine, J.P. (Jim)
Dewfield, A. (Adam)
Dexter, M.C. (Martin)
Dodd, D. (David)
Dorr, S.J. (Steve)
Drysdale, D. (Darren)
East, R. (Roger)
Eastwood, P. (Peter)
Ebbage, M. (Martin)
Edwards, C.D. (Clive)
Enright, D.J. (Dave)
Evans, E.M. (Eddie)
Evans, R.J. (Russell)
Evetts, G.S. (Gary)
Faulkner, I.L. (Ian)
Foulkes, G.W. (Gary)
Foster, D. (Dave)
Francis, C.J. (Chris)
Friend, K.A. (Kevin)
Gagen, S.L. (Simon)
Garratt, A.M. (Andy)
Garrett, L.P. (Lee)
Gibbs, P.N. (Phil)
Gosling, I.J. (Ian)
Gould, R. (Ray)
Graham, F. (Fred)
Greaves, A.J. (Alan)
Green, A.J. (Tony)
Green, R. (Russell)
Habgood, S.D. (Steve)
Hancox, N. (Neil)

Harris, I.R. (Ian)
Harris, M.A. (Martin)
Harvey, A.C. (Andrew)
Harwood, C.N. (Colin)
Hawken, M.A. (Mike)
Hawkes, K.J. (Kevin)
Haxby, M.D. (Mike)
Head, S.C. (Stephen)
Hewitt, R.T. (Richard)
Hills, C.J. (Colin)
Hilton, G. (Gary)
Hine, D.J. (David)
Hogg, A.S. (Andy)
Holbrook, J.H. (John)
Horton, A.J. (Tony)
Horwood, G.D. (Graham)
Howes, T.P. (Tim)
Hubbard, J.R. (Jim)
Hughes, M.H. (Mike)
Hutchinson, S.M. (Mark)
Ilderton, E.L. (Eddie)
Ingram, K.R. (Kevin)
Ives, G.L. (Gary)
Ives, M. (Mark)
James, R.G. (Ron)
Jones, L.C. (Laurence)
Jones, N.L. (Neil)
Kellett, D.G. (Gary)
Kettle, T.M. (Trevor)
King, E.A. (Eddie)
Kinseley, N. (Nick)
Kirkup, P.J. (Peter)
Lawson, K.D. (Keith)
Lee, R. (Ray)
Lewis, G.J. (Gary)
Lewis, R.L. (Robert)
Lockhart, R. (Bob)
Lomas, W.D. (Wayne)
McCallum, D.A. (Dave)
McCoy, M.T. (Michael)
McGee, A. (Tony)
McGuffog, P. (Paul)
McIntosh, W.A. (Wayne)
Malone, B. (Brendan)
Marriner, A.M. (Andre)
Martin, A.J. (Andy)
Martin, E.A.C. (Edward)
Martin, P.C. (Paul)
Martin, R.W. (Rob)
Mason, L.S. (Lee)
Massey, T. (Trevor)
Mattocks, K.J. (Kevin)
Maynard, M.A. (Mark)
Meads, C.J. (Colin)
Melin, P.W. (Paul)
Mellor, G.S. (Gary)
Merchant, K. (Kevin)
Miller, K.G. (Keith)
Miller, N.S. (Nigel)
Morrison, D.P. (Des)
Mullarkey, M. (Mike)
Murphy, M.E. (Michael)
Murphy, N. (Nigel)
Naylor, D. (Dave)
Nicholson, A.R. (Andy)
Nicholson, P.W. (Paul)
Nind, K.J. (Kevin)
Norman, P.V. (Paul)
Oliver, C.W. (Clive)
Page, A. (Andy)
Palmer, R. (Richard)
Parry, B. (Brian)
Pashley, R.A. (Rob)
Peacock, D. (David)
Pearce, J.E. (John)
Pearson, G.D. (Glenn)
Penn, A.M. (Andy)
Perkin, N.F. (Neil)
Perlejewski, A.J. (Andy)

Pike, K. (Kevin)
Pollard, T.J. (Trevor)
Pollock, R.M. (Bob)
Postles, M.D. (Martin)
Powell, K. (Ken)
Probert, L.W. (Lee)
Proctor-Green, S.R.M. (Shaun)
Ramsay, W. (William)
Ramsdale, P.A. (Paul)
Rawcliffe, A. (Allan)
Reeves, C.L. (Christopher)
Reynolds, K.S. (Keith)
Richards, D.C. (Cen)
Robinson, M.G. (Martin)
Rubery, S.P. (Steve)
Rushton, G.N. (Neale)
Russell, G. (Graham)
Russell, M. (Mike)
Sainsbury, A. (Andrew)
Sarginson, C.D. (Christopher)
Scarr, I.K. (Ian)
Sharp, P.R. (Phil)
Shaw, I.D. (Ian)
Shaw, M.A. (Mike)
Shaw, W. (Wright)
Sheffield, J.A. (Alan)
Short, M. (Michael)
Short, M.L. (Martyn)
Simpson, G.H. (George)
Singh, J. (Jarnail)
Smith, A.N. (Andrew)
Smith, R.G. (Robert)
Smith, R.H. (Richard)
Snartt, S.P. (Simon)
Spicer, D.R. (Darren)
Steans, R.J. (Rob)
Stokes, J.D. (John)
Stott, G.T. (Gary)
Stroud, K.P. (Keith)
Sutton, G.J. (Gary)
Swarbrick, N.D. (Neil)
Sygmuta, B.C. (Barry)
Tanner, S.J. (Steve)
Tarry, E.J. (Eddie)
Tattan, J.F. (James)
Taylor, J.T. (Joe)
Thiarra, S.S. (Sukhdev)
Thorpe, M. (Mike)
Tiffin, R. (Russell)
Tincknell, S.W. (Steve)
Tingey, M. (Mike)
Tomlinson, S.D. (Stephen)
Toms, W. (Wendy)
Townsend, K.N. (Keith)
Turner, G.B. (Glenn)
Unsworth, D. (David)
Vosper, P.A. (Paul)
Wade, B. (Barrie)
Wallace, G. (Gary)
Warrent, G.J. (Graeme)
Webb, A.J. (Alf)
West, M. (Malcolm)
Whitby, D. (Dave)
Whitehouse, I. (Ian)
Whitestone, D. (Dean)
Wilkins, A.M. (Andy)
Wilkinson, K. (Keith)
Williams, M.A. (Andy)
Williamson, I.G. (Ian)
Wilson, S.M. (Stuart)
Wood, D. (David)
Wood, P.M. (Paul)
Woodward, I.J. (Irvine)
Woolmer, K.A. (Andy)
Wright, K.K. (Kevin)
Yates, N.A. (Neil)
Yerby, M.S. (Martin)
Young, G.R. (Gary)

FOOTBALL AND THE LAW

Football and the Law last season moved forward at four different levels: in crime, damages, discrimination and trade mark areas.

Criminal activities hit the headlines with the off-field allegations against the Leeds United internationals, Lee Bowyer and Jonathan Woodgate. At the end of eight weeks evidence concerning city centre activities, the trial at Hull Crown Court was cut short before the jury retired to consider its verdict because the *Sunday Mirror* had published an article including an interview with the victim's father, who was quoted as saying that the alleged assault at the heart of the case, had clearly been racially motivated. That had not been considered or discussed before the jury after legal argument at the start of the trial. The judge ruled that if the jurors had read the article, it could have prejudiced the verdict. As the judge said:

"It is, to put it mildly, not at all desirable that a crime and therefore a suspect, should be labelled a racist when it is the prosecution submission they are no such thing ... The whole misleading issue of a racial motivation which the prosecution and defence have sought to exercise has been revived and placed before the jury in highly emotive terms",

adding that there was

"a clear and substantial risk of prejudice raised by the article",

and that justice would not be served if the trial continued.

In due course, the newspaper's publisher publicly stated that it had

"acknowledged to the Attorney-General that the article published on 8 April could be said to have been in contempt as a breach of the strict liability rule",

which creates a substantial risk that the course of justice will be seriously impeded or prejudiced, so watch this space next year for the re-trial.

On the other side of the Pennines at Birkenhead County Court, an amateur soccer player recovered £18,000 damages for injuries and financial loss from a broken tibia and fibula, which caused the referee in a minor Sunday League game to show the offender a red card. The claim in negligence was on the same basis for which Gordon Watson of Bradford City successfully received nearly £1m, against Kevin Gray and Huddersfield Town last year. Because the victim was not a registered player at the time of his injury, he was unable to claim upon the club's insurance policy. As a student, he lost a year's income, and a claim for an award against the Criminal Injuries Comeosnat on board was initially refused, but is subject to an appeal on the issue whether sufficient intention existed to establish criminal liability.

In comparable circumstances when a 3rd XV rugby player lost an eye in a rugby line-out, his appeal succeeded with the appropriate supporting evidence to establish a criminal intent.

The key point about the case is that the law does not differentiate between professional and amateur player when compensation claims arise from playing injuries; and clubs as well as players, should always consider and take advice when sufficient insurance cover exists before any steps on to the field. Indeed, the unsuccessful defendant was reported to have said he may have to sell his house to meet the claim and costs.

Still in the north-west, James Hussaney of Chester City not only obtained an award of £2,500 for injury to feelings from racial abuse at an employment tribunal. In due course he succeeded before an Employment Appeal Tribunal because insufficient reasons had been given for his complaint about victimisation from not offering him a professional contract after his membership of the club's youth squad, which was of mixed race.

Finally, Arsenal experienced another giant-killing opponent when it failed to prove that the seller of memorabilia and souvenirs had passed off to the public as Arsenal merchandise and infringed its trade marks by what he had been selling for over 30 years in and outside Highbury Stadium. To prove the passing off, Arsenal would have had to produce evidence or confusion among the public concerned with the purchases, which it did not; and the trade mark issue was sufficiently inconclusive that it will have to be resolved by the European Court of Justice, which is where the Bosman case opened up a Pandora's Box of complex legal and actual rulings.

Arthur Rowe, the Spurs push and run manager of half a century ago, with Billy Nicholson in the team, and who later brought Danny Blanchflower to White Hart Lane, used to say, football is a simple game; the players make it difficult. Today he would have to include insurance, racism and trading.

EDWARD GRAYSON
Founder President, British Association for Sport and Law.

The Football Stadia Improvement Fund
supporter of the football foundation

Continuing the work of the now defunct Football Trust, the FSIF has already spent over £30m improving grounds at all levels up to, and including, Division 1 of the Nationwide. Funded by the FA Premier League, The FA, Sport England and the Government the FSIF was launched in July last year by the Prime Minister, Tony Blair and Foundation chairman Lord Pendry.

The Football Stadia Improvement Fund's key objectives are to provide a safe and secure environment for fans and to fund improvements to football grounds at the lower levels, delivering modern family, community and disabled facilities.

Grants include:

Bournemouth	£3m	Redevelopment of Dean Court
Telford United	£400,000	To build a new stadium in the town
Cambridge United	£2m	To develop new North and South stands
Preston North End	£1m	To develop the new North Stand
Forest Green Rovers	£100,000	To build a new East Terrace and improve spectator facilities
Cirencester Town	£200,000	The development of a new stadium
Darlington	£1.2m	To build a new stadium
Cheltenham Town	£1m	To build a new stand
Hartlepool United	£1,112,968	To develop a new East stand and a new South and West stand
Plymouth Argyle	£1.8	To build a new all seater stadium

Football Foundation
football's biggest supporter

"Encouraging clubs to invest in their local community is one of the key aims of the Football Foundation. Sport, particularly football, has a proven track record in increasing educational standards, reducing crime rates and promoting a healthier lifestyle."
The Rt Hon Tom Pendry, Chairman, Football Foundation

With an annual budget of £60m the Football Foundation is the country's biggest sporting charity and is committed to revitalising the grass roots of our National Game. Launched in July last year the Football Foundation is funded by the FA Premier League, The FA, Sport England and the Government.

Our fully inclusive grant procedure is designed to cover all of our funding regimes, from schools projects and ethnic community officers to providing brand new pitches and changing facilities for football clubs up and down the country. Our aim is to promote the game of football as a force for good in society.

We have established education and community projects with organisations throughout England, using clubs as centres for learning and as a focal point for their neighbourhood.

No-one is excluded from our community programmes, we have put in place football development officers up and down the country, promoting the women's game and encouraging ethnic community involvement who have often found themselves marginalized through a lack of adequate facilities and opportunities to participate.

Our grass roots development programme is dedicated to providing the very best in facilities. No-one should have to play on sub-standard pitches or change in run down dressing rooms.

Grants include:

Buckhurst Hill Junior Sports Club, Epping Forest, Essex	£174,000	To build a new clubhouse (4 changing rooms, kitchen and social areas)
Milbourne St Andrews Sports Club, Dorset	£256,927	To provide a new pavilion (4 changing rooms, 2 officials rooms, showers, toilets, disabled facilities and social area) senior pitch, two junior pitches, 2 mini soccer pitches and car parking facilities
North Herts College, Shephalbury	£850,000	To provide a new complex incorporating a floodlit all weather pitch, pitch improvements, a new pavilion (including changing rooms, fitness room, showers and toilets and a social area). 70% of use will be for community needs, 10% for College needs and 20% for SBFC requirements
Norton Hill School, Midsomer Norton, Somerset	£105,000	To provide a full floodlit artificial pitch together with changing facilities at the school. The facilities will also be used by other schools in the area and by Norton Radstock College
Gateshead Metropolitan Borough Council	£174,121	To provide a new floodlit astroturf football pitch in the Windmill Hills area of the town. This new pitch will provide better footballing opportunities for people in the area and will stimulate growth in the take-up of the game amongst women and girls. The new pitch will also be used as a training base for local junior teams
Notts County FITC	£262,134	To fund programme delivering an individually designed educational and practical projects in a stimulating and safe environment for children aged 14–16 who had been excluded from school.
Stanley House Youth Academy	£126,200	A football development programme to address the issues of social exclusion among young people in the Toxteth/Granby area of Liverpool.

To find out more information about the work of the Football Foundation, or to receive one of our application forms visit our website www.footballfoundation.org.uk or telephone us on 020 7534 4210.

FOOTBALL CLUB CHAPLAINCY

FOOTBALL CHAPLAINCY – A MINISTRY PACKED WITH SURPRISES

Every clergyman will confirm that it is not only aspects of Christian teaching that are surprising (e.g. the King of all creation becoming a helpless, defenceless baby) but our ministry is packed with surprises too. And nowhere is this more apparent than among the football chaplains.

For example, the veterans among us are absolutely delighted but astonished at the fact that our ministry is leading British football clubs, which a dozen or so years ago was certainly unusual if no longer a rarity, has become a familiar feature of the game – so much so that by now it is the clubs which aren't benefiting in one way or another from the ministry of a chaplain who are the odd ones out!

The reaction of football clubs themselves and that of members of their staffs, to their chaplain's involvement in the Adidas Football Scholarship Scheme has also been a cause of some amused surprise among our fraternity. Some readers will know that the Professional Footballers Association has asked the clubs to involve their chaplains in the teaching of certain of the modules in the detailed, three-year curriculum which the young men now follow upon joining a Football or Premier League club, or to appoint one to do so. In some instances the chaplain has not only been able to fulfil this request with real flair, but has helped with other areas too, and done so in such a way that club officers and young footballers alike have been delighted by his communication skills. But then of course, these men have been in the communications business all their ministry, and involving them in this way is like playing a Cup tie on *our* ground – no wonder we've taken to it like ducks to water and are sometimes surprised at the pleasure and approval our efforts in this respect have evoked at our clubs

There's also been a most appealing surprise for some of our chaplains in the ecclesiastical realm. Originally most bishops looked with some disdain at parsons being involved as chaplains at major football clubs, but nowadays several prelates have actually given enthusiastic encouragement to their men who are so engaged! Free church leaders tended to be more open-minded about football chaplaincy from the start but, recently, one bishop, moving to a new diocese where there are two senior League outfits, was given a club scarf for each of them by the chaplain of the club in the city he was leaving – and to our delighted surprise, the old boy took the gesture in good part and is understood to have been seen at games with them both!

THE REV

OFFICIAL CHAPLAINS TO FA PREMIERSHIP AND FOOTBALL LEAGUE CLUBS
Rev Steven Hawkins—Bristol Rovers; Rev Catherine Bell—Luton T; Rev Richard Chewter—Exeter C; Rev Peter Bye—Carlisle U; Rev Ken Howles—Blackburn Rovers; Rev David Langdon—QPR; Rev Andrew Taggart—Torquay U; Rev Gary Piper—Fulham; Rev David Jeans—Sheffield W; Rev Peter Amos—Barnsley; Rev Nigel Sands—Crystal Palace; Rev Barry Kirk—Reading; Rev Graham Spencer—Leicester C; Rev David Bunbury—Bradford C; Rev Philip Miller—Ipswich T; Rev John Boyers—Manchester U; Rev Allen Bagshawe—Hull C; Rev Martin Butt—Walsall; Rev David Tully—Newcastle U; Rev Steve Riley and Capt Andrew Vertigan—Leeds U; Rev Derek Cleave—Bristol City; Rev Fr Alan Poulter and Fr Gerald Courell—Tranmere R; Rev Brian Rice—Hartlepool U; Rev Matt Baker and Rev Jeffrey Heskins—Charlton Ath; Revs Andy Cowley and John Graham—Watford; Rev Owen Beament—Millwall; Rev Michael Chantry—Oxford U; Rev Elwin Cockett—West Ham U; Rev Michael Futens—Derby C; Rev Mick Woodhead—Sheffield U; Rev Ken Hawkins—Birmingham C; Rev Alan Comfort—Leyton Orient; Rev Simon Stevenette—Swindon Town; Rev John Hall-Matthews—Wolverhampton W; Rev Canon Michael Hunter—Grimsby T; Rev Steve Collis—Port Vale; Rev Chris Cullwick—York C; Rev Ken Baker—Northampton T; Rev Mark Hirst—Burnley; Rev Tony Porter—Manchester C; Rev Richard Hayton—Gillingham; Rev Piers Lane—Darlington; Rev Clive Andrews—Notts Co; Fr Andrew McMahon—Southampton; Rev Chris Nelson—Preston North End; Rev Henry Corbett and Rev Harry Ross—Everton; Rev Paul Brown—Wrexham; Rev Jeff Howden—Plymouth Argyle; Rev Mike Pusey—Portsmouth; Rev Alan Hayday—Scunthorpe U; Rev Tim Welch—Shrewsbury T; Rev James Booth—Southend U; Rev Philip Hearn—Kidderminster H; Rev David Ottley—Bury; Capt Nigel Tansley—Crewe Alex; Rev Billy Montgomery—Stockport Co; Rev Ken Hipkiss—W.B.A.; Canon Roger Knight—Rushden & Diamonds.

The chaplains hope that those who read this page will see the value and benefit of chaplaincy work in football and will take appropriate steps to spread the word where this is possible. They would also like to thank the editors of the Rothmans Yearbook *for their continued support for this specialist and growing area of work.*

The following addresses may be helpful: SCORE (Sports Chaplaincy Offering Resources and Encouragement), PO Box 123, Sale, Manchester M33 4ZA and Christians in Sport, PO Box 93, Oxford OX2 7YP.

OBITUARIES

Jose Aguas (b Angola c30; d 00) Accomplished forward who scored for Benfica in both the 1961 and 1962 European Cup final victories – against Barcelona and Real Madrid respectively.

Peter Aird (b Glencraig 29.08.21; d 06.12.00) Tough but fair centre half who played for Hibernian and East Fife, before winding down his playing career with Caerphilly in Wales. Peter was a member of Hibs' Scottish Championship-winning squad of 1947–48. He also appeared in the Victory Cup final of 1946 when Hibernian lost to Rangers and in the 1947 Scottish Cup final when Aberdeen beat Hibs 2-1. His elder brother, Willie, was a striker with Greenock Morton and Queen of the South.

Andy Aitken (d 08.06.00) Scottish amateur of the 1940s who played for Queen's Park, Third Lanark and Hamilton Academicals. Andy was a member of the Great Britain side that finished fourth in the 1948 Olympics Games tournament in London. He scored in England's 5-3 defeat by Denmark in the third place play-off match.

Ronnie Allen (b Fenton 15.01.29; d Great Wyrley 09.06.01) Prolific centre forward who netted 231 goals in 457 appearances in all competitions for West Bromwich Albion. Ronnie began with Port Vale, making his debut in an FA Cup 1st Round tie against Wellington Town in November 1945 and turning professional the following April. He started on the right wing, but later settled into his true vocation as a goal-getter par excellence. He was a two-footed striker blessed with a powerful shot in both feet, a penchant for the swift volley, the knack of beating big defenders to a header and a cool expertise from the penalty spot. He moved from Vale Park to the Hawthorns in March 1950, scoring in his first match against Wolves, and continuing to find the net with alarming regularity throughout eleven seasons with WBA. The highlight came in 1954 when, against the odds, the Baggies beat Preston 3-2 in the FA Cup final, with Allen scoring twice (one penalty). His 208 League goals remained a club record until 1978. Whilst with West Brom, he played five times for England, scoring twice. Ronnie left the Hawthorns in May 1961 and joined Crystal Palace, scoring 34 goals in 100 League games before turning to coaching with Wolves in 1965. He became manager at Molineux in '66 and led the club back into the top flight two years later. He later managed Athletic Bilbao, Sporting Lisbon, Walsall, West Brom (twice), the Saudi Arabian national team and Panathinaikos.

Juanito Alonso (b Spain c28; d Ferrol, Spain 08.00) Real Madrid goalkeeper who played in the first three European Cup finals (1956 to 1958), with Real recording victories in each. In the 1958 final, a 3-2 extra time victory against AC Milan in Brussels, Alonso became the first 'keeper to captain a European Cup winning side. He made five international appearances for Spain.

George Armstrong (b Felling 09.08.44; d Hemel Hempstead 31.10.00) Winger 'Geordie' Armstrong was ever present throughout Arsenal's remarkable double-winning success of 1970–71. He scored seven times in the League campaign and created many of the 71 First Division goals amassed by the Gunners that season. Indeed, it was from Armstrong's cross that Ray Kennedy headed home the winner against Spurs that clinched the title on the last day of the League programme. Five days later George was in the Arsenal side that completed the double with a 2-1 extra time victory over Liverpool in the FA Cup final at Wembley. In the previous season he had played in both legs of the European Fairs Cup final, in which Arsenal beat Anderlecht with a 4-3 aggregate to gather their first trophy since winning the League in 1952–53. Armstrong joined Arsenal in August 1961, making his League debut six months later in a 1-0 victory over Blackpool at Bloomfield Road. His first goal came in the last game of the '61–62 season, a 3-2 home defeat by Everton. He remained with the Gunners until September 1977, having made a then club record 621 appearances in all competitions and with 68 goals to his name. But his reputation at Highbury was largely built upon his abilities as a creator of goals – especially from the by-line – along with his undeniable stamina, prodigious energy and speed on the ball. A former England Youth international, he collected five caps at Under-23 level while at Highbury and many were surprised that he did not make the breakthrough into the senior side. He next joined Leicester City, making 14 League appearances before moving on in September 1978 to Stockport County where his playing career ended after a single season. After coaching with Aston Villa, Fulham and Middlesbrough as well as in the non-league game and abroad, George returned to Arsenal in 1990. He died after collapsing during a Gunners training session.

Viktor Bannikov (b c39; d c04.01) Former USSR goalkeeper who understudied Lev Yashin at the 1966 World Cup finals in England. Following the dissolution of the Soviet Union Bannikov became president of Ukraine's Football Federation.

Jim Baxter (b Hill of Beath 28.09.39; d Glasgow 14.04.01) Sir Alex Ferguson, once a team-mate of Jim Baxter's at Ibrox, called him 'the greatest-ever Scottish footballer'. Most would agree with the compliment – as a creative midfielder 'Slim' Jim had it all, and then some. The road to fame, if not fortune, began in Kirkaldy in April 1957 when Raith Rovers secured his services by paying a few hundred pounds to his former junior club Crossgates Primrose. News quickly spread of the phenomenal new talent performing at Stark's Park and the inevitable step into the Big Time occurred when Rangers came calling in June 1960. By the end of his first Ibrox term (1960–61) Baxter had two major honours under his belt, the League Championship and the Scottish Cup (along with appearances in both legs of Rangers' European Cup-Winners Cup final defeat by Fiorentina). Two more League medals were to come, as were three Scottish Cup wins and three more League Cup successes – all achieved by 1965. He made his full debut for Scotland against Northern Ireland in November 1960, the first of 34 caps. Uppermost among his performances in national colours was his 'toying' with England at Wembley in 1967 when Scotland won 3-2, thus inflicting the World Champions' first defeat since gaining the title ten months earlier. And he was in his element in 1963 when playing alongside the likes of Ferenc Puskas, Alfredo Di Stefano, Uwe Seeler et al, for the Rest of the World against England in the FA Centenary celebration match. Jim travelled south of the border in May 1965 to join his ex-Scotland boss Ian McColl, then in charge at Sunderland. The Roker stay lasted until December '67 when Baxter moved further south to Nottingham Forest. His experience of English League football was not particularly happy or successful and in 1969 he returned to Rangers on a free transfer. Never one to relish the rigours of the training pitch, a discipline demanded of him by the Rangers managerial regime, Jim retired at 30. He went into the pub trade as a genial mein host with one hand on the beer pump, the other hovering over the self-destruct button. The cavalier attitude that had once helped to make him such a flamboyant player now served the over indulgent side of his nature, which eventually took its toll. But Jim Baxter will be remembered not for the excesses of his private life, rather for the abundance of talent that was plainly evident whenever he had a football at his feet.

Cyril Beech (b Tamworth 13.03.25; d Merthyr Tydfil 04.05.01) Staffordshire-born left-winger who spent his first class playing career with Welsh clubs Swansea City and Newport County. Cyril joined the Swans from non-league Merthyr Tydfil in August 1949 and made 133 League appearances (29 goals). He was renowned at the Vetch Field for his speed on the ball – it was said of him: 'If he gets the ball in Swansea, you won't stop him till he gets to Oystermouth!' He moved on to Newport in the 1955 close season and made 39 further League appearances (8 goals) before returning to the non-league game first with Worcester City then with Hereford. In later years he became a scout for Swansea.

Pierre Bolangi (b c83; d Aldershot 09.08.00) A Charlton Athletic Youth Academy player who tragically drowned whilst Charlton's scholars were undergoing a training exercise with the Army.

James Bowie (b Aberdeen 09.08.24; d Essex 08.00) Busy, bustling inside forward whose career flourished during the Second World War – he played for Chelsea in their 1942–43 League Cup South final triumph over Charlton at Wembley. In peacetime he made 76 League appearances and scored 18 goals for the Blues before moving to neighbouring Fulham in January 1951. Fourteen months later he joined Brentford and stayed until the summer of '52 when he moved on to Watford. His four-season tenure at Vicarage Road was to produce his most prolific figures: 39 goals in 125 Third Division (South) outings. Knee problems cost him his first team place and he entered the non-league game.

Bill Bradbury (b Matlock 03.04.33; d c99) Inside forward who began as a half back with Coventry in 1950. He moved to Birmingham City in November 1954 scoring twice in his three appearances for them as they pushed for promotion out of Division Two (eventually going up as champions ahead of Luton). Instead of sampling life in the top flight, Bill was next transferred to Hull where he enjoyed his most prolific form, scoring 82 League goals in 178 outings, mainly in the Third Division (North). In 1959–59, his 30 goals in 45 games helped the Tigers to promotion as runners-up in the new Third Division. In February 1960 he moved on to Bury and later played for Workington and Southport, before entering non-league soccer with Wigan Athletic.

Shay Brennan (b Manchester 06.05.37; d Waterford 09.06.00) Former 'Busby Babe' who came to the fore immediately after the Munich air disaster. Manchester-born of Irish parentage, he joined United straight from school initially as an inside forward, the position he occupied in the club's FA Youth Cup winning side of 1955. Shay was still waiting in the Old Trafford wings when the Munich tragedy decimated United's squad in February 1958. Suddenly he found himself in the spotlight and performing an unfamiliar left flank role in an FA Cup 5th Round tie against Sheffield Wednesday. He became the hero of the hour, scoring twice in United's 3-0 victory. He netted again in the semi-final replay victory over Fulham at Highbury (United won 5-3), but was not selected for the final against Bolton. Five years later, having been injured prior to the semi-final, he again missed out on a cup final place in United's victory against Leicester. By then he was an established right back and went on to enjoy success with League championship medals in 1964–65 (as an ever-present) and 1966–67 – and a European Cup winners' medal in 1968 when United beat Benfica at Wembley. He collected the first of 19 international caps for the Republic of Ireland against Spain in 1965. His Manchester United career finished in 1969–70 after 359 appearances in all competitions for the club. His playing days wound down as player/manager at Waterford. Heart problems led to Shay's eventual retirement from the game.

Chick Brodie (b Duntocher 22.02.37; d 04.00) Goalkeeper who started with Manchester City in 1954, although he did not make a first team appearance for the Maine Road club. He joined Gillingham in July 1957, making 18 League appearances before transferring to Aldershot the following summer. After 95 League games for the Shots he joined Wolves in February 1961 but made just one appearance in the old gold (a 2-1 win against Manchester United). That September saw him move again, this time to Northampton where he collected a Third Division championship medal in 1962–63 as the Cobblers continued their climb through the divisions. His last club was Brentford for whom he kept goal for seven seasons, making 199 first team appearances. Chick's retirement was brought about in most unfortunate circumstances; he severely injured a knee in a collision with a loose dog during a match.

'Canito' (Jose Cano Lopez) (b Spain c56; d Spain 11.00) Spanish international midfielder who represented his country in the Moscow Olympics of 1980. 'Canito' played for Barcelona.

Ron Challis (b Barkham c32; d Tonbridge 01.01) Top class referee whose career began in 1952 and ended in 1981. Ron ran the line in the 1975 FA Cup final (West Ham v Fulham) and took charge of the 1979 event (Arsenal v Manchester United).

Harry Clarke (b Woodford 23.02.23; d 16.04.00) Stalwart centre half in Arthur Rowe's 'push and run' Tottenham team of the early-50s. Harry (christened Henry Alfred) joined Second Division Spurs from Southern League Lovells Athletic in March 1949, having previously gained experience with the RAF Command XI. He made his League debut in a 2-1 victory over Luton at White Hart Lane shortly after signing and he never looked back. At 6' 3" – he was once described as a 'shy giant' – Clarke was a cool, commanding figure both in the air and on the ground, attributes that were vital to Tottenham's dashing style. His first major honour came in 1949–50 when Spurs topped the Second Division table; his second came a year later as Rowe's team pushed and ran its way to the League Championship. In the following season, they were runners-up to Manchester United, but by then other sides were getting the measure of their method and Tottenham's glory days were numbered for the time being. Harry made one full international appearance for England, in a World Cup qualifying match/Home International victory against Scotland at Hampden Park in April 1954; he also gained a single 'B' cap. He hung up his boots in 1956–57, after 322 League and Cup games for Spurs. He became a coach at White Hart Lane and later managed at non-league level.

Jack Cowan (b Canada c27; d Canada 12.00) Canadian-born full back Jack Cowan joined Dundee in 1949 and spent five seasons in the Scottish League, gaining a League Cup winners medal and a Scottish Cup runners-up medal in 1951–52. In 1954, after 115 League appearances for Dundee he returned to Canada, against the club's wishes. He found further success in his homeland with the Vancouver Halecoes and became an established Canadian international.

Stan Cullis (b Ellesmere Port 25.10.16; d 27.02.01) Stan Cullis might have become a Wanderer with Bolton as he had a trial period at Burnden Park in his teens. Instead he became a Wolverhampton Wanderer in February 1934 and, under the ever-watchful eye of Major Frank Buckley, he developed into a solid and creative wing half renowned for his heading ability; for a certain coolness on the ball and for the accuracy of his long passes. He was in the Wolves line-up that lost 4-1 to Portsmouth in the 1939 FA Cup final. Ten years later when Wolves beat Leicester 3-1 at Wembley, Cullis was their manager. In between those two landmark matches, he had played 12 times for England in peacetime (and 20 times during the war) and had three times captained Wolves agonisingly close to the League title. In August 1947, after retiring due to injury, he became assistant manager at Wolverhampton and a year later succeeded Ted Vizard in the Molineux hot seat. Stan was a pioneering boss who instilled a direct and highly effective style of play into the side and encouraged the club to arrange fixtures against exotic foreign opposition in the days before the European Cup. He was the driving force that steered Wolves through their most successful period. After the Cup final victory of 1949 came three League championships, in 1953–54, 1957–58 and 1958–59; Wolves were also League runners-up three times during his 17 seasons tenure and they beat Blackburn 3-0 in the 1960 FA Cup final.

Willie Cunningham (b Hill of Beath 22.02.25; d 11.00) Scottish international full back who became a pivotal figure in Preston's potent side of the 1950s. Willie arrived at Deepdale from Airdrieonians in July 1949, having previously played for Dunfermline. He made his Preston debut in August 1949, in a 2-0 home win against Grimsby in Division Two. In 1950–51 he was prominent as North End returned to the top flight as Second Division champions. Two seasons later Preston lost out on the League Championship to Arsenal; both had 54 points, but the Gunners boasted a superior goal average of 1.51 against Preston's 1.41. Cunningham's near misses continued as North End finished third in 1956–57 and were again runners-up in '57–58. The FA Cup was no kinder to him in 1954, when Preston were firm favourites to beat West Brom in the final but lost 3-2. Willie gained eight international caps and was Scotland's skipper at the 1954 World Cup finals in Switzerland. After a spell as Preston's assistant coach, he became player/manager at Southport in March 1964, leaving that post a year later.

Terence Curran (b Staines 26.06.40; d 05.00) Inside forward who was an amateur on the books at Tottenham. He joined Brentford in September 1957, making five League appearances before moving into the non-league game.

Stan Cullis

John Dick (b Glasgow 19.03.30; d Chigwell 09.00) Whilst serving in the RAF at Colchester, John played at inside forward for Crittall Athletic where he was noticed by both Tottenham and West Ham. It was the Hammers who captured his signature, just ahead of an offer from White Hart Lane. His League debut came in August 1953, a 5-0 victory over Lincoln in Division Two at Upton Park. He stayed for ten seasons, netting 153 League goals and helping the Hammers into the top flight in 1957–58, as Second Division champions. He scored 21 goals in the promotion push and formed a deadly duo with Vic Keeble who netted 19 in the campaign. International recognition came in April 1959 when John won his only cap, against England at Wembley (he also collected a single Scotland 'B' cap). He left West Ham in September 1962 and headed for Brentford in a £17,500 transfer, helping them – with 23 goals – to the Fourth Division title and an instant return to Division Three. In 1965 he went into non-league football and was later involved with West Ham's coaching system.

Didi (Waldir Pereira) (b c1930; d c04.01) Supreme midfielder who became a double World Cup winner with Brazil – in 1958 (when he scored in the semi-final against France and was named player of the tournament) and in 1962. Didi had previously impressed in the 1954 finals when Brazil's journey was ended by Hungary in the so-called 'Battle of Berne' quarter-final. He had a spell in Europe with Real Madrid and later coached Peru to the 1970 World Cup finals.

Peter Dubovsky (b Slovakia c72; d Thailand 06.00) Real Oviedo player who died whilst diving in Thailand.

Jack Dyson (b Oldham 08.07.34; d Oldham 11.00) Manchester City centre forward and Lancashire opening batsman. Jack arrived at Maine Road from Nelson in May 1952 and by 1955 was in regular contention for the inside left spot. He scored City's second goal in their 3-1 FA Cup final victory over Birmingham in 1956. He represented England at Under-23 level, but sadly his senior football career was curtailed by injury when he was 25. However, he continued playing first class cricket until the age of 30 and later moved to Scotland where he resumed his cricket and football at a lower level.

Maurice Evans (b Didcot 22.09.36; d Reading 18.08.00) A wing half of distinction (later a right back), Maurice joined Reading in September 1953. He made his Royals debut in October 1955, in a 1-1 draw with Southampton at Elm Park in Division Three (South). He went on to complete 407 League appearances and score 13 League goals in a 15 year, one-club playing career in which he was never booked. After a spell as player-manager with non-league Andover, he was appointed coach at Shrewsbury in 1968. Four years later he succeeded Harry Gregg in the Gay Meadow hot seat and remained until the Shrews relegation to Division Four in 1974. A return to Reading followed, first as coach then, in May 1977, as manager. Success came in 1978–79 when Evans led Reading to the Fourth Division championship, the club's first title since 1925–26. In January 1984, by which time Reading were back in the lower division, he was unexpectedly sacked – an experience that made him reluctant to return to management. However, following a spell as Youth Development Officer at fast-rising Oxford United, he was persuaded to take over the reins at the Manor Ground in June '85. His acceptance ultimately led to his finest moment as a manager when he led Oxford to League Cup success with a 3-0 victory over QPR in the 1986 final at Wembley.

Joe Fagan (b Liverpool 12.03.21; d 30.06.01) Joe Fagan's brief managerial tenure at Anfield provided continuity to Liverpool's remarkable success story in the 1970s and '80s. A former member of the famous 'Boot Room' team and Liverpool's assistant manager since July 1974, Joe succeeded Bob Paisley as team boss in June 1983 at the age of 62, thus becoming the oldest debutant League manager. He then led the Reds to three major trophies in his first season in charge, thus becoming the first English manager to achieve such a treble. The 1983–84 League Cup was secured with a 1-0 victory in a replayed final against Everton at Maine Road. The League championship was won ahead of Southampton; and the European Cup was won on penalties against AS Roma in Rome. In 1984–85 Liverpool were challenging for honours as usual, but were destined to finish as runners-up to Everton in the League and as semi-finalists in the FA Cup. In the end their trophy hopes rested on success in the European Cup final against Juventus in Brussels on 29 May 1985, just days after Joe had announced his intended retirement. As history tragically records, the match at the Heysel Stadium turned to disaster when rioting broke out and resulted in the loss of 39 lives. The distress and dismay on Joe's face was plain to see as he attempted to quell the trouble by pleading with the rioters. In the aftermath of the disaster English clubs were denied further European competition until 1990–91. It was a sad note on which to end Joe's distinguished career. As a player he had been a mainstay of Manchester City's half back line in the first four post-war seasons. He then had a spell in non-league football with Altrincham and Nelson before returning briefly to Third Division (North) action with Bradford Park Avenue. After a spell as Rochdale's trainer, his long association with Liverpool began in 1958 and continued into the fabulously successful era that was to follow, first under the leadership of Bill Shankly and then Bob Paisley. After Joe's two seasons in charge, the legacy of success was handed to Kenny Dalglish who in turn continued the tradition.

John Farquhar (b c24; d Glasgow 22.11.00) Six foot-plus amateur who first emerged as an attacker with Queen's Park during the Second World War. His development as a player was interrupted by his military call up and he later delayed turning professional in hopeful anticipation of selection for Great Britain's 1948 Olympic team. John joined Morton later in '48 and spent five seasons at Cappielow Park, but his career was curtailed by a serious knee injury.

Benny Fenton (b West Ham 28.10.18; d Dorset 29.07.00) Like his elder brother Ted, Benny Fenton started out with his local club West Ham (prior to the war the two brothers played together in the claret-and-blue). After 21 first team appearances, Benny went to Millwall on a free transfer in 1939, appearing as an inside forward many times during wartime, also guesting for a number of other clubs. A move to Charlton came in January 1947 and with it an eventual switch to wing half. Being 'cup tied' meant he was not in contention for a place in the Addicks' 1948 FA Cup final team, but he went on to complete 264 First Division appearances and score 22 goals between 1947 and 1955. In February '55 he became player/manager at Colchester United, also taking on the captain's role and re-energising the 'U's in the process. Fenton hung up his boots in 1958 after adding 103 more League games and 22 more goals to his totals. He remained at Layer Road as manager until October 1963 when he took over at Leyton Orient – a tenure that was to last just over a year in which time he was unable to improve the club's fortunes. In 1966 he took over the managerial reins at his old club Millwall, building a difficult to beat, defence-orientated side. Under Fenton's guidance, the Lions missed promotion to the top flight by a whisker in 1971–72. He gave up the post in October 1974 and returned to another of his old clubs, Charlton, where he served in a number of administrative roles.

Hocine Gacemi (b Algeria c76; d Paris 05.00) Talented striker who suffered a fractured skull during a match between Jeunesse Sportive Kabilye and USMA Annaba in Algeria. He lost his life after an operation in Paris.

Alberto Gallardo (b c41; d 01) Forward who played for Peru in the 1970 World Cup finals, and was with Cagliari for a while. As a coach he took Sporting Cristal to the Peruvian title in 1989.

Jimmy Golder (b Manchester 28.03.55; d c03.00) Midfielder who played one League game as a substitute for Stockport County against Bury.

Pablo Hernan Gomez (b Argentina c78; d Mexico 01) Argentinian-born striker who played for Pachuca in Mexico. He was killed in a car accident in Central Mexico; his wife also died in the tragedy.

Johnny Gordon (b Portsmouth 11.09.31; d 26.05.01) Inside forward who started out with Portsmouth in January 1949 and went on to complete 209 League appearances (69 goals) in his first spell with the club. In September 1958 he was transferred to Birmingham City and played almost 100 League games for the Blues before returning to Fratton Park in March '61 for a further six seasons, adding 234 more League (37 goals) games to his Pompey tally.

J. R. P. Gordon (b Inverness c30; d Dundee 21.11.00) A top class referee for 18 seasons, John Gordon officiated at two games during the 1978 World Cup finals in Argentina and wielded the whistle in several other international tournaments. He was in charge of Scotland's Centenary Cup Final of 1973, when Rangers beat Celtic 3-2.

Catalin Haldan (b Bucharest 03.02.76; d Romania 10.00) A talented midfielder with Dinamo Bucharest and Romania, Catalin had collected eight full international caps by the time of his untimely death at the age of 24. The tragedy occurred during a friendly fixture between Dinamo and Oltenita. He was a member of Romania's Euro 2000 squad.

Tony Harris (b Glasgow c23; d 25.08.00) Right winger (later a right half) with Aberdeen whom he joined in 1946 after impressing as an amateur with Queen's Park during the war. He played in the 1947 Scottish Cup final when Aberdeen beat Hibernian 2-1, and in the 1953 final when the Dons lost 1-0 to Rangers in a replay.

Archie Hill (b Chesterfield 12.11.21; d Chesterfield 09.99) Winger who played one League match for Chesterfield, at Leeds in 1948, after impressing in wartime football. Archie (christened Arthur) was the son of Harold Hill the former Notts County, Sheffield Wednesday and Chesterfield player.

Ron Jewell (b Plymouth 06.12.20; d Yealmpton 14.02.00) Former Plymouth Argyle amateur inside forward who joined Torquay United in September 1946 and played in a single League game (a 2-2 draw at Reading).

John Kelly (b Paisley 21.02.21; d Glasgow 01.01) John's promising career with Celtic was curtailed almost before it began, by the outbreak of World War II. A talented right winger he moved on to Morton in 1941 eventually gaining international recognition with a wartime appearance for Scotland against England in 1945. After the war he joined Barnsley for a then club record £4,000, after saying farewell to his former employers with a last-gasp goal that earned Morton a 4-3 victory over Queen's Park. Barnsley switched him to the left wing and he gained two full Scotland caps in that position in 1948. However, his progress was hampered for almost two years by a severe knee injury. When the Tykes were relegated to the Third Division (North) in 1952–53, he joined Falkirk and returned briefly to Morton in 1955 before moving to Halifax in '56. His playing career wound down with Portadown and he later worked as a Barnsley scout.

Jim Kilgannon (b Bannockburn c38; d Bannockburn 24.07.00) Hailing from a footballing family, right half Jim Kilgannon started out with Falkirk but found success with Stirling Albion as a member of their 1960–61 Second Division Championship-winning side. He also played for Dumbarton, Montrose, East Stirlingshire, Clydebank, Berwick Rangers and Alloa Athletic. He was in the Berwick side that knocked Glasgow Rangers out of the Scottish Cup in 1967.

Harry Kinsell (b Cannock 31.05.31; d 09.00) Left back who turned professional with West Brom in 1938. During the War he guested for Blackpool and was in their League North Cup final side of 1943–44, losing over two legs to Aston Villa. After West Brom's promotion to the top flight in 1948–49, Harry joined Bolton but stayed less than a year before moving on to Reading in May 1950. Eight months later he arrived at West Ham where he stayed for five seasons in the Second Division, making 101 League appearances and scoring two League goals.

Alf Kirchen (b Shouldham 28.04.13; d 18.08.99) Goal-getting right winger who impressed with Norwich City in 1933–34 and was subsequently signed by Arsenal in 1935. He scored two goals against Spurs on his Gunners' debut, a 6-0 victory that contributed to Arsenal's championship-winning campaign of 1934–35 (although Alf did not make enough appearances to warrant a medal). Thirty-three League appearances and 18 goals in 1936–37 earned him a place on England's highly successful three-games tour of Scandinavia on which he scored in a 6-0 victory against Norway and in an 8-0 drubbing of Finland. Alf won a championship medal in the following season as the Gunners pipped Wolves to the post. He represented Arsenal in two wartime cup finals and made three wartime international appearances for England. A knee injury in 1943 brought his playing career to an end. In peacetime he became a coach with Norwich and was later a director at Carrow Road. He was also a successful farmer.

Pedro Lavoura (b Portugal c74; d Portugal 08.00) Talented Sporting Braga midfielder who died in a road accident.

Thomas Lechner (b Germany c79; d Germany 00) Young Kaiserslautern star and German Under-21 international who died in a motorcycle accident.

Billy Liddell (b Dunfermline 10.01.22; d 03.07.01) As a teenager Billy Liddell was studying to become an accountant while playing football with Scottish junior team Lochgelly Violet. Partick Thistle and Hamilton Academicals were keeping tabs on the lad, when fellow Scot Matt Busby recommended him to his club, Liverpool. Billy was adamant that if he were to sign on at Anfield then he must be allowed to continue with his studies and to work for a local accountancy firm. The club also had to meet certain moral standards, as the youngster had been raised a strict Presbyterian. With the formalities settled Billy became a Liverpool professional in April 1939. The war (in which he served in the RAF) delayed his first class debut until 5 January 1946, in the 1st leg of Liverpool's FA Cup 3rd Round encounter with Chester, a 2-0 victory with Billy scoring the opening goal. In 1946–47, the first Football League season after the hostilities, Liddell played 35 games at outside left and contributed seven goals as Liverpool took the title ahead of Manchester United and Wolves (a lifelong teetotaller, he refused to partake of the celebratory champagne when the task was completed). Billy had played for Scotland in wartime internationals, but made his official dark blues debut against Wales at Wrexham in October 1946 and went on to complete 28 appearances for his country; he also represented Great Britain in two games against The Rest of Europe. In 1950 he appeared in the FA Cup Final when the Anfielders lost 2-0 to Arsenal at Wembley. A remarkably fit, ferociously fast and totally fair individual, Billy occupied the centre forward role in his later seasons and played on until 1959. By then Liverpool – or 'Liddellpool' as they were dubbed in his heyday – were in the Second Division with Bill Shankly at the helm and planning the Anfield revolution. In the course of his fine career Billy had shattered the club's appearance record with 539 games in all competitions (a tally later bettered by Ian Callaghan) and had netted an incredible 219 first class goals. He had been appointed a Justice of the Peace in 1958 and after hanging up his boots he devoted his life to that office, as well as to lay preaching, Sunday School teaching and accountancy for the Students' Union at Liverpool University.

George Ludford (b Barnet 22.03.15; d Enfield 02.01.01) George played the majority of his matches for Spurs during the Second World War and also guested for eight other London clubs. Included in this list was an appearance for Millwall in the 1945 League South Cup final defeat by Chelsea at Wembley. Originally a centre forward, he later became a wing half, then a full back. His peacetime figures for Tottenham show 75 League games and seven League goals. He became a highly successful manager with non-league Enfield.

Peter McKay (b Newburgh 23.02.25; d Corby 23.11.00) Goal ace Peter McKay joined Dundee United from Newburgh West End in 1949. He went on to break United's scoring record with 158 successful strikes, a Tannadice target that still remains untouched. In May 1954 he moved on to Burnley, where it took a while before he regained his scoring touch. But, once his confidence had returned, he went on to net 36 League goals in two seasons before returning to Scotland with St Mirren in 1957. Peter later became a part-time player with Corby Town.

Bob McPhail (b Barrhead 25.10.05; d Glasgow 24.08.00) Former Scottish Schoolboys star who played for Airdrieonians in their 1924 Scottish Cup final success against Hibernian. In April 1927 he moved to Rangers and became an Ibrox favourite for the next 14 years. As a goalscoring inside left he went on to collect six more cup-winners' medals and nine Scottish championship medals with the Gers. In addition he also gained 17 Scottish caps, including a two-goal match-winning performance against England at Hampden Park in 1937.

John McPhail (b Glasgow 27.12.23; d Glasgow 08.11.00) 'Hooky' McPhail had his own special place in Celtic folklore, as the player who scored the winning goal against Motherwell at Hampden Park in 1951 – the strike gave the Bhoys their first Scottish Cup success in 14 years. The versatile McPhail arrived at Parkhead in 1941 from Strathclyde and became a professional player despite an early bout of tuberculosis. He won a Scottish League championship medal with Celtic in 1953–54 and gained five caps for Scotland between 1950 and 1954.

Willie Maddren (b Billingham 11.01.51; d Stockton 29.08.00) The young Willie Maddren was invited to a trial by Leeds United, but injury prevented his attending and the opportunity passed him by. Subsequently Leeds' loss became Middlesbrough's gain when he signed for the Ayresome Park club in June 1968. He was employed initially as a striker (he made a scoring debut against Bury in April 1969), later as a central defender especially prominent in Boro's Second Division championship-winning team of 1973–74. Willie gained five Under-23 caps for England and many felt that his blend of aggression and determination, allied to an instinctive reading of the game, would lead to full international honours. Indeed, that might have been the case if not for a career-ending knee injury suffered in 1977. He turned to coaching first with Hartlepool, later with Middlesbrough. In June 1984 he was appointed manager at debt-stricken Ayresome Park, an arrangement destined to end in bitterness and acrimony. For the last five years of his life Willie suffered from motor neurone disease.

Steve Malcolm (b Jamaica c71; d Jamaica 01) Highly experienced Jamaican international (76 caps) who appeared in the France 98 World Cup finals, against Argentina and Japan. Steve was killed in a car accident near Montego Bay, shortly after appearing in an international match against Bulgaria in Kingston.

George Millington (b Aston 01.11.11; d Telford 27.10.00) Wing half who debuted in the League with Halifax Town in 1934–35 after being on the books of four other clubs. Following a spell with non-league Runcorn he moved to Bristol Rovers in 1936, playing in three League matches. George's playing career ended when he suffered a broken leg. He later worked as a physiotherapist.

Stan Montgomery (b Silvertown, London 07.07.20; d Cardiff 06.10.00) After five League games for Hull City, centre half Stan Montgomery returned southwards to join Southend in September 1946. He made 96 League appearances for the Essex resort side before heading west to join Cardiff City in December 1948. He became a Bluebirds regular and was a vital factor in their promotion to the top flight in 1951–52, as Second Division runners-up to Sheffield Wednesday. In 1955 he joined non-league Worcester City and later returned briefly to League action with Newport County. Stan also played cricket for Glamorgan.

Bobby Murdoch (b Bothwell 17.08.44; d Glasgow 15.05.01) Legendary midfielder and a mainstay of Jock Stein's successful Celtic side of the 1960s and '70s. Bobby started out with non-league Cambuslang Rangers from where he was snapped-up by Celtic, first on a trial basis in 1959 then as a full-timer in 1961. It was a wise decision by the club as Murdoch went on to make 291 League appearances and score 61 goals in the green-and-white – initially as an inside forward, later settling into the right half role in which his supreme pass-making abilities were used to optimum effect. As he was amassing those impressive personal figures, Celtic dominated the Scottish scene and spread their wings over Europe. Bobby collected no less than eight consecutive Scottish League title medals between 1966 and 1973. He was in the team that lifted the European Cup in Lisbon in 1967 when Celtic beat Inter Milan, thereby becoming the first British club to win that trophy. He was also in the Bhoys line-up when they lost to Feyenoord after extra time in the 1970 European Cup final in Milan. He gained four Scottish Cup winners medals and was prominent as Celtic took the Scottish League Cup from 1966 to 1970 inclusively. He made his full international debut in Scotland's 1-0 victory over Italy in November 1965 and scored two goals against Wales in his second appearance, a 4-1 success at Hampden Park. He went on to gain 12 caps and score five times for his country. In September 1973 Murdoch moved to Middlesbrough and was influential in their 1973–74 Second Division title success. He was appointed Boro's Youth team coach in 1976 and became the club's manager five years later when they were in dire financial straits, a factor which undoubtedly contributed to their relegation from the top flight in his only full season in charge.

Mike North (b c60; d Southend 16.04.01) Poole-based referee who died in hospital after collapsing during the Southend United v Mansfield Town Third Division fixture on 16 April 2001.

Pedro Peqaloza (b Mexico c80; d Mexico 12.00) Pedro was killed in a motoring accident in Central Mexico. He had been an up and coming midfielder with Pumas UNAM.

Harold Phipps (b Dartford 15.01.15; d 12.00) After an illustrious footballing career in the army, Harold joined Charlton in 1943 as an amateur. He was certainly in the right place at the right time, as Charlton were to appear in the first two post-war FA Cup finals and he was selected for defensive duty on both occasions. The first game, against Derby County in 1946, went into extra time before Charlton were defeated. A year later the Addicks faced Burnley in the final, and again the action went to an extra period – this time Charlton triumphed with a 1-0 scoreline. Phipps remained a consistent and versatile defender at the Valley until taking his talents to Watford in June 1952 and playing a further 47 League games before his first class career came to a close.

James Phiri (b c69; d 01) Zambia's goalkeeper in the 1994 and 1996 African Nations Cup.

John Pritchard (b Meriden 30.01.13; d Beccles 05.00) Winger who began with Coventry in October 1935 after impressing with Exhall Colliery. In June 1937, after only a handful of appearances, he moved south to Crystal Palace for whom he played 30 League games before moving on again, to relegation-threatened Manchester City in March '38. After the war he joined Southend, scoring eight League goals in 71 appearances before entering the non-league scene.

Bobby Reid (b Dundee 18.11.36; d Kirkaldy 29.07.00) Boisterous Scottish-born goalkeeper whose professional career began in Wales. After 18 appearances for Swansea City between 1957 and 1959, Bobby returned to his homeland to join Raith Rovers with whom he enjoyed a lifelong association in a number of roles.

Peter Robinson (b Manchester 29.01.22; d 09.00) Wing half who joined Manchester City in June 1940 and played for them in numerous wartime matches, also guesting for QPR and Aldershot while serving in the Army. After a single League appearance for City in the 1946–47 campaign, he moved on to Chesterfield where his stay was ultimately an unhappy one. After a brief spell with non-league Buxton Peter joined Notts County in February 1950 for the most productive period of his career in which he made 82 League appearances and netted one League goal before ending his first class career in 1952–53.

David Rocastle (b Lewisham 02.05.67; d 31.03.01) 'Rocky' Rocastle started out as an Arsenal apprentice and turned professional with the Gunners in December 1984. He made his League debut in 0-0 draw with Newcastle in September 1985. Within two seasons he was a Highbury favourite and one of the most exciting attacking midfielders in the Football League. He collected a League Cup winners medal when Arsenal beat Liverpool 2-1 at Wembley in 1987 and followed that with two championship medals, in 1988–89 and 1990–91. His full England debut came against Denmark when Bobby Robson introduced him as his first new cap of the 1988–89 season. Prior to that David had collected 14 Under-21 caps, the same number he would achieve at senior level. In August 1992 after completing 204 League appearances and scoring 14 League goals for Arsenal, a £2 million transfer took his talents to the then reigning champions Leeds. His stay at Elland Road lasted 18 months before another £2 million move took him to Manchester City where he helped to avoid relegation from the top flight. In August '94 he returned to London, this time with Glenn Hoddle's Chelsea for £1.25 million. After a productive first season at Stamford Bridge, he missed the majority of 1995–96 due to a broken toe. Next came a loan spell at Norwich, followed by another at Hull. He then played club football in Malaysia. David was diagnosed with non-Hodgkin's lymphoma in February 2001. His nine year-old son, Ryan, was Arsenal's mascot for the 2001 FA Cup final at the Millennium Stadium in Cardiff.

Don Roper (b Botley 14.12.22; d 08.06.01) Hampshire-born Don Roper had a footballing pedigree – his grandfather played for Chesterfield, his father for Huddersfield. Spotted in local football, young Don was signed by Southampton in June 1940 and was a prolific goalscorer throughout the war, first as a striker, later converting to the right wing role. In peacetime he continued to impress for the Saints and an inevitable move came in August 1947 when Arsenal paid £20,000 for his services – although it took eleven evaluations of the player before manager Tom Whittaker would sanction the purchase. Over the next decade it proved to be money well spent by the Gunners. In his first Highbury season Don collected a championship medal, making 40 League appearances and scoring ten goals as Arsenal won the 1947–48 title with a seven points margin ahead of Manchester United. He was not selected for the 1950 FA Cup final, but he was in the side that lost to Newcastle at Wembley two years later. His second title medal came in 1952–53 after 41 appearances and 14 goals in Arsenal's seventh title success (on goal average ahead of Preston). In all he played in 297 League games and scored 88 League goals for the Gunners. In January 1957 Southampton fans were delighted when he returned to the Dell as skipper for two seasons, adding 80 League appearances and a further 32 goals to his League figures. Don later played in non-league football in Dorset. He was also a cricketer of note and once played in a single first class game for Hampshire.

Dave Russell (b Methill c14; d Cheshire 12.06.00) David W. Russell gained a Scottish Cup winners medal with East Fife when they beat Kilmarnock 4-2 in the replayed final of 1938. He then joined Sheffield Wednesday and was hoping for a productive playing career after a promising first season in the blue-and-white stripes – then war broke out and he joined the RAF. Over 30 when peacetime resumed he turned to coaching and led the Danish Olympic team to the bronze medal position in London in 1948. He later managed Bury to the 1960–61 Third Division title and Tranmere Rovers to promotion out of Division Four in 1966–67. He became General Manager at Prenton Park in 1970.

Jimmy Scarth (b North Shields 26.08.26; d Hertford 12.12.00) Following service in the Royal Navy, Jimmy played as an inside forward for north-east side Percy Main from where he was snapped up by Tottenham in August 1948. After only seven first team games and three goals in three-and-a-half years with Spurs, he moved to Gillingham where things were destined to happen more quickly for him – in more ways than one. On 1 November 1952 he became the scorer of the fastest hat trick yet recorded in British football. He achieved this feat within two minutes, for Gillingham against Leyton Orient in a 3-2 victory in Division Three (South). In all he made 139 League appearances and scored 25 League goals for the Gills. In 1957–58 Jimmy won a Southern League championship medal with Gravesend & Northfleet. He continued playing in Sunday league soccer until his late-sixties.

Len Shackleton (b Bradford 03.05.22; d Cumbria 28.11.00) As outspoken as he was outstanding, Leonard Francis Shackleton will be remembered as one of English football's great entertainers. He was an inside forward capable of controlling the ball from any angle; a player whose skills were a match for any of his ultra-talented contemporaries; a goalscorer of genius; and a showman, often exasperating for team-mates and opponents alike. Yet, his illustrious career almost failed to take-off. After a trial period at Arsenal the slightly built Yorkshire lad was advised to find alternative employment since, in the opinion of manager George Allison, he wasn't up to Highbury standards and probably never would be. That was in 1939 and, after a brief spell with the works team of the London Paper Mills in Dartford, the cheeky youngster returned home to Bradford. There he was snapped-up by Bradford Park Avenue manager David Steele who offered professional terms in December 1940. Throughout the war Shackleton was a guest player for numerous clubs, including appearances on the same day for Bradford PA and Bradford City; one game in Leeds, the other in Huddersfield. He made his official League debut in Division Two, a 1-1 draw at Chesterfield in August 1946 but played just six more games in Park Avenue's colours. Having requested a transfer he was quickly sold for £13,000 to Newcastle United. On 5 October 1946 he took his place in the Magpies forward line in a Second Division encounter with Newport County at St James's Park – and proceeded to find the net no less than six times in a 13-0 victory. This astonishing feat set a club and Second Division record. Len finished the 1946–47 campaign with 19 League goals from 32 appearances, as Newcastle took fifth place in the table. He contributed a further seven goals in 25 League games to the club's promotion push in 1947–48, but by the time their place in the top flight was confirmed he had moved on, to nearby Sunderland, having endured an unhappy time since that remarkable debut match for the Magpies. The £20,050 fee was a record and Sunderland had won his signature ahead of several other clubs, including Arsenal who now acknowledged the folly of that opinion made almost a decade earlier. Shackleton represented England in an unofficial wartime international against Scotland in May 1946 but had to wait until September 1948 for his first official call-up, a 0-0

Len Shackleton

draw with Denmark in Copenhagen. Considering his immense talents it is surprising that he collected only four further caps over the next six years (perhaps not so surprising on reflection, given the plodding conservatism of the selectors). Three of those games were victories against Wales, the fourth was a 3-1 win against West Germany in December 1954, in which he scored a stunning individual goal. He was to remain at Roker Park until the autumn of 1957. During his tenure the club did not win a title, nor did they reach the cup final – although they came close to both on occasion – but they were always entertaining, especially when Len Shackleton was in the side. In 1957 a severe ankle injury brought his playing days to a close. Coaching or management were out of the question for the man whose 1955 autobiography *The Clown Prince of Soccer* had included the now famous wordless chapter to effectively illustrate his judgement of 'The Average Director's Knowledge of Football'. Instead he turned to journalism and continued to make astute observations on the game, initially for the *Daily Express*, later for the *Sunday People*.

John Shaw (b Annathill 29.11.12; d Glasgow 06.00) Dubbed 'Tiger' Shaw by the Ibrox faithful, this rock solid full back was a mainstay of Rangers' post-war 'Iron Curtain' defence. He was club captain, too, and collected four championships, three Scottish Cups and two Scottish League Cups – included in that array of honours was the double of 1949–50, achieved in his 38th year (he played on until he was 42). The Tiger also roared his way to four Scottish caps, making his international debut in a 1-1 draw with England in April 1947. He stayed with Rangers in various capacities for some 50 years. John was the elder brother of Hibernian and Scotland defender David Shaw (1917–1977).

John Simpson (b Hull 27.10.18; d Weighton 21.06.00) Tough tackling left back who began with Hull City as an amateur after impressing in local football. In 1939 he turned professional with Huddersfield. He played in wartime matches and skippered the Southern Command XI. His League debut came in 1947, against Blackpool, but he made just five appearances for The Terriers before transferring to York City in March 1948 at the age of 30. By the time he retired in 1954 he had amassed 207 League appearances for the Minstermen. He later worked variously as physiotherapist, trainer or manager with Hull, Hartlepool and Cambridge United.

Brian Skingley (b Ilford 20.08.37; d 08.99) Full back who between 1955 and 1959 was on the books of three major clubs – Bristol Rovers, Crystal Palace and QPR – although he only appeared in the League with Palace. He then enjoyed spells with several Southern League sides and had the distinction of scoring Gravesend & Northfleet's equaliser in a 1-1 draw with Second Division Sunderland in the FA Cup 4th Round in 1962–63 (Sunderland won the replay 5-2 at Roker Park).

Billy Sperrin (b Wood Green 09.04.22; d Sawbridgeworth 21.06.00) Inside forward who joined Brentford after gaining experience with Tottenham as an amateur, also as a guest player for half-a-dozen teams in wartime football and in the non-league game with Finchley and Guildford City. He scored 27 League goals in 90 League appearances for Brentford between 1949 and 1956. Billy was the younger brother of Jimmy Sperrin (1920–2000).

Jimmy Sperrin (b Wood Green 10.07.20; d Luton 10.05.00) Elder brother of Billy Sperrin (1922–2000), Jimmy played for Spurs during the war, but in peacetime made his name in non-league circles, most notably as a winger with Finchley and St Albans.

Alec Stock (b Peasedown St John 30.03.17; d 16.04.01) Yeovil Town v Sunderland: FA Cup 4th Round 1949. It should have been a foregone conclusion. The First Division giants couldn't lose against the Southern League minnows, or so the theory went. But the theorists had reckoned without Yeovil's player/manager, a then largely unknown quantity called Alec Stock. He had been an inside forward on the books of Spurs, Charlton and QPR before the war and had guested for a number of other clubs during the hostilities. He joined Yeovil in 1946 and knew how to use the infamous sloping pitch at the Huish to his team's advantage, at least that was the gist of what was reported in the sporting pages before the build-up to the 3rd Round tie at home to Bury. 'By the time Bury arrived the entire country thought we played on the side of a house,' he said later. Bury came, saw the slope and were conquered. So too were mighty Sunderland, with Stock scoring the opening goal in what ended as a 2-1 victory after extra time. No matter that Yeovil lost 8-0 at Manchester United in the next round – they

had already written their own special chapter in the history of the game and the cup run had suitably boosted the club's bank balance. The manager's stock had risen in the process and he was soon off to Leyton Orient. He led the 'O's on exciting cup jaunts in 1951–52 and 1953–54, and to the Third Division (South) title in 1955–56 – there was a 53 days spell as Arsenal's assistant manager implausibly squeezed into that campaign as well. In August 1957 he went to Italy to take charge, albeit briefly, at AS Roma before returning again to Brisbane Road. In the summer of 1959 he took the reins at QPR, leading them into the Second Division and winning the first-ever League Cup final in 1966–67. A year later he steered the west London side into the First Division, but resigned as manager before Rangers began their first-ever top-flight campaign. Stock's next stop was Luton Town where once again he won promotion, as 1969–70 Third Division runners-up. In the summer of 1972 he returned to London as manager of Fulham, where he signed the likes of Alan Mullery and later Bobby Moore who formed the backbone of the Cottagers' side that reached the 1975 all-London FA Cup final in which they lost to West Ham. Alec Stock was a fine tactician, not only on the pitch, but also in the transfer market. His shrewd eye ensnared not only Mullery and Moore in the twilight of their playing careers, but also the likes of Rodney Marsh and Malcolm Macdonald when they were in the ascendant. Alec became a QPR director in 1977 and later managed at Bournemouth.

Reg Stone (b c27; d Bristol 01.07.00) Former policeman who was a highly respected administrator in the west country. Reg worked in various capacities for the Bristol Suburban League and was eventually made life vice president. He was also a life member of the Gloucestershire FA and a former chairman and vice-president of the Bristol Referees Association.

Karl Kalle Svensson (b Hanaskog Sweden 11.11.25; d Helsingborg 15.07.00) Sweden's goalkeeper in the 1958 World Cup final against Brazil, and one of his country's most experienced players. Svensson also won a third place medal with Sweden at the 1950 finals and Olympic bronze in 1952. In all he collected 73 international caps. His extensive club career included 639 appearances for Helsingborgs IF, a club record.

Tommy Tighe (b Edinburgh 12.08.34; d c04.00) An inside forward with Hibernian and Dunfermline, Tommy (christened Terence) later switched to wing half with Accrington Stanley. He made 117 League appearances and scored 20 League goals for Stanley between 1957 and 1960. In December 1960 he moved on to Crewe, staying until the summer of '63 when he joined Southport, his last League club. His playing career wound down in non-league circles with Runcorn and Great Harwood.

Derek Trevis (b Birmingham 09.09.42; d California 00) Derek's career began at Villa Park in 1962, although he did not make a first team breakthrough there. In March 1964 he joined Colchester and made his League debut against Mansfield. A combative midfielder he became club captain, was a major factor in the 'U's promotion to Division Three in 1965–66 and, in all, made 196 League appearances for the Essex side. A move to Walsall followed in September 1968, producing six goals in 65 League appearances before he joined Lincoln in July 1970. Trevis served in a variety of positions in 108 League games for the Sincil Bank side. His English career ended at Stockport in 1973–74. He then moved to the USA, playing for the Philadelphia Atoms, San Diego Jaws, Las Vegas Quicksilver and Philadelphia Fury. Derek died in Sacramento.

George Waites (b Stepney 12.03.38; d 24.08.00) Right-sided forward who had two spells with Leyton Orient. The first began in December 1958 after his signing from Harwich & Parkeston. Between January 1961 and July '62 he was a regular member of the Norwich City forward line, netting eleven goals in 36 League games before returning to Orient, who were newly-promoted to the top flight. However, he was largely kept out of first team contention by the consistent form of Phil White (see below) and after just two further appearances for the 'O's in 1962, George moved on to Brighton that December and suffered relegation to the Football League basement five months later. His first class career ended at Millwall from where he entered the non-league game with Gravesend & Northfleet.

Jack Walker (b Blackburn 19.05.29; d 17.08.00) The Man Who Transformed Blackburn Rovers. Local lad Jack had supported the Ewood Park side since childhood and was delighted when they reached the 1960 FA Cup final against Wolves. By then he was a successful businessman having, together with his brother, revitalised his family's sheet metal works during the previous nine years. In the 27 years that followed Rovers' Wembley appearance the club slipped from the heights, but Walker's support never wavered and in 1987 he became actively involved behind the scenes at Ewood Park. Three years later, having sold his business for a reported £330 million, he purchased a majority share in Blackburn Rovers FC and became a vice-president of the club. Everyone in the game knew of Walker's lofty ambitions, but it was the surprise appointment of ex-Liverpool boss Kenny Dalglish as Rovers manager in October 1991 that underlined the seriousness of his intent. In May 1992 Dalglish led Rovers into the newly created Premier League via a Wembley play-off victory against Leicester. The club's next coup was the £3.2 million signing of star striker Alan Shearer from Southampton. After that Blackburn went from strength to strength. Three seasons later they were champions; Ewood Park had been improved almost beyond recognition; and Jack Walker's dream was fulfilled.

Colin Webster (b Cardiff 17.06.32; d Swansea 01.03.01) Centre forward who would probably have been aboard Manchester United's ill-fated flight home from Belgrade in February 1958, had it not been for a bout of debilitating flu. Colin joined United in May 1952, from Cardiff City with whom he had served his apprenticeship but had not made a League appearance. He made his first team debut in a 1-1 draw with Portsmouth at Fratton Park in November 1953. In the following campaign he bagged eight League goals in 17 appearances; and in United's title winning campaign of 1955–56 he netted four times in 15 games to earn a medal. United were top dogs again the following season, in which Colin made just five appearances. By the time of the Munich air crash, he had played just a handful of games in the 1957–58 League campaign and he had scored twice against Shamrock Rovers in the Preliminary Round of the European Cup and once against Dukla Prague in the 1st Round. After the crash, he was fully involved in the makeshift side that served for the remainder of United's season. Like Shay Brennan (who sadly included in these obituaries) he lined-up in United's emotional first match after the tragedy, in the FA Cup 5th Round against Sheffield Wednesday. In the 6th Round he scored the winning goal in a replay against West Brom. Unlike Brennan, Webster did play in that year's final when United lost 2-0 to Bolton. That summer he represented Wales in their Best of British showing in the World Cup finals, reaching the quarter-finals in Sweden before elimination by eventual champions Brazil. Then at the start of 1958–59 he played just seven more League games for Manchester United, before returning to Wales with Swansea for whom he scored 65 League goals in 159 appearances up to March 1963. His first class playing career ended in Wales, with 31 games for Newport County.

Phil White (b Fulham 29.12.30; d 00) A quicksilver right winger and a one-club-man, Phil joined Leyton Orient in 1953 after impressing with non-league Wealdstone. In 1955–56 his form was a vital element in Orient's Division Three (South) championship success. Six seasons later he was again prominent as the 'O's took the Second Division runners-up spot behind Liverpool and ahead of Sunderland. Unfortunately injury kept him out of contention for a place in the top flight where Orient stayed for just a single season. It was said that things might have been different had he been available. It was also reckoned that he would have fared better at a bigger club – but Phil once declined an offer from Liverpool in order to stay at Brisbane Road. He finally retired in 1963–64 after 217 League games and 28 League goals for Orient.

George Wright (b Ramsgate 19.03.30; d c09.00) Full back who joined West Ham from Margate in February 1951, making his first team debut seven months later against Hull City in Division Two. He retained his place until ousted by the consistency of John Bond. George represented London in the away leg of the inaugural Inter Cities Fairs Cup final against Barcelona in May 1958 (a 6-0 defeat for the Londoners who lost 8-2 on aggregate). In the same month he made the short journey to Leyton Orient with whom he made 87 League appearances and scored his only League goal (a penalty against Middlesbrough). He was in the 'O's side that won promotion to the top flight as Second Division runners-up in 1961–62. However, he was destined not to play in the higher strata as he was transferred to Gillingham that summer. His Football League career wound down with just four appearances for the Gills, but he played on in Kent with Ramsgate, his hometown club.

THE FA BARCLAYCARD PREMIERSHIP and NATIONWIDE FOOTBALL LEAGUE FIXTURES 2001–2002

Saturday, 11 August 2001

Nationwide Football League Division 1
Bradford v Barnsley
Gillingham v Preston
Grimsby v Crewe
Man City v Watford
Millwall v Norwich
Nottm Forest v Sheff Utd
Rotherham v Crystal Palace
Stockport v Coventry
Walsall v West Brom
Wimbledon v Birmingham
Wolverhampton v Portsmouth

Nationwide Football League Division 2
Blackpool v Reading
Cambridge Utd v Brighton
Cardiff v Wycombe
Chesterfield v Colchester
Huddersfield v Bournemouth
Northampton v Bristol City
Port Vale v Notts County
QPR v Stoke
Swindon v Peterborough
Tranmere v Bury
Wigan v Brentford
Wrexham v Oldham

Nationwide Football League Division 3
Bristol Rovers v Torquay
Carlisle v Luton
Cheltenham v Leyton Orient
Exeter v Hull
Hartlepool v Mansfield
Kidderminster v Scunthorpe
Lincoln City v Halifax
Macclesfield v Swansea
Oxford Utd v Rochdale
Plymouth v Shrewsbury
Southend v Darlington
York v Rushden & D'monds

Sunday, 12 August 2001

Nationwide Football League Division 1
Sheff Wed v Burnley

Thursday, 16 August 2001

Nationwide Football League Division 3
Rushden & D'monds v Lincoln City

Saturday, 18 August 2001

FA Barclaycard Premiership
Charlton v Everton
Derby v Blackburn
Leeds v Southampton
Leicester v Bolton
Liverpool v West Ham
Middlesbrough v Arsenal
Sunderland v Ipswich
Tottenham v Aston Villa

Nationwide Football League Division 1
Barnsley v Nottm Forest
Burnley v Wimbledon
Crewe v Sheff Wed
Crystal Palace v Stockport
Norwich v Man City
Portsmouth v Bradford
Preston v Walsall
Sheff Utd v Gillingham
Watford v Rotherham
West Brom v Grimsby

Nationwide Football League Division 2
Bournemouth v Blackpool
Brentford v Port Vale
Brighton v Wigan
Bristol City v Swindon
Bury v QPR
Colchester v Tranmere
Notts County v Cambridge Utd
Oldham v Chesterfield
Peterborough v Cardiff
Reading v Huddersfield
Stoke v Northampton
Wycombe v Wrexham

Nationwide Football League Division 3
Darlington v Kidderminster
Halifax v Exeter
Hull v Plymouth
Leyton Orient v Carlisle
Luton v Cheltenham
Mansfield v Southend
Rochdale v Macclesfield
Scunthorpe v Bristol Rovers
Shrewsbury v Hartlepool
Swansea v Oxford Utd
Torquay v York

Nationwide Football Conference
Boston Utd v Margate
Chester v Woking
Dag & Red v Southport
Dover v Telford
Farnborough v Doncaster
Hereford v Barnet
Leigh RMI v Hayes
Morecambe v Nuneaton
Scarborough v Forest Green
Stevenage v Stalybridge
Yeovil v Northwich

Sunday, 19 August 2001

FA Barclaycard Premiership
Chelsea v Newcastle
Man Utd v Fulham

Nationwide Football League Division 1
Birmingham v Millwall
Coventry v Wolverhampton

Monday, 20 August 2001

FA Barclaycard Premiership
Everton v Tottenham

Tuesday, 21 August 2001

FA Barclaycard Premiership
Arsenal v Leeds
Bolton v Middlesbrough
Ipswich v Derby

Nationwide Football Conference
Barnet v Dover
Doncaster v Leigh RMI
Hayes v Stevenage
Margate v Dag & Red
Northwich v Scarborough
Nuneaton v Hereford
Southport v Chester
Stalybridge v Morecambe
Telford v Yeovil
Woking v Boston Utd

Wednesday, 22 August 2001

FA Barclaycard Premiership
Aston Villa v Charlton
Blackburn v Man Utd
Fulham v Sunderland
Newcastle v Leicester

Nationwide Football Conference
Forest Green v Farnborough

Thursday, 23 August 2001

Nationwide Football League Division 1
Rotherham v Sheff Utd

Friday, 24 August 2001

Nationwide Football League Division 1
Bradford v Coventry

Saturday, 25 August 2001

FA Barclaycard Premiership
Arsenal v Leicester
Blackburn v Tottenham
Everton v Middlesbrough
Fulham v Derby
Ipswich v Charlton
Southampton v Chelsea
West Ham v Leeds

Nationwide Football League Division 1
Gillingham v Barnsley
Grimsby v Preston
Man City v Crewe
Millwall v Burnley
Nottm Forest v Crystal Palace
Sheff Wed v West Brom
Stockport v Portsmouth
Walsall v Birmingham
Wimbledon v Norwich
Wolverhampton v Watford

Nationwide Football League Division 2
Blackpool v Wycombe
Cambridge Utd v Stoke
Cardiff v Bournemouth
Chesterfield v Brentford
Huddersfield v Bury
Northampton v Notts County
Port Vale v Peterborough
QPR v Reading
Swindon v Oldham
Tranmere v Brighton
Wigan v Bristol City
Wrexham v Colchester

Nationwide Football League Division 3
Bristol Rovers v Luton
Carlisle v Hull
Cheltenham v Mansfield
Exeter v Scunthorpe
Hartlepool v Darlington
Kidderminster v Torquay
Lincoln City v Swansea
Macclesfield v Rushden & D'monds
Oxford Utd v Shrewsbury
Plymouth v Rochdale
Southend v Halifax
York v Leyton Orient

Nationwide Football Conference
Barnet v Scarborough
Doncaster v Yeovil
Forest Green v Boston Utd
Hayes v Chester

Margate v Leigh RMI
Northwich v Stevenage
Nuneaton v Dover
Southport v Farnborough
Stalybridge v Hereford
Telford v Dag & Red
Woking v Morecambe

Sunday, 26 August 2001
FA Barclaycard Premiership
Aston Villa v Man Utd
Newcastle v Sunderland

Monday, 27 August 2001
FA Barclaycard Premiership
Bolton v Liverpool

Nationwide Football League Division 1
Barnsley v Rotherham
Birmingham v Stockport
Burnley v Man City
Coventry v Nottm Forest
Norwich v Sheff Wed
Portsmouth v Grimsby
Preston v Wimbledon
Sheff Utd v Wolverhampton
Watford v Walsall
West Brom v Gillingham

Nationwide Football League Division 2
Brentford v Cambridge Utd
Brighton v Blackpool
Bury v Swindon
Colchester v Port Vale
Notts County v Chesterfield
Peterborough v Huddersfield
Stoke v Tranmere
Wycombe v QPR

Nationwide Football League Division 3
Darlington v Bristol Rovers
Halifax v Oxford Utd
Hull v Kidderminster
Leyton Orient v Hartlepool
Luton v Southend
Mansfield v Macclesfield
Rochdale v Exeter
Rushden & D'monds v Plymouth
Scunthorpe v Lincoln City
Swansea v Cheltenham
Torquay v Carlisle

Nationwide Football Conference
Chester v Nuneaton
Dag & Red v Woking
Dover v Forest Green
Farnborough v Barnet
Hereford v Southport
Leigh RMI v Northwich
Morecambe v Telford
Scarborough v Margate
Stevenage v Doncaster
Yeovil v Hayes

Tuesday, 28 August 2001
Nationwide Football League Division 1
Crewe v Millwall
Crystal Palace v Bradford

Nationwide Football League Division 2
Bournemouth v Wigan
Bristol City v Cardiff
Oldham v Northampton
Reading v Wrexham

Nationwide Football League Division 3
Shrewsbury v York

Wednesday, 29 August 2001
Nationwide Football Conference
Boston Utd v Stalybridge

Thursday, 30 August 2001
Nationwide Football League Division 2
QPR v Bristol City

Friday, 31 August 2001
Nationwide Football League Division 1
Gillingham v Crystal Palace

Nationwide Football League Division 2
Cardiff v Brentford
Northampton v Brighton
Wrexham v Bury

Saturday, 1 September 2001
Nationwide Football League Division 1
Grimsby v Barnsley
Man City v Sheff Utd
Millwall v Watford
Nottm Forest v Birmingham
Rotherham v Coventry
Sheff Wed v Preston
Stockport v West Brom
Walsall v Norwich
Wimbledon v Portsmouth
Wolverhampton v Crewe

Nationwide Football League Division 2
Blackpool v Stoke
Cambridge Utd v Bournemouth
Chesterfield v Peterborough
Port Vale v Reading
Swindon v Colchester
Tranmere v Oldham
Wigan v Notts County

Nationwide Football League Division 3
Bristol Rovers v Shrewsbury
Carlisle v Rochdale
Cheltenham v Torquay
Exeter v Luton
Hartlepool v Hull
Kidderminster v Mansfield
Lincoln City v Darlington
Macclesfield v Scunthorpe
Oxford Utd v Rushden & D'monds
Plymouth v Swansea
Southend v Leyton Orient
York v Halifax

Nationwide Football Conference
Barnet v Chester
Doncaster v Dover
Forest Green v Dag & Red
Hayes v Morecambe
Margate v Hereford
Northwich v Boston Utd
Nuneaton v Yeovil
Southport v Stevenage
Stalybridge v Farnborough
Telford v Leigh RMI
Woking v Scarborough

Sunday, 2 September 2001
Nationwide Football League Division 1
Bradford v Burnley

Nationwide Football League Division 2
Huddersfield v Wycombe

Monday, 3 September 2001
Nationwide Football Conference
Dover v Hayes
Stevenage v Nuneaton

Tuesday, 4 September 2001
Nationwide Football Conference
Chester v Telford
Dag & Red v Barnet
Farnborough v Margate
Hereford v Forest Green
Leigh RMI v Southport
Morecambe v Northwich
Scarborough v Stalybridge
Yeovil v Woking

Wednesday, 5 September 2001
Nationwide Football Conference
Boston Utd v Doncaster

Saturday, 8 September 2001
FA Barclaycard Premiership
Chelsea v Arsenal
Derby v West Ham
Leeds v Bolton
Leicester v Ipswich
Liverpool v Aston Villa
Man Utd v Everton
Middlesbrough v Newcastle
Sunderland v Blackburn

Nationwide Football League Division 1
Barnsley v Stockport
Birmingham v Sheff Wed
Burnley v Rotherham
Coventry v Grimsby
Crewe v Walsall
Crystal Palace v Millwall
Norwich v Nottm Forest
Portsmouth v Gillingham
Preston v Wolverhampton
Sheff Utd v Bradford
West Brom v Man City

Nationwide Football League Division 2
Bournemouth v Swindon
Brentford v Tranmere
Brighton v QPR
Bristol City v Port Vale
Bury v Wigan
Colchester v Northampton
Notts County v Wrexham
Oldham v Blackpool
Peterborough v Cambridge Utd
Reading v Cardiff
Stoke v Huddersfield
Wycombe v Chesterfield

Nationwide Football League Division 3
Darlington v Carlisle
Halifax v Macclesfield
Hull v York
Leyton Orient v Bristol Rovers
Luton v Oxford Utd
Mansfield v Lincoln City
Rochdale v Kidderminster
Rushden & D'monds v Southend
Scunthorpe v Hartlepool
Shrewsbury v Cheltenham
Swansea v Exeter
Torquay v Plymouth

Nationwide Football Conference
Barnet v Southport
Boston Utd v Yeovil
Doncaster v Woking
Farnborough v Chester
Forest Green v Morecambe
Hereford v Dover
Leigh RMI v Stevenage
Margate v Telford
Northwich v Nuneaton
Scarborough v Hayes
Stalybridge v Dag & Red

Sunday, 9 September 2001
FA Barclaycard Premiership
Charlton v Fulham
Tottenham v Southampton

Nationwide Football League Division 1
Watford v Wimbledon

Monday, 10 September 2001
Nationwide Football Conference
Dover v Boston Utd
Stevenage v Scarborough

Tuesday, 11 September 2001
Nationwide Football Conference
Chester v Stalybridge
Dag & Red v Hereford
Hayes v Forest Green
Morecambe v Barnet
Nuneaton v Leigh RMI
Southport v Northwich

Telford v Doncaster
Woking v Margate
Yeovil v Farnborough

Friday, 14 September 2001
Nationwide Football League Division 2
Wrexham v Brighton

Nationwide Football League Division 3
Mansfield v Shrewsbury

Saturday, 15 September 2001
FA Barclaycard Premiership
Aston Villa v Sunderland
Bolton v Southampton
Derby v Leicester
Everton v Liverpool
Fulham v Arsenal
Middlesbrough v West Ham
Newcastle v Man Utd

Nationwide Football League Division 1
Barnsley v Crewe
Bradford v Gillingham
Burnley v Walsall
Grimsby v Nottm Forest
Man City v Birmingham
Portsmouth v Crystal Palace
Preston v Millwall
Rotherham v Norwich
Sheff Utd v Coventry
Watford v West Brom
Wimbledon v Sheff Wed
Wolverhampton v Stockport

Nationwide Football League Division 2
Bournemouth v Bury
Bristol City v Colchester
Cambridge Utd v Cardiff
Huddersfield v Blackpool
Northampton v Chesterfield
Notts County v Brentford
Oldham v Peterborough
QPR v Port Vale
Stoke v Reading
Swindon v Tranmere
Wycombe v Wigan

Nationwide Football League Division 3
Cheltenham v Carlisle
Exeter v Oxford Utd
Kidderminster v Plymouth
Leyton Orient v Rushden & D'monds
Lincoln City v Bristol Rovers
Macclesfield v Hull
Rochdale v Scunthorpe
Southend v Hartlepool
Swansea v Halifax
Torquay v Darlington
York v Luton

Nationwide Football Conference
Chester v Boston Utd
Dag & Red v Leigh RMI
Dover v Stalybridge
Hayes v Doncaster
Morecambe v Hereford
Nuneaton v Forest Green
Southport v Margate
Stevenage v Farnborough
Telford v Barnet
Woking v Northwich
Yeovil v Scarborough

Sunday, 16 September 2001

FA Barclaycard Premiership
Charlton v Leeds
Ipswich v Blackburn
Tottenham v Chelsea

Monday, 17 September 2001

FA Barclaycard Premiership
Leicester v Middlesbrough

Nationwide Football League Division 1
Nottm Forest v Rotherham

Tuesday, 18 September 2001
FA Barclaycard Premiership
Arsenal v Newcastle

Nationwide Football League Division 1
Birmingham v Burnley
Crewe v Wimbledon
Crystal Palace v Grimsby
Gillingham v Wolverhampton
Millwall v Barnsley
Norwich v Watford
Stockport v Sheff Utd
Walsall v Portsmouth
West Brom v Preston

Nationwide Football League Division 2
Blackpool v QPR
Brentford v Bristol City
Brighton v Stoke
Bury v Wycombe
Cardiff v Northampton
Chesterfield v Wrexham
Colchester v Oldham
Peterborough v Bournemouth
Port Vale v Swindon
Reading v Cambridge Utd
Tranmere v Notts County
Wigan v Huddersfield

Nationwide Football League Division 3
Bristol Rovers v Southend
Carlisle v York
Darlington v Leyton Orient
Exeter v Plymouth
Halifax v Mansfield
Hartlepool v Cheltenham
Hull v Rochdale
Luton v Lincoln City
Oxford Utd v Macclesfield
Rushden & D'monds v Torquay
Scunthorpe v Swansea
Shrewsbury v Kidderminster

Nationwide Football Conference
Barnet v Hayes
Doncaster v Nuneaton
Farnborough v Dover
Hereford v Yeovil
Leigh RMI v Chester
Margate v Stevenage
Northwich v Telford
Scarborough v Morecambe
Stalybridge v Southport

Wednesday, 19 September 2001
FA Barclaycard Premiership
Blackburn v Bolton
Chelsea v Charlton
Leeds v Everton
Liverpool v Fulham
Southampton v Ipswich
Sunderland v Tottenham
West Ham v Aston Villa

Nationwide Football League Division 1
Coventry v Man City
Sheff Wed v Bradford

Nationwide Football Conference
Boston Utd v Dag & Red
Forest Green v Woking

Thursday, 20 September 2001
Nationwide Football League Division 1
Nottm Forest v Bradford

Friday, 21 September 2001
Nationwide Football League Division 1
Walsall v Wolverhampton

Nationwide Football League Division 2
Tranmere v Wrexham

Saturday, 22 September 2001
FA Barclaycard Premiership
Arsenal v Bolton

Blackburn v Everton
Chelsea v Middlesbrough
Leicester v Fulham
Liverpool v Tottenham
Man Utd v Ipswich
Sunderland v Charlton

Nationwide Football League Division 1
Coventry v Portsmouth
Crewe v Watford
Crystal Palace v Barnsley
Gillingham v Rotherham
Millwall v Sheff Utd
Norwich v Burnley
Sheff Wed v Man City
Stockport v Grimsby
West Brom v Wimbledon

Nationwide Football League Division 2
Blackpool v Cambridge Utd
Brentford v Oldham
Brighton v Bournemouth
Bury v Stoke
Cardiff v Huddersfield
Chesterfield v Swindon
Colchester v Notts County
Peterborough v Bristol City
Port Vale v Northampton
Reading v Wycombe
Wigan v QPR

Nationwide Football League Division 3
Bristol Rovers v York
Carlisle v Lincoln City
Darlington v Exeter
Halifax v Leyton Orient
Hartlepool v Kidderminster
Hull v Swansea
Luton v Torquay
Oxford Utd v Southend
Plymouth v Macclesfield
Rushden & D'monds v Cheltenham
Scunthorpe v Mansfield
Shrewsbury v Rochdale

Nationwide Football Conference
Barnet v Northwich
Boston Utd v Hayes
Chester v Dag & Red
Doncaster v Morecambe
Dover v Yeovil
Forest Green v Southport
Hereford v Stevenage
Leigh RMI v Farnborough
Scarborough v Nuneaton
Stalybridge v Margate
Woking v Telford

Sunday, 23 September 2001

FA Barclaycard Premiership
Leeds v Derby
West Ham v Newcastle

Nationwide Football League Division 1
Birmingham v Preston

Monday, 24 September 2001

FA Barclaycard Premiership
Southampton v Aston Villa

Tuesday, 25 September 2001
Nationwide Football League Division 1
Barnsley v Coventry
Bradford v Stockport
Burnley v Crewe
Grimsby v Gillingham
Portsmouth v West Brom
Rotherham v Sheff Wed
Sheff Utd v Crystal Palace
Wimbledon v Millwall
Wolverhampton v Nottm Forest

Nationwide Football League Division 2
Bournemouth v Reading
Bristol City v Tranmere
Cambridge Utd v Wigan
Huddersfield v Chesterfield

Northampton v Blackpool
Notts County v Peterborough
Oldham v Bury
QPR v Cardiff
Swindon v Brentford
Wrexham v Port Vale
Wycombe v Brighton

Nationwide Football League Division 3
Cheltenham v Bristol Rovers
Exeter v Rushden & D'monds
Kidderminster v Oxford Utd
Leyton Orient v Luton
Lincoln City v Hartlepool
Macclesfield v Darlington
Mansfield v Hull
Rochdale v Halifax
Southend v Carlisle
Swansea v Shrewsbury
Torquay v Scunthorpe
York v Plymouth

Wednesday, 26 September 2001
Nationwide Football League Division 1
Man City v Walsall
Preston v Norwich
Watford v Birmingham

Nationwide Football League Division 2
Stoke v Colchester

Friday, 28 September 2001
Nationwide Football League Division 1
Barnsley v Portsmouth

Nationwide Football League Division 3
Southend v Cheltenham

Saturday, 29 September 2001
FA Barclaycard Premiership
Aston Villa v Blackburn
Bolton v Sunderland
Charlton v Leicester
Derby v Arsenal
Everton v West Ham
Middlesbrough v Southampton
Tottenham v Man Utd

Nationwide Football League Division 1
Bradford v Grimsby
Crewe v Birmingham
Crystal Palace v Sheff Wed
Gillingham v Coventry
Man City v Wimbledon
Nottm Forest v Stockport
Rotherham v Wolverhampton
Sheff Utd v Norwich
Walsall v Millwall
West Brom v Burnley

Nationwide Football League Division 2
Blackpool v Wigan
Brentford v Colchester
Cambridge Utd v QPR
Cardiff v Brighton
Chesterfield v Tranmere
Huddersfield v Bristol City
Northampton v Swindon
Oldham v Notts County
Reading v Bury
Stoke v Bournemouth
Wrexham v Peterborough
Wycombe v Port Vale

Nationwide Football League Division 3
Bristol Rovers v Oxford Utd
Darlington v Rushden & D'monds
Exeter v Macclesfield
Hartlepool v Carlisle
Hull v Halifax
Kidderminster v Swansea
Leyton Orient v Torquay
Lincoln City v York
Plymouth v Luton
Rochdale v Mansfield
Scunthorpe v Shrewsbury

Nationwide Football Conference
Dag & Red v Scarborough
Farnborough v Boston Utd
Hayes v Hereford
Margate v Barnet
Morecambe v Dover
Northwich v Forest Green
Nuneaton v Woking
Southport v Doncaster
Stevenage v Chester
Telford v Stalybridge
Yeovil v Leigh RMI

Sunday, 30 September 2001
FA Barclaycard Premiership
Fulham v Chelsea
Ipswich v Leeds
Newcastle v Liverpool

Nationwide Football League Division 1
Watford v Preston

Tuesday, 2 October 2001
Nationwide Football Conference
Barnet v Yeovil
Dag & Red v Stevenage
Hereford v Farnborough
Margate v Hayes
Morecambe v Leigh RMI
Northwich v Doncaster
Nuneaton v Southport
Scarborough v Chester
Telford v Boston Utd
Woking v Dover

Wednesday, 3 October 2001
Nationwide Football Conference
Forest Green v Stalybridge

Thursday, 4 October 2001
Nationwide Football League Division 2
Tranmere v Blackpool

Friday, 5 October 2001
Nationwide Football League Division 1
Burnley v Watford
Grimsby v Rotherham
Portsmouth v Nottm Forest
Preston v Bradford
Stockport v Gillingham

Nationwide Football League Division 2
Bournemouth v Oldham
Brighton v Brentford
Port Vale v Cambridge Utd
Wigan v Stoke

Nationwide Football League Division 3
Halifax v Scunthorpe
Mansfield v Leyton Orient
Rushden & D'monds v Hartlepool
Shrewsbury v Hull
Torquay v Southend

Saturday, 6 October 2001
Nationwide Football League Division 1
Birmingham v West Brom
Coventry v Crystal Palace
Millwall v Man City
Wimbledon v Walsall
Wolverhampton v Barnsley

Nationwide Football League Division 2
Bristol City v Chesterfield
Colchester v Reading
Notts County v Wycombe
Swindon v Wrexham

Nationwide Football League Division 3
Carlisle v Bristol Rovers
Cheltenham v Lincoln City
Luton v Darlington
Oxford Utd v Plymouth
Swansea v Rochdale
York v Exeter

Nationwide Football Conference
Boston Utd v Scarborough
Chester v Margate
Doncaster v Forest Green
Dover v Northwich
Farnborough v Dag & Red
Hayes v Nuneaton
Leigh RMI v Hereford
Southport v Telford
Stalybridge v Barnet
Stevenage v Woking
Yeovil v Morecambe

Sunday, 7 October 2001
Nationwide Football League Division 1
Norwich v Crewe
Sheff Wed v Sheff Utd

Nationwide Football League Division 2
Bury v Cardiff
Peterborough v Northampton
QPR v Huddersfield

Nationwide Football League Division 3
Macclesfield v Kidderminster

Monday, 8 October 2001
Nationwide Football Conference
Dover v Dag & Red
Stevenage v Telford

Tuesday, 9 October 2001
Nationwide Football Conference
Chester v Hereford
Doncaster v Barnet
Farnborough v Nuneaton
Hayes v Woking
Leigh RMI v Forest Green
Southport v Scarborough
Stalybridge v Northwich
Yeovil v Margate

Wednesday, 10 October 2001
Nationwide Football Conference
Boston Utd v Morecambe

Thursday, 11 October 2001
Nationwide Football League Division 1
West Brom v Millwall

Friday, 12 October 2001
Nationwide Football League Division 1
Rotherham v Portsmouth

Nationwide Football League Division 2
Cardiff v Wigan

Saturday, 13 October 2001
FA Barclaycard Premiership
Bolton v Newcastle
Charlton v Middlesbrough
Chelsea v Leicester
Ipswich v Everton
Liverpool v Leeds
Southampton v Arsenal
Sunderland v Man Utd

Nationwide Football League Division 1
Barnsley v Birmingham
Bradford v Wolverhampton
Crewe v Preston
Crystal Palace v Wimbledon
Gillingham v Norwich
Man City v Stockport
Nottm Forest v Burnley
Sheff Utd v Grimsby
Watford v Sheff Wed

Nationwide Football League Division 2
Blackpool v Colchester
Brentford v Peterborough
Cambridge Utd v Bury
Chesterfield v Port Vale
Huddersfield v Brighton
Northampton v Tranmere

Oldham v Bristol City
Reading v Swindon
Stoke v Notts County
Wrexham v QPR
Wycombe v Bournemouth

Nationwide Football League Division 3
Bristol Rovers v Macclesfield
Darlington v Mansfield
Exeter v Carlisle
Hartlepool v York
Hull v Torquay
Kidderminster v Cheltenham
Leyton Orient v Shrewsbury
Lincoln City v Oxford Utd
Plymouth v Halifax
Rochdale v Rushden & D'monds
Scunthorpe v Luton
Southend v Swansea

Nationwide Football Conference
Barnet v Leigh RMI
Dag & Red v Yeovil
Forest Green v Stevenage
Hereford v Boston Utd
Margate v Doncaster
Morecambe v Chester
Northwich v Hayes
Nuneaton v Stalybridge
Scarborough v Dover
Telford v Farnborough
Woking v Southport

Sunday, 14 October 2001
FA Barclaycard Premiership
Aston Villa v Fulham
Blackburn v West Ham

Monday, 15 October 2001
FA Barclaycard Premiership
Tottenham v Derby

Friday, 19 October 2001
Nationwide Football League Division 1
Norwich v West Brom

Saturday, 20 October 2001
FA Barclaycard Premiership
Arsenal v Blackburn
Derby v Charlton
Everton v Aston Villa
Fulham v Ipswich
Leicester v Liverpool
Man Utd v Bolton
West Ham v Southampton

Nationwide Football League Division 1
Birmingham v Bradford
Burnley v Barnsley
Grimsby v Watford
Millwall v Nottm Forest
Portsmouth v Sheff Utd
Sheff Wed v Walsall
Stockport v Rotherham
Wimbledon v Gillingham
Wolverhampton v Crystal Palace

Nationwide Football League Division 2
Bournemouth v Brentford
Brighton v Oldham
Bristol City v Wycombe
Bury v Chesterfield
Colchester v Cambridge Utd
Notts County v Reading
Peterborough v Blackpool
Port Vale v Stoke
QPR v Northampton
Tranmere v Huddersfield
Wigan v Wrexham

Nationwide Football League Division 3
Carlisle v Kidderminster
Cheltenham v Exeter
Halifax v Bristol Rovers
Luton v Rochdale
Macclesfield v Lincoln City

Mansfield v Plymouth
Oxford Utd v Scunthorpe
Rushden & D'monds v Hull
Shrewsbury v Darlington
Swansea v Leyton Orient
Torquay v Hartlepool
York v Southend

Nationwide Football Conference
Barnet v Boston Utd
Chester v Doncaster
Dag & Red v Nuneaton
Farnborough v Hayes
Hereford v Scarborough
Leigh RMI v Woking
Margate v Northwich
Southport v Dover
Stalybridge v Yeovil
Stevenage v Morecambe
Telford v Forest Green

Sunday, 21 October 2001
FA Barclaycard Premiership
Leeds v Chelsea
Newcastle v Tottenham

Nationwide Football League Division 1
Coventry v Crewe
Preston v Man City

Nationwide Football League Division 2
Swindon v Cardiff

Monday, 22 October 2001
FA Barclaycard Premiership
Middlesbrough v Sunderland

Tuesday, 23 October 2001
Nationwide Football League Division 1
Birmingham v Gillingham
Burnley v Crystal Palace
Man City v Grimsby
Millwall v Bradford
Norwich v Portsmouth
Preston v Sheff Utd
Walsall v Rotherham
Watford v Nottm Forest
West Brom v Wolverhampton
Wimbledon v Coventry

Nationwide Football League Division 2
Brentford v Bury
Bristol City v Bournemouth
Chesterfield v Stoke
Colchester v Wycombe
Northampton v Huddersfield
Notts County v Brighton
Oldham v Reading
Peterborough v QPR
Port Vale v Cardiff
Swindon v Cambridge Utd
Tranmere v Wigan
Wrexham v Blackpool

Nationwide Football League Division 3
Exeter v Bristol Rovers
Halifax v Luton
Hull v Leyton Orient
Kidderminster v York
Macclesfield v Hartlepool
Mansfield v Torquay
Oxford Utd v Carlisle
Plymouth v Lincoln City
Rochdale v Cheltenham
Scunthorpe v Southend
Shrewsbury v Rushden & D'monds
Swansea v Darlington

Wednesday, 24 October 2001
FA Barclaycard Premiership
Southampton v Liverpool
West Ham v Chelsea

Nationwide Football League Division 1
Crewe v Stockport
Sheff Wed v Barnsley

Friday, 26 October 2001
Nationwide Football League Division 1
Grimsby v Birmingham

Nationwide Football League Division 3
Cheltenham v Scunthorpe

Saturday, 27 October 2001
FA Barclaycard Premiership
Aston Villa v Bolton
Charlton v Liverpool
Everton v Newcastle
Fulham v Southampton
Ipswich v West Ham
Man Utd v Leeds
Sunderland v Arsenal
Tottenham v Middlesbrough

Nationwide Football League Division 1
Barnsley v West Brom
Bradford v Watford
Coventry v Sheff Wed
Gillingham v Walsall
Portsmouth v Preston
Rotherham v Wimbledon
Sheff Utd v Crewe
Stockport v Millwall
Wolverhampton v Burnley

Nationwide Football League Division 2
Blackpool v Chesterfield
Bournemouth v Notts County
Brighton v Colchester
Bury v Peterborough
Cambridge Utd v Northampton
Cardiff v Tranmere
Huddersfield v Wrexham
QPR v Oldham
Reading v Brentford
Stoke v Bristol City
Wigan v Port Vale
Wycombe v Swindon

Nationwide Football League Division 3
Carlisle v Halifax
Darlington v Hull
Hartlepool v Oxford Utd
Leyton Orient v Rochdale
Lincoln City v Exeter
Luton v Swansea
Rushden & D'monds v Mansfield
Southend v Kidderminster
Torquay v Shrewsbury
York v Macclesfield

Sunday, 28 October 2001
FA Barclaycard Premiership
Derby v Chelsea

Nationwide Football League Division 1
Crystal Palace v Norwich
Nottm Forest v Man City

Nationwide Football League Division 3
Bristol Rovers v Plymouth

Monday, 29 October 2001
FA Barclaycard Premiership
Blackburn v Leicester

Tuesday, 30 October 2001
Nationwide Football League Division 1
Bradford v Wimbledon
Crystal Palace v West Brom
Gillingham v Burnley
Grimsby v Norwich
Portsmouth v Birmingham
Rotherham v Crewe
Sheff Utd v Watford
Stockport v Walsall
Wolverhampton v Millwall

Wednesday, 31 October 2001
Nationwide Football League Division 1
Barnsley v Man City
Coventry v Preston
Nottm Forest v Sheff Wed

Saturday, 3 November 2001

FA Barclaycard Premiership
Bolton v Everton
Leeds v Tottenham
Leicester v Sunderland
Middlesbrough v Derby
Newcastle v Aston Villa
Southampton v Blackburn
West Ham v Fulham

Nationwide Football League Division 1
Birmingham v Rotherham
Crewe v Bradford
Man City v Gillingham
Millwall v Coventry
Norwich v Wolverhampton
Preston v Stockport
Sheff Wed v Portsmouth
Walsall v Crystal Palace
Watford v Barnsley
Wimbledon v Grimsby

Nationwide Football League Division 2
Brentford v Blackpool
Bristol City v Brighton
Chesterfield v Cambridge Utd
Colchester v Bournemouth
Northampton v Reading
Notts County v QPR
Oldham v Huddersfield
Peterborough v Wigan
Port Vale v Bury
Swindon v Stoke
Tranmere v Wycombe

Nationwide Football League Division 3
Exeter v Southend
Halifax v Darlington
Hull v Cheltenham
Kidderminster v Bristol Rovers
Macclesfield v Carlisle
Mansfield v Luton
Oxford Utd v York
Plymouth v Hartlepool
Rochdale v Torquay
Scunthorpe v Leyton Orient
Shrewsbury v Lincoln City
Swansea v Rushden & D'monds

Nationwide Football Conference
Boston Utd v Southport
Doncaster v Stalybridge
Dover v Stevenage
Forest Green v Margate
Hayes v Telford
Morecambe v Dag & Red
Northwich v Farnborough
Nuneaton v Barnet
Scarborough v Leigh RMI
Woking v Hereford
Yeovil v Chester

Sunday, 4 November 2001

FA Barclaycard Premiership
Arsenal v Charlton
Chelsea v Ipswich
Liverpool v Man Utd

Nationwide Football League Division 1
Burnley v Sheff Utd
West Brom v Nottm Forest

Nationwide Football League Division 2
Wrexham v Cardiff

Friday, 9 November 2001

Nationwide Football League Division 2
Wigan v Colchester

Saturday, 10 November 2001

Nationwide Football League Division 1
Birmingham v Crystal Palace
Burnley v Portsmouth
Crewe v Gillingham
Man City v Wolverhampton
Millwall v Rotherham

Norwich v Bradford
Preston v Barnsley
Sheff Wed v Grimsby
Walsall v Nottm Forest
Watford v Stockport
West Brom v Coventry
Wimbledon v Sheff Utd

Nationwide Football League Division 2
Blackpool v Swindon
Bournemouth v Wrexham
Brighton v Port Vale
Bury v Northampton
Cambridge Utd v Oldham
Cardiff v Chesterfield
Huddersfield v Notts County
QPR v Tranmere
Reading v Bristol City
Stoke v Brentford
Wycombe v Peterborough

Nationwide Football League Division 3
Bristol Rovers v Rochdale
Carlisle v Mansfield
Cheltenham v Plymouth
Darlington v Oxford Utd
Hartlepool v Exeter
Leyton Orient v Kidderminster
Lincoln City v Hull
Luton v Shrewsbury
Rushden & D'monds v Halifax
Southend v Macclesfield
Torquay v Swansea
York v Scunthorpe

Nationwide Football Conference
Barnet v Woking
Chester v Forest Green
Dag & Red v Northwich
Farnborough v Morecambe
Hereford v Doncaster
Leigh RMI v Dover
Margate v Nuneaton
Southport v Yeovil
Stalybridge v Hayes
Stevenage v Boston Utd
Telford v Scarborough

Saturday, 17 November 2001

FA Barclaycard Premiership
Aston Villa v Middlesbrough
Blackburn v Liverpool
Derby v Southampton
Everton v Chelsea
Fulham v Newcastle
Man Utd v Leicester
Sunderland v Leeds
Tottenham v Arsenal

Nationwide Football League Division 1
Barnsley v Wimbledon
Bradford v Walsall
Coventry v Burnley
Crystal Palace v Crewe
Gillingham v Watford
Grimsby v Millwall
Nottm Forest v Preston
Portsmouth v Man City
Rotherham v West Brom
Sheff Utd v Birmingham
Stockport v Norwich

Sunday, 18 November 2001

FA Barclaycard Premiership
Ipswich v Bolton

Nationwide Football League Division 1
Wolverhampton v Sheff Wed

Monday, 19 November 2001

FA Barclaycard Premiership
Charlton v West Ham

Tuesday, 20 November 2001

Nationwide Football League Division 2
Blackpool v Notts County

Bournemouth v Port Vale
Bury v Bristol City
Cambridge Utd v Wrexham
Cardiff v Colchester
Huddersfield v Brentford
QPR v Swindon
Reading v Tranmere
Wigan v Chesterfield
Wycombe v Northampton

Nationwide Football League Division 3
Bristol Rovers v Mansfield
Carlisle v Shrewsbury
Cheltenham v Macclesfield
Darlington v Rochdale
Hartlepool v Halifax
Leyton Orient v Oxford Utd
Lincoln City v Kidderminster
Luton v Hull
Rushden & D'monds v Scunthorpe
Southend v Plymouth
Torquay v Exeter
York v Swansea

Wednesday, 21 November 2001

Nationwide Football League Division 2
Brighton v Peterborough
Stoke v Oldham

Friday, 23 November 2001

Nationwide Football League Division 3
Mansfield v York
Swansea v Hartlepool

Saturday, 24 November 2001

FA Barclaycard Premiership
Bolton v Fulham
Chelsea v Blackburn
Leeds v Aston Villa
Leicester v Everton
Liverpool v Sunderland
Middlesbrough v Ipswich
Newcastle v Derby
Southampton v Charlton
West Ham v Tottenham

Nationwide Football League Division 1
Burnley v Grimsby
Crewe v Nottm Forest
Man City v Rotherham
Millwall v Gillingham
Norwich v Barnsley
Preston v Crystal Palace
Sheff Wed v Stockport
Walsall v Sheff Utd
Watford v Portsmouth
West Brom v Bradford
Wimbledon v Wolverhampton

Nationwide Football League Division 2
Brentford v QPR
Bristol City v Blackpool
Chesterfield v Bournemouth
Colchester v Bury
Northampton v Wigan
Notts County v Cardiff
Oldham v Wycombe
Peterborough v Reading
Port Vale v Huddersfield
Swindon v Brighton
Tranmere v Cambridge Utd
Wrexham v Stoke

Nationwide Football League Division 3
Exeter v Leyton Orient
Halifax v Torquay
Hull v Bristol Rovers
Kidderminster v Rushden & D'monds
Macclesfield v Luton
Oxford Utd v Cheltenham
Plymouth v Carlisle
Rochdale v Lincoln City
Scunthorpe v Darlington
Shrewsbury v Southend

Nationwide Football Conference
Boston Utd v Leigh RMI
Doncaster v Dag & Red
Dover v Chester
Forest Green v Barnet
Hayes v Southport
Morecambe v Margate
Northwich v Hereford
Nuneaton v Telford
Scarborough v Farnborough
Woking v Stalybridge
Yeovil v Stevenage

Sunday, 25 November 2001

FA Barclaycard Premiership
Arsenal v Man Utd

Nationwide Football League Division 1
Birmingham v Coventry

Friday, 30 November 2001

Nationwide Football League Division 3
Hartlepool v Rochdale

Saturday, 1 December 2001

FA Barclaycard Premiership
Aston Villa v Leicester
Blackburn v Middlesbrough
Charlton v Newcastle
Derby v Liverpool
Fulham v Leeds
Ipswich v Arsenal
Man Utd v Chelsea
Sunderland v West Ham
Tottenham v Bolton

Nationwide Football League Division 1
Barnsley v Sheff Wed
Bradford v Millwall
Coventry v Wimbledon
Crystal Palace v Burnley
Gillingham v Birmingham
Grimsby v Man City
Nottm Forest v Watford
Rotherham v Walsall
Sheff Utd v Preston
Stockport v Crewe

Nationwide Football League Division 2
Bournemouth v Tranmere
Bristol City v Notts County
Bury v Brighton
Cardiff v Oldham
Huddersfield v Cambridge Utd
Peterborough v Stoke
Port Vale v Blackpool
QPR v Colchester
Reading v Chesterfield
Wigan v Swindon
Wrexham v Northampton
Wycombe v Brentford

Nationwide Football League Division 3
Carlisle v Scunthorpe
Cheltenham v Halifax
Darlington v York
Hull v Oxford Utd
Kidderminster v Luton
Leyton Orient v Plymouth
Mansfield v Swansea
Rushden & D'monds v Bristol Rovers
Shrewsbury v Exeter
Southend v Lincoln City
Torquay v Macclesfield

Nationwide Football Conference
Barnet v Hereford
Doncaster v Farnborough
Forest Green v Scarborough
Hayes v Leigh RMI
Margate v Boston Utd
Northwich v Yeovil
Nuneaton v Morecambe
Southport v Dag & Red
Stalybridge v Stevenage
Telford v Dover
Woking v Chester

Sunday, 2 December 2001

FA Barclaycard Premiership
Everton v Southampton

Nationwide Football League Division 1
Portsmouth v Norwich
Wolverhampton v West Brom

Saturday, 8 December 2001

FA Barclaycard Premiership
Blackburn v Leeds
Charlton v Tottenham
Derby v Bolton
Fulham v Everton
Ipswich v Newcastle
Leicester v Southampton
Liverpool v Middlesbrough
Man Utd v West Ham
Sunderland v Chelsea

Nationwide Football League Division 1
Barnsley v Walsall
Birmingham v Norwich
Bradford v Rotherham
Crystal Palace v Man City
Grimsby v Wolverhampton
Nottm Forest v Gillingham
Portsmouth v Crewe
Preston v Burnley
Sheff Wed v Millwall
Stockport v Wimbledon
West Brom v Sheff Utd

Sunday, 9 December 2001

FA Barclaycard Premiership
Arsenal v Aston Villa

Nationwide Football League Division 1
Coventry v Watford

Wednesday, 12 December 2001

FA Barclaycard Premiership
Man Utd v Derby

Friday, 14 December 2001

Nationwide Football League Division 2
Brighton v Reading

Saturday, 15 December 2001

FA Barclaycard Premiership
Aston Villa v Ipswich
Bolton v Charlton
Chelsea v Liverpool
Everton v Derby
Leeds v Leicester
Middlesbrough v Man Utd
Newcastle v Blackburn
Southampton v Sunderland
Tottenham v Fulham
West Ham v Arsenal

Nationwide Football League Division 1
Burnley v Stockport
Crewe v West Brom
Gillingham v Sheff Wed
Millwall v Portsmouth
Norwich v Coventry
Rotherham v Preston
Sheff Utd v Barnsley
Walsall v Grimsby
Watford v Crystal Palace

Nationwide Football League Division 2
Blackpool v Cardiff
Brentford v Wrexham
Cambridge Utd v Bristol City
Chesterfield v QPR
Colchester v Peterborough
Northampton v Bournemouth
Notts County v Bury
Oldham v Wigan
Stoke v Wycombe
Swindon v Huddersfield
Tranmere v Port Vale

Nationwide Football League Division 3
Bristol Rovers v Hartlepool
Exeter v Kidderminster
Halifax v Shrewsbury
Lincoln City v Torquay
Luton v Rushden & D'monds
Macclesfield v Leyton Orient
Oxford Utd v Mansfield
Plymouth v Darlington
Rochdale v Southend
Scunthorpe v Hull
Swansea v Carlisle
York v Cheltenham

Nationwide Football Conference
Boston Utd v Woking
Chester v Southport
Dag & Red v Margate
Dover v Barnet
Farnborough v Forest Green
Hereford v Nuneaton
Leigh RMI v Doncaster
Morecambe v Stalybridge
Scarborough v Northwich
Stevenage v Hayes
Yeovil v Telford

Sunday, 16 December 2001

Nationwide Football League Division 1
Man City v Bradford
Wimbledon v Nottm Forest
Wolverhampton v Birmingham

Wednesday, 19 December 2001

Nationwide Football League Division 2
Stoke v Cardiff

Friday, 21 December 2001

Nationwide Football League Division 1
Portsmouth v Stockport

Nationwide Football League Division 2
Brentford v Northampton
Brighton v Chesterfield
Notts County v Swindon
Oldham v Port Vale

Nationwide Football League Division 3
Hull v Southend
Mansfield v Exeter
Shrewsbury v Macclesfield

Saturday, 22 December 2001

FA Barclaycard Premiership
Charlton v Blackburn
Chelsea v Bolton
Derby v Aston Villa
Leeds v Newcastle
Leicester v West Ham
Man Utd v Southampton
Middlesbrough v Fulham
Sunderland v Everton
Tottenham v Ipswich

Nationwide Football League Division 1
Barnsley v Gillingham
Birmingham v Walsall
Burnley v Millwall
Coventry v Bradford
Crewe v Man City
Crystal Palace v Nottm Forest
Norwich v Wimbledon
Preston v Grimsby
Sheff Utd v Rotherham
Watford v Wolverhampton
West Brom v Sheff Wed

Nationwide Football League Division 2
Bournemouth v QPR
Bristol City v Wrexham
Bury v Blackpool
Colchester v Huddersfield
Peterborough v Tranmere
Reading v Wigan
Wycombe v Cambridge Utd

Nationwide Football League Division 3
Darlington v Cheltenham
Halifax v Kidderminster
Leyton Orient v Lincoln City
Luton v Hartlepool
Rochdale v York
Rushden & D'monds v Carlisle
Scunthorpe v Plymouth
Swansea v Bristol Rovers
Torquay v Oxford Utd

Sunday, 23 December 2001

FA Barclaycard Premiership
Liverpool v Arsenal

Wednesday, 26 December 2001

FA Barclaycard Premiership
Arsenal v Chelsea
Aston Villa v Liverpool
Blackburn v Sunderland
Bolton v Leeds
Everton v Man Utd
Fulham v Charlton
Ipswich v Leicester
Newcastle v Middlesbrough
Southampton v Tottenham
West Ham v Derby

Nationwide Football League Division 1
Bradford v Sheff Utd
Gillingham v Portsmouth
Grimsby v Coventry
Man City v West Brom
Millwall v Crystal Palace
Nottm Forest v Norwich
Rotherham v Burnley
Sheff Wed v Birmingham
Stockport v Barnsley
Walsall v Crewe
Wimbledon v Watford
Wolverhampton v Preston

Nationwide Football League Division 2
Blackpool v Oldham
Cambridge Utd v Brentford
Cardiff v Reading
Chesterfield v Wycombe
Huddersfield v Peterborough
Northampton v Colchester
Port Vale v Bristol City
QPR v Brighton
Swindon v Bournemouth
Tranmere v Stoke
Wigan v Bury
Wrexham v Notts County

Nationwide Football League Division 3
Bristol Rovers v Leyton Orient
Carlisle v Darlington
Cheltenham v Shrewsbury
Exeter v Swansea
Hartlepool v Scunthorpe
Kidderminster v Rochdale
Lincoln City v Mansfield
Macclesfield v Halifax
Oxford Utd v Luton
Plymouth v Torquay
Southend v Rushden & D'monds
York v Hull

Nationwide Football Conference
Barnet v Stevenage
Doncaster v Scarborough
Forest Green v Yeovil
Hayes v Dag & Red
Margate v Dover
Northwich v Chester
Nuneaton v Boston Utd
Southport v Morecambe
Stalybridge v Leigh RMI
Telford v Hereford
Woking v Farnborough

Saturday, 29 December 2001

FA Barclaycard Premiership
Arsenal v Middlesbrough

Aston Villa v Tottenham
Blackburn v Derby
Bolton v Leicester
Everton v Charlton
Fulham v Man Utd
Ipswich v Sunderland
Newcastle v Chelsea
Southampton v Leeds
West Ham v Liverpool

Nationwide Football League Division 1
Bradford v Crystal Palace
Gillingham v West Brom
Grimsby v Portsmouth
Man City v Burnley
Millwall v Crewe
Nottm Forest v Coventry
Rotherham v Barnsley
Sheff Wed v Norwich
Stockport v Birmingham
Walsall v Watford
Wimbledon v Preston
Wolverhampton v Sheff Utd

Nationwide Football League Division 2
Blackpool v Brighton
Cambridge Utd v Peterborough
Cardiff v Bristol City
Chesterfield v Notts County
Huddersfield v Stoke
Northampton v Oldham
Port Vale v Colchester
QPR v Wycombe
Swindon v Bury
Tranmere v Brentford
Wigan v Bournemouth
Wrexham v Reading

Nationwide Football League Division 3
Bristol Rovers v Darlington
Carlisle v Torquay
Cheltenham v Swansea
Exeter v Rochdale
Hartlepool v Leyton Orient
Kidderminster v Hull
Lincoln City v Scunthorpe
Macclesfield v Mansfield
Oxford Utd v Halifax
Plymouth v Rushden & D'monds
Southend v Luton
York v Shrewsbury

Nationwide Football Conference
Boston Utd v Forest Green
Chester v Hayes
Dag & Red v Telford
Dover v Nuneaton
Farnborough v Southport
Hereford v Stalybridge
Leigh RMI v Margate
Morecambe v Woking
Scarborough v Barnet
Stevenage v Northwich
Yeovil v Doncaster

Tuesday, 1 January 2002

FA Barclaycard Premiership
Charlton v Ipswich
Chelsea v Southampton
Leeds v West Ham
Leicester v Arsenal
Liverpool v Bolton
Man Utd v Newcastle
Middlesbrough v Everton
Sunderland v Aston Villa
Tottenham v Blackburn

Nationwide Football League Division 1
Barnsley v Grimsby
Birmingham v Nottm Forest
Burnley v Bradford
Coventry v Rotherham
Crewe v Wolverhampton
Crystal Palace v Gillingham
Norwich v Walsall
Portsmouth v Wimbledon
Preston v Sheff Wed

Sheff Utd v Man City
Watford v Millwall
West Brom v Stockport

Nationwide Football League Division 2
Bournemouth v Cambridge Utd
Brentford v Cardiff
Brighton v Northampton
Bristol City v QPR
Bury v Wrexham
Colchester v Swindon
Notts County v Wigan
Oldham v Tranmere
Peterborough v Chesterfield
Reading v Port Vale
Stoke v Blackpool
Wycombe v Huddersfield

Nationwide Football League Division 3
Darlington v Lincoln City
Halifax v York
Hull v Hartlepool
Leyton Orient v Southend
Luton v Exeter
Mansfield v Kidderminster
Rochdale v Carlisle
Rushden & D'monds v Oxford Utd
Scunthorpe v Macclesfield
Shrewsbury v Bristol Rovers
Swansea v Plymouth
Torquay v Cheltenham

Nationwide Football Conference
Boston Utd v Nuneaton
Chester v Northwich
Dag & Red v Hayes
Dover v Margate
Farnborough v Woking
Hereford v Telford
Leigh RMI v Stalybridge
Morecambe v Southport
Scarborough v Doncaster
Stevenage v Barnet
Yeovil v Forest Green

Wednesday, 2 January 2002

FA Barclaycard Premiership
Derby v Fulham

Saturday, 5 January 2002

Nationwide Football League Division 2
Bournemouth v Cardiff
Brentford v Chesterfield
Brighton v Tranmere
Bristol City v Wigan
Bury v Huddersfield
Colchester v Wrexham
Notts County v Northampton
Oldham v Swindon
Peterborough v Port Vale
Reading v QPR
Stoke v Cambridge Utd
Wycombe v Blackpool

Nationwide Football League Division 3
Darlington v Hartlepool
Halifax v Southend
Hull v Carlisle
Leyton Orient v York
Luton v Bristol Rovers
Mansfield v Cheltenham
Rochdale v Plymouth
Rushden & D'monds v Macclesfield
Scunthorpe v Exeter
Shrewsbury v Oxford Utd
Swansea v Lincoln City
Torquay v Kidderminster

Nationwide Football Conference
Barnet v Dag & Red
Doncaster v Boston Utd
Forest Green v Hereford
Hayes v Dover
Margate v Farnborough
Northwich v Morecambe
Nuneaton v Stevenage
Southport v Leigh RMI

Stalybridge v Scarborough
Telford v Chester
Woking v Yeovil

Saturday, 12 January 2002
FA Barclaycard Premiership
Arsenal v Liverpool
Aston Villa v Derby
Blackburn v Charlton
Bolton v Chelsea
Everton v Sunderland
Fulham v Middlesbrough
Ipswich v Tottenham
Newcastle v Leeds
Southampton v Man Utd
West Ham v Leicester

Nationwide Football League Division 1
Bradford v Portsmouth
Gillingham v Sheff Utd
Grimsby v West Brom
Man City v Norwich
Millwall v Birmingham
Nottm Forest v Barnsley
Rotherham v Watford
Sheff Wed v Crewe
Stockport v Crystal Palace
Walsall v Preston
Wimbledon v Burnley
Wolverhampton v Coventry

Nationwide Football League Division 2
Blackpool v Bournemouth
Cambridge Utd v Notts County
Cardiff v Peterborough
Chesterfield v Oldham
Huddersfield v Reading
Port Vale v Brentford
QPR v Bury
Swindon v Bristol City
Tranmere v Colchester
Wigan v Brighton
Wrexham v Wycombe

Nationwide Football League Division 3
Bristol Rovers v Scunthorpe
Carlisle v Leyton Orient
Cheltenham v Luton
Exeter v Halifax
Hartlepool v Shrewsbury
Kidderminster v Darlington
Lincoln City v Rushden & D'monds
Macclesfield v Rochdale
Oxford Utd v Swansea
Plymouth v Hull
Southend v Mansfield
York v Torquay

Sunday, 13 January 2002
Nationwide Football League Division 2
Northampton v Stoke

Saturday, 19 January 2002
FA Barclaycard Premiership
Charlton v Aston Villa
Chelsea v West Ham
Derby v Ipswich
Leeds v Arsenal
Leicester v Newcastle
Liverpool v Southampton
Man Utd v Blackburn
Middlesbrough v Bolton
Sunderland v Fulham
Tottenham v Everton

Nationwide Football League Division 1
Barnsley v Bradford
Birmingham v Wimbledon
Burnley v Sheff Wed
Coventry v Stockport
Crewe v Grimsby
Crystal Palace v Rotherham
Norwich v Millwall
Portsmouth v Wolverhampton
Preston v Gillingham
Sheff Utd v Nottm Forest

Watford v Man City
West Brom v Walsall

Nationwide Football League Division 2
Bournemouth v Huddersfield
Brentford v Wigan
Brighton v Cambridge Utd
Bristol City v Northampton
Bury v Tranmere
Colchester v Chesterfield
Notts County v Port Vale
Oldham v Wrexham
Peterborough v Swindon
Reading v Blackpool
Stoke v QPR
Wycombe v Cardiff

Nationwide Football League Division 3
Darlington v Southend
Halifax v Lincoln City
Hull v Exeter
Leyton Orient v Cheltenham
Luton v Carlisle
Mansfield v Hartlepool
Rochdale v Oxford Utd
Rushden & D'monds v York
Scunthorpe v Kidderminster
Shrewsbury v Plymouth
Swansea v Macclesfield
Torquay v Bristol Rovers

Nationwide Football Conference
Boston Utd v Northwich
Chester v Barnet
Dag & Red v Forest Green
Dover v Doncaster
Farnborough v Stalybridge
Hereford v Margate
Leigh RMI v Telford
Morecambe v Hayes
Scarborough v Woking
Stevenage v Southport
Yeovil v Nuneaton

Wednesday, 23 January 2002
Nationwide Football League Division 2
Blackpool v Bury
Cambridge Utd v Wycombe
Cardiff v Stoke
Chesterfield v Brighton
Huddersfield v Colchester
Northampton v Brentford
Port Vale v Oldham
QPR v Bournemouth
Swindon v Notts County
Tranmere v Peterborough
Wigan v Reading
Wrexham v Bristol City

Nationwide Football League Division 3
Bristol Rovers v Swansea
Carlisle v Rushden & D'monds
Cheltenham v Darlington
Exeter v Mansfield
Hartlepool v Luton
Kidderminster v Halifax
Lincoln City v Leyton Orient
Macclesfield v Shrewsbury
Oxford Utd v Torquay
Plymouth v Scunthorpe
Southend v Hull
York v Rochdale

Friday, 25 January 2002
Nationwide Football Conference
Doncaster v Stevenage

Saturday, 26 January 2002
Nationwide Football League Division 2
Blackpool v Tranmere
Brentford v Brighton
Cambridge Utd v Port Vale
Cardiff v Bury
Chesterfield v Bristol City
Huddersfield v QPR
Northampton v Peterborough

Oldham v Bournemouth
Reading v Colchester
Stoke v Wigan
Wrexham v Swindon
Wycombe v Notts County

Nationwide Football League Division 3
Bristol Rovers v Carlisle
Darlington v Luton
Exeter v York
Hartlepool v Rushden & D'monds
Hull v Shrewsbury
Kidderminster v Macclesfield
Leyton Orient v Mansfield
Lincoln City v Cheltenham
Plymouth v Oxford Utd
Rochdale v Swansea
Scunthorpe v Halifax
Southend v Torquay

Nationwide Football Conference
Barnet v Farnborough
Forest Green v Dover
Hayes v Yeovil
Margate v Scarborough
Northwich v Leigh RMI
Nuneaton v Chester
Southport v Hereford
Stalybridge v Boston Utd
Telford v Morecambe
Woking v Dag & Red

Tuesday, 29 January 2002
FA Barclaycard Premiership
Bolton v Man Utd
Charlton v Derby
Ipswich v Fulham
Sunderland v Middlesbrough

Nationwide Football League Division 1
Barnsley v Wolverhampton
Bradford v Preston
Crewe v Norwich
Crystal Palace v Coventry
Gillingham v Stockport
Rotherham v Grimsby
Sheff Utd v Sheff Wed
Walsall v Wimbledon
Watford v Burnley
West Brom v Birmingham

Wednesday, 30 January 2002
FA Barclaycard Premiership
Aston Villa v Everton
Blackburn v Arsenal
Chelsea v Leeds
Liverpool v Leicester
Southampton v West Ham
Tottenham v Newcastle

Nationwide Football League Division 1
Man City v Millwall
Nottm Forest v Portsmouth

Friday, 1 February 2002
Nationwide Football League Division 3
Cheltenham v Southend

Saturday, 2 February 2002
FA Barclaycard Premiership
Arsenal v Southampton
Derby v Tottenham
Everton v Ipswich
Fulham v Aston Villa
Leeds v Liverpool
Leicester v Chelsea
Man Utd v Sunderland
Middlesbrough v Charlton
Newcastle v Bolton
West Ham v Blackburn

Nationwide Football League Division 1
Birmingham v Crewe
Burnley v West Brom
Coventry v Gillingham
Grimsby v Bradford

Millwall v Walsall
Norwich v Sheff Utd
Portsmouth v Barnsley
Preston v Watford
Sheff Wed v Crystal Palace
Stockport v Nottm Forest
Wimbledon v Man City
Wolverhampton v Rotherham

Nationwide Football League Division 2
Bournemouth v Stoke
Brighton v Cardiff
Bristol City v Huddersfield
Bury v Reading
Colchester v Brentford
Notts County v Oldham
Peterborough v Wrexham
Port Vale v Wycombe
QPR v Cambridge Utd
Swindon v Northampton
Tranmere v Chesterfield
Wigan v Blackpool

Nationwide Football League Division 3
Carlisle v Hartlepool
Halifax v Hull
Luton v Plymouth
Macclesfield v Exeter
Mansfield v Rochdale
Oxford Utd v Bristol Rovers
Rushden & D'monds v Darlington
Shrewsbury v Scunthorpe
Swansea v Kidderminster
Torquay v Leyton Orient
York v Lincoln City

Nationwide Football Conference
Boston Utd v Telford
Chester v Scarborough
Doncaster v Northwich
Dover v Woking
Farnborough v Hereford
Hayes v Margate
Leigh RMI v Morecambe
Southport v Nuneaton
Stalybridge v Forest Green
Stevenage v Dag & Red
Yeovil v Barnet

Saturday, 9 February 2002
FA Barclaycard Premiership
Aston Villa v Chelsea
Bolton v West Ham
Charlton v Man Utd
Derby v Sunderland
Everton v Arsenal
Fulham v Blackburn
Ipswich v Liverpool
Middlesbrough v Leeds
Newcastle v Southampton
Tottenham v Leicester

Nationwide Football League Division 1
Barnsley v Burnley
Bradford v Birmingham
Crewe v Coventry
Crystal Palace v Wolverhampton
Gillingham v Wimbledon
Man City v Preston
Nottm Forest v Millwall
Rotherham v Stockport
Sheff Utd v Portsmouth
Walsall v Sheff Wed
Watford v Grimsby
West Brom v Norwich

Nationwide Football League Division 2
Blackpool v Peterborough
Brentford v Bournemouth
Cambridge Utd v Colchester
Cardiff v Swindon
Chesterfield v Bury
Huddersfield v Tranmere
Northampton v QPR
Oldham v Brighton
Reading v Notts County
Stoke v Port Vale

Wrexham v Wigan
Wycombe v Bristol City

Nationwide Football League Division 3
Bristol Rovers v Halifax
Darlington v Shrewsbury
Exeter v Cheltenham
Hartlepool v Torquay
Hull v Rushden & D'monds
Kidderminster v Carlisle
Leyton Orient v Swansea
Lincoln City v Macclesfield
Plymouth v Mansfield
Rochdale v Luton
Scunthorpe v Oxford Utd
Southend v York

Nationwide Football Conference
Barnet v Stalybridge
Dag & Red v Farnborough
Forest Green v Doncaster
Hereford v Leigh RMI
Margate v Chester
Morecambe v Yeovil
Northwich v Dover
Nuneaton v Hayes
Scarborough v Boston Utd
Telford v Southport
Woking v Stevenage

Friday, 15 February 2002
Nationwide Football League Division 3
Swansea v Southend

Saturday, 16 February 2002
Nationwide Football League Division 1
Birmingham v Barnsley
Burnley v Nottm Forest
Coventry v Walsall
Grimsby v Sheff Utd
Millwall v West Brom
Norwich v Gillingham
Portsmouth v Rotherham
Preston v Crewe
Sheff Wed v Watford
Stockport v Man City
Wimbledon v Crystal Palace
Wolverhampton v Bradford

Nationwide Football League Division 2
Bournemouth v Wycombe
Brighton v Huddersfield
Bristol City v Oldham
Bury v Cambridge Utd
Colchester v Blackpool
Notts County v Stoke
Peterborough v Brentford
Port Vale v Chesterfield
QPR v Wrexham
Swindon v Reading
Tranmere v Northampton
Wigan v Cardiff

Nationwide Football League Division 3
Carlisle v Exeter
Cheltenham v Kidderminster
Halifax v Plymouth
Luton v Scunthorpe
Macclesfield v Bristol Rovers
Mansfield v Darlington
Oxford Utd v Lincoln City
Rushden & D'monds v Rochdale
Shrewsbury v Leyton Orient
Torquay v Hull
York v Hartlepool

Nationwide Football Conference
Boston Utd v Hereford
Chester v Morecambe
Doncaster v Margate
Dover v Scarborough
Farnborough v Telford
Hayes v Northwich
Leigh RMI v Barnet
Southport v Woking
Stalybridge v Nuneaton
Stevenage v Forest Green
Yeovil v Dag & Red

Friday, 22 February 2002
Nationwide Football League Division 2
Tranmere v Swindon

Nationwide Football League Division 3
Hull v Macclesfield

Saturday, 23 February 2002
FA Barclaycard Premiership
Arsenal v Fulham
Blackburn v Ipswich
Chelsea v Tottenham
Leeds v Charlton
Leicester v Derby
Liverpool v Everton
Man Utd v Aston Villa
Southampton v Bolton
Sunderland v Newcastle
West Ham v Middlesbrough

Nationwide Football League Division 1
Birmingham v Watford
Coventry v Barnsley
Crewe v Burnley
Crystal Palace v Sheff Utd
Gillingham v Bradford
Millwall v Wimbledon
Norwich v Preston
Nottm Forest v Grimsby
Sheff Wed v Rotherham
Stockport v Wolverhampton
Walsall v Man City
West Brom v Portsmouth

Nationwide Football League Division 2
Blackpool v Huddersfield
Brentford v Notts County
Brighton v Wrexham
Bury v Bournemouth
Cardiff v Cambridge Utd
Chesterfield v Northampton
Colchester v Bristol City
Peterborough v Oldham
Port Vale v QPR
Reading v Stoke
Wigan v Wycombe

Nationwide Football League Division 3
Bristol Rovers v Lincoln City
Carlisle v Cheltenham
Darlington v Torquay
Halifax v Swansea
Hartlepool v Southend
Luton v York
Oxford Utd v Exeter
Plymouth v Kidderminster
Rushden & D'monds v Leyton Orient
Scunthorpe v Rochdale
Shrewsbury v Mansfield

Nationwide Football Conference
Barnet v Doncaster
Dag & Red v Dover
Forest Green v Leigh RMI
Hereford v Chester
Margate v Yeovil
Morecambe v Boston Utd
Northwich v Stalybridge
Nuneaton v Farnborough
Scarborough v Southport
Telford v Stevenage
Woking v Hayes

Tuesday, 26 February 2002
Nationwide Football League Division 1
Barnsley v Crystal Palace
Bradford v Nottm Forest
Burnley v Birmingham
Grimsby v Stockport
Portsmouth v Coventry
Preston v West Brom
Rotherham v Gillingham
Sheff Utd v Millwall
Watford v Norwich
Wimbledon v Crewe
Wolverhampton v Walsall

Nationwide Football League Division 2
Bournemouth v Brighton
Bristol City v Peterborough
Cambridge Utd v Blackpool
Huddersfield v Cardiff
Northampton v Port Vale
Notts County v Colchester
Oldham v Brentford
QPR v Wigan
Swindon v Chesterfield
Wrexham v Tranmere
Wycombe v Reading

Nationwide Football League Division 3
Cheltenham v Hartlepool
Kidderminster v Shrewsbury
Leyton Orient v Darlington
Lincoln City v Luton
Macclesfield v Oxford Utd
Mansfield v Halifax
Plymouth v Exeter
Rochdale v Hull
Southend v Bristol Rovers
Swansea v Scunthorpe
Torquay v Rushden & D'monds
York v Carlisle

Wednesday, 27 February 2002
Nationwide Football League Division 1
Man City v Sheff Wed

Nationwide Football League Division 2
Stoke v Bury

Friday, 1 March 2002
Nationwide Football League Division 3
Swansea v Hull

Saturday, 2 March 2002
FA Barclaycard Premiership
Aston Villa v West Ham
Bolton v Blackburn
Charlton v Chelsea
Derby v Man Utd
Everton v Leeds
Fulham v Liverpool
Ipswich v Southampton
Middlesbrough v Leicester
Newcastle v Arsenal
Tottenham v Sunderland

Nationwide Football League Division 1
Barnsley v Millwall
Bradford v Sheff Wed
Burnley v Norwich
Grimsby v Crystal Palace
Man City v Coventry
Portsmouth v Walsall
Preston v Birmingham
Rotherham v Nottm Forest
Sheff Utd v Stockport
Watford v Crewe
Wimbledon v West Brom
Wolverhampton v Gillingham

Nationwide Football League Division 2
Bournemouth v Peterborough
Bristol City v Brentford
Cambridge Utd v Reading
Huddersfield v Wigan
Northampton v Cardiff
Notts County v Tranmere
Oldham v Colchester
QPR v Blackpool
Stoke v Brighton
Swindon v Port Vale
Wrexham v Chesterfield
Wycombe v Bury

Nationwide Football League Division 3
Cheltenham v Rushden & D'monds
Exeter v Darlington
Kidderminster v Hartlepool
Leyton Orient v Halifax
Lincoln City v Carlisle
Macclesfield v Plymouth

Mansfield v Scunthorpe
Rochdale v Shrewsbury
Southend v Oxford Utd
Torquay v Luton
York v Bristol Rovers

Nationwide Football Conference
Chester v Leigh RMI
Dag & Red v Boston Utd
Dover v Farnborough
Hayes v Barnet
Morecambe v Scarborough
Nuneaton v Doncaster
Southport v Stalybridge
Stevenage v Margate
Telford v Northwich
Woking v Forest Green
Yeovil v Hereford

Tuesday, 5 March 2002
FA Barclaycard Premiership
Arsenal v Derby
Leeds v Ipswich
Sunderland v Bolton

Nationwide Football League Division 1
Birmingham v Man City
Crewe v Barnsley
Crystal Palace v Portsmouth
Gillingham v Grimsby
Millwall v Preston
Norwich v Rotherham
Stockport v Bradford
Walsall v Burnley
West Brom v Watford

Nationwide Football League Division 2
Blackpool v Northampton
Brentford v Swindon
Brighton v Wycombe
Bury v Oldham
Cardiff v QPR
Chesterfield v Huddersfield
Colchester v Stoke
Peterborough v Notts County
Port Vale v Wrexham
Reading v Bournemouth
Tranmere v Bristol City
Wigan v Cambridge Utd

Nationwide Football League Division 3
Bristol Rovers v Cheltenham
Carlisle v Southend
Darlington v Macclesfield
Halifax v Rochdale
Hartlepool v Lincoln City
Hull v Mansfield
Luton v Leyton Orient
Oxford Utd v Kidderminster
Plymouth v York
Rushden & D'monds v Exeter
Scunthorpe v Torquay
Shrewsbury v Swansea

Wednesday, 6 March 2002
FA Barclaycard Premiership
Blackburn v Aston Villa
Chelsea v Fulham
Leicester v Charlton
Liverpool v Newcastle
Man Utd v Tottenham
Southampton v Middlesbrough
West Ham v Everton

Nationwide Football League Division 1
Coventry v Sheff Utd
Nottm Forest v Wolverhampton
Sheff Wed v Wimbledon

Saturday, 9 March 2002
Nationwide Football League Division 1
Barnsley v Sheff Utd
Birmingham v Wolverhampton
Bradford v Man Utd
Coventry v Norwich
Crystal Palace v Watford

Grimsby v Walsall
Nottm Forest v Wimbledon
Portsmouth v Millwall
Preston v Rotherham
Sheff Wed v Gillingham
Stockport v Burnley
West Brom v Crewe

Nationwide Football League Division 2
Bournemouth v Northampton
Bristol City v Cambridge Utd
Bury v Notts County
Cardiff v Blackpool
Huddersfield v Swindon
Peterborough v Colchester
Port Vale v Tranmere
QPR v Chesterfield
Reading v Brighton
Wigan v Oldham
Wrexham v Brentford
Wycombe v Stoke

Nationwide Football League Division 3
Carlisle v Swansea
Cheltenham v York
Darlington v Plymouth
Hartlepool v Bristol Rovers
Hull v Scunthorpe
Kidderminster v Exeter
Leyton Orient v Macclesfield
Mansfield v Oxford Utd
Rushden & D'monds v Luton
Shrewsbury v Halifax
Southend v Rochdale
Torquay v Lincoln City

Nationwide Football Conference
Barnet v Morecambe
Boston Utd v Dover
Doncaster v Telford
Farnborough v Yeovil
Forest Green v Hayes
Hereford v Dag & Red
Leigh RMI v Nuneaton
Margate v Woking
Northwich v Southport
Scarborough v Stevenage
Stalybridge v Chester

Saturday, 16 March 2002
FA Barclaycard Premiership
Aston Villa v Arsenal
Bolton v Derby
Chelsea v Sunderland
Everton v Fulham
Leeds v Blackburn
Middlesbrough v Liverpool
Newcastle v Ipswich
Southampton v Leicester
Tottenham v Charlton
West Ham v Man Utd

Nationwide Football League Division 1
Burnley v Preston
Crewe v Portsmouth
Gillingham v Nottm Forest
Man City v Crystal Palace
Millwall v Sheff Wed
Norwich v Birmingham
Rotherham v Bradford
Sheff Utd v West Brom
Walsall v Barnsley
Watford v Coventry
Wimbledon v Stockport
Wolverhampton v Grimsby

Nationwide Football League Division 2
Blackpool v Port Vale
Brentford v Wycombe
Brighton v Bury
Cambridge Utd v Huddersfield
Chesterfield v Reading
Colchester v QPR
Northampton v Wrexham
Notts County v Bristol City
Oldham v Cardiff
Stoke v Peterborough

Swindon v Wigan
Tranmere v Bournemouth

Nationwide Football League Division 3
Bristol Rovers v Rushden & D'monds
Exeter v Shrewsbury
Halifax v Cheltenham
Lincoln City v Southend
Luton v Kidderminster
Macclesfield v Torquay
Oxford Utd v Hull
Plymouth v Leyton Orient
Rochdale v Hartlepool
Scunthorpe v Carlisle
Swansea v Mansfield
York v Darlington

Nationwide Football Conference
Chester v Farnborough
Dag & Red v Stalybridge
Dover v Hereford
Hayes v Scarborough
Morecambe v Forest Green
Nuneaton v Northwich
Southport v Barnet
Stevenage v Leigh RMI
Telford v Margate
Woking v Doncaster
Yeovil v Boston Utd

Friday, 22 March 2002
Nationwide Football League Division 2
Cardiff v Wrexham

Nationwide Football League Division 3
Hartlepool v Macclesfield

Nationwide Football Conference
Doncaster v Hayes

Saturday, 23 March 2002
FA Barclaycard Premiership
Arsenal v West Ham
Blackburn v Newcastle
Charlton v Bolton
Derby v Everton
Fulham v Tottenham
Ipswich v Aston Villa
Leicester v Leeds
Liverpool v Chelsea
Man Utd v Middlesbrough
Sunderland v Southampton

Nationwide Football League Division 1
Barnsley v Watford
Bradford v Crewe
Coventry v Birmingham
Crystal Palace v Walsall
Gillingham v Millwall
Grimsby v Wimbledon
Nottm Forest v West Brom
Portsmouth v Sheff Wed
Rotherham v Man City
Sheff Utd v Burnley
Stockport v Preston
Wolverhampton v Norwich

Nationwide Football League Division 2
Blackpool v Brentford
Bournemouth v Bristol City
Brighton v Notts County
Bury v Port Vale
Cambridge Utd v Swindon
Huddersfield v Northampton
QPR v Peterborough
Reading v Oldham
Stoke v Chesterfield
Wigan v Tranmere
Wycombe v Colchester

Nationwide Football League Division 3
Bristol Rovers v Exeter
Carlisle v Oxford Utd
Cheltenham v Rochdale
Darlington v Swansea
Leyton Orient v Hull
Lincoln City v Plymouth

Luton v Halifax
Rushden & D'monds v Shrewsbury
Southend v Scunthorpe
Torquay v Mansfield
York v Kidderminster

Nationwide Football Conference
Barnet v Telford
Boston Utd v Chester
Farnborough v Stevenage
Forest Green v Nuneaton
Hereford v Morecambe
Leigh RMI v Dag & Red
Margate v Southport
Northwich v Woking
Scarborough v Yeovil
Stalybridge v Dover

Friday, 29 March 2002
Nationwide Football League Division 1
Watford v Bradford

Nationwide Football League Division 2
Northampton v Bury

Nationwide Football League Division 3
Halifax v Carlisle

Saturday, 30 March 2002
FA Barclaycard Premiership
Arsenal v Sunderland
Bolton v Aston Villa
Chelsea v Derby
Leeds v Man Utd
Leicester v Blackburn
Liverpool v Charlton
Middlesbrough v Tottenham
Newcastle v Everton
Southampton v Fulham
West Ham v Ipswich

Nationwide Football League Division 1
Birmingham v Grimsby
Burnley v Wolverhampton
Crewe v Sheff Utd
Man City v Nottm Forest
Millwall v Stockport
Norwich v Crystal Palace
Preston v Portsmouth
Sheff Wed v Coventry
Walsall v Gillingham
Watford v Bradford
West Brom v Barnsley
Wimbledon v Rotherham

Nationwide Football League Division 2
Brentford v Stoke
Bristol City v Reading
Chesterfield v Cardiff
Colchester v Brighton
Notts County v Bournemouth
Oldham v Cambridge Utd
Peterborough v Wycombe
Port Vale v Wigan
Swindon v Blackpool
Tranmere v QPR
Wrexham v Huddersfield

Nationwide Football League Division 3
Exeter v Lincoln City
Halifax v Carlisle
Hull v Darlington
Kidderminster v Southend
Macclesfield v York
Mansfield v Rushden & D'monds
Oxford Utd v Hartlepool
Plymouth v Bristol Rovers
Rochdale v Leyton Orient
Scunthorpe v Cheltenham
Shrewsbury v Torquay
Swansea v Luton

Nationwide Football Conference
Boston Utd v Barnet
Doncaster v Chester
Dover v Southport
Forest Green v Telford

Hayes v Farnborough
Morecambe v Stevenage
Northwich v Margate
Nuneaton v Dag & Red
Scarborough v Hereford
Woking v Leigh RMI
Yeovil v Stalybridge

Monday, 1 April 2002
FA Barclaycard Premiership
Blackburn v Southampton
Charlton v Arsenal
Derby v Middlesbrough
Everton v Bolton
Fulham v West Ham
Ipswich v Chelsea
Man Utd v Liverpool
Sunderland v Leicester
Tottenham v Leeds

Nationwide Football League Division 1
Barnsley v Preston
Bradford v Norwich
Coventry v West Brom
Crystal Palace v Birmingham
Gillingham v Crewe
Grimsby v Sheff Wed
Nottm Forest v Walsall
Portsmouth v Burnley
Rotherham v Millwall
Sheff Utd v Wimbledon
Stockport v Watford
Wolverhampton v Man City

Nationwide Football League Division 2
Blackpool v Wrexham
Bournemouth v Colchester
Brighton v Bristol City
Bury v Brentford
Cardiff v Port Vale
Huddersfield v Oldham
QPR v Notts County
Reading v Northampton
Stoke v Swindon
Wigan v Peterborough
Wycombe v Tranmere

Nationwide Football League Division 3
Bristol Rovers v Kidderminster
Carlisle v Macclesfield
Cheltenham v Hull
Darlington v Halifax
Hartlepool v Plymouth
Leyton Orient v Scunthorpe
Lincoln City v Shrewsbury
Luton v Mansfield
Rushden & D'monds v Swansea
Southend v Exeter
Torquay v Rochdale
York v Oxford Utd

Nationwide Football Conference
Barnet v Nuneaton
Chester v Yeovil
Dag & Red v Morecambe
Farnborough v Northwich
Hereford v Woking
Leigh RMI v Scarborough
Margate v Forest Green
Southport v Boston Utd
Stalybridge v Doncaster
Stevenage v Dover
Telford v Hayes

Tuesday, 2 April 2002
FA Barclaycard Premiership
Aston Villa v Newcastle

Nationwide Football League Division 2
Bournemouth v Colchester
Cambridge Utd v Chesterfield

Saturday, 6 April 2002
FA Barclaycard Premiership
Arsenal v Tottenham
Bolton v Ipswich

Chelsea v Everton
Leeds v Sunderland
Leicester v Man Utd
Middlesbrough v Aston Villa
Newcastle v Fulham
Southampton v Derby
West Ham v Charlton

Nationwide Football League Division 1
Birmingham v Portsmouth
Burnley v Gillingham
Crewe v Crystal Palace
Man City v Barnsley
Millwall v Wolverhampton
Norwich v Grimsby
Preston v Coventry
Sheff Wed v Nottm Forest
Walsall v Stockport
Watford v Sheff Utd
West Brom v Rotherham
Wimbledon v Bradford

Nationwide Football League Division 2
Brentford v Huddersfield
Bristol City v Bury
Chesterfield v Wigan
Colchester v Cardiff
Northampton v Wycombe
Notts County v Blackpool
Oldham v Stoke
Peterborough v Brighton
Port Vale v Bournemouth
Swindon v QPR
Wrexham v Cambridge Utd

Nationwide Football League Division 3
Exeter v Torquay
Halifax v Hartlepool
Hull v Luton
Kidderminster v Lincoln City
Macclesfield v Cheltenham
Mansfield v Bristol Rovers
Oxford Utd v Leyton Orient
Plymouth v Southend
Rochdale v Darlington
Scunthorpe v Rushden & D'monds
Shrewsbury v Carlisle
Swansea v York

Nationwide Football Conference
Boston Utd v Stevenage
Doncaster v Hereford
Dover v Leigh RMI
Forest Green v Chester
Hayes v Stalybridge
Morecambe v Farnborough
Northwich v Dag & Red
Nuneaton v Margate
Scarborough v Telford
Woking v Barnet
Yeovil v Southport

Sunday, 7 April 2002
FA Barclaycard Premiership
Liverpool v Blackburn

Nationwide Football League Division 2
Tranmere v Reading

Saturday, 13 April 2002
FA Barclaycard Premiership
Aston Villa v Leeds
Blackburn v Chelsea
Charlton v Southampton
Derby v Newcastle
Everton v Leicester
Fulham v Bolton
Ipswich v Middlesbrough
Man Utd v Arsenal
Sunderland v Liverpool
Tottenham v West Ham

Nationwide Football League Division 1
Barnsley v Norwich
Bradford v West Brom
Coventry v Millwall
Crystal Palace v Preston
Gillingham v Man City
Grimsby v Burnley
Nottm Forest v Crewe
Portsmouth v Watford
Rotherham v Birmingham
Sheff Utd v Walsall
Stockport v Sheff Wed
Wolverhampton v Wimbledon

Nationwide Football League Division 2
Blackpool v Bristol City
Bournemouth v Chesterfield
Brighton v Swindon
Bury v Colchester
Cambridge Utd v Tranmere
Cardiff v Notts County
Huddersfield v Port Vale
QPR v Brentford
Reading v Peterborough
Stoke v Wrexham
Wigan v Northampton
Wycombe v Oldham

Nationwide Football League Division 3
Bristol Rovers v Hull
Carlisle v Plymouth
Cheltenham v Oxford Utd
Darlington v Scunthorpe
Hartlepool v Swansea
Leyton Orient v Exeter
Lincoln City v Rochdale
Luton v Macclesfield
Rushden & D'monds v Kidderminster
Southend v Shrewsbury
Torquay v Halifax
York v Mansfield

Nationwide Football Conference
Barnet v Forest Green
Chester v Dover
Dag & Red v Doncaster
Farnborough v Scarborough
Hereford v Northwich
Leigh RMI v Boston Utd
Margate v Morecambe
Southport v Hayes
Stalybridge v Woking
Stevenage v Yeovil
Telford v Nuneaton

Saturday, 20 April 2002
FA Barclaycard Premiership
Arsenal v Ipswich
Bolton v Tottenham
Chelsea v Man Utd
Leeds v Fulham
Leicester v Aston Villa
Liverpool v Derby
Middlesbrough v Blackburn
Newcastle v Charlton
Southampton v Everton
West Ham v Sunderland

Nationwide Football League Division 2
Brentford v Reading
Bristol City v Stoke
Chesterfield v Blackpool
Colchester v Wigan
Northampton v Cambridge Utd
Notts County v Huddersfield
Oldham v QPR
Peterborough v Bury
Port Vale v Brighton
Swindon v Wycombe
Tranmere v Cardiff
Wrexham v Bournemouth

Nationwide Football League Division 3
Exeter v Hartlepool
Halifax v Rushden & D'monds
Hull v Lincoln City
Kidderminster v Leyton Orient
Macclesfield v Southend
Mansfield v Carlisle
Oxford Utd v Darlington
Plymouth v Cheltenham
Rochdale v Bristol Rovers
Scunthorpe v York
Shrewsbury v Luton
Swansea v Torquay

Nationwide Football Conference
Barnet v Margate
Boston Utd v Farnborough
Chester v Stevenage
Doncaster v Southport
Dover v Morecambe
Forest Green v Northwich
Hereford v Hayes
Leigh RMI v Yeovil
Scarborough v Dag & Red
Stalybridge v Telford
Woking v Nuneaton

Sunday, 21 April 2002
Nationwide Football League Division 1
Birmingham v Sheff Utd
Burnley v Coventry
Crewe v Rotherham
Man City v Portsmouth
Millwall v Grimsby
Norwich v Stockport
Preston v Nottm Forest
Sheff Wed v Wolverhampton
Walsall v Bradford
Watford v Gillingham
West Brom v Crystal Palace
Wimbledon v Barnsley

Saturday, 27 April 2002
FA Barclaycard Premiership
Aston Villa v Southampton
Bolton v Arsenal
Charlton v Sunderland
Derby v Leeds
Everton v Blackburn
Fulham v Leicester
Ipswich v Man Utd
Middlesbrough v Chelsea
Newcastle v West Ham
Tottenham v Liverpool

Nationwide Football Conference
Dag & Red v Chester
Farnborough v Leigh RMI
Hayes v Boston Utd
Margate v Stalybridge
Morecambe v Doncaster
Northwich v Barnet
Nuneaton v Scarborough
Southport v Forest Green
Stevenage v Hereford
Telford v Woking
Yeovil v Dover

Saturday, 11 May 2002
FA Barclaycard Premiership
Arsenal v Everton
Blackburn v Fulham
Chelsea v Aston Villa
Leeds v Middlesbrough
Leicester v Tottenham
Liverpool v Ipswich
Man Utd v Charlton
Southampton v Newcastle
Sunderland v Derby
West Ham v Bolton

FA BARCLAYCARD PREMIERSHIP FIXTURES 2001–2002

Home \ Away	Arsenal	Aston Villa	Blackburn R	Bolton W	Charlton Ath	Chelsea	Derby Co	Everton	Fulham	Ipswich T	Leeds U	Leicester C	Liverpool	Manchester U	Middlesbrough	Newcastle U	Southampton	Sunderland	Tottenham H	West Ham U
Arsenal	—	9.12	20.10	22.9	4.11	26.12	5.3	11.5	23.2	20.4	21.8	25.8	12.1	25.11	29.12	18.9	2.2	30.3	6.4	23.3
Aston Villa	16.3	—	29.9	27.10	22.8	9.2	12.1	30.1	14.10	15.12	13.4	1.12	26.12	26.8	17.11	2.4	27.4	15.9	29.12	2.3
Blackburn R	30.1	6.3	—	19.9	12.1	13.4	29.12	22.9	11.5	23.2	8.12	29.10	17.11	22.8	1.12	23.3	1.4	26.12	25.8	14.10
Bolton W	27.4	30.3	2.3	—	15.12	12.1	16.3	3.11	24.11	6.4	26.12	29.12	27.8	29.1	21.8	13.10	15.9	29.9	20.4	9.2
Charlton Ath	1.4	19.1	22.12	23.3	—	2.3	29.1	18.8	9.9	1.1	16.9	29.9	27.10	9.2	13.10	1.12	13.4	27.4	8.12	19.11
Chelsea	8.9	11.5	24.11	22.12	19.9	—	30.3	6.4	6.3	4.11	30.1	13.10	27.10	20.4	22.9	19.8	1.1	16.3	23.2	19.1
Derby Co	29.9	22.12	18.8	8.12	20.10	28.10	—	23.3	2.1	19.1	27.4	15.9	1.12	2.3	1.4	13.4	17.11	9.2	2.2	8.9
Everton	9.2	20.10	27.4	1.4	13.4	17.11	15.12	—	16.3	2.2	2.3	13.4	15.9	26.12	25.8	27.10	2.12	12.1	20.8	29.9
Fulham	15.9	2.2	9.2	13.4	26.12	30.9	25.8	8.12	—	20.10	1.12	27.4	2.3	29.12	12.1	17.11	27.10	22.8	23.3	1.4
Ipswich T	1.12	23.3	16.9	18.11	25.8	1.4	21.8	13.10	29.1	—	30.9	26.12	9.2	27.4	13.4	8.12	2.3	29.12	12.1	27.10
Leeds U	19.1	24.11	16.3	8.9	23.2	21.10	23.9	19.9	20.4	5.3	—	15.12	2.2	30.3	17.9	22.12	18.8	6.4	3.11	1.1
Leicester C	1.1	20.4	30.3	18.8	6.3	2.2	23.2	23.2	22.9	8.9	23.3	—	20.10	4.11	17.9	19.1	8.12	3.11	11.5	22.12
Liverpool	23.12	8.9	7.4	1.1	30.3	2.2	20.4	23.2	19.9	11.5	13.10	30.1	—	4.11	17.9	6.3	19.1	24.11	22.9	18.8
Manchester U	13.4	23.2	19.1	20.10	11.5	1.12	12.12	8.9	19.8	22.9	27.10	17.11	1.4	—	23.3	1.1	22.12	2.2	6.3	8.12
Middlesbrough	18.8	6.4	20.4	19.1	2.2	27.4	3.11	1.1	22.12	24.11	9.2	2.3	16.3	15.12	—	8.9	29.9	22.10	30.3	15.9
Newcastle U	2.3	3.11	24.9	2.2	29.12	20.4	24.11	30.3	6.4	16.3	12.1	22.8	30.9	15.9	26.12	—	9.2	26.8	21.10	27.4
Southampton	13.10	24.9	3.11	23.2	24.11	25.8	6.4	20.4	30.3	19.9	29.12	16.3	24.10	12.1	6.3	11.5	—	15.12	30.3	30.1
Sunderland	27.10	1.1	8.9	5.3	22.9	8.12	11.5	22.12	19.1	18.8	17.11	1.4	13.4	13.10	29.1	23.2	23.3	—	19.9	1.12
Tottenham H	17.11	18.8	1.1	1.12	16.3	16.9	14.10	19.1	15.12	22.12	1.4	9.2	27.4	29.9	27.10	30.1	9.9	2.3	—	13.4
West Ham U	15.12	19.9	2.2	11.5	6.4	24.10	26.12	6.3	3.11	30.3	25.8	12.1	29.12	16.3	23.2	23.9	22.10	20.4	24.11	—

NATIONWIDE FOOTBALL LEAGUE FIXTURES 2001–2002

DIVISION ONE

	Barnsley	Birmingham C	Bradford C	Burnley	Coventry C	Crewe Alex	Crystal Palace	Gillingham	Grimsby T	Manchester C	Millwall	Norwich C	Nottingham F	Portsmouth	Preston NE	Rotherham U	Sheffield U	Sheffield W	Stockport Co	Walsall	Watford	WBA	Wimbledon	Wolverhampton W
Barnsley	—	13.10	19.1	9.2	25.9	15.9	26.2	22.12	1.1	31.10	2.3	13.4	18.8	28.9	1.4	27.8	9.3	1.12	8.9	8.12	23.3	27.10	17.11	29.1
Birmingham C	16.2	—	20.10	18.9	25.11	2.2	10.11	23.10	30.3	5.3	19.8	8.12	1.1	6.4	23.9	3.11	21.4	8.9	27.8	22.12	23.2	6.10	19.1	9.3
Bradford C	11.8	9.2	—	2.9	24.8	23.3	29.12	15.9	29.9	9.3	1.12	1.4	26.2	12.1	29.1	8.12	26.12	2.3	25.9	17.11	27.10	13.4	30.10	13.10
Burnley	20.10	26.2	9.2	—	21.4	25.9	23.10	6.4	24.11	27.8	22.12	2.3	16.2	10.11	16.3	8.9	4.11	19.1	15.12	15.9	5.10	2.2	18.8	30.3
Coventry C	23.2	23.3	22.12	17.11	—	21.10	9.2	29.1	8.9	19.9	13.4	26.9	2.3	21.4	16.2	1.9	27.10	15.9	1.12	8.9	8.12	1.4	1.12	19.8
Crewe Alex	5.3	29.9	3.11	21.10	21.10	—	6.4	10.11	19.1	22.12	28.8	17.11	23.2	25.9	12.1	16.2	30.10	27.10	12.1	2.3	15.12	5.10	1.1	1.9
Crystal Palace	22.9	1.4	29.12	23.10	9.2	6.4	—	1.1	18.9	8.12	23.3	27.10	22.12	5.3	2.2	31.8	23.2	2.3	2.2	23.3	9.3	30.10	13.10	9.2
Gillingham	25.8	1.12	23.2	13.4	2.2	1.4	31.8	—	5.3	23.3	26.12	13.10	15.9	26.2	11.8	22.9	16.2	1.4	29.1	21.4	20.10	12.1	9.2	18.9
Grimsby T	1.9	26.10	29.9	24.11	8.9	1.4	18.9	5.3	—	30.1	17.11	30.10	9.2	29.12	25.8	22.9	16.2	1.4	26.2	9.3	20.10	25.9	23.3	8.12
Manchester C	6.4	15.9	9.3	29.12	19.9	25.8	16.3	3.11	23.10	—	30.1	11.8	28.10	21.4	9.2	24.11	17.11	27.10	16.2	30.3	8.9	2.2	1.1	1.4
Millwall	18.9	19.8	1.12	22.12	13.4	28.8	23.3	24.11	5.3	30.1	—	11.8	5.10	21.4	30.1	10.11	1.9	27.2	16.3	2.2	11.10	25.9	23.2	6.4
Norwich C	24.11	20.9	23.10	22.9	15.12	7.10	30.3	16.2	6.4	6.10	19.1	—	8.9	23.10	5.3	5.3	22.9	27.8	21.4	1.1	18.9	19.10	22.12	3.11
Nottingham F	12.1	1.9	20.9	13.10	29.12	13.4	2.2	8.12	23.2	27.8	9.2	30.1	—	30.1	17.11	17.9	11.8	31.10	29.9	1.4	18.9	23.3	9.3	6.3
Portsmouth	2.2	30.10	18.8	1.4	26.2	8.12	15.9	8.9	30.1	21.4	5.10	5.10	5.10	—	27.10	16.2	20.10	23.3	21.12	2.3	13.4	25.9	1.1	19.1
Preston NE	10.11	2.3	16.2	6.4	1.9	16.2	24.11	19.1	26.9	21.4	15.12	5.3	27.10	30.3	—	9.3	23.10	1.1	3.11	18.8	2.2	26.2	27.8	8.9
Rotherham U	29.12	16.3	8.9	26.12	1.9	30.10	11.8	26.2	23.3	1.9	2.3	15.12	1.12	12.10	15.12	—	23.8	25.9	9.2	1.12	12.1	17.11	27.10	29.9
Sheffield U	15.12	8.9	23.3	26.12	15.9	27.10	25.9	18.8	13.10	1.1	26.2	2.3	19.1	9.2	1.12	22.12	—	29.1	2.3	13.4	30.10	16.3	1.4	27.8
Sheffield W	24.10	19.9	12.8	12.1	30.3	12.1	2.2	9.3	10.11	22.9	27.10	6.4	1.9	3.11	1.9	23.2	7.10	—	24.11	20.10	16.2	25.8	6.3	21.4
Stockport C	26.12	29.12	5.3	1.12	11.8	1.12	12.1	5.10	22.9	16.2	27.10	17.11	22.2	25.8	23.3	20.10	18.9	13.4	—	30.10	1.4	1.9	8.12	23.2
Walsall	16.3	25.8	21.4	5.3	14.10	16.3	3.11	30.3	15.12	23.2	29.9	1.9	10.11	13.9	30.9	24.11	6.4	9.2	6.4	—	29.12	1.9	1.4	20.9
Watford	3.11	29.3	5.3	29.1	16.3	2.3	15.12	21.4	19.1	1.1	1.1	10.11	24.11	24.11	30.9	18.8	6.4	13.10	10.11	24.11	—	15.9	9.9	22.12
WBA	30.3	29.1	24.11	29.9	10.11	9.3	21.4	27.8	1.1	2.2	11.10	9.2	23.2	18.9	18.9	6.4	8.12	22.12	1.1	19.1	5.3	—	22.9	23.10
Wimbledon	21.4	11.8	6.4	12.1	24.10	26.2	16.2	20.10	3.11	25.9	2.2	1.9	16.12	1.9	29.12	30.3	10.11	15.9	16.3	6.10	26.12	2.3	—	24.11
Wolverhampton W	6.10	16.12	16.2	27.10	12.1	1.9	20.10	2.3	16.3	1.4	30.10	25.9	26.12	11.8	26.12	2.2	29.12	18.11	15.9	26.2	25.8	2.12	13.4	—

NATIONWIDE FOOTBALL LEAGUE FIXTURES 2001–2002

DIVISION TWO

	Blackpool	AFC Bournemouth	Brentford	Brighton & HA	Bristol C	Bury	Cambridge U	Cardiff C	Chesterfield	Colchester U	Huddersfield T	Northampton T	Notts Co	Oldham Ath	Peterborough U	Port Vale	QPR	Reading	Stoke C	Swindon T	Tranmere R	Wigan Ath	Wrexham	Wycombe W
Blackpool	—	12.1	3.11	27.8	24.11	22.1	22.9	15.12	27.10	13.10	23.2	5.3	20.11	26.12	9.2	16.3	18.9	11.8	1.9	10.11	26.1	29.9	1.4	25.8
AFC Bournemouth	18.8	—	20.10	26.2	23.3	15.9	1.1	25.8	3.11	2.4	11.8	6.4	27.10	5.10	2.3	18.9	22.12	25.9	5.3	8.9	1.12	19.1	28.8	16.2
Brentford	3.11	9.2	—	26.1	19.1	23.10	27.8	1.1	30.3	6.4	20.11	22.1	15.9	22.9	13.10	20.4	24.11	29.12	5.3	25.9	11.8	5.3	2.2	16.3
Brighton & HA	27.8	26.2	26.1	—	31.8	26.1	30.3	3.11	22.1	20.4	13.10	31.8	23.10	9.2	6.4	20.4	26.12	9.3	27.10	25.8	2.2	25.8	14.9	25.9
Bristol C	24.11	22.9	18.9	1.4	—	6.4	9.3	29.12	26.1	15.9	29.9	11.8	25.8	16.2	26.2	22.9	30.3	2.3	20.4	5.3	25.8	5.3	12.1	9.2
Bury	22.12	23.2	23.10	26.1	6.4	—	20.4	13.10	2.2	2.3	25.8	29.12	15.12	5.3	20.10	31.8	11.8	23.2	25.9	11.8	27.2	1.12	31.8	2.3
Cambridge U	26.2	1.9	27.8	30.3	9.3	20.4	—	2.2	29.12	13.10	24.11	8.9	1.12	26.2	5.3	22.12	3.11	20.10	23.2	15.12	11.8	2.3	5.3	16.2
Cardiff City	9.3	25.8	1.1	3.11	29.12	13.10	2.2	—	22.1	19.1	9.2	27.10	26.12	5.3	25.9	1.4	15.9	2.3	13.10	22.9	20.11	9.11	30.3	4.11
Chesterfield	20.4	3.11	30.3	22.1	26.1	2.2	29.12	22.1	—	11.8	22.12	28.8	13.4	23.2	12.1	1.4	5.3	26.12	23.10	9.2	27.10	12.10	22.3	11.8
Colchester U	16.2	11.8	6.4	20.4	15.9	2.3	13.10	20.11	11.8	—	22.12	23.3	25.8	18.9	1.9	27.8	16.3	6.10	5.3	1.1	18.8	20.4	18.9	5.3
Huddersfield T	15.9	20.11	20.11	13.10	29.9	25.8	24.11	9.2	22.12	22.12	—	23.3	25.8	10.11	15.12	27.8	16.3	12.1	29.12	29.9	9.2	2.3	5.1	23.10
Northampton T	25.9	15.12	22.1	31.8	11.8	29.12	8.9	27.10	28.8	23.3	11.11	—	29.12	10.11	1.9	19.1	3.11	20.10	27.10	20.11	13.10	9.3	1.2	2.9
Notts Co	6.4	30.3	15.9	23.10	25.8	15.12	1.12	26.12	13.4	25.8	11.11	29.9	—	2.2	25.9	19.1	20.4	23.10	1.1	21.12	2.3	1.1	8.9	6.10
Oldham Ath	8.9	26.1	22.9	9.2	16.2	5.3	26.2	5.3	3.11	29.12	11.1	2.2	29.9	—	15.9	21.12	20.4	23.10	6.4	5.1	1.1	15.12	19.1	24.11
Peterborough U	20.10	18.9	13.10	6.4	26.2	20.10	5.1	5.3	1.9	23.3	26.12	26.1	25.9	15.9	—	5.1	23.10	24.11	25.8	13.4	22.12	3.10	29.9	30.3
Port Vale	1.12	6.4	20.4	20.4	22.9	31.8	22.12	22.9	26.12	26.12	1.9	12.1	5.3	21.12	25.8	—	23.2	1.9	20.10	18.9	9.3	30.3	5.3	2.2
QPR	2.3	22.1	24.11	26.12	30.3	11.8	3.11	15.9	6.4	20.4	26.1	27.10	25.9	20.4	23.10	23.2	—	25.8	11.8	20.11	10.11	22.12	27.8	29.12
Reading	19.1	5.3	27.10	9.3	2.3	23.2	26.1	1.12	18.9	23.10	24.11	1.1	13.10	23.3	13.4	16.3	5.1	—	25.8	13.10	20.11	22.12	16.2	26.2
Stoke C	1.1	29.9	10.11	24.11	27.10	25.9	30.3	19.12	23.3	26.9	1.9	15.12	11.8	23.3	16.3	9.2	19.1	15.9	—	1.4	15.9	16.3	6.10	9.3
Swindon T	30.3	26.12	29.12	24.11	20.4	27.2	5.1	21.10	26.2	2.2	20.10	16.2	18.9	30.3	30.3	15.12	6.4	7.4	26.12	—	22.2	23.10	21.9	27.10
Tranmere R	4.10	16.3	11.8	25.8	5.3	29.12	29.12	16.2	5.10	9.11	18.9	13.4	22.2	27.10	1.4	15.12	30.3	22.1	5.10	15.9	—	23.10	21.9	23.2
Wigan Ath	2.2	29.12	11.8	12.1	25.8	31.8	3.11	1.9	30.3	9.11	9.3	1.9	26.12	23.3	1.9	27.10	22.9	2.1	5.10	23.10	23.3	—	20.10	23.2
Wrexham	23.10	20.4	9.3	14.9	12.1	11.8	20.11	1.2	30.3	25.8	21.9	9.3	26.2	20.10	29.9	25.9	16.2	28.8	13.4	26.1	26.2	9.2	—	12.1
Wycombe W	5.1	13.10	1.12	25.9	9.2	2.3	22.1	4.11	23.2	5.3	21.9	13.4	26.1	13.4	10.11	29.7	27.8	26.2	9.3	27.10	1.4	15.9	18.8	—

NATIONWIDE FOOTBALL LEAGUE FIXTURES 2001–2002

DIVISION THREE

Home \ Away	Bristol R	Carlisle U	Cheltenham T	Darlington	Exeter C	Halifax T	Hartlepool U	Hull C	Kidderminster H	Leyton Orient	Lincoln C	Luton T	Macclesfield T	Mansfield T	Oxford U	Plymouth Arg	Rochdale	Rushden & D	Scunthorpe U	Shrewsbury T	Southend U	Swansea C	Torquay U	York C
Bristol R	—	26.1	6.10	24.9	27.8	23.10	20.10	9.3	24.11	3.11	8.9	15.9	5.1	16.2	6.4	2.2	30.3	20.4	1.12	18.8	1.1	26.2	22.12	19.1
Carlisle U	6.10	—	15.9	8.9	13.10	29.3	29.9	5.1	9.2	18.8	2.3	19.1	3.11	20.4	23.10	24.11	1.1	22.12	16.3	6.4	24.9	15.12	27.8	26.2
Cheltenham T	24.9	22.1	—	20.10	22.9	27.10	26.2	1.4	10.11	19.1	26.1	12.1	20.11	23.2	13.4	10.11	22.9	2.3	26.10	9.3	1.12	29.12	1.9	9.3
Darlington	27.8	8.9	22.9	—	12.1	1.4	2.3	27.10	18.9	5.1	20.4	23.2	26.2	24.11	9.3	9.3	20.11	29.9	13.4	25.8	5.1	1.12	22.1	1.12
Exeter C	23.10	13.10	—	22.9	—	18.8	6.4	11.8	15.12	24.11	22.9	23.10	29.9	22.3	27.8	16.2	5.3	20.4	26.1	16.3	3.11	26.12	6.4	26.1
Halifax T	20.10	29.3	18.9	3.11	25.8	—	6.4	2.2	22.9	23.10	30.3	19.1	8.9	18.9	27.10	16.2	5.3	26.1	5.10	26.2	5.1	23.2	13.4	1.1
Hartlepool U	9.3	29.9	25.8	3.11	1.1	—	1.1	1.9	27.8	23.3	29.12	23.10	16.3	11.8	27.10	1.4	30.11	18.9	26.1	26.12	5.10	13.4	9.2	13.10
Hull C	24.11	5.1	1.9	1.1	2.2	1.9	—	29.12	23.3	10.11	29.9	24.9	16.3	22.3	27.10	18.9	30.11	24.11	26.12	26.1	23.2	13.4	9.2	8.9
Kidderminster H	3.11	9.2	—	27.8	10.11	22.9	20.4	23.3	—	20.4	22.12	24.9	26.1	26.1	24.9	15.9	18.9	24.11	1.4	13.10	1.1	29.9	25.8	23.10
Leyton Orient	8.9	18.8	19.1	2.3	27.8	22.1	24.9	23.3	10.11	—	22.12	24.9	9.3	9.2	20.11	15.9	27.10	13.4	12.1	1.4	16.3	9.2	29.9	5.1
Lincoln C	15.9	2.3	26.1	1.9	27.10	11.8	23.3	10.11	20.11	22.1	—	26.2	13.4	9.2	20.11	23.3	13.4	12.1	1.4	13.10	16.3	25.8	15.12	23.2
Luton T	5.1	19.1	18.8	23.3	1.1	23.3	24.9	20.11	16.3	5.3	19.1	—	13.4	1.4	8.9	2.2	20.10	15.12	16.2	22.1	27.8	27.10	22.9	23.2
Macclesfield T	16.2	3.11	6.4	5.1	21.12	26.2	16.2	12.1	25.8	1.9	6.4	—	16.3	29.12	9.3	27.8	22.9	30.3	1.9	14.9	2.3	11.8	16.3	30.3
Mansfield T	6.4	20.4	5.1	16.2	23.2	20.4	19.1	24.9	5.3	5.10	16.2	18.9	27.8	—	9.3	20.10	2.3	1.9	2.3	14.9	25.8	1.12	23.10	23.11
Oxford U	2.2	23.10	24.11	26.2	23.2	15.12	16.3	23.2	6.4	16.3	2.3	15.12	22.9	9.2	—	6.10	11.8	1.9	20.10	22.1	22.9	12.1	22.1	3.11
Plymouth Arg	30.3	24.11	1.4	6.4	5.1	6.4	23.2	16.3	29.9	22.1	26.1	9.2	22.9	9.2	26.1	—	25.8	29.12	22.1	21.1	15.12	26.1	26.12	5.3
Rochdale	20.4	1.1	6.4	15.12	27.8	24.9	26.2	26.2	8.9	30.3	24.11	5.3	12.1	2.2	5.1	27.8	—	13.10	15.9	2.3	15.12	26.1	3.11	22.12
Rushden & D	1.12	22.12	2.2	2.2	5.3	23.2	16.8	8.9	13.4	3.11	24.11	9.2	22.9	22.9	19.1	1.1	27.8	—	20.11	23.3	8.9	1.4	18.9	19.1
Scunthorpe U	18.8	16.3	30.3	24.11	5.1	26.1	8.9	20.10	13.4	3.11	27.8	13.10	22.9	5.1	1.1	27.8	23.2	6.4	—	29.9	23.10	18.9	5.3	20.4
Shrewsbury T	1.1	6.4	8.9	20.10	18.8	9.3	16.2	5.10	18.9	16.2	3.11	21.12	10.11	23.2	19.1	19.1	22.9	23.10	2.2	—	24.11	5.3	30.3	28.8
Southend U	26.2	24.9	11.8	25.8	1.4	15.9	22.1	22.1	27.10	1.9	29.12	29.12	10.11	12.1	2.3	20.11	9.3	26.12	23.3	13.4	—	13.10	26.1	9.2
Swansea C	22.12	15.12	8.9	15.9	8.9	23.10	6.4	1.3	2.2	20.10	5.1	30.3	16.3	19.1	18.8	1.1	6.10	3.11	26.2	24.9	15.2	—	20.4	6.4
Torquay U	19.1	27.8	1.1	13.4	15.9	13.4	16.3	16.2	5.1	2.2	9.3	2.3	1.12	23.3	22.12	8.9	1.4	26.2	24.9	27.10	5.10	10.11	—	18.8
York C	2.3	26.2	15.12	16.3	6.10	1.9	16.2	26.12	23.3	25.8	2.2	15.9	13.4	13.4	1.4	24.9	22.1	11.8	10.11	29.12	20.10	20.11	12.1	—

THE SCOTTISH PREMIERSHIP and FOOTBALL LEAGUE FIXTURES 2001–2002

Reproduced under Copyright Licence No. PRINT/ALL/8010.
Copyright © The Scottish Premier League Limited/The Scottish Football League 2001.

Saturday, 28 July 2001
Scottish Premier League
Aberdeen v Rangers
Celtic v St Johnstone
Dundee Utd v Dundee
Dunfermline v Motherwell
Hibernian v Kilmarnock
Livingston v Hearts

Saturday, 4 August 2001
Scottish Premier League
Dundee v Hibernian
Hearts v Aberdeen
Kilmarnock v Celtic
Motherwell v Dundee Utd
Rangers v Livingston
St Johnstone v Dunfermline
Scottish League Division 1
Airdrie v Raith
Clyde v Inverness CT
Falkirk v Ayr
Partick v St Mirren
Ross County v Arbroath

Scottish League Division 2
Berwick v Alloa
Forfar v Clydebank
Hamilton v Queen of South
Morton v Stenhousemuir
Stranraer v Cowdenbeath

Scottish League Division 3
Dumbarton v Brechin
East Fife v Albion
Elgin v East Stirling
Montrose v Queens Park
Stirling v Peterhead

Saturday, 11 August 2001
Scottish Premier League
Celtic v Hearts
Dundee v Livingston
Dunfermline v Rangers
Hibernian v Aberdeen
Motherwell v Kilmarnock
St Johnstone v Dundee Utd

Scottish League Division 1
Arbroath v Airdrie
Ayr v Ross County
Inverness CT v Falkirk
Raith v Partick
St Mirren v Clyde

Scottish League Division 2
Alloa v Morton
Clydebank v Hamilton
Cowdenbeath v Berwick
Queen of South v Forfar
Stenhousemuir v Stranraer

Scottish League Division 3
Albion v Stirling

Brechin v East Fife
East Stirling v Montrose
Peterhead v Dumbarton
Queens Park v Elgin

Saturday, 18 August 2001
Scottish Premier League
Aberdeen v Motherwell
Dundee Utd v Dunfermline
Hearts v Dundee
Kilmarnock v St Johnstone
Livingston v Celtic
Rangers v Hibernian

Scottish League Division 1
Airdrie v Ayr
Clyde v Arbroath
Falkirk v St Mirren
Partick v Inverness CT
Ross County v Raith

Scottish League Division 2
Berwick v Clydebank
Forfar v Stenhousemuir
Hamilton v Cowdenbeath
Morton v Queen of South
Stranraer v Alloa

Scottish League Division 3
Dumbarton v Queens Park
East Fife v East Stirling
Elgin v Albion
Montrose v Peterhead
Stirling v Brechin

Saturday, 25 August 2001
Scottish Premier League
Dundee Utd v Kilmarnock
Dunfermline v Hearts
Hibernian v Celtic
Motherwell v Livingston
Rangers v Dundee
St Johnstone v Aberdeen

Scottish League Division 1
Arbroath v Partick
Ayr v Raith
Falkirk v Clyde
Ross County v Airdrie
St Mirren v Inverness CT

Scottish League Division 2
Cowdenbeath v Alloa
Hamilton v Forfar
Morton v Stranraer
Queen of South v Clydebank
Stenhousemuir v Berwick

Scottish League Division 3
Brechin v Albion
Dumbarton v Montrose
East Fife v Peterhead
Elgin v Stirling
Queens Park v East Stirling

Saturday, 8 September 2001
Scottish Premier League
Aberdeen v Kilmarnock
Celtic v Dunfermline
Dundee v St Johnstone
Hearts v Rangers
Livingston v Dundee Utd
Motherwell v Hibernian

Scottish League Division 1
Airdrie v St Mirren
Clyde v Ross County
Inverness CT v Arbroath
Partick v Ayr
Raith v Falkirk

Scottish League Division 2
Alloa v Stenhousemuir
Berwick v Hamilton
Clydebank v Morton
Forfar v Cowdenbeath
Stranraer v Queen of South

Scottish League Division 3
Albion v Queens Park
East Stirling v Dumbarton
Montrose v Brechin
Peterhead v Elgin
Stirling v East Fife

Saturday, 15 September 2001
Scottish Premier League
Aberdeen v Dundee Utd
Dundee v Celtic
Hibernian v Dunfermline
Kilmarnock v Hearts
Rangers v Motherwell
St Johnstone v Livingston

Scottish League Division 1
Airdrie v Falkirk
Ayr v St Mirren
Partick v Clyde
Raith v Arbroath
Ross County v Inverness CT

Scottish League Division 2
Alloa v Clydebank
Cowdenbeath v Queen of South
Morton v Forfar
Stenhousemuir v Hamilton
Stranraer v Berwick

Scottish League Division 3
Dumbarton v Albion
East Stirling v Peterhead
Elgin v East Fife
Montrose v Stirling
Queens Park v Brechin

Tuesday, 18 September 2001
Scottish League Division 1
Arbroath v Ayr
Clyde v Airdrie

Falkirk v Partick
St Mirren v Ross County

Scottish League Division 2
Berwick v Morton
Forfar v Alloa
Hamilton v Stranraer
Queen of South v Stenhousemuir

Scottish League Division 3
Albion v East Stirling
Brechin v Elgin
East Fife v Montrose
Peterhead v Queens Park

Wednesday, 19 September 2001
Scottish League Division 1
Inverness CT v Raith

Scottish League Division 2
Clydebank v Cowdenbeath

Scottish League Division 3
Stirling v Dumbarton

Saturday, 22 September 2001
Scottish Premier League
Celtic v Aberdeen
Dundee Utd v Rangers
Dunfermline v Livingston
Hibernian v St Johnstone
Kilmarnock v Dundee
Motherwell v Hearts

Scottish League Division 1
Airdrie v Inverness CT
Arbroath v Falkirk
Ayr v Clyde
Raith v St Mirren
Ross County v Partick

Scottish League Division 2
Alloa v Hamilton
Berwick v Queen of South
Morton v Cowdenbeath
Stenhousemuir v Clydebank
Stranraer v Forfar

Scottish League Division 3
Dumbarton v Elgin
East Stirling v Stirling
Montrose v Albion
Peterhead v Brechin
Queens Park v East Fife

Saturday, 29 September 2001
Scottish Premier League
Dundee v Aberdeen
Dunfermline v Kilmarnock
Hearts v Dundee Utd
Livingston v Hibernian
Rangers v Celtic
St Johnstone v Motherwell

Scottish League Division 1
Clyde v Raith
Falkirk v Ross County
Inverness CT v Ayr
Partick v Airdrie
St Mirren v Arbroath

Scottish League Division 2
Clydebank v Stranraer
Cowdenbeath v Stenhousemuir
Forfar v Berwick
Hamilton v Morton
Queen of South v Alloa

Scottish League Division 3
Albion v Peterhead
Brechin v East Stirling
East Fife v Dumbarton
Elgin v Montrose
Stirling v Queens Park

Sunday, 30 September 2001
Scottish Premier League
Rangers v Celtic

Saturday, 13 October 2001
Scottish Premier League
Dundee Utd v Hibernian
Dunfermline v Dundee
Hearts v St Johnstone
Livingston v Aberdeen
Motherwell v Celtic
Rangers v Kilmarnock

Scottish League Division 1
Arbroath v Ross County
Ayr v Falkirk
Inverness CT v Clyde
Raith v Airdrie
St Mirren v Partick

Scottish League Division 2
Alloa v Berwick
Clydebank v Forfar
Cowdenbeath v Stranraer
Queen of South v Hamilton
Stenhousemuir v Morton

Scottish League Division 3
Albion v East Fife
Brechin v Dumbarton
East Stirling v Elgin
Peterhead v Stirling
Queens Park v Montrose

Saturday, 20 October 2001
Scottish Premier League
Aberdeen v Dunfermline
Celtic v Dundee Utd
Dundee v Motherwell
Hibernian v Hearts
Kilmarnock v Livingston
St Johnstone v Rangers

Scottish League Division 1
Airdrie v Arbroath
Clyde v St Mirren
Falkirk v Inverness CT
Partick v Raith
Ross County v Ayr

Scottish League Division 2
Berwick v Cowdenbeath
Forfar v Queen of South
Hamilton v Clydebank
Morton v Alloa
Stranraer v Stenhousemuir

Scottish League Division 3
Dumbarton v Peterhead
East Fife v Brechin
Elgin v Queens Park
Montrose v East Stirling
Stirling v Albion

Saturday, 27 October 2001
Scottish Premier League
Aberdeen v Hearts
Celtic v Kilmarnock

Dundee Utd v Motherwell
Dunfermline v St Johnstone
Hibernian v Dundee
Livingston v Rangers

Scottish League Division 1
Arbroath v Inverness CT
Ayr v Partick
Falkirk v Raith
Ross County v Clyde
St Mirren v Airdrie

Scottish League Division 2
Cowdenbeath v Forfar
Hamilton v Berwick
Morton v Clydebank
Queen of South v Stranraer
Stenhousemuir v Alloa

Scottish League Division 3
Brechin v Montrose
Dumbarton v East Stirling
East Fife v Stirling
Elgin v Peterhead
Queens Park v Albion

Saturday, 3 November 2001
Scottish Premier League
Dundee v Dundee Utd
Hearts v Livingston
Kilmarnock v Hibernian
Motherwell v Dunfermline
Rangers v Aberdeen
St Johnstone v Celtic

Scottish League Division 1
Airdrie v Ross County
Clyde v Falkirk
Inverness CT v St Mirren
Partick v Arbroath
Raith v Ayr

Scottish League Division 2
Alloa v Cowdenbeath
Berwick v Stenhousemuir
Clydebank v Queen of South
Forfar v Hamilton
Stranraer v Morton

Scottish League Division 3
Albion v Brechin
East Stirling v Queens Park
Montrose v Dumbarton
Peterhead v East Fife
Stirling v Elgin

Saturday, 10 November 2001
Scottish League Division 1
Airdrie v Clyde
Ayr v Arbroath
Partick v Falkirk
Raith v Inverness CT
Ross County v St Mirren

Scottish League Division 2
Berwick v Stranraer
Clydebank v Alloa
Forfar v Morton
Hamilton v Stenhousemuir
Queen of South v Cowdenbeath

Scottish League Division 3
Albion v Dumbarton
Brechin v Queens Park
East Fife v Elgin
Peterhead v East Stirling
Stirling v Montrose

Saturday, 17 November 2001

Scottish Premier League
Aberdeen v Hibernian
Dundee Utd v St Johnstone
Hearts v Celtic
Kilmarnock v Motherwell
Livingston v Dundee
Rangers v Dunfermline

Scottish League Division 1
Arbroath v Raith
Clyde v Partick
Falkirk v Airdrie
Inverness CT v Ross County
St Mirren v Ayr

Saturday, 24 November 2001

Scottish Premier League
Celtic v Rangers
Dundee v Hearts
Dunfermline v Dundee Utd
Hibernian v Livingston
Motherwell v Aberdeen
St Johnstone v Kilmarnock

Scottish League Division 1
Airdrie v Partick
Arbroath v St Mirren
Ayr v Inverness CT
Raith v Clyde
Ross County v Falkirk

Scottish League Division 2
Alloa v Forfar
Cowdenbeath v Clydebank
Morton v Berwick
Stenhousemuir v Queen of South
Stranraer v Hamilton

Scottish League Division 3
Dumbarton v Stirling
East Stirling v Albion
Elgin v Brechin
Montrose v East Fife
Queens Park v Peterhead

Saturday, 1 December 2001

Scottish Premier League
Aberdeen v St Johnstone
Celtic v Hibernian
Dundee v Rangers
Hearts v Dunfermline
Kilmarnock v Dundee Utd
Livingston v Motherwell

Scottish League Division 1
Clyde v Ayr
Falkirk v Arbroath
Inverness CT v Airdrie
Partick v Ross County
St Mirren v Raith

Scottish League Division 2
Clydebank v Stenhousemuir
Cowdenbeath v Morton
Forfar v Stranraer
Hamilton v Alloa
Queen of South v Berwick

Scottish League Division 3
Albion v Montrose
Brechin v Peterhead
East Fife v Queens Park
Elgin v Dumbarton
Stirling v East Stirling

Saturday, 8 December 2001

Scottish Premier League
Dundee Utd v Livingston
Dunfermline v Celtic
Hibernian v Motherwell
Kilmarnock v Aberdeen
Rangers v Hearts
St Johnstone v Dundee

Scottish League Division 1
Arbroath v Clyde
Ayr v Airdrie
Inverness CT v Partick
Raith v Ross County
St Mirren v Falkirk

Saturday, 15 December 2001

Scottish Premier League
Celtic v Dundee
Dundee Utd v Aberdeen
Dunfermline v Hibernian
Hearts v Kilmarnock
Livingston v St Johnstone
Motherwell v Rangers

Scottish League Division 1
Airdrie v Raith
Clyde v Inverness CT
Falkirk v Ayr
Partick v St Mirren
Ross County v Arbroath

Scottish League Division 2
Alloa v Queen of South
Berwick v Forfar
Morton v Hamilton
Stenhousemuir v Cowdenbeath
Stranraer v Clydebank

Scottish League Division 3
Dumbarton v East Fife
East Stirling v Brechin
Montrose v Elgin
Peterhead v Albion
Queens Park v Stirling

Saturday, 22 December 2001

Scottish Premier League
Aberdeen v Celtic
Dundee v Kilmarnock
Hearts v Motherwell
Livingston v Dunfermline
Rangers v Dundee Utd
St Johnstone v Hibernian

Wednesday, 26 December 2001

Scottish Premier League
Aberdeen v Dundee
Celtic v Livingston
Dundee Utd v Hearts
Hibernian v Rangers
Kilmarnock v Dunfermline
Motherwell v St Johnstone

Scottish League Division 1
Airdrie v St Mirren
Clyde v Ross County
Inverness CT v Arbroath
Partick v Ayr
Raith v Falkirk

Scottish League Division 2
Alloa v Stranraer
Clydebank v Berwick

Cowdenbeath v Hamilton
Queen of South v Morton
Stenhousemuir v Forfar

Scottish League Division 3
Albion v Elgin
Brechin v Stirling
East Stirling v East Fife
Peterhead v Montrose
Queens Park v Dumbarton

Saturday, 29 December 2001

Scottish Premier League
Dundee Utd v Celtic
Dunfermline v Aberdeen
Hearts v Hibernian
Livingston v Kilmarnock
Motherwell v Dundee
Rangers v St Johnstone

Scottish League Division 1
Arbroath v Partick
Ayr v Raith
Falkirk v Clyde
Ross County v Airdrie
St Mirren v Inverness CT

Scottish League Division 2
Berwick v Alloa
Forfar v Clydebank
Hamilton v Queen of South
Morton v Stenhousemuir
Stranraer v Cowdenbeath

Scottish League Division 3
Dumbarton v Brechin
East Fife v Albion
Elgin v East Stirling
Montrose v Queens Park
Stirling v Peterhead

Wednesday, 2 January 2002

Scottish Premier League
Aberdeen v Livingston
Celtic v Motherwell
Dundee v Dunfermline
Hibernian v Dundee Utd
Kilmarnock v Rangers
St Johnstone v Hearts

Scottish League Division 1
Airdrie v Falkirk
Ayr v St Mirren
Partick v Clyde
Raith v Arbroath
Ross County v Inverness CT

Scottish League Division 2
Alloa v Stenhousemuir
Berwick v Hamilton
Clydebank v Morton
Forfar v Cowdenbeath
Stranraer v Queen of South

Scottish League Division 3
Albion v Queens Park
East Stirling v Dumbarton
Montrose v Brechin
Peterhead v Elgin
Stirling v East Fife

Saturday, 12 January 2002

Scottish Premier League
Dundee v Hibernian
Hearts v Aberdeen
Kilmarnock v Celtic

Motherwell v Dundee Utd
Rangers v Livingston
St Johnstone v Dunfermline

Scottish League Division 1
Arbroath v Ayr
Clyde v Airdrie
Falkirk v Partick
Inverness CT v Raith
St Mirren v Ross County

Scottish League Division 2
Cowdenbeath v Alloa
Hamilton v Forfar
Morton v Stranraer
Queen of South v Clydebank
Stenhousemuir v Berwick

Scottish League Division 3
Brechin v Albion
Dumbarton v Montrose
East Fife v Peterhead
Elgin v Stirling
Queens Park v East Stirling

Saturday, 19 January 2002

Scottish Premier League
Aberdeen v Rangers
Celtic v St Johnstone
Dundee Utd v Dundee
Dunfermline v Motherwell
Hibernian v Kilmarnock
Livingston v Hearts

Scottish League Division 1
Airdrie v Inverness CT
Arbroath v Falkirk
Ayr v Clyde
Raith v St Mirren
Ross County v Partick

Scottish League Division 2
Berwick v Morton
Clydebank v Cowdenbeath
Forfar v Alloa
Hamilton v Stranraer
Queen of South v Stenhousemuir

Scottish League Division 3
Albion v East Stirling
Brechin v Elgin
East Fife v Montrose
Peterhead v Queens Park
Stirling v Dumbarton

Wednesday, 23 January 2002

Scottish Premier League
Celtic v Hearts
Dundee v Livingston
Dunfermline v Rangers
Hibernian v Aberdeen
Motherwell v Kilmarnock
St Johnstone v Dundee Utd

Saturday, 26 January 2002

Scottish League Division 2
Alloa v Clydebank
Cowdenbeath v Queen of South
Morton v Forfar
Stenhousemuir v Hamilton
Stranraer v Berwick

Scottish League Division 3
Dumbarton v Albion
East Stirling v Peterhead
Elgin v East Fife

Montrose v Stirling
Queens Park v Brechin

Wednesday, 30 January 2002

Scottish Premier League
Aberdeen v Motherwell
Dundee Utd v Dunfermline
Hearts v Dundee
Kilmarnock v St Johnstone
Livingston v Celtic
Rangers v Hibernian

Saturday, 2 February 2002

Scottish Premier League
Dundee Utd v Kilmarnock
Dunfermline v Hearts
Hibernian v Celtic
Motherwell v Livingston
Rangers v Dundee
St Johnstone v Aberdeen

Scottish League Division 1
Clyde v Raith
Falkirk v Ross County
Inverness CT v Ayr
Partick v Airdrie
St Mirren v Arbroath

Scottish League Division 2
Clydebank v Stranraer
Cowdenbeath v Stenhousemuir
Forfar v Berwick
Hamilton v Morton
Queen of South v Alloa

Scottish League Division 3
Albion v Peterhead
Brechin v East Stirling
East Fife v Dumbarton
Elgin v Montrose
Stirling v Queens Park

Saturday, 9 February 2002

Scottish Premier League
Aberdeen v Kilmarnock
Celtic v Dunfermline
Dundee v St Johnstone
Hearts v Rangers
Livingston v Dundee Utd
Motherwell v Hibernian

Scottish League Division 1
Airdrie v Ayr
Clyde v Arbroath
Falkirk v St Mirren
Partick v Inverness CT
Ross County v Raith

Scottish League Division 2
Alloa v Hamilton
Berwick v Queen of South
Morton v Cowdenbeath
Stenhousemuir v Clydebank
Stranraer v Forfar

Scottish League Division 3
Dumbarton v Elgin
East Stirling v Stirling
Montrose v Albion
Peterhead v Brechin
Queens Park v East Fife

Saturday, 16 February 2002

Scottish Premier League
Aberdeen v Dundee Utd

Dundee v Celtic
Hibernian v Dunfermline
Kilmarnock v Hearts
Rangers v Motherwell
St Johnstone v Livingston

Scottish League Division 1
Arbroath v Airdrie
Ayr v Ross County
Inverness CT v Falkirk
Raith v Partick
St Mirren v Clyde

Scottish League Division 2
Alloa v Morton
Clydebank v Hamilton
Cowdenbeath v Berwick
Queen of South v Forfar
Stenhousemuir v Stranraer

Scottish League Division 3
Albion v Stirling
Brechin v East Fife
East Stirling v Montrose
Peterhead v Dumbarton
Queens Park v Elgin

Saturday, 23 February 2002

Scottish League Division 2
Berwick v Clydebank
Forfar v Stenhousemuir
Hamilton v Cowdenbeath
Morton v Queen of South
Stranraer v Alloa

Scottish League Division 3
Dumbarton v Queens Park
East Fife v East Stirling
Elgin v Albion
Montrose v Peterhead
Stirling v Brechin

Saturday, 2 March 2002

Scottish Premier League
Celtic v Aberdeen
Dundee Utd v Rangers
Dunfermline v Livingston
Hibernian v St Johnstone
Kilmarnock v Dundee
Motherwell v Hearts

Scottish League Division 1
Airdrie v Ross County
Clyde v Falkirk
Inverness CT v St Mirren
Partick v Arbroath
Raith v Ayr

Scottish League Division 2
Alloa v Cowdenbeath
Berwick v Stenhousemuir
Clydebank v Queen of South
Forfar v Hamilton
Stranraer v Morton

Scottish League Division 3
Albion v Brechin
East Stirling v Queens Park
Montrose v Dumbarton
Peterhead v East Fife
Stirling v Elgin

Saturday, 9 March 2002

Scottish Premier League
Dundee v Aberdeen
Dunfermline v Kilmarnock

Hearts v Dundee Utd
Livingston v Hibernian
Rangers v Celtic
St Johnstone v Motherwell

Scottish League Division 1
Arbroath v Inverness CT
Ayr v Partick
Falkirk v Raith
Ross County v Clyde
St Mirren v Airdrie

Scottish League Division 2
Cowdenbeath v Forfar
Hamilton v Berwick
Morton v Clydebank
Queen of South v Stranraer
Stenhousemuir v Alloa

Scottish League Division 3
Brechin v Montrose
Dumbarton v East Stirling
East Fife v Stirling
Elgin v Peterhead
Queens Park v Albion

Saturday, 16 March 2002
Scottish Premier League
Aberdeen v Dunfermline
Celtic v Dundee Utd
Dundee v Motherwell
Hibernian v Hearts
Kilmarnock v Livingston
St Johnstone v Rangers

Scottish League Division 1
Airdrie v Clyde
Ayr v Arbroath
Partick v Falkirk
Raith v Inverness CT
Ross County v St Mirren

Scottish League Division 2
Berwick v Stranraer
Clydebank v Alloa
Forfar v Morton
Hamilton v Stenhousemuir
Queen of South v Cowdenbeath

Scottish League Division 3
Albion v Dumbarton
Brechin v Queens Park
East Fife v Elgin
Peterhead v East Stirling
Stirling v Montrose

Saturday, 23 March 2002
Scottish Premier League
Dundee Utd v Hibernian
Dunfermline v Dundee
Hearts v St Johnstone
Livingston v Aberdeen
Motherwell v Celtic
Rangers v Kilmarnock

Scottish League Division 1
Arbroath v Raith
Clyde v Partick
Falkirk v Airdrie
Inverness CT v Ross County
St Mirren v Ayr

Scottish League Division 2
Alloa v Forfar
Cowdenbeath v Clydebank
Morton v Berwick
Stenhousemuir v Queen of South
Stranraer v Hamilton

Scottish League Division 3
Dumbarton v Stirling
East Stirling v Albion
Elgin v Brechin
Montrose v East Fife
Queens Park v Peterhead

Saturday, 30 March 2002
Scottish League Division 1
Clyde v Ayr
Falkirk v Arbroath
Inverness CT v Airdrie
Partick v Ross County
St Mirren v Raith

Scottish League Division 2
Clydebank v Stenhousemuir
Cowdenbeath v Morton
Forfar v Stranraer
Hamilton v Alloa
Queen of South v Berwick

Scottish League Division 3
Albion v Montrose
Brechin v Peterhead
East Fife v Queens Park
Elgin v Dumbarton
Stirling v East Stirling

Saturday, 6 April 2002
Scottish League Division 1
Airdrie v Partick
Arbroath v St Mirren
Ayr v Inverness CT
Raith v Clyde
Ross County v Falkirk

Scottish League Division 2
Alloa v Queen of South
Berwick v Forfar
Morton v Hamilton
Stenhousemuir v Cowdenbeath
Stranraer v Clydebank

Scottish League Division 3
Dumbarton v East Fife
East Stirling v Brechin
Montrose v Elgin
Peterhead v Albion
Queens Park v Stirling

Saturday, 13 April 2002
Scottish League Division 1
Arbroath v Ross County
Ayr v Falkirk
Inverness CT v Clyde
Raith v Airdrie
St Mirren v Partick

Scottish League Division 2
Alloa v Berwick
Clydebank v Forfar
Cowdenbeath v Stranraer
Queen of South v Hamilton
Stenhousemuir v Morton

Scottish League Division 3
Albion v East Fife
Brechin v Dumbarton
East Stirling v Elgin
Peterhead v Stirling
Queens Park v Montrose

Saturday, 20 April 2002
Scottish League Division 1
Airdrie v Arbroath
Clyde v St Mirren
Falkirk v Inverness CT
Partick v Raith
Ross County v Ayr

Scottish League Division 2
Berwick v Cowdenbeath
Forfar v Queen of South
Hamilton v Clydebank
Morton v Alloa
Stranraer v Stenhousemuir

Scottish League Division 3
Dumbarton v Peterhead
East Fife v Brechin
Elgin v Queens Park
Montrose v East Stirling
Stirling v Albion

Saturday, 27 April 2002
Scottish League Division 1
Arbroath v Clyde
Ayr v Airdrie
Inverness CT v Partick
Raith v Ross County
St Mirren v Falkirk

Scottish League Division 2
Alloa v Stranraer
Clydebank v Berwick
Cowdenbeath v Hamilton
Queen of South v Morton
Stenhousemuir v Forfar

Scottish League Division 3
Albion v Elgin
Brechin v Stirling
East Stirling v East Fife
Peterhead v Montrose
Queens Park v Dumbarton

OTHER FIXTURES 2001–2002

July 2001
1 Sun   UEFA Intertoto Cup 2 (1)
9/10 Sat/Sun UEFA Intertoto Cup 2 (2)
14/15 Sat/Sun UEFA Intertoto Cup 3 (1)
21 Sat   UEFA Intertoto Cup 3 (2)
25 Wed   UEFA Intertoto Cup SF (1)
    UEFA Women's U18 Championship Final
    Round commences

August 2001
1 Wed   UEFA Intertoto Cup SF (2)
7 Tue   UEFA Intertoto Cup Final (1)
7/8 Tue/Wed UEFA Champions League 3Q (1)
11 Sat   Football League commences
12 Sun   F.A. Charity Shield
14 Tue   U21 Friendly International –
    venue & ko tbc
15 Wed   Friendly International –
    England v Netherlands
    (*at Tottenham Hotspur FC*)
18 Sat   Premier League commences
    Football Conference commences
21 Tue   UEFA Intertoto Cup Final (2)
21/22 Tue/Wed UEFA Champions League 3Q (2)
22 Wed   Worthington Cup 1
24 Fri   UEFA Super Cup
25 Sat   F.A. Cup sponsored by AXA EP
31 Fri   UEFA U21 Qualifier – Germany v England
    venue & ko tbc

September 2001
1 Sat   FIFA World Cup Qualifier –
    Germany v England (*at Bayern Munich FC*)
    F.A. Cup sponsored by AXA P
    AXA F.A. Youth Cup 1Q*
4 Tue   UEFA U21 Qualifier – England v Albania
    venue & ko tbc
5 Wed   FIFA World Cup Qualifier –
    (*at Newcastle United FC*)
    England v Albania
8 Sat   F.A. Carlsberg Vase 1Q
9 Sun   AXA F.A. Women's Cup 1Q
11/12 Tue/Wed UEFA Champions League –
    Group Stage 1 – Match Day 1
12 Wed   Worthington Cup 2
13 Thu   UEFA Cup 1 (1)
14 Fri   World U17 Championship commences –
    Trinidad & Tobago
15 Sat   F.A. Cup sponsored by AXA 1Q
18/19 Tue/Wed UEFA Champions League –
    Group Stage 1 – Match Day 2
22 Sat   F.A. Carlsberg Vase 2Q
    AXA F.A. Youth Cup 2Q*
25/26 Tue/Wed UEFA Champions League –
    Group Stage 1 – Match Day 3
27 Thu   UEFA Cup 1 (2)
29 Sat   F.A. Cup sponsored by AXA 2Q
30 Sun   World U17 Championship ends
    AXA F.A. Women's Cup 2Q

October 2001
5 Fri   UEFA U21 Qualifier – England v Greece
    venue & ko tbc
6 Sat   FIFA World Cup Qualifier –
    England v Greece
    (*at Manchester United FC*)
    AXA F.A. Youth Cup 3Q*
    F.A. County Youth Cup 1*
7 Sun   F.A. Umbro Sunday Cup 1

10 Wed   Worthington Cup 3
13 Sat   F.A. Cup sponsored by AXA 3Q
16/17 Tue/Wed UEFA Champions League –
    Group Stage 1 – Match Day 4
18 Thu   UEFA CUP 2 (1)
20 Sat   F.A. Carlsberg Vase 1P
23/24 Tue/Wed UEFA Champions League –
    Group Stage 1 – Match Day 5
27 Sat   F.A. Cup sponsored by AXA 4Q
    AXA F.A. Youth Cup 1P*
28 Sun   AXA F.A. Women's Cup 3Q
30/31 Tue/Wed UEFA Champions League –
    Group Stage 1 – Match Day 6

November 2001
1 Thu   UEFA Cup 2 (2)
3 Sat   F.A. Umbro Trophy 1
4 Sun   F.A. Umbro Sunday Cup 2
10 Sat   F.A. Carlsberg Vase 2P
    AXA F.A. Youth Cup 2P*
    F.A. County Youth Cup 2*
11 Sun   AXA F.A. Women's Cup 1P
17 Sat   F.A. Cup sponsored by AXA 1P
20/21 Tue/Wed UEFA Champions League –
    Group Stage 2 – Match Day 7
22 Thu   UEFA Cup 3 (1)
27 Tue   EU/SA Cup
28 Wed   Worthington Cup 4

December 2001
1 Sat   F.A. Umbro Trophy 2
2 Sun   F.A. Umbro Sunday Cup 3
4/5 Tue/Wed UEFA Champions League –
    Group Stage 2 – Match Day 8
6 Thu   UEFA Cup 3 (2)
8 Sat   F.A. Cup sponsored by AXA 2P
    F.A. Carlsberg Vase 3P
    AXA F.A. Youth Cup 3P*
9 Sun   AXA F.A. Women's Cup 2P
12 Wed   Worthington Cup 5
15 Sat   F.A. County Youth Cup 3*
24 Mon   Christmas Eve
25 Tue   Christmas Day
26 Wed   Boxing Day

January 2002
1 Tue   New Year's Day
5 Sat   F.A. Cup sponsored by AXA 3P
6 Sun   AXA F.A. Women's Cup 3P
9 Wed   Worthington Cup SF (1)
12 Sat   F.A. Umbro Trophy 3
13 Sun   F.A. Umbro Sunday Cup 4
19 Sat   F.A. Carlsberg Vase 4P
    AXA F.A. Youth Cup 4P*
23 Wed   Worthington Cup SF (2)
26 Sat   F.A. Cup sponsored by AXA 4P
27 Sun   AXA F.A. Women's Cup 4P

February 2002
2 Sat   F.A. Umbro Trophy 4
3 Sun   F.A. County Youth Cup 4*
9 Sat   F.A. Umbro Sunday Cup 5
10 Sun   F.A. Carlsberg Vase 5P
12/13 Tue/Wed International Friendly dates
16 Sat   F.A. Cup sponsored by AXA 5P
    AXA F.A. Youth Cup 5P*
19/20 Tue/Wed UEFA Champions League –
    Group Stage 2 – Match Day 9

21 Thu	UEFA Cup 4 (1)
23 Sat	F.A. Umbro Trophy 5
24 Sun	Worthington Cup Final
26/27 Tue/Wed	UEFA Champions League – Group Stage 2 – Match Day 10
28 Thu	UEFA Cup 4 (2)

March 2002

2 Sat	F.A. Carlsberg Vase 6P
3 Sun	F.A. Umbro Sunday Cup SF
9 Sat	F.A. Cup sponsored by AXA 6P
	AXA F.A. Youth Cup SF*
	F.A. County Youth Cup SF*
10 Sun	AXA F.A. Women's Cup 6P
12/13 Tue/Wed	UEFA Champions League – Group Stage 2 – Match Day 11
14 Thu	UEFA Cup QF (1)
16 Sat	F.A. Umbro Trophy 6
19/20 Tue/Wed	UEFA Champions League – Group Stage 2 – Match Day 12
21 Thu	UEFA Cup QF (2)
23 Sat	F.A. Carlsberg Vase SF (1)
26/27 Tue/Wed	International Friendly dates
29 Fri	Good Friday
30 Sat	F.A. Carlsberg Vase SF (2)
	AXA F.A. Youth Cup SF (1)*
31 Sun	Easter Sunday

April 2002

1 Mon	Easter Monday
2/3 Tue/Wed	UEFA Champions League – QF (1)
4 Thu	UEFA Cup SF (1)
6 Sat	F.A. Umbro Trophy SF (1)
7 Sun	AXA F.A. Women's Cup SF

9/10 Tue/Wed	UEFA Champions League – QF (2)
11 Thu	UEFA Cup SF (2)
13 Sat	F.A. Umbro Trophy SF (2)
	AXA F.A. Youth Cup SF (2)*
14 Sun	F.A. Cup sponsored by AXA SF
16/17 Tue/Wed	International Friendly dates
20 Sat	Football League finishes
23/24 Tue/Wed	UEFA Champions League – SF (1)
27 Sat	AXA F.A. Youth Cup Final
28 Sun	Football League Play-Off SF (1)
30/1 Tue/Wed	UEFA Champions League – SF (2)

May 2002

1 Wed	Football League Play-Off SF (2)
2 Thu	AXA F.A. Youth Cup Final (1) - tbc
4 Sat	
6 Mon	Bank Holiday
	AXA F.A. Women's Cup Final – tbc
7 Tue	AXA F.A. Youth Cup Final (2) – tbc
8 Wed	UEFA Cup Final
10-12 Fri/Sun	Football League Play-Off Finals
15 Wed	UEFA Champions League Final
31 Fri	World Cup 2002 commences

June 2002

30 Sun	World Cup 2002 Final

To be confirmed:
F.A. Cup sponsored by AXA Final
F.A. Umbro Trophy Final
F.A. Carlsberg Vase Final
F.A. Umbro Sunday Cup Final

* = Closing date of Round

STOP PRESS

Copa America off and on – but Argentina and Canada quit and Brazil eliminated ... FIFA to experiment with goal judges but face massive losses on ISL collapse ... Spurs lose their Sol to Arsenal ... Zidane in world record £47.7m Real Madrid move ... Man U pay British record £28.1m for a 'little witch' ... New transfer regulations imminent ... England U-17's flop ... Eriksson lookalike Platt gets U-21 job, Forest take Hart, Roy McFarland in at Torquay ... Barry and Bohs Euro bonus ... Cameroon, Tunisia, South Africa and Senegal qualify for WC 2002 ... Carlisle crisis ... Man U stand closure averted ... Everton eye new ground ...

Arsenal: Francis Jeffers (Everton) £10m; Giovanni Van Bronckhorst (Rangers) £8.5m; Richard Wright (Ipswich T) £6m; Junichi Inamoto (Gamba Osaka) £4m; Sol Campbell (Tottenham H) Free; **Aston Villa:** Olof Mellberg (Santander) £5m; Mustapha Hadji (Coventry C) – deal includes Julian Joachim + £2m; Peter Schmeichel (Sporting Lisbon) Free; Hassan Kachloul (Southampton) Free; **Blackburn R:** Corrado Grabbi (Ternana) £6.75m; Kerimoglou Tugay (Rangers) £1.3m; Gordon Greer (Clyde) £200,000; Alan Mahon (Sporting Lisbon) £1.5m; **Bolton W:** Henrik Pedersen (Silkeborg) £650,000; Nicky Southall (Gillingham) Free; Djibril Diawara (Torino) Loan; Akinori Nishizawa (Cerezo Osaka) Loan; **Charlton Ath:** Jason Euell (Wimbledon) £4.75m; Shaun Bartlett (Zurich) £2m; **Chelsea:** Frank Lampard (West Ham U) £11m; Emmanuel Petit (Barcelona) £7.5m; William Gallas (Marseille) £6.2m; **Everton:** Tomasz Radzinski (Anderlecht) £4.5m; Alan Stubbs (Celtic) Free; **Fulham:** Luis Boa Morte (Southampton) £1.7m; Matt Clarke (Bradford C) Loan; Abdeslan Ouaddou (Nancy) £2m; **Ipswich T:** Pablo Counago (Celta Vigo) Free; Andy Marshall (Norwich C) Free; Tommy Miller (Hartlepool U) £800,000; Chris Hogg (York C) £150,000; **Leeds U:** Robbie Keane (Internazionale) £11m; **Leicester C:** Dennis Wise (Chelsea) £1.6m; Ian Walker (Tottenham H) £2.5m; Ashley Lyth (Scarborough) £100,000; **Liverpool:** John Arne Riise (Monaco) £4.6m; **Manchester U:** Juan Sebastian Veron (Lazio) £28.1m; Ruud Van Nistelrooy (PSV Eindhoven) £19m; Roy Carroll (Wigan Ath) £2.5m; **Middlesbrough:** Szilard Nemeth (Inter Bratislava) Free; Gareth Southgate (Aston Villa) £6.5m; **Newcastle U:** Craig Bellamy (Coventry C) £6.5m; Robbie Elliott (Bolton W) Free; **Southampton:** Rory Delap (Derby Co) £4m; Anders Svensson (Elfsborg) £500,000; Jacinta Ela Eyene (Espanyol) Free; **Sunderland:** Lilian Laslandes (Bordeaux) £3.6m; Nicolas Medina (Argentinos Juniors) £3.5m; David Bellion (Cannes) Free; Baki Mercimek (Haarlem) Free; **Tottenham H:** Goran Bunjevcevic (Red Star Belgrade) £4m; Christian Ziege (Liverpool) £4m; Gustavo Poyet (Chelsea) £1.5m; Teddy Sheringham (Manchester U) Free; Jose Antonio Chamot (AC Milan) Free; Shwan Jalal (Hastings T) Free; **West Ham U:** David James (Aston Villa) £3.5m; Sebastian Schemmel (Metz) £465,000.

Other moves completed and pending: Mark Kennedy, Manchester C to Wolverhampton W £2m; Eyal Berkovic, Celtic to Manchester C £1.5m; Peter Crouch, QPR to Portsmouth £1.5m; Neil Shipperley, Barnsley to Wimbledon £750,000; Spencer Prior, Manchester C to Cardiff C £700,000; Mark Rivers, Crewe Alex to Norwich C £600,000; Richard Cresswell, Leicester C to Preston NE £500,000; Neil Emblen, Wolverhampton W to Norwich C £500,000; Lawrie Dudfield, Leicester C to Hull C £250,000; Gary Alexander, Swindon T to Hull C £200,000; Neil Alexander, Livingston to Cardiff C £200,000; Stuart Campbell, Leicester C to Grimsby T £200,000; Darren Currie, Barnet to Wycombe W £200,000; Jermaine Darlington, QPR to Wimbledon £200,000; Clint Easton, Watford to Norwich C £200,000; Paul Crichton, Burnley to Norwich C £150,000; Scott Dobie, Carlisle U to WBA £150,000; Gary Fletcher, Northwich Vic to Leyton Orient £150,000; Phillip Jevons, Everton to Grimsby T £150,000; Andy Holt, Oldham Ath to Hull C £150,000; Paul Peschisolido, Fulham to Sheffield U £150,000; Sam Stockley, Barnet to Oxford U £150,000; Ryan Williams, Chesterfield to Hull C £150,000; Tony Hackworth, Leeds U to Notts Co £120,000; Carl Griffiths, Leyton Orient to Luton £65,000; Matthew Glennon, Bolton W to Hull C £50,000; Mark Freeman, Cheltenham T to Boston U £15,000; Colin Alcide, York C to Cambridge C; Mark Angel, Darlington to Boston U; Stuart Balmer, Wigan Ath to Oldham Ath; Michael Bingham, Blackburn R to Mansfield T; Matthew Bloomer, Grimsby T to Hull C; Peter Handyside, Grimsby T to Stoke C; Scott Kerr, Bradford C to Hull C; Dominic Ludden, Preston NE to Halifax T; Mark McGregor, Wrexham to Burnley; Paul McGregor, Plymouth Arg to Northampton T; Paul McLaren, Luton T to Sheffield W; Stephen McPhee, Coventry C to Port Vale; Craig Midgley, Hartlepool U to Halifax T; Nicky Mohan, Stoke C to Hull C; Mark Monington, Rochdale to Boston U; Tommy Mooney, Watford to Birmingham C; Paul Morgan, Preston NE to Lincoln C; John O'Kane, Bolton W to Blackpool; Paul Pettinger, Rotherham U to Lincoln C; Ben Petty, Stoke C to Hull C; Geoffrey Pitcher, Kingstonian to Brighton & HA; Michael Pollitt, Chesterfield to Rotherham U; Ben Smith, Yeovil T to Southend U; Nico Vaesen, Huddersfield T to Birmingham C; Philip Warner, Southampton to Cambridge U; Kevin Dixon, Leeds U to Barnsley; Steve Cosgrove, Manchester U to Motherwell; Jay Richardson, Chelsea to Exeter C; Layton Maxwell, Liverpool to Cardiff C; Ian Armstrong, Liverpool to Port Vale; Stuart Reddington, Chelsea to Mansfield T; Stuart Pearce, West Ham U to Manchester C; Stephen Hughes, Everton to Watford; Dave McEwen, Tottenham H to QPR; Stevland Angus, West Ham U to Cambridge U; Terrell Forbes, West Ham U to QPR; Marc Whiteman, Manchester U to Bury; Michael Rose, Manchester U to Chester C; Amos Foyewa, West Ham U to Bournemouth.

Leaving the country: Nelson Vivas, Arsenal to Internazionale; Stefan Malz, Arsenal to Kaiserslautern; Carsten Fredgaard, Sunderland to FC Copenhagen; Alberto Mendez, Arsenal to Racing Club; Christian Karembeu, Middlesbrough to Olympiakos; Bernard Lambourde, Chelsea to Bastia.

Euro round-up: Inter-Toto: Carmarthen T, Cliftonville, Cork C and Dundee exit; Aston Villa and Newcastle U third round winners. European Cup: Barry Town beat Shamkir, Bohemians beat Levadia, but Linfield sunk by Torpedo Kutaisi.

Finally: Leading Scorers do not include Charity Shield (page 572). Wolverhampton W record transfer fee received £5m from Leicester C for Ade Akinbiyi, July 2000.

Now you can buy any of these other bestselling sports titles from your bookshop or *direct from the publisher.*

FREE P&P AND UK DELIVERY
(Overseas and Ireland £3.50 per book)

Playfair Football Annual 2001–2002	Glenda Rollin and Jack Rollin	£5.99
The Autobiography	Gareth Edwards	£7.99
The Autobiography	John Barnes	£6.99
Crossing the Line	Charlie Brooks	£7.99
Ultra Nippon	Jonathan Birchall	£7.99
Barmy Army	Dougie Brimson	£6.99
Vinnie	Vinnie Jones	£6.99
Formula One Uncovered	Derick Allsop	£7.99
Manchester United Ruined My Life	Colin Shindler	£5.99
God Save the Team	Eddy Brimson	£6.99
Dark Trade	Donald McRae	£7.99
A Lot of Hard Yakka	Simon Hughes	£6.99
Left Foot Forward	Garry Nelson	£6.99

TO ORDER SIMPLY CALL THIS NUMBER

01235 400 414

or e-mail <u>orders@bookpoint.co.uk</u>

Prices and availability subject to change without notice.